P9-DFQ-426

FINLAND 18

UNION OF SOVIET SOCIALIST REPUBLICS
48

BALTIC STATES 53

EUROPEAN U.S.S.R. 52

ROM. 45

45

45

45

GREECE

TURKEY 62

CYPRUS 62

SYR. 62

IRAQ 66

IRAN 66

AFGHAN. 68

68

MONGOLIA 77

CHINA 77

N. KOREA 80

S. KOREA 80

JAPAN 81

KUWAIT 58

PAKISTAN

NEPAL 68

BH.

TAIWAN 77

EGYPT 110

SAUDI ARABIA 58

BAH. QATAR 58

U.A.E. 58

OMAN 58

INDIA 68

BANG. 68

BURMA 72

LAOS

HONG KONG 78

PACIFIC OCEAN
Page 87

CHAD 110

SUDAN 110

YEMEN 58

P.D.R. YEMEN 58

THAILAND 72

CAMB. 72

VIETNAM 72

PHILIPPINES 82

GUAM 86

110

DJIB. 110

ETHIOPIA 110

SRI LANKA 68

BRUNEI

AFR. REP.

UGANDA 114

KENYA 114

SOMALIA 115

MALAYSIA 72

SING. 72

PAPUA NEW GUINEA 84

ZAIRE 114

RWA. BUR. 114

TANZANIA 114

SEYCHELLES 119

ASIA
Page 54

INDONESIA 85

SOLOMON IS. 86

SAMOA 86

ZAMBIA 114

FIJI 86

ZIMBABWE 119

MOZAMBIQUE 119

MADAGASCAR 119

MAURITUS RÉUNION 119

NORTHERN TERRITORY 93

QUEENSLAND 95

NEW CALEDONIA 86

BOTSWANA 119

WESTERN AUSTRALIA 92

SOUTH AUSTRALIA 94

SWAZILAND 119

NEW SOUTH WALES 96

SOUTH AFRICA 119

LESOTHO 119

VICTORIA 96

NEW ZEALAND 100

TASMANIA 99

AUSTRALIA
Page 88

NORWAY 18

FINLAND 18

SWEDEN 18

UNITED KINGDOM 10

SCOTLAND 15

DENMARK 21

BALTIC STATES 53

EUROPEAN U.S.S.R. 52

IRELAND 17

ENGLAND 13

WALES

NETH. 27

EAST GER. 22

POLAND 47

BELG. LUX.

WEST GERMANY

CZECH. 41

FRANCE 28

SWITZ. 39

AUST. 41

HUN. 41

ROMANIA 45

ITALY

MON.

YUGOSLAVIA 45

AND.

34

BULGARIA 45

ALB. 45

PORTUGAL 32

SPAIN 33

MEDITERRANEAN 36

GREECE 45

TURKEY 62

CYPRUS 62

SYRIA 62

IRAN 66

TUNISIA 106

MALTA 34

LEBANON 62

ISRAEL

IRAQ 66

MOROCCO 106

ALGERIA 106

LIBYA 110

EGYPT 110

JORDAN 65

SAUDI ARABIA 58

HAMMOND®
WORLD ATLAS

HAMMOND® CITATION

WORLD

ATLAS

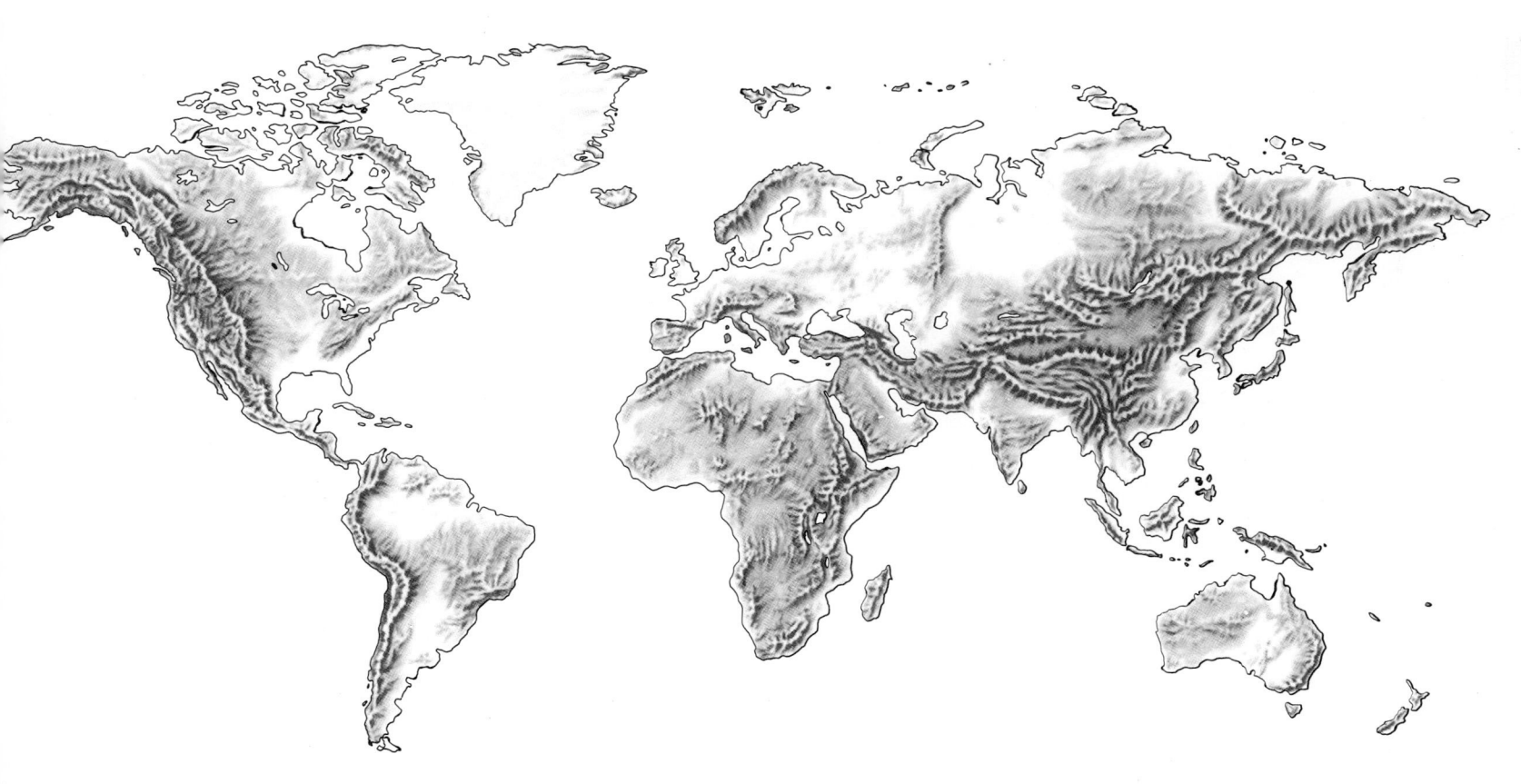

HAMMOND INCORPORATED   MAPLEWOOD, NEW JERSEY 07040

Hammond Publications Advisory Board

Library of Congress Cataloging-in-Publication Data
Hammond Incorporated.
   Hammond citation world atlas.
   Rev. ed. of: Citation world atlas / Hammond
Incorporated. c 1988.
   Includes indexes.
   1. Atlases. I. Hammond Incorporated. Citation
world atlas. II. Title. III. Title: Citation world
atlas.
G1021.H267   1988   912   87-675134
ISBN 0-8437-1258-9 (thumb-indexed)
ISBN 0-8437-1253-8 (paperback)

Contents

Introduction to the World Atlas

The current edition of the Hammond World Atlas features an outstanding new section devoted to THE PHYSICAL WORLD — a series of terrain maps of land forms and ocean floors. These physical maps were originally produced as sculptured terrain models, thus simulating the earth's surface in a highly realistic manner. The three-dimensional effect is both instructive and pleasing to the eye.

As in previous editions, the atlas is organized to make the retrieval of information as simple and quick as possible. The guiding principle in organizing the atlas material has been to present separate subjects on *separate* maps. In this way, each individual map topic is shown with the greatest degree of clarity, unencumbered with extraneous information that is best revealed on separate maps. Of equal importance from the standpoint of good atlas design is the treatment of all current information on a given country or state as a single atlas unit. Thus, the basic reference map of an area is accompanied on adjacent pages by all supplementary information pertaining to that area. For example, the detailed index for a given map always appears on the same page as, or on the pages immediately following, the reference map. This same map index provides population data for the many cities, towns and villages shown on the map. Highlight information on the area, i.e., the total population and area, the capital, the highest point, is listed in the summary fact listings accompanying each unit. An adjacent locator map relates the subject area to the larger world beyond. A three-dimensional picture of the area is exhibited by means of the accompanying full-color topographic map. A separate economic map defines the vital agricultural, industrial and mineral resources of the area. In the case of the foreign maps, the flag of each independent nation appears on the appropriate page. Finally, certain country units contain special subject maps dealing with the history, climate, demography and vegetation of the area.

An important feature of the atlas is the addition of ZIP codes to the index entries for each of the legion of communities shown on the state maps. With the exception of the U.S. Postal Service directories of limited availability, the ZIP code listings herein are the most extensive published.

The back of the book contains a second type of index. This is a multi-paged "A-to-Z" index of places that appear on the maps. The use of this map index is essential when the name of a place is known but its country, state, or province is unknown.

Of course, the maps have been thoroughly updated. These revisions echo the new nations, shifting boundaries and the fluid internal divisions of many countries. New communities generated by the opening up of resources in the developing nations are also noted. Up-to-date geographical information, both foreign and domestic, is received daily by the atlas editors. A worldwide correspondence and thorough research brings to the atlas user the latest geographical and demographic information obtainable.

In closing it may be said that the atlas has truly been designed for contemporary use. Just as the information presented on the following pages is as current and up to date as the editors and cartographers could issue it, so the design and organization has been as well planned as possible to create a work useful to present generations.

President
HAMMOND INCORPORATED

Introduction to the Maps and Indexes

The following notes have been added to aid the reader in making the best use of this atlas. Though he may be familiar with maps and map indexes, the publisher believes that a quick review of the material below will add to his enjoyment of this reference work.

Arrangement — The Plan of the Atlas. The atlas has been designed with maximum convenience for the user as its obejective. Part I of the atlas is devoted to the physical world — terrain maps of land forms and the sea floor. Part II contains the general political reference maps, area by area. All geographically related information pertaining to a country or region appears on adjacent pages, eliminating the task of searching throughout the entire volume for data on a given area. Thus, the reader will find, conveniently assembled, political, topographic, economic and special maps of a political area or region, accompanied by detailed map indexes, statistical data, and illustrations of the national flags of the area.

The sequence of country units in this American-designed atlas is international in arrangement. Units on the world as a whole are followed by a section on the polar regions which, in turn, is followed by pages devoted to Europe and its countries. Every continent map is accompanied by special population distribution, climatic and vegetation maps of that continent. Following the maps of the European continent and its countries, the geographic sequence plan proceeds as follows: Asia, the Pacific and Australia, Africa, South America, North America, and ends with detailed coverage on the United States.

Political Maps — The Primary Reference Tool. The most detailed maps in each country unit are the *political maps*. It is our feeling that the reader is likely to refer to these maps more often than to any other in the book when confronted by such questions as — Where? How big? What is it near? Answering these common queries is the function of the political maps. Each political map stresses *political* phenomena — countries, internal political divisions, boundaries, cities and towns. The major political unit or units, shown on the map, are banded in distinctive colors for easy identification and delineation. First-order political subdivisions (states, provinces, counties on the state maps) are shown, scale permitting.

The reader is advised to make use of the *legend* appearing under the title on each political map. Map *symbols*, the special "language" of maps, are explained in the legend. Each variety of dot, circle, star or interrupted line has a special meaning which should be clearly understood by the user so that he may interpret the map data correctly.

Each country has been portrayed at a *scale* commensurate with its political, areal, economic or tourist importance. In certain cases, a whole map unit may be devoted to a single nation if that nation is considered to be of prime interest to most atlas users. In other cases, several nations will be shown on a single map if, as separate entities, they are of lesser relative importance. Areas of dense settlement and important significance within a country have been enlarged and portrayed in inset maps inserted on the margins of the main map. The scale of each map is indicated as a fractional representation (1:1,000,000). The reader is advised to refer to the linear or "bar" scale appearing on each map or map inset in order to determine the distance between points.

The *projection* system used for each map is noted near the title of the map. Map projections are the special graphic systems used by cartographers to render the curved three-dimensional surface of the globe on a flat surface. Optimum map projections determined by the attributes of the area have been used by the publishers for each map in the atlas.

A word here as to the choice of place names on the maps. Throughout the atlas names appear, with a few exceptions, in their local official spellings. However, conventional Anglicized spellings are used for major geographical divisions and for towns and topographic features for which English forms exist; i.e., "Spain" instead of "España" or "Munich" instead of "München." Names of this type are normally followed by the local official spelling in parentheses. As an aid to the user the indexes are cross-referenced for all current and most former spellings of such names.

Names of cities and towns in the United States follow the forms listed in the *Post Office Directory* of the United States Postal Service. Domestic physical names follow the decisions of the Board on Geographic Names, U.S. Department of the Interior, and of various state geographic name boards.

It is the belief of the publishers that the boundaries shown in a general reference atlas should reflect current geographic and political realities. This policy has been followed consistently in the atlas. The presentation of *de facto* boundaries in cases of territorial dispute between various nations does not imply the political endorsement of such boundaries by the publisher, but simply the honest representation of boundaries as they exist at the time of the printing of the atlas maps.

Indexes — Pinpointing a Location. Each political map is accompanied by a comprehensive index of the place names appearing on the map. If you are unfamiliar with the location of a particular geographical place and wish to find its position within the confines of the subject area of the map, consult the map index as your first step. The name of the feature sought will be found in its proper alphabetical sequence with a key reference letter-number combination corresponding to its location on the map. After noting the key reference letter-number combination for the place name, turn to the map. The place name will be found within the square formed by the two lines of latitude and the two lines of longitude which enclose the co-ordinates — i.e., the marginal letters and numbers. The diagram below illustrates the system of indexing.

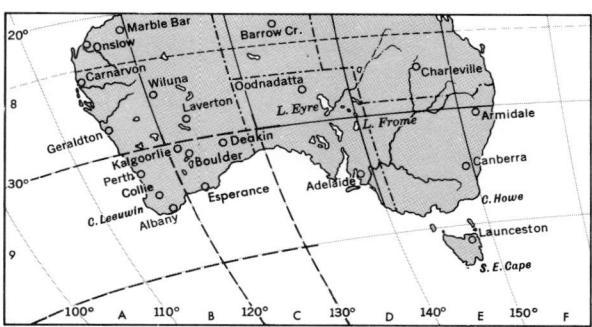

In the case of maps consisting entirely of insets, the place name is found near the intersection point of the imaginary lines connecting the co-ordinates at right angles. See below.

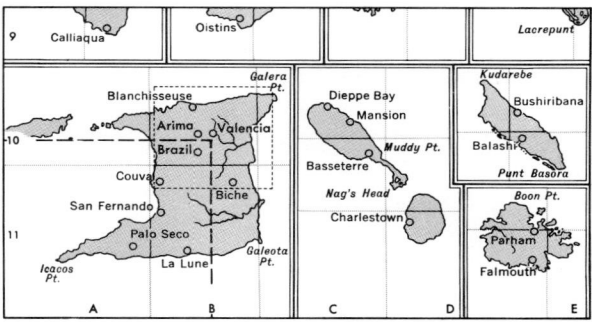

Where space on the map has not permitted giving the complete form of the place name, the complete form is shown in the index. Where a place is known by more than one name or by various spellings of the same name, the different forms have been included in the index. Physical features are listed under their proper names and not according to their generic terms; that is to say, Rio Negro will be found under Negro and not under Rio Negro. On the other hand, Rio Grande will be found under Rio Grande. Accompanying most index entries for cities and towns, and for other political units, are *population figures* for the particular entries. The large number of population figures in the atlas makes this work one of the most comprehensive statistical sources available to the public today. The population the various nations. Dates and sources for the population figures are listed in the Gazetteer-Index of the World following this section.

Population and area figures for countries and major political units are listed in bold type *fact lists* on the margins of the indexes. In addition, the capital, largest city, highest point, monetary unit, principal languages and the prevailing religions of the country concerned are also listed. The Gazetteer-Index of the World on the following pages provides a quick reference index for countries and other important areas. Though population and area figures for each major unit area also found in the map section, the Gazetteer-Index provides a conveniently arranged statistical comparison contained in five pages. As mentioned, dates and sources of the population figures appearing in the country indexes are also listed in this section.

All index entries for cities and towns in the indexes accompanying individual state maps for the United States are preceded by a five-digit postal ZIP code number applying to the community. A dagger (†) designates those places that do not possess a post office. The ZIP code number listed in such cases refers to that of the nearest post office. An asterisk (*) marks those larger cities which are divided into multiple ZIP code areas. Using the single ZIP code number listed in such cases will direct your letter to the proper city with dispatch. However, if the precise ZIP code number of the address within the city is needed, it is suggested that the reader refer to the latest National ZIP Code Directory at his local post office. This detailed guide lists every street in a multiple ZIP code city with the proper ZIP code for the street.

Relief Maps. Accompanying each political map is a relief map of the area. These are in addition to the terrain maps of land forms in Part I of the atlas. The purpose of the relief map is to illustrate the surface configuration (TOPOGRAPHY) of the region. A shading technique in color simulates the relative ruggedness of the terrain — plains, plateaus, valleys, hills and mountains. Graded colors, ranging from greens for lowlands, yellows for intermediate elevations to browns in the highlands, indicate the height above sea level of each part of the land. A vertical scale at the margin of the map shows the approximate height in meters and feet represented by each color.

Economic Maps — Agriculture, Industry and Resources. One of the most interesting features that will be found in each country unit is the economic map. From this map one can determine the basic activities of a nation as expressed through its economy. A perusal of the map yields a full understanding of the area's economic geography and natural resources.

The agricultural economy is manifested in two ways: color bands and commodity names. The color bands express broad categories of *dominant land use*, such as, cereal belts, forest lands, livestock range lands, nonagricultural wastes. The red commodity names, on the other hand, pinpoint the areas of production of *specific crops*; i.e., wheat, cotton, sugar beets, etc.

Major mineral occurrences are denoted by standard letter symbols appearing in blue. The relative size of the letter symbols signifies the relative importance of the deposit.

The manufacturing sector of the economy is presented by means of diagonal line patterns expressing the various *industrial areas* of consequence within a country.

The fishing industry is represented by names of commercial fish species appearing offshore in blue letters. Major waterpower sites are designated by blue symbols.

The publishers have tried to make this work the most comprehensive and useful atlas available, and it is hoped that it will prove a valuable reference work. Any constructive suggestions from the reader will be welcomed.

Sources and Acknowledgements

A multitude of sources goes into the making of a large-scale reference work such as this. To list them all would take many pages and would consume space better devoted to the maps and reference materials themselves. However, certain general sources were very useful in preparing this work and are listed below.

STATISTICAL OFFICE OF THE UNITED NATIONS.
Demographic Yearbook. New York. Issued annually.

STATISTICAL OFFICE OF THE UNITED NATIONS.
Statistical Yearbook. New York. Issued annually.

THE GEOGRAPHER, U.S. DEPARTMENT OF STATE.
International Boundary Study papers. Washington. Various dates.

THE GEOGRAPHER, U.S. DEPARTMENT OF STATE.
Geographic Notes. Washington. Various dates.

UNITED STATES BOARD ON GEOGRAPHIC NAMES.
Decisions on Geographic Names in the United States. Washington. Various dates.

UNITED STATES BOARD ON GEOGRAPHIC NAMES.
Official Standard Names Gazetteers. Washington. Various dates.

CANADIAN PERMANENT COMMITTEE ON GEOGRAPHICAL NAMES.
Gazetteer of Canada series. Ottawa. Various dates.

UNITED STATES POSTAL SERVICE.
National Five Digit ZIP Code and Post Office Directory. Washington. Issued annually.

UNITED STATES POSTAL SERVICE.
Postal Bulletin. Washington. Issued weekly.

UNITED STATES DEPARTMENT OF THE INTERIOR. BUREAU OF MINES.
Minerals Yearbook. 4 vols. Washington. Various dates.

UNITED STATES GEOLOGICAL SURVEY.
Elevations and distances in the United States. Reston, Va. 1980.

CARTACTUAL.
Cartactual — Topical Map Service. Budapest. Issued bimonthly.

AMERICAN GEOGRAPHICAL SOCIETY.
Focus. New York. Issued ten times a year.

THE AMERICAN UNIVERSITY.
Foreign Area Studies. Washington. Various dates.

CENTRAL INTELLIGENCE AGENCY.
General reference maps. Washington. Various dates.

A sample list of sources used for specific countries follows:

Afghanistan
CENTRAL STATISTICS OFFICE.
Preliminary Results of the First Afghan Population Census 1979. Kabul.

Albania
DREJTORIA E STATISTIKES.
1979 Census. Tiranë.

Argentina
INSTITUTO NACIONAL DE ESTADISTICA Y CENSOS.
Censo Nacional de Población y Vivienda 1980. Buenos Aires.

Australia
AUSTRALIAN BUREAU OF STATISTICS.
Census of Population and Housing 1981. Canberra.

Brazil
FUNDACAO INSTITUTO BRASILEIRO DE GEOGRAFIA E ESTATISTICA.
IX Recenseamento Geral do Brasil 1980. Rio de Janeiro.

Canada
STATISTICS CANADA.
1981 Census of Canada. Ottawa.

Cuba
COMITE ESTATAL DE ESTADISTICAS.
Censo de Población y Viviendas 1981. Havana.

Hungary
HUNGARIAN CENTRAL STATISTICAL OFFICE.
1980 Census. Budapest.

Indonesia
BIRO PUSAT STATISTIK.
Sensus Penduduk 1980. Jakarta.

Kuwait
CENTRAL OFFICE OF STATISTICS.
1980 Census. Al Kuwait.

New Zealand
DEPARTMENT OF STATISTICS.
New Zealand Census of Population and Dwellings 1981. Wellington.

Panama
DIRECCIÓN DE ESTADISTICA Y CENSO.
Censos Nacionales de 1980. Panamá.

Papua New Guinea
BUREAU OF STATISTICS.
National Population Census 1980. Port Moresby.

Philippines
NATIONAL CENSUS AND STATISTICS OFFICE.
1980 Census of Population. Manila.

Saint Lucia
CENSUS OFFICE.
1980 Population Census. Castries.

Singapore
DEPARTMENT OF STATISTICS.
Census of Population 1980. Singapore.

U.S.S.R.
CENTRAL STATISTICAL ADMINISTRATION.
1979 Census. Moscow.

United States
BUREAU OF THE CENSUS.
1980 Census of Population. Washington.

Vanuatu
CENSUS OFFICE.
1979 Population Census. Port Vila.

Zambia
CENTRAL STATISTICAL OFFICE.
1980 Census of Population and Housing. Lusaka.

Gazetteer-Index of the World

This alphabetical list of continents, countries, states, colonial possessions and other major geographical areas provides a quick reference to their area in square miles and square kilometers, population, capital or chief town, map page number and index key thereon. The last name indicates the square on the respective page in which the name may be found. An indication of the population sources used is also included, and refers both to the total figures given in this Gazetteer-Index and to the populations appearing in greater detail with the maps throughout the atlas. The population figures used in each case are the latest reliable figures obtainable. A glance at the sources will show that the dates vary considerably throughout the world. In certain areas where no census has ever been taken, we must rely on official estimates. In other areas where censuses have been taken at infrequent intervals, we again rely on estimates. The key to the abbreviations used in the Gazetteer-Index follows:

aut = autonomous	est = estimates	reg = regions
boro = boroughs	excl = excluding	rep = republics
cap = capital	FC = final census	S.S.R. = Soviet Socialist Republic
CE = census (undetermined)	gov = governorates	terr = territories; territory
CIA = U.S. Central Intelligence	incl = including	TP = total population
Agency	isl = islands	U.K. = United Kingdom
cit = cities	met = metropolitan	UN = United Nations
co = counties	OE = official estimate	U.S.A. = United States of America
com = communes	oth = other populations	U.S.S.R. = Union of Soviet
dept = departments	par = parishes	Socialist Republics
dist = districts	PC = preliminary census	ws = with suburbs
div = divisions	prov = provinces; provincial	

Country	Area Square Miles	Area Square Kilometers	Population	Capital or Chief Town	Page and Index Ref.	Sources of Population Data
*Afghanistan	250,775	649,507	15,540,000	Kabul	68/A 2	79 PC
Africa	11,707,000	30,321,130	469,000,000	....	102/......	80 UN est
Alabama, U.S.A.	51,705	133,916	3,893,888	Montgomery	195/......	80 FC & OE
Alaska, U.S.A.	591,004	1,530,700	401,851	Juneau	196/......	80 FC & OE
*Albania	11,100	28,749	2,590,600	Tiranë	45/E 5	TP—79 PC; cit over 6,000—70 OE; oth—63 OE
Alberta, Canada	255,285	661,185	2,237,724	Edmonton	182/......	81 FC
*Algeria	919,591	2,381,740	17,422,000	Algiers	106/D 3	77 PC
American Samoa	77	199	32,297	Pago Pago	87/J 7; 86/......	80 FC
Andorra	188	487	31,000	Andorra la Vella	33/G 1	TP—79 OE; cap—75 OE
*Angola	481,351	1,246,700	7,078,000	Luanda	114/C 6	TP—80 UN est; oth—70 FC
Anguilla	35	91	6,519	The Valley	156/F 3	74 FC
Antarctica	5,500,000	14,245,000	....	....	5/......	....
*Antigua and Barbuda	171	443	75,000	St. John's	161/E11; 156/G 3	TP—80 OE; oth—70 FC
*Argentina	1,072,070	2,776,661	28,438,000	Buenos Aires	143/......	TP—82 OE; oth—80 PC
Arizona, U.S.A.	114,000	295,260	2,718,425	Phoenix	198/......	80 FC & OE
Arkansas, U.S.A.	53,187	137,754	2,286,435	Little Rock	202/......	80 FC & OE
Armenian S.S.R., U.S.S.R.	11,506	29,800	3,031,000	Erivan	52/F 6	TP, cit over 50,000—79 PC; oth—70 FC
Aruba	75	193	66,790	Oranjestad	161/E 9	TP—86 OE; cap—72 est
Ascension Island, St. Helena	34	88	719	Georgetown	102/A 5	76 FC
Ashmore & Cartier Islands, Australia	61	159	....	(Canberra, Austr.)	88/C 2	....
Asia	17,128,500	44,362,815	2,633,000,000	....	54/......	80 est
*Australia	2,966,136	7,682,300	14,576,330	Canberra	88/......	81 FC
Australian Capital Territory	927	2,400	221,609	Canberra	96/E 4	81 FC
*Austria	32,375	83,851	7,507,000	Vienna	40/B 3	TP—80 OE; cap, cit over 100,000—73 OE; oth—71 FC
Azerbaidzhan S.S.R., U.S.S.R.	33,436	86,600	6,028,000	Baku	52/G 6	TP, cit over 50,000—79 PC; oth—70 FC
Azores Islands, Portugal	902	2,335	264,400	Ponta Delgada; Angra do Heroísmo; Horta	32/......	TP—77 OE; oth—70 FC & PC
*Bahamas	5,382	13,939	209,505	Nassau	156/C 1	80 PC
*Bahrain	240	622	358,857	Manama	58/F 4	TP—81 PC; oth—71 FC
Baker Island, U.S.A.	1	2.6	....	....	87/J 5	....
Balearic Islands, Spain	1,936	5,014	558,287	Palma	33/H 3	70 FC
*Bangladesh	55,126	142,776	87,052,024	Dhaka	68/G 4	TP—81 PC; oth—74 FC
*Barbados	166	430	248,983	Bridgetown	161/B 8	80 PC
Belau (Palau)	188	487	12,116	Koror	86/D 5	80 FC
*Belgium	11,781	30,513	9,855,110	Brussels	27/E 7	TP—80 OE; oth—70 FC (com)
*Belize	8,867	22,966	144,857	Belmopan	154/C 2	TP, cap, cit over 1,000—80 PC; oth—70 PC
*Benin	43,483	112,620	3,338,240	Porto-Novo	106/E 6	TP—79 PC; cap, Cotonou—75 OE; oth—73 OE
Bermuda	21	54	67,761	Hamilton	156/H 3	80 PC
*Bhutan	18,147	47,000	1,298,000	Thimphu	68/G 3	TP—80 UN est; oth—70 OE
*Bolivia	424,163	1,098,582	5,600,000	La Paz; Sucre	136/......	TP—80 OE; cap, dept, dept cap—76 FC; oth—50 FC
Bonaire, Neth. Antilles	112	291	8,087	Kralendijk	161/E 9	TP—71 FC; cap—72 est
Bophuthatswana (rep.), South Africa	15,570	40,326	1,200,000	Mmabatho	119/D 5	TP—78 est; oth—70 FC
*Botswana	224,764	582,139	819,000	Gaborone	119/C 4	TP—80 OE; cap, Francistown—74 OE; Selebi-Pikwe—75 FC; oth—71 FC
Bouvet Island	22	57	....	....	5/D 1	....
*Brazil	3,284,426	8,506,663	119,098,992	Brasília	132/......	80 PC
British Columbia, Canada	366,253	948,596	2,744,467	Victoria	184/......	81 FC
British Indian Ocean Terr.	29	75	2,000	(London, U.K.)	54/L10	78 est
British Virgin Islands	59	153	11,006	Road Town	157/H 1	TP—80 FC; oth—70 FC
Brunei	2,226	5,765	192,832	Bandar Seri Begawan	85/E 4	81 PC
*Bulgaria	42,823	110,912	8,862,000	Sofia	45/F 4	TP—80 OE; oth—75 PC
*Burkina Faso	105,869	274,200	6,908,000	Ouagadougou	106/D 6	TP—80 UN est; oth—75 FC, 73 OE
*Burma	261,789	678,034	32,913,000	Rangoon	72/B 2	TP—79 OE; states, div. cit over 100,000—73 PC; oth—53 FC
*Burundi	10,747	27,835	4,021,910	Bujumbura	114/E 4	79 PC
*Byelorussian S.S.R. (White Russian S.S.R.), U.S.S.R.	80,154	207,600	9,560,000	Minsk	52/C 4	TP, cit over 50,000—79 PC; oth—70 FC
California, U.S.A.	158,706	411,049	23,667,565	Sacramento	204/......	80 FC & OE
*Cambodia (Kampuchea)	69,898	181,036	5,200,000	Phnom Penh	72/E 4	TP—79 CIA est; cap—80 est
*Cameroon	183,568	475,441	8,503,000	Yaoundé	114/B 2	TP—80 OE; cit over 21,000—76 FC; Ebolowa, oth—70 OE
*Canada	3,851,787	9,976,139	24,343,181	Ottawa	162/......	81 FC
Canary Islands, Spain	2,808	7,273	1,170,224	Las Palmas; Santa Cruz	32/B 4	70 FC
Cape Province, South Africa	261,705	677,816	5,543,506	Cape Town	118/C 6	TP—80 PC; oth—70 FC
*Cape Verde	1,557	4,033	324,000	Praia	106/B 8	TP—80 UN est; oth—70 PC
Cayman Islands	100	259	18,000	Georgetown	156/B 3	TP—81 OE; oth—79 FC

*Member of the United Nations.

Gazetteer-Index of the World

Country	Area Square Miles	Square Kilometers	Population	Capital or Chief Town	Page and Index Ref.	Sources of Population Data
Celebes, Indonesia	72,986	189,034	7,732,383	Ujung Pandang	85/G 6	71 PC
*Central African Republic	242,000	626,780	2,284,000	Bangui	114/C 2	TP—79 est; oth—75 FC
Central America	197,480	511,475	21,000,000	....	154/......	79 OE
Ceylon, see Sri Lanka						
*Chad	495,752	1,283,998	4,309,000	N'Djamena	111/C 4	TP—78 OE; oth—72 OE
Channel Islands	75	194	133,000	St. Helier; St. Peter Port	13/E 8	TP—81 OE; oth—71 FC
*Chile	292,257	756,946	11,275,440	Santiago	138/......	TP—82 PC; cit (part)—79 OE; oth—70 FC & PC
*China, People's Rep. of	3,691,000	9,559,690	958,090,000	Peking (Beijing)	77/......	TP, prov, Peking, Shanghai, Tianjin—78 OE; oth—70 est
China, Republic of (Taiwan)	13,971	36,185	16,609,961	Taipei	77/K 7	TP, cap, Penghu Isl., cit over 300,000—77 OE; oth—70 OE
Christmas Island, Australia	52	135	3,184	Flying Fish Cove	54/M11	80 OE
Ciskei (rep.), S. Africa	2,988	7,740	635,631	Bisho	119/D 6	80 PC
Clipperton Island	2	5.2	....	....	146/H 8	....
Cocos (Keeling) Islands, Australia	5.4	14	555	West Island	54/N11	81 PC
*Colombia	439,513	1,138,339	27,520,000	Bogotá	126/......	TP—80 OE; oth—73 PC
Colorado, U.S.A.	104,091	269,596	2,889,735	Denver	208/......	80 FC & OE
*Comoros	719	1,862	290,000	Moroni	119/G 2	TP—78 est; cap—75 OE; oth—66 FC
*Congo, Republic of	132,046	342,000	1,537,000	Brazzaville	114/B 4	TP—80 UN est; cap—74 FC; oth—74 PC
Connecticut, U.S.A.	5,018	12,997	3,107,576	Hartford	210/......	80 FC & OE
Cook Islands	91	236	17,695	Avarua	87/K 7	81 PC
Coral Sea Islands, Australia	8.5	22	....	....	88/J 3	
Corsica, France	3,352	8,682	289,842	Ajaccio; Bastia	28/B 6	75 FC
*Costa Rica	19,575	50,700	2,245,000	San José	154/E 5	TP—80 OE; oth—73 FC
*Cuba	44,206	114,494	9,706,369	Havana	158/......	TP—81 PC; prov, cap—81 PC; oth—81 & 70 PC
Curaçao, Neth. Antilles	178	462	145,430	Willemstad	161/G 7	TP—71 FC; cap—75 OE
*Cyprus	3,473	8,995	629,000	Nicosia	62/E 5	TP—80 OE; oth—73 FC, 72 OE
*Czechoslovakia	49,373	127,876	15,276,799	Prague	41/C 2	TP—80 PC; cap, cit over 100,000—75 OE; rep, reg—74 OE; oth—75 OE, 70 FC
Delaware, U.S.A.	2,044	5,294	594,317	Dover	245/R 3	80 FC & OE
*Denmark	16,629	43,069	5,124,000	Copenhagen	21/......	TP—80 OE; oth—75 OE, 71 OE, 70 FC
District of Columbia, U.S.A.	69	179	638,432	Washington	244/F 5	80 FC
*Djibouti	8,880	23,000	386,000	Djibouti	111/H 5	TP—79 est; cap—73 OE
*Dominica	290	751	74,089	Roseau	161/E 7	TP—80 PC; oth—70 FC
*Dominican Republic	18,704	48,443	5,647,977	Santo Domingo	158/D 6	81 PC
*East Germany (German Democratic Republic)	41,768	108,179	16,737,000	Berlin (East)	22/......	TP—80 OE; oth—75 OE
*Ecuador	109,483	283,561	8,644,000	Quito	128/C 3	TP—81 OE; oth—74 FC
*Egypt	386,659	1,001,447	41,572,000	Cairo	110/E 2	TP—80 OE; oth—76 PC
*El Salvador	8,260	21,393	4,813,000	San Salvador	154/C 4	TP—80 OE; oth—71 OE
England, U.K.	50,516	130,836	46,220,955	London	13/......	TP—81 PC; co, cap (boro & ws)—76 OE; cit—76 & 73 OE; oth—71 FC
*Equatorial Guinea	10,831	28,052	244,000	Malabo	114/A 3	TP—79 est; terr—68 OE; oth—60 FC
Estonian S.S.R., U.S.S.R.	17,413	45,100	1,466,000	Tallinn	52/C 3; 53/......	TP, cit over 50,000—79 PC; oth—70 FC
*Ethiopia	471,776	1,221,900	31,065,000	Addis Ababa	110/G 5	TP—80 OE; cap, Asmara—78 OE; prov—72 OE; oth—72 & 71 OE
Europe	4,057,000	10,507,630	676,000,000	....	7/......	80 est
Faeroe Islands, Denmark	540	1,399	41,969	Tórshavn	21/B 2	77 FC
Falkland Islands & Dependencies	6,198	16,053	1,813	Stanley	120/E 8; 143/D 7	76 FC
*Fiji	7,055	18,272	588,068	Suva	87/H 8; 86/......	80 FC
*Finland	130,128	337,032	4,788,000	Helsinki	18/O 6	TP—80 OE; prov—75 OE; oth—75 OE, 70 FC
Florida, U.S.A.	58,664	151,940	9,746,342	Tallahassee	212/......	80 FC & OE
*France	210,038	543,998	53,788,000	Paris	28/......	TP—80 OE; oth—75 FC
French Guiana	35,135	91,000	73,022	Cayenne	131/E 3	82 FC
French Polynesia	1,544	4,000	137,382	Papeete	87/L 8	77 FC
*Gabon	103,346	267,666	551,000	Libreville	114/B 4	TP—80 UN est; oth—70 FC
*Gambia	4,127	10,689	601,000	Banjul	106/A 6	TP—80 OE; oth—73 FC
Gaza Strip	139	360	400,000	Gaza	65/A 4	TP—76 OE; oth—67 CE
Georgia, U.S.A.	58,910	152,577	5,463,105	Atlanta	217/......	80 FC & OE
Georgian S.S.R., U.S.S.R.	26,911	69,700	5,015,000	Tbilisi	52/F 6	TP, cit over 50,000—79 PC; oth—70 FC
*Germany, East (German Democratic Republic)	41,768	108,179	16,737,000	Berlin (East)	22/......	TP—80 OE; oth—75 OE
*Germany, West (Federal Republic)	95,985	248,601	61,658,000	Bonn	22/......	TP—80 OE; states, cap—76 OE; oth—76 OE, 70 FC
*Ghana	92,099	238,536	11,450,000	Accra	106/D 7	TP—80 OE; oth—70 FC
Gibraltar	2.28	5.91	29,760	Gibraltar	33/D 4	79 OE
*Great Britain & Northern Ireland (United Kingdom)	94,399	244,493	55,672,000	London	10/......	TP—81 OE (see England, Wales, Scotland, Northern Ireland)
*Greece	50,944	131,945	9,599,000	Athens	45/F 6	TP—80 OE; oth—71 FC
Greenland	840,000	2,175,600	49,773	Nuuk (Godthåb)	4/B12	TP—80 OE
*Grenada	133	344	103,103	St. George's	161/D 9; 156/G 4	TP, cap—81 OE; oth—70 FC
Guadeloupe & Dependencies	687	1,779	328,400	Basse-Terre	161/A 5; 156/F 4	82 FC
Guam	209	541	105,979	Agaña	87/E 4; 86/......	80 FC
*Guatemala	42,042	108,889	7,262,419	Guatemala	154/B 3	TP—80 OE; oth—73 FC
*Guinea	94,925	245,856	5,143,284	Conakry	106/B 6	TP, cap (ws), Kankan, Kindia, Labé—72 FC; oth—67 OE
*Guinea-Bissau	13,948	36,125	777,214	Bissau	106/A 6	79 PC
*Guyana	83,000	214,970	793,000	Georgetown	131/B 3	TP—80 OE; cap, cit over 10,000—70 FC; oth—60 FC
*Haiti	10,694	27,697	5,053,792	Port-au-Prince	158/C 5	82 PC
Hawaii, U.S.A.	6,471	16,760	964,691	Honolulu	218/......	80 FC & OE
Heard & McDonald Islands, Australia	113	293	....	....	2/N 8	....
Holland, see Netherlands						
*Honduras	43,277	112,087	3,691,000	Tegucigalpa	154/D 3	TP—80 OE; oth—74 FC
Hong Kong	403	1,044	5,022,000	Victoria	77/H 7; 78/......	TP—81 PC; oth—76 FC
Howland Island, U.S.A.	1	2.6	....	....	87/J 5	....
*Hungary	35,919	93,030	10,709,536	Budapest	41/D 3	TP, cap, co—80 PC; oth—80 PC, 70 FC
*Iceland	39,768	103,000	228,785	Reykjavík	21/B 1	TP—80 PC; oth—70 FC
Idaho, U.S.A.	83,564	216,431	944,038	Boise	220/......	80 FC & OE

Gazetteer-Index of the World

Country	Area Square Miles	Area Square Kilometers	Population	Capital or Chief Town	Page and Index Ref.	Sources of Population Data
Illinois, U.S.A.	56,345	145,934	11,426,596	Springfield	222/......	80 FC & OE
*India	1,269,339	3,287,588	683,810,051	New Delhi	68/D 4	TP & states—81 PC; oth—71 FC
Indiana, U.S.A.	36,185	93,719	5,490,260	Indianapolis	227/......	80 FC & OE
*Indonesia	788,430	2,042,034	147,490,298	Jakarta	85/D 7	TP—80 PC; cit—80 PC & 71 PC; isls.—71 PC
Iowa, U.S.A.	56,275	145,752	2,913,808	Des Moines	229/......	80 FC & OE
*Iran	636,293	1,648,000	37,447,000	Tehran	66/F 4	TP—80 OE; div, cit over 50,000—76 PC; oth—66 FC & PC, 56 FC
*Iraq	172,476	446,713	12,767,000	Baghdad	66/C 4	TP—79 OE; oth—65 & 57 FC
*Ireland	27,136	70,282	3,440,427	Dublin	17/......	TP—81 PC; oth—71 FC
Ireland, Northern, U.K.	5,452	14,121	1,543,000	Belfast	17/F 2	TP—81 OE; dist—76 OE; cap, Londonderry—73 OE; oth—71 FC
Isle of Man	227	588	64,000	Douglas	13/C 3	TP—80 OE; oth—71 FC
*Israel	7,847	20,324	3,878,000	Jerusalem	65/B 4	TP—80 OE; cap, cit over 100,000—77 OE; dist, cit over 5,000—72 PC; oth—61 FC
*Italy	116,303	301,225	57,140,000	Rome	34/......	TP—80 OE; oth—71 FC
*Ivory Coast	124,504	322,465	7,920,000	Yamoussoukro	106/C 7	TP—79 OE; oth—75 PC
*Jamaica	4,411	11,424	2,184,000	Kingston	158/......	TP—80 OE; oth—70 & 60 FC
Jan Mayen	144	373	....	....	6/D 1	....
*Japan	145,730	377,441	117,057,485	Tokyo	81/......	TP—80 PC; oth—75 FC
Jarvis Island, U.S.A.	1	2.6	....	....	87/K 6	....
Java, Indonesia	48,842	126,500	73,712,411	Jakarta	85/J 2	71 PC
Johnston Atoll	.91	2.4	327	....	87/K 4	80 FC
*Jordan	35,000	90,650	2,152,273	Amman	65/D 3	TP—79 PC; cap, cit over 100,000—77 OE; gov, cit 9,000-100,000—73 OE; oth—61 FC
*Kampuchea (Cambodia)	69,898	181,036	5,200,000	Phnom Penh	72/E 4	TP—79 CIA est; cap—80 est
Kansas, U.S.A.	82,277	213,097	2,364,236	Topeka	232/......	80 FC & OE
Kazakh S.S.R., U.S.S.R.	1,048,300	2,715,100	14,684,000	Alma-Ata	48/G 5	TP, cit over 50,000—79 PC; oth—70 FC
Kentucky, U.S.A.	40,409	104,659	3,660,257	Frankfort	237/......	80 FC & OE
*Kenya	224,960	582,646	15,327,061	Nairobi	115/G 3	TP—79 PC; oth—69 FC
Kermadec Islands	13	33	5	....	87/J 9	81 FC
Kingman Reef	0.1	0.26	....	....	87/K 5	....
Kirgiz S.S.R., U.S.S.R.	76,641	198,500	3,529,000	Frunze	48/H 5	TP, cit over 50,000—79 PC; oth—70 FC
Kiribati	291	754	56,213	Bairiki	87/J 6	TP—78 FC; oth—73 FC
Korea, North	46,540	120,539	17,914,000	P'yŏngyang	80/D 3	TP—80 UN est; cap—76 OE; Hamhŭng—72 OE; oth—70 OE
Korea, South	38,175	98,873	37,448,836	Seoul	80/D 5	TP—80 PC; oth—75 FC & PC
*Kuwait	6,532	16,918	1,355,827	Al Kuwait	58/E 4	80 PC
*Laos	91,428	236,800	3,721,000	Vientiane	72/D 3	TP—80 UN est; cap—66 FC; oth—58 OE
Latvian S.S.R., U.S.S.R.	24,595	63,700	2,521,000	Riga	52/B 3; 53/......	TP, cit over 50,000—79 PC; oth—70 FC
*Lebanon	4,015	10,399	3,161,000	Beirut	62/F 6	TP—80 UN est; cap—70 FC; Tarabulus—64 OE; oth—61 OE
*Lesotho	11,720	30,355	1,339,000	Maseru	119/D 5	TP—80 OE; oth—80 est
*Liberia	43,000	111,370	1,873,000	Monrovia	106/C 7	TP—80 OE; oth—74 FC
*Libya	679,358	1,759,537	2,856,000	Tripoli	110/B 2	TP—79 OE; oth—73 FC & PC
Liechtenstein	61	158	25,220	Vaduz	39/J 2	80 PC
Lithuanian S.S.R., U.S.S.R.	25,174	65,200	3,398,000	Vilna	52/B 3; 53/......	TP, cit over 50,000—79 PC; oth—70 FC
Louisiana, U.S.A.	47,752	123,678	4,206,312	Baton Rouge	238/......*	80 FC & OE
*Luxembourg	999	2,587	364,000	Luxembourg	27/J 9	TP—79 OE; cap—74 OE; oth—70 FC
Macau	6	16	271,000	Macau	77/H 7	TP—78 OE; cap—70 FC
*Madagascar	226,657	587,041	8,742,000	Antananarivo	119/H 3	TP—80 UN est; prov, cap, cit over 40,000—75 PC; oth—71 OE
Madeira Islands, Portugal	307	796	262,800	Funchal	32/A 2	TP—77 OE; oth—70 FC & PC
Maine, U.S.A.	33,265	86,156	1,125,027	Augusta	243/......	80 FC & OE
*Malawi	45,747	118,485	5,968,000	Lilongwe	114/F 6	TP—80 OE; oth—77 PC
Malaya, Malaysia	50,806	131,588	11,138,227	Kuala Lumpur	72/D 6	TP, states, Kuala Lumpur—80 PC; cit over 100,000—70 FC; oth—70 PC
*Malaysia	128,308	332,318	13,435,588	Kuala Lumpur	72/D 6; 85/E 4	TP, states, Kuala Lumpur—80 PC; Kuching, Kota Kinabalu, cit over 100,000—70 FC; oth—70 PC
*Maldives	115	298	143,046	Male	54/L 9	78 FC
*Mali	464,873	1,204,021	6,906,000	Bamako	106/C 6	TP—80 OE; oth—76 FC
*Malta	122	316	343,970	Valletta	34/E 7	TP, cit—79 OE; oth—73 OE
Man, Isle of	227	588	64,000	Douglas	13/C 3	TP—80 OE; oth—71 FC
Manitoba, Canada	250,999	650,087	1,026,241	Winnipeg	179/......	81 FC
Marquesas Islands, French Polynesia	492	1,274	5,419	Atuona	87/N 6	77 FC
Marshall Islands	70	181	30,873	Majuro	87/G 4	80 FC
Martinique	425	1,101	328,566	Fort-de-France	161/D 5	82 FC
Maryland, U.S.A.	10,460	27,091	4,216,975	Annapolis	245/......	80 FC & OE
Massachusetts, U.S.A.	8,284	21,456	5,737,037	Boston	249/......	80 FC & OE
*Mauritania	419,229	1,085,803	1,634,000	Nouakchott	106/B 5	TP—80 UN est; oth—76 PC
*Mauritius	790	2,046	959,000	Port Louis	119/G 5	TP—80 OE; cap—77 OE; Curepipe, Quatre Bornes—74 OE; oth—72 PC
Mayotte	144	373	47,300	Dzaoudzi	119/G 2	TP—78 CE; cap—66 FC
*Mexico	761,601	1,972,546	67,395,826	Mexico City	150/......	TP, states, cap—80 PC; cap (ws), Guadalajara (ws), Monterrey (ws)—78 OE; oth—70 FC
Michigan, U.S.A.	58,527	151,585	9,262,078	Lansing	250/......	80 FC & OE
Micronesia, Federated States of	....	....	73,160	Kolonia	87/E 5	TP—80 FC
Midway Islands	1.9	4.9	453	....	87/J 3	80 FC
Minnesota, U.S.A.	84,402	218,601	4,075,970	St. Paul	255/......	80 FC & OE
Mississippi, U.S.A.	47,689	123,515	2,520,638	Jackson	256/......	80 FC & OE
Missouri, U.S.A.	69,697	180,515	4,916,759	Jefferson City	261/......	80 FC & OE
Moldavian S.S.R., U.S.S.R.	13,012	33,700	3,947,000	Kishinev	52/C 5	TP, cit over 50,000—79 PC; oth—70 FC
Monaco	368 acres	149 hectares	25,029	Monaco	28/G 6	75 FC
*Mongolia	606,163	1,569,962	1,594,800	Ulaanbaatar	77/E 2	TP—79 PC; prov, cap, Darhan—77 OE; oth—69 FC
Montana, U.S.A.	147,046	380,849	786,690	Helena	262/......	80 FC & OE
Montserrat	40	104	12,073	Plymouth	157/G 3	80 PC
*Morocco	172,414	446,550	20,242,000	Rabat	106/C 2	TP—80 OE; oth—71 FC
*Mozambique	303,769	786,762	12,130,000	Maputo	119/E 4	TP, prov, cap—80 PC; oth—70 FC
Namibia (South-West Africa)	317,827	823,172	1,200,000	Windhoek	118/B 3	TP—74 est; oth—70 PC
Natal, South Africa	33,578	86,967	5,722,215	Pietermaritzburg	119/E 5	TP—80 PC; oth—70 PC
Nauru	7.7	20	7,254	Yaren (district)	87/G 6	77 PC
Navassa Island	2	5	....	....	156/C 3	....
Nebraska, U.S.A.	77,355	200,349	1,569,825	Lincoln	264/......	80 FC & OE
*Nepal	54,663	141,577	14,179,301	Kathmandu	68/E 3	TP—81 PC; oth—71 FC
*Netherlands	15,892	41,160	14,227,000	The Hague; Amsterdam	27/F 5	TP—81 OE; oth—76 OE (com)

Gazetteer-Index of the World

Country	Area Square Miles	Square Kilometers	Population	Capital or Chief Town	Page and Index Ref.	Sources of Population Data
Netherlands Antilles	390	1,010	246,000	Willemstad	156/E 4	TP—78 OE; Willemsted—75 OE; oth—72 est.
Nevada, U.S.A.	110,561	286,353	800,493	Carson City	266/......	80 FC & OE
New Brunswick, Canada	28,354	73,437	696,403	Fredericton	170/......	81 FC
New Caledonia & Dependencies	7,335	18,998	133,233	Nouméa	87/G 8	76 FC
Newfoundland, Canada	156,184	404,517	567,681	St. John's	166/......	81 FC
New Hampshire, U.S.A.	9,279	24,033	920,610	Concord	268/......	80 FC & OE
New Hebrides, see Vanuatu						
New Jersey, U.S.A.	7,787	20,168	7,364,823	Trenton	273/......	80 FC & OE
New Mexico, U.S.A.	121,593	314,926	1,302,981	Santa Fe	274/......	80 FC & OE
New South Wales, Australia	309,498	801,600	5.126,217	Sydney	96/B 2	81 FC
New York, U.S.A.	49,108	127,190	17,558,072	Albany	276/......	80 FC & OE
*New Zealand	103,736	268,676	3,175,737	Wellington	100/......	TP, inc. places, isls.—81 FC; oth—76 FC
*Nicaragua	45,698	118,358	2,703,000	Managua	154/D 4	TP—80 OE; oth—71 PC
*Niger	489,189	1,267,000	5,098,427	Niamey	106/F 5	TP, cap, Maradi, Tahoua, Zinder—77 PC; oth—72 OE
*Nigeria	357,000	924,630	82,643,000	Lagos	106/F 6	TP—79 OE; prov—63 FC; oth—75 & 71 OE
Niue	100	259	3,578	Alofi	87/K 7	79 OE
Norfolk Island, Australia	13.4	34.6	2,175	Kingston	88/L 5	81 FC
North America	9,363,000	24,250,170	370,000,000	....	146/......	80 UN est
North Carolina, U.S.A.	52,669	136,413	5,881,813	Raleigh	281/......	80 FC & OE
North Dakota, U.S.A.	70,702	183,118	652,717	Bismarck	282/......	80 FC & OE
Northern Ireland, U.K.	5,452	14,121	1,543,000	Belfast	17/F 2	TP—81 OE; dist—76 OE; cap, Londonderry—73 OE; oth—71 FC
Northern Marianas	184	477	16,780	Capitol Hill	87/E 4	80 FC
Northern Territory, Australia	519,768	1,346,200	123,324	Darwin	93/......	81 FC
North Korea	46,540	120,539	17,914,000	P'yŏngyang	80/D 3	TP—80 UN est; cap—76 OE; Hamhŭng—72 OE; oth—70 OE
Northwest Territories, Canada	1,304,896	3,379,683	45,741	Yellowknife	187/G 3	81 FC
*Norway	125,053	323,887	4,092,000	Oslo	18/F 7	TP—80 OE; co, Svalbard—76 OE; oth—76 OE, 70 FC
Nova Scotia, Canada	21,425	55,491	847,442	Halifax	168/......	81 FC
Oceania	3,292,000	8,526,280	23,000,000	....	87/......	80 UN est
Ohio, U.S.A.	41,330	107,045	10,797,624	Columbus	284/......	80 FC & OE
Oklahoma, U.S.A.	69,956	181,186	3,025,290	Oklahoma City	288/......	80 FC & OE
*Oman	120,000	310,800	891,000	Muscat	58/G 6	TP—80 UN est; cap, Matrah—66 OE; Salala—68 OE
Ontario, Canada	412,580	1,068,582	8,625,107	Toronto	175, 177/......	81 FC
Orange Free State, South Africa	49,866	129,153	1,833,216	Bloemfontein	119/D 5	TP—80 PC; oth—70 FC
Oregon, U.S.A.	97,073	251,419	2,633,149	Salem	291/......	80 FC & OE
Orkney Islands, Scotland	376	974	17,675	Kirkwall	15/E 1	TP—76 OE; oth—71 FC
Pacific Islands, Territory of the	533	1,380	132,929	Saipan	87/F 5	80 FC
*Pakistan	310,403	803,944	83,782,000	Islamabad	68/B 3	TP—81 PC; Abbottabad, Bannu, cit over 50,000—72 PC; oth—61 FC
Palau (Belau)	188	487	12,116	Koror	86/D 5	80 FC
Palmyra Atoll	3.85	1			87/K 5	....
*Panama	29,761	77,082	1,830,175	Panamá	154/G 6	TP, cit over 1,600—80 PC; oth—70 FC
*Papua New Guinea	183,540	475,369	3,010,727	**Port Moresby**	85/B 7; 87/E 6	80 PC
Paracel Islands	....	....	....		85/E 2	
*Paraguay	157,047	406,752	2,973,000	Asunción	144/......	TP—79 OE; oth—72 PC
Pennsylvania, U.S.A.	45,308	117,348	11,863,895	Harrisburg	294/......	80 FC & OE
Persia, see Iran						
*Peru	496,222	1,285,215	17,031,221	Lima	128/......	81 PC
*Philippines	115,707	299,681	48,098,460	Manila	82/......	80 FC
Pitcairn Islands	18	47	54	Adamstown	87/O 8	81 FC
*Poland	120,725	312,678	35,815,000	Warsaw	47/......	TP—81 OE; prov, cap, Cracow, Łódź—75 OE; oth—70 FC
*Portugal	35,549	92,072	9,933,000	Lisbon	32/B 3	TP—80 OE; cap (ws)—76 OE; oth—70 FC & PC
Prince Edward Island, Canada	2,184	5,657	122,506	Charlottetown	168/E 2	81 FC
Puerto Rico	3,515	9,104	3,196,520	San Juan	161/......	80 FC
*Qatar	4,247	11,000	220,000	Doha	58/F 4	TP—80 UN est; cap—79 OE
Québec, Canada	594,857	1,540,680	6,438,403	Québec	172, 174/......	81 FC
Queensland, Australia	666,872	1,727,200	2,295,123	Brisbane	95/......	81 FC
Réunion	969	2,510	491,000	St-Denis	119/F 5	TP—80 OE; oth—74 FC
Rhode Island, U.S.A.	1,212	3,139	947,154	Providence	249/H 5	80 FC & OE
Rhodesia, see Zimbabwe						
*Romania	91,699	237,500	22,048,305	Bucharest	45/F 3	79 OE
Russian S.F.S.R., U.S.S.R.	6,592,812	17,075,400	137,551,000	Moscow	48/D 4	TP, cit over 50,000—79 PC; oth—70 FC
*Rwanda	10,169	26,337	4,819,317	Kigali	114/E 4	78 PC
Sabah, Malaysia	29,300	75,887	1,002,608	Kota Kinabalu	85/F 4	TP—80 PC; Kota Kinabalu—70 FC; oth—70 PC
*Saint Christopher and Nevis	104	269	44,404	**Basseterre**	156/F 3; 161/C11	TP, isl, cap—80 PC; oth—70 FC
Saint Helena & Dependencies	162	420	5,147	Jamestown	102/B 6	76 FC
*Saint Lucia	238	616	115,783	Castries	161/G 6	80 PC
Saint Pierre & Miquelon	93.5	242	6,034	Saint-Pierre	166/C 4	82 FC
*Saint Vincent & the Grenadines	150	388	124,000	Kingstown	161/A 8; 157/G 4	TP—80 OE; oth—70 FC
Sakhalin, U.S.S.R.	29,500	76,405	655,000	Yuzhno-Sakhalinsk	48/P 4	TP, cit over 50,000—79 PC; oth—70 FC
*Salvador, El	8,260	21,393	4,813,000	San Salvador	154/C 4	TP—80 OE; oth—71 FC
San Marino	23.4	60.6	19,149	San Marino	34/D 3	TP—76 FC; oth—77 OE
*São Tomé e Príncipe	372	963	85,000	São Tomé	106/F 8	TP—80 UN est; oth—70 PC
Sarawak, Malaysia	48,202	124,843	1,294,753	Kuching	85/E 5	TP—80 PC; Kuching—70 FC; oth—70 PC
Sardinia, Italy	9,301	24,090	1,450,483	Cagliari	34/B 4	71 FC
Saskatchewan, Canada	251,699	651,900	968,313	Regina	181/......	81 FC
*Saudi Arabia	829,995	2,149,687	8,367,000	Riyadh	58/D 4	TP—80 UN est; oth—74 PC
Scotland, U.K.	30,414	78,772	5,117,146	Edinburgh	15/......	TP—81 PC; reg—75 OE; cit—75 & 73 OE, 71 FC; oth—71 FC
*Senegal	75,954	196,720	5,508,000	Dakar	106/A 5	TP—79 OE; oth—76 PC
*Seychelles	145	375	63,000	Victoria	119/H 5	TP—79 OE; oth—77 FC
Shetland Islands, Scotland	552	1,430	18,494	Lerwick	15/G 2	TP—76 OE; oth—73 OE & 71 FC
Siam, see Thailand						
Sicily, Italy	9,926	25,708	4,628,918	Palermo	34/D 6	71 FC
*Sierra Leone	27,925	72,325	3,470,000	Freetown	106/B 7	TP—80 UN est; cap, Bo, Kenema, Makeni—74 PC; oth—63 FC
*Singapore	226	585	2,413,945	Singapore	72/F 6	80 FC
Society Islands, French Polynesia	677	1,753	117,703	Papeete	87/L 7	77 FC
*Solomon Islands	11,500	29,785	221,000	**Honiara**	87/G 6; 86/......	TP—79 OE; oth—76 FC
*Somalia	246,200	637,658	3,645,000	Mogadishu	115/H 3	TP—80 UN est; prov, cap—75 PC; oth—69, 68, 67, 63 & 62 OE

Gazetteer-Index of the World

Country	Area Square Miles	Area Square Kilometers	Population	Capital or Chief Town	Page and Index Ref.	Sources of Population Data
*South Africa	455,318	1,179,274	23,771,970	Cape Town; Pretoria	118/C 5	TP (excl Transkei, Bophuthatswana, Venda), prov—80 PC; Transkei, Bophuthatswana—78 est; Venda—79 est; oth—70 FC
South America	6,875,000	17,806,250	245,000,000	....	120/......	80 UN est
South Australia, Australia	379,922	984,000	1,285,033	Adelaide	94/......	81 FC
South Carolina, U.S.A.	31,113	80,583	3,121,833	Columbia	296/......	80 FC & OE
South Dakota, U.S.A.	77,116	199,730	690,768	Pierre	298/......	80 FC & OE
South Korea	38,175	98,873	37,448,836	Seoul	80/D 5	TP—80 PC; oth—75 FC & PC
South-West Africa (Namibia)	317,827	823,172	1,200,000	Windhoek	118/B 3	TP—74 est; oth—70 PC
*Spain	194,881	504,742	37,430,000	Madrid	33/......	TP—80 OE; met areas—75 OE; oth—70 FC
Spratly Island	....	....			85/E 4	
*Sri Lanka	25,332	65,610	14,850,001	Colombo	68/E 7	TP—81 PC; cap, Jaffna—73 OE; oth—71 FC
*Sudan	967,494	2,505,809	18,691,000	Khartoum	110/E 4	TP—80 OE; cap, prov, prov cap—73 PC; oth—73 PC, 72 OE
Sumatra, Indonesia	164,000	424,760	19,360,400	Medan	84/B 5	71 PC
*Suriname	55,144	142,823	354,860	Paramaribo	131/C 3	TP, cap—80 PC; dist—71 PC; oth—64 FC
Svalbard, Norway	23,957	62,049	3,431	Longyearbyen	18/C 2	76 OE
*Swaziland	6,705	17,366	547,000	Mbabane	119/E 5	TP—80 OE; oth—76 FC
*Sweden	173,665	449,792	8,320,000	Stockholm	18/J 8	TP—81 OE; oth—75 FC
Switzerland	15,943	41,292	6,365,960	Bern	39/......	TP—80 FC; cantons—78 OE; cap, cit over 100,000 (& ws)—74 OE; cit (com) over 30,000 (& ws)—73 OE; oth—70 FC
*Syria	71,498	185,180	8,979,000	Damascus	62/G 5	TP—80 OE; oth—70 FC
Tadzhik S.S.R., U.S.S.R.	55,251	143,100	3,801,000	Dushanbe	48/G 6	TP, cit over 50,000—79 PC; oth—70 FC
Tahiti, French Polynesia	402	1,041	95,604	Papeete	87/L 7	77 FC
Taiwan	13,971	36,185	16,609,961	Taipei	77/K 7	TP, cap, Penghu Isl., cit over 300,000—77 OE; oth—70 OE
*Tanzania	363,708	942,003	17,527,560	Dar es Salaam	114/F 5	TP—78 PC; div, cap, cit over 17,000—78 PC; oth—67 FC
Tasmania, Australia	26,178	67,800	418,957	Hobart	99/......	81 FC
Tennessee, U.S.A.	42,144	109,153	4,591,120	Nashville	237/......	80 FC & OE
Texas, U.S.A.	266,807	691,030	14,229,288	Austin	303/......	80 FC & OE
*Thailand	198,455	513,998	46,455,000	Bangkok	72/D 3	TP—80 OE; oth—70 FC
Tibet, China	463,320	1,200,000	1,790,000	Lhasa	76/C 5	TP—78 OE; oth—70 est
*Togo	21,622	56,000	2,472,000	Lomé	106/E 7	TP—79 OE; oth—70 FC
Tokelau	3.9	10	1,575	Fakaofo	87/J 6	TP—76 FC; oth—72 FC
Tonga	270	699	90,128	Nuku'alofa	87/J 8	76 PC
Transkei (rep.), South Africa	16,910	43,797	2,000,000	Umtata	119/D 6	TP—80 est; oth—70 FC
Transvaal, South Africa	109,621	283,918	10,673,033	Pretoria	119/D 4	TP—80 PC; oth—70 FC
*Trinidad and Tobago	1,980	5,128	1,067,108	Port-of-Spain	157/G 5; 161/A10	80 PC
Tristan da Cunha, St. Helena	38	98	251	Edinburgh	2/J 7	79 OE
Tuamotu Archipelago, French Polynesia	341	883	9,052	Apataki	87/M 7	77 FC
*Tunisia	63,378	164,149	6,367,000	Tunis	106/F 1	TP—79 OE; oth—75 FC
*Turkey	300,946	779,450	45,217,556	Ankara	62/D 3	TP—80 PC; oth—75 FC
Turkmen S.S.R., U.S.S.R.	188,455	488,100	2,759,000	Ashkhabad	48/F 6	TP, cit over 50,000—79 PC; oth—70 FC
Turks and Caicos Islands	166	430	7,436	Cockburn Town, Grand Turk	156/D 2	80 PC
Tuvalu	9.78	25.33	7,349	Fongafale, Funafuti	87/H 6	79 FC
*Uganda	91,076	235,887	12,630,076	Kampala	114/F 3	TP, cap—80 PC; oth—69 FC
*Ukrainian S.S.R., U.S.S.R.	233,089	603,700	49,755,000	Kiev	52/D 5	TP, cit over 50,000—79 PC; oth—70 FC
*Union of Soviet Socialist Republics	8,649,490	22,402,179	262,436,227	Moscow	48/......	TP, S.S.R., cit over 50,000—79 PC; oth—70 FC
*United Arab Emirates	32,278	83,600	1,040,275	Abu Dhabi	58/F 5	TP—80 PC; oth—79 OE
*United Kingdom	94,399	244,493	55,672,000	London	10/......	TP—81 OE (see England, Wales, Scotland, Northern Ireland)
*United States of America	3,623,420	9,384,658	226,504,825	Washington	188/......	80 FC & OE
*Upper Volta (Burkina Faso)	105,869	274,200	6,908,000	Ouagadougou	106/D 6	TP—80 UN est; oth—75 FC, 73 OE
*Uruguay	72,172	186,925	2,899,000	Montevideo	145/......	TP—80 OE; oth—75 PC
Utah, U.S.A.	84,899	219,888	1,461,037	Salt Lake City	304/......	80 FC & OE
Uzbek S.S.R., U.S.S.R.	173,591	449,600	15,391,000	Tashkent	48/G 5	TP, cit over 50,000—79 PC; oth—70 FC
*Vanuatu	5,700	14,763	112,596	Vila	87/G 7	79 FC
Vatican City	108.7 acres	44 hectares	728	....	34/B 6	78 OE
Venda (rep.), South Africa	2,510	6,501	450,000	Thohoyandou	119/E 4	79 est
*Venezuela	352,143	912,050	14,313,000	Caracas	124/......	TP—81 OE; oth—71 FC
Vermont U.S.A.	9,614	24,900	511,456	Montpelier	268/......	80 FC & OE
Victoria, Australia	87,876	227,600	3,832,443	Melbourne	96/B 5	81 FC
*Vietnam	128,405	332,569	52,741,766	Hanoi	72/E 3	TP—79 FC; cap, Haiphong, Ho Chi Minh City—79 PC; oth cit over 100,000 (north)—70 est, (south)—73 & 71 OE; oth—69 OE, 60 FC
Virginia, U.S.A.	40,767	105,587	5,346,818	Richmond	307/......	80 FC & OE
Virgin Islands, British	59	153	11,006	Road Town	157/H 1	TP—80 FC; oth—70 FC
Virgin Islands, U.S.A.	132	342	96,569	Charlotte Amalie	161/A 4	80 FC
Wake Island	2.5	6.5	302	Wake Islet	87/G 4	80 FC
Wales, U.K.	8,017	20,764	2,790,462	Cardiff	13/D 5	TP—81 PC; co—76 OE; cit—76 & 73 OE; par—71 FC
Wallis and Futuna	106	275	9,192	Mata Utu	87/J 7	76 FC
Washington, U.S.A.	68,139	176,480	4,132,180	Olympia	310/......	80 FC & OE
West Bank	2,100	5,439	c. 800,000	....	65/C 3	TP—81 est; oth—67 CE & 61 FC
Western Australia, Australia	975,096	2,525,500	1,273,624	Perth	92/......	81 FC
Western Sahara	102,703	266,000	76,425	....	106/B 3	70 FC
*Western Samoa	1,133	2,934	158,130	Apia	87/J 7	81 PC
*West Germany (Federal Republic)	95,985	248,601	61,658,000	Bonn	22/......	TP—80 OE; states, cap—76 OE; oth—76 OE, 70 FC
West Virginia, U.S.A.	24,231	62,758	1,950,279	Charleston	312/......	80 FC & OE
*White Russian S.S.R. (Byelo-russian S.S.R.), U.S.S.R.	80,154	207,600	9,560,000	Minsk	52/C 4	TP, cit over 50,000—79 PC; oth—70 FC
Wisconsin, U.S.A.	56,153	145,436	4,705,521	Madison	317/......	80 FC & OE
World	(land) 57,970,000	150,142,300	4,415,000,000	....	1, 2/......	80 UN est
Wyoming, U.S.A.	97,809	253,325	469,557	Cheyenne	319/......	80 FC & OE
*Yemen, People's Democratic Republic of	111,101	287,752	1,969,000	Aden	58/E 7	TP—81 PC; oth—75 FC
*Yemen Arab Republic	77,220	200,000	6,456,189	San a	58/D 6	TP—80 OE; Mukalla, Seiyun—76 OE; cap—73 OE; Saihut—60 OE
*Yugoslavia	98,766	255,804	22,471,000	Belgrade	45/C 3	TP—81 OE; oth—71 FC
Yukon Territory, Canada	207,075	536,324	23,153	Whitehorse	186/E 3	81 FC
*Zaire	905,063	2,344,113	28,291,000	Kinshasa	114/D 4	TP—80 OE; prov, cap—70 FC; oth—70 FC & PC
*Zambia	290,586	752,618	5,679,808	Lusaka	114/E 7	80 PC
*Zimbabwe	150,803	390,580	7,360,000	Harare	119/D 3	TP—80 OE; cap, cit over 12,000—77 OE; oth—69 FC

Glossary of Abbreviations

A

A. A. F. — Army Air Field
Acad. — Academy
A. C. T. — Australian Capital Territory
adm. — administration; administrative
A. F. B. — Air Force Base
Afgh., Afghan. — Afghanistan
Afr. — Africa
Ala. — Alabama
Alb. — Albania
Alg. — Algeria
Alta. — Alberta
Amer. — American
Amer. Samoa — American Samoa
And. — Andorra
Ant., Antarc. — Antarctica
Ant. & Bar. — Antigua and Barbuda
Ar. — Arabia
arch. — archipelago
Arg. — Argentina
Ariz. — Arizona
Ark. — Arkansas
A. S. S. R. — Autonomous Soviet
    Socialist Republic
Aust. — Austria
Aust. Cap. Terr. — Australian Capital
    Territory
Austr., Austral. — Australian, Australia
aut. — autonomous
Aut. Obl. — Autonomous Oblast

B

B. — bay
Bah. — Bahamas
Barb. — Barbados
Battlef. — Battlefield
Bch. — Beach
Belg. — Belgium
Berm. — Bermuda
Bol. — Bolivia
Bots. — Botswana
Br. — Branch
Br. — British
Braz. — Brazil
Br. Col. — British Columbia
Br. Ind. Oc. Terr. — British Indian
    Ocean Territory
Bulg. — Bulgaria

C

C. — cape
Calif. — California
Can. — Canada
can. — canal
cap. — capital
Cent. Afr. Rep. — Central African
    Republic
Cent. Amer. — Central America
C. G. Sta. — Coast Guard Station
C. H. — Court House
chan. — channel
Chan. Is. — Channel Islands
Chem. Ctr. — Chemical Center
co. — county
C. of G. H. — Cape of Good Hope
Col. — Colombia
Colo. — Colorado
comm. — commissary
Conn. — Connecticut
cont. — continent
cord. — cordillera (mountain range)
C. Rica — Costa Rica
C. S. — County Seat
C. Verde — Cape Verde
Czech. — Czechoslovakia

D

D. C. — District of Columbia
Del. — Delaware
Dem. — Democratic
Den. — Denmark
depr. — depression
dept. — department
des. — desert
dist., dist's — district, districts
div. — division
Dom. Rep. — Dominican Republic

E

E. — East
Ec., Ecua. — Ecuador
E. Ger. — East Germany
elec. div. — electoral division
El Salv. — El Salvador
Eng. — England
Equat. Guinea, Eq. Guin — Equatorial
    Guinea

escarp. — escarpment
est. — estuary
Eth. — Ethiopia

F

Falk. Is. — Falkland Islands
Fin. — Finland
Fk., Fks. — Fork, Forks
Fla. — Florida
for. — forest
Fr. — France, French
Fr. Gui. — French Guiana
Fr. Poly. — French Polynesia
Ft. — Fort

G

G. — gulf
Ga. — Georgia
Game Res. — Game Reserve
Ger. — Germany
geys. — geyser
Gibr. — Gibraltar
glac. — glacier
gov. — governorate
Gr. — Group
Greenl. — Greenland
Gren. — Grenada
Gt. Brit. — Great Britain
Guad. — Guadeloupe
Guat. — Guatemala
Guinea-Biss. — Guinea-Bissau
Guy. — Guyana

H

har., harb., hbr. — harbor
hd. — head
highl. — highland, highlands
Hist. — Historic, Historical
Hond. — Honduras
Hts. — Heights
Hung. — Hungary

I

i., isl. — island, isle
I. C. — independent city
Ice., Icel. — Iceland
Ida. — Idaho
Ill. — Illinois
Ind. — Indiana
ind. city — independent city
Indon. — Indonesia
Ind. Res. — Indian Reservation
int. div. — internal division
inten. — intendency
Int'l — International
Ire. — Ireland
is., isls. — islands
Isr. — Israel
isth. — isthmus
Iv. Coast — Ivory Coast

J

Jam. — Jamaica
Jct. — Junction

K

Kans. — Kansas
Ky. — Kentucky

L

L. — Lake, Loch, Lough
La. — Louisiana
Lab. — Laboratory
lag. — lagoon
Ld. — Land
Leb. — Lebanon
Les. — Lesotho
Liecht. — Liechtenstein
Lux. — Luxembourg

M

Mad., Madag. — Madagascar
Man. — Manitoba
Mart. — Martinique
Mass. — Massachusetts
Maur. — Mauritania
Md. — Maryland
met. area — metropolitan area
Mex. — Mexico
Mich. — Michigan
Minn. — Minnesota
Miss. — Mississippi
Mo. — Missouri
Mon. — Monument
Mong. — Mongolia
Mont. — Montana
Mor. — Morocco

Moz., Mozamb. — Mozambique
mt. — mount
mtn. — mountain

N

N., No., North. — North, Northern
N. Amer. — North America
Nam., Namib. — Namibia
N. A. S. — Naval Air Station
Nat'l — National
Nat'l Cem. — National Cemetery
Nat'l Mem. Park — National Memorial
    Park
Nat'l Mil. Park — National Military
    Park
Nat'l Pkwy. — National Parkway
Nav. Base — Naval Ease
Nav. Sta. — Naval Station
N. B., N. Br. — New Brunswick
N. C. — North Carolina
N. Dak. — North Dakota
Nebr. — Nebraska
Neth. — Netherlands
Neth. Ant. — Netherlands Antilles
Nev. — Nevada
New Bruns. — New Brunswick
New Cal., New Caled. — New Caledonia
Newf. — Newfoundland
New Hebr. — New Hebrides
N. H. — New Hampshire
Nic. — Nicaragua
N. Ire. — Northern Ireland
N. J. — New Jersey
N. Mex. — New Mexico
Nor. — Norway, Norwegian
North. — Northern
North. Terr., No. Terr. — Northern
    Territory
    (Australia)
N. S. — Nova Scotia
N. S. W., N.S. Wales — New South Wales
N. W. T., N. W. Terrs. — Northwest
    Territories
    (Canada)
N. Y. — New York
N. Z., N. Zealand — New Zealand

O

Obl. — Oblast
O. F. S. — Orange Free State
Okla. — Oklahoma
Okr. — Okrug
Ont. — Ontario
Ord. Depot — Ordnance Depot
Oreg. — Oregon

P

Pa. — Pennsylvania
Pac. Is. — Pacific Islands,
    Territory of the
Pak. — Pakistan
Pan. — Panama
Papua N. G. —Papua New Guinea
Par. — Paraguay
par. — parish
passg. — passage
P.D.R. Yemen — People's Democratic
    Republic of Yemen
P. E. I. — Prince Edward Island
pen. — peninsula
Phil., Phil. Is. — Philippines
Pk. — Park
pk. — peak
plat. — plateau
P. N. G. — Papua New Guinea
Pol. — Poland
Port. — Portugal, Portuguese
Pr. Edward I. — Prince Edward Island
pref. — prefecture
P. Rico — Puerto Rico
prom. — promontory
prov. — province, provincial
pt. — point

Q

Que. — Québec
Queens. — Queensland

R

R. — River
ra. — range
Rec., Recr. — Recreation, Recreational
reg. — region
Rep. — Republic
res. — reservoir
Res. — Reservation, Reserve
R. I. — Rhode Island

riv. — river
Rom. — Romania

S

S. — South
Sa. — Sierra, Serra
S. Afr., S. Africa — South Africa
salt dep. — salt deposit
salt des. — salt desert
S. Amer. — South America
São T. & Pr. — São Tomé
    and Príncipe
Sask. — Saskatchewan
Saudi Ar. — Saudi Arabia
S. Aust., S. Austral. — South Australia
S. C. — South Carolina
Scot. — Scotland
Sd. — Sound
S. Dak. — South Dakota
Sen. — Senegal
sen. dist. — senatorial district
Seych. — Seychelles
S. F. S. R. — Soviet Federated Socialist
    Republic
Sing. — Singapore
S. Leone — Sierra Leone
S. Marino — San Marino
Sol. Is. — Solomon Islands
Sp. — Spanish
Spr., Sprs. — Spring, Springs
S. S. R. — Soviet Socialist Republic
St., Ste. — Saint, Sainte
Sta. — Station
St. Chris.-Nevis — Saint Christopher-
    Nevis
St. P. & M. — Saint Pierre and
    Miquelon
St. Vin. & Grens. — St. Vincent & The
    Grenadines
str., strs. — strait, straits
Sur. — Suriname
S. W. Afr. — South-West Africa
Swaz. — Swaziland
Switz. — Switzerland

T

Tanz. — Tanzania
Tas. — Tasmania
Tenn. — Tennessee
terr., terrs. — territory, territories
Tex. — Texas
Thai. — Thailand
trad. — traditional
Trin. & Tob. — Trinidad and Tobago
Tun. — Tunisia
twp. — township

U

U. A. E. — United
    Arab Emirates
U. K. — United Kingdom
Upp. Volta — Upper Volta
urb. area — urban area
Urug. — Uruguay
U. S. — United States
U. S. S. R. — Union of Soviet Socialist
    Republics

V

Va. — Virginia
Ven., Venez. — Venezuela
V. I. (Br.) — Virgin Islands (British)
V. I. (U. S.) — Virgin Islands (U. S.)
Vic. — Victoria
Viet. — Vietnam
Vill. — Village
vol. — volcano
Vt. — Vermont

W

W. — West, Western
Wash. — Washington
W. Aust., W. Austral. — Western
    Australia
W. Ger. — West Germany
W. Indies — West Indies
Wis. — Wisconsin
W. Samoa — Western Samoa
W. Va. — West Virginia
Wyo. — Wyoming

Y

Yugo. — Yugoslavia
Yukon — Yukon Territory

Z

Zim. — Zimbabwe

Index to Terrain Maps

on pages X through XXXII

This index contains only names of land and ocean physical features. Names of towns, internal divisions and countries are not included. The entry name is followed by a letter-number combination which refers to the area on the map in which the name will be found. The number following the map reference for the entry refers, not to the page on which the entry will be found, but to the map plate number.

Index continued

HAMMOND®
THE PHYSICAL WORLD
Terrain Maps of Land Forms and Ocean Floors

CONTENTS

RELIEF MODELS BY ERNST G. HOFMANN, ASSISTED BY RAFAEL MARTINEZ

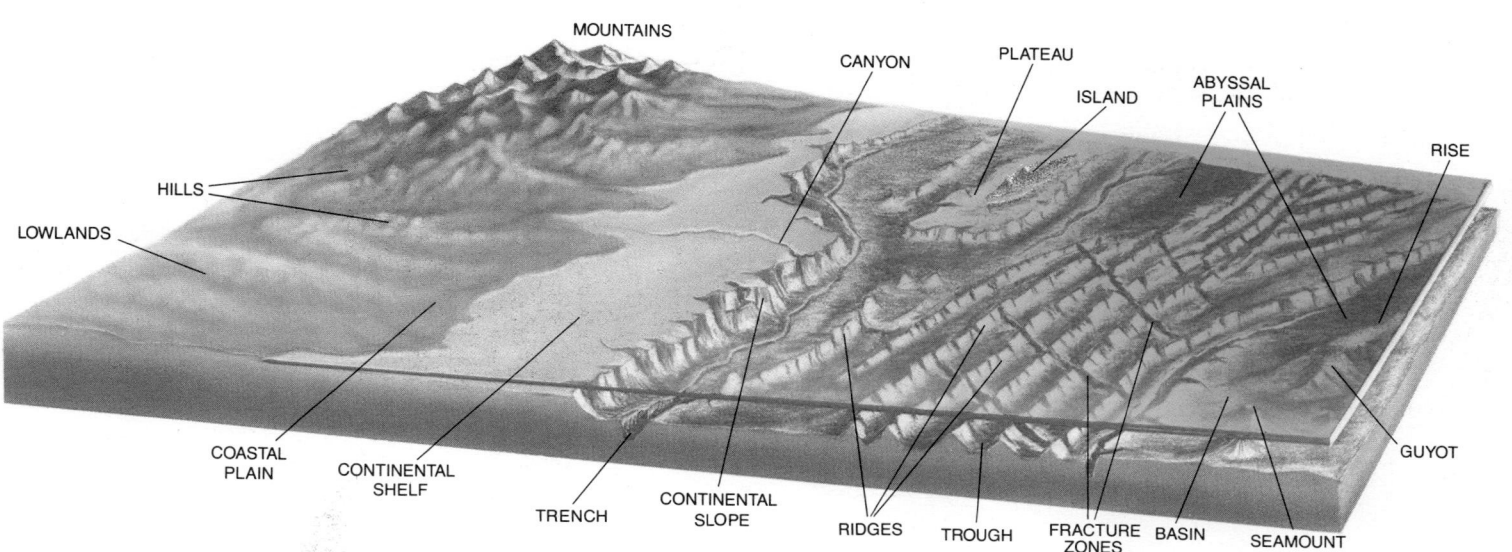

The oblique view diagram above is designed to provide a detailed view of the ocean floor as if seen through the depth of the sea. Graduating blue tones are used to contrast ocean floor depths: from light blue to represent shallow continental shelves to dark blues in the greater depths. Land relief is shown in conventional hypsometric tints.

In this dramatic collection of topographic maps of continents, oceans and major regions of the world, Hammond introduces a revolutionary new technique in cartography.

While most maps depicting terrain are created from painted artwork that is then photographed, Hammond now premiers the use of a remarkable sculptured model mapping technique created by one of our master cartographers.

The process begins with the sculpting of large scale three-dimensional models. Once physical details have been etched on the models and refinements completed, relief work is checked for accurate elevation based on a vertical scale exaggerated for visual effect.

Finished models are airbrushed and painted, then photographed using a single northwesterly light source to achieve a striking three-dimensional effect. The result is the dynamic presentation of mountain ranges and peaks on land, and canyons, trenches and seamounts on the ocean floor. Never before have maps conveyed such rich beauty while providing a realistic representation of the world as we know it.

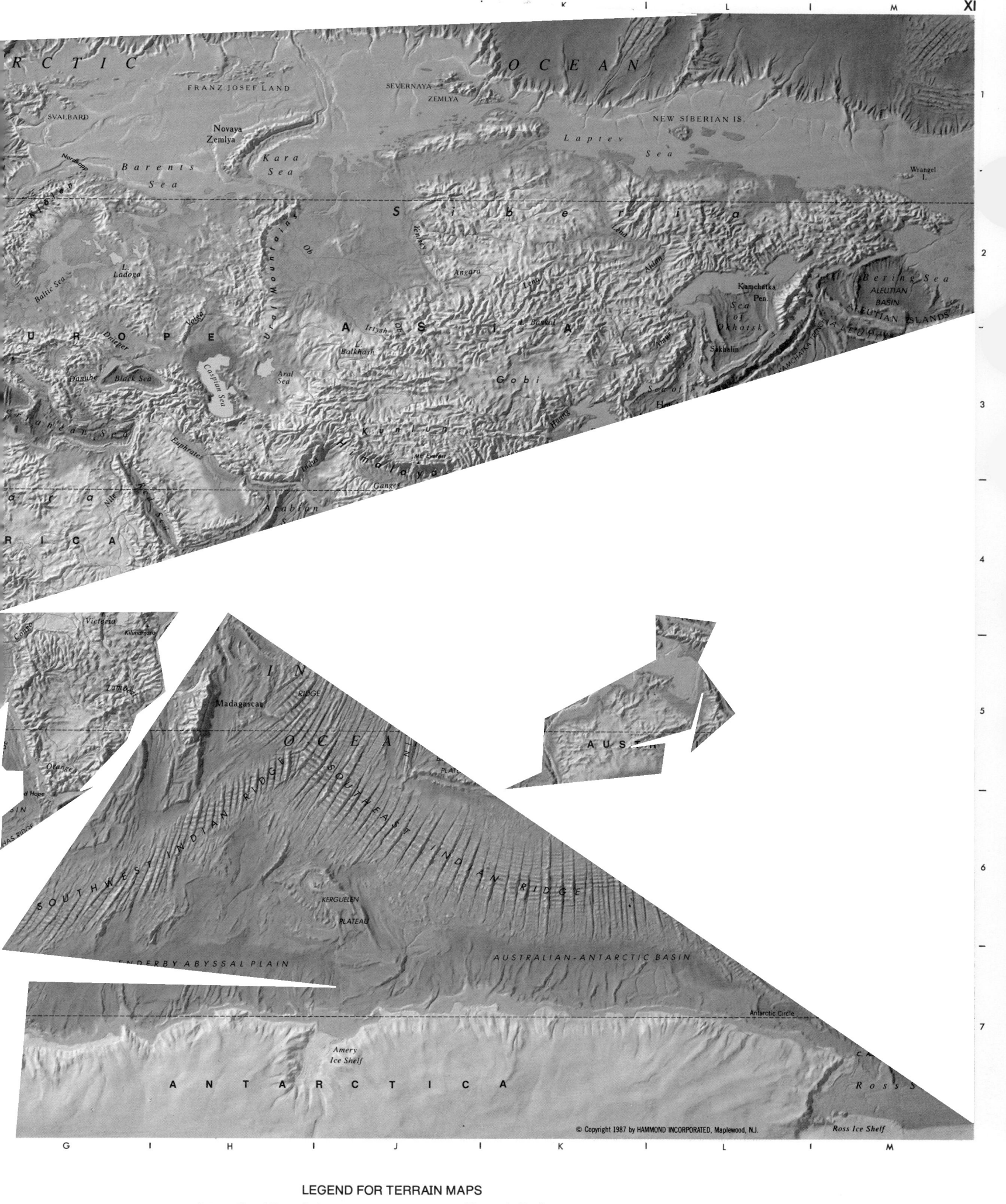

A R C T I C O C E A N

FRANZ JOSEF LAND
SEVERNAYA
ZEMLYA
NEW SIBERIAN IS.
SVALBARD
Novaya
Zemlya
Kara
Sea
Laptev
Sea
Nordkapp
Barents
Sea
Wrangel
I.
Kjølen
S i b e r i a
Ob
Yenisei
Lena
L. Ladoga
Aldan
Baltic Sea
Angara
Kamchatka
Pen.
Bering Sea
ALEUTIAN
BASIN
E U R O P E
Ural Mountains
A S I A
Sea
of
Okhotsk
ALEUTIAN ISLANDS
KAMCHATKA PEN.
Volga
Irtysh
Ob
Lena
Baykal
Danube
Black Sea
Balkhash
Sakhalin
Dnieper
Caspian Sea
Aral
Sea
Gobi
Sea
of
Japan
A F R I C A
Euphrates
Kunlun
Huang
Nile
Himalaya
Mt. Everest
Tibet
Indus
Arabian
Sea
Ganges

Congo
Victoria
Kilimanjaro
Zambezi
I N D I A N
Madagascar
RIDGE
O C E A N
A U S T R A L I A
PLATEAU
Orange
SOUTHEAST INDIAN RIDGE
Good Hope
SOUTHWEST INDIAN RIDGE
ATLAS RIDGE
KERGUELEN
PLATEAU
ENDERBY ABYSSAL PLAIN
AUSTRALIAN-ANTARCTIC BASIN
Antarctic Circle
Amery
Ice Shelf
A N T A R C T I C A
Ross S
CA
© Copyright 1987 by HAMMOND INCORPORATED, Maplewood, N.J.
Ross Ice Shelf

LEGEND FOR TERRAIN MAPS

International Boundaries   —··—   Mountain Peaks   ▲
State and Provincial Boundaries   —·—·   National Capitals   ⊛
Other Boundaries   — — — —   Other Capitals   ◉
Canals   ——⊢——

WORLD | Plate 1

Plate 2 | EUROPE

© Copyright 1987 by HAMMOND INCORPORATED, Maplewood, N.J.

| 0 | 100 | 200 | 300 | 400 | 500 MILES |
| 0 | 100 | 200 | 300 | 400 | 500 KILOMETERS |

WESTERN EUROPE | Plate 3

0 100 200 300 400 500 MILES
0 100 200 300 400 500 KILOMETERS

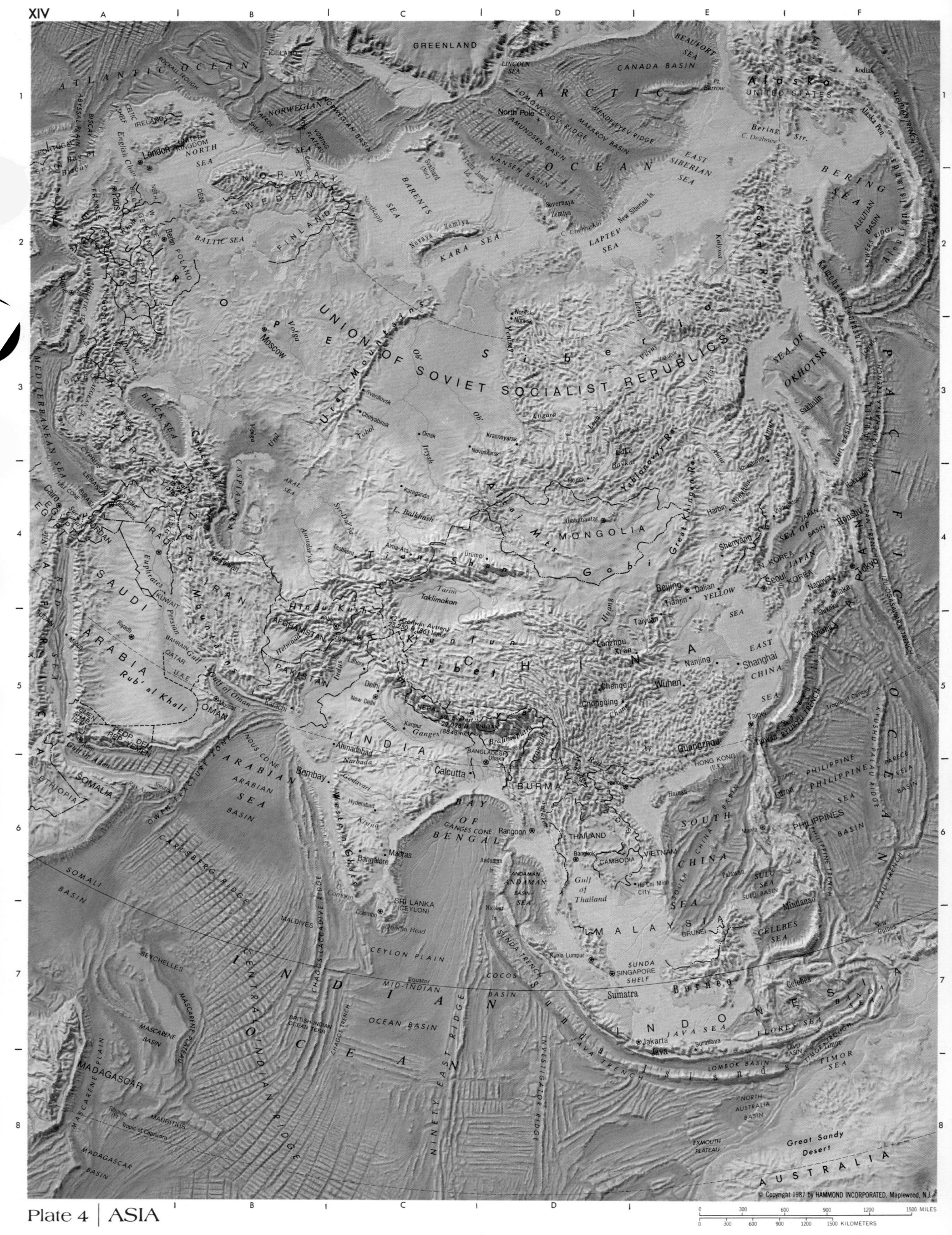

Plate 4 | ASIA

0	300	600	900	1200	1500 MILES

0	300	600	900	1200	1500 KILOMETERS

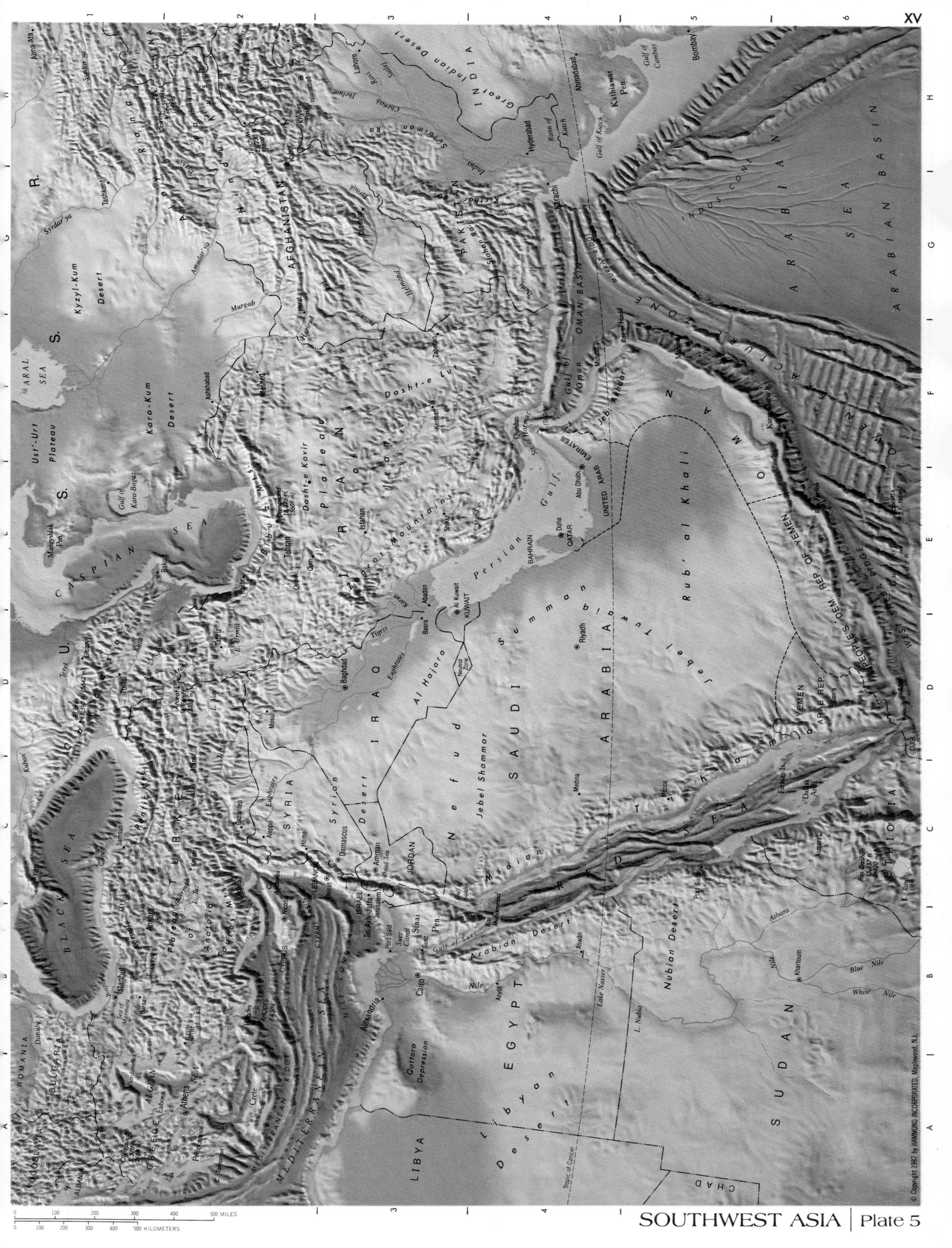

SOUTHWEST ASIA | Plate 5

© Copyright 1982 by HAMMOND INCORPORATED, Maplewood, N.J.

0   100   200   300   400   500 MILES
0   100   200   300   400   500 KILOMETERS

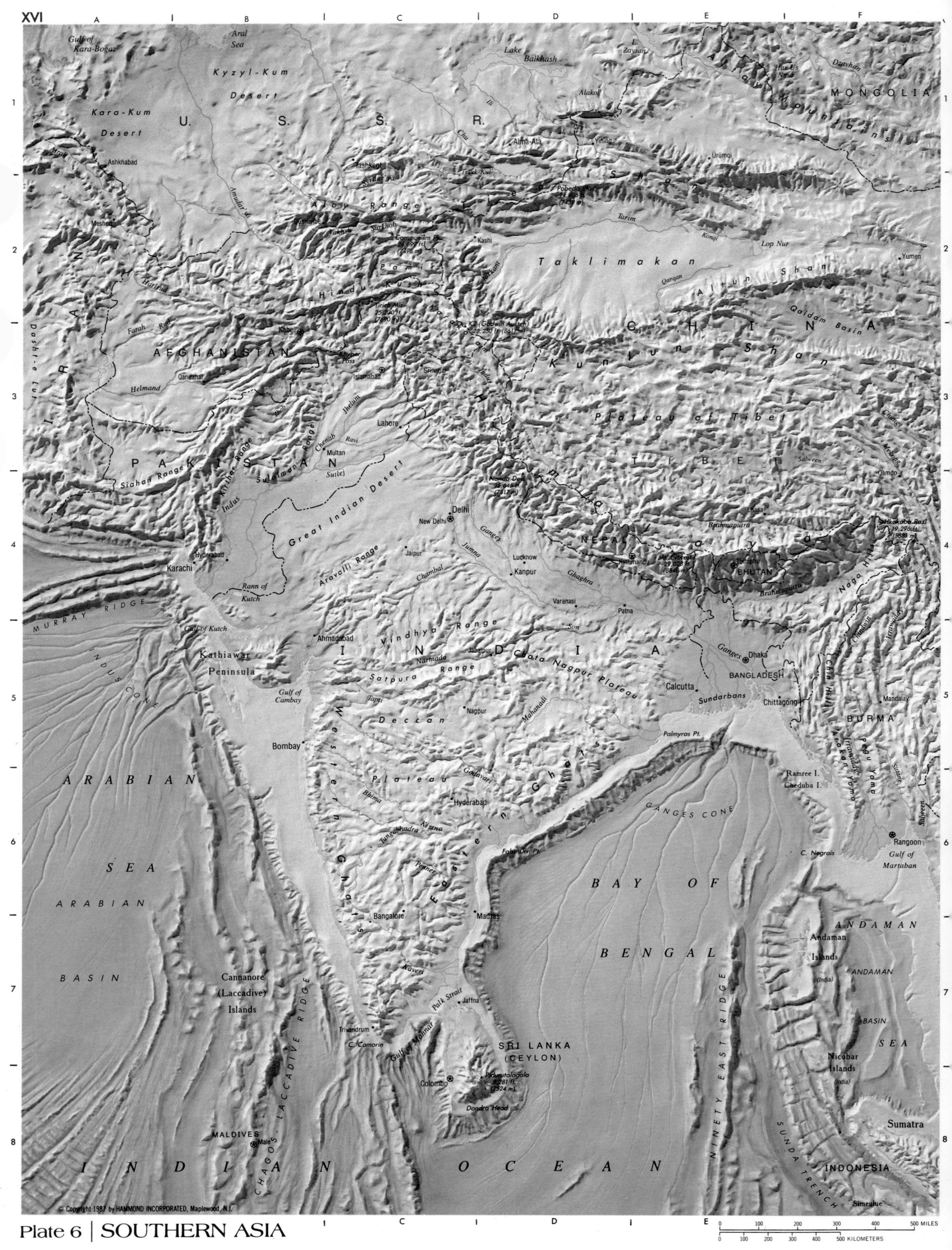

Plate 6 | SOUTHERN ASIA

© Copyright 1987 by HAMMOND INCORPORATED, Maplewood, N.J.

| 0 | 100 | 200 | 300 | 400 | 500 MILES |

| 0 | 100 | 200 | 300 | 400 | 500 KILOMETERS |

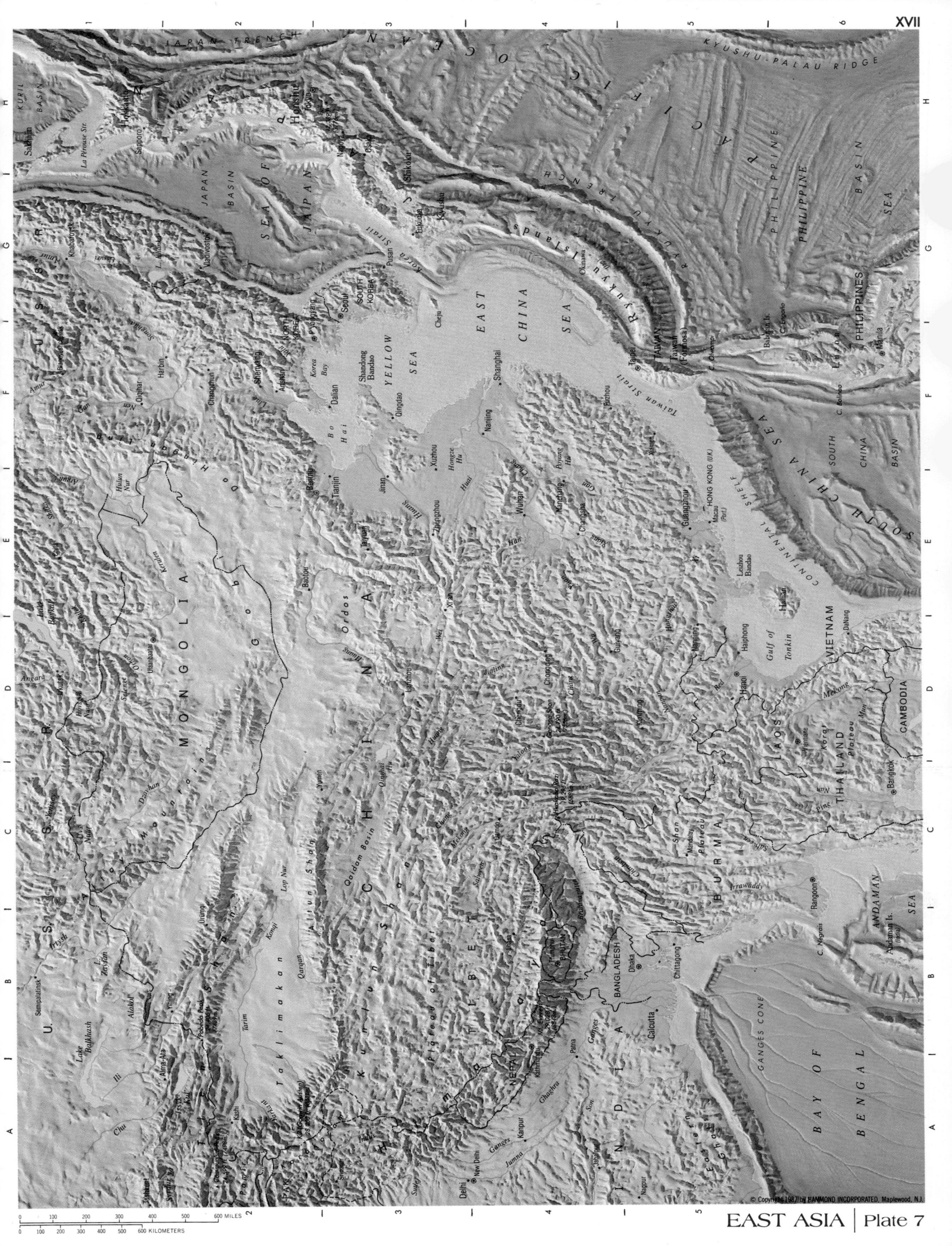

EAST ASIA | Plate 7

0   100   200   300   400   500   600 MILES

0   100   200   300   400   500   600 KILOMETERS

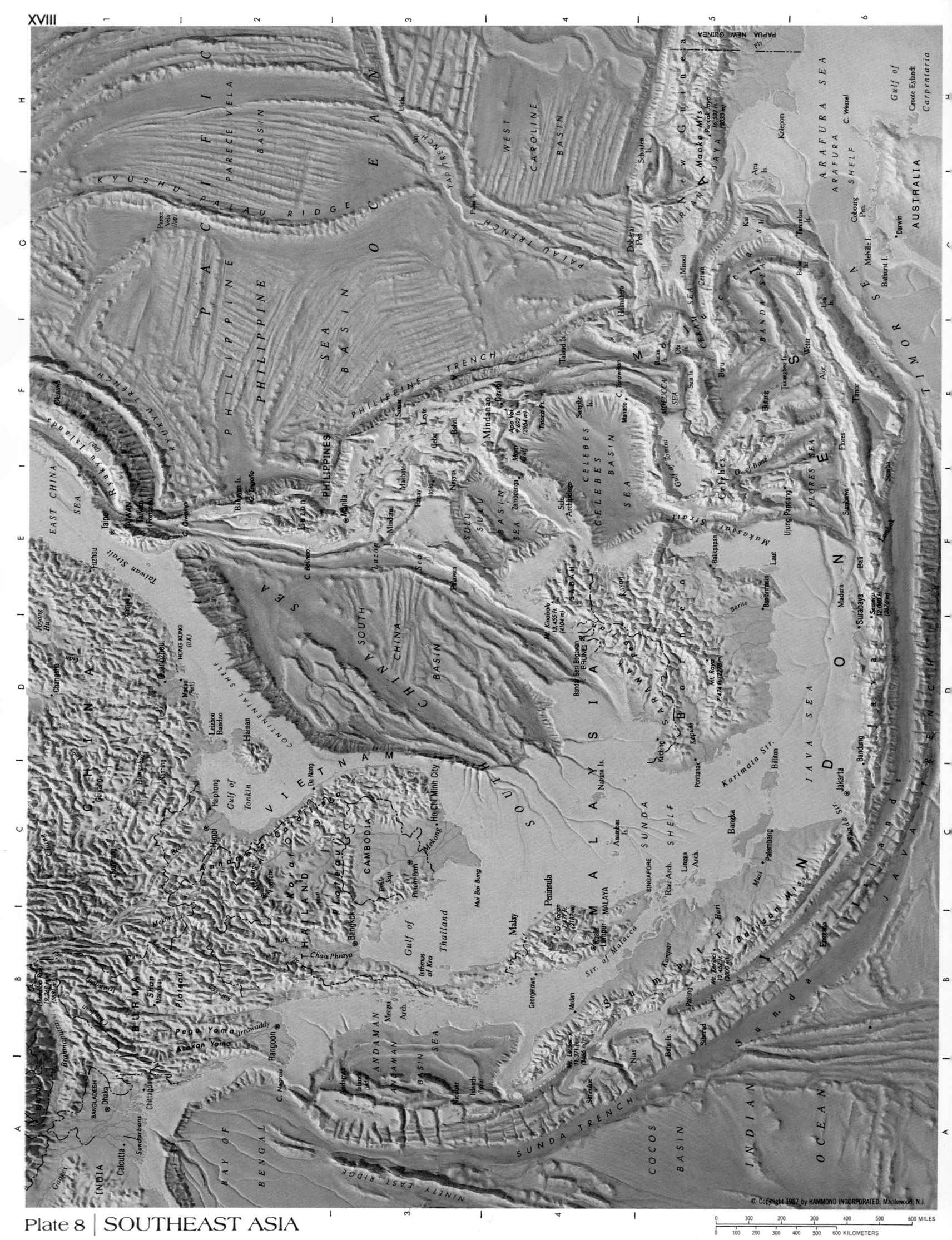

Plate 8 | SOUTHEAST ASIA

| 0 | 100 | 200 | 300 | 400 | 500 | 600 MILES |
| 0 | 100 | 200 | 300 | 400 | 500 | 600 KILOMETERS |

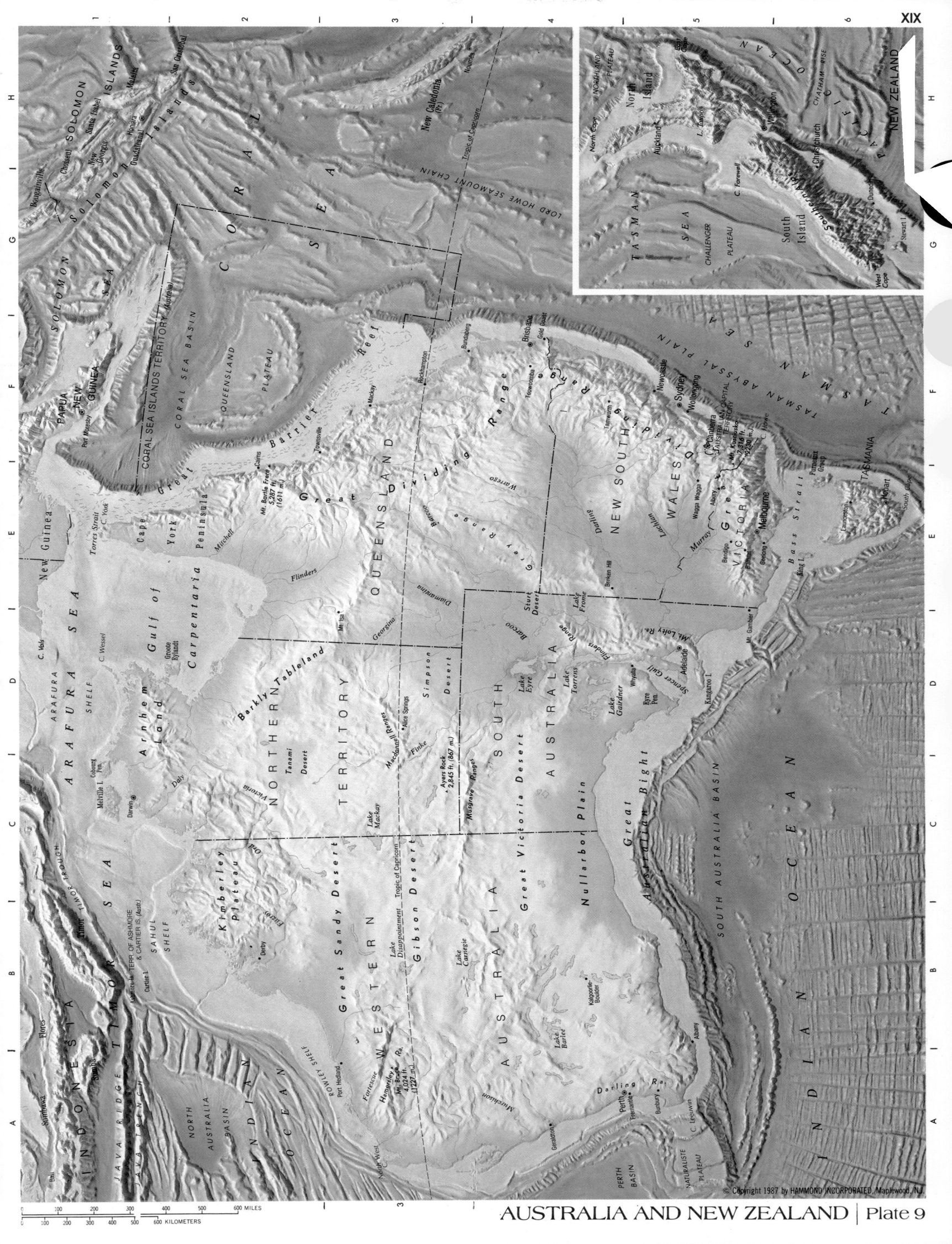

SOLOMON ISLANDS

SOLOMON SEA

Bougainville
Choiseul
SOLOMON
New Georgia
Santa Isabel
Malaita
San Cristobal
Guadalcanal
Honiara

C O R A L   S E A

New Caledonia (Fr.)

Tropic of Capricorn

LORD HOWE SEAMOUNT CHAIN

PAPUA NEW GUINEA
Port Moresby

New Guinea

CORAL SEA ISLANDS TERRITORY (Australia)

CORAL SEA BASIN

QUEENSLAND PLATEAU

Great Barrier Reef

Bundaberg
Brisbane
Gold Coast

Rockhampton

Mackay

Townsville

Cairns
Mt. Bartle Frere
5,287 ft.
(1611 m.)

Toowoomba

Newcastle
Sydney
Wollongong

NEW SOUTH WALES

Darling

Tamworth

Wagga Wagga

Murray

CANBERRA
AUSTRALIAN CAPITAL TERRITORY
Mt. Kosciusko
7,316 ft.
(2230 m.)

Great

TASMAN
SEA

TASMANIA
Launceston
Hobart

Bass Strait
King I.

VICTORIA
Melbourne
Geelong
Bendigo

Broken Hill

Mt. Gambier

Lake
Frome

Sturt
Desert

Great
Dividing
Range

Warrego

Barcoo

Gulf of Carpentaria
ARAFURA SEA
C. Vols
C. Wessel
Groote Eylandt

Cape York Peninsula
Mitchell
Torres Strait
C. York
Flinders

Arnhem
Land
Cobourg Pen.
Melville I.
Darwin

Daly

QUEENSLAND

Diamantina

Georgina

Mt. Isa

NORTHERN TERRITORY

Barkly Tableland

Tanami
Desert

MacDonnell Ranges
Alice Springs
Finke

Simpson
Desert

Ayers Rock
2,845 ft. (867 m.)

Musgrave Ranges

SOUTH

AUSTRALIA

Lake
Eyre

Lake
Torrens

Lake
Gairdner

Flinders
Range

Mt. Lofty Ra.
Adelaide
Whyalla
Eyre
Pen.

Spencer Gulf
Kangaroo I.

Great Australian Bight

Nullarbor Plain

AUSTRALIAN ABYSSAL PLAIN

SOUTH AUSTRALIA BASIN

Great Victoria Desert

Kimberley
Plateau
Derby

Ord

Fitzroy

SAHUL
SHELF

ROWLEY SHELF

Great Sandy Desert

Lake
Disappointment

Gibson Desert

Lake
Carnegie

WESTERN
AUSTRALIA

Tropic of Capricorn

Lake
Mackay

TIMOR SEA
TERR. OF ASHMORE & CARTIER (Austr.)
Cartier I.

INDONESIA
Timor
Flores
Sumbawa

JAVA RIDGE
JAVA TRENCH

NORTH AUSTRALIA BASIN

I N D I A N   O C E A N

North West C.
Port Hedland
Hamersley
Mt. Bruce
4,024 ft.
(1227 m.)
Fortescue

Murchison
Darling Ra.

Lake
Barlee

Kalgoorlie-
Boulder

Lake
Austin

Geraldton
Perth
Fremantle
Bunbury
Albany
C. Leeuwin

PERTH
BASIN

NATURALISTE
PLATEAU

NEW ZEALAND

PACIFIC OCEAN

North Cape
NORTHLAND
PLATEAU
Auckland
North
Island
L. Taupo
Wellington
C. Farewell

CHATHAM RISE

LORD HOWE RISE

TASMAN
SEA
CHALLENGER
PLATEAU
West Cape
South
Island
Christchurch
Dunedin
Stewart I.

Southern Alps

© Copyright 1987 by HAMMOND INCORPORATED, Maplewood, N.J.

AUSTRALIA AND NEW ZEALAND | Plate 9

100   200   300   400   500   600 MILES
100 200 300 400 500 600 KILOMETERS

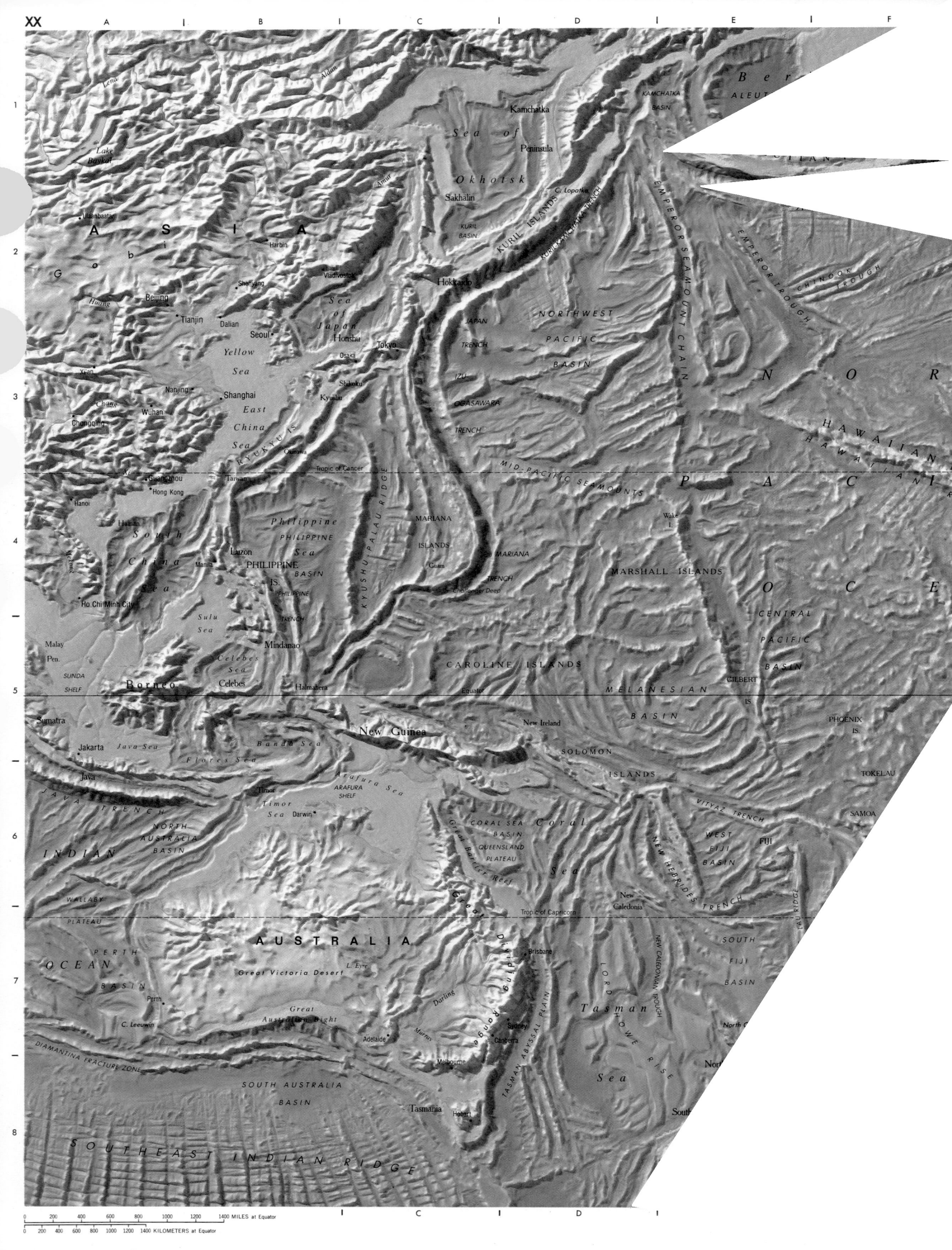

A · I · B · I · C · I · D · I · E · I · F

1

ASIA

G

o
b
i

Lena

Lake
Baykal

Ulaanbaatar

Aldan

Kamchatka

KAMCHATKA
BASIN

Ber

ALEU

2

Harbin

Shenyang

Vladivostok

Beijing

Dalian

Tianjin

Huang

Xi'an

Amur

Sea
of
Japan

Sea of

Okhotsk

Sakhalin

KURIL
BASIN

Hokkaido

C. Lopatka

Peninsula

KURIL ISLANDS

KURIL-KAMCHATKA TRENCH

EMPEROR SEAMOUNT CHAIN

EMPEROR TROUGH

CHINOOK TROUGH

N O R

N

O R

3

Yellow
Sea

Seoul

Osaka

Honshu

Tokyo

Shikoku

Kyushu

Chang

Wuhan

Nanjing

Shanghai

Chongqing

East
China
Sea

RYUKYU IS.

Okinawa

JAPAN

TRENCH

IZU

OGASAWARA

TRENCH

NORTHWEST

PACIFIC

BASIN

MID-PACIFIC SEAMOUNTS

P A C

HAWAIIAN

HAWAII AN I

Tropic of Cancer

Taiwan

4

Hanoi

Hainan

Guangzhou

Hong Kong

South

China

Sea

Ho Chi Minh City

Malay
Pen.

Mekong

Sulu
Sea

SUNDA
SHELF

Luzon

Manila

PHILIPPINE
IS.

PHILIPPINE

TRENCH

Mindanao

Celebes
Sea

Philippine
Sea

PHILIPPINE

PHILIPPINE
SEA
BASIN

KYUSHU-PALAU RIDGE

MARIANA

ISLANDS

Guam

MARIANA

TRENCH

Challenger Deep

Wake
I.

MARSHALL ISLANDS

CENTRAL

PACIFIC

BASIN

O C E

5

Borneo

Celebes

Halmahera

Equator

CAROLINE ISLANDS

MELANESIAN

GILBERT

IS

BASIN

Sumatra

Jakarta

Java

Java Sea

JAVA

TRENCH

Flores Sea

Banda Sea

New Guinea

New Ireland

SOLOMON

ISLANDS

PHOENIX
IS.

TOKELAU

6

INDIAN

NORTH
AUSTRALIA
BASIN

WALLABY

PLATEAU

Timor

Timor
Sea

Darwin

Arafura Sea

ARAFURA
SHELF

CORAL SEA
BASIN

QUEENSLAND
PLATEAU

Great Barrier Reef

Coral
Sea

Coral

NEW HEBRIDES

TRENCH

VITYAZ TRENCH

WEST

FIJI

BASIN

FIJI

SAMOA

New
Caledonia

LAU RIDGE

Tropic of Capricorn

7

OCEAN

PERTH

BASIN

Perth

C. Leeuwin

AUSTRALIA

Great Victoria Desert

L. Eyre

Great
Australian Bight

Adelaide

Darling

Murray

Melbourne

Brisbane

Sydney

Canberra

Dividing Range

Great

TASMAN ABYSSAL PLAIN

Tasman

Sea

Howe

RISE

LORD

NEW CALEDONIAN TROUGH

SOUTH
FIJI
BASIN

North C

Nor

South

DIAMANTINA FRACTURE ZONE

SOUTH AUSTRALIA
BASIN

Tasmania

Hobart

8

SOUTHEAST INDIAN RIDGE

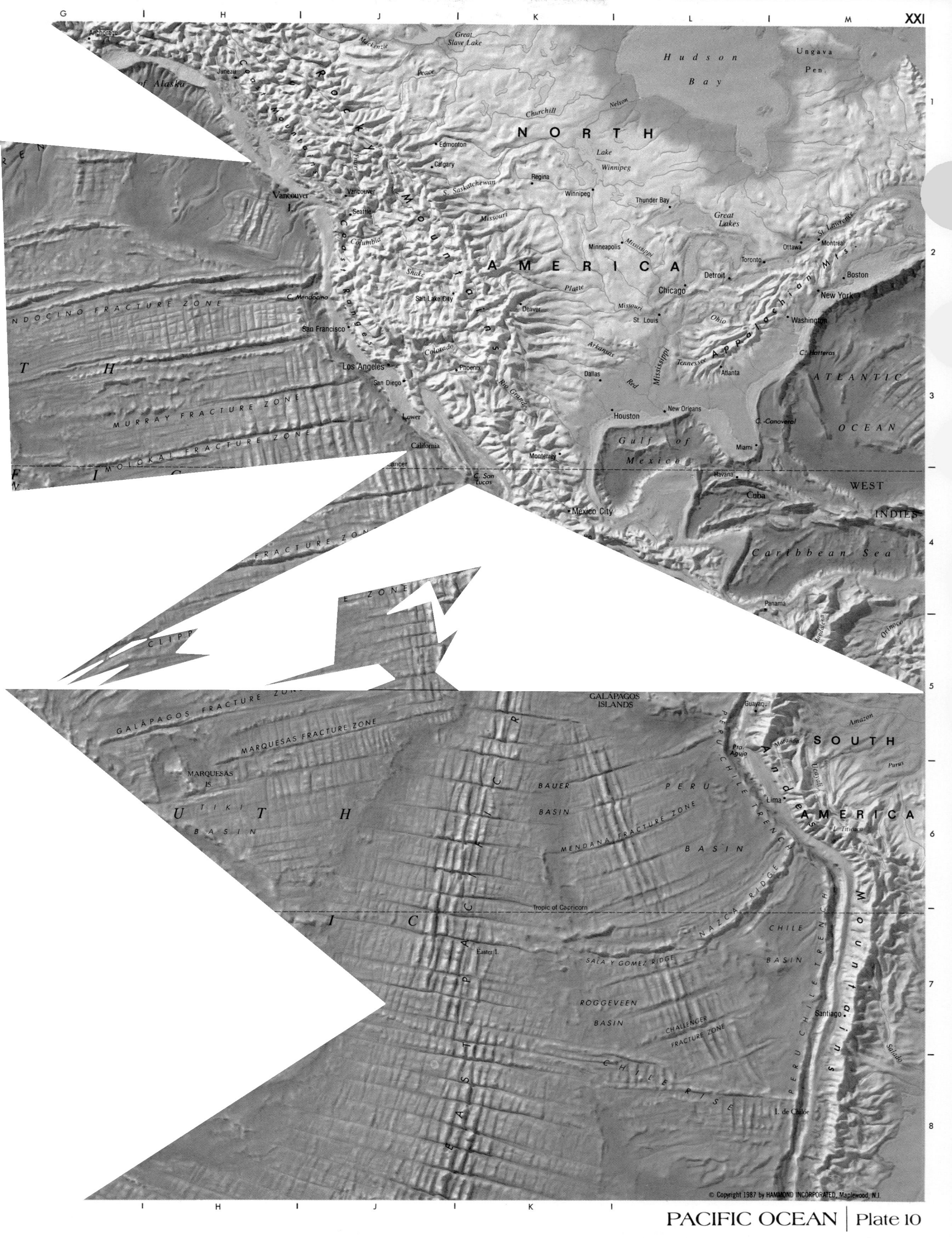

G I H I J I J I K I L I M I M

Anchorage

Juneau
Mackenzie
Great
Slave Lake

Hudson
Bay
Ungava
Pen.

of Alaska
Peace
Churchill
Nelson

Coast Mountains
NORTH

Edmonton
Lake
Winnipeg

Vancouver
Calgary

Vancouver
I.
Regina
Winnipeg
Thunder Bay
Great
Lakes
St. Lawrence
Montreal

Seattle
S. Saskatchewan
AMERICA
Minneapolis
Mississippi
Ottawa
Toronto
Boston

Columbia
Missouri
Detroit

C. Mendocino
Snake
Chicago
New York

NDOCINO FRACTURE ZONE
Salt Lake City
Platte
Missouri
St. Louis
Ohio
Washington

San Francisco
Denver
Arkansas
Tennessee
Appalachian Mts.
C. Hatteras
ATLANTIC

T   H
Colorado
Atlanta

Coast Ranges
Los Angeles
Phoenix
Dallas
Red
Mississippi
OCEAN

MURRAY FRACTURE ZONE
San Diego
Rio Grande
Houston
New Orleans
C. Canaveral

Lower
Monterrey
Miami

MOLOKAI FRACTURE ZONE
California
Gulf of
Havana
WEST

F   I
Cancer
C. San
Mexico
Cuba
INDIES

Lucas

Mexico City
Caribbean Sea

FRACTURE ZONE

E ZONE
Panama

CLIPP
Orinoco
Magdalena

GALÁPAGOS
ISLANDS
Guayaquil
Amazon

GALÁPAGOS FRACTURE ZONE
Marañón
SOUTH

MARQUESAS FRACTURE ZONE
Pta.
Aguja
Ucayali
Purus

MARQUESAS
IS.
BAUER
BASIN
PERU
AMERICA

U   TIKI T   H
BASIN
MENDAÑA FRACTURE ZONE
BASIN
L. Titicaca

BASIN
Lima

Tropic of Capricorn
NAZCA RIDGE
CHILE

I   C
Easter I.
BASIN

SALA Y GOMEZ RIDGE

RÖGGEVEEN
CHALLENGER
Santiago

BASIN
FRACTURE ZONE

CHILE RISE
I. de Chiloé

Salado

G I H I J I K I L I I

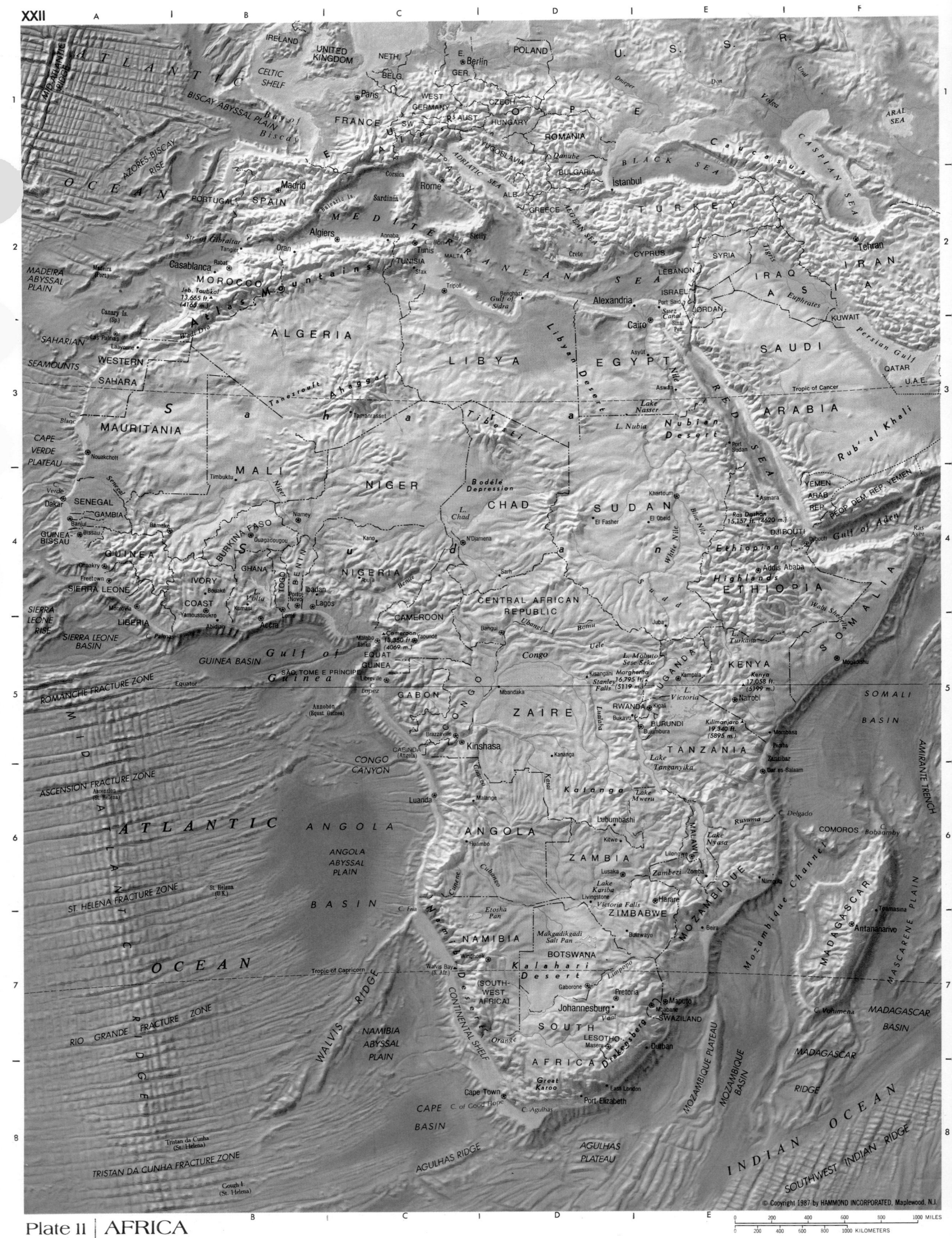

Plate II | AFRICA

| | | | 200 | 400 | 600 | 800 | 1000 MILES |
| | | 200 | 400 | 600 | 800 | 1000 KILOMETERS |

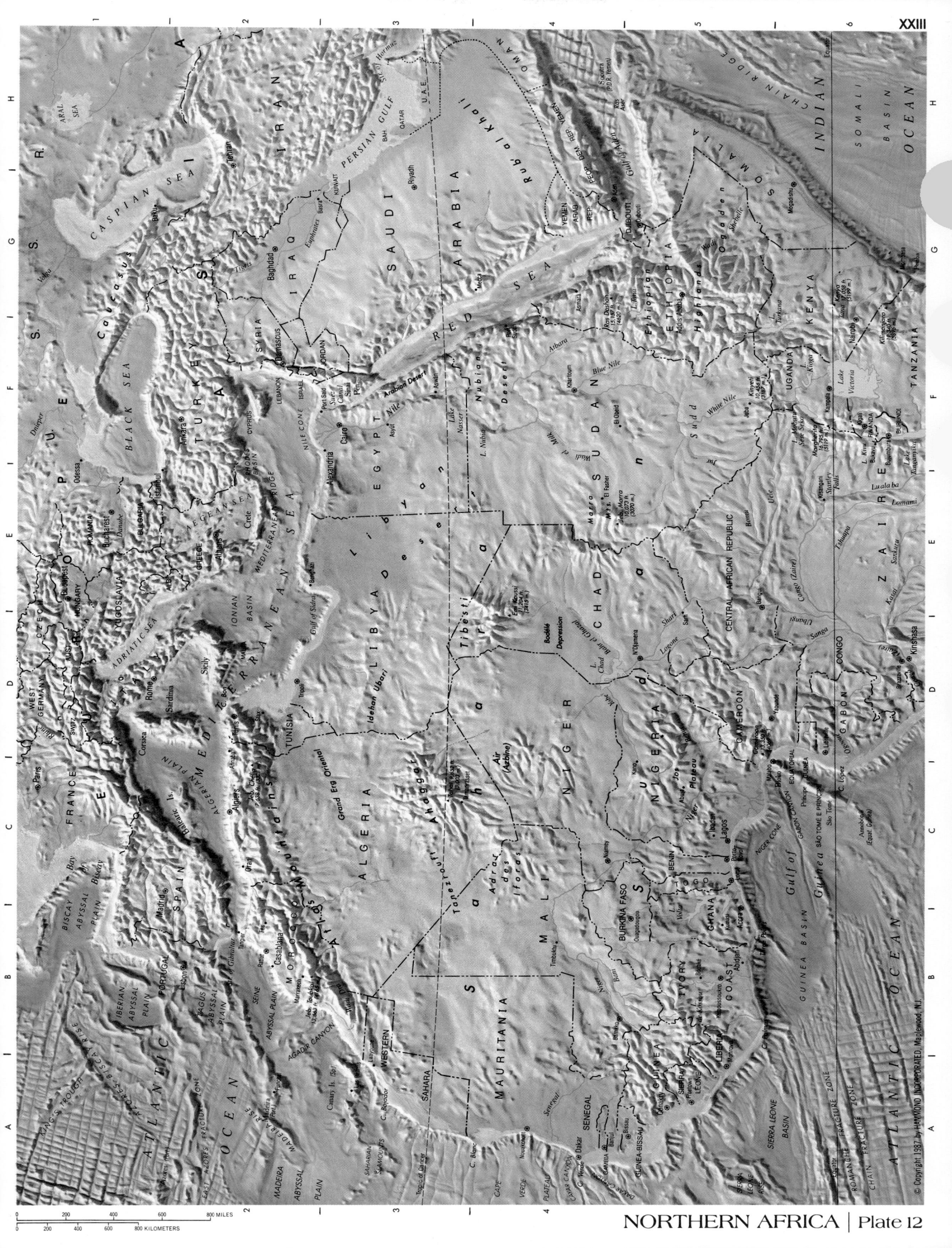

0   200   400   600   800 MILES
0   200   400   600   800 KILOMETERS

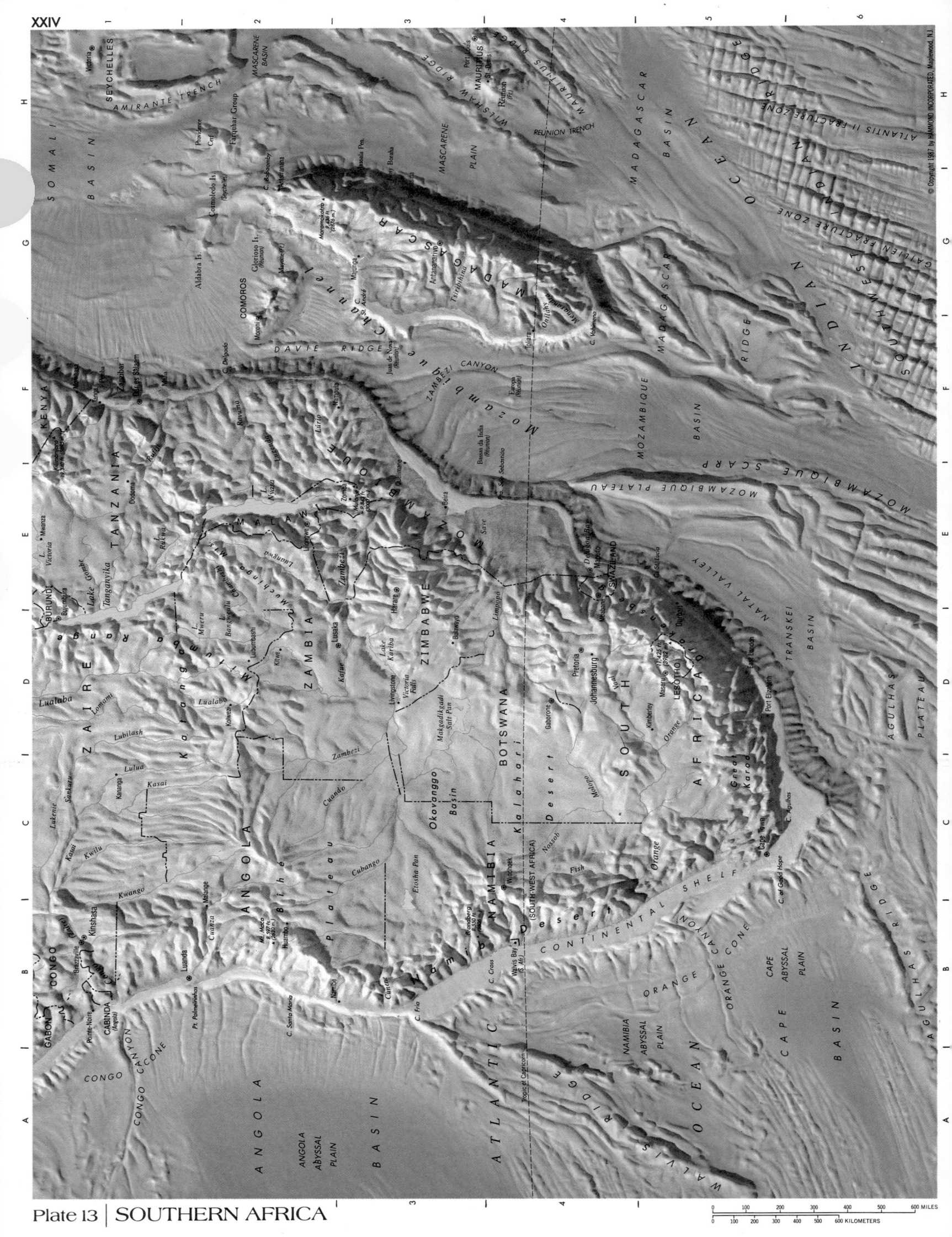

Plate 13 | SOUTHERN AFRICA

SOUTH AMERICA | Plate 14

© Copyright 1987 by HAMMOND INCORPORATED, Maplewood, N.J.

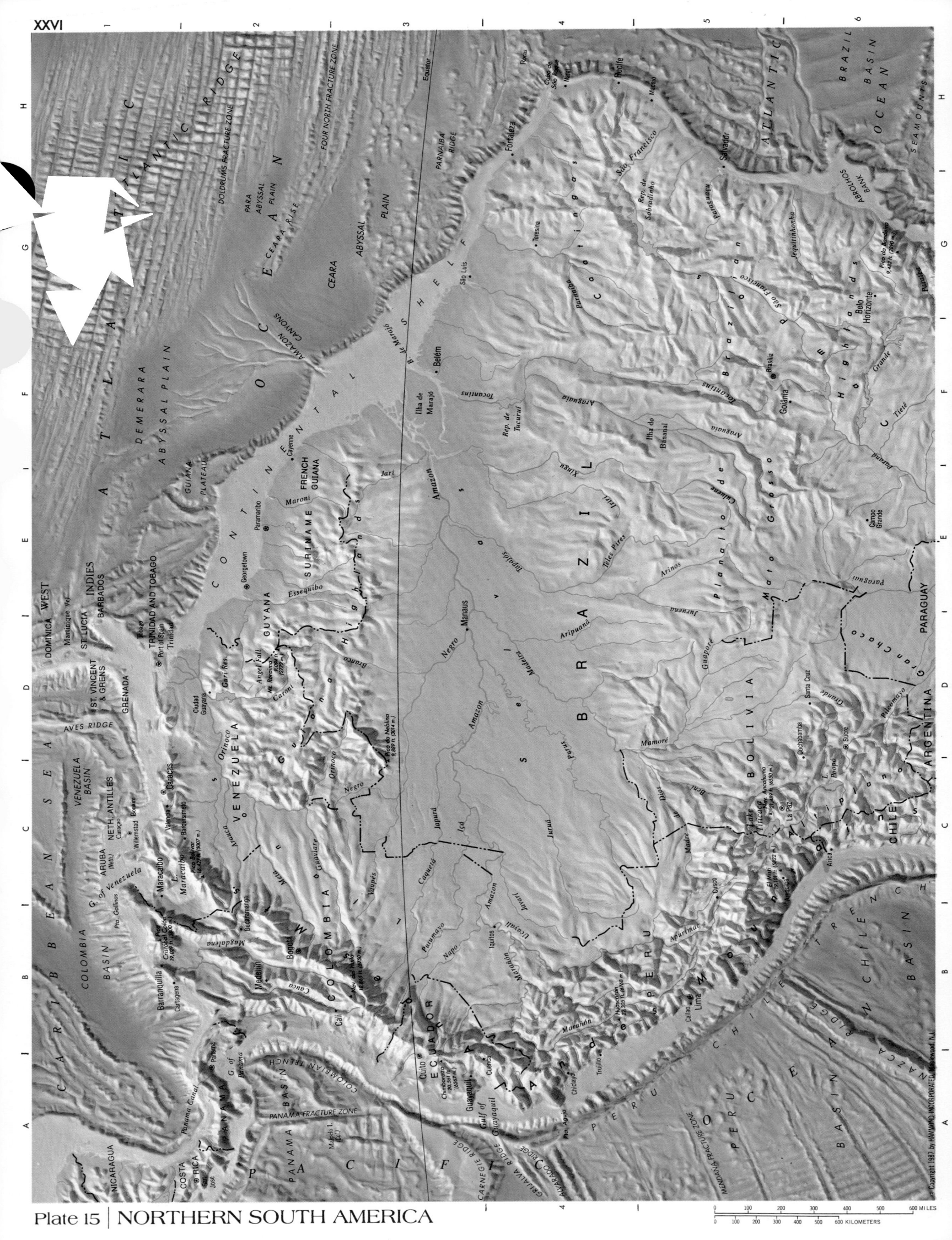

Plate 15 | NORTHERN SOUTH AMERICA

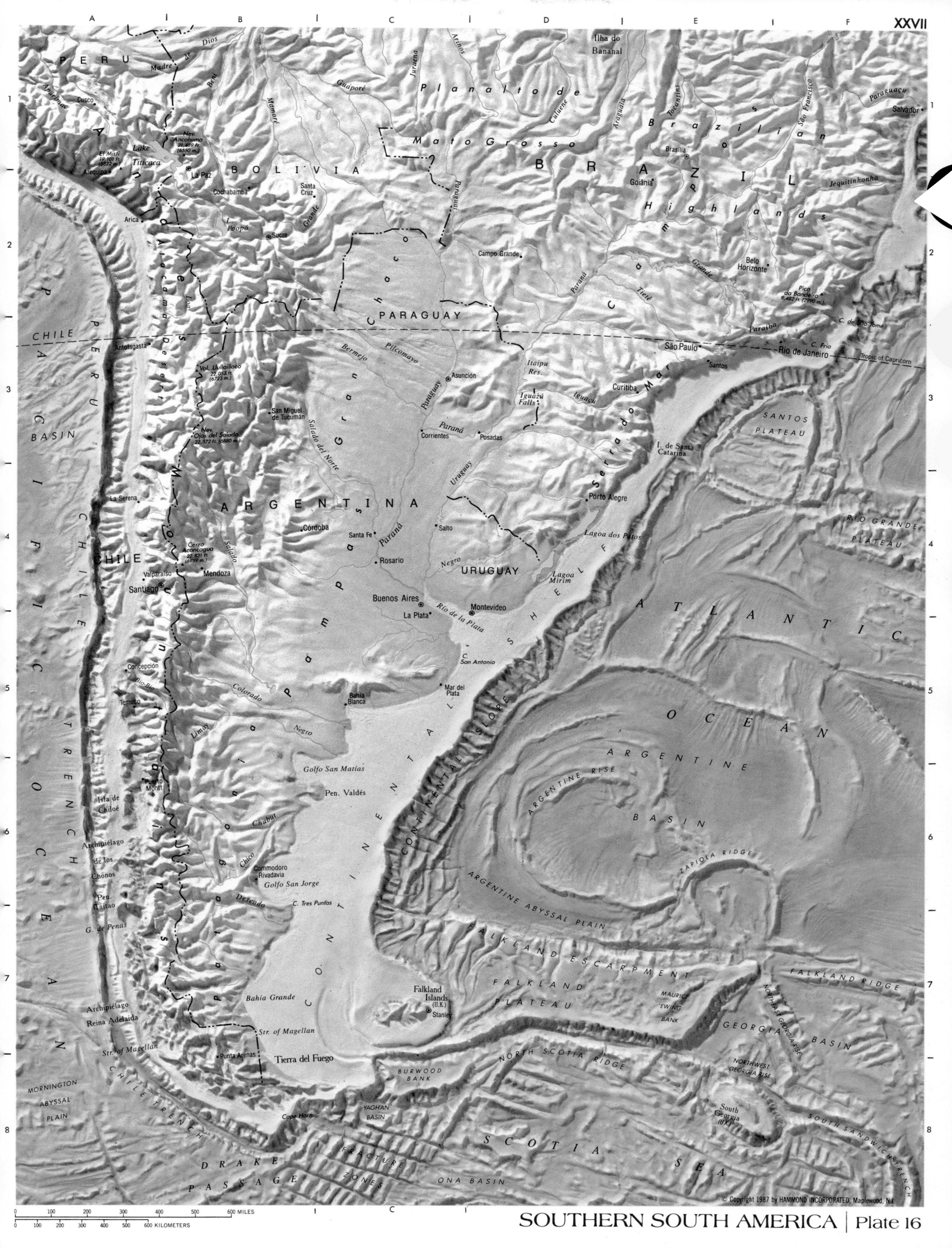

SOUTHERN SOUTH AMERICA | Plate 16

© Copyright 1987 by HAMMOND INCORPORATED, Maplewood, N.J.

Plate 17 | NORTH AMERICA

CANADA | Plate 18

0   100   200   300   400   500   600 MILES
0   100   200   300   400   500   600 KILOMETERS

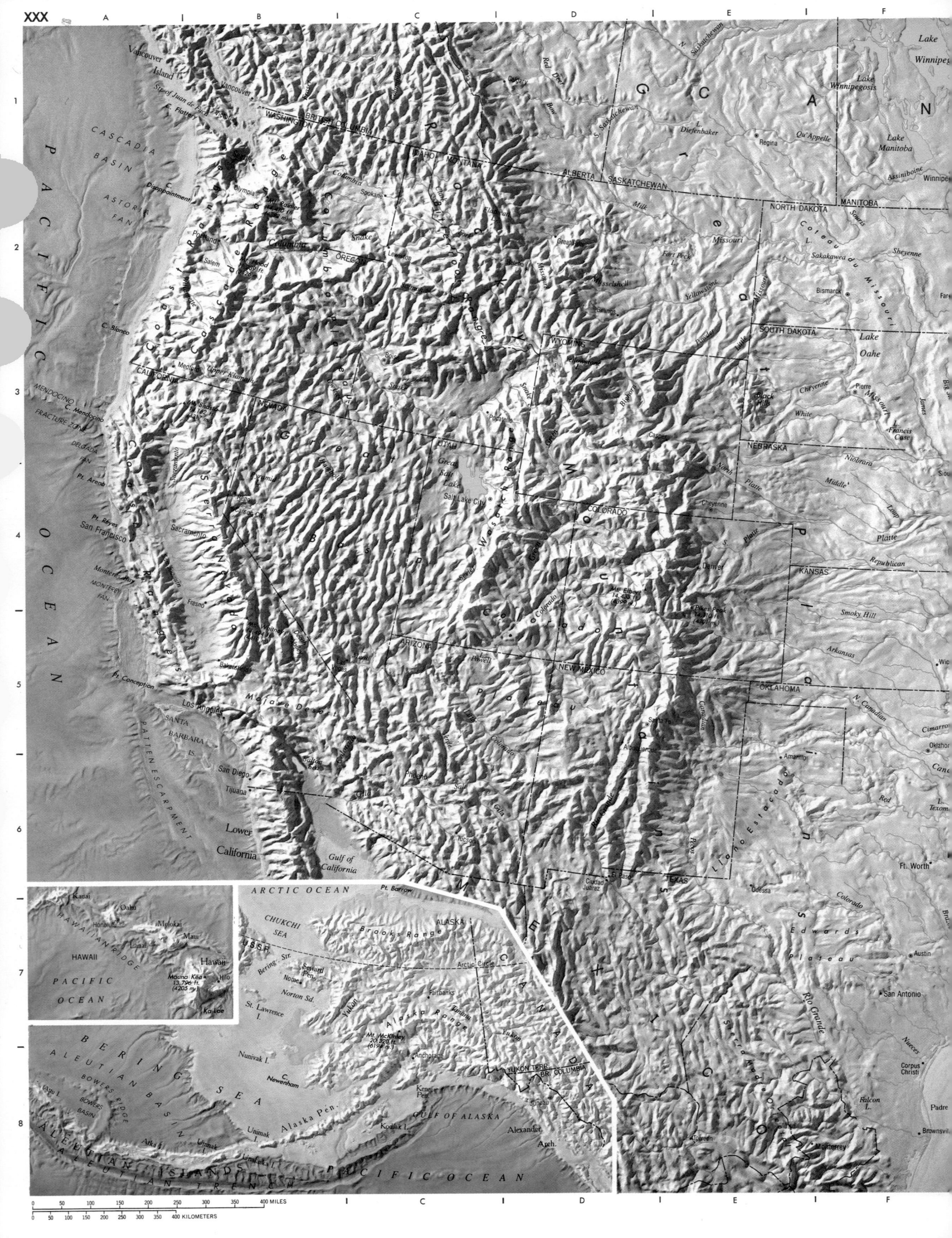

James
Bay

CANADA

Severn

Ogoki

Albany

*Lac
Seul*

*L.
Nipigon*

Missinaibi

Abitibi

Harricana

L.
Mistassini

L. St-Jean

Île d'Anticosti

Gulf of
St. Lawrence

Gaspé Pen.

Saguenay

St. Lawrence

NEW BRUNSWICK

P.E.I.

*Lake of
the Woods*

Rainy

*Red
Lakes*

Thunder Bay

I. Royale

Keweenaw
Pen.

Lake Superior

Marquette

MAINE

Québec

Fredericton

Bay of Fundy

NOVA
SCOTIA

St Croix

Mississippi

WISCONSIN

L.
Winnebago

Manitoulin
I.

Georgian Bay

Sudbury

QUEBEC
ONTARIO

Ottawa

Montreal

VERMONT

L.
Champlain

Montpelier

N.H.

Augusta

Portland

C. Sable

Minneapolis

St. Paul

SOTA

Green
Bay

Madison

Milwaukee

Lake Michigan

Muskegon

Lake
Huron

Saginaw Bay

Toronto

Lake Ontario

Rochester

Buffalo

London

Albany

MASS.

Boston

C. Cod

GEORGES
BANK

CONN.

Providence

Hartford

R.I.

Nantucket I.

Martha's
Vineyard

Wisconsin

Iowa

Cedar

ILLINOIS

Fox

Grand

Lansing

Detroit

Lake Erie

Cleveland

NEW YORK

PENNSYLVANIA

Allegheny

Susquehanna

New York

Long I.

Des Moines

Davenport

Illinois

Chicago

MICHIGAN
INDIANA

OHIO

Toledo

Akron

Pittsburgh

Harrisburg

N.J.

Trenton

Philadelphia

HUDSON
CANYON

Des Moines

Ft.
Wayne

Wabash

Columbus

Scioto

W. VA.

Potomac

MD.

Baltimore

Dover

C. May

Delaware Bay

DEL.

MISSOURI

Mississippi

Springfield

Indianapolis

Cincinnati

Ohio

Washington

Annapolis

Chesapeake
Bay

Grand

St.
Louis

Ohio

White

Louisville

Frankfort

Charleston

Kanawha

Richmond

James

Norfolk

CONTINENTAL

SHELF

ATLANTIC

Kansas
City

Missouri

Jefferson City

Green

Cumberland

Clinch

VIRGINIA

Roanoke

Roanoke

Neuse

Raleigh

C. Hatteras

Pamlico Sound

OCEAN

Ozark

Neosho

Plateau

ARKANSAS

KENTUCKY

Kentucky
Lake

Nashville

Black

Cumberland

NORTH CAROLINA

Charlotte

C. Lookout

BLAKE RIDGE

Arkansas

Memphis

TENNESSEE

Chattanooga

Mt. Mitchell
6,684 ft.
(2037 m.)

GEORGIA

S.CAROLINA

C. Fear

Columbia

C. Fear

Little Rock

White

MISSISSIPPI

ALABAMA

Tennessee

Coosa

Atlanta

Savannah

Ouachita

Mississippi

Yazoo

Jackson

Birmingham

Tombigbee

Chattahoochee

Montgomery

Oconee

Ocmulgee

Charleston

Savannah

BLAKE

Sabine

LOUISIANA

Red

Shreveport

Pearl

Alabama

FLORIDA

Altamaha

PLATEAU

BAHAMA RIDGE

Toledo
Bend
Res.

Jackson

Mobile

Tallahassee

Jacksonville

St. John

Baton Rouge

CONTINENTAL

SHELF

C. Blas

C. San Blas

New Orleans

Galveston
Bay

Delta of the
Mississippi

MISSISSIPPI
FAN

Florida

Orlando

C. Canaveral

Tampa

Grand
Bahama

Great
Abaco

CONTINENTAL

GULF   OF   MEXICO

SIGSBEE ESCARPMENT

Tampa Bay

Peninsula

L.
Okeechobee

Miami

BAHAMAS

Nassau

New
Providence

Eleuthera

Cat I.

San Salvador

Andros I.

Great
Exuma

Long I.

FLORIDA KEYS

C. Sable

Straits of Florida

GREAT BAHAMA BANK

Acklins I.

Copyright 1987 by HAMMOND INCORPORATED, Maplewood, N.J.

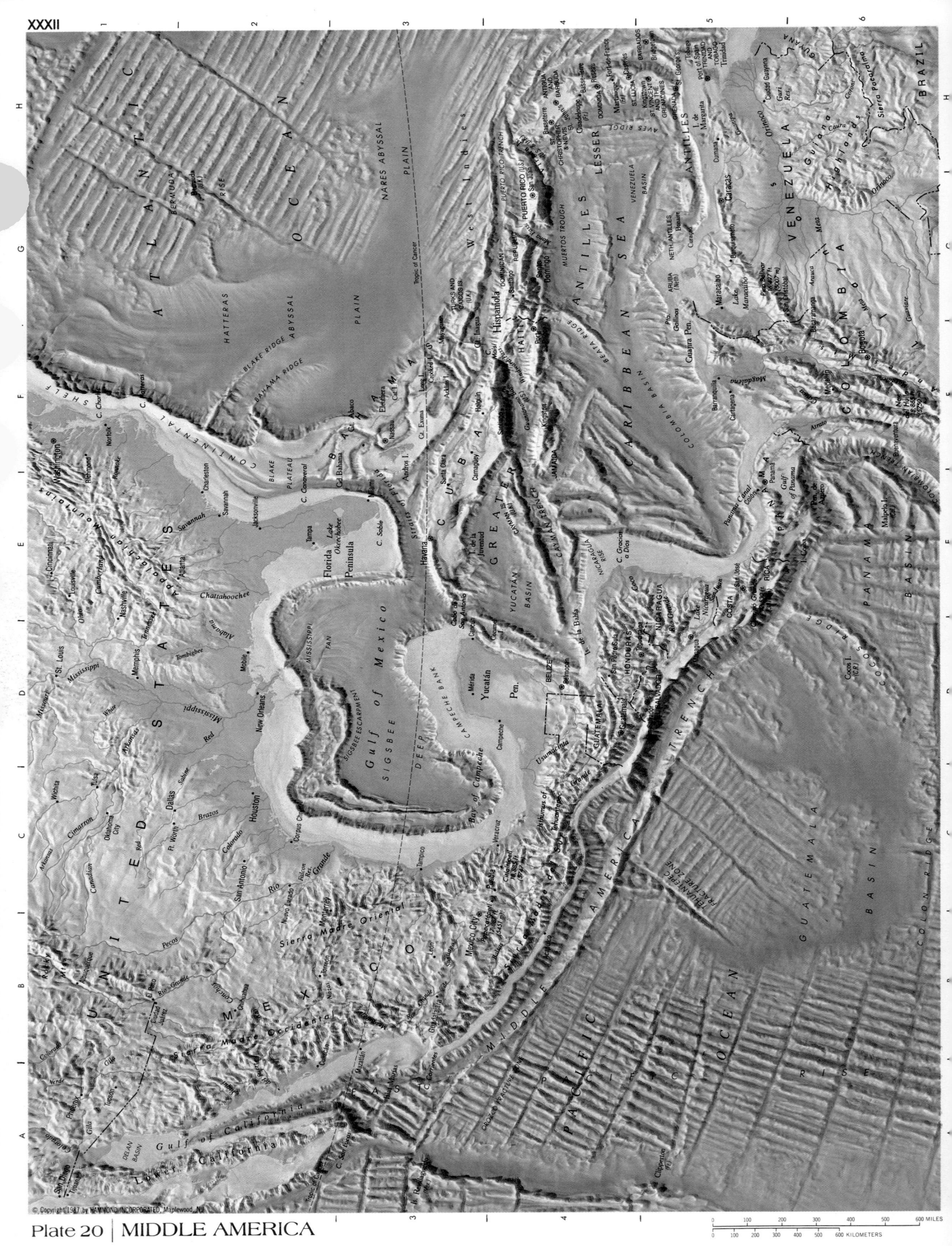

Plate 20 | MIDDLE AMERICA

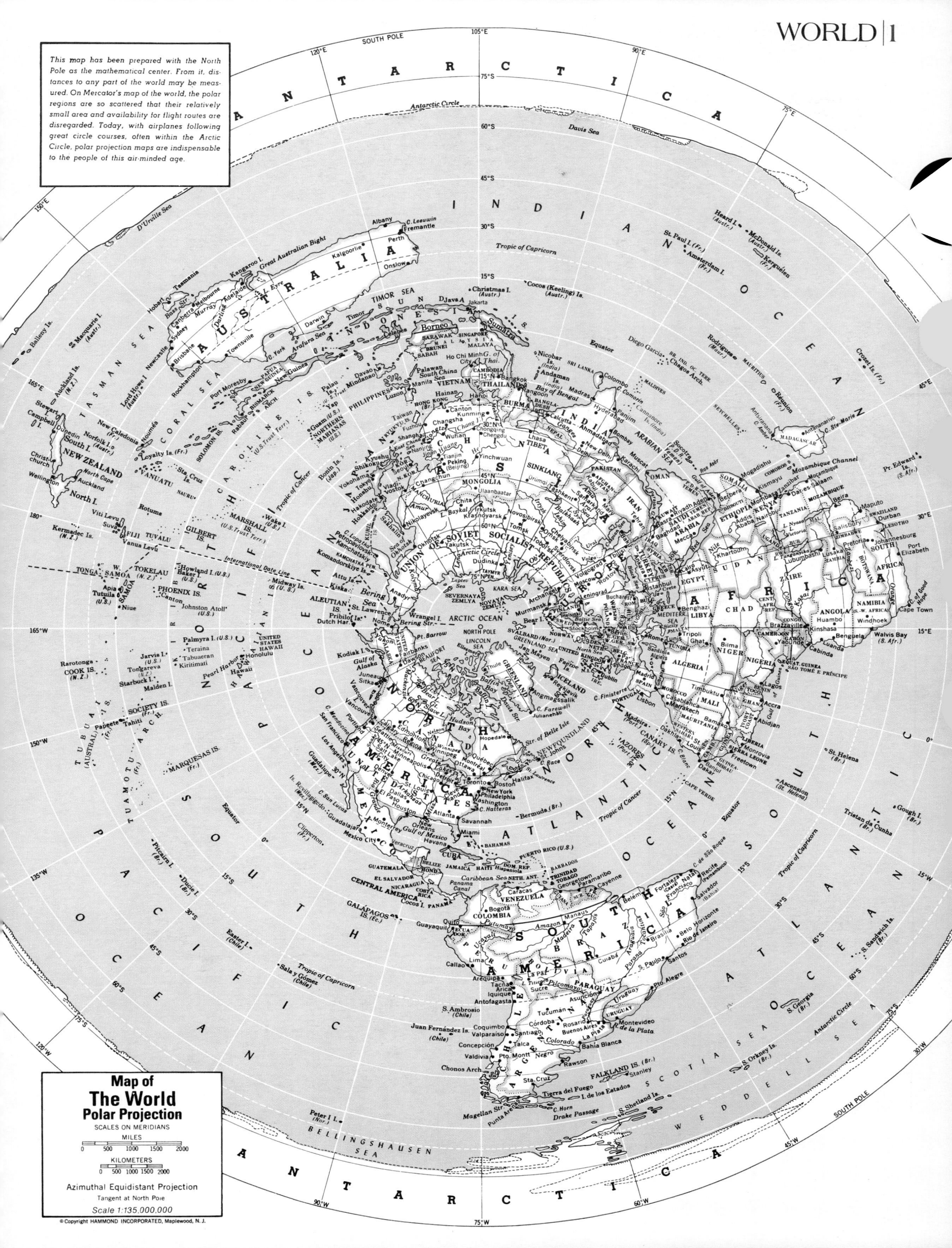

This map has been prepared with the North Pole as the mathematical center. From it, distances to any part of the world may be measured. On Mercator's map of the world, the polar regions are so scattered that their relatively small area and availability for flight routes are disregarded. Today, with airplanes following great circle courses, often within the Arctic Circle, polar projection maps are indispensable to the people of this air-minded age.

Map of
The World
Polar Projection

SCALES ON MERIDIANS

MILES

0   500   1000   1500   2000

KILOMETERS

0 500 1000 1500 2000

Azimuthal Equidistant Projection

Tangent at North Pole

Scale 1:135,000,000

© Copyright HAMMOND INCORPORATED, Maplewood, N.J.

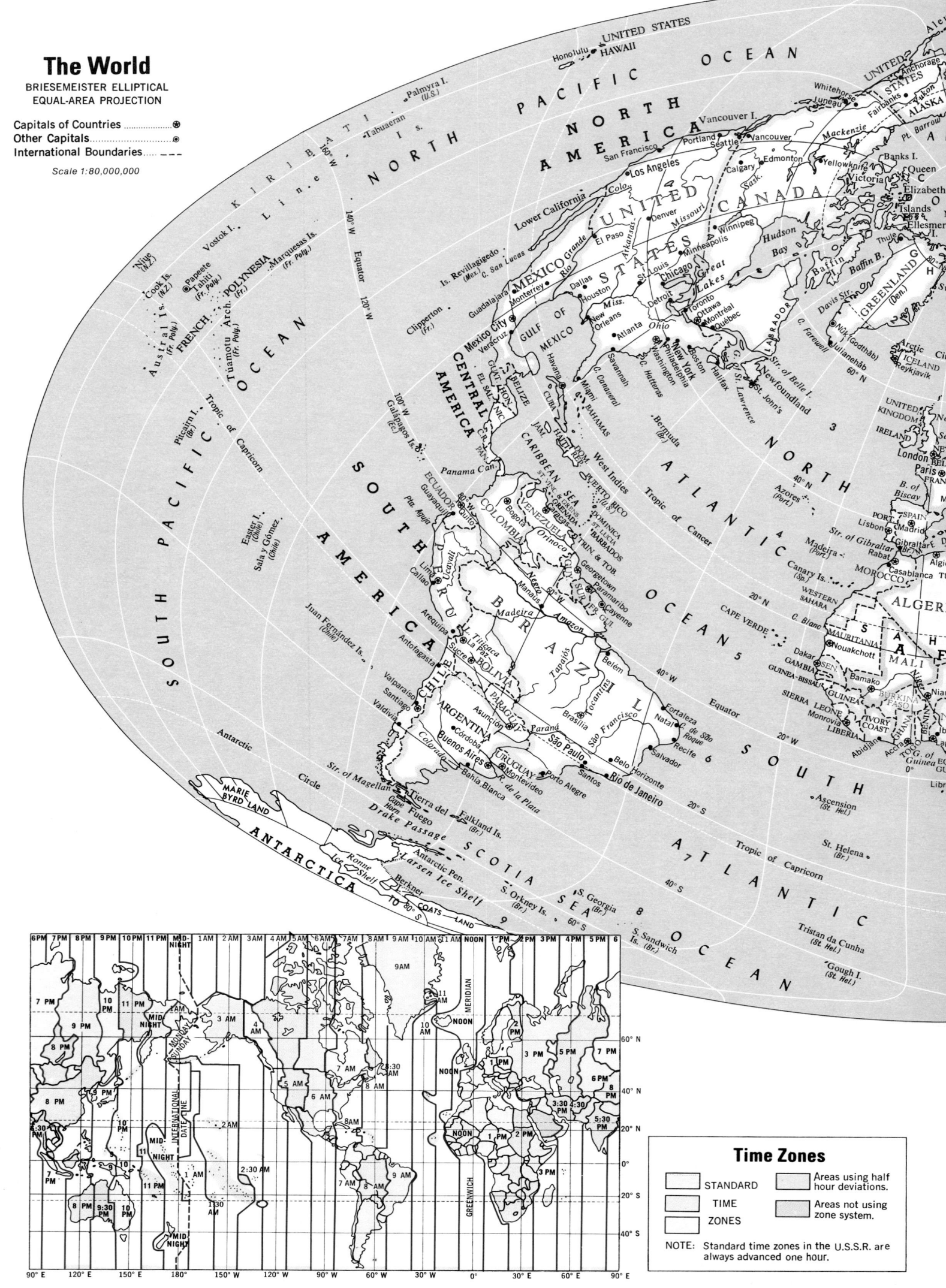

The World

**BRIESEMEISTER ELLIPTICAL
EQUAL-AREA PROJECTION**

Capitals of Countries .... ⊛
Other Capitals .... ⊛
International Boundaries ..... ▬ ▬

Scale 1:80,000,000

Time Zones

STANDARD
TIME
ZONES

Areas using half
hour deviations.

Areas not using
zone system.

NOTE: Standard time zones in the U.S.S.R. are
always advanced one hour.

LAND AREA 57,970,000 sq. mi.
(150,142,300 sq. km.)
WATER AREA 139,781,000 sq. mi.
(362,032,790 sq. km.)
TOTAL SURFACE AREA 197,751,000 sq. mi.
(512,175,090 sq. km.)
POPULATION 4,415,000,000

Antarctica
AZIMUTHAL EQUIDISTANT PROJECTION
Scale 1:62,000,000

© Copyright HAMMOND INCORPORATED, Maplewood, N.J.

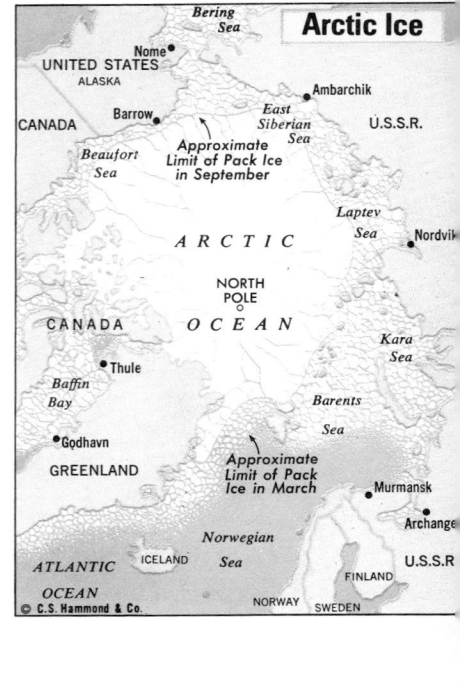

Arctic Ice

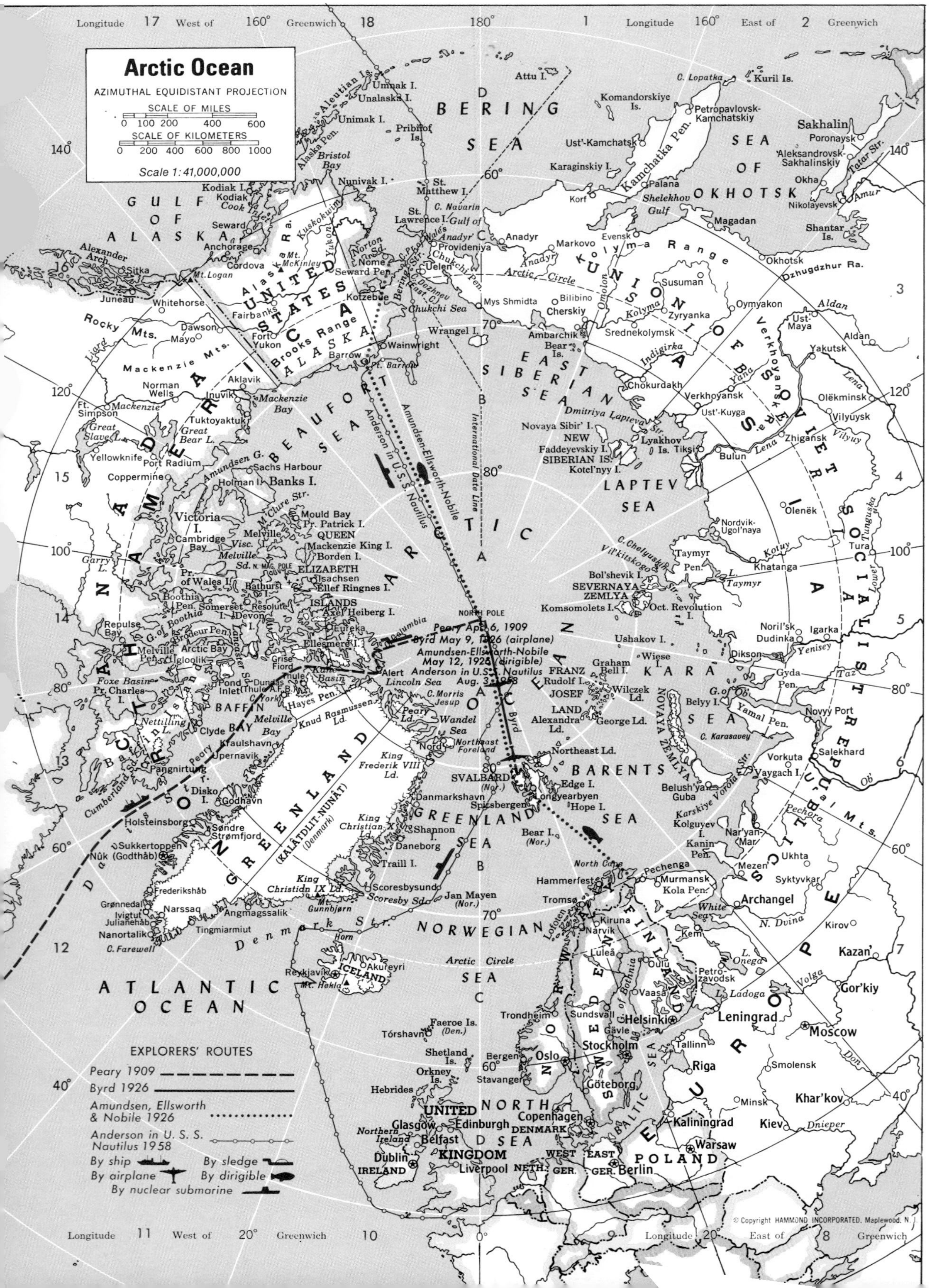

Arctic Ocean

AZIMUTHAL EQUIDISTANT PROJECTION

SCALE OF MILES
0 100 200 400 600

SCALE OF KILOMETERS
0 200 400 600 800 1000

Scale 1:41,000,000

EXPLORERS' ROUTES

Peary 1909
Byrd 1926
Amundsen, Ellsworth & Nobile 1926
Anderson in U.S.S. Nautilus 1958
By ship — By sledge
By airplane — By dirigible
By nuclear submarine

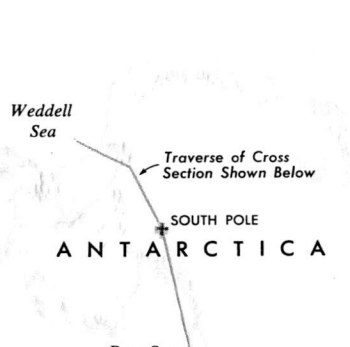

Traverse of Cross Section Shown Below

Antarctic Cross Section: Weddell Sea to Ross Sea

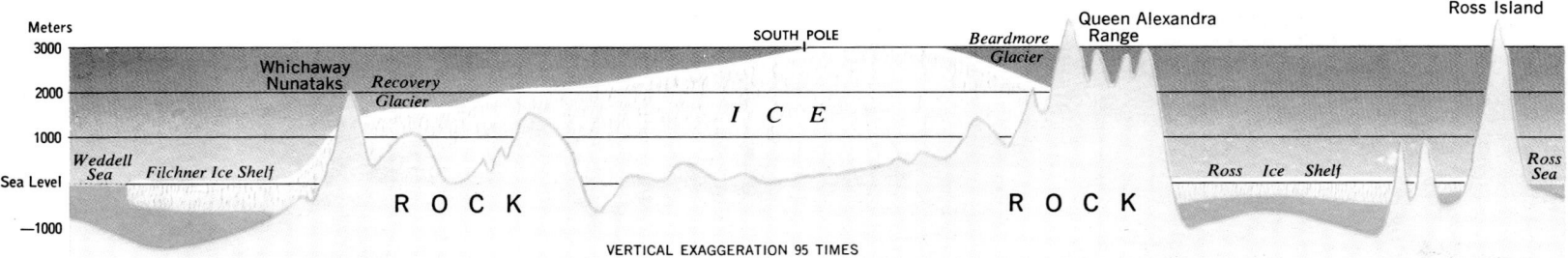

VERTICAL EXAGGERATION 95 TIMES

Information Based on American Geographical Society's "Antarctic Map Folio Series"

Europe

POLYCONIC PROJECTION

SCALE OF MILES

0 100 200 300 400

KILOMETERS

0 100 200 300 400

Capitals of Countries .... ⊛

Other Capitals .... ⊙

International Boundaries .... ━ ∙ ━

Internal Boundaries .... ━ ∙∙ ━

Canals .... ━━

Scale 1:20,800,000

AREA 4,057,000 sq. mi.
(10,507,630 sq. km.)
POPULATION 676,000,000
LARGEST CITY Paris
HIGHEST POINT El'brus 18,510 ft.
(5,642 m.)
LOWEST POINT Caspian Sea -92 ft.
(-28 m.)

Population Distribution

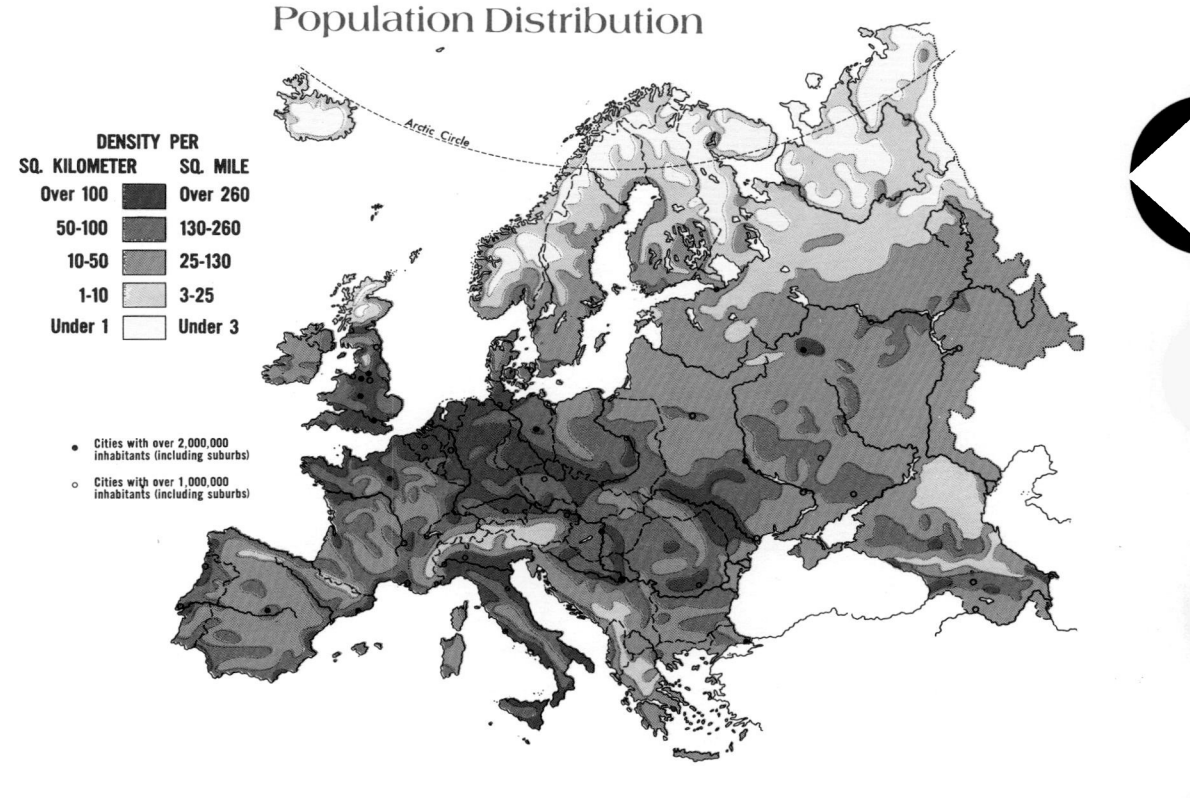

DENSITY PER

SQ. KILOMETER	SQ. MILE
Over 100	Over 260
50-100	130-260
10-50	25-130
1-10	3-25
Under 1	Under 3

• Cities with over 2,000,000
inhabitants (including suburbs)

○ Cities with over 1,000,000
inhabitants (including suburbs)

Vegetation

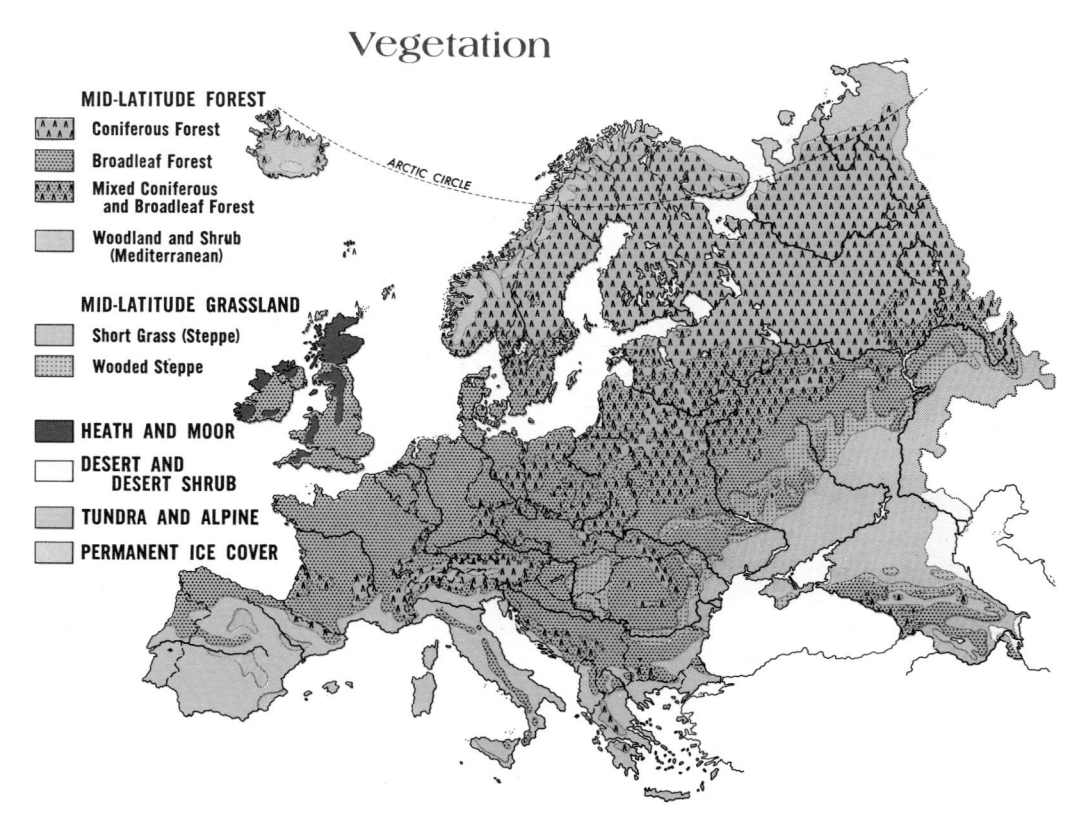

MID-LATITUDE FOREST

Coniferous Forest

Broadleaf Forest

Mixed Coniferous
and Broadleaf Forest

Woodland and Shrub
(Mediterranean)

MID-LATITUDE GRASSLAND

Short Grass (Steppe)

Wooded Steppe

HEATH AND MOOR

**DESERT AND
DESERT SHRUB**

TUNDRA AND ALPINE

PERMANENT ICE COVER

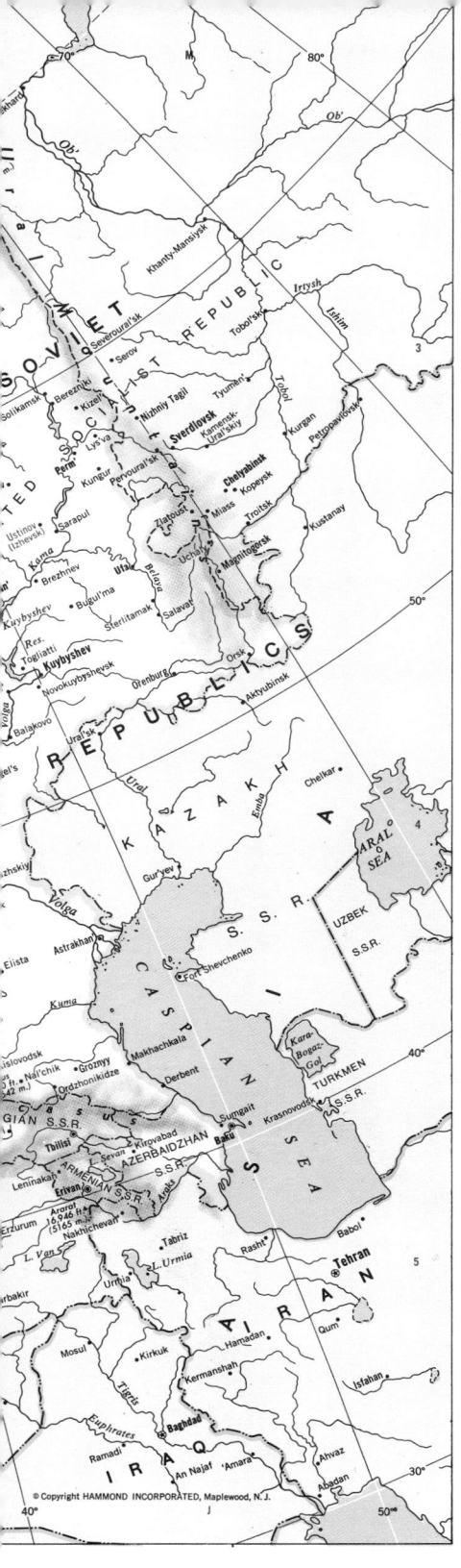

© Copyright HAMMOND INCORPORATED, Maplewood, N.J.

30° 20° 10° 0° 10° 20° 30° 40° 50°

60°

NORWEGIAN

Horn

Fontur

ICELAND

Reykjavik

Arctic Circle

SEA

Nordkapp

BARENTS

Kolguyev I.

Sørøy Hammerfest

Kanin Pen.

Chelskaya Bay

Vesterålen

Kola Pen.

Murmansk

WHITE SEA

Archangel

Lofoten

Kiruna

Vestfjord

Pechora

Faeroe Is. *(Den.)*

Trondheim

Oulu

FINLAND

Northern Dvina

Shetland Is.

Glittertind 8,110 ft. (2,472 m.)

Bergen

Sundsvall

Tampere

Lake Onega

Hebrides

Orkney Is.

Moray Firth

Hardangerfjord

Oslo

Glomma

Lake Ladoga

Helsinki

Leningrad

UNION OF

Ben Nevis 4,406 ft. (1,343 m.)

Aberdeen

NORTH SEA

Skagerrak

Västerås

Åland Is.

Stockholm

Hiiumaa

Gulf of Finland

Volga

Gor'kiy

U.K. Belfast

Glasgow

UNITED

Lindesnes

Göteborg

Saaremaa

Riga

Moscow

Western Dvina

SOCIAL

IRELAND

Dublin

IRISH SEA

Liverpool

KINGDOM

DENMARK

Gotland

Copenhagen

BALTIC SEA

Minsk

50°

C. Clear

Birmingham

St. Georges Chan.

Bornholm

Rügen

Gdańsk

ATLANTIC

Land's End

London

English Channel

Frisian Is.

NETHERLANDS

Amsterdam

Hamburg

Elbe

EAST

Berlin

POLAND

Vistula

Warsaw

Łódź

Kiev

Khar'kov

Land's End

Channel Is. *(U.K.)*

Le Havre

BELGIUM

Brussels

Cologne

Weser

GERMANY

Leipzig

Oder

Cracow

L'vov

Dnieper

Donetsk

OCEAN

Nantes

Seine

Paris

LUX.

GERMANY

Stuttgart

Prague

CZECHOSLOVAKIA

Brno

Carpathian Mts.

Don

Loire

Rhine

Danube

Prut

SEA OF AZOV

Finistère

Bordeaux

Dordogne

Rhône

Munich

LIECH.

Bern

SWITZ.

Vienna

AUSTRIA

Graz

Budapest

HUNGARY

Cluj-Napoca

ROMANIA

Odessa

Crimea

Krasnodar

Bay of Biscay

Garonne

Lyon

Turin

Genoa

Zagreb

Venice

Sava

Belgrade

Bucharest

BLACK SEA

40°

Porto

Douro

Bilbao

Pyrenees

MONACO

SAN MARINO

ADRIATIC SEA

YUGOSLAVIA

Danube

Balkan Mts.

Lisbon

SPAIN

Madrid

Tagus

Guadiana

Barcelona

Corsica

VATICAN CITY

Rome

Sofia

Skopje

BULGARIA

Istanbul

Bosporus

PORTUGAL

C. de São Vicente

Valencia

Balearic Is.

Minorca

Sardinia

Naples

TYRRHENIAN SEA

Tirane

ALB.

Thessaloniki

Sea of Marmara

Ankara

TURKEY

Cádiz

Málaga

Ibiza

Majorca

Palermo

IONIAN SEA

Dardanelles

Lésvos

Tangier

GIBRALTAR *(U.K.)*

Str. of Gibraltar

Algiers

Oran

MEDITERRANEAN

C. Teulada

Sicily

Etna 11,053 ft. (3,369 m.)

C. Bon

Athens

AEGEAN SEA

Euboía

Izmir

Rabat

Casablanca

MOROCCO

Constantine

ALGERIA

Tunis

C. Passero

MALTA Valletta

C. Tainaron

Rhodes

Crete

CYPRUS

Nicosia

LEBANON

Beirut

AFRICA

TUNISIA

SEA

Longitude West of Greenwich 0° Longitude East of Greenwich 10° 20° 30°

Vegetation / Relief

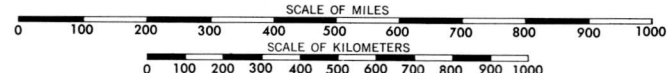

SCALE OF MILES

0 100 200 300 400 500 600 700 800 900 1000

SCALE OF KILOMETERS

0 100 200 300 400 500 600 700 800 900 1000

Capitals of Countries .... ⊛

International Boundaries .... —·—·—

Canals ....

Depths in Fathoms

COLOR KEY

Forest | Woodland and Scrub | Grassland | Forest and Grassland | Cropland | Desert | Tundra and Alpine | Ice and Snow | Grassland and Scrub | Scrub and Fernlands

Rainfall

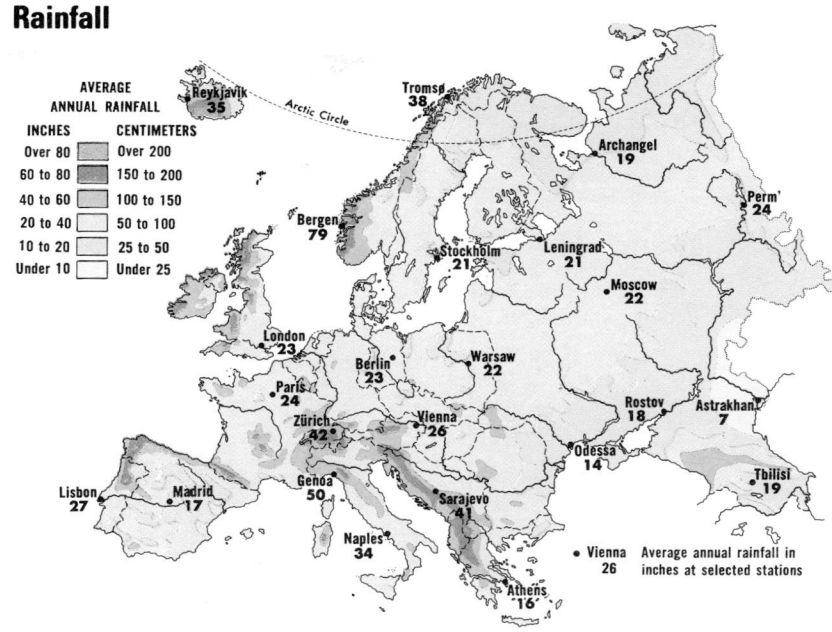

AVERAGE ANNUAL RAINFALL

INCHES	CENTIMETERS
Over 80	Over 200
60 to 80	150 to 200
40 to 60	100 to 150
20 to 40	50 to 100
10 to 20	25 to 50
Under 10	Under 25

Reykjavík 35 · Tromsø 38 · Archangel 19 · Perm' 24 · Bergen 79 · Stockholm 21 · Leningrad 21 · Moscow 22 · London 23 · Berlin 23 · Warsaw 22 · Paris 24 · Zürich 42 · Vienna 26 · Rostov 18 · Astrakhan 7 · Odessa 14 · Lisbon 27 · Madrid 17 · Genoa 50 · Sarajevo 41 · Tbilisi 19 · Naples 34 · Athens 16

• Vienna   Average annual rainfall in
  26   inches at selected stations

Average January Temperature

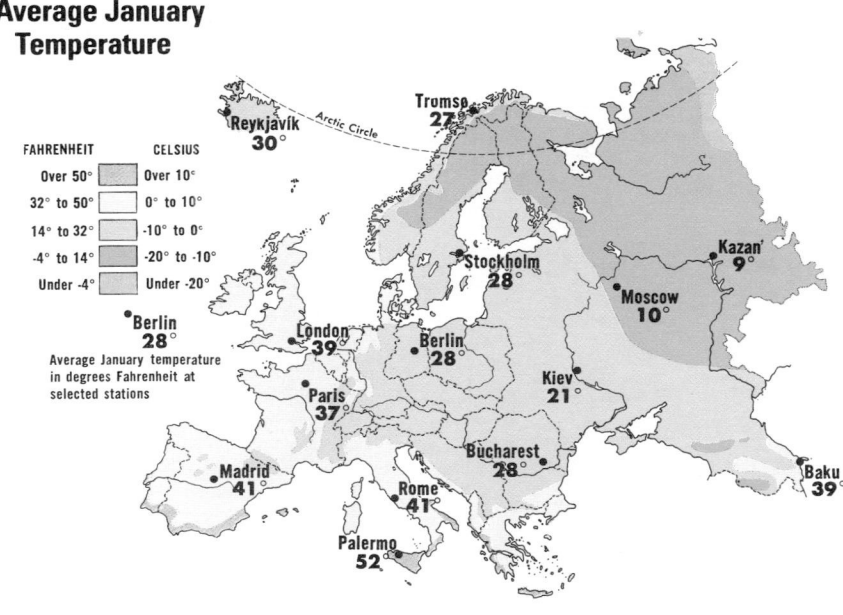

FAHRENHEIT	CELSIUS
Over 50°	Over 10°
32° to 50°	0° to 10°
14° to 32°	-10° to 0°
-4° to 14°	-20° to -10°
Under -4°	Under -20°

Reykjavík 30° · Tromsø 27° · Kazan' 9° · Stockholm 28° · Moscow 10° · Berlin 28° · London 39° · Berlin 28° · Kiev 21° · Paris 37° · Madrid 41° · Bucharest 28° · Baku 39° · Rome 41° · Palermo 52°

Average January temperature
in degrees Fahrenheit at
selected stations

Average July Temperature

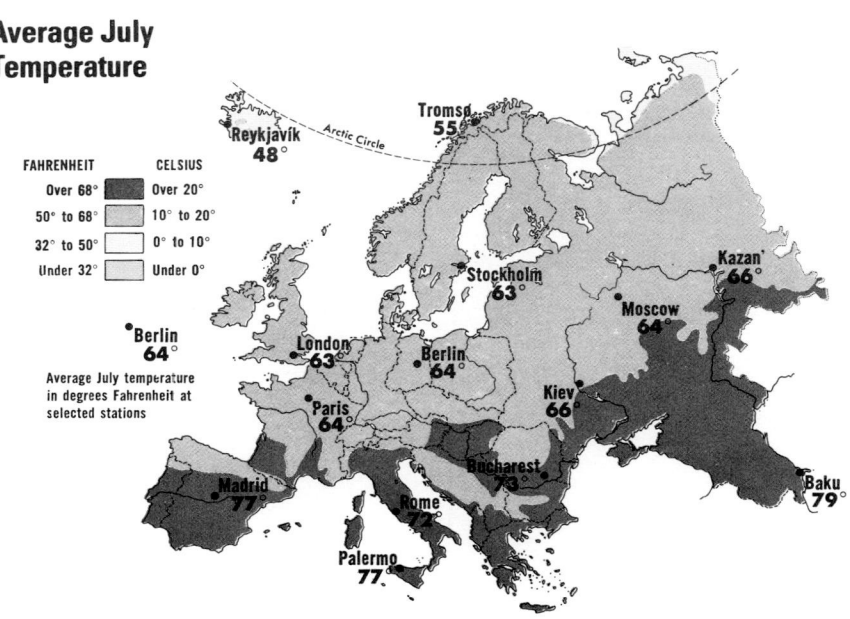

FAHRENHEIT	CELSIUS
Over 68°	Over 20°
50° to 68°	10° to 20°
32° to 50°	0° to 10°
Under 32°	Under 0°

Reykjavík 48° · Tromsø 55° · Kazan' 66° · Stockholm 63° · Moscow 64° · Berlin 64° · London 63° · Berlin 64° · Kiev 66° · Paris 64° · Bucharest 73° · Baku 79° · Madrid 77° · Rome 72° · Palermo 77°

Average July temperature
in degrees Fahrenheit at
selected stations

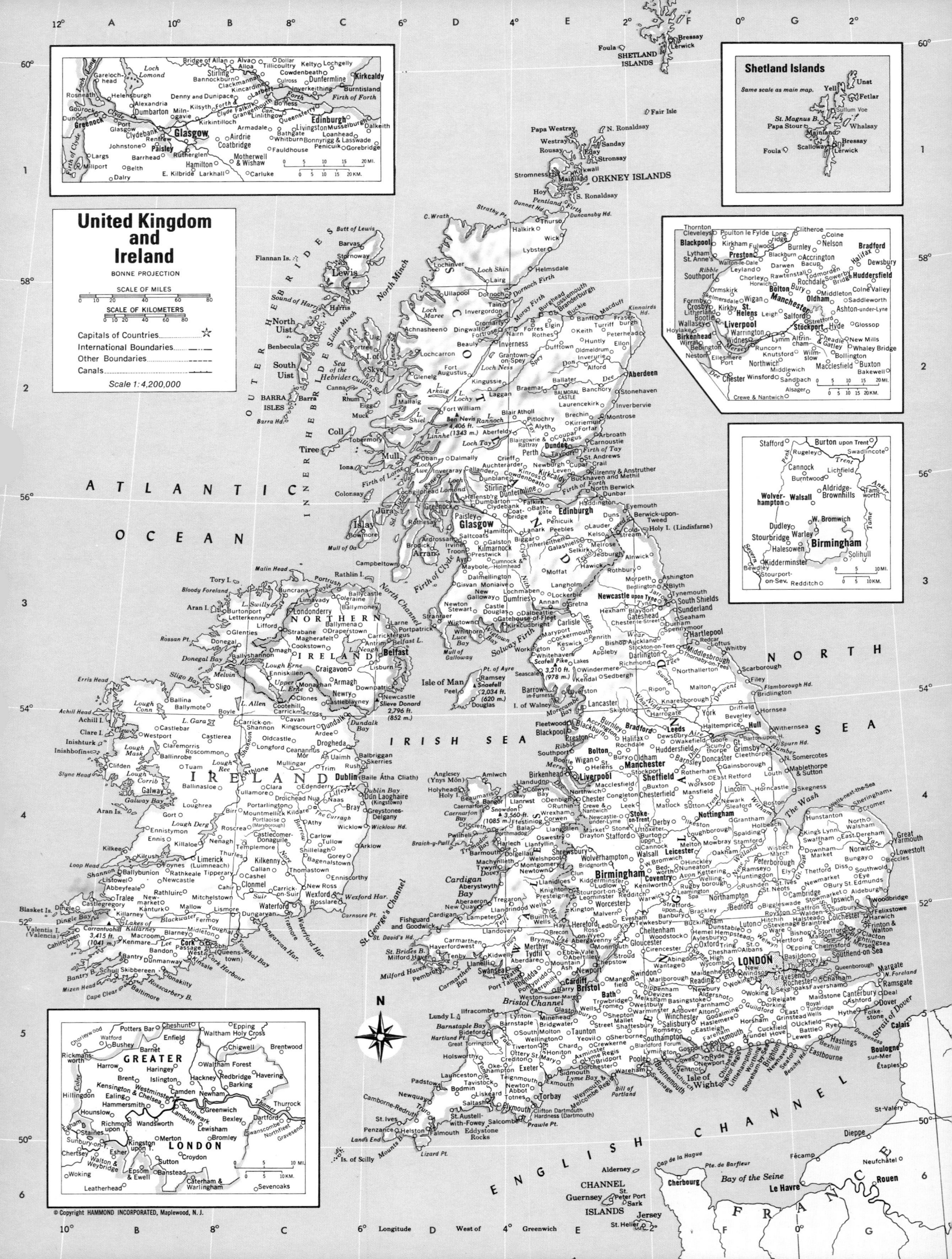

United Kingdom and Ireland

BONNE PROJECTION

SCALE OF MILES

SCALE OF KILOMETERS

Capitals of Countries..........★
International Boundaries..........
Other Boundaries..........
Canals..........

Scale 1 : 4,200,000

Shetland Islands

Same scale as main map.

GREATER LONDON

© Copyright HAMMOND INCORPORATED, Maplewood, N.J.

UNITED KINGDOM

AREA 94,399 sq. mi. (244,493 sq. km.)
POPULATION 55,672,000
CAPITAL London
LARGEST CITY London
HIGHEST POINT Ben Nevis 4,406 ft. (1,343 m.)
MONETARY UNIT pound sterling
MAJOR LANGUAGES English, Gaelic, Welsh
MAJOR RELIGIONS Protestantism, Roman Catholicism

IRELAND

AREA 27,136 sq. mi. (70,282 sq. km.)
POPULATION 3,440,427
CAPITAL Dublin
LARGEST CITY Dublin
HIGHEST POINT Carrantuohill 3,415 ft. (1,041 m.)
MONETARY UNIT Irish pound
MAJOR LANGUAGES English, Gaelic (Irish)
MAJOR RELIGION Roman Catholicism

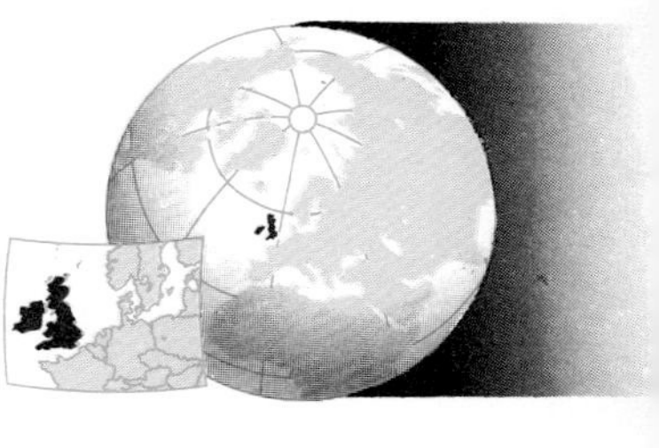

ENGLAND

COUNTIES

Avon, 920,200 E 6
Bedfordshire, 491,700 G 5
Berkshire, 659,000 F 6
Buckinghamshire, 512,000 G 6
Cambridgeshire, 563,000 G 5
Cheshire, 916,400 E 4
Cleveland, 567,900 F 3
Cornwall, 405,200 C 7
Cumbria, 473,600 D 3
Derbyshire, 887,600 F 5
Devon, 942,100 D 7
Dorset, 575,800 E 7
Durham, 610,400 F 3
East Sussex, 655,600 H 7
Essex, 1,426,200 H 6
Gloucestershire, 491,500 E 6
Greater London, 7,028,200 H 8
Greater Manchester, 2,684,100 H 2
Hampshire, 1,456,100 F 6
Hereford and Worcester, 594,200 E 5
Hertfordshire, 937,300 G 6
Humberside, 848,600 G 4
Isle of Wight, 111,300 F 7
Isles of Scilly, 1,900 A 7
Kent, 1,448,100 H 6
Lancashire, 1,375,500 E 4
Leicestershire, 837,900 F 5
Lincolnshire, 524,500 G 4
London, Greater, 7,028,200 H 8
Manchester, Greater, 2,684,100 H 2
Merseyside, 1,578,000 G 2
Norfolk, 662,500 H 5
Northamptonshire, 505,900 G 5
Northumberland, 287,300 E 2
North Yorkshire, 653,000 F 3
Nottinghamshire, 977,500 F 4
Oxfordshire 541,800 F6
Shropshire (Salop) 359,000 E5
Somerset 404,400 E6
South Yorkshire 1,318,300 F4
Staffordshire 997,600 E5
Suffolk 577,600 H5
Surrey 1,002,900 G6
Sussex, East 655,600 H7
Sussex, West 623,400 G7
Tyne and Wear 1,182,900 H3
Warwickshire 471,000 F5
West Midlands 2,743,300 F5
West Sussex 623,400 G7
West Yorkshire 2,072,500 J1
Wiltshire 512,800 E6
Yorkshire, North 653,000 F3
Yorkshire, South 1,318,300 F4
Yorkshire, West 2,072,500 J1

CITIES and TOWNS

Abingdon, 20,130 F 6
Accrington, 36,470 H 1
Adwick le Street, 17,650 K 2
Aldeburgh, 2,750 J 5
Aldershot, 33,750 G 8
Aldridge Brownhills, 89,370 E 5
Alfreton, 21,560 F 4
Alnwick, 7,300 F 2
Altrincham, 40,800 H 2
Amersham, ⊙17,254 G 7
Andover, 27,620 F 6
Appleby, 2,240 E 3
Arnold, 35,090 F 4
Arundel, 2,390 G 7
Ashford, 36,380 H 6
Ashington, 24,720 F 2
Ashton-under-Lyne, 48,500 H 2
Axminster, ⊙4,515 D 7
Aycliffe, ⊙20,203 F 3
Aylesbury, 41,420 G 7
Bacup, 14,990 H 1
Bakewell, 4,100 J 2
Banbury, 31,060 F 5
Banstead, 44,100 H 8
Barking, 153,800 H 8
Barnet, 305,200 H 7
Barnsley, 74,730 J 2
Barnstaple, 17,820 D 6
Barrow-in-Furness, 73,400 D 3
Barton-upon-Humber, 7,750 G 4
Basildon, 135,720 J 8
Basingstoke, 60,910 F 6
Bath, 83,100 E 6
Batley, 41,630 J 1
Battle, ⊙4,987 H 7
Bebington, 62,500 G 2
Bedford, 74,390 G 5
Bedlington, 27,200 F 2
Bedworth, 41,600 F 5
Beeston and Stapleford, 65,360 F 5
Benfleet, 49,180 J 8
Bentley with Arksey, 22,320 F 4
Berkhamsted, 15,920 G 7
Beverley, 16,920 G 4
Bexhill, 34,680 H 7
Bexley, 213,500 H 8
Biddulph, 18,720 H 2
Birkenhead, 135,750 G 2
Birmingham, 1,058,800 F 5
Bishop Auckland, 32,940 E 3
Bishop's Stortford, 21,720 H 6
Blackburn, 101,670 H 1
Blackpool, 149,000 G 1
Blaydon, 31,940 H 3
Blyth, 35,390 F 2
Bodmin, 10,430 C 7
Bognor Regis, 34,620 G 7
Boldon, 24,430 J 3
Bolton, 154,480 H 2
Bootle 71,160 G2
Boston 26,700 G5
Bournemouth 144,100 F7
Bracknell† 34,067 G8
Bradford 458,900 J1
Braintree and Bocking 26,300 H6
Brent 256,500 H8
Brentwood 58,690 J8
Bridgwater 26,700 E6
Bridlington 26,920 G3
Bridport 6,660 E7
Brigg 4,870 G4
Brighouse 35,320 J1
Brightlingsea 7,170 J6
Brighton 156,500 G7
Bristol 416,300 E6
Broadstairs and Saint Peter's 21,670 J6
Bromley 299,100 H8
Bromsgrove 41,430 E5
Buckfastleigh 2,870 C7
Buckingham 5,290 G6
Bude-Stratton 5,750 C7
Bungay 4,120 J5
Burgess Hill 20,030 G7
Burnham-on-Crouch 4,920 H6
Burnley 74,300 H1
Burntwood† 23,088 F5
Burton upon Trent 49,480 F5
Bury 69,550 H2
Bury Saint Edmunds 26,800 H5
Bushey 24,500 H7
Buxton 20,050 J2
Caister-on-Sea† 6,287 J5
Camborne-Redruth 43,970 B7
Cambridge 106,400 G5
Camden 185,800 H8
Cannock 56,440 E5
Canterbury 115,600 H6
Canvey Island 29,550 J8

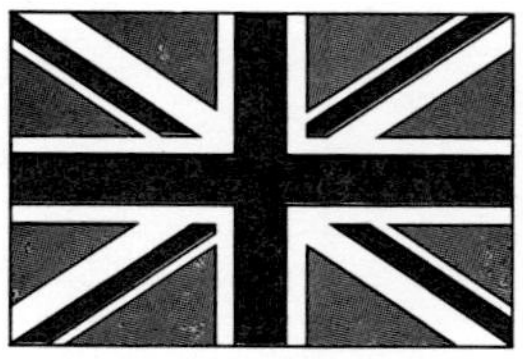

UNITED KINGDOM

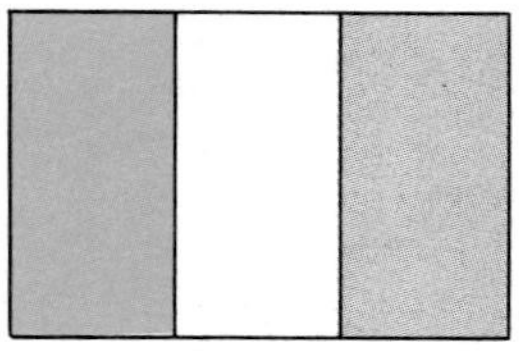

IRELAND

Carlisle, 99,600 D 3
Carlton, 46,690 F 5
Caterham and Warlingham, 35,840 H 8
Chatham, 59,550 J 8
Cheadle and Gatley, 62,460 H 2
Chelmsford, 58,320 J 7
Cheltenham, 75,910 E 6
Chertsey, 45,070 G 8
Chesham, 20,830 G 7
Cheshunt, 45,750 H 7
Chester, 117,200 G 2
Chesterfield, 69,480 J 2
Chester-le-Street, 20,720 J 3
Chichester, 20,940 G 7
Chigwell, 54,220 H 8
Chippenham, 18,550 E 6
Chorley, 31,800 G 2
Christchurch, 31,610 F 7
Cirencester, 14,500 E 6
Clacton, 39,380 J 6
Clay Cross, 9,630 J 2
Cleator Moor, ⊙7,686 D 3
Cleethorpes, 37,200 H 4
Clevedon, 15,140 D 6
Clun, ⊙1,261 D 6
Coalville, 28,740 F 5
Cockermouth, 6,480 D 3
Colchester, 79,600 H 6
Colne, 19,030 H 1
Colne Valley, 21,190 J 2
Congleton, 21,500 H 2
Consett, 35,080 H 3
Corby, 48,850 G 5
Coventry, 336,800 F 5
Cowes, 19,190 F 7
Crawley, 72,600 G 6
Crewe and Nantwich, 98,100 E 4
Cromer, 5,720 J 5
Crook and Willington, 21,120 E 3
Crosby, 56,750 G 2
Croydon, 330,600 H 8
Cuckfield, 26,500 G 6
Darlington, 85,120 F 3
Dartford, 44,130 J 8
Darton, 15,710 J 2
Darwen, 29,290 H 1
Deal, 26,840 J 6
Dearne, 24,780 K 2
Denton, 38,110 H 2
Derby, 213,700 F 5
Dewsbury, 50,560 J 1
Didcot, ⊙14,277 F 6
Doncaster, 81,530 F 4
Dorking, 22,410 G 8
Dover, 34,160 J 6
Downham Market, 4,120 H 5
Droitwich, 13,950 E 5
Dronfield, 20,000 J 2
Dudley, 187,110 E 5
Dunstable, 32,090 G 6
Durham, 88,800 J 3
Ealing, 293,800 H 8
Eastbourne, 73,200 H 7
East Grinstead, 19,420 G 6
Eastleigh, 46,340 F 7
East Retford, 18,260 G 4
Egham, 30,320 G 8
Egremont, ⊙7,253 D 3
Eling, ⊙20,006 F 7
Ellesmere, ⊙2,630 E 5
Ellesmere Port, 63,870 G 2
Enfield, 260,900 H 7
Epsom and Ewell, 70,700 G 8
Esher, 63,970 H 8
Eston, ⊙46,219 F 3
Eton, 4,950 G 8
Evesham, 14,090 F 5
Exeter, 93,300 D 7
Exminster, ⊙3,181 D 7
Exmouth, 26,840 D 7
Falmouth, 17,530 B 7
Fareham, 86,300 F 7
Farnborough, 43,520 G 8
Farnham, 33,140 G 8
Farnworth, 26,110 H 2
Faversham, 15,010 H 6
Felixstowe, 19,460 J 6
Felling, 38,990 J 3
Filey, 5,660 G 3
Fleet, 22,930 G 8
Fleetwood, 30,070 D 4
Folkestone, 45,610 J 6
Formby, 24,850 G 2
Framlingham, ⊙2,258 J 5
Frimley and Camberley, 47,390 G 8
Fulwood, 22,910 G 1
Gainsborough, 17,440 G 4
Gateshead, 91,230 J 3
Gillingham, Dorset, ⊙4,050 E 6
Gillingham, Kent, 93,900 J 8
Glastonbury, 6,580 E 6
Glossop, 24,820 J 2
Gloucester, 91,600 E 6
Godalming, 18,840 G 8
Golborne, 28,720 G 2
Goole, 17,920 G 4
Gosport, 82,300 F 7
Grange, 3,520 E 3

ENGLAND

AREA 50,516 sq. mi. (130,836 sq. km.)
POPULATION 46,220,955
CAPITAL London
LARGEST CITY London
HIGHEST POINT Scafell Pike 3,210 ft. (978 m.)

WALES

AREA 8,017 sq. mi. (20,764 sq. km.)
POPULATION 2,790,462
CAPITAL Cardiff
LARGEST CITY Cardiff
HIGHEST POINT Snowdon 3,560 ft. (1,085 m.)

SCOTLAND

AREA 30,414 sq. mi. (78,772 sq. km.)
POPULATION 5,117,146
CAPITAL Edinburgh
LARGEST CITY Glasgow
HIGHEST POINT Ben Nevis 4,406 ft. (1,343 m.)

NORTHERN IRELAND

AREA 5,452 sq. mi. (14,121 sq. km.)
POPULATION 1,543,000
CAPITAL Belfast
LARGEST CITY Belfast
HIGHEST POINT Slieve Donard 2,796 ft. (852 m.)

Grantham 27,830 G5
Gravesend 53,500 J8
Great Grimsby 93,800 G4
Great Torrington 3,430 C7
Great Yarmouth 49,410 J5
Greenwich 207,200 H8
Guildford 58,470 G8
Guisborough 14,860 F3
Hackney 192,500 H8
Hale 17,080 H2
Halesowen 54,120 E5
Halifax 88,580 J1
Haltemprice 54,850 G4
Haltwhistle† 3,511 E2
Hammersmith 170,000 H8
Haringey 228,200 H8
Harlow 79,160 H7
Harrogate 64,620 F4
Harrow 200,200 B5
Hartlepool 97,100 F3
Harwich 15,280 J6
Haslingden 15,140 H1
Hastings 74,600 H7
Hatfield† 25,359 H7
Havant and Waterloo 112,430 G7
Haverhill 14,550 H5
Havering 239,200 J8
Hayle† 5,378 B7
Hazel Grove and Bramhall 40,400 H2
Heanor 24,590 F4
Hebburn 23,150 J3
Hedon 3,010 G4
Hemel Hempstead 71,150 G7
Hereford 47,800 E5
Hertford 20,760 H7
Hetton 16,810 J3
Hexham 9,820 E3
Heywood 31,720 H2
High Wycombe 61,190 G8
Hillingdon 230,800 G8
Hinckley 49,310 F5
Hinderwell† 2,551 G3
Hitchin 29,190 G6
Hoddesdon 27,510 H7
Holmfirth 19,790 J2
Horley† 18,593 H8
Hornsea 7,280 G4
Horsham 26,770 G6
Horwich 16,670 G2
Houghton-le-Spring 33,150 J3
Hounslow, 199,100 G 8
Hove, 72,000 G 7
Hoylake, 32,000 G 2
Hoyland Nether, 15,500 J 2
Hucknall, 27,110 F 4
Huddersfield, 130,060 J 2
Hugh Town, ⊙1,958 A 8
Hull, 276,600 G 4
Hunstanton, 4,140 H 5
Huntingdon and Godmanchester, 17,200 G 5
Huyton-with-Roby, 65,950 G 2
Hyde, 37,040 H 2
Ilfracombe, 9,350 C 6
Ilkeston, 33,690 F 5
Immingham, ⊙10,259 G 4
Ipswich, 121,500 J 5
Islington, 171,600 H 8
Jarrow, 28,510 J 3
Kendal, 22,440 E 3
Kenilworth, 19,730 F 5
Kensington and Chelsea, 161,400 G 8
Keswick, 4,790 D 3
Kettering, 44,480 G 5
Keynsham, 18,970 E 6
Kidderminster, 49,960 E!
Kidsgrove, 22,690 E 4
King's Lynn, 29,990 H 5
Kingston upon Thames, 135,600 H 8
Kingswood, 30,450 E 6
Kirkburton, 20,320 J 2
Kirkby, 59,100 G 2
Kirkby Lonsdale, ⊙1,506 E 3
Kirkby Stephen, ⊙1,539 E 3
Knutsford, 14,840 H 2
Lambeth, 290,300 H 8
Lancaster, 126,300 E 3
Leatherhead, 40,830 G 8
Leeds, 744,500 J 1
Leek, 19,460 H 2
Leicester, 289,400 F 5
Leigh, 46,390 H 2
Leighton-Linslade, 22,590 F 7
Letchworth, 31,520 G 6
Lewes, 14,170 H 7
Lewisham, 237,300 H 8
Leyland, 23,690 G 1
Lichfield, 23,690 F 5
Lincoln, 73,700 G 4
Liskeard, 5,360 C 7
Litherland, 23,530 G 2
Littlehampton, 20,320 G 7

(continued on following page)

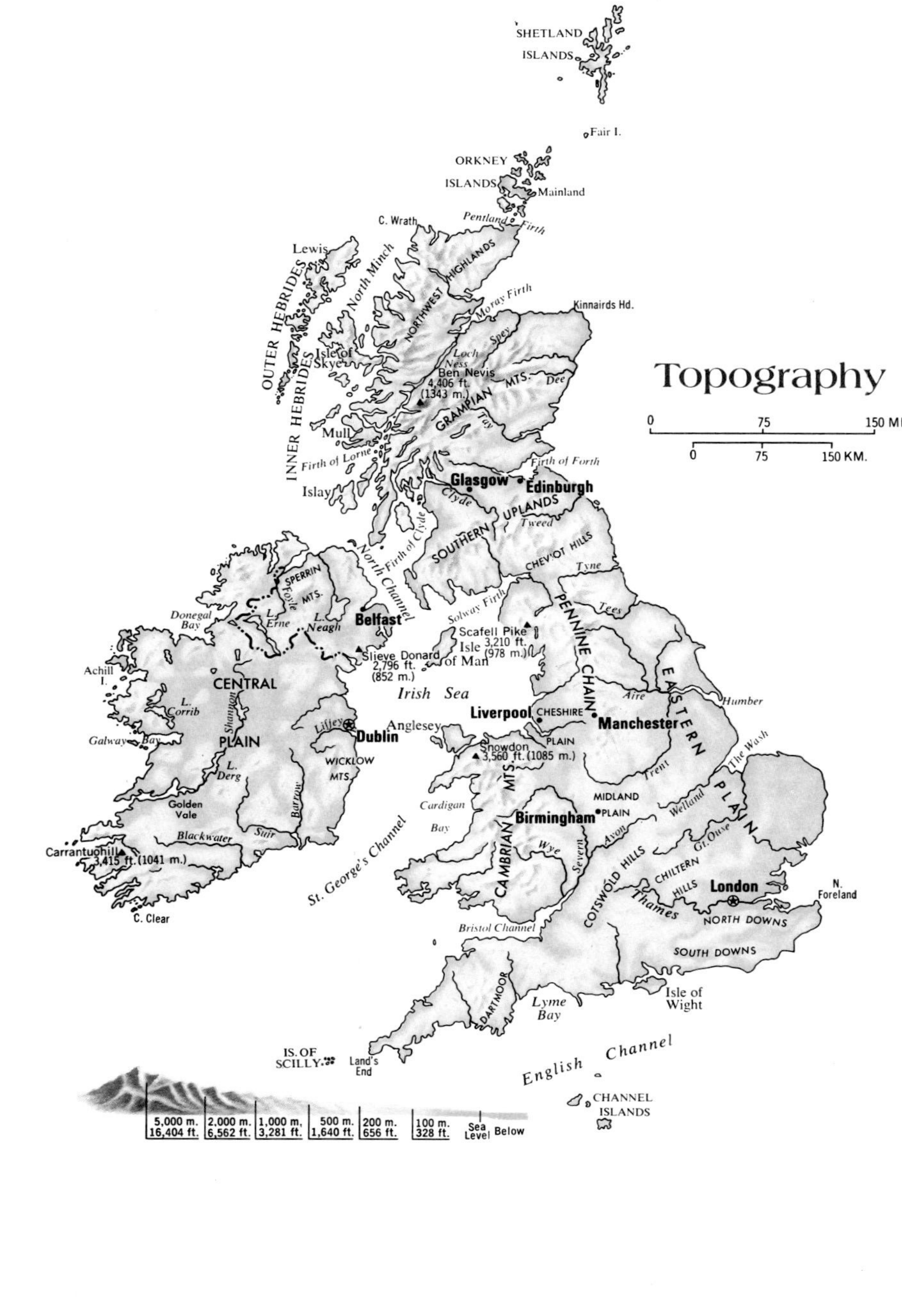

Topography
0 75 150 MI.
0 75 150 KM.
SHETLAND ISLANDS
Fair I.
ORKNEY ISLANDS
Mainland
C. Wrath
Pentland Firth
Lewis
OUTER HEBRIDES
North Minch
NORTHWEST HIGHLANDS
Moray Firth
Kinnairds Hd.
Spey
Isle of Skye
Loch Ness
Ben Nevis 4,406 ft. (1343 m.)
GRAMPIAN MTS.
Dee
INNER HEBRIDES
Mull
Firth of Lorne
Firth of Forth
Glasgow
Edinburgh
Islay
Clyde
SOUTHERN UPLANDS
Tweed
CHEVIOT HILLS
Tyne
North Firth of Clyde
North Channel
SPERRIN MTS.
Foyle
Donegal Bay
L. Erne
L. Neagh
Belfast
Solway Firth
Scafell Pike 3,210 ft. (978 m.)
Tees
PENNINE CHAIN
Isle of Man
Slieve Donard 2,796 ft. (852 m.)
Achill I.
CENTRAL
L. Corrib
Shannon
PLAIN
Galway Bay
Irish Sea
Liffey
Dublin
Anglesey
Liverpool
CHESHIRE PLAIN
Manchester
Aire
Humber
EASTERN PLAIN
The Wash
L. Derg
WICKLOW MTS.
Snowdon 3,560 ft. (1085 m.)
Trent
Golden Vale
Barrow
Cardigan Bay
MIDLAND PLAIN
Birmingham
Welland
Gt. Ouse
Blackwater
Suir
CAMBRIAN MTS.
Wye
Severn
Avon
CHILTERN HILLS
Carrantuohill 3,415 ft. (1041 m.)
St. George's Channel
COTSWOLD HILLS
London
N. Foreland
Thames
C. Clear
Bristol Channel
NORTH DOWNS
SOUTH DOWNS
DARTMOOR
Lyme Bay
Isle of Wight
IS. OF SCILLY
Land's End
English Channel
CHANNEL ISLANDS
5,000 m. 16,404 ft.
2,000 m. 6,562 ft.
1,000 m. 3,281 ft.
500 m. 1,640 ft.
200 m. 656 ft.
100 m. 328 ft.
Sea Level
Below

Liverpool, 539,700 G 2
Loftus, 7,850 G 3
London (cap.), 7,028,200 H 8
London, ★12,332,900 H 8
Long Eaton, 33,560 F 5
Longbenton, 50,120 J 3
Looe, 4,060 C 7
Loughborough, 49,010 F 5
Lowestoft, 53,260 J 5
Ludlow, ⊙7,466 E 5
Luton, 164,500 G 6
Lydd, 4,670 H 7
Lyme Regis, 3,460 E 7
Lymington, 36,780 F 7
Lynton, 1,770 D 6
Lytham Saint Anne's, 42,120 G 1
Mablethorpe and Sutton, 6,750 H 4
Macclesfield, 45,420 H 2
Maidenhead, 48,210 G 8
Maidstone, 72,110 J 8
Maldon, 14,350 H 6
Malmesbury, 2,550 E 6
Malton, 4,010 G 3
Malvern, 30,420 E 5
Manchester, 490,000 H 2
Mangotsfield, 23,000 E 6
Mansfield, 58,450 K 2
Mansfield Woodhouse, 25,400 F 4
March, 14,560 H 5
Margate, 50,290 J 6
Market Harborough, 15,230 G 5
Marlborough, 6,370 F 6
Matlock, 20,300 J 2
Melton Mowbray, 20,680 G 5
Merton, 169,400 H 8
Middlesbrough, 153,900 F 3
Middleton, 53,340 H 2
Middlewich, 7,600 H 2
Mildenhall, ⊙9,269 H 5
Millom, ⊙7,101 D 3
Milton Keynes, 89,900 F 5
Minehead, 8,230 D 6
Moretonhampstead, ⊙1,440 C 7
Morpeth, 14,450 F 2
Mundesley, ⊙1,536 J 5
Nelson, 31,220 H 1
Neston, 18,210 G 2
Newark, 24,760 G 4
Newbury, 24,850 F 6
Newcastle upon Tyne, 295,800 H 3
Newcastle-under-Lyme, 75,940 E 4
Newham, 228,900 H 8
Newhaven, 9,970 H 7
Newport, 22,430 F 7
New Romney, 3,830 J 7
Newton Abbot, 19,940 D 7
Newton-le-Willows, 21,780 H 2
New Windsor, 29,660 G 8
Northallerton F 3
Northam, 8,310 C 6
Northampton, 128,290 F 5
Northfleet, 27,150 J 8
North Sunderland, ⊙1,725 F 2
Northwich, 17,710 H 2
Norton, 5,580 G 3
Norton-Radstock, 15,900 E 6
Norwich, 119,200 J 5
Nottingham, 280,300 F 5
Nuneaton, 69,210 F 5
Oadby, 20,700 F 5
Oakham, 7,280 G 5
Okehampton, 4,000 D 7
Oldham, 103,690 H 2
Ormskirk, 28,860 G 2
Oswaldtwistle, 14,270 H 1
Oxford, 117,400 F 6
Padstow, ⊙2,802 B 7
Penryn, 5,660 B 7
Penzance, 19,360 B 7
Peterborough, 118,900 G 5
Peterlee, ⊙21,846 J 3
Plymouth, 259,100 C 7
Polperro, ⊙1,491 C 7
Poole, 110,600 E 7
Porlock, ⊙1,290 D 6
Portishead, 9,680 E 6
Portland, 14,860 E 7
Portslade-by-Sea, 18,040 G 7
Portsmouth, 198,500 F 7
Potters Bar, 24,670 H 7
Poulton-le-Fylde, 16,340 G 1
Preston, 94,760 G 1
Prestwich, 32,850 H 2
Queenborough, 31,550 H 6
Radcliffe, 29,630 H 2
Ramsbottom, 16,710 H 2
Ramsgate, 40,090 J 6
Rawtenstall, 20,950 H 1
Rayleigh, 26,740 J 8
Reading, 131,200 G 8
Redbridge, 231,600 H 8
Redcar, ⊙46,325 F 3
Redditch, 44,750 E 5
Reigate, 55,600 H 8
Richmond upon Thames, 166,800 H 8
Rickmansworth, 29,030 G 8
Ripley, 18,060 F 4
Rochdale, 93,780 H 2
Rochester, 56,030 J 8
Rothbury, ⊙1,818 E 2
Rotherham, 84,770 K 2
Royal Leamington Spa, 44,950 F 5
Royal Tunbridge Wells, 44,800 H 6
Rugby, 60,380 F 5
Rugeley, 24,440 E 5
Runcorn, 42,730 G 2
Rushden, 21,840 G 5
Ryde, 23,170 F 7
Rye, 4,530 H 7
Ryton, 15,170 H 3
Saddleworth, 21,340 J 2
Saint Agnes, ⊙4,747 B 7
Saint Albans, 123,800 H 7
Saint Austell-with-Fowey, 32,710 C 7
Saint Columb Major, ⊙3,953 B 7
Saint Helens, 104,890 G 2
Saint Ives, Cornwall, 9,760 B 7
Saint Neots, 17,940 G 5
Salcombe, 2,370 D 7
Sale, 59,060 H 2
Salford, 261,100 H 2
Salisbury, 35,460 F 6
Saltburn and Marske-by-the-Sea, 21,170 G 3
Sandbach, 14,280 H 2
Sandown-Shanklin, 14,800 F 7
Sandwich, 4,420 J 6
Saxmundham, 1,820 J 5
Scarborough, 43,300 G 3
Scunthorpe, 68,100 G 4
Seaford, 18,020 H 7
Seaham, 22,470 J 3
Seascale, ⊙2,106 D 3
Seaton, 4,500 D 7
Seaton Valley, 35,880 J 3
Sedbergh, ⊙2,741 E 3
Selsey, ⊙6,491 G 7
Sevenoaks, 18,160 J 8
Shaftesbury, 4,180 E 7
Sheffield, 558,000 J 2
Sherborne, 9,230 E 7
Sheringham, 4,940 J 5
Shildon, 15,360 F 3
Shoreham-by-Sea, 19,620 G 7
Shrewsbury, 56,120 E 5
Silloth, ⊙2,662 D 3
Sittingbourne and Milton, 32,830 H 6
Skelmersdale, 35,850 G 2
Skelton and Brotton, 15,930 G 3
Sleaford, 8,050 G 5
Slough, 89,060 G 8
Solihull, 108,230 F 5
Southampton, 213,700 F 7
Southend-on-Sea, 159,300 H 6
Southport, 86,030 G 1
South Shields, 96,900 J 3
Southwark, 224,900 H 8
Southwold, 1,960 J 5
Sowerby Bridge, 15,700 H 1
Spalding, 17,040 G 5
Spenborough, 41,460 J 1
Spennymoor, 19,050 F 3
Stafford, 54,860 E 5
Staines, 56,380 G 8
Stamford, 14,980 G 5
Stanley, 42,280 H 3
Staveley, 17,620 K 2
Stevenage, 72,600 G 6
Stockport, 138,350 H 2
Stockton-on-Tees, 165,400 F 3
Stoke-on-Trent, 256,200 E 4
Stourbridge, 56,530 E 5
Stourport-on-Severn, 19,430 E 5
Stowmarket, 9,020 J 5
Stratford-upon-Avon, 20,080 F 5
Stretford, 52,450 H 2
Stroud, 19,600 E 6
Sudbury, 8,860 H 5
Sunbury-on-Thames, 40,070 G 8
Sunderland, 214,820 J 3
Sutton, 166,700 H 8
Sutton Bridge, ⊙3,113 H 5
Sutton in Ashfield, 40,330 K 2
Swadlincote, 21,060 F 5
Swanage, 8,000 E 7
Swindon, 90,680 F 6
Tamworth, 46,960 F 5
Taunton, 37,570 D 6
Tavistock, ⊙7,620 C 7
Telford, ⊙79,451 E 5
Tenbury, ⊙2,151 E 5
Tewkesbury, 9,210 E 6
Thetford, 15,690 H 5
Thirsk, ⊙2,884 F 3
Thornaby-on-Tees, ⊙42,385 F 3
Thorne, ⊙16,694 F 4
Thornton Cleveleys, 27,090 G 1
Thurrock, 127,700 J 8
Tiverton, 16,190 D 7
Todmorden, 14,540 H 1
Tonbridge, 31,410 H 8
Torbay, 109,900 D 7
Torpoint, 6,840 C 7
Tower Hamlets, 146,100 H 8
Tow Law, 2,460 H 4
Trowbridge, 20,120 E 6
Truro, 15,690 B 7
Turton, 22,800 H 2
Tynemouth, 67,090 J 3
Upton upon Severn, ⊙2,048 E 5
Urmston, 44,130 H 2
Uttoxeter, 9,100 E 5
Ventnor, 6,980 F 7
Wainfleet All Saints, ⊙1,116 H 4
Wakefield, 306,500 J 2
Wallasey, 94,520 G 2
Wallsend, 45,490 J 3
Walsall, 182,430 E 5
Waltham Forest, 223,700 H 8
Waltham Holy Cross, 14,810 H 7
Walton and Weybridge, 51,270 G 8
Walton-le-Dale, 27,660 G 1
Wandsworth, 284,600 H 8
Wantage, 8,490 F 6
Ware, 14,900 H 7
Wareham, 4,630 E 7
Warley, 161,260 E 5
Warminster, 14,440 E 6
Warrington, 65,320 G 2
Warwick, 17,870 F 5
Washington, 27,720 J 3
Watchet, 2,980 D 6
Watford, 77,000 H 7
Wellingborough, 39,570 G 5
Wells, 8,960 E 6
Wells-next-the-Sea, 2,450 H 5
Welwyn, 39,900 H 7
Wem, ⊙3,411 E 5
West Bridgford, 28,340 F 5
West Bromwich, 162,740 F 5
West Mersea, 4,730 H 6
Westminster, 216,100 H 8
Weston-super-Mare, 51,960 D 6
Weymouth and Melcombe Regis, 41,080 E 7
Whickham, 29,710 J 3
Whitchurch, ⊙7,142 E 5
Whitehaven, 26,260 D 3
Whitley Bay, 37,010 J 3
Widnes, 58,330 G 2
Wigan, 80,920 G 2
Wigston, 31,650 F 5
Wilmslow, 31,250 H 2
Wilton, 4,090 F 6
Winchester, 88,900 F 6
Windermere, 7,860 E 3
Winsford, 26,920 G 2
Wirral, 27,510 G 2
Wisbech, 16,990 H 5
Witham, 19,730 H 6
Withernsea, 6,300 H 4
Wivenhoe, 5,630 J 6
Woking, 79,300 G 8
Wokingham, 22,390 G 8
Wolverhampton, 266,400 E 5
Wombwell, 17,850 K 2
Woodhall Spa, 2,420 G 4
Woodley and Sandford, ⊙24,581 G 8
Woodstock, 2,070 F 6
Wooler, ⊙1,833 F 2
Worcester, 73,900 E 5
Workington, 28,260 D 3
Worksop, 36,590 F 4
Worsbrough, 15,180 J 2
Worsley, 49,530 H 2
Worthing, 89,100 G 7
Wymondham, 9,390 J 5
Yateley, ⊙16,505 G 8
Yeovil, 26,180 E 7
York, 101,900 F 4

OTHER FEATURES

Aire (riv.) F 4
Atlantic Ocean A 7
Avon (riv.) F 5
Avon (riv.) F 7
Axe Edge (mt.) H 2
Barnstaple (bay) C 6
Beachy (head) H 7
Bigbury (bay) C 7
Blackwater (riv.) H 6
Bristol (chan.) C 6
Brown Willy (mt.) C 7
Cheviot (hills) E 2
Cheviot, The (mt.) E 2
Chiltern (hills) G 6
Cleveland (hills) F 3
Colne (riv.) G 8
Cornwall (cape) B 7
Cotswold (hills) E 6
Cross Fell (mt.) E 3
Cumbrian (mts.) D 3
Dart (riv.) D 7
Dartmoor National Park C 7
Dee (riv.) D 4
Derwent (riv.) G 3
Derwent (riv.) H 3
Don (riv.) F 4
Dorset Heights (hills) E 7
Dove (riv.) J 2
Dover (str.) J 7
Dungeness (prom.) J 7
Dunkery (hill) D 6
Eddystone (rocks) C 7
Eden (riv.) E 3
English (chan.) D 8
Esk (riv.) D 2
Exe (riv.) D 7
Exmoor National Park D 6
Fens, The (reg.) G 5
Flamborough (head) G 3
Formby (head) G 2
Foulness Island (pen.) J 6
Gibraltar (pt.) H 4
Great Ouse (riv.) H 5
Hartland (pt.) C 6
High Willhays (mt.) C 7
Hodder (riv.) H 1
Holderness (pen.), 43,900 G 4
Holy (isl.), 189 F 2
Humber (riv.) G 4
Irish (sea) B 4
Kennet (riv.) F 6
Lake District National Park D 3
Land's End (prom.) B 7
Lea (riv.) G 6
Lincoln Wolds (hills) G 4
Lindisfarne (Holy) (isl.), 189 F 2
Liverpool (bay) D 4
Lizard, The (pen.), 7,371 B 8
Lundy (isl.), 49 C 6
Lune (riv.) E 3
Lyme (bay) D 7
Manacle (pt.) C 7
Medway (riv.) H 6
Mendip (hills) E 6
Mersea (isl.), 4,423 J 6
Mersey (riv.) G 2
Morecambe (bay) D 3
Mounts (bay) B 7
Naze, The (prom.) J 6
Nene (riv.) H 5
New (for.) F 6
North (sea) J 4
North Downs (hills) G 6
North Foreland (prom.) J 6
Northumberland National Park E 2
North York Moors National Park G 3
Orford Ness (prom.) J 5
Ouse (riv.) G 4
Ouse (riv.) G 6
Parrett (riv.) E 6
Peak District National Park F 4
Peak, The (mt.) J 2
Peel Fell (mt.) E 2
Pennine Chain (range) E 3
Plymouth (sound) C 7
Portland, Bill of (pt.) E 7
Prawle (pt.) D 7
Purbeck, Isle of (pen.), 39,500 F 7
Ribble (riv.) E 4
Saint Alban's (head) F 7
Saint Bees (head) D 3
Saint Martin's (isl.), 106 A 8
Saint Mary's (isl.), 1,958 A 8
Scafell Pike (mt.) D 3
Scilly (isls.), 1,900 A 7
Selsey Bill (prom.) G 7
Severn (riv.) E 6
Sheppey (isl.), 31,550 J 6
Sherwood (for.) F 4
Skiddaw (mt.) D 3
Solent (chan.) F 7
Solway (firth) D 3
South Downs (hills) G 7
Spithead (chan.) F 7
Spurn (head) H 4
Stonehenge (ruins) F 6
Stour (riv.) E 7
Stour (riv.) H 6
Stour (riv.) J 6
Swale (riv.) F 3
Tamar (riv.) C 7
Taw (riv.) D 7
Tees (riv.) F 3
Test (riv.) F 6
Thames (riv.) H 6
Tintagel (head) C 7
Torridge (riv.) C 7
Trent (riv.) G 4
Tresco (isl.), 246 A 8
Tweed (riv.) E 2
Tyne (riv.) F 3
Ure (riv.) F 3
Ver (riv.) H 7
Walney, Isle of (isl.), 11,241 D 3
Wash, The (bay) H 5
Weald, The (reg.) H 6
Wear (riv.) F 3
Weaver (riv.) G 2
Welland (riv.) G 5
Wey (riv.) G 6
Wharfe (riv.) E 3
Wirral (pen.), 432,900 G 2
Witham (riv.) G 4
Wolds, The (hills) G 4
Wye (riv.) D 5
Wyre (riv.) G 1
Yare (riv.) J 5
Yorkshire Dales National Park E 3

CHANNEL ISLANDS

CITIES and TOWNS

Saint Anne E 8
Saint Helier (cap.), Jersey, ⊙28,135 E 8
Saint Peter Port (cap.), Guernsey, ⊙16,303 E 8
Saint Sampson's, ⊙6,534 E 8

OTHER FEATURES

Alderney (isl.), 1,686 E 8
Guernsey (isl.), 51,351 E 8
Herm (isl.), 96 E 8
Jersey (isl.), 72,629 E 8
Sark (isl.), 590 E 8

ISLE of MAN

CITIES and TOWNS

Castletown, 2,620 C 3
Douglas (cap.), 20,389 C 3
Laxey, 1,170 C 3
Michael, 408 C 3
Onchan, 4,807 C 3
Peel, 3,081 C 3
Port Erin, 1,714 C 3
Port Saint Mary, 1,508 C 3
Ramsey, 5,048 C 3

OTHER FEATURES

Ayre (pt.) C 3
Calf of Man (isl.) C 3
Langness (prom.) C 3
Snaefell (mt.) C 3
Spanish (head) C 3

WALES

COUNTIES

Clwyd, 376,000 D 4
Dyfed, 323,100 C 6
Gwent, 439,600 D 6
Gwynedd, 225,100 C 4
Mid Glamorgan, 540,400 D 6
Powys, 101,500 D 5
South Glamorgan, 389,200 A 7
West Glamorgan, 371,900 D 6

CITIES and TOWNS

Aberaeron, 1,340 C 5
Abercarn, 18,370 B 6
Aberdare, 38,030 A 6
Abertillery, 20,550 B 6
Amlwch, 3,630 C 4
Bala, 1,650 D 5
Bangor, 16,030 C 4
Barmouth, 2,070 C 5
Barry, 42,780 B 7
Beaumaris, 2,090 C 4
Bedwellty, 25,460 B 6
Bethesda, 4,180 D 4
Betws-y-Coed, 720 D 4
Brecknock (Brecon), 6,460 D 6
Brecon, 6,460 D 6
Bridgend, 14,690 A 7
Brynmawr, 5,970 B 6
Builth Wells, 1,480 D 5
Burry Port, 5,990 C 6
Caernarfon, 8,840 C 4
Caerphilly, 42,190 B 6
Cardiff, 281,500 B 7
Cardigan, 3,830 C 5
Chepstow, 8,260 E 6
Chirk, ⊙3,564 D 5
Colwyn Bay, 25,370 D 4
Criccieth, 1,590 C 5
Cwmamman, 3,950 D 6
Cwmbran, 32,980 B 6
Denbigh, 8,420 D 4
Dolgellau, 2,430 D 5
Ebbw Vale, 25,670 B 6
Ffestiniog, 5,510 D 5
Fishguard and Goodwick, 5,020 B 5
Flint, 15,070 G 2
Gelligaer, 33,820 A 6
Harlech, ⊙332 C 5
Haverfordwest, 8,930 B 6
Hawarden, ⊙20,389 G 2
Hay, 1,200 D 5
Holywell, 8,570 G 2
Kidwelly, 3,090 C 6
Knighton, 2,190 D 5
Llandeilo, 1,780 C 6
Llandovery, 2,040 D 5
Llandrindod Wells, 3,460 D 5
Llandudno, 17,700 D 4
Llanelli, 25,870 C 6
Llanfairfechan, 3,800 D 4
Llangefni, 4,070 C 4
Llangollen, 3,050 D 5
Llanguicke, ⊙15,029 D 6
Llanidloes, 2,390 D 5
Llantrisant, ⊙27,490 A 7
Llanwrtyd Wells, 460 D 5
Llwchwr, 27,530 D 6
Machynlleth, 1,830 D 5
Maesteg, 21,100 D 6
Menai Bridge, 2,730 C 4
Merthyr Tydfil, 61,500 A 6
Milford Haven, 13,960 B 6
Mold, 8,700 G 2
Montgomery, 1,000 D 5
Mountain Ash, 27,710 A 6
Mynyddislwyn, 15,590 B 6
Narberth, 970 C 6
Neath, 27,280 D 6
Nefyn, ⊙2,086 C 5
Newcastle Emlyn, 690 C 5
Newport, Dyfed, ⊙1,062 C 5
Newport, Gwent, 110,090 B 6
New Quay, 760 C 5
Newtown, 6,400 D 5
Neyland, 2,690 B 6
Ogmore and Garw, 19,680 A 6
Pembroke, 14,570 C 6
Penarth, 24,180 B 7
Penmaenmawr, 4,050 C 4
Pontypool, 36,710 B 6
Pontypridd, 34,180 A 6
Porthcawl, 14,980 D 6
Porthmadog, 3,900 C 5
Port Talbot, 58,200 D 6
Prestatyn, 15,480 D 4
Presteigne, 1,330 D 5
Pwllheli, 4,020 C 5
Rhondda, 85,400 A 6
Rhyl, 22,150 D 4
Risca, 15,780 B 6
Ruthin, 4,780 D 4
Saint David's, ⊙1,638 B 6
Swansea, 190,800 C 6
Tenby, 4,930 C 6
Tredegar, 17,450 B 6
Tywyn, 3,850 C 5
Welshpool, 7,370 D 5
Wrexham, 39,530 E 4

OTHER FEATURES

Anglesey (isl.), 64,500 C 4
Aran Fawddwy (mt.) C 5
Bardsey (isl.), 9 C 5
Berwyn (mts.) D 5
Black (mts.) D 6
Braich-y-Pwll (prom.) C 5
Brecon Beacons (mt.) D 6
Brecon Beacons National Park D 6
Caldy (isl.), 70 C 6
Cambrian (mts.) D 5
Cardigan (bay) C 5
Carmarthen (bay) C 6
Cemmaes (head) C 5
Dee (riv.) D 4
Dovey (riv.) D 5
Ely (riv.) B 7
Gower (pen.), 17,220 C 6
Great Ormes (head) C 4
Holy (isl.), 13,715 C 4
Lleyn (pen.), 25,800 C 5
Menai (str.) C 4
Milford Haven (inlet) B 6
Pembrokeshire Coast National Park C 6
Plynlimon (mt.) D 5
Preseli (mts.) C 6
Radnor (for.) D 5
Rhymney (riv.) B 6
Saint Brides (bay) B 6
Saint David's (head) B 6
Saint George's (chan.) B 5
Saint Gowans (head) C 6
Severn (riv.) E 5
Snowdon (mt.) D 4
Snowdonia National Park D 4
Taff (riv.) B 7
Teifi (riv.) C 5
Towy (riv.) D 6
Tremadoc (bay) C 5
Usk (riv.) B 6
Wye (riv.) D 5
Ynys Môn (Anglesey) (isl.), 64,500 C 4

★Population of met. area.
⊙Population of parish.

SCOTLAND

(map on page 15)

REGIONS

Borders, 99,409 E 5
Central, 269,281 D 4
Dumfries and Galloway, 143,667 E 5
Fife, 336,339 E 4
Grampian, 448,772 F 3
Highland, 182,044 D 3
Lothian, 754,008 E 5
Orkney (islands area), 17,675 E 1
Shetland (islands area), 18,494 F 2
Strathclyde, 2,504,909 C 4
Tayside, 401,987 E 4
Western Isles (islands area), 29,615 A 3

CITIES and TOWNS

Aberchirder, 877 F 3
Aberdeen, 210,362 F 3
Aberdour, 1,576 D 1
Aberfeldy, 1,552 E 4
Aberfoyle, 793 D 4
Aberlady, 737 F 4
Aberlour, 842 E 3
Abernethy, 776 E 4
Aboyne, 1,040 F 3
Acharacle, ⊙764 C 4
Achiltibuie, ⊙1,564 C 3
Achnasheen, ⊙1,078 C 3
Ae, 239 E 5
Airdrie, 38,491 C 2
Alexandria, 9,758 A 1
Alford, 764 F 3
Alloa, 13,558 C 1
Alness, 2,560 D 3
Altnaharra, ⊙1,227 D 2
Alva, 4,593 C 1
Alyth, 1,738 E 4
Ancrum, 266 F 5
Annan, 6,250 E 6
Annat, ⊙550 C 3
Annbank Station, 2,530 D 5
Applecross, ⊙550 C 3
Arbroath, 22,706 F 4
Ardavasar, ⊙449 B 3
Ardersier, 942 E 3
Ardgay, 193 D 3
Ardrishaig, 946 C 4
Ardrossan, 11,072 D 5
Armadale, 7,200 C 2
Arrochar, 543 D 4
Ascog, 230 A 2
Auchenblae, 339 F 4
Auchencairn, 215 E 6
Auchinleck, 4,883 D 5
Auchterarder, 1,738 E 4
Auchtermuchty, 1,426 E 4
Auldearn, 405 E 3
Aviemore, 1,224 E 3
Avoch, 776 D 3
Ayr, 47,990 D 5
Ayton, 410 F 5
Bailivanish, 347 A 3
Baillieston, 7,671 B 2
Balallan, 283 B 2
Balerno, 3,576 D 2
Balfron, 1,149 B 1
Ballantrae, 262 C 5
Ballater, 981 F 3
Ballingry, 4,332 D 1
Ballinluig, 188 E 4
Balloch, Highland, 572 D 3
Balloch, Strathclyde, 1,484 B 1
Baltasound, 246 G 2
Banchory, 2,435 F 3
Banff, 3,832 F 3
Bankfoot, 868 E 4
Bankhead, 1,492 F 3
Bannockburn, 5,889 C 1
Barrhead, 18,736 B 2
Barrhill, 236 D 5
Barvas, 279 B 2
Bathgate, 14,038 C 2
Bayble, 543 B 2
Bearsden, 25,128 B 2
Beattock, 309 E 5
Beauly, 1,141 D 3
Beith, 5,859 D 5
Bellsbank, 3,066 D 5
Bellshill, 18,166 C 2
Berriedale, ⊙1,927 E 2
Bieldside, 1,137 F 3
Biggar, 1,718 E 5
Birnam, 659 E 4
Bishopbriggs, 21,570 B 2
Bishopton, 2,931 B 2
Blackburn, 7,636 C 2
Blackford, 529 E 4
Blair Atholl, 437 E 4
Blairgowrie and Rattray, 5,681 E 4
Blanefield, 835 B 1
Blantyre, 13,992 B 2
Blyth Bridge, ⊙441 E 5
Bo'ness, 12,959 C 1
Boat of Garten, 406 E 3
Boddam, 1,429 G 3
Bonar Bridge, 519 D 3
Bonhill, 4,385 B 1
Bonnybridge, 5,701 C 1
Bonnyrigg and Lasswade, 7,429 D 2
Bowmore, 947 B 5
Braemar, 394 E 3
Breasclete, 234 B 2
Brechin, 6,759 F 4
Bridge of Allan, 4,638 C 1
Bridge of Don, 4,086 F 3
Bridge of Weir, 4,724 A 2
Brightons, 3,106 C 1
Broadford, 310 B 3
Brodick, 630 C 5
Brora, 1,436 E 2
Broxburn, 7,776 D 1
Buchlyvie, 412 B 1
Buckhaven and Methil, 17,930 F 4
Buckie, 8,145 E 3
Bucksburn, 6,567 F 3
Bunessan, ⊙585 B 4
Burghead, 1,321 E 3
Burnmouth, 300 F 5
Burntisland, 5,626 D 1
Cairndow, ⊙874 D 4
Cairnryan, 199 D 6
Callander, 1,805 D 4
Cambuslang, 14,607 B 2
Campbeltown, 6,428 C 5
Cannich, 203 D 3
Canonbie, 234 F 5
Caol, 3,719 C 4
Carbost, ⊙772 B 3
Cardenden, 6,802 D 1
Carloway, 178 B 2
Carluke, 8,864 E 5
Carnoustie, 6,838 F 4
Carnwath, 1,246 E 5
Carradale, 262 C 5
Carrbridge, 416 E 3
Carron, 2,626 C 1
Carsphairn, 186 D 5
Castlebay, 284 A 4
Castle Douglas, 3,384 E 6
Castle Kennedy, 307 D 6
Castletown, 902 E 2
Catrine, 2,681 D 5
Cawdor, 111 E 3
Chirnside, 888 F 5
Chryston, 8,322 C 2
Clackmannan, 3,248 C 1
Clarkston, 8,404 B 2
Closeburn, 225 E 5
Clovulin, ⊙315 C 4
Clydebank, 47,538 B 2
Coalburn, 1,460 E 5
Coatbridge, 50,806 C 2
Cockburnspath, 233 F 5
Cockenzie and Port Seton, 3,539 D 1
Coldingham, 423 F 5
Coldstream, 1,393 F 5
Coll, 305 B 2
Colmonell, 218 D 5
Comrie, 1,119 E 4
Connel, 300 C 4
Cononbridge, 914 D 3
Corpach, 1,296 C 4
Coupar Angus, 2,010 E 4
Cove and Kilcreggan, 1,402 A 1
Cove Bay, 765 F 3
Cowdenbeath, 10,215 D 1
Cowie, 2,751 C 1
Craigellachie, 382 E 3
Craignure, ⊙544 C 4
Crail, 1,033 F 4
Crawford, 384 E 5
Creetown, 769 D 6
Crieff, 5,718 E 4
Crimond, 313 G 3
Crinan, ⊙462 C 4
Cromarty, 492 E 3
Crosshill, 535 D 5
Crossmichael, 317 D 6
Cruden Bay, 528 G 3
Cullen, 1,199 F 3
Culross, 504 C 1
Cults, 3,336 F 3
Cumbernauld, 41,200 C 1
Cumnock and Holmhead, 6,298 D 5
Cupar, 6,607 E 4
Currie, 6,764 D 2
Dailly, 1,258 D 5
Dalbeattie, 3,659 E 6
Daliburgh, 261 A 3
Dalkeith, 9,713 D 2
Dalmally, 283 D 4
Dalmellington, 1,949 D 5
Dalry, 5,833 D 5
Dalrymple, 1,336 D 5
Darvel, 3,177 D 5
Daviot, ⊙513 D 3
Denholm, 581 F 5
Denny and Dunipace, 10,424 C 1
Dervaig, ⊙1,081 B 4
Dingwall, 4,275 D 3
Dollar, 2,573 E 4
Dornoch, 880 D 3
Douglas, 1,843 E 5
Doune, 859 D 4
Drongan, 3,609 D 5
Drumbeg, ⊙833 C 2
Drummore, 336 D 6
Drumnadrochit, 359 D 3
Drymen, 659 B 1
Dufftown, 1,481 E 3
Dumbarton, 25,469 B 1
Dumfries, 29,259 E 5
Dunbar, 4,609 F 4
Dunbeath, 161 E 2
Dunbeg, 939 C 4
Dunblane, 5,222 E 4
Dundee, 194,732 F 4
Dundonald, 2,256 D 5
Dunfermline, 52,098 D 1
Dunkeld, 273 E 4
Dunning, 564 E 4
Dunoon, 8,759 A 2
Dunragit, 323 D 6
Duns, 1,812 F 5
Duntochter, 3,532 B 2
Dunure, 452 D 5
Dunvegan, 301 B 3
Dyce, 2,733 F 3
Eaglesfield, 581 E 5
Eaglesham, 2,788 D 5
Earlston, 1,415 F 5
East Calder, 2,690 D 2
East Kilbride, 71,200 B 2
East Linton, 882 F 5
Eastriggs, 1,455 E 5
Ecclefechan, 844 E 5
Edinburgh (cap.), 470,085 D 1
Edzell, 658 F 4
Elderslie, 5,204 B 2
Elgin, 17,042 E 3
Elie and Earlsferry, 807 F 4
Ellon, 2,855 F 3
Embo, 260 E 3
Errol, 762 E 4
Evanton, 562 D 3
Eyemouth, 2,704 F 5
Fairlie, 1,029 D 5
Falkirk, 36,901 C 1
Falkland, 998 E 4
Fallin, 3,159 C 1
Fauldhouse, 5,247 C 2
Ferness, ⊙287 E 3
Ferryden, 740 F 4
Findhorn, 664 E 3
Findochty, 1,229 E 3
Fintry, 296 B 1
Fochabers, 1,238 E 3
Forfar, 11,179 F 4
Forres, 5,317 E 3
Fort Augustus, 670 D 3
Forth, 2,929 C 2
Fortrose, 1,150 D 3
Fort William, 4,370 C 4
Foyers, 276 D 3
Fraserburgh, 10,930 G 3
Friockheim, 807 F 4
Furnace, 220 C 4
Fyvie, 405 F 3
Gairloch, 125 C 3
Galashiels, 12,808 F 5
Galston, 4,256 D 5
Gardenstown, 892 F 3
Garelochhead, 1,552 A 1
Gargunnock, 457 B 1
Garlieston, 385 D 6
Garmouth, 352 E 3
Garrabost, 307 B 2
Gartmore, 253 B 1
Gatehouse-of-Fleet, 835 D 6
Giffnock, 10,987 B 2
Gifford, 575 F 5
Girvan, 7,597 D 5
Glamis, 190 F 4
Glasgow, 880,617 B 2
Glasgow, ★1,674,789 B 2
Glenbarr, ⊙691 C 5
Glencaple, 275 E 5
Glencoe, 195 C 4
Glenelg, ⊙1,468 C 3
Glenluce, 725 D 6
Glenrothes, 31,400 E 4
Golspie, 1,374 E 3
Gordon, 320 F 5
Gorebridge, 3,426 D 2
Gourock, 11,192 A 1
Grangemouth, 24,430 C 1
Grantown-on-Spey, 1,578 E 3
Greenlaw, 574 F 5
Greenock, 67,275 A 2
Gretna, 1,907 E 5
Gullane, 1,701 F 4
Haddington, 6,767 F 5
Halkirk, 679 E 2
Hamilton, 45,495 C 2
Hamnavoe, 307 G 2
Harthill, 4,712 C 2
Hatton, 315 G 3
Hawick, 16,484 F 5
Heathhall, 1,365 E 5
Helensburgh, 13,327 A 1
Helmsdale, 727 E 2
Hill of Fearn, 233 D 3
Hillside, 692 F 4
Hillswick, ⊙696 G 2
Hopeman, 1,248 E 3
Huntly, 4,078 F 3
Hurlford, 4,294 D 5
Inchnadamph, ⊙833 D 2
Innellan, 922 A 2
Innerleithen, 2,293 E 5
Insch, 881 F 3
Inveraray, 473 C 4
Inverbervie, 853 F 4
Invercassley, ⊙1,067 D 3
Invergordon, 2,386 D 3
Invergowrie, 1,389 E 4
Inverie, ⊙1,468 C 3
Inverkeithing, 6,102 D 1
Inverness, 35,801 D 3
Inverurie, 5,534 F 3
Irvine, 48,500 D 5
Isle of Whithorn, 222 D 6
Jedburgh, 3,953 F 5
John O'Groats, 195 E 2
Johnshaven, 544 F 4
Johnstone, 23,251 B 2
Kames, 230 C 5
Keiss, 344 E 2
Keith, 4,192 F 3
Kelso, 4,934 F 5
Kelty, 6,573 D 1
Kemnay, 1,042 F 3
Kenmore, 211 E 4
Kilbarchan, 2,669 A 2
Kilbirnie, 8,259 A 2
Kilchoan, ⊙764 B 4
Kildonan, ⊙1,105 E 2
Killearn, 1,086 B 1
Killin, 600 D 4
Kilmacolm, 3,348 A 2
Kilmarnock, 50,175 D 5
Kilmaurs, 2,518 D 5
Kilninver, ⊙247 C 4
Kilrenny and Anstruther, 2,951 F 4
Kilsyth, 10,210 B 1
Kilwinning, 8,460 D 5
Kinbrace, ⊙1,105 E 2
Kincardine, 3,278 C 1
Kinghorn, 2,163 D 1
Kingussie, 1,036 D 3
Kinlochewe, ⊙1,794 C 3
Kinlochleven, 1,243 D 4
Kinloch Rannoch, 241 D 4
Kinloss, 2,378 E 3
Kinross, 2,829 E 4
Kintore, 970 F 3
Kippen, 529 B 1
Kirkcaldy, 50,207 D 1
Kirkcolm, 346 C 6
Kirkconnel, 3,318 E 5
Kirkcowan, 354 D 6
Kirkcudbright, 2,690 E 6
Kirkhill, 210 D 3
Kirkintilloch, 26,664 B 2
Kirkmuirhill, 2,575 E 5
Kirkton of Glenisla, ⊙331 E 4
Kirkwall, 4,777 E 2
Kirriemuir, 4,295 E 4
Kyleakin, 268 C 3
Kyle of Lochalsh, 687 C 3
Kylestrome, ⊙745 D 2
Ladybank, 1,216 E 4
Laggan, 393 D 3
Lairg, 572 D 2
Lamlash, 613 C 5
Lanark, 8,842 E 5
Langholm, 2,509 E 5
Larbert, 4,922 C 1
Largs, 9,461 A 2
Larkhall, 15,926 E 5
Lauder, 639 F 5
Laurencekirk, 1,416 F 4

(continued)

England and Wales

CONIC PROJECTION

MILES

KILOMETERS

Capitals of Countries .... ⊛
Administrative Centers .... ⊛
Other Capitals .... ⊙
Canals ....

International Boundaries ___ ___
County Boundaries ___ ___
Other Boundaries ....

The administrative centers
for MID GLAMORGAN,
NORTHUMBERLAND and SURREY
are Cardiff,
Newcastle upon Tyne and Kingston upon Thames,
respectively.

Scale 1:2,886,000

© Copyright HAMMOND INCORPORATED, Maplewood, N.J.

Lennoxtown, 3,070 ....B 1
Lerwick, 6,195 ....G 2
Leslie, 3,303 ....E 4
Lesmahagow, 3,906 ....E 5
Leswalt, 237 ....C 6
Letham, 804 ....F 4
Leuchars, 2,482 ....F 4
Leurbost, 461 ....B 2
Leven, 9,507 ....F 4
Leverburgh, 223 ....B 3
Lhanbryde, 1,184 ....E 3
Lilliesleaf, 212 ....F 5
Limekilns, 812 ....D 1
Linlithgow, 6,098 ....C 1
Linwood, 10,510 ....B 2
Lionel, 187 ....B 2
Livingston, 21,900 ....C 2
Loanhead, 5,971 ....D 2
Lochailort, ⊙673 ....C 4
Lochaline, 213 ....C 4
Lochans, 355 ....D 6
Locharbriggs, 2,561 ....E 5
Lochawe, 200 ....C 4
Lochboisdale, 382 ....A 3
Lochcarron, 204 ....C 3
Lochgelly, 7,754 ....D 1
Lochgilphead, 1,217 ....C 4
Lochgoilhead, 216 ....D 4
Lochinver, 283 ....C 2
Lochmaben, 1,304 ....E 5
Lochmaddy, 307 ....A 3
Lochore, 2,994 ....D 1
Lochwinnoch, 2,064 ....A 2
Lockerbie, 3,135 ....E 5
Lossiemouth and Branderburgh, 5,817 ....E 3
Lumsden, 248 ....F 3
Luncarty, 584 ....E 4
Lybster, 554 ....E 2
Lyness, ⊙454 ....E 2
Macduff, 3,682 ....F 3
Machrihanish, 212 ....C 5
Maidens, 536 ....D 5
Mallaig, 903 ....C 4
Markinch, 2,366 ....E 4
Mauchline, 3,612 ....D 5
Maud, 634 ....F 3
Maybole, 4,703 ....D 5
Mayfield, 8,232 ....D 2
Meigle, 357 ....E 4
Melrose, 2,197 ....F 5
Melvaig, ⊙1,794 ....C 3
Methlick, 315 ....F 3
Methven, 806 ....E 4
Mid Yell, 220 ....G 2
Millport, 1,161 ....A 2
Milnathort, 1,099 ....E 4
Milngavie, 10,846 ....B 1
Minnigaff, 658 ....D 6
Mintlaw, 657 ....F 3
Moffat, 2,041 ....E 5
Moniaive, 342 ....E 5
Monifieth, 7,100 ....F 4
Montrose, 4,704 ....F 4
Morar, 184 ....C 4
Motherwell and Wishaw, 72,991 ....C 2
Muirkirk, 2,607 ....E 5
Muir of Ord, 1,339 ....D 3
Musselburgh, 17,045 ....D 2
Muthill, 672 ....E 4
Nairn, 5,821 ....E 3
Neilston, 4,358 ....B 2
Nethy Bridge, 431 ....E 3
New Abbey, 339 ....E 6
Newarthill, 7,003 ....C 2
Newburgh, Fife, 2,124 ....E 4
Newburgh, Grampian, 447 ....G 3
Newcastleton, 903 ....F 5
New Cumnock, 5,077 ....D 5
New Deer, 601 ....F 3
New Galloway, 337 ....D 5
Newmains, 6,847 ....C 2
Newmarket, 613 ....B 2
Newmill, 449 ....E 3
Newmilns and Greenholm, 3,509 ....D 5
New Pitsligo, 1,125 ....F 3
Newport-on-Tay, 3,762 ....F 4
New Scone, 3,830 ....E 4
Newtongrange, 4,555 ....D 2
Newton Mearns, 6,901 ....B 2
Newtonmore, 894 ....D 3
Newton Stewart, 1,983 ....D 6
Newtown Saint Boswells, 1,101 ....F 5
Newtyle, 664 ....E 4
North Berwick, 4,317 ....F 4
North Tolsta, 527 ....B 2
Oakley, 3,499 ....C 1
Oban, 6,515 ....C 4
Old Kilpatrick, 3,256 ....B 2
Oldmeldrum, 1,103 ....F 3
Oykel Bridge, ⊙742 ....D 3
Paisley, 94,833 ....B 2
Palnackie, 225 ....E 6
Patna, 2,867 ....D 5
Peebles, 6,049 ....E 5
Penicuik, 10,476 ....D 2
Penpont, 364 ....E 5
Perth, 43,098 ....E 4
Peterculter, 3,226 ....F 3
Peterhead, 14,846 ....G 3
Pierowall, ⊙735 ....E 1
Pitlochry, 2,468 ....E 4
Pitmedden, 313 ....F 3
Pittenweem, 1,548 ....F 4
Plockton, 288 ....C 3
Poolewe, ⊙1,794 ....C 3
Port Appin, ⊙2,172 ....C 4
Port Askaig, ⊙1,795 ....B 5
Port Bannatyne, 730 ....A 2
Port Charlotte, 240 ....B 5
Port Ellen, 932 ....B 5
Port Glasgow, 22,189 ....A 2
Portgordon, 814 ....F 3
Portknockie, 1,217 ....F 3
Portmahomack, 226 ....E 3
Portpatrick, 643 ....C 6
Portree, 1,374 ....B 3
Portsoy, 1,717 ....F 3
Port William, 517 ....D 6
Prestonpans, 3,272 ....D 1
Prestwick, 13,218 ....D 5
Queensferry, 5,339 ....D 1
Reay, 283 ....E 2
Renfrew, 18,880 ....B 2
Renton, 3,443 ....A 1
Rhu, 1,540 ....A 1
Rhynie, 333 ....F 3
Rigside, 1,195 ....E 5
Rosehearty, 1,220 ....F 3
Rosneath, 946 ....A 1
Rothes, 1,240 ....E 3
Rothesay, 6,285 ....A 2
Rutherglen, 24,091 ....B 2
Saint Abbs, 203 ....F 5
Saint Andrews, 12,837 ....F 4
Saint Combs, 738 ....G 3
Saint Cyrus, 340 ....F 4
Saint Margaret's Hope, 210 ....F 2
Saint Monance, 1,205 ....F 4
Saline, 831 ....C 1
Saltcoats, 14,861 ....D 5
Sandbank, 850 ....A 1
Sandhead, 248 ....D 6
Sandwick, 603 ....B 2
Sanquhar, 2,030 ....D 5
Sauchie, 6,082 ....C 1
Scalasaig, ⊙137 ....B 4
Scalloway, 896 ....G 2
Scarinish, ⊙875 ....B 4
Scourie, ⊙745 ....C 2
Scrabster, 273 ....E 2
Selkirk, 5,635 ....F 5
Shader, 258 ....B 2
Shawbost, 458 ....B 2
Shieldaig, ⊙550 ....C 3
Shotts, 9,512 ....C 2
Skateraw, 674 ....F 3
Skelmorlie, 1,535 ....A 2
Skipness, ⊙765 ....C 5
Slamannan, 1,584 ....C 2
Spean Bridge, 235 ....D 4
Springholm, 340 ....E 5
Stanley, 1,385 ....E 4
Stenhousemuir, 8,203 ....C 1
Stevenston, 11,786 ....D 5
Stewarton, 5,165 ....D 5
Stirling, 29,799 ....C 1
Stonehaven, 4,837 ....F 4
Stonehouse, 7,900 ....D 5
Stornoway, 5,371 ....B 2
Stow, 485 ....F 5
Strachan, ⊙390 ....F 3
Strachur Bay, ⊙678 ....C 4
Stranraer, 10,174 ....C 6
Strathaven, 5,464 ....D 5
Strathpeffer, 874 ....D 3
Strichen, 962 ....F 3
Stromeferry, ⊙1,724 ....C 3
Stromness, 1,680 ....E 2
Strontian, ⊙764 ....C 4
Struan, ⊙772 ....B 3
Swinton, 235 ....F 5
Tain, 2,057 ....D 3
Tarbert, Strathclyde, 1,391 ....C 5
Tarbert, W. Isles, 479 ....B 3
Tarbolton, 2,224 ....D 5
Tarland, 452 ....F 3
Tayport, 2,848 ....F 4
Thornhill, Central, 443 ....D 4
Thornhill, Dumf. & Gall., 1,510 ....E 5
Thurso, 9,113 ....E 2
Tillicoultry, 4,320 ....C 1
Tobermory, 652 ....B 4
Tolob, ⊙2,033 ....G 2
Tomatin, 214 ....D 3
Tomintoul, 306 ....E 3
Torphins, 499 ....F 3
Tradespark, 425 ....E 3
Tranent, 7,212 ....F 5
Troon, 11,656 ....D 5
Tullibody, 6,082 ....C 1
Turriff, 3,051 ....F 3
Tweedsmuir, ⊙105 ....E 5
Twynholm, 274 ....D 6
Tyndrum, ⊙1,153 ....D 4
Uddingston, 5,278 ....B 2
Uig, Highland, 103 ....B 3
Uig, W. Isles, ⊙1,948 ....A 2
Ullapool, 807 ....C 3
Uphall, 3,035 ....C 1
Viewpark, 9,812 ....C 2
Walkerburn, 842 ....F 5
Watten, 347 ....E 2
Wemyss Bay, 323 ....A 2
West Barns, 659 ....F 5
West Calder, 2,005 ....C 2
West Kilbride, 3,883 ....D 5
West Linton, 705 ....D 2
Whitburn, 11,647 ....C 2
Whitehills, 875 ....F 3
Whithorn, 990 ....D 6
Whiting Bay, 352 ....C 5
Wick, 7,804 ....E 2
Wigtown, 1,118 ....D 6
Winchburgh, 2,409 ....D 1
Yetholm, 435 ....F 5

OTHER FEATURES

A'Chralaig (mt.) ....C 3
Ailsa Craig (isl.), 3 ....C 5
Almond (riv.) ....E 4
Annan (riv.) ....E 5
Appin (dist.), 2,006 ....C 4
Ardgour (dist.), 315 ....C 4
Ardle (riv.) ....E 4
Ardnamurchan (pen.), 764 ....B 4
Argyll (dist.), 4,940 ....C 4
Arkaig, Loch (lake) ....C 4
Arran (isl.), 3,564 ....C 5
Askival (mt.) ....B 4
Assynt (dist.), 833 ....C 2
Athol (dist.), 1,082 ....D 4
Atlantic Ocean ....B 2
Avon (riv.) ....C 1
Avon (riv.) ....E 3
Awe, Loch (lake) ....C 4
Ayr (riv.) ....D 5
Ayr, Heads of (cape) ....D 5
Badenoch (dist.), 2,717 ....D 4
Baleshare (isl.), 64 ....A 3
Balmoral Castle ....E 3
Barra (sound) ....A 3
Barra (isl.), 1,005 ....A 4
Barra (head) ....A 4
Barra Isles (isls.), 1,092 ....A 4
Battock (mt.) ....F 4
Beauly (riv.) ....D 3
Beinn Dearg (mt.) ....D 3
Beinn a Ghlo (mt.) ....E 4
Bell Rock (isl.), 3 ....F 4
Ben Alder (mt.) ....D 4
Ben Avon (mt.) ....E 3
Benbecula (isl.), 1,355 ....A 3
Ben Cruachan (mt.) ....C 4
Ben Lawers (mt.) ....D 4
Ben Lui (mt.) ....D 4
Ben Macdhui (mt.) ....E 3
Ben Mhor (mt.) ....A 3
Ben More (mt.) ....B 4
Ben More (mt.) ....D 4
Ben More Assynt (mt.) ....D 2
Ben Nevis (mt.) ....D 4
Bernera (isl.), 276 ....B 2
Berneray (isl.), 131 ....A 3
Berneray (isl.), 6 ....A 4
Bidean nam Bian (mt.) ....D 4
Black Isle (pen.), 7,209 ....D 3
Blackwater (res.) ....D 4
Boisdale, Loch (inlet) ....A 3
Bracadale, Loch (inlet) ....B 3
Braemar (dist.), 7,624 ....E 3
Breadalbane (dist.), 3,649 ....D 4
Bressay (isl.), 248 ....G 2
Broad (bay) ....B 2
Broad Law (mt.) ....E 5
Broom, Loch (inlet) ....C 3
Brough Ness (prom.) ....F 2
Buchan (dist.), 40,089 ....F 3
Buddon Ness (prom.) ....F 4
Burray (isl.), 209 ....F 2
Burrow (head) ....D 6
Bute (isl.), 8,423 ....C 5
Bute (sound) ....C 5
Butt of Lewis (prom.) ....B 2
Cairn Gorm (mt.) ....E 3
Cairngorm (mts.) ....E 3
Cairn Toul (mt.) ....E 3
Caledonian (canal) ....D 3
Canna (isl.), 22 ....B 3
Carn Ban (mt.) ....D 3
Carn Eige (mt.) ....C 3
Carrick (dist.), 21,425 ....D 5
Carron (riv.) ....C 1
Carron (riv.) ....C 3
Cheviot (hills) ....F 5
Cheviot, The (mt.) ....F 5
Clisham (mt.) ....B 3
Clyde (riv.) ....D 5
Clyde (firth) ....D 5
Coll (isl.), 144 ....B 4
Colonsay (isl.), 137 ....B 4
Copinsay (isl.), 3 ....F 2
Cowal (dist.), 15,548 ....C 4
Creag Meagaidh (mt.) ....D 4
Cromarty (firth) ....D 3
Cuillin (hills) ....B 3
Cuillin (sound) ....B 3
Dee (riv.) ....D 5
Dee (riv.) ....F 3
Dennis (head) ....F 1
Deveron (riv.) ....F 3
Don (riv.) ....F 3
Doon (riv.) ....D 5
Dornoch (firth) ....E 3
Duirinish (dist.), 1,085 ....B 3
Duncansby (head) ....F 2
Dunnet (head) ....E 2
Earn (riv.) ....E 4
Earn, Loch (lake) ....D 4
Eday (isl.), 179 ....F 1
Eddrachillis (bay) ....C 2
Eden (riv.) ....F 4
Egilsay (isl.), 39 ....F 1
Eigg (isl.), 69 ....B 4
Eil, Loch (lake) ....C 4
Eishort, Loch (inlet) ....B 3
Enard (bay) ....C 2
Eriboll, Loch (inlet) ....D 2
Ericht, Loch (lake) ....D 4
Eriskay (isl.), 219 ....A 3
Erisort, Loch (inlet) ....B 2
Esk (riv.) ....F 5
Etive, Loch (inlet) ....C 4
Ewe, Loch (inlet) ....C 3
Eye (pen.), 850 ....B 2
Fair Isle (isl.), 65 ....F 3
Fetlar (isl.), 88 ....G 2
Fife Ness (prom.) ....F 4
Findhorn (riv.) ....E 3
Flannan (isls.), 3 ....A 2
Formartine (dist.), 10,768 ....F 3
Forth (riv.) ....B 1
Forth (firth) ....F 4
Forth and Clyde (canal) ....B 2
Foula (isl.), 33 ....F 2
Fyne, Loch (inlet) ....C 5
Galloway (dist.), 54,972 ....D 5
Galloway, Mull of (prom.) ....D 6
Gare Loch (inlet) ....A 1
Garioch (dist.), 6,863 ....F 3
Garry, Loch (lake) ....D 3
Gigha (isl.), 174 ....C 5
Girdle Ness (prom.) ....G 3
Glass (riv.) ....D 3
Glen More (dist.), 55,035 ....D 3
Goat Fell (mt.) ....C 5
Gometra (isl.), 10 ....B 4
Grampian (mts.) ....D 4
Great Cumbrae (isl.), 1,296 ....A 2
Gruinard (bay) ....C 3
Hallandale (riv.) ....E 2
Harris (sound) ....A 3
Harris (dist.), 2,175 ....B 3
Hebrides (sea) ....B 3
Hebrides, Inner (isls.), 14,881 ....B 4
Hebrides, Outer (isls.), 29,615 ....A 3
Helmsdale (riv.) ....E 2
Herma Ness (prom.) ....G 2
Holy (isl.), 10 ....C 5
Holy Loch (inlet) ....A 1
Hoy (isl.), 419 ....E 2
Inchcape (Bell Rock) (isl.), 3 ....F 4
Inchkeith (isl.), 3 ....D 1
Indaal, Loch (inlet) ....B 5
Inner (sound) ....C 3
Inner Hebrides (isls.), 14,881 ....B 4
Iona (isl.), 145 ....B 4
Isla (riv.) ....E 4
Islay (isl.), 3,816 ....B 5
Jura (isl.), 210 ....C 5
Jura (sound) ....C 5
Katrine, Loch (lake) ....D 4
Kerrera (isl.), 27 ....C 4
Kilbrannan (sound) ....C 5
Kinnairds (head) ....G 3
Kintyre (pen.), 10,077 ....C 5
Kintyre, Mull of (prom.) ....C 5
Knapdale (dist.), 4,082 ....C 5
Kyle of Tongue (inlet) ....D 2
Laggan (bay) ....B 5
Lammermuir (hills) ....F 5
Lennox (hills) ....B 1
Leven (lake) ....E 4
Leven, Loch (inlet) ....D 4
Lewis (dist.), 20,047 ....B 2
Liddel Water (riv.) ....F 5
Linnhe, Loch (inlet) ....C 4
Lismore (isl.), 166 ....C 4
Little Minch (sound) ....B 3
Lochaber (dist.), 13,813 ....D 4
Lochnagar (mt.) ....E 4
Lochy, Loch (lake) ....D 3
Lomond, Loch (lake) ....D 4
Long, Loch (inlet) ....D 4
Lorne (dist.), 12,162 ....C 4
Lorne (firth) ....C 4
Loyal, Loch (lake) ....D 2
Luce (bay) ....D 6
Luing (isl.), 151 ....C 4
Lyon (riv.) ....D 4
Machers, The (pen.), 6,192 ....D 6
Mainland (isl.), 12,747 ....E 1
Mainland (isl.), 12,944 ....G 2
Mar (dist.), 23,931 ....F 3
Maree, Loch (lake) ....C 3
May, Isle of (isl.), 10 ....F 4
Merrick (mt.) ....D 5
Minginish (dist.), 772 ....B 3
Moidart (dist.), 155 ....C 4
Monach (sound) ....A 3
Monadhliath (mts.) ....D 3
Moorfoot (hills) ....E 5
Moray (firth) ....E 3
Moriston (riv.) ....D 3
Morven (dist.), 398 ....C 4
Morven (mt.) ....E 2
Muck (isl.), 24 ....B 4
Muckle Flugga (isl.), 3 ....G 2
Mull (isl.), 2,024 ....C 4
Mull (head) ....F 1
Mull (sound) ....C 4
Nairn (riv.) ....D 3
na Keal, Loch (inlet) ....B 4
Naver (riv.) ....D 2
Ness, Loch (lake) ....D 3
Nevis, Loch (inlet) ....C 3
Nith (riv.) ....E 5
North (chan.) ....C 5
North (sound) ....F 1
North (sound) ....G 4
North Esk (riv.) ....F 4
North Minch (sound) ....B 3
North Ronaldsay (isl.), 134 ....F 1
North Uist (isl.), 1,469 ....A 3
Oa, Mull of (prom.) ....B 5
Ochil (hills) ....E 4
Oich (riv.) ....D 3
Orchy (riv.) ....D 4
Orkney (isls.), 17,675 ....F 1
Oronsay (isl.), 2 ....B 4
Outer Hebrides (isls.), 29,615 ....A 3
Oykel (riv.) ....D 3
Pabbay (isl.), 4 ....A 3
Papa Stour (isl.), 24 ....F 2
Papa Westray (isl.), 106 ....F 1
Paps of Jura (mt.) ....C 5
Park (dist.), 210 ....B 2
Peel Fell (mt.) ....F 5
Pentland (hills) ....D 2
Pentland (firth) ....E 2
Pladda (isl.), 2 ....C 5
Quoich, Loch (lake) ....C 3
Raasay (isl.), 163 ....C 3
Rannoch (dist.), 1,177 ....D 4
Rannoch, Loch (lake) ....D 4
Rhinns, The (pen.), 8,295 ....C 6
Roag, Loch (inlet) ....B 2
Rona (isl.), 3 ....B 3
Ross of Mull (pen.), 585 ....B 4
Rousay (isl.), 181 ....E 1
Rudha Hunish (cape) ....B 3
Rudh Re (cape) ....C 3
Rum (isl.), 40 ....B 3
Ryan, Loch (inlet) ....C 5
Saint Kilda (isl.), 65 ....A 2
Saint Magnus (bay) ....F 2
Sanda (isl.), 9 ....C 5
Sanday (isl.), 11 ....B 3
Sanday (isl.), 592 ....F 1
Scalpay (isl.), 483 ....B 3
Scalpay (isl.), 5 ....C 3
Scapa Flow (chan.) ....E 2
Scarp (isl.), 12 ....A 2
Scridain, Loch (inlet) ....B 4
Scurdie Ness (prom.) ....F 4
Seaforth, Loch (inlet) ....B 3
Seil (isl.), 326 ....C 4
Sgurr a Choire Ghlais (mt.) ....D 3
Sgurr Alasdair (mt.) ....B 3
Sgurr Mor (mt.) ....C 3
Sgurr na Lapaich (mt.) ....C 3
Shapinsay (isl.), 346 ....F 1
Shetland (isls.), 18,494 ....G 2
Shiant (sound) ....B 3
Shiel, Loch (lake) ....C 4
Shin (falls) ....D 3
Shin, Loch (lake) ....D 2
Shona (isl.), 17 ....C 4
Sidlaw (hills) ....E 4
Sinclair's (bay) ....E 2
Skye, Isle of (isl.), 7,183 ....B 3
Sleat (pt.) ....B 4
Sleat (dist.), 449 ....C 3
Small Isles (isls.), 171 ....B 4
Snizort, Loch (inlet) ....B 3
Soay (isl.), 5 ....B 3
Solway (firth) ....E 6
South Esk (riv.) ....F 4
South Ronaldsay (isl.), 776 ....F 2
South Uist (isl.), 2,281 ....A 3
Spean (riv.) ....D 4
Spey (riv.) ....E 3
Start (pt.) ....F 1
Stinchar (riv.) ....D 5
Strathbogie (dist.), 7,959 ....F 3
Strathmore (valley) ....E 4
Strathspey (dist.), 6,668 ....E 3
Strathy (pt.) ....E 2
Stroma (isl.), 8 ....E 2
Stronsay (isl.), 436 ....F 1
Sumburgh (head) ....G 2
Sunart, Loch (inlet) ....C 4
Swona (isl.), 3 ....E 2
Taransay (isl.), 5 ....A 3
Tarbat Ness (prom.) ....E 3
Tarbert, East Loch (inlet) ....B 3
Tarbert, Loch (inlet) ....B 5
Tarbert, West Loch (inlet) ....A 3
Tay (riv.) ....E 4
Tay (firth) ....F 4
Tay, Loch (lake) ....D 4
Teith (riv.) ....D 4
Teviot (riv.) ....F 5
Thurso (riv.) ....E 2
Tiree (isl.), 875 ....B 4
Tolsta (head) ....B 2
Tor Ness (prom.) ....E 2
Torridon, Loch (inlet) ....C 3
Trossachs, The (valley) ....D 4
Trotternish (dist.), 1,948 ....B 3
Tweed (riv.) ....F 5
Tyne (riv.) ....F 5
Ulva (isl.), 23 ....B 4
Unst (isl.), 1,124 ....G 2
Vaternish (dist.), 162 ....B 3
Vatersay (isl.), 77 ....A 4
West Burra (isl.), 501 ....G 2
Westray (firth) ....E 1
Westray (isl.), 735 ....E 1
Whalsay (isl.), 870 ....G 2
White Coomb (mt.) ....E 5
Wigtown (bay) ....D 6
Wrath (cape) ....C 2
Wyre (isl.), 36 ....F 1
Yarrow (riv.) ....E 5
Yell (isl.), 1,143 ....G 2
Ythan (riv.) ....F 3

★Population of met. area
⊙Population of parish.

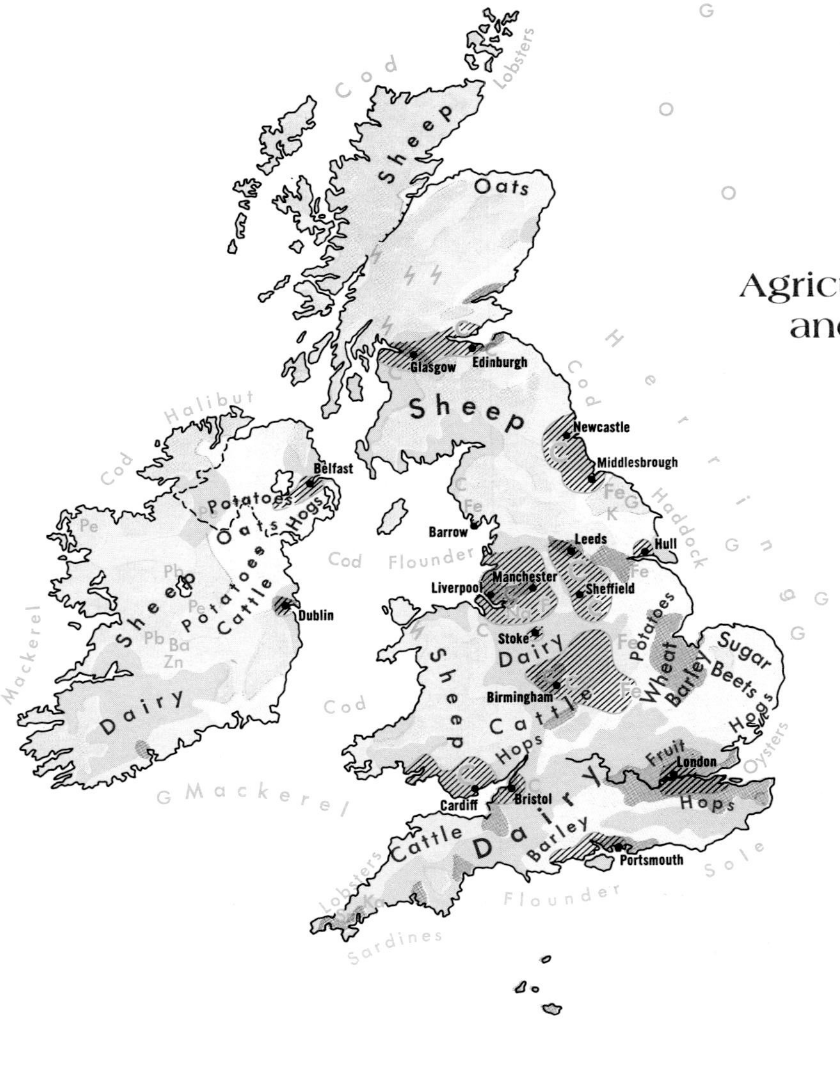

Agriculture, Industry and Resources

DOMINANT LAND USE

- Cereals (chiefly oats, barley)
- Truck Farming, Horticulture
- Dairy, Mixed Farming
- Livestock, Mixed Farming
- Pasture Livestock

MAJOR MINERAL OCCURRENCES

Ba	Barite	Na	Salt
C	Coal	O	Petroleum
F	Fluorspar	Pb	Lead
Fe	Iron Ore	Pe	Peat
G	Natural Gas	Sn	Tin
K	Potash	Zn	Zinc
Ka	Kaolin (china clay)		

Water Power
Major Industrial Areas

Scotland

CONIC PROJECTION

MILES

KILOMETERS

Capital .... ⊛
Regional Centers .... ◉
Canals ....

International Boundaries _____
Regional Boundaries _____
Other Boundaries _____

Scale 1:1,850,000
© Copyright HAMMOND INCORPORATED, Maplewood, N.J.

Former Counties

1 CLACKMANNAN
2 DUNBARTON
3 KINROSS
4 MIDLOTHIAN
5 PEEBLES
6 RENFREW
7 SELKIRK
8 STIRLING
9 W. LOTHIAN

Shetland Islands

IRELAND

Carlow 34,237 H6
Cavan 52,618 G4
Clare 75,008 D6
Cork 352,883 D7
Donegal 108,344 K2
Dublin 852,219 J5
Galway 149,223 D5
Kerry 112,772 B7
Kildare 71,977 H5
Kilkenny 61,473 G6
Laois 45,259 G6
Leitrim 28,360 E3
Leix (Laois) 45,259 G6
Limerick 140,459 D7
Longford 28,250 F4
Louth 74,951 J4
Mayo 109,525 C4
Meath 71,729 H4
Monaghan 46,242 H3
Offaly 51,829 F5
Roscommon 53,519 E4
Sligo 50,275 D3
Tipperary 123,565 F6
Waterford 77,315 F7
Westmeath 53,570 G5
Wexford 86,351 H7
Wicklow 66,295 J5

CITIES and TOWNS

Abbeydorney, 188 B 7
Abbeyfeale, 1,337 C 7
Abbeylara, ‡290 F 4
Abbeyleix, 1,033 G 6
Achill Sound, ‡1,163 B 4
Aclare, ‡336 D 3
Adare, 545 D 6
Aghada-Farsid-Rostellan, 461 E 8
Aghadoe, ‡497 B 7
Aghagower, ‡693 C 4
Ahascragh, 221 E 5
Annagry, 201 E 1
Annascaul, 236 B 7
An Uaimh, 4,605 H 4
An Uaimh, *6,665 H 4
Ardagh, Limerick, 213 C 7
Ardagh, Longford, ‡974 F 4
Ardara, 683 E 2
Ardee, *3,183 H 4
Ardee, 3,096 H 4
Ardfert, 286 B 7
Ardfinnan, 510 F 7
Ardmore, 233 F 8
Ardrahan, ‡239 D 5
Arklow, 6,948 J 6
Arthurstown, 1,188 H 7
Arva, 370 F 4
Ashford, 341 J 5
Askeaton, 844 D 6
Athboy, 705 H 4
Athea, 328 C 7
Athenry, 1,240 D 5
Athleague, ‡955 E 4
Athlone, 9,825 F 5
Athlone, *11,611 F 5
Athy, 4,270 H 6
Athy, *4,654 H 6
Aughrim, 451 J 6
Avoca, ‡620 J 6
Bagenalstown (Muinebeag), 2,321 H 6
Baile Átha Cliath (Dublin) (cap.), 567,866 K 5
Bailieborough, 1,293 G 4
Balbriggan, 3,741 J 4
Balla, 293 C 4
Ballaghaderreen, 1,121 E 4
Ballina, Mayo, 6,063 C 3
Ballina, *6,369 C 3
Ballina, Tipperary, 336 E 6
Ballinagh, 459 G 4
Ballinakill, 300 G 6
Ballineen D 8
Ballinamore, 808 F 3
Ballinasloe, 5,969 E 5
Ballincollig-Carrigrohane, 2,110 D 8
Ballindine, 232 C 4
Ballingarry, Limerick, 422 D 7
Ballingarry, Tipperary, ‡574 F 6
Ballinlough, 242 D 4
Ballinrobe, 1,272 C 4
Ballintober, ‡867 E 4
Ballintra, 197 E 2
Ballisodare, 486 E 3
Ballivor, 287 H 4
Ballybay, 754 G 3
Ballybay, *1,159 G 3
Ballybofey-Stranorlar, 2,214 F 2
Ballybunion, 1,287 B 7
Ballycanew, ‡460 J 6
Ballycarney, ‡294 J 6
Ballycastle, ‡724 C 3
Ballyconnell, 421 F 3
Ballycotton, 389 F 8
Ballydehob, 253 C 8
Ballyduff, 406 B 7
Ballygar, 359 E 4
Ballygeary, 725 J 7
Ballyhaise, 274 G 3
Ballyhaunis, 1,093 D 4
Ballyheigue, 450 B 7
Ballyjamesduff, 673 G 4
Ballylanders, 266 E 7
Ballylongford, 504 B 6
Ballymahon, 707 F 4
Ballymakeery, 272 C 8
Ballymore, ‡447 F 5
Ballymore Eustace, 433 J 5
Ballymote, 952 D 3
Ballyporeen, ‡810 E 7
Ballyragget, 519 G 6
Ballyroan, ‡478 G 6
Ballyshannon, 2,325 E 3
Ballytore, ‡580 H 5
Baltimore, 200 C 9
Baltinglass, 909 H 6
Baltray, 236 J 4
Banagher, 1,052 F 5
Bandon, 2,257 D 8
Bandon, *4,071 D 8
Bannow, ‡798 H 7
Bansha, 184 E 7
Bantry, 2,579 C 8
Barna, ‡1,734 C 5
Belmullet, 744 B 3
Belturbet, 1,092 G 3
Bennettsbridge, 367 G 6
Birr, 3,319 F 5
Birr, *3,881 F 5
Blanchardstown, 3,279 H 5
Blarney, 1,128 D 8
Blessington, 637 J 5
Boherbue, 372 C 7
Borris, 430 H 6
Borris-in-Ossory, 276 F 6
Borrisokane, 769 E 6
Borrisoleigh, 471 E 6
Boyle, 1,727 E 4
Boyle, *1,939 E 4
Bray, 14,467 K 5
Bray, *15,841 K 5
Brí Chualann (Bray), 14,467 K 5
Broadford, 226 C 7
Brosna, 250 C 7
Bruff, 547 D 7
Bruree, 243 D 7
Bunbeg-Derrybeg, 878 E 1
Bunclody-Carrickduff, 929 H 6
Buncrana, 2,955 G 1
Buncrana, *3,334 G 1
Bundoran, 1,337 E 3
Burtonport, ‡1,288 E 2
Buttevant, 1,045 D 7
Cahir, 1,747 F 7
Cahirciveen, 1,547 A 8
Callan, 1,283 G 7
Camolin, 306 J 6
Campile, 231 H 7
Cappamore, 567 E 6
Cappawhite, 305 E 6
Cappoquin, 872 F 7
Carbury, ‡894 H 5
Carlingford, 559 J 3
Carlow, 9,588 H 6
Carlow, *10,399 H 6
Carndonagh, 1,146 G 1
Carnew, 570 H 6
Carrickmacross, 2,100 H 4
Carrickmacross, *2,475 H 4
Carrick-on-Shannon, 1,854 F 4
Carrick-on-Suir, 5,006 F 7
Carrigaholt, ‡493 B 6
Carrigaline, 951 E 8
Carrigallen, 230 F 4
Carrigart, ‡753 F 1
Carrigtwohill, 622 E 8
Carrowkeel, ‡326 G 1
Cashel, 2,692 F 7
Castlebar, 5,979 C 4
Castlebar, *6,476 C 4
Castlebellingham, 407 J 4
Castleblayney, 2,118 H 3
Castleblayney, *2,395 H 3
Castlecomer-Donaguile, 1,244 G 6
Castledermot, 583 H 6
Castlefin, 610 F 2
Castlegregory, 216 A 7
Castleisland, 1,929 B 7
Castlemartyr, 491 E 8
Castlepollard, 693 G 4
Castlerea, 1,752 D 4
Castletown, ‡504 F 6
Castletownbere, 812 B 8
Castletownroche, 399 D 7
Castletownshend, 170 C 9
Causeway, 215 B 7
Cavan, 3,273 G 4
Cavan, *4,312 G 3
Ceanannus Mór, 2,391 G 4
Ceanannus Mór, *2,653 G 4
Celbridge, 1,568 H 5
Charlestown-Bellahy, 677 D 4
Charleville (Rathluirc), 2,232 D 7
Clara, 2,156 F 5
Claregalway, ‡594 D 5
Claremorris, 1,718 C 4
Clashmore, ‡379 F 8
Clifden, 790 B 5
Cloghan, 404 F 5
Clogh-Chatsworth, 324 G 6
Clogheen, 530 F 7
Clogherhead, 649 J 4
Clonakilty, 2,430 D 8
Clonaslee, 285 F 5
Clondalkin, 7,009 J 5
Clonegal, 202 H 6
Clones, 2,164 G 3
Clonfert, ‡430 E 5
Clonmany, ‡936 G 1
Clonmel, 11,622 F 7
Clonmel, *12,291 F 7
Clonmellon, 328 H 4
Clonroche, 222 H 7
Clontuskert, 351 E 4
Cloone, ‡460 F 4
Cloughjordan, 480 E 6
Cloyne, 654 E 8
Coachford, 290 D 8
Cobh, 6,076 E 8
Cobh, *7,141 E 8
Coill Dubh, 920 H 5
Collon, 262 J 4
Collooney, 546 E 3
Cong, 233 C 4
Convoy, 654 F 2
Coolaney, ‡352 D 3
Coolgreany, ‡603 J 6
Cootehill, 1,415 G 3
Cootehill, *1,542 G 3
Cork, 128,645 E 8
Cork, *134,430 E 8
Corofin, 342 C 6
Courtmacsherry, 210 D 8
Courtown Harbour, 291 J 6
Creeslough, 269 F 1
Crookhaven, ‡400 B 9
Croom, 756 D 6
Crosshaven, 1,222 E 8
Crossmolina, 1,077 C 3
Crusheen, ‡405 D 6
Culdaff, ‡621 G 1
Daingean, 492 G 5
Delvin, 223 G 4
Dingle, 1,401 A 7
Doaghbeg, ‡701 F 1
Donabate, 426 J 5
Donegal, 1,725 F 2
Doneraile, 799 D 7
Dooagh-Keel, 649 A 4
Doon, 387 E 7
Douglas, ‡4,448 D 8
Drimoleague, 415 C 8
Drishane, ‡1,548 C 7
Drogheda, 19,762 J 4
Drogheda, *20,095 J 4
Droichead Nua, 5,053 H 5
Droichead Nua, *6,444 H 5
Dromahair, 177 E 3
Drumcar, ‡1,215 J 4
Drumconrath, ‡1,044 H 4
Drumkeerin, ‡467 E 3
Drumlish, 205 F 4
Drumshanbo, 576 E 3
Dublin (cap.), 567,866 K 5
Dublin, *679,748 K 5
Duleek, 658 J 4
Duncannon, 228 H 7
Dundalk, 21,672 H 3
Dundalk, *23,816 H 3
Dunfanaghy, 303 F 1
Dungarvan, 5,583 F 7
Dungloe, 940 E 2
Dunkineely, 288 E 2
Dun Laoghaire, 53,171 K 5
Dun Laoghaire, *98,379 K 5
Dunlavin, 423 H 5
Dunleer 855 J4
Dunmanway 1,392 C8
Dunmore 522 D4
Dunmore East 656 G7
Dunshaughlin⊙ 283 H5
Durrow, Laois 596 G6
Durrow, Offaly⊙ 441 F5
Easky 184 D3
Edenderry 2,953 G5
Edenderry* 3,116 G5
Elphin 489 E4
Emyvale 281 G3
Ennis 5,972 D6
Ennis* 10,840 D6
Enniscorthy 5,704 J7
Enniscorthy* 6,642 J7
Enniskerry 772 J5
Ennistymon 1,013 C6
Eyrecourt 314 E5
Fahan⊙ 1,023 G1
Falcarragh 506 E1
Feakle⊙ 398 D6
Fenit 360 B7
Ferbane 1,064 F5
Fermoy 3,237 E7
Fermoy* 4,033 E7
Ferns 712 J6
Fethard, Tipperary 1,064 F7
Fethard, Wexford⊙ 637 H7
Foxford 868 C4
Foynes 624 C6
Frankford (Kilcormac) 1,089 F5
Frenchpark⊙ 693 E4
Freshford 585 G6
Galbally 258 E7
Galway 27,726 C5
Galway* 29,375 C5
Geashill⊙ 751 G5
Glandore⊙ 695 C8
Glanmire-Riverstown 1,113 E8
Glanworth 335 E7
Glenamaddy 315 D4
Glenbeigh 266 B7
Glencolumbkille⊙ 787 D2
Glengarriff 244 C8
Glenties 734 E2
Glenville⊙ 264 D7
Glin 623 C6
Golden⊙ 640 F7
Gorey 2,946 J6
Gorey* 3,024 J6
Gormanston⊙ 1,384 J4
Gort 975 D5
Gowran 402 G6
Graiguenamanagh-Tinnahinch 1,303 H6
Granard 1,054 F4
Greencastle 322 H1
Greenore 882 J4
Greystones-Delgany 4,517 K5
Gurteen 165 D3
Hacketstown 574 H6
Headford 673 C5
Holycross⊙ 902 F6
Hospital 525 E7
Inchigeelagh⊙ 516 C8
Inishannon 190 D8
Inistioge 179 G7
Inniscrone 582 C3
Johnstown 303 G6
Kanturk 2,063 D7
Keel-Dooagh 649 A4
Kells⊙ 423 G6
Kells (Ceanannus Mór) 2,391 G4
Kenmare 903 B8
Kilbaha⊙ 471 B6
Kilbeggan 635 G5
Kilcar 273 D2
Kilcock 827 H5
Kilconnell⊙ 629 E5
Kilcoole 679 K5
Kilcormac 1,089 F5
Kilcullen 880 H5
Kildare 3,137 H5
Kildysart 239 C6
Kilfenora⊙ 441 C6
Kilfinane 561 D7
Kilgarvan 228 B8
Kilkee 1,287 B6
Kilkelly 225 D4
Kilkenny 9,838 G6
Kilkenny* 13,306 G6
Killala 368 C3
Killaloe 871 E6
Killarney 7,184 C7
Killarney* 7,541 C7
Killavullen 221 D7
Killenaule 592 F6
Killeshandra 432 F3
Killimor 221 E5
Killinaboy⊙ 297 C6
Killorglin 1,150 B7
Killucan-Rathwire 290 G4
Killybegs 1,094 E2
Kilmacrennan 274 F1
Kilmacthomas 396 G7
Kilmallock 1,170 D7
Kilmeadan⊙ 262 G7
Kilmihil 284 C6
Kilmaganny 181 G7
Kilmore Quay 273 H7
Kilmurry⊙ 387 C6
Kilnaleck 273 G4
Kilronan 243 B5
Kilrush 2,671 C6
Kilsheelan⊙ 665 F7
Kiltimagh 978 C4
Kilworth 360 E7
Kingscourt 1,016 H4
Kingstown (Dún Laoghaire) 53,171 K5
Kinlough 160 E3
Kinnegad 362 G5
Kinnitty⊙ 420 F5
Kinsale 1,622 D8
Kinsale* 1,989 D8
Kinvara 293 D5
Knightstown 236 A8
Knock⊙ 1,202 D4
Knocklong 248 D7
Knocknagashel 168 C7
Labasheeda⊙ 468 C6
Laghy⊙ 625 E2
Lahinch 455 C6
Lanesborough-Ballyleague 906 F4
Laracor⊙ 404 H4
Laytown-Bettystown-Mornington 1,882 J4
Leenane⊙ 271 B4
Leighlinbridge 379 H6
Leitrim⊙ 544 F3
Leixlip 2,402 H5
Letterkenny 4,930 F2
Letterkenny* 5,207 F2
Lifford 1,121 F2
Limerick 57,161 D6
Limerick* 63,002 D6
Liscarroll 231 D7
Lisdoonvarna 459 C5
Lismore 884 F7
Lismore⊙ 1,041 F7
Listowel 3,021 C7
Littleton 322 F6
Longford 3,876 F4
Longford* 4,791 F4
Lorrha⊙ 685 E5
Loughrea 3,075 E5
Louisburgh 310 B4
Louth 208 J4
Lucan-Doddsborough 4,245 J5
Luimneach (Limerick) 57,161 D6
Lusk 553 J4
Macroom 2,256 C8
Malahide 3,834 J5
Malin⊙ 552 G1
Mallow 5,901 D7
Mallow* 6,506 D7
Manorhamilton 858 E3
Manulla⊙ 660 C4
Maryborough (Portlaoise) 3,902 G5
Maynooth 1,296 H5
Meathas Truim 546 G4
Midleton 3,075 E8
Midleton* 4,666 E8
Milford 763 F1
Millstreet 1,319 D7
Milltown 260 A7
Miltown-Malbay 677 C6
Minard⊙ 397 A7
Mitchelstown 2,783 E7
Moate 1,378 F5
Mohill 868 F4
Monaghan 5,256 G3
Monasterevan 1,619 H5
Moneygall 282 F6
Monivea⊙ 405 D5
Mooncoin 413 G7
Mount Bellew 275 D5
Mountcharles 445 E2
Mountmellick 2,595 G5
Mountmellick* 2,864 G5
Mountrath 1,098 F5
Moville 1,089 G1
Moycullen⊙ 498 C5
Moynalty⊙ 583 H4
Muff 240 G1
Muinebeag 2,321 H6
Mullagh 293 H4
Mullaghmore⊙ 629 D3
Mullinahone 262 F7
Mullinavat 343 G7
Mullingar 6,790 G4
Mullingar* 9,245 G4
Naas 5,078 H5
Navan (An Uaimh) 4,605 H4
Nenagh 5,085 E6
Nenagh* 5,174 E6
Newbliss⊙ 547 G3
Newbridge (Droichead Nua) 5,053 H5
Newcastle 2,549 D7
Newcastle* 2,680 D7
Newmarket 886 C7
Newmarket-on-Fergus 1,052 D6
New Pallas⊙ 1,271 E6
Newport, Mayo 420 C4
Newport, Tipperary 582 E6
New Ross 4,775 H7
New Ross* 5,153 H7
Newtown Forbes⊙ 495 F4
Newtownmountkennedy 882 J5
Newtownsandes 268 C6
O'Briensbridge-Montpelier 237 D6
Oldcastle 759 G4
Old Leighlin⊙ 309 G6
Oola 348 E6
Oranmore 440 D5
Oughterard 628 C5
Passage East 408 G7
Passage West 2,709 E8
Patrickswell 415 D6
Pettigo 332 F2
Piltown 456 G7
Portarlington 3,117 G5
Portlaoise 3,902 G5
Portlaoise* 6,470 G5
Portlaw 1,166 G7
Portmarnock 1,726 J5
Portumna 913 E5
Queenstown (Cóbh) 6,076 E8
Rahan⊙ 531 F5
Ramelton 807 F1
Raphoe 945 F2
Rathangan 868 G5
Rathcoole 1,740 J5
Rathcormac 191 E7
Rathdowney 892 F6
Rathdrum 1,141 J6
Rathgormuck⊙ 231 F7
Rathkeale 1,543 D7
Rathluirc 2,232 D7
Rathmore 437 C7
Rathmullen 486 F1
Rathnew-Merrymeeting 954 J6
Rathowen⊙ 294 F4
Rathvilly 230 H6
Ratoath 300 J5
Riverstown 236 E3
Rockcorry 233 H3
Rosapenna⊙ 822 F1
Roscommon 1,556 E4
Roscommon* 2,821 E4
Roscrea 3,855 F6
Rosscarbery 309 C8
Rosses Point 464 D3
Rosslare 588 J7
Rosslare Harbour (Ballygeary) 725 J7
Roundstone 204 A5
Roundwood 260 J5
Rush 2,633 J4
Saint Johnston 463 F2
Scarriff 619 E6
Schull 457 B8
Scotstown 264 H3
Shanagolden 231 C6
Shannon Airport 3,657 D6
Shannon Bridge 188 F5
Shercock 313 G4
Shillelagh 246 J6
Shinrone 365 F5
Shrule 288 C4
Sixmilebridge 567 D6
Skerries 3,044 J4
Skibbereen 2,104 C8
Slane 483 H4
Sligo 14,080 E3
Sligo* 14,456 E3
Sneem 285 B8
Spiddal⊙ 819 C5
Stepaside 748 J5
Stradbally, Laois 891 G5
Stradbally, Waterford 158 F7
Strokestown 563 E4
Swanlinbar 257 F3
Swinford 1,105 C4
Swords 4,133 J5
Taghmon 369 H7
Tallaght 6,174 J5
Tallow, 883 F 7
Tarbert, 485 C 6
Teltown, ‡739 H 4
Templemore, 2,174 F 6
Templetuohy, 197 F 6
Termonfeckin, 328 J 4
Thomastown, 1,270 G 7
Thurles, 6,840 F 6
Thurles, *7,087 F 6
Timoleague, 257 D 8
Tinahely, 450 H 6
Tipperary, 4,631 E 7
Tipperary, *4,717 E 7
Toomevara, 272 E 6
Tralee, 12,287 B 7
Tralee, *13,263 B 7
Tramore, 3,792 G 7
Trim, 1,700 H 4
Trim, *2,255 H 4
Tuam, 3,808 D 4
Tuam, *4,952 D 4
Tubbercurry, 959 D 3
Tulla, 415 D 6
Tullamore, 6,809 G 5
Tullamore, *7,474 G 5
Tullaroan, ‡301 G 6
Tullow, 1,838 H 6
Tullow, *1,945 H 6
Tynagh, ‡452 E 5
Tyrrellspass, 289 G 5
Urlingford, 652 F 6
Virginia, 583 G 4
Waterford, 31,968 G 7
Waterford, *33,676 G 7
Waterville, 547 A 8
Westport, 3,023 C 4
Wexford, 11,849 H 7
Wexford, *13,293 H 7
Whitegate, 370 E 8
Wicklow, 3,786 K 6
Wicklow, *3,915 K 6
Woodenbridge, ‡620 J 6
Woodford, 198 E 5
Youghal, 5,445 F 8
Youghal, *5,626 F 8

OTHER FEATURES

Achill (isl.), 3,129 A 4
Allen (lake) E 3
Allen, Bog of (marsh) H 5
Aran (isl.), 773 D 2
Aran (isls.), 1,499 B 5
Arklow (bank) K 6
Arrow (lake) E 3
Awbeg (riv.) D 7
Ballinskelligs (bay) A 8
Ballycotton (bay) F 8
Ballyheige (bay) B 7
Ballyhoura (hills) E 7
Ballyteige (bay) H 7
Bandon (riv.) D 8
Bann (riv.) J 6
Bantry (bay) B 8
Barrow (riv.) H 7
Baurtregaum (mt.) A 7
Bear (isl.), 288 B 8
Blacksod (bay) A 3
Blackstairs (mt.) H 6
Blackwater (riv.) D 7
Blackwater (riv.) H 4
Blasket (isls.) A 7
Bloody Foreland (prom.) E 1
Blue Stack (mts.) E 2
Boderg (lake) E 4
Boggeragh (mts.) D 7
Boyne (riv.) J 4
Brandon (head) A 7
Bride (riv.) E 7
Broad Haven (harb.) B 3
Brosna (riv.) F 5
Bull, The (isl.), 5 A 8
Caha (mts.) B 8
Carlingford (inlet) J 3
Carnsore (pt.) J 7
Carrantuohill (mt.) B 7
Clare (riv.) C 5
Clare (isls.), 168 A 4
Clear (cape) B 9
Clear (isl.), 192 C 9
Clew (bay) B 4
Comeragh (mts.) F 7
Conn (lake) C 3
Connacht (prov.), 390,902 C 4
Connemara (dist.), 7,599 B 5
Cork (harb.) E 8
Corrib (lake) C 5
Courtmacsherry (bay) D 8
Curragh, The H 5
Dee (riv.) H 4
Deel (riv.) D 7
Deele (riv.) F 2
Derg (lake) E 6
Derravaragh (lake) G 4
Derryveagh (mts.) E 2
Dingle (bay) A 7
Donegal (bay) D 3
Drum (hills) F 7
Dublin (bay) J 5
Dundalk (bay) J 4
Dunmanus (bay) B 8
Dursey (isl.), 38 A 8
Ennell (lake) G 5
Erne (riv.) F 3
Errigal (mt.) E 1
Erris (head) A 3
Fanad (head) F 1
Fastnet Rock (isl.), 3 B 9
Feale (riv.) C 7
Fergus (riv.) D 6
Finn (riv.) F 2
Finn (riv.) G 3
Flesk (riv.) C 7
Foyle (inlet) G 1
Foyle (riv.) G 2
Galley (head) D 9
Galtee (mts.) E 7
Galtymore (mt.) E 7
Galway (bay) C 5
Gara (lake) D 4
Garadice (lake) F 3
Gill (lake) E 3
Glyde (riv.) H 4
Golden Vale (plain) E 7
Gorumna (isl.), 1,108 B 5
Gowna (lake) G 4
Grand (canal) G 5
Greenore (pt.) J 7
Gweebarra (bay) D 2
Hags (head) B 6
Helvick (head) G 7
Hook (head) H 7
Horn (head) E 1
Iar Connacht (dist.), 10,774 C 5
Inishbofin (isl.), 236 A 4
Inishbofin (isl.), 103 E 1
Inisheer (isl.), 313 B 5
Inishmaan (isl.), 319 C 5
Inishmore (isl.), 864 B 5
Inishowen (head) H 1
Inishowen (pen.), 24,109 G 1
Inishtrahull (isl.), 3 G 1
Inishturk (isls.), 83 A 4
Inny (riv.) A 8
Inny (riv.) F 4
Inver (bay) E 2
Ireland's Eye (isl.) K 5
Irish (sea) K 4
Joyce's Country (dist.), 2,021 B 4
Kenmare (riv.) A 8
Kerry (head) A 7
Key (lake) E 3
Kilkieran (bay) B 5
Killala (bay) C 3
Killary (harb.) A 4
Kinsale (harb.) E 8
Kippure (mt.) J 5
Knockboy (mt.) B 8
Knockmealdown (mts.) F 7
Lady's Island Lake (inlet) J 7
Lambay (isl.), 24 K 4
Laune (riv.) B 7
Leane (lake) B 7
Leane (lake) G 4
Lee (riv.) D 8
Leinster (mt.) H 6
Leinster (prov.), 1,498,140 G 5
Lettermullan (isl.), 221 B 5
Liffey (riv.) H 5
Liscannor (bay) B 6
Long Island (bay) B 9
Loop (head) A 6
Lugnaquillia (mt.) J 5
Macgillicuddy's Reeks (mts.) B 7
Macnean (lake) F 3
Maigue (riv.) D 6
Maine (riv.) C 7
Malin (head) F 1
Mask (lake) C 4
Maumturk (mts.) B 5
Melvin (lake) E 3
Mizen (head) B 9
Moher (cliffs) B 6
Monavullagh (mts.) F 7
Moy (riv.) C 3
Mulkear (riv.) E 6
Mullaghareirk (mts.) C 7
Mulroy (bay) F 1
Munster (prov.), 882,002 D 7
Mweelrea (mt.) B 4
Mweenish (isl.), 198 B 5
Nagles (mts.) E 7
Nenagh (riv.) E 6
Nephin (mt.) C 3
Nore (riv.) G 7
North (sound) B 5
Omey (isl.), 34 A 5
Oughter (lake) G 3
Ovoca (riv.) J 6
Owenmore (riv.) D 3
Owey (isl.), 51 D 1
Paps, The (mt.) C 7
Partry (mts.) C 4
Pollaphuca (res.) J 5
Punchestown H 5
Rathlin O'Birne (isl.), 3 C 2
Ree (lake) F 5
Roaringwater (bay) B 9
Rosses (bay) D 1
Rosskeeragh (pt.) D 3
Royal (canal) G 4
Saint Finan's (bay) A 8
Saint George's (chan.) K 7
Saint John's (pt.) D 2
Saltee (isls.) H 7
Seven (heads) D 8
Seven Hogs, The (isls.) A 7
Shannon (riv.) E 6
Sheeffry (hills) B 4
Sheelin (lake) G 4
Sheep Haven (harb.) F 1
Sheeps (head) B 8
Sherkin (isl.), 82 C 9
Silvermine (mts.) E 6
Slaney (riv.) H 7
Slieve Aughty (mts.) D 5
Slieve Bloom (mts.) F 5
Slieve Gamph (mts.) D 3
Slievenaman (mt.) F 7
Sligo (bay) D 3
Slyne (head) A 5
South (sound) C 5
Stacks (mts.) B 7
Suck (riv.) E 5
Suir (riv.) G 7
Swilly (inlet) F 1
Tara (hill) H 4
Tory (isl.), 273 E 1
Tory (sound) E 1
Tralee (bay) B 7
Trawbreaga (bay) F 1
Ulster (part) (prov.), 207,204 G 2
Valencia (Valentia) (isl.), 770 A 8
Valentia (isl.), 770 A 8
Waterford (harb.) G 7
Wexford (bay) J 7
Wicklow (head) K 6
Wicklow (mts.) J 6
Youghal (bay) F 8

NORTHERN IRELAND

DISTRICTS

Antrim, 37,600 J 2
Ards, 52,100 K 2
Armagh, 47,500 H 3
Ballymena, 52,200 J 2
Ballymoney, 22,700 J 1
Banbridge, 28,800 J 3
Belfast, 368,200 J 2
Carrickfergus, 27,500 K 2
Castlereagh, 63,600 K 2
Coleraine, 44,900 H 1
Cookstown, 27,500 H 2
Craigavon, 71,200 J 3
Down, 48,800 K 3
Dungannon, 43,000 H 3
Fermanagh, 50,900 F 3
Larne, 29,000 K 2
Limavady, 25,000 H 1
Lisburn, 80,800 J 2
Londonderry, 86,600 G 2
Magherafelt, 32,200 H 2
Mourne (Newry and Mourne), 75,300 J 3
Moyle, 13,400 J 1
Newtownabbey, 71,500 J 2
North Down, 59,600 K 2
Omagh, 41,800 G 2
Strabane, 35,500 G 2

CITIES and TOWNS

Ahoghill, ‡1,929 J 2
Annalong, 1,001 K 3
Antrim, 8,351 J 2
Ardglass, 1,052 K 3
Armagh, 13,606 H 3
Armoy, ‡1,051 J 1
Augher, ‡1,986 G 3
Aughnacloy, ‡1,885 H 3
Ballycastle, 2,899 J 1
Ballyclare, 5,155 J 2
Ballygawley, ‡2,165 G 3
Ballykelly, 1,116 G 1
Ballymena, 23,386 J 2
Ballymoney, 5,697 J 1
Ballynahinch, 3,485 J 3
Banbridge, 7,968 J 3
Bangor, 35,260 K 2
Belfast (cap.), 353,700 J 2
Belfast, *551,940 J 2
Bellaghy, ‡2,265 H 2
Belleek, ‡2,487 E 3
Beragh, ‡2,137 G 2
Bessbrook, 2,619 J 3
Brookeborough, ‡2,534 G 3
Broughshane, 1,288 J 2
Bushmills, 1,288 J 1
Caledon, ‡1,828 H 3
Carnlough, 1,416 J 2
Carrickfergus, 16,603 K 2
Carrowdore, 2,548 K 2
Castledawson, 1,162 H 2
Castlederg, 1,766 F 2
Castlewellan, 1,488 K 3
Claudy, ‡2,507 G 2
Clogher, ‡1,888 G 3
Coalisland, 3,614 H 2
Coleraine, 16,354 H 1
Comber, 5,575 K 2
Cookstown, 6,965 H 2
Craigavon, 12,740 J 3
Crossgar, 1,098 K 3
Crossmaglen, 1,085 H 3
Crumlin, 1,450 J 2
Cullybackey, 1,649 J 2
Derrygonnelly, ‡2,539 F 3
Dervock, ‡1,191 J 1
Donaghadee, 4,008 K 2
Downpatrick, 7,918 K 3
Draperstown, ‡2,247 H 2
Dromore, Banbridge, 2,848 J 3
Dromore, Omagh, ‡2,224 G 3
Drumquin, ‡1,982 F 2
Dundrum, ‡2,245 K 3
Dungannon, 8,190 H 3
Dungiven, 1,536 H 2
Dunnamanagh, ‡2,242 G 2
Ederny and Kesh, ‡2,497 F 2
Enniskillen, 9,679 F 3
Feeny, ‡1,459 H 2
Fintona, 1,190 G 3
Fivemiletown, ‡1,649 G 3
Garvagh, ‡2,363 H 2
Gilford, 1,592 J 3
Glenarm, ‡1,728 J 2
Glenavy, ‡2,360 J 2
Glynn, ‡1,872 K 2
Gortin, ‡2,033 G 2
Greyabbey, ‡2,646 K 2
Hillsborough, 1,021 J 3
Holywood, 9,892 K 2
Irvinestown, 1,457 F 3
Keady, 2,145 H 3
Kells, ‡2,560 J 2
Kesh, ‡2,497 F 3
Kilkeel, 4,090 K 3
Killough, ‡3,295 K 3
Killyleagh, 2,359 K 3
Kilrea, 1,196 H 2
Kircubbin, 1,075 K 3
Larne, 18,482 K 2
Limavady, 6,004 H 1
Lisburn, 31,836 J 2
Lisnaskea, 1,443 G 3
Londonderry, 51,200 G 2
Loughbrickland, ‡2,056 J 3
Maghera, 2,085 H 2
Magherafelt, 4,704 H 2
Markethill, ‡2,352 H 3
Millisle, 1,172 K 2
Moneymore, 1,178 H 2
Moy, ‡2,349 H 3
Moygashel, 1,086 H 3
Newcastle, 4,647 K 3
Newry, 20,279 J 3
Newtownabbey, 58,114 K 2
Newtownards, 15,484 K 2
Newtownbutler, ‡2,663 G 3
Newtownhamilton, ‡1,936 H 3
Newtownstewart, 1,433 G 2
Omagh, 14,594 G 2
Pomeroy, ‡1,786 H 2
Portaferry, 1,730 K 3
Portavogie, 1,310 K 3
Portglenone, ‡2,061 H 2
Portrush, 5,376 H 1
Portstewart, 5,085 H 1
Randalstown, 2,799 J 2
Rathfriland, 1,886 J 3
Rostrevor, 1,617 J 3
Saintfield, ‡2,198 K 3
Sion Mills, 1,588 G 2
Sixmilecross, ‡1,980 G 2
Stewartstown, ‡1,759 H 2
Strabane, 9,413 G 2
Strangford, ‡1,987 K 3
Tandragee, 1,725 J 3
Tempo, ‡2,282 G 3
Trillick, ‡2,167 G 3
Warrenpoint, 4,291 J 3
Whitehead, 2,642 K 2

OTHER FEATURES

Bann (riv.) H 2
Belfast (inlet) K 2
Blackwater (riv.) H 2
Bush (riv.) H 1
Derg (riv.) F 2
Divis (mt.) J 2
Dundrum (bay) K 3
Erne (lake) F 3
Foyle (inlet) G 1
Foyle (riv.) G 2
Giant's Causeway H 1
Lagan (riv.) K 2
Larne (inlet) K 2
Magee, Island (pen.), 1,581 K 2
Magilligan (pt.) H 1
Main (riv.) J 2
Mourne (mts.) J 3
Mourne (riv.) G 2
Neagh (lake) H 2
North (chan.) K 1
Rathlin (isl.), 109 J 1
Red (bay) K 1
Roe (riv.) H 1
Saint John's (pt.) K 3
Slieve Donard (mt.) K 3
Sperrin (mts.) G 2
Strangford (inlet) K 3
Torr (head) K 1
Ulster (part) (prov.), 1,537,200 G 2
Upper Lough Erne (lake) F 3

*City and suburbs.
‡Population of district.

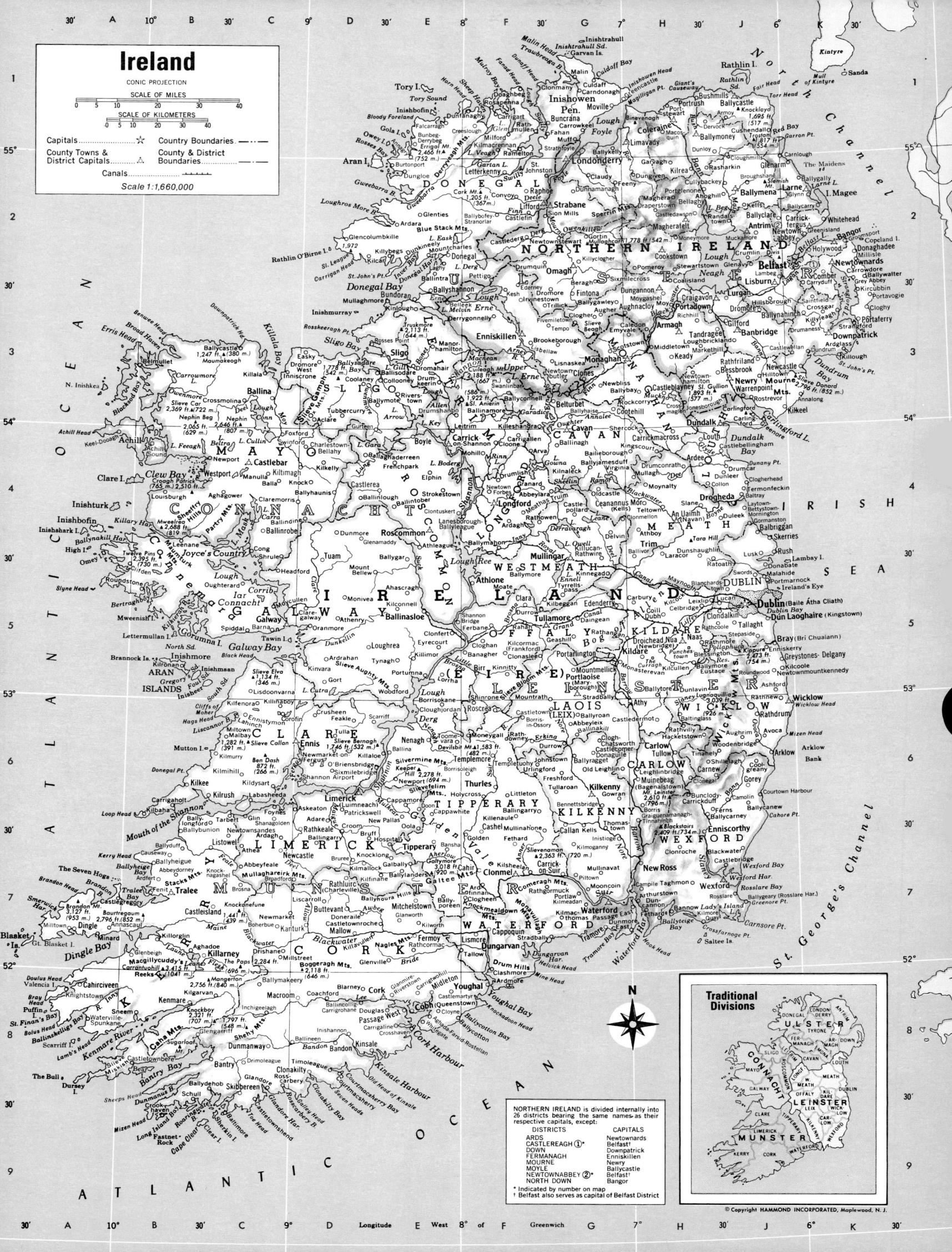

Norway, Sweden, Finland and Denmark

CONIC PROJECTION

SCALE OF MILES

SCALE OF KILOMETERS

Capitals of Countries .... ☆
Administrative Centers .... △
International Boundaries .... — · —
Internal Boundaries .... — · · —
Canals ....

SUBDIVISIONS
Indicated by Numbers
Counties in NORWAY
1 Akershus .... G 6
2 Vestfold .... G 7
3 Østfold .... G 7
4 Oslo .... G 7

Oslo is the administrative
center for Akershus and
Oslo County.

Counties in SWEDEN
5 Göteborg och
  Bohus .... G 7
6 Västmanland ..... K 7
7 Södermanland ... K 7
8 Östergötland ..... H J 7
9 Malmöhus .... H J 5
10 Kristianstad ..... J 8

NORWEGIAN SEA

Svalbard

NORWEGIAN SEA

STOCKHOLM

ATLANTIC OCEAN

ARCTIC OCEAN

BARENTS SEA

GULF OF BOTHNIA

BALTIC SEA

Gulf of Finland

Gulf of Riga

DENMARK

NETH.

WEST GERMANY

GERMANY

POLAND

U. S. S. R.

© Copyright HAMMOND INCORPORATED, Maplewood, N.J.

AREA 125,053 sq. mi. (323,887 sq. km.)
POPULATION 4,092,000
CAPITAL Oslo
LARGEST CITY Oslo
HIGHEST POINT Glittertinden 8,110 ft. (2,472 m.)
MONETARY UNIT krone
MAJOR LANGUAGE Norwegian
MAJOR RELIGION Protestantism

AREA 173,665 sq. mi. (449,792 sq. km.)
POPULATION 8,320,000
CAPITAL Stockholm
LARGEST CITY Stockholm
HIGHEST POINT Kebnekaise 6,946 ft. (2,117 m.)
MONETARY UNIT krona
MAJOR LANGUAGE Swedish
MAJOR RELIGION Protestantism

AREA 130,128 sq. mi. (337,032 sq. km.)
POPULATION 4,788,000
CAPITAL Helsinki
LARGEST CITY Helsinki
HIGHEST POINT Haltiatunturi 4,343 ft. (1,324 m.)
MONETARY UNIT markka
MAJOR LANGUAGES Finnish, Swedish
MAJOR RELIGION Protestantism

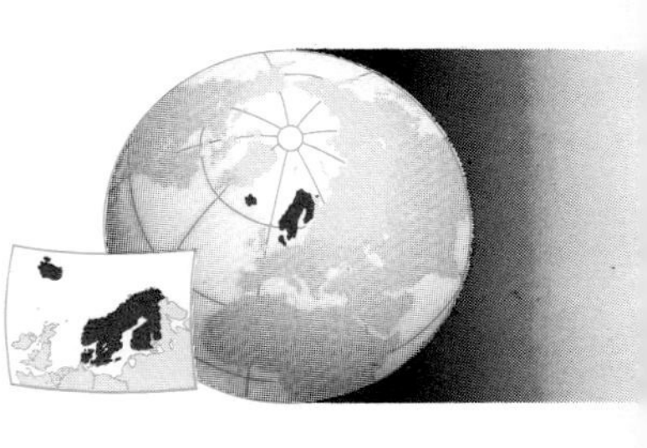

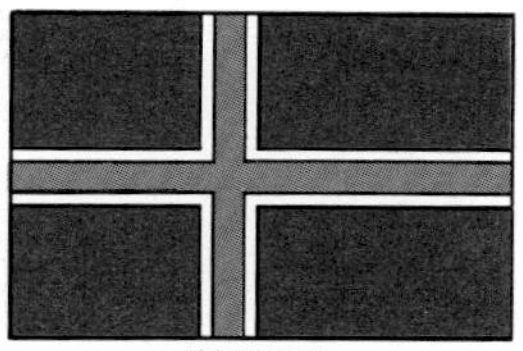

NORWAY

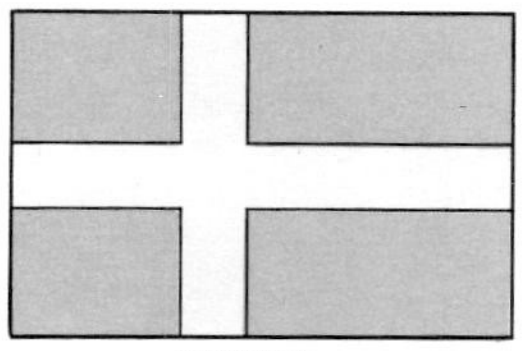

SWEDEN

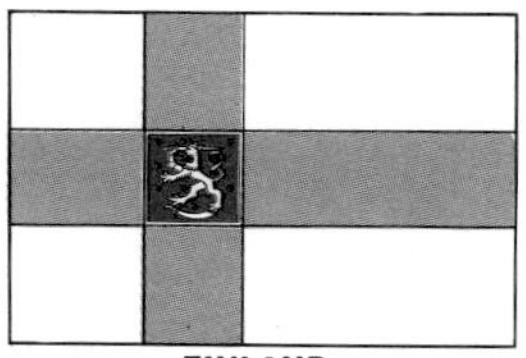

FINLAND

FINLAND

PROVINCES

Ahvenanmaa 22,380	L6
Åland (Ahvenanmaa) 22,380	L6
Häme 662,500	O6
Keski-Suomi 241,770	O5
Kuopio 252,023	P5
Kymi 346,478	Q6
Lappi 196,792	P3
Mikkeli 211,453	P6
Oulu 406,309	P4
Pohjois-Karjala 179,065	Q5
Turku ja Pori 697,988	N6
Uusimaa 1,085,625	O6
Vaasa 425,283	N5

CITIES and TOWNS

Äänekoski 10,725	O5
Åbo (Turku) 164,857	N6
Alavus 10,285	N5
Borgå 18,740	O6
Ekenäs 7,391	N6
Espoo 117,090	O6
Forssa 18,442	N6
Haapajärvi 7,791	O5
Hämeenlinna 40,761	O6
Hamina 11,055	P6
Hangö 10,374	N7
Hanko (Hangö) 10,374	N7
Harjavalta 8,445	M6
Heinola 15,350	P6
Helsinki (cap.) 502,961	O6
Helsinki* 794,746	O6
Huutokoski† 6,458	P5
Hyvinkää 35,865	O6
Iisalmi 21,159	P5
Ikaalinen 8,364	N6
Imatra 35,590	Q6
Ivalo 2,661	P2
Jakobstad 20,397	N5
Jämsä 12,526	O6
Järvenpää 16,259	O6
Joensuu 41,429	R5
Jyväskylä 61,209	O5
Jyväskylä* 84,185	O5
Kajaani 20,583	P4
Kalajoki 3,624	N4
Kankaanpää 12,564	M6
Karhula 21,834	P6
Karis 8,152	N6
Karjaa (Karis) 8,152	N6
Karkkila 8,678	N6
Kauniainien 6,219	O6
Kauttua 3,297	M6
Kelloselkä† 8,200	Q3
Kemi 27,893	O4
Kemijärvi 12,951	P3
Kerava 19,966	O6
Kokemäki 10,188	N6
Kokkola 22,096	N5
Kotka 34,026	P6
Kotka* 60,235	P6
Kouvola 29,383	P6
Kouvola* 59,507	P6
Kristiinankaupunki (Kristinestad) 9,331	N5
Kristinestad 9,331	N5
Kuhmo 4,150	Q4
Kuopio 71,684	Q5
Kurikka 11,177	M5
Kuusamo 4,449	Q4
Kuusankoski 22,342	P6
Lahti 94,864	O6
Lahti* 112,129	O6
Lappeenranta 52,682	P6
Lapua 15,189	N5
Lieksa 20,274	R5
Loimaa 6,575	N6
Lovisa 8,674	P6
Maarianhamina (Mariehamn) 9,574	M7
Mänttä 7,910	O6
Mariehamn 9,574	M7
Mikkeli 27,112	P6
Naantali 7,814	M6
Nokia 22,308	N6
Nurmes 11,721	Q5
Nykarleby 7,408	N5
Oulainen 7,322	O4
Oulu 93,707	O4
Oulu* 103,044	O4
Outokumpu 10,736	Q5
Parainen 10,170	M6
Parkano 8,518	N6
Pieksämäki 12,923	P5
Pietarsaari (Jakobstad) 20,397	N5
Pori 80,343	M6
Pori* 86,635	M6
Posio† 6,205	Q3
Pudasjärvi† 12,594	P4
Raahe 15,379	O4
Raisio 14,271	M6
Rauma 29,081	M6
Riihimäki 24,106	O6
Rovaniemi 28,411	O3
Saarijärvi 2,714	O5
Salo 19,176	N6
Savonlinna 28,336	Q6
Seinäjoki 22,123	N5
Sodankylä 3,304	P3
Sotkamo 2,316	Q4
Suolahti 5,936	O5
Suonenjoki 9,286	P5
Tammisaari (Ekenäs) 7,391	N6
Tampere 168,118	N6
Tampere* 220,920	N6
Toijala 8,080	N6
Tornio 19,971	O4
Turku 164,857	N6
Turku* 217,423	N6
Turtola† 5,852	O3
Ulvila† 8,040	N6
Uusikaarlepyy (Nykarleby) 7,408	N5
Uusikaupunki 11,915	M6
Vaasa 54,402	M5
Vaasa* 58,224	M5
Valkeakoski 22,588	N6
Vammala 16,363	N6
Varkaus 24,450	Q5
Vasa (Vaasa) 54,402	M5
Vuotso† 10,186	P2
Ylivieska 10,827	O4

OTHER FEATURES

Åland (isls.)	L6
Baltic (sea)	K9
Bothnia (gulf)	M5
Finland (gulf)	P7
Hailuoto (isl.)	O4
Haltiatunturi (mt.)	M2
Hangöudd (prom.)	N7
Haukivesi (lake)	Q5
Iijoki (riv.)	O4
Inari (lake)	P2
Ivalojoki (riv.)	P2
Juojärvi (lake)	Q5
Kalajoki (riv.)	O4
Kallavesi (lake)	P5
Karlö (Hailuoto) (isl.)	O4
Keitele (lake)	O5
Kemijärvi (lake)	Q3
Kemijoki (riv.)	O3
Kiantajärvi (lake)	Q4
Kilpisjärvi (lake)	M2
Kitinen (riv.)	P3
Kivijärvi (lake)	O5
Koitere (lake)	R5
Kuusamojärvi (lake)	Q4
Längelmävesi (lake)	O6
Lapland (reg.)	O2
Lappajärvi (lake)	O5
Lapuanjoki (riv.)	N5
Lestijärvi (lake)	O5
Lokka (res.)	Q3
Muojärvi (lake)	R4
Muonio (riv.)	M2
Näsijärvi (lake)	O6
Onkivesi (lake)	P5
Orihvesi (lake)	Q5
Oulujärvi (lake)	P4
Oulujoki (riv.)	O4
Ounasjoki (riv.)	O3
Päijänne (lake)	O6
Pielinen (lake)	Q5
Puruvesi (lake)	Q6
Puulavesi (lake)	P5
Pyhäjärvi (lake)	O5
Pyhäjärvi (lake)	M6
Saimaa (lake)	Q6
Siikajoki (riv.)	O4
Simojärvi (lake)	P3
Simojoki (riv.)	O4
Tana (riv.)	P2
Tornio (riv.)	O3
Vallgrund (isl.)	M5
Ylikitka (lake)	Q3

NORWAY

COUNTIES

Akershus 355,196	G6
Aust-Agder 86,216	E7
Buskerud 209,684	F6
Finnmark 79,373	O2
Hedmark 183,465	G6
Hordaland 386,492	E6
Møre og Romsdal 231,944	E5
Nordland 243,233	J3
Nord-Trøndelag 122,886	H4
Oppland 178,259	F6
Oslo (city) 462,732	D3
Østfold 228,546	G7
Rogaland 287,653	E7
Sogn og Fjordane 103,135	E6
Sør-Trøndelag 241,361	G5
Telemark 158,853	F7
Troms 144,111	L2
Vest-Agder 131,659	E7
Vestfold 182,433	G7

CITIES and TOWNS

Ålesund 40,868	D5
Ålgård 2,322	D7
Alta 5,582	N2
Åndalsnes 2,574	F5
Årdalstangen 2,360	F6
Arendal 11,701	F7
Arendal* 21,228	F7
Årnes 2,267	G6
Askim 8,413	E4
Bamble† 7,031	F7
Barentsburg	C2
Bergen 213,434	D6
Bodø 31,077	J3
Borge† 3,294	H2
Brønnøysund 3,130	G4
Dombås 1,114	F5
Drammen 50,777	C4
Drammen* 56,521	C4
Drøbak 4,538	D4
Eidsvoll 2,906	G6
Eigersund 11,379	D7
Elverum 7,391	G6
Farsund 8,908	E7
Flekkefjord 8,750	E7
Flora 8,822	D6
Fredrikstad 29,024	D4
Fredrikstad* 51,141	D4
Gjøvik 25,963	G6
Grimstad 13,091	F7
Halden 27,087	G7
Hamar 16,418	G6
Hamar* 25,138	G6
Hammerfest 7,610	N1
Hammerfest* 8,005	N1
Harstad 21,125	K2
Haugesund 27,386	D7
Haugesund* 29,277	D7
Hermansverk 706	E6
Holmestrand 8,246	C4
Holmsbu 273	D4
Honningsvag 3,780	O1
Horten 13,746	D4
Horten* 17,246	D4
Kirkenes 4,466	Q2
Kongsberg 19,854	F7
Kongsvinger 16,146	H6
Kopervik 4,221	D7
Kornsjø† 6,079	G7
Kragerø 5,249	F7
Kristiansand 59,488	F8
Kristiansund 18,847	E5
Kvinnherad† 2,898	E6
Larvik 9,097	C4
Larvik* 19,202	C4
Lenvik† 11,098	L2
Levanger 5,066	G5
Lillehammer 21,248	F6
Lillesand 3,028	F7
Lillestrøm† 11,550	E3
Longyearbyen	D2
Lysaker† 81,612	D3
Mandal 11,579	E7
Meråker† 2,907	G5
Mo 21,033	J3
Molde 20,334	E5
Mosjøen 9,341	H4
Moss 25,786	D4
Moss* 27,430	D4
Mysen 3,760	G7
Namsos 11,452	G4
Narvik 19,582	K2
Nesttun† 11,519	D6
Nittedal† 8,889	D3
Notodden 12,970	F7
Nøtterøy 11,944	D4
Ny-Ålesund	C2
Odda 7,401	E6
Oppdal 2,173	F5
Orkanger 3,685	F5
Oslo (cap.) 462,732	D3
Oslo* 645,413	D3
Porsgrunn 31,709	G7
Rakkestad 2,392	G7
Ringerike 30,156	C3
Risør 6,560	F7
Rjukan 5,334	F7
Røros 3,041	G5
Sandefjord 33,350	C4
Sandnes 33,934	D7
Sandvika† 34,337	C3
Sarpsborg 12,889	D4
Sarpsborg* 36,449	D4
Selje† 3,386	D5
Ski 9,081	D4
Skien 47,105	F7
Stavanger 86,639	D7
Stavern 2,604	D4
Steinkjer 20,553	G4
Stor-Elvdal† 2,993	G6
Sunndalsøra 5,114	F5
Sveagruva	D2
Svolvaer 3,942	J2
Tønsberg 9,964	D4
Tønsberg* 36,374	D4
Tromsø 43,830	L2
Trondheim 134,910	F5
Ullensvang† 2,326	E6
Vadsø 6,019	Q1
Vardø 3,875	R1
Vik 1,019	E6
Volda 3,511	E5
Voss 5,944	E6

OTHER FEATURES

Alsten (isl.)	H4
Andøya (isl.)	J2
Barduelv (riv.)	L2
Bellsund	C2
Bjørnafjorden (fjord)	D6
Bjornøya (isl.)	D3
Boknafjord (fjord)	D7
Bremanger (isl.)	D6
Dønna (isl.)	H3
Dovrefjell (hills)	F5
Edgeøya (isl.)	E2
Femundsjø (lake)	G5
Folda (fjord)	G4
Folda (fjord)	J3
Frohavet (bay)	F5
Frøya (isl.)	F5
Glittertinden (mt.)	F6
Hardangervidda (plat.)	E6
Hardangerfjord (fjord)	D7
Hinlopenstreten (str.)	C1
Hinnøya (isl.)	K2
Hitra (isl.)	F5
Hopen (isl.)	E2
Isfjorden (fjord)	C2
Jostedalsbreen (glac.)	E6
Kjölen (mts.)	K3
Kongsfjorden (fjord)	B2
Kvaløya (isl.)	O1
Lågen (riv.)	G6
Laksefjorden (fjord)	P1
Langøy (isl.)	J2
Lapland (reg.)	K2
Leka (isl.)	G4
Lindesnes (cape)	E8
Lista (pen.)	E7
Lofoten (isls.)	H2
Lopphavet (bay)	M1
Magerøya (isl.)	P1
Moskenesøya (isl.)	H3
Namsen (riv.)	H4
Nordaustlandet (isl.)	D1
Nordfjord (fjord)	E6
Nordkapp (pt.)	C1
Nordkinn (headland)	Q1
Nordkinn (pen.)	P1
North Cape (Nordkapp) (pt.)	P1
Norwegian (sea)	F3
Ofotfjorden (fjord)	K2
Oslofjord (fjord)	D4
Otra (riv.)	E7
Otterøya (isl.)	E5
Pasvikelv (riv.)	Q2
Platen, Kapp (pt.)	D1
Porsangen (fjord)	O1
Rana (fjord)	H3
Rauma (riv.)	F5
Ringvassøy (isl.)	L2
Romsdalsfjorden (fjord)	E5
Saltfjorden (fjord)	J3
Seiland (isl.)	N1
Senja (isl.)	K2
Skagerrak (str.)	F8
Smøla (isl.)	E5
Sognafjorden (fjord)	D6
Sørkapp (pt.)	C2
Sorøya (isl.)	N1
Spitsbergen (isl.)	C2
Storfjorden (fjord)	D2
Sulitjelma (mt.)	J3
Svalbard (isls.)	C3
Tana (riv.)	P1
Tanafjord (fjord)	Q1
Tokke (riv.)	F7
Trondheimsfjorden (fjord)	G5
Tyrifjord (lake)	C3
Vaerøy (isl.)	H3
Vagåvatn (lake)	F6
Vannøy (isl.)	L1
Varangerhalvøya (pen.)	Q1
Varangerfjord (fjord)	Q2
Vega (isl.)	G4
Vesterålen (isls.)	J2
Vestfjord (fjord)	H3
Vestvågøya (isl.)	H3
Vikna (isls.)	G4

SWEDEN

COUNTIES

Älvsborg 418,150	H7
Blekinge 155,391	J8
Gävleborg 294,595	K6
Göteborg och Bohus 714,660	G7
Gotland 54,447	L8
Halland 219,767	H8
Jämtland 133,559	J5
Jönköping 301,905	H8
Kalmar 240,768	K8
Kopparberg 281,082	J6
Kristianstad 272,090	J8

(continued on following page)

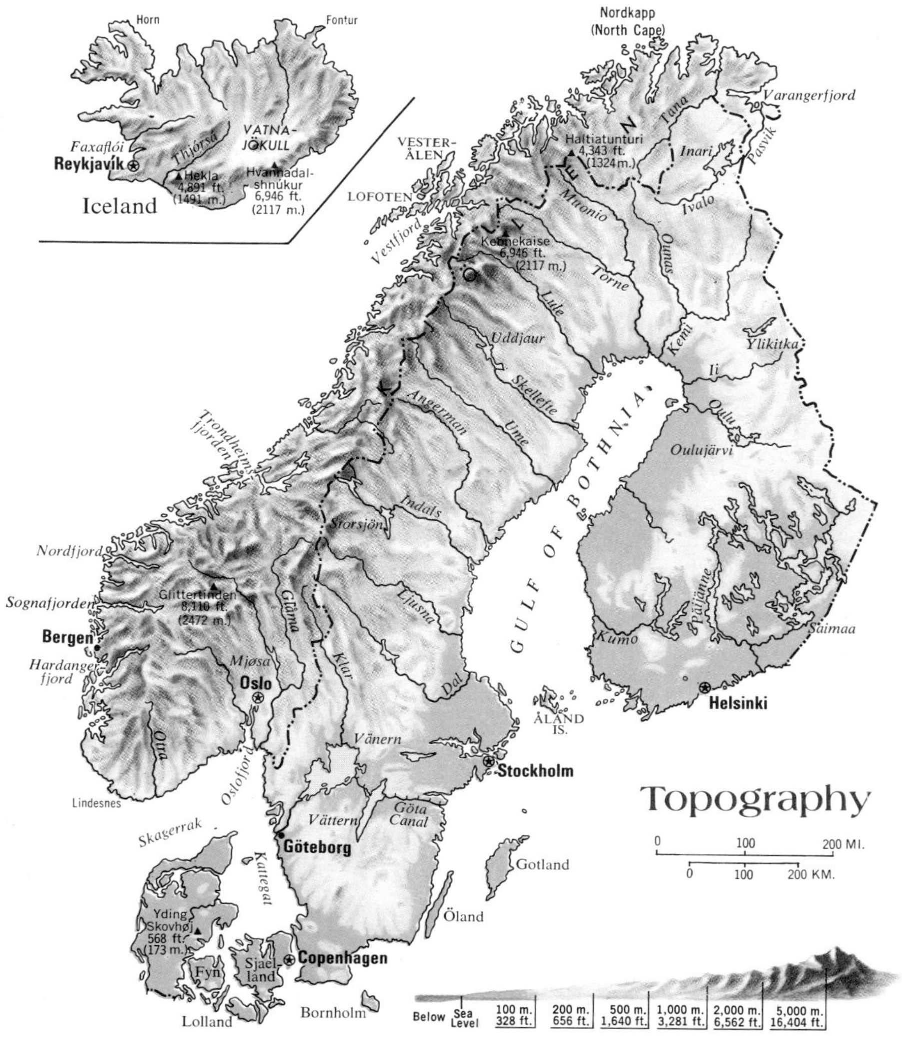
Horn
Fontur
Faxaflói
Reykjavík
Thjórsá
VATNA-JÖKULL
Hekla 4,891 ft. (1491 m.)
Iceland
Nordkapp (North Cape)
Varangerfjord
VESTERÅLEN
LOFOTEN
Haltiatunturi 4,343 ft. (1324 m.)
Inari
Tana
Pasvik
Vestfjord
Kebnekaise 6,946 ft. (2117 m.)
Muonio
Ivalo
Ounas
Torne
Lule
Kemi
Ylikitka
Uddjaur
Ii
Skellefte
Ume
Ångerman
Oulu
Oulujärvi
GULF OF BOTHNIA
Trondheimsfjorden
Indals
Storsjön
Nordfjord
Sognafjorden
Glittertinden 8,110 ft. (2472 m.)
Bergen
Glåma
Ljusna
Hardangerfjord
Mjøsa
Oslo
Klar
Dal
Päijänne
Kumo
Saimaa
Helsinki
ÅLAND IS.
Otra
Vänern
Stockholm
Lindesnes
Oslofjord
Skagerrak
Vättern
Göta Canal
Göteborg
Kattegat
Gotland
Öland
Yding Skovhøj 568 ft. (173 m.)
Fyn
Sjælland
Copenhagen
Lolland
Bornholm
Topography
0 100 200 MI.
0 100 200 KM.
Below Sea Level
100 m. 328 ft.
200 m. 656 ft.
500 m. 1,640 ft.
1,000 m. 3,281 ft.
2,000 m. 6,562 ft.
5,000 m. 16,404 ft.

Agriculture, Industry and Resources

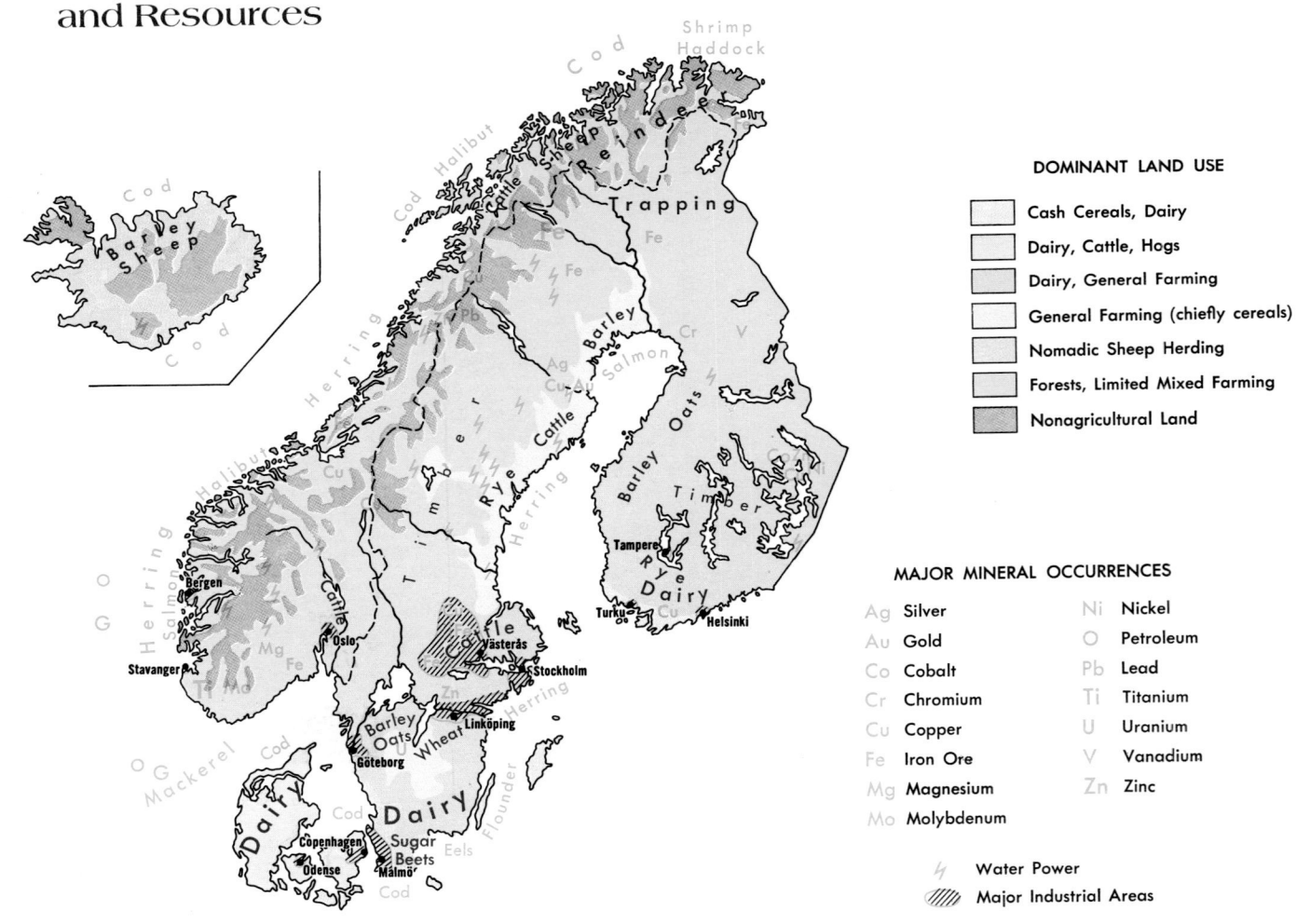

DOMINANT LAND USE

- Cash Cereals, Dairy
- Dairy, Cattle, Hogs
- Dairy, General Farming
- General Farming (chiefly cereals)
- Nomadic Sheep Herding
- Forests, Limited Mixed Farming
- Nonagricultural Land

MAJOR MINERAL OCCURRENCES

Ag	Silver	Ni	Nickel
Au	Gold	O	Petroleum
Co	Cobalt	Pb	Lead
Cr	Chromium	Ti	Titanium
Cu	Copper	U	Uranium
Fe	Iron Ore	V	Vanadium
Mg	Magnesium	Zn	Zinc
Mo	Molybdenum		

Water Power
Major Industrial Areas

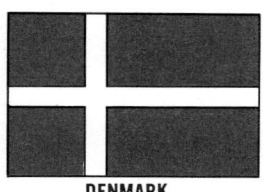

DENMARK

ICELAND

DENMARK

AREA 16,629 sq. mi. (43,069 sq. km.)
POPULATION 5,124,000
CAPITAL Copenhagen
LARGEST CITY Copenhagen
HIGHEST POINT Yding Skovhøj
568 ft. (173 m.)
MONETARY UNIT krone
MAJOR LANGUAGE Danish
MAJOR RELIGION Protestantism

ICELAND

AREA 39,768 sq. mi. (103,000 sq. km.)
POPULATION 228,785
CAPITAL Reykjavík
LARGEST CITY Reykjavík
HIGHEST POINT Hvannadalshnúkur
6,952 ft. (2,119 m.)
MONETARY UNIT króna
MAJOR LANGUAGE Icelandic
MAJOR RELIGION Protestantism

Denmark and Iceland

CONIC PROJECTION

SCALE OF MILES

SCALE OF KILOMETERS

Capitals of Countries .... ★
Capitals of Counties (amter) .... △
International Boundaries ....
Internal Boundaries ....

Scale 1:2,300,000

Denmark is divided into fourteen Counties plus Copenhagen and Frederiksberg communes.

© Copyright HAMMOND INCORPORATED, Maplewood, N.J.

[Map of Denmark, Iceland, Faeroe Islands, and Bornholm with geographic place names]

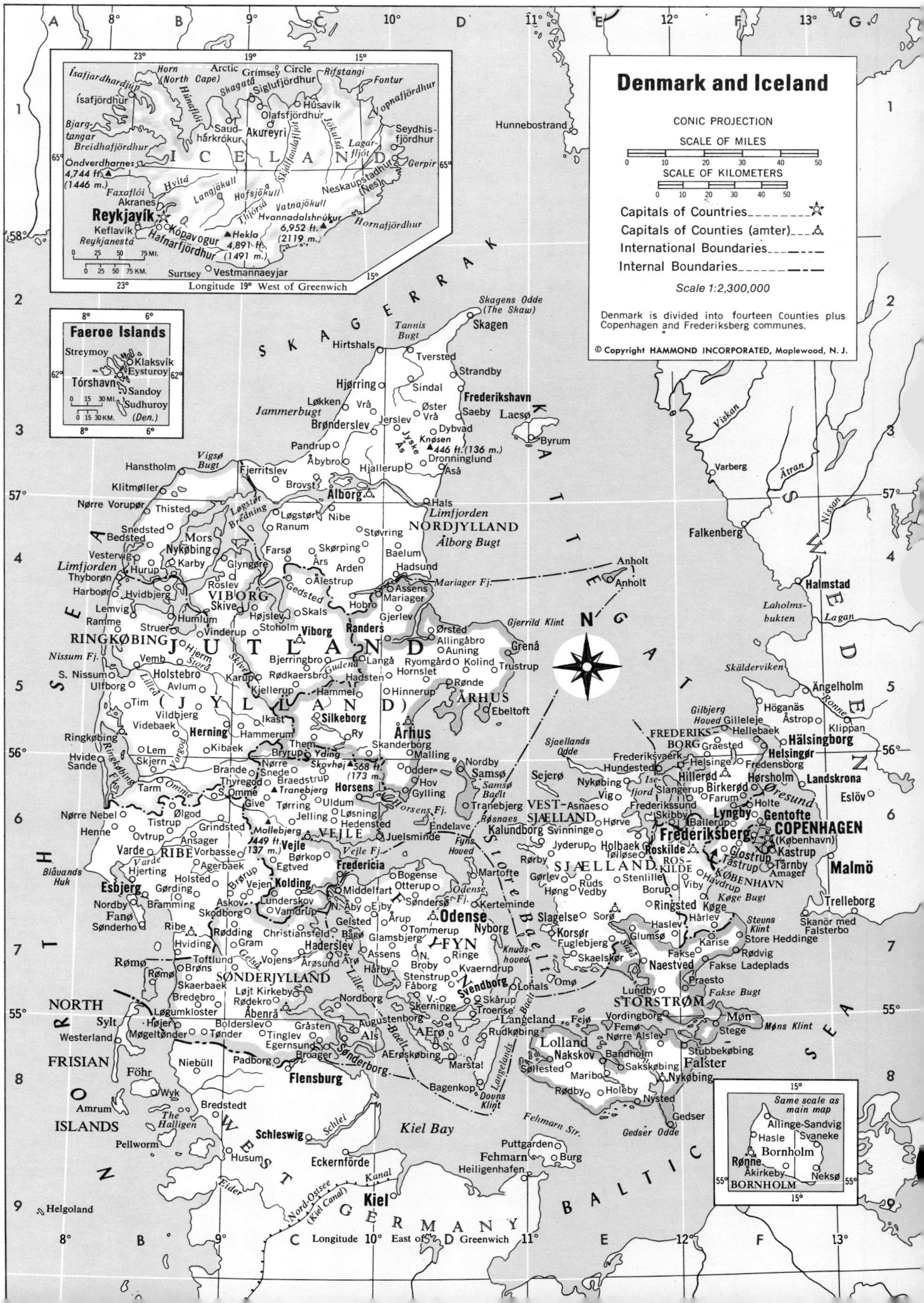

AREA 95,985 sq. mi. (248,601 sq. km.)
POPULATION 61,658,000
CAPITAL Bonn
LARGEST CITY Berlin (West)
HIGHEST POINT Zugspitze 9,718 ft. (2,962 m.)
MONETARY UNIT Deutsche mark
MAJOR LANGUAGE German
MAJOR RELIGIONS Protestantism, Roman
Catholicism

AREA 41,768 sq. mi. (108,179 sq. km.)
POPULATION 16,737,000
CAPITAL Berlin (East)
LARGEST CITY Berlin (East)
HIGHEST POINT Fichtelberg 3,983 ft. (1,214 m.)
MONETARY UNIT East German mark
MAJOR LANGUAGE German
MAJOR RELIGIONS Protestantism, Roman
Catholicism

WEST GERMANY

EAST GERMANY

Topography

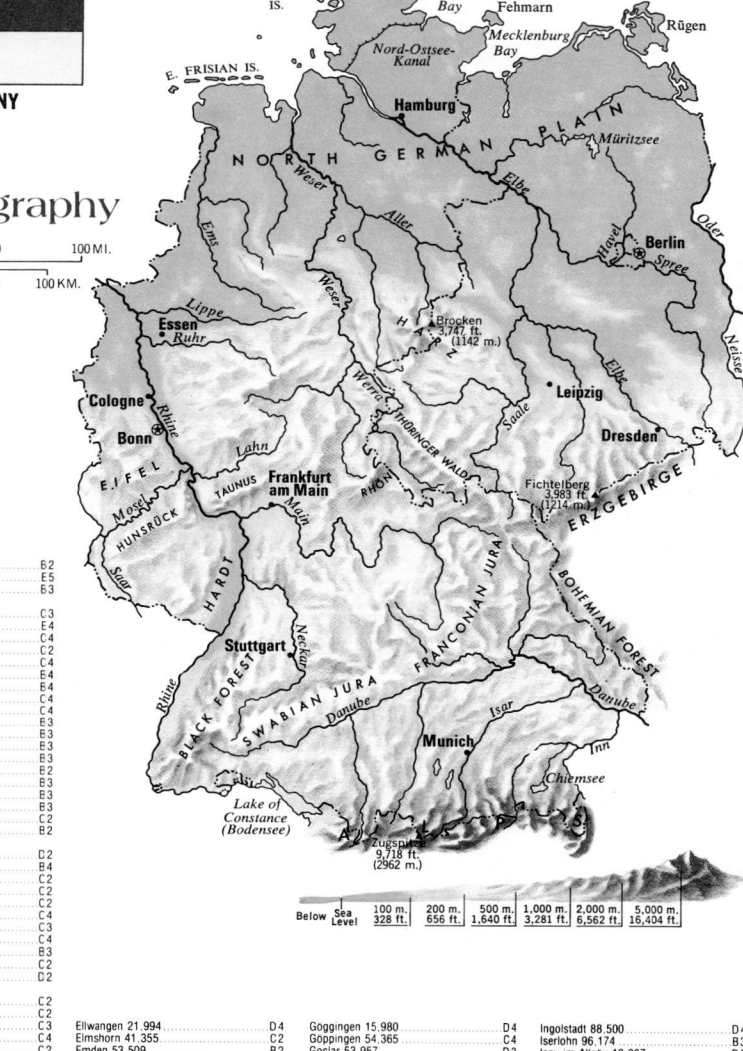

0   50   100 MI.
0   50   100 KM.

Below Sea Level	100 m. 328 ft.	200 m. 656 ft.	500 m. 1,640 ft.	1,000 m. 3,281 ft.	2,000 m. 6,562 ft.	5,000 m. 16,404 ft.

EAST GERMANY

DISTRICTS

Berlin 1,094,147	F4
Cottbus 872,242	F3
Dresden 1,845,459	E3
Erfurt 1,247,213	D3
Frankfurt 688,637	F2
Gera 738,847	E3
Halle 1,890,187	D3
Karl-Marx-Stadt 1,994,115	E3
Leipzig 1,457,817	E3
Magdeburg 1,297,881	D2
Neubrandenburg 628,686	E2
Potsdam 1,124,892	E2
Rostock 867,806	E1
Schwerin 592,334	D2
Suhl 550,497	D3

CITIES and TOWNS

Aken 11,742	D3
Altenburg 51,193	E3
Angermünde 11,786	F2
Anklam 19,099	E2
Annaberg-Buchholz 26,561	E3
Apolda 28,649	D3
Arnstadt 29,462	D3
Aschersleben 36,674	D3
Aue 32,622	E3
Auerbach 18,168	E3
Bad Doberan 12,541	D1
Bad Dürrenberg 15,192	D3
Bad Langensalza 166,282	D3
Bad Salzungen 17,277	D3
Barth 12,069	E1
Bautzen 45,851	F3
Bergen 13,244	E1
Berlin, East (cap.) 1,094,147	F4
Bernau bei Berlin 15,749	E2
Bernburg 44,428	D3
Bischofswerda 11,540	F3
Bitterfeld 27,062	E3
Blankenburg am Harz 18,784	D3
Borzenburg an der Elbe 12,428	D2
Borna 21,807	E3
Brandenburg 94,071	E2
Burg bei Magdeburg 29,027	D2
Calbe 15,096	D3
Chemnitz	
(Karl-Marx-Stadt) 303,811	E3
Coswig, Dresden 22,149	E3
Coswig, Halle 12,473	E3
Cottbus 94,293	F3
Crimmitschau 28,845	E3
Delitzsch 24,076	E3
Demmin 17,270	E2
Dessau 100,820	E3
Döbeln 27,624	E3
Dresden 507,692	F3
Ebersbach 12,694	F3
Eberswalde-Finow 47,141	F2
Eilenburg 22,245	E3
Eisenach 49,954	D3
Eisenberg 13,450	D3
Eisenhüttenstadt 46,455	F2
Eisleben 29,297	D3
Elsterwerda 20,979	E3
Falkensee 25,295	E2
Finsterwalde 22,466	E3
Forst 28,084	F3
Frankfurt an der Oder 70,817	F2
Freiberg 50,815	E3
Freital 46,061	F3
Friedland	E2
Fürstenwalde 31,065	F2
Gardelegen 12,987	D2
Genthin 15,916	E2
Gera 113,108	E3
Glauchau 30,927	E3
Görlitz 84,658	F3
Gotha 59,243	D3
Greifswald 53,940	E1
Greiz 37,612	E3
Grevesmühlen 12,005	D2
Grimma 17,100	E3
Grimmen 14,571	E1
Großenhain 18,712	E3
Großräschen 12,889	E3
Guben	
(Wilhelm-Pieck-Stadt) 32,731	F3
Güstrow 36,824	D2
Halberstadt 46,669	D3
Haldensleben 19,194	D2
Halle 241,425	D3
Halle-Neustadt 67,956	D3
Havelberg	D2
Heidenau 21,315	F3
Heiligenstadt 13,931	D3
Hennigsdorf bei Berlin 24,853	E2
Hettstedt 20,291	D3
Hildburghausen 11,372	D3
Hoyerswerda 64,904	F3
Ilmenau 22,021	D3
Jena 99,431	D3
Johanngeorgenstadt 10,328	E3
Jüterbog 13,477	E3
Kamenz 18,221	F3
Karl-Marx-Stadt 303,811	E3
Kleinmachnow 14,059	E4
Klingenthal 13,614	E3
Königs Wusterhausen 11,825	E2

Köpenick 130,987	F4
Köthen 35,451	E3
Kühlungsborn	D1
Lauchhammer 26,939	E3
Leipzig 570,972	E3
Lichtenberg 192,063	F4
Limbach-Oberfrohna 25,706	E3
Löbau 18,077	F3
Lübben 14,224	E3
Lübbenau 22,350	E3
Luckenwalde 28,544	E3
Ludwigslust 13,280	D2
Magdeburg 276,089	D2
Markkleeberg 22,380	E3
Meerane 25,037	E3
Meiningen 26,134	D3
Meissen 43,561	E3
Merseburg 54,269	D3
Meuselwitz 13,585	E3
Mittweida 19,259	E3
Mühlhausen	
(Thomas-Müntzer-Stadt) 44,106	D3
Nauen 11,940	E2
Naumburg 36,358	D3
Neubrandenburg 59,971	E2
Neuenhagen bei Berlin 12,603	F4
Neuruppin 24,888	E2
Neustrelitz 27,074	E2
Nordhausen 44,442	D3
Oelsnitz 15,084	E3
Oelsnitz im Erzgebirge 16,063	E3
Olbernhau 13,479	E3
Oranienburg 24,452	E2
Oschatz 18,974	E3
Oschersleben 17,377	D2
Pankow 136,527	F4
Parchim 22,907	D2
Pasewalk 15,099	F2
Peenemünde	E1
Perleberg 15,029	D2
Pirna 49,771	E3
Plauen 80,353	E3
Pössneck 18,469	E3
Potsdam 117,236	E2
Prenzlau 22,738	E2
Pritzwalk 11,887	E2
Quedlinburg 29,796	D3
Radeberg 18,528	E3
Radebeul 38,383	E3
Rathenow 32,011	E2
Reichenbach 27,440	E3
Ribnitz-Damgarten 17,254	E1
Riesa 49,989	E3
Rosslau 16,920	E3
Rostock 210,167	E1
Rudolstadt 31,698	D3
Saalfeld 33,648	D3
Salzwedel 21,741	D2
Sangerhausen 32,721	D3
Sassnitz 13,925	E1
Schkeuditz 15,585	E3
Schmalkalden 15,017	D3
Schmölln 13,406	E3
Schneeberg 20,376	E3
Schönebeck 45,197	D3
Schwarzenberg 20,372	E3
Schwerin 104,984	D2
Sebnitz 13,470	F3
Senftenberg 29,953	F3
Sömmerda 20,712	D3
Sondershausen 23,383	D3
Sonneberg 29,193	D3
Spremberg 22,862	F3
Stassfurt 26,225	D3
Stendal 39,647	D2
Stralsund 72,167	E1
Strausberg 21,334	F2
Suhl 36,642	D3
Tangermünde 12,898	D2
Teltow 16,171	E4
Templin 11,718	E2
Thale 17,248	D3
Thomas-Müntzer-Stadt 44,106	D3
Torgau 21,613	E3
Torgelow 14,320	F2
Treptow 127,448	F4
Ueckermünde 11,423	F2
Waldheim 11,925	E3
Waltershausen 13,893	D3
Waren 22,921	E2
Weida 11,816	E3
Weimar 63,144	D3
Weissenfels 43,191	D3
Weissensee 78,451	F3
Weisswasser 28,910	F3
Werdau 22,249	E3
Wernigerode 34,658	D3
Wilhelm-Pieck-Stadt 32,731	F3
Wismar 56,765	D1
Wittenberg 51,364	E3
Wittenberge 32,907	D2
Wolfen 27,570	D3
Wolgast 16,384	E1
Wurzen 20,501	E3
Zehdenick 12,651	E2
Zeitz 44,582	E3
Zella-Mehlis 16,301	D3
Zerbst 19,356	E3
Zeulenroda 13,452	E3
Zittau 42,298	F3
Zwickau 123,069	E3

OTHER FEATURES

Altmark (reg.)	D2
Arkona (cape)	E1

Baltic (sea)	E1
Black Elster (riv.)	E3
Brandenburg (reg.)	E2
Elbe (riv.)	D2
Elde (riv.)	D2
Elster, Black (riv.)	E3
Elster, White (riv.)	E3
Erzgebirge (mts.)	E3
Fichtelberg (mt.)	E3
Harz (mts.)	D3
Havel (riv.)	E2
Lusatia (reg.)	F3
Mecklenburg (bay)	D1
Mecklenburg (reg.)	E2
Mulde (riv.)	E3
Neisse (riv.)	F3
Oder (riv.)	F2
Peene (riv.)	E2
Pomerania (reg.)	E2
Pomeranian (bay)	F1
Rhön (mts.)	D3
Rügen (isl.)	E1
Saale (riv.)	D3
Saxony (reg.)	E3
Spree (riv.)	F3
Spreewald (for.)	F3
Thüringer Wald (for.)	D3
Thuringia (reg.)	D3
Ücker (riv.)	E2
Unstrut (riv.)	D3
Usedom (isl.)	F1
Warnow (riv.)	D2
Werra (riv.)	D3
White Elster (riv.)	E3

WEST GERMANY

STATES

Baden-Württemberg 9,152,700	C4
Bavaria 10,810,400	D4
Berlin (West) (free city) 1,984,800	E4
Bremen 716,800	C2
Hamburg 1,717,400	D2
Hesse 5,549,800	C3
Lower Saxony 7,238,500	C2
North Rhine-Westphalia 17,129,600	B3
Rhineland-Palatinate 3,665,800	B4
Saarland 1,096,300	B4
Schleswig-Holstein 2,582,400	C1

CITIES and TOWNS

Aachen 242,453	B3
Aalen 64,735	D4
Aarau 27,126	B2
Ahlen 54,214	B3
Ahrensburg 24,964	D2
Alfeld 24,273	C2
Alsdorf 47,473	B3
Alsfeld 18,091	C3
Altena 26,753	B3
Altona	C2
Alzey 15,190	C4
Amberg 46,934	D4
Andernach 27,132	B3
Ansbach 39,117	D4
Arnsberg 80,287	C3
Arolsen 15,619	C3
Aschaffenburg 55,398	C4
Augsburg 249,943	D4
Aurich 34,194	B2
Backnang 29,614	C4
Bad Berleburg 20,415	C3
Bad Driburg 17,478	C3
Bad Dürkheim 16,133	C4
Bad Ems 10,487	B3
Baden-Baden 49,718	C4
Bad Gandersheim 11,614	D3
Bad Harzburg 25,786	D3
Bad Hersfeld 29,248	C3
Bad Homburg vor der Höhe 51,196	C3
Bad Honnef 20,903	B3
Bad Kissingen 22,279	D3
Bad Kreuznach 42,588	B4
Bad Lauterberg im Harz 14,715	D3
Bad Mergentheim 19,895	C4
Bad Münstereifel 14,340	B3
Bad Nauheim 25,916	C3
Bad Oldesloe 19,640	D2
Bad Pyrmont 21,896	C3
Bad Reichenhall 13,048	E5
Bad Salzuflen 50,934	C2
Bad Schwartau 18,696	D2
Bad Segeberg 13,320	D2
Bad Tölz 12,458	D5
Bad Waldsee 14,296	C5
Bad Wildungen 15,418	C3
Bad Wimpfen 5,536	C4
Baiersbronn 14,845	C4
Balingen 29,310	C4
Bamberg 74,236	D4
Barsinghausen 32,873	C2
Bassum 14,113	C2
Bayreuth 67,035	D4
Bayrischzell 1,639	E5
Bebra 15,740	C3
Bendorf 15,943	B3
Bensheim 32,653	C4

Bentheim 13,681	B2
Berchtesgaden 8,558	E5
Bergisch Gladbach 99,517	B3
Berleburg (Bad Berleburg) 20,415	C3
Berlin (West) 1,984,837	E4
Biberach an der Riss 28,891	C4
Bielefeld 316,058	C2
Bietigheim-Bissingen 34,042	C4
Bingen 24,541	B4
Birkenfeld 5,883	B4
Blaubeuren 11,652	C4
Böblingen 40,547	C4
Bocholt 65,460	B3
Bochum 414,842	B3
Bonn (cap.) 283,711	B3
Boppard 16,888	B3
Borghorst 17,238	B3
Borken 30,212	B3
Bornheim 32,847	B3
Bottrop 101,495	B3
Brake 18,089	C2
Bramsche 24,119	B2
Braunschweig (Brunswick) 268,519	D2
Breisach am Rhein 9,230	B4
Bremen 572,969	C2
Bremerhaven 143,836	C2
Bremervörde 17,565	C2
Bretten 22,140	C4
Brilon 24,595	C3
Bruchsal 38,929	C4
Brühl 44,305	B3
Brunsbüttel 11,451	C2
Brunswick 268,519	D2
Buchholz in der Nordheide 25,713	C2
Bückeburg 21,393	C2
Büdingen 16,845	C3
Bühl 21,596	C4
Bünde 40,021	C2
Burg auf Fehmarn 5,874	D1
Burghausen 16,892	E4
Burgsteinfurt 31,367	B2
Butzbach 20,592	C3
Buxtehude 30,249	C2
Calw 22,970	C4
Castrop-Rauxel 82,373	B3
Celle 74,347	D2
Cham 12,423	E4
Charlottenburg 201,732	E4
Clausthal-Zellerfeld 16,690	D3
Cloppenburg 19,757	B2
Coburg 46,244	D3
Coesfeld 30,617	B3
Cologne 1,013,771	B3
Crailsheim 24,506	D4
Cuxhaven 60,353	C2
Dachau 33,207	D4
Dahlem	E4
Darmstadt 137,018	C4
Deggendorf 25,188	E4
Delmenhorst 71,488	C2
Detmold 65,629	C3
Diepholz 14,201	C2
Dillenburg 14,068	C3
Dillingen 21,369	B4
Dillingen an der Donau 11,601	D4
Dingolfing 13,325	E4
Dinkelsbühl 10,034	D4
Donaueschingen 17,578	C5
Donauwörth 17,077	D4
Dorsten 65,718	B3
Dortmund 630,609	B3
Duderstadt 23,255	D3
Dudweiler 27,877	B4
Duisburg 591,635	B3
Dülmen 37,013	B3
Düren 87,774	B3
Düsseldorf 664,336	B3
Eberbach 15,834	C4
Eckernförde 22,938	D1
Ehingen 21,600	C4
Eichstätt 13,080	D4
Einbeck 29,821	D3
Eiserfeld 22,346	C3

Ellwangen 21,994	D4
Elmshorn 41,355	C2
Emden 53,509	B2
Emmendingen 24,722	B4
Emmerich 29,113	B3
Emsdetten 30,195	B2
Erlangen 100,671	D4
Eschwege 24,882	D3
Eschweiler 53,603	B3
Espelkamp 22,670	C2
Esslingen am Neckar 95,298	C4
Ettlingen 35,159	C4
Euskirchen 43,558	B3
Eutin 17,701	D1
Fellbach 42,591	C4
Flensburg 93,213	C1
Forchheim 23,430	D4
Frankenberg-Eder 15,337	C3
Frankenthal 43,684	C4
Frankfurt am Main 636,157	C4
Frechen 41,453	B3
Freiburg im Breisgau 175,371	B5
Freising 31,524	D4
Freudenstadt 19,454	C4
Friedberg 24,762	C3
Friedrichshafen 51,544	C5
Fritzlar 15,079	C3
Fulda 58,976	C3
Furtwangen im Schwarzwald 11,071	C5
Fürstenfeldbruck 27,194	D4
Fürth 101,639	D4
Füssen 10,506	D5
Gaggenau 28,846	C4
Garbsen 56,337	C2
Garmisch-Partenkirchen 26,831	D5
Gatow	E4
Geesthacht 24,745	D2
Geislingen an der Steige 28,693	C4
Geldern 24,082	B3
Gelnhausen 17,889	C3
Gelsenkirchen 322,584	B3
Georgsmarienhütte 30,259	B2
Geretsried 17,330	D5
Germersheim 12,041	C4
Gerolstein 6,857	B3
Gifhorn 31,635	D2
Glückstadt 12,159	C2
Goch 28,213	B3

Göggingen 15,980	D4
Göppingen 54,365	C4
Goslar 53,957	D3
Göttingen 123,797	D3
Greven 27,479	B2
Grevenbroich 56,392	B3
Griesheim 19,548	C4
Gronau 40,527	B2
Gummersbach 49,316	B3
Günzburg 13,528	D4
Gunzenhausen 13,565	D4
Gütersloh 77,128	C3
Haar 18,824	D4
Hagen 229,224	B3
Haltern 29,750	B3
Hamburg 1,717,383	D2
Hameln 61,066	C2
Hamm 172,210	B3
Hammelburg 12,350	C3
Hanau 86,676	C3
Hannover 552,955	C2
Harburg-Wilhelmsburg	C2
Hassloch 17,752	C4
Haunstetten 21,810	D4
Hechingen 15,926	C4
Heide 21,918	C1
Heidelberg 129,368	C4
Heidenheim an der Brenz 49,943	D4
Heilbronn 113,177	C4
Helmstedt 28,095	D2
Hennef 27,815	B3
Herford 64,385	C2
Herne 190,561	B3
Hildesheim 105,290	D2
Hockenheim 16,890	C4
Hof 54,357	D3
Hofgeismar 13,380	C3
Holzminden 23,650	C3
Homburg 44,986	B4
Horb 9,776	C4
Horn-Bad Meinberg 16,927	C3
Höxter 32,759	C3
Hückelhoven 34,865	B3
Hünfeld 13,873	C3
Hürth 51,692	B3
Husum 24,984	C1
Ibbenbüren 42,202	B2
Idar-Oberstein 37,179	B4
Immenstadt im Allgäu 13,720	C5

Ingolstadt 88,500	D4
Iserlohn 96,174	B3
Isny im Allgäu 12,367	D5
Itzehoe 35,077	C2
Jever 12,096	B2
Jülich 31,564	B3
Kaiserslautern 100,886	B4
Karlsruhe 280,448	C4
Kassel 205,534	C3
Kaufbeuren 42,224	D5
Kehl 29,861	B4
Kelheim 11,996	D4
Kempten 56,944	D5
Kerpen an der 20,971	B3
Kiel 262,164	D1
Kirchheim unter Teck 31,666	C4
Kitzingen 19,116	D4
Kleve 44,043	B3
Koblenz 118,394	B3
Köln (Cologne) 1,013,771	B3
Königswinter 34,586	B3
Konstanz 70,152	C5
Korbach 22,998	C3
Kornwestheim 27,771	C4
Krefeld 228,463	B3
Kreuztal 30,473	C3
Kronach 11,538	D3
Kulmbach 25,711	D3
Lage 31,724	C3
Lahnstein 19,725	B3
Lahr 35,570	B4
Lampertheim 31,993	C4
Landau in der Pfalz 37,661	C4
Landsberg am Lech 15,862	D4
Landshut 55,858	E4
Langen 30,227	C4
Langenfeld 41,564	B3
Lauenburg an der Elbe 11,077	D2
Lauf an der Pegnitz 19,443	D4
Lauingen 8,778	D4
Leer 32,785	B2
Lehrte 38,272	D2
Lemgo 39,664	C2
Lengerich 20,836	B2
Leverkusen 165,947	B3
Lichtenfels 13,719	D3
Limburg an der Lahn 28,606	C3
Lindau 23,930	C5

(continued on following page)

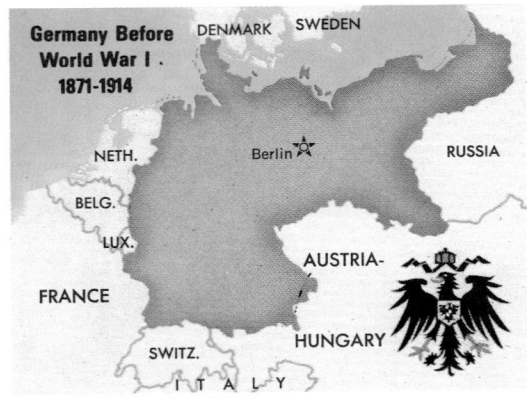

Germany Before World War I 1871-1914

Germany Between Wars 1919-1937

Occupied Germany 1945-1949

Agriculture, Industry and Resources

DOMINANT LAND USE

- Wheat, Sugar Beets
- Cereals (chiefly rye, oats, barley)
- Potatoes, Rye
- Dairy, Livestock
- Mixed Cereals, Dairy
- Truck Farming
- Grapes, Fruit
- Forests

MAJOR MINERAL OCCURRENCES

Ag	Silver	K	Potash
Ba	Barite	Lg	Lignite
C	Coal	Na	Salt
Cu	Copper	O	Petroleum
Fe	Iron Ore	Pb	Lead
G	Natural Gas	U	Uranium
Gr	Graphite	Zn	Zinc

⚡ Water Power

▨ Major Industrial Areas

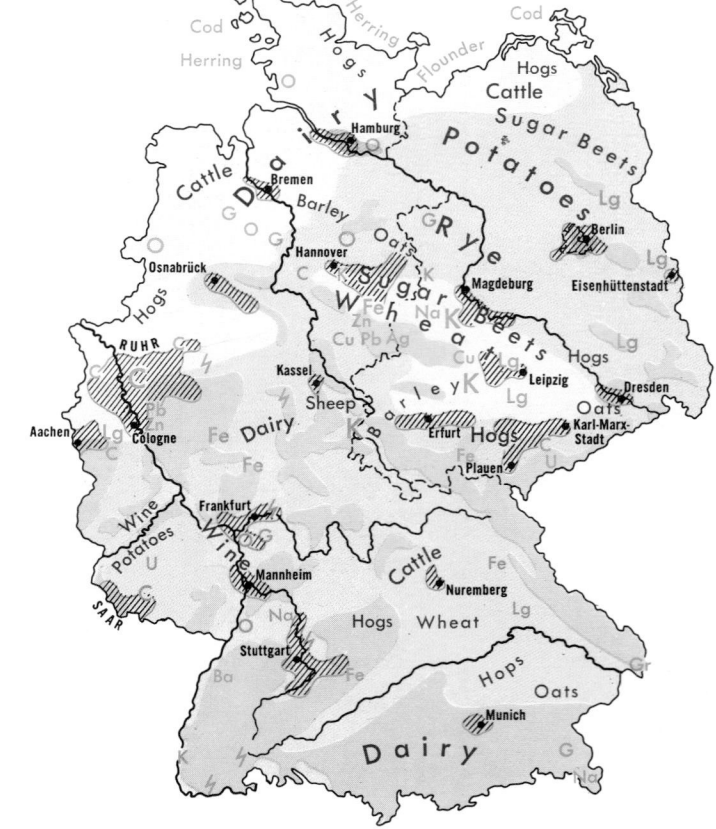

AREA 15,892 sq. mi. (41,160 sq. km.)
POPULATION 14,227,000
CAPITALS The Hague, Amsterdam
LARGEST CITY Amsterdam
HIGHEST POINT Vaalserberg 1,056 ft. (322 m.)
MONETARY UNIT guilder (florin)
MAJOR LANGUAGE Dutch
MAJOR RELIGIONS Protestantism, Roman Catholicism

AREA 11,781 sq. mi. (30,513 sq. km.)
POPULATION 9,855,110
CAPITAL Brussels
LARGEST CITY Brussels (greater)
HIGHEST POINT Botrange 2,277 ft. (694 m.)
MONETARY UNIT Belgian franc
MAJOR LANGUAGES French (Walloon), Flemish
MAJOR RELIGION Roman Catholicism

AREA 999 sq. mi. (2,587 sq. km.)
POPULATION 364,000
CAPITAL Luxembourg
LARGEST CITY Luxembourg
HIGHEST POINT Ardennes Plateau 1,825 ft. (556 m.)
MONETARY UNIT Luxembourg franc
MAJOR LANGUAGES Luxembourgeois (Letzeburgisch), French, German
MAJOR RELIGION Roman Catholicism

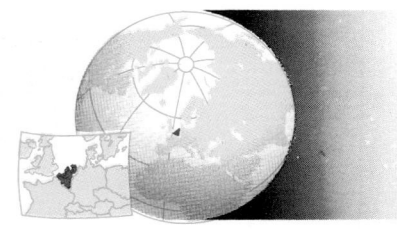

NETHERLANDS

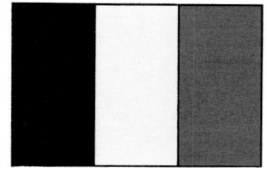

BELGIUM

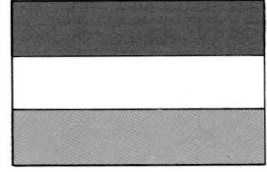

LUXEMBOURG

Agriculture, Industry and Resources

DOMINANT LAND USE

- Dairy, Truck Farming
- Cash Crops, Livestock
- Mixed Cereals, Dairy
- Specialized Horticulture
- Grapes, Wine
- Forests
- Sand Dunes

MAJOR MINERAL OCCURRENCES

- C Coal
- Fe Iron Ore
- G Natural Gas
- Na Salt
- O Petroleum

////// Major Industrial Areas

BELGIUM

PROVINCES

Antwerp 1,533,249	F6
Brabant 2,176,373	F7
East Flanders 1,310,117	D7
Hainaut 1,317,453	D7
Liège 1,008,905	H7
Limburg 652,547	G7
Luxembourg 217,310	G9
Namur 380,561	F8
West Flanders 1,054,429	B7

CITIES and TOWNS†

Aalst 46,659	D7
Aalter 9,173	C6
Aarlen (Arlon) 13,745	H9
Aarschot 12,474	F7
Aat (Ath) 11,842	D7
Aiken 8,677	G7
Alost (Aalst) 46,659	D7
Amay 7,617	G7
Andenne 8,091	G8
Anderlecht 103,796	B9
Anderlues 12,176	E8
Ans 7	H7
Antoing 3,426	C7
Antwerp 224,543	E6
Antwerp* 928,000	E6
Antwerpen (Antwerp) 224,543	E6
Ardooie 7,081	C7
Arendonk 9,919	G6
Arlon 13,745	H9
As 5,496	H6
Asse 6,583	E7
Ath 11,842	D7
Attert	H9
Aubange 3,761	H9
Audenarde (Oudenaarde) 26,615	D7
Auderghem 34,546	C9
Auvelais 8,287	F8
Aywaille 3,850	H8
Baerle-Hertog	F6
Balen 15,110	G6
Basse-Sambre	F8
Bastenaken (Bastogne) 6,816	H9
Bastogne 6,816	H9
Beernem	C6
Beloeil	D7
Berchem 50,241	F6
Berchem-Sainte-Agathe 19,087	B9
Bergen (Mons) 59,362	E8
Beringen	G6
Bertogne	H8
Bertrix 4,562	G9
Beveren 15,913	E6
Bilzen 7,178	G7
Binche 10,096	E8
Blankenberge 13,969	C6
Bocholt 6,497	H6
Boom 16,584	E6
Borgerhout 49,002	E6
Borgloon 3,412	G7
Borgworm (Waremme) 10,956	G7
Bourg-Léopold (Leopoldsburg) 9,593	G6
Boussu 11,474	D8
Braine-l'Alleud 18,531	E7
Braine-le-Comte 11,957	D7
Brecht	F6
Bredene 9,244	B6
Bree 10,389	H6
Bruges 117,220	C6
Brugge (Bruges) 117,220	C6
Brussels (cap.)* 1,054,970	C9
Bruxelles (Brussels)	
(cap.)* 1,054,970	C9
Cerfontaine	E8
Charleroi 23,689	E8
Charleroi* 458,000	E8
Chastre	F7
Châtelet 14,752	F8
Chièvres 3,283	D7
Chimay 3,288	E8
Ciney 7,536	G9
Comblain-au-Pont 3,582	G8
Comines 8,192	B7
Courcelles 17,015	E8
Courtrai (Kortrijk) 44,961	C7
Couvin 4,234	F8
Damme	C6
De Haan	C6
Deinze 16,711	D7
Denderleeuw 9,925	E7
Dendermonde 22,119	E6
De Panne 6,985	B6
Dessel 7,505	G6
Destelbergen	D6
Deurne 80,766	F6
Diest 10,799	F7
Diksmuide 6,669	B6
Dilbeek 15,108	B9
Dilsen 9,747	H6
Dinant 9,747	G8
Dison 8,466	H7
Dixmude (Diksmuide) 6,669	B6
Doische	F8
Doornik (Tournai) 32,794	C7
Dour 10,059	D8
Drogenbos 4,840	B10
Duffel 13,802	F6
Durbuy	H8
Ecaussinnes 6,630	E7
Edingen (Enghien) 4,115	D7
Eeklo 19,144	D6
Egheezée	F7
Eigenbrakel (Braine-l'Alleud) 18,531	E7
Ekeren 27,648	E6
Ellezelles 3,556	D7
Enghien 4,115	D7
Erezée	G8
Erquelinnes 4,471	E8
Esneux 6,183	H7
Essen 10,795	F6
Estampuis	C7
Etterbeek 51,030	B9
Eupen 14,879	J7
Evere 26,957	C9
Evergem 12,886	D6
Farciennes	F8
Fermelmont	F7
Ferrières	H8
Flémalle 8,135	G7
Fleurus 8,523	F8
Florennes 4,107	F8
Forest 55,135	B9
Fosses-La-Ville 3,972	F8
Frameries 11,224	D8
Froidchapelle	E8
Furnes (Veurne) 9,496	B6
Ganshoren 21,147	B9
Geel 29,346	F6
Geldenaken (Jodoigne) 4,132	F7
Gembloux-sur-Orneau 11,249	F7
Genk 57,913	H7
Gent (Ghent) 148,860	D6
Geraardsbergen 17,533	D7
Gerpinnes	F8
Ghent 148,860	D6
Ghent* 477,000	D6
Gistel	B6
Gooik	E7
Gouvy	H8
Grammont (Geraardsbergen) 17,533	D7
Grez-Doiceau	F7
Grimbergen	E7
Haacht 4,436	F7
Habay	H9
Hal (Halle) 20,017	E7
Halen 5,322	G7
Halle 20,017	E7
Hamme 17,559	E6
Hamois	G8
Hamont-Achel 6,893	H6
Hannut (Hannut) 7,232	G7
Hannut 7,232	G7
Harelbeke 18,498	C7
Hasselt 39,663	G7
Hastière	F8
Heist-Knokke 27,582	C6
Heist-op-den-Berg 13,472	F6
Hensies	D8
Herentals 18,639	F6
Herne	E7
Herselt 7,412	F6
Herstal 29,600	H7
Herve 4,118	H7
Heuvelland	B7
Hoboken 33,693	E6
Hoei (Huy) 12,736	G8
Hoeselt 6,884	G7
Honnelles	D8
Hoogstraten 4,381	F6
Hotton	G8
Huy 12,736	G8
Ichtegem	B6
Ieper 20,825	B7
Ingelmunster 10,245	C7
Ittre	E7
Ixelles 86,450	C9
Izegem 22,928	C7
Jabbeke	C6
Jemappes 18,632	D8
Jette 40,013	B9
Jodoigne 4,132	F7
Kalmthout 12,724	F6
Kapellen 13,352	E6
Kasterlee	F6
Kinrooi	H6
Knokke-Heist 27,582	C6
Koekelare 7,807	B6
Koekelberg 17,570	B9
Koksijde	B6
Kontich 14,432	E6
Kortemark 5,904	C6
Kortrijk 44,961	C7
Kraainem 11,390	C9
La Louvière 23,310	E8
La Louvière* 113,259	E8
Lanaken 8,659	H7
Landen 5,740	G7
Langemark-Poelkapelle 5,457	B7
Lasne	F7
Lede 10,316	D7
Léglise	H9
Leopoldsburg 9,593	G6
Le Roeulx	E8
Lessen (Lessines) 8,906	D7
Lessines 8,906	D7
Leuven 30,623	F7
Leuze-en-Hainaut 7,185	D7
Libin	G9
Libramont-Chevigny 2,975	G9
Lichtervelde 7,459	C6
Liedekerke 10,482	D7
Liège 145,573	H7
Liège* 622,000	H7
Lier 28,416	F6
Lierre (Lier) 28,416	F6
Limburg 3,762	J7
Limburg (Limbourg) 3,762	J7
Linkebeek 4,265	C10
Linter	G7
Lochristi	D6
Lokeren 26,740	D6
Lommel 21,984	G6
Lontzen	H9
Looz (Borgloon) 3,412	G7
Lo-Reninge	B7
Louvain (Leuven) 30,623	F7
Luik (Liège) 145,573	H7
Lummen	G7
Maaseik 8,622	H6
Maasmechelen	H7
Machelen 7,057	C9
Maldegem 14,474	C6
Malines (Mechelen) 65,466	F6
Malmédy 6,464	J8
Manage	E7
Manhay	H8
Marche-en-Famenne 4,567	G8
Marchin 4,206	G8
Mechelen 65,466	F6
Meerhout 8,567	G6
Meise	E7
Menen 22,037	B7
Menin (Menen) 22,037	B7
Merchtem 8,998	E7
Merelbeke 13,837	D7
Merksem 39,768	E6
Merksplas 5,065	F6
Messancy 3,150	H9
Mettet 3,372	F8
Meulebeke 10,458	C7
Middelkerke	B6
Moeskroen (Mouscron) 37,311	C7
Mol 28,823	G6
Molenbeek-Saint-Jean 68,411	B9
Momignies	E8
Moorslede	B7
Mortsel 28,012	E6
Mouscron 37,311	C7
Namen (Namur) 32,269	F8
Namur 32,269	F8
Nassogne	G8
Nazareth	D7
Neerpelt 8,771	G6
Neufchâteau 2,670	G9
Nevele	D6
Nieuport (Nieuwpoort) 8,273	B6
Nieuwpoort 8,273	B6
Nijvel (Nivelles) 16,126	E7
Ninove 12,428	D7
Nivelles 16,126	E7
Ohey	G8
Onhaye	F8
Oostende (Ostend) 71,227	B6
Oostkamp 8,999	C6
Opwijk 9,699	E7
Ostend 71,227	B6
Oudenaarde 26,615	D7
Oudenburg	B6
Oud-Turnhout 9,245	F6
Oupeye	H7
Overijse 16,181	F7
Overpelt 10,470	G6
Paliseul	G9
Peer 7,201	G6
Péruwelz 7,878	D8
Philippeville 2,076	F8
Plombières	H7
Pont-à-Celles	E8
Poperinge 12,671	B7
Profondeville	F8
Putte 6,953	F6
Quaregnon 17,688	D8
Quévy	D8
Quiévrain 5,510	D8
Raeren 3,655	J7
Ravels	F6
Rebecq 3,744	E7
Renaix (Ronse) 25,056	D7
Rendeux	H8
Retie 6,619	G6
Rochefort 4,357	G8
Roeselare 40,428	C7
Ronse 25,056	D7
Roulers (Roeselare) 40,428	C7
Rouvroy	G9
Ruislede	C6
Sainte-Ode	H8
Saint-Georges-sur-Meuse 6,003	G7
Saint-Gilles 55,055	B9
Saint-Hubert 3,091	G8
Saint-Josse-ten-Noode 23,633	C9
Saint-Nicolas	
Saint-Trond (Sint-Truiden) 21,473	G7
Saint-Vith (Sankt Vith) 3,001	J8
Sankt Vith 3,001	J8
Schaerbeek 118,950	C9
Schoten 29,914	F6
Seraing 40,545	H7
's-Gravenbrakel (Braine-le-Comte) 11,957	D7
Sint-Laurens	D6
Sint-Niklaas 49,214	E6

(continued on following page)

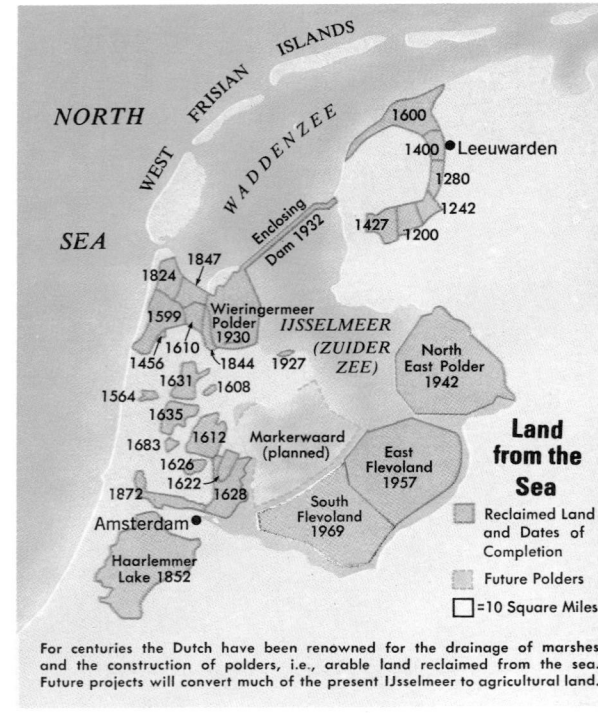

Land from the Sea

■ Reclaimed Land and Dates of Completion

□ Future Polders

☐ =10 Square Miles

For centuries the Dutch have been renowned for the drainage of marshes and the construction of polders, i.e., arable land reclaimed from the sea. Future projects will convert much of the present IJsselmeer to agricultural land.

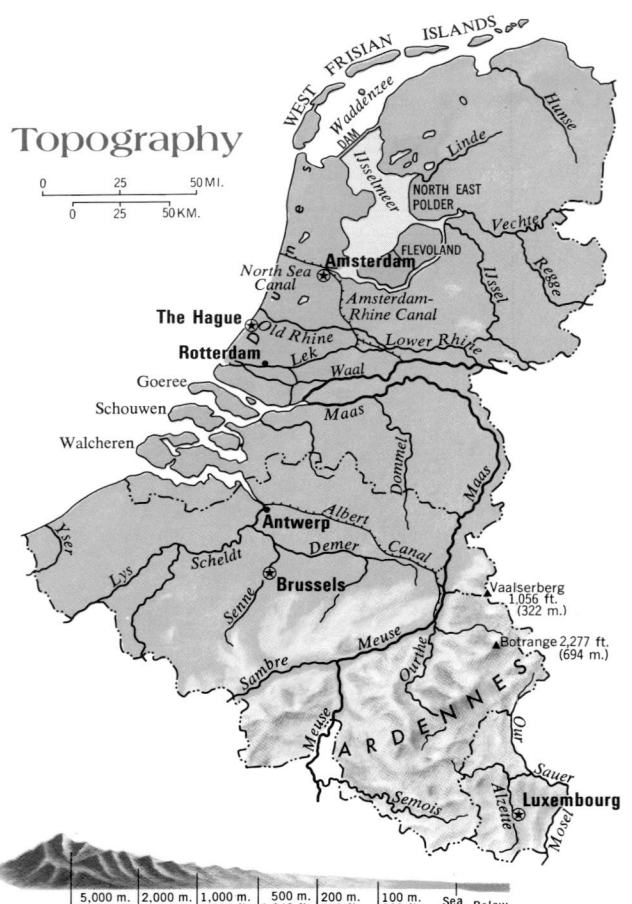

Topography

0 — 25 — 50 MI.

0 — 25 — 50 KM.

| 5,000 m. 16,404 ft. | 2,000 m. 6,562 ft. | 1,000 m. 3,281 ft. | 500 m. 1,640 ft. | 200 m. 656 ft. | 100 m. 328 ft. | Sea Level | Below |

Netherlands, Belgium and Luxembourg

CONIC PROJECTION

SCALE OF MILES

SCALE OF KILOMETRES

Capitals of Countries
Provincial Capitals
International Boundaries
Provincial Boundaries
Canals

© Copyright HAMMOND INCORPORATED, Maplewood, N.J.

AMSTERDAM

BRUSSELS

© Copyright HAMMOND INCORPORATED, Maplewood, N.J.

Paris and Environs

France
CONIC PROJECTION

SCALE OF MILES

SCALE OF KILOMETERS

Capitals of Countries .... ☆
Capitals of Departments .... △
International Boundaries ....
Department Boundaries ....
Canals ....

Scale 1:4,750,000

Corsica
Same Scale as Main Map

© Copyright HAMMOND INCORPORATED, Maplewood, N.J.

AREA 210,038 sq. mi. (543,998 sq. km.)
POPULATION 53,788,000
CAPITAL Paris
LARGEST CITY Paris
HIGHEST POINT Mont Blanc 15,771 ft. (4,807 m.)
MONETARY UNIT franc
MAJOR LANGUAGE French
MAJOR RELIGION Roman Catholicism

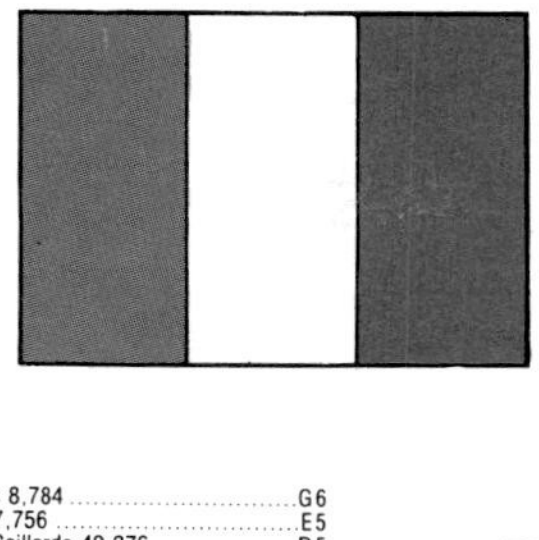

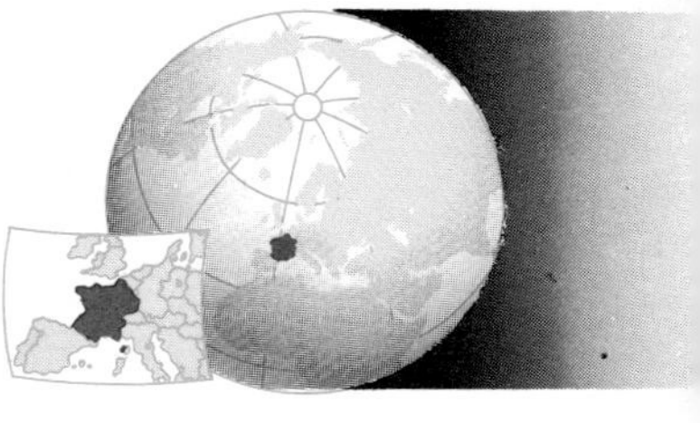

DEPARTMENTS

Ain 376,477 F4
Aisne 533,862 E3
Allier 378,406 E4
Alpes-de-Haute-Provence 112,178 G5
Alpes-Maritimes 816,681 G6
Ardèche 257,065 F5
Ardennes 309,306 F3
Ariège 137,857 D6
Aube 284,823 E3
Aude 272,366 E6
Aveyron 278,306 E5
Bas-Rhin 882,121 G3
Belfort (terr.) 128,125 G4
Bouches-du-Rhône 1,632,974 F6
Calvados 560,967 C3
Cantal 166,549 E5
Charente 337,064 D5
Charente-Maritime 497,859 C5
Cher 316,350 E4
Corrèze 240,363 D5
Corse du Sud 128,634 B6
Côte-d'Or 456,070 F4
Côtes-du-Nord 525,556 B3
Creuse 146,214 D4
Deux-Sèvres 335,829 C4
Dordogne 373,179 D5
Doubs 471,082 G4
Drôme 361,847 F5
Essonne 923,063 E3
Eure 422,952 D3
Eure-et-Loir 335,151 D3
Finistère 804,088 A3
Gard 494,575 F6
Gers 175,366 D6
Gironde 1,061,480 C5
Haute-Corse 161,208 B6
Haute-Garonne 777,431 D6
Haute-Loire 205,491 E5
Haute-Marne 212,304 F3
Hautes-Alpes 97,358 G5
Haute-Saône 222,254 G4
Haute-Savoie 447,795 G5
Hautes-Pyrénées 227,222 D6
Haute-Vienne 352,149 D5
Haut-Rhin 635,209 G4
Hauts-de-Seine 1,438,930 A2
Hérault 648,202 E6
Ille-et-Vilaine 702,199 C3
Indre 248,523 D4
Indre-et-Loire 478,601 D4
Isère 860,339 F5
Jura 238,856 F4
Landes 288,323 C5
Loire 742,396 F5
Loire-Atlantique 934,499 C4
Loiret 490,189 E4
Loir-et-Cher 283,686 D4
Lot 150,778 D5
Lot-et-Garonne 292,616 D5
Lozère 74,825 E5
Maine-et-Loire 629,849 C4
Manche 451,662 C3
Marne 530,399 F3
Mayenne 261,789 C3
Meurthe-et-Moselle 722,588 G3
Meuse 203,904 F3
Morbihan 563,588 B4
Moselle 1,006,373 G3
Nièvre 245,212 E4
Nord 2,510,738 E2
Oise 606,320 E3
Orne 293,523 C3
Paris (city) 2,299,830 B2
Pas-de-Calais 1,403,035 E2
Puy-de-Dôme 580,033 E5
Pyrénées-Atlantiques 534,748 C6
Pyrénées-Orientales 299,506 E6
Rhône 1,429,647 F5
Saône-et-Loire 569,810 F4
Sarthe 490,385 D3
Savoie 305,118 G5
Seine-et-Marne 755,762 E3
Seine-Saint-Denis 1,322,127 C1
Somme 538,462 E3
Tarn 338,024 E6
Tarn-et-Garonne 183,314 D5
Val-de-Marne 1,215,713 C1
Val-d'Oise 840,885 E3
Var 626,093 G6
Vaucluse 390,446 F6
Vendée 450,641 C4
Vienne 357,366 D4
Vosges 397,957 G3
Yonne 299,851 E4
Yvelines 1,082,255 D3

CITIES and TOWNS

Abbeville 25,252 D2
Agde 9,856 E6
Agen 33,763 D5
Aix-en-Provence 91,665 F6
Aix-les-Bains 21,884 G5
Ajaccio 47,065 B7
Albert 11,746 E2
Albertville 16,630 G5
Albi 43,942 E6
Alençon 32,917 D3
Alès 33,315 E5
Ambérieu-en-Bugey 9,294 F5
Amboise 10,498 D4
Amiens 129,453 D3
Ancenis 6,689 C4
Angers 136,603 C4
Angoulême 46,293 D5
Annecy 53,058 G5
Annonay 19,234 F5
Antibes 44,226 G6
Antony 57,450 B2
Apt 9,735 F6
Arcachon 13,856 C5
Argentan 16,063 D3
Argenteuil 101,542 A1
Arles 37,337 F6
Armentières 23,850 E2
Arras 45,804 E2
Asnières-sur-Seine 75,328 A1
Aubagne 26,145 F6
Aubenas 11,967 F5
Aubervilliers 72,859 B1
Auch 18,767 D6
Audincourt 18,570 G4
Aulnay-sous-Bois 77,982 B1
Auray 10,006 B4
Aurignac 744 D6
Aurillac 29,458 E5
Autun 19,441 F4
Auxerre 36,039 E4
Auxonne 6,414 F4
Avallon 8,518 E4
Avignon 73,482 F6
Avion 22,860 E2
Avranches 10,128 C3
Ax-les-Thermes 1,456 D6
Bagnères-de-Bigorre 9,080 D6
Bagnolet 35,858 B2
Bagnols-sur-Cèze 13,111 F5
Barbizon 1,189 E3
Barcelonnette 2,523 G5
Barfleur 701 C3
Bar-le-Duc 19,188 F3
Bar-sur-Aube 7,227 F3
Bastia 45,387 B6
Bayeux 13,381 C3
Bayonne 41,281 C6
Beaucaire 10,189 F6
Beaune 16,386 F4
Beauvais 53,493 E3
Belfort 54,469 G4
Belley 6,612 F5
Berck 14,104 D2
Bergerac 25,488 D5
Bernay 9,928 D3
Besançon 119,803 G4
Béthune 26,208 E2
Béziers 79,213 E6
Biarritz 27,453 C6
Blois 49,134 D4
Bobigny 43,041 B1
Bogny-sur-Meuse 6,845 F3
Bolbec 12,347 D3
Bondy 48,285 B1
Bonneville 6,717 G4
Bordeaux 220,830 C5
Boulogne-Billancourt 103,527 A2
Boulogne-sur-Mer 48,309 D2
Bourg-en-Bresse 40,052 F4
Bourges 75,200 E4
Bourgoin-Jallieu 18,504 F5
Bressuire 9,778 C4
Brest 163,940 A3
Briançon 8,523 G5
Brignoles 8,784 G6
Brioude 7,756 E5
Brive-la-Gaillarde 49,276 D5
Bruay-en-Artois 25,544 E2
Caen 116,987 C3
Cahors 19,288 D5
Calais 73,009 D2
Caluire-et-Cuire 43,024 F5
Cambrai 38,706 E2
Cannes 70,226 G6
Carcassonne 38,887 D6
Carmaux 11,970 E5
Carpentras 20,169 F5
Castelnaudary 8,947 E6
Castelsarrasin 6,562 D6
Castres 41,037 E6
Cavaillon 17,383 F6
Châlons-sur-Marne 50,870 F3
Chalon-sur-Saône 55,495 F4
Chambéry 52,286 F5
Chambord 166 D4
Chamonix-Mont-Blanc 6,246 G5
Champigny-sur-Marne 80,189 C2
Chantilly 10,517 E3
Charenton-le-Pont 20,383 B2
Charleville-Mézières 59,513 F3
Chartres 38,574 D3
Châteaubriant 12,417 C4
Château-du-Loir 5,598 D4
Châteaudun 14,634 D3
Château-Gontier 8,301 C4
Châteauroux 53,166 D4
Château-Thierry 13,379 E3
Châtellerault 33,811 D4
Châtillon 26,562 B2
Châtillon-sur-Seine 7,367 F4
Chatou 26,415 A1
Chaumont 26,568 F3
Chauny 14,324 E3
Chelles 24,192 C1
Cherbourg 31,333 C3
Chinon 5,378 D4
Choisy-le-Roi 38,629 B2
Cholet 49,887 C4
Clamart 52,881 A2
Clermont 7,834 E3
Clermont-Ferrand 153,379 E5
Clichy 47,731 B1
Cluny 4,335 F4
Cluses 12,713 G4
Cognac 21,567 C5
Colmar 58,585 G3
Colombes 83,241 A1
Commentry 8,074 E4
Commercy 6,918 F3
Compiègne 37,009 E3
Concarneau 15,096 A4
Cosne-Cours-sur-Loire 9,768 E4
Coudekerque-Branche 24,702 E2
Coulommiers 11,363 E3
Courbevoie 54,391 A1
Coutances 8,286 C3
Creil 31,893 E3
Crépy-en-Valois 10,661 E3
Créteil 58,665 B2
Cusset 13,672 E4
Dax 18,019 C6
Deauville 5,655 C3
Decazeville 9,318 E5
Decize 6,853 E4
Denain 26,096 E2
Dieppe 25,607 D3

Topography

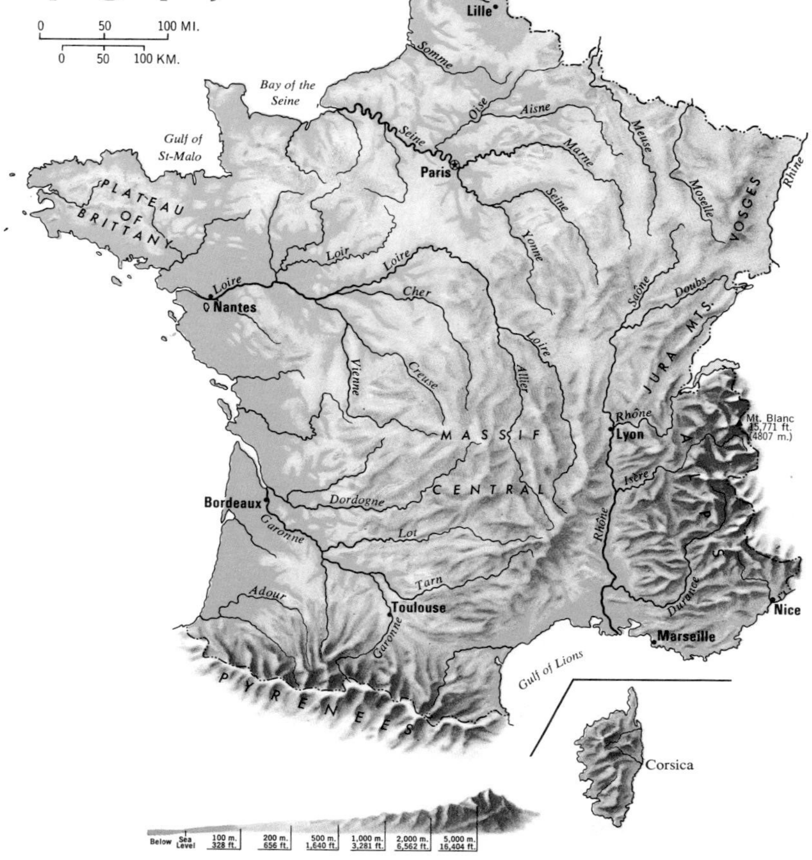
0 50 100 MI.
0 50 100 KM.
Lille
Somme
Bay of the Seine
Seine
Oise
Aisne
Gulf of St-Malo
Marne
Meuse
Moselle
VOSGES
Rhine
Paris
PLATEAU OF BRITTANY
Seine
Yonne
Loir
Loire
Saône
Doubs
Loire
Nantes
Cher
JURA MTS.
Vienne
Creuse
Allier
Loire
Rhône
Lyon
Mt. Blanc 15,771 ft. (4807 m.)
MASSIF CENTRAL
Isère
Bordeaux
Dordogne
Garonne
Lot
Rhône
ALPS
Tarn
Adour
Toulouse
Garonne
Durance
Nice
Marseille
Gulf of Lions
PYRENEES
Corsica
Below Sea Level
100 m. 328 ft.
200 m. 656 ft.
500 m. 1,640 ft.
1,000 m. 3,281 ft.
2,000 m. 6,562 ft.
5,000 m. 16,404 ft.

Historic Provinces

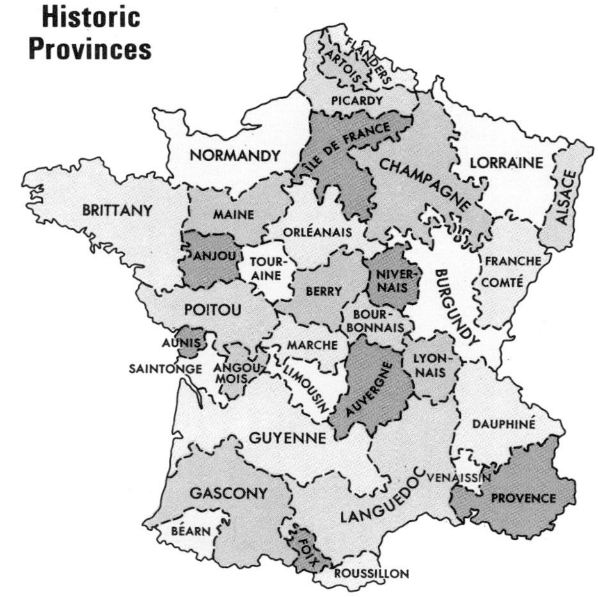
FLANDERS
ARTOIS
PICARDY
NORMANDY
ÎLE DE FRANCE
CHAMPAGNE
LORRAINE
ALSACE
BRITTANY
MAINE
ORLÉANAIS
ANJOU
TOUR-AINE
BERRY
NIVER-NAIS
FRANCHE COMTÉ
BURGUNDY
POITOU
BOUR-BONNAIS
AUNIS
MARCHE
SAINTONGE
ANGOU-MOIS
LIMOUSIN
AUVERGNE
LYON-NAIS
DAUPHINÉ
GUYENNE
VENAISSIN
GASCONY
LANGUEDOC
PROVENCE
BÉARN
FOIX
ROUSSILLON

A resident of the city of Caen thinks of himself as a Norman rather than as a citizen of the modern department of Calvados. In spite of the passing of nearly two centuries, the historic provinces which existed before 1790 command the local patriotism of most Frenchmen.

Digne 13,140 G5
Digoin 10,449 F4
Dijon 149,899 F4
Dinan 13,303 B3
Dinard 9,211 B3
Dôle 28,109 F4
Domrémy-la-Pucelle 190 F3
Douai 43,954 E2
Douarnenez 17,851 A3
Doullens 6,806 E2
Draguignan 19,653 G6
Drancy 64,258 B1
Dreux 31,503 D3
Dunkirk (Dunkerque) 78,171 E2
Elbeuf 18,642 D3
Épernay 29,286 E3
Épinal 39,000 G3
Épinay-sur-Seine 46,458 B1
Erstein 6,494 G3
Étampes 18,810 E3
Étaples 10,423 D2
Eu 8,349 D3
Évreux 46,181 D3
Évry 15,300 E3
Falaise 8,133 C3
Fécamp 20,835 D3
Figeac 8,675 D5
Firminy 23,776 F5
Flers 18,590 C3
Foix 9,569 D6
Fontainebleau 16,436 E3
Fontenay-le-Comte 12,301 C4
Fontenay-sous-Bois 46,200 C2
Forbach 24,812 G3
Fougères 26,260 C3
Fourmies 15,318 F2
Fréjus 27,805 G6
Gagny 36,714 C1
Gaillac 7,653 D6
Gap 24,962 G5
Gardanne 8,175 F6
Gennevilliers 50,154 B1
Gentilly 16,843 B2
Gex 3,959 G4
Gien 13,817 E4
Gif 10,866 E3
Gisors 7,591 D3
Givet 7,787 F2
Givors 19,356 F5
Granville 12,869 C3
Grasse 24,260 G6
Graulhet 11,099 E6
Gray 8,718 F4
Grenoble 165,431 F5
Guebwiller 10,477 G4
Guéret 14,418 D4
Guingamp 9,269 B3
Guise 6,642 E3
Haguenau 23,023 G3
Harfleur 9,857 D3
Hautmont 19,130 F2
Hayange 8,479 F3
Hazebrouck 18,867 E2
Hendaye 9,404 C6
Hénin-Beaumont 26,296 E2
Hennebont 8,978 B4
Héricourt 8,481 G4
Hirson 11,909 F3
Honfleur 8,995 D3
Hyères 29,366 G6
Issoire 13,560 E5
Issoudun 15,065 D4
Issy-les-Moulineaux 47,355 A2
Istres 10,127 F6
Ivry-sur-Seine 62,804 B2
Joigny 10,825 E3
La Baule-Escoublac 13,854 B4
La Ciotat 29,290 F6
La Courneuve 37,917 B1
La Flèche 12,743 C4
La Grand-Combe 9,406 E5
L'Aigle 9,198 D3
Landerneau 13,983 B3
Langres 10,745 F4
Lannion 13,692 B3
Laon 27,420 E3
La Pallice C4
La Rochelle 72,936 C4
La Roche-sur-Yon 40,789 C4
La Seyne-sur-Mer 50,059 F6
Laval 50,734 C3
Lavelanet 9,278 E6
Le Blanc 7,431 D4
Le Blanc-Mesnil 49,062 B1
Le Bourget 10,520 B1
Le Cateau 8,680 E2
Le Chesnay 24,590 A2
Le Creusot 31,643 F4
Le Havre 216,917 C3
Le Mans 150,289 C3
Lens 39,973 E2
Le Puy 24,793 F5
Les Andelys 7,524 D3
Les Sables-d'Olonne 17,157 B4
Le Teil 7,993 F5
Le Tréport 6,463 D2
Levallois-Perret 52,460 A1
Lézignan-Corbières 6,929 E6
Libourne 21,265 C5
Liévin 33,040 E2
Lille 171,010 E2
Limoges 136,059 D5
Limoux 9,595 E6
Lisieux 24,972 D3
Livry-Gargan 32,879 C1
Lodève 7,131 E6
Longwy 20,107 F3
Lons-le-Saunier 20,897 F4
Lorient 68,655 B4
Loudéac 7,173 B3
Loudun 7,060 D4
Lourdes 17,685 C6
Louviers 17,919 D3
Luçon 8,834 C4
Lunel 12,392 E6
Lunéville 22,438 G3
Lure 8,538 G4
Luxeuil-les-Bains 10,061 G4
Lyon 454,265 F5
Mâcon 39,130 F4
Maisons-Alfort 53,963 B2
Maisons-Laffitte 23,465 A1
Malakoff 34,100 A2
Manosque 17,256 G6
Mantes-la-Jolie 42,408 D3
Marmande 13,223 C5
Marseille 901,421 F6
Martigues 26,850 F6
Maubeuge 34,152 F2
Mayenne 11,278 C3
Mazamet 13,148 E6
Meaux 41,831 E3
Mehun-sur-Yèvre 6,533 E4
Melun 36,913 E3
Mende 10,040 E5
Menton 24,736 G6
Metz 110,939 G3
Meudon 31,294 A2
Millau 20,401 E5
Mimizan 6,826 C5
Mirecourt 7,160 G3
Moissac 7,403 D5
Montargis 18,021 E3
Montauban 35,344 D5
Montbard 7,477 F4
Montbéliard 29,968 G4
Montbrison 9,945 E5
Montceau-les-Mines 28,093 F4
Mont-de-Marsan 24,812 C6
Mont-Dore 2,074 E5
Montélimar 25,422 F5
Montfort 2,701 C3
Montigny-les-Metz 24,208 G3
Montluçon 56,337 E4
Montmédy 1,859 F3
Montpellier 178,136 E6
Montreuil, Seine-Saint-Denis 96,441 B2
Montrouge 40,189 B2
Mont-Saint-Michel 88 C3
Morlaix 15,919 B3
Morteau 6,515 G4
Moulins 25,856 E4
Moyeuvre-Grande 12,448 G3
Mulhouse 116,494 G4
Muret 13,041 D6
Nancy 106,906 G3
Nanterre 94,441 A1
Nantes 252,537 C4
Narbonne 36,525 E6
Nemours 11,159 E3
Neufchâteau 8,582 F3
Neuilly-sur-Seine 65,941 A1
Nevers 45,122 E4
Nice 331,002 G6
Nîmes 123,914 F6
Niort 59,297 C4
Nogent-le-Rotrou 12,284 D3
Noisy-le-Sec 37,674 B1
Noyon 13,784 E3
Oloron-Sainte-Marie 11,616 C6
Orange 19,847 F5
Orléans 88,503 D3
Orly 26,090 B2
Orthez 9,639 C6
Oullins 27,731 F5
Oyonnax 22,548 F4
Pamiers 12,906 D6
Pantin 42,651 B1
Paray-le-Monial 11,523 F4
Paris (cap.) 2,291,554 B2
Parthenay 12,549 C4
Pau 81,560 C6
Périgueux 34,779 D5
Péronne 8,358 E3
Perpignan 101,198 E6
Pessac 50,333 C5
Pézenas 6,768 E6
Pithiviers 9,976 E3
Poitiers 78,739 D4
Pont-à-Mousson 14,461 G3
Pontarlier 17,778 G4
Pontivy 9,478 B3
Pont-l'Abbe 6,618 A4
Pontoise 26,702 E3
Port-de-Bouc 20,448 F6
Port-Saint-Louis-du-Rhône 9,649 F6
Port-Vendres 5,448 E6
Privas 9,385 F5
Provins 12,281 E3
Puteau 35,366 A2
Quimper 50,856 A4
Quimperlé 9,783 B4
Rambouillet 18,446 D3
Redon 9,528 C4
Reims 177,320 E3
Remiremont 10,250 G3
Rennes 194,094 C3

(continued on following page)

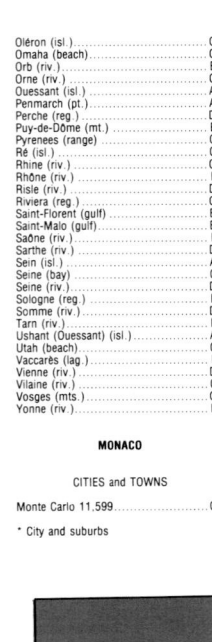
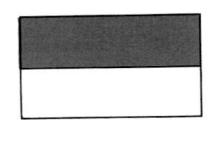

Wine Regions

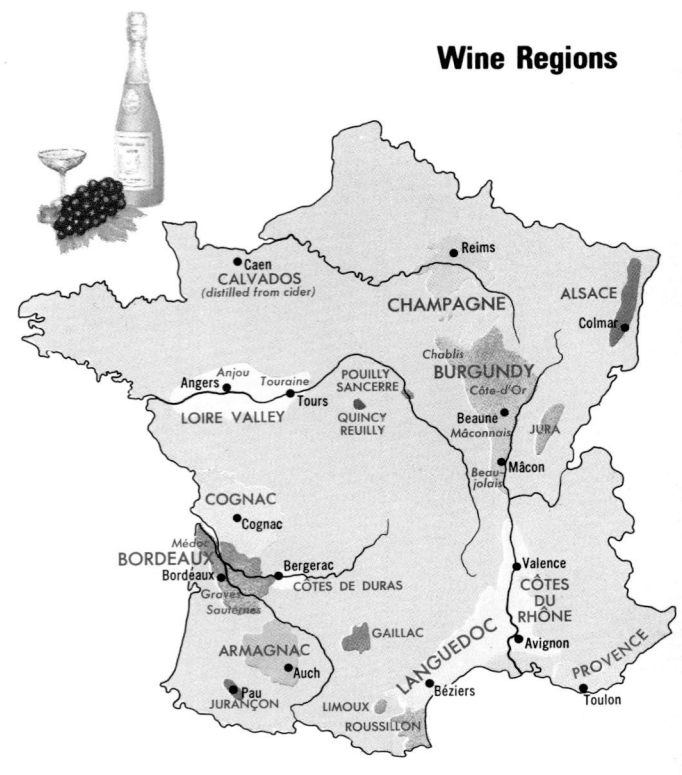

MONACO

AREA 368 acres
(149 hectares)
POPULATION 25,029

Climate, soil and variety of grape planted determine the quality of wine. Long, hot and fairly dry summers with cool, humid nights constitute an ideal climate. The nature of the soil is such a determining influence that identical grapes planted in Bordeaux, Burgundy and Champagne, will yield wines of widely different types.

Agriculture, Industry and Resources

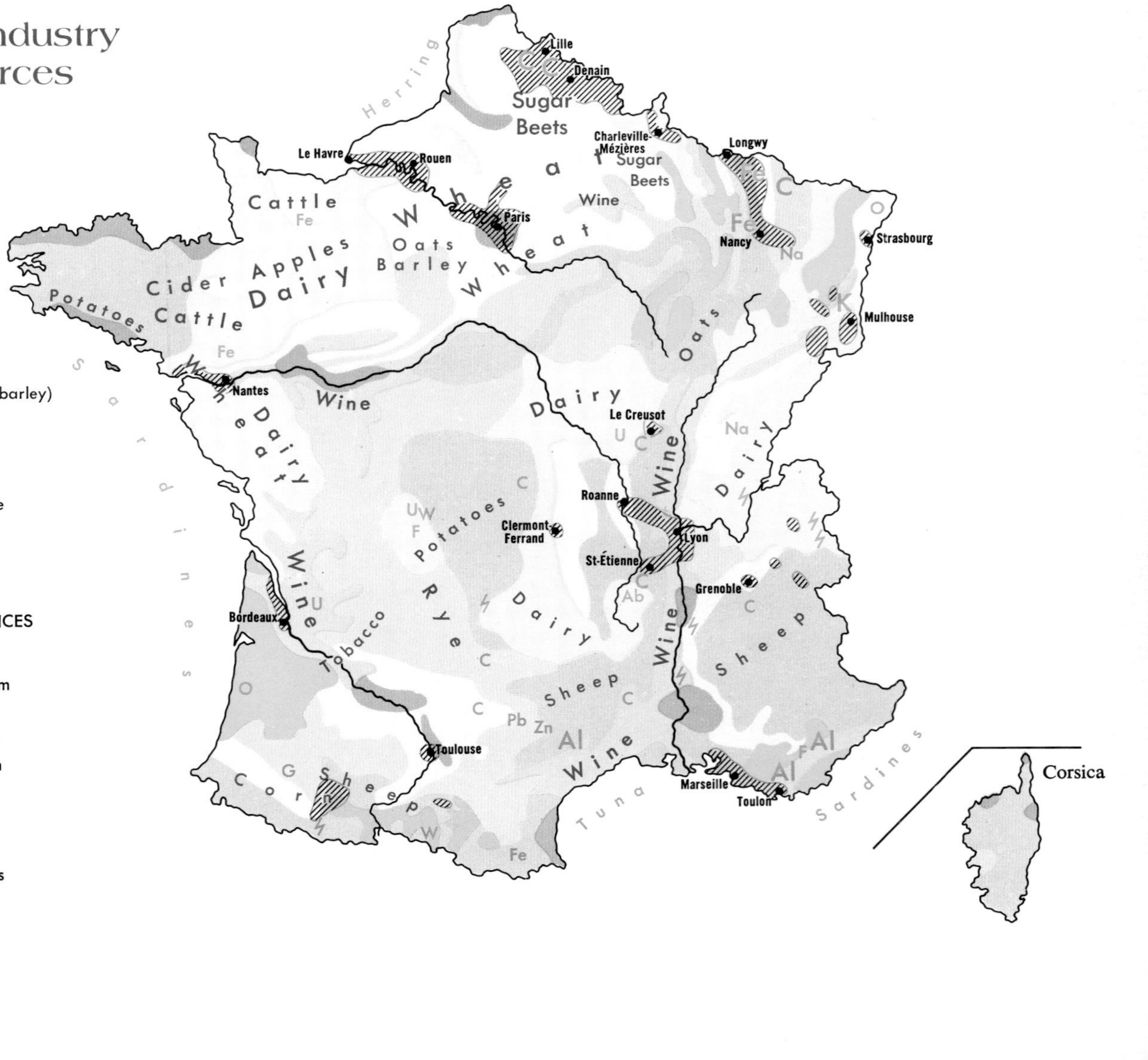

DOMINANT LAND USE

- Cereals (chiefly wheat)
- Cereals (chiefly rye, oats, barley)
- Dairy
- Pasture Livestock
- Truck Farming, Horticulture
- Grapes, Wine
- Forests

MAJOR MINERAL OCCURRENCES

Ab	Asbestos	Na	Salt
Al	Bauxite	O	Petroleum
C	Coal	Pb	Lead
F	Fluorspar	U	Uranium
Fe	Iron Ore	W	Tungsten
G	Natural Gas	Zn	Zinc
K	Potash		

⚡ Water Power
▨ Major Industrial Areas

Corsica

Agriculture, Industry and Resources

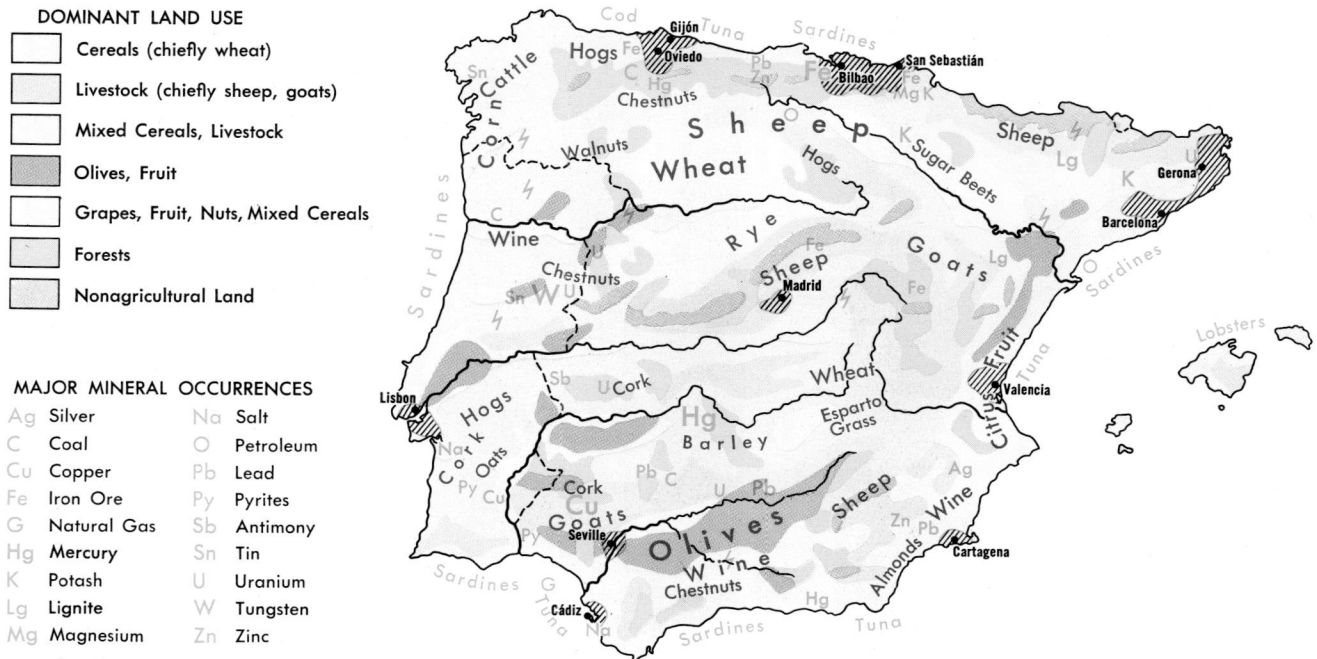

DOMINANT LAND USE

- Cereals (chiefly wheat)
- Livestock (chiefly sheep, goats)
- Mixed Cereals, Livestock
- Olives, Fruit
- Grapes, Fruit, Nuts, Mixed Cereals
- Forests
- Nonagricultural Land

MAJOR MINERAL OCCURRENCES

Ag	Silver	Na	Salt
C	Coal	O	Petroleum
Cu	Copper	Pb	Lead
Fe	Iron Ore	Py	Pyrites
G	Natural Gas	Sb	Antimony
Hg	Mercury	Sn	Tin
K	Potash	U	Uranium
Lg	Lignite	W	Tungsten
Mg	Magnesium	Zn	Zinc

⚡ Water Power

▨ Major Industrial Areas

ANDORRA

SPAIN

PORTUGAL

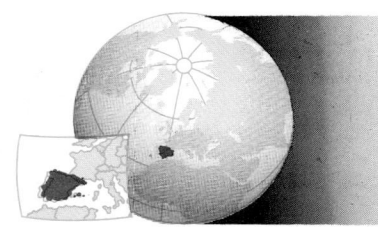

SPAIN

AREA 194,881 sq. mi. (504,742 sq. km.)
POPULATION 37,430,000
CAPITAL Madrid
LARGEST CITY Madrid
HIGHEST POINT Pico de Teide 12,172 ft. (3,710 m.)
(Canary Is.); Mulhacén 11,411 ft. (3,478 m.)
(mainland)
MONETARY UNIT peseta
MAJOR LANGUAGES Spanish, Catalan, Basque,
Galician, Valencian
MAJOR RELIGION Roman Catholicism

ANDORRA

AREA 188 sq. mi. (487 sq. km.)
POPULATION 31,000
CAPITAL Andorra la Vella
MONETARY UNITS French franc, Spanish peseta
MAJOR LANGUAGE Catalan
MAJOR RELIGION Roman Catholicism

PORTUGAL

AREA 35,549 sq. mi. (92,072 sq. km.)
POPULATION 9,933,000
CAPITAL Lisbon
LARGEST CITY Lisbon
HIGHEST POINT Malhão da Estrela
6,532 ft. (1,991 m.)
MONETARY UNIT escudo
MAJOR LANGUAGE Portuguese
MAJOR RELIGION Roman Catholicism

GIBRALTAR

AREA 2.28 sq. mi. (5.91 sq. km.)
POPULATION 29,760
CAPITAL Gibraltar
MONETARY UNIT pound sterling
MAJOR LANGUAGES English, Spanish
MAJOR RELIGION Roman Catholicism

(continued on following page)

Topography

0   50   100 MI.
0   50   100 KM.

Cape Finisterre — CANTABRIAN MTS. — Bilbao — PYRENEES — Pico de Aneto 11,168 ft. (3404 m.) — Saragossa — Barcelona — Minorca — Majorca — Ibiza — C. de la Nao — BALEARIC ISLANDS — Gulf of Valencia — Valencia — Madrid — SA. DE GUADARRAMA — Matilhão da Estrela 6,532 ft. (1991 m.) — Porto — Douro — Mino — Sil — Esla — Duero — Tormes — Tagus — Lisbon — Sado — Guadiana — SIERRA MORENA — Córdoba — Genil — Seville — Guadalquivir — Gulf of Cádiz — Cape St. Vincent — Mulhacén 11,411 ft. (3478 m.) — SA. NEVADA — Málaga — Europa Pt.

| Below Sea Level | 100 m. 328 ft. | 200 m. 656 ft. | 500 m. 1,640 ft. | 1,000 m. 3,281 ft. | 2,000 m. 6,562 ft. | 5,000 m. 16,404 ft. |

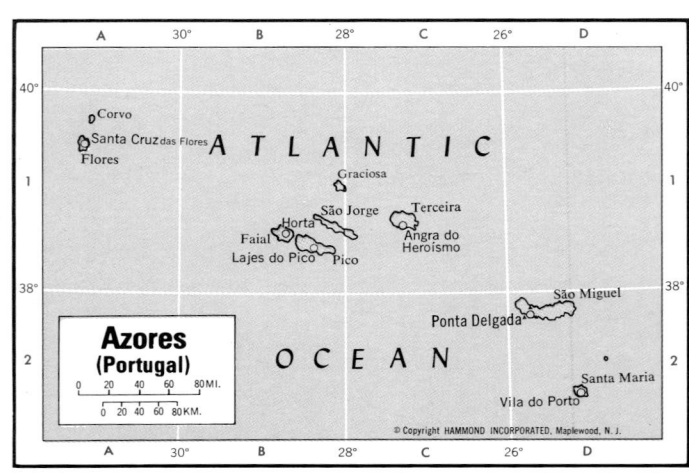

Azores (Portugal)

0   20   40   60   80MI.
0   20   40   60   80KM.

ATLANTIC OCEAN

Corvo — Santa Cruz das Flores — Flores — Graciosa — São Jorge — Terceira — Horta — Faial — Pico — Lajes do Pico — Angra do Heroísmo — São Miguel — Ponta Delgada — Santa Maria — Vila do Porto

© Copyright HAMMOND INCORPORATED, Maplewood, N.J.

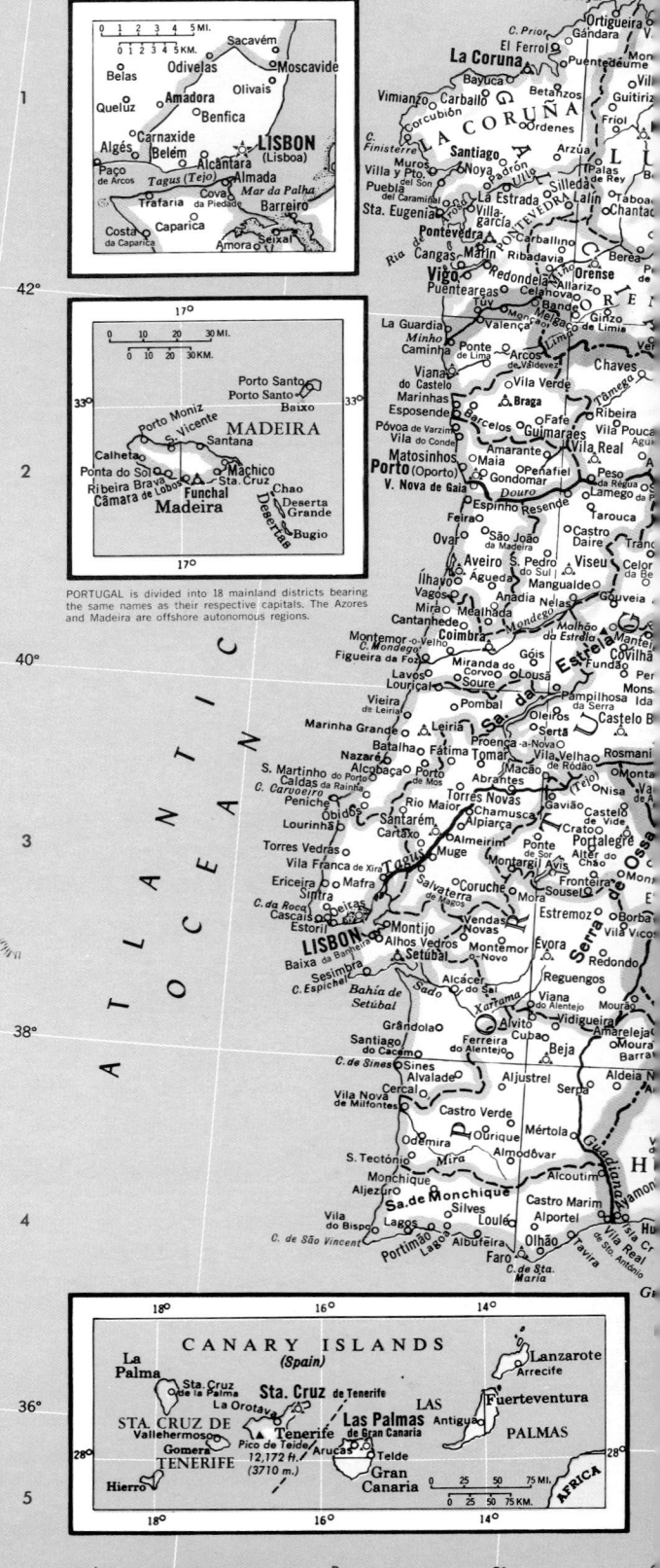

PORTUGAL is divided into 18 mainland districts bearing the same names as their respective capitals. The Azores and Madeira are offshore autonomous regions.

MADEIRA

Porto Santo — Porto Santo Baixo — Porto Moniz — S. Vicente — Santana — Calheta — Ponta do Sol — Ribeira Brava — Câmara de Lobos — Funchal — Machico — Sta. Cruz — Chão — Deserta Grande — Bugio

CANARY ISLANDS (Spain)

La Palma — Sta. Cruz de la Palma — La Orotava — STA. CRUZ DE TENERIFE — Pico de Teide 12,172 ft. (3710 m.) — Tenerife — Gomera — Vallehermoso — Hierro — GRAN CANARIA — Arucas — LAS PALMAS — Telde — Lanzarote — Arrecife — Fuerteventura — Antigua — AFRICA

0   25   50   75 MI.
0   25   50   75 KM.

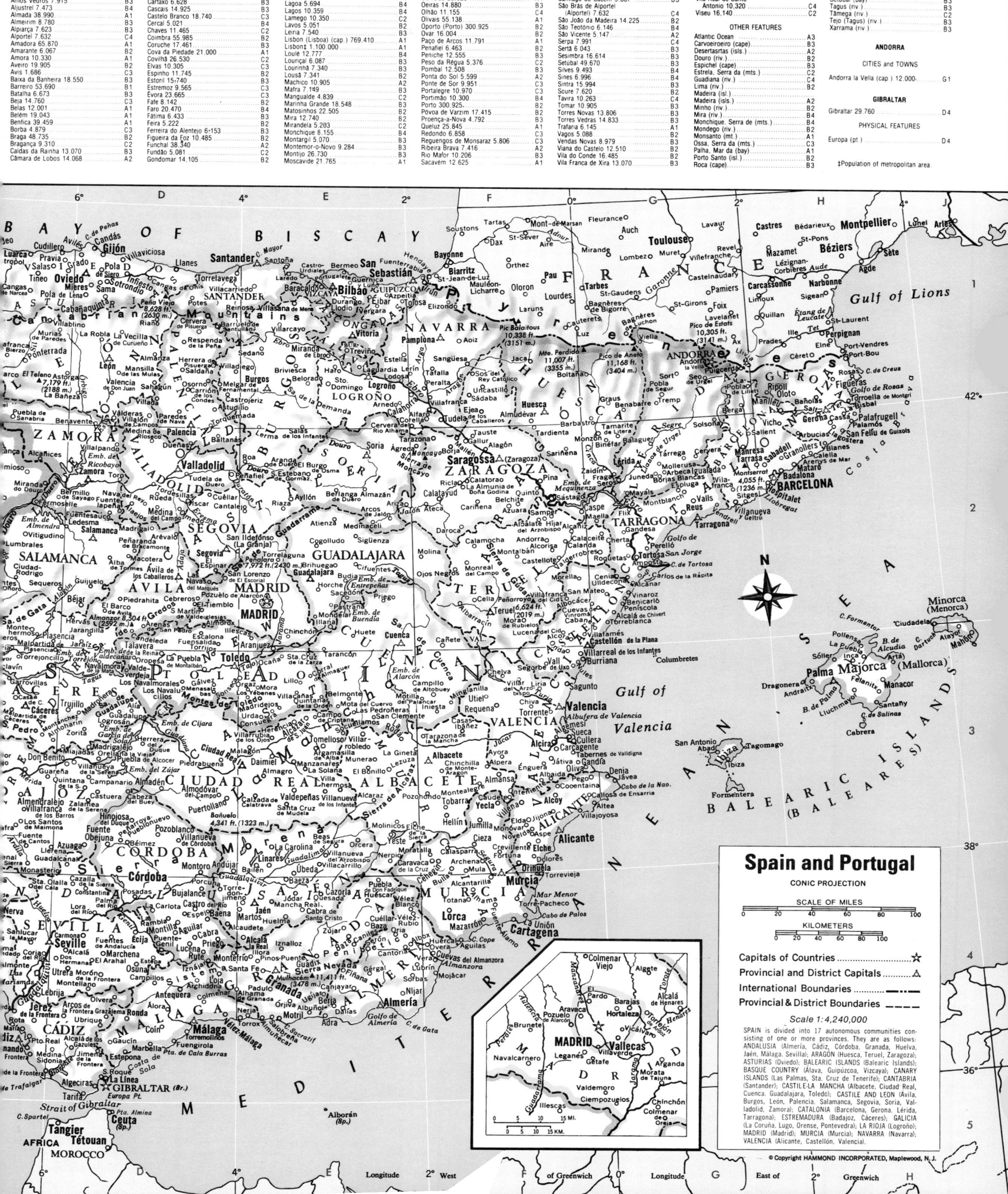

Spain and Portugal

CONIC PROJECTION

SCALE OF MILES
0 20 40 60 80 100

KILOMETERS
0 20 40 60 80 100

Capitals of Countries ....☆
Provincial and District Capitals ....△
International Boundaries ....━ ─ ━
Provincial & District Boundaries ....─ ─ ─

Scale 1:4,240,000

SPAIN is divided into 17 autonomous communities consisting of one or more provinces. They are as follows: ANDALUSIA (Almería, Cádiz, Córdoba, Granada, Huelva, Jaén, Málaga, Sevilla); ARAGÓN (Huesca, Teruel, Zaragoza); ASTURIAS (Oviedo); BALEARIC ISLANDS (Balearic Islands); BASQUE COUNTRY (Álava, Guipúzcoa, Vizcaya); CANARY ISLANDS (Las Palmas, Sta. Cruz de Tenerife); CANTABRIA (Santander); CASTILE-LA MANCHA (Albacete, Ciudad Real, Cuenca, Guadalajara, Toledo); CASTILE AND LEON (Avila, Burgos, León, Palencia, Salamanca, Segovia, Soria, Valladolid, Zamora); CATALONIA (Barcelona, Gerona, Lérida, Tarragona); ESTREMADURA (Badajoz, Cáceres); GALICIA (La Coruña, Lugo, Orense, Pontevedra); LA RIOJA (Logroño); MADRID (Madrid); MURCIA (Murcia); NAVARRA (Navarra); VALENCIA (Alicante, Castellón, Valencia).

© Copyright HAMMOND INCORPORATED, Maplewood, N.J.

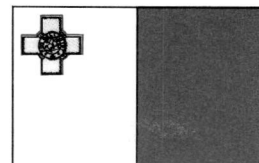
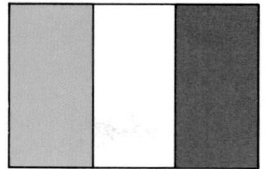
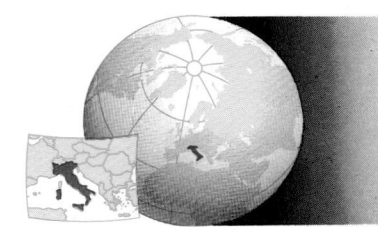

VATICAN CITY

AREA 108.7 acres
(44 hectares)
POPULATION 728

SAN MARINO

AREA 23.4 sq. mi.
(60.6 sq. km.)
POPULATION
19,149

MALTA

AREA 122 sq. mi. (316 sq. km.)
POPULATION 343,970
CAPITAL Valletta
LARGEST CITY Sliema
HIGHEST POINT 787 ft. (240 m.)
MONETARY UNIT Maltese pound
MAJOR LANGUAGES Maltese, English
MAJOR RELIGION Roman Catholicism

ITALY

AREA 116,303 sq. mi.
(301,225 sq. km.)
POPULATION 57,140,000
CAPITAL Rome
LARGEST CITY Rome
HIGHEST POINT Dufourspitze
(Mte. Rosa) 15,203 ft. (4,634 m.)
MONETARY UNIT lira
MAJOR LANGUAGE Italian
MAJOR RELIGION Roman Catholicism

Topography

0   50   100   150 MI.

0   50   100   150 KM.

Below Sea Level | 100 m. 328 ft. | 200 m. 656 ft. | 500 m. 1,640 ft. | 1,000 m. 3,281 ft. | 2,000 m. 6,562 ft. | 5,000 m. 16,404 ft.

(continued on following page)

Sabaudia 4.501 D4
Saint Vincent 3.737 A2
Sala Consilina 8.177 E4
Salemi 10.180 D6
Salerno 146.534 E4
Salsomaggiore Terme 13.677 B2
Saluzzo 13.929 A2
Sambiase 10.567 F5
San Bartolomeo in Galdo 6.943 E4
San Benedetto del
  Tronto 40.108 E3
San Cataldo 19.609 D6
San Giovanni in Fiore 16.116 F5
San Giovanni in
  Persiceto 12.151 C2
San Marco in Lamis 15.817 E4
San Miniato 3.245 C3
Sannicandro Garganico 17.939 E4
San Remo 47.684 A3
Sansepolcro 11.443 C3
San Severino Marche 6.447 D3
San Severo 49.622 E4
Santa Maria Capua
  Vetere 31.077 E4
Sant'Elpidio a Mare 4.446 E3
Santeramo in Colle 19.758 F4
San Vito 3.901 B5
San Vito al Tagliamento 6.328 D1
San Vito dei Normanni 18.447 F4
San Vito Romano 3.256 F6
Saronno 32.477 B2
Sarroch 3.560 B5
Sassari 94.312 B4
Sassuolo 33.451 C2
Savigliano 14.036 A2
Savona 76.274 B2
Schio 27.890 C1
Sciacca 29.803 D6
Scicli 18.405 E6
Segni 7.193 F7
Senigallia 25.413 D3
Sesto Fiorentino 41.636 C3
Sestri Levante 18.331 B2
Settebagni 5.022 F6
Sezze 7.043 D4
Siderno 8.023 F5
Siena 56.539 C3
Siniscola 6.149 B4
Sinnai 8.499 B5
Siracusa (Syracuse) 93.006 E6
Sondrio 19.724 B1
Sora 14.031 D4
Soresina 9.300 C2
Sorrento 13.078 E4
Sorso 10.741 B4
Spoleto 18.013 D3
Squinzano 14.053 G4
Stresa 3.758 B2
Sulmona 18.221 D3
Susa 5.773 A2
Suzzara 12.013 C2
Syracuse 93.006 E6
Taormina 6.696 E6
Taranto 205.158 F4
Tarquinia 10.300 C3
Tauriano 12.198 B4
Tempo Pausania 10.382 B4
Teramo 31.163 D3
Termini Imerese 24.085 D6
Termoli 13.986 E3
Terni 75.873 D3
Terracina 24.092 D4
Terralba 8.551 B5
Tirano 7.413 C1
Tivoli 28.393 F6
Todi 5.705 D3
Tolentino 11.642 D3
Torino (Turin) 1.181.698 A2
Torre Annunziata 71.068 E4
Torre del Greco 74.752 E4
Torremaggiore 16.171 E4
Tortona 24.165 B2
Trani 40.508 F4
Trapani 90.305 D5
Trento 64.272 C1
Treviglio 21.920 B2
Treviso 87.447 D2
Tricase 10.481 G5
Trieste 257.259 E2
Trino 8.722 B2
Turin 1.181.698 A2
Udine 97.544 D2
Umbertide 6.640 D3
Urbino 7.735 D3
Valdagno 20.342 C2
Valenza 20.533 B2
Valmontone 6.543 F6
Varallo Pombia 3.118 B2
Varazze 11.676 B2
Varese 65.978 B2
Vasto 17.295 E3
Venafro 5.156 E4
Venezia (Venice) 108.082 D2
Venice 108.082 D2
Venosa 10.993 F4
Ventimiglia 20.343 A3
Verbania 29.894 B2
Vercelli 54.934 B2
Veroli 2.793 D4
Verona 227.032 C2
Viadana 6.667 C2
Viareggio 49.965 C3
Vicenza 99.451 C2
Vigevano 3.005 B2
Vigevano 62.855 B2
Villadolid 12.651 B2
Villafranca di Verona 11.762 C2
Viterbo 39.291 D4
Vittoria 43.673 E6
Vittorio Veneto 25.476 D1
Vizzini 9.583 E6
Voghera 37.316 B2
Volterra 10.732 C3
Zagarolo 4.232 F7

OTHER FEATURES

Adda (riv.) B2
Adige (riv.) C2
Adriatic (sea) E3
Alicudi (isl.) E5
Apennines, Central (range) D3
Apennines, Northern (range) B2
Apennines, Southern (range) E4
Arno (riv.) C3
Asinara (isl.) B4
Bernina, Piz (peak) B1
Blanc (mt.) A2
Bolsena (lake) C3
Bonifacio (str.) B4
Bracciano (lake) D3
Brenner (pass) C1
Capraia (isl.) B3
Capri (isl.) E4
Carbonara (cape) B5
Carnic Alps (range) D1
Castellammare (gulf) D5
Circeo (cape) D4
Como (lake) B1
Cottian Alps (range) A2
Dolomite Alps (range) C1
Dora Baltea (riv.) A2
Dora Riparia (riv.) A2
Egadi (isls.) C6
Elba (isl.) C3
Etna (vol.) E6
Favignana (isl.) D6

Filicudi (isl.) E5
Gaeta (gulf) D4
Garda (lake) C2
Gennargentu, Monti del (mt.) B5
Genoa (gulf) B2
Giannutri (isl.) C3
Giglio (isl.) C3
Gorgona (isl.) B3
Graian Alps (range) A2
Gran Paradiso (mt.) A2
Great Saint Bernard (pass) A2
Ionian (sea) F6
Ischia (isl.) D4
Julian Alps (range) D1
Lampedusa (isl.) D7
Lepontine Alps (range) B1
Levanzo (isl.) D5
Ligurian (sea) B3
Linosa (isl.) E8
Lipari (isl.) E5
Lipari (isls.) B1
Maggiore (lake) B1
Manfredonia (gulf) F4
Marettimo (isl.) C6
Maritime Alps (range) A2
Marmolada (mt.) C1
Mediterranean (sea) B6
Messina (str.) E5
Metauro (riv.) D3
Mincio (riv.) C2
Montecristo (isl.) C3
Nera (riv.) D3
Oglio (riv.) C2
Ombrone (riv.) C3
Oristano (gulf) B5
Orosei (gulf) B4
Ortles (range) C1
Otranto (str.) G5
Ötztal Alps (range) C1
Panarea (isl.) E5
Panaro (riv.) C2
Pantelleria (isl.) D7
Pelagie (isls.) D7
Pennine Alps (range) A2
Pianosa (isl.) C3
Piave (riv.) D2
Po (riv.) D2
Pompeii (ruins) E4
Pontine (isls.) D4
Ponza (isl.) D4
Rosa (mt.) A2
Salina (isl.) E5
Salso (riv.) D6
Santa Maria di Leuca (cape) G5
Sant'Antioco (pen.) B5
Sant'Eufemia (gulf) F5
Sardinia (isl.) B4
Sicily (isl.) D6
Sicily (str.) D6
Simplon (tunnel) A1
Spartivento (cape) B5
Spartivento (cape) F6
Squillace (gulf) F5
Stromboli (isl.) E5
Taglamento (riv.) D1
Tanaro (riv.) B2
Taranto (gulf) F5
Testa del Gargano (cape) F4
Tiber (riv.) D3
Trasimeno (lake) D3
Tremiti (isls.) E3
Trieste (gulf) D2
Tuscan (arch.) B3
Tyrrhenian (sea) C4
Ustica (isl.) D5
Vaticano (cape) E5
Venice (gulf) D2
Ventotene (isl.) D4

Vesuvius (vol.) E4
Viso (mt.) A2
Volturno (riv.) E4
Vulcano (isl.) E5

MALTA

CITIES and TOWNS

Sliema 20.095 E7
Valletta (cap.) 14.042 E7
Victoria 5.249 E6

SAN MARINO

CITIES and TOWNS

San Marino (cap.) 4.628 D3
San Marino* 5.410 D3

VATICAN CITY

Vatican City 728 B6

*City and suburbs.

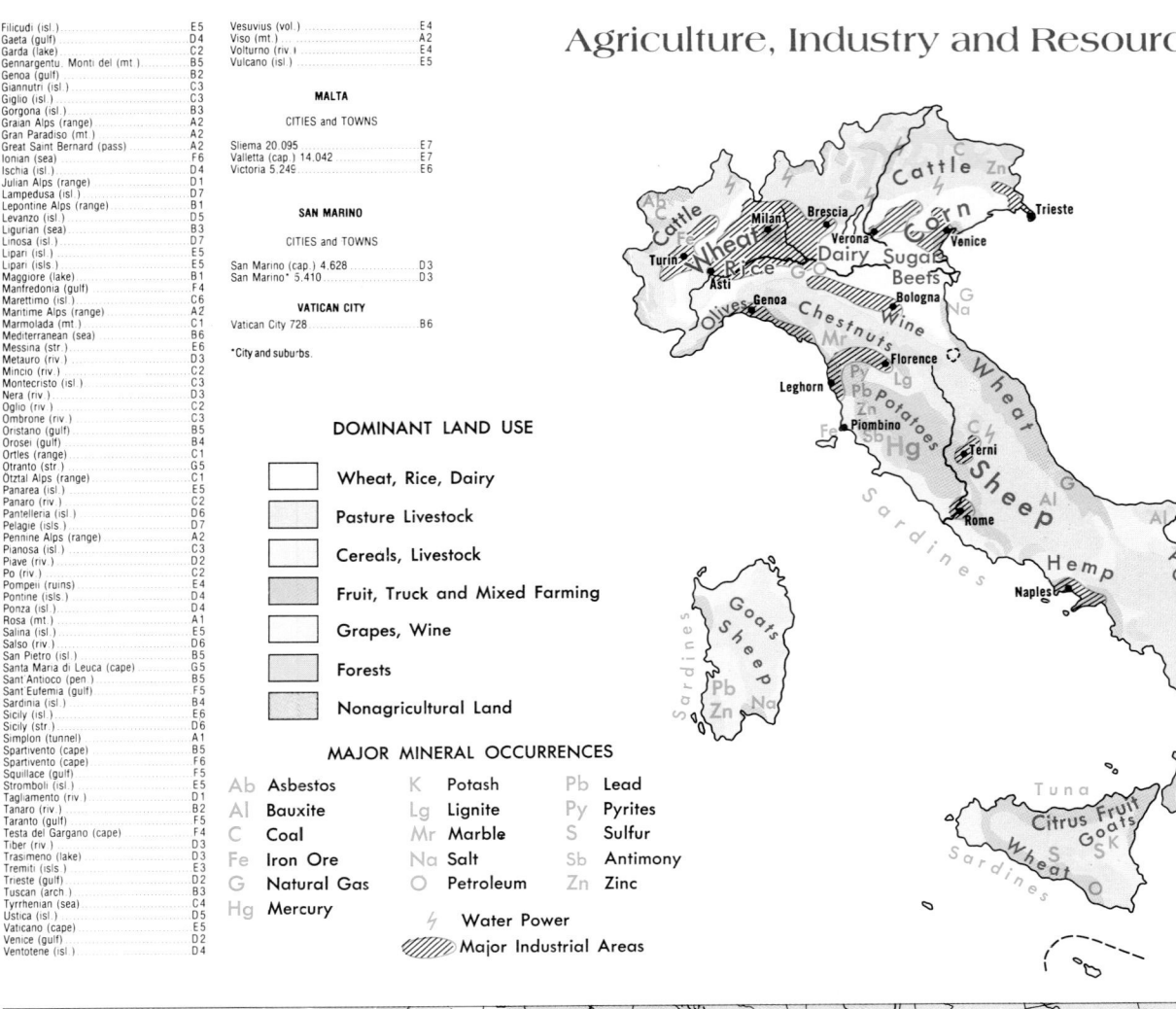

Agriculture, Industry and Resources

DOMINANT LAND USE

- Wheat, Rice, Dairy
- Pasture Livestock
- Cereals, Livestock
- Fruit, Truck and Mixed Farming
- Grapes, Wine
- Forests
- Nonagricultural Land

MAJOR MINERAL OCCURRENCES

Ab Asbestos
Al Bauxite
C Coal
Fe Iron Ore
G Natural Gas
Hg Mercury

K Potash
Lg Lignite
Mr Marble
Na Salt
O Petroleum

Pb Lead
Py Pyrites
S Sulfur
Sb Antimony
Zn Zinc

⚡ Water Power
▨ Major Industrial Areas

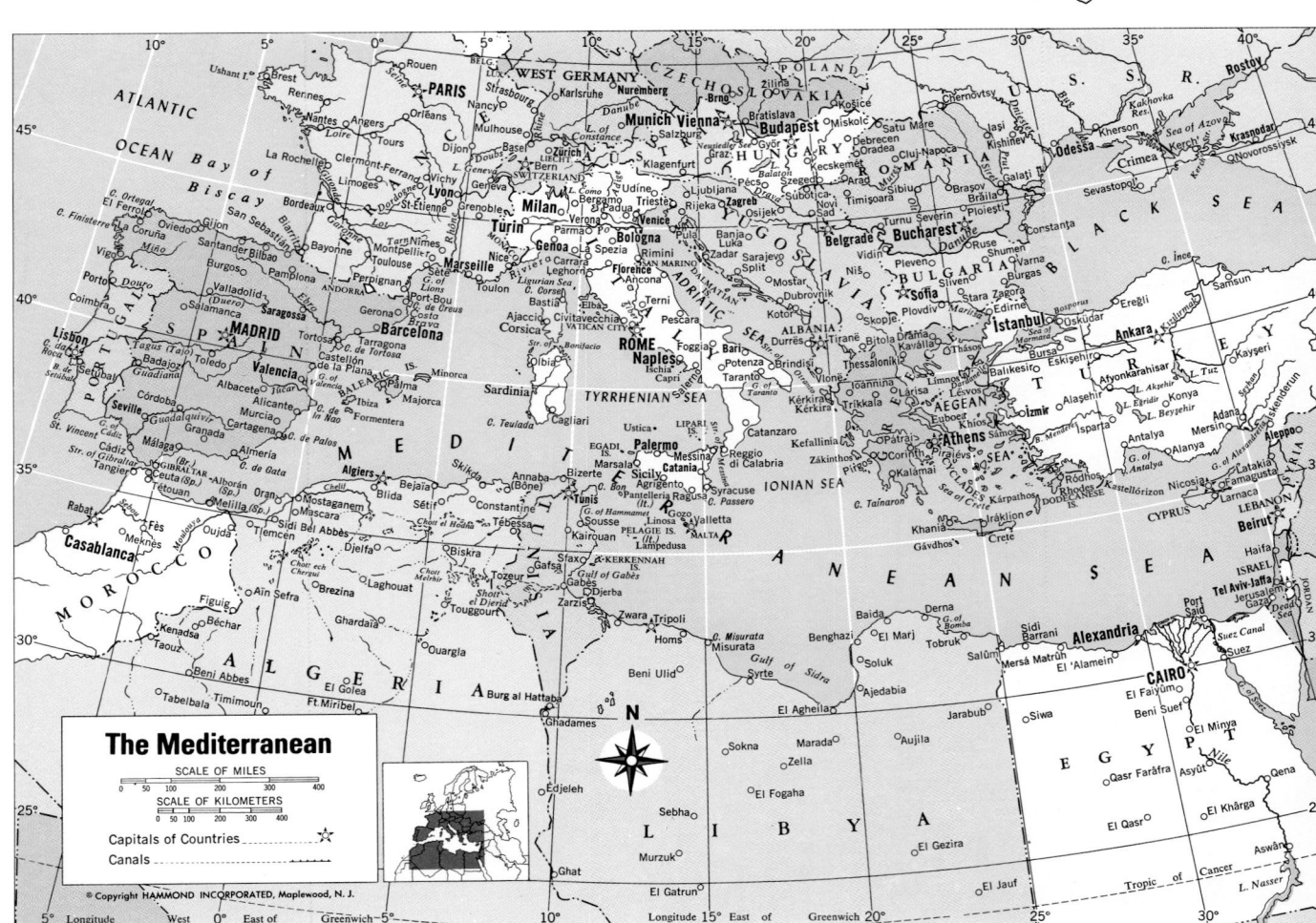

The Mediterranean

SCALE OF MILES
0 50 100 200 300 400

SCALE OF KILOMETERS
0 50 100 200 300 400

Capitals of Countries .... ☆
Canals

© Copyright HAMMOND INCORPORATED, Maplewood, N.J.

SWITZERLAND

AREA 15,943 sq. mi. (41,292 sq. km.)
POPULATION 6,365,960
CAPITAL Bern
LARGEST CITY Zürich
HIGHEST POINT Dufourspitze
(Mte. Rosa) 15,203 ft. (4,634 m.)
MONETARY UNIT Swiss franc
MAJOR LANGUAGES German, French,
Italian, Romansch
MAJOR RELIGIONS Protestantism,
Roman Catholicism

LIECHTENSTEIN

AREA 61 sq. mi. (158 sq. km.)
POPULATION 25,220
CAPITAL Vaduz
LARGEST CITY Vaduz
HIGHEST POINT Grauspitze 8,527 ft.
(2,599 m.)
MONETARY UNIT Swiss franc
MAJOR LANGUAGE German
MAJOR RELIGION Roman Catholicism

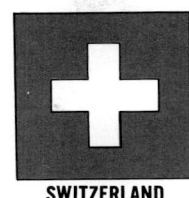

SWITZERLAND

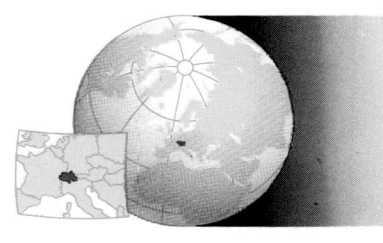

LIECHTENSTEIN

Languages

German
French
Italian
Romansch

Switzerland is a multilingual nation with four official languages. 70% of the people speak German, 19% French, 10% Italian and 1% Romansch.

SWITZERLAND

CANTONS

Aargau 442,400	F2
Appenzell, Ausser Rhoden 46,700	H2
Appenzell, Inner Rhoden 13,500	H2
Baselland 219,500	E2
Baselstadt 209,700	E1
Bern 920,900	D2
Fribourg 181,600	D3
Geneva (Genève) 338,600	B4
Glarus 35,700	H3
Graubünden (Grisons) 164,300	H3
Grisons (Graubünden) 164,300	H3
Jura 67,200	D2
Lucerne (Luzern) 292,900	F2
Luzern 292,900	F2
Neuchâtel 162,200	C3
Nidwalden 26,900	F3
Obwalden 25,400	F3
Sankt Gallen 385,000	H2
Schaffhausen 69,300	G1
Schwyz 93,100	G2
Soleure (Solothurn) 221,800	E2
Solothurn 221,800	E2
Thurgau 183,500	H1
Ticino 264,400	G4
Uri 34,000	G3
Valais 214,000	D4
Vaud 523,500	B3
Zug 73,600	G2
Zürich 1,117,300	G2

CITIES and TOWNS

Aadorf 3,022	G2
Aarau 16,881	F2
Aarau* 51,800	F2
Aarberg 3,122	D2
Aarburg 5,943	E2
Adelboden 3,326	E3
Adliswil 15,920	F2
Aeschi bei Spiez 1,402	E3
Affoltern am Albis 7,363	F2
Affoltern im Emmental 1,223	E2
Aigle 6,532	C4
Airolo 2,140	G3
Alle 1,615	D2
Allschwil 17,638	D1
Alpnach 3,277	F3
Altdorf 8,647	G3
Altstätten 9,084	J2
Amriswil 7,601	H1
Andelfingen 1,453	G1
Andermatt 1,589	G3
Appenzell 5,217	H2
Arbedo-Castione 2,456	G4
Arbon 12,227	H1
Arbon* 15,400	H1
Ardon 1,498	D4
Arosa 2,717	J3
Arth 7,580	F2
Ascona 4,086	G4
Attalens 1,116	C3
Au 4,944	J2
Aubonne 1,983	B4
Avenches 2,235	D3
Baar 14,074	F2
Baden 14,115	F2
Baden* 66,800	F2
Bad Ragaz 3,713	H2
Balerna 3,885	G5
Balsthal 5,607	E2
Bärtswil 2,733	G2
Basel 199,600	E1
Basel* 379,700	E1
Bassecourt 2,985	D2
Bätterkinden 1,757	E2

Bauma 3,159	G2
Beatenberg 1,263	E3
Beinwil am See 2,520	F2
Belfaux 1,075	D3
Bellinzona 16,979	H4
Bellinzona* 31,000	H4
Belp 6,981	D3
Berg 1,039	H1
Bern (cap.) 154,700	D3
Bern* 285,300	D3
Beromünster 1,552	F2
Bettlach 4,046	D2
Bex 5,069	D4
Biasca 4,696	H4
Biberist 7,769	D2
Biel 63,400	D2
Biel*89,900	D2
Bière 1,252	B3
Binningen 15,344	D1
Bischofszell 4,233	H1
Blumenstein 1,049	E3
Bodio 1,425	G4
Bolligen 26,121	E2
Boltigen 1,519	D3
Bonaduz 1,289	H3
Boncourt 1,528	C2
Bönigen 1,738	E3
Boswil 1,904	F2
Boudry 4,372	C3
Brittnau 2,888	E2
Broc 1,842	D3
Brugg 8,635	F2
Brusio 1,344	K4
Bubendorf 2,070	E2
Bubikon 3,244	G2
Buchs 8,454	H2
Bülach 11,043	G1
Bulle 7,556	D3
Buochs 3,232	F3
Büren an der Aare 3,085	D2
Burgdorf 15,888	E2
Burgdorf* 18,400	E2
Bürglen, Thurgau 1,920	H1
Bürglen, Uri 3,401	G3
Bussigny-près-Lausanne 4,509	B3
Bütschwil 3,270	H2
Carouge 14,055	B4
Castagnola 4,430	G4
Cazis 1,687	H3
Cernier 1,717	C2
Chalais 1,651	E4
Cham 8,209	F2
Chamoson 2,049	D4
Charmey 1,155	D3
Château-d'Oex 3,203	D4
Châtel-Saint-Denis 2,842	C3
Chêne-Bougeries 8,670	B4
Chavornay 1,521	C3
Chexbres 1,607	C3
Chiasso 8,868	G5
Chippis 1,561	E4
Chur 32,400	J3
Churwalden 1,052	J3
Claro 1,143	G4
Collombey-Muraz 2,279	C4
Collonge-Bellerive 3,541	B4
Conthey 4,259	D4
Coppet 1,097	B4
Corcelles-près-Payerne 1,256	C3
Corgémont 1,645	D2
Cossonay 1,529	B3
Courgenay 1,954	D2
Courrendlin 2,656	D2
Courroux 1,788	D2
Courtelary 1,462	D2
Courtételle 1,864	D2
Couvet 3,481	C3
Cully 1,535	C4
Davos 10,238	J3
Degersheim 3,400	H2
Delémont 11,797	D2
Derendingen 4,917	E2
Dielsdorf 2,691	F1
Diemtigen 1,913	D3
Diepoldsau 3,311	J2
Diessenhofen 2,532	G1
Dietikon 22,705	F2
Disentis-Muster 2,319	G3
Domat-Ems 5,701	H3
Dombresson 1,109	C2
Dornach 5,258	D2
Döttingen 3,380	F1
Dübendorf 19,639	G2
Düdingen 4,932	D2
Dürnten 4,820	G2
Dürrenroth 1,084	E2
Ebnat-Kappel 5,131	H2
Echallens 1,643	C3
Ecublens 6,379	B3
Egg 5,250	G2
Eggiwil 2,391	E3
Eglisau 2,160	G1
Egnach 3,466	H1

Agriculture, Industry and Resources

DOMINANT LAND USE

Cereals, Dairy
Pasture Livestock
General Farming, Livestock
Fruit, Truck, Mixed Farming
Forests
Nonagricultural Land

⚡ Water Power
Major Industrial Areas

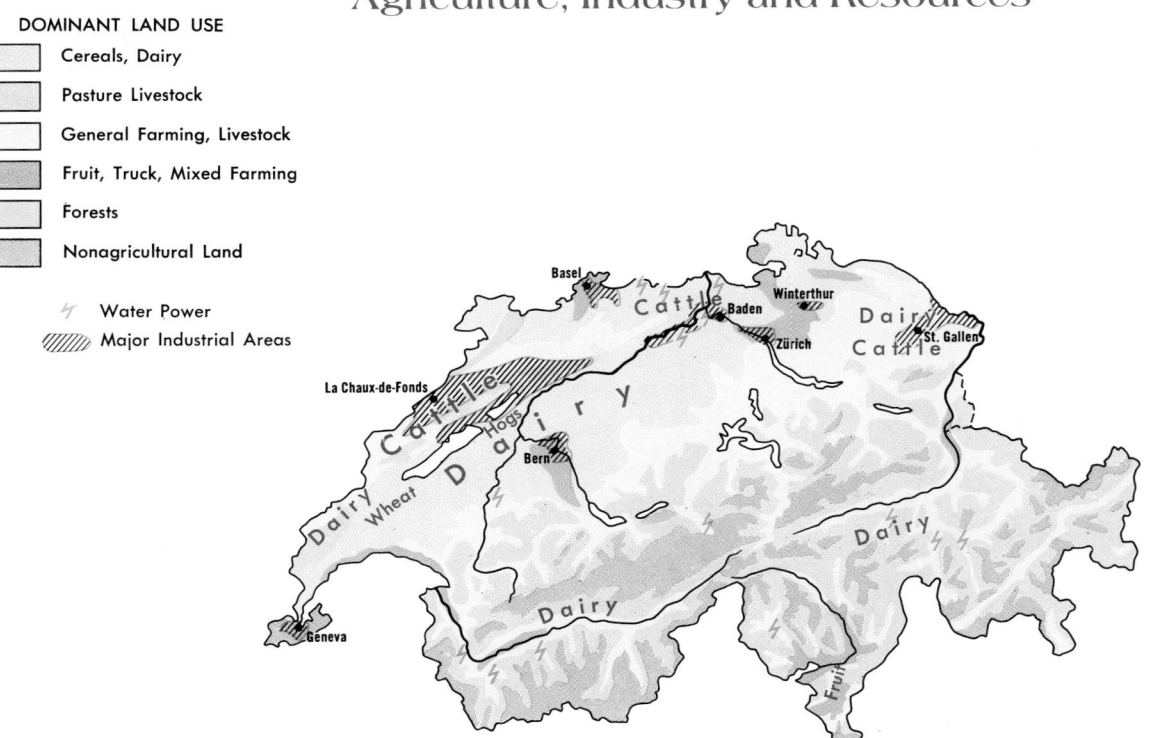

(continued on following page)

Topography

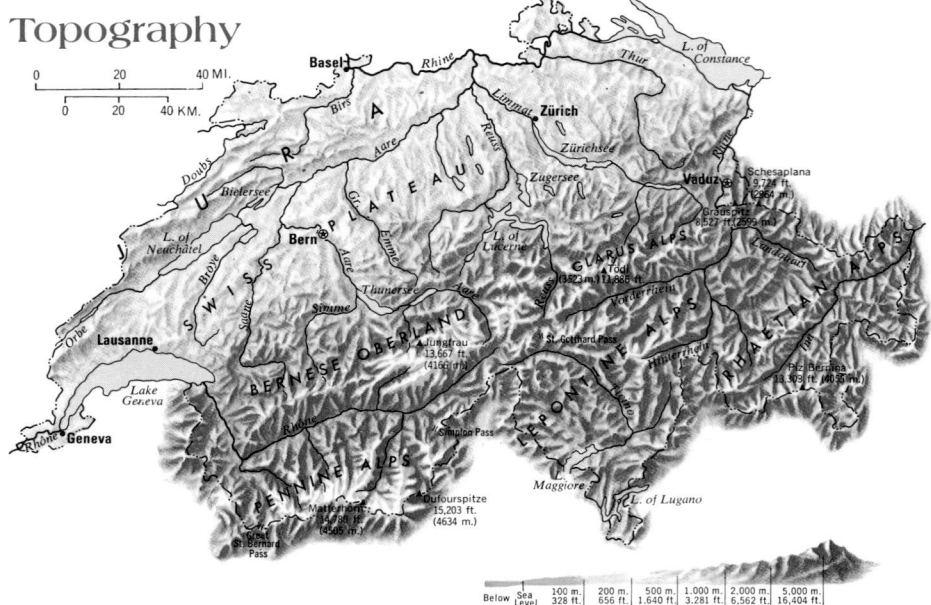

Below Sea Level | 100 m. 328 ft. | 200 m. 656 ft. | 500 m. 1,640 ft. | 1,000 m. 3,281 ft. | 2,000 m. 6,562 ft. | 5,000 m. 16,404 ft.

Switzerland and Liechtenstein

CONIC PROJECTION

SCALE OF MILES

0 5 10 20 30

SCALE OF KILOMETERS

0 5 10 20 30 40 50

Capitals of Countries .... ☆
Capitals of Cantons .... ◉
International Boundaries .... ▬ ▬ ▬
Canals .... ⌁⌁⌁

Scale 1:1,140,000

© Copyright HAMMOND INCORPORATED, Maplewood, N.J.

AUSTRIA

PROVINCES

Burgenland 272,119 .... D3
Carinthia 525,728 .... B3
Lower Austria 1,414,161 .... C2
Salzburg 401,766 .... B3
Styria 1,192,442 .... C3
Tirol 540,771 .... A3
Upper Austria 1,223,444 .... C2
Vienna (city) 1,614,841 .... D2
Vorarlberg 271,473 .... A3

CITIES and TOWNS†

Admont 3,126 .... C3
Allentsteig 2,783 .... C2
Altheim 4,766 .... B2
Althofen 3,886 .... C3
Amstetten 13,330 .... C2
Andau 3,058 .... D3
Arnoldstein 6,740 .... C3
Aspang Markt 2,316 .... D3
Attnang-Puchheim 7,837 .... B2
Bregenz 22,839 .... A3
Baden 22,631 .... D2
Badgastein 5,228 .... B3
Bad Goisern 6,360 .... C3
Bad Hofgastein 5,525 .... B3
Bad Ischl 12,740 .... B3
Bad Leonfelden 2,712 .... C2
Bad Sankt-Leonhard im
  Lavanttal 4,882 .... C3
Berndorf 8,371 .... D2
Bischofshofen 9,417 .... B3
Bludenz 12,050 .... A3
Bramberg am Wildkogel 3,129 .... B3
Braunau am Inn 16,432 .... B2
Bregenz 22,839 .... A3
Bruck an der Leitha 7,506 .... D2
Bruck an der Mur 16,359 .... C3
Deutsch Feistritz 3,820 .... C3
Deutschkreutz 3,673 .... D3
Deutsch Landsberg 6,614 .... C3
Deutsch Wagram 4,481 .... D2
Dornbirn 33,810 .... A3
Ebenfurth 2,272 .... D2
Ebensee 9,413 .... B3
Eferding 3,014 .... C2
Eggenburg 3,730 .... C2
Ehrwald 2,198 .... A3

Horn 6,264 .... C2
Hüttenberg 3,251 .... C3
Imst 5,855 .... A3
Innsbruck 115,800 .... A3
Innsbruck* 167,200 .... A3
Jenbach 5,868 .... A3
Jennersdorf 4,210 .... D3
Judenburg 11,346 .... C3
Kapfenberg 26,001 .... C3
Kappl 2,156 .... A3
Kaprun 2,604 .... B3
Kindberg 6,128 .... C3
Kirchdorf an der Krems 3,471 .... C3
Kitzbühel 7,995 .... B3
Klagenfurt 74,326 .... C3
Klagenfurt* 112,600 .... C3
Klosterneuburg 21,912 .... D2
Knittelfeld 14,517 .... C3
Köflach 12,612 .... C3
Königswiesen 2,921 .... C2
Korneuburg 8,892 .... D2
Kössen 2,764 .... B3
Kötschach-Mauthen 3,740 .... B3
Krems an der Donau 21,733 .... C2
Kufstein 12,766 .... A3
Kundl 3,020 .... A3
Laa an der Thaya 5,455 .... D2
Laakirchen 7,664 .... B3
Lambach 3,301 .... C2
Landeck 7,288 .... A3
Längenfeld 2,838 .... A3
Langenlois 4,957 .... C2
Langenwang 4,071 .... C3
Lavamünd 4,120 .... C3
Leibnitz 6,681 .... C3
Lenzing 5,385 .... B3
Leoben 35,153 .... C3
Lienz 11,696 .... B3
Liezen 6,244 .... C3
Lilienfeld 3,126 .... C3
Linz 205,700 .... C2
Linz* 356,500 .... C2
Lustenau 15,239 .... A3
Mannersdorf am
  Leithagebirge 4,012 .... D3
Marchegg 2,678 .... D2
Mariazell 2,298 .... C3
Matrei in Osttirol 4,003 .... B3
Mattersburg 5,417 .... D3
Mattighofen 4,344 .... B2
Mauerkirchen 2,237 .... B2
Mautern in Steiermark 2,536 .... C3

Sankt Valentin 8,715 .... C2
Sankt Veit an der Glan 11,047 .... C3
Scheibbs 4,419 .... C2
Schärding 5,874 .... B2
Schladming 3,460 .... B3
Schrems 3,393 .... C2
Schruns 3,607 .... A3
Schwarzach im Pongau 3,616 .... B3
Schwaz 10,253 .... A3
Schwechat 14,997 .... D2
Schwertberg 3,881 .... C2
Sierning 4,610 .... C2
Sillian 1,988 .... B3
Solbad Hall in Tirol 12,335 .... A3
Spital am Pyhrn 2,315 .... C3
Spittal an der Drau 13,690 .... B3
Steinach 2,696 .... A3
Steyr 40,578 .... C2
Stockerau 12,634 .... C2
Strassburg 2,850 .... C3
Tamsweg 5,060 .... B3
Telfs 6,589 .... A3
Ternitz 10,287 .... D3
Traiskirchen 8,878 .... D2
Traun 20,843 .... C2
Trieben 4,639 .... C3
Trofaiach 8,731 .... C3
Tulln 7,705 .... C2
Velden am Wörthersee 7,306 .... C3
Vienna (cap.) 1,700,000 .... D2
Vienna* 1,858,700 .... D2
Villach 50,979 .... B3
Vöcklabruck 10,627 .... B2
Voitsberg 11,094 .... C3
Völkermarkt 10,772 .... C3
Vorderberg 2,508 .... C3
Waidhofen an der Thaya 4,200 .... C2
Waidhofen an der Ybbs 5,218 .... C3
Weitensfeld-Flattnitz 5,206 .... C3
Weitra 3,250 .... C2
Weiz 8,241 .... C3
Wels 47,279 .... C2
Weyer Markt 2,518 .... C3
Wien (Vienna) (cap.) 1,700,000 .... D2
Wiener Neustadt 34,774 .... D3
Wildon 2,002 .... C3
Wilhelmsburg 5,417 .... C3
Wolfsberg 31,176 .... C3
Wörgl 7,811 .... A3
Ybbs an der Donau 6,422 .... C2

Zams 3,120 .... A3
Zell am See 7,456 .... B3
Zell am Ziller 1,882 .... A3
Zeltweg 8,431 .... C3
Zirl 4,157 .... A3
Zistersdorf 3,412 .... D2
Zwettl-Niederösterreich 11,624 .... C2

OTHER FEATURES

Allgäu Alps (mts.) A3
Bavarian Alps (mts.) A3
Bodensee (Constance) (lake) A3
Brenner (pass) A3
Carnic Alps (mts.) B3
Constance (lake) A3
Danube (riv.) C2
Donau (Danube) (riv.) C3
Drau (riv.) B3
Enns (riv.) C3
Grossglockner (mt.) B3
Hohe Tauern (range) B3
Inn (riv.) B2
Karawanken (range) C3
March (riv.) D2
Mühlviertel (reg.) C2
Mur (riv.) C3
Neusiedler (lake) D3
Niedere Tauern (range) B3
Ötztal Alps (mts.) A3
Raab (riv.) C3
Rhine (riv.) A3
Salzach (riv.) B2
Salzkammergut (reg.) B3
Semmering (pass) C3
Thaya (riv.) C2
Traun (riv.) C2
Wildspitze (mt.) A3
Zugspitze (mt.) A3

CZECHOSLOVAKIA

REPUBLICS

Czech Socialist Rep. 9,964,338 .... B1
Slovak Socialist Rep. 4,670,409 .... E2

REGIONS

Bratislava (city) 333,000 .... D2
Jihočeský 662,002 .... D2
Jihomoravský 1,966,850 .... D2
Praha (city) 1,161,200 .... C1

Severočeský 1,122,035 .... C1
Severomoravský 1,849,286 .... D2
Středočeský 1,193,041 .... C2
Středoslovenský 1,436,351 .... E2
Východočeský 1,214,581 .... D2
Východoslovenský 1,298,481 .... F2
Západočeský 865,094 .... D2
Západoslovenský 1,610,542 .... D2

CITIES and TOWNS

Aš 120,000 .... B1
Austerlitz (Slavkov) D2
Bánovce nad Bebravou 11,400 .... E2
Banská Bystrica 53,000 .... E2
Banská Štiavnica 7,486 .... E2
Bardejov 17,400 .... F2
Benešov 11,100 .... C2
Beroun 17,600 .... C2
Bílina 17,800 .... B1
Blansko 13,800 .... D2
Boskovice 8,531 .... D2
Brandýs nad Labem-Stará
  Boleslav 333,000 .... C1
Bratislava 333,000 .... D2
Břeclav 21,100 .... D2
Brezno 14,800 .... E2
Brno 335,700 .... D2
Broumov 7,782 .... D1
Bruntál 12,300 .... D2
Bystřice nad
  Pernštejnem 6,471 .... D2
Bytča 6,922 .... E2

Čadca 16,800 .... E2
Čáslav 10,200 .... C2
Česká Lípa 18,600 .... C1
Česká Třebová 14,700 .... D2
České Budějovice 80,800 .... C2
Český Brod 6,640 .... C2
Český Krumlov 12,000 .... C2
Cheb 27,000 .... B1
Chomutov 44,200 .... B1
Chotěboř 6,692 .... D2
Chrudim 18,800 .... D2
Detva 13,100 .... E2
Dobříš 6,378 .... C2
Dobruška 5,779 .... D1
Dolný Kubín 9,900 .... E2
Domažlice 9,100 .... B2
Dubnica nad Váhom 11,300 .... E2
Duchcov 9,712 .... B1
Dunajská Streda 13,000 .... D3
Dvory nad Žitavou 5,847 .... E3
Dvůr Králové nad
  Labem 16,800 .... D1
Falknov (Sokolov) 23,900 .... B1
Fiľakovo 7,822 .... E2
Frýdek-Místek 43,800 .... E2
Frýdlant v.
  Čechách 5,948 .... C1

Frýdlant nad
  Ostravicí 6,250 .... E2
Galanta 12,300 .... D2
Gottwaldov 84,300 .... D2
Handlová 16,200 .... E2
Havířov 85,000 .... E2
Havlíčkův Brod 19,200 .... D2
Hlinsko 8,890 .... D2
Hlohovec 15,200 .... D2
Hlučín 15,300 .... E2
Hodonín 22,600 .... D2
Holešov 9,091 .... D2
Holíč 7,602 .... D2
Holice 6,151 .... D2
Horažďovice C2
Hořice v.
  Podkrkonoší 7,715 .... D1
Horná Štubňa E2
Horní Benešov D2
Horní Lištná E2
Hořovice 5,665 .... C2
Horšovský Týn B2
Hostinné D1
Hradec Králové 85,600 .... C1
Hranice 13,300 .... D2
Hrinová 7,800 .... E2
Hronov 9,767 .... D1
Hrušovany D2
Humenné 22,200 .... F2
Humpolec 7,810 .... D2
Hurbanovo E3
Hustopeče D2
Ilava E2
Ivančice 7,314 .... D2

Topography

Eisenerz 11,563 .... C3
Eisenkappel-Vellach 3,761 .... C3
Eisenstadt 10,059 .... D3
Enns 9,622 .... C2
Feldbach 3,887 .... C3
Feldkirch 21,214 .... A3
Feldkirchen in
  Kärnten 11,188 .... B3
Ferlach 7,621 .... C3
Fieberbrunn 3,651 .... B3
Fohnsdorf 11,169 .... C3
Frankenmarkt 2,960 .... B3
Frauenkirchen 2,749 .... D3
Freistadt 5,956 .... C2
Freidberg 2,504 .... C3
Friesach 7,257 .... C3
Frohnleiten 5,081 .... C3
Fulpmes 2,553 .... A3
Fürstenfeld 6,054 .... C3
Gaming 4,181 .... C3
Gänserndorf 4,211 .... D2
Gleisdorf 4,921 .... C3
Gloggnitz 7,178 .... C3
Gmünd, Carinthia 2,267 .... B3
Gmünd, Lower Austria 6,323 .... C2
Gmunden 12,270 .... B3
Golling an der Salzach 3,089 .... B3
Götzis 7,931 .... A3
Gratwein 2,747 .... C3
Graz 251,900 .... C3
Graz* 314,200 .... C3
Grein 2,767 .... C2
f2Griesskirchen 4,519 .... B2
Grosssiegharts 3,288 .... C2
Grünburg 3,775 .... C2
Güssing 3,675 .... D3
Haag 5,060 .... C2
Hainburg an der Donau 6,009 .... D2
Hainfeld 3,897 .... C3
Hallein 14,371 .... B3
Hallstatt 1,303 .... B3
Hartberg 5,702 .... C3
Haslach an der Mühl 2,636 .... C2
Heidenreichstein 4,340 .... C2
Heiligenblut 1,324 .... B3
Hermagor-Presseggersee 7,531 .... B3
Herzogenburg 7,299 .... C2
Hohenau an der March 3,591 .... D2
Hohenberg 2,016 .... C3
Hohenems 11,487 .... A3
Hollabrunn 6,563 .... C2
Hopfgarten in Nordtirol 4,784 .... B3

Mauthausen 4,419 .... C2
Mauthen-Kötschach 3,750 .... B3
Mayrhofen 3,174 .... A3
Melk 5,108 .... C2
Mistelbach an der Zaya 6,306 .... D2
Mittersill 4,361 .... B3
Mödling 18,712 .... D2
Mondsee 2,141 .... B3
Murau 2,710 .... C3
Mürzzuschlag 11,564 .... C3
Neuberg an der Mürz 2,183 .... C3
Neumarkt am Wallersee 3,267 .... B3
Neunkirchen 10,922 .... D3
Neusiedl am See 3,999 .... D3
Neustift im Stubaital 2,789 .... A3
Ober Grafendorf 4,109 .... C2
Oberndorf bei Salzburg 3,293 .... B3
Obervellach 2,426 .... B3
Oberwart 5,661 .... D3
Paternion 5,805 .... B3
Perg 4,872 .... C2
Peuerbach 2,161 .... B2
Pfunds 2,043 .... A3
Pinkafeld 4,610 .... D3
Pöchlarn 3,199 .... C2
Pörtschach am
  Wörthersee 2,511 .... C3
Poysdorf 5,714 .... D2
Pregarten 3,249 .... C2
Raabs an der Thaya 4,194 .... C2
Radenthein 6,847 .... B3
Radkersburg 2,000 .... C3
Radstadt 3,585 .... B3
Rankweil 8,440 .... A3
Rechnitz 3,412 .... D3
Reichenau an der Rax 4,053 .... C3
Retz 4,780 .... C2
Ried im Innkreis 10,534 .... B2
Rottenmann 4,781 .... C3
Saalfelden am Steinernen
  Meer 10,172 .... B3
Salzburg 122,100 .... B3
Salzburg* 213,430 .... B3
Sankt Aegyd am Neuwalde 3,165 .... C3
Sankt Anton am Arlberg 2,086 .... A3
Sankt Johann in Tirol 5,942 .... B3
Sankt Michael im Lungau 2,839 .... B3
Sankt Michael in
  Obersteiermark 3,717 .... C3
Sankt Michael im Lungau 2,839 .... C3
Sankt Paul im Lavanttal 6,721 .... C3
Sankt Pölten 43,300 .... C2

AREA 32,375 sq. mi. (83,851 sq. km.)
POPULATION 7,507,000
CAPITAL Vienna
LARGEST CITY Vienna
HIGHEST POINT Grossglockner
   12,457 ft. (3,797 m.)
MONETARY UNIT schilling
MAJOR LANGUAGE German
MAJOR RELIGION Roman Catholicism

AREA 49,373 sq. mi. (127,876 sq. km.)
POPULATION 15,276,799
CAPITAL Prague
LARGEST CITY Prague
HIGHEST POINT Gerlachovka 8,707 ft.
   (2,654 m.)
MONETARY UNIT koruna
MAJOR LANGUAGES Czech, Slovak
MAJOR RELIGIONS Roman Catholicism,
   Protestantism

AREA 35,919 sq. mi. (93,030 sq. km.)
POPULATION 10,709,536
CAPITAL Budapest
LARGEST CITY Budapest
HIGHEST POINT Kékes 3,330 ft.
   (1,015 m.)
MONETARY UNIT forint
MAJOR LANGUAGE Hungarian
MAJOR RELIGIONS Roman Catholicism,
   Protestantism

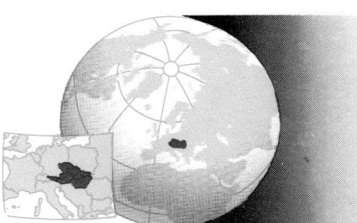

AUSTRIA

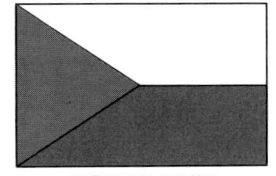

CZECHOSLOVAKIA

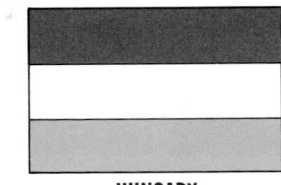

HUNGARY

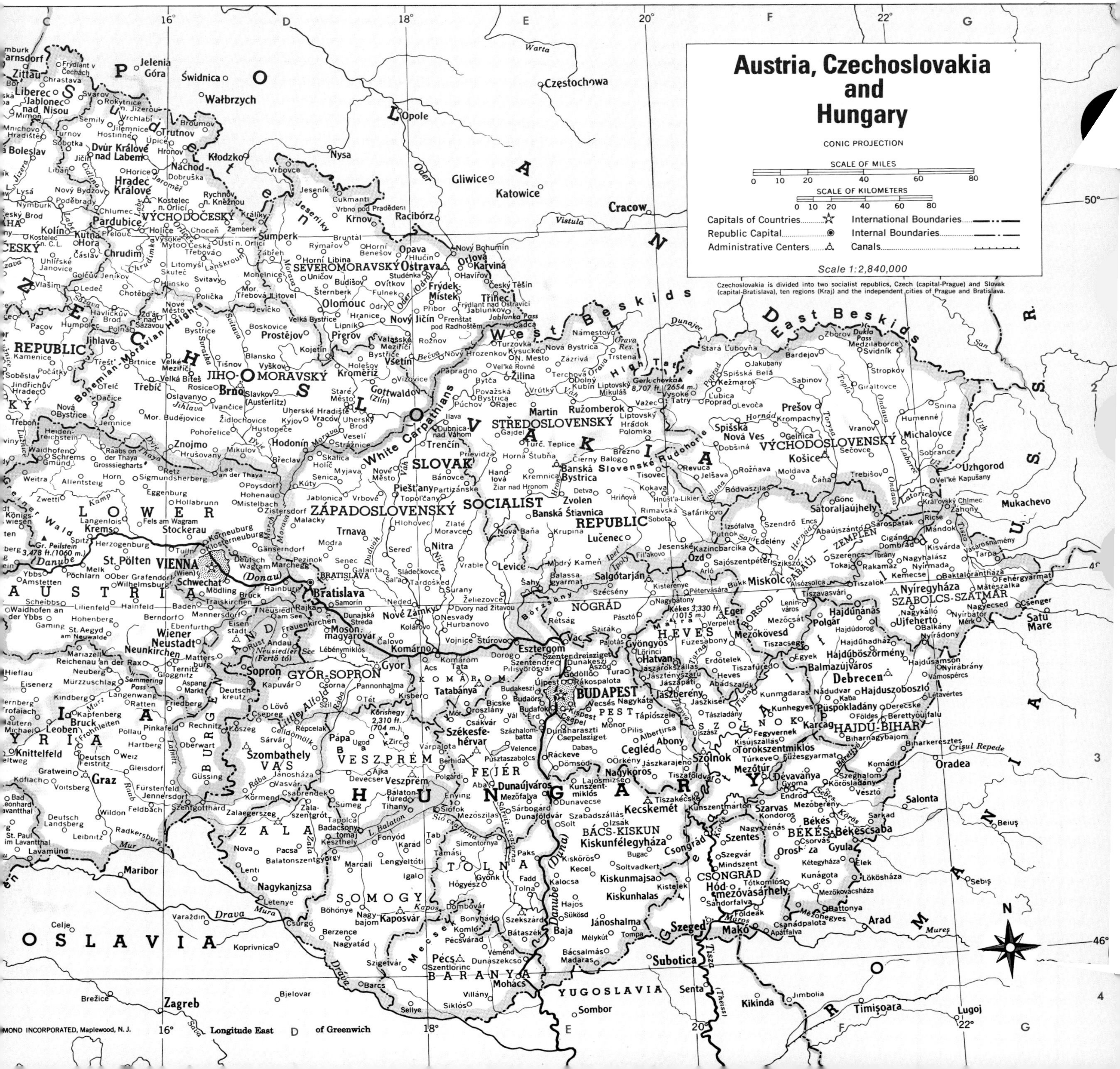

Austria, Czechoslovakia and Hungary

CONIC PROJECTION

SCALE OF MILES
0   10   20   40   60   80

SCALE OF KILOMETERS
0 10 20   40   60   80

Capitals of Countries.........☆   International Boundaries........
Republic Capital...............◉   Internal Boundaries...........
Administrative Centers........⌂   Canals......................

Scale 1:2,840,000

Czechoslovakia is divided into two socialist republics, Czech (capital-Prague) and Slovak
(capital-Bratislava), ten regions (Kraj) and the independent cities of Prague and Bratislava.

MOND INCORPORATED, Maplewood, N.J.   16°   **Longitude East**   D   of Greenwich   18°   E   20°   F   22°   G

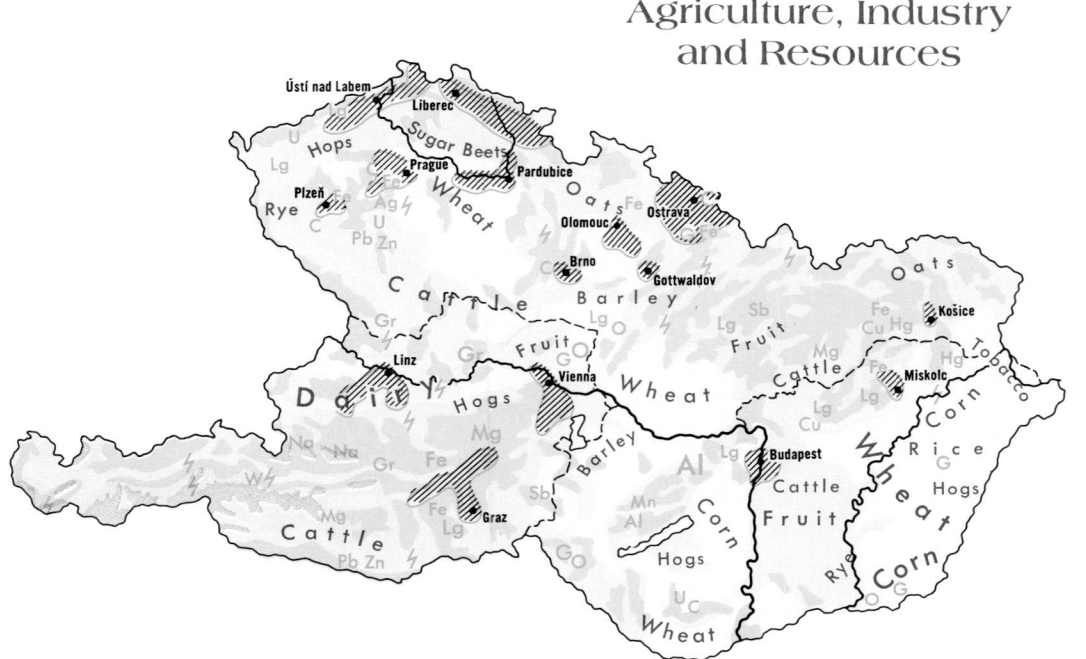

Agriculture, Industry and Resources

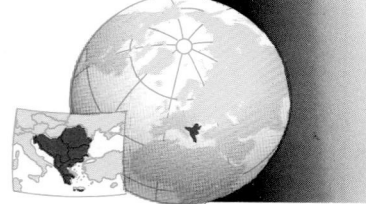

YUGOSLAVIA

AREA 98,766 sq. mi. (255,804 sq. km.)
POPULATION 22,471,000
CAPITAL Belgrade
LARGEST CITY Belgrade
HIGHEST POINT Triglav 9,393 ft. (2,863 m.)
MONETARY UNIT Yugoslav dinar
MAJOR LANGUAGES Serbo-Croatian, Slovenian, Macedonian, Montenegrin, Albanian
MAJOR RELIGIONS Eastern Orthodoxy, Roman Catholicism, Islam

ALBANIA

AREA 11,100 sq. mi. (28,749 sq. km.)
POPULATION 2,590,600
CAPITAL Tiranë
LARGEST CITY Tiranë
HIGHEST POINT Korab 9,026 ft. (2,751 m.)
MONETARY UNIT lek
MAJOR LANGUAGE Albanian
MAJOR RELIGIONS Islam, Eastern Orthodoxy, Roman Catholicism

ROMANIA

AREA 91,699 sq. mi. (237,500 sq. km.)
POPULATION 22,048,305
CAPITAL Bucharest
LARGEST CITY Bucharest
HIGHEST POINT Moldoveanul 8,343 ft. (2,543 m.)
MONETARY UNIT leu
MAJOR LANGUAGES Romanian, Hungarian
MAJOR RELIGION Eastern Orthodoxy

BULGARIA

AREA 42,823 sq. mi. (110,912 sq. km.)
POPULATION 8,862,000
CAPITAL Sofia
LARGEST CITY Sofia
HIGHEST POINT Musala 9,597 ft. (2,925 m.)
MONETARY UNIT lev
MAJOR LANGUAGE Bulgarian
MAJOR RELIGION Eastern Orthodoxy

GREECE

AREA 50,944 sq. mi. (131,945 sq. km.)
POPULATION 9,599,000
CAPITAL Athens
LARGEST CITY Athens
HIGHEST POINT Olympus 9,570 ft. (2,917 m.)
MONETARY UNIT drachma
MAJOR LANGUAGE Greek
MAJOR RELIGION Eastern (Greek) Orthodoxy

BULGARIA

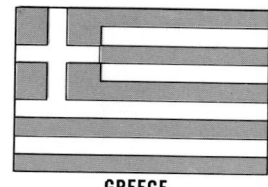

GREECE

YUGOSLAVIA

ALBANIA

ROMANIA

Agriculture, Industry and Resources

DOMINANT LAND USE

- Cereals (chiefly wheat, corn)
- Mixed Farming, Horticulture
- Pasture Livestock
- Tobacco, Cotton
- Grapes, Wine
- Forests
- Nonagricultural Land

MAJOR MINERAL OCCURRENCES

Ab	Asbestos	Mg	Magnesium
Ag	Silver	Mn	Manganese
Al	Bauxite	Mr	Marble
C	Coal	Na	Salt
Cr	Chromium	Ni	Nickel
Cu	Copper	O	Petroleum
Fe	Iron Ore	Pb	Lead
G	Natural Gas	Sb	Antimony
Hg	Mercury	U	Uranium
Lg	Lignite	Zn	Zinc

⚡ Water Power
▨ Major Industrial Areas

(continued on following page)

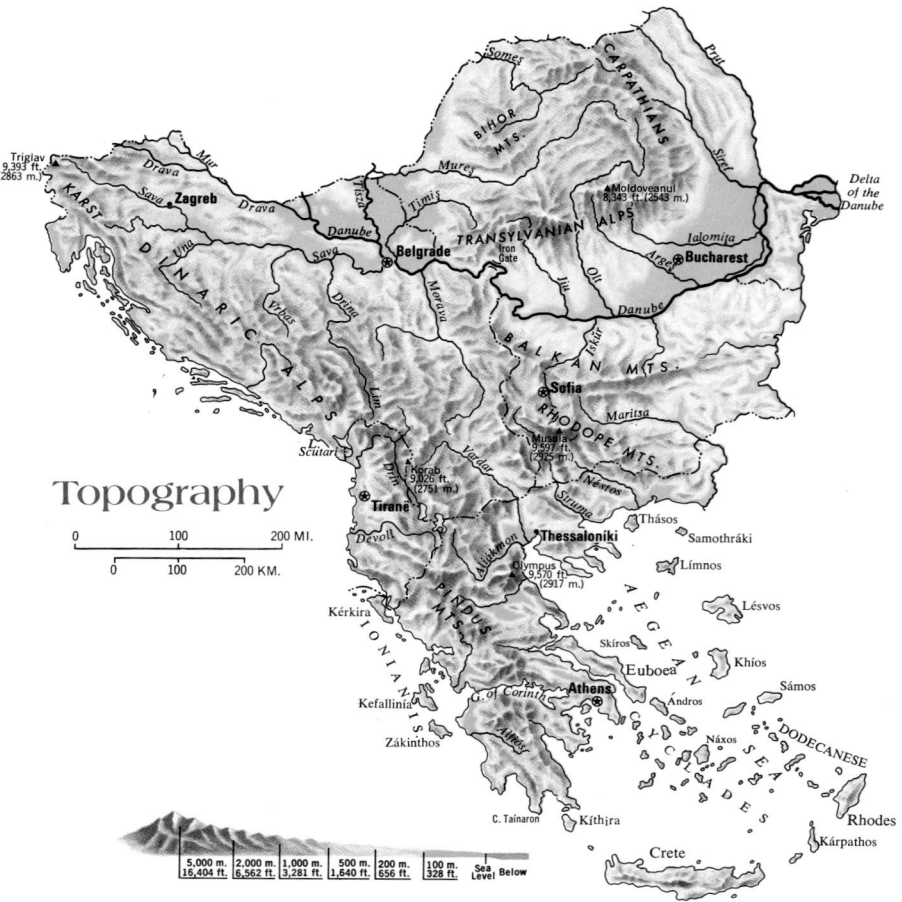

Topography

```
0      100      200 MI.
0    100    200 KM.
```

```
5,000 m.   2,000 m.   1,000 m.   500 m.   200 m.   100 m.   Sea
16,404 ft.  6,562 ft.  3,281 ft.  1,640 ft.  656 ft.  328 ft.  Level   Below
```

The Balkan States

CONIC PROJECTION

SCALE OF MILES

0 25 50 75 100 125 150 175

SCALE OF KILOMETERS

0 25 50 75 100 125 150 175

Capitals of Countries — ☆
Administrative Centers — △
International Boundaries — —·—·—
Major Internal Boundaries — —··—··—
Minor Internal Boundaries — ········
Canals — —·—·—

Scale 1 : 6,150,000

BULGARIA and GREECE are divided into counties and departments, respectively. Because of the scale no attempt has been made to delimit and name these sub-divisions; their administrative centers have, however, been designated.

The larger divisions named in Greece are well-known geographical regions, without administrative function.

ROMANIA consists of thirty-nine counties and three cities of regional status, Bucharest, Constanța and Petroșeni. Scale does not permit delimiting these counties.

ALBANIA is divided into twenty-seven districts. Scale does not permit the delimitation of these divisions.

YUGOSLAVIA is a federation of six republics. The Serbian republic includes an autonomous province (Vojvodina), and an autonomous region (Kosovo).

© Copyright HAMMOND INCORPORATED, Maplewood, N. J.

Topography

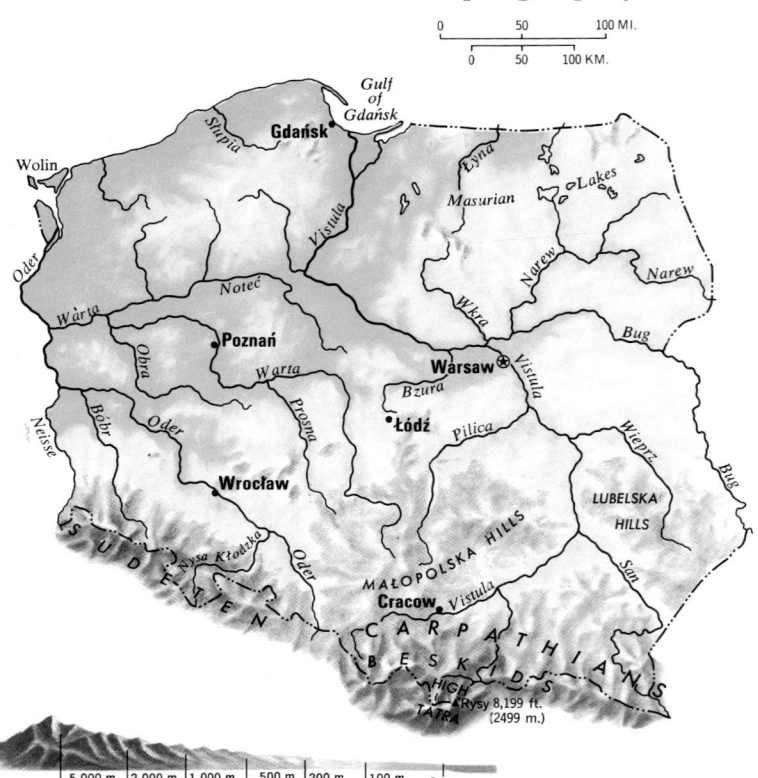

0 50 100 MI.
0 50 100 KM.

5,000 m. 2,000 m. 1,000 m. 500 m. 200 m. 100 m. Sea Below
16,404 ft. 6,562 ft. 3,281 ft. 1,640 ft. 656 ft. 328 ft. Level

Rysy 8,199 ft. (2499 m.)

Agriculture, Industry and Resources

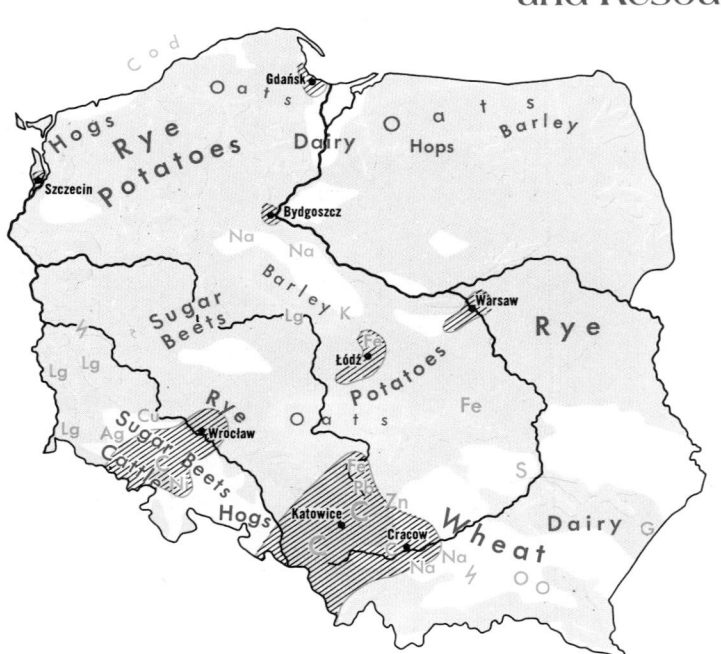

MAJOR MINERAL OCCURRENCES

Ag Silver
C Coal
Cu Copper
Fe Iron Ore
G Natural Gas
K Potash
Lg Lignite

Na Salt
Ni Nickel
O Petroleum
Pb Lead
S Sulfur
Zn Zinc

 Water Power
Major Industrial Areas

DOMINANT LAND USE

Cereals (chiefly wheat)

Rye, Oats, Barley, Potatoes

General Farming, Livestock

Forests

Poland 1938

0 50 100 MILES

Poland 1945

0 50 100 MILES

AREA 120,725 sq. mi. (312,678 sq. km.)
POPULATION 35,815,000
CAPITAL Warsaw
LARGEST CITY Warsaw
HIGHEST POINT Rysy 8,199 ft.
(2,499 m.)
MONETARY UNIT zloty
MAJOR LANGUAGE Polish
MAJOR RELIGION Roman Catholicism

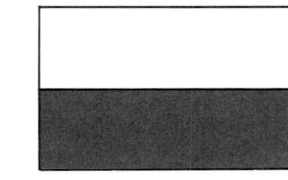

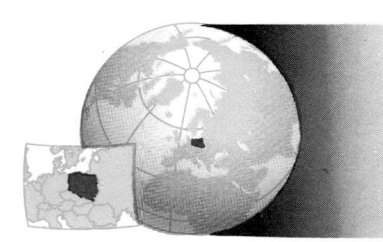

Braniewo 12.100	D1
Breslau (Wrocław) 461.900	C3
Brieg (Brzeg) 30.780	C3
Brodnica 17.300	D2
Brzeg 30.780	C3
Brzesko 9.701	E4
Busko Zdrój 11.100	E3
Bydgoszcz 280.460	C2
Bytom 186.993	A3
Bytów 10.642	C1
Chełm 38.789	F3
Chełmno 17.906	C2
Chełmza 14.200	C2
Chodzież 14.100	C2
Chojnice 23.500	C2
Chojnów 11.000	B3
Chorzów 151.338	B4
Choszczno 9.800	B2
Chrzanów 28.500	E4
Ciechanów 29.300	E2
Cieplice	
Śląskie-Zdrój 15.400	B3
Cieszyn 25.234	D4
Cracow 651.300	E4
Czechowice-Dziedzice 25.400	D4
Częstochowa 187.613	D3
Dąbrowa Górnicza 61.660	B3
Danzig (Gdańsk) 364.285	C1
Darłowo 11.200	C1
Dębica 22.900	E4
Dęblin 14.600	E3
Dębno 10.700	B2
Działdowo 10.100	E2
Dzierżoniów 32.800	C3
Elbing (Elbląg) 89.835	D1
Ełk 27.188	F2
Gdańsk 364.285	C1
Gdynia 190.125	D1
Giżycko 18.200	E1
Gleiwitz (Gliwice) 170.912	A4
Głogów (Głogau) 20.226	C3
Głowno 12.800	D3
Głubczyce 11.300	C3
Głuchołazy 13.200	C3
Gniezno 50.643	C2
Golenów 14.600	B2
Gorlice 15.200	E4
Gorzów Wielkopolski 74.267	B2
Gostyń 13.000	C3
Gostynin 12.000	D2
Grajewo 11.200	F2
Grodzisk Mazowiecki 20.400	E2
Grójec 10.300	E3
Grudziądz 75.511	D2
Grünberg (Zielona	
Góra) 59.700	B3
Gryfice 13.200	B2
Gubin (Guben) 14.600	B3
Hajnowka m4.345	F2
Hindenburg (Zabrze) 199.400	A4
Hirschberg (Jelenia	
Góra) 55.720	B3
Hrubieszów 14.999	F3
Iława 16.400	D2
Inowrocław 54.817	D2

Jarocin 18.100	C3
Jarosław 29.000	F4
Jasło 17.025	E4
Jastrzębie Zdrój 34.400	D3
Jaworzno 63.271	B4
Jędrzejów 13.264	E3
Jelenia Góra 55.720	B3
Kalisz 81.227	D3
Kamienna Góra 21.000	B3
Kartuzy 10.558	C1
Katowice 303.264	B4
Kędzierzyn-Koźle 45.600	C3
Kępno 10.151	C3
Kętrzyn 19.300	E1
Kielce 125.952	E3
Kłobuck 12.600	D3
Kłodzko 26.000	C3
Kluczbork 18.000	C3
Knurów 28.400	A4
Kolberg (Kołobrzeg) 25.419	B1
Koło 13.100	D2
Kołobrzeg 25.419	B1
Końskie 13.100	E3
Konstantynów	
Łódzki 12.800	D3
Kościan 18.700	C3
Kościerzyna 18.914	C1
Köslin (Koszalin) 64.414	C1
Kostrzyn 11.200	B2
Koszalin 64.414	C1
Kraków (Cracow) 651.300	E4
Krapkowice 13.800	D3
Kraśnik Fabryczny 14.600	E3
Krasnystaw 12.495	F3
Krosno 26.500	E4
Krotoszyn 21.900	C3
Krynica 11.000	E4
Küstrin 11.200	B2
Kutno 30.000	D2
Kwidzin 23.104	D2
Łańcut 12.049	F3
Landsberg (Gorzów	
Wielkopolski) 74.267	B2
Łaziska Górne 10.800	A4
Lębork 25.000	C1
Łęczyca 13.900	D2
Legionowo 20.800	E2
Legnica 75.843	C3
Leszczyny 12.200	A4
Leszno 33.890	C3
Libiąż 10.600	D3
Lidzbark Warmiński 12.900	E1
Liegnitz (Legnica) 75.843	C3
Lipno 10.900	D2
Łódź 777.800	D3
Łomża 25.500	F2
Łowicz 20.400	D2
Lubań 17.200	B3
Lubartów 10.000	F3
Lubin 28.400	C3
Lublin 235.937	F3
Lubliniec 19.800	C3
Luboń 16.400	C2
Lubsko 12.600	B3
Łuków 15.500	F3
Piekary Śląskie 36.300	B4
Piła 43.778	C2

Międzyrzec Podlaski 13.500	F3
Międzyrzecz 14.900	B2
Mielec 21.300	E3
Mikołów 21.300	B4
Mińsk Mazowiecki 24.200	E2
Mława 20.007	E2
Mońki 9.560	F2
Morąg 9.681	E2
Mrągowo 13.400	E2
Myślenice 12.100	E4
Mysłowice 44.737	C4
Myszków 18.000	D3
Nakło nad Notecią 16.800	C2
Namysłów 11.076	C3
Neisse (Nysa) 31.837	C3
Nidzica 9.642	E2
Nisko 10.000	E3
Nowa Ruda 18.100	C3
Nowa Sól 33.300	B3
Nowy Dwór Mazowiecki 16.900	E2
Nowy Sącz 41.103	E4
Nowy Targ 21.900	E4
Nysa 31.837	C3
Oborniki 10.200	C2
Oława 17.746	C3
Olecko 9.600	F1
Oleśnica 27.500	C3
Olkusz 15.800	D3
Olsztyn 94.119	E2
Opoczno 12.168	E3
Opole 86.510	C3
Oppeln 86.510	C3
Orzesze 9.600	A4
Ostróda 21.300	D2
Ostrołęka 21.981	E2
Ostrów Mazowiecka 15.000	E2
Ostrów Wielkopolski 49.530	C3
Ostrowiec	
Świętokrzyski 49.958	E3
Oświęcim 41.000	D3
Otwock 39.863	E2
Ozorków 18.100	D2
Pabianice 62.275	D3

Pionki 13.600	E3
Piotrków Trybunalski 59.683	D3
Pleszew 13.348	C3
Płock 71.727	D2
Płońsk 11.619	E2
Police 12.700	B2
Poznań 469.085	C2
Prudnik 20.300	C3
Pruszcz Gdański 13.000	D1
Pruszków 42.961	E2
Przasnysz 11.100	E2
Przemyśl 53.228	F4
Puck 9.500	D1
Puławy 34.800	F3
Pułtusk 12.600	E2
Rabka 10.700	E4
Raciborz 40.418	C3
Radom 158.640	E3
Radomsko 31.179	D3
Ratibor (Racibórz) 40.418	C3
Rawa Mazowiecka 9.800	E3
Rawicz 14.100	C3
Ruda Śląska 142.407	B4
Rumia 23.300	D1
Rybnik 43.415	D3
Rypin 10.029	D2
Rzeszów 82.192	F4
Sandomierz 16.800	E3
Sanok 21.600	F4
Schneidemühl (Piła) 36.600	C2
Schweidnitz	
(Świdnica) 47.542	C3
Siedlce 38.983	F2
Siemianowice	
Śląskie 67.278	B4
Sieradz 38.500	D3
Sierpc 12.700	D2
Skarżysko-Kamienna 39.194	E3
Skawina 15.900	D4
Skierniewice 25.590	E2
Sławno 10.700	C1
Słubice 12.000	B2
Słupsk 68.311	C1

Sochaczew 20.500	E2
Sokółka 10.023	F2
Sokół Podolski 9.569	F2
Sopot 47.573	D1
Sosnowiec 144.652	B4
Śrem 15.600	C3
Środa Śląska 10.259	C3
Środa Wielkopolska 14.800	C2
Stalowa Wola 29.768	F3
Starachowice 42.807	E3
Stargard Szczeciński 44.400	B2
Starogard Gdański 33.400	D2
Stary Sącz 57.400	E4
Stettin (Szczecin) 337.294	B2
Stolp (Słupsk) 68.311	C1
Strzegom 14.000	C3
Strzelce Opolskie 14.700	C3
Strzelin 9.800	C3
Sulechów 10.200	B2
Suwałki 25.360	F1
Swarzędz 12.100	C2
Świdnica 47.542	C3
Świdnik 21.900	F3
Świdwin 12.500	B2
Świebodzin 18.500	B3
Świebodzin 14.900	B2
Świętochłowice 57.633	A4
Świnoujście	
(Swinemünde) 27.900	B1
Szamotuły 14.600	C2
Szczecin 337.294	B2
Szczecinek 28.600	C2
Szczytno 17.371	E2
Szprotawa 11.200	B3
Szreniawa 18.800	E4
Tarnów 85.514	E4
Tarnowskie Góry 34.200	A3
Tczew 40.794	D1
Tomaszów Lubelski 12.329	F4
Tomaszów Mazowiecki 54.911	E3
Toruń 129.152	D2
Trzcianka 10.900	C2
Trzebinia-Siersza	C4

Turek 18.500	D2
Tychy 71.384	B4
Ustka 9.900	C1
Wąbrzeźno 11.800	D2
Wadowice 11.700	D4
Wągrowiec 15.600	C2
Wałbrzych 125.048	C3
Wałcz 18.900	C2
Waldenburg	
(Wałbrzych) 125.048	C3
Warsaw (Warszawa)	
(cap.) 1.377.100	E2
Wejherowo 33.600	D1
Wieliczka 13.600	D3
Wieluń 14.300	D3
Wisła 9.800	D4
Włocławek 77.169	D2
Wodzisław Śląski 25.600	D4
Wolin 35.458	B2
Wołomin 24.000	E2
Wołów 10.500	C3
Wrocław 523.318	C3
Września 17.800	C2
Wschowa 10.000	C3
Zabrze 197.214	A4
Ząbkowice Śląskie 13.800	C3
Zagań 21.400	B3
Zakopane 27.039	D4
Zambrów 14.082	F2
Zamość 34.734	F3
Żary 28.300	B3
Zawiercie 39.410	D3
Zduńska Wola 29.066	D3
Zgierz 42.838	D3
Zgorzelec 28.400	B3
Zięice 9.700	C3
Zielona Góra 73.156	B3
Złocieniec 10.100	C2
Złotoryja 12.200	C3
Złotów 11.600	C2
Żnin 9.600	C2
Żyrardów 33.196	E2
Żywiec 22.400	D4

OTHER FEATURES

Baltic (sea)	B1
Beskids (range)	D4
Brda (riv.)	C2
Brynica (riv.)	B3
Bug (riv.)	F2
Danzig (Gdańsk) (gulf)	D1
Dukla (pass)	E4
Dunajec (riv.)	E4
Gwda (riv.)	C2
Hel (pen.)	D1
High Tatra (range)	D4
Kłodnica (riv.)	A4
Lyna (riv.)	E1
Mamry, Jezioro (lake)	E1
Masurian (lakes)	E2
Narew (riv.)	E2
Neisse (riv.)	B3
Noteć (riv.)	C2
Nysa Kłodzka (riv.)	C3
Nysa Łużycka (Neisse)	
(riv.)	B2
Oder (riv.)	B2
Orava (riv.)	D4
Pilica (riv.)	D3
Pomeranian (bay)	B1
Prosna (riv.)	C3
Przemsza (riv.)	B4
Rysy (mt.)	E4
San (riv.)	F3
Słupia (riv.)	C1
Śniardwy, Jezioro (lake)	E2
Sudeten (mts.)	B3
Uznam (Usedom) (isl.)	B1
Vistula (riv.)	D1
Warma (riv.)	D1
Warta (riv.)	D2
Wieprz (riv.)	F3
Wisła (Vistula) (riv.)	D2
Wkra (riv.)	E2
Wolin (Wollin) (isl.)	B2

48

AREA 8,649,490 sq. mi. (22,402,179 sq. km.)
POPULATION 262,436,227
CAPITAL Moscow
LARGEST CITY Moscow
HIGHEST POINT Communism Peak 24,599 ft. (7,498 m.)
MONETARY UNIT ruble
MAJOR LANGUAGES Russian, Ukrainian, White Russian, Uzbek, Azerbaidzhani, Tatar, Georgian, Lithuanian, Armenian, Yiddish, Latvian, Mordvinian, Kirgiz, Tadzhik, Estonian, Kazakh, Moldavian (Romanian), German, Chuvash, Turkmenian, Bashkir
MAJOR RELIGIONS Eastern (Russian) Orthodoxy, Islam, Judaism, Protestantism (Baltic States)

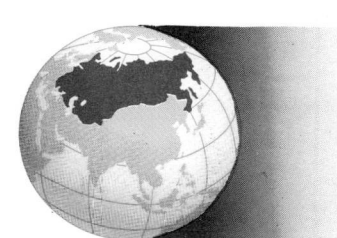

UNION REPUBLICS

	AREA (sq. mi.)	AREA (sq. km.)	POPULATION	CAPITAL and LARGEST CITY
RUSSIAN S.F.S.R.	6,592,812	17,075,400	137,551,000	Moscow 7,831,000
KAZAKH S.S.R.	1,048,300	2,715,100	14,684,000	Alma-Ata 910,000
UKRAINIAN S.S.R.	233,089	603,700	49,755,000	Kiev 2,144,000
TURKMEN S.S.R.	188,455	488,100	2,759,000	Ashkhabad 312,000
UZBEK S.S.R.	173,591	449,600	15,391,000	Tashkent 1,780,000
WHITE RUSSIAN S.S.R.	80,154	207,600	9,560,000	Minsk 1,262,000
KIRGIZ S.S.R.	76,641	198,500	3,529,000	Frunze 533,000
TADZHIK S.S.R.	55,251	143,100	3,801,000	Dushanbe 494,000
AZERBAIDZHAN S.S.R.	33,436	86,600	6,028,000	Baku 1,022,000
GEORGIAN S.S.R.	26,911	69,700	5,015,000	Tbilisi 1,066,000
LITHUANIAN S.S.R.	25,174	65,200	3,398,000	Vilna 481,000
LATVIAN S.S.R.	24,595	63,700	2,521,000	Riga 835,000
ESTONIAN S.S.R.	17,413	45,100	1,466,000	Tallinn 430,000
MOLDAVIAN S.S.R.	13,012	33,700	3,947,000	Kishinev 503,000
ARMENIAN S.S.R.	11,506	29,800	3,031,000	Erivan 1,019,000

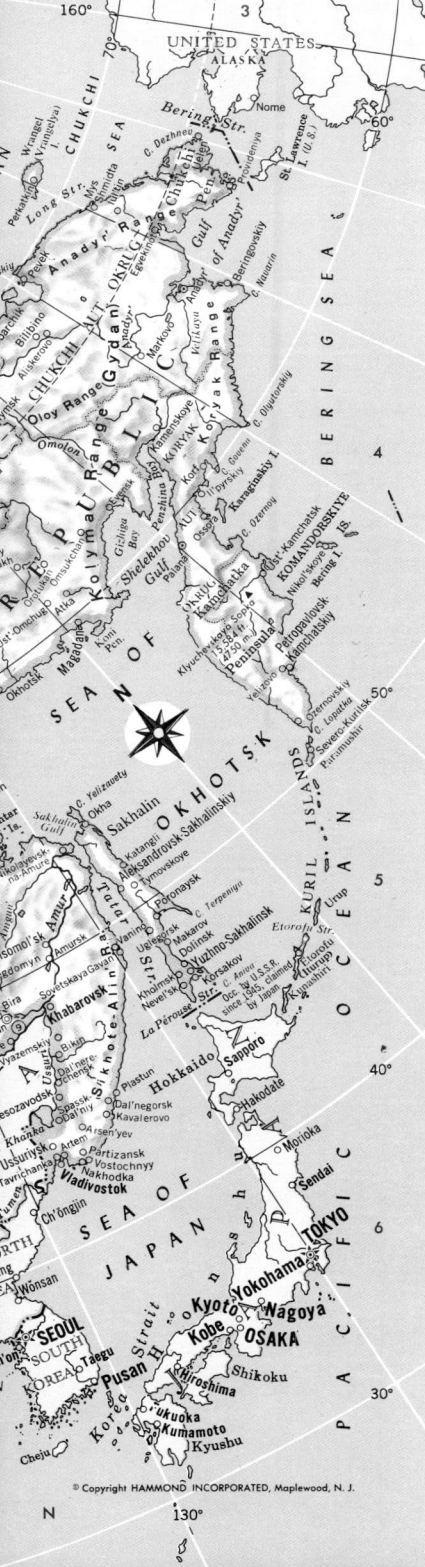

Topography

Nyandoma 23,366 . . . . . E3
Nyurba M3
Obluch'ye 17,000 . . . . . N5
Odessa 1,046,000 . . . . . D5
Okha 30,890 . . . . . P4
Okhotsk P4
Olëkminsk N3
Olënek M3
Omsk 1,014,000 . . . . . H4
Omsukchan Q3
Omutninsk 28,777 . . . . . F4
Onega 25,047 . . . . . D3
Ordzhonikidze 279,000 . . . . . E5
Orel 305,000 . . . . . D4
Orenburg 459,000 . . . . . F4
Orotukan Q3
Orsk 247,000 . . . . . F4
Osh 169,000 . . . . . H5
Ostrogozhsk 29,921 . . . . . D4
Oymyakon O3
Ozernovskiy Q4
Palana 2,735 . . . . . R4
Panfilov 19,173 . . . . . H5
Pärnu 51,000 . . . . . C4
Partizansk 48,345 . . . . . O5
Pavlodar 273,000 . . . . . H4
Pechenga D2
Pechora 56,000 . . . . . F3
Peleduy M4
Penza 483,000 . . . . . E4
Perkatkin T2
Perm' 999,000 . . . . . F4
Pervoural'sk 129,000 . . . . . F4
Petropavlovsk 207,000 . . . . . G4
Petropavlovsk-Kamchatskiy 215,000 . . . . . R4
Petrovsk-Zabaykal'skiy 28,313 . . . . . L4
Petrozavodsk 234,000 . . . . . D3
Pevek S3
Pikol'skiy 32,862 . . . . . G5
Pinsk 90,000 . . . . . C4
Plastun O5
Podol'sk 202,000 . . . . . D4
Pokrovsk N3
Poligus K3
Poltava 279,000 . . . . . D5
Polyarnyy 15,321 . . . . . D3
Ponoy E3
Poronaysk 23,610 . . . . . P5
Prikumsk 35,768 . . . . . E5
Progress 10,000 . . . . . O5
Prokop'yevsk 266,000 . . . . . J4
Provideniya T3
Przheval'sk 51,000 . . . . . H5
Pskov 176,000 . . . . . C4
Pushkin 90,000 . . . . . C4
Raychikhinsk 25,157 . . . . . N5
Riga 835,000 . . . . . C4
Rostov-na-Donau 934,000 . . . . . E5
Rovno 179,000 . . . . . C4
Rubtsovsk 157,000 . . . . . J4
Ruch'i E3
Rudnyy 110,000 . . . . . G4
Ryazan' 453,000 . . . . . E4
Rybach'ye H5
Rybinsk (Andropov) 239,000 . . . . . D4
Rzhev 69,000 . . . . . D4
Saksaul'sky F5
Salekhard 21,929 . . . . . G3
Sal'sk 57,000 . . . . . E5
Samagaltay K4
Samarkand 477,000 . . . . . G6
Sangar N3
Saran' 55,000 . . . . . H5
Saransk 263,000 . . . . . E4
Sarapul 107,000 . . . . . F4
Saratov 856,000 . . . . . E4
Sarkand 18,296 . . . . . J5
Segezha 28,810 . . . . . D3
Semipalatinsk 283,000 . . . . . H4
Serakhs G6
Serov 101,000 . . . . . G4
Serpukhov 140,000 . . . . . D4
Sevastopol' 301,000 . . . . . D5
Severobaykal'sk M4
Severodvinsk 197,000 . . . . . E3
Severo-Kuril'sk 8,000 . . . . . Q4
Severoural'sk 29,880 . . . . . G3
Severo-Yeniseysk K3
Shadrinsk 82,000 . . . . . G4
Shakhtinsk 50,000 . . . . . H5
Shakhty 209,000 . . . . . E5
Shar'ya 25,788 . . . . . E4
Shchuchinsk 40,432 . . . . . H4
Shenkursk E3
Shevchenko 111,000 . . . . . F5
Shilka 16,065 . . . . . M4
Shimanovsk 16,880 . . . . . N4
Shushenskoye 10,000 . . . . . K4
Šiauliai 118,000 . . . . . C4
Siktyakh N3
Simferopol' 302,000 . . . . . D5
Skovorodino 10,000 . . . . . N4
Slavgorod 32,908 . . . . . H4
Slobodskoy 34,374 . . . . . E4
Slyudyanka 20,639 . . . . . L4
Smolensk 276,000 . . . . . D4
Snezhnogorsk J3
Sochi 287,000 . . . . . D5
Sokol 48,253 . . . . . E4
Solikamsk 101,000 . . . . . F3
Sortavala 22,188 . . . . . C3
Sosnogorsk 24,688 . . . . . F3
Sosnovo-Ozerskoye M4
Sovetskaya Gavan' 28,455 . . . . . P5
Spassk-Dal'niy 53,000 . . . . . O5
Srednekolymsk Q3
Sretensk 16,000 . . . . . M4
Stalingrad (Volgograd) 929,000 . . . . . E5
Stavropol' 258,000 . . . . . E5
Stepanakert 30,293 . . . . . E6
Sterlitamak 220,000 . . . . . F4
Strezhevoy H3
Sukhana M3
Sukhumi 114,000 . . . . . D5
Sumy 228,000 . . . . . D4
Suntar M3
Surgut 107,000 . . . . . H3
Susuman 12,000 . . . . . P3
Sverdlovsk 1,211,000 . . . . . F4
Svobodnyy 75,000 . . . . . N4
Syktyvkar 171,000 . . . . . F3
Syzran' 178,000 . . . . . E4
Taganrog 276,000 . . . . . D5
Takhiatash F5
Takhta-Bazar G6
Taksimo M4
Taldy-Kurgan 88,000 . . . . . H5
Talgar 31,273 . . . . . H5
Tallinn 430,000 . . . . . C4
Tambey G2
Tambov 270,000 . . . . . E4
Tara 22,358 . . . . . H4
Tarko-Sale H3
Tartu 105,000 . . . . . C4
Tashauz 84,000 . . . . . F5
Tashkent 1,780,000 . . . . . G5
Tatarsk 29,589 . . . . . H4
Tavda G4
Tayshet 34,232 . . . . . K4
Tazovskiy J3
Tbilisi 1,066,000 . . . . . E5
Tedzhen 25,708 . . . . . F6
Tekeli 29,846 . . . . . H5
Temirtau 213,000 . . . . . H4
Termez 57,000 . . . . . G6
Ternopol' 144,000 . . . . . C5
Tiksi N2
Tobol'sk 62,000 . . . . . G4
Togliatti (Tol'yatti) 502,000 . . . . . F4
Tokmak 59,000 . . . . . H5

Tommot 8,000 . . . . . N4
Tomsk 421,000 . . . . . J4
Tot'ma E4
Troitsk 88,000 . . . . . G4
Tselinograd 234,000 . . . . . H4
Tskhinvali 30,311 . . . . . E5
Tula 514,000 . . . . . D4
Tulun 52,000 . . . . . L4
Tura 3,528 . . . . . L3
Turan K4
Turgay G5
Turkestan 67,000 . . . . . G5
Tynda N4
Tyumen' 359,000 . . . . . G4
Uelen T3
Ufa 969,000 . . . . . F4
Uglegorsk 17,921 . . . . . P5
Ukhta 87,000 . . . . . F3
Ulan-Ude 300,000 . . . . . L4
Ul'yanovsk 464,000 . . . . . E4
Ural'sk 167,000 . . . . . F4
Uray 17,385 . . . . . G3
Urgench 100,000 . . . . . G5
Ushtobe 24,484 . . . . . H5
Usol'ye-Sibirskoye 103,000 . . . . . L4
Ussuriysk 147,000 . . . . . O5
Ust'-Ilimsk 69,000 . . . . . L4
Ustinov 549,000 . . . . . F4
Ust'-Kamchatsk 10,000 . . . . . R4
Ust'-Kamenogorsk 274,000 . . . . . J5
Ust'-Kut 50,000 . . . . . L4
Ust'-Kuyga O3
Ust'-Maya O3
Ust'-Nera P3
Ust'-Omchug P3
Ust'-Olenëk M2
Ust'-Ordynskiy 10,693 . . . . . L4
Ust'-Port J2
Vanavara L3
Vanino 15,401 . . . . . P5
Velikiye Luki 102,000 . . . . . D4
Velikiy Ustyug 36,737 . . . . . E3
Vel'sk 21,899 . . . . . E3
Ventspils 40,467 . . . . . B4
Verkhnevilyuysk N3
Verkniy At-Uryakh Q3
Verkhoyansk 2,000 . . . . . N3
Vilna (Vilnius) 481,000 . . . . . C4
Vilyuysk N3
Vinnitsa 314,000 . . . . . C5
Vitebsk 297,000 . . . . . D4
Vitimskiy M4
Vladimir 296,000 . . . . . D4
Vladivostok 550,000 . . . . . O5
Volgograd 929,000 . . . . . E5
Volochanka K2
Vologda 237,000 . . . . . E4
Vorkuta 100,000 . . . . . G3
Voronezh 783,000 . . . . . E4
Voroshilovgrad 463,000 . . . . . E5
Vostochnyy O5
Votkinsk 90,000 . . . . . F4
Voy-Vozh 10,000 . . . . . F3
Vyazemskiy 18,365 . . . . . O5
Vyborg 76,000 . . . . . C3
Vyshniy Volochek 72,000 . . . . . D4
Yakutsk 152,000 . . . . . N3
Yalutorsk 25,426 . . . . . G4
Yamsk Q4
Yaroslavl' 597,000 . . . . . D4
Yartsevo J4
Yelets 112,000 . . . . . D4
Yelizovo 10,000 . . . . . Q4
Yeniseysk 19,880 . . . . . K4
Yermak 28,133 . . . . . H4
Yermentau 15,276 . . . . . H4
Yesil' 15,000 . . . . . G4
Yessey L3
Yoshkar-Ola 201,000 . . . . . E4
Yurga 78,000 . . . . . J4
Yuzhno-Sakhalinsk 140,000 . . . . . P5
Zabaykal'sk M5
Zakamensk 10,000 . . . . . L4
Zaozernyy 27,216 . . . . . K4
Zaporozh'ye 781,000 . . . . . D5
Zarafshan G5
Zavitinsk 19,009 . . . . . O4
Zaysan 10,000 . . . . . J5
Zeya 16,684 . . . . . N4
Zhatay O3
Zhdanov 503,000 . . . . . D5
Zheleznogorsk-Ilimskiy 22,179 . . . . . L4
Zhigalovo L4
Zhigansk N3
Zhitomir 244,000 . . . . . C4
Zima 41,567 . . . . . L4
Zlatoust 198,000 . . . . . F4
Zyryanka Q3

OTHER FEATURES

Alakol' (lake) J5
Alazeya (riv.) Q3
Aldan (plat.) N4
Aldan (riv.) O3
Alexandra Land (isl.) E1
Altay (mts.) J5
Amga (riv.) O3
Amgun' (riv.) O4
Amudar'ya (riv.) G5
Amur (riv.) O4
Anabar (riv.) M2
Anadyr' (gulf) T3
Anadyr' (range) S3
Anadyr' (riv.) S3
Angara (riv.) K4
Aral (sea) F5
Arctic Ocean K1
Argun (riv.) M4
Arkticheskiy Institut (isls.) H2
Atrek (riv.) F6
Ayon (isl.) R2
Azov (sea) D5
Balkhash (lake) H5
Baltic (sea) B4
Barents (sea) D2
Baykal (lake) L4
Baykal (mts.) L4
Beloye (lake) D3
Belyy (isl.) G2
Bering (isl.) R4
Bering (sea) S4
Bering (strait) U3
Bet-Pak-Dala (des.) H5
Black (sea) D5
Bol'shevik (isl.) K2
Bol'shoy Lyakhovskiy (isl.) P2
Bolvanskiy Nos (cape) G2
Bratsk (res.) L4
Caspian (sea) F6
Caucasus (mts.) E5
Chelyuskin (cape) M2
Cherskiy (range) P3
Chu (riv.) H5
Chukchi (pen.) T3
Chukchi (sea) T2
Chulym (riv.) J4
Chuna (riv.) K4
Chunya (riv.) K3
Communism (peak) H6
Crimea (pen.) D5
Dezhnev (cape) T3
Dmitriya Lapteva (strait) O2
Dnieper (riv.) D5
Dniester (riv.) C5
Don (riv.) E5
Donets (riv.) D5
Dulgalakh (riv.) O3
Dvina, Northern (riv.) E3

Agriculture, Industry and Resources

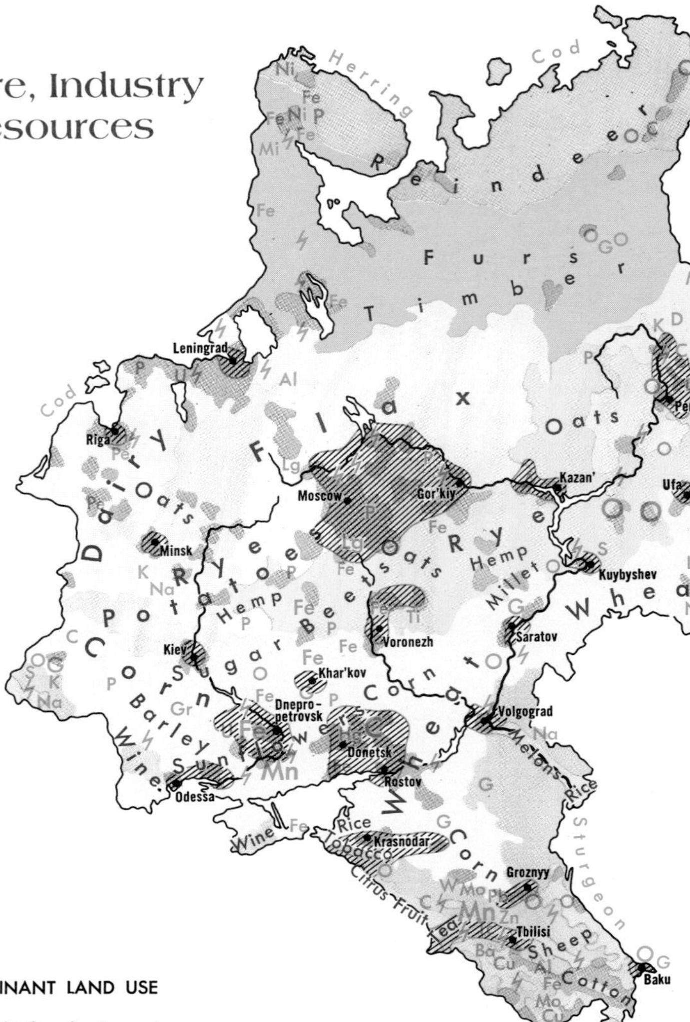

DOMINANT LAND USE

- Cereals (chiefly wheat, corn)
- Cereals (chiefly wheat, rye, oats)
- Dairy, Hogs, Livestock
- Livestock, Dairy
- Pasture Livestock
- Truck Farming, Potatoes, Vegetables, Dairy
- Flax, Dairy, Potatoes
- Cotton
- Vineyards, Orchards, Horticulture
- Sheep Herding, Limited Agriculture
- Forests
- Nonagricultural Land

MAJOR MINERAL OCCURRENCES

Ab	Asbestos	Hg	Mercury	Pb	Lead
Al	Bauxite	K	Potash	Pe	Peat
Au	Gold	Lg	Lignite	Pt	Platinum
Ba	Barite	Mg	Magnesium	S	Sulfur, Pyrites
C	Coal	Mi	Mica	Tc	Talc
Cr	Chromium	Mn	Manganese	Ti	Titanium
Cu	Copper	Mo	Molybdenum	U	Uranium
D	Diamonds	Na	Salt	V	Vanadium
Fe	Iron Ore	Ni	Nickel	W	Tungsten
G	Natural Gas	O	Petroleum	Zn	Zinc
Gr	Graphite	P	Phosphates		

Water Power — Major Industrial Areas

Dvina, Western (riv.) C4
Dzhugdzhur (range) O4
East Siberian (sea) S2
Emba (riv.) F5
Etorofu (Iturup) (isl.) P5
Faddeyevskiy (isl.) P2
Finland (gulf) C4
Franz Josef Land (isls.) F1
George Land (isl.) E1
Gizhiga (bay) Q3
Govena (cape) R4
Graham Bell (isl.) G1
Gyda (pen.) H2
Gydan (Kolyma) (range) Q3
Hiiumaa (isl.) C4
Ili (riv.) H5
Imandra (lake) D3
Indigirka (riv.) P3
Irtysh (riv.) H4
Ishim (riv.) G4
Issyk-Kul' (lake) H5
Japan (sea) O6
Kakhovka (res.) D5
Kamchatka (pen.) Q4
Kanin (pen.) E3
Kanin Nos (cape) E3
Kara (sea) G2
Kara-Bogaz-Gol (gulf) F5
Karaginskiy (isl.) R4
Kara-Kum (canal) F6
Kara-Kum (des.) F5
Karskiye Vorota (strait) F2
Khanka (lake) O5

Kharasavey (cape) G2
Kheta (riv.) K2
Klyuchevskaya Sopka (vol.) Q4
Kola (pen.) D3
Kolguyev (isl.) E3
Kolyma (range) Q3
Kolyma (riv.) Q3
Komandorskiye (isls.) R4
Komsomolets (isl.) L1
Koni (pen.) Q4
Koryak (range) S3
Kotel'nyy (isl.) O2
Kotuy (riv.) L3
Kuma (riv.) E5
Kura (riv.) E6
Kuril (isls.) P5
Kuybyshev (res.) F4
Kyzyl-Kum (des.) G5
Ladoga (lake) D3
La Pérouse (str.) P5
Laptev (sea) N2
Lena (riv.) N3
Little Yenisey (riv.) K4
Long (str.) S2
Lopatka (cape) Q4
Lower Tunguska (riv.) K3
Lyatkhovskiye (isls.) O2
Mangyshlak (pen.) F5
Markha (riv.) M3
Matochkin Shar (str.) F2
Maya (riv.) O4
Mezen' (riv.) E3

Murgab (riv.) G6
Nadym (riv.) H3
Narodnaya (mt.) G3
Navarin (cape) T3
New Siberian (isls.) P2
Northern Dvina (riv.) E3
Novaya Sibir' (isl.) Q2
Novaya Zemlya (isls.) F2
Ob' (gulf) H3
Ob' (riv.) G3
October Revolution (isl.) L2
Oka (riv.) L4
Okhotsk (sea) P4
Olëkma (riv.) N4
Olënek (bay) N2
Olënek (riv.) M3
Oloy (range) R3
Olyutorskiy (cape) S4
Omolon (riv.) Q3
Omoloy (riv.) O3
Onega (lake) D3
Onega (riv.) D3
Ozernoy (cape) R4
Paramushir (isl.) Q4
Pechora (riv.) F3
Peipus (lake) C4
Penzhina (bay) R3
Pioner (isl.) J2
Pobeda (peak) J5
Pur (riv.) H3
Pyasina (riv.) J2
Riga (gulf) C4

Rybachiy (pen.) D2
Rybinsk (res.) D4
Saaremaa (isl.) B4
Sakhalin (gulf) P4
Sakhalin (isl.) P4
Sannikova (str.) O2
Sary Su (riv.) H5
Sayan (mts.) K4
Selemdzha (riv.) O4
Sergeya Kirova (isls.) J2
Severnaya Zemlya (isls.) L1
Shantar (isls.) O4
Shelagskiy (cape) R2
Shelekhov (gulf) Q4
Siberia (reg.) 38,524,000 . . . . . M3
Sikhote-Alin' (range) O5
Stanovoy (range) N4
Stony Tunguska (riv.) K3
Syrdar'ya (riv.) G5
Tannu-Ola (range) K5
Tatar (str.) P4
Taymyr (lake) K2
Taymyr (pen.) L2
Taymyr (riv.) K2
Taz (riv.) J3
Tengiz (lake) G4
Terpeniye (cape) P5
Tobol (riv.) G4
Tsimlyansk (res.) E5
Tym (riv.) J3
Tyung (riv.) M3
Uda (riv.) O4

Ulutau (mts.) . . . . . G
Ural (mts.) . . . . . F
Ural (riv.) . . . . . F
Urup (isl.) . . . . . O
Ussuri (riv.) . . . . . O
Ust'-Urt (plat.) . . . . . F
Vakh (riv.) . . . . . J
Velikaya (riv.) . . . . . S
Verkhoyansk (range) . . . . . N
Vil'kitskogo (str.) L
Vilyuy (range) . . . . . M
Vilyuy (res.) . . . . . M
Vilyuy (riv.) L
Vitim (riv.) . . . . . M
Volga (riv.) . . . . . E
Western Dvina (riv.) C
White (sea) . . . . . D
Wiese (isl.) . . . . . H
Wilczek Land (isl.) . . . . . G
Wrangel (isl.) . . . . . T
Yablonovyy (range) . . . . . M
Yamal (pen.) . . . . . G
Yana (riv.) . . . . . O
Yelizavety (cape) . . . . . P
Yenisey (riv.) . . . . . J
Zaysan (lake) . . . . . J
Zeya (riv.) . . . . . N
Zhelaniye (cape) . . . . . H

*City and suburbs.

Agriculture, Industry and Resources

DOMINANT LAND USE

- Cereals (chiefly wheat, corn)
- Livestock, Dairy
- Truck Farming, Potatoes, Vegetables, Dairy
- Cotton
- Sheep Herding, Limited Agriculture
- Forests
- Nonagricultural Land

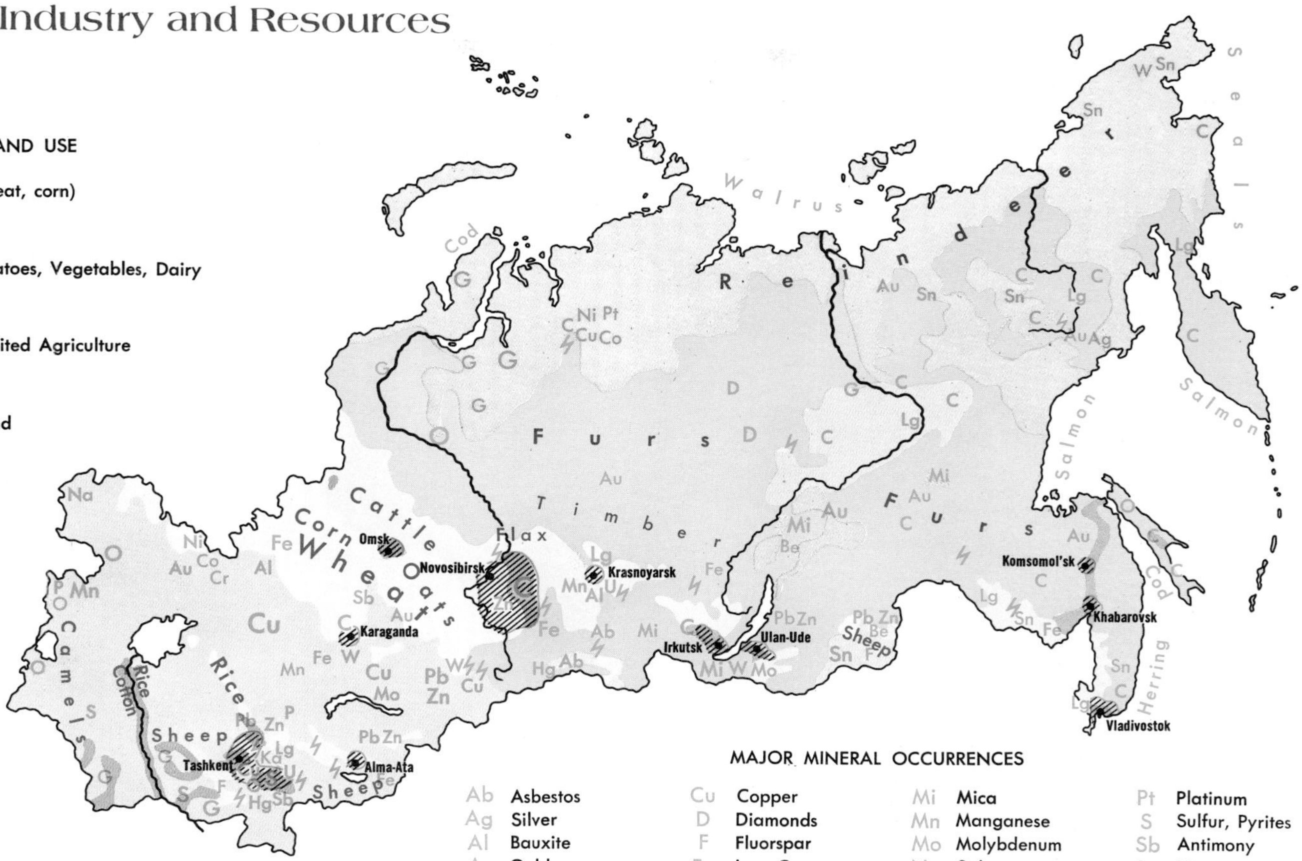

MAJOR MINERAL OCCURRENCES

Ab	Asbestos	Cu	Copper	Mi	Mica	Pt	Platinum
Ag	Silver	D	Diamonds	Mn	Manganese	S	Sulfur, Pyrites
Al	Bauxite	F	Fluorspar	Mo	Molybdenum	Sb	Antimony
Au	Gold	Fe	Iron Ore	Na	Salt	Sn	Tin
Be	Beryl	G	Natural Gas	Ni	Nickel	U	Uranium
C	Coal	Hg	Mercury	O	Petroleum	W	Tungsten
Co	Cobalt	Ka	Kaolin	P	Phosphates	Zn	Zinc
Cr	Chromium	Lg	Lignite	Pb	Lead		

⚡ Water Power   ▨ Major Industrial Areas

U.S.S.R.—Railroads and Navigation

Principal Railroads
Navigable Rivers
Canals
Main Sea Routes
Major Russian Ports ⚓

SCALE OF MILES
0   500   1000

SCALE OF KILOMETERS
0   500   1000

© Copyright HAMMOND INCORPORATED, Maplewood, N.J.

(continued on following page)

Union of Soviet Socialist Republics
European Part

CONIC PROJECTION
SCALE OF MILES
0 50 100 200 300
SCALE OF KILOMETERS
0 50 100 200 300

National Capitals	.... ★
Capitals of Union Republics	.... ⬡
Administrative Centers	.... △
International boundaries	....
Union Republic boundaries	....
A.S.S.R., Oblast, Kray boundaries	....
Autonomous Oblast boundaries	....
Autonomous Okrug boundaries	....

Scale 1:13,250,000

The government of the United States has not recognized the incorporation of Estonia, Latvia and Lithuania into the Soviet Union, nor does it recognize as final the de facto western limit of Polish administration in Germany (the Oder-Neisse line).

Administrative Divisions bear same names as their respective Capitals or Centers, except:

Abkhaz A.S.S.R.	Sukhumi	F6
Adygey Aut. Oblast	Maykop	F6
Adzhar A.S.S.R.	Batumi	F6
Bashkir A.S.S.R.	Ufa	J4
Chechen-Ingush A.S.S.R.	Groznyy	G6
Chuvash A.S.S.R.	Cheboksary	G3
Crimean Oblast	Simferopol'	D6
Dagestan A.S.S.R	Makhachkala	G6
Kabardin-Balkar A.S.S.R.	Nal'chik	F6
Kalmuck A.S.S.R.	Elista	F5
Karachay-Cherkess Aut. Obl.	Cherkessk	F6
Karelian A.S.S.R.	Petrozavodsk	D2
Komi A.S.S.R.	Syktyvkar	H2
Komi-Permyak Aut. Okrug	Kudymkar	H3
Mari A.S.S.R.	Yoshkar-Ola	G3
Mordvinian A.S.S.R.	Saransk	G4
Nagorno-Karabakh Aut. Obl.	Stepanakert	G7
Nenets Aut. Okrug	Nar'yan-Mar	H1
North Ossetian A.S.S.R.	Ordzhonikidze	F6
South Ossetian Aut. Obl.	Tskhinvali	F6
Tatar A.S.S.R.	Kazan'	G3
Trans-Carpathian Oblast	Uzhgorod	B5
Udmurt A.S.S.R.	Ustinov	H3
Volyn Oblast	Lutsk	C4

© Copyright HAMMOND INCORPORATED, Maplewood, N.J.

U.S.S.R. — EUROPEAN

UNION REPUBLICS

Armenian S.S.R. 3,031,000 F6
Azerbaidzhan S.S.R. 6,028,000 G6
Estonian S.S.R 1,466,000 C3
Georgian S.S.R. 5,015,000 F6
Latvian S.S.R 2,521,000 B3
Lithuanian S.S.R. 3,398,000 B3
Moldavian S.S.R. 3,947,000 C5
Russian S.F.S.R. 137,551,000 F3
Ukrainian S.S.R. 49,755,000 D5
White Russian S.S.R. 9,560,000 C4

INTERNAL DIVISIONS

Abkhaz A.S.S.R. 505,000 F6
Adygey Aut. Obl. 405,000 F6
Adzhar A.S.S.R. 354,000 F6
Bashkir A.S.S.R. 3,849,000 J4
Chechen-Ingush A.S.S.R. 1,154,000 G6
Chuvash A.S.S.R. 1,292,000 G3
Crimean Oblast 2,183,000 D6
Dagestan A.S.S.R. 1,628,000 G6
Kabardin-Balkar A.S.S.R. 674,000 F6
Kalmuck A.S.S.R. 294,000 F5
Karachay-Cherkess Aut. Obl. 368,000 F6
Karelian A.S.S.R. 736,000 D2
Komi A.S.S.R. 1,119,000 H2
Komi-Permyak Aut. Okr. 173,000 H3
Mari A.S.S.R. 703,000 G3
Mordvinian A.S.S.R. 991,000 G4
Nagorno-Karabakh Aut. Obl. 161,000 G7
Nakhichevan' A.S.S.R. 239,000 F7
Nenets Aut. Okr. 47,000 H1
North Ossetian A.S.S.R. 597,000 F6
South Ossetian Aut. Obl. 98,000 F6
Tatar A.S.S.R. 3,436,000 G3
Trans-Carpathian Oblast 1,155,000 B5
Udmurt A.S.S.R. 1,494,000 H3
Volyn Oblast 1,015,000 C4

CITIES and TOWNS

Abdulino 26,010 H4
Agdam 21,277 G6
Agryz 19,267 H3
Akhaltsikhe 18,972 F6
Akhtubinsk 43,466 G5
Akhty G6
Akhtyrka 41,354 E4
Akkerman (Belgorod-Dnestrovskiy) 32,928 D5
Alagir 18,161 F6
Alatyr' 43,499 G4
Alaverdi 21,311 F6
Aleksandriya 82,000 D5
Aleksandrovsk 18,286 J3
Alekseyevka 25,562 E4
Aleksin 67,000 E4
Ali-Bayramly 33,828 G7
Al'met'yevsk 110,000 H3
Alushta 22,016 D6
Amderma K1
Anapa 29,900 E6
Andropov 239,000 E3
Apatity 62,000 D1
Apsheronsk 32,867 F6
Archangel (Arkhangel'sk) 385,000 F2
Armavir 162,000 F5
Arzamas 93,000 F3
Astara G7
Astrakhan' 461,000 G5
Atkarsk 28,881 G4
Azov 75,000 E5
Bakhchisaray 15,912 D6
Baku 1,022,000 H6
Balakhna 36,542 F3
Balaklava D6
Balakovo 152,000 G4
Balashov 93,000 F4
Baltiysk 20,300 A4
Baranovichi 131,000 C4
Barysh 20,792 G4
Bataysk 90,000 E5
Batumi 123,000 F6
Belaya Tserkov' 151,000 C5
Belebey 32,460 H4
Belev 17,733 E4
Belgorod 240,000 E4
Belgorod-Dnestrovskiy 32,928 D5
Belomorsk 16,595 D2
Belorechensk 35,970 E6
Beloretsk 71,000 J4
Belozersk E3
Bel'tsy 125,000 C5
Belush'ya Guba H1
Bendery 101,000 C5
Berdichev 80,000 C5
Berdyansk 122,000 E5
Beregovo 27,308 B5
Berezniki 185,000 J3
Beslan 26,893 F6
Bezhetsk 30,030 E3
Birsk 29,607 J3
Bobrov 17,977 F4
Bobruysk 192,000 C4
Bologoye 33,949 D3
Bor 63,000 F3
Borislav 33,800 B5
Borisoglebsk 68,000 F4
Borisov 112,000 C4
Borovichi 60,000 D3
Brest 177,000 B4
Brezhnev 301,000 H3
Bryansk 394,000 D4
Bugul'ma 80,000 H4
Buguruslan 54,000 H4
Buturlinovka 21,643 F4
Buy 29,946 F3
Buynaksk 37,946 G6
Buzuluk 76,000 H4
Bykhov 17,371 C4
Cēsis 17,696 C3
Chadyr-Lunga 20,474 C5
Chapayevsk 85,000 G4
Chaykovskiy 48,034 H3
Cheboksary 308,000 G3
Cherepovets 266,000 E3
Cherkassy 228,000 D5
Cherkessk 91,000 F6
Chernigov 238,000 D4
Chernovtsy 219,000 C5
Chernushka 21,106 J3
Chervonograd 55,000 B4
Chiatura 25,474 F6
Chistopol' 64,000 H3
Chortkov 19,183 B5
Chudovo D3
Chusovoy 56,000 J3
Danilov 17,500 E3
Dankov 20,030 E4
Daugavpils 116,000 C3
Davlekanovo 20,123 H4
Derbent 70,000 G6
Dimitrovgrad 106,000 G4
Dneprodzerzhinsk 250,000 D5
Dnepropetrovsk 1,066,000 D5
Dobrush 16,809 D4
Dobryanka 18,349 J3
Donetsk 1,021,000 E5
Drogobych 66,000 B5
Dubna 55,000 E3
Dubna E4
Dubno 25,442 C4
Dvinsk (Daugavpils) 116,000 C3
Dyat'kovo 26,825 D4
Dzerzhinsk 257,000 F3
Dzhankoy 43,459 D5
Dzhul'fa G7
Echmiadzin 31,819 F6
Elektrostal' 139,000 E3
Elista 70,000 F5
El'ton G5
Engel's 161,000 G4
Erivan 1,019,000 F6
Fastov 51,000 C4
Feodosiya 76,000 D5
Frolovo 33,398 F5
Furmanov 40,155 F3
Gagra 23,025 E6
Galich 19,374 F3
Gandzha (Kirovabad) 232,000 G6
Gatchina 75,000 C3
Gay 28,250 J4
Gaysin 23,741 C5
Gdov C3
Gelendzhik 29,086 E6
Genichesk 20,031 E5
Georgiu-Dezh 52,000 E4
Glazov 81,000 H3
Glubokoye C3
Glukhov 27,096 D4
Gomel' 383,000 D4
Gori 56,000 F6
Gorki 22,117 D4
Gor'kiy 1,344,000 F3
Gorlovka 336,000 E5
Gorodets 34,229 F3
Gremikha E1
Gremyachinsk 29,975 J3
Grodno 195,000 B4
Groznyy 375,000 G6
Gryazi 41,292 F4
Gubakha 33,243 J3
Gubkin 65,000 E4
Gudauta F6
Gudermes 32,445 G6
Gukovo 68,000 F5
Gus'-Khrustal'nyy 72,000 F3
Imishli 17,839 G7
Inta 51,000 K1
Inza 19,060 G4
Ishimbay 57,000 J4
Ivano-Frankovsk 150,000 B5
Ivanovo 465,000 E3
Izberbash 17,299 G6
Izhevsk (Ustinov) 549,000 H3
Izmail 83,000 C5
Izyum 61,000 E5
Jēkabpils 22,440 C3
Jelgava 68,000 B3
Jurmala 61,000 B3
Kadiyevka (Stakhanov) 108,000 E5
Kafan 29,916 G7
Kagul 26,249 C5
Kakhovka 28,472 D5
Kalach 18,475 F4
Kalach-na-Donu 20,795 F5
Kalinin 412,000 E3
Kaliningrad, Kaliningrad 355,000 B4
Kaliningrad, Moscow Oblast 133,000 E3
Kalinkovichi 23,918 C4
Kaluga 265,000 E4
Kalush 60,000 B5
Kamenets-Podol'skiy 81,000 C5
Kamenka 30,067 F4
Kamensk-Shakhtinskiy 72,000 F5
Kamyshin 112,000 F4
Kanash 40,682 G3
Kandalaksha 42,656 D1
Kapsukas 28,763 B4
Karachayevsk F6
Karachev 15,972 E4
Kashin 17,678 E3
Kasimov 33,066 F4
Kaspiysk 38,990 G6
Kaunas 370,000 B4
Kazan' 993,000 G3
Kazatin 26,649 C5
Kem' 21,025 D2
Kerch' 157,000 E5
Keret' D1
Khachmas 22,313 G6
Khadyzhensk 17,856 E6
Khar'kov 1,444,000 E5
Khasavyurt 65,000 G6
Khashuri 24,469 F6
Kherson 319,000 D5
Khmel'nitskiy 172,000 C5
Khotin 10,319 C5
Khust 23,810 B5
Khvalynsk 16,249 G4
Kiev 2,144,000 D4
Kiliya 24,276 C5
Kimovsk 44,490 E4
Kimry 58,000 E3
Kinel' 39,373 H4
Kineshma 101,000 F3
Kirishi 27,252 D3
Kirov, Kaluga 29,355 D4
Kirov, Kirov 390,000 G3
Kirovabad 232,000 G6
Kirovakan 146,000 G6
Kirovo-Chepetsk 71,000 H3
Kirovograd 237,000 D5
Kirovsk 38,484 D1
Kirsanov 21,795 F4
Kishinev 503,000 C5
Kislovodsk 101,000 F6
Kizel 46,264 J3
Kizlyar 29,745 G6
Klaipeda 176,000 B3
Klintsy 67,000 D4
Kobrin 24,935 B4
Kobuleti 18,051 F6
Kohtla-Järve 73,000 C3
Kolomiya 52,000 B5
Kolomna 147,000 E4
Kolpino 114,000 D3
Kommunarsk 120,000 E5
Komrat 21,369 C5
Komsomol'skiy 17,078 K1
Kondopoga 27,908 D2
Königsberg (Kaliningrad) 355,000 B4
Konotop 82,000 D4
Konstantinovka 112,000 E5
Korenovsk 26,323 E5
Korosten' 65,000 C4
Korostyshev 21,153 C4
Koryazhma 33,230 G2
Kostopol' 17,548 C4
Kostroma 255,000 F3
Kotel'nich 29,196 G3
Kotel'nikovo 19,063 F5
Kotlas 61,000 G2
Kotovo 20,553 G4
Kotovsk, Odessa 36,463 C5
Kotovsk, Tambov 33,347 F4
Kovel' 33,351 C4
Kovrov 143,000 F3
Kovylkino 17,300 F4
Kramatorsk 178,000 E5
Krasnoarmeysk 60,000 G4
Krasnodar 560,000 E6
Krasnograd 18,386 E5
Krasnokamsk 56,000 H3
Krasnoslobodsk 17,749 G5
Krasnovishersk J2
Krasnyy Kut 17,087 G4

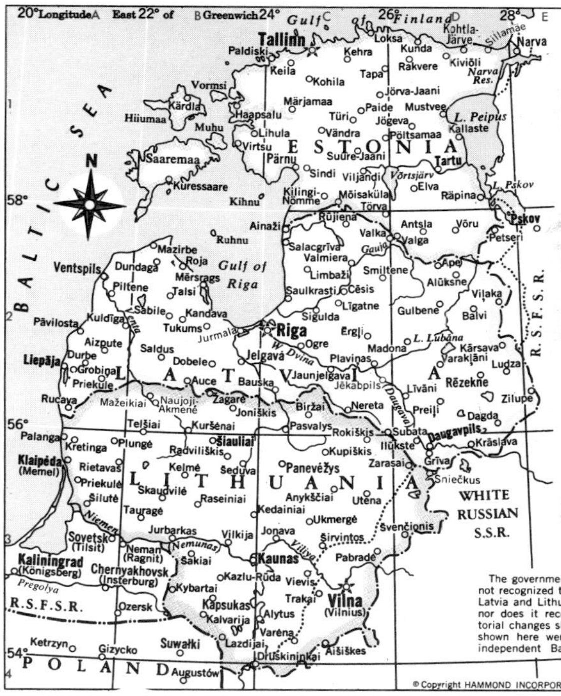

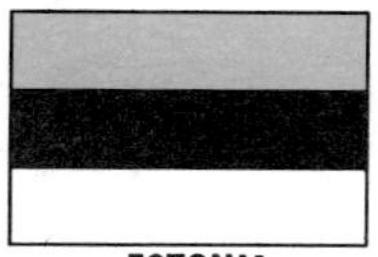

ESTONIA

LATVIA

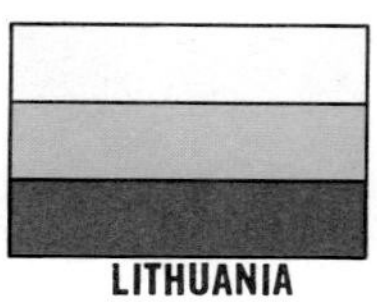

LITHUANIA

The government of the United States has not recognized the incorporation of Estonia, Latvia and Lithuania into the Soviet Union, nor does it recognize other post-war territorial changes shown on this map. The flags shown here were the official flags of the independent Baltic States prior to 1939.

The Baltic States

SCALE OF MILES 0 25 50 75 100
SCALE OF KILOMETERS 0 30 60 90 120 150 180

Capitals ☆
International Boundaries
Union Republic Boundaries
Prewar boundaries of the Baltic States where divergent from present boundaries

BALTIC STATES

Alytus 55,000 C3
Biržai 11,400 C2
Cēsis 17,696 C2
Daugava (Western Dvina) (riv.) D2
Daugavpils 116,000 D3
Dobele 10,100 B2
Druskininkai 11,200 C3
Dvina, Western (riv.) C2
Finland (gulf) D1
Gauja (riv.) C2
Haapsalu 11,483 B1
Hiiumaa (isl.) B1
Jēkabpils 22,400 C2
Jelgava 68,000 B2
Jonava 14,400 C3
Jurmala 61,000 B2
Kapsukas 28,763 B3
Kaunas 370,000 C3
Kedainiai 19,677 C3
Kihnu (isl.) B1
Kingisepp (Kuressaare) 12,140 B1
Kiviõli 11,153 D1
Klaipeda 176,000 A3
Kohtla-Järve 73,000 D1
Kretinga 13,000 A3
Kuldīga 12,300 A2
Kuressaare 12,140 B1
Kuršenai 11,500 B2
Liepāja 108,000 A2
Lubāna (lake) D2
Mažeikiai 13,400 A2
Memel (Klaipeda) 176,000 A3
Muhu (isl.) B1
Narva 73,000 E1
Naujoji-Akmene 10,200 B2
Niemen (riv.) A3
Ogre 15,708 C2
Panevežys 102,000 C3
Pärnu 51,000 C1
Peipus (lake) D1
Plunge 13,600 B3
Radviliškis 16,841 B3
Rakvere 17,891 D1
Rēzekne 30,803 D2
Riga (cap.), Latvia 835,000 C2
Riga (gulf) B2
Saaremaa (isl.) B1
Saldus 10,000 B2
Šiauliai 118,000 B3
Sillamäe 13,505 D1
Šilute 12,400 A3
Tallinn (cap.), Estonia 430,000 C1
Tapa 10,037 C1
Tartu 105,000 D1
Taurage 19,461 B3
Telšiai 20,220 B2
Tukums 14,800 B2
Ukmerge 21,663 C3
Utena 13,300 C3
Valga 16,795 D2
Valmiera 20,331 C2
Venta (riv.) B2
Ventspils 40,467 A2
Viliya (riv.) C3
Viljandi 20,814 C1
Vilna (Vilnius) (cap.) Lithuania 481,000 C3
Vormosi (isl.) B1
Võrtsjärv (lake) D1
Võru 15,398 D2
Western Dvina (riv.) C2

Krasnyy Luch 106,000 E5
Krasnyy Sulin 41,684 F5
Kremenchug 210,000 D5
Krichev 25,682 D4
Krivoy Rog 650,000 D5
Krolevets 18,307 D4
Kronshtadt 39,477 C3
Kropotkin 70,000 F5
Krymsk 41,430 E5
Kuba 18,871 G6
Kudymkar 26,350 H3
Kulebaki 46,252 F3
Kumertau 52,000 J4
Kunda C3
Kungur 80,000 J3
Kupyansk 30,055 E5
Kuressaare 12,140 B3
Kursk 375,000 E4
Kutaisi 194,000 F6
Kuvandyk 22,914 J4
Kuybyshev 1,216,000 H4
Kuznetsk 94,000 G4
Kuzomen' E1
Labinsk 54,000 F6
Lakhdenpokh'ya C2
Lebedin 29,240 D4
Leninakan 207,000 F6
Leningrad 4,073,000 C3
Leningrad* 4,588,000 C3
Leninogorsk 54,000 H4
Lenkoran' 35,505 G7
L'gov 25,110 E4
Lida 66,000 C4
Liepāja 108,000 B3
Likhoslavl' E3
Lipetsk 396,000 E4
Lisichansk 119,000 E5
Livny 37,290 E4
Lodeynoye Pole 19,632 D2
Lozovaya 53,000 E5
Lubny 54,000 D4
Luga 31,905 C3
Lutsk 137,000 B4
L'vov (Lwów) 667,000 B5
Lys'va 75,000 J3
Lyubertsy 160,000 E3
Lyubotin 33,324 E4
Lyudinovo 33,871 D4
Makeyevka 436,000 E5
Makhachkala 251,000 G6
Makharadze 21,679 F6
Malaya Vishera 15,381 D3
Malgobek 20,548 F6
Manturovo 21,510 F3
Marganets 50,000 E5
Mariupol' (Zhdanov) 503,000 E5
Marks 17,132 G4
Maykop 128,000 F6
Mednogorsk 38,024 J4
Medvezh'yegorsk 17,465 D2
Melenki 18,545 F3
Meleuz 24,851 J4
Melitopol' 161,000 D5
Memel (Klaipeda) 176,000 B3
Merefa 29,985 E5
Mezen' F1
Michurinsk 101,000 F4
Mikhaylovka 58,000 F4
Millerovo 34,627 F5
Mineral'nye Vody 67,000 F6
Mingechaur 60,000 G6
Minsk 1,262,000 C4
Minsk* 1,276,000 C4
Mirgorod 28,407 D5
Mogilev 290,000 C4
Mogilev-Podol'skiy 26,051 C5
Molodechno 73,000 C4
Molotov (Perm') 999,000 J3
Monchegorsk 51,000 D1
Morshansk 44,245 F4
Moscow (Moskva) (cap.) 7,831,000 E3
Moscow* 8,011,000 E3
Mozhaysk 20,321 E3
Mozhga 38,930 H3
Mozyr' 73,000 C4
Mtsensk 27,833 E4
Mukachevo 72,000 B5
Murmansk 381,000 D1
Murom 114,000 F3
Mytishchi 141,000 E3
Nakhichevan' 33,279 F7
Nal'chik 207,000 F6
Narva 73,000 C3
Nar'yan-Mar 16,864 H1
Neftekamsk 70,000 J3
Nelidovo 29,813 D3
Nerekhta 25,722 F3
Nevel' 17,804 D3
Nevinnomyssk 104,000 F6
Nezhin 70,000 D4
Nikel' 21,299 C1
Nikolayev 440,000 D5
Nikol'sk 20,740 G4
Nikopol' 146,000 D5
Nizhnekamsk 134,000 H3
Nizhniy Lomov 17,460 F4
Nizhniy Novgorod (Gor'kiy) 1,344,000 F3
Nosovka 19,430 D4
Novaya Kakhovka 52,000 D5
Novgorod 186,000 D3
Novgorod-Severskiy D4
Novoanninskiy 20,461 F4
Novocherkassk 183,000 F5
Novograd-Volynskiy 41,194 C4
Novogrudok 19,374 C4
Novokuybyshevsk 109,000 G4
Novomoskovsk 147,000 E4
Novopolotsk 67,000 C3
Novorossiysk 159,000 E6
Novoshakhtinsk 104,000 E5
Novotroitsk 95,000 J4
Novoukrainka 19,554 D5
Novouzensk G4
Novovolynsk 41,187 B4
Novovyatsk 26,408 G3
Novozybkov 34,433 D4
Nurlat 17,533 H4
Nyandoma 23,366 F2
Nytva 17,491 H3
Nyuvchim H2
Obninsk 73,000 E3
Ochamchira 18,718 F6
Odessa 1,046,000 D5
Oktyabr'sk 33,981 G4
Oktyabr'skiy 88,000 H4
Okulovka 19,194 D3
Olenegorsk 21,485 D1
Olonets D2
Omutninsk 28,777 H3
Onega 25,047 E2
Ordzhonikidze 279,000 F6
Orel 305,000 E4
Orenburg 459,000 J4
Orgeyev 25,798 C5
Orsha 112,000 C4
Orsk 247,000 J4
Osa 15,038 J3
Osipenko (Berdyansk) 122,000 E5
Osipovichi 19,705 C4
Ostashkov 23,419 D3
Ostrogozhsk 29,921 E4
Ostrov 22,369 C3
Otradnyy 44,426 H4
Panevežys 102,000 B3
Pärnu 51,000 C3
Pavlograd 107,000 E5
Pavlovo 68,000 F3
Pechenga D1
Pechora 56,000 J1
Penza 483,000 G4
Perm' 999,000 J3
Pervomaysk 72,000 D5
Petrokrepost' D3
Petrovsk 30,953 G4
Petrozavodsk 234,000 D2
Petsamo (Pechenga) D1
Pinsk 90,000 C4
Podol'sk 202,000 E3
Podporozh'ye 21,545 D2
Pokhvistnevo 26,125 H4
Polonnoye 22,484 C4
Polotsk 71,000 C3
Poltava 279,000 D5
Polyarnyy 15,321 D1
Ponoy F1
Poti 45,979 F6
Povenets E2
Povorino 20,591 F4
Prikumsk 35,768 F6
Priluki 65,000 D4
Primorsk C2
Primorsko-Akhtarsk 25,981 E5
Priozersk 16,652 D2
Privolzhskiy 23,041 G4
Priyutovo 21,051 H4
Prokhladnyy 40,074 F6
Pskov 176,000 C3
Pugachev 33,963 G4
Pushkin 90,000 C3
Pyatigorsk 110,000 F6
Rabocheostrovsk D1
Rakhov B5
Rakvere 17,891 C3
Rasskazovo 40,038 F4
Razdan 26,833 G6
Rechitsa 60,000 C4
Reni 19,625 C5
Revel (Tallinn) 430,000 B3
Rēzekne 30,803 C3
Riga 835,000 B3
Romny 53,000 D4
Roslavl' 56,000 D4
Rossosh' 36,438 E4
Rostov 30,815 E3
Rostov-na-Donu 934,000 F5
Rovno 179,000 C4
Rtishchevo 37,146 F4
Rubezhnoye 66,000 E5
Rustavi 129,000 G6
Ruzayevka 41,084 F4
Ryazan' 453,000 E4
Ryazhsk 25,425 F4
Rybinsk (Andropov) 239,000 E3
Rybnitsa 32,266 C5
Rzhev 69,000 D3
Safonovo 53,000 D3
Saki 24,208 D5
Salavat 137,000 H4
Sal'sk 57,000 F5
Sal'yany 24,228 G7
Samara (Kuybyshev) 1,216,000 H4
Sambor 29,253 B5
Saransk 263,000 G4
Sarapul 107,000 H3
Saratov 856,000 G4
Sasovo 27,228 F4
Segezha 28,810 D2
Semenov 23,633 F3
Semiluki 18,221 E4
Sengiley G4
Serdobol (Sortavala) 22,188 D2
Serdobsk 33,783 F4
Sergach 22,509 F3
Serpukhov 140,000 E4
Sevastopol' 301,000 D6
Severodonetsk 113,000 E5
Severodvinsk 197,000 E2
Severomorsk 50,000 D1
Shakhty 209,000 F5
Shakhun'ya 20,009 G3
Shar'ya 25,788 G3
Shchekino 70,000 E4
Shchigry 17,133 E4
Sheki 43,158 G6
Shemakha 17,986 G6
Shepetovka 38,707 C4
Shostka 82,000 D4
Shpola 19,806 D5
Shumerlya 33,816 G3
Shuya 72,000 F3
Šiauliai 118,000 B3
Sibay 37,656 J4
Simferopol' 302,000 D6
Skadovsk D5
Skopin 24,429 F4
Slantsy 41,146 C3
Slavuta 25,573 C4
Slavyansk 140,000 E5
Slavyansk-na-Kubani 54,000 E5
Slobodskoy 34,374 H3
Slonim 30,279 B4
Slutsk 35,609 C4
Smela 62,000 D5
Smolensk 276,000 D4
Sochi 287,000 E6
Sokol 48,243 F3
Soligorsk 65,000 C4
Solikamsk 101,000 J3
Sol'-Iletsk 22,227 J4
Sorochinsk 23,235 H4
Soroki 21,924 C5
Sortavala 22,188 D2
Sosnogorsk 24,688 H2
Sovetsk (Tilsit) 38,456 B4
Sovetsk 17,027 G3
Stakhanov 108,000 E5
Stalingrad (Volgograd) 929,000 F5
Staraya Russa 34,577 D3
Staryy Oskol 115,000 E4
Stavropol' 258,000 F5
Stepanakert 30,293 G7
Sterlitamak 220,000 J4
Stupino 70,000 E4
Sudak E6
Sukhumi 114,000 F6
Sumgait 190,000 G6
Sumy 228,000 E4
Svetlogorsk 55,000 C4
Svetlograd 40,265 F5
Syktyvkar 171,000 H2
Syzran' 178,000 G4
Taganrog 276,000 E5
Tallinn 430,000 B3
Tambov 270,000 F4
Tartu 105,000 C3
Taurage 19,461 B3
Tbilisi 1,066,000 F6
Telavi 21,179 G6
Telšiai 20,220 B3
Temryuk 23,172 E5
Ternopol' 144,000 C5
Teykovo 41,607 E3
Tiflis (Tbilisi) 1,066,000 F6
Tighina (Bendery) 101,000 C5
Tikhoretsk 64,000 F5
Tikhvin 59,000 D3
Tilsit (Sovetsk) 38,456 B4
Timashevsk 29,055 E5
Tiraspol' 139,000 D5
Togliatti (Tol'yatti) 502,000 G4
Tokmak 59,000 E5
Toropets 16,863 D3
Torzhok 45,443 D3
Troitsko-Pechorsk J2
Tskhinvali 30,311 F6
Tuapse 60,000 E6
Tula 514,000 E4
Tutayev 16,839 E3
Tuymazy 37,021 H4
Tver (Kalinin) 412,000 E3
Tyrnyauz 18,253 F6
Uchaly 21,808 J4
Ufa 969,000 J4
Uglich 35,463 E3
Ukmerge 21,663 C3
Ul'yanovsk 464,000 G4
Uman' 79,000 D5
Unecha 21,749 D4
Ungeny 17,228 C5
Uryupinsk 38,192 F4
Usinsk J1
Usman' 20,150 E4
Ustinov 549,000 H3
Uvarovo 24,946 F4
Uzhgorod 91,000 B5
Uzlovaya 65,000 E4
Valga 16,795 C3
Valmiera 20,331 C3
Valuyki 29,093 E4
Vasil'kov 26,741 D4
Velikiye Luki 102,000 D3
Velikiy Ustyug 36,737 F2
Vel'sk 21,899 F2
Ventspils 40,467 B3
Vereshchagino 23,585 H3
Vichuga 52,000 F3
Viipuri (Vyborg) 76,000 C2
Vileyka C4
Vilna (Vilnius) 481,000 C4
Vinnitsa 314,000 C5
Vinogradov 20,580 B5
Vitebsk 297,000 C3
Vladimir 296,000 F3
Vladimir-Volynskiy 28,412 B4
Volgodonsk 91,000 F5
Volgograd 929,000 F5
Volkhov 47,025 D3
Volkovysk 28,266 B4
Vologda 237,000 F3
Vol'sk 66,000 G4
Volzhsk 52,000 G3
Volzhskiy 209,000 G5
Vorkuta 100,000 K1
Voronezh 783,000 E4
Voroshilovgrad 463,000 E5
Voskresensk 76,000 E3
Votkinsk 90,000 H3
Voznesensk 36,457 D5
Vyatskiye Polyany 32,729 H3
Vyaz'ma 52,000 D3
Vyborg 76,000 C2
Vyksa 54,000 F3
Vyshniy Volochek 72,000 D3
Yalta 80,000 D6
Yanaul 20,115 J3
Yaroslavl' 597,000 E3
Yartsevo 36,662 D3
Yefremov 53,000 E4
Yelabuga 31,728 H3
Yelets 112,000 E4
Yenakiyevo 114,000 E5
Yershov 21,731 G4
Yessentuki 78,000 F6
Yevlakh 29,462 G6
Yevpatoria 93,000 D5
Yeysk 71,000 E5
Yoshkar-Ola 201,000 G3
Yur'yevets 20,144 F3
Zagorsk 107,000 E3
Zapolyarnyy 22,084 D1
Zaporozh'ye 781,000 E5
Zelenodol'sk 85,000 G3
Zelenokumsk 29,691 F6
Zernograd 20,324 F5
Zhdanov 503,000 E5
Zheleznodorozhnyy 76,000 H2
Zheleznogorsk 65,000 E4
Zhigulevsk 52,130 G4
Zhitomir 244,000 C4
Zhlobin 25,359 D4
Zhmerinka 36,195 C5
Zhodino 22,083 C4
Zhovtnevoye 31,102 D5
Znamenka 27,393 D5
Zolotonosha 27,639 D5
Zugdidi 39,896 F6
Zuyevka 17,001 H3

OTHER FEATURES

Apsheron (pen.) H6
Araks (riv.) G7
Azov (sea) E5
Baltic (sea) B3
Barents (sea) E1
Belaya (riv.) H3
Beloye (lake) E2
Black (sea) D6
Bug (riv.) B4
Bug (riv.) D5
Caspian (sea) G6
Caucasus (mts.) F6
Crimea (pen.) D5
Desna (riv.) D4
Dnieper (riv.) D5
Dniester (riv.) C5
Don (riv.) F5
Donets (riv.) E5
Dvina (bay) E2
Dvina, Northern (riv.) F2
Dvina, Western (riv.) C3
Dykh-Tau (mt.) F6
El'brus (mt.) F6
Finland (gulf) C3
Hiiumaa (isl.) B3
Il'men' (lake) D3
Imandra (lake) D1
Kakhovka (res.) D5
Kama (riv.) H2
Kandalaksha (gulf) D1
Kanin (pen.) G1
Kara (sea) K1
Karskiye Vorota (str.) J1
Kazbek (mt.) F6
Khoper (riv.) F4
Kola (pen.) E1
Kolguyev (isl.) G1
Kuban' (riv.) E5
Kura (riv.) G6
Kuybyshev (res.) G4
Ladoga (lake) D2
Lapland (reg.) D1
Mezen' (riv.) G1
Moksha (riv.) F4
Narodnaya (mt.) J1
Niemen (riv.) B4
Novaya Zemlya (isls.) H1
Oka (riv.) F4
Onega (bay) E2
Onega (lake) E2
Onega (riv.) E2
Pechora (riv.) H1
Peipus (lake) C3
Pripet (marshes) C4
Pripyat' (riv.) C4
Prut (riv.) C5
Riga (gulf) B3
Rybachiy (pen.) D1
Rybinsk (res.) E3
Saaremaa (isl.) B3
Samara (riv.) H4
Sevan (lake) G6
Seym (riv.) D4
Sura (riv.) G4
Svir' (riv.) D2
Timan (ridge) G1
Tsil'ma (riv.) H1
Tsimlyansk (res.) F5
Tuloma (riv.) D1
Ural (mts.) J2
Ural (riv.) J4
Usa (riv.) K1
Valday (hills) D3
Vaygach (isl.) K1
Velikaya (riv.) C3
Volga (riv.) G5
Volga-Don (canal) F5
Volgograd (res.) G5
Volkhov (riv.) D3
Vorskla (riv.) E4
Vyatka (riv.) H3
Vychegda (riv.) G2
Vyg (lake) E2
White (sea) E1
Yamantau (mt.) J4
Yugorskiy (pen.) K1

*City and suburbs.

Asia

LAMBERT AZIMUTHAL EQUAL-AREA PROJECTION

SCALE OF MILES
0 100 200   400   600   800   1000   1200

SCALE OF KILOMETERS
0   200 400 600 800 1000 1200

Capitals of Countries .... ⊛
Other Capitals .... ◉
International Boundaries ....
Other Boundaries ....
Canals ....

Scale 1:46,500,000

© Copyright HAMMOND INCORPORATED, Maplewood, N.J.

Population Distribution

AREA 17,128,500 sq. mi.
(44,362,815 sq. km.)
POPULATION 2,633,000,000
LARGEST CITY Tokyo
HIGHEST POINT Mt. Everest 29,028 ft.
(8,848 m.)
LOWEST POINT Dead Sea -1,296 ft.
(-395 m.)

Vegetation

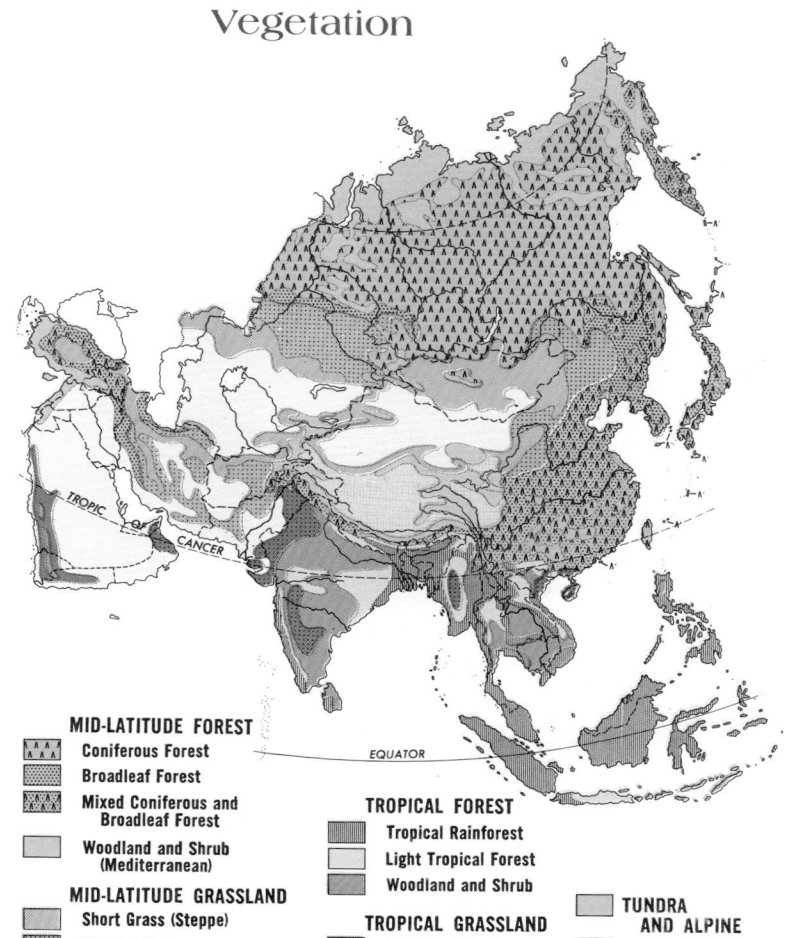

DENSITY PER

SQ. KILOMETER	SQ. MILE
Over 100	Over 260
50-100	130-260
10-50	25-130
1-10	3-25
Under 1	Under 3

• Cities with over 2,000,000 inhabitants (including suburbs)

○ Cities with over 1,000,000 inhabitants (including suburbs)

MID-LATITUDE FOREST
- Coniferous Forest
- Broadleaf Forest
- Mixed Coniferous and Broadleaf Forest
- Woodland and Shrub (Mediterranean)

MID-LATITUDE GRASSLAND
- Short Grass (Steppe)
- Wooded Steppe

DESERT AND DESERT SHRUB

TROPICAL FOREST
- Tropical Rainforest
- Light Tropical Forest
- Woodland and Shrub

TROPICAL GRASSLAND
- Grass and Shrub (Savanna)
- Wooded Savanna

TUNDRA AND ALPINE

UNCLASSIFIED HIGHLANDS

Average January Temperature

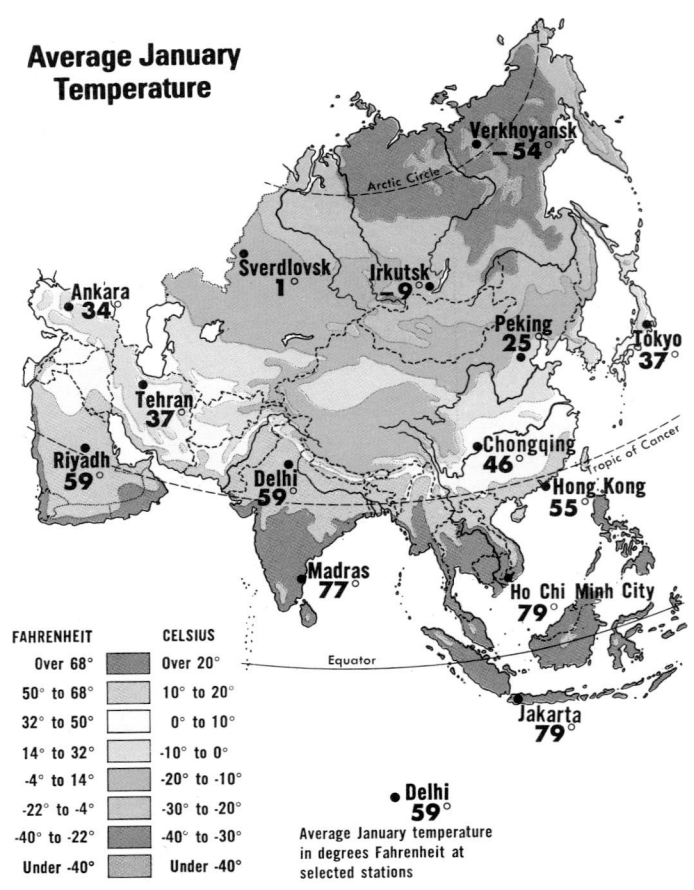

Verkhoyansk -54°

Sverdlovsk 1°   Irkutsk -9°

Ankara 34°

Peking 25°   Tokyo 37°

Tehran 37°

Riyadh 59°   Delhi 59°   Chongqing 46°

Hong Kong 55°

Madras 77°

Ho Chi Minh City 79°

Jakarta 79°

FAHRENHEIT	CELSIUS
Over 68°	Over 20°
50° to 68°	10° to 20°
32° to 50°	0° to 10°
14° to 32°	-10° to 0°
-4° to 14°	-20° to -10°
-22° to -4°	-30° to -20°
-40° to -22°	-40° to -30°
Under -40°	Under -40°

● Delhi 59°
Average January temperature in degrees Fahrenheit at selected stations

Average July Temperature

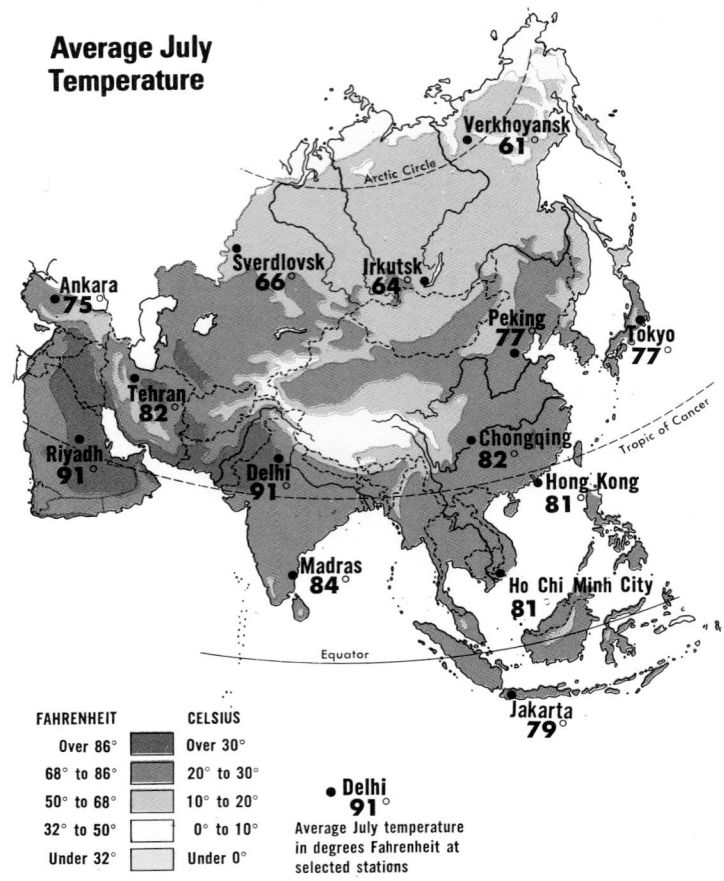

Verkhoyansk 61°

Sverdlovsk 66°   Irkutsk 64°

Ankara 75°

Peking 77°   Tokyo 77°

Tehran 82°

Riyadh 91°   Delhi 91°   Chongqing 82°

Hong Kong 81°

Madras 84°

Ho Chi Minh City 81°

Jakarta 79°

FAHRENHEIT	CELSIUS
Over 86°	Over 30°
68° to 86°	20° to 30°
50° to 68°	10° to 20°
32° to 50°	0° to 10°
Under 32°	Under 0°

● Delhi 91°
Average July temperature in degrees Fahrenheit at selected stations

Rainfall

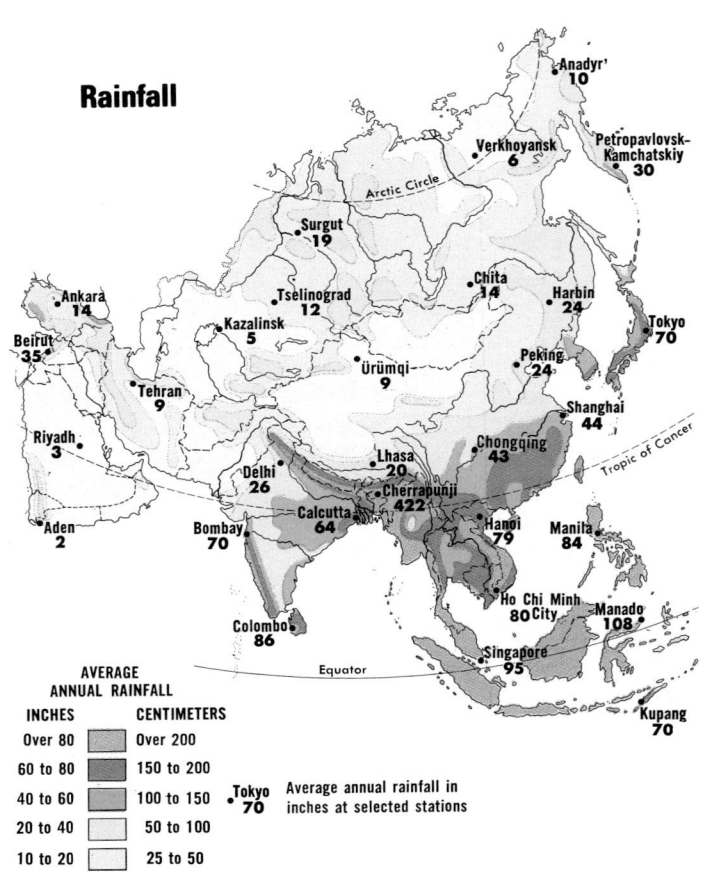

Anadyr' 10

Verkhoyansk 6   Petropavlovsk-Kamchatskiy 30

Surgut 19

Chita 14   Harbin 24   Tokyo 70

Tselinograd 12

Kazalinsk 5

Ürümqi 9   Peking 24

Shanghai 44

Tehran 9   Lhasa 20   Chongqing 43

Riyadh 3

Delhi 26   Cherrapunji 422

Ankara 14

Beirut 35

Aden 2   Bombay 70   Calcutta 64   Hanoi 79   Manila 84

Colombo 86   Ho Chi Minh City 80   Manado 108

Singapore 95

Kupang 70

AVERAGE ANNUAL RAINFALL

INCHES	CENTIMETERS
Over 80	Over 200
60 to 80	150 to 200
40 to 60	100 to 150
20 to 40	50 to 100
10 to 20	25 to 50
Under 10	Under 25

● Tokyo 70
Average annual rainfall in inches at selected stations

Vegetation / Relief

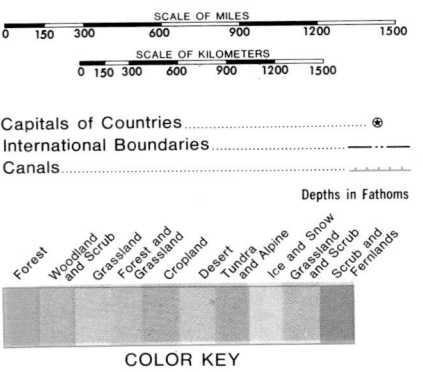

SCALE OF MILES
0 150 300 600 900 1200 1500

SCALE OF KILOMETERS
0 150 300 600 900 1200 1500

Capitals of Countries .... ⊛
International Boundaries ....
Canals ....

Depths in Fathoms

Forest | Woodland and Scrub | Grassland | Forest and Grassland | Cropland | Desert | Tundra and Alpine | Ice and Snow | Grassland and Scrub | Scrub and Fernlands

COLOR KEY

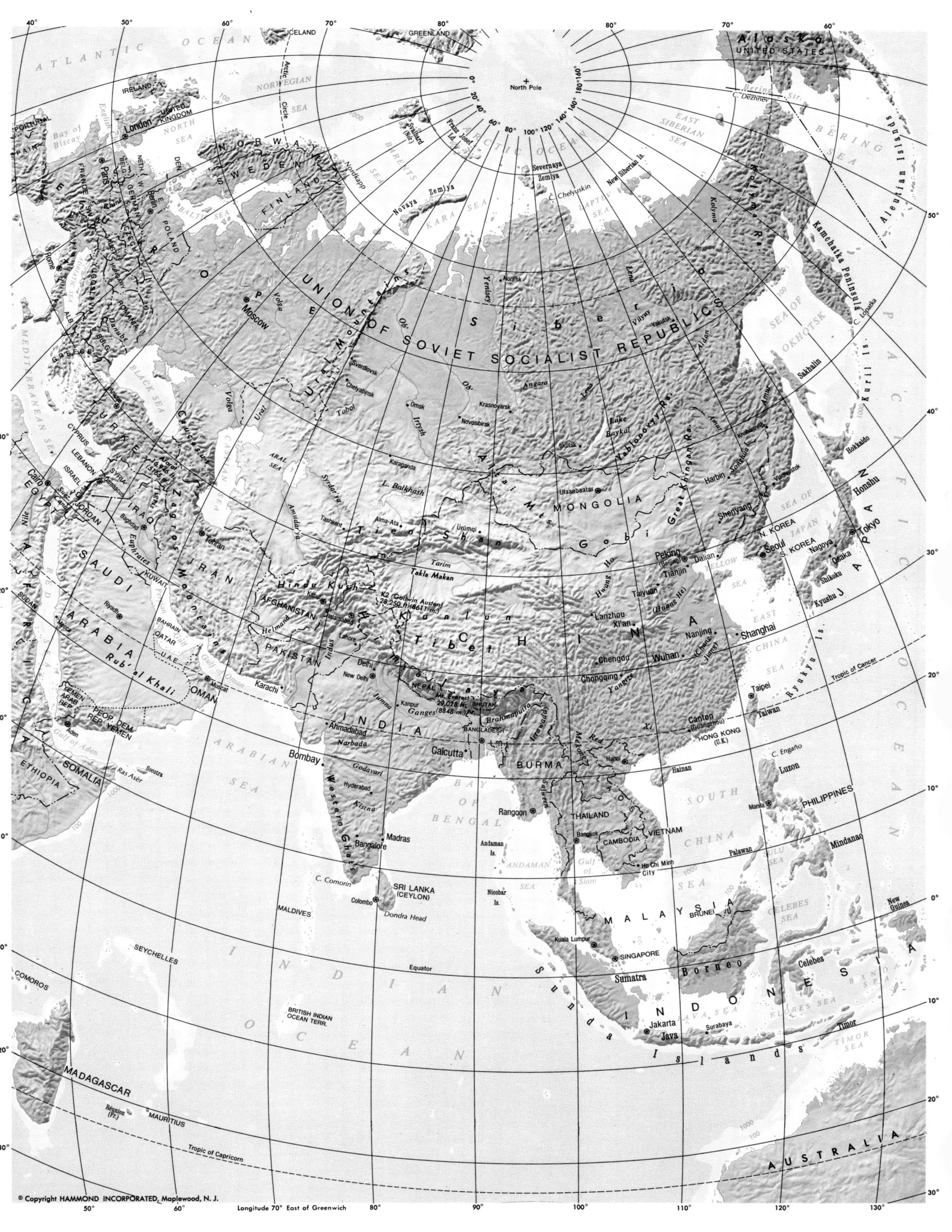

ATLANTIC OCEAN

ICELAND

GREENLAND

North Pole

Alaska
UNITED STATES

NORWEGIAN SEA

Arctic Circle

ARCTIC OCEAN

EAST SIBERIAN SEA

BERING SEA

Aleutian Islands

IRELAND

UNITED KINGDOM

London

NORTH SEA

PORTUGAL

Bay of Biscay

France Paris

BALTIC SEA

BELG. W. GERMANY

NETH.

Rhine

Berlin

DEN.

POLAND

Rome

YUGOSLAVIA

Danube

ALB.

GREECE

MEDITERRANEAN SEA

BLACK SEA

TURKEY

CYPRUS

LEBANON

ISRAEL

SYRIA

JORDAN

Damascus

Baghdad

IRAQ

Tigris

Euphrates

KUWAIT

BAHRAIN

QATAR

U.A.E.

SAUDI ARABIA

Riyadh

Mecca

Rub' al Khali

YEMEN ARAB REP.

PEOP. DEM. REP. YEMEN

Aden

Gulf of Aden

SUDAN

ETHIOPIA

SOMALIA

Ras Aser

Socotra

RED SEA

EGYPT

Cairo

Nile

SWEDEN

FINLAND

Nordkapp

U S S R

NORWAY

Moscow

Volga

Ural Mountains

Sverdlovsk

Chelyabinsk

Ob

Tobol

Irtysh

Omsk

Novosibirsk

Karaganda

L. Balkhash

ARAL SEA

Syrdar'ya

Tashkent

Alma-Ata

CASPIAN SEA

Volga

CAUCASUS

Tehran

IRAN

Zagros Mountains

Elburz Mts.

AFGHANISTAN

Kabul

Helmand

PAKISTAN

Hindu Kush

Islamabad

Lahore

Indus

Karachi

Muscat

OMAN

Gulf of Oman

ARABIAN SEA

MALDIVES

SEYCHELLES

COMOROS

MADAGASCAR

Réunion (Fr.)

MAURITIUS

BRITISH INDIAN OCEAN TERR.

INDIAN OCEAN

Tropic of Capricorn

Equator

Novaya Zemlya

KARA SEA

Yenisey

Noril'sk

Severnaya Zemlya

C. Chelyuskin

LAPTEV SEA

New Siberian Is.

S i b e r i a

UNION OF SOVIET SOCIALIST REPUBLICS

Ob

Angara

Lena

Vilyuy

Yakutsk

Krasnoyarsk

Irkutsk

Lake Baykal

Yablonovyy Rs.

Altai Mts.

Alma-Ata

Ürümqi

Tien Shan

Tarim

Takla Makan

K u n l u n

Kolyma

Kamchatka Peninsula

C. Lopatka

SEA OF OKHOTSK

Amur

Khabarovsk

Sakhalin

Kuril Is.

Aldan

MONGOLIA

Ulaanbaatar

Gobi

Great Khingan Rs.

Harbin

Changchun

Vladivostok

SEA OF JAPAN

Hokkaido

Honshu

JAPAN

Tokyo

Nagoya

Osaka

Kyushu

Shikoku

N. KOREA

Seoul

S. KOREA

Shenyang

Peking (Beijing)

Tianjin

Dalian

YELLOW SEA

Taiyuan

Hwang Ho (Huang He)

Lanzhou

Xi'an

C H I N A

Chengdu

Chongqing

Nanjing

Wuhan

Shanghai

Yangtze

EAST CHINA SEA

Ryukyu Is.

Tropic of Cancer

Taipei

TAIWAN

Xi

Canton (Guangzhou)

HONG KONG (U.K.)

Hainan

C. Engaño

Luzon

PACIFIC OCEAN

Bering Str.

Dezhnev

C A U C A S U S

Ararat (5165 ft.)

K2 (Godwin Austen) 28,250 ft. (8611 m.)

Delhi

New Delhi

Jumna

Ganges

Kanpur

NEPAL

Mt. Everest 29,028 ft. (8848 m.)

BHUTAN

H i m a l a y a s

Brahmaputra

BANGLADESH

Calcutta

I N D I A

Ahmadabad

Narbada

Bombay

Godavari

Hyderabad

Kistna

Bangalore

Madras

Western Ghats

C. Comorin

SRI LANKA (CEYLON)

Colombo

Dondra Head

BAY OF BENGAL

Andaman Is.

ANDAMAN SEA

Nicobar Is.

BURMA

Irrawaddy

Salween

Rangoon

Mekong

Red R.

Hanoi

THAILAND

Bangkok

CAMBODIA

VIETNAM

Ho Chi Minh City

Gulf of Siam

SOUTH CHINA SEA

Palawan

SULU SEA

Manila

PHILIPPINES

Mindanao

CELEBES SEA

MALAYSIA

BRUNEI

Kuala Lumpur

SINGAPORE

Sumatra

Borneo

Celebes

Sunda Islands

JAVA SEA

Jakarta

Java

Surabaya

FLORES SEA

BANDA SEA

Timor

TIMOR SEA

I N D O N E S I A

New Guinea

AUSTRALIA

Longitude 70° East of Greenwich

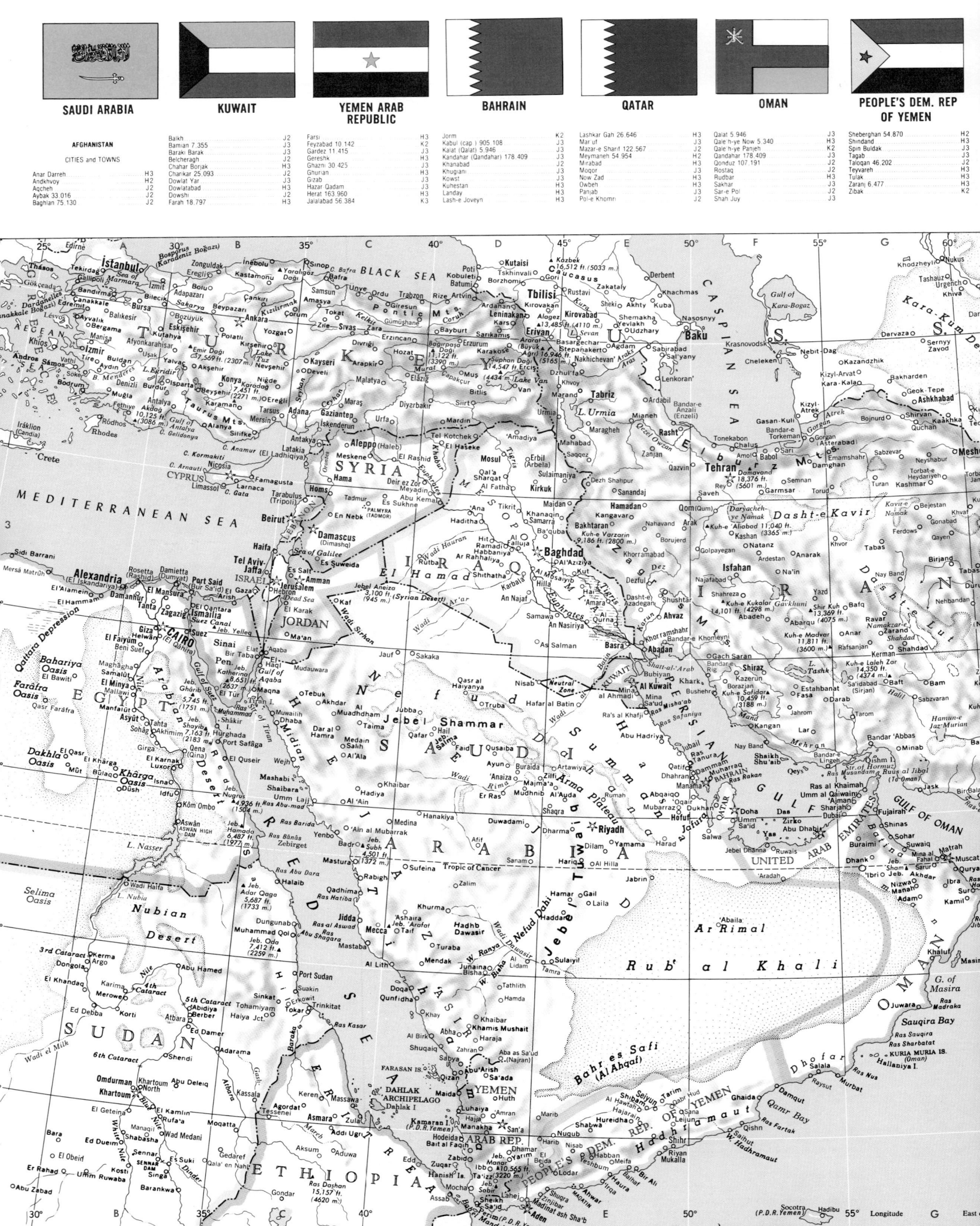

SAUDI ARABIA   **KUWAIT**   **YEMEN ARAB REPUBLIC**   **BAHRAIN**   **QATAR**   **OMAN**   **PEOPLE'S DEM. REP OF YEMEN**

AFGHANISTAN

CITIES and TOWNS

Anar Darreh	H3	Balkh	J2
Andkhvoy	H2	Bamian 7.355	J3
Aqcheh	J2	Baraki Barak	J3
Aybak 33.016	J2	Belcheragh	J2
Baghlan 75.130	J2	Chahar Borjak	H3
		Charikar 25.093	J3
		Dowlat Yar	J3
		Dowlatabad	J2
		Dowshi	J2
		Farah 18.797	H3

Farsi	J2	Jorm	K2
Feyzabad 10.142	K2	Kabul (cap) 905.108	J3
Gardez 11.415	J3	Kalat (Qalat) 5.946	J3
Gereshk	H3	Kandahar (Qandahar) 178.409	J3
Ghazni 30.425	J3	Khanabad	J2
Ghuran	H3	Khugiani	J3
Gizab	J3	Kowst	J3
Hazar Qadam	J3	Kuhestan	H3
Herat 163.960	H3	Landay	H3
Jalalabad 56.384	K3	Lash-e Joveyn	H3

Lashkar Gah 26.646	H3	Qalat 5.946	J3
Mar uf	K2	Qale h-ye Now 5.340	H3
Mazar-e Sharif 122.567	J2	Qale h-ye Panjeh	K2
Meymaneh 54.954	H2	Qandahar 178.409	J3
Mirabad	J3	Qonduz 107.191	J2
Mogor	J3	Rostaq	J2
Now Zad	J3	Rudbar	H3
Owbeh	J3	Sakhar	J3
Panjab	J3	Sar-e Pol	J2
Pol-e Khomri	J2	Shah Juy	J3

Sheberghan 54.870	H2		
Shindand	H3		
Spin Buldak	K3		
Tagab	J3		
Taloqan 46.202	J2		
Teyvareh	H3		
Tulak	H3		
Zaranj 6.477	H3		
Zibak	K2		

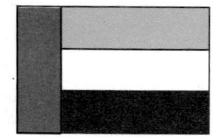

UNITED ARAB EMIRATES
OTHER FEATURES

Farah Rud (riv.)	H3
Gowd-e Zerreh (depr.)	H4
Harirud (riv.)	H3
Helmand (riv.)	J3
Hindu Kush (mts.)	J2
Kabul (riv.)	K3
Konar (riv.)	K2
Lurah (riv.)	J3

Margow, Dasht-e (des.)	H3
Murghab (riv.)	H2
Namaksar (salt lake)	H3
Paropamisus (mts.)	H3
Rigestan (reg.)	H3

BAHRAIN
CITIES and TOWNS

GAZA STRIP
CITIES and TOWNS

Gaza* 118.272	B3

Manama (cap.) 88.785	F4
Muharraq 37.732	F4

IRAN
CITIES and TOWNS

Abadan 296.081	E3
Abadeh 16.000	F3
Abarqu 8.000	F3
Ahvaz 329.006	E3

Amol 68.782	F2
Anar 463	G3
Anarak 2.038	F3
Arak 114.507	E3
Ardabil 147.404	E2
Ardestan 5.868	F3
Asterabad (Gorgan) 88.348	F2
Babol 67.790	F2
Bafq 5.000	G3
Baft 6.000	G4

(continued on following page)

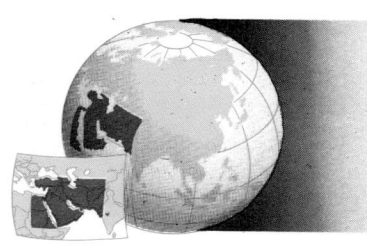

SAUDI ARABIA

AREA 829,995 sq. mi.
(2,149,687 sq. km.)
POPULATION 8,367,000
CAPITAL Riyadh
MONETARY UNIT Saudi riyal
MAJOR LANGUAGE Arabic
MAJOR RELIGION Islam

KUWAIT

AREA 6,532 sq. mi. (16,918 sq. km.)
POPULATION 1,355,827
CAPITAL Al Kuwait
MONETARY UNIT Kuwaiti dinar
MAJOR LANGUAGE Arabic
MAJOR RELIGION Islam

YEMEN ARAB REPUBLIC

AREA 77,220 sq. mi. (200,000 sq. km.)
POPULATION 6,456,189
CAPITAL San'a
MONETARY UNIT Yemeni rial
MAJOR LANGUAGE Arabic
MAJOR RELIGION Islam

BAHRAIN

AREA 240 sq. mi. (622 sq. km.)
POPULATION 358,857
CAPITAL Manama
MONETARY UNIT Bahraini dinar
MAJOR LANGUAGE Arabic
MAJOR RELIGION Islam

QATAR

AREA 4,247 sq. mi. (11,000 sq. km.)
POPULATION 220,000
CAPITAL Doha
MONETARY UNIT Qatari riyal
MAJOR LANGUAGE Arabic
MAJOR RELIGION Islam

OMAN

AREA 120,000 sq. mi. (310,800 sq. km.)
POPULATION 891,000
CAPITAL Muscat
MONETARY UNIT Omani rial
MAJOR LANGUAGE Arabic
MAJOR RELIGION Islam

PEOPLE'S DEM. REP. OF YEMEN

AREA 111,101 sq. mi. (287,752 sq. km.)
POPULATION 1,969,000
CAPITAL Aden
MONETARY UNIT Yemeni dinar
MAJOR LANGUAGE Arabic
MAJOR RELIGION Islam

UNITED ARAB EMIRATES

AREA 32,278 sq. mi. (83,600 sq. km.)
POPULATION 1,040,275
CAPITAL Abu Dhabi
MONETARY UNIT dirham
MAJOR LANGUAGE Arabic
MAJOR RELIGION Islam

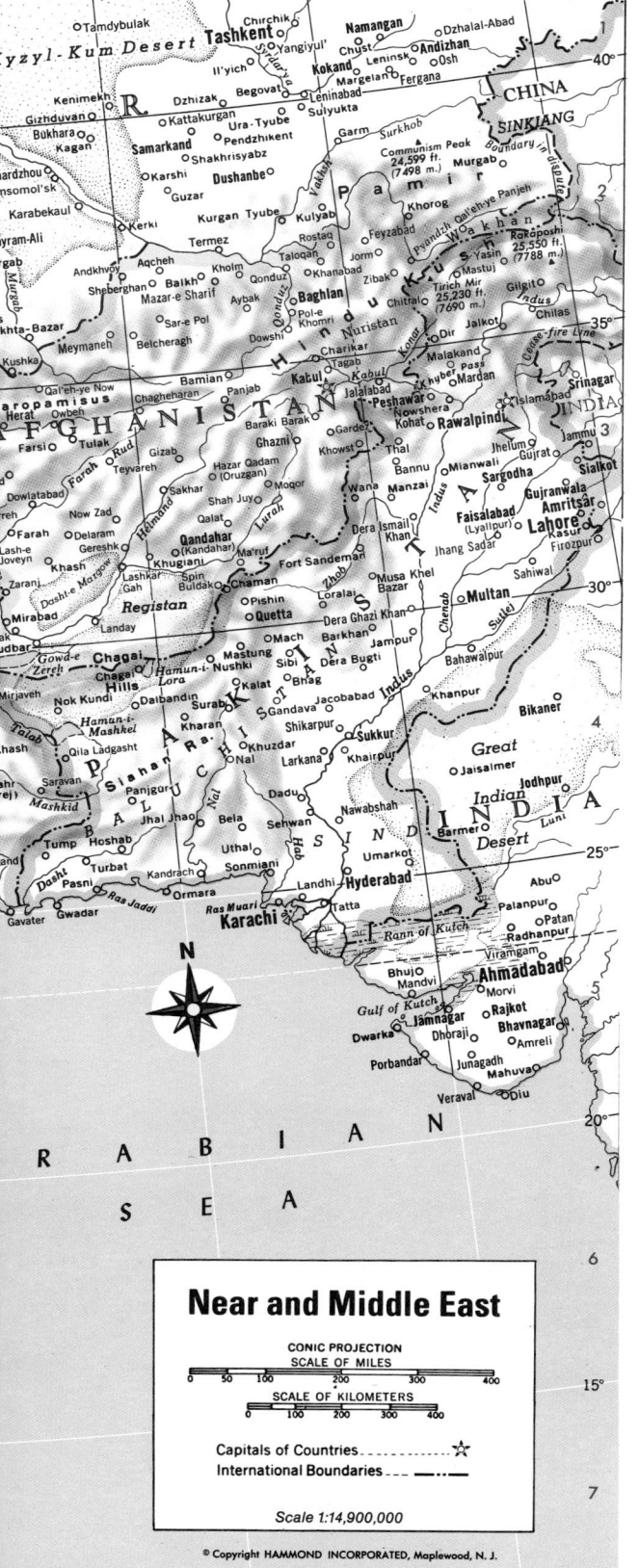

Topography

Near and Middle East

CONIC PROJECTION
SCALE OF MILES
0 50 100 200 300 400
SCALE OF KILOMETERS
0 100 200 300 400

Capitals of Countries .... ☆
International Boundaries ___ ___ ___

Scale 1:14,900,000

® Copyright HAMMOND INCORPORATED, Maplewood, N. J.

Bakhtaran 290,861 E3
Bam 22,000 G4
Bampur 1,585 H4
Bandar 'Abbas 89,103 G4
Bandar-e Anzali (Enzeli) 55,978 E2
Bandar-e Khomeyni 6,000 E3
Bandar-e Lengeh 4,920 F4
Bandar-e Rig 1,889 F4
Bandar-e Torkeman 13,000 F2
Bejestan 3,823 G3
Birjand 25,854 G3
Bojnurd 31,248 G2
Borazjan 20,000 F4
Borujerd 100,103 E3
Bushehr 57,681 F4
Chah Bahar 1,800 H4
Chalus 15,000 F2
Damghan 13,000 F2
Darab 13,000 G4
Dasht-e Azadegan 21,000 E3
Dashtiari H4
Dezful 110,287 E3
Dezh Shahpur 1,384 E2
Emamshahr 30,767 G2
Enzeli 55,978 E2
Estahbanat 18,187 F4
Fahrej (Iranshahr)5,000 H4
Fasa 19,000 F4
Ferdows 11,000 G3
Gach Saran F3
Garmsar 4,723 F2
Golpayegan 20,515 F3
Gonabad 8,000 G3
Gorgan 88,348 F2
Hamadan 155,846 E3
Iranshahr 5,000 H4
Isfahan 671,825 F3
Jahrom 38,236 F4
Kangan 2,682 F4
Kangavar 9,414 E3
Kashan 84,545 F3
Kashmar 17,000 G2
Kazerun 51,309 F4
Kerman 140,309 G3
Khash 7,439 H4
Khorramabad 104,928 E3
Khorramshahr 146,709 E3
Khvoy 70,040 E2
Lar 22,000 F4
Mahabad 28,610 E2
Maragheh 60,820 E2
Marand 24,000 E2
Meshed 670,180 H2
Mianeh 28,447 E2
Minab 4,228 G2
Mirjaveh 11,000 H4
Nahavand 24,000 E3
Na‘in 5,925 F3
Najafabad 76,236 F3
Nasratabad (Zabol) 20,000 H3
Natanz 4,370 F3
Nehbandan 2,130 G3
Neyshabur 59,101 G2
Nikshahr H4
Pahlevi (Enzeli) 55,978 E2
Qasr-e Qand 1,879 H4
Qayen 6,000 G3
Qazvin 138,527 E2
Qom 246,831 F3
Quchan 29,133 G2
Qum (Qom) 246,831 F3
Rafsanjan 21,000 G3
Rasht 187,203 E2
Ravar 5,074 G3
Rey 102,825 F2
Reza‘iyeh (Urmia) 163,991 D2
Sabzevar 69,174 G2
Sabzvaran 7,000 G4
Sai'dabad 20,000 G4
Sanandaj 95,834 E2
Saqqez 17,000 E2
Saravan H4
Sari 70,936 F2
Saveh 17,565 F2
Semnan 31,058 F2
Shahdad 2,777 G3
Shahreza 34,220 F3
Shiraz 416,408 F4
Shirvan 11,000 G2
Shustar 24,000 E3
Sirjan (Sai'dabad) 20,000 G4
Tabas 10,000 G3
Tabas-Masina (Tabas) 466 H3
Tabriz 598,576 E2
Tarom 394 G4
Tehran (cap.) 4,496,159 F2
Tonekabon 12,000 F2
Torbat-e Heydariyeh 30,106 G2
Torbat-e Jam 13,000 H2
Torud 721 F2
Turan G2
Turbat-i-Shaikh Jam 13,000 H2
Urmia 163,991 D2
Yazd 135,978 F3
Yazdan H3
Zabol 20,000 H3
Zahedan 92,628 H4
Zanjan 99,967 E2
Zarand 5,000 G3

OTHER FEATURES

Araks (riv.) E2
Atrek (riv.) G2
Bazman, Kuh-e (mt.) H4
Damavand (mt.) F2
Dez (riv.) E3
Elburz (mts.) F2
Gavkhuni (lake) F3
Gorgan (riv.) F2
Halil (riv.) G4
Jaz Murian, Hamun-e (marsh) G4
Karun (riv.) E3
Kavir, Dasht-e (salt des.) G3
Kavir-e Namak (salt des.) G3
Lut, Dasht-e (des.) G3
Maidani, Ras (cape) G4
Mand Rud (riv.) F4
Mashkid (riv.) H4
Mehran (riv.) F4
Namak, Daryacheh-ye (salt lake) F3
Namaksar (salt lake) H3
Namakzar-e Shahdad (salt lake) G3
Oman (gulf) G5
Persian (gulf) F4
Qeys (isl.) F4
Qezel Owzan (riv.) E2
Qeshm (isl.) G4
Safidar, Kuh-e (mt.) F4
Shaikh Shua'ib (isl.) F4
Shir Kuh (mt.) F3
Taftan, Kuh-e (mt.) H4
Talab (riv.) H4
Tashk (lake) F4
Urmia (lake) E2
Zagros (mts.) E3

IRAQ

CITIES and TOWNS

Al'Aziziya 7,450 E3
Al Falluja 38,072 D3
Al Fathat 15,329 D2
Al Musaiyib 15,955 D3
Al Qurna 5,638 E3
'Amadiya 2,578 D2
'Amara 64,847 E3
'Ana 15,729 D3
An Najaf 128,096 D3
An Nasiriya 60,405 E3
Arbela (Erbil) 90,320 D2
Ar Rahhaliya 1,579 D3
As Salman 3,584 E3
Baghdad (cap.) 502,503 E3
Baghdad* 1,745,328 E3
Baq'uba 34,575 D3
Basra 313,327 E3
Erbil 90,320 D2
Habbaniya 14,405 D3
Haditha 6,870 D3
Hai 16,988 E3
Hilla 84,717 D3
Hit 9,131 D3
Karbal'a 83,301 D3
Khanaqin 23,522 D3
Kirkuk 167,413 D2
Kirkuk* 176,794 D2
Kut 42,116 E3
Maidan 354 E3
Mosul 315,157 D2
Qala' Sharqat 2,434 D2
Ramadi 28,723 D3
Rutba 5,091 D3
Samarra 24,746 D3
Samawa 33,473 D3
Shithatha 2,326 D3
Sulaimaniya 86,822 E2
Tikrit 9,921 D3

OTHER FEATURES

'Aneiza, Jebel (mt.) C3
'Ara'r, Wadi (dry riv.) D3
Batin, Wadi al (dry riv.) E4
Euphrates (riv.) E3
Hauran, Wadi (dry riv.) D3
Mesopotamia (reg.) D3
Syrian (El Hamad) (des.) D3
Tigris (riv.) E3

KUWAIT

CITIES and TOWNS

Al Kuwait (cap.) 181,774 E4
Mina al Ahmadi E4
Mina Saud E4

OTHER FEATURES

Bubiyan (isl.) E4
Persian (gulf) F4

OMAN

CITIES and TOWNS

Adam G5
Buraimi G5
Dhank G5
Ibra G5
I'bri G5
Juwara G6
Kamil G5
Khaluf G5
Khasab G4
Manah G5
Masqat (Muscat) (cap.) 7,500 G5
Matrah 15,000 G5
Mina al Fahal G5
Murbat G6
Muscat (cap.) 7,500 G5
Nizwa G5
Quryat G5
Raysut (Risut) F6
Salala 4,000 F6
Sarur G5
Shinas G5
Sohar G5
Sur G5
Suwaiq G5

OTHER FEATURES

Akhdar, Jebel (range) G5
Batina (reg.) G5
Dhofar (reg.) F6
Hadd, Ras al (cape) G5
Jibsh, Ras (cape) G5
Kuria Muria (isls.) G6
Madraka, Ras (cape) G6
Masira (gulf) G6
Masira (isl.) G5
Musandam, Ras (cape) G4
Nus, Ras (cape) G6
Oman (gulf) G5
Oman (reg.) G5
Ruus al Jibal (dist.) G4
Sauqira (bay) G6
Sauqira, Ras (cape) G6
Sham, Jebel (mt.) G5
Sharbatat, Ras (cape) G6

QATAR

CITIES and TOWNS

Doha (cap.) 150,000 F4
Dukhan F4
Umm Sa'id F5

OTHER FEATURES

Persian (gulf) F4
Rakan, Ras (cape) F4

SAUDI ARABIA

CITIES and TOWNS

Aba as Sau'd 47,501 D6
'Abaila F5
Abha 30,150 D6
Abqaiq E4
Abu 'Arish D6
Abu Hadriya E4
'Ain al Mubarrak C5
Al 'Ain C4
Al 'Ala C4
Al 'Auda E4
Al Birk D6
Al Hilla E5
Al Lidam D5
Al Lith C5
Al Muadhdam C4
'Anaiza D4
Artawiya E4
'Ashaira D5
Ayun D4
Badr C5
Buraida 69,940 D4
Dam D5
Dammam 127,844 F4
Dar al Hamra C4
Dhaba C4
Dhahran E4
Dharma E5
Dilam E5
Doqa D6
Duwadami D5
Er Ras D4
Faid D4
Gail E5
Haddar E5
Hadiya C4
Hafar al Batin E4
Hail 40,502 D4
Hamar E5
Hamda D6
Hanakiya D5
Haql C4
Harad E5
Haraja D6
Hariq E5
Hofuf 101,271 E4
Jabrin E5
Jauf C4
Jidda 561,104 C5
Jizan (Qizan) 32,812 D6
Jubail F4
Jubba D4
Junaina D5
Kaf C3
Khaibar, 'Asir D5
Khaibar, Hejaz C4
Khamis Mushait 49,581 D6
Khay D6
Khurma D5
Laila E5
Majmaa' D4
Maqna C4
Marib E6
Mastaba C5
Mastura C5
Mecca 366,801 C5
Medain Salih C4
Medina 198,186 D5
Mendak D5
Mina Sau'd E4
Mubarraz 54,325 E4
Mudhnib D4
Muwailih C4
Najran (Aba as Sau'd) 47,501 D6
Nisab D4
O'qair E4
Qadhima C5
Qafar D4
Qasr al Haiyanya D4
Qatif E4
Qizan 32,812 D6
Qunfidha D6
Qusaiba D4
Rabigh C5
Ra's al Khafji E4
Ras Tanura F4
Riyadh (cap.) 666,840 E5
Rumah E4
Sabya D6
Sakaka D4
Salwa F5
Shaqra D4
Shuqaiq D6
Sufeina D5
Sulaiyil E5
Taif 204,857 D5
Taima C4
Tamra E5
Tathlith D6
Tebuk (Tabuk) 74,825 C4
Truba D4
Turaba D5
Umm Lajj C4
Wejh C4
Yamama E5
Yenbo C5
Zahran D6
Zalim D5
Zilfi E4

OTHER FEATURES

Abu-Mad, Ras (cape) C5
'Aneiza, Jebel (mt.) C3
Aqaba (gulf) C4
Arafat, Jebel (mt.) D5
'Ara'r, Wadi (dry riv.) D3
Arma (plat.) E4
Aswad, Ras al (cape) C5
Bahr es Safi (des.) E6
Barida, Ras (cape) C5
Bisha, Wadi (dry riv.) D5
Dahana (des.) E4
Dawasir, Wadi (dry riv.) E5
Dawasir, Hadhb (range) D5
Farasan (isls.) D6
Hatiba, Ras (cape) C5
Jafura (des.) F5
Mashabi (isl.) C4
Midian (dist.) C4
Mishaa'b, Ras (cape) E4
Nefud (des.) D4
Nefud Dahi (des.) D5
Persian (gulf) F4
Ranya, Wadi (dry riv.) D5
Red (sea) C5
Rima, Wadi (dry riv.) D4
Rimal, Ar (des.) F5
Rub al Khali (des.) F5
Safaniya, Ras (cape) E4
Salma, Jebel (mts.) D4
Shaibara (isl.) C4
Shammar, Jebel (plat.) D4
Sirhan, Wadi (dry riv.) C3
Subh, Jebel (mt.) C5
Summan (plat.) E4
Tihama (reg.) C5
Tiran (isl.) C4
Tiran (str.) C4
Tuwaiq, Jebel (range) E5

UNITED ARAB EMIRATES

CITIES and TOWNS

Abu Dhabi (cap.) 347,000 F5
'AJman G4
'Aradah F5
Buraimi G5
Dubai F4
Fujairah G4
Jebel Dhanna F5
Ras al Khaimah G4
Ruwais F5
Sharjah F4
Umm al Qaiwain G4

OTHER FEATURES

Das (isl.) F4
Oman (gulf) G5
Yas (isl.) F5
Zirko (isl.) F5

WEST BANK

CITIES and TOWNS

Hebron 38,309 C3

OTHER FEATURES

Dead (sea) C3

YEMEN ARAB REP.

CITIES and TOWNS

'Amran D6
Bait al Faqih D7
Dhamar 19,467 D7
El Beida 5,975 E7
Hajja 5,814 D6
Harib E7
Hodeida 80,314 D7
Huth D6
Ibb 19,066 D7
Luhaiya D6
Marib 292 D6
Mocha D7
Saa'da 4,252 D6
Sana' (cap.) 134,588 D6
Sheikh Sai'd D7
Tai'zz 78,642 D7
Yarim D7
Zabid D7

OTHER FEATURES

Hanish (isls.) D7
Manar, Jebel (mt.) D7
Mandeb, Bab el (str.) D7
Red (sea) C5
Sabir, Jebel (mt.) D7
Tihama (reg.) C5
Zuqar (isl.) D7

YEMEN, PEOPLE'S DEM. REPUBLIC OF

CITIES and TOWNS

Aden (cap.) 240,370 E7
Ahwar E7
Balhaf E7
Bir 'Ali E7
Damqut F6
Ghaida F6
Habban E7
Hadibu F7
Hajarain E6
Haura E7
Hureidha E6
I'rqa E7
Lahej E7
Leijun E6
Lodar E7
Madinat ash Shab' E7
Meifa E7
Mukalla 45,000 E7
Nisab E7
Nuqub E6
Qishn F6
Riyan E7
Saihut F6
Seiyun 20,000 E6
Shabwa E6
Shibam E6
Shihr E7
Shuqra E7
Tarim E6
Yeshbum E7
Zinjibar E7

OTHER FEATURES

Fartak, Ras (cape) F6
Hadhramaut (dist.) E7
Hadhramaut, Wadi (dry riv.) F7
Kamaran (isl.) D6
Perim (isl.) D7
Socotra (isl.) F7

*City and suburbs.

Agriculture, Industry and Resources

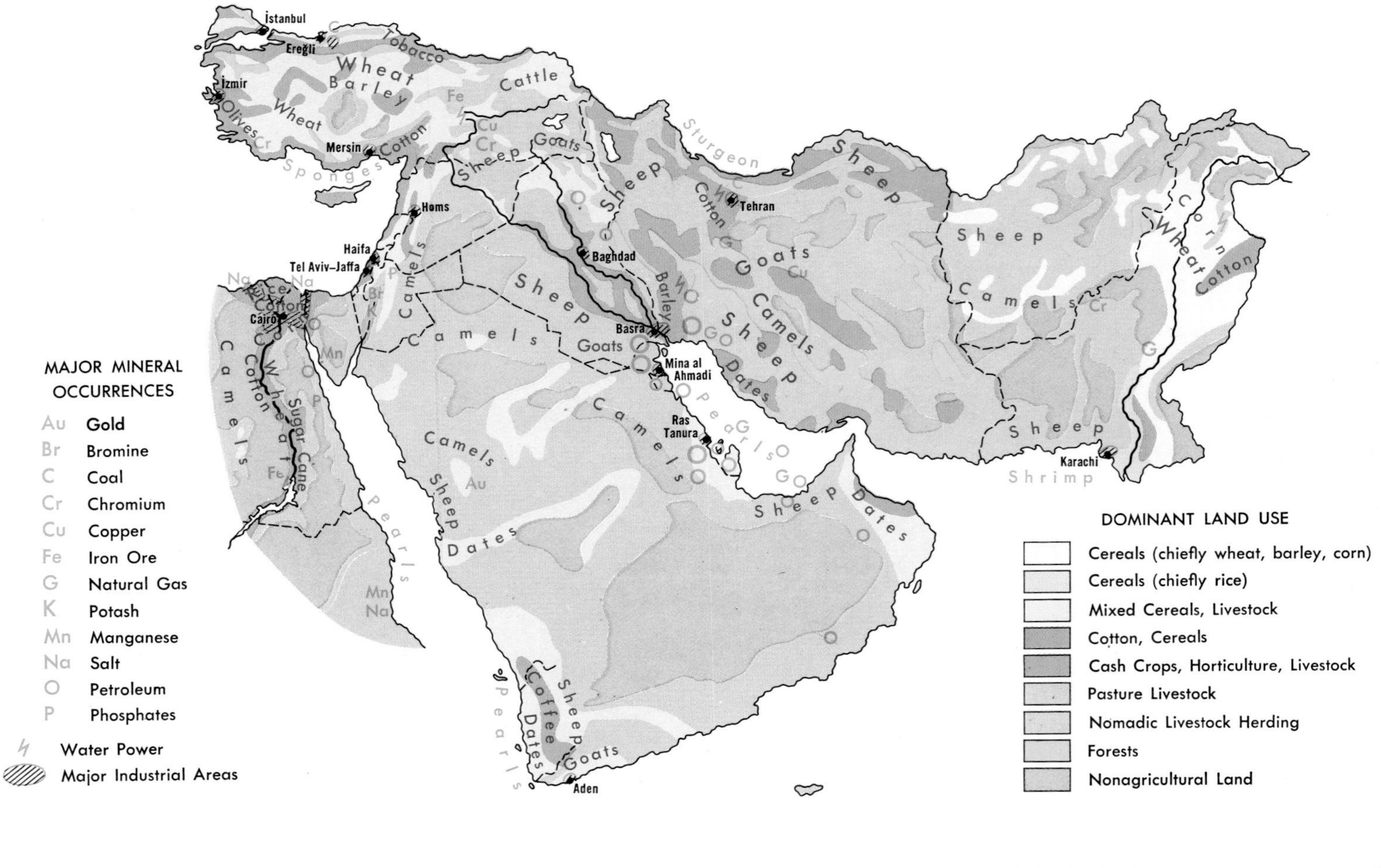

İstanbul
Ereğli
İzmir
Mersin
Homs
Haifa
Tel Aviv–Jaffa
Cairo
Baghdad
Tehran
Basra
Mina al Ahmadi
Ras Tanura
Karachi
Aden
Wheat
Barley
Cattle
Tobacco
Olives
Cotton
Sponges
Sheep
Goats
Sturgeon
Camels
Dates
Pearls
Sugar Cane
Corn
Coffee
Shrimp
MAJOR MINERAL OCCURRENCES
Au Gold
Br Bromine
C Coal
Cr Chromium
Cu Copper
Fe Iron Ore
G Natural Gas
K Potash
Mn Manganese
Na Salt
O Petroleum
P Phosphates
Water Power
Major Industrial Areas
DOMINANT LAND USE
Cereals (chiefly wheat, barley, corn)
Cereals (chiefly rice)
Mixed Cereals, Livestock
Cotton, Cereals
Cash Crops, Horticulture, Livestock
Pasture Livestock
Nomadic Livestock Herding
Forests
Nonagricultural Land

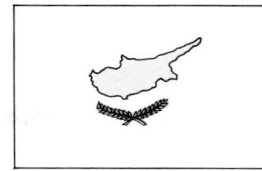
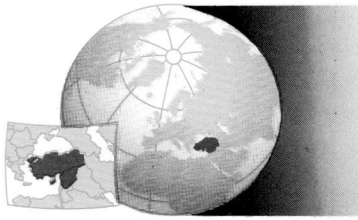

TURKEY **SYRIA** **LEBANON** **CYPRUS**

TURKEY
AREA 300,946 sq. mi.
   (779,450 sq. km.)
POPULATION 45,217,556
CAPITAL Ankara
LARGEST CITY Istanbul
HIGHEST POINT Ararat 16,946 ft.
   (5,165 m.)
MONETARY UNIT Turkish lira
MAJOR LANGUAGE Turkish
MAJOR RELIGION Islam

SYRIA
AREA 71,498 sq. mi. (185,180 sq. km.)
POPULATION 8,979,000
CAPITAL Damascus
LARGEST CITY Damascus
HIGHEST POINT Hermon 9,232 ft.
   (2,814 m.)
MONETARY UNIT Syrian pound
MAJOR LANGUAGES Arabic, French,
   Kurdish, Armenian
MAJOR RELIGIONS Islam, Christianity

LEBANON
AREA 4,015 sq. mi. (10,399 sq. km.)
POPULATION 3,161,000
CAPITAL Beirut
LARGEST CITY Beirut
HIGHEST POINT Qurnet es Sauda
   10,131 ft. (3,088 m.)
MONETARY UNIT Lebanese pound
MAJOR LANGUAGES Arabic, French
MAJOR RELIGIONS Christianity, Islam

CYPRUS
AREA 3,473 sq. mi. (8,995 sq. km.)
POPULATION 629,000
CAPITAL Nicosia
LARGEST CITY Nicosia
HIGHEST POINT Troödos 6,406 ft. (1,953 m.)
MONETARY UNIT Cypriot pound
MAJOR LANGUAGES Greek, Turkish, English
MAJOR RELIGIONS Eastern (Greek) Orthodoxy,
   Islam

(continued on following page)

Agriculture, Industry and Resources

DOMINANT LAND USE

- ☐ Cereals (chiefly wheat, barley), Livestock
- ▨ Cash Crops, Horticulture, Livestock
- ☐ Pasture Livestock
- ▨ Nomadic Livestock Herding
- ☐ Forests
- ☐ Nonagricultural Land

MAJOR MINERAL OCCURRENCES

Ab	Asbestos	Na	Salt
Al	Bauxite	O	Petroleum
C	Coal	P	Phosphates
Cr	Chromium	Pb	Lead
Cu	Copper	Py	Pyrites
Fe	Iron Ore	Sb	Antimony
Hg	Mercury	Zn	Zinc
Mg	Magnesium		

⚡ Water Power
▨ Major Industrial Areas

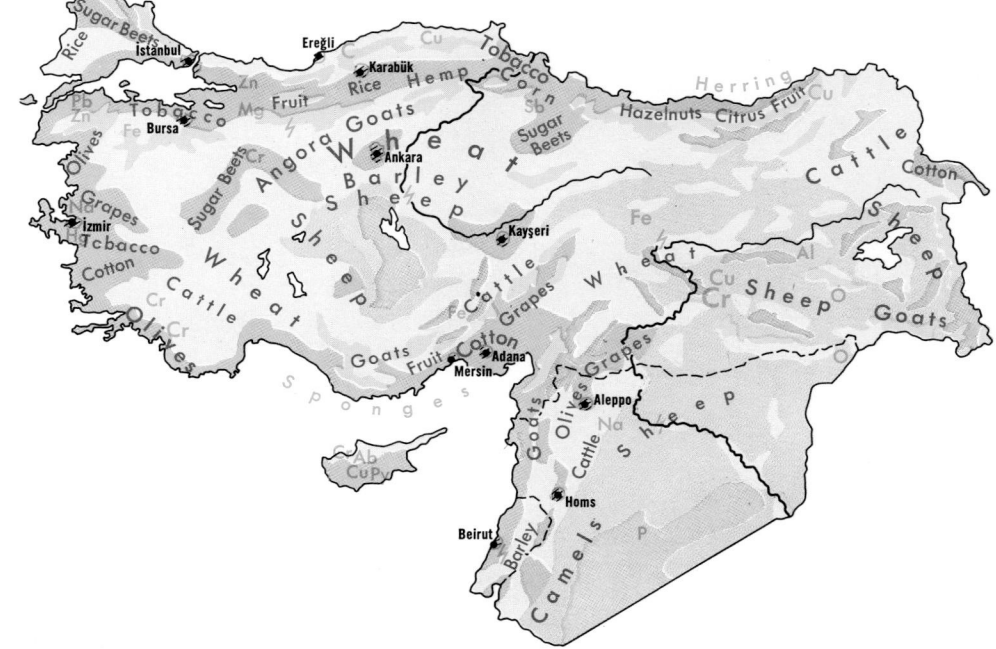

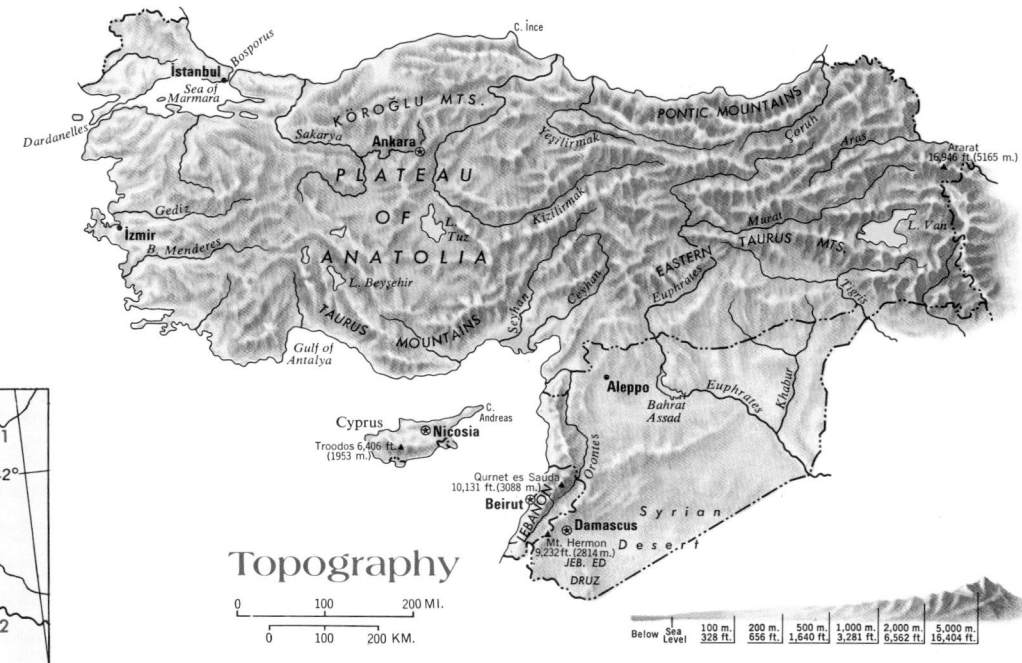

Topography

Scale 0 — 100 — 200 MI.
0 — 100 — 200 KM.

| Below Sea Level | 100 m. 328 ft. | 200 m. 656 ft. | 500 m. 1,640 ft. | 1,000 m. 3,281 ft. | 2,000 m. 6,562 ft. | 5,000 m. 16,404 ft. |

Hayrabolu 12.331	B2	Islâhiye 20.683	G4
Hazro 4.896	J3	Isparta 62.870	D4
Hekimhan 11.818	G3	Ispir 3.929	J2
Hendek 15.291	D2	Istanbul 2.547.364	D6
Hilvan 6.473	H4	Ivrindi 3.730	B3
Hınıs 10.226	J3	Izmir 636.834	B3
Hisarönu 4.485	E2	Izmit 165.483	C2
Hizan 2.545	K3	Iznik 11.614	C2
Hopa 9.089	J2	Kadıköy 354.957	D6
Horasan 7.724	K2	Kadinhani 11.802	E3
Hozat 5.796	H3	Kadirli 34.779	F4
İçel (Mersin) 152.236	F4	Kağithane 164.448	D6
İdil 4.862	J4	Kağizman 11.517	K3
Iğdir 29.542	K3	Kâhta 15.602	H4
Ilgaz 6.624	E2	Kalan 11.637	H3
Ilgın 11.830	D3	Kale 3.399	C4
Ilıca 8.947	J3	Kalecik 4.707	E2
İmranlı 5.667	H2	Kandira 10.187	D2
İncesu 7.089	F3	Kangal 5.937	G3
İnebolu 6.824	E2	Karabük 69.182	E2
İnegöl 37.805	C2	Karacabey 21.648	C2
İnönü 4.152	D3	Karahallı 5.539	C3
İpsala 6.829	B2	Karaisali 2.316	F4
İpsile 2.328	J3	Karakoçan 5.604	H3
İskenderun 107.437	G4	Karaköse (Ağri) 35.284	K3
İskilip 16.588	F2		

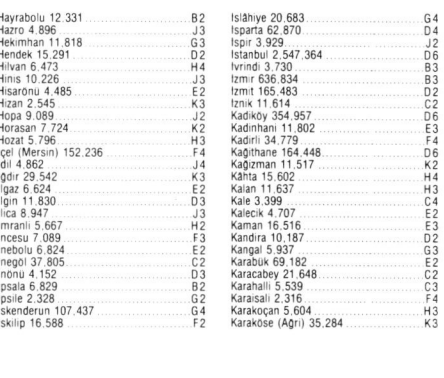

Karaman 43.759	E4	Muğla 24.178	C4	Silvan 29.599	J3	Yeşilyurt 7.451	H3
Karamanli 5.904	C4	Muradiye 6.334	K3	Simav 11.601	C3	Yildizeli 7.043	G3
Karapinar 19.589	E4	Muş 27.761	J3	Sincanli 3.847	D3	Yozgat 32.501	F3
Karasu 11.600	D2	Mustafakemalpaşa 27.706	C3	Sindirgi 7.818	C3	Yüksekova 7.329	L4
Karataş 5.598	F4	Mut 11.466	E4	Sinop 16.098	F2	Yumurtalık 2.442	F4
Karayaka 4.242	G2	Mutki 2.815	J3	Şiran 5.048	H2	Yunak 6.187	D3
Karayazi 3.595	J3	Muttalip 3.917	D3	Şirnak 10.587	K4	Yusufeli 3.050	J2
Kargi 5.021	E2	Nallihan 7.883	D2	Şirvan 5.166	K3	Zara 10.376	G3
Karliova 3.631	J3	Narman 4.607	J2	Sivas 149.201	G3	Zeytinburnu 123.548	D6
Kars 54.892	K2	Nazilli 52.176	C4	Sivaslı 4.394	C3	Zeytindağ 3.517	B3
Karşiyaka 171.600	B3	Nevşehir 30.203	F3	Siverek 40.990	H4	Zile 32.157	F2
Kartal 53.073	D6	Niğde 31.844	F4	Sivrihisar 8.713	D3	Zivarik 2.703	E3
Kaş 2.493	C4	Niksar 19.156	G2	Smyrna (Izmir) 636.834	B3	Zonguldak 90.221	D2
Kastamonu 29.993	F2	Nizip 36.190	G4	Söğüt 5.329	D3		
Kavak, Çanakkale 3.932	A2	Nusaybin 23.684	J4	Söke 35.407	B4	OTHER FEATURES	
Kavak, Samsun 3.964	F2	Ödemiş 37.364	C3	Solhan 7.014	J3		
Kayseri 207.037	F3	Of 10.376	J2	Soma 23.713	B3	Abydos (ruins)	B6
Kazanli 4.461	E4	Oğuzeli 7.194	G4	Sorgun 14.081	F3	Aci (lake)	C4
Kazimkarabekir 4.086	E4	Oltu 10.093	J2	Şuhut 8.154	D3	Adalar (isl.)	D6
Keban 5.800	H3	Ömerli 4.738	J4	Sulakyurt 4.311	E2	Aegean (sea)	A3
Keçiborlu 7.096	D3	Ordu 47.481	H2	Sultandağı 4.017	D3	Ağri, Büyük (Ararat) (mt.)	L3
Keles 2.423	C3	Orhaneli 3.335	C3	Sultanham 5.112	E3	Akdağ (mt.)	C4
Kelkit 6.928	H2	Orhangazi 12.181	C2	Suluova 21.278	F2	Aladağ (mt.)	C4
Kemah 3.038	H3	Orta 3.596	E2	Sungurlu 21.641	F2	Alexandretta (gulf)	F4
Kemaliye 3.014	H3	Ortaca 8.604	C4	Sürmene 8.096	J2	Amanos (mts.)	G4
Kemalpaşa 7.572	J2	Ortakaraviran 3.856	E4	Sürüç 20.395	H4	Anamur (cape)	E5
Kemerburgaz 7.234	C2	Ortaköy, Çorum 2.657	F2	Suşehri 10.863	H2	Anatolia (reg.)	D3
Kemhisar 6.205	F4	Ortaköy, Niğde 6.371	F3	Susurluk 14.000	C2	Anatolia (reg.)	D3
Kepsut 4.704	C3	Osmancik 11.921	F2	Susuz 5.006	K2	Antalya (gulf)	D4
Keşan 27.088	B2	Osmaneli 4.789	D2	Sütçüler 2.721	D4	Anti-Taurus (mts.)	G3
Keşap 5.264	H2	Osmaniye 61.581	F4	Taşkent 7.098	E4	Araks (riv.)	K2
Keşkin 10.540	E3	Ovacik, Tunceli 2.248	H3	Taşköprü 8.146	F2	Ararat (mt.)	L3
Kığı 5.598	J3	Ozalp 4.188	L3	Taşlıçay 3.684	K3	Arpa (riv.)	K2
Kilimli 26.649	D2	Palu 5.489	H3	Taşova 6.516	F2	Baba (cape)	A3
Kilis 54.055	G4	Pasinler 14.267	J3	Tatvan 29.728	J3	Bati Firat (riv.)	H3
Kinik 11.785	B3	Patnos 15.918	K3	Tavşanli 19.575	C3	Beyşehir (lake)	D4
Kiraz 5.284	C3	Pazar, Rize 8.856	J2	Tefenni 4.280	C4	Black (sea)	E1
Kirikhan 38.118	G4	Pazar, Tokat 4.337	G2	Tekirdağ 41.257	B2	Bosporus (str.)	C2
Kirikkale 137.874	E3	Pazarcik 15.943	G4	Tercan 6.068	J3	Bozcaada (isl.)	A3
Kirklareli 33.285	B2	Pertek 4.176	H3	Terme 15.660	F2	Burgaz (gulf)	D6
Kirşehir 41.415	F3	Perşembe 8.701	H2	Tire 30.864	B3	Büyük Ağri (Ararat) (mt.)	L3
Kizilcahamam 7.050	E2	Pertek 4.176	H3	Tirebolu 7.385	H2	Çanakkale Boğazi (Dardanelles) (str.)	B6
Kizilhisar 11.119	C3	Pervari 4.521	K4	Tokat 48.588	G2	Çandarli (gulf)	B3
Kizilitepe 21.531	J4	Pinarbaşi 9.503	G3	Tomarza 6.648	F3	Çanik (mts.)	G2
Kiziliran 3.260	E4	Pinarhisar 10.523	B2	Tomük 7.660	F4	Ceyhan (riv.)	F4
Kocaeli (Izmit) 165.483	D2	Polatli 35.267	E3	Tonya 10.544	H2	Cilo Dağı (mt.)	K4
Koçarli 5.182	B4	Posof 2.209	J1	Torbali 17.237	B3	Çoruh (riv.)	J2
Konya 246.727	E4	Pozanti 5.408	F4	Tortum 4.110	J2	Dardanelles (str.)	B6
Korkuteli 10.334	D4	Pülümür 3.442	H3	Torul 3.221	H2	Dicle (riv.)	J4
Köyceğiz 4.612	C4	Pütürge 4.878	H4	Tosya 17.515	F2	Eastern Taurus (mts.)	J3
Koyulhisar 3.861	G2	Refahiye 6.570	H3	Trabzon 97.210	H2	Ephesus (ruins)	B3
Kozakli 6.200	F3	Reşadiye 9.022	G2	Trebizond (Trabzon) 97.210	H2	Erciyas Dağı (mt.)	F3
Kozan 32.045	F4	Reyhanli 25.749	G4	Tunceli (Kalan) 11.637	H3	Ergene (riv.)	B2
Kozlu 27.322	D2	Rize 36.044	J2	Turgutlu 47.009	B3	Euphrates (Firat) (riv.)	G4
Kozluk 6.197	J3	Şabanözü 3.442	E2	Turhal 39.170	F2	Firat (riv.)	G4
Küçükköy 56.411	C2	Safranbolu 14.793	E2	Türkeli 2.194	F2	Gediz (riv.)	C3
Kula 10.807	C3	Sağanca 9.040	D2	Türkoğlu 9.207	G4	Gelidonya (cape)	D4
Kulp 4.474	J3	Saphane 3.919	C3	Tutak 4.325	K3	Gökçeada (isl.)	A2
Kulu 11.707	E3	Sarayköy 10.513	C4	Tuzluca 5.209	K3	Goksu (riv.)	E4
Kumkale 1.752	B6	Sarayönü 8.946	E3	Tuzlukçu 4.613	D3	Helles (cape)	B6
Kumluca 7.704	D4	Sarigöl 6.979	C3	Ula 5.117	C4	Heybeli (isl.)	D6
Küre 2.378	E2	Sarikamiş 21.262	K2	Ulaş 2.469	G3	Ilium (ruins)	B6
Kurşunlu 6.562	E2	Sarikaya 5.160	F3	Ulubey 4.214	C3	Imbros (Gökçeada) (isl.)	A2
Kurtalan 7.001	J3	Sarıköy 4.695	C2	Uluborlu 10.016	D3	Ince (cape)	F1
Kuşadasi 10.269	B4	Sarioğlan 3.245	F3	Uludere 4.060	K4	Istranca (mts.)	B2
Kütahya 82.442	C3	Sariyer 79.329	D5	Ulukişla 6.336	F4	Kaçkar Dağı (mt.)	J2
Kuyucak 6.039	C4	Sariz 3.591	G3	Umurbey 2.754	C6	Karadeniz Boğazi (Bosporus) (str.)	C2
Küre 6.785	E2	Şarkikaraağaç 4.772	D3	Ünye 23.366	G2	Karasu-Aras (mts.)	J3
Lâpseki 3.727	C6	Şarkişla 12.763	G3	Urfa 132.934	H4	Kelkit (riv.)	G2
Lice 8.625	J3	Şarköy 5.396	B2	Ürgüp 6.758	F3	Kerme (gulf)	B4
Lüleburgaz 32.401	B2	Sason 3.211	J3	Urla 13.903	B3	Keşiş Tepesi (mt.)	H3
Madenköy 15.151	H3	Savaştepe 7.179	B3	Uşak 58.578	C3	Kizilirmak (riv.)	F2
Mağara 4.314	G3	Şavşat 3.078	J1	Üsküdar 202.957	D6	Koca (riv.)	C3
Mahmudiye 5.240	D3	Şavur 4.983	J4	Üzümlü 4.365	J3	Köroğlu (mts.)	E2
Malatya 154.505	H3	Maraş (Kahramanmaraş) 135.782	G4	Uzunköprü 27.005	B2	Küre (mts.)	E2
Malazgirt 13.094	K3	Mardin 36.629	J4	Vakfikebir 12.556	H2	Mandalya (gulf)	B4
Maikara 14.399	H3	Marmaris 5.596	C4	Van 63.663	K3	Marmara (sea)	C2
Maltepe 66.343	D6	Mazgirt 3.141	H3	Varto 5.572	J3	Marmara (isl.)	B2
Manavgat 10.804	D4	Mazidağı 4.842	J4	Vezirköprü 11.705	F2	Menderes, Büyük (riv.)	C4
Manisa 78.114	B3	Mecitözü 6.066	F2	Viranşehir 26.244	H4	Meriç (riv.)	B2
Manyas 4.410	B3	Menemen 18.464	B3	Vize 8.203	B2	Murat (riv.)	H3
		Mengen 2.459	D2	Yahyalı 13.738	F4	Pontic (mts.)	H2
		Meriç 3.922	B2	Yalova, Istanbul 27.289	C2	Porsuk (riv.)	D3
		Mersin 152.236	F4	Yalvaç 18.305	D3	Prinkipo (Adalar) (isl.)	D6
		Merzifon 30.801	F2	Yaprakli 3.020	E2	Sakarya (riv.)	C2
		Mesudiye 4.294	G2	Yatağan 4.903	C4	Seyhan (riv.)	F4
		Midyat 16.905	J4	Yayladağı 4.471	G4	Simav (riv.)	C3
		Midye 2.003	B2	Yenice, Çanakkale 4.004	B3	Sinop (cape)	F1
		Mihalıççık 4.004	D3	Yenice, İçel 4.106	F4	Sultan (mts.)	D3
		Milas 17.929	B4	Yenice, Zonguldak 5.791	D2	Süphan Dağı (mt.)	J3
		Mucur 9.398	F3	Yeniceoba 5.740	E3	Taurus (mts.)	D4
		Mudanya 8.399	C2	Yeniköy, Istanbul	D5	Tigris (Dicle) (riv.)	J4
		Mudurnu 3.905	D2	Yenimahalle 198.643	E4	Troy (Ilium) (ruins)	B6
				Yenişehir 15.188	C2	Tuz (lake)	E3
				Yerkesik 2.381	C4	Van (lake)	K3
				Yerköy 19.927	F3	Yeşilirmak (riv.)	G2
				Yeşilhisar 10.429	F3		
				Yeşilköy	D6		
				Yeşilova, Burdur 3.685	C4		
				Yeşilova, Niğde 5.237	E3		

*City and suburbs

Turkey, Syria, Lebanon and Cyprus

© Copyright HAMMOND INCORPORATED, Maplewood, N.J.

SCALE OF MILES
0 — 25 — 50 — 75 — 100 — 125 — 150

SCALE OF KILOMETERS
0 — 25 — 50 — 75 — 100 — 125 — 150

Capitals of Countries ☆   Capitals of Provinces △

Provincial Boundaries

Scale 1:5,440,000

Topography

0   40   80 MI.

0   40   80 KM.

Meiron 3,963 ft. (1208 m.)
C. Carmel
Haifa
L. Tiberias (Sea of Galilee)
Yarmuk
GHOR
Tel Aviv-Jaffa
Hadera
Jordan
Zurqa
Jabbok
Soreq
Jerusalem
Amman
Dead Sea
El Ghor
Mujib
Syrian Desert
Beersheba
Besor
Negev
Tsin
Hasa
Esh Sheba
ARDES SAUWAN
Arava
Paran
EL JAFR
Jebel Ramm 5,755 ft. (1754 m.)

Below Sea Level	100 m. 328 ft.	200 m. 656 ft.	500 m. 1,640 ft.	1,000 m. 3,281 ft.	2,000 m. 6,562 ft.	5,000 m. 16,404 ft.

ISRAEL

DISTRICTS

Central 572,300 ....B3
Haifa 480,800 ....C2
Jerusalem 338,600 ....B4
Northern 473,700 ....C2
Southern 351,300 ....B5
Tel Aviv 905,100 ....B3

CITIES and TOWNS

Acre 34,400 ....C2
Afiqim 1,243 ....D2
'Afula 17,400 ....C2
Ahuzzam 407 ....B4
Akko (Acre) 34,400 ....C2
Arad 5,400 ....C5
'Arrabe 6,000 ....C2
Ashdod 40,500 ....B4
Ashdod Yaa'qov 1,197 ....D2
Ashqelon 43,100 ....A4
Atlit 1,516 ....B2
Avihayil 579 ....B2
Bat Shelomo 218 ....B2
Bat Yam 124,100 ....B3
Be'eri 390 ....A5
Be'er Menuha D5
Beersheba (Be'er
  Sheva) 101,000 ....B5
Be'er Tuveya 602 ....B4
Beit Guvrin B4
Bene Beraq 74,100 ....B3
Bet Qama 228 ....B5
Bet She'an 11,300 ....D3
Bet Shemesh 10,100 ....B4
Binyamina 2,701 ....B2
Carmel C2
Dafna 577 ....D1
Dalyat al-Karmel 6,200 ....B2
Dan 498 ....D1
Dimona 23,700 ....C5
Dor 195 ....B2
E'in Gedi C5
E'in Harod 1,372 ....C2
Elat D6
Elath (Elat) 12,800 ....D6
El 'Auja C5
Elyakim 568 ....B2
Elyashiv 435 ....B3
Even Yehuda 3,464 ....B3
Gal'on 356 ....B4
Gat 430 ....B4
Gedera 5,400 ....B4
Gerofit D6
Gesher 360 ....C2
Gesher Haziv 238 ....C1
Gevara'm 283 ....B4
Gilat 561 ....B5
Ginnosar 473 ....D2
Giv'atayim 48,500 ....B3
Giv'at Brenner 1,505 ....B4
Giv'at Hayyim 1,360 ....B3
Habonim 189 ....B2
Hadera 31,900 ....B3
Haifa 227,800 ....B2
Haifa* 367,400 ....B2
Hatseva D5
Hazerim 127 ....B5

Hazor Hagelilit D2
Helez 466 ....B4
Herzeliyya 41,200 ....B3
Hod Hasharon 13,500 ....B3
Hodiyya 400 ....B4
Holon 121,200 ....B3
Iksal 2,156 ....C2
Jerusalem (cap.) 376,000 ....C4
Jish 1,498 ....C1
Kafar Kanna 5,200 ....C2
Kafr Yasif 2,975 ....C2
Karkur-Pardes Hanna 13,600 ....C3
Kefar Blum 565 ....D1
Kefar Gila'di 701 ....C1
Kefar Ruppin 306 ....D3
Kefar Sava 26,500 ....B3
Kefar Vitkin 808 ....B3
Kefar Zekhariya 420 ....B4
Kinneret 909 ....D2
Lod (Lydda) 30,500 ....B4
Lydda 30,500 ....B4
Magen 149 ....A5
Maa'lot-Tarshiha C1
Makiya D1
Mash 'Abbe Sade 238 ....B6
Mavqi'm 177 ....B4
Megiddo C2
Metula 261 ....D1
Migdal 688 ....C2
Migdal Ha E'meq C2
Mikhmoret 608 ....B3
Mishmar Hanegev*336 ....B5
Mishmar Hayarden D1
Mivtahim 398 ....A5
Mizpe Ramon 331 ....D5
Moza Illit 219 ....C4
Mughar 4,010 ....B4
Muqeible 459 ....C2
Nahariyya 24,000 ....C1
Nazareth 33,300 ....C2
Nazerat I'lit C2
Negba 453 ....B4
Nes Ziyyona 11,700 ....B4
Netanya 70,700 ....B3
Netivot B5
Nevatim 436 ....B5
Newe Yam 211 ....B2
Newe Zohar C5
Nir Yitzhaq 209 ....A5
Nizzanim 479 ....B4
Otaqim B5
O'mer B5
Oron C6
Or Yehuda B4
Pardes Hanna-Karkur 13,600 ....B2
Peduyim 361 ....B5
Petah Tiqwa 112,000 ....B3
Qadima 2,937 ....B3
Qalansuwa B3
Qedma 157 ....B4
Qiryat Atta C2
Qiryat Bialik 18,000 ....B2
Qiryat Gat 19,200 ....B4
Qiryat Mal'akhi B4
Qiryat Motzkin 17,600 ....B2
Qiryat Shemona 15,200 ....C1
Qiryat Tivo'n 9,800 ....C2
Qiryat Yam 19,800 ....C2
Raa'nana 14,900 ....B3
Ramat Gan 120,900 ....B3

Ramat Hasharon 20,100 ....B3
Rame 2,986 ....C2
Ramla 34,100 ....B4
Rehovot 39,200 ....B4
Rei'm 155 ....A5
Revadim 175 ....B4
Revivim 258 ....D5
Rishon Le Ziyyon 51,900 ....B4
Rosh Ha 'Ayin B3
Rosh Pinna 700 ....D1
Ruhama 497 ....B4
Saa'd 418 ....B4
Safad (Zefat) 13,600 ....C2
Sakhnin 8,400 ....C2
Sede Boger D5
Sederot B4
Sedom C5
Sedot Yam 511 ....B2
Shave Ziyyon 269 ....B2
Shefara'm 11,800 ....C2
Shefayim 614 ....B3
Shoval 393 ....B5
Tayibe 11,700 ....C3
Tel Aviv-Jaffa 343,300 ....B3
Tel Aviv-Jaffa* 1,219,900 ....B3
Tiberias 23,800 ....C2
Tirat Hakarmel 14,400 ....B2
Tirat Zevi 353 ....D3
Tur'an 2,304 ....C2
Umm el Fahm 13,300 ....C2
Urim 203 ....B5
Uzza 487 ....B4
Yad Mordekhai 416 ....A4
Yagur 1,266 ....C2
Yahav D5
Yavne 10,100 ....B4
Yavne'el 1,580 ....D2
Yehud 8,900 ....B3
Yeroham 5,800 ....B6
Yesodot 293 ....B4
Yesud Hamaa'la 428 ....D1
Yiftah D1
Yirka 2,715 ....C2
Yotvata D5
Zavdi'el 396 ....B4
Ze'olim 148 ....A5
Zefat 13,600 ....C2
Zikhron Yaa'qov 6,500 ....C2
Zippori 241 ....C2

OTHER FEATURES

Aqaba (gulf) D6
'Araba, Wadi (valley) D5
Beer Sheva' (dry riv.) B5
Besor (riv.) B5
Carmel (cape) B2
Carmel (mt.) C2
Dead (sea) C4
Galilee, Sea of (Tiberias)
  (lake) D2
Galilee (reg.) C2
Gerar (dry riv.) B5
Hadera (dry riv.) B3
Haniqra, Rosh (cape) C1
Jordan (riv.) D3
Judaea (reg.) B5
Lakhish (dry riv.) B4
Meiron (mt.) C1
Negev (reg.) D5

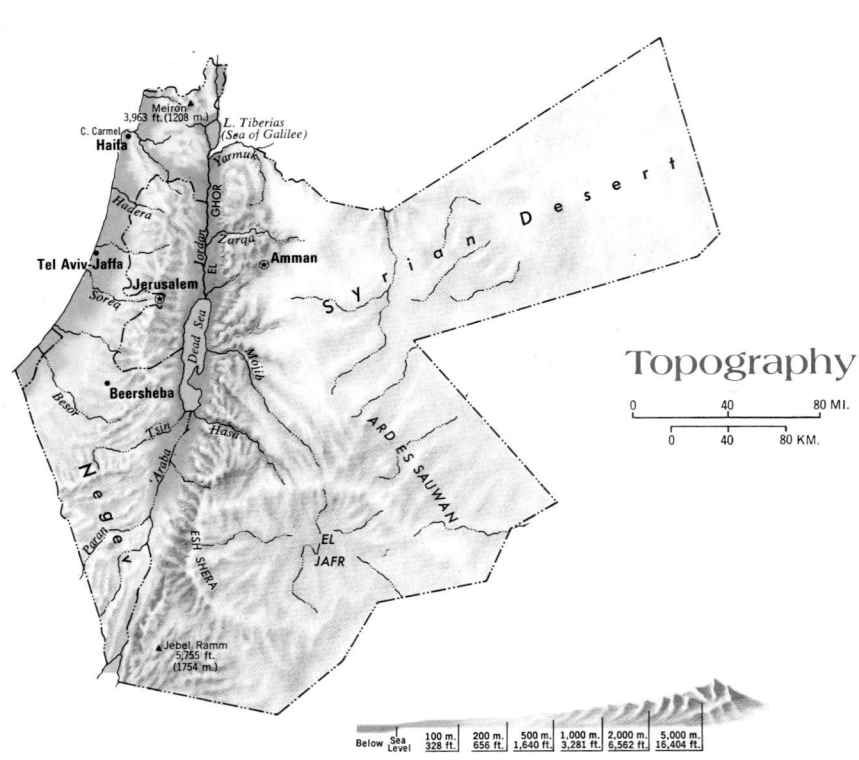

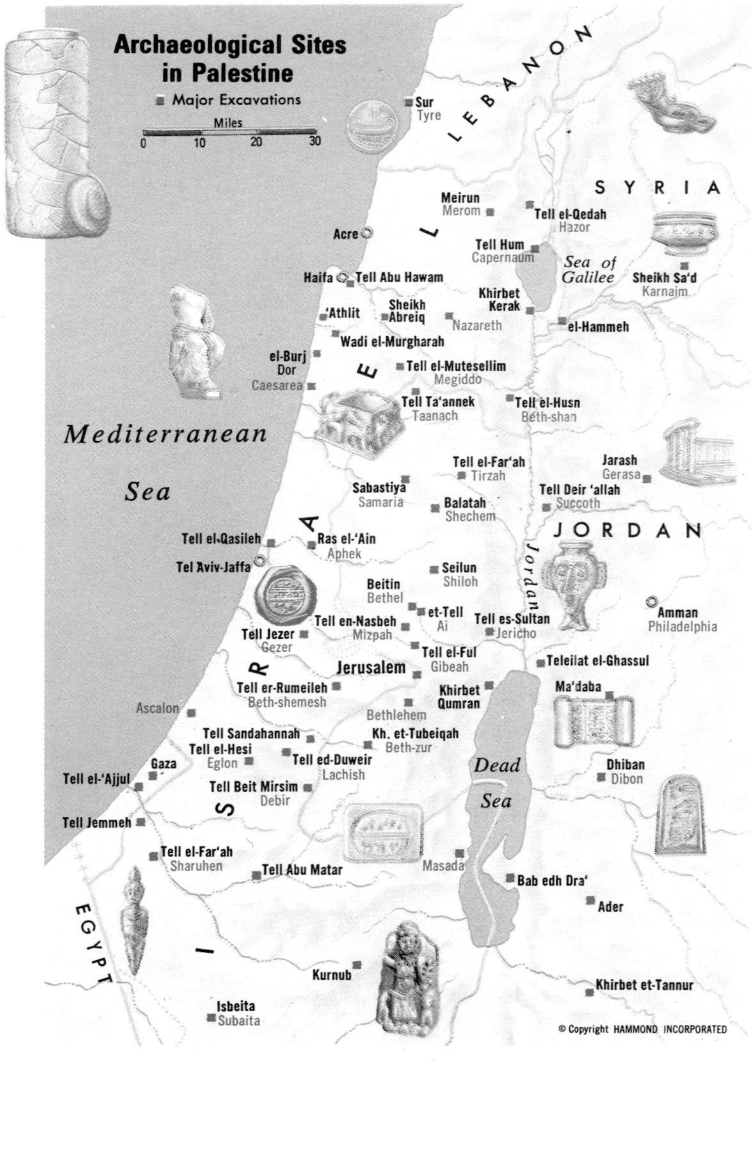

Archaeological Sites in Palestine

■ Major Excavations

0   10   20   30
Miles

LEBANON
SYRIA
Mediterranean Sea
JORDAN
EGYPT
ISRAEL

Sur
Tyre
Meirun / Merom
Acre
Tell el-Qedah / Hazor
Tell Hum / Capernaum
Sheikh Sa'd / Karnajm
Sea of Galilee
Haifa / Tell Abu Hawam
'Athlit
Sheikh Abreiq
Khirbet Kerak
Wadi el-Murgharah
Nazareth
el-Hammeh
el-Burj / Dor
Caesarea
Tell el-Mutesellim / Megiddo
Tell Ta'annek / Taanach
Tell el-Husn / Beth-shan
Tell el-Far'ah / Tirzah
Jarash / Gerasa
Sabastiya / Samaria
Tell Deir 'alla / Succoth
Balatah / Shechem
Tell el-Qasileh
Ras el-'Ain / Aphek
Tel Aviv-Jaffa
Seilun / Shiloh
Beitin / Bethel
et-Tell / Ai
Tell es-Sultan / Jericho
Amman / Philadelphia
Tell Jezer / Gezer
Tell en-Nasbeh / Mizpah
Tell el-Ful / Gibeah
Jerusalem
Teleilat el-Ghassul
Tell er-Rumeileh / Beth-shemesh
Khirbet Qumran
Ma'daba
Bethlehem
Ascalon
Tell Sandahannah
Kh. et-Tubeiqah / Beth-zur
Tell el-Hesi / Eglon
Tell ed-Duweir / Lachish
Gaza
Dhiban / Dibon
Tell el-'Ajjul
Tell Beit Mirsim / Debir
Tell Jemmeh
Dead Sea
Tell el-Far'ah / Sharuhen
Tell Abu Matar
Masada
Bab edh Dra'
Ader
Kurnub
Isbeita / Subaita
Khirbet et-Tannur

© Copyright HAMMOND INCORPORATED

Agriculture, Industry and Resources

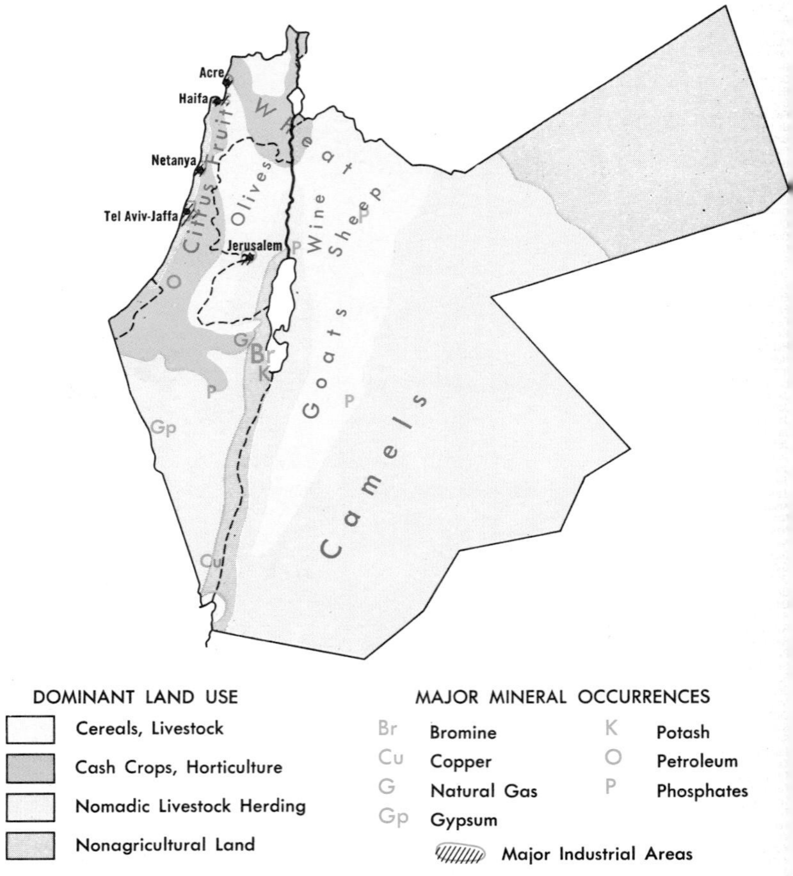

Acre
Haifa
Netanya
Tel Aviv-Jaffa
Jerusalem
Citrus Fruit
Olives
Wheat
Wine
Sheep
Goats
Camels
G
Br
K
P
Gp
Cu

DOMINANT LAND USE

☐ Cereals, Livestock
▨ Cash Crops, Horticulture
☐ Nomadic Livestock Herding
▨ Nonagricultural Land

MAJOR MINERAL OCCURRENCES

Br Bromine   K Potash
Cu Copper   O Petroleum
G   Natural Gas   P Phosphates
Gp Gypsum

▨ Major Industrial Areas

ISRAEL

JORDAN

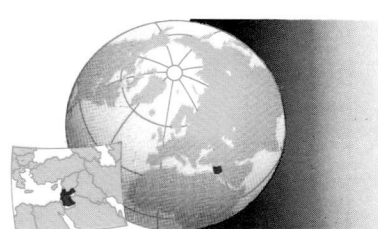

ISRAEL

AREA 7,847 sq. mi. (20,324 sq. km.)
POPULATION 3,878,000
CAPITAL Jerusalem
LARGEST CITY Tel Aviv-Jaffa
HIGHEST POINT Meiran 3,963 ft.
　(1,208 m.)
MONETARY UNIT shekel
MAJOR LANGUAGES Hebrew, Arabic
MAJOR RELIGIONS Judaism, Islam,
　Christianity

JORDAN

AREA 35,000 sq. mi.
　(90,650 sq. km.)
POPULATION 2,152,273
CAPITAL Amman
LARGEST CITY Amman
HIGHEST POINT Jeb. Ramm 5,755 ft.
　(1,754 m.)
MONETARY UNIT Jordanian dinar
MAJOR LANGUAGE Arabic
MAJOR RELIGION Islam

Qishon (riv.) C2
Ramon (mt.) D5
Rubin (dry riv.) B4
Tabor (mt.) C2
Tiberias (lake) D2
Yarmuk (riv.) D2
Yarqon (riv.) B3

GAZA STRIP

CITIES and TOWNS

Abasan 1,481 .... A5
Bani Suheila 7,561 .... A5
Beit Hanun 4,756 .... A4
Deir el Balah 10,854 ...... A5
Deir el Balah* 18,118 ..... A5
Gaza 87,793 .... A5
Gaza* 118,272 .... A5
Jabaliya 10,508 .... A4
Jabaliya* 43,604 .... A4
Khan Yunis 29,522 .... A5
Khan Yunis* 52,997 .... A5
Rafah 10,812 .... A5
Rafah* 49,812 .... A5

WEST BANK

CITIES AND TOWNS

'Ajja 1,322 .... C3
'Anabta 3,426 .... C2
Anin 914 .... C2
'Anza 807 .... C3
'Aqqaba 1,127 .... C3
'Aqraba 2,501 .... C4
Ariha (Jericho) 5,312 ..... C4
'Arraba 4,231 .... C4
Arura 849 .... C3
Attil 3,808 .... C3
Beit Fajjar 2,474 .... C4
Beit Hanina 1,177 .... C4
Beit Jala 6,041 .... C4
Beit Lahm (Bethlehem) 14,439 ... C4
Beit Nuba 1,350 .... C4
Beit Sahur 5,380 .... C4
Bethlehem 14,439 .... C4
Biddu 1,259 .... C4
Birqin 2,036 .... C3
Bir Zeit 2,311 .... C3
Burqa 2,477 .... C3
Deir Ballut 1,058 .... C3
Deir Sharaf 973 .... C3
Duma 524 .... C4
Dura 4,954 .... C4
El Bira 9,674 .... C4
El Bira* 13,037 .... C4
El Khalil (Hebron) 38,309 ... C4
Er Rihiya 679 .... C4
Ez Zababida 1,474 .... B5
Falama 162 .... C3
Halhul 6,041 .... C4
Haris 641 .... C4
Hebron 38,309 .... C4
Idna 3,713 .... B4
I'mwas 1,955 .... C4
Jaba 2,817 .... C3
Jalama 784 .... C3
Jalbun 914 .... C3
Jalud 221 .... C3
Jenin 8,346 .... C3
Jenin* 13,365 .... C3
Jericho 5,312 .... C4
Jericho* 6,931 .... C4
Jifna 655 .... C4
Kharas 1,364 .... C4
Nablus (Nablus) 41,799 ... C3
Nahhalin 1,109 .... C4
Nil'in 1,227 .... C3
Qabalan 1,970 .... C3
Qabatiya 6,005 .... C3
Qaffin 2,480 .... C3
Qalqiliya 8,926 .... C3
Qibya 926 .... C3
Rafidiya 1,123 .... C3
Ramallah 12,134 .... C4
Rammun 1,198 .... C4
Rantis 897 .... C3
Salfit 3,201 .... C3
Samu 3,784 .... C5
Shuf'at 14,000 .... C4
Shuweika 2,332 .... C3
Silat Dhahr 2,104 .... C3
Sinjil 1,823 .... C3
Siris 1,285 .... C3
Tammun 2,952 .... C3
Tarqumiya 2,412 .... C4
Tubas 5,262 .... C3
Tulkarm 10,255 .... C3
Tulkarm* 15,275 .... C3
Tur 12,200 .... C4
Yab'ad 4,857 .... C3
Yabrud 277 .... C4
Yatta 7,281 .... C5
Zububa 633 .... C2

OTHER FEATURES

Golan Heights D1
West Bank C3

JORDAN

GOVERNORATES

El Asima 1,000,000 ...... D4
El Balqa 113,000 .... D4
El Karak 93,000 .... E5
Irbid 506,000 .... D3
Ma'an 62,000 .... D5

CITIES and TOWNS

'Ajlun 42,000 .... D3
Amman (cap.) 711,850 ... D4
'Anjara 3,163 .... D3
'Aqaba 15,000 .... D6
Bala'ma 769 .... E3
Baqura 3,042 .... D3
Damiya 483 .... D3
Dana 844 .... E5
Deir Abu Sa'id 1,927 ... D3
Dhira' D5
El 'Al 492 .... D4
El Husn 3,728 .... D3
El Karak 10,000 .... D4
El Kitta 987 .... D3
El Madwar 164 .... E3
El Mafraq 15,500 .... E3
El Majdal 259 .... D3
El Quweira 268 .... D6
El Yaduda 251 .... D4
Er Rafid 787 .... D2
Er Ramtha 19,000 ...... E2
Er Rumman 293 .... D3
Er Ruseifa 6,200 .... E3
Esh Shaubak 01 .... D5
Es Sahab 2,580 .... E4
Es Salt 24,000 .... D3
Es Sukhna 649 .... D3
Et Tafila* 17,000 ...... E5
Et Taiyiba 2,606 ...... D3
Ez Zarqa' 263,400 ..... E3
Harima 635 .... D3
Hawara 2,342 .... D2
Hisban 718 .... D4
I'bbin 1,364 .... D3
Irbid 136,770 .... D2
Jabir 132 .... E2
Jarash 29,000 .... D3
Kitim 1,026 .... D3
Kufrinja 3,922 .... D3
Kuraiyima D3
Maa'd 125 .... D3
Maa'n 9,500 .... E5
Ma'daba 22,600 ...... D4
Main 1,271 .... D4
Manja 353 .... D4
Mazra C5
Nau'r 2,382 .... D4
Nitil 348 .... D4
Qumeim 955 .... D2
Ra's en Naqb 225 .... E6
Safi D5
Safut 4,210 .... D3
Samar 716 .... D3
Sarih 3,390 .... D3
Shunat Nimrin 109 ... D4
Subeihi 514 .... D3
Suf D3
Suweilih 3,457 ..... D4
Suweima 315 .... D4
Um Jauza 582 ...... D4
Wadi es Sir 4,455 ... D4
Wadi Musa 654 ..... E5
Waqqas 2,321 ...... D2
Zuweiza 126 .... D4

OTHER FEATURES

'Ajlun (range) D3
Aqaba (gulf) D6
'Araba, Wadi (valley) ... D5
Dead (sea) D4
Ebal (mt.) C4
El Ghor (reg.) C6
El Lisan (pen.) D5
Hasa, Wadi el (dry riv.) ... D5
Jordan (riv.) C5
Judaea (reg.) C4
Khirbet Qumran (site) ... C4
Mashash, Wadi (dry riv.) ... D4
Nebo (mt.) D4
Petra (ruins) D5
Ramm, Jebel (mt.) ... D6
Samaria (reg.) C3
Shallala, Wadi esh (dry riv.) ... C4
Shu'eib, Wadi (dry riv.) ... C4
Tell 'Asur (mt.) .. C4
Yabis, Wadi el (dry riv.) ... D3
Zarqa' (riv.) D3

*City and suburbs.
⊙ Population of subdivision.

Israel and Jordan

CYLINDRICAL PROJECTION

© Copyright HAMMOND INCORPORATED, Maplewood, N.J.

SCALE OF MILES
0　5　10　15　20　25　30

SCALE OF KILOMETERS
0　5　10　15　20　25　30

Capitals of Countries _____ ☆
Internal Capitals _____ ⊙
International Boundaries _____
Internal Boundaries _____

Scale 1:1,325,000

IRAN

INTERNAL DIVISIONS

Azerbaijan, East
(prov.) 3,194,543 ....E1
Azerbaijan, West
(prov.) 1,404,875 ....D1
Bakhtaran (prov.) 1,016,199 ....E3
Bakhtiari
(governorate) 394,300 ......F4
Boyer Ahmediyeh and Kohkiluyeh
(governorate) 244,750 ......G5
Bushehr (prov.) 345,427 ......G6
Central (Markazi)
(prov.) 6,921,283 ....G3
Esfahan (Isfahan)
(prov.) 1,974,938 ....H4
Fars (prov.) 2,020,947 ......H6
Gilan (prov.) 1,577,800 ......F2
Hamadan (governorate) 1,086,512 ...F3
Hormozgan (governorate) 463,419 ...J7
Ilam (governorate) 244,222 ....E4
Isfahan (prov.) 1,974,938 ......H4
Kerman (prov.) 1,088,045 ......K6
Khorasan (prov.) 3,266,650 ....K3
Khuzestan (prov.) 2,176,612 ....F5
Kordestan (Kurdistan)
(prov.) 781,889 ....E3
Lorestan (Luristan)
(governorate) 924,848 ......F4
Mazandaran (prov.) 2,384,226 ....H2
Semnan (governorate) 485,875 ...J3
Sistan and Baluchestan
(prov.) 659,297 ....M6
Yazd (governorate) 356,218 ....J5
Zanjan (governorate) 579,000 ....F2

CITIES and TOWNS

Abadan 296,081 ....F5
Abadeh 16,000 ....H5
Abarqu 8,000 ....H5
Abhar 24,000 ....F2
Agha Jari 24,195 ....F5
Ahar 24,000 ....E1
Ahvaz (Ahwaz) 329,006 ....F5
Amol 68,782 ....H2
Anarak 2,038 ....H4
Aradan 8,978 ....H3
Arak 114,507 ....F4
Ardakan 8,978 ....H4
Ardestan 5,868 ....H4
Asadabad 7,000 ....F3
Asterabad (Gorgan) 88,348 ...J2
Babol 67,790 ....H2
Babol Sar 7,237 ....H2
Baft 6,000 ....K6
Bafq 24,000 ....J5
Bam 22,000 ....L6
Bandar 'Abbas 89,103 ......J7
Bandar-e Anzali
(Enzeli) 55,978 ....F2
Bandar-e Deylam 3,691 ......G5
Bandar-e Khomeyni 6,000 ....F5
Bandar-e Lengeh 4,920 ......J7
Bandar-e Mas hur 17,000 ....G6
Bandar-e Rig 1,889 ....G6
Bandar-e Torkeman 13,000 ....H2
Bandar Shahpur 6,000 ......F5
Bastak 2,473 ....J7
Bastam 3,296 ....J2
Behbehan 39,874 ....G5
Behshahr 26,032 ....H2

Bejestan 3,823 ....K3
Bijar 12,000 ....E2
Birjand 25,854 ....L4
Bojnurd 31,246 ....K2
Borazjan 20,000 ....G6
Borujerd 100,103 ....F4
Bostan 4,619 ....F5
Bowkan 9,000 ....E2
Bushehr (Bushire) 57,681 ....G6
Chalus 15,000 ....G2
Damavand 5,319 ....H3
Damghan 13,000 ....J2
Darab 5,000 ....J6
Darab 4,609 ....G4
Darreh Gaz 11,000 ....L2
Dehkhvareqan 6,000 ......D2
Delijan 6,000 ....G4
Dezful 110,287 ....F4
Dizful (Dezful) 110,287 ......F4
Duzdab (Zahedan) 92,628 ....M6
Emamshahr 30,767 ....J2
Enzeli 55,978 ....F2
Eslamabad (Iranshahr) 671,820 ..E3
Eslamabad 12,000 ....E3
Eslamabad 18,187 ....J6
Eshtehard 18,187 ....J6
Evaz 6,064 ....J7
Fahrej (Iranshahr) 5,000 ......M7
Fariman 8,000 ....L3
Farrahabad 3,532 ....G6
Fasa 19,000 ....H6
Firuzabad 8,718 ....H6
Firuzkuh 4,684 ....H3
Fowman 9,000 ....F2
Gach Saran 31,000 ....G5

Ganaveh 9,000 ....G6
Garmsar 4,723 ....H3
Gavater M8
Ghaemshahr 63,289 ......H2
Golpayegan 20,515 ....G4
Golshan (Tabas) 10,000 ....K4
Gomishan 6,000 ....J2
Gonbad-e Kavus 59,868 ....J2
Gonbadli 531 ....M2
Gorgan (Gurgan) 88,348 ....J2
Haft Gel 10,000 ....F5
Hamadan 155,846 ....F3
Hashtpar 5,000 ....F2
Hormoz 2,569 ....J7
Huzgan 4,722 ....F5
Ilam 15,000 ....E4
Iranshahr 5,000 ....M7
Isfahan (Isfahan) 671,825 ....H4
Jahrom 38,236 ....H6
Jajarm 3,641 ....K2
Jask 1,976 ....K8
Kakhk 4,043 ....L3
Kangan 2,682 ....G6
Kangavar 9,414 ....F3
Karaj 138,774 ....G3
Kashan 84,545 ....G3
Kashmar 17,000 ....L3
Kazerun 51,309 ....G6
Kazvin (Qazvin) 138,527 ....F3
Kerman 140,309 ....K6
Khaf 5,000 ....L3
Khalkhal 5,422 ....F2
Khash 7,439 ....M6
Khiyav 9,000 ....E1
Khoman 3,054 ....F2
Khomeinishar 46,836 ......G4

Khorramabad 104,928 ......F4
Khorramshahr 146,709 ......F5
Khvaf 5,000 ....L3
Khvonsar 10,947 ....G4
Khvor 2,912 ....J4
Khvoy (Khoi) 70,040 ......D1
Kord Kuy 9,855 ....J2
Lahijan 25,725 ....F2
Lar 22,000 ....J7
Mahabad 28,610 ....D2
Mahallat 12,000 ....G4
Mahan 8,000 ....K5
Maku 16,000 ....D1
Malamir (Izeh) 1,983 ......F5
Maragheh 60,820 ....D2
Marand 24,000 ....D1
Marv Dasht 25,498 ....H6
Mashhad (Meshed) 670,180 ...L2
Masjed Soleyman 77,161 ....F5
Medishahr 9,000 ....J2
Mehran 664 ....E4
Meshed 670,180 ....L2
Meshed-i-Sar (Babol
Sar) 12,000 ....H2
Meybod 15,000 ....J4
Miandowab 19,000 ....E2
Mianeh 28,447 ....E2
Minab 4,228 ....K7
Mirjaveh 11,000 ....M6
Nae in 5,925 ....H4
Naft-e Shah 3,043 ....D4
Najafabad 76,236 ....G4
Naraq 2,725 ....G4
Nasratabad (Zaboli) 20,000 ...M5
Nayband 4,370 ....H4
Neyriz 16,114 ....J6
Neyshabur 59,101 ....L2

Nishapur (Neyshabur) 59,101 ..L2
Nosratabad 20,000 ....L6
Now Shahr 8,000 ....G2
Orumiyeh (Urmia) 163,991 ....D2
Oshnoviyeh 5,000 ....D2
Pahlevi (Enzeli) 55,978 ......F2
Pazanan 81 ....F5
Qayen 6,000 ....L3
Qayen 6,000 ....J4
Qazvin 138,527 ....F2
Qom 246,831 ....G3
Qorveh 2,929 ....E3
Quchan 29,133 ....K2
Qum (Qom) 246,831 ......G3
Rafsanjan 21,000 ....K5
Ramhormoz 9,000 ....F5
Rasht 187,203 ....F2
Ravar 5,074 ....K5
Rasht (Rasht) 187,203 ......F2
Rey 102,825 ....G3
Reza'iyeh (Urmia) 163,991 ....D2
Rigan 8,255 ....L6
Rud Sar 7,460 ....F2
Sabzevar 69,174 ....K2
Sabzvaran 7,000 ....K6
Saeendey 4,195 ....L2
Sakht-Sar 12,000 ....G2
Salmas 13,161 ....D1
Sanandaj 95,834 ....E3
Saqqez 17,000 ....E2
Sarab 16,000 ....E1
Sarakhs 3,461 ....M2
Saravan 4,012 ....N7
Sari 70,936 ....H2
Savanat (Estahbanat) 18,187 ..J6
Saveh 17,565 ....G3
Semnan 31,058 ....H3

Shadegan 6,000 ....F5
Shahdad 2,777 ....L5
Shahista (Saravan) 4,012 ....N7
Shahreza 34,220 ....H4
Shahr Kord 24,000 ....G4
Shahrud (Emamshahr) 30,767 ..J2
Sharafkhaneh 1,260 ....D1
Shiraz 416,408 ....H6
Shirvan 11,000 ....K2
Shush 1,433 ....F5
Shushtar 24,000 ....F5
Sinneh (Sanandaj) 95,834 ....E3
Sirjan (Sai'dabad) 20,000 ....J6
Sivand 1,811 ....H6
Songor 10,453 ....F3
Sufian 2,914 ....D1
Sultanabad (Kashmar) 17,000 ..L3
Tabas 10,000 ....K4
Tabriz 598,576 ....D2
Taft 7,000 ....J5
Takestan 13,485 ....F2
Takistan 57,486 ....F2
Tehran (cap.) 4,496,159 ....G3
Tonekabon 12,000 ....G2
Torbat-e Heydariyeh 30,106 ...L3
Torbat-i-Jam 13,000 ....M3
Tuysarkan 12,000 ....F3
Urmia 163,991 ....D2
Varamin 11,183 ....G3
Yazd (Yezd) 135,978 ......J5
Yazd-e Khvast 3,544 ....H5
Zabol 20,000 ....M5
Zahedan 92,628 ....M6
Zanjan 99,967 ....F2
Zarand 5,000 ....K5
Zarqam 7,000 ....F5
Zenjan (Zanjan) 99,967 ......F2

Iran and Iraq

CONIC PROJECTION

SCALE OF MILES

0 25 50 100 150 200

SCALE OF KILOMETERS

0 25 50 100 150 200

Capitals of Countries..............☆
Capitals of Provinces.............△
Capitals of Governorates..........◉
International Boundaries...........
Provincial Boundaries.............
Governorate Boundaries...........

Scale 1:8,160,000

© Copyright HAMMOND INCORPORATED, Maplewood, N.J.

Iran consists of fifteen provinces
called ostans. Attached to seven of
these provinces are eight governorates.

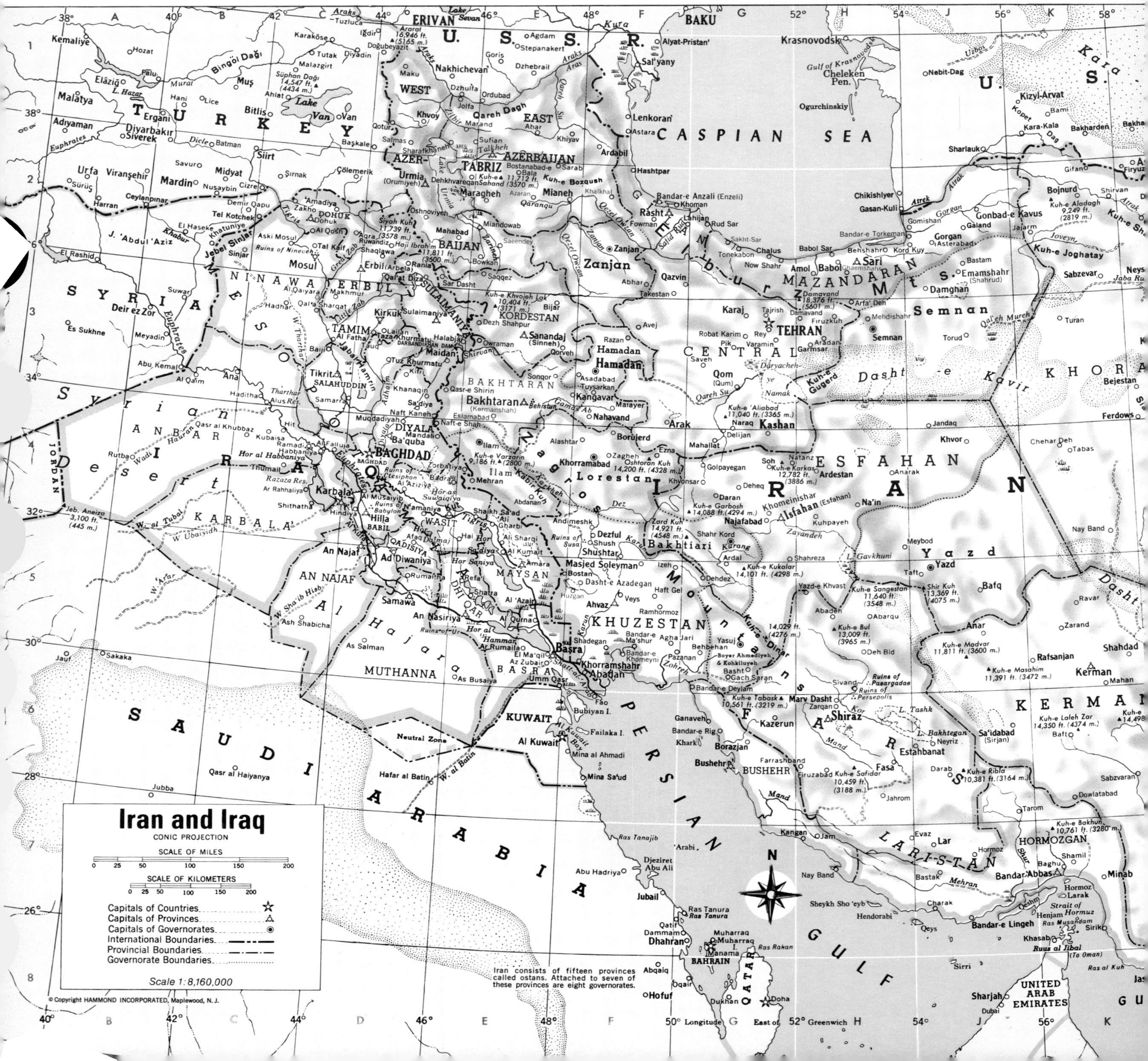

OTHER FEATURES

Aji Chai (riv.) E1
A'rabi (isl.) G7
Araks (Aras) (riv.) E1
Atrak (Atrek) (riv.) J2
Bakhtegan (lake) J6
Baluchistan (reg.) M7
Bampur (riv.) M7
Behistun (ruins) E3
Caspian (sea) G1
Damavand (Demavend) (mt.) H3
Dez (riv.) F4
Elburz (mts.) G2
Farsi (isl.) G7
Gorgan (riv.) J2
Hari Rud (riv.) M3
Karkheh (riv.) E4
Karun (riv.) F5
Kashaf Rud (riv.) M2
Khark (Kharg) (isl.) G6
Kuh (cape) K8
Kurang (riv.) G4
Laristan (reg.) J7
Makran (reg.) M8
Mand Rud (riv.) G6
Mehran (riv.) H7
Namaksar (lake) M4
Nezwar (mt.) H3
Oman (gulf) M8
Pasargadae (ruins) H5
Persepolis (ruins) H6
Persian (gulf) G6
Qareh Su (riv.) E1
Qareh Su (riv.) G3
Qeshm (isl.) J7
Qezel Owzam (riv.) F2
Safid Rud (riv.) F2

Shaikh Shua'ib (isl.) H7
Shelagh (riv.) M5
Shirvan (riv.) E3
Shur (riv.) J7
Siah Kuh (mt.) L3
Silup (riv.) M8
Susa (ruins) F4
Talab (riv.) N6
Tashk (lake) J6
Urmia (lake) D2
Zagros (mts.) E4
Zarineh (riv.) E2
Zilbir (riv.) D1
Zohreh (riv.) F5

IRAQ
GOVERNORATES

Anbar B4
An Najaf C5
Babil D4
Baghdad D4
Basra E5
Dhi Qar E5
Diyala D4
Dohuk C2
Erbil C3
Karbala B4
Maysan E5
Muthanna D5
Ninawa B3
Qadisiya D4
Salahuddin D3
Sulaimaniya D3
Tamin D3
Wasit D4

CITIES and TOWNS

Ad Diwaniya 60,553 .... D5
A'faq 5,390 .... D4
Al A'ziziya 7,450 .... D4
Al Falluja 38,072 .... C4
Al Fathat 15,329 .... C3
A'li Gharbi 15,456 .... E4
A'li Sharqi 8,398 .... E4
Al Kufa 30,862 .... D4
Al Musaiyib 15,955 .... D4
Al Qa'im 3,372 .... B3
Al Qaiyara 3,060 .... C3
Al Qosh 3,863 .... C2
Al Qurna 5,638 .... E5
A'madiya 2,578 .... C2
A'mara 64,847 .... E5
A'na 15,729 .... B3
An Najaf 128,096 .... D5
An Nasiriya 60,405 .... D5
A'qra 8,659 .... D2
Arbela (Erbil) 90,320 .... D2
Aski Mosul 643 .... C2
As Salman 1,789 .... D5
Az Zubair 41,408 .... E5
Badra 3,564 .... D4
Baghdad (cap.) 502,503 .... D4
Baghdad* 1,745,328 .... D4
Baiji 6,785 .... C3
Baq'uba 34,575 .... D4
Basra 313,327 .... E5
Dohuk 16,998 .... C2
Erbil 90,320 .... D2
Fao 15,399 .... F6
Habbaniya 14,405 .... C4
Haditha 6,870 .... C3
Hai 16,988 .... E4
Halabja 11,206 .... D3
Hilla 84,717 .... D4
Hindiya 16,436 .... C4
Hit 9,131 .... C4
Karbal'a 83,301 .... C4
Khanaqin 23,522 .... D3
Kifri 8,500 .... D3
Kirkuk 167,413 .... D3
Kirkuk* 176,794 .... D3
Kubaisa 4,023 .... C4
Kut 42,116 .... D4
Makhmur 2,556 .... C3
Mandali 11,262 .... D4
Mosul 315,157 .... C2
Muqdadiyah 12,181 .... D4
Naft Kaneh D3
Na'maniya 11,943 .... D4
Qal'at Diza 6,250 .... D2
Ramadi 28,723 .... C4
Rania 4,090 .... D2
Refai 7,681 .... E5
Rumaitha 10,222 .... D5
Rutba 5,091 .... B4
Ruwandiz 5,801 .... D2
Sad'iya 5,285 .... D4
Samarra 24,746 .... D3
Samawa 33,473 .... D5
Shaikh Saa'd 2,958 .... E4
Shaqlawa 6,814 .... D2
Shatra 18,822 .... E5
Sinjar 7,942 .... B2
Sulaimaniya 86,822 .... D3
Tal Kaif 7,482 .... C2
Taza Khurmatu 2,681 .... D3
Tikrit 9,921 .... C3
Tuz Khurmatu 13,860 .... D3
Zakho 14,790 .... C2

OTHER FEATURES

Adhaim (riv.) D3
Aneiza, Jebel (mt.) A4
A'rab, Shatt-al- (riv.) F5
A'ra'r, Wadi (dry riv.) B5
Babylon (ruins) D4
Batin, Wadi al (dry riv.) E6
Ctesiphon (ruins) D4
Darbandikhan (dam) D3
Euphrates (riv.) D4
Great Zab (riv.) C3
Hauran, Wadi (dry riv.) B4
Little Zab (riv.) C3
Mesopotamia (reg.) B3
Nineveh (ruins) C2
Sad'iya, Hor (lake) E4
Saniya, Hor (lake) E5
Shai'b Hisb, Wadi (dry riv.) C5
Sinjar, Jebel (mts.) B2
Siyah Kuh (mt.) D2
Syrian (des.) B4
Tigris (riv.) E4
Ubaiyidh, Wadi (dry riv.) B5
Ur (ruins) E5

*City and suburbs.
†Population of commune.

IRAN

IRAQ

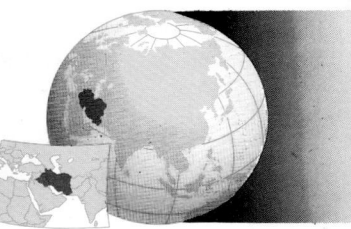

AREA 636,293 sq. mi. (1,648,000 sq. km.)
POPULATION 37,447,000
CAPITAL Tehran
LARGEST CITY Tehran
HIGHEST POINT Damavand 18,376 ft. (5,601 m.)
MONETARY UNIT Iranian rial
MAJOR LANGUAGES Persian, Azerbaijani, Kurdish
MAJOR RELIGION Islam

AREA 172,476 sq. mi. (446,713 sq. km.)
POPULATION 12,767,000
CAPITAL Baghdad
LARGEST CITY Baghdad
HIGHEST POINT Haji Ibrahim 11,811 ft. (3,600 m.)
MONETARY UNIT Iraqi dinar
MAJOR LANGUAGES Arabic, Kurdish
MAJOR RELIGION Islam

Topography

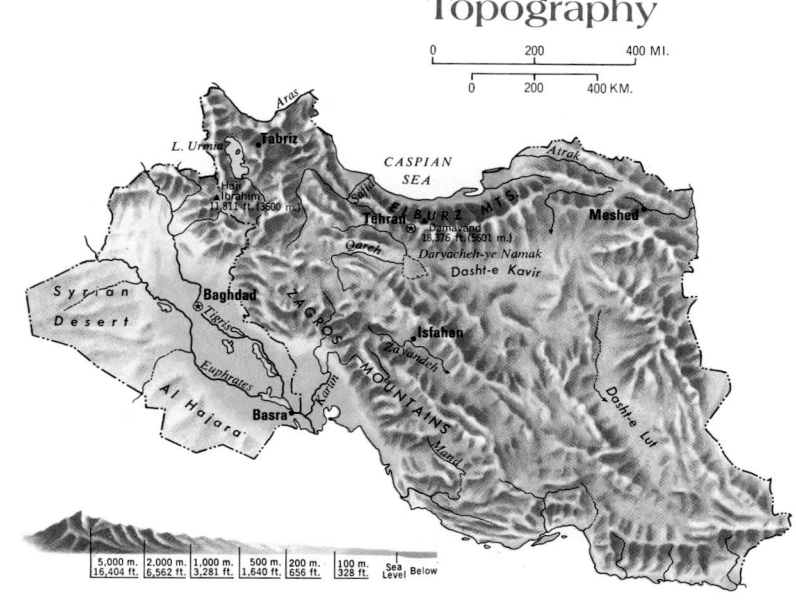

Agriculture, Industry and Resources

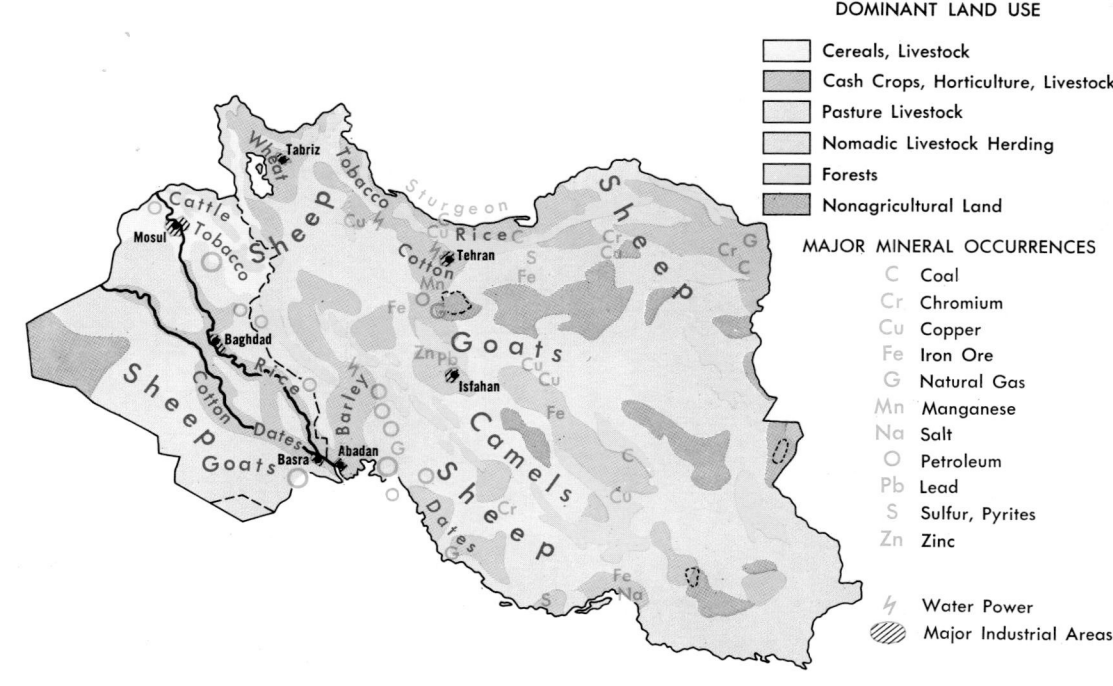

DOMINANT LAND USE

- Cereals, Livestock
- Cash Crops, Horticulture, Livestock
- Pasture Livestock
- Nomadic Livestock Herding
- Forests
- Nonagricultural Land

MAJOR MINERAL OCCURRENCES

- C Coal
- Cr Chromium
- Cu Copper
- Fe Iron Ore
- G Natural Gas
- Mn Manganese
- Na Salt
- O Petroleum
- Pb Lead
- S Sulfur, Pyrites
- Zn Zinc

- Water Power
- Major Industrial Areas

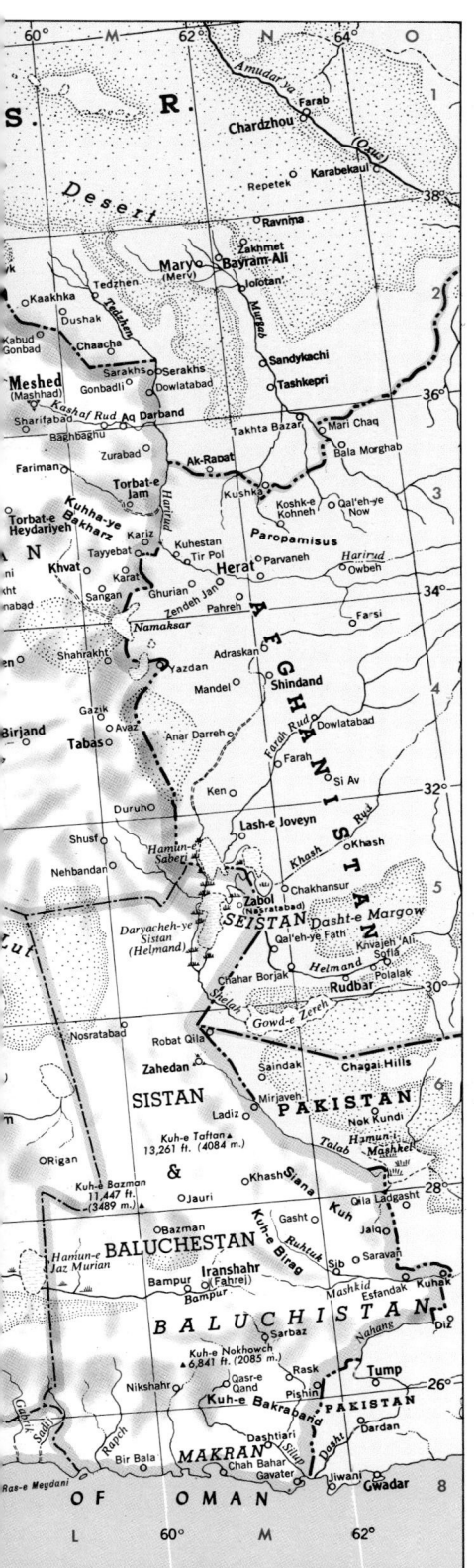

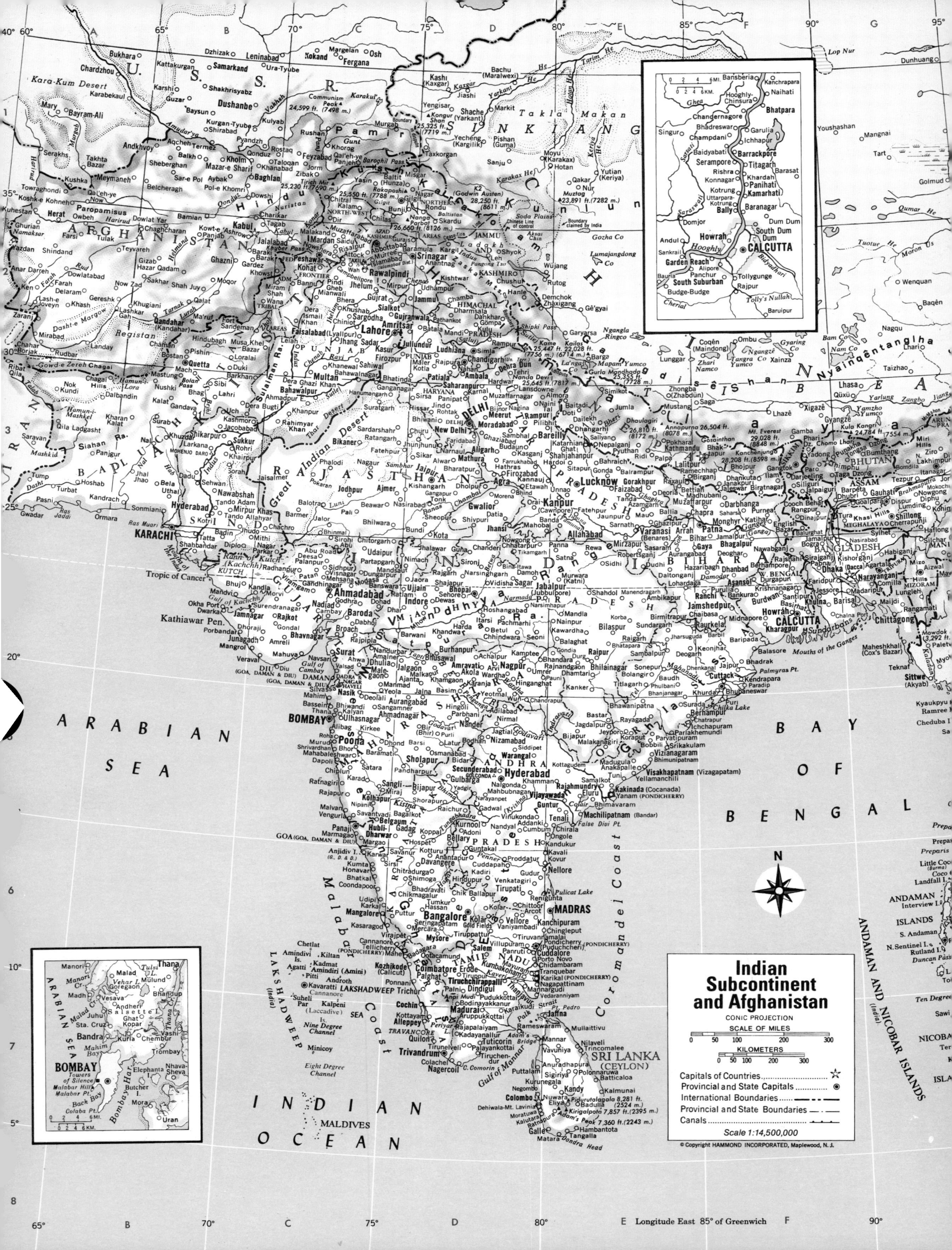

Indian Subcontinent and Afghanistan

CONIC PROJECTION

SCALE OF MILES

KILOMETERS

Capitals of Countries .... ☆
Provincial and State Capitals .... ◉
International Boundaries .... — · —
Provincial and State Boundaries ... — — —
Canals .... — · —

Scale 1:14,500,000

© Copyright HAMMOND INCORPORATED, Maplewood, N.J.

INDIA

AREA 1,269,339 sq. mi. (3,287,588 sq. km.)
POPULATION 683,810,051
CAPITAL New Delhi
LARGEST CITY Calcutta (greater)
HIGHEST POINT Nanda Devi 25,645 ft. (7,817 m.)
MONETARY UNIT Indian rupee
MAJOR LANGUAGES Hindi, English, Bihari, Telugu,
 Marathi, Bengali, Tamil, Gujarati, Rajasthani,
 Kanarese, Malayalam, Oriya, Punjabi, Assamese,
 Kashmiri, Urdu
MAJOR RELIGIONS Hinduism, Islam, Christianity,
 Sikhism, Buddhism, Jainism, Zoroastrianism, Animism

PAKISTAN

AREA 310,403 sq. mi. (803,944 sq. km.)
POPULATION 83,782,000
CAPITAL Islamabad
LARGEST CITY Karachi
HIGHEST POINT K2 (Godwin Austen)
 28,250 ft. (8,611 m.)
MONETARY UNIT Pakistani rupee
MAJOR LANGUAGES Urdu, English, Punjabi,
 Pushtu, Sindhi, Baluchi, Brahui
MAJOR RELIGIONS Islam, Hinduism, Sikhism,
 Christianity, Buddhism

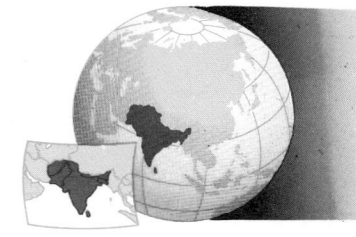

SRI LANKA (CEYLON)

AREA 25,332 sq. mi.
 (65,610 sq. km.)
POPULATION 14,850,001
CAPITAL Colombo
LARGEST CITY Colombo
HIGHEST POINT Pidurutalagala
 8,281 ft. (2,524 m.)
MONETARY UNIT Sri Lanka rupee
MAJOR LANGUAGES Sinhala, Tamil,
 English
MAJOR RELIGIONS Buddhism,
 Hinduism, Christianity, Islam

AFGHANISTAN

AREA 250,775 sq. mi.
 (649,507 sq. km.)
POPULATION 15,540,000
CAPITAL Kabul
LARGEST CITY Kabul
HIGHEST POINT Nowshak
 24,557 ft. (7,485 m.)
MONETARY UNIT afghani
MAJOR LANGUAGES Pushtu, Dari,
 Uzbek
MAJOR RELIGION Islam

NEPAL

AREA 54,663 sq. mi.
 (141,577 sq. km.)
POPULATION 14,179,301
CAPITAL Kathmandu
LARGEST CITY Kathmandu
HIGHEST POINT Mt. Everest
 29,028 ft. (8,848 m.)
MONETARY UNIT Nepalese rupee
MAJOR LANGUAGES Nepali,
 Maithili, Tamang, Newari, Tharu
MAJOR RELIGIONS Hinduism,
 Buddhism

MALDIVES

AREA 115 sq. mi. (298 sq. km.)
POPULATION 143,046
CAPITAL Male
LARGEST CITY Male
HIGHEST POINT 20 ft. (6 m.)
MONETARY UNIT Maldivian rupee
MAJOR LANGUAGE Divehi
MAJOR RELIGION Islam

BHUTAN

AREA 18,147 sq. mi.
 (47,000 sq. km.)
POPULATION 1,298,000
CAPITAL Thimphu
LARGEST CITY Thimphu
HIGHEST POINT Kula Kangri
 24,784 ft. (7,554 m.)
MONETARY UNIT ngultrum
MAJOR LANGUAGES Dzongka,
 Nepali
MAJOR RELIGIONS Buddhism,
 Hinduism

BANGLADESH

AREA 55,126 sq. mi.
 (142,776 sq. km.)
POPULATION 87,052,024
CAPITAL Dhaka
LARGEST CITY Dhaka
HIGHEST POINT Keokradong
 4,034 ft. (1,230 m.)
MONETARY UNIT taka
MAJOR LANGUAGES Bengali,
 English
MAJOR RELIGIONS Islam,
 Hinduism Christianity

INDIA PAKISTAN SRI LANKA (CEYLON) BHUTAN

AFGHANISTAN MALDIVES BANGLADESH NEPAL

(continued on following page)

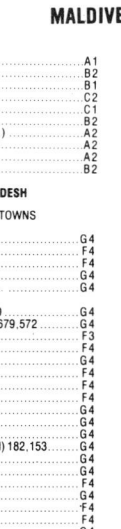

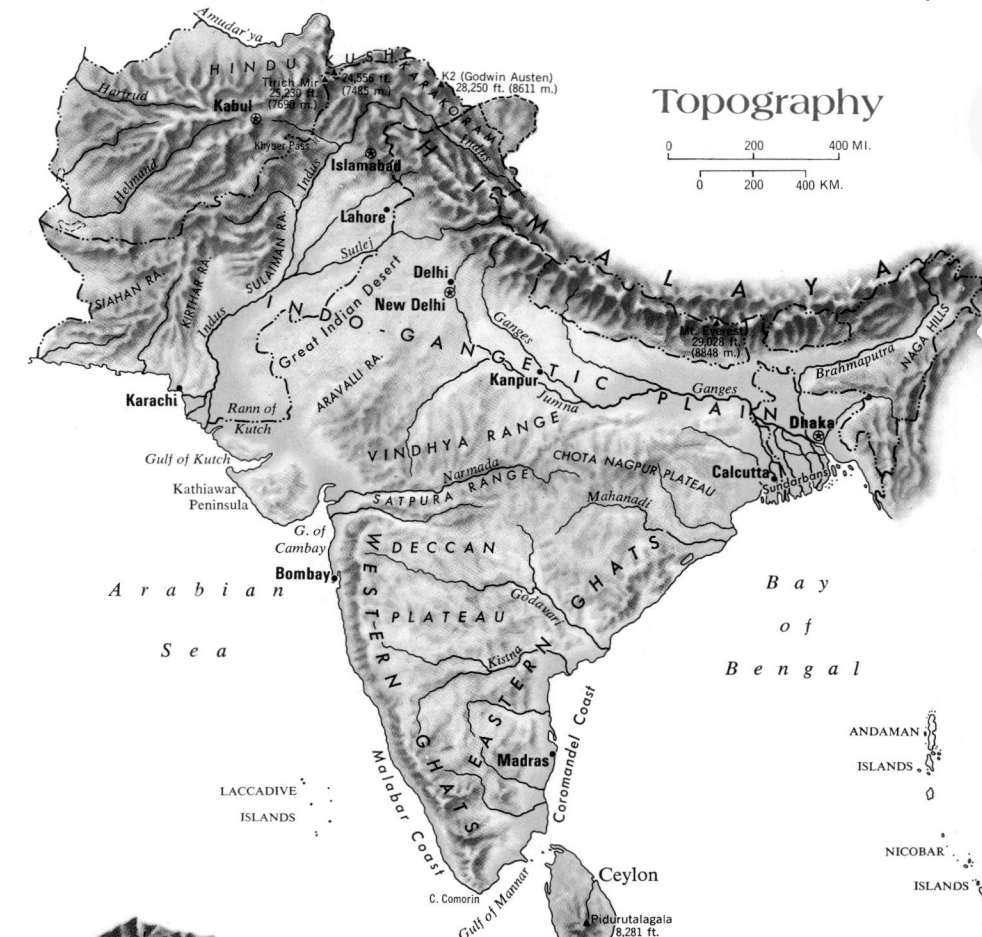

Topography

| 0 | 200 | 400 MI. |

| 0 | 200 | 400 KM. |

| 5,000 m. | 2,000 m. | 1,000 m. | 500 m. | 200 m. | 100 m. | Sea | Below |
| 16,404 ft. | 6,562 ft. | 3,281 ft. | 1,640 ft. | 656 ft. | 328 ft. | Level | |

Assam (state) 19,902,826 G3
Bihar (state) 69,823,154 F4
Chandigarh (terr.) 450,061 D2
Dadra and Nagar Haveli (terr.) 103,677 C4
Delhi (terr.) 6,196,414 D3
Goa, Daman and Diu (terr.) 1,082,117 C4
Gujarat (state) 33,960,905 C4
Haryana (state) 12,850,902 D3
Himachal Pradesh (state) 4,237,569 D2
Jammu and Kashmir (state) 5,981,600 D2
Karnataka (state) 37,043,451 D6
Kerala (state) 25,403,217 D6
Lakshadweep (terr.) 40,237 C6
Madhya Pradesh (state) 52,131,717 D4
Maharashtra (state) 62,693,898 C5
Manipur (state) 1,433,691 G4
Meghalaya (state) 1,327,874 G3
Mizoram (terr.) 487,774 G4
Nagaland (state) 773,281 G3
Orissa (state) 26,272,054 E5
Pondicherry (terr.) 604,136 E6
Punjab (state) 16,669,755 D2
Rajasthan (state) 34,102,912 C3
Sikkim (state) 315,682 F3
Tamil Nadu (state) 48,297,456 D6
Tripura (state) 2,060,189 G4
Uttar Pradesh (state) 110,858,019 D3
West Bengal (state) 54,485,560 F4

CITIES and TOWNS

Abu 9,840 C4
Abu Road 25,331 C4
Achalpur 42,326 D4
Addanki 10,223 D5
Adilabad 30,368 D5
Adoni 85,311 D5
Agartala 59,625 G4
Agartala□ 100,264 G4
Agra 591,917 D3
Agra□ 634,622 D3
Ahmadabad 1,591,832 C4
Ahmadabad□ 1,741,522 C4
Ahmadnagar 118,236 C5
Ahmadnagar□ 148,405 C5
Aizwal 31,740 G4
Ajanta D4
Ajmer 262,851 C3
Akola 168,438 D4
Alibag 11,913 C5
Aligarh 252,314 D3
Alipore F2
Allahabad 490,622 E3
Allahabad□ 513,036 E3
Alleppey-Cochin 160,166 D7
Almora 19,671 D3
Along 3,524 G3
Alwar 100,378 D3
Amalner 55,544 C4
Ambala 83,633 D2
Ambala□ 186,168 D2
Ambikapur 23,087 E4
Amravati 193,800 D4
Amreli 39,520 C4
Amritsar 407,628 C2
Amritsar□ 458,029 C2
Anakapalle 57,273 E5
Anantapur 80,069 D6
Anantnag 27,643 D2
Andheri B7
Andul 3,602 F2
Arcot 30,230 D6
Arrah 92,919 E3
Aruppukkottai 62,223 D7
Arvi 26,494 D4
Asansol 155,968 F4
Asansol□ 241,792 F4
Aurangabad, Bihar 18,714 E4
Aurangabad, Maharashtra 150,483 D5
Aurangabad□ 165,253 D5
Azamgarh 40,963 E3
Badagara 53,938 D6
Bagalkot 51,746 D5
Bahraich 73,931 E3
Baidyabati 54,130 F1
Balaghat 27,872 E4
Balasore 46,239 F4
Ballia 47,101 E3
Bally 38,892 F1
Balotra 17,595 C3
Balrampur 36,191 E3
Balurghat 67,088 F3
Banda 50,575 D3
Bandar (Machilipatnam) 112,612 E5
Bandra B7
Bangalore 1,540,741 D6
Bangalore□ 1,653,779 D6
Bankura 79,129 F4
Bansberia 61,748 F1
Banswara 27,363 C4
Baramati 27,912 C5
Baramula 26,334 C2
Baranagar 136,842 F1
Barasat 42,642 F1
Barbil 24,342 F4
Bareilly 296,248 D3
Bareilly□ 326,106 D3
Baripada 28,725 F4
Barmer 38,630 C3
Baroda (Vadodara) 466,696 C4
Barpeta 26,479 G3
Barrackpore 96,889 F1
Barrackpore□ 198,255 F1
Barsi 62,374 D5
Baruipur 20,501 F2
Barwani 22,099 D4
Basim 32,496 D4
Basirhat 63,816 F4
Bassein 30,594 C5
Bastar E5
Batala 58,200 D2
Baudh 8,891 E4
Bauria 10,610 E2
Beawar 66,114 C3
Belgaum 192,427 C5
Belgaum□ 213,872 C5
Bellary 125,183 D5
Benares (Varanasi) 583,856 E3
Berhampore 72,605 F4
Berhampur 117,662 F5
Bettiah 51 018 E3
Betul 30,862 D4
Bhadrak 40,487 F4
Bhadravati 40,203 D6
Bhadravati□ 101,358 D6
Bhadreswar 45,586 F1
Bhagalpur 172,202 F4
Bhandara 39,423 E4
Bhandup B7
Bhanjanagar 12,353 E4
Bharatpur 68,036 D3
Bharuch 91,589 C4
Bhatapara 20,980 E4
Bhatinda 53,684 C2
Bhatkal 18,732 C6
Bhatpara 204,750 F1
Bhavnagar 225,358 C4
Bhavnagar□ 225,974 C4
Bhawanipatna 22,808 E5
Bhilai 157,173 E4
Bhilwara 82,155 C3
Bhimavaram 63,762 E5
Bhimunipatnam 14,291 E5
Bhind 42,371 D3
Bhinmal 14,050 C3
Bhir (Bir) 49,965 D5
Bhiwandi 79,576 C5
Bhiwani 73,086 D3
Bhopal 298,022 D4
Bhor 10,708 C5
Bhubaneswar 105,491 F4
Bhuj 52,177 B4
Bhusawal 96,800 D4
Bhusawal□ 104,708 D4
Bidar 50,670 D5
Bihar 100,046 F3
Bijapur, Karnataka 103,931 D5
Bijapur, Madhya Pradesh 5,289 E5
Bijnor 43,290 D3
Bikaner 188,518 C3
Bikaner□ 208,894 C3
Bilaspur 98,410 E4
Bina-Itawa 33,106 D4
Bir 49,965 D5
Birmitrapur 28,063 E4
Bobbili 30,649 E5
Bodhan 37,589 D5
Bodinayakkanur 54,176 D6
Bolangir 35,748 E4
Bombay (Greater)* 5,970,575 B7
Bomdila 2,264 G3
Broach (Bharuch) 91,589 C4
Budaun 72,204 D3
Budge-Budge 51,039 F2
Bundi 34,279 D3
Burdwan 143,318 F4
Burhanpur 105,246 D4
Calcutta 3,148,746 F2
Calcutta□ 7,031,382 F2
Calicut (Kozhikode) 333,979 D6
Cambay 62,097 C4
Cannanore 55,162 C6
Cawnpore (Kanpur) 1,154,388 E3
Chaibasa 35,386 F4
Chamba 11,814 D2
Champdani 58,596 F1
Chanderi 10,294 D4
Chandernagore 75,238 F1
Chandigarh 218,743 D2
Chandigarh□ 232,940 D2
Chandrapur 75,134 D5
Chapra 83,101 F3
Chatrapur 10,835 F5
Chembur B7
Cherrapunji⊙ 83,987 G3
Chhatarpur 32,271 D4
Chhindwara 53,492 D4
Chidambaram 48,811 E6
Chik Ballapur 29,227 D6
Chikmagalur 41,639 D6
Chingleput 38,419 E6
Chiplun 20,942 C5
Chirala 54,487 E5
Chitorgarh 25,917 C4
Chitradurga 50,254 D6
Chittoor 63,035 D6
Churachandpur 8,706 G4
Churu 52,502 D3
Chushul D2
Cocanada (Kakinada) 164,200 E5
Cochin-Alleppey 439,066 D6
Coimbatore 356,368 D6
Coimbatore□ 736,203 D6
Colachel 18,819 D7
Cooch Behar 53,684 F3
Coondapoor 23,831 C6
Cuddalore 101,335 E6
Cuddapah 66,195 D6
Cumbum 9,745 D5
Cuttack 194,068 F4
Cuttack□ 205,759 F4
Dabhoi 37,892 C4
Daltonganj 32,367 E4
Damoh 59,489 D4
Dapoli 6,296 C5
Darbhanga 132,059 F3
Darjeeling 42,873 F3
Datia 36,439 D3
Davangere 121,110 D6
Deesa 28,324 C4
Dehra Dun 166,073 D2
Dehra Dun□ 203,464 D2
Delhi 3,287,883 D3
Delhi□ 3,647,023 D3
Demchok D2
Deogarh, Orissa 8,906 E4
Deoghar, Bihar 40,356 F4
Deolali 55,436 C5
Deoria 38,161 E3
Dewas 51,545 D4
Dhamtari 34,546 E4
Dhanbad 79,838 F4
Dhanbad□ 434,031 F4
Dhar 36,172 C4
Dharmsala 10,939 D2
Dharwar-Hubli 379,166 C5
Dhenkanal 19,615 E4
Dholpur 31,865 D3
Dhond 16,583 C5
Dhoraji 59,773 C4
Dhubri 36,503 G3
Dhulia 137,129 C4
Dibrugarh 80,348 G3
Digboi 16,538 H3
Dindigul 128,429 D6
Diphu 10,200 G3
Dispur 1,725 G3
Diu 6,214 C4
Dohad 44,506 C4
Domjor 10,896 F1
Dudhi 5,084 E4
Dum Dum 31,363 F1
Dum Dum□ 273,812 F1
Dungarpur 19,773 C4
Durg 67,892 E4
Durgapur 206,638 F4
Dwarka 17,801 B4
Eluru 127,023 E5
English Bazar 61,335 F3
Erode 105,111 D6
Etawah 85,894 D3
Faizabad-cum-Ayodhya 102,835 E3
Faridabad 85,762 D3
Farrukhabad-cum-Fatehgarh 102,768 D3
Farrukhabad-cum-Fatehgarh□ 110,835 D3
Fatehpur, Rajasthan 34,929 C3
Fatehpur, Uttar Pradesh 54,665 E3
Firozabad 133,863 D3
Firozpur 49,545 C2
Gadag-Betgeri 95,426 D5
Gadwal 21,828 D5
Gandhinagar 24,055 C4
Ganganagar 90,042 C3
Gangapur 27,453 D3
Gangtok 12,000 F3
Garden Reach 154,913 F2
Garulia 44,271 F1
Gauhati 123,783 G3
Gauhati□ 200,377 G3
Gaya 179,884 F4
Ghat Kopar 34,256 B7
Ghaziabad 118,836 D3
Ghaziabad□ 127,700 D3
Ghazipur 45,635 E3
Goalpara 16,703 G3
Godhra 66,403 C4
Gonda 52,662 E3
Gondal 54,928 C4
Gondia 77,992 E4
Gorakhpur 230,911 E3
Goregaon B7
Gudur 33,778 D6
Gulbarga 145,588 D5
Guna 40,006 D4
Guntakal 66,320 D5
Guntur 269,991 D5
Gurais D2
Gwalior 384,772 D3
Gwalior□ 406,140 D3
Haflong 5,197 G3
Hanle D2
Hanumangarh 30,017 C3
Harda 28,504 D4
Hardoi 46,639 E3
Hardwar 77,864 D2
Hassan 51,325 D6
Hathras 74,349 D3
Hazaribagh 54,818 F4
Hindupur 42,959 D6
Hinganghat 44,349 D4
Hingoli 31,948 D5
Hissar 89,437 D3
Honavar 12,444 C6
Hooghly-Chinsura 105,241 F1
Hoshangabad 27,011 D4
Hospet 65,196 D5
Howrah 737,877 F2
Hubli-Dharwar 379,166 C5
Hyderabad 1,607,396 D5
Hyderabad□ 1,796,339 D5
Ichchapuram 15,850 F5
Ichhapur 11,975 F1
Imphal 100,366 G4
Indore 543,381 D4
Indore□ 560,936 D4
Itanagar⊙ 18,787 G3
Itarsi 44,191 D4
Jabalpur 426,224 D4
Jabalpur□ 534,845 D4
Jagdalpur 31,344 E5
Jagtial 30,900 D5
Jaipur 615,258 D3
Jaipur□ 636,768 D3
Jaisalmer 16,578 C3
Jajpur 16,707 F4
Jalgaon 106,711 D4
Jalna 91,099 D4
Jalor 15,478 C3
Jalpaiguri 55,159 F3
Jamalpur 61,731 F3
Jammu 155,338 D2
Jammu□ 164,207 D2
Jamnagar 214,816 B4
Jamnagar□ 227,640 B4
Jamshedpur 341,576 F4
Jamshedpur□ 456,146 F4
Jaora 37,235 D4
Jaunpur 80,737 E3
Jeypore 34,319 E5
Jhalawar 20,035 D4
Jhansi 173,292 D3
Jhansi□ 198,135 D3
Jharsuguda 24,727 E4
Jhunjhunu 32,024 D3
Jind 38,161 D3
Jodhpur 317,612 C3
Jorhat 30,247 G3
Jubbulpore (Jabalpur) 426,224 D4
Juhu B7
Jullundur 296,106 D2
Jullundur□ 329,830 D2
Junagadh 95,485 B4
Kadayanallur 50,295 D7
Kadiri 33,810 D6
Kakinada 164,200 E5
Kalyan 99,547 C5
Kamarhati 169,404 F1
Kamptee 53,412 D4
Kanchipuram 110,657 E6
Kanchrapara 78,768 F1
Kandla 17,995 C4
Kandukur 16,654 E5
Kanker 9,278 E4
Kannauj 28,187 D3
Kanpur 1,154,388 E3
Kanpur□ 1,275,242 E3
Karad 42,329 C5
Karaikudi 55,449 D7
Karanja 31,150 D4
Kargil 2,390 D2
Karikal 26,080 E6
Karkal 18,593 C6
Karnal 92,784 D3
Karwar 27,770 C6
Kasaragod 34,984 C6
Kasganj 46,467 D3
Katarnian Ghat E3
Katihar 67,014 F3
Katni (Murwara) 54,864 E4
Kavali 29,616 E6
Kavaratti 4,420 C6
Kawardha 11,226 E4
Kendrapara 20,079 F4
Keonjhar 19,340 F4
Khamgaon 53,692 D4
Khamman 56,919 D5
Khandwa 84,517 D4
Kharagpur 61,783 F4
Khardah 32,302 F1
Khurda 15,879 F4
Kirkee 65,497 C5
Kishangarh 37,405 D3
Kishtwar 5,276 D2
Kohima 21,545 G3
Kolar 43,418 D6
Kolar Gold Fields 76,112 D6
Kolhapur 259,050 C5
Konnagar 34,424 F1
Koppal 27,277 D5
Koraput 21,505 E5
Korba 30,963 E4
Kota 212,991 D3
Kottaguden 75,542 E5
Kottayam 59,714 D7
Kotturu 12,873 D6
Kovur 16,846 E6
Kozhikode 333,979 D6
Krishnanagar 85,923 F4
Kulu 8,958 D2
Kumbakonam 113,130 D6
Kumta 19,112 C6
Kurla B7
Kurnool 136,710 D5
Laful⊙ 8,161 G7
Lansdowne 6,670 D3
Latur 70,156 D5
Leh 5,519 D2
Lohardaga 17,087 E4
Lucknow 749,239 E3
Lucknow□ 813,982 E3
Ludhiana 397,850 D2
Ludhiana□ 401,176 D2
Lumding 29,253 G3
Lungleh 6,019 G4
Machilipatnam 112,612 E5
Madh B7
Madhubani 32,919 F3
Madras 2,469,449 E6
Madras□ 3,169,930 E6
Madugula 8,376 E5
Madurai 549,114 D7
Madurai□ 711,501 D7
Mahabaleshwar 7,318 C5
Mahbubnagar 51,756 D5
Mahe 8,972 D6
Mahim 11,344 C5
Mahoba 29,707 D3
Mahuva 39,497 C4
Malad B6
Malakanagiri 7,494 E5
Malegaon 191,847 C4
Maler Kotla 48,536 D2
Malkapur 35,476 D4
Malvan 17,579 C5
Mandi 16,849 D2
Mandla 24,406 E4
Mandsaur 52,347 C4
Mandvi 27,849 B4
Manendragarh 11,936 E4
Mangalore 165,174 C6
Mangrol 27,183 B4
Manmad 29,571 C4
Mannargudi 42,783 E6
Manori B6
Margao 41,655 C5
Marmagao 44,065 C5
Mathura 132,028 D3
Mau 64,058 E3
Mayuram 60,195 D6
Meerut 270,993 D3
Mehsana 51,598 C4
Mercara 19,357 D6
Mhow 59,037 D4
Midnapore 71,326 F4
Miraj 77,606 D5
Mirzapur-cum-Vindhyachal 105,939 E4
Modasa 22,483 C4
Mokokchung 17,423 G3
Monghyr 102,474 F3
Mora B7
Moradabad 258,590 D3
Morena 44,901 D3
Morvi 60,976 C4
Mulund B6
Murud 11,210 C5
Murwara 54,864 E4
Muzaffarnagar 114,783 D3
Muzaffarpur 126,379 E3
Mysore 355,685 D6
Nadiad 108,269 C4
Nagapattinam 68,026 E6
Nagaur 36,448 C3
Nagercoil 141,288 D7
Nagina 37,066 D3
Nagpur 866,076 D4
Nagpur□ 930,459 D4
Nahan 16,017 D2
Naihati 82,080 F1
Naini Tal 23,986 D3
Nainpur 14,683 E4
Nalgonda 33,126 D5
Nander 126,538 D5
Nandurbar 54,070 C4
Nandyal 63,193 D5
Narayanpet 21,744 D5
Narnaul 31,875 D3
Narsimhapur 25,552 D4
Narsinghgarh 13,814 D4
Nasik 176,091 C5
Nasirabad 25,732 C3
Navsari 72,979 C4
Nellore 133,590 E6
New Delhi (cap.) 301,801 D3
Nhava-Sheva B7
Nimach 47,113 D4
Nipani 35,116 C5
Nirmal 28,529 D5
Nizamabad 115,640 D5
North Lakhimpur 20,094 G3
Nova Goa (Panaji) 34,953 C5
Nowgong, Assam 56,537 G3
Nowgong, Madhya Pradesh 10,248 D3
Okha Port 10,687 B4
Ongole 53,330 E5
Ootacamund 63,310 D6
Orai 42,513 D3
Osmanabad 27,279 D5
Pachmarhi 1,212 D4
Palanpur 42,114 C4
Palayankottai 70,070 D7
Palghat 95,788 D6
Pali 49,834 C3
Palni 49,575 D6
Panaji 34,953 C5
Panchur 59,021 F2
Pandharpur 53,638 D5
Panihati 148,046 F1
Panipat 87,981 D3
Panna 22,316 E4
Panruti 34,065 D6
Paradip F4
Parbhani 61,570 D5
Parlakhemundi 26,917 E5
Partapgarh 17,402 C4
Parvatipuram 30,025 E5
Pasighat 5,116 G3
Patan 64,519 C4
Pathankot 76,355 D2
Patiala 148,686 D2
Patiala□ D2
Patna 473,001 F3
Patna□ F3
Pauni 17,781 E4
Phalodi 17,379 C3
Phulbani 10,677 E4
Pilibhit 68,273 D3
Pokaran 7,769 C3
Pondicherry 90,537 E6
Ponnani 35,723 D6
Poona (Pune)□ C5
Porbandar 96,881 B4
Porbandar□ B4
Port Blair 26,218 G6
Porto Novo 17,412 E6
Proddatur 70,822 D6
Puduchcheri (Pondicherry) 90,537 E6
Pudukkottai 66,384 D6
Pune 856,105 C5
Puri 72,674 F5
Purli 31,078 D5
Purnea 56,484 F3
Purulia 57,708 F4
Puttur 17,483 D6
Quilon 124,208 D7
Radhanpur 18,360 C4
Raichur 79,831 D5
Raigarh 46,745 E4
Raipur 174,518 E4
Raipur□ E4
Rajahmundry 165,912 E5
Rajahmundry□ E5
Rajapalaiyam 86,952 D7
Rajapur 9,017 C5
Rajgarh 11,475 D4
Rajkot 300,612 C4
Rajnandgaon 41,183 E4
Rajpipla 25,769 C4
Rajpur 34,393 F2
Rajpura 14,840 D2
Rameswarem 16,755 D7
Rampur, Him. Pradesh 2,623 D2
Rampur, Uttar Pradesh 161,417 D3
Ranchi 175,934 F4
Ratangarh 31,506 C3
Ratlam 106,666 C4
Ratnagiri 37,551 C5
Raurkela 47,076 F4
Raxaul 12,064 E3
Rayagada 25,064 E5
Renigunta 8,567 E6
Rewa 69,182 E4
Rishra 63,486 F1
Robertsganj 7,093 E4
Roha 8,631 C5
Rohtak 124,783 C5
Sadiya⊙ 64,252 H3

British India
U.S.S.R.
GILGIT AGENCY
AFGHANISTAN
KASHMIR & JAMMU
N.W. FRONTIER PROV.
PUNJAB
PUNJAB STATES
BALUCHISTAN
BAHAWALPUR (PUNJ. ST.)
TIBET
CHINA
IRAN
DELHI
RAMPUR
NEPAL
UNITED PROVINCES
SIKKIM
BHUTAN
ASSAM
PUNJ. ST.
RAJPUTANA
AJMER-MERWARA
SIND
Gwadar (Oman)
GWALIOR
Brahmaputra
Ganges
E. ST.
KHASI HILLS
BENARES
BIHAR
MANIPUR
WESTERN INDIA
CENTRAL INDIA
EASTERN STATES
BENGAL
TRIPURA (E. ST.)
Chandernagore (Fr.)
BURMA
Arabian Sea
GUJARAT ST.
BOMBAY
CENTRAL PROVINCES
BERAR
ORISSA ST.
ORISSA
Diu (Port.)
Damão (Port.)
Bay of Bengal
HYDERABAD
DECCAN STATES
Yanaon (Fr.)
Gôa (Port.)
MADRAS
MYSORE
COORG
Bangalore (Br.)
Mahé (Fr.)
Pondichéry (Fr.)
Karikal (Fr.)
M. ST.
Laccadive Islands (Madras)
Cochin (Br.)
MADRAS STATES
CEYLON
Andaman Islands (Br.)
Nicobar Islands (Br.)
British India. *The provinces of British India were directly administered by Britain. A few areas were leased from the Indian princes.*
Indian States. *The Indian States, sometimes referred to as the "Native" or "Princely States," were under the nominal control of maharajas or other hereditary princes.*
Possessions of Other Countries in India
State or Provincial Boundaries
Other Internal Boundaries

sagar 118.574 ... D4
aharanpur 225.396 ... D3
aharsa 23.217 ... F3
... D6
alem 308.716 ... E5
amalkot 34.607 ... E5
ambalpur 64.675 ... D3
ambhal 86.323 ... D3
angamner 28.594 ... C5
angli 115.138 ... C5
ankral 11.300 ... C2
anta Cruz ... B7
antipur 61.166 ... F4
ardarshahr 37.703 ... E3
arnath ... E3
asaram 48.282 ... E4
aau 66.433 ... C5
atna 57.531 ... E4
avanvati 16.873 ... C5
avanur 18.302 ... D6
aw 13.504 ... G7
ecunderabad 250.636 ... D5
ecunderabad 345.052 ... D5
ehon 38.396 ... D4
eeampore 102.023 ... F1
eringapatam 14.100 ... C6
hahjahanpur 135.604 ... E3
hahdol 28.490 ... D4
heopur 16.418 ... D3
hillong 87.659 ... H3
himoga 102.709 ... D6
hivpuri 42.120 ... D3
holapur 398.361 ... D5
horapur 21.056 ... D5
hyok ... D2
hbsagar 27.426 ... H3
hddipet 26.296 ... D5
hdhpur 40.521 ... C4
hkar 70.987 ... D3
hilchar 52.596 ... G4
hliguri 97.484 ... F3
hlvassa ... C4
hmla 55.368 ... D2
hngur 10.957 ... F1
hrohi 18.774 ... C4
hronj 22.413 ... D4
hrsa 48.808 ... D3
hrsi 28.576 ... D6
htapur 66.715 ... C5
honepur 8.084 ... E4
outh Dum Dum 174.538 ... F2
outh Suburban 272.600 ... F2
rikakulam 45.179 ... E5
rinagar 403.413 ... D2
rinagar 423.253 ... D2
rivardhan 12.342 ... C5
undargarh 17.244 ... E4
urada 9.833 ... C4
urat 471.656 ... C4
uratgarh 14.491 ... C3
urendranagar 66.667 ... C4
anda 41.611 ... D2
ehri 5.480 ... D2
ellicherry 68.759 ... C6
enali 102.937 ... E5
ezpur 39.870 ... G3

Tezu 3.055 ... H3
Thana 170.675 ... B6
Thanjavur 140.547 ... D6
Tikamgarh 27.007 ... D4
Tinsukia 54.911 ... H3
Tiruchchirappalli 307.400 ... D6
Tiruchchirappalli 464.624 ... D6
Tiruchendur 18.126 ... D7
Tirunelveli 108.498 ... D7
Tirupati 65.843 ... D6
Tiruppattur 40.357 ... D6
Tiruppur 113.302 ... D6
Tiruvannamalai 61.370 ... D6
Titagarh 88.218 ... F1
Titlagarh 14.504 ... E4
Toibalawe ... F2
Tollygunge ... F2
Tonk 55.866 ... D4
Tranquebar 17.318 ... D6
Trichur 76.241 ... D6
Trivandrum 409.627 ... D7
Trombay ... B7
Tumkur 70.476 ... D6
Tuni 28.344 ... E5
Tura 15.489 ... G3
Tuticorin 155.310 ... D7
Udaipur 161.278 ... C4
Udhampur 16.392 ... D2
Udipi 29.753 ... C6
Ujjain 203.278 ... D4
Ulhasnagar 168.462 ... C5
Ummer 27.092 ... D4
Unnao 38.195 ... E3
Uran 12.616 ... B7
Uttarpara-Kotrung 67.568 ... F1
Vadodara 466.696 ... C4
Vadodara 467.487 ... C4
Valsad 43.254 ... C4
Vaniyambadi 51.810 ... D6
Varanasi 583.856 ... E3
Varanasi 606.721 ... E3
Vashi
Vedaranniyam 21.471 ... E6
Vellore 139.082 ... D6
Vellore 178.554 ... D6
Vengurla 11.805 ... C5
Venkatagiri 17.546 ... D6
Veraval 58.771 ... B7
Vesava ... B7
Vidisha 43.212 ... D4
Vijayawada 317.258 ... D5
Villupuram 60.242 ... D6
Vinukonda 16.259 ... D5
Virajpet 9.782 ... C6
Viramgam 43.790 ... C4
Visakhapatnam 352.504 ... E5
Visnagar 34.863 ... C4
Vizianagaram 86.608 ... E5
Warangal 207.520 ... D5
Wardha 69.037 ... D4
Wun 24.455 ... D5
Yadgir 32.756 ... D5
Yanam 8.291 ... E5
Yellamanchili 15.318 ... E5
Yeola 24.533 ... C4
Yeotmal 64.836 ... D4

OTHER FEATURES

Abor (hills) ... G3
Adam's Bridge (sound) ... D7
Agatti (isl.) ... C6
Amindivi (isl.) ... C6
Amindivi (isls.) ... C6
Amini (Amindivi) (isl.) ... C6
Andaman (isls.) ... G6
Andaman (sea) ... G6
Androth (isl.) ... C6
Anjidiv (Angedeva) (isl.) ... C6
Arabian (sea) ... B5
Back (bay) ... B7
Bengal, Bay of (sea) ... F5
Berar (reg.) ... D4
Brahmaputra (riv.) ... G3
Butcher (isl.) ... B7
Cambay (gulf) ... C4
Cannanore (isls.) ... C6
Car Nicobar (isl.) ... G7
Chambal (riv.) ... D3
Chenab (riv.) ... C3
Chetlat (isl.) ... C6
Chilka (lake) ... E5
Coco (chan.) ... G6
Colaba (pt.) ... B7
Colair (lake) ... D5
Comorin (cape) ... D7
Coromandel Coast (reg.) ... E6
Daman (dist.) ... C4
Deccan (plat.) ... D4
Diu (dist.) ... C4
Eastern Ghats (mts.) ... D6
Elephanta (isl.) ... B7
Ganga (Ganges) (riv.) ... F3
Ganges, Mouths of the (delta) ... F4
Ganges (riv.) ... F3
Ghaghra (riv.) ... E3
Goa (dist.) ... C5
Godavari (riv.) ... C5
Golconda (ruins) ... D5
Great (chan.) ... G7
Great Indian (des.) ... C3
Great Nicobar (isl.) ... G7
Himalaya (mts.) ... D2
Hindu Kush (mts.) ... F2
Hooghly (riv.) ... F2
Indus (riv.) ... B3
Jhelum (riv.) ... C2
Jumna (riv.) ... E3
Kadmat (isl.) ... C6
Kalpeni (isl.) ... C7
Kamet (mt.) ... D2
Kanchenjunga (mt.) ... F3
Karakoram (mts.) ... D1
Kaveri (riv.) ... D6
Khakchn (Kutch) (gulf) ... B4
Khasi (hills) ... G3
Kiltan (isl.) ... C6
Kistna (Krishna) (riv.) ... D5
Kunlun (range) ... D1
Kutch, Rann of (salt marsh) ... B4
Laccadive (Cannanore) (isls.) ... C6
Ladakh (reg.) ... D2
Little Andaman (isl.) ... G6
Little Nicobar (isl.) ... G7
Mahanadi (riv.) ... E4

Malabar (hill) ... B7
Malabar Coast (reg.) ... C6
Mannar (gulf) ... D7
Middle Andaman (isl.) ... G6
Minicoy (isl.) ... C7
Miri (hills) ... H3
Mishmi (hills) ... H3
Nancowry (isl.) ... G7
Narmada (riv.) ... D4
North Andaman (isl.) ... G6
Palk (str.) ... D7
Penganga (riv.) ... D5
Periyar (lake) ... D7
Pitti (isl.) ... C6
Pulicat (lake) ... D6
Salsette (isl.) ... B7
Sambhar (lake) ... D3
Satpura (range) ... D4
Shipki (pass) ... D2
South Andaman (isl.) ... G6
Sundarbans (reg.) ... F4
Sutlej (riv.) ... C3
Ten Degree (chan.) ... G7
Towers of Silence ... B7
Travancore (reg.) ... D7
Tungabhadra (riv.) ... D5
Vindhya (range) ... D4
Western Ghats (mts.) ... C5
Zaskar (mts.) ... D2

MALDIVES

Maldives 143.046 ... C7

NEPAL

CITIES and TOWNS

Bhaktapur 40.112 ... F3
Bhaktapur 110.157 ... F3
Biratnagar 45.100 ... F3
Birganj 12.999 ... E3
Dhangarhi ... E3
Ilam 7.299 ... F3
Jaleswar ... F3
Janakpur 14.294 ... F3
Jumla 122.753 ... E3
Kathmandu (cap.) 150.402 ... E3
Kathmandu 353.752 ... E3
Lalitpur 59.049 ... E3
Lalitpur 154.998 ... E3
Mustang 26.944 ... E3
Nepalganj 23.523 ... E3
Pokhara 20.611 ... E3
Pyuthan 137.338 ... E3
Ridi ... E3
Sallyan 141.457 ... E3
Simikot ... E3

OTHER FEATURES

Annapurna (mt.) ... E3
Bheri (riv.) ... E3
Dhaulagiri (mt.) ... E3
Everest (mt.) ... F3
Himalaya (mts.) ... D2
Kanchenjunga (mt.) ... F3

PAKISTAN

PROVINCES

Azad Kashmir ... C2
Baluchistan 2.409.000 ... B3
Federal Administrated Tribal Areas ... C2
Islamabad District 235.000 ... C2
Northern Areas ... D1
North-West Frontier 10.909.000 ... C2
Punjab 37.374.000 ... C2
Sind 13.965.000 ... B3

CITIES and TOWNS

Abbottabad 47.011 ... C2
Ahmadpur East 32.423 ... C3
Attock ... C2
Badin 6.387 ... B4
Bahawalnagar 36.290 ... C3
Bahawalpur 133.956 ... C3
Baltit ... C1
Bannu 43.795 ... C2
Barkhan 930 ... B3
Bhag 4.316 ... B3
Bhera 17.992 ... C2
Bostan ... B2
Buni ... C1
Campbellpore 19.041 ... C2
Chachro ... C3
Chagai 41.263 ... A3
Chaman 12.208 ... B2
Chilas ... C1
Chiniot 69.124 ... C2
Chitral ... C1
Dadu 19.142 ... B3
Dalbandin 1.724 ... A3
Dera Ghazi Khan 71.429 ... C2
Dera Ismail Khan 59.892 ... C2
Diplo ... B4
Dir ... C1
Duki 464 ... B2
Faisalabad 822.263 ... C2
Fort Sandeman 8.058 ... B2
Ghizar ... C1
Gilgit ... C1
Gujranwala 360.419 ... C2
Gujrat 100.581 ... C2
Gwadar 8.146 ... A4
Hindubagh 2.217 ... B2
Hoshab ... A3
Hunza (Baltit) ... C1
Hyderabad 628.310 ... B3
Islamabad (cap.) 77.318 ... C2
Jacobabad 57.292 ... B3
Jhal Jhao ... B3
Jhang Sadar 135.722 ... C2
Jhelum 63.653 ... C2
Jhudo 6.950 ... B3
Kalam ... C1
Kalat 5.321 ... B3
Kandrach ... A3
Karachi 3.498.634 ... B4
Karachi 3.650.000 ... B4
Kashmor ... C3
Kasur 102.531 ... C2
Khairpur 34.144 ... B3
Khanewal 67.617 ... C2
Kharan 31.465 ... A3
Kharan Kalat 2.692 ... A3

Khushab 24.851 ... C2
Kohat 64.634 ... C2
Kotri 20.262 ... B3
Ladgasht (Qila Ladgasht) ... A3
Lahore 2.165.372 ... C2
Lahri ... B3
Larkana 71.943 ... B3
Leiah 19.608 ... C2
Loralai 5.519 ... B2
Lyallpur (Faisalabad) 822.263 ... C2
Mach 4.921 ... B3
Makaland ... C2
Mardan 115.218 ... C2
Mastung 5.962 ... B3
Mianwali 31.398 ... C2
Miram Shah ... C2
Mirpur ... B3
Mirpur Khas 81.617 ... B3
Misgar ... C1
Mithi ... C4
Multan 542.195 ... C2
Multan 723.000 ... C2
Murree 13.486 ... C2
Musa Khel Bazar 429 ... B2
Muzaffarabad ... C2
Nagar ... D1
Nagar Parkar ... C4
Nal ... B3
Nawabshah 80.779 ... B3
Nok Kundi 861 ... A3
Nowshera 56.117 ... C2
Nushki 3.153 ... B3
Ormara ... A3
Panjgur 2.032 ... A3
Pasni 7.483 ... A3
Peshawar 268.366 ... C2
Pindi Gheb 12.416 ... C2
Pishin 2.906 ... B2
Qila Ladgasht ... A3
Quetta 156.000 ... B2
Rahimyar Khan 74.407 ... C3
Rawalpindi 615.392 ... C2
Ribat Qila ... A3
Risalpur Cantonment 11.291 ... C2
Rohri 19.072 ... B3
Rondu ... D1
Sahiwal 106.213 ... C2
Saidu 15.920 ... C2
Sargodha 201.407 ... C2
Sehwan 4.169 ... B3
Shahbandar ... B4
Shikarpur 70.301 ... B3
Sialkot 203.779 ... C2
Sibi 13.327 ... B3
Skardu ... D1
Sonmiani ... B3
Sorah ... B3
Sui 1.082 ... B3
Sukkur 158.876 ... B3
Surab ... B3
Tando Bahawal ... B3
Tando Adam 31.246 ... B3
Tando Allahyar ... B3
Tatta 12.786 ... B4
Tump ... A3
Turbat 4.578 ... A3
Uch 5.483 ... B3
Uthal ... B3
Wah 107.671 ... C2
Wana ... C2
Yasin ... C1

OTHER FEATURES

Arabian (sea) ... B5
Bolan (pass) ... B3
Chagai (hills) ... A3
Chenab (riv.) ... C2
Hindu Kush (mts.) ... B1
Indus (riv.) ... B3
Jhelum (riv.) ... C2
K2 (mt.) ... D1
Konar (riv.) ... C1
Kutch, Rann of (salt marsh) ... B4
Mohenjo Daro (ruins) ... B3
Muari, Ras (cape) ... B4
Ravi (riv.) ... C2
Siahan (range) ... A3
Sulaiman (range) ... B3
Sutlej (riv.) ... C3
Talab (riv.) ... A3
Taxila (ruins) ... C2
Tirich Mir (mt.) ... C1
Zhob (riv.) ... B2

SRI LANKA (CEYLON)

CITIES and TOWNS

Anuradhapura 34.836 ... E7
Badulla 34.658 ... E7
Batticaloa 36.761 ... E7
Colombo (cap.) 618.000 ... D7
Colombo 852.098 ... D7
Dehiwala-Mt. Lavinia 154.785 ... D7
Galle 72.720 ... D7
Hambantota 6.908 ... E7
Jaffna 112.000 ... E7
Kalmunai 19.176 ... E7
Kandy 93.602 ... E7
Kurunegala 25.189 ... E7
Mannar 11.157 ... E7
Matara 36.641 ... E7
Moratuwa 96.489 ... D7
Mullaittivu 4.930 ... E7
Negombo 57.115 ... D7
Nilaveli 4.556 ... E7
Nuwara Eliya 16.347 ... E7
Polonnaruwa 9.551 ... E7
Puttalam 17.982 ... D7
Ratnapura 29.116 ... D7
Sri Jayawar... 1.446 ... E7
Tangalla 8.748 ... E7
Trincomalee 41.780 ... E7
Vavuniya 15.639 ... E7

OTHER FEATURES

Adam's (peak) ... E7
Adam's Bridge (shoals) ... D7
Dondra (head) ... E7
Kirigalpota (mt.) ... E7
Mannar (gulf) ... D7
Palk (str.) ... D7
Pedro (pt.) ... E6
Pidurutalagala (mt.) ... E7

*City and suburbs.
⊙Population of district.
□Population of urban areas.

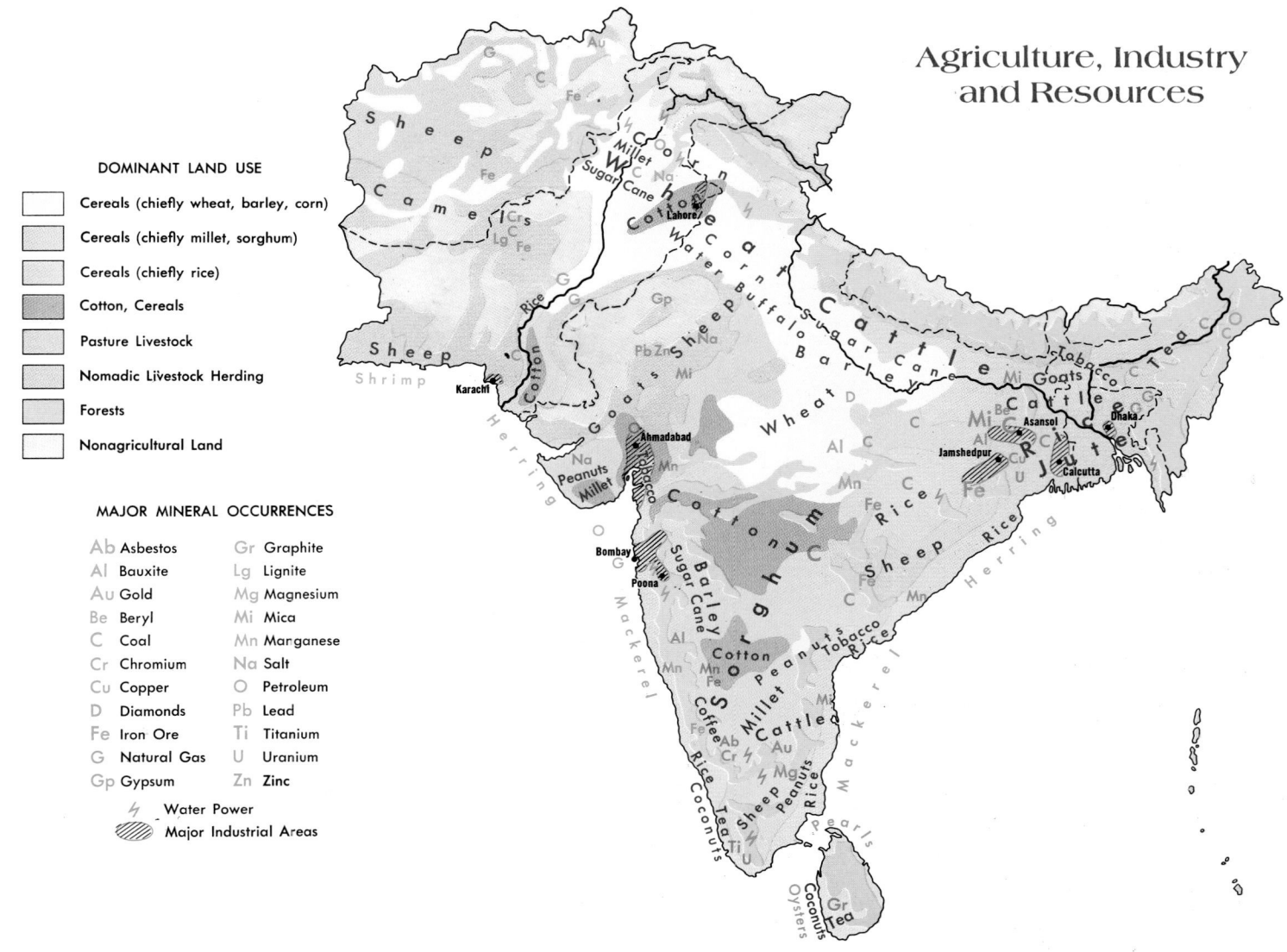

Agriculture, Industry and Resources

DOMINANT LAND USE

- Cereals (chiefly wheat, barley, corn)
- Cereals (chiefly millet, sorghum)
- Cereals (chiefly rice)
- Cotton, Cereals
- Pasture Livestock
- Nomadic Livestock Herding
- Forests
- Nonagricultural Land

MAJOR MINERAL OCCURRENCES

Ab	Asbestos	Gr	Graphite
Al	Bauxite	Lg	Lignite
Au	Gold	Mg	Magnesium
Be	Beryl	Mi	Mica
C	Coal	Mn	Marganese
Cr	Chromium	Na	Salt
Cu	Copper	O	Petroleum
D	Diamonds	Pb	Lead
Fe	Iron Ore	Ti	Titanium
G	Natural Gas	U	Uranium
Gp	Gypsum	Zn	Zinc

⚡ Water Power
Major Industrial Areas

Burma, Thailand, Indochina and Malaya

CONIC PROJECTION

SCALE OF MILES

SCALE OF KILOMETERS

International Boundaries _____
Division and State Boundaries _____
Capitals of Countries _____☆
Division and State Capitals _____◉

Scale 1:10,000,000

© Copyright HAMMOND INCORPORATED, Maplewood, N.J.

Longitude East 96° of Greenwich

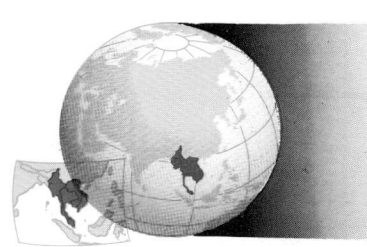

BURMA

AREA   261,789 sq. mi. (678,034 sq. km.)
POPULATION   32,913,000
CAPITAL   Rangoon
LARGEST CITY   Rangoon
HIGHEST POINT   Hkakabo Razi 19,296 ft.
   (5,881 m.)
MONETARY UNIT   kyat
MAJOR LANGUAGES   Burmese, Karen, Shan,
   Kachin, Chin, Kayah, English
MAJOR RELIGIONS   Buddhism, tribal religions

THAILAND

AREA   198,455 sq. mi. (513,998 sq. km.)
POPULATION   46,455,000
CAPITAL   Bangkok
LARGEST CITY   Bangkok
HIGHEST POINT   Doi Inthanon 8,452 ft.
   (2,576 m.)
MONETARY UNIT   baht
MAJOR LANGUAGES   Thai, Lao, Chinese,
   Khmer, Malay
MAJOR RELIGIONS   Buddhism, tribal religions

LAOS

AREA   91,428 sq. mi. (236,800 sq. km.)
POPULATION   3,721,000
CAPITAL   Vientiane
LARGEST CITY   Vientiane
HIGHEST POINT   Phou Bia 9,252 ft. (2,820 m.)
MONETARY UNIT   kip
MAJOR LANGUAGE   Lao
MAJOR RELIGIONS   Buddhism, tribal religions

CAMBODIA

AREA   69,898 sq. mi. (181,036 sq. km.)
POPULATION   5,200,000
CAPITAL   Phnom Penh
LARGEST CITY   Phnom Penh
HIGHEST POINT   5,948 ft. (1,813 m.)
MONETARY UNIT   riel
MAJOR LANGUAGE   Khmer (Cambodian)
MAJOR RELIGION   Buddhism

VIETNAM

AREA   128,405 sq. mi. (332,569 sq. km.)
POPULATION   52,741,766
CAPITAL   Hanoi
LARGEST CITY   Ho Chi Minh City (Saigon)
HIGHEST POINT   Fan Si Pan 10,308 ft.
   (3,142 m.)
MONETARY UNIT   dong
MAJOR LANGUAGES   Vietnamese, Thai,
   Muong, Meo, Yao, Khmer, French,
   Chinese, Cham
MAJOR RELIGIONS   Buddhism, Taoism,
   Confucianism, Roman Catholicism,
   Cao-Dai

MALAYSIA

AREA   128,308 sq. mi. (332,318 sq. km.)
POPULATION   13,435,588
CAPITAL   Kuala Lumpur
LARGEST CITY   Kuala Lumpur
HIGHEST POINT   Mt. Kinabalu 13,455 ft.
   (4,101 m.)
MONETARY UNIT   ringgit
MAJOR LANGUAGES   Malay, Chinese, English,
   Tamil, Dayak, Kadazan
MAJOR RELIGIONS   Islam, Confucianism,
   Buddhism, tribal religions, Hinduism,
   Taoism, Christianity, Sikhism

SINGAPORE

AREA   226 sq. mi. (585 sq. km.)
POPULATION   2,413,945
CAPITAL   Singapore
LARGEST CITY   Singapore
HIGHEST POINT   Bukit Timah 581 ft. (177 m.)
MONETARY UNIT   Singapore dollar
MAJOR LANGUAGES   Chinese, Malay, Tamil,
   English, Hindi
MAJOR RELIGIONS   Confucianism, Buddhism,
   Taoism, Hinduism, Islam, Christianity

Topography

0   200   400 MI.
0   200   400 KM.

5,000 m. | 2,000 m. | 1,000 m. | 500 m. | 200 m. | 100 m. | Sea
16,404 ft. | 6,562 ft. | 3,281 ft. | 1,640 ft. | 656 ft. | 328 ft. | Level | Below

BURMA

INTERNAL DIVISIONS

Arakan (state) 1,710,913	B3
Chin (state) 323,094	B2
Irrawaddy (div.) 4,152,521	B3
Kachin (state) 735,144	C1
Karen (state) 865,218	C3
Kayah (state) 126,492	C3
Magwe (div.) 2,632,144	B2
Mandalay (div.) 3,662,312	B2
Mon (state) 1,313,111	C3
Pegu (div.) 3,174,109	C3
Rangoon (div.) 3,186,886	C3
Sagaing (div.) 3,115,502	B1
Shan (state) 3,178,214	C2
Tenasserim (div.) 717,607	C4

CITIES and TOWNS

Akyab (Sittwe) 42,329	B2
Allanmyo 15,580	B3
Amarapura 11,268	B2
Amherst 6,000	C3
An	B3
Anin	C4
Bassein 126,045	B3
Bhamo 9,821	C1
Chauk 24,466	B2
Danubyu	B3
Falam	B2
Fort Hertz (Putao)	C1
Gawai	C1
Gokteik	C2
Gwa	B3
Gyobingauk 9,922	C3
Haka	B2
Henzada 61,972	B3
Hmawbi 23,032	C3
Homalin	B1
Hsenwi	C2
Hsipaw	C2
Htawgaw	C1
Insein 143,625	C3
Kamaing	C1
Karathuri	C5
Katha 7,648	C1
Kawludo	C3
Kawthaung 1,520	C5
Keng Hkam	C2
Keng Tung	C2
Koma	C4
Kunlong	C2
Kyaikto 13,154	C3
Kya-in Seikkyi	C3
Kyangin 6,073	B3
Kyaukme	C2
Kyaukpadaung 5,480	B2
Kyaukpyu 7,335	B3
Kyaukse 8,659	C2
Labutta 12,982	B3
Lai-hka	C2
Lamu	B3
Lashio	C2
Lenya	C5
Letpadan 15,896	C3
Lewe	B3
Loi-kaw	C3
Lonton	B1
Magwe 13,270	B2
Maingkwan	C1
Maliwun	C5
Mandalay 418,008	C2
Man Hpang	C2
Martaban 5,661	C3
Ma-ubin 23,362	B3
Maungdaw 3,772	B2
Mawkmai	C2
Mawlaik 2,993	B2
Mawlu	C1
Maymyo 22,287	C2
Meiktila 19,474	B2
Mergui 33,697	C4
Minbu 9,096	B2

Minhla 6,470	B3
Mogaung 2,920	C1
Mogok 8,334	C2
Mohnyin	C1
Möng Hsat	C3
Möng Mau	C3
Möng Mit	C2
Möng Pan	C2
Möng Si	C2
Möng Tön	C2
Möng Tung	C2
Monywa 26,279	B2
Moulmein 171,977	C3
Mudon 20,136	C3
Myanaung 11,155	B3
Myaungmya 24,532	B3
Myingyan 36,439	B2
Myitkyina 12,382	C1
Myohaung 6,534	B2
Naba	B1
Namhkam	C2
Namlan	C2
Namtu	C2
Natmauk	B2
Okkan 14,443	B3
Okpo 12,155	C3
Pakokku 30,943	B2
Palaw 5,596	C4
Paletwa	B2
Pantha	B2
Papun	C3
Pasawng	C3
Paungde 17,286	B3
Pegu 47,378	C3
Prome (Pye) 36,997	B3
Putao	C1
Pyapon 19,174	B3
Pye 36,997	B3
Pyinmana 22,025	C3
Pyu 10,443	C3
Rangoon (cap.) 1,586,422	C3
Rangoon* 2,055,365	C3
Rathedaung 2,969	B2
Sadon	C1
Sagaing 15,382	B2
Samka	C2
Sandoway 5,172	B3
Shingbwiyang	B1
Shwebo 17,827	B2
Shwenyaung	C2
Singkaling Hkamti	B1
Singu 4,027	C2
Sinlumkaba	C1
Sittwe 42,329	B2
Sumprabum	C1
Syriam 15,296	C3
Taungdwingyi 16,233	C2
Taunggyi	C2
Tavoy 40,312	C4
Tharrawaddy 8,977	C3
Thaton 38,047	C3
Thaungdut	B1
Thayetmyo 11,649	B3
Thazi 7,531	C2
Thongwa 10,829	C3
Toungoo 31,589	C3
Wakema 20,716	B3
Yamethin 11,167	C2
Yandoon 15,245	B3
Ye 12,852	C4
Yenangyaung 24,416	B2
Yesagyo 7,880	B2
Ye-u 5,307	B2
Ywathit	C3
Zadi	C4
Zalun 899	B3

OTHER FEATURES

Amya (pass)	C4
Andaman (sea)	B4
Arakan Yoma (mts.)	B3
Ataran (riv.)	C3
Bengal, Bay of (sea)	B3
Bentinck (isl.)	C5

(continued on following page)

(vertical tabs at left: BURMA, THAILAND, LAOS, CAMBODIA, VIETNAM, MALAYSIA, SINGAPORE)

Agriculture, Industry and Resources

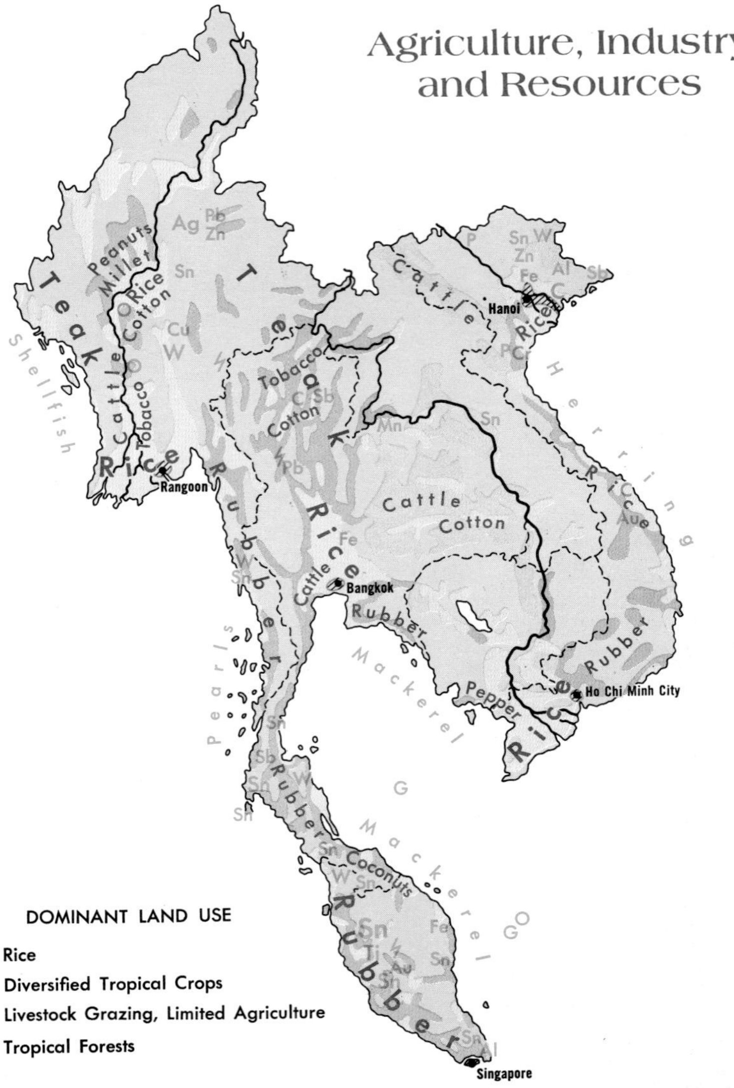

DOMINANT LAND USE

- Rice
- Diversified Tropical Crops
- Livestock Grazing, Limited Agriculture
- Tropical Forests

MAJOR MINERAL OCCURRENCES

Ag	Silver	Cu	Copper	O	Petroleum	Sn	Tin
Al	Bauxite	Fe	Iron Ore	P	Phosphates	Ti	Titanium
Au	Gold	G	Natural Gas	Pb	Lead	W	Tungsten
C	Coal	Mn	Manganese	Sb	Antimony	Zn	Zinc
Cr	Chromium						

Water Power — Major Industrial Areas

Bilauktaung (range) C4
Chaukan (pass) C1
Cheduba (isl.) B3
Chin (hills) B2
Chindwin (riv.) B2
Coco (chan.) B4
Combermere (bay) B3
Daung Kyun (isl.) C4
Dawna (range) C3
Great Coco (isl.) B4
Great Tenasserim (riv.) C4
Heinze Chaung (bay) C4
Heywood (chan.) B3
Hka, Nam (riv.) C2
Hkakabo Razi (mt.) C1
Indawgyi (lake) C1
Inle (lake) C2
Irrawaddy (riv.) B3
Irrawaddy, Mouths of the (delta) B4
Kadan Kyun (isl.) C4
Kaladan (riv.) B2
Kalegauk (isl.) C4
Khao Luang (mt.) C5
Lanbi Kyun (isl.) C5
Launglon Bok (isls.) C4
Loi Leng (mt.) C2
Manipur (riv.) B2
Martaban (gulf) C4
Mekong (riv.) D2
Mergui (arch.) C5
Mon (riv.) B2
Mu (riv.) B2
Negrais (cape) B3
Pakchan (riv.) C5
Pangsau (pass) C1
Pawn, Nam (riv.) C2
Pegu Yoma (mts.) B3
Preparis (isl.) B4
Ramree (isl.) B3
Salween (riv.) C3
Shan (plat.) C2
Sittang (riv.) C3
Taungthonton (mt.) B1
Tavoy (pt.) C4
Tenasserim (isl.) C4
Teng, Nam (riv.) C2
Three Pagodas (pass) C4
Victoria (mt.) B2

CAMBODIA (KAMPUCHEA)

CITIES and TOWNS

Batdambang (Battambang) D4
Choam Khsant E4
Kampong Cham E4
Kampong Chhnang D4
Kampong Khleang E4
Kampong Saom D5
Kampong Spoe E5
Kampong Thum E4
Kampong Trabek E5
Kampot E5
Kaoh Nhek E4
Kracheh E4
Krong Kaoh Kong D4
Krong Keb E5
Kulen E4
Lumphat E4
Moung Roessei D4
Pailin D4
Paoy Pet D4
Phnom Penh (cap.) c. 300,000 E5
Phnum Tbeng Meanchey E4
Phsar Ream D5
Phumi Banam E5
Phumi Phsar E4
Phumi Prek Kak E4
Phumi Samraong D4
Pouthisat D4
Prek Pouthi E5
Prey Veng E5
Pursat (Pouthisat) D4
Rovieng Tbong E4
Sambor E4
Senmonoron E4
Siempang E4
Siemreab D4
Sisophon D4
Sre Ambel D5
Sre Khtum E4
Stoeng Treng E4
Suong E5
Svay Rieng E5
Takev E5
Virochey E4

OTHER FEATURES

Angkor Wat (ruins) E4
Dangrek (mts.) D4
Drang, Ia (riv.) E4
Joncs (plain) E5
Khong, Se (riv.) E4
Kong, Kaoh (isl.) D5
Mekong (riv.) E4
Rung, Kaoh (isl.) D5
San, Se (riv.) E4
Sen, Stoeng (riv.) E4
Srepok (riv.) E4
Tang, Kaoh (isl.) D5
Thailand (gulf) D5
Tonle Sap (lake) D4
Wai, Poulo (isls.) D5

LAOS

CITIES and TOWNS

Attapu 2,750 E4
Ban Khon E4
Ban Lahanam E3
Borikan D3
Champasak 3,500 E4
Dônghén E3
Khamkeut⊙ 31,206 E3
Louang Namtha 1,459 D2
Louangphrabang 7,596 D3
Muang Hinboun 1,750 E3
Muang Kènthao D3
Muang Khammoun 5,500 E3
Muang Không 1,750 E4
Muang Khôngxédôn 2,000 E4
Muang Khoua D2
Muang May E4
Muang Ou Tai D2
Muang Paktha D2
Muang Phin E3
Muang Tahoi E3
Muang Vapi E4
Muang Xaignabouri (Sayaboury) 2,500 D3
Mounlapamôk E4
Napè E3
Nong Het E3
Pakxé 8,000 E4
Phiafai⊙ 17,216 E4
Phôngsali 2,500 D2
San Nua (Sam Neua) 3,000 E2
Saravan 2,350 E4
Savannakhét 8,500 E3
Sayaboury (Muang Xaignabouri) 2,500 D3
Thakhek (Muang Khammouan) 5,500 E3
Tourakom D3
Viangchan (Vientiane) 132,253 D3
Vientiane (cap.) 132,253 D3
Xiangkhoang 3,500 D3

OTHER FEATURES

Bolovens (plat.) E4
Hou, Nam (riv.) D2
Jars (plain) D3
Mekong (riv.) D3
Ou, Nam (riv.) D2
Phou Bia (mt.) D3
Phou Cô Pi (mt.) E3
Phou Loi (mt.) D2
Rao Co (mt.) E3
Se Khong (riv.) E4
Tha, Nam (riv.) D2
Xianghoang (plat.) D3

MALAYA, MALAYSIA*

STATES

Federal Territory 937,875 D7
Johor (Johore) 1,601,504 D7
Kedah 1,102,200 D6
Kelantan 877,575 D6
Melaka 453,153 D7
Negeri Sembilan 563,955 D7
Pahang 770,644 D7
Perak 1,762,288 D6
Perlis 147,726 D6
Pinang (Penang) 911,586 D6
Selangor 1,467,441 D7
Terengganu 542,280 D6

CITIES and TOWNS

Alor Gajah 2,222 D7
Alor Setar 66,260 D6
Bandar Maharani (Muar) 61,218 D7
Bandar Penggaram (Batu Pahat) 53,291 D7
Batu Gajah 10,692 D6
Batu Pahat 53,291 D7
Bentong 22,683 D7
Butterworth 61,187 D6
Chukai 12,514 D6
Gemas 5,214 D7
George Town (Pinang) 269,603 C6
Ipoh 247,953 D6
Johor Baharu (Johore Bharu) 136,234 F5
Kampar 26,591 D6
Kangar 8,758 D6
Kelang 113,611 D7
Keluang 43,272 D7
Kota Baharu 55,124 D6
Kota Tinggi 8,725 F5
Kuala Dungun 17,560 D6
Kuala Lipis 9,270 D6
Kuala Lumpur (cap.) 451,977 D7
Kuala Lumpur* 937,875 D7
Kuala Pilah 12,508 D7
Kuala Rompin 1,384 D7
Kuala Selangor 3,132 D7
Kuala Terengganu 53,320 D6
Kuantan 43,358 D7
Kulai 11,841 F5
Lumut 3,255 D6
Malacca (Melaka) 87,160 D7
Mawai F5
Melaka 87,160 D7
Mersing 18,246 E7
Muar 61,218 D7
Pekan 4,682 D7
Pekan Nanas 9,003 E5
Pinang (George Town) 269,603 C6
Pontian Kechil 8,349 E5
Port Dickson 10,300 D7
Port Kelang D7
Port Weld 3,233 D6
Raub 18,433 D7
Segamat 17,796 D7
Seremban 80,921 D7
Sungai Petani 35,959 C6
Taiping 54,645 D6
Tanah Merah 7,012 D6
Telok Anson 44,524 D6
Tumpat 10,673 D6

OTHER FEATURES

Aur, Pulau (isl.) E7
Belumut, Gunong (mt.) D7
Gelang, Tanjong (pt.) D6
Johor, Sungai (riv.) F5
Johore (str.) E6
Kelantan, Sungai (riv.) D6
Langkawi, Pulau (isl.) C6
Ledang, Gunong (mt.) D7
Lima, Pulau (isl.) F6
Malacca (str.) D7
Malay (pen.) D6
Pahang, Sungai (riv.) D7
Pangkor, Pulau (isl.) D6
Perak, Gunong (mt.) D6
Perhentian, Kepulauan (isls.) D6
Pulai, Sungai (riv.) E5
Ramunia, Tanjong (pt.) F6
Redang, Pulau (isl.) D6
Sedili Kechil, Tanjong (pt.) F5
Tahan, Gunong (mt.) D6
Temiang, Bukit (mt.) D6
Tenggol, Pulau (isl.) D6
Tinggi, Pulau (isl.) E7

SINGAPORE

CITIES and TOWNS

Jurong 50,974 E6
Nee Soon 37,641 F6
Serangoon 89,558 F6
Singapore (cap.) 2,413,945 F6

OTHER FEATURES

Keppel (harb.) F6
Main (str.) F6
Singapore (str.) F6
Tekong Besar, Pulau (isl.) F6

THAILAND (SIAM)

CITIES and TOWNS

Ang Thong 7,267 C4
Ayutthaya (Phra Nakhon Si Ayutthaya) 37,213 D4
Ban Aranyaprathet 12,276 D4
Bangkok (cap.) 1,867,297 D4
Bangkok* 2,495,312 D4
Bang Lamung D4
Bang Saphan C5
Ban Kantang 9,247 C6
Ban Kapong C5
Ban Khlong Yai D5
Ban Kui Nua D4
Ban Ngon D3
Ban Pak Phanang 13,590 D5
Banphot Phisai C3
Ban Pua D3
Ban Sattahip D4
Ban Tha Uthen D3
Bua Chum D4
Buriram 16,431 D4
Chachoengsao 22,106 D4
Chai Badan D4
Chai Buri D3
Chainat 9,944 D4
Chaiya C5
Chaiyaphum 12,540 D4
Chang Khoeng C3
Chanthaburi 15,479 D4
Chiang Dao C3
Chiang Khan D3
Chiang Mai 83,729 C3
Chiang Rai 13,927 C3
Chiang Saen C2
Chon Buri 39,367 D4
Chumphon 11,643 C5
Den Chai C3
Hat Yai 47,953 C6
Hot C3
Hua Hin 21,426 D4
Kalasin 14,960 D3
Kamphaeng Phet 12,378 C3
Kanchanaburi 16,397 C4
Khanu C3
Khemmarat E4
Khon Kaen 29,431 D3
Khorat (Nakhon Ratchasima) 66,071 D4
Krabi 8,764 C5
Krung Thep (Bangkok) (cap.) 1,867,297 D4
Kumphawapi D3
Lae D3
Lampang 40,100 C3
Lamphun 11,309 C3
Lang Suan 4,020 C5
Loei 10,137 D3
Lom Sak 10,597 D3
Lop Buri 23,112 D4
Mae Hong Son 3,981 C3
Maha Sarakham 19,707 D3
Mukdahan E3
Nakhon Nayok 8,185 D4
Nakhon Pathom 34,300 C4
Nakhon Phanom 20,385 D3
Nakhon Ratchasima 66,071 D4
Nakhon Sawan 46,853 D4
Nakhon Si Thammarat 40,671 D5
Nan 17,738 D3
Nang Rong D4
Narathiwat 21,256 D6
Ngao D3
Nong Khai 21,150 D3
Pattani 21,938 D6
Phanat Nikhom 10,514 D4
Phangnga 5,738 C5
Phatthalung 13,336 D6
Phayao 20,346 C3
Phet Buri 27,755 C4
Phetchabun 6,240 D3
Phichai D3
Phichit 10,814 D3
Phitsanulok 33,883 D3
Phon Phisai D3
Phrae 17,555 D3
Phra Nakhon Si Ayutthaya 37,213 D4
Phuket 34,362 C6
Phutthaisong D4
Prachin Buri 14,167 D4
Prachuap Khiri Khan 9,075 D5
Pran Buri D4
Rahaeng (Tak) 16,317 C3
Ranong 10,301 C5
Rat Buri 32,271 C4
Rayong 14,846 D4
Roi Et 20,242 D4
Rong Kwang D3
Sakon Nakhon 18,943 E3
Samut Prakan 46,632 D4
Samut Sakhon 33,619 D4
Samut Songkhram 23,574 C4
Sara Buri 25,025 D4
Satun 7,315 C6
Sawankhalok 8,387 C3
Selaphum E3
Sing Buri 9,050 D4
Singora (Songkhla) 41,193 D6
Sisaket 13,662 E4
Songkhla 41,193 D6
Sukhothai 15,488 D3
Suphan Buri 18,768 C4
Surat Thani 24,923 C5
Surin 16,342 D4
Suwannaphum D4
Tak 16,317 C3
Takua Pa 7,825 C5
Thoen C3
Thon Buri 628,015 D4
To Mo D6
Trang 32,985 C6
Trat 7,917 D4
Ubon 40,650 E4
Udon Thani 56,218 D3
Uthai Thani 10,525 C4
Uttaradit 12,022 D3
Warin Chamrap 21,520 E4
Yala 30,051 D6
Yasothon 12,079 D4

OTHER FEATURES

Amya (pass) C4
Bilauktaung (range) C4
Chang, Ko (isl.) D4
Chao Phraya, Mae Nam (riv.) D4
Chi, Mae Nam (riv.) D3
Dangrek (Dong Rak) (mts.) D4
Doi Inthanon (mt.) C3
Doi Pha Hom Pok (mt.) C2
Doi Pia Fai (mt.) D4
Kao Prawa (mt.) C3
Khao Luang (mt.) C5
Khwae Noi, Mae Nam (riv.) C4
Kra (isth.) C5
Kut, Ko (isl.) D5
Laem Pho (cape) D6
Laem Talumphuk (cape) D5
Lanta, Ko (isl.) C6
Luang (mt.) C5
Mae Klong, Mae Nam (riv.) C4
Mekong (riv.) E3
Mun, Mae Nam (riv.) D4
Nan, Mae Nam (riv.) D3
Nong Lahan (lake) D3
Pakchan (riv.) C5
Pa Sak, Mae Nam (riv.) D4
Phangan, Ko (isl.) D5
Phuket, Ko (isl.) C5
Ping, Mae Nam (riv.) C3
Samui (str.) D5
Samui, Ko (isl.) D5
Siam (Thailand) (gulf) D5
Tao, Ko (isl.) C5
Tapi, Mae Nam (riv.) C5
Terutao, Ko (isl.) C6
Tha Chin, Mae Nam (riv.) C4
Thale Luang (lag.) D6
Thalu, Ko (isls.) C5
Three Pagodas (pass) C4
Wang, Mae Nam (riv.) C3

VIETNAM

CITIES and TOWNS

An Loc (Binh Long) 15,276 E5
An Nhon F4
An Tuc (An Khe) F4
Ap Long Ha F5
Ap Vinh Hao F5
Bac Can E2
Bac Giang E2
Bac Lieu 53,841 E5
Bac Ninh 22,560 E2
Ba Don E3
Bai Thuong E3
Ban Me Thuot 68,771 F4
Bao Ha D2
Bao Lac E2
Bien Hoa 87,135 E5
Binh Long (An Loc) 15,276 E5
Binh Son F4
Bo Duc E4
Bong Son (Hoai Nhon) F4
Cam Ranh 118,111 F5
Can Tho 182,424 E5
Cao Bang E2
Cao Lanh 16,482 E5
Chau Phu 37,175 E5
Chu Lai F4
Con Cuong E3
Cua Rao E3
Da Lat 105,072 F5
Dam Doi E5
Da Nang 492,194 E3
Dien Bien Phu D2
Dong Hoi E3
Duong Dong D5
Gia Dinh E5
Go Cong 33,191 E5
Ha Giang E2
Haiphong* 1,279,067 E2
Hanoi (cap.)* 2,570,905 E2
Ha Tien E5
Ha Tinh E3
Hau Bon E4
Hoa Binh E2
Hoa Da F5
Hoai Nhon F4
Ho Chi Minh City (Saigon)* 3,419,678 E5
Hoi An 45,059 F4
Hoi Xuan E2
Hon Chong E5
Hon Gai 100,000 E2
Hue 209,043 E3
Huong Khe E3
Ke Bao E2
Khanh Hoa F4
Khanh Hung 59,015 E5
Khe Sanh E3
Kien Hung E5
Kontum 33,554 E4
Lac Giao (Ban Me Thuot) 68,771 E4
Lai Chau D2
Lang Son 15,071 E2
Lao Cai E2
Loc Ninh E5
Long Xuyen 72,658 E5
Mo Duc F4
Mong Cai E2
Muong Khuong E2
My Tho 119,892 E5
Nam Dinh E2
Nghia Lo D2
Nha Trang 216,227 F4
Ninh Binh E3
Phan Rang 33,377 F5
Phan Thiet 80,122 F5
Phu Cuong 28,267 E5
Phu Lang Thuong (Bac Giang) E2
Phuc Loi E3
Phu Dien E3
Phu Ly E2
Phu My F4
Phu Qui E3
Phu Rieng E5
Phu Tho 10,888 E2
Phu Vinh 48,485 E5
Pleiku 23,720 E4
Quang Nam E4
Quang Ngai 14,119 F4
Quang Tri 15,874 E3
Quang Yen E2
Quan Long 59,331 E5
Qui Nhon 213,757 F4
Rach Gia 104,161 E5
Ron E3
Sa Dec 51,867 E5
Saigon (Ho Chi Minh City)* 3,419,678 E5
Song Cau F4
Son Ha F4
Son La D2
Son Tay 19,213 E2
Tam Ky 38,532 F4
Tam Quan F4
Tan An 38,082 E5
Tay Ninh 22,957 E5
Thai Binh 14,739 E2
Thai Nguyen E2
Thanh Hoa 31,211 E3
Thanh Tri E5
That Khe E2
Tien Yen E2
Tra Vinh (Phu Vinh) 48,485 E5
Truc Giang 68,629 E5
Trung Khanh Phu E2
Tuyen Quang E2
Tuy Hoa 63,552 F4
Van Hoa E2
Van Ninh F4
Van Yen E2
Vinh 43,954 E3
Vinh Long 30,667 E5
Vinh Yen E2
Vu Liet E3
Vung Tau 108,436 E5
Xuan Loc
Yen Bai

OTHER FEATURES

Bach Long Vi, Dao (isl.)
Ba Den, Nui (mt.)
Bai Bung, Mui (Ca Mau) (pt.)
Black (riv.)
Ca Mau (Mui Bai Bung) (pt.)
Cam Ranh, Vinh (bay)
Cat Ba, Dao (isl.)
Chon May, Vung (bay)
Cu Lao, Hon (isls.)
Deux Frères, Les (isls.)
Dinh, Mui (cape)
Fan Si Pan (mt.)
Ia Drang (riv.)
Joncs (plain)
Kontum (plat.)
Khoai, Hon (isl.)
Lang Bian, Nui (mts.)
Lay, Mui (cape)
Mekong, Mouths of the (delta)
Nam Tram, Mui (cape)
Nightingale (Bach Long Vi) (isl.)
Panjang, Hon (Hon Tho Chau) (isl.)
Phu Quoc, Dao (isl.)
Rao Co (mt.)
Red (riv.)
Se San (riv.)
Sip Song Chau Thai (mts.)
Song Ba (riv.)
Song Ca (riv.)
Song Cai (riv.)
South China (sea)
Tonkin (gulf)
Varella, Mui (cape)
Wai, Poulo (isls.)
Yang Sin, Chu (mt.)

*See Southeast Asia, p. 85 for other part of Malaysia.

*City and suburbs.
⊙Population of district.

CHINA (MAINLAND)

AREA 3,691,000 sq. mi. (9,559,690 sq. km.)
POPULATION 958,090,000
CAPITAL Peking (Beijing)
LARGEST CITY Shanghai
HIGHEST POINT Mt. Everest 29,028 ft.
(8,848 m.)
MONETARY UNIT yuan
MAJOR LANGUAGES Chinese, Chuang, Uigur,
Yi, Tibetan, Miao, Mongol, Kazakh
MAJOR RELIGIONS Confucianism, Buddhism,
Taoism, Islam

CHINA (TAIWAN)

AREA 13,971 sq. mi. (36,185 sq. km.)
POPULATION 16,609,961
CAPITAL Taipei
LARGEST CITY Taipei
HIGHEST POINT Yü Shan 13,113 ft. (3,997 m.)
MONETARY UNIT new Taiwan yüan (dollar)
MAJOR LANGUAGES Chinese, Formosan
MAJOR RELIGIONS Confucianism, Buddhism,
Taoism, Christianity, tribal religions

MONGOLIA

AREA 606,163 sq. mi. (1,569,962 sq. km.)
POPULATION 1,594,800
CAPITAL Ulaanbaatar
LARGEST CITY Ulaanbaatar
HIGHEST POINT Tabun Bogdo 14,288 ft.
(4,355 m.)
MONETARY UNIT tughrik
MAJOR LANGUAGES Khalkha Mongolian,
Kazakh (Turkic)
MAJOR RELIGION Buddhism

HONG KONG

AREA 403 sq. mi. (1,044 sq. km.)
POPULATION 5,022,000
CAPITAL Victoria
MONETARY UNIT Hong Kong dollar
MAJOR LANGUAGES Chinese, English
MAJOR RELIGIONS Confucianism, Buddhism,
Christianity

MACAU

AREA 6 sq. mi. (16 sq. km.)
POPULATION 271,000
CAPITAL Macau
MONETARY UNIT pataca
MAJOR LANGUAGES Chinese, Portuguese
MAJOR RELIGIONS Confucianism, Buddhism,
Taoism, Christianity

CHINA (MAINLAND)

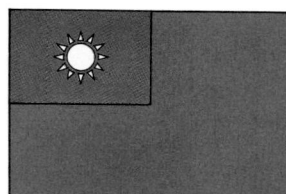

CHINA (TAIWAN)

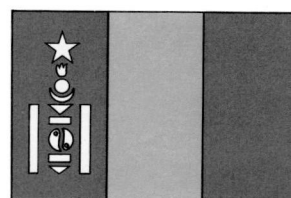

MONGOLIA

CHINA

PROVINCES

Anhui (Anhwei) 47,130,000	J5
Chekiang (Zhejiang) 37,510,000	K6
Fujian (Fukien) 24,500,000	J6
Gansu (Kansu) 18,730,000	E3
Guangdong (Kwangtung) 55,930,000	H7
Guangxi Zhuangzu (Kwangsi Chuang Aut. Reg.) 34,020,000	G7
Guizhou (Kweichow) 26,860,000	G6
Heilongjiang (Heilungkiang) 33,760,000	K2
Hebei (Hopei) 50,570,000	J4
Henan (Honan) 70,660,000	H5
Hubei (Hupei) 45,750,000	H5
Hunan 51,660,000	H6
Inner Mongolian Aut. Reg. (Nei Monggol) 8,900,000	H3
Jiangxi (Kiangsi) 31,830,000	J6
Jiangsu (Kiangsu) 58,340,000	K5
Jilin (Kirin) 24,740,000	L3
Kansu (Gansu) 18,730,000	E3
Kiangsi (Jiangxi) 31,830,000	J6
Kiangsu (Jiangsu) 58,340,000	K5
Kirin (Jilin) 24,740,000	L3
Kwangsi Chuang Aut. Reg. (Guangxi Zhuang) 34,020,000	G7
Kwangtung (Guangdong) 55,930,000	H7
Kweichow (Guizhou) 26,860,000	G6
Liaoning 37,430,000	K3
Nei Monggol (Inner Mongolian Aut. Reg.) 8,900,000	H3
Ningxia Huizu (Ningsia Hui Aut. Reg.) 3,660,000	F3
Qinghai (Tsinghai) 3,650,000	E4
Shaanxi (Shensi) 27,790,000	G5
Shanxi (Shansi) 24,340,000	H4
Shandong (Shantung) 71,600,000	J4
Sichuan (Szechwan) 97,070,000	F5
Sinkiang-Uigur Aut. Reg. (Xinjiang Uygur) 12,330,000	B3
Taiwan 16,609,961	K7
Tibet Aut. Reg. (Xizang) 1,790,000	B5
Tsinghai (Qinghai) 3,650,000	E4
Xinjiang Uygur (Sinkiang-Uigur Aut. Reg.) 12,330,000	B3
Xizang (Tibet Aut. Reg.) 1,790,000	B5
Yunnan 30,920,000	F7
Zhejiang (Chekiang) 37,510,000	K6

CITIES and TOWNS†

Aba	F5
Abagnar (Silinhot)	J3
Aihui (Aigun) (Heihe)	L1
Aksu (Aqsu)	B3
Altay	C2
Alxa Youqi	F4
Alxa Zuoqi	F4
Amoy (Xiamen) 400,000	J7
Ankang	G5
Anqing (Anking) 160,000	J5
Anshan 1,500,000	K3
Anshun	G6
Antu	L3
Anxi	E3
Anyang 225,000	H4
Aqsu (Aksu)	B3
Aratürük (Yiwu)	D3
Ar Horqin	K3
Arixang (Wenquan)	B3
Artux (Atushi)	A4
Bachu (Maralwexi)	A4
Baicheng, Jilin	K2
Baicheng (Bay), Xinjiang Uygur	B3
Bairin Zuoqi	J3
Baoding (Paoting) 350,000	J4
Baoji (Paoki) 275,000	G5
Baoshan	E7
Baoting	G8
Baotou (Paotow) 800,000	G3
Bargrax (Bohu)	C3
Batang	E5
Bay (Baicheng)	B3
Bayan Bobo	G3
Ba Xian	J4
Bei'an (Pehan) 130,000	L2
Beihai (Pakhoi) 175,000	G7
Beijing (Peking) (cap.) ●8,000,000	J3
Bengbu (Pengpu) 400,000	J5
Benxi (Penki) 750,000	K3
Bohu (Bagrax)	C3
Bole	B3
Bortala (Bole)	B3
Boshan	J4
Bo Xian (Pohsien)	J5
Butha	K2
Cangzhou (Tsangchow)	J4
Canton (Guangzhou) 2,300,000	H7
Chamdo (Qamdo)	E5
Changchih (Changzhi)	H4
Changchow (Changzhou) 400,000	J5
Changchow (Zhangzhou)	J7
Changchun 1,500,000	K3
Changde (Changteh) 225,000	H6
Changhua 137,236	K7
Changji	C3
Changjiang	G7
Changsha 850,000	H6
Changteh (Changde) 225,000	H6
Changyeh (Zhangye)	F4
Changzhi (Changchih)	H4
Changzhou (Changchow) 400,000	J5
Chankiang (Zhanjiang) 220,000	H7
Chao'an (Chaochow)	J7
Chaotung (Zhaotong)	F6
Chaoyang, Liaoning	J3
Chaoyang, Guangdong	J7
Charkhlia (Ruoqiang)	C4
Chefoo (Yantai) 180,000	K4
Chengchow (Zhengzhou) 1,500,000	H5
Chengde (Chengteh) 200,000	J3
Chengdu (Chengtu) 2,000,000	F5
Chen Xian	H6
Cherchen (Qiemo)	C4
Chiai 238,713	K7
Chifeng	J3
Chinchow (Jinzhou) 750,000	K3
Chindu	E5
Chinkiang (Zhenjiang) 250,000	J5
Chinsi (Jinxi)	K3
Chinwangtao (Qinhuangdao) 400,000	K4
Chishui	G6
Chongqing (Chungking) 3,500,000	G6
Chüanchow (Quanzhou) 130,000	J7
Chuchow (Zhuzhou) 350,000	H6
Chuguchak (Tacheng)	B2
Chumatien (Zhumadian)	H5
Chungshing	K7
Chungking (Chongqing) 3,500,000	G6
Chungshan (Zhongshan) 135,000	H7
Da'an (Talai)	K2
Dali	E6
Dalian 1,480,240	K4
Danba	F5
Dandong (Tantung) 450,000	K3
Dan Xian	G8
Da Qaidam	E4
Danba	F5
Daqing 758,430	L2
Datong, Liaoning	F4
Datong (Tatung), Shanxi 300,000	H3
Da Xian	G5
Dazhai	H4
Dengkou	G3
Deyang	F5
Dezhou (Tehchow)	J4
Dingxing	H4
Dongchuan	F6
Dongfang	G8
Dongsheng	H4
Dongtai	K5
Dorbiljin (Emin)	B2
Dukou	F6
Dulan	E4
Dunhua (Tunhwa)	L3
Dunhuang	E3
Duolun	J3
Dushan	G6
Duyun (Tuyün)	G6
Ejin	F3
Emin (Dorbiljin)	B2
Ergun Youqi	K1
Ergun Zuoqi	K1
Ertai	C2
Fatshan (Foshan)	H7

(continued on following page)

Map: China and Mongolia Transportation

China and Mongolia
Transportation

Railroads	————
Under Construction	– – – –
Connecting Roads	————
Navigable Rivers	————
Canals	————
Major Seaports	‡

© Copyright HAMMOND INCORPORATED, Maplewood, N.J.

Foochow (Fuzhou) 900,000 ... J6
Foshan (Fatshan) ... H7
Fowyang (Fuyang) ... J5
Fushun 1,700,000 ... K3
Fusingchen (Simao) ... F7
Fu Xian ... K4
Fu Xian, Shaanxi ... G4
Fuyang (Fuyang) 350,000 ... J5
Fuyu (Fusin) ... K3
Fuyu, Heilongjiang ... K2
Fuyu, Jilin ... L2
Fuyu, Heilongjiang ... M2
Fuyuan, Yunnan ... F6
Fuyun ... C2
Fuzhou (Foochow)
  Fujian 900,000 ... J6
Fuzhou, Jiangxi ... J6
Ganzhou (Kanchow) 135,000 ... H6
Garyarsa (Gartok) ... B5
Gejiu (Kokiu) 250,000 ... F7
Golmud (Golmo) ... D4
Gonghe ... F4
Guangyuan ... G5
Guan Xian ... F5
Guangzhou (Canton) 2,300,000 ... H7
Guilin (Kweilin) 225,000 ... G6
Guiyang (Kweiyang)
  Guizhou 1,500,000 ... G6
Guiyang, Hunan ... H6
Gulja (Yining) 160,000 ... B3
Guma (Pishan) ... A4
Guyang ... G3
Guyuan ... G4
Gyaca ... C6
Gyangzê ... C6
Habahe ... C2
Haikou (Hoihow) 500,000 ... H7
Hailar ... J2
Hami (Kumul) ... D3
Hancheng ... G5
Hanchung (Hanzhong) 120,000 ... G5
Handan (Hantan) 500,000 ... H4
Hangzhou (Hangchow) 1,100,000 ... J5
Hantan (Handan) 500,000 ... H4
Hanzhong (Hanchung) 120,000 ... G5
Harbin 2,750,000 ... M2
Hebi ... H4
Hechuan (Hochwan) ... G5
Hefei (Hofei) 400,000 ... J5
Hegang (Hokang) 350,000 ... L2
Heihe (Aihui) (Aigun) ... L1
Hekou ... K7
Hengchun ... J7
Hengshan ... G4
Hengyang 310,000 ... H6
Hepu (Hoppo) ... G7
Hexigten ... J3
Hezuo ... F5
Hochwan (Hechuan) ... G5
Hofei (Hefei) 400,000 ... J5
Hohhot (Huhehot) 700,000 ... H3
Hoihow (Haikou) 500,000 ... H7
Hokang (Hegang) 350,000 ... L2
Hoppo (Hepu) ... G7
Horqin Youyi Qianqi
  (Ulanhot) 100,000 ... K2
Houma ... H4
Hsüchang (Xuchang) ... H5

Huadian ... L3
Huaibei ... J5
Huaide (Hwaiteh) ... K3
Huainan 350,000 ... J5
Hualien ... K7
Huangling ... G4
Huangshi 200,000 ... J5
Huangzhong ... F4
Huhehot (Hohhot) 700,000 ... H3
Huizhou ... H7
Hulin ... M2
Hunchun ... M3
Hunjiang ... L3
Hwainan (Huainan) 350,000 ... J5
Hwaiteh (Huaide) ... K3
Hwangshih (Huangshi) 200,000 ... J5
Ichang (Yichang) 150,000 ... H5
Ichun (Yichun) 200,000 ... L2
Ilan ... K7
Ipin (Yibin) 275,000 ... F6
Jemnay ... C2
Jiamusi (Kiamusze) 275,000 ... M2
Ji'an (Kian) 100,000 ... J6
Jiangmen (Kongmoon) 150,000 ... H7
Jian'ou ... J6
Jiaozuo (Tsiaotso) 300,000 ... H4
Jiaxing (Kashing) ... K5
Jiayuguan ... E4
Jieyang ... J7
Jilin (Kirin) 1,200,000 ... L3
Jinan (Tsinan) 1,500,000 ... J4
Jingdezhen
  (Kingtehchen) 300,000 ... J6
Jinghong ... F7
Jingxi ... G7
Jing Xian, Anhui ... J5
Jing Xian, Hunan ... H6
Jingyuan ... F4
Jinhua (Kinhwa) ... J6
Jining (Tsining), Nei
  Monggol 160,000 ... H3
Jining (Tsining), Shandong ... J4
Jinshi (Tsingshih) 100,000 ... H6
Jinxi (Chinsi) ... K3
Jinzhou (Chinchow) 750,000 ... K3
Jiujiang (Kiukiang) 120,000 ... J6
Jiuquan (Kiuchuan) ... E4
Jixi (Kisi) 350,000 ... M2
Juichin (Ruijin) ... J6
Jun Xian ... H5
Kaba (Habahe) ... C2
Kaifeng 330,000 ... H4
Kailu ... K3
Kaiyuan, Liaoning ... K3
Kaiyuan, Yunnan ... F7
Kalgan (Zhangjiakou) 1,000,000 ... J3
Kanchow (Ganzhou) 135,000 ... H6
Kangding ... F5
Kaohsiung 1,028,334 ... K7
Karakax (Kara Kash) (Moyu) ... A4
Karamay ... B2
Karghalik (Yecheng) ... A4
Kashi (Kashgar) 175,000 ... A4
Kashing (Jiaxing) ... K5
Kaxgar (Kashi) 175,000 ... A4
Keelung 342,604 ... K6
Kenli ... J4
Keriya (Yutian) ... B4
Khotan (Hotan) ... B4

Kiamusze (Jiamusi)
  275,000 ... M2
Kian (Ji'an) 100,000 ... J6
Kienyang (Qianyang) ... H6
Kingtehchen (Jingdezhen)
  300,000 ... J6
Kinhwa (Jinhua) ... J6
Kirin (Jilin) 1,200,000 ... L3
Kisi (Jixi) 350,000 ... M2
Kiuchüan (Jiuquan) ... E4
Kiukiang (Jiujiang) 120,000 ... J6
Koku (Gejiu) 250,000 ... F7
Kongmoon (Jiangmen)
  150,000 ... H7
Korla ... C3
Kuldja (Yining) 160,000 ... B3
Kumul (Hami) ... D3
Künes (Xinyuan) ... B3
Kunming 1,700,000 ... F6
Kuqa ... C3
Kuytun ... C3
Kwangchow (Canton)
  2,300,000 ... H7
Kweilin (Guilin) 225,000 ... G6
Kweisiu (Hohhot) 700,000 ... H3
Kweiyang (Guiyang)
  1,500,000 ... G6
Lanzhou (Lanchow) 1,500,000 ... F4
Lenghu ... D4
Leshan (Loshan) 250,000 ... F6
Lhasa 175,000 ... D6
Lhazê (Lhatse) ... C6
Lianyungang (Lienyünkang)
  300,000 ... J5
Liaoyang 250,000 ... K3
Liaoyuan 300,000 ... L3
Lijiang ... F6
Linfen ... H4
Lingling ... H6
Linhe ... G3
Linqing (Lintsing) ... J4
Linxi ... J3
Linxia (Linsia) ... F4
Luzhou (Luchow) 250,000 ... G6
Loho (Luohe) ... H5
Longjiang ... K2
Lopnur (Yuli) ... C3
Loshan (Leshan) 250,000 ... F6
Luoyang (Loyang) 750,000 ... J5
Lu'an ... J5
Luchow (Luzhou) 225,000 ... G6
Lüda (Dalian) 1,480,240 ... K4
Luohe ... H5
Luoyang (Loyang) 750,000 ... J5
Lüshun ... K4
Luxi ... F7
Luzhou (Luchow) 225,000 ... G6
Ma'anshan ... J5
Manas ... C3
Manchouli (Manzhouli) ... J2
Maoming (Mowming) ... H7
Maralwexi (Bachu) ... A4
Mengcheng ... J5
Mengzi ... F7
Mianyang, Hubei ... H5
Mianyang, Sichuan ... F5
Minfeng (Niya) ... B4
Mingshui, Gansu ... E3
Mingshui, Heilongjiang ... L2
Minle ... F4
Mowming (Maoming) ... H7
Moyu (Karakax) ... A4

Mudanjiang (Mutankiang) 400,000 ... M3
Mukden (Shenyang) 3,750,000 ... K3
Muli ... F6
Naggu ... D5
Nanchang 900,000 ... J6
Nanchong (Nanchung) 275,000 ... G5
Nanjing (Nanking) 2,000,000 ... J5
Nanning 375,000 ... G7
Nanping ... J6
Nantong 300,000 ... K5
Nanyang ... H5
Napo ... G6
Neijiang (Neikiang) 240,000 ... G6
Nenjiang ... L2
Ningbo (Ningpo) 350,000 ... K6
Ningpo (Ningbo) 350,000 ... K6
Ningxia (Yinchuan,
  Yinchwan) 175,000 ... G4
Niya (Minfeng) ... B4
Ongniud ... K1
Orogen ... K1
Paicheng (Baicheng) ... K2
Pakhoi (Beihai) 175,000 ... G7
Paoki (Baoji) 275,000 ... G5
Paoting (Baoding) 350,000 ... J4
Paotow (Baotou) 800,000 ... G3
Pehan (Bei'an) 130,000 ... L2
Peking (Beijing)
  (cap.) •8,500,000 ... J3
Pengbu (Bengbu) 400,000 ... J5
Penki (Benxi) 750,000 ... K3
Pingdingshan ... H5
Pingliang ... G4
Pingtung 165,360 ... K7
Pingxiang, Guangxi Zhuangzu ... G7
Pingxiang, Jiangxi ... H6
Piqan (Shanshan) ... D3
Pishan (Guma) ... A4
Pohsien (Bo Xian) ... J5
Qamdo ... E5
Qarkilik (Ruoqiang) ... C4
Qargan (Qiemo) ... C4
Qianyang (Kienyang) ... H6
Qiemo (Qargan) ... C4
Qingdao (Tsingtao) 1,900,000 ... K4
Qingjiang, Jiangxi ... J6
Qingjiang 110,000 ... J6
Qinhuangdao
  (Chinwangdao) 400,000 ... K4
Qionghai ... H8
Qiqihar (Tsitsihar) 1,500,000 ... K2
Qitai ... D3
Qog ... G3
Qoqek (Tacheng) ... B2
Quanzhou (Chüanchow) 130,000 ... J7
Qu Xian, Sichuan ... G5
Qu Xian, Zhejiang ... J6
Quxü ... D6
Ruijin (Juichin) ... J6
Ruoqiang (Qarkilik) ... C4
Rutog ... B5
Sanmenxia ... H5
Sanming ... J6
Sêrtar ... F5
Shache (Yarkand) ... A4
Shangdu ... H3
Shangdu ... J3
Shanghai 10,980,000 ... K5
Shangqiu (Shangkiu) 250,000 ... J5

Shangrao (Shangjao) 100,000 ... J6
Shangshui 100,000 ... H5
Shanshan (Piqan) ... D3
Shantou (Swatow) 400,000 ... J7
Shaoguan (Shiukwan) 125,000 ... H6
Shaoxing (Shaohing) 225,000 ... K5
Shaoyang 275,000 ... H6
Shashi 125,000 ... H5
Shenyang (Mukden) 3,750,000 ... K3
Shigatse (Xigazê) ... C6
Shihezi (Shihhotzu) ... C3
Shijiazhuang
  (Shihkiachwang) 1,500,000 ... J4
Shiquanhe ... A5
Shiukwan (Shaoguan) 125,000 ... H6
Shiyan ... H5
Shizuishan (Shihsuishan) ... G4
Shuangcheng ... L2
Shuangyashan 150,000 ... M2
Shuo Xian ... H4
Siakwan (Xiaguan) ... F6
Sian (Xi'an) 1,900,000 ... G5
Siangtan (Xiangtan) 150,000 ... H6
Siangtan (Xiangtan) 300,000 ... H6
Sienyang (Xianyang) 125,000 ... G5
Silinhot (Abnagar) ... J3
Simao (Fusingchen) ... F7
Sinchu 208,038 ... K7
Sining (Xining) 250,000 ... F4

Sinsiang (Xinxiang) 300,000 ... H4
Sinyang (Xinyang) 125,000 ... H5
Siping (Szeping) 180,000 ... K3
Soche (Shache) ... A4
Soochow (Suzhou) 1,300,000 ... K5
Suao ... K7
Süchow (Suzhou) 1,500,000 ... M3
Suifenhe ... M3
Suihua ... L2
Suining ... G5
Suzhou (Soochow) 1,300,000 ... K5
Swatow (Shantou) 400,000 ... J7
Szeping (Siping) 180,000 ... K3
Tacheng (Qoqek) ... B2
Tai'an ... J4
Taichow (Taizhou) ... J5
Taichung 565,255 ... K7
Taigu ... H4
Tainan 541,390 ... K7
Taipei 2,108,193 ... K7
Taitung ... K7
Taiyuan 2,725,000 ... H4
Taizhou (Taichow) 275,000 ... K5
Talai (Da'an, Dalai) ... K2
Tali (Dali) ... E6
Tangshan 1,200,000 ... J4
Tantung (Dandong) 450,000 ... K3
Tao'an ... K2
Taoyuan 105,841 ... K6

Tart ... D4
Tatung (Datong) 300,000 ... H3
Taxkorgan ... A4
Tehchow (Dezhou) ... J4
Tengchong ... E6
Tianjin (Tientsin) 7,210,000 ... J4
Tianjin ... J4
Tianshui 100,000 ... F5
Tieling ... K3
Tianshui (Tianshui) 100,000 ... F5
Tientsin (Tianjin) 7,210,000 ... J4
Tingri ... C6
Togtoh ... H3
Toksu (Xinhe) ... C3
Toksun ... D3
Tongchuan (Tungchwan) ... G4
Tonghua (Tunghwa) 275,000 ... L3
Tongjiang (Tungkiang) ... M2
Tongliao ... K3
Tongling ... J5
Tongxin ... G4
Tongyu ... K3
Tsangchow (Cangzhou) ... J4
Tsiaotso (Jiaozuo) 300,000 ... H4
Tsinan (Jinan) 1,500,000 ... J4
Tsingshih (Jinshi) 100,000 ... H6
Tsingtao (Qingdao) 110,000 ... K4
Tsingtao (Qingdao) 1,900,000 ... K4
Tsining (Jining) 160,000 ... H3

Topography

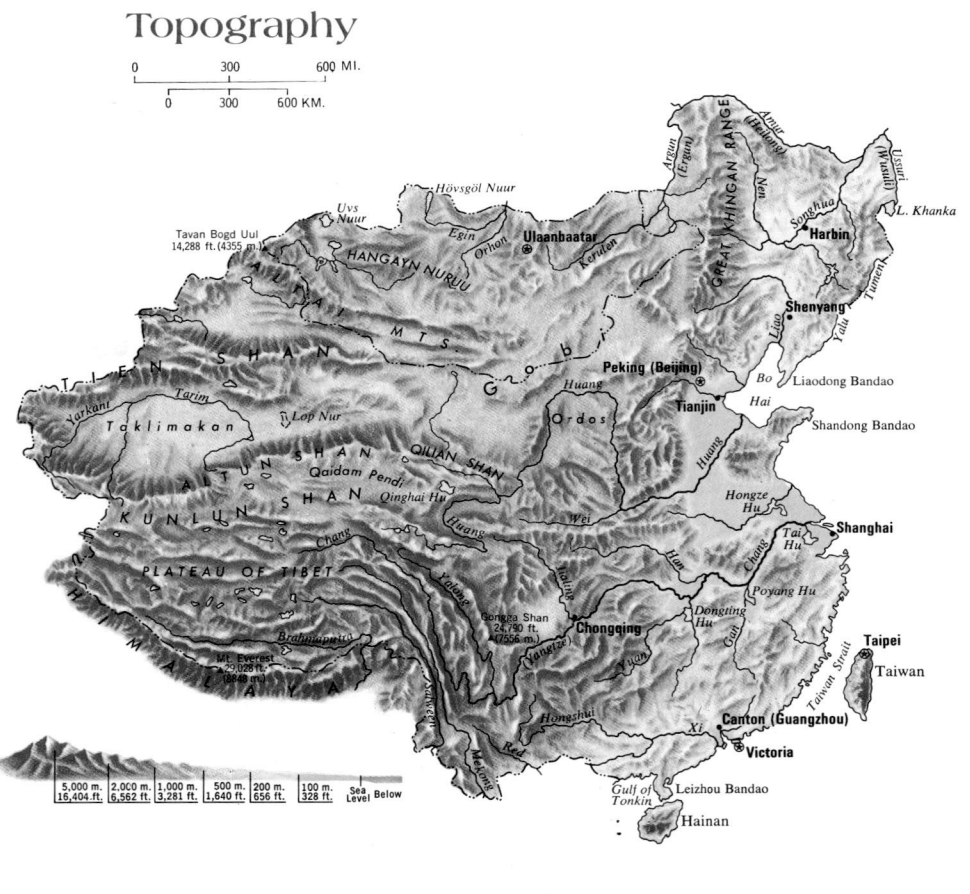

0   300   600 MI.
0   300   600 KM.

5,000 m. | 2,000 m. | 1,000 m. | 500 m. | 200 m. | 100 m. | Sea
16,404 ft. | 6,562 ft. | 3,281 ft. | 1,640 ft. | 656 ft. | 328 ft. | Level
Below

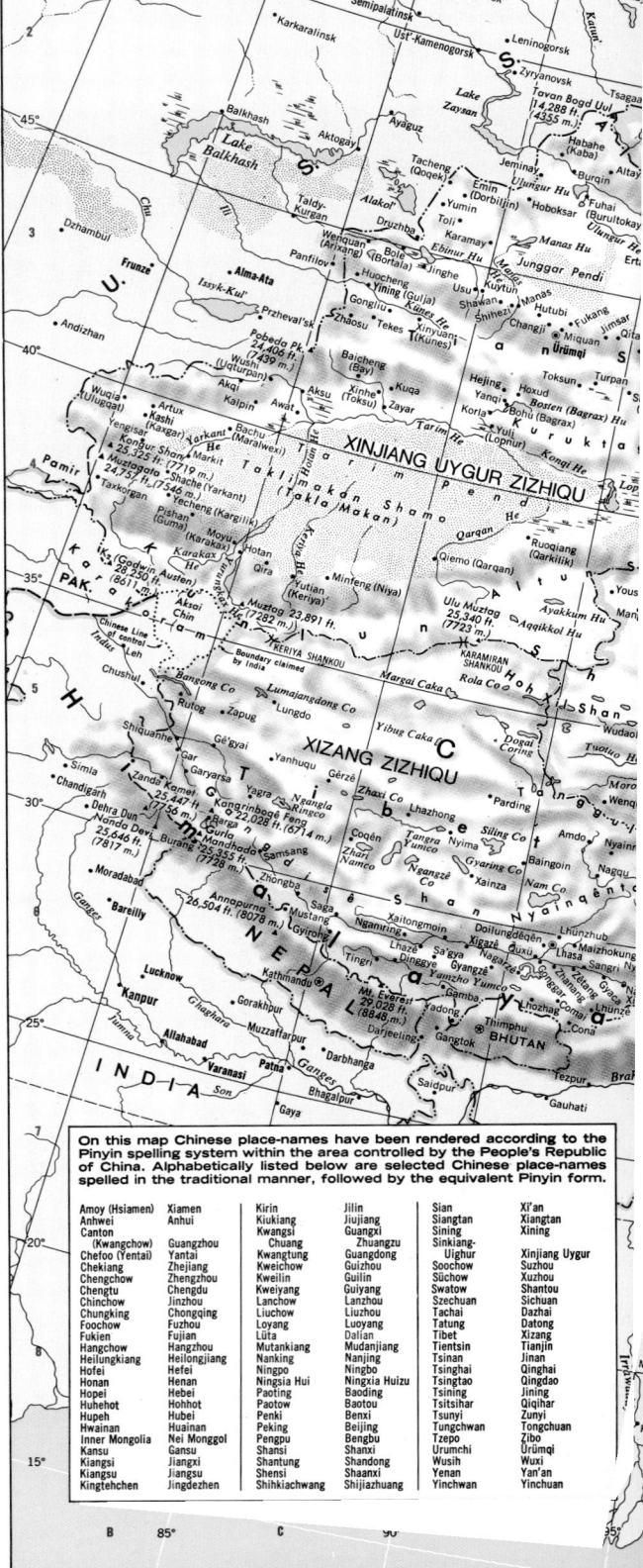

On this map Chinese place-names have been rendered according to the Pinyin spelling system within the area controlled by the People's Republic of China. Alphabetically listed below are selected Chinese place-names spelled in the traditional manner, followed by the equivalent Pinyin form.

Amoy (Hsiamen)	Xiamen	Kirin	Jilin	Sian	Xi'an
Anhwei	Anhui	Kiukiang	Jiujiang	Siangtan	Xiangtan
Canton		Kwangsi	Guangxi	Sining	Xining
(Kwangchow)	Guangzhou	Chuang	Zhuangzu	Sinkiang-	
Chefoo (Yentai)	Yantai	Kwangtung	Guangdong	Uighur	Xinjiang Uygur
Chekiang	Zhejiang	Kweichow	Guizhou	Soochow	Suzhou
Chengchow	Zhengzhou	Kweilin	Guilin	Süchow	Xuzhou
Chengtu	Chengdu	Kweiyang	Guiyang	Swatow	Shantou
Chinchow	Jinzhou	Lanchow	Lanzhou	Szechuan	Sichuan
Chungking	Chongqing	Liuchow	Liuzhou	Tachai	Dazhai
Foochow	Fuzhou	Loyang	Luoyang	Tatung	Datong
Fukien	Fujian	Lüta	Dalian	Tibet	Xizang
Hangchow	Hangzhou	Mutankiang	Mudanjiang	Tientsin	Tianjin
Heilungkiang	Heilongjiang	Nanking	Nanjing	Tsinan	Jinan
Hofei	Hefei	Ningsia Hui	Ningxia Huizu	Tsinghai	Qinghai
Honan	Henan	Ningpo	Ningbo	Tsingtao	Qingdao
Hopei	Hebei	Paoting	Baoding	Tsining	Jining
Huhehot	Hohhot	Paotow	Baotou	Tsitsihar	Qiqihar
Hupeh	Hubei	Penki	Benxi	Tsunyi	Zunyi
Hwainan	Huainan	Peking	Beijing	Tungchwan	Tongchuan
Inner Mongolia	Nei Monggol	Pengpu	Bengbu	Urumchi	Ürümqi
Kansu	Gansu	Shansi	Shanxi	Wusih	Wuxi
Kiangsi	Jiangxi	Shantung	Shandong	Yenan	Yan'an
Kiangsu	Jiangsu	Shensi	Shaanxi	Yinchwan	Yinchuan
Kingtehchen	Jingdezhen	Shihkiachwang	Shijiazhuang		

Tsining (Jining), Shandong	J4	Wenzhou 250,000	J6
Tsitsihar (Qiqihar) 1,500,000	K2	Wuchang	L3
Tsunyi (Zunyi) 275,000	G6	Wuchow (Wuzhou) 150,000	H7
Tumen	M3	Wuchuan, Guizhou	G6
Tungchwan (Tongchuan)	G5	Wuchuan, Nei Monggol	H3
Tunghwa (Tonghua) 275,000	L3	Wuchung (Wuzhong)	G4
Tungkiang (Tongjiang)	M2	Wuhai	G4
Tungliao (Tongliao)	K3	Wuhan 4,250,000	H5
Tunhwa (Dunhua)	L3	Wuhing (Wuxing) 160,000	K5
Tunxi (Tunki)	J6	Wuhu 300,000	J5
Turpan (Turfan)	C3	Wuqi	H4
Tuyün (Duyun)	G6	Wuqia	A4
Tzepo (Zibo) 1,750,000	J4	Wushi	A4
Uch Turfan (Wushi)	A3	Wushi (Wuxi) 900,000	J5
Ulanhot (Horqin Youyi		Wutai	H4
Qianqi) 250,000	K2	Wuwei	F4
Uluqchat (Wuqia)	A4	Wuxi (Wusih) 900,000	K5
Urümqi (Urumchi) 500,000	C3	Wuxing (Wuhing) 160,000	K5
Usu	B3	Wuyuan	G3
Wanning	H8	Wuzhong (Wuchung)	G4
Wanxian (Wanhsien) 175,000	H5	Wuzhou (Wuchow) 150,000	H7
Weichang	J3	Xiaguan (Siakwan)	E6
Weifang (Weifang) 260,000	J4	Xiamen (Amoy) 400,000	J7
Weihai (Weihaiwei)	K4	Xi'an (Sian) 1,900,000	G5
Weixi	E6	Xiangfan (Siangfan) 150,000	H5
Weixin	F6	Xiangtan (Siangtan) 300,000	H6
Wenchow (Wenzhou) 250,000	J6	Xianyang (Sienyang) 125,000	G5
Wenquan, Qinghai	D5	Xiapu (Siapu)	K6
Wenquan, Xinjiang Uygur	B3	Xichang (Sichang)	F6
Wenzhou 250,000	J6	Xibin	F3

Xigazê (Shigatse)	C6	Yichang (Ichang) 150,000	H5
Ximiao	F3	Yichun, Jiangxi	J6
Xin Barag Zuoqi	J2	Yichun, Heilongjiang 200,000	L2
Xingtai (Singtai)	H4	Yidu, Hubei	H5
Xinhe (Toksu)	B3	Yidu, Shandong	J4
Xining (Sining) 250,000	F4	Yinchuan (Ningsia) 175,000	G4
Xinxiang (Sinsiang) 300,000	H4	Yingkou 215,000	K3
Xinyang (Sinyang) 125,000	H5	Yining 160,000	B3
Xinyuan (Künes)	B3	Yiwu (Aratürük)	D3
Xiugang (Hsüchang)	H5	Yong'an (Yenan)	H6
Xugut	K2	Yongxin	H6
Xuzhou (Süchow) 1,500,000	J5	Yueyang	H6
Ya'an 100,000	F6	Yuli (Lopnur)	C3
Yadong	C6	Yulin, Guangxi Zhuangzu	G7
Yancheng	K5	Yulin, Shanxi	G4
Yanchuan (Yangchuan) 210,000	J5	Yumen 325,000	E4
Yangi		Yuncheng	H4
Yangjiang	G7	Yungxien	F4
Yanji (Yenki) 130,000	L3	Yushu (Chuchow) 350,000	H6
Yangquan (Yangchuan) 350,000	H4	Yutze (Yuci)	H4
Yanyuan (Yangchuan) 210,000	H4	Yushu, Jilin	L3
Ya Xian	G8	Yushu, Qinghai	E5
Yecheng	A4	Yutian, Hebei	H4
Yenan (Yan'an)	G4	Yutian, Xinjiang Uygur	B4
Yenki (Yanji) 130,000	L3	Yutze (Yuci)	H4
Yibin (Ipin) 275,000	F6	Yangzhou 250,000	J6
		Yushu, Jilin	E5
		Zunhua	J3

Zhangzhou (Changchow)	J7	Bagrax (Bosten Hu) (lake)	C3
Zhanjiang (Chankiang) 220,000	H7	Bangong Co (lake)	A5
Zhaodong	K2	Bashi (chan.)	K7
Zhaoqing	F6	Bayan Har Shan (range)	E5
Zhaosu	B3	Bo Hai (gulf)	J4
Zhaotong (Chaotung)	F6	Bosten (Bagrax) Hu (lake)	C3
Zhengzhou (Chengchow) 1,500,000	H5	Da Hinggan Ling (range)	J3
Zhenjiang (Chinkiang) 250,000	J5	Chang Jiang (Yangtze) (riv.)	K5
Zhenyuan	G6	Dian Chi (lake)	F7
Zhongba	B6	Dongsha (isl.)	J7
Zhongdian	E5	Dongting Hu (lake)	H6
Zhongshan (Chungshan) 135,000	H7	East China (sea)	L6
Zhongwei	F4	Ebinur Hu (lake)	B2
Zhumadian (Chumatien)	H5	Ergun He (Argun') (riv.)	K1
Zhushan	G7	Er Hai (lake)	F6
Zhuzhou (Chuchow) 350,000	H6	Everest (mt.)	C6
Zigong (Tzepo) 1,750,000	F6	Fen He (riv.)	H4
Zigong (Tzekung) 350,000	H7	Formosa (Taiwan) (str.)	J7
Zinhui		Formosa (Taiwan) (isl.)	J7
Zunyi (Tsunyi) 275,000	G6	Gandisê Shan (range)	B5
OTHER FEATURES		Gaoyou Hu (lake)	J5
		Genghis Khan Wall (ruin)	H2
Altun Shan (range)	C4	Gobi (des.)	G3
Alxa Shamo (des.)	F4	Gongga Shan (mt.)	F6
Amur (Heilong Jiang) (riv.)	L2	Grand (canal)	J5
A'nyêmaqên Shan (mts.)	E5	Great Wall (ruins)	G4, J
Aqqikkol Hu (lake)	C4	Gurla Mandhata (mt.)	B5
Argun' (Ergun He) (riv.)	K1	Hailar He (riv.)	K2
		Hainan (isl.)	H8

Hangzhou Wan (bay)	K5
Han Shui (riv.)	H5
Heilong Jiang (Amur) (riv.)	L2
Himalaya (mts.)	C6
Hongshui He (riv.)	G7
Hotan (Khotan) (riv.)	B4
Hotan He (riv.)	B4
Huang He (Yellow) (riv.)	J4
Hulun Nur (lake)	J2
Hungtow (isl.)	K7
Inner Mongolia (reg.)	H3
Jinmen (Quemoy) (isl.)	J7
Jinsha Jiang (Yangtze) (riv.)	E5
Junggar Pendi (desert basin)	B5
Kangrinboqê Feng (mt.)	B5
Karakiran Shankou (pass)	C4
Karamiran Shankou (pass)	C4
Khanka (lake)	M3
Kongur Shan (mt.)	A4
Kunlun Shan (range)	B3
Kunlun Shan (range)	C3
Lancang Jiang (riv.)	F7
Leizhou Bandao (pen.)	G7
Liaodong Bandao (pen.)	K3
Liao He (riv.)	K3
Lop Nor (Lop Nur) (lake)	D3
Manas He (riv.)	C3
Manas Hu (lake)	C2

(continued on following page)

China and Mongolia

SCALE OF MILES
0 100 200 300 400 500
SCALE OF KILOMETERS
0 100 200 300 400 500

Capitals of Countries......⊛   International Boundaries _____
Provincial Capitals......⊛   Provincial Boundaries _____
Canals _____   Walls ~~~~~~~

Scale 1:19,100,000

© Copyright HAMMOND INCORPORATED, Maplewood, N.J.

† Populations of mainland cities, excluding Peking (Beijing), Shanghai and Tianjin (Tientsin), courtesy of Kingsley Davis,
Office of Int'l Pop. and Research, Inst. of Int'l Studies Univ. of California.

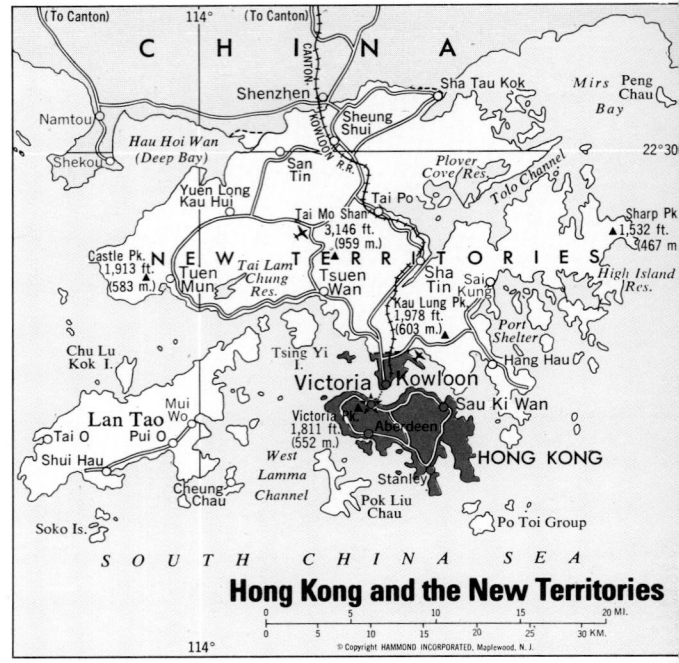

Hong Kong and the New Territories

Agriculture, Industry and Resources

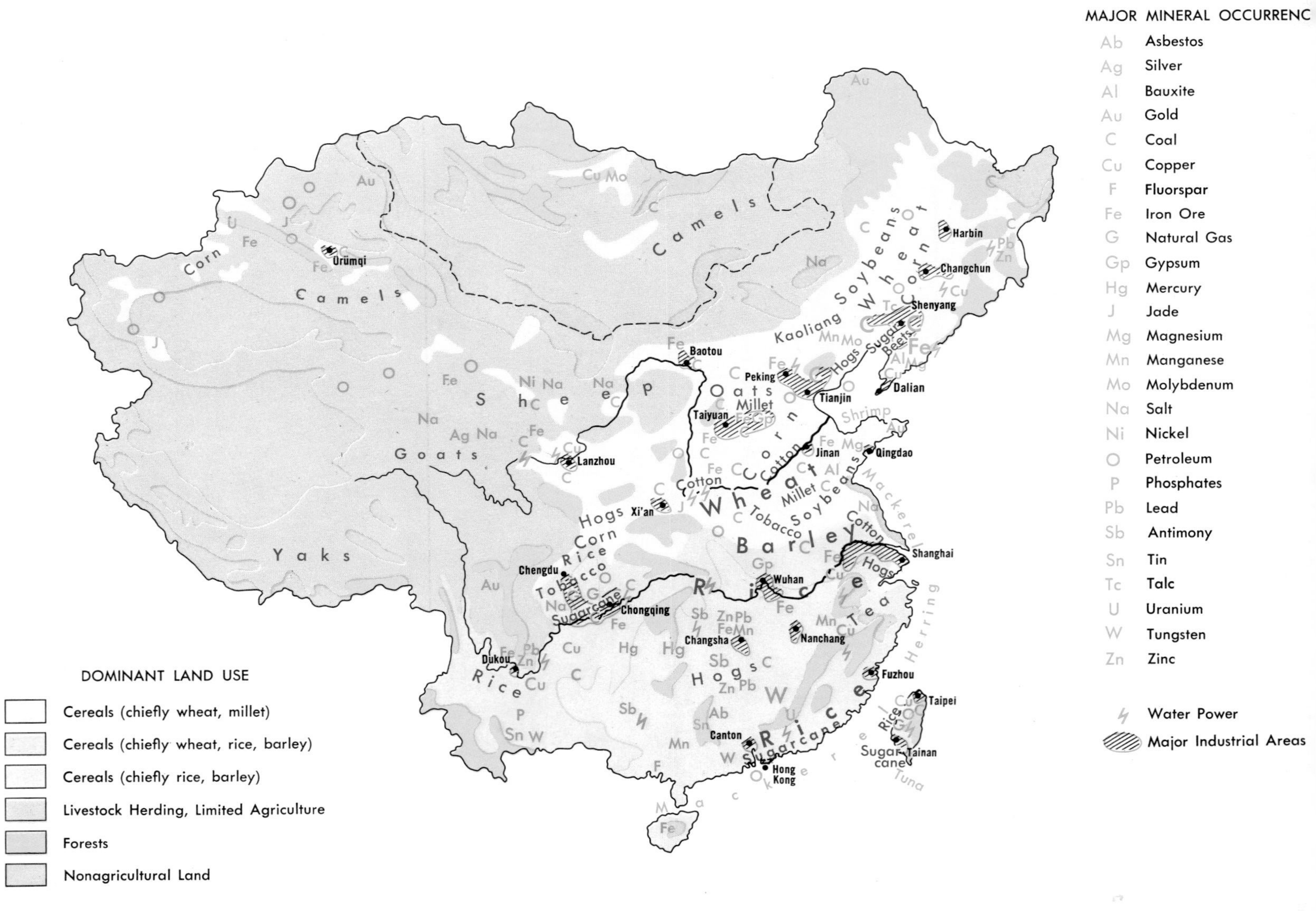

DOMINANT LAND USE

- Cereals (chiefly wheat, millet)
- Cereals (chiefly wheat, rice, barley)
- Cereals (chiefly rice, barley)
- Livestock Herding, Limited Agriculture
- Forests
- Nonagricultural Land

MAJOR MINERAL OCCURRENC

Ab	Asbestos
Ag	Silver
Al	Bauxite
Au	Gold
C	Coal
Cu	Copper
F	Fluorspar
Fe	Iron Ore
G	Natural Gas
Gp	Gypsum
Hg	Mercury
J	Jade
Mg	Magnesium
Mn	Manganese
Mo	Molybdenum
Na	Salt
Ni	Nickel
O	Petroleum
P	Phosphates
Pb	Lead
Sb	Antimony
Sn	Tin
Tc	Talc
U	Uranium
W	Tungsten
Zn	Zinc

⚡ Water Power

▨ Major Industrial Areas

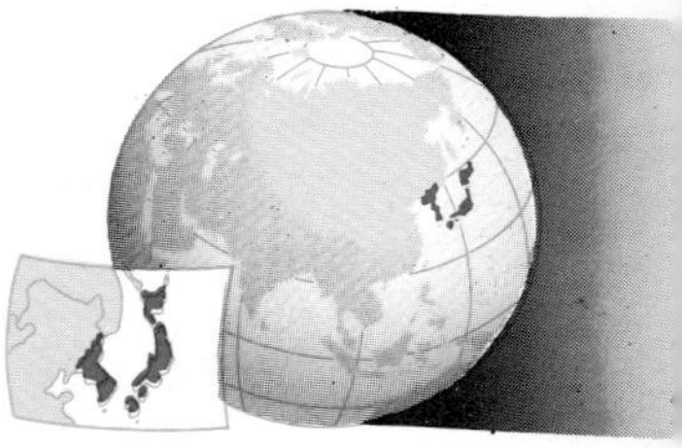

AREA 145,730 sq. mi. (377,441 sq. km.)
POPULATION 117,057,485
CAPITAL Tokyo
LARGEST CITY Tokyo
HIGHEST POINT Fuji 12,389 ft. (3,776 m.)
MONETARY UNIT yen
MAJOR LANGUAGE Japanese
MAJOR RELIGIONS Buddhism, Shintoism

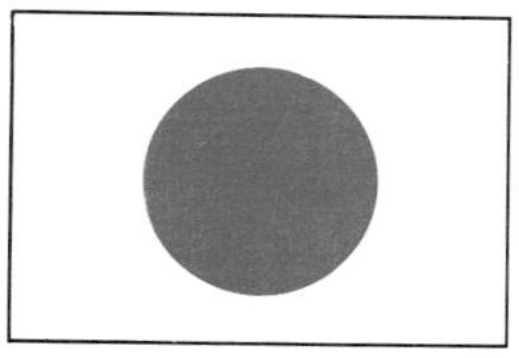

AREA 46,540 sq. mi. (120,539 sq. km.)
POPULATION 17,914,000
CAPITAL P'yŏngyang
LARGEST CITY P'yŏngyang
HIGHEST POINT Paektu 9,003 ft. (2,744 m.)
MONETARY UNIT won
MAJOR LANGUAGE Korean
MAJOR RELIGIONS Confucianism, Buddhism, Ch'ondogyo

AREA 38,175 sq. mi. (98,873 sq. km.)
POPULATION 37,448,836
CAPITAL Seoul
LARGEST CITY Seoul
HIGHEST POINT Halla 6,398 ft. (1,950 m.)
MONETARY UNIT won
MAJOR LANGUAGE Korean
MAJOR RELIGIONS Confucianism, Buddhism, Ch'ondogyo, Christianity

JAPAN

NORTH KOREA

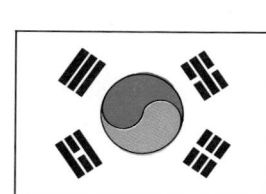

SOUTH KOREA

Agriculture, Industry and Resources

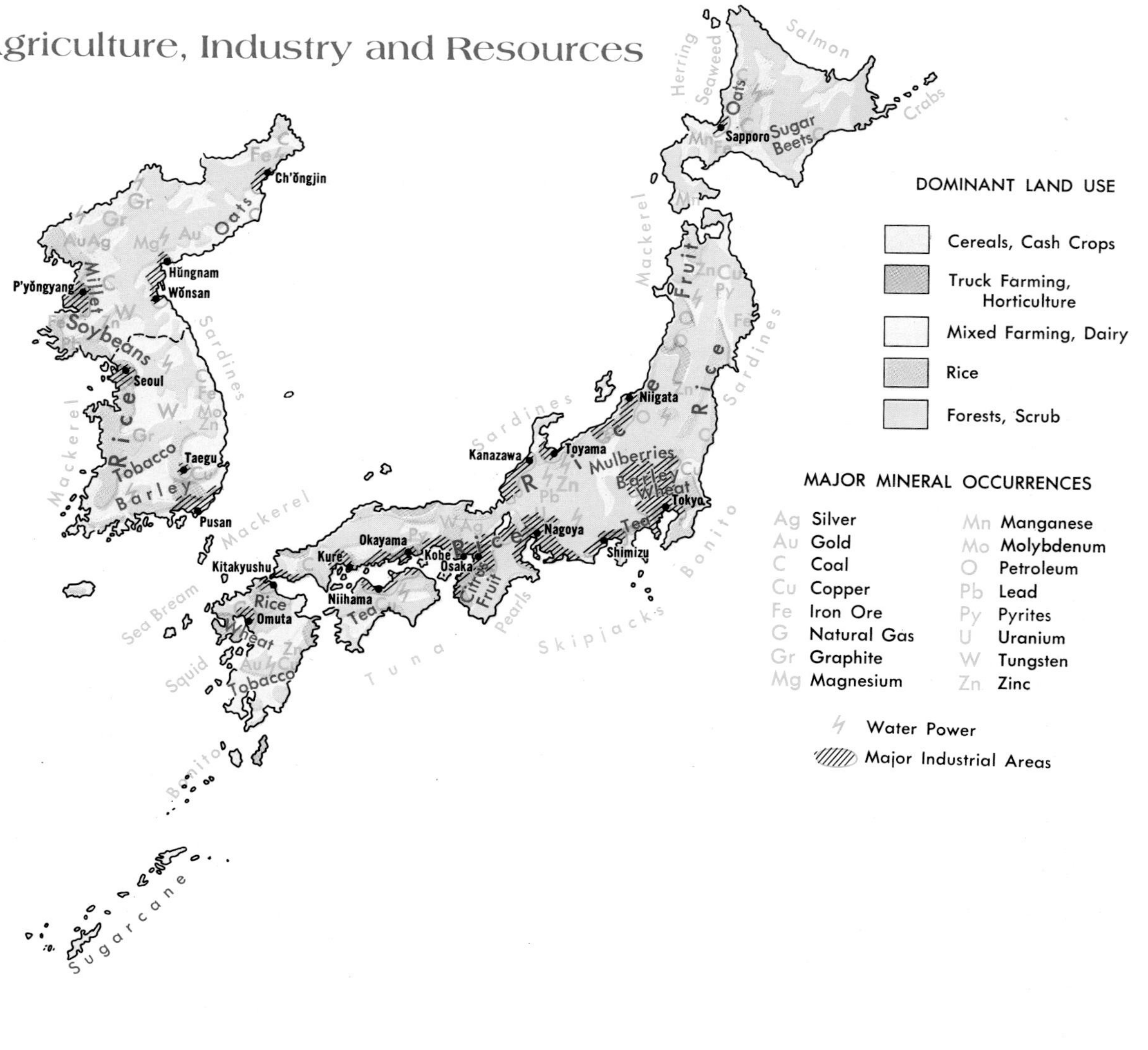

DOMINANT LAND USE

- Cereals, Cash Crops
- Truck Farming, Horticulture
- Mixed Farming, Dairy
- Rice
- Forests, Scrub

MAJOR MINERAL OCCURRENCES

Ag Silver
Au Gold
C Coal
Cu Copper
Fe Iron Ore
G Natural Gas
Gr Graphite
Mg Magnesium
Mn Manganese
Mo Molybdenum
O Petroleum
Pb Lead
Py Pyrites
U Uranium
W Tungsten
Zn Zinc

⚡ Water Power
▨ Major Industrial Areas

(continued on following page)

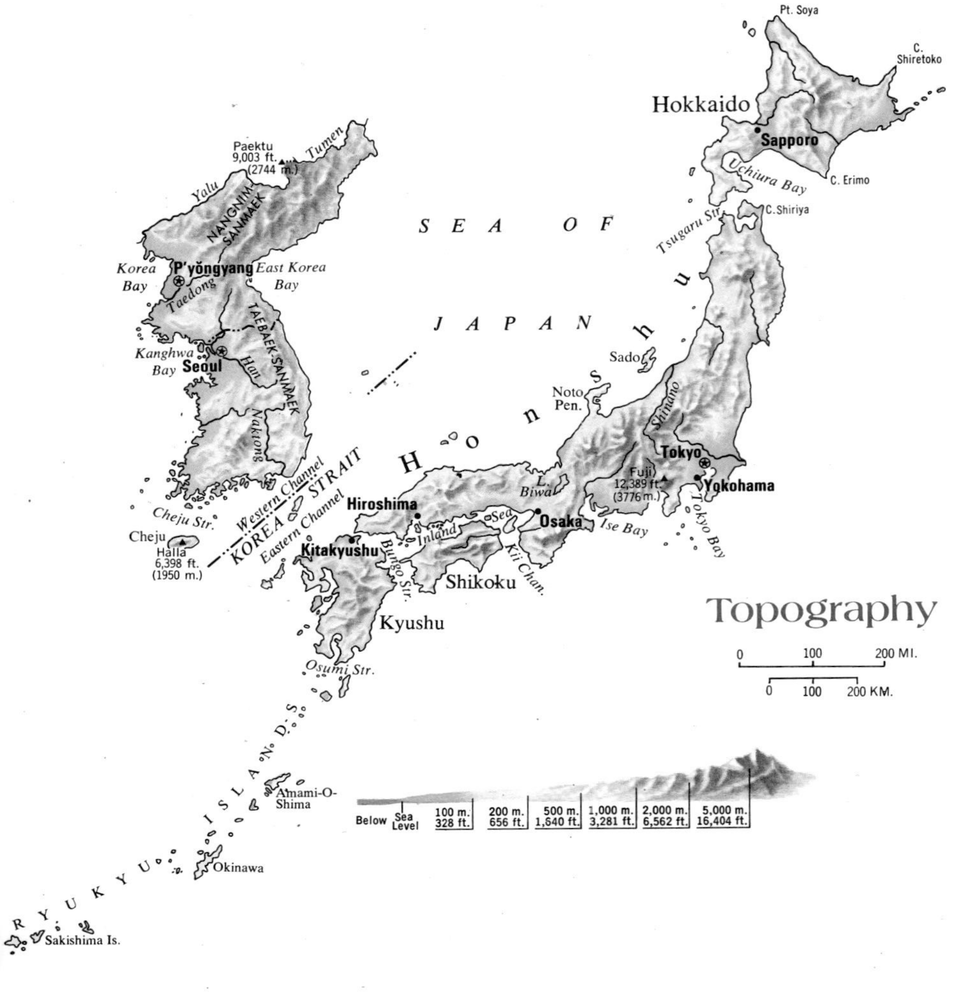
Pt. Soya
C. Shiretoko
Hokkaido
Sapporo
C. Erimo
Uchiura Bay
C.Shiriya
Tsugaru Str.
Paektu
9,003 ft.
(2744 m.)
Tumen
Yalu
NANGNIM SANMAEK
Korea Bay
P'yŏngyang
East Korea Bay
Taedong
TAEBAEK SANMAEK
Kanghwa Bay
Seoul
Han
Naktong
SEA OF JAPAN
Honshu
Sado
Noto Pen.
Shinano
Tokyo
Fuji
12,389 ft.
(3776 m.)
Yokohama
Tokyo Bay
L. Biwa
Osaka
Ise Bay
Kii Chan.
Western Channel
KOREA STRAIT
Eastern Channel
Cheju Str.
Cheju
Halla
6,398 ft.
(1950 m.)
Hiroshima
Kitakyushu
Inland Sea
Bungo Str.
Shikoku
Kyushu
Osumi Str.
Topography
0 100 200 MI.
0 100 200 KM.
Amami-O-Shima
RYUKYU ISLANDS
Okinawa
Sakishima Is.
Below Sea Level
100 m. 328 ft.
200 m. 656 ft.
500 m. 1,640 ft.
1,000 m. 3,281 ft.
2,000 m. 6,562 ft.
5,000 m. 16,404 ft.

Nishinoomote 24,266 .... E8
Nobeoka 134,521 .... E7
Noboribetsu 50,885 .... K2
Noda 78,193 .... P2
Nogata 58,551 .... E7
Nose 9,749 .... J7
Noshiro 59,215 .... J3
Noto 15,815 .... H5
Numata 45,255 .... J5
Numazu 199,325 .... J6
Obama 33,890 .... G6
Obihiro 141,774 .... L2
Oda 37,449 .... F6
Odate 71,828 .... K3
Odawara 173,519 .... J6
Ofunato 39,632 .... K4
Oga 39,619 .... J4
Ogaki 140,424 .... H6
Ogi 4,717 .... J5
Ohata 12,632 .... K3
Oita 320,237 .... E7
Ojiya 44,375 .... J5
Okawa 50,395 .... E7
Okaya 61,776 .... H5
Okayama 513,471 .... F6
Okazaki 234,510 .... H6
Omagari 40,581 .... K4
Omiya 327,698 .... O2
Omu 7,407 .... L1
Omura, Bonin Is. 1,507 .... M3
Omura, Nagasaki 60,919 .... E7
Omuta 165,969 .... E7
Onagawa 16,945 .... K4
Ono 41,918 .... H6
Onoda 43,804 .... E6
Onomichi 102,951 .... F6
Osaka 2,778,987 .... J8
Ota 110,723 .... J5
Otaru 184,406 .... K2
Otawara 42,332 .... K5
Otofuke 26,933 .... L2
Otsu 191,481 .... J7
Owase 31,797 .... H6
Oyabe 35,791 .... H5
Oyama 120,264 .... J5
Ozu 37,294 .... F7
Rausu 8,249 .... M1
Rikuzentakata 29,439 .... K4
Rumoi 36,882 .... K2
Ryotsu 22,110 .... J4
Ryugasaki 40,565 .... P2
Sabae 57,252 .... H5
Saga 152,258 .... E7
Sagamihara 377,398 .... O2
Saigo 14,409 .... F5
Saiki 52,863 .... E7
Saito 37,054 .... E7
Sakado 51,232 .... O2
Sakai, Ibaraki 24,347 .... P1
Sakai, Osaka 750,688 .... J8
Sakaide 67,624 .... G6
Sakaiminato 35,821 .... F6
Sakata 97,723 .... J4
Saku 56,143 .... J5
Sakurai 54,314 .... J8
Sanda 35,261 .... H7
Sanjo 81,806 .... J5
Sapporo 1,240,613 .... K2
Sarufutsu 3,552 .... L1
Sasebo 250,729 .... D7
Satte 43,083 .... O1
Sawara 48,670 .... K6
Sayama 98,548 .... O2
Sendai, Kagoshima 61,788 .... E8
Sendai, Miyagi 615,473 .... K4
Setouchi 15,290 .... O5
Settsu 76,704 .... J8
Shari 15,996 .... M2
Shibata 74,025 .... J5
Shibetsu 30,028 .... M2
Shimabara 45,179 .... E7
Shimamoto 22,404 .... J7
Shimizu 243,049 .... J6
Shimoda 31,700 .... J6
Shimonoseki 266,593 .... E6
Shingu 39,023 .... H7
Shinjo 42,227 .... K4
Shiogama 59,235 .... K4
Shirakawa 42,685 .... K5
Shiranuka 14,897 .... M2
Shiroishi 40,862 .... K4
Shizunai 24,833 .... L2
Shizuoka 446,952 .... H6
Shobara 23,867 .... F6
Soka 167,177 .... O2
Soma 37,551 .... K5
Sonobe 14,827 .... J7
Suita 300,956 .... J7
Sukagawa 54,922 .... K5
Sukumo 25,340 .... F7
Sumoto 44,137 .... G6
Sunagawa 26,023 .... K2
Susaki 31,019 .... F7
Suttsu 6,511 .... J2
Suwa 49,594 .... H6
Suzu 28,238 .... H5
Suzuka 141,829 .... H6
Tachikawa 138,129 .... O2
Tagawa 61,464 .... E7
Tajimi 68,901 .... H6
Takaishi 66,824 .... H8
Takamatsu 298,999 .... F6
Takaoka 169,621 .... H5
Takarazuka 162,624 .... H7
Takasaki 211,348 .... J5
Takatsuki 330,570 .... J7
Takayama 60,504 .... H5
Takefu 65,012 .... G6
Takikawa 50,090 .... K2
Tanabe, Kyoto 30,022 .... J7
Tanabe, Wakayama 66,999 .... G7
Tateyama 56,139 .... K6
Tendo 48,082 .... K4
Tenri 62,909 .... J8
Teshio 6,509 .... K1
Toba 29,346 .... H6
Tobetsu 17,351 .... K2
Togane 33,406 .... K6
Toi 6,983 .... J6
Tojo 13,796 .... F6
Tokamachi 50,211 .... J5
Tokorozawa 196,870 .... O2
Tokunoshima 35,391 .... O5
Tokushima 239,281 .... G7
Tokuyama 106,967 .... F6
Tokyo (cap.) 8,646,520 .... O2
Tokyo* 11,673,554 .... O2
Tomakomai 132,477 .... K2
Tomiyama 7,389 .... O3
Tondabayashi 91,393 .... J8
Tosa 30,679 .... F7
Tosashimizu 24,856 .... F7
Tosu 50,733 .... E7
Tottori 122,312 .... G6
Towada 54,365 .... K3
Toyama 290,143 .... H5
Toyohashi 284,585 .... H6
Toyonaka 398,384 .... J7
Toyooka 46,210 .... G6
Toyota 248,774 .... H6
Tsu 139,538 .... H6
Tsubame 43,265 .... J5
Tsuchiura 104,028 .... J5
Tsuruga 60,205 .... G6
Tsuruoka 95,932 .... J4
Tsuyama 79,907 .... F6
Ube 161,969 .... E6
Ueda 105,151 .... J5
Ugo 21,956 .... K4
Uji 133,405 .... J7
Uozu 48,419 .... H5
Urakawa 20,213 .... L2
Urawa 331,145 .... O2
Ushibuka 24,250 .... D7
Usuki 39,163 .... F7
Utsunomiya 344,420 .... K5
Uwajima 70,428 .... F7
Wajima 33,234 .... H5
Wakasa 6,989 .... G6
Wakayama 389,717 .... G6
Wakkanai 55,464 .... K1
Warabi 76,311 .... O2
Yaizu 94,102 .... J6
Yakumo 19,260 .... J2
Yamagata 219,773 .... K4
Yamaguchi 106,099 .... E6
Yamato 145,881 .... O2
Yamatokoriyama 71,001 .... J8
Yamatotakada 58,637 .... J8
Yao 261,639 .... J8
Yatabe 22,225 .... P2
Yatsushiro 103,691 .... E7
Yawata 50,132 .... J7
Yawatahama 45,259 .... F7
Yoichi 25,816 .... K2
Yokawa 8,015 .... H7
Yokkaichi 247,001 .... H6
Yokohama 2,621,771 .... O3
Yokosuka 389,557 .... O3
Yokote 43,030 .... K4
Yonago 118,332 .... F6
Yonezawa 91,974 .... K5
Yono 71,044 .... O2
Yubari 50,131 .... L2
Yubetsu 6,693 .... L1
Yukuhashi 53,750 .... E7
Yuzawa 38,005 .... K4
Zushi 56,298 .... O3

OTHER FEATURES

Abashiri (riv.) M1
Agano (riv.) J4
Akan National Park M2
Amakusa (isls.) D7
Amami (isls.) N5
Amami-O-Shima (isl.) N5
Ara (riv.) O2
Asahi (mt.) J4
Asama (mt.) J5
Ashizuri (cape) F7
Aso (mt.) E7
Aso National Park E7
Atsumi (bay) H6
Awa (isl.) J4
Awaji (isl.) H8
Bandai (mt.) K5
Bandai-Asahi National Park J4
Biwa (lake) H6
Bonin (isls.) M3
Boso (pen.) K6
Bungo (strait) F7
Chichi (isl.) M3
Chichibu-Tama National Park J6
Chokai (mt.) J4
Chubu-Sangaku National Park H5
Dai (mt.) F6
Daimanji (mt.) F5
Daio (cape) H6
Daisen-Oki National Park F6
Daisetsu (mt.) L2
Daisetsu-Zan National Park L2
Dogo (isl.) F5
Dozen (isls.) F5
East China (sea) C8
Edo (riv.) P2
Erimo (cape) L3
Esan (pt.) K3
Etorofu (isl.) N1
Fuji (mt.) J6
Fuji (riv.) J6
Fuji-Hakone-Izu National Park H6
Gassan (mt.) J4
Goto (isls.) D7
Habomai (isls.) N2
Hachiro (lag.) J3
Haha (isl.) M3
Hakken (mt.) H6
Haku (mt.) H5
Hakusan National Park H5
Harima (sea) G6
Hida (riv.) H6
Hodaka (mt.) H5
Hokkaido (isl.) L2
Honshu (isl.) J5
Ie (isl.) N6
Iheya (isl.) N6
Iki (isl.) D7
Ina (riv.) H7
Inawashiro (lake) K5
Inubo (cape) K6
Iriomote (isl.) K7
Iro (cape) J6
Ise (bay) H6
Ise-Shima National Park H6
Ishigaki (isl.) L7
Ishikari (bay) K2
Ishikari (riv.) L2
Ishizuchi (mt.) F7
Iwaki (mt.) K3
Iwate (mt.) K4
Iwo (isl.) M4
Iyo (sea) E7
Izu (isls.) J6
Izu (pen.) J6
Japan (sea) G4
Joshinetsu-Kogen National Park J5
Kagoshima (bay) E8
Kamui (cape) K2
Kariba (mt.) K2
Kasumiga (lag.) K5
Kazan-retto (Volcano) (isls.) M4
Kerama (isls.) M6
Kii (chan.) G7
Kikai (isl.) O5
Kino (riv.) G6
Kirishima-Yaku National Park E7
Kita Iwo (isl.) M4
Kitakami (riv.) K4
Komaga (mt.) K2
Koshiki (isls.) D8
Kuchino (isl.) O4
Kuju (mt.) E7
Kume (isl.) M6
Kunashiri (isl.) N1
Kutcharo (lake) M2
Kyushu (isl.) E7
Meakan (mt.) L2
Minami Iwo (isl.) M5
Miura (pen.) O3
Miyako (isl.) L7
Miyako (isls.) L7
Mogami (riv.) K4
Motsuta (cape) J2
Muko (isl.) M3
Muko (riv.) H7
Muroto (pt.) G7
Mutsu (bay) K3
Naka (riv.) K5
Nampo-Shoto (isls.) M3
Nansei Shoto (Ryukyu) (isls.) M6
Nantai (mt.) J5
Nasu (mt.) J5
Nemuro (strait) M1
Nii (isl.) J6
Nikko National Park J5
Nishino (isl.) M3
Nojima (cape) K6
Nosappu (pt.) N2
Noto (pen.) H5
Nyudo (cape) J4
Oani (riv.) K3
Obitsu (riv.) P3
Oga (pen.) J4
Ogasawara-gunto (Bonin) (isls.) M3
Okhotsk (sea) M1
Oki (isls.) F5
Okinawa (isl.) N6
Okinawa (isls.) N6
Okinoerabu (isl.) N5
Okushiri (isl.) J2
Oma (cape) K3
Omono (riv.) J4
Ono (riv.) E7
Ontake (mt.) H6
Osaka (bay) H8
O-Shima (isl.) J6
Osumi (isls.) E8
Osumi (pen.) E8
Osumi (str.) E8
Otakine (mt.) K5
Rikuchu-Kaigan National Park L4
Rishiri (isl.) K1
Ryukyu (isls.) L7
Sado (isl.) J4
Sagami (bay) O3
Sagami (riv.) O2
Sagami (sea) J6
Saikai National Park D7
Sakishima (isls.) K7
San'in Kaigan National Park G6
Sata (cape) E8
Setonaikai National Park H7
Shikoku (isl.) F7
Shikotan (isl.) N2
Shikotsu (lake) K2
Shikotsu-Toya National Park K2
Shimane (pen.) F6
Shimokita (pen.) K3
Shinano (riv.) J5
Shiono (cape) H7
Shiragami (cape) J3
Shirane (mt.) J5
Shirane (mt.) H6
Shiretoko (cape) M1
Shiriya (cape) K3
Soya (pt.) L1
Suo (sea) E7
Suruga (bay) J6
Suwanose (isl.) O4
Suzu (pt.) H5
Takeshima (isls.) F5
Tama (riv.) O2
Tanega (isl.) E8
Tappi (cape) K3

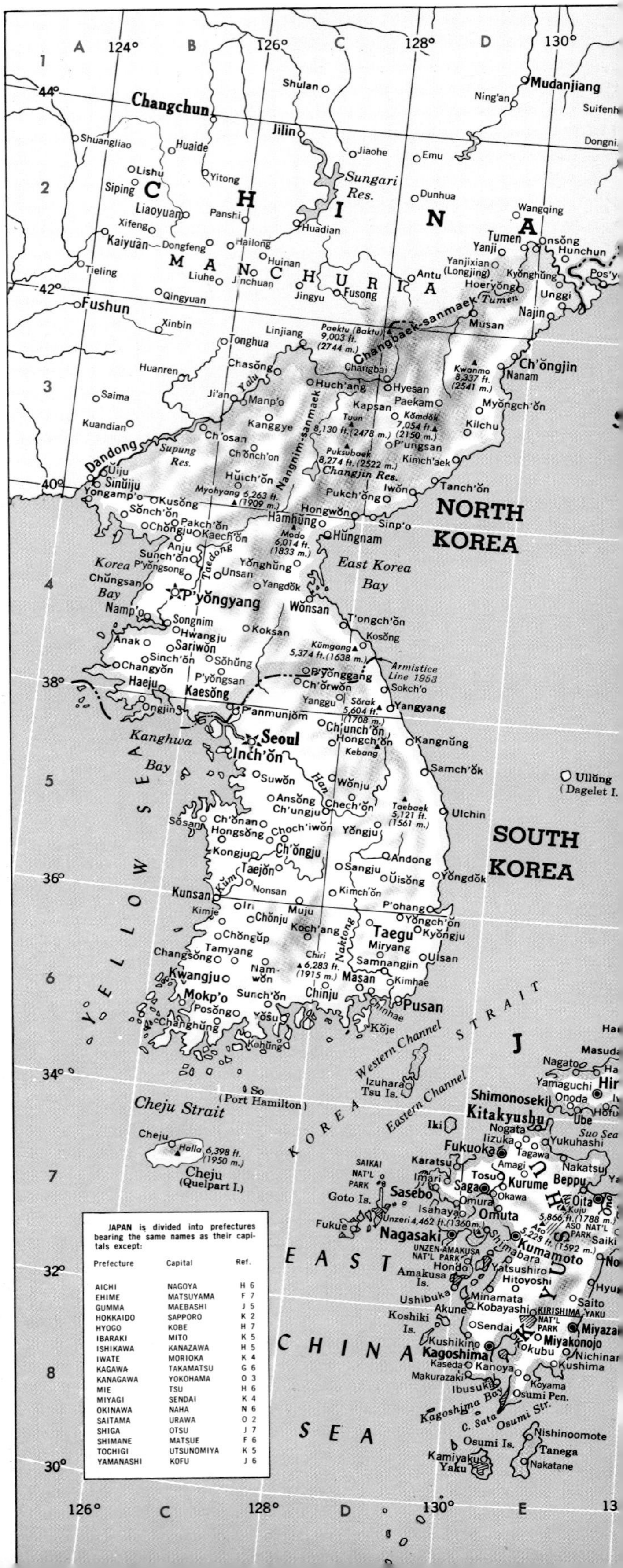
124° 126° 128° 130°
Changchun
Jilin
Mudanjiang
CHINA
MANCHURIA
Paektu (Baktu)
9,003 ft.
(2744 m.)
Changbaek-sanmaek
Nangnim-sanmaek
Yalu
Dandong
Sinŭiju
Supung Res.
Changjin Res.
Hamhŭng
Hŭngnam
NORTH KOREA
Korea Bay
East Korea Bay
P'yŏngyang
Wŏnsan
Armistice Line 1953
Kaesŏng
Panmunjŏm
Seoul
Inch'ŏn
Kanghwa Bay
Han
YELLOW SEA
Ullŭng
(Dagelet I.)
SOUTH KOREA
Taejŏn
Kunsan
Taegu
Naktong
Kwangju
Mokp'o
Masan
Pusan
KOREA STRAIT
Western Channel
Eastern Channel
Cheju Strait
Cheju
Halla 6,398 ft.
(1950 m.)
Cheju
(Quelpart I.)
EAST CHINA SEA
Tsu Is.
Shimonoseki
Kitakyushu
Fukuoka
Sasebo
Nagasaki
Kumamoto
Kagoshima
Miyakonojo
Osumi Is.
Tanega
Yaku

JAPAN is divided into prefectures bearing the same names as their capitals except:

Prefecture	Capital	Ref.
AICHI	NAGOYA	H 6
EHIME	MATSUYAMA	F 7
GUMMA	MAEBASHI	J 5
HOKKAIDO	SAPPORO	K 2
HYOGO	KOBE	H 7
IBARAKI	MITO	K 5
ISHIKAWA	KANAZAWA	H 5
IWATE	MORIOKA	K 4
KAGAWA	TAKAMATSU	G 6
KANAGAWA	YOKOHAMA	O 3
MIE	TSU	H 6
MIYAGI	SENDAI	K 4
OKINAWA	NAHA	N 6
SAITAMA	URAWA	O 2
SHIGA	OTSU	J 7
SHIMANE	MATSUE	F 6
TOCHIGI	UTSUNOMIYA	K 5
YAMANASHI	KOFU	J 6

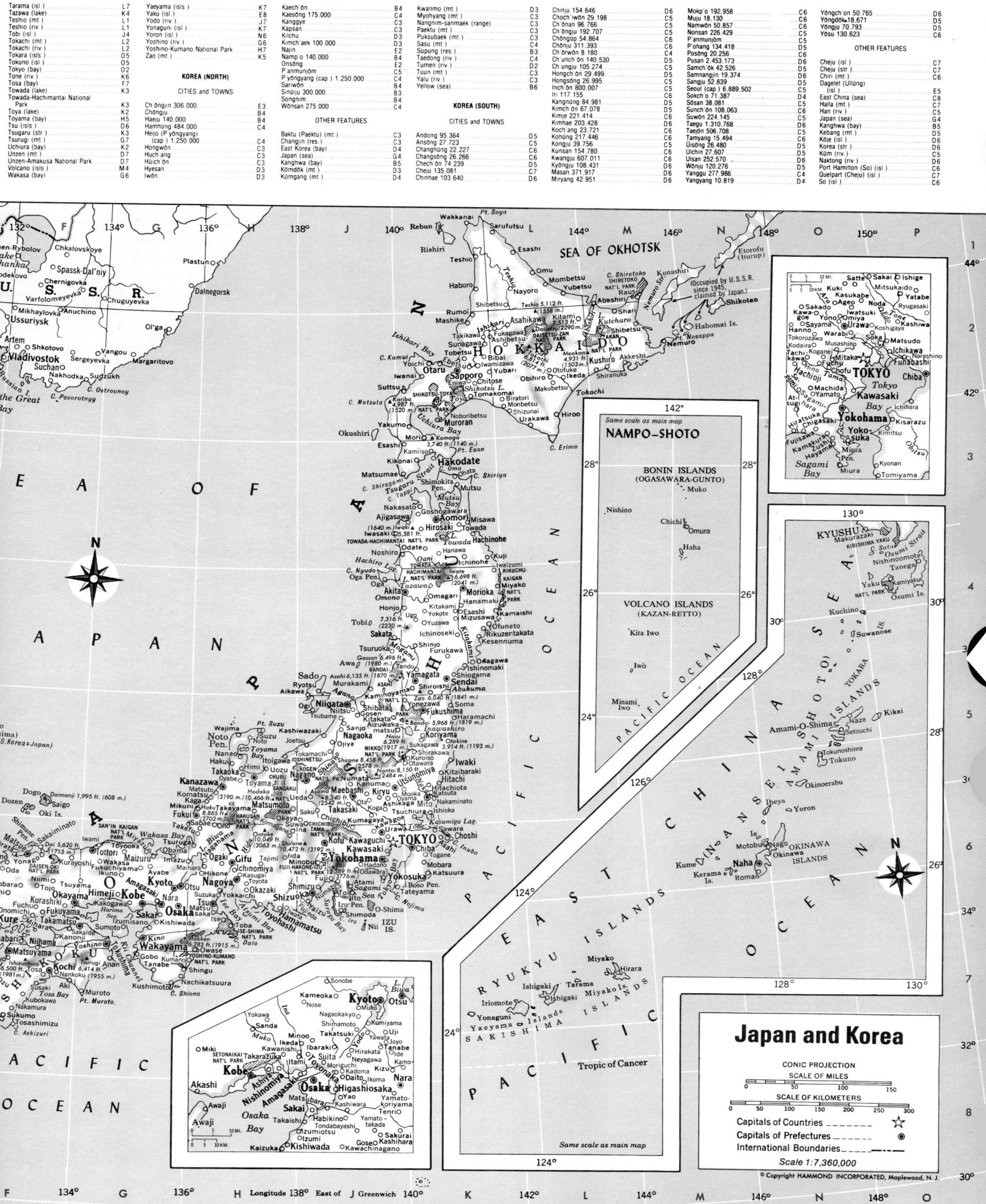

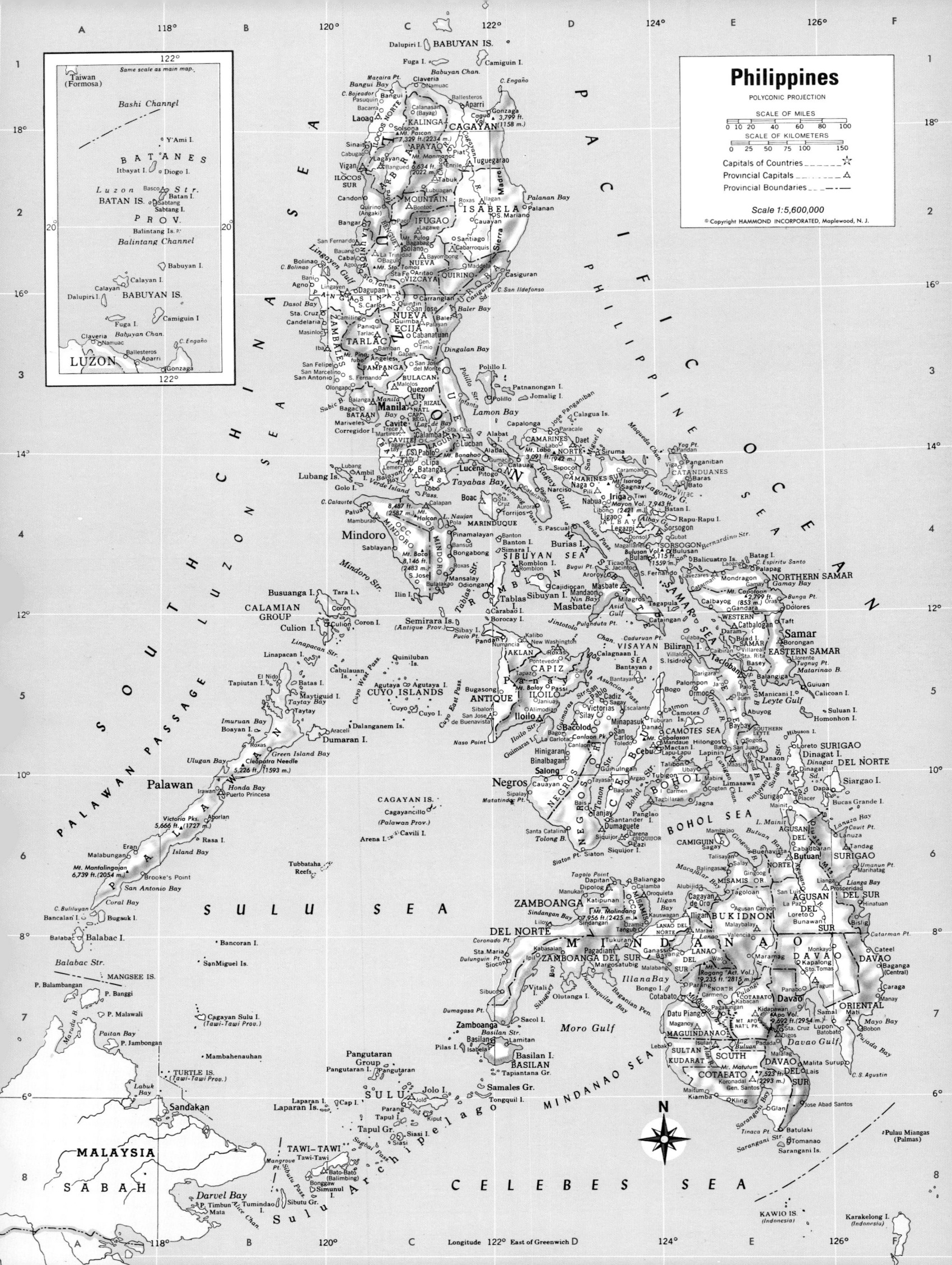

Philippines
POLYCONIC PROJECTION

SCALE OF MILES
0 10 20 40 60 80 100

SCALE OF KILOMETERS
0 25 50 75 100 150

Capitals of Countries _____ ☆
Provincial Capitals _____ △
Provincial Boundaries _____

Scale 1:5,600,000

© Copyright HAMMOND INCORPORATED, Maplewood, N.J.

LUZON

Taiwan (Formosa)

Bashi Channel

BATANES

Y'Ami I.
Itbayat I.   Diogo I.

Luzon   Str.
BATAN IS.   Basco   Batan I.
PROV.   Sabtang   Sabtang I.

Balintang Is.
Balintang Channel

Babuyan I.

Calayan I.

Dalupiri I.   BABUYAN IS.
Fuga I.

Camiguin I.

Claveria   Babuyan Chan.
Namuac
Ballesteros
Aparri   C. Engaño
Gonzaga

Same scale as main map.

PROVINCES

Abra 160,198 . . . . C2
Agusan del Norte 365,421 . . E6
Agusan del Sur 631,634 . . . . E6
Aklan 324,563 . . . . D5
Albay 809,177 . . . . D4
Antique 344,879 . . . . D5
Aurora 107,145 . . . . C3
Basilan 201,407 . . . . D7
Bataan 323,254 . . . . C3
Batanes 12,091 . . . . A2
Batangas 1,174,201 . . . . . . C4
Benguet 354,751 . . . . C2
Bohol 806,031 . . . . E6
Bukidnon 631,634 . . . . E6
Bulacan 1,098,046 . . . . C3
Cagayan 711,476 . . . . C1
Camarines Norte 368,007 . . . D3
Camarines Sur 1,099,346 . . D4
Camiguin 57,126 . . . . E6
Capiz 492,231 . . . . D5
Catanduanes 175,247 . . . . . E4
Cavite 771,320 . . . . C3
Cebu 2,091,602 . . . . D5
Davao 725,153 . . . . E7
Davao del Sur 1,133,599 . . . E7
Davao Oriental 339,931 . . . . F7
Eastern Samar 320,637 . . . . E5
Ifugao 111,368 . . . . C2
Ilocos Norte 390,666 . . . . . . C1
Ilocos Sur 443,591 . . . . C2
Iloilo 1,433,641 . . . . D5
Isabela 870,604 . . . . C2
Kalinga-Apayao 185,063 . . . . C1
Laguna 973,104 . . . . C3
Lanao del Norte 461,049 . . . E6
Lanao del Sur 404,971 . . . . . E7
La Union 452,578 . . . . C2
Leyte 1,302,648 . . . . E5
Maguindanao 536,546 . . . . . E7
Manila 5,925,884 . . . . C3
Marinduque 173,715 . . . . . . C4
Masbate 584,526 . . . . D4
Misamis Occidental 386,328 D6
Misamis Oriental 690,032 . . . E6
Mountain 103,052 . . . . C2
National Capital Region (Manila) 5,925,884 . . . . . . C3
Negros Occidental 1,930,301 . . . . D6
Negros Oriental 819,399 . . . D6
North Cotabato 564,599 . . . . E7
Northern Samar 378,516 . . . E4
Nueva Ecija 1,069,409 . . . . . C3
Nueva Vizcaya 241,690 . . . . . C2
Occidental Mindoro 222,431 C4
Oriental Mindoro 448,938 . . . C4
Palawan 371,782 . . . . B6
Pampanga 1,181,590 . . . . . . C3
Pangasinan 1,636,057 . . . . . C3
Quezon 1,129,277 . . . . C3
Quirino 83,230 . . . . C2
Rizal 555,533 . . . . C3
Romblon 193,174 . . . . D4
Siquijor 70,300 . . . . D6
Sorsogon 500,685 . . . . E4
South Cotabato 770,473 . . . . E7
Southern Leyte 298,294 . . . . E5
Sultan Kudarat 303,784 . . . . E7
Sulu 360,588 . . . . C7
Surigao del Norte 363,414 . . F5
Surigao del Sur 377,647 . . . . F6
Tarlac 638,457 . . . . C3
Tawi-Tawi 194,651 . . . . B8
Western Samar 501,439 . . . . E5
Zambales 444,037 . . . . C3
Zamboanga del Norte 588,015 . . . . D6
Zamboanga del Sur 1,183,845 . . . . D7

CITIES and TOWNS

Angeles 188,834 . . . . C3
Aparri 45,070 . . . . C1
Bacolod 262,415 . . . . D5
Bagac 13,109 . . . . C3
Bago 99,631 . . . . D5
Baguio 119,009 . . . . C2
Balanga 39,132 . . . . C3
Baler 18,349 . . . . C3
Balimbing (Bato-Bato) 22,189 . . . . C8
Bamban 26,072 . . . . C3
Basco 4,341 . . . . A2
Batangas 143,570 . . . . C4
Bato-Bato 22,189 . . . . C8
Baybay 74,640 . . . . E5
Bislig 81,615 . . . . F6
Boac 37,005 . . . . C4
Bontoc 17,091 . . . . C2
Burauen 48,058 . . . . E5
Butuan 172,489 . . . . E6
Cabanatuan 138,298 . . . . . . C3
Cabarroguis 17,450 . . . . C2
Cadiz 129,632 . . . . D5
Cagayan de Oro 227,312 . . . E6
Calamba 121,175 . . . . C3
Calbayog 106,719 . . . . E4
Carigara 34,377 . . . . E5
Cauayan 70,017 . . . . D6
Cavite 87,666 . . . . C3
Cebu 490,281 . . . . D5
Cotabato 83,871 . . . . D7
Dagupan 98,344 . . . . C2
Davao 610,375 . . . . E7
Digos 70,065 . . . . E7
Escalante 71,293 . . . . D5
General Santos 149,396 . . . . E7
Gingoog 79,937 . . . . E6
Guihulngan 84,156 . . . . D5
Guimba 58,847 . . . . C3
Iba 22,791 . . . . B3
Ilagan 79,336 . . . . C2
Iligan 167,358 . . . . E6
Iloilo 244,827 . . . . D5
Infanta 27,914 . . . . C3
Jaro 29,739 . . . . E5
Jolo 52,429 . . . . C8
Koronadal 80,566 . . . . E7
Lagawe 15,075 . . . . C2
Lapu-Lapu 98,723 . . . . E5
Legazpi 99,766 . . . . D4
Ligao 69,860 . . . . D4
Lingayen 65,187 . . . . C2
Lipa 121,166 . . . . C4
Lucena 107,880 . . . . C4
Maganoy 45,845 . . . . E7
Mainit 18,078 . . . . E6
Malabang 18,955 . . . . D7
Malolos 95,699 . . . . C3
Mandaue 110,590 . . . . E5
Manila (cap.) 1,630,485 . . . . C3
Mariveles 48,594 . . . . C3
Mati 78,178 . . . . F7
Naga 90,712 . . . . D4
Olongapo 156,430 . . . . C3
Ormoc 104,978 . . . . E5
Ozamiz 77,832 . . . . D6
Pagadian 80,861 . . . . D7
Palo 31,124 . . . . E5
Palompon 40,242 . . . . E5
Panabo 71,098 . . . . E7
Prosperidad 33,824 . . . . F6
Puerto Princesa 60,234 . . . . B6
Quezon City 1,165,865 . . . . . C3
Romblon 24,251 . . . . D4
Roxas 81,183 . . . . D5
Sagay 99,118 . . . . D5
San Antonio 42,969 . . . . B3
San Carlos, Negros Occ. 91,627 . . . . D5
San Carlos, Pangasinan 101,243 . . . . C3
San Fernando, La Union 68,410 . . . . C2
San Fernando, Pampanga 110,891 . . . . C3
San Jose 64,254 . . . . C3
San Jose del Monte 90,732 . C3
San Pablo 131,655 . . . . C3
Santa Fe 6,338 . . . . C2
Santiago 69,877 . . . . C2
Silay 111,131 . . . . D5
Siquijor 17,533 . . . . D6
Surigao 79,745 . . . . E6
Tacloban 102,523 . . . . E5
Tagaytay 16,322 . . . . C3
Tagum 86,201 . . . . E7
Tarlac 175,691 . . . . C3
Toledo 91,668 . . . . D5
Tuguegarao 73,507 . . . . C2
Zamboanga 343,722 . . . . C7

OTHER FEATURES

Agusan (riv.) E6
Alabat (isl.) D3
Apo (vol.) E7
Babuyan (isl.) B2
Balabac (isl.) A7
Balayan (bay) C4
Balintang (chan.) A2
Baloy (mt.) D5
Bantayan (isl.) D5
Banton (isl.) D4
Bashi (chan.) A1
Basilan (isl.) D7
Batan, Albay (isl.) E4
Batan, Batanes (isl.) B2
Batan (isls.) A2
Bay, Laguna de (lake) C3
Biliran (isl.) E5
Bohol (isl.) E6
Bojeador (cape) C1
Borocay (isl.) D5
Bucas Grande (isl.) F6
Bugsuk (isl.) A6
Bululiyan (cape) A6
Bunga (pt.) E4
Burias (isl.) D4
Busuanga (isl.) B4
Cabalasan (mt.) E5
Cabulauan (isls.) C5
Cagayan (isls.) C6
Cagayan (riv.) C2
Cagayan Sulu (isl.) B7
Cagua (vol.) D1
Calagua (isls.) D3
Calamian Group (isls.) B4
Calayan (isl.) A2
Calicoan (isl.) E5
Camiguin, Cagayan (isl.) . . . B3
Camiguin, Camiguin (isl.) . . . E6
Camotes (isls.) E5
Camotes (sea) E5
Canigao (chan.) E5
Canlaon (peak) D5
Capotoan (mt.) E4
Carabao (isl.) D4
Catanduanes (isl.) E4
Cebu (isl.) D5
Celebes (sea) D8
Cleopatra Needle (mt.) B5
Coron (isl.) C5
Corregidor (isl.) C3
Culion (isl.) B5
Cuyo (isl.) C5
Cuyo (isls.) C5
Daram (isl.) E5
Davao (gulf) E7
Dinagat (isl.) E5
Diuata (mts.) E6
Dumanquilas (bay) D7
Dumaran (isl.) C5
Engaño (cape) D1
Espiritu Santo (cape) E4
Fuga (isl.) A3
Guimaras (isl.) D5
Halcon (mt.) C4
Hibuson (isl.) E5
Homonhon (isl.) E5
Honda (bay) B6
Iligan (bay) E6
Ilin (isl.) C4
Illana (bay) D7
Imuruan (bay) B5
Island (bay) B6
Itbayat (isl.) A2
Jintotolo (chan.) D5
Jolo (isl.) C7
Jomalig (isl.) D3
Lagonoy (gulf) E4
Lamon (bay) C3
Lanao (lake) E7
Laparan (isls.) B8
Lapinin (isl.) E5
Leyte (gulf) E5
Leyte (isl.) E5
Limasawa (isl.) E6
Linapacan (isl.) B5
Lingayen (gulf) C2
Lubang (isls.) B4
Luzon (isl.) C3
Luzon (str.) A2
Macajalar (bay) E6
Malindang (mt.) D6
Mangsee (isls.) A7
Manila (bay) C3
Mantalingajan (mt.) A6
Maqueda (chan.) D3
Maraira (pt.) C1
Marinduque (isl.) C4
Masbate (isl.) D4
Mayon (vol.) D4
Maytiguid (isl.) B5
Mindanao (isl.) D7
Mindanao (riv.) E7
Mindoro (isl.) C4
Mindoro (str.) C4
Mompog (passg.) D4
Moro (gulf) D7
Mount Apo National Park . . . E7
Naso (pt.) C5
Negros (isl.) D6
Olutanga (isl.) D7
Pacsan (mt.) C2
Palawan (isl.) B6
Palawan (passg.) A6
Panaon (isl.) E5
Panay (isl.) D5
Panglao (isl.) D6
Pangutaran (isl.) C7
Pangutaran Group (isls.) . . . C7
Patnanongan (isl.) D3
Philippine (sea) D3
Pilas (isl.) C7
Pinatubo (mt.) C3
Polillo (isl.) C3
Pujada (bay) F7
Pulangi (riv.) E7
Ragang (vol.) E7
Ragay (gulf) D4
Rapu-Rapu (isl.) E4
Romblon (isl.) D4
Sabtang (isl.) B2
Sacol (isl.) D7
Samal (isl.) E7
Samales Group (isls.) D7
Samar (isl.) E5
Samar (sea) E4
San Agustin (cape) F7
San Bernardino (str.) E4
San Miguel (bay) D3
San Pedro (bay) E5
Santo Tomas (mt.) C2
Semirara (isls.) C5
Siargao (isl.) F6
Sibay (isl.) C5
Sibuguey (bay) D7
Sibutu Group (isls.) B8
Sibuyan (isl.) D4
Sibuyan (sea) D4
Sierra Madre (mt.) D2
Simunul (isl.) B8
Siquijor (isl.) D6
South China (sea) B3
Subic (bay) C3
Sulu (arch.) B8
Sulu (sea) B6
Suluan (isl.) F5
Surigao (str.) E6
Taal (lake) C4
Tablas (isl.) D4
Tablas (str.) C4
Tagapula (isl.) E4
Tagolo (pt.) D6
Tanon (str.) D6
Tapul (isl.) C8
Tapul Group (isls.) C8
Tara (isl.) C4
Tawi-Tawi (isl.) B8
Tayabas (bay) C4
Ticao (isl.) D4
Tinaca (pt.) E8
Tongquil (isl.) D8
Tumindao (isl.) B8
Turtle (isls.) B7
Verde Island (passg.) C4
Victoria (peaks) B6
Visayan (sea) D5

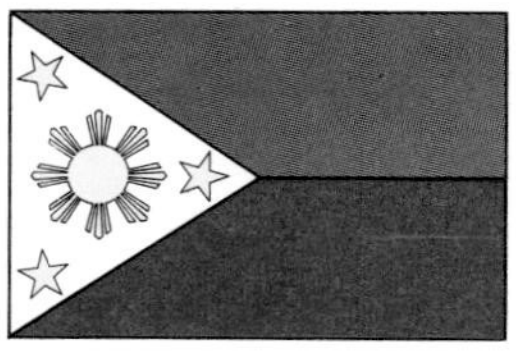

AREA 115,707 sq. mi. (299,681 sq. km.)
POPULATION 48,098,460
CAPITAL Manila
LARGEST CITY Manila
HIGHEST POINT Apo 9,692 ft. (2,954 m.)
MONETARY UNIT piso
MAJOR LANGUAGES Pilipino (Tagalog), English, Spanish, Bisayan, Ilocano, Bikol
MAJOR RELIGIONS Roman Catholicism, Islam, Protestantism, tribal religions

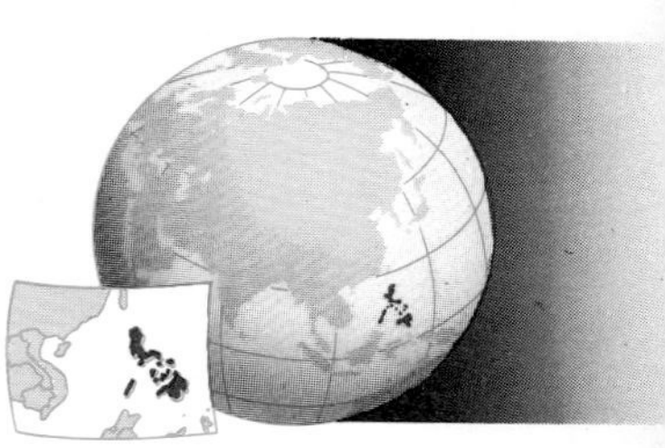

Topography

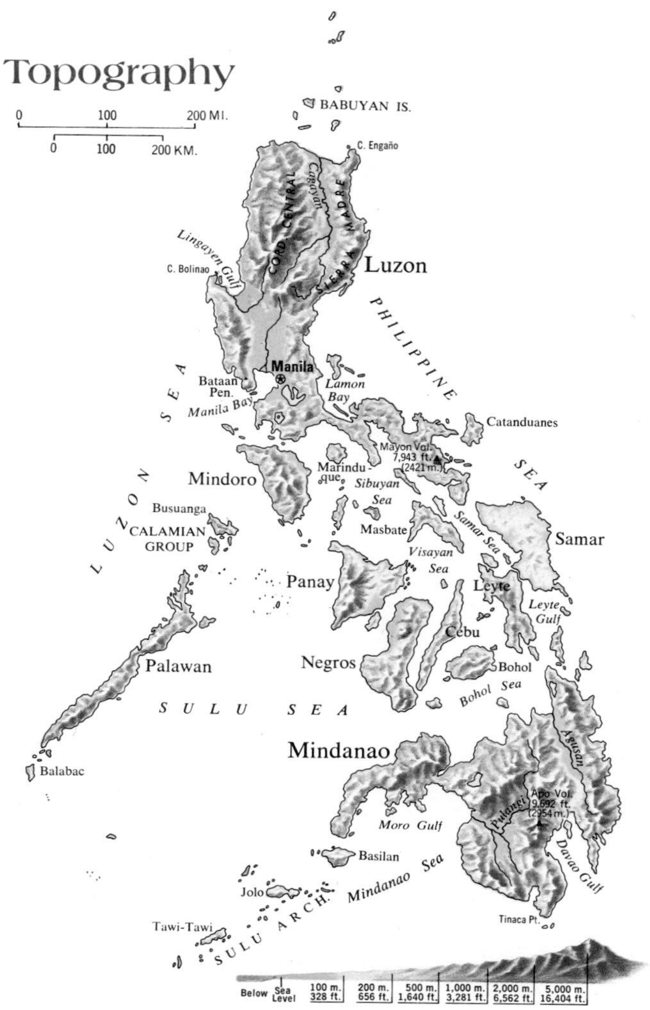

Agriculture, Industry and Resources

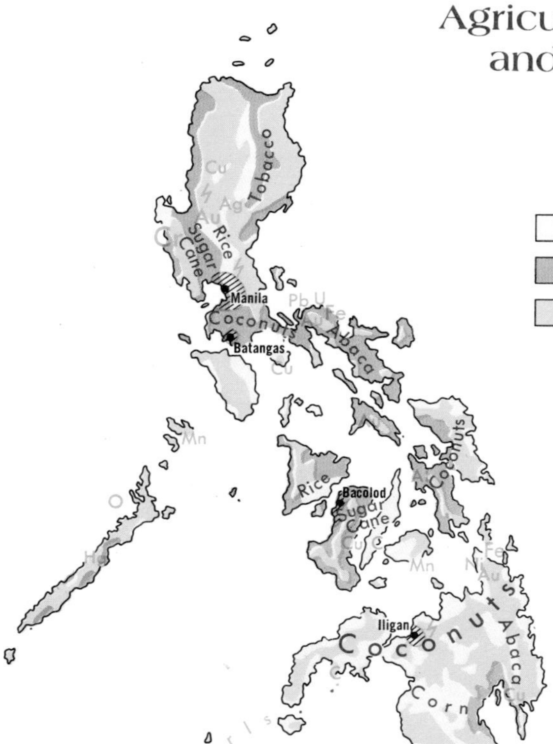

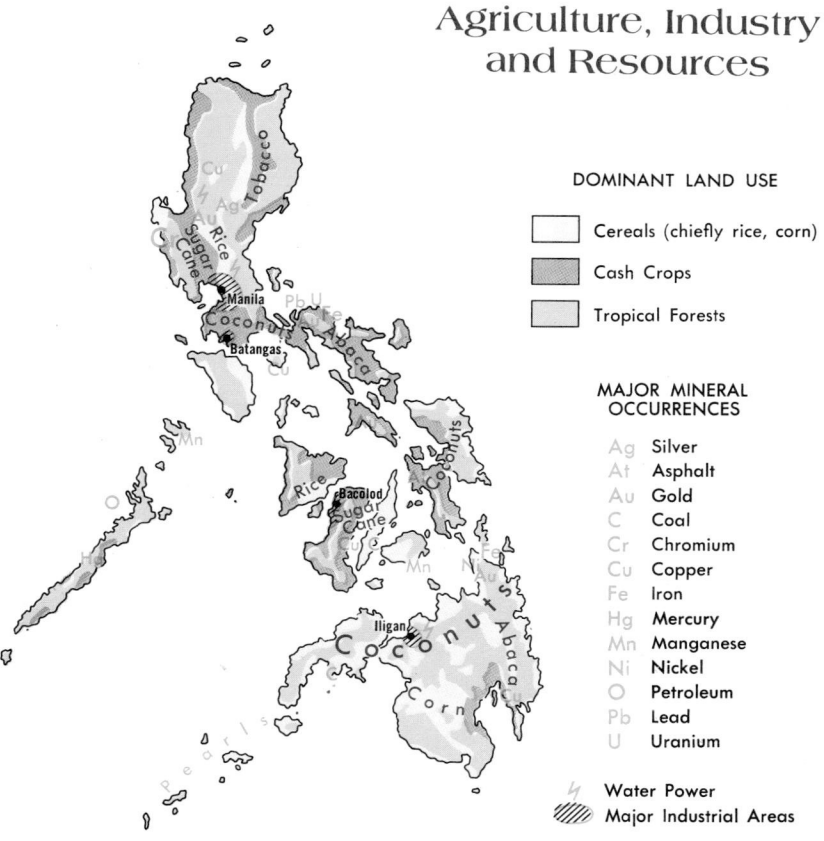

DOMINANT LAND USE

Cereals (chiefly rice, corn)
Cash Crops
Tropical Forests

MAJOR MINERAL OCCURRENCES

Ag Silver
At Asphalt
Au Gold
C Coal
Cr Chromium
Cu Copper
Fe Iron
Hg Mercury
Mn Manganese
Ni Nickel
O Petroleum
Pb Lead
U Uranium

Water Power
Major Industrial Areas

BRUNEI

CITIES and TOWNS

Bandar Seri Begawan 63,868 E4
Seria 23,511 .... E5

INDONESIA

CITIES and TOWNS

Adaut J7
Agats K7
Ambon (Amboina) 208,898 ... H6
Amuntai F6
Amurang G5
Atambua G7
Aubá H7
Baa G8
Bagansiapiapi C5
Balikpapan 280,675 .... F6
Banda Aceh 72,090 .... A4
Bandanaira H6
Bandung 1,462,637 .... H2
Banggai G6
Banjarmasin 381,286 .... E6
Banyumas J2
Batang J2
Batavia (Jakarta) (cap.) 6,503,449 ..... H1
Baukau H7
Bekasi H2
Belawan B5
Bengkulu 64,783 .... C6
Beo H5
Biak K6
Binjai 76,464 .... B5
Bintuhan C6
Blitar 78,503 .... K2
Bogor 247,409 .... H2
Bojonegoro J2
Bukittinggi 70,771 .... B6
Bula J6
Bulukumba G7
Buntok F6
Cianjur H2
Cimahi H2
Cirebon 223,776 .... H2
Demta L6
Denpasar E7
Dili H7
Djambi (Jambi) 230,373 ..... C6
Djokjakarta (Yogyakarta) 398,727 ..... J2
Dobo J7
Donggala F6
Enaratoli K6
Ende G7
Fakfak J6
Garut H2
Gorontalo 97,628 .... G5
Hollandia (Jayapura) K6
Indramayu H2
Jailolo H5
Jakarta (cap.) 6,503,449 ... H1
Jambi 230,373 .... C6
Jayapura (Hollandia) K6
Jogjakarta (Yogyakarta) 398,727 ..... J2
Jombang K2
Kaimana J6
Kampung Baru (Tolitoli) G5
Kediri 221,820 .... K2
Kendari G6
Kepi K7
Ketapang E6
Kokonau K6
Kolonodale G6
Kotabaharu E6
Kotabaru F6
Kotawaringin E6
Kragen K2
Kupang G8
Kutaraja (Banda Aceh) 72,090 ..... A4
Labuha H6
Labuhan G2
Laiwui H6
Larantuka G7
Lekitobi G6
Longiram F5
Madiun 150,562 .... K2
Magelang 123,484 .... J2
Majalengka H2
Makassar (Ujung Pandang) 709,038 ..... F7
Malang 511,780 .... K2
Malili G6
Manado 217,159 .... G5
Manokwari J6
Maumere G7
Medan 1,378,955 .... B5
Menggala D6
Merauke K7
Mindiptana L7
Mojokerto 68,849 .... K2
Muarasiberut B6
Nangatayap E6
Pacitan J2
Padang 480,922 .... B6
Padangpanjang 34,517 .... B6
Padangsidempuan B5
Pakanbaru 186,262 .... C5
Palangkaraya 60,447 .... E6
Palembang 787,187 .... D6
Pangkalanbuun E6
Pangkalpinang 90,096 .... D6
Parepare 86,450 .... F6
Pasangkayu F6
Pasuruan 95,864 .... K2
Payakumbuh 78,836 .... C6
Pekalongan 132,558 .... J2
Pemalang J2
Pematangsiantar 150,376 .... B5
Pinrang F6
Plaju D6
Pontianak 304,778 .... D6
Probolinggo 100,296 .... K2
Purbolinggo J2
Raha G6
Rantauprapat C5
Rembang K2
Sabang, Celebes F5
Sabang, Weh 23,821 .... B4
Salatiga 85,849 .... J2
Samarinda 264,718 .... F6
Sampit E6
Sarmi K6
Sawahlunto 13,561 .... C6
Seba G8
Semarang 1,026,671 .... J2
Semitau E5
Serui K6
Sibolga 59,897 .... B5
Sigli B4
Sinabang B5
Singaraja F7
Solo (Surakarta) 469,888 ... J2
Solok 31,724 .... C6
Sorong J6
Sragen J2
Subang H2
Sukabumi 109,994 .... H2
Sumbawa Besar F7
Sumedang H2
Surabaya 2,027,913 .... K2
Surakarta 469,888 .... J2
Tanahmerah K7
Tanjungbalai 41,894 .... C5
Tanjungkarang 284,275 ...... D7
Tanjungpinang C5
Tanjungselor F5
Tarakan F5
Tebingtinggi 92,087 .... B5
Tegal 131,728 .... J2
Telukbayur C6
Tepa H7
Terempa D5
Tjilatjap (Cilicap) H2
Tjirebon (Cirebon) 223,776 ... H2
Tolitoli G5
Tuban K2
Ujung Pandang 709,038 ...... F7
Vikeke H7
Wahai H6
Waigama H6
Wajabula H5
Waren K6
Weda H5
Wonreli H7
Yogyakarta 398,727 .... J2

OTHER FEATURES

Anambas (isls.) 29,572 ..... D5
Arafura (sea) J8
Aru (isls.) 34,195 .... K7
Babar (isl.) H7
Bali (isl.) 2,074,438 ...... F7
Banda (sea) H7
Banggai (arch.) 169,025 ... G6
Bangka (isl.) 298,017 ...... D6
Banyak (isls.) 1,980 .... B5
Barisan (mts.) C6
Barito (riv.) E6
Batu (isls.) 16,390 .... B6
Bawean (isl.) 64,551 .... K1
Belitung (Billiton) (isl.) 128,694 ..... D6
Berau (bay) J6
Biak (isl.) K6
Billiton (isl.) 128,694 .... D6
Binongko (isl.) 11,549 ..... G7
Bone (gulf) G7
Borneo (isl.) E5
Bosch, van den (cape) J6
Bunguran (Great Natuna) (isl.) D5
Buru (isl.) 23,034 .... H6
Butung (isl.) 188,173 ...... G6
Celebes (Sulawesi) (isl.) 7,732,383 ..... G5
Celebes (sea) G5
Cenderawasih (bay) K6
Dampier (str.) J6
Digul (riv.) K7
Doberai (pen.) J6
Enggano (isl.) 1,082 .... C7
Ewab (Kai) (isls.) 108,328 .. J7
Flores (isl.) 860,328 ...... G7
Flores (sea) F7
Frederik Hendrik (Kolepom) (isl.) K7
Geelvink (Cenderawasih) (bay) K6
Great Kai (isl.) 38,748 .... J7
Halmahera (isl.) 122,521 ... H5
Irian Jaya (reg.) 923,440 .. J6
Jambuair (cape) B4
Jamursba (cape) J5
Java (head) C7
Java (isl.) 73,712,411 ..... J2
Java (sea) D6
Jaya, Puncak (mt.) K6
Jayawijaya (range) K6
Jemaja (isl.) 5,628 .... D5
Kabaena (isl.) G7
Kai (isls.) 108,328 .... J7
Kalao (isl.) G7
Kalaotoa (isl.) G5
Kalimantan (reg.) 4,956,865. E5
Kangean (isl.) F7
Kapuas (riv.) D6
Karakelong (isl.) H5
Karimata (arch.) 9,398 ..... D6
Karimunjawa (isls.) 5,025 .. J1
Kerinci (mt.) C6
Kisar (isl.) H7
Komodo (isl.) 30,407 .... F7
Krakatau (Rakata) (isl.) ... C7
Laut (isl.) 55,711 .... F6
Leuser (mt.) B5
Lingga (arch.) 46,658 ...... D5
Lingga (isl.) 18,027 .... D6
Lombok (isl.) 1,581,193 .... F7
Madura (isl.) 1,509,774 .... K2
Mahakam (riv.) F6
Makassar (str.) F6
Malacca (str.) C5
Mamberamo (riv.) K6
Maoke (mts.) K6
Mapia (isls.) J5
Mentawai (isls.) 30,107 .... B6
Misool (isl.) J6
Molucca (sea) H6
Moluccas (isls.) 944,240 ... H6
Morotai (isl.) 27,333 ...... H5
Muli (str.) K7
Müller (mts.) E5
Muna (isl.) 156,186 .... G7
Musi (riv.) C6
Natuna (isls.) 23,893 ...... D5
Ngunju (cape) F8
Nias (isl.) 356,093 .... B5
Numfoor (isl.) J6
Obi (isls.) 12,437 .... H6
Ombai (str.) H7
Pantar (isl.) 28,259 .... G7
Perkam (cape) K6
Puting, Borneo (cape) E6
Puting, Sumatra (cape) C7
Raja Ampat Group (isls.) ... H6
Rakata (isl.) C7
Rantekombola (mt.) F6
Raya (mt.) E6
Riau (arch.) 483,230 .... C5
Rokan (riv.) C5
Roti (isl.) 76,270 .... G8
Salawati (isl.) J6
Sangihe (isl.) H5
Sangihe (isls.) 183,000 .... G5
Sawu (isls.) 51,002 .... G8
Sawu (sea) G7
Schouten (isls.) 110,148 ... K6
Schwaner (mts.) E6
Sebuku (bay) F5
Selatan (cape) E6
Selayar (isl.) 92,342 ...... G7
Semeru (mt.) K2
Siau (isl.) 46,801 .... H5
Siberut (str.) B6
Simeulue (isl.) 29,147 ..... A5
Singkep (isl.) 28,631 ...... D6
Sipura (isl.) 6,051 .... B6
Slamet (mt.) J2
Sorikmerapi (mt.) B5
South Natuna (isls.) D5
Sudirman (range) K6
Sula (isls.) 36,922 .... H6
Sulawesi (isl.) 7,732,383 .. G6
Sumatra (isl.) 19,360,400 .. B5
Sumba (isl.) 291,190 .... F7
Sumba (str.) F7
Sumbawa (isl.) 621,140 ..... F7
Sunda (str.) C7
Tahulandang (isl.) 21,493 .. H5
Talaud (isls.) 46,395 ...... H5
Taliabu (isl.) 18,303 ...... G6
Tambelan (isls.) 4,032 ..... D5
Tanimbar (isls.) 55,405 .... J7
Tariku (riv.) K6
Tidore (isl.) 28,655 .... H5
Timor (reg.) 1,435,527 ..... H7
Timor (sea) H7
Toba (lake) B5
Tolo (gulf) G6
Tomini (gulf) G6
Tukangbesi (isls.) 73,106 .. G7
Vals (cape) K7
Vogelkop (Doberai) (pen.) .. J6
Waigeo (isl.) J5
Wakde (isl.) K6
Wangiwangi (isl.) 28,469 ... G7
We (isl.) B4
Wetar (isl.) H7
Yapen (isl.) 50,888 .... K6

MALAYSIA

STATES

North Borneo (Sabah) 1,002,608 ..... F3
Sarawak 1,294,753 .... E5

CITIES and TOWNS

Beaufort 2,709 .... F4
Bintulu 4,424 .... E5
Kabong E5
Kampong Sibuti E5
Kapit 1,929 .... E5
Keningau 2,037 .... F4
Kota Kinabalu 40,939 .... F4
Kuching 63,535 .... E5
Kudat 5,089 .... F4
Labuan 7,216 .... E4
Lahad Datu 5,169 .... F5
Lamag F4
Marudi 4,700 .... E5
Miri 35,702 .... E5
Mukah 1,717 .... E5

Topography

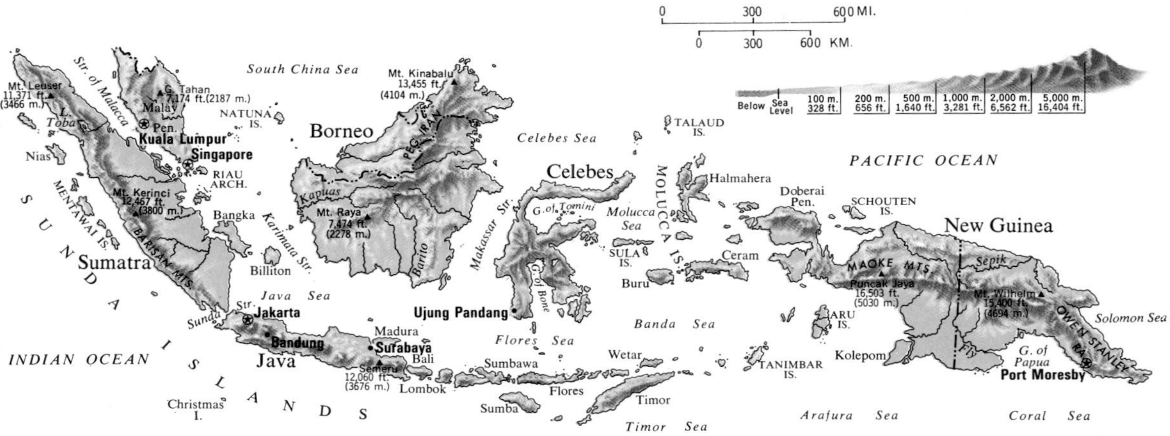
0 300 600 MI.
0 300 600 KM.
Below Sea Level
100 m. 328 ft.
200 m. 656 ft.
500 m. 1,640 ft.
1,000 m. 3,281 ft.
2,000 m. 6,562 ft.
5,000 m. 16,404 ft.
South China Sea
Mt. Kinabalu 13,455 ft. (4104 m.)
Borneo
Celebes Sea
TALAUD IS.
Celebes
Halmahera
PACIFIC OCEAN
Doberai Pen.
SCHOUTEN IS.
New Guinea
Sumatra
Singapore
Kuala Lumpur
Mt. Kerinci 12,467 ft. (3800 m.)
Mt. Raya 7,474 ft. (2278 m.)
Bangka
Billiton
Java Sea
Jakarta
Bandung
Java
Madura
Surabaya
Bali
Lombok
Ujung Pandang
Flores Sea
Banda Sea
Ceram
Buru
Sumbawa
Flores
Wetar
Timor
Sumba
TANIMBAR IS.
ARU IS.
Kolepom
Puncak Jaya 16,503 ft. (5030 m.)
Port Moresby
Solomon Sea
INDIAN OCEAN
Christmas I.
Arafura Sea
Timor Sea
Coral Sea

Agriculture, Industry and Resources

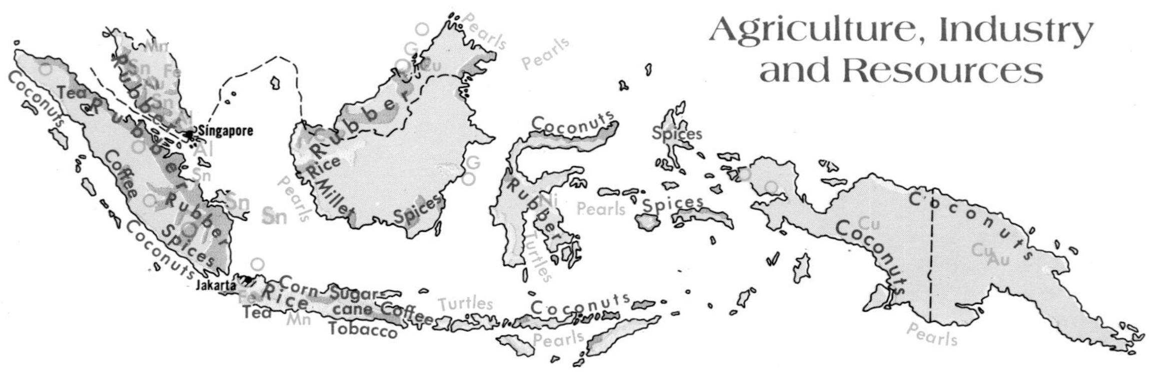
Singapore
Jakarta
Rubber
Rice
Millet
Coconuts
Coffee
Spices
Tea
Sugar cane
Tobacco
Corn
Pearls
Turtles

DOMINANT LAND USE

- Cereals (chiefly rice, corn)
- Diversified Tropical Crops
- Forests

MAJOR MINERAL OCCURRENCES

Al	Bauxite	Cu	Copper	Mn	Manganese	O	Petroleum
Au	Gold	Fe	Iron Ore	Ni	Nickel	Sn	Tin
C	Coal	G	Natural Gas				

Major Industrial Areas

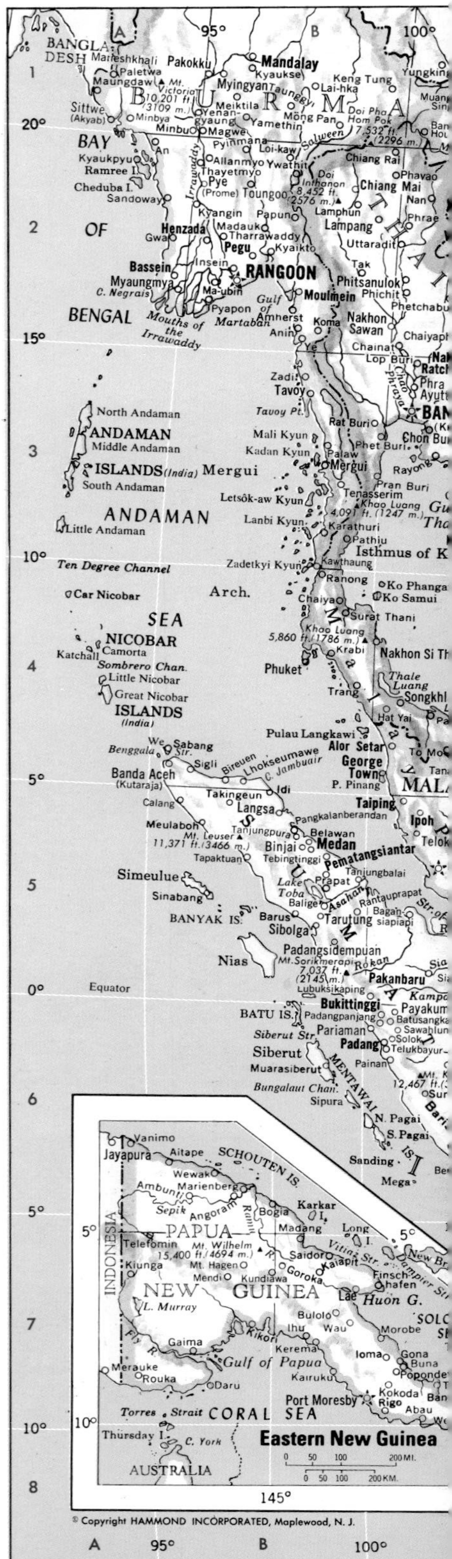
BANGLADESH
Mandalay
BAY OF BENGAL
RANGOON
Moulmein
ANDAMAN ISLANDS (India)
North Andaman
Middle Andaman
South Andaman
Little Andaman
ANDAMAN SEA
Ten Degree Channel
Car Nicobar
NICOBAR ISLANDS (India)
Great Nicobar
Mergui
Isthmus of Kra
Phuket
Banda Aceh (Kutaraja)
Medan
George Town
Taiping
Ipoh
Simeulue
Sibolga
Nias
Padang
Pakanbaru
Siberut
Equator
Eastern New Guinea
Jayapura
SCHOUTEN IS.
PAPUA NEW GUINEA
INDONESIA
Madang
Lae
Huon G.
Gulf of Papua
Port Moresby
CORAL SEA
Torres Strait
AUSTRALIA
Thursday I.
A
B
95°
100°
145°

© Copyright HAMMOND INCORPORATED, Maplewood, N. J.

...par 1,855 ....F4
...anau 2,024 ....F4
...andakan 42,413 ....F4
...ematan D5
...emporna 3,371 ....F5
...erian 2,209 ....E5
...au 50,635 ....E5
...imanggang 8,445 ......E5
...uai F5
...awau 24,247 ....F5
...weston F4

OTHER FEATURES

...alambangan (isl.) F4
...anggi (isl.) F4
...an (mts.) E5
...inabalu (mt.) F4
...abuan (isl.) 17,189 ...F4
...abuk (bay) F4
...ajang (riv.) E5
...irik (cape) E5

PAPUA NEW GUINEA

CITIES and TOWNS

...bau C7
...itape 3,368 ....B6
...mbunti 1,035 ....B6
...ngoram 1,846 ....B6

Baniara C7
Bogia 755 ....B6
Bulolo 6,730 ....B7
Buna C7
Daru 7,127 ....C7
Finschhaffen 756. .....C7
Gaima C8
Gehua C8
Gona C7
Goroka 18,511 ....B7
Ihu 541 ....C7
Ioma C7
Kaiapit 515 ....B7
Kairuku B7
Kerema 3,389 ....C7
Kikori 763 ....B7
Kiunga 1,407 ....B7
Kokoda C7
Kundiawa 4,299 ......B7
Lae 61,617 ....B7
Madang 21,335 ....B7
Marienberg B6
Mendi 4,130 ....B7
Morobe C7
Mount Hagen 13,441 ..B7
Popondetta 6,429 .....C7
Port Moresby
  (cap.) 123,624 .....B7
Rouka B7
Saidor 500 ....B7
Samarai 864 ....C8

Telefomin B7
Vanimo 3,071 ....B6
Wau 2,349 ....C7
Wedau C7
Wewak 19,890 ....B6

OTHER FEATURES

Dampier (str.) C7
D'Entrecasteaux (isls.) .C7
Fly (riv.) A7
Huon (gulf) C7
Karkar (isl.) B6
Kiriwina (isl.) B7
Long (isl.) B7
Louisiade (arch.) D8
Milne (bay) C8
Misima (isl.) C8
New Britain (isl.) 148,773 .C7
Ramu (riv.) B7
Rossel (isl.) D8
Schouten (isls.) B6
Sepik (riv.) B6
Solomon (sea) C8
Tagula (isl.) C8
Torres (str.) A7
Trobriand (isls.) C7
Vitiaz (str.) B7
Woodlark (isl.) C7

✶See page 74 for other
Malaysian entries.

INDONESIA

AREA 788,430 sq. mi. (2,042,034 sq. km.)
POPULATION 147,490,298
CAPITAL Jakarta
LARGEST CITY Jakarta
HIGHEST POINT Puncak Jaya 16,503 ft.
  (5,030 m.)
MONETARY UNIT rupiah
MAJOR LANGUAGES Bahasa Indonesia,
  Indonesian and Papuan languages,
  English
MAJOR RELIGIONS Islam, tribal religions,
  Christianity, Hinduism

PAPUA NEW GUINEA

AREA 183,540 sq. mi. (475,369 sq. km.)
POPULATION 3,010,727
CAPITAL Port Moresby
LARGEST CITY Port Moresby
HIGHEST POINT Mt. Wilhelm 15,400 ft.
  (4,694 m.)
MONETARY UNIT kina
MAJOR LANGUAGES pidgin English,
  Hiri Motu, English
MAJOR RELIGIONS Tribal religions,
  Christianity

BRUNEI

AREA 2,226 sq. mi. (5,765 sq. km.)
POPULATION 192,832
CAPITAL Bandar Seri Begawan
LARGEST CITY Bandar Seri Begawan
HIGHEST POINT Pagon 6,070 ft.
  (1,850 m.)
MONETARY UNIT Brunei Dollar
MAJOR LANGUAGES Malay, English,
  Chinese
MAJOR RELIGIONS Islam, Buddhism,
  Christianity, tribal religions

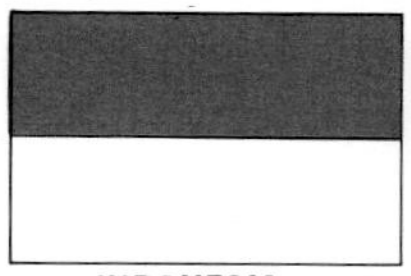

INDONESIA

PAPUA NEW GUINEA

BRUNEI

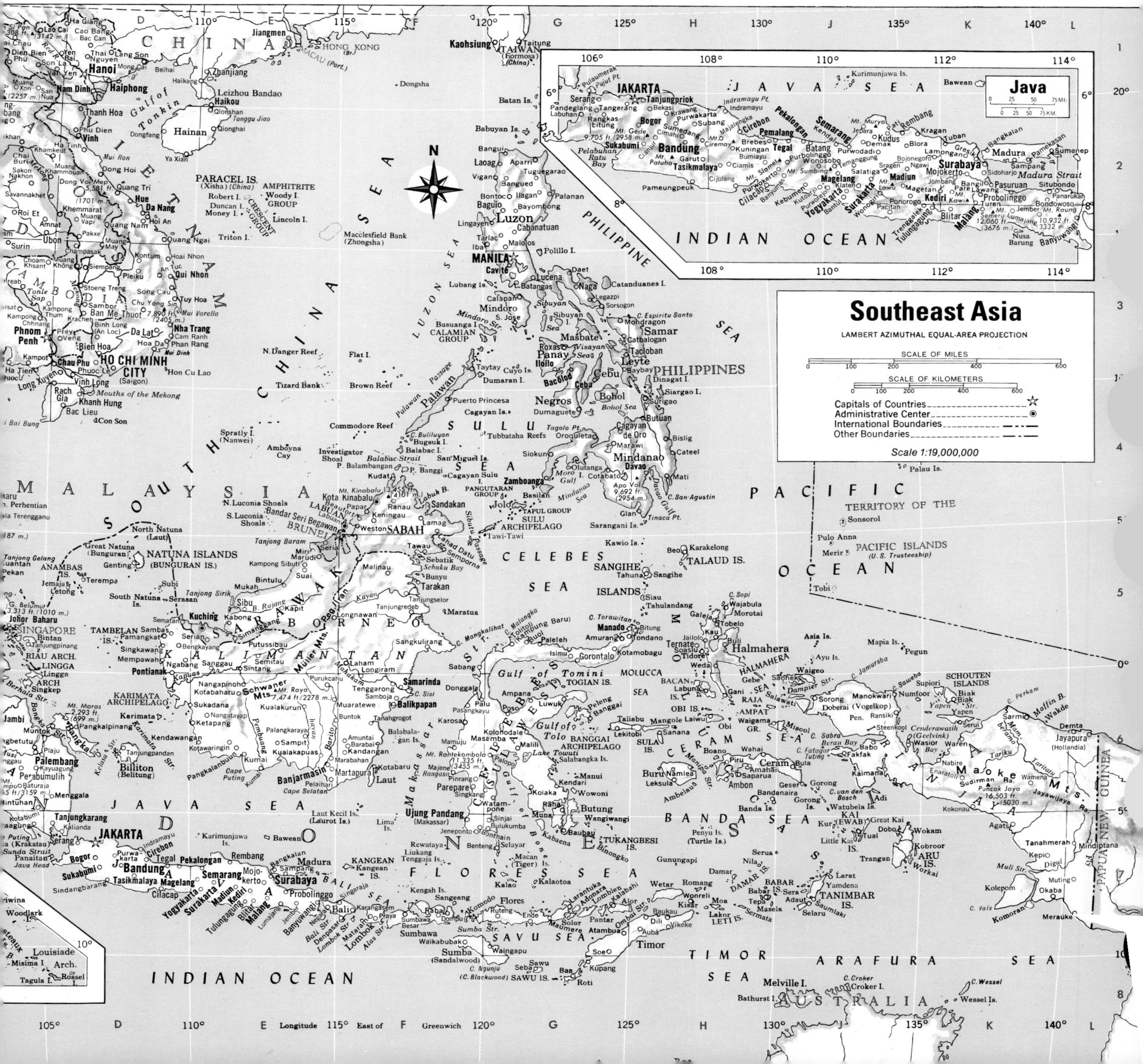

FIJI

AREA 7,055 sq. mi. (18,272 sq. km.)
POPULATION 588,068
CAPITAL Suva
LARGEST CITY Suva
HIGHEST POINT Tomaniivi 4,341 ft.
(1,323 m.)
MONETARY UNIT Fijian dollar
MAJOR LANGUAGES Fijian, Hindi, English
MAJOR RELIGIONS Protestantism, Hinduism

KIRIBATI

AREA 291 sq. mi. (754 sq. km.)
POPULATION 56,213
CAPITAL Bairiki (Tarawa)
HIGHEST POINT (on Banaba I.) 285 ft. (87 m.)
MONETARY UNIT Australian dollar
MAJOR LANGUAGES I-Kiribati, English
MAJOR RELIGIONS Protestantism, Roman
Catholicism

NAURU

AREA 7.7 sq. mi. (20 sq. km.)
POPULATION 7,254
CAPITAL Yaren (district)
MONETARY UNIT Australian dollar
MAJOR LANGUAGES Nauruan, English
MAJOR RELIGION Protestantism

SOLOMON ISLANDS

AREA 11,500 sq. mi. (29,785 sq. km.)
POPULATION 221,000
CAPITAL Honiara
HIGHEST POINT Mount Popomanatseu
7,647 ft. (2,331 m.)
MONETARY UNIT Solomon Islands dollar
MAJOR LANGUAGES English, pidgin English,
Melanesian dialects
MAJOR RELIGIONS Tribal religions,
Protestantism, Roman Catholicism

TONGA

AREA 270 sq. mi. (699 sq. km.)
POPULATION 90,128
CAPITAL Nuku'alofa
LARGEST CITY Nuku'alofa
HIGHEST POINT 3,389 ft. (1,033 m.)
MONETARY UNIT pa'anga
MAJOR LANGUAGES Tongan, English
MAJOR RELIGION Protestantism

TUVALU

AREA 9.78 sq. mi. (25.33 sq. km.)
POPULATION 7,349
CAPITAL Fongafale (Funafuti)
HIGHEST POINT 15 ft. (4.6 m.)
MONETARY UNIT Australian dollar
MAJOR LANGUAGES English, Tuvaluan
MAJOR RELIGION Protestantism

Abaiang (atoll) 3,296	H 5
Abemama (atoll) 2,300	H 5
Adamstown (cap.), Pitcairn Is. 54	N 8
Admiralty (isls.)	E 6
Agaña (cap.), Guam 896	E 4
Agrihan (isl.)	E 4
Ailinglapalap (atoll) 1,385	G 5
Ailuk (atoll) 413	H 4
Aitutaki (isl.) 2,348	K 7
Alofi (cap.), Niue 960	K 7
Alotau 4,310	E 7
Ambrym (isl.) 6,324	H 7
American Samoa 32,297	J 7
Anaa (atoll) 444	M 7
Angaur (isl.) 243	D 5
Apataki (atoll)	M 7
Apia (cap.), W. Samoa 33,100	J 7
Arno (atoll) 1,487	H 5
Arorae (atoll) 1,626	H 6
Atafu (atoll) 577	J 6
Atiu (isl.) -1,225	L 8
Austral (isls.) 5,208	L 8
Avarua (cap.), Cook Is.	L 8
Babelthuap (isl.) 10,391	D 5
Bairiki (cap.), Kiribati 1,777	H 5
Baker (isl.)	J 5
Banaba (isl.) 2,314	G 6
Banks (isls.) 3,158	G 7
Belau (Palau) 12,116	D 5
Belep (isls.) 624	G 7
Bellona (reefs)	G 8
Beru (atoll) 2,318	H 6
Bikini (atoll)	G 4
Bismarck (arch.) 218,339	E 6
Bonin (isls.) 1,879	E 3
Bora-Bora (isl.) 2,572	L 7
Bougainville (isl.) 71,761	F 6
Bounty (isls.)	H 10
Bourail 3,149	G 8
Butaritari (atoll) 2,971	H 5
Canton (isl.)	J 6
Capitol Hill (cap.), No. Marianas 592	E 4
Caroline (isl.)	M 7
Caroline (isls.)	E 5
Chichi (isl.)	E 3
Choiseul (isl.) 10,349	F 6
Christmas (Kiritimati) 674	L 5
Cook (isls.) 17,695	K 7
Coral (sea)	F 7
Danger (Pukapuka) (atoll) 797	K 7
Daru 7,127	E 6
Disappointment (isls.) 373	N 7
Ducie (isl.)	O 8
Easter (isl.) 1,598	Q 8
Ebon (atoll) 887	G 5
Efate (isl.) 18,038	H 7
Enderbury (isl.)	J 6
Enewetak (Eniwetok) (atoll) 542	G 4
Erromanga (isl.) 945	H 7
Espíritu Santo (isl.) 16,220	G 7
Fais (isl.) 207	E 5
Fakaofo (atoll) 654	J 6
Fanning (Tabuaeran) 340	L 5
Faraulep (atoll) 132	E 5
Fatuhiva (isl.) 386	N 7
Fiji 588,068	H 8
Flint (isl.)	L 7
Fly (riv.)	E 6
Fongafale (cap.), Tuvalu	H 6
French Polynesia 137,382	L 8
Funafuti (atoll) 2,120	H 6
Futuna (Hoorn) (isls.) 3,173	J 7
Gambier (isls.) 556	N 8
Gardner (isl.)	J 6
Gilbert (isls.) 47,711	H 6
Greenwich (Kapingamarangi) (atoll) 508	F 5
Guadalcanal (isl.) 46,619	F 7
Guam (isl.) 105,979	E 4
Hall (isls.) 647	F 5
Hawaiian (isls.) 964,691	J 3
Henderson (isl.)	O 8
Hivaoa (isl.) 1,159	N 6
Honiara (cap.), Solomon Is. 14,942	F 6
Hoorn (isls.) 3,173	J 7
Howland (isl.)	J 5
Huahine (isl.) 3,140	L 7
Hull (isl.)	J 6
Huon (gulf)	E 6
Ifalik (atoll) 389	E 5
Iwo (isl.)	E 3
Jaluit (atoll) 1,450	G 5
Jarvis (isl.)	K 6
Johnston (atoll) 327	K 4
Kadavu (Kandavu) (isl.) 8,699	H 7
Kapingamarangi (atoll) 508	F 5
Kavieng 4,633	E 6
Kermadec (isls.) 5	J 9
Kieta 3,491	F 6
Kimbe 4,662	E 6
Kingman (reef)	K 5
Kiribati 57,500	J 6
Kirimati (isl.) 674	L 5
Kolonia (cap.), Micronesia 5,549	F 5
Koror (cap.), Belau 6,222	D 5
Kosrae (isl.) 5,491	F 5
Kwajalein (atoll) 6,624	G 5
Lae 61,617	E 6
Lau Group (isls.) 14,452	J 7
Lavongai (isl.)	E 6
Lifu (isl.) 7,585	G 8
Line (isls.)	K 5
Little Makin (atoll) 1,445	H 5
Lord Howe (Ontong Java) (isl.) 1,082	G 6
Lord Howe (isl.) 287	G 9
Lorengau 3,986	E 6
Louisiade (arch.)	F 7
Loyalty (isls.) 14,518	G 8
Luganville 4,935	G 7
Madang 21,335	E 6

Majuro (atoll) (cap.), Marshall Is. 8,583	H 5
Makin (Butaritari) (atoll) 2,971	H 5
Malaita (atoll) 50,912	G 6
Malden (isl.)	L 6
Malekula (isl.) 15,931	G 7
Maloelap (atoll) 763	H 5
Mangaia (isl.) 1,364	L 8
Mangareva (isl.) 556	N 8
Manihiki (atoll) 405	K 7
Manua (isls.) 1,459	K 7
Manus (isl.) 25,844	F 6
Marcus (isl.)	F 3
Maré (isl.) 4,156	G 8
Marianas, Northern 16,780	E 4
Mariana Trench	E 4
Marquesas (isls.) 5,419	N 6
Marshall Islands 30,873	G 4
Marutea (atoll)	N 8
Mata Utu (cap.), Wallis and Futuna 558	J 7
Mauke (isl.) 684	L 8
Melanesia (reg.)	F 6
Micronesia (reg.)	E 4
Micronesia, Federated States of 73,160	F 5
Midway (isls.) 453	J 3
Mili (atoll) 763	H 5
Moen (isl.) 10,351	F 5
Moorea (isl.) 5,788	L 7

Mururoa (isl.)	M 8
Nadi 6,938	H 7
Namonuito (atoll) 783	E 5
Namorik (atoll) 617	G 5
Nanumea (atoll) 844	H 6
Nauru 7,254	G 6
Ndeni (isl.) 4,854	G 7
New Britain (isl.) 148,773	F 6
New Caledonia 133,233	G 8
New Caledonia (isl.) 118,715	G 8
New Georgia 16,472	F 6
New Guinea (isl.)	D 6
New Ireland (isl.) 65,657	F 6
Ngatik (atoll) 560	F 5
Ngulu (atoll) 21	D 5
Niuatoputapu (isl.) 1,650	J 7
Niue (isl.) 3,578	K 7
Niutao (atoll) 866	H 6
Nomoi (isls.) 1,879	F 5
Nonouti (atoll) 2,223	H 6
Norfolk Island (terr.) 2,175	G 8
Northern Marianas 16,780	E 4
Nouméa (cap.), New Caled. 56,078	G 8
Nouméa '74,335	G 8
Nui (atoll) 603	H 6
Nuku'alofa (cap.), Tonga 18,356	J 8
Nukuhiva (isl.) 1,484	N 6
Ocean (Banaba) (isl.) 2,314	G 6

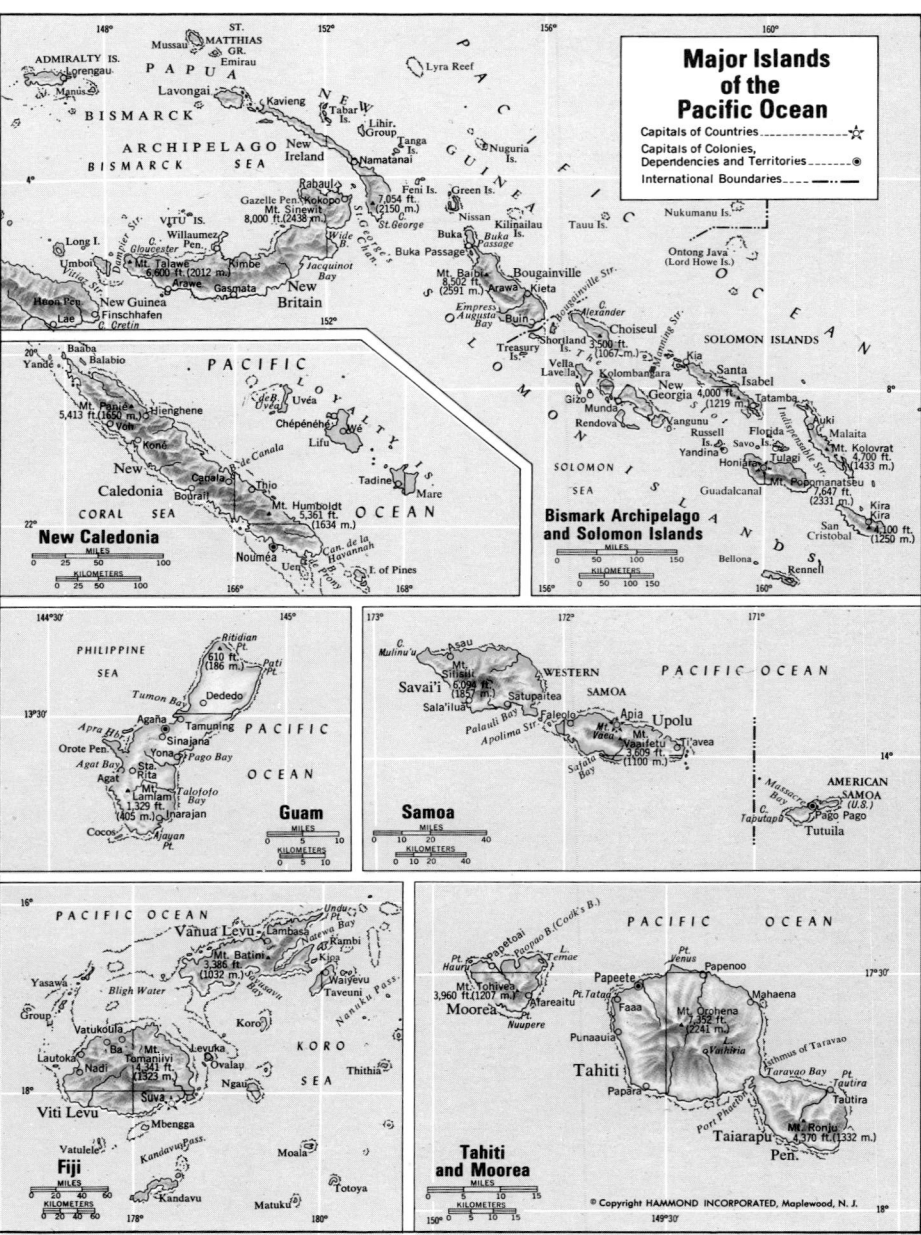

Major Islands of the Pacific Ocean

Capitals of Countries ☆
Capitals of Colonies, Dependencies and Territories ◉
International Boundaries

New Caledonia

Bismark Archipelago and Solomon Islands

Guam

Samoa

Fiji

Tahiti and Moorea

© Copyright HAMMOND INCORPORATED, Maplewood, N.J.

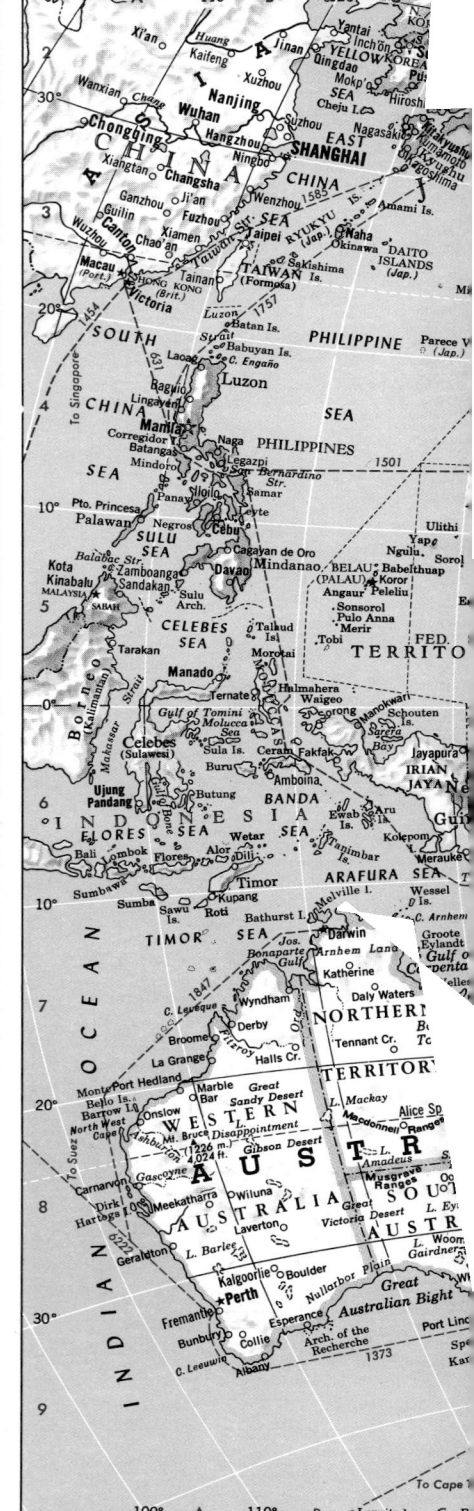

VANUATU

AREA 5,700 sq. mi. (14,763 sq. km.)
POPULATION 112,596
CAPITAL Vila
HIGHEST POINT Mt. Tabwemasana
  6,165 ft. (1,879 m.)
MONETARY UNIT vatu
MAJOR LANGUAGES Bislama, English,
  French
MAJOR RELIGIONS Christian, animist

WESTERN SAMOA

AREA 1,133 sq. mi. (2,934 sq. km.)
POPULATION 158,130
CAPITAL Apia
LARGEST CITY Apia
HIGHEST POINT Mt. Silisili 6,094 ft.
  (1,857 m.)
MONETARY UNIT tala
MAJOR LANGUAGES Samoan, English
MAJOR RELIGIONS Protestantism,
  Roman Catholicism

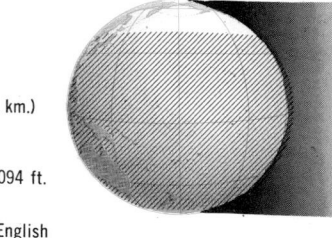

FIJI   TONGA

KIRIBATI   TUVALU

NAURU   VANUATU

SOLOMON ISLANDS   WESTERN SAMOA

Pacific Ocean

LAMBERT AZIMUTHAL EQUAL-AREA PROJECTION

©Copyright HAMMOND INCORPORATED, Maplewood, N.J.

NAUTICAL MILES
0 200 400 600 800 1000 1200

STATUTE MILES
0 200 400 600 800 1000 1200

KILOMETERS
0 200 400 600 800 1000 1200

Capitals of Countries .... ☆
Capitals of Colonies,
  Dependencies, States and Territories .★
Administrative Centers .... ◉

International Boundaries ......
Internal Boundaries ......
Railroads ......
Distances Between Points .. 5444
  (nautical miles)

Scale 1:50,000,000

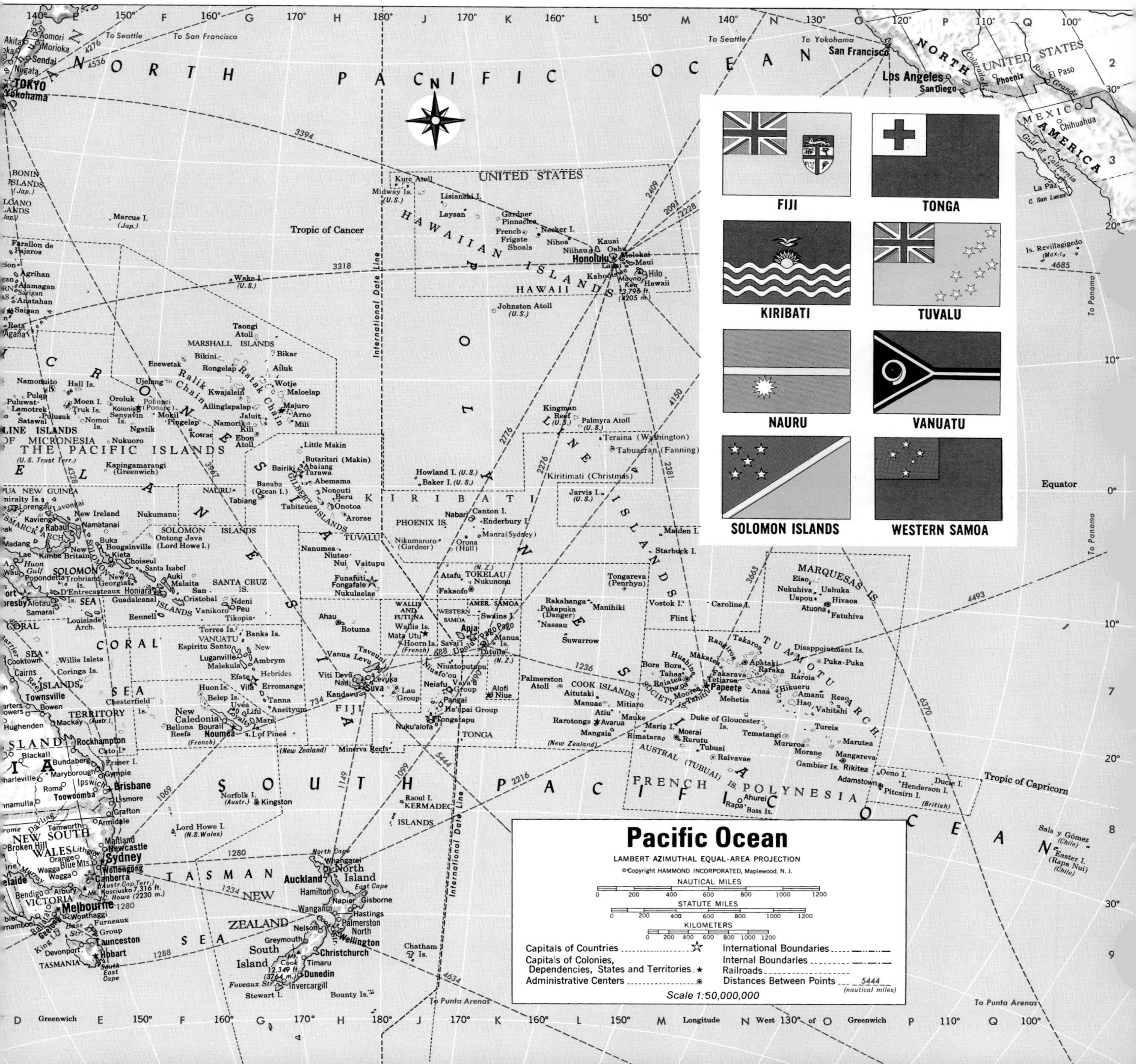

Australia

CONIC PROJECTION

MILES

KILOMETERS

Capital of Country .... ⊛   State & Territorial Capitals .... ◉

International Boundaries........   State & Territorial Boundaries........

Scale 1:19,000,000

© Copyright HAMMOND INCORPORATED, Maplewood, N.J.

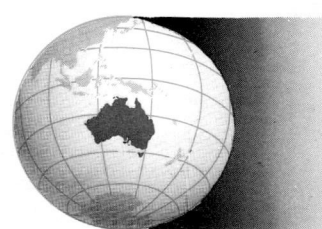

AREA   2,966,136 sq. mi. (7,682,300 sq. km.)
POPULATION   14,576,330
CAPITAL   Canberra
LARGEST CITY   Sydney
HIGHEST POINT   Mt. Kosciusko 7,310 ft.
   (2,228 m.)
LOWEST POINT   Lake Eyre -39 ft. (-12 m.)
MONETARY UNIT   Australian dollar
MAJOR LANGUAGE   English
MAJOR RELIGIONS   Protestantism,
   Roman Catholicism

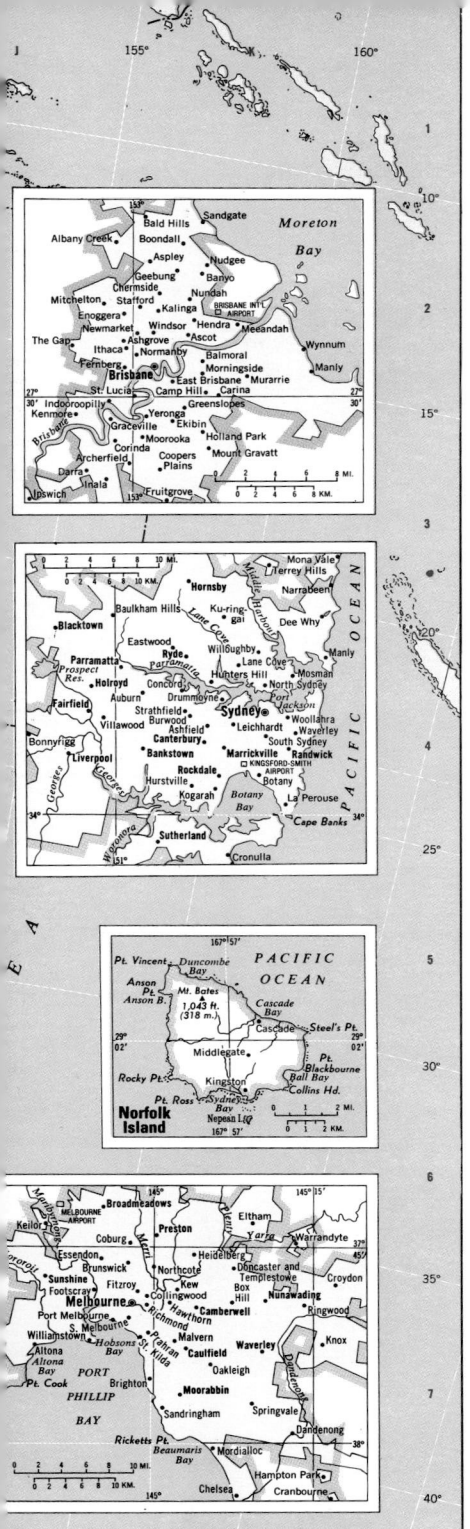

Population Distribution

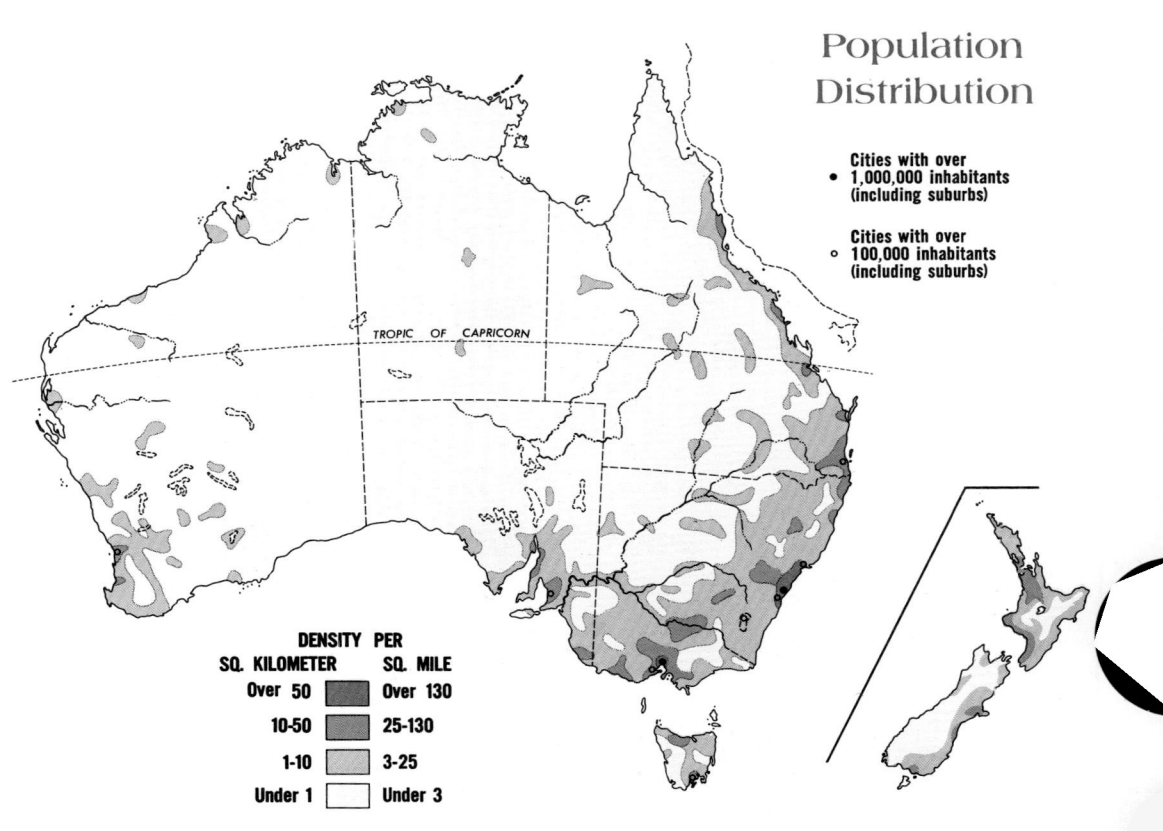

● Cities with over
  1,000,000 inhabitants
  (including suburbs)

○ Cities with over
  100,000 inhabitants
  (including suburbs)

DENSITY PER

SQ. KILOMETER	SQ. MILE
Over 50	Over 130
10-50	25-130
1-10	3-25
Under 1	Under 3

Vegetation

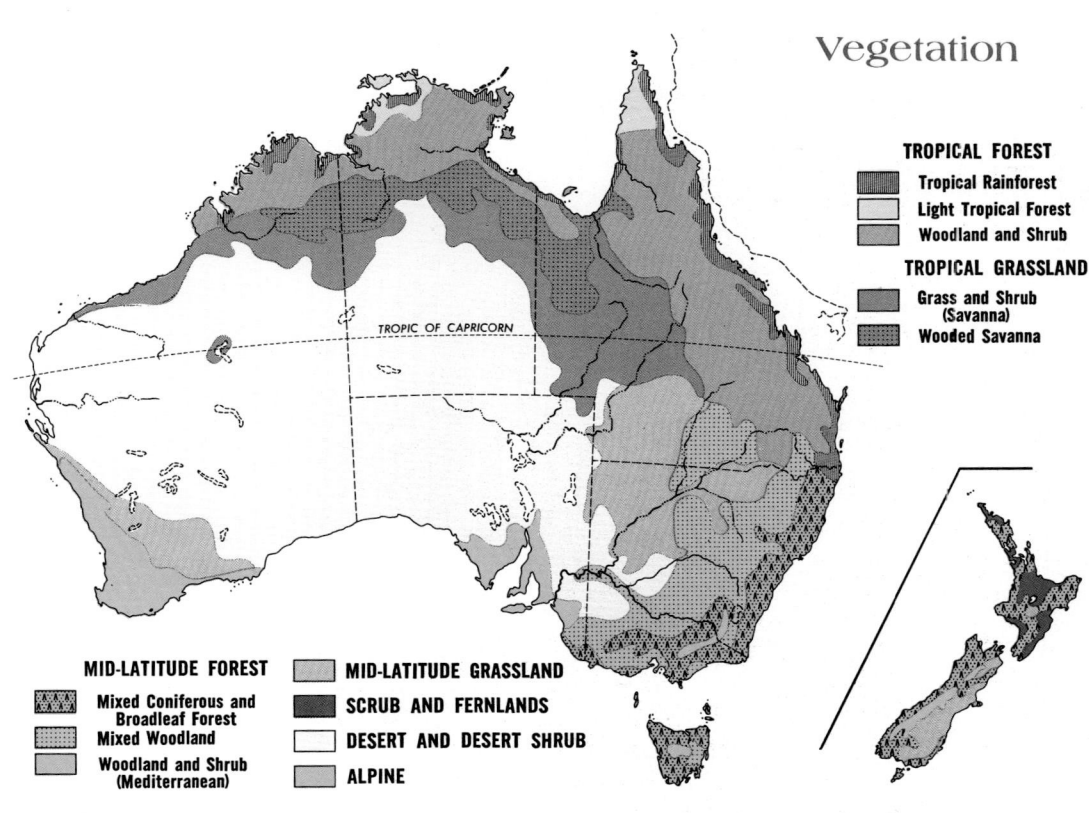

TROPICAL FOREST

- Tropical Rainforest
- Light Tropical Forest
- Woodland and Shrub

TROPICAL GRASSLAND

- Grass and Shrub (Savanna)
- Wooded Savanna

MID-LATITUDE FOREST

- Mixed Coniferous and Broadleaf Forest
- Mixed Woodland
- Woodland and Shrub (Mediterranean)

MID-LATITUDE GRASSLAND

SCRUB AND FERNLANDS

DESERT AND DESERT SHRUB

ALPINE

Average January Temperature

FAHRENHEIT	CELSIUS
Over 86°	Over 30°
68° to 86°	20° to 30°
50° to 68°	10° to 20°
32° to 50°	0° to 10°
Under 32°	Under 0°

Darwin 83°
Derby 88°
Onslow 85°
Cairns 81°
Alice Springs 82°
Brisbane 77°
Kalgoorlie 78°
Broken Hill 79°
Perth 74°
Adelaide 72°
Sydney 70°
Albany 63°
Melbourne 67°
Hobart 62°
Auckland 66°
Dunedin 60°

Tropic of Capricorn

• Sydney 70° Average January temperature in degrees Fahrenheit at selected stations

Average July Temperature

FAHRENHEIT	CELSIUS
Over 68°	20° to 30°
50° to 68°	10° to 20°
32° to 50°	0° to 10°
Under 32°	Under 0°

Darwin 76°
Derby 72°
Onslow 63°
Cairns 70°
Alice Springs 52°
Brisbane 59°
Kalgoorlie 52°
Broken Hill 51°
Perth 55°
Adelaide 52°
Sydney 54°
Albany 53°
Melbourne 49°
Hobart 46°
Auckland 52°
Dunedin 43°

Tropic of Capricorn

• Sydney 54° Average July temperature in degrees Fahrenheit at selected stations

Rainfall

AVERAGE ANNUAL RAINFALL	
INCHES	CENTIMETERS
Over 80	Over 200
60 to 80	150 to 200
40 to 60	100 to 150
20 to 40	50 to 100
10 to 20	25 to 50
Under 10	Under 25

Thursday Island 66
Darwin 60
Derby 23
Tennant Creek 15
Cairns 86
Cloncurry 19
Mackay 63
Onslow 12
Tropic of Capricorn
Alice Springs 12
William Creek 5
Brisbane 45
Geraldton 19
Kalgoorlie 9
Broken Hill 9
Perth 36
Adelaide 20
Albury 28
Sydney 47
Albany 37
Melbourne 26
Hobart 25
Auckland 48
Hokitika 116
Wellington 48
Dunedin 36

• Sydney 47 Average annual rainfall in inches at selected stations

DOMINANT LAND USE

- Cereals (chiefly wheat), Livestock
- Dairy, Truck Farming
- Cash Crops, Horticulture, Fruit
- Pasture Livestock
- Range Livestock
- Forests
- Nonagricultural Land

MAJOR MINERAL OCCURRENCES

Ab	Asbestos	Na	Salt
Ag	Silver	Ni	Nickel
Al	Bauxite	O	Petroleum
Au	Gold	Op	Opals
C	Coal	P	Phosphates
Cu	Copper	Pb	Lead
D	Diamonds	S	Sulfur, Pyrites
Fe	Iron Ore	Sb	Antimony
G	Natural Gas	Sn	Tin
Gp	Gypsum	Ti	Titanium
Lg	Lignite	U	Uranium
Ls	Limestone	W	Tungsten
Mg	Magnesium	Zn	Zinc
Mi	Mica	Zr	Zirconium
Mn	Manganese		

⚡ Water Power
/// Major Industrial Areas

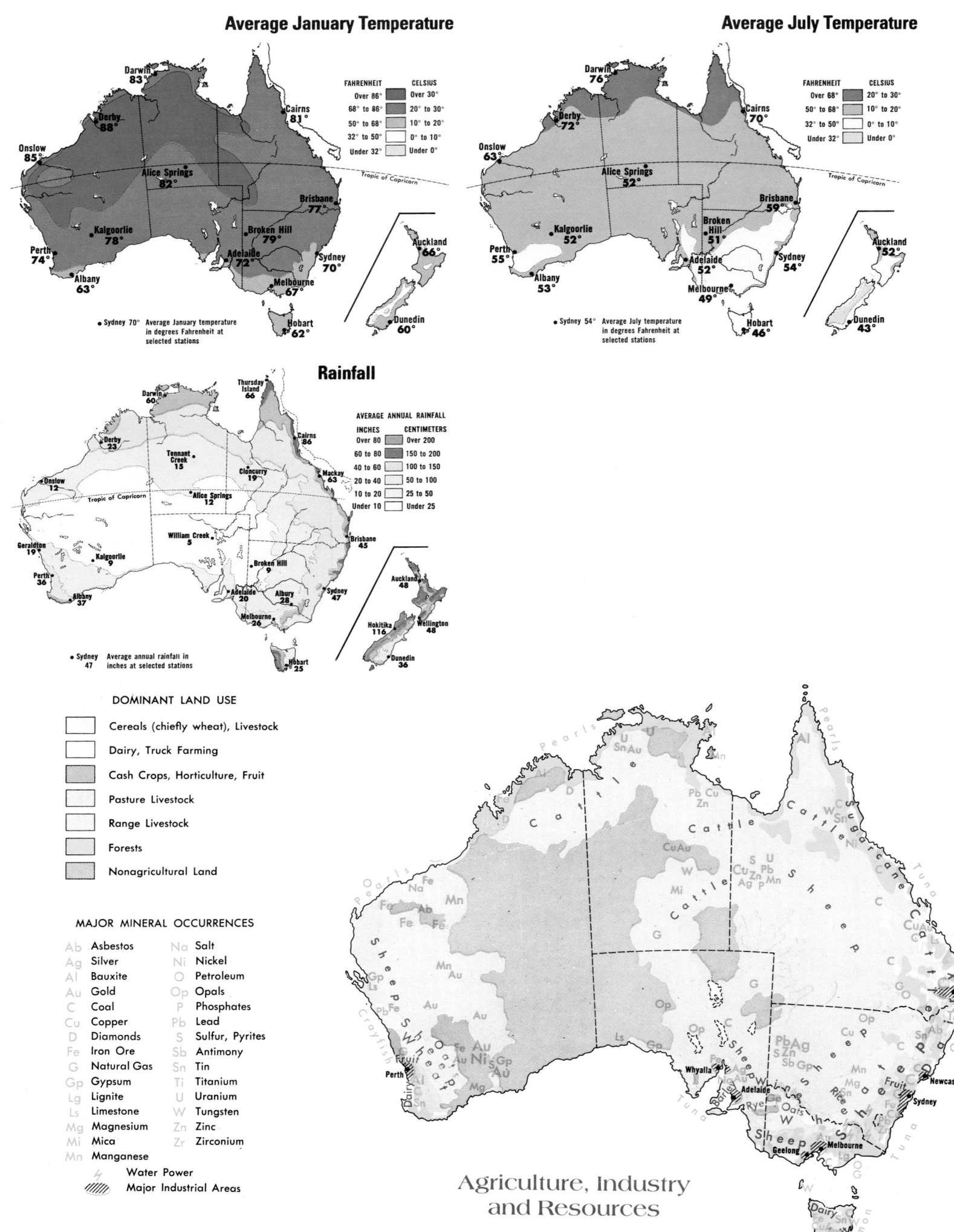

Agriculture, Industry and Resources

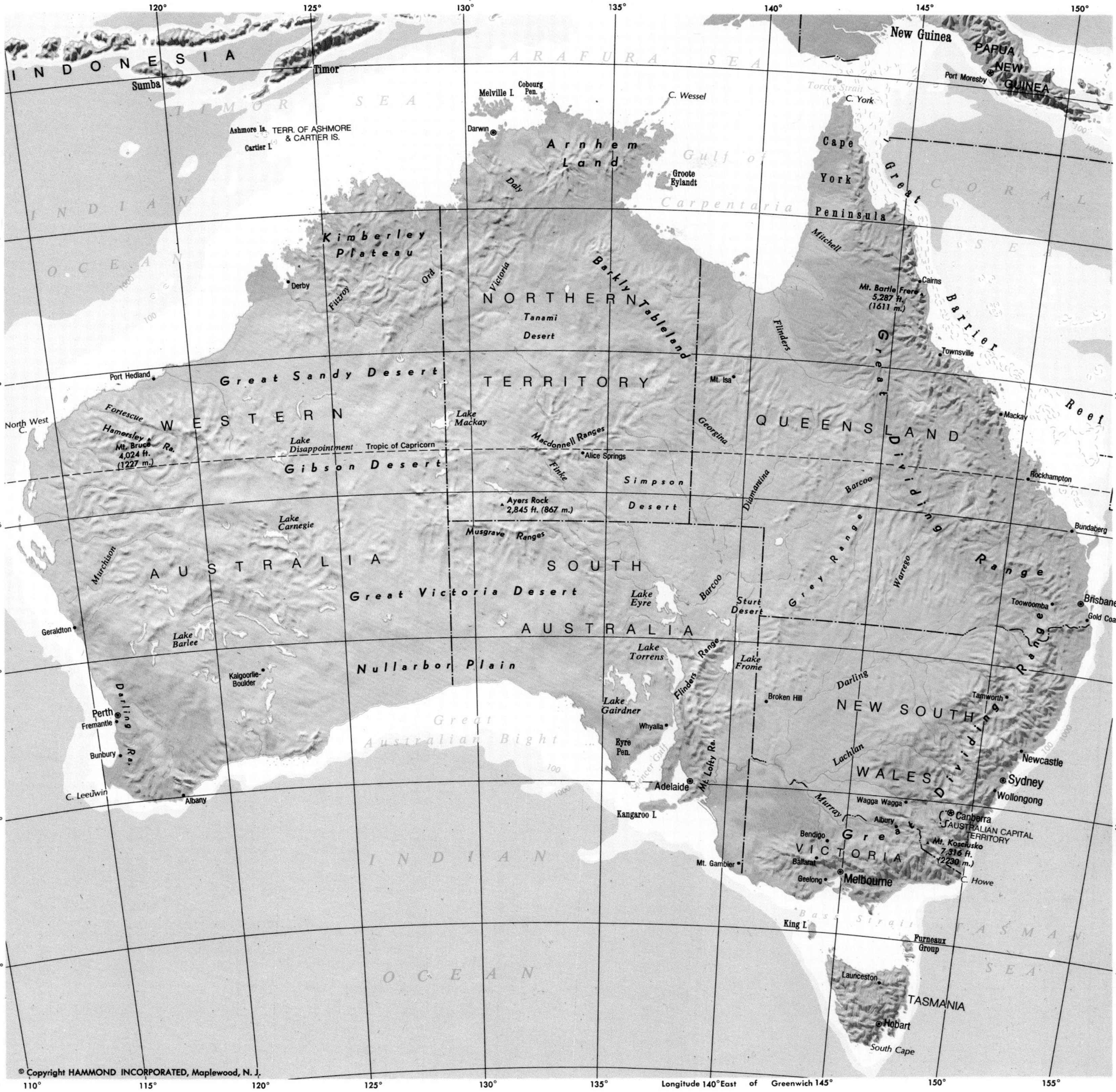

INDONESIA
Sumba
Timor

ARAFURA SEA
Melville I.
Cobourg Pen.
C. Wessel

Ashmore Is. TERR. OF ASHMORE & CARTIER IS.
Cartier I.

Darwin
Arnhem Land
Groote Eylandt

Gulf of Carpentaria

New Guinea
PAPUA NEW GUINEA
Port Moresby

Torres Strait
C. York
Cape York Peninsula

Great Barrier Reef

CORAL

Kimberley Plateau
Derby
Fitzroy
Ord
Victoria
Daly

NORTHERN
Barkly Tableland

Mitchell
Flinders

Mt. Bartle Frere 5,287 ft. (1611 m.)
Cairns

Port Hedland
North West C.
Fortescue
Hamersley Ra.
Mt. Bruce 4,024 ft. (1227 m.)

Great Sandy Desert
Tanami Desert

WESTERN

TERRITORY

Lake Mackay

Macdonnell Ranges

Mt. Isa

QUEENSLAND

Georgina

Townsville

Mackay

Lake Disappointment
Tropic of Capricorn
Gibson Desert

Alice Springs
Finke
Simpson

Barcoo

Grey Range

Rockhampton

AUSTRALIA
Lake Carnegie

Ayers Rock 2,845 ft. (867 m.)

Desert
Diamantina

Warrego

Great Dividing Range

Bundaberg

Musgrave Ranges

SOUTH

Geraldton
Murchison

Great Victoria Desert
Lake Eyre

AUSTRALIA

Barcoo
Sturt Desert

Toowoomba
Brisbane
Gold Coast

Lake Barlee

Kalgoorlie-Boulder

Nullarbor Plain

Lake Torrens

Lake Frome

NEW SOUTH

Darling
Broken Hill

Tamworth

Perth
Fremantle
Darling Ra.

Great Australian Bight

Lake Gairdner
Whyalla
Eyre Pen.

Flinders Range

WALES

Lachlan

Newcastle
Sydney
Wollongong

Bunbury

C. Leeuwin
Albany

Spencer Gulf
Adelaide
Mt. Lofty Ra.

Murray
Wagga Wagga
Albury

Canberra
AUSTRALIAN CAPITAL TERRITORY

Kangaroo I.

Bendigo
Ballarat
VICTORIA
Geelong
Melbourne
Mt. Gambier

Great
Mt. Kosciusko 7,316 ft. (2230 m.)
C. Howe

INDIAN

OCEAN

King I.

Bass Strait
Furneaux Group

TASMAN SEA

Launceston
TASMANIA

Hobart
South Cape

© Copyright HAMMOND INCORPORATED, Maplewood, N. J.

Longitude 140° East of Greenwich 145°

Vegetation / Relief

SCALE OF MILES
0 100 200 300 400 500 600

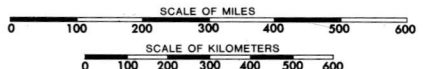
SCALE OF KILOMETERS
0 100 200 300 400 500 600

Capital of Country..........................⊛
State and Territorial Capitals................⊛
International Boundaries.....................
State and Territorial Boundaries............
Depths in Fathoms

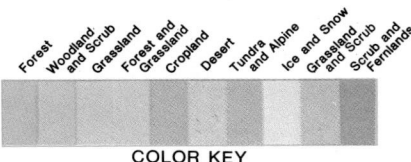
Forest
Woodland and Scrub
Grassland
Forest and Grassland
Cropland
Desert
Tundra and Alpine
Ice and Snow
Grassland and Scrub
Scrub and Fernlands
COLOR KEY

AREA 975,096 sq. mi.
(2,525,500 sq. km.)
POPULATION 1,273,624
CAPITAL Perth
LARGEST CITY Perth
HIGHEST POINT Mt. Bruce 4,024 ft.
(1,227 m.)

Topography

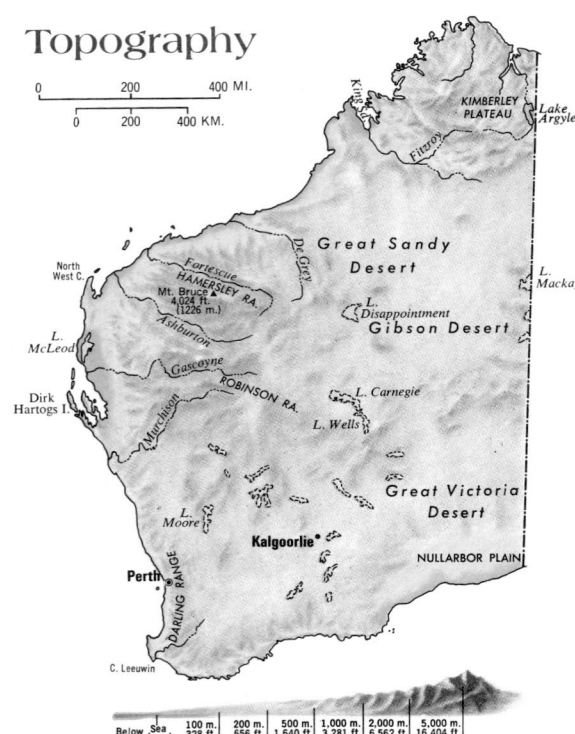

| 0 | 200 | 400 MI. |
| 0 | 200 | 400 KM. |

KIMBERLEY PLATEAU — L. Argyle — Fitzroy — Great Sandy Desert — L. Mackay — Gibson Desert — L. Disappointment — HAMERSLEY RA. — Mt. Bruce 4,024 ft. (1226 m.) — North West C. — FORTESCUE — Ashburton — L. McLeod — Gascoyne — ROBINSON RA. — L. Carnegie — L. Wells — Dirk Hartogs I. — Murchison — L. Moore — Great Victoria Desert — DARLING RANGE — Kalgoorlie — NULLARBOR PLAIN — Perth — C. Leeuwin

| | Below Sea Level | 100 m. 328 ft. | 200 m. 656 ft. | 500 m. 1,640 ft. | 1,000 m. 3,281 ft. | 2,000 m. 6,562 ft. | 5,000 m. 16,404 ft. |

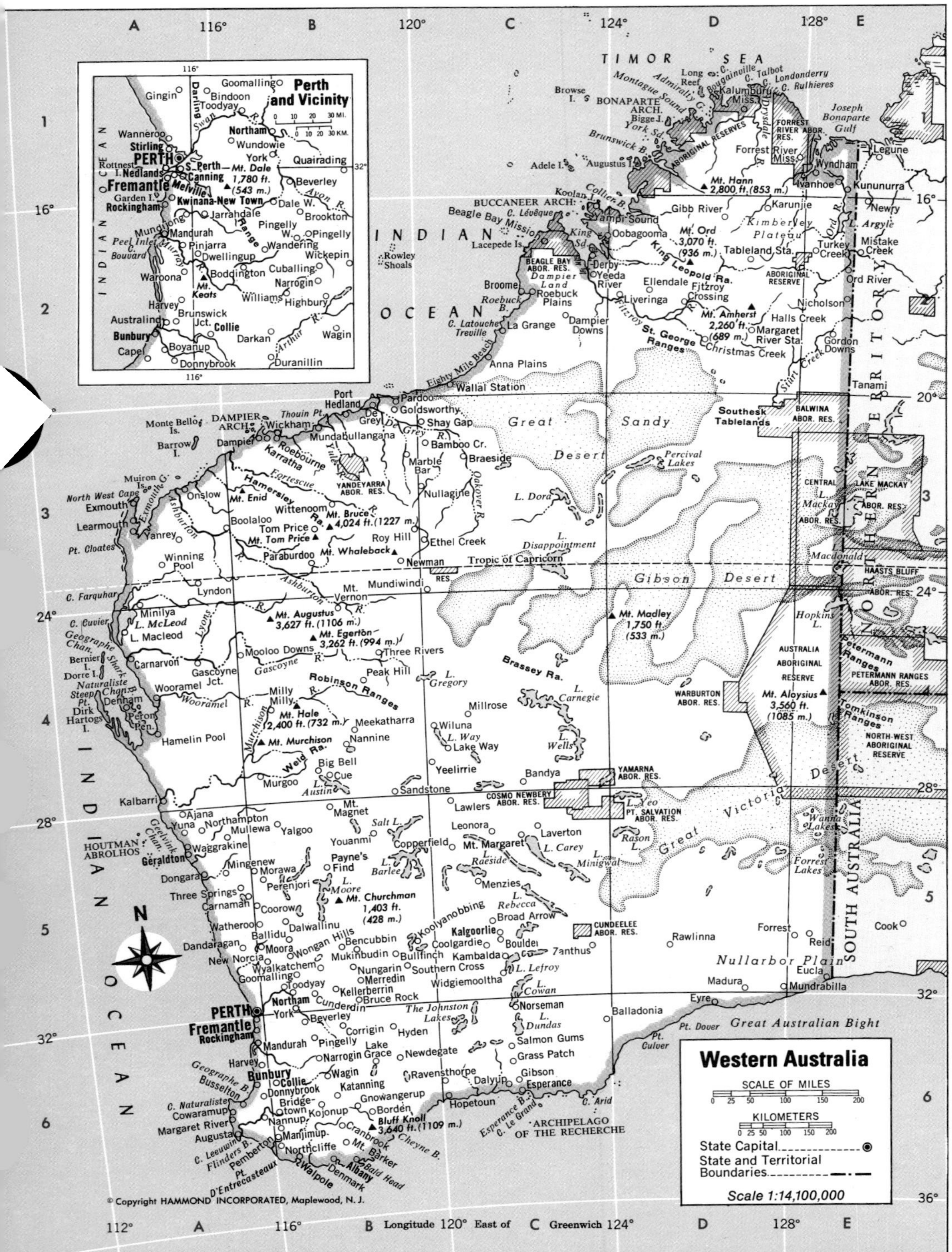

CITIES and TOWNS

Albany 15,222 . . . . B6
Augusta 588 . . . . A6
Australind 1,681 . . . . A2
Balladonia D6
Beverley 756 . . . . B1
Boddington 367 . . . . B2
Boulder-Kalgoorlie 19,848 . . C5
Boyanup 365 . . . . A2
Bridgetown 1,521 . . . . B6
Brookton 595 . . . . B2
Broome 3,666 . . . . C2
Bruce Rock 565 . . . . B5
Brunswick Junction 889 . . . A2
Bunbury 21,749 . . . . A2
Busselton 6,463 . . . . A6
Canning 52,816 . . . . A1
Capel 680 . . . . A2
Carnamah 422 . . . . A5
Carnarvon 5,053 . . . . A4
Collie 7,667 . . . . B2
Coolgardie 891 . . . . C5
Coorow 226 . . . . B5
Corrigin 841 . . . . B6
Cranbrook 316 . . . . B6
Cuballing ○647 . . . . B2
Cue 320 . . . . B4
Cunderdin 731 . . . . B5
Dalwallinu 639 . . . . B5
Dampier 2,471 . . . . B3
Dandaragan ○1,748 . . . . . . B2
Darkan 242 . . . . B2
Denham 402 . . . . A4
Denmark 985 . . . . B6
Derby 2,933 . . . . C2
Dongara-Port Denison 1,155 . A5
Donnybrook 1,197 . . . . A2
Dwellingup 453 . . . . B2
Esperance 6,375 . . . . C6
Eucla E5
Exmouth 2,583 . . . . A3
Fitzroy Crossing D2
Fremantle 22,484 . . . . A1
Geraldton 20,895 . . . . A4
Gingin 382 . . . . A1
Gnowangerup 872 . . . . B6
Goldsworthy 923 . . . . B3
Goomalling 600 . . . . B1
Halls Creek 966 . . . . D2
Harvey 2,479 . . . . A2
Hopetoun C6
Hyden B6
Jarrahdale 315 . . . . B2
Kalbarri 820 . . . . A4
Kalgoorlie 9,145 . . . . C5
Kalgoorlie-Boulder 19,848 . . C5
Kambalda 4,463 . . . . C5
Karratha 8,341 . . . . B3
Katanning 4,413 . . . . B6
Kellerberrin 1,091 . . . . B5
Kojonup 544 . . . . B6
Koolyanobbing 277 . . . . . . B5
Kununurra 2,081 . . . . E2
Kwinana New Town 12,355 . . A1
Lake Grace 575 . . . . B6
Laverton 872 . . . . C5
Learmonth A3
Leonora 524 . . . . C5
Madura D5
Mandurah 10,978 . . . . A2

Manjimup 4,150 . . . . B6
Marble Bar 357 . . . . C3
Margaret River 798 . . . . . . A6
Meekatharra 989 . . . . B4
Melville 61,211 . . . . A1
Menzies 232 . . . . C5
Merredin 3,520 . . . . B5
Mingenew 368 . . . . A5
Moora 1,677 . . . . B5
Morawa 694 . . . . B5
Mount Barker 1,519 . . . . . . B6
Mount Magnet 618 . . . . B5
Mukinbudin 370 . . . . B5
Mullewa 918 . . . . A5
Mundijong 356 . . . . A2
Nannup 552 . . . . B6
Narrogin 4,969 . . . . B2
Nedlands 20,257 . . . . A1
Newman 3,466 . . . . B3
New Norcia A5
Norseman 1,895 . . . . C6
Northam 6,791 . . . . B1
Northampton 750 . . . . A5
Northcliffe B6
Nungarin ○332 . . . . B5
Onslow 594 . . . . A3
Pannawonica 1,170 . . . . . . B3
Paraburdoo 2,357 . . . . B3
Pardoo B3
Pemberton 871 . . . . A6
Perenjori 257 . . . . B5
Perth (cap.) 809,035 . . . . . A1
Perth *898,918 . . . . A1
Pingelly 937 . . . . B2
Pinjarra 1,336 . . . . A2
Port Denison-Dongara 1,155 . A5
Port Hedland 12,948 . . . . . B3
Quairading 741 . . . . B1
Ravensthorpe 327 . . . . B6
Rockingham 24,932 . . . . . . A2
Roebourne 1,688 . . . . B3

Sandstone ○133 . . . . B4
Shay Gap 853 . . . . C3
Southern Cross 798 . . . . . . B5
South Perth 31,524 . . . . . . A1
Stirling 161,858 . . . . A1
Three Springs 638 . . . . A5
Tom Price 3,540 . . . . B3
Toodyay 560 . . . . B1
Turkey Creek 212 . . . . E2
Wagin 1,488 . . . . B2
Walpole 291 . . . . B6
Wandering ○470 . . . . B2
Wanneroo 6,745 . . . . A1
Waroona 1,462 . . . . A2
Wickepin 267 . . . . B2
Wickham 2,387 . . . . B3
Williams 453 . . . . B2
Wiluna 221 . . . . C4
Wittenoom 247 . . . . B3
Wongan Hills 947 . . . . B5
Wundowie 720 . . . . B1
Wyalkatchem 453 . . . . B5
Wyndham 1,509 . . . . E1
Yalgoo ○315 . . . . B5
Yampi Sound C2
York 1,136 . . . . B1

OTHER FEATURES

Adele (isl.) C1
Admiralty (gulf) D1
Aloysius (mt.) E4
Argyle (lake) E2
Arid (cape) C6
Ashburton (riv.) A3
Augustus (mt.) B4
Austin (lake) B4
Australia Aboriginal Res. . . . E4
Bald (head) B6
Balwina Aboriginal Res. E3
Barlee (lake) B5
Barrow (isl.) A3
Beaglebay Aboriginal Res. . . C2
Bluff Knoll (mt.) B6
Bonaparte (arch.) D1
Bougainville (cape) D1
Brassey (range) C4
Bruce (mt.) B3
Brunswick (bay) D1
Buccaneer (arch.) C2
Carey (lake) C5
Carnegie (lake) C4
Central Aboriginal Res. E3
Churchman (mt.) B5
Collier (bay) C1
Cosmo Newbery Aboriginal
  Res. C5
Cowan (lake) C5
Cundeelee Aboriginal Res. . . C5
Dale (mt.) A2
Dampier (arch.) B3
Dampier Land (reg.) C2
Darling (range) A1
De Grey (riv.) B3
D'Entrecasteaux (pt.) A6
Dirk Hartogs (isl.) A4
Disappointment (lake) C3
Drysdale (riv.) D1
Dundas (lake) C6
Egerton (mt.) B4
Eighty Mile (beach) C2
Enid (mt.) B3
Esperance (bay) C6

Exmouth (gulf) A3
Fitzroy (riv.) D2
Flinders (bay) A6
Forrest River Aboriginal Res. . D1
Fortescue (riv.) B3
Garden (isl.) A1
Gascoyne (riv.) B4
Geelvink (chan.) A5
Geographe (bay) A6
Geographe (chan.) A4
Gibson (des.) D3
Great Australian (bight) E6
Great Sandy (des.) C3
Great Victoria (des.) D5
Hamersley (range) B3
Hann (mt.) D1
Hopkins (lake) E4
Houtman Abrolhos (isls.) . . . A5
Indian Ocean A5
Johnston, The (lakes) C6
Joseph Bonaparte (gulf) . . . E1
Kimberley (plat.) C2
King (sound) C2
King Leopold (range) C2
Koolan (isl.) C1
Leeuwin (cape) C6
Le Grand (cape) C6
Lévêque (cape) C1
Londonderry (cape) D1
Lyons (riv.) A4
Macdonald (lake) E3
Mackay (lake) E3
Mackay (lake) E4
McLeod (lake) A4
Minigwal (lake) C5
Monte Bello (isls.) A3
Moore (lake) B5
Murchison (riv.) A4
Murray (riv.) A2
Naturaliste (cape) A6
Naturaliste (chan.) A4
North West (cape) A3
North-West Aboriginal Res. . . E4
Nullarbor (plain) D6
Oakover (riv.) C3
Ord (mt.) D2
Ord (riv.) E2
Percival (lakes) D3
Peron (pen.) A4
Petermann (ranges) E4
Rason (lake) C5
Rebecca (lake) C5
Recherche (arch.) C6
Robinson (ranges) B4
Roebuck (bay) C2
Rottnest (isl.) A1
Saint George (ranges) D2
Shark (bay) A4
Southesk Tablelands D2
Sturt (creek) D2
Timor (sea) D1
Tomkinson (ranges) E4
Wanna (lakes) D5
Warburton Aboriginal Res. . . D4
Way (lake) C4
Weld (range) B4
Wells (lake) C4
Whaleback (mt.) B3
Wooramel (riv.) A4
York (sound) D1

○ Population of district.
*Population of met. area.

Western Australia

SCALE OF MILES

KILOMETERS

State Capital . . . . ◉
State and Territorial
Boundaries . . . . ▬ ▬

Scale 1:14,100,000

© Copyright HAMMOND INCORPORATED, Maplewood, N.J.

CITIES and TOWNS

Adelaide River	B2
Aileron	C7
Alice Springs 18,395	D7
Alyangula 1,181	E2
Angurugu 597	E3
Anthony Lagoon	D4
Areyonga	C8
Arltunga	D7
Avon Downs	E5
Bamyili-Beswick 685	C3
Banka Banka	C5
Barrow Creek	D6
Batchelor	B2
Bathurst Island 1,032	B1
Birdum	C3
Birrimbah	B2
Birrindudu	A5
Borroloola 420	E4
Bundooma	D8
Burramurra	E6
Charlotte Waters	D8
Claravale	B3
Coniston	C7
Coolibah	B3
Creswell Downs	E4
Croker Island Mission	C1
Daly River	B2
Daly Waters	C4
Darwin (cap.) 56,482	B2
Docker River 217	A8
Elliott	C4
Epenarra	D6
Erldunda	C8
Eva Downs	D5
Ewaninga	D7
Goulburn Island 277	C1
Gove (Nhulunbuy) 3,879	E2
Harts Range	D7
Hatches Creek	D6
Helen Springs	C5
Henbury	C8
Hermannsburg 541	C7
Hooker Creek 671	B5
Humpty Doo	B2
Katherine 3,737	B3
Kildurk	A4
Koolpinyah	B2
Kulgera	C8
Kurundi	D6
Lake Nash	E6
Larrimah	C3
Legune	B4
Limbunya	B4
Lucy Creek	E7
Mainoru	C3
Maningrida 702	C2
Mataranka	C3
Milingimbi 564	D2
Mistake Creek	A4
Montejinnie	C4
Mount Cavenagh	C8
Mount Doreen	B7
Murray Downs	D6
Napperby	C7
Newcastle Waters	C4
Nhulunbuy 3,879	E2
Numbulwar 422	D3
Oenpelli 452	C2
O. T. Downs	D4
Papunya 635	B7
Pine Creek 214	C2
Plenty River Mine	D7
Port Keats 819	A3
Powell Creek	C5
Rankine Store	E5
Robinson River	E4
Rockhampton Downs	D5
Rodinga	D8
Rum Jungle	B2
Santa Teresa 479	D8
Soudan	E6
Stirling Station	C6
Tanami	A5
Tarlton Downs	E7
Tea Tree Well	C7
Tennant Creek 3,118	C5
The Granites	B6
Top Springs	C4
Ucharonidge	D4
Umbakumba 247	E3
Umbeara	C8
Urapunga	D3
Utopia	D7
Victoria River Downs	B4
Warrabri 459	D6
Warrego 991	C5
Wave Hill	B4
White Quartz Hill	D7
Willeroo	B3
Willowra	C6
Wollogorang	F4
Yambah	C7
Yirrkala 543	E2
Yuendumu 687	B7

OTHER FEATURES

Amadeus (lake)	B8
Arafura (sea)	D1
Arnhem (cape)	E2
Arnhem Land (reg.)	D2
Arnhem Land Aboriginal Res.	C2
Arnold (riv.)	D3
Ayers Rock Nat'l Park	B8
Barkly Tableland	D4
Bathurst (isl.)	A1
Beagle (gulf)	A2
Beatrice (cape)	E3
Bennett (lake)	B7
Beswick Aboriginal Res.	C3
Bickerton (isl.)	E2
Blaze (pt.)	A2
Carpentaria (gulf)	E3
Central Wedge (mt.)	C7
Clarence (str.)	B2
Cobourg (pen.)	C1
Conner (mt.)	B8
Croker (cape)	C1
Daly (riv.)	B2
Daly River Aboriginal Res.	A2
Davenport (mt.)	B7
Dundas (str.)	B1
East Alligator (riv.)	C2
Ehrenberg (range)	B7
Elcho (isl.)	D1
Finke (riv.)	C8
Fitzmaurice (riv.)	B3
Ford (cape)	A2
Georgina (riv.)	E6
Goulburn (isls.)	C1
Goyder (riv.)	D2
Groote Eylandt (isl.) 2,230	E3
Haasts Bluff Aboriginal Res.	B7
Hale (riv.)	D8
Hanson (riv.)	C6
Hay (dry riv.)	E7
Hogarth (mt.)	E6
Hopkins (lake)	A8
Joseph Bonaparte (gulf)	A3
Katherine (riv.)	C3
Lake MacKay Aboriginal Res.	A6
Lander (riv.)	C6
Leisler (mt.)	A7
Limmen (bight)	D3
Limmen Bight (riv.)	D4
Macdonald (lake)	B7
Macdonnell (ranges)	C7
MacKay (lake)	A7
Mann (riv.)	D2
Marshall (riv.)	D7
Melville (bay)	E2
Melville (isl.)	B1
Mount Olga Nat'l Park	B8
Murchison (range)	D6
Napier (mt.)	A4
Neale (lake)	A8
Newcastle (creek)	C4
Nicholson (riv.)	E5
Olga (mt.)	B8
Peron (isls.)	A2
Petermann (ranges)	A8
Petermann Ranges Aboriginal Res.	A8
Port Darwin (inlet)	B2
Ranken (riv.)	E6
Robinson (riv.)	E4
Roper (riv.)	C3
Sandover (riv.)	D6
Simpson (des.)	E8
Singleton (mt.)	B6
Sir Edward Pellew Group (isls.)	E3
South Alligator (riv.)	C2
Stanley (mt.)	B7
Stewart (cape)	D1
Stirling (creek)	A4
Sturt (plain)	C4
Tanami (des.)	C5
Timor (sea)	A2
Todd (riv.)	D8
Vanderlin (isl.)	E3
Van Diemen (cape)	A1
Van Diemen (gulf)	B1
Victoria (riv.)	B3
Wagait Aboriginal Res.	B2
Warwick (chan.)	E2
Wessel (cape)	E1
Wessel (isls.)	E1
West Baines (riv.)	A4
White (lake)	A6
Woods (lake)	C4
Young (mt.)	D3
Ziel (mt.)	C7

AREA 519,768 sq. mi. (1,346,200 sq. km.)
POPULATION 123,324
CAPITAL Darwin
LARGEST CITY Darwin
HIGHEST POINT Mt. Ziel 4,955 ft. (1,510 m.)

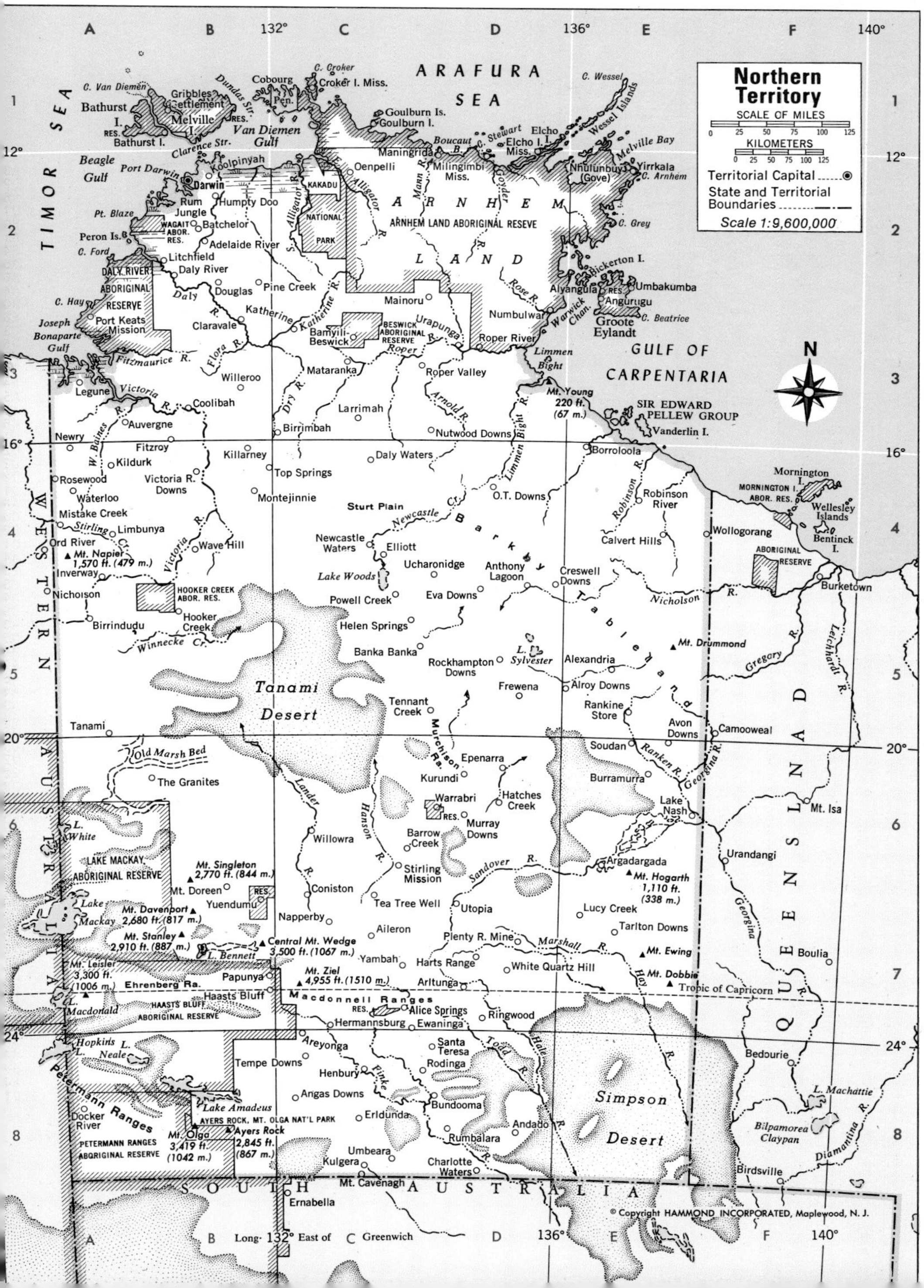

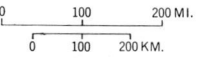

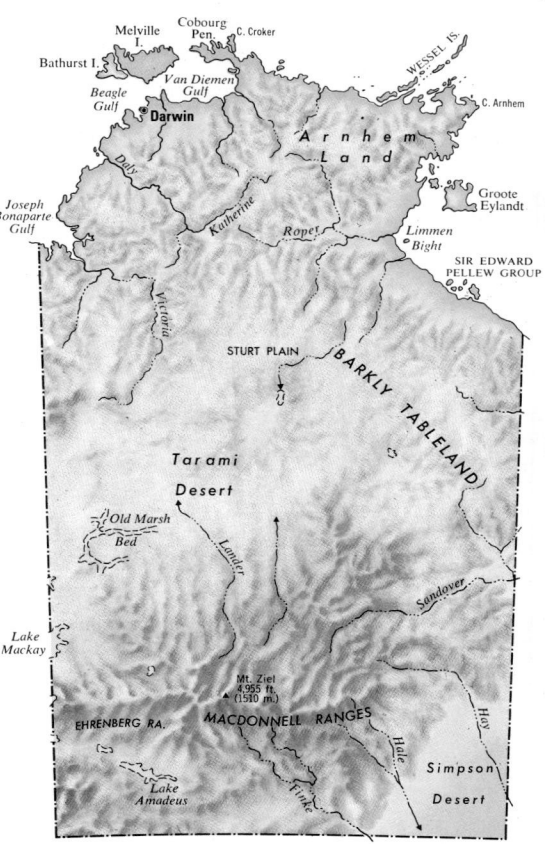

Topography

© Copyright HAMMOND INCORPORATED, Maplewood, N.J.

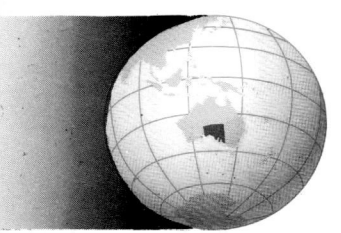

AREA 379,922 sq. mi. (984,000 sq. km.)
POPULATION 1,285,033
CAPITAL Adelaide
LARGEST CITY Adelaide
HIGHEST POINT Mt. Woodroffe 4,970 ft.
(1,515 m.)

CITIES and TOWNS

Adelaide (cap.) 882,520 .... B6
Adelaide *931,886 .... B6
Andamooka 402 .... E4
Angaston 1,753 .... F6
Balaklava 1,306 .... F6
Barmera 2,014 .... G6
Beachport 357 .... F7
Berri 3,419 .... G6
Birdwood 397 .... C7
Blinman F4
Bordertown 2,138 ...... G7
Brighton 19,441 .... A8
Burnside 37,593 .... B8
Burra 1,222 .... F5
Campbelltown 43,084 ... B7
Ceduna 2,794 .... D5
Clare 2,381 .... F5
Cleve 827 .... E5
Coober Pedy 2,078 ..... D3
Cowell 626 .... E5
Crafters-Bridgewater 9,764 .. B8
Crystal Brook 1,240 .... E5
Cummins 767 .... D6
Edithburgh 359 .... E6
Elizabeth 32,608 ...... B7
Elliston ○1,345 .... D5
Enfield 66,797 .... B7
Gawler 9,433 .... B6
Gladstone 680 .... F5
Glenelg 13,306 .... A8
Gumeracha 387 .... C7
Hahndorf 1,274 .... C8
Hawker 351 .... F4
Hindmarsh 7,593 ...... A7
Iron Knob 398 .... E5
Jamestown 1,384 ...... F5
Kadina 2,943 .... E5
Kapunda 1,340 .... F6
Keith 1,147 .... G7
Kensington and Norwood
8,950 .... B8
Kimba 862 .... E5
Kingscote 1,236 ...... E6
Kingston 1,325 .... G7
Lameroo 599 .... G6
Laura 504 .... F5
Leigh Creek 1,635 .... F4
Lobethal 1,522 .... C7
Lock 213 .... D5
Loxton 3,100 .... G6
Lyndoch 539 .... C6
Maitland 1,085 .... E6
Mannum 1,984 .... F6
Marion 66,580 .... A8
Marree E3
Meadows 388 .... B8
Meningie 807 .... F6
Millicent 5,255 ...... F7
Minlaton 865 .... E6
Mitcham 60,309 ...... B8
Moonta 1,751 .... E5
Mount Barker 4,190 ... C8
Mount Gambier 18,193 . G7
Murray Bridge 8,664 .. F6
Nairne 706 .... C8
Nangwarry 758 ...... G7

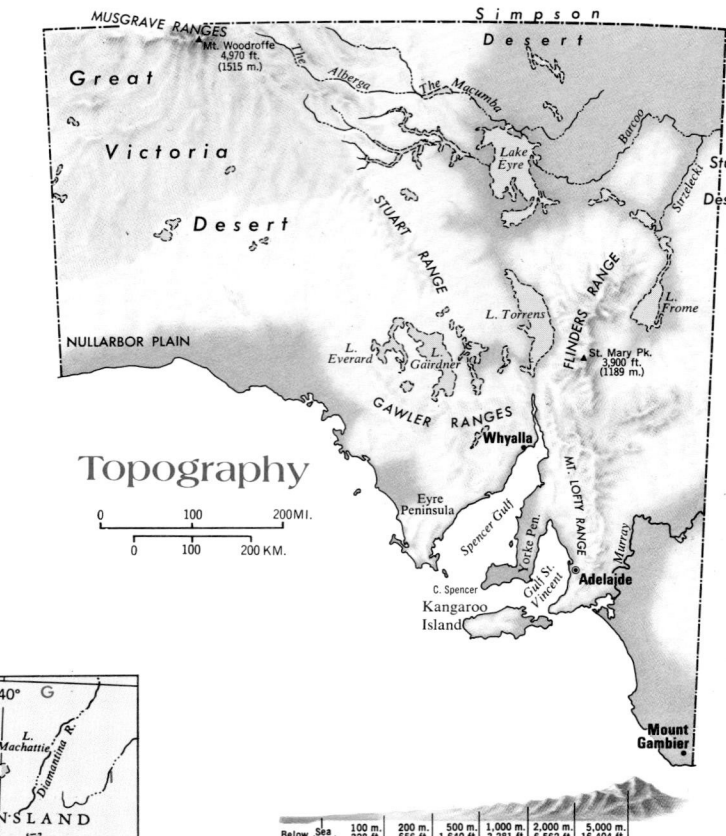

Topography

0 100 200 MI.
0 100 200 KM.

Below Sea Level | 100 m. 328 ft. | 200 m. 656 ft. | 500 m. 1,640 ft. | 1,000 m. 3,281 ft. | 2,000 m. 6,562 ft. | 5,000 m. 16,404 ft.

Naracoorte 4,758 ...... G7
Noarlunga 60,928 ...... A8
Nuriootpa 2,851 .... F6
Oodnadatta D2
Orroroo 604 .... F5
Payneham 16,502 ..... B7
Penola 1,205 .... G7
Peterborough 2,575 ... F5
Pinnaroo 731 .... G6
Port Adelaide 35,407 .. A7
Port Augusta 15,566 .. E5
Port Broughton 587 ... F5
Port Lincoln 9,846 ... E6
Port Pirie 14,695 .... F5
Prospect 18,591 ..... B7
Quorn 1,049 .... F5
Renmark 3,475 ...... G5
Robe 590 .... F7
Salisbury 86,451 .... B7
Snowtown 492 ...... E5
Strathalbyn 1,756 ... F6
Streaky Bay 985 .... D5
Tailem Bend 1,677 .. F6
Tanunda 2,621 ..... C6
Tea Tree Gully 67,237 . B7
Thebarton 9,208 ... A7
Tumby Bay 933 .... E6
Unley 35,844 ...... B8
Uraidla 303 .... B8
Victor Harbor 4,522 . F6
Virginia 353 ...... B7
Waikerie 1,629 .... F6
Wallaroo 2,043 .... E5
West Torrens 45,099 . A8
Whyalla 30,518 .... E5
Williamstown 495 .. C7
Willunga 667 ..... F6
Wilmington 227 ... F6
Woodside 724 .... C8
Woodville 77,634 . A7
Woomera 1,658 ... E4
Wudinna 572 .... D5
Yorketown 713 ... E6

OTHER FEATURES

Acraman (lake) D5
Alberga, The (riv.) D2
Alexandrina (lake) F6
Anxious (bay) D5
Arckaringa (creek) D2
Barcoo (creek) F3
Birksgate (range) A2
Blanche (lake) F3
Brady (mt.) D3
Cadibarrawirracanna (lake) . D3
Callabonna (lake) F3
Catastrophe (cape) ... D6
Coffin (bay) D6
Coffin Bay (pen.) D6
Coopers (Barcoo) (creek) . F3
Coorong, The (lag.) ... F6
Dey Dey (lake) B3
Encounter (bay) F6
Everard (lake) D4
Everard (ranges) C2
Eyre (pen.) D5
Eyre North (lake) ... E3
Eyre South (lake) ... E3
Finke (riv.) C1

Flinders (range) G7
Frome (lake) G4
Gairdner (lake) E4
Gawler (ranges) E5
Gawler (riv.) B6
Gilles (lake) E5
Goyders (lag.) E2
Great Australian (bight) . A5
Great Victoria (des.) .. B3
Gregory (lake) F3
Hack (mt.) F4
Hamilton, The (riv.) .. D2
Harris (lake) D4
Head of Bight (bay) .. C5
Indian Ocean B6
Investigator (str.) ... E6
Investigator Group (isls.) . D6
Island (lag.) E4
Jaffa (cape) G7
Kangaroo (isl.) 3,515 . E6
Lacepede (bay) F7
Lofty (mt.) C8
Macfarlane (lake) ... E4
Macumba, The (riv.) .. D2
Maurice (lake) B3
Meramangye (lake) .. C3
Morris (mt.) B2
Murray (res.) B7
Musgrave (ranges) .. A1
Neales, The (riv.) .. D3
Northumberland (cape) . G7
Nukey Bluff (mt.) ... E5
Nullarbor (plain) ... B4
Nuyts (arch.) D6
Nuyts (cape) D6
Peera Peera Poolanna (lake) . E2
Saint Mary (peak) .. F4
Saint Vincent (gulf) . E6
Serpentine (lakes) .. A3
Simpson (des.) E1
Sir Joseph Banks Group (isls.) . E6
Spencer (cape) E6
Spencer (gulf) E5
Stevenson, The (riv.) . D2
Streaky (bay) C5
Strzelecki (creek) . G3
Stuart (range) D3
Sturt (des.) F2
The Alberga (riv.) . D2
The Coorong (lag.) . F6
The Hamilton (riv.) . D2
The Macumba (riv.) . D2
The Neales (riv.) . D3
The Stevenson (riv.) . D2
The Warburton (riv.) . D3
Thistle (isl.) E6
Torrens (lake) E4
Torrens (lake) F5
Warburton, The (riv.) . D3
Wilkinson (lakes) . C3
Woodroffe (mt.) .. B2
Yalata Aboriginal Res. . C5
Yarle (lakes) C4
Yorke (pen.) E6

○ Population of district.
*Population of met. area.

South Australia

SCALE OF MILES
KILOMETERS

State Capital .... ◉
State and Territorial
Boundaries .... ━ ━ ━
Scale 1:9,790,000

© Copyright HAMMOND INCORPORATED, Maplewood, N.J.

Adelaide and Vicinity

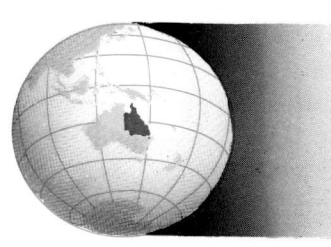

CITIES and TOWNS

ramac 428	C4
rcherfield 785	D3
scot 4,298	E2
therton 4,196	C3
yr 8,787	C3
almoral 2,915	E2
arcaldine 1,432	C4
eaudesert 3,780	E6
iloela 4,643	D5
irdsville	A5
lackall 1,609	C5
lackwater 5,434	D4
oulia 292	A4
owen 7,663	D4
risbane (cap.) 689,378	D2
risbane *1,028,527	D2
ucasia 1,356	D4
undaberg 32,560	D5
urketown 210	A3
airns 48,557	C3
aloundra 16,758	E5
amooweal 251	A3
amp Hill 8,999	E3
apella 660	D4
ardwell 1,249	C3
harleville 3,523	C5
harters Towers 6,823	C4
hermside 6,892	E3
herbourg 963	D5
ollinsville 2,756	C4
ooktown 913	C2
oorinda 4,894	D3
oopers Plains 4,492	D3
roydon ○255	B3
unnamulla 1,627	C5
alby 8,784	D5
irranbandi 480	D6
ast Brisbane 4,853	E3
dsvold 613	D5
merald 4,628	C4
sk 676	E5
atton 4,190	E5
ayndah 1,708	D5
eebung 4,850	E2
eorgetown 319	B3
adstone 22,083	D4
old Coast 135,437	E6
oondiwindi 3,576	D6
ordonvale 2,375	C3
reenslopes 7,219	E3
ympie 10,768	E5

Hervey Bay 13,569	E5
Holland Park 7,363	E3
Home Hill 3,138	C3
Hughenden 1,657	B4
Inala 17,383	D3
Indooroopilly 7,959	D3
Ingham 5,598	C3
Injune 407	D5
Innisfail 7,933	C3
Ipswich 68,297	E5
Isisford ○605	C5
Jandowae 781	D5
Jericho ○1,177	C4
Julia Creek 602	B4
Karumba 670	A3
Kilcoy 1,257	E5
Kingaroy 5,134	D5
Longreach 2,971	B4
Mackay 35,361	D4
Mareeba 6,309	C3
Marian 796	D4
Maroochydore-Mooloolaba 17,460	E5
Maryborough 20,111	E5
Mary Kathleen 830	A4
McKinlay ○1,477	B4
Millmerran 1,107	D5
Mitchell 1,171	C5
Mitchelton 5,810	D2
Monto 1,397	D5
Moorooka 8,740	D3
Moranbah 4,362	C9
Mossman 1,614	C3
Mount Isa 23,679	A4
Moura 2,871	D4
Murgon 2,327	D5
Nambour 7,965	E5
Newmarket 3,520	D2
Normanton 926	B3
Nundah 7,358	E2
Proserpine 3,058	C4
Quilpie 694	C5
Ravenshoe 915	C3
Redcliffe 42,223	E5
Richmond 784	B4
Rockhampton 50,146	D4
Roma 5,706	D5
Saint George 2,204	D5
Saint Lucia 6,075	D3
Sandgate 6,776	D3
Sarina 2,815	D4
Springsure 774	D5
Stafford (Stafford Heights) 13,731	D2
Stanthorpe 3,966	D6
Tara 864	D5

Taroom 688	D5
Tewantin-Noosa 9,965	E5
Theodore 643	D5
Thursday Island 2,283	B1
Toowoomba 63,401	D5
Townsville 86,112	C3
Tully 2,728	C3
Walkerston 1,277	D4
Warwick 8,853	D6
Weipa 2,433	B2
Windsor 6,119	D2
Winton 1,259	B4
Wynnum 10,794	E5

Yeppoon 6,447	D4
Yeronga 4,579	D3

OTHER FEATURES

Albatross (bay)	B2
Archer (riv.)	B2
Balonne (riv.)	D6
Banks (isl.)	B1
Barcoo (creek)	B5
Barkly Tableland	A4
Bartle Frere (mt.)	C3
Beal (range)	B5

AREA 666,872 sq. mi. (1,727,200 sq. km.)
POPULATION 2,295,123
CAPITAL Brisbane
LARGEST CITY Brisbane
HIGHEST POINT Mt. Bartle Frere 5,287 ft. (1,611 m.)

Topography

Belyando (riv.)	C4
Broad (sound)	D4
Bulloo (lake)	B6
Bulloo (riv.)	B6
Bunker Group (isls.)	E4
Burdekin (riv.)	C3
Cape York (pen.)	B2
Capricorn (chan.)	D4
Capricorn Group (isls.)	E4
Carnarvon (range)	D5
Carpentaria (gulf)	A2
Cloncurry (riv.)	B4
Coopers (Barcoo) (creek)	B5
Coral (sea)	C1
Culgoa (riv.)	C6
Cumberland (isls.)	D4
Curtis (isl.)	D4
Darling Downs	D5
Dawson (riv.)	D5
Diamantina (riv.)	B4
Drummond (range)	C4
Duifken (pt.)	B2
Endeavour (str.)	B1

Fitzroy (riv.)	D4
Flinders (riv.)	B3
Fraser (isl.)	E5
Georgina (riv.)	A4
Gilbert (riv.)	B3
Great Dividing (range)	C4
Gregory (range)	C3
Gregory (riv.)	A3
Grey (range)	C5
Hamilton (riv.)	B4
Hervey (bay)	E5
Hinchinbrook (isl.)	C3
Hook (isl.)	D4
Leichhardt (riv.)	A3
Machattie (lake)	B5
Macintyre (riv.)	D6
Maranoa (riv.)	C5
Mary (riv.)	E5
Melville (cape)	C2
Mitchell (riv.)	B2
Moreton (bay)	E5
Moreton (isl.)	E5
Mornington (isl.)	A3

Norman (riv.)	B3
Northern Peninsula Aboriginal Res.	B1
Prince of Wales (isl.)	B1
Princess Charlotte (bay)	C2
Sandy (cape)	E5
Selwyn (range)	B4
Simpson (des.)	A5
Sturt (des.)	B3
Suttor (riv.)	C4
Swain (reefs)	E4
Thompson (riv.)	B5
Torres (str.)	B1
Warrego (range)	C5
Warrego (riv.)	C5
Wellesley (isls.)	A3
Whitsunday (isl.)	D4
Willies (range)	C6
Yamma Yamma (lake)	B5
York (cape)	B1

○ Population of district.
*Population of met. area.

Cobbadah F2
Coffs Harbour 16,020 . . . . . G2
Collarenebri 602 . . . . . E1
Collie E2
Comboyne G2
Concord 23,926 . . . . . J3
Condobolin 3,355 . . . . . D3
Conoble C3
Coogee K3
Coolah 878 . . . . . E2
Coolamon 1,088 . . . . . D4
Cooma 7,978 . . . . . E5
Coonabarabran 3,001 . . . . . E2
Coonamble 3,090 . . . . . E2
Cootamundra 6,540 . . . . . D4
Copmanhurst ○2,857 . . . . . G1
Coraki 895 . . . . . G1
Coramba 202 . . . . . G2
Corowa-Wahgunyah 3,390 . . D4
Cowra 7,900 . . . . . E3
Crescent Head 944 . . . . . G2
Cronulla J4
Crookwell 2,063 . . . . . E4
Cudal 400 . . . . . E3
Cullburra-Orient Point 2,068 . F4
Culcairn 1,027 . . . . . D4
Cullen Bullen 231 . . . . . F3
Cumnock 252 . . . . . E3
Curlewis 487 . . . . . F2
Dareton 612 . . . . . B4
Darlington Point 599 . . . . . C4
Deepwater 260 . . . . . F1
Dee Why K3
Delegate 347 . . . . . E5
Delungra 332 . . . . . F1
Deniliquin 7,354 . . . . . C4
Denman 1,122 . . . . . F3
Dorrigo 1,192 . . . . . G2
Drummoyne 30,961 . . . . . J3
Dubbo 23,986 . . . . . E3
Dunedoo 836 . . . . . E3
Dungalear Station D1
Dungog 2,126 . . . . . F3
Eden 3,107 . . . . . E5
Emmaville 503 . . . . . F1
Ermeran Station D3
Eugowra 577 . . . . . E3
Evans Head 1,802 . . . . . G1

NEW SOUTH WALES

AREA 309,498 sq. mi. (801,600 sq. km.)
POPULATION 5,126,217
CAPITAL Sydney
LARGEST CITY Sydney
HIGHEST POINT Mt. Kosciusko 7,310 ft. (2,228 m.)

VICTORIA

AREA 87,876 sq. mi. (227,600 sq. km.)
POPULATION 3,832,443
CAPITAL Melbourne
LARGEST CITY Melbourne
HIGHEST POINT Mt. Bogong 6,508 ft. (1,984 m.)

Topography

Fairfield 129,557 . . . . . H3
Finley 2,193 . . . . . C4
Forbes 8,029 . . . . . E3
Forest Hill 1,977 . . . . . D4
Forster-Tuncurry 9,261 . . . . . G3
Frederickton 616 . . . . . G2
Ganmain 650 . . . . . D4
Gerringong 1,775 . . . . . F4
Geurie 290 . . . . . E3
Gilgai 257 . . . . . F1
Gilgandra 2,700 . . . . . E2
Gilgunnia C3
Glen Innes 6,052 . . . . . F1
Glenreagh 233 . . . . . G2
Gloucester 2,488 . . . . . F2
Goodooga 248 . . . . . D1
Goolgowi 245 . . . . . C3
Gooloogong 221 . . . . . E3
Goombalie C1
Goulburn 21,755 . . . . . E4
Grafton 17,005 . . . . . G1
Grenfell 2,070 . . . . . E3
Greta-Branxton 2,849 . . . . . F3
Greta East 398 . . . . . F3
Griffith 13,187 . . . . . C4
Gulargambone 457 . . . . . E2
Gulgong 1,740 . . . . . E3
Gundagai 2,308 . . . . . D4
Gunnedah 8,909 . . . . . F2
Gunning 438 . . . . . E4
Guyra 1,840 . . . . . F2
Hanwood 306 . . . . . C4
Harrington 1,183 . . . . . G2
Hay 2,958 . . . . . C4
Henty 883 . . . . . D4
Hillston 999 . . . . . C3
Holbrook 1,276 . . . . . D4
Holroyd 80,116 . . . . . H3
Hornsby 111,081 . . . . . J3
Howlong 1,072 . . . . . D4
Hunters Hill 12,537 . . . . . J3
Hurstville 64,910 . . . . . J4
Huskisson 2,296 . . . . . F4
Iluka 1,362 . . . . . G1
Inverell 9,734 . . . . . F1
Ivanhoe 517 . . . . . C3
Jerilderie 1,075 . . . . . C4
Jindabyne 1,602 . . . . . E5
Junee 3,993 . . . . . D4
Kandos 1,626 . . . . . F3
Karpakora B3
Katoomba-Wentworth Falls 13,942 . . . . . F3
Keewong C3
Kempsey 9,037 . . . . . G2
Kendall 522 . . . . . G2
Khancoban 515 . . . . . E5
Kiama 7,717 . . . . . F4
Kinalung B3
Kogarah 46,322 . . . . . J4
Koorawatha 262 . . . . . E4
Kootingal 731 . . . . . F2
Ku-ring-gai 101,501 . . . . . J3
Kurri Kurri-Weston 12,795 . . F3
Kyogle 3,070 . . . . . G1
Lake Cargelligo 1,240 . . . . . D3
Lane Cove 29,113 . . . . . J3
Leeton 6,498 . . . . . D4
Leichhardt 57,332 . . . . . J3
Lette B4
Lidcombe J3
Lightning Ridge 1,112 . . . . . E1
Lismore 24,033 . . . . . G1
Lithgow 12,793 . . . . . F3
Liverpool 92,715 . . . . . H4
Lockhart 923 . . . . . D4
Macksville 2,352 . . . . . G2
Maclean 2,593 . . . . . G1
Maitland 38,865 . . . . . F3
Manildra 520 . . . . . E3
Manilla 1,884 . . . . . F2
Manly 37,080 . . . . . K3
Maroubra K3
Marrickville 83,448 . . . . . J3
Marsden D3
Marsden Park 518 . . . . . H3
Marulan 330 . . . . . E4
Mathoura 582 . . . . . C4
Melrose D3
Mendooran 325 . . . . . E2
Menindee 455 . . . . . B3
Merimbula 2,899 . . . . . F5
Merriwa 943 . . . . . F3
Millthorpe 607 . . . . . E5
Milpa B2
Milperra H4
Milton 740 . . . . . F4
Mittagong 4,266 . . . . . F4
Moama C5
Mogil Mogil E1
Molong 1,374 . . . . . E3
Mona Vale K2
Moree 10,459 . . . . . E1
Morisset 1,593 . . . . . F3
Moruya 2,003 . . . . . F4
Mosman 26,200 . . . . . J3
Moss Vale 4,415 . . . . . F4
Mossgiel C4
Moulamein 396 . . . . . C4
Mount Arrowsmith A2
Mount Drysdale C2
Mount Hope C3
Mudgee 6,015 . . . . . E3
Mullumbimby 2,234 . . . . . G1
Mungindi 707 . . . . . E1
Murrumburrah 2,070 . . . . . E4
Murrurundi 861 . . . . . F2
Murwillumbah 7,807 . . . . . G1
Muswellbrook 8,548 . . . . . F3
Nabiac 363 . . . . . G3
Nambucca Heads 4,053 . . . . . G2
Narellan 2,104 . . . . . F3
Narooma 2,758 . . . . . F5
Narrabeen K3
Narrabri 7,296 . . . . . E2
Narrandera 5,013 . . . . . D4
Narromine 2,994 . . . . . E3
New Angledool E1
Newcastle 135,207 . . . . . F3
Newcastle †389,237 . . . . . F3
Nimmitabel 257 . . . . . E5
North Sydney 48,500 . . . . . J3
Nowra-Bomaderry 17,887 . . . F4
Nundle 235 . . . . . F2
Nymboida ○2,044 . . . . . G1
Nyngan 2,485 . . . . . D2
Oaklands 283 . . . . . D4
Oberon 1,937 . . . . . E3
Old Bar 970 . . . . . G2
Orange 27,626 . . . . . E3
Pallamallawa 340 . . . . . F1
Pambula 604 . . . . . E5
Parkes 9,047 . . . . . E3
Parramatta 130,943 . . . . . H3
Peak Hill 1,037 . . . . . E3
Penrith 108,720 . . . . . F3
Perthville 639 . . . . . E3
Picton 1,817 . . . . . F4
Pilliga 206 . . . . . E2
Popiltah A3
Portland 1,980 . . . . . E3
Port Kembla F4
Port Macquarie 19,581 . . . . . G2
Queanbeyan 19,383 . . . . . E4
Quirindi 2,851 . . . . . F2
Randwick 116,202 . . . . . J3
Raymond Terrace 7,548 . . . . . F3
Richmond-Windsor 15,491 . . F3
Rockdale 83,719 . . . . . J4

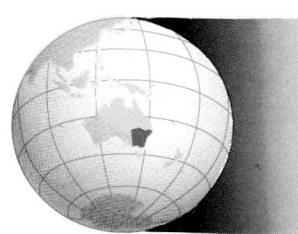

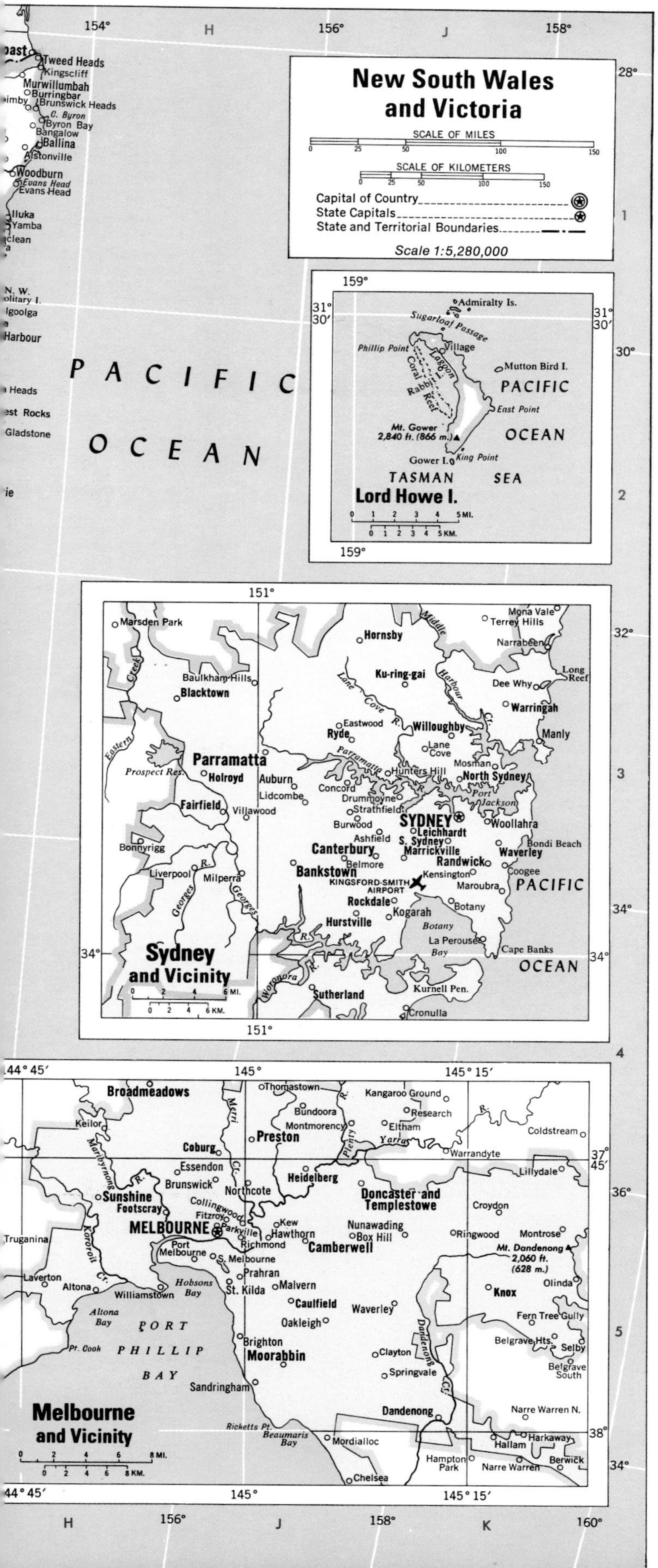

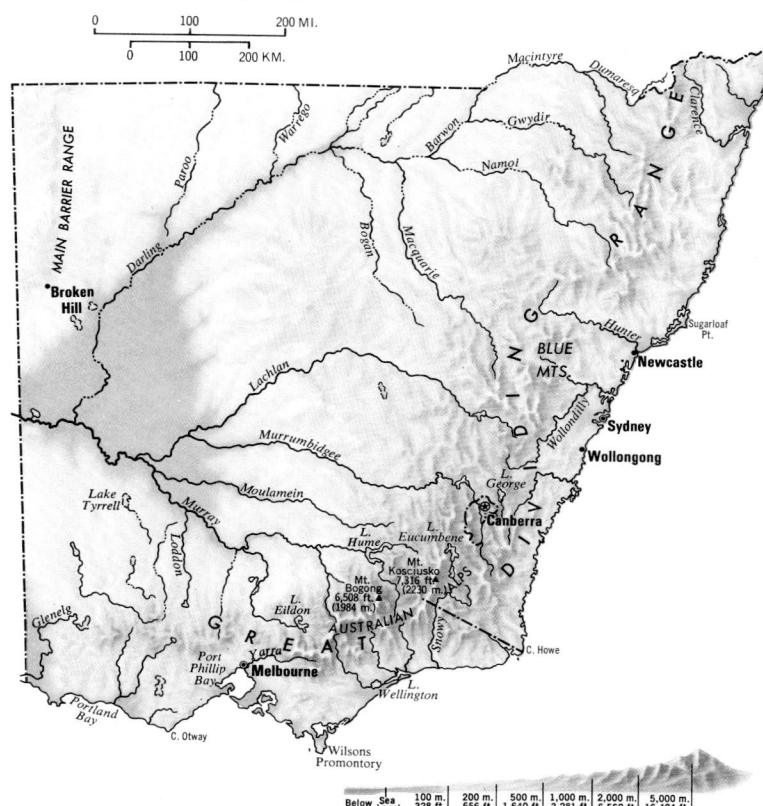

(continued on following page)

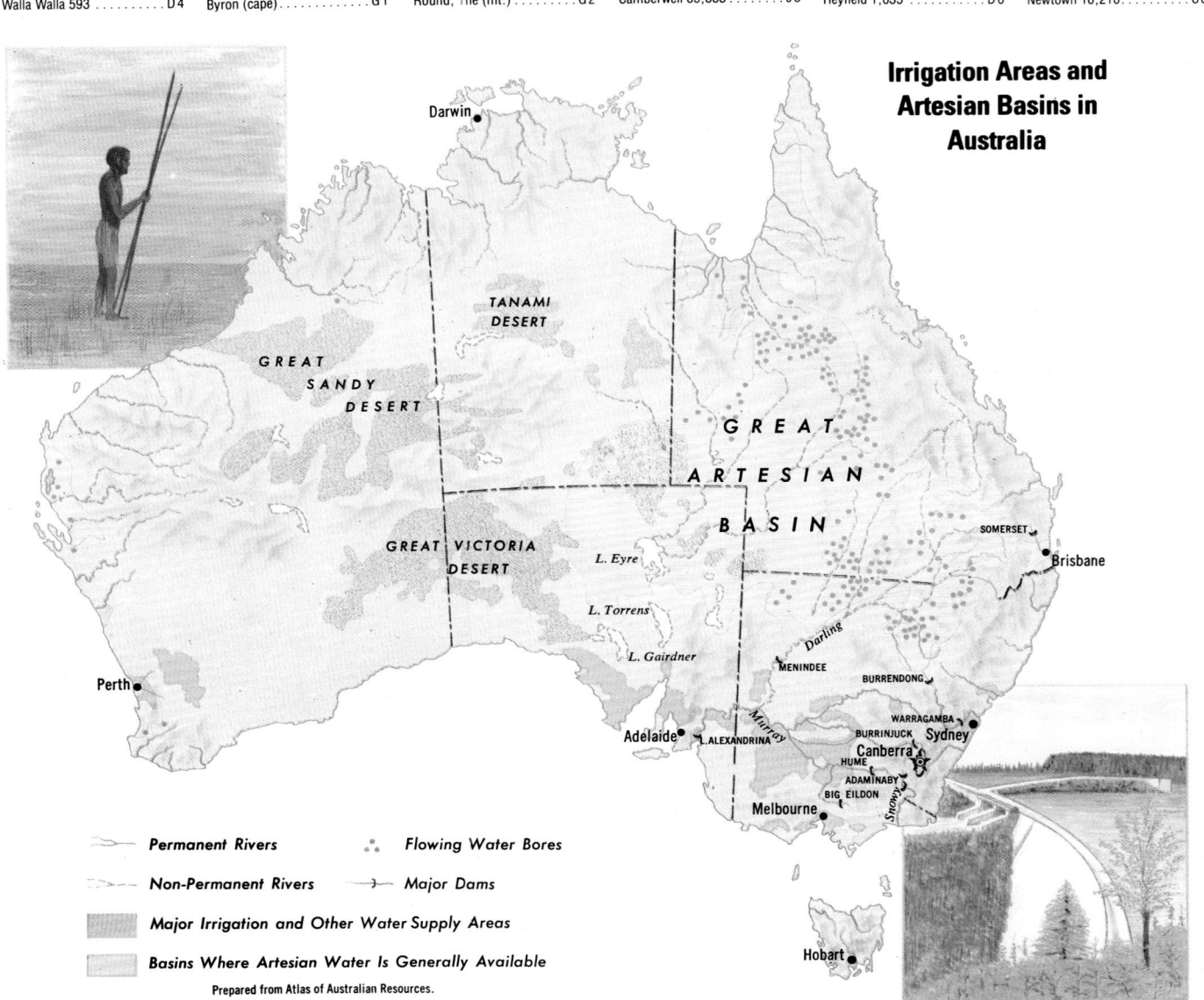

Irrigation Areas and Artesian Basins in Australia

Darwin

TANAMI DESERT

GREAT SANDY DESERT

GREAT ARTESIAN BASIN

GREAT VICTORIA DESERT

L. Eyre

L. Torrens

L. Gairdner

Perth

SOMERSET

Brisbane

MENINDEE

BURRENDONG

Murray

Darling

Adelaide

L. ALEXANDRINA

WARRAGAMBA

BURRINJUCK

Sydney

HUME

Canberra

ADAMINABY

BIG EILDON

Snowy

Melbourne

Hobart

Permanent Rivers
Non-Permanent Rivers
Major Irrigation and Other Water Supply Areas
Basins Where Artesian Water Is Generally Available
Flowing Water Bores
Major Dams

Prepared from Atlas of Australian Resources.

Topography

0   30   60 MI.

0   30   60 KM.

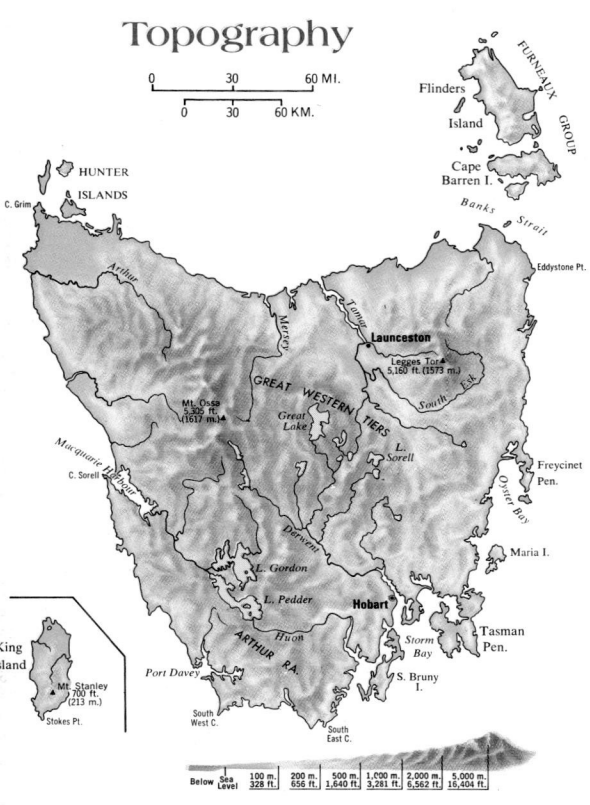

Below Sea Level | 100 m. 328 ft. | 200 m. 656 ft. | 500 m. 1,640 ft. | 1,000 m. 3,281 ft. | 2,000 m. 6,562 ft. | 5,000 m. 16,404 ft.

TASMANIA

AREA 26,178 sq. mi. (67,800 sq. km.)
POPULATION 418,957
CAPITAL Hobart
LARGEST CITY Hobart
HIGHEST POINT Mt. Ossa 5,305 ft.
(1,617 m.)

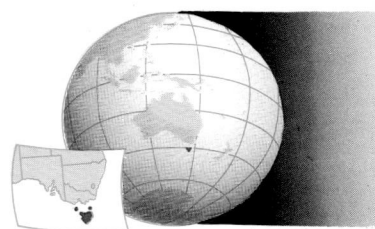

Forth (riv.) C3
Frankland (cape) D1
Frankland (range) B4
Franklin (riv.) B4
Frenchmans Cap (mt.) B4
Freycinet (pen.) E4
Furneaux Group (isls.) 1,039 E1
Gordon (lake) C4
Gordon (riv.) B4
Great (lake) C3
Great Western Tiers (mts.) . . C3
Grim (cape) A2
Hartz (mt.) C5
Hibbs (pt.) B4
Hogan Group (isl.) D1
Hummock (isl.) D2
Hunter (isl.) A2
Hunter (isls.) B2
Huon (riv.) C5
Indian Ocean A4
Kent Group (isls.) D1
King (isl.) 2,592 . . . . A1

King (riv.) B4
King William (lake) C4
Lake (riv.) D3
Legges Tor (mt.) D3
Leven (riv.) C3
Lofty (range) B3
Low Rocky (pt.) B4
Lyell (mt.) B4
Maatsuyker (isls.) C5
Macquarie (harb.) B4
Macquarie (riv.) D3
Maria (isl.) E4
Marion (bay) E4
Mersey (riv.) C3
Munro (mt.) E2
Naturaliste (cape) E2
Nive (riv.) C4
Norfolk (bay) D4
North (pt.) E1
North Bruny (isl.) D5
North Esk (riv.) D3
Ossa (mt.) C3

Ouse (riv.) C4
Oyster (bay) E4
Pedder (riv.) B4
Phoques (bay) A1
Picton (mt.) C5
Pieman (riv.) B3
Pillar (cape) E5
Port Davey (inlet) B5
Portland (cape) D2
Ramsey (mt.) B3
Raoul (cape) D5
Reid (rapid) B1
Ringarooma (bay) D2
Robbins (isl.) B2
Saint Clair (lake) C4
Saint Helens (pt.) E3
Saint Vincent (cape) B5
Savage (riv.) B3
Schouten (isl.) E4
Sorell (cape) B4
Sorell (lake) D4
South (cape) C5

South Bruny (isl.) D5
South East (cape) C5
South Esk (riv.) D3
South West (cape) B5
Stanley (mt.) A1
Stokes (pt.) A1
Storm (bay) D5
Strzelecki (mt.) D2
Tamar (riv.) D3
Tasman (head) D5
Tasman (pen.) E5
Tasman (sea) E4
Three Hummock (isl.) B2
Vansittart (isl.) E2
West (pt.) A2
West Sister (isl.) D1
Wickham (cape) A1

○ Population of district.
*Population of met. area.

CITIES and TOWNS

Adventure Bay D5
Avoca D3
Bagdad D4
Beaconsfield 898 . . . . C3
Beauty Point 998 . . . . C3
Bell Bay C3
Bicheno 674 . . . . E3
Boat Harbour B2
Bothwell 356 . . . . C4
Bracknell 347 . . . . C3
Branxholm 273 . . . . D3
Bridgewater 6,880 . . . . . . D4
Bridport 885 . . . . D3
Brighton 9,441 . . . . D4
Burnie 19,994 . . . . B3
Campbell Town 879 . . . . . . D4
Chudleigh C3
Colebrook D4
Cressy 640 . . . . C3
Currie 859 . . . . A1
Cygnet 715 . . . . C5
Deloraine 1,923 . . . . C3
Derwent Bridge C4
Devonport 21,424 . . . . C3
Dover 570 . . . . C5
Dunalley 203 . . . . D4
Evandale 614 . . . . D3
Exeter 353 . . . . C3
Fingal 424 . . . . E3
Forth 273 . . . . C3
Franklin 479 . . . . C5
Geeveston 860 . . . . C5
George Town 5,592 . . . . . . C3
Glenorchy 41,019 . . . . D4
Gormanston 126 . . . . B4
Gowrie Park C3
Grassy 780 . . . . B1
Gravelly Beach 535 . . . . . . C3
Hadspen 908 . . . . D3
Hagley 232 . . . . C3
Hamilton 2,488 . . . . C4
Heybridge 395 . . . . B3
Hobart (cap.) 128,603 . . . . D4
Hobart *168,359 . . . . D4
Huonville-Ranelagh 1,347 . . C5
Kettering 288 . . . . D4
Kingston 8,556 . . . . D4
Latrobe 2,401 . . . . C3
Lauderdale 2,117 . . . . D4
Launceston 31,273 . . . . . . C3
Launceston *64,555 . . . . . . C3
Legana 964 . . . . C3
Lilydale 308 . . . . D3
Longford 2,027 . . . . C3
Luina 522 . . . . B3
Margate 476 . . . . D4
Maydena 461 . . . . C4
Meander C3
Mole Creek 303 . . . . C3
New Norfolk 6,243 . . . . . . D4
Nubeena 225 . . . . D5
Oatlands 545 . . . . D4
Orford 378 . . . . D4
Penguin 2,616 . . . . C3
Perth 1,229 . . . . C3
Poatina C3
Port Sorell 859 . . . . C3
Queenstown 3,714 . . . . . . B4
Railton 857 . . . . C3
Richmond 587 . . . . D4
Ridgley 452 . . . . B3

Ringarooma 223 . . . . D3
Rosebery 2,675 . . . . B3
Ross 289 . . . . D4
Rossarden 365 . . . . D3
Saint Helens 1,005 . . . . . . E3
Saint Marys 653 . . . . E3
Sassafras C3
Savage River 1,141 . . . . . . B3
Scottsdale 2,002 . . . . D3
Sheffield 945 . . . . C3
Smithton 3,378 . . . . A2
Snug 684 . . . . D5
Sorell-Midway Point 2,544 . . D4
Stanley 603 . . . . B2
Storeys Creek D3
Strahan 402 . . . . B4
Strathgordon C4
Sulphur Creek 367 . . . . . . C3
Swansea 428 . . . . D4
Tarraleah 498 . . . . C4
Temma A3
Triabunna 924 . . . . D4
Tullah 1,894 . . . . B3
Ulverstone 9,413 . . . . C3
Waratah 342 . . . . B3
Wesley Vale C3
Westbury 1,161 . . . . C3
Whitemark D2
Woodbridge 259 . . . . D5
Wynyard 4,582 . . . . B3
Zeehan 1,750 . . . . B3

OTHER FEATURES

Anderson (bay) D2
Anne (mt.) C4
Anser Group (isls.) C1
Arthur (lake) D4
Arthur (range) C5
Arthur (riv.) B3
Babel (isl.) E1
Banks (str.) D2
Barn Bluff (mt.) B3
Barren (cape) E2
Bass (str.) C1
Bathurst (gulf) C5
Cape Barren (isl.) E2
Chappell (isls.) D2
Circular (gulf) B2
Clarke (isl.) E2
Clyde (riv.) D4
Cox (bight) C5
Cradle (mt.) B3
Cradle Mt. Lake St. Clair
   Nat'l Park B3
Crescent (lake) D4
Curtis Group (isls.) C1
D'Aguilar (range) B4
Davey (riv.) B4
Deal (isl.) D1
Dee (riv.) C4
Denison (range) C4
D'Entrecasteaux (chan.) . . . D5
Derwent (riv.) D4
East Sister (isl.) E1
Echo (lake) C4
Eddystone (pt.) E2
Elliott (bay) B5
Fires (bay) E3
Flinders (isl.) 2,150 . . . . . . D1
Florence (riv.) C4
Forestier (chan.) E4
Forestier (pen.) E4

Tasmania

MILES
0   10   20   30

KILOMETERS
0   10   20   30

State Capital . . . . ◉
State Boundaries . . . . ___
Scale 1:3,000,000

© Copyright HAMMOND INCORPORATED, Maplewood, N.J.

New Zealand

CONIC PROJECTION

SCALE OF MILES

0   50   100   150

SCALE OF KILOMETERS

0   50   100   150

Capital of Country .... ☆

Scale 1:5,700,000

© Copyright HAMMOND INCORPORATED, Maplewood, N.J.

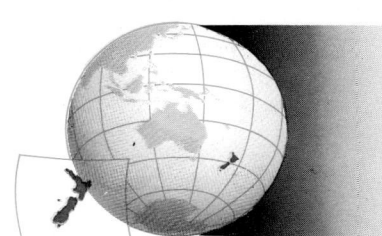

AREA 103,736 sq. mi. (268,676 sq. km.)
POPULATION 3,175,737
CAPITAL Wellington
LARGEST CITY Auckland
HIGHEST POINT Mt. Cook 12,349 ft.
(3,764 m.)
MONETARY UNIT New Zealand dollar
MAJOR LANGUAGES English, Maori
MAJOR RELIGIONS Protestantism,
Roman Catholicism

Topography

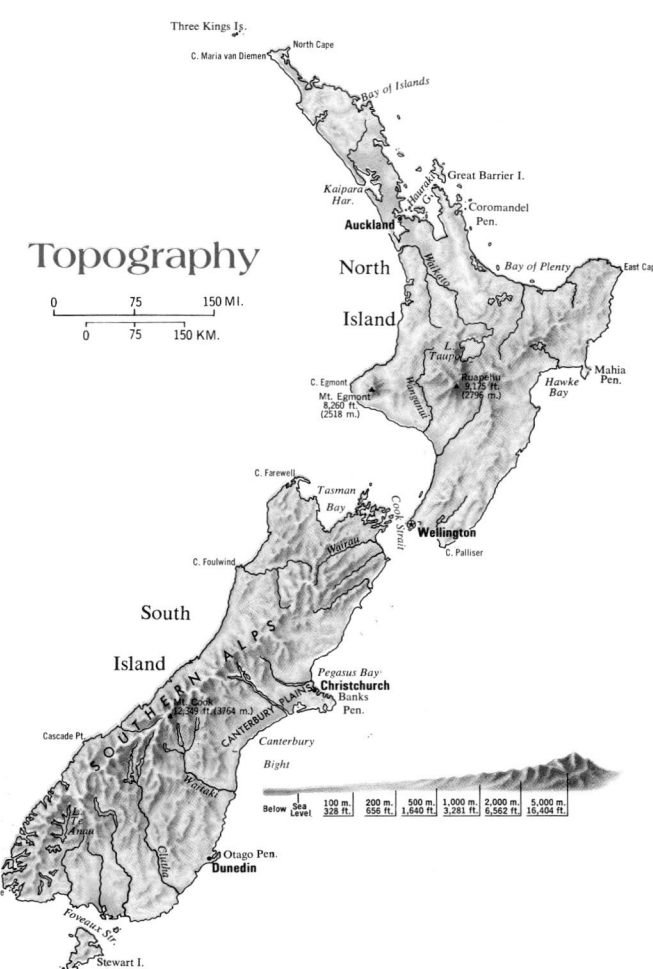

0 75 150 MI.
0 75 150 KM.

Below Sea Level | 100 m. 328 ft. | 200 m. 656 ft. | 500 m. 1,640 ft. | 1,000 m. 3,281 ft. | 2,000 m. 6,562 ft. | 5,000 m. 16,404 ft.

Wellington †321,004 ..... A3
Wellsford 1,621 .... E2
Westport 4,686 .... C4
Whakatane 12,286 ...... F2
Whangamata 1,566 ..... F2
Whangarei 36,550 ...... E1
Whangarei †40,212 ..... E1
Whitianga 1,960 .... E2
Winton 2,035 .... B7
Woodville 1,647 .... F4

OTHER FEATURES

Arthur's (pass) C5
Aspiring (mt.) B6
Banks (pen.) D5
Bream (bay) E1
Brett (cape) E1
Buller (riv.) D4
Campbell (cape) E4
Canterbury (bight) D6
Cascade (pt.) B6
Chatham (isls.) 751 .... D7
Cloudy (bay) E4
Clutha (riv.) B6
Coleridge (lake) C5
Colville (cape) E2
Cook (mt.) C5
Cook (str.) E4
Coromandel (pen.) F2
Devil River (peak) D4
D'Urville (isl.) D4
Dusky (sound) A6
East (cape) G2
Egmont (cape) D3
Egmont (mt.) D3
Ellesmere (lake) D5
Farewell (cape) D4
Foulwind (cape) C4
Fournier (cape) E7
Foveaaux (str.) A7
Golden (bay) D4
Great Barrier (isl.) 572 ... E2
Haast (pass) B6
Hauraki (gulf) C1
Hawke (bay) F3
Hikurangi (mt.) G2
Hokianga (harb.) D1
Huiarau (range) F3
Hutt (riv.) C2
Islands (bay) E1
Jackson (bay) B5
Kaikoura (range) D5
Kaimanawa (range) ... E3
Kaipara (harb.) D2
Karamea (bight) C4
Kawhia (harb.) E3
Kidnappers (cape) ... F3
Mahia (pen.) G3
Manapouri (lake) A6
Manukau (harb.) B1
Maria van Diemen (cape) D1
Mataura (riv.) B6
Mercury (isls.) F2
Milford (sound) A6
Needles (pt.) E2
Nicholson, Port (inlet) . B3
Ninety Mile (beach) .. D1
North (cape) D1
North (isl.) 2,322,989 .. F1
North Taranaki (bight) . D3
Otago (pen.) C6
Owen (mt.) D4
Palliser (cape) E4
Pegasus (bay) D5
Pitt (isl.) E7
Plenty (bay) F2
Port Nicholson (inlet) . B3
Port Pegasus (inlet) . B7
Pukaki (lake) B6
Puysegur (pt.) A7
Rakaia (riv.) C5
Rangitata (riv.) C5
Rangitikei (riv.) ... E3
Raukumara (range) .. F3
Reinga (cape) D1
Resolution (isl.) ... A6
Richmond (range) .. D4
Rocks (pt.) C4
Rotorua (lake) F3
Ruahine (range) F4
Ruapehu (mt.) E3
Ruapuke (isl.) B7
South (cape) A7
South (isl.) 852,748 .. B5
Southern Alps (range) . C5
South Taranaki (bight) . D3
Spenser (mts.) D5
Stewart (isl.) 600 ... A7
Tararua (range) E4
Tasman (bay) D4
Tasman (mt.) C5
Tasman (mts.) D4
Tasman (sea) B4
Taupo (lake) F3
Tauroa (pt.) D1

Te Anau (lake) A6
Tekapo (lake) C5
Terawhiti (cape) ... A3
Thames (firth) E2
Three Kings (isls.) . D1
Turakirae (head) ... B3
Una (mt.) D5
Waiheke (isl.) 3,223 . E2
Waikato (riv.) E2
Waimakariri (riv.) .. D5
Waipa (riv.) E2
Wairau (riv.) D4
Waitaki (riv.) C6
Waitemata (harb.) .. B1
Wakatipu (lake) ... B6
Wanaka (lake) B6
Wanganui (riv.) ... E3
West (cape) A6
Whitcombe (mt.) ... C5

†Population of urban area.

Agriculture, Industry and Resources

CITIES and TOWNS

Albany 2,001 .... B1
Alexandra 4,348 ..... B6
Ashburton 14,151 .... C5
Ashhurst 1,906 ...... E4
Auckland 144,963 .... B1
Auckland †769,558 ... B1
Balclutha 4,495 ..... B7
Belmont 2,402 ...... B2
Birkenhead 21,324 ... B1
Blenheim 17,849 .... D4
Bluff 2,720 .... B7
Bulls 1,839 .... E4
Cambridge 8,514 .... E2
Carterton 3,971 .... E4
Christchurch 164,680 . D5
Christchurch †289,959 . D5
Cromwell 2,364 .... B6
Dannevirke 5,663 ... F4
Dargaville 4,747 ... D1
Devonport 10,410 ... C1
Dunedin 77,176 .... C6
Dunedin †107,445 ... C6
Eastbourne 4,561 ... B3
East Coast Bays 28,866 . B1
Edgecumbe 1,929 ... F2
Ellerslie 5,404 .... B1
Eltham 2,411 ..... E3
Fairfield 1,849 .... C6
Featherston 2,458 .. E4
Feilding 11,522 .... E4
Foxton 2,719 ..... E4
Geraldine 2,128 ... C6
Gisborne 29,986 ... G3
Gisborne †32,062 .. G3
Glen Eden 9,406 ... B1
Glenfield 3,691 ... B1
Gore 9,185 ...... B7
Green Bay 3,035 ... B1
Green Island 6,899 . C7
Greymouth 8,103 .. C5
Greytown 1,797 ... E4
Half Moon Bay (Oban) 2,448 B7
Hamilton 91,109 ... E2
Hamilton †97,907 .. E2
Hastings 36,083 ... F3
Hastings †52,563 .. F3
Havelock North 8,507 . F3
Hawera 8,400 .... E3
Helensville 1,360 .. B1
Henderson 6,645 .. B1
Heretaunga-Pinehaven 6,171 C2
Hokitika 3,414 ... C5
Hornby 8,215 .... D5
Howick 13,866 ... C1
Huntly 6,534 .... E2
Hutt (Upper and Lower)
†131,257 .... B2
Inglewood 2,839 ... E3

Invercargill 49,446 .... B7
Invercargill †53,868 ... B7
Kaiapoi 4,894 ...... D5
Kaikohe 3,663 ..... D1
Kaikoura 2,180 .... D5
Kaitaia 4,737 ..... D1
Kawerau 8,593 .... F2
Kumeu 3,414 ..... B1
Levin 14,652 ..... E4
Lower Hutt 63,245 .. B2
Lyttelton 3,184 ... D5
Manukau 159,362 .. C1
Marton 4,858 .... E4
Masterton 18,785 .. E4
Mataura 2,345 .... B7
Milton 2,193 ..... B7
Morrinsville 5,080 .. E2
Mosgiel 9,264 .... C6
Motueka 4,693 .... D4
Mount Albert 26,462 . B1
Mount Eden 18,305 . B1
Mount Maunganui 11,391 . E2
Mount Roskill 33,577 . B1
Mount Wellington 19,528 . C1
Murupara 2,964 ... F3
Napier 48,314 .... F3
Napier †51,330 ... F3
Nelson 33,304 .... D4
Nelson †43,121 ... D4
New Lynn 10,445 .. B1
New Plymouth 36,048 . D3
New Plymouth †44,095 . D3
Ngaruawahia 4,435 . E2
Northcote 10,061 .. B1
Oamaru 13,043 .... C6
Oban (Half Moon Bay) 2,448 B7
Onehunga 15,386 .. C1
One Tree Hill 11,078 . B1
Opotiki 3,388 .... F2
Orewa 5,552 ..... E2
Otahuhu 10,298 ... C1
Otaki 4,301 ..... E4
Otorohanga 2,574 . E3
Paeroa 3,702 .... E2
Pahiatua 2,599 ... E4
Paihia 1,740 .... D1
Palmerston North 60,105 . E4
Palmerston North †66,691 . E4
Papakura 22,473 .. E2
Papatoetoe 21,700 . C1
Patea 1,938 ..... E3
Petone 8,113 .... B2
Picton 3,220 .... D4
Pinehaven (Heretaunga-
Pinehaven) 6,171 ... C2
Porirua 41,104 ... B2
Port Chalmers 2,917 . C6
Pukekohe 9,070 .. E2
Putaruru 4,222 ... E3
Queenstown 3,367 . B6

Raetihi 1,247 ...... E3
Raglan 1,414 ..... E2
Rangiora 6,385 .... D5
Reefton 1,200 .... C5
Richmond 6,847 ... D4
Riverton 1,479 ... B7
Rotorua 38,157 ... F3
Rotorua †48,314 .. F3
Runanga 1,264 ... C5
Russell 932 ..... E1
Saint Kilda 6,147 . C7
Shannon 1,465 ... E4
Stratford 5,518 ... E3
Taihape 2,586 ... E3
Takapuna 64,844 .. B1
Tapanui 1,042 ... B6
Taradale 4,681 ... F3
Taumarunui 6,541 . E3
Taupo 13,651 .... F3
Tauranga 37,099 .. F2
Tauranga †53,097 . F2
Tawa 12,216 .... B2
Te Anau 2,610 ... A6
Te Aroha 3,331 .. E2
Te Atatu 14,713 .. B1
Te Awamutu 7,922 . E3
Te Kauwhata 842 . E2
Te Kuiti 4,795 ... E3
Te Puke 4,577 ... F2
Thames 6,456 ... E2
The Hermitage ... C5
Timaru 28,412 ... C6
Timaru †29,225 .. C6
Titirangi 8,426 .. B1
Tokoroa 18,713 .. F3
Tuakau 1,982 ... E2
Tuatapere 884 ... A7
Turangi 5,517 ... E3
Upper Hutt 31,405 . B2
Waihi 3,538 .... E2
Waikanae 4,818 . E4
Waikouaiti 858 .. C6
Waimate 3,393 .. C6
Wainuiomata 19,192 . B3
Waipawa 1,732 .. F4
Waipukurau 3,648 . F4
Wairoa 5,439 ... F3
Waitangi D7
Waitara 6,012 .. D3
Waitemata 87,452 . B1
Waiuku 3,654 ... E2
Waanaka 1,155 .. B6
Wanganui 37,012 . E3
Wanganui †39,595 . E3
Warkworth 1,734 . E2
Washdyke 949 .. C6
Waverley 1,239 .. E3
Wellington (cap.) 135,688 . A3

DOMINANT LAND USE

Mixed Farming, Livestock
Dairy
Truck Farming, Horticulture
Pasture Livestock (chiefly sheep)
Livestock Herding
Forests
Nonagricultural Land

MAJOR MINERAL OCCURRENCES

C Coal
G Natural Gas
J Jade
Ka Kaolin
Lg Lignite
O Petroleum
U Uranium

🗲 Water Power
▨ Major Industrial Areas

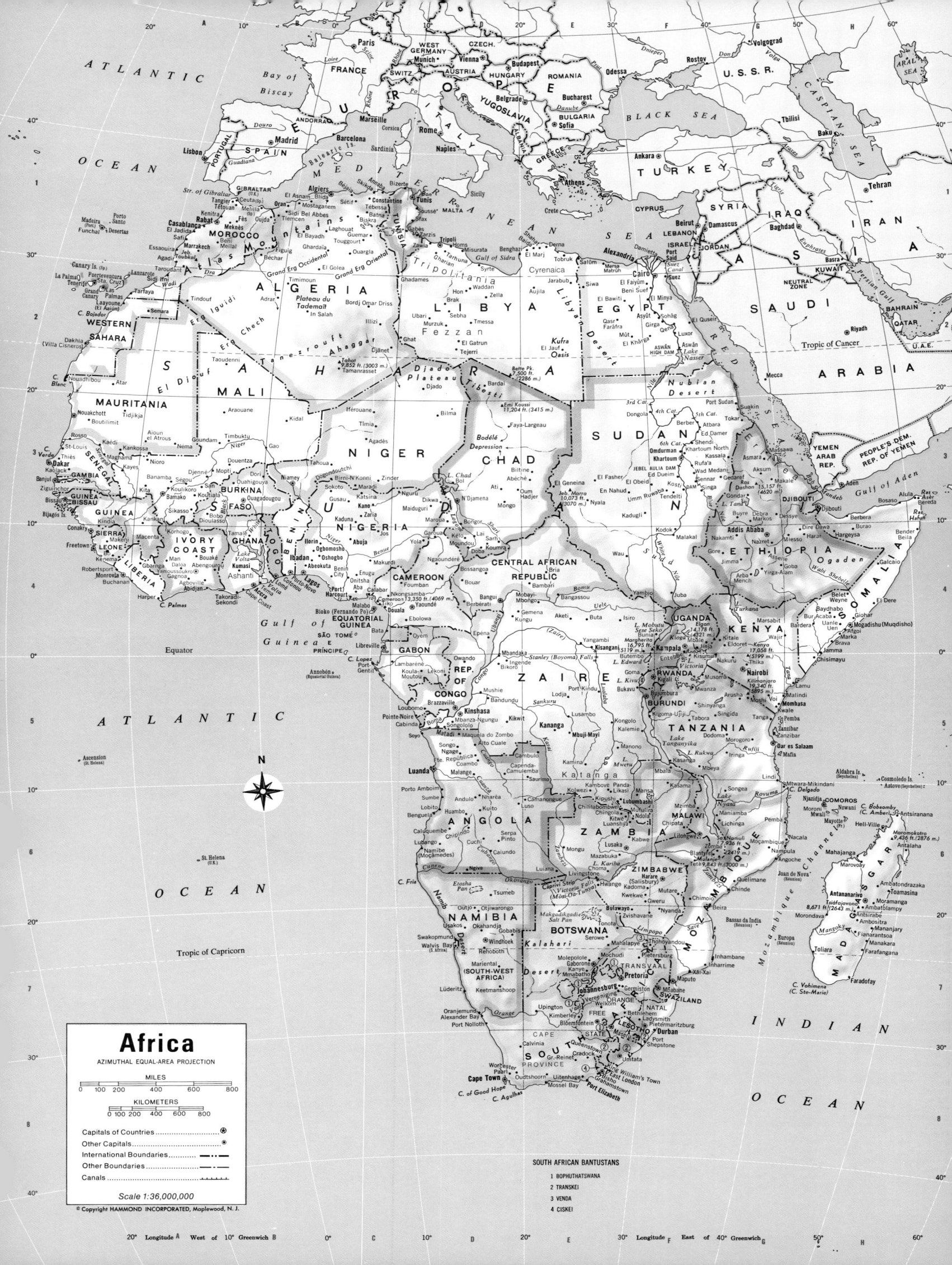

AREA 11,707,000 sq. mi. (30,321,130 sq. km.)
POPULATION 469,000,000
LARGEST CITY Cairo
HIGHEST POINT Kilimanjaro 19,340 ft.
  (5,895 m.)
LOWEST POINT Lake Assal, Djibouti -512 ft.
  (-156 m.)

Population Distribution

Vegetation

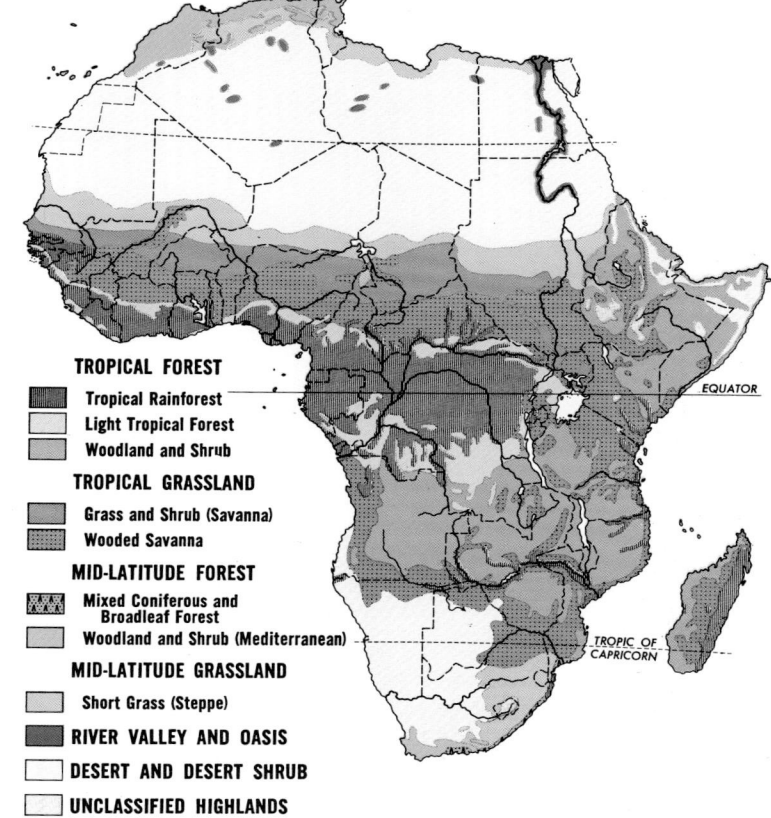

DENSITY PER

SQ. KILOMETER	SQ. MILE
Over 100	Over 260
50-100	130-260
10-50	25-130
1-10	3-25
Under 1	Under 3

• Cities with over 1,000,000
  inhabitants (including suburbs)

○ Cities with over 350,000
  inhabitants (including suburbs)

TROPICAL FOREST
- Tropical Rainforest
- Light Tropical Forest
- Woodland and Shrub

TROPICAL GRASSLAND
- Grass and Shrub (Savanna)
- Wooded Savanna

MID-LATITUDE FOREST
- Mixed Coniferous and Broadleaf Forest
- Woodland and Shrub (Mediterranean)

MID-LATITUDE GRASSLAND
- Short Grass (Steppe)

RIVER VALLEY AND OASIS

DESERT AND DESERT SHRUB

UNCLASSIFIED HIGHLANDS

TROPIC OF CANCER
EQUATOR
TROPIC OF CAPRICORN

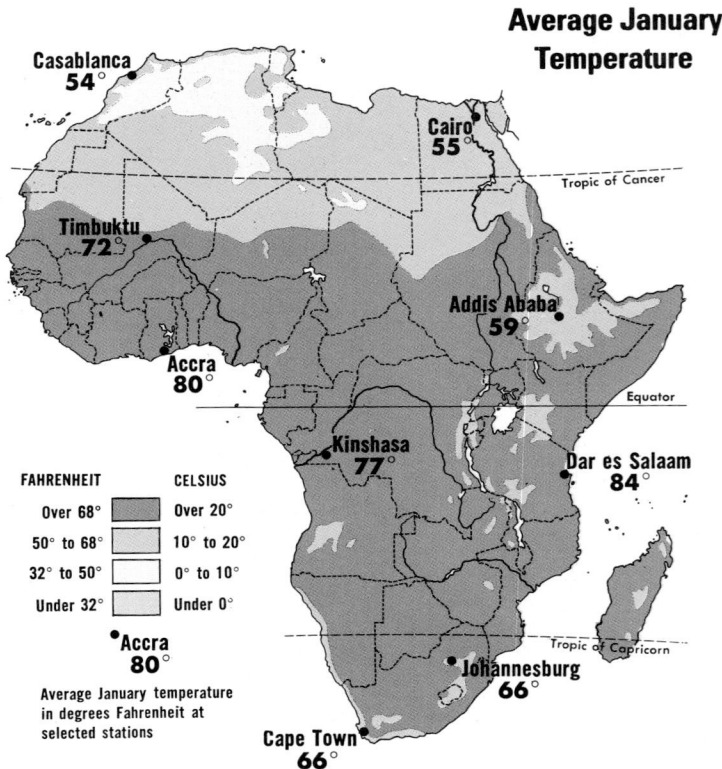

Average January Temperature

Casablanca 54°
Cairo 55°
Timbuktu 72°
Addis Ababa 59°
Accra 80°
Kinshasa 77°
Dar es Salaam 84°
Johannesburg 66°
Cape Town 66°

FAHRENHEIT	CELSIUS
Over 68°	Over 20°
50° to 68°	10° to 20°
32° to 50°	0° to 10°
Under 32°	Under 0°

● Accra 80°
Average January temperature in degrees Fahrenheit at selected stations

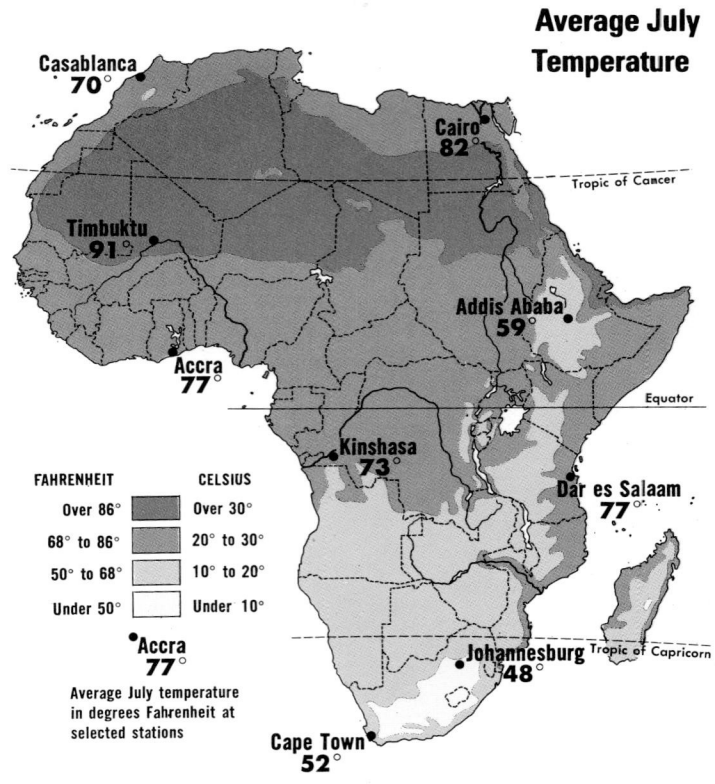

Average July Temperature

Casablanca 70°
Cairo 82°
Timbuktu 91°
Addis Ababa 59°
Accra 77°
Kinshasa 73°
Dar es Salaam 77°
Johannesburg 48°
Cape Town 52°

FAHRENHEIT	CELSIUS
Over 86°	Over 30°
68° to 86°	20° to 30°
50° to 68°	10° to 20°
Under 50°	Under 10°

● Accra 77°
Average July temperature in degrees Fahrenheit at selected stations

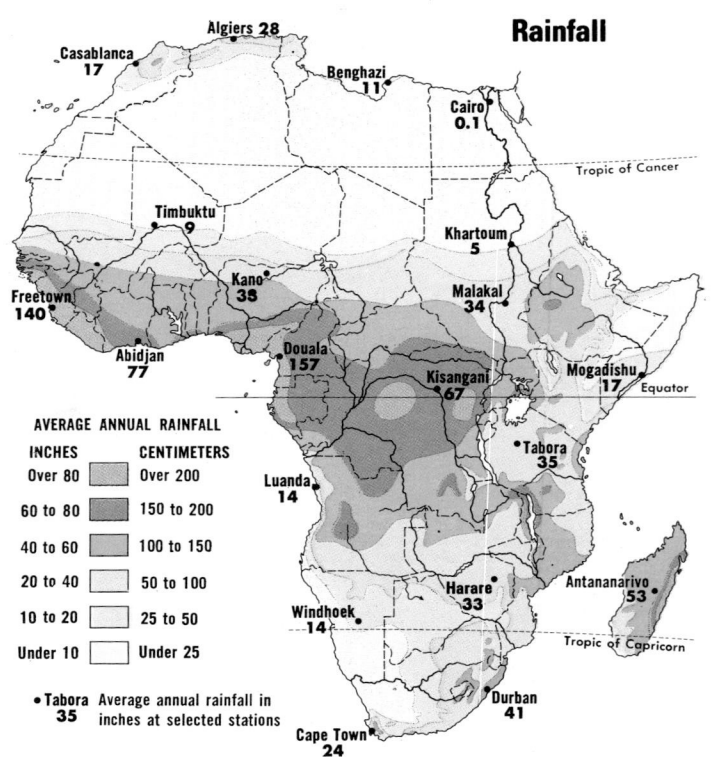

Rainfall

Algiers 28
Casablanca 17
Benghazi 11
Cairo 0.1
Timbuktu 9
Khartoum 5
Kano 38
Malakal 34
Freetown 140
Abidjan 77
Douala 157
Kisangani 67
Mogadishu 17
Tabora 35
Luanda 14
Harare 33
Antananarivo 53
Windhoek 14
Durban 41
Cape Town 24

AVERAGE ANNUAL RAINFALL

INCHES	CENTIMETERS
Over 80	Over 200
60 to 80	150 to 200
40 to 60	100 to 150
20 to 40	50 to 100
10 to 20	25 to 50
Under 10	Under 25

● Tabora 35   Average annual rainfall in inches at selected stations

Vegetation / Relief

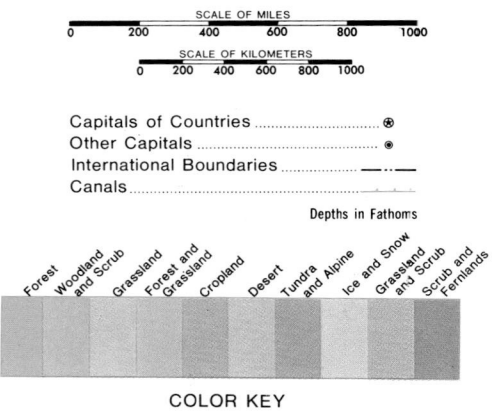

SCALE OF MILES
0   200   400   600   800   1000

SCALE OF KILOMETERS
0   200   400   600   800   1000

Capitals of Countries .... ⊛
Other Capitals .... ⊛
International Boundaries .... ━ ━
Canals ....

Depths in Fathoms

Forest
Woodland and Scrub
Grassland
Forest and Grassland
Cropland
Desert
Tundra and Alpine
Ice and Snow
Grassland and Scrub
Scrub and Fernlands

COLOR KEY

Longitude 10° West of Greenwich   0°   Longitude 10° East of Greenwich

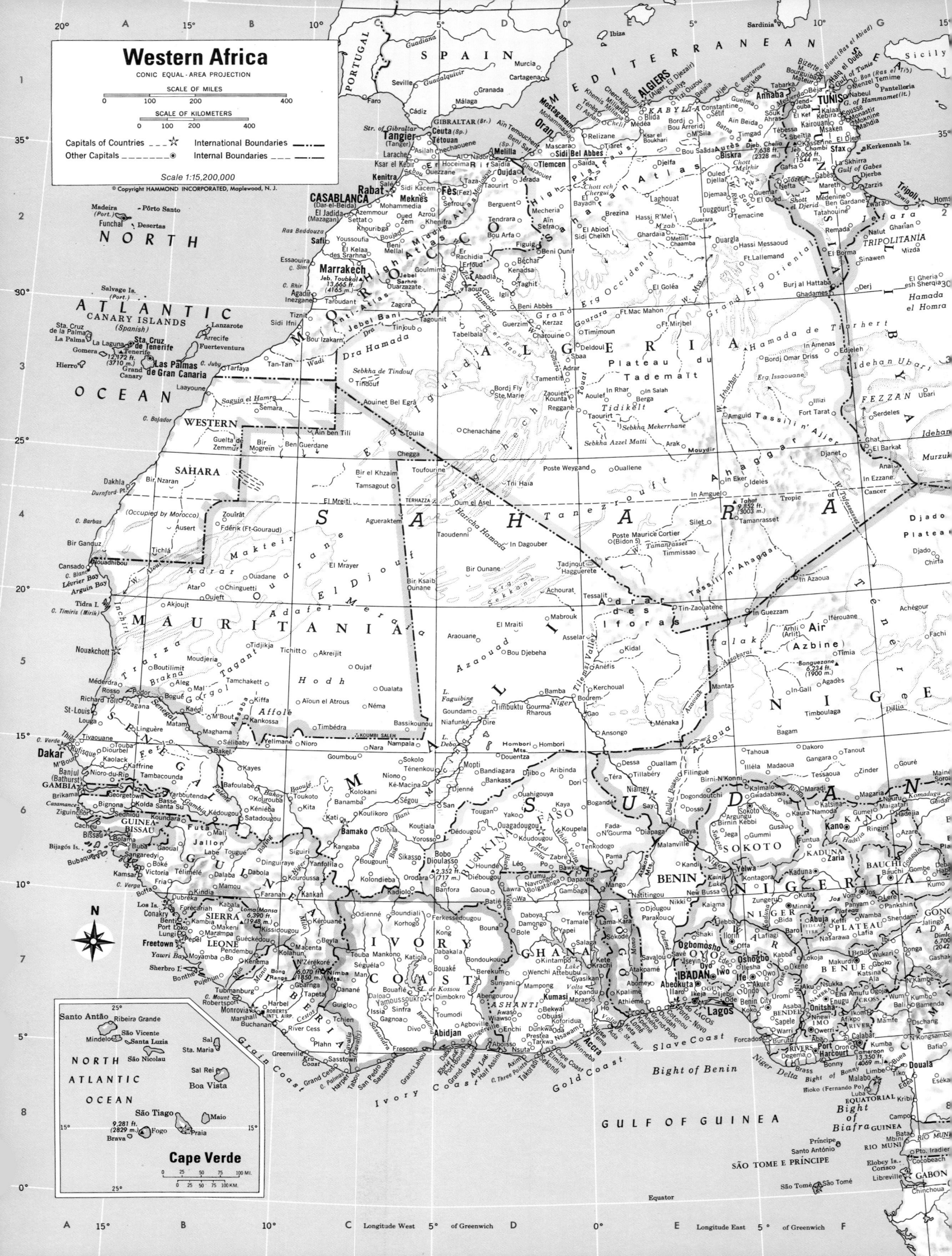

Western Africa

CONIC EQUAL-AREA PROJECTION

SCALE OF MILES

0 100 200 400

SCALE OF KILOMETERS

0 100 200 400

Capitals of Countries ___ ☆   International Boundaries _____
Other Capitals _____ ◉   Internal Boundaries ___

Scale 1:15,200,000

© Copyright HAMMOND INCORPORATED, Maplewood, N.J.

Cape Verde

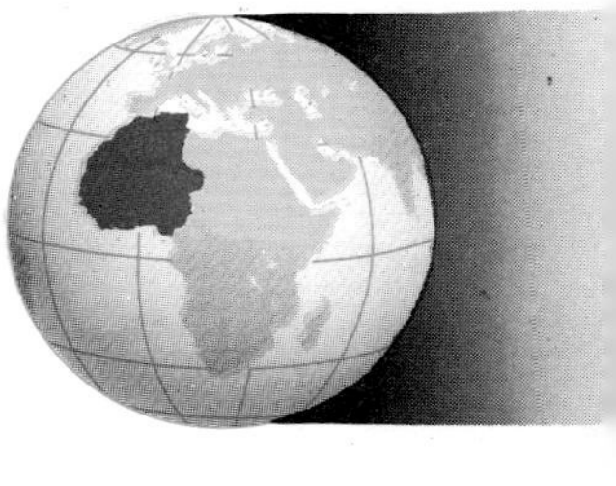

ALGERIA

AREA 919,591 sq. mi. (2,381,740 sq. km.)
POPULATION 17,422,000
CAPITAL Algiers
LARGEST CITY Algiers
HIGHEST POINT Tahat 9,852 ft. (3,003 m.)
MONETARY UNIT Algerian dinar
MAJOR LANGUAGES Arabic, Berber, French
MAJOR RELIGION Islam

BENIN

AREA 43,483 sq. mi. (112,620 sq. km.)
POPULATION 3,338,240
CAPITAL Porto-Novo
LARGEST CITY Cotonou
HIGHEST POINT Atakora Mts. 2,083 ft. (635 m.)
MONETARY UNIT CFA franc
MAJOR LANGUAGES Fon, Somba, Yoruba, Bariba, French, Mina, Dendi
MAJOR RELIGIONS Tribal religions, Islam, Roman Catholicism

CAPE VERDE

AREA 1,557 sq. mi. (4,033 sq. km.)
POPULATION 324,000
CAPITAL Praia
LARGEST CITY Praia
HIGHEST POINT 9,281 ft. (2,829 m.)
MONETARY UNIT Cape Verde escudo
MAJOR LANGUAGE Portuguese
MAJOR RELIGION Roman Catholicism

GAMBIA

AREA 4,127 sq. mi. (10,689 sq. km.)
POPULATION 601,000
CAPITAL Banjul
LARGEST CITY Banjul
HIGHEST POINT 100 ft. (30 m.)
MONETARY UNIT dalasi
MAJOR LANGUAGES Mandingo, Fulani, Wolof, English, Malinke
MAJOR RELIGIONS Islam, tribal religions, Christianity

GHANA

AREA 92,099 sq. mi. (238,536 sq. km.)
POPULATION 11,450,000
CAPITAL Accra
LARGEST CITY Accra
HIGHEST POINT Togo Hills 2,900 ft. (884 m.)
MONETARY UNIT cedi
MAJOR LANGUAGES Twi, Fante, Dagbani, Ewe, Ga, English, Hausa, Akan
MAJOR RELIGIONS Tribal religions, Christianity, Islam

GUINEA

AREA 94,925 sq. mi. (245,856 sq. km.)
POPULATION 5,143,284
CAPITAL Conakry
LARGEST CITY Conakry
HIGHEST POINT Nimba Mts. 6,070 ft. (1,850 m.)
MONETARY UNIT syli
MAJOR LANGUAGES Fulani, Mandingo, Susu, French
MAJOR RELIGIONS Islam, tribal religions

GUINEA-BISSAU

AREA 13,948 sq. mi. (36,125 sq. km.)
POPULATION 777,214
CAPITAL Bissau
LARGEST CITY Bissau
HIGHEST POINT 689 ft. (210 m.)
MONETARY UNIT Guinea-Bissau escudo
MAJOR LANGUAGES Balante, Fulani, Crioulo, Mandingo, Portuguese
MAJOR RELIGIONS Islam, tribal religions, Roman Catholicism

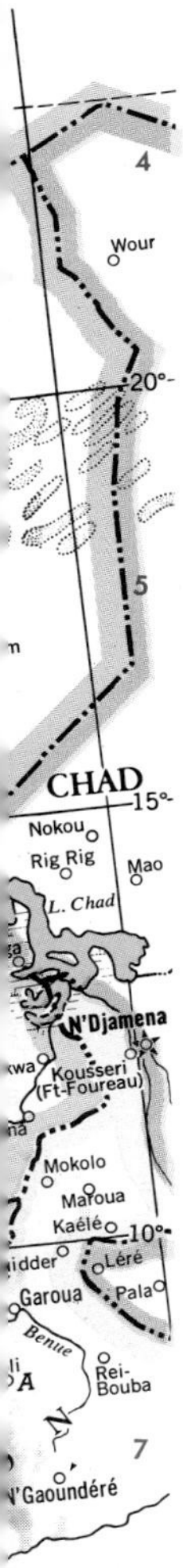

IVORY COAST

AREA 124,504 sq. mi. (322,465 sq. km.)
POPULATION 7,920,000
CAPITAL Yamoussoukro
LARGEST CITY Abidjan
HIGHEST POINT 5,745 ft. (1,751 m.)
MONETARY UNIT CFA franc
MAJOR LANGUAGES Bale, Bete, Senufu, French, Dioula
MAJOR RELIGIONS Tribal religions, Islam

LIBERIA

AREA 43,000 sq. mi. (111,370 sq. km.)
POPULATION 1,873,000
CAPITAL Monrovia
LARGEST CITY Monrovia
HIGHEST POINT Wutivi 5,584 ft. (1,702 m.)
MONETARY UNIT Liberian dollar
MAJOR LANGUAGES Kru, Kpelle, Bassa, Vai, English
MAJOR RELIGIONS Christianity, tribal religions, Islam

MALI

AREA 464,873 sq. mi. (1,204,021 sq. km.)
POPULATION 6,906,000
CAPITAL Bamako
LARGEST CITY Bamako
HIGHEST POINT Hombori Mts. 3,789 ft. (1,155 m.)
MONETARY UNIT Mali franc
MAJOR LANGUAGES Bambara, Senufu, Fulani, Soninke, French
MAJOR RELIGIONS Islam, tribal religions

MAURITANIA

AREA 419,229 sq. mi. (1,085,803 sq. km.)
POPULATION 1,634,000
CAPITAL Nouakchott
LARGEST CITY Nouakchott
HIGHEST POINT 2,972 ft. (906 m.)
MONETARY UNIT ouguiya
MAJOR LANGUAGES Arabic, Wolof, Tukolor, French
MAJOR RELIGION Islam

MOROCCO

AREA 172,414 sq. mi. (446,550 sq. km.)
POPULATION 20,242,000
CAPITAL Rabat
LARGEST CITY Casablanca
HIGHEST POINT Jeb. Toubkal 13,665 ft. (4,165 m.)
MONETARY UNIT dirham
MAJOR LANGUAGES Arabic, Berber, French
MAJOR RELIGIONS Islam, Judaism, Christianity

NIGER

AREA 489,189 sq. mi. (1,267,000 sq. km.)
POPULATION 5,098,427
CAPITAL Niamey
LARGEST CITY Niamey
HIGHEST POINT Banguezane 6,234 ft. (1,900 m.)
MONETARY UNIT CFA franc
MAJOR LANGUAGES Hausa, Songhai, Fulani, French, Tamashek, Djerma
MAJOR RELIGIONS Islam, tribal religions

NIGERIA

AREA 357,000 sq. mi. (924,630 sq. km.)
POPULATION 82,643,000
CAPITAL Lagos
LARGEST CITY Lagos
HIGHEST POINT Dimlang 6,700 ft. (2,042 m.)
MONETARY UNIT naira
MAJOR LANGUAGES Hausa, Yoruba, Ibo, Ijaw, Fulani, Tiv, Kanuri, Ibibio, English, Edo
MAJOR RELIGIONS Islam, Christianity, tribal religions

SÃO TOMÉ E PRÍNCIPE

AREA 372 sq. mi. (963 sq. km.)
POPULATION 85,000
CAPITAL São Tomé
LARGEST CITY São Tomé
HIGHEST POINT Pico 6,640 ft. (2,024 m.)
MONETARY UNIT dobra
MAJOR LANGUAGES Bantu languages, Portuguese
MAJOR RELIGIONS Tribal religions, Roman Catholicism

SENEGAL

AREA 75,954 sq. mi. (196,720 sq. km.)
POPULATION 5,508,000
CAPITAL Dakar
LARGEST CITY Dakar
HIGHEST POINT Futa Jallon 1,640 ft. (500 m.)
MONETARY UNIT CFA franc
MAJOR LANGUAGES Wolof, Peul (Fulani), French, Mende, Mandingo, Dida
MAJOR RELIGIONS Islam, tribal religions, Roman Catholicism

SIERRA LEONE

AREA 27,925 sq. mi. (72,325 sq. km.)
POPULATION 3,470,000
CAPITAL Freetown
LARGEST CITY Freetown
HIGHEST POINT Loma Mts. 6,390 ft. (1,947 m.)
MONETARY UNIT leone
MAJOR LANGUAGES Mende, Temne, Vai, English, Krio (pidgin)
MAJOR RELIGIONS Tribal religions, Islam, Christianity

TOGO

AREA 21,622 sq. mi. (56,000 sq. km.)
POPULATION 2,472,000
CAPITAL Lomé
LARGEST CITY Lomé
HIGHEST POINT Agou 3,445 ft. (1,050 m.)
MONETARY UNIT CFA franc
MAJOR LANGUAGES Ewe, French, Twi, Hausa
MAJOR RELIGIONS Tribal religions, Roman Catholicism, Islam

TUNISIA

AREA 63,378 sq. mi. (164,149 sq. km.)
POPULATION 6,367,000
CAPITAL Tunis
LARGEST CITY Tunis
HIGHEST POINT Jeb. Chambi 5,066 ft. (1,544 m.)
MONETARY UNIT Tunisian dinar
MAJOR LANGUAGES Arabic, French
MAJOR RELIGION Islam

BURKINA FASO (UPPER VOLTA)

AREA 105,869 sq. mi. (274,200 sq. km.)
POPULATION 6,908,000
CAPITAL Ouagadougou
LARGEST CITY Ouagadougou
HIGHEST POINT 2,352 ft. (717 m.)
MONETARY UNIT CFA franc
MAJOR LANGUAGES Mossi, Lobi, French, Samo, Gourounsi
MAJOR RELIGIONS Islam, tribal religions, Roman Catholicism

WESTERN SAHARA

AREA 102,703 sq. mi. (266,000 sq. km.)
POPULATION 76,425
HIGHEST POINT 2,700 ft. (823 m.)
MAJOR LANGUAGE Arabic
MAJOR RELIGION Islam

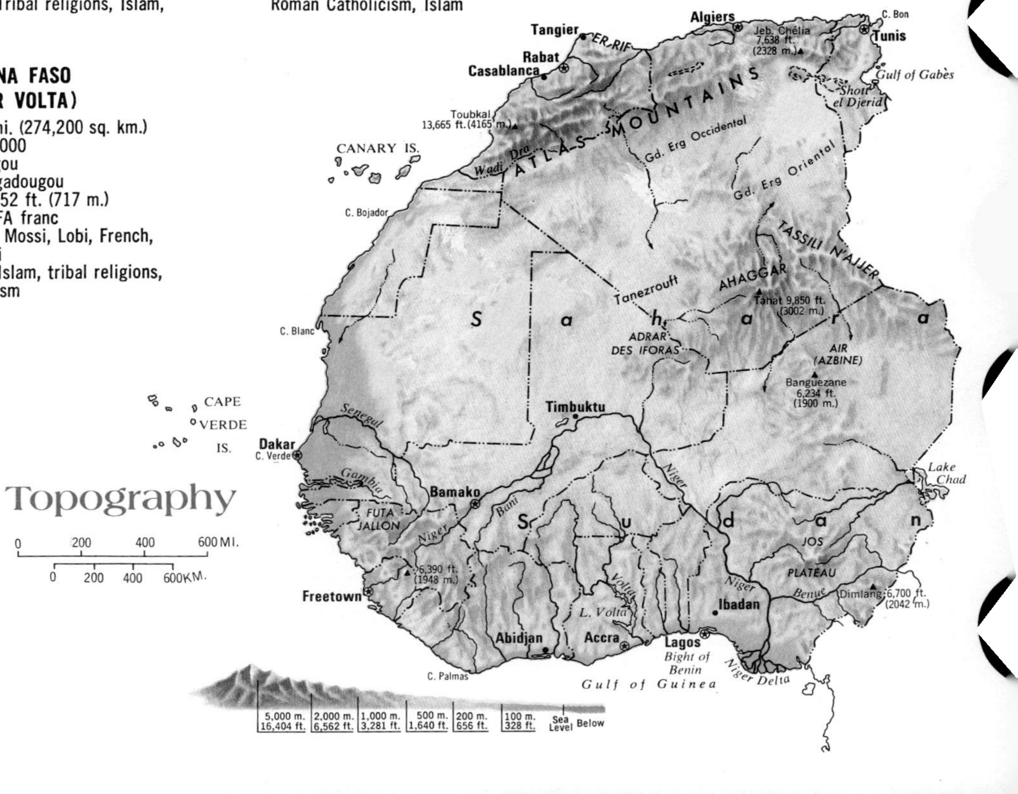

Topography

0 200 400 600 MI.
0 200 400 600 KM.

| 5,000 m. 16,404 ft. | 2,000 m. 6,562 ft. | 1,000 m. 3,281 ft. | 500 m. 1,640 ft. | 200 m. 656 ft. | 100 m. 328 ft. | Sea Level | Below |

ALGERIA
CITIES and TOWNS

Abadla 12,200 ... D2
Adrar 22,800 ... D3
Aïn Belda 26,976 ... F1
Aïn Sefra 22,400 ... D2
Aïn Temouchent 42,000 ... D1
Algiers (cap.) 1,365,400 ... E1
Amguid ... F3
Annaba 255,900 ... F1
Aoulef 17,200 ... E3
Arak ... E3
Batna 112,100 ... F1
Béchar 72,800 ... D2
Bejaïa 89,500 ... F1
Beni Abbès 5,000 ... D2
Beni Ounif 7,500 ... D2
Beni Saf 30,700 ... D1
Berga ... E3
Bidon 5 (Poste Maurice
  Cordier) ... E4
Biskra 90,500 ... F2
Blida 160,900 ... E1
Bône (Annaba) 255,900 ... F1
Bordj Bou Arreridj 65,000 ... E1
Bordj Fly Sainte Marie ... D3
Bordj Omar Driss 1,900 ... F3
Boufarik 50,000 ... E1
Bougie (Bejaïa) 89,500 ... F1
Bou Saâda 50,000 ... E1
Brezina 10,000 ... E2
Charouine ... D3
Chenachane ... D3
Cherchell 36,800 ... E1
Constantine 335,100 ... F1
Deldoul ... E3
Dellys 29,700 ... E1
Djanet 5,300 ... F4
Djelfa 51,000 ... E2
Djemaa 34,600 ... F2
Edjeleh ... F3
El Abiod Sidi Cheikh 15,300 ... E2
El Asnam 106,100 ... E1
El Bayadh 38,500 ... E2
El Djezair (Algiers)
  (cap.) 1,365,400 ... E1
El Goléa 24,400 ... E2
El Oued 72,100 ... F2
Fort Lallemand ... F3
Fort MacMahon ... E3
Fort Miribel ... E3
Fort Tarat ... F3
Ghardaïa 70,500 ... E2
Ghazaouet 25,900 ... D2
Guelma 60,100 ... F2
Guemar ... F2
Guerara 22,300 ... E2
Guerzim ... D3
Hassi Messaoud ... F2
Hassi R'Mel ... E2
Ideles ... F4
Igli 3,400 ... D2
Illizi 4,600 ... F3
In Amenas 4,200 ... F3
In Amguel ... E4
In Eker ... F4
In Guezzam ... E5
In Rhar ... E3
In Salah 18,800 ... E3
Jijel 49,800 ... F1
Kenadsa 7,600 ... D2
Kerzaz 2,900 ... D3
Khemis Miliana 57,800 ... E1
Ksar el Boukhari 41,200 ... E1
Laghouat 59,200 ... E2
Mascara 62,300 ... D1
Mecheria 22,600 ... D2
Médéa 72,300 ... E1
Metlili Chaamba 21,300 ... E2
Miliana 36,400 ... E1
Mohammadia 53,700 ... D1
Mostaganem 101,600 ... D1
M'Sila 49,100 ... E1
Oran 491,900 ... D1
Orléansville (El
  Asnam) 106,100 ... E1
Ouallene ... E4
Ouargla 77,400 ... F2
Ouled Djellal 22,700 ... F2
Philippeville (Skikda) 107,700 ... F1
Poste Maurice Cordier ... E4
Poste Weygand ... D4
Reggane 11,300 ... D3
Relizane 60,000 ... D1
Salda 62,100 ... E2
Sbaa ... D3
Sétif 144,200 ... F1
Sidi Bel-Abbès 116,000 ... D1
Silet ... E4
Skikda 107,700 ... F1
Souk Ahras 60,200 ... F1
Tabelbala 3,100 ... D3
Taghit 3,500 ... D2
Tamanrasset 23,200 ... F4
Tamentit ... E3
Taourirt ... E3
Tébessa 67,200 ... F1
Temacine ... F2
Ténès 30,100 ... E1
Tiaret 62,900 ... E1
Tiguentourine ... F3
Timgad 9,800 ... F1
Timimoun 20,500 ... E3
Tindouf 6,500 ... C3
Tinjoub ... C3
Tin-Zaouatene ... E5
Tizi Ouzou 73,100 ... E1
Tlemcen 109,400 ... D2
Touggourt 75,600 ... F2
Zaouiet Kounta 13,800 ... D3

OTHER FEATURES

Adrar des Iforas (plat.) ... E5
Ahaggar (range) ... F4
Anal (well) ... G4
Aouinet Bel Egrâ (well) ... C3
Atlas (mts.) ... E2
Aurès (lag.) ... F1
Azzel Mati, Sebkha (lake) ... E3
Bougaroun (cape) ... F1
Chech, Erg (des.) ... D3
Chelia (mt.) ... F1
Chelif (riv.) ... E1
Chergui, Chott Ech
  (salt lake) ... E2
Gourara (oasis) ... E3
Grand Erg Occidental (des.) ... E2
Grand Erg Oriental (des.) ... F2
Guir Hamada (des.) ... D2
High Plateaus (ranges) ... D2
Iguidi, Erg (des.) ... C3
In Ezzane (well) ... G4
Irharhar, Wadi (dry riv.) ... F3
Issaouane Erg (des.) ... F3
Kabylia (reg.) ... E1
Mediterranean (sea) ... F1
Medjerda (riv.) ... F1
Melrhir, Chott (salt lake) ... F2
Mouydir (mts.) ... E3
Mya, Wadi (dry riv.) ... F2
M'zab (oasis) ... E2
Raoui, Erg el (des.) ... D3
Rhir, Wadi (dry riv.) ... F2
Sahara (des.) ... E4
Saharan Atlas (ranges) ... E2
Saoura, Wadi (dry riv.) ... D3

Souf (oasis) ... F2
Tademaït, Plateau du
  (plat.) ... E3
Tafassasset, Wadi (dry riv.) ... F4
Tahat (mt.) ... F4
Tamanrasset, Wadi (dry riv.) ... E4
Tanezrouft (des.) ... E4
Tassili N Ahaggar (plat.) ... E4
Tassili N Ajjer (plat.) ... F3
Tidikelt (oasis) ... E3
Timmissao (well) ... E4
Tindouf, Sebkha de
  (salt lake) ... C3
Tinrhert, Hamada de (des.) ... F3
Tni Haïa (well) ... D4
Touat (oasis) ... E3
Touila (well) ... C3

BENIN
CITIES and TOWNS

Abomey 38,000 ... E7
Cotonou 178,000 ... E7
Djougou ... E7
Grand-Popo ... E7
Kandi ... E6
Lokossa 6,000 ... E7
Malanville ... E6
Natitingou 49,000 ... E6
Nikki ... E7
Ouidah ... E7
Parakou 21,000 ... E7
Porto-Novo (cap.) 104,000 ... E7
Savalou ... E7
Savé ... E7

OTHER FEATURES

Atakora (mts.) ... E6
Benin (bight) ... E8
Guinea (gulf) ... E8
Mono (riv.) ... E7
Niger (riv.) ... E6
Ouémé (riv.) ... E7
Slave Coast (reg.) ... E7
Sudan (reg.) ... E6

CAPE VERDE
CITIES and TOWNS

Mindelo 28,797 ... A7
Praia (cap.) 21,494 ... B8
Ribeira Grande 1,892 ... B7
Sal Rei 1,296 ... B8
Santa Maria 956 ... B8

OTHER FEATURES

Boa Vista (isl.) ... B8
Brava (isl.) ... B8
Fogo (isl.) ... B8
Maio (isl.) ... B8
Sal (isl.) ... B7
Santa Luzia (isl.) ... B8
Santo Antão (isl.) ... A7
São Nicolau (isl.) ... B8
São Tiago (isl.) ... B8
São Vicente (isl.) ... B7

GAMBIA
CITIES and TOWNS

Banjul (cap.) 39,476 ... A6
Basse Santa Su 2,899 ... B6
Brikama 9,483 ... A6
Georgetown 2,510 ... A6

GHANA
CITIES and TOWNS

Accra (cap.) 564,194 ... D7
Accra* 738,498 ... D7
Ada 4,285 ... E7
Akuse 3,791 ... E7
Attebubu 6,630 ... D7
Awaso 5,449 ... D7
Axim 8,107 ... D8
Bawku 20,567 ... D6
Bekwai 11,287 ... D7
Berekum 14,296 ... D7
Bole 4,772 ... D7
Bolgatanga 18,896 ... D6
Damongo 7,760 ... D7
Dunkwa 15,437 ... D7
Elmina 11,401 ... D8
Enchi 4,382 ... D7
Gambaga 3,730 ... D6
Gyasikan 6,403 ... D7
Half Assini 5,429 ... D8
Ho 24,199 ... E7
Keta 14,446 ... E7
Kete Krachi 5,097 ... D7
Kintampo 7,149 ... D7
Koforidua 46,235 ... D7
Kumasi 260,286 ... D7
Kumasi* 345,117 ... D7
Lawra 2,709 ... D6
Mampong 13,895 ... D7
Mpraeso 5,908 ... D7
Navrongo ... D6
Nsawam 25,518 ... D7
Nsuta 3,854 ... D7
Obuasi 31,005 ... D7
Oda 20,957 ... D7
Prestea 15,143 ... D7
Salaga 6,413 ... D7
Sekondi 33,713 ... D8
Sekondi-Takoradi* 160,868 ... D8
Sunyani 23,780 ... D7
Takoradi 58,161 ... D8
Tamale 83,653 ... D7
Tarkwa 14,702 ... D7
Tema 60,767 ... E7
Tumu 4,366 ... D6
Wa 21,374 ... D6
Wenchi 13,836 ... D7
Wiawso 5,558 ... D7
Winneba 30,778 ... D7
Yapei 1,203 ... D7
Yendi 22,072 ... D7

OTHER FEATURES

Ashanti (reg.) ... D7
Benin (bight) ... E8
Black Volta (riv.) ... D6
Gold Coast (reg.) ... D8
Guinea (gulf) ... E8
Oti (riv.) ... E7
Red Volta (riv.) ... D6
Saint Paul (cape) ... D7
Three Points (cape) ... D8
Volta (lake) ... E7
Volta (riv.) ... E7
White Volta (riv.) ... D6

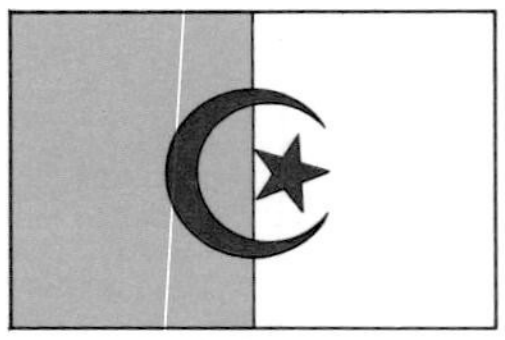

ALGERIA  **BENIN** 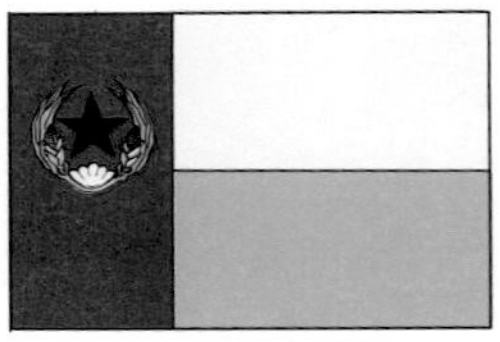 **CAPE VERDE** 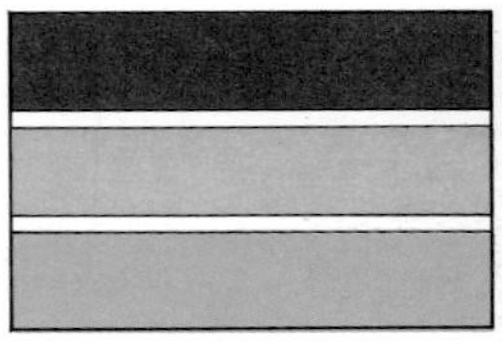 **GAMBIA**

GHANA 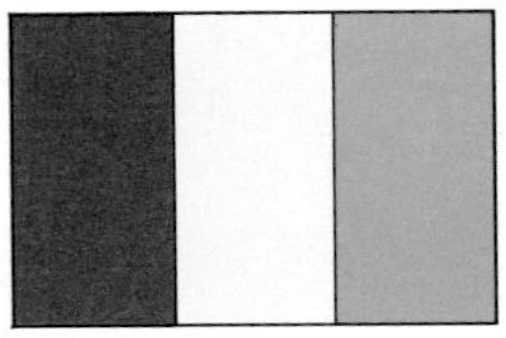 **GUINEA** 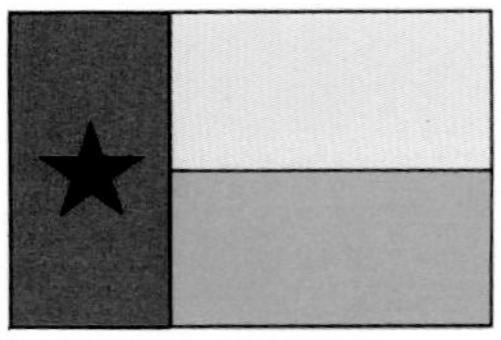 **GUINEA-BISSAU** 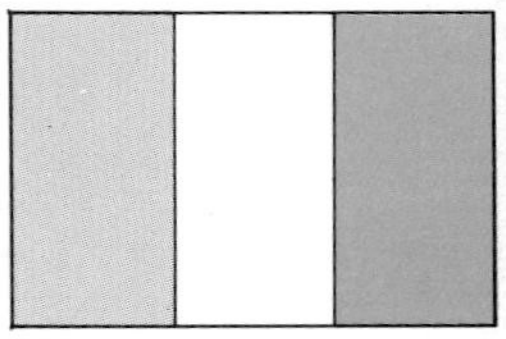 **IVORY COAST**

LIBERIA 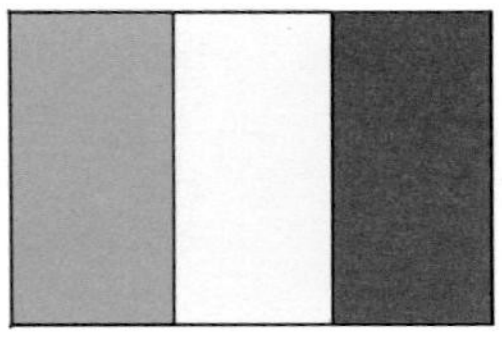 **MALI**  **MAURITANIA**  **MOROCCO**

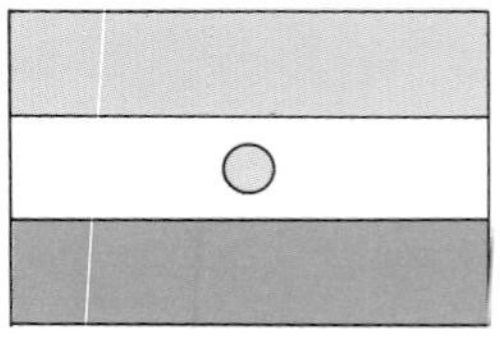

NIGER 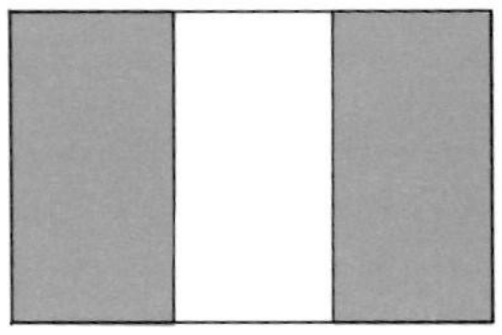 **NIGERIA**  **SÃO TOMÉ E PRÍNCIPE**  **SENEGAL**

SIERRA LEONE  **TOGO**  **TUNISIA**  **BURKINA FASO (UPPER VOLTA)**

GUINEA
CITIES and TOWNS

Beyla ... C7
Boffa ... B6
Boké ... B6
Conakry (cap.)* 525,671 ... B7
Dabola ... C7
Dalaba ... B6
Dinguiraye ... C6
Dubréka ... B7
Faranah ... C6
Forécariah ... B7
Fria ... B6
Gaoual ... B6
Guéckédou ... B7
Kamsar ... B6
Kankan 85,310 ... C6
Kérouané ... C7
Kissidougou ... C6
Koundara 6,000 ... B6
Kouroussa ... C6
Labé 79,670 ... B6
Macenta ... C7
Mali ... B6
N'Zérékoré 23,000 ... C7
Siguiri ... C6
Télimélé 12,000 ... B6
Tougué ... C6
Victoria ... B6

OTHER FEATURES

Bafing (riv.) ... B6
Bakoy (riv.) ... C6
Futa Jallon (reg.) ... B6
Los (isls.) ... B7
Milo (riv.) ... C7
Moa (riv.) ... B7
Niger (riv.) ... C7
Nimba (lag.) ... C7
Verga (cape) ... B6

GUINEA-BISSAU
CITIES and TOWNS

Bissau (cap.) 109,486 ... A6
Bolama 9,133 ... A6
Bubaô 6,706 ... B6
Bubaque 8,441 ... A6
Cacheu 15,194 ... A6

OTHER FEATURES

Bijagós (isls.) ... A6

IVORY COAST
CITIES and TOWNS

Abengourou 31,239 ... D7
Abidjan 685,828 ... D7
Aboisso 14,272 ... D7
Agbonville 27,192 ... D7
Bouaflé 15,917 ... D7
Bouaké 173,248 ... D7
Bouna 5,787 ... D7
Boundiali 9,869 ... C7
Dabakala 3,272 ... D7
Daloa 23,870 ... C7
Dalaa 60,958 ... C7
Danané 19,872 ... C7
Dimbokro 30,986 ... D7
Divo 37,896 ... C7
Ferkéssédougou 25,307 ... C7
Fresco 1,865 ... C7
Gagnoa 42,362 ... C7
Grand-Bassam 25,808 ... D7
Grand-Lahou 4,070 ... C7
Guiglo 10,441 ... C7
Issia 11,143 ... C7
Katiola 21,559 ... C7
Kong 2,551 ... C7
Korhogo 47,657 ... C7
Man 50,315 ... C7
Mankono 6,570 ... C7
Odienné 13,864 ... C6
Port-Bouet 72,616 ... D7
San Pedro 27,616 ... C8
Sassandra 9,404 ... C7
Séguéla 12,587 ... C7
Sinfra 16,399 ... C7
Tabou 7,255 ... C8
Touba 5,256 ... C6
Toumodi 12,983 ... C7
Yamoussoukro (cap.) 50,000 ... C7

OTHER FEATURES

Aby (lag.) ... D8
Bagoé (riv.) ... C6
Bandama (riv.) ... C7
Baoulé (riv.) ... C6
Black Volta (riv.) ... D6
Cavally (riv.) ... C7
Comoé (riv.) ... D7
Ebrié (lag.) ... D8
Guinea (gulf) ... D8
Ivory Coast (reg.) ... C8
Kossou, Lac de (lake) ... C7
Nimba (lag.) ... C7
Sassandra (riv.) ... C7

LIBERIA
CITIES and TOWNS

Buchanan 23,999 ... B7
Gbarnga 6,896 ... C7
Grand Cess ... C8
Greenville 8,462 ... C8
Harbel 11,445 ... B7
Nioro 11,617 ... C8
Harper 10,627 ... C8
Kolahun ... B7
Marshall ... B7
Monrovia (cap.) 166,507 ... B7
Plahn ... B7
River Cess 2,041 ... C7
Robertsport 2,562 ... B7
Sasstown ... C8

Tapeta 3,927 ... C7
Tchien 6,094 ... C7
Tubmanburg 14,089 ... B7

OTHER FEATURES

Bong (range) ... B7
Cavalla (riv.) ... C7
Cestos (riv.) ... C7
Grain Coast (reg.) ... B8
Kru Coast (reg.) ... C8
Mano (riv.) ... B7
Mount (cape) ... B7
Nimba (lag.) ... C7
Palmas (cape) ... C8
Roberts Field Int'l Airport ... C7

MALI
CITIES and TOWNS

Anéfis ... E5
Ansongo 3,485 ... E5
Araouane ... D5
Bafoulabé 2,163 ... B6
Bamako (cap.) 404,022 ... C6
Bamba ... D5
Banamba 6,776 ... C6
Bandiagara 8,920 ... D6
Bankass 3,229 ... D6
Bou Djebeha ... D5
Bougouni 17,246 ... C6
Bourem 4,538 ... D5
Diola 4,953 ... C6
Dire 8,941 ... D5
Djenné 10,251 ... C6
Douentza 6,746 ... D6
Gao 30,714 ... E5
Goundam 10,262 ... D5
Gourma-Rharous 4,671 ... D5
Hombori ... D5
Kadiolo 3,991 ... C6
Kangaba 3,184 ... C6
Kati 24,991 ... C6
Kayes 44,736 ... B6
Ké-Macina 5,426 ... C6
Kéniéba 4,510 ... B6
Kerchoual ... E5
Kidal 3,308 ... E5
Kita 17,538 ... B6
Kolokani 8,923 ... C6
Kolondiéba 5,882 ... C6
Koulikoro 16,376 ... C6
Kourouba ... B6
Koutiala 27,497 ... C6
Mabrouk ... D5
Ménaka 3,693 ... E5
Mopti 53,885 ... C6
Nampala ... C5
Nara 6,091 ... C5
Niafunké 6,399 ... C5
Niono 12,290 ... C6
Nioro 11,617 ... C5
San 22,962 ... C6
Satadougou ... B6
Ségou 64,890 ... C6
Sikasso 47,030 ... C6
Sokolo ... C6
Taoudenni ... D4
Ténenkou 4,708 ... C6
Tessalit ... E4

Timbuktu (Tombouctou) 20,483 ... D5
Toukoto ... C6
Yantolila 3,809 ... C6
Yelimané 1,481 ... C5
Yorosso 2,390 ... C6

OTHER FEATURES

Achourat (well) ... D4
Adrar des Iforas (plat.) ... E5
Asselar (well) ... E5
Azaouad (reg.) ... D5
Azaouak (dry riv.) ... E5
Bafing (riv.) ... B6
Bagoé (riv.) ... C6
Bakoy (riv.) ... B6
Bani (riv.) ... C6
Baoulé (dry riv.) ... C6
Baoulé (riv.) ... C6
Bir Ounane (well) ... D4
Chech, Erg (des.) ... D4
Debo (lake) ... D5
El Mraïti (well) ... D5
Faguibine (lake) ... D5
Falémé (riv.) ... B6
Haricha Hamada (des.) ... D4
Hombori (mts.) ... D5
In Dagouber (well) ... D4
Macina (depr.) ... C6
Niger (riv.) ... D5
Oum el Asel (well) ... D4
Sahara (des.) ... D4
Sekkane, Erg (des.) ... D4
Sudan (reg.) ... B5
Tadjnout Hagguerete (well) ... D4
Terhazza (ruins) ... D4
Tilemsi (valley) ... E5
Toufourine (well) ... D4

MAURITANIA
CITIES and TOWNS

Aioun el Atrous ... C5
Akjoujt 8,044 ... B5
Akreïjit ... C5
Aleg 6,415 ... B5
Atar 16,326 ... B4
Bassikounou ... C5
Bir Mogreïn ... B3
Boutilimit 7,261 ... B5
Bogué 8,056 ... B5
Chinguetti ... B4
Fderik (Fort-Gouraud) 2,160 ... B4
Kaédi 20,848 ... B5
Kankossa ... B5
Kiffa 10,629 ... B5
Maghama ... B5
M'Bout ... B5
Médardra ... A5
Néma 8,232 ... C5
Nouakchott (cap.) 134,986 ... A5
Nouadhibou 21,961 ... A4
Ouadane ... B4
Oualata ... C5
Oujeft ... B4
Rosso 16,466 ... A5
Sélibaby 5,994 ... B5
Tamchakett ... B5

Tamsagout ... C4
Tazadit ... B4
Tichitt ... C5
Tidjikja 7,870 ... B5
Timbédra 5,317 ... C5
Zouîrât 17,474 ... B4

OTHER FEATURES

Adafer (reg.) ... B5
Adrar (reg.) ... B4
Affolé (reg.) ... B5
Agueraktem (well) ... C3
Aïn ben Tili (well) ... C3
Arguin (bay) ... A4
Assaba (reg.) ... B5
Atoui, Wadi (dry riv.) ... B4
Ben Guerdane (well) ... D4
Bir el Khzaim (well) ... D4
Blanc (cape) ... A4
Brakna (reg.) ... B5
Chegga (well) ... C4
Dhout, El (des.) ... C4
El Mrayer (well) ... C4
El Mrelti (well) ... D5
Gorgol (reg.) ... B5
Hodh (reg.) ... C5
Iguidi, Erg (des.) ... C3
Inchiri (reg.) ... A5
Koumbi Saleh (ruins) ... C5
Lévrier (bay) ... A4
Makteïr (des.) ... B4
Meraia (reg.) ... C5
Mirik (Timiris) (cape) ... A5
Ouarane (reg.) ... B4
Sahara (des.) ... C4
Senegal (riv.) ... B5
Tagant (reg.) ... B5
Tidra (isl.) ... A4
Timiris (cape) ... A5
Touila (well) ... C3
Trarza (reg.) ... A5

MOROCCO
CITIES and TOWNS

Agadir 61,192 ... C2
Al Hoceima 18,686 ... D1
Asilah 14,074 ... C1
Azemmour 17,182 ... C2
Azrou 20,756 ... C2
Beni Mellal 53,825 ... C2
Berguent 3,356 ... D2
Bou Arfa ... D2
Bou Izakarn 2,342 ... C3
Boujad 18,838 ... C2
Casablanca 1,505,373 ... C2
Chechaouene 15,362 ... D1
Dar-el-Beïda
  (Casablanca) 1,506,373 ... C2
El Jadida 55,501 ... C2
El Kelaa des Srarhna 17,163 ... C2
Erfoud 5,400 ... D2
Er Rachidia 16,*75 ... D2
Essaouira 30,061 ... B2
Fédala (Mohammedia) 70,392 ... C2
Fès (Fez) 325,327 ... D2
Figuig 13,660 ... D2
Goulmima 4,056 ... C2
Inezgane 11,495 ... C2

Agriculture, Industry and Resources

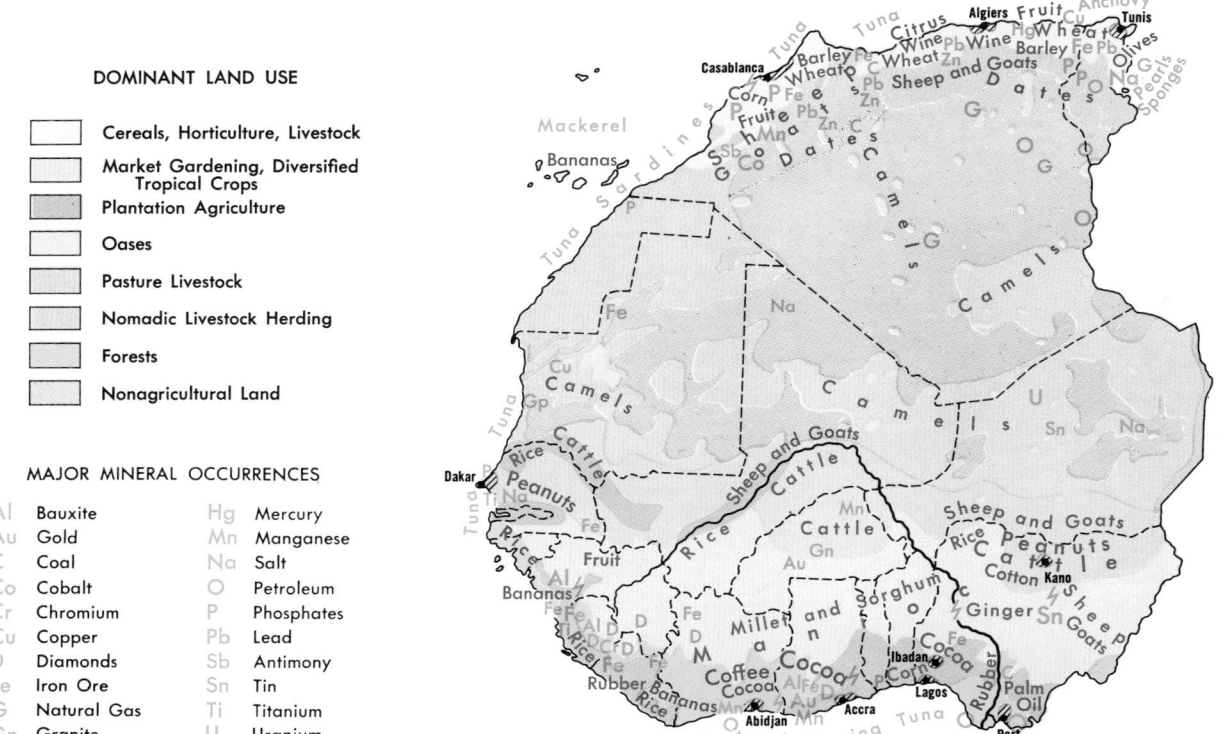

DOMINANT LAND USE

- Cereals, Horticulture, Livestock
- Market Gardening, Diversified Tropical Crops
- Plantation Agriculture
- Oases
- Pasture Livestock
- Nomadic Livestock Herding
- Forests
- Nonagricultural Land

MAJOR MINERAL OCCURRENCES

Al	Bauxite	Hg	Mercury
Au	Gold	Mn	Manganese
C	Coal	Na	Salt
Co	Cobalt	O	Petroleum
Cr	Chromium	P	Phosphates
Cu	Copper	Pb	Lead
D	Diamonds	Sb	Antimony
Fe	Iron Ore	Sn	Tin
G	Natural Gas	Ti	Titanium
Gn	Granite	U	Uranium
Gp	Gypsum	Zn	Zinc

⚡ Water Power
Major Industrial Areas

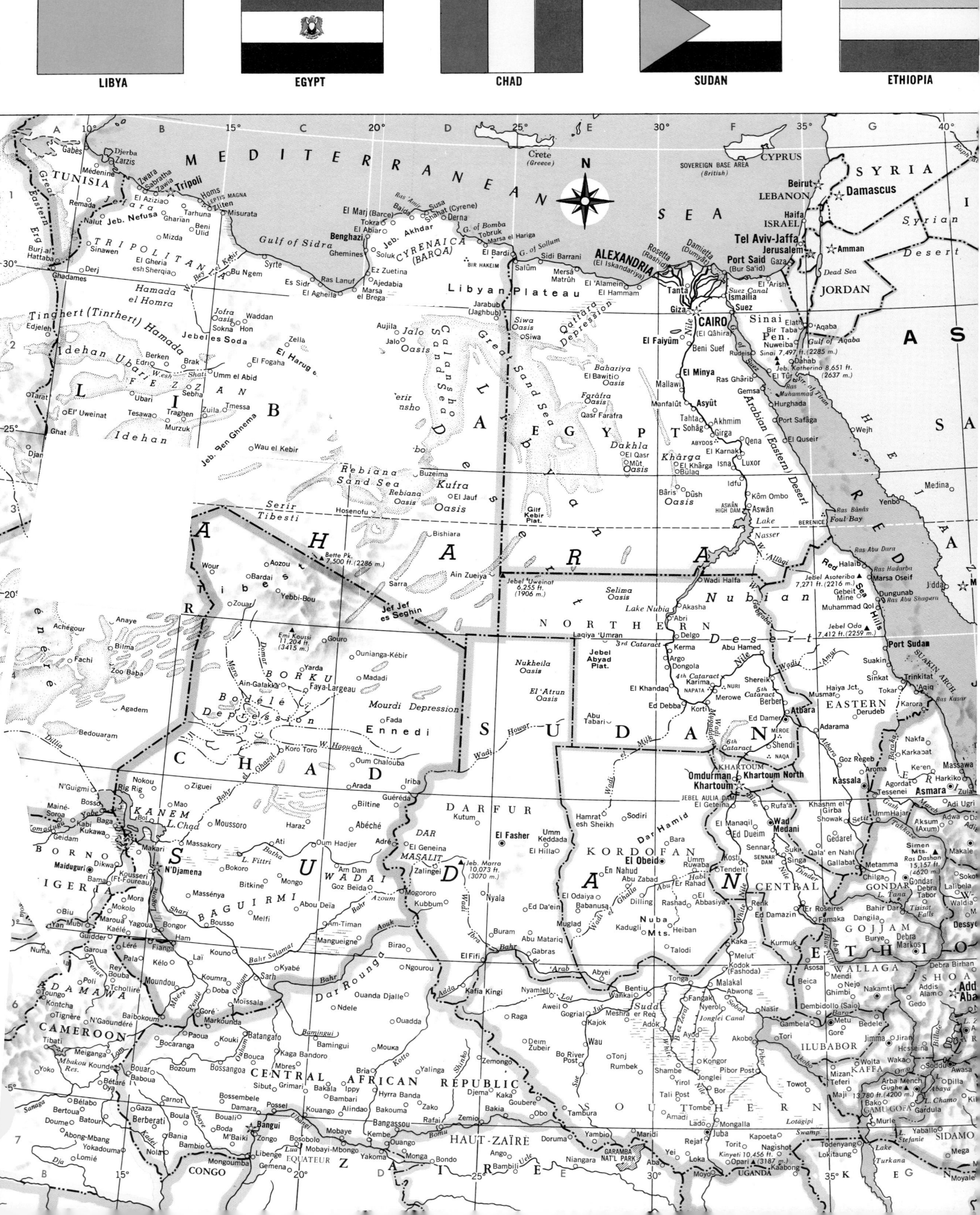

LIBYA **EGYPT** **CHAD** **SUDAN** **ETHIOPIA**

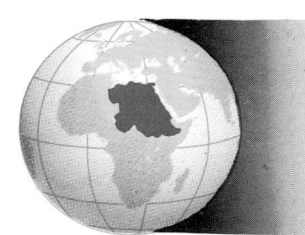

DJIBOUTI

LIBYA

AREA 679,358 sq. mi. (1,759,537 sq. km.)
POPULATION 2,856,000
CAPITAL Tripoli
LARGEST CITY Tripoli
HIGHEST POINT Bette Pk. 7,500 ft. (2,286 m.)
MONETARY UNIT Libyan dinar
MAJOR LANGUAGES Arabic, Berber
MAJOR RELIGION Islam

EGYPT

AREA 386,659 sq. mi. (1,001,447 sq. km.)
POPULATION 41,572,000
CAPITAL Cairo
LARGEST CITY Cairo
HIGHEST POINT Jeb. Katherina 8,651 ft. (2,637 m.)
MONETARY UNIT Egyptian pound
MAJOR LANGUAGE Arabic
MAJOR RELIGIONS Islam, Coptic Christianity

CHAD

AREA 495,752 sq. mi. (1,283,998 sq. km.)
POPULATION 4,309,000
CAPITAL N'Djamena
LARGEST CITY N'Djamena
HIGHEST POINT Emi Koussi 11,204 ft. (3,415 m.)
MONETARY UNIT CFA franc
MAJOR LANGUAGES Arabic, Bagirmi, French, Sara, Massa, Moudang
MAJOR RELIGIONS Islam, tribal religions

SUDAN

AREA 967,494 sq. mi. (2,505,809 sq. km.)
POPULATION 18,691,000
CAPITAL Khartoum
LARGEST CITY Khartoum
HIGHEST POINT Jeb. Marra 10,073 ft. (3,070 m.)
MONETARY UNIT Sudanese pound
MAJOR LANGUAGES Arabic, Dinka, Nubian, Beja, Nuer
MAJOR RELIGIONS Islam, tribal religions

ETHIOPIA

AREA 471,776 sq. mi. (1,221,900 sq. km.)
POPULATION 31,065,000
CAPITAL Addis Ababa
LARGEST CITY Addis Ababa
HIGHEST POINT Ras Dashan 15,157 ft. (4,620 m.)
MONETARY UNIT birr
MAJOR LANGUAGES Amharic, Gallinya, Tigrinya, Somali, Sidamo, Arabic, Ge'ez
MAJOR RELIGIONS Coptic Christianity, Islam

DJIBOUTI

AREA 8,880 sq. mi. (23,000 sq. km.)
POPULATION 386,000
CAPITAL Djibouti
LARGEST CITY Djibouti
HIGHEST POINT Moussa Ali 6,768 ft. (2,063 m.)
MONETARY UNIT Djibouti franc
MAJOR LANGUAGES Arabic, Somali, Afar, French
MAJOR RELIGIONS Islam, Roman Catholicism

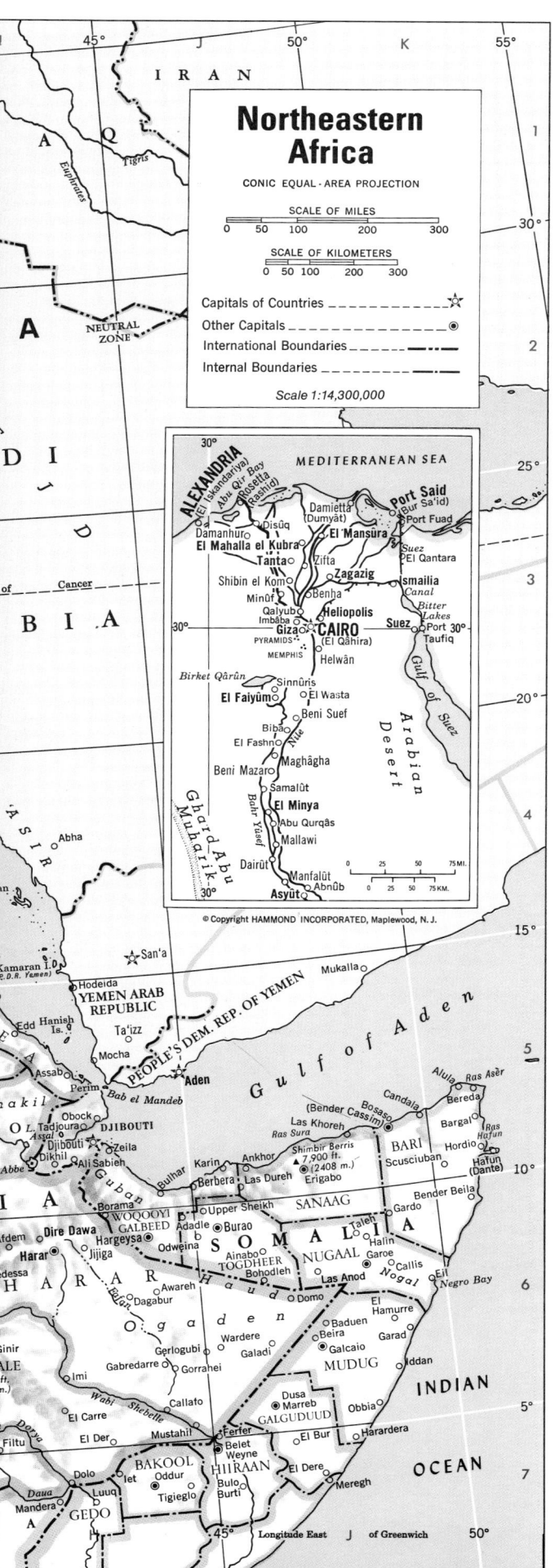

CHAD

CITIES and TOWNS

Abéché 28,100	D5
Abou Dela	D5
Adré	D5
Ain-Galakka	C4
Am-Dam	D5
Am-Timan 4,200	D5
Arada	D4
Ati 7,500	C5
Baïbokoum 5,500	C6
Bardai	C3
Biltine 3,900	D5
Bitkine 5,000	C5
Bokoro 6,500	C5
Bol 2,500	B5
Bongor 14,300	C5
Bousso 4,500	C5
Doba 13,300	C6
Fada	D4
Faya-Largeau 6,800	C3
Fianga 10,000	C6
Goré	C6
Gouro	C3
Guéréda	D5
Ham	C5

Haraz	C5
Iriba	D4
Kélo 16,800	C6
Koro Toro	C4
Koumra 17,000	C6
Kouno	C5
Kyabé 5,000	C6
Lal 10,400	C6
Léré	B6
Madadi	D4
Mangueigne	C6
Mao 4,900	C5
Massakory	C5
Massénya	C5
Melfi	C5
Mogororo	C5
Moïssala 5,100	C6
Mongo 8,300	C5
Moundou 39,600	C6
Moussoro 7,700	C5
N'Djamena (cap.) 179,000	C5
Nokou	B5
Oum Chalouba	D4
Oum Hadjer 5,600	D5
Ounianga-Kébir	D3
Pala 13,200	C6
Rig Rig	B5
Sarh 43,700	C6
Wour	C3
Yarda	C4

Yebbi-Bou	C3
Ziguei	C5
Zouar	C3

OTHER FEATURES

Azoum, Bahr	D5
Baguirmi (reg.)	C5
Bahr el Ghazal (dry riv.)	C5
Batha (riv.)	C5
Bodélé (depr.)	C4
Borku 72	C4
Chad (lake)	C4
Domar (dry riv.)	C4
Emi Koussi (mt.)	C4
Ennedi (plat.)	D4
Fittri (lake)	C5
Haouach, Wadi (dry riv.)	C4
Jef Jef es Seghin (plat.)	D3
Kanem (reg.)	C5
Logone (riv.)	C6
Maro (dry riv.)	C4
Mbéré (riv.)	C6
Mourdi (depr.)	D4
Ouham (riv.)	C6
Pende (riv.)	C6
Sahara (des.)	C3
Salamat, Bahr (riv.)	C6
Sara (riv.)	C6
Shari (riv.)	C5

Sudan (reg.)	C5
Tibesti (mts.)	C3
Wadai (reg.)	D5

DJIBOUTI

CITIES and TOWNS

Ali Sabieh	H5
Dikhil	H5
Djibouti (cap.) 96,000	H5
Obock	H5
Tadjoura	H5

OTHER FEATURES

Abbe (lake)	H5
Aden (gulf)	J5
Bab el Mandeb (str.)	H5

EGYPT

CITIES and TOWNS

Abnûb 39,343	J4
Abu Qurqâs	J4
Akhmim 53,234	F2
Alexandria 2,318,655	J2

(continued on following page)

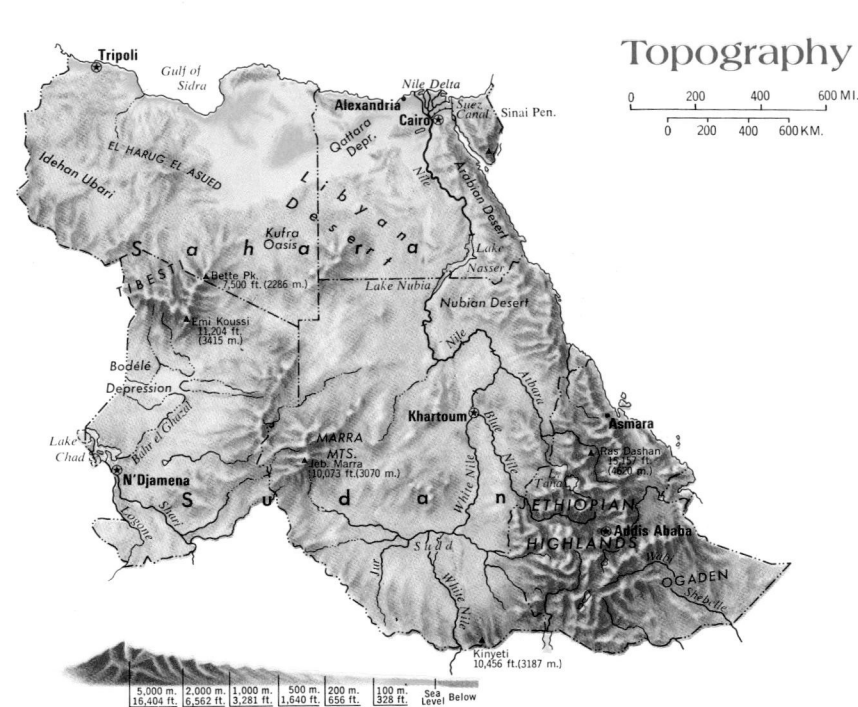

Topography

(continued on following page)

Aswân 144,377	F3
Asyût 213,983	J4
Bâris	F3
Benha 88,992	J3
Beni Mazar 39,373	J4
Beni Suef 118,148	J3
Biba 33,074	J4
Bûlaq	F2
Bur Sai'd (Port Said) 262,620	K2
Cairo (cap.) 5,084,463	J3
Dahab	F2
Dairût 31,624	J4
Damanhur 188,927	J3
Damietta 93,546	J3
Disûq 58,650	J3
Dumyât (Damietta) 93,546	J3
Dûsh	F3
El A'lamein	E1
El A'rish	F1
El Bawiti	E2
El Faiyûm 167,081	J3
El Fashn 33,506	J4
El Hammam 6,588	E1
El Iskandariya (Alexandria) 2,318,655	J2
El Karnak	F2
El Khârga 26,375	F2
El Mahalla el Kubra 292,853	J3
El Mansûra 257,866	K3
El Minya 146,423	J4
El Qâhira (Cairo) (cap.) 5,084,463	J3
El Qantara 919	K3
El Qasr	E2
El Quseir 12,297	F2
El Tûr	F2
El Wasta 17,659	J3
Gemsa	F2
Girga 51,110	F2
Giza 1,246,713	J3
Heliopolis	J3
Helwân	J3
Hurghada	F2
Idfu 34,858	F3
Imbâba	J3
Ismailia 145,978	K3
Isna 34,186	F2
Karnak (El Karnak)	F2
Kôm Ombo 44,531	F3
Luxor 92,748	F2
Maghâgha 40,802	J4
Mallawi 74,256	J4
Manfalût 41,126	J4
Mersá Matrûh 27,857	E1
Minûf 55,131	J3
Mût 8,032	E2
Nuweiba	F2
Port Fuad	K3
Port Safâga	F2
Port Said 262,620	K2
Port Taufiq	K3
Qalyub 62,739	J3
Qasr Farâfra	E2
Qena 94,013	F2
Ras Ghârib	F2
Rashid (Rosetta) 42,962	J2
Rudeis	F2
Salûm 4,161	E1
Samalût 48,146	J4
Shibin el Kom 102,844	J3
Sidi Barrani 1,574	E1
Sinnûris 42,022	J3
Siwa 4,999	E2
Sohâg 101,758	F2
Suez 194,001	K3
Tahta 45,242	F2
Tanta 284,636	J3
Zagazig 202,637	K3
Zifta 50,410	J3

OTHER FEATURES

Abu Qir (bay)	J2
Abydos (ruins)	F2
A'llaqi, Wadi (dry riv.)	F3
A'qaba (gulf)	G2
Arabian (des.)	F2
Aswân (dam)	F3
Aswân High (dam)	F3
Bahariya (oasis)	E2
Bahr Yusef (stream)	J4
Bânâs, Ras (cape)	G3
Berenice (ruins)	F3
Birket Qârûn (lake)	J3
Bir Taba (well)	F2
Bitter (lkes)	K3
Dakhla (oasis)	E2
Eastern (Arabian) (des.)	F2
El Sollum (gulf)	E1
Farâfra (oasis)	E2
Foul (bay)	G3
Ghard Abu Muharik (des.)	J4
Gilf Kebir (plat.)	E3
Great Sand Sea (des.)	D2
Katherina, Jebel (mt.)	F2
Khârga (oasis)	F2
Libyan (des.)	E2
Libyan (plat.)	E1
Mediterranean (sea)	E1
Memphis (ruins)	J3
Muhammad, Ras (cape)	F2
Nasser (lake)	F3
Nile (riv.)	F2
Pyramids (ruins)	J3
Qattara (depr.)	E2
Red (sea)	G3
Sahara (des.)	E3
Sinai (mt.)	F2
Sinai (pen.)	F2
Siwa (oasis)	E2
Suez (canal)	K3
Suez (gulf)	F2
Tiran (str.)	F2
U'weinat, Jebel (mt.)	E3

ETHIOPIA

PROVINCES

Arusi 852,900	G6
Bale 707,800	H6
Eritrea 1,947,600	G4
Gamu-Gofa 698,800	G6
Gojjam 1,750,100	G5
Gondar 1,355,800	G5
Harar 3,359,200	H6
Ilubabor 688,800	F6
Kaffa 1,693,000	G6
Shoa 5,369,500	G6
Sidamo 2,479,800	G7
Tigre 1,828,900	H5
Wallaga 1,269,100	G6
Wallo 2,459,900	H5

CITIES and TOWNS

Addis Ababa (cap.) 1,196,300	G6
Addis Alam 5,500	G6
Adigrat 9,400	G5
Adi Ugri 12,800	G5
Adwa 16,400	G5
Afdem	H6
Agordat	G4
Aksum 12,800	G5
Ankober	H6
Arba Mench 7,660	G6
Asmara 393,800	G4
Asosa	F5
Assab 16,000	H5
Asselle 19,390	G6
Awareh	H6
Awasa 16,790	G6
Awash	H6
Axum (Aksum) 12,800	G5
Bahir Dar 25,100	G5
Burye	G5
Callafo	H6
Chilga	G5
Dagabur	H6
Dallol	G5
Dangila	G5
Debra Birhan 16,700	G6
Debra Markos 30,260	G5
Debra Tabor 8,700	G5
Dembidollo 7,600	F6
Dessye 49,750	G5
Dilla 13,800	G6
Dire Dawa 63,700	H6
Dolo	H7
Domo	J6
Edd	H5
El Carre	H6
El Der	H6
Filtu	H6
Gabredarre	H6
Galadi	J6
Gambela	F6
Gardula 5,800	G6
Gedo	G6
Gerlogubi	H6
Ghimbi 8,300	G6
Ginir	H6
Goba 13,500	H6
Gondar 38,600	G5
Gore 8,500	G6
Gorrahei	H6
Harar 48,440	H6
Harkiko	G4
Hosseina 8,500	G6
Imi	H6
Jijiga 8,000	H6
Jimma 47,360	G6
Jiran	G6
Karkabat	G4
Keren	G4
Kibre Mengist 8,300	G6
Lalibela	G5
Magdala	G5
Maji	G6
Makale 30,780	G5
Massawa 19,800	G4
Mega	G7
Mendi	G6
Mersa Fatma	H5
Metamma	G5
Metu	G6
Miesso	H6
Mizan Teferi	G6
Moyale	G7
Murle	G6
Mustahil	H6
Nakamti 18,310	G6
Nakfa	G4
Nazret 42,900	G6
Negelli 8,800	G6
Nejo	G6
Saio (Dembidollo) 7,600	F6
Soddu 11,900	G6
Sokota	G5
Tessenei	G4
Thio	H5
Tori	F6
Umm Hajar	G5
Waka	G6
Waldia 9,600	G5
Wardere	J6
Wolta	G6
Yaballo	G6
Zula	G4

OTHER FEATURES

Abay (riv.)	G5
Abaya (lake)	G6
Akobo (riv.)	F6
Assale (lake)	H5
Atbara (riv.)	G4
Awash (riv.)	H5
Bale (mt.)	G6
Baraka (riv.)	G4
Baro (riv.)	G6
Billate (riv.)	G6
Blue Nile (Abay) (riv.)	G5
Buri (pen.)	H4
Chamo (lake)	G6
Dahlak (arch.)	H4
Dahlak (isl.)	H4
Danakil (reg.)	H5
Dawa (riv.)	G7
Fafan (riv.)	H6
Ganale Dorya (riv.)	H6
Gash Mareb (riv.)	G5
Gughe (mt.)	G6
Haud (reg.)	J6
Kasar, Ras (cape)	G4
Ogaden (reg.)	H6
Omo (riv.)	G6
Ras Dashan (mt.)	G5
Red (sea)	H4
Rudolf (Turkana) (lake)	G7
Simen (mts.)	G5
Stefanie (lake)	G7
Takkaze (riv.)	G5
Tana (lake)	G5
Tisisat (fall)	G5
Turkana (lake)	G7
Wabi (riv.)	H6
Wabi Shebelle (riv.)	H6
Zwai (lake)	G6

LIBYA

CITIES and TOWNS

Ajedabia○ 53,170	D1
Aujila○ 6,695	D2
Baida○ 59,765	D1
Barce (El Marj)○ 55,444	D1
Benghazi (cap.)○ 286,943	C1
Beni Ulid○ 19,113	B1
Berken	B2
Brak○ 12,507	B2
Bu Ngem	C1
Cyrene (Shahat)○ 17,157	D1
Derj○ 2,152	B1
Derna○ 44,145	D1
Edri	B2
El Abiar○ 17,685	D1
El Agheila	C1
El Azizia○ 34,077	B1
El Bardi○ 4,330	D1
El Barkat○ 2,139	B3
El Fogaha	C2
El Gatrun	B3
El Gezira	D2
El Jauf○ 6,481	D3
El Marj○ 55,444	D1
El' Uweinat	B2
Es Sidr○ 706	C1
Ez Zuetina○ 7,256	D1
Ghadames○ 6,172	A2
Gharîan○ 65,224	B1
Ghat○ 6,924	B3
Ghemines○ 4,313	C1
Homs○ 66,890	B1
Hon○ 2,766	C2
Jaghbub (Jarabub)○ 1,436	D2
Jalo	D2
Jarabub○ 1,436	D2
Marada○ 3,201	C2
Marsa el Brega○ 2,618	D1
Marsa el Hariga○ 5,043	D1
Mekili	D1
Misurata○ 102,439	C1
Mizda○ 11,472	B1
Murzuk○ 22,185	B2
Nalut○ 23,535	B1
Ras Lanuf○ 1,990	C1
Sabrathaa○ 30,836	B1
Sebha○ 35,879	B2
Shahat○ 17,157	D1
Sinawen○ 1,549	B1
Sokna○ 3,757	C2
Soluk○ 6,501	D1
Susa	D1
Syrte○ 22,797	C1
Tarhuna○ 52,657	B1
Tejerri	B3
Tesawa	B2
Tmessa	C2
Tobruk○ 58,384	D1
Tokra○ 10,714	D1
Traghen	B2
Tripoli (cap.)○ 550,438	B1
Ubari○ 19,132	B2
Umm el Abid	C2
Waddan○ 5,347	C2
Wau el Kebir	C2
Zawia○ 72,092	B1
Zella○ 4,835	C2
Zliten○ 58,981	C1
Zuila	C2
Zwara○ 15,078	B1

OTHER FEATURES

Ain Zueiya (well)	D3
Akhdar, Jebel (mts.)	D1
A'mir, Ras (cape)	D1
Barqa (Cyrenaica) (reg.)	D1
Ben Ghnema, Jebel (mts.)	C2
Bette (peak)	C3
Bey el Kebir, Wadi (dry riv.)	B1
Bir Hakeim (ruins)	D1
Bishiara (well)	D3
Bomba (gulf)	D1
Buzeima (well)	D3
Calansho Sand Sea (des.)	D2
Calansho, Serir (des.)	D2
Cyrenaica (reg.)	D1
Fezzan (reg.)	B2
Great Sand Sea (des.)	D2
Harug el Asued, El (mts.)	C2
Homra, Hamada el (des.)	B2
Hosenofu (well)	D3
Idehan Ubari (des.)	B2
Idehan Murzuk (des.)	B2
Jalo (oasis)	D2
Jefara (reg.)	B1
Jef Jef es Seghin (plat.)	D3
Jofra (oasis)	C2
Kufra (oasis)	D3
Leptis Magna (ruins)	B1
Libyan (des.)	D2
Libyan (plat.)	D1
Mediterranean (sea)	C1
Nefusa, Jebel (mts.)	B1
Rebiana○ (oasis)	D3
Rebiana Sand Sea (des.)	D3
Sahara (des.)	C3
Sarra (well)	D3
Shati, Wadi esh (dry riv.)	B2
Sidra (gulf)	C1
Soda, Jebel es (mts.)	C2
Tazerbo○ (oasis)	D2
Tibesti, Serir (des.)	C3
Tinghert Hamada (Tinrhert) (des.)	B2
Tripolitania (reg.)	B1
U'weinat, Jebel (mt.)	E3
Zelten, Jebel (mts.)	D2

SUDAN

PROVINCES

Central	F5
Darfur	D5
Eastern	G4
Khartoum	F4
Kordofan	E5
Northern	E3
Southern	E6

CITIES and TOWNS

A'bri	F3
Abu Hamed	F4
Abu Matariq	E5
Abu Zabad	E5
Abwong	F6
Abyei	E6
Adarama	G4
Adok	F6
Akasha	F3
Akobo	F6
Amadi	F6
A'qiq	G4
Argo	F4
Aroma	G4
Atbara 66,000	F4
Aweil	E6
Ayod	F6
Babanusa	E5
Bara	F5
Bentiu	E6
Berber	F4
Bor	F6
Bo River Post	E6
Buram	E5
Damazin (Ed Damazin) 12,000	F5
Deim Zubeir	E6
Delgo	F3
Derudeb	G4
Dilling	E5
Dongola 6,000	F4
Dungunab	G3
Ed Dae'in	E5
Ed Damer 17,000	F4
Ed Damazin 12,000	F5
Ed Debba	F4
Ed Dueim 27,000	F5
El Abbasiya	F5
El Fasher 52,000	E5
El Fifi	D5
El Geneina 33,000	D5
El Geteina	F5
El Hilla	E5
El Khandaq	E4
El Managil	F5
El Obeid 90,000	E5
El Odaiya	E5
En Nahud 23,000	E5
Er Rahad	F5
Er Roseires	F5
Famaka	F5
Fangak	F6
Fashoda (Kodok)	F6
Gabras	E5
Gallabat	G5
Gebeit Mine	G3
Gedaref 92,000	G5
Gogrial	E6
Goz Regeb	G4
Haiya Junction	G4
Halaib	G3
Heiban	F5
Jonglei	F6
Juba 57,000	F7
Kadugli 18,000	E5
Kafia Kingi	D6
Kajok	E6
Kaka	F5
Kapoeta	F7
Karima	F4
Karora	G4
Kassala 99,000	G4
Kerma	F4
Khartoum (cap.) 334,000	F4
Khartoum North 151,000	F4
Khashm el Girba	G5
Kodok	F6
Kongor	F6
Korti	F4
Kosti 57,000	F5
Kubbum	D5
Kurmuk	F5
Kutum	D5
Lado	F6
Loka	F7
Malakal 35,000	F6
Maridi	E7
Marsa Oseif	G3
Melut	F5
Merowe	F4
Meshra er Req	E6
Mongalla	F6
Muglad	E5
Muhammad Qol	G3
Musmar	G4
Nagishot	F7
Nasir	F6
Nimule	F7
Nyala 60,000	E5
Nyamlell	E6
Nyerol	F6
Omdurman 299,000	F4
Opari	F7
Pibor Post	F6
Port Sudan 133,000	G4
Qalae'n Nahl	F5
Raga	E6
Rashad	F5
Rejaf	F7
Renk	F5
Rufaa'	F5
Rumbek 17,000	E6
Sennar	F5
Shambe	F6
Shendi	F4
Shereik	F4
Showak	G5
Singa	F5
Sinkat	G4
Sodiri	E5
Suakin	G4
Suki	F5
Tali Post	F6
Talodi	F5
Tambura	E6
Tendelti	F5
Tokar	G4
Tombe	F6
Tonga	F6
Tonj	E6
Torit	F7
Towot	F6
Trinkitat	G4
Umm Keddada	E5
Umm Ruwaba	F5
Wadi Halfa	F3
Wad Medani 107,000	F5
Wankai	E6
Wau 53,000	E6
Yambio 7,000	E7
Yei	F7
Yirol	F6
Zalingei	D5

OTHER FEATURES

Abu Dara, Ras (cape)	G3
Abu Habl, Wadi (dry riv.)	F5
Abu Shagara, Ras (cape)	G3
Abu Tabari (well)	E4
Adda (riv.)	D6
Akobo (riv.)	F6
A'mur, Wadi (dry riv.)	G4
Asoteriba, Jebel (mt.)	G3
Atbara (riv.)	G4
Bahr Azoum (riv.)	D5
Bahr el A'rab (riv.)	E6
Bahr ez Zeraf (riv.)	F6
Baraka (riv.)	G4
Blue Nile (riv.)	F5
Dar Hamid (reg.)	F5
Dar Masalit (reg.)	D5
Dinder (riv.)	F5
El A'trun (oasis)	E4
Fifth Cataract	F4
Fourth Cataract	F4
Gabgaba, Wadi (dry riv.)	F3
Gezira, El (reg.)	F5
Ghalla, Wadi el (dry riv.)	E5
Hadarba, Ras (cape)	G3
Howar, Wadi (dry riv.)	E4
Ibra, Wadi (dry riv.)	D5
Jebel Abyad (plat.)	E4
Jebel Aulia (dam)	F4
Jur (riv.)	E6
Kasar, Ras (cape)	G4
Kinyeti (mt.)	F7
Laqiya U'mran (well)	E3
Libyan (des.)	E3
Lol (dry riv.)	E6
Lotagipi Swamp (plain)	F6
Marra, Jebel (mt.)	D5
Meroe (ruins)	F4
Milk, Wadi el (dry riv.)	E4
Muqaddam, Wadi (dry riv.)	F4
Napata (ruins)	F4
Naqa (ruins)	F4
Nile (riv.)	F4
Nuba (mts.)	E5
Nubia (lake)	F3
Nubian (des.)	F3
Nukheila (oasis)	E4
Nuri (ruins)	F4
Oda, Jebel (mt.)	G3
Pibor (riv.)	F6
Red (sea)	G3
Sahara (des.)	E3
Second Cataract	F3
Selima (oasis)	E3
Sennar (dam)	F5
Setit (riv.)	G5
Sixth Cataract	F4
Sobat (riv.)	F6
Suakin (arch.)	G4
Sudan (reg.)	E5
Sudd (swamp)	F6
Sue (riv.)	E6
Third Cataract	E4
U'weinat, Jebel (mt.)	E3
White Nile (riv.)	F5

○Population of sub-distr ct or division.

Agriculture, Industry and Resources

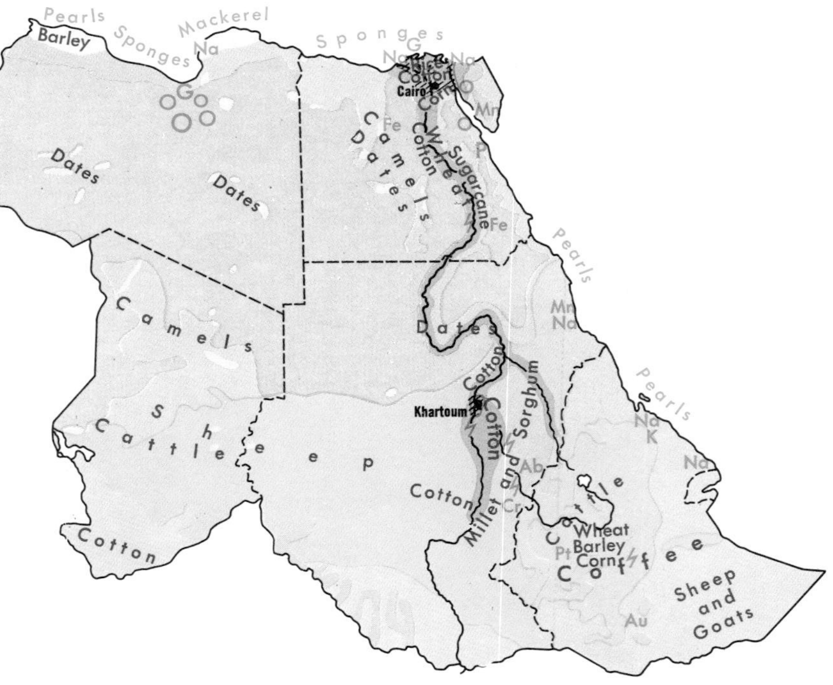

DOMINANT LAND USE

- Cereals, Horticulture, Livestock
- Cash Crops, Mixed Cereals
- Cotton, Cereals
- Market Gardening, Diversified Tropical Crops
- Plantation Agriculture
- Oases
- Pasture Livestock
- Nomadic Livestock Herding
- Forests
- Nonagricultural Land

MAJOR MINERAL OCCURRENCES

Ab	Asbestos	Mn	Manganese
Au	Gold	Na	Salt
Cr	Chromium	O	Petroleum
Fe	Iron Ore	P	Phosphates
G	Natural Gas	Pt	Platinum
K	Potash		

Water Power

Major Industrial Areas

ANGOLA

AREA 481,351 sq. mi. (1,246,700 sq. km.)
POPULATION 7,078,000
CAPITAL Luanda
LARGEST CITY Luanda
HIGHEST POINT Mt. Moco 8,593 ft. (2,620 m.)
MONETARY UNIT kwanza
MAJOR LANGUAGES Mbundu, Kongo, Lunda, Portuguese
MAJOR RELIGIONS Tribal religions, Roman Catholicism

BURUNDI

AREA 10,747 sq. mi. (27,835 sq. km.)
POPULATION 4,021,910
CAPITAL Bujumbura
LARGEST CITY Bujumbura
HIGHEST POINT 8,858 ft. (2,700 m.)
MONETARY UNIT Burundi franc
MAJOR LANGUAGES Kirundi, French, Swahili
MAJOR RELIGIONS Tribal religions, Roman Catholicism, Islam

CAMEROON

AREA 183,568 sq. mi. (475,441 sq. km.)
POPULATION 8,503,000
CAPITAL Yaoundé
LARGEST CITY Douala
HIGHEST POINT Cameroon 13,350 ft. (4,069 m.)
MONETARY UNIT CFA franc
MAJOR LANGUAGES Fang, Bamileke, Fulani, Duala, French, English
MAJOR RELIGIONS Tribal religions, Christianity, Islam

CENTRAL AFRICAN REP.

AREA 242,000 sq. mi. (626,780 sq. km.)
POPULATION 2,284,000
CAPITAL Bangui
LARGEST CITY Bangui
HIGHEST POINT Gao 4,659 ft. (1,420 m.)
MONETARY UNIT CFA franc
MAJOR LANGUAGES Banda, Gbaya, Sangho, French
MAJOR RELIGIONS Tribal religions, Christianity, Islam

CONGO

AREA 132,046 sq. mi. (342,000 sq. km.)
POPULATION 1,537,000
CAPITAL Brazzaville
LARGEST CITY Brazzaville
HIGHEST POINT Leketi Mts. 3,412 ft. (1,040 m.)
MONETARY UNIT CFA franc
MAJOR LANGUAGES Kikongo, Bateke, Lingala, French
MAJOR RELIGIONS Christianity, tribal religions, Islam

EQUATORIAL GUINEA

AREA 10,831 sq. mi. (28,052 sq. km.)
POPULATION 244,000
CAPITAL Malabo
LARGEST CITY Malabo
HIGHEST POINT 9,868 ft. (3,008 m.)
MONETARY UNIT ekuele
MAJOR LANGUAGES Fang, Bubi, Spanish
MAJOR RELIGIONS Tribal religions, Christianity

GABON

AREA 103,346 sq. mi. (267,666 sq. km.)
POPULATION 551,000
CAPITAL Libreville
LARGEST CITY Libreville
HIGHEST POINT Ibounzi 5,165 ft. (1,574 m.)
MONETARY UNIT CFA franc
MAJOR LANGUAGES Fang and other Bantu languages, French
MAJOR RELIGIONS Tribal religions, Christianity, Islam

KENYA

AREA 224,960 sq. mi. (582,646 sq. km.)
POPULATION 15,327,061
CAPITAL Nairobi
LARGEST CITY Nairobi
HIGHEST POINT Kenya 17,058 ft. (5,199 m.)
MONETARY UNIT Kenya shilling
MAJOR LANGUAGES Kikuyu, Luo, Kavirondo, Kamba, Swahili, English
MAJOR RELIGIONS Tribal religions, Christianity, Hinduism, Islam

MALAWI

AREA 45,747 sq. mi. (118,485 sq. km.)
POPULATION 5,968,000
CAPITAL Lilongwe
LARGEST CITY Blantyre
HIGHEST POINT Mulanje 9,843 ft. (3,000 m.)
MONETARY UNIT Malawi kwacha
MAJOR LANGUAGES Chichewa, Yao, English, Nyanja, Tumbuka, Tonga, Ngoni
MAJOR RELIGIONS Tribal religions, Islam, Christianity

RWANDA

AREA 10,169 sq. mi. (26,337 sq. km.)
POPULATION 4,819,317
CAPITAL Kigali
LARGEST CITY Kigali
HIGHEST POINT Karisimbi 14,780 ft. (4,505 m.)
MONETARY UNIT Rwanda franc
MAJOR LANGUAGES Kinyarwanda, French, Swahili
MAJOR RELIGIONS Tribal religions, Roman Catholicism, Islam

SOMALIA

AREA 246,200 sq. mi. (637,658 sq. km.)
POPULATION 3,645,000
CAPITAL Mogadishu
LARGEST CITY Mogadishu
HIGHEST POINT Surud Ad 7,900 ft. (2,408 m.)
MONETARY UNIT Somali shilling
MAJOR LANGUAGES Somali, Arabic, Italian, English
MAJOR RELIGION Islam

TANZANIA

AREA 363,708 sq. mi. (942,003 sq. km.)
POPULATION 17,527,560
CAPITAL Dar es Salaam
LARGEST CITY Dar es Salaam
HIGHEST POINT Kilimanjaro 19,340 ft. (5,895 m.)
MONETARY UNIT Tanzanian shilling
MAJOR LANGUAGES Nyamwezi-Sukuma, Swahili, English
MAJOR RELIGIONS Tribal religions, Christianity, Islam

UGANDA

AREA 91,076 sq. mi. (235,887 sq. km.)
POPULATION 12,630,076
CAPITAL Kampala
LARGEST CITY Kampala
HIGHEST POINT Margherita 16,795 ft. (5,119 m.)
MONETARY UNIT Ugandan shilling
MAJOR LANGUAGES Luganda, Acholi, Teso, Nyoro, Soga, Nkole, English, Swahili
MAJOR RELIGIONS Tribal religions, Christianity, Islam

ZAIRE

AREA 905,063 sq. mi. (2,344,113 sq. km.)
POPULATION 28,291,000
CAPITAL Kinshasa
LARGEST CITY Kinshasa
HIGHEST POINT Margherita 16,795 ft. (5,119 m.)
MONETARY UNIT zaire
MAJOR LANGUAGES Tshiluba, Mongo, Kikongo, Kingwana, Zande, Lingala, Swahili, French
MAJOR RELIGIONS Tribal religions, Christianity

ZAMBIA

AREA 290,586 sq. mi. (752,618 sq. km.)
POPULATION 5,679,808
CAPITAL Lusaka
LARGEST CITY Lusaka
HIGHEST POINT Sunzu 6,782 ft. (2,067 m.)
MONETARY UNIT Zambian kwacha
MAJOR LANGUAGES Bemba, Tonga, Lozi, Luvale, Nyanja, English
MAJOR RELIGIONS Tribal religions

ANGOLA

BURUNDI

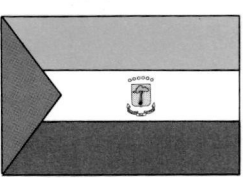
CAMEROON

CENTRAL AFRICAN REP.

CONGO

EQUATORIAL GUINEA

GABON

KENYA

MALAWI

RWANDA

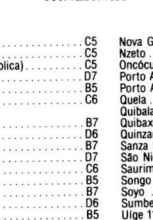
SOMALIA

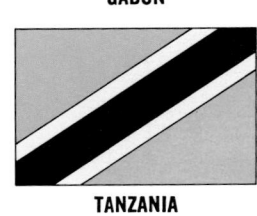
TANZANIA

UGANDA

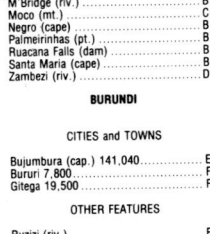
ZAIRE

ZAMBIA

ANGOLA

DISTRICTS

go 68,885	B5
guela 474,897	B6
550,337	C6
inda 80,857	B5
ndo Cubango 112,073	C7
anza-Norte 298,062	B5
anza-Sul 458,592	C6
ene 147,394	C7
ambo 837,627	C6
la 497,470	B6
nda 491,704	B5
da Norte 210,000	C6
da Sul 98,000	D5
ange 558,630	D6
ico 213,119	D6
mbe 53,058	B7
e 386,037	B5
e 41,766	B5

CITIES and TOWNS

a Chicapa	C6
o Cuale	B5
briz	C6
ulo	C6
a dos Tigres	B7
a Farta	B6
ombo	B6
a Vista	B5
mbe	B5
guela 40,996	B6
la 8,894	B5
inda 21,124	B6
onda	C5
uso	C7
undo	C6
ulo	B6
uquembe	C6
nacupa 5,740	D5
nanongue	D5
mbulo	C6
gamba	C7
pelongo	D7
penda-Camulemba	C5
ssai	D6
ssamba	D5
ete	B5
umbela	B6
angola	B6
kito	D6
ombo	D6
a 2,784	B7
ange	B7
nguar	C6
pindo	B7
tado	B7
tembo	C6
tembo	C5
ango	C5
chi	C6
lo	C5
to-Cuanavale	C7
ma	B6
mba	C6
ico	D7
mbe Grande	B6
ndo	B5
gares	C6
te República	C5

Foz do Cunene	B7
Gabela 6,930	B6
Gambos	B6
Golungo Alto	B5
Huambo 61,885	C6
Iona	B7
Kalandula	C5
Kassinga	C7
Kuito 18,941	C6
Lobito 59,528	B6
Lóvua	C5
Longa	C6
Luacano	D5
Luachimo	D5
Luana	C6
Lucira	B6
Luiana	D7
Lukapa	D5
Macondo	D6

Malange 31,599	C5
Maquela do Zombo	C5
Massango (Forte República)	D7
Mavinga	D7
Mbanza Congo 4,002	B5
Menongue 3,023	C6
Moçâmedes (Namibe) 12,076	B7
Muconda	D6
Mucope	B7
Mucusso	D7
Munhango	D6
Muxima	B5
Namibe 12,076	B7
Nana Candundo	D6
Ndalatando 7,342	B5
N'gage 2,548	C5
Ngiva	B7
Nganga (Sumbe) 7,911	B6
Nharêa	C6
Nóqui	B5

Nova Gaia	C5
Nzeto	B5
Oncócua	B7
Porto Alexandre 8,235	B7
Porto Amboim	B6
Quela	C5
Quibala	B6
Quibaxe	B5
Quinzau	B5
Sanza Pombo	C5
São Nicolau	B6
Saurimo 12,901	D5
Songo	C5
Soyo	B5
Sumbe 7,911	B6
Uige 11,972	C5
Vila Guilherme Capelo	B5
Xangongo	B7

OTHER FEATURES

Bero (riv.)	B7
Chicapa (riv.)	D5
Chiumbe (riv.)	D5
Congo (riv.)	C4
Coporolo (riv.)	B6
Cuando (riv.)	C7
Cuango (riv.)	C5
Cuanza (riv.)	C5
Cubango (riv.)	C7
Cuito (riv.)	C7
Cunene (riv.)	B7
Cunene (dam)	B7
Cuvo (riv.)	B6
Kasai (riv.)	D5
Loange (riv.)	C5
Loge (riv.)	B5
Lungwebungu (riv.)	D6
Matala (dam)	B6

M'Bridge (riv.)	B5
Moco (mt.)	C6
Negro (cape)	B5
Palmeirinhas (pt.)	B5
Ruacana Falls (dam)	B7
Santa Maria (cape)	B6
Zambezi (riv.)	D6

BURUNDI

CITIES and TOWNS

Bujumbura (cap.) 141,040	E4
Bururi 7,800	F4
Gitega 19,500	F4

OTHER FEATURES

Ruzizi (riv.)	E4
Tanganyika (lake)	E5

CAMEROON

CITIES and TOWNS

Abong-Mbang 6,000	B3
Ambam 4,000	B3
Bafia 12,000	B2
Bali	A2
Bafoussam 62,239	B2
Bamenda 48,111	B2
Banyo	B2
Batouri 7,000	B3
Bélabo	B3
Bengbis	B3
Bertoua 10,000	B3
Bétaré-Oya	B2
Bonabéri	A3

(continued on following page)

Kounde ... B2
Mbaïki 12,346 ... C3
Mbres 2,622 ... C2
Mobaye 4,220 ... D3
Mouka ... D2
Ndele 5,858 ... D2
Ngourou ... E2
Nola 6,703 ... C3
Obo 3,978 ... E2
Ouadda 3,009 ... D2
Paoua 7,052 ... C2
Possel ... C2
Sibut 13,341 ... C2
Zako ... D2
Zemio 3,259 ... D2

Zemongo ... E2

OTHER FEATURES

Bamingui (riv.) ... C2
Bomu (riv.) ... D3
Dar Rounga (reg.) ... D2
Gao (mt.) ... C2
Kadeï (riv.) ... C3
Kotto (riv.) ... D2
Mbéré (riv.) ... B2
Ouham (riv.) ... C2
Pendé (riv.) ... C2
Sanga (riv.) ... C3

Sara (riv.) ... C2
Shari (riv.) ... C2
Shinko (riv.) ... D2
Ubangi (riv.) ... C3

CONGO

CITIES and TOWNS

Abala ... C4
Boko ... C4
Brazzaville (cap.) 298,967 ... B4
Boundji ... C4
Djambala ... B4

Dongou ... C3
Enyellé ... C3
Epéna ... C3
Etoumbi ... B3
Ewo ... B4
Gamboma ... C4
Ikelemba ... C3
Impfondo ... C3
Kellé ... B4
Kibangou ... B4
Kindama ... C4
Kinkala ... B4
Komono ... B4
Loubomo 29,600 ... B4
Loudima ... B4

Madingo-Kayes ... B4
Madingou ... B4
Makoua ... C3
Mbinda ... B4
Mindouli ... B4
Mossaka ... C4
Mossendjo ... B4
M'Pouya ... C4
Nkayi 30,600 ... B4
Okoyo ... C3
Ouesso ... C3
Owando ... C4
Oyo ... C4
Pangala ... B4
Pointe-Noire 141,700 ... B4
Sembé ... B3
Sibiti ... B4
Souanké ... B3
Zanaga ... B4

Tchibanga 14,001 ... B4

OTHER FEATURES

Crystal (mts.) ... B4
Ibounzi (mt.) ... B4
Ivindo (riv.) ... B3
Lopez (cape) ... A4
N'Dogo (lag.) ... B4
N'Gounié (riv.) ... B4
N'Komi (lag.) ... A4
Ogooué (riv.) ... A4
Onangué (lake) ... A4
Pongara (pt.) ... A3

KENYA

PROVINCES

Central 1,675,647 ... G4
Coast 944,082 ... G4
Eastern 1,907,301 ... G4
Nairobi 509,286 ... G4
North-Eastern 245,757 ... G3
Nyanza 2,122,045 ... G4
Rift Valley 2,210,289 ... G3
Western 1,328,298 ... G3

CITIES and TOWNS

Buna ... G3
Bunyala ... F3
Bura ... H4
Eldoret 18,196 ... G4
El Wak ... H3
Embu 3,928 ... G4
Fort Hall 4,750 ... G4
Galole 3,609 ... G4
Garba Tula ... G4
Garissa ... G4
Garsen ... G4
Gilgil 4,178 ... G4
Isiolo 8,201 ... G4
Kakamega 6,244 ... F3
Kaningo ... G4
Kericho 10,144 ... G4
Kiambu 2,776 ... G4
Kilifi 2,662 ... H4
Kipini ... H4
Kisii 6,080 ... F4
Kisumu 32,431 ... F3
Kitale 11,573 ... G3
Kitui 3,071 ... G4
Kolbio ... H4
Konza ... G4
Laisamis ... G3
Lamu 7,403 ... H4
Lodwar ... G3
Lokitaung 4,090 ... G3
Loigorien ... G4
Machakos 6,312 ... G4
Magadi ... G4
Malindi 10,757 ... H4
Mambrui ... H4
Maralal 3,878 ... G3
Marsabit 6,635 ... G3
Meru 4,475 ... G4
Moyale ... G3
Mombasa 247,073 ... G4
Nairobi (cap.) 509,286 ... G4
Naivasha 6,920 ... G4
Nakuru 47,151 ... G4
Namanga ... G4
Nanyuki 11,624 ... G4
Narok 2,608 ... G4
North Horr ... G3
South Horr ... G3
Taveta ... G4
Thika 18,387 ... G4
Thomson's Falls 7,602 ... G3
Todenyang ... G3
Tsavo ... G4
Vanga ... G4
Voi 5,313 ... G4
Wajir ... H3
Wamba 2,650 ... G3

EQUATORIAL GUINEA

TERRITORIES

Bioko 78,000 ... A3
Rio Muni 203,000 ... B3

CITIES and TOWNS

Bata 27,024 ... B3
Luba 19,933 ... A3
Malabo (cap.) 37,237 ... A3
Mbini 14,503 ... A3

OTHER FEATURES

Biafra (bight) ... A3
Bioko (isl.) ... A3
Corisco (isl.) ... A3
Elobey (isls.) ... A3
Fernando Po (Bioko) (isl.) ... A3

GABON

CITIES and TOWNS

Banda ... B4
Bitam 5,936 ... B3
Booué ... B3
Chinchoua ... B3
Cocobeach ... B3
Fougamou ... B4
Franceville 9,345 ... B4
Iguéla ... A4
Kango ... B3
Kemboma ... B3
Koula-Moutou 8,032 ... B4
Lalara ... B3
Lambaréné 17,770 ... B4
Lastoursville ... B4
Lekoni ... B4
Libreville (cap.) 105,080 ... A3
Makokou 5,005 ... B3
Mayumba ... A4
M'Bigou ... B4
Médouneu ... B3
Mekambo ... B3
Mimongo ... B4
Minvoul ... B3
Mitzic ... B3
Moanda 10,709 ... B4
Mouila 15,016 ... B4
Mounana 4,000 ... B4
N'Dendé ... B4
N'Djolé ... B4
Nyanga ... A4
Okondja ... B4
Owendo ... A4
Oyem 12,455 ... B3
Port-Gentil 48,190 ... A4
Setté-Cama ... A4

OTHER FEATURES

Daua (riv.) ... H3
Elgon (mt.) ... F3
Formosa (bay) ... H4
Galana (riv.) ... G4
Gedi (ruins) ... G4
Kavirondo (gulf) ... F4
Kenya (mt.) ... G4
Lak Dera (dry riv.) ... H3
Lorian (swamp) ... H3
Natron (lake) ... G4
Nyiru (mt.) ... G3
Patta (isl.) ... H4

Rudolf (Turkana) (lake) ... G3
Tana (riv.) ... G4
Tsavo Nat'l Park ... G4
Turkana (lake) ... G3
Victoria (lake) ... F4
Winam (bay) ... F4

MALAWI

CITIES and TOWNS

Bandawe ... F6
Blantyre 222,153 ... F7
Chilumba ... F6
Chipoka ... F7
Chiromo ... F7
Chitipa 3,079 ... F6
Dedza 5,448 ... F6
Karonga 11,873 ... F6
Kasungu ... F6
Lilongwe (cap.) 102,924 ... F6
Livingstonia ... F6
Mangochi 3,341 ... G6
Mzimba 4,962 ... F6
Nkhata Bay 4,024 ... F6
Nkhotakota 10,312 ... F6
Nsanje 6,091 ... G7
Rumphi 3,998 ... F6
Salima 4,646 ... F6
Thyolo 4,186 ... F7
Zomba 21,000 ... G7

OTHER FEATURES

Chilwa (lake) ... G7
Malawi (Nyasa) (lake) ... F6
Mulanje (mts.) ... G7
Nyasa (lake) ... F6
Shire (riv.) ... G7

RWANDA

CITIES and TOWNS

Butare 21,691 ... E4
Cyangugu 7,042 ... E4
Gisenyi 12,436 ... E4
Kigali (cap.) 117,749 ... F4
Nyabisindu 8,587 ... F4

OTHER FEATURES

Kagera Nat'l Park ... F4
Karisimbi (mt.) ... E4
Kivu (lake) ... E4
Ruzizi (riv.) ... E4
Virunga (range) ... E4

SOMALIA

PROVINCES

Bakool 100,000 ... H3
Bari 155,000 ... J1
Bay 302,000 ... H3
Galguduud 182,000 ... J2
Gedo 212,000 ... H3
Hiiraan 147,000 ... J3
Jubbada Hoose 246,000 ... H3
Mogadiscio 371,000 ... J3
Mudug 215,000 ... J2
Nugaal 85,000 ... J2
Sanaag 146,000 ... J1
Shabeellaha Dhexe 237,000 ... J3
Shabeellaha Hoose 398,000 ... H3
Togdheer 258,000 ... J2
Woqooyi Galbeed 440,000 ... H1

CITIES and TOWNS

Adadle ... H2
Afgoi ... J3
Afmadu 2,580 ... H3
Alula ... K1
Ankhor ... J1
Audegle ... J2
Baduen ... J2
Barawa (Brava) ... H3
Bardera ... H3
Bargal ... K1
Baydhabo 14,962 ... H3
Belet Weyne 11,426 ... J3
Bender Beila ... K2
Bender Cassim (Bosaso) ... J1
Berbera 12,219 ... J1
Bereda ... K1
Bircao ... H4
Bohodleh ... J2
Borama 3,244 ... H1

(continued on following page)

Topography

0   200   400   600 MI.
0 200 400 600 KM.

Central Africa

CYLINDRICAL EQUAL-AREA PROJECTION

SCALE OF MILES
0 50 100   200   300
SCALE OF KILOMETERS
0 50 100   200   300

Capitals of Countries ____ ☆
Other Capitals ____ ◉
International Boundaries ____
Internal Boundaries ____

Scale 1:13,800,000

© Copyright HAMMOND INCORPORATED, Maplewood, N.J.

Bosaso J1
Brava 6,167 H3
Bulhar H1
Bulo Burti 5,247 J3
Bur Acaba H3
Burao 12,617 J2
Callis J2
Candala J1
Chisimayu 17,872 H4
Chiambone H4
Coriole 4,341 H3
Dante (Hafun) K1
Dif H3
Dinsor H3
Dusa Marreb J2
Eil J2
El Athale (Itala) J3
El Bur J3
El Dere J3
El Hamurre J2
Erigabo 4,279 J1
Ferfer J2
Galcaio J2
Garad J2
Garbahaarrey H3
Gardo J2
Garoe J2
Giohar 13,156 J3
Gobwen H4
Hafun K1
Halin J2
Harardera J3
Hargeysa 40,254 H2
Hordio K1
Iddan J2
Iet H3
Itala J3
Jamama 5,408 H3
Jilib 3,232 H3
Karin J1
Kismayu (Chisimayu) 17,872 H4
Las Dureh J1
Luuq H3
Margherita (Jamama) H3
Marka (Merka) 17,708 H3
Mogadishu (cap.) 371,000 J3
Muqdisho (Mogadishu) (cap.) 371,000 J3
Obbia J2
Oddur H3
Taleh J2
Uanle Uen H3
Upper Sheikh J2
Villabruzzi (Johar) J3
Zeila 1,226 H1

OTHER FEATURES

Aden (gulf) J1
Asèr, Ras (cape) K1
Giuba (riv.) H3
Guban (reg.) H1
Hafun, Ras (cape) K1
Haud (plat.) J2
Lak Dera (dry riv.) H3
Negro (bay) J2
Nogal (reg.) J2
Shimbir Berris (mt.) J1
Sura, Ras (cape) J1
Surud Ad (mt.) J1
Webi Shabelle (riv.) H3

TANZANIA

REGIONS

Arusha 928,478 G4
Dar es Salaam 851,222 G5
Dodoma 971,921 G5
Iringa 922,801 G5
Kagera 1,009,379 F4
Kigoma 648,950 F4
Kilimanjaro 902,394 G4
Lindi 527,902 G5
Mara 723,295 F4
Mbeya 1,080,241 F5
Morogoro 939,190 G5
Mtwara 771,726 G5
Mwanza 1,443,418 F4
Pemba 205,870 H5
Pwani (Coast) 516,949 G5
Rukwa 451,897 F5
Ruvuma 564,113 G6
Shinyanga 1,323,482 F4
Singida 614,030 F5
Tabora 818,049 F5
Tanga 1,088,592 G5
Zanzibar Mjini 143,616 G5
Zanzibar Shambani North 77,424 G5
Zanzibar Shambani South 52,325 G5

CITIES and TOWNS

Arusha 55,281 G4
Babati G4
Bagamoyo 5,112 G5
Bukoba 20,430 F4
Chake Chake 4,862 H5
Dar es Salaam (cap.) 757,346 G5
Dodoma 45,703 G5
Geita 3,066 F4
Handeni G5
Ifakara G5
Iringa 57,182 G5
Itigi F5
Kahama 3,211 F4
Kaliua F5
Kanga G5
Karema F5
Kasanga F5
Kasulu F4
Kibara F4
Kibaya G5
Kibondo F4
Kigoma-Ujiji 50,044 E4
Kilosa 4,458 G5
Kilwa Kivinje 2,790 G5
Kilwa Masoko G5
Kinyangiri G4
Kipili F5
Kisiju G5
Kitunda F5
Kizimkazi G5
Kondoa 4,514 G4
Kongwa G5
Korogwe 6,675 G5
Lindi 27,308 G5
Liuli F6
Liwale G5
Longido G4
Mahenge G5
Makumbako G5
Manda F6
Manyoni G5
Masasi G6
Mbamba Bay G6
Mbeya 76,606 F5
Mbulu G4
Mchinga H5
Mohoro G5
Mombo G4
Morogoro 61,890 G5
Moshi 52,223 G4
Mpanda F5
Mtakuja F5
Mtwara-Mikindani 48,510 H6
Murongo F4
Musoma 32,658 F4
Muwale F5
Mwadui 7,383 F4
Mwanza 110,611 F4
Mwaya F5
Mwesi F5
Nachingwea 3,751 G6
Newala G6
Ngara F4
Njombe F5
Pangani 2,955 G5
Rungwa F5
Sadani G5
Same G4
Sekenke F4
Shinyanga 21,703 F4
Singida 29,252 F4
Songea 17,954 G6
Sumbawanga 28,586 F5
Tabora 67,392 F5
Tanga 103,409 G4
Tukuyu 4,089 F5
Tunduru G6
Urambo F4
Utete G5
Uvinza F5
Wete 8,469 G4
Zanzibar 110,669 G5

OTHER FEATURES

Eyasi (lake) F4
Great Ruaha (riv.) G5
Juani (isl.) G5
Kalambo (falls) F5
Kanzi (cape) G5
Kilimanjaro (mt.) G4
Kilombero (riv.) G5
Mafia (isl.) H5
Manyara (lake) G4
Masai (steppe) G4
Mbarangandu (riv.) G5
Mbemkuru (riv.) G5
Meru (mt.) G4
Mikumi Nat'l Park G5
Natron (lake) G4
Ngorongoro (crater) F4
Njombe (riv.) F5
Nyasa (lake) F6
Olduvai Gorge (canyon) G4
Pangani (riv.) G4
Pemba (isl.) H5
Rovuma (riv.) G6
Rufiji (riv.) G5
Ruaha Nat'l Park F5
Rukwa (lake) F5
Rungwa (riv.) F5
Rungwe (mt.) F5
Serengeti Nat'l Park F4
Tanganyika (lake) E5
Tarangire Nat'l Park G4
Victoria (lake) F4
Wami (riv.) G5
Wembere (riv.) F4
Zanzibar (isl.) G5

UGANDA

CITIES and TOWNS

Arua 10,837 F3
Atura F3
Butiaba 261 F3
Entebbe 21,096 F4
Fort Portal 7,947 F3
Gulu 18,170 F3
Hoima 2,339 F3
Jinja 52,509 F3
Kabale 8,234 E4
Kampala (cap.) 478,895 F3
Kasese 7,213 F3
Kilembe F3
Kitgum 3,242 F3
Lira 7,340 F3
Masaka 12,987 F4
Masindi 2,100 F3
Mbale 23,544 F3
Mbarara 16,078 F4
Moroto 5,488 F3
Moyo 2,656 F3
Mubende 6,004 F3
Rhino Camp 198 F3
Soroti 8,130 F3
Tororo 15,977 F3

OTHER FEATURES

Albert (Mobuto Sese Seko) (lake) F3
Edward (lake) E4
Elgon (mt.) F3
George (lake) F4
Kabalega (falls) F3
Kagalega Nat'l Park F3
Kidepo Nat'l Park F3
Kioga (lake) F3
Margherita (mt.) E3
Mobuto Sese Seko (lake) F3
Owen Falls (dam) F3
Ruwenzori (range) E3
Sese (isls.) F4
Victoria (lake) F4
Virunga (range) E4
Virunga Nat'l Park F4

ZAIRE

PRUVINCES

Bandundu 2,600,556 C4
Bas-Zaïre 1,504,361 B4
Equateur 2,431,812 D3
Haut-Zaïre 3,356,419 E3
Kasai-Occidental 2,433,861 D4
Kasai-Oriental 1,872,231 D5
Kinshasa 1,323,039 C4
Kivu 3,361,883 E4
Shaba 2,753,714 E5

CITIES and TOWNS

Aba 7,600 F3
Abumombazi D3
Aketi 17,200 D3
Andoma E3
Ango E3
Ankoro E5
Bagata C4
Balangala D3
Bambesa E3
Bambili E3
Banalia E3
Banana B5
Bandundu 74,467 C4
Baraka E4
Basankusu C3
Basoko 9,100 D3
Basongo D4
Befale D3
Bena-Dibele D4
Beni 22,800 E3
Bikoro C4
Boende 12,800 D4
Bokote D4
Bokungu D4
Bolobo 10,300 C4
Bolomba 7,200 C3
Boma 61,100 B5
Bomboma C3
Bomongo C3
Bondo 10,000 D3
Bongandanga 12,900 D3
Bosobolo 11,100 D3
Budjala C3
Bukama E5
Bukavu 134,861 E4
Bulungu 16,300 C4
Bumba 34,700 D3
Bunia 28,800 E3
Bunkeya 5,100 E6
Businga 11,000 D3
Busu-Djanoa D3
Buta 19,800 D3
Butembo 27,800 E3
Dekese D4
Demba 22,000 D5
Dibaya 11,400 D5
Dibaya-Lubue 7,900 C4
Dilolo 14,000 D6
Dimbelenge D5
Djolu D3
Djugu F3
Dongo C3
Doruma E3
Dungu 9,100 E3
Etoile E6
Faradje 10,400 E3
Feshi C5
Fizi E4
Gandajika 60,100 D5
Gemena 37,300 D3
Goma 48,600 E4
Gungu C5
Idiofa C4
Ikela D4
Ilebo 32,200 D4
Imese C3
Ingende C4
Inongo 14,800 C4
Irumu 9,300 E3
Isangi D3
Isiro 49,300 E3
Kabalo 22,600 E5
Kabambare E4
Kabare 12,600 E4
Kabinda 60,500 D5
Kabongo 6,500 E5
Kahemba C5
Kalehe E4
Kalemie 62,300 E5
Kalima 27,500 E4
Kama 17,700 E4
Kambove 18,900 E6
Kamina 56,300 D5
Kampene 14,600 E4
Kananga 428,960 D5
Kanda-Kanda D5
Kaniama D5
Kapanga D5
Kasaji D6
Kasangulu 11,900 C4
Kasenga E6
Kasenyi E3
Kasese E4
Kasongo 37,800 E4
Kasongo-Lunda C5
Katako-Kombe D4
Katenga E5
Kazumba D5
Kenge 17,500 C4
Kiambi E5
Kibombo E4
Kikwit 111,960 C5
Kilembe C5
Kilwa E5
Kilo E3
Kinda D5
Kiniama E6
Kinshasa (cap.) 1,323,039 C4
Kipushi 32,900 E6
Kiri C4
Kirundu E4
Kisangani 229,596 E3
Kole, Kasai-Oriental D4
Kole, Haut-Zaïre E3
Kolwezi 81,600 E6
Komba D3
Kongolo 14,800 E5
Kungu C3
Kutu 10,000 C4
Kwamouth C4
Libenge 12,500 C3
Likasi, Panda- 146,394 E6
Likati D3
Lisala D3
Lodja 20,300 D4
Lokolama D4
Lomela D4
Loto D4
Luashi D6
Lubefu D4
Lubero E4
Lubudi 6,000 E5
Lubumbashi 318,000 E6
Lubutu E4
Luebo 21,800 D5
Luishia E6
Luiza D5
Lukolela, Equateur C4
Lukolela, Kasai-Oriental D5
Lukula 9,400 B5
Luozi 7,000 B5
Lusambo 13,100 D4
Makanza C3
Malemba-Nkulu E5
Mambasa 7,400 E3
Mangai 15,200 C4
Manono 44,500 E5
Masi-Manimba 6,300 C4
Masisi E4
Matadi 110,436 B5
Mbandaka 107,910 C3
Mbanza-Ngungu 55,800 C5
Mbuji-Mayi 256,154 D5
Mitwaba E5
Moanda 6,400 B5
Mobayi-Mbongo D3
Moliro E5
Monga D3
Monkoto D4
Mulongo E5
Mungbere E3
Mushie 13,700 C4
Mutshatsha D6
Muyumba E5
Mwadingusha E6
Mwanza E5
Mweka 24,900 D4
Mwene-Ditu 71,200 D5
Mwenga E4
Niangara 9,200 E3
Niemba E5
Nyunzu 11,300 E5
Opala D4
Oshwe C4
Panda-Likasi 146,394 E6
Pangi E4
Penge D5
Poko E3
Popokabaka C5
Port Kindu 42,800 E4
Punia E4
Pweto E5
Rutshuru E4
Sakania E6
Sampwe E5
Sandoa D5
Seke-Banza B5
Sentery 24,300 E5
Shabunda 6,900 E4
Songololo 4,600 B5
Tenke E6
Titule E3
Tshela 10,700 B4
Tshikapa 38,900 D5
Tshofa D5
Ubundu 6,300 E4
Uvira 15,900 E4
Virunga 21,900 E5
Waka D3
Walikale E4
Wamba 11,500 E3
Watsa 21,300 E3
Yahuma D3
Yakoma D3
Yangambi 22,600 D3
Zongo C3

OTHER FEATURES

Albert (Mobuto Sese Seko) (lake) F3
Aruwimi (riv.) E3
Bomu (riv.) D3
Boyoma (Stanley) (falls) D3
Chicapa (riv.) D5
Congo (riv.) C4
Edward (lake) E4
Elila (riv.) E4
Fimi (riv.) C4
Garamba Nat'l Park E3
Giri (riv.) C3
Itimbiri (riv.) D3
Ituri (for.) E3
Karisimbi (mt.) E4
Kasai (riv.) C4
Kivu (lake) E4
Kwa (riv.) C4
Kwango (riv.) C5
Kwilu (riv.) C5
Lindi (riv.) E3
Livingstone (falls) B5
Loange (riv.) C5
Lokoro (riv.) C4
Lomami (riv.) D4
Lomela (riv.) D4
Lowa (riv.) E4
Lua (riv.) C3
Lualaba (riv.) E4
Luapula (riv.) E
Lubilash (riv.) D
Lufira (riv.) E
Luilaka (riv.) C
Lukenie (riv.) D
Lukuga (riv.) E
Lulua (riv.) D
Luvua (riv.) E
Mai-Ndombe (lake) C
Malebo (Stanley Pool) (lake) C
Margherita (mt.) E
Marungu (mts.) E
Mobuto Sese Seko (lake) F
Mweru (lake) E
Ruwenzori (range) E
Ruzizi (riv.) E
Salonga Nat'l Park D
Sankuru (riv.) D
Stanley (falls) D
Stanley Pool (lake) C
Tanganyika (lake) E
Tshuapa (riv.) D
Tumba (lake) C
Ubangi (riv.) C
Uele (riv.) E
Ulindi (riv.) E
Upemba (lake) E
Upemba Nat'l Park E
Virunga (range) E
Virunga Nat'l Park E
Zaire (Congo) (riv.) C

ZAMBIA

CITIES and TOWNS

Abercorn (Mbala) 11,179
Bancroft (Chililabombwe) 61,928
Broken Hill (Kabwe) 143,635
Chibwe
Chilanga 12,503
Chililabombwe 61,928
Chingola 145,869
Chinsali 4,211
Chipata 32,291
Choma 17,943
Fort Rosebery (Mansa) 34,801
Isoka 6,832
Kabompo 5,357
Kabwe 143,635
Kafue 29,794
Kalabo 7,398
Kalomo 5,878
Kaoma 6,731
Kapiri Mposhi 13,677
Kasama 38,093
Kasempa 3,063
Kataba
Kawambwa 7,235
Kitwe 314,794
Lealui
Livingstone 71,987
Luanshya 132,164
Lundazi 4,083
Lusaka (cap.) 538,469
Luwingu 3,763
Mansa 34,801
Mazabuka 29,602
Mbala 11,179
Mkushi 4,104
Mongu 24,919
Monze 13,141
Mpika 25,880
Mporokoso 6,008
Mpulungu 6,354
Mufulira 149,778
Mulobezi 2,589
Mumbwa 7,570
Mwinilunga 3,169
Nakonde 4,599
Namwala 3,008
Ndola 282,439
Petauke 7,531
Senanga 7,204
Serenje 6,008
Sesheke 3,500
Solwezi 15,032
Zambezi 8,166

OTHER FEATURES

Bangweulu (lake)
Barotseland (reg.)
Chambeshi (riv.)
Cuando (riv.)
Dongwe (riv.)
Kabompo (riv.)
Kafue (riv.)
Kafue Nat'l Park
Kalambo (falls)
Kariba (dam)
Kariba (lake)
Luangwa (riv.)
Luapula (riv.)
Lungwebungu (riv.)
Mosi-Oa-Tunya (Victoria) (falls)
Mulungushi (dam)
Mweru (lake)
Sunzu (mt.)
Tanganyika (lake)
Victoria (falls)
Zambezi (riv.)

Agriculture, Industry and Resources

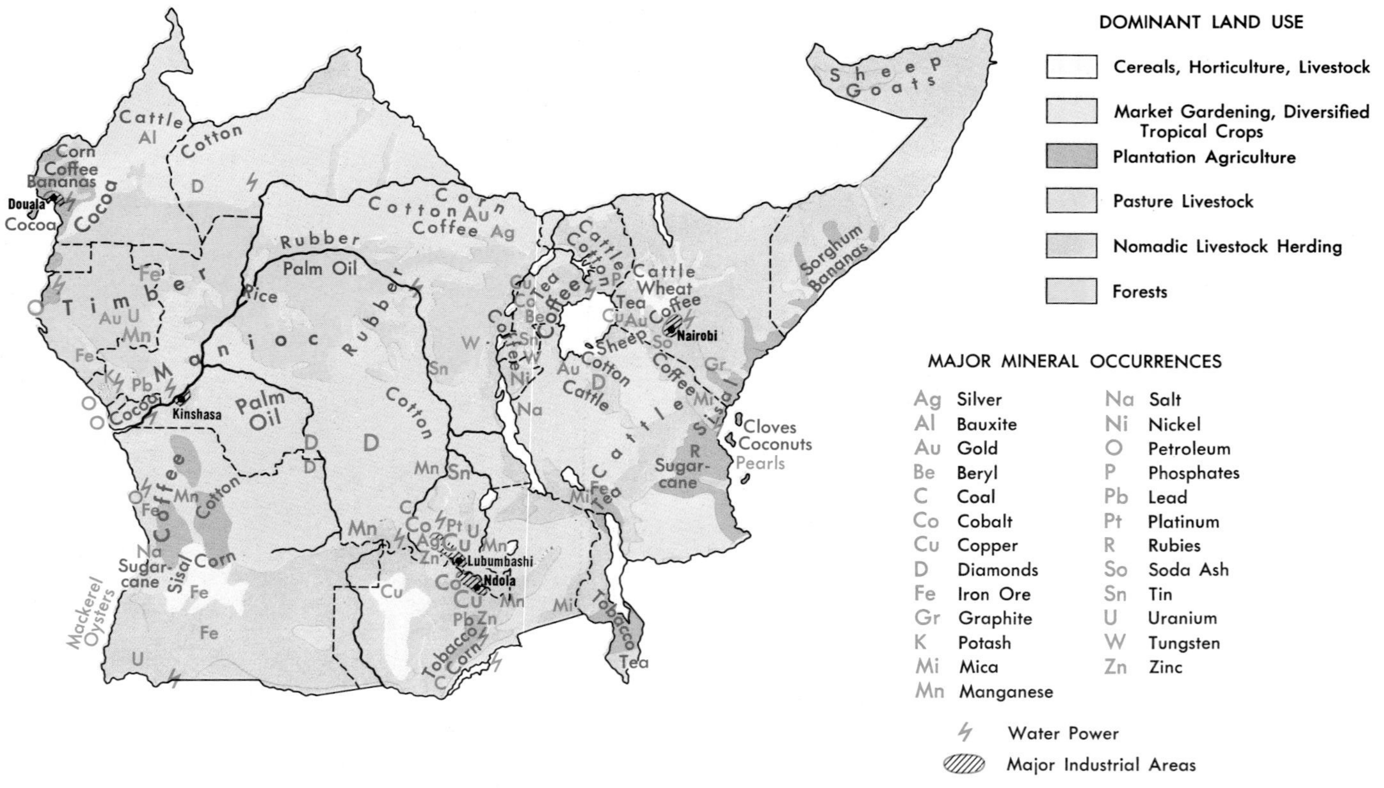
DOMINANT LAND USE
Cereals, Horticulture, Livestock
Market Gardening, Diversified Tropical Crops
Plantation Agriculture
Pasture Livestock
Nomadic Livestock Herding
Forests
MAJOR MINERAL OCCURRENCES
Ag Silver
Al Bauxite
Au Gold
Be Beryl
C Coal
Co Cobalt
Cu Copper
D Diamonds
Fe Iron Ore
Gr Graphite
K Potash
Mi Mica
Mn Manganese
Na Salt
Ni Nickel
O Petroleum
P Phosphates
Pb Lead
Pt Platinum
R Rubies
So Soda Ash
Sn Tin
U Uranium
W Tungsten
Zn Zinc
Water Power
Major Industrial Areas
Douala
Kinshasa
Nairobi
Lubumbashi
Ndola
Sheep Goats
Cattle
Corn Coffee Bananas
Cocoa
Cotton
Rubber
Palm Oil
Timber
Manioc
Rice
Coffee
Sisal
Sugar-cane
Tea
Wheat
Sorghum Bananas
Cloves Coconuts Pearls
Mackerel Oysters
Tobacco

NAMIBIA (SOUTH-WEST AFRICA)

AREA 317,827 sq. mi. (823,172 sq. km.)
POPULATION 1,200,000
CAPITAL Windhoek
LARGEST CITY Windhoek
HIGHEST POINT Brandberg 8,550 ft.
(2,606 m.)
MONETARY UNIT rand
MAJOR LANGUAGES Ovambo, Hottentot,
Herero, Afrikaans, English
MAJOR RELIGIONS Tribal religions,
Protestantism

SOUTH AFRICA

AREA 455,318 sq. mi. (1,179,274 sq. km.)
POPULATION 23,771,970
CAPITALS Cape Town, Pretoria
LARGEST CITY Johannesburg
HIGHEST POINT Injasuti 11,182 ft. (3,408 m.)
MONETARY UNIT rand
MAJOR LANGUAGES Afrikaans, English,
Xhosa, Zulu, Sesotho
MAJOR RELIGIONS Protestantism,
Roman Catholicism, Islam, Hinduism,
tribal religions

LESOTHO

AREA 11,720 sq. mi. (30,355 sq. km.)
POPULATION 1,339,000
CAPITAL Maseru
LARGEST CITY Maseru
HIGHEST POINT 11,425 ft. (3,482 m.)
MONETARY UNIT loti
MAJOR LANGUAGES Sesotho, English
MAJOR RELIGIONS Tribal religions,
Christianity

BOTSWANA

AREA 224,764 sq. mi. (582,139 sq. km.)
POPULATION 819,000
CAPITAL Gaborone
LARGEST CITY Francistown
HIGHEST POINT Tsodilo Hill 5,922 ft.
(1,805 m.)
MONETARY UNIT pula
MAJOR LANGUAGES Setswana, Shona,
Bushman, English, Afrikaans
MAJOR RELIGIONS Tribal religions,
Protestantism

MOZAMBIQUE

AREA 303,769 sq. mi. (786,762 sq. km.)
POPULATION 12,130,000
CAPITAL Maputo
LARGEST CITY Maputo
HIGHEST POINT Mt. Binga 7,992 ft.
(2,436 m.)
MONETARY UNIT metical
MAJOR LANGUAGES Makua, Thonga,
Shona, Portuguese
MAJOR RELIGIONS Tribal religions,
Roman Catholicism, Islam

SWAZILAND

AREA 6,705 sq. mi. (17,366 sq. km.)
POPULATION 547,000
CAPITAL Mbabane
LARGEST CITY Manzini
HIGHEST POINT Emlembe 6,109 ft.
(1,862 m.)
MONETARY UNIT lilangeni
MAJOR LANGUAGES siSwati, English
MAJOR RELIGIONS Tribal religions,
Christianity

ZIMBABWE

AREA 150,803 sq. mi. (390,580 sq. km.)
POPULATION 7,360,000
CAPITAL Harare
LARGEST CITY Harare
HIGHEST POINT Mt. Inyangani 8,517 ft.
(2,596 m.)
MONETARY UNIT Zimbabwe dollar
MAJOR LANGUAGES English, Shona,
Ndebele
MAJOR RELIGIONS Tribal religions,
Protestantism

MADAGASCAR

AREA 226,657 sq. mi. (587,041 sq. km.)
POPULATION 8,742,000
CAPITAL Antananarivo
LARGEST CITY Antananarivo
HIGHEST POINT Maromokotro 9,436 ft.
(2,876 m.)
MONETARY UNIT Madagascar franc
MAJOR LANGUAGES Malagasy, French
MAJOR RELIGIONS Tribal religions,
Roman Catholicism, Protestantism

COMOROS

AREA 719 sq. mi. (1,862 sq. km.)
POPULATION 290,000
CAPITAL Moroni
LARGEST CITY Moroni
HIGHEST POINT Karthala 7,746 ft.
(2,361 m.)
MONETARY UNIT CFA franc
MAJOR LANGUAGES Arabic, French,
Swahili
MAJOR RELIGION Islam

MAURITIUS

AREA 790 sq. mi. (2,046 sq. km.)
POPULATION 959,000
CAPITAL Port Louis
LARGEST CITY Port Louis
HIGHEST POINT 2,711 ft. (826 m.)
MONETARY UNIT Mauritian rupee
MAJOR LANGUAGES English, French,
French Creole, Hindi, Urdu
MAJOR RELIGIONS Hinduism, Christianity,
Islam

SEYCHELLES

AREA 145 sq. mi. (375 sq. km.)
POPULATION 63,000
CAPITAL Victoria
LARGEST CITY Victoria
HIGHEST POINT Morne Seychellois
2,993 ft. (912·m.)
MONETARY UNIT Seychellois rupee
MAJOR LANGUAGES English, French,
Creole
MAJOR RELIGION Roman Catholicism

RÉUNION

AREA 969 sq. mi. (2,510 sq. km.)
POPULATION 491,000
CAPITAL St-Denis

MAYOTTE

AREA 144 sq. mi. (373 sq. km.)
POPULATION 47,300
CAPITAL Dzaoudzi

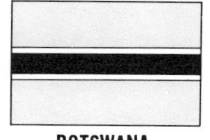

ZIMBABWE

BOTSWANA

SOUTH AFRICA

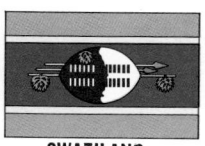

LESOTHO

SWAZILAND

MOZAMBIQUE

COMOROS

MADAGASCAR

MAURITIUS

SEYCHELLES

Agriculture, Industry and Resources

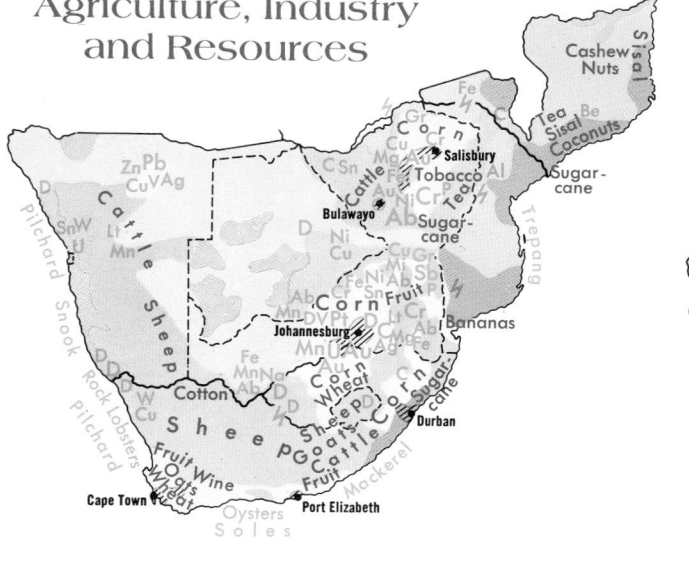

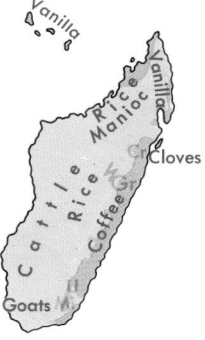

DOMINANT LAND USE

- Cereals, Horticulture, Livestock
- Market Gardening, Diversified Tropical Crops
- Plantation Agriculture
- Pasture Livestock
- Nomadic Livestock Herding
- Forests
- Nonagricultural Land

MAJOR MINERAL OCCURRENCES

Ab	Asbestos	Cu	Copper	Mn	Manganese	Sb	Antimony
Ag	Silver	D	Diamonds	Na	Salt	Sn	Tin
Al	Bauxite	Fe	Iron Ore	Ni	Nickel	U	Uranium
Au	Gold	Gr	Graphite	P	Phosphates	V	Vanadium
Be	Beryl	Lt	Lithium	Pb	Lead	W	Tungsten
C	Coal	Mg	Magnesium	Pt	Platinum	Zn	Zinc
Cr	Chromium	Mi	Mica				

⚡ Water Power
▨ Major Industrial Areas

BOTSWANA

CITIES and TOWNS

Bobonong 2,184	D4
Dibete 1,599	D4
Dinokwe 560	D4
Francistown 22,000	D4
Gaborone (cap.) 21,000	D4
Ghanzi 1,198	C3
Gumare 689	C3
Kalkfontein 1,532	C4
Kang 1,151	C4
Kanye 10,664	C5
Kasane 1,476	D3
Lehututu 988	C4
Lephepe 1,355	D4
Lobatse 11,936	D5
Machaneng 725	D4
Mahalapye 12,056	D4
Maun 9,614	C4
Mochudi 6,945	D4
Molepolole 9,448	C4
Nata 873	D4
Orapa 1,269	D4
Palapye 5,217	D4
Ramotswa 7,991	C4
Selebi-Pikwe 20,572	D4
Serowe 15,723	D4
Shakawe 1,767	C3
Shashe 1,337	D4
Shoshong 3,132	D4
Tonota 4,494	D4
Tsau 427	C4
Tshabong 983	C5
Tshane 604	C4

OTHER FEATURES

Chobe (riv.)	C3
Kalahari (des.)	C4
Limpopo (riv.)	D4
Makgadikgadi (salt pan)	D3
Molopo (riv.)	C5
Ngami (lake)	C4
Ngamiland (reg.)	C3
Nossob (riv.)	B4
Okovango (swamps)	C3
Orange (riv.)	B5
Shashe (riv.)	D4
Tati (riv.)	D4

COMOROS

CITIES and TOWNS

Fomboni 3,229	G2
Mitsamiouli 3,196	G2
Moroni (cap.) 12,000	G2
Mutsamudu 7,652	G2

OTHER FEATURES

Anjouan (Nzwani) (isl.) 83,486	G2
Grand Comoro (Njazidja) (isl.) 118,443	G2
Moheli (Mwali) (isl.) 9,525	G2

LESOTHO

CITIES and TOWNS

Leribe 5,200	D5
Mafeteng 4,600	D5
Maseru (cap.) 71,500	D5
Mohaleshoek 3,600	D6

MADAGASCAR

PROVINCES

Antananarivo 2,167,973	H3
Antsiranana 597,982	H2
Fianarantsoa 1,804,365	H4
Mahajanga 819,750	H3
Toamasina 1,179,660	H3
Toliara 1,034,114	G4

CITIES and TOWNS

Ambalavao 6,988	H4
Ambanja 12,258	H2
Ambato Boeny 3,317	H3
Ambatofinandrahana 2,161	H4
Ambatolampy 11,539	H3
Ambatomainty 1,276	H3
Ambatondrazaka 18,044	H3
Ambilobe 9,415	H2
Amboasary 2,420	H4
Ambodifototra 1,112	J3
Ambohimahasoa 5,851	H4
Ambositra 16,780	H4
Ambovombe 1,375	H5
Ampanihy 2,262	G4
Analalava 5,184	H2
Andapa 6,275	H2
Andilamena 3,512	H3
Androka 1,068	G5
Ankazoabo 1,677	G4
Antalaha 17,541	J2
Antananarivo (cap.) 451,808	H3
Antsalova 2,202	G3
Antsirabe 32,979	H3
Antsiranana 40,443	H2
Antsohihy 8,721	H2
Arivonimamo 8,497	H3
Bealanana 2,299	H2
Befandriana 3,004	H3
Bekily 1,933	G4
Belo-Tsiribihina 4,403	G3
Bereroha 1,742	G4
Besalampy 2,874	G3
Betioky 3,964	G4
Betroka 3,943	H4
Brickaville (Vohibinany) 1,741	H3
Diégo-Suarez (Antsiranana) 40,443	H2
Fandriana 4,139	H4
Faradofay 13,805	H5
Farafangana 10,817	H4
Fenoarivo, Toamasina 7,696	H3
Fianarantsoa 68,054	H4
Fort-Dauphin (Faradofay) 13,805	H5
Foulpointe	H3
Hell-Ville 6,183	H2
Ifanadiana 1,111	H4
Ihosy 4,521	H4
Ivohibe 1,254	H4
Madirovalo 3,991	H3
Maevatanana 7,197	H3
Mahabo 4,941	G4
Mahanoro 5,041	H3
Maintirano 6,375	G3
Majunga 65,864	H3
Manakara 19,768	H4
Mananara 3,253	J3
Mananjary 14,638	H4
Mandabe 1,757	G4
Mandritsara 6,826	H3
Manja 4,151	G4
Manombo 2,908	G4
Maroantsetra 6,645	J3
Marovoay 20,253	H3

(continued on following page)

Topography

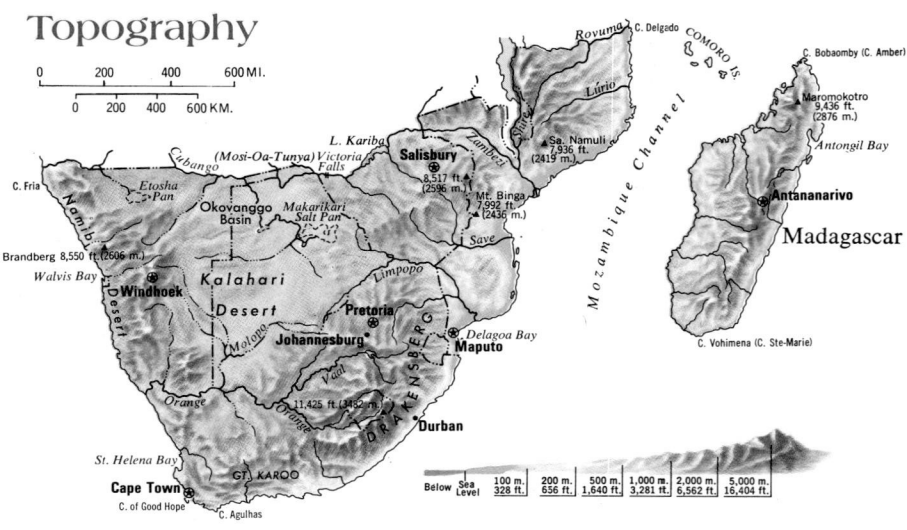

Madagascar

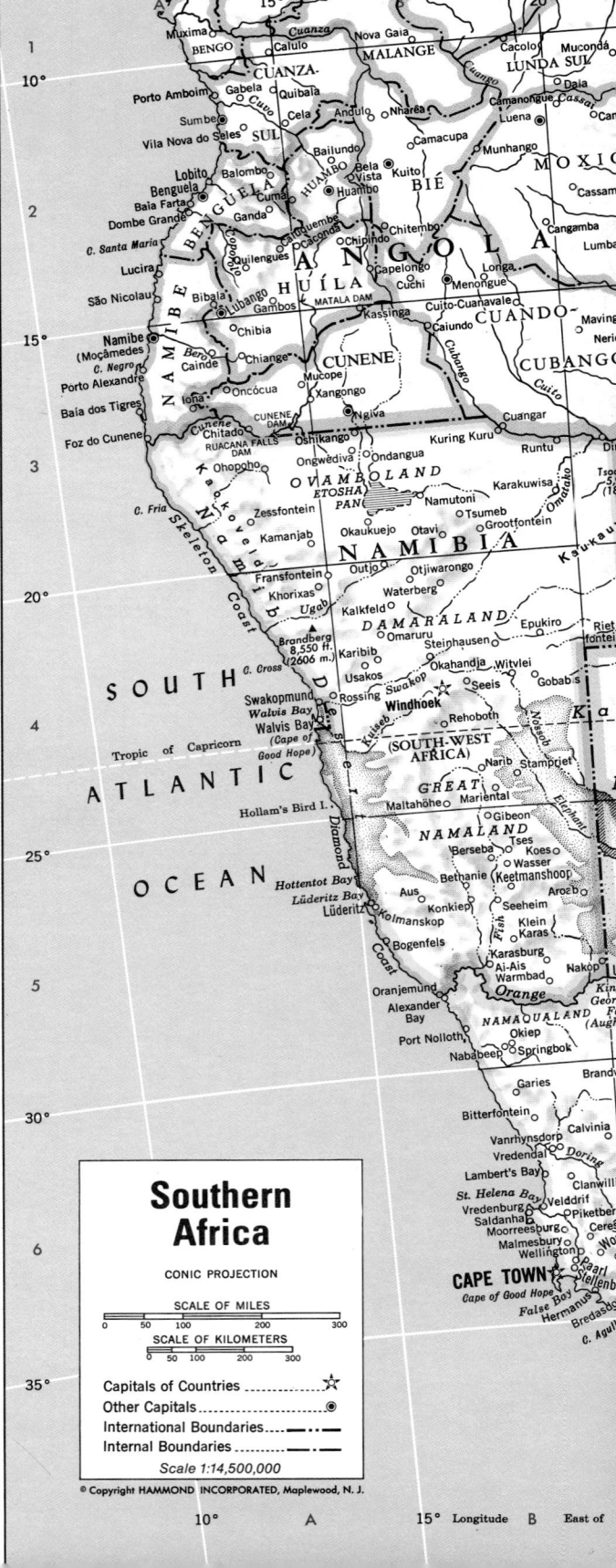

Potchefstroom 57.443 .... D5
Potgietersrus 6.667 .... D4
Pretoria (cap.) 545.450 .... D5
Pretoria[*] 573.283 .... D5
Prieska 8.521 .... C5
Prince Albert 3.346 .... C6
Queenstown 39.304 .... D6
Randburg 43.257 .... H6
Randfontein 50.481 .... H6
Reitz 5.650 .... D5
Rensburg 2.042 .... J7
Richards Bay 598 .... E5
Richmond 3.185 .... C6
Riversdale 6.165 .... C6
Robertson 10.237 .... C6
Rustenburg 22.303 .... D5
Saldanha 4.994 .... B6
Senekal 9.124 .... D5
Sesfontein 2.731 .... H6
Simonstown 12.137 .... E7
Sishen 2.692 .... C5
Somerset East 10.383 .... D6
Somerset West 11.828 .... F6
Soweto 602.043 .... H6
Springbok 4.357 .... B5
Springs 142.812 .... J6
Springs[□] 146.831 .... J6

Standerton 21.038 .... D5
Stanger 11.064 .... E5
Stellenbosch 29.955 .... F6
Stutterheim 12.077 .... D6
Sundra 2.088 .... J6
Swellendam 6.423 .... C6
Taung 1.316 .... C5
Tembisa 81.821 .... H6
Thabazimbi 6.711 .... D4
Thohoyandou E4
Tzaneen 4.331 .... E4
Ubombo 3.697 .... E5
Uitenhage 70.517 .... C6
Ulundi E5
Umtata 25.216 .... D6
Umzimkulu 1.817 .... D6
Upington 28.632 .... C5
Vaalpos 5.699 .... C5
Vanderbijl Park 78.754 .... D5
Vanrhynsdorp 2.279 .... B6
Veldrif 3.361 .... B6
Venterspos G6
Vereeniging 172.549 .... H6
Vereeniging[□] 200.078 .... D5
Victoria West 3.949 .... C6
Villiersdorp 2.349 .... G7

Vishoek 6.721 .... E7
Volksrust 10.238 .... D5
Vrede 6.309 .... H6
Vredenburg 6.094 .... B6
Vredendal 5.377 .... B6
Vryburg 16.916 .... C5
Vryheid 16.992 .... E5
Walvis Bay 21.725 .... A4
Warmbad 8.343 .... D5
Warrenton 9.614 .... C5
Waterval-Bo 6.951 .... H7
Welkom 67.472 .... D5
Wellington 17.092 .... B6
Westonaria 36.253 .... H7
Willowmore 3.740 .... C6
Winburg 6.761 .... D5
Witbank 37.456 .... D5
Wolmaransstad 7.219 .... D5
Worcester 41.198 .... B6
Zastron 4.483 .... D6
Zeerust 6.972 .... D5
Zwelitsha 7.890 .... D6

OTHER FEATURES

Addo Nat'l Park D6
Agulhas (cape) B6
Bot (riv.) G7

Bredasdorp Nat'l Park C6
Cape (pen.) E7
Crocodile (riv.) H6
Drakensberg (range) D6
False (bay) F7
Good Hope (cape) E7
Great Fish (riv.) D6
Great Karoo (reg.) C6
Great Kei (riv.) D6
Griqualand West (reg.) C5
Groote (riv.) C6
Hartbees (riv.) C5
Kalahari Gemsbok Nat'l Park B5
King George's (falls) D6
Klip (riv.) H7
Kruger Nat'l Park E4
Limpopo (riv.) D4
Molopo (riv.) C5
Mountain Zebra Nat'l Park D6
Olifants (riv.) D4
Orange (riv.) B5
Palmiet (riv.) F7
Plettenberg (bay) C6
Pondoland (reg.) D6
Robben (isl.) E6
Royal Natal Nat'l Park D5
Saint Helena (bay) B6
Saint Lucia (lake) E5

Sak (riv.) C6
Sand (riv.) D5
Slangkop (pt.) D4
Sneeuwkop (mt.) F6
Table (bay) E6
Table (mt.) E6
Walvis (bay) A4
Witwatersberg (range) G6
Witwatersrand (reg.) H7
Zonderend (riv.) G6
Zululand (reg.) E5

SWAZILAND

CITIES and TOWNS

Manzini 28.837 .... E5
Mbabane (cap.) 23.109 .... E5
Siteki 1.362 .... E5

ZIMBABWE

CITIES and TOWNS

Beitbridge 1.986 .... E4
Bindura 17.000 .... E3

Bulawayo 359.000 .... D3
Chegutu 12.000 .... E3
Chimanimani 667 .... E3
Chinhoyi 25.000 .... E3
Chipinge 2.350 .... E4
Chivhu 1.669 .... E3
Dete 2.473 .... D3
Gwaai 2.710 .... D3
Gwanda 2.049 .... D3
Gweru 68.000 .... D3
Harare (Salisbury) (cap.) 601.000 .... E3
Hwange 33.000 .... D3
Inyanga 733 .... E3
Kadoma 32.000 .... D3
Kariba 3.943 .... D3
Kwekwe 54.000 .... D3
Marondera 23.000 .... E3
Masvingo 22.000 .... E4
Matopos 11.330 .... D3
Mount Darwin 904 .... E3
Mutare 61.000 .... E3
Mvuma 1.525 .... D3
Mwenezi 7.830 .... E4
Plumtree 2.041 .... D3
Rusape 5.286 .... E3
Salisbury (Harare) (cap.) 601.000 .... E3
Shamva 785 .... E3
Shurugwi 8.387 .... E3

Tuli 340 .... D4
West Nicholson 1.929 .... D4
Zvishavane 20.000 .... E4

OTHER FEATURES

Inyanga Nat'l Park E3
Kariba (lake) D3
Lundi (riv.) E4
Mashonaland (reg.) 1.875.700 .... E3
Matabeleland (reg.) 969.220 .... D3
Mazoe (riv.) E3
Mushandike Nat'l Park D4
Sabi (riv.) E3
Shangani (riv.) D3
Umvukwe (range) E3
Victoria (falls) D3
Zambezi (riv.) E3
Zimbabwe Nat'l Park E4

*City and suburbs.
†Population of parish.
○Population of subdivision.
□Population of urban area.

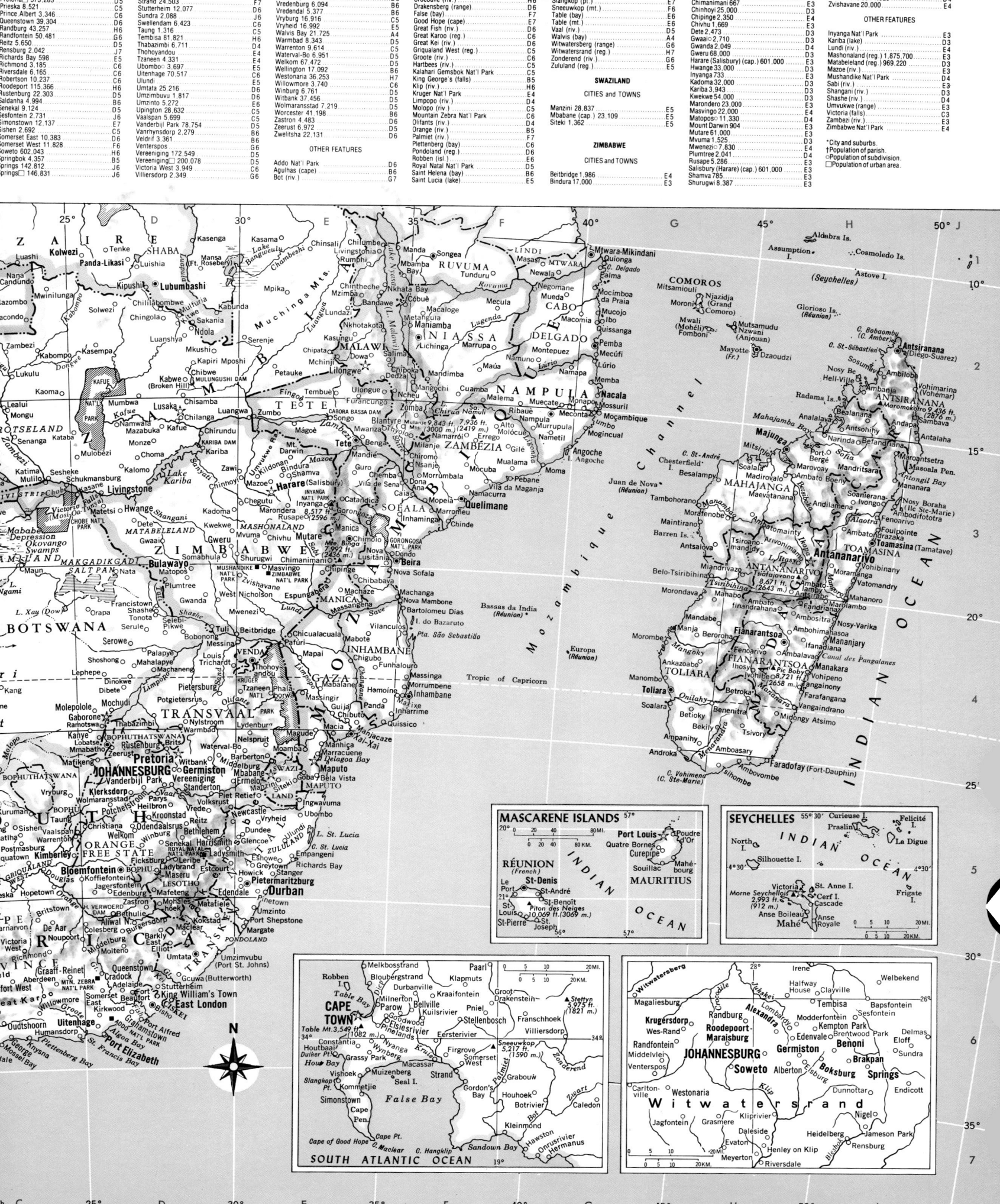

Population Distribution

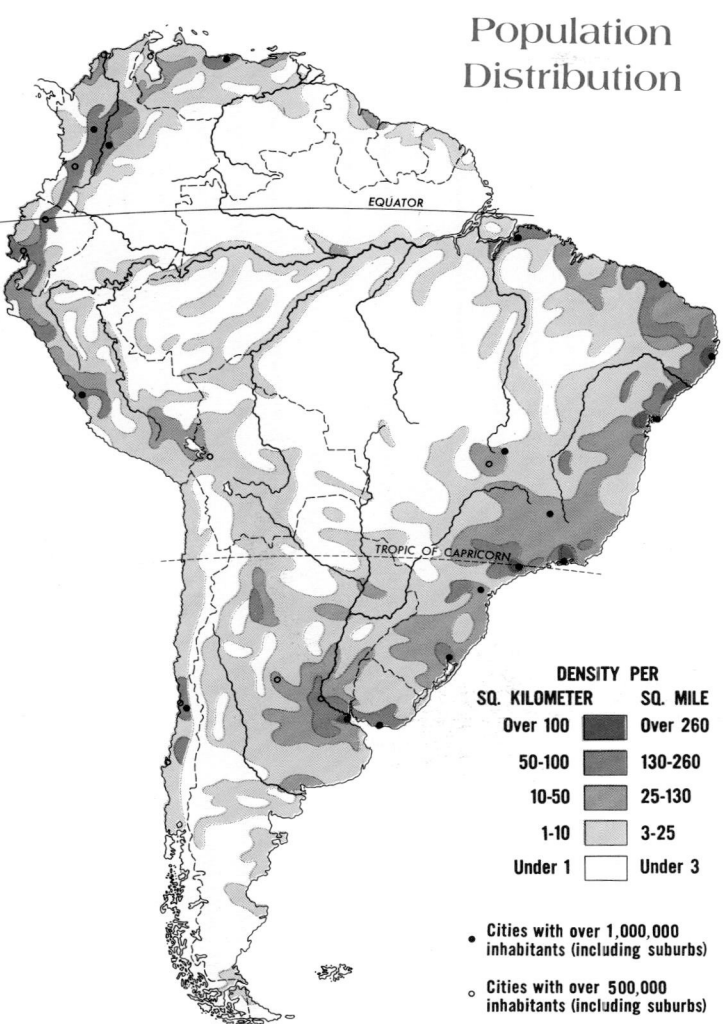

EQUATOR

TROPIC OF CAPRICORN

AREA 6,875,000 sq. mi. (17,806,250 sq. km.)
POPULATION 245,000,000
LARGEST CITY São Paulo
HIGHEST POINT Cerro Aconcagua 22,831 ft. (6,959 m.)
LOWEST POINT Salina Grande -131 ft. (-40 m.)

Vegetation

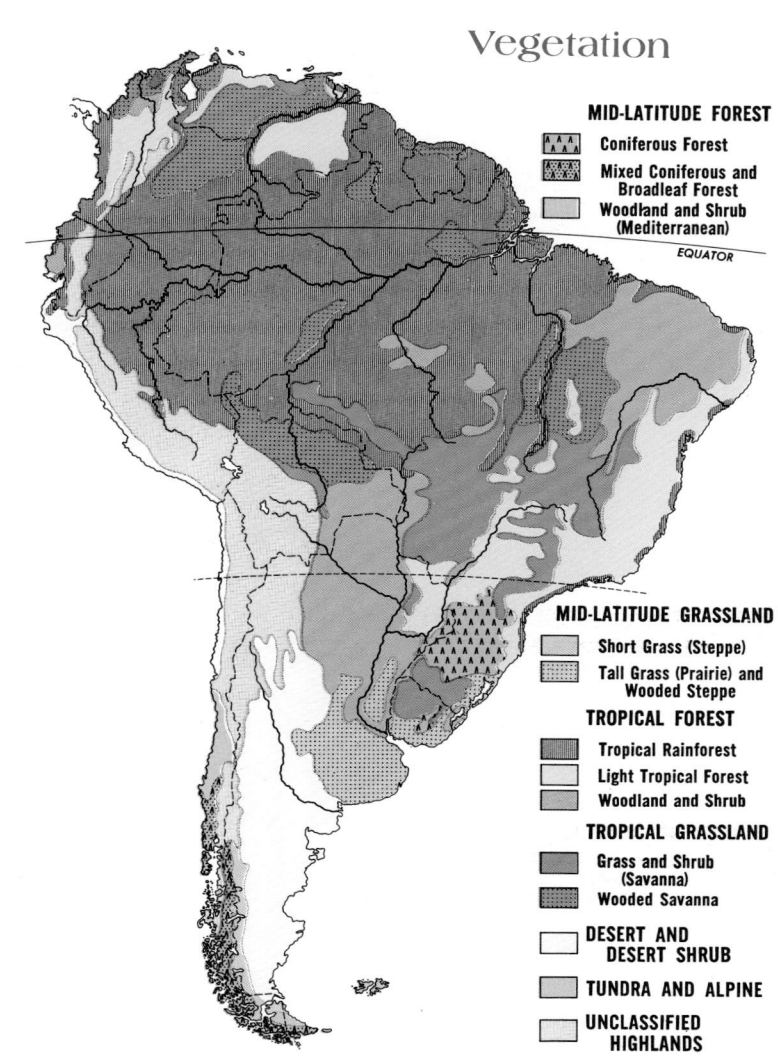

EQUATOR

DENSITY PER

SQ. KILOMETER	SQ. MILE
Over 100	Over 260
50-100	130-260
10-50	25-130
1-10	3-25
Under 1	Under 3

• Cities with over 1,000,000 inhabitants (including suburbs)

○ Cities with over 500,000 inhabitants (including suburbs)

MID-LATITUDE FOREST
- Coniferous Forest
- Mixed Coniferous and Broadleaf Forest
- Woodland and Shrub (Mediterranean)

MID-LATITUDE GRASSLAND
- Short Grass (Steppe)
- Tall Grass (Prairie) and Wooded Steppe

TROPICAL FOREST
- Tropical Rainforest
- Light Tropical Forest
- Woodland and Shrub

TROPICAL GRASSLAND
- Grass and Shrub (Savanna)
- Wooded Savanna

DESERT AND DESERT SHRUB

TUNDRA AND ALPINE

UNCLASSIFIED HIGHLANDS

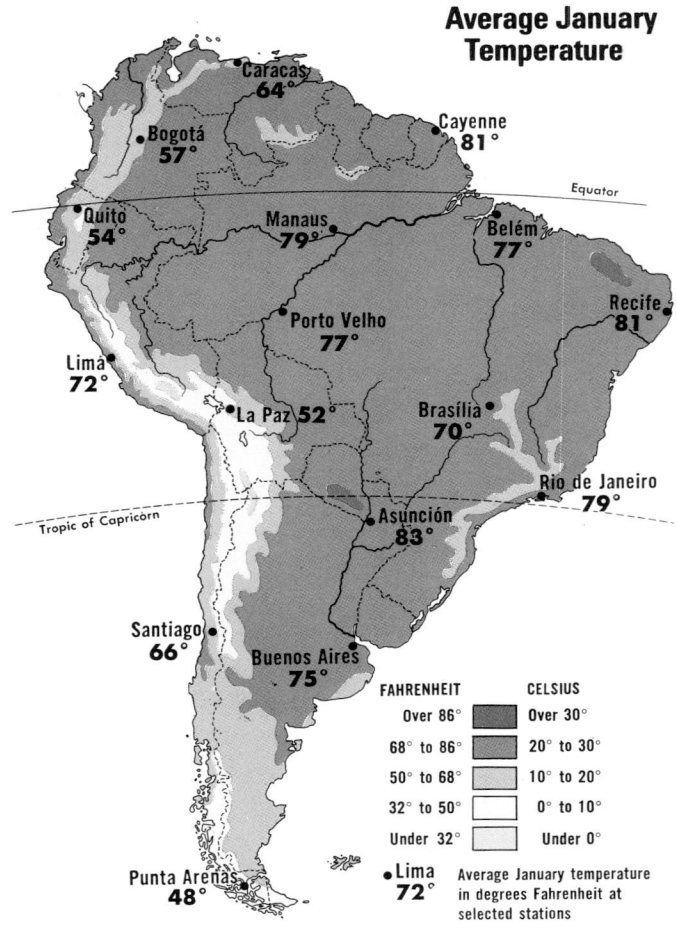

Average January Temperature

Caracas 64°
Bogotá 57°
Cayenne 81°
Quito 54°
Manaus 79°
Belém 77°
Lima 72°
Porto Velho 77°
Recife 81°
La Paz 52°
Brasília 70°
Rio de Janeiro 79°
Asunción 83°
Santiago 66°
Buenos Aires 75°
Punta Arenas 48°

Equator
Tropic of Capricorn

FAHRENHEIT	CELSIUS
Over 86°	Over 30°
68° to 86°	20° to 30°
50° to 68°	10° to 20°
32° to 50°	0° to 10°
Under 32°	Under 0°

● Lima 72° Average January temperature in degrees Fahrenheit at selected stations

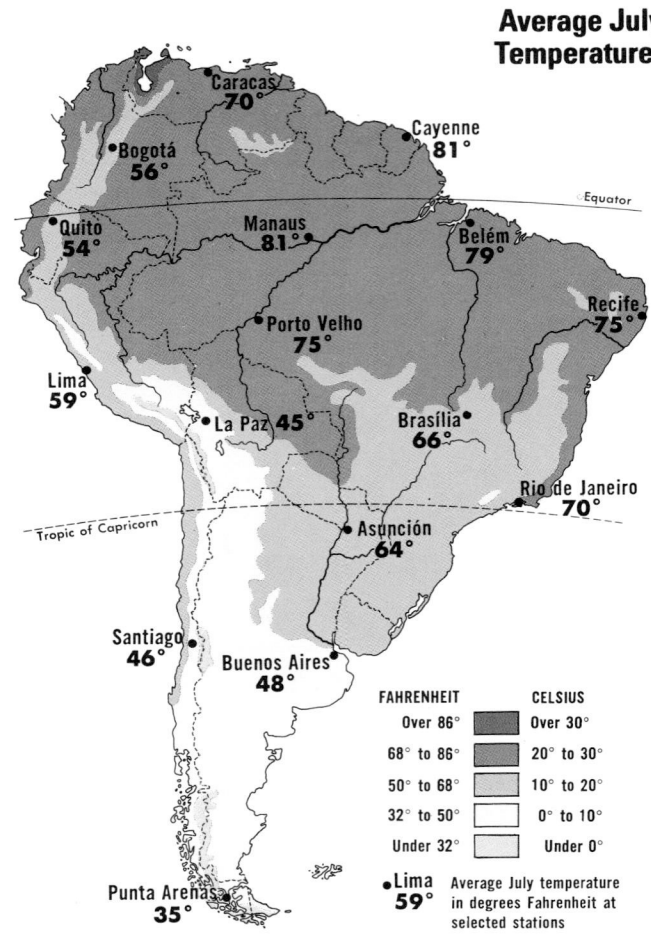

Average July Temperature

Caracas 70°
Bogotá 56°
Cayenne 81°
Quito 54°
Manaus 81°
Belém 79°
Lima 59°
Porto Velho 75°
Recife 75°
La Paz 45°
Brasília 66°
Rio de Janeiro 70°
Asunción 64°
Santiago 46°
Buenos Aires 48°
Punta Arenas 35°

Equator
Tropic of Capricorn

FAHRENHEIT	CELSIUS
Over 86°	Over 30°
68° to 86°	20° to 30°
50° to 68°	10° to 20°
32° to 50°	0° to 10°
Under 32°	Under 0°

● Lima 59° Average July temperature in degrees Fahrenheit at selected stations

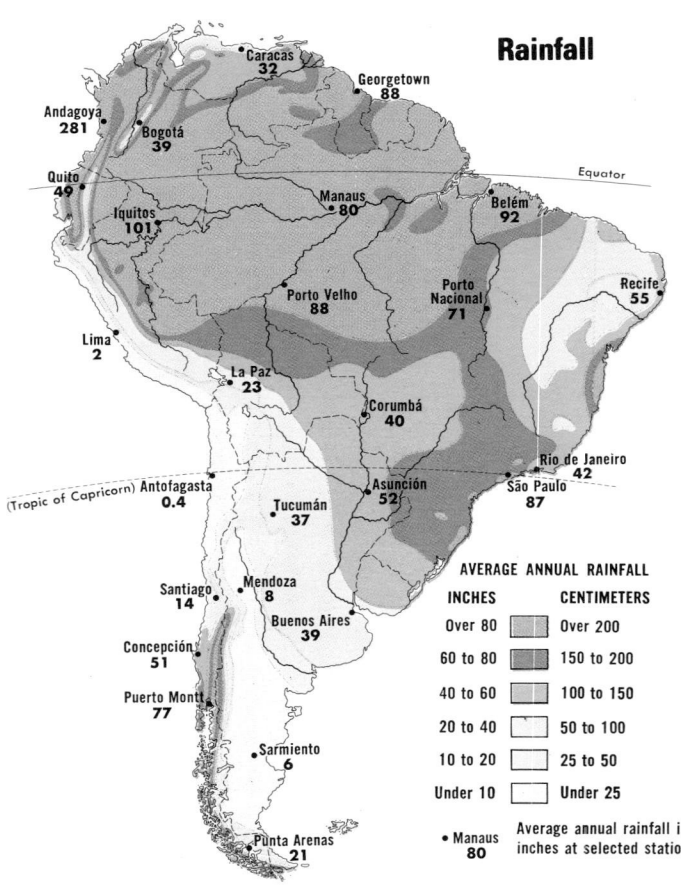

Rainfall

Caracas 32
Georgetown 88
Andagoya 281
Bogotá 39
Quito 49
Manaus 80
Belém 92
Iquitos 101
Porto Velho 88
Porto Nacional 71
Recife 55
Lima 2
La Paz 23
Corumbá 40
Rio de Janeiro 42
(Tropic of Capricorn) Antofagasta 0.4
Tucumán 37
Asunción 52
São Paulo 87
Santiago 14
Mendoza 8
Concepción 51
Buenos Aires 39
Puerto Montt 77
Sarmiento 6
Punta Arenas 21

Equator

AVERAGE ANNUAL RAINFALL

INCHES	CENTIMETERS
Over 80	Over 200
60 to 80	150 to 200
40 to 60	100 to 150
20 to 40	50 to 100
10 to 20	25 to 50
Under 10	Under 25

● Manaus 80 Average annual rainfall in inches at selected stations

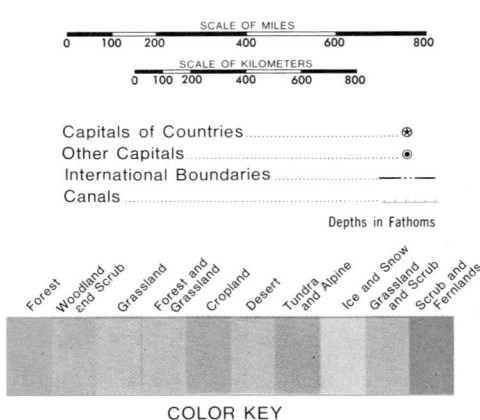

Vegetation / Relief

SCALE OF MILES
0 100 200 400 600 800

SCALE OF KILOMETERS
0 100 200 400 600 800

Capitals of Countries .... ⊕
Other Capitals .... ⊙
International Boundaries ....
Canals ....

Depths in Fathoms

Forest
Woodland and Scrub
Grassland
Forest and Grassland
Cropland
Desert
Tundra and Alpine
Ice and Snow
Grassland Scrub and
Scrub and Fernlands

COLOR KEY

CARIBBEAN SEA

Pta. Gallinas
G. of Venezuela
ARUBA (Neth.)
NETH. ANTILLES
Curaçao
Bonaire
Willemstad
BARBADOS
GRENADA
West Indies
Tobago
TRINIDAD & TOBAGO
Port of Spain
Trinidad

PANAMÁ
Panamá Canal
Panamá
Colón

ATLANTIC OCEAN

Barranquilla
Maracaibo
Caracas
L. Maracaibo
Pico Bolívar
16,427 ft. (5007 m.)

Medellín
Bucaramanga
Bogotá
COLOMBIA
Cali
Cúcuta

VENEZUELA
Orinoco
Guri Res.
Arauca
Meta
Angel Falls
Mt. Roraima
9,094 ft.
(2772 m.)
Georgetown
Paramaribo
Cayenne

GUYANA
SURINAME
FRENCH GUIANA

Guiana Highlands

Ciudad Guayana

ECUADOR
Quito
Chimborazo
20,561 ft.
(6267 m.)
Guayaquil
Gulf of Guayaquil
Pta. Aguja

Putumayo
Caquetá
Vaupés
Pico Phelps
Pico da Neblina
9,889 ft.
(3014 m.)
Negro
Içá
Japurá
Iquitos
Amazon
Yavarí
Juruá
Selvas
Purus
Madeira
Manaus
Amazon
Belém
I. de Marajó
Baía de Marajó
São Luís
Equator
Fortaleza

PERU
Trujillo
Huascarán
22,205 ft.
(6768 m.)
Callao
Lima
Cusco

Ucayali
Marañón
Tapajós
Xingu
Tocantins
Teresina
Cabo de São Roque
Natal

BRAZIL
Planalto de
Mato Grosso
Brasília
Goiânia
Recife
Maceió

BOLIVIA
Nev. Ancohuma
21,489 ft.
(6550 m.)
La Paz
Cochabamba
Lake Titicaca
Arequipa
Arica
Lake Poopó
Sucre

Brazilian Highlands
São Francisco
Salvador
Jequitinhonha
Belo Horizonte
Pico da Bandeira
9,482 ft. (2890 m.)
Paraguaçu

Antofagasta
Tropic of Capricorn
Volcán Llullaillaco
22,057 ft.
(6723 m.)
San Miguel de Tucumán
Nev. Ojos del Salado
22,572 ft.
(6880 m.)

PARAGUAY
Campo Grande
Asunción
ITAIPU DAM
Iguazú Falls
Iguaçu

Paraná
Tietê
C. de São Tomé
C. Frio
São Paulo
Santos
Rio de Janeiro
Curitiba
I. de Santa Catarina

Pilcomayo
Bermejo
Salado del Norte
Gran Chaco

I. de San Félix (Chile)
I. San Ambrosio (Chile)

CHILE
Cerro Aconcagua
22,831 ft. (6959 m.)
Valparaíso
Santiago
Mendoza
Córdoba
Santa Fé
Rosario
Porto Alegre
Lagoa dos Patos
Lagoa Mirim

I. Alejandro Selkirk
I. Robinson Crusoe
Juan Fernandez Is.
(Chile)

URUGUAY
Negro
Buenos Aires
La Plata
Montevideo
Río de la Plata
C. San Antonio

ARGENTINA
Pampas
Salado
Colorado
Negro
Concepción
Bahía Blanca
Limay

PACIFIC OCEAN

Puerto Montt
Isla de Chiloé
Golfo San Matías
Pen. Valdés
ATLANTIC OCEAN

Archipiélago de los Chonos
Chubut
Golfo San Jorge
C. Tres Puntas
Pen. Taitao
Deseado
G. de Penas

PATAGONIA

Archipiélago Reina Adelaida
Bahía Grande
Str. of Magellan
Punta Arenas
Tierra del Fuego

Falkland Islands
(U.K.)
Stanley

Cape Horn

Longitude West of Greenwich

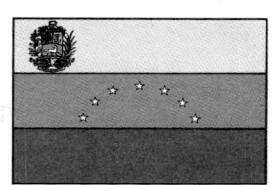

AREA 352,143 sq. mi. (912,050 sq. km.)
POPULATION 14,313,000
CAPITAL Caracas
LARGEST CITY Caracas
HIGHEST POINT Pico Bolívar 16,427 ft. (5,007 m.)
MONETARY UNIT Bolívar
MAJOR LANGUAGE Spanish
MAJOR RELIGION Roman Catholicism

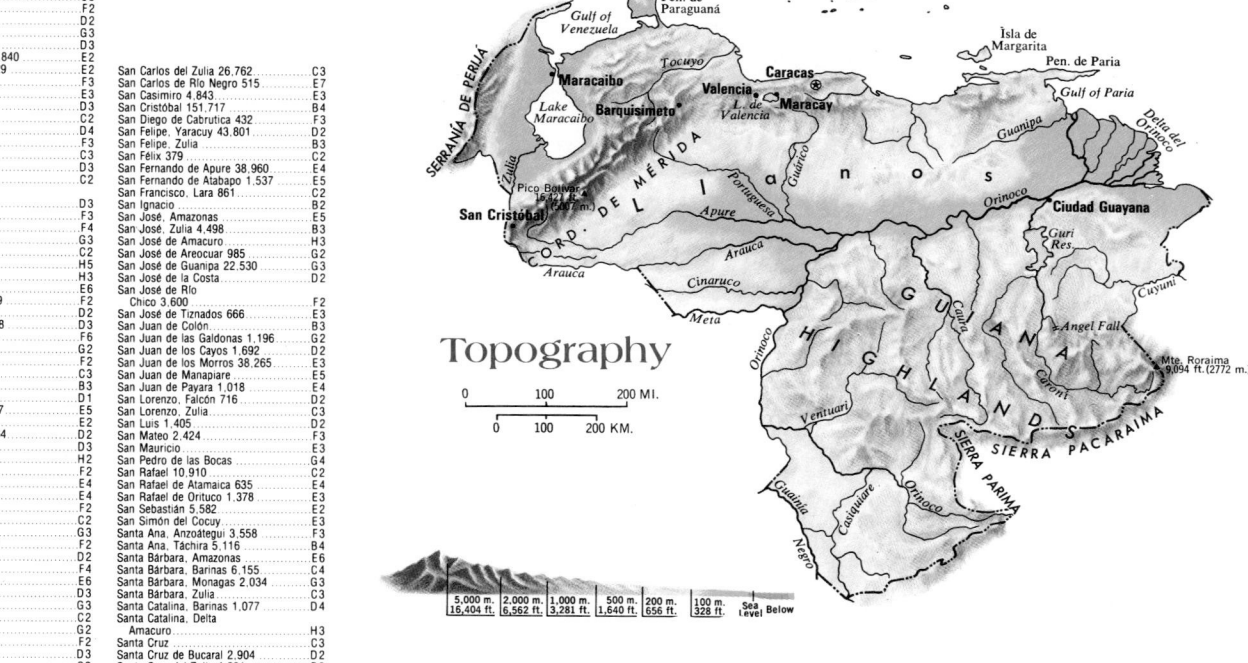

Topography

0   100   200 MI.
0   100   200 KM.

5,000 m. | 2,000 m. | 1,000 m. | 500 m. | 200 m. | 100 m. | Sea | Below
16,404 ft. | 6,562 ft. | 3,281 ft. | 1,640 ft. | 656 ft. | 328 ft. | Level

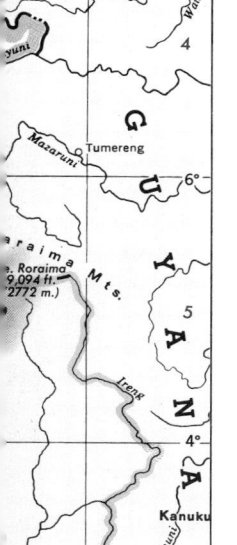

Agriculture, Industry and Resources

MAJOR MINERAL OCCURRENCES

Al   Bauxite
Au   Gold
C   Coal
D   Diamonds
Fe   Iron Ore
G   Natural Gas
Mn   Manganese
Na   Salt
O   Petroleum

⚡   Water Power
▨   Major Industrial Areas

DOMINANT LAND USE

Diversified Tropical Crops (chiefly plantation agriculture)
Upland Cultivated Areas
Upland Livestock Grazing, Limited Agriculture
Extensive Livestock Ranching
Forests

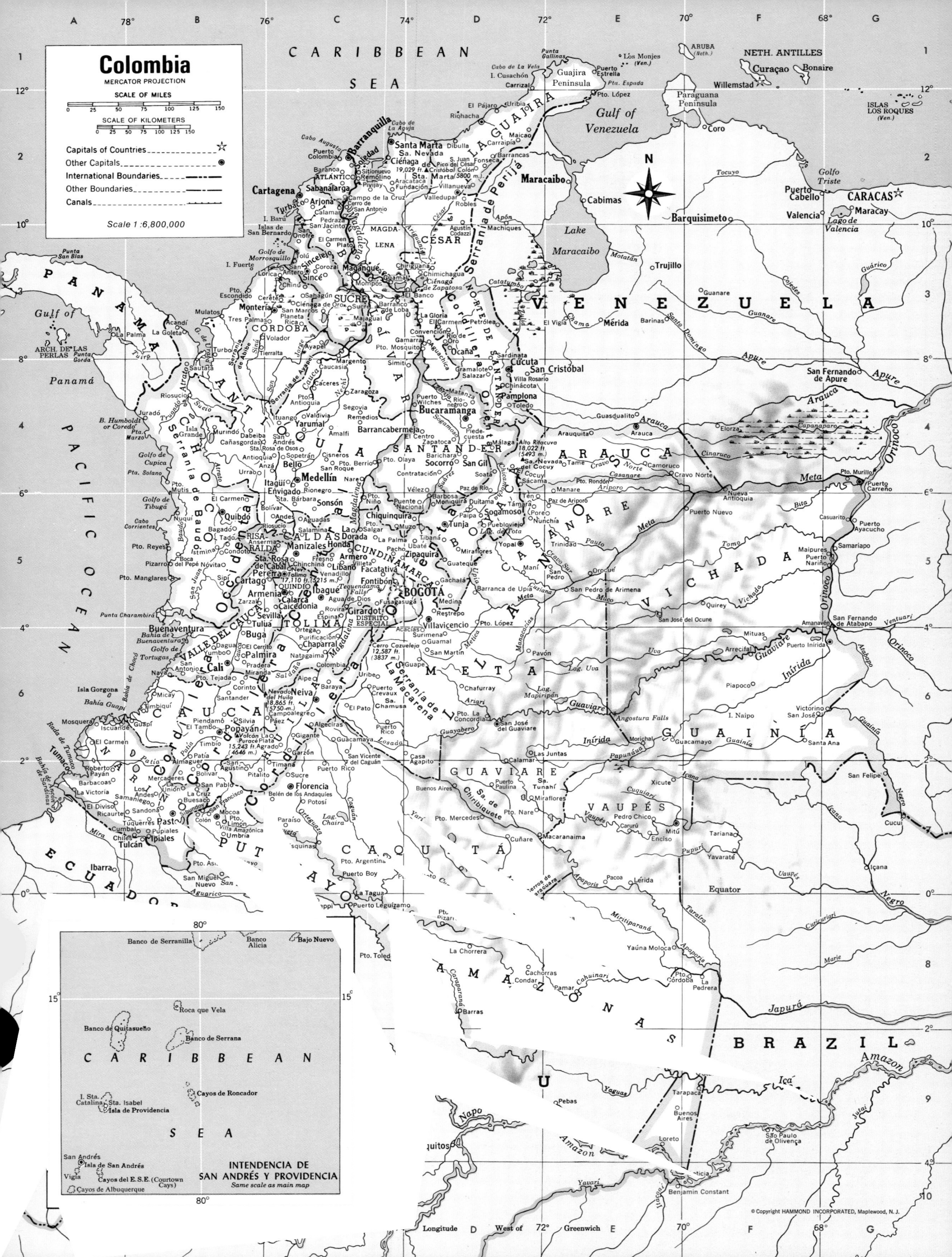

Colombia

MERCATOR PROJECTION

SCALE OF MILES

0 25 50 75 100 125 150

SCALE OF KILOMETERS

0 25 50 75 100 125 150

Capitals of Countries _ _ _ _ _ _ _ ★
Other Capitals _ _ _ _ _ _ _ _ _ _ ⊙
International Boundaries _ _ _ _ _ _
Other Boundaries _ _ _ _ _ _ _ _ _
Canals _ _ _ _ _ _ _ _ _ _ _ _ _

Scale 1 : 6,800,000

INTENDENCIA DE
SAN ANDRÉS Y PROVIDENCIA
Same scale as main map

© Copyright HAMMOND INCORPORATED, Maplewood, N.J.

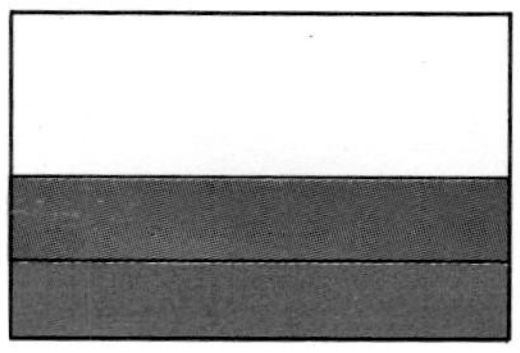

AREA 439,513 sq. mi. (1,138,339 sq. km.)
POPULATION 27,520,000
CAPITAL Bogotá
LARGEST CITY Bogotá
HIGHEST POINT Pico Cristóbal Colón 19,029 ft. (5,800 m.)
MONETARY UNIT Colombian peso
MAJOR LANGUAGE Spanish
MAJOR RELIGION Roman Catholicism

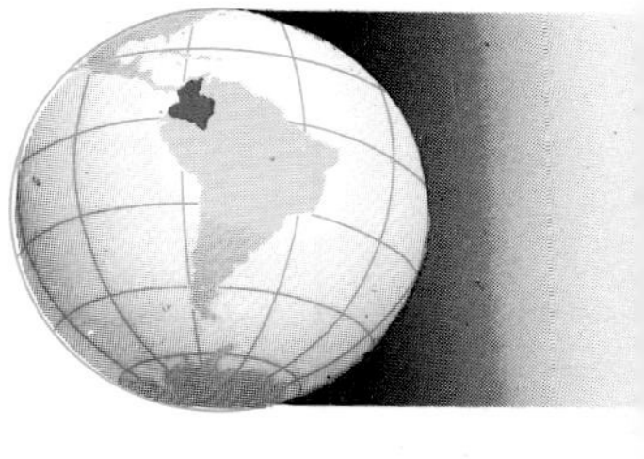

INTERNAL DIVISIONS

Amazonas (comm.) 6,825 ... D8
Antioquia (dept.) 2,976,153 ... B4
Arauca (inten.) 19,884 ... E4
Atlántico (dept.) 958,560 ... C2
Bolívar (dept.) 802,407 ... C3
Boyacá (dept.) 1,084,766 ... D5
Caldas (dept.) 700,954 ... C5
Caquetá (inten.) 57,103 ... C7
Casanare (inten.) ... B3
Cauca (dept.) 603,894 ... B6
César (dept.) 339,843 ... D3
Chocó (dept.) 201,915 ... B4
Córdoba (dept.) 645,478 ... C3
Cundinamarca (dept.) 1,106,626 ... C5
Distrito Especial 2,855,065 ... C5
Guainía (comm.) 1,792 ... F6
Guajira, La (dept.) 180,520 ... D2
Guaviare (comm.) ... D7
Huila (dept.) 469,834 ... C6
La Guajira (dept.) 180,520 ... D2
Magdalena (dept.) 536,122 ... C3
Meta (dept.) 245,176 ... D6
Nariño (dept.) 807,112 ... B7
Norte de Santander (dept.) 693,298 ... D3
Putumayo (inten.) 22,916 ... C7
Quindío (dept.) 321,677 ... C5
Risaralda (dept.) 452,626 ... B5
San Andrés y Providencia (inten.) 22,719 ... B10
Santander (dept.) 1,130,977 ... D4
Sucre (dept.) 354,412 ... C3
Tolima (dept.) 903,520 ... C5
Valle del Cauca (dept.) 2,204,722 ... B6
Vaupés (comm.) 6,923 ... E7
Vichada (comm.) 2,172 ... F5

CITIES and TOWNS

Acacías 9,238 ... D6
Acandí 2,358 ... B3
Agrado 2,771 ... C6
Aguachica 16,771 ... D3
Aguadas 9,995 ... C5
Agua de Dios 9,689 ... C5
Agustín Codazzi 21,932 ... D3
Aipe 3,794 ... C6
Algeciras 5,022 ... C6
Almaguer 1,518 ... B7
Amalfi 6,494 ... C4
Andes 14,957 ... C5
Anserma 15,559 ... B5
Antioquia 6,841 ... B4
Anzá 647 ... C4
Aracataca 7,511 ... D2
Arauca 7,613 ... E4
Arauquita 1,096 ... E4
Arjona 20,571 ... C2
Armenia 135,615 ... B5
Armero 19,567 ... C5
Ayapel 7,475 ... C3
Bagadó 1,575 ... B5
Baranoa 18,397 ... C2
Baraya 2,581 ... C6
Barbacoas 4,653 ... A7
Barbosa 7,960 ... D5
Barichara 2,548 ... D4
Barrancabermeja 87,191 ... C4
Barrancas 2,979 ... D2
Barranco de Loba 2,215 ... C3
Barranquilla 661,009 ... C2
Belén de los Andaquíes 2,190 ... C7
Bello 115,119 ... C4
Bogotá (cap.) 2,696,270 ... D5
Bogotá* 2,855,065 ... D5
Bolívar, Antioquia 13,259 ... C5
Bucaramanga 291,661 ... D4
Buenaventura 115,770 ... B6
Buesaco 2,763 ... B7
Buga 71,016 ... B6
Cáceres 7,154 ... C4
Caicedonia 23,567 ... C5
Calamar, Bolívar 5,867 ... C2
Calarcá 29,349 ... C5
Cali 898,253 ... B6
Campoalegre 11,799 ... C6
Campo de la Cruz 13,137 ... C2
Cañasgordas 3,900 ... B4
Cartagena 292,512 ... C2
Cartago 69,154 ... B5
Caucasia 19,348 ... C4
Cereté 18,788 ... C3
Cerro de San Antonio 3,394 ... C2
Chaparral 14,546 ... C6
Chimichaqua 6,382 ... D3
Chinácota 4,478 ... D4
Chinchiná 24,891 ... C5
Chinú 10,023 ... C3
Chiquinquirá 21,727 ... C5
Chiriguaná 6,611 ... D3
Ciénaga 42,546 ... C2
Ciénaga de Oro 10,607 ... C3
Cisneros 7,226 ... C4
Colombia 2,903 ... C6
Colón 1,306 ... B7
Condoto 4,798 ... B5
Contratación 3,057 ... D4
Convención 7,545 ... D3
Corinto 6,933 ... B6
Corozal 17,419 ... C3
Cravo Norte 771 ... F4
Cúcuta 219,772 ... D4
Cumbal 2,891 ... B7
Dabeiba 7,600 ... B4
Dagua 5,392 ... B6
Duitama 36,551 ... D5
El Banco 20,756 ... D3
El Carmen, Chocó 1,879 ... B5
El Carmen, Norte de Santander 2,362 ... D3
El Carmen de Bolívar 23,392 ... C3
El Cerrito 17,357 ... B6
El Cocuy 2,740 ... D4
El Tambo 2,179 ... B6
Envigado 63,584 ... C4
Espinal 32,475 ... C5
Facatativá 27,892 ... C5
Florencia 31,817 ... C7
Fonseca 9,988 ... D2
Fresno 8,141 ... C5
Fundación 17,497 ... C2
Fusagasugá 25,456 ... C5
Gachalá 1,364 ... D5
Gamarra 5,071 ... D3
Garzón 13,783 ... C6
Gigante 4,880 ... C6
Girardot 59,165 ... C5
Gramalote 2,880 ... D4
Guamal, Magdalena 4,986 ... C3
Guamal, Meta 2,854 ... D6
Guapí 5,005 ... B6
Guateque 6,032 ... D5
Honda 21,506 ... C5
Ibagué 176,223 ... C5
Inírida 1,792 ... F6
Ipiales 30,871 ... B7
Iscuandé 561 ... A6
Istmina 5,575 ... B5
Itagüí 96,972 ... C4
Ituango 5,561 ... C4
Juradó 935 ... B4
La Cruz 4,353 ... B7
La Dorada 30,962 ... C5
La Gloria 2,632 ... D3
La Palma 5,430 ... C5
La Plata 8,047 ... C6
La Unión 5,392 ... B7
Leticia 6,285 ... F10
Líbano 19,132 ... C5
Lorica 18,251 ... C3
Los Andes 1,414 ... B7
Magangué 34,396 ... C3
Maicao 21,645 ... D2
Majagual 2,329 ... C3
Málaga 10,645 ... D4
Maní 951 ... D5
Manizales 199,904 ... C5
Matanza 1,211 ... D4
Medellín 1,070,924 ... C4
Medina 1,436 ... D5
Mercaderes 3,877 ... B7
Miraflores, Boyacá 3,584 ... D5
Miraflores, Vaupés 536 ... D7
Miranda 6,439 ... B6
Mitú 1,637 ... E7
Mocoa 6,221 ... B7
Mompós 14,076 ... C3
Moniquirá 5,711 ... D5
Montería 89,583 ... B3
Morichal ... E6
Mosquera 594 ... A6
Murindó 485 ... B4
Muzo 1,823 ... D5
Natagaima 7,772 ... C6
Neiva 105,476 ... C6
Nóvita 802 ... B5
Nunchía 437 ... D5
Nuquí 1,115 ... B5
Ocaña 38,352 ... D3
Orocué 1,011 ... E5
Ortega 5,150 ... C6
Pacho 6,786 ... C5
Páez 2,098 ... C6
Paipa 4,260 ... D5
Palmira 140,481 ... B6
Pamplona 31,817 ... D4
Pasto 119,339 ... B7
Patía 5,306 ... B6
Paz de Ariporo 2,584 ... E5
Paz de Río 3,464 ... D4
Pedraza 1,872 ... C2
Pereira 174,128 ... C5
Piedecuesta 17,308 ... D4
Piendamó 5,046 ... B6
Pitalito 15,049 ... B7
Pivijay 10,172 ... C2
Planeta Rica 12,932 ... C3
Plato 18,589 ... C3
Popayán 77,669 ... B6
Pore 389 ... D5
Pradera 15,732 ... B6
Puente Nacional 4,317 ... D5
Puerto Asís 6,364 ... B7
Puerto Berrío 19,579 ... C4
Puerto Carreño 2,172 ... G4
Puerto Colombia 9,255 ... C2
Puerto Escondido 1,368 ... B3
Puerto Leguízamo 3,179 ... C8
Puerto López, Meta 4,948 ... D5
Puerto Murillo ... G4
Puerto Mutis ... B4
Puerto Nare ... D7
Puerto Paulina ... D7
Puerto Rico, Caquetá 4,853 ... C7
Puerto Rondón 1,010 ... E4
Puerto Salgar 6,396 ... C5
Puerto Tejada 18,315 ... B6
Puerto Wilches 5,282 ... D4
Pupiales 2,723 ... B7
Purificación 8,164 ... C6
Quibdó 28,040 ... B5
Remedios 4,681 ... C4
Remolino 3,408 ... C2
Restrepo 2,704 ... D5
Ricaurte 1,205 ... A7
Río de Oro 2,985 ... D3
Riohacha 19,604 ... D2
Rionegro, Antioquia 22,654 ... C4
Rionegro, Santander 3,491 ... D4
Riosucio, Caldas 11,619 ... C5
Riosucio, Chocó 2,184 ... B4
Roberto Payán 445 ... A7
Robles 5,422 ... D2
Rovira 5,105 ... C5
Sabanalarga 26,542 ... C2
Sácama 69 ... D4
Sahagún 18,717 ... C3
Salamina 12,136 ... C5
Salazar 2,791 ... D4
Samaniego 4,790 ... B7
San Agustín 4,532 ... B7
San Andrés, Antioquia 2,003 ... C4
San Andrés, San Andrés y Providencia 14,428 ... A9
San Antero 7,129 ... C3
Sandoná 7,222 ... B7
San Francisco 1,654 ... B7
San Gil 21,679 ... D4
San Jacinto 13,459 ... C3
San José del Guaviare 4,138 ... D6
San Juan del César 9,468 ... D2
San Marcos 10,415 ... C3
San Martín 8,281 ... D6
San Onofre 7,899 ... C3
San Pablo 3,662 ... B7
San Roque 4,972 ... C4
Santa Bárbara 11,848 ... C5
Santa Marta 102,484 ... D2
Santander 13,625 ... B6
Santa Rosa de Cabal 28,368 ... C5
Santa Rosa de Osos 8,593 ... C4
San Vicente del Caguán 3,182 ... C6
Sardinata 3,726 ... D3
Segovia 10,000 ... C4
Sevilla 31,143 ... C5
Sibundoy 2,853 ... B7
Silvia 3,045 ... B6
Simití 3,062 ... C4
Sincé 11,909 ... C3
Sincelejo 68,797 ... C3
Sipí 153 ... B5
Sitionuevo 5,919 ... C2
Soatá 4,294 ... D4
Socorro 15,596 ... D4
Sogamoso 48,891 ... D5
Soledad 64,469 ... C2
Sonsón 15,990 ... C5
Sopetrán 5,223 ... C4
Tadó 3,102 ... B5
Támara 947 ... D5
Tame 4,811 ... E4
Tibaná 1,100 ... D5
Tierralta 7,950 ... C3
Timaná 4,262 ... C7
Timbío 4,755 ... B6
Timbiquí 1,048 ... B6
Toledo 2,942 ... D4
Tolú 9,118 ... C3
Trinidad 729 ... E5
Tuluá 86,736 ... B5
Tumaco 38,742 ... A7
Tunja 51,620 ... D5
Túquerres 12,058 ... B7
Turbaco 19,360 ... C2
Turbo 16,070 ... B3
Ubaté 7,716 ... D5
Uribia 2,193 ... D2
Urrao 8,577 ... B4
Valdivia 4,318 ... C4
Valledupar 87,425 ... D2
Vélez 8,241 ... D4
Venadillo 8,383 ... C5
Villanueva 9,836 ... D2
Villa Rosario 8,668 ... D4
Villavicencio 82,869 ... D5
Villeta 6,507 ... C5
Yarumal 21,333 ... C4
Yopal 5,851 ... D5
Yumbo 28,011 ... B6
Zapatoca 6,258 ... D4
Zaragoza 9,660 ... C4
Zarzal 21,370 ... B5
Zipaquirá 25,413 ... D5

OTHER FEATURES

Abibe, Serranía de, (mts.) ... B3
Aguarico, (riv.) ... B7
Aguja, La, (cape) ... C2
Albuquerque, (cays) ... A10
Alicia, (bank) ... B8
Alto Ritacuva, (mt.) ... D4
Amazon, (riv.) ... E9
Ancón de Sardinas, (bay) ... A7
Angostura, (falls) ... E6
Apaporis, (riv.) ... F8
Araracuara, Cerros de, (mts.) ... E7
Arauca, (riv.) ... E4
Ariari, (riv.) ... D6
Ariguaní, (riv.) ... D3
Ariporo, (riv.) ... E4
Atabapo, (riv.) ... G6
Atrato, (riv.) ... B4
Augusta, (cape) ... C2
Ayapel, Serranía de, (mts.) ... C4
Bajo Nuevo, (shoal) ... C8
Barú, (isl.) ... C2
Baudó, Serranía de, (mts.) ... B5
Baudó, (riv.) ... B5
Bita, (riv.) ... F5
Buenaventura, (bay) ... B6
Caguán, (riv.) ... C7
Cahuinari, (riv.) ... E8
Caquetá, (riv.) ... E8
Caraparaná, (riv.) ... D8
Casanare, (riv.) ... E4
Catatumbo, (riv.) ... D3
Cauca, (riv.) ... C4
Cazueleja, Cerro, (mt.) ... C6
Central, Cordillera, (range) ... C5
César, (riv.) ... D2
Chaira, Laguna, (lake) ... C7
Chamusa, Sierra, (mts.) ... C6
Charambirá, (pt.) ... B5
Chicamocha, (riv.) ... D4
Chiribiquete, Sierra de, (mts.) ... D7
Cinaruco, (riv.) ... F4
Chocó, (bay) ... B6
Cocuy, Sierra Nevada del, (mts.) ... D4
Coredó (Humboldt), (bay) ... B4
Corrientes, (cape) ... B5
Courtown (Este Sudeste), (cays) ... A10
Cravo Norte, (riv.) ... E4
Cravo Sur, (riv.) ... E5
Cristóbal Colón, Pico, (peak) ... D2
Cuemaní, (riv.) ... D7
Cupica, (gulf) ... B4
Cuquiari, (riv.) ... E7
Cusachón, (isl.) ... D1
Cusiana, (riv.) ... D5
Espada, (pt.) ... E1
Este Sudeste, (cays) ... A10
Fuerte, (isl.) ... B3
Gallinas, (pt.) ... E1
Gorgona, (isl.) ... A6
Grande, (isl.) ... B4
Grande, Salto, (falls) ... D8
Guainía, (riv.) ... F6
Guajira, (pen.) ... E1
Guapi, (bay) ... A6
Guaviare, (riv.) ... F6
Guayabero, (riv.) ... D6
Huila, Nevado del, (mt.) ... C6
Humboldt, (bay) ... B4
Igara-Paraná, (riv.) ... D8
Inírida, (riv.) ... F6
Isana, (riv.) ... F7
La Aguja, (cape) ... C2
La Macarena, Serranía de, (mts.) ... D6
La Vela, (cape) ... D1
Lebrija, (riv.) ... D4
Llanos, (plains) ... D5
Losada, (riv.) ... C6
Macarena, Serranía de La, (mts.) ... D6
Magdalena, (riv.) ... C3
Manacacías, (riv.) ... D6
Mapiripán, Laguna, (lake) ... E6
Marzo, (pt.) ... B4
Mesai, (riv.) ... D7
Meta, (riv.) ... E5
Metica, (riv.) ... D6
Mira, (riv.) ... A7
Miritiparaná, (riv.) ... E8
Morrosquillo, (gulf) ... C3
Muco, (riv.) ... E5
Naipo, (isl.) ... F6
Nechí, (riv.) ... C4
Negro, (riv.) ... G7
Occidental, Cordillera, (range) ... B5
Oriental, Cordillera, (range) ... D5
Orinoco, (riv.) ... G5
Orteguaza, (riv.) ... C7
Papunáua, (riv.) ... E6
Papurí, (riv.) ... F7
Patía, (riv.) ... B6
Pauto, (riv.) ... E5
Perijá, Serranía de, (mts.) ... D2
Providencia, (isl.) ... B9
Puracé, (vol.) ... B6
Putumayo, (riv.) ... E9
Quitasueño, (bank) ... A8
Roca que Vela, (cay) ... B8
Roncador, (cays) ... B9
Saldaña, (riv.) ... C6
Salto Grande, (falls) ... D8
San Andrés, (isl.) ... A10
San Bernardo, (isls.) ... C3
San Jorge, (riv.) ... C3
San Juan, (riv.) ... B5
San Miguel, (riv.) ... B7
Santa Catalina, (isl.) ... A9
Santa Marta, Sierra Nevada de, (range) ... D2
Serrana, (bank) ... B9
Serranilla, (bank) ... B8
Sinú, (riv.) ... B3
Sogamoso, (riv.) ... D4
Solano, (pt.) ... B4
Suárez, (riv.) ... D4
Sucio, (riv.) ... B4
Taraíra, (riv.) ... F8
Tequendama, (falls) ... C5
Tibugá, (gulf) ... B5
Tolima, Nevada del, (mt.) ... C5
Tomo, (riv.) ... F5
Tortugas, (gulf) ... B6
Tota, Laguna de, (lake) ... D5
Truandó, (riv.) ... B4
Tumaco, Rada de, (bay) ... A6
Tunahí, Sierra, (mts.) ... E7
Upía, (riv.) ... D5
Urabá, (gulf) ... B3
Uva, Laguna, (lake) ... E6
Uva, (riv.) ... E6
Vaupés, (riv.) ... E7
Vela, La, (cape) ... D1
Vela, Roca que, (cay) ... B8
Vichada, (riv.) ... F5
Viglá, (cay) ... A10
Yarí, (riv.) ... D8
Zapatosa, Ciénaga de, (swamp) ... D3

*City and suburbs.

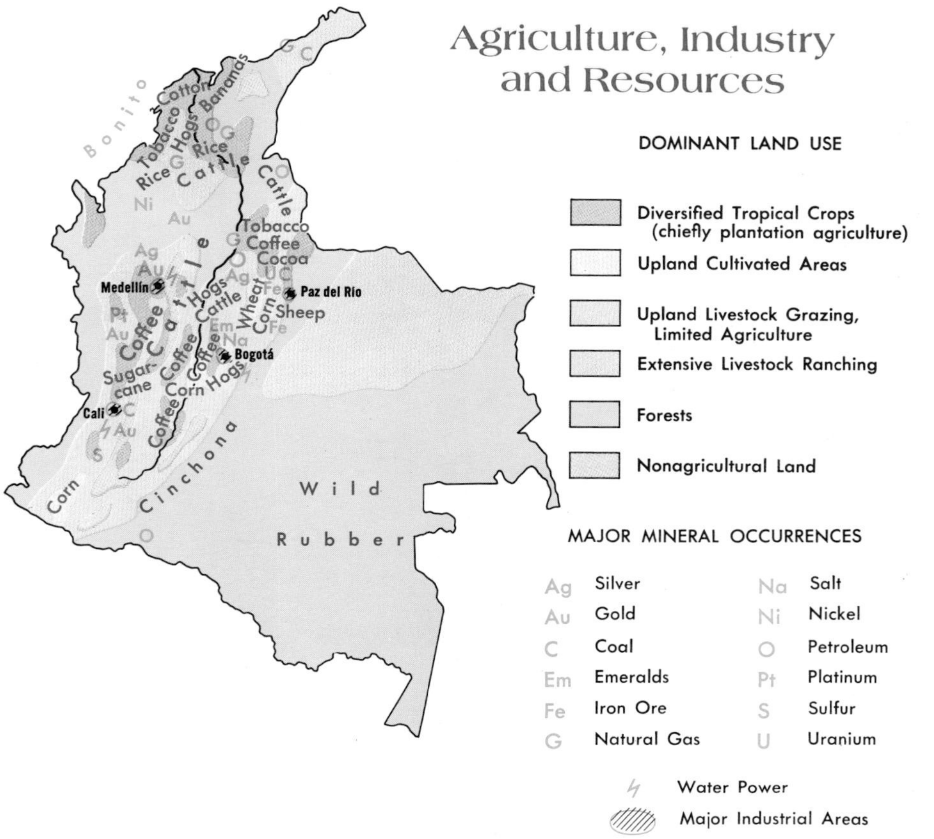
Agriculture, Industry and Resources
DOMINANT LAND USE
Diversified Tropical Crops (chiefly plantation agriculture)
Upland Cultivated Areas
Upland Livestock Grazing, Limited Agriculture
Extensive Livestock Ranching
Forests
Nonagricultural Land
MAJOR MINERAL OCCURRENCES
Ag Silver
Au Gold
C Coal
Em Emeralds
Fe Iron Ore
G Natural Gas
Na Salt
Ni Nickel
O Petroleum
Pt Platinum
S Sulfur
U Uranium
Water Power
Major Industrial Areas
Medellín
Paz del Río
Bogotá
Cali
Bonito
Cotton
Tobacco
Bananas
Rice
Hogs
Cattle
Coffee
Cocoa
Wheat
Corn
Sheep
Sugar-cane
Cinchona
Wild Rubber

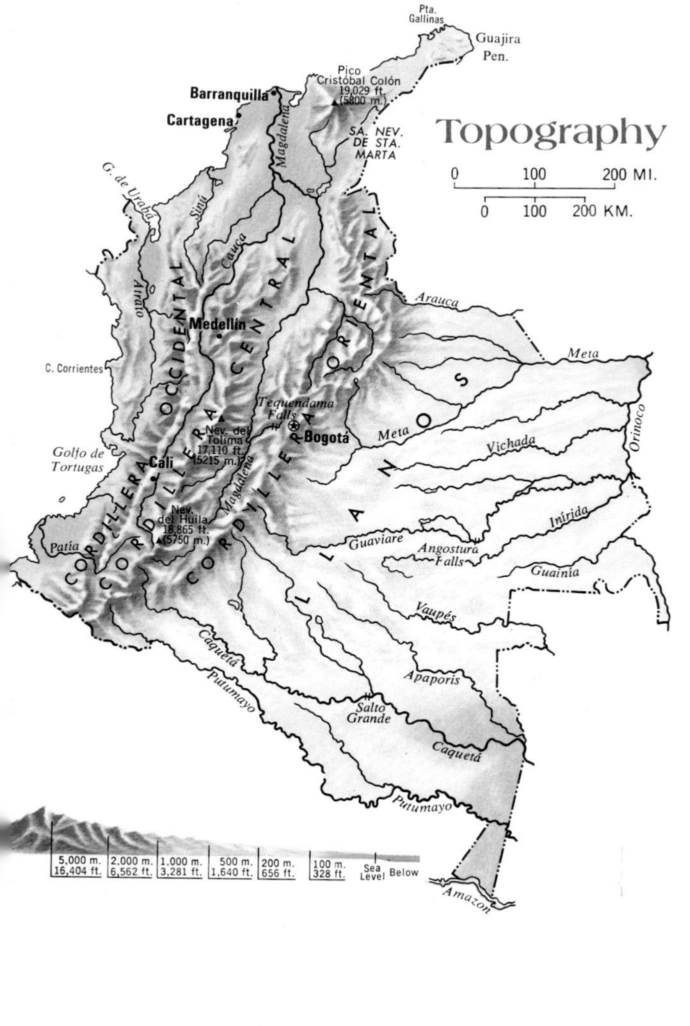
Topography
0 100 200 MI.
0 100 200 KM.
Pta. Gallinas
Guajira Pen.
Pico Cristóbal Colón 19,029 ft. (5800 m.)
Barranquilla
Cartagena
SA. NEV. DE STA. MARTA
Magdalena
G. de Urabá
Sinú
Cauca
Atrato
Medellín
C. Corrientes
Arauca
Meta
Tequendama Falls
Nev. del Tolima 17,110 ft. (5215 m.)
Bogotá
Cali
Golfo de Tortugas
Nev. del Huila 18,865 ft. (5750 m.)
Patía
Vichada
Orinoco
Inírida
Guaviare
Angostura Falls
Guainía
Vaupés
Apaporis
Caquetá
Putumayo
Salto Grande
Amazon
CORDILLERA OCCIDENTAL
CORDILLERA CENTRAL
CORDILLERA ORIENTAL
LLANOS
5,000 m. 16,404 ft.
2,000 m. 6,562 ft.
1,000 m. 3,281 ft.
500 m. 1,640 ft.
200 m. 656 ft.
100 m. 328 ft.
Sea Level
Below

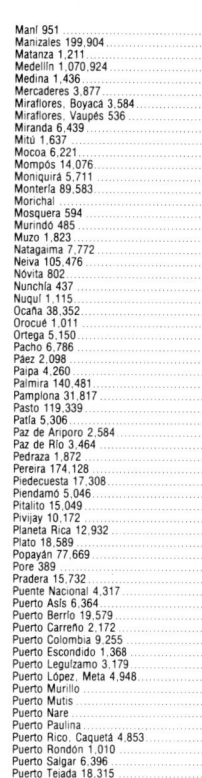

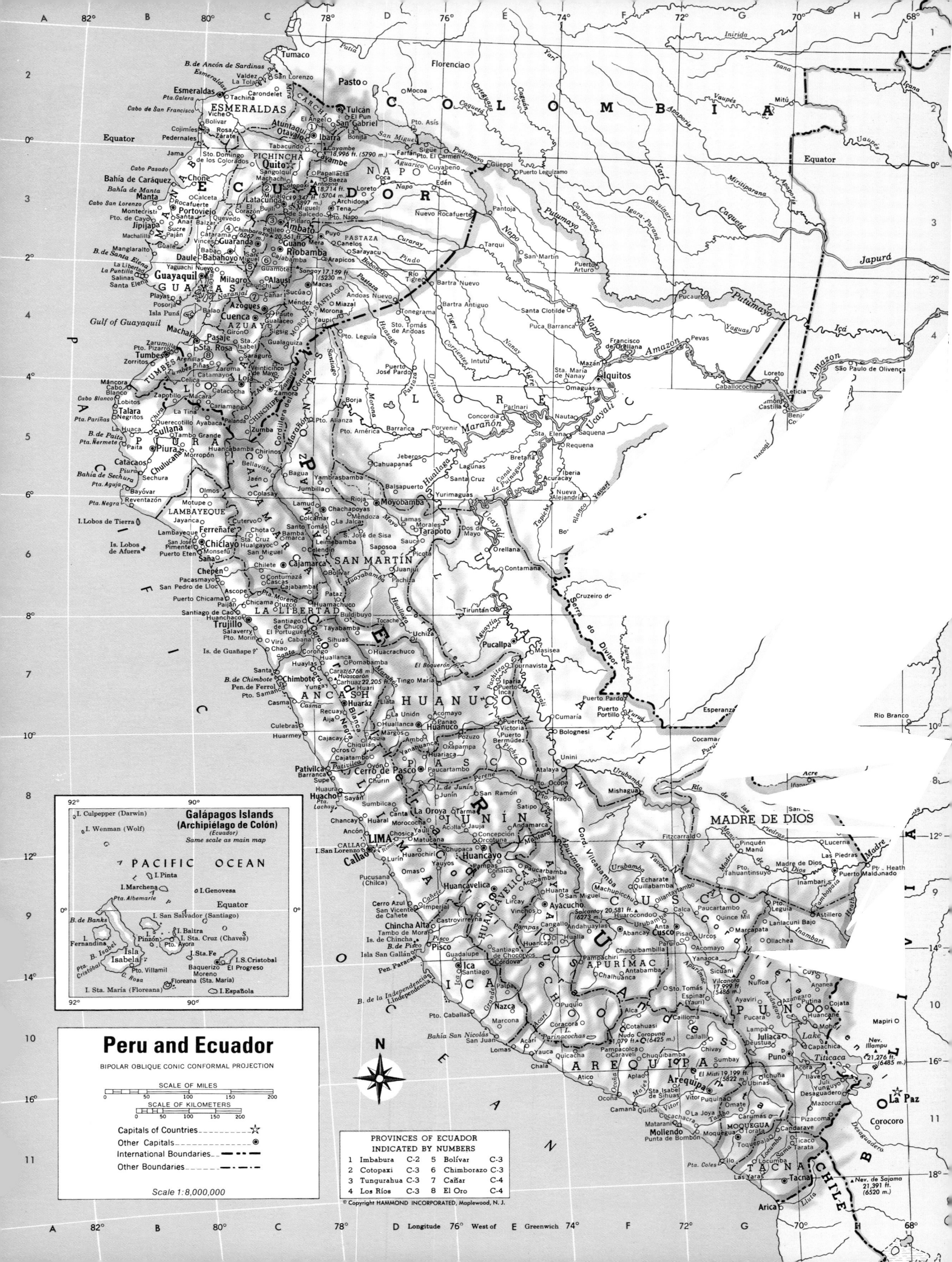

Peru and Ecuador

BIPOLAR OBLIQUE CONIC CONFORMAL PROJECTION

SCALE OF MILES

0   50   100   150   200

SCALE OF KILOMETERS

0   50   100   150   200

Capitals of Countries .... ★

Other Capitals .... ◉

International Boundaries ----·----

Other Boundaries ------------

Scale 1:8,000,000

Galápagos Islands
(Archipiélago de Colón)
(Ecuador)
Same scale as main map

PACIFIC OCEAN

PROVINCES OF ECUADOR
INDICATED BY NUMBERS

1 Imbabura	C-2	5 Bolívar	C-3
2 Cotopaxi	C-3	6 Chimborazo	C-3
3 Tungurahua	C-3	7 Cañar	C-4
4 Los Ríos	C-3	8 El Oro	C-4

© Copyright HAMMOND INCORPORATED, Maplewood, N. J.

Longitude 76° West of Greenwich

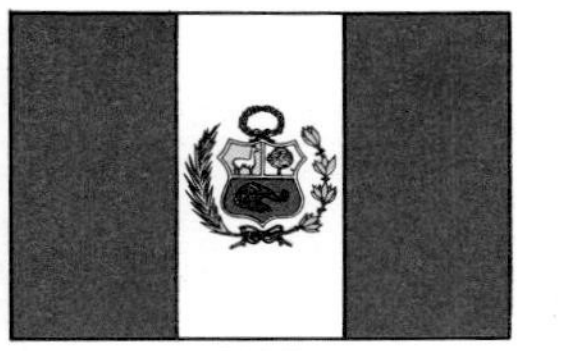

PERU

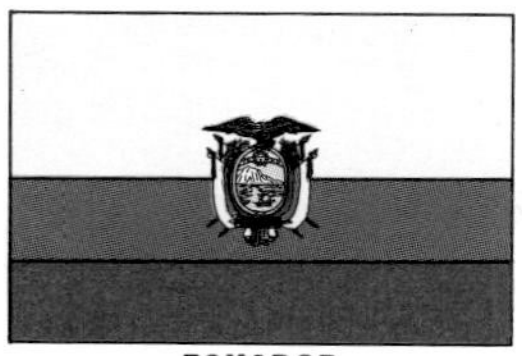

ECUADOR

PERU

AREA 496,222 sq. mi. (1,285,215 sq. km.)
POPULATION 17,031,221
CAPITAL Lima
LARGEST CITY Lima
HIGHEST POINT Huascarán 22,205 ft. (6,768 m.)
MONETARY UNIT sol
MAJOR LANGUAGES Spanish, Quechua, Aymara
MAJOR RELIGION Roman Catholicism

ECUADOR

AREA 109,483 sq. mi. (283,561 sq. km.)
POPULATION 8,644,000
CAPITAL Quito
LARGEST CITY Guayaquil
HIGHEST POINT Chimborazo 20,561 ft. (6,267 m.)
MONETARY UNIT sucre
MAJOR LANGUAGES Spanish, Quechua
MAJOR RELIGION Roman Catholicism

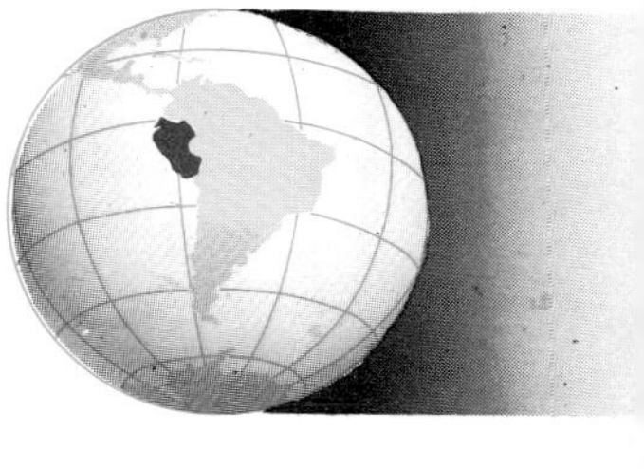

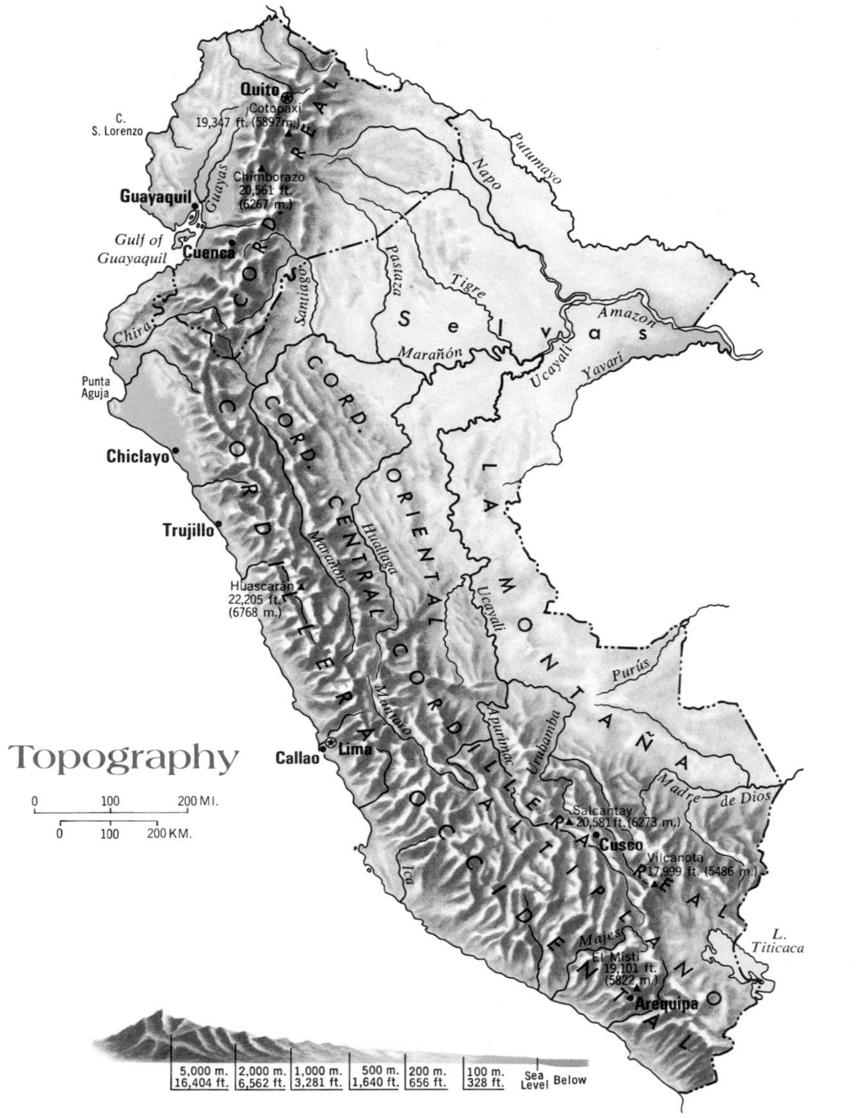

PERU

DEPARTMENTS

Amazonas 256,460 C5
Ancash 815,646 D7
Apurímac 321,936 F10
Arequipa 702,308 F10
Ayacucho 500,732 E9
Cajamarca 1,044,689 C6
Callao (prov.) 446,730 D9
Cusco 829,294 F9
Huancavelica 346,460 E9
Huánuco 481,924 D7
Ica 431,442 E10
Junín 848,993 E8
La Libertad 960,537 C6
Lambayeque 683,425 B6
Lima 4,738,266 D8
Loreto 446,316 E5
Madre de Dios 36,555 G8
Moquegua 99,287 G11
Pasco 221,219 E8
Piura 1,168,442 B5
Puno 893,586 G10
San Martín 319,670 D6
Tacna 133,240 G11
Tumbes 103,979 B4
Ucayali 200,085 E6

CITIES and TOWNS

Abancay 19,807 F9
Acarí 4,907 E10
Acobamba 2,156 E9
Acolla 5,717 E8
Acomayo, Cusco 1,419 G9
Acomayo, Huánuco 2,883 E7
Acora 1,910 H11
Acuracay 1,282 F5
Aija 1,843 D7
Alca 755 F10
Ambo 3,060 D8
Ananea 668 H10
Ancón 8,610 D8
Andahuaylas 7,654 F9
Andamarca 470 E8
Anta 3,703 F9
Antabamba 2,223 F10
Aplao 1,941 F11
Aquia 970 D8
Arequipa 107,858 G11
Arequipa* 447,431 G11
Ascope 12,070 C6
Astillero H9
Atalaya 2,229 E8
Atico 2,316 F11
Ayabaca 4,543 C5
Ayacucho 68,535 F9
Ayaviri 11,067 G10
Azángaro 7,658 H10
Bagua 9,735 C5
Balsapuerto 164 D5
Bambamarca 6,867 C6
Barranca, Lima 31,312 C8
Barranca, Loreto 1,351 D5
Bartra Antiguo E4
Bartra Nuevo E4
Bayóvar B5
Bellavista 4,906 C5
Bolívar 1,106 D6
Bolognesi F6
Bolognesi 661 F8
Borja 215 D5
Bretaña 1,035 E5
Buldibuyo 582 D7
Cabana 1,804 C7
Cabo Blanco B5
Cahuapanas 304 D5
Cailloma 1,187 G10
Cajabamba 7,282 C6
Cajacay 668 D8
Cajamarca 60,280 C6
Cajatambo 1,721 D8
Calca 6,112 G9
Callalli 819 G10
Callao 260,581 D9
Callao* 441,374 D9
Camaná 11,386 F11
Candarave 1,207 G11
Cangallo 1,584 E9
Canta 3,431 D8
Capachica 307 H10
Caraz 6,376 D7
Caravelí 1,827 F10
Carhuás 3,147 D7
Carumás 1,031 G11
Cascas 2,638 C6
Casma 12,725 C7
Castrovirreyna 1,749 E9
Catacaos 30,927 B5
Celendín 8,538 D6
Cerro Azul 2,314 D9
Cerro de Pasco 71,558 D8
Chachapoyas 11,919 D6
Chala 1,646 E10
Chalhuanca 3,071 F10
Chancay 18,993 D8
Chao C7
Chepén 29,919 C6
Chicama 11,160 C6
Chiclayo 280,244 C6
Chilca (Pucusana) 3,329 D9
Chilete 2,537 C6
Chimbote 216,406 C7
Chincha Alta 237,475 D9
Chiquián 3,521 D8
Chirinos 1,061 C5
Chivay 3,296 G10
Chosica D8
Chota 8,299 C6
Chulucanas 34,977 B5
Chupaca 5,422 E9
Chuquibamba 2,630 F10
Chuquibambilla 2,147 F9
Churín 1,801 D8
Cocachacra 5,985 G11
Cocama G8
Cojata 888 H10
Colasay 721 C5
Colcamar 1,216 D6
Conaica 1,154 E9
Concepción 7,129 E8
Concordia 1,372 E5
Contamana 5,718 E6
Contumazá 2,491 C6
Coracora 4,598 F10
Córdova 453 E10
Corongo 1,762 D7
Cotahuasi 1,301 F10
Culebras C7
Cumaría F7
Cusco (Cuzco) 85,044 F9
Cusco* 181,604 F9
Cutervo 6,890 C6
Cuyocuyo 1,101 H10
Desaguadero 2,682 H11
Deustua 544 G10
Dos de Mayo 574 E6
Echarate 1,071 F9
El Portugués C7
Esperanza 375 G7
Espinar 6,381 G10
Ferreñafe 22,200 C6
Francisco de Orellana 445 F4
Guadalupe 7,613 E9
Güeppi E3
Huacho 43,402 D8
Huacrachuco 1,210 D7
Hualgayoc 1,691 C6
Hualla 4,042 F9
Huallanca, Ancash 930 D7
Huallanca, Huánuco 4,806 D7
Huamachuco 8,273 D6
Huancabamba 4,393 C5
Huancané 5,227 H10
Huancapi 2,539 E9
Huancavelica 20,889 E9
Huancayo 165,132 E9
Huanchaco 6,005 C7
Huanta 11,213 E9
Huánuco 52,628 E7
Huaral 34,235 D8
Huaráz 45,116 D7
Huari 2,344 D7
Huariaca 2,671 E8
Huarmey 11,094 C8
Huarochirí 1,828 D9
Huarocondo 2,498 F9
Huaura 9,338 D8
Huaylas 1,344 C7
Iberia 2,307 F5
Ica 111,087 E10
Ichuña 277 G11
Ilave 9,891 H11
Ilo 31,549 G11
Imperial 20,894 D9
Iñapari 188 H8
Intutu 746 E4
Iparia 278 E7
Iquitos 173,629 F4
Jaén 24,356 C5
Jauja 14,630 E8
Jayanca 6,401 B6
Jeberos 1,493 D5
Juanjuí 9,324 D6
Juli 5,575 H11
Juliaca 77,976 G10
Jumbilla 1,035 C5
Junín 8,988 E8
Lagunas 4,601 E5
La Huaca 5,161 B5
La Jalca 1,769 D6
La Joya 5,000 G11
Lamas 8,937 D6
Lambayeque 23,746 B6
Lampa 4,319 G10
Lamud 2,405 C6
Lanlacuni Bajo 405 G9
La Oroya 33,305 D8
Las Piedras H9
Las Yaras 759 G11
La Unión 2,828 D7
Leimebamba 1,957 D6
Lima (cap.) 375,957 D8
Lima* 3,968,972 D8
Limbani 728 H10
Lircay 5,213 E9
Llata 2,922 D7
Lobitos 2,975 B5
Locumba 369 G11
Lomas 287 E10
Lucerna H9
Lurín 14,405 D9
Machupicchu 544 F9
Macusani 3,389 G10
Madre de Dios 660 G9
Máncora 5,358 B5
Manú 234 G9
Marcapata 369 G9
Marcona 25,962 E10
Margos 1,622 D8
Masisea 1,586 E7
Matarani F11
Matucana 4,196 D8
Mavila H8
Mazán 281 F4
Mazocruz 1,580 H11
Mendoza 1,902 D6
Mishagua F8
Moho 2,560 H10
Mollendo 21,206 F11
Monsefú 17,186 C6
Moquegua 21,488 G11
Morales 4,370 D6
Morococha 11,234 D8
Morropón 7,611 C5
Motupe 3,411 C6
Moyobamba 14,319 D6
Nauta 4,083 F5
Nazca 22,756 E10
Negritos 12,476 B5
Nuñoa 3,613 G10
Ocoña 1,062 F11
Ocros 1,037 D8
Ollachea 1,308 G9
Ollantaytambo 1,500 F9
Olmos 7,946 C5
Omaguas F5
Omas 249 D9
Omate 1,131 G11
Orcotuna 3,359 E8
Orellana 2,886 E6
Otuzco 5,765 C6
Oxapampa 5,233 E8
Oyón 6,279 D8
Pacasmayo 17,588 C6
Pachiza 889 D6
Paiján 12,699 C6
Paita 18,749 B5
Palpa 3,393 E10
Pampachiri 428 F10
Pampacolca 2,010 F10
Pampas 3,850 E9
Panao 1,363 E7
Pantoja 457 E3
Parinari 375 E5
Paruro 1,727 F9
Pataz 759 D6
Paucarbamba 534 E9
Paucartambo, Cusco 1,620 G9
Paucartambo, Pasco 3,497 E8
Pevas 1,325 G4
Picota 2,288 D6
Pimentel 9,129 B6
Pinquén G9
Pisac 1,566 G9
Pisco 53,414 D9
Piura 186,354 B5
Pizacoma 400 H11
Pomabamba 2,489 D7
Porvenir E5
Pozuzo 326 E8
Puca Barranca E4
Pucallpa 91,953 E7
Pucará 2,268 G10
Pucaurco 628 G4
Pucusana 3,329 D9
Puerto Alianza D5
Puerto América 240 D5
Puerto Arturo F3
Puerto Bermúdez 1,133 E8
Puerto Caballas E10
Puerto Chicama 3,136 C6
Puerto Eten 2,575 B6
Puerto Inca 1,286 E7
Puerto José Pardo D4
Puerto Leguía, Loreto D4
Puerto Leguía, Puno G9
Puerto Maldonado 12,609 H9
Puerto Morín C7
Puerto Ocopa 1,088 E8
Puerto Pardo F7
Puerto Pizarro B4
Puerto Portillo 86 F7
Puerto Prado 328 E8
Puerto Samanco 1,435 C7
Puerto Tahuantinsuyo G9
Puerto Victoria E7
Puno 66,477 G10
Punta de Bombón 4,647 F11
Punta Moreno C6
Puquina 1,026 G11
Puquio 8,099 F10
Putina 5,414 H10
Querecotillo 10,637 B5
Quicacha 255 F10
Quilca 235 F11
Quillabamba 16,837 F9
Quince Mil G9
Ramón Castilla 1,811 G5
Recuay 2,764 D7
Requena 8,270 F5
Reventazón B6
Rioja 9,876 D6
Salaverry 5,539 C7
Saña 40,144 C6
Sandia 1,682 H10
San José 4,070 B6
San José de Sisa 3,782 D6
San Juan E10
San Lorenzo 124 H8
San Martín E3
San Miguel, Ayacucho 1,440 F9
San Miguel, Cajamarca 1,798 C6
San Pedro de Lloc 11,463 C6
San Ramón 7,145 E8
Santa 20,490 C7
Santa Clotilde 1,068 E4
Santa Cruz, Cajamarca 2,739 C6
Santa Cruz, Loreto 449 E5
Santa Elena 368 F5
Santa María de Nanay 294 F4
Santiago 5,092 E10
Santiago de Cao 22,119 C6
Santiago de Chocorvos 525 E9
Santiago de Chuco 5,189 C7
Santo Tomás, Amazonas 1,093 C6
Santo Tomás, Cusco 2,755 G10
Santo Tomás de Andoas 272 D4
San Vicente de Cañete 15,277 D9
Saposoa 4,541 D6
Saquena 2,755 F5
Satipo 9,208 E8
Sauce 2,263 D6
Sayán 5,129 D8
Sechura 11,724 B5
Sicuani 21,176 G10
Sihuas 2,178 D7
Sullana 80,947 B5
Sumbay G10
Sumbilca 1,155 D8
Supe 10,061 D8
Tacna 92,640 G11
Tahuamanu 2,619 H8
Talara 55,122 B5
Tambo de Mora 2,790 D9
Tambo Grande 10,087 B5
Tamshiyacu 2,040 F5
Tarapoto 33,429 D6
Tarata 2,624 H11
Tarma 34,369 E8
Tarqui E3
Tayabamba 1,649 D7
Ticaco 781 H11
Tingo María 25,030 D7
Tiruntán 723 E6
Tocache 5,940 D7
Tonegrama D4
Topará D9
Toquepala G11
Torata 6,320 G11
Tournavista E7
Trujillo 354,557 C7
Tumbes 48,187 B4
Ubinas 422 G11
Uchiza 2,471 D7
Unini F8
Urcos 4,155 G9
Urubamba 4,686 F9
Vinchos 735 E9
Virú 6,587 C7
Vitor 416 G11
Yambrasbamba 277 D5
Yanahuanca 5,109 D8
Yanaoca 1,152 G10
Yauca 1,805 E10
Yauli 1,020 D8
Yauyos 1,296 E9
Yunguyo 7,253 H11
Yurimaguas 22,858 E5
Zarumilla 9,713 B4
Zorritos 4,497 B4

OTHER FEATURES

Acarí (riv.) E10
Aguaytía (riv.) E7
Aguja (pt.) B5
Amazon (riv.) F4
Andes, Cordillera de los (mts.) F10
Apurímac (riv.) F9
Azángaro (riv.) G10
Azul, Cordillera (mts.) E7
Blanca, Cordillera (mts.) D7
Blanco (cape) B5
Blanco (riv.) F6
Boquerón, El (pass) E7
Cañete (riv.) D9
Casma (riv.) C7
Chimbote (bay) C7
Chincha (isls.) D9
Coles (pt.) G11
Cóndor, Cordillera del (range) C5
Coropuna, Nudo (mt.) F10
Corrientes (riv.) E4
El Boquerón (pass) E7
El Misti (mt.) G11
Ene (riv.) E8
Ferrol (pen.) C7
Grande (riv.) E10
Guañape (isls.) C7
Heath (riv.) H9
Huallaga (riv.) D5
Huasaga (riv.) D4
Huascarán (mt.) D7
Huayabamba (riv.) D6
Ica (riv.) E10
Inambari (riv.) H9
Independencia (bay) D10
Independencia (isl.) D10
Junín (lake) E8
Juruá (riv.) F7
Lachay (pt.) D8
Lobos de Afuera (isls.) B6
Lobos de Tierra (isl.) B6
Locumba (riv.) G11
Madre de Dios (riv.) G9
Majes (riv.) F11
Mantaro (riv.) E8
Manú (riv.) G8
Marañón (riv.) E5
Mayo (riv.) D6
Misti, El (mt.) G11
Montaña, La (reg.) F8
Morona (riv.) D5
Nanay (riv.) E4
Napo (riv.) F4
Negra, Cordillera (mts.) D7
Negra (pt.) B6
Ñermete (pt.) B5
Occidental, Cordillera (range) F10
Ocoña (riv.) F11
Oriental, Cordillera (range) H10
Pachitea (riv.) E7
Paita (bay) B5
Pampas (riv.) E9
Paracas (pen.) D9
Parinacochas (lake) F10
Pariñas (pt.) B5
Pastaza (riv.) D5
Pativilca (riv.) D8
Perené (riv.) E8
Pichis (riv.) E8
Piedras, Las (riv.) G8
Pisco (bay) D9
Pisco (riv.) D9
Piura (riv.) B5
Puinagua, Canal de (riv.) E5
Purús (riv.) G8
Putumayo (riv.) G4
Rímac (riv.) D9
Salcantay (mt.) F9
Sama (riv.) G11
San Gallán (isl.) D9
San Lorenzo (isl.) D9
San Nicolás (bay) E10
Santa (riv.) C7
Santiago (riv.) D4
Sechura (bay) B5
Tahuamanu (riv.) H8
Tambo (riv.) G11
Tambopata (riv.) H9
Tapiche (riv.) E6
Tigre (riv.) E4
Titicaca (lake) H10
Tumbes (riv.) B4
Ucayali (riv.) F5

(continued on following page)

Agriculture, Industry and Resources

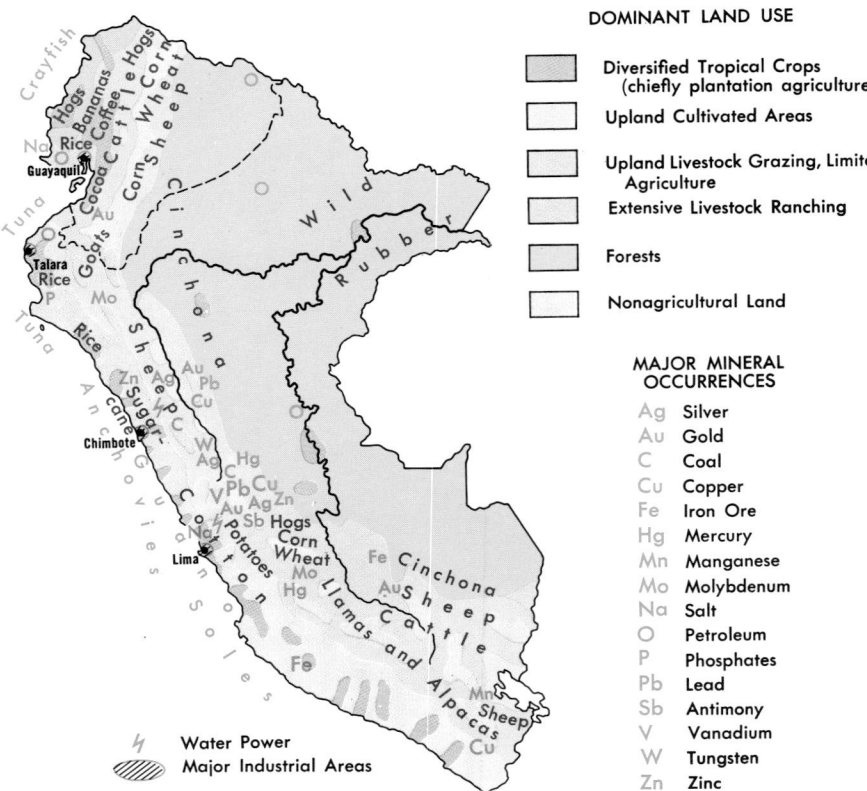

DOMINANT LAND USE

- Diversified Tropical Crops (chiefly plantation agriculture)
- Upland Cultivated Areas
- Upland Livestock Grazing, Limited Agriculture
- Extensive Livestock Ranching
- Forests
- Nonagricultural Land

MAJOR MINERAL OCCURRENCES

- Ag   Silver
- Au   Gold
- C   Coal
- Cu   Copper
- Fe   Iron Ore
- Hg   Mercury
- Mn   Manganese
- Mo   Molybdenum
- Na   Salt
- O   Petroleum
- P   Phosphates
- Pb   Lead
- Sb   Antimony
- V   Vanadium
- W   Tungsten
- Zn   Zinc

⚡ Water Power

▨ Major Industrial Areas

Agriculture, Industry and Resources

DOMINANT LAND USE

- Diversified Tropical Crops (chiefly plantation agriculture)
- Extensive Livestock Ranching
- Forests

MAJOR MINERAL OCCURRENCES

- Al   Bauxite
- Au   Gold
- D   Diamonds
- Mn   Manganese

⚡ Water Power

GUYANA

AREA 83,000 sq. mi. (214,970 sq. km.)
POPULATION 793,000
CAPITAL Georgetown
LARGEST CITY Georgetown
HIGHEST POINT Mt. Roraima 9,094 ft. (2,772 m.)
MONETARY UNIT Guyana dollar
MAJOR LANGUAGES English, Hindi
MAJOR RELIGIONS Christianity, Hinduism, Islam

SURINAME

AREA 55,144 sq. mi. (142,823 sq. km.)
POPULATION 354,860
CAPITAL Paramaribo
LARGEST CITY Paramaribo
HIGHEST POINT Julianatop 4,200 ft. (1,280 m.)
MONETARY UNIT Suriname guilder
MAJOR LANGUAGES Dutch, Hindi, Indonesian
MAJOR RELIGIONS Christianity, Islam, Hinduism

FRENCH GUIANA

AREA 35,135 sq. mi. (91,000 sq. km.)
POPULATION 73,022
CAPITAL Cayenne
LARGEST CITY Cayenne
HIGHEST POINT 2,723 ft. (830 m.)
MONETARY UNIT French franc
MAJOR LANGUAGE French
MAJOR RELIGIONS Roman Catholicism, Protestantism

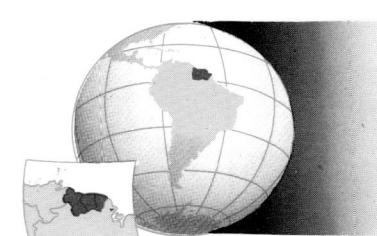

Courantyne (riv.)	C3
Cuyuni (riv.)	B2
Demerara (riv.)	B3
Enwarak (mt.)	B3
Essequibo (riv.)	B3
Great (fall)	B3
Ireng (riv.)	B3
Kaieteur (fall)	B3
Kamaria (falls)	B2
Kuyuwini (riv.)	B4
Kwitaro (riv.)	B4
Leguan (isl.)	B2
Marudi (mts.)	B5
Mazaruni (riv.)	A2
Moruka (riv.)	B2
New (riv.)	C4
Pakaraima (mts.)	A3
Playa (pt.)	B1
Pomeroon (riv.)	B2
Potaro (riv.)	B3
Puruni (riv.)	B2
Roraima (mt.)	A3
Rupununi (riv.)	B4
Sororieng (mt.)	B2
Surwakwima (fall)	B2
Takutu (riv.)	B4
Venamo (mt.)	A3
Waini (riv.)	B2
Wenamu (riv.)	A2

SURINAME

DISTRICTS

Brokopondo 17,763	D4
Commewijne 18,740	D3
Coronie 3,251	C3
Marowijne 25,911	D4
Nickerie 35,178	C3
Para 16,635	D3
Paramaribo 102,297	D2
Saramacca 13,554	C3
Suriname 151,585	D2

CITIES and TOWNS

Ajoewa	C4
Alalapadu	C4

Albina 1,000	D3
Asidonhoppo	D4
Berg en Dal	D3
Bitagron	C3
Brokopondo	D3
Burnside	C2
Calcutta 1,100	C3
Cottica	D4
Domburg 1,200	D3
Groningen 600	D2
Huwelijkszorg	C2
Kwakoegron	D3
Lelydorp 300	D3
Majoli	D4
Mariënburg 3,500	D2
Moengo 2,100	D3
Nieuw-Amsterdam 1,400	D2
Nieuw-Nickerie 7,400	C2
Paramaribo (cap.) ⊙ 167,905	D2
Paranam	D3
Totness 1,300	C3
Uitkijk	D3
Wageningen 800	C3
Zanderij	D3

OTHER FEATURES

Bakhuys (mts.)	C3
Coeroeni (riv.)	C4
Commewijne (riv.)	D3
Coppename (riv.)	C3
Corantijn (riv.)	C3
Cottica (riv.)	D3
Eilerts de Haan (mts.)	C4
Frederik Willem IV (falls)	C4
Kayser (mts.)	C4
Lely (mts.)	D3
Litani (riv.)	D4
Marowijne (riv.)	D3
Nickerie (riv.)	C3
Orange (mts.)	D4
Saramacca (riv.)	D3
Sipwliwini (riv.)	D4
Suriname (riv.)	D3
Tapanahoni (riv.)	D3
Toekomstig (res.)	C3
Van Blommestein (lake)	D3
Wilhelmina (mts.)	C4

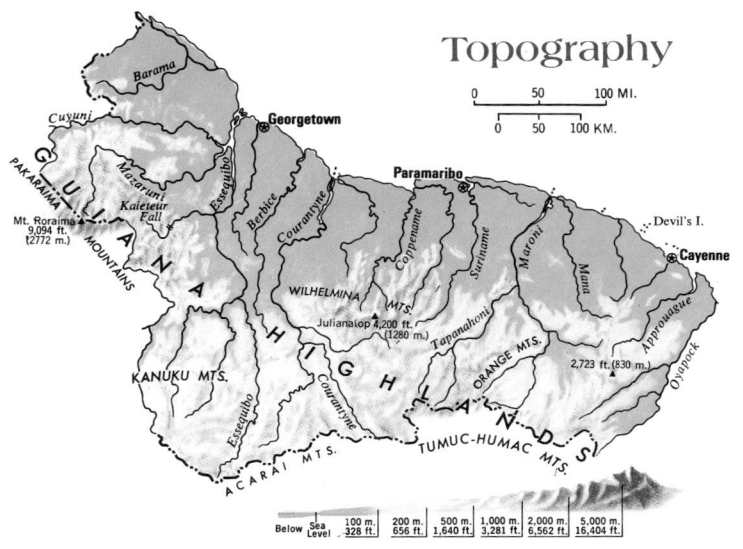

Topography

0   50   100 MI.
0   50   100 KM.

Below Sea Level	100 m. 328 ft.	200 m. 656 ft.	500 m. 1,640 ft.	1,000 m. 3,281 ft.	2,000 m. 6,562 ft.	5,000 m. 16,404 ft.

GUYANA

SURINAME

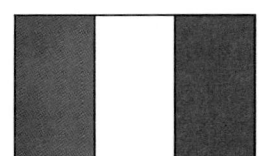

FRENCH GUIANA

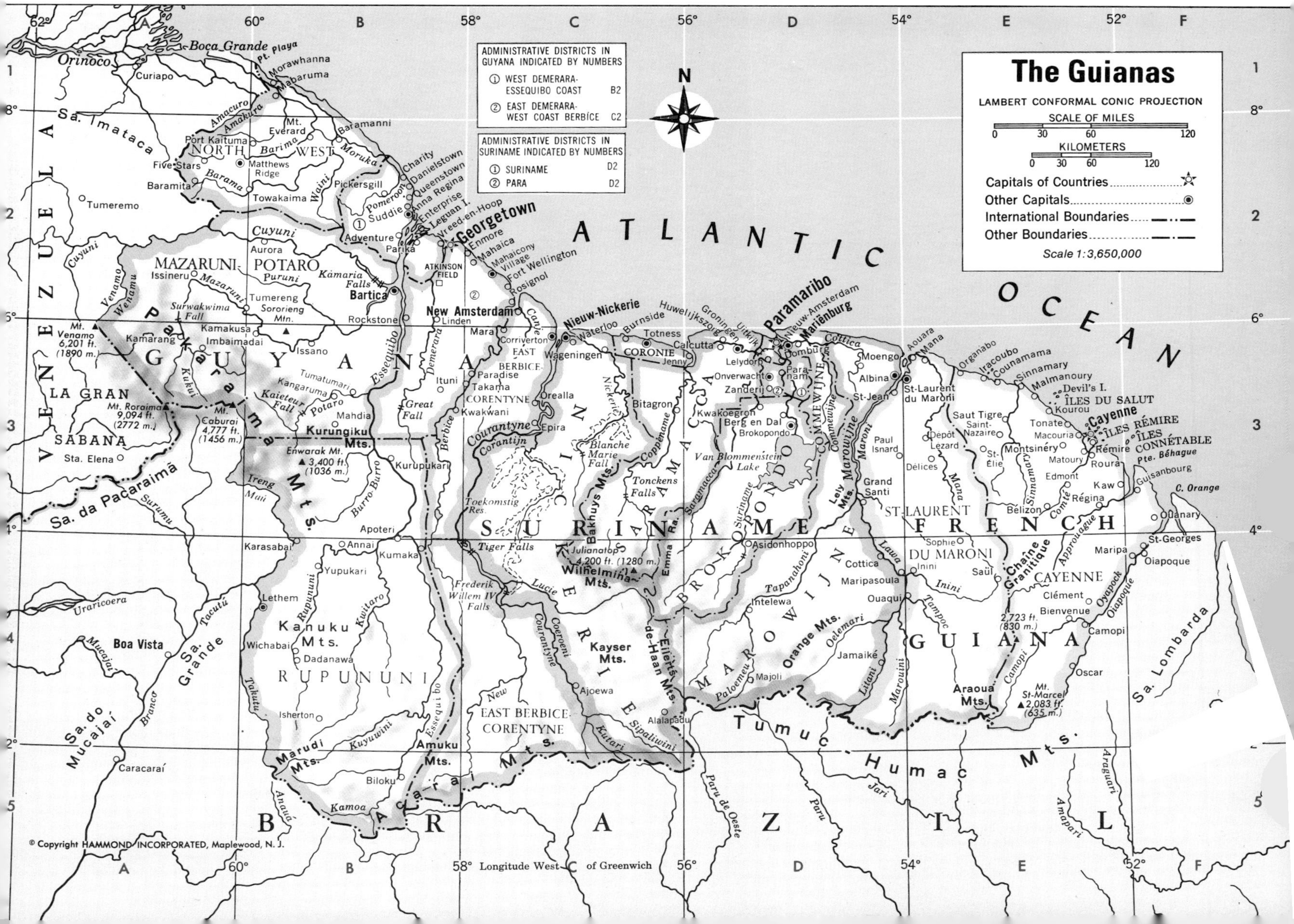

ADMINISTRATIVE DISTRICTS IN GUYANA INDICATED BY NUMBERS
① WEST DEMERARA-ESSEQUIBO COAST B2
② EAST DEMERARA-WEST COAST BERBICE C2

ADMINISTRATIVE DISTRICTS IN SURINAME INDICATED BY NUMBERS
① SURINAME D2
② PARA D2

The Guianas

LAMBERT CONFORMAL CONIC PROJECTION

SCALE OF MILES
0   30   60   120

KILOMETERS
0   30   60   120

Capitals of Countries .... ☆
Other Capitals .... ⊙
International Boundaries .... —·—·—
Other Boundaries .... —··—··—

Scale 1:3,650,000

© Copyright HAMMOND INCORPORATED, Maplewood, N.J.

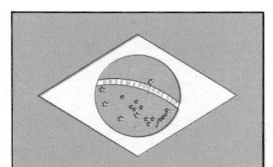

AREA 3,284,426 sq. mi. (8,506,663 sq. km.)
POPULATION 119,098,992
CAPITAL Brasília
LARGEST CITY São Paulo (greater)
HIGHEST POINT Pico da Neblina 9,889 ft.
(3,014 m.)
MONETARY UNIT cruzado
MAJOR LANGUAGE Portuguese
MAJOR RELIGION Roman Catholicism

Topography

5,000 m. / 2,000 m. / 1,000 m. / 500 m. / 200 m. / 100 m. / Sea Level / Below
16,404 ft. / 6,562 ft. / 3,281 ft. / 1,640 ft. / 656 ft. / 328 ft.

0   200   400 MI.
0   200   400 KM.

(continued on following page)

Pinhal (Espírito Santo do Pinhal) 23,235 .... *C3
Pinheiro 19,556 .... E3
Piquete 10,316 .... *D3
Piracanjuba 11,151 .... D7
Piracicaba 179,395 .... *C3
Piracuruca 9,419 .... F3
Piraí do Sul 13,709 .... *B4
Piraju 16,288 .... B3
Pirapora 31,533 .... E7
Pirassununga 32,510 .... *C2
Pires do Rio 16,659 .... D7
Piripiri 29,497 .... F4
Pitangui 12,116 .... *D1
Piúí 17,327 .... *D2
Poções 16,036 .... F6
Poconé 12,960 .... B7
Poços de Caldas 81,448 .... *C2
Pombal 14,831 .... G4
Pompéia 11,282 .... *A3
Ponta Grossa 171,111 .... *B4
Ponta Porã 25,807 .... C8
Ponte Nova 34,807 .... *E2
Porangatu 21,192 .... D6
Porto Alegre 1,108,883 ... D10
Porto Alegre †2,232,370 .. D10
Porto Feliz 19,680 .... *C3
Porto Nacional 19,052 ...... E5
Porto Seguro 5,007 .... G7
Porto União 19,426 .... D9
Porto Velho 101,644 ...... H10
Pouso Alegre 50,517 ...... *D3
Presidente Dutra 14,506 .... E4
Presidente Prudente 127,623 .... D8
Presidente Venceslau 26,720 D8
Propriá 19,034 .... G5
Promissão 15,333 .... *B2
Prudentópolis 8,645 .... D9
Quaral 15,091 .... C10
Quixadá 25,149 .... G4
Quixeramobim 14,387 ...... F4
Raposos 11,078 .... *E2
Raul Soares 10,055 .... *E2
Recife 1,184,215 .... H5
Recife †2,348,362 .... H5
Registro 28,702 .... *C4
Remanso 13,067 .... F5
Resende 36,633 .... *D3
Ribamar (São José de Ribamar) 17,560 .... F3
Ribeirão Preto 300,704 .... *C2
Rio Bonito 20,561 .... *E3
Rio Branco 87,462 .... G10
Rio Claro 103,174 .... *C3
Rio de Janeiro 5,093,237 .. *E3
Rio de Janeiro †9,018,637 . *E3
Rio do Sul 33,408 .... D9
Rio Grande 124,706 ...... D11
Rio Negro 15,851 .... D9
Rio Pardo 18,370 .... C10
Rio Pomba 9,319 .... *E2
Rio Tinto 12,511 .... H4
Rio Verde 47,639 .... D7
Rio Verde de Mato Grosso 10,001 .... C7
Rosário 11,669 .... F3
Rosário do Sul 30,753 ...... C10
Russas 16,259 .... G4
Sabará 22,883 .... *E1
Sacramento 10,524 .... *C1
Salgueiro 25,915 .... G5
Salinas 12,613 .... F7
Salinópolis 10,395 .... E3
Salto 42,351 .... *C3
Salvador 1,496,276 .... G6
Salvador †1,772,018 ...... G6
Santa Cruz 13,172 .... G4
Santa Cruz do Rio Pardo 20,507 .... *B3
Santa Cruz do Sul 52,050 .. C10
Santa Helena de Goiás 20,067 .... D7
Santa Leopoldina 1,217 .... G7
Santa Maria 151,202 ...... C10
Santa Maria da Vitória 16,294 .... F6
Santana do Ipanema 15,311 . G5
Santana do Livramento 58,165 .... C10
Santarém 101,534 .... C3
Santa Rita do Sapucaí 15,005 .... *D3
Santa Vitória do Palmar 14,758 .... C11
Santiago 30,406 .... C10
Santo Amaro 29,627 ...... G6
Santo Ângelo 50,161 ...... C10
Santo André 549,278 ...... *C3
Santo Antônio da Platina 21,284 .... *A3
Santos 411,023 .... *C3
Santos Dumont 31,053 .... *E2
São Bento 9,607 .... E3
São Bernardo do Campo 381,261 .... *C3
São Borja 41,598 .... C10
São Carlos 109,231 .... *C3
São Cristóvão 11,720 ...... G5
São Fidélis 11,713 .... *F2
São Francisco 12,011 ...... E6
São Francisco do Sul 13,914 .... E9
São Gabriel 40,497 .... C10
São Gonçalo 221,278 ...... F8
São João da Boa Vista 45,712 .... *C2
São João del Rei 53,401 .... *D2
São João dos Patos 12,848 . F4
São João Nepomuceno 12,752 .... *E2
São Joaquim da Barra 26,273 .... *C2

São José 37,562 .... D9
São José do Rio Pardo 21,914 .... *C2
São José do Rio Preto 171,982 .... *B2
São José dos Campos 268,073 .... *D3
São José dos Pinhais 53,422 .... D9
São Leopoldo 94,864 ...... D10
São Lourenço 23,047 ...... *D3
São Lourenço do Sul 13,251 .... C10
São Luís 182,466 .... F3
São Luís Gonzaga 29,188 .. C10
São Manuel 17,028 .... *B3
São Mateus 22,522 .... G7
São Miguel do Guamá 9,929 E3
São Miguel dos Campos 18,495 .... G5
São Paulo 7,033,529 .... *C3
São Paulo †12,588,439 .... *C3
São Paulo de Olivença 3,102 G9
São Raimundo Nonato 8,574 F5
São Roque 26,118 .... *C3
São Sebastião 11,065 ...... *D3
São Sebastião do Paraíso 28,482 .... *C2
São Vicente 192,770 .... *C4
Senador Pompeu 10,109 .... G4
Sena Madureira 6,668 ...... G10
Senhor do Bonfim 33,811 .. F5
Serra do Navio 415 .... F3
Serra Talhada 28,912 ...... G4
Serrinha 23,920 .... G5
Sertânia 11,410 .... G5
Sete Lagoas 94,502 .... E7
Sobral 69,072 .... G3
Socorro 12,111 .... *C3
Sorocaba 254,718 .... *C3
Soure 11,306 .... D3
Taguatinga 480,109 .... D6
Taquaritinga 28,018 .... *B2
Tarauacá 6,889 .... G10
Tatuí 44,816 .... *C3
Taubaté 155,371 .... E8
Tefé 14,670 .... G9
Teófilo Otoni 83,108 .... F7
Teresina 339,264 .... F4
Teresópolis 78,782 .... *E3
Tijucas 8,979 .... D9
Timon 55,318 .... F4
Tocantinópolis 8,427 .... D4
Touros H4

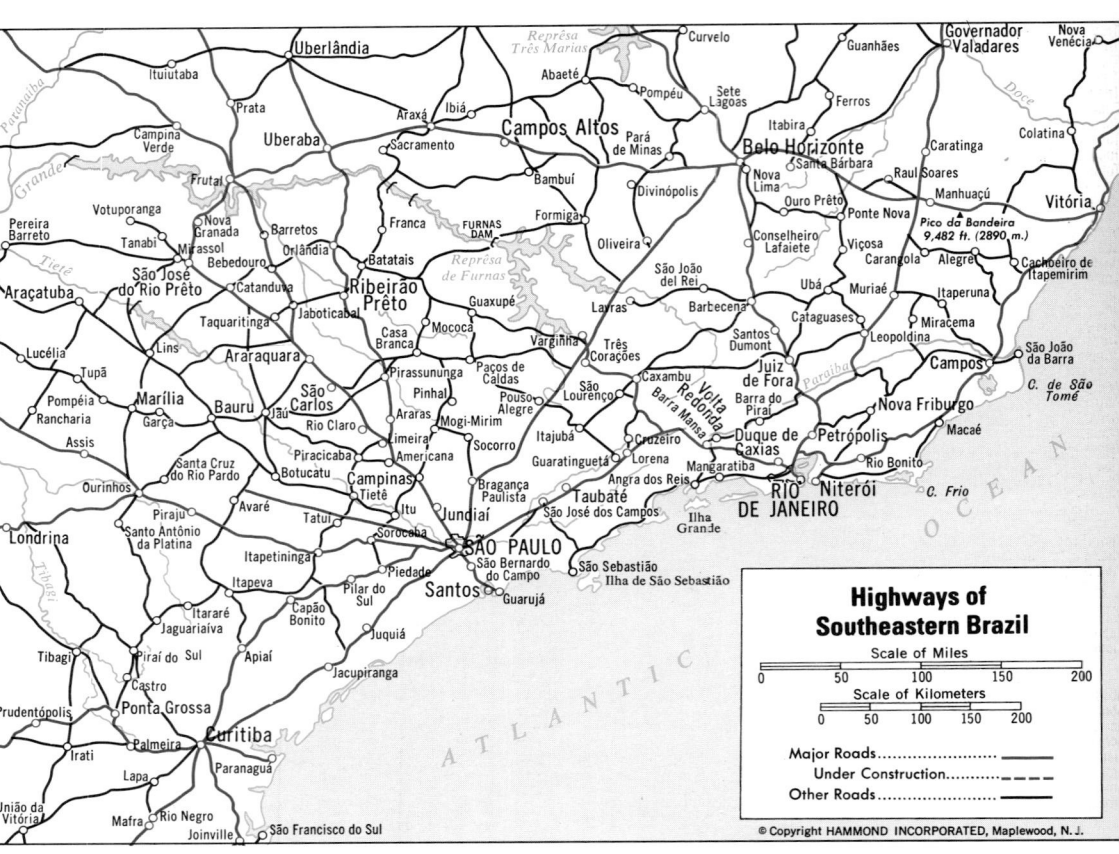

Highways of Southeastern Brazil

Scale of Miles
0   50   100   150   200

Scale of Kilometers
0   50   100   150   200

Major Roads ....
Under Construction............
Other Roads ....

© Copyright HAMMOND INCORPORATED, Maplewood, N.J.

Agriculture, Industry and Resources

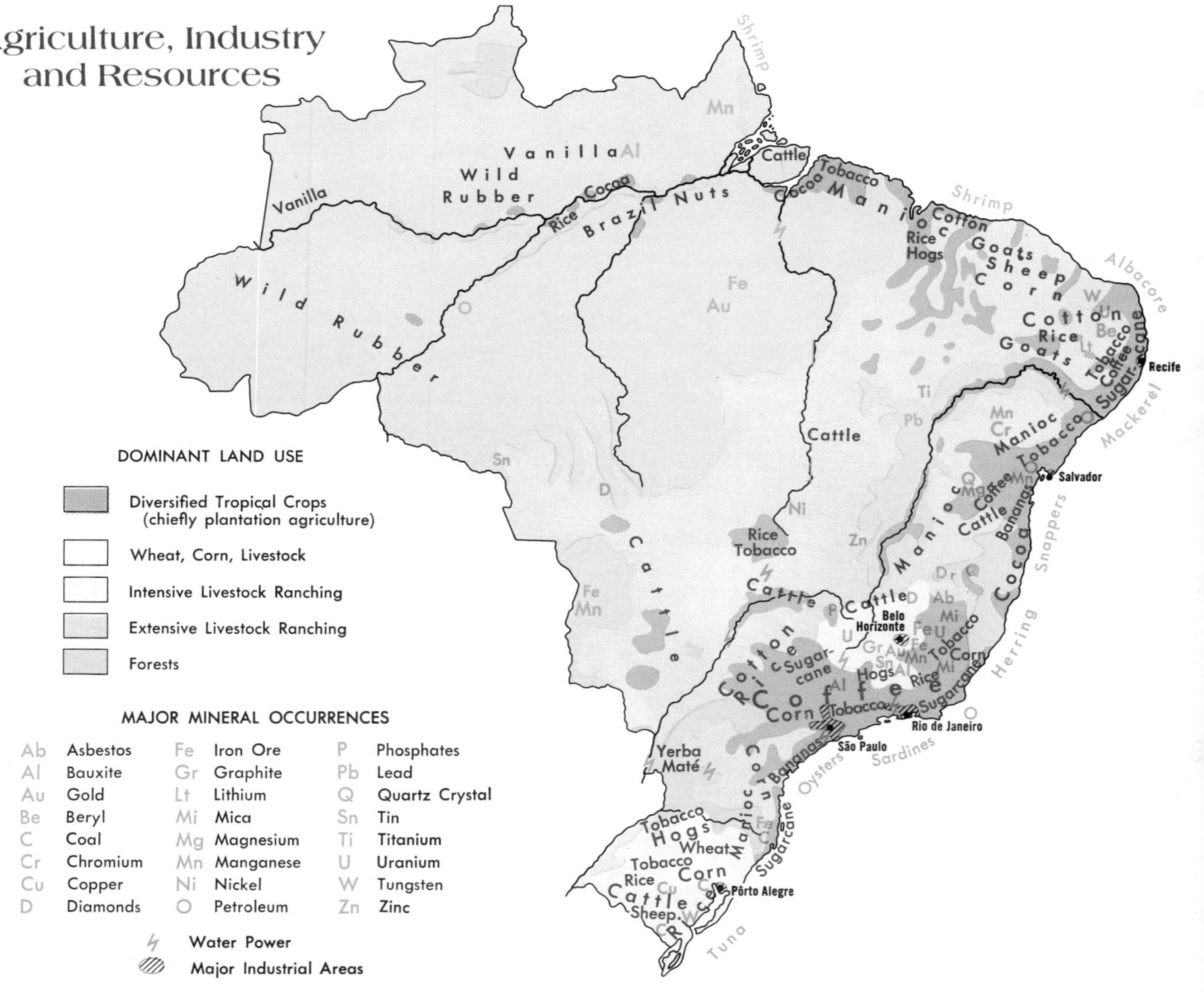

DOMINANT LAND USE

Diversified Tropical Crops (chiefly plantation agriculture)

Wheat, Corn, Livestock

Intensive Livestock Ranching

Extensive Livestock Ranching

Forests

MAJOR MINERAL OCCURRENCES

Ab	Asbestos	Fe	Iron Ore	P	Phosphates
Al	Bauxite	Gr	Graphite	Pb	Lead
Au	Gold	Lt	Lithium	Q	Quartz Crystal
Be	Beryl	Mi	Mica	Sn	Tin
C	Coal	Mg	Magnesium	Ti	Titanium
Cr	Chromium	Mn	Manganese	U	Uranium
Cu	Copper	Ni	Nickel	W	Tungsten
D	Diamonds	O	Petroleum	Zn	Zinc

Water Power

Major Industrial Areas

Três Corações 36,179	*D2	Anauá (riv.)	B2
Três Lagoas 45,171	C8	Aporé (riv.)	D7
Três Pontas 24,225	*D2	Araguaia (riv.)	D4
Três Rios 47,497	*E3	Araguari (riv.)	D2
Trindade 22,321	D7	Araruama (lake)	*E3
Tubarão 64,585	D10	Arinos (riv.)	B5
Tucuruí 27,209	D3	Aripuanã (riv.)	A4
Tupã 44,450	*A2	Armando Laydner (res.)	*B3
Tupanciretã 13,103	C10	Bailique (isl.)	D2
Tutóia 4,766	F3	Balsas (riv.)	E5
Ubá 43,080	*E2	Bananal (isl.)	D5
Ubaitaba 9,413	G6	Bandeira, Pico da (mt.)	*E2, F8
Ubatuba 23,078	*D3	Braço Maior do Araguaia	
Uberaba 180,296	*C1	(riv.)	D5
Uberlândia 230,400	E7	Braço Menor do Araguaia	D6
Unaí 28,148	E7	Branco (riv.)	H8
União 9,396	F3	Buzios (cape)	*F3
União da Vitória 22,682	D9	Cananéia (riv.)	B4
União dos Palmares 20,876	H5	Capim (riv.)	D3
Jruaçu 19,607	D6	Carajás, Serra dos (range)	D4
Jruçuí 6,047	E4	Cardoso (isl.)	*C4
Jruguaiana 79,059	B10	Cassiporé (cape)	D2
Vacaria 37,370	D10	Caviana (isl.)	D2
Valença 34,231	*E3	Chavantes, Serra dos	
Varginha 57,448	*D2	(range)	D5
Viana 9,753	E3	Claro (riv.)	D7
Viçosa 9,843	G5	Comprida (isl.)	*C4
Viçosa 29,198	*E2	Cuiabá (riv.)	B7
Vigia 14,749	E3	Culuene (riv.)	C6
Vila Velha Argolas 74,166	F8	Curuá (riv.)	C4
Vilhena 12,565	H10	Doce (riv.)	*E2, F7
Visconde dos Rio Branco		Dois Irmãos, Serra (range)	F5
17,295	*E2	Espigão Mestre (Geral	
Vitória 144,143	*D2	de Goiás) (range)	E6
Vitória da Conquista 125,717	F6	Espinhaço, Serra do (range)	F7
Vitória de Santo Antão		Estrondo, Serra do (range)	D4
62,890	G4	Feia (lake)	*F3
Volta Redonda 177,772	*D3	Feio (riv.)	*B2
Votuporanga 44,169	*B2	Formosa, Serra (range)	C5
Xapuri 3,122	G10	Frio (riv.)	*F3
Xique-Xique 17,625	F5	Furnas (dam)	*C2
		Geral de Goiás, Serra	
OTHER FEATURES		(range)	E6
Abacaxis (riv.)	B4	Gi-Paraná (riv.)	H10
Abunã (riv.)	G10	Gradaús, Serra dos (range)	D4
Acaraí, Serra do (range)	B2	Grajaú (riv.)	E4
Acre (riv.)	G10	Grande (isl.)	*D3
Aiama (lake)	H9	Grande (riv.)	*B2, E8
Aimambaí, Serra de (range)	C7	Guanabara (bay)	*E3
Amapari (riv.)	C3	Guaporé (riv.)	H10
Amazon (riv.)	C3		

Gurguéia (riv.)	E5	Orange (cape)	D1
Gurupi, Serra do (range)	E4	Órgãos (range)	*E3
Gurupi (riv.)	E3	Oyapock (riv.)	C2
Ibicuí (riv.)	C10	Pacajá Grande (riv.)	D4
Içá (riv.)	G9	Pacaraimã, Serra da (mts.)	H8
Iguaçu (riv.)	C9	Papagaio (riv.)	B6
Iguazú (falls)	C9	Pará (riv.)	D3
Ilha Grande (bay)	*D3	Paracatu (riv.)	E7
Iriri (riv.)	C4	Paraguaçu (riv.)	F6
Itaipu (dam)	C9	Paraguai (riv.)	B8
Itapecuru (riv.)	F4	Paraíba (riv.)	*E2
Itapetinga (riv.)	B3	Paraná (riv.)	C8
Itapicuru (riv.)	G5	Paranapanema (riv.)	*B3, C8
Itararé (riv.)	*B3	Paranapiacaba (range)	*B4
Ivaí (riv.)	C8	Paranatinga (riv.)	C6
Jaculpe (riv.)	F5	Pardo (riv.)	*B2, D8
Jaguaribe (riv.)	G4	Pardo (riv.)	F6
Jamanxim (riv.)	C4	Parecis, Serra dos (range)	B6
Japurá (riv.)	G9	Parnaíba (riv.)	F3
Jauari, Serra (mts.)	C3	Paru (riv.)	C3
Javari (riv.)	F9	Patos (lag.)	D10
Jequitinhonha (riv.)	F7	Penitente, Serra do (range)	E5
Juruá (riv.)	G10	Piauí, Serra do (range)	F5
Juruena (riv.)	B5	Piauí (riv.)	F5
Jutaí (riv.)	G9	Purus (riv.)	H9
Mar, Serra do (range)	*C4, E9	Ribeira (riv.)	*B4
Mapuera (riv.)	B4	Roncador, Serra do (range)	D5
Maracá (isl.)	C3	Ronuro (riv.)	C6
Marajó (bay)	E2	Roosevelt (riv.)	A5
Marajó (isl.) 147,895	D3	Santa Catarina (isl.) 138,556	E9
Mato Grosso, Planalto de		São Lourenço (riv.)	C7
(plat.)	B6	São Marcos (bay)	F3
Maués-Açu (riv.)	B4	São Roque (cape)	H4
Mearim (riv.)	E4	São Francisco (riv.)	*D2, G5
Mexiana (isl.)	D2	São Sebastião (isl.) 5,724	*D3, D3
Miranda (riv.)	B8	São Tomé (cape)	F8
Mirim (lag.)	C11	Sapucaí (riv.)	*D2
Mogi Guaçu (riv.)	*C2	Sepetiba (bay)	*D3
Mortes (Manso) (riv.)	C6	Sete Quedas (falls)	C9
Neblina, Pico da (peak)	H8	Sete Quedas (Grande) (isl.)	C8
Negro (riv.)	H9	Sobradinho (res.)	F5
Norte, Serra do (range)	B5	Sono (riv.)	E5
Oiapoque (Oyapock) (riv.)	C2	Sul (chan.)	D2
		Tacutu (riv.)	B2
		Tapajós (riv.)	B4
		Taquari (riv.)	C7
		Tefé (riv.)	G9
		Teles Pires (riv.)	B5

Tibagi (riv.)	*A4	Turvo (riv.)	*B2	Verde (riv.)	C7
Tietê (riv.)	*B2, D8	Uaupés (riv.)	G9	Verdinho (riv.)	D7
Tiracambu, Serra (range)	E3	Uaricoera (riv.)	H8	Xavantes (res.)	*B3
Tocantins (riv.)	D3	Urubu (riv.)	A3	Xingu (riv.)	C3
Tombador, Serra do (range)	B6	Urubupungá (dam)	C8		
Trombetas (riv.)	B3	Urucún, Morro do (mt.)	B7	†Population of met. area.	
Tucutú (riv.)	D4	Uruguai (riv.)	C9	*preceding reference indicates	
Tumucumaque, Serra de		Vasa Barris (riv.)	G5	that the name will be found on	
(range)	C2	Velhas (riv.)	E7	S.E. Brazil map, page 135.	

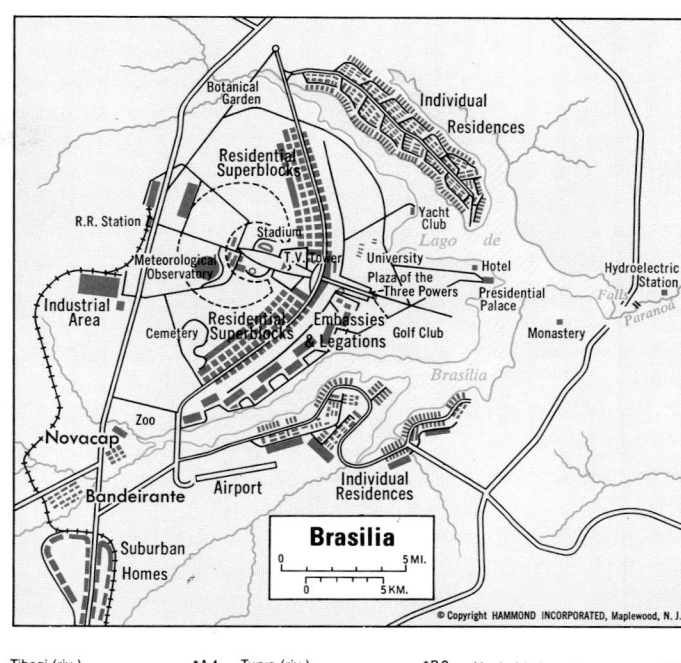

Brasilia

0 _____ 5 MI.

0 _____ 5 KM.

© Copyright HAMMOND INCORPORATED, Maplewood, N.J.

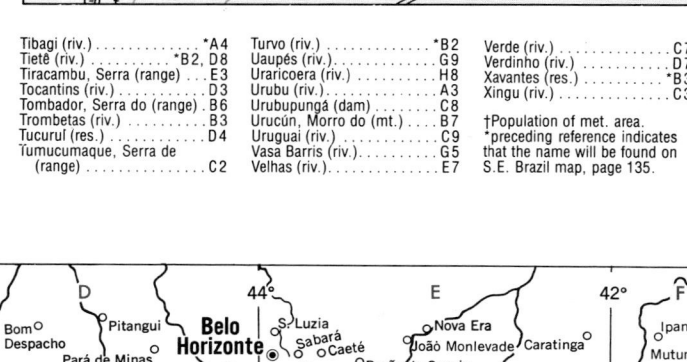

Southeastern Brazil

POLYCONIC PROJECTION

SCALE OF MILES

0   25   50   100   150

SCALE OF KILOMETERS

0   25 50   100   150

State Capitals .... ◉

State Boundaries .... ▬ ▬ ▬

Scale 1:4,480,000

© Copyright HAMMOND INCORPORATED, Maplewood, N.J.

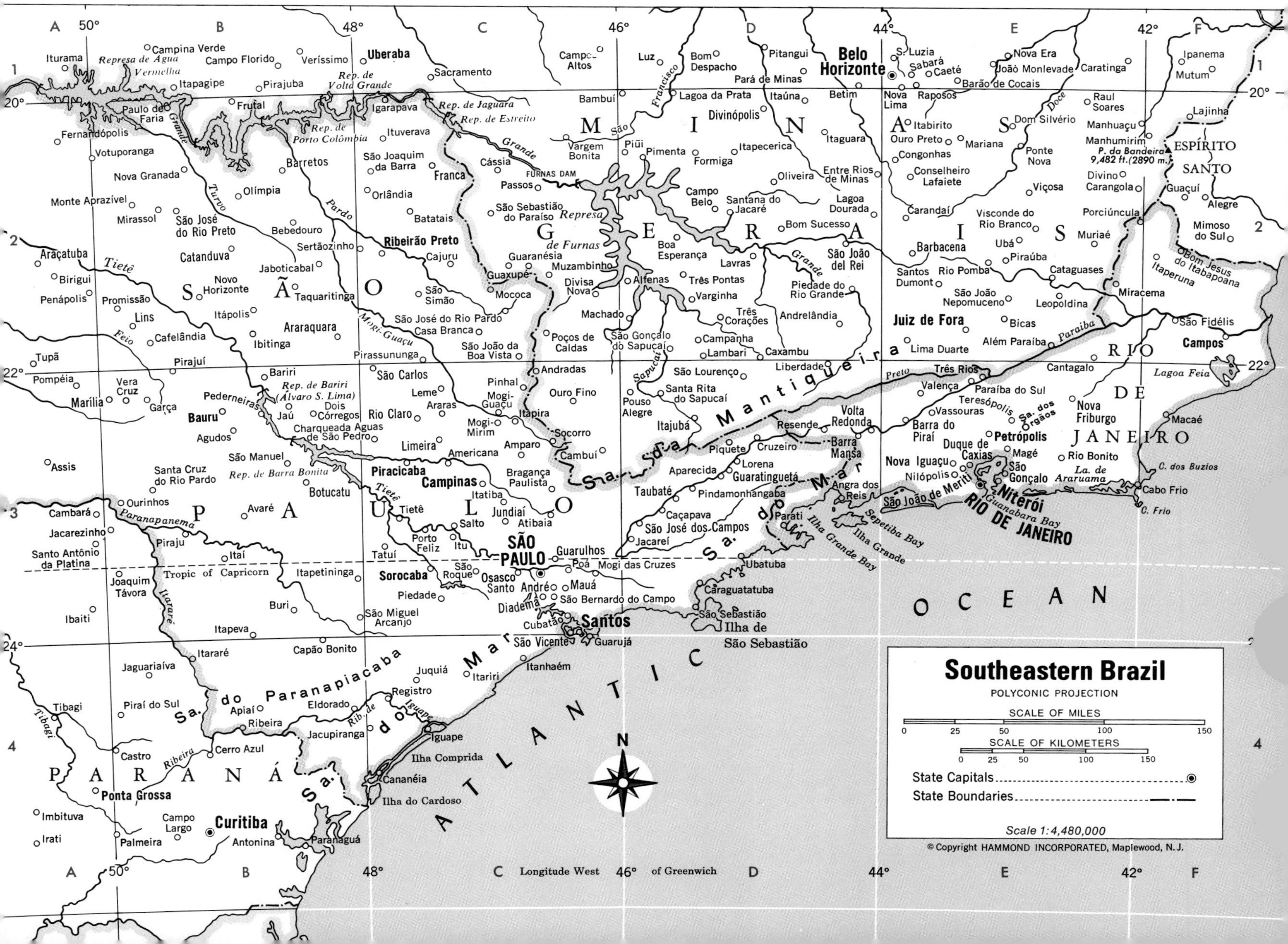

DEPARTMENTS

Beni, El 168,367 .... C3
Chuquisaca 358,516 .... C6
Cochabamba 720,952 ...... C5
El Beni 168,367 .... C3
La Paz 1,465,078 .... A4
Oruro 310,409 .... A6
Pando 34,493 .... B2
Potosí 657,743 .... B7
Santa Cruz 710,724 .... E5
Tarija 187,204 .... D7

CITIES and TOWNS

Abapó 466 .... D6
Aracchilla 208 .... C7
Achacachi 3,621 .... A5
Aiquile 3,465 .... C6
Alcalá 236 .... C6
Alejandría‡ 198 .... C3
Alto Seco‡ 3,414 .... D6
Amarete 992 .... A4
Ananea 302 .... A4
Ancoraimes 769 .... A4
Andamarca‡ 5,187 .... B6
Añimbo 443 .... C7
Anzaldo 1,056 .... C5

Apolo 1,043 .... A4
Aracat 3,537 .... B5
Arampampa 829 .... B5
Arani 2,200 .... B5
Arcopongot 2,223 .... B5
Aromat 873 .... B5
Arque 1,254 .... B5
Arroyo Grande A2
Ascención (Añez) D4
Asunción A2
Asunta 45 .... A4
Atén 199 .... A4
Atocha‡ 3,964 .... B7
Ayacucho 729 .... D5
Ayata 479 .... A4

Azurduy 1,234 .... C6
Barrera B3
Baures 592 .... D3
Bella Flor A2
Bella Vista E3
Berenguela‡ 2,412 .... A5
Betanzos 1,097 .... C6
Bolívar B3
Bolpebra A2
Boyuibe 537 .... D6
Buena Vista, Santa Cruz . D5
Cabezas 298 .... D6
Cachuela Esperanza 1,073 . C2
Caiza 838 .... C7
Cajuata 447 .... B5

Calacoto 415 .... A5
Calamarca 802 .... A5
Callapa 636 .... A5
Camacho‡ 875 .... A5
Camargo 1,609 .... C7
Camatindi‡ 297 .... D7
Camiri 4,969 .... D6
Candelaria‡ 468 .... F5
Canquella 148 .... A5
Capinota 1,734 .... B5
Capirenda D7
Caquiaviri 760 .... A5
Carabuco 626 .... A4
Caracollo 909 .... B5
Caranaví‡ 525 .... B4

Carandaiti 1,403 .... D7
Caraparí 351 .... D7
Carmen‡ 845 .... B2
Cataricagua 3,240 ...... B6
Cavani 249 .... B5
Caviñas‡ 1,011 .... B3
Chacomani 159 .... A6
Chacoma‡ 330 .... A6
Chaguaya 643 .... C7
Challaccollo 284 .... B5
Challana‡ 1,206 .... B4
Challapata 2,529 .... B6
Chapacerat 152 .... A2
Chaquí 291 .... C6
Charagua 1,185 .... D6

Charaña 794 .... A5
Chayanta 1,272 .... B6
Chiguana 154 .... B7
Chijijo 27 .... A5
Chivet 336 .... B5
Chocaya 444 .... B6
Choquecota‡ 1,976 .... A6
Chulumani 2,362 ...... B4
Chuma 931 .... A4
Chuquichambi‡ 1,094 . A6
Chuquichuqui‡ 1,892 .. C6
Cliza 3,121 .... B5
Cobija 3,650 .... A2
Cocani‡ 658 .... C6
Cocapata‡ 2,855 ...... B5

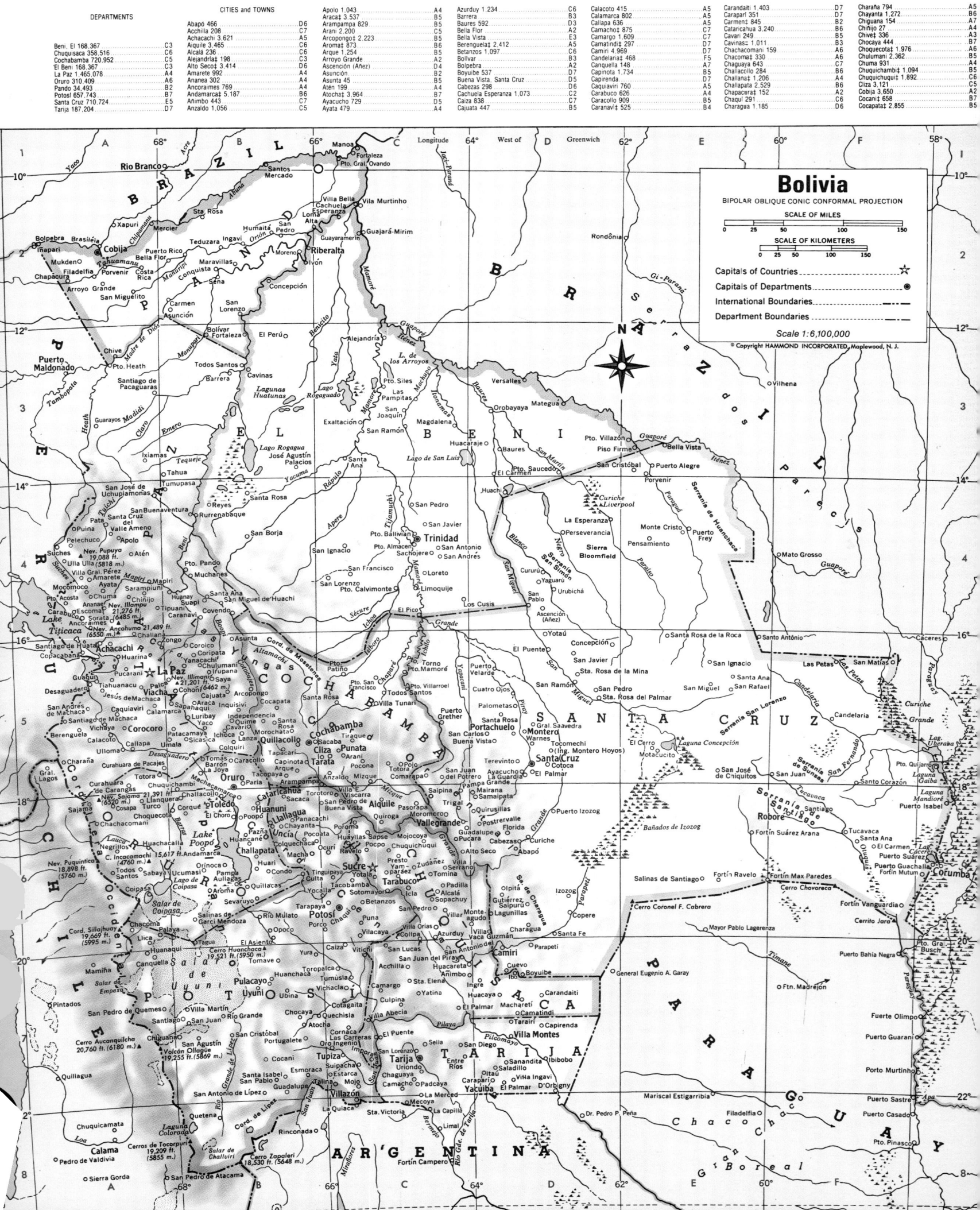

Cochabamba 204,684 C5
Cohoni 890 B5
Coipasa‡ 202 A6
Collpa 481 C6
Colquechaca 1,070 B6
Colquiri 806 B5
Comarapa 1,096 C5
Concepción, El Beni‡ 61 B2
Concepción, Santa Cruz 1,056 D5
Condo‡ 5,525 B6
Conquista‡ 1,162 B2
Copacabana 1,981 A5
Copere D6
Coripata 1,647 B5
Cornaca 264 C7
Corocoro 4,431 A5
Coroico 2,235 B5
Corque 423 B6
Cosapa 297 A6
Costa Rica‡ 43 A2
Cotagaita 1,353 C7
Cotoca 915 D5
Covendo 71 B4
Cuatro Ojos‡ 465 D5
Cuevo 902 D7
Culpina 981 C7
Culta‡ 4,412 B6
Curahuara de Carangas 235 A5
Curahuara de Pacajes 510 A5
Curiche 257 D6
Cururú D4
Desaguadero 201 A5
D'Orbigny‡ 214 D7
El Asiento B6
El Carmen, El Beni 232 D3
El Carmen, Santa Cruz F6
El Cerro 117 E5
El Choro 224 B6
El Palmar, Chuquisaca‡ 772 D7
El Palmar, Santa Cruz 437 D5
El Palmar, Tarija 832 D7
El Perú B3
El Pico C4
El Puente, Santa Cruz‡ 1,185 D5
El Puente, Tarija‡ 1,310 C7
Entre Ríos 1,011 C7
Escoma 220 A4
Esmoraca‡ 1,137 B7
Estarca‡ 2,331 C7
Exaltación, El Beni 405 C3
Filadelfia‡ 942 A2
Florida, Santa Cruz 128 D6
Fortaleza‡ 765 B3
Fortaleza C1
Fortín Campero‡ 87 C8
Fortín Max Paredes F6
Fortín Mutum F6
Fortín Ravelo E6
Fortín Suárez Arana F6
Fortín Vanguardia F6
General Saavedra 1,006 D5
Guadalupe, Potosí 71 B7
Guadalupe, Santa Cruz 2,355 C6
Guaqui 2,266 A5
Guayaramerín 1,470 C2
Huacaraje 673 D3
Huacareta 239 C7
Huacaya 229 D7
Huachacalla 801 A6
Huachi D4
Huanaqui 359 A7
Huanay 574 B4
Huancané 148 B6
Huanchaca B7
Huanuni 5,696 B6
Huari 1,070 B6
Huarina 1,151 A5
Huayllas 206 C6
Humaitá‡ 429 B2
Ibibobo D7
Ibo D7
Ichoca 591 B5
Icla 196 C6
Impora 274 C7
Independencia 1,742 B5
Ingavi‡ 111 B2
Ingeniero Montero Hoyos (Tocomechi) 575 D5
Ingre 162 D7
Inquisivi 530 B5
Irupana 1,937 B5
Itaú 102 D7
Ivón‡ 772 C2
Ixiamas 292 A3
Izozog‡ 2,759 D6
Jesús de Machaca 529 A5
José Agustín Palacios‡ 2,273 B3
La Capilla‡ 1,870 C8
La Esmeralda D8
La Esperanza D4
La Guardia 470 D5
Lagunillas 840 D6
La Joya 401 B5
La Merced‡ 688 C8
Lanza 526 B5
La Paz (cap.) 635,283 B5
Las Carreras 155 C7
Las Pampitas‡ 71 C3
Las Petas‡ 383 F5
Limal‡ 524 C8
Limoquije C4
Llallagua 6,719 B6
Llanquera 613 A6
Llica 560 A6
Loma Alta B2
Loreto 589 C4
Los Cusis D4
Luribay 392 B5
Macha 1,050 B6
Machacamarca 1,746 B5
Macharetí‡ 1,164 D7
Magdalena 1,724 C3
Mairana 508 D6
Manoa C1
Mapiri 289 B4
Maravillas B2
Mateguá 38 D3
Mecoya‡ 585 C8
Mercier‡ 272 B2
Mizque 870 C5
Mocomoco 977 A4
Mojo 469 C7
Mojocoya 498 C6
Monteagudo 971 D6
Monte Cristo E4
Montero 2,713 D5
Moreno B2
Morochata 461 B5
Moromoro 556 C6
Motacucito‡ 585 E5
Muchanes B4
Mukden‡ 84 A2
Negrillos 85 A6
Ocurí 1,531 C6
Opoco B6
Orinoca‡ 2,380 B6
Orobayaya‡ 1,132 D3
Oro Ingenio‡ 945 C7
Oruro 124,213 B5
Padcaya 324 C7
Padilla 2,462 C6
Palaya 300 A6
Palca 887 A5
Palometas‡ 3,453 D5
Pampa Aullagas‡ 1,834 B6
Pampa Grande 727 D5
Panacachi 952 B6
Paria 335 B5
Pasorapa 1,016 C6
Pata 122 A4
Patacamaya 1,278 B5
Pazña 671 B6
Pelechuco 873 A4
Pensamiento E4
Perseverancia D4
Piso Firme D3
Pocoata 859 B6
Pocona 518 C5
Pocpo‡ 2,791 C6
Pojo 1,047 C5
Poopó 736 B6
Porco 817 B6
Poroma 171 C6
Portachuelo 2,456 D5
Portugalete‡ 1,590 B7
Porvenir, Pando‡ 846 A2
Porvenir, Santa Cruz E4
Postrervalle 750 D6
Potosí 77,397 C6
Presto 725 C6
Pucara 762 C6
Pucarani 1,041 A5
Puerto Acosta 1,302 A4
Puerto Alegre E3
Puerto Almacen 358 C4
Puerto Ballivián C4
Puerto Calvimonte C4
Puerto Frey E4
Puerto General Ovando 50
Puerto Grether C5
Puerto Guachalla F6
Puerto Heath‡ 570 A3
Puerto Isabel F6
Puerto Izozog D6
Puerto Mamoré C5
Puerto Pando B4
Puerto Patiño C5
Puerto Quijarro G5
Puerto Rico‡ 539 B2
Puerto San Francisco C5
Puerto Saucedo D3
Puerto Siles 357 C3
Puerto Suárez 1,159 F6
Puerto Torno C5
Puerto Velarde D5
Puerto Villarroel C5
Puerto Villazón D3
Puina A4
Pulacayo 7,984 B7
Puna 852 C6
Punata 5,014 C5
Quechisla 171 C7
Queteña 183 B8
Quillacas 1,170 B6
Quillacollo 9,123 B5
Quime 1,256 B5
Quiroga‡ 3,467 C6
Quirusillas 433 D6
Ravelo 907 C6
Reyes 1,404 B4
Riberalta 6,549 C2
Río Grande 281 B7
Río Mulato 381 B6
Roboré 3,715 F6
Rurrenabaque 1,225 B4
Sabaya 649 A6
Sacaba 2,752 C5
Sacaca 1,778 B6
Sachojere 401 C4
Saipina 573 C6
Sajama 231 A6
Saladillo‡ 1,315 D7
Salinas de Garci Mendoza 335 B6
Salinas de Santiago E6
Samaipata 1,656 D6
San Agustín‡ 810 B7
Sanandita 379 D7
San Andrés 399 C4
San Andrés de Machaca 101 A5
San Antonio, El Beni 436 C4
San Antonio de Lípez‡ 177 B7
San Antonio del Parapetí 497 D7
San Borja 708 B4
San Buenaventura 307 A4
San Carlos 570 D5
San Cristóbal, Potosí‡ 1,200 B7
San Cristóbal, Santa Cruz E3
San Diego‡ 773 D7
San Francisco, El Beni 185 C4
San Ignacio, El Beni 1,757 C4
San Ignacio, Santa Cruz 1,819 E5
San Javier, El Beni 233 C4
San Javier, Santa Cruz 564 D5
San Joaquín 1,959 C3
San José de Chiquitos 1,933 E5
San José de Uchupiamonas 277 A4
San Juan, Potosí 131 B7
San Juan, Santa Cruz‡ 1,482 F5
San Juan del Piray 541 C7
San Juan del Potrero 263 C5
San Lorenzo, El Beni 496 C4
San Lorenzo, Pando‡ 317 B2
San Lorenzo, Tarija 785 C7
San Lucas 925 C7
San Matías 887 F5
San Miguel 502 E5
San Miguel de Huachi 25 B4
San Miguelito A2
San Pablo, Potosí 11 B7
San Pablo, Santa Cruz D4
San Pedro, Chuquisaca 182 C6
San Pedro, El Beni 262 C4
San Pedro, Pando‡ 312 B2
San Pedro, Santa Cruz 80 D5
San Pedro de Buena Vista 1,094 C6
San Pedro de Quemes‡ 290 A7
San Rafael‡ 1,282 E5
San Ramón, El Beni 1,161 C3
San Ramón, Santa Cruz 379 D5
Santa Ana, El Beni 2,225 C3
Santa Ana, La Paz 171 B4
Santa Ana, Santa Cruz 275 E5
Santa Ana, Santa Cruz 663 F6
Santa Cruz, Santa Cruz 254,682 D5
Santa Cruz del Valle Ameno 442 A4
Santa Elena‡ 4,474 C7
Santa Fe D6
Santa Isabel‡ 323 B7
Santa Rosa, Cochabamba‡ 942 B5
Santa Rosa, Cochabamba‡ 276 C5
Santa Rosa, El Beni 765 B4
Santa Rosa, Pando‡ 105 B2
Santa Rosa, Santa Cruz 995 D5
Santa Rosa de la Mina 99 D5
Santa Rosa de la Roca 101 E5
Santa Rosa del Palmar 441 E5
Santiago, Potosí 172 A7
Santiago, Santa Cruz 765 F6
Santiago de Huata 948 A5
Santiago de Machaca 218 A5
Santiago de Pacaguaras A3
Santo Corazón‡ 963 F5
Santos Mercado B1
Sapahaqui 55 B5
Sapse‡ 89 C6
Sarampiuni 138 A4
Saya 339 B5
Sella C7
Sena‡ 660 B2
Sevaruyo 475 B6
Sicasica 1,486 B5
Sopachuy 713 C6
Sorata 2,087 A4
Sotomayor 510 C6
Suapi‡ 1,750 B4
Suches‡ 231 A4
Sucre (cap.) 63,625 C6
Suipacha‡ 2,701 C7
Tacobamba‡ 6,933 C6
Tacopaya 795 B5
Tagua B6
Tahua B3
Talina 122 B7
Tapacarí 980 B5
Tarabuco 2,833 C6
Tarairí‡ 394 D7
Tarapaya 357 B6
Tarata 3,016 C5
Tarija 38,916 C7
Teduzara‡ 271 B2
Terevinto‡ 3,790 D5
Tiahuanacu 1,227 A5
Tinguipaya 766 C6
Tipuani‡ 1,216 B4
Tiraque 1,390 C5
Tocomechi 575 D5
Todos Santos, Cochabamba 408 C5
Todos Santos, La Paz B3
Todos Santos, Oruro 68 A6
Toledo 3,273 B6
Tomás Barrón 1,852 B5
Tomave 201 B7
Tomina 708 C6
Toropalca‡ 199 B7
Torotoro 1,233 C6
Totora, Cochabamba C5
Totora, Oruro A5
Trigal 749 C6
Trinidad, El Beni 27,487 C4
Trinidad, Pando‡ 332 B2
Tucavaca F6
Tumupasa 349 B4
Tumusla‡ 526 C7
Tupiza 8,248 C7
Turco 131 A6
Ubina‡ 462 B7
Ucumasi‡ 1,040 B6
Ulla Ulla 52 A4
Ulloma 116 A5
Umala 481 B5
Uncía 4,507 B6
Uriondo 860 C7
Urubichá 1,369 D4
Uyuni 6,968 B7
Vallegrande 5,094 C6
Versalles 83 D3
Viacha 6,607 A5
Vichacla 317 C7
Vichaya 422 A5
Vilacaya 200 C6
Villa Abecia 539 C7
Villa Bella 88 C2
Villa E. Viscarra 658 C6
Villa General Pérez 802 A4
Villa Ingavi 122 D7
Villa Martín 543 B7
Villa Montes 3,105 D7
Villa Orías 404 C6
Villar 322 C6
Villa Serrano 1,570 C6
Villa Tunari 510 C5
Villa Vaca Guzmán 699 D6
Villazón 6,261 C7
Vitichi 1,515 C7
Warnes 1,571 D5
Yaco 835 B5
Yacuiba 5,027 D7
Yaguarú D4
Yamparaéz 725 C6
Yanacachi‡ 1,964 B5
Yatina‡ 1,850 C7
Yocalla‡ 1,814 B6
Yotala 1,554 C6
Yotaú D5
Yura 136 B7
Zongo 141 B5
Zudáñez 1,868 C6

OTHER FEATURES

Abuná (riv.) B2
Altamachi (riv.) B5
Ancohuma, Nevada (mt.) A4
Apere (riv.) C4
Arroyas, Los (lake) C3
Barras (riv.) B6
Baures (riv.) D3
Beni (riv.) B2
Benicito (riv.) C3
Bermejo (riv.) C8
Blanco (riv.) D4
Bloomfield, Sierra (mts.) D4
Boopi (riv.) B4
Cáceres (lag.) G6
Candelaria (riv.) F5
Capitán Ustarés, Cerro (mt.) E6
Central, Cordillera (range) C6
Challviri (salt dep.) B8
Chaparé (riv.) C5
Charagua, Sierra de (mts.) D6
Chipamanu (riv.) A2
Chovoreca, Cerro (mt.) F6
Claro (riv.) A3
Coipasa (lake) B6
Coipasa (salt dep.) A6
Colorada (lag.) A8
Concepción (lag.) E5
Coronel F. Gabrera E6
Cotacajes (riv.) B5
Desaguadero (riv.) B5
Emero (riv.) B3
Empexa (salt dep.) A7
Gaiba (lag.) F5
Grande (marsh) F5
Grande (riv.) C4
Grande (riv.) C6
Grande de Lípez (riv.) B7
Guaporé (riv.) C3
Heath (riv.) A3
Huanchaca, Cerro (mt.) B7
Huanchaca, Serranía de (mts.) E4
Huatunas (lag.) B3
Ichilo (riv.) C5
Ichoa (riv.) C4
Illampu, Nevada (mt.) A4
Illimani, Nevada (mt.) B5
Incacamachi, Cerro (mt.) A6
Isiboro (riv.) C5
Iténez (Guaporé) (riv.) C3
Itonamas (riv.) C3
Izozog (swamp) E6
Jara, Cerrito (mt.) F6
Las Yungas (reg.) B5
Lauca (riv.) A6
Lípez, Cordillera de (range) B8
Liverpool (swamp) D4
Machupo (riv.) C3
Madidi (riv.) A3
Madre de Diós (riv.) A3
Mamoré (riv.) C2
Mandioré (lag.) F6
Manuripi (riv.) B2
Mizque (riv.) C6
Mosetenes, Cordillera de (range) B5
Negro (riv.) D4
Occidental, Cordillera (range) A6
Ollagüe (vol.) B7
Oriental, Cordillera (range) C5
Ortón (riv.) B2
Otuquis (riv.) F6
Paraguá (riv.) E4
Paraguay (riv.) F7
Parapetí (riv.) D6
Petas, Las (riv.) F5
Pilaya (riv.) C7
Pilcomayo (riv.) D7
Piray (riv.) D5
Poopó (lake) B6
Pupuya, Nevada (mt.) A4
Puquintica, Nevado (mt.) A6
Rápulo (riv.) C4
Real, Cordillera (range) A5
Rogagua (lake) B3
Rogaguado (lake) C3
Sajama, Nevada (mt.) A6
San Fernando (riv.) F5
San Juan (riv.) C7
San Lorenzo, Serranía (mts.) E5
San Luis (lake) C3
San Martín (riv.) D3
San Miguel (riv.) D4
San Simón, Serranía (mts.) D4
Santiago, Serranía de (mts.) F6
Sécure (riv.) C4
Sillajhuay, Cordillera (mt.) A6
Suches (riv.) A4
Sunsas, Serranía de (mts.) F5
Tahuamanu (riv.) A2
Tarija, Rio Grande de (riv.) C8
Tequeje (riv.) B3
Tijamuchi (riv.) C4
Titicaca (lake) A4
Tocorpuri, Cerros de (mt.) A8
Tucavaca (riv.) F6
Tuichi (riv.) A4
Uberaba (lag.) G5
Uyuni (salt dep.) B7
Yacuma (riv.) B3
Yapacani (riv.) C5
Yata (riv.) C3
Yungas, Las (reg.) B5
Zapaleri, Cerro (mt.) B8

‡Population of canton.

AREA 424,163 sq. mi. (1,098,582 sq. km.)
POPULATION 5,600,000
CAPITALS La Paz, Sucre
LARGEST CITY La Paz
HIGHEST POINT Nevada Ancohuma 21,489 ft. (6,550 m.)
MONETARY UNIT Bolivian peso
MAJOR LANGUAGES Spanish, Quechua, Aymara
MAJOR RELIGION Roman Catholicism

Topography

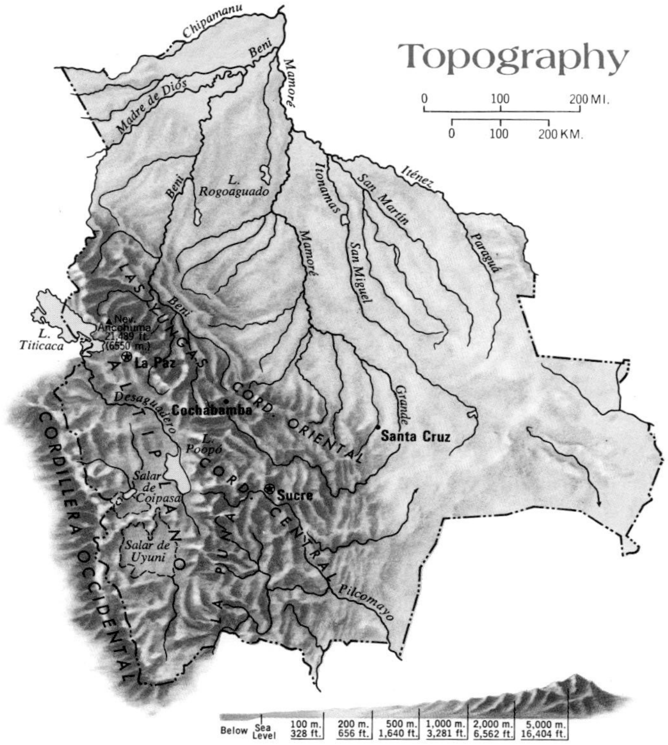

0 100 200 MI.
0 100 200 KM.
Chipamanu
Beni
Mamoré
Madre de Diós
Itonamas
Iténez
San Martín
San Miguel
Paraguá
L. Rogoaguado
L. Titicaca
Nev. Ancohuma 21,489 ft. (6550 m.)
La Paz
Cochabamba
Santa Cruz
Sucre
Desaguadero
L. Poopó
Salar de Coipasa
Salar de Uyuni
Grande
Pilcomayo
CORDILLERA OCCIDENTAL
CORD. ORIENTAL
CORD. CENTRAL
Below Sea Level
100 m. 328 ft.
200 m. 656 ft.
500 m. 1,640 ft.
1,000 m. 3,281 ft.
2,000 m. 6,562 ft.
5,000 m. 16,404 ft.

Agriculture, Industry and Resources

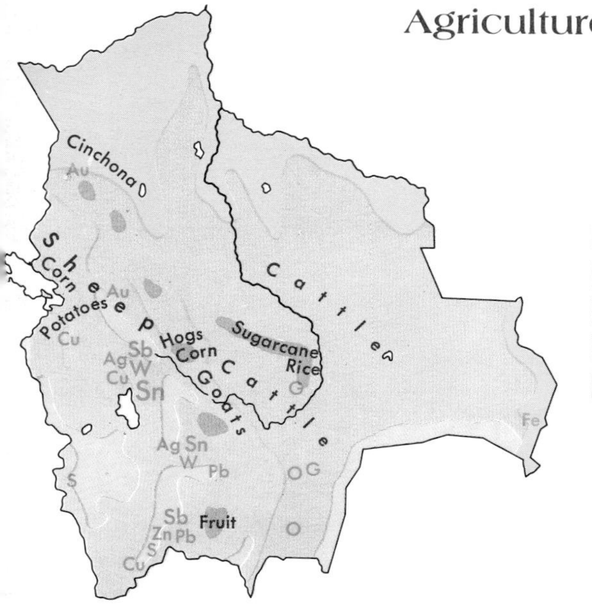

Cinchona
Sheep
Corn
Potatoes
Hogs
Corn
Goats
Cattle
Sugarcane
Rice
Fruit
Au
Cu
Sb
Ag
W
Sn
Pb
Zn
S
G
O
Fe

DOMINANT LAND USE

- Diversified Tropical Crops (chiefly plantation agriculture)
- Upland Cultivated Areas
- Upland Livestock Grazing, Limited Agriculture
- Extensive Livestock Ranching
- Forests
- Nonagricultural Land

MAJOR MINERAL OCCURRENCES

Ag	Silver	G	Natural Gas	Sb	Antimony
Au	Gold	O	Petroleum	Sn	Tin
Cu	Copper	Pb	Lead	W	Tungsten
Fe	Iron Ore	S	Sulfur	Zn	Zinc

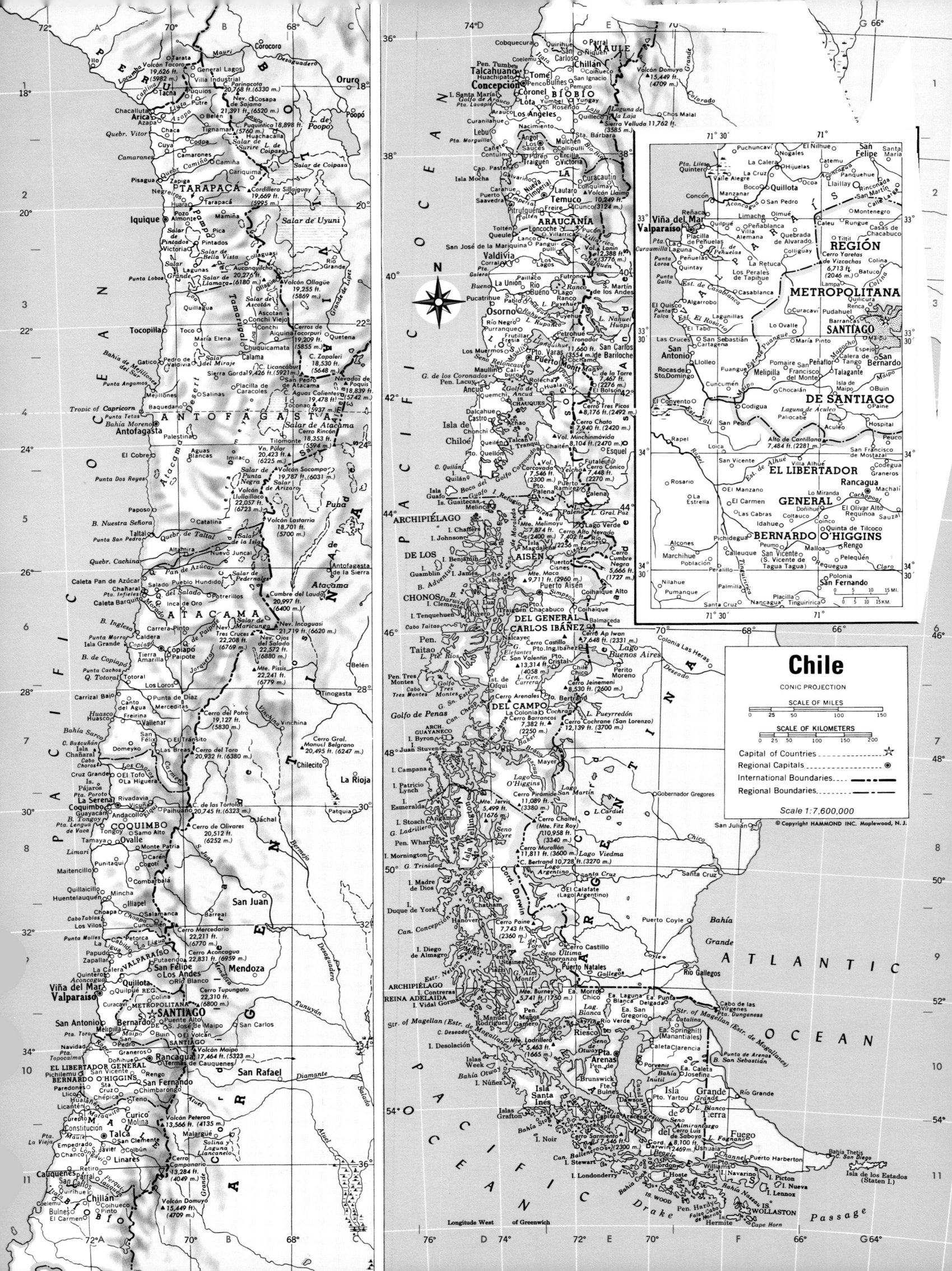

AREA 292,257 sq. mi. (756,946 sq. km.)
POPULATION 11,275,440
CAPITAL Santiago
LARGEST CITY Santiago
HIGHEST POINT Ojos del Salado 22,572 ft. (6,880 m.)
MONETARY UNIT Chilean escudo
MAJOR LANGUAGE Spanish
MAJOR RELIGION Roman Catholicism

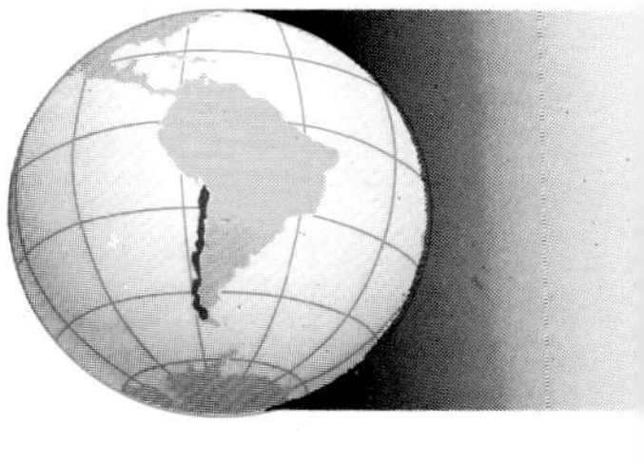

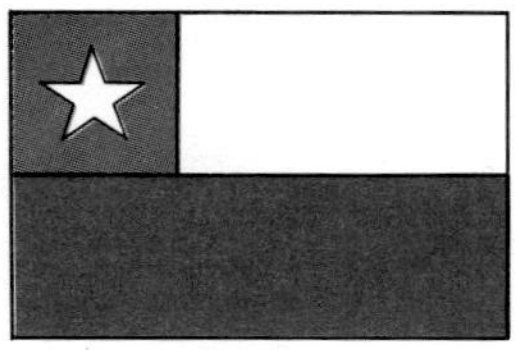

Topography

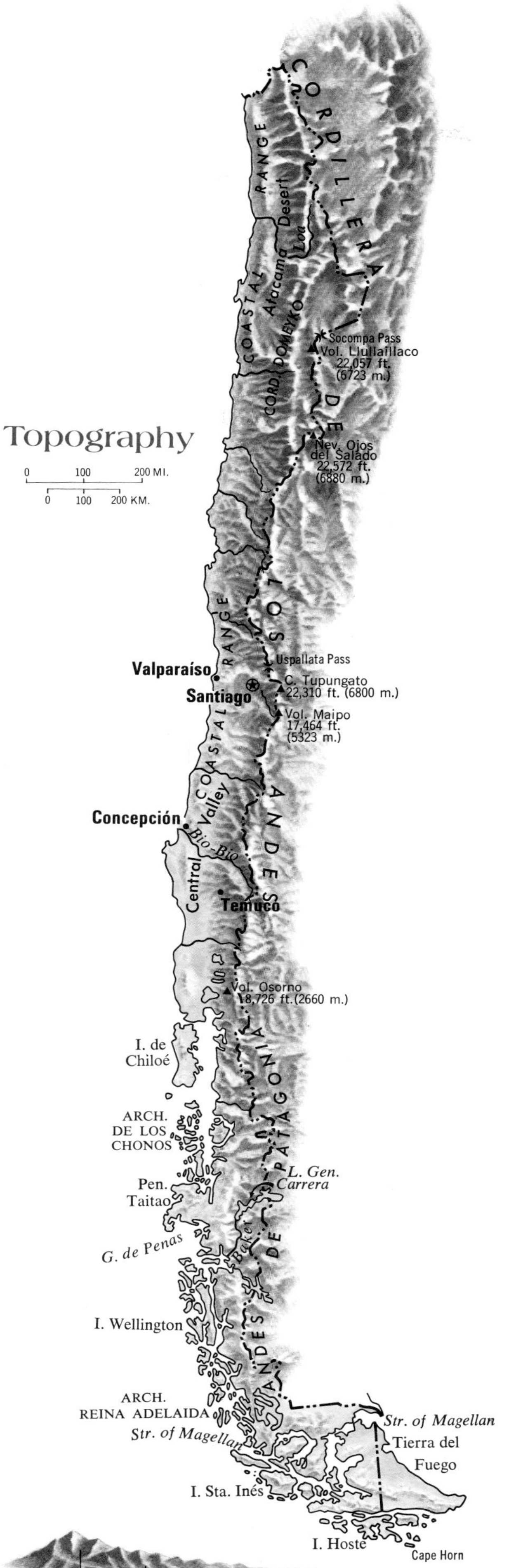

0 100 200 MI.
0 100 200 KM.
CORDILLERA DE LOS ANDES
COASTAL RANGE
Atacama Desert
Loa
CORD. DOMEYKO
Socompa Pass
Vol. Llullaillaco 22,057 ft. (6723 m.)
Nev. Ojos del Salado 22,572 ft. (6880 m.)
Valparaíso
Santiago
Uspallata Pass
C. Tupungato 22,310 ft. (6800 m.)
Vol. Maipo 17,464 ft. (5323 m.)
COASTAL RANGE
Central Valley
Concepción
Bío Bío
Temuco
Vol. Osorno 8,726 ft.(2660 m.)
I. de Chiloé
ARCH. DE LOS CHONOS
Pen. Taitao
L. Gen. Carrera
Baker
G. de Penas
ANDES DE PATAGONIA
I. Wellington
ARCH. REINA ADELAIDA
Str. of Magellan
Str. of Magellan
Tierra del Fuego
I. Sta. Inés
I. Hoste
Cape Horn

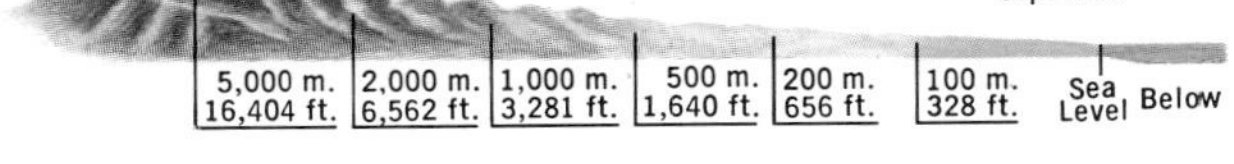

5,000 m. 16,404 ft.
2,000 m. 6,562 ft.
1,000 m. 3,281 ft.
500 m. 1,640 ft.
200 m. 656 ft.
100 m. 328 ft.
Sea Level
Below

REGIONS

Aisén del General Carlos Ibáñez del Campo 65,478 . . . . . E6
Antofagasta 341,203 . . . . . B4
Atacama 183,071 . . . . . B6
Biobío 1,516,552 . . . . . E1
Coquimbo 419,178 . . . . . A8
El Libertador General Bernardo O'Higgins 584,989 . . . . . A10
La Araucanía 692,924 . . . . . E2
Los Lagos 843,430 . . . . . D3
Magallanes 132,333 . . . . . E10
Maule 723,224 . . . . . A11
Santiago, Región Metropolitana de (Santiago Metropolitan Region) 4,294,938 . . . . . A9
Tarapacá 273,427 . . . . . B2
Valparaíso 1,204,693 . . . . . A9

CITIES and TOWNS

Achao ○11,501 . . . . . D4
Aguas Blancas ○203 . . . . . B4
Algarrobo ○3,941 . . . . . F3
Ancud 11,900 . . . . . D4
Andacollo 6,000 . . . . . A8
Angol 42,670 . . . . . D1
Antofagasta 125,100 . . . . . A4
Arauco 5,400 . . . . . D1
Arica 87,700 . . . . . A1
Ascotán B3
Barrancas ○184,241 . . . . . G3
Belén ○925 . . . . . B1
Buin 11,800 . . . . . G4
Bulnes 6,900 . . . . . E1
Cabildo 5,800 . . . . . A9
Calama 45,900 . . . . . B3
Calbuco ○21,673 . . . . . D4
Caldera ○3,268 . . . . . A6
Calera de Tango ○6,198 . . G4
Calle Larga ○7,172 . . . . . G2
Cañete 7,900 . . . . . D2
Carahue ○12,733 . . . . . D2
Cartagena ○7,124 . . . . . F3
Casablanca 5,500 . . . . . F3
Casas de Chacabuco G2
Castro 11,200 . . . . . D4
Catalina ○1,637 . . . . . B5
Catemu ○8,728 . . . . . G2
Cauquenes 20,200 . . . . . A11
Cerro Castillo ○537 . . . . . E9
Cerro Manantiales F10
Chaitén ○4,067 . . . . . E4
Chañaral ○36,949 . . . . . A6
Chanco ○12,433 . . . . . A11
Chépica ○11,199 . . . . . A10
Chillán 128,515 . . . . . A11
Chimbarongo 5,300 . . . . . A10
Chonchi ○8,911 . . . . . D4
Chuquicamata 22,100 . . . . . B3
Cobquecura ○6,298 . . . . . D1
Cochamó ○5,042 . . . . . E3
Codegua ○6,757 . . . . . G4
Codpa ○950 . . . . . B1
Coelemu 5,400 . . . . . D1
Coihaique 32,129 . . . . . E6
Coihueco ○17,276 . . . . . A11
Coinco ○4,942 . . . . . G5
Colbún ○12,924 . . . . . A11
Colina 7,400 . . . . . G3
Collipulli 7,200 . . . . . E2
Coltauco ○11,857 . . . . . F5
Combarbalá ○17,332 . . . . . A8
Concepción 206,226 . . . . . D1
Constitución 11,500 . . . . . A11
Contulmo ○13,987 . . . . . D2
Copiapó 45,200 . . . . . B6
Coquimbo 73,953 . . . . . A8
Coronel 37,300 . . . . . D1
Corral ○5,533 . . . . . D3
Cunco ○18,836 . . . . . E2
Curacautín 9,800 . . . . . E2
Curacaví 5,800 . . . . . G3
Curanilahue 13,200 . . . . . D1
Curepto ○13,020 . . . . . A10
Curicó 41,300 . . . . . A10
Dalcahue ○7,084 . . . . . D4
Domeiko A7
Doñihue ○8,837 . . . . . G5
El Carmen ○13,226 . . . . . A11
El Monte 7,000 . . . . . G4
El Quisco ○2,152 . . . . . E3
El Tabo ○2,180 . . . . . F3
El Tofo A7
Empedrado ○7,887 . . . . . A11
Ercilla ○8,061 . . . . . E2
Estancia Caleta Josefina ○1,042 . . . . . F10
Estancia Morro Chico ○785 . E9
Estancia San Gregorio ○1,156 . . . . . E9
Estancia Springhill (Cerro Manantiales) F10
Freire ○23,313 . . . . . E2
Freirina ○5,523 . . . . . A7
Fresia ○15,359 . . . . . D3
Frutillar ○12,721 . . . . . D3
Futaleufú ○2,366 . . . . . E4
Futrono ○7,109 . . . . . E3
Galvarino ○9,495 . . . . . D2
General Lagos ○810 . . . . . B1
Graneros 8,900 . . . . . G5
Guayacán A8
Hijuelas ○7,128 . . . . . F2
Hualañé ○6,912 . . . . . A10
Huara ○1,934 . . . . . B2
Huasco ○4,971 . . . . . A7
Illapel 12,200 . . . . . A8
Inca de Oro 1,406 . . . . . B6
Iquique 64,500 . . . . . A2
Isla de Maipo ○12,903 . . . . G4
La Calera 24,600 . . . . . F2
La Cruz ○8,907 . . . . . F2
La Estrella ○3,707 . . . . . F5
Lago Ranco ○12,767 . . . . . E3
Lagunas ○5,653 . . . . . B3
La Higuera ○6,991 . . . . . A7
La Ligua 7,500 . . . . . A9
Lampa ○10,220 . . . . . G3
Lanco 5,200 . . . . . D2
Las Cabras ○12,119 . . . . . F5
La Serena 99,908 . . . . . A8
La Unión 15,200 . . . . . D3
Lautaro 11,900 . . . . . E2
Lebu 12,500 . . . . . D1
Licantén ○6,354 . . . . . A10
Limache 15,200 . . . . . F2
Linares 37,900 . . . . . A11
Llay-Llay 9,700 . . . . . G2
Loica F4
Loncoche ○17,539 . . . . . D2
Longaví ○15,909 . . . . . A11
Lonquimay ○9,524 . . . . . E2
Los Andes 23,500 . . . . . B9
Los Ángeles 49,500 . . . . . D1
Los Lagos ○14,934 . . . . . D3
Los Muermos ○9,296 . . . . . D3
Los Sauces ○7,613 . . . . . D2
Los Vilos ○10,453 . . . . . A9
Lota 48,100 . . . . . D1
Machalí 5,800 . . . . . G5
Maipú ○117,872 . . . . . G3
Malloa ○9,742 . . . . . G5
Marchigüe ○4,451 . . . . . F5
María Elena 5,900 . . . . . B3
María Pinto ○5,980 . . . . . G3
Maullín ○14,544 . . . . . D4
Mejillones ○3,333 . . . . . A4
Melipilla 23,900 . . . . . F4
Mincha ○11,329 . . . . . A8
Molina 9,400 . . . . . A10
Monte Patria ○18,927 . . . . A8
Mulchén 13,700 . . . . . E1
Nacimiento ○17,651 . . . . . D1
Nancagua ○11,076 . . . . . F6
Navidad ○6,618 . . . . . A10
Negreiros ○1,144 . . . . . B2
Ñiquén ○13,640 . . . . . E1
Nogales ○18,529 . . . . . F2
Nueva Imperial 8,000 . . . . . D2
Olivar Alto ○5,414 . . . . . G5
Ollagüe B3
Olmué ○8,804 . . . . . F2
Osorno 68,800 . . . . . D3
Ovalle 31,700 . . . . . A8
Paihuano ○6,048 . . . . . B8
Paillaco 5,200 . . . . . D3
Paine ○21,876 . . . . . G4
Palena ○2,508 . . . . . E5
Palmilla ○7,965 . . . . . F6
Panguipulli 5,700 . . . . . E2
Panquehue ○4,230 . . . . . G2
Papudo ○2,594 . . . . . A9
Paredones ○7,404 . . . . . A10
Parral 17,000 . . . . . A11
Pedro de Valdivia 6,200 . . . B4
Pemuco ○7,577 . . . . . E1
Peñaflor 15,500 . . . . . G4
Penco ○33,962 . . . . . D1
Peñuelas F3
Petorca ○8,343 . . . . . A9
Petrohué E3
Peumo ○11,308 . . . . . F5
Pica ○1,487 . . . . . B2
Pichidegua ○13,550 . . . . . F5
Pichilemu ○8,042 . . . . . A10
Pinto ○8,687 . . . . . A11
Pisagua ○1,880 . . . . . A2
Pitrufquén 7,800 . . . . . D2
Placilla ○6,441 . . . . . F6
Porvenir ○4,000 . . . . . E10
Potrerillos 5,800 . . . . . B6
Pozo Almonte ○1,798 . . . . . B2
Puchuncaví ○7,542 . . . . . F2
Pucón 18,000 . . . . . E2
Pudahuel G3
Pueblo Hundido 6,200 . . . . . B6
Puente Alto 65,100 . . . . . B10
Puerto Aisén 17,848 . . . . . E6
Puerto Cisnes ○2,800 . . . . . E5
Puerto Ingeniero Ibáñez ○1,900 . . . . . E6
Puerto Montt 119,059 . . . . . E4
Puerto Natales 17,280 . . . . . E9
Puerto Quellón ○7,734 . . . . . D4
Puerto Varas 10,900 . . . . . E3
Puerto Williams ○949 . . . . F11
Pumanque ○3,137 . . . . . F6
Punitaqui ○16,167 . . . . . A8
Punta Arenas 2,140 . . . . . E10
Purén ○11,604 . . . . . D2
Purranque 5,900 . . . . . D3
Putaendo ○12,806 . . . . . A9
Putre ○855 . . . . . B1
Puyehue E3
Queilén ○6,055 . . . . . D4
Quemchi ○6,707 . . . . . D4
Quilicura 8,100 . . . . . G3
Quillagua B3
Quilleco ○16,043 . . . . . E1
Quillota 36,500 . . . . . F2
Quilpué 40,600 . . . . . F2
Quinta de Tilcoco ○6,513 . . G5
Quintero 9,900 . . . . . F2
Quirihue ○11,178 . . . . . E1
Rancagua 140,589 . . . . . G5
Renca ○67,168 . . . . . G3
Rengo 12,400 . . . . . G5
Requínoa ○10,730 . . . . . G5
Retiro ○15,146 . . . . . A11
Rinconada San Martín ○4,118 . . . . . G2
Río Blanco B9
Río Bueno 9,600 . . . . . D3
Río Negro 5,100 . . . . . D3
Río Verde ○554 . . . . . E10
Rocas de Santo Domingo ○4,114 . . . . . F4
Rosario ○3,383 . . . . . F5
Salamanca ○18,741 . . . . . A9
Samo Alto ○5,689 . . . . . A8
San Antonio 46,700 . . . . . F3
San Bernardo ○117,766 . . . G4
San Carlos 17,000 . . . . . E1
San Clemente ○23,273 . . . A11
San Felipe 26,100 . . . . . G2
San Fernando 23,600 . . . . . G6
San Francisco de Mostazal ○11,439 . . . . . G4
San Ignacio ○13,523 . . . . . E1
San Javier 10,800 . . . . . A11
San José de Maipo ○9,601 . . . . . B10
San Pablo ○7,978 . . . . . D3
San Pedro ○8,255 . . . . . F4
San Pedro de Atacama C4
San Rosendo ○14,337 . . . . . E1
Santa Bárbara ○14,345 . . . . . E1
Santa Cruz 8,600 . . . . . F6
Santa María ○8,162 . . . . . G2
Santiago (cap.) 3,614,947 . . G3
Santiago *3,672,374 . . . . . G3
San Vicente F4
San Vicente (San Vicente de Tagua Tagua) ○28,333 F5
Sierra Gorda ○8,805 . . . . . B4
Talagante 16,500 . . . . . G4
Talca 133,160 . . . . . A11
Talcahuano 148,300 . . . . . D1
Taltal 6,400 . . . . . A5
Tamaya A8
Tarapacá B2
Temuco 197,232 . . . . . E2
Teno ○17,675 . . . . . A10
Termas de Cauquenes B10
Tierra Amarilla ○7,899 . . . . A6
Tiltil ○9,198 . . . . . G2
Toco ○8,734 . . . . . B3
Toconao C4
Tocopilla 22,000 . . . . . A3
Toltén ○16,265 . . . . . D2
Tomé 29,600 . . . . . D1
Traiguén 11,400 . . . . . D2
Valdivia 115,536 . . . . . D3
Vallenar 26,800 . . . . . A7
Valparaíso 271,580 . . . . . E2
Victoria 16,500 . . . . . D2
Vicuña 5,100 . . . . . A8
Villa Alemana 29,600 . . . . . F2
Villa Alhué ○5,078 . . . . . G4
Villarrica 25,091 . . . . . E2
Viña del Mar 281,361 . . . . . F2
Yumbel ○21,858 . . . . . E1
Yungay ○10,725 . . . . . E1
Zapallar ○2,894 . . . . . A9
Zapiga B2

OTHER FEATURES

Aconcagua (riv.) F2
Aculeo (lag.) G4
Adventure (bay) D5
Aguas Calientes, Cerro (mt.) C4
Almirantazgo (bay) F11
Almirante Montt (gulf) D9
Ancud (gulf) D4
Angamos (isl.) D8
Angamos (pt.) A4
Ap Iwan, Cerro (mt.) E6
Arauco (gulf) D1
Arenales, Cerro (mt.) D7
Atacama (des.) B4
Atacama, Salar de (salt dep.) C4
Aucanquilcha, Cerro (mt.) . . B3
Azapa, Quebrada (riv.) B1
Baker (riv.) D7
Ballenero (chan.) E11
Bascuñán (cape) A7
Beagle (chan.) E11
Bella Vista, Salar de (salt dep.) B3
Benjamín (isl.) D5
Bío-Bío (riv.) E2
Blanca (lag.) E10
Blanco (lake) F10
Bravo (riv.) D7
Brunswick (pen.) E10
Bueno (riv.) D3
Buenos Aires (lake) E6
Byron (isl.) D7
Cachapoal (riv.) G5
Cachina, Quebrada (riv.) A5
Cachos (pt.) A6
Calafquén (lake) E3
Camarones (riv.) A2
Camiña, Quebrada (riv.) B2
Campana (isl.) D7
Campanario, Cerro (mt.) . . A10
Capitán Aracena (isl.) E10
Carmen (riv.) B7
Castillo, Cerro (mt.) E6
Catalina (pt.) F10
Chaffers (isl.) D5
Chaltel, Cerro (mt.) E8
Chañaral (isl.) A7
Chatham (isl.) D9
Chauques (isls.) D4
Cheap (chan.) D7
Chiloé (isl.) 119,286 . . . . . D4
Choapa (riv.) A9
Chonos (arch.) D6
Choros (cape) A7
Cisnes (riv.) E5
Clarence (isl.) E10
Clemente (isl.) D6
Cochrane (lake) E7
Cochrane, Cerro (mt.) E7
Cockburn (chan.) E11
Concepción (chan.) D9
Cónico, Cerro (mt.) E4
Contreras (isl.) D9
Cook (bay) E11
Copiapó (bay) A6
Copiapó (riv.) A6
Corcovado (gulf) D4
Corcovado (vol.) D5
Coronados (gulf) D4
Curaumilla (pt.) E2
Darwin (bay) D6
Darwin, Cordillera (mts.) . . . D8
Darwin, Cordillera (mts.) . . E11

(continued on following page)

Agriculture, Industry and Resources

DOMINANT LAND USE

- Cereals, Livestock
- Mediterranean Agriculture (cereals, fruit, livestock)
- Pasture Livestock
- Extensive Livestock Ranching
- Limited Seasonal Grazing
- Forests
- Nonagricultural Land

MAJOR MINERAL OCCURRENCES

Ag	Silver	Hg	Mercury
Au	Gold	Id	Iodine
C	Coal	Mn	Manganese
Cu	Copper	Mo	Molybdenum
Fe	Iron Ore	N	Nitrates
G	Natural Gas	Na	Salt
Gp	Gypsum	O	Petroleum
		S	Sulfur

⚡ Water Power   ▨ Major Industrial Areas

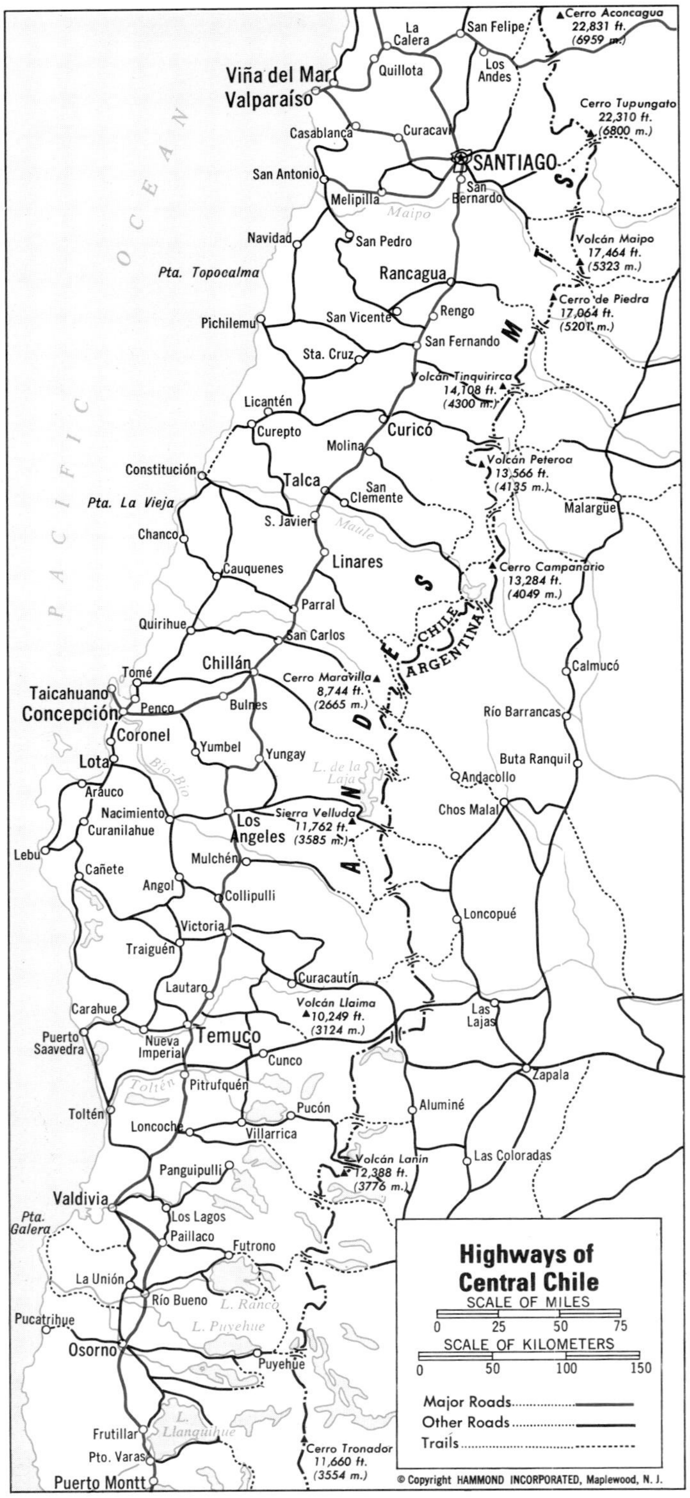

Highways of Central Chile

SCALE OF MILES
0   25   50   75

SCALE OF KILOMETERS
0   50   100   150

Major Roads ——————
Other Roads ——————
Trails ··············

© Copyright HAMMOND INCORPORATED, Maplewood, N. J.

PROVINCES

Buenos Aires 10,796,036...D 4
Catamarca 206,204...C 2
Chaco 692,410...D 2
Chubut 262,196...C 5
Córdoba 2,407,135...D 3
Corrientes 657,716...E 2
Distrito Federal 2,908,001...H 7
Entre Ríos 902,241...E 3
Formosa 292,479...D 1
Jujuy 408,514...C 1
La Pampa 207,132...C 4
La Rioja 163,342...C 2
Mendoza 1,187,305...C 4
Misiones 579,579...F 2
Neuquén 241,904...C 4
Río Negro 383,896...C 5
Salta 662,369...D 1
San Juan 469,973...C 3
San Luis 212,837...C 3
Santa Cruz 114,479...C 6
Santa Fe 2,457,188...D 3
Santiago del Estero 652,318...D 2
Tierra del Fuego, Antártida,
  e Islas del Atlántico
  Sur 29,451...C 7
Tucumán 968,066...C 2

CITIES and TOWNS

Abra Pampa 2,929...C 1
Adolfo Alsina 7,707...D 4

Aguaray 4,802...D 1
Aguilares 20,286...C 2
Aimogasta 4,640...C 2
Alberti 6,440...G 7
Alcorta 5,818...F 6
Algarrobo del Águila...C 4
Allen 14,041...C 4
Alpachiri 1,657...D 4
Alta Gracia 30,628...D 3
Aluminé 1,560...B 4
Alvear 5,419...E 2
Ameghino 2,775...D 3
Añatuya 15,025...D 2
Andalgalá 6,853...C 2
Antofagasta de la Sierra...C 2
Apóstoles 11,252...E 2
Arrecifes 17,719...F 7
Arroyo Seco 12,886...F 6
Ascensión 3,031...F 7
Avellaneda 330,654...G 7
Ayacucho 12,363...E 4
Azul 43,582...E 4
Bahía Blanca 220,765...D 4
Bahía Bustamante...C 6
Bahía Thetis...C 7
Balcarce 28,985...E 4
Balnearia 4,531...D 3
Baradero 20,103...G 6
Barrancas 3,602...F 6
Barranqueras...E 2
Barreal 2,739...C 3
Basavilbaso 7,657...G 6
Belén 7,411...C 2

Bella Vista, Corrientes
  14,229...E 2
Bella Vista, Tucumán 9,177...D 2
Bell Ville 26,559...D 3
Bolívar 16,382...D 4
Bovril 4,735...G 5
Bragado 27,101...F 7
Buenos Aires (cap.)
  2,908,001...H 7
Buenos Aires *9,927,404...H 7
Cafayate 5,048...C 2
Calafate...B 7
Calchaquí 5,958...F 5
Caleta Olivia 20,141...C 6
Camarones...C 5
Campana 51,498...G 6
Cañada de Gómez 24,706...F 6
Canals 6,627...D 3
Cañuelas 14,831...G 7
Carcarañá 11,121...F 6
Carlos Casares 13,236...F 7
Carlos Tejedor 4,421...D 4
Carmen de Areco 7,882...F 7
Carmen de Patagones
  13,981...D 5
Casilda 23,492...F 6
Castelli 4,507...H 7
Catamarca 88,432...C 2
Caucete 14,512...C 3
Ceres 10,743...D 2
Chabás 5,156...F 6
Chacabuco 26,492...F 7
Chajarí 15,242...G 5

Chamical 6,333...C 3
Charadai 1,078...D 2
Charata 13,070...D 2
Chascomús 21,864...H 7
Chepes 4,775...C 3
Chicoana 1,844...C 2
Chilecito 14,010...C 2
Chivilcoy 43,779...F 7
Choele-Choel 6,191...C 4
Chos-Malal 4,823...C 4
Cinco Saltos 15,094...C 4
Cipolletti 40,123...C 4
Clorinda 21,008...E 2
Colón, Buenos Aires 16,070...F 6
Colón, Entre Ríos 11,648...G 6
Colonia Las Heras 3,176...C 6
Comandante Fontana 4,468...D 2
Comandante Luis Piedrabuena
  2,492...C 6
Comodoro Rivadavia 96,865...C 6
Concepción 29,359...C 2
Concepción de
  la Sierra 2,778...E 2
Concepción del
  Uruguay 46,065...G 6
Concordia 93,618...G 5
Constanza 1,313...G 6
Córdoba 982,018...D 3
Coronda 11,554...F 6
Coronel Brandsen 10,484...H 7
Coronel Dorrego 10,661...D 4
Coronel Pringles 16,592...D 4
Coronel Suárez 16,359...D 4

AREA 1,072,070 sq. mi. (2,776,661 sq. km.)
POPULATION 28,438,000
CAPITAL Buenos Aires
LARGEST CITY Buenos Aires
HIGHEST POINT Cerro Aconcagua 22,831 ft.
  (6,959 m.)
MONETARY UNIT austral
MAJOR LANGUAGE Spanish
MAJOR RELIGION Roman Catholicism

Agriculture, Industry and Resources

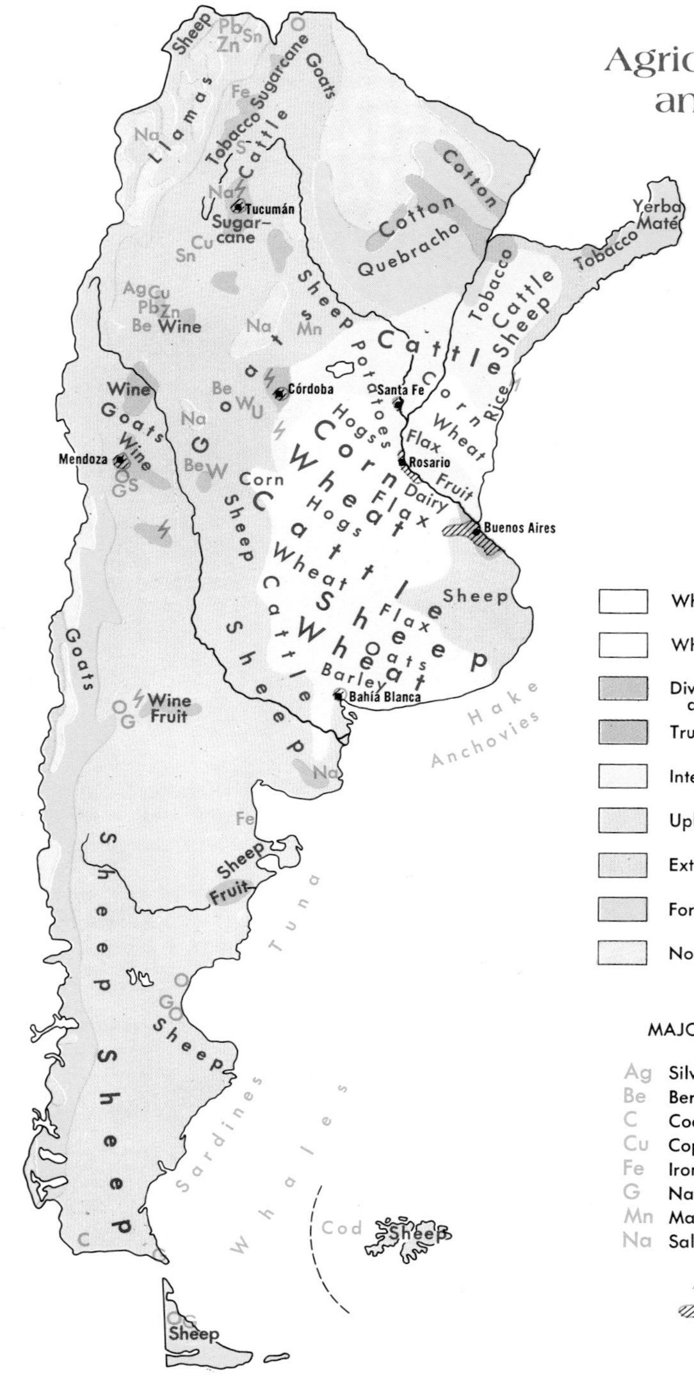

DOMINANT LAND USE

Wheat, Livestock

Wheat, Corn, Livestock

Diversified Tropical Crops (chiefly plantation agriculture)

Truck Farming, Horticulture, Special Crops

Intensive Livestock Ranching

Upland Livestock Grazing, Limited Agriculture

Extensive Livestock Ranching

Forests

Nonagricultural Land

MAJOR MINERAL OCCURRENCES

Ag Silver
Be Beryl
C Coal
Cu Copper
Fe Iron Ore
G Natural Gas
Mn Manganese
Na Salt

O Petroleum
Pb Lead
S Sulfur
Sn Tin
U Uranium
W Tungsten
Zn Zinc

⚡ Water Power
▨ Major Industrial Areas

Coronel Vidal 4,774...E 4
Corral de Bustos 8,613...D 3
Corrientes 179,590...E 2
Cosquín 13,929...D 3
Crespo 10,668...F 6
Cruz del Eje 23,473...C 3
Curuzú Cuatiá 24,955...G 5
Cutral-Có 25,870...C 4
Daireaux 8,150...D 4
Deán Funes 16,306...D 3
Diamante 13,464...F 6
Dolavon 1,778...C 5
Dolores 19,307...E 4
Eduardo Castex 5,397...D 4
El Bolsón 5,001...B 5
Eldorado 22,821...F 2
El Maitén 2,350...B 5
Elortondo 4,939...F 6
El Quebrachal 2,202...D 2
Embarcación 9,016...D 1
Empedrado 4,732...E 2
Escobar 70,829...G 7
Esperanza 22,838...F 5
Esquel 17,228...B 5
Esquina 10,380...G 5
Famatina 1,237...C 2
Federación 7,259...G 5
Felipe Yofré 1,140...G 4
Fernández 6,062...D 2
Fiambalá 1,201...C 2
Firmat 13,588...F 6
Formosa 95,067...E 2
Fortín Olmos 1,101...F 4
Frías 20,901...D 2
Gaimán 2,651...C 5
Gálvez 14,711...F 6
General Acha 7,647...C 4
General Alvear, Buenos Aires
  5,481...F 7
General Alvear,
  Mendoza 21,250...C 3
General Arenales 3,332...F 7
General Belgrano 10,909...G 7
General Conesa 3,566...C 5
General Galarza 3,057...C 6
General Güemes 15,534...D 1
General José de
  San Martín 16,296...E 2
General Juan Madariaga
  13,409...E 4
General La Madrid 5,154...D 4
General Las Heras 6,005...G 7
General Paz 5,127...H 7
General Pico 30,180...D 4
General Ramírez 5,393...F 6
General Roca 38,296...C 4
General San Martín, Buenos
  Aires 384,306...G 7
General San Martín,
  La Pampa 2,168...D 4
General Viamonte 10,112...F 7
General Villegas 11,307...D 4
Gobernador Crespo 2,972...F 5
Godoy Cruz 141,553...C 3
Goya 47,357...G 4
Gualeguay 24,883...G 6
Gualeguaychú 51,057...G 6
Guandacol 1,351...C 2
Hasenkamp 2,804...F 5
Helvecia 3,927...F 5
Hernandarias 3,002...F 5
Hernando 8,619...D 3
Huinca Renancó 7,187...D 3
Humahuaca 3,963...C 1
Humberto (Humberto
  Primo) 4,163...F 5
Ibarreta 5,262...D 2
Ibicuy 3,082...G 6
Ingeniero Huergo 3,385...C 4
Ingeniero Jacobacci 4,045...C 5
Ingeniero Luiggi 3,002...D 4
Intendente Alvear 3,640...D 4
Itatí 3,269...E 2

Ituzaingó 8,687...E 2
Jáchal 8,832...C 3
Jesús María 17,594...D 3
Joaquín V. González 6,054...D 2
Juárez 11,798...E 4
Jujuy 124,487...C 1
Junín 62,080...F 7
Junín de los Andes 5,638...B 4
La Banda 46,994...D 2
Laboulaye 16,883...D 3
La Carlota 8,614...D 3
La Cruz 4,132...E 2
La Cumbre 6,110...C 3
La Falda 12,502...D 3
Laguna Paiva 11,129...F 5
Lanús 465,891...H 7
La Paz, Entre Ríos 14,920...G 5
La Paz, Mendoza 4,604...C 3
La Plata 560,341...H 7
Laprida 6,495...D 4
La Quiaca 8,289...C 1
La Rioja 66,826...C 2
Larroque 3,147...F 5
Las Flores 18,287...E 4
Las Lomitas 4,047...D 1
Las Palmas 5,061...E 2
Las Parejas 7,430...F 6
Las Rosas 9,725...F 6
Las Varillas 10,605...D 3
La Toma 4,325...C 3
Lincoln 19,009...F 7
Loberia 8,898...E 4
Lobos 20,798...G 7
Lomas de Zamora 508,620...G 7
Lucas González 3,015...G 6
Luján 38,919...G 7
Lules 11,391...C 2
Maciel 4,066...F 6
Magdalena 7,135...H 7
Maipú 7,289...E 4
Malabrigo 3,294...F 4
Malargüe 9,496...C 4
Maquinchao 1,299...C 5
Marcos Juárez 19,827...D 3
Mar del Plata 407,024...E 4
Máximo Paz 3,216...F 6
Mburucuyá 3,044...E 2
Médanos 4,511...D 4
Mendoza 596,796...C 3
Mercedes, Buenos Aires
  46,581...G 7
Mercedes, Corrientes
  20,603...G 4
Mercedes, San Luis 50,856...C 3
Merlo 293,059...G 7
Metán 18,928...D 2
Miramar 15,473...E 4
Monte Caseros 18,247...G 5
Monte Quemado 4,707...D 2
Monteros 15,832...C 2
Morón 596,769...G 7
Morteros 11,456...D 3
Navarro 7,176...G 7
Necochea 50,939...E 4
Neuquén 90,037...C 4
Nogoyá 15,862...F 6
Norquincó...B 5
Nueve de Julio 26,608...F 7
Oberá 27,311...F 2
Olavarría 63,686...D 4
Oliva 9,231...D 3
Palo Santo 3,088...E 2
Paraná 159,581...F 5
Paso de Los Libres 24,112...E 2
Pedro Luro 3,142...D 4
Pehuajó 25,613...D 4
Pellegrini 3,940...D 4
Pergamino 68,989...F 6
Pico Truncado 9,626...C 6
Pigüé 10,793...D 4
Pilar 3,805...F 5
Pirané 9,039...E 2
Plaza Huincul 7,988...B 4

(continued on following page)

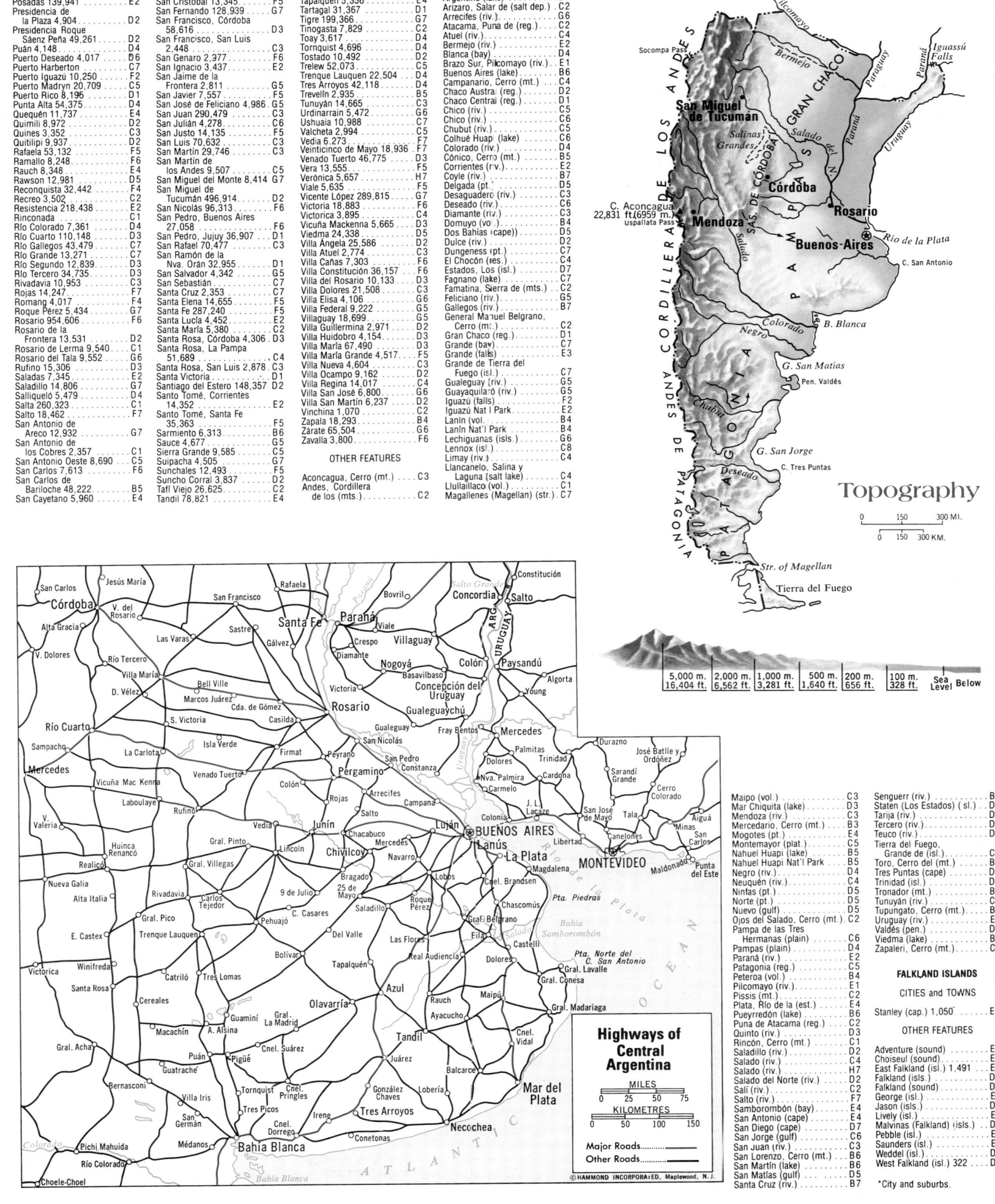

Posadas 139,941 . . . . E2
Presidencia de
la Plaza 4,904 . . . . D2
Presidencia Roque
Sáenz Peña 49,261 . . . . . D2
Puán 4,148 . . . . D4
Puerto Deseado 4,017 . . . . D6
Puerto Harberton C7
Puerto Iguazú 10,250 . . . . . F2
Puerto Madryn 20,709 . . . . . C5
Puerto Rico 8,195 . . . . D1
Punta Alta 54,375 . . . . D4
Quequén 11,737 . . . . E4
Quimili 8,972 . . . . D2
Quines 3,352 . . . . C3
Quitilipi 9,937 . . . . D2
Rafaela 53,132 . . . . F5
Ramallo 8,248 . . . . F6
Rauch 8,348 . . . . E4
Rawson 12,981 . . . . D5
Reconquista 32,442 . . . . . . F4
Recreo 3,502 . . . . C2
Resistencia 218,438 . . . . . . E2
Rinconada C1
Río Colorado 7,361 . . . . . . D4
Río Cuarto 110,148 . . . . . . D3
Río Gallegos 43,479 . . . . . C7
Río Grande 13,271 . . . . . . C7
Río Segundo 12,839 . . . . . D3
Río Tercero 34,735 . . . . . . D3
Rivadavia 10,953 . . . . C3
Rojas 14,247 . . . . F7
Romang 4,017 . . . . F4
Roque Pérez 5,434 . . . . . . G7
Rosario 954,606 . . . . F6
Rosario de la
Frontera 13,531 . . . . . . D2
Rosario de Lerma 9,540 . . . . C1
Rosario del Tala 9,552 . . . . G6
Rufino 15,306 . . . . D3
Saladas 7,345 . . . . E2
Saladillo 14,806 . . . . G7
Salliqueló 5,479 . . . . D4
Salta 260,323 . . . . C1
Salto 18,462 . . . . F7
San Antonio de
Areco 12,932 . . . . G7
San Antonio de
los Cobres 2,357 . . . . . . C1
San Antonio Oeste 8,690 . . . C5
San Carlos 7,613 . . . . F6
San Carlos de
Bariloche 48,222 . . . . . . B5
San Cayetano 5,960 . . . . . . E4

San Cristóbal 13,345 . . . . . . F5
San Fernando 128,939 . . . . . G7
San Francisco, Córdoba
58,616 . . . . D3
San Francisco, San Luis
2,448 . . . . C3
San Genaro 2,977 . . . . F6
San Ignacio 3,437 . . . . E2
San Jaime de la
Frontera 2,811 . . . . G5
San Javier 7,557 . . . . F5
San José de Feliciano 4,986 . . G5
San Juan 290,479 . . . . C3
San Julián 4,278 . . . . C6
San Justo 14,135 . . . . F5
San Luis 70,632 . . . . C3
San Martín 29,746 . . . . C3
San Martín de
los Andes 9,507 . . . . . . C5
San Miguel del Monte 8,414 . . G7
San Miguel de
Tucumán 496,914 . . . . . . C2
San Nicolás 96,313 . . . . . . F6
San Pedro, Buenos Aires
27,058 . . . . F6
San Pedro, Jujuy 36,907 . . . . D1
San Rafael 70,477 . . . . C3
San Ramón de la
Nva. Orán 32,955 . . . . . . D1
San Salvador 4,342 . . . . . . G5
San Sebastián C7
Santa Cruz 2,353 . . . . C7
Santa Elena 14,655 . . . . . . F5
Santa Fe 287,240 . . . . F5
Santa Lucía 4,452 . . . . C3
Santa María 5,380 . . . . C2
Santa Rosa, Córdoba 4,306 . . D3
Santa Rosa, La Pampa
51,689 . . . . C4
Santa Victoria C1
Santiago del Estero 148,357 . . D2
Santo Tomé, Corrientes
14,352 . . . . E2
Santo Tomé, Santa Fe
35,363 . . . . F5
Sarmiento 6,313 . . . . B6
Sauce 4,677 . . . . G5
Sierra Grande 9,585 . . . . . . C5
Suipacha 4,505 . . . . G7
Sunchales 12,493 . . . . F5
Suncho Corral 3,837 . . . . . . D2
Tafi Viejo 26,625 . . . . C2
Tandil 78,821 . . . . E4

Tapalquén 5,356 . . . . E4
Tartagal 31,367 . . . . D1
Tigre 199,366 . . . . G7
Tinogasta 7,829 . . . . C2
Toay 3,617 . . . . D4
Tornquist 4,696 . . . . D4
Tostado 10,492 . . . . D2
Trelew 52,073 . . . . C5
Trenque Lauquen 22,504 . . . . D4
Tres Arroyos 42,118 . . . . . . E4
Trevelín 2,935 . . . . B5
Tunuyán 14,665 . . . . C3
Urdinarrain 5,472 . . . . G6
Ushuaia 10,988 . . . . C7
Valcheta 2,994 . . . . C5
Vedia 6,273 . . . . F6
Veinticinco de Mayo 18,936 . . F7
Venado Tuerto 46,775 . . . . . F6
Vera 13,555 . . . . E2
Verónica 5,657 . . . . H7
Viale 5,635 . . . . F5
Vicente López 289,815 . . . . . G7
Victoria 18,883 . . . . F5
Victorica 3,895 . . . . C4
Vicuña Mackenna 5,665 . . . . C3
Viedma 24,338 . . . . D5
Villa Ángela 25,586 . . . . . . D2
Villa Atuel 2,774 . . . . C3
Villa Cañas 7,303 . . . . F6
Villa Constitución 36,157 . . . . F6
Villa del Rosario 10,133 . . . . D3
Villa Dolores 21,508 . . . . . . C3
Villa Elisa 4,106 . . . . G6
Villa Federal 9,222 . . . . G5
Villaguay 18,699 . . . . G5
Villa Guillermina 2,971 . . . . . D2
Villa Huidobro 4,154 . . . . . . D3
Villa María 67,490 . . . . D3
Villa María Grande 4,517 . . . . F5
Villa Nueva 4,604 . . . . D3
Villa Ocampo 9,162 . . . . . . D2
Villa Regina 14,017 . . . . . . C4
Villa San José 6,800 . . . . . . G6
Villa San Martín 6,237 . . . . . D2
Vinchina 1,070 . . . . C2
Zapala 18,293 . . . . B4
Zárate 65,504 . . . . G6
Zavalla 3,800 . . . . F6

OTHER FEATURES

Aconcagua, Cerro (mt.) C3
Andes, Cordillera
de los (mts.) C2

Argentino (lake) B7
Arizaro, Salar de (salt dep.) . . C2
Arrecifes (riv.) G6
Atacama, Puna de (reg.) C2
Atuel (riv.) C4
Bermejo (riv.) E2
Blanca (bay) D4
Brazo Sur, Pilcomayo (riv.) . . . E1
Buenos Aires (lake) B6
Campanario, Cerro (mt.) C4
Chaco Austral (reg.) D2
Chaco Central (reg.) D1
Chico (riv.) C5
Chico (riv.) C5
Chico (riv.) C5
Chubut (riv.) C5
Colhué Huap (lake) C6
Colorado (riv.) D4
Cónico, Cerro (mt.) B5
Corrientes (riv.) E2
Coyle (riv.) B7
Delgada (pt.) D5
Desaguadero (riv.) C3
Deseado (riv.) C6
Diamante (riv.) C3
Domuyo (vol.) B4
Dos Bahías (cape)) D5
Dulce (riv.) D2
Dungeness (pt.) C7
El Chocón (res.) C4
Estados, Los (isl.) D7
Fagnano (lake) C7
Famatina, Sierra de (mts.) . . . C2
Feliciano (riv.) G5
Gallegos (riv.) B7
General Manuel Belgrano,
Cerro (mt.) C2
Gran Chaco (reg.) D1
Grande (bay) C7
Grande (falls) E3
Grande de Tierra del
Fuego (riv.) C7
Gualeguay (riv.) G5
Guayaquilaró (riv.) G5
Iguazú (falls) F2
Iguazú Nat'l Park E2
Lanín (vol.) B4
Lanín Nat'l Park B4
Lechiguanas (isls.) G6
Lennox (isl.) C8
Limay (riv.) C4
Llancanelo, Salina y
Laguna (salt lake) C4
Llullaillaco (vol.) C1
Magallanes (Magellan) (str.) . . C7

Maipo (vol.) C3
Mar Chiquita (lake) D3
Mendoza (riv.) C3
Mercedario, Cerro (mt.) B3
Mogotes (pt.) E4
Montemayor (plat.) C5
Nahuel Huapi (lake) B5
Nahuel Huapi Nat'l Park B5
Negro (riv.) D4
Neuquén (riv.) C4
Ninfas (pt.) D5
Norte (pt.) D5
Nuevo (gulf) D5
Ojos del Salado, Cerro (mt.) . . C2
Pampa de las Tres
Hermanas (plain) C6
Pampas (plain) D4
Paraná (riv.) E2
Patagonia (reg.) C5
Peteroa (mt.) B4
Pilcomayo (riv.) E1
Pissis (mt.) C2
Plata, Río de la (est.) E4
Pueyrredón (lake) B6
Puna de Atacama (reg.) C2
Quinto (riv.) D3
Rincón, Cerro (mt.) C1
Saladillo (riv.) D2
Salado (riv.) C4
Salado (riv.) H7
Salado del Norte (riv.) D2
Sali (riv.) C2
Salto (riv.) F7
Samborombón (bay) E4
San Antonio (cape) E4
San Diego (cape) D7
San Jorge (gulf) C6
San Juan (riv.) C3
San Lorenzo, Cerro (mt.) B6
San Martín (lake) B6
San Matías (gulf) D5
Santa Cruz (riv.) B7

Senguerr (riv.) B6
Staten (Los Estados) (sl.) . . . D7
Tarija (riv.) . . . . D
Tercero (riv.) . . . . D
Teuco (riv.) . . . . D
Tierra del Fuego,
Grande de (isl.) C
Toro, Cerro del (mt.) . . . . . . B
Tres Puntas (cape) C
Trinidad (isl.) . . . . D
Tronador (mt.) . . . . B
Tunuyán (riv.) C
Tupungato, Cerro (mt.) C
Uruguay (riv.) . . . . E
Valdés (pen.) . . . . D
Viedma (lake) . . . . B
Zapaleri, Cerro (mt.) C

FALKLAND ISLANDS

CITIES and TOWNS

Stanley (cap.) 1,050 . . . . . . E

OTHER FEATURES

Adventure (sound) . . . . E
Choiseul (sound) . . . . E
East Falkland (isl.) 1,491 . . . . E
Falkland (isls.) . . . . E
Falkland (sound) . . . . E
George (isl.) . . . . E
Jason (isls.) . . . . E
Lively (isl.) . . . . E
Malvinas (Falkland) (isls.) . . . E
Pebble (isl.) . . . . E
Saunders (isl.) . . . . E
Weddel (isl.) . . . . E
West Falkland (isl.) 322 . . . . E

*City and suburbs.

Topography

0   150   300 MI.

0   150   300 KM.

5,000 m. | 2,000 m. | 1,000 m. | 500 m. | 200 m. | 100 m. | Sea
16,404 ft. | 6,562 ft. | 3,281 ft. | 1,640 ft. | 656 ft. | 328 ft. | Level   Below

Highways of Central Argentina

MILES
0   25   50   75

KILOMETRES
0   50   100   150

Major Roads . . . .
Other Roads . . . .

© HAMMOND INCORPORATED, Maplewood, N.J.

Paraguay

CONIC PROJECTION

SCALE OF MILES
0 20 40 60 80 100 120 140

SCALE OF KILOMETERS
0 20 40 60 80 100 120 140

Capitals of Countries .... ☆
Capitals of Departments .... ◉
International Boundaries ....
Department Boundaries ....

Scale 1:6,740,000

© Copyright HAMMOND INCORPORATED, Maplewood, N.J.

PARAGUAY

DEPARTMENTS

Alto Paraguay	C2
Alto Paraná	E4
Amambay	D3
Asunción	A4
Boquerón	B3
Caaguazú	D-E4
Caazapá	D-E5
Canendiyu	E4
Centra	D4
Chaco	B-C2
Concepción	D3
Cordillera	D4
Guaira	D4
Itapúa	E5
Misiones	D5
Ñeembucú	C-D5
Nueva Asunción	B2
Paraguari	D4-5
Presidente Hayes	D4-5
San Pedro	D4

CITIES and TOWNS

Abal '.507	E4
Acahay 1.937	B5
Alberdi 2.346	B5
Altos 1.441	B4
Antequera 1.281	D4
Areguá 3.941	B4
Arroyos y Esteros 1.253	B4
Asunción (cap) 387.676	A4
Atyrá 1.427	B4
Ayolas 309	A4
Belén 1.219	D3
Bella Vista 3.101	D3
Bella Vista 1.421	E5
Benjamín Aceval 2.877	C4
Buena Vista 1.353	D4
Caacupé 7.278	B5
Caaguazú 7.950	D4
Caapucú 1.400	D5
Caazapá 3.132	D5
Caballero 1.225	B5
Cap atá 2.827	B4
Capitán Bado 915	E3
Capitán Meza 375	E5
Caraguatay 1.439	B4
Carapeguá 3.416	B5
Carayaó 1.190	C4
Carmen del Paraná 1.980	D5
Cerrito 958	D5
Ciudad Presidente Stroessner 7.085	E4
Concepción 19.392	D3
Coronel Bogado 3.973	D5
Coronel Martínez 1.598	B5
Coronel Oviedo 13.786	C5
Co'onel Oviedo 1.112	C5
Desmochados 551	C5
Doctor Cecilio Báez 1.300	D4
Doctor Juan L. Mallorquin 1.913	E4
Doctor Juan Manuel Frutos 1.494	E4
Doctor M. Irala 468	D4
Emboscada 1.222	B4
Encarnación 23.343	E5
Escobar 548	B5
El sebio Ayala 4.328	B4
Fernando de la Mora 36.834	A4
Filadelfia 1.438	B3
Fram 1.090	E5
Fuerte Olimpo 3.063	C2
General Artigas 3.542	D9
General Elizardo Aquino 1.304	D4
General Eugenio A. Garay 740	A2
Guarambaré 3.640	B5
Hernandarias 3.898	E4
Hohenau 1.121	E5
Horqueta 4.328	D3
Hugo Stroessner 536	C4
Humaitá 938	C5
Isla Pucú 1.766	B4
Isla Umbú 236	C5
Ita 7.041	B5
Itacurubí 1.997	B5
Itacurubí del Rosario 2.467	D4
Itapé 1.376	C5
Itaquyry	E4
Itaugua 3.767	B5
Iturbe 3.413	C5
Jesús 1.495	E5
Juan de Mena 1.027	D4
La Colmena 1.804	B5
Lambaré 31.656	A4
Laureles 435	D5
Lima 1.098	D3
Limpio 2.219	B4
Loreto 1.258	D3
Luque 13.921	B4
Maciel 376	D5
Mariano Roque Alonso 1.492	A4
Mariscal Estigarribia 3.150	B3
Mayor Martínez 324	C5

Mayor Pablo Lagerenza	B
Mbocayaty 925	D
Mbuyapey 1.560	E
Nacunday 380	E
Natalicio Talavera 1.228	D
Nueva Germania 572	D
Nueva Italia 1.517	D
Numi 941	D
Paraguari 5.036	D
Paso de Patria 698	D
Pedro Juan Caballero 21.033	F
Pilar 12.506	C
Pirayú 2.698	B
Piribebuy 4.497	B
Primero de Marzo 696	D
Puerto Casado 4.078	D
Puerto Guaraní 302	C
Puerto Pinasco 5.477	D
Puerto Presidente Franco 4.152	E
Puerto Sastre 160	D
Quiindy 2.664	D
Quyquyo 928	D
Roque González de Santa Cruz 1.375	B
Rosario 4.165	D
Salto del Guairá	E
San Antonio 4.906	A
San Bernardino 949	B
San Cosme y Damián 602	D
San Estanislao 4.753	D
San Ignacio 6.116	D
San Joaquín 536	D
San José 3.102	B
San Juan Bautista 6.457	D
San Juan Bautista de Ñeembucú 688	C
San Juan Nepomuceno 2.974	D
San Lázaro 1.767	C
San Lorenzo 11.616	A
San Miguel 1.030	D
San Patricio 1.130	D
San Pedro 3.186	D
San Salvador 1.393	D
Santa Elena 1.439	D
Santa María 793	D
Santa Rosa 3.736	D
Santiago 1.265	D
Sapucal 1.864	B
Tacuaras 193	C
Tacuatí 836	D
Tavaí 472	D
Tebicuary Mí 183	C
Tobatí 4.983	B
Trinidad 837	E
Unión 1.286	D
Valenzuela 1.108	B
Valle Mí 1.318	D
25 de Diciembre 439	D
Villa Florida 1.261	D
Villa Franca 359	C
Villa Hayes 4.749	B
Villa Oliva 564	C
Villarrica 17.687	D
Villeta 3.156	A
Yabebyry 797	C
Yaguarón 3.368	B
Yataity 1.159	D
Ybycuí 1.736	D
Ybytymí 816	D
Yegros 1.051	D
Ygatimí 396	E
Yhú 964	D
Ypacaraí 5.195	B
Ypé Jhú 645	E
Yuty 2.392	D

OTHER FEATURES

Acaray (riv)	E
Alto Paraná (riv)	D
Amambay, Cordillera de (mts)	D-E
Apa (riv)	D
Chaco Boreal (reg)	B2
Chovoreca (mt)	B
Confuso (riv)	B
Coronel F. Cabrera (mt)	B
González, Riacho (riv)	B
Gran Chaco (reg)	B
Iguazú (falls)	E
Itaipu (res)	E
Jara (hill)	B
Mbaracayú, Cordillera de (mts)	E
Monday (riv)	E
Montelindo (riv)	D
Mosquito, Riacho (riv)	D
Negro (riv)	B
Paraguay (riv)	C
Pilcomayo (riv)	B
Tebicuary (riv)	C
Timane (riv)	B
Vera (lag)	E
Verde (riv)	B

Agriculture, Industry and Resources

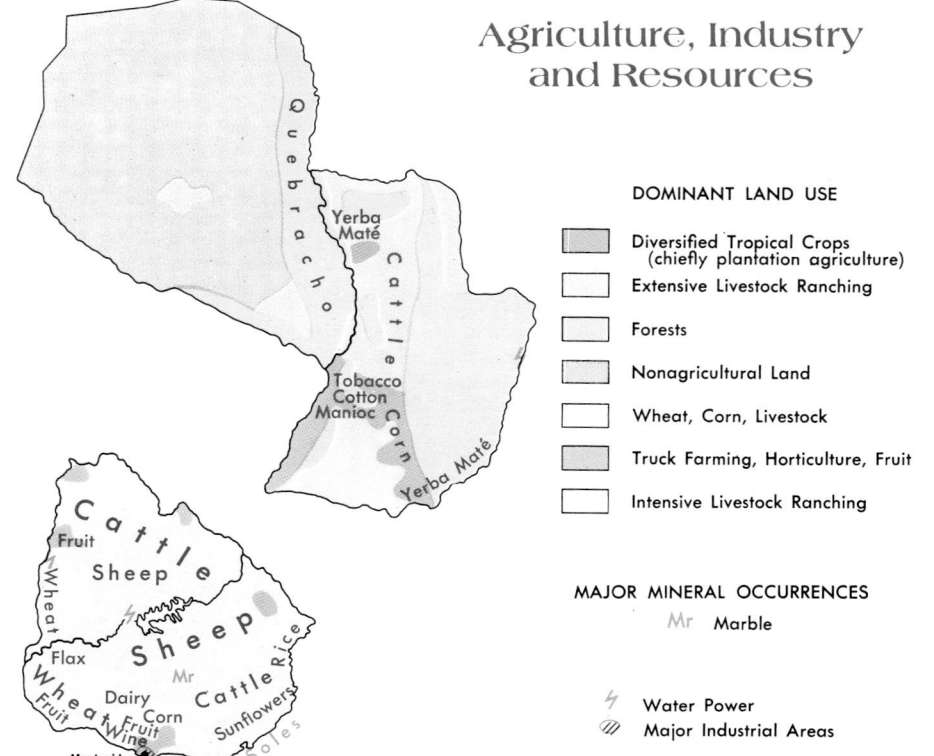

DOMINANT LAND USE

- Diversified Tropical Crops (chiefly plantation agriculture)
- Extensive Livestock Ranching
- Forests
- Nonagricultural Land
- Wheat, Corn, Livestock
- Truck Farming, Horticulture, Fruit
- Intensive Livestock Ranching

MAJOR MINERAL OCCURRENCES

Mr Marble

Water Power

Major Industrial Areas

Topography

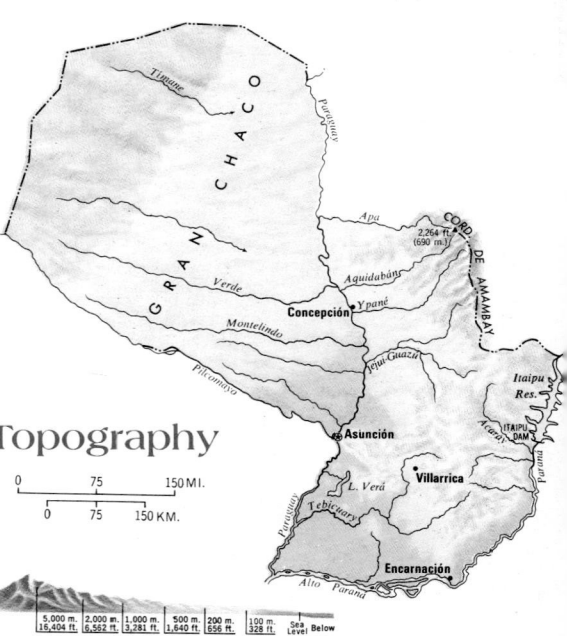

0 75 150 MI.
0 75 150 KM.

5,000 m. / 16,404 ft. — 2,000 m. / 6,562 ft. — 1,000 m. / 3,281 ft. — 500 m. / 1,640 ft. — 200 m. / 656 ft. — 100 m. / 328 ft. — Sea Level — Below

URUGUAY

DEPARTMENTS

Artigas 52,843 .... B1
Canelones 258,195 .... D5
Cerro Largo 71,023 .... E3
Colonia 105,350 .... B5
Durazno 53,635 .... C3
Flores 23,530 .... C4
Florida 63,987 .... D4
Lavalleja 65,823 .... D5
Maldonado 61,259 .... E5
Montevideo 1,202,757 .... B7
Paysandú 88,029 .... B3
Río Negro 46,861 .... B3
Rivera 77,086 .... D2
Rocha 55,097 .... E4
Salto 92,183 .... B2
San José 79,563 .... C5
Soriano 77,906 .... B4
Tacuarembó 76,964 .... D3
Treinta y Tres 43,419 .... E4

CITIES and TOWNS

Aceguá 930 .... E2
Achar 606 .... C3
Agraciada 638 .... A4
Aguas Corrientes 992 .... A6
Aiguá 2,470 .... E5
Algorta 1,372 .... B3
Artigas 29,256 .... C1
Atlántida 2,268 .... B6
Balneario El Tesoro E5
Balneario La Barra E5
Balneario Solís 288 .... D5
Baltasar Brum 1,753 .... B1
Belén 2,129 .... B1
Bella Unión 7,778 .... B1
Bernabé Rivera 540 .... B1
Blanquillo 1,053 .... D3
Cañada Nieto 503 .... B4
Canelones 15,938 .... B6
Cardal 847 .... C5
Cardona 4,126 .... B4
Cardozo 143 .... C3
Carlos Reyles 961 .... C4
Carmelo 13,631 .... A4
Carmen 2,318 .... D4
Carrasco B7
Castillos 6,446 .... F5
Casupá 2,265 .... D5
Cebollatí 1,233 .... F4
Cerrillos 1,690 .... A6
Cerro Chato, Treinta y Tres 1,850 .... D4
Chamizo 486 .... D5
Chuy 4,472 .... F4
Colón, Lavalleja 367 .... E4
Colonia 16,895 .... B5
Colonia Lavalleja C2
Colonia Rossel y Rius 130 .... D4
Colonia Valdense 2,113 .... B5
Conchillas 748 .... B5
Constitución 3,217 .... A2
Costa Azul 453 .... E5
Cufré 430 .... B5
Cuñapirú D2
Curtina 723 .... C3
Diez y Nueve (19) de Abril 308 .... E5
Diez y Ocho (18) de Julio 742 .... F4
Dolores 12,771 .... A4
Durazno 25,811 .... C4
Egaña 667 .... B4
Empalme Olmos 2,084 .... B6
Estación Atlántida 1,845 .... B6
Estación Migues 241 .... C6
Florida 25,030 .... C5
Fortaleza de Santa Teresa F5
Fraile Muerto 2,468 .... E3
Fray Bentos 19,569 .... A4
Fray Marcos 1,573 .... D5
Garzón 258 .... E5
General Enrique Martínez 973 .... F4
Goñi 278 .... C4
Grecco 447 .... B3
Guichón 4,720 .... B3
Ituzaingó 717 .... A6
Javier de Viana 286 .... C1
Joanico 692 .... B6
Joaquín Suárez, Canelones 3,517 .... B6
José Batlle y Ordóñez 2,044 .... D4
José Enrique Rodó 1,334 .... B4
José Pedro Varela 3,541 .... E4
Juan L. Lacaze 11,133 .... B5
Julio María Sanz E4
a Bolsa C1
La Coronilla 571 .... F4
La Cruz 633 .... C4
a Cuchilla F3
a Floresta C7
a Lata E2
La Paloma 1,558 .... F5
La Paz, Canelones 14,402 .... B6
a Paz, Colonia B5
a Pedrera 116 .... F5
ascano 6,043 .... E4
as Flores 403 .... D5
a Sierra D5
as Piedras 53,983 .... B6
as Toscas 893 .... E3
bertad 6,071 .... C5
orenzo Geyres 474 .... B3
Mal Abrigo 209 .... C5
Maldonado 22,159 .... D6
Mariscala 1,393 .... E5
Mazangano E3
Melo 38,260 .... E3
Mercedes 34,667 .... B4
Merinos 403 .... C3
Miguelete 533 .... B5
Migues 2,183 .... C6
Minas 35,433 .... D5
Minas de Corrales 2,518 .... D2
Montes 2,217 .... D5
Montevideo (cap.) 1,173,254 .... B7
Nico Pérez D4
Nueva Helvecia 8,598 .... B5
Nueva Palmira 6,934 .... A4
Nuevo Berlín 1,970 .... B3
Ombúes de Lavalle 1,689 .... B4
Ombúes de Oribe C4
Palmitas 1,332 .... B4
Pan de Azúcar 4,862 .... D5
Pando 16,184 .... B6
Paso de la Laguna, Salto B2
Paso de la Laguna, Tacuarembó D3
Paso de León B1
Paso del Borracho D2
Paso del Cerro 317 .... C2
Paso de los Toros 13,178 .... C3
Paso Potrero C2
Paysandú 62,412 .... A3
Peralta C3
Piedra Sola 233 .... C3
Piedras Coloradas 487 .... B3
Piñera 261 .... C3
Pintado, Artigas C1
Piraraja 774 .... E4
Piriápolis 5,221 .... D5
Porvenir 705 .... B3
Progreso 8,257 .... B6
Pueblo del Sauce E4
Pueblo Nuevo B2
Punta del Este 6,914 .... E6
Quebracho 1,514 .... B2
Reboledo 373 .... D4
Rio Branco 5,697 .... F3
Rivera 49,013 .... D1
Rocha 21,612 .... E5
Rodríguez 1,575 .... C5
Rosario 8,302 .... B5
Salto 72,94 .... B2
San Antonio, Canelones 1,122 .... B6
San Bautista 1,472 .... B6
San Carlos 16,883 .... E5
San Gregorio, San José C4
San Gregorio, Tacuarembó 2,892 .... D3
San Jacinto 2,292 .... C6
San Javier 1,583 .... A3
San José de Mayo 28,427 .... C5
San Ramón 6,570 .... D5
San Servando F3
Santa Catalina 885 .... B4
Santa Clara de Olimar 2,867 .... D3
Santa Lucía 14,101 .... B6
Santa Rosa 2,736 .... B6
Santiago Vázquez 1,323 .... A7
Sarandí del Yi 6,326 .... D4
Sarandí de Navarro 259 .... C3
Sarandí Grande 5,598 .... C4
Sauce, Canelones 3,942 .... B6
Sauce del Yi D4
Saucedo B2
Sequeira C1
Solís 356 .... D5
Solís de Mataojo 1,763 .... D5
Soriano 1,125 .... A4
Tacuarembó 34,152 .... D2
Tala 3,611 .... D5
Tambores 1,534 .... C2
Toledo 3,127 .... B6
Tomás Gomensoro 2,105 .... B1
Totoral C3
Tranqueras 3,922 .... D2
Treinta y Tres 25,757 .... E4
Tres Bocas B2
Tres Islas E3
Trinidad 17,598 .... B4
Tupambaé 1,039 .... E3
Unión B7
Valentines 153 .... E4
Veinticinco (25) de Agosto 1,891 .... A6
Veinticinco (25) de Mayo 1,744 .... C5
Velázquez 1,042 .... E5
Vergara 2,822 .... E3
Vichadero 1,989 .... E2
Villa Darwin 507 .... B4
Villa del Cerro A7
Young 11,080 .... B3
Zapicán 764 .... E4
Zapucay D2

OTHER FEATURES

Aiguá (riv.) E4
Alférez (riv.) E5
Arapey Chico (riv.) B1
Arapey Grande (riv.) B2
Belén (range) C1
Bonete (dam) C3
Brava (pt.) B7
Cañas (range) C2
Caraguatá (riv.) D3
Castillos (lag.) F5
Cebollatí (riv.) F4
Cordobés (riv.) D3
Cuareim (riv.) B1
Cuñapirú, Arroyo (riv.) D2
Daymán (range) B2
Daymán (riv.) B2
Durazno, Grande del (range) D4
Espinillo (pt.) A7
Este (pt.) D6
Flores (isl.) D5
Garzón (lag.) E5
Grande (range) D4
Grande, Arroyo (riv.) B4
Grande Inferior (range) C4
Haedo (range) C2
India Muerta (riv.) E4
José Ignacio (lag.) E5
Lobos (isl.) E6
Maciel, Arroyo (riv.) C4
Merín (lag.) F4
Mirador Nacional (mt.) D5
Negra (lag.) F5
Negra (range) D2
Negro (riv.) B4
Negro, Arroyo (riv.) B3
Olimar Grande (riv.) E4
Pando (riv.) B6
Parao (riv.) E3
Plata, La (riv.) B5
Polonio (cape) F5
Quequay Chico (riv.) B3
Quequay Grande (riv.) B3
Río Negro (res.) D3
Rocha (lag.) E5
Salto Grande (falls) A2
San José (riv.) C4
San Miguel (swamp) F4
San Salvador (riv.) B4
Santa Ana (range) D2
Santa Lucía (riv.) D5
Santa Lucía Chico (riv.) D4
Santa María (cape) F5
Sauce (lag.) D5
Sopas, Arroyo (riv.) C2
Tacuarembó (riv.) D2
Tacuarí (riv.) E3
Tigre (isl.) A7
Uruguay (riv.) A3
Yaguarón (riv.) F3
Yi (riv.) B4

PARAGUAY

AREA 157,047 sq. mi. (406,752 sq. km.)
POPULATION 2,973,000
CAPITAL Asunción
LARGEST CITY Asunción
HIGHEST POINT Amambay Range 2,264 ft. (690 m.)
MONETARY UNIT guaraní
MAJOR LANGUAGES Spanish, Guaraní
MAJOR RELIGION Roman Catholicism

URUGUAY

AREA 72,172 sq. mi. (186,925 sq. km.)
POPULATION 2,899,000
CAPITAL Montevideo
LARGEST CITY Montevideo
HIGHEST POINT Mirador Nacional 1,644 ft. (501 m.)
MONETARY UNIT Uruguayan peso
MAJOR LANGUAGE Spanish
MAJOR RELIGION Roman Catholicism

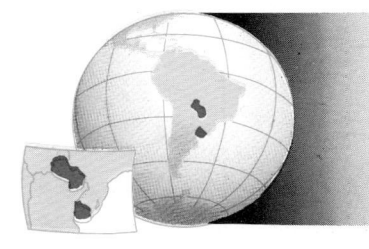

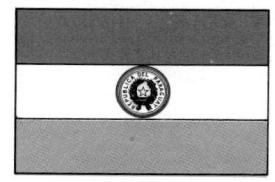

PARAGUAY

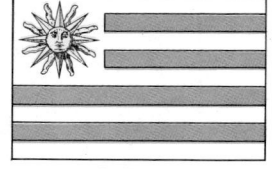

URUGUAY

Topography
Rivera
Salto
Salto Grande
Paysandú
Mercedes
Montevideo
Cuareim
Arapey
Grande
CUCH. DE SANTA ANA
CUCH. DE HAEDO
Trinidad Hito 1,237 ft. (377 m.)
Negro
Embalse del R. Negro
Yaguarón
Uruguay
Yí
CUCHILLA GRANDE
Cebollatí
Lag. Merín
Sta. Lucía
Río de la Plata
Mirador Nacional 1,644 ft. (501 m.)
Pta. Brava
Pta. del Este
0 50 100 MI.
0 50 100 KM.
Below Sea Level
100 m. 328 ft.
200 m. 656 ft.
500 m. 1,640 ft.
1,000 m. 3,281 ft.
2,000 m. 6,562 ft.
5,000 m. 16,404 ft.

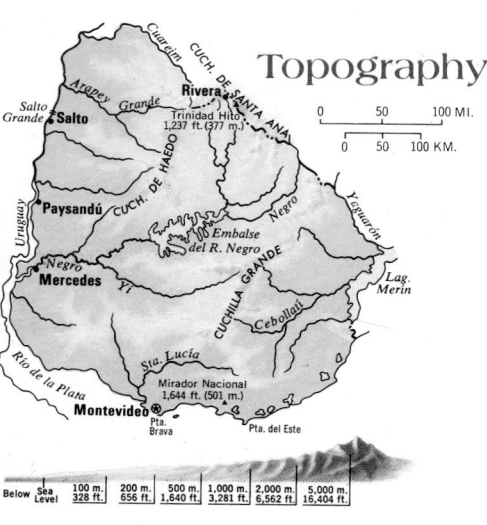

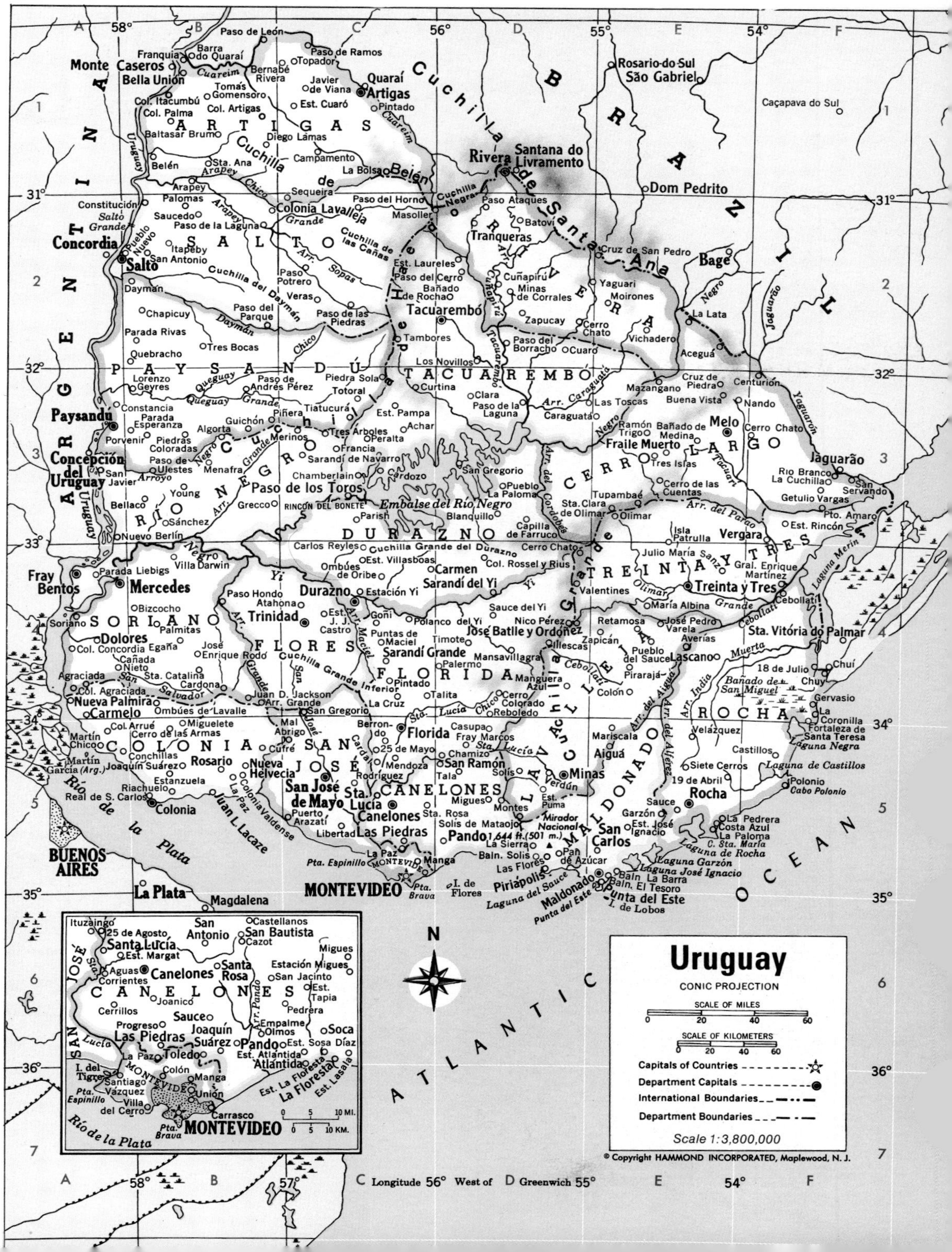

Uruguay
CONIC PROJECTION
SCALE OF MILES
0 20 40 60
SCALE OF KILOMETERS
0 20 40 60
Capitals of Countries
Department Capitals
International Boundaries
Department Boundaries
Scale 1:3,800,000
© Copyright HAMMOND INCORPORATED, Maplewood, N. J.
ATLANTIC OCEAN
BRAZIL
ARGENTINA
MONTEVIDEO
BUENOS AIRES
Río de la Plata
Longitude 56° West of Greenwich 55°

North America

LAMBERT AZIMUTHAL EQUAL-AREA PROJECTION

MILES
0 100 200 400 600 800

KILOMETERS
0 100 200 400 600 800

Capitals of Countries .... ⦿
Other Capitals .... ◉
International Boundaries .... —·—·—
Other Boundaries .... — — —

Scale 1:36,600,000

© Copyright HAMMOND INCORPORATED, Maplewood, N.J.

Population Distribution

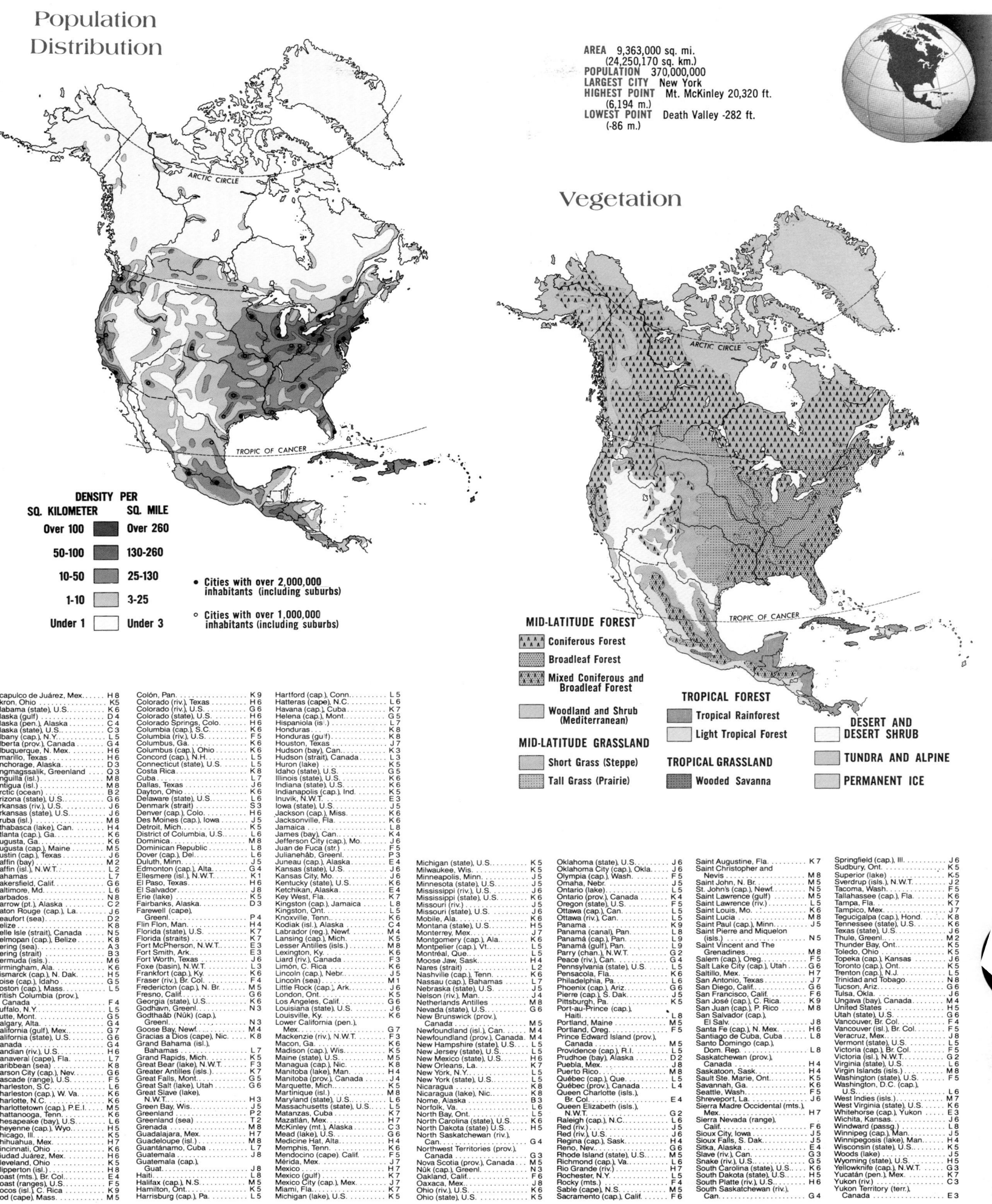

ARCTIC CIRCLE

TROPIC OF CANCER

AREA 9,363,000 sq. mi.
(24,250,170 sq. km.)
POPULATION 370,000,000
LARGEST CITY New York
HIGHEST POINT Mt. McKinley 20,320 ft.
(6,194 m.)
LOWEST POINT Death Valley -282 ft.
(-86 m.)

Vegetation

ARCTIC CIRCLE

TROPIC OF CANCER

DENSITY PER

SQ. KILOMETER	SQ. MILE
Over 100	Over 260
50-100	130-260
10-50	25-130
1-10	3-25
Under 1	Under 3

• Cities with over 2,000,000 inhabitants (including suburbs)

○ Cities with over 1,000,000 inhabitants (including suburbs)

MID-LATITUDE FOREST
- Coniferous Forest
- Broadleaf Forest
- Mixed Coniferous and Broadleaf Forest
- Woodland and Shrub (Mediterranean)

MID-LATITUDE GRASSLAND
- Short Grass (Steppe)
- Tall Grass (Prairie)

TROPICAL FOREST
- Tropical Rainforest
- Light Tropical Forest

TROPICAL GRASSLAND
- Wooded Savanna

DESERT AND DESERT SHRUB

TUNDRA AND ALPINE

PERMANENT ICE

Average January Temperature

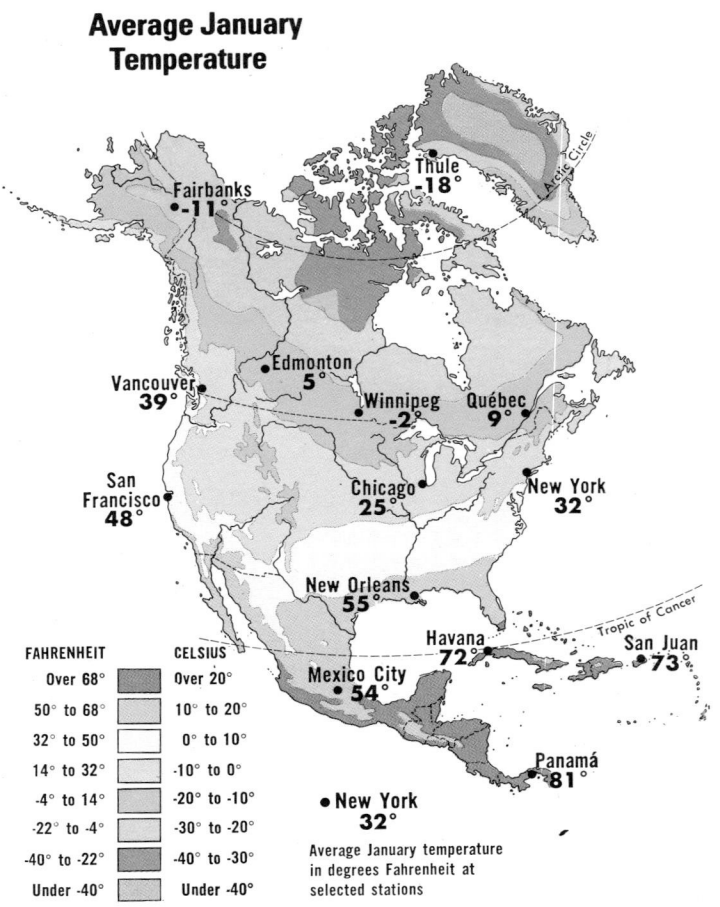

Thule -18°
Fairbanks -11°
Edmonton 5°
Vancouver 39°
Winnipeg -2°
Québec 9°
San Francisco 48°
Chicago 25°
New York 32°
New Orleans 55°
Havana 72°
San Juan 73°
Mexico City 54°
Panamá 81°

FAHRENHEIT		CELSIUS
Over 68°		Over 20°
50° to 68°		10° to 20°
32° to 50°		0° to 10°
14° to 32°		-10° to 0°
-4° to 14°		-20° to -10°
-22° to -4°		-30° to -20°
-40° to -22°		-40° to -30°
Under -40°		Under -40°

● New York 32°

Average January temperature in degrees Fahrenheit at selected stations

Average July Temperature

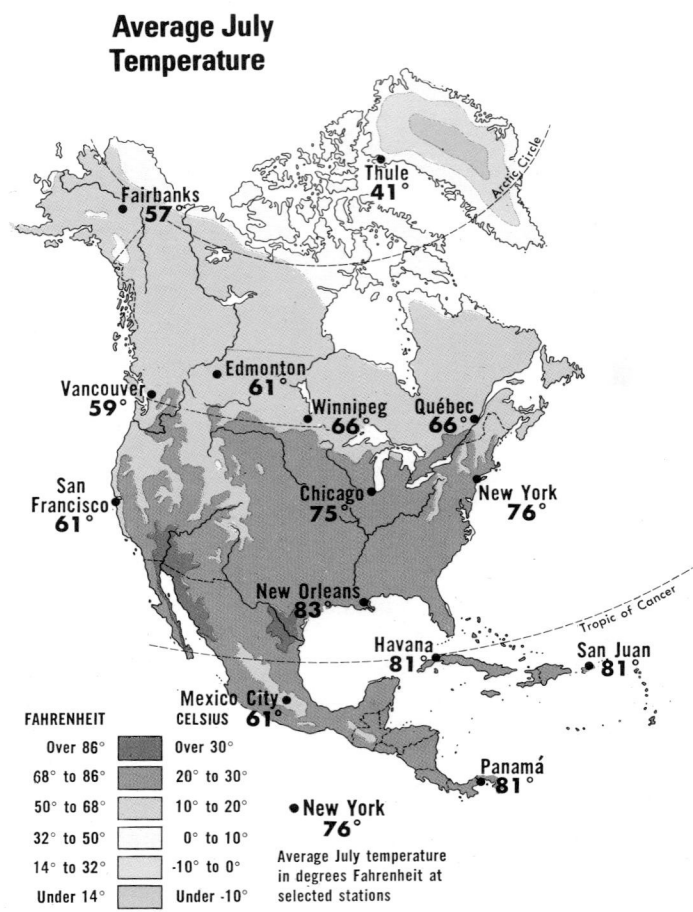

Thule 41°
Fairbanks 57°
Edmonton 61°
Vancouver 59°
Winnipeg 66°
Québec 66°
San Francisco 61°
Chicago 75°
New York 76°
New Orleans 83°
Havana 81°
San Juan 81°
Mexico City 61°
Panamá 81°

FAHRENHEIT		CELSIUS
Over 86°		Over 30°
68° to 86°		20° to 30°
50° to 68°		10° to 20°
32° to 50°		0° to 10°
14° to 32°		-10° to 0°
Under 14°		Under -10°

● New York 76°

Average July temperature in degrees Fahrenheit at selected stations

Rainfall

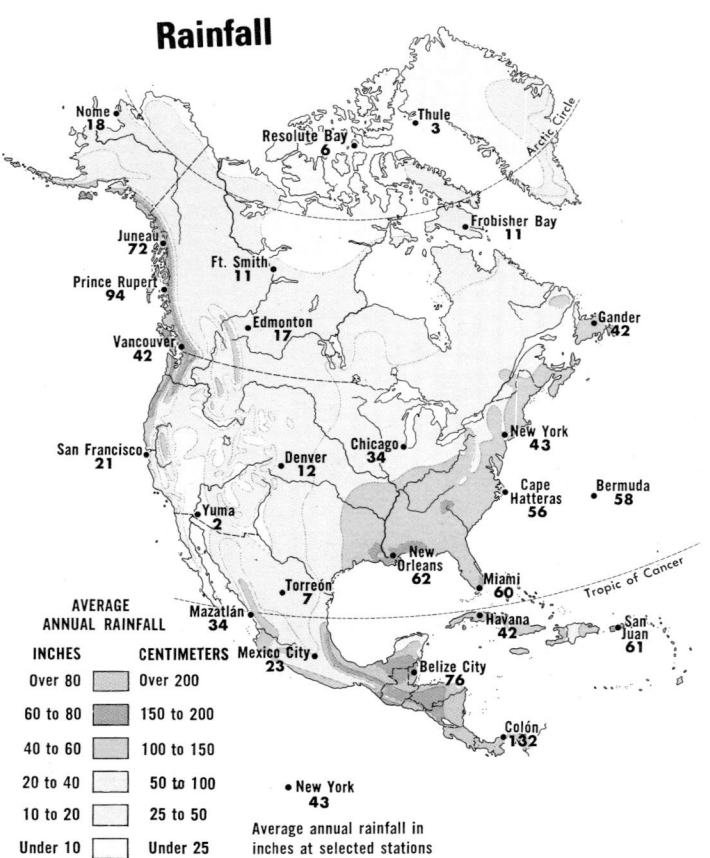

Nome 18
Thule 3
Resolute Bay 6
Juneau 72
Ft. Smith 11
Frobisher Bay 11
Prince Rupert 94
Edmonton 17
Gander 42
Vancouver 42
San Francisco 21
Denver 12
Chicago 34
New York 43
Yuma 2
Cape Hatteras 56
Bermuda 58
Torreón 7
New Orleans 62
Miami 60
Mazatlán 34
Havana 42
San Juan 61
Mexico City 23
Belize City 76
Colón 132

AVERAGE ANNUAL RAINFALL

INCHES		CENTIMETERS
Over 80		Over 200
60 to 80		150 to 200
40 to 60		100 to 150
20 to 40		50 to 100
10 to 20		25 to 50
Under 10		Under 25

● New York 43

Average annual rainfall in inches at selected stations

Vegetation / Relief

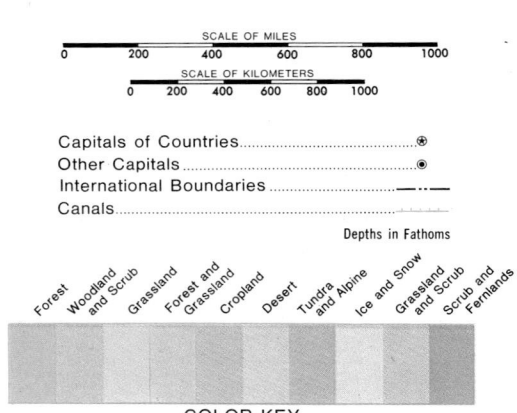

SCALE OF MILES
0 200 400 600 800 1000

SCALE OF KILOMETERS
0 200 400 600 800 1000

Capitals of Countries .... ⊛
Other Capitals .... ◎
International Boundaries .... ———
Canals ....

Depths in Fathoms

Forest
Woodland and Scrub
Grassland
Forest and Grassland
Cropland
Desert
Tundra and Alpine
Ice and Snow
Grassland and Scrub
Scrub and Fernlands

COLOR KEY

Longitude 90° West of Greenwich

Topography

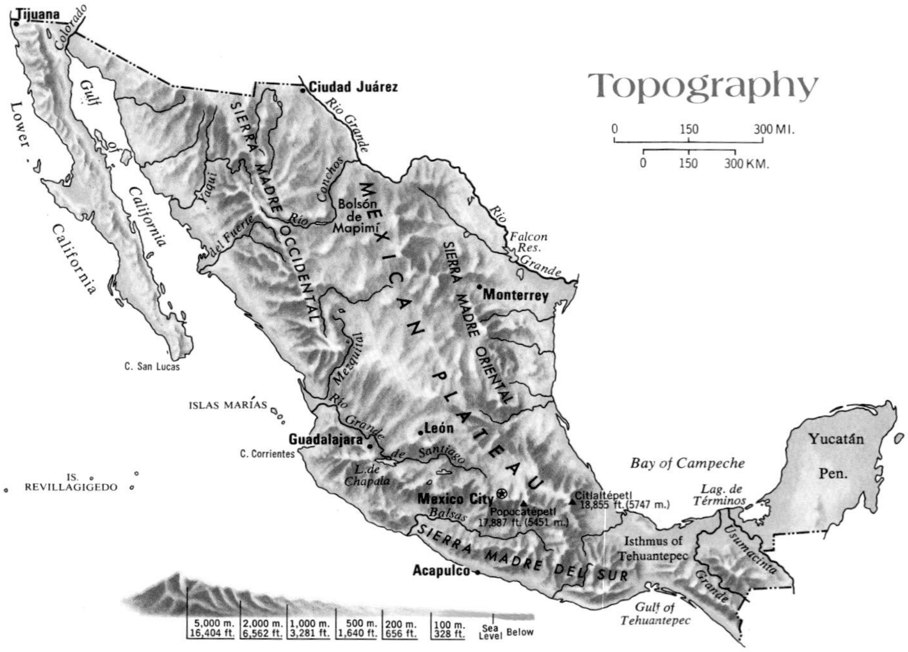

STATES

- Aguascalientes 504,300 H6
- Baja California 1,227,400 B1
- Baja California Sur 221,000 C3
- Campeche 371,800 O7
- Chiapas 2,097,500 N8
- Chihuahua 1,935,100 F2
- Coahuila 1,561,000 H3
- Colima 339,400 G7
- Distrito Federal 9,377,300 L1
- Durango 1,160,300 G4
- Guanajuato 3,045,600 J6
- Guerrero 2,174,200 J8
- Hidalgo 1,518,200 K6
- Jalisco 4,296,500 H6
- México 7,542,300 K7
- Michoacán 3,049,400 H7
- Morelos 931,400 K7
- Nayarit 729,500 G6
- Nuevo León 2,463,500 K4
- Oaxaca 2,517,500 L8
- Puebla 3,285,300 L7
- Querétaro 730,900 J6
- Quintana Roo 209,900 P7
- San Luis Potosí 1,669,900 J5
- Sinaloa 1,882,200 F4
- Sonora 1,498,100 D2
- Tabasco 1,150,000 N7
- Tamaulipas 1,924,900 K4
- Tlaxcala 548,500 N1
- Veracruz 5,263,800 L7
- Yucatán 1,034,300 P6
- Zacatecas 1,144,700 H5

CITIES and TOWNS

- Acala 11,483 N8
- Acámbaro 32,257 J7
- Acaponeta 11,844 G5
- Acapulco de Juárez 309,254 K8
- Acatlán de Osorio 7,624 K7
- Acatzingo de Hidalgo 6,905 N2
- Acayucan 21,173 M8
- Aconchi 1,596 D2
- Actopan, Hidalgo 11,037 K6
- Actopan, Veracruz 2,265 Q1
- Agua Dulce 21,060 M7
- Agualeguas 2,502 J3
- Agua Prieta 20,754 E1
- Aguascalientes 181,277 H6
- Aguililla 5,715 H7
- Ahome 4,182 E4
- Ahuacatitlán 6,436 L1
- Ahuacatlán 5,350 G6
- Ahumada 6,466 F1
- Ajalpan 8,238 L7
- Alamo 9,954 L6
- Álamos 4,269 E3
- Aldama, Chihuahua 6,047 G2
- Aldama, Tamaulipas 3,033 L5
- Aljojuca 3,204 O1
- Allende, Coahuila 11,076 J2
- Allende, Nuevo León 9,914 J4
- Almoloya del Río 3,714 K1
- Altamira 6,053 L5
- Altar 2,519 D1
- Altepexi 6,661 L7
- Alto Lucero 3,698 P1
- Altotonga 6,754 P1
- Alvarado 15,592 M7
- Amatlán de los Reyes 3,664 P2
- Amealco 2,960 K6
- Ameca 21,018 H6
- Amecameca de Juárez 16,276 L1
- Amozoc de Mota 9,203 N2
- Anáhuac, Chihuahua 10,886 F2
- Anáhuac, Nuevo León 8,168 J3
- Angostura 2,663 E4
- Antiguo Morelos 1,569 K5
- Apan 13,705 M1
- Apatzingán de la Constitución 44,849 H7
- Apizaco 21,189 N1
- Aquiles Serdán 2,565 G2
- Aramberri 1,786 J5
- Arandas 18,934 H6
- Arcelia 10,024 J7
- Ario de Rosales 8,774 J7
- Arizpe 1,736 D1
- Armería 10,616 G7
- Arriaga 13,193 N8
- Arteaga 5,324 H7
- Ascensión 4,104 E1
- Asunción Nochixtlán 3,235 L8
- Atlixco 41,967 M2
- Atotonilco el Alto 16,271 H6
- Atoyac de Álvarez 8,874 J8
- Autlán de Navarro 20,398 G7
- Axochiapan 8,283 M2
- Ayutla de los Libres 3,618 K8
- Azcapotzalco 534,554 L1
- Azoyú 3,446 K8
- Bacadéhuachi 1,514 E2
- Bacalar 2,121 P7
- Bachíniva 1,809 F2
- Bácum 2,668 D3
- Bahía Tortugas 1,457 B3
- Balancán de Domínguez 3,669 O8
- Bamoa 5,866 E4
- Banderilla 3,488 P1
- Baviácora 2,049 E2
- Benjamín Hill 5,366 D1
- Bernardino de Sahagún 12,327 M1
- Boca del Río 2,354 Q2
- Bolonchén de Rejón 2,342 O7
- Buenaventura 3,924 F2
- Burgos 673 K4
- Cabo San Lucas 1,534 E5
- Cacahoatán 5,079 N9
- Cadereyta Jiménez 13,586 K4
- Calkiní 6,870 O6
- Calnali 3,318 K6
- Calpulálpan 8,659 M1
- Calvillo 6,453 H6
- Campeche 69,506 O7
- Cananea 17,518 D1
- Canatlán 5,983 G4
- Cancún 326 Q6
- Candela 1,689 J3
- Candelaria 1,982 O7
- Cañitas de Felipe Pescador 4,885 H5
- Capulhuac de Mirafuentes 8,289 K1
- Carbo 2,804 D2
- Cárdenas, San Luis Potosí 12,020 K6
- Cárdenas, Tabasco 15,643 N8
- Carichic 1,520 F2
- Castaños 8,996 J3
- Catemaco 11,786 M7
- Ceballos 2,937 H3
- Cedral 4,057 J5
- Celaya 79,977 J6
- Celestún 1,490 O6
- Cerritos 10,421 J5
- Cerro Azul 20,259 L6
- Chahuites 5,218 M8
- Chalchihuites 1,894 G5
- Chalco de Díaz Covarrubias 12,172 M1
- Champotón 6,606 O7
- Charcas 10,491 J5
- Chetumal 23,685 Q7
- Chiapa de Corzo 8,571 N8
- Chiautempan 12,327 N1
- Chietla 4,602 M2
- Chignahuapan 3,805 N1
- Chihuahua 327,313 F2
- Chilapa de Álvarez 9,204 K8
- Chilpancingo de los Bravos 36,193 K8
- China, Nuevo León 4,958 K4
- Chocomán 5,114 P2
- Choix 2,503 E3
- Cholula de Rivadavia 15,399 M1
- Cihuatlán 9,451 G7
- Cintalapa de Figueroa 12,036 N8
- Ciudad Acuña (Villa Acuña) 30,276 J2
- Ciudad Altamirano 8,694 J7
- Ciudad Camargo, Chihuahua 24,030 G3
- Ciudad Camargo, Tamaulipas 5,953 K3
- Ciudad del Carmen 34,656 N7
- Ciudad Delicias 52,446 G2
- Ciudad del Maíz 5,241 K5
- Ciudad de Río Grande 11,651 H5
- Ciudad Guerrero 3,110 F2
- Ciudad Guzmán 48,166 H7
- Ciudad Hidalgo, Chiapas 4,105 N9
- Ciudad Hidalgo, Michoacán 24,692 J7
- Ciudad Juárez 424,135 F1
- Ciudad Lerdo 19,803 H4
- Ciudad Madero 115,302 L5
- Ciudad Mante 51,247 K5
- Ciudad Mendoza 18,696 O2
- Ciudad Miguel Alemán 11,259 K3
- Ciudad Obregón 144,795 E3
- Ciudad Río Bravo 39,018 K4
- Ciudad Satélite 35,083 L1
- Ciudad Serdán 9,581 O2
- Ciudad Valles 47,587 K5
- Ciudad Victoria 83,897 K5
- Coalcomán de Matamoros 4,875 H7
- Coatepec 21,542 P1
- Coatetelco 5,268 L2
- Coatzacoalcos 69,753 M7
- Coatzingo 3,038 N2
- Cocorit 4,478 E3
- Colima 58,450 H7
- Colón 3,346 K6
- Colotlán 6,135 H5
- Comala 5,592 H7
- Comalcalco 14,963 N7
- Comitán de Domínguez 21,249 O8
- Compostela 9,801 G6
- Concepción del Oro 8,144 J4
- Concordia 3,947 G5
- Contla 7,517 N1
- Copala 3,783 K8
- Coquimatlán 6,212 G7
- Córdoba 78,495 P2
- Cosalá 2,279 F4
- Cosamaloapan de Carpio 19,766 M7
- Cosautlán de Carvajal 2,039 P1
- Coscomatepec de Bravo 6,023 P2
- Coslo 2,680 H5
- Costa Rica 11,795 F4
- Cotija de la Paz 9,178 H7
- Coyoacán 339,446 L1
- Coyotepec 8,888 L1
- Coyuca de Benítez 6,328 J8
- Coyuca de Catalán 2,926 J7
- Coyutla 3,726 L6
- Cozumel 5,858 Q6
- Creel 2,449 E3
- Cuatrociénagas de Carranza 5,523 H3
- Cuauhtémoc 26,598 F2
- Cuautepec de Hinojosa 5,501 K6
- Cuautitlán de Romero Rubio 11,439 L1
- Cuautla Morelos 13,946 L2
- Cuencamé de Ceniceros 3,774 H4
- Cuernavaca 239,813 L2
- Cuicatlán 2,733 L8
- Cuitlahuac 4,813 P2
- Culiacán 228,001 F4
- Cumpas 2,395 E1
- Cunduacán 4,397 N7
- Dimas 2,194 F5
- Doctor Arroyo 4,290 K5
- Dolores Hidalgo de la Independencia Naci 16,849 J6
- Durango 182,633 G1
- Dzibalchén 1,917 P7
- Dzidzantún 7,064 P6
- Dzitbalché 4,393 P6
- Ebano 17,489 K5
- Ecatepec de Morelos 11,899 L1
- Ejutla de Crespo 5,263 L8
- Eldorado 8,115 E4
- El Fuerte 7,179 E3
- El Porvenir 3,030 G1
- El Potosí 2,032 J4
- El Salto 7,818 G5
- El Zacatón 2,686 J5
- Empalme 24,927 D2
- Encarnación de Díaz 10,474 H6
- Ensenada 77,687 A1
- Escalón 2,998 G3
- Escarcega 7,248 O7
- Escuinapa de Hidalgo 16,442 G5
- Escuintla 4,111 N9
- Esperanza, Puebla 4,258 O2
- Esperanza, Sonora 11,762 E3
- Espita 5,394 Q6
- Esqueda 1,458 E1
- Etchojoa 4,398 E3
- Ezequiel Montes 3,139 K6
- Fortín de las Flores 9,358 P2
- Francisco I. Madero 12,613 H4
- Fresnillo de González Echererría 44,475 H5
- Frontera 10,066 N7
- Galeana, Nuevo León 3,429 J4
- General Bravo 2,894 K4
- General Cepeda 3,486 J4
- General Terán 5,354 K4
- Gómez Farías 3,030 F2
- Gómez Palacio 79,650 G4
- González 6,440 K5
- Guadalajara 1,478,383 H6
- Guadalajara* 2,343,034 H6
- Guadalupe, Nuevo León 51,899 K4
- Guadalupe, Zacatecas 13,246 H5
- Guadalupe Bravo 3,333 F1
- Guadalupe Victoria, Durango 7,931 H4
- Guadalupe Victoria, Puebla 3,946 O1
- Guamúchil 17,151 E4
- Guanajuato 36,809 J6
- Guasave 26,080 E4
- Guaymas 57,492 D3
- Gustavo Díaz Ordaz 10,154 K3
- Gutiérrez Zamora 9,099 L6
- Halachó 4,804 O6
- Hecelchakán 4,279 O6
- Hermosillo 232,691 D2
- Heroica Caborca 20,771 C1
- Heroica Nogales 52,108 D1
- Hidalgo, Tamaulipas 2,450 K4
- Hidalgo del Parral (Parral) 57,619 G3
- Hopelchén 3,699 P7
- Huajuapan de León 13,822 L8
- Huamantla 15,565 N1
- Huaquechula 2,294 M2
- Huatabampo 18,506 D3
- Huatusco de Chicuellar 9,501 P2
- Huauchinango 16,826 L6
- Huautla de Jiménez 6,132 L7
- Huehuetlán el Chico 2,667 M2
- Huejotzingo 8,552 M1
- Huejutla 6,854 K6
- Huetamo 9,333 J7
- Hueyotlipan de Hidalgo 2,353 M1
- Huimanguillo 7,075 N8
- Huitzilán 3,573 O1
- Huitzuco de los Figueroa 9,406 K7
- Huixcolotla 4,039 N2
- Huixtepec 5,927 L8
- Huixtla 15,737 N9
- Hunucmá 8,020 O6
- Ignacio de la Llave 3,962 Q2
- Iguala de la Independencia 45,355 K7
- Imuris 1,958 D1
- Irapuato 135,596 J6
- Isla Mujeres 2,663 Q6
- Isla, Veracruz 8,075 M7
- Ixmiquilpan 6,048 K6
- Ixtapa J8
- Ixtapalapa 522,095 L1
- Ixtenco 5,035 N1
- Ixtepec 14,025 M8
- Ixtlán del Río 10,986 G6
- Izamal 9,749 P6
- Izúcar de Matamoros 21,164 M2
- Jala 4,535 G6
- Jalacingo 3,427 P1
- Jalapa Enríquez 161,352 P1
- Jalpa 9,904 H6
- Jalpa de Méndez 4,785 N7
- Jalpan 1,878 K6
- Jáltipan de Morelos 15,170 M8
- Jantetelco 2,015 L2
- Jaumave 3,072 K5
- Jerez de García Salinas 20,325 H5
- Jico 7,269 P1
- Jilotepec de Abasolo 4,252 K7
- Jiménez, Chihuahua 18,095 G3
- Joachín 3,918 Q2
- Jojutla de Juárez 14,438 L2
- Jonacatepec 3,868 M2
- Jonuta 2,746 N7
- José Cardel 5,396 Q1
- Juan Aldama 9,667 H4
- Juchipila 6,328 H6
- Juchitán de Zaragoza 30,218 M8
- Kantunilkin 1,970 Q6
- La Barca 18,055 H6
- La Barra de Navidad 1,829 G7
- La Concordia 3,559 N9
- La Cruz, Sinaloa 4,218 F5
- Lagos de Moreno 33,782 J6
- La Huerta 4,328 G7
- La Paz, Baja California Sur 46,011 D5
- La Paz, San Luis Potosí 3,735 J5
- La Piedad Cavadas 34,963 H6
- Las Choapas 20,166 M7
- Las Hadas G7
- Las Nieves 2,262 G3
- Las Rosas 7,658 N8
- León 468,887 J6
- Lerdo de Tejada 11,628 M8
- Lerma 4,158 O7
- Libres 4,830 O1
- Linares 24,456 K4
- Llera de Canales 3,564 K5
- Loma Bonita 15,804 M7
- Loreto, Baja California 2,570 D4
- Loreto, Zacatecas 7,132 J5
- Los Mochis 67,953 E4
- Los Reyes de Salgado 19,452 H7
- Macuspana 12,293 N8
- Madera 9,759 F2
- Magdalena de Kino 10,281 D1
- Maltrata 5,457 O2
- Manzanillo 20,777 G7
- Mapastepec 5,907 N9
- Mapimí 2,737 G4
- Martínez de la Torre 17,203 L6
- Mascota 5,674 G6
- Matamoros, Coahuila 15,125 H4
- Matamoros, Tamaulipas 165,124 L4
- Matehuala 28,799 J5
- Matías Romero 13,200 M8
- Maxcanú 6,505 O6
- Mazatlán 147,010 F5
- Melchor Múzquiz 18,868 H3
- Melchor Ocampo del Balsas 4,766 H8
- Meoquí 12,308 G2
- Mérida 233,912 P6
- Metepec 4,625 M2
- Metlatonoc 1,870 K8
- Mexicali 317,228 B1
- Mexico City (cap.) 9,377,300 L1
- Mexico City* 13,993,866 L1
- Miacatlán 3,980 K2
- Mier 5,636 K3
- Miguel Auza 9,303 H4
- Minatitlán 68,397 M8
- Mineral del Monte 8,887 K6
- Miquihuana 1,971 J5
- Misantla 8,799 P1
- Miahuatlán de Porfirio Díaz 5,714 L8
- Mocorito 3,993 F4
- Moctezuma, San Luis Potosí 1,734 J5
- Moctezuma, Sonora 2,700 E2
- Monclova 78,134 J3
- Montemorelos 18,642 K4
- Monterrey 1,006,221 J4
- Monterrey* 1,923,402 J4
- Morelia 199,099 J7
- Morelos 4,241 J2
- Morelos Cañada 2,288 O2
- Moroleón 25,620 J6
- Motozintla de Mendoza 4,682 N9
- Motul de Felipe Carillo Puerto 12,949 P6
- Muna 5,491 P6
- Naco 3,580 D1
- Nacozari 2,976 E1
- Nadadores 2,461 H3
- Naica 7,190 G2
- Namiquipa 4,875 F2
- Nanacamilpa 6,356 M1
- Naolinco de Victoria 4,365 P1
- Naranjos 14,732 L6
- Naucalpan de Juárez 9,425 L1
- Nautla 1,935 L6
- Nava 4,097 J2
- Navojoa 43,817 E3
- Navolato 12,799 E4
- Nazas 2,881 G4
- Netzahualcóyotl 580,436 L1
- Nieves 3,966 H5
- Nochistlán 8,780 H6
- Nogales 14,254 P2
- Nombre de Dios 3,188 G5
- Nopalucan de la Granja 3,002 O1
- Nueva Casas Grandes 20,023 F1
- Nueva Ciudad Guerrero 3,300 K3
- Nueva Italia de Ruiz 14,718 J7
- Nueva Rosita 34,706 J2
- Nuevo Ideal 5,252 G4
- Nuevo Laredo 184,622 J3
- Oaxaca de Juárez 114,948 L8
- Ocampo, Coahuila 1,613 H3
- Ocampo, Tamaulipas 4,801 K5
- Ocosingo 2,946 O8
- Ocotlán 35,361 H6
- Ocotlán de Morelos 5,882 L8
- Ojinaga 12,757 G2
- Ojocaliente 7,582 H5
- Ometepec 7,342 K8
- Oriental 6,009 O1
- Orizaba 105,150 P2
- Otumba de Gómez Farías 3,198 M1
- Oxkutzcab 8,182 P6
- Ozuluama 2,851 L6
- Ozumba de Alzate 6,876 M1
- Pachuca de Soto 83,892 K6
- Padilla 4,581 K5
- Palenque 2,595 O8
- Palizada 2,332 O7
- Palomas 2,129 F1

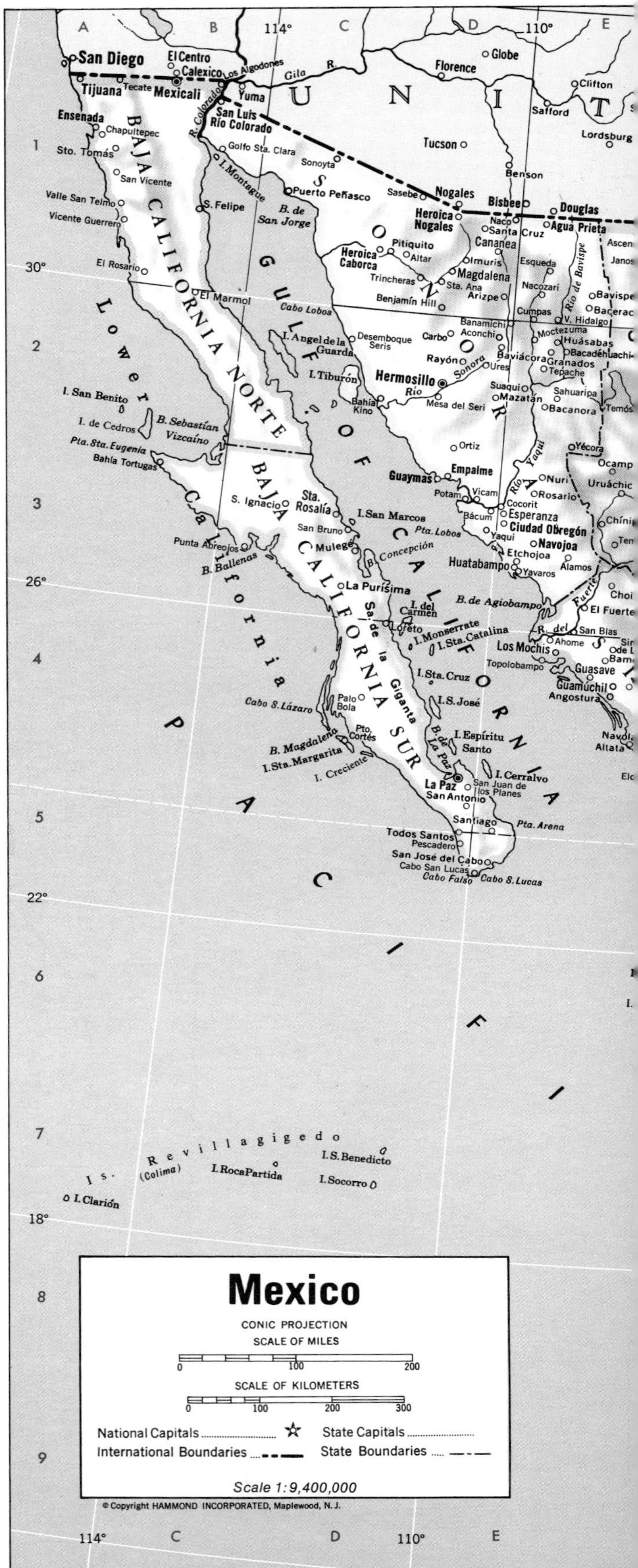

(continued on following page)

AREA 761,601 sq. mi. (1,972,546 sq. km.)
POPULATION 67,395,826
CAPITAL Mexico City
LARGEST CITY Mexico City
HIGHEST POINT Citlaltépetl 18,855 ft.
(5,747 m.)
MONETARY UNIT Mexican peso
MAJOR LANGUAGE Spanish
MAJOR RELIGION Roman Catholicism

States Indicated by Numbers
1 Tlaxcala
2 Morelos
3 Distrito Federal
4 México
5 Hidalgo
6 Querétaro
7 Guanajuato
8 Aguascalientes
9 Nayarit
10 Colima

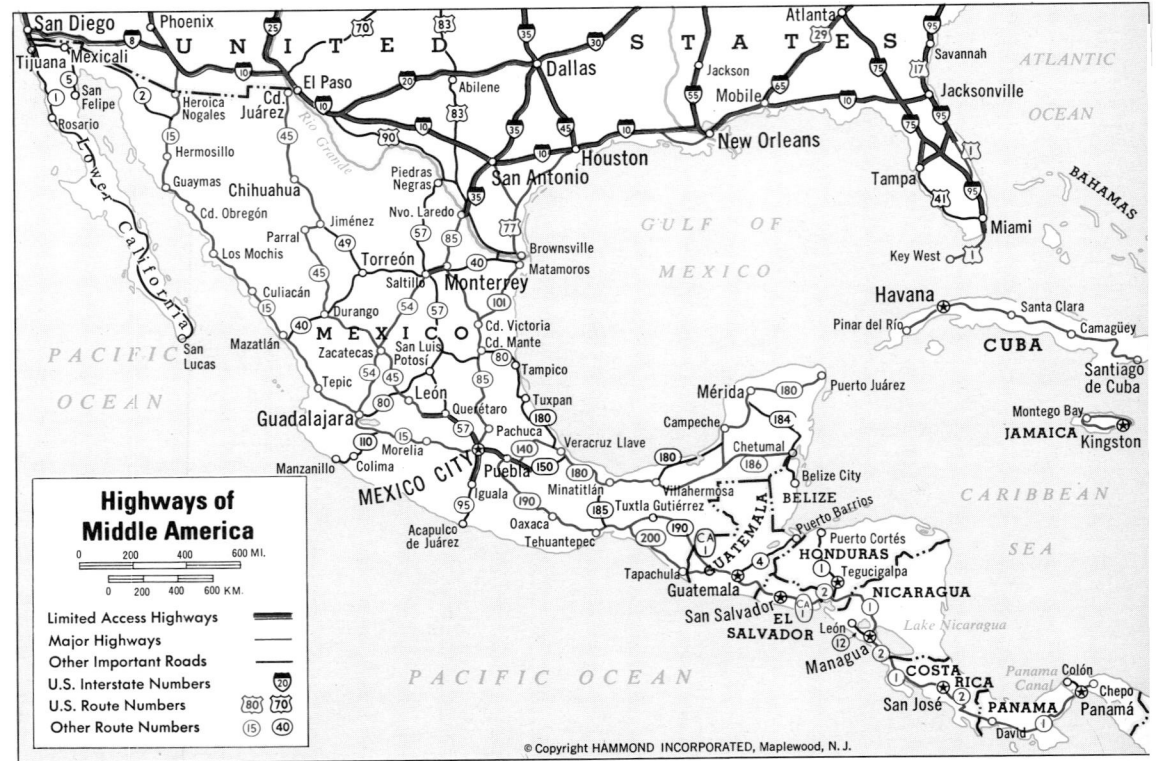

Highways of Middle America

0   200   400   600 MI.
0   200   400   600 KM.

Limited Access Highways
Major Highways
Other Important Roads
U.S. Interstate Numbers
U.S. Route Numbers
Other Route Numbers

© Copyright HAMMOND INCORPORATED, Maplewood, N.J.

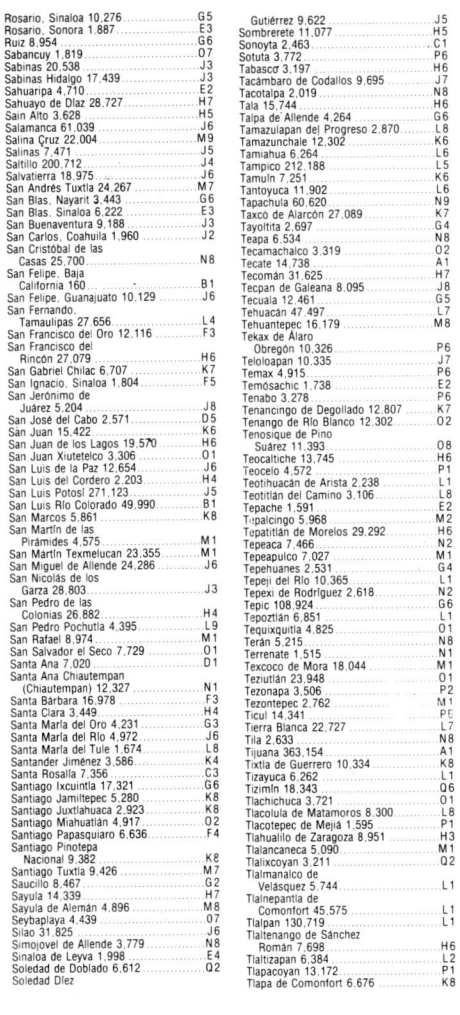

Agriculture, Industry and Resources

DOMINANT LAND USE

Wheat, Livestock
Cereals (chiefly corn), Livestock
Diversified Tropical Cash Crops
Cotton, Mixed Cereals
Livestock, Limited Agriculture
Range Livestock
Forests
Nonagricultural Land

Water Power
Major Industrial Areas

MAJOR MINERAL OCCURRENCES

Ag	Silver	G	Natural Gas	O	Petroleum
Au	Gold	Gr	Graphite	Pb	Lead
C	Coal	Hg	Mercury	S	Sulfur
Cu	Copper	Mn	Manganese	Sb	Antimony
F	Fluorspar	Mo	Molybdenum	Sn	Tin
Fe	Iron Ore	Na	Salt	W	Tungsten
				Zn	Zinc

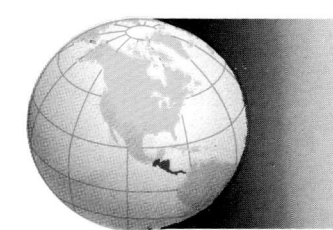

GUATEMALA

AREA 42,042 sq. mi. (108,889 sq. km.)
POPULATION 7,262,419
CAPITAL Guatemala
LARGEST CITY Guatemala
HIGHEST POINT Tajumulco 13,845 ft. (4,220 m.)
MONETARY UNIT quetzal
MAJOR LANGUAGES Spanish, Quiché
MAJOR RELIGION Roman Catholicism

BELIZE

AREA 8,867 sq. mi. (22,966 sq. km.)
POPULATION 144,857
CAPITAL Belmopan
LARGEST CITY Belize City
HIGHEST POINT Victoria Peak 3,681 ft. (1,122 m.)
MONETARY UNIT Belize dollar
MAJOR LANGUAGES English, Spanish, Mayan
MAJOR RELIGIONS Roman Catholicism, Protestantism

EL SALVADOR

AREA 8,260 sq. mi. (21,393 sq. km.)
POPULATION 4,813,000
CAPITAL San Salvador
LARGEST CITY San Salvador
HIGHEST POINT Santa Ana 7,825 ft. (2,385 m.)
MONETARY UNIT colón
MAJOR LANGUAGE Spanish
MAJOR RELIGION Roman Catholicism

HONDURAS

AREA 43,277 sq. mi. (112,087 sq. km.)
POPULATION 3,691,000
CAPITAL Tegucigalpa
LARGEST CITY Tegucigalpa
HIGHEST POINT Las Minas 9,347 ft. (2,849 m.)
MONETARY UNIT lempira
MAJOR LANGUAGE Spanish
MAJOR RELIGION Roman Catholicism

NICARAGUA

AREA 45,698 sq. mi. (118,358 sq. km.)
POPULATION 2,703,000
CAPITAL Managua
LARGEST CITY Managua
HIGHEST POINT Cerro Mocotón 6,913 ft. (2,107 m.)
MONETARY UNIT córdoba
MAJOR LANGUAGE Spanish
MAJOR RELIGION Roman Catholicism

COSTA RICA

AREA 19,575 sq. mi. (50,700 sq. km.)
POPULATION 2,245,000
CAPITAL San José
LARGEST CITY San José
HIGHEST POINT Chirripó Grande 12,530 ft. (3,819 m.)
MONETARY UNIT colón
MAJOR LANGUAGE Spanish
MAJOR RELIGION Roman Catholicism

PANAMA

AREA 29,761 sq. mi. (77,082 sq. km.)
POPULATION 1,830,175
CAPITAL Panamá
LARGEST CITY Panamá
HIGHEST POINT Vol. Baru 11,401 ft. (3,475 m.)
MONETARY UNIT balboa
MAJOR LANGUAGE Spanish
MAJOR RELIGION Roman Catholicism

Agriculture, Industry and Resources

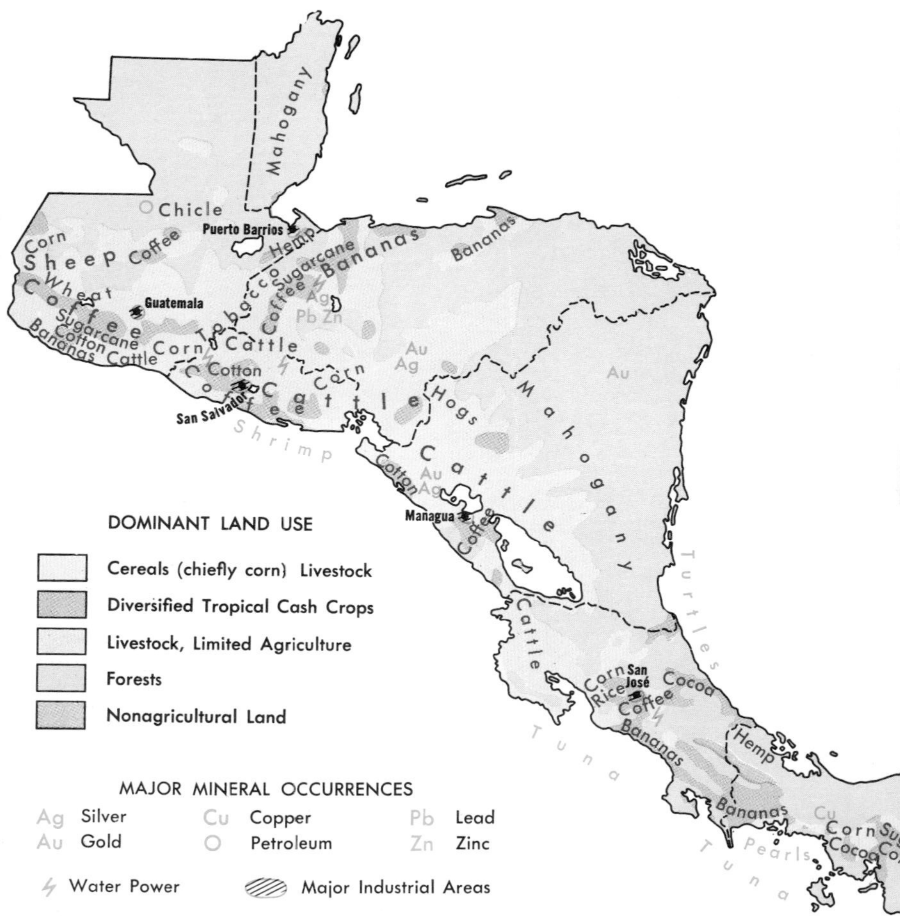

Chicle
Puerto Barrios
Mahogany
Bananas
Corn
Sheep
Coffee
Wheat
Guatemala
Sugarcane
Cotton
Cattle
Tobacco
Hemp
Ag
Pb Zn
Au
San Salvador
Shrimp
Hogs
Managua
Turtles
Colón
Panamá
San José
Rice
Cocoa
Tuna
Pearls
Cu
DOMINANT LAND USE
Cereals (chiefly corn) Livestock
Diversified Tropical Cash Crops
Livestock, Limited Agriculture
Forests
Nonagricultural Land
MAJOR MINERAL OCCURRENCES
Ag Silver
Au Gold
Cu Copper
O Petroleum
Pb Lead
Zn Zinc
Water Power
Major Industrial Areas

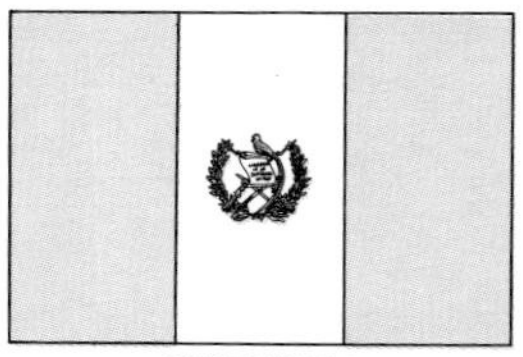

GUATEMALA

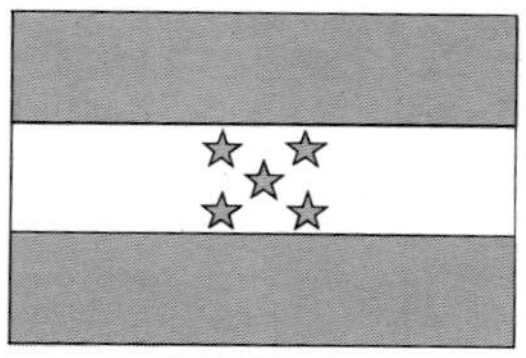

HONDURAS

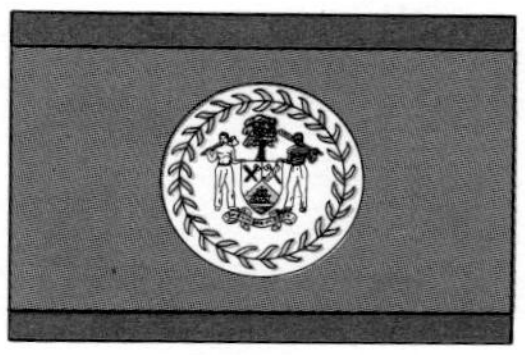

BELIZE

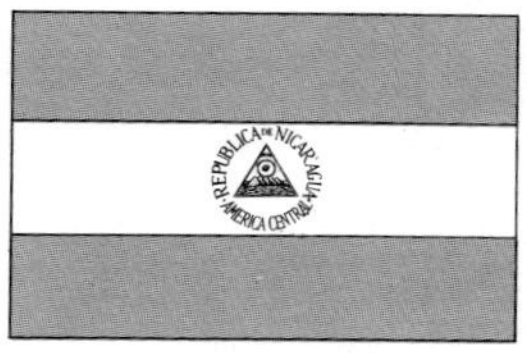

NICARAGUA

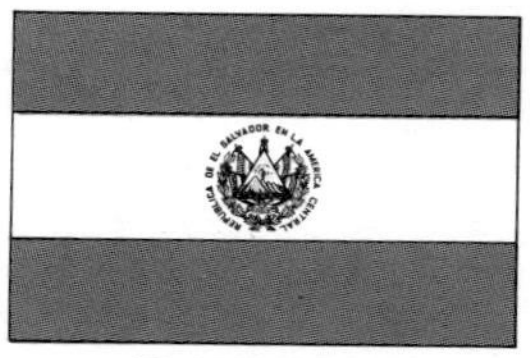

EL SALVADOR

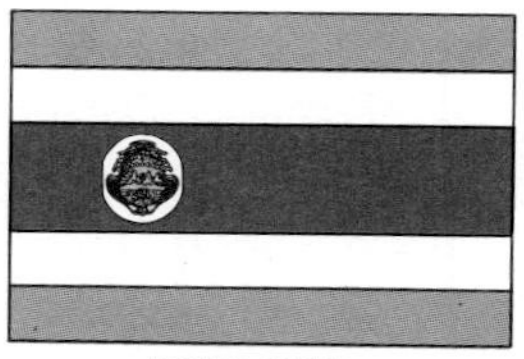

COSTA RICA

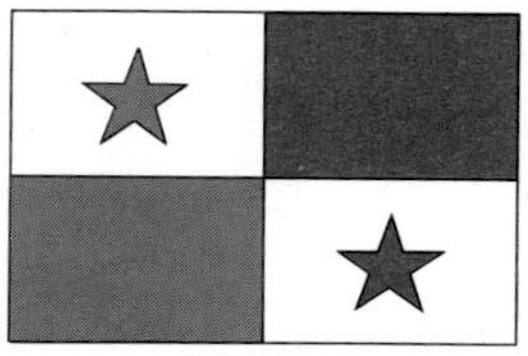

PANAMA

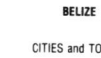

BELIZE

CITIES and TOWNS

Belize City 39,887 ..... C2
Belize City* 50,925 ..... C2
Belmopan (cap.) 2,932 ..... C2
Corozal Town 6,862 ..... C1
Hattieville 904 ..... C2
Libertad 856 ..... C1
Orange Walk Town 8,441 ..... C1
Punta Gorda 2,219 ..... C2
San Ignacio 5,606 ..... C2
Stann Creek Town 6,627 ..... C2

OTHER FEATURES

Ambergris (cay) D1
Belize (riv.) C2
Bokel (cay) D2
Glover (reef) D2
Half Moon (cay) D2
Hondo (riv.) C1
Honduras (gulf) D2
Mauger (cay) D2
New (riv.) C2
Saint Georges (cay) D2
Sarstún (riv.) C3
Turneffe (isls.) D2

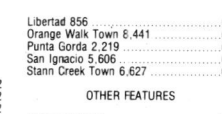

COSTA RICA

CITIES and TOWNS

Alajuela 33,122 ..... E6
Atenas 1,728 ..... E6
Bagaces 2,129 ..... E5
Boruca⊙ 1,892 ..... F6
Buenos Aires⊙ 302 ..... F6
Cañas 6,053 ..... E5
Cartago 21,753 ..... F6
Ciudad Quesada 9,754 ..... E5
Esparta 4,699 ..... E5
Filadelfia 2,958 ..... E5
Golfito 6,962 ..... F6
Grecia 8,355 ..... E5
Guácimo 1,168 ..... F5
Guápiles 3,524 ..... F5
Heredia 22,700 ..... E5
Las Juntas 1,129 ..... E5
Liberia 10,802 ..... E5
Limón 29,621 ..... F6
Miramar 1,673 ..... E5
Nicoya 7,474 ..... E5
Orotina 3,170 ..... E6
Palmares 3,083 ..... F6
Paraíso 8,446 ..... F6
Puerto Cortés 2,070 ..... F6
Puntarenas 26,331 ..... E6
Quepos 2,155 ..... E6
San José (cap.) 215,441 ..... F5
San José* 391,107 ..... F5
San Marcos 917 ..... E6
San Ramón 9,245 ..... E5
Santa Cruz 5,777 ..... E5
Santo Domingo 5,148 ..... F6
Siquirres 4,361 ..... F5
Turrialba 12,151 ..... F6

(continued on following page)

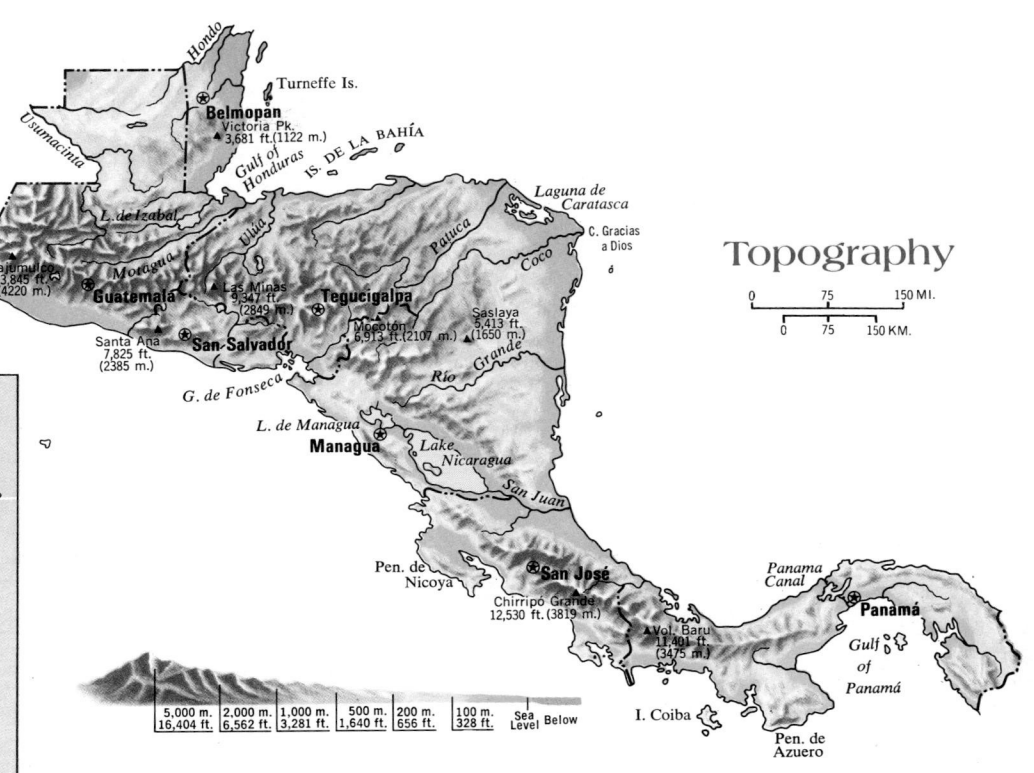

Topography

0 75 150 MI.

0 75 150 KM.

Turneffe Is.

Belmopan
Victoria Pk.
3,681 ft.(1122 m.)

Gulf of Honduras

IS. DE LA BAHÍA

Laguna de Caratasca

C. Gracias a Dios

L. de Izabal

Tajumulco
13,845 ft.
(4220 m.)

Guatemala

Minas
2,347 ft.

Tegucigalpa

Saslaya
5,413 ft.
(1650 m.)

Santa Ana
7,825 ft.
(2385 m.)

San Salvador

Mocorón
6,913 ft.(2107 m.)

G. de Fonseca

Río Grande

L. de Managua

Managua

Lake Nicaragua

San Juan

Pen. de Nicoya

San José

Chirripó Grande
12,530 ft. (3819 m.)

Vol. Barú
11,401 ft.
(3475 m.)

Panamá

Panama Canal

Gulf of Panamá

I. Coiba

Pen. de Azuero

| 5,000 m. 16,404 ft. | 2,000 m. 6,562 ft. | 1,000 m. 3,281 ft. | 500 m. 1,640 ft. | 200 m. 656 ft. | 100 m. 328 ft. | Sea Level | Below |

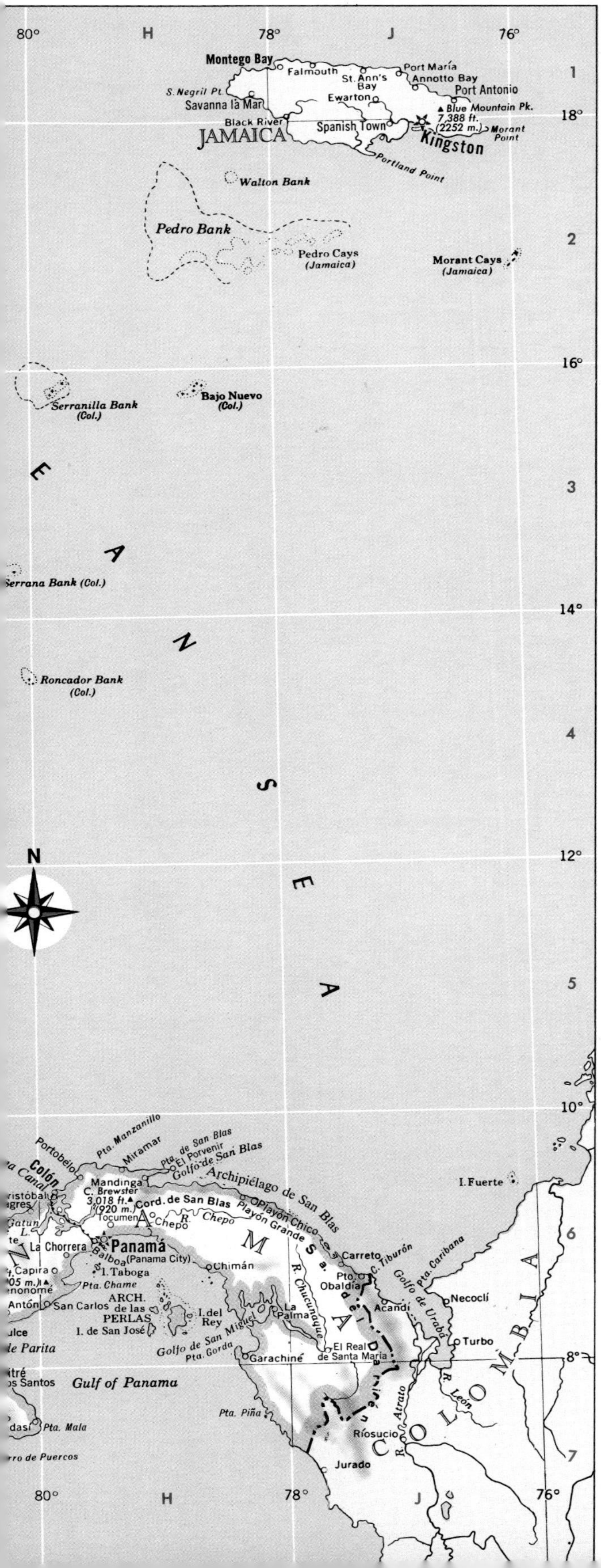

JAMAICA

80° H 78° J 76°

Montego Bay
Falmouth
St. Ann's Bay
Annotto Bay
Port María
Port Antonio
Port Maria
S. Negril Pt.
Savanna la Mar
Black River
Spanish Town
Ewarton
Kingston
Blue Mountain Pk.
7,388 ft.
(2252 m.)
Morant Point
Portland Point

1
18°

Walton Bank

Pedro Bank

Pedro Cays (Jamaica)

Morant Cays (Jamaica)

2

16°

Serranilla Bank (Col.)
Bajo Nuevo (Col.)

C A R I B B E A N   S E A

Serrana Bank (Col.)

3

14°

Roncador Bank (Col.)

4

12°

N

5

10°

COLOMBIA

Pta. Manzanillo
Pta. de San Blas
Pta. de San Blas
Pto. de Porvenir
Golfo de San Blas
Archipiélago de San Blas
Playón Chico
Portobelo
Colón
Miramar
C. Brewster
Cristóbal
Mandinga
3,018 ft.
(920 m.)
Cord. de San Blas
Tocumen
Chepo
I. Fuerte
La Chorrera
Panamá (Panama City)
Balboa
Pta. Chame
ARCH. de las PERLAS
I. del Rey
I. de San José
Carreto
C. Tiburón
Pta. Piña
Chimán
Pta. Garachiné
Pta. Gorda
Golfo de San Miguel
Golfo de Urabá
Turbo
Necoclí
Acandí
Garachiné
El Real de Santa María
R. Chucunaque
Jurado
Ríosucio
Atrato
6
8°
7

80° H 78° J 76°

Gulf of Panama

N E

CUBA

HAITI

DOMINICAN REPUBLIC

JAMAICA

TRINIDAD AND TOBAGO

BARBADOS

GRENADA

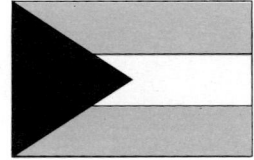
BAHAMAS

DOMINICA

ST. LUCIA

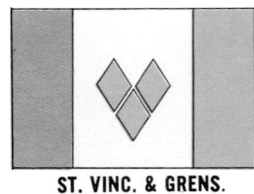
ST. VINC. & GRENS.

ANTIGUA AND BARBUDA

CUBA

AREA 44,206 sq. mi. (114,494 sq. km.)
POPULATION 9,706,369
CAPITAL Havana
LARGEST CITY Havana
HIGHEST POINT Pico Turquino
6,561 ft. (2,000 m.)
MONETARY UNIT Cuban peso
MAJOR LANGUAGE Spanish
MAJOR RELIGION Roman Catholicism

HAITI

AREA 10,694 sq. mi. (27,697 sq. km.)
POPULATION 5,053,792
CAPITAL Port-au-Prince
LARGEST CITY Port-au-Prince
HIGHEST POINT Pic La Selle 8,793 ft. (2,680 m.)
MONETARY UNIT gourde
MAJOR LANGUAGES Creole French, French
MAJOR RELIGION Roman Catholicism

DOMINICAN REPUBLIC

AREA 18,704 sq. mi. (48,443 sq. km.)
POPULATION 5,647,977
CAPITAL Santo Domingo
LARGEST CITY Santo Domingo
HIGHEST POINT Pico Duarte
10,417 ft. (3,175 m.)
MONETARY UNIT Dominican peso
MAJOR LANGUAGE Spanish
MAJOR RELIGION Roman Catholicism

JAMAICA

AREA 4,411 sq. mi. (11,424 sq. km.)
POPULATION 2,184,000
CAPITAL Kingston
LARGEST CITY Kingston
HIGHEST POINT Blue Mountain Peak
7,402 ft. (2,256 m.)
MONETARY UNIT Jamaican dollar
MAJOR LANGUAGE English
MAJOR RELIGIONS Protestantism,
Roman Catholicism

PUERTO RICO

AREA 3,515 sq. mi. (9,104 sq. km.)
POPULATION 3,196,520
CAPITAL San Juan
MONETARY UNIT U.S. dollar
MAJOR LANGUAGES Spanish, English
MAJOR RELIGION Roman Catholicism

NETHERLANDS ANTILLES

AREA 390 sq. mi. (1,010 sq. km.)
POPULATION 246,000
CAPITAL Willemstad
MONETARY UNIT Antilles guilder
MAJOR LANGUAGES Dutch, Papiamento, English
MAJOR RELIGIONS Roman Catholicism,
Protestantism

BERMUDA

AREA 21 sq. mi. (54 sq. km.)
POPULATION 67,761
CAPITAL Hamilton
MONETARY UNIT Bermuda dollar
MAJOR LANGUAGE English
MAJOR RELIGION Protestantism

ARUBA

AREA 75 sq. mi (193 sq. km.)
POPULATION 66,790
CAPITAL Oranjestad
MONETARY UNIT Aruba guilder
MAJOR LANGUAGES Dutch, Papiamento
MAJOR RELIGION Roman Catholic

ANGUILLA

Anguilla (isl.) 6,519	F3

ANTIGUA and BARBUDA

Antigua (isl.) 76,213	G3
Barbuda (isl.) 1,071	G3
Caribbean (sea)	B4
Codrington 1,071	G3
Falmouth 1,134	F3
Redonda (isl.)	F3
Saint John's (cap.) 21,814	G3

ARUBA

Aruba (isl.) 66,790	E4

BAHAMAS

Acklins (isl.) 616	C2
Andros (isl.) 8,397	B1
Atwood (Samana) (cay)	D2
Berry (isls.) 509	B1
Biminis, The (isls.) 1,432	B1
Caicos (passg.)	D2
Cat (isl.) 2,143	C1
Cay Sal (bank)	B2
Crooked (isl.) 517	C2
Eleuthera (isl.) 8,326	C1
Exuma (isls.)	C1
Flamingo (cay)	C2
Freeport 22,301	B1
Grand Bahama (isl.) 33,102	B1
Great Abaco (isl.) 7,324	C1
Great Bahama (bank)	B1
Great Exuma (isl.)	C1
Great Inagua (isl.) 939	D2
Great Isaac (isl.)	B1

Gun (cay)	B1
Harbour (isl.)	C1
Little Inagua (isl.)	D2
Long (cay) 33	C2
Long (isl.) 3,353	C2
Mayaguana (isl.) 476	D2
Mira Por Vos (cays)	C2
Nassau (cap.) 135,437	C1
New Providence (isl.) 135,437	C1
Old Bahama (chan.)	B2
Plana (cays)	D2
Ragged (isl.) 146	C2
Rum (cay)	C2
Samana (cay)	D2
San Salvador (isl.)	D1
Santarén (chan.)	B1
Tongue of the Ocean (chan.)	C1
Verde (cay)	C2
Watling (San Salvador) (isl.)	C1

BARBADOS

Bridgetown (cap.) 7,552	G4
Speightstown	G4

BERMUDA

Bermuda (isls.)	H3
Castle (harb.)	H2
Great (sound)	G3
Hamilton (cap.) 1,617	G3
Harrington (sound)	H3
Ireland (isl.)	G3
North (rapid)	H2
Saint Davids (isl.)	H2
Saint George 1,647	H2
Saint George's (cap.)	H2
Somerset (isl.)	G3

CAYMAN ISLANDS

Bartlett Deep	B3
Cayman Brac (isl.) 1,603	B3
George Town (cap.) 7,617	B3
Grand Cayman (isl.) 15,000	B3
Little Cayman (isl.) 74	B3
Misteriosa (bank)	A3

CUBA

Bayamo 109,201	C2
Camaguey 245,235	C2
Cienfuegos 107,396	B2
Florida (str.)	B1
Guanabacoa 89,741	B2
Guantánamo 178,129	C2
Havana (cap.) 1,924,886	A2
Holguin 190,155	C2
Juventud (Pines) (isl.) 57,879	A2
Manzanillo 95,420	C2
Marianao ○127,563	A2
Matanzas 103,302	B2
Pinar del Rio 104,598	A2
San Felipe (cays)	A2
Santa Clara 175,113	B2
Santiago de Cuba 362,432	C3
Windward (passg.)	C3

DOMINICA

Portsmouth 2,329	G4
Roseau (cap.) 9,968	G4

DOMINICAN REPUBLIC

La Romana 91,571	E3
San Francisco de Macoris 64,906	E3
San Pedro de Macoris 78,562	E3
Santiago 278,638	D3
Santo Domingo (cap.) 1,313,172	E3

GRENADA

Carriacou (isl.) 6,052	G4
Gouyave 2,498	F4
Grenadines (isls.)	G4
Saint George's (cap.) 6,463	F5

GUADELOUPE

Basse-Terre 13,397	F4
Saint-Barthélemy (isl.) 3,059	F3
Saint Martin 6,072	F3

HAITI

Cap-Haitien 64,406	D3
Gonaives 34,209	D3
Port-au-Prince (cap.) 449,831	D3
Gonâve (isl.)	D3
Jamaica (chan.)	C3
Tortuga (isl.)	D2

JAMAICA

Blue Mountain (peak)	C3
Jamaica (chan.)	C3
Kingston (cap.) 106,791	C3
Montego Bay 43,521	B3
Pedro (cays)	C3
Savanna-la-Mar ·1,759	B3

MARTINIQUE

Fort-de-France (cap.) 96,649	G4
Saint-Pierre 4,923	G4
Pelée (vol.)	G4

MONTSERRAT

Plymouth (cap.) 1,623	F3

NETHERLANDS ANTILLES

Bonaire (isl.)	E4
Curaçao (isl.)	E4
Oranjestad 10,100	D4
Saba (isl.)	F3
Saint Eustatius (isl.)	F3
Saint Martin (Sint Maarten) (isl.)	F3
Willemstad (cap.) 95,000	E4

PUERTO RICO

Bayamón 185,087	G1
Caguas 87,214	G1
Culebra (isl.) 1,265	G1
Mayagüez 82,968	F1
Mona (passg.)	E3
Ponce 161,739	F1

San Juan (cap.) 424,600	G1
Vieques (isl.) 7,662	G1

SAINT CHRISTOPHER and NEVIS

Basseterre (cap.) 14,725	F3
Nevis (isl.) 9,300	F3
Saint Christopher (isl.) 35,104	F3

SAINT LUCIA

Castries (cap.) ·42,770	G4
Vieux Fort ·10,675	G4

SAINT VINCENT and THE GRENADINES

Bequia (isl.)	G4
Georgetown 1,100	G4
Grenadines (isls.) 8,371	G4
Kingstown (cap.) 17,117	G4

TRINIDAD and TOBAGO

Port-of-Spain (cap.) 67,978	G5
Scarborough 6,057	G5
Tobago (isl.) 39,695	G5
Trinidad (isl.) 1,020,130	G5

TURKS and CAICOS ISLANDS

Caicos (isls.) 4,008	D2
Cockburn Harbour	D2
Grand Caicos (isl.) 371	D2
Grand Turk (isl.) 3,146	D2
Providenciales (isl.) 979	D2
Turks (isls.) 3,348	D2

VIRGIN ISLANDS (British)

Anegada (isl.) 89	H1
Jost Van Dyke (isl.) 135	G1
Road Town (cap.) 2,200	H1
Tortola (isl.) 9,257	H1
Virgin Gorda (isl.) 1,443	H1

VIRGIN ISLANDS (U.S.)

Charlotte Amalie (cap.) 11,842	H1
Christiansted 2,914	H2
Fredriksted 1,046	G2
Saint Croix (isl.) 49,725	H2
Saint John (isl.) 2,472	H1
Saint Thomas (isl.) 44,372	G1

WEST INDIES

Antilles, Greater (isls.)	B2
Antilles, Lesser (isls.)	E4
Aves (Bird) (isl.)	F4
Hispaniola (isl.)	D2
Leeward (isls.)	F3
Navassa (isl.)	C3
Windward (isls.)	G4

● Population of district.
○ Population of municipality.

Topography

0 100 200 MI.
0 100 200 KM.

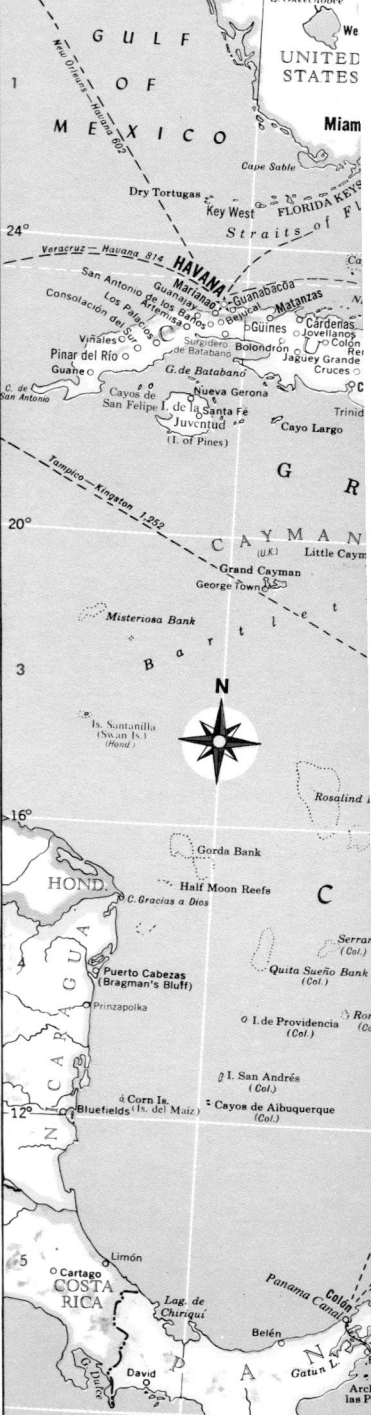

TRINIDAD AND TOBAGO

AREA 1,980 sq. mi. (5,128 sq. km.)
POPULATION 1,067,108
CAPITAL Port of Spain
LARGEST CITY Port of Spain
HIGHEST POINT Mt. Aripo 3,084 ft. (940 m.)
MONETARY UNIT Trinidad and Tobago dollar
MAJOR LANGUAGES English, Hindi
MAJOR RELIGIONS Roman Catholicism,
    Protestantism, Hinduism, Islam

ST. CHRISTOPHER & NEVIS

BARBADOS

AREA 166 sq. mi. (430 sq. km.)
POPULATION 248,983
CAPITAL Bridgetown
LARGEST CITY Bridgetown
HIGHEST POINT Mt. Hillaby 1,104 ft.
    (336 m.)
MONETARY UNIT Barbadian dollar
MAJOR LANGUAGE English
MAJOR RELIGION Protestantism

BAHAMAS

AREA 5,382 sq. mi. (13,939 sq. km.)
POPULATION 209,505
CAPITAL Nassau
LARGEST CITY Nassau
HIGHEST POINT Mt. Alvernia 206 ft. (63 m.)
MONETARY UNIT Bahamian dollar
MAJOR LANGUAGE English
MAJOR RELIGIONS Roman Catholicism,
    Protestantism

GRENADA

AREA 133 sq. mi. (344 sq. km.)
POPULATION 103,103
CAPITAL St. George's
LARGEST CITY St. George's
HIGHEST POINT Mt. St. Catherine
    2,757 ft. (840 m.)
MONETARY UNIT East Caribbean dollar
MAJOR LANGUAGES English, French patois
MAJOR RELIGIONS Roman Catholicism,
    Protestantism

DOMINICA

AREA 290 sq. mi. (751 sq. km.)
POPULATION 74,089
CAPITAL Roseau
HIGHEST POINT Morne Diablotin
    4,747 ft. (1,447 m.)
MONETARY UNIT Dominican dollar
MAJOR LANGUAGES English, French patois
MAJOR RELIGIONS Roman Catholicism,
    Protestantism

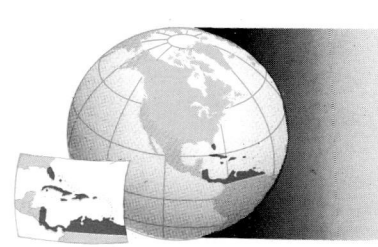

SAINT LUCIA

AREA 238 sq. mi. (616 sq. km.)
POPULATION 115,783
CAPITAL Castries
HIGHEST POINT Mt. Gimie 3,117 ft. (950 m.)
MONETARY UNIT East Caribbean dollar
MAJOR LANGUAGES English, French patois
MAJOR RELIGIONS Roman Catholicism,
    Protestantism

SAINT VINCENT AND THE GRENADINES

AREA 150 sq. mi. (388 sq. km.)
POPULATION 124,000
CAPITAL Kingstown
HIGHEST POINT Soufrière 4,000 ft. (1,219 m.)
MONETARY UNIT East Caribbean dollar
MAJOR LANGUAGE English
MAJOR RELIGIONS Protestantism,
    Roman Catholicism

ANTIGUA AND BARBUDA

AREA 171 sq. mi. (443 sq. km.)
POPULATION 75,000
CAPITAL St. John's
HIGHEST POINT Boggy Peak 1,319 ft. (402 m.)
MONETARY UNIT East Caribbean dollar
MAJOR LANGUAGE English
MAJOR RELIGION Protestantism

SAINT CHRISTOPHER & NEVIS

AREA 104 sq. mi. (269 sq. km.)
POPULATION 44,404
CAPITAL Basseterre
HIGHEST POINT Mt. Misery 4,314 ft.
    (1,315 m.)
MONETARY UNIT East Caribbean dollar
MAJOR LANGUAGE English
MAJOR RELIGIONS Protestantism,
    Roman Catholicism

The West Indies

CONIC PROJECTION

SCALE OF MILES
0   50   100   150   200

SCALE OF KILOMETERS
0   50   100   200   300

Capitals ----------- ☆

Scale 1:11,200,000
Distances are given in Nautical Miles

Puerto Rico

Bermuda Islands

© Copyright HAMMOND INCORPORATED, Maplewood, N.J.

Longitude 70° West of Greenwich

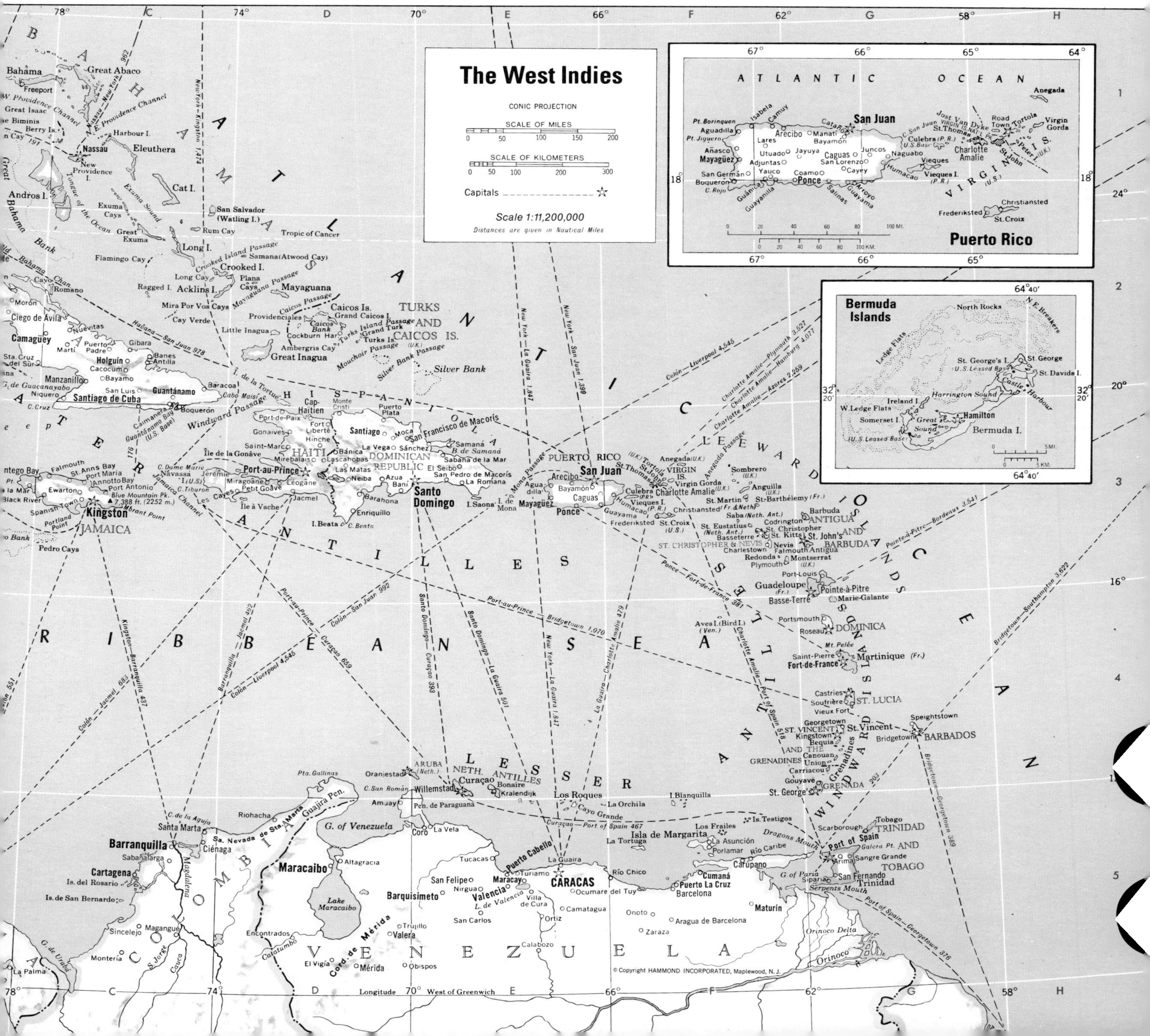

CUBA

PROVINCES

Camagüey 664,566 . . . . G2
Ciego de Ávila 320,961 . . . . . . F2
Cienfuegos 326,412 . . . . E2
Granma 739,335 . . . . H4
Guantánamo 466,609 . . . . K4
Habana 1,924,886 . . . . C1
Habana, La (Havana)
 586,029 . . . . C1
Holguín 911,034 . . . . J3
Juventud (municipio
 especial) 57,879 . . . . C2
Las Tunas 436,341 . . . . H4
Matanzas 557,628 . . . . D1
Pinar del Río 640,740 . . . . . . A2
Sancti Spíritus 399,700 . . . . . F2
Santiago de Cuba 909,506 . . . H4
Villa Clara 764,743 . . . . E1

CITIES and TOWNS

Abreus 14,267 . . . . D2
Agramonte 4,603 . . . . D1
Aguada de Pasajeros 20,219 . . D2
Alacranes 4,959 . . . . D1
Alonso Rojas 1,427 . . . . B2
Alquízar 12,691 . . . . C1
Altagracia 1,722 . . . . G3
Alto Songo-La Maya 25,188 . . J4

Amarillas 2,767 . . . . D2
Amazonas 1,066 . . . . F2
Antilla 10,052 . . . . J3
Arroyo Blanco 1,431 . . . . F2
Artemisa 45,689 . . . . B1
Báez 4,178 . . . . E2
Báguanos 12,678 . . . . J3
Bahía Honda 16,901 . . . . B1
Baire 4,879 . . . . H4
Banao 803 . . . . F2
Banes 38,905 . . . . J3
Baracoa 36,702 . . . . K4
Baraguá 12,633 . . . . F2
Bauta 26,826 . . . . C1
Bayamo 109,201 . . . . H4
Bejucal 15,649 . . . . C1
Bolondrón 5,840 . . . . D1
Buenaventura 4,711 . . . . H3
Buenavista 1,303 . . . . F2
Buey Arriba 8,017 . . . . H4
Cabaiguán 36,544 . . . . E2
Cabañas 4,897 . . . . B1
Cabezas 5,262 . . . . D1
Cacocum 14,145 . . . . H3
Caibarién 32,094 . . . . F2
Caimanera 6,664 . . . . K4
Calabazar de Sagua 9,023 . . . E1
Calimete 19,925 . . . . D1
Camagüey 245,235 . . . . G3
Camajuaní 26,653 . . . . E2
Campechuela 20,743 . . . . G4
Canasí 1,637 . . . . C1

Candelaria 10,810 . . . . B1
Cárdenas 65,585 . . . . D1
Cartagena 2,166 . . . . D2
Cascajal 3,530 . . . . E1
Cauto del Embarcadero 949 . . H4
Cauto el Cristo 1,626 . . . . J3
Central Amancio Rodríguez
 22,506 . . . . G3
Central Bolivia 6,301 . . . . F2
Central Brasil 4,904 . . . . E1
Central Cándido González
 3,414 . . . . G3
Central Colombia 16,799 . . . . F2
Central Frank País 9,066 . . . . K3
Central Guatemala 5,584 . . . . J3
Central Haití 3,609 . . . . G3
Central Los Reynaldos 3,997 J4
Central Loynaz Echevarría
 3,245 . . . . G3
Central Manuel Tames 7,864 K4
Céspedes 6,634 . . . . G2
Chambas 19,877 . . . . F2
Chaparra 8,428 . . . . H3
Cidra 3,567 . . . . D1
Ciego de Ávila 80,010 . . . . . . F2
Cienfuegos 107,396 . . . . D2
Colón 47,010 . . . . D1
Condado 33,115 . . . . E1
Consolación del Norte 4,681 . B1
Consolación del Sur 34,334 . . B2
Contramaestre 44,991 . . . . . . G3
Corralillo 15,822 . . . . D1

Cruces 20,324 . . . . E2
Cueto 23,183 . . . . J3
Cumanayagua 25,338 . . . . E2
Daiquirí J4
Delicias 10,562 . . . . H3
Dos Caminos 3,772 . . . . J4
Dos Ríos 1,786 . . . . J4
El Caney 3,921 . . . . J4
El Cobre 3,952 . . . . J4
El Santo 2,473 . . . . E1
Encrucijada 23,029 . . . . E1
Esmeralda 17,205 . . . . G1
Esperanza 9,241 . . . . E2
Florencia 6,979 . . . . F2
Florida 43,881 . . . . G3
Fomento 17,310 . . . . E2
Gaspar 2,682 . . . . F2
Gibara 23,137 . . . . J3
Guáimaro 29,712 . . . . G3
Guanabacoa 89,741 . . . . C1
Guanajay 21,042 . . . . B1
Guane 14,126 . . . . A2
Guantánamo 178,129 . . . . K4
Guaro 3,086 . . . . J3
Guasimal 3,057 . . . . F2
Guayabal 3,703 . . . . G3
Guayos 6,753 . . . . F2
Güines 51,691 . . . . C1
Güira de Melena 19,851 . . . . . C1
Guisa 15,182 . . . . H4
Havana (cap.) 1,924,886 . . . . C1
Herradura 3,762 . . . . B1

Holguín 190,155 . . . . J3
Ignacio Agramonte 1,487 . . . . G3
Imías 4,491 . . . . K4
Isabela de Sagua 3,721 . . . . . E1
Jagüey Grande 30,205 . . . . . . D2
Jamaica 5,128 . . . . K4
Jaruco 16,844 . . . . C1
Jatibonico 17,047 . . . . F2
Jíbaro 1,263 . . . . F2
Jiguaní 25,069 . . . . H4
Jobabo 14,899 . . . . H3
Jovellanos 35,043 . . . . D1
La Coloma 3,462 . . . . B2
La Maya-Alto Songo 25,188 . J4
Las Martinas 4,511 . . . . A2
Limonar 9,629 . . . . D1
Los Arabos 10,664 . . . . E1
Los Palacios 21,884 . . . . B1
Lugareño 4,396 . . . . G2
Mabay 6,176 . . . . H4
Maceo 2,652 . . . . H3
Majagua 9,110 . . . . F2
Manacas 5,914 . . . . E1
Manatí 11,054 . . . . H3
Manguito 2,914 . . . . D1
Manicaragua 33,900 . . . . E2
Mantua 9,165 . . . . A2
Manzanillo 95,420 . . . . H4
Mapos (Amazonas) 1,066 . . . F2
Mariano 127,563 . . . . C1
Mariel 24,115 . . . . B1
Martí 11,474 . . . . D1

Matanzas 103,302 . . . . C1
Máximo Gómez, Ciego
 de Ávila 5,116 . . . . F2
Máximo Gómez, Matanzas
 4,970 . . . . D1
Mayajigua 4,425 . . . . F2
Mayarí 54,699 . . . . J3
Mayarí Arriba 2,302 . . . . J4
Media Luna 13,794 . . . . G4
Mendoza 2,914 . . . . A2
Meneses 4,768 . . . . F2
Minas 17,675 . . . . G2
Minas de Matahambre
 14,976 . . . . A1
Moa 28,696 . . . . K3
Morón 40,396 . . . . F2
Nicaro 9,506 . . . . J3
Niquero 15,544 . . . . G4
Nueva Gerona 17,175 . . . . . . B2
Nuevitas 35,103 . . . . G2
Orozco 4,256 . . . . B1
Palma Soriano 66,222 . . . . . . J4
Palmira 19,680 . . . . E2
Pedro Betancourt 22,915 . . . . D1
Perico 20,633 . . . . D1
Pilón 10,194 . . . . H4
Pinar del Río 104,598 . . . . . . B2
Placetas 46,038 . . . . E2
Primero Enero 14,807 . . . . . . F2
Puerto Esperanza 3,499 . . . . . A1
Puerto Padre 46,806 . . . . H3
Quemado de Güines 11,208 E1

Rancho Veloz 3,966 . . . . D1
Ranchuelo 34,255 . . . . E2
Regla 38,491 . . . . C1
Remedios 27,722 . . . . E2
Repúbliica Dominicana
 2,540 . . . . F2
Río Cauto 19,550 . . . . H4
Rodas 16,350 . . . . E2
Sagua de Tánamo 15,327 . . . K3
Sagua la Grande 52,315 . . . . E1
San Andrés 2,127 . . . . G2
San Antonio de los Baños
 28,137 . . . . C1
Sancti Spíritus 79,542 . . . . . . F2
San Diego de los Baños
 1,430 . . . . B1
San Germán 12,362 . . . . J3
San José de las Lajas
 37,149 . . . . C1
San José de los Ramos
 1,726 . . . . D1
San Juan y Martínez 13,227 . B2
San Luis, Pinar del Río
 5,677 . . . . B2
San Luis, Santiago de Cuba
 32,826 . . . . J4
San Nicolás 12,368 . . . . C1
San Ramón 2,676 . . . . H4
Santa Clara 175,113 . . . . E2
Santa Cruz del Norte
 15,239 . . . . C1

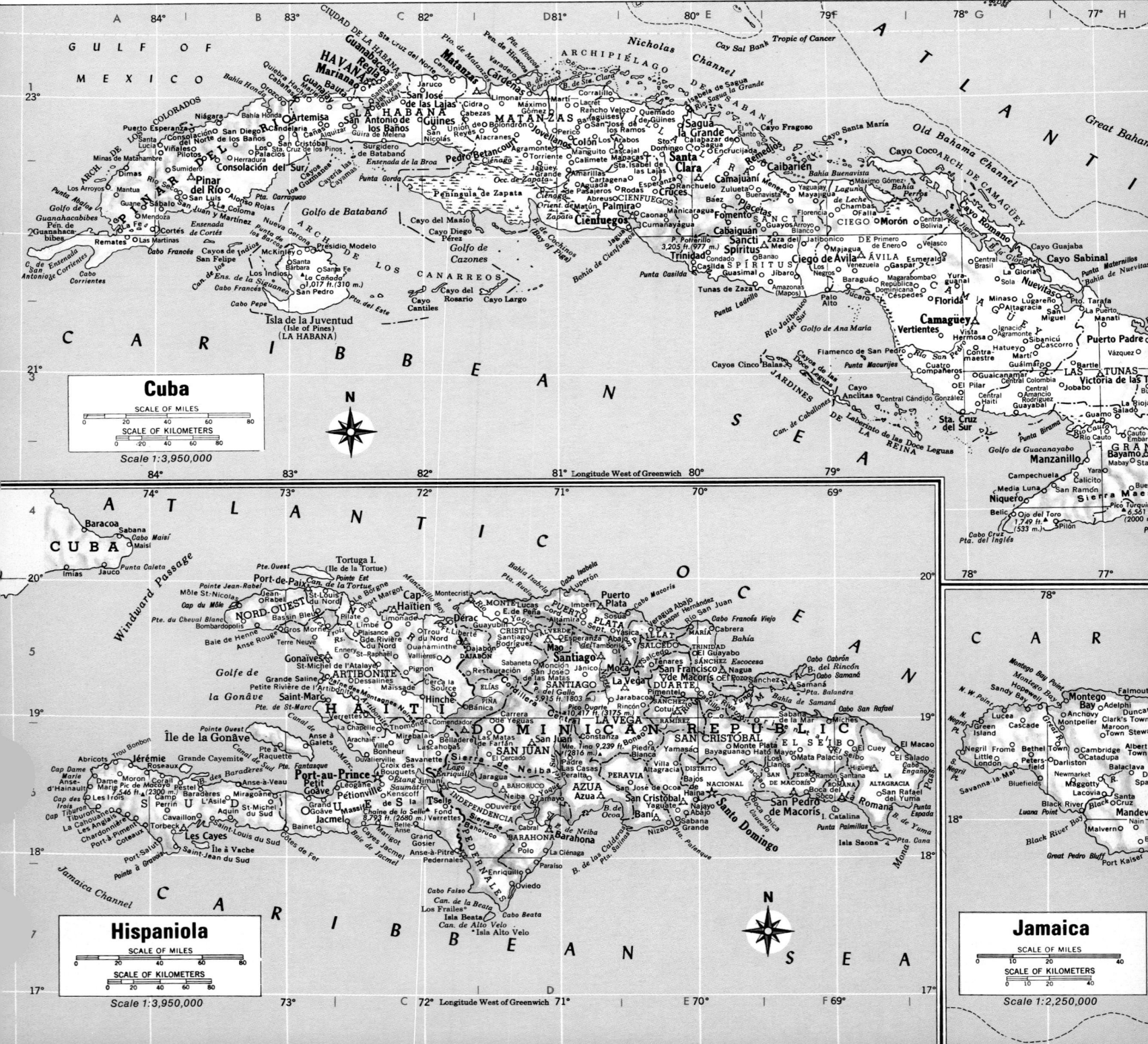

Cuba

SCALE OF MILES
0   20   40   60   80

SCALE OF KILOMETERS
-20   0   20   40   60   80

Scale 1:3,950,000

Hispaniola

SCALE OF MILES
0   20   40   60   80

SCALE OF KILOMETERS
0   20   40   60   80

Scale 1:3,950,000

Jamaica

SCALE OF MILES
0   10   20   40

SCALE OF KILOMETERS
0   10   20   40

Scale 1:2,250,000

Santa Cruz de los Pinos 3,545 .... B1
Santa Cruz del Sur 27,142 . G3
Santa Fe 3,925 .... B2
Santa Isabel de las Lajas 7,279 .... E2
Santa Lucía 3,734 .... J3
Santa Rita 6,358 .... H4
Santiago de Cuba 362,432 . J4
Santiago de las Vegas 29,325 .... C1
Santo Domingo 32,950 ... E1
Sibanicú 14,252 .... G3
Sola 2,436 .... G2
Sumidero 980 .... A2
Surgidero de Batabanó 11,533 .... C1
Tacajó 4,469 .... J3
Torriente 1,759 .... D11
Trinidad 42,080 .... E2
Unión de Reyes 28,422 .. C1
Varadero 14,737 .... D1
Vázquez 3,851 .... H3
Velasco 5,618 .... H3
Venezuela 13,744 .... F2
Vertientes 25,178 .... G3
Victoria de las Tunas 87,522 H3
Viñales 2,049 .... A1
Yaguajay 30,720 .... F2
Yara 238,891 .... H4
Zaza del Medio 7,495 .... F2
Zulueta 5,425 .... E2

OTHER FEATURES

Abalos (pt.) A2
Ana María (gulf) F3
Anclitas (cay) F3
Batabanó (gulf) C2
Birama (bay) G4
Broa (inlet) C1
Buenavista (bay) F2
Caballones (chan.) F3
Camagüey (arch.) G2
Cantiles (cay) C3
Cárdenas (bay) D1
Carraguao (bay) B2
Casilda (bay) E2
Cauto (riv.) H3
Cayamas (cays) C2
Cazones (gulf) C2
Cienfuegos (bay) D2
Cinco Balas (cays) E3
Cochinos (bay) D2
Coco (cay) G1
Corrientes (cape) A2
Corrientes (inlet) A2
Cortés (inlet) B2
Cristal, Sierra del (mts.) . J3
Cruz (cape) G4
Diego Pérez (cay) C2
Doce Leguas (cays) F3
Este (pt.) C3
Fragoso (cay) F1
Francés (cape) A2

Gorda (pt.) C2
Gran Piedra (mt.) J4
Guacanayabo (gulf) G4
Guajaba (cay) G2
Guanahacabibes (gulf) ... A2
Guanahacabibes (pen.) ... A2
Guantánamo (bay) J4
Guantánamo Bay U.S. Nav. Reserve K4
Guárico (pt.) K3
Guzmanes (cays) B2
Hicacos (pen.) D1
Hicacos (pt.) D1
Honda (bay) B1
Indios (chan.) E5
Inglés (pt.) G4
Jardines de la Reina (arch.) . F3
Jatibonico del Sur (riv.) . F3
Jigüey (bay) G2
Juventud, Isla de la (Pines) (isl.) 57,879 ...... B3
Laberinto de las Doce Leguas (cays) F3
Ladrillo (pt.) E3
Largo (cay) D2
Leche (lag.) F2
Los Barcos (pt.) B2
Los Canarreos (arch.) ... C2
Los Colorados (arch.) ... A1
Lucrecia (cape) J3
Macurijes (pt.) F3
Maestra, Sierra (mts.) .. H4
Maisí (cape) K4
Mangle (pt.) J3
Maslo (cay) C2
Matanzas (bay) D1
Nicholas (chan.) E1
Nipe (bay) J3
Nuevitas (bay) H2
Ojo del Toro (mt.) G4
Old Bahama (chan.) G1
Pepe (cape) B3
Perros (bay) G2
Pigs (Cochinos) (bay) ... D2
Pines (Isla de la Juventud) (isl.) 7,879 .... B3
Potrerillo (peak) E2
Quemado (pt.) K4
Romano (cay) G2
Rosario (cay) C2
Sabana (arch.) E1
Sabinal (cay) H2
Sagua la Grande (riv.) .. E1
San Antonio (cape) A2
San Felipe (cays) B2
San Pedro (riv.) G3
Santa Clara (bay) D1
Santa María (cay) F1
Siguanea (bay) B2
Tabacal (pt.) H4
Toa, Cuchillas de (mts.) . K4
Tortuguilla (pt.) K4
Turquino (peak) H4
Zapata (pen.) C2
Zapata Occidental (swamp) . D2
Zapata Oriental (swamp) . D2

DOMINICAN REPUBLIC
PROVINCES

Azua 142,770 .... D6

Bahoruco 78,636 .... D6
Barahona 137,160 .... D6
Dajabón 57,709 .... D5
Distrito Nacional 1,550,739 . E6
Duarte 235,544 .... E5
Elías Piña 65,384 ...... C5
El Seibo 157,866 .... F6
Espaillat 164,017 ...... E5
Independencia 38,768 ... D6
La Altagracia 100,112 .. F6
La Romana 109,769 ...... F6
La Vega 385,043 .... D6
María Trinidad Sánchez 112,629 .... E5
Monte Cristi 83,407 .... D5
Pedernales 17,006 ...... D7
Peravia 168,123 .... E6
Puerto Plata 206,757 ... D5
Salcedo 99,191 .... E5
Samaná 65,699 .... E5
Sánchez Ramírez 126,567 . E5
San Cristóbal 446,132 .. E6
San Juan 239,957 .... D6
San Pedro de Macorís 152,890 .... F6
Santiago 550,372 .... D5
Santiago Rodríguez 55,411 . D5
Valverde 100,319 .... D5

CITIES and TOWNS

Altamira 2,759 .... D5
Azua 31,481 .... D6
Bajos de Haina 33,135 .. E6
Baní 36,705 .... E6
Barahona 49,334 .... D6
Bonao 44,486 .... E5
Cabrera 2,542 .... E5
Comendador 5,962 .... C6
Constanza 15,141 .... D6
Cotuí 16,688 .... E5
Dajabón 8,808 .... D5
El Seibo 13,511 .... F6
Hato Mayor 17,859 ...... F6
Higüey 33,501 .... F6
Imbert 5,315 .... D5
Jarabacoa 13,416 .... D5
Jimaní 3,327 .... C6
La Romana 91,571 .... F6
La Vega 52,432 .... E5
Luperón 2,500 .... D5
Mao 33,527 .... D5
Moca 31,176 .... D5
Monción 3,344 .... D5
Nagua 20,912 .... E5
Puerto Plata 45,348 .... D5
Sabana de la Mar 9,983 . F5
Sabaneta 9,170 .... D5
Samaná 5,023 .... F5
Sánchez 7,919 .... E5
San Cristóbal 58,520 ... E6
San Francisco de Macorís 64,906 .... E5
San Juan 49,764 .... D6
San Pedro de Macorís 78,562 .... F6
Santiago 278,638 .... D5
Santo Domingo (cap.) 1,313,172 .... E6
Tenares 4,065 .... E5
Villa Altagracia 20,890 . E6

OTHER FEATURES

Alto Velo (chan.) C7
Alto Velo (isl.) D7
Balandra (pt.) F5
Beata (cape) C7
Beata (chan.) C7
Beata (isl.) F7
Cabrón (cape) F5
Calderas (bay) F6
Cana (pt.) F6
Catalina (isl.) F6
Caucedo (capee) E6
Central, Cordillera (range) . D5
Duarte (peak) D5
Engaño (cape) F6
Enriquillo (lake) C6
Escocesa (bay) E5
Espada (pt.) E5
Falso (cape) C7
Francés Viejo (cape) ... F5
Gallo (mt.) D5
Isabela (bay) D5
Isabela (cape) D5
Los Frailes (isl.) C7
Macorís (cape) E5
Manzanillo (bay) C5
Mona (passg.) F6
Neiba (bay) D6
Neiba, Sierra de (mts.) . D6
Ocoa (bay) D6
Oriental, Cordillera (range) . F6
Palenque (pt.) E6
Palmillas (pt.) E6
Rincón (bay) F5
Rucia (pt.) D5
Salinas (pt.) E6
Samaná (bay) F5
Samaná (cape) F5
San Rafael (cape) C6
Saona (isl.) F6
Septentrional, Cordillera (range) D5
Tina (mt.) D6
Yaque del Norte (riv.) . D5
Yaque del Sur (riv.) ... D6
Yuma (pt.) F6
Yuna (riv.) E5

HAITI
DEPARTMENTS

Artibonite C5
Nord C5
Nord-Ouest B5
Ouest C6
Sud A6

CITIES and TOWNS

Anse-à-Galets 3,623 .... B6
Anse-d'Hainault 5,220 .. A6
Aquin 3,820 .... B6
Cap-Haïtien 64,406 ..... C5
Croix des Bouquets 4,365 . C6
Dame Marie 4,320 .... A6
Dérac 1,300 .... C5

Dessalines 7,984 .... C5
Fort Liberté 5,012 ..... C5
Gonaïves 34,209 .... B5
Grande Rivière du Nord 6,007 .... C5
Gros Morne 4,739 .... B5
Hinche 10,070 .... C5
Jacmel 13,730 .... C6
Jérémie 18,493 .... A6
Kenscoff 2,605 .... C6
Lascahobas 3,805 .... C6
Léogâne 5,782 .... C6
Les Cayes 34,090 .... B6
Limbé 10,476 .... C5
Miragoâne 4,327 .... B6
Mirebalais 6,069 .... C6
Ouanaminthe 7,276 ...... C5
Pétionville 35,333 ..... C6
Petite Rivière de l'Artibonite 10,099 .... B5
Petit Goâve 7,310 ...... C6
Pignon 4,576 .... C5
Port-au-Prince (cap.) 449,831 .... C6
Port-de-Paix 15,540 .... B5
Saint-Louis du Nord 7,203 . B5
Saint-Marc 24,165 ...... C5
Saint-Michel de l'Atalaye 7,559 .... C5
Saint-Raphaël 3,889 .... C5
Trou du Nord 7,637 ..... C5
Verrettes 3,670 .... C5

OTHER FEATURES

Artibonite (riv.) C5
Baradères (bay) B6
Cheval Blanc (pt.) B5
Dame Marie (cape) A6
Est (pt.) C4
Fantasque (pt.) B6
Gonâve (gulf) B5
Gonâve (isl.) B6
Grande Cayemite (isl.) . A6
Gravois (pt.) A7
Irois (bay) A6
Jean-Rabel (pt.) B5
Macaya (mt.) A6
Manzanillo (bay) C5
Môle (cape) B5
Noires (mts.) B6
Ouest (pt.) B4
Ouest (pt.) B6
Saint-Marc (chan.) B5
Saint-Marc (pt.) B5
Saumâtre (lake) C6
Selle (peak) C6
Sud (chan.) B6
Tortue (chan.) C5
Tortue (Tortuga) (isl.) . B5
Tortuga (isl.) B5
Trois-Rivières (riv.) .. B5
Vache (isl.) B6
Windward (passg.) A5

JAMAICA
CITIES and TOWNS

Alley J7

Alligator Pond H6
Anchovy 2,558 .... H5
Annotto Bay K6
Bamboo 2,971 .... J6
Bath K6
Black River 2,701 ...... H6
Bog Walk J6
Bowden K6
Browns Town 5,479 ...... J6
Bull Savanna-Junction 5,110 .... H6
Cambridge 2,449 .... H6
Catadupa H6
Christiana H6
Discovery Bay 1,814 .... J5
Falmouth 3,937 .... H5
Green Island G6
Hope Bay K6
Kingston (cap.) 106,791 . K6
Kingston *516,865 ...... J7
Linstead J6
Lucea 3,635 .... G5
Mandeville 14,421 ...... H6
Maroon Town 2,717 ...... H6
May Pen 26,074 .... J6
Montego Bay 43,521 ..... H5
Montpelier H6
Morant Bay 7,465 .... K7
Negril G6
Ocho Rios 5,851 .... J6
Oracabessa J5
Port Antonio 10,538 .... K6
Port Kaiser H7
Port Maria 5,259 .... J6
Port Morant K6
Saint Ann's Bay 7,101 .. J5
Saint Margaret's Bay ... K6
Savanna-la-Mar 11,759 .. G6
Spanish Town 40,731 .... J6
Williamsfield H6

OTHER FEATURES

Black (riv.) H6
Black River (bay) G6
Blue (mts.) J6
Blue Mountain (peak) ... K6
Galina (pt.) J6
Grande (riv.) K6
Great (riv.) H6
Great Pedro Bluff (prom.) . H6
Long (bay) H7
Luana (pt.) G6
Minho (riv.) J6
Montego (bay) G5
Montego Bay ((pt.)) G5
North East (pt.) K6
North Negril (pt.) G6
North West (pt.) G5
Old Harbour (bay) J6
Portland (pt.) J7
Sir John's (peak) K6
South East (pt.) K6
South Negril (pt.) G6

*City and Suburbs.
○ Population of municipality.

LEGEND

Capitals of Countries _____ ☆
Provincial Capitals _____ △
International Boundaries _____
Provincial Boundaries _____

© Copyright HAMMOND INCORPORATED, Maplewood, N.J.

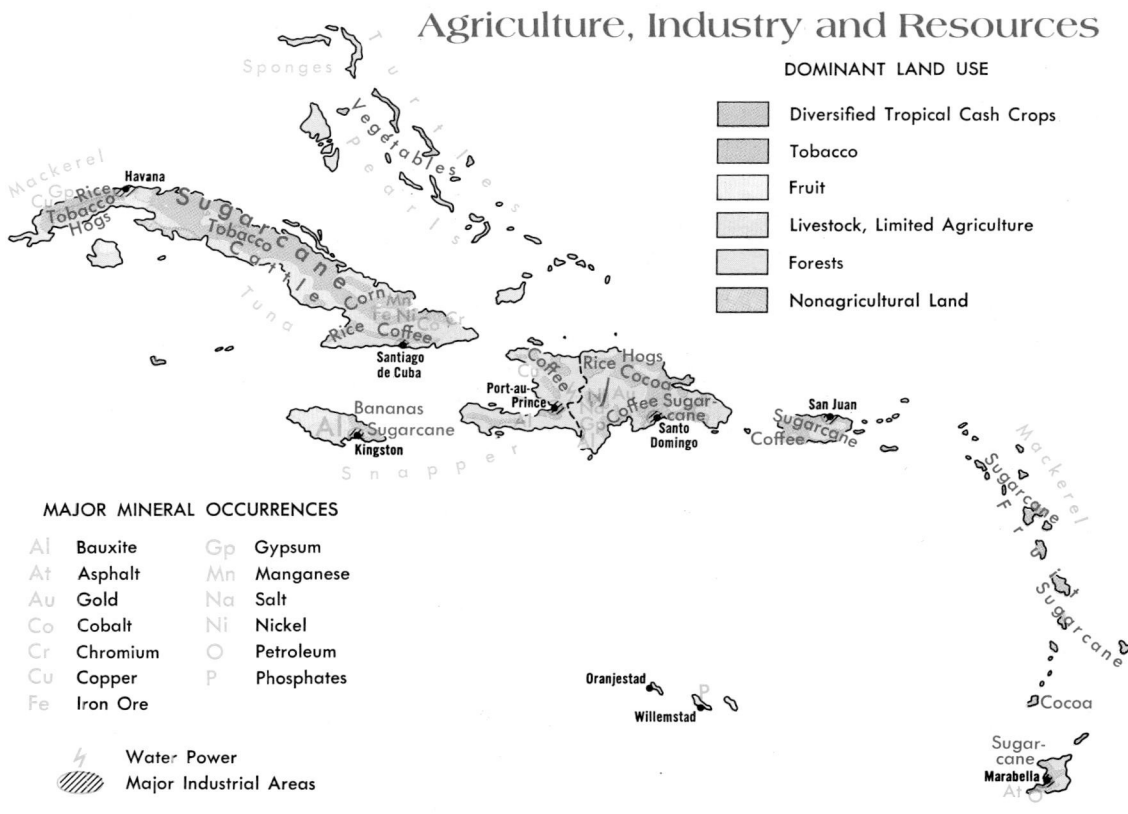

Agriculture, Industry and Resources

DOMINANT LAND USE

Diversified Tropical Cash Crops
Tobacco
Fruit
Livestock, Limited Agriculture
Forests
Nonagricultural Land

MAJOR MINERAL OCCURRENCES

Al Bauxite
At Asphalt
Au Gold
Co Cobalt
Cr Chromium
Cu Copper
Fe Iron Ore

Gp Gypsum
Mn Manganese
Na Salt
Ni Nickel
O Petroleum
P Phosphates

⚡ Water Power
▨ Major Industrial Areas

PUERTO RICO

DISTRICTS

Aguadilla A1
Arecibo C1
Bayamón D1
Guayama D2
Humacao E2
Mayagüez B2
Ponce C2
San Juan D1

CITIES and TOWNS

Adjuntas 5,239 . . . . . B2
Aguada 5,025 . . . . . A1
Aguadilla 22,039 . . . . . A1
Aguas Buenas 3,766 . . . . . E2
Aibonito 9,331 . . . . . D2
Añasco 5,646 . . . . . A1
Ángeles ○2,817 . . . . . B2
Arecibo 48,779 . . . . . B1
Arroyo 8,435 . . . . . E3
Bahomamey A1
Bajadero 3,678 . . . . . C1
Barceloneta 4,502 . . . . . C1
Barranquitas 3,618 . . . . . D2
Bayamón 185,087 . . . . . D1
Boquerón ○3,675 . . . . . A3
Cabo Rojo 10,292 . . . . . A2
Caguas 87,214 . . . . . E2
Caguas †156,819 . . . . . E2
Camuy 3,834 . . . . . B1
Carolina 147,835 . . . . . E1
Cataño 26,243 . . . . . D1
Cayey 23,305 . . . . . D2
Ceiba 4,973 . . . . . F2
Central Aguirre 1,049 . . . . . D3
Ciales 3,582 . . . . . C1
Cidra 6,069 . . . . . D2
Coamo 12,851 . . . . . D2
Comerío 5,736 . . . . . D2
Coquí 3,018 . . . . . D3
Corozal 5,889 . . . . . D1
Coto Laurel ○5,192 . . . . . C2
Culebra (Dewey) 938 . . . . . G1
Dorado 10,203 . . . . . D1
Ensenada B3
Esperanza 1,130 . . . . . G2
Fajardo 26,928 . . . . . F1
Florida 3,641 . . . . . C1
Guánica 9,628 . . . . . B3
Guayama 21,097 . . . . . E3
Guayanilla 6,163 . . . . . B3
Guaynabo 65,075 . . . . . D1
Gurabo 7,645 . . . . . E2
Hatillo 5,019 . . . . . B1
Hato Rey E1
Hormigüeros 12,031 . . . . . A2
Humacao 19,147 . . . . . E2
Isabela 12,087 . . . . . A1
Isabel Segunda 2,330 . . . . . G2
Jayuya 3,588 . . . . . C2
Jobos 4,194 . . . . . D3
Juana Díaz 10,469 . . . . . C2
Juncos 7,851 . . . . . E2
Lajas 4,275 . . . . . A2
Lares 5,224 . . . . . B2
Las Piedras 4,857 . . . . . E2
Levittown 31,613 . . . . . D1
Loíza 3,932 . . . . . E1
Loíza Aldea E1
Luquillo 4,531 . . . . . F1
Manatí 17,347 . . . . . C1
Maricao 1,390 . . . . . B2
Mayagüez 82,968 . . . . . A2
Mayagüez †98,155 . . . . . A2
Moca 3,960 . . . . . A1
Naguabo 4,135 . . . . . F2
Naranjito 2,849 . . . . . D1
Palmer 1,566 . . . . . F1
Palo Seco 1,172 . . . . . D1
Parguera A3
Patillas 3,172 . . . . . E2
Peñuelas 4,235 . . . . . B2
Playa de Fajardo F1
Playa de Humacao ○5,573 . . F2
Ponce 161,739 . . . . . C3
Ponce †168,272 . . . . . C3
Puerto Nuevo D1
Puerto Real 2,390 . . . . . A2
Puerto Real (Playa de Fajardo) F1
Punta Santiago (Playa de Humacao) ○5,573 . . . . . F2
Quebradillas 3,770 . . . . . B1
Río Blanco 1,433 . . . . . F2
Río Grande 12,047 . . . . . E1
Río Piedras E1
Rosario A2
Sabana Grande 7,435 . . . . . B2
Sabana Seca 11,431 . . . . . D1
Salinas 6,220 . . . . . D3
San Antonio 2,681 . . . . . A1
San Germán 13,054 . . . . . A2
San Juan (cap.) 424,600 . . . E1
San Juan †1,081,193 . . . . . E1
San Lorenzo 8,880 . . . . . E2
San Sebastián 10,619 . . . . . B1
Santa Isabel 6,948 . . . . . C3
Santurce E1
Tallaboa 1,059 . . . . . B3
Toa Alta 4,427 . . . . . D1
Toa Baja 1,992 . . . . . D1
Trujillo Alto 41,141 . . . . . E1
Utuado 11,113 . . . . . B2
Vega Alta 10,582 . . . . . D1
Vega Baja 18,233 . . . . . D1
Vieques (Isabel Segunda) 2,330 . . . . . G2
Villalba 3,469 . . . . . C2
Yabucoa 6,797 . . . . . E2
Yauco 14,594 . . . . . B2

OTHER FEATURES

Aguadilla (bay) A1
Algarrobo (pt.) A2
Añasco (bay) A1
Arenas (pt.) F2
Bauta (riv.) C2
Bayamón (riv.) D1
Boquerón (bay) A3
Borinquen (pt.) A1
Cabullones (pt.) C3
Caja de Muertos (isl.) C3
Camuy (riv.) B1
Canovanas (riv.) E1
Caonillas (lake) C2
Carite (lake) E2
Carraízo (lake) E1
Cayey, Sierra de (mts.) D2
Central, Cordillera (range) . . C2
Cerro Gordo (pt.) D1
Coamo (res.) D3
Coamo (riv.) D3
Culebra (isl.) 1,265 . . . . . G1
Culebrinas (riv.) A1
Culebrita (isl.) G2
El Toro (mt.) F2
El Yunque (mt.) F1
Este (pt.) G2
Fajardo (riv.) F1
Figuras (pt.) E3
Fosforescente (bay) A3
Grande de Añasco (riv.) B2
Grande de Arecibo (riv.) C1
Grande de Loíza (riv.) E1
Grande de Manatí (riv.) C1
Guajataca (lake) B1
Guanajibo (pt.) A2
Guanajibo (riv.) A2
Guánica (lake) B3
Guaniquilla (pt.) A2
Guayabal (lake) C2
Guayanés (pt.) F2
Guayanés (riv.) E2
Guayanilla (bay) B3
Guayo (lake) B2
Guilarte (mt.) B2
Honda (bay) F2
Jacaguas (riv.) C2
Jaicoa, Cordillera (mts.) B1
Jiguero (pt.) A1
Jobos (bay) D3
Lima (pt.) F2
Luquillo, Sierra de (mts.) . . . E2
Manglillo (pt.) B3
Mayagüez (bay) A2
Miquillo (pt.) F1
Molinos (pt.) G1
Mona (passg.) A2
Negra (pt.) G2
Nigua (riv.) D2
Ola Grande (pt.) D3
Palmas Altas (pt.) C1
Patillas (lake) E2
Petrona (pt.) D3
Pirata (mt.) F2
Plata (riv.) D2
Puerca (pt.) F2
Puerto Medio Mundo (bay) . . F2
Punta, Cerro de (mt.) C2
Ramey A.F.B. A1
Rincón (bay) A2
Rojo (cape) A3
Roosevelt Road Naval Res. . . F2
Salinas (pt.) D1
San José (lag.) E1
San Juan, Cabezas de (prom.) F1
San Juan Nat'l Hist. Site . . . D1
Soldado (pt.) G2
Sucia (bay) A3
Tanamá (riv.) B1
Toro, El (mt.) F2
Torrecilla (lag.) E1
Tortuguero (lag.) D1
Tuna (pt.) E3
Vacía Talega (pt.) E1
Vieques (isl.) 7,662 . . . . . G2
Vieques (passg.) F2
Vieques (sound) G2
Yagüez (riv.) A2
Yauco (lake) B2
Yeguas ((pt.) F3

ANTIGUA

CITIES and TOWNS

All Saints 1,796 . . . . . E11
Cedar Grove 1,460 . . . . . E11
Falmouth 1,134 . . . . . E11
Freetown 1,250 . . . . . E11
Jennings 1,370 . . . . . D11
Liberta 2,394 . . . . . E11
Old Road 1,244 . . . . . D11
Parham 1,570 . . . . . E11
Saint John's (cap.) 21,814 . E11
Willikies 1,843 . . . . . E11

OTHER FEATURES

Antigua (isl.) 76,213 . . . . . E11
Boggy (peak) D11
Boon (pt.) E11
Green (isl.) E11
Guiana (isl.) E11
Long (isl.) E11
Saint John's (harb.) C11
Standfast (pt.) E11
Willoughby (bay) E11

ARUBA

CITIES and TOWNS

Aresji D9
Balashi E10
Bubali D10
Bushiribana E10
Druif D1
Oranjestad (cap.) Aruba 10,100 . . . . . D10
Sint Nicolaas E10
Westpunt D10

OTHER FEATURES

Aruba (isl.) 66,790 . . . . . E9
Basora (pt.) E10
Jamanota (mt.) E10
Paarden (bay) D10
Palm (beach) D10

BARBADOS

CITIES and TOWNS

Bathsheba B8
Belleplaine B8
Bridgetown (cap.) 7,552 . . . B9
Carlton B8
Cave Hill B9
Checker Hall B8
Codrington B8
Crab Hill B8
Crane C9
Drax Hall B8
Ellerton B9
Greenland B8
Holetown B8
Kendal B8
Lodge Hill B8
Marchfield B9
Mount Standfast B8
Oistins B9
Rose Hill B8
Rouen B9
Saint Lawrence B9
Saint Martins C9
Scarboro B9
Seawell B9
Six Mens B8
Speightstown B8
Spring Hall B8
Welchman Hall B8

OTHER FEATURES

Carlisle (bay) B9
Hillaby (mt.) B8
Long (bay) B9
North (pt.) B8
Oistins (bay) B9
Pelican (isl.) B9
Ragged (pt.) C8
Sam Lord's Castle C9
South (pt.) B9

DOMINICA

CITIES and TOWNS

Barroui 1,480 . . . . . E6
Castle Bruce 1,975 . . . . . F6
Coulihaut 1,735 . . . . . E6
Delice F7
Grand Bay 3,152 . . . . . F7
Hampstead E5
La Plaine F6
Mahout 2,095 . . . . . E6
Marigot 3,183 . . . . . F6
Petit Soufrière F6
Portsmouth 2,329 . . . . . E5
Rosalie F6
Roseau (cap.) 9,968 . . . . . E7
Roseau *16,035 . . . . . E7
Saint Joseph 2,643 . . . . . E6
Salybia F6
Soufrière E7
Vieille Case E5
Wesley 2,002 . . . . . F5

OTHER FEATURES

Capuchin (cape) E5
Carib Reserve F6
Clyde (riv.) F6
Crumpton (pt.) F5
Diablotin, Morne (mt.) E6
Dominica (passg.) E5
Douglas (bay) E5
Grand (bay) F7
Jaquet (pt.) E5
Layou (riv.) E6
Martinique (passg.) E7
Micotrin (mt.) F6
Pagoua (bay) F6
Prince Rupert (bay) E5
Scotts (head) E7
Soufrière (bay) E7
Trois Pitons, Morne (mt.) . . E6

GRENADA

CITIES and TOWNS

Gouyave 2,498 . . . . . C8
Grand Roy C8
Grenville 1,723 . . . . . D8
Hermitage D8
La Taste D8
Marquis D8
Mount Tivoli D8
Saint George's (cap.) 6,463 . C9
Saint George's *34,624 . . . C9
Sauteurs 605 . . . . . D8
Victoria 1,673 . . . . . D8
Woodford C8

OTHER FEATURES

Bedford (pt.) D8
David (pt.) D8
Great Bacolet (pt.) D8
Green (isl.) D8
Grenville (bay) D8
Gros (pt.) C8
Halifax (harb.) C8
Irvin's (bay) D8
Les Tantes (isls.) D7
Molinière (pt.) C8
Prickly (pt.) C9
Ronde (isl.) D7
Saint Catherine (mt.) D8
Saline (pt.) C9
Sinai (mt.) D8
Telescope (pt.) D8

GUADELOUPE
Total Population 329,017

CITIES and TOWNS

Anse-Bertrand 1,921 . . . . . A5
Baie-Mahault 5,874 . . . . . A6
Baillif 3,844 . . . . . A7
Bananier A7
Basse-Terre (cap.) 13,397 . . . A7
Bouillante 1,821 . . . . . A6
Bourg-des-Saintes 907 . . . . . A7
Capesterre 7,541 . . . . . A7
Ferry A6
Gosier 13,741 . . . . . B6
Gourbeyre 5,637 . . . . . A7
Goyave 1,709 . . . . . A6
Grand-Bourg 3,249 . . . . . B7
Lamentin 2,319 . . . . . A6
Les Abymes 51,837 . . . . . B6
Morne-à-l'Eau 9,457 . . . . . A6
Moule 9,800 . . . . . B6
Petit-Bourg 5,097 . . . . . A6
Petit-Canal 1,581 . . . . . A6
Pigeon A6
Pointe-à-Pitre 25,151 . . . . . B6
Pointe-Noire 2,180 . . . . . A6
Port-Louis 4,517 . . . . . B5
Saint-Claude 6,755 . . . . . A7
Sainte-Anne 11,527 . . . . . B6
Sainte-Marguerite B6
Sainte-Marie A6
Sainte-Rose 4,805 . . . . . A6
Saint-François 3,141 . . . . . B6
Trois-Rivières 7,881 . . . . . A7
Vieux-Fort 1,073 . . . . . B7
Vieux-Habitants 4,065 . . . . . A7

OTHER FEATURES

Allègre (pt.) A6
Antigues (pt.) A5
Basse-Terre (isl.) 138,777 . . A6
Châteaux (pt.) B6
Constant, Morne (hill) B7
Désirade, La (isl.) 1,602 . . . B6
Fajou (isl.) A6
Grand Cul-de-Sac Marin (bay) A6
Grande-Terre (isl.) B6
Grande Vigie (pt.) B5
Grand-Îlet (isl.) A7
Guadeloupe (isl.) 167,896 . . B6
Guadeloupe (passg.) A5
Guadeloupe Nat'l Park A6
Kahouanne (isl.) A6
Marie-Galante (isl.) 13,757 . B7
Nord (pt.) B7
Nord-Est (bay) B6
Petit Cul-de-Sac Marin (bay) A6
Petite-Terre (isls.) B6
Saintes (chan.) A7
Saintes (isls.) 2,901 . . . . . A7
Salée (riv.) A6
Sans Toucher (mt.) A6
Soufrière (mt.) A7
Terre-de-Bas (isl.) 1,427 . . . A7
Terre-de-Haut (isl.) 1,453 . . A7
Vieux-Fort (pt.) A7

MARTINIQUE
Total Population 330,220

CITIES and TOWNS

Ajoupa-Bouillon 1,569 . . . . . C5
Basse-Pointe 2,163 . . . . . C5
Bellefontaine 818 . . . . . C6
Case-Pilote 1,776 . . . . . C6
Ducos 4,429 . . . . . D6
Fond-Saint-Denis 962 . . . . . C6
Fort-de-France (cap.) 96,649 . . . . . C6
Grand' Rivière 1,053 . . . . . C5
Gros-Morne 1,976 . . . . . D6
La Trinité 3,380 . . . . . D6
Le Carbet 2,321 . . . . . C6
Le François 2,940 . . . . . D6
Le Lamentin 6,872 . . . . . D6
Le Lorrain 2,024 . . . . . D6
Le Marin 2,651 . . . . . D7
Le Morne-Rouge 2,650 . . . . . C5
Le Prêcheur 1,350 . . . . . C5
Le Robert 3,610 . . . . . D6
Le Saint-Esprit 3,947 . . . . . D6
Les Trois-Îlets 1,484 . . . . . D6
Le Vauclin 3,054 . . . . . D6
Macouba 1,142 . . . . . C5
Marigot 1,765 . . . . . D5
Rivière-Pilote 1,587 . . . . . D7
Rivière-Salée 1,859 . . . . . D7
Sainte-Luce 1,502 . . . . . D7
Sainte-Marie 3,966 . . . . . D5
Saint-Joseph 2,052 . . . . . D6
Saint-Pierre 4,923 . . . . . C6
Schoelcher 16,412 . . . . . C6

OTHER FEATURES

Cabet, Pitons du (mt.) C6
Cabrits (isl.) D7
Caravelle (pen.) D6
Cul-de-Sac du Marin (bay) . . D7
Diable (pt.) D5
Ferré (cape) E7
Fort-de-France (bay) C6
Galion (bay) D6
Lézarde (riv.) D6
Long (isl.) D6
Lorrain (riv.) D5
Martinique (passg.) C5
Pelée (vol.) C5
Pilote (riv.) D7
Ramiers (isl.) C6
Ramville (isl.) D6
Robert (harb.) D6
Rose (pt.) D6
Saint-Martin (cape) C5
Saint-Pierre (bay) C6
Salines (pt.) D7
Salomon (pt.) C7
Vauclin (mt.) D6

NETHERLANDS ANTILLES

CITIES and TOWNS

Ascension F8
Bacuna E8
Boven Bolivia E8
Dokterstuin F8
Emmastad F9
Entrejo E8
Fontein E8
Groot Sint Joris G9
Hato G8
Kralendijk (cap.), Bonaire 2,500 . . . . . E8
Lagoen F8
Montanja di Reij G9
New Port G9
Noord di Salinja E8
Onima E8
Otrabanda F9
Patrick F8
Rincon E8
Rooi E8
Santa Barbara G9
Santa Catharina G9
Savonet F8
Sint Kruis F8
Sint Martha F8
Sint Michiel F9
Sint Willebrordus F8
Terra Corra E8
Westpunt F8
Willemstad (cap.) 95,000 . . . F9
Willemstad *130,000 . . . . . F9

OTHER FEATURES

Bonaire (isl.) 8,087 . . . . . E9
Bullen (bay) F8
Caracas (bay) G9
Curaçao (isl.) 145,430 . . . . . G7
Goto (lake) D8
Kanon (pt.) G9
Klein Bonaire (isl.) E8
Kudarebe (pt.) D9
Lac (bay) D9
Lacre (pt.) E9
Malmok (mt.) E8
Noord (pt.) D8
Noord (pt.) F8
Pekelmeer (lake) E9
Piscadera (bay) F9
Schottegat (bay) G9
Sint Anna (bay) F9
Sint Christoffel (mt.) F8
Sint Joris (bay) G9
Slag (bay) D8
Vierkant (pt.) E8

SAINT CHRISTOPHER and NEVIS

CITIES and TOWNS

Basseterre (cap.) 14,725 . . C10
Cayon C10
Charlestown 1,326 . . . . . C11
Cotton Ground 471 . . . . . C11
Dieppe Bay C10
Frigate Bay C10
Gingerland D11
Golden Rock C10
Newcastle D11
Old Road Town C10
Sadlers Village C10
Sandy Point 862 . . . . . C10
Tabernacle C10
Zion Hill D11

OTHER FEATURES

Brimstone (hill) C10
Dogwood (pt.) D11
Fort (pt.) C11
Great Salt (pond) D10
Heldens (pt.) C10
Horse Shoe (pt.) C11
Misery (mt.) C10
Monkey (hill) C10
Narrows, The (str.) D11
Nevis (isl.) 9,300 . . . . . D11
Nevis (peak) D11
North Friars (bay) D10
Pinney's (beach) D11
Saint Christopher (Saint Kitts) (isl.) 35,104 . . . . . D10
South Friars (bay) C10

SAINT LUCIA

CITIES and TOWNS

Anse la Raye •5,007 . . . . . F6
Canaries •2,075 . . . . . G6
Castries (cap.) •42,770 . . . G6
Choc G5
Choiseul •6,382 . . . . . F7
Dauphin G5
Dennery •9,654 . . . . . G6
Gros Islet •10,329 . . . . . G5
Laborie •6,944 . . . . . G7
Marigot G6
Marquis G6
Micoud •12,264 . . . . . G6
Preslin G6
Soufrière •7,456 . . . . . F6
Vieux Fort •10,675 . . . . . G7

OTHER FEATURES

Beaumont (pt.) F6
Canaries, Piton (mt.) G6
Cannelles (pt.) G7
Cannelles (riv.) G6
Cap (pt.) G5
Choc (bay) G5
Fond d'Or (bay) G6
Gimie (mt.) G6
Grand Caille (pt.) F6
Grand Cul de Sac (riv.) G6
Gros Islet (bay) G5
Gros Piton (mt.) G6
La Sorcière (mt.) G6
Maria (isls.) G7
Ministre (pt.) G7
Moule-à-Chique (cape) G7
Petit Piton (mt.) G6
Pigeon (isl.) G5
Port Castries (harb.) G6
Port Praslin (bay) G6
Roseau (riv.) G6
Saint Lucia (chan.) G5
Saint Vincent (chan.) G7
Savannes (bay) G7
Sorcière, La (mt.) G6
Soufrière (bay) F6
Vierge (pt.) G6

SAINT VINCENT and THE GRENADINES

CITIES and TOWNS

Barrouallie 1,298 . . . . . A9
Calliaqua 627 . . . . . A9
Camden Park A9
Colonarie A9
Georgetown 1,100 . . . . . A8
Kingstown (cap.) 17,117 . . . A9
Kingstown *23,330 . . . . . A9
Layou 1,147 . . . . . A9
Wallibu A8

OTHER FEATURES

Colonarie (pt.) A9
Cumberland (bay) A8
Dark (head) A8
De Volet (pt.) A8
Espagnol (pt.) A8
Greathead (bay) A9
Kingstown (bay) A9
Owia (bay) A8
Porter (pt.) A8
Richmond (peak) A8
Saint Andrew (mt.) A9
Saint Vincent (passg.) A8
Soufrière (mt.) A8
Yambou (head) A9

TRINIDAD and TOBAGO

CITIES and TOWNS

Arima 11,390 . . . . . B10
Arouca B10
Basse Terre B11
Biche B10
Blanchisseuse B10
California A11
Carapichaima B10
Caroni B10
Cedros A11
Chaguanas 6,122 . . . . . B10
Chaguaramas A10
Couva 3,635 . . . . . B10
Cunapo B10
Flanagin Town B10
Fullarton A11
Fyzabad 1,564 . . . . . A11
Grande Rivière B10
Guaico B10
Guayaguayare B11
La Brea 1,487 . . . . . A11
Marabella 18,158 . . . . . A11
Matelot B10
Matura B10
Mayaro 2,638 . . . . . B11
Moruga B11
Mucurapo A10
Palo Seco A11
Peñal 3,606 . . . . . B11
Point Fortin 6,538 . . . . . A11
Port-of-Spain (cap.) 67,978 . . . . . A10
Princes Town 8,288 . . . . . B11
Redhead B10
Rio Claro 2,423 . . . . . B11
Saint Joseph 4,132 . . . . . B10
Saint Joseph B11
San Fernando 33,490 . . . . . A11
San Francique A11
Sangre Grande 8,948 . . . . . B1
San Juan A10
Sans Souci B10
Siparia 5,773 . . . . . B11
Tabaquite 2,309 . . . . . B11
Talparo B10
Toco 1,287 . . . . . B10
Tunapuna 10,251 . . . . . B10
Upper Manzanilla B1
Valencia B10
Waterloo A10

OTHER FEATURES

Aripo, El Cerro del (mt.) . . B10
Boca Grande (passg.) A10
Chacachacare (isl.) A10
Chupara (pt.) B10
Cocos (bay) B10
Dragons Mouth (str.) A10
El Tucuche (mt.) B10
Erin (bay) A11
Galeota (pt.) B11
Galera (pt.) C10
Guapo (bay) A11
Guatuaro (pt.) B11
Icacos (pt.) A11
Maracas (bay) C10
Pitch (lake) A11

VIRGIN ISLANDS (Br.)

CITIES and TOWNS

Road Town (cap.) 2,200 . . . D3
West End C4

OTHER FEATURES

Flanagan (passg.) D4
Frenchman (cay) C4
Great Thatch (isl.) C4
Great Tobago (isl.) B3
Jost Van Dyke (isl.) 135 . . . C3
Little Tobago (isl.) B3
Narrows, The (str.) C4
Norman (isl.) D4
Peter (isl.) D4
Road (bay) D3
Sage (mt.) D4
Sir Francis Drake (chan.) . . . D4
Tortola (isl.) 9,257 . . . . . D3

VIRGIN ISLANDS (U.S.)

CITIES and TOWNS

Bethlehem E4
Canebay E3
Charlotte Amalie (cap.) 11,842 . . . . . B4
Christiansted 2,914 . . . . . F4
Cruz Bay 1,928 . . . . . C4
Diamond F4
Eastend D4
Emmaus C4
Fredensdal F4
Frederiksted 1,046 . . . . . E4
Grove Place 3,599 . . . . . E4
Kingshill F4
Longford F4
Negro Bay E4

OTHER FEATURES

Altona (lag.) F4
Annaly (bay) E3
Baron Bluff (prom.) E3
Bordeaux (mt.) C4
Brass (isls.) B4
Buck (isl.) G3
Buck Island (chan.) F3
Buck Island Reef Nat'l Mon. . G3
Butler (bay) E4
Caneel (bay) B4
Capella (isls.) B5
Christiansted Nat'l Hist. Site . F4
Coral (bay) C4
Crown (mt.) A4
Dutch Cap (cay) A4
Eagle (mt.) E4
East (pt.) G4
Flanagan (passg.) D4
Flat (cays) A4
Grass (pt.) G4
Great (pond) F4
Great Pond (bay) F4
Green (cay) F4
Hams Bluff (prom.) E3
Hans Lollik (isls.) B4
Hassel (isl.) B4
Jersey (bay) B4
Krause Lagoon (chan.) F4
Leeward (passg.) B4
Long (pt.) B4
Long (pt.) E4
Lovango (cay) C4
Magens (bay) B4
Maho (bay) C4
Narrows, The (str.) C4
Nulliberg (mt.) B4
Perseverance (bay) A4
Picara (pt.) B4
Pillsbury (sound) B4
Privateer (pt.) D4
Pull (pt.) F3
Ram (head) C5
Red (pt.) D4
Reef (bay) C4
Saba (isl.) A4
Saint Croix (isl.) 49,725 . . . G4
Saint James (isls.) B4
Saint John (isl.) 2,472 . . . . C4
Saint Thomas (harb.) B4
Saint Thomas (isl.) 44,372 . . A4
Salt (cay) A4
Salt (riv.) F4
Salt River (bay) F3
Sandy (pt.) D4
Savana (isl.) A4
Southwest (cape) E4
Tague (bay) G4
Thatch (cay) B4
Turner Hole (bay) G4
U.S. Nav. Air Sta. A4
Virgin (str.) A4
Virgin Isls. Nat'l Park C4
Water (isl.) A4
Westend Saltpond (lag.) E4

*City and suburbs.
• Population of district.
†Population of met. area.
○ Population of municipality.

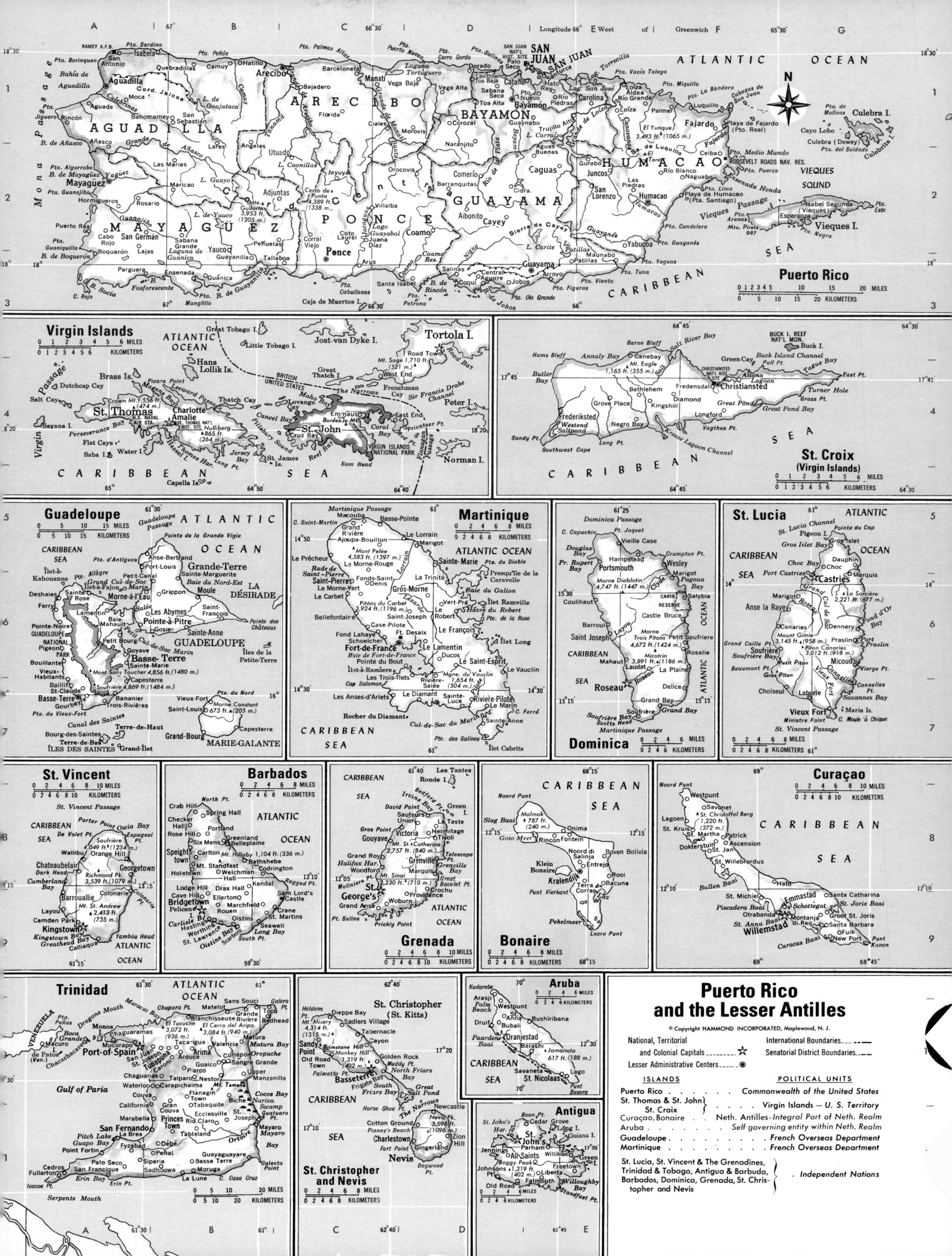

Puerto Rico and the Lesser Antilles

© Copyright HAMMOND INCORPORATED, Maplewood, N.J.

National, Territorial and Colonial Capitals ☆   International Boundaries
Lesser Administrative Centers ◉   Senatorial District Boundaries

ISLANDS	POLITICAL UNITS
Puerto Rico	Commonwealth of the United States
St. Thomas & St. John	Virgin Islands — U. S. Territory
St. Croix	
Curaçao, Bonaire	Neth. Antilles-Integral Part of Neth. Realm
Aruba	Self governing entity within Neth. Realm
Guadeloupe	French Overseas Department
Martinique	French Overseas Department

St. Lucia, St. Vincent & The Grenadines,
Trinidad & Tobago, Antigua & Barbuda,
Barbados, Dominica, Grenada, St. Christopher and Nevis

Independent Nations

Canada

CONIC PROJECTION

SCALE OF MILES
0 50 100 200 300

SCALE OF KILOMETERS
0 50 100 200 300 500

Capitals of Countries .... ☆
Provincial & Territorial Capitals .... △
Administrative Centers .... ⊙
International Boundaries .... —·—·—
Provincial Boundaries .... ———
Regional Boundaries .... ·········

Scale 1:19,600,000

© Copyright HAMMOND INCORPORATED, Maplewood, N. J.

Abitibi (lake), Ont. . . . . H 6
Aklavik, N.W.T. 721 . . . . C 2
Albany (riv.), Ont. . . . . H 5
Alberta (prov.) 2,237,724 . . . . E 5
Amherst, N.S. 9,684 . . . . K 6
Amos, Que. 9,421 . . . . J 6
Anticosti (isl.), Que. . . . . K 6
Athabasca (lake) . . . . F 4
Athabasca (riv.), Alta. . . . . E 4
Axel Heiberg (isl.), N.W.T. . . . N 3
Baffin (reg.), N.W.T. 8,300 . . . G 1
Baffin (bay), N.W.T. . . . . J 1
Baffin (isl.), N.W.T. . . . . J 1
Baker Lake, N.W.T. 954 . . . . . . G 3
Banff Nat'l Park, Alta. . . . . E 5
Banks (isl.), N.W.T. . . . . D 1
Bathurst, N. Br. 15,705 . . . . . . K 6
Belle Isle (str.), Newf. . . . . L 5
Bonavista, Newf. 4,460 . . . . . . L 6
Boothia (pen.), N.W.T. . . . . . . G 1
Brandon, Man. 36,242 . . . . F 6
British Columbia (prov.)
  2,744,467 . . . . D 4
Cabot (str.) . . . . K 6
Calgary, Alta. 592,743 . . . . E 5
Cambridge Bay, N.W.T. 815 . . F 2
Camrose, Alta. 12,570 . . . . E 5
Cape Breton (isl.), N.S. . . . . . . K 6
Cartwright, Newf. 658 . . . . L 5
Channel-Port aux Basques,
  Newf. 5,988 . . . . L 6
Charlottetown (cap.), P.E.I.
  15,282 . . . . K 6
Chatham, N. Br. 6,779 . . . . K 6

Chesterfield Inlet, N.W.T. 249 . G 3
Chibougamau, Que. 10,732 . . J 6
Chicoutimi, Que. 60,064 . . . . . J 6
Chidley (cape), Newf. . . . . K 3
Chilliwack, Br. Col. 040,642 . . D 6
Churchill, Man. 1,186 . . . . G 4
Coast (mts.) . . . . C 4
Coppermine, N.W.T. 809 . . . . E 2
Corner Brook, Newf. 24,339 . . K 6
Cornwall, Ont. 46,144 . . . . J 7
Cranbrook, Br. Col. 15,915 . . . K 3
Cree (lake), Sask. . . . . F 4
Dartmouth, N.S. 62,277 . . . . . K 7
Dauphin, Man. 8,971 . . . . F 5
Davis (str.), N.W.T. . . . . K 1
Dawson, Yukon 697 . . . . C 3
Devon (isl.), N.W.T. . . . . M 3
Drumheller, Alta. 6,508 . . . . . E 5
Edmonton (cap.), Alta.
  532,246 . . . . E 5
Edmundston, N. Br. 12,044 . . K 6
Ellesmere (isl.), N.W.T. . . . . . N 3
Eskimo Point, N.W.T. 1,022 . . G 3
Estevan, Sask. 9,174 . . . . F 6
Finlay (riv.), Br. Col. . . . . D 4
Flin Flon, Man. -Sask. 8,261 . F 4
Fogo (isl.), Newf. . . . . L 6
Fort-Chimo, Que. . . . . K 4
Fort Frances, Ont. 8,906 . . . . G 6
Fort Franklin, N.W.T. 521 . . . . D 2
Fort-George, Que. 2,222 . . . . J 5
Fort McMurray, Alta. 31,000 . E 4
Fort McPherson, N.W.T. 632 . C 2
Fort Nelson, Br. Col. 3,724 . . D 4
Fort Providence, N.W.T. 605 . E 3

Fort Saskatchewan, Alta.
  12,169 . . . . E 5
Fort Simpson, N.W.T. 980 . . . D 3
Fort Smith (reg.), N.W.T.
  22,384 . . . . E 3
Fort Smith, N.W.T. 2,298 . . . . E 3
Foxe (basin), N.W.T. . . . . J 2
Franklin (dist.), N.W.T. . . . . . . H 1
Fraser (riv.), Br. Col. . . . . D 5
Fredericton, N. Br. 43,723 . . . K 6
Frobisher Bay, N.W.T. 2,333 . K 3
Fundy (bay) . . . . K 7
Gander, Newf. 10,404 . . . . L 6
Gaspé, Que. 17,261 . . . . K 6
Georgian (bay), Ont. . . . . H 6
Geraldton, Ont. 2,956 . . . . . . H 6
Glace Bay, N.S. 21,466 . . . . . L 6
Goose Bay, Newf. 7,103 . . . . . K 5
Gouin (res.), Que. . . . . J 6
Grand Falls, Newf. 8,765 . . . . L 6
Grande Prairie, Alta. 24,263 . E 4
Great Bear (lake), N.W.T. . . . . D 2
Great Slave (lake), N.W.T. . . . E 3
Guelph, Ont. 71,207 . . . . H 7
Halifax (cap.), N.S. 114,594. . K 7
Hamilton, Ont. 306,434 . . . . . H 7
Harbour Grace, Newf. 2,988 . L 6
Havre-St-Pierre, Que. 3,200 . K 5
Hay River, N.W.T. 2,863 . . . . E 3
Hearst, Ont. 5,533 . . . . H 6
Hecate (str.), Br. Col. . . . . C 5
Hull, Que. 56,225 . . . . J 6
Magdalen (isls.), Que. . . . . . . K 6
Manicouagan (riv.), Que. . . . . K 5
Manitoba (lake), Man. . . . . . . G 5
Manitoba (prov.) 1,026,241 . G 5
Iroquois Falls, Ont. 6,339 . . . H 6

Jasper Nat'l Park, Alta. . . . . . . E 5
Jonquière, Que. 60,354 . . . . . J 6
Juan de Fuca (str.), Br. Col. . D 6
Kamloops, Br. Col. 64,048. . . D 5
Kane (basin), N.W.T. . . . . N 3
Kapuskasing, Ont. 12,014 . . . H 6
Keewatin (reg.), N.W.T. 4,327 G 2
Kelowna, Br. Col. 59,196 . . . . E 6
Kenora, Ont. 9,817 . . . . G 5
Kingston, Ont. 52,616 . . . . . . J 7
Kirkland Lake, Ont. 12,219 . . H 6
Kitikmeot (reg.), N.W.T. 3,245 F 1
Kitimat, Br. Col. 12,462 . . . . . D 5
Kluane (lake), Yukon . . . . B 3
Kootenay (lake), Br. Col. . . . . E 6
Labrador (reg.), Newf. . . . . . . K 4
Lacombe, Alta. 5,591 . . . . E 5
Lake Harbour, N.W.T. 252 . . . J 3
Lake Louise, Alta. 355 . . . . . . E 5
Lancaster (sound), N.W.T. . . . H 1
Leduc, Alta. 12,471 . . . . E 5
Lesser Slave (lake), Alta. . . . . E 4
Lethbridge, Alta. 54,072 . . . . E 6
Liard (riv.) . . . . D 3
Lloydminster, Alta.-Sask.
  15,031 . . . . E 5
Logan (mt.), Yukon . . . . B 3
London, Ont. 254,280 . . . . . . H 7
Lunenburg, N.S. 3,014 . . . . . . K 7
Mackenzie (dist.), N.W.T. . . . . C 2
Mackenzie (riv.), N.W.T. . . . . . C 2
Magdalen (isls.), Que. . . . . . . K 6
Manicouagan (riv.), Que. . . . . K 5
Manitoba (lake), Man. . . . . . . G 5
Manitoba (prov.) 1,026,241 . G 5

Manitoulin (isl.), Ont. . . . . H 6
Maple Creek, Sask. 2,470 . . . F 6
Marathon, Ont. 2,271 . . . . H 6
Mayo, Yukon 398 . . . . C 3
M'Clintock (chan.), N.W.T. . . . F 1
Medicine Hat, Alta. 40,380 . . E 5
Melville, Sask. 5,092 . . . . F 5
Melville (isl.), N.W.T. . . . . E 1
Merritt, Br. Col. 6,110 . . . . D 5
Minto (lake), Que. . . . . J 4
Mistassibi (riv.), Que. . . . . J 5
Mistassini (riv.), Que. . . . . J 5
Mistassini (lake), Que. . . . . . . J 5
Moncton, N. Br. 54,743 . . . . . K 6
Mont-Joli, Que. 6,359 . . . . . . K 6
Mont-Laurier, Que. 8,405 . . . J 6
Montréal, Que. 980,354 . . . . J 6
Moose Jaw, Sask. 33,941 . . . F 6
Moosomin, Sask. 2,579 . . . . . F 5
Moosonee, Ont. 1,433 . . . . . . H 5
Morden, Man. 4,579 . . . . G 6
Nain, Newf. 938 . . . . K 4
Nanaimo, Br. Col. 47,069 . . . D 6
Nares (str.), N.W.T. . . . . N 3
Nelson, Br. Col. 9,143 . . . . . . E 6
Nelson (riv.), Man. . . . . G 4
New Brunswick (prov.)
  696,423 . . . . K 6
Newfoundland (isl.) . . . . L 6
Newfoundland (prov.) 567,681 L 5
New Westminster, Br. Col.
  38,550 . . . . D 6
Niagara Falls, Ont. 70,960 . . J 7
Norman Wells, N.W.T. 420. . . D 2
North Battleford, Sask.
  14,030 . . . . F 5

North Bay, Ont. 51,268. . . . . . J 6
North Magnetic Pole . . . . F 1
North Saskatchewan (riv.) . . . D 5
N. Vancouver, Br. Col. 33,952 D 6
Northwest Territories 45,741 . E 2
Nova Scotia (prov.) 847,422 . K 7
Okanagan (lake), Br. Col. . . . D 6
Ontario (prov.) 8,625,107 . . . H 5
Ottawa (cap.), Canada
  295,163 . . . . J 6
Ottawa (riv.) . . . . J 6
Owen Sound, Ont. 19,883 . . . H 7
Pangnirtung, N.W.T. 839 . . . . K 2
Parry (chan.), N.W.T. . . . . . . E-H 1
Parry Sound, Ont. 6,124 . . . . J 6
Peace (riv.), Alta. . . . . E 4
Peace River, Alta. 5,907. . . . . E 4
Peel (riv.) . . . . C 2
Pelly (riv.), Yukon . . . . C 3
Pembroke, Ont. 14,026 . . . . . J 6
Péribonca (riv.), Que. . . . . J 5
Peterborough, Ont. 60,620 . . J 7
Portage la Prairie, Man.
  13,086 . . . . G 5
Port Radium, N.W.T. 56 . . . . . E 2
Poste-de-la-Baleine, Que.
  435 . . . . J 4
Povungnituk, Que. . . . . J 3
Prince Albert, Sask. 31,380. . F 5
Prince Albert Nat'l Park, Sask. F 5
Prince Edward Island (prov.)
  122,506 . . . . K 6
Prince George, Br. Col.
  67,559 . . . . D 5

Prince Patrick (isl.), N.W.T. . . M 3
Prince Rupert, Br. Col. 16,197 C 5
Québec (prov.) 6,438,403 . . . J 6
Québec (cap.), Que. 166,474 . J 6
Queen Charlotte (isls.), Br.
  Col. C 5
Queen Elizabeth (isls.),
  N.W.T. . . . . M 3
Quesnel, Br. Col. 8,240 . . . . . D 5
Race (cape), Newf. . . . . L 6
Rainy (lake), Ont. . . . . G 6
Rainy River, Ont. 1,061 . . . . . G 6
Rankin Inlet, N.W.T. 1,109 . . G 3
Ray (cape), Newf. . . . . L 6
Red Deer, Alta. 46,393. . . . . . E 5
Regina (cap.), Sask. 162,613 . F 5
Reindeer (lake) . . . . F 4
Revelstoke, Br. Col. 5,544 . . . E 5
Riding Mountain Nat'l Park,
  Man. . . . . F 5
Rimouski, Que. 29,120 . . . . . K 6
Rivière-du-Loup, Que. 13,459 K 6
Roberval, Que. 11,429 . . . . . . J 6
Robson (mt.), Br. Col. . . . . . . D 5
Rocky (mts.) . . . . D 4
Rocky Mountain House, Alta.
  4,698 . . . . E 5
Rouyn, Que. 17,224 . . . . J 6
Sable (cape), N.S. . . . . K 7
Sable (isl.), N.S. . . . . L 7
Saint Elias (mt.), Yukon . . . . . B 3
Saint John, N. Br. 80,521. . . . K 6
St. John's (cap.), Newf.
  83,770 . . . . L 6
Saint Lawrence (riv.) . . . . K 6

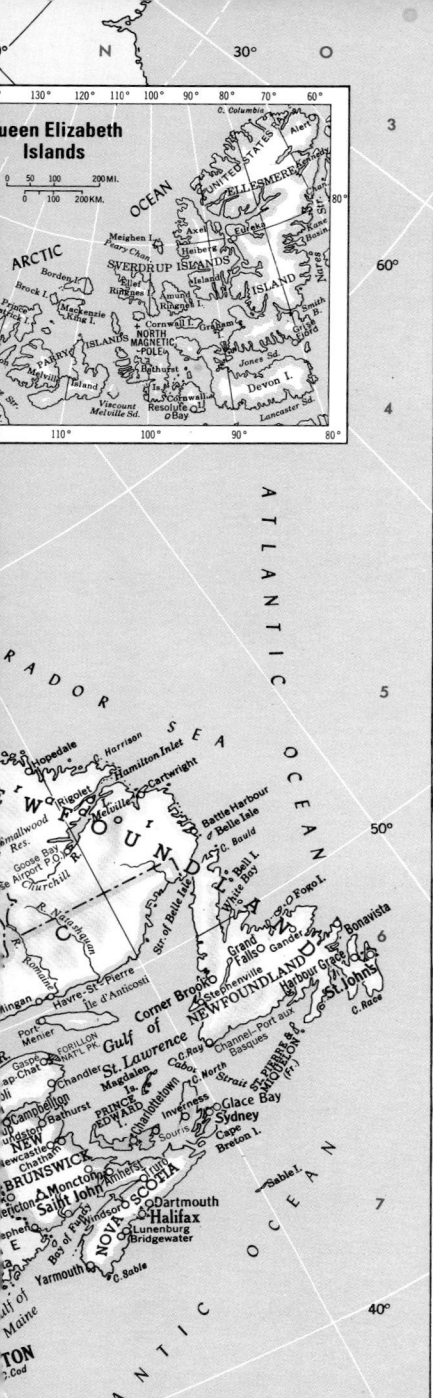

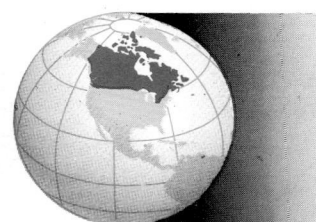

AREA 3,851,787 sq. mi. (9,976,139 sq. km.)
POPULATION 24,343,181
CAPITAL Ottawa
LARGEST CITY Montréal
HIGHEST POINT Mt. Logan 19,524 ft. (5,951 m.)
MONETARY UNIT Canadian dollar
MAJOR LANGUAGES English, French
MAJOR RELIGIONS Protestantism, Roman Catholicism

Population Distribution

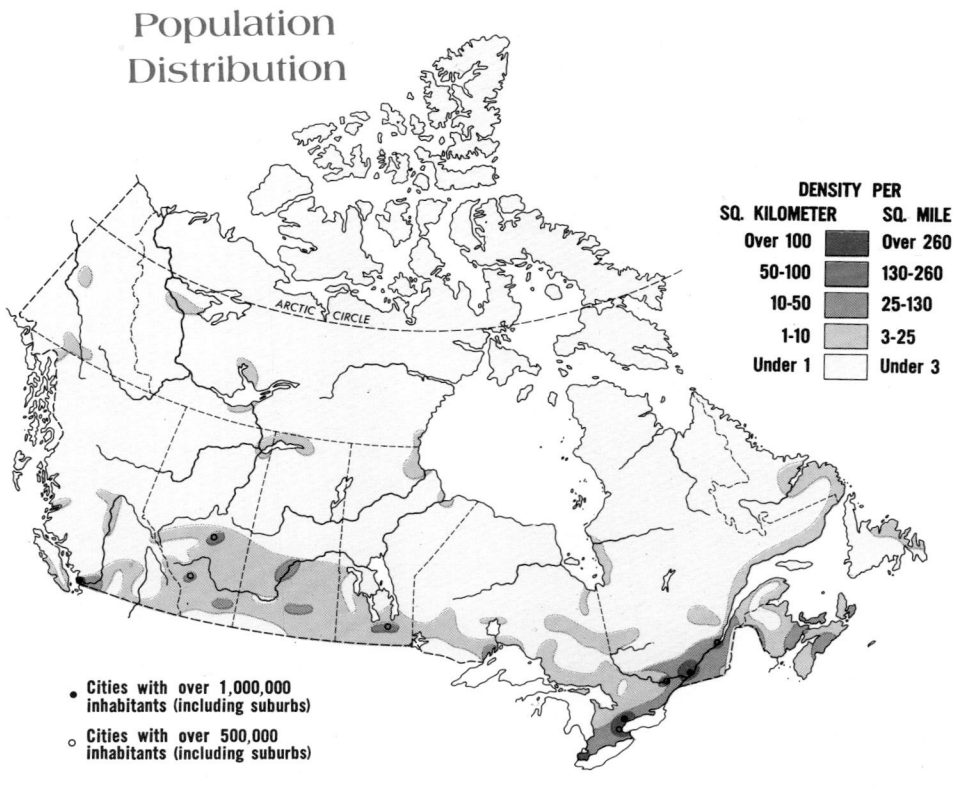

DENSITY PER	
SQ. KILOMETER	SQ. MILE
Over 100	Over 260
50-100	130-260
10-50	25-130
1-10	3-25
Under 1	Under 3

• Cities with over 1,000,000 inhabitants (including suburbs)

○ Cities with over 500,000 inhabitants (including suburbs)

Vegetation

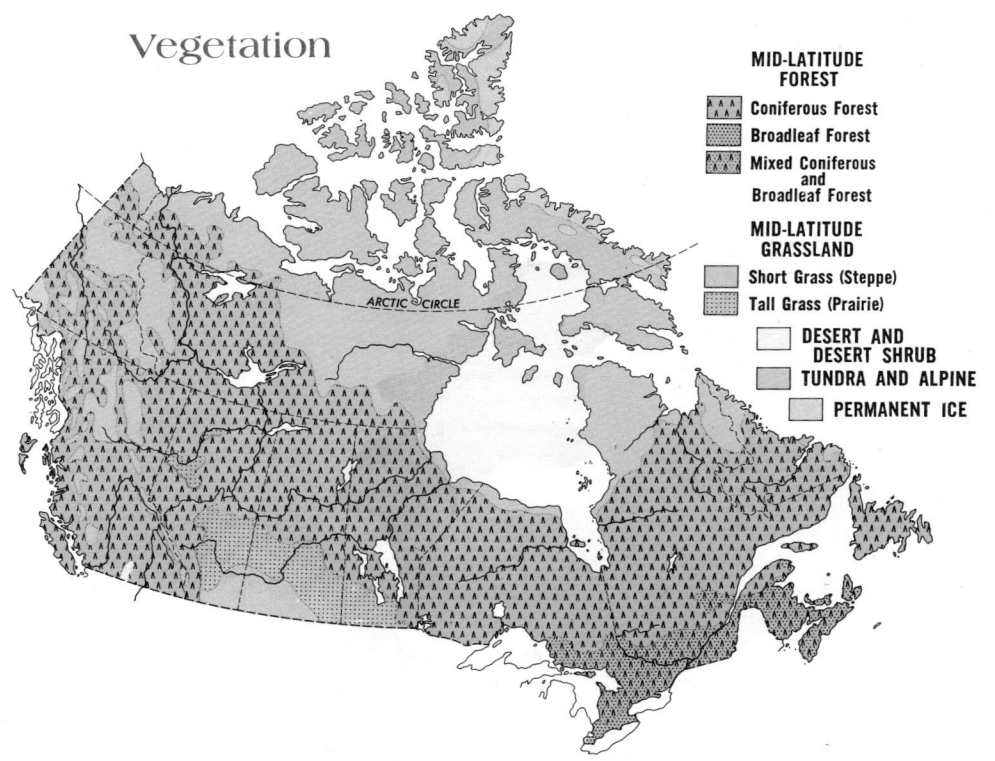

MID-LATITUDE FOREST
Coniferous Forest
Broadleaf Forest
Mixed Coniferous and Broadleaf Forest

MID-LATITUDE GRASSLAND
Short Grass (Steppe)
Tall Grass (Prairie)

DESERT AND DESERT SHRUB
TUNDRA AND ALPINE
PERMANENT ICE

Saint Pierre & Miquelon (isls.)
  6,041 . . . . L 6
Sarnia, Ont. 50,892 . . . . H 7
Saskatchewan (prov.) 968,313 F 5
Saskatchewan (riv.). . . . . F 5
Saskatoon, Sask. 154,210 . . . . F 5
Sault Sainte Marie, Ont.
  82,697 . . . . H 6
Schefferville, Que. 1,997 . . . . K 5
Selkirk, Man. 10,037 . . . . . . G 5
Sept-Îles (Seven Is.), Que.
  29,262 . . . . K 5
Shawinigan, Que. 23,011 . . . . J 6
Sherbrooke, Que. 74,075 . . . . J 7
Sioux Lookout, Ont. 3,074. . . . H 5
Skeena (riv.), Br. Col. . . . . . . D 5
Slave (riv.). . . . . F 4
Smallwood (res.), Newf. . . . . . K 5
Southampton (isl.), N.W.T. . . . . I 2
Stettler, Alta. 5,136 . . . . . . E 5
Stewart (riv.), Yukon . . . . . . C 3
Stikine (riv.), Br. Col. . . . . . . C 3
Sudbury, Ont. 91,829 . . . . . . H 6
Swift Current, Sask. 14,747 . . F 5
Sydney, N.S. 29,444. . . . . . . K 6
Terrace, Br. Col. ○10,914. . . . D 5
The Pas, Man. 6,390 . . . . . . F 5
Thompson, Man. 14,288 . . . . G 4
Thunder Bay, Ont. 112,486 . . H 6
Timmins, Ont. 46,114. . . . . . H 6
Toronto (cap.), Ont. 599,217 . H 7
Trail, Br. Col. 9,599 . . . . . . E 6
Trois-Rivières, Que. 50,466. . J 6
Truro, N.S. 12,552. . . . . K 6
Tuktoyaktuk, N.W.T. 772. . . . . C 2

Val-d'Or, Que. 21,371. . . . . . J 6
Vancouver, Br. Col. 414,281 . . D 6
Vancouver (isl.), Br. Col. . . . . D 6
Vanderhoof, Br. Col. 2,323. . . . D 5
Végreville, Alta. 5,251 . . . . . . E 5
Vernon, Br. Col. 19,987 . . . . . E 5
Victoria (cap.), Br. Col. 64,379 D 6
Victoria (isl.), N.W.T. . . . . . . E 1
Wabush, Newf. 3,155 . . . . . . K 5
Waterton-Glacier International
  Peace Park, Alta. . . . . E 6
Wetaskiwin, Alta. 9,597 . . . . . E 5
Weyburn, Sask. 9,523 . . . . . . F 6
Whitehorse (cap.), Yukon
  14,814 . . . . C 3
Williams Lake, Br. Col. 8,362 . D 5
Williston (lake), Br. Col. . . . . D 4
Windsor, N.S. 3,646 . . . . . . K 7
Windsor, Ont. 192,083 . . . . . H 7
Winnipeg (cap.), Man.
  564,473. . . . . G 6
Winnipeg (lake), Man.. . . . . . G 5
Winnipegosis (lake), Man.. . . . F 5
Wood Buffalo Nat'l Park, Alta. . E 4
Woods (lake). . . . . G 6
Wrigley, N.W.T. 137. . . . . . . D 3
Yarmouth, N.S. 7,475. . . . . . K 7
Yellowknife (cap.), N.W.T.
  9,483 . . . . E 3
Yoho Nat'l Park, Br. Col. . . . . E 5
York Factory, Man. . . . . G 4
Yorkton, Sask. 15,339 . . . . . F 5
Yukon Territory 23,153. . . . . . C 3

○Population of municipality.

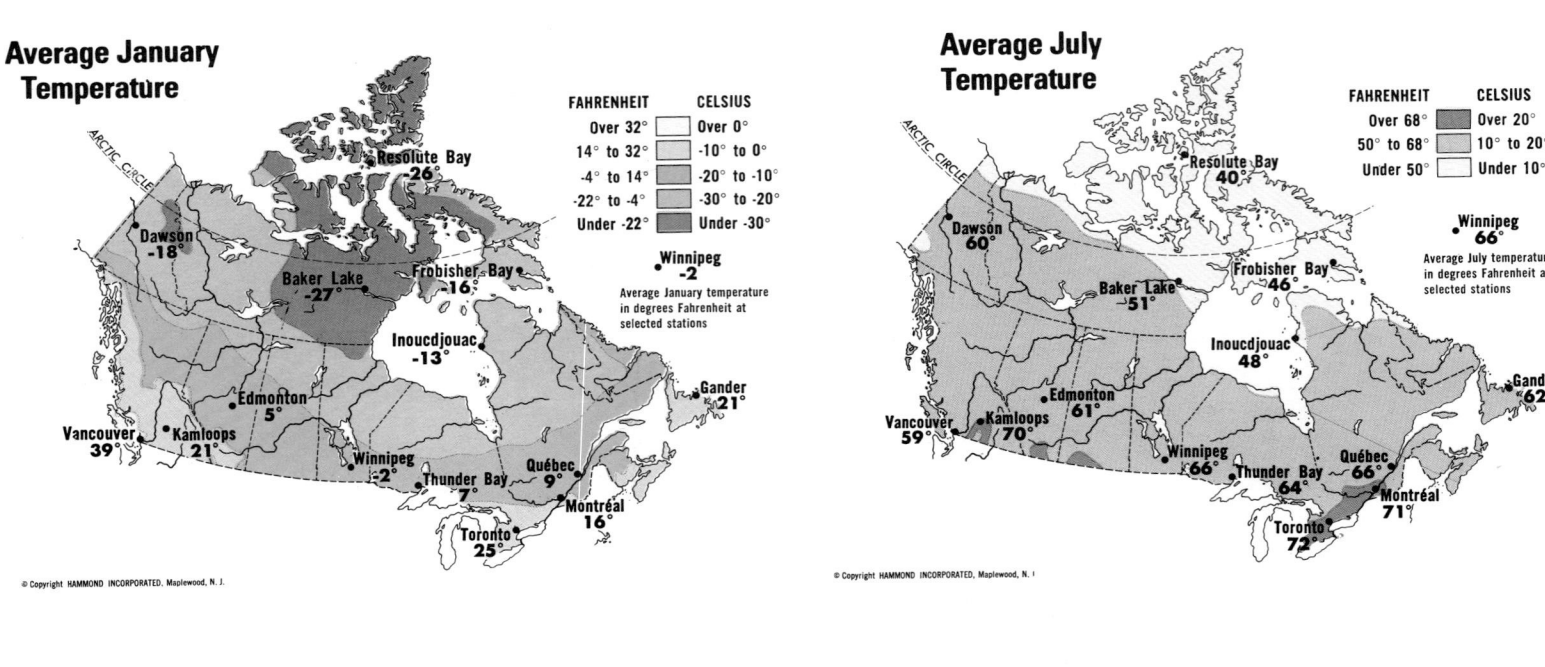

Average January Temperature

FAHRENHEIT	CELSIUS
Over 32°	Over 0°
14° to 32°	-10° to 0°
-4° to 14°	-20° to -10°
-22° to -4°	-30° to -20°
Under -22°	Under -30°

Resolute Bay -26°

Dawson -18°

Baker Lake -27°

Frobisher Bay -16°

Winnipeg -2°

Average January temperature in degrees Fahrenheit at selected stations

Inoucdjouac -13°

Gander 21°

Edmonton 5°

Vancouver 39°

Kamloops 21°

Winnipeg -2°

Thunder Bay 7°

Québec 9°

Montréal 16°

Toronto 25°

© Copyright HAMMOND INCORPORATED, Maplewood, N. J.

Average July Temperature

FAHRENHEIT	CELSIUS
Over 68°	Over 20°
50° to 68°	10° to 20°
Under 50°	Under 10°

Resolute Bay 40°

Dawson 60°

Winnipeg 66°

Baker Lake 51°

Frobisher Bay 46°

Average July temperature in degrees Fahrenheit at selected stations

Inoucdjouac 48°

Gander 62°

Edmonton 61°

Vancouver 59°

Kamloops 70°

Winnipeg 66°

Thunder Bay 64°

Québec 66°

Montréal 71°

Toronto 72°

© Copyright HAMMOND INCORPORATED, Maplewood, N. J.

Agriculture, Industry and Resources

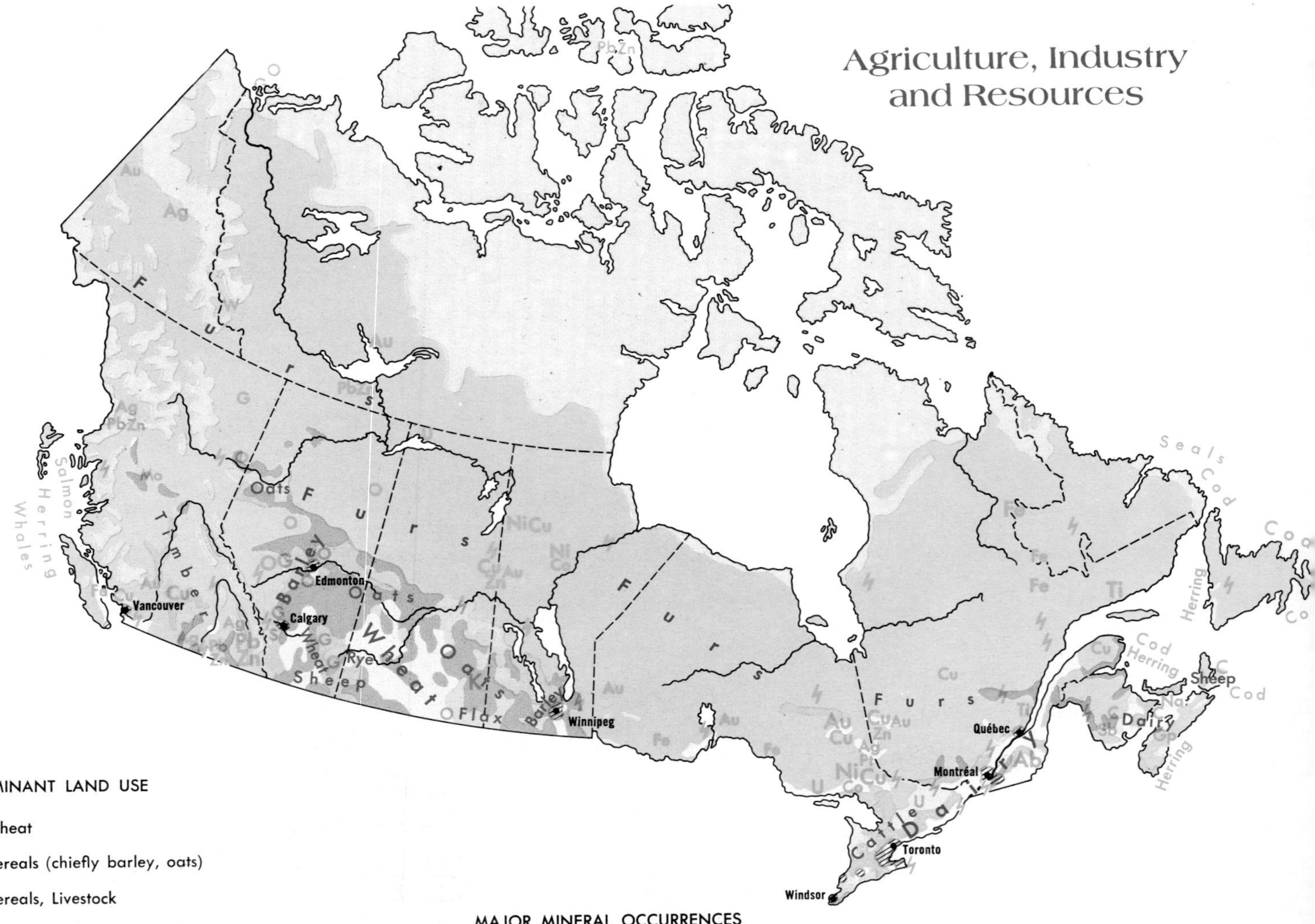

DOMINANT LAND USE

- Wheat
- Cereals (chiefly barley, oats)
- Cereals, Livestock
- General Farming, Livestock
- Dairy
- Fruit, Vegetables
- Pasture Livestock
- Range Livestock
- Forests
- Nonagricultural Land

MAJOR MINERAL OCCURRENCES

Ab	Asbestos	Fe	Iron Ore	Ni	Nickel	Sb	Antimony
Ag	Silver	G	Natural Gas	O	Petroleum	Ti	Titanium
Au	Gold	Gp	Gypsum	Pb	Lead	U	Uranium
C	Coal	K	Potash	Pt	Platinum	W	Tungsten
Co	Cobalt	Mo	Molybdenum	S	Sulfur	Zn	Zinc
Cu	Copper	Na	Salt				

Water Power

Major Industrial Areas

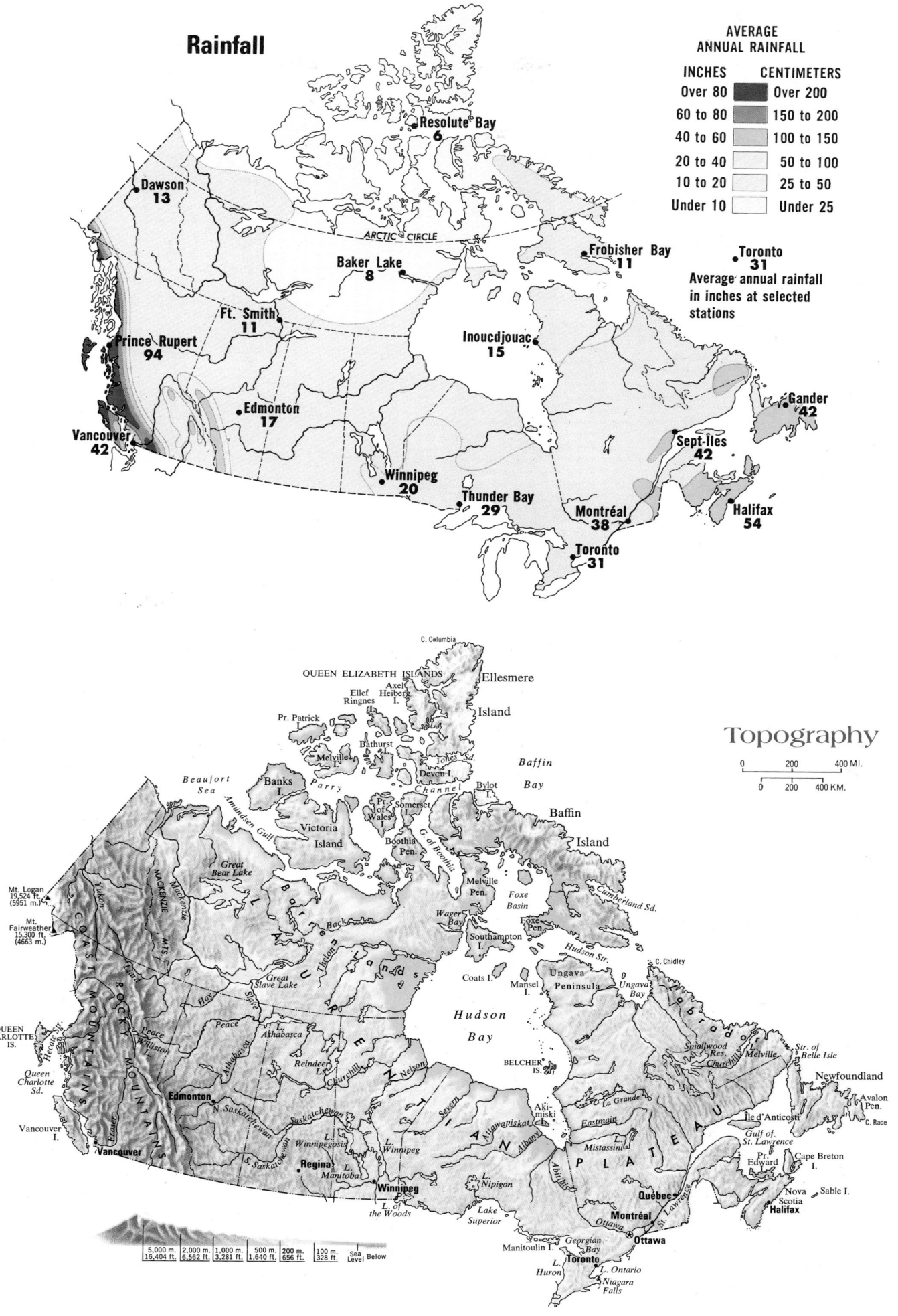

Rainfall

AVERAGE
ANNUAL RAINFALL

INCHES	CENTIMETERS
Over 80	Over 200
60 to 80	150 to 200
40 to 60	100 to 150
20 to 40	50 to 100
10 to 20	25 to 50
Under 10	Under 25

Resolute Bay
6

Dawson
13

ARCTIC CIRCLE

Frobisher Bay
11

Toronto
31

Baker Lake
8

Average annual rainfall
in inches at selected
stations

Ft. Smith
11

Inoucdjouac
15

Prince Rupert
94

Gander
42

Edmonton
17

Sept-Îles
42

Vancouver
42

Winnipeg
20

Thunder Bay
29

Montréal
38

Halifax
54

Toronto
31

Topography

C. Columbia

QUEEN ELIZABETH ISLANDS   Ellesmere

Ellef   Axel
Ringnes   Heiberg I.

Pr. Patrick

Island

Bathurst
I.

Jones Sd.

Baffin

Melville
I.

Devon I.

Bay

Beaufort
Sea

Banks
I.

Parry   Channel

Bylot
I.

0	200	400 MI.
0	200	400 KM.

Amundsen Gulf

Pr. of
Wales
I.

Somerset
I.

Baffin

Victoria
Island

Boothia
Pen.

G. of Boothia

Island

Mt. Logan
19,524 ft.
(5951 m.)

MACKENZIE

Great
Bear Lake

Melville
Pen.

Foxe
Basin

Cumberland Sd.

Mt.
Fairweather
15,300 ft.
(4663 m.)

Back

Wager
Bay

Foxe
Pen.

Hudson Str.

C. Chidley

Great
Slave Lake

Southampton
I.

Ungava
Peninsula

Ungava
Bay

QUEEN
CHARLOTTE
IS.

Hecate Str.

Liard

Hay

Stave

Coats I.

Mansel
I.

Hudson

Queen
Charlotte
Sd.

Peace
Williston

Peace

Reindeer
L.

Athabasca

Churchill

Nelson

Bay

BELCHER
IS.

Smallwood
Res.

Melville

Str. of
Belle Isle

Vancouver
I.

Edmonton

N. Saskatchewan

Churchill

Newfoundland

Vancouver

Trout

Saskatchewan

Severn

Aki-
miski

La Grande

Avalon
Pen.

C. Race

Regina

L.
Winnipegosis

S. Saskatchewan

L.
Winnipeg

Algawapiskat

Albany

Eastmain

L.
Mistassini

PLATEAU

Île d'Anticosti

Gulf of
St. Lawrence

Cape Breton
I.

Winnipeg

L.
Manitoba

L. of
the Woods

Lake
Superior

L.
Nipigon

Abitibi

Québec

St. Lawrence

Pr.
Edward

Nova
Scotia
Halifax

Sable I.

Montréal

Ottawa

Ottawa

Manitoulin I.

Georgian
Bay

Toronto

L. Ontario

Niagara
Falls

L.
Huron

5,000 m. 16,404 ft.	2,000 m. 6,562 ft.	1,000 m. 3,281 ft.	500 m. 1,640 ft.	200 m. 656 ft.	100 m. 328 ft.	Sea Level	Below

Newfoundland including Labrador

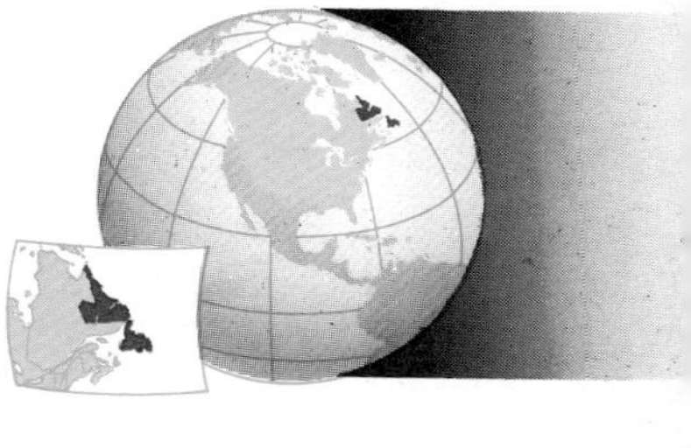

AREA 156,184 sq. mi. (404,517 sq. km.)
POPULATION 567,681
CAPITAL St. John's
LARGEST CITY St. John's
HIGHEST POINT in Torngat Mountains 5,420 ft. (1,652 m.)
SETTLED IN 1610
ADMITTED TO CONFEDERATION 1949
PROVINCIAL FLOWER Pitcher Plant

Agriculture, Industry and Resources

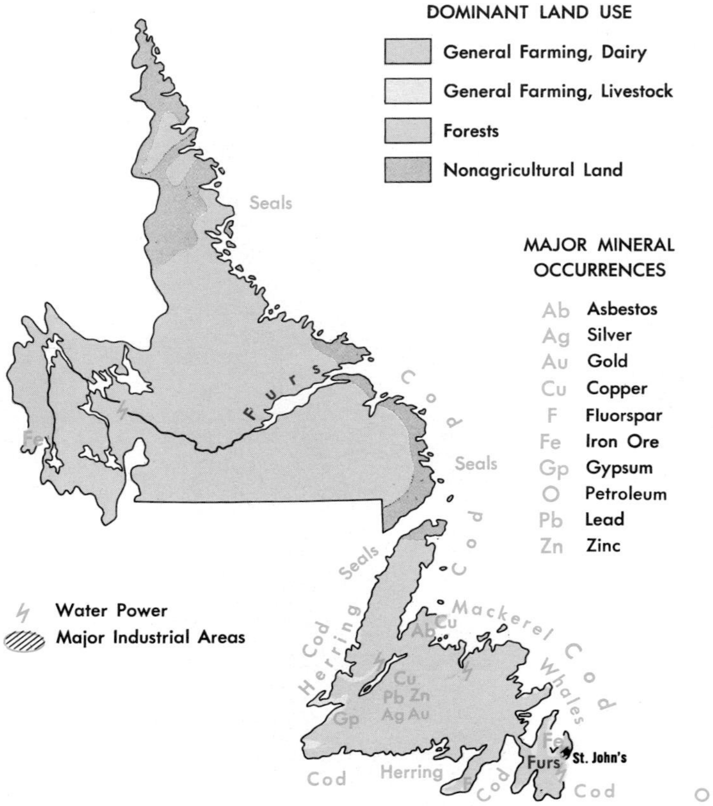
DOMINANT LAND USE
General Farming, Dairy
General Farming, Livestock
Forests
Nonagricultural Land
MAJOR MINERAL OCCURRENCES
Ab Asbestos
Ag Silver
Au Gold
Cu Copper
F Fluorspar
Fe Iron Ore
Gp Gypsum
O Petroleum
Pb Lead
Zn Zinc
Water Power
Major Industrial Areas
Seals
Furs
Cod
Herring
Mackerel
Whales
St. John's

NEWFOUNDLAND

CITIES and TOWNS

dmiral's Beach 362 . . . D2
dmiral's Cove 99 . . . D2
nchor Point 368 . . . C3
quaforte 200 . . . D2
rgentia 93 . . . C2
rnold's Cove 1,124 . . . C2
vondale 890 . . . D2
adger 1,090 . . . C4
adger's Quay-Valleyfield-Pool's Island 1,566 . . . D4
aie Verte 2,491 . . . C4
attle Harbour . . . C3
auline 423 . . . D2
ay Bulls 1,081 . . . D2
ay de Verde 786 . . . D2
ay L'Argent 483 . . . D4
ay Roberts 4,512 . . . D2
ellburns 147 . . . C3
elleoram 565 . . . C4
ellevue 286 . . . D2
de Arm 339 . . . C3
g Pond 167 . . . D2
rchy Bay 707 . . . D4
rd Cove 400 . . . C3
shop's Falls 4,395 . . . C4
ack Tickle 194 . . . C3
ackhead Road 1,855 . . . D2
aketown 617 . . . D2
oomfield 715 . . . D2
onavista 4,460 . . . D2
otwood 4,074 . . . C4
anch 462 . . . D2
igus 898 . . . D2
oad Cove 198 . . . D2
ooklyn 197 . . . D2
ownsdale 199 . . . D2
uchans 1,655 . . . C4
inyan's Cove 590 . . . C2
irgeo 2,504 . . . C4
irin 2,904 . . . C4
irnt Islands 991 . . . C4
irnt Point 260 . . . D2
alvert 482 . . . D2
ampbellton 703 . . . D4
ape Broyle 698 . . . D2
ape Ray 484 . . . C4
aplin Cove 150 . . . D2
arbonear 5,335 . . . D2
armanville 966 . . . D4
artwright 658 . . . C3
atalina 1,162 . . . D2
avendish 343 . . . D2
ampney's West 141 . . . D2
ance Cove 498 . . . D2
ange Islands 580 . . . D4
annel-Port aux Basques 5,988 . . . C4
apel Arm 689 . . . D2
arlottetown 330 . . . D2
arlottetown 250 . . . C3
urchill Falls 936 . . . B3
arenville 2,878 . . . C2
arke's Beach 1,009 . . . D2
droy 346 . . . C4
linet 318 . . . D2
lliers 819 . . . D2
me By Chance 337 . . . C2
nception Harbour 917 . . . D2
nche 464 . . . C3
ok's Harbour 388 . . . C3
rner Brook 24,339 . . . C4
Cow Head 695 . . . C4
Cox's Cove 980 . . . C4
Cupids 706 . . . D2
Daniell's Harbour 614 . . . C3
Dark Cove 1,344 . . . D4
Davis Inlet 240 . . . B2
Deep Bight 243 . . . C2
Deer Lake 4,348 . . . C4
Dildo 877 . . . D2
Dunville 1,817 . . . D2
Durrell 1,145 . . . D4
Eastport 597 . . . D1
Elliston 527 . . . D2
Embree 846 . . . C4
Englee 998 . . . C3
English Harbour 118 . . . D2
English Harbour West 327 . . . C4
Fermeuse 584 . . . D2
Ferryland 795 . . . D2
Flat Bay 322 . . . C4
Flat Rock 808 . . . D2
Fleur de Lys 616 . . . C3
Flowers Cove 459 . . . C3
Fogo 1,105 . . . D4
Forteau 520 . . . C3
Fortune 2,473 . . . C4
Fox Harbour 280 . . . C3
Fox Harbour 538 . . . D2
François 219 . . . C4
Freshwater 1,276 . . . C2
Freshwater 209 . . . D2
Gambo 2,932 . . . D4
Gander 10,404 . . . D4
Garnish 761 . . . C4
Gaskiers-Point la Haye 505 . . . D2
Gaultois 558 . . . C4
Georges Brook 356 . . . D2
Glenwood 1,129 . . . D4
Glovertown 2,165 . . . C1
Goobies 185 . . . D2
Goose Bay-Happy Valley 7,103 . . . B3
Gooseberry Cove 195 . . . C2
Goose Cove 134 . . . C2
Goose Cove 368 . . . C3
Goulds 4,242 . . . D2
Grand Bank 3,901 . . . C4
Grand Falls 8,765 . . . C4
Grates Cove 275 . . . D2
Green Island Cove 222 . . . C3
Green's Harbour 785 . . . D2
Greenspond 423 . . . D4
Grey River 234 . . . C4
Gull Island 362 . . . D2
Hampden 838 . . . C4
Hant's Harbour 542 . . . D2
Happy Adventure 352 . . . D2
Happy Valley-Goose Bay 7,103 . . . B3
Harbour Breton 2,464 . . . C4
Harbour Deep 278 . . . C3
Harbour Grace 2,988 . . . D2
Harbour Main-Chapel Cove-Lakeview 1,303 . . . D2
Hare Bay 1,520 . . . D4
Hawke's Bay 553 . . . C3
Head of Bay d'Espoir 586 . . . C4
Heart's Content 625 . . . D2
Heart's Delight-Islington 899 D2
Heart's Desire 416 . . . D2
Heatherton 328 . . . C4
Hermitage 863 . . . C4
Hickman's Harbour 479 . . . D2
Hillview 295 . . . D2
Hodge's Cove 438 . . . D2
Holyrood 1,789 . . . D2
Hopedale 425 . . . B2
Howley 456 . . . C4
Isle aux Morts 1,238 . . . C4
Jackson's Arm 623 . . . C4
Jeffrey's 276 . . . C4
Jerseyside 641 . . . B3
Job's Cove 201 . . . D2
Joe Batt's Arm-Barr'd Islands 1,155 . . . D4
Keels 129 . . . D1
Kelligrews (Foxtrap-Greeleytown-Peachtown-Kelligrews) 2,292 . . . D2
Kilbride 5,014 . . . D2
King's Cove 253 . . . D1
King's Point 825 . . . C4
Kippens 1,219 . . . C4
Labrador City 11,538 . . . A3
Lamaline 548 . . . C4
L'Anse-au-Clair 267 . . . C3
L'Anse-au-Loup 589 . . . C3
L'Anse au Meadow 66 . . . C3
La Poile 186 . . . C4
Lark Harbour 783 . . . C4
La Scie 1,422 . . . C4
Lawn 999 . . . C4
Lethbridge 686 . . . D2
Lewisporte 3,963 . . . C4
Little Bay Islands 407 . . . C4
Little Catalina 750 . . . D2
Little Heart's Ease 467 . . . D2
Lodge Bay 124 . . . C3
Long Harbour-Mount Arlington Heights 660 . . . D2
Lourdes 932 . . . C4
Lower Island Cove 415 . . . D2
Lumsden 645 . . . D4
Main Brook 514 . . . C3
Makkovik 347 . . . C2
Markland 344 . . . D2
Mary's Harbour 408 . . . C3
Marystown 6,299 . . . D4
McCallum 243 . . . C4
Melrose 416 . . . D2
Middle Arm, Green Bay 575 . . . C4
Millertown 228 . . . C4
Milltown-Head of Bay d'Espoir 1,376 . . . C4
Milton 258 . . . C2
Mobile 171 . . . D2
Mount Carmel-Mitchell's Brook-St. Catherine's 699 . . . D2
Mount Pearl 11,543 . . . D2
Musgrave Harbour 1,554 . . . D4
Musgravetown 635 . . . C2
Nain 938 . . . B2
New Bonaventure 106 . . . D2
New Chelsea 144 . . . D2
New Harbour 777 . . . D2
Newmans Cove 231 . . . D2
New Perlican 350 . . . D2
Newtown 511 . . . D4
Nippers Harbour 259 . . . C4
Norman's Cove-Long Cove 1,152 . . . D2
Norris Arm 1,216 . . . C4
Norris Point 1,033 . . . C4
North Harbour 151 . . . D2
North River 245 . . . D2
North West Brook 279 . . . C2
North West River 515 . . . B3
O'Donnells 280 . . . D2
Old Bonaventure 111 . . . D2
Old Perlican 709 . . . D2
Paradise 2,861 . . . D2
Parkers Cove 424 . . . D4
Parson's Pond 605 . . . C3
Pasadena 2,685 . . . C4
Patrick's Cove 155 . . . C2
Perry's Cove 141 . . . D2
Peterview 1,119 . . . C4
Petites 108 . . . C4
Petley 147 . . . D2
Petty Harbour-Maddox Cove 853 . . . D2
Picadilly 524 . . . C4
Pinware River 201 . . . C3
Placentia 2,204 . . . C2
Plate Cove 474 . . . D2
Point La Haye 195 . . . D2
Point Lance 141 . . . C2
Point Leamington 848 . . . C4
Point Verde 296 . . . C2
Pollards Point 502 . . . C4
Port au Bras 366 . . . D4
Port au Choix 1,311 . . . C3
Port au Port 603 . . . C4
Port Blandford 702 . . . C2
Port Hope Simpson 581 . . . C3
Port Kirwan 164 . . . D2
Port Rexton 489 . . . D2
Port Saunders 769 . . . C3
Portugal Cove 2,361 . . . D2
Portugal Cove South 371 . . . D2
Port Union 671 . . . D2
Postville 223 . . . B3
Pouch Cove 1,522 . . . D2
Princeton 204 . . . D2
Raleigh 373 . . . C3
Ramea 1,386 . . . C4
Red Bay 316 . . . C3
Red Head Cove 225 . . . D2
Rencontre East 230 . . . C4
Renews-Cappahayden 578 . . . D2
Rigolet 271 . . . C3
Riverhead 431 . . . D2
River of Ponds 304 . . . C3
Robert's Arm 1,005 . . . C4
Rocky Harbour 1,273 . . . C4
Roddickton 1,142 . . . C3
Rose Blanche-Harbour le Cou 975 . . . C4
Rushoon 520 . . . D4
Saint Alban's 1,968 . . . C4
Saint Andrew's 262 . . . C4
Saint Anthony 3,107 . . . C3
Saint Brendan's 468 . . . D4
Saint Bride's 599 . . . C2
Saint George's 1,756 . . . C4
St, John's (cap.) 83,770 . . . D2
Saint Joseph's 262 . . . D2
Saint Lawrence 2,012 . . . C4
Saint Lunaire-Griquet 1,010 . . . C3
Saint Mary's 701 . . . D2
Saint Paul's 454 . . . C4
Saint Phillips 1,365 . . . D2
Saint Shotts 239 . . . D2
Saint Vincent's-Saint Stephens-Peter's River 796 . . . D2
Sally's Cove 100 . . . C4
Salmon Cove 786 . . . D2
Seal Cove 751 . . . C3
Seal Cove-White Bay 498 . . . C4
Seldom-Little Seldom 560 . . . D4
Ship Harbour 265 . . . D2
Shoal Cove 223 . . . C3
Shoal Harbour 1,000 . . . C2
South Branch 264 . . . C4
South Brook, Hall's Bay Dist. 786 . . . C4
South Brook, Humber Dist. 477 . . . C4
Southern Harbour 772 . . . C2
South River 645 . . . D2
Spaniard's Bay 2,125 . . . D2
Springdale 3,501 . . . C4
Stephenville 8,876 . . . C4
Stephenville Crossing 2,172 . C4
Summerford 1,198 . . . C4
Summerville 346 . . . D2
Sunnyside 703 . . . D2
Sweet Bay 204 . . . D2
Swift Current 329 . . . C2
Terrenceville 796 . . . D4
Tilting 427 . . . D4
Torbay 3,394 . . . D2
Tors Cove 355 . . . D2
Traytown 383 . . . D1
Trepassey 1,473 . . . D2
Trinity 522 . . . D2
Trinity 375 . . . D4
Trout River 759 . . . C4
Twillingate 1,506 . . . C4
Upper Island Cove 2,025 . . . D2
Victoria 1,870 . . . D2
Wabana 4,254 . . . D2
Wabush 3,155 . . . A3
Wesleyville 1,125 . . . D4
Western Bay 463 . . . D2
West Saint Modeste 273 . . . C3
Whitbourne 1,233 . . . D2
Wild Cove 152 . . . C3
Windsor 5,747 . . . C4
Winterton 753 . . . D2
Witless Bay 907 . . . D2

OTHER FEATURES

Alexis (riv.) . . . C3
Anguille (cape) . . . C4
Annieopscotch (mts.) . . . C4
Ashuanipi (lake) . . . A3
Ashuanipi (riv.) . . . A3
Atikonak (lake) . . . B3
Attikamagen (lake) . . . A3
Avalon (pen.) . . . D2
Barachois Pond Prov. Park . . . C4
Bauld (cape) . . . C3
Bell (isl.) . . . C3
Bell (isl.) . . . D2
Belle Isle (isl.) . . . C3
Belle Isle (str.) . . . C3
Blackhead (bay) . . . D2
Bonavista (bay) . . . D1
Bonavista (cape) . . . D1
Bonne (bay) . . . C4
Branch (riv.) . . . C2
Broyle (cape) . . . D2
Bull Arm (inlet) . . . D2
Burin (pen.) . . . C4
Butter Pot Prov. Park . . . D2
Cabot (str.) . . . B4
Canada (bay) . . . C3
Chidley (cape) . . . B1
Churchill (falls) . . . B3
Churchill (riv.) . . . B3
Cirque (mt.) . . . B2
Clode (sound) . . . D2
Conception (bay) . . . D2
Deep (inlet) . . . B2
Double Mer (lake) . . . C3
Dyke (lake) . . . A3
Eagle (riv.) . . . C3
Espoir (bay) . . . C4
Exploits (riv.) . . . C4
Fogo (isl.) . . . D4
Fortune (bay) . . . C4
Freels (cape) . . . D3
Gander (lake) . . . D4
Gander (riv.) . . . D4
Glover (isl.) . . . C4
Goose (riv.) . . . B3
Grand (lake) . . . B3
Grand (lake) . . . C4
Grates (pt.) . . . D2
Great Colinet (isl.) . . . D2
Grey (isls.) . . . C3
Groais (isl.) . . . C3
Gros Morne (mt.) . . . C4
Gros Morne Nat'l Park . . . C4
Groswater (bay) . . . C3
Hamilton (inlet) . . . C3
Hamilton (sound) . . . D4
Hare (bay) . . . C3
Hawke (hills) . . . D2
Hebron (fjord) . . . B2
Hermitage (bay) . . . C4
Holyrood (bay) . . . D2
Horse (isls.) . . . C3
Horse Chops (head) . . . D2
Humber (riv.) . . . C4
Ingornachoix (bay) . . . C3
Ireland's Eye (isl.) . . . D2
Islands (bay) . . . C4
Kaipokok (bay) . . . B2
Kanairiktok (riv.) . . . B3
Kaumajet (mts.) . . . B2
Kingurutik (mesa) . . . B2
Labrador (reg.) . . . B2
Labrador (sea) . . . C2
La Manche Valley Prov. Park D2
La Poile (bay) . . . C4
Little Mecatina (riv.) . . . B3
Long (isl.) . . . C2
Long (lake) . . . A3
Long (pt.) . . . C4
Long Range (mts.) . . . C4
Main Topsail (mt.) . . . C4
Makkovik (cape) . . . C2
McLelan (str.) . . . B1
Mealy (lake) . . . C3
Meelpaeg (lake) . . . C4
Melville (lake) . . . C3
Menihek (lakes) . . . A3
Merasheen (isl.) . . . C2
Mistaken (pt.) . . . D2
Mistastin (lake) . . . B2
Nachvak (fjord) . . . B2
Naskaupi (riv.) . . . B3
Newfoundland (isl.) . . . C4
Newman (sound) . . . D2
New World (isl.) . . . C4
Norman (cape) . . . C3
North Aulatsivik (isl.) . . . B2
Notre Dame (bay) . . . C4
Okak (bay) . . . B2
Ossokmanuan (res.) . . . B3
Petitsikapau (lake) . . . A3
Pine (cape) . . . D2
Pinware (riv.) . . . C3
Pistolet (bay) . . . C3
Placentia (bay) . . . C2
Ponds (isl.) . . . C3
Port au Port (bay) . . . C4
Port au Port (pen.) . . . C4
Port Manvers (harb.) . . . B2
Race (cape) . . . D2
Ramah (bay) . . . B2
Ramea (isls.) . . . C4
Random (isl.) . . . D2
Random (sound) . . . D2
Ray (cape) . . . C4
Red (isl.) . . . C2
Red Indian (lake) . . . C4
Red Wine (riv.) . . . B3
Rocky (riv.) . . . D2
Round (pond) . . . C4
Saglek (bay) . . . B2
Saint Francis (cape) . . . D2
Saint George (cape) . . . C4
Saint George's (bay) . . . C4
Saint John (bay) . . . C3
Saint John (cape) . . . C3
Saint Lawrence (gulf) . . . B4
Saint Lewis (cape) . . . C3
Saint Mary's (bay) . . . C2
Saint Mary's (cape) . . . C2
Saint Michaels (bay) . . . C3
Salmonier (riv.) . . . D2
Sandwich (bay) . . . C3
Shabogamo (lake) . . . A3
Shoal (bay) . . . D2
Smallwood (res.) . . . B3
Smith (sound) . . . D2
South Aulatsivik (isl.) . . . B2
Spear (cape) . . . D2
Squires Mem. Park . . . C4
Swale (isl.) . . . D1
Terra Nova (riv.) . . . C2
Terra Nova Nat'l Park . . . D2
Territok (cape) . . . B2
Thoresby (mt.) . . . B2
Torbay (pt.) . . . D2
Torngat (mts.) . . . B2
Trespassey (bay) . . . D2
Trinity (bay) . . . D2
Tunungayualok (isl.) . . . B2
Ukasiksalik (isl.) . . . B2
Victoria (lake) . . . C4
White (bay) . . . C3
White Bear (lake) . . . C4
White Handkerchief (cape) . . . B2

SAINT PIERRE and MIQUELON

CITIES and TOWNS

Saint-Pierre (cap.) 5,415 . . . C4

OTHER FEATURES

Miquelon (isl.) 626 . . . C4
Saint Pierre (isl.) 5,415 . . . C4

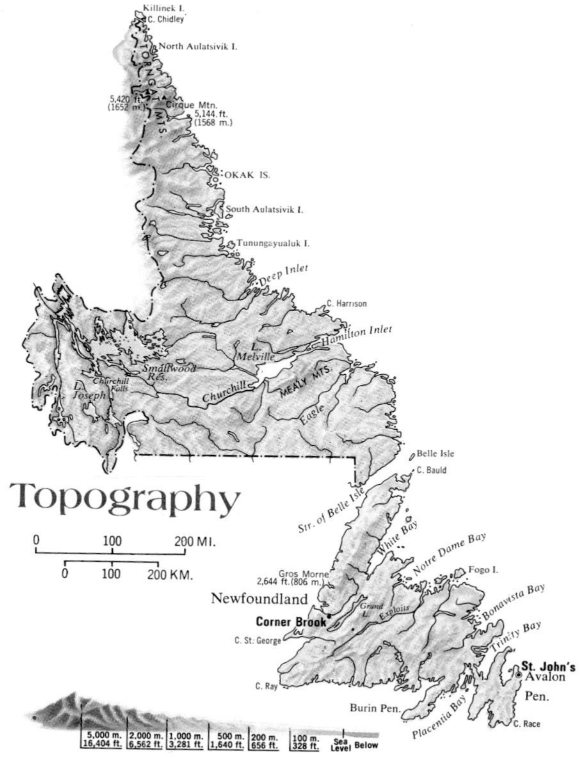
Topography
0 100 200 MI.
0 100 200 KM.
Killinek I.
C. Chidley
North Aulatsivik I.
Cirque Mtn.
OKAK IS.
South Aulatsivik I.
Tunungayualok I.
Deep Inlet
C. Harrison
Hamilton Inlet
Melville
Smallwood Res.
Churchill
MEALY MTS.
Eagle
Belle Isle
C. Bauld
Str. of Belle Isle
White Bay
Notre Dame Bay
Fogo I.
Gros Morne
Newfoundland
Corner Brook
C. St. George
Grand L.
Exploits
Bonavista Bay
Trinity Bay
St. John's
Avalon Pen.
C. Ray
Burin Pen.
Placentia Bay
C. Race
5,000 m. 16,404 ft.
2,000 m. 6,562 ft.
1,000 m. 3,281 ft.
500 m. 1,640 ft.
200 m. 656 ft.
100 m. 328 ft.
Sea Level
Below

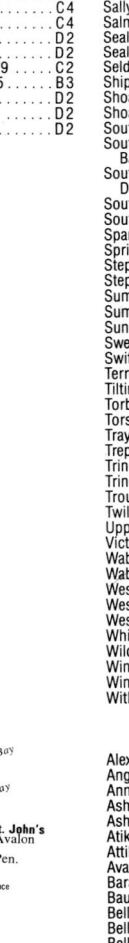

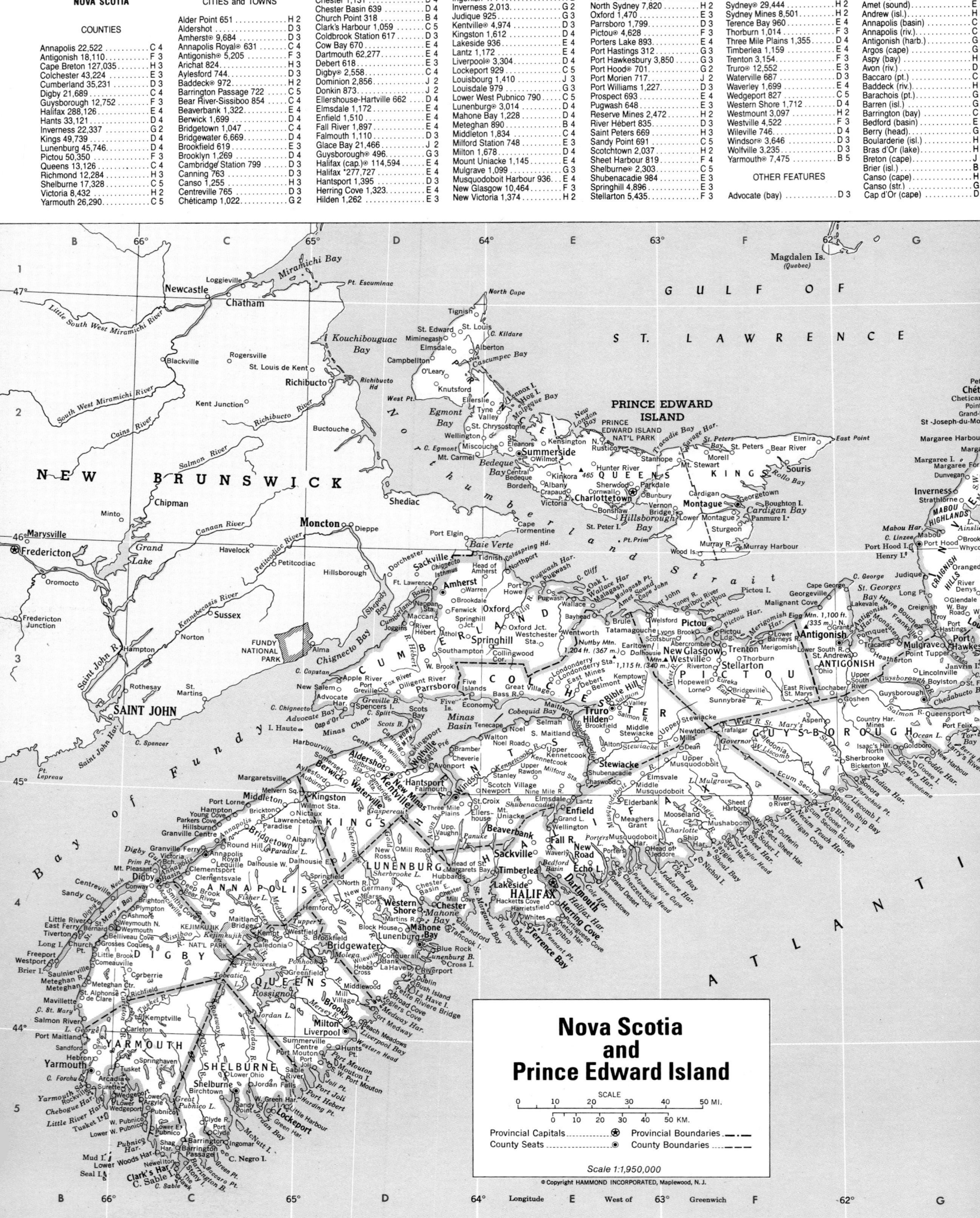

Nova Scotia and Prince Edward Island

SCALE

0   10   20   30   40   50 MI.

0   10   20   30   40   50 KM.

Provincial Capitals . . . . ⊛   Provincial Boundaries . . _ . . _ . .
County Seats . . . . ⊙   County Boundaries . . _ _ _ _ _

Scale 1:1,950,000

© Copyright HAMMOND INCORPORATED, Maplewood, N.J.

PRINCE EDWARD ISLAND
AREA 2,184 sq. mi. (5,657 sq. km.)
POPULATION 122,506
CAPITAL Charlottetown
LARGEST CITY Charlottetown
HIGHEST POINT 465 ft. (142 m.)
SETTLED IN 1720
ADMITTED TO CONFEDERATION 1873
PROVINCIAL FLOWER Lady's Slipper

NOVA SCOTIA
AREA 21,425 sq. mi. (55,491 sq. km.)
POPULATION 847,442
CAPITAL Halifax
LARGEST CITY Halifax
HIGHEST POINT Cape Breton Highlands 1,747 ft. (532 m.)
SETTLED IN 1605
ADMITTED TO CONFEDERATION 1867
PROVINCIAL FLOWER Trailing Arbutus or Mayflower

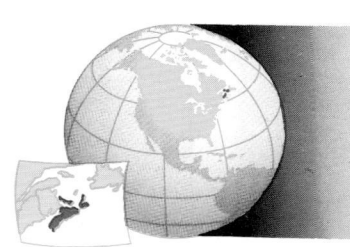

Topography

Scale: 0 — 30 — 60 MI.
0 — 30 — 60 KM.

Below Sea Level | 100 m. 328 ft. | 200 m. 656 ft. | 500 m. 1,640 ft. | 1,000 m. 3,281 ft. | 2,000 m. 6,562 ft. | 5,000 m. 16,404 ft.

Agriculture, Industry and Resources

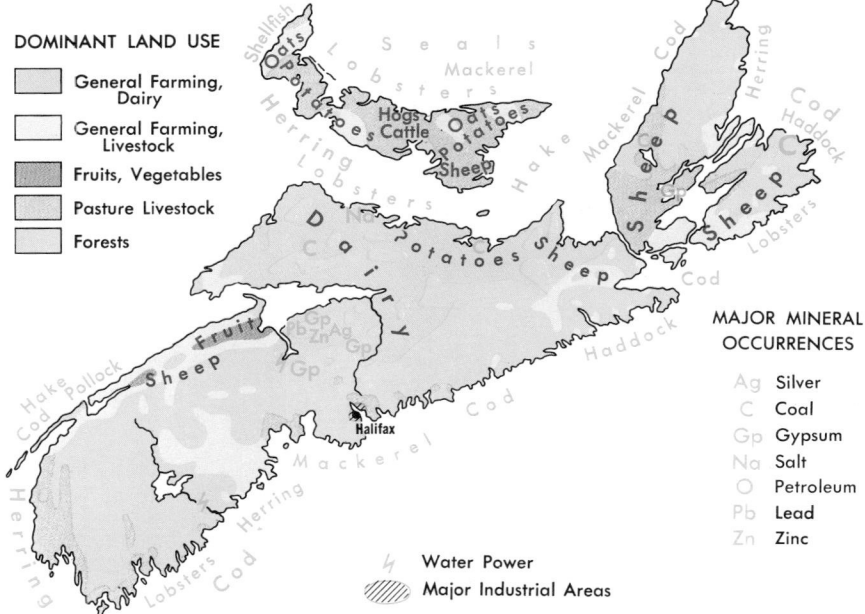

DOMINANT LAND USE

- General Farming, Dairy
- General Farming, Livestock
- Fruits, Vegetables
- Pasture Livestock
- Forests

MAJOR MINERAL OCCURRENCES

- Ag Silver
- C Coal
- Gp Gypsum
- Na Salt
- O Petroleum
- Pb Lead
- Zn Zinc

⚡ Water Power
▨ Major Industrial Areas

New Brunswick

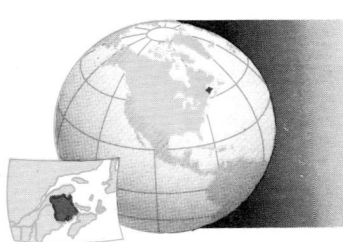

AREA   28,354 sq. mi. (73,437 sq. km.)
POPULATION   696,403
CAPITAL   Fredericton
LARGEST CITY   Saint John
HIGHEST POINT   Mt. Carleton 2,690 ft.
    (820 m.)
SETTLED IN   1611
ADMITTED TO CONFEDERATION   1867
PROVINCIAL FLOWER   Purple Violet

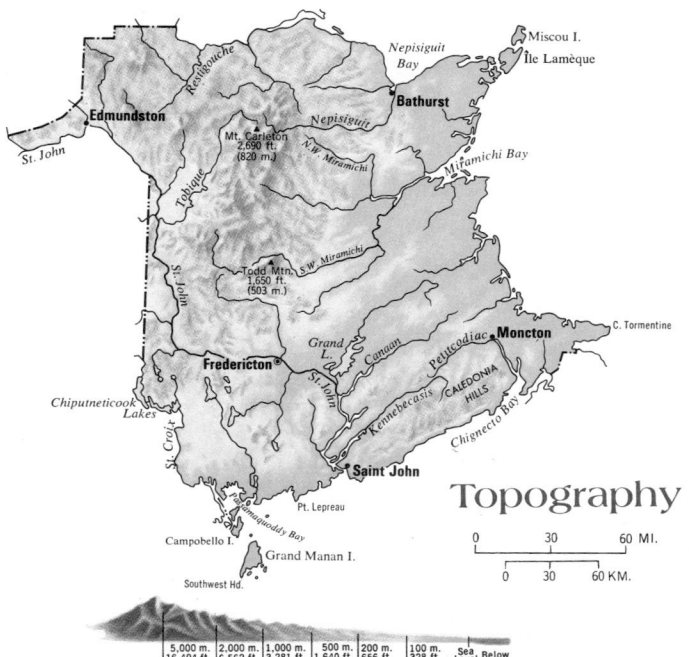

Topography

0   30   60 MI.

0   30   60 KM.

5,000 m. | 2,000 m. | 1,000 m. | 500 m. | 200 m. | 100 m. | Sea | Below
16,404 ft. | 6,562 ft. | 3,281 ft. | 1,640 ft. | 656 ft. | 328 ft. | Level

Agriculture, Industry and Resources

DOMINANT LAND USE

- Cereals, Livestock
- Dairy
- Potatoes
- General Farming, Livestock
- Pasture Livestock
- Forests

MAJOR MINERAL OCCURRENCES

Ag   Silver   Pb   Lead
C   Coal   Sb   Antimony
Cu   Copper   Zn   Zinc

⚡   Water Power
▨   Major Industrial Areas

Topography

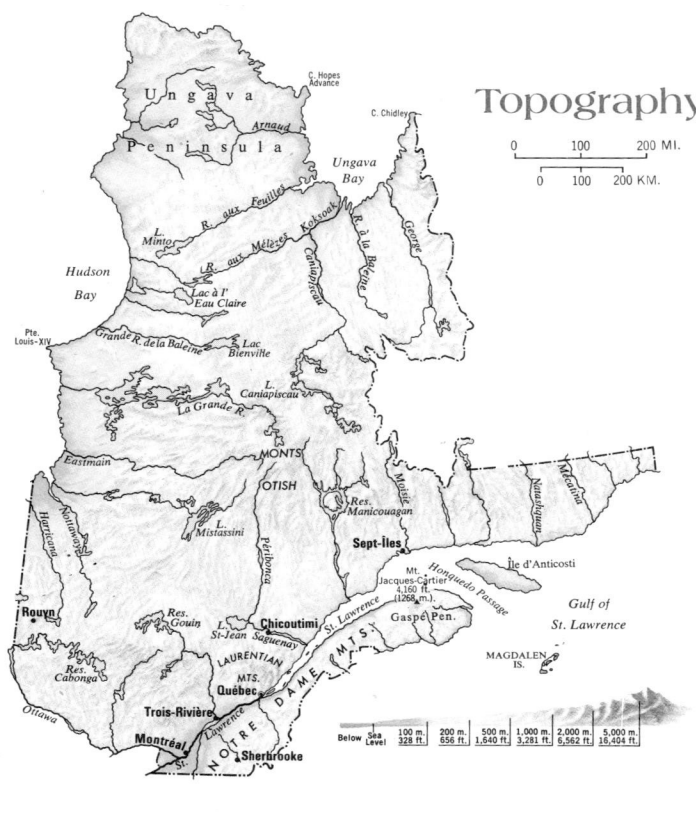

0 100 200 MI.

0 100 200 KM.

Below Sea Level | 100 m. 328 ft. | 200 m. 656 ft. | 500 m. 1,640 ft. | 1,000 m. 3,281 ft. | 2,000 m. 6,562 ft. | 5,000 m. 16,404 ft.

COUNTIES

Argenteuil 32,454	C 4
Arthabaska 59,277	F 3
Bagot 26,840	E 4
Beauce 73,427	G 3
Beauharnois 54,034	C 4
Bellechasse 23,559	G 3
Berthier 31,096	C 3
Bonaventure 40,487	C 2
Brome 17,436	E 4
Chambly 307,090	J 4
Champlain 119,595	D 4
Charlevoix-Est 17,448	G 2
Charlevoix-Ouest 14,172	G 2
Châteauguay 59,968	D 4
Chicoutimi 174,441	F 1
Compton 20,536	F 4
Deux-Montagnes 71,252	C 4
Dorchester 33,949	C 3
Drummond 69,770	E 4
Frontenac 26,814	G 4
Gaspé-Est 41,173	D 1
Gaspé-Ouest 18,943	C 1
Gatineau 54,229	B 3
Hull 131,213	B 4
Huntingdon 16,953	C 4
Iberville 23,180	D 4
Île-de-Montréal 1,760,122	H 4
Île-Jésus 268,335	H 4
Joliette 60,384	C 3
Kamouraska 28,642	H 2
Labelle 34,395	B 3
Lac-Saint-Jean-Est 47,891	F 1
Lac-Saint-Jean-Ouest 62,952	E 1
Laprairie 105,962	H 4
L'Assomption 109,705	D 4
Lévis 94,104	J 3
L'Islet 22,062	G 2
Lotbinière 29,653	F 3
Maskinongé 20,763	D 4
Matane 29,955	B 1
Matapédia 23,715	B 2
Mégantic 57,892	F 3
Missisquoi 36,161	D 4
Montcalm 27,557	C 3
Montmagny 25,622	G 3
Montmorency No. 1 23,048	F 2
Montmorency No. 2 6,436	F 3
Napierville 13,562	D 4
Nicolet 33,513	E 3
Papineau 37,975	B 4
Pontiac 20,283	A 3
Portneuf 58,843	E 3
Québec 458,980	F 3
Richelieu 53,058	D 4
Richmond 40,871	E 4
Rimouski 69,099	J 1
Rivière-du-Loup 41,250	H 2
Rouville 42,391	D 4
Saguenay 115,881	H 1
Saint-Hyacinthe 55,888	D 4
Saint-Jean 55,576	D 4
Saint-Maurice 107,703	D 3
Shefford 70,733	E 4
Sherbrooke 115,983	E 4

Agriculture, Industry and Resources

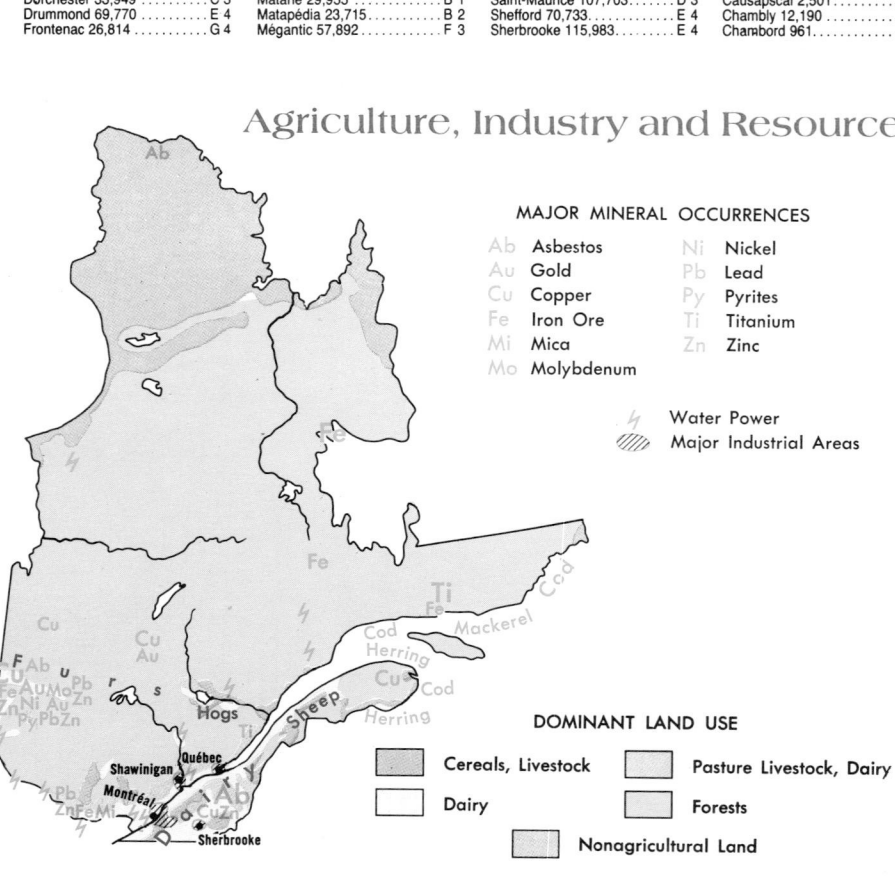

MAJOR MINERAL OCCURRENCES

Ab	Asbestos		Ni	Nickel
Au	Gold		Pb	Lead
Cu	Copper		Py	Pyrites
Fe	Iron Ore		Ti	Titanium
Mi	Mica		Zn	Zinc
Mo	Molybdenum			

⚡ Water Power

▨ Major Industrial Areas

DOMINANT LAND USE

▨ Cereals, Livestock

▨ Pasture Livestock, Dairy

☐ Dairy

▨ Forests

▨ Nonagricultural Land

(Index columns)

Soulanges 15,429	C 4
Stanstead 38,186	F 4
Témiscouata 52,570	J 2
Terrebonne 193,865	H 4
Vaudreuil 50,043	C 4
Verchères 63,353	J 4
Wolfe 15,635	F 4
Yamaska 14,797	E 3

CITIES and TOWNS

Acton Vale 4,371	E 4
Albanel 992	E 1
Alma◎ 26,322	F 1
Amqui◎ 4,048	B 2
Ancienne-Lorette 12,935	H 3
Angers	B 4
Anjou 37,346	H 4
Annaville 712	E 3
Armagh 878	G 3
Arthabaska◎ 6,827	F 3
Arvida	F 1
Asbestos 7,967	F 4
Ascot Corner 847	F 4
Audet 760	G 4
Ayer's Cliff◎ 810	E 4
Aylmer 26,695	B 4
Baie-Comeau 12,866	A 1
Baie-d'Urfé 3,674	G 4
Baie-Saint-Paul◎ 3,961	G 2
Baie-Trinité 749	B 1
Beaconsfield 19,613	H 4
Beauceville 4,302	G 3
Beauharnois◎ 7,025	D 4
Beaumont 791	F 3
Beauport 60,447	J 3
Beaupré 2,740	G 2
Bécancour◎ 10,247	E 3
Bedford◎ 2,832	E 4
Beebe Plain 1,072	E 4
Bélair (Val-Bélair) 12,695	H 3
Beloeil 17,540	D 4
Bernierville 2,120	F 3
Berthier-en-Bas 562	G 3
Berthierville◎ 4,049	D 3
Bic 2,994	J 1
Biencourt 824	J 2
Black Lake 5,148	F 3
Blainville 14,682	H 4
Boischatel 3,345	J 3
Bois-des-Filion 4,943	H 4
Bolduc 1,565	G 4
Bonaventure 1,371	C 2
Boucherville 29,704	J 4
Bromont 2,731	E 4
Bromptonville 3,035	F 4
Brossard 52,232	H 4
Brownsburg 2,875	C 4
Buckingham 7,992	B 4
Cabano 3,291	J 2
Cacouna 1,160	H 2
Calumet 612	C 4
Candiac 8,502	J 4
Cap-à-l'Aigle 819	G 2
Cap-Chat 3,464	B 1
Cap-de-la-Madeleine 32,626	E 3
Caplan-Rivière Caplan 1,139	C 2
Cap-Saint-Ignace 1,485	G 2
Cap-Santé 671	F 3
Carignan 4,544	J 4
Carleton 2,710	C 2
Causapscal 2,501	B 2
Chambly 12,190	J 4
Chambord 961	E 1
Chandler 3,946	D 2
Charlemagne 4,827	H 4
Charlesbourg 68,326	J 3
Charny 8,240	J 3
Châteauguay 36,928	H 4
Château-Richer◎ 3,628	F 3
Chénéville 633	B 4
Chicoutimi◎ 60,064	G 1
Chicoutimi-Jonquière *135,172	G 1
Chute-aux-Outardes 2,280	A 1
Clermont 3,621	G 2
Coaticook 6,271	F 4
Coleraine 1,660	F 4
Compton 728	F 4
Contrecoeur 5,449	D 4
Cookshire◎ 1,480	F 4
Coteau-du-Lac 1,247	C 4
Coteau-Landing◎ 1,386	C 4
Côte-Saint-Luc 27,531	H 4
Courcelles 608	G 4
Courville	J 3
Cowansville 12,240	E 4
Crabtree 1,950	D 4
Danville 2,200	E 4
Daveluyville 1,257	E 3
Deauville 942	E 4
Dégelis 3,477	J 2
Delisle 4,011	F 1
Delson 4,935	H 4
Desbiens 1,541	E 1
Deschaillons-sur-Saint-Laurent 950	E 3
Deschambault 977	E 3
Deschênes	B 4
Deux-Montagnes 9,944	H 4
Didyme 667	E 1
Disraëli 3,181	F 4
Dolbeau 8,766	E 1
Dollard-des-Ormeaux 39,940	H 4
Donnacona 5,731	F 3
Dorion 5,749	C 4
Dorval 17,727	H 4
Dosquet 703	F 3
Douville	D 4
Drummondville◎ 27,347	E 4
Drummondville-Sud 9,220	E 4
Dunham 2,887	E 4
Durham-Sud 1,045	E 4
East Angus 4,016	F 4
East Broughton 1,397	F 4
East Broughton Station 1,302	F 3
Eastman 612	E 4
Entrelacs 1,735	C 3
Farnham 6,498	E 4
Ferme-Neuve 2,266	B 3
Forestville 4,271	H 1
Frampton 824	G 3
Francoeur 1,422	F 3
Gaspé 17,261	D 1
Gatineau 74,988	B 4
Giffard	J 3
Girardville 1,128	E 1
Gracefield 869	A 3
Granby 38,069	E 4
Grand'Mère 15,442	E 3
Grande-Rivière 4,420	D 2
Grandes-Bergeronnes 748	H 1
Grande-Vallée 700	D 1
Greenfield Park 18,527	J 4
Grenville 1,417	C 4
Gros-Morne 672	C 1
Hampstead 7,598	H 4
Ham-Sud◎ 62	F 4
Hauterive 13,995	A 1
Hébertville 2,515	F 1
Hébertville-Station 1,442	F 1
Hemmingford 737	D 4
Henryville 595	D 4
Howick 639	D 4
Hudson 4,414	C 4
Hull 56,225	B 4
Huntingdon◎ 3,018	C 4
Île-Perrot 5,945	G 4
Iberville◎ 8,587	D 4
Inverness◎ 329	F 3
Joliette◎ 16,987	D 3
Jonquière 60,354	F 1
Jonquière-Chicoutimi *135,172	F 1
Kingsey Falls 818	E 4
Kirkland 10,476	H 4
Knowlton (Lac-Brome)◎ 4,316	E 4
La Baie 20,935	G 1
Labelle 1,534	C 3
Lac-à-la-Croix 1,017	F 1
Lac-Alouette-Lac-Brière 1,356	D 4
Lac-au-Saumon 1,332	B 2
Lac-aux-Sables 838	E 3
Lac-Beauport 3,123	F 3
Lac-Bouchette 1,703	E 1
Lac-Carré 717	C 3
Lac-des-Écorces 766	B 3
Lac-Drolet 1,120	G 4
Lac-Etchemin 2,729	G 3
Lachenaie 8,631	D 4
Lachine 37,521	H 4
Lachute◎ 11,729	C 4
Lac-Mégantic◎ 6,119	G 4
Lacolle 1,319	D 4
Lac-Saint-Charles 5,837	H 3
Lafontaine 4,799	C 4
La Guadeloupe 1,692	F 4
La Malbaie 4,030	G 2
Lambton 1,559	F 4
L'Annonciation 2,384	C 3
Lanoraie (Lanoraie-d'Autry) 1,613	D 4
La Pêche 4,977	B 4
La Pérade 1,039	E 3
La Pocatière 4,560	H 2
La Prairie◎ 10,627	J 4
La Providence	E 4
Larouche 662	F 1
La Salle 76,299	H 4
Maria 1,178	C 2
L'Ascension 1,287	F 1
L'Assomption◎ 4,844	D 4
La Station-du-Coteau 892	C 4
Laterrière 788	F 1
La Tuque 11,556	E 2
Laurentides 1,947	D 4
Laurier-Station 1,123	F 3
Laurierville 939	F 3
Lauzon 13,362	J 3
Laval 268,335	H 4
Lavaltrie 2,053	D 4
L'Avenir 1,116	E 4
Lawrenceville 562	E 4
Le Moyne 6,137	J 4
L'Épiphanie 2,971	D 4
Léry 2,239	H 4
Lévis 17,895	J 3
Lennoxville 3,922	F 4
Les Méchins 803	B 1
Linière 1,168	G 3
L'Islet 1,070	G 2
L'Islet-sur-Mer 774	G 2
L'Isle-Verte 1,142	G 1
Longueuil 124,320	J 4
Loretteville◎ 15,060	H 3
Lorraine 6,881	H 4
Louiseville◎ 3,735	E 3
Luceville 1,524	J 1
Lyster 830	F 3
Magog 13,604	E 4
Maniwaki◎ 5,424	B 3
Manseau 626	E 3
Maple Grove 2,009	H 4
Marieville◎ 4,877	D 4
Mascouche 20,345	H 4
Maskinongé 1,005	E 3
Masson 4,264	B 4
Massueville 671	E 4
Matane◎ 13,612	B 1
Matapédia 586	C 2
Melocheville 1,892	C 4
Mercier 6,352	H 4
Metabetchouan 3,406	F 1
Mirabel◎ 14,080	H 4
Mistassini 6,682	E 1
Montauban 557	E 3
Mont-Carmel 807	H 2
Montcerf 570	A 3
Montebello 1,229	B 4
Mont-Joli 6,359	J 1
Montmagny◎ 12,405	G 3
Montréal◎ 980,354	H 4
Montréal *2,828,349	H 4
Montréal-Est 3,778	J 4
Montréal-Nord 94,914	H 4
Mont-Rolland 1,517	C 4
Mont-Royal 19,247	H 4
Mont-Saint-Hilaire 10,066	D 4
Morin Heights 592	C 4
Murdochville 3,396	C 1
Nantes 1,167	F 4

Québec Southern Part

SCALE

0 5 10 20 30 40 MI.

0 5 10 20 30 40 KM.

Scale 1:2,250,000

National Capital ⊛
Provincial Capital ⊛
County Seats ◉
International Boundaries ———

Provincial & State Boundaries ———
County Boundaries ———

Napierville⊙ 2,343 .... D 4
Neuville 996 .... F 3
New Carlisle⊙ 1,292 ...... D 2
New Richmond 4,257 ...... C 2
Nicolet 4,880 .... E 3
Nominingue 881 .... B 3
Normandin 4,041 .... E 1
North Hatley 689 .... H 4
Notre-Dame-de-la-Doré 1,064 .. E 1
Notre-Dame-des-Laurentides .. H 3
Notre-Dame-des-Prairies
6,150 .... D 3
Notre-Dame-du-Bon-Conseil
1,089 .... E 4
Notre-Dame-du-Lac⊙ 2,258 .. J 2
Nouvelle 669 .... C 2
Oka 1,538. .... E 4
Omerville 1,398 .... E 4
Ormstown 1,659 .... D 4
Orsainville .... H 3
Otis 673 .... G 1
Otterburn Park 4,268 ..... H 4
Outremont 24,338 .... H 4
Pabos 1,295 .... D 2
Pabos-Mills 1,565 .... D 2
Papineauville⊙ 1,481 ..... C 4
Paspébiac 1,914 .... D 2
Percé⊙ 4,839 .... D 1
Petit-Cap 1,023 .... H 3
Petite-Matane 1,065 ...... B 1
Petit-Saguenay (Saint-
François-d'Assise) 804 ... G 1
Pierrefonds 38,390 ...... H 4
Pierreville 1,212 .... E 3

Pincourt 8,750 .... D 4
Pintendre 1,849 .... J 3
Plaisance 748 .... B 4
Plessisville 7,249 .... F 3
Pohénégamooke 3,702 ... H 2
Pointe-à-la-Croix 1,481 ... C 2
Pointe-au-Père 796 ..... J 1
Pointe-au-Pic 1,054 ..... G 2
Pointe-aux-Outardes 1,056.. A 1
Pointe-aux-Trembles 36,270 .. J 4
Pointe-Calumet 2,935 .... G 4
Pointe-Claire 24,571 ..... H 4
Pointe-Gatineau .... B 4
Pointe-Lebel 1,573 ...... A 1
Pont-Rouge 3,580 .... F 3
Port-Alfred 8,621 .... G 1
Portneuf 1,333 .... F 3
Portneuf-sur-Mer (Rivière-
Portneuf-sur-Mer) 1,255 .. H 1
Price 2,273. .... A 1
Princeville 4,023 .... E 3
Proulxville 588 .... F 4
Québec (cap.) 166,474 ... H 3
Québec *576,075 .... H 3
Quyon 744 .... A 4
Rawdon 2,958 .... D 3
Repentigny 34,419 ...... J 4
Richelieu 1,832 .... D 4
Richmond⊙ 3,568 ...... E 3
Rigaud 2,268 .... C 4
Rimouski 29,120 .... J 1
Rimouski-Est 2,506 ..... J 1
Ripon 620 .... B 4

Rivière-à-Pierre 615 ..... E 3
Rivière-au-Renard 2,211 .. D 1
Rivière-Bleue 1,690 ..... J 2
Rivière-Bois-Clair 604 ... F 3
Rivière-du-Loup 13,459 .. H 2
Rivière-du-Moulin .... G 1
Rivière-Éternité 659 ..... G 1
Rivière-Portneuf-Portneuf-sur-
Mer 1,255 .... H 1
Robertsonville 1,987 .... F 3
Roberval⊙ 11,429 ...... E 1
Rock Island 1,179 ...... E 4
Rosemère 7,778 .... H 4
Rougemont 972 .... D 4
Roxboro 6,292 .... H 4
Roxton Falls 1,245 ..... E 4
Sacré-Coeur-de-Saguenay
1,678 .... H 1
Saint-Adelme 618 ...... B 1
Saint-Adelphe 1,159 .... E 3
Saint-Adolphe-d'Howard
1,686. .... C 4
Saint-Adrien 597 ...... F 4
Saint-Agapitville 2,954 .. F 3
Saint-Aimé-des-Lacs 861 .. G 2
Saint-Alban 673. ...... E 3
Saint-Alexandre-de-
Kamouraska 1,048 .... H 2
Saint-Alexis-des-Monts 1,984. D 3
Saint-Amable 2,424 .... J 4
Saint-Ambroise 3,606 ... F 1
Saint-Anaclet 1,377 .... J 1
Saint-André-Avellin 1,312 .. B 4
Saint-André-Est 1,293 ... C 4

Saint-Anselme 1,808 .... F 3
Saint-Antoine 7,012 .... H 4
Saint-Antonin 941 ..... H 2
Saint-Aubert 884 ...... G 2
Saint-Augustin-de-Québec
2,475 .... E 3
Saint-Basile-Sud 1,719 .. F 3
Saint-Basile-le-Grand 7,658 .. J 4
Saint-Benjamin 1,027 ... G 3
Saint-Bernard 585 ...... F 2
Saint-Bernard-sur-Mer 711 .. G 2
Saint-Boniface-de-Shawinigan
3,164 .... D 3
Saint-Bruno 2,580 ..... F 1
Saint-Bruno-de-Montarville
22,880 .... J 4
Saint-Camille-de-Bellechasse
1,744 .... G 3
Saint-Casimir 1,133 .... E 3
Saint-Césaire 2,935 .... D 4
Saint-Charles 1,019 .... G 3
Saint-Charles-de-Mandeville
1,392 .... D 3
Saint-Chrysostome 1,018 .. D 4
Saint-Côme 660 .... D 3
Saint-Constant 9,938 ... H 4
Saint-Cyprien 860 ..... J 2
Saint-Cyrille 1,041 ..... E 4
Saint-Damien-de-Buckland
1,522 .... G 3
Saint-David 5,380 ..... D 4
Saint-David-de-Falardeau
1,876 .... F 1
Saint-Denis 861 .... D 4

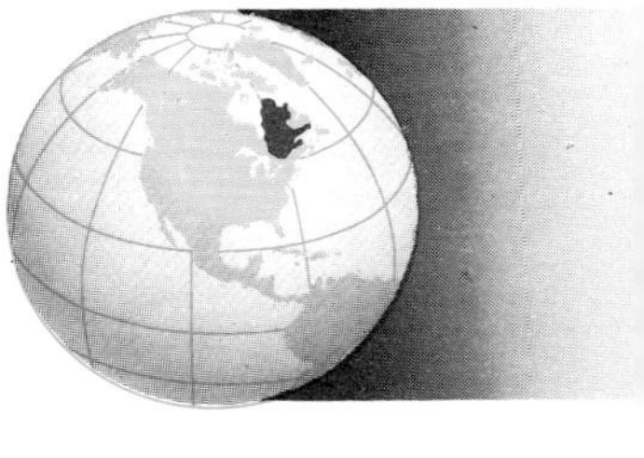

Saint-Dominique 2,068 ..... E 4
Saint-Donat-de-Montcalm
1,521 .... C 3
Sainte-Adèle 4,675 ...... C 4
Sainte-Agathe 709 ...... F 3
Sainte-Agathe-des-Monts
5,641 .... C 3
Sainte-Anne-de-Beaupré
3,292 .... F 2
Sainte-Anne-de-Bellevue
3,981 .... H 4
Sainte-Anne-des-Monts⊙
6,062 .... C 1
Sainte-Anne-des-Plaines
4,258 .... H 4
Sainte-Anne-du-Lac 686 .. B 3
Sainte-Aurélie 1,045. .... G 3
Sainte-Blandine 849 ..... J 1

Sainte-Catherine 1,474 .... F 3
Sainte-Claire 1,566. ...... G 3
Sainte-Croix 1,814 .... F 3
Sainte-Félicité 711 .... B 1
Sainte-Foy 68,883 .... H 3
Sainte-Geneviève 2,573 ... H 4
Sainte-Geneviève-de-
Batiscan⊙ 356 .... E 3
Sainte-Hélène-de-Bagot
1,328 .... E 4
Sainte-Hénédine⊙ 639 ... F 3
Sainte-Julie-de-Verchères
14,343 .... J 4
Sainte-Julienne⊙ 750 .... D 4
Sainte-Justine 1,080 ..... G 3
Saint-Élie 639 .... E 3
Saint-Elzéar 743 .... F 3
Sainte-Marie 8,937 ..... G 3

Sainte-Martine⊙ 2,196 .... D 4
Saint-Émile 5,216. ...... H 3
Sainte-Monique 705 ..... F 1
Sainte-Perpétue-de-l'Islet
1,232 .... H 2
Saint-Éphrem-de-Tring 973 .. G 3
Saint-Épiphane 647 ..... H 2
Sainte-Pudentienne 866 ... E 4
Sainte-Rosalie 2,862 .... E 4
Saint-Esprit 1,068. ...... D 4
Sainte-Thérèse 18,750 ... H 4
Sainte-Thérèse-Ouest
(Boisbriand) 13,471 .... H 4
Sainte-Thècle 1,703 ..... E 3
Saint-Étienne-de-Grès 845.. E 3
Saint-Étienne-de-Lauzon
1,218 .... J 3

AREA 594,857 sq. mi. (1,540,680 sq. km.)
POPULATION 6,438,403
CAPITAL Québec
LARGEST CITY Montréal
HIGHEST POINT Mont D'Iberville 5,420 ft.
(1,652 m.)
SETTLED IN 1608
ADMITTED TO CONFEDERATION 1867
PROVINCIAL FLOWER White Garden Lily

Gaspé Peninsula

0 5 10 20 30 40 MI.

0 5 10 20 30 40 KM.

COUNTIES
(indicated by numbers:)

No.	County	Grid
1	Iberville	D4
2	Napierville	D4
3	Rouville	D4
4	St-Hyacinthe	D4
5	Île-de-Montréal	D4
6	Deux-Montagnes	C4
7	Laprairie	D4
8	Beauharnois	D4
9	Châteauguay	D4
10	Île-Jésus	C4
11	Richelieu	D4
12	Vaudreuil	C4

Internal divisions represent Municipal Counties

© Copyright HAMMOND INCORPORATED, Maplewood, N.J.

Saint-Eustache 29,716......H 4
Saint-Fabien 1,361......J 1
Saint-Félicien 9,058......E 1
Saint-Félix-de-Valois 1,462..D 3
Saint-Ferréol-les-Neiges
 1,758......G 2
Saint-Flavien 734......F 3
Saint-François-de-Sales 831..E 1
Saint-Gilles® 942..E 4
Saint-Fulgence 950......G 1
Saint-Gabriel-de-Rimouski
 779......J 1
Saint-Gédéon, Frontenac
 1,569......F 4
Saint-Gédéon, Lac-St-Jean-E.
 1,000......F 1
Saint-Georges, Beauce
 10,342......G 4
Saint-Georges, Champlain
 3,344......E 3
Saint-Georges-Ouest 6,378..G 3
Saint-Germain-de-Grantham
 1,373......E 4
Saint-Gervais 973......F 3
Saint-Gilles 912......E 4
Saint-Grégoire (Mont-St-
 Grégoire)® 740......D 4
Saint-Henri 1,970......J 3
Saint-Honoré, Beauce 1,116..G 4
Saint-Honoré, Chicoutimi
 1,790......F 1
Saint-Hubert 60,573......J 4
Saint-Hubert-de-Témiscouata
 871......J 2
Saint-Hyacinthe® 38,246...D 4
Saint-Isidore 811......F 3
Saint-Isidore-de-Laprairie 769 D 4
Saint-Jacques 2,152......D 4
Saint-Jacques-le-Mineur
 1,203......H 4
Saint-Jean-Chrysostome
 6,930......J 3
Saint-Jean-de-Dieu 1,377...J 1
Saint-Jean-de-Matha 931...D 3
Saint-Jean-Port-Joli 1,813..G 2
Saint-Jean-sur-Richelieu®
 35,640......D 4
Saint-Jérôme 25,123......H 4
Saint-Joachim 1,139......G 2
Saint-Joseph-de-Beauce
 3,216......G 3
Saint-Joseph-de-Sorel 2,545.C 3
Saint-Jovite 3,841......C 3
Saint-Lambert 20,557......J 4
Saint-Laurent 65,900......H 4

Saint-Lazare 731......G 3
Saint-Léonard 79,429......H 4
Saint-Léonard-d'Aston 992..E 3
Saint-Léon-de-Chicoutimi 749 F 1
Saint-Léon-de-Standon 816..G 3
Saint-Léon-le-Grand 722....B 2
Saint-Liboire® 746......E 4
Saint-Louis-de-Gonzague
 615......D 4
Saint-Louis-de-Terrebonne
 14,172......H 4
Saint-Louis-du-Ha! Ha! 809..H 2
Saint-Luc 8,815......D 4
Saint-Luc-de-Matane 598...B 1
Saint-Marc-des-Carrières
 925......F 3
Saint-Méthode-de-Frontenac
 963......G 3
Saint-Michel-de-Bellechasse
 1,584......F 3
Saint-Michel-des-Saints
 962......D 3
Saint-Nazaire-de-Chicoutimi
 962......F 1
Saint-Nérée 970......G 3
Saint-Nicolas 5,074......J 3
Saint-Noël 666......B 1
Saint-Odilon 580......G 3
Saint-Omer 718......C 2
Saint-Ours 625......D 4
Saint-Pacôme 1,996......H 2
Saint-Pamphile 3,428......H 3
Saint-Pascal® 2,763......H 2
Saint-Paul-de-Montminy 602..G 3
Saint-Paulin 663......D 3
Saint-Paul-l'Ermite (Le
 Gardeur) 8,312......J 4
Saint-Philippe-de-Néri 715...H 2
Saint-Pie 1,725......E 4
Saint-Pierre 5,305......H 4
Saint-Pierre-d'Orléans 880...G 3
Saint-Polycarpe 602......C 4
Saint-Prime 2,522......E 1
Saint-Prosper-de-Dorchester
 2,150......G 3
Saint-Raphaël® 1,346......G 3
Saint-Raymond 3,605......F 3
Saint-Rédempteur 4,463....J 3
Saint-Régis 1,370......C 4
Saint-Rémi 5,146......D 4
Saint-Roch-de-l'Achigan
 1,160......D 4
Saint-Roch-de-Richelieu
 1,650......D 4
Saint-Romuald-d'Etchemin®
 9,849......J 3

Saint-Sauveur-des-Monts
 2,348......C 4
Saint-Siméon 1,152......G 2
Saint-Simon 602......H 1
Saint-Stanislas 1,443......E 3
Saint-Sylvère 1,006......E 3
Saint-Timothée 2,113......D 4
Saint-Tite 3,031......E 3
Saint-Tite-des-Caps 626....G 2
Saint-Ubald 1,605......E 3
Saint-Urbain-de-Charlevoix
 1,079......G 2
Saint-Victor 1,104......G 3
Saint-Zacharie 1,284......G 3
Saint-Zotique 1,774......C 4
Sault-au-Mouton 828......H 1
Sawyerville 939......F 4
Sayabec 1,721......B 2
Scotstown 762......F 4
Senneville 1,221......G 4
Shannon 3,488......F 3
Shawbridge 942......E 3
Shawinigan 23,011......E 3
Shawinigan-Sud 11,325......E 3
Shawville 1,608......A 4
Sherbrooke® 74,075......E 4
Sherrington 614......D 4
Sillery 12,825......J 3
Sorel® 20,347......D 4
Squatec 1,000......J 2
Stanstead Plain 1,093......E 4
Sutton 1,599......E 4
Tadoussac® 900......H 1
Templeton......B 4
Terrebonne 11,769......H 4
Thetford Mines 19,965......F 3
Thurso 2,780......B 4
Tourelle (Tourelle-Grand-
 Tourelle) 942......C 1
Tourville 659......H 2
Tracy 12,843......D 3
Tring-Jonction 1,315......F 3
Trois-Pistoles 4,445......H 1
Trois-Rivières 50,466......E 3
Trois-Rivières *111,453......E 3
Trois-Rivières-Ouest 13,107..E 3
Upton 926......E 4
Val-Barrette 609......B 3
Val-Brillant 687......B 1
Valcourt 2,601......E 4
Val-David 2,336......C 3
Vallée-Jonction 1,200......G 3
Valleyfield (Salaberry-de-
 Valleyfield) 29,574......C 4
Vanier 10,725......J 3

Varennes 8,764......J 4
Vaudreuil® 4,473......J 4
Verchères® 4,473......J 4
Verdun 61,287......H 4
Victoriaville 21,838......F 3
Villeneuve......H 4
Warwick 2,847......F 3
Waterloo® 4,664......E 4
Waterville 1,397......F 4
Weedon-Centre 1,263......F 4
Westmount 20,480......H 4
Wickham 2,043......E 4
Windsor 5,233......E 4
Wottonville 673......F 4
Yamachiche 1,258......E 3

OTHER FEATURES

Alma (isl.)......F 1
Aylmer (lake)......F 4
Baskatong (res.)......B 3
Batiscan (riv.)......E 2
Bécancour (riv.)......F 3
Bonaventure (isl.)......D 1
Bonaventure (riv.)......C 1
Brome (lake)......E 4
Brompton (lake)......E 4
Cascapédia (riv.)......C 1
Chaleur (bay)......C 2
Champlain (lake)......D 4
Chaudière (riv.)......G 4
Chic-Chocs (mts.)......C 1
Chicoutimi (riv.)......F 2
Coudres (isl.)......G 2
Deschênes (lake)......A 4
Deux Montagnes (lake)......H 4
Ditton (riv.)......F 4
Forillon Nat'l Park......D 1
Fort Chambly Nat'l Hist. Park J 4
Gaspé (bay)......D 1
Gaspé (cape)......D 1
Gaspé (pen.)......D 2
Gaspésie Prov. Park......C 1
Gatineau (riv.)......B 3
Îles (lake)......B 3
Jacques-Cartier (mt.)......C 1
Jacques-Cartier (riv.)......F 2
Kénogami (lake)......F 1
Kiamika (lake)......B 3
La Maurice Nat'l Park......D 3
Laurentides Prov. Park......D 3
Lièvre (riv.)......B 4
Lièvres (isl.)......H 2
Maskinongé (riv.)......D 3
Matane (riv.)......B 1
Matane Prov. Park......B 1

Matapédia (riv.)......B 2
Mégantic (lake)......G 4
Memphremagog (lake)......E 4
Mercier (dam)......A 3
Métabetchouane (riv.)......F 1
Mille Îles (riv.)......H 4
Montmorency (riv.)......F 2
Mont-Tremblant Prov. Park..C 3
Nicolet (riv.)......E 3
Nominingue (lake)......B 3
Nord (riv.)......C 4
Orléans (isl.)......F 3
Ottawa (riv.)......B 3
Ouareau (riv.)......D 3
Ouelle (riv.)......H 2
Patapédia (riv.)......B 2
Péribonca (riv.)......F 1
Petite Nation (riv.)......B 4
Prairies (riv.)......H 4
Rimouski (riv.)......J 1
Ristigouche (riv.)......B 2
Saguenay (riv.)......G 1
Sainte-Anne (lake)......F 1
Sainte-Anne (riv.)......G 2
Saint-François (lake)......F 4
Saint-François (riv.)......E 1
Saint-Jean (lake)......E 1
Saint Lawrence (gulf)......D 2
Saint Lawrence (riv.)......H 1
Saint-Louis (lake)......H 4
Saint-Maurice (riv.)......E 2
Saint-Pierre (lake)......E 3
Shawinigan (riv.)......E 3
Shipshaw (riv.)......F 1
Soeurs (isl.)......H 4
Témiscouata (lake)......H 2
Tremblant (lake)......C 3
Trente et un Milles (lake)....B 3
Verte (isl.)......H 1
Yamaska (riv.)......E 4
York (riv.)......D 1

®County seat.
*Population of metropolitan area.

QUÉBEC, NORTHERN

INTERNAL DIVISIONS

Abitibi (county) 93,529......B 3
Abitibi (terr.)......B 3
Berthier (county) 31,096....D 3
Bonaventure (county) 40,487.D 3
Champlain (county) 119,595..C 3
Charlevoix-Est (co.) 17,448..C 3

Charlevoix-Ouest (county)
 14,172......C 3
Chicoutimi (county) 174,441..C 2
Gaspé-Est (county) 41,173...E 3
Gaspé-Ouest (county) 18,943 D 3
Gatineau (county) 54,229....B 3
Joliette (county) 60,384.....C 3
Lac-Saint-Jean-Est (county)
 47,891......C 3
Lac-Saint-Jean-Ouest
 (county) 62,952......C 3
Maskinongé (county) 20,763..C 3
Matane (county) 29,955......D 3
Matapédia (county) 23,715...D 3
Mistassini (terr.)......B 3
Montcalm (county) 27,557...B 3
Montmorency No. I (county)
 23,048......C 3
Nouveau-Québec (terr.)......E 1
Pontiac (county) 20,283.....B 3
Portneuf (county) 58,843....C 3
Québec (county) 458,980....C 3
Rimouski (county) 69,099....D 3
Saguenay (county) 115,881..D 2
Saint-Maurice (co.) 107,703..C 3
Témiscamingue (co.) 52,570..B 3

CITIES and TOWNS

Alma® 26,322......C 3
Amos® 9,421......B 3
Baie-Comeau 12,866......D 3
Baie-du-Poste 1,690......C 2
Chicoutimi® 60,064......C 3
Gaspé 17,261......E 3
Hauterive 13,995......D 3
Jonquière 60,354......C 3
Lévis 17,895......C 3
La Tuque 11,556......C 3
Manicouagan......D 3
Maniwaki® 5,424......B 3
Matane® 13,612......D 3
Mistassini (Baie-du-Poste)
 1,690......C 2
Mont-Laurier® 8,405......B 3
Montmagny 12,405......C 3
New Carlisle® 781......B 3
Nouveau-Comptoir......B 2
Percé® 4,839......E 3
Port-Cartier-Ouest......D 3
Port-Menier® 275......E 3
Povungnituk 745......E 1
Québec (cap.)® 166,474....C 3
Rimouski® 29,120......D 3
Rivière-au-Tonnerre 480.....D 2
Rivière-du-Loup 13,459......D 3

Rouyn 17,224......B 3
Sept-Îles 29,262......D 2
Seven Islands (Sept-Îles)
 29,262......D 2
Shawinigan 23,011......C 3
Tadoussac 900......C 3
Val d'Or 21,371......B 3
Ville-Marie 2,651......B 3

OTHER FEATURES

Allard (riv.)......E 2
Anticosti (isl.)......E 3
Baleine, Grand Rivière de la
 (riv.)......B 3
Bell (riv.)......B 3
Betsiamites (riv.)......C 3
Bienville (lake)......C 2
Broadback (riv.)......B 3
Cabonga (res.)......B 3
Caniapiscau (riv.)......D 1
Eastmain (riv.)......B 3
Eau Claire (lake)......C 1
Feuilles (riv.)......C 1
Gaspésie Prov. Park......F 2
George (riv.)......C 1
Gouin (res.)......B 3
Grande Rivière, La (riv.)....B 2
Honguedo (passage)......E 3
Hudson (bay)......A 1
Hudson (str.)......C 1
Jacques-Cartier (passage)...D 3
James (bay)......A 2
Koksoak (riv.)......C 1
Laurentides Prov. Park......C 3
Louis-XIV (pt.)......A 2
Manicouagan (res.)......D 2
Minto (lake)......E 1
Mistassibi (riv.)......C 2
Mistassini (riv.)......C 2
Moisie (riv.)......D 2
Natashquan (riv.)......D 2
Nottaway (riv.)......B 2
Nouveau-Québec (crater)....F 1
Otish (mts.)......C 2
Ottawa (riv.)......B 3
Péribonca (riv.)......C 3
Plétipi (lake)......C 2
Saguenay (riv.)......C 3
Saint-Jean (lake)......C 3
Saint Lawrence (gulf)......D 3
Saint Lawrence (riv.)......D 3
Ungava (pen.)......E 1

®County seat.
*Population of metropolitan area.

© Copyright HAMMOND INCORPORATED, Maplewood, N.J.

Northern Québec

SCALE
0   50   100   150   200 MI.
0   50   100   150   200 KM.

Provincial Capital............⊛   Provincial Boundaries....—..—
County Seats...................○   County Boundaries..........——
International Boundaries....—···—   Territorial Boundaries.....——

Scale 1:8,400,000

ONTARIO, NORTHERN

INTERNAL DIVISIONS

Algoma (terr. dist.) 133,553...D 3
Cochrane (terr. dist.) 96,875...C 2
Kenora (terr. dist.) 59,421...C 2
Manitoulin (terr. dist.) 11,001...D 3
Nipissing (terr. dist.) 80,268...E 3
Parry Sound (terr. dist.)
33,528...E 3
Rainy River (terr. dist.) 22,798...B 3
Renfrew (county) 87,484...E 3
Sudbury (reg. munic.)
159,779...D 3
Sudbury (terr. dist.) 27,068...D 3
Thunder Bay (terr. dist.)
153,997...C 3
Timiskaming (terr. dist.)
41,288...D 3

CITIES and TOWNS

Chalk River 1,010...E 3
Elliot Lake 16,723...D 3
Fort Albany 482...D 2
Fort Frances⊙ 8,906...B 3
Kapuskasing 12,014...D 3
Kenora⊙ 9,817...B 3
Kirkland Lake 12,219...D 3
Moose Factory 1,452...D 2
Moosonee 1,433...D 2
Nickel Centre 12,318...D 3
North Bay⊙ 51,268...E 3
Pembroke⊙ 14,026...E 3
Sault Sainte Marie⊙ 82,697...D 3
Sudbury 91,829...D 3
Thunder Bay⊙ 112,486...C 3
Timmins 46,114...D 3
Valley East 20,433...D 3

OTHER FEATURES

Abitibi (lake)...E 3
Abitibi (riv.)...D 2
Albany (riv.)...C 2
Algonquin Prov. Park...E 3
Asheweig (riv.)...C 2
Attawapiskat (lake)...C 2
Attawapiskat (riv.)...C 2
Basswood (lake)...B 3
Berens (riv.)...A 2
Big Trout (lake)...B 2
Black Duck (riv.)...C 1
Bloodvein (riv.)...A 2
Caribou (lake)...C 3

Cobham (riv.)...A 2
Eabamet (lake)...C 2
Ekwan (riv.)...C 2
English (riv.)...B 2
Fawn (riv.)...C 2
Finger (lake)...B 2
Georgian (bay)...D 3
Hannah (bay)...D 2
Henrietta Maria (cape)...D 1
Hudson (bay)...D 1
Huron (lake)...D 3
James (bay)...D 2
Kapiskau (riv.)...D 2
Kapuskasing (riv.)...D 3
Kenogami (riv.)...C 2
Kesagami (riv.)...E 2
Lake of the Woods (lake)...B 3
Lake Superior Prov. Park...D 3
Little Current (riv.)...C 2
Long (lake)...C 3
Manitoulin (isl.)...D 3
Mattagami (lake)...D 3
Michipicoten (isl.)...D 3
Mille Lacs (lake)...B 3
Missinaibi (lake)...D 3
Missinaibi (riv.)...D 2
Missisa (lake)...C 2
Nipigon (lake)...C 3
Nipissing (lake)...E 3
North (chan.)...D 3
North Caribou (lake)...B 2
Nungesser (lake)...B 2
Ogidaki (mt.)...D 3
Ogoki (riv.)...C 3
Opazatika (riv.)...D 3
Opinnagau (riv.)...D 2
Otoskwin (riv.)...B 2
Ottawa (riv.)...E 3
Pipestone (riv.)...B 2
Polar Bear Prov. Park...C 2
Pukaskwa Prov. Park...C 3
Quetico Prov. Park...B 3
Rainy (lake)...B 3
Red (lake)...B 2
Sachigo (lake)...B 2
Saganaga (lake)...B 3
Saint Ignace (isl.)...C 3
Saint Joseph (lake)...B 2
Sandy (lake)...B 2
Savant (lake)...B 2
Seine (riv.)...B 3
Seul (lake)...B 2
Severn (lake)...B 2
Severn (riv.)...B 2
Shamattawa (riv.)...C 2
Shibogama (lake)...C 2

Sibley Prov. Park...C 3
Slate (isls.)...C 3
Stout (lake)...B 2
Superior (lake)...C 3
Sutton (lake)...D 2
Sutton (riv.)...D 2
Timagami (lake)...D 3
Timiskaming (lake)...E 3
Trout (lake)...B 2
Wabuk (pt.)...D 1
Winisk (lake)...C 2
Winisk (riv.)...C 2
Winnipeg (riv.)...A 2
Woods (lake)...B 3

ONTARIO

INTERNAL DIVISIONS

Algoma (terr. dist.) 133,553...J 5
Brant (county) 104,427...D 4
Bruce (county) 60,020...C 3
Cochrane (terr. dist.) 96,875...J 4
Dufferin (county) 31,145...D 3
Dundas (county) 18,946...J 2
Durham (reg. munic.) 283,639 F 3
Elgin (county) 69,707...C 5
Essex (county) 312,467...B 5
Frontenac (county) 108,133...H 3
Glengarry (county) 20,254...K 2
Grenville (county) 27,176...J 3
Grey (county) 73,824...D 3
Haldimand-Norfolk (reg.
munic.) 89,456...E 5
Haliburton (county) 11,361...F 2
Halton (reg. munic.) 253,883...E 4
Hamilton-Wentworth (reg.
munic.) 411,445...D 4
Hastings (county) 106,883...G 3
Huron (county) 56,127...C 4
Kenora (terr. dist.) 59,421...G 5
Kent (county) 107,022...B 5
Lambton (county) 123,445...B 5
Lanark (county) 45,676...H 3
Leeds (county) 53,765...H 3
Lennox and Addington
(county) 33,040...G 3
Manitoulin (terr. dist.) 11,001...B 2
Middlesex (county) 318,184...C 4
Muskoka (dist. munic.)
38,370...E 3
Niagara (reg. munic.) 368,288 E 4
Nipissing (terr. dist.) 80,268...E 3
Northumberland (county)
64,966...G 3

Ottawa-Carleton (reg. munic.)
546,849...J 2
Oxford (county) 85,920...D 4
Parry Sound (terr. dist.)
33,528...D 2
Peel (reg. munic.) 490,731...E 4
Perth (county) 66,096...C 4
Peterborough (county)
102,452...F 3
Prescott (county) 30,365...K 2
Prince Edward (county)
22,336...G 3
Rainy River (terr. dist.) 22,798 G 5
Renfrew (county) 87,484...G 2
Russell (county) 22,412...J 2
Simcoe (county) 225,071...E 3
Stormont (county) 61,927...K 2
Sudbury (reg. munic.)
159,779...K 6
Sudbury (terr. dist.) 27,068...J 5
Thunder Bay (terr. dist.)
153,997...H 5
Timiskaming (terr. dist.)
41,288...K 5
Toronto (metro. munic.)
2,137,395...K 4
Victoria (county) 47,854...F 3
Waterloo (reg. munic.)
305,496...D 4
Wellington (county) 129,432...D 4
York (reg. munic.) 252,053...E 4

CITIES and TOWNS

Ailsa Craig 765...C 4
Ajax 25,475...J 4
Alban 342...D 1
Alexandria 3,271...K 2
Alfred 1,057...K 2
Alliston 4,712...E 3
Almonte 3,855...H 2
Alvinston 736...B 5
Amherstburg 5,685...A 5
Amherst View 6,110...H 3
Ancaster 14,428...D 4
Angus 3,085...E 3
Apsley 264...F 3
Arkona 473...C 4
Armstrong 378...H 4
Arnprior 5,828...H 2
Aroland 291...H 4
Arthur 1,700...D 4
Astorville 340...E 1
Athens 948...J 3
Atherley 366...E 3
Atikokan 4,452...G 5

Atwood 723...D 4
Aurora 16,267...J 3
Avonmore 273...K 2
Aylmer 5,254...C 5
Ayr 1,295...D 4
Ayton 424...D 3
Baden 945...D 4
Bala 577...E 2
Bancroft 2,329...G 2
Barrie⊙ 38,423...E 3
Barry's Bay 1,216...G 2
Batawa 430...G 3
Bath 1,071...H 3
Bayfield 649...C 4
Beachburg 682...H 2
Beachville 917...D 4
Beardmore 583...H 5
Beaverton 1,952...E 3
Beeton 1,989...E 3
Belle River 3,561...B 5
Belleville⊙ 34,881...G 3
Belmont 831...C 5
Bethany 365...F 3
Bewdley 508...F 3
Binbrook 306...E 4
Blackstock 720...F 3
Blenheim 4,044...C 5
Blind River 3,444...J 5
Bloomfield 718...G 4
Blyth 926...C 4
Bobcaygeon 1,625...F 3
Bonfield 540...E 1
Bothwell 915...C 5
Bourget 1,057...J 2
Bracebridge⊙ 9,063...E 2
Bradford 7,370...E 3
Braeside 492...H 2
Brampton⊙ 149,030...J 4
Brantford⊙ 74,315...D 4
Bridgenorth 1,633...F 3

Brigden 635...B 5
Brighton 3,147...G 3
Britt 419...D 2
Brockville⊙ 19,896...J 3
Bruce Mines 635...J 5
Brussels 962...C 4
Burford 1,461...D 4
Burgessville 302...D 4
Burk's Falls 922...E 2
Burlington 114,853...E 4
Cache Bay 665...D 1
Caesarea 551...F 3
Calabogie 256...H 2
Caledon 26,645...E 4
Callander 1,158...E 1
Cambridge 77,183...D 4
Campbellford 3,409...G 3
Cannington 1,623...E 3
Capreol 3,845...K 5
Caramat 265...H 5
Cardinal 1,753...J 3
Carleton Place 5,626...H 2
Carlisle 781...D 4
Carlsbad Springs 616...J 2
Carp 707...H 2
Cartier 590...J 5
Casselman 1,675...J 2
Castleton 346...F 3
Chalk River 1,010...G 1
Chapleau 3,243...J 5
Charing Cross 443...B 5
Chatham⊙ 40,952...B 5
Chatsworth 383...D 3
Cherry Valley 289...G 4
Chesley 1,840...C 3
Chesterville 1,430...J 2
Chute-à-Blondeau 365...K 2
City View...J 2
Clarence Creek 796...J 2
Clarksburg 508...D 3

Clifford 645...D 4
Clinton 3,081...C 4
Cobalt 1,759...K 5
Cobden 997...H 2
Coboconk 426...F 3
Cobourg⊙ 11,385...F 4
Cochrane⊙ 4,848...K 5
Colborne 1,796...G 4
Colchester 711...B 6
Coldwater 964...E 3
Collingwood 12,064...D 3
Comber 667...B 5
Consecon 295...G 3
Cookstown 918...E 3
Cornwall⊙ 46,144...K 2
Cottam 404...B 5
Courtland 647...D 5
Courtright 1,024...B 5
Crediton 370...C 4
Creemore 1,182...D 3
Crysler 540...J 2
Cumberland 518...J 2
Cumberland Beach-Bramshot-
Buena Vista 679...E 3
Dashwood 426...C 4
Deep River 5,095...G 1
Delaware 481...C 5
Delhi 4,043...D 5
Delta 360...H 3
Deseronto 1,740...G 3
Douglas 303...H 2
Drayton 809...D 4
Dresden 2,550...B 5
Drumbo 476...D 4
Dryden 6,640...G 4
Dublin 295...C 4
Dubreuilville △988...J 5
Dundalk 1,250...D 3
Dundas 19,586...D 4
Dungannon 284...C 4
Dunnville 11,353...E 5
Durham 2,458...D 3
Dutton 1,115...C 5
Earlton 1,028...K 5
East York 101,974...J 4
Echo Bay 786...J 5
Eden Mills 318...D 4
Eganville 1,245...G 2
Egmondville 465...C 4
Elgin 327...H 3
Elk Lake 526...K 5
Elliot Lake 16,723...B 1
Elmira 7,063...D 4
Elmvale 1,183...E 3
Elmwood 364...C 3
Elora 2,666...D 4
Embro 727...C 4
Embrun 1,883...J 2
Emeryville-Puce 1,611...B 5
Emo 762...F 5
Englehart 1,689...K 5
Enterprise 357...H 3
Erieau 430...C 5
Erin 2,313...D 4
Espanola 5,836...J 5
Essex 6,295...B 5
Etobicoke 298,713...J 4
Everett 570...E 3
Exeter 3,732...C 4
Fauquier 561...J 5
Fenelon Falls 1,701...F 3
Fergus 6,064...D 4
Field 462...E 1
Finch 353...J 2
Fingal 380...C 5
Fitzroy Harbour 446...H 2
Flesherton 565...D 3
Foleyet 484...J 5
Fordwich 365...C 4
Forest 2,671...C 4
Formosa 393...C 3
Fort Erie 24,096...E 5
Fort Frances⊙ 8,906...F 5
Foxboro 597...G 3
Frankford 1,919...G 3
Fraserdale 303...J 5
Freelton 307...D 4
Gananoque 4,863...H 3
Garden Village 270...E 1
Geraldton 2,956...H 5
Glencoe 1,694...C 5
Glen Miller 639...G 3
Glen Robertson 378...K 2
Glen Walter 710...K 2
Goderich⊙ 7,322...C 4
Gogama 652...J 5
Goodwood 335...E 3
Gore Bay⊙ 777...B 2
Gorrie 468...C 4
Grafton 409...G 4
Grand Bend 680...C 4
Grand Valley 1,226...D 4
Granton 315...C 4
Gravenhurst 8,532...E 3
Greely 567...J 2
Green Valley 459...K 2
Grimsby 15,797...E 4
Guelph⊙ 71,207...D 4

(continued on following page)

AREA 412,580 sq. mi. (1,068,582 sq. km.)
POPULATION 8,625,107
CAPITAL Toronto
LARGEST CITY Toronto
HIGHEST POINT in Timiskaming Dist.
2,275 ft. (693 m.)
SETTLED IN 1749
ADMITTED TO CONFEDERATION 1867
PROVINCIAL FLOWER White Trillium

Northern Ontario

SCALE

0 25 50   100   150   200 MI.

0 25 50   100   150 200 KM.

Provincial Capital ...... ⊛ Provincial and
County Seats ......⊙ State Boundaries ___·___
International Boundaries ___··___ County Boundaries ___·___

Scale 1:8,550,000

© Copyright HAMMOND INCORPORATED, Maplewood, N.J.

Longitude West B of Greenwich

Ontario
Central Part

© Copyright HAMMOND INCORPORATED, Maplewood, N.J.

Index (continued)

Saint Jacobs 1,189	D 4	
Saint Mary's 4,883	C 4	
Saint Thomas® 28,165	C 5	
Saint Williams 442	D 5	
Salem 825	D 4	
Sarnia® 50,892	B 5	
Sauble Beach 729	C 3	
Sault Sainte Marie® 82,697	J 5	
Scarborough 443,353	K 4	
Schomberg 923	J 3	
Schreiber 1,968	H 5	
Scotland 600	D 4	
Seaforth 2,114	C 4	
Searchmont 384	J 5	
Sebringville 579	C 4	
Seeleys Bay 503	H 3	
Shakespeare 602	D 4	
Shallow Lake 418	C 3	
Shannonville 314	H 3	
Shanty Bay 358	E 3	
Sharbot Lake 495	H 3	
Shedden 292	C 5	
Shelburne 2,862	D 3	
Simcoe® 14,326	D 5	
Sioux Lookout 3,074	G 4	
Sioux Narrows 394	F 5	
Smithfield 349	G 3	
Smiths Falls 8,831	H 3	
Smithville 1,936	E 4	
Smooth Rock Falls 2,352	J 5	
Sombra 420	B 5	
Southampton 2,830	C 3	
South Mountain 285	J 3	
South River 1,109	E 2	
Spanish 1,063	J 5	
Sparta 283	C 5	

Spencerville 438	J 3	
Springfield 555	C 5	
Springford 309	D 5	
Stayner 2,530	E 3	
Stirling 1,638	G 3	
Stittsville 2,652	J 2	
Stoney Creek 36,762	E 4	
Stoney Point 1,090	B 5	
Straffordville 752	D 5	
Stratford® 26,262	C 4	
Strathroy 8,748	C 5	
Sturgeon Falls 6,045	E 1	
Sudbury® 91,829	K 5	
Sudbury *149,923	K 5	
Sunderland 703	E 3	
Sundridge 734	E 2	
Sydenham 595	H 3	
Tamworth 402	H 3	
Tara 687	C 3	
Tavistock 1,885	D 4	
Tecumseh 6,364	B 5	
Teeswater 1,026	C 3	
Terrace Bay 2,639	H 5	
Thamesford 1,920	C 4	
Thamesville 961	C 5	
Thedford 694	C 4	
Thessalon 1,620	J 5	
Thornbury 1,435	D 3	
Thorndale 581	C 4	
Thornton 414	E 3	
Thorold 15,412	E 4	
Thunder Bay® 112,486	H 5	
Thunder Bay *121,379	H 5	
Tilbury 4,298	B 5	
Tillsonburg 10,487	D 5	
Timmins 46,114	J 5	

Tiverton 806	C 3	
Tobermory 282	C 2	
Toronto (cap.)® 599,217	K 4	
Toronto *2,998,947	K 4	
Tottenham 3,022	E 3	
Trenton 15,085	G 3	
Trout Creek 652	E 2	
Turkey Point 407	D 5	
Tweed 1,574	G 3	
Udora 375	E 3	
Union 485	C 5	
Uxbridge 4,209	E 3	
Valley East 20,433	J 5	
Vanier 18,792	J 2	
Vankleek Hill 1,774	K 2	
Vars 527	J 2	
Vaughan 29,674	J 4	
Vermilion Bay 505	G 4	
Verner 1,076	D 1	
Vernon 303	J 2	
Verona 754	H 3	
Victoria Harbour 1,125	E 3	
Vienna 369	D 5	
Virginiatown 1,010	K 5	
Vittoria 420	D 5	
Wabigoon 268	G 5	
Walden 10,139	J 5	
Walkerton® 4,682	C 3	
Wallaceburg 11,506	B 5	
Wardsville 450	C 5	
Warkworth 618	G 3	
Warren 579	D 1	
Warsaw 314	F 3	
Warsaw Beach 4,705	D 4	
Washago 569	E 3	
Waterloo 49,428	D 4	
Watford 1,402	C 5	
Waubaushene 878	E 3	
Wawa 4,206	J 5	
Webbwood 519	C 1	
Welcome 293	F 4	
Welland 454,448	E 5	
Wellesley 997	D 4	
Wellington 1,082	G 4	
Wendover 326	J 2	
West Lorne 1,258	C 5	
Westmeath 262	H 2	
Westport 621	H 3	
Wheatley 1,638	B 5	
Whitby® 36,698	F 4	
Whitchurch-Stouffville 13,557	J 3	
White River △1,006	J 5	
Whitney 766	F 2	
Wiarton 2,074	C 3	
Wikwemikong 1,030	C 2	
Williamsburg 407	J 3	
Williamsford 256	D 3	
Williamstown 328	K 2	
Winchester 2,001	J 2	
Windsor® 192,083	B 5	
Windsor *246,110	B 5	
Wingham 2,897	C 4	
Wolfe Island 271	H 3	
Woodstock® 26,603	D 4	
Woodville 575	F 3	
Wroxeter 350	C 4	
Wyoming 1,682	B 5	
Yarker 319	H 3	
York 134,617	J 4	
Zephyr 330	E 3	
Zurich 795	C 4	

OTHER FEATURES

Abitibi (riv.)	J 5	
Algonquin Prov. Park	F 2	
Amherst (isl.)	H 3	
Balsam (lake)	F 3	
Barrie (isl.)	B 1	
Bays (lake)	F 2	
Big Rideau (lake)	H 3	
Black (riv.)	E 3	
Bruce (pen.)	C 2	
Buckhorn (lake)	F 3	
Cabot (head)	C 2	
Charleston (lake)	J 3	
Christian (isl.)	D 3	
Clear (lake)	F 3	
Cockburn (isl.)	A 2	
Couchiching (lake)	E 3	
Croker (cape)	D 3	

Don (riv.)	J 4	
Doré (lake)	G 2	
Douglas (pt.)	C 3	
Erie (lake)	E 5	
Flowerpot (isl.)	C 2	
French (riv.)	D 1	
Georgian (bay)	D 2	
Georgian Bay Is.		
Nat'l Park	C 2, D 3	
Georgina (isl.)	E 3	
Grand (riv.)	D 4	
Humber (riv.)	J 3	
Hurd (cape)	C 2	
Huron (lake)	B 3	
Ipperwash Prov. Park	C 5	
Joseph (lake)	E 2	
Killarney Prov. Park	C 1	
Killbear Point Prov. Park	D 2	
Lake of the Woods (lake)	F 5	

Lake Superior Prov. Park	J 5	
Lonely (isl.)	C 2	
Long (pt.)	D 5	
Long Point (bay)	D 5	
Madawaska (riv.)	G 2	
Magnetawan (riv.)	D 2	
Main (chan.)	C 2	
Manitou (lake)	C 2	
Manitoulin (isl.)	B 2	
Mattagami (riv.)	J 5	
Michipicoten (isl.)	H 5	
Missinaibi (riv.)	J 5	
Mississagi (riv.)	A 1	
Mississippi (lake)	H 2	
Muskoka (lake)	E 2	
Niagara (riv.)	E 4	
Nipigon (lake)	H 5	
Nipissing (lake)	E 1	
North (chan.)	A 1	
Nottawasaga (bay)	D 3	
Ogidaki (mt.)	J 5	
Ontario (lake)	G 4	
Opeongo (lake)	F 2	
Ottawa (riv.)	H 2	
Owen (sound)	D 3	
Panache (lake)	C 1	
Parry (isl.)	D 2	
Parry (sound)	D 2	
Pelee (pt.)	B 6	
Petre (pt.)	G 4	
Point Pelee Nat'l Park	B 5	
Presqu'ile Prov. Park	G 4	
Pukaskwa Prov. Park	H 5	
Quetico Prov. Park	G 5	

Rainy (lake)	G 5	
Rice (lake)	F 3	
Rideau (lake)	H 3	
Rondeau Prov. Park	C 5	
Rosseau (lake)	E 2	
Saint Clair (lake)	B 5	
Saint Clair (riv.)	B 5	
Saint Lawrence (lake)	K 3	
Saint Lawrence (riv.)	J 3	
Saint Lawrence Is. Nat'l Park	J 3	
Saugeen (riv.)	C 3	
Scugog (lake)	F 3	
Seul (lake)	G 4	
Severn (riv.)	E 3	
Sibley Prov. Park	H 5	
Simcoe (lake)	E 3	
South (bay)	C 2	
Spanish (riv.)	C 1	
Stony (lake)	G 3	
Superior (lake)	H 5	
Sydenham (riv.)	B 5	
Thames (riv.)	B 5	
Theano (pt.)	J 5	
Thousand (isls.)	H 3	
Timagami (lake)	K 5	
Trout (lake)	E 1	
Vernon (lake)	E 2	
Walpole (isl.)	B 5	
Welland (canal)	E 5	
Woods (lake)	F 5	

®County seat.
*Population of metropolitan area.
△Population of town or township.

Topography

Scale: 0 — 100 — 200 MI. / 0 — 100 — 200 KM.

Below Sea Level | 100 m. 328 ft. | 200 m. 656 ft. | 500 m. 1,640 ft. | 1,000 m. 3,281 ft. | 2,000 m. 6,562 ft. | 5,000 m. 16,404 ft.

Ontario Southern Part

SCALE
0 10 20 30 40 50 MI.
0 10 20 30 40 50 KM.

National Capital ⊛ Provincial & State
Provincial Capital ⊛   Boundaries
County Seats ◉ County Boundaries – – –
International   Canals
Boundaries

Scale 1:2,620,000

Agriculture, Industry and Resources

DOMINANT LAND USE

- Cereals, Cash Crops, Livestock
- Dairy
- General Farming, Livestock
- Fruits, Vegetables
- Pasture Livestock
- Forests
- Nonagricultural Land

MAJOR MINERAL OCCURRENCES

Ab	Asbestos	Mg	Magnesium
Ag	Silver	Mr	Marble
Au	Gold	Na	Salt
Co	Cobalt	Ni	Nickel
Cu	Copper	Pb	Lead
Fe	Iron Ore	Pt	Platinum
G	Natural Gas	U	Uranium
Gr	Graphite	Zn	Zinc

⚡ Water Power
▨ Major Industrial Areas

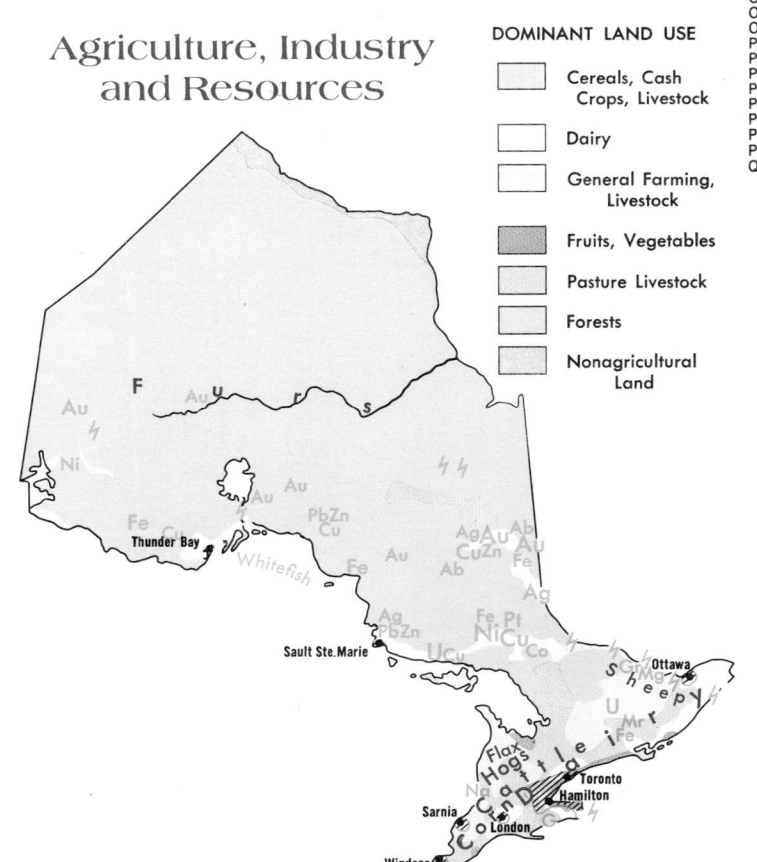

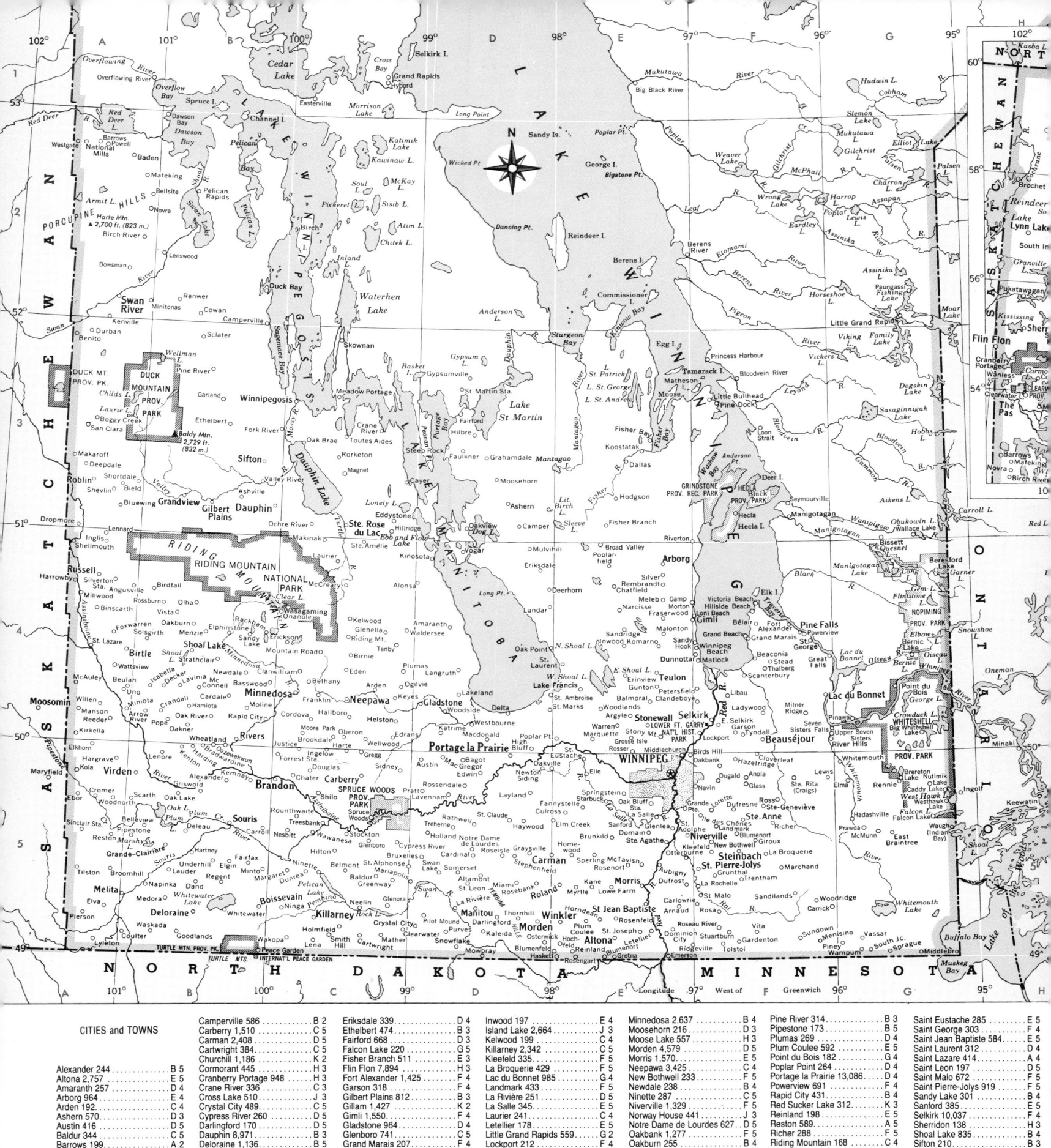

CITIES and TOWNS

Manitoba
Northern Part

0 40 80 120 MI.
0 40 80 120 KM.

HUDSON BAY

Manitoba
Southern Part

SCALE

0 5 10 20 40 60 MI.
0 5 10 20 40 60 KM.

Provincial Capital .... ✹
International Boundaries ─ ∙ ─ ∙ ─
Provincial Boundaries ─ ─ ─ ─

Scale 1:2,340,000

© Copyright HAMMOND INCORPORATED, Maplewood, N.J.

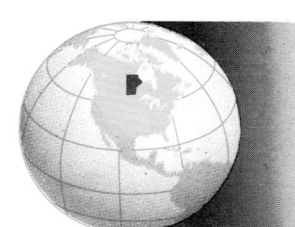

AREA 250,999 sq. mi. (650,087 sq. km.
POPULATION 1,026,241
CAPITAL Winnipeg
LARGEST CITY Winnipeg
HIGHEST POINT Baldy Mtn. 2,729 ft.
   (832 m.)
SETTLED IN 1812
ADMITTED TO CONFEDERATION 1870
PROVINCIAL FLOWER Prairie Crocus

The Pas 6,390	H 3
Thicket Portage 195	J 3
Thompson 14,288	J 2
Treherne 743	D 5
Tyndall 421	F 4
Virden 2,940	A 5
Vita 364	F 5
Wabowden 655	J 3
Wallace Lake ●2,044	G 3
Wanless 193	H 3
Warren 459	E 4
Waskada 239	B 5
Wawanesa 492	C 5
Whitemouth 320	F 4
Whitewater ●856	B 5
Winkler 5,046	E 5
Winnipeg (cap.) 564,473	E 5
Winnipeg *584,842	E 5
Winnipeg Beach 565	F 4
Winnipegosis 855	B 3
Woodlands 185	E 4
Wooodridge 170	G 5
York Landing 229	J 2

OTHER FEATURES

Aikens (lake)	G 3
Anderson (lake)	D 2
Anderson (pt.)	F 3
Armit (lake)	A 2
Assapan (riv.)	G 2
Assiniboine (riv.)	C 5
Assinika (lake)	G 2
Assinika (riv.)	G 2
Atim (lake)	C 2
Baldy (mt.)	B 3
Basket (lake)	C 3
Beaverhill (lake)	J 3
Berens (isl.)	E 2
Berens (riv.)	F 2
Bernic (lake)	G 4
Big Sand (lake)	H 2
Bigstone (lake)	J 3
Bigstone (pt.)	E 2
Bigstone (riv.)	J 3
Birch (isl.)	C 2
Black (isl.)	F 3
Black (riv.)	F 4
Bloodvein (riv.)	F 3
Bonnet (lake)	G 4
Buffalo (bay)	G 5
Burntwood (riv.)	J 2
Caribou (riv.)	J 1
Carroll (lake)	G 3
Cedar (lake)	B 1
Channel (isl.)	B 2
Charron (lake)	G 2
Childs (lake)	A 3
Chitek (lake)	C 2
Churchill (cape)	K 2
Churchill (riv.)	J 2
Clear (lake)	C 4
Clearwater Lake Prov. Park	H 3
Cobham (riv.)	G 1
Cochrane (riv.)	H 2
Commissioner (isl.)	E 2
Cormorant (lake)	H 3
Cross (bay)	C 1
Cross (lake)	J 3
Crowduck (lake)	G 4
Dancing (pt.)	D 2
Dauphin (lake)	C 3
Dauphin (riv.)	D 3
Dawson (bay)	B 2
Dog (lake)	D 3
Dogskin (lake)	F 3
Duck Mountain Prov. Park	B 3
Eardley (lake)	F 2

East Shoal (lake)	E 4
Ebb and Flow (lake)	C 3
Egg (isl.)	E 3
Elbow (lake)	G 4
Elk (isl.)	F 4
Elliot (lake)	G 2
Etawney (lake)	J 2
Etomami (riv.)	F 2
Falcon (lake)	G 5
Family (lake)	G 3
Fisher (bay)	E 3
Fisher (riv.)	E 3
Fishing (lake)	G 2
Flintstone (lake)	G 4
Fox (riv.)	K 2
Gammon (riv.)	G 3
Garner (lake)	G 4
Gem (lake)	G 4
George (isl.)	E 2
George (lake)	G 4
Gilchrist (creek)	F 2
Gilchrist (lake)	G 2
Gods (lake)	K 3
Gods (riv.)	K 3
Granville (lake)	H 2
Grass (riv.)	J 3
Grass River Prov. Park	H 3
Grindstone Prov. Rec. Park	F 3
Gunisao (lake)	F 3
Gypsum (lake)	D 3
Harrop (lake)	G 2
Harte (mt.)	A 2
Hayes (riv.)	K 3
Hecla (isl.)	F 3
Hecla Prov. Park	F 3
Hobbs (lake)	G 3
Horseshoe (lake)	G 2
Hubbart (pt.)	K 2
Hudson (bay)	K 2
Hudwin (lake)	G 1
Inland (lake)	C 2
International Peace Garden	B 5
Island (lake)	K 3
Katimik (lake)	C 2
Kawinaw (lake)	C 2
Kinwow (bay)	E 2
Kississing (lake)	H 2
Knee (lake)	J 3
Lake of the Woods (lake)	H 5
La Salle (riv.)	E 5
Laurie (lake)	A 3
Leaf (riv.)	F 2
Lewis (lake)	G 2
Leyond (riv.)	F 3
Little Birch (lake)	E 3
Lonely (lake)	C 3
Long (lake)	G 4
Long (pt.)	D 1
Long (pt.)	D 4
Manigotagan (lake)	G 4

Manigotagan (riv.)	G 3
Manitoba (lake)	D 4
Mantagao (riv.)	E 3
Marshy (lake)	B 5
McKay (lake)	C 2
McPhail (riv.)	F 2
Minnedosa (riv.)	B 4
Moar (lake)	G 2
Molson (lake)	J 3
Moose (isl.)	E 3
Morrison (lake)	C 1
Mossy (riv.)	C 3
Mukutawa (lake)	D 2
Mukutawa (riv.)	E 1
Muskeg (bay)	G 6
Nejanilini (lake)	J 1
Nelson (riv.)	J 2
Nopiming Prov. Park	G 4
Northern Indian (lake)	J 2
North Knife (lake)	J 2
North Seal (riv.)	H 2
North Shoal (lake)	E 4
Nueltin (lake)	H 1
Oak (lake)	B 5
Obukowin (lake)	G 3
Oiseau (lake)	G 4
Oiseau (riv.)	G 4
Overflow (bay)	A 1
Overflowing (riv.)	A 1
Owl (riv.)	K 2
Oxford (lake)	J 3
Paint (lake)	J 2
Palsen (riv.)	G 2
Pelican (bay)	B 2
Pelican (lake)	B 2
Pelican (lake)	C 5
Pembina (hills)	D 5
Pembina (riv.)	C 5
Peonan (pt.)	D 3
Pickerel (lake)	C 2
Pigeon (riv.)	F 2
Pipestone (creek)	A 5
Plum (creek)	B 5
Plum (lake)	B 5
Poplar (riv.)	F 2
Porcupine (hills)	A 2
Portage (bay)	D 3
Punk (isl.)	F 3
Quesnel (lake)	G 4
Rat (riv.)	F 5
Red (riv.)	F 4
Red Deer (lake)	A 2
Red Deer (riv.)	A 2
Reindeer (isl.)	E 2
Reindeer (lake)	H 2
Riding (mt.)	B 4
Riding Mountain Nat'l Park	B 4
Rock (lake)	C 5
Ross (isl.)	J 3
Sagemace (bay)	B 3

Saint Andrew (lake)	E 3
Saint George (lake)	E 3
Saint Martin (lake)	D 3
Saint Patrick (lake)	E 3
Sale (riv.)	E 5
Sandy (isls.)	D 2
Sasaginnigak (lake)	G 3
Seal (riv.)	J 2
Selkirk (isl.)	C 1
Setting (lake)	H 3
Shoal (lake)	G 5
Shoal (riv.)	B 2
Sipiwesk (lake)	J 3
Sisib (lake)	C 2
Sleeve (lake)	E 3
Slemon (lake)	G 1
Snowshoe (lake)	G 4
Soul (lake)	C 2
Souris (riv.)	B 5
Southern Indian (lake)	H 2
South Knife (riv.)	J 2
South Seal (riv.)	J 2
Split (lake)	J 2
Spruce (isl.)	B 1
Spruce Woods Prov. Park	C 5
Stevenson (lake)	J 3
Sturgeon (bay)	E 3
Swan (lake)	A 3
Swan (lake)	D 5
Swan (riv.)	A 3
Tadoule (lake)	J 2
Tamarack (isl.)	F 3
Tatnam (cape)	K 2
Traverse (bay)	F 4
Turtle (mts.)	B 5
Turtle (riv.)	C 3
Turtle Mountain Prov. Park	B 5
Valley (lake)	B 3
Vickers (lake)	F 3
Viking (lake)	G 3
Wanipigow (riv.)	G 3
Washow (bay)	F 3
Waterhen (lake)	C 2
Weaver (lake)	F 2
Wellman (lake)	B 3
West Hawk (lake)	G 5
West Shoal (lake)	E 4
Whitemouth (lake)	G 5
Whitemouth (riv.)	G 5
Whiteshell Prov. Park	G 4
Whitewater (lake)	B 5
Wicked (pt.)	D 2
Winnipeg (lake)	E 2
Winnipeg (riv.)	G 4
Winnipegosis (lake)	C 2
Woods (lake)	H 5
Wrong (lake)	F 2

*Population of metropolitan area.
●Population of rural municipality.

Topography

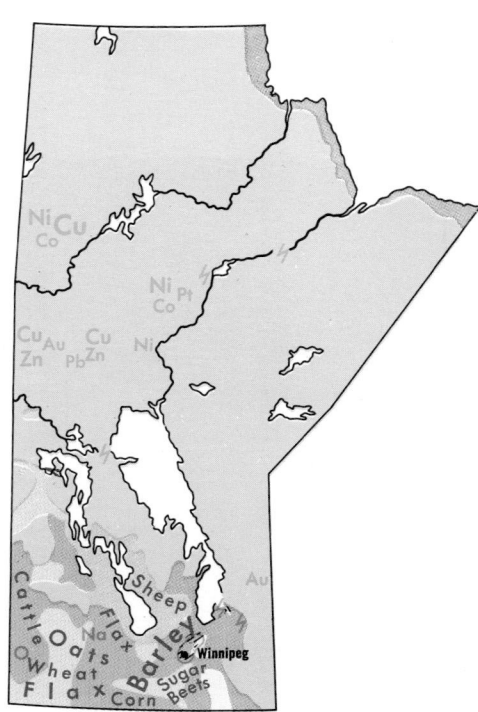

Below Sea Level 100 m. 328 ft. 200 m. 656 ft. 500 m. 1,640 ft. 1,000 m. 3,281 ft. 2,000 m. 6,562 ft. 5,000 m. 16,404 ft.

Agriculture, Industry and Resources

DOMINANT LAND USE

Cereals (chiefly barley, oats)

Cereals, Livestock

Dairy

Livestock

Forests

Nonagricultural Land

MAJOR MINERAL OCCURRENCES

Au Gold   Ni Nickel
Co Cobalt   O   Petroleum
Cu Copper   Pb Lead
Na Salt   Pt Platinum
               Zn Zinc

⚡ Water Power
▨ 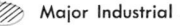 Major Industrial Areas

Topography

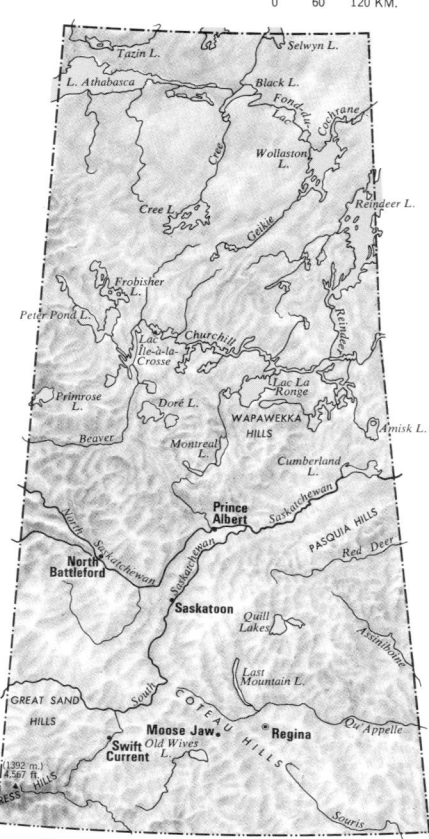

0   60   120 MI.
0   60   120 KM.

5,000 m. 16,404 ft. | 2,000 m. 6,562 ft. | 1,000 m. 3,281 ft. | 500 m. 1,640 ft. | 200 m. 656 ft. | 100 m. 328 ft. | Sea Level | Below

OTHER FEATURES

CITIES and TOWNS

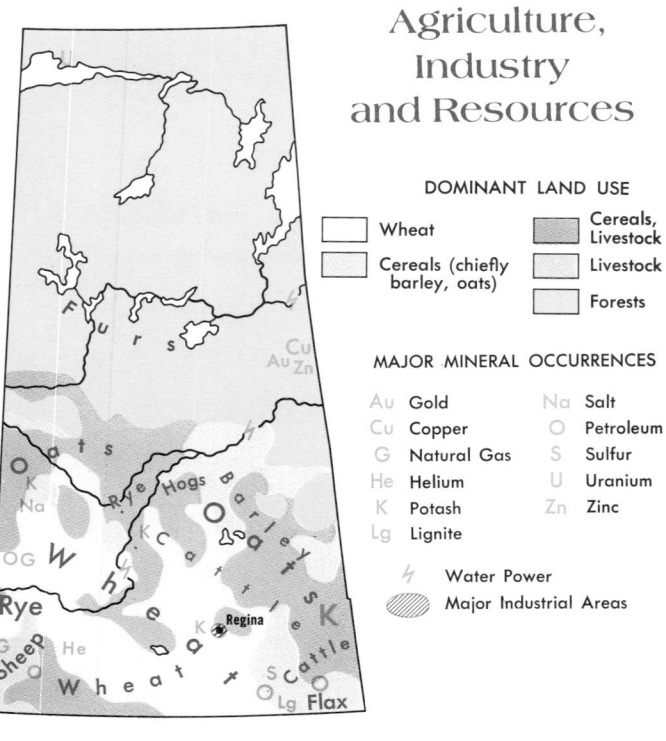

Agriculture, Industry and Resources

DOMINANT LAND USE

- Wheat
- Cereals (chiefly barley, oats)
- Cereals, Livestock
- Livestock
- Forests

MAJOR MINERAL OCCURRENCES

Au	Gold	Na	Salt
Cu	Copper	O	Petroleum
G	Natural Gas	S	Sulfur
He	Helium	U	Uranium
K	Potash	Zn	Zinc
Lg	Lignite		

⚡ Water Power
▨ Major Industrial Areas

AREA 251,699 sq. mi. (651,900 sq. km.)
POPULATION 968,313
CAPITAL Regina
LARGEST CITY Regina
HIGHEST POINT Cypress Hills 4,567 ft.
  (1,392 m.)
SETTLED IN 1774
ADMITTED TO CONFEDERATION 1905
PROVINCIAL FLOWER Prairie Lily

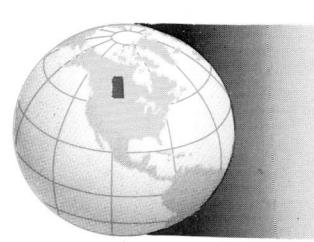

*Population of metropolitan area.
•Population of rural municipality.

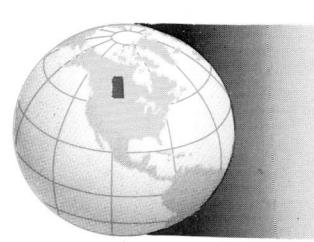

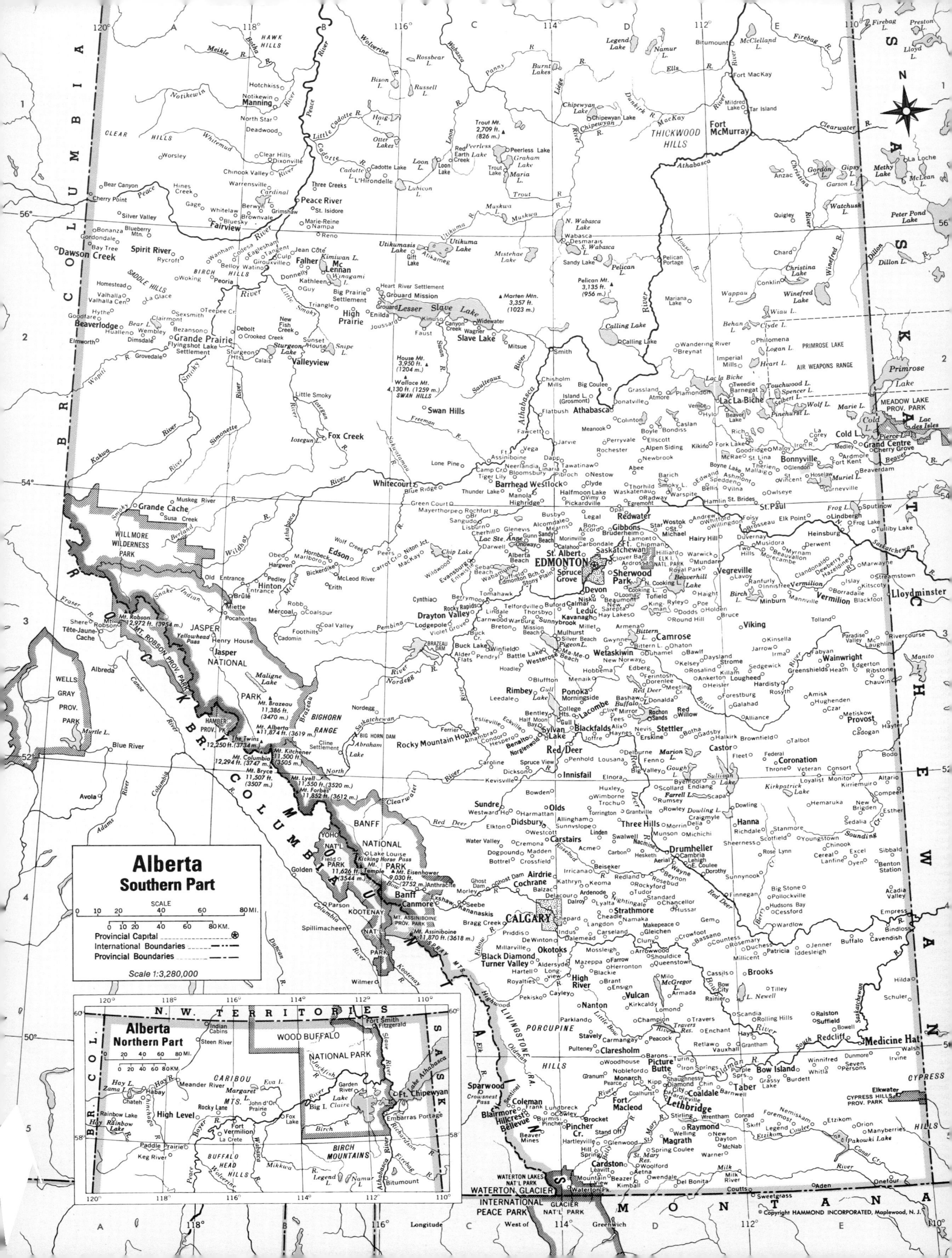

Alberta
Southern Part

SCALE

0 10 20 40 60 80 MI.

0 10 20 40 60 80 KM.

Provincial Capital . . . . ⊛
International Boundaries . . . . . . —·—
Provincial Boundaries . . . . —·—

Scale 1:3,280,000

Alberta
Northern Part

0 20 40 60 80 MI.

0 20 40 60 80 KM.

© Copyright HAMMOND INCORPORATED, Maplewood, N.J.

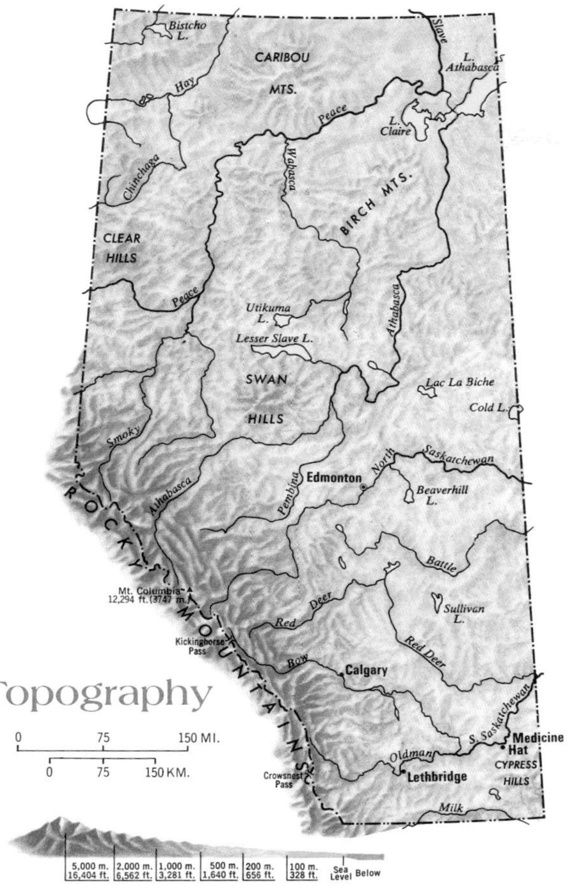
Bistcho L.
CARIBOU MTS.
Hay
Slave
L. Athabasca
Peace
L. Claire
Wabasca
BIRCH MTS.
Chinchaga
CLEAR HILLS
Peace
Utikuma L.
Lesser Slave L.
Athabasca
SWAN HILLS
Lac La Biche
Cold L.
Smoky
North Saskatchewan
Athabasca
Edmonton
Pembina
Beaverhill L.
Battle
Mt. Columbia 12,294 ft. (3747 m.)
Red Deer
Sullivan L.
Kickinghorse Pass
Red Deer
Bow
Calgary
ROCKY MOUNTAINS
S. Saskatchewan
Medicine Hat
CYPRESS HILLS
Oldman
Lethbridge
Crowsnest Pass
Milk
0 75 150 MI.
0 75 150 KM.
5,000 m. 16,404 ft.
2,000 m. 6,562 ft.
1,000 m. 3,281 ft.
500 m. 1,640 ft.
200 m. 656 ft.
100 m. 328 ft.
Sea Level
Below

Topography

AREA 255,285 sq. mi. (661,185 sq. km.)
POPULATION 2,237,724
CAPITAL Edmonton
LARGEST CITY Edmonton
HIGHEST POINT Mt. Columbia 12,294 ft. (3,747 m.)
SETTLED IN 1861
ADMITTED TO CONFEDERATION 1905
PROVINCIAL FLOWER Wild Rose

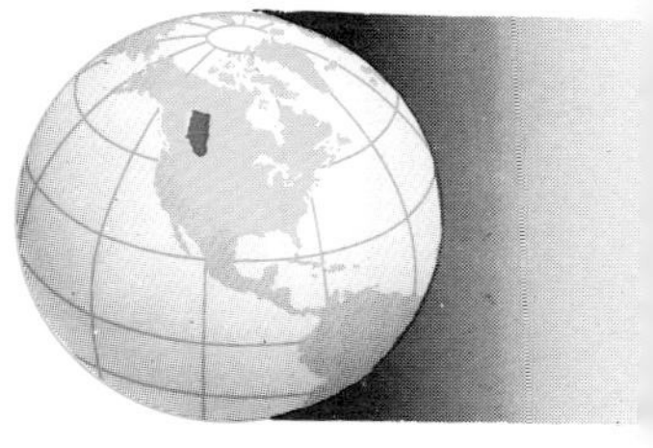

CITIES and TOWNS

Acme 457	D 4
Airdrie 8,414	C 4
Alberta Beach 485	C 3
Alix 837	D 3
Andrew 548	D 3
Antler Lake 334	D 3
Ardmore 224	E 2
Arrowwood 156	D 4
Athabasca 1,731	D 2
Banff 4,208	C 4
Barnwell 359	D 5
Barons 315	D 4
Barrhead 3,736	C 2
Bashaw 875	D 3
Bassano 1,200	D 4
Bawlf 350	D 3
Beaumont 2,638	D 3
Beaverlodge 1,937	A 2
Beiseker 580	D 4
Bentley 823	C 3
Berwyn 557	B 1
Big Valley 360	D 3
Black Diamond 1,444	C 4
Blackfalds 1,488	D 3
Blackfoot 220	E 3
Blackie 298	D 4
Bon Accord 1,376	D 3
Bonnyville 4,454	E 2
Bowden 989	C 4
Bow Island 1,491	E 5
Boyle 638	D 2
Bragg Creek 505	C 4
Breton 552	C 3
Brooks 9,421	E 4
Bruce 88	E 3
Bruderheim 1,136	D 3
Burdett 220	E 5
Calgary 592,743	C 4
Calgary *592,743	C 4
Calmar 1,003	D 3
Camrose 12,570	D 3
Canmore 3,484	C 4
Carbon 434	D 4
Cardston 3,267	D 5
Carmangay 266	D 4
Caroline 436	C 3
Carseland 484	D 4
Carstairs 1,587	D 4
Castor 1,123	D 3
Cereal 249	E 4
Champion 339	D 4
Chauvin 298	E 3
Chipman 266	D 3
Clairmont 469	A 2
Claresholm 3,493	D 4
Clive 364	D 3
Clyde 364	D 2
Coaldale 4,579	D 5
Coalhurst 882	D 5
Cochrane 3,544	C 4
Cold Lake 2,110	E 2
College Heights 267	D 3
Consort 632	E 3
Cooking Lake 218	D 3
Coronation 1,309	E 3
Coutts 400	D 5
Cowley 304	D 5
Cremona 382	C 4
Crossfield 1,217	C 4
Daysland 679	D 3
Delburne 574	D 3
Desmarais 260	D 2
Devon 3,885	D 3
Didsbury 3,095	C 4
Donalda 280	D 3
Donnelly 336	B 2
Drayton Valley 5,042	C 3
Drumheller 6,508	D 4
Duchess 429	E 4
East Coulee 218	D 4
Eckville 870	C 3
Edgerton 387	E 3
Edmonton (cap.) 532,246	D 3
Edmonton *657,057	D 3
Edmonton Beach 280	C 3
Edson 5,835	B 3
Elk Point 1,022	E 3
Elnora 249	D 3
Entwistle 462	C 3
Erskine 259	D 3
Evansburg 779	C 3
Exshaw 353	C 4
Fairview 2,869	A 1
Falher 1,102	B 2
Faust 399	C 2
Foremost 568	E 5
Forestburg 924	E 3
Fort Assiniboine 207	C 2
Fort Chipewyan 944	C 5
Fort Macleod 3,139	D 5
Fort McKay 267	E 1
Fort McMurray 31,000	E 1
Fort Saskatchewan 12,169	D 3
Fort Vermilion 752	B 5
Fox Creek 1,978	B 2
Fox Lake 634	B 5
Gibbons 2,276	D 3
Gift Lake 428	C 2
Girouxville 325	B 2
Gleichen 381	D 4
Glendon 430	E 2
Glenwood 259	D 5
Grand Centre 3,146	E 2
Grande Cache 4,523	A 3
Grande Prairie 24,263	A 2
Granum 399	D 5
Grimshaw 2,316	B 1
Grouard Mission 221	C 2
Hanna 2,806	E 4
Hardisty 641	E 3
Hay Lakes 302	D 3
Heisler 212	D 3
High Level 2,194	A 5
High Prairie 2,506	B 2
High River 4,792	D 4
Hines Creek 575	A 1
Hinton 8,342	B 3
Holden 430	D 3
Hughenden 267	E 3
Hythe 639	A 2
Innisfail 5,247	D 3
Innisfree 255	E 3
Irma 474	E 3
Irricana 558	D 4
Irvine 360	E 5
Jasper 3,269	B 3
John d'Or Prairie 437	B 5
Joussard 330	B 2
Killam 1,005	E 3
Kinuso 285	C 2
Kitscoty 497	E 3
Lac La Biche 2,007	E 2
Lacombe 5,591	D 3
La Crete 479	B 5
Lake Louise 355	B 4
Lamont 1,563	D 3
Leduc 12,471	D 3
Legal 1,022	D 3
Lethbridge 54,072	D 5
Linden 407	D 4
Little Buffalo Lake 253	B 1
Lloydminster 8,997	E 3
Longview 301	C 4
Lougheed 226	E 3
Lundbreck 244	C 5
Magrath 1,576	D 5
Manning 1,173	B 1
Mannville 788	E 3
Marlboro 211	B 3
Marwayne 500	E 3
Mayerthorpe 1,475	C 3
McLennan 1,125	B 2
Medicine Hat 40,380	E 4
Milk River 894	D 5
Millet 1,120	D 3
Mirror 507	D 3
Monarch 212	D 5
Morinville 4,657	D 3
Morrin 244	D 4
Mundare 604	D 3
Myrnam 397	E 3
Nacmine 369	D 4
Nampa 334	B 1
Nanton 1,641	D 4
New Norway 291	D 3
New Sarepta 417	D 3
Nobleford 534	D 5
North Calling Lake 234	D 2
Okotoks 3,847	C 4
Olds 4,813	D 4
Onoway 621	C 3
Oyen 975	E 4
Peace River 5,907	B 1
Penhold 1,531	D 3
Picture Butte 1,404	D 5
Pincher Creek 3,757	D 5
Plamondon 259	D 2
Pollockville 19	E 4
Ponoka 5,221	D 3
Provost 1,645	E 3
Rainbow Lake 504	A 5
Ralston 357	E 4
Raymond 2,837	D 5
Redcliff 3,876	E 4
Red Deer 46,393	D 3
Redwater 1,932	D 3
Rimbey 1,685	C 3
Robb 230	B 3
Rockyford 329	D 4
Rocky Mountain House 4,698	C 3
Rosemary 328	E 4
Rycroft 649	A 2
Ryley 483	D 3
Saint Albert 31,996	D 3
Saint Paul 4,884	E 3
Sangudo 398	C 3
Sedgewick 879	E 3
Sexsmith 1,180	A 2
Shaughnessy 270	D 5
Sherwood Park 29,285	D 3
Slave Lake 4,506	C 2
Smith 216	D 2
Smoky Lake 1,074	D 2
Spirit River 1,104	A 2
Spruce Grove 10,326	D 3
Standard 379	D 4
Stavely 504	D 4
Stettler 5,136	D 3
Stirling 688	D 5
Stony Plain 4,839	C 3
Strathmore 2,986	D 4
Strome 281	E 3
Sundre 1,742	C 4
Swan Hills 2,497	C 2
Sylvan Lake 3,779	C 3
Taber 5,988	E 5
Thorhild 576	D 2
Thorsby 737	C 3
Three Hills 1,787	D 4
Tilley 345	E 4
Tofield 1,504	D 3
Trochu 880	D 4
Turner Valley 1,311	C 4
Two Hills 1,193	E 3
Valleyview 2,061	B 2
Vauxhall 1,049	D 4
Vegreville 5,251	E 3
Vermilion 3,766	E 3
Veteran 314	E 3
Viking 1,232	E 3
Vilna 345	E 2
Vulcan 1,489	D 4
Wabamun 662	C 3
Wabasca 701	D 2
Wainwright 4,266	E 3
Warburg 501	C 3
Warner 477	D 5
Waskatenau 290	D 2
Wembley 1,169	A 2
Westlock 4,424	C 2
Wetaskiwin 9,597	D 3
Whitecourt 5,585	C 2
Wildwood 441	C 3
Willingdon 366	E 3
Youngstown 297	E 4

OTHER FEATURES

Abraham (lake)	B 3
Alberta (mt.)	B 3
Assiniboine (mt.)	C 4
Athabasca (lake)	C 5
Athabasca (riv.)	D 1
Banff Nat'l Park	B 4
Battle (riv.)	D 3
Bear (lake)	A 2
Beaver (riv.)	E 2
Beaverhill (lake)	D 3
Behan (lake)	E 2
Belly (riv.)	D 5
Berland (riv.)	A 3
Berry (creek)	E 4
Biche (lake)	E 2
Big (isl.)	B 5
Big Horn (dam)	B 3
Bighorn (range)	B 3
Birch (hills)	A 2
Birch (lake)	E 3
Birch (mts.)	B 5
Birch (riv.)	B 5
Bison (lake)	B 1
Bittern (lake)	D 3
Botha (riv.)	B 1
Bow (riv.)	D 4
Boyer (riv.)	A 5
Brazeau (mt.)	B 3
Brazeau (riv.)	B 3
Buffalo (lake)	D 3
Buffalo Head (hills)	B 5
Burnt (lakes)	C 1
Cadotte (lake)	B 1
Cadotte (riv.)	B 1
Calling (lake)	D 2
Canal (creek)	E 5
Cardinal (lake)	B 1
Caribou (mts.)	B 5
Chinchaga (riv.)	A 5
Chip (lake)	C 3
Chipewyan (lake)	D 1
Chipewyan (riv.)	D 1
Christina (lake)	E 2
Christina (riv.)	E 1
Claire (lake)	B 5
Clear (hills)	A 1
Clearwater (riv.)	C 4
Clearwater (riv.)	E 1
Clyde (lake)	E 2
Cold (lake)	E 2
Columbia (mt.)	B 3
Crowsnest (pass)	C 5
Cypress (hills)	E 5
Cypress Hills Prov. Park	E 5
Dillon (riv.)	E 2
Dowling (lake)	D 4
Dunkirk (riv.)	D 1
Eisenhower (mt.)	C 4
Elbow (riv.)	C 4
Elk Island Nat'l Park	D 3
Ells (riv.)	D 1
Etzikom Coulee (riv.)	E 5
Eva (lake)	B 5
Farrell (lake)	D 4
Firebag (riv.)	E 1
Forbes (mt.)	B 4
Freeman (riv.)	C 2
Frog (lake)	E 3
Garson (lake)	E 1
Gipsy (lake)	E 1
Gordon (lake)	E 1
Gough (lake)	D 3
Graham (lake)	C 1
Gull (lake)	C 3
Haig (lake)	B 1
Hawk (hills)	B 1
Hay (lake)	A 5
Hay (riv.)	A 5
Heart (lake)	E 2
Highwood (riv.)	C 4
House (mt.)	C 2
House (riv.)	D 2
Iosegun (lake)	B 2
Iosegun (riv.)	B 2
Jackfish (riv.)	B 5
Jasper Nat'l Park	A 3
Kakwa (riv.)	A 2
Kickinghorse (pass)	B 4
Kimiwan (lake)	B 2
Kirkpatrick (lake)	E 4
Kitchener (mt.)	B 3
Legend (lake)	D 1
Lesser Slave (lake)	C 2
Liége (riv.)	D 1
Little Bow (riv.)	D 4
Little Cadotte (riv.)	B 1
Little Smoky (riv.)	B 2
Livingstone (range)	C 4
Logan (lake)	E 2
Loon (lake)	C 1
Loon (riv.)	C 1
Lubicon (lake)	C 1
Lyell (mt.)	B 4
MacKay (riv.)	D 1
Maligne (lake)	B 3
Margaret (lake)	B 5
Marie (lake)	E 2
Marion (lake)	D 3
Marten (mt.)	C 2
McClelland (lake)	E 1
McGregor (lake)	D 4
McLeod (riv.)	B 3
Meikle (riv.)	A 1
Mikkwa (riv.)	B 5
Milk (riv.)	D 5
Mistehae (lake)	C 2
Muriel (lake)	E 2
Muskwa (lake)	C 1
Muskwa (riv.)	C 1
Namur (lake)	D 1
Newell (lake)	E 4
Nordegg (riv.)	C 3
North Saskatchewan (riv.)	E 3
North Wabasca (lake)	D 1
Notikewin (riv.)	A 1
Oldman (riv.)	D 5
Otter (lakes)	B 1
Pakowki (lake)	E 5
Panny (riv.)	C 1
Peace (riv.)	B 1
Peerless (lake)	C 1
Pelican (lake)	D 2
Pelican (mts.)	D 2
Pembina (riv.)	C 3
Pigeon (lake)	D 3
Pinehurst (lake)	E 2
Porcupine (hills)	C 4
Primrose (lake)	E 2
Rainbow (lake)	A 5
Red Deer (lake)	D 3
Red Deer (riv.)	D 4
Richardson (riv.)	C 5
Rocky (mts.)	B-C 4
Rosebud (riv.)	D 4
Russell (lake)	C 1
Saddle (hills)	A 2
Sainte Anne (lake)	C 3
Saint Mary (res.)	D 5
Saint Mary (riv.)	D 5
Saulteaux (riv.)	C 2
Seibert (lake)	E 2
Simonette (riv.)	A 2
Slave (riv.)	C 5
Smoky (riv.)	A 2
Snake Indian (riv.)	A 3
Snipe (lake)	B 2
Sounding (creek)	E 4
South Saskatchewan (riv.)	E 4
South Wabasca (lake)	D 2
Spencer (lake)	E 2
Spray (mts.)	C 4
Sturgeon (lake)	B 2
Sullivan (lake)	D 3
Swan (hills)	C 2
Swan (riv.)	C 2
Temple (mt.)	B 4
The Twins (mt.)	B 3
Thickwood (hills)	D 1
Touchwood (lake)	E 2
Travers (res.)	D 4
Trout (mt.)	C 1
Trout (riv.)	C 1
Utikuma (lake)	C 2
Utikuma (riv.)	C 1
Utikumasis (lake)	C 2
Vermilion (riv.)	E 3
Wabasca (riv.)	C 1
Wallace (mt.)	C 2
Wapiti (riv.)	A 2
Wappau (lake)	E 2
Watchusk (lake)	E 1
Waterton-Glacier Int'l Peace Park	C 5
Waterton Lakes Nat'l Park	C 5
Whitemud (riv.)	A 1
Wildhay (riv.)	B 3
Willmore Wilderness Prov. Park	A 3
Winagami (lake)	B 2
Winefred (lake)	E 2
Winefred (riv.)	E 2
Wolf (lake)	E 2
Wolverine (riv.)	B 1
Wood Buffalo Nat'l Park	B 5
Yellowhead (pass)	A 3
Zama (lake)	A 5

*Population of metropolitan area.

Agriculture, Industry and Resources

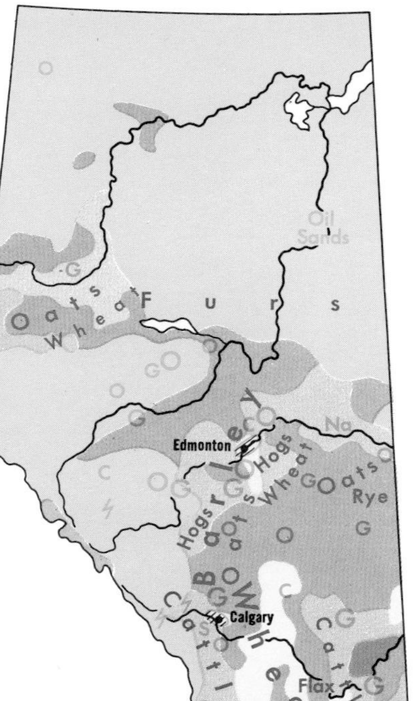
Oil Sands
Furs
Oats
Wheat
Edmonton
Na
Hogs
Barley
Oats
Wheat
Rye
Calgary
Cattle
Flax
Sheep
Sugar Beets

DOMINANT LAND USE

- Wheat
- Cereals (chiefly barley, oats)
- Cereals, Livestock
- Dairy
- Pasture Livestock
- Range Livestock
- Forests
- Nonagricultural Land

MAJOR MINERAL OCCURRENCES

- C Coal
- G Natural Gas
- Na Salt
- O Petroleum
- S Sulfur
- Water Power
- Major Industrial Areas

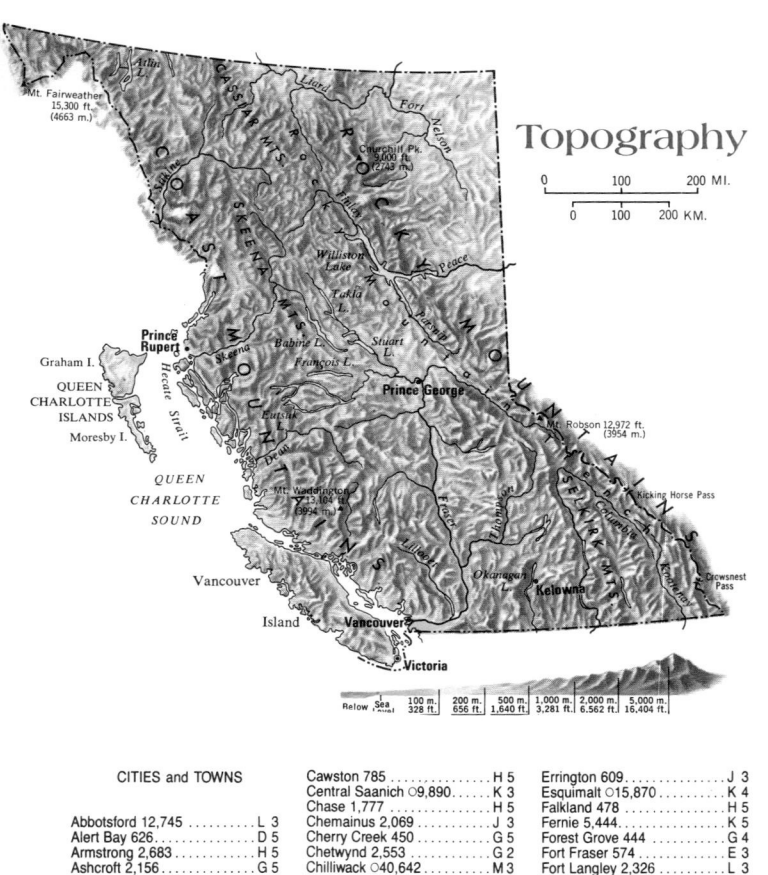

Topography

0 100 200 MI.
0 100 200 KM.

Below Sea Level | 100 m. 328 ft. | 200 m. 656 ft. | 500 m. 1,640 ft. | 1,000 m. 3,281 ft. | 2,000 m. 6,562 ft. | 5,000 m. 16,404 ft.

CITIES and TOWNS

Abbotsford 12,745 .... L 3
Alert Bay 626 .... D 5
Armstrong 2,683 .... H 5
Ashcroft 2,156 .... G 5
Ashton Creek 452 .... H 5
Balfour 472 .... J 5
Barlow 441 .... F 3
Barrière 1,370 .... H 4
Blueberry Creek 635 .... J 5
Blue River 384 .... H 4
Boston Bar 498 .... G 5
Bowen Island 1,125 .... K 3
Brackendale 1,719 .... F 5
Burnaby ○136,494 .... K 3
Burns Lake 1,777 .... D 3
Cache Creek 1,308 .... G 5
Campbell River 15,370 .... E 5
Canal Flats 919 .... K 5
Canyon 698 .... J 5
Cassiar 1,045 .... K 2
Castlegar 6,902 .... J 5
Cawston 785 .... H 5
Central Saanich ○9,890 .... K 3
Chase 1,777 .... H 5
Chemainus 2,069 .... J 3
Cherry Creek 450 .... G 5
Chetwynd 2,553 .... G 2
Chilliwack ○40,642 .... M 3
Clearwater 1,461 .... G 4
Clinton 804 .... G 4
Coldstream ○6,450 .... H 5
Comox 6,607 .... H 2
Coquitlam ○61,077 .... K 3
Courtenay 8,992 .... E 5
Cranbrook 15,915 .... K 5
Creston 4,190 .... J 5
Crofton 1,303 .... J 3
Cultus Lake 481 .... M 3
Cumberland 1,947 .... E 5
Dawson Creek 11,373 .... G 2
Delta ○74,692 .... K 3
Duncan 4,228 .... J 3
Elkford 3,126 .... K 5
Enderby 1,816 .... H 5
Erickson 972 .... J 5
Errington 609 .... J 3
Esquimalt ○15,870 .... K 4
Falkland 478 .... H 5
Fernie 5,444 .... K 5
Forest Grove 444 .... G 4
Fort Fraser 574 .... E 3
Fort Langley 2,326 .... L 3
Fort Nelson 3,724 .... M 2
Fort Saint James 2,284 .... E 3
Fort Saint John 13,891 .... G 2
Fraser Lake 1,543 .... E 3
Fruitvale 1,904 .... J 5
Gabriola 1,627 .... J 3
Galiano 669 .... K 3
Ganges 1,118 .... K 3
Gibsons 2,594 .... K 3
Gold River 2,225 .... D 5
Golden 3,476 .... J 4
Grand Forks 3,486 .... H 6
Granisle 1,430 .... D 3
Greenwood 856 .... H 5
Hagensborg 350 .... D 4
Harrison Hot Springs 569 .... M 3
Hatzic 1,055 .... L 3

Hazelton 393 .... D 2
Hedley 426 .... G 5
Holberg 444 .... C 5
Honeymoon Bay 474 .... J 3
Hope 3,205 .... M 3
Hornby Island 474 .... H 2
Horsefly 430 .... G 4
Houston 3,147 .... D 3
Hudson Hope 984 .... F 2
Invermere 1,969 .... J 5
Kaleden 998 .... H 5
Kamloops 64,048 .... G 5
Kaslo 854 .... J 5
Kelowna 59,196 .... H 5
Kent ○3,394 .... M 3
Keremeos 830 .... G 5
Kimberley 7,375 .... K 5
Kitimat 12,462 .... C 3
Kitsault 554 .... C 2
Kitwanga 369 .... D 2
Lac La Hache 647 .... G 4
Ladysmith 4,558 .... J 3
Lake Cowichan 2,391 .... J 3
Langley 15,124 .... L 3
Lantzville 969 .... J 3
Likely 425 .... G 4
Lillooet 1,725 .... G 5
Lion's Bay 1,078 .... K 3
Logan Lake 2,637 .... G 5
Lumby 1,266 .... H 5
Lytton 428 .... G 5
Mackenzie 5,797 .... F 2
Mackenzie ○5,890 .... F 2
Malakwa 392 .... H 5
Maple Bay 393 .... K 3
Maple Ridge ○32,232 .... L 3
Masset 1,569 .... B 3
Matsqui ○42,001 .... L 3
Mayne 546 .... K 3
McBride 641 .... G 3
Merritt 6,110 .... G 5
Midway 633 .... H 6
Mill Bay 583 .... K 3
Mission ○20,056 .... L 3
Mission City 9,948 .... L 3
Montrose 1,229 .... J 5
Nakusp 1,495 .... J 5
Nanaimo 47,069 .... J 3
Naramata 876 .... H 5
Nelson 9,143 .... J 5
New Denver 642 .... J 5
New Hazelton 792 .... D 2
New Westminster 38,550 .... K 3
Nicomen Island 360 .... L 3
Nootka .... D 5
North Cowichan ○18,210 .... J 3
North Pender Island 906 .... K 3
North Saanich ○6,117 .... K 3
North Vancouver 33,952 .... K 3
North Vancouver ○65,367 .... K 3
Oak Bay ○16,990 .... K 4
Okanagan Falls 1,030 .... H 5
Okanagan Landing 834 .... H 5
Okanagan Mission .... H 5
Old Barkerville 11 .... G 3
Oliver 1,893 .... H 5
One Hundred Mile House 1,925 .... G 4
Osoyoos 2,738 .... H 5
Oyama 430 .... H 5
Parksville 5,216 .... J 3
Peachland ○2,865 .... G 5

Penticton 23,181 .... H 5
Pitt Meadows ○6,209 .... L 3
Port Alberni 19,892 .... H 3
Port Alice 1,668 .... D 5
Port Clements 380 .... B 3
Port Coquitlam 27,535 .... L 3
Port Edward 989 .... B 3
Port Hardy ○3,778 .... D 5
Port McNeill 2,474 .... D 5
Port Moody 14,917 .... L 3
Pouce-Coupé 821 .... G 2
Powell River ○13,423 .... E 5
Prince George 67,559 .... F 3
Prince Rupert 16,197 .... B 3
Princeton 3,051 .... G 5
Qualicum Beach 2,844 .... J 3
Queen Charlotte 1,070 .... A 3
Quesnel 8,240 .... F 4
Radium Hot Springs 419 .... J 5
Revelstoke 5,544 .... J 5
Richmond ○96,154 .... K 3
Roberts Creek 926 .... J 3
Robson 1,008 .... J 5
Rossland 3,967 .... H 6
Royston 754 .... H 2
Saanich ○78,710 .... K 3
Salmo 1,169 .... J 5
Salmon Arm 1,946 .... H 5
Salmon Arm ○10,780 .... H 5
Saltair 1,356 .... J 3
Sandspit 794 .... B 3
Sayward 482 .... D 5
Sechelt 1,096 .... J 2
Shawnigan Lake 419 .... J 3
Shoreacres 555 .... J 5
Sicamous 1,057 .... H 5
Sidney 7,946 .... K 3
Slocan 351 .... J 5
Slocan Park 414 .... J 5
Smithers 4,570 .... D 3
Sointula 567 .... D 5
Sooke 852 .... J 4
Sorrento 659 .... H 5
South Hazelton 500 .... D 2
South Wellington 620 .... J 3
Spallumcheen 4,213 .... H 5
Sparwood 3,267 .... K 5
Sproat Lake 440 .... H 3
Squamish 1,590 .... F 5
Stewart ○1,456 .... C 2
Summerland ○7,473 .... G 5
Surrey ○147,138 .... K 3
Tahsis 1,739 .... D 5
Taylor 966 .... G 2
Telkwa 840 .... D 3
Terrace 8,893 .... C 3
Terrace ○10,914 .... C 3
Thornhill 4,281 .... C 3
Thrums 360 .... J 5
Tofino 705 .... E 5
Trail 9,599 .... J 6
Ucluelet 1,593 .... E 6
Union Bay 601 .... H 2
Valemount 1,130 .... H 4
Vancouver 414,281 .... K 3
Vancouver (Greater)
 *1,169,831 .... K 3
Vanderhoof 2,323 .... E 3
Vavenby 479 .... H 4
Vernon 19,987 .... H 5
Victoria (cap.) 64,379 .... K 4
Victoria *233,481 .... K 4
Warfield 1,969 .... J 5
Wasa 345 .... K 5
Wells 417 .... G 3
Westbank 1,271 .... H 5
West Vancouver ○35,728 .... K 3
Westwold 409 .... G 5
Whistler ○1,365 .... F 5
White Rock 13,550 .... K 3
Williams Lake 8,362 .... F 4
Wilson Creek 611 .... J 2
Windermere 611 .... K 5
Winlaw 435 .... J 5
Woss Lake 395 .... D 5
Wynndel 566 .... J 5
Yarrow 1,201 .... M 3
Youbou 965 .... G 5

OTHER FEATURES

Adams (lake) .... H 4
Adams (riv.) .... H 4
Alberni (inlet) .... H 3
Alsek (riv.) .... H 1
Aristazabal (isl.) .... C 4
Assiniboine (mt.) .... K 5
Atlin (lake) .... J 1
Azure (lake) .... G 4
Babine (lake) .... E 3
Babine (riv.) .... D 2
Banks (isl.) .... B 3
Barkley (sound) .... E 6
Beale (cape) .... E 6
Beatton (riv.) .... G 1
Bella Coola (riv.) .... D 4
Bennett, W.A.C. (dam) .... F 2
Birkenhead Lake Prov. Park .... F 5
Bowron Lake Prov. Park .... G 3
Bowser (lake) .... C 2
Brooks (pen.) .... D 5
Browning Entrance (str.) .... B 3
Bryce (mt.) .... H 4
Bugaboo Glacier Prov. Park .... J 5
Bulkley (riv.) .... D 3
Burke (chan.) .... D 4
Burnaby (isl.) .... B 4
Bute (inlet) .... E 5
Caamaño (sound) .... C 4
Calvert (isl.) .... D 5
Canim (lake) .... G 4
Canoe (riv.) .... H 4
Cariboo (mts.) .... G 3
Carpenter (lake) .... F 5
Carp Lake Prov. Park .... F 3
Cassiar (mts.) .... K 2
Castle (mt.) .... A 2

Charlotte (lake) .... E 4
Chatham (sound) .... B 3
Chehalis (lake) .... L 3
Chilcotin (riv.) .... E 4
Chilko (lake) .... F 4
Chilko (riv.) .... E 4
Chilkoot (pass) .... J 1
Chuchi (lake) .... E 2
Churchill (peak) .... L 2
Clayoquot (sound) .... D 5
Clearwater (lake) .... G 4
Clearwater (riv.) .... G 4
Coast (mts.) .... D 3
Columbia (lake) .... K 5
Columbia (mt.) .... J 4
Columbia (riv.) .... H 4
Cook (cape) .... C 5
Cowichan (lake) .... J 3
Crowsnest (pass) .... K 5
Cypress Prov. Park .... K 3
Dean (chan.) .... D 4
Dean (riv.) .... D 4
Dease (lake) .... K 2
Dease (riv.) .... K 2
Devils Thumb (mt.) .... A 1
Dixon Entrance (chan.) .... A 3
Douglas (chan.) .... C 3
Duncan (riv.) .... J 5
Dundas (isl.) .... B 3
Elk (riv.) .... K 5
Elk Lakes Prov. Park .... K 5
Eutsuk (lake) .... D 3
Fairweather (mt.) .... H 1

Cathedral Prov. Park .... H 5
Finlay (riv.) .... E 1
Fitzhugh (sound) .... D 4
Flathead (riv.) .... K 6
Flores (isl.) .... D 5
Fontas (riv.) .... M 2
Forbes (mt.) .... J 4
Fort Nelson (riv.) .... M 2
François (lake) .... D 3
Fraser (lake) .... E 3
Fraser (riv.) .... G 4
Fraser Reach (chan.) .... C 3
Galiano (isl.) .... K 3
Gardner (canal) .... C 3
Garibaldi Prov. Park .... F 5
Georgia (str.) .... J 3
Germansen (lake) .... E 2
Gil (isl.) .... C 3
Glacier Nat'l Park .... J 4
Golden Ears Prov. Park .... L 2
Gordon (riv.) .... J 3
Graham (isl.) .... A 3
Graham Reach (chan.) .... C 3
Grenville (chan.) .... C 3
Halfway (riv.) .... F 2
Hamber Prov. Park .... H 4
Harrison (lake) .... M 2
Hawkesbury (isl.) .... C 3
Hazelton (mts.) .... C 2
Hecate (str.) .... B 3
Hobson (lake) .... H 4
Homathko (riv.) .... E 4
Horsefly (riv.) .... G 4

Agriculture, Industry and Resources

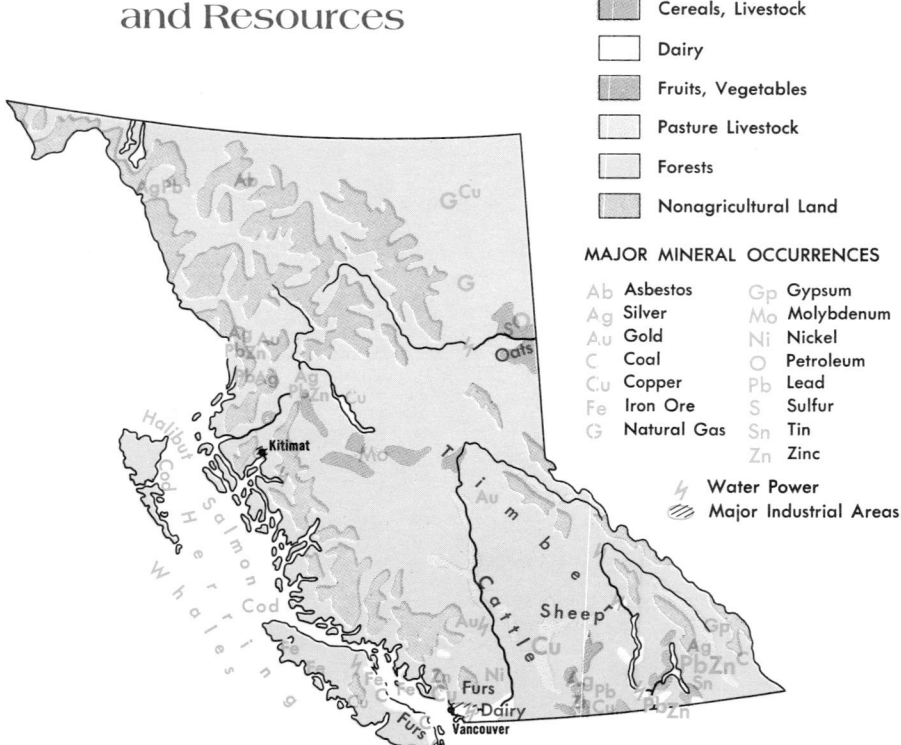

DOMINANT LAND USE

Cereals, Livestock
Dairy
Fruits, Vegetables
Pasture Livestock
Forests
Nonagricultural Land

MAJOR MINERAL OCCURRENCES

Ab Asbestos
Ag Silver
Au Gold
C Coal
Cu Copper
Fe Iron Ore
G Natural Gas
Gp Gypsum
Mo Molybdenum
Ni Nickel
O Petroleum
Pb Lead
S Sulfur
Sn Tin
Zn Zinc

⚡ Water Power
Major Industrial Areas

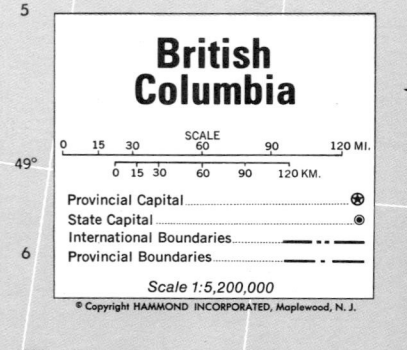

British Columbia

SCALE
0 15 30 60 90 120 MI.
0 15 30 60 90 120 KM.

Provincial Capital .... ⊛
State Capital .... ◉
International Boundaries .... —·—·—
Provincial Boundaries .... ———

Scale 1:5,200,000

© Copyright HAMMOND INCORPORATED, Maplewood, N.J.

Howe (sound)	K 2	Louise (isl.)	B 4	Nootka (sound)
Hunter (isl.)	C 4	Lower Arrow (lake)	H 5	North Thompson (riv.)
Inklin (riv.)	J 2	Lyell (isl.)	B 4	Observatory (inlet)
Inzana (lake)	E 3	Lyell (mt.)	J 4	Okanagan (lake)
Isaac (lake)	G 3	Mabel (lake)	H 5	Okanagan Mtn. Prov. Park
Iskut (riv.)	B 2	Mahood (lake)	G 4	Okanogan (riv.)
Jervis (inlet)	E 5	Malaspina (str.)	J 2	Omineca (mts.)
John Jay (mt.)	B 2	Manning Prov. Park	G 5	Omineca (riv.)
Johnstone (str.)	D 5	Masset (inlet)	A 3	Ootsa (lake)
Juan de Fuca (str.)	J 4	McCauley (isl.)	B 3	Owikeno (lake)
Kates Needle (mt.)	A 1	McGregor (riv.)	G 3	Pacific Rim Nat'l Park
Kechika (riv.)	L 2	Meziadin (lake)	C 2	Pa'snip (riv.)
Kenney (dam)	E 3	Milbanke (sound)	C 4	Peace (riv.)
Kettle (riv.)	H 5	Moberly (lake)	F 2	Pend Oreille (riv.)
Kicking Horse (pass)	J 4	Monashee (mts.)	H 4	Petitot (riv.)
King (isl.)	D 4	Moresby (isl.)	B 4	Pinchi (lake)
Klinaklini (riv.)	E 4	Morice (lake)	D 3	Pine (riv.)
Kloch (lake)	E 2	Morice (riv.)	D 3	Pitt (isl.)
Knight (inlet)	E 5	Mount Assiniboine Prov. Park	K 5	Pitt (lake)
Knox (cape)	A 3	Mount Edziza Prov. Park and		Porcher (isl.)
Kokanee Glacier Prov. Park	J 5	Rec. Area	B 1	Portland (canal)
Koocanusa (lake)	K 6	Mount Revelstoke Nat'l Park	H 4	Portland (inlet)
Kootenay (lake)	J 5	Mount Robson Prov. Park	G 3	Price (riv.)
Kootenay (riv.)	K 5	Muncho Lake Prov. Park	L 2	Princess Royal (isl.)
Kootenay Nat'l Park	J 4	Murray (riv.)	G 3	Principe (chan.)
Kotcho (lake)	M 2	Murtle (lake)	H 4	Prophet (riv.)
Kotcho (riv.)	M 2	Muskwa (riv.)	M 2	Purcell (mts.)
Kunghit (isl.)	B 4	Nanika (dam)	D 3	Quatsino (sound)
Kyuquot (sound)	D 5	Nass (riv.)	C 2	Queen Charlotte (isls.)
Langara (isl.)	A 3	Nation (riv.)	F 2	Queen Charlotte (sound)
Laredo (sound)	C 4	Nechako (riv.)	E 3	Queen Charlotte (str.)
Liard (riv.)	L 2	Nitinat (lake)	H 3	Queens (sound)
Lillooet (riv.)	F 5	Nootka (isl.)	D 5	Quesnel (lake)

Nootka (sound)	D 5	Quesnel (riv.)	F 4	
North Thompson (riv.)	G 4	Rivers (inlet)	D 4	
Observatory (inlet)	C 2	Robson (mt.)	H 3	
Okanagan (lake)	H 5	Rocky (mts.)	F 2	
Okanagan Mtn. Prov. Park	G 5	Roderick (isl.)	C 4	
Okanogan (riv.)	H 6	Rose (pt.)	B 3	
Omineca (mts.)	E 2	Saint James (cape)	B 4	
Omineca (riv.)	E 2	Salmon (riv.)	J 2	
Ootsa (lake)	D 3	Salmon (riv.)	F 3	
Owikeno (lake)	D 4	Salmon Arm (inlet)	J 2	
Pacific Rim Nat'l Park	E 6	San Juan (riv.)	J 3	
Pa'snip (riv.)	E 2	Schoen Lake Prov. Park	J 4	
Peace (riv.)	G 2	Scott (cape)	C 5	
Pend Oreille (riv.)	J 6	Scott (isls.)	C 5	
Petitot (riv.)	M 2	Seechelt (inlet)	J 2	
Pinchi (lake)	E 3	Seechelt (pen.)	J 2	
Pine (riv.)	F 2	Selkirk (mts.)	J 4	
Pitt (isl.)	C 3	Seymour (inlet)	J 2	
Pitt (lake)	J 2	Sheslay (riv.)	B 1	
Porcher (isl.)	B 3	Shuswap (lake)	H 4	
Portland (canal)	B 2	Sikanni Chief (riv.)	F 1	
Portland (inlet)	C 3	Silver Star Prov. Park	H 4	
Price (riv.)	E 3	Sir Sandford (mt.)	H 4	
Princess Royal (isl.)	C 3	Skagit (riv.)	G 6	
Principe (chan.)	C 3	Skeena (mts.)	C 2	
Prophet (riv.)	M 2	Skeena (riv.)	B 3	
Purcell (mts.)	J 5	Skidegate (inlet)	B 3	
Quatsino (sound)	C 5	Slocan (lake)	J 5	
Queen Charlotte (isls.)	B 3	Smith (sound)	D 4	
Queen Charlotte (sound)	C 4	South Bentinck Arm (inlet)	D 4	
Queen Charlotte (str.)	D 5	Stave (lake)	L 3	
Queens (sound)	C 4	Stephens (isl.)	B 3	
Quesnel (lake)	G 4	Stikine (riv.)	B 1	
		Stone Mountain Prov. Park	L 2	

Strathcona Prov. Park	E 5	Three Guardsmen (mt.)	H 1	Vancouver (isl.)	D 5
Stuart (lake)	E 3	Thutade (lake)	D 2	Virago (sound)	A 3
Sustut (riv.)	D 2	Tiedemann (mt.)	E 4	Waddington (mt.)	E 4
Tagish (lake)	J 1	Toad (riv.)	L 2	Wapiti (riv.)	H 3
Tahtsa (lake)	D 3	Toba (inlet)	J 2	Wells Gray Prov. Park	H 4
Takla (lake)	D 2	Tochcha (lake)	E 3	West Road (riv.)	E 3
Taku (riv.)	B 1	Top Of The World Prov. Park	K 5	Whitesail (lake)	D 3
Tatlatui (lake)	D 2	Trembleur (lake)	E 3	Williston (lake)	F 2
Tatlayoko (lake)	D 4	Troitsa (lake)	D 3	Work (chan.)	C 3
Tchentlo (lake)	E 2	Tumeka (lake)	C 1	Yellowhead (pass)	H 4
Teslin (lake)	K 1	Turnagain (riv.)	K 2	Yoho Nat'l Park	J 4
Tetachuck (lake)	D 3	Tuya (riv.)	K 2		
Texada (isl.)	J 2	Tweedsmuir Prov. Park	D 3		
Tezzeron (lake)	E 3	Upper Arrow (lake)	H 5	*Population of metropolitan area.	
Thompson (riv.)	G 5	Valdes (isl.)	K 3	◦Population of municipality.	

AREA 366,253 sq. mi. (948,596 sq. km.)
POPULATION 2,744,467
CAPITAL Victoria
LARGEST CITY Vancouver
HIGHEST POINT Mt. Fairweather 15,300 ft. (4,663 m.)
SETTLED IN 1806
ADMITTED TO CONFEDERATION 1871
PROVINCIAL FLOWER Dogwood

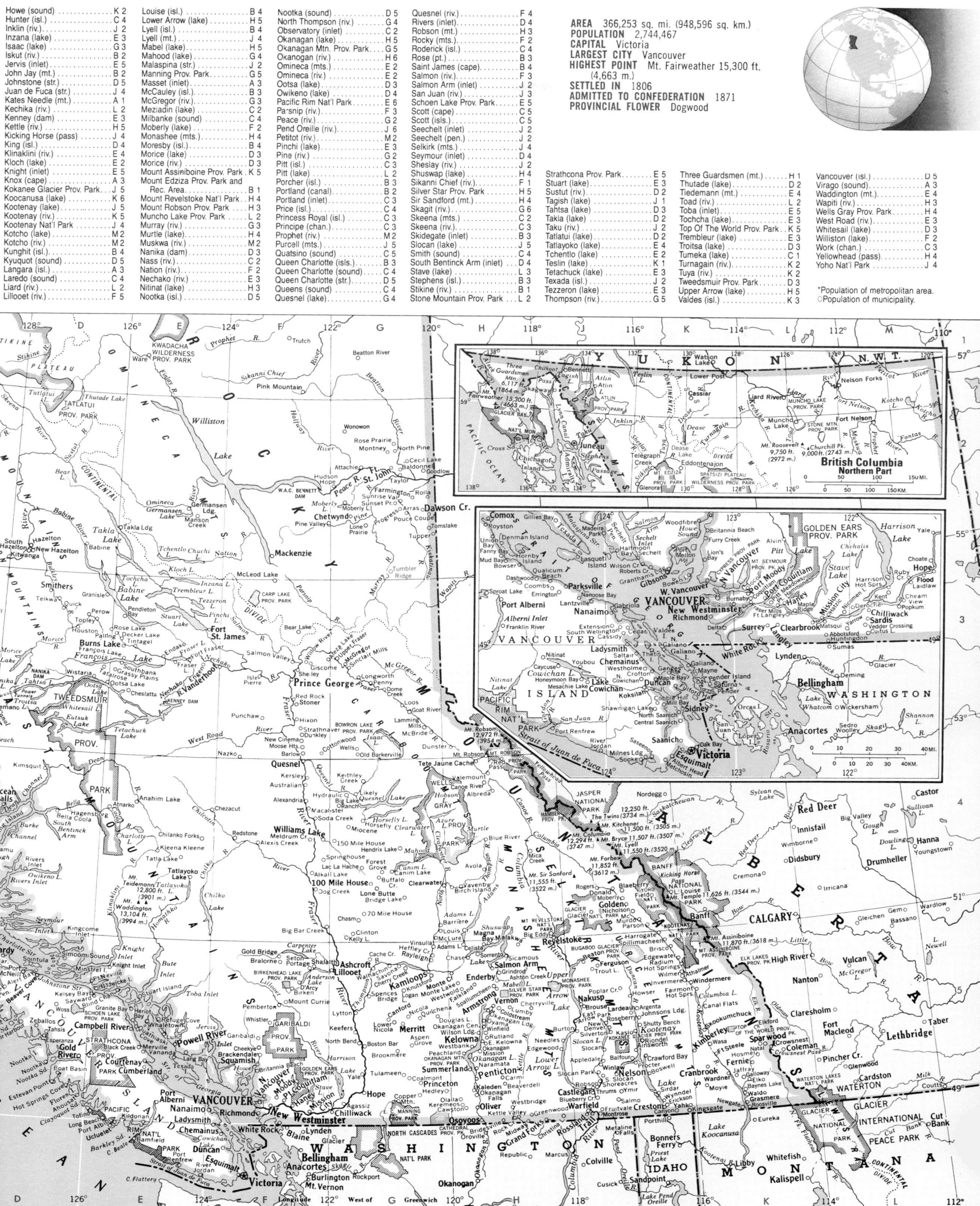

NORTHWEST TERRITORIES

DISTRICTS

Baffin 8,300 .... J2
Fort Smith 22,384 .... G3
Inuvik 7,485 .... F3
Keewatin 4,327 .... J3
Kitikmeot 3,245 .... G2

CITIES and TOWNS

Aklavik 721 .... E3
Alert M1
Amadjuak L3
Arctic Bay 375 ...... K2
Arctic Red River 120 .. E3
Baker Lake 954 ...... J3
Bathurst Inlet 20 .... H3
Bay Chimo 60 .... H3
Bell Rock G3
Broughton Island 378 . M3
Buffalo River Junction . G3
Cambridge Bay 815 ... G3
Cape Dorset 784 ..... L3
Cape Dyer M3
Cape Smith L3
Chesterfield Inlet 249 . K3
Clyde (Clyde River) 443 . M2
Colville Lake 57 ..... F3
Coppermine 809 ..... G3
Coral Harbour 429 ... K3
Detah 143 .... G3
Dory Point G3
Enterprise 46 ...... G3
Eskimo Point 1,022 .. J3
Eureka K2
Fort Franklin 521 ... F3
Fort Good Hope 463 .. F3
Fort Liard 405 ..... F3
Fort McPherson 632 .. E3
Fort Norman 286 .... F3
Fort Providence 605 .. G3
Fort Resolution 480 .. G3
Fort Simpson 980 ... F3
Fort Smith 2,298 ... G4
Frobisher Bay 2,333 .. M3
Gjoa Haven 523 .... J3
Grise Fiord 106 .... K2
Hall Beach 349 .... K3
Hay River 2,863 .... G3
Holman Island 300 .. G2
Igloolik 746 ...... K3
Inuvik 3,147 ...... E3
Isachsen H2
Jean-Marie River 69 . F3
Kakisa 36 .... G3
Kipisa 43 .... M3
Lac la Martre 268 ... G3
Lake Harbour 252 ... L3
Mould Bay F2
Nahanni Butte 85 ... F3
Nanisivik 261 ..... K2
Norman Wells 420 .. F3
Pangnirtung 839 ... M3
Paulatuk 174 ..... F3
Pelly Bay 257 .... K3
Pine Point 1,861 ... G3
Pond Inlet 705 .... L2
Port Burwell M3
Port Radium 56 ... G3
Rae-Edzo 1,378 ... G3
Rae Lakes 200 .... G3
Rankin Inlet 1,109 .. J3
Reliance 15 ...... H3
Repulse Bay 352 ... K3
Resolute Bay 168 .. J2

Resolution Island M3
Rocher River G3
Sachs Harbour 161 .... F2
Salt River G3
Sawmill Bay G3
Snare Lake 69 ...... G3
Snowdrift 253 ...... G3
Spence Bay 431 .... J3
Trout Lake 59 ..... F3
Tuktoyaktuk 772 ... E3
Tungsten 320 ..... F3
Whale Cove 188 ... J3
Wrigley 137 ...... F3
Yellowknife (cap.) 9,483 ... G3

OTHER FEATURES

Adelaide (pen.) J3
Admiralty (inlet) K2
Air Force (isl.) L3
Akpatok (isl.) M3
Amadjuak (lake) L3
Amund Ringnes (isl.) . J2
Amundsen (gulf) F2
Anderson (riv.) F3
Arctic Red (riv.) E3
Artillery (lake) H3
Axel Heiberg (isl.) .. J2
Aylmer (lake) H3
Back (riv.) J3
Baffin (bay) M2
Baffin (isl.) L2
Baker (lake) J3
Banks (isl.) F2
Barbeau (peak) ... L1
Barrow (str.) J2
Bathurst (cape) .. F2
Bathurst (inlet) .. H3
Bathurst (isl.) ... H2
Beaufort (sea) ... D2
Bellot (str.) J2
Boothia (gulf) ... K3
Boothia (pen.) ... J2
Borden (isl.) ... G2
Borden (pen.) ... K2
Brodeur (pen.) .. K2
Bruce (mts.) ... L2
Buchan (gulf) .. L2
Burnside (riv.) . G3
Byam Martin (chan.) . H2
Byam Martin (isl.) .. H2
Bylot (isl.) L2
Camsell (riv.) ... G3
Challenger (mts.) . L1
Chantrey (inlet) .. J3
Chesterfield (inlet) . J3
Chidley (cape) ... M3
Clinton-Colden (lake) . H3
Clyde (inlet) M2
Coats (isl.) K3
Coburg (isl.) L2
Columbia (cape) .. M1
Colville (lake) ... F3
Committee (bay) .. K3
Contwoyto (lake) . H3
Coppermine (riv.) . G3
Cornwall (isl.) ... J2
Cornwallis (isl.) .. J2
Coronation (gulf) . G3
Croker (bay) K2
Crown Prince Frederik (isl.) . K3
Cumberland (pen.) . M3
Cumberland (sound) . M3
Dalhousie (cape) .. E2
Davis (str.) M3
Dease (str.) H3

Denmark (bay) H2
Devon (isl.) K2
Dolphin and Union (str.) . G3
Dubawnt (lake) H3
Dubawnt (riv.) H3
Dundas (pen.) G2
Dyer (cape) M3
Eclipse (sound) L2
Eglinton (isl.) F2
Ellef Ringnes (isl.) . H2
Ellesmere (isl.) ... K2
Ennadai (lake) ... H3
Eskimo (lakes) ... E3
Eureka (sound) ... K2
Evans (str.) K3
Exeter (sound) ... M3
Fisher (str.) K3
Fosheim (pen.) .. K1
Foxe (basin) L3
Foxe (chan.) K3
Foxe (pen.) L3
Franklin (bay) ... F2
Franklin (mts.) .. F3
Franklin (str.) .. J2
Frobisher (bay) .. M3
Frozen (str.) K3
Fury and Hecla (str.) . K3
Gabriel (str.) ... M3
Garry (lake) H3
Gods Mercy (bay) . K3
Great Bear (lake) . F3
Great Bear (riv.) . F3
Great Slave (lake) . G3
Greely (fjord) ... K1
Grinnell (pen.) .. J2
Hadley (bay) H2
Hall (basin) M1
Hall (pen.) M3
Hayes (riv.) J3
Hazen (lake) L1
Hazen (str.) G2
Henik (lakes) ... J3
Henry Kater (cape) . M3
Home (bay) M3
Hood (riv.) G3
Horn (mts.) G3
Hornaday (riv.) .. F3
Horton (riv.) F3
Hottah (lake) ... G3
Hudson (bay) ... K3
Hudson (str.) ... L3
Isachsen (cape) . H2
James Ross (str.) . J3
Jenny Lind (isl.) . H3
Jens Munk (isl.) . K3
Jones (sound) ... K2
Kaminuriak (lake) . J3
Kane (basin) ... L2
Kasba (lake) H3
Kazan (riv.) H3
Keele (riv.) F3
Keith Arm (inlet) . F3
Kellett (cape) ... F2
Kellett (str.) ... G2
Kennedy (chan.) . M1
Kent (pen.) H3
King Christian (isl.) . H2
King William (isl.) . J3
Lady Ann (str.) .. K2
La Martre (lake) . G3
Lancaster (sound) . K2
Lands End (cape) . F2
Larsen (sound) .. J2
Liard (riv.) F4
Lincoln (sea) M1
Liverpool (bay) .. E2
Lockhart (riv.) .. H3

Lougheed (isl.) H2
Lyon (inlet) K3
MacKay (lake) G3
Mackenzie (bay) E3
Mackenzie (mts.) ... E3
Mackenzie (riv.) ... F3
Mackenzie King (isl.) . G2
Macmillan (pass) ... F3
Maguse (lake) J3
Makinson (inlet) .. L2
Mansel (isl.) K3
Marian (lake) ... G3
Markham (inlet) .. L1
McLeod (bay) ... G3
M'Clintock (chan.) . H2
M'Clure (str.) ... G2
McTavish Arm (inlet) . G3
Meighen (isl.) ... H1
Melville (isl.) ... G2
Melville (pen.) .. K3
Mercy (cape) ... M3
Mills (lake) G3
Minto (inlet) ... G2
Mistake (bay) .. J3
Nahanni Nat'l Park . F3
Nansen (sound) . J1
Nares (str.) L2
Navy Board (inlet) . K2
Nelson Head (prom.) . F2
Nettilling (lake) . L3

Nonacho (lake) H3
North Arm (inlet) G3
North Magnetic Pole .. H2
Norwegian (bay) ... J2
Nottingham (isl.) .. L3
Nueltin (lake) H3
Ommanney (bay) .. H2
Padloping (isl.) .. M3
Parry (bay) K3
Parry (chan.) ... G2
Parry (isls.) ... G2
Parry (pen.) ... F2
Peary (chan.) .. H1
Peel (sound) ... J2
Pelly (bay) J3
Penny (str.) ... J2
Point (lake) ... G3
Pond (inlet) ... L2
Prince Albert (pen.) . G2
Prince Albert (sound) . G2
Prince Charles (isl.) . L3
Prince Gustav Adolf (sea) . H2
Prince of Wales (isl.) . J2
Prince of Wales (str.) . G2
Prince Patrick (isl.) . F2
Prince Regent (inlet) . K2
Queen Elizabeth (isls.) . H1
Queen Maud (gulf) . H3
Queens (chan.) .. J2
Raanes (pen.) ... K2

Topography

0   200   400 MI.

0   200   400 KM.

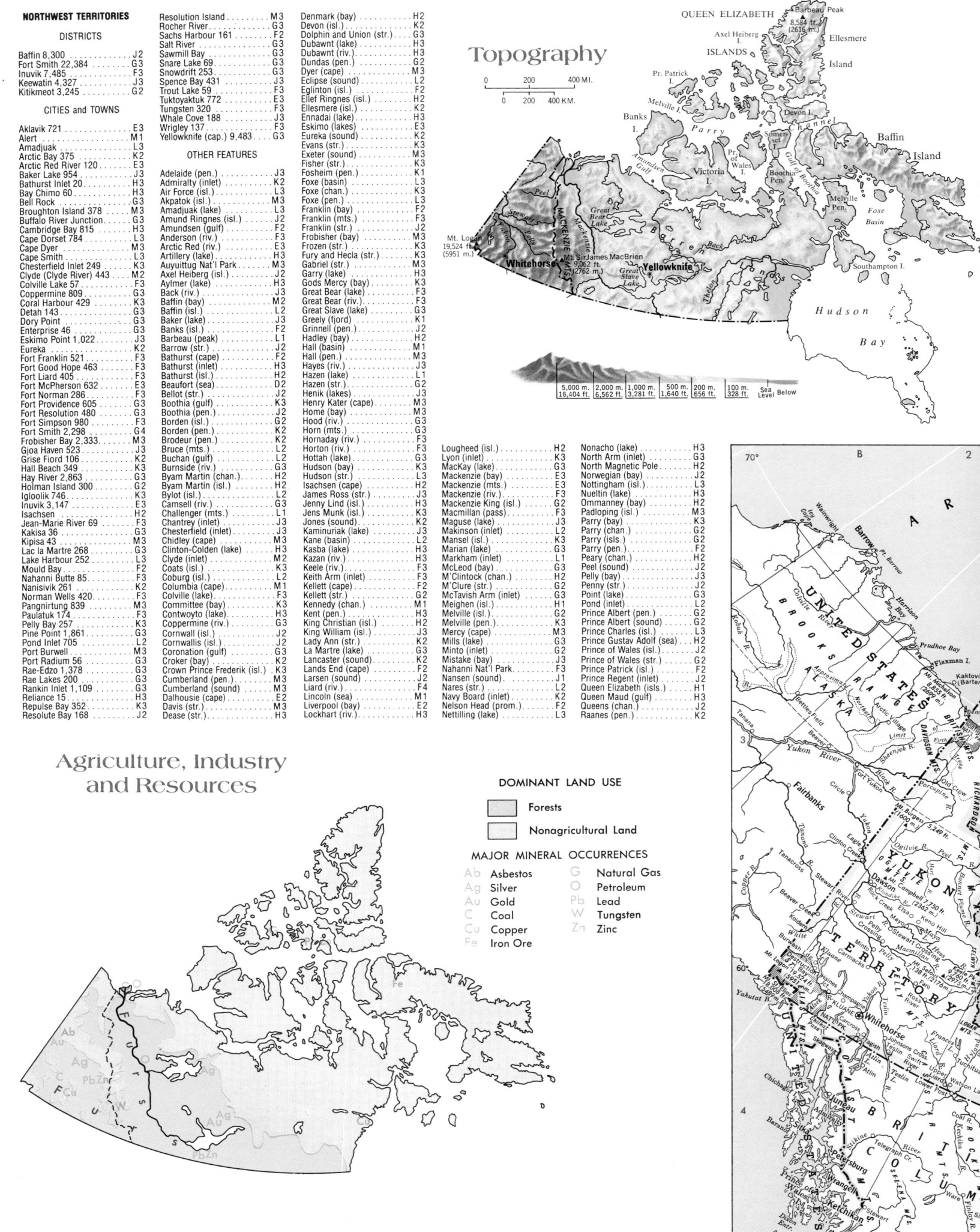

5,000 m. / 16,404 ft.   2,000 m. / 6,562 ft.   1,000 m. / 3,281 ft.   500 m. / 1,640 ft.   200 m. / 656 ft.   100 m. / 328 ft.   Sea Level   Below

QUEEN ELIZABETH
Barbeau Peak
8,534 ft.
(2615 m.)
Axel Heiberg
I.
Ellesmere
ISLANDS
Island
Pr. Patrick
I.
Melville I.
Devon I.
Banks
I.
Parry
Channel
Baffin
Gulf
of
Boothia
Island
Amundsen
Gulf
Victoria
I.
Pr.
of
Wales
I.
Boothia
Pen.
Somer-
set
Melville
Pen.
Foxe
Basin
Great Bear
Lake
Barren
Back
Southampton I.
Mt. Logan
19,524 ft.
(5951 m.)
Whitehorse
Mt. Sir James MacBrien
9,062 ft.
(2762 m.)
Great
Slave
Lake
Yellowknife
Thelon
Hudson
Bay

Agriculture, Industry and Resources

DOMINANT LAND USE

Forests

Nonagricultural Land

MAJOR MINERAL OCCURRENCES

Ab Asbestos
Ag Silver
Au Gold
C   Coal
Cu Copper
Fe Iron Ore

G   Natural Gas
O   Petroleum
Pb Lead
W   Tungsten
Zn Zinc

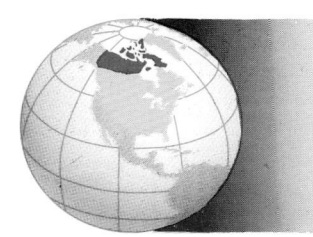

Rae (isth.)	K3	Sverdrup (chan.)	J1
Rae (riv.)	G3	Sverdrup (isls.)	J1
Rae (str.)	J3	Talbot (inlet)	L2
Ramparts (riv.)	E3	Taltson (riv.)	G3
Resolution (isl.)	M3	Tathlina (lake)	G3
Richard Collinson (inlet)	G2	Tha-anne (riv.)	J3
Richards (isl.)	E3	Thelon (riv.)	H3
Richardson (mts.)	E3	Thlewiaza (riv.)	H3
Robeson (chan.)	M1	Trout (lake)	F3
Roes Welcome (sound)	K3	Ungava (bay)	M4
Rowley (isl.)	K3	Vansittart (isl.)	K3
Royal Geographical Society (isls.)	J3	Victoria (isl.)	G2
Russell (isl.)	J2	Victoria (str.)	H3
Sabine (pen.)	H2	Viscount Melville (sound)	G2
Salisbury (isl.)	L3	Wager (bay)	J3
Seahorse (pt.)	L3	Wales (isl.)	K3
Selwyn (lake)	H4	Walsingham (cape)	M3
Sherman (inlet)	J3	Wellington (chan.)	J2
Simpson (pen.)	K3	Wholdaia (lake)	H3
Sir James MacBrien (mt.)	F3	Winter (harb.)	H2
Slave (riv.)	G3	Wollaston (pen.)	G2
Smith (bay)	K3	Wood Buffalo Nat'l Park	G3
Smith (cape)	L3	Wynniatt (bay)	G2
Smith (sound)	L2	Yathkyed (lake)	J3
Snare (riv.)	G3	Yellowknife (riv.)	G3
Snowbird (lake)	H3		
Somerset (isl.)	J2	**YUKON TERRITORY**	
South (bay)	K3		
Southampton (isl.)	K3	**CITIES and TOWNS**	
South Nahanni (riv.)	F3		
Stallworthy (cape)	J1	Beaver Creek 90	D3
Steensby (inlet)	L2	Burwash Landing 73	D3
Stefansson (isl.)	H2	Carcross 216	E3
		Carmacks •256	E3

YUKON TERRITORY

AREA 207,075 sq. mi.
(536,324 sq. km.)
POPULATION 23,153
CAPITAL Whitehorse
LARGEST CITY Whitehorse
HIGHEST POINT Mt. Logan 19,524 ft.
(5,951 m.)
SETTLED IN 1897
ADMITTED TO CONFEDERATION 1898
PROVINCIAL FLOWER Fireweed

NORTHWEST TERRITORIES

AREA 1,304,896 sq. mi. (3,379,683 sq. km.)
POPULATION 45,741
CAPITAL Yellowknife
LARGEST CITY Yellowknife
HIGHEST POINT Mt. Sir James MacBrien
9,062 ft. (2,762 m.)
SETTLED IN 1800
ADMITTED TO CONFEDERATION 1870
PROVINCIAL FLOWER Mountain Avens

Champagne	E3	Old Crow 243	E3
Clinton Creek	D3	Pelly Crossing 182	E3
Cowley	E3	Rock Creek 59	E3
Dawson 697	E3	Ross River 294	E3
Destruction Bay 45	E3	Stewart Crossing 20	D3
Elsa 336	E3	Stewart River	D3
Faro 1,652	E3	Swift River 24	E3
Haines Junction •366	E3	Tagish 89	E3
Johnson's Crossing 13	E3	Teslin •310	E3
Keno Hill 88	E3	Tuchitua Lake	F3
Koidern	D3	Upper Liard 130	F3
Mayo 398	E3	Watson Lake •748	E3
Minto	E3	Whitehorse (cap.) 14,814	E3

OTHER FEATURES

Alsek (riv.)	E3	Kluane Nat'l Park	E3	Porcupine (riv.)	E3
Bonnet Plume (riv.)	D3	Liard (riv.)	E3	Richardson (mts.)	E3
British (mts.)	D3	Logan (mt.)	D3	Rocky (mts.)	F4
Campbell (mt.)	E3	Logan (mts.)	F3	Saint Elias (mt.)	D3
Cassiar (mts.)	E3	Mackenzie (mts.)	E3	Saint Elias (mts.)	D3
Frances (lake)	F3	Macmillan (riv.)	E3	Selous (mt.)	E3
Herschel (isl.)	E3	Mayo (lake)	E3	Selwyn (riv.)	E3
Hess (riv.)	E3	Northern Yukon Nat'l Pk.	E3	Stewart (riv.)	E3
Hyland (riv.)	F3	Ogilvie (mts.)	E3	Teslin (lake)	E4
Keele (peak)	E3	Ogilvie (riv.)	E3	Teslin (riv.)	E3
Klondike (riv.)	E3	Peel (riv.)	E3	White (riv.)	D3
Kluane (lake)	E3	Pelly (mts.)	E3	Yukon (riv.)	E3
		Pelly (riv.)	E3	• Population of district.	

United States

POLYCONIC PROJECTION

SCALE OF MILES

SCALE OF KILOMETERS

Capitals of Countries .... ☆
State Capitals .... △
International Boundaries .... —·—·—

Scale 1:17,400,000

© Copyright HAMMOND INCORPORATED, Maplewood, N.J.

GULF OF MEXICO

Akron, Ohio‡ 660,328	K2	
Alabama (state) 3,890,061	J4	
Alaska (state) 400,481	C5	
Alaska (gulf), Alaska	D6	
Alaska (range), Alaska	C5	
Albany (cap.), N.Y.‡ 795,019	M2	
Albuquerque, N. Mex.‡ 454,499	E3	
Aleutian (isls.), Alaska	D6	
Allentown, Pa.‡ 636,714	L2	
Anchorage, Alaska‡ 173,017	D6	
Annapolis (cap.), Md. 31,740	L3	
Ann Arbor, Mich.‡ 264,748	K2	
Appalachian (mts.)	K3	
Appleton, Wis.‡ 291,325	J2	
Arizona (state) 2,717,866	D4	
Arkansas (state) 2,285,513	H3	
Arkansas (riv.)	H3	
Atlanta (cap.), Ga.‡ 2,029,618	K4	
Atlantic City, N.J.‡ 194,119	M3	
Attu (isl.), Alaska	D6	
Augusta, Ga.‡ 327,372	K4	
Augusta (cap.), Maine 21,819	N2	
Austin (cap.), Texas‡ 536,450	G4	
Bakersfield, Calif.‡ 403,089	C3	
Baltimore, Md.‡ 2,174,023	L3	
Baton Rouge (cap.), La.‡ 493,973	H4	
Beaumont, Texas‡ 375,497	H4	
Bering (sea), Alaska	C6	
Bering (str.), Alaska	C6	
Bighorn (riv.)	E2	
Binghamton, N.Y.‡ 301,336	L2	
Birmingham, Ala.‡ 847,360	J4	
Bismarck (cap.), N. Dak.‡ 79,988	G1	
Bitterroot (range)	D2	
Black Hills, S. Dak.	F2	
Boise (cap.), Idaho‡ 173,076	D2	
Borah (peak), Idaho	D2	

Boston (cap.), Mass.‡ 2,763,357	M2	
Bridgeport, Conn.‡ 395,455	M2	
Brazos (riv.), Texas	G4	
Brooks (range), Alaska	C5	
Buffalo, N.Y.‡ 1,242,573	L2	
California (state) 23,668,562	B3	
Canadian (riv.)	F3	
Canaveral (Kennedy) (cape), Fla.	L5	
Canton, Ohio‡ 404,421	K2	
Cape Fear (riv.), N.C.	L4	
Carson City (cap.), Nev. 32,022	C3	
Cascade (range)	B1	
Cedar Rapids, Iowa‡ 169,775	H2	
Champlain (lake)	M2	
Charleston, S.C.‡ 430,301	L4	
Charleston (cap.), W. Va.‡ 269,595	K3	
Charlotte, N.C.‡ 637,218	L3	
Chattahoochee (riv.)	K4	
Chattanooga, Tenn.‡ 426,540	J3	
Chesapeake (bay)	L3	
Cheyenne (cap.), Wyo. 47,283	F2	
Cheyenne (riv.)	F2	
Chicago, Ill.‡ 7,102,328	J2	
Cimarron (riv.)	G3	
Cincinnati, Ohio‡ 1,401,403	K3	
Cleveland, Ohio‡ 1,898,720	K2	
Coast (ranges)	A3	
Cod (cape), Mass.	N2	
Colorado (state) 2,888,834	E3	
Colorado (riv.)	D4	
Colorado (riv.), Texas	G4	
Colorado Springs, Colo.‡ 317,458	F3	
Columbia (riv.)	B1	
Columbia (cap.), S.C.‡ 408,176	L4	
Columbus, Ga.‡ 239,196	K4	

Columbus (cap.), Ohio‡ 1,093,293	K3	
Concord (cap.), N.H. 30,400	M2	
Connecticut (state) 3,107,576	M2	
Connecticut (riv.)	M2	
Corpus Christi, Texas‡ 326,228	G5	
Cumberland (riv.)	J3	
Dallas, Texas‡ 2,974,878	G4	
Davenport, Iowa‡ 383,958	H2	
Dayton, Ohio‡ 830,070	K3	
Death Valley (depr.), Calif.	C3	
Delaware (state) 595,225	L3	
Delaware (bay)	M3	
Denver (cap.), Colo.‡ 1,619,921	F3	
Des Moines (cap.), Iowa‡ 338,048	H2	
Detroit, Mich.‡ 4,352,762	K2	
District of Columbia 637,651	L3	
Dover (cap.), Del. 23,512	L3	
Duluth, Minn.‡ 266,650	H1	
Durham, N.C.‡ 530,673	L3	
Elbert (mt.), Colo.	E3	
El Paso, Texas‡ 479,899	E4	
Erie, Pa.‡ 279,780	K2	
Erie (lake)	K2	
Eugene, Oreg.‡ 275,225	B2	
Evansville, Ind.‡ 309,408	J3	
Everglades, The (swamp), Fla.	L3	
Fayetteville, N.C.‡ 247,160	L3	
Flint, Mich.‡ 521,589	K2	
Florida (state) 9,739,992	K5	
Florida (keys), Fla.	K6	
Fort Smith, Ark.‡ 203,269	H3	
Fort Wayne, Ind.‡ 382,961	J2	
Fort Worth, Texas 385,141	G4	
Frankfort (cap.), Ky. 25,973	K3	
Fresno, Calif.‡ 515,013	C3	
Galveston, Texas‡ 195,940	H5	
Gary, Ind.‡ 642,781	J2	

Georgia (state) 5,464,265	K4	
Gila (riv.)	D4	
Glacier Nat'l Park, Mont.	D1	
Golden Gate (chan.), Calif.	B3	
Grand Canyon Nat'l Park, Ariz.	D3	
Grand Rapids, Mich.‡ 601,680	K2	
Great Salt (lake), Utah	D2	
Greensboro, N.C.‡ 827,385	L3	
Greenville, S.C.‡ 568,758	K4	
Harrisburg (cap.), Pa.‡ 446,072	L2	
Hartford (cap.), Conn.‡ 726,114	M2	
Hatteras (cape), N.C.	M3	
Havasu (lake)	D4	
Hawaii (state) 965,000	F6	
Hawaii (isl.), Hawaii	G6	
Honolulu (cap.), Hawaii‡ 762,874	F6	
Houston, Texas‡ 2,905,350	G5	
Huntington, W. Va.‡ 311,350	K3	
Huntsville, Ala.‡ 308,593	J4	
Huron (lake)	K2	
Idaho (state) 943,935	D2	
Illinois (state) 11,418,461	J2	
Indiana (state) 5,490,179	J3	
Aleutian (isls.), Alaska	D6	
Iowa (state) 2,913,387	H2	
Jackson (cap.), Miss.‡ 320,425	J4	
Jacksonville, Fla.‡ 737,519	K4	
Jefferson City (cap.), Mo. 33,619	H3	
Jersey City, N.J.‡ 556,972	M2	
Johnstown, Pa.‡ 264,506	L2	
Juneau (cap.), Alaska 19,528	E6	
Kalamazoo, Mich.‡ 279,192	J2	
Kansas (state) 2,363,208	G3	
Kansas City,		

Kans.-Mo.‡ 1,327,020	G3	
Kauai (isl.), Hawaii	E6	
Kentucky (state) 3,661,433	J3	
Kentucky (lake)	J3	
Knoxville, Tenn.‡ 476,517	K3	
Lancaster, Pa.‡ 362,346	L2	
Lansing (cap.), Mich.‡ 476,517	K2	
Las Vegas, Nev.‡ 461,816	C3	
Lawrence, Mass.‡ 281,981	M2	
Lexington, Ky.‡ 318,136	K3	
Lincoln (cap.), Nebr.‡ 192,884	G2	
Little Rock (cap.), Ark.‡ 393,494	H4	
Long (isl.), N.Y.	M2	
Long Beach, Calif. 361,334	C4	
Los Angeles, Calif.‡ 7,477,657	C4	
Louisiana (state) 4,203,972	H4	
Louisville, Ky.‡ 906,240	J3	
Lowell, Mass.‡ 233,410	M2	
Lubbock, Texas‡ 211,651	F4	
Macon, Ga.‡ 254,623	K4	
Madison (cap.), Wis.‡ 323,545	J2	
Maine (state) 1,124,660	N1	
Maryland (state) 4,216,446	L3	
Massachusetts (state) 5,737,037	M2	
Maui (isl.), Hawaii	F6	
Mauna Kea (mt.), Hawaii	G6	
Mauna Loa (mt.), Hawaii	G6	
May (cape), N.J.	M3	
McKinley (mt.), Alaska	C5	
Memphis, Tenn.‡ 912,887	J3	
Mendocino (cape), Calif.	A3	
Mexico (gulf)	J5	
Miami, Fla.‡ 1,625,979	K5	
Michigan (state) 9,258,344	J1	
Michigan (lake)	J2	
Milwaukee, Wis.‡ 1,397,143	J2	
Minneapolis, Minn.‡ 2,114,256	H1	

Minnesota (state) 4,077,148	H1	
Mississippi (state) 2,520,638	J4	
Mississippi (riv.)	H2	
Missouri (state) 4,917,444	H3	
Missouri (riv.)	H3	
Mitchell (mt.), N.C.	K3	
Mobile, Ala.‡ 442,819	J4	
Montana (state) 786,690	E1	
Montgomery (cap.), Ala.‡ 272,687	J4	
Nantucket (isl.), Mass.	N2	
Nashville (cap.), Tenn.‡ 850,505	J3	
Nebraska (state) 1,570,006	F2	
Nevada (state) 799,184	C3	
New Hampshire (state) 920,610	M2	
New Jersey (state) 7,364,158	M3	
New Mexico (state) 1,299,968	E4	
New Orleans, La.‡ 1,186,725	H5	
Newport News, Va.‡ 364,449	L3	
New York (state) 17,557,288	L2	
New York, N.Y.‡ 9,119,737	M2	
Norfolk, Va.‡ 806,691	L3	
North Carolina (state) 5,874,429	L3	
North Dakota (state) 652,695	F1	
Oahu (isl.), Hawaii	F5	
Oakland, Calif.‡ 3,252,721	B3	
Ohio (state) 10,797,419	K2	
Ohio (riv.)	J3	
Oklahoma (state) 3,025,266	G3	
Oklahoma City (cap.), Okla.‡ 834,088	G3	
Olympia (cap.), Wash.‡ 124,264	B1	
Olympic Nat'l Park, Wash.	B1	
Omaha, Nebr.‡ 570,399	G2	
Ontario (lake), N.Y.	L2	

Oregon (state) 2,632,663	B2	
Orlando, Fla.‡ 700,699	K5	
Ozark (mts.)	H3	
Paterson, N.J.‡ 447,585	M2	
Pennsylvania (state)	L2	
Pensacola, Fla.‡ 289,782	J4	
Peoria, Ill.‡ 365,864	J2	
Philadelphia, Pa.‡ 4,716,818	M2	
Phoenix (cap.), Ariz.‡ 1,508,030	D4	
Pierre (cap.), S. Dak. 11,793	F2	
Pikes (peak), Colo.	F3	
Pittsburgh, Pa.‡ 2,263,894	L2	
Platte (riv.), Nebr.	G2	
Pontchartrain (lake), La.	J5	
Portland, Maine‡ 183,625	N2	
Portland, Oreg.‡ 1,242,187	B1	
Potomac (riv.)	L3	
Providence (cap.), R.I.‡ 919,216	M2	
Racine, Wis.‡ 173,132	J2	
Raleigh (cap.), N.C.‡ 530,673	L3	
Rainier (mt.), Wash.	B1	
Red (riv.)	G4	
Red River of the North	G1	
Rhode Island (state) 947,154	M2	
Richmond (cap.), Va.‡ 632,015	L3	
Rio Grande (riv.)	F5	
Roanoke, Va.‡ 218,244	K3	
Rochester, N.Y.‡ 971,079	L2	
Rockford, Ill.‡ 279,514	J2	
Rocky (mts.)	E2	
Sacramento (cap.), Calif.‡ 1,014,002	B3	
Saginaw, Mich.‡ 224,548	K2	
Saint Clair (lake), Mich.	K2	
Saint Lawrence, N.Y.	N1	
Saint Louis, Mo.‡ 2,355,276	H3	

AREA 3,623,420 sq. mi.
(9,384,658 sq. km.)
POPULATION 226,504,825
CAPITAL Washington
LARGEST CITY New York
HIGHEST POINT Mt. McKinley 20,320 ft.
(6,194 m.)
MONETARY UNIT U.S. dollar
MAJOR LANGUAGE English
MAJOR RELIGIONS Protestantism,
Roman Catholicism, Judaism

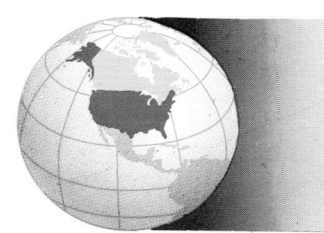

Population Distribution

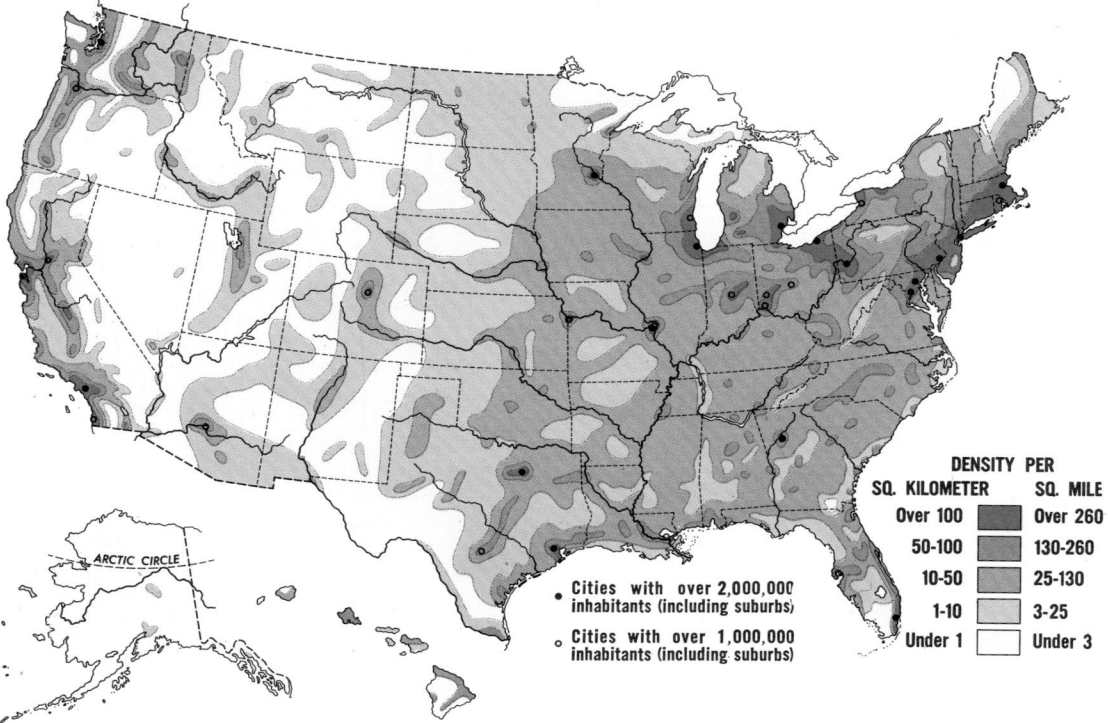

DENSITY PER

SQ. KILOMETER	SQ. MILE
Over 100	Over 260
50-100	130-260
10-50	25-130
1-10	3-25
Under 1	Under 3

● Cities with over 2,000,000 inhabitants (including suburbs)
○ Cities with over 1,000,000 inhabitants (including suburbs)

Vegetation

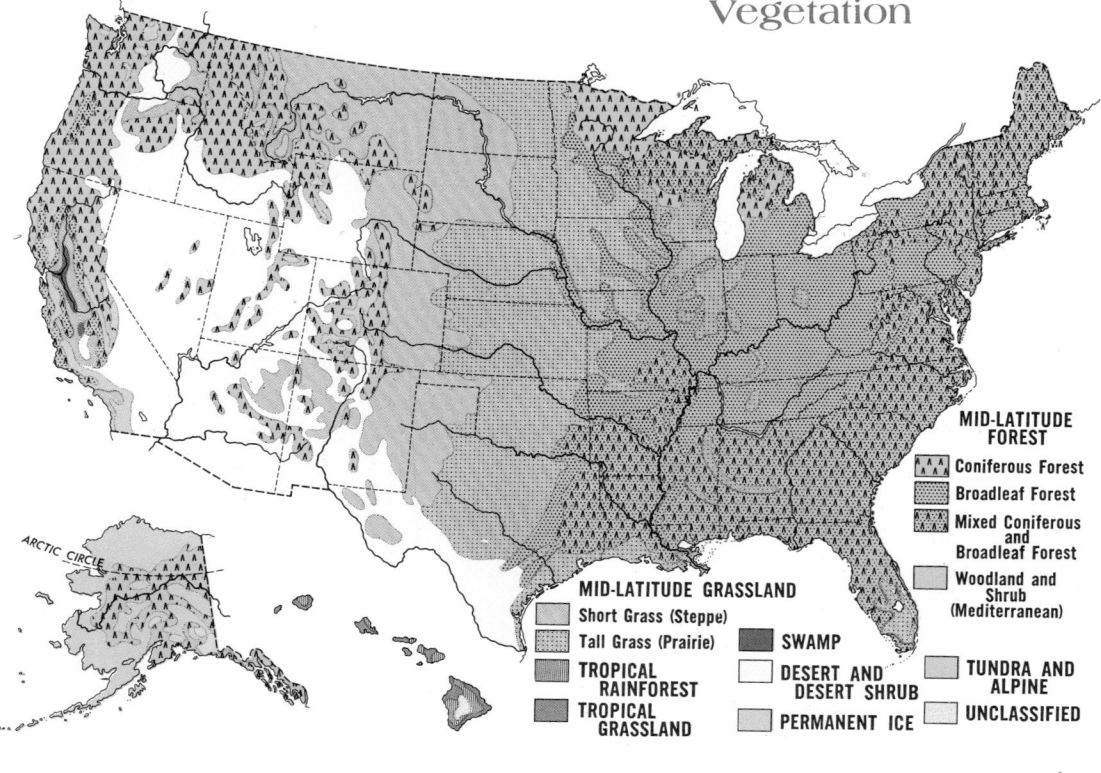

MID-LATITUDE FOREST
▲▲▲ Coniferous Forest
Broadleaf Forest
Mixed Coniferous and Broadleaf Forest
Woodland and Shrub (Mediterranean)

MID-LATITUDE GRASSLAND
Short Grass (Steppe)
Tall Grass (Prairie) SWAMP
TROPICAL RAINFOREST DESERT AND DESERT SHRUB TUNDRA AND ALPINE
TROPICAL GRASSLAND PERMANENT ICE UNCLASSIFIED

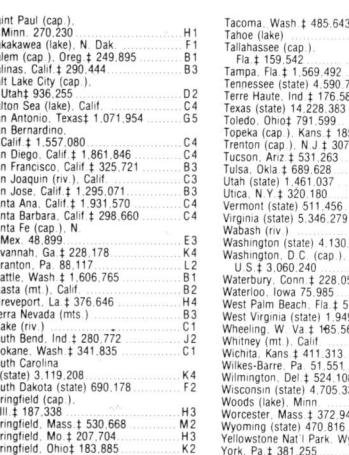

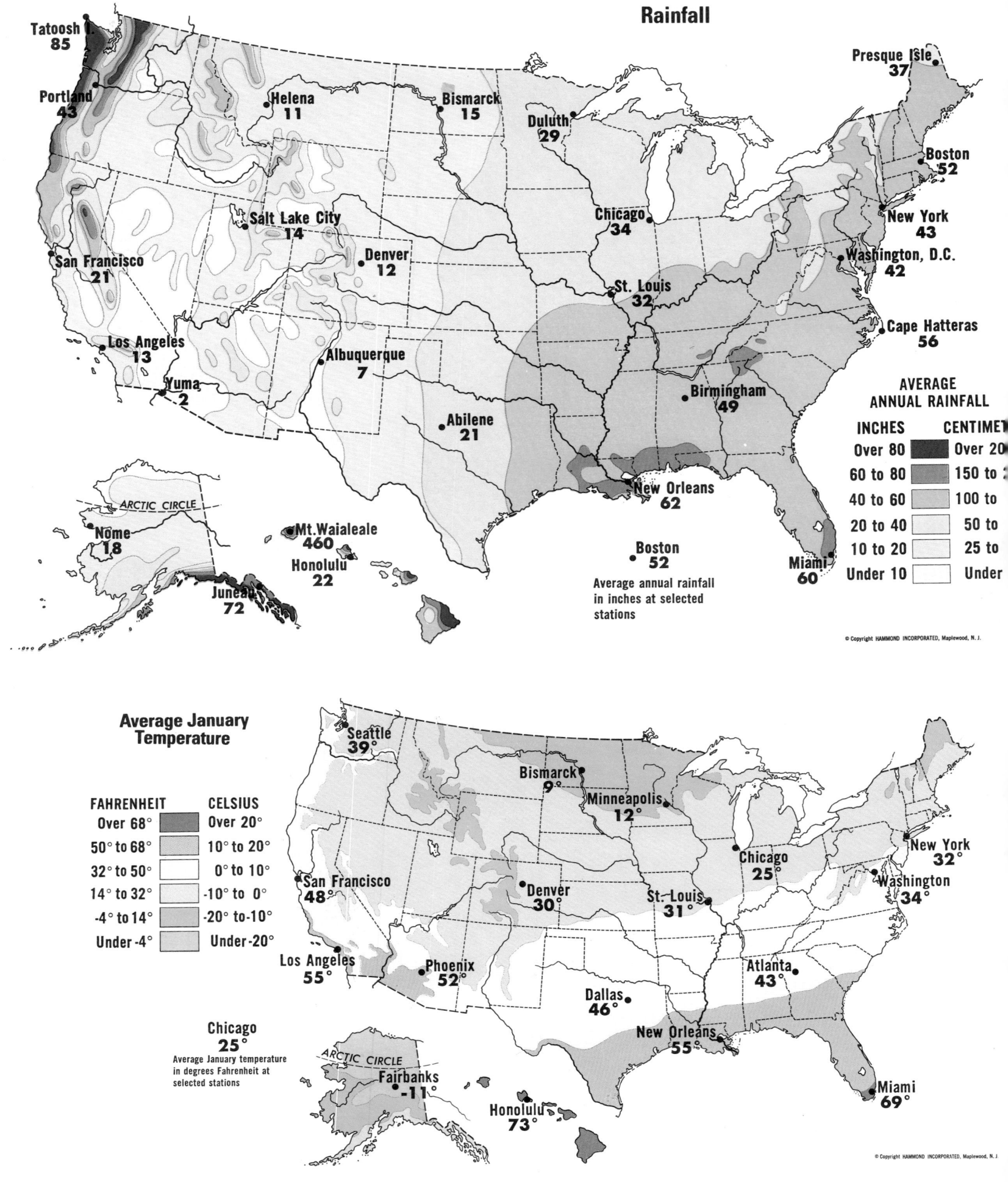

Rainfall

Tatoosh I.
85

Portland
43

Helena
11

Bismarck
15

Duluth
29

Presque Isle
37

Boston
52

New York
43

Washington, D.C.
42

Chicago
34

Salt Lake City
14

Denver
12

St. Louis
32

San Francisco
21

Los Angeles
13

Yuma
2

Albuquerque
7

Abilene
21

Birmingham
49

Cape Hatteras
56

New Orleans
62

Miami
60

ARCTIC CIRCLE

Nome
18

Mt. Waialeale
460

Honolulu
22

Juneau
72

Boston
52

Average annual rainfall
in inches at selected
stations

AVERAGE ANNUAL RAINFALL

INCHES	CENTIMET
Over 80	Over 20
60 to 80	150 to
40 to 60	100 to
20 to 40	50 to
10 to 20	25 to
Under 10	Under

© Copyright HAMMOND INCORPORATED, Maplewood, N.J.

Average January Temperature

Seattle
39°

Bismarck
9°

Minneapolis
12°

New York
32°

Chicago
25°

Washington
34°

San Francisco
48°

Denver
30°

St. Louis
31°

Los Angeles
55°

Phoenix
52°

Atlanta
43°

Dallas
46°

New Orleans
55°

Miami
69°

FAHRENHEIT	CELSIUS
Over 68°	Over 20°
50° to 68°	10° to 20°
32° to 50°	0° to 10°
14° to 32°	-10° to 0°
-4° to 14°	-20° to -10°
Under -4°	Under -20°

Chicago
25°

Average January temperature
in degrees Fahrenheit at
selected stations

ARCTIC CIRCLE

Fairbanks
-11°

Honolulu
73°

© Copyright HAMMOND INCORPORATED, Maplewood, N.J.

Topography

200   400 MI.

0   200   400 KM.

PACIFIC OCEAN

C. Flattery
Seattle
Mt. St. Helens
9,564 ft.
(2549 m.)
Mt. Rainier 14,410 ft.
(4392 m.)
Snake
COLUMBIA PLATEAU
COAST RANGE
CASCADE RANGE
BITTERROOT RANGE
ROCKY MOUNTAINS
Columbia
Missouri
Fort Peck Lake
Yellowstone
GREAT
Rainy
Lake Superior
Keweenaw Pen.
St. Lawrence
L. Champlain
Gulf of Maine
Boston
C. Cod

Sacramento
SIERRA NEVADA
Great Salt Lake
Great Basin
Lake Mead
COLORADO PLATEAU
Denver
Mt. Elbert
14,431 ft. (4399 m.)
N. Platte
Platte
Lake Oahe
Lake Sakakawea
Red
James
Missouri
Des Moines
Wisconsin
Lake Michigan
Lake Huron
Lake Erie
Lake Ontario
Niagara Falls
Minneapolis
Milwaukee
Chicago
Detroit
Cleveland
New York
Long Island
Philadelphia
ATLANTIC

San Francisco
Central Valley
Mt. Whitney
14,495 ft. (4418 m.)
PLAINS
Kansas City
Missouri
St. Louis
Illinois
Ohio
Wabash
Indianapolis
Washington
Chesapeake Bay
ATLANTIC

Pt. Conception
SANTA BARBARA IS.
Mojave Desert
Los Angeles
Grand Canyon
Colorado
Lake Powell
Arkansas
OZARK PLATEAU
Tennessee
Mt. Mitchell
6,684 ft. (2037 m.)
APPALACHIAN MOUNTAINS
ALLEGHENY MTS.
C. Hatteras
OCEAN

San Diego
Phoenix
PLATEAU
Gila
Rio Grande
Canadian
Red
Memphis
Wheeler L.
Atlanta
Savannah
Chattahoochee
C. Fear

ARCTIC OCEAN
BROOKS RANGE
LLANO ESTACADO
Pecos
Brazos
EDWARDS PLATEAU
Colorado
Dallas
Red
Mississippi
COASTAL PLAIN
ATLANTIC COASTAL PLAIN
Jacksonville
C. Canaveral

0 200 400 MI.
0 200 400 KM.
St. Lawrence I.
Yukon
Tanana
Mt. McKinley
20,320 ft. (6194 m.)
Anchorage
Gulf of Alaska
Kodiak I.
ALEXANDER ARCHIPELAGO
BERING SEA
Bering Str.
Alaska Pen.
Aleutian Islands
Kauai
HAWAIIAN ISLANDS
PACIFIC OCEAN
Oahu
Molokai
Honolulu
Maui
Mauna Kea
13,796 ft. (4205 m.)
Hawaii
0 50 100 MI.
0 50 100 KM.
Houston
New Orleans
Mississippi Delta
Gulf of Mexico
L. Okeechobee
The Everglades
FLORIDA KEYS
Miami

5,000 m. 16,404 ft. | 2,000 m. 6,562 ft. | 1,000 m. 3,281 ft. | 500 m. 1,640 ft. | 200 m. 656 ft. | 100 m. 328 ft. | Sea Level | Below

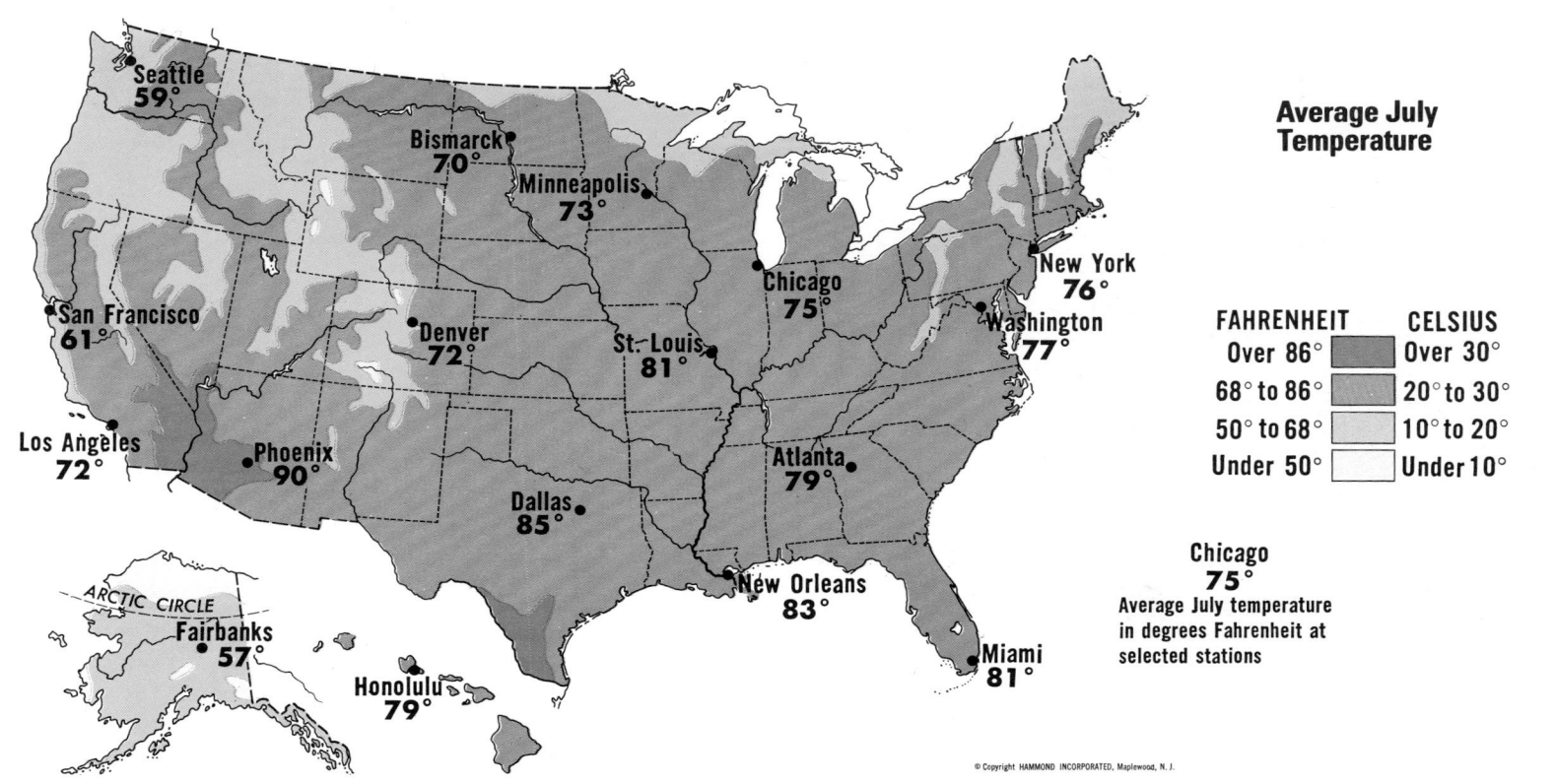

Average July Temperature

Seattle 59°
Bismarck 70°
Minneapolis 73°
Chicago 75°
New York 76°
Washington 77°
San Francisco 61°
Denver 72°
St. Louis 81°
Los Angeles 72°
Phoenix 90°
Atlanta 79°
Dallas 85°
New Orleans 83°
Miami 81°
Fairbanks 57°
Honolulu 79°

FAHRENHEIT	CELSIUS
Over 86°	Over 30°
68° to 86°	20° to 30°
50° to 68°	10° to 20°
Under 50°	Under 10°

Chicago 75°

Average July temperature in degrees Fahrenheit at selected stations

ARCTIC CIRCLE

© Copyright HAMMOND INCORPORATED, Maplewood, N.J.

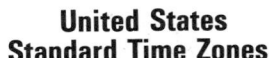

United States Standard Time Zones

U. S. STANDARD TIME ZONES
Established by the Uniform Time Act
PACIFIC STANDARD TIME
MOUNTAIN STANDARD TIME
CENTRAL STANDARD TIME
EASTERN STANDARD TIME
ATLANTIC STD. TIME
ALASKA STANDARD TIME
HAWAII-ALEUTIAN STD. TIME
HAWAII-ALEUTIAN STANDARD TIME
PACIFIC OCEAN
ATLANTIC OCEAN
Gulf of Mexico
UNITED STATES
CANADA
MEXICO
PUERTO RICO
Long. West of Greenwich
SCALE OF MILES

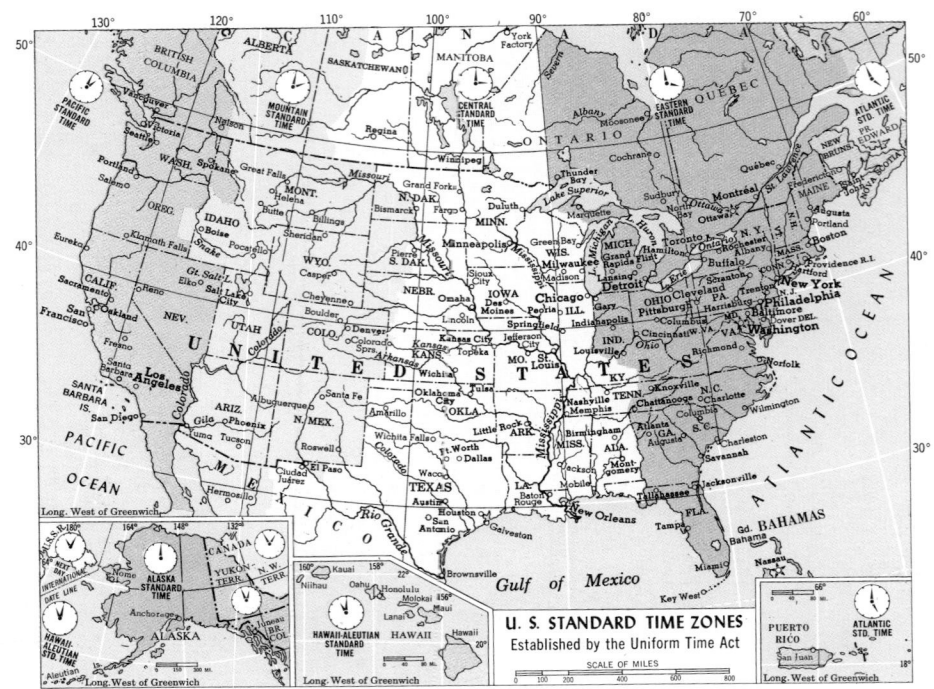

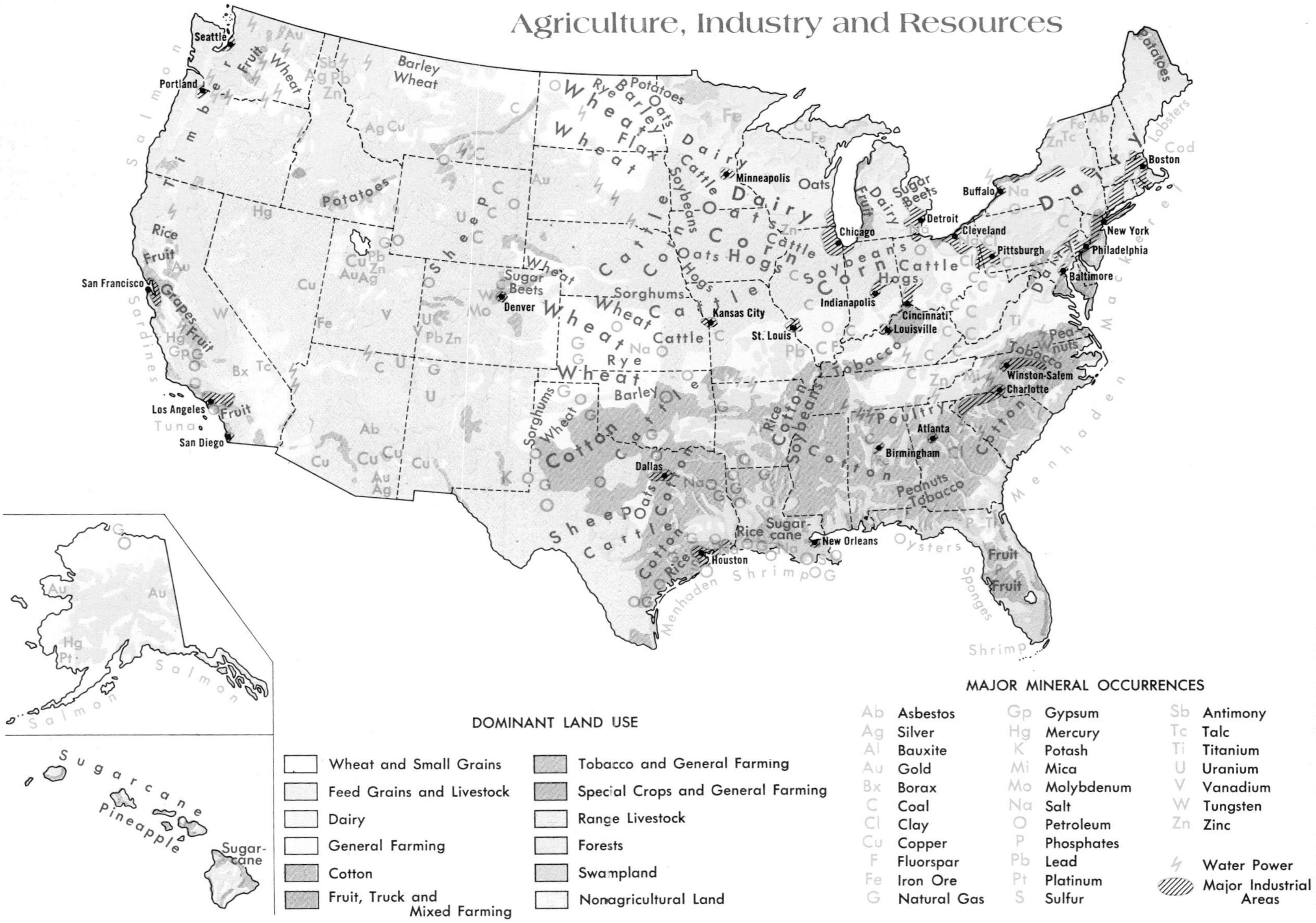

Agriculture, Industry and Resources
DOMINANT LAND USE
Wheat and Small Grains
Feed Grains and Livestock
Dairy
General Farming
Cotton
Fruit, Truck and Mixed Farming
Tobacco and General Farming
Special Crops and General Farming
Range Livestock
Forests
Swampland
Nonagricultural Land
MAJOR MINERAL OCCURRENCES
Ab Asbestos
Ag Silver
Al Bauxite
Au Gold
Bx Borax
C Coal
Cl Clay
Cu Copper
F Fluorspar
Fe Iron Ore
G Natural Gas
Gp Gypsum
Hg Mercury
K Potash
Mi Mica
Mo Molybdenum
Na Salt
O Petroleum
P Phosphates
Pb Lead
Pt Platinum
S Sulfur
Sb Antimony
Tc Talc
Ti Titanium
U Uranium
V Vanadium
W Tungsten
Zn Zinc
Water Power
Major Industrial Areas

AREA 51,705 sq. mi. (133,916 sq. km.)
POPULATION 3,893,888
CAPITAL Montgomery
LARGEST CITY Birmingham
HIGHEST POINT Cheaha Mtn. 2,407 ft. (734 m.)
SETTLED IN 1702
ADMITTED TO UNION December 14, 1819
POPULAR NAME Heart of Dixie; Cotton State; Yellowhammer State
STATE FLOWER Camellia
STATE BIRD Yellowhammer

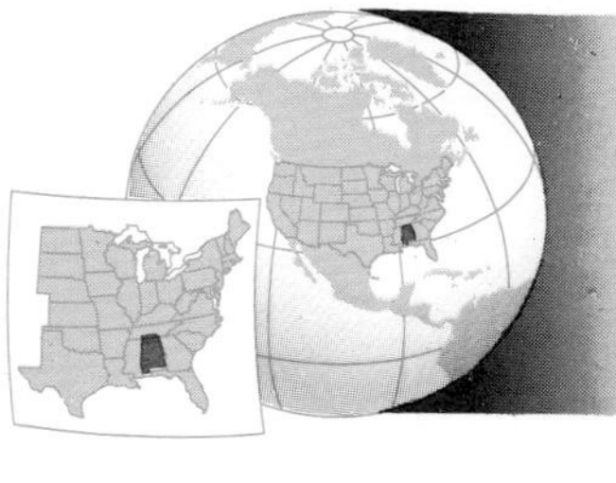

COUNTIES

Autauga 32,259 ..... E5
Baldwin 78,556 ..... C9
Barbour 24,756 ..... H7
Bibb 15,723 ..... D5
Blount 36,459 ..... E2
Bullock 10,596 ..... G6
Butler 21,680 ..... E7
Calhoun 119,761 ..... G3
Chambers 39,191 ..... H5
Cherokee 18,760 ..... G2
Chilton 30,612 ..... E5
Choctaw 16,839 ..... B6
Clarke 27,702 ..... C7
Clay 13,703 ..... G4
Cleburne 12,595 ..... G3
Coffee 38,533 ..... G8
Colbert 54,519 ..... C1
Conecuh 15,884 ..... E8
Coosa 11,377 ..... F5
Covington 36,850 ..... F8
Crenshaw 14,110 ..... F7
Cullman 61,642 ..... E2
Dale 47,821 ..... G8
Dallas 53,981 ..... D6
De Kalb 53,658 ..... G2
Elmore 43,390 ..... F5
Escambia 38,440 ..... D8
Etowah 103,057 ..... F2
ayette 18,809 ..... C3
ranklin 28,350 ..... C2
eneva 24,253 ..... G8
reene 11,021 ..... C5
ale 15,604 ..... C5
enry 15,302 ..... H7
ouston 74,632 ..... H8
ackson 51,407 ..... F1
efferson 671,324 ..... E3
amar 16,453 ..... B3
auderdale 80,546 ..... C1
awrence 30,170 ..... D1
ee 76,283 ..... H5
imestone 46,005 ..... E1
owndes 13,253 ..... E6
acon 26,829 ..... G6
adison 196,966 ..... E1
arengo 25,047 ..... C6
arion 30,041 ..... C2
arshall 65,622 ..... F2
obile 364,980 ..... B9
onroe 22,651 ..... D7
ontgomery 197,038 ..... F6
organ 90,231 ..... E2
erry 15,012 ..... D5
ickens 21,481 ..... B4
ike 28,050 ..... G7
andolph 20,075 ..... H4
ussell 47,356 ..... H6
aint Clair 41,205 ..... F3
helby 66,298 ..... E4
umter 16,908 ..... B5
alladega 73,826 ..... F4
allapoosa 38,676 ..... G5
uscaloosa 137,541 ..... C4
alker 68,660 ..... D3
ashington 16,821 ..... B8
ilcox 14,755 ..... D7
inston 21,953 ..... D2

CITIES and TOWNS

p — Name/Pop. — Key

36310 Abbeville⊙ 3,155 ..... H7
35440 Abernant 405 ..... D4
35005 Adamsville 2,498 ..... D3
35540 Addison 746 ..... D2
35006 Adger 400 ..... D4
35441 Akron 604 ..... C5
35007 Alabaster 7,079 ..... E4
35950 Albertville 12,039 ..... F2
35115 Aldrich 500 ..... E4
35010 Alexander City 13,807 ..... G5
36250 Alexandria 600 ..... G3
35442 Aliceville 3,207 ..... B4
35013 Allgood 387 ..... F3
36501 Alma 500 ..... C8
35952 Altoona 928 ..... F2
36420 Andalusia⊙ 10,415 ..... E8
35610 Anderson 405 ..... D1
36201 Anniston⊙ 29,523 ..... G3
Anniston‡ 116,936 ..... G3
5016 Arab 5,967 ..... E2
5805 Ardmore 1,096 ..... E1
5173 Argo 600 ..... E3
6311 Ariton 844 ..... G7
5033 Arkadelphia 150 ..... E3
5541 Arley 276 ..... D2
5035 Ashby 500 ..... E4
6312 Ashford 2,165 ..... H8
6251 Ashland⊙ 2,052 ..... G4
5953 Ashville⊙ 1,489 ..... F3
5611 Athens⊙ 14,558 ..... E1
6503 Atmore 8,789 ..... C8
35954 Attalla 7,737 ..... F2
36830 Auburn 28,471 ..... H5
36003 Autaugaville 843 ..... E6
†36312 Avon 433 ..... H8
36505 Axis 500 ..... B9
†36420 Babbie 553 ..... F8
35019 Baileyton 396 ..... E2
36005 Banks 160 ..... G7
†36532 Barnwell 700 ..... C10
36507 Bay Minette⊙ 7,455 ..... C9
36509 Bayou La Batre 2,005 ..... B10
35543 Bear Creek 353 ..... C2
36425 Beatrice 558 ..... D7
35544 Beaverton 360 ..... B3
†35653 Belgreen 500 ..... C2
35545 Belk 308 ..... C3
36901 Bellamy 700 ..... B6
35615 Belle Mina 675 ..... E1
36313 Bellwood 400 ..... G8
36785 Benton 74 ..... E6
35546 Berry 916 ..... C3
35020 Bessemer 31,729 ..... D4
†36872 Beulah 500 ..... H5
36006 Billingsley 106 ..... E5
*35201 Birmingham⊙ 284,413 ..... D3
Birmingham‡ 847,360 ..... D3
36314 Black 156 ..... G8
35031 Blountsville 1,509 ..... E2
36201 Blue Mountain 284 ..... G3
†36017 Blue Springs 112 ..... G7
35957 Boaz 7,151 ..... F2
35443 Boligee 164 ..... C5
35032 Bon Air 118 ..... F4
36511 Bon Secour 850 ..... C10
†35120 Branchville 365 ..... F3
36009 Brantley 1,151 ..... F7
35034 Brent 2,862 ..... D5
36426 Brewton⊙ 6,680 ..... D8
35740 Bridgeport 2,974 ..... G1
35020 Brighton 5,308 ..... D4
35548 Brilliant 871 ..... C2
35036 Brookside 1,409 ..... E3
35444 Brookwood 492 ..... D4
36010 Brundidge 3,213 ..... G7
36725 Burkville 250 ..... E6
36431 Burnt Corn 60 ..... D7
36904 Butler⊙ 1,882 ..... B6
†36767 Cahaba 75 ..... D6
35040 Calera 2,035 ..... E4
†36047 Calhoun 950 ..... F6
36513 Calvert 600 ..... B8
36726 Camden⊙ 2,406 ..... D7
36850 Camp Hill 1,628 ..... G5
†36502 Canoe 560 ..... D8
†36726 Canton Bend 300 ..... D6
35549 Carbon Hill 2,452 ..... D3
35041 Cardiff 140 ..... E3
†36420 Carolina 203 ..... E8
35447 Carrollton⊙ 1,104 ..... B4
†36023 Carrville 820 ..... G5
†36548 Carson 400 ..... C8
36432 Castleberry 847 ..... D8
35959 Cedar Bluff 1,129 ..... G2
35960 Centre⊙ 2,351 ..... G2
35042 Centreville⊙ 2,504 ..... D5
36518 Chatom⊙ 1,122 ..... B8
35043 Chelsea 600 ..... E4
35616 Cherokee 1,589 ..... C1
36611 Chickasaw 7,402 ..... B9
35044 Childersburg 5,084 ..... F4
36254 Choccolocco 500 ..... G3
36905 Choctaw 600 ..... B6
†36550 Chrysler 400 ..... C8
36521 Chunchula 700 ..... B9
36522 Citronelle 2,841 ..... B8
35045 Clanton⊙ 5,832 ..... E5
†36322 Clayhatchee 560 ..... G8
36015 Clayton⊙ 1,589 ..... G7
35049 Cleveland 487 ..... E3
36017 Clio 1,224 ..... G7
35449 Coaling 400 ..... D4
36523 Coden 600 ..... B10
36318 Coffee Springs 339 ..... G8
36524 Coffeeville 448 ..... B7
35452 Coker 800 ..... C4
35961 Collinsville 1,383 ..... G2
36319 Columbia 881 ..... H8
35051 Columbiana⊙ 2,655 ..... E4
36020 Coosada 980 ..... F5
35550 Cordova 3,123 ..... D3
35453 Cottondale 500 ..... D4
36320 Cottonwood 1,352 ..... H8
†35172 County Line 199 ..... E3
†36467 County Line 124 ..... F8
35618 Courtland 456 ..... D1
36321 Cowarts 418 ..... H8
36435 Coy 950 ..... D7
36525 Creola 1,652 ..... B9
36906 Cromwell 650 ..... B6
35962 Crossville 1,222 ..... G2
36907 Cuba 486 ..... B6
35055 Cullman⊙ 13,084 ..... E2
36852 Cusseta 650 ..... H5
36853 Dadeville⊙ 3,263 ..... G5
36322 Daleville 4,250 ..... G8
36526 Daphne 3,406 ..... C9
36528 Dauphin Island 950 ..... B10
36256 Daviston 334 ..... G4
36731 Dayton 113 ..... C6
*35601 Decatur⊙ 42,002 ..... D1
36257 De Armanville 350 ..... G3
36732 Demopolis 7,678 ..... C6
35552 Detroit 326 ..... B2
35062 Dora 2,327 ..... D3
*36303 Dothan⊙ 48,750 ..... H8
35553 Double Springs⊙ 1,057 ..... D2
35964 Douglas 116 ..... F2
36028 Dozier 494 ..... F7
35744 Dutton 276 ..... G1
36426 East Brewton 3,012 ..... E8
36024 Eclectic 1,124 ..... F5
36261 Edwardsville 207 ..... H3
36323 Elba⊙ 4,355 ..... F8
36530 Elberta 491 ..... C10
35554 Eldridge 230 ..... C3
35620 Elkmont 429 ..... E1
36025 Elmore 600 ..... F5
35458 Elrod 746 ..... C4
35063 Empire 600 ..... D3
36330 Enterprise 18,033 ..... G8
35460 Epes 399 ..... B5
35461 Ethelsville 95 ..... B4
36027 Eufaula 12,097 ..... H7
†36340 Eunola 169 ..... G8
35462 Eutaw⊙ 2,444 ..... C5
35621 Eva 185 ..... E2
36401 Evergreen⊙ 4,171 ..... E8
36439 Excel 385 ..... D8
35746 Fackler 250 ..... G1
36854 Fairfax 3,776 ..... H5
35064 Fairfield 13,242 ..... E4
36532 Fairhope 7,286 ..... C10
35208 Fairview 450 ..... E2
35622 Falkville 1,310 ..... E2
36738 Faunsdale 174 ..... C6
35555 Fayette⊙ 5,287 ..... C3
36855 Five Points 197 ..... H4
35966 Flat Rock 750 ..... G1
†35601 Flint City 673 ..... D1
36441 Flomaton 1,882 ..... D8
36442 Florala 2,165 ..... F8
*35630 Florence⊙ 37,029 ..... C1
Florence‡ 135,023 ..... C1
36535 Foley 4,003 ..... C10
35214 Forestdale 10,814 ..... E3
36740 Forkland 429 ..... C5
36031 Fort Davis 500 ..... G6
36032 Fort Deposit 1,519 ..... E7
36856 Fort Mitchell 900 ..... H6
35967 Fort Payne⊙ 11,485 ..... G2
35463 Fosters 400 ..... C4
36444 Franklin 133 ..... G6
36445 Frisco City 1,424 ..... D8
36539 Fruitdale 500 ..... B8
36262 Fruithurst 239 ..... G3
36446 Fulton 606 ..... C7
35068 Fultondale 6,217 ..... E3
35971 Fyffe 1,305 ..... G2
*35901 Gadsden⊙ 47,565 ..... G2
Gadsden‡ 103,057 ..... G2
35464 Gainesville 207 ..... B5
35972 Gallant 475 ..... F2
36038 Gantt 314 ..... E8
35070 Garden City 655 ..... E2
35071 Gardendale 7,928 ..... E3
35973 Gaylesville 192 ..... G2
†35459 Geiger 200 ..... B5
36340 Geneva⊙ 4,866 ..... G8
36033 Georgiana 1,993 ..... E7
35974 Geraldine 911 ..... G2
36908 Gilbertown 218 ..... B7
35559 Glen Allen 312 ..... C3
35905 Glencoe 4,648 ..... G3
36034 Glenwood 341 ..... F7
†35010 Goldville 89 ..... G4
†36024 Good Hope 1,442 ..... E2
35072 Goodwater 1,895 ..... F4
35466 Gordo 2,112 ..... C4
36343 Gordon 362 ..... H8
†35580 Gorgas 500 ..... D3
36035 Goshen 365 ..... F7
†36482 Gosport 500 ..... C7
36541 Grand Bay 3,185 ..... B10
35747 Grant 632 ..... F1
35073 Graysville 2,642 ..... D3
35074 Green Pond 750 ..... D4
36744 Greensboro⊙ 3,248 ..... C5
36037 Greenville⊙ 7,807 ..... E7
†36350 Grimes 298 ..... H8
36451 Grove Hill⊙ 1,912 ..... C7
35563 Guin 2,418 ..... C3
36542 Gulf Shores 1,349 ..... C10
35976 Guntersville⊙ 7,041 ..... F2
35748 Gurley 735 ..... F1
†35563 Gu-Win 266 ..... C3
35564 Hackleburg 883 ..... C2
†36319 Haleburg 106 ..... H8
35565 Haleyville 5,306 ..... C2

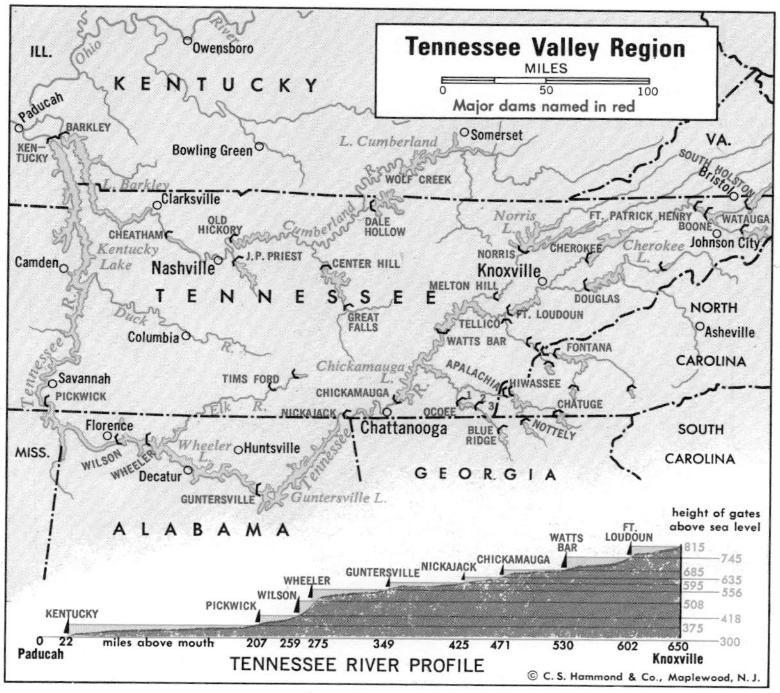

Tennessee Valley Region
MILES
0 50 100
Major dams named in red
ILL.
KENTUCKY
Owensboro
Paducah
BARKLEY
KEN-TUCKY
Bowling Green
L. Cumberland
Somerset
WOLF CREEK
VA.
SOUTH HOLSTON
Bristol
L. Barkley
Clarksville
OLD HICKORY
DALE HOLLOW
Norris L.
FT. PATRICK HENRY
BOONE
WATAUGA
CHEATHAM
Kentucky Lake
J. P. PRIEST
CENTER HILL
NORRIS
CHEROKEE
Cherokee L.
Johnson City
Camden
Nashville
Knoxville
TENNESSEE
MELTON HILL
DOUGLAS
NORTH
GREAT FALLS
TELLICO
FT. LOUDOUN
Asheville
Columbia
WATTS BAR
FONTANA
CAROLINA
Duck R.
Chickamauga L.
Savannah
PICKWICK
TIMS FORD
CHICKAMAUGA
HIWASSEE
Elk R.
NICKAJACK
OCOEE
CHATUGE
Florence
Chattanooga
BLUE RIDGE
NOTTELY
SOUTH CAROLINA
MISS.
WILSON
WHEELER
Wheeler L.
Huntsville
Decatur
GEORGIA
GUNTERSVILLE
Guntersville L.
ALABAMA
height of gates above sea level
WATTS BAR
FT. LOUDOUN
CHICKAMAUGA
NICKAJACK
GUNTERSVILLE
WHEELER
WILSON
PICKWICK
KENTUCKY
815
745
685
635
595
556
508
418
375
300
0 22 miles above mouth 207 259 275 349 425 471 530 602 650
Paducah
Knoxville
TENNESSEE RIVER PROFILE
© C. S. Hammond & Co., Maplewood, N. J.

35570 Hamilton⊙ 5,093 ..... C2
†35989 Hammondville 369 ..... G1
35077 Hanceville 2,220 ..... E2
36039 Hardaway 600 ..... G6
35078 Harpersville 934 ..... F4
36344 Hartford 2,647 ..... G8
35640 Hartselle 8,858 ..... E2
36858 Hatchechubbee 840 ..... H6
†35672 Hatton 950 ..... D1
35079 Hayden 268 ..... E3
36040 Hayneville⊙ 592 ..... E6
35750 Hazel Green 1,503 ..... E1
36345 Headland 3,327 ..... H8
†36558 Healing Springs 100 ..... B7
†36420 Heath 354 ..... F8
36264 Heflin⊙ 3,014 ..... G3
35080 Helena 2,130 ..... E4
35978 Henagar 1,188 ..... G1
35979 Higdon 925 ..... G1
†35013 Highland Lake 210 ..... F3
35643 Hillsboro 278 ..... D1
†36201 Hobson City 1,268 ..... G3
35571 Hodges 250 ..... C2
35903 Hokes Bluff 3,216 ..... G3
35082 Hollins 500 ..... F4
35083 Holly Pond 493 ..... E2
35752 Hollywood 1,110 ..... G1
35209 Homewood 21,412 ..... E4
†35216 Hoover 19,792 ..... E4
36043 Hope Hull 975 ..... F6
†36467 Horn Hill 186 ..... F8
35020 Hueytown 13,478 ..... D4
*35801 Huntsville⊙ 142,513 ..... E1
Huntsville‡ 308,593 ..... E1
36860 Hurtsboro 752 ..... H6
35981 Ider 698 ..... G1
35210 Irondale 6,510 ..... E3
36545 Jackson 6,073 ..... C8
36861 Jacksons Gap 800 ..... G5
36265 Jacksonville 9,735 ..... G3
35501 Jasper⊙ 11,894 ..... D3
35085 Jemison 1,828 ..... E5
35573 Kansas 267 ..... C3
35574 Kennedy 604 ..... B3
35645 Killen 747 ..... D1
35091 Kimberly 1,043 ..... E3
†36301 Kinsey 1,239 ..... H8
36453 Kinston 604 ..... F8
36862 Lafayette⊙ 3,647 ..... H5
†35986 Lakeview 441 ..... G2
36863 Lanett 6,897 ..... H5
36864 Langdale 2,034 ..... H5
†35768 Larkinsville 425 ..... F1
36911 Lavaca 500 ..... B6
35094 Leeds 8,638 ..... E3
35983 Leesburg 116 ..... G2
35646 Leighton 1,218 ..... D1
36548 Leroy 699 ..... B8
35647 Lester 117 ..... D1
†36322 Level Plains 867 ..... G8
35648 Lexington 884 ..... D1
†36420 Libertyville 141 ..... F8
35096 Lincoln 2,081 ..... F3
36748 Linden⊙ 2,773 ..... C6
36266 Lineville 2,257 ..... G4
35020 Lipscomb 3,741 ..... E4
36912 Lisman 638 ..... B6
†36876 Little Shawmut 2,793 ..... H5
†35653 Littleville 1,262 ..... C1
35470 Livingston⊙ 3,187 ..... B5
36865 Loachapoka 335 ..... G5
36455 Lockhart 547 ..... F8
35097 Locust Fork 488 ..... E3
†35137 Longview 475 ..... E4
36048 Louisville 791 ..... G7
36751 Lower Peach Tree 926 ..... C7
36752 Lowndesboro 207 ..... E6
36551 Loxley 804 ..... C9
36049 Luverne⊙ 2,639 ..... F7
35575 Lynn 554 ..... C2
35758 Madison 4,057 ..... E1
36348 Madrid 172 ..... H8
36555 Magnolia Springs 800 ..... C10
36349 Malvern 558 ..... G8
36750 Maplesville 754 ..... E5
35112 Margaret 757 ..... F3
36756 Marion⊙ 4,467 ..... D5
35114 Maylene 500 ..... E4
35111 McCalla 657 ..... E4
36552 McCullough 500 ..... D8
36553 McIntosh 319 ..... B8
36456 McKenzie 605 ..... E7
†35442 Memphis 95 ..... B4
35984 Mentone 476 ..... G1
35759 Meridianville 1,403 ..... F1
35228 Midfield 6,203 ..... E4
36350 Midland City 1,903 ..... H8
36053 Midway 593 ..... H6
†35150 Mignon 2,054 ..... F4
36054 Millbrook 3,101 ..... F6
35576 Millport 1,287 ..... B3
36558 Millry 956 ..... B7
36761 Minter 450 ..... D6
*36601 Mobile⊙ 200,452 ..... B9
Mobile‡ 442,819 ..... B9
36460 Monroeville⊙ 5,674 ..... D7
†35804 Monrovia 500 ..... E1
35115 Montevallo 3,965 ..... E4
*36101 Montgomery (cap.)⊙ 178,857 ..... F6
Montgomery‡ 272,687 ..... F3
36559 Montrose 750 ..... C9
†35125 Moody 1,840 ..... F3
35649 Mooresville 58 ..... E1
35116 Morris 623 ..... E3
35650 Moulton⊙ 3,197 ..... D2
35474 Moundville 1,310 ..... C5
†35957 Mountainboro 266 ..... F2
35223 Mountain Brook 19,718 ..... E4
36560 Mount Vernon 1,038 ..... B8
36268 Munford 700 ..... F3
35660 Muscle Shoals 8,911 ..... C1
36763 Myrtlewood 252 ..... C6
36764 Nanafalia 500 ..... B6
36303 Napier Field 493 ..... H8
35578 Nauvoo 259 ..... D3
†35049 Nectar 367 ..... E3
36765 Newbern 307 ..... C5
36351 New Brockton 1,392 ..... G8
35760 New Hope 1,546 ..... F1
35761 New Market 680 ..... F1
†35010 New Site 340 ..... G4
36352 Newton 1,540 ..... G8
36353 Newville 814 ..... H8
35086 North Johns 243 ..... D4
35476 Northport 14,291 ..... C4
36866 Notasulga 876 ..... G5
35006 Oak Grove 638 ..... F4
36766 Oak Hill 63 ..... D7
35579 Oakman 770 ..... D3
35120 Odenville 724 ..... F3
36271 Ohatchee 860 ..... G3
35121 Oneonta⊙ 4,824 ..... E3
†36467 Onycha 147 ..... F8
36801 Opelika⊙ 21,896 ..... H5
36467 Opp 7,204 ..... F8
36561 Orange Beach 600 ..... C10
36767 Orrville 349 ..... D6
35763 Owens Cross Roads 804 ..... E1
36203 Oxford 8,939 ..... G3
36360 Ozark⊙ 13,188 ..... G8
35764 Paint Rock 221 ..... F1
35580 Parrish 1,583 ..... D3
35124 Pelham 6,759 ..... E4
35125 Pell City⊙ 6,616 ..... F3
36916 Pennington 355 ..... B6
36562 Perdido 500 ..... C8
36471 Peterman 600 ..... D7
36062 Petrey 93 ..... F7
36867 Phenix City⊙ 26,928 ..... H6
35581 Phil Campbell 1,549 ..... C2
†35447 Pickensville 132 ..... B4
36272 Piedmont 5,544 ..... G3
36371 Pinckard 771 ..... G8
36768 Pine Apple 298 ..... E7
36769 Pine Hill 510 ..... C7
35765 Pisgah 699 ..... G1
36758 Plantersville 650 ..... E5
35127 Pleasant Grove 7,102 ..... D4
36564 Point Clear 1,812 ..... C10
†36441 Pollard 144 ..... D8

(continued on following page)

Agriculture, Industry and Resources

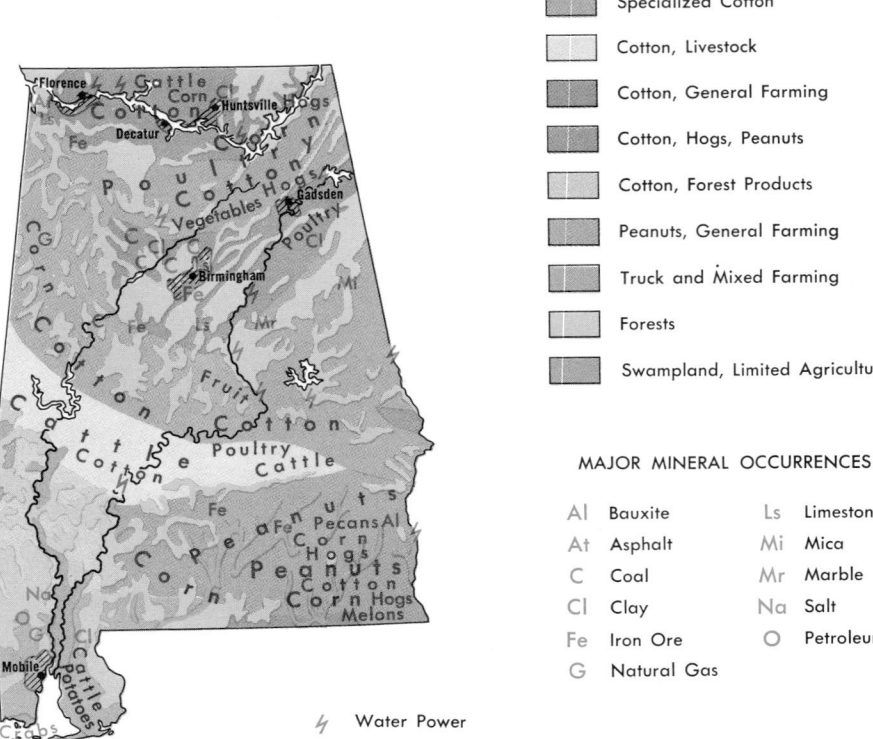

DOMINANT LAND USE

- Specialized Cotton
- Cotton, Livestock
- Cotton, General Farming
- Cotton, Hogs, Peanuts
- Cotton, Forest Products
- Peanuts, General Farming
- Truck and Mixed Farming
- Forests
- Swampland, Limited Agriculture

MAJOR MINERAL OCCURRENCES

Al	Bauxite	Ls	Limestone
At	Asphalt	Mi	Mica
C	Coal	Mr	Marble
Cl	Clay	Na	Salt
Fe	Iron Ore	O	Petroleum
G	Natural Gas		

⚡ Water Power

◯ Major Industrial Areas

Topography

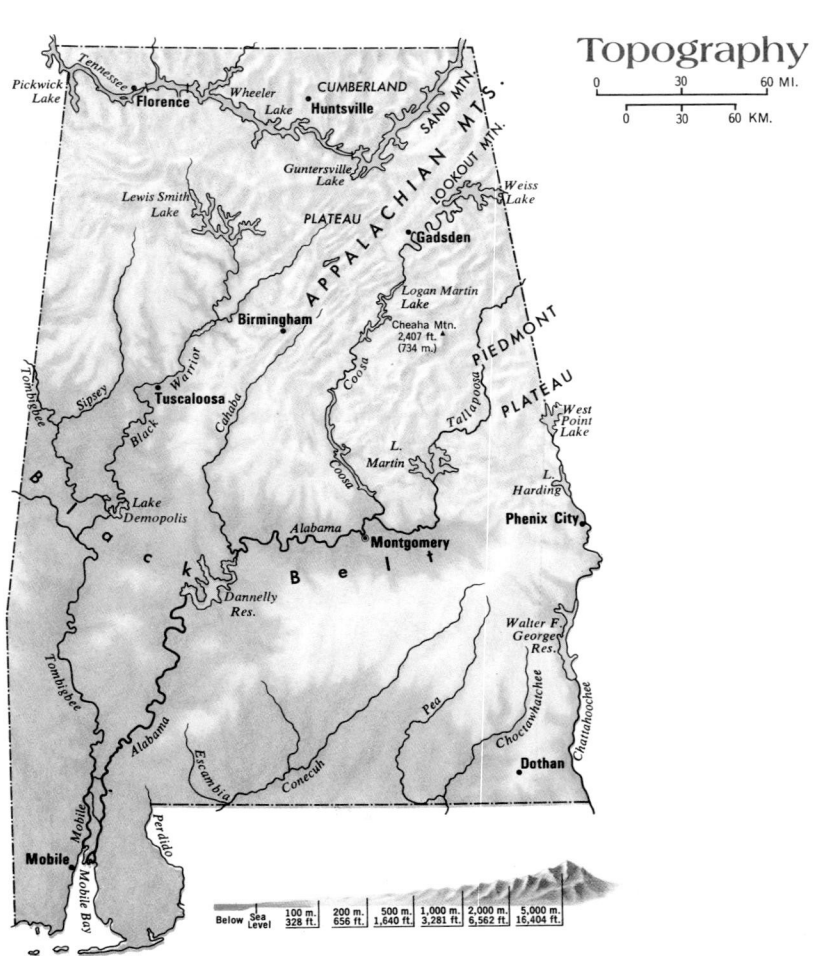

0   30   60 MI.
0   30   60 KM.

Below Sea Level | 100 m. 328 ft. | 200 m. 656 ft. | 500 m. 1,640 ft. | 1,000 m. 3,281 ft. | 2,000 m. 6,562 ft. | 5,000 m. 16,404 ft.

Alabama

SCALE
0 5 10 20 30 40 MI.

0 5 10 20 30 40 KM.

State Capitals .... ⊛
County Seats .... ⊙
Major Limited Access Hwys. ━━━

Scale 1:1,930,000

© Copyright HAMMOND INCORPORATED, Maplewood, N. J.

CITIES and TOWNS

Zip Name/Pop. Key

†99609 Akolmiut (Kasigluk) 641.. F2
99554 Alakanuk 522 .... E2
*99501 Anchorage⊙ 174,431 ...... B1
       Anchorage‡ 174,431 ...... B1
†99760 Anderson 517 .... H2
99723 Barrow 2,207 .... G1
99559 Bethel 3,576 .... F2
99704 Clear 504 .... J2
99701 College 4,043 .... J1
99574 Cordova 1,879 .... D1
99921 Craig 527 .... M2
99737 Delta Junction 945 .... J2
99576 Dillingham 1,563 .... G3
†99685 Dutch Harbor 250 .... E4
99581 Emanguk (Emmonak) 567 E2
99701 Fairbanks⊙ 22,645 .... J1
99740 Fort Yukon 619 .... J1
99741 Galena 765 .... G2
99588 Glennallen 511 .... D1
99827 Haines 993 .... M1
99603 Homer 2,209 .... B2
99829 Hoonah 680 .... M1

99604 Hooper Bay 627 .... E2
99801 Juneau (cap.)⊙ 19,528 .. N1
99830 Kake 555 .... M1
99609 Kasigluk 641 .... F2
99611 Kenai 4,324 .... B1
99901 Ketchikan 7,198 .... N2
99615 Kodiak 4,756 .... H3
99752 Kotzebue 2,054 .... F1
†99901 Mountain Point 396 ..... N2
99632 Mountain Village 583 .... E2
99762 Nome⊙ 2,301 .... E2
99763 Noorvik 492 .... F1
99645 Palmer 2,141 .... C1
99833 Petersburg 2,821 .... N2
99660 Saint Paul Island 551 .... D3
99661 Sand Point 625 .... G3
99664 Seward 1,843 .... C1
99835 Sitka 7,803 .... N2
99840 Skagway 768 .... M1
99669 Soldotna 2,320 .... B1
99503 Spenard C1
99672 Sterling 919 .... B1
99780 Tok 589 .... K2
99685 Unalakleet 623 .... G2
99685 Unalaska 1,322 .... E4
99686 Valdez 3,079 .... D1
99929 Wrangell 2,184 .... N2
99689 Yakutat 449 .... L3

OTHER FEATURES

Adak (isl.) L4
Admiralty (isl.) M1
Afognak (isl.) H3
Agattu (isl.) J3
Akutan (isl.) E4
Alaska (gulf) K3
Alaska (range) H2
Aleutian (isls.) J4
Aleutian (range) G3
Alexander (arch.) L1
Amchitka (isl.) K4
Amlia (passage) L4
Amukta (isl.) D4
Andreanof (isls.) L4
Atka (isl.) L4
Attu (isl.) J3
Baird (mts.) F1
Baranof (isl.) M1
Barrow (pt.) G1
Bear (mt.) K2
Beaufort (sea) K1
Becharof (lake) G3
Bering (glac.) K2
Bering (sea) D2
Bering (str.) E1
Blackburn (mt.) K2
Bona (mt.) K2
Bristol (bay) F3
British (mts.) K1
Brooks (range) G1
Chandalar (riv.) J1
Chatham (str.) M1
Chichagof (isl.) M1
Chignik (bay) G3
Chilkoot (pass) M1
Chirikof (isl.) G3

Chitina (riv.) K2
Christian (riv.) M2
Chugash (mts.) C1
Chukchi (sea) E1
Clarence (str.) N2
Clark (lake) H2
Coast (mts.) N1
Columbia (glac.) C1
Colville (riv.) G1
Constantine (cape) G3
Cook (inlet) B1
Cook (mt.) K2
Copper (riv.) J2
Cordova (bay) M2
Coronation (isl.) M2
Cross (sound) L1
Dease (riv.) H1
Decision (cape) M2
Denali Nat'l Park H2
Devils Paw (mt.) N1
Dixon Entrance (chan.) .. M2
Douglas (mt.) H3
Dry (bay) L3
Eielson A.F.B. 5,232 ..... J2
Elmendorf A.F.B. B1
Endicott (mts.) H1
Etolin (isl.) N2
Fairweather (cape) L1
Fairweather (mt.) L1
Firth (riv.) K1
Foraker (mt.) H2
Fort Davis E2
Fort Greely 1,635 .... J2
Fort Richardson C1

Fort Wainwright J1
Four Mountains (isls.) .. E4
Fox (isls.) E4
Frederick (sound) N1
Gates of the Arctic Nat'l
  Park H1
Glacier (bay) M1
Glacier Bay Nat'l Park .. M1
Goodhope (bay) F1
Great Sitkin (isl.) L4
Guyot (glac.) K2
Hagemeister (isl.) F3
Halkett (cape) H1
Hall (isl.) D2
Harding Icefield C2
Harrison (bay) H1
Hayes (mt.) J2
Hazen (bay) E2
Hinchinbrook (isl.) D1
Hoonah (sound) M1
Hope (pt.) E1
Howard (pass) G1
Icy (bay) K3
Icy (cape) F1
Icy (pt.) L1
Icy (str.) M1
Iliamna (lake) G3
Iliamna (vol.) H2
Innoko (riv.) G2
Kachemak (bay) B2
Kanaga (isl.) L4
Kates Needle (mt.) N1
Katmai (vol.) H3
Katmai Nat'l Park H3

Kayak (isl.) K3
Kenai (lake) C2
Kenai (mt.) C2
Kenai (pen.) C2
Kenai Fjords Nat'l Park . H3
Kennedy Entrance (str.) . E1
King (isl.) E1
Kiska (isl.) J4
Kiska (vol.) J4
Klondike Gold Rush Nat'l Hist.
  Park N1
Knight (isl.) C1
Knik Arm (inlet) H1
Kobuk (riv.) F1
Kobuk Valley Nat'l Park . F1
Kodiak (isl.) H3
Kotzebue (sound) F1
Koyukuk (riv.) G1
Krusenstern (cape) F1
Kuiu (isl.) M2
Kuskokwim (bay) F3
Kuskokwim (mts.) G2
Kuskokwim (riv.) G2
Kvichak (bay) G2
Lake Clark Nat'l Park ... H2
Lisburne (cape) E1
Little Diomede (isl.) E1
Little Sitkin (isl.) J4
Lynn Canal (inlet) M1
Makushin (vol.) E4
Malaspina (glac.) K3
Marcus Baker (mt.) H3
Marmot (isl.) H3
Matanuska (riv.) C1

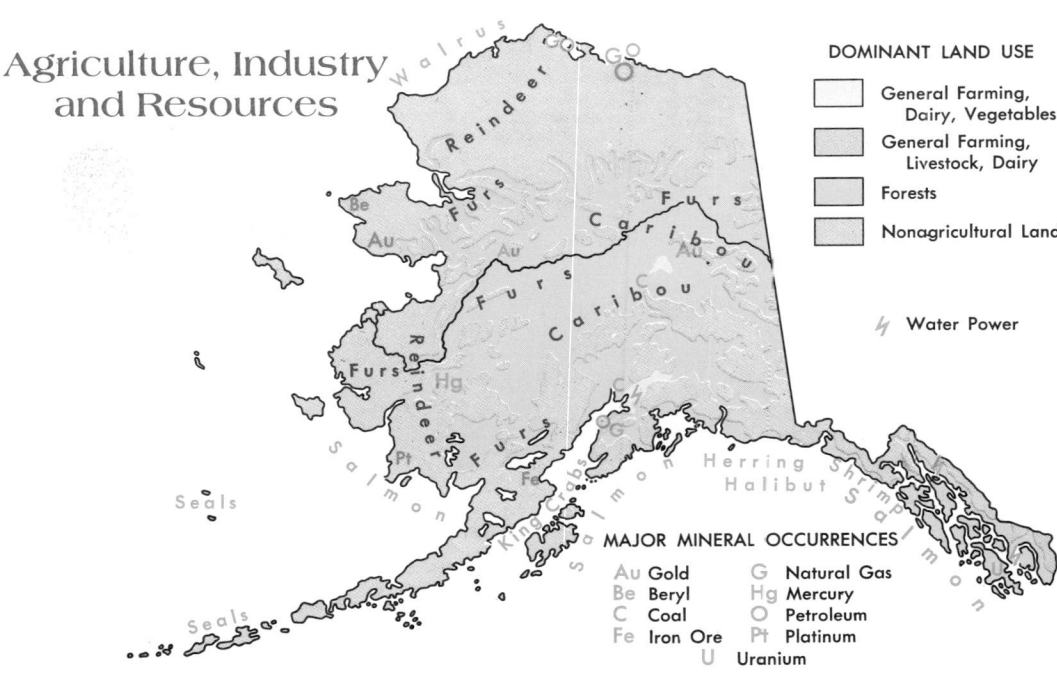

Agriculture, Industry and Resources

DOMINANT LAND USE

- General Farming, Dairy, Vegetables
- General Farming, Livestock, Dairy
- Forests
- Nonagricultural Land

⚡ Water Power

MAJOR MINERAL OCCURRENCES

Au Gold   G   Natural Gas
Be Beryl   Hg Mercury
C   Coal   O   Petroleum
Fe Iron Ore   Pt Platinum
            U   Uranium

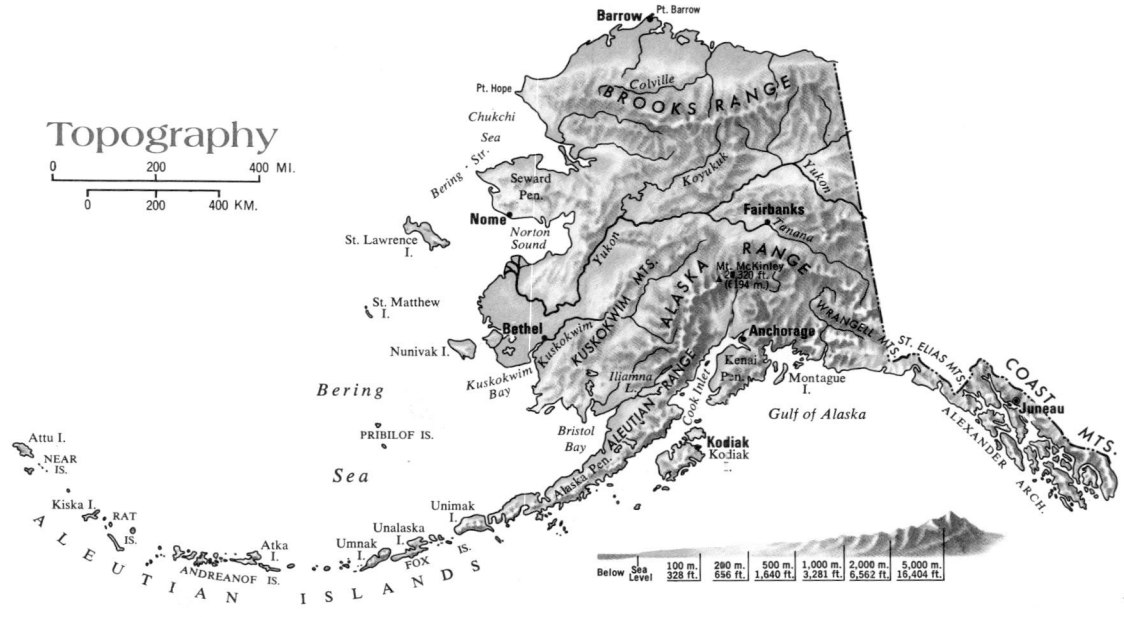

Topography

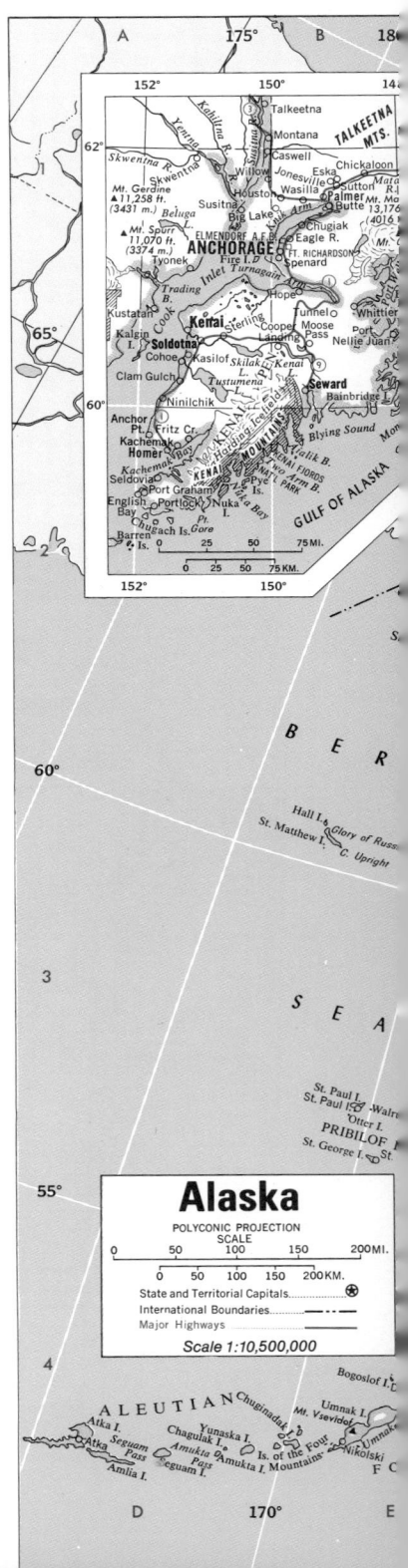

Alaska

POLYCONIC PROJECTION
SCALE

State and Territorial Capitals .... ⊛
International Boundaries .... ─ ─ ─
Major Highways

Scale 1:10,500,000

McKinley (mt.)	H2	Portland Canal (inlet)	N2
Meade (riv.)	G1	Port Moller (inlet)	F3
Mendenhall (cape)	E3	Port Wells (inlet)	C1
Mentasta (pass)	K2	Pribilof (isls.)	D3
Merrill (pass)	H2	Prince of Wales (cape)	E1
Michelson (mt.)	K1	Prince of Wales (isl.)	N2
Middleton (isl.)	J3	Prince William (sound)	D1
Misty Fjords Nat'l Mon.	N2	Prudhoe (bay)	J1
Mitkof (isl.)	N2	Rat (isls.)	K4
Montague (isl.)	D1	Redoubt (vol.)	H2
Muir (glac.)	M1	Revillagigedo (chan.)	N2
Mulchatna (riv.)	G2	Revillagigedo (isl.)	N2
Muzon (cape)	M2	Romanzof (cape)	E2
Naknek (lake)	G3	Sagavanirktok (riv.)	J1
Near (isls.)	H3	Saint Elias (cape)	K3
Nelson (isl.)	E2	Saint Elias (mts.)	L2
Newenham (cape)	F3	Saint George (isl.)	D3
Noatak (riv.)	F1	Saint Lawrence (isl.)	D2
Norton (riv.)	F2	Saint Matthew (isl.)	D2
Norton (sound)	E2	Saint Paul (isl.)	D3
Nowitna (riv.)	H2	Salisbury (sound)	M1
Nuka (bay)	C2	Sanak (isl.)	F4
Nunivak (isl.)	E3	Sanford (mt.)	K2
Nushagak (riv.)	G2	Schwatka (mts.)	G1
Nuyakuk (lake)	F3	Seguam (isl.)	K4
Ommaney (cape)	M2	Selawik (lake)	F1
Otter (isl.)	D3	Semichi (isls.)	H3
Pastol (bay)	F2	Semidi (isls.)	G3
Pavlof (bay)	F3	Semisopochnoi (isl.)	K4
Pavlof (vol.)	F3	Seward (pen.)	E1
Philip Smith (mts.)	J1	Seymour (canal)	N1
Porcupine (riv.)	K1	Sheenjek (riv.)	K1
Port Clarence (inlet)	E1	Shelikof (str.)	H3
Port Heiden (inlet)	G3	Shemya (isl.)	J3

Shishaldin (vol.)	E4	Turnagain Arm (inlet)	B1
Shumagin (isls.)	G4	Tustumena (lake)	C1
Shuyak (isl.)	H3	Two Arm (bay)	C2
Sitka (sound)	M1	Ugashik (lkes)	G3
Sitka Nat'l Hist. Park	M1	Umnak (isl.)	E4
Sitkinak (str.)	H3	Umnak (passage)	E4
Skilak (lake)	C1	Unalaska (isl.)	E4
Smith (bay)	H1	Unga (isl.)	F3
Spencer (cape)	L1	Unimak (isl.)	E4
Stephens (passage)	N1	Unimak (passage)	F4
Stevenson Entrance (str.)	H3	Utukok (riv.)	F1
Stikine (riv.)	N2	Valley of Ten Thousand Smokes	G3
Stikine (str.)	N2	Vancouver (cape)	E2
Stony (riv.)	G2	Veniaminof (crater)	F3
Stuart (isl.)	F2	Vsevidof (mt.)	E4
Suemez (isl.)	M2	Walrus (isl.)	E3
Sumner (str.)	M2	Walrus (isls.)	F3
Susitna (riv.)	B1	Waring (mts.)	G1
Sutwik (isl.)	G3	West Point (mt.)	K2
Taku (glac.)	N1	White (pass)	N1
Taku (riv.)	N1	White (riv.)	K2
Talkeetna (mts.)	J2	White Mountains Nat'l Rec. Area	J1
Tanaga (isl.)	K4	Witherspoon (mt.)	C1
Tanaga (vol.)	K4	Wrangell (cape)	H3
Tanana (riv.)	J2	Wrangell (isl.)	N2
Taylor (mts.)	G2	Wrangell (mts.)	K2
Tazlina (lake)	D1	Wrangell-St. Elias Nat'l Park	K2
Tazlina (riv.)	D1	Yakobi (isl.)	M1
Teshekpuk (lake)	H1	Yakutat (bay)	K3
Tigalda (isl.)	F4	Yentna (riv.)	A1
Tikchik (lkes)	G2	Yukon (riv.)	F2
Togiak (bay)	F3		
Tugidak (isl.)	G3		

⊙ Court House
‡Population of metropolitan area.
† Zip of nearest p.o.
* Multiple zips.

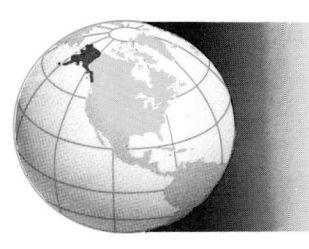

AREA 591,004 sq. mi. (1,530,700 sq. km.)
POPULATION 401,851
CAPITAL Juneau
LARGEST CITY Anchorage
HIGHEST POINT Mt. McKinley 20,320 ft. (6194 m.)
SETTLED IN 1801
ADMITTED TO UNION January 3, 1959
POPULAR NAME Great Land; Last Frontier
STATE FLOWER Forget-me-not
STATE BIRD Willow Ptarmigan

HAMMOND INCORPORATED, Maplewood, N. J.

Arizona

SCALE

0 5 10   20   30   40   50   60 MI.

0 5 10 20 30 40 50 60 KM.

State Capitals................⊛

County Seats................◉

Major Limited Access Hwys._____

Scale 1:2,700,000

© Copyright HAMMOND INCORPORATED, Maplewood, N.J.

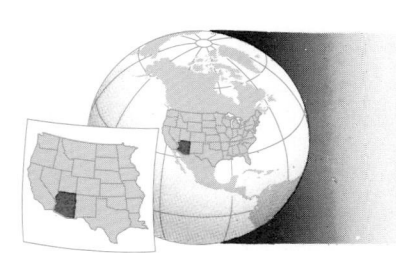

AREA   114,000 sq. mi. (295,260 sq. km.)
POPULATION 2,718,425
CAPITAL Phoenix
LARGEST CITY Phoenix
HIGHEST POINT Humphreys Pk. 12,633 ft.
    (3851 m.)
SETTLED IN 1752
ADMITTED TO UNION February 14, 1912
POPULAR NAME Grand Canyon State
STATE FLOWER Saguaro Cactus Blossom
STATE BIRD Cactus Wren

Agriculture, Industry and Resources

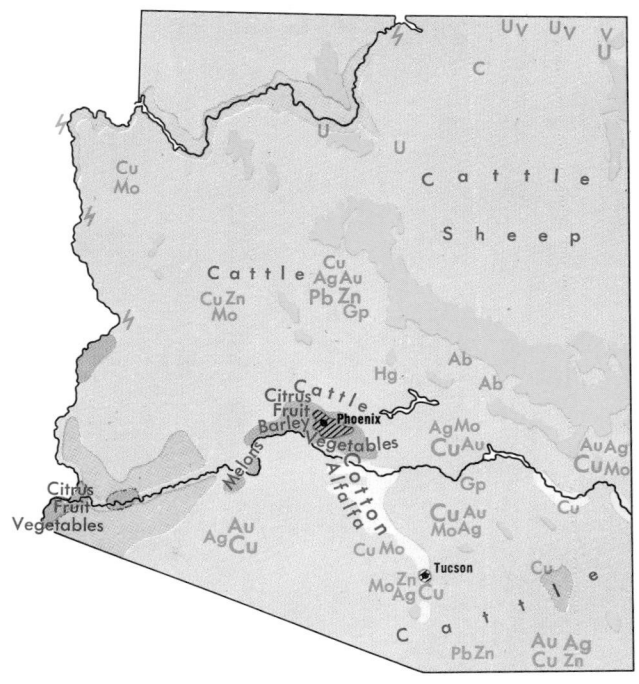

MAJOR MINERAL OCCURRENCES

Ab	Asbestos	Cu	Copper	Pb	Lead
Ag	Silver	Gp	Gypsum	U	Uranium
Au	Gold	Hg	Mercury	V	Vanadium
C	Coal	Mo	Molybdenum	Zn	Zinc

DOMINANT LAND USE

Fruit, Truck and Mixed Farming

Cotton and Alfalfa

General Farming, Livestock, Special Crops

Range Livestock

Forests

Nonagricultural Land

⚡ Water Power

▨ Major Industrial Areas

COUNTIES

Apache 52,108	F3
Cochise 85,686	F7
Coconino 75,008	C3
Gila 37,080	E5
Graham 22,862	E6
Greenlee 11,406	F5
La Paz· 13,100	A5
Maricopa 1,509,052	C5
Mohave 55,865	A3
Navajo 67,629	E3
Pima 531,443	D6
Pinal 90,918	D6
Santa Cruz 20,459	E7
Yavapai 68,145	C4
Yuma· 81,800	A6

·1982 official estimate.

CITIES and TOWNS

Zip	Name/Pop.	Key
†85333	Agua Caliente 60	B6
85320	Aguila 900	B5
85321	Ajo 5,189	C6
85920	Alpine 450	F5
85640	Amado 75	D7
85220	Apache Junction 9,935	D5
†85901	Aripine 25	E4
85601	Arivaca 400	D7
85223	Arizona City 825	D6
85625	Arizona Sunsites 825	F7
85322	Arlington 950	C5
86320	Ash Fork 800	C3

85323	Avondale 8,168	C5
†85333	Aztec 20	B6
86321	Bagdad 2,331	B4
85221	Bapchule 400	D5
86015	Bellemont 210	D3
85602	Benson 4,190	E7
85603	Bisbee⊙ 7,154	F7
85324	Black Canyon City 600	C4
85922	Blue 50	F5
†85643	Bonita 20	E6
85325	Bouse 500	A5
85605	Bowie 600	F6
85326	Buckeye 3,434	C5
86430	Bullhead	
	City-Riviera 10,364	A3
†86301	Bumble Bee 15	C4
85530	Bylas 1,175	E5
†85530	Calva 10	E5
86020	Cameron 600	D3
86322	Camp Verde 1,125	D4
†86022	Cane Beds 30	B2
85331	Carefree 986	C5
†85640	Carmen 200	D7
85222	Casa Grande 14,971	D6
85329	Cashion 3,014	C5
†85342	Castle Hot Springs 50	C5
85331	Cave Creek 1,589	D5
85531	Central 300	F6
†85501	Central Heights-Midland	
	City 2,791	E5
86502	Chambers 500	F3
85224	Chandler 29,673	D5
†86327	Cherry 20	C4
86503	Chinle 2,815	F2

86323	Chino Valley 2,858	C4
86431	Chloride 225	A3
†85292	Christmas 201	E5
85911	Cibecue 100	E4
86324	Clarkdale 1,512	C4
85532	Claypool 2,362	E5
†85934	Clay Springs 500	E4
†86326	Clemenceau 300	C4
85533	Clifton⊙ 4,245	F5
85606	Cochise 150	F6
86021	Colorado City 350	B2
85924	Concho 100	F4
85332	Congress 800	C4
†85640	Continental 250	D7
85228	Coolidge 6,851	D6
†85542	Coolidge Dam 42	E5
†86505	Cornfields 200	F3
86325	Cornville 425	D4
85230	Cortaro 375	D6
86326	Cottonwood 4,550	D4
86333	Crown King 100	C4
85333	Dateland 100	B6
86430	Davis Dam 125	A3
86327	Dewey 100	C4
†86047	Dilkon 90	E3
86441	Dolan Springs 870	A3
85364	Dome 48	A6
†85643	Dos Cabezas 30	F6
85607	Douglas 13,058	F7
85609	Dragoon 150	F6
85534	Duncan 603	F6
85925	Eagar 2,791	F4
85535	Eden 89	F6
85334	Ehrenburg 93	A5

(continued on following page)

Topography

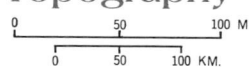

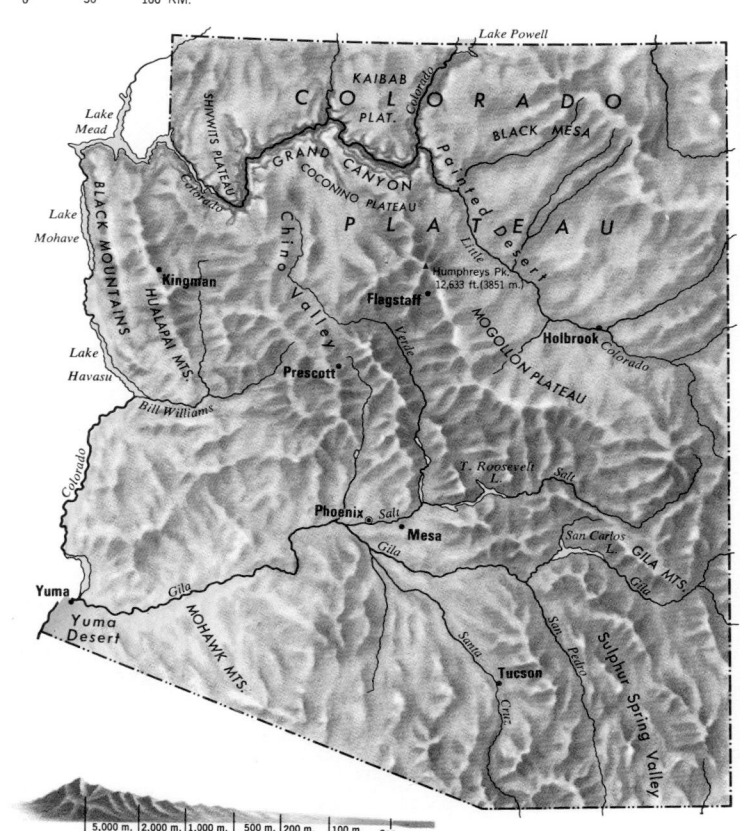

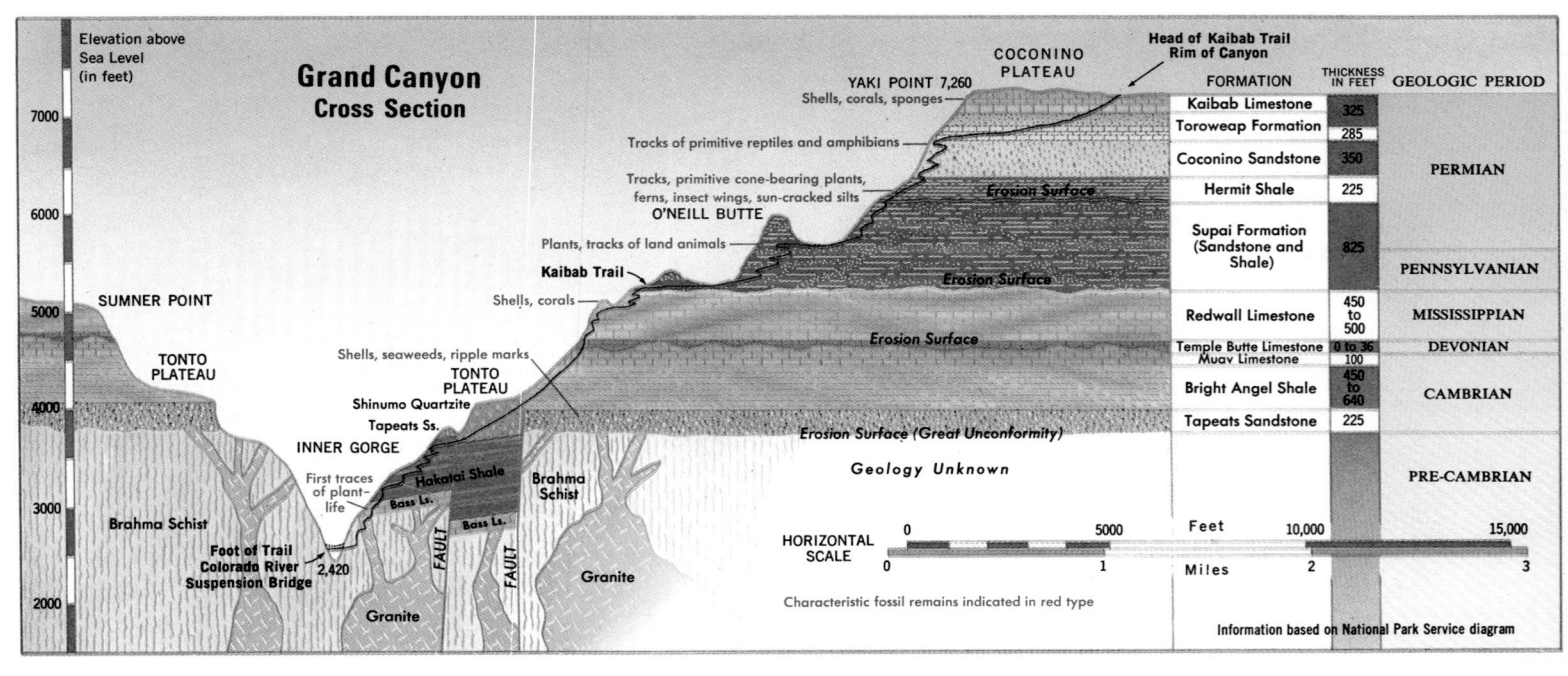

Grand Canyon Cross Section

Elevation above Sea Level (in feet)

FORMATION	THICKNESS IN FEET	GEOLOGIC PERIOD
Kaibab Limestone	325	PERMIAN
Toroweap Formation	285	
Coconino Sandstone	350	
Hermit Shale	225	
Supai Formation (Sandstone and Shale)	825	PENNSYLVANIAN
Redwall Limestone	450 to 500	MISSISSIPPIAN
Temple Butte Limestone	0 to 36	DEVONIAN
Muav Limestone	100	
Bright Angel Shale	450 to 640	CAMBRIAN
Tapeats Sandstone	225	
Geology Unknown		PRE-CAMBRIAN

Head of Kaibab Trail
Rim of Canyon
COCONINO PLATEAU
YAKI POINT 7,260
Shells, corals, sponges
Tracks of primitive reptiles and amphibians
Erosion Surface
Tracks, primitive cone-bearing plants, ferns, insect wings, sun-cracked silts
O'NEILL BUTTE
Plants, tracks of land animals
Kaibab Trail
Erosion Surface
Shells, corals
Erosion Surface
SUMNER POINT
Shells, seaweeds, ripple marks
TONTO PLATEAU
Shinumo Quartzite
Tapeats Ss.
TONTO PLATEAU
Erosion Surface (Great Unconformity)
INNER GORGE
First traces of plant-life
Hakatai Shale
Bass Ls.
Brahma Schist
Brahma Schist
Bass Ls.
FAULT
FAULT
Foot of Trail
Colorado River Suspension Bridge 2,420
Granite
Granite

HORIZONTAL SCALE
Feet: 0   5000   10,000   15,000
Miles: 0   1   2   3

Characteristic fossil remains indicated in red type

Information based on National Park Service diagram

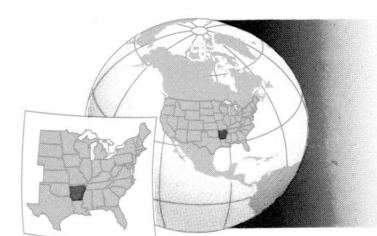

AREA 53,187 sq. mi. (137,754 sq. km.)
POPULATION 2,286,435
CAPITAL Little Rock
LARGEST CITY Little Rock
HIGHEST POINT Magazine Mtn. 2,753 ft. (839 m.)
SETTLED IN 1685
ADMITTED TO UNION June 15, 1836
POPULAR NAME Land of Opportunity
STATE FLOWER Apple Blossom
STATE BIRD Mockingbird

COUNTIES

Arkansas 24,175 ....H5
Ashley 26,538 ....G7
Baxter 27,409 ....F1
Benton 78,115 ....B1
Boone 26,067 ....D1
Bradley 13,803 ....F7
Calhoun 6,079 ....E6
Carroll 16,203 ....C1
Chicot 17,793 ....H7
Clark 23,326 ....D5
Clay 20,616 ....K1
Cleburne 16,909 ....F2
Cleveland 7,868 ....F6
Columbia 26,644 ....D7
Conway 19,505 ....E3
Craighead 63,239 ....J2
Crawford 36,892 ....B2
Crittenden 49,499 ....K3
Cross 20,434 ....J3
Dallas 10,515 ....E6
Desha 19,760 ....H6
Drew 17,910 ....G6
Faulkner 46,192 ....F3
Franklin 14,705 ....C2
Fulton 9,975 ....G1
Garland 70,531 ....D4
Grant 13,008 ....F5
Greene 30,744 ....J1
Hempstead 23,635 ....C6
Hot Spring 26,819 ....E5
Howard 13,459 ....C5
Independence 30,147 .....G2
Izard 10,768 ....G1
Jackson 21,646 ....H2
Jefferson 90,718 ....G5
Johnson 17,423 ....C2
Lafayette 10,213 ....C7
Lawrence 18,447 ....H1
Lee 15,539 ....J4
Lincoln 13,369 ....G6
Little River 13,952 ....B6
Logan 20,144 ....C3
Lonoke 34,518 ....G4
Madison 11,373 ....C1
Marion 11,334 ....E1
Miller 37,766 ....C7
Mississippi 59,517 ....K2
Monroe 14,052 ....H4
Montgomery 7,771 ....C4
Nevada 11,097 ....D6
Newton 7,756 ....D2
Ouachita 30,541 ....E6
Perry 7,266 ....E4
Phillips 34,772 ....J5
Pike 10,373 ....C5
Poinsett 27,032 ....J2
Polk 17,007 ....B5
Pope 39,021 ....D3
Prairie 10,140 ....G4
Pulaski 340,613 ....F4
Randolph 16,834 ....H1
Saint Francis 30,858 .....J3
Saline 53,161 ....E4
Scott 9,685 ....B4
Searcy 8,847 ....E2
Sebastian 95,172 ....B3
Sevier 14,060 ....B6
Sharp 14,607 ....G1
Stone 9,022 ....F2
Union 48,573 ....E7
Van Buren 13,357 ....E2
Washington 100,494 .....B2
White 50,835 ....G3
Woodruff 11,222 ....H3
Yell 17,026 ....D3

CITIES and TOWNS

Zip	Name/Pop.	Key
72001	Adona 230	E3
72002	Alexander 223	F4
72410	Alicia 246	H2
72820	Alix 225	C3
†72046	Allport 295	G4
72921	Alma 2,755	B3
72003	Almyra 294	H5
72611	Alpena 344	D1
72004	Altheimer 1,231	G5
72821	Altus 441	C3
72005	Amagon 126	H2
71921	Amity 859	D5
71922	Antoine 194	D5
71923	Arkadelphia⊙ 10,005	D5
71630	Arkansas City⊙ 668	H6
72310	Armorel 500	L2
71822	Ashdown⊙ 4,218	B6
72513	Ash Flat⊙ 524	G1
72823	Atkins 3,002	E3
72311	Aubrey 267	J4
72006	Augusta⊙ 3,496	H3
72007	Austin 269	G4
72711	Avoca 256	B1
72010	Bald Knob 2,756	G3
71631	Banks 216	F6

72922	Barber 35	B3
72923	Barling 3,761	B3
72313	Bassett 243	K2
72924	Bates	B4
72501	Batesville⊙ 8,263	G2
72411	Bay 1,605	J2
71720	Bearden 1,191	E6
72613	Beaver	C1
72012	Beebe 3,599	G3
72014	Beedeville 183	H3
†72712	Bella Vista 2,589	B1
†72601	Bellefonte 393	D1
72824	Belleville 571	D3
71823	Ben Lomond 155	B6
72015	Benton⊙ 17,717	E4
72712	Bentonville⊙ 8,756	B1
72615	Bergman 320	E1
72616	Berryville⊙ 2,966	C1
†72764	Bethel Heights 296	B1
72016	Bigelow 373	E3
72617	Big Flat 150	F1
72413	Biggers 363	J1
72017	Biscoe 486	H4
72414	Black Oak 309	K2
72415	Black Rock 848	H1
†71960	Black Springs 92	C5
71825	Blevins 314	C6
65611	Blue Eye 43	D1
72826	Blue Mountain 112	C3
71722	Bluff City 292	D6
72315	Blytheville⊙ 23,844	L2
†71858	Bodcaw 197	D6
†72901	Bonanza 553	B3
72416	Bono 967	J2
72927	Booneville⊙ 3,718	C3
72020	Bradford 950	G3
71826	Bradley 790	C7
72928	Branch 353	C3
72021	Brinkley 4,909	H4
72417	Brookland 840	J2
72022	Bryant 2,682	F4
71827	Buckner 436	D7
72619	Bull Shoals 1,312	E1
72321	Burdette 328	L2
72023	Cabot 4,806	F4
72322	Caldwell 283	J3
71828	Cale 110	D6
72519	Calico Rock 1,046	F1
71724	Calion 638	E7
71701	Camden⊙ 15,356	E6
†72201	Cammack Village 920	E4
†72473	Campbell Station 297	H2
72419	Caraway 1,165	K2
72024	Carlisle 2,567	G4
71725	Carthage 568	E5
72025	Casa 179	D3
72421	Cash 285	J2
72026	Casscoe 297	H4
72521	Cave City 1,634	G2
72718	Cave Springs 429	B1
72932	Cedarville 375	B2
72719	Centerton 425	B1
72829	Centerville 300	D3
†72923	Central City 339	B3
72933	Charleston⊙ 1,748	B3
†72525	Cherokee Village-Hidden Valley 4,058	G1
72324	Cherry Valley 729	J3
72934	Chester 139	B2
71726	Chidester 342	D6
72029	Clarendon⊙ 2,361	H4
72325	Clarkedale 300	K3
72830	Clarksville⊙ 5,237	D3
72031	Clinton⊙ 1,284	F2
72832	Coal Hill 859	C3
72476	College City 432	J1
72326	Colt 378	J3
71831	Columbus 265	C6
72523	Concord 234	G2
72032	Conway⊙ 20,375	F3
72524	Cord 250	H2
72626	Cotter 920	E1
72036	Cotton Plant 1,323	H3
71937	Cove 391	B5
72037	Coy 183	G4
72327	Crawfordsville 685	K3
71635	Crossett 6,706	G7
71728	Curtis 300	D6
72526	Cushman 556	G2
†71950	Daisy 177	C5
72039	Damascus 307	F3
72833	Danville⊙ 1,698	D3
72834	Dardanelle⊙ 3,621	D3
72424	Datto 112	J1
72722	Decatur 1,013	A1
72425	Delaplaine 161	J1
71940	Delight 431	C5
72426	Dell 310	K2
†72821	Denning 238	C3
71832	De Queen⊙ 4,594	B5
71638	Dermott 4,731	H7
72040	Des Arc⊙ 2,001	G4
72041	De Valls Bluff⊙ 738	H4
72042	De Witt⊙ 3,928	H5

72644	Diamond City 650	E1
72043	Diaz 1,192	H2
71833	Dierks 1,249	B5
71941	Donaldson 300	E5
72837	Dover 948	D3
71639	Dumas 6,091	H6
72935	Dyer 608	B3
72330	Dyess 446	K2
72331	Earle 3,517	K3
71701	East Camden 632	E6
72332	Edmondson 344	K3
72333	Elaine 991	J5
71730	El Dorado⊙ 25,270	E7
72727	Elkins 579	C1
72728	Elm Springs 781	B1
71740	Emerson 444	D7
71835	Emmet 475	D6
72046	England 3,081	G4
72047	Enola 186	F3
71640	Eudora 3,840	H7
72632	Eureka Springs⊙ 1,989	C1
72532	Evening Shade 397	G1
72633	Everton 134	E1
72730	Farmington 1,283	B1
72701	Fayetteville⊙ 36,608	B1
	Fayetteville-Springdale 07	B1
†71747	Felsenthal 220	F7
72429	Fisher 302	J2
72634	Flippin 1,072	E1
71742	Fordyce⊙ 5,175	F6
71836	Foreman 1,377	B6
72335	Forrest City⊙ 13,803	J3
*72901	Fort Smith⊙ 71,626	B3
	Fort Smith‡ 203,269	B3
71837	Fouke 614	C7
71642	Fountain Hill 352	G7
†72016	Fourche 51	E4
72536	Franklin 253	G1
72017	Fredonia (Biscoe) 486	H4
71942	Friendship 163	E5
71838	Fulton 326	C6
72732	Garfield 187	C1
71839	Garland 660	C7
72052	Garner 216	G3
72635	Gassville 859	F1
72733	Gateway 75	B1
71840	Genoa 350	C7
72734	Gentry 1,468	A1
72636	Gilbert 43	E2
72055	Gillett 927	H5
71841	Gillham 252	B5
72339	Gilmore 503	K3
72340	Goodwin 225	J4
†72315	Gosnell 3,215	K2
71643	Gould 1,671	G6
71644	Grady 488	G5
71944	Grannis 349	B5
72838	Gravelly 300	C4
72736	Gravette 1,218	B1
72058	Greenbrier 1,423	F3
72638	Green Forest 1,609	D1
72737	Greenland 622	B1
72430	Greenway 317	K1
72936	Greenwood⊙ 3,317	B3
72067	Greers Ferry 558	F2
72060	Griffithville 254	G3
72431	Grubbs 546	H2
72540	Guion 177	G2
†71923	Gum Springs 255	D5
71743	Gurdon 2,707	D6
72061	Guy 209	F3
72937	Hackett 505	B3
†71638	Halley	H6
71646	Hamburg⊙ 3,394	G7
71744	Hampton⊙ 1,627	F6
72542	Hardy 643	H1
71745	Harrell 302	F7
72432	Harrisburg⊙ 1,921	J2
72601	Harrison⊙ 9,567	D1
72938	Hartford 613	B3
72840	Hartman 517	C3
†72015	Haskell 1,074	E4
71945	Hatfield 410	B5
72842	Havana 352	D3
72341	Haynes 359	J4
72064	Hazen 1,636	G4
72543	Heber Springs⊙ 4,589	G2
72843	Hector 449	E3
72342	Helena⊙ 9,598	J4
72065	Hensley 500	F4
71647	Hermitage 378	F7
72347	Hickory Ridge 478	J3
72067	Higden 45	F2
72068	Higginson 333	G3
†72734	Highfill 92	B1
72738	Hindsville	C1
72069	Holly Grove 754	H4
†72958	Hon 250	B4
71801	Hope⊙ 10,290	C6
71842	Horatio 989	B3
72512	Horseshoe Bend 1,909	G1
71901	Hot Springs National Park⊙ 35,781	D4
72070	Houston 183	E3

(continued on following page)

Agriculture, Industry and Resources

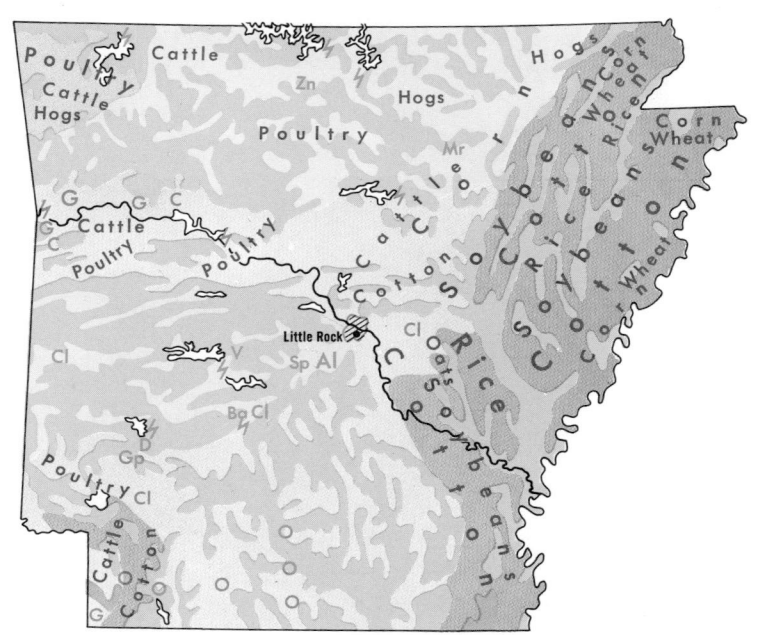

DOMINANT LAND USE

- Fruit and Mixed Farming
- Specialized Cotton
- Cotton, General Farming
- Rice, General Farming
- General Farming, Livestock, Truck Farming, Cotton
- Forests
- Swampland, Limited Agriculture

MAJOR MINERAL OCCURRENCES

Al	Bauxite	Gp	Gypsum
Ba	Barite	Mr	Marble
C	Coal	O	Petroleum
Cl	Clay	Sp	Soapstone
D	Diamonds	V	Vanadium
G	Natural Gas	Zn	Zinc
ϟ	Water Power	▨	Major Industrial Areas

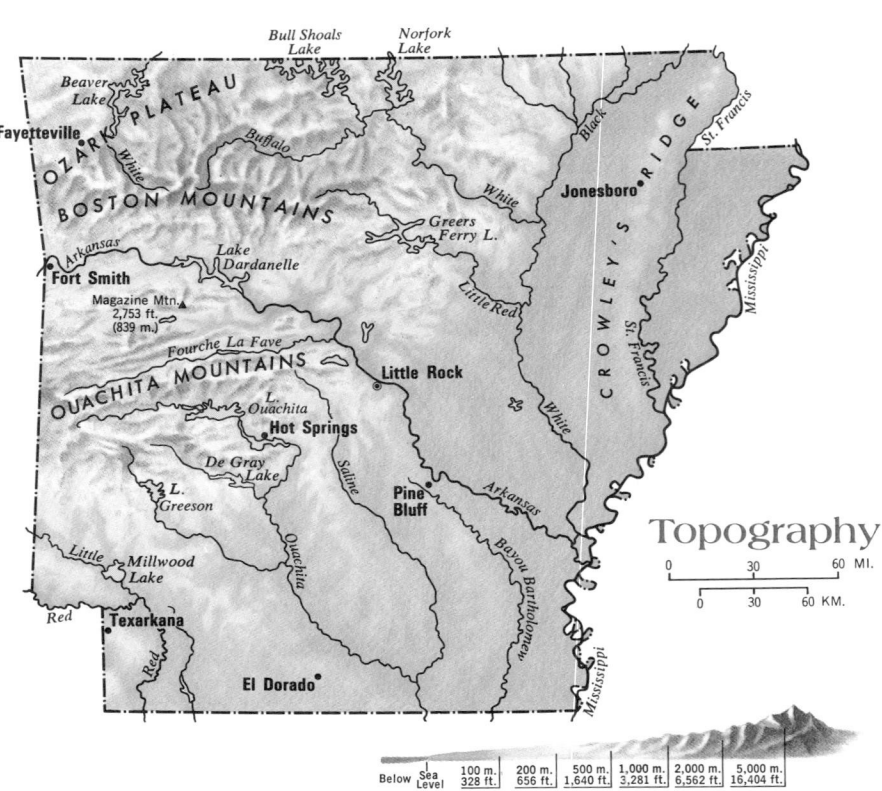

Topography

Magazine Mtn.
2,753 ft.
(839 m.)

100 m. 200 m. 500 m. 1,000 m. 2,000 m. 5,000 m.
Below Sea Level 328 ft. 656 ft. 1,640 ft. 3,281 ft. 6,562 ft. 16,404 ft.

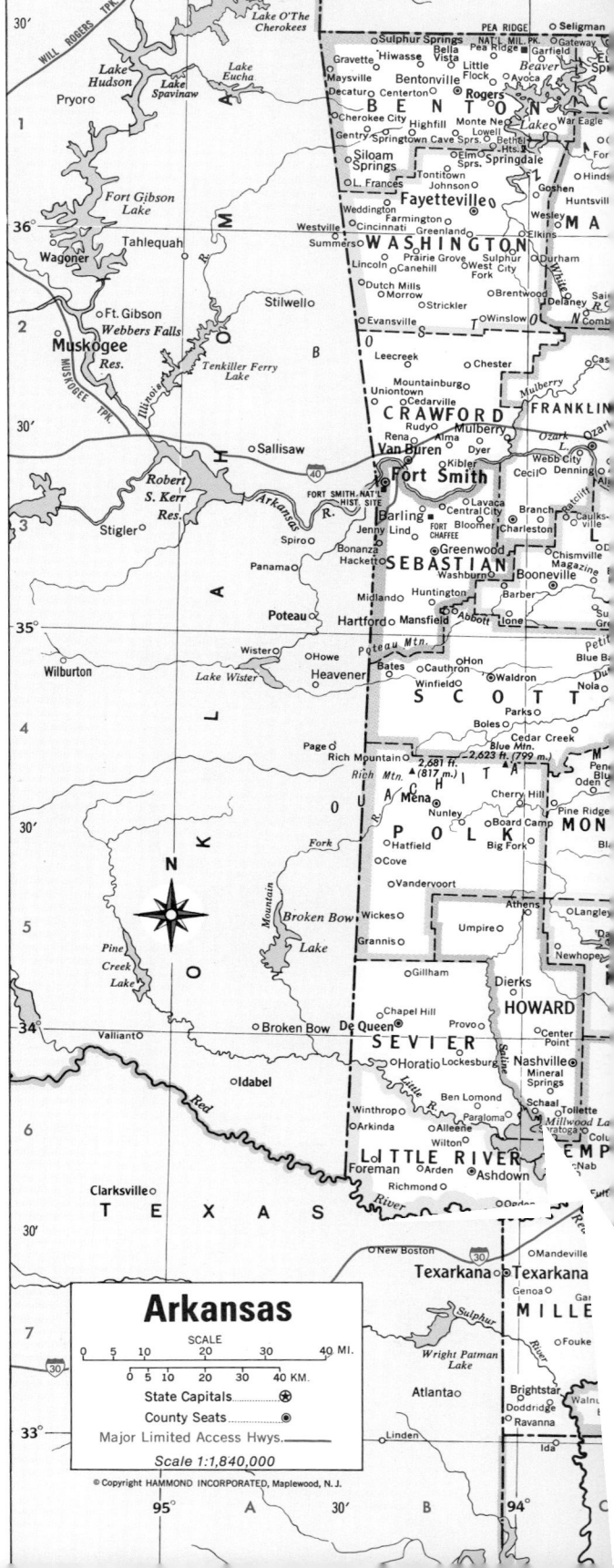

Arkansas

SCALE
0 5 10 20 30 40 MI.
0 5 10 20 30 40 KM.

State Capitals ⊛
County Seats ⊙
Major Limited Access Hwys.
Scale 1:1,840,000

California

SCALE
0 10 20 40 60 80 MI.
0 10 20 40 60 80 KM.
State Capitals ⊛
County Seats ◉
Canals
Major Limited Access Hwys.
Scale 1: 4,400,000

San Francisco
and Vicinity

0 5 10 15 20MI.
0 5 10 15 20KM.

Sacramento
and Vicinity

0 5 10 15 20MI.
0 5 10 15 20KM.

Los Angeles
and Vicinity

0 5 10 15 20MI.
0 5 10 15 20KM.

© Copyright HAMMOND INCORPORATED, Maplewood, N.J.

AREA 158,706 sq. mi. (411,049 sq. km.)
POPULATION 23,667,565
CAPITAL Sacramento
LARGEST CITY Los Angeles
HIGHEST POINT Mt. Whitney 14,494 ft. (4418 m.)
SETTLED IN 1769
ADMITTED TO UNION September 9, 1850
POPULAR NAME Golden State
STATE FLOWER Golden Poppy
STATE BIRD California Valley Quail

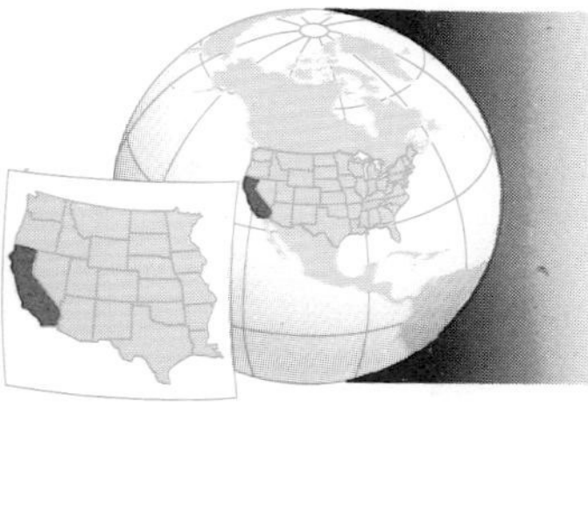

COUNTIES

Alameda 1,105,379 .... D6
Alpine 1,097 .... F5
Amador 19,314 .... E5
Butte 143,851 .... D4
Calaveras 20,710 .... E5
Colusa 12,791 .... C4
Contra Costa 656,380 .... D6
Del Norte 18,217 .... B2
El Dorado 85,812 .... E5
Fresno 514,229 .... E7
Glenn 21,350 .... C4
Humboldt 108,514 .... B3
Imperial 92,110 .... K10
Inyo 17,895 .... H7
Kern 403,089 .... G8
Kings 73,738 .... G8
Lake 36,366 .... C4
Lassen 21,661 .... E3
Los Angeles 7,477,503 .... G9
Madera 63,116 .... F6
Marin 222,592 .... C5
Mariposa 11,108 .... E6
Mendocino 66,738 .... B4
Merced 134,558 .... E6
Modoc 8,610 .... E2
Mono 8,577 .... F5
Monterey 290,444 .... D7
Napa 99,199 .... C5
Nevada 51,645 .... E4
Orange 1,932,709 .... H10
Placer 117,247 .... E4
Plumas 17,340 .... E4
Riverside 663,199 .... J10
Sacramento 783,381 .... D5
San Benito 25,005 .... D7
San Bernardino 895,016 .... J9
San Diego 1,861,846 .... J10
San Francisco (city county) 678,974 .... J2
San Joaquin 347,342 .... D6
San Luis Obispo 155,435 .... E8
San Mateo 587,329 .... J3
Santa Barbara 298,694 .... E9
Santa Clara 1,295,071 .... D6
Santa Cruz 188,141 .... C6
Shasta 115,715 .... C3
Sierra 3,073 .... E4
Siskiyou 39,732 .... C2
Solano 235,203 .... D5
Sonoma 299,681 .... C5
Stanislaus 265,900 .... D6
Sutter 52,246 .... D4
Tehama 38,888 .... C3
Trinity 11,858 .... B3
Tulare 245,738 .... G7
Tuolumne 33,928 .... F5
Ventura 529,174 .... F9
Yolo 113,374 .... D5
Yuba 49,733 .... D4

CITIES and TOWNS

Zip *Name/Pop.* *Key*

94501 Alameda 63,852 .... J2
94507 Alamo 8,505 .... K2
94706 Albany 15,130 .... J2
*91801 Alhambra 64,615 .... C10
92001 Alpine 5,368 .... J11
91001 Altadena 40,983 .... C10
96101 Alturas⊙ 3,025 .... E2
†95116 Alum Rock 16,890 .... L3
*92801 Anaheim 219,494 .... D11
Anaheim-Santa Ana-Garden Grove‡ 1,931,570 .... D11
96007 Anderson 7,381 .... C3
95222 Angels Camp 2,302 .... E5
94508 Angwin 3,526 .... C5
94509 Antioch 42,683 .... L1
92307 Apple Valley 14,305 .... H9
95003 Aptos 7,039 .... K4
91006 Arcadia 45,994 .... C10
95521 Arcata 12,850 .... A3
95825 Arden-Arcade 87,570 .... B8
93420 Arroyo Grande 11,290 .... E8
90701 Artesia 14,301 .... C11
93203 Arvin 6,863 .... G8
†94577 Ashland 13,983 .... K2
95413 Asti 75 .... C5
93422 Atascadero 16,232 .... E8
94025 Atherton 7,797 .... K3
95301 Atwater 17,530 .... E6
95603 Auburn⊙ 7,540 .... C8
90704 Avalon 2,022 .... G10
93204 Avenal 4,137 .... E8
91702 Azusa 29,380 .... D10
*93301 Bakersfield⊙ 105,735 .... G8
Bakersfield‡ 403,089 .... G8
91706 Baldwin Park 50,554 .... D10
92220 Banning 14,020 .... J10
92311 Barstow 17,690 .... H9
†93402 Baywood Park-Los Osos 10,933 .... E8
92223 Beaumont 6,818 .... J10
90201 Bell 25,450 .... C11
90706 Bellflower 53,441 .... C11
90201 Bell Gardens 34,117 .... C11
94002 Belmont 24,505 .... J3
94510 Benicia 15,376 .... K1
95005 Ben Lomond 7,238 .... K4
*94701 Berkeley 103,328 .... J2
*90210 Beverly Hills 32,367 .... B10
92315 Big Bear Lake J9
93920 Big Sur 500 .... D7
93514 Bishop 3,333 .... G6
92316 Bloomington 18,888 .... E10
92225 Blythe 6,805 .... L10
94923 Bodega Bay 800 .... B5
93516 Boron 2,040 .... H8
92004 Borrego Springs 1,405 .... J10
95006 Boulder Creek 5,662 .... J4
92227 Brawley 14,946 .... K11
92621 Brea 27,913 .... D11
94513 Brentwood 4,434 .... L2
93517 Bridgeport⊙ 525 .... F5
94005 Brisbane 2,969 .... J2
95605 Broderick-Bryte 10,194 .... B8
*90622 Buena Park 64,165 .... D11
*91501 Burbank 84,625 .... C10
94010 Burlingame 26,173 .... J2
96013 Burney 3,187 .... D3
92231 Calexico 14,412 .... K11
93505 California City 2,743 .... H8
94515 Calistoga 3,879 .... C5
93745 Calwa 6,640 .... F7
93010 Camarillo 37,797 .... F9
95008 Campbell 26,910 .... K3
*91303 Canoga Park B10
92624 Capistrano Beach 6,168 .... H10
95010 Capitola 9,095 .... K4
92007 Cardiff-by-the-Sea 10,054 .... H10
92008 Carlsbad 35,490 .... H10
93923 Carmel 4,707 .... D7
93924 Carmel Valley 4,013 .... D7
95608 Carmichael 43,108 .... C8
93013 Carpinteria 10,835 .... F9
90745 Carson 81,221 .... C11
94546 Castro Valley 44,011 .... K2
95012 Castroville 4,396 .... D7
92234 Cathedral City 4,130 .... J10
96019 Central Valley 3,424 .... C3
95307 Ceres 13,281 .... D6
†90701 Cerritos 53,020 .... C11
†94541 Cherryland 9,425 .... K2
95926 Chico 26,603 .... D4
Chico‡ 143,851 .... D4
†93555 China Lake 4,275 .... H8
95309 Chinese Camp 150 .... E6
91710 Chino 40,165 .... D10
*92010 Chula Vista 83,927 .... J11
95610 Citrus Heights 85,911 .... C8
91711 Claremont 30,950 .... D10
95425 Cloverdale 3,989 .... B5
93612 Clovis 33,021 .... F7
92236 Coachella 9,129 .... J10
93210 Coalinga 6,593 .... E7
95713 Colfax 981 .... E4
92324 Colton 15,201 .... E10
95932 Colusa⊙ 4,075 .... C4
90022 Commerce 10,509 .... C10
*90220 Compton 81,286 .... C11
*94520 Concord 103,255 .... K1
93212 Corcoran 6,454 .... F7
96021 Corning 4,745 .... C4
91720 Corona 37,791 .... E11
92118 Coronado 18,790 .... H11
94925 Corte Madera 8,074 .... J2
*92626 Costa Mesa 82,562 .... D11
94928 Cotati 3,346 .... C5
*91722 Covina 33,751 .... D10
95531 Crescent City⊙ 3,075 .... A2
92325 Crestline 6,715 .... H9
90201 Cudahy 17,984 .... C11
90230 Culver City 38,139 .... B10
95014 Cupertino 34,265 .... K3
93615 Cutler 3,149 .... F7
90630 Cypress 40,391 .... D11
*94014 Daly City 78,519 .... H2
92629 Dana Point 10,602 .... H10
94526 Danville 26,446 .... K2
95616 Davis 36,640 .... B8
93215 Delano 16,491 .... F8
95315 Delhi 2,832 .... E6
92014 Del Mar 5,017 .... H11
92240 Desert Hot Springs 5,941 .... J9
93618 Dinuba 9,907 .... F7
95620 Dixon 7,541 .... B9
93620 Dos Palos 3,121 .... E6
*90240 Downey 82,602 .... C11
95936 Downieville⊙ 500 .... E4
91010 Duarte 16,766 .... D10
94566 Dublin 13,496 .... K2
93219 Earlimart 4,578 .... F8
90022 East Los Angeles 100,017 .... C10
*92020 El Cajon 73,892 .... J11
92243 El Centro⊙ 23,996 .... K11
94530 El Cerrito 22,731 .... J2
95630 El Dorado Hills 3,453 .... C8
94018 El Granada 3,582 .... H3
95624 Elk Grove 10,959 .... B9
*91731 El Monte 79,494 .... D10
†93030 El Rio 5,674 .... F9
90245 El Segundo 13,752 .... B11
92630 El Toro 38,153 .... E11
94608 Emeryville 3,714 .... J2
92024 Encinitas 10,796 .... H10
91316 Encino B10
95320 Escalon 3,127 .... E6
*92025 Escondido 64,355 .... J10
95501 Eureka⊙ 24,153 .... A3
93221 Exeter 5,606 .... F7
94930 Fairfax 7,391 .... H1
94533 Fairfield⊙ 58,099 .... K1
95628 Fair Oaks 22,602 .... C8
92028 Fallbrook 14,041 .... H10
93223 Farmersville 5,544 .... F7
95018 Felton 4,564 .... K4
93015 Fillmore 9,602 .... G9
93622 Firebaugh 3,740 .... E7
95828 Florin 16,523 .... B8
95630 Folsom 11,003 .... C8
92335 Fontana 37,107 .... E10
†93268 Ford City 3,392 .... F8
95437 Fort Bragg 5,019 .... B4
†95421 Fort Ross 30 .... B5
95540 Fortuna 7,591 .... A3
94404 Foster City 23,287 .... J2
92708 Fountain Valley 55,080 .... D11
95019 Freedom 6,416 .... L4
*94536 Fremont 131,945 .... K3
*93706 Fresno⊙ 217,289 .... F7
Fresno‡ 515,013 .... F7
*92631 Fullerton 102,034 .... D11
95632 Galt 5,514 .... C9
*90747 Gardena 45,165 .... C11
*92640 Garden Grove 123,307 .... D11
95020 Gilroy 21,641 .... D6
92509 Glen Avon Heights 8,444 .... E10
*91201 Glendale 139,060 .... C10
91740 Glendora 38,500 .... D10
93926 Gonzales 2,891 .... D7
91344 Granada Hills B10
92324 Grand Terrace 8,498 .... E10
95945 Grass Valley 6,697 .... D4
93308 Greenacres 5,381 .... F8
93927 Greenfield 4,181 .... D7
95948 Gridley 3,982 .... D4
93433 Grover City 8,827 .... E8
93434 Guadalupe 3,629 .... E9
95322 Gustine 3,142 .... D6
94019 Half Moon Bay 7,282 .... H3
93230 Hanford⊙ 20,958 .... F7
90250 Hawthorne 56,447 .... C11
*94541 Hayward 94,342 .... K2
95448 Healdsburg 7,217 .... B5
92343 Hemet 22,454 .... H10
94547 Hercules 5,963 .... J1
90254 Hermosa Beach 18,070 .... B11
92345 Hesperia 13,540 .... H9
92346 Highland 10,908 .... H9
94010 Hillsborough 10,372 .... J2
95023 Hollister⊙ 11,488 .... D7
90028 Hollywood C10
92250 Holtville 4,399 .... K11
†91720 Home Gardens 5,783 .... E11
95326 Hughson 2,943 .... E6
*92646 Huntington Beach 170,505 .... C11
90255 Huntington Park 46,223 .... C11
92251 Imperial 3,451 .... K11
92032 Imperial Beach 22,689 .... H11
93526 Independence⊙ 748 .... H7
92201 Indio 21,611 .... J10
*90301 Inglewood 94,245 .... B11
92713 Irvine 62,134 .... D11
95642 Jackson⊙ 2,331 .... C9
†94701 Kensington 5,342 .... J2
93630 Kerman 4,002 .... E7
93930 King City 5,495 .... D7
93631 Kingsburg 5,115 .... F7
91011 La Canada 20,153 .... C10
91214 La Crescenta-Montrose 16,531 .... C10
94549 Lafayette 20,879 .... K2
*92651 Laguna Beach 17,901 .... G10
92653 Laguna Hills 33,600 .... D11
92677 Laguna Niguel 12,237 .... H10
90631 La Habra 45,232 .... D11
92037 La Jolla H11
92352 Lake Arrowhead 6,272 .... H9
92330 Lake Elsinore 5,982 .... F11
93240 Lake Isabella 3,428 .... G8
95453 Lakeport⊙ 3,675 .... C4
*90712 Lakewood 74,654 .... C11
92041 La Mesa 50,308 .... H11
90638 La Mirada 40,986 .... D11
93241 Lamont 9,616 .... G8
93534 Lancaster 48,027 .... G9
*91744 La Puente 30,882 .... D10
94939 Larkspur 11,064 .... H1
95330 Lathrop 3,717 .... D6
91750 La Verne 23,508 .... D10
90260 Lawndale 23,460 .... B11
92045 Lemon Grove 20,780 .... J11
93245 Lemoore 8,832 .... F7
†92311 Lenwood 2,974 .... H9
92024 Leucadia 9,478 .... H10
95648 Lincoln 4,132 .... B8
†95901 Linda 10,225 .... D4
93247 Lindsay 6,924 .... F7
95953 Live Oak 3,103 .... D4
†95073 Live Oak 11,482 .... K4
94550 Livermore 48,349 .... L2
95334 Livingston 5,326 .... E6
95240 Lodi 35,221 .... C9
92354 Loma Linda 10,694 .... F10
90717 Lomita 18,807 .... C11
93436 Lompoc 26,267 .... E9
*90801 Long Beach 361,334 .... C11
90720 Los Alamitos 11,529 .... D11
94022 Los Altos 25,769 .... K3
94022 Los Altos Hills 7,421 .... J3
*90001 Los Angeles⊙ 2,966,850 .... C10
Los Angeles-Long Beach‡ 7,477,657 .... C10
93635 Los Banos 10,341 .... E6
95030 Los Gatos 26,906 .... K4
†93402 Los Osos-Baywood Park 10,933 .... E8
90262 Lynwood 48,548 .... C11
93637 Madera⊙ 21,732 .... E7
90265 Malibu B10
93546 Mammoth Lakes 3,929 .... G6
90266 Manhattan Beach 31,542 .... B11
95336 Manteca 24,925 .... D6
93933 Marina 20,647 .... D7
95338 Mariposa⊙ 1,150 .... F6
94553 Martinez⊙ 22,582 .... K1
95901 Marysville⊙ 9,898 .... D4
90201 Maywood 21,810 .... C10
93250 McFarland 5,151 .... F8
93023 Meiners Oaks-Mira Monte 9,512 .... F9
93640 Mendota 5,038 .... E7
94025 Menlo Park 26,369 .... J3
95340 Merced⊙ 36,499 .... E6
94030 Millbrae 20,058 .... J2
94941 Mill Valley 12,967 .... H2
95035 Milpitas 37,820 .... L3
91752 Mira Loma 8,707 .... E10
92691 Mission Viejo 50,666 .... D11
*95350 Modesto⊙ 106,602 .... D6
Modesto‡ 265,902 .... D6
93501 Mojave 2,886 .... G8
91016 Monrovia 30,531 .... D10
91763 Montclair 22,628 .... D10
90640 Montebello 52,929 .... C10
93940 Monterey 27,558 .... D7
91754 Monterey Park 54,338 .... C10
95030 Monte Sereno 3,434 .... K4
91214 Montrose-La Crescenta 16,531 .... C10
93021 Moorpark 4,030 .... G9
94556 Moraga 15,014 .... K2
95037 Morgan Hill 17,060 .... L4
93442 Morro Bay 9,064 .... D8
*94042 Mountain View 58,655 .... K3
96067 Mount Shasta 2,837 .... C5
92405 Muscoy 6,188 .... E10
94558 Napa⊙ 50,879 .... C5
92050 National City 48,772 .... J11
92363 Needles 4,120 .... L9
95959 Nevada City⊙ 2,431 .... D4
94560 Newark 32,126 .... K3
91321 Newhall 12,029 .... G9
95360 Newman 2,785 .... D6
*92660 Newport Beach 62,556 .... D11
93444 Nipomo 5,247 .... E8
91760 Norco 21,126 .... E11
95660 North Highlands 37,825 .... B8
*91601 North Hollywood B10
90650 Norwalk 85,286 .... C11
94947 Novato 43,916 .... H1
95361 Oakdale 8,474 .... E6
*94601 Oakland⊙ 339,337 .... J2
93022 Oak View 4,671 .... F9
93445 Oceano 4,478 .... E8
92054 Oceanside 76,698 .... H10
93308 Oildale 23,382 .... F8
93023 Ojai 6,816 .... F9
*91761 Ontario 88,820 .... D10
†95060 Opal Cliffs 5,041 .... K4
*92666 Orange 91,450 .... D11
93646 Orange Cove 4,026 .... F7
94563 Orinda 16,825 .... J2
95963 Orland 4,031 .... C4
93647 Orosi 4,076 .... F7
95965 Oroville⊙ 8,683 .... D4
93030 Oxnard 108,195 .... F9
Oxnard-Simi Valley-Ventura‡ 529,899 .... F9
94553 Pacheco-Vine Hill 6,129 .... K1
94044 Pacifica 36,866 .... H2
93950 Pacific Grove 15,755 .... C7
93550 Palmdale 12,277 .... G9
92260 Palm Desert 11,801 .... J10
92262 Palm Springs 32,366 .... J10
*94301 Palo Alto 55,225 .... K3
90274 Palos Verdes Estates 14,376 .... B11
95969 Paradise 22,571 .... D4
90723 Paramount 36,407 .... C11
93648 Parlier 2,902 .... F7
*91101 Pasadena 118,072 .... C10
93446 Paso Robles 9,163 .... E8
95363 Patterson 3,908 .... D6
93953 Pebble Beach C7
92370 Perris 6,827 .... F11
94952 Petaluma 33,834 .... H1
90660 Pico Rivera 53,387 .... C10
94611 Piedmont 10,498 .... J2
94564 Pinole 14,253 .... J1
93449 Pismo Beach 5,364 .... E8
94565 Pittsburg 33,034 .... L1
92670 Placentia 35,041 .... D11
95667 Placerville⊙ 6,739 .... C8
94523 Pleasant Hill 25,124 .... K2
94566 Pleasanton 35,160 .... L2
*91766 Pomona 92,742 .... D10
93257 Porterville 19,707 .... G7
93041 Port Hueneme 17,803 .... F9
94025 Portola Valley 3,939 .... J3
92064 Poway 32,263 .... J11
93534 Quartz Hill 7,421 .... G9
95971 Quincy⊙ 4,451 .... E4
92065 Ramona 8,173 .... J10
95670 Rancho Cordova 42,881 .... C8
91730 Rancho Cucamonga 55,250 .... E10
92270 Rancho Mirage 6,281 .... J10
90274 Rancho Palos Verdes 36,577 .... B11
92067 Rancho Santa Fe 4,014 .... H10
96080 Red Bluff⊙ 9,490 .... C3
96001 Redding⊙ 41,995 .... C3
Redding○ 80
92373 Redlands 43,619 .... H9
*90277 Redondo Beach 57,102 .... B11
*94061 Redwood City⊙ 54,951 .... J3
93654 Reedley 11,071 .... F7
92376 Rialto 37,474 .... E10
*94801 Richmond 74,676 .... J1
93555 Ridgecrest 15,929 .... H8
95562 Rio Dell 2,687 .... A3
95673 Rio Linda 7,359 .... B8
94571 Rio Vista 3,142 .... L1
95366 Ripon 3,509 .... D6
95367 Riverbank 5,695 .... E6
*92501 Riverside⊙ 170,591 .... E11
Riverside-San Bernardino-Ontario‡ 1,557,080 .... E11
95677 Rocklin 7,344 .... B8
94572 Rodeo 8,286 .... J1
94928 Rohnert Park 22,965 .... C5
90274 Rolling Hills 2,049 .... B11
90274 Rolling Hills Estates 7,701 .... B11
91770 Rosemead 42,604 .... C10
95678 Roseville 24,347 .... B8
94957 Ross 2,801 .... H1
92509 Rubidoux 17,048 .... E10

(continued on following page)

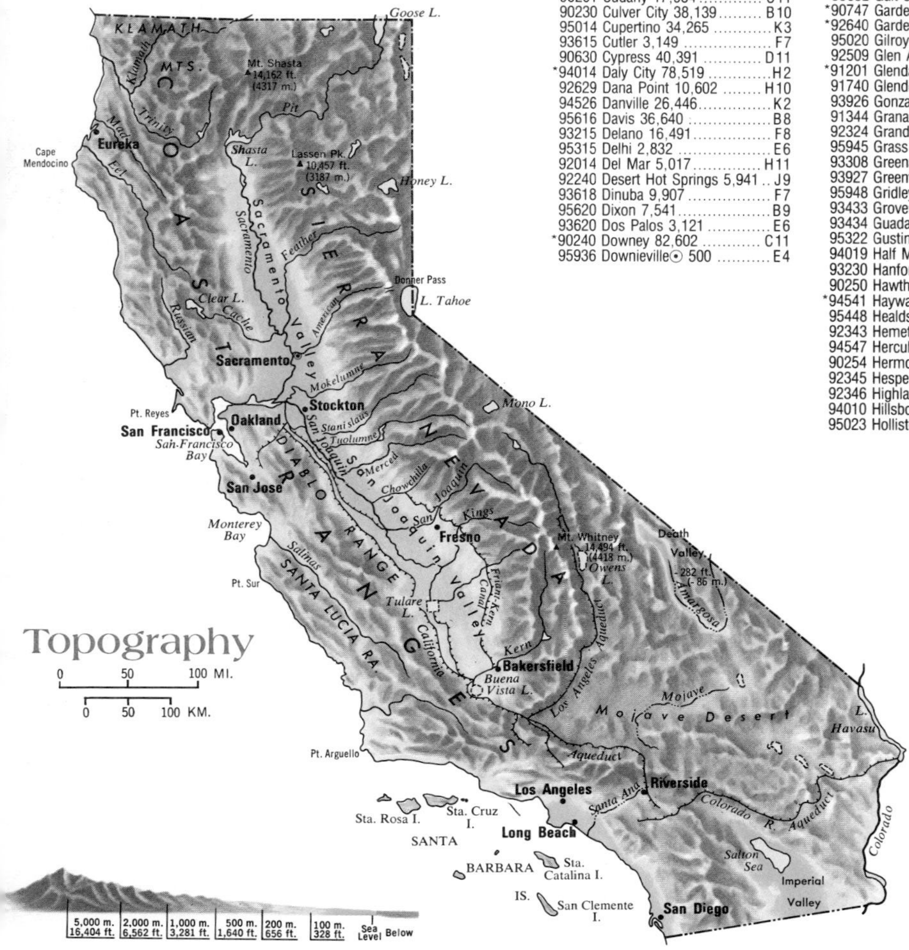

Goose L.
KLAMATH
MTS.
Mt. Shasta 14,162 ft. (4317 m.)
Pit
Trinity
Eureka
Cape Mendocino
Eel
Shasta L.
Lassen Pk. 10,457 ft. (3187 m.)
Honey L.
Sacramento
Feather
Donner Pass
L. Tahoe
Clear L.
Russian
Cache
American
Sacramento
Mokelumne
Mono L.
Pt. Reyes
Oakland
Stockton
San Francisco
San Francisco Bay
Tuolumne
Merced
Chowchilla
San Jose
Monterey Bay
Fresno
Kings
Mt. Whitney 14,494 ft. (4418 m.)
Death Valley
Owens L.
-282 ft. (-86 m.)
Salinas
Pt. Sur
Tulare L.
Kern
Bakersfield
Buena Vista L.
Los Angeles Aqueduct
Mojave Desert
L. Havasu
Pt. Arguello
Los Angeles
Riverside
Colorado R. Aqueduct
Sta. Rosa I.
Sta. Cruz I.
SANTA BARBARA IS.
Long Beach
Sta. Catalina I.
San Clemente I.
Salton Sea
Imperial Valley
San Diego
Colorado
Topography
0 50 100 MI.
0 50 100 KM.
5,000 m. 16,404 ft.
2,000 m. 6,562 ft.
1,000 m. 3,281 ft.
500 m. 1,640 ft.
200 m. 656 ft.
100 m. 328 ft.
Sea Level
Below

Agriculture, Industry and Resources

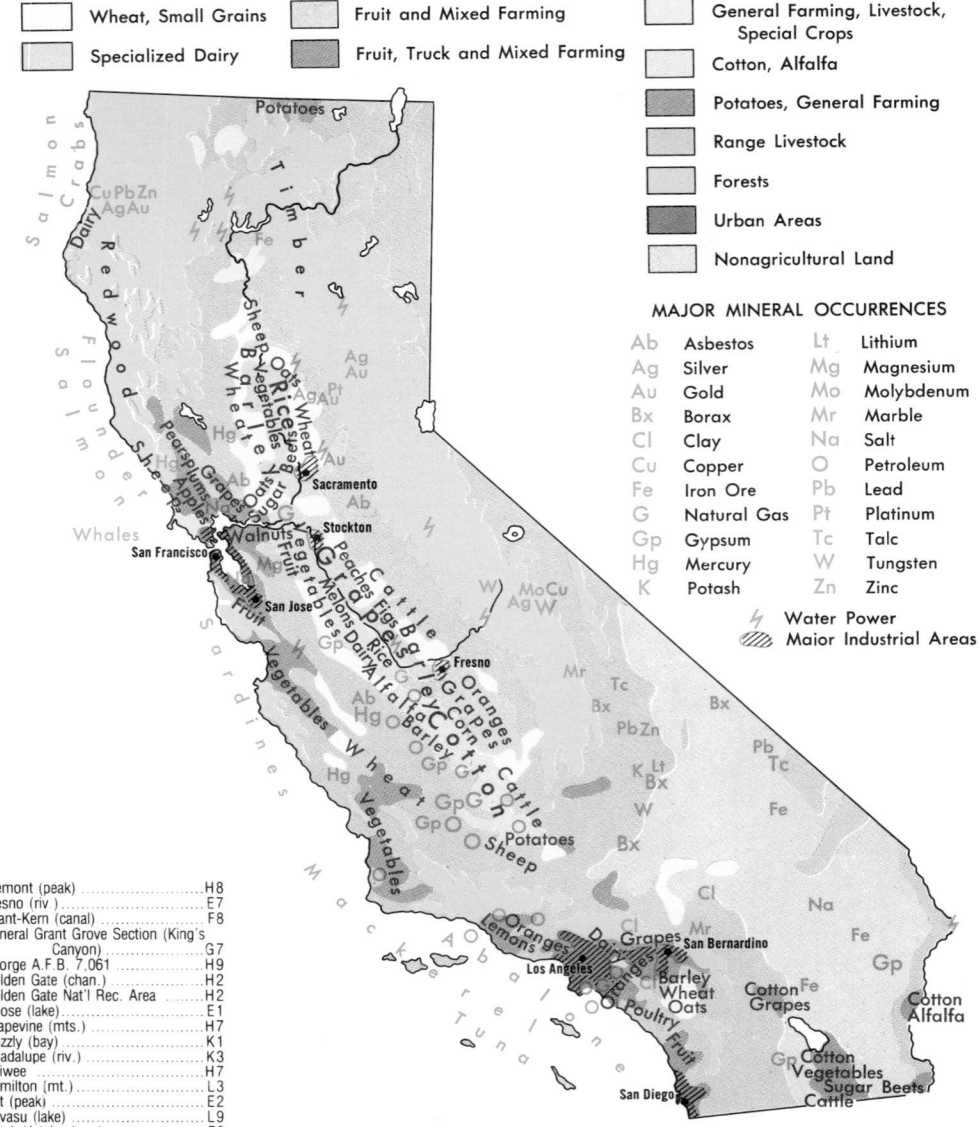

DOMINANT LAND USE

☐ Wheat, Small Grains	☐ Fruit and Mixed Farming
☐ Specialized Dairy	☐ Fruit, Truck and Mixed Farming
☐ General Farming, Livestock, Special Crops
☐ Cotton, Alfalfa
☐ Potatoes, General Farming
☐ Range Livestock
☐ Forests
☐ Urban Areas
☐ Nonagricultural Land

MAJOR MINERAL OCCURRENCES

Ab	Asbestos	Lt	Lithium
Ag	Silver	Mg	Magnesium
Au	Gold	Mo	Molybdenum
Bx	Borax	Mr	Marble
Cl	Clay	Na	Salt
Cu	Copper	O	Petroleum
Fe	Iron Ore	Pb	Lead
G	Natural Gas	Pt	Platinum
Gp	Gypsum	Tc	Talc
Hg	Mercury	W	Tungsten
K	Potash	Zn	Zinc

⚡ Water Power
▨ Major Industrial Areas

AREA 104,091 sq. mi. (269,596 sq. km.)
POPULATION 2,889,735
CAPITAL Denver
LARGEST CITY Denver
HIGHEST POINT Mt. Elbert 14,433 ft. (4399 m.)
SETTLED IN 1858
ADMITTED TO UNION August 1, 1876
POPULAR NAME Centennial State
STATE FLOWER Rocky Mountain Columbine
STATE BIRD Lark Bunting

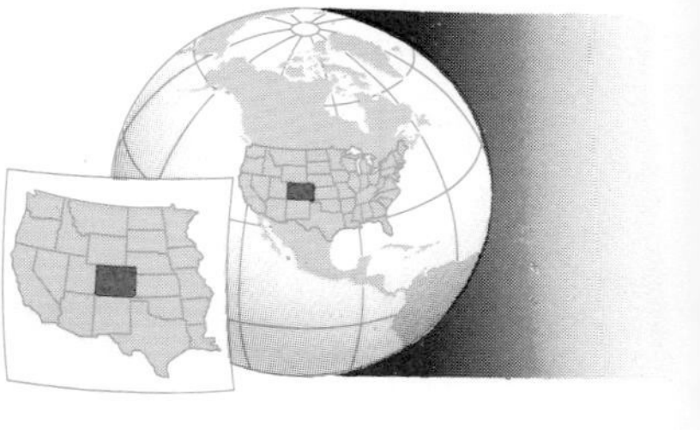

COUNTIES

Adams 245,944 .... L3
Alamosa 11,799 .... H7
Arapahoe 293,621 .... L3
Archuleta 3,664 .... E8
Baca 5,419 .... O8
Bent 5,945 .... N7
Boulder 189,625 .... J2
Chaffee 13,227 .... G5
Cheyenne 2,153 .... O5
Clear Creek 7,308 .... H3
Conejos 7,794 .... G8
Costilla 3,071 .... J8
Crowley 2,988 .... M6
Custer 1,528 .... J6
Delta 21,225 .... D5
Denver 492,365 .... K3
Dolores 1,658 .... C7
Douglas 25,153 .... K4
Eagle 13,320 .... F3
Elbert 6,850 .... L4
El Paso 309,424 .... K5
Fremont 28,676 .... J5
Garfield 22,514 .... C3
Gilpin 2,441 .... H3
Grand 7,475 .... G2
Gunnison 10,689 .... E5
Hinsdale 408 .... E7
Huerfano 6,440 .... K7
Jackson 1,863 .... G1
Jefferson 371,741 .... J3
Kiowa 1,936 .... O6
Kit Carson 7,599 .... O4
Lake 8,830 .... G4
La Plata 27,195 .... D8
Larimer 149,184 .... H1
Las Animas 14,897 .... L8
Lincoln 4,663 .... M5
Logan 19,800 .... N1
Mesa 81,530 .... B5
Mineral 804 .... F7
Moffat 13,133 .... C1
Montezuma 16,510 .... B8
Montrose 24,352 .... C6
Morgan 22,513 .... M2
Otero 22,567 .... M7
Ouray 1,925 .... D6
Park 5,333 .... H4
Phillips 4,542 .... P1
Pitkin 10,338 .... F4
Prowers 13,070 .... P7
Pueblo 125,972 .... K6
Rio Blanco 6,255 .... C3
Rio Grande 10,511 .... G7
Routt 13,404 .... E1
Saguache 3,935 .... G6
San Juan 833 .... D7
San Miguel 3,192 .... C6
Sedgwick 3,266 .... P1
Summit 8,848 .... G3
Teller 8,034 .... J5
Washington 5,304 .... N3
Weld 123,438 .... L1
Yuma 9,682 .... P2

CITIES and TOWNS

Zip *Name/Pop.* *Key*

80101 Agate 90 .... M4
81020 Aguilar 624 .... K8
80720 Akron⊙ 1,716 .... N2
81101 Alamosa⊙ 6,830 .... H8
80510 Allenspark 200 .... J2
80420 Alma 132 .... G4
81210 Almont 135 .... F5
80721 Amherst 85 .... P1
80801 Anton 55 .... N3
81120 Antonito 1,103 .... H8
80802 Arapahoe 300 .... P5
81021 Arlington 37 .... N6
80804 Arriba 236 .... N4
†81323 Arriola 56 .... B8
*80001 Arvada 84,576 .... J3
81611 Aspen⊙ 3,678 .... F4
80722 Atwood 100 .... N1
80610 Ault 1,056 .... K1
*80010 Aurora 158,588 .... K3
81410 Austin D5
81620 Avon 640 .... F3
81022 Avondale 750 .... L6
80421 Bailey 150 .... H4
†80624 Barnesville 20 .... L2
81621 Basalt 529 .... E4
81122 Bayfield 724 .... D8
81411 Bedrock 45 .... B6
†80758 Beecher Island 5 .... P3
80512 Bellvue 250 .... J1
80102 Bennett 942 .... L3
80513 Berthoud 2,362 .... J2
†80438 Berthoud Pass 40 .... H3
80805 Bethune 149 .... P4
81023 Beulah 650 .... K6
80908 Black Forest 3,372 .... K4
80422 Black Hawk 232 .... J3
81123 Blanca 252 .... H8
†80424 Blue River 230 .... G4
†81155 Bonanza 8 .... G6
81024 Boncarbo 200 .... K8
80423 Bond 65 .... F3
81025 Boone 431 .... L6
*80301 Boulder⊙ 76,685 .... J2
†81428 Bowie 18 .... D5
80821 Boyero 12 .... N5
81026 Brandon 30 .... P6
81027 Branson 73 .... M8
80424 Breckenridge⊙ 818 .... G4
80611 Briggsdale 85 .... L1
80601 Brighton⊙ 12,773 .... K3
81028 Bristol 200 .... P6
†81212 Brookside 178 .... J6
80020 Broomfield 20,730 .... J3
80723 Brush 4,082 .... M2
†80742 Buckingham 5 .... L1
81211 Buena Vista 2,075 .... G5
80425 Buffalo Creek 150 .... J4
80807 Burlington⊙ 3,107 .... P4
80426 Burns 100 .... F3
80103 Byers 490 .... L3
81320 Cahone 200 .... B7
80808 Calhan 541 .... L4
81029 Campo 185 .... O8
81212 Canon City⊙ 13,037 .... J6
81124 Capulin 600 .... G8
81623 Carbondale 2,084 .... E4
80612 Carr 49 .... K1
80909 Cascade 950 .... K5
80104 Castle Rock⊙ 3,921 .... K4
81413 Cedaredge 1,184 .... D5
81125 Center 1,630 .... G7
80427 Central City⊙ 329 .... J3
81126 Chama 239 .... J8
81030 Cheraw 233 .... N6
80810 Cheyenne Wells⊙ 950 .... P5
81127 Chimney Rock 76 .... E8
81031 Chivington 20 .... O6
81128 Chromo 115 .... F8
81220 Cimarron 50 .... D6
80428 Clark 20 .... F1
81520 Clifton 5,223 .... C4
80429 Climax 975 .... G4
81221 Coal Creek 190 .... J6
81222 Coaldale 153 .... H6
80430 Coalmont 50 .... F1
81032 Cokedale 90 .... K8
81624 Collbran 344 .... C4
†81401 Colona 54 .... D6
81019 Colorado City 411 .... K6
*80901 Colorado Springs⊙ 214,821 .... K5
Colorado Springs‡ 317,458 .... K5
†80428 Columbine 12 .... E1
80022 Commerce City 16,234 .... K3
80432 Como 30 .... H4
81129 Conejos⊙ 200 .... G8
80812 Cope 110 .... O3
†80611 Cornish 15 .... L2
81321 Cortez⊙ 7,095 .... B8
81223 Cotopaxi 250 .... H6
80434 Cowdrey 80 .... G1
81625 Craig⊙ 8,133 .... D2
81415 Crawford 268 .... D5
81130 Creede⊙ 610 .... E7
81224 Crested Butte 959 .... E5
81131 Crestone 54 .... H7
80813 Cripple Creek⊙ 655 .... J5
80726 Crook 177 .... O1
81033 Crowley 192 .... M6
81055 Cuchara 43 .... J8
80514 Dacono 2,321 .... K2
†80728 Dailey 20 .... O1
81630 De Beque 279 .... C4
†80135 Deckers 4 .... J4
80105 Deer Trail 463 .... M3
†81059 Delhi 10 .... M7
81132 Del Norte⊙ 1,709 .... G7
81416 Delta⊙ 3,931 .... D5
*80201 Denver (cap.)⊙ 492,365 .... K3
Denver‡ 1,619,921 .... K3
†81054 Deora 2 .... O7
80435 Dillon 337 .... H3
81610 Dinosaur 313 .... B2
80814 Divide 700 .... J5
81323 Dolores 802 .... C8
81324 Dove Creek⊙ 826 .... A7
†81239 Doyleville 75 .... F6
80515 Drake 300 .... J2
81301 Durango⊙ 11,649 .... D8
81036 Eads⊙ 878 .... O6
81631 Eagle⊙ 950 .... F3
80615 Eaton 1,932 .... K1
80727 Eckley 262 .... P2
80214 Edgewater 4,766 .... J3
81632 Edwards 250 .... F3
81325 Egnar 50 .... B7
80106 Elbert 200 .... L4
†80466 Eldora 100 .... H3
80107 Elizabeth 789 .... K4
81633 Elk Springs 18 .... C2
80438 Empire 423 .... H3
†80110 Englewood 30,021 .... K3
80516 Erie 1,254 .... K2
80517 Estes Park 2,703 .... J2
†81433 Eureka 25 .... D7
80620 Evans 5,063 .... K2
80439 Evergreen 6,376 .... J3
80440 Fairplay⊙ 421 .... H4
81037 Farisita 116 .... J7
†80221 Federal Heights 7,846 .... J3
80520 Firestone 1,204 .... K2
†80810 Firstview 6 .... O5
80815 Flagler 550 .... N4
80728 Fleming 388 .... O1
81226 Florence 2,987 .... J6
80816 Florissant 130 .... J5
80521 Fort Collins⊙ 65,092 .... J1
Fort Collins‡ 149,184 .... J1
81133 Fort Garland 700 .... J8
80621 Fort Lupton 4,251 .... K2
81038 Fort Lyon 500 .... N6
80701 Fort Morgan⊙ 8,768 .... M2
80817 Fountain 8,324 .... K5
81039 Fowler 1,227 .... L6
80441 Foxton 12 .... J4
80116 Franktown 200 .... K4
80442 Fraser 470 .... H3
80530 Frederick 855 .... K2
80820 Freshwater (Guffey) 24 .... H5
80443 Frisco 1,221 .... G3
81521 Fruita 2,810 .... B4
80622 Galeton 200 .... K1
81134 Garcia 75 .... J8
81040 Gardner 100 .... J7
81227 Garfield 30 .... G5
81522 Gateway 350 .... B5
80818 Genoa 165 .... N4
80444 Georgetown⊙ 830 .... H3
80623 Gilcrest 1,025 .... K2
80624 Gill 250 .... L2
81634 Gilman 160 .... G3
81523 Glade Park 100 .... B5
†80485 Glendevey 50 .... H1
80532 Glen Haven 110 .... H2
81601 Glenwood Springs⊙ 4,637 .... E4
80401 Golden⊙ 12,237 .... J3
†80653 Goodrich 85 .... M2
†80480 Gould 12 .... G2
81041 Granada 557 .... P6
80446 Granby 963 .... H2
81501 Grand Junction⊙ 27,956 .... B4
80447 Grand Lake 382 .... H2
81228 Granite 47 .... G4
80448 Grant 50 .... H4
80631 Greeley⊙ 53,006 .... K2
Greeley‡ 123,438 .... K2
†80118 Greenland 21 .... K4
80819 Green Mountain Falls 607 .... K5
†81640 Greystone 2 .... B1
80729 Grover 158 .... L1
80820 Guffey 24 .... H5
81042 Gulnare 6 .... K8
81230 Gunnison⊙ 5,785 .... E5
81637 Gypsum 743 .... F3
80730 Hale 4 .... P3
81638 Hamilton 100 .... D2
81043 Hartman 122 .... P6
80449 Hartsel 69 .... H4
81044 Hasty 150 .... O6
81045 Haswell 126 .... N6
80731 Haxtun 1,014 .... O1
81639 Hayden 1,720 .... E2
80732 Hereford 50 .... L1
81326 Hesperus 250 .... C8
80733 Hillrose 213 .... N2
81232 Hillside 79 .... H6
81046 Hoehne 400 .... L8
81047 Holly 969 .... P6
80734 Holyoke⊙ 2,092 .... P1
81136 Hooper 71 .... H7
81419 Hotchkiss 849 .... D5
80451 Hot Sulphur Springs⊙ 405 .... H2
81233 Howard 200 .... H6
80641 Hoyt 60 .... L2
80642 Hudson 698 .... K2
80821 Hugo⊙ 776 .... N4
80533 Hygiene 450 .... J2
80452 Idaho Springs 2,077 .... H3
80735 Idalia 125 .... P3
81137 Ignacio 667 .... D8
80736 Iliff 218 .... N1
80455 Jamestown 223 .... J2
†81082 Jansen 267 .... K8
81138 Jaroso 50 .... H8
80456 Jefferson 50 .... H4
80822 Joes 100 .... O3
80534 Johnstown 1,535 .... K2
80737 Julesburg⊙ 1,528 .... P1
80823 Karval 51 .... N5
80643 Keenesburg 541 .... L2
†80729 Keota 4 .... L1
80644 Kersey 913 .... L2
81049 Kim 100 .... N8
80117 Kiowa⊙ 206 .... L4
80824 Kirk 30 .... P3
80825 Kit Carson 278 .... O5
80459 Kremmling 1,296 .... G2
†80832 Kutch 2 .... M5
80026 Lafayette 8,935 .... K3
†81132 La Garita 10 .... G7
80739 Laird 105 .... P2
81140 La Jara 858 .... H8
81050 La Junta⊙ 8,388 .... M7
81235 Lake City⊙ 206 .... E6
80827 Lake George 500 .... J5
80215 Lakewood 113,808 .... J3
81052 Lamar⊙ 7,713 .... O6
80535 Laporte 950 .... J1
80118 Larkspur 141 .... K4
80645 La Salle 1,929 .... K2
81054 Las Animas⊙ 2,818 .... N6
†81151 Lasauces 150 .... H8
†81153 Lavalley 237 .... J8
81055 La Veta 611 .... J8
†80452 Lawson 108 .... H3
†81625 Lay 40 .... D2
81420 Lazear 60 .... D5
80461 Leadville⊙ 3,879 .... G4
†81323 Lebanon 50 .... B8
81327 Lewis 150 .... B8
80828 Limon 1,805 .... M4
†81212 Lincoln Park 2,984 .... J6
80740 Lindon 60 .... N3
*80120 Littleton⊙ 28,631 .... K3
80536 Livermore 150 .... J1
†80601 Lochbuie 895 .... K2
†80701 Log Lane Village 709 .... M2
81524 Loma 265 .... B4
80501 Longmont 42,942 .... J2
†80135 Longview 10 .... J4
80027 Louisville 5,593 .... J3
80131 Louviers 300 .... K4
80537 Loveland 30,244 .... J2
80646 Lucerne 135 .... K2
†81054 Lycan 4 .... P7
80540 Lyons 1,137 .... J2
81525 Mack 380 .... B4
81421 Maher 75 .... D5
†80461 Malta 200 .... G4
81141 Manassa 945 .... H8
81328 Mancos 870 .... C8
80829 Manitou Springs 4,475 .... J5
81058 Manzanola 459 .... M6
†81623 Marble 30 .... E4
81329 Marvel 176 .... C8
80541 Masonville 200 .... J2
†80649 Masters 50 .... L2
80830 Matheson 120 .... M4
81640 Maybell 130 .... C2
81057 McClave 125 .... O6
80463 McCoy 62 .... F3
80542 Mead 356 .... K2
81641 Meeker⊙ 2,356 .... D2
81642 Meredith 47 .... F4
80741 Merino 255 .... N2
81005 Mesa 120 .... C4
81330 Mesa Verde National Park 45 .... C8
81142 Mesita 70 .... H8
80543 Milliken 1,506 .... K2
80477 Milner 196 .... F2
81645 Minturn 1,060 .... G3

(continued on following page)

Agriculture, Industry and Resources

DOMINANT LAND USE

- Specialized Wheat
- Wheat, Range Livestock
- Wheat, Grain Sorghums, Range Livestock
- Dry Beans, General Farming
- Sugar Beets, Dry Beans, Livestock, General Farming
- Fruit, Mixed Farming
- General Farming, Livestock, Special Crops
- Range Livestock
- Forests
- Urban Areas
- Nonagricultural Land

MAJOR MINERAL OCCURRENCES

Ag	Silver	Mi	Mica
Au	Gold	Mo	Molybdenum
Be	Beryl	Mr	Marble
C	Coal	O	Petroleum
Cl	Clay	Pb	Lead
Cu	Copper	U	Uranium
F	Fluorspar	V	Vanadium
Fe	Iron Ore	W	Tungsten
G	Natural Gas	Zn	Zinc

Water Power
Major Industrial Areas

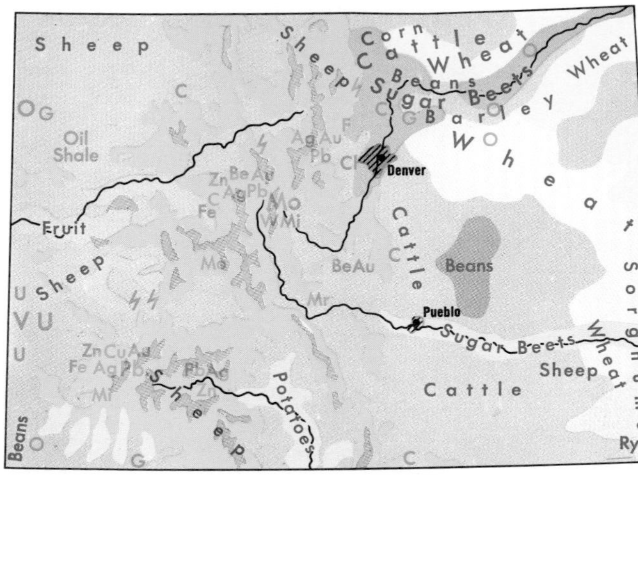

Topography

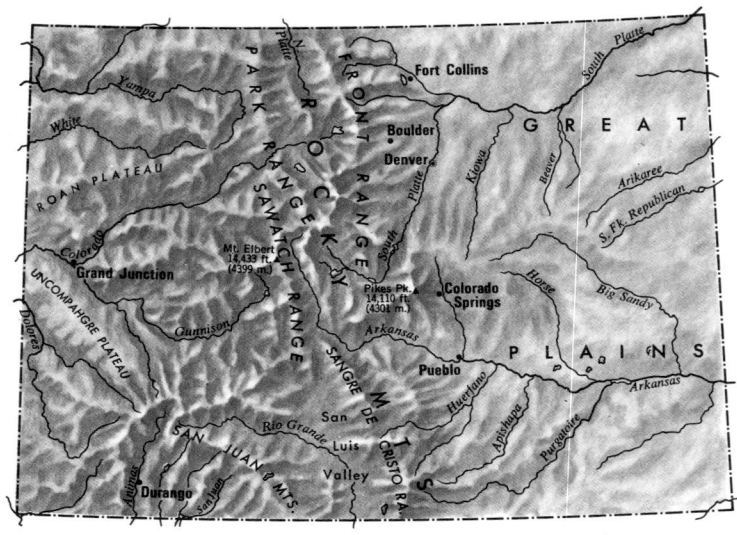

Below Sea Level | 100 m. 328 ft. | 200 m. 656 ft. | 500 m. 1,640 ft. | 1,000 m. 3,281 ft. | 2,000 m. 6,562 ft. | 5,000 m. 16,404 ft.

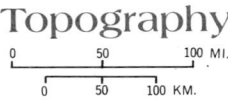

81646 Molina 200 ....D4	80473 Rand 50 ....G2	81334 Towaoc 300 ....B8
81144 Monte Vista 3,902 ......G7	81648 Rangely 2,113 ......B2	81080 Towner 61 ....P6
†80435 Montezuma 6 ....H3	80742 Raymer (New Raymer) 80 .M1	81081 Trinchera 30 ......M8
81401 Montrose⊙ 8,722 ......D6	81649 Red Cliff 409 ......G4	81082 Trinidad⊙ 9,663 ......L8
80132 Monument 690 ......K4	80545 Red Feather Lakes 150 ...H1	†80864 Truckton 30 ......L5
80465 Morrison 478 ....J3	†81326 Red Mesa 100 ......C8	81251 Twin Lakes 40 ......G4
81146 Mosca 100 ....H7	†81623 Redstone 115 ......E4	81084 Two Buttes 84 ......P7
81236 Nathrop 150 ....H5	81431 Redvale 300 ......B6	81059 Tyrone 9 ......L8
81422 Naturita 819 ....B6	81066 Red Wing 200 ......J7	81436 Uravan 500 ......B6
80466 Nederland 1,212 ......H3	81332 Rico 76 ......C7	81064 Utleyville 2 ......O8
81647 New Castle 563 ......E3	81432 Ridgway 369 ......D6	81657 Vail 2,261 ......G3
80742 New Raymer 80 ......M1	81650 Rifle 3,215 ......D3	†81082 Valdez 12 ......K8
†81054 Ninaview 2 ....N7	†81650 Rio Blanco 4 ......C3	80755 Vernon 50 ......P3
80544 Niwot 500 ....J2	81244 Rockvale 338 ......J6	80860 Victor 265 ......J5
†81022 North Avondale 110 ......L6	81067 Rocky Ford 4,804 ......M6	81087 Vilas 118 ......P8
80233 Northglenn 29,847 ......K3	80652 Roggen 100 ......L2	81155 Villa Grove 37 ......G6
†81050 North La Junta 1,076 ......N7	81148 Romeo 308 ......G8	81088 Villegreen 6 ......M8
81423 Norwood 478 ....C6	80833 Rush 40 ......L5	81001 Vineland 100 ......K6
81424 Nucla 1,027 ....B6	81069 Rye 232 ......K7	80548 Virginia Dale 2 ......J1
80648 Nunn 295 ....K1	81149 Saguache⊙ 656 ......G6	80861 Vona 94 ......O4
80467 Oak Creek 929 ......F2	†81236 Saint Elmo 75 ......H6	81130 Wagon Wheel Gap 20 ......F7
81237 Ohio 100 ....F5	81201 Salida⊙ 44,870 ......H6	80480 Walden⊙ 947 ......G1
81425 Olathe 1,262 ....D5	81150 San Acacio 30 ......J8	81089 Walsenburg⊙ 3,945 ......K7
81062 Olney Springs 253 ......M6	81151 Sanford 687 ......H8	81090 Walsh 884 ......P8
81426 Ophir 38 ....D7	†81069 San Isabel 82 ......K7	80481 Ward 129 ......H2
80649 Orchard 79 ....L2	81152 San Luis⊙ 842 ......J8	80653 Weldona 200 ......M2
†81501 Orchard Mesa 4,876 ......C4	81153 San Pablo 150 ......J8	80549 Wellington 1,215 ......K1
81063 Ordway⊙ 1,135 ......M6	81248 Sargents 31 ......F6	81252 Westcliffe⊙ 324 ......H6
†81120 Ortiz 163 ....H8	†81430 Sawpit 41 ......D7	†80135 Westcreek 2 ......J4
80743 Otis 534 ....O2	80911 Security-Widefield 18,768 ..K5	80030 Westminster 50,211 ......J3
81427 Ouray⊙ 684 ....D6	80135 Sedalia 200 ......K4	81091 Weston 150 ......K8
80744 Ovid 439 ....P1	80749 Sedgwick 258 ......O1	81253 Wetmore 150 ......J6
80745 Padroni 100 ....N1	81070 Segundo 200 ......K8	80033 Wheat Ridge 30,293 ......J3
†81147 Pagosa Junction 15 ......E8	80834 Seibert 180 ......O4	81527 Whitewater 300 ......C5
†81147 Pagosa Springs⊙ 1,331 ..E8	80546 Severance 102 ......K1	80654 Wiggins 531 ......L2
81526 Palisade 1,551 ....C4	80475 Shawnee 100 ......H4	80862 Wild Horse 13 ......N5
80133 Palmer Lake 1,130 ......J4	†80110 Sheridan 5,377 ......J3	81092 Wiley 425 ......O6
80746 Paoli 81 ....P1	81071 Sheridan Lake 87 ......P6	81226 Williamsburg 72 ......J6
81428 Paonia 1,425 ....D5	81652 Silt 923 ......D4	80550 Windsor 4,277 ......J2
81635 Parachute 338 ....C4	81249 Silver Cliff 280 ......J6	80482 Winter Park 480 ......H3
81429 Paradox 250 ....B6	80476 Silver Plume 140 ......H3	81655 Wolcott 30 ......F3
†81212 Parkdale 21 ....H6	80498 Silverthorne 989 ......G3	80863 Woodland Park 2,634 ......J4
80134 Parker 200 ....K4	81433 Silverton⊙ 794 ......D7	80757 Woodrow 24 ......M3
81239 Parlin 100 ....F6	80835 Simla 494 ......M4	81656 Woody Creek 400 ......F4
80468 Parshall 80 ....G2	81653 Slater 10 ......E1	80758 Wray⊙ 2,131 ......P2
80747 Peetz 220 ....N1	81654 Snowmass 999 ......E4	80483 Yampa 472 ......F2
81240 Penrose 500 ....K6	80750 Snyder 200 ......M2	81335 Yellow Jacket 115 ......B7
80831 Peyton 30 ....K4	81434 Somerset 200 ......E5	80864 Yoder 25 ......L5
80469 Phippsburg 300 ......F2	81154 South Fork 500 ......F7	80759 Yuma 2,824 ......O2
80650 Pierce 878 ....K1	81073 Springfield⊙ 1,657 ......O8	
80470 Pine 100 ....J4	81074 Starkville 127 ......L8	
80471 Pinecliffe 375 ....J3	80477 Steamboat Springs⊙ 5,098.F2	**OTHER FEATURES**
†81001 Pinon 50 ....K6	80751 Sterling⊙ 11,385 ......N1	
81241 Pitkin 59 ....F5	80754 Stoneham 35 ......M1	Adams (mt.) H6
81430 Placerville 50 ....D6	81075 Stonington 27 ......P8	Adobe Creek (res.) N6
†81624 Plateau City 35 ......D4	80136 Strasburg 1,005 ......L3	Air Force Academy 8,655 ......K5
†80743 Platner 30 ....N2	80836 Stratton 705 ......O4	Alamosa (creek) G8
80651 Platteville 1,662 ......K2	81076 Sugar City 306 ......M6	Alva B. Adams (tunnel) H2
81331 Pleasant View 300 ......B7	81640 Sunbeam 19 ......C1	Animas (riv.) D8
81242 Poncha Springs 321 ......G6	†80027 Superior 208 ......J3	Antero (mt.) G5
†81226 Portland 17 ....K6	81077 Swink 668 ......M7	Antero (res.) H5
†81427 Portland D6	80478 Tabernash 250 ......H3	Antora (peak) G6
81243 Powderhorn 100 ......F6	81435 Telluride⊙ 1,047 ......D7	Apishapa (riv.) L8
81064 Pritchett 183 ....O8	†80461 Tennessee Pass 5 ......G4	Arapaho Nat'l Rec. Area G2
†80736 Proctor 25 ....N1	81250 Texas Creek 80 ......H6	Arapahoe (peak) H2
81065 Pryor 50 ....K8	†81082 Thatcher 50 ......L7	Arikaree (riv.) O3
*81001 Pueblo⊙ 101,686 ......K6	80229 Thornton 40,343 ......K3	Arkansas (riv.) P6
Pueblo‡ 125,972 ......K6	†81137 Tiffany 50 ......D8	Arkansas Divide (mts.) L4
80472 Radium 22 ....G3	81034 Timpas 25 ......M7	Baker (mt.) H2
80832 Ramah 119 ....L4	†81210 Tincup 8 ......F5	Bald (mt.) H4
80473 Rand 50 ....G2	80479 Toponas 55 ......F2	Bear (peak) P8
81648 Rangely 2,113 ....B2		Beaver (creek) M3
		Bennett (peak) G7

Bent's Old Fort Nat'l Hist. Site M6	Cochetopa (creek) F6	Evans (mt.) H3
Big Grizzly (creek) G1	Colorado (riv.) A5	Florissant Fossil Beds Nat'l Mon. J5
Big Sandy (creek) N4	Colorado Nat'l Mon. B4	Fort Carson 19,399 ......K5
Big Thompson (riv.) H2	Conejos (peak) G8	Fountain (creek) K6
Bijou (creek) L3	Conejos (riv.) G8	Frenchman (creek) P1
Black Canyon of the Gunnison Nat'l Mon. D5	Crestone (peak) H7	Frenchman, North Fork (creek) O1
Black Squirrel (creek) L5	Crow (creek) L1	Frenchman, South Fork (creek) O1
Blanca (peak) H7	Culebra (peak) H8	Front (range) H1
Blue (mt.) B2	Culebra (range) J8	Gore (range) G3
Blue (riv.) G3	Curecanti Nat'l Rec. Area F6	Graham (peak) E8
Blue Mesa (res.) E5	Del Norte (riv.) B2	Granby (lake) H2
Bonny (res.) P3	De Weese (plat.) J6	Great Sand Dunes Nat'l Mon. H7
Box Elder (creek) K4	Dinosaur Nat'l Mon. B2	Green (riv.) A1
Cache la Poudre (riv.) H1	Disappointment (creek) B7	Green Mountain (res.) G3
Cameron (peak) H1	Dolores (riv.) B5	Gunnison (riv.) B4
Camp Hale G4	Douglas (creek) B3	Gunnison (tunnel) D6
Carbon (peak) E5	Eagle (riv.) E3	Gunnison, North Fork (riv.) D5
Castle (peak) F5	Elbert (mt.) G4	Hale, Camp G4
Cebolla (creek) E6	El Diente (peak) C7	Handies (peak) E7
Chacuaco (creek) M8	Eleven Mile Canyon (res.) H5	Harvard (mt.) G5
Cheesman (lake) J4	Elk (riv.) F1	Hermosa (peak) D7
Clay (creek) O7	Empire (res.) L2	Hesperus (mt.) C8
	Ent A.F.B. K5	Holy Cross (mt.) F4
	Ethel (mt.) F1	

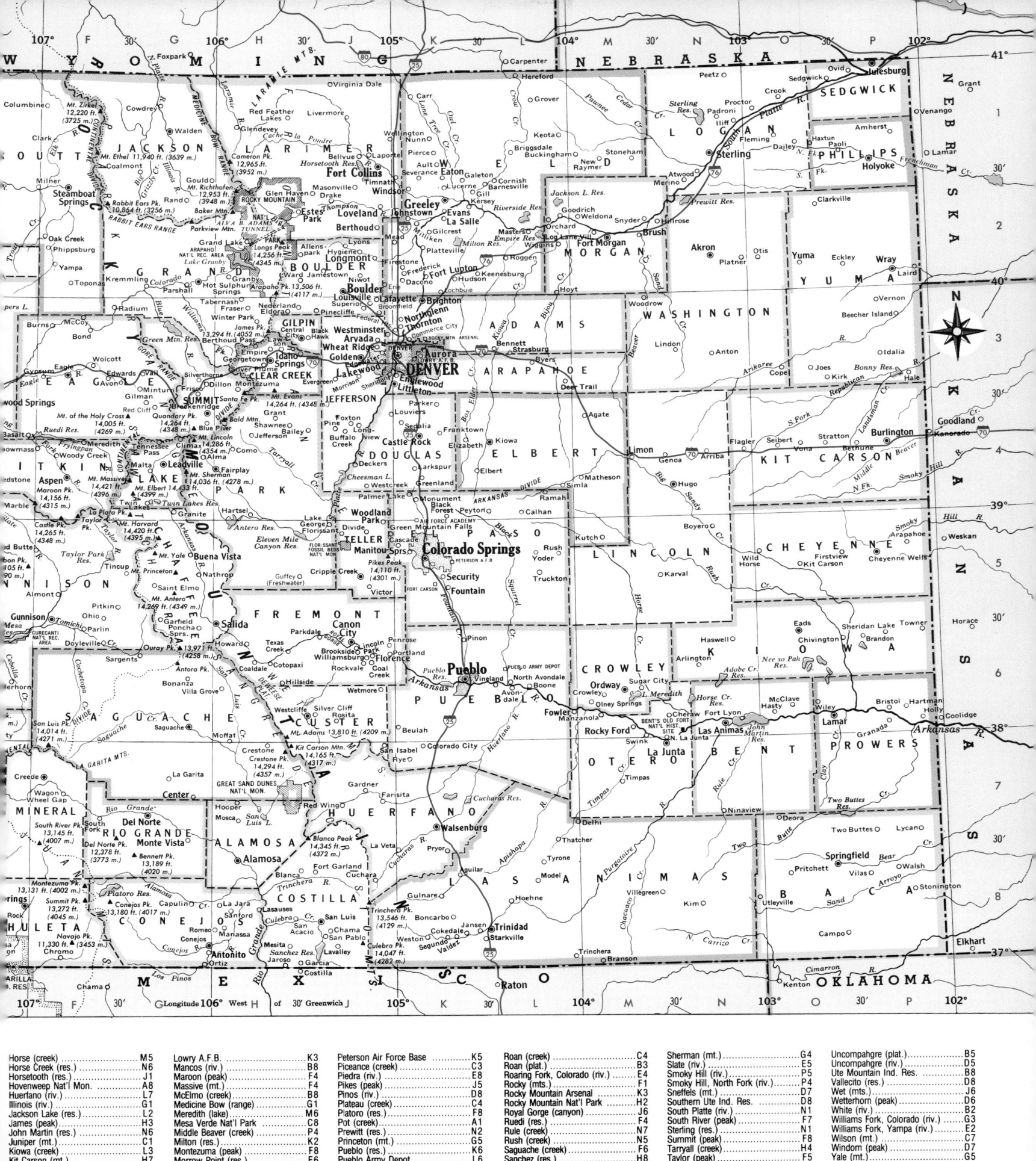

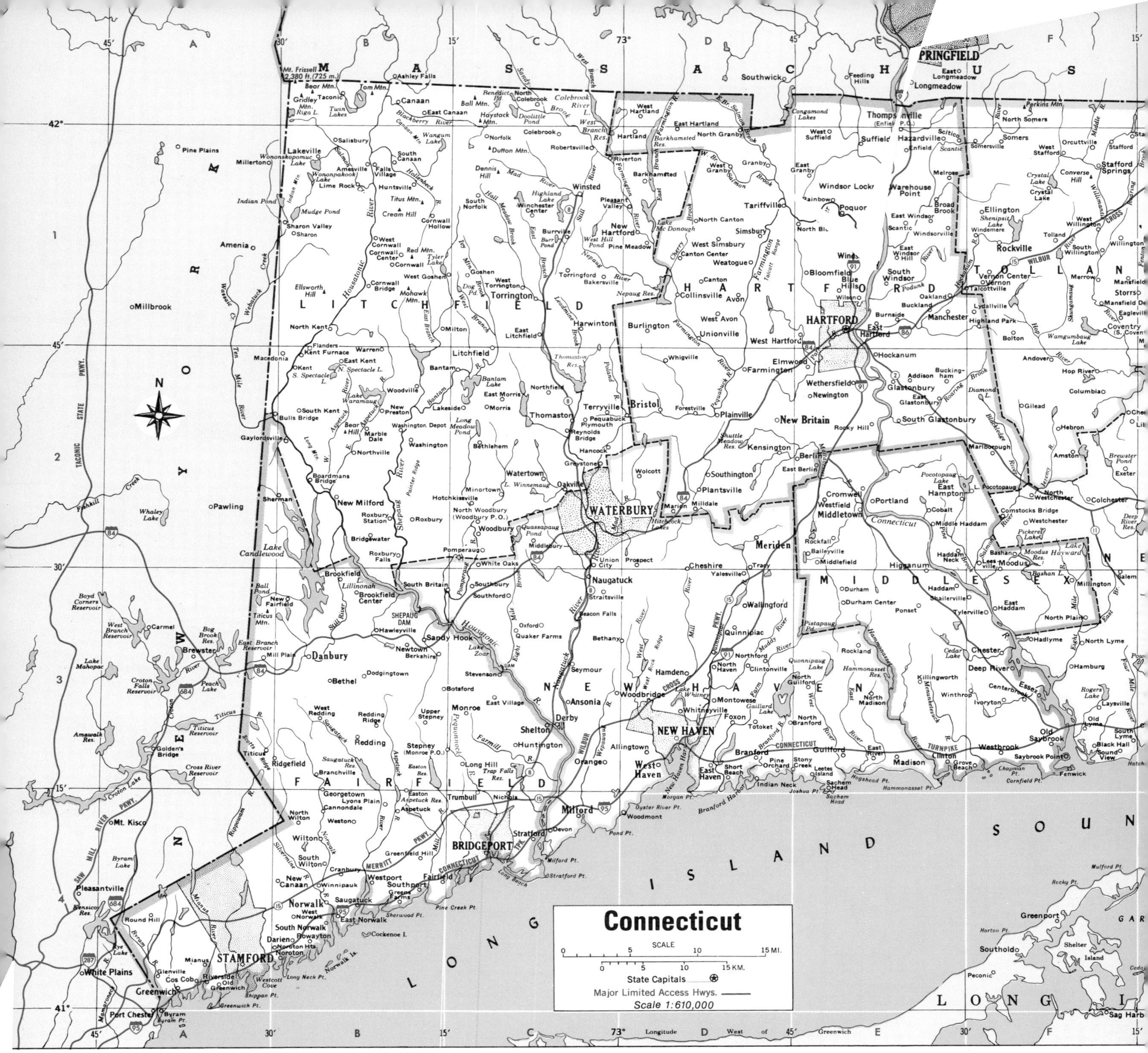

Connecticut

SCALE

0 — 5 — 10 — 15 MI.

0 5 10 15 KM.

State Capitals .... ⊛

Major Limited Access Hwys. ——

Scale 1:610,000

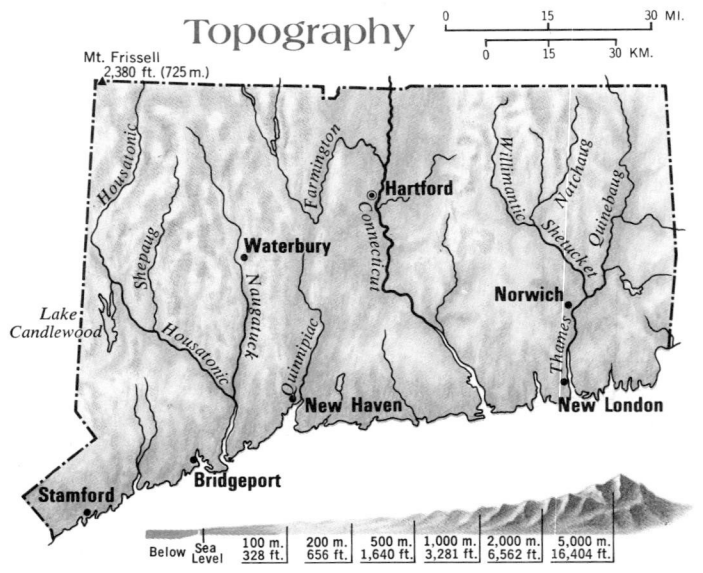

Topography

Mt. Frissell
2,380 ft. (725 m.)

0 — 15 — 30 MI.

0 15 30 KM.

Hartford

Waterbury

New Haven

New London

Norwich

Bridgeport

Stamford

Lake Candlewood

	100 m.	200 m.	500 m.	1,000 m.	2,000 m.	5,000 m.
Below Sea Level	328 ft.	656 ft.	1,640 ft.	3,281 ft.	6,562 ft.	16,404 ft.

COUNTIES

	Key
Fairfield 807,143	B3
Hartford 807,766	D1
Litchfield 156,769	B1
Middlesex 129,017	E3
New Haven 761,337	D3
New London 238,409	G2
Tolland 114,823	F1
Windham 92,312	H1

CITIES and TOWNS

Zip	Name/Pop.	Key
06230	Abington 600	G1
06231	Amston 900	F2
06232	Andover○ 2,144	F2
06401	Ansonia 19,039	C3
06278	Ashford○ 3,221	G1
06278	Ashford P.O. (Warrenville) 500	G1
†06241	Attawaugan 400	H1
06001	Avon○ 11,201	D1
06001	Avon 1,434	D1
06233	Ballouville 800	H1
06330	Baltic	G2
06750	Bantam 860	B2
†06063	Barkhamsted○ 2,935	D1
†06423	Bashan 90	F2
06403	Beacon Falls○ 3,995	C3
06037	Berlin 15,121	E2
†06501	Bethany○ 4,330	C3
06801	Bethel 16,004	B3
06801	Bethel 8,755	B3
06751	Bethlehem○ 2,573	C2
06751	Bethlehem 1,762	C2
06002	Bloomfield 18,608	E1
06112	Blue Hills	E1
06040	Bolton○ 3,951	F1
06404	Botsford 400	C3
06016	Broad Brook	E1
06804	Brookfield○ 12,872	B3
06234	Brooklyn○ 5,691	H1
06013	Burlington○ 5,660	D1
06830	Byram	A4
06018	Canaan○ 1,002	B1
06018	Canaan 1,160	B1
†06897	Cannondale 400	B4
06331	Canterbury○ 3,426	H2
06019	Canton○ 7,635	D1
06019	Canton 1,680	D1
06409	Centerbrook 800	F3
06332	Central Village 950	H2
06235	Chaplin○ 1,793	G1
06410	Cheshire○ 21,788	D2
06410	Cheshire 5,722	D2
06412	Chester○ 3,068	F3
06412	Chester 1,388	F3
06413	Clinton○ 11,195	E3
06413	Clinton 3,168	E3
06414	Cobalt 700	E2
06415	Colchester○ 7,761	F2
06415	Colchester 3,190	F2
06021	Colebrook○ 1,221	C1
06022	Collinsville 2,555	D1
06237	Columbia○ 3,386	F2
06753	Cornwall○ 1,288	B1
06807	Cos Cob	A4
06238	Coventry○ 8,895	F1
06416	Cromwell○ 10,265	E2
06810	Danbury 60,470	B3
	Danbury‡ 146,405	B3
06239	Danielson 4,553	H1
06820	Darien○ 18,892	B4
06241	Dayville	H1
06417	Deep River○ 3,994	F3
06417	Deep River 2,495	F3
06418	Derby 12,346	C3
06422	Durham○ 5,143	E2
06422	Durham 2,641	E2
06023	East Berlin 950	E2
†06239	East Brooklyn 1,251	H1
06024	East Canaan 800	B1
06242	Eastford○ 1,028	G1
06025	East Glastonbury 300	E2
06026	East Granby○ 4,102	E1
06423	East Haddam○ 5,621	F3
06424	East Hampton○ 8,572	E2

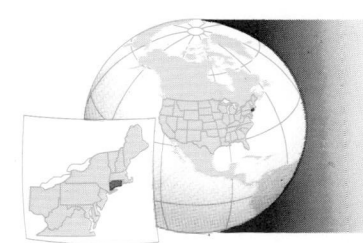

AREA 5,018 sq. mi. (12,997 sq. km.)
POPULATION 3,107,576
CAPITAL Hartford
LARGEST CITY Bridgeport
HIGHEST POINT Mt. Frissell (S. Slope) 2,380 ft. (725 m.)
SETTLED IN 1635
ADMITTED TO UNION January 9, 1788
POPULAR NAME Constitution State; Nutmeg State
STATE FLOWER Mountain Laurel
STATE BIRD Robin

06351 Lisbon○ 3,279	G2
06759 Litchfield○ 7,605	C2
06759 Litchfield 1,489	C2
†06378 Lords Point 500	H3
06443 Madison 14,031	E3
06443 Madison 2,069	E3
06040 Manchester○ 49,761	E1
06040 Manchester 31,058	E1
†06250 Mansfield○ 20,634	F1
06250 Mansfield Center 1,043	G1
06777 Marble Dale 300	B2
06444 Marion 900	D2
06447 Marlborough○ 4,746	F2
06447 Marlborough 1,039	F2
†06382 Massapeag 350	G3
06252 Mechanicsville 425	H1
06450 Meriden 57,118	D2
Meriden‡ 57,118	D2
06762 Middlebury○ 5,995	C2
06455 Middlefield○ 3,796	E2
06456 Middle Haddam 325	E2
06457 Middletown 39,040	E2
06460 Milford 49,101	C4
06467 Milldale 975	D2
†06759 Milton 600	C1
06468 Monroe○ 14,010	C3
06468 Monroe P.O. (Stepney)	C3
06353 Montville○ 16,455	G3
06353 Montville 1,711	G3
06469 Moodus 1,179	F2
06354 Moosup 3,308	H2
06763 Morris○ 1,996	C2
06355 Mystic 2,333	H3
06770 Naugatuck 26,456	C3
*06050 New Britain 73,840	E2
New Britain‡ 142,241	E2
06840 New Canaan○ 17,931	B4
06810 New Fairfield○ 11,260	B3
06057 New Hartford○ 4,884	C1
06057 New Hartford 1,310	C1
*06501 New Haven 126,109	D3
New Haven-West	
Haven‡ 417,592	D3
06111 Newington○ 28,841	E2
06320 New London 28,842	G3
New London-Norwich‡	
248,554	G3
06776 New Milford○ 19,420	B2
06776 New Milford 5,186	B2
06777 New Preston 1,209	B2
06470 Newtown○ 19,107	B3
06470 Newtown 2,022	B3
06357 Niantic 3,151	G3
06340 Noank 1,406	G3
06058 Norfolk○ 2,156	C1
06471 North Branford 11,554	E3
06778 Northfield 600	C2
06254 North Franklin 500	G2
06060 North Granby 450	D1
06255 North Grosvenor	
Dale 1,856	H1
†06437 North Guilford 500	E3
06473 North Haven○ 22,080	D3
06359 North Stonington 4,219	H3
06256 North Windham 200	G1
*06850 Norwalk 77,767	B4
06360 Norwich 38,074	G2
06370 Oakdale 608	G3
06779 Oakville 8,737	C2
06371 Old Lyme○ 6,159	F3

06372 Old Mystic 600	H3
06475 Old Saybrook○ 9,287	F3
06475 Old Saybrook 1,857	F3
06373 Oneco 550	H2
06477 Orange○ 13,237	C3
06483 Oxford○ 6,634	C3
06379 Pawcatuck 5,216	H3
06781 Pequabuck 642	C2
06374 Pine Meadow 400	D1
†06405 Pine Orchard 300	D3
06374 Plainfield○ 12,774	H2
06374 Plainfield 2,799	H2
06062 Plainville○ 16,401	D2
06063 Pleasant Valley 300	C1
†06385 Pleasure Beach 1,356	G3
06782 Plymouth○ 10,732	C2
06258 Pomfret○ 2,775	H1
†06340 Poquonock Bridge 2,549	G3
06480 Portland○ 8,383	E2
06480 Portland 5,914	E2
06712 Prospect○ 6,807	D2
06260 Putnam○ 8,580	H1
06260 Putnam 6,855	H1
06375 Quaker Hill 2,052	G3
06262 Quinebaug 1,088	H1
06875 Redding○ 7,272	B3
06876 Redding Ridge 550	B3
06877 Ridgefield○ 20,120	B3
06877 Ridgefield 6,066	B3
06065 Riverton 250	D1
06481 Rockfall 900	E2
†06066 Rockville○	F1
06067 Rocky Hill 14,559	E2
06263 Rogers 650	H1
06783 Roxbury○ 1,468	B2
06415 Salem○ 2,335	F3
06068 Salisbury○ 3,896	B1
06264 Scotland○ 1,072	G2
06483 Seymour○ 13,434	C3
06069 Sharon○ 2,623	B1
06484 Shelton 31,314	C3
06784 Sherman○ 2,281	B2
06070 Simsbury○ 21,161	D1
06070 Simsbury 5,488	D1
06071 Somers○ 8,473	F1
06071 Somers 1,643	F1
06072 Somersville 750	F1
06487 South Britain 390	B3
06488 Southbury○ 14,156	C3
†06238 South Coventry	
(Coventry) 3,769	F1
06073 South Glastonbury	E2
06489 Southington○ 36,879	D2
06785 South Kent 450	B2
06265 South Willington 450	F1
06266 South Windham 1,399	G2
06074 South Windsor○ 17,198	E1
06267 South Woodstock 1,319	G1
06075 Stafford○ 9,268	F1
06076 Stafford Springs 3,392	F1
06077 Staffordville 500	G1
*06901 Stamford 102,453	A4
Stamford‡ 198,854	A4
†06468 Stepney	B3
06377 Sterling○ 1,791	H2
06491 Stevenson 300	C3
06378 Stonington○ 16,220	H3
06378 Stonington 1,228	H3
06268 Storrs 11,394	F1
06497 Stratford○ 50,541	C4

06078 Suffield○ 9,294	E1
06078 Suffield 1,122	E1
06079 Taconic 400	B1
06380 Taftville	G2
06081 Tariffville 1,324	D1
06786 Terryville 5,234	C2
06787 Thomaston○ 6,276	C2
06277 Thompson○ 8,141	H1
†06082 Thompsonville	E1
06084 Tolland○ 9,694	F1
06790 Torrington 30,987	C1
06611 Trumbull○ 32,989	C4
06382 Uncasville 1,597	G3
†06076 Union○ 546	G1
06066 Vernon○ 27,974	F1
06383 Versailles 540	G2
06384 Voluntown○ 1,637	H2
06492 Wallingford 37,274	D3
06492 Wallingford 17,821	D3
06754 Warren○ 1,027	B2
†06278 Warrenville 500	G1
06793 Washington○ 3,657	B2
06794 Washington Depot 900	B2
*06701 Waterbury 103,266	C2
Waterbury‡ 228,178	C2
06385 Waterford○ 17,843	G3
06385 Waterford 2,736	G3
06795 Watertown 19,489	C2
06089 Weatogue 2,249	D1
06498 Westbrook○ 5,216	F3
06498 Westbrook 2,035	F3
06796 West Cornwall 425	B1
06090 West Granby 567	D1
06107 West Hartford○ 61,301	D1
06516 West Haven 53,184	D3
06388 West Mystic 3,364	H3
06883 Weston○ 8,284	B4
06880 Westport○ 25,290	B4
06896 West Redding 500	B3
06092 West Simsbury 2,140	D1
06109 Wethersfield○ 26,013	E2
06517 Whitneyville	D3
06226 Willimantic 14,652	G2
†06279 Willington○ 4,694	F1
06897 Wilton○ 15,351	B4
06094 Winchester○ 10,841	C1
06094 Winchester Center 350	C1
06280 Windham○ 21,062	G2
06095 Windsor○ 25,204	E1
06095 Windsor 17,517	E1
06096 Windsor Locks○ 12,190	E1
06097 Windsorville 450	E1
06098 Winsted 8,092	C1
06417 Winthrop 750	E3
06716 Wolcott○ 13,008	D2
†06515 Woodbridge○ 7,761	D3
06798 Woodbury○ 6,942	C2
06798 Woodbury 1,290	C2
†06460 Woodmont 1,797	D4
06281 Woodstock○ 5,117	H1

OTHER FEATURES

Aspetuck (res.)	B4
Bantam (lake)	C2
Barkhamsted (res.)	D1
Bear (mt.)	B1
Byram (riv.)	A4
Candlewood (lake)	A2
Coast Guard Academy	G3

Colebrook River (lake)	C1
Congamond (lkes)	E1
Connecticut (riv.)	E2
Dennis (hill)	C1
Easton (res.)	B3
Eight Mile (riv.)	F3
Farmington (riv.)	D1
French (riv.)	H1
Frissell (mt.)	B1
Gaillard (lake)	D3
Gardner (lake)	G2
Hammonasset (pt.)	E3
Hammonasset (res.)	E3
Haystack (mt.)	C1
Highland (lake)	C1
Hockanum (riv.)	E1
Hop (riv.)	F1
Housatonic (riv.)	C3
Lillinonah (lake)	B3
Little (riv.)	G2
Long Island (sound)	C4
Mad (riv.)	C1
Mashapaug (lake)	G1
Mason (isl.)	H3
Mattabesset (riv.)	E2
Mianus (riv.)	A4
Mohawk (mt.)	B1
Moosup (riv.)	H2
Mount Hope (riv.)	G1
Mudge (pond)	B1
Mystic (riv.)	H3
Natchaug (riv.)	G1
Naugatuck (riv.)	C3
Nepaug (res.)	D1
Niantic (riv.)	G3
Norwalk (riv.)	B4
Pachaug (pond)	H2
Pawcatuck (riv.)	H3
Pequabuck (riv.)	D2
Pequonnock (riv.)	C4
Pocotopaug (lake)	E2
Quaddick (res.)	H1
Quinebaug (riv.)	H2
Quinnipiac (riv.)	D3
Rippowam (riv.)	A4
Sachem (head)	E4
Salmon (brook)	D1
Salmon (riv.)	F2
Saugatuck (res.)	B3
Scantic (riv.)	E1
Shenipsit (lake)	F1
Shepaug (riv.)	B2
Shetucket (riv.)	G2
Silvermine (riv.)	B4
Spectacle (lkes)	B2
Still (riv.)	B1
Still (riv.)	C1
Talcott (range)	E1
Thames (riv.)	G3
Thomaston (res.)	C2
Titicus (riv.)	A3
Trap Falls (res.)	C3
Twin (lkes)	B1
Wamgumbaug (lake)	F1
Waramaug (lake)	B2
West Rock Ridge (hills)	D3
Willimantic (riv.)	F1
Wononskopomuc (lake)	B1
Yantic (riv.)	G2

‡Population of metropolitan area.
○Population of town or township.
† Zip of nearest p.o. * Multiple zips.

06424 East Hampton 2,152	E2
06108 East Hartford 52,563	E1
06027 East Hartland 900	D1
06512 East Haven 25,028	D3
06243 East Killingly 900	H1
06333 East Lyme○ 13,870	G3
†06763 East Morris 800	C2
06612 Easton○ 5,962	B4
†06088 East Windsor○ 8,925	E1
06028 East Windsor Hill 500	E1
06244 East Woodstock 400	H1
06029 Ellington○ 9,711	F1
06082 Enfield○ 42,695	E1
06082 Enfield 8,151	E1
06426 Essex○ 5,078	F3
06426 Essex 2,501	F3
06245 Fabyan 600	H1
06430 Fairfield○ 54,849	B4
06031 Falls Village 600	B1
06032 Farmington○ 16,407	D2
06334 Fitchville 400	G2
†06254 Franklin○ 1,592	G2
06335 Gales Ferry 1,191	G3
06755 Gaylordsville 960	A2
06829 Georgetown 1,834	B4
06336 Gilman 350	G2
06337 Glasgo 450	H2
06033 Glastonbury○ 24,327	E2
06033 Glastonbury 7,049	E2
06756 Goshen○ 1,706	C1
06035 Granby○ 7,956	D1
06035 Granby 1,912	D1

06830 Greenwich○ 59,578	A4
06246 Grosvenor Dale 700	H1
06340 Groton○ 41,062	G3
06340 Groton 10,086	G3
06437 Guilford○ 17,375	E3
06437 Guilford 2,555	E3
06438 Haddam○ 6,383	E3
06439 Hadlyme 450	F3
06514 Hamden○ 51,071	D3
06247 Hampton○ 1,322	G1
06350 Hanover 500	G2
*06101 Hartford (cap.) 136,392	E1
Hartford‡ 726,114	E1
†06091 Hartland○ 1,416	D1
06791 Harwinton○ 4,889	C1
06791 Harwinton 3,293	C1
06440 Hawleyville 600	B3
06082 Hazardville 5,436	F1
06248 Hebron○ 5,453	F2
06441 Higganum 1,660	E2
†06040 Highland Park 500	F1
06351 Jewett City 3,294	H2
06037 Kensington 7,502	D2
06757 Kent○ 2,505	B2
†06241 Killingly○ 14,519	H1
†06413 Killingworth○ 3,976	E3
†06424 Lake Pocotopaug 2,137	F2
06758 Lakeside 350	B2
06249 Lebanon○ 4,762	G2
06339 Ledyard○ 13,735	G3
†06437 Leetes Island 500	E3
†06039 Lime Rock 350	B1

Agriculture, Industry and Resources

DOMINANT LAND USE

Specialized Dairy

Dairy, Poultry, Mixed Farming

Forests

Urban Areas

MAJOR MINERAL OCCURRENCES

Cl Clay   Mi Mica

Major Industrial Areas

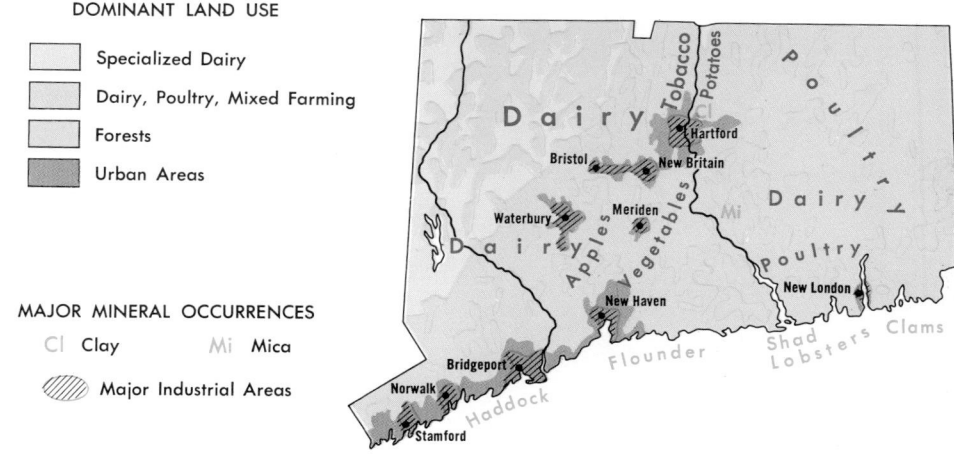

© Copyright HAMMOND INCORPORATED, Maplewood, N.J.

Florida

SCALE
0 5 10 20 30 40 50 MI.
0 5 10 20 30 40 50 KM.

State Capitals................⊛
County Seats.................◉
Canals.......................
Major Limited Access Hwys.....

Scale 1:2,550,000

Western Part of Florida
Same scale as main map

© Copyright HAMMOND INCORPORATED, Maplewood, N.J.

Longitude   West of   Greenwich

AREA 58,664 sq. mi. (151,940 sq. km.)
POPULATION 9,746,342
CAPITAL Tallahassee
LARGEST CITY Jacksonville
HIGHEST POINT (Walton County) 345 ft. (105 m.)
SETTLED IN 1565
ADMITTED TO UNION March 3, 1845
POPULAR NAME Sunshine State; Peninsula State
STATE FLOWER Orange Blossom
STATE BIRD Mockingbird

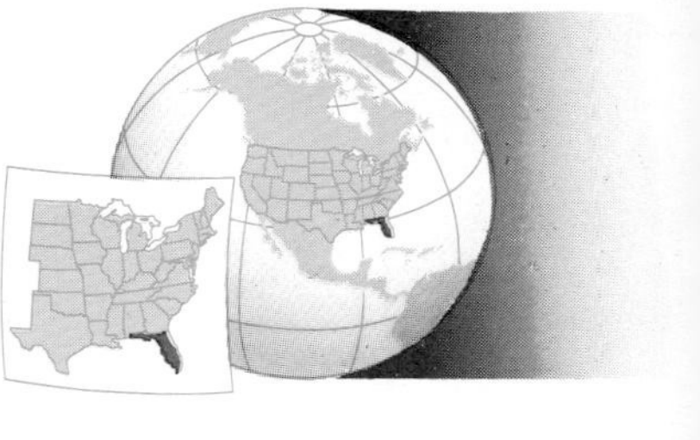

Topography

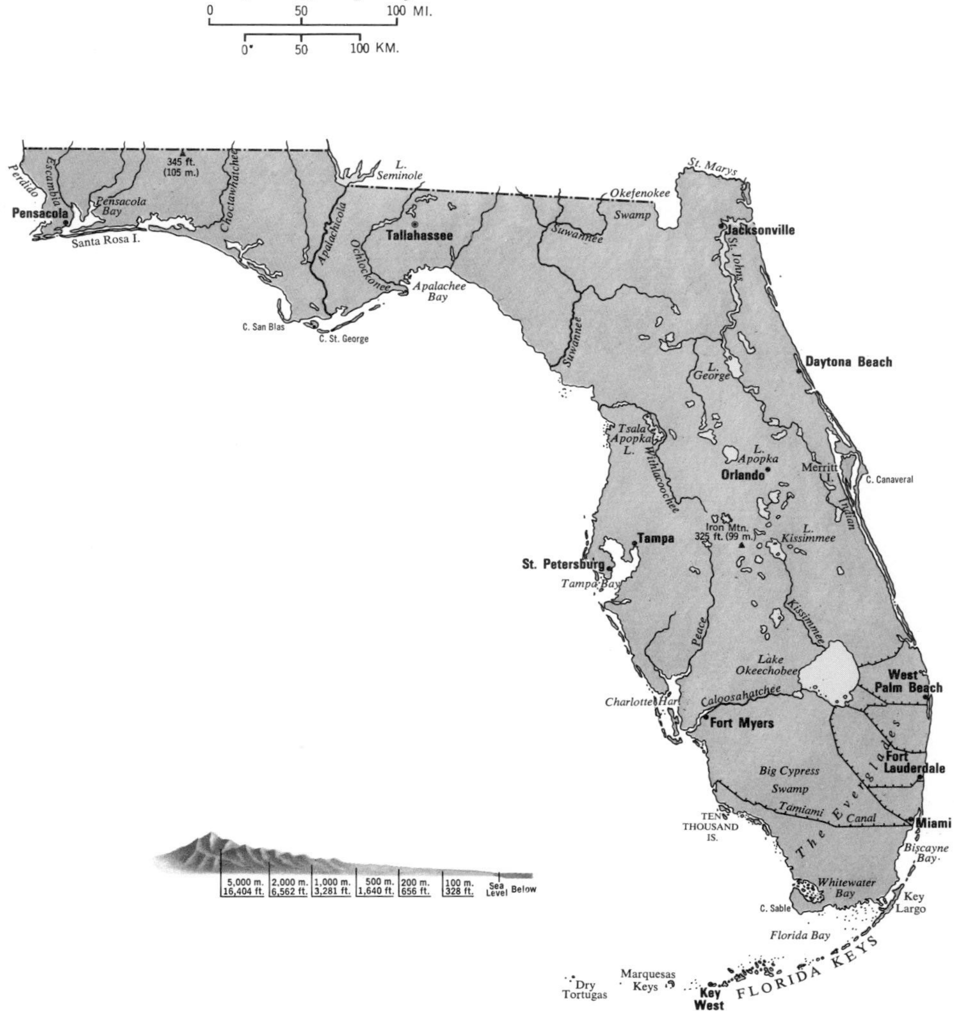

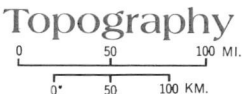

COUNTIES

lachua 151,348 ... D2
aker 15,289 ... D1
ay 97,740 ... C6
radford 20,023 ... D2
revard 272,959 ... F3
roward 101,820 ... F5
alhoun 9,294 ... D6
harlotte 58,460 ... E5
itrus 54,703 ... D3
lay 67,052 ... E2
ollier 85,791 ... E5
olumbia 35,399 ... D1
ade 1,625,781 ... F6
e Soto 19,039 ... E4
ixie 7,751 ... C2
uval 571,003 ... E1
scambia 233,794 ... B6
agler 10,913 ... E2
anklin 7,661 ... B2
adsden 41,565 ... B1
ilchrist 5,767 ... D2
lades 5,992 ... E5
ulf 10,658 ... D7
amilton 8,761 ... D1
ardee 19,379 ... E4
endry 18,599 ... E5
ernando 44,4693
ighlands 47,526 ... E4
illsborough 646,960 ... D4
olmes 14,723 ... C5
dian River 59,896 ... F4
ackson 39,154 ... D5
efferson 10,703 ... C1
afayette 4,035 ... C2
ake 104,870 ... E3
ee 205,266 ... E5
eon 148,655 ... B1
evy 19,870 ... D2
berty 4,260 ... B1
adison 14,894 ... C1
Manatee 148,442 ... D4
Marion 122,488 ... D2
Martin 64,014 ... F4
Monroe 63,188 ... E7
Nassau 32,894 ... E1
Okaloosa 109,920 ... C6
Okeechobee 20,264 ... F4
Orange 471,016 ... E3
Osceola 49,287 ... E3
Palm Beach 576,863 ... F5
Pasco 193,643 ... D3
Pinellas 728,531 ... D4
Polk 321,652 ... E4
Putnam 50,549 ... E2
Saint Johns 51,303 ... E2
Saint Lucie 87,182 ... F4
Santa Rosa 55,988 ... B6
Sarasota 202,251 ... D4
Seminole 179,752 ... E3
Sumter 24,272 ... D3
Suwannee 22,287 ... C1
Taylor 16,532 ... C1
Union 10,166 ... D1
Volusia 258,762 ... E2
Wakulla 10,887 ... B1
Walton 21,300 ... C6
Washington 14,509 ... C6

CITIES and TOWNS

Zip *Name/Pop.* *Key*

32615 Alachua 3,561 ... D2
32420 Alford 548 ... D6
32701 Altamonte Springs 22,028 . E3
32421 Altha 478 ... A1
33820 Alturas 900 ... E4
33501 Anna Maria 1,537 ... D4
32320 Apalachicola⊙ 2,565 ... A2
33570 Apollo Beach 4,014 ... C3
32703 Apopka 6,019 ... E3
33821 Arcadia⊙ 6,002 ... E4
32618 Archer 1,230 ... D2
33502 Aripeka 450 ... D3
32705 Astatula 755 ... E3
32233 Atlantic Beach 7,847 ... E1
33823 Auburndale 6,501 ... E3
33825 Avon Park 8,026 ... E4
32807 Azalea Park 8,301 ... E3
32530 Bagdad 1,479 ... B6
32234 Baldwin 1,526 ... E1
†33101 Bal Harbour 2,973 ... C4
33830 Bartow⊙ 14,780 ... E4
32423 Bascom 134 ... A1
†33101 Bay Harbor Islands 4,869 .. B4
†32786 Bay Lake 74 ... E3
33504 Bay Pines 5,757 ... B3
33507 Bayshore Gardens 14,945 .. D4
†33578 Bee Ridge 3,313 ... D4
32619 Bell 227 ... D2
33540 Belleair 3,673 ... B2
†33540 Belleair Beach 1,643 ... B2
33540 Belleair Bluffs 2,522 ... B3
†33540 Belleair Shores 80 ... B3
33430 Belle Glade 16,535 ... F5
†33430 Belle Glade Camp 1,645 ... F5
†32801 Belle Isle 2,848 ... E3
32620 Belleview 1,913 ... D2
†32036 Beverly Beach 217 ... E2
33152 Biscayne Park 3,088 ... B4
†32801 Bithlo 3,143 ... E3
32424 Blountstown⊙ 2,632 ... A1
33921 Boca Grande 900 ... D5
*33432 Boca Raton 49,505 ... F5
32425 Bonifay⊙ 2,534 ... C5
33923 Bonita Springs 5,435 ... E5
33834 Bowling Green 2,310 ... E4
*33435 Boynton Beach 35,624 ... F5
*33506 Bradenton⊙ 30,170 ... D4
Bradenton‡ 148,442 ... D4
33510 Bradenton Beach 1,595 ... D4
33835 Bradley 1,108 ... D4
33511 Brandon 41,826 ... D4
32008 Branford 622 ... D2
†33435 Briny Breezes 387 ... G5
32321 Bristol⊙ 1,044 ... B1
†33314 Broadview Park 6,022 ... B4
32621 Bronson⊙ 853 ... D2
32622 Brooker 429 ... D2
33512 Brooksville⊙ 5,582 ... D3
†33311 Browardale 7,409 ... B4
32010 Bunnell⊙ 1,816 ... E2
33513 Bushnell⊙ 983 ... D3
32011 Callahan 869 ... E1
32401 Calloway 7,154 ... D6
32426 Campbellton 336 ... D5
32624 Candler 275 ... E2
32920 Cape Canaveral 5,733 ... F3
33904 Cape Coral 32,103 ... E5
33055 Carol City 47,349 ... B4
Carrabelle 1,304 ... B2
32427 Caryville 633 ... C6
32707 Casselberry 15,247 ... E3
†32401 Cedar Grove 1,104 ... D6
32625 Cedar Key 700 ... C2
33514 Center Hill 751 ... D3
32535 Century 495 ... B5
†33950 Charlotte Harbor 2,084 ... E5
32324 Chattahoochee 5,332 ... B1
32626 Chiefland 1,986 ... D2
32428 Chipley⊙ 3,330 ... D6
†32548 Cinco Bayou 202 ... B6
*33515 Clearwater⊙ 85,528 ... B2
32711 Clermont 5,461 ... E3
†33950 Cleveland 2,417 ... E5
33440 Clewiston 5,219 ... E5
32922 Cocoa 16,096 ... F3
32931 Cocoa Beach 10,926 ... F3
†33060 Coconut Creek 6,288 ... F5
33521 Coleman 1,022 ... D3
33328 Cooper City 10,140 ... B4
†33559 Coral Cove 2,042 ... D4
33134 Coral Gables 43,241 ... B5
33060 Coral Springs 37,349 ... F5
33522 Cortez 3,821 ... D4
32431 Cottondale 1,056 ... D6
32327 Crawfordville⊙ 1,110 ... B1
32012 Crescent City 1,722 ... E2
32536 Crestview⊙ 7,617 ... C6
32628 Cross City⊙ 2,154 ... C2
32629 Crystal River 2,778 ... D3
33157 Cutler Ridge 20,886 ... F6
33880 Cypress Gardens 8,043 ... E3
†33472 Cypress Quarters 1,479 ... F4
33525 Dade City⊙ 4,923 ... D3
33004 Dania 11,811.B4
33837 Davenport 1,509 ... E3
33314 Davie 20,877 ... B4
*32014 Daytona Beach 54,176 ... F2
Daytona Beach‡ 258,762 .. F2
32016 Daytona Beach Shores 1,324 ... F2
32713 De Bary 4,980 ... E3
33441 Deerfield Beach 39,193 ... F5
32433 De Funiak Springs⊙ 5,563 C6
32720 De Land⊙ 15,354 ... E2
32028 De Leon Springs 1,669 ... E2
*33444 Delray Beach 34,325 ... F5
32725 Deltona 15,710 ... E3
32541 Destin 3,672 ... C6
33527 Dover 2,354 ... D4
33838 Dundee 2,227 ... E3
33528 Dunedin 30,203 ... B2
32630 Dunnellon 1,427 ... D2
33839 Eagle Lake 1,678 ... E4
†33601 East Lake-Orient Park 5,612 ... C2
†33940 East Naples 12,127 ... E5
32031 East Palatka 1,613 ... E2
32328 Eastpoint 1,246 ... B2
32751 Eatonville 2,185 ... E3
32437 Ebro 233 ... C6
32032 Edgewater 6,726 ... F3
†32801 Edgewood 1,034 ... E3
†33614 Egypt Lake 11,932 ... C2
33531 Elfers 11,396 ... D3
†33101 El Portal 1,819 ... B4
33533 Englewood 9,633 ... D5
32504 Ensley 14,422 ... B6
32425 Esto 304 ... C5
32726 Eustis 9,453 ... E3
33929 Everglades City 524 ... E6
32634 Fairfield 450 ... D2
†32693 Fanning Springs (Suwannee Riv.) 314 ... D2
32948 Fellsmere 1,161 ... F4
32034 Fernandina Beach⊙ 7,224 . E1
32922 Five Points 1,691 ... D1
32036 Flagler Beach 2,208 ... E2
32636 Floral City 1,181 ... D3
33034 Florida City 6,174 ... F6
†32960 Florida Ridge 4,988 ... F4
†33472 Fort Drum 70 ... F4
*33301 Fort Lauderdale⊙ 153,279. C4
Fort Lauderdale-Hollywood‡ 1,014,043 .. C4
33841 Fort Meade 5,546 ... E4
*33901 Fort Myers⊙ 36,638 ... E5
Fort Myers-Cape Coral‡ 205,266 ... E5
33931 Fort Myers Beach 5,753 ... E5
33842 Fort Ogden 900 ... E4
*33450 Fort Pierce⊙ 33,802 ... F4
32548 Fort Walton Beach 20,829 C6
Fort Walton Beach‡ 109,920 ... C6
32038 Fort White 386 ... D2
32438 Fountain 900 ... D6
32439 Freeport 669 ... C6
33843 Frostproof 2,995 ... E4
32731 Fruitland Park 2,259 ... D3
33578 Fruitville 3,070 ... D4
*32601 Gainesville⊙ 81,371 ... D2
Gainesville‡ 151,348 ... D2
32732 Geneva 1,120 ... E3
33534 Gibsonton 7,219 ... C3
32960 Gifford 6,240 ... F4
32040 Glen Saint Mary 462 ... D1
†33160 Golden Beach 612 ... C4
33999 Golden Gate 4,327 ... E5
†33444 Golf 110 ... F5
32560 Gonzalez 6,084 ... B6
33933 Goodland 600 ... E6
†32502 Goulding 5,352 ... B6
33170 Goulds 7,078 ... F6
32440 Graceville 2,918 ... D5
32442 Grand Ridge 591 ... A1
33463 Greenacres City 8,843 ... F5
32043 Green Cove Springs⊙ 4,154 ... E2
32330 Greensboro 562 ... B1
32331 Greenville 1,096 ... C1
32443 Greenwood 577 ... A1
32332 Gretna 1,448 ... B1
33533 Grove City 1,932 ... D5
32736 Groveland 1,992 ... E3
32561 Gulf Breeze 5,478 ... B6
33737 Gulfport 11,180 ... B3
†33444 Gulf Stream 475 ... F5
†33301 Hacienda Village 126 ... B4
33844 Haines City 10,799 ... E3
33009 Hallandale 36,517 ... B4
32044 Hampton 466 ... D2
33440 Harlem 2,669 ... F5
32045 Hastings 636 ... E2
32333 Havana 2,782 ... B1
32640 Hawthorne 1,303 ... D2
32642 Hernando 1,653 ... D3
*33010 Hialeah 145,254 ... B4
†33010 Hialeah Gardens 2,700 ... B4
33431 Highland Beach 2,030 ... F5
33846 Highland City 1,555 ... E4
32401 Highland Park 184 ... E4
32643 High Springs 2,491 ... D2
32405 Hiland Park 4,763 ... C6
†33827 Hillcrest Heights 177 ... E4
32046 Hilliard 1,869 ... E1
†33060 Hillsboro Beach 1,554 ... F5
33455 Hobe Sound 6,822 ... F4
32047 Hollister 980 ... E2
32017 Holly Hill 9,953 ... E2
*33020 Hollywood 121,323 ... B4
33509 Holmes Beach 4,023 ... D4
*33030 Homestead 20,668 ... F6
32646 Homosassa 1,426 ... D3
32648 Horseshoe Beach 304 ... C2
32334 Hosford 750 ... B1
32737 Howey In The Hills 626 ... E3
33568 Hudson 5,799 ... D3
†33460 Hypoluxo 573 ... F5
33934 Immokalee 11,038 ... E5
32903 Indialantic 2,883 ... F3
†33139 Indian Creek 103 ... B4
†32901 Indian Harbour Beach 5,967 ... F3
32960 Indian River Shores 1,254 . F4
33535 Indian Rocks Beach 3,717 . B3
†33535 Indian Shores 984 ... B3
33456 Indiantown 3,383 ... F4
32649 Inglis 1,173 ... D2
32048 Interlachen 848 ... E2
32650 Inverness⊙ 4,095 ... D3
33036 Islamorada 1,441 ... F7
†33101 Islandia 12 ... F6
*32201 Jacksonville⊙ 540,920 ... E1
Jacksonville‡ 737,519 ... E1
32250 Jacksonville Beach 15,462 . E1
†33568 Jasmine Estates 11,995 ... D3
32052 Jasper⊙ 2,093 ... D1
32565 Jay 633 ... B5
32053 Jennings 749 ... C1
33457 Jensen Beach 6,639 ... F4
†32901 June Park 4,051 ... F3
†33404 Juno Beach 1,142 ... F5
33458 Jupiter 9,868 ... F5
†33455 Jupiter Island 364 ... F4
33849 Kathleen 1,866 ... D3
33156 Kendall 73,758 ... B5
33709 Kenneth City 4,344 ... B3
33149 Key Biscayne 6,313 ... B5
33051 Key Colony Beach 977 ... F7
33037 Key Largo 7,447 ... F6
32656 Keystone Heights 1,056 ... E2
33040 Key West⊙ 24,382 ... E7
32741 Kissimmee⊙ 15,487 ... E3
33935 La Belle⊙ 2,287 ... E5
33537 Lacoochee 1,720 ... D3
32658 La Crosse 170 ... D2
32659 Lady Lake 1,193 ... E3
33850 Lake Alfred 3,134 ... E3
†32830 Lake Buena Vista 98 ... E3
32054 Lake Butler⊙ 1,830 ... D1
†33601 Lake Carroll 13,012 ... C2
32055 Lake City⊙ 9,257 ... D1
32744 Lake Helen 2,047 ... E3
*33801 Lakeland 47,406 ... D3
Lakeland-Winter Haven‡ 321,652 ... D3
†33612 Lake Magdalene 13,331 ... D3
32746 Lake Mary 2,853 ... E3
33403 Lake Park 6,909 ... F5
33852 Lake Placid 963 ... E4
33853 Lake Wales 8,466 ... E4
*33460 Lake Worth 27,048 ... G5
33539 Land O'Lakes 4,515 ... D3
33462 Lantana 8,048 ... F5
*33540 Largo 58,977 ... B3
33308 Lauderdale-by-the-Sea 2,639 ... C3
†33313 Lauderdale Lakes 25,426 ... B3
33313 Lauderhill 37,271 ... B3
33545 Laurel 6,368 ... D4
32567 Laurel Hill 610 ... C5
32058 Lawtey 692 ... D1
†33050 Layton 88 ... F7
†33301 Lazy Lake 31 ... B3
32059 Lee 297 ... C1
32748 Leesburg 13,191 ... E3
33936 Lehigh Acres 9,604 ... E5
33033 Leisure City 17,905 ... F6
†33614 Leto 9,003 ... C2
33064 Lighthouse Point 11,488 ... F5
32060 Live Oak⊙ 6,732 ... D1
32662 Lochloosa 450 ... E2
33548 Longboat Key 4,843 ... D4
32750 Longwood 10,029 ... E3
33549 Lutz 5,555 ... D3
32444 Lynn Haven 6,239 ... C6
32063 Macclenny⊙ 3,851 ... D1

(continued on following page)

33738 Madeira Beach 4,520 ....B3
32340 Madison⊙ 3,487 ....C1
32751 Maitland 8,763 ....E3
32950 Malabar 1,118 ....F3
32445 Malone 897 ....A1
33550 Mango 6,493 ....D4
33050 Marathon 7,568 ....E7
33937 Marco (Marco Island) 4,679 ....E6
33063 Margate 35,900 ....F5
32446 Marianna⊙ 7,006 ....A1
†32084 Marineland 31 ....E2
32569 Mary Esther 3,530 ....B6
32753 Mascotte 1,112 ....E3
32066 Mayo⊙ 891 ....C1
32664 McIntosh 404 ....D2
†33101 Medley 537 ....B4
*32901 Melbourne 46,536 ....F3
Melbourne-Titusville-Cocoa‡ 272,959 ....F3
32951 Melbourne Beach 2,713 ....F3
†33301 Melrose Park 5,672 ....B4
†33561 Memphis 5,501 ....D4
32952 Merritt Island 30,708 ....F3
32410 Mexico Beach 632 ....D6
*33101 Miami⊙ 346,931 ....B5
Miami‡ 1,625,979 ....B5
33139 Miami Beach 96,298 ....C5
†33101 Miami Lakes 9,809 ....B4
33153 Miami Shores 9,244 ....B4
33166 Miami Springs 12,350 ....B5
32667 Micanopy 737 ....D2
†32960 Micco 3,585 ....F4
32343 Midway 950 ....B1
32570 Milton⊙ 7,206 ....B6
32754 Mims 7,583 ....F3
32755 Minneola 851 ....E3
33023 Miramar 32,813 ....B4
32577 Molino 1,456 ....B6
32344 Monticello⊙ 2,994 ....C1
32756 Montverde 397 ....E3
33471 Moore Haven⊙ 1,250 ....E5
32757 Mount Dora 5,883 ....E3
33860 Mulberry 2,932 ....E4
33938 Murdock 272 ....D4
32506 Myrtle Grove 14,238 ....B6
*33940 Naples⊙ 17,581 ....E5
†33940 Naples Park 5,438 ....E5
33032 Naranja 10,381 ....F6
32233 Neptune Beach 5,248 ....E1
32669 Newberry 1,826 ....D2
*33552 New Port Richey 11,196 ....D3
32069 New Smyrna Beach 13,557 ....F2
32578 Niceville 8,543 ....C6
33555 Nokomis 3,108 ....D4
32452 Noma 113 ....C5
†33169 Norland 19,471 ....B4
33141 North Bay Village 4,920 ....B4
33903 North Fort Myers 22,808 ....E5
†33063 North Lauderdale 18,653 ....B3
33161 North Miami 42,566 ....B4
33161 North Miami Beach 36,481 ....C4
33940 North Naples 7,950 ....E5
33403 North Palm Beach 11,344 ....F5
33595 North Port 6,205 ....D4
†33708 North Redington Beach 1,156 ....B3
32759 Oak Hill 938 ....F3
32760 Oakland 658 ....E3
33334 Oakland Park 23,035 ....B3
*32670 Ocala⊙ 37,170 ....D2
Ocala‡ 122,488 ....D2
†33457 Ocean Breeze Park 469 ....F4
33444 Ocean Ridge 1,355 ....F5
32761 Ocoee 7,803 ....E3
33163 Ojus 17,344 ....B4
32762 Okahumpka 900 ....D3
33472 Okeechobee⊙ 4,225 ....F4
33557 Oldsmar 2,608 ....B2
33558 Oneco 6,417 ....D4
33054 Opa Locka 14,460 ....B4
32763 Orange City 2,795 ....E3
32073 Orange Park 8,766 ....E1
†32970 Orchid 42 ....F4
*32801 Orlando⊙ 128,291 ....E3
Orlando‡ 700,699 ....E3
32074 Ormond Beach 21,378 ....E2
32074 Ormond-by-the-Sea 7,665 ....E2
33559 Osprey 1,660 ....D4
32683 Otter Creek 167 ....D2
32765 Oviedo 3,074 ....E3
32570 Pace 5,006 ....B6
33476 Pahokee 6,346 ....F5
†32036 Painters Hill 40 ....E2
32077 Palatka⊙ 10,175 ....E2
32905 Palm Bay 18,560 ....F3
33480 Palm Beach 9,729 ....G4
†33403 Palm Beach Gardens 14,407 ....F5
†33404 Palm Beach Shores 1,232 ....G5
33490 Palm City 2,177 ....F4
32037 Palm Coast 2,837 ....E2
33561 Palmetto 8,637 ....D4
33563 Palm Harbor 5,215 ....D3
33619 Palm River-Clair Mel 14,447 ....C3
†32901 Palm Shores 77 ....F3
33460 Palm Springs 8,166 ....F5
*32401 Panama City⊙ 33,346 ....C6
Panama City‡ 97,740 ....C6
32407 Panama City Beach 2,148 ....C6
32401 Parker 4,298 ....C6
†33441 Parkland 545 ....F5
32538 Paxton 659 ....C5
†33023 Pembroke Park 4,783 ....B4
33024 Pembroke Pines 35,776 ....B4
32079 Penney Farms 630 ....E2
†33010 Pennsuco 15 ....B4
*32501 Pensacola⊙ 57,619 ....B6
Pensacola‡ 289,782 ....B6
33157 Perrine 16,129 ....F6
32347 Perry⊙ 8,254 ....C1
32080 Pierson 1,085 ....E2
32808 Pine Hills 35,771 ....E3
33565 Pinellas Park 32,811 ....B3
33317 Plantation 48,653 ....B4
33566 Plant City 17,064 ....D3
33868 Polk City 576 ....E3
32081 Pomona Park 791 ....E2
*33060 Pompano Beach 52,618 ....F5
32455 Ponce de Leon 454 ....C6
†32019 Ponce Inlet 1,003 ....F2
33952 Port Charlotte 25,770 ....D5
32019 Port Orange 18,756 ....F2
33568 Port Richey 2,165 ....D3
32456 Port Saint Joe 4,027 ....D6
33452 Port Saint Lucie 14,690 ....F4
33492 Port Salerno 4,511 ....F4
33032 Princeton 10,381 ....F6
*33950 Punta Gorda⊙ 6,797 ....E5
32351 Quincy⊙ 8,591 ....B1
32083 Raiford 259 ....D1
32686 Reddick 657 ....D2
33708 Redington Beach 1,708 ....B3
†33708 Redington Shores 2,142 ....B3
†33158 Richmond Heights 8,577 ....F6
†33301 Riverland 5,919 ....B4
33404 Riviera Beach 26,489 ....G5
32955 Rockledge 11,877 ....F3
32957 Roseland 1,607 ....F4
33570 Ruskin 5,117 ....C3
33572 Safety Harbor 6,461 ....B2
32084 Saint Augustine⊙ 11,985 ....E2
32084 Saint Augustine Beach 1,289 ....E2
32769 Saint Cloud 7,840 ....E3
33956 Saint James City 1,298 ....D5
33574 Saint Leo 917 ....D3
33452 Saint Lucie 593 ....F4
32355 Saint Marks 286 ....B1
*33701 Saint Petersburg 238,647 ....B3
33736 Saint Petersburg Beach 9,354 ....B3
†33508 Samoset 5,747 ....D4
†32069 Samsula 1,971 ....E2
33576 San Antonio 529 ....D3
32771 Sanford⊙ 23,176 ....E3
33957 Sanibel 3,363 ....D5
*33577 Sarasota⊙ 48,868 ....D4
Sarasota‡ 202,251 ....D4
†33577 Sarasota Springs 13,860 ....D4
32935 Satellite Beach 9,163 ....F3
32775 Scottsmoor 900 ....F3
†33301 Sea Ranch Lakes 584 ....C3
32958 Sebastian 2,831 ....F4
33870 Sebring⊙ 8,736 ....E4
33584 Seffner 6,493 ....D4
33542 Seminole 4,586 ....B3
†33457 Sewalls Point 1,187 ....F4
32579 Shalimar 390 ....C6
32959 Sharpes 4,149 ....F3
32688 Silver Springs 1,082 ....D2
32460 Sneads 1,690 ....B1
32358 Sopchoppy 444 ....B1
33493 South Bay 3,886 ....F5
32021 South Daytona 11,252 ....F2
33143 South Miami 10,944 ....B5
†33157 South Miami Heights 23,559 ....F6
33707 South Pasadena 4,188 ....B3
†32901 South Patrick Shores 9,816 ....F3
†32401 Southport 1,992 ....C6
33452 South Port Saint Lucie (Port Saint Lucie 14,690 ....F4
33595 South Venice 8,075 ....D4
32690 Sparr 902 ....D2
32401 Springfield 7,220 ....D6
32091 Starke⊙ 5,306 ....D2
33494 Stuart⊙ 9,467 ....F4
33586 Sun City D4
†33570 Sun City Center 5,605 ....C3
†33450 Sunland Gardens F4
33160 Sunny Isles 12,564 ....C4
33313 Sunrise 39,681 ....B4
33154 Surfside 3,763 ....B4
32692 Suwannee (Fanning Sprs.) 314 ....C2
†33144 Sweetwater 8,251 ....B5
†32043 Switzerland 3,906 ....E1
32809 Taft 900 ....E3
*32301 Tallahassee (cap.)⊙ 81,548 ....B1
Tallahassee‡ 159,542 ....B1
†33321 Tamarac 29,376 ....B3
*33601 Tampa⊙ 271,523 ....C2
Tampa-Saint Petersburg‡ 1,569,492 ....C2
*33589 Tarpon Springs 13,251 ....D3
32778 Tavares⊙ 4,103 ....E3
33070 Tavernier 1,834 ....F6
33617 Temple Terrace 11,097 ....C2
33458 Tequesta 3,685 ....F5
33905 Tice 6,645 ....E5
32780 Titusville⊙ 31,910 ....F3
33740 Treasure Island 6,316 ....B3
32693 Trenton⊙ 1,131 ....D2
32784 Umatilla 1,872 ....E3
33620 University 24,514 ....C2
32580 Valparaiso 6,142 ....C6
*33595 Venice 12,153 ....D4
32462 Vernon 885 ....C6
32960 Vero Beach⊙ 16,176 ....F4
†33166 Virginia Gardens 2,098 ....B5
32970 Wabasso 2,157 ....F4
†32327 Wakulla 225 ....B1
32694 Waldo 993 ....D2
†32456 Ward Ridge 104 ....D6
32507 Warrington 15,792 ....B6
†32055 Watertown 3,804 ....D1
33873 Wauchula⊙ 2,986 ....E4
32463 Wausau 347 ....D6
33877 Waverly 1,208 ....E4
33597 Webster 856 ....D3
†33512 Weeki Wachee 8 ....D3
32093 Welaka 492 ....E2
32935 West Eau Gallie 2,591 ....F3
†32901 West Melbourne 5,078 ....F3
†33101 West Miami 6,076 ....B5
*33401 West Palm Beach⊙ 63,305 ....F5
West Palm Beach-Boca Raton‡ 573,125 ....F5
†32502 West Pensacola 24,371 ....B6
32464 Westville 343 ....C6
†33165 Westwood Lakes 11,478 ....B5
32465 Wewahitchka⊙ 1,742 ....D6
†32465 White City 4,110 ....F4
32096 White Springs 781 ....D1
32785 Wildwood 2,665 ....D3
32696 Williston 2,240 ....D2
33334 Wilton Manors 12,742 ....B3
33598 Wimauma 1,477 ....D4
32786 Windermere 1,302 ....E3
33880 Winter Haven 21,119 ....E3
*32789 Winter Park 22,339 ....E3
†32801 Winter Springs 10,475 ....E3
32362 Woodville 1,768 ....B1
32697 Worthington Springs 220 ....D2
32698 Yankeetown 600 ....D2
32097 Yulee 3,168 ....E1
32798 Zellwood 1,760 ....E3
33599 Zephyrhills 5,742 ....D3
33890 Zolfo Springs 1,495 ....E4

OTHER FEATURES

Alapaha (riv.) C1
Alligator (lake) E3
Amelia (isl.) E1
Anastasia (isl.) E2
Anclote (keys) D3
Apalachee (bay) B2
Apalachicola (bay) B2
Apalachicola (riv.) A1
Apopka (lake) E3
Arbuckle (lake) E4
Aucilla (riv.) C1
Banana (riv.) F3
Beresford (lake) E3
Big Cypress (swamp) E5
Big Cypress Nat'l Preserve E5
Biscayne (bay) F6
Biscayne (key) B5
Biscayne Nat'l Park F6
Blackwater (riv.) B6
Blue Cypress (lake) F4
Boca Chica (key) E7
Boca Ciega (bay) B3
Boca Grande (key) D7
Bryant (lake) E2
Caloosahatchee (riv.) E5
Captiva (isl.) D5
Casey (key) D4
Castillo de San Marcos Nat'l Mon. E2
Cecil Field Naval Air Sta. E1
Charlotte (harb.) D5
Chattahoochee (riv.) B1
Chipola (riv.) D6
Choctawhatchee (riv.) C6
Crescent (lake) E2
Cumberland Island Nat'l Seashore E1
Cypress (lake) E3
De Soto Nat'l Mem. D4
Dead (lake) D6
Dexter (lake) E2
Dog (isl.) B2
Dorr (lake) E2
Dry Tortugas (keys) D7
Dumfoundling (bay) C4
East (pt.) E6
Eglin A.F.B. 7,574 ....C6
Egmont (key) D4
Elliott (key) F6
Escambia (riv.) B6
Estero (isl.) E5
Eureka (res.) E2
Everglades, The (swamp) F6
Everglades Nat'l Park F6
Fenholloway (riv.) C1
Florida (bay) F6
Florida (cape) F6
Florida (keys) E7
Florida (strs) F7
Fort Caroline Nat'l Mem. E1
Fort Jefferson Nat'l Mon. C7
Fort Matanzas Nat'l Mon. E2
Gasparilla (isl.) D5
George (lake) E2
Grassy (key) F7
Gulf Island Nat'l Seashore B6
Harney (lake) F3
Hart (lake) E3
Hillsborough (bay) C3
Hillsborough (canal) F5
Hillsborough (riv.) C2
Homosassa (isls.) D3
Homestead A.F.B. 7,594 ....F6
Iamonia (lake) B1
Indian (riv.) F3
Iron (mt.) E4
Istokpoga (lake) E4
Jackson (lake) B1
Jackson (lake) E4
Jacksonville Naval Air Sta. E1
John F. Kennedy Space Center F3
June in Winter (lake) E4
Kennedy (Canaveral) (cape) F3
Kerr (lake) E2
Key Largo (key) F6
Key Vaca (key) E7
Key West Naval Air Sta. E7
Kissimmee (lake) E4
Kissimmee (riv.) E4
Largo (key) F6
Levy (lake) D2
Lochloosa (lake) D2
Long (key) B3
Long (key) F7
Longboat (key) D4
Lower Matecumbe (key) F7
Lowery (lake) E3
MacDill A.F.B. C3
Manatee (riv.) D4
Marco (isl.) E6
Marian (lake) E4
Marquesas (keys) D7
Matanzas (inlet) E2
Mayport Naval Air Sta. E1
McCoy A.F.B. E3
Merritt (isl.) F3
Mexico (gulf) C4
Miami (canal) F5
Miami (riv.) B5
Miccosukee (lake) ....B
Monroe (lake) ....E
Mosquito (lag.) ....F
Mullet (key) ....D
Myakka (riv.) ....D
Nassau (riv.) ....E
Nassau (sound) ....E
New (riv.) ....B
New (riv.) ....D
Newnans (lake) ....D
North Merritt (isl.) ....F
North New River (canal) ....F
Ochlockonee (riv.) ....B
Okaloacoochee Slough (swamp) ....E
Okeechobee (lake) ....F
Okefenokee (swamp) ....D
Oklawaha (riv.) ....E
Old Rhodes (key) ....F
Old Tampa (bay) ....B
Olustee (riv.) ....D
Orange (lake) ....D
Patrick A.F.B. 2,843 ....F
Peace (riv.) ....E
Pensacola (bay) ....B
Pensacola Naval Air Sta. ....B
Perdido (riv.) ....B
Pine (isl.) ....D
Pine Island (sound) ....D
Pine Log (creek) C
Pinellas (pt.) C
Piney (isl.) ....B
Piney (pt.) C
Placid (lake) ....E
Plantation (key) ....F
Poinsett (lake) ....F
Ponce de Leon (bay) ....E
Port Everglades (harb.) C
Port Tampa (harb.) ....B
Reedy (lake) ....E
Romano (cape) ....E
Sable (cape) ....E
Saint Andrew (pt.) ....D
Saint George (cape) ....A
Saint George (isl.) ....E
Saint George (sound) ....B
Saint Johns (riv.) ....E
Saint Joseph (bay) ....D
Saint Joseph (pt.) ....D
Saint Lucie (canal) ....
Saint Lucie (inlet) ....
Saint Marys (riv.) ....D
Saint Marys Entrance (inlet) ....E
Saint Vincent (isl.) ....D
San Blas (cape) ....D
Sand (key) ....E
Sands (key) ....
Sanibel (isl.) ....D
Santa Fe (lake) ....D
Santa Fe (riv.) ....D
Santa Rosa (isl.) ....
Santa Rosa (sound) ....E
Sarasota (pt.) ....D
Seminole (lake) ....
Seminole Ind. Res. ....
Seminole Ind. Res. ....
Shark (pt.) ....
Shoal (riv.) ....
Snake Creek (canal) ....
South New River (canal) ....
Stafford (lake) ....
Sugarloaf (key) ....
Suwannee (riv.) ....
Suwannee (sound) ....
Talbot (isl.) ....
Talquin (lake) ....
Tamiami (canal) ....
Tampa (bay) ....
Ten Thousand (isls.) ....
Torch (key) ....
Treasure (isl.) ....
Tsala Apopka (lake) ....
Tyndall A.F.B. 4,542 ....
Upper Matecumbe (key) ....
Vaca (key) ....
Virginia (key) ....
Waccasassa (bay) ....
Waccasassa (riv.) ....
Washington (lake) ....
Weir (lake) ....
Weohyakapka (lake) ....
West Palm Beach (canal) ....
Whitewater (bay) ....
Whiting Field Naval Air Sta. ....
Wimico (lake) ....
Winder (lake) ....
Withlacoochee (riv.) ....
Withlacoochee (riv.) ....
Yale (lake) ....
Yellow (riv.) ....

⊙County seat.
‡Population of metropolitan area.
† Zip of nearest p.o. * Multiple zi

Agriculture, Industry and Resources

Cotton
Peanuts
Corn
Hogs
Pensacola
Oysters
Red Snapper
Mullet
Groupers
Crabs
Sponges
Tobacco
Peanuts
Jacksonville
Potatoes
Cattle
Menhaden
Mackerel
Vegetables
Melons
Oranges
Grapefruit
Orlando
Tampa
St. Petersburg
Cattle
Oranges
Citrus Fruit
Kingfish
Vegetables
W. Palm Beach
Sugar-cane
Shrimp
Clams
Miami
Lobsters
DOMINANT LAND USE
Fruit, Truck & Mixed Farming
Truck & Mixed Farming
Truck Farming
Cotton, Tobacco, Hogs, Peanuts
Peanuts, General Farming
General Farming, Forest Products, Truck Farming, Cotton
Livestock Grazing
Forests
Swampland, Limited Agriculture
Urban Areas
Nonagricultural Land
MAJOR MINERAL OCCURRENCES
Cl Clay
Ls Limestone
O Petroleum
P Phosphates
Pe Peat
Ti Titanium
Zr Zirconium
Water Power
Major Industrial Areas

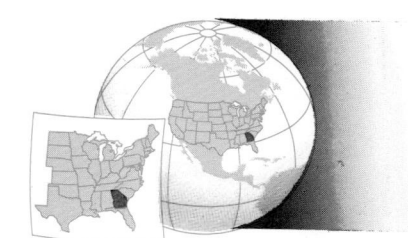

AREA 58,910 sq. mi. (152,577 sq. km.)
POPULATION 5,463,105
CAPITAL Atlanta
LARGEST CITY Atlanta
HIGHEST POINT Brasstown Bald 4,784 ft.
(1458 m.)
SETTLED IN 1733
ADMITTED TO UNION January 2, 1788
POPULAR NAME Empire State of the South;
Peach State
STATE FLOWER Cherokee Rose
STATE BIRD Brown Thrasher

COUNTIES

ppling 15,565	H7
tkinson 6,141	G8
acon 9,379	G7
aker 3,808	D8
aldwin 34,686	F4
arrow 21,293	E2
artow 40,760	C2
en Hill 16,000	F7
errien 13,525	F8
bb 151,085	E5
eckley 10,767	F6
rantley 8,701	J8
rooks 15,255	E9
ryan 10,175	K6
ulloch 35,785	J6
urke 19,349	J4
utts 13,665	E4
alhoun 5,717	C7
amden 13,371	J9
andler 7,518	H6
arroll 56,346	B3
atoosa 36,991	B1
harlton 7,343	H9
hatham 202,226	K6
hattahoochee 21,732	C6
hattooga 21,856	B1
herokee 51,699	D2
larke 74,498	F3
ay 3,553	B7
ayton 150,357	D3
nch 6,660	G9
Cobb 297,694	C3
Coffee 26,894	G8
Colquitt 35,376	E8
Columbia 40,118	H3
Cook 13,490	F8
Coweta 39,268	C4
Crawford 7,684	E5
Crisp 19,489	E7
Dade 12,318	A1
Dawson 4,774	D2
Decatur 25,495	C9
De Kalb 483,024	D3
Dodge 16,955	F6
Dooly 10,826	E6
Dougherty 100,978	D7
Douglas 54,573	C3
Early 13,158	C8
Echols 2,297	G9
Effingham 18,327	K6
Elbert 18,758	G2
Emanuel 20,795	H5
Evans 8,428	J6
Fannin 14,748	D1
Fayette 29,043	C4
Floyd 79,800	B2
Forsyth 27,958	D2
Franklin 15,185	F2
Fulton 589,904	D3
Gilmer 11,110	D1
Glascock 2,382	G4
Glynn 54,981	J8
Gordon 30,070	C2
Grady 19,845	D9
Greene 11,391	F3
Gwinnett 166,903	D2
Habersham 25,020	E1
Hall 75,649	E2
Hancock 9,466	G4
Haralson 18,422	B3
Harris 15,464	C5
Hart 18,585	F2
Heard 6,520	B4
Henry 36,309	D4
Houston 77,605	E6
Irwin 8,988	F7
Jackson 25,343	E2
Jasper 7,553	E4
Jeff Davis 11,473	G7
Jefferson 18,403	H4
Jenkins 8,841	J5
Johnson 8,660	G5
Jones 16,579	E5
Lamar 12,215	D4
Lanier 5,654	F8
Laurens 36,990	G6
Lee 11,684	D7
Liberty 37,583	J7
Lincoln 6,949	H3
Long 4,524	J7
Lowndes 67,972	F9
Lumpkin 10,762	D1
Macon 14,003	D6
Madison 17,747	F2
Marion 5,297	C6
McDuffie 18,546	H4
McIntosh 8,046	K7
Meriwether 21,229	C4
Miller 7,038	C8
Mitchell 21,114	D8
Monroe 14,610	E4
Montgomery 7,011	G6
Morgan 11,572	F3
Murray 19,685	C1
Muscogee 170,108	C6
Newton 34,489	E3
Oconee 12,427	F3
Oglethorpe 8,929	F3
Paulding 26,042	C3
Peach 19,151	E5
Pickens 11,652	D2
Pierce 11,897	H8
Pike 8,937	D4
Polk 32,386	B3
Pulaski 8,950	E6
Putnam 10,295	F4
Quitman 2,357	B7
Rabun 10,466	F1
Randolph 9,599	C7
Richmond 181,629	H4
Rockdale 36,747	D3
Schley 3,433	D6
Screven 14,043	J5
Seminole 9,057	C9
Spalding 47,899	D4
Stephens 21,763	F1
Stewart 5,896	C6
Sumter 29,360	D6
Talbot 6,536	C5
Taliaferro 2,032	G3
Tattnall 18,134	J6
Taylor 7,902	D5
Telfair 11,445	G7
Terrell 12,017	D7
Thomas 38,098	E9
Tift 32,862	E7
Toombs 22,592	H6
Towns 5,638	E1
Treutlen 6,087	G6
Troup 50,003	B4
Turner 9,510	E7
Twiggs 9,354	F5
Union 9,390	E1
Upson 25,998	D5
Walker 56,470	B1
Walton 31,211	E3
Ware 37,180	H8
Warren 6,583	G4
Washington 18,842	G4
Wayne 20,750	J7
Webster 2,341	C6
Wheeler 5,155	G6
White 10,120	E1
Whitfield 65,780	B1
Wilcox 7,682	F7
Wilkes 10,951	G3
Wilkinson 10,368	F5
Worth 18,064	E8

CITIES and TOWNS

Zip	Name/Pop.	Key
31001	Abbeville⊙ 985	F7
30101	Acworth 3,648	C2
30103	Adairsville 1,739	C2
31620	Adel⊙ 5,592	F8
31002	Adrian 756	G5
30410	Ailey 579	G6
30411	Alamo⊙ 993	G6
31622	Alapaha 771	F8
*31701	Albany⊙ 74,550	D7
	Albany‡ 112,456	D7
†30204	Aldora 139	D4
31301	Allenhurst 606	J7
31003	Allentown 321	F5
31510	Alma⊙ 3,819	G7
30201	Alpharetta 3,128	D2
30412	Alston 111	H6
30510	Alto 618	E2
†30161	Alto Park	B2
31512	Ambrose 360	G7
31709	Americus⊙ 16,120	D6
31711	Andersonville 267	D6
30802	Appling⊙ 150	H3
31712	Arabi 376	E7
30104	Aragon 855	B2
†30549	Arcade 223	E2
†31520	Arco	J8
31623	Argyle 206	G8
31713	Arlington 1,572	C8
30619	Arnoldsville 187	F3
31714	Ashburn⊙ 4,766	E7
*30601	Athens⊙ 42,549	F3
	Athens‡ 130,015	F3
*30301	Atlanta (cap.)⊙ 425,022	K1
	Atlanta‡ 2,029,618	K1
31715	Attapulgus 623	D9
30203	Auburn 692	E2
*30901	Augusta⊙ 47,532	J4
	Augusta‡ 327,372	J4
30001	Austell 3,939	J1
†30557	Avalon 200	F1
30803	Avera 248	G4
30002	Avondale Estates 1,313	L1
31716	Baconton 763	D8
31717	Bainbridge⊙ 10,553	C9
30511	Baldwin 1,080	E2
30107	Ball Ground 640	D2
30204	Barnesville⊙ 4,887	D4
31625	Barney 146	E8
30413	Bartow 357	G5
31720	Barwick 413	E9
31513	Baxley⊙ 3,586	H7
†31554	Beach	G8
30414	Bellville 173	H6
31721	Benevolence 138	C7
†30136	Berkeley Lake 503	D3
31722	Berlin 538	E8
30620	Bethlehem 281	E3
†31901	Bibb City 667	B5
30621	Bishop 172	F3
31516	Blackshear⊙ 3,222	H8
30512	Blairsville⊙ 530	E1
31723	Blakely⊙ 5,880	C8
31302	Bloomingdale 1,855	K6
30513	Blue Ridge⊙ 1,376	D1
31724	Bluffton 132	C7
30805	Blythe 367	H4
30622	Bogart 819	E3
31626	Boston 1,424	E9
30623	Bostwick 357	E3
30108	Bowdon 1,743	B3
30516	Bowersville 318	G2
30624	Bowman 890	G2
30517	Braselton 308	E2
†30153	Braswell 282	C3
30110	Bremen 3,966	B3
31725	Brinson 274	C9
31726	Bronwood 524	D7
30415	Brooklet 1,035	J6
30205	Brooks 199	D4
31519	Broxton 1,711	G7
31520	Brunswick⊙ 17,605	K8
30113	Buchanan⊙ 1,019	B3
30625	Buckhead 219	F3
31803	Buena Vista⊙ 1,544	C6
30518	Buford 6,578	D2
31006	Butler⊙ 1,959	D5
31007	Byromville 567	E6
31008	Byron 1,661	E5
31009	Cadwell 353	G6
31728	Cairo⊙ 8,777	D9
30701	Calhoun⊙ 5,335	C1
30807	Camak 283	G4
31730	Camilla⊙ 5,414	D8
30520	Canon 704	F2
30114	Canton⊙ 3,601	C2
30203	Carl 239	E3
30627	Carlton 291	F2
30521	Carnesville⊙ 465	F2
30117	Carrollton⊙ 14,078	C3
30120	Cartersville⊙ 9,247	C2
30124	Cave Spring 883	B2
31627	Cecil 280	F8
30125	Cedartown⊙ 8,619	B2
30601	Center 330	F2
31028	Centerville 2,622	E5
†30217	Centralhatchee 240	B4
†31816	Chalybeate Springs 265	C5
30341	Chamblee 7,137	K1
30705	Chatsworth⊙ 2,493	C1
31011	Chauncey 350	F6
31012	Chester 409	F6
30707	Chickamauga 2,232	B1
30523	Clarkesville⊙ 1,348	F1
30021	Clarkston 4,539	L1
30417	Claxton⊙ 2,694	J6
30525	Clayton⊙ 1,838	F1
30527	Clermont 300	E2
30528	Cleveland⊙ 1,578	E1
31734	Climax 407	D9
31735	Cobb	E7
30420	Cobbtown 494	H6
31014	Cochran⊙ 5,121	F6
30710	Cohutta 407	C1
30628	Colbert 498	F2
31736	Coleman 164	C7
30337	College Park 24,632	K2
30421	Collins 639	H6
31737	Colquitt⊙ 2,065	C8
*31901	Columbus⊙ 169,441	C6
	Columbus‡ 239,196	C6
30629	Comer 930	F2
30529	Commerce 4,092	E2
30206	Concord 317	D4
*30207	Conyers⊙ 6,567	D3
31738	Coolidge 736	E8
31015	Cordele⊙ 11,184	E7
30531	Cornelia 3,203	E1
31739	Cotton 122	D8
30209	Covington⊙ 10,586	E3
30711	Crandall	C1
30630	Crawford 498	F3
30631	Crawfordville⊙ 594	G3
†31771	Crosland	E8
31016	Culloden 281	D5
30130	Cumming⊙ 2,094	D2
31805	Cusseta⊙ 1,218	C6
31740	Cuthbert⊙ 4,340	C7
30211	Dacula 1,577	E3
30533	Dahlonega⊙ 2,844	D1
30423	Daisy 174	J6
30132	Dallas⊙ 2,440	C3
30720	Dalton⊙ 20,743	C1
31741	Damascus 403	C8
30633	Danielsville⊙ 354	F2
31017	Danville 529	F5
31305	Darien⊙ 1,731	K8
31601	Dasher 659	F9
31018	Davisboro 433	G5
31742	Dawson⊙ 5,699	D7
30534	Dawsonville⊙ 342	D2
30808	Dearing 539	H4
*30030	Decatur⊙ 18,404	K1
†31501	Deenwood	H8
31082	Deepstep 120	G4
30535	Demorest 1,130	F1
31532	Denton 286	G7
31743	De Soto 248	D7
31019	Dexter 527	G6
30537	Dillard 238	F1
31629	Dixie 259	E9
†31520	Dock Junction (Arco)	J8
31744	Doerun 1,062	E8
31745	Donalsonville⊙ 3,320	C8
30340	Doraville 7,414	K1
31533	Douglas⊙ 10,980	G7
*30133	Douglasville⊙ 7,641	C3
31021	Dublin⊙ 16,083	G5
31022	Dudley 425	F5
30136	Duluth 2,956	D2
31630	Du Pont 267	G9
†31830	Durand 206	C5
31021	East Dublin 2,916	G5
30539	East Ellijay 469	C1

(continued on following page)

Agriculture, Industry and Resources

DOMINANT LAND USE

- Specialized Cotton
- Cotton, General Farming
- Cotton, Tobacco, Hogs, Peanuts
- Peanuts, General Farming
- General Farming, Livestock, Fruit, Tobacco
- General Farming, Forest Products, Cotton, Truck Farming
- Forests
- Swampland, Limited Agriculture
- Urban Areas

MAJOR MINERAL OCCURRENCES

- Al Bauxite
- Ba Barite
- C Coal
- Cl Clay
- Fe Iron Ore
- Gn Granite
- Mi Mica
- Mn Manganese
- Mr Marble
- Sl Slate
- Tc Talc
- Ti Titanium

⚡ Water Power   ///// Major Industrial Areas

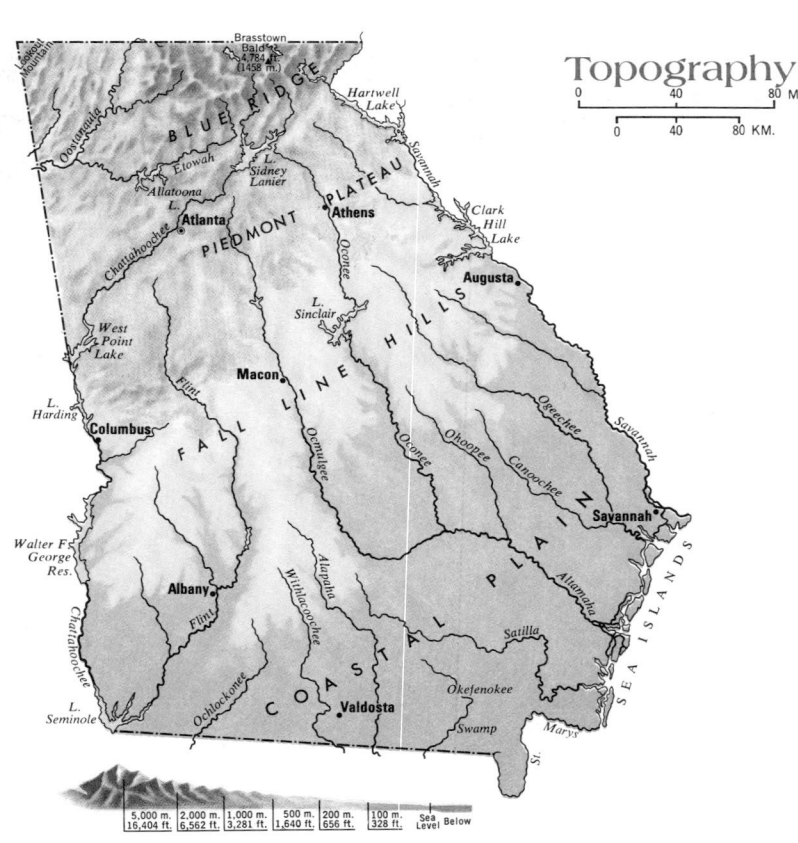

Topography

0   40   80 MI.

0   40   80 KM.

Brasstown Bald 4,784 ft. (1458 m.)

BLUE RIDGE

Hartwell Lake

 Outourga Mountains

Oostanaula

Etowah

Allatoona L.

L. Sidney Lanier

Chattahoochee

Atlanta

PIEDMONT

PLATEAU

Athens

Oconee

Savannah

Clark Hill Lake

Augusta

West Point Lake

L. Sinclair

FALL LINE HILLS

Flint

Ocmulgee

Oconee

Ohoopee

Canoochee

Ogeechee

Savannah

L. Harding

Columbus

Macon

Chattahoochee

COASTAL PLAIN

Flint

Albany

Withlacoochee

Alapaha

Satilla

Altamaha

SEA ISLANDS

Savannah

L. Seminole

Ochlockonee

Valdosta

Okefenokee Swamp

Marys

St. Marys

5,000 m. 16,404 ft. | 2,000 m. 6,562 ft. | 1,000 m. 3,281 ft. | 500 m. 1,640 ft. | 200 m. 656 ft. | 100 m. 328 ft. | Sea Level | Below

Georgia

SCALE

1:2,210,000

State Capitals ⊛

County Seats ⊙

Major Limited Access Hwys. ▬▬

© Copyright HAMMOND INCORPORATED, Maplewood, N.J.

COUNTIES

Hawaii 92,053 .... K7
Honolulu 762,565 .... D3
Kalawao 144 .... G1
Kauai 39,082 .... A1
Maui 70,847 .... J1

CITIES and TOWNS

Zip	Name/Pop.	Key
96701	Aiea 32,879	B3
96821	Aina Haina	F2
	Ala Moana 96,820	C4
96703	Anahola 915	C1
†96706	Barbers Point 1,373	E2
96704	Captain Cook 2,008	G5
96705	Eleele 580	C2
96706	Ewa 2,637	A4
96706	Ewa Beach 14,369	A4
†96701	Foster Village	B3
†96714	Haena 200	C1
96708	Haiku 619	J2
96710	Hakalau	J4
†96711	Halawa, Hawaii 50	G3
†96748	Halawa, Molokai 15	H1
†96701	Halawa Heights	B3
96712	Haleiwa 2,412	E1
†96718	Halfway House 150	H6
96787	Haliimaile 741	J2
†96713	Hamoa 35	K2
96713	Hana 643	K2
96714	Hanalei 483	C1
96715	Hanamaulu 3,227	C1
96716	Hanapepe 1,417	C2
96717	Hauula 2,997	E1
96825	Hawaii Kai	F2
96718	Hawaii Nat'l Park 250	J6
96719	Hawi 795	G3
96824	Hickam Housing 4,425	B4
96720	Hilo⊙ 35,269	J5
96725	Holualoa 1,243	G5
96726	Honaunau 950	G6
96727	Honokaa 1,936	H4
†96761	Honokahua 309	H1
*96801	Honolulu (cap.)⊙ 365,048	C4
	Honolulu‡ 762,874	C4
96728	Honomu 559	J4
96729	Hoolehua	G1
†96706	Iroquois Point 3,915	A4
96730	Kaaawa 959	F1
†96761	Kaanapali 541	H2
†96793	Kahakuloa 75	J1
†96801	Kahala	D5
†96744	Kahaluu 2,925	E2
96731	Kahuku 935	E1
96732	Kahului 12,978	J2
96740	Kailua (Kailua Kona), Hawaii 4,751	F5
96734	Kailua, Oahu 35,812	F2
96740	Kailua Kona 4,751	F5
†96750	Kainaliu 512	G5
96741	Kalaheo 2,500	C2
96742	Kalaupapa⊙ 170	G1
†96754	Kalihiwai 40	C1
†96748	Kaluaaha 20	H1
†96748	Kamalo 60	H1
96743	Kamuela 1,179	G3
96744	Kaneohe 29,919	F2
96746	Kapaa 4,467	D1
96755	Kapaau 612	G3
96817	Kapalama	C4
96747	Kaumakani 888	C2
96748	Kaunakakai 2,231	G1
†96708	Kaupakulua 600	K2
†96713	Kaupo 65	K2
96743	Kawaihae 50	G4
†96712	Kawailoa 200	E1
96749	Keaau 775	J5
96750	Kealakekua 1,033	G5
96751	Kealia, Kauai 300	D1
†96708	Keanae 280	K2
96752	Kekaha 3,260	C2
96753	Kihei 5,644	J2
96754	Kilauea 895	C1
†96713	Kipahulu 75	K2
†96713	Koali 60	K2
†96755	Kohala (Kapaau) 612	G3
†96708	Kokomo 500	K2
96756	Koloa 1,457	C2
†96756	Koloa Landing	C2
96757	Kualapuu 502	G1
†96775	Kukaiau 75	H4
96727	Kukuihaele 332	H3
96790	Kula 800	J2
96759	Kunia 550	E2
96760	Kurtistown 900	J5
96761	Lahaina 6,095	H2
96762	Laie 4,643	E1
96763	Lanai City 2,092	H2
96764	Laupahoehoe 500	J4
96765	Lawai 950	C2
96766	Lihue⊙ 4,000	C2
†96779	Lower Paia 1,500	J1
†96719	Mahukona 2	G3
†96792	Maili 5,026	D2
†96792	Makaha 6,582	D2
96706	Makakilo 7,691	E2
96768	Makawao 2,900	K2
96769	Makaweli 500	B2
†96790	Makena 100	J2
96822	Makiki	C4
96770	Maunaloa 633	G1
†96744	Maunawili 5,239	F2
96789	Mililani Town 21,365	E2
96828	Moiliili	C4
†96734	Mokapu 11,615	F2
96771	Mountainview 540	J5
96772	Naalehu 1,168	H7
†96713	Nahiku 50	K2
96792	Nanakuli 8,185	D2
†96761	Napili-Honokowai 2,446	H1
96773	Ninole 75	J4
†96781	Onomea 10	J4
96774	Ookala 401	J4
96775	Paauhau 350	H4
96776	Paauilo 755	H4
96777	Pahala 1,619	H6
96778	Pahoa 923	J5
96779	Paia	J2
96780	Papaaloa	J4
96781	Papaikou 1,567	J5
†96781	Paukaa 544	J5
†96708	Pauwela 468	K2
†96708	Peahi 308	K2
96782	Pearl City 42,575	B3
96783	Pepeekeo	J4
†96756	Poipu 685	C2
†96714	Princeville 500	C1
96766	Puhi 991	C2
96788	Pukalani 3,950	J2
†96748	Pukoo 50	H1
†96713	Puuiki 75	K2
96784	Puunene 572	J2
†96801	Puunui	C4
96786	Schofield Barracks 18,851	E2
96779	Spreckelsville 350	J1
†96708	Ulumalu 201	K2
†96776	Umikoa 25	H4
96785	Volcano 400	J6
96786	Wahiawa 16,911	E2
†96788	Waiakoa	J2
96816	Waialae	D4
†96731	Waialee 50	E1
†96748	Waialua, Molokai 30	H1
96791	Waialua, Oahu 4,051	E1
96792	Waianae 7,941	D2
†96793	Waihee 413	J2
†96793	Waikapu 698	J2
96815	Waikiki	C4
†96748	Wailau 20	H1
†96710	Wailea, Hawaii 150	J4
†96790	Wailea, Maui 1,124	J2
†96746	Wailua 1,587	D2
96793	Wailuku⊙ 10,260	J2
96795	Waimanalo 3,562	F2
†96795	Waimanalo Bch. 4,161	F2
†96743	Waimea (Kamuela), Hawaii 1,179	G3
96796	Waimea, Kauai 1,569	B2
†96720	Wainaku 1,045	J5
†96714	Wainiha 175	C1
96797	Waipahu 29,139	A3
†96786	Waipio Acres 4,091	E2
†96786	Whitmore Village 2,318	E1

OTHER FEATURES

Alalakeiki (chan.) J3
Alenuihaha (chan.) E7

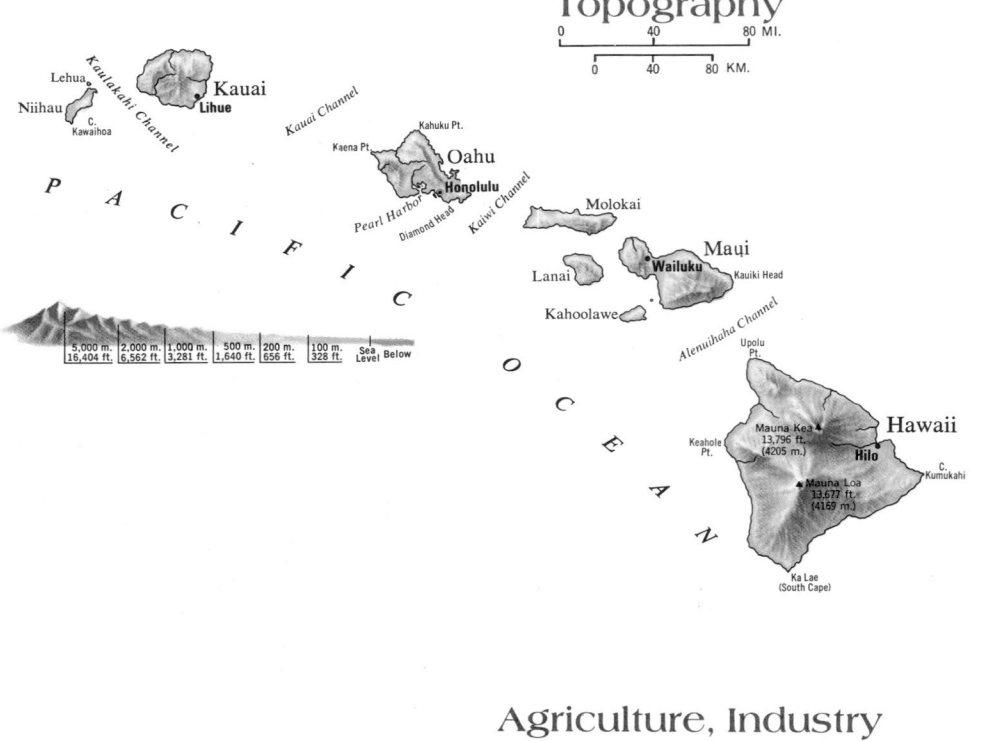

Topography

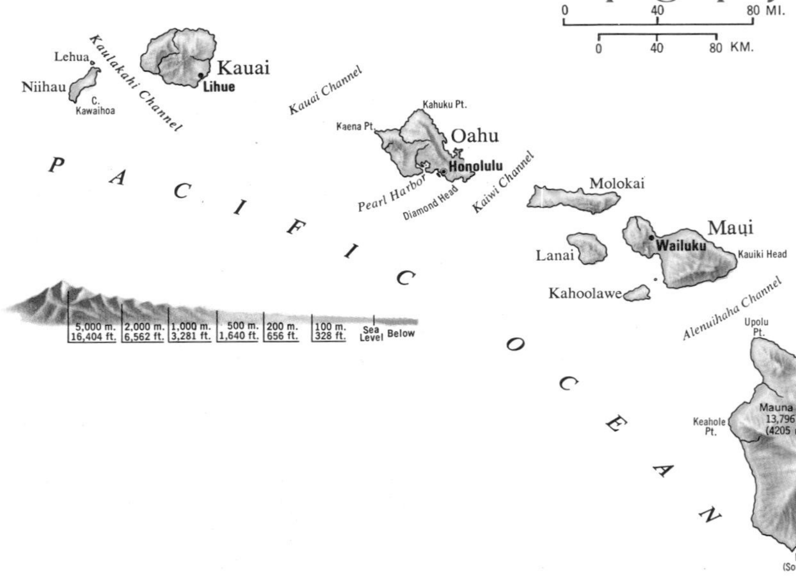

Agriculture, Industry and Resources

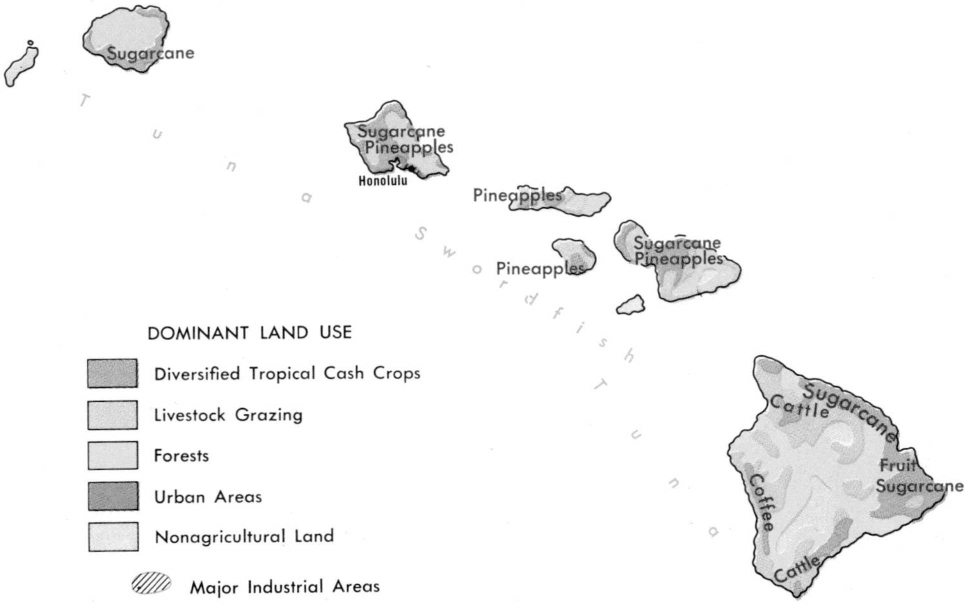

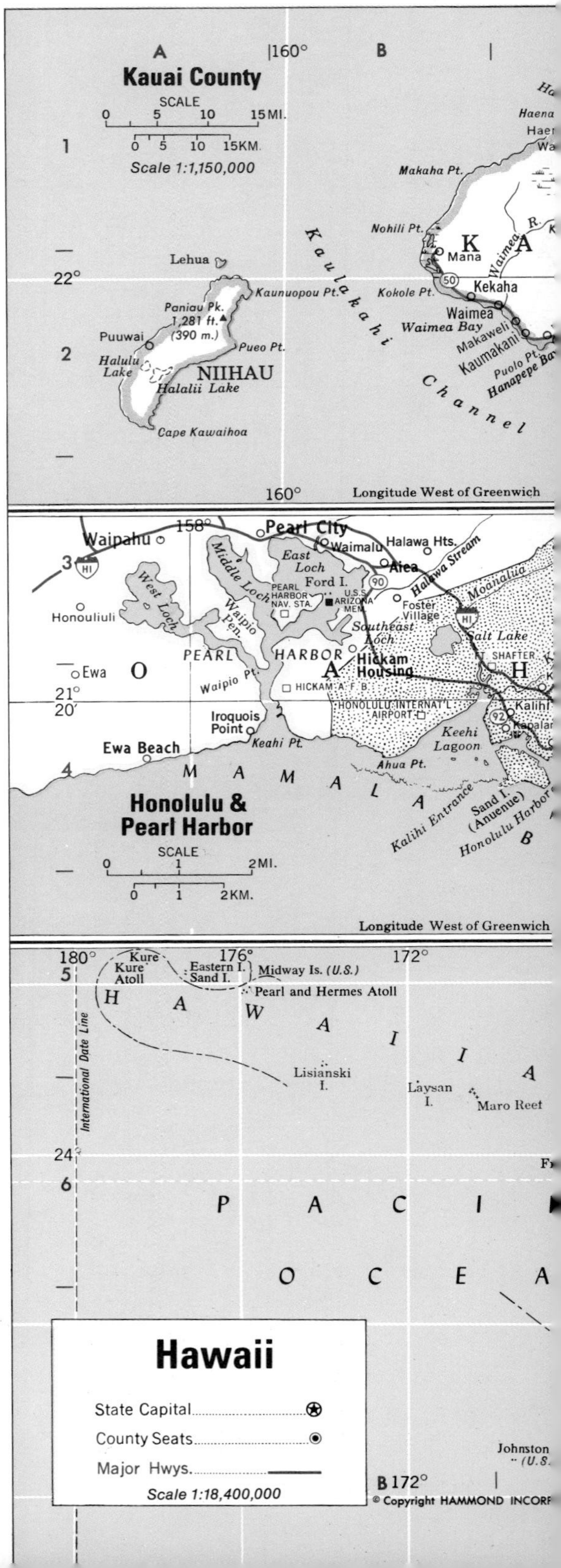

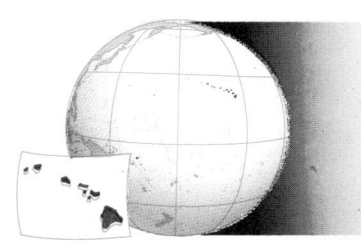

AREA 6,471 sq. mi. (16,760 sq. km.)
POPULATION 964,691
CAPITAL Honolulu
LARGEST CITY Honolulu
HIGHEST POINT Mauna Kea 13,796 ft. (4205 m.)
SETTLED IN —
ADMITTED TO UNION August 21, 1959
POPULAR NAME Aloha State
STATE FLOWER Hibiscus
STATE BIRD Nene (Hawaiian Goose)

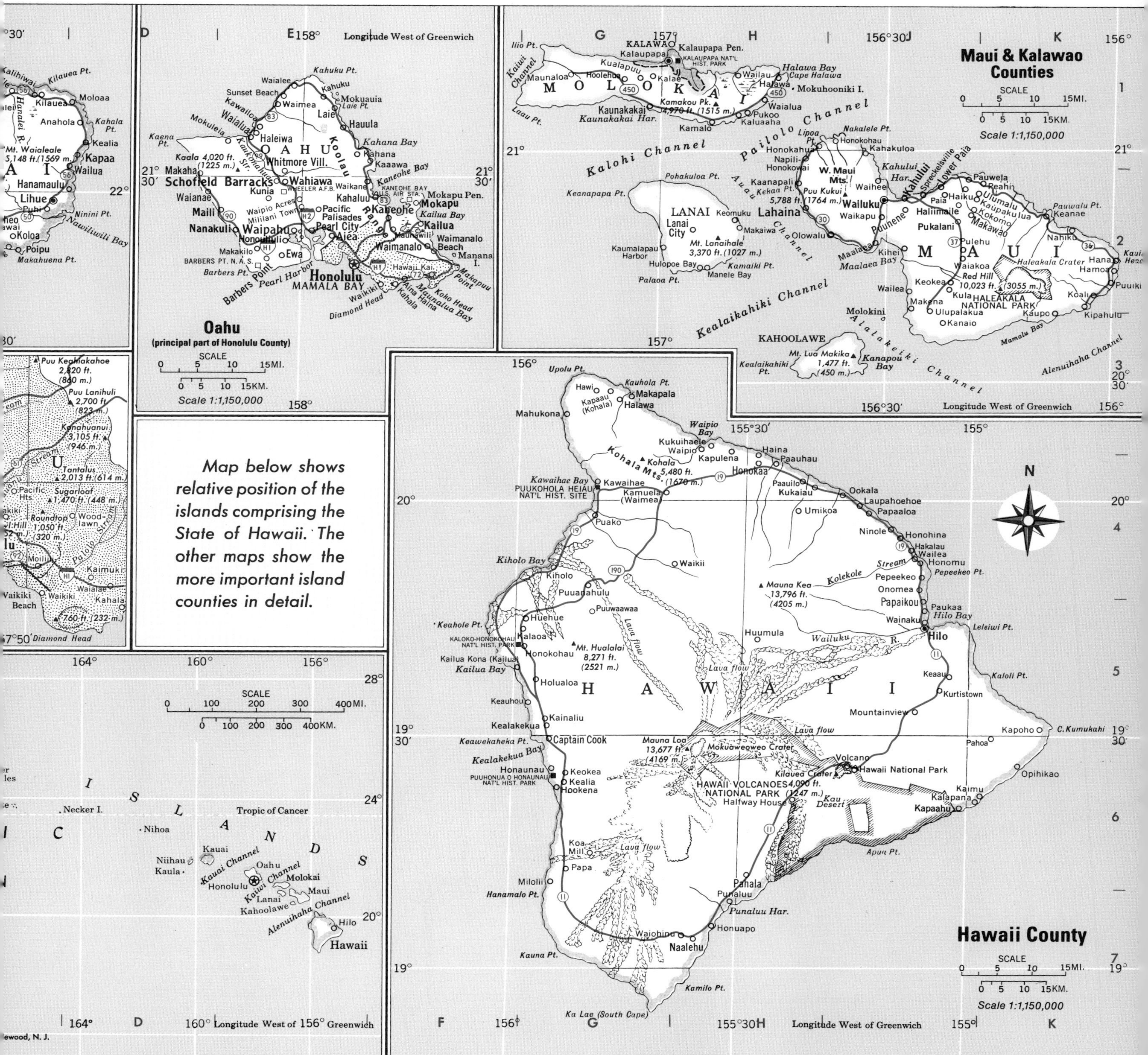

Maui & Kalawao Counties

Scale 1:1,150,000

Oahu
(principal part of Honolulu County)

Scale 1:1,150,000

Map below shows relative position of the islands comprising the State of Hawaii. The other maps show the more important island counties in detail.

Hawaii County

Scale 1:1,150,000

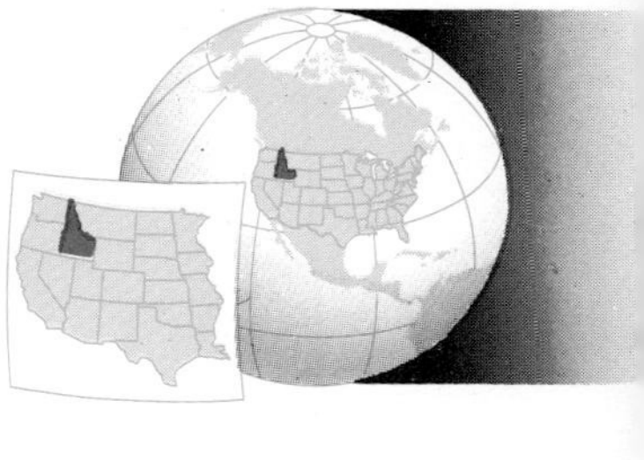

AREA 83,564 sq. mi. (216,431 sq. km.)
POPULATION 944,038
CAPITAL Boise
LARGEST CITY Boise
HIGHEST POINT Borah Pk. 12,662 ft. (3859 m.)
SETTLED IN 1842
ADMITTED TO UNION July 3, 1890
POPULAR NAME Gem State
STATE FLOWER Syringa
STATE BIRD Mountain Bluebird

COUNTIES

Ada 173,036 B6
Adams 3,347 B5
Bannock 65,421 F7
Bear Lake 6,931 G7
Benewah 8,292 B2
Bingham 36,489 F6
Blaine 9,841 D6
Boise 2,999 C6
Bonner 24,163 B1
Bonneville 65,980 G6
Boundary 7,289 B1
Butte 3,342 E6
Camas 818 D6
Canyon 83,756 B6
Caribou 8,695 G7
Cassia 19,427 E7
Clark 798 F5
Clearwater 10,390 C3
Custer 3,385 D5
Elmore 21,565 C6
Franklin 8,895 G7
Fremont 10,813 G5
Gem 11,972 B6
Gooding 11,874 D6
Idaho 14,769 C4
Jefferson 15,304 F6
Jerome 14,840 D7
Kootenai 59,770 B2
Latah 28,749 B3
Lemhi 7,460 D4
Lewis 4,118 B3
Lincoln 3,436 D6
Madison 19,480 G6
Minidoka 19,718 E7
Nez Perce 33,220 B3
Oneida 3,258 F7
Owyhee 8,272 B7
Payette 15,825 B5
Power 6,844 F7
Shoshone 19,226 B2
Teton 2,897 G6
Twin Falls 52,927 D7
Valley 5,604 C5
Washington 8,803 B5

CITIES and TOWNS

Zip Name/Pop. Key

83210 Aberdeen 1,528 F7
83350 Acequia 100 E7
83311 Albion 286 E7
83211 American Falls⊙ 3,626 E7
†83401 Ammon 4,669 G6
83213 Arco⊙ 1,241 E6
83214 Arimo 338 F7
83420 Ashton 1,219 G5
83801 Athol 312 B2
83217 Bancroft 505 G7
83218 Basalt 414 F6
83313 Bellevue 1,016 D6
83221 Blackfoot⊙ 10,065 F6
83314 Bliss 208 D7
83223 Bloomington 212 G7
*83701 Boise (cap.)⊙ 102,160 B6
Boise‡ 173,036 B6
83805 Bonners Ferry⊙ 1,906 B1
83806 Bovill 289 B3
83316 Buhl 3,629 D7
83318 Burley⊙ 8,761 E7
83213 Butte City 93 E6
83605 Caldwell⊙ 17,699 B6
83610 Cambridge 428 B5
83611 Cascade⊙ 945 C5
83321 Castleford 191 C7
83226 Challis⊙ 758 D5
†83851 Chatcolet 181 B2
83202 Chubbuck 7,052 F7
83811 Clark Fork 449 B1
83227 Clayton 43 D5
83228 Clifton 208 F7
83814 Coeur d'Alene⊙ 20,054 B2
83522 Cottonwood 941 B3
83612 Council⊙ 917 B5
83523 Craigmont 617 B3
†83622 Crouch 69 B5
83524 Culdesac 261 B3
†83814 Dalton Gardens 1,795 B2
83232 Dayton 368 F7
83823 Deary 539 B3
83323 Declo 276 E7
83324 Dietrich 101 D7
83615 Donnelly 139 B5
83234 Downey 645 F7
83422 Driggs⊙ 727 G6
83423 Dubois⊙ 413 F5
83616 Eagle 2,620 B6
†83836 East Hope 258 B1
83325 Eden 355 D7
83827 Elk River 265 B3
83617 Emmett⊙ 4,605 B6
83327 Fairfield⊙ 404 D6
83526 Ferdinand 144 B3
†83814 Fernan Lake 178 B2
83328 Filer 1,645 D7
83236 Firth 460 F6
83203 Fort Hall 750 F6
83237 Franklin 423 G7
83619 Fruitland 2,456 B6
†83704 Garden City 4,571 B6
83832 Genesee 791 B3
83239 Georgetown 544 G7
83623 Glenns Ferry 1,374 C7
83330 Gooding⊙ 2,949 D7
83241 Grace 1,216 G7
83624 Grand View 366 B7
83530 Grangeville⊙ 3,666 B4
83626 Greenleaf 663 B6
83332 Hagerman 602 D7
83333 Hailey⊙ 2,109 D6
83425 Hamer 93 F6
83334 Hansen 1,078 D7
83833 Harrison 260 B2
†83854 Hauser 305 A2
†83835 Hayden 2,586 B2
83835 Hayden Lake 273 B2
83335 Hazelton 496 E7
83336 Heyburn 2,889 E7
†83301 Hollister 167 D7
83628 Homedale 2,078 A6
83836 Hope 106 B1
83629 Horseshoe Bend 700 B6
†83854 Huetter 65 B2
83631 Idaho City⊙ 300 C6
*83401 Idaho Falls⊙ 39,590 F6
83245 Inkom 830 F7
83427 Iona 1,072 G6
83428 Irwin 113 G6
83429 Island Park 154 G5
83338 Jerome⊙ 6,891 D7
83535 Juliaetta 522 B3
83536 Kamiah 1,478 B3
83837 Kellogg 3,417 B2
83537 Kendrick 395 B3
83340 Ketchum 2,200 D6
83341 Kimberly 2,307 D7
83539 Kooskia 784 C3
83840 Kootenai 280 B1
83634 Kuna 1,767 B6
83540 Lapwai 1,043 B3
83246 Lava Hot Springs 467 F7
83464 Leadore 114 E5
83501 Lewiston⊙ 27,986 A3
83431 Lewisville 502 F6
83251 Mackay 541 E6
83252 Malad City⊙ 1,915 F7
83342 Malta 196 E7
83639 Marsing 786 B6
83638 McCall 2,188 C5
83250 McCammon 770 F7
83641 Melba 276 B6
83434 Menan 605 F6
83642 Meridian 6,658 B6
83644 Middleton 1,901 B6
83645 Midvale 205 B5
83343 Minidoka 101 E7
83254 Montpelier 3,107 G7
83255 Moore 210 E6
83843 Moscow⊙ 16,513 B3
83647 Mountain Home⊙ 7,540 C6
83845 Moyie Springs 386 B1
†83450 Mud Lake 243 F6
83846 Mullan 1,269 C2
83650 Murphy⊙ 200 B6
83344 Murtaugh 114 D7
83651 Nampa 25,112 B6
83436 Newdale 329 G6
83654 New Meadows 576 B4
83655 New Plymouth 1,186 B6
83543 Nezperce⊙ 517 B3
83656 Notus 437 B6
83346 Oakley 663 D7
†99156 Oldtown 257 A1
†83855 Onaway 254 B3
83544 Orofino⊙ 3,711 B3
83849 Osburn 2,220 B2
†83263 Oxford 66 F7
83261 Paris⊙ 707 G7
83438 Parker 262 G6
83660 Parma 1,820 B6
83347 Paul 940 E7
83661 Payette⊙ 5,448 B5
83545 Peck 209 B3
83546 Pierce 1,060 C3
83850 Pinehurst 2,183 B2
83851 Plummer 634 B2
*83201 Pocatello⊙ 46,340 F7
83852 Ponderay 399 B1
83854 Post Falls 5,736 A2
83855 Potlatch 819 A3
83263 Preston⊙ 3,759 G7
83856 Priest River 1,639 A1
83858 Rathdrum 1,369 A2
83548 Reubens 87 B3
83440 Rexburg⊙ 11,559 G6
83349 Richfield 357 D6
83442 Rigby⊙ 2,624 F6
83549 Riggins 527 B4
83443 Ririe 555 G6
83444 Roberts 466 F6
83271 Rockland 283 F7
83350 Rupert⊙ 5,476 E7
83445 Saint Anthony⊙ 3,212 G6
83272 Saint Charles 211 G7
83861 Saint Maries⊙ 2,794 B2
83467 Salmon⊙ 3,308 D4
83864 Sandpoint⊙ 4,460 B1
83274 Shelley 3,300 F6
83352 Shoshone⊙ 1,242 D7
†83650 Silver City 1 B6
83868 Smelterville 776 B2
83276 Soda Springs⊙ 4,051 G7
83869 Spirit Lake 834 A2
83278 Stanley 99 D5
83552 Stites 253 C3
83448 Sugar City 1,022 G6
83353 Sun Valley 545 D6
83449 Swan Valley 135 G6
83870 Tensed 113 B2
83451 Teton 559 G6
83452 Tetonia 191 G6
83871 Troy 820 B3
83301 Twin Falls⊙ 26,209 D7
83454 Ucon 833 F6
83455 Victor 323 G6
83873 Wallace⊙ 1,736 C2
†83837 Wardner 423 B2
83553 Weippe 828 C3
83672 Weiser⊙ 4,771 B5
83355 Wendell 1,974 D7
83286 Weston 310 F7
83554 White Bird 154 B4
83676 Wilder 1,260 A6
83555 Winchester 343 B3
83876 Worley 206 B2

OTHER FEATURES

Albeni Falls (dam) B1
Albion (mts.) E7
Allan (mt.) D4
American Falls (res.) F6
Anderson Ranch (res.) C6
Antelope (creek) E6
Arrowrock (res.) C6
Auger (falls) D7
Badger (peak) E7
Bald (mt.) D5
Bannock (creek) F7
Bannock (peak) F7
Bannock (range) F7
Bargamin (creek) C4
Battle (creek) B7
Bear (lake) G7
Bear (riv.) G7
Beaver (creek) F5
Beaverhead (mts.) E4
Big (creek) C4
Big Boulder (creek) B7
Big Elk (peak) G6
Big Hole (mts.) G6
Big Lost (riv.) E6
Big Southern (butte) E6
Big Wood (riv.) D6
Birch (creek) F5
Birch Creek (valley) E5
Bitterroot (range) D3
Blackfoot (res.) G7
Black Pine (mts.) E7
Blue Nose (mt.) D4
Boise (mts.) B6
Boise (riv.) B6
Borah (peak) E5
Boulder (mts.) D6
Brownlee (dam) B5
Bruneau (riv.) C7
Camas (creek) D5
Camas (creek) D6
Camas (creek) F5
Canyon (creek) C6
Cape Horn (mt.) C5
Caribou (mt.) G6
Caribou (range) G6
Cascade (res.) C5
Castle (creek) B7
Castle (peak) D5
Cedar Creek (peak) E7
Cedar Creek (res.) D7
Centennial (mts.) F5
Clearwater (mts.) C3
Clearwater (riv.) B3
Coeur d'Alene (lake) B2
Coeur d'Alene (mts.) C2
Coeur d'Alene (riv.) B2
Cottonwood (butte) C4
Craig (mts.) B4
Crane Creek (res.) B5
Craters of the Moon Nat'l Mon. E6
Deadwood (res.) C5
Deep (creek) B7
Deep (creek) F7
Deep Creek (mts.) F7
Diamond (peak) E5
Dworshak (res.) C3
East Sister (peak) C2
Eighteen Mile (peak) E5
Fish Creek (res.) E6
Fort Hall Ind. Res. F6
Goldstone (mt.) E4
Goose (creek) E7
Goose Creek (mts.) E7
Grand Canyon of the Snake River (canyon) B4
Grays (lake) G6
Grays Lake Outlet (creek) G6
Greylock (mt.) C6
Hayden (lake) B2
Hells (canyon) B4
Hells Canyon Nat'l Rec. Area B4
Henrys (lake) G5
Henrys Fork, Snake (riv.) G5
Hunter (peak) D3
Hyndman (peak) D6
Indian (creek) C5
Island Park (res.) G5
Jarbidge (riv.) C7
Johnson (creek) C5
Jordan (creek) A7
Kootenai (riv.) C1
Lemhi (pass) E5
Lemhi (range) E5
Lemhi (riv.) E5
Little Lost (riv.) E5
Little Owyhee (riv.) B7
Little Salmon (riv.) B4
Little Weiser (riv.) B5
Little Wood (riv.) D6
Lochsa (riv.) C3
Lolo (creek) C3
Lolo (pass) D3
Lone Pine (peak) D5
Lookout (mt.) D5
Lookout (mt.) F5
Lost River (range) E5
Lost Trail (pass) E4
Lowell (lake) B6
Lower Goose Creek (res.) D7
Lower Granite (lake) A3
Lucky Peak (lake) B6
Mackay (res.) E6
Magic (res.) D6
Malad (riv.) F7
Marsh (creek) F7
McGuire (mt.) D4
Meade (peak) G7
Meadow (creek) C4
Medicine Lodge (creek) F5
Middle Fork (peak) D5
Monument (peak) B4
Moose (creek) D3
Mores (creek) C6
Mormon (mt.) D4
Mountain Home (res.) C6
Mountain Home A.F.B. 6,403 C6
Moyie (riv.) B1
Mud (lake) F6
National Reactor Testing Sta. F6
Nez Perce Nat'l Hist. Park B-C3
North Fork (riv.) B7
Norton (peak) D6
Orofino (creek) C3
Owyhee (mts.) B6
Owyhee, East Fork (riv.) B7
Oxbow (dam) B5
Pack (riv.) B1
Pahsimeroi (riv.) E5
Palisades (res.) G6
Palouse (riv.) B3
Panther (creek) D4
Payette (lake) C4
Payette (mts.) B5
Payette (riv.) B6
Peale (mts.) G7
Pend Oreille (lake) B1
Pend Oreille (mt.) B1
Pend Oreille (riv.) A1
Pilot (peak) C4
Pilot (peak) C6
Pilot Knob (mt.) C4
Pinyon (peak) C5
Pioneer (mts.) D6
Portneuf (res.) F7
Pot (mt.) C3
Potlatch (riv.) B3
Priest (lake) B1
Priest (riv.) B1
Purcell (mts.) B1
Pyramid (peak) E4
Raft (riv.) E7
Rainbow (mt.) C4
Ranger (peak) D3
Rays (lake) F6
Red (riv.) C4
Redfish (lake) D5
Reynolds (creek) B6
Rhodes (peak) D3
Rocky (mts.) D1
Rocky Ridge (mt.) C3
Ryan (peak) D6
Saddle (mt.) D3
Saddle (mt.) F6
Sailor (creek) C7
Saint Joe (riv.) B2
Saint Maries (riv.) B2
Salmon (falls) C7
Salmon (riv.) B4
Salmon Falls (creek) D7
Salmon Falls Creek (res.) D7
Salmon River (mts.) C5
Sawtooth (range) C6
Sawtooth Nat'l Rec. Area D5
Secesh (riv.) C4
Selkirk (mts.) B1
Selway (riv.) C3
Seven Devils (mts.) B4
Shoshone (falls) D7
Sleeping Deer (mt.) D5
Smith (creek) B1
Smoky (mts.) D6
Snake (riv.) A3
Snake River (plain) D7
Snake River (range) G6
Spirit (lake) B2
Squaw (creek) B5
Squaw (peak) D4
Steamboat (mt.) C4
Steel (mt.) C6
Strike, C.J. (res.) C7
Sublett (mts.) E7
Sunset (peak) E6
Taylor (mt.) D5
Teton (riv.) G6
Thompson (peak) C5
Trinity (mt.) C6
Trout (creek) B1
Twin (falls) D7
Twin Peaks (mt.) D5
Walcott (lake) E7
Wasatch (range) G7
Waugh (mt.) D4
Weiser (riv.) B5
Western Shoshone Ind. Res. B7
White Knob (mts.) E6
Wickahoney (creek) C7
Willow (creek) G6
Wilson Lake (res.) D7
Yankee Fork, Salmon (riv.) D5
Yellowstone Nat'l Park G5

⊙County seat.
‡Population of metropolitan area.
† Zip of nearest p.o.
* Multiple zips.

Agriculture, Industry and Resources

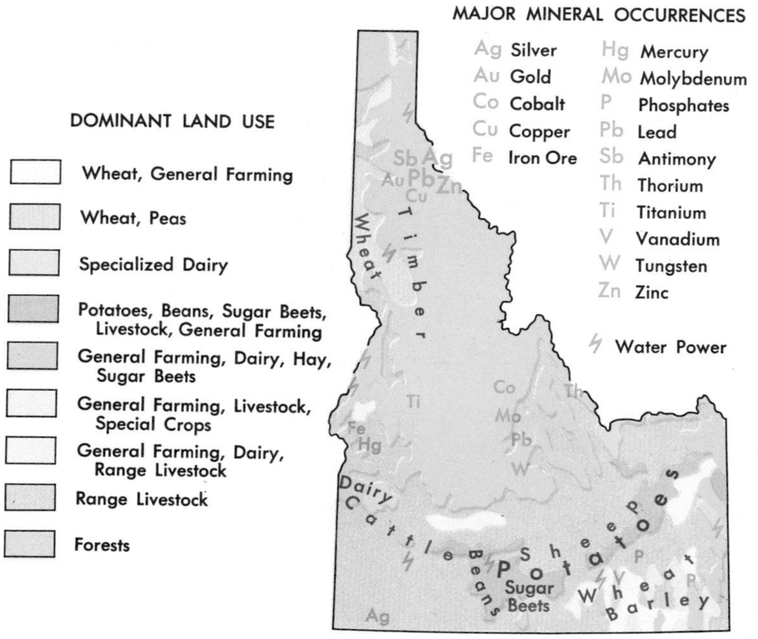
MAJOR MINERAL OCCURRENCES
Ag Silver
Au Gold
Co Cobalt
Cu Copper
Fe Iron Ore
Hg Mercury
Mo Molybdenum
P Phosphates
Pb Lead
Sb Antimony
Th Thorium
Ti Titanium
V Vanadium
W Tungsten
Zn Zinc
Water Power
DOMINANT LAND USE
Wheat, General Farming
Wheat, Peas
Specialized Dairy
Potatoes, Beans, Sugar Beets, Livestock, General Farming
General Farming, Dairy, Hay, Sugar Beets
General Farming, Livestock, Special Crops
General Farming, Dairy, Range Livestock
Range Livestock
Forests
Wheat
Timber
Dairy
Cattle
Sheep
Potatoes
Beans
Sugar Beets
Wheat
Barley

Illinois

SCALE
0 5 10 20 30 40 MI.
0 5 10 20 30 40 KM.

State Capitals ... ⊛
County Seats ... ⊙
Canals ...
Major Limited Access Hwys. ____

Scale 1:2,160,000

Chicago and Vicinity

Kentucky Lake © Copyright HAMMOND INCORPORATED, Maplewood, N.J.

Longitude West 90° of Greenwich

AREA 56,345 sq. mi. (145,934 sq. km.)
POPULATION 11,426,596
CAPITAL Springfield
LARGEST CITY Chicago
HIGHEST POINT Charles Mound 1,235 ft. (376 m.)
SETTLED IN 1720
ADMITTED TO UNION December 3, 1818
POPULAR NAME Prairie State; Land of Lincoln
STATE FLOWER Native Violet
STATE BIRD Cardinal

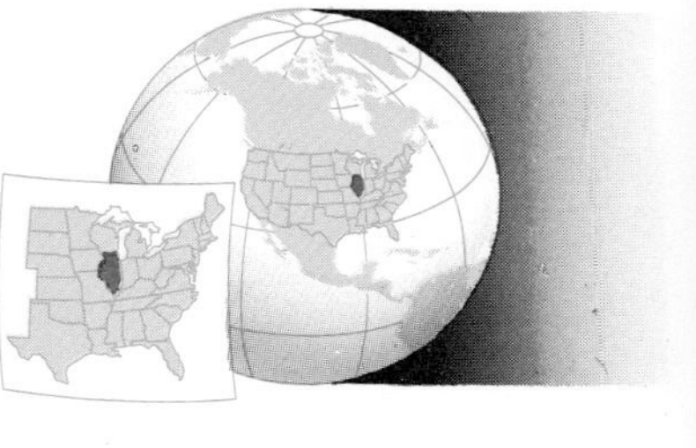

COUNTIES

County/Pop.	Key
Adams 71,622	B4
Alexander 12,264	D6
Bond 16,224	D5
Boone 28,630	E1
Brown 5,411	C4
Bureau 39,114	D2
Calhoun 5,867	C4
Carroll 18,779	D1
Cass 15,084	C4
Champaign 168,392	E3
Christian 36,446	D4
Clark 16,913	F4
Clay 15,283	E5
Clinton 32,617	D5
Coles 52,260	E4
Cook 5,253,655	F2
Crawford 20,818	F4
Cumberland 11,062	E4
De Kalb 74,624	E2
De Witt 18,108	E3
Douglas 19,774	E4
Du Page 658,835	E2
Edgar 21,725	F4
Edwards 7,961	E5
Effingham 30,944	E4
Fayette 22,167	D4
Ford 15,265	E3
Franklin 43,201	E5
Fulton 43,687	C3
Gallatin 7,590	E6
Greene 16,661	C4
Grundy 30,582	E2
Hamilton 9,172	E5
Hancock 23,877	B3
Hardin 5,383	E6
Henderson 9,114	C3
Henry 57,968	C2
Iroquois 32,976	F3
Jackson 61,522	D6
Jasper 11,318	E4
Jefferson 36,354	E5
Jersey 20,538	C4
Jo Daviess 23,520	C1
Johnson 9,624	E6
Kane 278,405	E2
Kankakee 102,926	F2
Kendall 37,202	E2
Knox 61,607	C3
Lake 440,372	E1
La Salle 112,033	E2
Lawrence 17,807	F5
Lee 36,328	D2
Livingston 41,381	E3
Logan 31,802	D3
Macon 131,375	E4
Macoupin 49,384	D4
Madison 247,691	D5
Marion 43,523	E5
Marshall 14,479	D2
Mason 19,492	D3
Massac 14,990	E6
McDonough 37,467	C3
McHenry 147,897	E1
McLean 119,149	E3
Menard 11,700	D3
Mercer 19,286	C2
Monroe 20,117	C5
Montgomery 31,686	D4
Morgan 37,502	C4
Moultrie 14,546	E4
Ogle 46,338	D1
Peoria 200,466	D3
Perry 21,714	D5
Piatt 16,581	E4
Pike 18,896	C4
Pope 4,404	E6
Pulaski 8,840	D6
Putnam 6,085	D2
Randolph 35,652	D5
Richland 17,587	E5
Rock Island 165,968	C2
Saint Clair 267,531	D5
Saline 28 448	E6
Sangamon 176,089	D4
Schuyler 8,365	C3
Scott 6,142	C4
Shelby 23 923	E4
Stark 7,389	D2
Stephenson 49,536	D1
Tazewell 132,078	D3
Union 17,765	D6
Vermilion 95,222	F3
Wabash 13,713	F5
Warren 21,943	C3
Washington 15,472	D5
Wayne 18,059	E5
White 17,864	E5
Whiteside 65,970	D2
Will 324,460	F2
Williamson 56,538	E6
Winnebago 250,884	D1
Woodford 33,320	D3

CITIES and TOWNS

Zip	Name/Pop.	Key
61410	Abingdon 4,210	C3
60101	Addison 29,826	B5
61230	Albany 1,014	C2
62806	Albion⊙ 2,285	E5
61231	Aledo⊙ 3,881	C2
61412	Alexis 1,076	C2
60102	Algonquin 5,834	E1
62207	Alorton 2,237	B2
61413	Alpha 815	C2
†60658	Alsip 17,134	B6
62411	Altamont 2,389	E4
62002	Alton 34,171	A2
61310	Amboy 2,377	D2
61232	Andalusia 1,238	C2
62906	Anna 5,408	D6
61234	Annawan 908	C2
60002	Antioch 4,419	E1
61910	Arcola 2,714	E4
62501	Argenta 994	E4
*60004	Arlington Heights 66,116	B5
61911	Arthur 2,122	E4
60911	Ashkum 735	E3
62612	Ashland 1,351	C4
62808	Ashley 658	D5
61912	Ashmore 883	F4
61006	Ashton 1,140	D2
62510	Assumption 1,283	E4
61501	Astoria 1,370	C3
62613	Athens 1,371	D4
61235	Atkinson 1,138	C2
61723	Atlanta 1,807	D3
61913	Atwood 1,464	E4
62615	Auburn 3,616	D4
62311	Augusta 764	C3
*60504	Aurora 81,293	E2
62907	Ava 811	D6
62216	Aviston 846	D5
61415	Avon 1,019	C3
†60015	Bannockburn 1,316	B5
60010	Barrington 9,029	A5
†60010	Barrington Hills 3,631	A5
62312	Barry 1,487	B4
60103	Bartlett 13,254	A5
61607	Bartonville 6,137	D3
60510	Batavia 12,574	E2
62618	Beardstown 6,338	C3
62219	Beckemeyer 1,119	D5
60401	Beecher 2,024	F2
*62220	Belleville⊙ 41,580	B3
60104	Bellwood 19,811	B5
61008	Belvidere⊙ 15,176	E1
61813	Bement 1,770	E4
62009	Benld 1,638	D4
60106	Bensenville 16,124	B5
62812	Benton⊙ 7,778	E6
60162	Berkeley 5,467	B5
60402	Berwyn 46,849	B6
62010	Bethalto 8,630	B2
61914	Bethany 1,550	E4
61420	Blandinsville 886	C3
60108	Bloomingdale 12,659	A5
61701	Bloomington⊙ 44,189	D3
	Bloomington-Normal‡ 119,149	D3
60406	Blue Island 21,855	B6
62513	Blue Mound 1,338	D4
62621	Bluffs 821	C4
60439	Bolingbrook 37,261	A6
60914	Bourbonnais 13,280	F2
60407	Braceville 721	E2
61421	Bradford 924	D2
60915	Bradley 11,008	F2
60408	Braidwood 3,429	E2
62230	Breese 3,516	D5
62417	Bridgeport 2,281	F5
60455	Bridgeview 14,155	B6
62012	Brighton 2,364	C4
61517	Brimfield 890	D3
60153	Broadview 8,618	B6
60513	Brookfield 19,395	B6
†62059	Brooklyn (Lovejoy) 1,233	A2
62910	Brookport 1,128	E6
61314	Buda 668	D2
†60090	Buffalo Grove 22,230	B5
62014	Bunker Hill 1,700	D4
60459	Burbank 28,462	B6
†60601	Burnham 4,030	C6
†60558	Burr Ridge 3,833	B6
61422	Bushnell 3,811	C3
61010	Byron 2,035	D1
62206	Cahokia 18,904	A3
62914	Cairo⊙ 5,931	D6
60409	Calumet City 39,697	C6
†60643	Calumet Park 8,788	C6
62915	Cambria 1,090	D6
61238	Cambridge⊙ 2,217	C2
62320	Camp Point 1,285	B3
61520	Canton 14,626	C3
61239	Carbon Cliff 1,578	C2
62901	Carbondale 26,414	D6
62626	Carlinville⊙ 5,439	D4
62231	Carlyle⊙ 3,388	D5
62821	Carmi⊙ 6,264	E5
†60187	Carol Stream 15,472	A5
60110	Carpentersville 23,272	E1
62917	Carrier Mills 2,268	E6
62016	Carrollton⊙ 2,816	C4
62918	Carterville 3,445	D6
62321	Carthage⊙ 2,978	B3
60013	Cary 6,640	E1
62420	Casey 3,026	F4
62232	Caseyville 4,308	B2
61817	Catlin 2,226	F3
61013	Cedarville 766	D1
†62801	Central City 1,505	D5
62801	Centralia 15,126	D5
62206	Centreville 9,747	B3
61818	Cerro Gordo 1,553	E4
61820	Champaign 58,133	E3
	Champaign-Urbana-Rantoul‡ 168,392	E3
62627	Chandlerville 842	C3
60410	Channahon 3,734	E2
61920	Charleston⊙ 19,355	E4
62629	Chatham 5,597	D4
60921	Chatsworth 1,187	E3
60922	Chebanse 1,191	F3
61726	Chenoa 1,847	E3
61016	Cherry Valley 946	D1
62233	Chester⊙ 8,401	D6
*60601	Chicago⊙ 3,005,072	C5
	Chicago‡ 7,102,328	C5
60411	Chicago Heights 37,026	C6
60415	Chicago Ridge 13,473	B6
61523	Chillicothe 6,176	D3
61924	Chrisman 1,413	F4
62822	Christopher 3,086	D6
60650	Cicero 61,232	B5
60924	Cissna Park 825	F3
60514	Clarendon Hills 6,870	B6
62824	Clay City 1,038	E5
62324	Clayton 889	B3
60927	Clifton 1,390	F3
61727	Clinton⊙ 8,014	E3
60416	Coal City 3,028	E2
61240	Coal Valley 3,800	C2
62920	Cobden 1,210	D6
62017	Coffeen 842	D4
62326	Colchester 1,729	C3
61728	Colfax 920	E3
62234	Collinsville 19,613	B2
61241	Colona 2,172	C2
62236	Columbia 4,269	C5
60112	Cortland 1,019	E2
62018	Cottage Hills	B2
62237	Coulterville 1,118	D5
†60525	Countryside 6,538	B6
62922	Creal Springs 845	E6
60431	Crest Hill 9,252	E2
†60445	Crestwood 10,852	B6
60417	Crete 5,417	F2
61611	Creve Coeur 6,851	D3
62827	Crossville 944	F5
60014	Crystal Lake 18,590	E1
61427	Cuba 1,648	C3
62330	Dallas City 1,408	B3
61320	Dalzell 824	D2
61732	Danvers 921	D3
61832	Danville⊙ 38,985	F3
†60559	Darien 14,536	B6
*62521	Decatur⊙ 94,081	E4
	Decatur‡ 131,375	E4
60015	Deerfield 17,430	B5
†60010	Deer Park 1,368	A5
60115	De Kalb 33,099	E2
61734	Delavan 1,973	D3
61322	Depue 1,873	D2
62924	De Soto 1,589	D6
*60016	Des Plaines 53,568	B5
62530	Divernon 1,081	D4
†60469	Dixmoor 4,175	C6
61021	Dixon⊙ 15,701	D2
60419	Dolton 24,766	C6
62926	Dongola 886	D6
60515	Downers Grove 42,572	A6
60118	Dundee (East and West Dundee) 6,169	E1
61525	Dunlap 824	D3
62239	Dupo 3,039	A3
62832	Du Quoin 6,594	D5
61024	Durand 1,073	D1
60420	Dwight 4,146	E2
60518	Earlville 1,382	E2
62024	East Alton 7,096	A2
†60411	East Chicago Heights 5,347	C6
61025	East Dubuque 2,194	C1
†60118	East Dundee (Dundee) 2,618	E1
61430	East Galesburg 928	C3
†60429	East Hazelcrest 1,362	C6
61244	East Moline 20,907	C2
61611	East Peoria 22,385	D3
*62201	East Saint Louis 55,200	A2
62531	Edinburg 1,231	D4
62025	Edwardsville⊙ 12,480	B2
62401	Effingham⊙ 11,270	E4
60119	Elburn 1,224	E2
62930	Eldorado 5,198	E6
60120	Elgin 63,981	E1
61028	Elizabeth 772	C1
62931	Elizabethtown⊙ 478	E6
60007	Elk Grove Village 28,907	B5
62932	Elkville 973	D6
60126	Elmhurst 44,276	B5
61529	Elmwood 2,117	D3
60635	Elmwood Park 24,016	B5
61738	El Paso 2,676	D3
62028	Elsah 990	C5
60421	Elwood 814	E2
62933	Energy 1,138	E6
62835	Enfield 890	E5
62934	Equality 831	E6
61250	Erie 1,725	C2
61530	Eureka⊙ 4,306	D3
*60201	Evanston 73,706	B5
62242	Evansville 863	D5
60642	Evergreen Park 22,260	B6
61739	Fairbury 3,544	E3
62837	Fairfield⊙ 5,954	E5
†62201	Fairmont City 2,313	B2
61841	Fairmount 851	F3
62208	Fairview Heights 12,414	B3
61842	Farmer City 2,252	E3
61531	Farmington 3,118	C3
62534	Findlay 868	E4
61843	Fisher 1,572	E3
61740	Flanagan 978	E3
62839	Flora 5,379	E5
60422	Flossmoor 8,423	B6
60130	Forest Park 15,177	B5
†60402	Forest View 764	B6
61741	Forrest 1,246	E3
61030	Forreston 1,384	D1
60020	Fox Lake 6,831	A4
60021	Fox River Grove 2,515	A5
60423	Frankfort 4,357	B6
61031	Franklin Grove 965	D2
60131	Franklin Park 17,507	B5
62243	Freeburg 2,989	D5
61032	Freeport⊙ 26,266	D1
61252	Fulton 3,936	C2
62935	Galatia 1,042	E6
61036	Galena⊙ 3,876	C1
61401	Galesburg⊙ 35,305	C3
61434	Galva 3,185	D2
60424	Gardner 1,322	E2
61254	Geneseo 6,373	C2
60134	Geneva⊙ 9,881	E2
60135	Genoa 3,276	E1
61846	Georgetown 4,220	F4
62245	Germantown 1,191	D5
60936	Gibson City 3,498	E3
61847	Gifford 848	E3
62033	Gillespie 3,740	D4
60938	Gilman 1,913	E3
62640	Girard 2,246	D4
61533	Glasford 1,201	D3
62034	Glen Carbon 5,197	B2
60022	Glencoe 9,200	B5
†60108	Glendale Heights 23,163	A5
60137	Glen Ellyn 23,717	A5
60025	Glenview 32,060	B5
60425	Glenwood 10,538	C6
62035	Godfrey	A2
62938	Golconda⊙ 960	E6
62939	Goreville 978	E6
62037	Grafton 1,024	C5
62942	Grand Tower 748	D6
†62701	Grandview 1,794	D4
62040	Granite City 36,815	A2
60940	Grant Park 1,038	F2
61326	Granville 1,537	D2
60030	Grayslake 5,260	B4
62844	Grayville 2,313	B4
62044	Greenfield 1,090	C4
†60048	Green Oaks 1,415	B4
†61241	Green Rock 3,324	C2
62428	Greenup 1,655	E4
61534	Green Valley 768	D3
62642	Greenview 830	D3
62246	Greenville⊙ 5,271	D5
61744	Gridley 1,246	E3
62340	Griggsville 1,301	C4
60031	Gurnee 7,179	B4
62341	Hamilton 3,509	B3
60140	Hampshire 1,735	E1
61256	Hampton 1,873	C2
61536	Hanna City 1,361	D3
61041	Hanover 1,069	C1
60103	Hanover Park 28,719	A5
62047	Hardin⊙ 1,107	C4
62946	Harrisburg⊙ 10,410	E6
62537	Harristown 1,456	D4
62048	Hartford 1,887	A2
60033	Harvard 5,126	E1
60426	Harvey 35,810	B6
60656	Harwood Heights 8,228	B5
62644	Havana⊙ 4,277	D3
†60047	Hawthorn Woods 1,658	B5
60429	Hazel Crest 13,973	B6
60034	Hebron 786	E1
†61832	Hegeler 1,853	F3
61327	Hennepin⊙ 716	D2
61537	Henry 2,740	D2
62948	Herrin 10,708	E6
60941	Herscher 1,214	E2
61745	Heyworth 1,598	E3
60457	Hickory Hills 13,778	B6
62249	Highland 7,122	D5
60035	Highland Park 30,611	B5
60040	Highwood 5,452	B5
62049	Hillsboro⊙ 4,408	D4
60162	Hillside 8,279	B5
60520	Hinckley 1,447	E2
60521	Hinsdale 16,726	B6
60525	Hodgkins 2,005	B6
60195	Hoffman Estates 37,272	A5
61849	Homer 1,279	F3
60456	Hometown 5,324	B6
60430	Homewood 19,724	B6
60942	Hoopeston 6,411	F3
61747	Hohedale 913	D3
61748	Hudson 929	E3

(continued on following page)

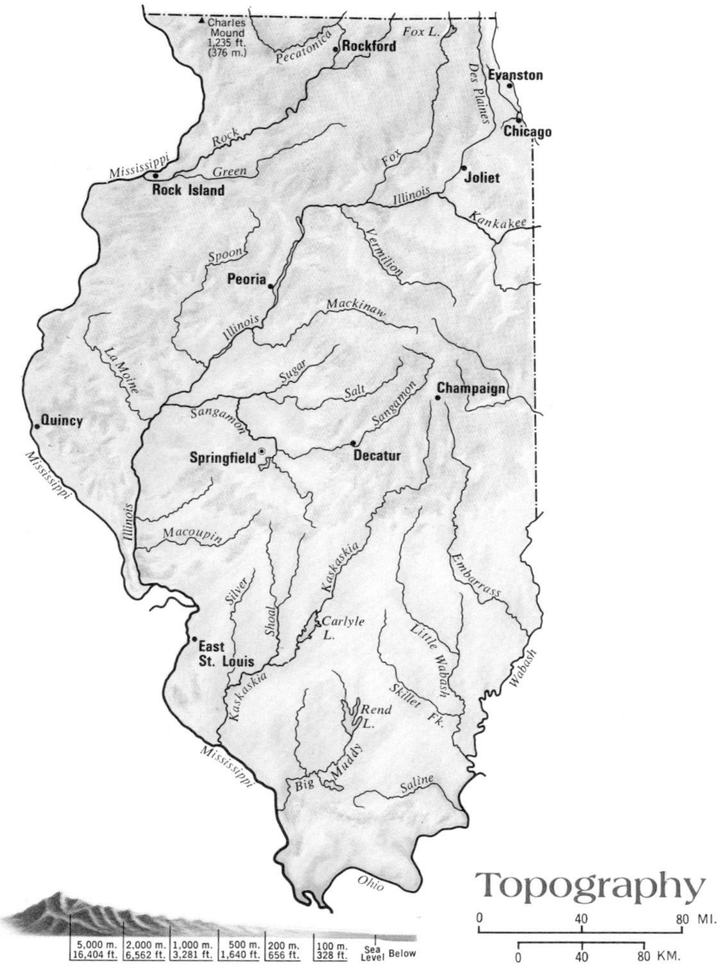

Topography

Agriculture, Industry and Resources

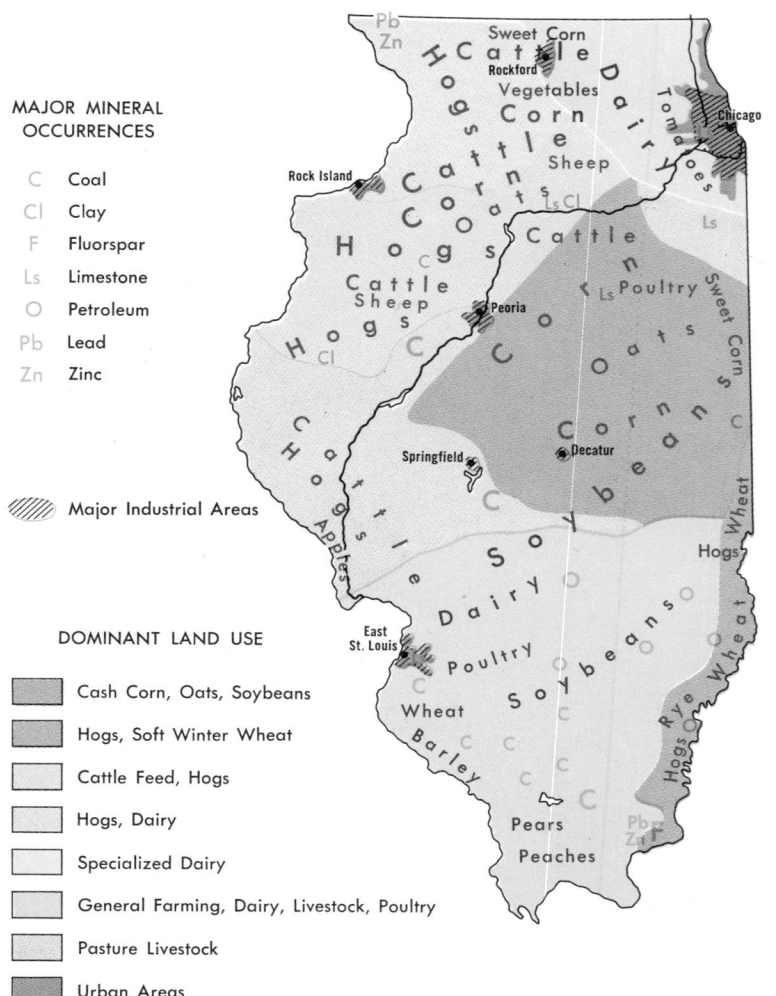

MAJOR MINERAL OCCURRENCES

C   Coal
Cl   Clay
F   Fluorspar
Ls   Limestone
O   Petroleum
Pb   Lead
Zn   Zinc

Major Industrial Areas

DOMINANT LAND USE

Cash Corn, Oats, Soybeans
Hogs, Soft Winter Wheat
Cattle Feed, Hogs
Hogs, Dairy
Specialized Dairy
General Farming, Dairy, Livestock, Poultry
Pasture Livestock
Urban Areas

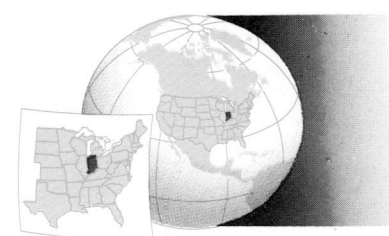

AREA 36,185 sq. mi. (93,719 sq. km.)
POPULATION 5,490,260
CAPITAL Indianapolis
LARGEST CITY Indianapolis
HIGHEST POINT 1,257 ft. (383 m.) (Wayne County)
SETTLED IN 1730
ADMITTED TO UNION December 11, 1816
POPULAR NAME Hoosier State
STATE FLOWER Peony
STATE BIRD Cardinal

COUNTIES

Adams 29,619 ...H3
Allen 294,335 ...G2
Bartholomew 65,088 ...F6
Benton 11,262 ...C3
Blackford 15,570 ...G4
Boone 36,446 ...E4
Brown 12,377 ...E6
Carroll 19,722 ...D3
Cass 40,936 ...E3
Clark 88,838 ...F8
Clay 24,862 ...C6
Clinton 31,545 ...E4
Crawford 9,820 ...E8
Daviess 27,836 ...C7
Dearborn 34,291 ...H6
Decatur 23,841 ...G6
De Kalb 33,606 ...H2
Delaware 128,587 ...G4
Dubois 34,238 ...D8
Elkhart 137,330 ...F1
Fayette 28,272 ...G5
Floyd 61,169 ...F8
Fountain 19,033 ...C4
Franklin 19,612 ...G6
Fulton 19,335 ...E2
Gibson 33,156 ...B8
Grant 80,934 ...F3
Greene 30,416 ...D6
Hamilton 82,027 ...E4
Hancock 43,939 ...F5
Harrison 27,276 ...E8
Hendricks 69,804 ...D5
Henry 53,336 ...G5
Howard 86,896 ...E4
Huntington 35,596 ...G3
Jackson 36,523 ...E7
Jasper 26,138 ...C2
Jay 23,239 ...G4
Jefferson 30,419 ...G7
Jennings 22,854 ...F7
Johnson 77,240 ...E6
Knox 41,838 ...C7
Kosciusko 59,555 ...F2
Lagrange 25,550 ...G1
Lake 522,965 ...C2
LaPorte 108,632 ...D1
Lawrence 4,272 ...E7
Madison 139,336 ...F4
Marion 765,233 ...E5
Marshall 39,155 ...E2
Martin 11,001 ...D7
Miami 39,820 ...E3
Monroe 98,785 ...D6
Montgomery 35,501 ...D4
Morgan 51,999 ...E6
Newton 14,844 ...C3
Noble 35,443 ...G2
Ohio 5,114 ...H7
Orange 18,677 ...E7
Owen 15,841 ...D6
Parke 16,372 ...C5
Perry 19,346 ...D8
Pike 12,465 ...C8
Porter 119,816 ...C2
Posey 26,414 ...B8
Pulaski 13,258 ...D2
Putnam 29,163 ...D5
Randolph 29,997 ...G4
Ripley 24,398 ...G6
Rush 19,604 ...G5
Saint Joseph 241,617 ...E1
Scott 20,422 ...F7
Shelby 39,887 ...F5
Spencer 19,361 ...C9
Starke 21,997 ...D2
Steuben 24,694 ...G1
Sullivan 21,107 ...C6
Switzerland 7,153 ...G7
Tippecanoe 121,702 ...D4
Tipton 16,819 ...E4
Union 6,860 ...H5
Vanderburgh 167,515 ...B8
Vermillion 18,229 ...C5
Vigo 112,385 ...C6
Wabash 36,640 ...F3
Warren 8,976 ...C4
Warrick 41,474 ...C8
Washington 21,932 ...E7
Wayne 76,058 ...G5
Wells 25,401 ...G3
White 23,867 ...D3
Whitley 26,215 ...G2

CITIES and TOWNS

Zip Name/Pop. Key

47240 Adams 250 ...F6
†46947 Adamsboro 325 ...E3
†46102 Advance 559 ...D5
46910 Akron 1,045 ...E2
47320 Albany 2,625 ...G4
46701 Albion⊙ 1,637 ...G2
†47283 Alert 102 ...F6
46001 Alexandria 6,028 ...F4
†46738 Altona 263 ...G2

47917 Ambia 274 ...C4
46911 Amboy 450 ...F3
†46131 Amity 200 ...E6
46103 Amo 444 ...D5
*46011 Anderson⊙ 64,695 ...F4
       Anderson‡ 139,336 ...F4
†47024 Andersonville 225 ...G5
46702 Andrews 1,243 ...F3
46703 Angola⊙ 5,486 ...G1
46030 Arcadia 1,801 ...E4
46704 Arcola 300 ...G2
†46624 Ardmore 800 ...E1
46501 Argos 1,547 ...E2
46104 Arlington 500 ...F5
46705 Ashley 841 ...G1
46031 Atlanta 657 ...E4
47918 Attica 3,841 ...C4
46502 Atwood 300 ...F2
46706 Auburn⊙ 8,122 ...G2
47001 Aurora 3,816 ...H6
47102 Austin 4,857 ...F7
47420 Avoca 400 ...D7
46105 Bainbridge 644 ...D5
46106 Bargersville 1,647 ...E5
47006 Batesville 4,152 ...G6
47920 Battle Ground 812 ...D3
47421 Bedford⊙ 14,410 ...E7
46107 Beech Grove 13,196 ...E5
†46526 Benton 220 ...F2
46711 Berne 3,300 ...H3
†46111 Bethany 127 ...E6
46301 Beverly Shores 864 ...C1
47512 Bicknell 4,713 ...C7
46713 Bippus 300 ...F3
47513 Birdseye 533 ...D8
†46406 Black Oak ...C1
47831 Blanford 500 ...B5
47138 Blocher 400 ...F7
47424 Bloomfield⊙ 2,705 ...D6
47832 Bloomingdale 409 ...C5
47401 Bloomington⊙ 52,044 ...D6
       Bloomington‡ 98,387 ...D6
†47360 Blountsville 213 ...G4
†46176 Blue Ridge 219 ...F5
46714 Bluffton⊙ 8,705 ...G3
46110 Boggstown 200 ...F5
46302 Boone Grove 220 ...C2
47601 Boonville⊙ 6,300 ...C8
47106 Borden 384 ...F8
47324 Boston 189 ...H5
47921 Boswell 810 ...C3
46504 Bourbon 1,522 ...E2
47833 Bowling Green 200 ...D6
47107 Bradford 350 ...E8
47834 Brazil⊙ 7,852 ...C5
46506 Bremen 3,565 ...E2
47836 Bridgeton 250 ...C5
†45030 Bright 450 ...H6
46720 Brimfield 292 ...G2
46913 Bringhurst 275 ...E3
46507 Bristol 1,203 ...F1
47922 Brook 926 ...C3
46111 Brooklyn 889 ...E5
†47250 Brooksburg 132 ...G7
47923 Brookston 1,701 ...D3
47012 Brookville⊙ 2,874 ...G6
46112 Brownsburg 6,242 ...E5
47220 Brownstown⊙ 2,704 ...F7
47325 Brownsville 250 ...H5
47516 Bruceville 646 ...C7
47326 Bryant 277 ...G3
47924 Buck Creek 225 ...D4
47647 Buckskin 200 ...C8
47925 Buffalo 500 ...D3
46914 Bunker Hill 984 ...E3
46508 Burket 260 ...F2
46915 Burlington 680 ...E4
47926 Burnettsville 496 ...D3
47222 Burney 300 ...F6
†46401 Burns Harbor 920 ...C1
46916 Burrows 250 ...E3
46721 Butler 2,509 ...H2
47223 Butlerville 300 ...F6
†46371 Byron 200 ...C5
†47362 Cadiz 180 ...G5
47327 Cambridge City 2,407 ...G5
46917 Camden 618 ...D3
47108 Campbellsburg 695 ...E7
47224 Canaan 90 ...G7
47519 Cannelburg 152 ...C7
47520 Cannelton⊙ 2,373 ...D9
47837 Carbon 307 ...C5
47838 Carlisle 717 ...C7
46032 Carmel 18,272 ...E5
46114 Cartersburg 300 ...E5
46115 Carthage 886 ...F5
47927 Cates 125 ...C4
47928 Cayuga 1,258 ...C5
47016 Cedar Grove 217 ...H6
46303 Cedar Lake 8,754 ...C2
47521 Celestine 150 ...D8
†47842 Centenary 150 ...B5
†46901 Center 310 ...E4
47840 Centerpoint 242 ...C6
46116 Centerton 250 ...E5
47330 Centerville 2,284 ...H5

47929 Chalmers 554 ...D3
47610 Chandler 3,043 ...C8
47111 Charlestown 5,596 ...F8
46117 Charlottesville 300 ...F5
†47138 Chelsea 200 ...F7
46017 Chesterfield 2,701 ...F4
46304 Chesterton 8,531 ...D1
47611 Chrisney 537 ...C8
46723 Churubusco 1,638 ...G2
47930 Clarks Hill 653 ...D4
47130 Clarksville 15,164 ...F8
47841 Clay City 883 ...C6
46510 Claypool 464 ...F2
47118 Clayton 703 ...D5
47426 Clear Creek 200 ...E6
†46737 Clear Lake 301 ...H1
47226 Clifford 310 ...F6
47842 Clinton 5,267 ...C5
46120 Cloverdale 1,357 ...D5
†47834 Cloverland 175 ...C6
47427 Coal City 225 ...D6
47845 Coalmont 450 ...C6
46121 Coatesville 474 ...D5
47931 Colburn 300 ...D3
46035 Colfax 823 ...D4
47978 Collegeville 1,059 ...C3
46725 Columbia City⊙ 5,091 ...G2
47201 Columbus⊙ 30,614 ...E6
47331 Connersville⊙ 17,023 ...G5
46919 Converse 1,279 ...F3
47228 Cortland 175 ...F7
46730 Corunna 304 ...G2
47112 Corydon⊙ 2,724 ...E8
47932 Covington⊙ 2,883 ...C4
†47302 Cowan 428 ...G4
47114 Crandall 176 ...E8

47522 Crane 250 ...D7
47933 Crawfordsville⊙ 13,325 ...D4
46732 Cromwell 458 ...F2
47229 Crothersville 1,747 ...F7
46307 Crown Point⊙ 16,455 ...C2
46511 Culver 1,601 ...E2
46229 Cumberland 3,375 ...E5
47612 Cynthiana 874 ...B8
47523 Dale 1,693 ...D8
47334 Daleville ...F4
47847 Dana 803 ...C5
46122 Danville⊙ 4,220 ...D5
47940 Darlington 811 ...D4
47618 Darmstadt 1,280 ...B8
47941 Dayton 781 ...D4
46733 Decatur⊙ 8,649 ...H3
47524 Decker 256 ...B7
†46917 Deer Creek 250 ...E3
46923 Delphi⊙ 3,042 ...D3
46310 Demotte 2,559 ...C2
46926 Denver 589 ...E3
47230 Deputy 200 ...F7
47302 Desoto 385 ...G4
47018 Dillsboro 1,038 ...G6
46513 Donaldson 320 ...E2
†47118 Doolittle Mills 200 ...D8
47335 Dublin 979 ...G5
47525 Dubois 550 ...D8
47848 Dugger 1,118 ...C6
†46304 Dune Acres 291 ...C1
47336 Dunkirk 3,180 ...G4
†46514 Dunlap 5,397 ...F1
47337 Dunreith 184 ...F5
47231 Dupont 392 ...G7
46311 Dyer 9,555 ...C1
†46074 Eagletown 306 ...E4
47942 Earl Park 469 ...C3
46312 East Chicago 39,786 ...C1

47019 East Enterprise 250 ...H7
†47370 East Germantown (Pershing) 438 ...G5
47338 Eaton 1,804 ...G4
47116 Eckerty 108 ...D8
47339 Economy 237 ...G5
†46011 Edgewood 2,215 ...F4
46124 Edinburgh 4,856 ...E6
47528 Edwardsport 459 ...C7
†47150 Edwardsville 700 ...F8
47613 Elberfeld 640 ...C8
47117 Elizabeth 178 ...F8
47232 Elizabethtown 603 ...F6
46514 Elkhart 41,305 ...F1
       Elkhart‡ 137,330 ...F1
47429 Ellettsville 3,328 ...D6
47529 Elnora 756 ...C7
47018 Elrod 200 ...G6
47901 Elston 500 ...D4
46036 Elwood 10,867 ...F4
46125 Eminence 200 ...D5
47118 English⊙ 633 ...E8
46524 Etna Green 522 ...E2
†47928 Eugene 400 ...B5
*47701 Evansville⊙ 130,496 ...C9
       Evansville‡ 309,408 ...C9
47531 Everton 500 ...G5
46126 Fairland 950 ...F5
†47842 Fairview Park 1,545 ...C5
47850 Farmersburg 1,240 ...C6
47340 Farmland 1,560 ...G4
†47421 Fayetteville 180 ...D7
47532 Ferdinand 2,192 ...D8
46129 Fillmore 550 ...D5
46128 Finly 400 ...F5
47234 Flat Rock 323 ...F6

46929 Flora 2,303 ...E3
47119 Floyds Knobs 500 ...F8
47851 Fontanet 325 ...C5
46039 Forest 400 ...E4
47648 Fort Branch 2,504 ...B8
46040 Fortville 2,787 ...F5
*46801 Fort Wayne⊙ 172,028 ...G2
       Fort Wayne‡ 382,961 ...G2
47341 Fountain City 839 ...H5
46130 Fountaintown 225 ...F5
47944 Fowler⊙ 2,319 ...C3
46930 Fowlerton 300 ...F4
47946 Francesville 944 ...D3
47649 Francisco 612 ...B8
46041 Frankfort⊙ 15,168 ...E4
46131 Franklin 11,563 ...E6
46044 Frankton 2,080 ...F4
47120 Fredericksburg 233 ...E8
47431 Freedom 100 ...D6
47535 Freelandville 600 ...C7
47235 Freetown 600 ...E7
46737 Fremont 1,180 ...H1
47432 French Lick 2,265 ...D7
46931 Fulton 393 ...E3
†47119 Galena 1,186 ...F8
46932 Galveston 1,822 ...E3
46738 Garrett 4,751 ...G2
*46401 Gary 151,953 ...C1
       Gary-Hammond-East Chicago‡ 642,781 ...C1
46933 Gas City 6,370 ...F4
47342 Gaston 1,150 ...G4
46740 Geneva 1,430 ...H3
47537 Gentryville 299 ...C8
47122 Georgetown 1,494 ...F8
46133 Glenwood 370 ...G5
†47567 Glezen 300 ...C8
46045 Goldsmith 235 ...E4

(continued on following page)

Agriculture, Industry and Resources

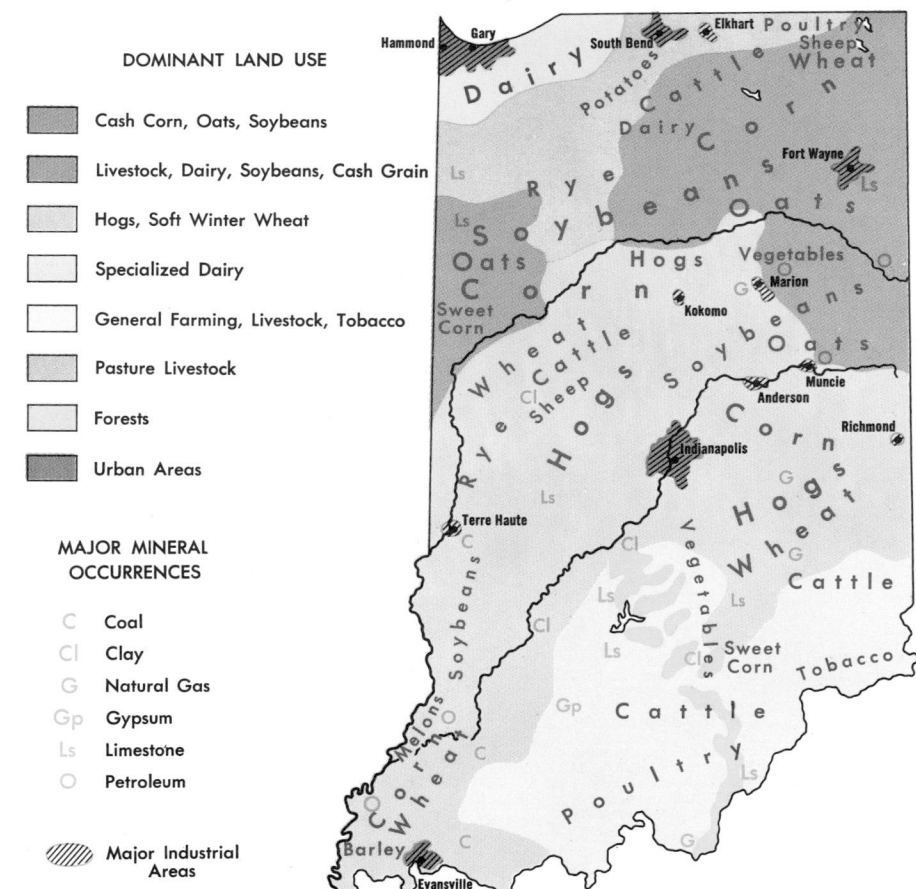

DOMINANT LAND USE

- Cash Corn, Oats, Soybeans
- Livestock, Dairy, Soybeans, Cash Grain
- Hogs, Soft Winter Wheat
- Specialized Dairy
- General Farming, Livestock, Tobacco
- Pasture Livestock
- Forests
- Urban Areas

MAJOR MINERAL OCCURRENCES

C   Coal
Cl Clay
G   Natural Gas
Gp Gypsum
Ls Limestone
○   Petroleum

Major Industrial Areas

47948 Goodland 1,200..............C3
46526 Goshen⊙ 19,665..............F1
47433 Gosport 729..............D6
46741 Grabill 658..............H2
47615 Grandview 670..............C9
46530 Granger 350..............E1
46135 Greencastle⊙ 8,403..............D5
†47025 Greendale 3,795..............H6
46140 Greenfield⊙ 11,299..............F5
47344 Greensboro 175..............G5
47240 Greensburg⊙ 9,254..............G6
47345 Greens Fork 426..............H5
46936 Greentown 2,265..............E4
47124 Greenville 537..............F8
46142 Greenwood 19,327..............E5
47616 Griffin 192..............B8
46319 Griffith 17,026..............C1
46144 Gwynneville 250..............F5
47346 Hagerstown 1,950..............G5
46742 Hamilton 587..............H1
46532 Hamlet 738..............D2
*46320 Hammond 93,714..............B1
46340 Hanna 550..............D2
47243 Hanover 4,054..............F7
47125 Hardinsburg 298..............E8
46743 Harlan 840..............H2
47853 Harmony 613..............C5
47434 Harrodsburg 400..............D6
47348 Hartford City⊙ 7,622..............G4
47244 Hartsville 379..............F6
47617 Hatfield 800..............C9
47639 Haubstadt 1,389..............B8
†47546 Haysville 600..............D8
46740 Hazleton 368..............B8
46341 Hebron 2,696..............C2
47436 Heltonville 400..............E7
46937 Hemlock 300..............F4
47126 Henryville 1,132..............F7
46322 Highland 25,935..............B1
47949 Hillsboro 561..............C4
47854 Hillsdale 500..............C5
46745 Hoagland 600..............H3
46342 Hobart 22,987..............C1
46047 Hobbs 200..............F4
47541 Holland 683..............C8
47023 Holton 487..............G6
46146 Homer 850..............F6
47246 Hope 2,185..............F6
†46069 Hortonville 240..............G4
46746 Howe 800..............G1
46747 Hudson 447..............H1
46552 Hudson Lake 1,347..............D1
46748 Huntertown 1,265..............G2
47542 Huntingburg 5,376..............D8
46750 Huntington⊙ 16,202..............G3
†46064 Huntsville 120..............G4
47437 Huron 250..............D7
47855 Hymera 1,054..............C6
47950 Idaville 655..............D3
*46201 Indianapolis (cap.)⊙
700,807..............E5
Indianapolis‡ 1,166,929..............E5
†46601 Indian Village 151..............E1
46048 Ingalls 909..............F5
47545 Ireland 600..............C8
46147 Jamestown 924..............D5
47438 Jasonville 2,497..............C6
47546 Jasper⊙ 9,097..............D8
†47130 Jeffersonville⊙ 21,220..............F8
†47565 Johnson 100..............B8
†46074 Jolietville 800..............E5
46938 Jonesboro 2,279..............F4
47247 Jonesville 213..............F6
46049 Kempton 410..............E4
46755 Kendallville⊙ 7,299..............G2
47351 Kennard 441..............G5
47951 Kentland⊙ 1,936..............C3
46939 Kewanna 711..............E3
46759 Keystone 204..............G3
46760 Kimmell 250..............F2
47952 Kingman 566..............C5
46345 Kingsbury 329..............D1
46346 Kingsford Heights 1,618..............D2
46050 Kirklin 662..............E4
46148 Knightstown 2,325..............F5
47857 Knightsville 763..............C6
46534 Knox⊙ 3,674..............D2
46901 Kokomo⊙ 47,808..............E4
Kokomo‡ 103,715..............E4
†46574 Koontz Lake 1,436..............D2
46347 Kouts 1,619..............C2
46348 La Crosse 713..............D2
47954 Ladoga 1,151..............D5
*47901 Lafayette⊙ 43,011..............D4
Lafayette-West Lafayette‡
121,702..............D4
46940 La Fontaine 946..............F3
46761 Lagrange⊙ 2,164..............F1
46941 Lagro 569..............F3
46157 Lake Hart 231..............E5
†46703 Lake James 400..............H1
46943 Laketon 500..............F3
46349 Lake Village 900..............C2
46536 Lakeville 629..............E1
46944 Landess 150..............F4
47136 Lanesville 570..............E8
46763 Laotto 361..............G2
46537 Lapaz 651..............E2
46051 Lapel 1,881..............F5
46350 LaPorte⊙ 21,796..............D1
46764 Larwill 286..............F2
47024 Laurel 819..............G6
46226 Lawrence 25,591..............E5
†47025 Lawrenceburg⊙ 4,403..............H6
47137 Leavenworth 356..............E8
46052 Lebanon⊙ 11,456..............D4
46538 Leesburg 629..............F2
46945 Leiters Ford 280..............E2
46765 Leo 500..............G2
47551 Leopold 175..............D8
46355 Leroy 400..............C2
†47232 Letts 247..............F6
47352 Lewisville 577..............G5
47138 Lexington..............F7
47353 Liberty⊙ 1,844..............H5
46766 Liberty Center 275..............G3
46946 Liberty Mills 200..............F2

46767 Ligonier 3,134..............F2
46769 Linden 700..............D4
46769 Linn Grove 175..............H3
47241 Linton 6,315..............C6
†46755 Lisbon 200..............G2
47139 Little York 150..............F7
46149 Lizton 456..............D5
46947 Logansport⊙ 17,731..............E3
†46360 Long Beach 2,262..............D1
47553 Loogootee 3,100..............D7
47354 Losantville 306..............G4
46356 Lowell 5,827..............C2
46950 Lucerne 135..............E3
†46601 Lydick..............E1
†47874 Lyford 400..............C5
47355 Lynn 1,250..............H4
47619 Lynnville 566..............C8
47443 Lyons 782..............C7
46951 Macy 282..............E3
47250 Madison⊙ 12,472..............G7
47555 Magnet 75..............D8
†47001 Manchester 250..............H6
46150 Manilla 350..............F5
†47872 Mansfield 200..............C5
†47443 Marco 150..............C7
47140 Marengo 892..............E8
47556 Mariah Hill 300..............D8
46151 Marietta 234..............F6
46952 Marion⊙ 35,874..............F3
46056 Markleville 427..............F5
47453 Marklee 975..............G3
46056 Markleville 427..............F5
46055 McCordsville 600..............F5
46151 Martinsville⊙ 11,311..............D6
46957 Matthews 745..............F4
46154 Maxwell 300..............F5
46055 McCordsville 600..............F5
47860 Mecca 482..............C5
47957 Medaryville 731..............D2
47260 Medora 853..............E7
47958 Mellott 294..............C4
47143 Memphis 300..............F8
46539 Mentone 973..............E2
47861 Merom 360..............B6
46410 Merrillville 27,677..............C2
47030 Metamora 350..............G6
†46703 Metz 200..............H1
46958 Mexico 850..............E3
46959 Miami 350..............E3
†49117 Michiana Shores 464..............D1
46360 Michigan City 36,850..............C1
46057 Michigantown 453..............E4
46540 Middlebury 1,665..............F1
47356 Middletown 2,978..............F4
47445 Midland 250..............C6
47031 Milan 1,566..............G6
46542 Milford 1,153..............F2
†47240 Milford 177..............F6
46543 Millersburg 809..............F1
47261 Millhousen 214..............G6
47145 Milltown 1,006..............E8
†47362 Millville 275..............G5
46156 Milroy 750..............G6
47357 Milton 729..............G5
46544 Mishawaka 40,201..............E1
47446 Mitchell 4,641..............E7
47358 Modoc 243..............G4
46771 Mongo 225..............G1
47959 Monon 1,540..............D3
46772 Monroe 739..............H3
47557 Monroe City 569..............C7
46157 Monroeville 1,372..............H3
46157 Monrovia 800..............E5
46960 Monterey 350..............D2
47862 Montezuma 1,352..............C5
47558 Montgomery 390..............C7
47960 Monticello⊙ 5,162..............D3
47962 Montmorenci 300..............D4
47359 Montpelier 1,995..............G3
47360 Mooreland 479..............G5
47032 Moores Hill 566..............G6
46158 Mooresville 5,349..............E5
46160 Morgantown 897..............E6
47963 Morocco 1,348..............C3
47033 Morris 350..............G6
46161 Morristown 989..............F5
†47327 Mount Auburn 192..............G5
47964 Mount Ayr 207..............C3
47361 Mount Summit 357..............G4
47620 Mount Vernon⊙ 7,656..............B9
46058 Mulberry 1,225..............D4
*47302 Muncie⊙ 77,216..............G4
Muncie‡..............G4
46321 Munster 20,671..............B1
47147 Nabb 150..............F7
47034 Napoleon 246..............G6
46550 Nappanee 4,694..............F2
47448 Nashville⊙ 705..............E6
†47421 Needmore 200..............E7
47150 New Albany⊙ 37,103..............F8
47449 Newberry 246..............C7
47630 Newburgh 2,906..............C9
46552 New Carlisle 1,439..............E1
47362 New Castle⊙ 20,056..............G5
†46342 New Chicago 3,284..............C1
47863 New Goshen 500..............B5
47631 New Harmony 945..............B8
46774 New Haven 6,714..............H2
47366 New Lisbon 300..............G5
†46979 New London 200..............E4
47965 New Market 608..............D5
46163 New Palestine 749..............F5
46553 New Paris 1,062..............F2
†47165 New Pekin 1,125..............F7
47263 New Point 296..............G6
47966 Newport⊙ 704..............C5
†47106 New Providence
(Borden) 384..............F8
47967 New Richmond 403..............D4
47968 New Ross 306..............D5
†46173 New Salisbury 350..............E8
47161 New Salisbury 350..............E8
47432 New Washington 136..............D8
47969 Newtown 277..............C4
47035 New Trenton 200..............H6
47162 New Washington 800..............F7
46961 New Waverly 162..............E3
46184 New Whiteland 4,502..............E5

†46122 New Winchester 180..............D5
46060 Noblesville⊙ 12,056..............F4
47266 North Judson 1,653..............D2
46554 North Liberty 1,211..............E1
46962 North Manchester 5,998..............F3
46165 North Salem 581..............D5
47805 North Terre Haute..............C5
47265 North Vernon 5,768..............F6
46555 North Webster 709..............F2
47960 Norway 300..............D3
46556 Notre Dame..............E1
47331 Nulltown 235..............G5
46965 Oakford 325..............F4
47660 Oakland City 3,301..............C8
47561 Oaktown 776..............C7
47562 Odon 1,463..............C7
†46401 Ogden Dunes 1,489..............C1
47036 Oldenburg 770..............G6
47451 Oolitic 1,495..............E7
46367 Otis 250..............D1
47163 Otisco 425..............F7
47970 Otterbein 1,118..............C4
47564 Otwell 600..............C8
47453 Owensburg 785..............D7
47665 Owensville 1,261..............B8
47971 Oxford 1,327..............C3
†46508 Palestine 800..............F2
47164 Palmyra 692..............E8
47454 Paoli⊙ 3,637..............E7
46166 Paragon 538..............D6
47368 Parker City 1,414..............G4
47666 Patoka 832..............B8
47455 Patricksburg 250..............D6
47038 Patriot 265..............H7
47865 Paxton 200..............C6
47165 Pekin 950..............E7
46064 Pendleton 2,130..............F5
47369 Pennville 805..............G4
†46011 Perkinsville 175..............F4
47974 Perrysville 532..............C4
47370 Pershing 438..............G5
†46975 Pershing 425..............E3
46970 Peru⊙ 13,764..............E3
47567 Petersburg⊙ 2,987..............C7
46778 Petroleum 212..............G3
46562 Pierceton 1,086..............F2
47866 Pimento 150..............C6
†46350 Pine Lake 1,676..............D1
47975 Pine Village 257..............C4
46167 Pittsboro 891..............D5
†46923 Pittsburg 175..............D3
46168 Plainfield 9,191..............E5
47568 Plainville 556..............C7
46779 Pleasant Lake 800..............H1
46563 Plymouth⊙ 7,693..............C2
47868 Poland 230..............D6
46781 Poneto 250..............G3
46368 Portage 27,409..............C1
46304 Porter 2,988..............C1
47371 Portland⊙ 7,074..............H4
47633 Poseyville 1,247..............B8
†46360 Pottawattamie Park 284..............C1
47869 Prairie Creek 275..............C6
48770 Prairieton 200..............B6
46782 Preble 150..............H3
†46164 Princes Lakes 937..............E6
47670 Princeton⊙ 8,976..............B8
46170 Putnamville 250..............D5
47456 Quincy 250..............D6
47573 Ragsdale 135..............C7
46737 Ray 200..............H1
†47274 Reddington 400..............F6
46171 Reelsville 210..............D5
47977 Remington 1,268..............C3
47978 Rensselaer⊙ 4,944..............C3
47980 Reynolds 350..............G6
47634 Richland 500..............C9
47374 Richmond⊙ 41,349..............H5
47380 Ridgeville 933..............G4
47871 Riley 269..............C6
47040 Rising Sun⊙ 2,478..............H7
46172 Roachdale 958..............D5
46974 Roann 548..............F3
46783 Roanoke 891..............G3
46975 Rochester⊙ 5,050..............E2
46977 Rockfield 300..............D3
47635 Rockport⊙ 2,590..............C9
47872 Rockville⊙ 2,785..............C5
46371 Rolling Prairie 550..............D1
47574 Rome 50..............D9
46784 Rome City 1,319..............G1
47981 Romney 250..............D4
47874 Rosedale 744..............C5
†46601 Roseland 832..............E1
†46310 Roselawn 200..............C2
46065 Rossville 1,148..............D4
46978 Royal Center 908..............E3
†47302 Royerton 300..............G4
46173 Russellville 376..............D5
46975 Russiaville 973..............E4
47575 Saint Anthony 470..............D8
47875 Saint Bernice 500..............C5
46785 Saint Joe 546..............H2
46383 Saint John 3,974..............C1
46373 Saint Leon 515..............H6
47876 Saint Mary-of-
the-Woods 920..............B6
†46556 Saint Marys..............E1
47577 Saint Meinrad 910..............D8
47272 Saint Paul 976..............F6
†47012 Saint Peter 175..............G6
†47620 Saint Philip 400..............B9
†47638 Saint Wendel 250..............B8
47167 Salem⊙ 5,290..............E7
47578 Sandborn 576..............C7
†47401 Sanders 65..............E6
46374 San Pierre 325..............D2
47579 Santa Claus 514..............D8

47382 Saratoga 338..............H4
†47283 Sardinia 133..............F6
46375 Schererville 13,209..............C2
46376 Schneider 364..............C2
47580 Schnellville 250..............D8
47273 Scipio 200..............F6
46636 Scircleville 125..............E4
47170 Scottsburg⊙ 5,068..............F7
47172 Sellersburg 3,211..............F8
47383 Selma 1,056..............G4
47274 Seymour 15,050..............F7
46068 Sharpsville 617..............E4
47879 Shelburn 1,259..............C6
46377 Shelby 700..............C2
46176 Shelbyville⊙ 14,989..............F6
47880 Shepardsville 325..............B5
46069 Sheridan 2,200..............E4
†47338 Shideler 275..............G4
46565 Shipshewana 466..............F1
47384 Shirley 919..............F5
†46797 Shirley City (Woodburn)
1,002..............H2
47581 Shoals⊙ 967..............D7
46566 Sidney 194..............F2
46982 Silver Lake 576..............F2
46983 Sims 250..............F3
†46142 Smith Valley..............E5
47458 Smithville 500..............D6
46984 Somerset 350..............F3
47683 Somerville 340..............C8
*46601 South Bend⊙ 109,727..............E1
South Bend‡ 280,772..............E1
46780 South Milford 270..............G1
46201 Southport 2,266..............E5
46787 South Whitley 1,575..............F2
†47355 Spartanburg 201..............H4
47172 Speed 800..............F8
46224 Speedway 12,641..............E5
†47808 Spelterville 200..............C5
47460 Spencer⊙ 2,732..............D6
46788 Spencerville 400..............G2
47385 Spiceland 940..............G5
†47374 Spring Grove 469..............H5
†46140 Spring Lake 236..............F5
47386 Springport 221..............G4
47462 Springville 279..............D7
47584 Spurgeon 250..............C8
47463 Stanford 200..............D6
46985 Star City 351..............D3
47982 State Line 233..............C4
47881 Staunton 607..............C6
47585 Stendal 175..............C8
47636 Stewartsville 225..............B8
46180 Stilesville 350..............D5
46351 Stillwell 225..............D1
47464 Stinesville 225..............D6
47983 Stockwell 310..............D4
47387 Straughn 331..............G5
46789 Stroh 350..............G1
47882 Sullivan⊙ 4,774..............C6
47388 Sulphur Springs 345..............G4
46379 Sumava Resorts 300..............C2
46070 Summitville 1,085..............F4
47041 Sunman 924..............G6
46987 Sweetser 944..............F3
47465 Switz City 300..............C6
46567 Syracuse 2,579..............F2
47280 Taylorsville 1,247..............F6
47586 Tell City 8,704..............D9
47637 Tennyson 331..............C8
*47801 Terre Haute⊙ 61,125..............C6
Terre Haute‡ 176,583..............C6
46381 Thayer 350..............C2
46071 Thorntown 1,468..............D4
†46975 Tiosa 100..............E2
46550 Tippecanoe 320..............E2
46072 Tipton⊙ 5,004..............E4
46571 Topeka 876..............F1
†46360 Town of Pines 962..............D1
46181 Trafalgar 466..............E6
†46360 Trail Creek 2,581..............D1
†46725 Tri Lakes 1,356..............G2
47588 Troy 350..............D9
46988 Twelve Mile 240..............E3
46572 Tyner 245..............E2
47177 Underwood 550..............F7
47390 Union City 3,908..............H4
46791 Uniondale 303..............G3
46382 Union Mills 650..............D2
47468 Unionville 225..............D6
47884 Universal 428..............C5
46989 Upland 3,335..............F4
47403 Urbana 400..............F3
†47130 Utica 501..............F8
47281 Vallonia 550..............E7
46383 Valparaiso⊙ 22,247..............C2
46991 Van Buren 935..............F3
47987 Veedersburg 2,261..............C4
47590 Velpen 375..............C8
47282 Vernon⊙ 329..............F7
47042 Versailles⊙ 1,560..............G6
47043 Vevay⊙ 1,343..............G7
47441 Vicksburg 175..............C6
†47170 Vienna 175..............F7
47591 Vincennes⊙ 20,857..............C7
46992 Wabash⊙ 12,985..............F3
47638 Wadesville 450..............B8
46573 Wakarusa 1,281..............F1
46182 Waldron 850..............F6
†47201 Walesboro 214..............F6
46574 Walkerton 2,051..............E2
†46802 Wallen 945..............G2
46994 Walton 1,202..............E3
46390 Wanatah 879..............D2
47293 Wanamaker 234..............G3
46580 Warsaw⊙ 10,647..............F2
47501 Washington⊙ 11,325..............C7
46793 Waterloo 1,951..............G2
†47130 Watson 200..............F8
47989 Waveland 559..............D5
46794 Wawaka 320..............F2
47392 Webster 350..............H5
47469 West Baden Springs 796..............D7
†47353 West College Corner 614..............H5
46074 Westfield 2,783..............E4

†45030 West Harrison 328..............H6
47906 West Lafayette 21,247..............D4
47991 West Lebanon 946..............C4
46995 West Middleton 327..............E4
47596 Westphalia 300..............C7
47992 Westpoint 375..............D4
47283 Westport 1,450..............F6
47885 West Terre Haute 2,806..............B6
46391 Westville 2,887..............D1
46392 Wheatfield 755..............C2
47597 Wheatland 532..............C7
46393 Wheeler 540..............C1
†47342 Wheeling 180..............G4
46184 Whiteland 1,956..............E5
46075 Whitestown 497..............E5
46394 Whiting 5,630..............C1
46186 Wilkinson 493..............F5
47470 Williams 350..............D7
47993 Williamsport⊙ 1,747..............C4
46996 Winamac⊙ 2,370..............D2
47394 Winchester⊙ 5,659..............G4
46076 Windfall 911..............F4
47994 Wingate 373..............C4
46590 Winona Lake 2,827..............F2
47598 Winslow 1,017..............C8
47995 Wolcott 923..............C3
46795 Wolcottville 890..............G1
46796 Wolflake 230..............F2
46797 Woodburn 1,002..............H2
†46624 Woodland 400..............E1
47471 Worthington 1,574..............C6
46595 Wyatt 250..............E1
†47630 Yankeetown 250..............C9
46798 Yoder 250..............H3
47396 Yorktown 3,945..............G4
46998 Young America 259..............E3
†47808 Youngstown 350..............C6
46799 Zanesville 575..............G3
46077 Zionsville 3,948..............E4

OTHER FEATURES

Anderson (riv.)..............D8
Bass (lake)..............D2
Beanblossom (creek)..............D6
Big (creek)..............B8
Big Blue (riv.)..............F5
Big Pine (creek)..............C3
Big Raccoon (creek)..............C5
Big Walnut (creek)..............D5
Blue (riv.)..............E8
Brookville (lake)..............G6
Buck (creek)..............F5
Busseron (creek)..............C7
Camp (creek)..............F6
Cedar (creek)..............G2
Clifty (creek)..............F6
Coal (creek)..............C4
Crooked (creek)..............D2
Cypress (pond)..............B8
Deer (creek)..............E3
Deer (creek)..............D4
Eagle (creek)..............E4
Eel (riv.)..............C6
Eel (riv.)..............F3
Elkhart (riv.)..............F1

Fawn (riv.)..............G1
Flatrock (creek)..............F5
Fort Benjamin Harrison..............E5
Freeman (lake)..............D3
Geist (res.)..............F5
George Rogers Clark Nat'l Hist.
Park..............B7
Graham (creek)..............F7
Grissom A.F.B. 4,676..............E3
Huntington (lake)..............F3
Indian (creek)..............E8
Indian (creek)..............C8
Indiana Dunes Nat'l Lakeshore..............C1
Iroquois (riv.)..............B3
Jefferson Proving Ground..............G7
Kankakee (riv.)..............C1
Lemon (lake)..............E6
Lincoln Boyhood Nat'l Mem...............C8
Little (riv.)..............G3
Little Elkhart (riv.)..............F1
Little Pigeon (creek)..............C9
Little Vermilion (riv.)..............C5
Lost (riv.)..............E7
Maria (creek)..............C7
Maumee (riv.)..............H2
Maxinkuckee (lake)..............E2
Michigan (lake)..............C1
Mill (creek)..............D6
Mississinewa (lake)..............F3
Mississinewa (riv.)..............F3
Monroe (lake)..............D6
Morse (res.)..............E4
Muscatatuck (riv.)..............E7
Ohio (riv.)..............B9
Patoka (riv.)..............D8
Pigeon (creek)..............C9
Pigeon (riv.)..............G1
Pipe (creek)..............F4
Prairie (creek)..............F6
Richland (creek)..............D6
Saint Joseph (riv.)..............E1
Saint Joseph (riv.)..............H2
Saint Marys (lake)..............G3
Saint Marys (riv.)..............H3
Salamonie (lake)..............G3
Salamonie (riv.)..............F3
Salt (creek)..............E7
Sand (creek)..............F6
Shafer (lake)..............D3
Silver (creek)..............F8
Sugar (creek)..............C5
Sugar (creek)..............D4
Sugar (creek)..............E4
Tippecanoe (riv.)..............E3
Vermilion (riv.)..............C4
Vernon Fork (creek)..............F7
Wabash (riv.)..............F3
Wawasee (lake)..............F2
White (riv.)..............C8
White, East Fork (riv.)..............E7
White, West Fork (riv.)..............C6
Whitewater (riv.)..............H5
Wildcat (creek)..............E4

⊙County seat.
‡Population of metropolitan area.
† Zip of nearest p.o.   * Multiple zips

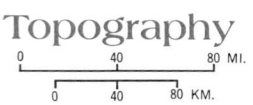

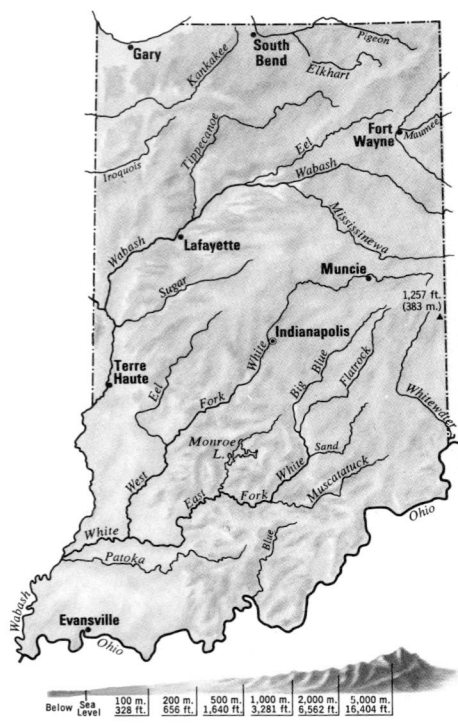

Topography

0   40   80 MI.

0   40   80 KM.

1,257 ft.
(383 m.)

Below Sea Level | 100 m. 328 ft. | 200 m. 656 ft. | 500 m. 1,640 ft. | 1,000 m. 3,281 ft. | 2,000 m. 6,562 ft. | 5,000 m. 16,404 ft.

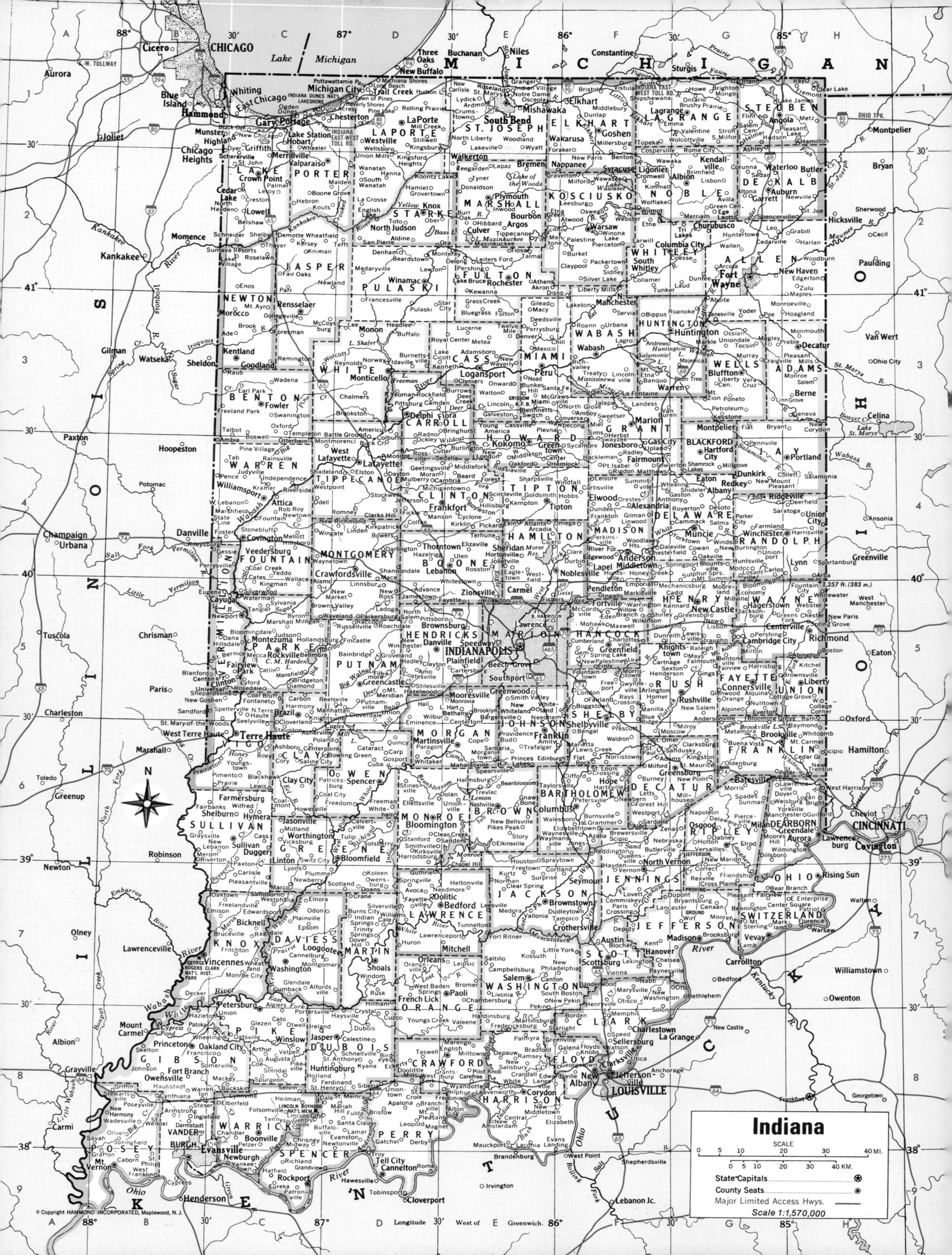

COUNTIES

Adair 9,509	E6
Adams 5,731	D6
Allamakee 15,108	L2
Appanoose 15,511	H7
Audubon 8,559	D5
Benton 23,649	J4
Black Hawk 137,961	J4
Boone 26,184	F5
Bremer 24,820	J3
Buchanan 22,900	K4
Buena Vista 20,774	C3
Butler 17,668	H3
Calhoun 13,542	D4
Carroll 22,951	D4
Cass 16,932	D6
Cedar 18,635	L5
Cerro Gordo 48,458	G2
Cherokee 16,238	B3
Chickasaw 15,437	J2
Clarke 8,612	F6
Clay 19,576	C2
Clayton 21,098	L3

Clinton 57,122	M5
Crawford 18,935	C4
Dallas 29,513	E5
Davis 9,104	J7
Decatur 9,794	F7
Delaware 18,933	L4
Des Moines 46,203	L7
Dickinson 15,629	C2
Dubuque 93,745	M4
Emmet 13,336	D2
Fayette 25,488	K3
Floyd 19,597	H2
Franklin 13,036	G3
Fremont 9,401	B7
Greene 12,119	E5
Grundy 14,366	H4
Guthrie 11,983	D5
Hamilton 17,862	F4
Hancock 13,833	F2
Hardin 21,776	G4
Harrison 16,348	B5
Henry 18,890	K6
Howard 11,114	J2
Humboldt 12,246	E3

Ida 8,908	C4
Iowa 15,429	J5
Jackson 22,503	M4
Jasper 36,425	G5
Jefferson 16,316	K6
Johnson 81,717	K5
Jones 20,401	L4
Keokuk 12,921	J6
Kossuth 21,891	E2
Lee 43,106	L7
Linn 169,775	K4
Louisa 12,055	L6
Lucas 10,313	G6
Lyon 12,896	A2
Madison 12,597	E6
Mahaska 22,867	H6
Marion 29,669	G6
Marshall 41,652	G4
Mills 13,406	B6
Mitchell 12,329	H2
Monona 11,692	B4
Monroe 9,209	H7
Montgomery 13,413	C6
Muscatine 40,436	L5

O'Brien 16,972	B2
Osceola 8,371	B2
Page 19,063	C7
Palo Alto 12,721	D2
Plymouth 24,743	A3
Pocahontas 11,369	D3
Polk 303,170	F5
Pottawattamie 86,561	B6
Poweshiek 19,306	H5
Ringgold 6,112	E7
Sac 14,118	C4
Scott 160,022	M5
Shelby 15,043	C5
Sioux 30,813	A2
Story 72,326	G4
Tama 19,533	H4
Taylor 8,353	D7
Union 13,858	E7
Van Buren 8,626	K7
Wapello 40,241	J6
Warren 34,878	F6
Washington 20,141	K6
Wayne 8,199	G7
Webster 45,953	E4

Winnebago 13,010	F2
Winneshiek 21,876	K2
Woodbury 100,884	B4
Worth 9,075	G2
Wright 16,319	F3

CITIES and TOWNS

Zip	Name/Pop.	Key
50601	Ackley 1,900	G3
50002	Adair 883	D6
50003	Adel⊙ 2,846	E5
50830	Afton 686	E6
52530	Agency 657	J7
52201	Ainsworth 547	K6
51001	Akron 1,517	A3
50510	Albert City 818	C3
50005	Albion 739	H4
52531	Albia⊙ 4,184	H6
50006	Alden 953	G4
50511	Algona⊙ 6,289	E2
50007	Alleman 307	F5
50008	Allerton 670	G7

Zip	Name/Pop.	Key
50602	Allison⊙ 1,132	H3
51002	Alta 1,720	C3
50603	Alta Vista 314	J2
51003	Alton 986	A3
50009	Altoona 5,764	G5
51230	Alvord 246	A2
52203	Amana 300	K5
50010	Ames 45,775	F4
52205	Anamosa⊙ 4,958	L4
52030	Andrew 349	M4
50020	Anita 1,153	D6
50021	Ankeny 15,429	F5
51004	Anthon 687	B4
50604	Aplington 1,027	H3
51430	Arcadia 454	C4
50606	Arlington 498	K3
50514	Armstrong 1,013	D2
51331	Arnolds Park 1,051	C2
51431	Arthur 288	C4
†52001	Asbury 2,017	M4
51232	Ashton 441	B2
52206	Atkins 678	K4
50022	Atlantic⊙ 7,789	D6

51433 Auburn 320 ....D4
50025 Audubon⊙ 2,841 ....D5
51005 Aurelia 1,143 ....C3
50607 Aurora 248 ....K3
51521 Avoca 1,650 ....C6
51515 Ayrshire 243 ....D2
50516 Badger 653 ....E3
50026 Bagley 370 ....E5
50517 Bancroft 1,082 ....E2
50027 Barnes City 266 ....H6
52533 Batavia 525 ....J7
51006 Battle Creek 919 ....B4
50028 Baxter 951 ....G5
50029 Bayard 637 ....D5
52534 Beacon 530 ....H6
50833 Bedford⊙ 1,692 ....D7
52208 Belle Plaine 2,903 .....J5
52031 Bellevue 2,450 ....M4
50421 Belmond 2,505 ....F3
52721 Bennett 458 ....L5
50032 Berwick 600 ....G5
52722 Bettendorf 27,381 .....N5
52535 Birmingham 410 ....K7
50034 Blairsburg 288 ....F4

52209 Blairstown 695 ....J5
52536 Blakesburg 404 ....H7
51523 Blencoe 247 ....A5
50836 Blockton 280 ....D7
52537 Bloomfield⊙ 2,849 ....J7
52726 Blue Grass 1,377 .....M5
50519 Bode 406 ....E3
52620 Bonaparte 489 ....K7
50035 Bondurant 1,283 ......G5
50036 Boone⊙ 12,602 ....F4
50040 Boxholm 267 ....E4
52210 Brandon 337 ....K4
51234 Boyden 708 ....B2
51436 Breda 502 ....C4
50837 Bridgewater 233 ......D6
52540 Brighton 804 ....K6
50611 Bristow 252 ....H3
50423 Britt 2,185 ....F2
51007 Bronson 289 ....A4
52211 Brooklyn 1,509 ....J5
52728 Buffalo 1,569 ....M6
50424 Buffalo Center 1,233 ..F2
52601 Burlington⊙ 29,529 ...L7
50522 Burt 689 ....E2

AREA 56,275 sq. mi. (145,752 sq. km.)
POPULATION 2,913,808
CAPITAL Des Moines
LARGEST CITY Des Moines
HIGHEST POINT (Osceola Co.) 1670 ft.
  (509 m.)
SETTLED IN 1788
ADMITTED TO UNION December 28, 1846
POPULAR NAME Hawkeye State
STATE FLOWER Wild Rose
STATE BIRD Eastern Goldfinch

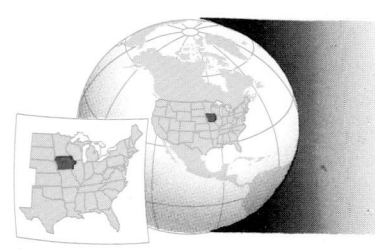

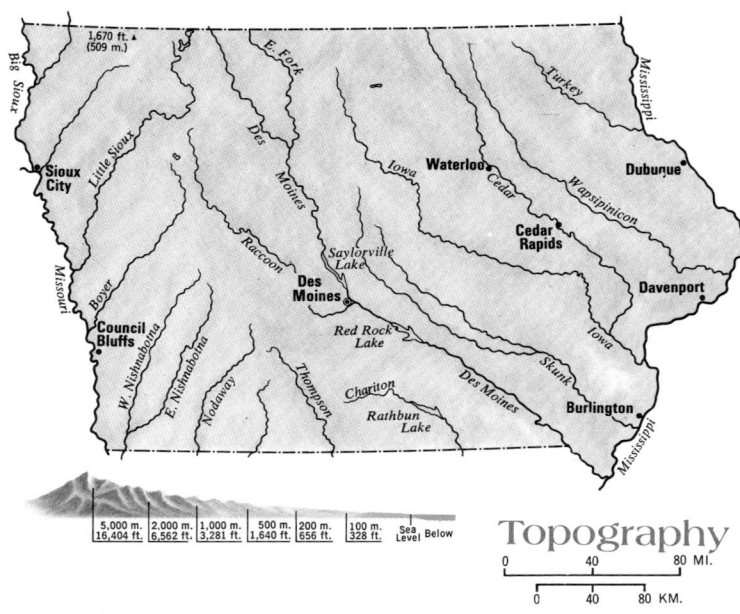

Topography

50044 Bussey 579 ....H6
52729 Calamus 452 ....M5
50523 Callender 446 ....E4
52132 Calmar 1,053 ....K2
52730 Camanche 4,725 ....N5
50046 Cambridge 732 ....G5
52542 Cantril 299 ....J7
50047 Carlisle 3,073 ....G6
51401 Carroll⊙ 9,705 ......D4
51525 Carson 716 ....C6
†68101 Carter Lake 3,438 ...B6
52033 Cascade 1,912 ....L4
50048 Casey 473 ....D5
50613 Cedar Falls 36,322 ...H3
*52401 Cedar Rapids⊙ 110,243 ..K5
  Cedar Rapids‡ 169,775 ...K5
52213 Center Point 1,591 ....K4
52544 Centerville⊙ 6,558 ...H7
52214 Central City 1,067 ....K4
50049 Chariton⊙ 4,987 .....G6
50616 Charles City⊙ 8,778 ..H2
52731 Charlotte 442 ....M5
51439 Charter Oak 615 ......C4
52215 Chelsea 376 ....J5
51012 Cherokee⊙ 7,004 .....B3
52135 Clermont 602 ....K3
52732 Clinton⊙ 32,828 .....N5
50318 Clive 6,064 ....F5
52217 Clutier 249 ....J4
52218 Coggon 639 ....L4
51636 Coin 316 ....C7
52035 Colesburg 463 ....L3
50054 Colfax 2,505 ....G5
51637 College Springs 307 ..C7
50055 Collins 481 ....G5
50056 Colo 808 ....G4
52737 Columbus City 367 ....L6
52738 Columbus Junction 1,429 ..L6
52739 Conesville 301 ....L6
50621 Conrad 1,133 ....H4
52220 Conroy 250 ....J5
50058 Coon Rapids 1,448 ....D5
52241 Coralville 7,687 .....K5
50841 Corning⊙ 1,939 .....D7
51016 Correctionville 935 ..B4
50430 Corwith 480 ....F3
50060 Corydon⊙ 1,818 .....G7
50431 Coulter 264 ....G3
51501 Council Bluffs⊙ 56,449 ..B6
52621 Crawfordsville 290 ...K6
51526 Crescent 547 ....B6
52136 Cresco⊙ 3,860 ......K2
50801 Creston⊙ 8,429 .....E6
50432 Crystal Lake 314 .....F2
50843 Cumberland 351 ......D6

51018 Cushing 270 ....B4
50529 Dakota City⊙ 1,072 ..E3
50062 Dallas 451 ....G6
50063 Dallas Center 1,360 ..E5
51019 Danbury 492 ....B4
52623 Danville 994 ....L7
*52801 Davenport⊙ 103,264 ..M5
  Davenport-Rock
  Island-Moline‡ 383,958 M5
50065 Davis City 327 ....F7
50530 Dayton 941 ....E4
52101 Decorah⊙ 7,991 .....K2
51440 Dedham 321 ....D5
52222 Deep River 323 ....J5
51527 Defiance 383 ....C5
52223 Delhi 511 ....L4
52037 Delmar 633 ....M4
51441 Deloit 345 ....C4
52550 Delta 482 ....J6
51442 Denison⊙ 6,675 .....C4
52624 Denmark 480 ....L7
50622 Denver 1,647 ....J3
*50301 Des Moines
  (cap.)⊙ 191,003 ......G5
  Des Moines‡ 338,048 ..G5
50069 De Soto 1,035 ....E5
50623 Dewar 230 ....J3
52742 De Witt 4,512 ....N5
50070 Dexter 685 ....E5
50845 Diagonal 362 ....E7
51333 Dickens 289 ....C2
50624 Dike 987 ....H4
52745 Dixon 230 ....M5
52746 Donahue 289 ....M5
52625 Donnellson 972 ....K7
51235 Doon 537 ....A2
52551 Douds 425 ....J7
51528 Dow City 616 ....B5
50071 Dows 771 ....F3
52001 Dubuque⊙ 62,321 ....M3
  Dubuque‡ 93,745 ......M3
50625 Dumont 815 ....H3
50532 Duncombe 504 ....E4
50626 Dunkerton 718 ....J3
51529 Dunlap 1,374 ....B5
52747 Durant 1,583 ....M5
52040 Dyersville 3,825 .....L3
52224 Dysart 1,355 ....J4
50533 Eagle Grove 4,324 ....F3
50072 Earlham 1,140 ....E6
51530 Earling 520 ....C5
52041 Earlville 844 ....L4
50535 Early 670 ....C4
52553 Eddyville 1,116 ......H6
52042 Edgewood 900 ....K3
52554 Eldon 1,255 ....J7
50627 Eldora⊙ 3,063 ......G4
52748 Eldridge 3,279 ....M5
52141 Elgin 702 ....K3
52043 Elkader⊙ 1,688 .....L3
50073 Elkhart 256 ....F5
51531 Elk Horn 746 ....C5
†50700 Elk Run Heights 1,186 ..J4
51532 Elliott 493 ....C6

50075 Ellsworth 480 ....F4
50628 Elma 714 ....J2
52227 Ely 425 ....K5
51533 Emerson 502 ....C6
50536 Emmetsburg⊙ 4,621 ..D2
52045 Epworth 1,380 ....M4
51638 Essex 1,001 ....C7
51334 Estherville⊙ 7,518 ..D2
50707 Evansdale 4,798 ......J4
51338 Everly 796 ....C2
50076 Exira 978 ....D5
50629 Fairbank 980 ....K3
52228 Fairfax 683 ....K5
52556 Fairfield⊙ 9,428 ....J6
52046 Farley 1,287 ....L4
52047 Farmersburg 276 ......L3
52626 Farmington 869 ....K7
50538 Farnhamville 461 .....D4
51639 Farragut 603 ....C7
52142 Fayette 1,515 ....K3
50539 Fenton 394 ....E2
50434 Fertile 372 ....G2
50435 Floyd 408 ....H2
50540 Fonda 863 ....D3
50846 Fontanelle 805 ....E6
50436 Forest City⊙ 4,270 ..F2
52144 Fort Atkinson 374 ....J2
50501 Fort Dodge⊙ 29,423 ..E4
52627 Fort Madison⊙ 13,520 ..L7
51340 Fostoria 261 ....C2
52630 Fredericksburg 1,075 ..J3
50631 Frederika 223 ....J3
52561 Fremont 730 ....H6
52749 Fruitland 461 ....L6
51020 Galva 420 ....C3
50103 Garden Grove 297 .....G7
52049 Garnavillo 723 ....L3
50438 Garner⊙ 2,908 ......F2
52229 Garrison 411 ....J4
50632 Garwin 626 ....H4
51237 George 1,241 ....B2
50105 Gilbert 805 ....F4
50634 Gilbertville 740 .....J4
50106 Gilman 642 ....H5
50541 Gilmore City 626 .....D3
50635 Gladbrook 910 ....H4
51534 Glenwood⊙ 5,280 ....B6
51443 Glidden 1,076 ....D4
50542 Goldfield 789 ....F4
52750 Goose Lake 274 ....N5
50543 Gowrie 1,089 ....E4
51342 Graettinger 923 ......D2
50440 Grafton 255 ....G2
50107 Grand Junction 970 ...E4
52751 Grand Mound 674 ......M5
52752 Grandview 473 ....L6
50109 Granger 619 ....F5
51022 Granville 336 ....B3
50848 Gravity 245 ....D7
52050 Greeley 313 ....L3
50636 Greene 1,332 ....H3
50849 Greenfield⊙ 2,243 ..D6
50111 Grimes 1,973 ....F5
50112 Grinnell 8,868 ....H5

(continued on following page)

Agriculture, Industry and Resources

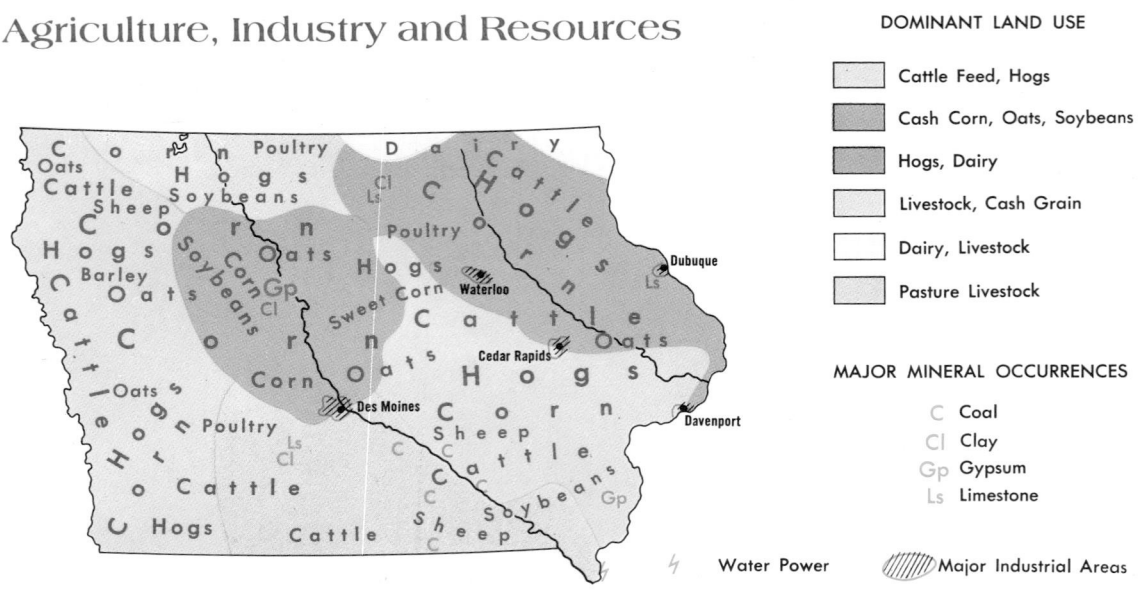

DOMINANT LAND USE

- Cattle Feed, Hogs
- Cash Corn, Oats, Soybeans
- Hogs, Dairy
- Livestock, Cash Grain
- Dairy, Livestock
- Pasture Livestock

MAJOR MINERAL OCCURRENCES

- C   Coal
- Cl   Clay
- Gp   Gypsum
- Ls   Limestone

↯ Water Power   ///// Major Industrial Areas

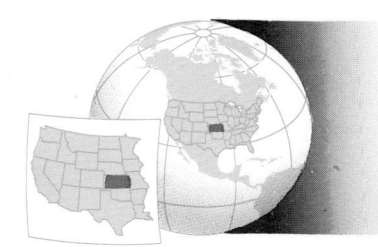

COUNTIES

Allen 15,654 ....G4
Anderson 8,749 ....G3
Atchison 18,397 ....G2
Barber 6,548 ....D4
Barton 31,343 ....D3
Bourbon 15,969 ....H4
Brown 11,955 ....G2
Butler 44,782 ....F4
Chase 3,309 ....F3
Chautauqua 5,016 ....F4
Cherokee 22,304 ....H4
Cheyenne 3,678 ....A2
Clark 2,599 ....C4
Clay 9,802 ....E2
Cloud 12,494 ....E2
Coffey 9,370 ....G3
Comanche 2,554 ....C4
Cowley 36,824 ....F4
Crawford 37,916 ....H4
Decatur 4,509 ....B2
Dickinson 20,175 ....E3
Doniphan 9,268 ....G2
Douglas 67,640 ....G3
Edwards 4,271 ....C4
Elk 3,918 ....F4
Ellis 26,098 ....C3
Ellsworth 6,640 ....D3
Finney 23,825 ....B3
Ford 24,315 ....C4
Franklin 22,062 ....G3
Geary 29,852 ....F3
Gove 3,726 ....B3
Graham 3,995 ....C2
Grant 6,977 ....A4
Gray 5,138 ....B4
Greeley 1,845 ....A3
Greenwood 8,764 ....F4
Hamilton 2,514 ....A3
Harper 7,778 ....D4
Harvey 30,531 ....E3
Haskell 3,814 ....B4
Hodgeman 2,269 ....C3
Jackson 11,644 ....G2
Jefferson 15,207 ....G2
Jewell 5,241 ....D2
Johnson 270,269 ....H3
Kearny 3,435 ....A3
Kingman 8,960 ....D4
Kiowa 4,046 ....C4
Labette 25,682 ....G4
Lane 2,472 ....B3
Leavenworth 54,809 .....G2
Lincoln 4,145 ....D2
Linn 8,234 ....H3
Logan 3,478 ....A3
Lyon 35,108 ....F3
Marion 13,522 ....E3
Marshall 12,787 ....F2
McPherson 26,855 ....E3
Meade 4,788 ....B4
Miami 21,618 ....H3
Mitchell 8,117 ....D2
Montgomery 42,281 .....G4
Morris 6,419 ....F3
Morton 3,454 ....A4
Nemaha 11,211 ....F2
Neosho 18,967 ....G4
Ness 4,498 ....C3
Norton 6,689 ....C2
Osage 15,248 ....G3
Osborne 5,959 ....D2
Ottawa 5,971 ....E2
Pawnee 8,065 ....C3
Phillips 7,406 ....C2
Pottawatomie 14,782 ....F2
Pratt 10,275 ....D4
Rawlins 4,105 ....A2
Reno 64,983 ....D4
Republic 7,569 ....E2
Rice 11,900 ....D3
Riley 63,505 ....F2
Rooks 7,006 ....C2
Rush 4,516 ....C3
Russell 8,868 ....D3
Saline 48,905 ....E3
Scott 5,782 ....B3
Sedgwick 367,088 ......E4
Seward 17,071 ....B4
Shawnee 154,916 ....G2
Sheridan 3,544 ....B2
Sherman 7,759 ....A2
Smith 5,947 ....D2
Stafford 5,694 ....D3
Stanton 2,339 ....A4
Stevens 4,736 ....A4
Sumner 24,928 ....E4
Thomas 8,451 ....A2
Trego 4,165 ....B2
Wabaunsee 6,867 ......F3
Wallace 2,045 ....A3
Washington 8,543 ......E2
Wichita 3,041 ....A3
Wilson 12,128 ....G4
Woodson 4,600 ....G4
Wyandotte 172,335 ....H2

CITIES and TOWNS

Zip Name/Pop. Key

67510 Abbyville 123 ....D4
67410 Abilene⊙ 6,572 ....E3
66830 Admire 158 ....F3
66930 Agenda 106 ....E2
67621 Agra 321 ....C2
67511 Albert 236 ....C3
67512 Alden 214 ....D3
67513 Alexander 116 ....C3
66833 Alma⊙ 214 ....F3
67401 Alma 925 ....F2
67622 Almena 517 ....C2
67330 Altamont 1,054 ....G4
66710 Altoona 564 ....G4
67623 Alton 135 ....D2
66835 Americus 915 ....F3

67001 Andale 538 ....E4
67002 Andover 2,801 ....E4
67003 Anthony⊙ 2,661 ....D4
66711 Arcadia 460 ....H4
67004 Argonia 587 ....E4
67005 Arkansas City 13,201 ..E4
67514 Arlington 631 ....D4
66712 Arma 1,676 ....H4
67831 Ashland⊙ 1,096 ......C4
67416 Assaria 414 ....E3
66002 Atchison⊙ 11,407 ....G2
66932 Athol 90 ....D2
67008 Atlanta 256 ....F4
67009 Attica 730 ....D4
67730 Atwood⊙ 1,665 ......B2
66402 Auburn 890 ....G3
67010 Augusta 6,968 ....E4
67417 Aurora 130 ....E2
66403 Axtell 470 ....F2
66404 Baileyville 130 ......F2
66006 Baldwin City 2,829 ...G3
67418 Barnard 163 ....D3
66933 Barnes 257 ....F2
67332 Bartlett 163 ....G4
66007 Basehor 1,483 ....G2
†66749 Bassett 31 ....G4
66713 Baxter Springs 4,730 ...H4
67516 Bazine 385 ....C3
66406 Beattie 316 ....F2
67013 Belle Plaine 1,706 ...E4
66935 Belleville⊙ 2,805 ....E2
67420 Beloit⊙ 4,367 ....D2
67519 Belpre 154 ....C4
66407 Belvue 212 ....F2
66714 Benedict 111 ....G4
67422 Bennington 579 .....E2
67016 Bentley 311 ....E4
67017 Benton 609 ....E4
66408 Bern 220 ....F2
67423 Beverly 171 ....E2
67731 Bird City 546 ......A2
67520 Bison 279 ....C3
66010 Blue Mound 319 ....H3
66411 Blue Rapids 1,280 ..F2
67018 Bluff City 95 ......E4
67625 Bogue 197 ....C2
66012 Bonner Springs 6,266 ..H2
67732 Brewster 327 ......A2
66716 Bronson 414 ......H4
67425 Brookville 259 ....E3
67521 Brownell 92 ......C3
67834 Bucklin 786 ......C4
66717 Buffalo 386 ......G4
67522 Buhler 1,188 .....E3
67626 Bunker Hill 124 ...D3
67019 Burden 518 ......F4
67523 Burdett 275 .....C3
66413 Burlingame 1,239 ..G3
66839 Burlington⊙ 2,901 ..G3
66840 Burns 224 ....F3
66936 Burr Oak 366 ....D2
67020 Burrton 976 .....E3
66841 Bushong 62 ......F3
67427 Bushton 388 .....D3
67021 Byers 47 ....D4
67022 Caldwell 1,401 ...E4
67023 Cambridge 113 ...F4
67333 Caney 2,284 .....G4
67428 Canton 926 .....E3
66414 Carbondale 1,518 ..G3
67429 Carlton 49 ......E3
66842 Cassoday 122 ...F3
67430 Cawker City 640 ..D2
67628 Cedar 53 ....D2
66843 Cedar Point 66 ..F3
67024 Cedar Vale 848 ..F4
66415 Centralia 486 ...F2
66720 Chanute 10,506 ..G4
67431 Chapman 1,255 ..E3
67524 Chase 753 .....D3
67334 Chautauqua 156 ..F4
67025 Cheney 1,404 ...E4
66724 Cherokee 775 ...H4
67335 Cherryvale 2,769 ..G4
67336 Chetopa 1,751 ..G4
67835 Cimarron⊙ 1,491 ..B4
66416 Circleville 164 ...G2
67525 Claflin 764 .....D3
67432 Clay Center⊙ 4,948 ..E2
67629 Clayton 102 ....B2
67026 Clearwater 1,684 ..E4
66937 Clifton 695 .....E2
67027 Climax 81 ......F4
66938 Clyde 909 .....E2
67028 Coats 153 .....D4
67337 Coffeyville 15,185 ..G4
67701 Colby⊙ 5,544 ...A2
67029 Coldwater⊙ 989 ..C4
67631 Collyer 151 ....B2
66015 Colony 474 ....G3
66725 Columbus⊙ 3,426 ..H4
67030 Colwich 935 ...E4
66901 Concordia⊙ 6,847 ..E2
67031 Conway Springs 1,313 ..E4
67836 Coolidge 82 ...A3
67837 Copeland 323 ..B4
66417 Corning 158 ...F2
67838 Cottonwood Falls⊙ 954 ..F3
66846 Council Grove⊙ 2,381 ..F3
66939 Courtland 377 ..E2
66727 Coyville 98 ....G4
66940 Cuba 286 .....E2
†67134 Cullison 154 ..D4
67435 Culver 167 ....E3
67035 Cunningham 540 ..D4
67632 Damar 204 ....C2
67036 Danville 71 ....E4
67340 Dearing 475 ...G4
67838 Deerfield 538 ..A4
66418 Delia 181 .....G2
67436 Delphos 570 ...E2
66419 Denison 156 ...G2
66017 Denton 156 ....G2
67037 Derby 9,786 ...E4
66018 De Soto 2,061 ..H3
67038 Dexter 366 ....F4
67839 Dighton⊙ 1,390 ..B3

67801 Dodge City⊙ 18,001 ..B4
67634 Dorrance 220 ....D3
67039 Douglass 1,450 ....F4
67437 Downs 1,324 ....D2
67635 Dresden 84 ....B2
66848 Dunlap 82 ....F3
67438 Durham 130 ....E3
66849 Dwight 320 ....F3
†66720 Earlton 79 ....G4
†67201 Eastborough 854 ...E4
66020 Easton 460 ....G2
66021 Edgerton 1,214 .....H3
67636 Edmond 56 ....C2
67342 Edna 537 ....G4
66113 Edwardsville 3,364 ..H2
66023 Effingham 634 ....G2
67041 Elbing 195 ....E3
67042 El Dorado⊙ 10,510 ..F4
†67361 Elgin 139 ....F4
67344 Elk City 404 ....G4
67345 Elk Falls 151 ......F4
67950 Elkhart⊙ 2,243 .....A4
67526 Ellinwood 2,508 ....D3
67637 Ellis 2,062 ....C3
67439 Ellsworth⊙ 2,465 ..D3
66850 Elmdale 109 ....F3

67732 Elsmore 104 ....G4
66024 Elwood 1,275 ....H2
66422 Emmett 223 ....F2
66801 Emporia⊙ 25,287 ....F3
67840 Englewood 111 ....C4
67841 Ensign 209 ....B4
67441 Enterprise 839 ......E3
66733 Erie⊙ 1,415 ....G4
66941 Esbon 234 ....D2
66423 Eskridge 603 ....F3
66025 Eudora 2,934 ....G3
67045 Eureka⊙ 3,425 ......F4
66424 Everest 331 ....G2
66425 Fairview 258 ....G2
†66101 Fairway 4,619 ......H2
67047 Fall River 173 ......G4
66851 Florence 729 ....E3
66026 Fontana 173 ....H3
67842 Ford 272 ....C4
66942 Formoso 166 ....D2
67843 Fort Dodge 400 .....C4
66027 Fort Leavenworth ...H2
66701 Fort Scott⊙ 8,893 ...H4
67844 Fowler 592 ....B4
66427 Frankfort 1,038 .....F2
66735 Franklin 400 ....H4

66736 Fredonia⊙ 3,047 ......G4
67049 Freeport 12 ....E4
66762 Frontenac 2,586 .....H4
66738 Fulton 194 ....H4
66739 Galena 3,587 ....H4
66740 Galesburg 181 ....G4
67443 Galva 651 ....E3
67846 Garden City⊙ 18,256 ..B4
67050 Garden Plain 775 ....E4
66030 Gardner 2,392 ....H3
67529 Garfield 277 ....C3
66032 Garnett⊙ 3,310 .....G3
66742 Gas 543 ....G4
67638 Gaylord 203 ....D2
66734 Gem 101 ....A2
67444 Geneseo 496 ....D3
67051 Geuda Springs 217 ..E4
66743 Girard⊙ 2,888 ......H4
67639 Glade 131 ....C2
67445 Glasco 710 ....E2
66446 Glen Elder 491 .....D2
67052 Goddard 1,427 .....E4
67053 Goessel 421 ....E3
66428 Goff 196 ....G2
67735 Goodland⊙ 5,708 ..A2
67640 Gorham 355 ......D3

67736 Gove⊙ 148 ....B3
67737 Grainfield 417 ....B2
†66441 Grandview Plaza 1,189 ..F2
66429 Grantville 220 ....G2
67530 Great Bend⊙ 16,608 ..D3
66033 Greeley 405 ....G3
67447 Green 155 ....E2
66943 Greenleaf 462 ....E2
67054 Greensburg⊙ 1,885 ..C4
67346 Grenola 335 ....F4
66852 Gridley 404 ....G3
67738 Grinnell 410 ....B2
67448 Gypsum 423 ....E3
66944 Haddam 239 ....E2
67056 Halstead 1,994 ......E4
67543 Hamilton 363 ....F4
66945 Hanover 802 ....F2
67849 Hanston 257 ....C3
67057 Hardtner 336 ....D4
67058 Harper 1,823 ....D4
66854 Hartford 551 ....F3
66431 Harveyville 280 ....F3
67347 Havana 169 ....G4
67543 Haven 1,125 ....E4
66432 Havensville 183 ....F2
67059 Haviland 770 ......C4

(continued on following page)

AREA 82,277 sq. mi. (213,097 sq. km.)
POPULATION 2,364,236
CAPITAL Topeka
LARGEST CITY Wichita
HIGHEST POINT Mt. Sunflower 4,039 ft. (1231 m.)
SETTLED IN 1831
ADMITTED TO UNION January 29, 1861
POPULAR NAME Sunflower State
STATE FLOWER Sunflower
STATE BIRD Western Meadowlark

Agriculture, Industry and Resources

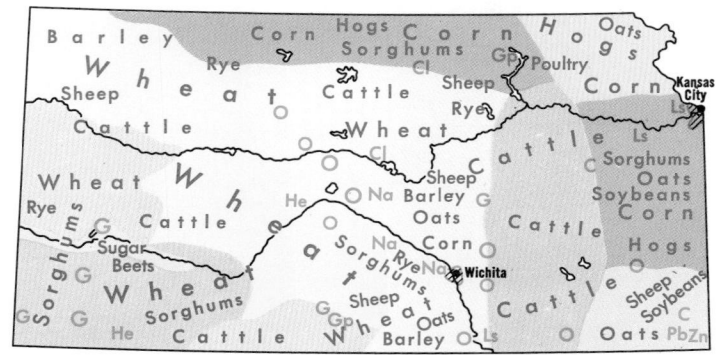

DOMINANT LAND USE

- Specialized Wheat
- Wheat, General Farming
- Wheat, Range Livestock
- Wheat, Grain Sorghums, Range Livestock
- Cattle Feed, Hogs
- Livestock, Cash Grain
- Livestock, Cash Grain, Dairy
- General Farming, Livestock, Cash Grain
- General Farming, Livestock, Special Crops
- Range Livestock

MAJOR MINERAL OCCURRENCES

C	Coal	Ls	Limestone
Cl	Clay	Na	Salt
G	Natural Gas	O	Petroleum
Gp	Gypsum	Pb	Lead
He	Helium	Zn	Zinc

⨈ Major Industrial Areas

67601 Hays⊙ 16,301 ....C3	67545 Hudson 157 ....D3	66039 Kincaid 192 ....G3	67073 Lehigh 189 ....E3	66053 Louisburg 1,744 ....H3	67745 McDonald 239 ....A2
67060 Haysville 8,006 ....E4	67951 Hugoton⊙ 3,165 ....A4	67068 Kingman⊙ 3,563 ....D4	66215 Lenexa 18,639 ....H2	66450 Louisville 207 ....F2	66501 McFarland 242 ....F2
67850 Healy 275 ....B3	67547 Kinsley⊙ 2,074 ....C4	67547 Kinsley⊙ 2,074 ....C4	67645 Lenora 444 ....C2	67648 Lucas 524 ....D2	66054 McLouth 700 ....G2
67061 Hazelton 143 ....D4	66748 Humboldt 2,230 ....G4	67070 Kiowa 1,409 ....D4	67074 Leon 667 ....F4	67649 Luray 295 ....D2	67460 McPherson⊙ 11,753 ....E3
67746 Hepler 165 ....H4	67452 Hunter 135 ....D2	67644 Kirwin 249 ....C2	66648 Leon 73 ....D4	67554 Lyons⊙ 4,134 ....D3	67864 Meade⊙ 1,777 ....B4
67449 Herington 2,930 ....E3	66038 Huron 107 ....G2	67859 Kismet 368 ....B4	66449 Leonardville 437 ....F2	67557 Macksville 546 ....C3	67104 Medicine Lodge⊙ 2,384 ....D4
67739 Herndon 220 ....B2	67501 Hutchinson⊙ 40,284 ....D3	67350 Labette 123 ....G4	67861 Leoti⊙ 1,869 ....A3	66860 Madison 1,099 ....F3	66510 Melvern 481 ....F3
67062 Hesston 3,013 ....E3	67301 Independence⊙ 10,598 ....G4	67548 La Crosse⊙ 1,618 ....C3	66857 Le Roy 701 ....G3	66955 Mahaska 287 ....E2	67746 Menlo 42 ....B2
66434 Hiawatha⊙ 3,702 ....G2	67853 Ingalls 274 ....B4	66040 La Cygne 1,025 ....H3	67552 Lewis 551 ....C4	67101 Maize 1,294 ....E4	66512 Meriden 707 ....G2
66035 Highland 954 ....G2	67546 Inman 947 ....E3	67860 Lakin 1,823 ....A4	67351 Liberty 174 ....G4	67463 Manchester 98 ....E2	66203 Merriam 10,794 ....H3
67642 Hill City⊙ 2,028 ....C2	66749 Iola⊙ 6,938 ....G3	67066 Iuka 235 ....D4	67901 Liberal⊙ 14,911 ....B4	66502 Manhattan⊙ 32,644 ....F2	67105 Milan 135 ....E4
67063 Hillsboro 2,717 ....E3	67065 Isabel 137 ....D4	66042 Lancaster 274 ....G2	67553 Liebenthal 163 ....C3	66956 Mankato⊙ 1,205 ....D2	66055 Mildred 64 ....G3
67544 Hoisington 3,678 ....D3	67066 Iuka 235 ....D4	66042 Lansing 5,307 ....H2	67455 Lincoln⊙ 1,599 ....E2	67862 Manter 205 ....A4	66514 Milford 465 ....F2
67851 Holcomb 816 ....B3	66948 Jamestown 440 ....E2	67549 Langdon 84 ....D4	66858 Lincolnville 235 ....F3	66507 Maple Hill 381 ....F2	67466 Miltonvale 588 ....E2
66946 Hollenberg 57 ....F2	67643 Jennings 194 ....B2	67643 Jennings 194 ....B2	67456 Lindsborg 3,155 ....E3	67754 Mapleton 121 ....H3	67467 Minneapolis⊙ 2,075 ....E2
67450 Holyrood 567 ....D3	67854 Jetmore⊙ 862 ....B3	66043 Lansing 5,307 ....H2	66953 Linn 483 ....E2	66861 Marion⊙ 1,951 ....F3	67865 Mineola 712 ....C4
67451 Hope 468 ....E3	66949 Jewell 589 ....E2	67072 Latham 148 ....F4	66052 Linwood 343 ....G2	67464 Marquette 639 ....E3	66205 Mission 8,643 ....H2
†67880 Horace 137 ....A3	67855 Johnson⊙ 1,244 ....A4	66044 Lawrence⊙ 52,738 ....G2	67457 Little River 529 ....E3	66508 Marysville⊙ 3,670 ....F2	67353 Moline 553 ....F4
66439 Horton 2,130 ....G2	66441 Junction City⊙ 19,305 ....F2	Lawrence‡ 67,640 ....G2	66458 Longford 109 ....E2	66862 Matfield Green 71 ....F3	67867 Montezuma 730 ....B4
67349 Howard⊙ 965 ....F4	67454 Kanopolis 729 ....D3	66048 Leavenworth⊙ 33,656 ....H2	67458 Long Island 187 ....C2	66509 Mayetta 287 ....G2	66755 Moran 643 ....G4
67740 Hoxie⊙ 1,462 ....B2	67453 Kanorado 217 ....A2	66206 Leawood 13,360 ....H3	67647 Long Island 187 ....C2	67103 Mayfield 128 ....E4	67468 Morganville 261 ....E2
*66101 Kansas City⊙ 161,148 ....H2	*66101 Kansas City⊙ 161,148 ....H2	66952 Lebanon 440 ....D2	67352 Longton 396 ....F4	67556 McCracken 292 ....C3	67650 Morland 223 ....B2
66440 Hoyt 536 ....G2	Kansas City‡ 1,327,020 ....H2	66856 Lebo 966 ....G3	67459 Lorraine 157 ....D3	66753 McCune 528 ....G4	66515 Morrill 336 ....G2
67067 Kechi 288 ....E4	66951 Kensington 681 ....C2	66050 Lecompton 576 ....G2	66859 Lost Springs 94 ....E3		66958 Morrowville 180 ....E2

Kansas

SCALE
0 5 10   20   30   40   50 MI.
0 5 10   20   30   40   50 KM.

⊛ State Capitals
⊙ County Seats
Major Limited Access Hwys.
Scale 1:2,250,000

© Copyright HAMMOND INCORPORATED, Maplewood, N.J.

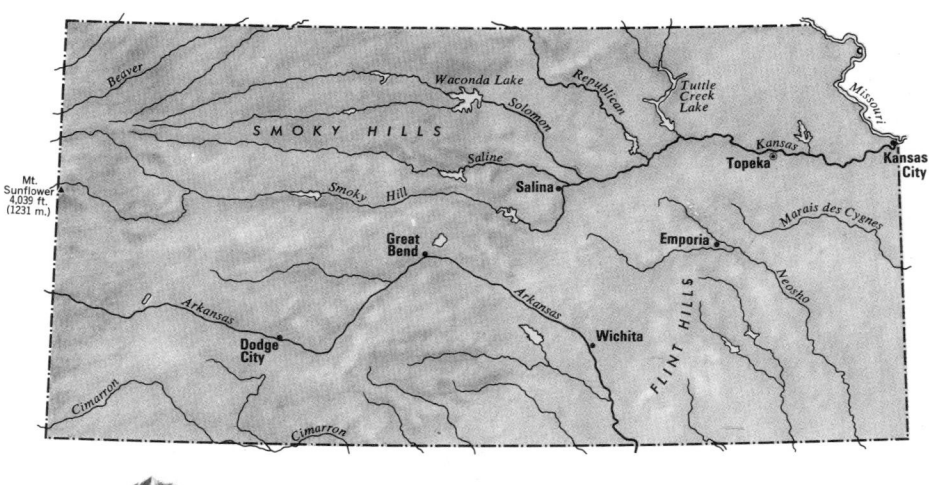

Topography

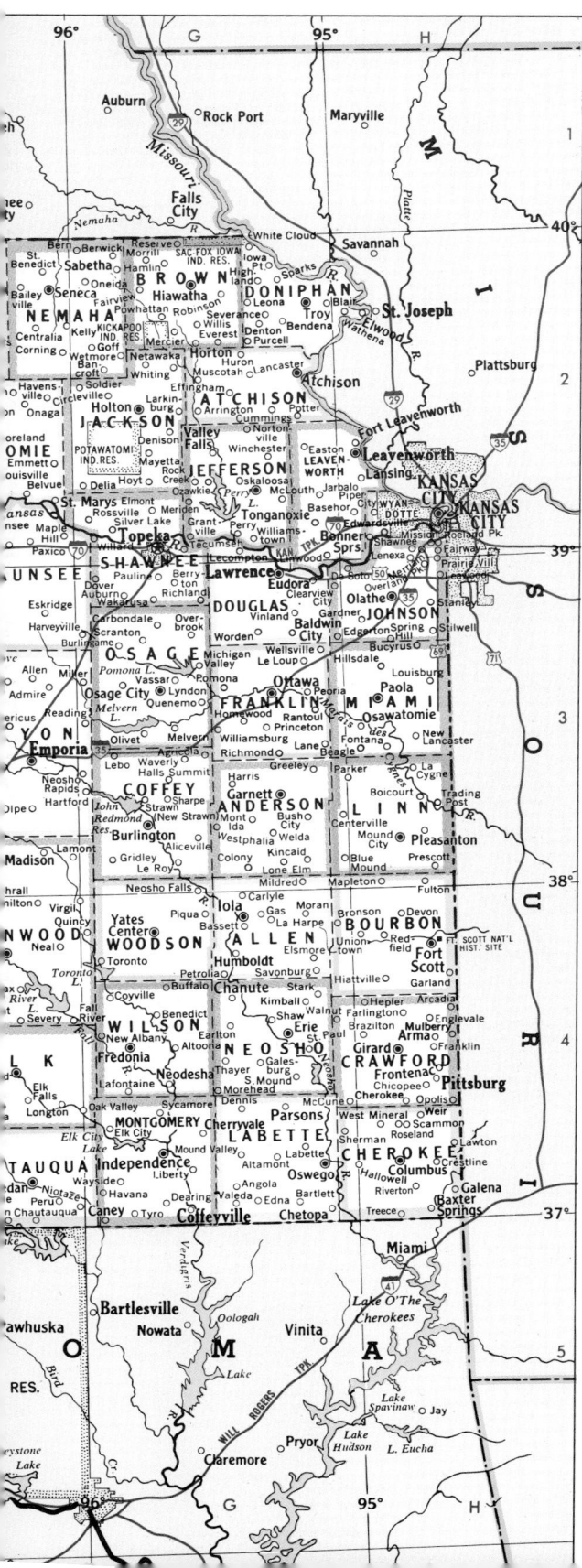

KENTUCKY

COUNTIES

Adair 15,233 .... L6
Allen 14,128 .... J7
Anderson 12,567 .... M5
Ballard 8,798 .... C6
Barren 34,009 .... K7
Bath 10,025 .... O4
Bell 34,330 .... O7
Boone 45,842 .... M3
Bourbon 19,405 .... N4
Boyd 55,513 .... R4
Boyle 25,066 .... M5
Bracken 7,738 .... N3
Breathitt 17,004 .... P5
Breckinridge 16,861 .... H5
Bullitt 43,346 .... K5
Butler 11,064 .... H6
Caldwell 13,473 .... F6
Calloway 30,031 .... E7
Campbell 83,317 .... N3
Carlisle 5,487 .... C7
Carroll 9,270 .... L3
Carter 25,060 .... P4
Casey 14,818 .... M6
Christian 66,878 .... F7
Clark 28,322 .... N4
Clay 22,752 .... O6
Clinton 9,321 .... L7
Crittenden 9,207 .... E6
Cumberland 7,289 .... L7
Daviess 85,949 .... G5
Edmonson 9,962 .... J6
Elliott 6,908 .... P4
Estill 14,495 .... O5
Fayette 204,165 .... N4
Fleming 12,323 .... O4
Floyd 48,764 .... R5
Franklin 41,830 .... M4
Fulton 8,971 .... C7
Gallatin 4,842 .... M3
Garrard 10,853 .... M5
Grant 13,308 .... M3
Graves 34,049 .... D7
Grayson 20,854 .... J5
Green 11,043 .... K6
Greenup 39,132 .... R3
Hancock 7,742 .... H5
Hardin 88,917 .... K5
Harlan 41,889 .... P7
Harrison 15,166 .... N4
Hart 15,402 .... K6
Henderson 40,849 .... F5
Henry 12,740 .... L4
Hickman 6,065 .... C7
Hopkins 46,174 .... F6
Jackson 11,996 .... N6
Jefferson 684,565 .... K4
Jessamine 26,065 .... M5
Johnson 24,432 .... R5
Kenton 137,058 .... M3
Knott 17,940 .... R6
Knox 30,239 .... O7
Larue 11,922 .... K5
Laurel 38,982 .... N6
Lawrence 14,121 .... R4
Lee 7,754 .... O5
Leslie 14,882 .... P6
Letcher 30,687 .... R6
Lewis 14,545 .... P3
Lincoln 19,053 .... M6
Livingston 9,219 .... E6
Logan 24,138 .... H7
Lyon 6,490 .... E6
Madison 53,352 .... N5
Magoffin 13,515 .... P5
Marion 17,910 .... L5
Marshall 25,637 .... E7
Martin 13,925 .... R5
Mason 17,765 .... O3
McCracken 61,310 .... D6
McCreary 15,634 .... N7
McLean 10,090 .... G5
Meade 22,854 .... J5
Menifee 5,117 .... O5
Mercer 19,011 .... M5
Metcalfe 9,484 .... K7
Monroe 12,353 .... K7
Montgomery 20,046 .... O4
Morgan 12,103 .... P5
Muhlenberg 32,238 .... G6
Nelson 27,584 .... K5
Nicholas 7,157 .... N4
Ohio 21,765 .... H6
Oldham 27,795 .... L4
Owen 8,924 .... M3
Owsley 5,709 .... O6
Pendleton 10,989 .... N3
Perry 33,763 .... P6
Pike 81,123 .... S6
Powell 11,101 .... O5
Pulaski 45,803 .... M6
Robertson 2,265 .... N3
Rockcastle 13,973 .... N6
Rowan 19,049 .... P4
Russell 13,708 .... L7
Scott 21,813 .... M4
Shelby 23,328 .... L4
Simpson 14,673 .... H7
Spencer 5,929 .... L4
Taylor 21,178 .... L6
Todd 11,874 .... G7
Trigg 9,384 .... F7
Trimble 6,253 .... L3
Union 17,821 .... F5
Warren 71,828 .... H6
Washington 10,764 .... L5
Wayne 17,022 .... M7
Webster 14,832 .... F5
Whitley 33,396 .... N7
Wolfe 6,698 .... O5
Woodford 17,778 .... M4

CITIES and TOWNS

Zip *Name/Pop.* *Key*

42202 Adairville 1,105 .... H7
42602 Albany⊙ 2,083 .... L7
41001 Alexandria⊙ 4,735 .... N3
41601 Allen 338 .... R5
42204 Allensville 170 .... G7
40223 Anchorage 1,726 .... L2
41101 Ashland 27,064 .... R4
Ashland-Huntington‡ 311,350 .... R4
42206 Auburn 1,467 .... H7
†40201 Audubon Park 1,571 .... J2
41002 Augusta 1,455 .... N3
41602 Auxier 900 .... R5
†40222 Bancroft 725 .... K1
41603 Banner 950 .... R5
†40201 Barbourmeade 1,038 .... K1
40906 Barbourville⊙ 3,333 .... O7
40004 Bardstown⊙ 6,155 .... L5
42023 Bardwell⊙ 988 .... D7
42024 Barlow 746 .... D6
41311 Beattyville⊙ 1,068 .... O5
42320 Beaver Dam 3,185 .... H6
40006 Bedford⊙ 835 .... L3
40359 Beechwood Village 1,462 .... K2
†40201 Bellemeade 918 .... L2
41073 Bellevue 7,678 .... S1
40807 Benham 936 .... R7
42025 Benton⊙ 3,700 .... E7
40403 Berea 8,226 .... N5
41003 Berry 287 .... N3
41605 Betsy Layne 975 .... R5
41124 Blaine 358 .... R4
40008 Bloomfield 954 .... L5
†40201 Blue Ridge Manor 465 .... L2
42713 Bonnieville 372 .... K6
†40403 Boone 300 .... N5
41314 Booneville⊙ 191 .... O6
42101 Bowling Green⊙ 40,450 .... H7
40009 Bradfordsville 331 .... L6
40108 Brandenburg⊙ 1,831 .... J4
†42025 Briensburg E7
†40201 Broadfields 311 .... K2
40409 Brodhead 686 .... N6
†41016 Bromley 844 .... S2
40109 Brooks 1,344 .... K4
41004 Brooksville⊙ 680 .... N3
†40201 Brownsboro Farm 790 .... L1
42210 Brownsville⊙ 674 .... J6
40218 Buechel 6,709 .... K2
40310 Burgin 1,008 .... M5
42717 Burkesville⊙ 2,051 .... L7
41005 Burlington⊙ 500 .... R2
42519 Burnside 775 .... M6
41006 Butler 663 .... N3
42211 Cadiz⊙ 1,661 .... F7
42327 Calhoun⊙ 1,080 .... G5
41007 California 135 .... N3
42029 Calvert City 2,388 .... E6
†40337 Camargo 1,301 .... K4
40011 Campbellsburg 714 .... L3
42718 Campbellsville⊙ 8,715 .... L6
41301 Campton⊙ 486 .... O5
42721 Caneyville 642 .... J6
40311 Carlisle⊙ 1,757 .... N4
41008 Carrollton⊙ 3,967 .... L3
42030 Carrsville 99 .... E6
†42459 Caseyville 43 .... E5
41129 Catlettsburg⊙ 3,005 .... R4
42127 Cave City 2,098 .... K6
†41522 Cedarville 81 .... S6
42328 Centertown 462 .... G6
42330 Central City 5,214 .... G6
42726 Clarkson 666 .... J6
42404 Clay 1,356 .... F6
40312 Clay City 1,276 .... O5
40313 Clearfield 1,250 .... P4
42031 Clinton⊙ 1,720 .... D7
40111 Cloverport 1,585 .... H5
†41501 Coal Run 348 .... R5
41076 Cold Spring 2,117 .... T2
42728 Columbia⊙ 3,710 .... L6
42032 Columbus 296 .... C7
41729 Combs 900 .... P6
41131 Concord 67 .... P3
40701 Corbin 8,075 .... N7
41010 Corinth 258 .... M3
42406 Corydon 874 .... F5
*41011 Covington 49,563 .... S2
40419 Crab Orchard 843 .... M6
†41016 Crescent Springs 1,951 .... R2
†41076 Crestview 528 .... S2
†41017 Crestview Hills 1,408 .... R2
40014 Crestwood 531 .... L4
41030 Crittenden 597 .... M3
42217 Crofton 823 .... G6
40823 Cumberland 3,712 .... R6
41031 Cynthiana⊙ 5,881 .... N4
40422 Danville⊙ 12,942 .... M5
42408 Dawson Springs 3,275 .... F6
41074 Dayton 6,979 .... T1
†40201 Devondale 1,164 .... K2
42036 Dexter E7
42409 Dixon⊙ 533 .... F5
†40243 Douglass Hills 4,384 .... L2
41034 Dover 305 .... O3
42337 Drakesboro 798 .... H6
41035 Dry Ridge 1,250 .... M3
42037 Dycusburg 64 .... E6
42410 Earlington 2,011 .... F6
42038 Eddyville⊙ 1,949 .... E6
†41017 Edgewood 7,230 .... S2
42129 Edmonton⊙ 1,401 .... K7
40117 Ekron 239 .... J5
42701 Elizabethtown⊙ 15,380 .... K5
41522 Elkhorn City 1,446 .... S6
42220 Elkton⊙ 1,815 .... G7
†41018 Elsmere 7,203 .... R2
40019 Eminence 2,260 .... L4
40826 Eolia 875 .... R6
41018 Erlanger 14,433 .... R2
40827 Essie 650 .... P6
42567 Eubank 207 .... M6
40828 Evarts 1,234 .... P7
41039 Ewing 144 .... O4
40118 Fairdale 7,315 .... K4
40020 Fairfield 169 .... L5
†41101 Fairview 198 .... S2
41040 Falmouth⊙ 2,482 .... N3
41524 Fedscreek 950 .... S6
42533 Ferguson 1,009 .... M6
†40222 Fincastle 804 .... L1
41139 Flatwoods 8,354 .... R4
41816 Fleming-Neon 1,195 .... R6
41041 Flemingsburg⊙ 2,835 .... O4
41042 Florence 15,586 .... R2
42343 Fordsville 561 .... H5
41527 Forest Hills 502 .... L2
40121 Fort Knox 31,055 .... K5
41017 Fort Mitchell 7,297 .... S2
41075 Fort Thomas 16,012 .... S2
†41011 Fort Wright 4,481 .... S2
41043 Foster 80 .... N3
42133 Fountain Run 340 .... K7
40601 Frankfort (cap.)⊙ 25,973 .... M4
42134 Franklin⊙ 7,738 .... J7
42411 Fredonia 535 .... E6
40322 Frenchburg⊙ 550 .... O5
†41175 Fullerton 950 .... P3
42041 Fulton 3,137 .... D7
42140 Gamaliel 456 .... K7
40324 Georgetown⊙ 10,972 .... M4
41044 Germantown 347 .... O3
41045 Ghent 439 .... L3
42044 Gilbertsville E7
42141 Glasgow⊙ 12,958 .... J7
41046 Glencoe 354 .... M3
†40222 Glenview 212 .... K1
†40222 Goose Creek 394 .... L1
42045 Grand Rivers 428 .... E7
†41005 Grant 150 .... M3
40327 Gratz 124 .... M4
†40201 Graymoor 1,167 .... K1
41143 Grayson⊙ 3,423 .... R4
42743 Greensburg⊙ 2,377 .... K6
41144 Greenup⊙ 1,386 .... R3
42345 Greenville⊙ 4,631 .... G6
42234 Guthrie 1,361 .... G7
42413 Hanson 485 .... G6
42048 Hardin 545 .... E7
40143 Hardinsburg⊙ 2,211 .... H5
41531 Hardy 900 .... S5
40831 Harlan⊙ 3,024 .... P7
40330 Harrodsburg⊙ 7,265 .... M5
42347 Hartford⊙ 2,512 .... H6
42348 Hawesville⊙ 1,036 .... H5
41701 Hazard⊙ 5,371 .... P6
42049 Hazel 465 .... E7
40949 Heidrick 400 .... O7
42420 Henderson⊙ 24,834 .... F5
42050 Hickman⊙ 2,894 .... C7
42051 Hickory D7
41076 Highland Heights 4,435 .... T2
41822 Hindman⊙ 876 .... R6
42152 Hiseville 349 .... K6
42748 Hodgenville⊙ 2,531 .... K5
†40228 Hollow Creek 1,023 .... K4
†41018 Hopeful Heights R2
42240 Hopkinsville⊙ 27,318 .... F7
42749 Horse Cave 2,045 .... K6
†40201 Houston Acres 608 .... K2
40437 Hustonville 339 .... M6
41749 Hyden⊙ 488 .... P6
41051 Independence⊙ 7,998 .... M3
†40201 Indian Hills 787 .... K1
41224 Inez⊙ 413 .... S5
40336 Irvine⊙ 2,889 .... O5
40146 Irvington 1,409 .... J5
42350 Island 532 .... G6
41642 Ivel 850 .... R5
41339 Jackson⊙ 2,651 .... P5
42629 Jamestown⊙ 1,441 .... L7
40299 Jeffersontown 15,795 .... L2
40337 Jeffersonville 1,528 .... O5
41537 Jenkins 3,271 .... R6
40440 Junction City 2,045 .... M5
40737 Keavy 900 .... N6
†41011 Kenton Vale 145 .... S2
42053 Kevil 382 .... D6
†40201 Kingsley 464 .... K2
42055 Kuttawa 560 .... E6
42056 La Center 1,044 .... C6
41643 Lackey R6
42254 La Fayette 160 .... F7
40031 La Grange⊙ 2,971 .... L4
†41017 Lakeside Park 3,038 .... R2
40444 Lancaster⊙ 3,365 .... M5
40342 Lawrenceburg⊙ 5,167 .... M4
40033 Lebanon⊙ 6,590 .... L5
40150 Lebanon Junction 1,581 .... K5
42754 Leitchfield⊙ 4,533 .... J6
42256 Lewisburg 972 .... G6
42351 Lewisport 1,832 .... H5
*40501 Lexington⊙ 204,165 .... N4
Lexington‡ 318,136 .... N4
42539 Liberty⊙ 2,206 .... M6
42352 Livermore 1,672 .... G5
40445 Livingston 334 .... N6
40036 Lockport 84 .... M4
40741 London⊙ 4,002 .... N6
42001 Lone Oak 443 .... D6
40037 Loretto 954 .... L5
41230 Louisa⊙ 1,832 .... R4
*40201 Louisville⊙ 298,840 .... J2
Louisville‡ 906,240 .... J2
40854 Loyall 1,210 .... P7
41016 Ludlow 4,959 .... S2
40855 Lynch 1,614 .... R7
†40201 Lynnview 1,157 .... K4
40040 Mackville 229 .... L5
42431 Madisonville⊙ 16,979 .... F6
40962 Manchester⊙ 1,838 .... O6
42064 Marion⊙ 3,392 .... E6
41649 Martin 827 .... R5
42066 Mayfield⊙ 10,705 .... D7
41056 Maysville⊙ 7,983 .... O3
41543 McAndrews 975 .... S5
42354 McHenry 582 .... H6
40447 McKee⊙ 759 .... O6
41835 McRoberts 1,106 .... R6
†40201 Meadow Vale 1,008 .... L1
41059 Melbourne 628 .... T2
†41060 Mentor 169 .... N3
40965 Middlesboro 12,251 .... O7
40243 Middletown 414 .... L2
40347 Midway 1,445 .... M4
40348 Millersburg 987 .... N4
40045 Milton 718 .... L3
†40201 Minor Lane Heights 1,882 .... K4
†40359 Monterey 186 .... M4
42633 Monticello⊙ 5,677 .... M7
†40223 Moorland 513 .... L2
40351 Morehead⊙ 7,789 .... P4
42437 Morganfield⊙ 3,781 .... E5
42261 Morgantown⊙ 2,000 .... H6
42440 Mortons Gap 1,201 .... F6
41064 Mount Olivet⊙ 346 .... N3
†40437 Mount Salem 50 .... M6
40353 Mount Sterling⊙ 5,820 .... N4
40456 Mount Vernon⊙ 2,334 .... N6
40047 Mount Washington 3,997 .... K4
41548 Mouthcard 900 .... S6
40155 Muldraugh 1,752 .... J5
42765 Munfordville⊙ 1,783 .... J6
42071 Murray⊙ 14,248 .... E7
42441 Nebo 269 .... F6
41840 Neon-Fleming 1,195 .... R6
40050 New Castle⊙ 832 .... L4
40051 New Haven 926 .... K5
*41071 Newport 21,587 .... S2
40356 Nicholasville⊙ 10,319 .... N5
†40201 Northfield 906 .... K1
40357 North Middletown 637 .... N4
42442 Nortonville 1,336 .... G6
42262 Oak Grove 2,088 .... G7
42159 Oakland 264 .... J6
41238 Oil Springs 900 .... P5
40219 Okolona 20,039 .... K4
41164 Olive Hill 2,539 .... P4
42301 Owensboro⊙ 54,450 .... G5
Owensboro‡ 85,949 .... G5
40359 Owenton⊙ 1,341 .... M3
40360 Owingsville⊙ 1,419 .... O4
42001 Paducah⊙ 29,315 .... D6
41240 Paintsville⊙ 3,815 .... R5
40361 Paris⊙ 7,935 .... N4
42160 Park City 614 .... J6
†41011 Park Hills 3,500 .... S2
†40201 Parkway Village 754 .... J2
42266 Pembroke 636 .... G7
40468 Perryville 841 .... M5
40056 Pewee Valley 982 .... L4
41553 Phelps 1,126 .... S6
41501 Pikeville⊙ 4,756 .... S6
42635 Pine Knot 1,389 .... M7
40977 Pineville⊙ 2,599 .... O7
†40201 Plantation 969 .... K1
40258 Pleasure Ridge Park 27,332 .... J4
40057 Pleasureville 837 .... L4
†42101 Plum Springs 393 .... J7
42367 Powderly 848 .... G6
41653 Prestonsburg⊙ 4,011 .... R5
†41008 Prestonville 205 .... L3
42445 Princeton⊙ 7,073 .... F6
40059 Prospect 1,981 .... K4
42450 Providence 4,434 .... F6
41169 Raceland 1,970 .... R3
40160 Radcliff 14,519 .... K5
40472 Ravenna 793 .... O5
40475 Richmond⊙ 21,705 .... N5
†40222 Riverwood 435 .... K1
42273 Rochester 289 .... H6

Agriculture, Industry and Resources

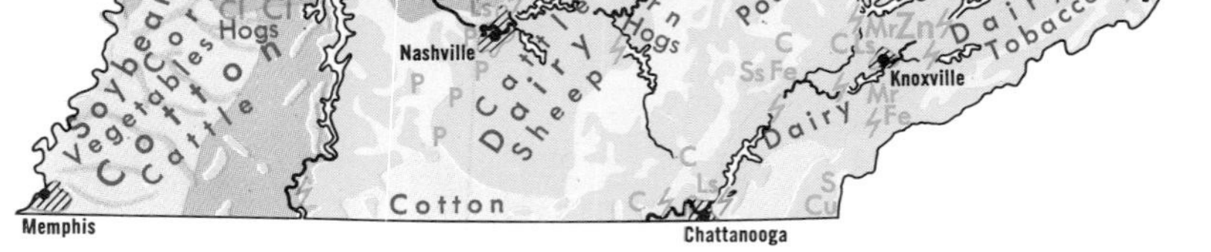

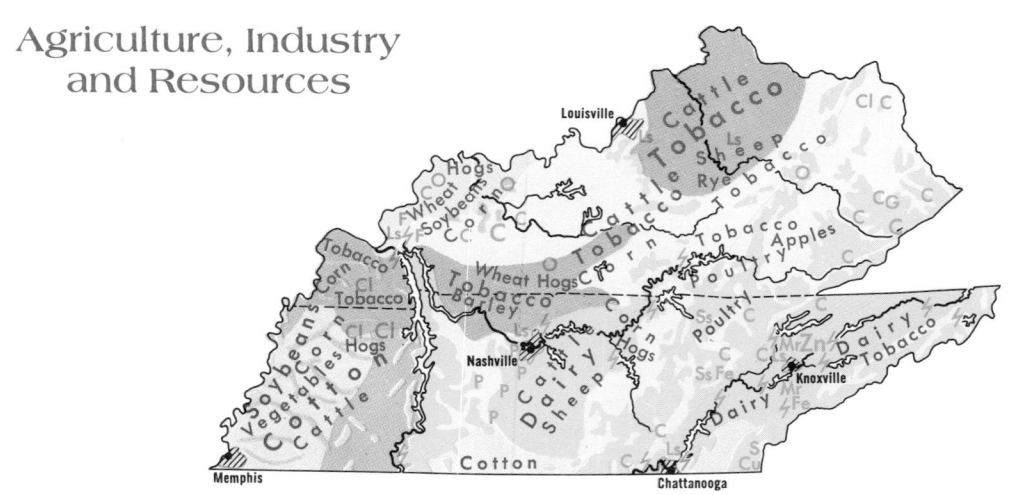

DOMINANT LAND USE

- Hogs, Soft Winter Wheat
- Tobacco, General Farming
- General Farming, Livestock, Tobacco
- General Farming, Livestock, Dairy
- General Farming, Livestock, Fruit, Tobacco
- Specialized Cotton
- Cotton, General Farming
- Cotton, Livestock
- Forests
- Swampland, Limited Agriculture

MAJOR MINERAL OCCURRENCES

C	Coal	G	Natural Gas	P	Phosphates
Cl	Clay	Ls	Limestone	S	Pyrites
Cu	Copper	Mr	Marble	Ss	Sandstone
F	Fluorspar	O	Petroleum	Zn	Zinc
Fe	Iron Ore				

Water Power   Major Industrial Areas

KENTUCKY

AREA 40,409 sq. mi. (104,659 sq. km.)
POPULATION 3,660,257
CAPITAL Frankfort
LARGEST CITY Louisville
HIGHEST POINT Black Mtn. 4,145 ft. (1263 m.)
SETTLED IN 1774
ADMITTED TO UNION June 1, 1792
POPULAR NAME Bluegrass State
STATE FLOWER Goldenrod
STATE BIRD Cardinal

TENNESSEE

AREA 42,144 sq. mi. (109,153 sq. km.)
POPULATION 4,591,120
CAPITAL Nashville
LARGEST CITY Memphis
HIGHEST POINT Clingmans Dome 6,643 ft. (2025 m.)
SETTLED IN 1757
ADMITTED TO UNION June 1, 1796
POPULAR NAME Volunteer State
STATE FLOWER Iris
STATE BIRD Mockingbird

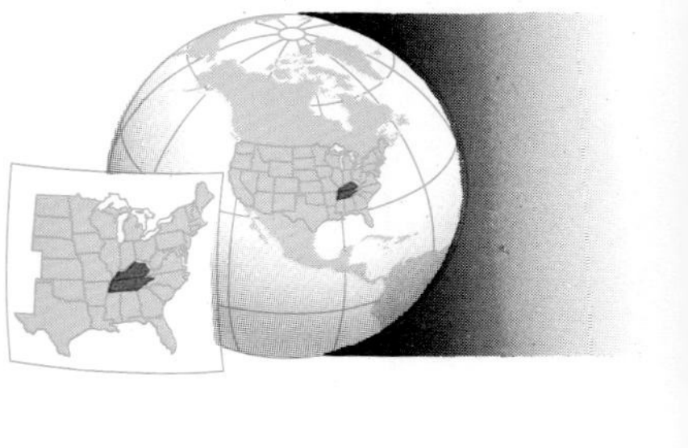

2369 Rockport 511 ... H6
201 Rolling Fields 731 ... K2
201 Rolling Hills 1,122 ... L1
169 Russell 3,824 ... R3
2642 Russell Springs 1,831 ... L6
2276 Russellville⊙ 7,520 ... H7
015 Ryland Heights 252 ... M3
2372 Sacramento 538 ... G6
370 Sadieville 253 ... M4
2453 Saint Charles 405 ... F6
207 Saint Matthews 13,519 ... K2
201 Saint Regis Park 1,735 ... K2
2078 Salem 833 ... E6
371 Salt Lick 347 ... O4
465 Salyersville⊙ 1,352 ... P5
083 Sanders 332 ... M3
171 Sandy Hook⊙ 627 ... P4
056 Sardis 198 ... O3
553 Science Hill 655 ... M6
164 Scottsville⊙ 4,278 ... J7
455 Sebree 1,516 ... F5
201 Seneca Gardens 748 ... K2
983 Sextons Creek 975 ... O6
374 Sharpsburg 339 ... O4
065 Shelbyville⊙ 5,329 ... L4
165 Shepherdsville⊙ 4,454 ... K4
216 Shively 16,819 ... K4
085 Silver Grove 1,260 ... T2
067 Simpsonville 642 ... L4
456 Slaughters 269 ... F6
764 Smilax 987 ... P6
068 Smithfield 137 ... L4
081 Smithland⊙ 512 ... E6
171 Smiths Grove 767 ... J6
501 Somerset⊙ 10,649 ... M6
776 Sonora 416 ... K5
374 South Carrollton 262 ... G6
071 Southgate 2,833 ... T2
174 South Portsmouth 900 ... P3
175 South Shore 1,525 ... R3
661 South Williamson 1,016 ... S5
086 Sparta 192 ... M3
458 Spottsville 914 ... G5
069 Springfield⊙ 3,179 ... L5
201 Springlee 498 ... K2
379 Stamping Ground 562 ... M4
484 Stanford⊙ 2,764 ... M5
380 Stanton⊙ 2,691 ... O5
647 Stearns 1,557 ... N7
567 Stone 900 ... S5
201 Strathmoor Village 466 ... J2
459 Sturgis 2,293 ... F5
011 Taylor Mill 4,509 ... S2
071 Taylorsville⊙ 801 ... L4
222 Thornhill 233 ... K1
189 Tollesboro 808 ... O3
167 Tompkinsville⊙ 4,366 ... K7
286 Trenton 465 ... G7
091 Union 601 ... M3
461 Uniontown 1,169 ... F5
784 Upton 731 ... K6
272 Valley Station 24,474 ... K4
179 Vanceburg⊙ 1,939 ... P3
265 Van Lear 2,035 ... R5
328 Verda 1,133 ... P7
383 Versailles⊙ 6,427 ... M4
773 Vicco 456 ... P6
017 Villa Hills 4,402 ... R2
175 Vine Grove 3,583 ... K5
063 Visalia 198 ... N3
373 Wallins Creek 459 ... O7
094 Walton 1,651 ... M3
095 Warsaw⊙ 1,328 ... M3
096 Washington 624 ... O3
085 Water Valley 395 ... D7
462 Waverly 434 ... F5
566 Wayland 601 ... R6
567 Weeksbury 850 ... R6
201 Wellington 653 ... K2
18 West Buechel 1,205 ... K2
72 West Liberty⊙ 1,381 ... P5
77 West Point 1,339 ... J4
01 West Somerset 850 ... M6
01 Westwood 5,973 ... R4
07 Westwood 826 ... L1
63 Wheatcroft 325 ... F5
69 Wheelwright 865 ... R6
90 Whick 280 ... P6
64 White Plains 859 ... G6
58 Whitesburg⊙ 1,525 ... R6
78 Whitesville 788 ... H5
53 Whitley City⊙ 1,683 ... N7
87 Wickliffe⊙ 1,034 ... C7
71 Wilders 633 ... S2
69 Williamsburg⊙ 5,560 ... N7
97 Williamstown⊙ 2,502 ... M3
78 Willisburg 235 ... L5
90 Wilmore 3,787 ... M5
91 Winchester⊙ 15,216 ... N5
01 Windy Hills 2,214 ... K1
88 Wingo 606 ... D7
71 Woodbine 900 ... N7
70 Woodburn 330 ... J7
01 Woodland Hills 839 ... L2
01 Woodlawn-Oakdale 4,722 ... D6
71 Woodlawn 331 ... T2
†40201 Woodlawn Park 1,052 ... K2
41183 Worthington 1,948 ... R3
41098 Worthville 272 ... L3
41144 Wurtland 1,301 ... R3

OTHER FEATURES

Abraham Lincoln Birthplace Nat'l Hist. Site ... K5
Barkley (dam) ... E6
Barkley (lake) ... F7
Barren (riv.) ... H6
Barren River (lake) ... J7
Beech Fork (riv.) ... L5
Big Sandy (riv.) ... R4
Black (mt.) ... R7
Buckhorn (lake) ... O6
Chaplin (riv.) ... L5
Clarks, East Fork (riv.) ... E7
Cove Run (lake) ... O4
Cumberland (lake) ... M7
Cumberland (mt.) ... P7
Cumberland (riv.) ... K8
Cumberland Gap Nat'l Hist. Park ... P7
Dale Hollow (lake) ... L7
Dewey (lake) ... R5
Dix (riv.) ... M5
Drakes (creek) ... J7
Dry (creek) ... R3
Eagle (creek) ... M3
Fishtrap (lake) ... S6
Fort Campbell ... G7
Grayson (lake) ... P4
Green (riv.) ... G6
Green River (lake) ... L6
Herrington (lake) ... M5
Hinkston (creek) ... N4
Kentucky (dam) ... E7
Kentucky (lake) ... E8
Kentucky (riv.) ... M3
Land Between The Lakes Rec. Area ... E7
Laurel River (lake) ... N6
Lexington Blue Grass Army Depot ... N5
Licking (riv.) ... N3
Mammoth Cave Nat'l Park ... J6
Mayfield (creek) ... C7
Mississippi (riv.) ... A10
Mud (riv.) ... H7
Nolin (lake) ... K6
Nolin (riv.) ... J6
Obion (creek) ... C7
Ohio (riv.) ... F5
Paint Lick (riv.) ... M5
Panther (creek) ... G5
Pine (mt.) ... O7
Pond (riv.) ... G6
Red (riv.) ... O5
Red (riv.) ... G7
Rockcastle (riv.) ... N6
Rolling Fork (riv.) ... L5
Rough (riv.) ... H5
Rough River (lake) ... J5
Salt (riv.) ... K5
Tennessee (riv.) ... D6
Tradewater (riv.) ... F6
Tug Fork (riv.) ... S5

TENNESSEE

COUNTIES

Anderson 67,346 ... N8
Bedford 27,916 ... J9
Benton 14,901 ... E8
Bledsoe 9,478 ... L9
Blount 77,770 ... O9
Bradley 67,547 ... M10
Campbell 34,923 ... N8
Cannon 10,234 ... J9
Carroll 28,285 ... E9
Carter 50,205 ... S8
Cheatham 21,616 ... G8
Chester 12,727 ... D10
Claiborne 24,595 ... O8
Clay 7,676 ... K7
Cocke 28,792 ... P9
Coffee 38,311 ... J9
Crockett 14,941 ... C9
Cumberland 28,676 ... L9
Davidson 477,811 ... H8
Decatur 10,857 ... E9
De Kalb 13,589 ... K9
Dickson 30,037 ... G8
Dyer 34,663 ... C8
Fayette 25,305 ... C10
Fentress 14,826 ... M8
Franklin 31,983 ... J10
Gibson 49,467 ... D9
Giles 24,625 ... G10
Grainger 16,751 ... O8
Greene 54,422 ... R8
Grundy 13,787 ... K10
Hamblen 49,300 ... P8
Hamilton 287,740 ... L10
Hancock 6,887 ... P7
Hardeman 23,873 ... C10
Hardin 22,280 ... E10
Hawkins 43,751 ... P8
Haywood 20,318 ... C9
Henderson 21,390 ... E9
Henry 28,656 ... E8
Hickman 15,151 ... G9
Houston 6,871 ... F8
Humphreys 15,957 ... F8
Jackson 9,398 ... K8
Jefferson 31,284 ... P8
Johnson 13,745 ... T7
Knox 319,694 ... O9
Lake 7,455 ... B8
Lauderdale 24,555 ... B9
Lawrence 34,110 ... G10
Lewis 9,700 ... F9
Lincoln 26,483 ... H10
Loudon 28,553 ... N9
Macon 15,700 ... J7
Madison 74,546 ... D9
Marion 24,416 ... K10
Marshall 19,698 ... H10
Maury 51,095 ... G9
McMinn 41,878 ... M10
McNairy 22,525 ... D10
Meigs 7,431 ... M9
Monroe 28,700 ... N10
Montgomery 83,342 ... G8
Moore 4,510 ... J10
Morgan 16,604 ... M8
Obion 32,781 ... C8
Overton 17,575 ... L8
Perry 6,111 ... F9
Pickett 4,358 ... M7
Polk 13,602 ... N10
Putnam 47,690 ... K8
Rhea 24,235 ... M9
Roane 48,425 ... M9
Robertson 37,021 ... H7
Rutherford 84,058 ... J9
Scott 19,259 ... M8
Sequatchie 8,605 ... L10
Sevier 41,418 ... O9
Shelby 777,113 ... B10
Smith 14,935 ... J8
Stewart 8,665 ... F7
Sullivan 143,968 ... S7
Sumner 85,790 ... J8
Tipton 32,930 ... B9
Trousdale 6,137 ... J8
Unicoi 16,362 ... S8
Union 11,707 ... O8
Van Buren 4,728 ... L9
Warren 32,653 ... K9
Washington 88,755 ... R8
Wayne 13,946 ... F10
Weakley 32,896 ... D8
White 19,567 ... L9
Williamson 58,108 ... H9
Wilson 56,064 ... J8

CITIES and TOWNS

Zip *Name/Pop.* *Key*

†38301 Adair 70 ... D9
37010 Adams 600 ... G7
38310 Adamsville 1,453 ... E10
38001 Alamo⊙ 2,615 ... C9
37701 Alcoa 6,870 ... N9
37012 Alexandria 689 ... J8
38501 Algood 2,406 ... K8
38504 Allardt 654 ... M8
37301 Altamont⊙ 679 ... K10
38449 Ardmore 835 ... H10
38002 Arlington 1,778 ... B10
37015 Ashland City⊙ 2,329 ... G8
37303 Athens⊙ 12,080 ... M10
38004 Atoka 691 ... B10
38220 Atwood 1,143 ... D9
37016 Auburntown 204 ... J9
37743 Baileyton 333 ... R8
†37650 Banner Hill 2,913 ... R8
38134 Bartlett 17,170 ... B10
38544 Baxter 1,411 ... K8
37305 Beersheba Springs 643 ... K10
37020 Bell Buckle 450 ... J9
37205 Belle Meade 3,182 ... H8
38006 Bells 1,571 ... C9
37307 Benton⊙ 1,115 ... M10
†37201 Berry Hill 1,113 ... H8
†37027 Berry's Chapel 2,703 ... H9
38315 Bethel Springs 873 ... D10
38221 Big Sandy 650 ... E8
37709 Blaine 1,147 ... O8
37660 Bloomingdale 12,088 ... R7
37617 Blountville⊙ 2,554 ... S7
37618 Bluff City 1,121 ... S8
38008 Bolivar⊙ 6,597 ... C10
38010 Braden 293 ... B10
38316 Bradford 1,146 ... D8
37027 Brentwood 9,431 ... H8
37710 Briceville 850 ... N8
38011 Brighton 976 ... B10
37620 Bristol 23,986 ... S7
38012 Brownsville⊙ 9,307 ... C9
38317 Bruceton 1,579 ... E8
37711 Bulls Gap 821 ... P8
38015 Burlison 386 ... B9
37029 Burns 777 ... G8
38549 Byrdstown⊙ 884 ... L7
37309 Calhoun 590 ... M10
38320 Camden⊙ 3,279 ... E8
37030 Carthage⊙ 2,672 ... K8
37714 Caryville 2,039 ... N8
37032 Cedar Hill 420 ... H7
38551 Celina⊙ 1,580 ... K7
†37110 Centertown 300 ... K9
37033 Centerville⊙ 2,824 ... G9
37034 Chapel Hill 861 ... H9
37310 Charleston 756 ... M10
37036 Charlotte⊙ 788 ... G8
*37401 Chattanooga⊙ 169,558 ... K10
Chattanooga‡ 426,540 ... K10
37642 Church Hill 4,110 ... R7
38324 Clarksburg 400 ... E9
37040 Clarksville⊙ 54,777 ... G7
Clarksville‡ 150,220 ... G7
37311 Cleveland⊙ 26,415 ... M10
38425 Clifton 773 ... F10
37716 Clinton⊙ 5,245 ... N8
37313 Coalmont 625 ... K10
37315 Collegedale 4,607 ... M10
38017 Collierville 7,839 ... B10
38450 Collinwood 1,064 ... F10
37663 Colonial Heights 6,744 ... R8
38401 Columbia⊙ 26,571 ... G9
37720 Concord 8,569 ... N9
38501 Cookeville⊙ 20,535 ... L8
37317 Copperhill 418 ... N10
37047 Cornersville 722 ... H10
38224 Cottage Grove 117 ... E8
38326 Counce 975 ... E10
38019 Covington⊙ 6,065 ... B9
37318 Cowan 1,790 ... K10
37723 Crab Orchard 1,065 ... M9
37049 Cross Plains 655 ... H7
38555 Crossville⊙ 6,394 ... L9
37050 Cumberland City 276 ... F8
37724 Cumberland Gap 263 ... O8
37725 Dandridge⊙ 1,383 ... O8
37321 Dayton⊙ 5,913 ... L9
37322 Decatur⊙ 1,069 ... M9
38329 Decaturville⊙ 1,004 ... E9
37324 Decherd 2,233 ... J10
38391 Denmark 51 ... D9
37055 Dickson 7,040 ... G8
37058 Dover⊙ 1,197 ... F8
37059 Dowelltown 341 ... K8
38559 Doyle 344 ... K9
38225 Dresden⊙ 2,256 ... D8
37326 Ducktown 583 ... N10
37327 Dunlap⊙ 3,681 ... L10
38330 Dyer 2,419 ... D8
38024 Dyersburg⊙ 15,856 ... C8
†37801 Eagleton Village 5,331 ... O9
37060 Eagleville 444 ... H9
37412 East Ridge 21,236 ... L11
†38367 Eastview 552 ... D10
37643 Elizabethton⊙ 12,431 ... S8
38455 Elkton 540 ... H10
38029 Ellendale 850 ... B10
37329 Englewood 1,840 ... M10
38332 Enville 287 ... E10
37061 Erin⊙ 1,614 ... F8
37650 Erwin⊙ 4,739 ... S8
37330 Estill Springs 1,324 ... J10
38456 Ethridge 548 ... G10
37331 Etowah 3,758 ... M10
37062 Fairview 3,648 ... G9
37656 Fall Branch 1,340 ... R8
37334 Fayetteville⊙ 7,559 ... H10
38334 Finger 245 ... D10
38030 Finley 1,014 ... B8
†37201 Forest Hills 4,516 ... H8
37064 Franklin⊙ 12,407 ... H9
38034 Friendship 763 ... C9
37737 Friendsville 694 ... N9
38337 Gadsden 683 ... D9
38562 Gainesboro⊙ 1,119 ... K8
37066 Gallatin⊙ 17,191 ... H8
38036 Gallaway 804 ... B10
†38019 Garland 301 ... B9
38037 Gates 729 ... C9
37738 Gatlinburg 3,210 ... O9
38138 Germantown 21,482 ... B10
38338 Gibson 458 ... D9
†38015 Gilt Edge 142 ... B9
38229 Gleason 1,335 ... D8
37072 Goodlettsville 8,327 ... H8
38563 Gordonsville 893 ... K8
38039 Grand Junction 360 ... C10
37338 Graysville 1,380 ... L10
37742 Greenback 546 ... N9
37073 Greenbrier 3,180 ... H8
37743 Greeneville⊙ 14,097 ... R8
38230 Greenfield 2,109 ... D8
37339 Gruetli 910 ... K10
38040 Halls 2,444 ... C9
37658 Hampton 2,236 ... S8
37748 Harriman 8,303 ... M9
37341 Harrison 6,206 ... L10
37752 Harrogate-Shawanee 2,530 ... O8
37074 Hartsville⊙ 2,674 ... J8
38340 Henderson⊙ 4,449 ... D10
37075 Hendersonville 26,561 ... H8
38041 Henning 638 ... B9
38231 Henry 295 ... E8
38042 Hickory Valley 252 ... C10
38462 Hohenwald⊙ 3,922 ... F9
38342 Hollow Rock 955 ... E8
38232 Hornbeak 452 ... C8
38044 Hornsby 401 ... D10
38343 Humboldt 10,209 ... D9
38344 Huntingdon⊙ 3,962 ... E8
37345 Huntland 983 ... J10
37756 Huntsville⊙ 519 ... N8
37078 Hurricane Mills 850 ... F9
38463 Iron City 482 ... F10
37757 Jacksboro⊙ 1,722 ... N8
38301 Jackson⊙ 49,131 ... D9
38556 Jamestown⊙ 2,364 ... M8
37347 Jasper⊙ 2,633 ... K10
37760 Jefferson City 5,612 ... P8
37762 Jellico 2,798 ... N7
37601 Johnson City 39,753 ... S8
Johnson City-Kingspoint-Bristol‡ 433,638 ... S8
37659 Jonesboro⊙ 2,829 ... R8
37921 Karns 1,173 ... N9
38233 Kenton 1,551 ... C8
†37347 Kimball 1,220 ... K10
*37660 Kingsport 32,027 ... R7
37763 Kingston⊙ 4,441 ... N9
37082 Kingston Springs 1,017 ... G8
*37901 Knoxville⊙ 175,045 ... O9
Knoxville‡ 476,517 ... O9
37083 Lafayette⊙ 3,808 ... J7
37766 La Follette 8,198 ... N8
38046 La Grange 185 ... C10
37769 Lake City 2,335 ... N8
†38134 Lakeland 612 ... B10
†37379 Lakesite 651 ... L10
†37138 Lakewood 2,325 ... H8
37086 La Vergne 5,495 ... H9
38464 Lawrenceburg⊙ 10,184 ... G10
37087 Lebanon⊙ 11,872 ... J8
37771 Lenoir City 5,446 ... N9
37091 Lewisburg⊙ 8,760 ... H10
38351 Lexington⊙ 5,934 ... E9
37095 Liberty 365 ... K8
37096 Linden⊙ 1,087 ... F9
38570 Livingston⊙ 3,372 ... L8
37097 Lobelville 993 ... F9
37350 Lookout Mountain 1,886 ... L11
38469 Loretto 1,612 ... G10
37774 Loudon⊙ 3,943 ... N9
37779 Luttrell 962 ... O8
37352 Lynchburg⊙ 668 ... J10
38472 Lynnville 383 ... G10
37354 Madisonville⊙ 2,884 ... N9
37355 Manchester⊙ 7,250 ... J10
38237 Martin 8,898 ... D8
37801 Maryville⊙ 17,480 ... O9
37806 Mascot 2,203 ... O8
38049 Mason 471 ... B10
38050 Maury City 989 ... C9
37807 Maynardville⊙ 924 ... O8
37101 McEwen 1,352 ... F8
38201 McKenzie 5,405 ... E8
38235 McLemoresville 311 ... D9
37110 McMinnville⊙ 10,683 ... K9
38355 Medina 687 ... D9
38356 Medon 169 ... D10
*38101 Memphis⊙ 646,174 ... B10
Memphis‡ 912,887 ... B10
38357 Michie 530 ... E10
38052 Middleton 596 ... D10
38358 Milan 8,083 ... D9
38359 Milledgeville 392 ... E10
38053 Millington 20,236 ... B10
38473 Minor Hill 564 ... G10
37119 Mitchellville 209 ... J7
37356 Monteagle 1,126 ... K10
38574 Monterey 2,610 ... L8
37357 Morrison 587 ... K9
†37660 Morrison City 2,032 ... R7
37814 Morristown⊙ 19,683 ... P8
38057 Moscow 499 ... C10
37818 Mosheim 1,539 ... R8
37683 Mountain City⊙ 2,125 ... T8
37642 Mount Carmel 3,764 ... R8
37122 Mount Juliet 2,879 ... H8
38474 Mount Pleasant 3,375 ... G9
38058 Munford 2,336 ... B10
37130 Murfreesboro⊙ 32,845 ... J9
*37201 Nashville (cap.)⊙ 455,651 ... H8
Nashville-Davidson‡ 850,505 ... H8
38059 Newbern 2,794 ... C8
†37380 New Hope 681 ... K11
37134 New Johnsonville 1,824 ... E8
37820 New Market 1,216 ... O8
37821 Newport⊙ 7,580 ... P9
37825 New Tazewell 1,677 ... O8
37826 Niota 765 ... M9
37360 Normandy 118 ... J10
37828 Norris 1,374 ... N8
37829 Oakdale 323 ... M9
†37201 Oak Hill 4,609 ... H8
38060 Oakland 472 ... B10
37830 Oak Ridge 27,662 ... N8
38240 Obion 1,282 ... C8
37840 Oliver Springs 3,659 ... N8
37841 Oneida 3,717 ... N7
37363 Ooltewah 950 ... M10
†37660 Orebank 1,284 ... R7
37141 Orlinda 382 ... H7
35740 Orme 181 ... K10
37365 Palmer 1,027 ... K10
38242 Paris⊙ 10,728 ... E8
37843 Parrottsville 118 ... P8
38363 Parsons 2,422 ... E9
37143 Pegram 1,081 ... H8
37144 Petersburg 681 ... H10
37845 Petros 1,286 ... M8
37846 Philadelphia 507 ... M9
37863 Pigeon Forge 1,822 ... O9
37367 Pikeville⊙ 2,085 ... L9
†38017 Piperton 746 ... B10
†37738 Pittman Center 488 ... P9
38578 Pleasant Hill 371 ... L9
37148 Portland 4,030 ... H7
37849 Powell 7,220 ... N8
†37397 Powells Crossroads 918 ... L10
38478 Pulaski⊙ 7,184 ... G10
38251 Puryear 624 ... E8
38367 Ramer 429 ... D10
37415 Red Bank 13,299 ... L10
37150 Red Boiling Springs 1,173 ... K7
†37641 Rheatown ... R8
†37380 Richard City 87 ... K11
38080 Ridgely 1,932 ... B8
†37401 Ridgeside 417 ... L10
37152 Ridgetop 1,225 ... H8
38063 Ripley⊙ 6,366 ... B9
38253 Rives 386 ... C8
37687 Roan Mountain 1,108 ... S8
37853 Rockford 567 ... O9
37854 Rockwood 5,767 ... M9
37857 Rogersville⊙ 4,368 ... P8
38053 Rosemark 950 ... B10
38066 Rossville 379 ... B10
37860 Russellville 1,069 ... P8
38369 Rutherford 1,378 ... C8
37861 Rutledge⊙ 1,058 ... P8
38481 Saint Joseph 897 ... G10
37373 Sale Creek 900 ... L10
38370 Saltillo 434 ... E10
38254 Samburg 465 ... C8
38371 Sardis 301 ... E10
38067 Saulsbury 156 ... C10
38372 Savannah⊙ 6,992 ... E10
38374 Scotts Hill 668 ... E10
38375 Selmer⊙ 3,979 ... D10
37862 Sevierville⊙ 4,556 ... P9
37375 Sewanee 2,298 ... K10
38255 Sharon 1,134 ... D8
37160 Shelbyville⊙ 13,530 ... H10
37376 Sherwood 900 ... K10
37377 Signal Mountain 5,818 ... L10
38377 Silerton 100 ... D10
37165 Slayden 69 ... G8
37166 Smithville⊙ 3,839 ... K9
37167 Smyrna 8,839 ... H9
37869 Sneedville⊙ 1,110 ... P7
37319 Soddy-Daisy 8,388 ... L10
38068 Somerville⊙ 2,264 ... C10
†37030 South Carthage 1,004 ... K8
†37311 South Cleveland 4,360 ... M10
†37716 South Clinton 1,671 ... N8
†42041 South Fulton 2,735 ... D8
37380 South Pittsburg 3,636 ... K10
37171 Southside 800 ... G8
38583 Sparta⊙ 4,864 ... K9
38585 Spencer⊙ 1,126 ... L9
37381 Spring City 1,951 ... M9
37172 Springfield⊙ 10,814 ... H8
37174 Spring Hill 989 ... H9
38069 Stanton 540 ... C10
38379 Stantonville 271 ... E10
†37660 Sullivan Gardens 2,513 ... R8
38483 Summertown 850 ... G10
37873 Surgoinsville 1,536 ... R8
37874 Sweetwater 4,725 ... N9
37877 Talbott 975 ... P8
37879 Tazewell⊙ 2,090 ... O8
37385 Tellico Plains 698 ... N10
37178 Tennessee Ridge 1,325 ... F8
38079 Tiptonville⊙ 2,438 ... B8
38381 Toone 355 ... D10
37882 Townsend 351 ... O9
37387 Tracy City 1,356 ... K10
38382 Trenton⊙ 4,601 ... D9
38258 Trezevant 921 ... D8
38259 Trimble 722 ... C8
38260 Troy 1,093 ... C8
37388 Tullahoma 15,800 ... J10
37743 Tusculum 1,242 ... R8
38261 Union City⊙ 10,436 ... C8
37181 Vanleer 401 ... G8
†37397 Victoria 800 ... K10
37394 Viola 149 ... K9

(continued on following page)

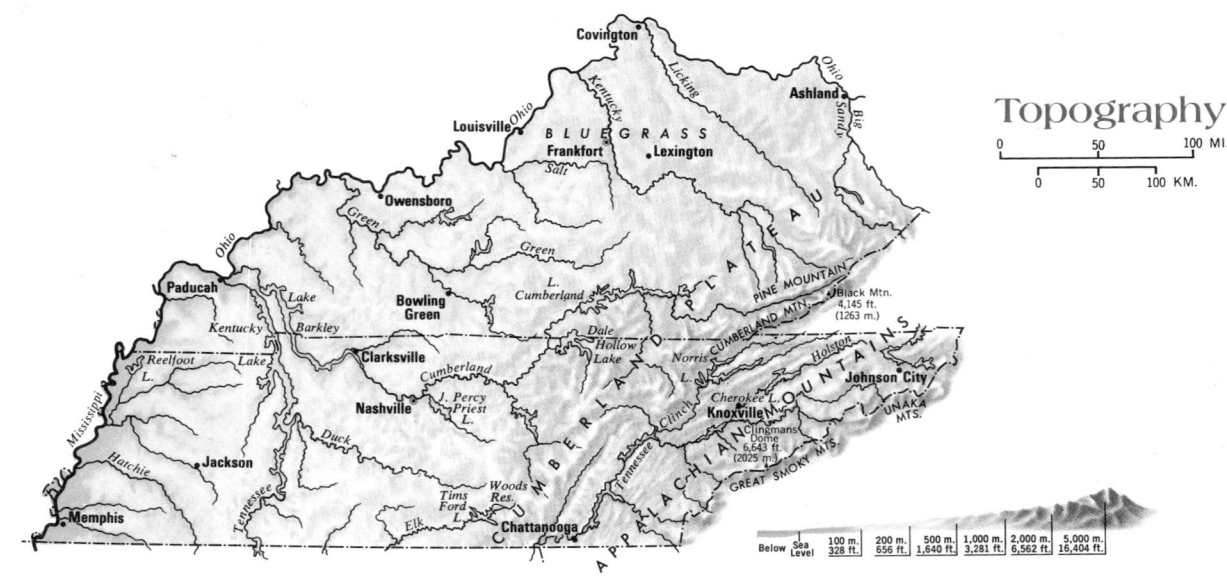

Topography

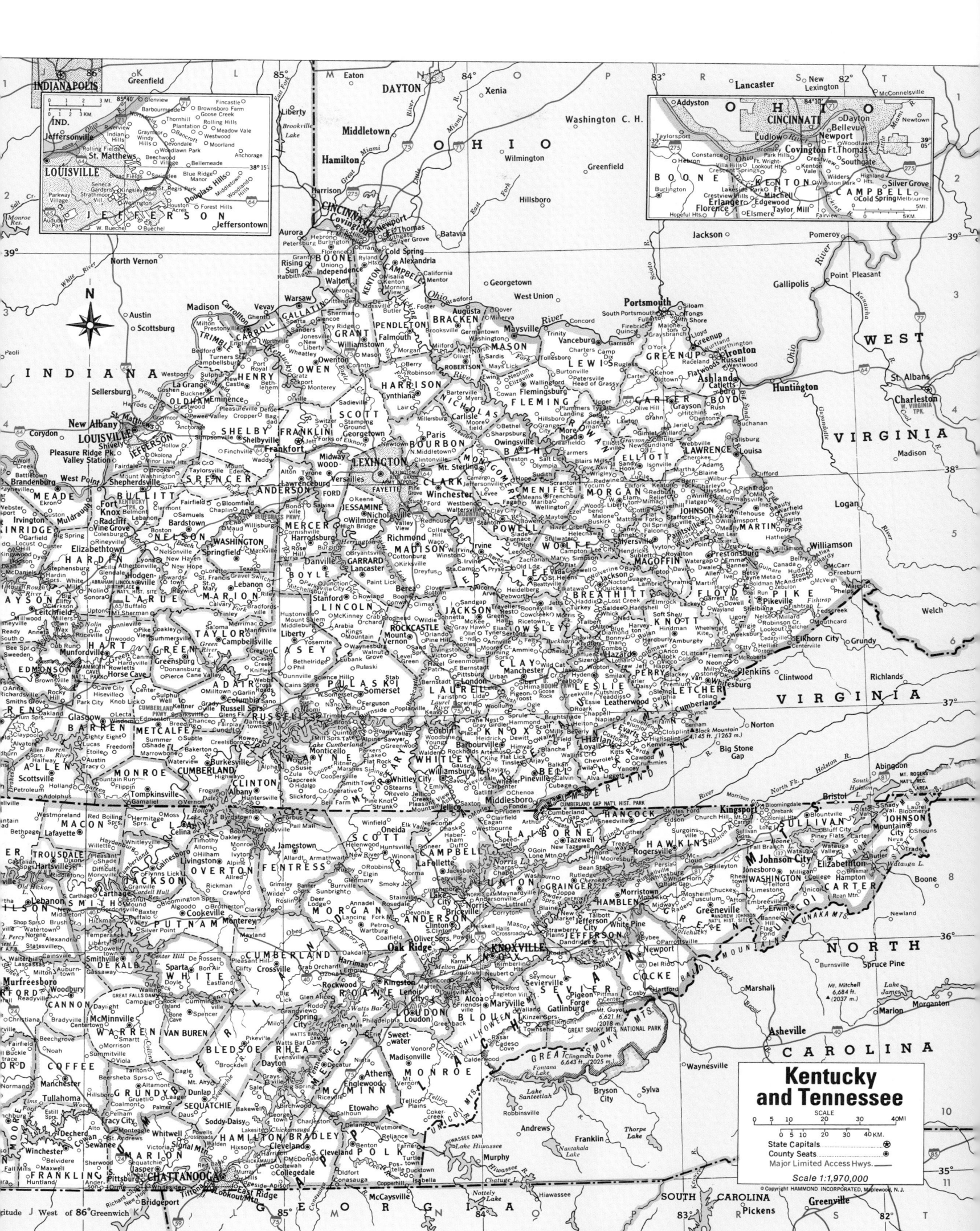

Kentucky and Tennessee

SCALE
0 5 10   20   30   40 MI.
0 5 10   20   30   40 KM.

State Capitals .... ⊛
County Seats .... ○
Major Limited Access Hwys. _____

Scale 1:1,970,000

© Copyright HAMMOND INCORPORATED, Maplewood, N.J.

Topography

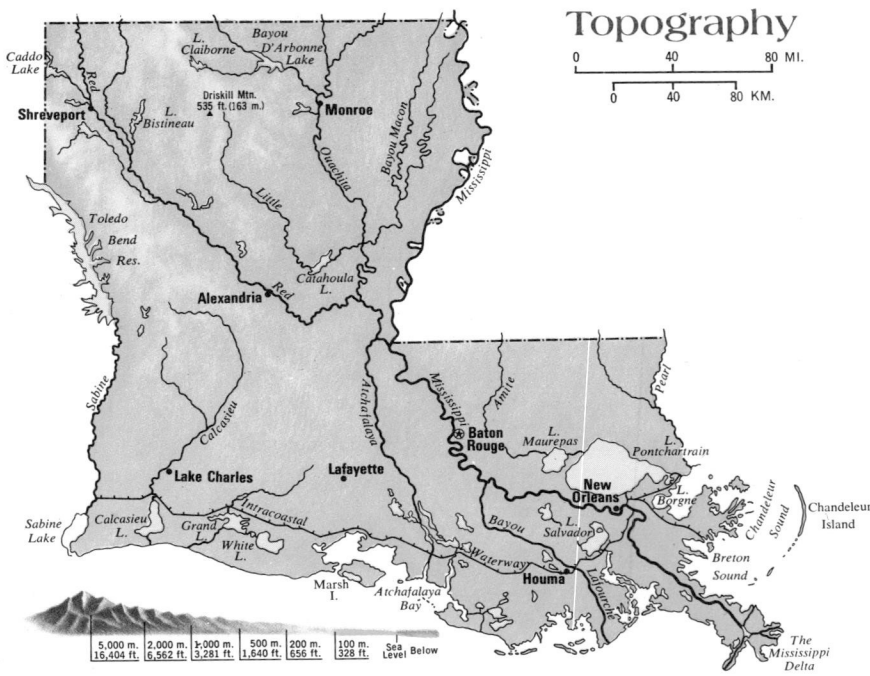

0   40   80 MI.

0   40   80 KM.

| 5,000 m. | 2,000 m. | 1,000 m. | 500 m. | 200 m. | 100 m. | Sea | Below |
| 16,404 ft. | 6,562 ft. | 3,281 ft. | 1,640 ft. | 656 ft. | 328 ft. | Level | |

PARISHES

Acadia 56,427	F6
Allen 21,390	E5
Ascension 50,068	J6
Assumption 22,084	H7
Avoyelles 41,393	G4
Beauregard 29,692	D5
Bienville 16,387	D2
Bossier 80,721	C1
Caddo 252,358	C1
Calcasieu 167,223	D6
Caldwell 10,761	F2
Cameron 9,336	D7
Catahoula 12,287	G3
Claiborne 17,095	D1
Concordia 22,981	G4
De Soto 25,727	C2
East Baton Rouge 366,191	K1
East Carroll 11,772	H1
East Feliciana 19,015	H5
Evangeline 33,343	F5
Franklin 24,141	G2
Grant 16,703	E3
Iberia 63,752	G7
Iberville 32,159	H6
Jackson 17,321	E2
Jefferson 454,592	K7
Jefferson Davis 32,168	E6
Lafayette 150,017	F6
Lafourche 82,483	K7
La Salle 17,004	F3
Lincoln 39,763	E1
Livingston 58,806	L2
Madison 15,975	H2
Morehouse 34,803	G1
Natchitoches 39,863	D3
Orleans 557,515	L6
Ouachita 139,241	F2
Plaquemines 26,049	L8
Pointe Coupee 24,045	G5
Rapides 135,282	E4
Red River 10,433	D2
Richland 22,187	G2
Sabine 25,280	C3
Saint Bernard 64,097	L7
Saint Charles 37,259	K7
Saint Helena 9,827	J5
Saint James 21,495	L3
Saint John the Baptist 31,924	M3
Saint Landry 84,128	F5
Saint Martin 40,214	G6
Saint Mary 64,253	H7
Saint Tammany 110,869	L4
Tangipahoa 80,698	K5
Tensas 8,525	H2
Terrebonne 94,393	J8
Union 21,167	F1
Vermilion 48,458	F7
Vernon 53,475	D4
Washington 44,207	K5
Webster 43,631	D1
West Baton Rouge 19,086	H6
West Carroll 12,922	H1
West Feliciana 12,186	H5
Winn 17,253	E3

CITIES and TOWNS

Zip	Name/Pop.	Key
70510	Abbeville⊙ 12,391	F7
70420	Abita Springs 1,072	L6
71316	Acme 235	G4
70710	Addis 1,320	J2
71401	Aimwell 55	G3
70421	Akers 150	N2

70711	Albany 857	M1
71301	Alexandria⊙ 51,565	E4
	Alexandria‡ 151,985	E4
†70458	Alton 500	L6
70340	Amelia 3,617	H7
70422	Amite⊙ 4,301	K5
71403	Anacoco 820	D4
70712	Angola 600	G5
70032	Arabi 10,248	P4
71001	Arcadia⊙ 3,403	E1
71218	Archibald 425	G2
70512	Arnaudville 1,679	G6
71002	Ashland 307	D2
71003	Athens 419	E1
71404	Atlanta 127	E3
70513	Avery Island 500	G7
70714	Baker 12,865	K1
70514	Baldwin 2,644	H7
71405	Ball 3,405	F4
70036	Barataria 1,123	K7
70515	Basile 2,635	E5
71219	Baskin 286	G2
71220	Bastrop⊙ 15,527	G1
70715	Batchelor 500	H5
*70801	Baton Rouge (cap.)⊙ 219,419	K2
	Baton Rouge‡ 493,973	K2
71004	Belcher 436	C1
70630	Bell City 400	D6
70037	Belle Chasse 5,412	O4
71406	Belmont 350	C3
71407	Bentley 120	E3
71006	Benton⊙ 1,864	C1
†70558	Bermuda 50	D3
71222	Bernice 1,956	E1
70342	Berwick 4,466	H7
71007	Bethany 300	B2
71008	Bienville 249	D2
71009	Blanchard 1,128	C1
70427	Bogalusa 16,976	L5
†71064	Bolinger 200	C1
71223	Bonita 503	G1
71320	Bordelonville 350	G4
70343	Bourg 2,073	J7
*71111	Bossier City 50,817	C1
71409	Boyce 1,198	E4
70040	Braithwaite 350	P4
70516	Branch 200	F6
70517	Breaux Bridge 5,922	G6
70718	Brittany 475	L3
70518	Broussard 2,923	F6
70719	Brusly 1,762	J2
71014	Bryceland 94	E2
71321	Buckeye 280	F4
71322	Bunkie 5,364	F5
70041	Buras-Triumph 4,137	L8
70519	Cade 175	G6
71410	Calhoun 263	E3
71225	Calhoun 350	F2
71416	Campti 1,037	K3
71016	Campti 1,198	D2
70522	Centerville 600	H7
70043	Chalmette⊙ 33,847	P4
†70767	Chamberlin 20	J1
71324	Chase 200	G2
70524	Chataignier 431	F5

71226	Chatham 714	F2
70344	Chauvin 3,338	J8
71325	Cheneyville 865	F4
71412	Chopin 175	E4
71227	Choudrant 809	F1
70525	Church Point 4,599	F6
71414	Clarence 612	E3
71415	Clarks 931	F2
71326	Clayton 1,204	H3
70722	Clinton⊙ 1,919	J5
71416	Cloutierville 100	E3
71417	Colfax⊙ 1,680	E3
71229	Collinston 439	G1
71418	Columbia⊙ 687	F2
70723	Convent⊙ 400	L3
71419	Converse 449	C3
†71107	Cooper Road	C1
71327	Cottonport 1,911	F5
71018	Cotton Valley 1,445	D1
71019	Coushatta⊙ 2,084	D2
70433	Covington⊙ 7,892	K5
†70510	Cow Island 200	F7
†70656	Cravens 200	E5
71020	Creston 135	E3
70526	Crowley⊙ 16,036	F6
71230	Crowville 400	G2
71021	Cullen 1,869	D1
70345	Cut Off 5,049	K7
71420	Cypress 55	D3
70046	Davant 50	L7
71233	Delta 295	J2
71232	Delhi 3,290	H2
70528	Delcambre 2,216	G7
70726	Denham Springs 8,563	L2
70633	De Quincy 3,966	D6
70634	De Ridder⊙ 11,057	D5
71421	Derry 75	E3
70030	Des Allemands 2,920	N4
70047	Destrehan 2,382	N4
†71055	Dixie Inn 453	D1
71422	Dodson 469	F1
70346	Donaldsonville⊙ 7,901	K3
70352	Donner 500	J7
71234	Downsville 213	F1
71023	Doyline 801	D1
70637	Dry Creek 300	D5
71423	Dry Prong 526	E3
71235	Dubach 1,161	E1
71024	Dubberly 421	D1
70353	Dulac 675	J8
71236	Dunn 225	G2
70728	Duplessis 500	K2
70529	Duson 1,253	F6
†71247	East Hodge 439	F1
71025	East Point 100	D2
71330	Echo 525	F4
70049	Edgard⊙ 400	M3
†71019	Edgefield 312	D2
71331	Effie 300	F4
70638	Elizabeth 454	E5
71424	Elmer 200	E4
71051	Elm Grove 100	C2
70532	Elton 1,450	E6
71425	Enterprise 375	G3
71332	Eola 47	F5
71237	Epps 672	G1
70533	Erath 2,133	F7
71238	Eros 158	F2
70534	Estherwood 691	F6
70730	Ethel 250	H5
70535	Eunice 12,479	F6
70639	Evans 500	D5
71333	Evergreen 272	F5
71240	Fairbanks 300	F1
71241	Farmerville⊙ 3,768	F1
70640	Fenton 491	E6

(continued)

Louisiana

SCALE

0   5   10   20   30   40 MI.

0   5   10   20   30   40 KM.

State Capitals	⊛
Parish Seats	⊙
Canals	
Major Limited Access Hwys.	

Scale 1:2,000,000

AREA 47,752 sq. mi. (123,678 sq. km.)
POPULATION 4,206,312
CAPITAL Baton Rouge
LARGEST CITY New Orleans
HIGHEST POINT Driskill Mtn. 535 ft. (163 m.)
SETTLED IN 1699
ADMITTED TO UNION April 30, 1812
POPULAR NAME Pelican State
STATE FLOWER Magnolia
STATE BIRD Eastern Brown Pelican

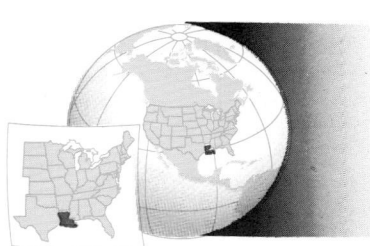

New Orleans, Baton Rouge and Vicinity

© Copyright HAMMOND INCORPORATED, Maplewood, N.J.

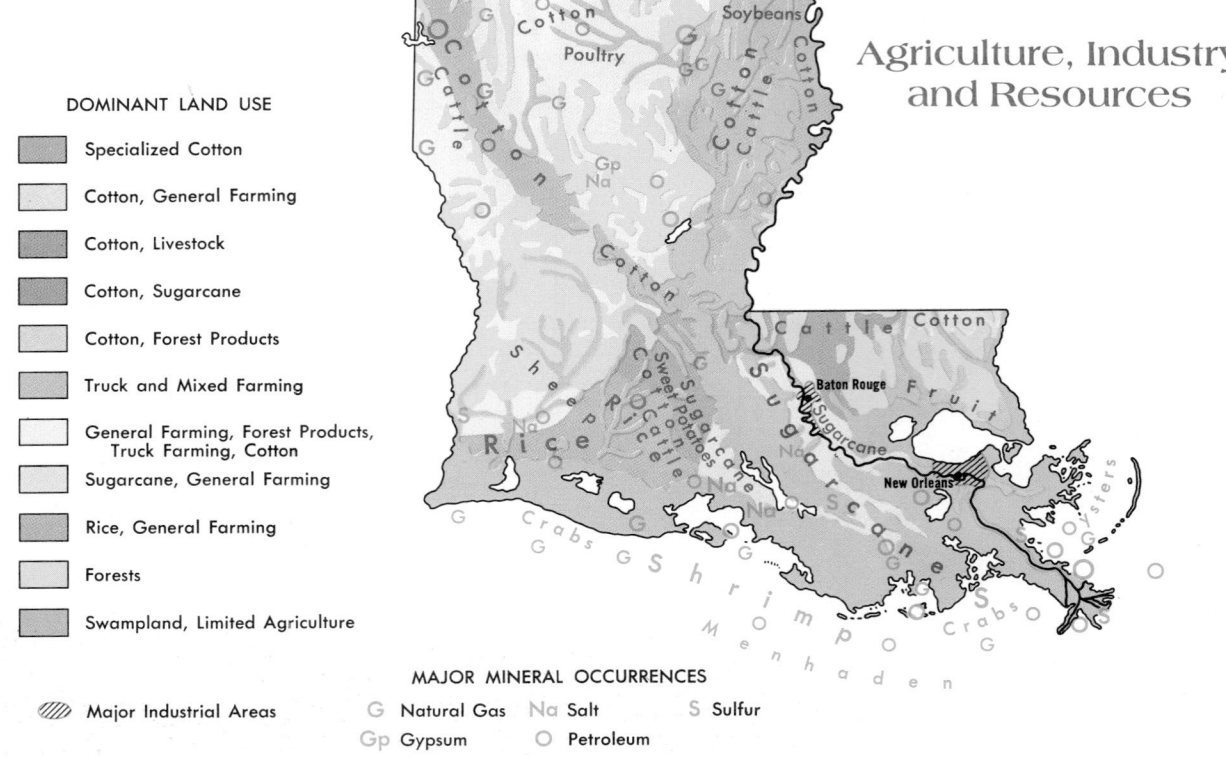

Agriculture, Industry and Resources

DOMINANT LAND USE

- Specialized Cotton
- Cotton, General Farming
- Cotton, Livestock
- Cotton, Sugarcane
- Cotton, Forest Products
- Truck and Mixed Farming
- General Farming, Forest Products, Truck Farming, Cotton
- Sugarcane, General Farming
- Rice, General Farming
- Forests
- Swampland, Limited Agriculture

MAJOR MINERAL OCCURRENCES

Major Industrial Areas   G Natural Gas   Na Salt   S Sulfur

Gp Gypsum   O Petroleum

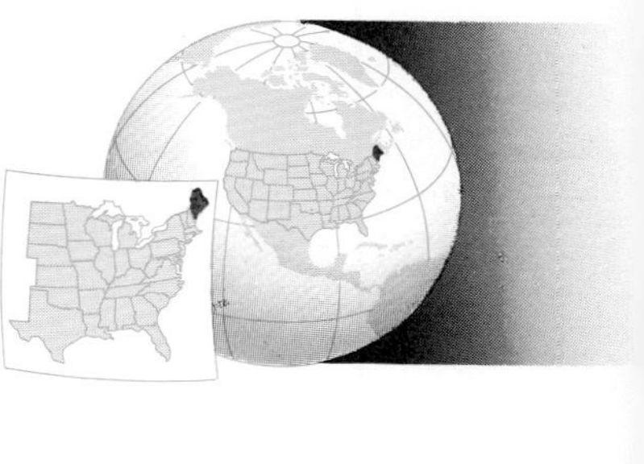

AREA 33,265 sq. mi. (86,156 sq. km.)
POPULATION 1,125,027
CAPITAL Augusta
LARGEST CITY Portland
HIGHEST POINT Katahdin 5,268 ft. (1606 m.)
SETTLED IN 1624
ADMITTED TO UNION March 15, 1820
POPULAR NAME Pine Tree State
STATE FLOWER White Pine Cone & Tassel
STATE BIRD Chickadee

COUNTIES

Androscoggin 99,657 .... C7
Aroostook 91,331 .... F2
Cumberland 215,789 .... C8
Franklin 27,098 .... B5
Hancock 41,781 .... G6
Kennebec 109,889 .... D7
Knox 32,941 .... E7
Lincoln 25,691 .... D7
Oxford 48,968 .... B7
Penobscot 137,015 .... F5
Piscataquis 17,634 .... E4
Sagadahoc 28,795 .... D7
Somerset 45,028 .... C4
Waldo 28,414 .... E6
Washington 34,963 .... H6
York 139,666 .... B9

CITIES and TOWNS

Zip *Name/Pop.* *Key*

04406 Abbot Village○ 576 .... D5
04001 Acton○ 1,228 .... B8
04606 Addison○ 1,061 .... H6
04910 Albion○ 1,551 .... E6
†04610 Alexander○ 385 .... H5
04002 Alfred○ 1,890 .... B9
†04774 Allagash○ 448 .... F1
†04938 Allens Mills 100 .... C6
04535 Alna○ 425 .... D7
†04468 Alton○ 468 .... F5
†04408 Amherst○ 203 .... G6
04216 Andover○ 850 .... B6
04911 Anson○ 2,226 .... D6
†04862 Appleton○ 818 .... E7
†04468 Argyle 225 .... F5
04732 Ashland○ 1,865 .... G2
04607 Ashville 36 .... G7
04912 Athens○ 802 .... D6
†04426 Atkinson○ 306 .... E5
04608 Atlantic 120 .... G7
04210 Auburn⊙ 23,128 .... C7
04330 Augusta (cap.)⊙ 21,819 ... D7
04408 Aurora○ 110 .... G6
04003 Bailey Island 500 .... D8
†04497 Bancroft○ 61 .... H4
04401 Bangor⊙ 31,643 .... F6
Bangor‡ 83,919 .... F6
04609 Bar Harbor○ 4,124 .... G7
04609 Bar Harbor 2,685 .... G7
†04619 Baring○ 308 .... J5
04004 Bar Mills 800 .... C8
04653 Bass Harbor 450 .... G7
04530 Bath⊙ 10,246 .... D8
†04915 Bayside F7
04611 Beals○ 695 .... H7
†04622 Beddington○ 36 .... H6
04915 Belfast⊙ 6,243 .... F7
04917 Belgrade○ 2,043 .... D7
†04915 Belmont○ 520 .... E7
04733 Benedicta○ 225 .... G4
†04937 Benton○ 2,188 .... D6
03901 Berwick○ 4,149 .... B9
03901 Berwick 2,378 .... B9
04217 Bethel○ 2,340 .... B7
04005 Biddeford 19,638 .... B9
04920 Bingham○ 1,184 .... D5
04920 Bingham 1,074 .... D5
04613 Birch Harbor 300 .... H7
04734 Blaine○ 922 .... H2
04734 Blaine-Mars Hill 1,921 .... H2
04614 Blue Hill○ 1,644 .... F7
04615 Blue Hill Falls 135 .... F7
04537 Boothbay○ 2,308 .... D8
04538 Boothbay Harbor 2,207 .... D8
04008 Bowdoinham○ 1,828 .... D7
†04481 Bowerbank○ 27 .... E5
04410 Bradford○ 888 .... F5
†04410 Bradford Center 105 .... F5
04411 Bradley○ 1,149 .... F6
04412 Brewer 9,017 .... F6
04735 Bridgewater○ 742 .... H3
04009 Bridgton○ 3,528 .... B7
04009 Bridgton 1,639 .... B7
†04990 Brighton○ 74 .... D5
04539 Bristol○ 2,095 .... D8
04616 Brooklin○ 619 .... F7
04921 Brooks○ 804 .... E6
04617 Brooksville○ 753 .... F7
04413 Brookton 175 .... H4
04010 Brownfield○ 767 .... B8
04414 Brownville○ 1,545 .... E5
04011 Brunswick○ 17,366 .... C8
04011 Brunswick 10,990 .... C8
04219 Bryant Pond 600 .... B7
†04232 Buckfield○ 1,333 .... C7
04618 Bucks Harbor 300 .... J6
04416 Bucksport○ 4,345 .... F6
04416 Bucksport 2,853 .... F6
04540 Burkettville 120 .... E7
04417 Burlington○ 322 .... G5
04922 Burnham○ 951 .... E6
†04093 Buxton○ 5,775 .... C8
†04275 Byron○ 114 .... B6
04619 Calais 4,262 .... J5
04923 Cambridge○ 445 .... E5
04843 Camden○ 4,584 .... F7
04843 Camden 3,743 .... F7
04924 Canaan○ 1,189 .... D6
04221 Canton○ 831 .... C7
03902 Cape Neddick 850 .... B9
04014 Cape Porpoise 500 .... C9
04736 Caribou 9,916 .... G2
04419 Carmel○ 1,695 .... E6
†04947 Carrabassett Valley○ 107 ... C5
†04487 Carroll○ 175 .... G5
†04224 Carthage○ 438 .... C6
†04465 Cary○ 229 .... H4
04015 Casco○ 2,243 .... B7
04421 Castine○ 1,304 .... F7
†04941 Center Montville 16 .... E7
†04623 Centerville○ 28 .... H6
†04757 Chapman○ 406 .... G2
04422 Charleston○ 1,037 .... F5
†04666 Charlotte○ 300 .... J5
04017 Chebeague Island 900 .... C8
†04345 Chelsea○ 2,522 .... D7
04622 Cherryfield○ 983 .... H6
†04458 Chester○ 434 .... F5
†04938 Chesterville○ 869 .... C6
†04478 Chesuncook 6 .... D3
04926 China○ 2,918 .... E7
†04239 Chisholm 1,796 .... C7
†04428 Clifton○ 462 .... G6
04927 Clinton○ 2,696 .... D6
04927 Clinton 1,305 .... D6
†04623 Columbia○ 275 .... H6
04623 Columbia Falls○ 517 .... H6
†04638 Cooper○ 105 .... H6
04624 Corea 375 .... H7
04928 Corinna○ 1,887 .... E6
04020 Cornish○ 1,047 .... B8
†04976 Cornville○ 838 .... D6
04625 Cranberry Isles○ 198 .... G7
†04610 Crawford○ 86 .... H5
†04015 Crescent Lake 325 .... C7
†04851 Criehaven 5 .... F8
04738 Crouseville 450 .... G2
†04747 Crystal○ 349 .... G4
04021 Cumberland Center○ 5,284. C8
04021 Cumberland Center 2,015 .. C8
04563 Cushing○ 795 .... E7
04626 Cutler○ 726 .... J6
04543 Damariscotta○ 1,493 .... E7
04543 Damariscotta-Newcastle 1,411 .... E7
04424 Danforth○ 826 .... H4
†04622 Deblois○ 44 .... H6
†04429 Dedham○ 841 .... F6
04627 Deer Isle○ 1,492 .... F7
04022 Denmark○ 672 .... B8
04628 Dennysville○ 296 .... J6
04929 Detroit○ 744 .... E6
04930 Dexter○ 4,286 .... E5
04930 Dexter 3,118 .... E5
04224 Dixfield○ 2,389 .... C6
04224 Dixfield 1,725 .... C6
04932 Dixmont○ 812 .... E6
04426 Dover-Foxcroft○ 4,323 .... E5
04426 Dover-Foxcroft⊙ 2,974 .... E5
†04426 Dover South Mills 54 .... E5
04342 Dresden○ 998 .... D7
†04747 Dyer Brook○ 275 .... G3
04739 Eagle Lake○ 1,019 .... F1
04226 East Andover 250 .... B6
04544 East Boothbay 800 .... D8
04427 East Corinth 525 .... F5
04227 East Dixfield 250 .... C6
04429 East Holden 600 .... F6
04027 East Lebanon 950 .... B9
04228 East Livermore 500 .... C7
04630 East Machias○ 1,233 .... J6
04430 East Millinocket○ 2,372 .... F4
04430 East Millinocket 2,361 .... F4
04740 Easton○ 1,305 .... H2
04028 East Parsonfield 400 .... B8
04229 East Peru 200 .... C7
†04210 East Poland 200 .... C7
04631 Eastport 1,982 .... K6
04231 East Stoneham 300 .... B7
†04607 East Sullivan 496 .... G6
†04220 East Sumner 120 .... C7
†04862 East Union 75 .... E7
†04428 Eddington○ 1,769 .... F6
†04556 Edgecomb○ 841 .... D8
03903 Eliot○ 4,948 .... B9
04605 Ellsworth⊙ 5,179 .... F6
04031 Emery Mills 100 .... B8
04433 Enfield○ 1,397 .... F5
04434 Etna○ 758 .... E6
04936 Eustis○ 582 .... B5
04435 Exeter○ 823 .... E6
†04938 Fairbanks 400 .... C6
04937 Fairfield○ 6,113 .... D6
04937 Fairfield 3,169 .... D6
04105 Falmouth○ 6,853 .... C8
04105 Falmouth 1,655 .... C8
†04345 Farmingdale○ 2,535 .... D7
†04345 Farmingdale 2,014 .... D7
04938 Farmington○ 6,730 .... C6
04938 Farmington⊙ 3,583 .... C6
04940 Farmington Falls 500 .... C6
†04349 Fayette○ 812 .... C7
04546 Five Islands 225 .... D8
04742 Fort Fairfield○ 4,376 .... H2
04742 Fort Fairfield 2,282 .... H2
04743 Fort Kent○ 4,826 .... F1
04743 Fort Kent 2,375 .... F1
04744 Fort Kent Mills 200 .... F1
04438 Frankfort○ 783 .... F6
04634 Franklin○ 979 .... G6
04941 Freedom○ 458 .... E7
04032 Freeport○ 5,863 .... C8
04032 Freeport 1,906 .... C8
04635 Frenchboro○ 43 .... G7
04745 Frenchville○ 1,450 .... G1
04547 Friendship○ 1,000 .... E7
04037 Fryeburg○ 2,715 .... A7
04037 Fryeburg 1,644 .... A7
04345 Gardiner 6,485 .... D7
04939 Garland○ 718 .... E5
04548 Georgetown○ 735 .... D8
†04217 Gilead○ 191 .... B7
†04401 Glenburn○ 2,319 .... F6
04846 Glen Cove 250 .... E7
04038 Gorham○ 10,101 .... C8
04038 Gorham 4,052 .... C8
†04607 Gouldsboro○ 1,574 .... H7
04746 Grand Isle○ 719 .... G1
04637 Grand Lake Stream○ 198 ... H5
04039 Gray○ 4,344 .... C8
†04408 Great Pond○ 45 .... G6
04236 Greene○ 3,037 .... C7
04441 Greenville○ 1,839 .... D5
04441 Greenville 1,640 .... D5
04442 Greenville Junction 650 .... D5
04443 Guilford○ 1,793 .... E5
04443 Guilford 1,235 .... E5
04347 Hallowell 2,502 .... D7
†04785 Hamlin○ 340 .... H1
04444 Hampden○ 5,250 .... F6
04444 Hampden 3,538 .... F6
04445 Hampden Highlands 950 ... F6
04640 Hancock○ 1,409 .... G6
04237 Hanover○ 256 .... B7
04942 Harmony○ 755 .... D6
†04011 Harpswell○ 3,796 .... D8
04643 Harrington○ 859 .... H6
04040 Harrison○ 1,667 .... B7
†04221 Hartford○ 480 .... C7
04943 Hartland○ 1,669 .... D6
04943 Hartland 1,041 .... D6
04446 Haynesville○ 169 .... G4
04238 Hebron○ 665 .... C7
†04401 Hermon○ 3,170 .... F6
04944 Hinckley 140 .... D6
04041 Hiram○ 1,067 .... B8
†04730 Hodgdon○ 1,084 .... H3
04042 Hollis Center○ 2,892 .... B8
04847 Hope○ 730 .... E7
04730 Houlton○ 6,766 .... H3
04730 Houlton⊙ 5,730 .... H3
04448 Howland○ 1,602 .... F5
04448 Howland 1,502 .... F5
04449 Hudson○ 797 .... F5
04644 Hulls Cove 200 .... G7
04747 Island Falls○ 981 .... G3
04645 Isle Au Haut○ 57 .... F7
04848 Islesboro○ 521 .... F7
04945 Jackman○ 1,003 .... C4
†04630 Jacksonville 200 .... J6
04239 Jay○ 5,080 .... C7
04348 Jefferson○ 1,616 .... D7
04648 Jonesboro○ 553 .... J6
04649 Jonesport○ 1,512 .... H6
04649 Jonesport 1,050 .... H6
04450 Kenduskeag○ 1,210 .... E6
04043 Kennebunk○ 6,621 .... B9
04043 Kennebunk 3,294 .... B9
†04043 Kennebunk Beach 200 .... C9
04046 Kennebunkport○ 2,952 .... C9
04046 Kennebunkport 1,685 .... C9
04349 Kents Hill 300 .... D7
04947 Kingfield○ 1,083 .... C6
04451 Kingman 281 .... G4
†04990 Kingsbury○ 4 .... D5
03904 Kittery○ 9,314 .... B9
03904 Kittery 5,465 .... B9
03905 Kittery Point 1,260 .... B9
†04986 Knox○ 558 .... E6
04453 La Grange○ 509 .... F5
†04463 Lake View○ 20 .... F5
†04605 Lamoine○ 953 .... G7
04455 Lee○ 688 .... G5
†04263 Leeds○ 1,463 .... C7
04456 Levant○ 1,117 .... F6
04240 Lewiston 40,481 .... C7
Lewiston-Auburn‡ 72,378 . C7
04949 Liberty○ 694 .... E7
04749 Lille 300 .... G1
04048 Limerick○ 1,356 .... B8
04750 Limestone○ 8,719 .... H2
04750 Limestone 1,334 .... H2
04049 Limington○ 2,203 .... B8
04457 Lincoln○ 5,066 .... G5
04457 Lincoln 3,524 .... G5
04849 Lincolnville○ 1,414 .... E7
04850 Lincolnville Center 200 .... E7
†04730 Linneus○ 752 .... H3
04250 Lisbon○ 8,769 .... C7
04250 Lisbon-Lisbon Center 1,865 .... C7
04252 Lisbon Falls 4,370 .... D7
04350 Litchfield○ 1,954 .... D7
†04627 Little Deer Isle 475 .... F7
04082 Little Falls-South Windham 1,366 .... C8
†04760 Littleton○ 1,009 .... H3
04253 Livermore○ 1,826 .... C7
04254 Livermore Falls○ 3,572 .... C7
04254 Livermore Falls 2,441 .... C7
04255 Locke Mills 600 .... B7
04051 Lovell○ 767 .... B7
†04433 Lowell○ 194 .... F5
04652 Lubec○ 2,045 .... K6
†04730 Ludlow○ 403 .... G3
04654 Machias○ 2,458 .... J6
04654 Machias⊙ 1,277 .... J6
04655 Machiasport○ 1,108 .... H6
†04451 Macwahoc○ 126 .... G4
04756 Madawaska○ 5,282 .... G1
04756 Madawaska 4,165 .... G1
04950 Madison○ 4,367 .... D6
04950 Madison 2,788 .... D6
†04966 Madrid○ 178 .... B6
†04942 Mainstream 100 .... D6
04351 Manchester○ 1,949 .... D7
04757 Mapleton○ 1,895 .... G2
04758 Mars Hill○ 1,892 .... H2
04758 Mars Hill-Blaine 1,921 .... H2
04759 Masardis○ 328 .... G3
04851 Matinicus 66 .... F8
04459 Mattawamkeag○ 1,000 .... G5
04256 Mechanic Falls○ 2,616 .... C7
04256 Mechanic Falls 2,198 .... C7
04657 Meddybemps○ 110 .... J5
†04453 Medford○ 163 .... F5
†04453 Medford Center 100 .... F5
04460 Medway○ 1,871 .... G4
04957 Mercer○ 448 .... D6
04257 Mexico○ 3,698 .... B6
04257 Mexico 3,207 .... B6
†04216 Middledam 10 .... B6
04658 Milbridge○ 1,306 .... H6
04461 Milford○ 2,160 .... F6
04461 Milford 1,688 .... F6
04462 Millinocket○ 7,567 .... F4

(continued on following page)

Agriculture, Industry and Resources

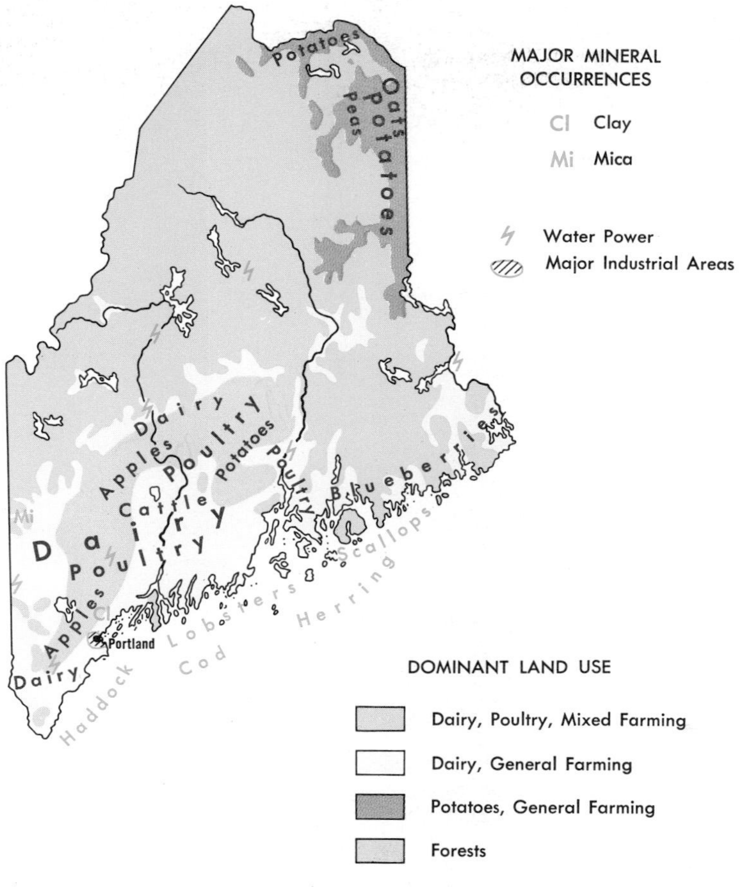

Potatoes
Oats
Peas
Potatoes
Dairy
Apples
Poultry
Potatoes
Cattle
Dairy
Poultry
Blueberries
Poultry
Dairy
Apples
Portland
Dairy
Lobsters
Scallops
Herring
Cod
Haddock
Mi
MAJOR MINERAL OCCURRENCES
Cl Clay
Mi Mica
Water Power
Major Industrial Areas
DOMINANT LAND USE
Dairy, Poultry, Mixed Farming
Dairy, General Farming
Potatoes, General Farming
Forests

Topography

0   30   60 MI.
0   30   60 KM.

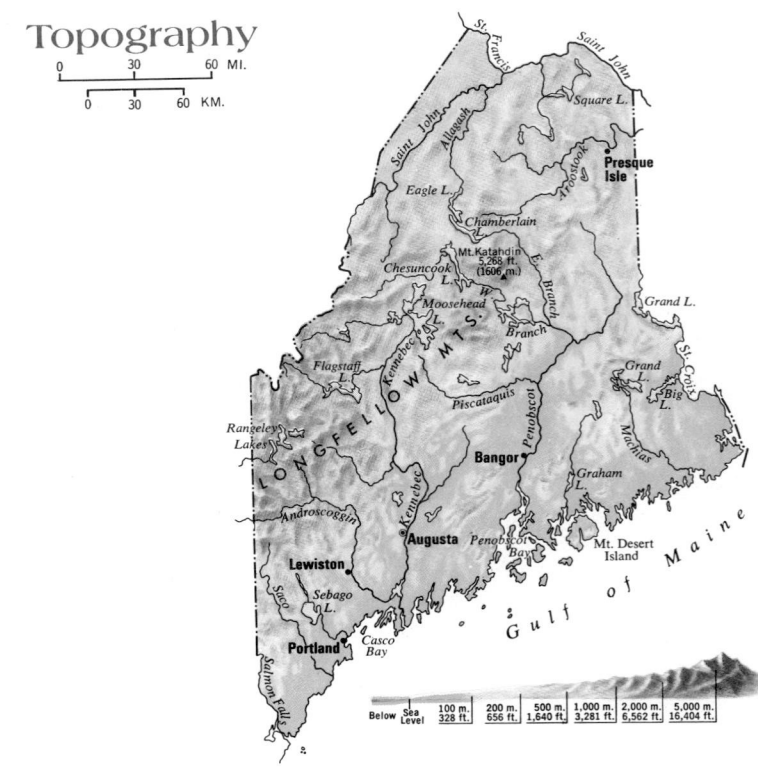

| Below Sea Level | 100 m. 328 ft. | 200 m. 656 ft. | 500 m. 1,640 ft. | 1,000 m. 3,281 ft. | 2,000 m. 6,562 ft. | 5,000 m. 16,404 ft. |

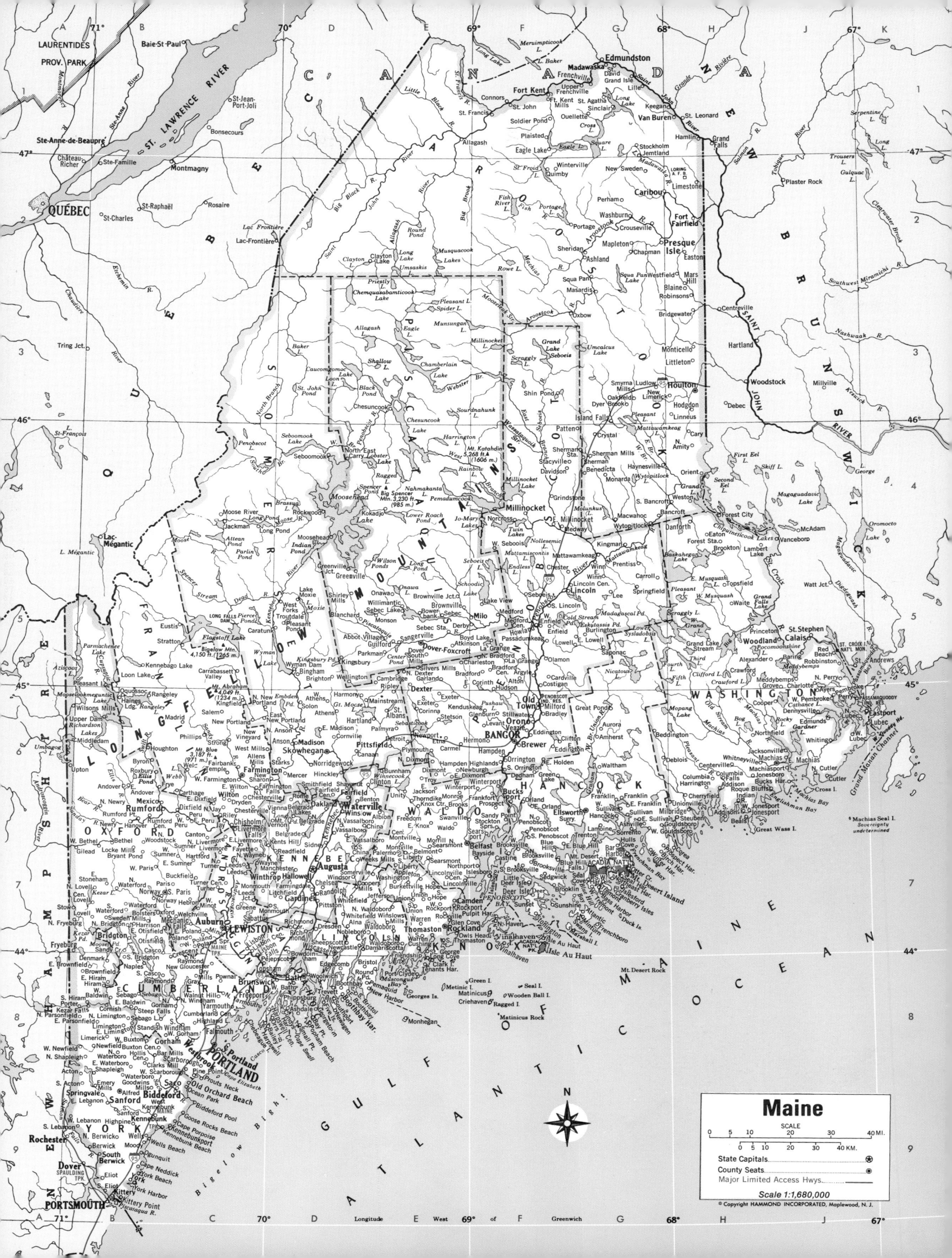

Maine

SCALE

0 5 10   20   30   40 MI.

0 5 10   20   30   40 KM.

State Capitals .... ⊗

County Seats .... ◉

Major Limited Access Hwys ....

Scale 1:1,680,000

© Copyright HAMMOND INCORPORATED, Maplewood, N.J.

MARYLAND
COUNTIES

Allegany 80,548	C2
Anne Arundel 370,775	M4
Baltimore 655,615	M3
Baltimore (city county) 786,775	M6
Calvert 34,638	M5
Caroline 23,143	P5
Carroll 96,356	K2
Cecil 60,430	P2
Charles 72,751	K6
Dorchester 30,623	O7
Frederick 114,792	J3
Garrett 26,498	A2
Harford 145,930	N2
Howard 118,572	L4
Kent 16,695	O3
Montgomery 579,053	J4
Prince Georges 665,071	L5
Queen Annes 25,508	P4
Saint Marys 59,895	M7
Somerset 19,188	R8
Talbot 25,604	O5
Washington 113,086	G2
Wicomico 64,540	R7
Worcester 30,889	S8

CITIES and TOWNS

Zip	Name/Pop.	Key
21001	Aberdeen 11,533	O2
21009	Abingdon 500	N3
21520	Accident 246	A2
20607	Accokeek 3,894	L6
*21401	Annapolis (cap.)⊙ 31,740	M5
20701	Annapolis Junction 775	M4
20608	Aquasco 950	L6
†21227	Arbutus 20,163	M4
†20785	Ardmore 500	G4
	Aspen Hill 47,455	K4
*21201	Baltimore 786,775	M3
	Baltimore‡ 2,174,023	M3
20610	Barstow 500	M6
21521	Barton 617	B2
21014	Bel Air⊙ 7,814	N2
20611	Bel Alton 800	L7
20705	Beltsville 12,760	G3
20612	Benedict 850	M6
21811	Berlin 2,162	T7
†20740	Berwyn Heights 3,135	G4
*20014	Bethesda 62,736	E4
21609	Bethlehem 500	P6
21610	Betterton 356	O3
20710	Bladensburg 7,691	G4
21523	Bloomington 486	B3
21713	Boonsboro 1,908	H2
†20027	Boulevard Heights 500	F5
20715	Bowie 33,695	L4
21612	Bozman 700	N5
20613	Brandywine 1,319	L6
20722	Brentwood 2,988	F4
21225	Brooklyn 11,508	M4
†21659	Brookview 78	P6
21716	Brunswick 4,572	H3
21717	Buckeystown 400	J3
21718	Burkittsville 202	H3
20618	Bushwood 750	L7
20731	Cabin	
	John-Brookmont 5,135	E4
20619	California 5,770	M7
†20705	Calverton 772	L4
21613	Cambridge⊙ 11,703	O6
20748	Camp Springs 16,118	G6
21401	Cape Saint Claire 6,022	N4
20743	Capitol Heights 3,271	G5
21024	Cardiff 475	N2
†20028	Carmody Hills-Pepper Mill	
	Village 5,571	G5
†21034	Castleton 750	N2
†21788	Catoctin Furnace 516	J2
21228	Catonsville 33,208	M3
21720	Cavetown 1,533	H2
21913	Cecilton 508	P3
21617	Centreville⊙ 2,018	O4
21816	Chance 600	P8
21914	Charlestown 720	P2
20622	Charlotte Hall 1,901	M7
21027	Chase 900	N3
20623	Cheltenham 950	L6
20732	Chesapeake Beach 1,408	N6
21915	Chesapeake City 899	P2
21619	Chester 950	N5
21620	Chestertown⊙ 3,300	O4
20785	Cheverly 5,751	G4
20815	Chevy Chase 12,232	E4
†20015	Chevy Chase Section	
	Four 3,189	E4
20783	Chillum 32,775	F4
21622	Church Creek 124	O6
21623	Church Hill 319	O4
21028	Churchville 500	N2
20734	Clarksburg 400	J4
21029	Clarksville 500	L4
21722	Clear Spring 477	G2
20624	Clements 800	L7
20735	Clinton 16,438	G6
21030	Cockeysville 17,013	M3
20904	Colesville 14,359	K4
20740	College Park 23,614	G4
†20722	Colmar Manor 1,286	F4
20626	Coltons Point 600	M8
21043	Columbia 52,518	L4
20627	Compton 500	M7
21723	Cooksville 497	K3
†20027	Coral Hills 11,602	G5
21524	Corriganville 1,020	C2
†20722	Cottage City 1,122	F4
†20611	Cox Station (Bel	
	Alton) 800	L7
21502	Cresaptown 4,645	C2
21817	Crisfield 2,924	P9
21114	Crofton 12,009	M4
21032	Crownsville 500	M4
21502	Cumberland⊙ 25,933	D2
	Cumberland‡ 107,782	D2

20750	Damascus 4,129	K3
20628	Dameron 759	N8
21034	Darlington 850	N2
†20760	Darnestown 950	J4
20751	Deale 3,008	M5
21821	Deal Island 800	P8
21550	Deer Park 486	A3
†20784	Defense Heights	G4
21875	Delmar 1,232	R7
21629	Denton⊙ 1,927	P5
20855	Derwood 413	K4
20753	Dickerson 530	J4
20747	District Heights 6,799	G5
20630	Drayden 400	N8
21222	Dundalk 71,293	N3
†20608	Eagle Harbor 45	M6
21631	East New Market 230	P6
21601	Easton⊙ 7,536	O5
21528	Eckhart Mines 1,333	C2
21822	Eden 800	R7
†21219	Edgemere 9,078	N4
21040	Edgewood 19,455	N3
†20781	Edmonston 1,109	F4
†21784	Eldersburg 4,959	L3
†21659	Eldorado 93	P6
21920	Elk Mills 550	P2
†21901	Elk Neck 700	P2
21921	Elkton⊙ 6,468	P2
21529	Ellerslie 950	C2
21043	Ellicott City⊙ 21,784	L3
21727	Emmitsburg 1,552	J2
21221	Essex 39,614	N3
21824	Ewell 595	O9
†20027	Fairmount Heights 1,616	G5
21047	Fallston 5,572	N2
21632	Federalsburg 1,952	P6
21061	Ferndale 14,314	M4
21048	Finksburg 950	L3
21634	Fishing Creek 595	N7
21530	Flintstone 400	D2
†20001	Forest Heights 2,999	F5
21050	Forest Hill 450	N2
†20028	Forestville 16,401	G5
20022	Fort Foote 750	F6
20744	Fort Washington	L6
21740	Fountain Head 1,745	G2
†21760	Foxville 175	H2
21701	Frederick⊙ 28,086	J3

21053	Freeland 500	M2
20758	Friendship 600	M6
21531	Friendsville 511	A2
21532	Frostburg 7,715	C2
21826	Fruitland 2,694	R7
21734	Funkstown 1,103	H2
20760	Gaithersburg 26,424	K4
21635	Galena 374	P3
†19973	Galestown 142	P6
20765	Galesville 600	M5
†21048	Gamber 500	L3
21054	Gambrills 460	M4
20766	Garrett Park 1,178	E3
21055	Garrison 950	L3
20767	Germantown 9,721	J4
†20801	Glenarden 4,993	G4
21061	Glen Burnie 37,263	M4
20768	Glen Echo 229	E4
21737	Glenelg 450	L3
21636	Goldsboro 188	P4
21163	Granite 950	L3
21536	Grantsville 498	B2
21638	Grasonville 1,910	O5
20770	Greenbelt 17,332	G4

21122	Green Haven 6,577	M4
21639	Greensboro 1,253	P5
21740	Hagerstown⊙ 34,132	G2
21532	Hagerstown‡ 113,086	G2
†21740	Halfway 8,659	G2
21074	Hampstead 1,293	L2
21750	Hancock 1,887	F2
21201	Hanover 500	M4
21077	Harmans 400	M4
21078	Havre de Grace 8,763	O2
21830	Hebron 714	R7
21640	Henderson 156	P4
†21111	Hereford 680	M2
21753	Highfield-Cascade 1,096	J2
21401	Highland Beach 8	M5
†20903	Hillandale 9,686	F4
20031	Hillcrest Heights 17,021	F5
21641	Hillsboro 180	P5
20636	Hollywood 950	M7
20637	Hughesville 1,208	L6
20639	Huntingtown 450	M6
21643	Hurlock 1,690	P6
†20780	Hyattsville 12,709	F4
20640	Indian Head 1,381	K6

†20685	Island Creek 400	M7
21084	Jarrettsville 1,485	M2
†21085	Joppatowne 11,348	N3
21756	Keedysville 476	H3
†20901	Kemp Mill	F3
20795	Kensington 1,822	E4
21087	Kingsville 2,824	N3
21538	Kitzmiller 387	B3
21758	Knoxville 500	H3
20785	Landover 5,374	G4
20784	Landover Hills 1,428	G4
20787	Langley Park 14,038	F4
20801	Lanham-Seabrook 15,814	G4
21227	Lansdowne-Baltimore	
	Highlands 16,759	M3
20646	La Plata⊙ 2,484	L6
*20810	Largo 5,557	G5
*20810	Laurel 12,103	L4
21502	La Vale-Narrows	
	Park 5,523	C2
20760	Laytonsville 195	K4
21761	Le Gore 500	J2
21740	Leitersburg 350	H2
20650	Leonardtown⊙ 1,448	M7

(continued)

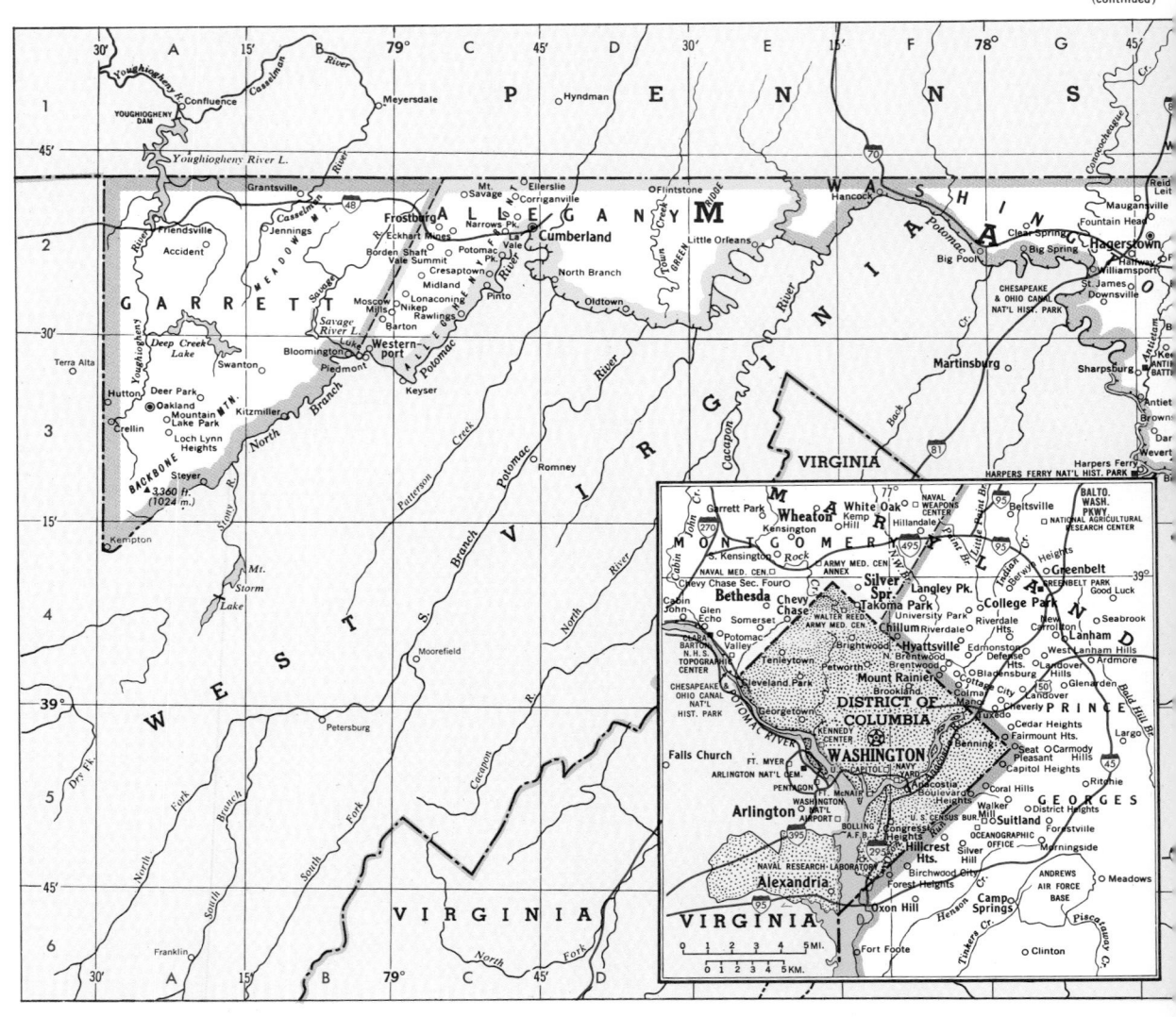

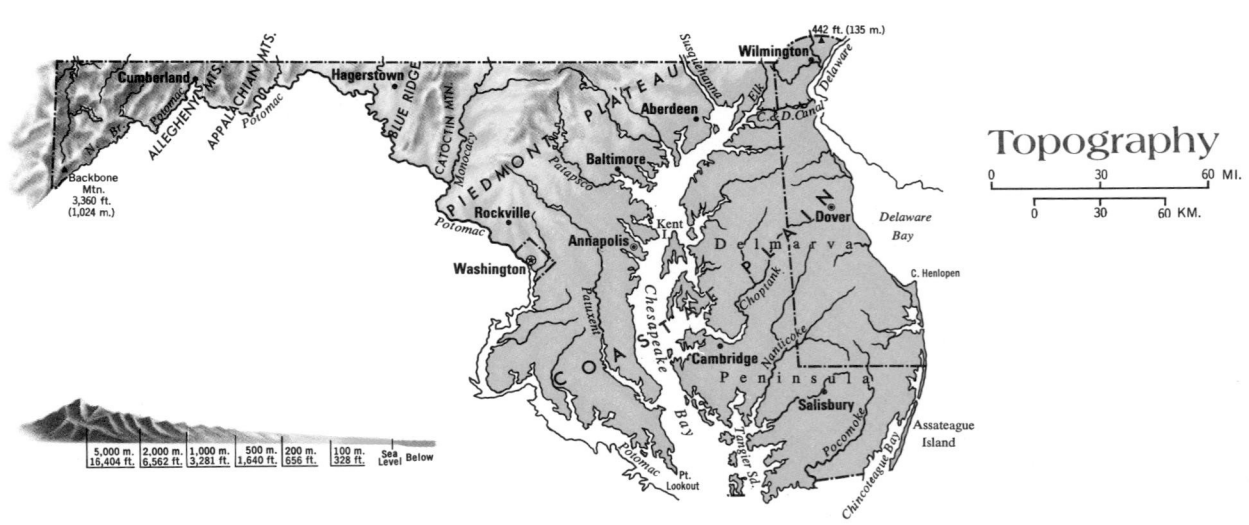

Topography

0   30   60 MI.

0   30   60 KM.

MARYLAND

AREA 10,460 sq. mi. (27,091 sq. km.)
POPULATION 4,216,975
CAPITAL Annapolis
LARGEST CITY Baltimore
HIGHEST POINT Backbone Mtn. 3,360 ft. (1024 m.)
SETTLED IN 1634
ADMITTED TO UNION April 28, 1788
POPULAR NAME Old Line State; Free State
STATE FLOWER Black-eyed Susan
STATE BIRD Baltimore Oriole

DELAWARE

AREA 2,044 sq. mi. (5,294 sq. km.)
POPULATION 594,317
CAPITAL Dover
LARGEST CITY Wilmington
HIGHEST POINT Ebright Road 442 ft. (135 m.)
SETTLED IN 1627
ADMITTED TO UNION December 7, 1787
POPULAR NAME First State; Diamond State
STATE FLOWER Peach Blossom
STATE BIRD Blue Hen Chicken

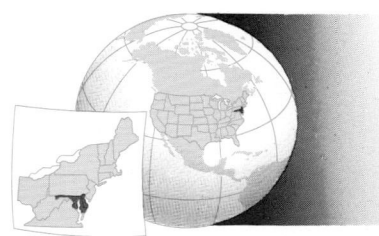

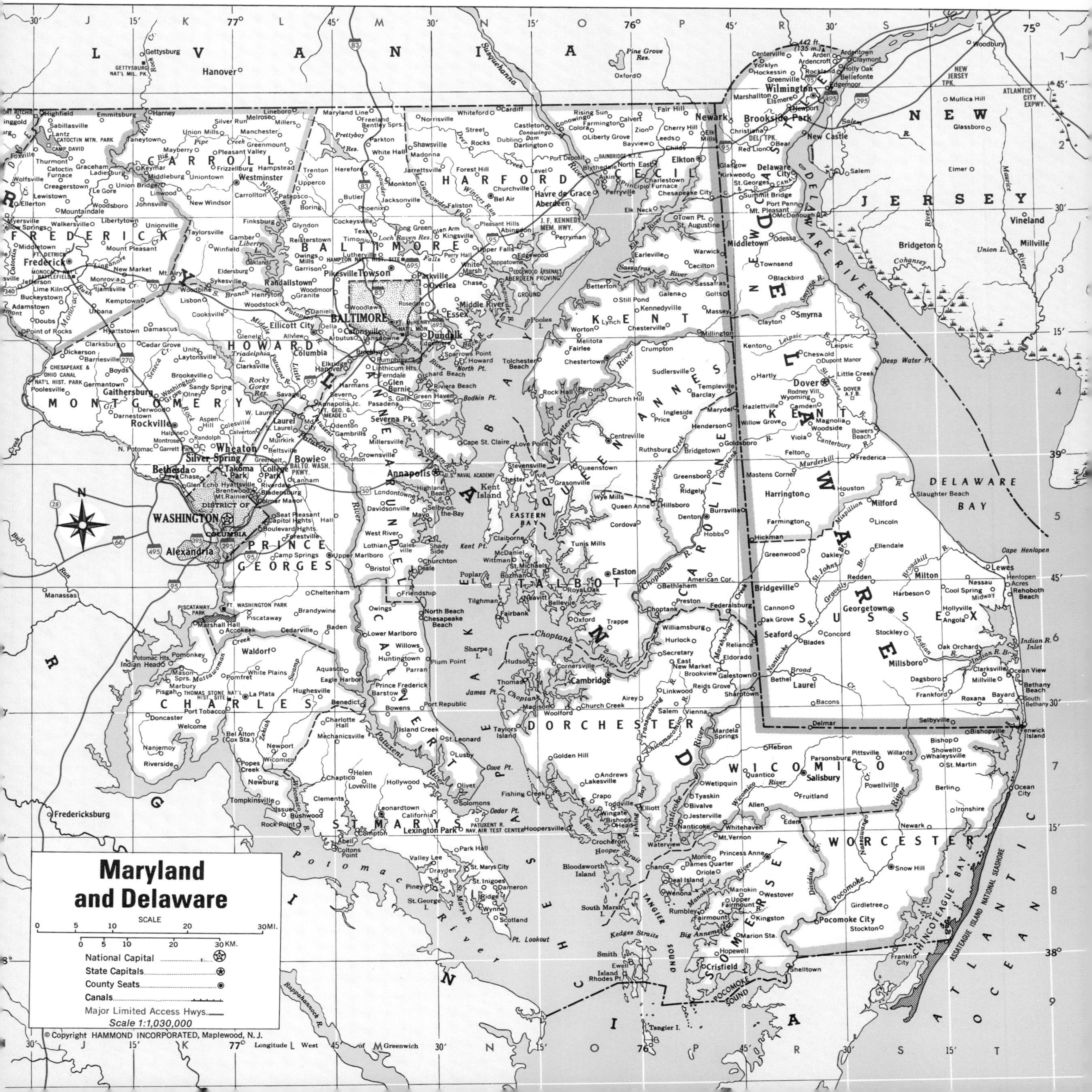

Maryland and Delaware

SCALE

0 5 10 20 30 MI.
0 5 10 20 30 KM.

National Capital ⊛
State Capitals ⊛
County Seats ⊙
Canals

Major Limited Access Hwys.

Scale 1:1,030,000

© Copyright HAMMOND INCORPORATED, Maplewood, N.J.

21701 Lewistown 600 .... J2
20653 Lexington Park 10,361 .... M7
21762 Libertytown 400 .... J3
21090 Linthicum Heights 7,457 .... M4
21766 Little Orleans 600 .... E2
†21550 Loch Lynn Heights 503 .... A3
21539 Lonaconing 1,420 .... C2
†21035 Londontowne 6,052 .... M4
21092 Long Green 1,626 .... M3
20656 Loveville 600 .... M7
21540 Luke 329 .... B3
21093 Lutherville-Timonium 16,871 .... M3
21648 Madison 350 .... O6
21102 Manchester 1,830 .... L2
20658 Marbury 1,189 .... K6
21837 Mardela Springs 320 .... P7
21838 Marion Station 400 .... R8
†20616 Marshall Hall 325 .... K6
21649 Marydel 152 .... P4
†21113 Maryland City 6,949 .... L4
21767 Maugansville 1,707 .... H2
21106 Mayo 2,795 .... M5
20659 Mechanicsville 784 .... M7
21220 Middle River 26,756 .... N3
21769 Middletown 1,748 .... J3
21542 Midland 601 .... C2
21108 Millersville 380 .... M4
21651 Millington 546 .... P3
†20028 Morningside 1,395 .... G5
†21701 Mountaindale 400 .... J2
21550 Mountain Lake Park 1,597 .... A3
21771 Mount Airy 2,450 .... K3
†21701 Mount Pleasant 400 .... J3
20822 Mount Rainier 7,361 .... F4
21545 Mount Savage 1,640 .... C2
†21853 Mount Vernon 900 .... P8
†20705 Muirkirk 950 .... L4
21773 Myersville 432 .... H3
21840 Nanticoke 450 .... P7
†21502 Narrows Park-La Vale 5,523 .... C2
21841 Newark 900 .... S7
20664 Newburg 550 .... L7
20784 New Carrollton 12,632 .... G4
21774 New Market 306 .... J3
21776 New Windsor 799 .... K2
20831 North Beach 1,504 .... N6
†20722 North Brentwood 580 .... F4
21901 North East 1,469 .... P2
†20854 North Potomac K4
21550 Oakland⊙ 1,994 .... A3
†21784 Oakland 2,242 .... L3
21842 Ocean City 4,946 .... T7
21113 Odenton 13,270 .... M4
†21228 Oella 600 .... L3
20832 Olney 13,026 .... K4
21206 Overlea 12,965 .... N3
20836 Owings 700 .... M6
21117 Owings Mills 9,526 .... L3
21654 Oxford 754 .... O6
20745 Oxon Hill 36,267 .... F6
20667 Park Hall 775 .... N8
21234 Parkville 35,159 .... M3
21122 Pasadena 7,439 .... M4
21128 Perry Hall 13,455 .... N3
21130 Perryman 1,819 .... O3
21903 Perryville 2,018 .... O2
21208 Pikesville 22,555 .... M3
20674 Piney Point 950 .... M8
†20735 Piscataway 500 .... L6
20640 Pisgah 650 .... K6
21850 Pittsville 519 .... S7
†21087 Pleasant Hills 2,790 .... N3
21851 Pocomoke City 3,558 .... R8
20675 Pomfret 600 .... L6
†20640 Pomonkey 410 .... K6
20837 Poolesville 3,428 .... J4
21904 Port Deposit 664 .... O2
20677 Port Tobacco 40 .... K6
20640 Potomac Heights 2,456 .... K6
†21502 Potomac Park-Bowling Green 2,275 .... C2
21852 Powellville 400 .... S7
21655 Preston 498 .... P6
20678 Prince Frederick⊙ 1,805 .... M6
21853 Princess Anne⊙ 1,499 .... P8
†21090 Pumphrey 5,666 .... M4
21657 Queen Anne 259 .... O5
21658 Queenstown 491 .... O5
21133 Randallstown 25,927 .... L3
21557 Rawlings 500 .... C2
21136 Reisterstown 19,385 .... L3
20680 Ridge 550 .... N8
21660 Ridgely 933 .... P5
21911 Rising Sun 1,160 .... O2
†20027 Ritchie 950 .... G5
†20840 Riverdale Heights G4
†21061 Riviera Beach 8,812 .... N4
21661 Rock Hall 1,511 .... O4
†21084 Rocks 450 .... N2
*20850 Rockville⊙ 43,811 .... K4
21779 Rohrersville 525 .... H3
21237 Rosedale 19,956 .... M3
†21758 Rosemont 305 .... H3
21662 Royal Oak 600 .... O6
21780 Sabillasville 450 .... J2
20684 Saint Inigoes 750 .... N8
21663 Saint Michaels 1,301 .... N5
21801 Salisbury⊙ 16,429 .... R7
20860 Sandy Spring-Ashton 2,659 .... K4
20863 Savage-Guilford 2,928 .... L4
20687 Scotland 475 .... N8
20801 Seabrook-Lanham 15,814 .... G4
20027 Seat Pleasant 5,217 .... G5
21664 Secretary 487 .... P6
†21037 Selby-on-the-Bay 3,125 .... N5
21144 Severn 20,147 .... M4
21146 Severna Park 21,253 .... M4
20867 Shady Side 2,877 .... M5
21782 Sharpsburg 721 .... G3
21861 Sharptown 654 .... R6
20023 Silver Hill-Suitland 32,164 .... F5
†21157 Silver Run 350 .... K2
*20901 Silver Spring 72,893 .... F4
21783 Smithsburg 833 .... H2
21863 Snow Hill⊙ 2,192 .... S8
†20015 Somerset 1,101 .... E4
†21113 South Gate 24,185 .... M4
†20795 South Kensington 9,344 .... E4
†20810 South Laurel 18,034 .... L4
21219 Sparrows Point N4
21666 Stevensville 500 .... N5
21667 Still Pond 350 .... O3
21864 Stockton 400 .... S8
21668 Sudlersville 443 .... P4
†20746 Suitland-Silver Hill 32,164 .... F5
21784 Sykesville 1,712 .... K3
20912 Takoma Park 16,231 .... F4
21787 Taneytown 2,618 .... K2
21669 Taylors Island 400 .... N7
21670 Templeville 96 .... P4
21788 Thurmont 2,934 .... J2
21671 Tilghman 979 .... N6
21093 Timonium-Lutherville 16,871 .... M3
21672 Toddville 500 .... O7
21204 Towson⊙ 51,083 .... M3
21673 Trappe 739 .... O6
†20780 Tuxedo 500 .... G5
21791 Union Bridge 927 .... K2
†20740 University Park 2,536 .... F4
21155 Upperco 500 .... L2
21867 Upper Fairmount 500 .... P8
21156 Upper Falls 550 .... N3
20870 Upper Marlboro⊙ 828 .... M5
20692 Valley Lee 600 .... M8
21869 Vienna 300 .... P7
20601 Waldorf 9,782 .... L6
†20023 Walker Mill 10,651 .... F5
21793 Walkersville 2,212 .... J3
21912 Warwick 550 .... P3
20880 Washington Grove 527 .... K4
20693 Welcome 438 .... K7
21562 Westernport 2,706 .... B3
†20784 West Lanham Hills 350 .... G4
21157 Westminster⊙ 8,808 .... L2
21871 Westover 450 .... R8
20902 Wheaton-Glenmont 48,598 .... E3
21160 Whiteford 500 .... N2
21161 White Hall 360 .... M2
21162 White Marsh 500 .... N3
†20901 White Oak 13,700 .... F3
20695 White Plains 5,167 .... L6
21874 Willards 540 .... S7
21795 Williamsport 2,153 .... G2
21676 Wittman 544 .... N5
21797 Woodbine 872 .... K3
21798 Woodsboro 506 .... J2
21163 Woodstock 700 .... L3
21677 Woolford 330 .... O7
21679 Wye Mills 315 .... O5
†20680 Wynne 450 .... N8
†21701 Yellow Springs 940 .... H3

OTHER FEATURES

Aberdeen Proving Ground 5,722 .... N3
Allegheny Front (mts.) C2
Andrews A.F.B. 10,064 .... G5
Antietam (creek) H2
Antietam Nat'l Battlefield H3
Army Chemical Center O3
Back (riv.) N4
Backbone (mt.) A3
Bainbridge N.T.C. O2
Bald Hill Branch (riv.) G4
Big Annemessex (riv.) P8
Big Pipe (creek) K2
Bloodsworth (isl.) O8
Blue Ridge (mts.) H3
Bodkin (pt.) N4
Bush (creek) J3
Cabin John (creek) E4
Camp David J2
Casselman (riv.) B2
Catoctin (creek) H3
Catoctin Mt. Park J2
Cedar (pt.) N7
Census Bureau F5
Chesapeake (bay) N7
Chesapeake and Delaware (canal) R2
Chesapeake and Ohio Canal Nat'l Hist. Park J4
Chester (riv.) O4
Chicamacomico (riv.) P7
Chincoteague (bay) S8
Choptank (riv.) O6
Clara Barton Nat'l Hist. Site E4
Conococheague (creek) G1
Conowingo (dam) O2
Cove (pt.) N7
Deep Creek (lake) A3
Deer (creek) N2
Dividing (creek) R8
Eastern (bay) N5
Elk (riv.) P3
Fishing (bay) O7
Fort Detrick J3
Fort George G. Meade 14,083 .... L4
Fort McHenry Nat'l Mon. M3
Fort Ritchie 1,754 .... H2
Fort Washington Park L6
Great Seneca (creek) J4
Greenbelt Park G4
Green Ridge (mts.) E2
Gunpowder (riv.) N3
Gunpowder Falls (creek) M2
Hampton Nat'l Hist. Site M3
Harpers Ferry Nat'l Hist. Park G3
Henson (creek) F6
Honga (riv.) O7
Hooper (str.) O8
Indian (creek) G4
James (pt.) N6
Kedges (strs) O8
Kent (isl.) N5
Kent (pt.) N5
Liberty (lake) L3
Linganore (creek) J3
Little Choptank (riv.) N6
Little Gunpowder Falls (creek) M2
Little Paint Branch (riv.) F4
Little Patuxent (riv.) L4
Loch Raven (res.) M3
Lookout (pt.) N8
Manokin (riv.) P8
Marshyhope (creek) P6
Mattawoman (creek) K6
Meadow (mt.) B2
Middle Patuxent (riv.) L3
Monocacy (riv.) J3
Monocacy Nat'l Battlefield J3
Nanticoke (riv.) P7
Nassawango (creek) S8
National Agricultural Research Center G3
Naval Academy, U.S. 5,367 .... N5
Naval Medical Center E4
Naval Weapons Center F3
North (pt.) N4
Oceanographic Office F5
Oxon Run (riv.) F5
Paint Branch (riv.) F4
Patapsco (riv.) M4
Patuxent (riv.) M7
Patuxent River Nav. Air Test Ctr. N7
Piscataway (creek) G6
Piscataway Park K6
Pocomoke (riv.) S8
Pocomoke (sound) P9
Pooles (isl.) O3
Poplar (isl.) N5
Potomac (riv.) M8
Prettyboy (res.) M2
Rock (creek) K4
Rocky Gorge (res.) L4
Saint George (isl.) M8
Saint Marys (riv.) N8
Sassafras (riv.) P3
Savage (riv.) B2
Savage River (lake) B2
Severn (riv.) N4
Sharps (isl.) N6
Smith (isl.) O8
South Marsh (isl.) O8
Susquehanna (riv.) N1
Tangier (sound) P8
Thomas Stone Nat'l Hist. Site K6
Tinkers (creek) F6
Topographic Center E4
Town (creek) E2
Transquaking (riv.) P7
Triadelphia (lake) L4
Tuckahoe (creek) P5
Walter Reed Army Med. Ctr. Annex E4
Wicomico (riv.) L7
Wicomico (riv.) R7
Winters Run (creek) N2
Youghiogheny (riv.) A3
Youghiogheny River (lake) A2
Zekiah Swamp (riv.) L7

DELAWARE

COUNTIES

Kent 98,219 .... R4
New Castle 398,115 .... R2
Sussex 97,983 .... S6

CITIES and TOWNS

Zip *Name/Pop.* *Key*

†19801 Arden 516 .... R1
†19810 Ardencroft 267 .... R1
†19810 Ardentown 307 .... S1
19809 Bellefonte 1,279 .... S1
19930 Bethany Beach 330 .... T6
19931 Bethel 197 .... R6
†19973 Blades 664 .... R6
†19962 Bowers Beach 198 .... S4
19993 Bridgeville 1,238 .... R6
19711 Brookside 15,255 .... R2
19934 Camden 1,757 .... R4
†19801 Centerville 800 .... R1
19936 Cheswold 269 .... R4
†19711 Christiana 500 .... R2
19937 Clarksville 350 .... T6
19703 Claymont 10,022 .... S1
19938 Clayton 1,216 .... R3
19930 Dagsboro 344 .... S6
19706 Delaware City 1,858 .... R2
19940 Delmar 948 .... R7
19901 Dover (cap.)⊙ 23,507 .... R4
†19901 Dupont Manor 1,059 .... R4
†19801 Edgemoor 7,397 .... S1
19941 Ellendale 361 .... S5
†19801 Elsmere 6,493 .... R2
19942 Farmington 141 .... R5
19943 Felton 547 .... R4
19944 Fenwick Island 114 .... T7
19945 Frankford 828 .... S6
19946 Frederica 864 .... S4
19947 Georgetown⊙ 1,710 .... S6
†19711 Glasgow 350 .... R2
19950 Greenwood 578 .... R5
19952 Harrington 2,405 .... R5
†19971 Henlopen Acres 176 .... T6
19707 Hockessin 950 .... R1
†19801 Holly Oak S1
19954 Houston 357 .... S5
19955 Kenton 243 .... R4
19708 Kirkwood 350 .... R2
19956 Laurel 3,052 .... R6
†19901 Leipsic 228 .... S4
19958 Lewes 2,197 .... T5
19960 Lincoln 757 .... S5
19961 Little Creek 230 .... S4
19962 Magnolia 197 .... R4
19709 Middletown 2,946 .... R3
19963 Milford 5,366 .... S5
19966 Millsboro 1,233 .... S6
19967 Millville 178 .... T6
19968 Milton 1,359 .... S5
19711 Newark 25,247 .... P2
19720 New Castle 4,907 .... R2
19804 Newport 1,167 .... R2
†19966 Oak Orchard 350 .... T6
19970 Ocean View 495 .... T6
19730 Odessa 384 .... R3
19971 Rehoboth Beach 1,730 .... T6
19901 Rodney Village 1,753 .... R4
19733 Saint Georges 450 .... R2
19973 Seaford 5,256 .... R6
19975 Selbyville 1,251 .... S7
†19963 Slaughter Beach 121 .... S5
19977 Smyrna 4,750 .... R3
†19930 South Bethany 115 .... T6
19734 Townsend 386 .... R3
19979 Viola 167 .... R4
*19801 Wilmington⊙ 70,195 .... R2
Wilmington‡ 524,108 .... R2
19980 Woodside 248 .... R4
19934 Wyoming 960 .... R4
19736 Yorklyn 600 .... R1

OTHER FEATURES

Broad (creek) R6
Broadkill (riv.) S5
Chesapeake and Delaware (canal) R2
Choptank (riv.) P5
Deep Water (pt.) S4
Delaware (bay) T5
Delaware (riv.) R3
Dover A.F.B. 4,391 .... S4
Henlopen (cape) T5
Indian (riv.) S6
Indian River (bay) T6
Indian River (inlet) T6
Leipsic (riv.) R4
Mispillion (riv.) S5
Murderkill (riv.) R5
Nanticoke (riv.) R6
Saint Jones (riv.) R4
Smyrna (res.) R3

DISTRICT OF COLUMBIA

CITIES and TOWNS

Zip *Name/Pop.* *Key*

20007 Georgetown E5
*20001 Washington, D.C. (cap.), U.S. 638,432 .... F5
Washington‡ 3,060,240 .... F5

OTHER FEATURES

Anacostia (riv.) F5
Bolling A.F.B. E5
Fort Lesley J. McNair E5
Kennedy Center A5
Naval Yard F5
U.S. Capitol F5
Walter Reed Army Med. Ctr. E4

⊙County seat.
‡Population of metropolitan area.
† Zip of nearest p.o.
* Multiple zips.

Agriculture, Industry and Resources

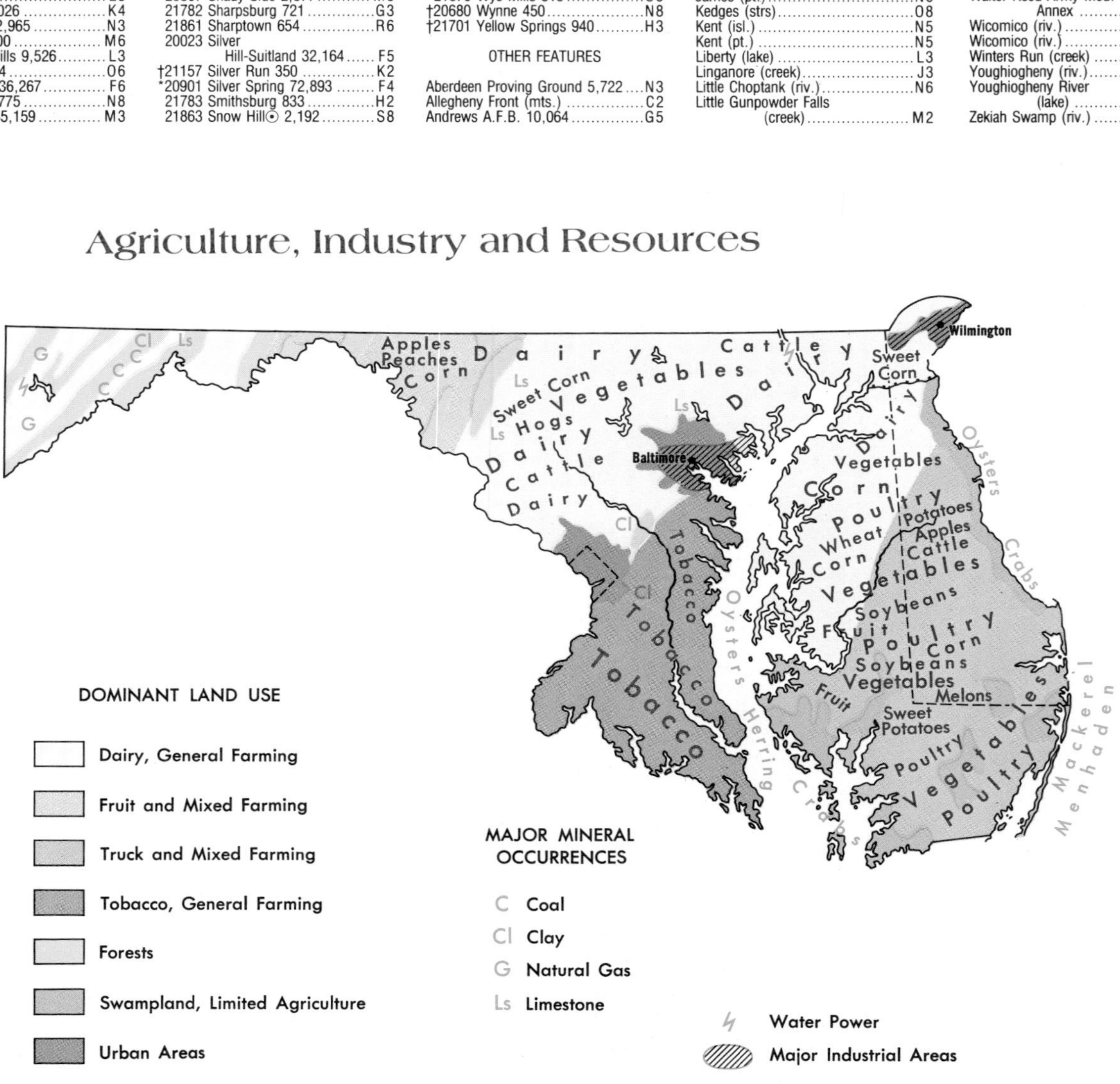
Apples
Peaches
Corn
Dairy
Cattle
Dairy
Sweet Corn
Wilmington
Sweet Corn
Vegetables
Hogs
Dairy
Cattle
Baltimore
Dairy
Vegetables
Corn
Poultry
Potatoes
Apples
Cattle
Wheat
Corn
Vegetables
Soybeans
Fruit
Poultry
Corn
Soybeans
Vegetables
Melons
Sweet Potatoes
Poultry
Vegetables
Poultry
Tobacco
Tobacco
Tobacco
Oysters
Oysters
Crabs
Herring
Crabs
Mackerel
Menhaden
Fruit
DOMINANT LAND USE
Dairy, General Farming
Fruit and Mixed Farming
Truck and Mixed Farming
Tobacco, General Farming
Forests
Swampland, Limited Agriculture
Urban Areas
MAJOR MINERAL OCCURRENCES
C Coal
Cl Clay
G Natural Gas
Ls Limestone
Water Power
Major Industrial Areas

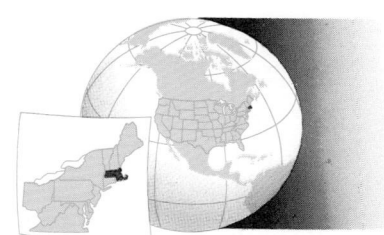

MASSACHUSETTS

AREA 8,284 sq. mi. (21,456 sq. km.)
POPULATION 5,737,037
CAPITAL Boston
LARGEST CITY Boston
HIGHEST POINT Mt. Greylock 3,491 ft.
(1064 m.)
SETTLED IN 1620
ADMITTED TO UNION February 6, 1788
POPULAR NAME Bay State; Old Colony
STATE FLOWER Mayflower
STATE BIRD Chickadee

RHODE ISLAND

AREA 1,212 sq. mi. (3,139 sq. km.)
POPULATION 947,154
CAPITAL Providence
LARGEST CITY Providence
HIGHEST POINT Jerimoth Hill 812 ft.
(247 m.)
SETTLED IN 1636
ADMITTED TO UNION May 29, 1790
POPULAR NAME Little Rhody; Ocean State
STATE FLOWER Violet
STATE BIRD Rhode Island Red

Agriculture, Industry and Resources

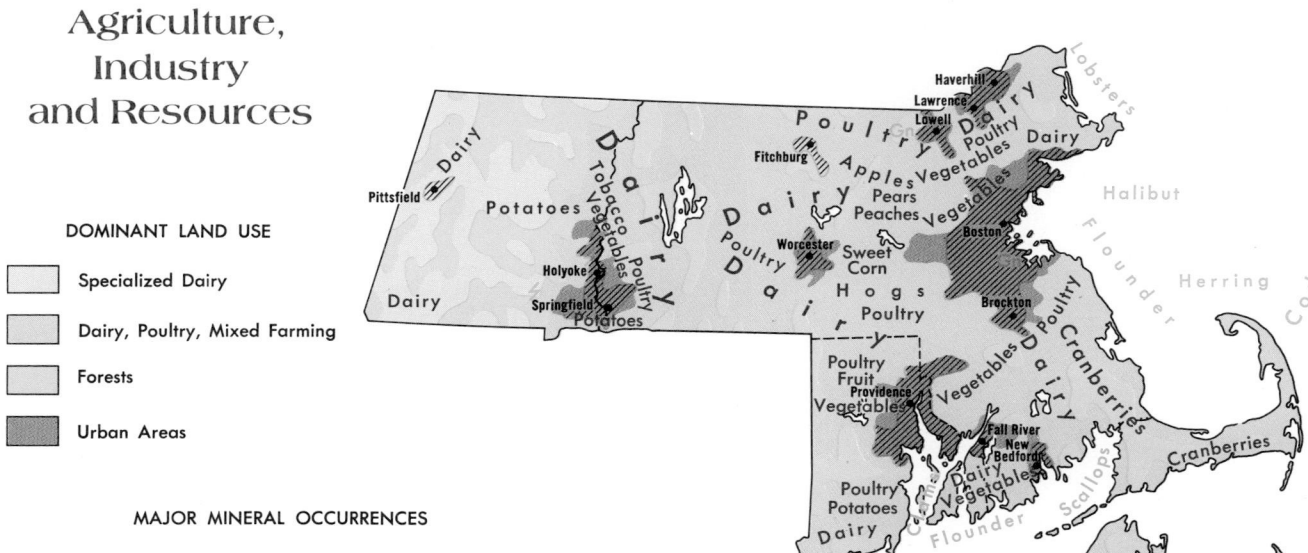

DOMINANT LAND USE

- Specialized Dairy
- Dairy, Poultry, Mixed Farming
- Forests
- Urban Areas

MAJOR MINERAL OCCURRENCES

Gn   Granite

⚡ Water Power   ▨ Major Industrial Areas

MASSACHUSETTS

COUNTIES

Barnstable 147,925 ....N6
Berkshire 145,110 ....B3
Bristol 474,641 ....K5
Dukes 8,942 ....M7
Essex 633,632 ....L2
Franklin 64,317 ....D2
Hampden 443,018 ....D4
Hampshire 138,813 ....D3
Middlesex 1,367,034 ....J3
Nantucket 5,087 ....O7
Norfolk 606,587 ....K4
Plymouth 405,437 ....L5
Suffolk 650,142 ....K3
Worcester 646,352 ....G3

CITIES and TOWNS

Zip   Name/Pop.   Key

02351 Abington○ 13,517 ....L4
01720 Acton○ 17,544 ....J3
02743 Acushnet○ 8,704 ....L6
01220 Adams○ 10,381 ....B2
01220 Adams 6,857 ....B2
01001 Agawam○ 26,271 ....D4
†01261 Alford○ 394 ....A4
01913 Amesbury○ 13,971 ....L1
01913 Amesbury 12,236 ....L1
01002 Amherst○ 33,229 ....E3
01002 Amherst 17,773 ....E3
01810 Andover○ 26,370 ....K2
01810 Andover 8,445 ....K2
02174 Arlington○ 48,219 ....C6
01430 Ashburnham○ 4,075 .....G2
01430 Ashburnham 900 ....G2
01431 Ashby○ 2,311 ....G2
01330 Ashfield○ 1,458 ....C2
01721 Ashland○ 9,165 ....J3
01331 Athol○ 10,634 ....F2
01331 Athol 8,708 ....F2
02703 Attleboro 34,196 ....J5
01501 Auburn○ 14,845 ....G4
02322 Avon○ 5,026 ....K4
*01432 Ayer○ 6,993 ....H2
*01432 Ayer 3,165 ....H2
01436 Baldwinville○ 1,709 ......F2
02630 Barnstable○ 30,898 ......N6
02630 Barnstable○ 2,033 ....N6
01005 Barre○ 4,102 ....F3
01005 Barre 1,136 ....F3
01223 Becket○ 1,339 ....B3
01730 Bedford 13,067 ....B6
01007 Belchertown○ 8,339 .....E3
01007 Belchertown 2,531 ....E3
02019 Bellingham 14,300 ....J4
02019 Bellingham 4,454 ....J4
02178 Belmont○ 26,100 ....C6
*02780 Berkley○ 2,731 ....K5
01503 Berlin○ 2,215 ....H3

01337 Bernardston○ 1,750 ......D2
01915 Beverly 37,655 ....E5
01821 Billerica○ 36,727 ....J2
01504 Blackstone○ 6,570 ....H4
01008 Blandford○ 1,038 ....C4
01740 Bolton○ 2,530 ....H3
01009 Bondsville 1,906 ....E4
*02101 Boston (cap.)⊙ 562,994...D7
       Boston‡ 2,763,357 ....D7
02532 Bourne○ 13,874 ....M6
02532 Bourne 2,678 ....M6
01719 Boxborough○ 3,126 ......H3
01921 Boxford○ 5,374 ....L2
01921 Boxford 1,841 ....L2
01505 Boylston○ 3,470 ....H3
02184 Braintree○ 36,337 ....D8
02020 Brant Rock-Ocean
       Bluff 4,055 ....M4
02631 Brewster○ 5,226 ....O5
02631 Brewster 1,744 ....O5
02324 Bridgewater○ 17,202 ....K5
02324 Bridgewater 6,781 ....K5
01010 Brimfield○ 2,318 ....F4
*C2401 Brockton 95,172 ....K4
       Brockton‡ 169,374 ....K4
01506 Brookfield○ 2,397 ....F4
01506 Brookfield 1,037 ....F4
02146 Brookline○ 55,062 ....C7
01338 Buckland○ 1,864 ....C2
01803 Burlington 23,486 ....C5
02532 Buzzards Bay 3,375 ....M5
02138 Cambridge○ 95,322 ....C7
02021 Canton○ 18,182 ....C8
01741 Carlisle○ 3,306 ....J2
02330 Carver○ 6,988 ....M5
02632 Centerville 3,640 ....N6
01339 Charlemont○ 1,149 ....C2
01507 Charlton○ 6,719 ....F4
02633 Chatham○ 6,071 ....P6
02633 Chatham 1,922 ....P6
01824 Chelmsford○ 31,174 ......J2
02150 Chelsea 25,431 ....D6
01225 Cheshire○ 3,124 ....B2
01011 Chester○ 1,123 ....C3
01012 Chesterfield○ 1,000 ......C3
*01013 Chicopee 55,112 ....D4
02535 Chilmark○ 489 ....M7
†02054 Clicquot-Mills 3,777 .....A8
01510 Clinton○ 12,771 ....H3
01778 Cochituate 6,126 ....A7
02025 Cohasset○ 7,174 ....F7
01340 Colrain○ 1,552 ....D2
01742 Concord○ 16,293 ....B6
01341 Conway○ 1,213 ....D2
†01772 Cordaville 1,384 ....H3
01026 Cummington○ 657 ....C3
01226 Dalton○ 6,797 ....B3
01923 Danvers○ 24,100 ....D5
02714 Dartmouth○ 23,966 ......K6
02026 Dedham○ 25,298 ....C7
01342 Deerfield○ 4,517 ....D2
02638 Dennis○ 12,360 ....O5

01035 Hadley○ 4,125 ....D3
02338 Halifax○ 5,513 ....L5
01936 Hamilton○ 6,960 ....L2
01036 Hampden○ 4,745 ....E4
01237 Hancock○ 643 ....A2
02339 Hanover○ 11,358 ....L4
02341 Hanson○ 8,617 ....L4
02341 Hanson 2,120 ....L4
01037 Hardwick○ 2,272 ....F3
01451 Harvard○ 12,170 ....H2
02645 Harwich○ 8,971 ....O6
02645 Harwich 4,399 ....O6
01038 Hatfield○ 3,045 ....D3
01038 Hatfield 1,251 ....D3
01830 Haverhill 46,865 ....K1
01346 Heath○ 482 ....C2
02043 Hingham○ 20,339 ....E8
02043 Hingham 5,742 ....E8
01235 Hinsdale○ 1,707 ....B3
02343 Holbrook○ 11,140 ....D8
01520 Holden○ 13,336 ....G3
01746 Holliston○ 12,622 ....A8
01040 Holyoke 44,678 ....D4
01747 Hopedale○ 3,905 ....H4
01747 Hopedale 2,810 ....H4
01748 Hopkinton○ 7,114 ....J4
01748 Hopkinton 2,542 ....J4
01236 Housatonic 1,314 ....A3
01452 Hubbardston○ 1,797 .....F3
01749 Hudson○ 16,408 ....H3
01749 Hudson 14,156 ....H3
02045 Hull○ 9,714 ....E7
01050 Huntington○ 1,804 ....C4
02601 Hyannis 9,118 ....N6
01938 Ipswich○ 11,158 ....L2
01938 Ipswich 4,548 ....L2
02364 Kingston○ 7,362 ....M5
02364 Kingston 4,405 ....M5
02346 Lakeville○ 5,931 ....L5
02346 Lakeville 1,948 ....L5
01523 Lancaster○ 6,334 ....H3
01237 Lanesboro○ 3,131 ....A2
*01840 Lawrence○ 63,175 ....K2
       Lawrence-Haverhill‡
       281,981 ....K2
01238 Lee○ 6,247 ....B3
01238 Lee 2,140 ....B3
01524 Leicester○ 9,446 ....G4
01240 Lenox○ 6,523 ....A3
01240 Lenox 2,684 ....A3
01453 Leominster 34,508 ....G2
01054 Leverett○ 1,471 ....E3
02173 Lexington○ 29,479 ....B6
*01301 Leyden○ 498 ....D2
01773 Lincoln○ 7,098 ....B6
01460 Littleton○ 6,970 ....J2
*01460 Littleton Common 3,109...J2
01106 Longmeadow○ 16,301 ..D4
*01850 Lowell○ 92,418 ....J2
       Lowell‡ 233,410 ....J2
01056 Ludlow○ 18,150 ....E4

01462 Lunenburg○ 8,405 ....H2
01462 Lunenburg 1,789 ....H2
01940 Lynnfield○ 11,267 ....D5
*01901 Lynn 78,471 ....D6
02148 Malden 53,386 ....D6
01944 Manchester○ 5,424 ......F5
02048 Mansfield○ 13,453 ....J4
02048 Mansfield 6,786 ....J4
01945 Marblehead○ 20,126 .....E7
02738 Marion○ 3,932 ....L6
02738 Marion 1,438 ....L6
01752 Marlborough 30,617 ......H3
02050 Marshfield○ 20,916 ....M4
02050 Marshfield 4,421 ....M4
02051 Marshfield Hills 2,308 .....M4
02649 Mashpee○ 3,700 ....M6
02739 Mattapoisett○ 5,597 ......L6
02739 Mattapoisett 3,159 ....L6
01754 Maynard○ 9,590 ....J3
02052 Medfield○ 10,220 ....B8
02052 Medfield 6,108 ....B8
02155 Medford 58,076 ....C6
02053 Medway○ 8,447 ....J4
02176 Melrose 30,055 ....D6
01756 Mendon○ 3,108 ....H4
01860 Merrimac○ 4,451 ....L1
01844 Methuen○ 36,701 ....K2
02346 Middleboro○ 16,404 ......L5
02346 Middleboro 7,012 ....L5
01243 Middlefield○ 385 ....B3
01949 Middleton○ 4,135 ....K2
01757 Milford○ 23,390 ....H4
01757 Milford 21,730 ....H4
01527 Millbury○ 11,808 ....H4
01349 Millers Falls 1,101 ....E2
02054 Millis○ 6,908 ....A8
02054 Millis-Clicquot 3,777 ......A8
01529 Millville○ 1,693 ....H4
02186 Milton○ 25,860 ....D7
01057 Monson○ 7,315 ....E4
01057 Monson 2,167 ....E4
01351 Montague○ 8,011 ....E2
01245 Monterey○ 818 ....B4
02056 Norfolk○ 6,363 ....J4
01247 North Adams 18,063 .....B2
01059 North Amherst 5,616 .....E3
01060 Northampton○ 29,286 ...D3
01845 North Andover○ 20,129 ..K2

*02760 North Attleboro○ 21,095 ... J5
01532 Northborough○ 10,568 ...H3
01532 Northborough 5,670 ......H3
01534 Northbridge○ 12,246 .....H4
01535 North Brookfield○ 4,150...F3
01535 North Brookfield 2,543 ...F3
02764 North Dighton 1,174 ......K5
02651 North Eastham 1,318 .....O5
01360 Northfield○ 2,386 ....E2
01360 Northfield 1,182 ....E2
02358 North Pembroke 2,215 ...M4
02360 North Plymouth 3,250 ....L5
01864 North Reading 11,455 ....C5
02060 North Scituate 5,221 .....F8
02766 Norton 12,690 ....K5
02766 Norton 2,035 ....K5
02062 Norwood 29,711 ....B8
02557 Oak Bluffs○ 1,984 ....M7
02557 Oak Bluffs 1,124 ....M7
01068 Oakham○ 994 ....F3
02065 Ocean Bluff-Brant
       Rock 4,055 ....M4
†01566 Old Sturbridge
       Village 500 ....F4
02558 Onset 1,493 ....M6
01364 Orange○ 6,844 ....E2
01364 Orange 3,942 ....E2
02653 Orleans○ 5,306 ....O5
02653 Orleans 1,811 ....O5
02655 Osterville 1,799 ....N6
01253 Otis○ 963 ....B4
01540 Oxford○ 11,680 ....G4
01540 Oxford 6,369 ....G4
01069 Palmer○ 11,389 ....E4
01069 Palmer 3,854 ....E4
01612 Paxton○ 3,762 ....G3
01960 Peabody 45,976 ....E5
†01002 Pelham○ 1,112 ....E3
02359 Pembroke 13,487 ....L4
01463 Pepperell○ 8,061 ....H2
01463 Pepperell 2,076 ....H2
01366 Petersham○ 1,024 ....F3
†01331 Phillipston○ 953 ....F2
01866 Pinehurst 6,588 ....B5
01201 Pittsfield⊙ 51,974 ....A3
       Pittsfield‡ 90,505 ....A3
01070 Plainfield○ 425 ....C2
02762 Plainville○ 5,857 ....J4
02360 Plymouth 35,913 ....M5
02360 Plymouth○ 7,232 ....M5
02367 Plympton○ 1,974 ....L5
01541 Princeton○ 2,425 ....G3
02657 Provincetown○ 3,536 .....O4
02657 Provincetown 3,372 ......O4
02169 Quincy 84,743 ....D7
02368 Randolph○ 28,218 ....D8
02767 Raynham○ 9,085 ....K5
02768 Raynham Center 3,776 ...K5
01867 Reading○ 22,678 ....C5
02769 Rehoboth○ 7,570 ....K5
02151 Revere 42,423 ....D6

(continued on following page)

Boston and Vicinity

01266 West Stockbridge○ 1,280 .. A3
02575 West Tisbury○ 1,010...... M7
01587 West Upton-Upton 2,184... H4
02576 West Wareham 1,837...... L5
02090 Westwood○ 13,212...... B8
02673 West Yarmouth 3,852... N6
02188 Weymouth 55,601...... D8
01093 Whately○ 1,341...... D3
01588 Whitinsville 5,379...... H4
02382 Whitman○ 13,534...... L4
01095 Wilbraham 12,053...... E4
01095 Wilbraham 3,379...... E4
01096 Williamsburg 2,237...... C3
01267 Williamstown 8,741...... B2
01267 Williamstown 4,798...... B2
01887 Wilmington 17,471...... C5
01475 Winchendon 7,019...... F2
01475 Winchendon 4,030...... F2
01890 Winchester 20,701...... C6
01270 Windsor○ 598...... B2

02152 Winthrop○ 19,294...... D6
01801 Woburn 36,626...... C6
02543 Woods Hole 1,080...... M6
*01601 Worcester⊙ 161,799...... H3
　　　　Worcester‡ 372,940...... H3
01098 Worthington 932...... C3
02093 Wrentham 7,580...... J4
　　　　Yarmouth 18,449...... O6
02675 Yarmouth Port 2,490...... N6

OTHER FEATURES

Adams Nat'l Hist. Site......D7
Agawam (riv.)......M5
Allerton (pt.)......E7
Ann (cape)......M2
Ashmere (lake)......B3
Assabet (riv.)......H3
Assawompset (pond)......L5
Bachelor (brook)......D3

Berkshire (hills)......B4
Big (pond)......B4
Bigelow (bight)......M1
Blackstone (riv.)......G3
Blue (hills)......C8
Boston (bay)......E6
Boston (harb.)......D7
Boston Nat'l Hist. Park......D6
Brewster (isls.)......E7
Buel (lake)......A4
Buzzards (bay)......L7
Cambridge (res.)......B6
Cape Cod (bay)......N5
Cape Cod (canal)......N5
Cape Cod Nat'l Seashore......P5
Chappaquiddick (isl.)......N7
Charles (riv.)......D7
Chicopee (riv.)......C4
Cobble Mountain (res.)......C4
Cochituate (lake)......A7

Cod (cape)......O4
Concord (riv.)......J2
Congamond (lkes.)......D4
Connecticut (riv.)......D2
Cuttyhunk (isl.)......L7
Deer (isl.)......E7
Deerfield (riv.)......C2
East (pt.)......E6
East Chop (pt.)......M7
Eastern (pt.)......M2
Elizabeth (isls.)......L7
Everett (mt.)......A4
Falls (riv.)......D2
Fort Devens......H2
Fort Rodman......L6
Fresh (pond)......C6
Gammon (pt.)......N6
Gay Head (prom.)......L7
Grace (mt.)......E2
Great (pt.)......O7
Green (pt.)......B2
Greylock (mt.)......B2
Gurnet (pt.)......M4
Hingham (bay)......E7
Holyoke (range)......D3
Hoosac (range)......B2
Hoosic (riv.)......A1
Housatonic (riv.)......A4
Ipswich (riv.)......L2
John F. Kennedy Nat'l Hist.
　　Site......C7
Knightville (res.)......C3
Laurence G. Hanscom Field......B6
Little (riv.)......C4
Logan Internat'l Airport......D7
Long (isl.)......E7
Long (pt.)......O4
Long (pond)......L5
Lowell Nat'l Hist. Park......J2
Maine (gulf)......M2
Manhan (riv.)......D4
Manomet (pt.)......N5
Marblehead (neck)......F6
Martha's Vineyard (isl.)......M7
Massachusetts (bay)......M4
Merrimack (riv.)......K1
Mill (riv.)......C3
Mill (riv.)......D3
Millers (riv.)......E2
Minute Man Nat'l Hist. Park......B6
Mishaum (pt.)......L6
Monomonac (lake)......G2
Monomoy (isl.)......O6
Monomoy (pt.)......O6
Mount Hope (bay)......K6
Muskeget (chan.)......N7
Muskeget (isl.)......N7
Mystic (lake)......C6
Mystic (riv.)......C6
Nahant (bay)......E6
Nantucket (isl.)......O8
Nantucket (sound)......N6
Nashawena (isl.)......L7
Nashua (riv.)......H3
Naushon (isl.)......L7
Neponset (riv.)......C8
Nomans Land (isl.)......L7
Nonamesset (isl.)......M6
North (riv.)......D2
North (riv.)......L4
Onota (lake)......A3
Otis (res.)......B4

Otis A.F.B.......M6
Pasque (isl.)......L7
Plum (isl.)......L2
Plymouth (bay)......M5
Poge (cape)......N7
Pontoosuc (lake)......A3
Quabbin (res.)......E3
Quaboag (riv.)......F4
Quincy (bay)......D7
Quinebaug (riv.)......F4
Race (pt.)......N4
Salem Maritime Nat'l Hist.
　　Site......E5
Saugus Iron Works Nat'l Hist.
　　Site......D6
Shawshine (riv.)......K2
Silver (lake)......L4
South (riv.)......D2
Springfield Armory Nat'l Hist.
　　Site......D4
Squibnocket (pt.)......M7
Stillwater (riv.)......G3
Sudbury (res.)......H3
Sudbury (riv.)......A6
Swift (riv.)......F3
Taconic (mts.)......A2
Taunton (riv.)......K5
Thompson (isl.)......D7
Toby (mt.)......E3
Tom (mt.)......D4
Tuckernuck (isl.)......N7
Vineyard (sound)......L7
Wachusett (mt.)......G3
Wachusett (res.)......G3
Walden (pond)......A6
Ware (riv.)......F3
Watuppa (pond)......K6
Webster (lake)......G4
Wellfleet (harb.)......O5
West (riv.)......H4
West Branch, Farmington
　　(riv.)......B4
West Chop (pt.)......M7
Westfield (riv.)......C3
Westover A.F.B.......D4
Weweantic (riv.)......L5
Whitman (pt.)......G2
Winter I. Coast Guard Air Sta.......E5

RHODE ISLAND

COUNTIES

Bristol 46,942......J6
Kent 154,163......H6
Newport 81,383......K6
Providence 571,349......H5
Washington 93,317......H7

CITIES and TOWNS

Zip　　Name/Pop.　　Key
02804 Ashaway 1,747......G7
02806 Barrington○ 16,174......J6
02807 Block Island 620......H8
02808 Bradford 1,354......H7
02809 Bristol⊙ 20,128......J6
02863 Central Falls 16,995......J5
02816 Coventry○ 27,065......H6
02910 Cranston 71,992......J5
02818 East Greenwich⊙ 10,211 H6
02914 East Providence 50,980 .... J5

02822 Exeter○ 4,453......H6
02825 Foster○ 3,370......H5
02828 Greenville 7,516......H5
02830 Harrisville 1,224......H5
02832 Hope Valley 1,414......H6
02833 Hopkinton○ 6,406......H7
02835 Jamestown○ 4,040......J6
02835 Jamestown 2,156......J6
02881 Kingston 5,479......J7
02837 Little Compton○ 3,085......K6
02840 Middletown 17,216......J6
02882 Narragansett○ 12,088......J7
02882 Narragansett 3,342......J7
02840 Newport⊙ 29,259......J7
†02807 New Shoreham (Block
　　Island)○ 620......H8
02852 North Kingstown○
　　21,938......J6
02908 North Providence○
　　29,188......J5
02859 Pascoag 3,870......H5
*02860 Pawtucket 71,204......J5
02883 Peace
　　Dale-Wakefield 6,474 ....J7
*02871 Portsmouth○ 14,257......J6
*02901 Providence
　　(cap.)⊙ ⊙ 156,804......H5
　　Providence-Warwick-
　　Pawtucket‡ 919,216......H5
02878 Tiverton○ 13,526......K6
02878 Tiverton 7,653......K6
†02864 Valley Falls 10,892......J5
*02879 Wakefield-Peace
　　Dale 6,474......J7
02885 Warren○ 10,640......J6
*02886 Warwick 87,123......J6
02891 Westerly○ 18,580......G7
02891 Westerly⊙ 14,093......G7
02893 West Warwick 27,026......H6
02895 Woonsocket 45,914......J4

OTHER FEATURES

Black Rock (pt.)......H8
Block (isl.)......H8
Block Island (sound)......H8
Brenton (pt.)......J7
Conanicut (isl.)......J6
Dickens (pt.)......H8
Durfee (hill)......G5
Grace (pt.)......H8
Jerimoth (hill)......G5
Judith (pt.)......J7
Mount Hope (bay)......K6
Narragansett (bay)......J6
Noyes (pt.)......H7
Pawcatuck (riv.)......G7
Prudence (isl.)......J6
Rhode Island (isl.)......J6
Rhode Island (sound)......J7
Roger Williams Nat'l Mem.......J5
Sakonnet (pt.)......K7
Sakonnet (riv.)......K7
Sandy (pt.)......H8
Scituate (res.)......H5
Stillwater (res.)......C2
Touro Synagogue Nat'l Hist.
　　Site......J7
Watch Hill (pt.)......G7

⊙County seat (Shire town).
○Population of town or township.
‡Population of metropolitan area.
† Zip of nearest p.o.　* Multiple zips.

Massachusetts and Rhode Island

SCALE
0　5　10　15　20 MI.
0　5　10　15　20 KM.

State Capitals ......⊛
County Seats (Shire Towns) ......⊙
Canals ......
Major Limited Access Hwys. ......

Scale 1:970,000

© Copyright HAMMOND INCORPORATED, Maplewood, N.J.

Topography

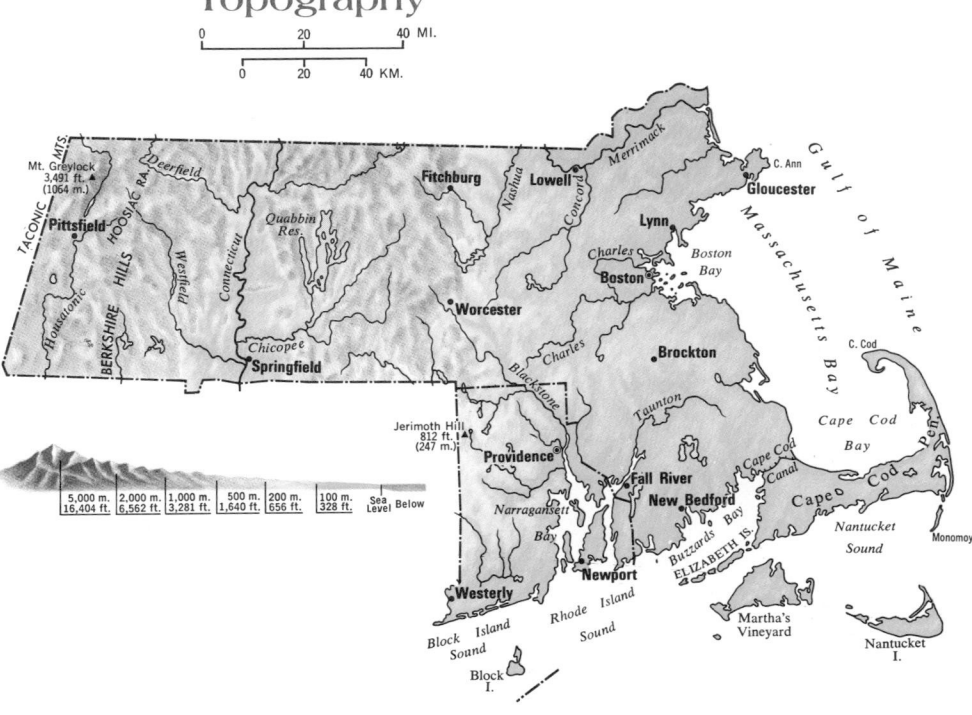

0　　20　　40 MI.
0　　20　　40 KM.

5,000 m. | 2,000 m. | 1,000 m. | 500 m. | 200 m. | 100 m. | Sea
16,404 ft. | 6,562 ft. | 3,281 ft. | 1,640 ft. | 656 ft. | 328 ft. | Level Below

Michigan

SCALE

State Capitals ⊛
County Seats ⊙
Canals
Major Limited Access Hwys.

Scale 1:2,360,000

© Copyright HAMMOND INCORPORATED, Maplewood, N.J.

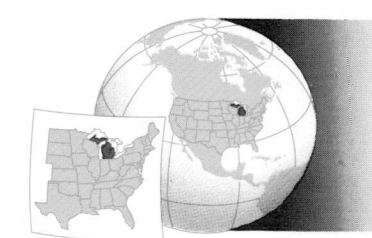

AREA 58,527 sq. mi. (151,585 sq. km.)
POPULATION 9,262,078
CAPITAL Lansing
LARGEST CITY Detroit
HIGHEST POINT Mt. Curwood 1,980 ft. (604 m.)
SETTLED IN 1650
ADMITTED TO UNION January 26, 1837
POPULAR NAME Wolverine State
STATE FLOWER Apple Blossom
STATE BIRD Robin

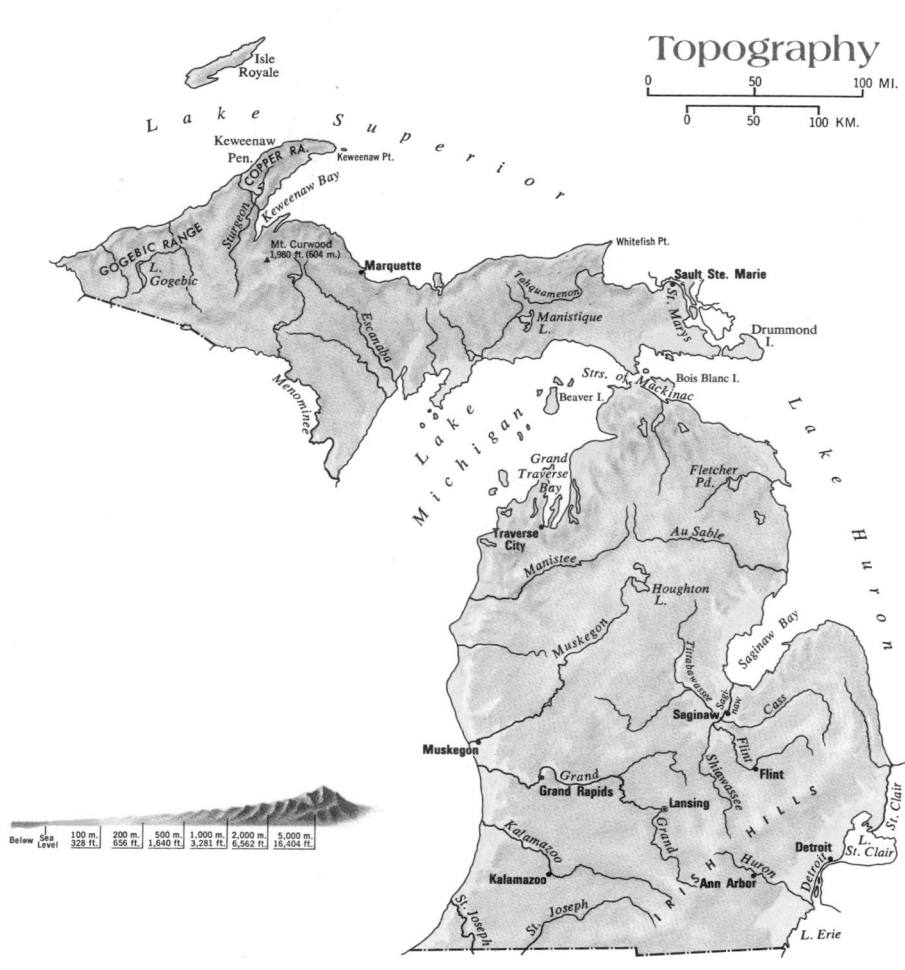

Topography

COUNTIES

Alcona 9,740 ... F4
Alger 9,225 ... C2
Allegan 81,555 ... D6
Alpena 32,315 ... F4
Antrim 16,194 ... D3
Arenac 14,706 ... F4
Baraga 8,484 ... A2
Barry 45,781 ... D6
Bay 119,881 ... E5
Benzie 11,205 ... C4
Berrien 171,276 ... C7
Branch 40,188 ... D7
Calhoun 141,557 ... D6
Cass 49,499 ... C7
Charlevoix 19,907 ... D3
Cheboygan 20,649 ... E3
Chippewa 29,029 ... E2
Clare 23,822 ... E5
Clinton 55,893 ... E6
Crawford 9,465 ... E4
Delta 38,947 ... C2
Dickinson 25,341 ... B2
Eaton 88,337 ... E6
Emmet 22,992 ... E3
Genesee 450,449 ... F5
Gladwin 19,957 ... E4
Gogebic 19,686 ... F2
Grand Traverse 54,899 ... D4
Gratiot 40,448 ... E5
Hillsdale 42,071 ... E7
Houghton 37,872 ... G1
Huron 36,459 ... F5
Ingham 275,520 ... E6
Ionia 51,815 ... D6
Iosco 28,349 ... F4
Iron 13,635 ... G2
Isabella 54,110 ... E5
Jackson 151,495 ... E6
Kalamazoo 212,378 ... D6
Kalkaska 10,952 ... D4
Kent 444,506 ... D5
Keweenaw 1,963 ... A1
Lake 7,711 ... D5
Lapeer 70,038 ... F5
Leelanau 14,007 ... D4
Lenawee 89,948 ... E7
Livingston 100,289 ... F6
Luce 6,659 ... D2
Mackinac 10,178 ... D2
Macomb 694,600 ... G6
Manistee 23,019 ... C4
Marquette 74,101 ... B2
Mason 26,365 ... C4
Mecosta 36,961 ... D5
Menominee 26,201 ... B3
Midland 73,578 ... E5
Missaukee 10,009 ... D4
Monroe 134,659 ... F7
Montcalm 47,555 ... D5
Montmorency 7,492 ... E3
Muskegon 157,589 ... C5
Newaygo 34,917 ... D5
Oakland 1,011,793 ... F6
Oceana 22,002 ... C5
Ogemaw 16,436 ... E4
Ontonagon 9,861 ... F1
Osceola 18,928 ... D5
Oscoda 6,858 ... E4
Otsego 14,993 ... E3
Ottawa 157,174 ... C6
Presque Isle 14,267 ... F3
Roscommon 16,374 ... E4
Saginaw 228,059 ... E5
Saint Clair 138,802 ... G6
Saint Joseph 56,083 ... D7
Sanilac 40,789 ... G5
Schoolcraft 8,575 ... C2
Shiawassee 71,140 ... E6
Tuscola 56,961 ... F5
Van Buren 66,814 ... C6
Washtenaw 264,748 ... F6
Wayne 2,337,891 ... F6
Wexford 25,102 ... D4

CITIES and TOWNS

Zip   Name/Pop.   Key
49220 Addison 655 ... E7
49221 Adrian⊙ 21,186 ... F7
48701 Akron 538 ... F5
†48763 Alabaster 46 ... F4
49224 Albion 11,059 ... E6
48001 Algonac 4,412 ... G6
49010 Allegan⊙ 4,576 ... D6
48101 Allen Park 34,196 ... B7
48801 Alma 9,652 ... E5
48003 Almont 1,857 ... F6
49707 Alpena⊙ 12,214 ... F3
*48103 Ann Arbor⊙ 107,966 ... F6
Ann Arbor‡ 264,748 ... F6
48005 Armada 1,392 ... G6
48806 Ashley 570 ... E5

49011 Athens 960 ... D6
49709 Atlanta⊙ 475 ... E3
48611 Auburn 1,921 ... F5
48703 Au Gres 768 ... F4
49012 Augusta 913 ... D6
†48750 Au Sable 1,240 ... F4
48413 Bad Axe⊙ 3,184 ... G5
49304 Baldwin⊙ 674 ... D5
48414 Bancroft 618 ... E6
49013 Bangor 2,001 ... C6
49908 Baraga 1,055 ... G1
49101 Baroda 627 ... C7
*49014 Battle Creek 35,724 ... D6
Battle Creek‡ 187,338 ... D6
48706 Bay City⊙ 41,593 ... F5
Bay City‡ 119,881 ... E5
48612 Beaverton 1,025 ... E5
†49423 Beechwood 2,333 ... C6
48809 Belding 5,634 ... D5
49615 Bellaire⊙ 1,063 ... D4
48111 Belleville 3,366 ... F6
49021 Bellevue 1,289 ... E6
49022 Benton Harbor 14,707 ... C6
Benton Harbor‡ 171,276 ... C6
†49022 Benton Heights 6,787 ... C6
48072 Berkley 18,637 ... B6
49103 Berrien Springs 2,042 ... C7
49911 Bessemer⊙ 2,553 ... F2
49617 Beulah⊙ 454 ... C4
†48010 Beverly Hills 11,598 ... B6
49307 Big Rapids⊙ 14,361 ... D5
48415 Birch Run 1,196 ... F5
*48008 Birmingham 21,689 ... B6
49228 Blissfield 3,107 ... F7
48013 Bloomfield Hills 3,985 ... B6
49026 Bloomingdale 537 ... C6
49712 Boyne City 3,348 ... E3
48615 Breckenridge 1,495 ... E5
49106 Bridgman 2,235 ... C7
48116 Brighton 4,268 ... F6
49229 Britton 693 ... F6
49028 Bronson 2,271 ... D7
49230 Brooklyn 1,110 ... E6
48416 Brown City 1,163 ... G5
49107 Buchanan 5,142 ... C7
48507 Burton 29,976 ... F6
48418 Byron 689 ... E6
49601 Cadillac⊙ 10,199 ... D4
49316 Caledonia 722 ... D6
49913 Calumet 1,013 ... A1
48014 Capac 1,377 ... G5
48117 Carleton 2,786 ... F6
48723 Caro⊙ 4,317 ... F5
48724 Carrollton 7,482 ... E5
48811 Carson City 1,229 ... E5
48419 Carsonville 622 ... G5
48725 Caseville 851 ... F5
49915 Caspian 1,038 ... G2
48726 Cass City 2,258 ... F5
49031 Cassopolis⊙ 1,933 ... C7
49319 Cedar Springs 2,615 ... D5
49233 Cement City 539 ... E6
48015 Center Line 9,293 ... B6
49622 Central Lake 895 ... D3
49032 Centreville⊙ 1,202 ... D7
49720 Charlevoix⊙ 3,296 ... D3
48813 Charlotte⊙ 8,251 ... E6
49721 Cheboygan⊙ 5,106 ... E3
48118 Chelsea 3,816 ... F6
48616 Chesaning 2,656 ... E5
48617 Clare 3,300 ... E5
48016 Clarkston 968 ... F6
48017 Clawson 15,103 ... B6
49034 Climax 619 ... D6
49236 Clinton 2,342 ... F6
48420 Clio 2,629 ... F5
49036 Coldwater⊙ 9,461 ... D7
48618 Coleman 1,429 ... E5
49038 Coloma 1,833 ... C6
49040 Colon 1,190 ... D7
48421 Columbiaville 953 ... F5
49041 Comstock⊙ 11,162 ... C6
49237 Concord 900 ... E6
49042 Constantine 1,680 ... D7
49404 Coopersville 2,889 ... C5
48817 Corunna⊙ 3,206 ... E5
48422 Croswell 2,073 ... G5
49508 Cutlerville 8,256 ... D6
48423 Davison 6,087 ... F5
*48120 Dearborn 90,660 ... B7
48127 Dearborn Heights 67,706 ... B7
49045 Decatur 1,915 ... C6
48427 Deckerville 887 ... G5
49238 Deerfield 957 ... F7
*48201 Detroit⊙ 1,203,339 ... B7
Detroit‡ 4,352,762 ... B7
†48161 Detroit Beach 2,112 ... F7
48820 De Witt 3,165 ... E6
48130 Dexter 1,524 ... F6
48821 Dimondale 1,008 ... E6
49406 Douglas 948 ... C6
49047 Dowagiac 6,307 ... C6
48020 Drayton Plains ... F6
49726 Drummond Island⊙ 746 ... F3

48428 Dryden 650 ... F6
48131 Dundee 2,575 ... F7
48429 Durand 4,241 ... E6
49924 Eagle River⊙ 20 ... A1
48021 East Detroit 38,280 ... B6
48623 East Freeland 1,364 ... E5
†49506 East Grand Rapids 10,914 ... D6
49727 East Jordan 2,185 ... D3
†49801 East Kingsford ... A3
48823 East Lansing 51,392 ... E6
48730 East Tawas 2,584 ... F4
†49001 Eastwood 7,186 ... D6
48827 Eaton Rapids 4,510 ... E6
49111 Eau Claire 573 ... C6
48229 Ecorse 14,447 ... B7
48829 Edmore 1,176 ... E5
49112 Edwardsburg 1,135 ... C7
49628 Elberta 556 ... C4
49629 Elk Rapids 1,504 ... D4
48731 Elkton 953 ... F5
48831 Elsie 1,022 ... E5
49829 Escanaba⊙ 14,355 ... C3
48732 Essexville 4,378 ... F5
49631 Evart 1,945 ... D5
48733 Fairgrove 691 ... F5
49022 Fair Plain 8,269 ... C6
*48024 Farmington 11,022 ... F6
48024 Farmington Hills 58,056 ... F6
48622 Farwell 804 ... E5
49408 Fennville 934 ... C6
48430 Fenton 8,098 ... F6
48220 Ferndale 26,227 ... B6
49409 Ferrysburg 2,440 ... C5
48134 Flat Rock 6,853 ... F6
*48501 Flint⊙ 159,611 ... F5
Flint‡ 521,589 ... F5
48433 Flushing 8,624 ... F5
48835 Fowler 1,021 ... E5
48836 Fowlerville 2,289 ... F6

48734 Frankenmuth 3,753 ... F5
49635 Frankfort 1,603 ... C4
48025 Franklin 2,864 ... B6
48026 Fraser 14,560 ... B6
49412 Freeland 1,364 ... E5
49412 Fremont 3,672 ... D5
49415 Fruitport 1,143 ... C5
49053 Galesburg 1,822 ... D6
49113 Galien 692 ... C7
48135 Garden City 35,640 ... F6
49735 Gaylord⊙ 3,011 ... E3
48173 Gibraltar 4,458 ... F6
49837 Gladstone 4,533 ... C3
48624 Gladwin⊙ 2,479 ... E5
49055 Gobles 816 ... D6
48438 Goodrich 1,135 ... F6
48439 Grand Blanc 6,848 ... F6
49417 Grand Haven⊙ 11,763 ... C5
48837 Grand Ledge 6,920 ... E6
*49501 Grand Rapids⊙ 181,843 ... D5
Grand Rapids‡ 601,680 ... D5
49418 Grandville 12,412 ... D6
49327 Grant 683 ... D5
49240 Grass Lake 962 ... E6
49738 Grayling⊙ 1,792 ... E4
48838 Greenville 8,019 ... D5
48138 Grosse Ile 9,320 ... B7
48236 Grosse Pointe 5,901 ... B7
†48236 Grosse Pointe
Farms 10,551 ... B6
†48236 Grosse Pointe Park 13,639 ... B7
†48236 Grosse Pointe
Shores 3,122 ... B6
49418 Grosse Pointe
Woods 18,886 ... B6
49841 Gwinn 1,408 ... B2
48212 Hamtramck 21,300 ... B6
49930 Hancock 5,122 ... G1

48441 Harbor Beach 2,000 ... G5
49740 Harbor Springs 1,567 ... D3
48225 Harper Woods 16,361 ... B6
48625 Harrison⊙ 1,700 ... E4
48740 Harrisville⊙ 559 ... F4
49420 Hart⊙ 1,888 ... C5
49057 Hartford 2,493 ... C6
48840 Haslett 7,025 ... E6
49058 Hastings⊙ 6,418 ... D6
48030 Hazel Park 20,914 ... B6
48626 Hemlock 1,362 ... E5
49421 Hesperia 876 ... D5
48203 Highland Park 27,909 ... B6
49242 Hillsdale⊙ 7,432 ... E7
49423 Holland 26,281 ... C6
48842 Holt 10,097 ... E6
49245 Homer 1,791 ... E6
49931 Houghton⊙ 7,512 ... G1
48629 Houghton Lake 2,449 ... E4
48630 Houghton Lake Heights ... E4
49329 Howard City 1,118 ... D5
48843 Howell⊙ 6,976 ... E6
49934 Hubbell 1,278 ... A1
49247 Hudson 2,545 ... E7
49426 Hudsonville 4,844 ... C6
48444 Imlay City 2,495 ... F6
48141 Inkster 35,190 ... B6
49643 Interlochen 600 ... D4
48846 Ionia⊙ 5,920 ... D6
49801 Iron Mountain⊙ 8,341 ... B3
49935 Iron River 2,426 ... G2
49938 Ironwood 7,741 ... F2
49849 Ishpeming 7,538 ... B2
48847 Ithaca⊙ 2,950 ... E5
*49201 Jackson⊙ 39,739 ... E6
Jackson‡ 151,495 ... E6
49428 Jenison 16,330 ... D6
49250 Jonesville 2,172 ... E6

*49001 Kalamazoo⊙ 79,722 ... D6
Kalamazoo-Portage‡
279,192 ... D6
49646 Kalkaska⊙ 1,654 ... D4
48030 Keego Harbor 3,083 ... F6
49330 Kent City 860 ... D5
49508 Kentwood 30,438 ... D6
48445 Kinde 600 ... G5
49801 Kingsford 5,290 ... A3
49649 Kingsley 664 ... D4
48848 Laingsburg 1,145 ... E6
49651 Lake City⊙ 843 ... D4
49945 Lake Linden 1,181 ... A1
†49039 Lake Michigan Beach 2,001 ... C6
48849 Lake Odessa 2,171 ... D6
48035 Lake Orion 2,907 ... F6
48850 Lakeview 1,139 ... E6
†49440 Lakewood Club 695 ... C5
48144 Lambertville 6,341 ... F7
49946 L'Anse⊙ 2,500 ... G1
*48901 Lansing (cap.) 130,414 ... E6
Lansing-East
Lansing‡ 468,482 ... E6
48446 Lapeer⊙ 6,198 ... F5
49913 Laurium 2,678 ... A1
49064 Lawrence 903 ... C6
49065 Lawton 1,558 ... D6
49654 Leland⊙ 776 ... D3
48449 Lennon 600 ... E5
49251 Leslie 2,110 ... E6
48450 Lexington 765 ... G5
48742 Lincoln 361 ... F4
48146 Lincoln Park 45,105 ... B7
48451 Linden 2,174 ... F6
49252 Litchfield 1,353 ... E6
*48150 Livonia 104,814 ... F6
49331 Lowell 3,707 ... D6
49431 Ludington⊙ 8,937 ... C5

(continued on following page)

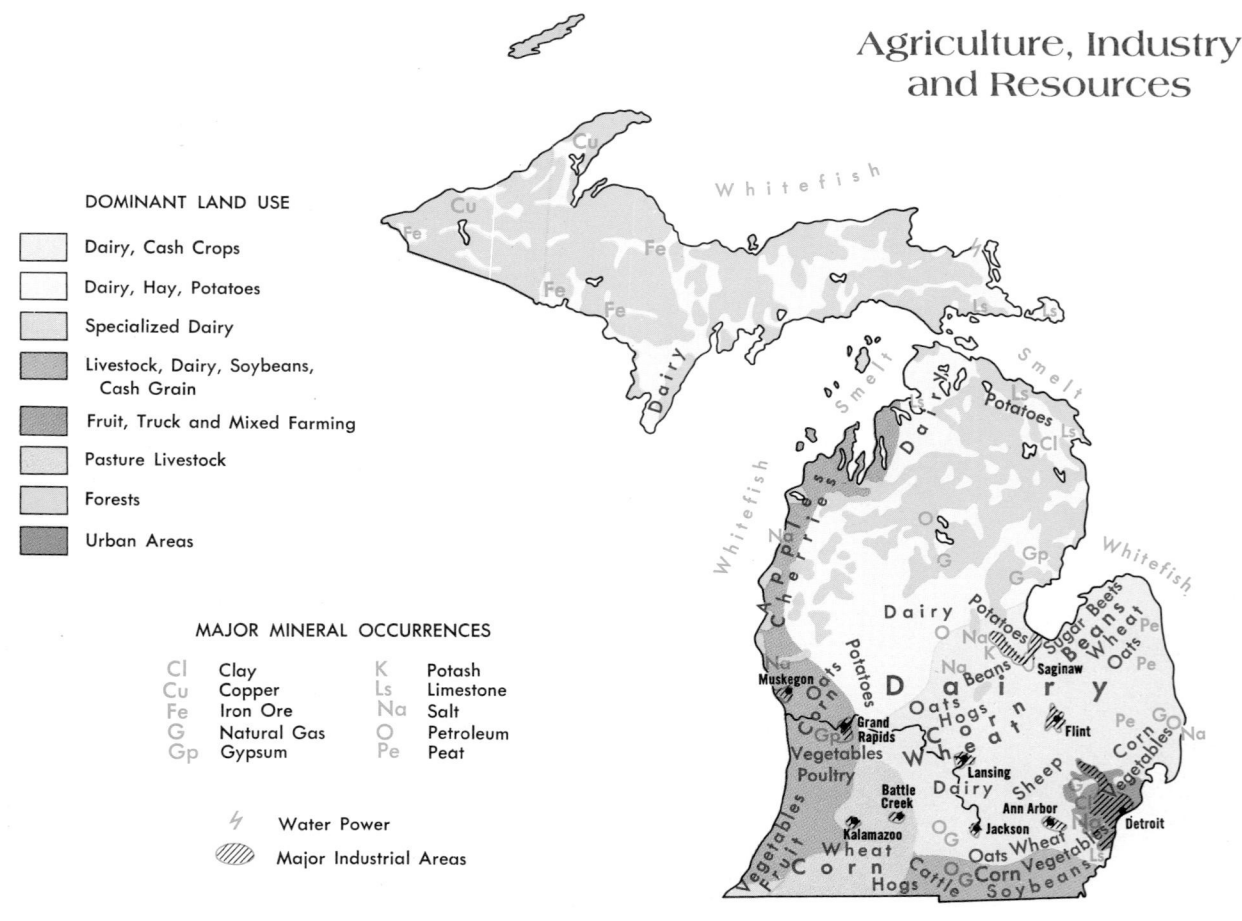

Agriculture, Industry and Resources

DOMINANT LAND USE

Dairy, Cash Crops

Dairy, Hay, Potatoes

Specialized Dairy

Livestock, Dairy, Soybeans, Cash Grain

Fruit, Truck and Mixed Farming

Pasture Livestock

Forests

Urban Areas

MAJOR MINERAL OCCURRENCES

Cl   Clay   K   Potash
Cu   Copper   Ls   Limestone
Fe   Iron Ore   Na   Salt
G   Natural Gas   O   Petroleum
Gp   Gypsum   Pe   Peat

Water Power

Major Industrial Areas

AREA 84,402 sq. mi. (218,601 sq. km.)
POPULATION 4,075,970
CAPITAL St. Paul
LARGEST CITY Minneapolis
HIGHEST POINT Eagle Mtn. 2,301 ft. (701 m.)
SETTLED IN 1805
ADMITTED TO UNION May 11, 1858
POPULAR NAME North Star State; Gopher State
STATE FLOWER Pink & White Lady's-Slipper
STATE BIRD Common Loon

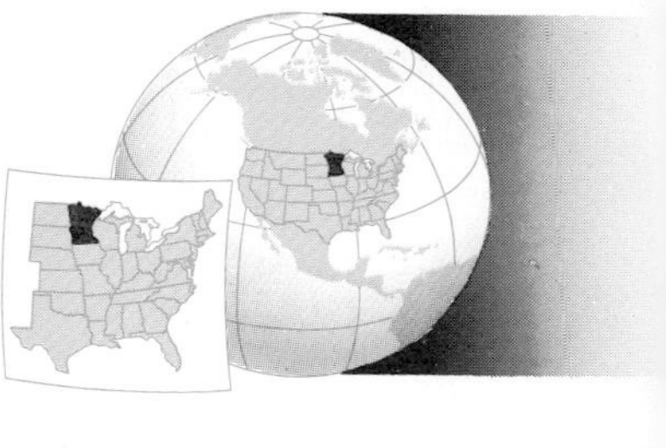

COUNTIES

Aitkin 13,404 ... E4
Anoka 195,998 ... E5
Becker 29,336 ... C4
Beltrami 30,982 ... C2
Benton 25,187 ... D5
Big Stone 7,716 ... B5
Blue Earth 52,314 ... D6
Brown 28,645 ... D6
Carlton 29,936 ... F4
Carver 37,046 ... E6
Cass 21,050 ... D4
Chippewa 14,941 ... C5
Chisago 25,717 ... F5
Clay 49,327 ... B4
Clearwater 8,761 ... C3
Cook 4,092 ... H3
Cottonwood 14,854 ... C6
Crow Wing 41,722 ... D4
Dakota 194,279 ... E6
Dodge 14,773 ... F7
Douglas 27,839 ... C5
Faribault 19,714 ... D7
Fillmore 21,930 ... F7
Freeborn 36,329 ... E7
Goodhue 38,749 ... F6
Grant 7,171 ... B5
Hennepin 941,411 ... E5
Houston 18,382 ... G7
Hubbard 14,098 ... D3
Isanti 23,600 ... E5
Itasca 43,069 ... E3
Jackson 13,690 ... C7
Kanabec 12,161 ... E5
Kandiyohi 36,763 ... C5
Kittson 6,672 ... B2
Koochiching 17,571 ... E2
Lac qui Parle 10,592 ... B6
Lake 13,043 ... G3
Lake of the Woods 3,764 ... D2
Le Sueur 23,434 ... E6
Lincoln 8,207 ... B6
Lyon 25,207 ... C6
Mahnomen 5,535 ... C3
Marshall 13,027 ... B2
Martin 24,687 ... D7
McLeod 29,657 ... D6
Meeker 20,594 ... D5
Mille Lacs 18,430 ... E5
Morrison 29,311 ... D4
Mower 40,390 ... F7
Murray 11,507 ... C6
Nicollet 26,929 ... D6
Nobles 21,840 ... C7
Norman 9,379 ... B3
Olmsted 92,006 ... F7
Otter Tail 51,937 ... C4
Pennington 15,258 ... B2
Pine 19,871 ... F4
Pipestone 11,690 ... B6
Polk 34,844 ... B3
Pope 11,657 ... C5
Ramsey 459,784 ... E5
Red Lake 5,471 ... B3
Redwood 19,341 ... C6
Renville 20,401 ... C6
Rice 46,087 ... E6
Rock 10,703 ... B7
Roseau 12,574 ... C2
Saint Louis 222,229 ... F3
Scott 43,784 ... E6
Sherburne 29,908 ... E5
Sibley 15,448 ... D6
Stearns 108,161 ... D5
Steele 30,328 ... E7
Stevens 11,322 ... B5
Swift 12,920 ... C5
Todd 24,991 ... D4
Traverse 5,542 ... B5
Wabasha 19,335 ... F6
Wadena 14,192 ... D4
Waseca 18,448 ... E6
Washington 113,571 ... F5
Watonwan 12,361 ... D7
Wilkin 8,454 ... B4
Winona 46,256 ... G6
Wright 58,681 ... D5
Yellow Medicine 13,653 ... B6

CITIES and TOWNS

Zip *Name/Pop.* *Key*

56510 Ada⊙ 1,971 ... B3
55909 Adams 797 ... F7
56110 Adrian 1,336 ... C7
55001 Afton 2,550 ... F6
56430 Ah-Gwah-Ching 400 ... D3
56431 Aitkin⊙ 1,770 ... E4
56433 Akeley 486 ... D3
56307 Albany 1,569 ... D5
56207 Alberta 145 ... B5
56007 Albert Lea⊙ 19,200 ... E7
55301 Albertville 564 ... E5
56009 Alden 687 ... E7
56308 Alexandria⊙ 7,608 ... C5
56111 Alpha 180 ... D7
55910 Altura 354 ... G6
56710 Alvarado 385 ... B2
56010 Amboy 606 ... D7
†55303 Andover 9,387 ... E5
55302 Annandale 1,568 ... D5
55303 Anoka⊙ 15,634 ... E5
56208 Appleton 1,842 ... C5
†55124 Apple Valley 21,818 ... G6
56713 Argyle 741 ... B2
55307 Arlington 1,779 ... D6
56309 Ashby 486 ... C4
55704 Askov 350 ... F4
56209 Atwater 1,128 ... D5
56511 Audubon 383 ... C4
55705 Aurora 2,670 ... F3
55912 Austin⊙ 23,020 ... E7
56114 Avoca 201 ... C7
56310 Avon 804 ... D5
55706 Babbitt 2,435 ... G3
56435 Backus 255 ... D4
56714 Badger 320 ... B2
56621 Bagley⊙ 1,321 ... C3
56115 Balaton 752 ... C6
56514 Barnesville 2,207 ... B4
55707 Barnum 464 ... F4
56311 Barrett 388 ... B5
56515 Battle Lake 708 ... C4
56623 Baudette⊙ 1,170 ... D2
†56401 Baxter 2,625 ... D4
55003 Bayport 2,932 ... F5
56211 Beardsley 344 ... B5
55601 Beaver Bay 283 ... G3
56116 Beaver Creek 260 ... B7
55308 Becker 601 ... E5
56312 Belgrade 805 ... C5
†55027 Bellechester 220 ... F6
56011 Belle Plaine 2,754 ... E6
56212 Bellingham 290 ... B5
56214 Belview 438 ... C6
56601 Bemidji⊙ 10,949 ... D3
56626 Bena 153 ... D3
56215 Benson⊙ 3,656 ... C5
56437 Bertha 510 ... C4
55005 Bethel 272 ... E5
56117 Bigelow 249 ... C7
56627 Big Falls 490 ... E2
56628 Bigfork 457 ... E3
55309 Big Lake 2,210 ... E5
56118 Bingham Lake 222 ... C7
55310 Bird Island 1,372 ... D6
55708 Biwabik 1,428 ... F3
56630 Blackduck 653 ... D3
†55433 Blaine 28,558 ... G5
56216 Blomkest 200 ... D6
55917 Blooming Prairie 1,969 ... E7
55420 Bloomington 81,831 ... G6
56013 Blue Earth⊙ 4,132 ... D7
56518 Bluffton 206 ... C4
56519 Borup 160 ... B3
55709 Bovey 813 ... E3
56314 Bowlus 276 ... D5
56218 Boyd 329 ... C6
55006 Braham 1,015 ... E5
56401 Brainerd⊙ 11,489 ... D4
†55056 Branch 1,866 ... F5
56315 Brandon 473 ... C5
56520 Breckenridge⊙ 3,909 ... B4
†56472 Breezy Point 384 ... D4
56119 Brewster 559 ... C7
56014 Bricelyn 487 ... E7
55429 Brooklyn Center 31,230 ... G5
†55444 Brooklyn Park 43,332 ... G5
56715 Brooks 173 ... B3
56316 Brooten 647 ... C5
56438 Browerville 693 ... D4
55918 Brownsdale 691 ... F7
56219 Browns Valley 887 ... B5
55919 Brownsville 418 ... G7
55312 Brownton 697 ... D6
56317 Buckman 171 ... D5
55313 Buffalo⊙ 4,560 ... E5
55314 Buffalo Lake 782 ... D6
55713 Buhl 1,284 ... F3
55337 Burnsville 35,674 ... E6
56318 Burtrum 177 ... D5
56120 Butterfield 634 ... D7
55920 Byron 1,715 ... F6
55921 Caledonia⊙ 2,691 ... G7
56521 Callaway 238 ... C3
55716 Calumet 469 ... E3
55008 Cambridge⊙ 3,287 ... E5
56522 Campbell 286 ... B4
56220 Canby 2,143 ... B6
55009 Cannon Falls 2,653 ... F6
55922 Canton 386 ... F7
56319 Carlos 364 ... C5
55718 Carlton⊙ 862 ... F4
55315 Carver 642 ... E6
56633 Cass Lake 1,001 ... D3
55012 Center City⊙ 458 ... F5
†55038 Centerville 734 ... E5
56121 Ceylon 543 ... D7
55316 Champlin 9,006 ... G5
56122 Chandler 344 ... C7
55317 Chanhassen 6,359 ... F6
55318 Chaska⊙ 8,346 ... F6
55923 Chatfield 2,055 ... F7
55013 Chisago City 1,634 ... E5
55719 Chisholm 5,930 ... E3
56221 Chokio 559 ... B5
55014 Circle Pines 3,321 ... G5
56222 Clara City 1,574 ... C6
55924 Claremont 591 ... E6
56440 Clarissa 663 ... C4
56223 Clarkfield 1,171 ... C6
56016 Clarks Grove 620 ... E7
56634 Clearbrook 579 ... C3
55319 Clear Lake 266 ... E5
55320 Clearwater 379 ... D5
56224 Clements 227 ... D6
56017 Cleveland 699 ... E6
56523 Climax 273 ... B3
56225 Clinton 622 ... B5
56226 Clontarf 196 ... C5
55720 Cloquet 11,142 ... F4
†55068 Coates 207 ... E6
55321 Cokato 2,056 ... D5
56320 Cold Spring 2,294 ... D5
55722 Coleraine 1,116 ... E3
55322 Cologne 545 ... E6
55421 Columbia Heights 20,029 ... G5
56019 Comfrey 548 ... D6
56020 Conger 183 ... E7
55723 Cook 800 ... F3
55433 Coon Rapids 35,826 ... G5
†55340 Corcoran 4,252 ... F5
56228 Cosmos 571 ... D6
55016 Cottage Grove 18,994 ... F6
56229 Cottonwood 924 ... C6
56021 Courtland 399 ... D6
55726 Cromwell 229 ... F4
56716 Crookston⊙ 8,628 ... B3
56441 Crosby 2,218 ... D4
56442 Crosslake 1,064 ... E4
†55428 Crystal 25,543 ... G5
55323 Crystal Bay (Orono) 6,845 ... F5
56123 Currie 359 ... C6
56323 Cyrus 334 ... C5
55925 Dakota 350 ... G7
56324 Dalton 248 ... C4
56230 Danube 590 ... C6
56231 Danvers 152 ... C5
56022 Darfur 139 ... D6
55324 Darwin 282 ... D5
55325 Dassel 1,066 ... D5
56232 Dawson 1,901 ... B6
55327 Dayton 4,070 ... E5
55391 Deephaven 3,716 ... G5
56527 Deer Creek 392 ... C4
56636 Deer River 907 ... E3
56444 Deerwood 580 ... E4
56233 De Graff 179 ... C5
55328 Delano 2,480 ... E5
56023 Delavan 262 ... D7
†55110 Dellwood 751 ... F5
56528 Dent 167 ... C4
56501 Detroit Lakes⊙ 7,106 ... C4
55926 Dexter 279 ... F7
56529 Dilworth 2,585 ... B4
55927 Dodge Center 1,816 ... F6
56235 Donnelly 317 ... B5
55929 Dover 312 ... F7
*55801 Duluth⊙ 92,811 ... F4
Duluth-Superior‡ 266,650 ... F4
56236 Dumont 173 ... B5
55019 Dundas 422 ... E6
56127 Dunnell 216 ... D7
55111 Eagan 20,700 ... G6
56446 Eagle Bend 593 ... D4
56024 Eagle Lake 1,470 ... E6
†55005 East Bethel 6,626 ... E5
56721 East Grand Forks 8,537 ... B3
†56401 East Gull Lake 586 ... D4
56025 Easton 283 ... E7
56237 Echo 334 ... C6
55344 Eden Prairie 16,263 ... G6
55329 Eden Valley 763 ... D5
56128 Edgerton 1,123 ... B7
55424 Edina 46,073 ... G5
55931 Eitzen 226 ... G7
†55910 Elba 198 ... F6
56531 Elbow Lake⊙ 1,358 ... B5
55932 Elgin 667 ... F6
56533 Elizabeth 195 ... B4
55020 Elko 274 ... E6
55330 Elk River⊙ 6,785 ... E5
56026 Ellendale 555 ... E7
56129 Ellsworth 629 ... C7
56027 Elmore 882 ... D7
56325 Elrosa 214 ... C5
55731 Ely 4,820 ... G3
56028 Elysian 454 ... E6
56447 Emily 588 ... E4
56029 Emmons 465 ... E7
56534 Erhard 194 ... B4
56535 Erskine 585 ... B3
56326 Evansville 571 ... C4
55734 Eveleth 5,042 ... F3
55331 Excelsior 2,523 ... E6
55934 Eyota 1,244 ... F7
55332 Fairfax 1,405 ... D6
56031 Fairmont⊙ 11,506 ... D7
55113 Falcon Heights 5,291 ... G5
55021 Faribault⊙ 16,241 ... E6
55024 Farmington 4,370 ... E6
56641 Federal Dam 192 ... D3
56536 Felton 264 ... B3
56537 Fergus Falls⊙ 12,519 ... B4
56540 Fertile 869 ... B3
56448 Fifty Lakes 263 ... D4
55735 Finlayson 202 ... F4
56723 Fisher 453 ... B3
56328 Flensburg 256 ... D5
55736 Floodwood 648 ... E4
56329 Foley⊙ 1,606 ... D5
†56308 Forada 191 ... C5
55025 Forest Lake 4,596 ... F5
56330 Foreston 283 ... E5
56542 Fosston 1,599 ... C3
55935 Fountain 327 ... F7
56543 Foxhome 161 ... B4
55333 Franklin 512 ... D6
56544 Frazee 1,284 ... C4
56032 Freeborn 323 ... E7
56331 Freeport 563 ... D5
55432 Fridley 30,228 ... G5
56033 Frost 293 ... D7
56131 Fulda 1,308 ... C7
56332 Garfield 284 ... C5
56450 Garrison 174 ... E4
56132 Garvin 172 ... C6
56545 Gary 241 ... B3
55334 Gaylord⊙ 1,933 ... D6
56035 Geneva 417 ... E7
56239 Ghent 356 ... C6
55335 Gibbon 787 ... D6
55741 Gilbert 2,721 ... F3
56333 Gilman 156 ... E5
55336 Glencoe⊙ 4,396 ... D6
56036 Glenville 851 ... E7
56334 Glenwood⊙ 2,523 ... C5
56547 Glyndon 882 ... B4
55427 Golden Valley 22,775 ... G5
56644 Gonvick 362 ... C3
55027 Goodhue 657 ... F6
56725 Goodridge 191 ... C2
56037 Good Thunder 560 ... D6
55027 Goodview 2,567 ... G6
56240 Graceville 780 ... B5
56039 Granada 377 ... D7
55604 Grand Marais⊙ 1,289 ... G2
55936 Grand Meadow 965 ... F7
55744 Grand Rapids⊙ 7,934 ... E3
56241 Granite Falls⊙ 3,451 ... C6
55030 Grasston 123 ... E5
56726 Greenbush 817 ... B2
†55373 Greenfield 1,391 ... F5
55338 Green Isle 357 ... E6
56335 Greenwald 259 ... D5
56336 Grey Eagle 338 ... D5
56243 Grove City 596 ... D5
56727 Grygla 216 ... C2
56452 Hackensack 285 ... D4
56728 Hallock⊙ 1,405 ... A2
56548 Halstad 690 ... B3
55339 Hamburg 475 ... D6
55340 Hamel 2,623 ... F5
55304 Ham Lake 7,832 ... E5
55938 Hammond 178 ... F6
55031 Hampton 299 ... E6
56244 Hancock 877 ... C5
56245 Hanley Falls 265 ... C6
55341 Hanover 647 ... E5
56041 Hanska 429 ... D6
56134 Hardwick 279 ... B7
55939 Harmony 1,133 ... F7
55032 Harris 678 ... F5
56042 Hartland 322 ... E7
55033 Hastings⊙ 12,827 ... F6
56549 Hawley 1,634 ... B4
55940 Hayfield 1,243 ... F7
56043 Hayward 294 ... E7
55342 Hector 1,252 ... D6
56044 Henderson 739 ... E6
56136 Hendricks 737 ... B6
56550 Hendrum 336 ... B3
56551 Henning 832 ... C4
56248 Herman 600 ... B5
†55811 Hermantown 6,759 ... F4
56137 Heron Lake 783 ... C7
56453 Hewitt 299 ... C4
55746 Hibbing 21,193 ... F3
55748 Hill City 533 ... E4
56138 Hills 598 ... B7
55037 Hinckley 963 ... E4
56552 Hitterdal 253 ... B4

(continued on following page)

Agriculture, Industry and Resources

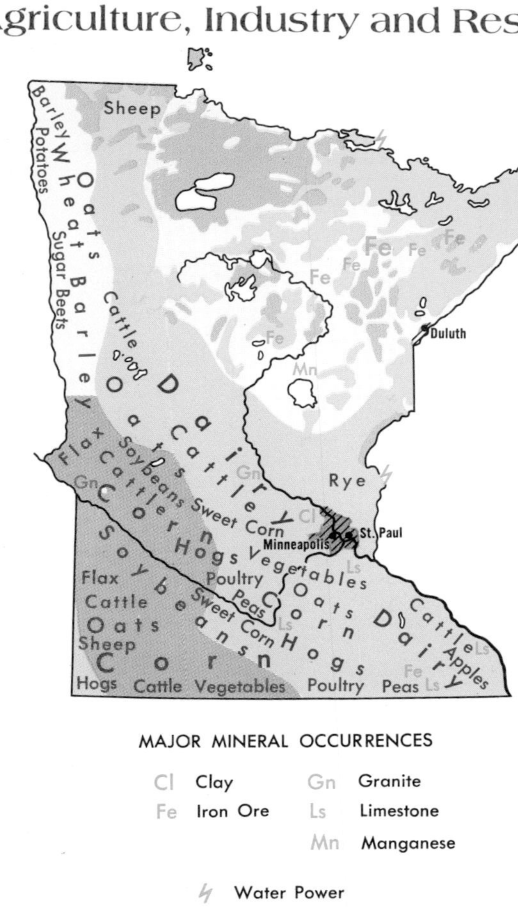

DOMINANT LAND USE

- Wheat, General Farming
- Dairy, Livestock
- Dairy, Hay, Potatoes
- Cattle Feed, Hogs
- Livestock, Cash Grain
- Forests
- Swampland, Limited Agriculture
- Urban Areas

MAJOR MINERAL OCCURRENCES

- Cl Clay
- Fe Iron Ore
- Gn Granite
- Ls Limestone
- Mn Manganese

- Water Power
- Major Industrial Areas

56339 Hoffman 631 C5
55941 Hokah 686 G7
56340 Holdingford 635 D5
56139 Holland 234 B6
56045 Hollandale 290 E7
56249 Holloway 142 C5
55343 Hopkins 15,336 G5
55943 Houston 1,057 G7
55349 Howard Lake 1,240 D5
55750 Hoyt Lakes 3,186 F3
55038 Hugo 3,771 E5
55350 Hutchinson 9,244 D6
†55359 Independence 2,640 F5
56649 International Falls⊙ 5,611 E2
55075 Inver Grove Heights 17,171 E6
56141 Iona 248 C7
56455 Ironton 537 D4
55040 Isanti 858 E5
56342 Isle 573 E4
56142 Ivanhoe⊙ 761 B6
56143 Jackson⊙ 3,797 C7
56048 Janesville 1,897 E6
56144 Jasper 731 B7
56145 Jeffers 437 C6
56456 Jenkins 219 D4
55352 Jordan 2,663 E6
56251 Kandiyohi 447 D5
56732 Karlstad 934 B2
56050 Kasota 739 D6
55944 Kasson 2,827 F6
55753 Keewatin 1,443 E3
56650 Kelliher 324 D3
55945 Kellogg 440 G6
55754 Kelly Lake 900 F3
56733 Kennedy 405 B2
56343 Kensington 331 C5
55946 Kenyon 1,529 E6
56252 Kerkhoven 761 C5
56051 Kiester 670 E7
56052 Kilkenny 177 E6
55353 Kimball 651 D5
55758 Kinney 447 F3
55947 La Crescent 3,674 G7
56054 Lafayette 507 D6
56149 Lake Benton 869 B6
56734 Lake Bronson 298 B2
55041 Lake City 4,505 F6
56055 Lake Crystal 2,078 D6
55042 Lake Elmo 5,296 F6
56150 Lakefield 1,845 C7
†55398 Lake Fremont (Zimmerman) 1,074 E5
55043 Lakeland 1,812 F6
56253 Lake Lillian 329 C6
56554 Lake Park 716 B4
†55043 Lake Saint Croix Beach 1,176 F6
†56401 Lake Shore 583 D4
55044 Lakeville 14,790 E6
56151 Lake Wilson 380 B7
56152 Lamberton 1,032 C6
56735 Lancaster 368 B2
55949 Lanesboro 923 G7
56461 Laporte 160 D3
†55744 La Prairie 536 E3
56344 Lastrup 150 D4
†55101 Lauderdale 1,985 G5
56057 Le Center⊙ 1,967 E6
55951 Le Roy 930 F7
55354 Lester Prairie 1,229 D6
56058 Le Sueur 3,763 E6
55952 Lewiston 1,226 G7
56060 Lewisville 273 D7
†55014 Lexington 2,150 G5
†55050 Lilydale 417 G5
55045 Lindstrom 1,972 F5
†55038 Lino Lakes 4,966 G5
56155 Lismore 276 B7
55355 Litchfield⊙ 5,904 D5
56345 Little Falls⊙ 7,250 D5
56653 Littlefork 918 E2
†56334 Long Beach 263 C5
55356 Long Lake 1,747 F5
56347 Long Prairie⊙ 2,859 D5
56655 Longville 191 D4
55046 Lonsdale 1,160 E6
55357 Loretto 297 F5
56349 Lowry 283 C5
56255 Lucan 262 C6
56156 Luverne⊙ 4,568 B7
55953 Lyle 576 F7
56157 Lynd 304 C6
55954 Mabel 861 G7
56062 Madelia 2,130 D6
56256 Madison⊙ 2,212 B5
56063 Madison Lake 592 E6
56158 Magnolia 234 B7
56557 Mahnomen⊙ 1,283 C3
55115 Mahtomedi 3,851 F5
56001 Mankato⊙ 28,651 E6
55955 Mantorville⊙ 705 F6
†55369 Maple Grove 20,525 G5
55358 Maple Lake 1,132 D5
55359 Maple Plain 1,421 F5
56065 Mapleton 1,516 E7
†55912 Mapleview 253 E7
55109 Maplewood 26,990 G5
55764 Marble 757 E3
56257 Marietta 279 B5
55047 Marine on Saint Croix 543 F5
56258 Marshall⊙ 11,161 C6
55360 Mayer 388 E6
56260 Maynard 428 C6
55956 Mazeppa 680 F6
55760 McGregor 447 E4
56556 McIntosh 681 C3
55761 McKinley 230 F3
55049 Medford 775 E6
55441 Medicine Lake 419 G5
†55340 Medina (Hamel) 2,623 F5
†56352 Meire Grove 174 C5
56352 Melrose 2,409 D5
56464 Menahga 980 C4
55050 Mendota 219 G5
†55050 Mendota Heights 7,288 G6
56736 Mentor 219 B3
56737 Middle River 349 B2
†55033 Miesville 179 F6
56262 Milan 417 C5
55957 Millville 186 F6
56263 Milroy 242 C6
56354 Miltona 187 C4
*55401 Minneapolis⊙ 370,951 G5
Minneapolis-Saint Paul‡ 2,114,256 G5
56264 Minneota 1,470 C6
55959 Minnesota City 265 G6
56068 Minnesota Lake 744 E7
55343 Minnetonka 38,683 G5
†55364 Minnetrista 3,236 F5
56265 Montevideo⊙ 5,845 C6
56069 Montgomery 2,349 E6
55362 Monticello 2,830 E5
55363 Montrose 762 E5
56560 Moorhead⊙ 29,998 B4
Moorhead-Fargo‡ 137,574 B4
55767 Moose Lake 1,408 F4
55051 Mora⊙ 2,890 E5
56266 Morgan 975 D6
56267 Morris⊙ 5,367 C5
55052 Morristown 639 E6
56270 Morton 549 C6
56466 Motley 444 D4
55364 Mound 9,280 E6
†55112 Mounds View 12,593 G5
55768 Mountain Iron 4,134 F3
56159 Mountain Lake 2,277 D7
56271 Murdock 343 C5
55769 Nashwauk 1,419 E3
56355 Nelson 209 C5
55053 Nerstrand 255 E6
56467 Nevis 332 D4
55366 New Auburn 331 D6
55112 New Brighton 23,269 G5
56738 Newfolden 384 B2
55367 New Germany 347 E6
†55428 New Hope 23,087 G5
56273 New London 812 C5
55054 New Market 286 E6
56356 New Munich 302 D5
55055 Newport 3,323 F6
56071 New Prague 2,952 E6
56072 New Richland 1,263 E7
56073 New Ulm⊙ 13,755 D6
56567 New York Mills 972 C4
56074 Nicollet 709 D6
56568 Nielsville 145 B3
56468 Nisswa 1,407 D4
55056 North Branch 1,597 F5
55057 Northfield 12,562 E6
56001 North Mankato 9,145 D6
†55101 North Oaks 2,846 G5
56661 Northome 312 D3
56275 North Redwood 206 D6
56075 Northrop 269 D7
55109 North Saint Paul 11,921 G5
55368 Norwood 1,219 E6
†55109 Oakdale 12,123 F5
56276 Odessa 177 B5
56160 Odin 134 D7
56569 Ogema 215 C3
56358 Ogilvie 423 E5
56161 Okabena 263 C7
56742 Oklee 536 C3
56277 Olivia⊙ 2,802 C6
56359 Onamia 691 E4
56162 Ormsby 181 D7
†55323 Orono 6,845 F5
55960 Oronoco 574 F6
55771 Orr 294 F2
56278 Ortonville⊙ 2,550 B5
56360 Osakis 1,355 C5
56744 Oslo 379 A2
55369 Osseo 2,974 G5
55961 Ostrander 293 F7
56571 Ottertail 239 C4
55060 Owatonna⊙ 18,632 E6
56469 Palisade 155 E4
56361 Parkers Prairie 917 C4
56470 Park Rapids⊙ 2,976 D4
56362 Paynesville 2,140 D5
56363 Pease 174 E5
†56472 Pelican Lakes (Breezy Point) 384 D4
56572 Pelican Rapids 1,867 B4
56078 Pemberton 208 E7
56279 Pennock 410 C5
56472 Pequot Lakes 681 D4
56573 Perham 2,086 C4
55962 Peterson 291 G7
†56364 Pierz 1,018 D5
56473 Pillager 341 D4
55063 Pine City⊙ 2,489 F5
55963 Pine Island 1,986 F6
56474 Pine River 881 D4
56164 Pipestone⊙ 4,887 B7
55964 Plainview 2,416 F6
55370 Plato 390 D6
56748 Plummer 353 B3
†55441 Plymouth 31,615 G5
56280 Porter 211 B6
55965 Preston⊙ 1,478 F7
55371 Princeton 3,146 E5
56281 Prinsburg 557 C6
55372 Prior Lake 7,284 E6
55810 Proctor 3,180 F4
55967 Racine 285 F7
56475 Randall 527 D4
55065 Randolph 351 E6
56668 Ranier 237 E2
56282 Raymond 723 C5
56750 Red Lake Falls⊙ 1,732 B3
55066 Red Wing⊙ 13,736 F6
56283 Redwood Falls⊙ 5,210 C6
56672 Remer 396 E3
56284 Renville 1,493 C6
56166 Revere 158 C6
56367 Rice 499 D5
55423 Richfield 37,851 G6
56368 Richmond 867 D5
55422 Robbinsdale 14,422 G5
55901 Rochester⊙ 57,890 F6
Rochester‡ 91,971 F6
55067 Rock Creek 890 F5
55373 Rockford 2,408 F5
56369 Rockville 597 D5
55374 Rogers 652 E5
55969 Rollingstone 528 G6
56371 Roscoe 154 D5
56751 Roseau⊙ 2,272 C2
55970 Rose Creek 371 F7
55068 Rosemount 5,083 E6
55113 Roseville 35,820 G5
56579 Rothsay 476 B4
56167 Round Lake 480 C7
56373 Royalton 660 D5
55069 Rush City 1,198 F5
55971 Rushford 1,478 G7
56168 Rushmore 387 C7
56169 Russell 412 C6
56170 Ruthton 328 B6
55778 Rutledge 185 F4
56580 Sabin 446 B4
56285 Sacred Heart 666 C6
55414 Saint Anthony 7,981 G5
55375 Saint Bonifacius 857 F5
55972 Saint Charles 2,184 F7
56080 Saint Clair 655 E6
56301 Saint Cloud⊙ 42,566 D5
Saint Cloud‡ 163,256 D5
55070 Saint Francis 1,184 E5
56554 Saint Hilaire 388 B2
56081 Saint James⊙ 4,346 D7
56374 Saint Joseph 2,994 D5
55426 Saint Louis Park 42,931 G5
56376 Saint Martin 220 D5
55376 Saint Michael 1,519 E5
*55101 Saint Paul (cap.)⊙ 270,230 G6
Saint Paul-Minneapolis‡ 2,114,256 G5
55071 Saint Paul Park 4,864 G6
56082 Saint Peter⊙ 9,056 E6
56375 Saint Stephen 453 D5
56755 Saint Vincent 141 A2
56083 Sanborn 518 C6
55072 Sandstone 1,594 F4
56377 Sartell 3,427 D5
56378 Sauk Centre 3,709 C5
56379 Sauk Rapids 5,793 D5
55337 Savage 3,954 G6
†55720 Scanlon 1,050 F4
56477 Sebeka 774 C4
55074 Shafer 180 F5
55379 Shakopee⊙ 9,941 F6
56581 Shelly 276 B3
56171 Sherburn 1,275 D7
56676 Shevlin 193 C3
†55112 Shoreview 17,300 G5
†55331 Shorewood 4,646 F5
55614 Silver Bay 2,917 G3
55381 Silver Lake 698 D6
†56001 Skyline 399 D6
56172 Slayton⊙ 2,420 C7
56085 Sleepy Eye 3,581 D6
†56345 Sobieski 219 D5
55382 South Haven 205 D5
56679 South International Falls 2,806 E2
55075 South Saint Paul 21,235 G6
56288 Spicer 909 C5
56087 Springfield 2,303 C6
55974 Spring Grove 1,275 G7
†55432 Spring Lake Park 6,477 E5
55384 Spring Park 1,465 F5
55975 Spring Valley 2,616 F7
56681 Squaw Lake 162 D3
55079 Stacy 996 E5
56479 Staples 2,887 D4
56381 Starbuck 1,224 C5
56173 Steen 153 B7
56757 Stephen 898 A2
55385 Stewart 616 D6
55976 Stewartville 3,925 F7
55082 Stillwater⊙ 12,290 F5
55988 Stockton 517 G6
56174 Storden 341 C6
56758 Strandquist 136 B2
55783 Sturgeon Lake 222 F4
†55075 Sunfish Lake 344 E6
56382 Swanville 295 D5
55786 Taconite 331 E3
56291 Taunton 177 B6
55084 Taylors Falls 623 F5
56683 Tenstrike 159 D3
56701 Thief River Falls⊙ 9,105 B2
†56319 Thomson 152 F4
†55331 Tonka Bay 1,354 F5
55790 Tower 640 F3
56175 Tracy 2,478 C6
56176 Trimont 805 D7
56088 Truman 1,392 D7
56089 Twin Lakes 210 E7
56584 Twin Valley 907 B3
55616 Two Harbors⊙ 4,039 G3
56178 Tyler 1,353 B6
56585 Ulen 514 B3
56586 Underwood 332 C4
56384 Upsala 400 D5
55979 Utica 249 G7
†55101 Vadnais Heights 5,111 G5
56587 Vergas 287 C4
55085 Vermillion 438 F6
56481 Verndale 504 C4
56090 Vernon Center 365 D7
56292 Vesta 360 C6
55386 Victoria 1,425 F6
56385 Villard 275 C5
55792 Virginia 11,056 F3
55981 Wabasha⊙ 2,372 G6
56293 Wabasso 745 C6
55387 Waconia 2,638 E6
56482 Wadena⊙ 4,699 C4
56386 Wahkon 271 E4
56387 Waite Park 3,496 D5
56091 Waldorf 249 E7
56484 Walker⊙ 970 D3
56180 Walnut Grove 753 C6
55982 Waltham 176 F7
55983 Wanamingo 717 F6
55743 Warba 150 E3
56762 Warren⊙ 2,105 B2
56763 Warroad 1,216 C2
56093 Waseca⊙ 8,219 E6
55388 Watertown 1,818 E6
56096 Waterville 1,717 E6
55389 Watkins 757 D5
56295 Watson 238 C5
56589 Waubun 390 C3
55390 Waverly 470 E5
55391 Wayzata 3,621 G5
56181 Welcome 855 D7
56097 Wells 2,777 E7
56590 Wendell 216 B4
56183 Westbrook 978 C6
55985 West Concord 762 F6
55118 West Saint Paul 18,527 G5
56296 Wheaton⊙ 1,969 B5
55110 White Bear Lake 22,538 G5
55090 Willernie 654 G5
56686 Williams 217 D2
56201 Willmar⊙ 15,895 C5
55795 Willow River 303 F4
56185 Wilmont 380 C7
56687 Wilton 176 D3
56101 Windom⊙ 4,666 C7
56592 Winger 200 B3
56098 Winnebago 1,869 D7
55987 Winona⊙ 25,075 G6
55395 Winsted 1,522 D6
55396 Winthrop 1,376 D6
55796 Winton 276 G3
56594 Wolverton 177 B4
†55798 Woodbury 10,297 F6
56297 Wood Lake 420 C6
56186 Woodstock 180 B7
56187 Worthington⊙ 10,243 C7
55797 Wrenshall 333 F4
55798 Wright 162 E4
55990 Wykoff 482 F7
55092 Wyoming 1,559 F5
55397 Young America 1,237 E6
55398 Zimmerman 1,074 E5
55991 Zumbro Falls 208 F6
55992 Zumbrota 2,129 F6

OTHER FEATURES

Ash (riv.) F2
Bald Eagle (lake) G3
Basswood (lake) E2
Battle (riv.) D3
Baudette (riv.) D2
Bear (riv.) E3
Bemidji (lake) D3
Benton (lake) B6
Big Fork (riv.) E2
Big Sandy (lake) E4
Big Stone (lake) B5
Birch (lake) G3
Black (riv.) D2
Blue Earth (riv.) D7
Bois de Sioux (riv.) B4
Bowstring (lake) E3
Buffalo (riv.) B4
Burntside (lake) F3
Cass (lake) D3
Cedar (riv.) F7
Chippewa (riv.) C5
Christina (lake) C4
Clearwater (riv.) C3
Cloquet (riv.) F4
Cobb (riv.) E7
Cottonwood (riv.) C6
Crooked (creek) F4
Crooked (lake) G2
Crow (riv.) F5
Crow Wing (riv.) D4
Cuyuna (range) D4
Dead (lake) C4
Deer (lake) E3
Des Moines (riv.) C7
Eagle (mt.) G2
East Swan (riv.) F3
Elbow (lake) C3
Emily (lake) C5
Fond du Lac Ind. Res. F4
Grand Portage Ind. Res. G2
Grand Portage Nat'l Mon. G2
Green (lake) D5
Greenwood (lake) G3
Gull (lake) D4
Heron (lake) C7
Hill (riv.) C3
Independence (lake) F5
Isabella (lake) G3
Itasca (lake) C3
Kabetogama (lake) E2
Kanaranzi (creek) C7
Kettle (riv.) F4
Knife (lake) G2
La Croix (lake) F2
Lac qui Parle (lake) C5
Lac qui Parle (riv.) B6
Lake of the Woods (lake) D1
Leaf (riv.) C4
Leech (lake) D3
Leech Lake Ind. Res. D3
Lida (lake) C4
Little Fork (riv.) E2
Little Rock (creek) C7
Long (lake) D4
Long (lake) F3
Long Prairie (riv.) D4
Lost (riv.) C3
Lower Red (lake) C3
Maple (lake) B3
Maple (riv.) E7
Marsh (lake) B5
Mary (lake) C5
Mesabi (range) E3
Middle (riv.) B2
Mille Lac Ind. Res. E4
Mille Lacs (lake) E4
Miltona (lake) C4
Minneapolis-Saint Paul Airport G5
Minnesota (riv.) E6
Minnetonka (lake) F5
Minnewaska (lake) C5
Misquah (hills) F2
Mississippi (riv.) D4
Moose (riv.) C2
Mud (lake) C2
Mud (riv.) C2
Muskeg (bay) C2
Mustinka (riv.) B5
Nemadji (riv.) F4
Nett (lake) E2
Nett Lake Ind. Res. E2
North (lake) F1
Otter Tail (lake) C4
Otter Tail (riv.) B4
Partridge (riv.) G3
Pelican (lake) C4
Pelican (lake) D4
Pelican (lake) F2
Pelican (riv.) B4
Pelican (riv.) F2
Pepin (lake) F6
Pigeon (riv.) G2
Pike (riv.) F3
Pipestone Nat'l Mon. B6
Pokegama (lake) E3
Pomme de Terre (riv.) C5
Poplar (riv.) C3
Prairie (riv.) E3
Rainy (lake) E2
Rainy (riv.) D2
Rapid (riv.) D2
Redeye (riv.) D4
Red Lake (riv.) B2
Red Lake Ind. Res. C2
Red River of the North (riv.) A2
Redwood (riv.) C6
Reno (lake) C5
Rice (lake) E4
Rock (riv.) B7
Root (riv.) G7
Roseau (riv.) B2
Rum (riv.) E5
Saganaga (lake) H2
Saint Croix (riv.) F5
Saint Louis (riv.) F4
Sand (creek) F5
Sand Hill (riv.) B3
Sarah (lake) F5
Schoolcraft (riv.) C3
Shakopee (creek) C5
Shell (riv.) C4
Shetek (lake) C6
Sleepy Eye (creek) C6
Snake (riv.) A2
Snake (riv.) E4
South Fowl (lake) G1
Star (lake) C4
Sturgeon (riv.) F3
Superior (lake) G3
Swan (lake) D6
Tamarac (riv.) A2
Tamarack (riv.) D2
Thief (lake) C2
Thief (riv.) B2
Traverse (lake) B5
Trout (lake) F2
Two Rivers (riv.) A1
Upper Red (lake) D2
Vermilion (lake) F3
Vermilion (range) F3
Vermilion (riv.) F2
Voyageurs Nat'l Park F2
Wabatawangang (lake) D3
West Swan (riv.) F3
White Earth Ind. Res. C3
Whiteface (riv.) F3
Whitefish (lake) D4
White Iron (lake) G3
Wild Rice (lake) F4
Wild Rice (riv.) B3
Willow (riv.) E4
Winnibigoshish (lake) D3
Woods (lake) D1
Zumbro (riv.) F6

⊙County seat.
‡Population of metropolitan area.
† Zip of nearest p.o. * Multiple zips.

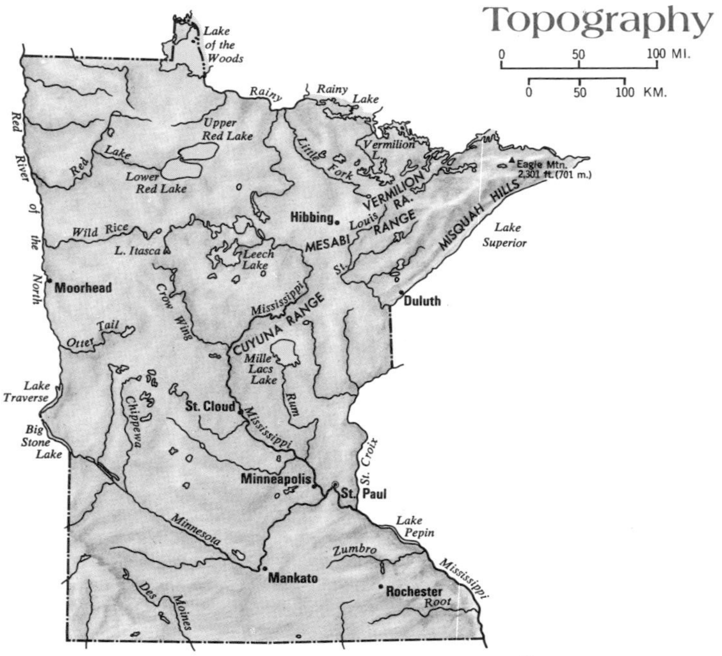
Topography
0 50 100 MI.
0 50 100 KM.
Lake of the Woods
Rainy
Rainy Lake
Upper Red Lake
Red Lake
Lower Red Lake
Vermilion
Eagle Mtn. 2,301 ft. (701 m.)
VERMILION RA.
MISQUAH HILLS
Little Fork
Red River of the North
Wild Rice
L. Itasca
Leech Lake
Hibbing
Louis
MESABI RANGE
Lake Superior
Moorhead
Crow Wing
Mississippi
Duluth
Otter Tail
CUYUNA RANGE
Mille Lacs Lake
Lake Traverse
Chippewa
Rum
St. Cloud
Big Stone Lake
St. Croix
Minneapolis
St. Paul
Minnesota
Lake Pepin
Zumbro
Mississippi
Mankato
Rochester
Root
Des Moines
Below Sea Level
100 m. 328 ft.
200 m. 656 ft.
500 m. 1,640 ft.
1,000 m. 3,281 ft.
2,000 m. 6,562 ft.
5,000 m. 16,404 ft.

Minnesota

SCALE
0 5 10 20 30 40 50 MI.
0 5 10 20 30 40 50 KM.

State Capitals ⊛
County Seats ⊙
Major Limited Access Hwys. ▬

Scale 1:2,300,000

Northeastern Part of Minnesota
Same scale as main map

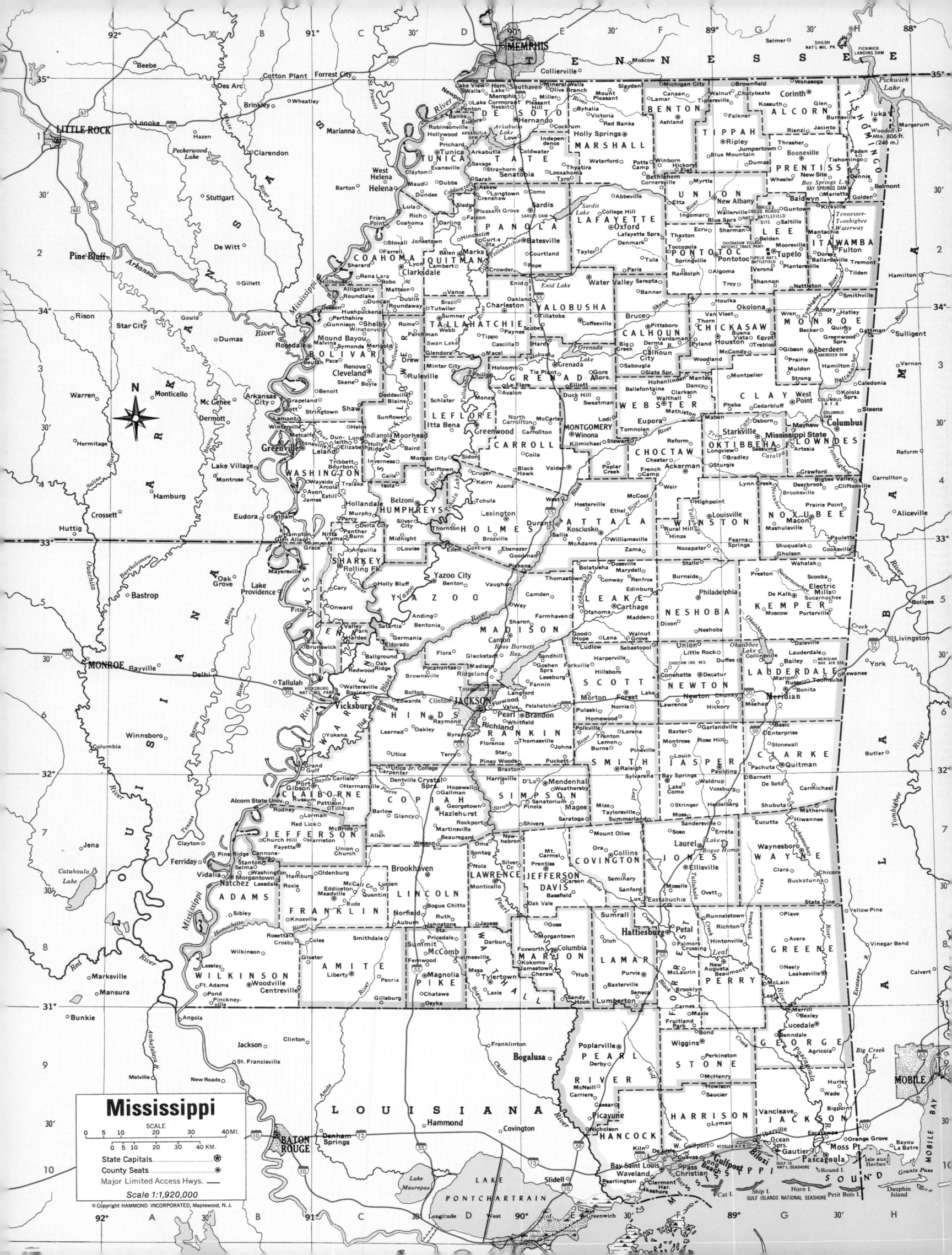

Mississippi

SCALE 1:1,920,000

SCALE				
0	5 10	20	30	40 MI.
0 5 10	20	30	40 KM.	

State Capitals ... ⊛
County Seats ... ◎
Major Limited Access Hwys. ———

© Copyright HAMMOND INCORPORATED, Maplewood, N.J.

COUNTIES

Adams 38,035 B8
Alcorn 33,036 G1
Amite 13,369 C8
Attala 19,865 E4
Benton 8,153 F1
Bolivar 45,965 C3
Calhoun 15,664 F3
Carroll 9,776 E4
Chickasaw 17,853 G3
Choctaw 8,996 F4
Claiborne 12,279 C7
Clarke 16,945 G6
Clay 21,082 G3
Coahoma 36,918 C2
Copiah 26,503 D7
Covington 15,927 E7
De Soto 53,930 E1
Forrest 66,018 F8
Franklin 8,208 C8
George 15,297 G9
Greene 9,827 G8
Grenada 21,043 E3
Hancock 24,537 E10
Harrison 157,665 F10
Hinds 250,998 D6
Holmes 22,970 D4
Humphreys 13,931 C4
Issaquena 2,513 B5
Itawamba 20,518 H2
Jackson 118,015 G9
Jasper 17,265 F6
Jefferson 9,181 B7
Jefferson Davis 13,846 E7
Jones 61,912 F7
Kemper 10,148 G5
Lafayette 31,030 E2
Lamar 23,821 E8
Lauderdale 77,285 G6
Lawrence 12,518 D7
Leake 18,790 E5
Lee 57,061 G2
Leflore 41,525 D3
Lincoln 30,174 D8
Lowndes 57,304 H4
Madison 41,613 D5
Marion 25,708 E8
Marshall 29,296 E1
Monroe 36,404 H3
Montgomery 13,366 E4
Neshoba 23,789 F5
Newton 19,944 F6
Noxubee 13,212 G4
Oktibbeha 36,018 G4
Panola 28,164 E2
Pearl River 33,795 E9
Perry 9,864 G8
Pike 36,173 D8
Pontotoc 20,918 F2
Prentiss 24,025 G1
Quitman 12,636 D2
Rankin 69,427 E6
Scott 24,556 E6
Sharkey 7,964 C5
Simpson 23,441 E7
Smith 15,077 E6
Stone 9,716 F9
Sunflower 34,844 C3
Tallahatchie 17,157 D3
Tate 20,119 E1
Tippah 18,739 G1
Tishomingo 18,434 H1
Tunica 9,652 D1
Union 21,741 F2
Walthall 13,761 D8
Warren 51,627 C6
Washington 72,344 C4
Wayne 19,135 G7
Webster 10,300 F3
Wilkinson 10,021 B8
Winston 19,474 F4
Yalobusha 13,139 E2
Yazoo 27,349 D5

CITIES and TOWNS

Zip *Name/Pop.* *Key*

38601 Abbeville 448 F2
39730 Aberdeen⊙ 7,184 H3
39735 Ackerman⊙ 1,567 F4
39096 Alcorn State University B7
38820 Algoma 175 G2
†39083 Allen 15 C7
38720 Alligator 256 C2
38821 Amory 7,307 H3
38721 Anguilla 950 C5
38722 Arcola 588 C4
38602 Arkabutla 400 D1
39736 Artesia 526 G4
38603 Ashland⊙ 532 F1
38604 Askew 300 D1
†39664 Auburn 500 C8
38912 Avalon 100 D3
38723 Avon 400 B4
39320 Bailey 320 G6
38724 Baird 150 C4
38824 Baldwyn 3,427 G2
†39156 Ballground 30 C5
38913 Banner 120 F2
†39083 Barlow 20 C7
†39330 Basic 60 G6
39421 Bassfield 325 E8
38606 Batesville⊙ 4,692 E2
†39343 Baxter 75 F6
†39455 Baxterville 100 E8
39520 Bay Saint Louis⊙ 7,891 F10
39422 Bay Springs⊙ 1,884 F7
39423 Beaumont 1,112 G8
†39191 Beauregard 185 D7
38825 Becker 350 G3
38826 Belden 241 G2
38609 Belen 400 D2
39737 Bellefontaine 400 F3
38827 Belmont 1,420 H1
39038 Belzoni⊙ 2,982 C4
†39450 Benndale 500 G9
38725 Benoit 499 C3
39039 Benton 350 D5
39040 Bentonia 518 D5
†38659 Bethlehem 210 F1
38726 Beulah 431 B3
39738 Bigbee Valley 370 H4
38914 Big Creek 146 F3
†39567 Bigpoint 350 H9
*39530 Biloxi 49,311 G10
Biloxi-Gulfport‡ 191,918 G10
†38917 Black Hawk 41 E4
38727 Blaine 75 C3
38610 Blue Mountain 867 G1
38828 Blue Springs 131 G2
†38614 Bobo 200 C2
39629 Bogue Chitto 575 D8
39041 Bolton 664 D6
39550 Bond 350 F9
†39301 Bonita 300 G6
38829 Booneville⊙ 6,199 G1
†38756 Bourbon 200 C4
†39180 Bovina 50 C6
38730 Boyle 888 C3
39042 Brandon⊙ 9,626 E6
39044 Braxton 172 D6
38963 Brazil 229 D2
39601 Brookhaven⊙ 10,800 C7
39425 Brooklyn 450 F8
39739 Brooksville 1,038 G4
†38683 Brownfield 125 G1
38915 Bruce 2,208 F3
39322 Buckatunna 500 G7
39630 Bude 1,092 C8
38833 Burnsville 889 H1
38611 Byhalia 757 E1
†39205 Byram 250 D6
†38754 Caile 30 C4
39740 Caledonia 497 H3
38916 Calhoun City 2,033 F3
39045 Camden 150 E5
38612 Canaan 200 F1
39046 Canton⊙ 11,116 D5
39049 Carlisle 425 C7
†39360 Carmichael 75 G7
39050 Carpenter 200 C6
39426 Carriere 900 E9
38917 Carrollton⊙ 338 E4
39427 Carson 400 E7
39051 Carthage⊙ 3,453 E5
39054 Cary 470 C5
38920 Cascilla 230 D3
39741 Cedarbluff 175 G3
39631 Centreville 1,844 B8
38684 Chalybeate 350 G1
38921 Charleston⊙ 2,878 D2
39632 Chatawa 300 D8
38731 Chatham 150 B4
39323 Chunky 277 G6
39055 Church Hill 350 B7
39324 Clara 275 G7
38614 Clarksdale⊙ 21,137 D2
39551 Clermont Harbor 550 F10
38732 Cleveland⊙ 14,524 C3
39056 Clinton 14,660 D6
38617 Coahoma 350 C2
†38632 Cockrum 150 E1
38922 Coffeeville⊙ 1,129 E3
38923 Coila 75 E4
38618 Coldwater 1,505 E1
†39638 Coles 150 C8
†38655 College Hill 150 E2
39428 Collins⊙ 2,131 E7
39325 Collinsville 700 G6
39429 Columbia⊙ 7,733 E8
39701 Columbus⊙ 27,383 H3
38619 Como 1,378 E1
39057 Conehatta 200 F6
†39051 Conway 25 E5
38834 Corinth⊙ 13,839 G1
†38659 Cornersville 65 F1
38620 Courtland 381 E2
†39095 Coxburg 300 D5
39743 Crawford 495 G4
38621 Crenshaw 1,019 D2
39633 Crosby 349 B8
38622 Crowder 789 D2
38924 Cruger 540 D4
39059 Crystal Springs 4,902 D7
†38606 Curtis Station 350 D2
39326 Daleville 210 G5
†39643 Darbun 100 D8
38623 Darling 275 D2
39327 Decatur⊙ 1,148 F6
†39739 Deerbrook 300 G4
39328 De Kalb⊙ 1,159 G5
†39571 De Lisle 450 F10
39061 Delta City 310 C4
†38655 Denmark 40 F2
38838 Dennis 150 H1
†39059 Dentville 175 C7
†39470 Derby 298 E9
38839 Derma 793 F3
†39532 D'Iberville 13,369 G10
39062 D'Lo 463 E7
38736 Doddsville 232 C3
38737 Drew 2,528 C3
38738 Dublin 100 C2
38925 Duck Hill 706 E3
†39337 Duffee 175 G6
38625 Dumas 312 G1
38740 Duncan 501 C2
38626 Dundee 600 D1
39063 Durant 2,889 E4
39436 Eastabuchie 200 F8
39064 Ebenezer 200 D5
38841 Ecru 687 F2
39634 Eddiceton 65 C8
39065 Eden 150 D5
39066 Edwards 1,515 C6
†39156 Eldorado 20 C5
39329 Electric Mills 100 G5
38742 Elizabeth 500 C4
38926 Elliott 200 E3
39437 Ellisville⊙ 4,652 F7
38927 Enid E2
39330 Enterprise 607 G6
†39440 Errata 85 F7
39552 Escatawpa 5,367 G10
39067 Ethel 486 F4
38627 Etta 75 F2
39744 Eupora 2,048 F3
†38676 Evansville 60 D1
38628 Falcon 260 D2
38629 Falkner 251 G1
38630 Farrell 300 C2
39069 Fayette⊙ 2,033 B7
39635 Fernwood 500 D8
39070 Fitler 175 B5
39071 Flora 1,507 D5
39073 Florence 1,111 D6
†39201 Flowood 943 D6
39074 Forest⊙ 5,229 F6
39076 Forkville 185 E6
39636 Fort Adams 75 B8
39483 Foxworth 800 E8
39745 French Camp 306 F4
38631 Friars Point 1,400 C2
39577 Fruitland Park 75 F9
38843 Fulton⊙ 3,238 H2
39077 Gallman D7
38844 Gattman 151 H3
39553 Gautier 8,917 G10
39078 Georgetown 343 D7
†39354 Gholson 50 G5
†39083 Glancy 25 C7
38846 Glen 100 H1
38744 Glen Allan 650 B4
38928 Glendora 220 D3
39638 Gloster 1,726 B8
†39110 Gluckstadt 150 D5
38847 Golden 292 H2
39079 Goodman 1,285 E5
38929 Gore Springs 125 E3
38745 Grace 325 C5
†38725 Grapeland 200 B3
38701 Greenville⊙ 40,613 B4
38930 Greenwood⊙ 20,115 D4
38848 Greenwood Springs 170 H3
38901 Grenada⊙ 12,641 E3
*39501 Gulfport⊙ 39,676 F10
38746 Gunnison 708 C3
38849 Guntown 359 G2
†39661 Hamburg 150 B7
39746 Hamilton 500 H3
†38901 Hardy 45 E3
39080 Harperville 200 E6
39081 Harriston 500 C7
39082 Harrisville 500 D7
†38821 Hatley 497 H3
39401 Hattiesburg⊙ 40,829 F8
39083 Hazlehurst⊙ 4,437 D7
39439 Heidelberg 1,098 F7
39086 Hermanville 750 C7
38632 Hernando⊙ 2,969 E1
†39192 Hesterville 25 E4
39332 Hickory 670 F6
38633 Hickory Flat 458 F1
39087 Hillsboro 800 E6
†38646 Hinchcliff 60 D2
†39462 Hintonville 300 F8
†39108 Hinze 30 F4
†39751 Hohenlinden 96 F3
38940 Holcomb 50 D3
38748 Hollandale 4,336 C4
39088 Holly Bluff 700 C5
38749 Holly Ridge 350 C4
38635 Holly Springs⊙ 7,285 E1
†38676 Hollywood 80 D1
†39648 Holmesville 50 D8
38637 Horn Lake 4,326 D1
38850 Houlka 710 G2
38851 Houston⊙ 3,747 G3
†39574 Howison 300 F9
†39429 Hub 80 E8
39555 Hurley 500 H9
†38774 Hushpuckena 60 C2
38638 Independence 150 E1
38751 Indianola⊙ 8,221 C4
†38652 Ingomar 150 F2
38753 Inverness 1,034 C4
38754 Isola 834 C4
38941 Itta Bena 2,904 D4
38852 Iuka⊙ 2,846 H1
†38865 Jacinto 65 H1
*39201 Jackson (cap.)⊙ 202,895 D6
Jackson‡ 320,425 D6
39641 Jayess 200 D8
38639 Jonestown 1,231 D2
†38829 Jumpertown 472 G1
†38924 Keirn 3 D4
†39364 Kewanee 250 H6
39747 Kilmichael 906 E4
39556 Kiln 800 F10
†39661 Knoxville 65 B8
39643 Kokomo 250 E8
†39740 Kolola Springs 100 H3
39090 Kosciusko⊙ 7,415 E4
38834 Kossuth 190 G1
38640 Lafayette Springs 80 F2
39092 Lake 524 F6
38641 Lake Cormorant 300 D1
39558 Lakeshore 550 F10
38642 Lamar 200 F1
38643 Lambert 1,624 D2
38755 Lamont 400 B3
39335 Lauderdale 600 G5
39440 Laurel⊙ 21,897 F7
39336 Lawrence 250 F6
39450 Leaf 250 G8
39451 Leakesville⊙ 1,120 G8
39093 Learned 113 C6
38756 Leland 6,667 C4
39094 Lena 231 E5
†39667 Lexie 40 D8
39095 Lexington⊙ 2,628 D4
39645 Liberty⊙ 669 C8
39337 Little Rock 70 F5
39560 Long Beach 7,967 F10
†39759 Longview 800 G4
39096 Lorman 350 B7
39338 Louin 338 F6
39097 Louise 400 C5
39339 Louisville⊙ 7,323 G4
†38632 Love 50 D1
39452 Lucedale⊙ 2,429 G9
39646 Lucien 75 C7
39098 Ludlow 350 E5
38644 Lula 394 C2
39455 Lumberton 2,217 E8
†39501 Lyman 500 F10
†39739 Lynn Creek 20 G4
38645 Lyon 531 D2
39750 Maben 855 F3
39341 Macon⊙ 2,396 G4
39109 Madden 450 F5
39110 Madison 2,241 D6
39111 Magee 3,497 E7
39652 Magnolia⊙ 2,461 D8
†38769 Malvina 100 C3
38855 Mantachie 732 H2
39751 Mantee 158 F3
38856 Marietta 298 H2
39342 Marion 771 G6
38646 Marks⊙ 2,260 D2
†39083 Martinsville 30 D7
†39051 Marydell 99 F5
39752 Mathiston 632 F3
38758 Mattson 200 C2
†39458 Maxie 233 F9
39113 Mayersville⊙ 378 B5
39753 Mayhew 150 G4
39107 McAdams 350 E4
†39144 McBride 2 C7
39647 McCall Creek 250 C7
38943 McCarley 250 E3
39648 McComb 12,331 D8
38854 McCondy 150 G3
39108 McCool 203 F4
39561 McHenry 660 F9
39456 McLain 688 G8
39457 McNeill 800 E9
39653 Meadville⊙ 575 C8
39114 Mendenhall⊙ 2,533 E7
39301 Meridian⊙ 46,577 G6
38759 Merigold 574 C3
†39667 Mesa 30 D8
38760 Metcalfe 952 B4
38647 Michigan City 350 F1
39115 Midnight 500 C4
38648 Mineral Wells 250 E1
38944 Minter City 150 D3
39762 Mississippi State G4
39116 Mize 363 E7
38945 Money 350 D3
39654 Monticello⊙ 1,834 D7
39754 Montpelier 175 G3
†39338 Montrose 120 F6
38857 Mooreville 200 G2
38761 Moorhead 2,358 C4
38946 Morgan City 319 D4
39484 Morgantown 325 E8
†39120 Morgantown 3,445 B7
39117 Morton 3,303 E6
†39328 Moscow 30 G5
39459 Moselle 525 F8
39460 Moss 253 F7
39563 Moss Point 18,998 G10
38762 Mound Bayou 2,917 C3
†39474 Mount Carmel 30 E7
39119 Mount Olive 993 E7
38649 Mount Pleasant 250 E1
38650 Myrtle 402 F1
39120 Natchez⊙ 22,015 B7
39461 Neely 270 G8
38651 Nesbit 366 D1
39365 Neshoba 250 F5
38858 Nettleton 1,911 G2
38652 New Albany⊙ 7,072 G2
39462 New Augusta⊙ 589 F8
39140 Newhebron 470 D7
38850 New Houlka (Houlka) 710 G2
38859 New Site 100 H1
39345 Newton 3,708 F6
39463 Nicholson 400 E10
38763 Nitta Yuma 150 C4
†39629 Norfield 75 C8
38947 North Carrollton 859 E3
39346 Noxapater 516 F5
38948 Oakland 540 E2
†39154 Oakley 133 D6
39656 Oak Vale E8
39564 Ocean Springs 14,504 G10
39141 Ofahoma 350 E5
38860 Okolona⊙ 3,409 G2
38654 Olive Branch 2,067 E1
†39482 Oloh 93 E8
†39654 Oma 200 D7
†39501 Orange Grove 13,476 H10
39657 Osyka 581 D8
39464 Ovett 600 F8
38655 Oxford⊙ 9,882 F2
38764 Pace 519 C3
39347 Pachuta 256 G6
38861 Paden 119 H1
†39401 Palmers Crossing 2,765 F8
38765 Panther Burn 300 C4
38738 Parchman 200 D3
38949 Paris 253 F2
39567 Pascagoula⊙ 29,318 G10
Pascagoula-Moss Point‡ 118,015 G10
39571 Pass Christian 5,014 F10
39144 Pattison 540 C7
†39348 Paulding⊙ 630 F6
39349 Paulette 230 H4
†38920 Paynes 100 D3
39028 Pearl 18,580 D6
39572 Pearlington 500 E10
39145 Pelahatchie 1,445 E6
39573 Perkinston 950 F9
†38746 Perthshire 25 C3
39465 Petal 8,476 F8
39755 Pheba 280 G3
39350 Philadelphia⊙ 6,434 F5
38950 Philipp 975 D3
†39476 Piave 150 G8
39466 Picayune 10,361 E9
39146 Pickens 1,386 E5
39148 Piney Woods 450 D6
39149 Pinola E7

(continued on following page)

AREA 47,689 sq. mi. (123,515 sq. km.)
POPULATION 2,520,638
CAPITAL Jackson
LARGEST CITY Jackson
HIGHEST POINT Woodall Mtn. 806 ft. (246 m.)
SETTLED IN 1716
ADMITTED TO UNION December 10, 1817
POPULAR NAME Magnolia State
STATE FLOWER Magnolia
STATE BIRD Mockingbird

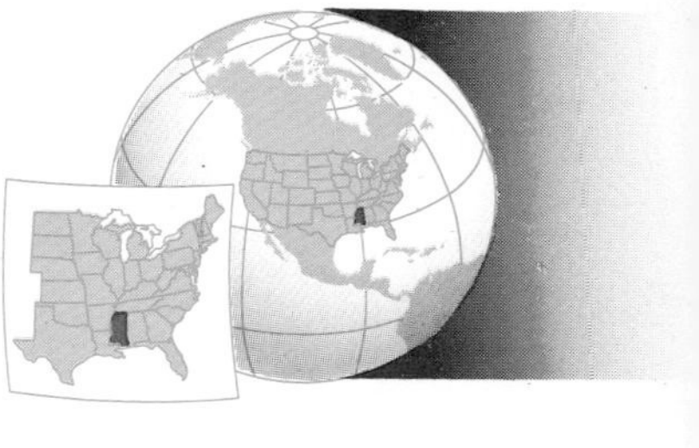

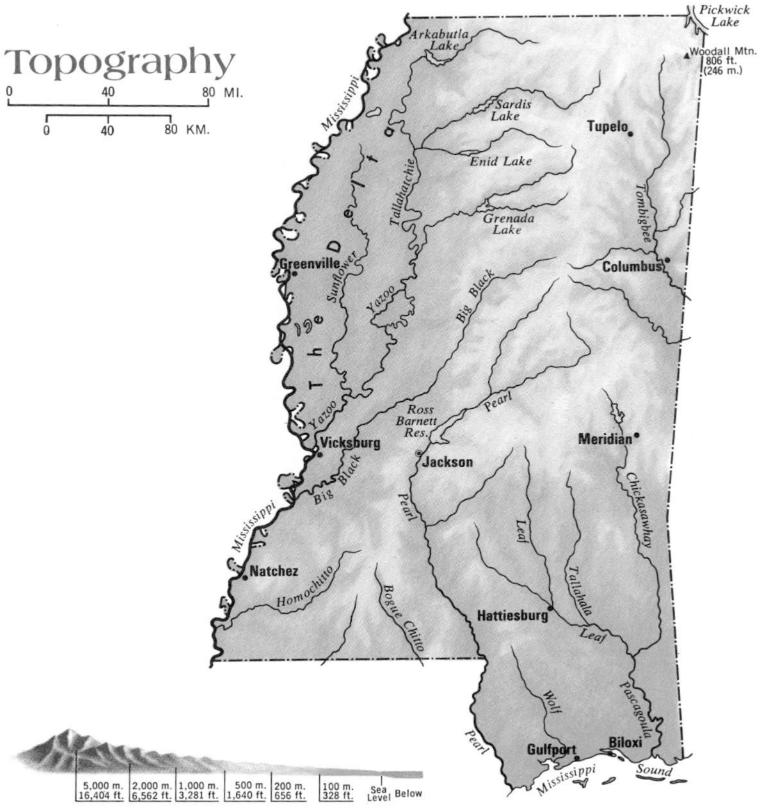

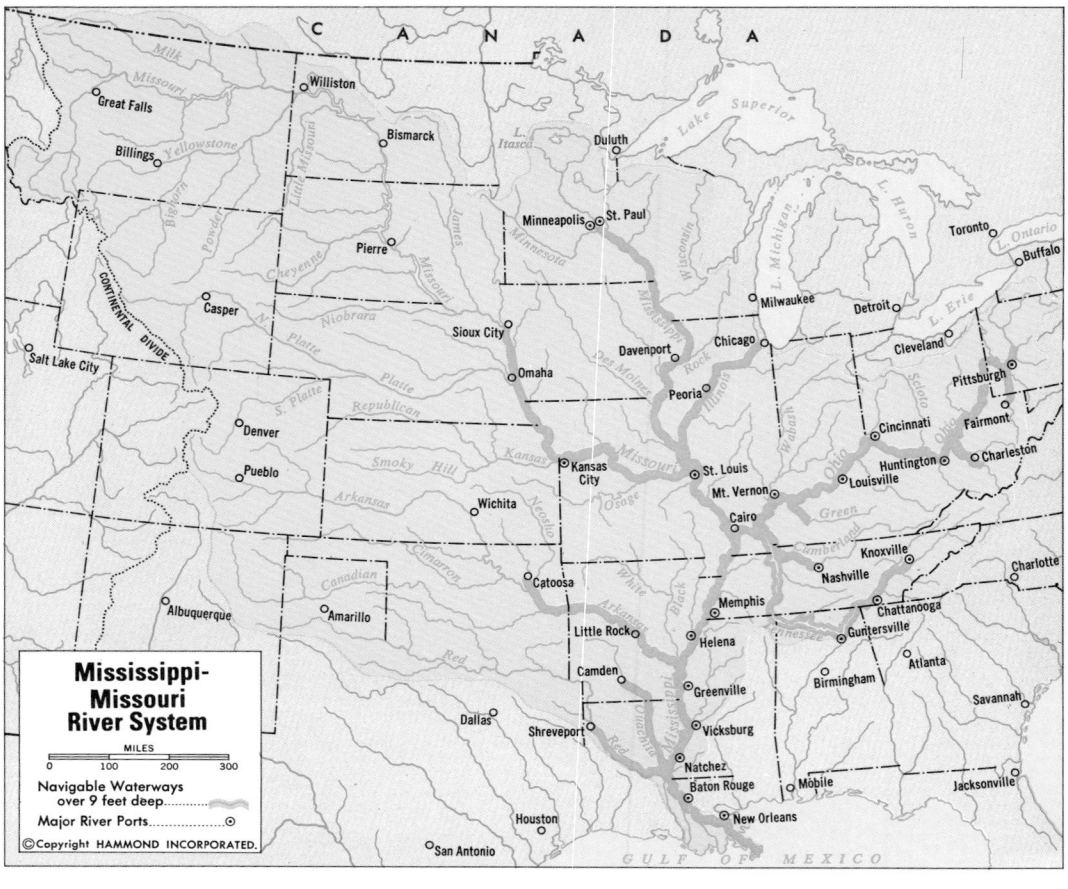

Mississippi-Missouri River System

MILES
0 100 200 300

Navigable Waterways over 9 feet deep.............
Major River Ports.............................⊙

©Copyright HAMMOND INCORPORATED.

Agriculture, Industry and Resources

DOMINANT LAND USE

- Specialized Cotton
- Cotton, Livestock
- Cotton, General Farming
- Cotton, Forest Products
- Truck and Mixed Farming
- Forests
- Swampland, Limited Agriculture

MAJOR MINERAL OCCURRENCES

- Cl Clay
- Fe Iron Ore
- G Natural Gas
- O Petroleum
- ///// Major Industrial Areas

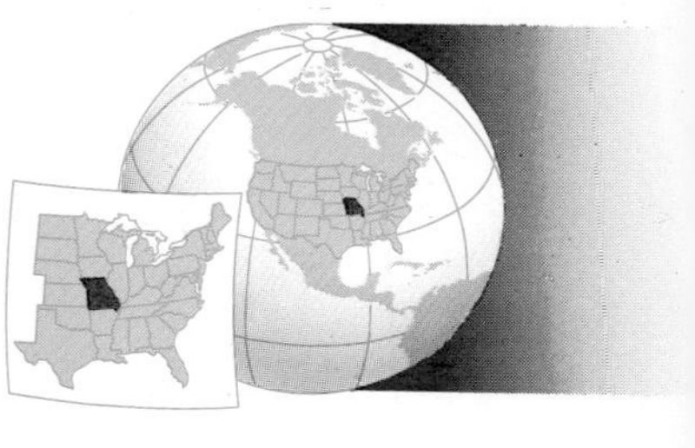

AREA 69,697 sq. mi. (180,515 sq. km.)
POPULATION 4,916,759
CAPITAL Jefferson City
LARGEST CITY St. Louis
HIGHEST POINT Taum Sauk Mtn. 1,772 ft. (540 m.)
SETTLED IN 1764
ADMITTED TO UNION August 10, 1821
POPULAR NAME Show Me State
STATE FLOWER Hawthorn
STATE BIRD Bluebird

COUNTIES

Adair 24,870 ... G2
Andrew 13,980 ... C3
Atchison 8,605 ... B2
Audrain 26,458 ... J4
Barry 24,408 ... E9
Barton 11,292 ... D7
Bates 15,873 ... D6
Benton 12,183 ... F6
Bollinger 10,301 ... M8
Boone 100,376 ... H4
Buchanan 87,888 ... C3
Butler 37,693 ... M9
Caldwell 8,660 ... E3
Callaway 32,252 ... J5
Camden 20,017 ... G6
Cape Girardeau 58,837 ... N8
Carroll 12,131 ... F4
Carter 5,428 ... L9
Cass 51,029 ... D5
Cedar 11,894 ... E7
Chariton 10,489 ... F3
Christian 22,402 ... F9
Clark 8,493 ... J2
Clay 136,488 ... D4
Clinton 15,916 ... D3
Cole 56,663 ... H6
Cooper 14,643 ... G5
Crawford 18,300 ... K7
Dade 7,383 ... E8
Dallas 12,096 ... F7
Daviess 8,905 ... E3
De Kalb 8,222 ... D3
Dent 14,517 ... J7
Douglas 11,594 ... G9
Dunklin 36,324 ... M10
Franklin 71,233 ... K6
Gasconade 13,181 ... J6
Gentry 7,887 ... D2
Greene 185,302 ... F8
Grundy 11,959 ... E2
Harrison 9,890 ... E2
Henry 19,672 ... E6
Hickory 6,367 ... F7
Holt 6,882 ... B2
Howard 10,008 ... G4
Howell 28,807 ... J9
Iron 11,084 ... L7
Jackson 629,266 ... R5
Jasper 86,958 ... D8
Jefferson 146,183 ... L6
Johnson 39,059 ... E5
Knox 5,508 ... H2
Laclede 24,323 ... G7
Lafayette 29,925 ... E4
Lawrence 28,973 ... E8
Lewis 10,901 ... J2
Lincoln 22,193 ... L4
Linn 15,495 ... F3
Livingston 15,739 ... E3
Macon 16,313 ... G3
Madison 10,725 ... M8
Maries 7,551 ... J6
Marion 28,638 ... J3
McDonald 14,917 ... D9
Mercer 4,685 ... E2
Miller 18,532 ... H6
Mississippi 15,726 ... O9
Moniteau 12,068 ... G5
Monroe 9,716 ... H3
Montgomery 11,537 ... K5
Morgan 13,807 ... G6
New Madrid 22,945 ... N9
Newton 40,555 ... D9
Nodaway 21,996 ... C2
Oregon 10,238 ... K9
Osage 12,014 ... J6
Ozark 7,961 ... H9
Pemiscot 24,987 ... N10
Perry 16,784 ... N7
Pettis 36,378 ... F5
Phelps 33,633 ... J7
Pike 17,568 ... K4
Platte 46,341 ... C4
Polk 18,822 ... F7
Pulaski 42,011 ... H7
Putnam 6,092 ... F2
Ralls 8,984 ... J3
Randolph 25,460 ... G3
Ray 21,378 ... E4
Reynolds 7,230 ... L8
Ripley 12,458 ... L9
Saint Charles 144,107 ... M2
Saint Clair 8,622 ... E6
Sainte Genevieve 15,180 ... M7
Saint Francois 42,600 ... M7
Saint Louis 973,896 ... O3
Saint Louis (city county) 453,085 ... P3
Saline 24,919 ... F4
Schuyler 4,979 ... G2
Scotland 5,415 ... H2
Scott 39,647 ... N8
Shannon 7,885 ... K8
Shelby 7,826 ... H3
Stoddard 29,009 ... N9
Stone 15,587 ... F9
Sullivan 7,434 ... F2
Taney 20,467 ... F9
Texas 21,070 ... J8
Vernon 19,806 ... D7
Warren 14,900 ... K5
Washington 17,983 ... L7
Wayne 11,277 ... L8
Webster 20,414 ... G8
Worth 3,008 ... D2
Wright 16,188 ... H8

CITIES and TOWNS

Zip *Name/Pop.* *Key*

64720 Adrian 1,484 ... D6
63730 Advance 1,054 ... N8
63123 Affton 23,181 ... P4
64401 Agency 419 ... C3
64830 Alba 474 ... D8
64402 Albany⊙ 2,152 ... D2
63430 Alexandria 417 ... K2
64001 Alma 445 ... E4
65606 Alton⊙ 721 ... K9
64421 Amazonia 314 ... C3
64723 Amsterdam 231 ... D6
64831 Anderson 1,237 ... D9
63620 Annapolis 370 ... L8
63820 Anniston 320 ... O9
64724 Appleton City 1,257 ... D6
63821 Arbyrd 704 ... M10
63621 Arcadia 683 ... L7
64725 Archie 753 ... D5
65230 Armstrong 360 ... G4
63010 Arnold 19,141 ... M6
65604 Ash Grove 1,157 ... E8
65010 Ashland 1,021 ... H5
63530 Atlanta 441 ... H3
63332 Augusta 308 ... L5
65605 Aurora 6,437 ... E9
65231 Auxvasse 858 ... J4
65608 Ava⊙ 2,761 ... G9
64010 Avondale 612 ... P5
63011 Ballwin 12,656 ... N3
64011 Bates City 199 ... E5
†65619 Battlefield 1,227 ... F8
†63101 Bella Villa 758 ... R4
63735 Bell City 539 ... N8
65013 Belle 1,233 ... J6
†63137 Bellefontaine Neighbors 12,082 ... R2
63333 Bellflower 403 ... K4
†63101 Bel-Nor 2,047 ... P2
†63101 Bel-Ridge 3,682 ... P2
64012 Belton 12,708 ... C5
63736 Benton⊙ 674 ... O8
63134 Berkeley 15,922 ... P2
63822 Bernie 1,975 ... M9
63823 Bertrand 688 ... O9
64424 Bethany⊙ 3,095 ... E2
63532 Bevier 733 ... G3
65610 Billings 911 ... F8
65438 Birch Tree 622 ... K9
63624 Bismarck 1,625 ... L7
65321 Blackburn 314 ... F4
†63031 Black Jack 5,293 ... R1
65014 Bland 662 ... J6
63825 Bloomfield⊙ 1,795 ... M9
63627 Bloomsdale 397 ... M6
64015 Blue Springs 25,927 ... R6
†64101 Blue Summit ... R5
65613 Bolivar⊙ 5,919 ... F7
63628 Bonne Terre 3,797 ... L7
65233 Boonville⊙ 6,959 ... G5
64723 Bosworth 394 ... F4
65441 Bourbon 1,259 ... K6
63334 Bowling Green⊙ 3,022 ... K4
65616 Branson 2,550 ... F9
63533 Brashear 332 ... H2
64624 Braymer 986 ... E3
64625 Breckenridge 523 ... E3
†63114 Breckenridge Hills 5,666 ... O2
63144 Brentwood 8,209 ... P3
63044 Bridgeton 18,445 ... O2
†63044 Bridgeton Terrace 334 ... O2
64628 Brookfield 5,555 ... F3
64630 Browning 368 ... F2
65236 Brunswick 1,272 ... F4
64631 Bucklin 713 ... G3
64016 Buckner 2,848 ... R5
65622 Buffalo⊙ 2,217 ... F7
65237 Bunceton 419 ... G5
63629 Bunker 673 ... K8
64428 Burlington Junction 657 ... B2
64730 Butler⊙ 4,107 ... D6
65689 Cabool 2,090 ... H8
64632 Cainsville 496 ... E2
65239 Cairo 315 ... H4
65323 Calhoun 427 ... E6
65018 California⊙ 3,381 ... H5
63534 Callao 326 ... G3
†63101 Calverton Park 1,717 ... P2
65020 Camdenton⊙ 2,303 ... G6
64429 Cameron 4,519 ... D3
63933 Campbell 2,134 ... M9
63828 Canalou 369 ... N9
63435 Canton 2,435 ... J2
63701 Cape Girardeau 34,361 ... O8
63829 Cardwell 831 ... M10
64834 Carl Junction 3,937 ... C8
64633 Carrollton⊙ 4,700 ... E4
64835 Carterville 1,973 ... D8
64836 Carthage⊙ 11,104 ... D8
63830 Caruthersville⊙ 7,958 ... N10
65625 Cassville⊙ 2,091 ... E9
65022 Cedar City 427 ... H5
63436 Center 669 ... J3
65023 Centertown 304 ... H5
63633 Centerville⊙ 241 ... L8
65240 Centralia 3,537 ... H4
63740 Chaffee 3,241 ... N8
65024 Chamois 546 ... J5
†63101 Charlack 1,537 ... P2
63834 Charleston⊙ 5,230 ... O9
64733 Chilhowee 349 ... E5
64601 Chillicothe⊙ 9,089 ... E3
63437 Clarence 1,147 ... H3
65243 Clark 304 ... H4
65025 Clarksburg 352 ... G5
64430 Clarksdale 278 ... D3
†63017 Clarkson Valley 1,435 ... N3
63336 Clarksville 585 ... K4
63837 Clarkton 1,228 ... M10
†64119 Claycomo 1,671 ... P5
63105 Clayton⊙ 14,273 ... P3
64734 Cleveland 485 ... C5
65631 Clever 551 ... F8
64735 Clinton⊙ 8,366 ... E6
65325 Cole Camp 1,022 ... F6
65201 Columbia⊙ 62,061 ... H5
Columbia‡ 100,376 ... H5
†63128 Concord 20,896 ... P4
64020 Concordia 2,129 ... E5
65632 Conway 601 ... G7
†63101 Cool Valley 2,084 ... P2
63839 Cooter 479 ... N10
64021 Corder 483 ... E4
†64501 Country Club Village 1,234 ... C3
64437 Craig 379 ... B2
65633 Crane 1,185 ... E9
64739 Creighton 301 ... D6
†63126 Crestwood 12,815 ... O3
63141 Creve Coeur 11,757 ... O2
65452 Crocker 979 ... H7
63019 Crystal City 3,618 ... M6
†63101 Crystal Lake Park 496 ... O3
65453 Cuba 2,120 ... K6
63339 Curryville 323 ... K4
64439 Dearborn 547 ... C3
64740 Deepwater 475 ... E6
64440 De Kalb 245 ... C3
†63135 Dellwood 6,200 ... R2
63744 Delta 524 ... N8
63636 Des Arc 237 ... L8
63601 Desloge 3,481 ... M7
63020 De Soto 5,993 ... L6
63131 Des Peres 8,254 ... O3
63841 Dexter 7,043 ... N9
64840 Diamond 766 ... D9
65459 Dixon 1,402 ... H6
63935 Doniphan⊙ 1,921 ... L9
†65550 Doolittle 701 ... J7
63536 Downing 462 ... H2
64742 Drexel 908 ... C6
64841 Duenweg 703 ... D8
†64801 Duquesne 1,252 ... D8
64442 Eagleville 364 ... D2
64443 Easton 313 ... C3
63845 East Prairie 3,713 ... O9
64444 Edgerton 584 ... C3
63537 Edina⊙ 1,520 ... H2
†63101 Edmundson 1,374 ... O2
65026 Eldon 4,342 ... G6
64744 El Dorado Springs 3,868 ... E7
63638 Ellington 1,215 ... L8
†63011 Ellisville 6,233 ... M3
63937 Ellsinore 362 ... L9
63343 Elsberry 1,272 ... L4
63639 Elvins 1,548 ... L7
65466 Eminence⊙ 614 ... K8
63344 Eolia 401 ... L4
63846 Essex 545 ... N9
†63601 Esther 1,038 ... M7
63025 Eureka 3,862 ... M4
65646 Everton 317 ... E8
63440 Ewing 400 ... J2
64024 Excelsior Springs 10,424 ... R4
65647 Exeter 588 ... D9
64446 Fairfax 835 ... B2
65648 Fair Grove 863 ... F8
65649 Fair Play 384 ... E7
63345 Farber 503 ... J4
63640 Farmington⊙ 8,270 ... M7
65248 Fayette⊙ 2,983 ... G4
63026 Fenton 2,417 ... O4
63135 Ferguson 24,740 ... P2
64163 Ferrelview 447 ... O4
63028 Festus 7,574 ... M6
64449 Fillmore 265 ... C2
63940 Fisk 450 ... M9
63601 Flat River 4,443 ... M7
*63031 Florissant 55,372 ... P1
65652 Fordland 569 ... G8
64451 Forest City 387 ... B3
65653 Forsyth⊙ 1,010 ... F9
63441 Frankford 443 ... K4
63645 Fredericktown⊙ 4,036 ... M7
65035 Freeburg 554 ... J6
64746 Freeman 485 ... C5
†63101 Frontenac 3,654 ... O3
65251 Fulton⊙ 11,046 ... J5
65655 Gainesville⊙ 707 ... G9
65656 Galena⊙ 423 ... F9
64640 Gallatin⊙ 2,063 ... E3
64641 Galt 323 ... F2
64747 Garden City 1,021 ... D5
63037 Gerald 921 ... K6
63848 Gideon 1,240 ... N10
64642 Gilman City 414 ... D2
64118 Gladstone 24,990 ... P5
65254 Glasgow 1,336 ... G4
†64068 Glenaire 541 ... R5
63122 Glendale 6,035 ... P3
64748 Golden City 900 ... D8
63843 Goodman 1,030 ... C9
63543 Gorin ... H2
64454 Gower 1,276 ... C3
64029 Grain Valley 1,327 ... S6
64844 Granby 1,908 ... D9
64030 Grandview 24,502 ... P6
64456 Grant City⊙ 1,068 ... D2
†63155 Grantwood Village 1,002 ... O4
65037 Gravois Mills ... G6
63545 Green City 719 ... F2
65661 Greenfield⊙ 1,394 ... E8
65332 Green Ridge 488 ... F5
63546 Greentop 538 ... H2
63944 Greenville⊙ 393 ... M8
64034 Greenwood 1,315 ... R6
64643 Hale 529 ... F3
65255 Hallsville 624 ... H4
64644 Hamilton 1,582 ... E3
†63101 Hanley Hills 2,439 ... P2
63401 Hannibal 18,811 ... K3
64035 Hardin 688 ... E4
64701 Harrisonville⊙ 6,372 ... D5
65667 Hartville⊙ 576 ... G8
63945 Harviell ... M9
63349 Hawk Point 386 ... K5
63851 Hayti 3,964 ... N10
†63851 Hayti Heights 1,023 ... N10
†63736 Haywood City 425 ... N9
*63042 Hazelwood 12,935 ... P2
64036 Henrietta 424 ... E4
63048 Herculaneum 2,293 ... M6
65041 Hermann⊙ 2,695 ... K5
65668 Hermitage⊙ 384 ... F7
65257 Higbee 817 ... H4
64037 Higginsville 4,595 ... E4
63350 High Hill 254 ... K5
63050 Hillsboro⊙ 1,508 ... L6
†63101 Hillsdale 2,247 ... R2
63852 Holcomb 632 ... N10
64040 Holden 2,195 ... E5
63853 Holland 295 ... N10
65672 Hollister 1,439 ... F9
64048 Holt 276 ... D4
65043 Holts Summit 2,540 ... H5
†63879 Homestown 306 ... N10
64461 Hopkins 634 ... C1
63855 Hornersville 704 ... M10
65483 Houston⊙ 2,157 ... J8
65333 Houstonia 327 ... F5
†64152 Houston Lake 280 ... O5
†63869 Howardville 536 ... N9
65674 Humansville 907 ... E7
64752 Hume 315 ... C6
63443 Hunnewell 235 ... J3
†63101 Huntleigh 428 ... O3
65259 Huntsville⊙ 1,657 ... H4
63547 Hurdland 227 ... H2
65486 Iberia 852 ... H6
63754 Illmo 1.368 ... O8

(continued on following page)

Agriculture, Industry and Resources

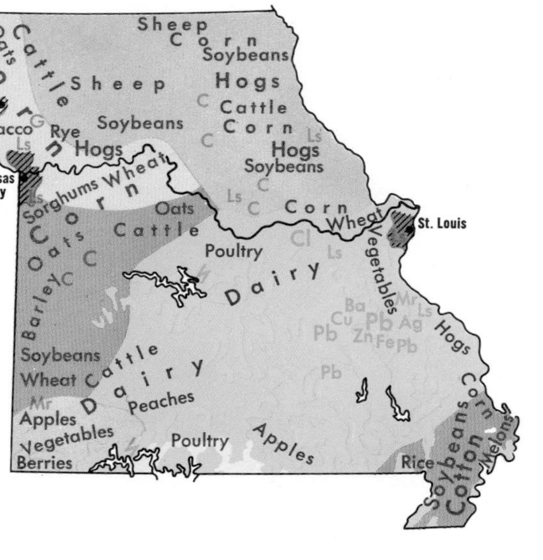

DOMINANT LAND USE

- Cattle Feed, Hogs
- Livestock, Cash Grain, Dairy
- Pasture Livestock
- Specialized Cotton
- General Farming, Dairy, Livestock, Poultry
- General Farming, Livestock, Truck Farming, Cotton
- Fruit and Mixed Farming
- Forests
- Urban Areas

MAJOR MINERAL OCCURRENCES

Ag	Silver	G	Natural Gas
Ba	Barite	Ls	Limestone
C	Coal	Mr	Marble
Cl	Clay	Pb	Lead
Cu	Copper	Zn	Zinc
Fe	Iron Ore		

Water Power — Major Industrial Areas

*64050 Independence⊙ 111,806...R5
63648 Irondale 349...L7
†64801 Iron Gates 314...C8
63650 Ironton⊙ 1,743...L7
63755 Jackson⊙ 7,827...N8
64648 Jamesport 651...E3
65046 Jamestown 317...G5
64755 Jasper 1,012...D8
65101 Jefferson City (cap.)⊙ 33,619...H5
63136 Jennings 17,026...R2
63351 Jonesboro 614...K5
64801 Joplin 39,023...C8
  Joplin‡ 127,513...C8
*63645 Junction City 238...M7
63445 Kahoka⊙ 2,101...J2
*64101 Kansas City 448,159...P5
  Kansas City‡ 1,327,020...P5
64060 Kearney 1,433...D4
63758 Kelso 455...O8
63857 Kennett⊙ 10,145...M10
65261 Keytesville⊙ 689...G4
64649 Kidder 265...D3
65686 Kimberling City 1,285...F9
64463 King City 1,063...C2
64650 Kingston⊙ 280...E3
64061 Kingsville 365...D5
63140 Kinloch 4,455...P2
63501 Kirksville⊙ 17,167...H2
63122 Kirkwood 27,987...O3
65336 Knob Noster 2,040...F5
63446 Knox City 281...H2
63447 La Belle 845...J2
64651 Laclede 445...F3
63352 Laddonia 726...J4
†63124 Ladue 9,376...P3
63448 La Grange 1,217...K2
64063 Lake Lotawana 1,875...R6
65049 Lake Ozark 427...G6
†63336 Lake Saint Louis 3,843...L4
63101 Lakeshire 1,593...P4
†64015 Lake Tapawingo 925...R6
†64152 Lake Waukomis 1,050...P5
64034 Lake Winnebago 681...R6
64759 Lamar⊙ 4,053...D8
65337 La Monte 1,054...F5
64847 Lanagan 440...C9
63548 Lancaster⊙ 855...H1
63549 La Plata 1,423...H2
64652 Laredo 340...E2
64760 Latour 84...D5
64062 Lawson 1,688...D4
†63640 Leadington 238...M7
63653 Leadwood 1,371...L7
65535 Leasburg 304...K6
65536 Lebanon⊙ 9,507...G7
64063 Lee's Summit 28,741...R6
64761 Leeton 604...E5
63125 Lemay 35,424...R4
64066 Levasy 235...S5
63452 Lewistown 502...J2
64067 Lexington⊙ 5,063...E4
64762 Liberal 701...D7
64068 Liberty⊙ 16,251...R5
65542 Licking 1,272...J8
63862 Lilbourn 1,463...N9
65338 Lincoln 819...F6
65051 Linn⊙ 1,211...J5
65052 Linn Creek 242...G6
64653 Linneus⊙ 421...F3
65682 Lockwood 971...E8
64070 Lone Jack 420...S6
63353 Louisiana 4,261...K4
64763 Lowry City 676...E6

63762 Lutesville 865...M8
63552 Macon⊙ 5,680...H3
65263 Madison 656...H4
64466 Maitland 415...B2
63863 Malden 6,096...M9
65339 Malta Bend 292...F4
65704 Mansfield 1,423...G8
63143 Maplewood 10,960...P3
63764 Marble Hill⊙ 601...N8
64658 Marceline 2,938...F3
65705 Marionville 1,920...E8
†63101 Marlborough 2,012...P3
63655 Marquand 397...M8
65340 Mayview⊙ 12,781...F4
65706 Marshfield⊙ 3,871...G8
63866 Marston 937...N9
63357 Marthasville 543...L5
65264 Martinsburg 309...J4
63043 Maryland Heights 5,676...O2
64468 Maryville⊙ 9,558...C2
63857 Matthews 547...N9
64469 Maysville⊙ 1,187...D3
64071 Mayview 291...E4
64659 Meadville 416...F3
63555 Memphis⊙ 2,105...H2
64660 Mendon 252...F3
64661 Mercer 442...F2
65058 Meta 336...H6
65265 Mexico⊙ 12,276...J4
63359 Middletown 268...J4
63556 Milan⊙ 1,947...F2
65707 Miller 795...E8
63952 Mill Spring 257...L8
64769 Mindenmines 318...C8
†63801 Miner 1,182...N9
63660 Mineral Point 358...L7
64072 Missouri City 343...R5
65270 Moberly 13,418...G4
65059 Mokane 293...J5
†63101 Moline Acres 2,774...R2
65708 Monett 6,148...E9
63456 Monroe City 2,557...J3
63361 Montgomery City⊙ 2,101...K5
63457 Monticello⊙ 134...J2
64770 Montrose 498...E6
63868 Morehouse 1,220...N9
63767 Morley 745...N8
65710 Morrisville 331...F8
64073 Mosby 284...R4
63362 Moscow Mills 484...K5
64470 Mound City 1,447...B2
65711 Mountain Grove 3,974...H8
65548 Mountain View 1,664...J8
64665 Mount Moriah 162...E2
65712 Mount Vernon⊙ 3,341...E8
†63088 Murphy 8,121...O4
65347 Napoleon 271...E4
63953 Naylor 602...L9
63964 Neelyville 474...M9
64850 Neosho⊙ 9,493...D9
64772 Nevada⊙ 9,044...D7
65063 New Bloomfield 519...J5
63558 New Cambria 246...G3
63363 New Florence 731...K5
65274 New Franklin 1,228...G4
†63736 New Hamburg...O8
64471 New Hampton 358...D2
63068 New Haven 1,581...K5
63459 New London⊙ 1,161...K3
63869 New Madrid⊙ 3,204...O9
65713 Niangua 376...G8

65714 Nixa 2,662...F8
64854 Noel 1,161...D9
64668 Norborne 931...E4
63121 Normandy 5,174...R2
64116 North Kansas City 4,507...P5
†64152 Northmoor 506...P5
65717 Norwood 391...H8
63559 Novinger 626...G2
64075 Oak Grove 4,067...S6
63080 Oak Grove 386...K6
†63101 Oakland 1,728...P3
63769 Oak Ridge 252...N7
†64116 Oakview 497...P5
63401 Oakwood 227...P5
64076 Odessa 3,608...E5
63366 O'Fallon 8,677...L5
63369 Old Monroe 272...L5
63124 Olivette 7,985...O2
63050 Olympian Village 774...M6
63771 Oran 1,266...N8
64473 Oregon⊙ 901...B2
64855 Oronogo 525...D8
64077 Orrick 922...D4
65065 Osage Beach 1,992...G6
64474 Osborn 381...D3
64776 Osceola⊙ 841...E6
65348 Otterville 472...G5
63114 Overland 19,620...O2
65066 Owensville 2,241...K6
65721 Ozark⊙ 2,980...F8
63069 Pacific 4,410...L5
†63101 Pagedale 4,542...P2
63461 Palmyra⊙ 3,469...J3
65275 Paris⊙ 1,598...J4
64152 Parkville 1,997...O5
64130 Parkway 254...L6
63870 Parma 1,081...N9
64670 Pattonsburg 502...D2
64078 Peculiar 1,571...R6
63462 Perry 836...J4
63775 Perryville⊙ 7,343...N7
63070 Pevely 2,732...M6
64476 Pickering 215...C2
63957 Piedmont 2,359...L8
65723 Pierce City 1,391...E9
65276 Pilot Grove 745...G5
63663 Pilot Knob 722...L7
63120 Pine Lawn 6,662...R2
64856 Pineville⊙ 504...D9
64079 Platte City⊙ 2,114...C4
†64152 Platte Woods 467...O5
64477 Plattsburg⊙ 2,095...D3
64080 Pleasant Hill 3,301...D5
65725 Pleasant Hope 354...F8
†64836 Pleasant Valley 1,545...R5
64671 Polo 583...D3
63901 Poplar Bluff⊙ 17,139...L9
63373 Portage Des Sioux 488...M5
63873 Portageville 3,470...N10
63664 Potosi⊙ 2,528...L7
65068 Prairie Home 279...G5
64673 Princeton⊙ 1,264...E2
64857 Purcell 322...D8
64674 Purdin 243...F3
65734 Purdy 928...E9
63960 Puxico 833...M9
63561 Queen City 783...H2
63961 Qulin 545...M9
†64101 Randolph 91...P5
64101 Ravenwood 436...C2
65555 Raymondville 388...J8
64083 Raymore 3,154...D5
64133 Raytown 31,759...P6
65737 Reeds Spring 461...F9

65738 Republic 4,485...E8
64779 Rich Hill 1,471...D6
55556 Richland 1,922...H7
64085 Richmond⊙ 5,499...D4
63117 Richmond Heights 11,516...P3
64481 Ridgeway 516...D2
63874 Risco 446...N9
†63601 Rivermines 414...L7
†63101 Riverside 3,206...O5
†63101 Riverview 3,367...R2
65279 Rocheport 272...H5
65740 Rockaway Beach 292...F9
63119 Rock Hill 5,702...P3
64482 Rock Port⊙ 1,511...B2
64780 Rockville 281...D6
65742 Rogersville 741...G8
65401 Rolla⊙ 13,303...J7
63091 Rosebud 326...K6
64483 Rosendale 223...C2
64484 Rushville 271...B3
65074 Russellville 667...H6
64864 Saginaw 467...C8

63074 Saint Ann 15,523...O2
63301 Saint Charles⊙ 37,379...N1
63077 Saint Clair 3,485...K6
63670 Sainte Genevieve⊙ 4,481...M6
65075 Saint Elizabeth 312...H6
†63101 Saint George 1,545...P4
65559 Saint James 3,328...J6
63114 Saint John 7,854...P2
*64501 Saint Joseph⊙ 76,691...C3
  Saint Joseph‡ 101,868...C3
*63101 Saint Louis⊙ 453,085...R3
  Saint Louis‡ 2,355,276...R3
†65101 Saint Martins 739...H5
63673 Saint Marys 565...M7
63366 Saint Paul 607...L5
63376 Saint Peters 15,700...M1
65583 Saint Robert 1,735...H7
63126 Sappington 11,388...O4
64862 Sarcoxie 1,381...D8
64485 Savannah⊙ 4,184...C3

64783 Schell City 327...D6
63780 Scott City 3,262...O8
65301 Sedalia⊙ 20,927...F5
65745 Seligman 508...D9
63876 Senath 1,728...M10
64865 Seneca 1,853...C9
65746 Seymour 1,535...G8
63468 Shelbina 2,169...H3
63469 Shelbyville⊙ 645...H3
64784 Sheldon 491...D7
†63101 Shrewsbury 5,077...P3
64088 Sibley 382...S5
63801 Sikeston 17,431...N9
63377 Silex 287...K4
64487 Skidmore 437...B2
65349 Slater 2,492...G4
65350 Smithton 551...F5
64089 Smithville 1,873...C4
64863 South West City 516...D9
†63138 Spanish Lake 20,632...R1
65753 Sparta 743...F9
65281 Spickard 389...F2

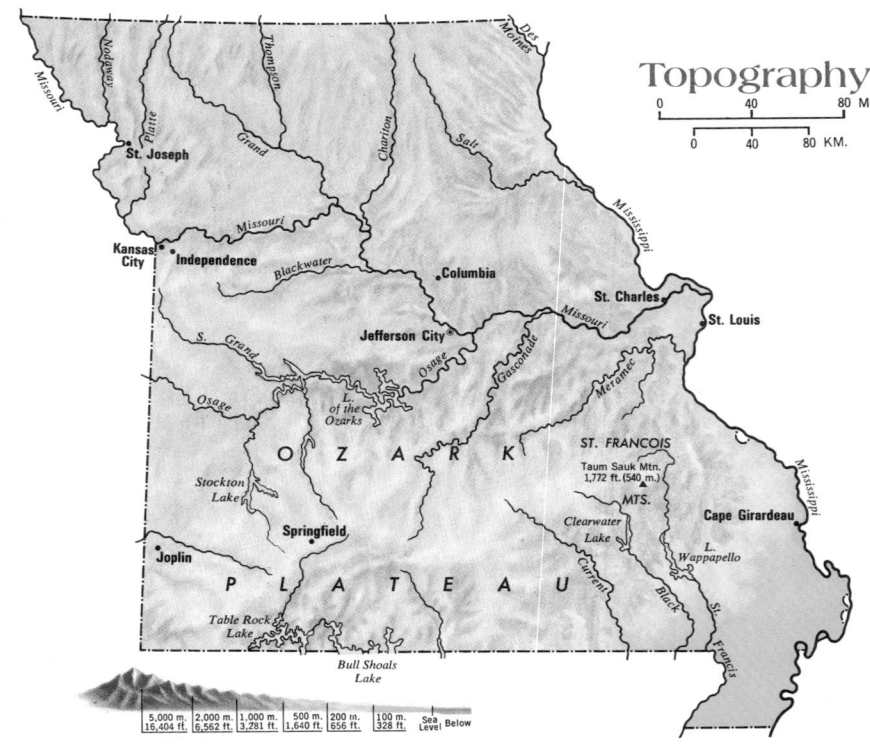

Topography

0   40   80 MI.

0   40   80 KM.

ST. FRANCOIS
Taum Sauk Mtn.
1,772 ft. (540 m.)
MTS.

5,000 m. | 2,000 m. | 1,000 m. | 500 m. | 200 m. | 100 m. | Sea Level
16,404 ft. | 6,562 ft. | 3,281 ft. | 1,640 ft. | 656 ft. | 328 ft. | Below

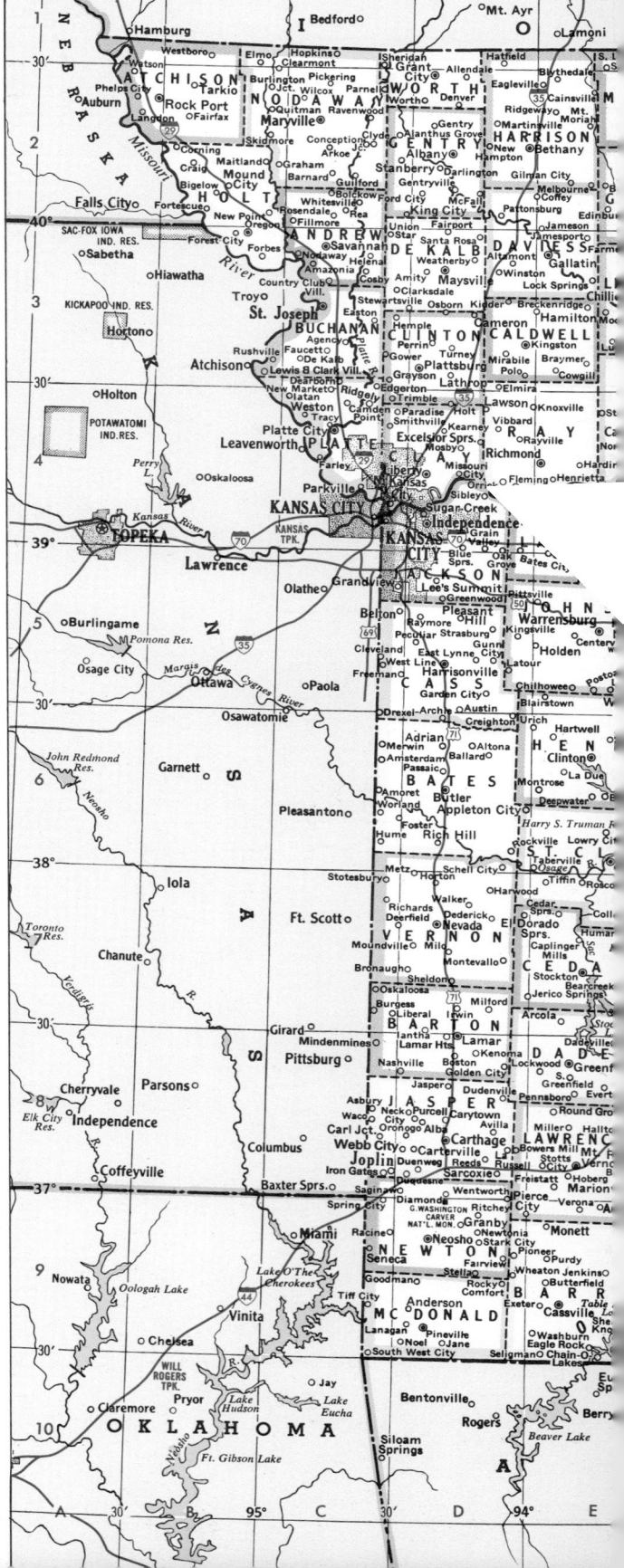

*65801 Springfield 133,116 .... F8
    Springfield‡ 207,704 ....F8
64489 Stanberry 1,387 ....C2
63877 Steele 2,419 ....N10
65565 Steeleville‡ 1,470 ....K7
64490 Stewartsville 832 ....C3
65785 Stockton 1,432 ....E7
65567 Stoutland 286 ....G7
65078 Stover 1,041 ....G6
65757 Strafford 1,121 ....F8
65284 Sturgeon 901 ....H4
64054 Sugar Creek 4,305 ....R5
63080 Sullivan 5,461 ....K6
65571 Summersville 551 ....J8
†63101 Sunset Hills 4,363 ....O4
65351 Sweet Springs 1,694 ....F5
65759 Taneyville 300 ....F9
65772 Taos 759 ....H5
64491 Tarkio 2,375 ....B2
†64063 Tarsney Lakes 329 ....R6
65791 Thayer 2,211 ....J9
†63025 Times Beach 2,041 ....N4

65081 Tipton 2,155 ....G5
†63101 Town and Country 3,187 ....O3
64079 Tracy 310 ....D7
64683 Trenton 6,811 ....E2
63379 Troy⊙ 2,624 ....L5
65082 Tuscumbia⊙ 241 ....H6
63088 Twin Oaks 426 ....N3
63084 Union⊙ 5,506 ....L6
64494 Union Star 423 ....C2
63565 Unionville⊙ 2,178 ....G2
63130 University City 42,738 ....P3
65767 Urbana 329 ....F7
64788 Urich 509 ....E6
63088 Valley Park 3,232 ....O3
63965 Van Buren⊙ 850 ....L8
63784 Vanduser 320 ....N9
65769 Verona 592 ....E9
65084 Versailles⊙ 2,406 ....G6
65566 Viburnum 836 ....K7
†63020 Victoria 375 ....M6

65582 Vienna⊙ 514 ....H6
†63101 Vinita Park 2,283 ....P2
64790 Walker 325 ....D7
65770 Walnut Grove 504 ....F8
†65101 Wardsville 535 ....H6
64093 Warrensburg⊙ 13,807 ....E5
63383 Warrenton⊙ 3,219 ....K5
65355 Warsaw⊙ 1,494 ....F6
†63101 Warson Woods 2,127 ....O3
63090 Washington 9,251 ....K5
64096 Waverly 941 ....E4
63472 Wayland 498 ....J2
65583 Waynesville⊙ 2,879 ....H7
†64152 Weatherby Lake 1,446 ....O5
65774 Weaubleau 464 ....F7
64870 Webb City 7,309 ....C8
63119 Webster Groves 23,097 ....P3
64097 Wellington 780 ....E4
63112 Wellston 4,495 ....R2
63384 Wellsville 1,546 ....K4
63385 Wentzville 3,193 ....L5
64498 Westboro 188 ....B1

64098 Weston 1,440 ....C4
65775 West Plains⊙
    7,741 ....J9
†63101 Westwood 319 ....O3
65779 Wheatland 364 ....F7
64874 Wheaton 548 ....C8
64688 Wheeling 379 ....F3
†63101 Wilbur Park 564 ....P3
65781 Willard 1,799 ....F8
63977 Williamsville 418 ....L9
65793 Willow Springs 2,215 ....H9
63834 Wilson City 309 ....O9
†63435 Winchester 2,237 ....N3
65360 Windsor 3,058 ....E5
63389 Winfield 592 ....L5
65588 Winona 1,050 ....K8
64689 Winston 246 ....D3
64024 Woods Heights 747 ....S4
†63101 Woodson Terrace 4,788 ....P2
63390 Wright City 1,179 ....K5
63474 Wyaconda 359 ....J2
63882 Wyatt 441 ....O9

OTHER FEATURES

Bagnell (dam) G6
Big (riv.) L6
Black (riv.) L10
Bull Shoals (lake) G10
Chariton (riv.) G1
Clearwater (lake) L8
Cuivre (riv.) N2
Current (riv.) K8
Des Moines (riv.) J1
Fort Leonard Wood 21,262 ....H7
Gasconade (riv.) H7
George Washington Carver Nat'l Mon. D9
Grand (riv.) F3
Jefferson Nat'l Expansion Mem. Nat'l His. R3
Lake City Arsenal R5
Meramec (riv.) N3
Mississippi (riv.) L4
Missouri (riv.) H5

Norfork (lake) H10
Osage (riv.) E6
Ozark (plat.) F9
Ozark Nat'l Scenic Riverways K8
Ozarks, Lake of the (lake) F6
Platte (riv.) C3
Pomme de Terre (lake) E7
Richards Gebaur A.F.B. 4,305 ....P6
Sac (riv.) E7
Saint Francis (riv.) M9
Salt (riv.) J3
Stockton (lake) E7
Table Rock (res.) E9
Taneycomo (lake) F9
Taum Sauk (mt.) L7
Wappapello (lake) L8
White (riv.) G10
Whiteman A.F.B. E5
Wilson's Creek Nat'l Battlefield F8
⊙County seat.
‡Population of metropolitan area.
† Zip of nearest p.o.   * Multiple zips.

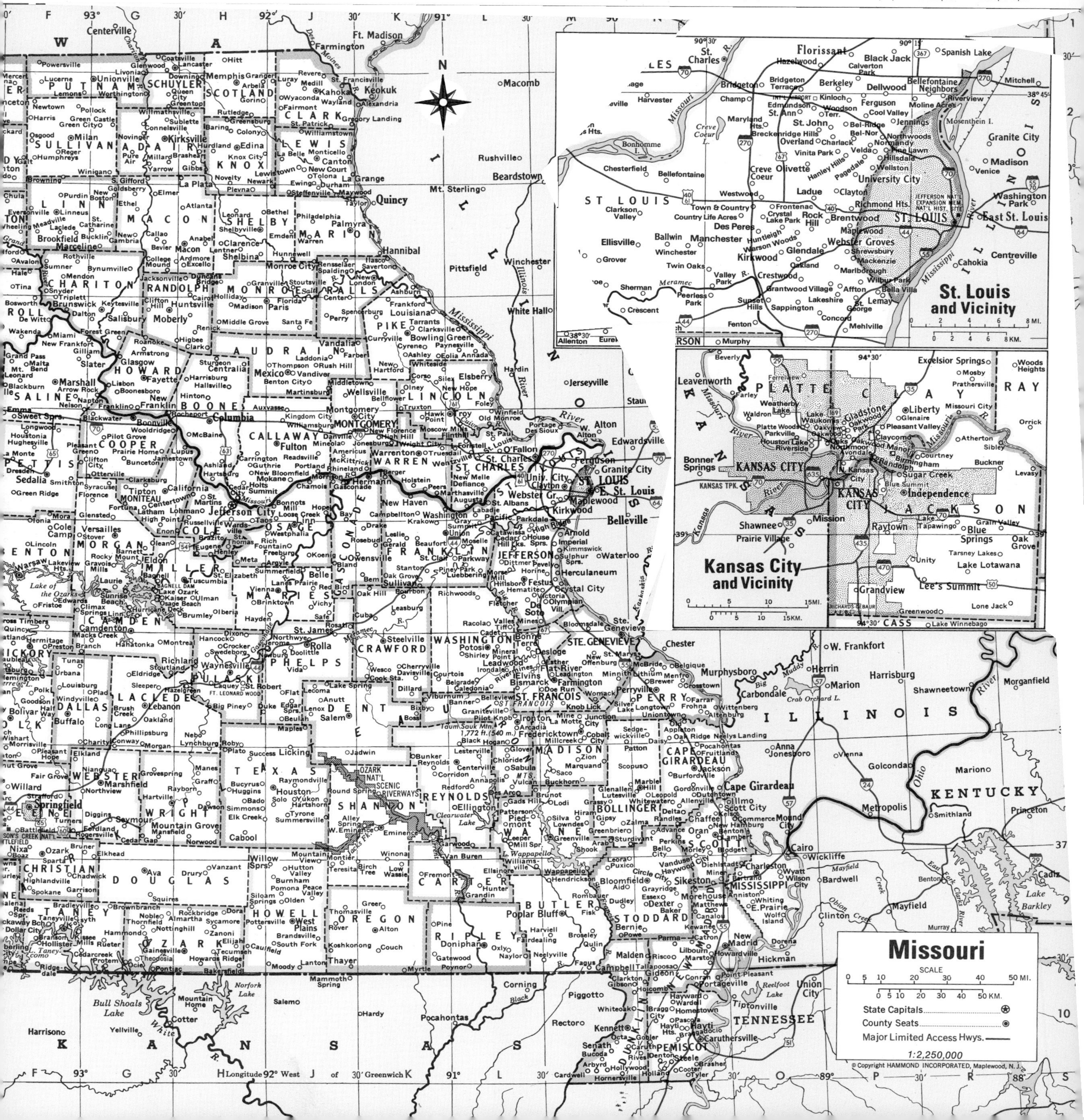

Missouri

SCALE
0 5 10   20   30   40   50 MI.
0 5 10 20 30 40 50 KM.

State Capitals ....⊛
County Seats ....⊙
Major Limited Access Hwys. ——

1:2,250,000
© Copyright HAMMOND INCORPORATED, Maplewood, N.J.

Agriculture, Industry and Resources

Wheat
Cattle
Barley
Wheat
Timber
Sb
Sheep
Pb
P
Gp
PbMnAg
Ag
CuZn
Au
Pb
Cattle
Tc
Th
Sugar Beets
Cattle

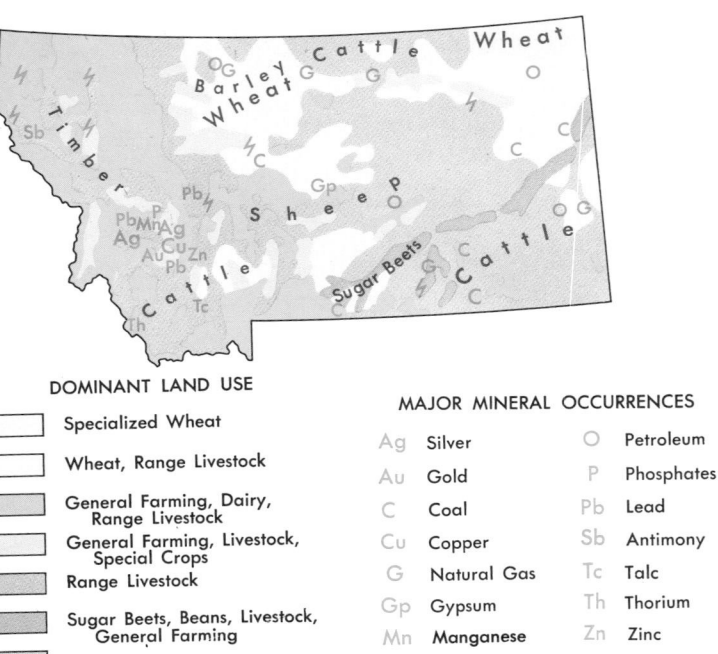

DOMINANT LAND USE

- Specialized Wheat
- Wheat, Range Livestock
- General Farming, Dairy, Range Livestock
- General Farming, Livestock, Special Crops
- Range Livestock
- Sugar Beets, Beans, Livestock, General Farming
- Forests

MAJOR MINERAL OCCURRENCES

Ag	Silver	O	Petroleum
Au	Gold	P	Phosphates
C	Coal	Pb	Lead
Cu	Copper	Sb	Antimony
G	Natural Gas	Tc	Talc
Gp	Gypsum	Th	Thorium
Mn	Manganese	Zn	Zinc

ϟ Water Power

COUNTIES

Beaverhead 8,186 .... C5
Big Horn 11,096 .... J5
Blaine 6,999 .... G2
Broadwater 3,267 .... E4
Carbon 8,099 .... G5
Carter 1,799 .... M5
Cascade 80,696 .... E3
Chouteau 6,092 .... F3
Custer 13,109 .... L4
Daniels 2,835 .... L2
Dawson 11,805 .... M3
Deer Lodge 12,518 .... C5
Fallon 3,763 .... M4
Fergus 13,076 .... G3
Flathead 51,966 .... B2
Gallatin 42,865 .... E5
Garfield 1,656 .... J3
Glacier 10,628 .... C2
Golden Valley 1,026 .... G4
Granite 2,700 .... C4
Hill 17,985 .... F2
Jefferson 7,029 .... D4
Judith Basin 2,646 .... F4
Lake 19,056 .... B3
Lewis and Clark 43,039 .... D3
Liberty 2,329 .... E2
Lincoln 17,752 .... A2
Madison 5,448 .... D5
McCone 2,702 .... L3
Meagher 2,154 .... F4
Mineral 3,675 .... B3
Missoula 76,016 .... C3
Musselshell 4,428 .... H4
Park 12,869 .... F5
Petroleum 655 .... H3
Phillips 5,367 .... J2
Pondera 6,731 .... D2
Powder River 2,520 .... L5
Powell 6,958 .... D4
Prairie 1,836 .... L4
Ravalli 22,493 .... B4
Richland 12,243 .... M3
Roosevelt 10,467 .... L2
Rosebud 9,899 .... K4
Sanders 8,675 .... A3
Sheridan 5,414 .... M2
Silver Bow 38,092 .... D5
Stillwater 5,598 .... G5
Sweet Grass 3,216 .... G5
Teton 6,491 .... D3
Toole 5,559 .... E2
Treasure 981 .... J4
Valley 10,250 .... K2
Wheatland 2,359 .... G4
Wibaux 1,476 .... M4
Yellowstone 108,035 .... H4
Yellowstone Nat'l Park 275 .... F6

CITIES and TOWNS

Zip	Name/Pop.	Key
59001	Absarokee 830	G5
59820	Alberton 368	B3
59710	Alder 120	D5
†59741	Amsterdam 130	E5
59711	Anaconda-Deer Lodge County⊙ 12,518	C4
59312	Angela 50	K4
59211	Antelope 83	M2
59821	Arlee 200	B3
59003	Ashland 600	K5
59410	Augusta 497	D3
59713	Avon 125	D4
59411	Babb 150	C2
59212	Bainville 245	M2
59313	Baker⊙ 2,354	M4
59006	Ballantine 380	J5
†59725	Bannack 2	C5
59613	Basin 350	D4
59007	Bearcreek 61	G5
59008	Belfry 300	H5
59714	Belgrade 2,336	E5
59412	Belt 825	E3
59314	Biddle 28	L5
59910	Big Arm 250	B3
59911	Bigfork 1,080	C2
59520	Big Sandy 835	G2
59011	Big Timber⊙ 1,690	G5
*59101	Billings⊙ 66,842	H5
	Billings‡ 108,035	H5
59012	Birney 100	K5
59414	Black Eagle 1,500	E3
59415	Blackfoot 100	D2
59823	Bonner-West Riverside 1,742	C4
59632	Boulder⊙ 1,441	E4
59521	Box Elder 300	F2
59715	Bozeman⊙ 21,645	E5
59416	Brady 450	E2
59014	Bridger 724	H5
59317	Broadus⊙ 712	L5
59015	Broadview 120	H4
59213	Brockton 374	M2
59417	Browning 1,226	C2
59016	Busby 700	J5
59701	Butte-Silver Bow County⊙ 37,205	D5
59720	Cameron 150	E5
59633	Canyon Creek 100	D4
†59347	Cartersville 115	K4
59421	Cascade 773	E3
59824	Charlo 250	B3
59522	Chester⊙ 963	E2
59523	Chinook⊙ 1,660	G2
59422	Choteau⊙ 1,798	D3
59215	Circle⊙ 931	L3
59634	Clancy 550	E4
59018	Clyde Park 283	F5
†59351	Coalwood 2	L5
59322	Cohagen 12	K3
59323	Colstrip 1,476	K5
59912	Columbia Falls 3,112	B2
59019	Columbus⊙ 1,439	G5
59826	Condon 300	C3
59827	Conner 420	B5
59425	Conrad⊙ 3,074	D2
59020	Cooke City 120	G5
59913	Coram 450	C2
59828	Corvallis 500	C4
59217	Crane 163	M3
59022	Crow Agency 975	J5
59218	Culbertson 887	M2
59024	Custer 300	J4
59427	Cut Bank⊙ 3,688	D2
59829	Darby 581	B4
59914	Dayton 140	B3
59830	De Borgia 300	A3
59025	Decker 150	K5
59722	Deer Lodge⊙ 4,023	D4
59430	Denton 356	G3

Montana
SCALE
0 5 10 20 40 60 MI.
0 5 10 20 40 60 KM.
State Capitals
County Seats
Major Limited Access Hwys.
Scale 1:3,450,000
© Copyright HAMMOND INCORPORATED, Maplewood, N.J.
110° Longitude West of 109° Greenwich

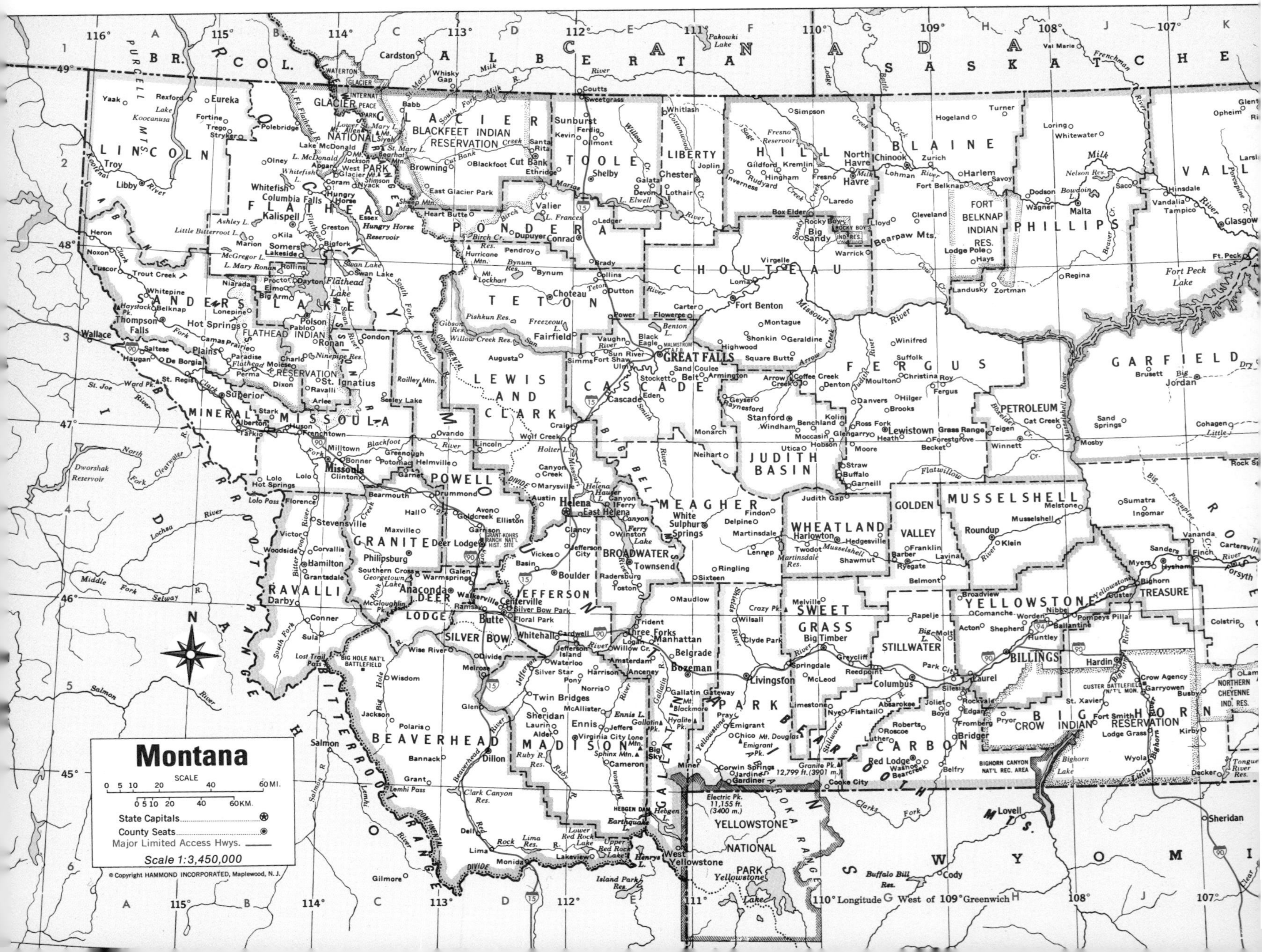

Topography

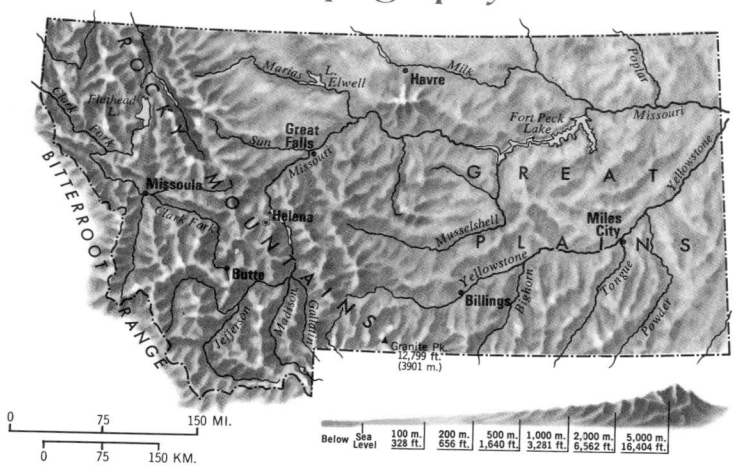

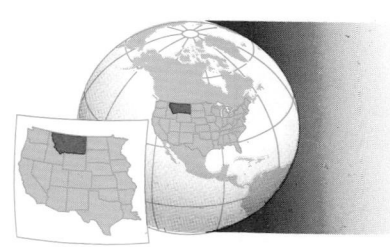

AREA 147,046 sq. mi. (380,849 sq. km.)
POPULATION 786,690
CAPITAL Helena
LARGEST CITY Billings
HIGHEST POINT Granite Pk. 12,799 ft. (3901 m.)
SETTLED IN 1809
ADMITTED TO UNION November 8, 1889
POPULAR NAME Treasure State; Big Sky Country
STATE FLOWER Bitterroot
STATE BIRD Western Meadowlark

59725 Dillon⊙ 3,976	D5
59727 Divide 275	D5
59831 Dixon 550	B3
59524 Dodson 158	H2
59832 Drummond 414	D4
59432 Dupuyer 105	D2
59433 Dutton 359	E3
59434 East Glacier Park 475	C2
59635 East Helena 1,647	E4
59026 Edgar 220	H5
59324 Ekalaka⊙ 620	M5
59728 Elliston 250	D4
59915 Elmo 250	B3
59729 Ennis 660	E5
59917 Eureka 1,119	B2
59436 Fairfield 650	D3
59221 Fairview 1,366	M3
59326 Fallon 225	L4
59222 Flaxville 142	L2
59833 Florence 700	B4
59441 Forestgrove 100	H3
59327 Forsyth⊙ 2,553	K4
†59526 Fort Belknap 185	H2
59442 Fort Benton⊙ 1,693	F3
59918 Fortine 250	A2
59443 Fort Shaw 200	E3
†59075 Fort Smith 300	J5
59225 Frazer 200	K2
59834 Frenchtown 300	B3
59226 Froid 323	M2
59029 Fromberg 469	H5
59444 Galata 100	E2
59730 Gallatin Gateway 600	E5
59030 Gardiner 600	F5
59731 Garrison 300	D4
59031 Garryowen 200	J5
59446 Geraldine 305	F3
59447 Geyser 125	F3
59525 Gildford 250	F2
59230 Glasgow⊙ 4,455	K2
59330 Glendive⊙ 5,978	M3
59733 Goldcreek 100	D4
59835 Grantsdale 500	B4
59032 Grass Range 139	H3
59401 Great Falls⊙ 56,725	E3
Great Falls‡ 80,696	E3
59836 Greenough 120	C4
59837 Hall 130	C4
59840 Hamilton⊙ 2,661	B4
59034 Hardin⊙ 3,300	J5
59526 Harlem 1,023	H2
59036 Harlowton⊙ 1,181	F4
59735 Harrison 94	E5
59842 Haugan 90	A3
59501 Havre⊙ 10,891	G2
59527 Hays 400	H2
59448 Heart Butte 300	C2
59601 Helena (cap.)⊙ 23,938	E4
59843 Helmville 250	C4
59450 Highwood 150	F3
59528 Hingham 186	F2
59241 Hinsdale 260	K2
59452 Hobson 261	G4
59845 Hot Springs 601	B3
59919 Hungry Horse 700	C2
59037 Huntley 250	H5
59846 Huson 97	B3
59038 Hysham⊙ 449	J4
59530 Inverness 150	F2
59336 Ismay 31	M4
59736 Jackson 210	C5
59638 Jefferson City 162	E4
59041 Joliet 580	H5
59531 Joplin 300	F2
59337 Jordan⊙ 485	J3
59453 Judith Gap 213	G4
59901 Kalispell⊙ 10,648	B2
59454 Kevin 208	E2
59920 Kila 350	B2
59338 Kinsey 100	L4
†59072 Klein 250	H4
59532 Kremlin 304	F2
59922 Lakeside 663	B2
59243 Lambert 203	M3
59043 Lame Deer 460	K5
59044 Laurel 5,481	H5
59046 Lavina 164	H4
59457 Lewistown⊙ 7,104	G4
59923 Libby⊙ 2,748	A2
59739 Lima 272	D6
59639 Lincoln 473	D4
59047 Livingston⊙ 6,994	F5
59050 Lodge Grass 771	J5
†59524 Lodge Pole 292	H2
59847 Lolo 2,418	B4
†59847 Lolo Hot Springs 25	B4
59460 Loma 200	F3
59225 Lustre 25	K2
59538 Malta⊙ 2,367	J2
59741 Manhattan 988	E5
59925 Marion 450	B2
59052 McLeod 150	G5
59247 Medicine Lake 408	M2
59743 Melrose 350	D5
59054 Melstone 238	H4
59055 Melville 100	F4
59301 Miles City⊙ 9,602	L4
59851 Milltown 300	C4
*59801 Missoula⊙ 33,388	C4
59463 Monarch 120	F3
59464 Moore 229	G4
59059 Musselshell 117	H4
59248 Nashua 495	K2
59465 Neihart 91	F4
†59501 North Havre 1,230	G2
59853 Noxon 800	A3
59927 Olney 200	B2
59250 Opheim 210	K2
59252 Outlook 122	M2
59854 Ovando 300	C3
59855 Pablo 500	B3
59856 Paradise 400	B3
59063 Park City 800	H5
59253 Peerless 110	L2
59467 Pendroy 100	D2
59858 Philipsburg⊙ 1,138	C4
59859 Plains 1,116	B3
59254 Plentywood⊙ 2,476	M2
59344 Plevna 191	M4
59860 Polson⊙ 2,798	B3
59064 Pompeys Pillar 300	J5
59747 Pony 130	E5
59255 Poplar 995	L2
59468 Power 159	E3
59929 Proctor 150	B3
59066 Pryor 146	H5
59641 Radersburg 104	E4
59863 Ravalli 150	B3
59068 Red Lodge⊙ 1,896	G5
59069 Reedpoint 160	G5
59258 Reserve 80	M2
59930 Rexford 130	A2
59259 Richey 417	L3
59642 Ringling 102	F4
59070 Roberts 312	G5
59931 Rollins 200	B3
59864 Ronan 1,530	C3
59347 Rosebud 259	K4
59072 Roundup⊙ 2,119	H4
59471 Roy 200	H3
59540 Rudyard 400	F2
59074 Ryegate⊙ 273	G4
59261 Saco 252	J2
59865 Saint Ignatius 877	C3
59866 Saint Regis 500	A3
59075 Saint Xavier 200	J5
59867 Saltese 90	A3
59472 Sand Coulee 600	E3
59473 Santa Rita 120	D2
59262 Savage 300	M3
59263 Scobey⊙ 1,382	L2
59868 Seeley Lake 900	C3
59474 Shelby⊙ 3,142	E2
59079 Shepherd 200	H5
59749 Sheridan 646	D5
59270 Sidney⊙ 5,726	M3
59751 Silver Star 125	D5
59477 Simms 200	E3
59932 Somers 700	B2
59479 Stanford⊙ 595	F3
59870 Stevensville 1,207	C4
59480 Stockett 500	E3
59933 Stryker 96	B2
59871 Sula 200	B5
59482 Sunburst 476	E2
59483 Sun River 300	E3
59872 Superior⊙ 1,054	B3
59911 Swan Lake 100	C3
59484 Sweetgrass 250	E2
59349 Terry⊙ 929	L4
59873 Thompson Falls⊙ 1,478	A3
59752 Three Forks 1,247	E5
59644 Townsend⊙ 1,587	E4
59874 Trout Creek 300	A3
59935 Troy 1,088	A2
59485 Twin Bridges 437	D5
59085 Twodot 285	F4
59486 Ulm 450	E3
59487 Vaughn 2,270	E3
59754 Victor 700	B4
59755 Virginia City⊙ 192	E5
59351 Volborg 125	L5
59701 Walkerville 887	D4
59756 Warmsprings 500	D4
59275 Westby 291	M2
59936 West Glacier 150	C2
59758 West Yellowstone 735	E6
59937 Whitefish 3,703	B2
59759 Whitehall 1,030	D5
59645 White Sulphur Springs⊙ 1,302	E4
59276 Whitetail 150	L2
59544 Whitewater 100	J2
59353 Wibaux⊙ 782	M3
59760 Willow Creek 150	E5
59086 Wilsall 250	F5
59489 Winifred 155	G3
59087 Winnett⊙ 207	H4
59647 Winston 120	E4
59761 Wisdom 140	C5
59762 Wise River 150	C5
59648 Wolf Creek 500	D3
59201 Wolf Point⊙ 3,074	L2
59088 Worden 600	H5
59089 Wyola 350	J5

OTHER FEATURES

Absaroka (range)	F5
Allen (mt.)	C2
Arrow (creek)	F3
Ashley (lake)	B2
Battle (creek)	G1
Bearhat (mt.)	C2
Bearpaw (mts.)	G2
Beartooth (mts.)	G5
Beaver (creek)	J2
Beaverhead (riv.)	D5
Benton (lake)	E3
Big (lake)	H5
Big Belt (mts.)	E4
Big Dry (creek)	K3
Big Hole (riv.)	C5
Big Hole Nat'l Battlefield	C5
Bighorn (lake)	H5
Bighorn (riv.)	J5
Bighorn Canyon Nat'l Rec. Area	H5
Big Muddy (riv.)	M2
Big Porcupine (creek)	J4
Birch (creek)	D2
Birch Creek (riv.)	D2
Bitterroot (range)	B4
Bitterroot (riv.)	B4
Blackfeet Ind. Res.	D2
Blackfoot (riv.)	C4
Blackmore (mt.)	F5
Bowdoin (lake)	J2
Boxelder (creek)	H3
Boxelder (creek)	M5
Bynum (res.)	D2
Cabinet (mts.)	A2
Canyon Ferry (lake)	E4
Clark Canyon (res.)	D6
Clark Fork (riv.)	A3
Clarks Fork, Yellowstone (riv.)	G6
Cottonwood (creek)	E2
Cow (creek)	G2
Crazy (peak)	F4
Crow Ind. Res.	H5
Custer Battlefield Nat'l Mon.	J5
Cut Bank (creek)	D2
Douglas (mt.)	F5
Earthquake (lake)	E6
Electric (peak)	F6
Elwell (lake)	E2
Emigrant (peak)	F5
Ennis (lake)	E5
Flathead (lake)	C3
Flathead (riv.)	B2
Flathead, North Fork (riv.)	B2
Flathead, South Fork (riv.)	C3
Flathead Ind. Res.	B3
Flatwillow (creek)	H4
Fort Belknap Ind. Res.	H2
Fort Peck (lake)	K3
Fort Union Trading Post Nat'l Hist. Site	N2
Frances (lake)	D2
Freezeout (lake)	D3
Frenchman (riv.)	J1
Fresno (res.)	F2
Gallatin (peak)	E5
Gallatin (riv.)	E5
Georgetown (lake)	C4
Gibson (res.)	D3
Glacier Nat'l Park	C2
Granite (peak)	F5
Grant-Kohrs Ranch Nat'l Hist. Site	D4
Hauser (lake)	E4
Haystack (peak)	A3
Hebgen (lake)	E6
Helena (lake)	E4
Holter (lake)	D4
Hungry Horse (res.)	C2
Hurricane (mt.)	D2
Hyalite (peak)	E5
Jackson (mt.)	C2
Jefferson (riv.)	D5
Judith (riv.)	G3
Koocanusa (lake)	A2
Kootenai (riv.)	A2
Lemhi (pass)	C6
Lewis (range)	C2
Lima (res.)	D6
Little Bighorn (riv.)	J5
Little Bitterroot (lake)	B2
Little Dry (creek)	K3
Little Missouri (riv.)	M5
Lockhart (mt.)	D3
Lodge (creek)	G1
Lolo (pass)	B4
Lone (mt.)	E5
Lost Trail (pass)	B5
Lower Red Rock (lake)	E6
Lower Saint Mary (lake)	C2
Madison (riv.)	E5
Malmstrom A.F.B. 6,675	E3
Marias (riv.)	D2
Martinsdale (res.)	F4
Mary Ronan (lake)	B3
McDonald (lake)	B2
McGloughlin (peak)	C4
McGregor (lake)	B3
Medicine (lake)	M2
Milk (riv.)	J2
Mission (range)	C3
Missouri (riv.)	L3
Musselshell (riv.)	J3
Nelson (res.)	J2
Ninepipe (res.)	C3
Northern Cheyenne Indian Reservation	K5
O'Fallon (creek)	L4
Pishkun (res.)	D3
Poplar (riv.)	L2
Porcupine (creek)	K2
Powder (riv.)	L4
Purcell (mts.)	A2
Railley (mt.)	C3
Red Rock (lkes.)	E6
Red Rock (riv.)	D6
Redwater (riv.)	L3
Rock (creek)	C4
Rocky (mts.)	D4
Rocky Boy's Ind. Res.	G2
Rosebud (creek)	K4
Ruby (riv.)	D5
Ruby River (res.)	D5
Sage (creek)	F2
Saint Mary (lake)	C2
Saint Mary (riv.)	C1
Sandy (creek)	F2
Sheep (mt.)	C2
Shields (riv.)	F4
Siyeh (mt.)	C2
Smith (riv.)	E3
Sphinx (mt.)	E5
Stillwater (riv.)	G5
Stimson (mt.)	C2
Sun (riv.)	D3
Swan (lake)	C3
Teton (riv.)	E3
Tongue (riv.)	K5
Upper Red Rock (lake)	E6
Ward (creek)	A3
Waterton-Glacier Int'l Peace Park	C2
Whitefish (lake)	B2
Willow (creek)	E2
Willow Creek (res.)	C2
Yellowstone (riv.)	M3
Yellowstone National Park	F6

⊙County seat.
‡Population of metropolitan area.
† Zip of nearest p.o.   * Multiple zips.

COUNTIES

Name/Pop.	Key
Adams 30,656	F4
Antelope 8,675	F2
Arthur 513	C3
Banner 918	A3
Blaine 867	E3
Boone 7,391	F3
Box Butte 13,696	A2
Boyd 3,331	F2
Brown 4,377	E2
Buffalo 34,797	E4
Burt 8,813	H3
Butler 9,330	G3
Cass 20,297	H4
Cedar 11,375	G2
Chase 4,758	C4
Cherry 6,758	C2
Cheyenne 10,057	A3
Clay 8,106	F4
Colfax 9,890	G3
Cuming 11,664	H3
Custer 13,877	E3
Dakota 16,573	H2
Dawes 9,609	A2
Dawson 22,304	E4
Deuel 2,462	B3
Dixon 7,137	H2
Dodge 35,847	H3
Douglas 397,038	H3
Dundy 2,861	C4
Fillmore 7,920	G4
Franklin 4,377	F4
Frontier 3,647	D4
Furnas 6,486	E4
Gage 24,456	H4
Garden 2,802	B3
Garfield 2,363	F3
Gosper 2,140	E4
Grant 877	C3
Greeley 3,462	F3
Hall 47,690	F4
Hamilton 9,301	F4
Harlan 4,292	E4
Hayes 1,356	C4
Hitchcock 4,079	C4
Holt 13,552	F2
Hooker 990	C3
Howard 6,773	F3
Jefferson 9,817	G4
Johnson 5,285	H4
Kearney 7,053	F4
Keith 9,364	C3
Keya Paha 1,301	E2
Kimball 4,882	A3
Knox 11,457	G2
Lancaster 192,884	H4
Lincoln 36,455	D4
Logan 983	D3
Loup 859	E3
Madison 31,382	G3
McPherson 593	C3
Merrick 8,945	F3
Morrill 6,085	A3
Nance 4,740	F3
Nemaha 8,367	J4
Nuckolls 6,726	F4
Otoe 15,183	H4
Pawnee 3,937	H4
Perkins 3,637	C4
Phelps 9,769	E4
Pierce 8,481	G2
Platte 28,852	G3
Polk 6,320	G3
Red Willow 12,615	D4
Richardson 11,315	J4
Rock 2,383	E2
Saline 13,131	G4
Sarpy 86,015	H3
Saunders 18,716	H3
Scotts Bluff 38,344	A3
Seward 15,789	G4
Sheridan 7,544	B2
Sherman 4,226	F3
Sioux 1,845	A2
Stanton 6,549	G3
Thayer 7,582	G4
Thomas 973	D3
Thurston 7,186	H2
Valley 5,633	E3
Washington 15,508	H3
Wayne 9,858	G2
Webster 4,858	F4
Wheeler 1,060	F3
York 14,798	G4

CITIES and TOWNS

Zip	Name/Pop.	Key
68301	Adams 395	H4
69210	Ainsworth⊙ 2,256	D2
68620	Albion⊙ 1,997	F3
68810	Alda 601	F4
68710	Allen 390	H2
69301	Alliance⊙ 9,920	A2
68920	Alma⊙ 1,369	E4
68304	Alvo 144	H4
68812	Amherst 269	E4
68814	Ansley 644	E3
68922	Arapahoe 1,107	E4
68815	Arcadia 412	F3
68002	Arlington 1,117	H3
69120	Arnold 813	D3
69121	Arthur⊙ 124	C3
68003	Ashland 2,274	H3
68713	Atkinson 1,521	E2
68305	Auburn⊙ 3,482	J4
68818	Aurora⊙ 3,717	F4
68924	Axtell 602	E4
68004	Bancroft 552	H2
68622	Bartlett⊙ 144	F3
69020	Bartley 342	D4
68714	Bassett⊙ 1,009	E2
68715	Battle Creek 948	G3
69334	Bayard 1,435	A3
68310	Beatrice⊙ 12,891	H4
68926	Beaver City⊙ 775	E4
68313	Beaver Crossing 458	G4
68716	Beemer 853	H3
68005	Bellevue 21,813	J3
68624	Bellwood 407	G3
69021	Benkelman⊙ 1,235	C4
68317	Bennet 523	H4
68007	Bennington 631	H3
68927	Bertrand 775	E4
69122	Big Springs 505	B3
68928	Bladen 298	F4
68008	Blair⊙ 6,418	H3
68718	Bloomfield 1,393	G2
68930	Blue Hill 883	F4
68318	Blue Springs 521	H4
68010	Boys Town 622	H3
68319	Bradshaw 373	G4
69123	Brady 377	D3
68821	Brewster⊙ 46	D3
69336	Bridgeport⊙ 1,668	A3
68822	Broken Bow⊙ 3,979	E3
69127	Brule 438	C3
68322	Bruning 330	G4
68823	Burwell⊙ 1,383	E3
68722	Butte⊙ 529	F2
68824	Cairo 737	F3
68825	Callaway 579	D3
69022	Cambridge 1,206	D4
68932	Campbell 441	F4
68015	Cedar Bluffs 632	H3
68016	Cedar Creek 311	H3
68627	Cedar Rapids 447	F3
68724	Center⊙ 123	G2
68826	Central City⊙ 3,083	F3
68017	Ceresco 836	H3
69337	Chadron⊙ 5,933	B2
68725	Chambers 390	F2
68827	Chapman 349	F3
69129	Chappell⊙ 1,095	B3
68327	Chester 435	G4
68628	Clarks 445	G3
68629	Clarkson 817	G3
68328	Clatonia 273	H4
68933	Clay Center⊙ 962	F4
68726	Clearwater 409	F2
†69343	Clinton 80	B2
68727	Coleridge 673	G2
68601	Columbus⊙ 17,328	G3
68329	Cook 341	H4
68331	Cortland 403	H4
69130	Cozad 4,453	E4
69339	Crawford 1,315	A2
68729	Creighton 1,341	G2
68333	Crete 4,872	G4
68730	Crofton 948	G2
69024	Culbertson 767	C4
69025	Curtis 1,014	D4
68731	Dakota City⊙ 1,440	H2
69131	Dalton 345	B3
68831	Dannebrog 356	F3
68335	Davenport 445	G4
68632	David City⊙ 2,514	G3
68020	Decatur 723	H2
68340	Deshler 997	G4
68341	De Witt 642	G4
68342	Diller 311	H4
69133	Dix 275	A3
68633	Dodge 815	H3
68832	Doniphan 696	F4
68343	Dorchester 611	G4
68634	Duncan 410	G3
68347	Eagle 832	H4
68935	Edgar 705	F4
68636	Elgin 807	F3
68022	Elkhorn 1,344	H3
68836	Elm Creek 862	E4
68349	Elmwood 598	H4
68937	Elwood⊙ 716	E4
68733	Emerson 874	H2
68350	Endicott 198	G4
69028	Eustis 460	D4
68735	Ewing 520	F2
68351	Exeter 807	G4
68352	Fairbury⊙ 4,885	G4
68938	Fairfield 543	G4
68354	Fairmont 767	G4
68355	Falls City⊙ 5,374	J4
69029	Farnam 268	D4
68358	Firth 384	H4
68023	Fort Calhoun 641	J3
68939	Franklin⊙ 1,167	E4
68025	Fremont⊙ 23,979	H3
68359	Friend 1,079	G4
68638	Fullerton⊙ 1,506	F3
68361	Geneva⊙ 2,400	G4
68640	Genoa 1,090	G3
69341	Gering⊙ 7,760	A3
68840	Gibbon 1,531	F4
68841	Giltner 400	F4
68941	Glenvil 363	F4
69343	Gordon 2,167	B2
69138	Gothenburg 3,479	D4
68801	Grand Island⊙ 33,180	F4
69140	Grant⊙ 1,270	C4
68842	Greeley⊙ 597	F3
68366	Greenwood 587	H3
68367	Gresham 320	G3
68028	Gretna 1,609	H3
68942	Guide Rock 344	F4
68738	Hadar 286	G2
68368	Hallam 290	H4
68843	Hampton 419	G4
69346	Harrison⊙ 361	A2
68739	Hartington⊙ 1,730	G2
68944	Harvard 1,217	F4
68901	Hastings⊙ 23,045	F4
69032	Hayes Center⊙ 231	C4
69347	Hay Springs 794	B2
68370	Hebron⊙ 1,906	G4
69348	Hemingford 1,023	A2
68371	Henderson 1,072	G4
68029	Herman 340	H3
69143	Hershey 633	D3
68372	Hickman 687	H4
68947	Hildreth 394	E4
68948	Holbrook 297	D4
68949	Holdrege⊙ 5,624	E4
68030	Homer 564	H2
68031	Hooper 932	H3
68740	Hoskins 306	G2
68641	Howells 677	H3
68376	Humboldt 1,176	J4
68642	Humphrey 799	G3
69350	Hyannis⊙ 336	C3
69033	Imperial⊙ 1,941	C4
69034	Indianola 856	D4
68743	Jackson 287	H2
68378	Johnson 341	J4
68955	Juniata 703	F4
68847	Kearney⊙ 21,158	E4
68956	Kenesaw 854	F4
68034	Kennard 372	H3
69145	Kimball⊙ 3,120	A3
69035	Lamar 60	C4
68745	Laurel 1,031	G2
†68046	La Vista 9,588	J3
68957	Lawrence 350	F4
68643	Leigh 509	G3
69147	Lewellen 368	B3
68850	Lexington⊙ 7,040	E4
*68501	Lincoln (cap.)⊙ 171,932	H4
	Lincoln‡ 192,884	H4
68644	Lindsay 383	G3
69149	Lodgepole 413	B3
69217	Long Pine 521	E2
68958	Loomis 447	E4
68037	Louisville 1,022	H3
68853	Loup City⊙ 1,368	E3
69352	Lyman 551	A3
68746	Lynch 357	F2
68038	Lyons 1,214	H3
68748	Madison⊙ 1,950	G3
69150	Madrid 284	C4
68402	Malcolm 355	H4
68854	Marquette 303	G4
69151	Maxwell 410	D3
69038	Maywood 332	D4
69001	McCook⊙ 8,404	D4
68401	McCool Junction 404	G4
68041	Mead 506	H3
68752	Meadow Grove 400	G2
68856	Merna 389	E3
68405	Milford 2,108	H4
68406	Milligan 332	G4
69356	Minatare 969	A3
68959	Minden⊙ 2,939	F4
69357	Mitchell 1,956	A3
68647	Monroe 294	G3
69358	Morrill 1,097	A3
69152	Mullen⊙ 720	C2
68409	Murray 465	J4
68410	Nebraska City⊙ 7,127	J4
68413	Nehawka 270	H4
68756	Neligh⊙ 1,893	G2
68961	Nelson⊙ 733	F4
68757	Newcastle 348	H2
68758	Newman Grove 930	G3
68760	Niobrara 419	G2
68962	Nora 24	G4
68701	Norfolk 19,449	G2
68649	North Bend 1,368	H3
68859	North Loup 405	F3
69101	North Platte⊙ 24,509	D3
68761	Oakdale 410	F2
68045	Oakland 1,393	H3
68415	Odell 322	H4
69153	Ogallala⊙ 5,638	C3
*68101	Omaha⊙ 313,911	J3
	Omaha‡ 570,399	J3
68763	O'Neill⊙ 4,049	F2
68764	Orchard 482	F2
68862	Ord⊙ 2,658	F3
68966	Orleans 527	E4
68651	Osceola⊙ 975	G3
69154	Oshkosh⊙ 1,057	B3
68765	Osmond 871	G2
68863	Overton 633	E4
68967	Oxford 1,109	E4
69040	Palisade 401	C4
68864	Palmer 487	F3
68418	Palmyra 512	H4
68046	Papillion⊙ 6,399	J3
68420	Pawnee City⊙ 1,156	H4
69155	Paxton 568	C3
68047	Pender⊙ 1,318	H2
68421	Peru 998	J4
68652	Petersburg 381	G3
68865	Phillips 405	F4
68767	Pierce⊙ 1,535	G2
68768	Pilger 400	G2
68769	Plainview 1,483	G2
68653	Platte Center 367	G3
68048	Plattsmouth⊙ 6,295	J3
68866	Pleasanton 349	E4
68424	Plymouth 506	G4
68654	Polk 440	G3
68770	Ponca⊙ 1,057	H2
68867	Poole	F4
69156	Potter 369	A3
68050	Prague 285	H3
68127	Ralston 5,143	J3
68771	Randolph 1,106	G2
68869	Ravenna 1,296	F4
68970	Red Cloud⊙ 1,300	F4
68658	Rising City 392	G3
69360	Rushville⊙ 1,217	B2
68660	Saint Edward 891	G3
68873	Saint Paul⊙ 2,094	F3
†68760	Santee 388	G2
68874	Sargent 828	E3
68661	Schuyler⊙ 4,151	G3
68875	Scotia 349	F3
69361	Scottsbluff 14,156	A3
68057	Scribner 1,011	H3
68434	Seward⊙ 5,713	H4
68662	Shelby 724	G3
68876	Shelton 1,046	F4
68436	Shickley 413	G4
69162	Sidney⊙ 6,010	B3
68663	Silver Creek 496	G3
68664	Snyder 387	H3
68776	South Sioux City 9,339	H2
68665	Spalding 645	F3
68777	Spencer 596	F2
68059	Springfield 782	H3
68778	Springview⊙ 326	E2
68779	Stanton⊙ 1,603	G3
68439	Staplehurst 306	G4
69163	Stapleton⊙ 340	D3
68442	Stella 289	J4
68443	Sterling 526	H4
69042	Stockville⊙ 45	D4
69043	Stratton 499	C4
68666	Stromsburg 1,290	G3
68780	Stuart 641	E2
68978	Superior 2,502	F4
69165	Sutherland 1,238	C3
68979	Sutton 1,416	G4
68446	Syracuse 1,638	H4
68447	Table Rock 393	H4

Agriculture, Industry and Resources

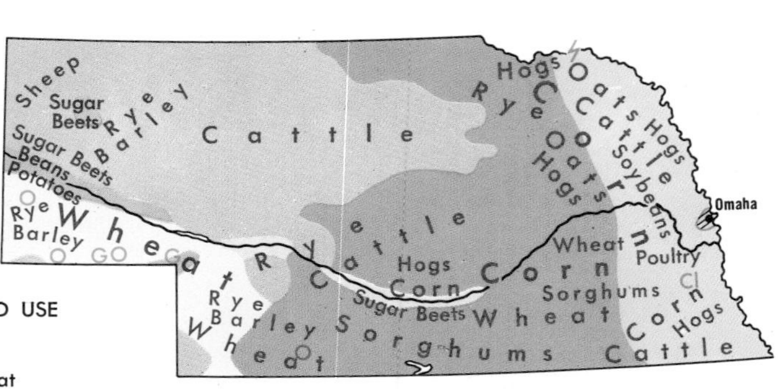

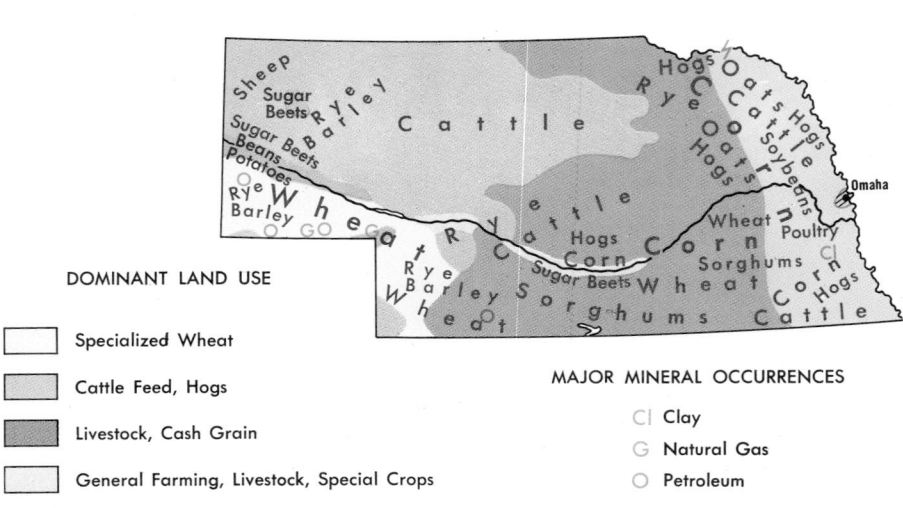

DOMINANT LAND USE

- Specialized Wheat
- Cattle Feed, Hogs
- Livestock, Cash Grain
- General Farming, Livestock, Special Crops
- Sugar Beets, Dry Beans, Livestock, General Farming
- Range Livestock

MAJOR MINERAL OCCURRENCES

- Cl Clay
- G Natural Gas
- ○ Petroleum
- Water Power
- Major Industrial Areas

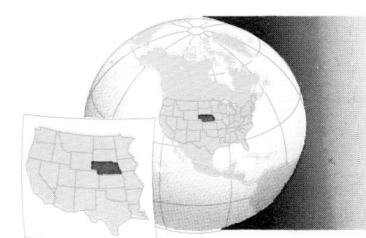

AREA 77,355 sq. mi. (200,349 sq. km.)
POPULATION 1,569,825
CAPITAL Lincoln
LARGEST CITY Omaha
HIGHEST POINT (Kimball Co.) 5,246 ft. (1654 n
SETTLED IN 1847
ADMITTED TO UNION March 1, 1867
POPULAR NAME Cornhusker State
STATE FLOWER Goldenrod
STATE BIRD Western Meadowlark

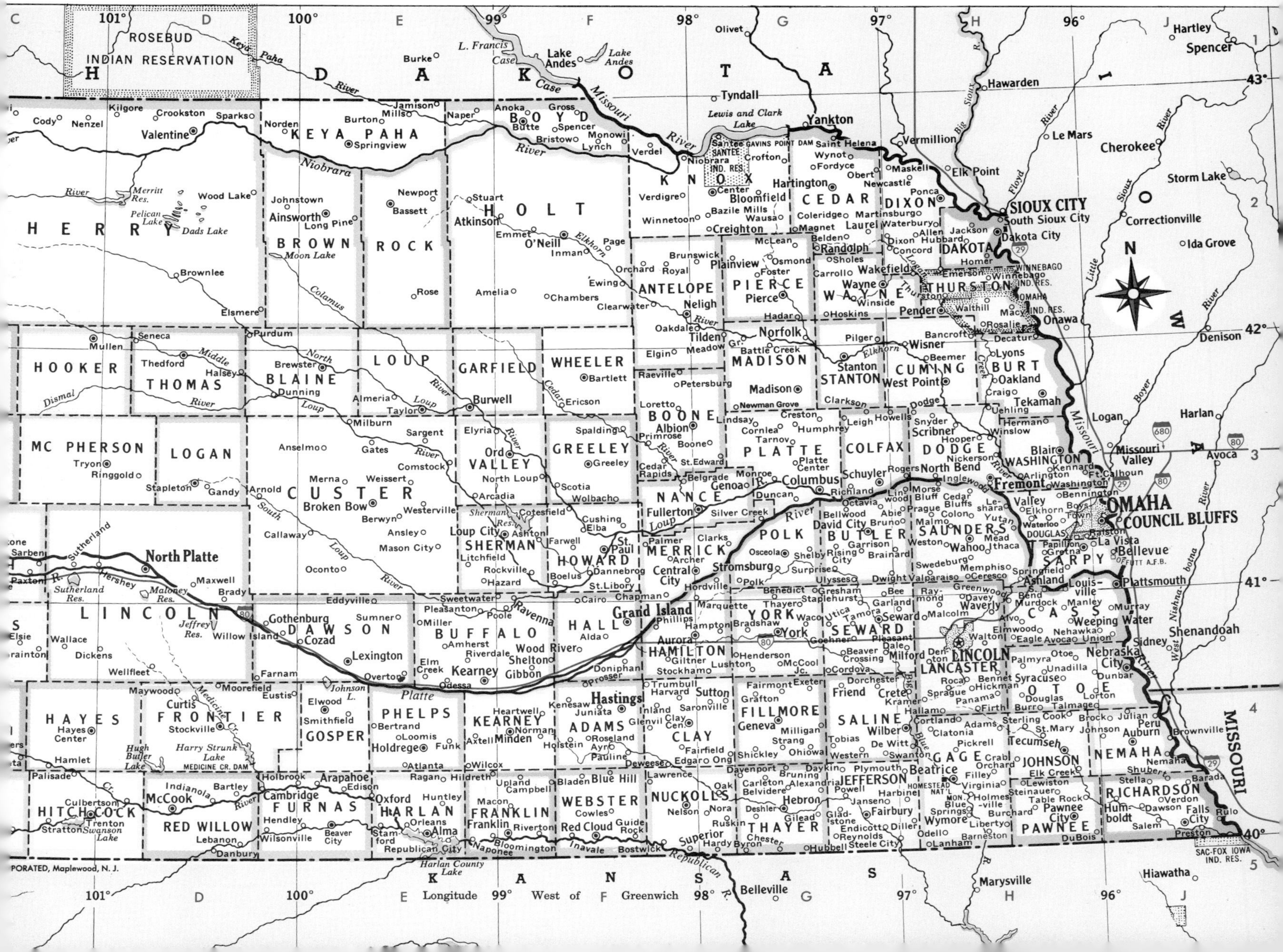

Topography

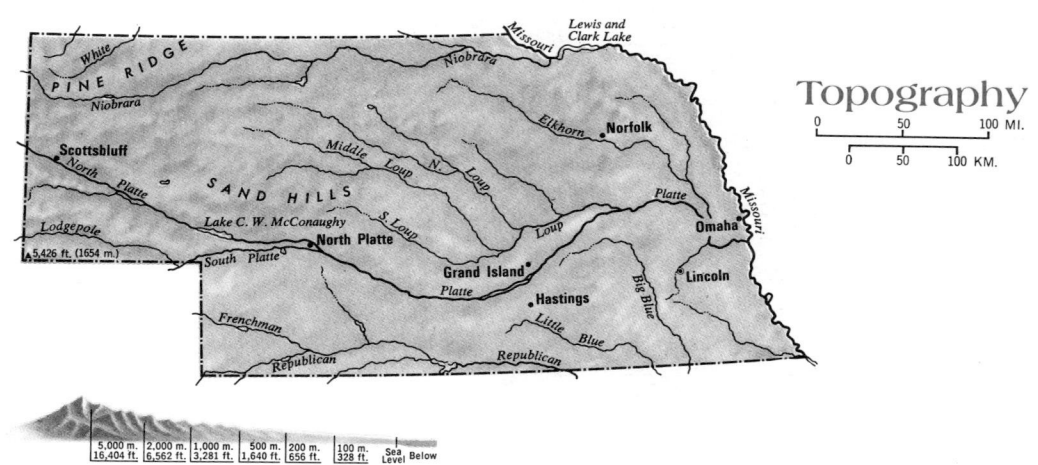

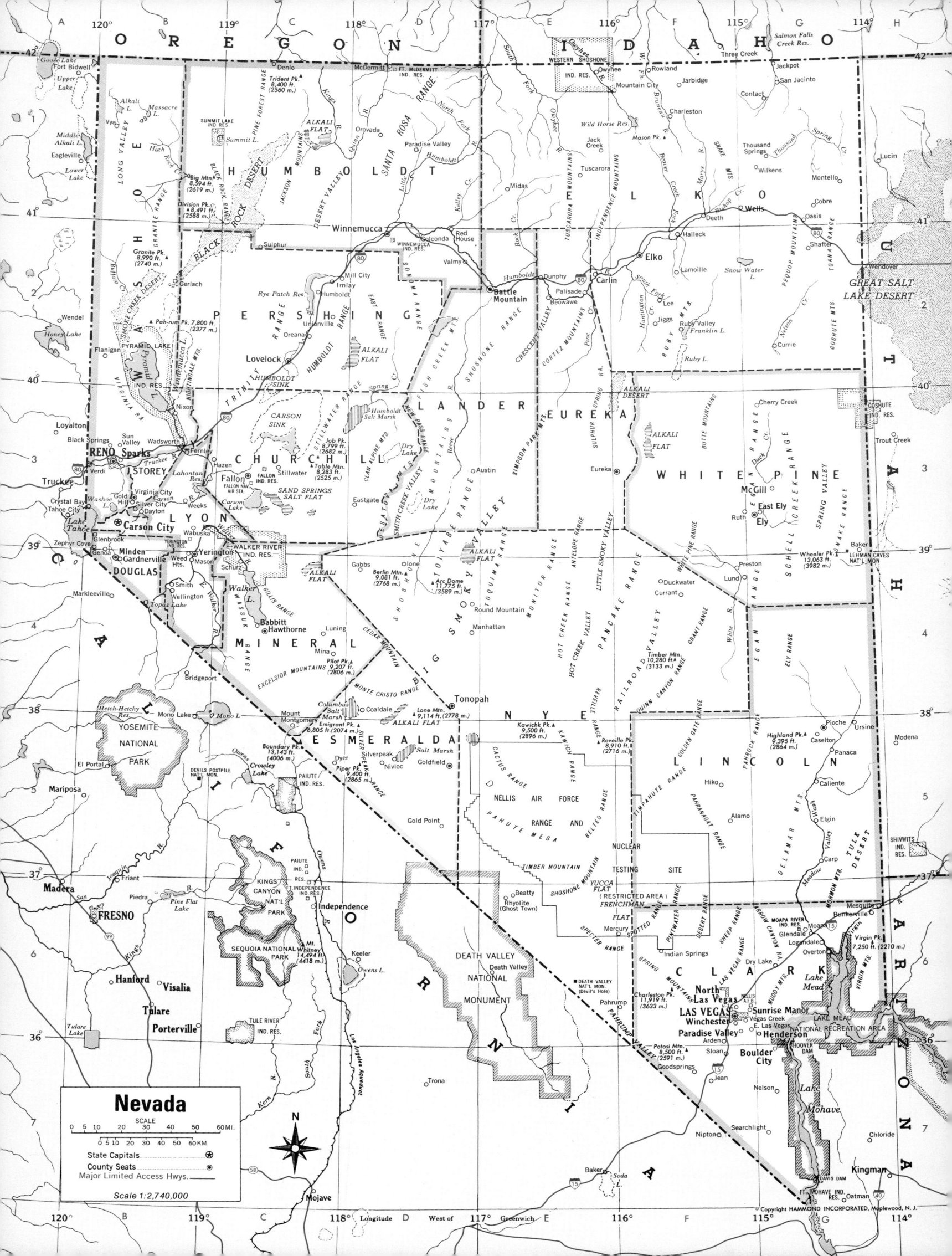

Nevada

SCALE

0 5 10 20 30 40 50 60MI.

0 5 10 20 30 40 50 60KM.

State Capitals ⊛

County Seats ⊙

Major Limited Access Hwys. ▬▬▬

Scale 1:2,740,000

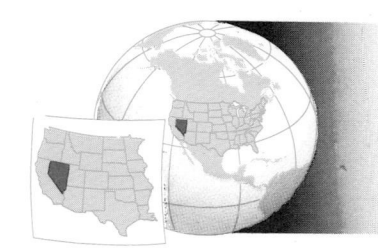

AREA 110,561 sq. mi. (286,353 sq. km.)
POPULATION 800,493
CAPITAL Carson City
LARGEST CITY Las Vegas
HIGHEST POINT Boundary Pk. 13,143 ft.
   (4006 m.)
SETTLED IN 1850
ADMITTED TO UNION October 31, 1864
POPULAR NAME Silver State; Sagebrush
   State
STATE FLOWER Sagebrush
STATE BIRD Mountain Bluebird

Agriculture, Industry and Resources

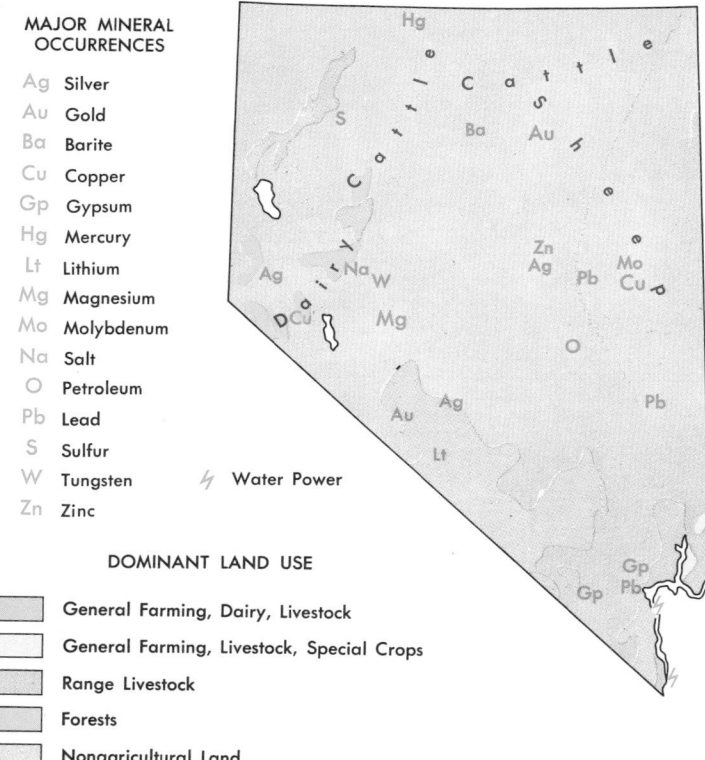

MAJOR MINERAL OCCURRENCES

Ag Silver
Au Gold
Ba Barite
Cu Copper
Gp Gypsum
Hg Mercury
Lt Lithium
Mg Magnesium
Mo Molybdenum
Na Salt
O Petroleum
Pb Lead
S Sulfur
W Tungsten   ⚡ Water Power
Zn Zinc

DOMINANT LAND USE

General Farming, Dairy, Livestock
General Farming, Livestock, Special Crops
Range Livestock
Forests
Nonagricultural Land

Topography

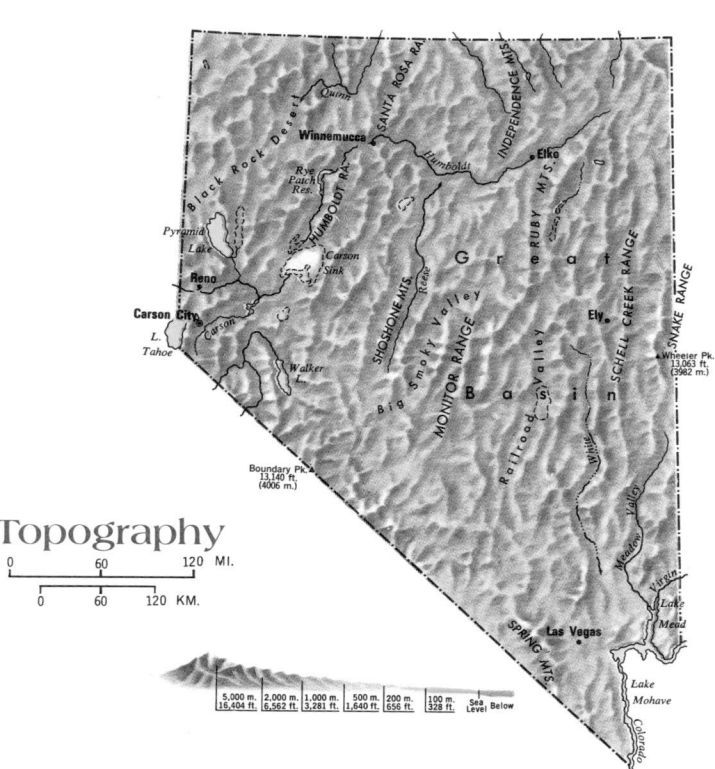

0   60   120 MI.
0   60   120 KM.

5,000 m. 2,000 m. 1,000 m. 500 m. 200 m. 100 m. Sea
16,404 ft. 6,562 ft. 3,281 ft. 1,640 ft. 656 ft. 328 ft. Level Below

COUNTIES

Carson City (city) 32,022	B3
Churchill 13,917	C3
Clark 463,087	F6
Douglas 19,421	B4
Elko 17,269	F1
Esmeralda 777	D5
Eureka 1,198	E3
Humboldt 9,434	C1
Lander 4,076	D3
Lincoln 3,732	F5
Lyon 13,594	B3
Mineral 6,217	C4
Nye 9,048	E4
Pershing 3,408	C2
Storey 1,503	B3
Washoe 193,623	B2
White Pine 8,167	F3

CITIES and TOWNS

Zip	Name/Pop.	Key
89001	Alamo 300	F5
89310	Austin 300	E3
89416	Babbitt	C4
89311	Baker 140	G3
89820	Battle Mountain⊙ 2,749	E2
89003	Beatty 600	E6
89821	Beowawe 77	E2
†89508	Black Springs 180	B3
89005	Boulder City 9,590	G7
89007	Bunkerville 300	G6
89008	Caliente 982	G5
89822	Carlin 1,232	E2
†89008	Carp 30	G5
89701	Carson City (cap.) 32,022	B3
†89043	Caselton	G5
†89301	Cherry Creek 80	G3
89402	Crystal Bay 6,225	A3
89403	Dayton 350	B3
89823	Deeth 125	F1
89404	Denio 35	C1
89314	Duckwater 80	F4
89010	Dyer 56	C5
89315	East Ely	G3
89112	East Las Vegas 6,449	F6
89801	Elko⊙ 8,758	F2
89301	Ely⊙ 4,882	G3
89316	Eureka⊙ 300	E3
89406	Fallon⊙ 4,262	C3
89408	Fernley 750	B3
89409	Gabbs 811	D4
89410	Gardnerville 1,610	B4
89411	Genoa 254	B4
89412	Gerlach 200	B2
89413	Glenbrook 800	B3
89414	Golconda 275	D2
89013	Goldfield⊙ 500	D5
89019	Goodsprings 80	F7
89824	Halleck 68	F2
89415	Hawthorne⊙ 3,741	C4
89417	Hazen 76	C3
89015	Henderson 24,363	G6
89017	Hiko 210	F5
†89418	Humboldt 14	C2
89418	Imlay 250	C2
89018	Indian Springs 500	F6
†89310	Ione 20	D4
†89834	Jack Creek	E1
89825	Jackpot 400	G1
89826	Jarbidge 11	F1
89019	Jean 125	F7
89828	Lamoille 100	F2
*89101	Las Vegas⊙ 164,674	F6
	Las Vegas‡ 461,816	F6
89829	Lee 125	F2
89021	Logandale 410	G6
89419	Lovelock⊙ 1,680	C2
89317	Lund 380	F4
89420	Luning 90	C4
89022	Manhattan 93	E4
†89447	Mason 200	B4
89421	McDermitt 240	D1
89318	McGill 1,419	G3
89023	Mercury 900	E6
89024	Mesquite 500	G6
89422	Mina 450	C4
89423	Minden⊙ 1,029	B4
89025	Moapa 275	G6
89830	Montello 100	G1
89831	Mountain City 100	F1
†89046	Nelson 75	G7
89424	Nixon 400	B3
89030	North Las Vegas 42,739	F6
89425	Orovada 200	D1
89040	Overton 1,111	G6
89041	Pahrump 400	E6
89042	Panaca 650	G5
89119	Paradise Valley 84,818	F6
89426	Paradise Valley 115	D1
89043	Pioche⊙ 850	G5
*89501	Reno⊙ 100,756	B3
	Reno‡ 193,623	B3
†89003	Rhyolite (Ghost Town) 8	E6
89045	Round Mountain 400	E4
89833	Ruby Valley 150	F2
89319	Ruth 455	F3
89427	Schurz 800	C4
89046	Searchlight 500	F7
89428	Silver City 150	B3
89047	Silverpeak 100	D5
89430	Smith 200	B4
89431	Sparks 40,780	B3
†89406	Stillwater 150	C3
†89445	Sulphur	C2
†89110	Sunrise Manor 44,155	F6
†89431	Sun Valley 8,822	B3
†89835	Thousand Springs	G1
89049	Tonopah⊙ 1,952	D4
89834	Tuscarora 24	E1
89438	Valmy 200	D2
89121	Vegas Creek	G6
†89109	Winchester 19,728	F6
89445	Winnemucca⊙ 4,140	D2
89440	Virginia City⊙ 750	B3
89442	Wadsworth 400	B3
89443	Weed Heights 8	B4
89444	Wellington 505	B4
89835	Wells 1,218	G1
89447	Yerington⊙ 2,021	B4
89448	Zephyr Cove 1,316	A3

OTHER FEATURES

Alkali (lake)	B1
Antelope (range)	E3
Arc Dome (mt.)	D4
Arrow Canyon (range)	G6
Beaver Creek Fork, Humboldt (riv.)	F1
Belted (range)	E5
Berlin (mt.)	D4
Big (mt.)	B1
Big Smoky (valley)	D4
Bishop (creek)	F1
Black Rock (des.)	B2
Black Rock (range)	B1
Boundary (peak)	C5
Buffalo (creek)	B2
Butte (mts.)	F3
Cactus (range)	E5
Carson (lake)	C3
Carson (riv.)	B3
Carson (sink)	C3
Cedar (mt.)	D4
Charleston (peak)	F6
Clan Alpine (mts.)	D3
Columbus Salt (marsh)	C4
Cortez (mts.)	E2
Crescent (valley)	E2
Davis (dam)	G7
Death Valley Nat'l Mon.	E6
Delamar (mts.)	G5
Desatoya (mts.)	D3
Desert (range)	F6
Desert (valley)	C1
Devil's Hole (Death Valley Nat'l Mon.)	E6
Division (peak)	B1
Duck (creek)	G3
East (range)	D2
East Walker (riv.)	B4
Egan (range)	G4
Ely (range)	G4
Emigrant (peak)	C5
Excelsior (mts.)	C4
Fallon Ind. Res.	C3
Fallon Nav. Air Sta.	C3
Fish Creek (mts.)	D2
Fort McDermitt Ind. Res.	D1
Fort Mohave Ind. Res.	G7
Franklin (lake)	F2
Frenchman Flat (basin)	F6
Gillis (range)	C4
Golden Gate (range)	F5
Goshute (mts.)	G2
Goshute Ind. Res.	G3
Granite (peak)	B1
Granite (range)	B2
Grant (range)	F4
Great Salt Lake (des.)	H2
High Rock (creek)	B1
Highland (peak)	G5
Hoover (dam)	G7
Hot Creek (range)	E4
Hot Creek (valley)	E4
Humboldt (range)	C2
Humboldt (riv.)	E2
Humboldt (sink)	C2
Humboldt Salt (marsh)	D3
Huntington (creek)	F2
Independence (mts.)	E1
Jackson (mts.)	C1
Job (peak)	C3
Kawich (peak)	E5
Kawich (range)	E5
Kelley (creek)	D1
Kings (riv.)	C1
Lahontan (res.)	B3
Lake Mead Nat'l Rec. Area	G6
Las Vegas (range)	F6
Lehman Caves Nat'l Mon.	G4
Little Humboldt (riv.)	D1
Little Smoky (valley)	E4
Lone (mt.)	D4
Long (valley)	B1
Marys (riv.)	F1
Mason (peak)	F1
Massacre (lake)	B1
Mead (lake)	G6
Meadow Valley Wash (riv.)	G5
Moapa River Ind. Res.	G6
Mohave (lake)	G7
Monitor (range)	E4
Monte Cristo (range)	D4
Mormon (mts.)	G5
Muddy (mts.)	G6
Nellis A.F.B. 7,476	F6
Nellis Air Force Range and Nuclear Testing Site	E5
Nelson (creek)	G2
New Pass (range)	D3
Nightingale (mts.)	B2
Owyhee (riv.)	E1
Pahranagat (range)	F5
Pahrock (range)	F5
Pah-rum (peak)	B2
Pahrump (valley)	F6
Pahute (mesa)	E5
Pancake (range)	F4
Pequop (mts.)	G2
Pilot (peak)	C4
Pine (creek)	E2
Pine Forest (range)	C1
Pintwater (range)	F6
Piper (peak)	D5
Potosi (mt.)	F7
Pyramid (lake)	B2
Pyramid Lake Ind. Res.	B2
Quinn (riv.)	D1
Quinn Canyon (range)	F4
Railroad (valley)	F4
Reese (riv.)	D3
Reveille (peak)	E4
Reveille (range)	E4
Ruby (lake)	F2
Ruby (mts.)	F2
Rye Patch (res.)	C2
Sand Springs (salt flat)	C3
Santa Rosa (range)	D1
Schell Creek (range)	G3
Sheep (range)	F6
Shoshone (mts.)	E6
Shoshone (mts.)	D3
Shoshone (range)	E2
Silver Peak (range)	D5
Simpson Park (mts.)	E3
Smith Creek (valley)	D3
Smoke Creek (des.)	B2
Snake (mts.)	F1
Snake (range)	G3
Snow Water (lake)	G2
Sonoma (range)	D2
Specter (range)	E6
Spotted (range)	F6
Spring (creek)	D2
Spring (mts.)	F6
Spring (valley)	G3
Stillwater (range)	C3
Sulphur Spring (range)	E3
Summit (lake)	C1
Summit Lake Ind. Res.	B1
Table (mt.)	C3
Tahoe (lake)	B3
Thousand Spring (creek)	G1
Timber (mt.)	F4
Timber (mt.)	E5
Timpahute (range)	F5
Toana (range)	G2
Toiyabe (range)	D3
Topaz (lake)	B4
Toquima (range)	E4
Trident (peak)	C1
Trinity (range)	C2
Truckee (riv.)	B3
Tule (des.)	G5
Tuscarora (mts.)	E1
Virgin (mts.)	G6
Virgin (peak)	G6
Virgin (riv.)	G6
Virginia (range)	B3
Walker (lake)	C4
Walker (riv.)	C3
Walker River Ind. Res.	C3
Washoe (lake)	B3
Wassuk (range)	C4
Western Shoshone Ind. Res.	E1
Wheeler (peak)	G4
White (riv.)	F4
White Pine (range)	F3
Wild Horse (res.)	E1
Winnemucca (lake)	B2
Winnemucca Ind. Res.	D2
Yerington Ind. Res.	B3
Yucca Flat (basin)	E6

⊙ County seat.
‡ Population of metropolitan area.
† Zip of nearest p.o.
* Multiple zips.

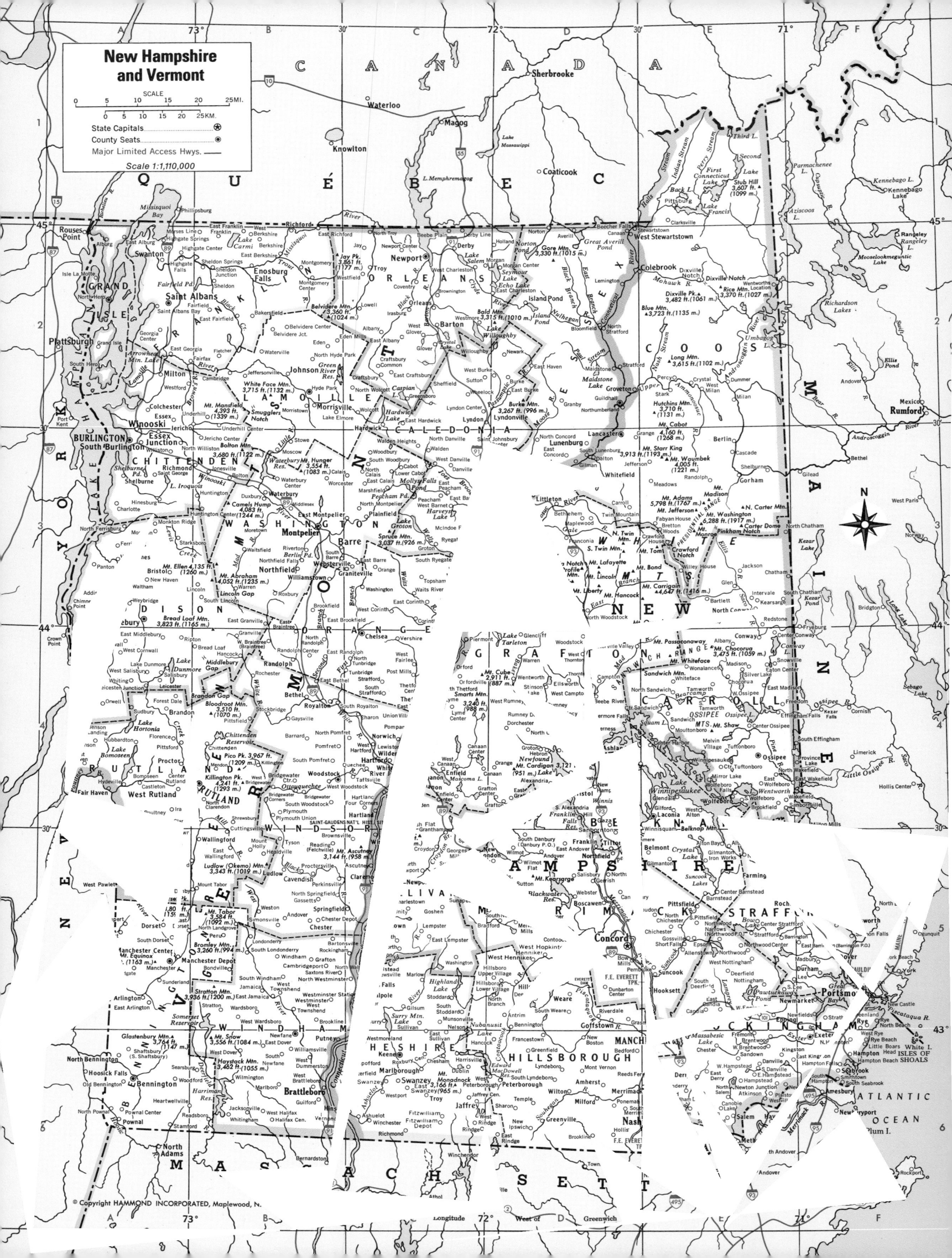

New Hampshire
and Vermont

SCALE

State Capitals ⊛
County Seats ⊚
Major Limited Access Hwys.

Scale 1:1,110,000

© Copyright HAMMOND INCORPORATED, Maplewood, N.

NEW HAMPSHIRE

AREA 9,279 sq. mi. (24,033 sq. km.)
POPULATION 920,610
CAPITAL Concord
LARGEST CITY Manchester
HIGHEST POINT Mt. Washington 6,288 ft. (1917 m.)
SETTLED IN 1623
ADMITTED TO UNION June 21, 1788
POPULAR NAME Granite State
STATE FLOWER Purple Lilac
STATE BIRD Purple Finch

VERMONT

AREA 9,614 sq. mi. (24,900 sq. km.)
POPULATION 511,456
CAPITAL Montpelier
LARGEST CITY Burlington
HIGHEST POINT Mt. Mansfield 4,393 ft. (1339 m.)
SETTLED IN 1764
ADMITTED TO UNION March 4, 1791
POPULAR NAME Green Mountain State
STATE FLOWER Red Clover
STATE BIRD Hermit Thrush

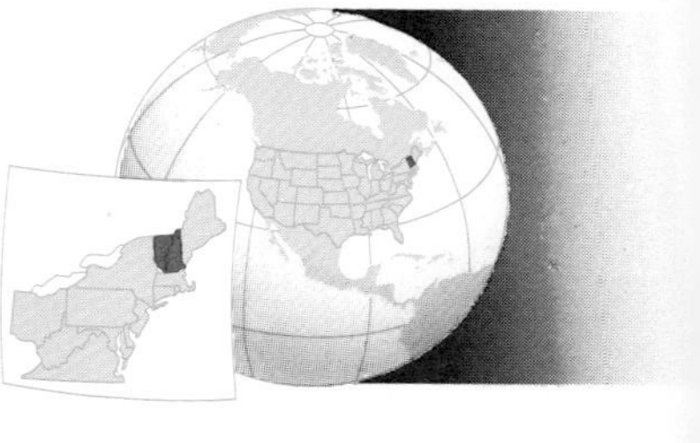

NEW HAMPSHIRE

COUNTIES

Belknap 42,884 .... D4
Carroll 27,931 .... E4
Cheshire 62,116 .... C6
Coos 35,147 .... E2
Grafton 65,806 .... D4
Hillsborough 276,608 .... D6
Merrimack 98,302 .... D5
Rockingham 190,345 .... E5
Strafford 85,408 .... E5
Sullivan 36,063 .... C5

CITIES and TOWNS

Zip *Name/Pop.* *Key*

03601 Acworth○ 590 .... C5
†03864 Albany○ 383 .... E4
†03222 Alexandria○ 706 .... D4
†03275 Allenstown○ 4,398 .... E5
03602 Alstead○ 1,461 .... C5
03809 Alton○ 2,440 .... E5
03810 Alton Bay 500 .... E5
03031 Amherst○ 8,243 .... D6
03216 Andover○ 1,587 .... D5
03440 Antrim○ 2,208 .... D5
03440 Antrim 1,142 .... D5
03217 Ashland○ 1,807 .... D4
03217 Ashland 1,479 .... D4
03441 Ashuelot 810 .... C6
03811 Atkinson○ 4,397 .... E6
03032 Auburn○ 2,883 .... E5
03218 Barnstead○ 2,292 .... E5
†03825 Barrington○ 4,404 .... F5
03812 Bartlett○ 1,566 .... E3
03740 Bath○ 761 .... D3
03102 Bedford○ 9,481 .... D6
03220 Belmont○ 4,026 .... E5
03442 Bennington○ 890 .... D5
†03785 Benton○ 333 .... D3
03570 Berlin 13,084 .... E3
03574 Bethlehem○ 1,784 .... D3
03301 Boscawen○ 3,435 .... D5
03221 Bradford○ 1,115 .... D5
†03833 Brentwood○ 2,004 .... E6
†03222 Bridgewater○ 606 .... D4
03222 Bristol○ 2,198 .... D4
03222 Bristol 1,258 .... D4
†03872 Brookfield○ 385 .... E4
03033 Brookline○ 1,766 .... D6
03223 Campton○ 1,694 .... D4
03741 Canaan○ 2,456 .... C4
03034 Candia○ 2,989 .... E5
03224 Canterbury○ 1,410 .... D5
†03595 Carroll○ 647 .... D3
03813 Center Conway 558 .... E4
03226 Center Harbor○ 808 .... E4
03814 Center Ossipee 800 .... E4
03603 Charlestown○ 4,417 .... C5
03603 Charlestown 1,294 .... C5
†04037 Chatham○ 189 .... E3
03036 Chester○ 2,006 .... E6
03443 Chesterfield○ 2,561 .... C6
†03258 Chichester○ 1,492 .... E5
03817 Chocorua 575 .... E4
03743 Claremont 14,557 .... C5
†05902 Clarksville○ 262 .... E1
03576 Colebrook○ 2,459 .... E2
03576 Colebrook 1,131 .... E2
03301 Concord (cap.)⊙ 30,400 ... D5
03229 Contoocook 1,499 .... D5
03818 Conway○ 7,158 .... E4
03818 Conway 1,781 .... E4
03746 Cornish Flat 450 .... C4
†03753 Croydon○ 457 .... C5
†03598 Dalton○ 672 .... D3
03230 Danbury○ 680 .... D4
03819 Danville○ 1,318 .... E6
03037 Deerfield○ 1,979 .... E5
†03244 Deering○ 1,041 .... D5
03038 Derry○ 18,875 .... E6
03038 Derry 12,248 .... E6
†03266 Dorchester○ 244 .... D4
03820 Dover⊙ 22,377 .... F5
03444 Dublin○ 1,303 .... C6
†03588 Dummer○ 390 .... E2
†03301 Dunbarton○ 1,174 .... D5
03824 Durham○ 10,652 .... F5
03824 Durham 8,448 .... F5
03231 East Andover 500 .... D5
03826 East Hampstead 900 .... E6
03827 East Kingston○ 1,135 .... F6
†03580 Easton○ 124 .... D3
03446 East Swanzey 500 .... C6
03832 Eaton (Eaton Center)○ 256 . E4
†03264 Ellsworth○ 53 .... D4
03748 Enfield○ 3,175 .... C4
03748 Enfield 1,581 .... C4
03042 Epping○ 3,460 .... E5
03042 Epping 1,384 .... E5
03234 Epsom○ 2,743 .... E5
03579 Errol○ 313 .... E2
03750 Etna 550 .... C4
03833 Exeter○ 11,024 .... F6
03833 Exeter⊙ 8,947 .... F6
03835 Farmington○ 4,630 .... E5
03835 Farmington 3,284 .... E5
03447 Fitzwilliam○ 1,795 .... C6
03043 Francestown○ 830 .... D6
03580 Franconia○ 743 .... D3
03235 Franklin 7,901 .... D5
03836 Freedom○ 720 .... E4
03044 Fremont○ 1,333 .... E6
†03246 Gilford○ 4,841 .... E4
03237 Gilmanton○ 1,941 .... E5
03448 Gilsum○ 652 .... C5
03838 Glen 600 .... E3
03045 Goffstown○ 11,315 .... D5
03581 Gorham○ 3,322 .... E3
03581 Gorham 2,180 .... E3
03752 Goshen○ 549 .... C5
03240 Grafton○ 739 .... D4
03753 Grantham○ 704 .... C5
03047 Greenfield○ 972 .... D6
03840 Greenland○ 2,129 .... F5
03048 Greenville○ 1,988 .... D6
03048 Greenville 1,447 .... D6
†03241 Groton○ 255 .... D4
03582 Groveton 1,389 .... D2
03754 Guild 500 .... C5
03841 Hampstead○ 3,785 .... E6
03842 Hampton○ 10,493 .... F6
03842 Hampton 6,779 .... F6
03844 Hampton Falls○ 1,372 .... F6
03449 Hancock○ 1,193 .... C6
03755 Hanover○ 9,119 .... C4
03755 Hanover 6,861 .... C4
03450 Harrisville○ 860 .... C6
03765 Haverhill○ 3,445 .... C3
03241 Hebron○ 349 .... D4
03242 Henniker○ 3,246 .... D5
03242 Henniker 1,538 .... D5
03243 Hill○ 736 .... D4
03244 Hillsboro○ 3,437 .... D5
03244 Hillsboro 1,797 .... D5
03451 Hinsdale○ 3,631 .... C6
03451 Hinsdale 1,546 .... C6
03245 Holderness○ 1,586 .... D4
03049 Hollis○ 4,679 .... D6
03106 Hooksett○ 7,303 .... E5
03106 Hooksett 1,868 .... E5
03301 Hopkinton○ 3,861 .... D5
03051 Hudson○ 14,022 .... E6
03051 Hudson 6,248 .... E6
03845 Intervale 725 .... E3
03846 Jackson○ 642 .... E3
03452 Jaffrey○ 4,349 .... C6
03452 Jaffrey 2,684 .... C6
03583 Jefferson○ 803 .... D3
03431 Keene⊙ 21,449 .... C6
03848 Kingston○ 4,111 .... E6
03246 Laconia⊙ 15,575 .... E4
03584 Lancaster○ 3,401 .... D3
03584 Lancaster⊙ 2,134 .... D3
†03585 Landaff○ 266 .... D3
†03602 Langdon○ 437 .... C5
03766 Lebanon 11,134 .... C4
†03857 Lee○ 2,111 .... F5
03606 Lempster○ 637 .... C5
03251 Lincoln○ 1,313 .... D3
03585 Lisbon○ 1,517 .... D3
03585 Lisbon 1,151 .... D3
†03051 Litchfield○ 4,150 .... E6
03561 Littleton○ 5,558 .... D3
03561 Littleton 4,480 .... D3
03053 Londonderry○ 13,598 .... E6
03301 Loudon○ 2,454 .... E5
†03585 Lyman○ 281 .... D3
03768 Lyme○ 1,289 .... C4
†03082 Lyndeborough○ 1,070 .... D6
†03820 Madbury○ 987 .... F5
03849 Madison○ 1,051 .... E4
*03101 Manchester 90,936 .... E6
Manchester‡ 160,767 .... E6
03455 Marlborough○ 1,846 .... C6
03455 Marlborough 1,184 .... C6
03456 Marlow○ 542 .... C5
03850 Melvin Village 450 .... E4
03253 Meredith○ 4,646 .... D4
03253 Meredith 1,202 .... D4
03770 Meriden 800 .... C4
03054 Merrimack○ 15,406 .... D6
†03887 Middleton○ 734 .... E5
03588 Milan○ 1,013 .... E2
03055 Milford○ 8,685 .... D6
03055 Milford 6,269 .... D6
03851 Milton○ 2,438 .... F5
03852 Milton Mills 450 .... F4
03771 Monroe○ 619 .... C3
03057 Mont Vernon○ 1,444 .... D6
03254 Moultonboro○ 2,206 .... E4
03060 Nashua⊙ 67,865 .... D6
Nashua‡ 114,221 .... D6
†03457 Nelson○ 442 .... C5
03070 New Boston○ 1,928 .... D6
03255 Newbury○ 961 .... C5
03854 New Castle○ 936 .... F5
03855 New Durham○ 1,183 .... E5
03856 Newfields○ 817 .... F5
03256 New Hampton○ 1,249 .... D4
†03801 Newington○ 716 .... F5
03071 New Ipswich○ 2,433 .... D6
03257 New London○ 2,935 .... D5
03257 New London 1,335 .... D5
03857 Newmarket○ 4,290 .... F5
03857 Newmarket 3,749 .... F5
03773 Newport○ 6,229 .... C5
03773 Newport⊙ 4,388 .... C5
03858 Newton○ 3,068 .... E6
03859 Newton Junction 450 .... E6
03860 North Conway 2,104 .... E3
†03276 Northfield○ 3,051 .... D5
†03276 Northfield-Tilton 2,574 .... D5
03862 North Hampton○ 3,425 .... F6
03590 North Stratford 600 .... D2
†03582 Northumberland○ 2,520 .... D2
03261 Northwood○ 2,175 .... E5
03262 North Woodstock 750 .... D3
03290 Nottingham○ 1,952 .... E5
†03741 Orange○ 197 .... D4
03777 Orford○ 928 .... C4
03864 Ossipee 2,465 .... E4
03076 Pelham○ 8,090 .... E6
†03275 Pembroke○ 4,861 .... E5
03458 Peterborough○ 4,895 .... D6
03458 Peterborough 2,568 .... D6
03779 Piermont○ 507 .... C4
03592 Pittsburg○ 780 .... E1
03263 Pittsfield○ 2,889 .... E5
03263 Pittsfield 1,584 .... E5
03781 Plainfield○ 1,749 .... C4
03865 Plaistow○ 5,609 .... E6
03264 Plymouth○ 5,094 .... D4
03264 Plymouth 3,628 .... D4
03801 Portsmouth 26,254 .... F5
Portsmouth-Dover-Rochester‡ 163,880 .... F5
03593 Randolph○ 274 .... E3
03077 Raymond○ 5,453 .... E5
03077 Raymond 1,192 .... E5
†03470 Richmond○ 518 .... C6
03461 Rindge○ 3,375 .... C6
03867 Rochester 21,560 .... E5
†03431 Roxbury○ 190 .... C6
03266 Rumney○ 1,212 .... D4
03870 Rye○ 4,508 .... F5
03871 Rye Beach 600 .... F6
03079 Salem○ 24,124 .... E6
03268 Salisbury○ 781 .... D5
03269 Sanbornton○ 1,679 .... D5
03872 Sanbornville 750 .... F4
03873 Sandown○ 2,057 .... E6
03270 Sandwich○ 905 .... E4
03874 Seabrook○ 5,917 .... F6
†03458 Sharon○ 184 .... D6
†03581 Shelburne○ 318 .... E3
03878 Somersworth 10,350 .... F5
†01913 South Hampton○ 660 .... F6
03462 Spofford 750 .... C6
†03284 Springfield○ 532 .... C4
†03582 Stark○ 470 .... E2
†03576 Stewartstown○ 943 .... E2
03464 Stoddard○ 482 .... C5
03884 Strafford○ 1,663 .... E5
†03590 Stratford○ 989 .... D2
03885 Stratham○ 2,507 .... F5
03585 Sugar Hill○ 397 .... D3
†03445 Sullivan○ 585 .... C5
03782 Sunapee○ 2,312 .... C5
03275 Suncook 4,698 .... D5
03431 Surry○ 656 .... C5
†03260 Sutton○ 1,091 .... D5
†03431 Swanzey○ 5,183 .... C6
03886 Tamworth○ 1,672 .... E4
03084 Temple○ 692 .... D6
†03285 Thornton○ 952 .... D4
03276 Tilton○ 3,387 .... D5
03276 Tilton-Northfield 2,574 .... D5
03465 Troy○ 2,131 .... C6
03465 Troy 1,318 .... C6
†03816 Tuftonboro○ 1,500 .... E4
03595 Twin Mountain 500 .... D3
†03743 Unity○ 1,092 .... C5
†03872 Wakefield○ 2,237 .... F4
03608 Walpole○ 3,188 .... C5
03278 Warner○ 1,963 .... D5
03279 Warren○ 650 .... D4
03280 Washington○ 411 .... C5
03223 Waterville Valley○ 180 .... D4
03281 Weare○ 3,232 .... D5
†03301 Webster○ 1,095 .... D5
03282 Wentworth○ 527 .... D4
†03579 Wentworths Location○ 49 .. E2
†03242 West Henniker 500 .... D5
03784 West Lebanon C4
03467 Westmoreland○ 1,452 .... C6
03597 West Stewartstown 700 .... E2
03469 West Swanzey 1,022 .... C6
03865 Westville 750 .... E6
03598 Whitefield○ 1,681 .... D3
03598 Whitefield 1,005 .... D3
†03287 Wilmot○ 725 .... D5
03287 Wilmot Flat 450 .... D5
03086 Wilton○ 2,669 .... D6
03086 Wilton 1,310 .... D6
03470 Winchester○ 3,465 .... C6

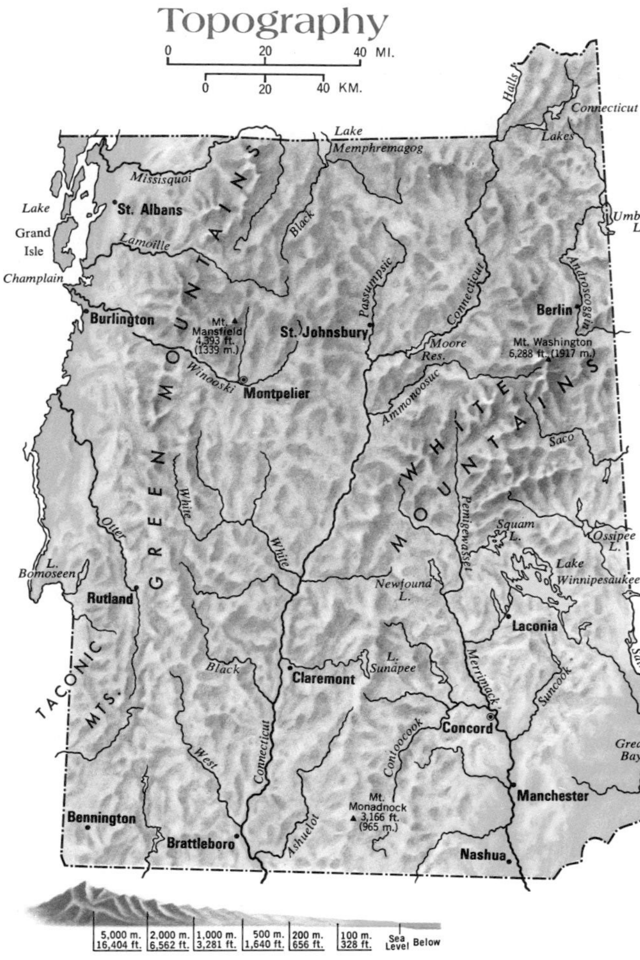
Topography
0 20 40 MI.
0 20 40 KM.
Lake Memphremagog
Missisquoi
St. Albans
Lake Champlain
Grand Isle
Lamoille
Burlington
Mt. Mansfield 4,393 ft. (1339 m.)
GREEN MOUNTAINS
Winooski
Montpelier
Black
Passumpsic
St. Johnsbury
Connecticut
Halls
Connecticut Lakes
Umbagog L.
Androscoggin
Berlin
Mt. Washington 6,288 ft. (1917 m.)
Moore Res.
Ammonoosuc
WHITE MOUNTAINS
Saco
White
Otter
L. Bomoseen
Rutland
Pemigewasset
Squam L.
Ossipee L.
Lake Winnipesaukee
Newfound L.
Laconia
TACONIC MTS.
Black
Claremont
L. Sunapee
Merrimack
Suncook
Salmon Falls
Concord
Contoocook
Great Bay
Portsmouth
West
Connecticut
Manchester
Bennington
Mt. Monadnock 3,166 ft. (965 m.)
Ashuelot
Brattleboro
Nashua
5,000 m. 16,404 ft.
2,000 m. 6,562 ft.
1,000 m. 3,281 ft.
500 m. 1,640 ft.
200 m. 656 ft.
100 m. 328 ft.
Sea Level
Below

03470 Winchester 1,732 .... C6
03087 Windham○ 5,664 .... E6
03289 Winnisquam 500 .... E5
03894 Wolfeboro○ 3,968 .... E4
03894 Wolfeboro 2,271 .... E4
03896 Wolfeboro Falls 600 .... E4
03293 Woodstock○ 1,008 .... D4
03785 Woodsville⊙ 1,195 .... C3

OTHER FEATURES

Adams (mt.) E3
Ammonoosuc (riv.) D3
Androscoggin (riv.) E2
Ashuelot (riv.) C6
Back (lake) E1
Baker (riv.) D4
Bearcamp (riv.) E4
Beaver (brook) E6
Belknap (mt.) E5
Blackwater (res.) D5
Blue (mt.) E2
Bond (mt.) E3
Bow (lake) E5
Cabot (mt.) E2
Cannon (mt.) D3
Cardigan (mt.) D4
Carrigain (mt.) E3
Carter Dome (mt.) E3
Chocorua (mt.) E4
Cocheco (riv.) E5
Cold (riv.) C5
Comerford (dam) D3
Connecticut (riv.) B6
Contoocook (riv.) D6
Conway (lake) E4
Crawford Notch (pass) E3
Croydon (peak) C5
Croydon Branch, Sugar (riv.) C5
Crystal (lake) E5
Cube (mt.) D4
Dixville (peak) E2
Dixville Notch (pass) E2
Edward MacDowell (res.) D6
Ellis (riv.) E3
Everett (dam) D5
Exeter (riv.) E6
First Connecticut (lake) E1
Francis (lake) E1
Franconia Notch (pass) D3
Franklin Falls (res.) D4
Gale (riv.) D3
Great (bay) F5
Halls (stream) E1
Hancock (mt.) D3
Highland (lake) C5
Hutchins (mt.) E2
Indian (stream) E1
Jefferson (mt.) E3
Kearsarge (mt.) D5
Kinsman (mt.) D3
Kinsman Notch (pass) D3
Lafayette (mt.) D3
Lamprey (riv.) E5
Liberty (mt.) D3
Lincoln (mt.) D3
Long (mt.) E2
Mad (riv.) D4
Madison (mt.) E3
Mascoma (lake) C4
Massabesic (lake) E6
Merrimack (riv.) D5
Merrymeeting (lake) E5
Mohawk (riv.) E2
Monadnock (mt.) C6
Monroe (mt.) E3
Moore (dam) D3
Moore (res.) D3
Moosilauke (mt.) D3
Nash (stream) E2
Newfound (lake) D4
North Carter (mt.) E3
North Twin (mt.) D3
Nubanusit (lake) C5
Osceola (mt.) E3
Ossipee (lake) E4
Ossipee (mts.) E4
Ossipee (riv.) F4
Passaconaway (mt.) E4
Pawtuckaway (pond) E5
Pease A.F.B. F5
Pemigewasset (riv.) D4
Perry (stream) E1
Pine (riv.) E4
Pinkham Notch (pass) E3
Piscataqua (riv.) F5
Piscataquog (riv.) D5
Presidential (range) E3
Rice (mt.) E2
Saco (riv.) E3
Saint-Gaudens Nat'l Hist. Site B4
Salmon Falls (riv.) F5

(continued on following page)

Agriculture, Industry and Resources

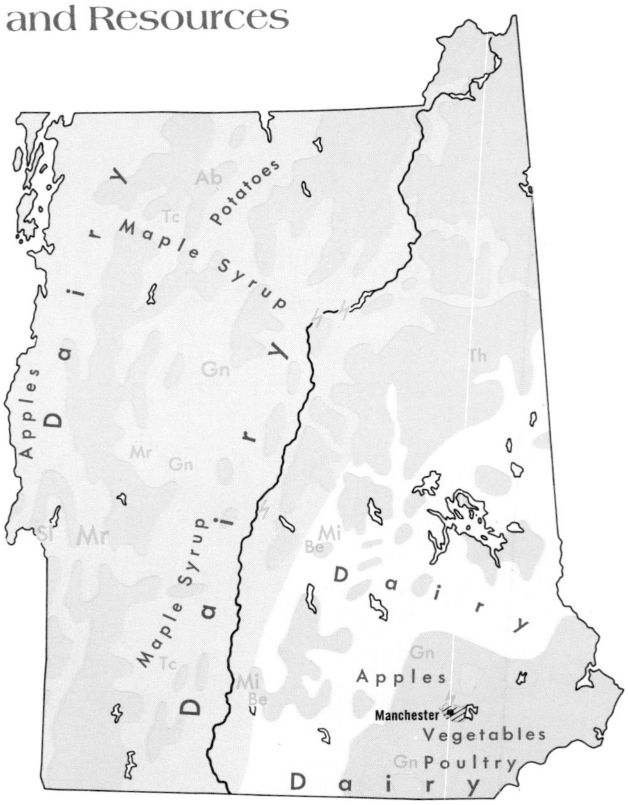

DOMINANT LAND USE

Specialized Dairy
Dairy, General Farming
Dairy, Poultry, Mixed Farming
Forests

Water Power
Major Industrial Areas

MAJOR MINERAL OCCURRENCES

Ab Asbestos
Be Beryl
Gn Granite
Mi Mica
Mr Marble
Sl Slate
Tc Talc
Th Thorium

Sandwich (mt.) E4
Sandwich (range) E4
Second (lake) E1
Shaw (mt.) E4
Shoals (isls.) F6
Smarts (mt.) C4
Souhegan (riv.) D6
South Twin (mt.) D3
Squam (lake) E4
Starr King (mt.) E3
Stub Hill (mt.) E1
Sugar (riv.) C5
Sunapee (lake) C5
Suncook (lkes) E5
Suncook (riv.) E5
Surry Mountain (lake) C5
Tarleton (lake) D4
Tecumseh (mt.) D4
Third (lake) E1
Tom (mt.) E3
Umbagog (lake) E2
Upper Ammonoosuc (riv.) E2
Warner (riv.) D5
Washington (mt.) E3
Waumbek (mt.) E3
Wentworth (lake) E4
White (isl.) F6
White (mts.) E3
Whiteface (mt.) E4
Wild Ammonoosuc (riv.) D3
Wilder (dam) C4
Winnipesaukee (lake) E4
Winnipesaukee (riv.) D5
Winnisquam (lake) D4

VERMONT

COUNTIES

Addison 29,406 .... A3
Bennington 33,345 .... A6
Caledonia 25,808 .... C2
Chittenden 115,534 .... A3
Essex 6,313 .... D2
Franklin 34,788 .... B2
Grand Isle 4,613 .... A2
Lamoille 16,767 .... B2
Orange 22,739 .... C3
Orleans 23,440 .... C2
Rutland 58,347 .... A4
Washington 52,393 .... B3
Windham 36,933 .... B5
Windsor 51,030 .... B4

CITIES and TOWNS

Zip *Name/Pop.* *Key*

05820 Albany○ 705 .... C2
05440 Alburg○ 1,352 .... A2
05440 Alburg 496 .... A2
†05143 Andover○ 350 .... B5
05250 Arlington○ 2,184 .... A5
05250 Arlington 1,309 .... A5
05441 Bakersfield○ 852 .... B2
05031 Barnard○ 790 .... B4
05821 Barnet○ 1,338 .... C3
05641 Barre 9,824 .... C3
05641 Barre○ 7,090 .... C3
05822 Barton○ 2,990 .... C2
05822 Barton 1,062 .... C2
05823 Beebe Plain 500 .... C2
05902 Beecher Falls 950 .... D2
05101 Bellows Falls 3,456 .... C5
05442 Belvidere○ 218 .... B2
05201 Bennington○ 15,815 .... A6
05201 Bennington⊙ 9,349 .... A6
05731 Benson○ 739 .... A4
†05476 Berkshire○ 1,116 .... B2
05032 Bethel○ 1,715 .... B4
05032 Bethel 1,016 .... B4
†03590 Bloomfield○ 188 .... D2
†05466 Bolton○ 715 .... B3
05732 Bomoseen 700 .... A4
05340 Bondville 500 .... B5
05033 Bradford○ 2,191 .... C3
05033 Bradford 831 .... C3
†05669 Braintree○ 1,065 .... B4
05733 Brandon○ 4,194 .... A4
05733 Brandon 1,925 .... A4
05301 Brattleboro○ 11,886 .... B6
05301 Brattleboro 8,596 .... B6
05034 Bridgewater○ 867 .... B4
05734 Bridport○ 997 .... A4
05443 Bristol○ 3,293 .... A3
05443 Bristol 1,793 .... A3
05036 Brookfield○ 959 .... B3
†05345 Brookline○ 310 .... B5
†05860 Brownington○ 708 .... C2
†05871 Burke○ 1,385 .... D2
05401 Burlington⊙ 37,712 .... A3
Burlington‡ 114,070 .... A3
05647 Cabot○ 958 .... C3
05647 Cabot 259 .... C3
05648 Calais○ 1,207 .... B3
05444 Cambridge○ 2,019 .... B2
05444 Cambridge 217 .... B2
05903 Canaan○ 1,196 .... D2
05735 Castleton○ 3,637 .... A4
05142 Cavendish○ 1,355 .... B5
05736 Center Rutland 465 .... A4
05445 Charlotte○ 2,561 .... A3
05038 Chelsea 1,091 .... C4
05143 Chester○ 2,791 .... B5
05143 Chester-Chester Depot 1,267 .... B5
05737 Chittenden○ 927 .... B4
†05759 Clarendon○ 2,372 .... A4
05446 Colchester○ 12,629 .... A2
05824 Concord○ 1,125 .... D3
05039 Corinth○ 904 .... C3
†05753 Cornwall○ 993 .... A4
05825 Coventry○ 674 .... C2
05826 Craftsbury○ 844 .... C2
05739 Danby○ 992 .... A5
05828 Danville○ 1,705 .... C3
05829 Derby○ 4,222 .... C2
05829 Derby (Derby Center) 598 .... C2
05830 Derby Line 874 .... C2
05251 Dorset○ 1,648 .... A5
†05676 Duxbury○ 877 .... B3
05252 East Arlington 600 .... A5
05649 East Barre-Graniteville 2,172 .... C3
05253 East Dorset 550 .... A5
05837 East Haven○ 280 .... D2
05740 East Middlebury 550 .... A4
05651 East Montpelier○ 2,205 .... B3
05741 East Poultney 450 .... A4
05742 East Wallingford 500 .... B5
05652 Eden○ 612 .... B2
05450 Enosburg Falls 1,207 .... B2
05451 Essex○ 14,392 .... A2
05452 Essex Junction 7,033 .... A3
05454 Fairfax○ 1,805 .... B2
05455 Fairfield○ 1,493 .... B2
05743 Fair Haven○ 2,819 .... A4
05743 Fair Haven 2,363 .... A4
05045 Fairlee○ 770 .... C4
05456 Ferrisburg○ 2,117 .... A3
†05444 Fletcher○ 626 .... B2
05745 Forest Dale 500 .... A4
05457 Franklin○ 1,006 .... B2
†05478 Georgia○ 2,818 .... A2
05904 Gilman 600 .... D3
05839 Glover○ 843 .... C2
05146 Grafton○ 604 .... B5
05840 Granby○ 70 .... D2
05458 Grand Isle○ 1,238 .... A2
05654 Graniteville-East Barre 2,172 .... C3
05747 Granville○ 288 .... B4
05841 Greensboro○ 677 .... C2
05046 Groton○ 667 .... C3
05905 Guildhall 202 .... D2
†05301 Guilford○ 1,532 .... B6
†05358 Halifax○ 488 .... B6
05748 Hancock○ 334 .... B4
05843 Hardwick○ 2,613 .... C2
05843 Hardwick 1,476 .... C2
05047 Hartford○ 7,963 .... C4
05048 Hartland○ 2,396 .... C4
†05459 Highgate○ 2,493 .... B2
05461 Hinesburg○ 2,690 .... A3
†05830 Holland○ 473 .... D2
05749 Hubbardton○ 490 .... A4
05462 Huntington○ 1,161 .... B3
05655 Hyde Park○ 2,021 .... B2
05655 Hyde Park⊙ 475 .... B2
05750 Hydeville 500 .... A4
†05777 Ira○ 354 .... A4
05845 Irasburg○ 870 .... C2
05846 Island Pond 1,216 .... D2
05463 Isle La Motte○ 393 .... A2
05342 Jacksonville 252 .... B6
05343 Jamaica○ 681 .... B5
†05859 Jay○ 302 .... C2
05464 Jeffersonville 491 .... B2
05465 Jericho○ 3,575 .... A2
05465 Jericho 1,340 .... A2
05656 Johnson○ 2,581 .... B2
05656 Johnson 1,393 .... B2
05751 Killington 700 .... B4
†05752 Leicester○ 803 .... A4
†03576 Lemington○ 108 .... D2
†05443 Lincoln○ 870 .... B3
05148 Londonderry○ 1,510 .... B5
05847 Lowell○ 573 .... C2
05149 Ludlow○ 2,414 .... B5
05149 Ludlow 1,352 .... B5
05906 Lunenburg○ 1,138 .... D3
05849 Lyndon○ 4,924 .... C2
05850 Lyndon Center C2
05851 Lyndonville 1,401 .... D2
†05905 Maidstone○ 100 .... D2
05254 Manchester○ 3,261 .... A5
05254 Manchester⊙ 563 .... A5
05255 Manchester Center 1,719 .... A5
05344 Marlboro○ 695 .... B6
05658 Marshfield○ 1,267 .... C3
05658 Marshfield 301 .... C3
†05701 Mendon○ 1,056 .... B4
05753 Middlebury○ 7,574 .... A3
05753 Middlebury⊙ 5,591 .... A3
†05602 Middlesex○ 1,235 .... B3
05757 Middletown Springs○ 603 .... A5
05468 Milton○ 6,829 .... A2
05468 Milton 1,411 .... A2
05469 Monkton○ 1,201 .... A3
05470 Montgomery○ 681 .... B2
05471 Montgomery Center 400 .... B2
05602 Montpelier (cap.)⊙ 8,241 .... B3
05660 Moretown○ 1,221 .... B3
05853 Morgan○ 460 .... D2
†05661 Morristown○ 4,448 .... B2
05661 Morrisville 2,074 .... B2
05758 Mount Holly○ 938 .... B5
†05739 Mount Tabor○ 211 .... B5
†05871 Newark○ 280 .... D2
05051 Newbury○ 1,699 .... C3
05051 Newbury 425 .... C3
05345 Newfane○ 1,129 .... B6
05345 Newfane⊙ 119 .... B6
05472 New Haven○ 1,217 .... A3
05855 Newport○ 1,319 .... C2
05855 Newport⊙ 4,756 .... C2
05257 North Bennington 1,685 .... A6
05663 Northfield○ 5,435 .... B3
05663 Northfield 2,033 .... B3
05664 Northfield Falls 600 .... B3
05052 North Hartland 500 .... C4
05474 North Hero 442 .... A2
05665 North Hyde Park 450 .... B2
05053 North Pomfret 400 .... B4
05260 North Pownal 700 .... A6
05150 North Springfield B5
05859 North Troy 717 .... C2
†05101 North Westminster 310 .... B5
05907 Norton○ 184 .... D2
05055 Norwich○ 2,398 .... C4
†05201 Old Bennington 353 .... A6
†05649 Orange○ 752 .... C3
05860 Orleans 983 .... C2
05760 Orwell○ 901 .... A4
†05491 Panton○ 537 .... A3
05761 Pawlet○ 1,244 .... A5
05862 Peacham○ 531 .... C3
05151 Perkinsville 187 .... B5
05152 Peru○ 312 .... B5
05762 Pittsfield○ 396 .... B4
05763 Pittsford○ 2,590 .... A4
05763 Pittsford 666 .... A4
05667 Plainfield○ 1,249 .... C3
05667 Plainfield 599 .... C3
05056 Plymouth○ 405 .... B4
†05067 Pomfret○ 856 .... B4
05058 Post Mills 500 .... C4
05764 Poultney○ 3,196 .... A4
05764 Poultney 1,554 .... A4
05261 Pownal○ 3,269 .... A6
05765 Proctor○ 1,998 .... A4
05153 Proctorsville 481 .... B5
05346 Putney○ 1,850 .... B6
05059 Quechee 900 .... C4
05060 Randolph○ 4,689 .... B4
05060 Randolph 2,217 .... B4
05062 Reading○ 647 .... B5
05350 Readsboro○ 638 .... B6
05350 Readsboro 402 .... B6
05476 Richford○ 2,206 .... B2
05476 Richford 1,471 .... B2
05477 Richmond○ 3,159 .... A3
05477 Richmond 865 .... A3
05766 Ripton○ 327 .... A4
05767 Rochester○ 1,054 .... B4
†05101 Rockingham○ 5,538 .... B5
05669 Roxbury○ 452 .... B3
†05068 Royalton○ 2,100 .... B4
05768 Rupert○ 605 .... A5
05701 Rutland○ 3,300 .... B4
05701 Rutland⊙ 18,436 .... B4
05042 Ryegate○ 1,000 .... C3
05478 Saint Albans○ 3,555 .... A2
05478 Saint Albans⊙ 7,308 .... A2
†05401 Saint George○ 677 .... A2
05819 Saint Johnsbury○ 7,938 .... D3
05819 Saint Johnsbury⊙ 7,150 .... D3
05863 Saint Johnsbury Center 400 .... D3
05769 Salisbury○ 881 .... A4
†05250 Sandgate○ 234 .... A5
05154 Saxtons River 593 .... B5
†05363 Searsburg○ 72 .... A6
05262 Shaftsbury○ 3,001 .... A6
05065 Sharon○ 828 .... C4
05866 Sheffield○ 435 .... C2
05482 Shelburne○ 5,000 .... A3
05483 Sheldon○ 1,618 .... B2
05770 Shoreham○ 972 .... A4
†05738 Shrewsbury○ 866 .... B4
05670 South Barre 1,301 .... B3
05401 South Burlington 10,679 .... A3
05486 South Hero○ 1,188 .... A2
05155 South Londonderry 500 .... B5
05068 South Royalton 700 .... C4
05069 South Ryegate 400 .... C3
05156 Springfield○ 10,190 .... B5
05156 Springfield 5,603 .... B5
05352 Stamford○ 773 .... A6
05487 Starksboro○ 1,336 .... A3
05772 Stockbridge○ 508 .... B4
05672 Stowe○ 2,991 .... B3
05672 Stowe 531 .... B3
05072 Strafford○ 731 .... C4
†05360 Stratton○ 122 .... B5
†05733 Sudbury○ 380 .... A4
†05250 Sunderland○ 768 .... A5
05867 Sutton○ 667 .... C2
05488 Swanton○ 5,141 .... A2
05488 Swanton 2,520 .... A2
05074 Thetford○ 2,188 .... C4
†05773 Tinmouth○ 406 .... A5
05076 Topsham○ 767 .... C3
05353 Townshend○ 849 .... B5
05868 Troy○ 1,498 .... C2
05077 Tunbridge○ 925 .... C4
05489 Underhill○ 2,172 .... B2
05490 Underhill Center 575 .... B2
05491 Vergennes 2,273 .... A3
05354 Vernon○ 1,175 .... B6
05079 Vershire○ 442 .... C4
05673 Waitsfield○ 1,300 .... B3
†05873 Walden○ 575 .... C3
05773 Wallingford○ 1,893 .... B5
05773 Wallingford 1,141 .... B5
†05491 Waltham○ 394 .... A3
05355 Wardsboro○ 505 .... B5
05674 Warren○ 956 .... B3
05675 Washington○ 855 .... C3
05676 Waterbury○ 4,465 .... B3
05676 Waterbury 1,892 .... B3
05492 Waterville○ 470 .... B2
05678 Websterville 700 .... B3
05774 Wells○ 815 .... A5
05081 Wells River 396 .... C3
05301 West Brattleboro 2,795 .... B6
05871 West Burke 338 .... C2
05356 West Dover 550 .... B6
05083 West Fairlee○ 427 .... C4
05874 Westfield○ 418 .... C2
05494 Westford○ 1,413 .... A2
05875 West Glover C2
†05743 West Haven○ 253 .... A4
05158 Westminster○ 2,493 .... C5
05158 Westminster 319 .... C5
†05860 Westmore○ 257 .... C2
05161 Weston○ 627 .... B5
05777 West Rutland○ 2,351 .... A4
05777 West Rutland 2,169 .... A4
05359 West Townshend 500 .... B5
†05753 Weybridge○ 667 .... A3
†05851 Wheelock○ 444 .... C2
05001 White River Junction 2,582 .... C4
05778 Whiting○ 379 .... A4
05361 Whitingham○ 1,043 .... B6
05088 Wilder 1,461 .... C4
05679 Williamstown○ 2,284 .... B3
05495 Williston○ 3,843 .... A3
05363 Wilmington○ 1,808 .... B6
†05359 Windham○ 223 .... B5
05089 Windsor○ 4,084 .... C5
05089 Windsor 3,478 .... C5
05404 Winooski 6,318 .... A2
05680 Wolcott○ 986 .... C2
05681 Woodbury○ 573 .... C3
†05201 Woodford○ 314 .... A6
05091 Woodstock○ 3,214 .... B4
05091 Woodstock⊙ 1,178 .... B4
05682 Worcester○ 727 .... B3

OTHER FEATURES

Abraham (mt.) B3
Arrowhead Mountain (lake) A2
Ascutney (mt.) C5
Bald (mt.) D2
Barton (riv.) C2
Batten Kill (riv.) A5
Belvidere (mt.) B2
Black (riv.) B5
Black (riv.) C2
Bloodroot (mt.) B4
Bolton (mt.) B3
Bomoseen (lake) A4
Brandon Gap (pass) B4
Bread Loaf (mt.) A3
Bromley (mt.) B5
Brown's (riv.) A2
Burke (mt.) D2
Camels Hump (mt.) B3
Carmi (lake) B2
Caspian (lake) C2
Champlain (lake) A2
Chittenden (res.) B4
Clyde (riv.) C2
Comerford (dam) D3
Connecticut (riv.) C4
Crystal (lake) C2
Dorset (peak) A5
Dunmore (lake) A4
Echo (lake) D2
Ellen (mt.) B3
Equinox (mt.) A5
Fairfield (pond) A2
Glastenbury (mt.) A6
Gore (mt.) D2
Green (mts.) B4
Green River (res.) B2
Groton (lake) C3
Hardwick (lake) C2
Harriman (res.) B6
Harveys (lake) C3
Haystack (mt.) B6
Hoosic (riv.) A6
Hortonia (lake) A4
Hunger (mt.) B3
Iroquois (lake) A3
Island (pond) D2
Jay (peak) B2
Joes (brook) C3
Killington (peak) B4
Lamoille (riv.) A2
Lewis (creek) A3
Lincoln Gap (pass) B3
Little (riv.) B3
Mad (riv.) B3
Maidstone (lake) D2
Mansfield (mt.) B2
Memphremagog (lake) C1
Mettawee (riv.) A5
Middlebury Gap (pass) B4
Mill (riv.) B4
Missisquoi (riv.) B2
Mollys Falls (pond) C3
Moore (dam) D3
Moore (res.) D3
Moose (riv.) D2
Norton (pond) D2
Nulhegan (riv.) D2
Ottauquechee (riv.) B4
Otter (creek) A3
Passumpsic (riv.) D2
Pico (peak) B4
Poultney (riv.) A4
Saint Catherine (lake) A5
Salem (lake) C2
Seymour (lake) D2
Shelburne (pond) A3
Smugglers Notch (pass) B2
Snow (mt.) B6
Somerset (res.) A5
Spruce (mt.) C3
Stratton (mt.) B5
Tabor (mt.) B5
Trout (riv.) B2
Waits (riv.) C3
Waterbury (res.) B3
Wells (riv.) C3
West (riv.) B5
White (riv.) C4
White Face (mt.) B2
Wilder (dam) C4
Willoughby (lake) D2
Winooski (riv.) B3

⊙County seat.
‡Population of metropolitan area.
○Population of town or township.
† Zip of nearest p.o. * Multiple zips

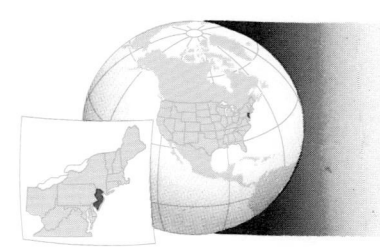

AREA 7,787 sq. mi. (20,168 sq. km.)
POPULATION 7,364,823
CAPITAL Trenton
LARGEST CITY Newark
HIGHEST POINT High Point 1,803 ft. (550 m.)
SETTLED IN 1617
ADMITTED TO UNION December 18, 1787
POPULAR NAME Garden State
STATE FLOWER Purple Violet
STATE BIRD Eastern Goldfinch

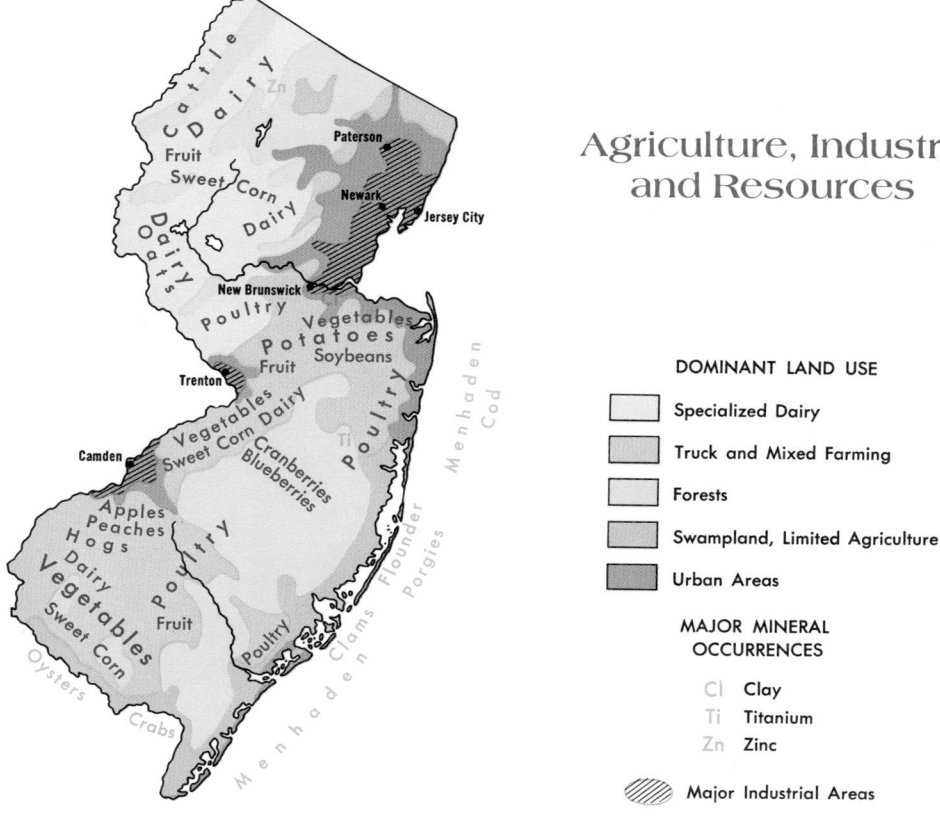

Agriculture, Industry and Resources

DOMINANT LAND USE

- Specialized Dairy
- Truck and Mixed Farming
- Forests
- Swampland, Limited Agriculture
- Urban Areas

MAJOR MINERAL OCCURRENCES

- Cl   Clay
- Ti   Titanium
- Zn   Zinc

Major Industrial Areas

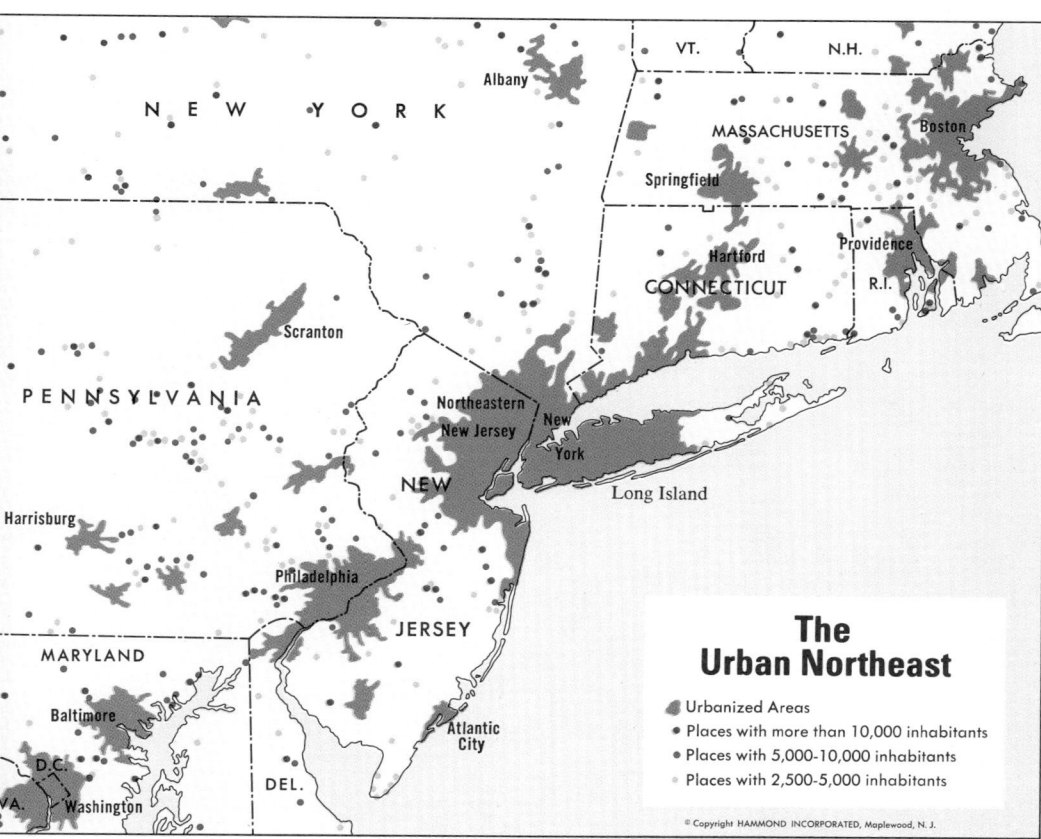

The Urban Northeast

- Urbanized Areas
- ● Places with more than 10,000 inhabitants
- ● Places with 5,000-10,000 inhabitants
- · Places with 2,500-5,000 inhabitants

© Copyright HAMMOND INCORPORATED, Maplewood, N. J.

COUNTIES

Atlantic 194,119		D5
Bergen 845,385		E2
Burlington 362,542		D4
Camden 471,650		D4
Cape May 82,266		D5
Cumberland 132,866		C5
Essex 851,116		E2
Gloucester 199,917		C4
Hudson 556,972		E2
Hunterdon 87,361		D2
Mercer 307,863		D3
Middlesex 595,893		E3
Monmouth 503,173		E3
Morris 407,630		D2
Ocean 346,038		E4
Passaic 447,585		E1
Salem 64,676		C4
Somerset 203,129		D2
Sussex 116,119		D1
Union 504,094		E2
Warren 84,429		C2

CITIES and TOWNS

Zip	Name/Pop.	Key
08201	Absecon 6,859	D5
07820	Allamuchy 600	D2
07401	Allendale 5,901	B1
07711	Allenhurst 912	F3
08501	Allentown 1,962	D3
08720	Allenwood	E3
08001	Alloway 1,370	C4
08865	Alpha 2,644	C2
07620	Alpine 1,549	C1
07821	Andover 892	D2
08801	Annandale 1,040	D2
07712	Asbury Park 17,015	F3
	Asbury Park-Long Branch‡ 503,173	F3
†08033	Ashland	B3
08004	Atco	D4
*08401	Atlantic City 40,199	E5
	Atlantic City‡ 194,119	E5
07716	Atlantic Highlands 4,950	F3
08106	Audubon 9,533	B3
†08106	Audubon Park 1,274	B3
08202	Avalon 2,162	D5
07001	Avenel	E2
07717	Avon By The Sea 2,337	E3
08005	Barnegat 1,012	E4
08006	Barnegat Light 619	E4
08007	Barrington 7,418	B3
07920	Basking Ridge	D2
08742	Bay Head 1,340	E3
07002	Bayonne 65,047	B2
08008	Beach Haven 1,714	E4
08722	Beachwood 7,687	E4
07921	Bedminster 2,469	D2
08502	Belle Mead	D2
07109	Belleville 35,367	B2
08031	Bellmawr 13,721	B3
07719	Belmar 6,771	E3
07823	Belvidere⊙ 2,475	C2
07621	Bergenfield 25,568	C1
07922	Berkeley Heights⊙ 12,549	E2
08009	Berlin 5,786	D4
07924	Bernardsville 6,715	D2
08010	Beverly 2,919	D3
08012	Blackwood 5,219	C4
07825	Blairstown⊙ 4,360	C2
07003	Bloomfield 47,792	B2
07403	Bloomingdale 7,867	E1
08804	Bloomsbury 864	C2
07603	Bogota 8,344	B2
07005	Boonton 8,620	E2
08505	Bordentown 4,441	D3
08805	Bound Brook 9,710	D2
07720	Bradley Beach 4,772	F3
07826	Branchville 870	D1
08723	Breton Woods	E3
08723	Brick⊙ 53,629	E3
08014	Bridgeport 750	C4
08302	Bridgeton⊙ 18,795	C5
08807	Bridgewater 29,175	D2
08730	Brielle 4,068	E3
08203	Brigantine 8,318	E5
08030	Brooklawn 2,133	B3
08015	Browns Mills 10,568	D4
08310	Buena 3,642	D4
08016	Burlington 10,246	D3
07405	Butler 7,616	E2
07006	Caldwell 7,624	B2
07830	Califon 1,023	D2
*08101	Camden⊙ 84,910	B3
†08701	Candlewood 6,750	E3
08204	Cape May 4,853	D6
08210	Cape May Court House⊙ 3,597	D5
07072	Carlstadt 6,166	B2
08069	Carneys Point 7,574	C4
07008	Carteret 20,598	E2
07009	Cedar Grove⊙ 12,600	B2
†08723	Cedarwood Park	E3

07928 Chatham 8,537		E2
08019 Chatsworth 700		D4
08879 Cheesequake		E3
*08034 Cherry Hill⊙ 68,785		B3
†08089 Chesilhurst 1,590		D4
07930 Chester 1,433		D2
†08505 Chesterfield⊙ 3,867		D3
†08077 Cinnaminson⊙ 16,072		B3
07066 Clark⊙ 16,699		A3
08020 Clarksboro		C4
08510 Clarksburg 800		E3
08312 Clayton 6,013		C4
08021 Clementon 5,764		D4
07010 Cliffside Park 21,464		C2
07721 Cliffwood		E3
*07011 Clifton 74,388		B2
08809 Clinton 1,910		D2
07624 Closter 8,164		C1
08108 Collingswood 15,838		B3
08213 Cologne 800		D4
07722 Colts Neck 950		E3
07832 Columbia 600		C2
08022 Columbus 800		D3
07961 Convent Station		E2
†08270 Corbin City 254		D5
†07821 Cranberry Lake 500		D2
08512 Cranbury 1,255		E3
07016 Cranford 24,573		E2
07626 Cresskill 7,609		C1
08515 Crosswicks 265		D3
07723 Deal 1,952		F3
08023 Deepwater 800		C4
08110 Delair		B3
08075 Delanco 3,730		D3
08075 Delran⊙ 14,811		B3
07627 Demarest 4,963		C1
08214 Dennisville 890		D5
07834 Denville⊙ 14,380		E2
08096 Deptford⊙ 23,473		B4
08317 Dorothy 900		D5
07801 Dover 14,681		D2
07628 Dumont 18,334		C1
08812 Dunellen 6,593		D2
08816 East Brunswick⊙ 37,711		E3
07936 East Hanover⊙ 9,319		E2
07734 East Keansburg		E3
08873 East Millstone 950		D3
†07100 East Newark 1,923		B2
*07017 East Orange 77,690		B2
07073 East Rutherford 7,849		B2
07724 Eatontown 12,703		E3
07020 Edgewater 4,628		C2
†08010 Edgewater Park⊙ 9,273		D3
*08817 Edison⊙ 70,193		E2
08215 Egg Harbor City 4,618		D4
07740 Elberon		F3
*07201 Elizabeth⊙ 106,201		B2
08318 Elmer 1,569		C4
†07407 Elmwood Park 18,377		B2
08204 Elwood 1,538		D4
07630 Emerson 7,793		B1
*07631 Englewood 23,701		C2
07632 Englewood Cliffs 5,698		C2
07726 Englishtown 976		E3
07021 Essex Fells 2,363		B2
08319 Estell Manor 848		D5
08025 Ewan 610		C4
07006 Fairfield⊙ 7,987		A2
07701 Fair Haven 5,679		E3
07410 Fair Lawn 32,229		B1
08320 Fairton 1,107		C5
07022 Fairview 10,519		C2
07023 Fanwood 7,767		E2
07931 Far Hills 677		D2
07727 Farmingdale 1,348		E3
†08505 Fieldsboro 597		D3
07836 Flanders		D2
08822 Flemington⊙ 4,132		D2
08518 Florence-Roebling 7,677		D3
07932 Florham Park 9,359		E2
†08037 Folsom 1,892		D4
08863 Fords		E2
08731 Forked River 900		E4
07024 Fort Lee 32,449		C2
07416 Franklin 4,486		D1
07417 Franklin Lakes 8,769		B1
†08823 Franklin Park⊙ 31,358		D3
08322 Franklinville		C4
07728 Freehold⊙ 10,020		E3
08825 Frenchtown 1,573		C2
07026 Garfield 26,803		B2
07027 Garwood 4,752		E2
08026 Gibbsboro 2,510		B4
08027 Gibbstown		C4
†08753 Gilford Park 6,528		E4
07933 Gillette		E2
08028 Glassboro 14,574		C4
08029 Glendora 5,632		B4
08826 Glen Gardner 834		D2
07028 Glen Ridge 7,855		B2
07452 Glen Rock 11,497		B1
08030 Gloucester City 13,121		B3
07435 Green Pond 800		E1
07935 Green Village 800		D2
08323 Greenwich⊙ 973		C5
08032 Grenloch 700		C4

(continued on following page)

07093 Guttenberg 7,340 .... C2
*07601 Hackensack⊙ 36,039 .... B2
07840 Hackettstown 8,850 .... D2
08033 Haddonfield 12,337 .... B3
08035 Haddon Heights 8,361 .... B3
08036 Hainesport○ 3,236 .... D4
07508 Haledon 6,607 .... B1
07419 Hamburg 1,832 .... D1
08690 Hamilton Square-
Mercerville 25,446 .... D3
08037 Hammonton 12,298 .... D4
08827 Hampton 1,614 .... D2
07640 Harrington Park 4,532 .... C1
07029 Harrison 12,242 .... B2
†08057 Hartford 650 .... D4
08008 Harvey Cedars 363 .... E4
07604 Hasbrouck Heights 12,166 .... B2
07641 Haworth 3,509 .... C1
07507 Hawthorne 18,200 .... B2
07730 Hazlet 23,013 .... E3
08828 Helmetta 955 .... E3
07421 Hewitt 950 .... E1
08829 High Bridge 3,435 .... D2
07422 Highland Lakes 2,888 .... E1
08904 Highland Park 13,396 .... D2
07732 Highlands 5,187 .... F3
08520 Hightstown 4,581 .... D3
07642 Hillsdale 10,495 .... B1
07205 Hillside○ 21,440 .... B2
†08083 Hi-Nella 1,250 .... B4
07030 Hoboken 42,460 .... C2
07423 Ho Ho Kus 4,129 .... B1
07733 Holmdel○ 8,447 .... E3
07843 Hopatcong 15,531 .... D2
07844 Hope 310 .... D2
08525 Hopewell 2,001 .... D3
07731 Howell○ 25,065 .... E3
†07712 Interlaken 1,037 .... E3
07845 Ironia D2
07111 Irvington 61,493 .... B2
08830 Iselin E2
08732 Island Heights 1,575 .... E4
08527 Jackson○ 25,644 .... E3
08831 Jamesburg 4,114 .... E3
*07301 Jersey City⊙ 223,532 .... B2
Jersey City‡ 556,972 .... B2
07734 Keansburg 10,613 .... E3
07032 Kearny 35,735 .... B2
08824 Kendall Park 7,419 .... D3
07033 Kenilworth 8,221 .... E2
07735 Keyport 7,413 .... E3
08528 Kingston D3
07405 Kinnelon 7,770 .... E2
07848 Lafayette 900 .... D1
07034 Lake Hiawatha E2
07849 Lake Hopatcong D2
08733 Lakehurst 2,908 .... E3
†07871 Lake Mohawk 8,498 .... D1
08701 Lakewood 22,863 .... E3
08530 Lambertville 4,044 .... D3
07850 Landing D2
08734 Lanoka Harbor E4
08021 Laurel Springs 2,249 .... B4
08879 Laurence Harbor 6,737 .... E3
08735 Lavallette 2,072 .... E4
08045 Lawnside 3,042 .... B3
08648 Lawrenceville 19,724 .... D3
08833 Lebanon 820 .... D2
07852 Ledgewood D2
08327 Leesburg 700 .... D5
07737 Leonardo E3
07605 Leonia 8,027 .... C2
07938 Liberty Corner D2
07035 Lincoln Park 8,806 .... A1
07738 Lincroft E3
07036 Linden 37,836 .... A3
08021 Lindenwold 18,196 .... B4
08221 Linwood 6,144 .... D5
07424 Little Falls○ 11,496 .... B2
07643 Little Ferry 9,399 .... B2
07739 Little Silver 5,548 .... F3
07039 Livingston○ 28,040 .... E2
07644 Lodi 23,956 .... B2
07740 Long Branch 29,819 .... F3
Long Branch-Asbury Park‡
503,173 .... F3
08403 Longport 1,249 .... D5
07853 Long Valley 1,682 .... D2
08048 Lumberton 600 .... D4
07071 Lyndhurst○ 20,326 .... B2
07939 Lyons D2
07940 Madison 15,357 .... E2
08049 Magnolia 4,881 .... B3
07430 Mahwah○ 12,127 .... E1
08328 Malaga 950 .... C4
08050 Manahawkin 1,469 .... E4
08736 Manasquan 5,354 .... E3
08738 Mantoloking 433 .... E3
08051 Mantua○ 9,193 .... C4
08835 Manville 11,278 .... D2
08052 Maple Shade○ 20,525 .... B3
07040 Maplewood○ 22,950 .... E2
08402 Margate City 9,179 .... E5
07746 Marlboro○ 17,560 .... E3
08053 Marlton 9,411 .... D4
08223 Marmora 650 .... D5
08836 Martinsville D2
07747 Matawan 8,837 .... E3
08330 Mays Landing⊙ 2,054 .... D5
07607 Maywood 9,895 .... B2
07428 McAfee 800 .... D1
†08232 McKee City 950 .... D5
08055 Medford D4
08055 Medford Lakes 4,958 .... D4
07945 Mendham 4,899 .... D2
08837 Menlo Park E2
08619 Mercerville-Hamilton
Square 25,446 .... D3
08109 Merchantville 3,972 .... B3
08840 Metuchen 13,762 .... E2
08846 Middlesex 13,480 .... E2
07748 Middletown○ 62,574 .... E3
07432 Midland Park 7,381 .... B1
08848 Milford 1,368 .... C2
07041 Millburn○ 19,543 .... E2
07946 Millington 975 .... D2
†08876 Millstone 530 .... D2
08850 Milltown 7,136 .... E3
08332 Millville 24,815 .... C5
†07801 Mine Hill○ 3,325 .... D2
08342 Mizpah 900 .... D5
07750 Monmouth Beach 3,318 .... F3
08852 Monmouth Junction 2,579 .... D3
07434 Monroe○ 15,858 .... E3
*07042 Montclair 38,321 .... B2
07645 Montvale 7,318 .... B1
07045 Montville○ 14,290 .... E2
†07070 Moonachie 2,706 .... B2
08057 Moorestown 13,695 .... B3
07950 Morris Plains 5,305 .... D2
07960 Morristown⊙ 16,614 .... D2
07046 Mountain Lakes 4,153 .... E2
07092 Mountainside 7,118 .... E2
07856 Mount Arlington 4,251 .... D2
08059 Mount Ephraim 4,863 .... B3
07970 Mount Freedom D2
08060 Mount Holly 10,818 .... D4
†08054 Mount Laurel○ 17,614 .... D4
†07828 Mount Olive○ 18,748 .... D2
08061 Mount Royal 900 .... C4
08062 Mullica Hill 1,050 .... C4
08087 Mystic Islands 4,929 .... E4
08063 National Park 3,552 .... B3
07752 Navesink E3
07753 Neptune○ 28,366 .... E3
07753 Neptune City 5,276 .... E3
07857 Netcong 3,557 .... D2
*07101 Newark⊙ 329,248 .... B2
Newark‡ 1,965,304 .... B2
*08901 New Brunswick⊙ 41,442 .... E3
New Brunswick-Perth
Amboy-Sayreville‡
595,893 .... E3
08533 New Egypt 2,111 .... E3
08344 Newfield 1,563 .... D4
07435 Newfoundland 900 .... D1
08224 New Gretna 800 .... E4
07646 New Milford 16,876 .... B1
07974 New Providence 12,426 .... E2
07860 Newton⊙ 7,748 .... D1
08346 Newtonville 950 .... D4
07976 New Vernon D2
07032 North Arlington 16,587 .... B2
07047 North Bergen○ 47,019 .... B2
08876 North Branch 610 .... D2
08902 North Brunswick○ 22,220 .... D3
†07006 North Caldwell 5,832 .... B2
08204 North Cape May 4,029 .... C6
08225 Northfield 7,795 .... D5
07508 North Haledon 8,177 .... B1
07060 North Plainfield 19,108 .... E2
07647 Northvale 5,046 .... F1
08260 North Wildwood 4,714 .... D6
07648 Norwood 4,413 .... C1
07110 Nutley 28,998 .... B2
07755 Oakhurst E3
07436 Oakland 13,443 .... B1
08107 Oaklyn 4,223 .... B3
08226 Ocean City 13,949 .... D5
08740 Ocean Gate 1,385 .... E4
07756 Ocean Grove F3
07757 Oceanport 5,888 .... F3
07439 Ogdensburg 2,737 .... D1
08857 Old Bridge 21,815 .... E3
07675 Old Tappan 4,168 .... C1
07649 Oradell 8,658 .... B1
*07050 Orange 31,136 .... B2
08723 Osbornsville E3
07863 Oxford 1,587 .... C2
07470 Packanack Lake B1
07650 Palisades Park 13,732 .... C2
08065 Palmyra 7,085 .... B3
07652 Paramus 26,474 .... B1
07656 Park Ridge 8,515 .... B1
07054 Parsippany-Troy
Hills○ 49,868 .... E2
07055 Passaic 52,463 .... E2
*07501 Paterson⊙ 137,970 .... B2
Paterson-Clifton-Passaic‡
447,585 .... B2
08066 Paulsboro 6,944 .... C4
07977 Peapack-Gladstone 2,038 .... D2
08067 Pedricktown C4
08068 Pemberton 1,198 .... D4
08534 Pennington 2,109 .... D3
08110 Pennsauken○ 33,775 .... B3
08069 Penns Grove 5,760 .... C4
08070 Pennsville 12,467 .... C4
07440 Pequannock○ 13,776 .... B1
*08861 Perth Amboy 38,951 .... E2
08865 Phillipsburg 16,647 .... C2
08741 Pine Beach 1,796 .... E4
07058 Pine Brook E2
08021 Pine Hill 8,684 .... D4
08854 Piscataway○ 42,223 .... D2
08071 Pitman 9,744 .... C4
*07060 Plainfield 45,555 .... E2
08536 Plainsboro D3
08232 Pleasantville 13,435 .... D5
08742 Point Pleasant 17,747 .... E3
08742 Point Pleasant Beach
5,415 .... E3
08240 Pomona 2,358 .... D5
07442 Pompton Lakes 10,660 .... A1
07444 Pompton Plains B1
07758 Port Monmouth E3
†07850 Port Morris 616 .... D2
07865 Port Murray 250 .... D2
08349 Port Norris 1,730 .... C5
08241 Port Republic 837 .... D4
08540 Princeton 12,035 .... D3
08550 Princeton Junction 2,419 .... D3
†07885 Prospect Park 5,142 .... B1
08072 Quinton 750 .... C4
*07065 Rahway 26,723 .... E2
†08054 Ramblewood 6,475 .... D4
07446 Ramsey 12,899 .... B1
†07801 Randolph○ 17,828 .... D2
08869 Raritan 6,128 .... D2
07701 Red Bank 12,031 .... E3
07657 Ridgefield 10,294 .... B2
07660 Ridgefield Park 12,738 .... B2
*07450 Ridgewood 25,208 .... B1
08551 Ringoes 682 .... D3
07456 Ringwood 12,625 .... E1
08242 Rio Grande 2,016 .... D5
07457 Riverdale 2,530 .... A1
07661 River Edge 11,111 .... B1
08075 Riverside○ 7,941 .... B3
08077 Riverton 3,068 .... B3
07675 River Vale○ 9,489 .... B1
07662 Rochelle Park○ 5,603 .... B2
07866 Rockaway 6,852 .... D2
07647 Rockleigh 192 .... C1
08553 Rocky Hill 717 .... D3
08554 Roebling-Florence 7,677 .... D3
08555 Roosevelt 835 .... E3
07068 Roseland 5,330 .... A2
07203 Roselle 20,641 .... B2
07204 Roselle Park 13,377 .... A2
08352 Rosenhayn 950 .... C5
†07876 Roxbury○ 18,878 .... D2
07760 Rumson 7,623 .... F3
08078 Runnemede 9,461 .... B3
*07070 Rutherford 19,068 .... B2
07662 Saddle Brook○ 14,084 .... B1
07458 Saddle River 2,763 .... B1
08079 Salem⊙ 6,959 .... C4
08872 Sayreville 29,969 .... E3
07076 Scotch Plains○ 20,774 .... E2
07760 Sea Bright 1,812 .... F3
08302 Seabrook 1,411 .... C5
08750 Sea Girt 2,650 .... E3
08243 Sea Isle City 2,644 .... D5
08751 Seaside Heights 1,802 .... E4
08752 Seaside Park 1,795 .... E4
07094 Secaucus 13,719 .... B2
07077 Sewaren E2
08080 Sewell C4
08353 Shiloh 604 .... C5
08008 Ship Bottom 1,427 .... E4
07078 Short Hills E2
07701 Shrewsbury 2,962 .... E3
08081 Sicklerville D4
08558 Skillman D3
08201 Smithville 70 .... E5
08083 Somerdale 5,900 .... B4
08244 Somers Point 10,330 .... D5
08876 Somerville⊙ 11,973 .... D2
08879 South Amboy 8,322 .... E3
†07719 South Belmar 1,566 .... E3
08880 South Bound Brook 4,331 .... E2
†08852 South Brunswick○ 17,127 .... E3
07079 South Orange○ 15,864 .... A2
07080 South Plainfield 20,521 .... E2
08882 South River 14,361 .... E3
08753 South Toms River 3,954 .... E4
07871 Sparta○ 13,333 .... D1
08884 Spotswood 7,840 .... E3
07081 Springfield○ 13,955 .... E2
07762 Spring Lake 4,215 .... F3
†07762 Spring Lake Heights 5,424 .... E3
07874 Stanhope 3,638 .... D2
08886 Stewartsville 950 .... C2
07980 Stirling E2
07460 Stockholm D1
08559 Stockton 643 .... D3
08247 Stone Harbor 1,187 .... D5
08084 Stratford 8,005 .... B4
†07747 Strathmore E3
07876 Succasunna 10,931 .... D2
07901 Summit 21,071 .... E2
08008 Surf City 1,571 .... E4
07461 Sussex 2,418 .... D1
08085 Swedesboro 2,031 .... C4
07878 Tabor E2
07666 Teaneck○ 39,007 .... B2
07670 Tenafly 13,552 .... C1
07608 Teterboro 19 .... B2
08086 Thorofare B4
08887 Three Bridges 750 .... D2
07724 Tinton Falls 7,740 .... E3
08753 Toms River⊙ 7,465 .... E4
07512 Totowa 11,448 .... B1
07082 Towaco E2
*08601 Trenton (cap.)⊙ 92,124 .... D3
Trenton‡ 307,863 .... D3
08087 Tuckerton 2,472 .... E4
07083 Union○ 50,184 .... A2
07735 Union Beach 6,354 .... E3
07087 Union City 55,593 .... C2
†07421 Upper Greenwood
Lake 2,734 .... E1
†07458 Upper Saddle River 7,958 .... B1
08406 Ventnor City 11,704 .... E5
07462 Vernon 800 .... E1
07044 Verona 14,166 .... B2
08251 Villas 5,909 .... D5
08088 Vincentown 900 .... D4
08360 Vineland 53,753 .... C5
Vineland-Millville-Bridgeton‡
132,866 .... C5
†08043 Voorhees○ 12,919 .... B3
07463 Waldwick 10,802 .... B1
07719 Wall○ 18,952 .... E3
07057 Wallington 10,741 .... B2
†07712 Wanamassa E3
07465 Wanaque 10,025 .... B1
08758 Waretown 1,175 .... E4
†07060 Warren○ 9,805 .... D2
07882 Washington 6,429 .... D2
07060 Watchung 5,290 .... E2
07470 Wayne○ 46,474 .... A1
07087 Weehawken○ 13,168 .... C2
08090 Wenonah 2,303 .... C4
07006 West Caldwell 11,407 .... A2
†08204 West Cape May 1,091 .... D6
08092 West Creek 827 .... E4
†08086 West Deptford○ 18,002 .... B3
*07090 Westfield 30,447 .... E2
07764 West Long Branch 7,380 .... F3
07480 West Milford 950 .... E1
08108 Westmont 15,875 .... B3
07093 West New York 39,194 .... C2
07052 West Orange 39,510 .... A2
07424 West Paterson 11,293 .... B2
08628 West Trenton D3
08093 Westville 4,786 .... B3
†08260 West Wildwood 360 .... D6
07675 Westwood 10,714 .... B1
07885 Wharton 5,485 .... D2

Topography

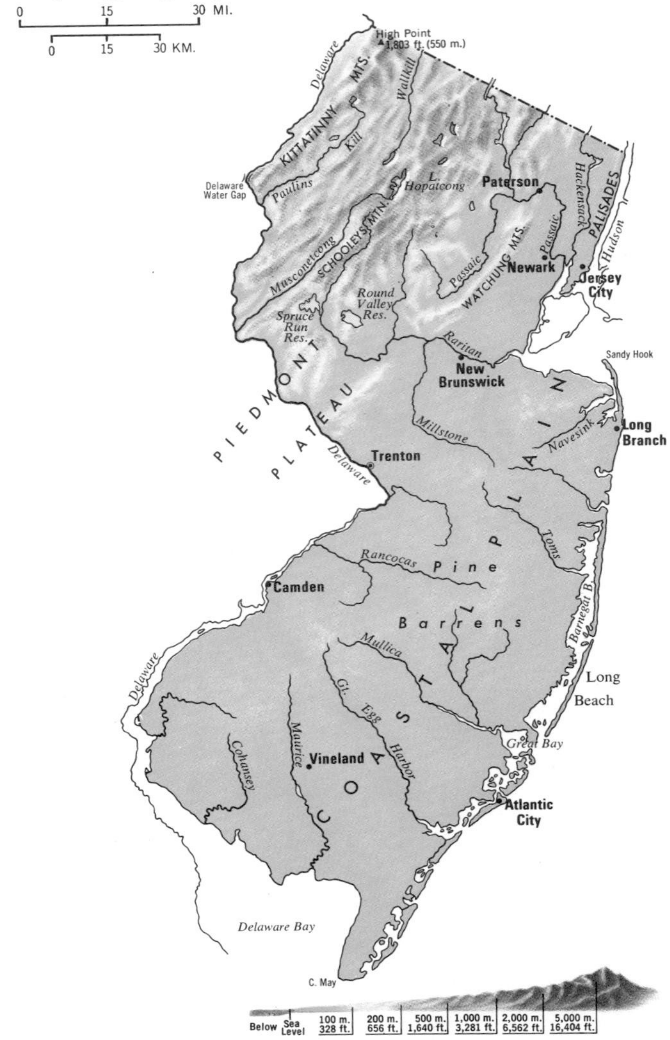

0 15 30 MI.
0 15 30 KM.
High Point 1,803 ft. (550 m.)
Delaware
KITTATINNY MTS.
Kill
Wallkill
Delaware Water Gap
Paulins
L. Hopatcong
Paterson
Hackensack
PALISADES
Hudson
Musconetcong
SCHOOLEYS MTN.
Passaic
Newark
Jersey City
WATCHUNG MTS.
Round Valley Res.
Spruce Run Res.
Raritan
Sandy Hook
New Brunswick
PIEDMONT PLATEAU
Millstone
Navesink
Long Branch
Trenton
Delaware
Toms
Rancocas
Pine
Camden
Barrens
Barnegat B.
Mullica
COASTAL PLAIN
Long Beach
Delaware
Gt. Egg Harbor
Maurice
Cohansey
Vineland
Great Bay
Atlantic City
Delaware Bay
C. May
Below Sea Level
100 m. 328 ft.
200 m. 656 ft.
500 m. 1,640 ft.
1,000 m. 3,281 ft.
2,000 m. 6,562 ft.
5,000 m. 16,404 ft.

07981 Whippany E2
08889 White House Station D2
†07866 White Meadow Lake 8,429 .... D2
08252 Whitesboro 1,583 .... D5
07765 Wickatunk 950 .... E3
08260 Wildwood 4,913 .... D6
08260 Wildwood Crest 4,149 .... D6
08094 Williamstown 5,768 .... D4
08046 Willingboro○ 39,912 .... D3
†07036 Winfield○ 1,785 .... B2
08270 Woodbine 2,809 .... D5
07095 Woodbridge○ 90,074 .... E2
08096 Woodbury⊙ 10,353 .... B4
08097 Woodbury Heights 3,460 .... B4
07675 Woodcliff Lake 5,644 .... B1
†08107 Wood-Lynne 2,578 .... B3
†07885 Woodport D2
07075 Wood-Ridge 7,929 .... B2
08098 Woodstown 3,250 .... C4
08562 Wrightstown 3,031 .... D3
07481 Wyckoff○ 15,500 .... B1
08620 Yardville 9,414 .... D3

OTHER FEATURES

Absecon (inlet) E5
Alloways (creek) C4
Arthur Kill (str.) B3
Atlantic Highlands (ridge) E3
Barnegat (bay) E4
Batsto (riv.) D4
Bayonne Military Ocean Terminal B2
Beach Haven (inlet) E4
Beaver (brook) C2
Ben Davis (pt.) C5
Big Flat (brook) D1
Big Timber (creek) C4
Boonton (res.) E2
Brigantine (inlet) E5
Budd (lake) D2
Canistear (res.) E1
Cedar (creek) E4
Clinton (res.) E1
Cohansey (riv.) C5
Cold Spring (inlet) D6
Cooper (riv.) B3
Corson (inlet) D5
Crosswicks (creek) D3
Culvers (lake) D1
Delaware (bay) C5
Delaware (riv.) D3
Delaware Water Gap Nat'l Rec.
Area C1
Earle Naval Weapons Sta. E3
Echo (lake) E1
Edison Nat'l Hist. Site A2
Egg Island (pt.) C5
Fort Dix 14,297 .... D3
Fort Hancock F3
Fort Monmouth E3
Gateway Nat'l Rec. Area E2
Great (bay) E4
Great Egg Harbor (inlet) E5
Greenwood (lake) E1
Hackensack (riv.) C1
Hereford (inlet) D5
High Point (mt.) D1
Hopatcong (lake) D2
Hudson (riv.) C1
Island (beach) E4
Kill Van Kull (str.) B2
Kittatinny (mts.) D1
Lakehurst Naval Air-Engineering
Center E3
Lamington (riv.) D2
Landing (creek) D4
Little Egg (harb.) E4
Lockatong (creek) C3
Long (beach) E4
Long Beach (isl.) E4
Lower New York (bay) E2
Manasquan (riv.) E3
Manumuskin (riv.) D5
Maurice (riv.) C4
May (cape) C6
McGuire A.F.B. 7,853 .... D3
Metedeconk (riv.) E3
Mill (creek) E4
Millstone (riv.) D3
Mohawk (lake) D1
Morristown Nat'l Hist. Park D2
Mullica (riv.) D4
Musconetcong (riv.) C2
Navesink (riv.) E3
Newark (bay) B2
Oak Ridge (res.) D1
Oldmans (creek) C4
Oradell (res.) B1
Oswego (riv.) E4
Owassa (lake) D1
Palisades C1
Passaic (riv.) E2
Paulins Kill (riv.) D1
Pennsauken (creek) B3
Pequest (riv.) D2
Picatinny Arsenal D2
Pohatcong (creek) C2
Pompton (lake) B1
Raccoon (creek) C4
Ramapo (riv.) E1
Rancocas (creek) D3
Raritan (bay) E3
Raritan (riv.) D2
Ridgeway Branch, Toms (riv.) E3
Round Valley (res.) D2
Saddle (riv.) B1
Salem (riv.) C4
Sandy Hook (spit) F3
Shoal Branch, Wading (riv.) D4
Spruce Run (res.) D2
Statue of Liberty Nat'l Mon. B2
Stony (brook) D3
Stow (creek) C5
Swartswood (lake) D1
Tappan (lake) C1
The Narrows (str.) E2
Toms (riv.) E3
Townsend (inlet) D5
Tuckahoe (riv.) D5
Union (lake) C5
Upper New York (bay) B2
Wading (riv.) D4
Wallkill (riv.) D1
Wanaque (res.) E1
Wawayanda (lake) E1

⊙County seat.
‡Population of metropolitan area.
○Population of town or township.
† Zip of nearest p.o. * Multiple zips.

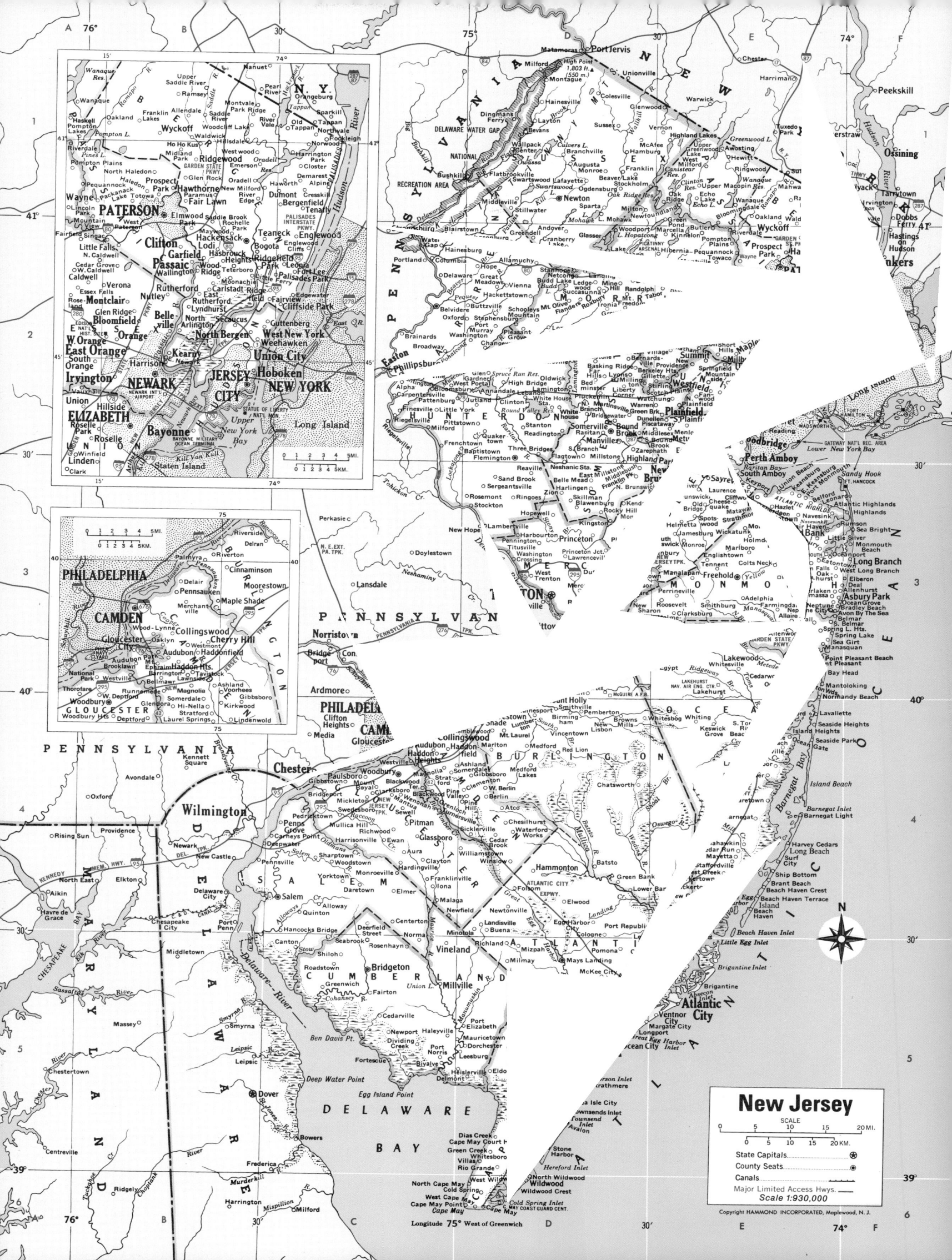

New Jersey

SCALE

0 5 10 15 20 MI.

0 5 10 15 20 KM.

State Capitals ⊛

County Seats ◉

Canals ┄┄┄

Major Limited Access Hwys. ▬▬

Scale 1:930,000

Copyright HAMMOND INCORPORATED, Maplewood, N.J.

Longitude 75° West of Greenwich

COUNTIES

Bernalillo 419,700 ....C4
Catron 2,720 ....A4
Chaves 51,103 ....E5
Cibola B3
Colfax 13,667 ....E2
Curry 42,019 ....F4
De Baca 2,454 ....E4
Dona Ana 96,340 ....C6
Eddy 47,855 ....E6
Grant 26,204 ....A5
Guadalupe 4,496 ....E4
Harding 1,090 ....F3
Hidalgo 6,049 ....A7
Lea 55,993 ....F6
Lincoln 10,997 ....D5

Los Alamos 17,599 ....C3
Luna 15,585 ....B6
McKinley 56,449 ....A3
Mora 4,205 ....E3
Otero 44,665 ....D6
Quay 10,577 ....F3
Rio Arriba 29,282 ....B2
Roosevelt 15,695 ....F4
Sandoval 34,799 ....C3
San Juan 81,433 ....A2
San Miguel
  22,751 ....D3
Santa Fe 75,360 ....C3
Sierra 8,454 ....B5
Socorro 12,566 ....C5
Taos 19,456 ....D2
Torrance 7,491 ....D4
Union 4,725 ....F2
Valencia 61,115 ....C4

CITIES and TOWNS

Zip	Name/Pop.	Key
87510	Abiquiu 500	C2
†87034	Acoma 150	B4
*87034	Acomita (Pueblo of Acoma) 975	B3
88310	Alamogordo⊙ 24,024	C6
*87101	Albuquerque⊙ 331,767 Albuquerque‡ 454,499	C3
87511	Alcalde 975	C2
87001	Algodones 195	C3
88312	Alto 285	D5
87512	Amalia 200	D2
88021	Anthony 3,285	C6
87711	Anton Chico 400	D3
87930	Arrey 367	B6
87930	Arroyo Hondo 400	D2

87514	Arroyo Seco 500	D2
88210	Artesia 10,385	E6
87410	Aztec⊙ 5,512	B2
88023	Bayard 3,036	A6
87002	Belen 5,617	C4
88314	Bent 294	D5
88024	Berino 600	C6
87004	Bernalillo⊙ 3,012	C3
87412	Blanco 200	B2
87413	Bloomfield 4,881	A2
87005	Bluewater 300	A3
87006	Bosque (Bosque Farms) 3,353	C4
87712	Buena Vista 178	D3
87515	Canjilon 380	C2
87516	Canones 300	C2
88316	Capitan 762	D5
88414	Capulin 100	F2
88220	Carlsbad⊙ 25,496	E6

88301	Carrizozo⊙ 1,222	D5
88007	Casa Blanca 560	B4
88113	Causey 81	F5
87518	Cebolla 100	C2
87008	Cedar Crest 600	C3
†87410	Cedar Hill 145	B2
88026	Central 1,968	A6
87010	Cerrillos 500	D2
87519	Cerro 400	D2
87713	Chacon 310	D2
87520	Chama 1,090	C2
88027	Chamberino 700	C6
87521	Chamisal 642	D2
87522	Chimayo 1,993	D3
87714	Cimarron 888	E2
88415	Clayton⊙ 2,968	F2
87715	Cleveland 450	D2
88028	Cliff 600	A6
88317	Cloudcroft 521	D6

88101	Clovis⊙ 31,194	F4
†87041	Cochiti 983	C3
88029	Columbus 414	B7
88416	Conchas Dam 240	E3
87523	Cordova 750	D2
88318	Corona 236	D4
87048	Corrales 2,791	C3
87524	Costilla 400	D2
87313	Crownpoint 1,134	A3
†86504	Crystal 200	A2
87013	Cuba 609	C2
87014	Cubero 300	B4
87821	Datil 150	B5
88030	Deming⊙ 9,964	B6
87933	Derry 175	B6
88418	Des Moines 178	F2
88230	Dexter 882	E5
87527	Dixon 800	D2
88032	Dona Ana 800	C6

New Mexico

88115 Dora 168 .... F5
87528 Dulce 1,648 .... B2
87718 Eagle Nest 202 .... D2
88116 Elida 202 .... F5
87529 El Prado 200 .... D2
87530 El Rito 475 .... C2
87531 Embudo 400 .... C2
88321 Encino 155 .... D4
87532 Espanola 6,803 .... C3
87016 Estancia⊙ 830 .... D4
88231 Eunice 2,970 .... F6
88033 Fairacres 700 .... C6
87401 Farmington 31,222 .... A2
†88041 Fierro 200 .... A6
87415 Flora Vista 500 .... A2
88118 Floyd 146 .... F4
88419 Folsom 73 .... F2
88036 Fort Bayard 400 .... A6
88323 Fort Stanton 80 .... D5
88119 Fort Sumner⊙ 1,421 .... E4
87316 Fort Wingate 800 .... A3
87416 Fruitland 800 .... A2
†87540 Galisteo 125 .... D3
87017 Gallina 420 .... C2
87301 Gallup⊙ 18,167 .... A3
87317 Gamerco 800 .... A3
87936 Garfield 600 .... B6
88038 Gila 350 .... A6
88324 Glencoe 125 .... D5
88039 Glenwood 220 .... A5
87535 Glorieta 300 .... D3
88120 Grady 122 .... F4
87020 Grants 11,439 .... B3
88424 Grenville 39 .... F2
87722 Guadalupita 300 .... D2
88232 Hagerman 936 .... E5
88041 Hanover 300 .... A6
87937 Hatch 1,028 .... B6
87537 Hernandez 500 .... C2
88325 High Rolls-Mountain Park 555 .... D5
88042 Hillsboro 175 .... B6
88240 Hobbs 29,153 .... F6
87723 Holman 400 .... D2
88336 Hondo 425 .... D5
88250 Hope 111 .... E6
87901 Hot Springs (Truth or Consequences)⊙ 5,219 .... B5
88121 House 117 .... F4
88043 Hurley 1,616 .... A6
87022 Isleta 1,246 .... C4
88252 Jal 2,675 .... F6
87023 Jarales 700 .... C4
87024 Jemez Pueblo 1,503 .... C3
87025 Jemez Springs 316 .... C3
87417 Kirtland 2,358 .... A2
87026 Laguna 900 .... B3
87027 La Jara 210 .... B2
88253 Lake Arthur 327 .... E5
88337 La Luz 1,194 .... C6
87539 La Madera 200 .... C2
88044 La Mesa 900 .... C6
87418 La Plata 150 .... A2
88001 Las Cruces⊙ 45,086 .... C6
Las Cruces‡ 96,340 .... C6
87701 Las Vegas⊙ 14,322 .... D3
87725 Ledoux 300 .... D3
87823 Lemitar 800 .... B4
88338 Lincoln 100 .... D5
87543 Llano 325 .... D2
88255 Loco Hills 375 .... F6
88426 Logan 735 .... F3
88045 Lordsburg⊙ 3,195 .... A6
87544 Los Alamos⊙ 11,039 .... C3

87031 Los Lunas⊙ 3,525 .... C4
†87101 Los Ranchos De Albuquerque 2,702 .... C3
88256 Loving 1,355 .... E6
88260 Lovington⊙ 9,727 .... F6
87547 Lumberton 175 .... C2
87824 Luna 200 .... A5
87825 Magdalena 1,022 .... B4
88263 Malaga 300 .... E6
87728 Maxwell 316 .... E2
88339 Mayhill 300 .... D6
†79901 Meadow Vista 3,377 .... C7
88124 Melrose 649 .... F4
87319 Mentmore 315 .... A3
88340 Mescalero 1,259 .... D5
88046 Mesilla 2,029 .... C6
88047 Mesilla Park C6
88048 Mesquite 500 .... C6
87320 Mexican Springs 150 .... A3
87729 Miami 112 .... E2
87021 Milan 3,747 .... B3
88049 Mimbres 300 .... B6
87731 Montezuma 250 .... D3
87939 Monticello 125 .... B5
88265 Monument 300 .... F6
87732 Mora⊙ D3
87035 Moriarty 1,276 .... D4
87733 Mosquero⊙ 197 .... F3
87036 Mountainair 1,170 .... C4
†87501 Nambe 1,017 .... D3
88430 Nara Visa 250 .... F3
87328 Navajo 920 .... A3
†87325 Newcomb 500 .... A2
87038 New Laguna 250 .... B4
88266 Oil Center 236 .... F6
87549 Ojo Caliente 600 .... D2
87735 Ojo Feliz 133 .... E2
87550 Ojo Sarco 380 .... D2
88052 Organ 300 .... C6
87040 Paguate 500 .... B3
87552 Pecos 885 .... D3
87041 Pena Blanca 700 .... C3
87553 Penasco 860 .... D2
87042 Peralta 400 .... C4
88343 Picacho 100 .... E5
88053 Pinos Altos 250 .... A6
87044 Ponderosa 300 .... C3
88130 Portales⊙ 9,940 .... F4
87045 Prewitt 300 .... B3
88432 Puerto de Luna 175 .... E4
87829 Quemado 450 .... A4
87556 Questa 1,202 .... D2
88054 Radium Springs 150 .... B6
87736 Rainsville 350 .... D2
87321 Ramah 574 .... A3
87557 Ranches of Taos 1,411 .... D2
87740 Raton⊙ 8,225 .... E2
87558 Red River 332 .... D2
87322 Rehoboth 200 .... A3
87830 Reserve⊙ 439 .... A5
87560 Ribera 84 .... D3
87940 Rincon 300 .... C6
87124 Rio Rancho 9,985 .... C3
87561 Rodarte 650 .... D2
88201 Roswell⊙ 39,676 .... E5
87562 Rowe 290 .... D3
87743 Roy 381 .... E3
88345 Ruidoso 4,260 .... D5
88346 Ruidoso Downs 949 .... D5
87941 Salem 400 .... B6
87831 San Acacia 286 .... B4
87832 San Antonio 359 .... B5
87564 San Cristobal 350 .... D2
87047 Sandia Park 450 .... C3

†87001 San Felipe Pueblo 1,465 .... C3
†87501 San Ildefonso 232 .... C3
88434 San Jon 341 .... F3
87565 San Jose 150 .... D3
87566 San Juan Pueblo 870 .... C2
88041 San Lorenzo 200 .... B6
87050 San Mateo 200 .... B3
88058 San Miguel 400 .... C6
88348 San Patricio 300 .... D5
87051 San Rafael 300 .... A3
87567 Santa Cruz 754 .... D2
87501 Santa Fe (cap.)⊙ 48,953 .... C3
†88041 Santa Rita 600 .... B6
88435 Santa Rosa⊙ 2,469 .... E4
87052 Santo Domingo Pueblo 2,082 .... C3
87053 San Ysidro 199 .... C3
87745 Sapello 600 .... D3
87055 Seboyeta 125 .... B3
87568 Sena 150 .... D3
87569 Serafina 225 .... D3
87420 Shiprock 7,237 .... A2
88061 Silver City⊙ 9,887 .... A6
87801 Socorro⊙ 7,173 .... C4
†87565 Soham 104 .... D3
87747 Springer 1,657 .... E2
87057 Tajique 145 .... C4
87571 Taos⊙ 3,369 .... D2
†87571 Taos Pueblo 900 .... D2
88267 Tatum 896 .... F5
87574 Tesuque 1,014 .... C3
88135 Texico 958 .... F4
87323 Thoreau 1,099 .... A3
87575 Tierra Amarilla⊙ 850 .... C2
87059 Tijeras 311 .... C3
87324 Toadlena 200 .... A2
87325 Tohatchi 1,011 .... A3
87060 Tome 500 .... C4
87577 Tres Piedras 200 .... D2
87578 Truchas 275 .... D2
†87701 Trujillo 148 .... E3
87901 Truth or Consequences⊙ 5,219 .... B5
88401 Tucumcari⊙ 6,765 .... F3
88352 Tularosa 2,536 .... C5
88003 University Park 4,353 .... C6
87579 Vadito 400 .... D2
88072 Vado 325 .... C6
88072 Valdez 300 .... D2
†87031 Valencia 500 .... C4
87581 Vallecitos 450 .... C2
88073 Vanadium 150 .... A6
88353 Vaughn 737 .... D4
87582 Velarde 950 .... C2
87583 Villanueva 500 .... D3
†88055 Virden 246 .... A6
87752 Wagon Mound 416 .... E2
87421 Waterflow 475 .... A2
87753 Watrous 175 .... D3
87544 White Rock 6,560 .... C3
88002 White Sands Missile Range 3,120 .... C6
87063 Willard 166 .... D4
87942 Williamsburg 433 .... B5
88136 Yeso 200 .... E4
87064 Youngsville 125 .... C2
†87053 Zia Pueblo 500 .... C3
87327 Zuni 5,551 .... A3

OTHER FEATURES

Abiquiu (res.) C2
Alamosa (riv.) B5
Animas (riv.) B1
Avalon (res.) E6
Aztec Ruins Nat'l Mon. A2
Baldy (peak) D3
Bandelier Nat'l Mon. C3
Big Burro (mts.) A6
Black (mt.) A6
Black (range) B5
Blanco (creek) F4
Bluewater (creek) B4
Bluewater (creek) D6
Bluewater (lake) A3
Boulder (lake) C2
Brazos (peak) C2
Burford (lake) C2
Caballo (res.) B6
Canadian (riv.) F3
Cannon A.F.B. 3,798 .... F4
Canyon Blanco (creek) B2
Capitan (mts.) D5
Capitan (peak) D5
Capulin Mountain Nat'l Mon. E2
Carlsbad Caverns Nat'l Park E6
Carrizo (creek) F2
Chaco (mesa) B3
Chaco (riv.) A2
Chaco Culture Nat'l Hist. Park B2
Chico Arroyo (creek) B3
Chivato (mesa) B3
Chupadera (mesa) C5
Chuska (mts.) A2
Cimarron (riv.) E2
Colorado, Arroyo (riv.) B4
Compañero, Arroyo (creek) B2
Conchas (lake) E3
Conchas (riv.) E3
Cookes (range) B6
Corrumpa (creek) F2
Costilla (peak) D2
Cuchillo Negro (creek) B5
Cuervo (creek) E3
Dark Canyon (creek) E6
Datil (mts.) B4
Dry Cimarron (riv.) F2
Eagle Nest (lake) D2
Elephant Butte (res.) B5
El Morro Nat'l Mon. A3
El Rito (riv.) C2
Fifteenmile Arroyo (creek) D4
Florida (mts.) B7
Fort Bliss Mil. Res. C6
Fort Union Nat'l Mon. E3
Gallinas (mts.) B4
Gallinas (riv.) E3
Gila (riv.) A6
Gila Cliff Dwellings Nat'l Mon. A5
Grouse (mt.) A5
Guadalupe (mts.) D6
Hatchet (mts.) A7
Holloman A.F.B. 7,245 .... C6
Hueco (mts.) D6
Jemez (riv.) C3
Jemez Canyon (res.) C3
Jicarilla Ind. Res. B2
Jornada del Muerto (valley) C5
Kirtland A.F.B. C3
Ladron (mts.) B4
La Plata (riv.) A1
Largo, Cañon (creek) B2
Las Animas (creek) B5
Llano Estacado (Staked) (plain) F5
Lucero (lake) C6
Macho, Arroyo del (creek) D5
Magdalena (mts.) B4
Manzano (mts.) C4
Manzano (peak) C4
McMillan (lake) E6
Mescalero (ridge) F6
Mescalero (valley) F5
Mescalero Apache Ind. Res. D5
Mimbres (mts.) B6
Mimbres (riv.) B6
Mogollon (mts.) A5
Mogollon Baldy (peak) A5
Montosa (mesa) E3
Mora (riv.) E3
Nacimiento (mts.) C3
Nacimiento (peak) C2
Navajo (res.) B2
Navajo Ind. Res. A2
North Truchas (peak) D3
Ocate (creek) E2
O'Keeffe Nat'l Hist. Site C2
Oscura (mts.) C5
Osha (peak) D3
Padilla (creek) D5
Pajarito (creek) A2
Pecos (riv.) E5
Pecos Nat'l Mon. D3
Peloncillo (mts.) A6
Perro (mts.) D4
Pinos, Rio de los (riv.) B2
Pintada Arroyo (creek) E4
Playas (lake) A7
Potrillo (mts.) B7
Pueblo Ind. Res. B4
Pueblo Ind. Res. D3
Pueblo Ind. Res. C4
Pueblo Ind. Res. D2
Puerco (riv.) A3
Red Bluff (lake) E7
Revuelto (creek) F3
Rio Brazos (riv.) C2
Rio Chama (riv.) C2
Rio Felix (riv.) E5
Rio Grande (riv.) C5
Rio Hondo (riv.) E5
Rio Penasco (riv.) E6
Rio Puerco (riv.) C4
Rio Salado (riv.) B4
Rocky (mts.) C1
Sacramento (mts.) D6
Salinas Nat'l Mon. C4
Salt (creek) E5
Salt (lake) F4
San Agustin (plains) B5
San Andres (mts.) C6
San Antonio (peak) C2
Sandia (peak) C3
San Francisco (riv.) A5
Sangre de Cristo (mts.) D3
San Jose (riv.) B3
San Juan (riv.) B2
San Mateo (mts.) B5
Seven Rivers (riv.) E6
Ship Rock (peak) A2
Sierra Blanca (peak) D5
Staked (Llano Estacado) (plain) F5
Sumner (lake) E4
Taylor (mt.) B3
Tecolote (creek) D3
Tequesquite (creek) E2
Thompson (peak) D3
Tierra Blanca (creek) B6
Tramperos (creek) F2
Tularosa (valley) C6
Ute (creek) F3
Ute (peak) D2
Ute (res.) F3
Ute Mountain Ind. Res. A1
Vermejo (riv.) E2
Wheeler (peak) D2
White Sands (des.) C5
White Sands Missile Range C5
White Sands Nat'l Mon. C6
Whitewater Baldy (mt.) A5
Wingate Army Depot A3
Yeso (creek) E4
Zuni (mts.) A3
Zuni (riv.) A3
Zuni Ind. Res. A3

⊙County seat.
‡Population of metropolitan area.
† Zip of nearest p.o. * Multiple zips.

AREA 121,593 sq. mi. (314,926 sq. km.)
POPULATION 1,302,981
CAPITAL Santa Fe
LARGEST CITY Albuquerque
HIGHEST POINT Wheeler Pk. 13,161 ft. (4011 m.)
SETTLED IN 1605
ADMITTED TO UNION January 6, 1912
POPULAR NAME Land of Enchantment
STATE FLOWER Yucca
STATE BIRD Road Runner

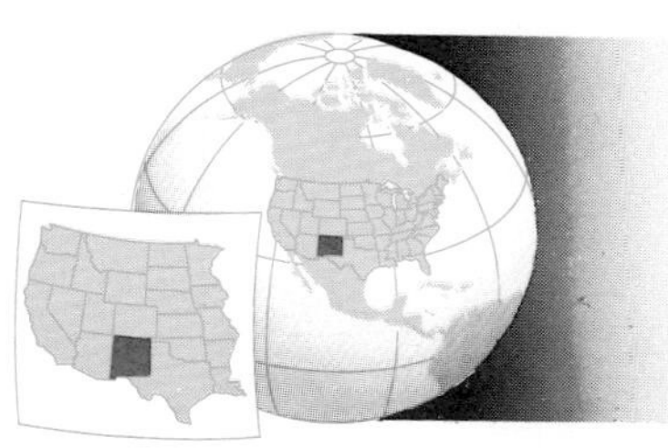

Topography

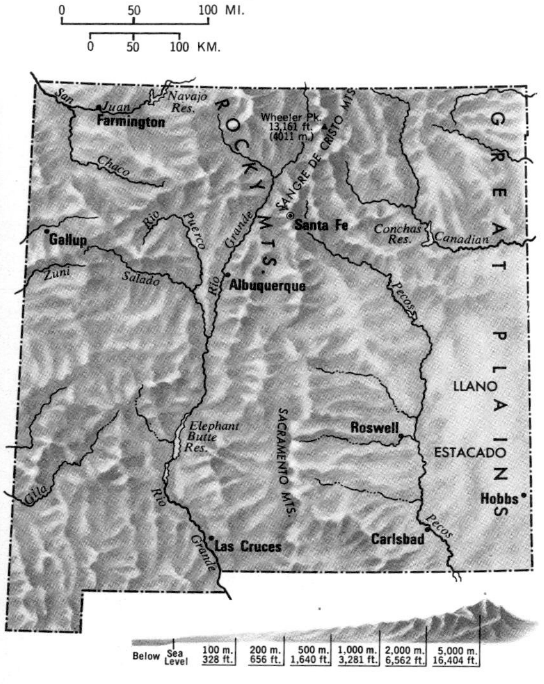
0 50 100 MI.
0 50 100 KM.
San Juan
Navajo Res.
Farmington
Wheeler Pk. 13,161 ft. (4011 m.)
ROCKY MTS.
SANGRE DE CRISTO MTS.
GREAT PLAINS
Chaco
Puerco
Rio Grande
Santa Fe
Conchas Res.
Canadian
Gallup
Zuni
Salado
Albuquerque
Pecos
LLANO
ESTACADO
Elephant Butte Res.
SACRAMENTO MTS.
Roswell
Gila
Hobbs
Las Cruces
Carlsbad
Below Sea Level
100 m. 328 ft.
200 m. 656 ft.
500 m. 1,640 ft.
1,000 m. 3,281 ft.
2,000 m. 6,562 ft.
5,000 m. 16,404 ft.

Agriculture, Industry and Resources

DOMINANT LAND USE

- Wheat, Grain Sorghums, Range Livestock
- General Farming, Livestock, Special Crops
- General Farming, Livestock, Cash Grain
- Dry Beans, General Farming
- Cotton, Forest Products
- Range Livestock
- Forests
- Nonagricultural Land

MAJOR MINERAL OCCURRENCES

Ag Silver
Au Gold
C Coal
Cu Copper
G Natural Gas
Gp Gypsum
K Potash
Mo Molybdenum
Mr Marble
Na Salt
O Petroleum
Pb Lead
U Uranium
V Vanadium
Zn Zinc
Water Power

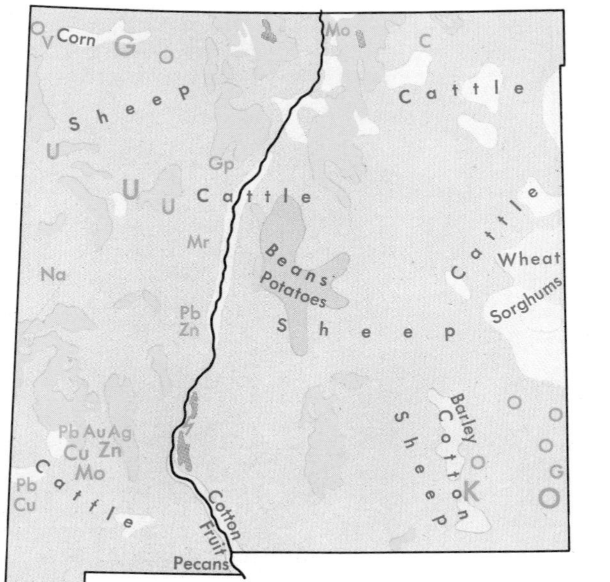
Corn
Sheep
Cattle
Wheat
Sorghums
Beans
Potatoes
Barley
Cotton
Fruit
Pecans
Pb Au Ag
Cu Zn
Mo

New York

SCALE
5 10 20 30 40 MI.
0 5 10 20 30 40 KM.

State Capitals........⊛
County Seats........⊙
Canals........
Major Limited Access Hwys.____

Scale 1:1,920,000

COUNTIES

Albany 285,909	M5	
Allegany 51,742	D6	
Bronx 1,168,972	N9	
Broome 213,648	J6	
Cattaraugus 85,697	C6	
Cayuga 79,894	G4	
Chautauqua 146,925	B6	
Chemung 97,656	G6	
Chenango 49,344	J6	
Clinton 80,750	N1	
Columbia 59,487	N6	
Cortland 48,820	H5	
Delaware 46,824	K6	
Dutchess 245,055	N7	
Erie 1,015,472	C5	
Essex 36,176	M2	
Franklin 44,929	M1	
Fulton 55,153	M4	
Genesee 59,400	D5	
Greene 40,861	M6	
Hamilton 5,034	L3	
Herkimer 66,714	L4	
Jefferson 88,151	J2	
Kings 2,230,936	N9	
Lewis 25,035	K3	
Livingston 57,006	E5	
Madison 65,150	J5	
Monroe 702,238	E4	
Montgomery 53,439	M5	
Nassau 1,321,582	N9	
New York 1,428,285	M9	
Niagara 227,354	C4	
Oneida 253,466	J4	
Onondaga 463,920	H5	
Ontario 88,909	F5	

Orange 259,603	M8	
Orleans 38,496	D4	
Oswego 113,901	H4	
Otsego 59,075	K5	
Putnam 77,193	N8	
Queens 1,891,325	N9	
Rensselaer 151,966	O5	
Richmond 352,121	M9	
Rockland 259,530	M8	
Saint Lawrence 114,254	K2	
Saratoga 153,759	N4	
Schenectady 149,946	M5	
Schoharie 29,710	M5	
Schuyler 17,686	G6	
Seneca 33,733	G5	
Steuben 99,217	F6	
Suffolk 1,284,231	P9	
Sullivan 65,155	L7	
Tioga 49,812	H6	
Tompkins 87,085	H6	
Ulster 158,158	M7	
Warren 54,854	N3	
Washington 54,795	O4	
Wayne 84,581	F4	
Westchester 866,599	N8	
Wyoming 39,895	D5	
Yates 21,459	F5	

CITIES and TOWNS

Zip	Name/Pop.	Key
13605	Adams 1,701	J3
14801	Addison 2,028	F6
14001	Akron 2,971	C4
†12201	Albany (cap.) ⊙ 101,727	N5
	Albany-Schenectady-Troy‡	
	795,019	N5
14411	Albion ⊙ 4,897	D4

14004	Alden 2,488	C5
13607	Alexandria Bay 1,265	J2
14802	Alfred 4,967	E6
14706	Allegany 2,078	C6
12009	Altamont 1,292	M5
11930	Amagansett 2,188	R9
11701	Amityville 9,076	O9
12010	Amsterdam 21,872	M5
14006	Angola 2,292	C5
14009	Arcade 2,052	D5
10502	Ardsley 4,183	O6
12603	Arlington 11,305	N7
12015	Athens 1,738	N6
11509	Atlantic Beach 1,775	P7
14011	Attica 2,659	D5
13021	Auburn ⊙ 32,548	G5
13026	Aurora 926	G5
12018	Averill Park 1,337	O5
14414	Avon 3,006	E5
*11702	Babylon 12,388	O9
13733	Bainbridge 1,603	J6
11510	Baldwin 31,630	R7
13027	Baldwinsville 6,446	H4
12020	Ballston Spa⊙ 4,711	N5
14020	Batavia⊙ 16,703	D5
14810	Bath⊙ 6,042	F6
11705	Bayport 9,282	O9
11706	Bay Shore 10,784	O9
11709	Bayville 7,034	R7
12508	Beacon 12,937	N7
11710	Bellmore 18,106	R7
11713	Bellport 2,809	P9
14813	Belmont⊙ 1,024	E6
11714	Bethpage 16,840	R7
14814	Big Flats 2,892	G6
*13901	Binghamton⊙ 55,860	J6
	Binghamton‡ 301,336	J6

13612	Black River 1,384	J3
14219	Blasdell 3,288	C5
14715	Bolivar 1,345	D6
13609	Boonville 2,344	K4
13613	Brasher	
	Falls-Winthrop 1,454	L1
11717	Brentwood 44,321	O9
13029	Brewerton 2,472	H4
10509	Brewster 1,650	N8
11932	Bridgehampton 1,941	R9
†12524	Brinckerhoff 3,030	N7
12025	Broadalbin 1,415	M4
14420	Brockport 9,776	D4
*10401	Bronx	
	(borough) 1,168,972	N9
10708	Bronxville 6,267	O7
*11201	Brooklyn	
	(borough) 2,230,936	N9
†11545	Brookville 3,290	R6
10511	Buchanan 2,041	N8
*14201	Buffalo⊙ 357,870	B5
	Buffalo‡ 1,242,573	B5
12413	Cairo 1,281	M6
14423	Caledonia 2,188	E5
12816	Cambridge 1,820	O4
13316	Camden 2,667	J4
13031	Camillus 1,298	H4
13317	Canajoharie 2,412	L5
14424	Canandaigua⊙ 10,419	F5
13032	Canastota 4,773	J4
14823	Caneadea 2,679	E6
13617	Canton⊙ 7,055	K1
10512	Carmel⊙ 27,948	N8
13619	Carthage 3,643	J3
12033	Castleton-on-Hudson 1,627	N5
12414	Catskill⊙ 4,718	N6
†14850	Cayuga Heights 3,170	H6

13035	Cazenovia 2,599	J5
11516	Cedarhurst 6,162	P7
14720	Celoron 1,405	B6
11720	Centereach 30,136	O9
11934	Center Moriches 5,703	P9
11722	Central Islip 19,734	O9
13036	Central Square 1,418	H4
10917	Central Valley 1,705	M8
12919	Champlain 1,410	N1
12037	Chatham 2,001	N6
14225	Cheektowaga 92,145	C5
12025	Chester 1,910	M8
13037	Chittenango 4,290	J4
14428	Churchville 1,399	E4
14031	Clarence 18,146	C5
13624	Clayton 1,816	H2
†12065	Clifton Park 23,989	N5
14432	Clifton Springs 2,039	F5
13323	Clinton 2,107	J4
14433	Clyde 2,491	G4
12043	Cobleskill 5,272	L5
12047	Cohoes 18,144	N5
10516	Cold Spring 2,161	N8
11724	Cold Spring Harbor 5,336	R6
†12201	Colonie 8,869	N5
11725	Commack 34,719	O9
13326	Cooperstown⊙ 2,342	L5
11726	Copiague 20,132	O9
12822	Corinth 2,702	N4
14830	Corning 12,953	F6
12518	Cornwall On Hudson 3,164	M8
13045	Cortland⊙ 20,138	H5
12051	Coxsackie 2,786	N6
10520	Croton-on-Hudson 6,889	N8
14727	Cuba 1,739	D6
11935	Cutchogue-New	
	Suffolk 2,788	P8
12929	Dannemora 3,770	N1

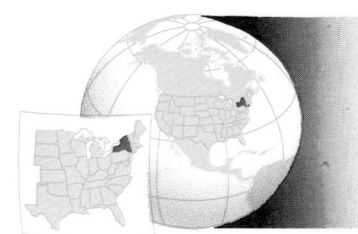

AREA 49,108 sq. mi. (127,190 sq. km.)
POPULATION 17,558,072
CAPITAL Albany
LARGEST CITY New York
HIGHEST POINT Mt. Marcy 5,344 ft. (1629 m.)
SETTLED IN 1614
ADMITTED TO UNION July 26, 1788
POPULAR NAME Empire State
STATE FLOWER Rose
STATE BIRD Bluebird

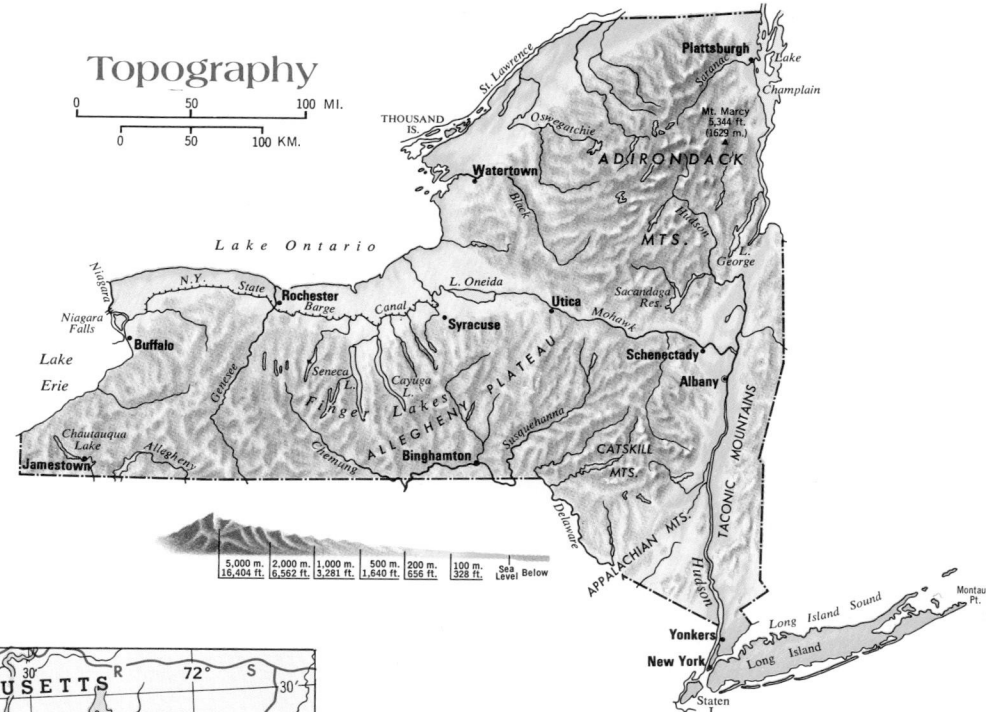

Topography

0   50   100 MI.

0   50   100 KM.

5,000 m. | 2,000 m. | 1,000 m. | 500 m. | 200 m. | 100 m. | Sea
16,404 ft. | 6,562 ft. | 3,281 ft. | 1,640 ft. | 656 ft. | 328 ft. | Level Below

14437 Dansville 4,979	E5	
11729 Deer Park 30,394	O9	
13753 Delhi⊙ 3,374	L6	
12054 Delmar 8,423	N5	
14043 Depew 19,819	C5	
13754 Deposit 1,897	K6	
13214 DeWitt 9,024	H4	
11746 Dix Hills 26,693	O9	
10522 Dobbs Ferry 10,053	O6	
13329 Dolgeville 2,602	L4	
12522 Dover Plains 1,753	O7	
14837 Dundee 1,556	F5	
14048 Dunkirk 15,310	B5	
14052 East Aurora 6,803	C5	
10709 Eastchester 20,305	P6	
11937 East Hampton 1,886	R9	
†11576 East Hills 7,160	R7	
11554 East Meadow 39,317	R7	
11731 East Northport 20,187	O9	
14445 East Rochester 7,596	F4	
11518 East Rockaway 10,917	R7	
13057 East Syracuse 3,412	H4	
14057 Eden 3,000	C5	
14058 Elba 750	D4	
12932 Elizabethtown⊙ 659	N2	
12428 Ellenville 4,405	M7	
14059 Elma 2,459	C5	
*14901 Elmira⊙ 35,327	G6	
Elmira‡ 97,656	G6	
14903 Elmira Heights 4,279	G6	
11003 Elmont 27,592	P7	
10523 Elmsford 3,361	O6	
11731 Elwood 11,847	O9	
13760 Endicott 14,457	H6	
13760 Endwell 13,745	H6	
14450 Fairport 5,970	F4	
†12601 Fairview 5,852	N7	
14733 Falconer 2,656	B6	
11735 Farmingdale 7,946	R7	
13066 Fayetteville 4,709	J4	
†12801 Fernwood 3,640	N4	
12524 Fishkill 1,555	N7	
††11901 Flanders-Riverside 5,400	P9	
*11001 Floral Park 16,805	P7	
10921 Florida 1,947	M8	
12068 Fonda⊙ 1,006	M5	
12937 Fort Covington 1,804	M1	
12828 Fort Edward 3,561	O4	
13339 Fort Plain 2,555	L5	
13340 Frankfort 2,995	K4	
11010 Franklin Square 29,051	R7	
14737 Franklinville 1,887	D6	
14063 Fredonia 11,126	B6	
11520 Freeport 38,272	R7	
14738 Frewsburg 1,908	B6	
14739 Friendship 1,461	D6	
13069 Fulton 13,312	H4	
11530 Garden City 22,927	R7	
14067 Gasport⊙ 1,339	C4	
14454 Geneseo⊙ 6,746	E5	
14456 Geneva 15,133	G5	
11542 Glen Cove 24,618	R6	
12801 Glens Falls 15,897	N4	
Glens Falls‡ 109,649	N4	
12078 Gloversville 17,836	M4	
10526 Golden's Bridge 1,367	N8	
10924 Goshen⊙ 4,874	M8	
13642 Gouverneur 4,285	K2	
14070 Gowanda 2,713	B6	
12832 Granville 2,696	O4	
*11020 Great Neck 9,168	P6	
14616 Greece 16,177	E4	
13778 Greene 1,747	J6	
12183 Green Island 2,696	N5	
11944 Greenport 2,273	P8	
12834 Greenwich 1,955	O4	
10925 Greenwood Lake 2,809	M8	
13073 Groton 2,313	H5	
12835 Hadley-Lake Luzerne 1,988	N4	
12086 Hagaman 1,331	M5	
14075 Hamburg 10,582	C5	
13346 Hamilton 3,725	J5	
11946 Hampton Bays 7,256	R9	
13783 Hancock 1,526	K7	
10528 Harrison 23,046	P6	
10530 Hartsdale 10,216	P6	
10706 Hastings On Hudson 8,573	O6	
11787 Hauppauge 20,960	O9	
10927 Haverstraw 8,800	M8	
10532 Hawthorne 5,010	O6	
*11550 Hempstead 40,404	R7	
13350 Herkimer⊙ 8,383	L4	
11557 Hewlett 6,986	P7	
†11557 Hewlett Harbor 1,331	P7	
*11801 Hicksville 43,245	R7	
12528 Highland 3,967	M7	
10928 Highland Falls 4,187	M8	
10931 Hillburn 926	M8	
*10977 Hillcrest 5,733	K8	
14468 Hilton 4,151	E4	
14080 Holland 1,347	C5	
14470 Holley 1,882	D4	
13077 Homer 3,635	H5	
14472 Honeoye Falls 2,410	F5	
12090 Hoosick Falls 3,609	O5	
12533 Hopewell Junction 1,754	N7	
14843 Hornell 10,234	E6	
14845 Horseheads 7,348	G6	
14744 Houghton 1,604	D6	
12534 Hudson⊙ 7,986	N6	
12839 Hudson Falls⊙ 7,419	O4	
11743 Huntington 21,727	R6	
11746 Huntington Station 28,769	R6	
12443 Hurley 4,892	M7	
12538 Hyde Park 2,550	N6	
13357 Ilion 9,450	K5	
11696 Inwood 8,228	P7	
14617 Irondequoit 57,648	E4	
10533 Irvington 5,774	O6	
11558 Island Park 4,847	R7	

(continued on following page)

11751 Islip 13,438 .... O9
14850 Ithaca⊙ 28,732 .... G6
*11401 Jamaica⊙ N9
14701 Jamestown 35,775 .... B6
11753 Jericho 12,739 .... R6
13790 Johnson City 17,126 .... J6
12095 Johnstown⊙ 9,360 .... M4
13080 Jordan 1,371 .... H4
12944 Keeseville 2,025 .... O2
14271 Kenmore 18,474 .... C5
12446 Kerhonkson 1,646 .... M7
12106 Kinderhook 1,377 .... N6
11754 Kings Park 16,131 .... O9
11024 Kings Point 5,234 .... P6
12401 Kingston⊙ 24,481 .... M7
14218 Lackawanna 22,701 .... B5
10512 Lake Carmel 7,295 .... N8
†14006 Lake Erie Beach 4,625 .... B5
12845 Lake George⊙ 1,047 .... N4
12449 Lake Katrine 2,011 .... M7
12846 Lake Luzerne-Hadley 1,988 N4
12946 Lake Placid 2,490 .... N2
12108 Lake Pleasant⊙ 700 .... M4
11040 Lake Success 2,396 .... P7
14750 Lakewood 3,941 .... B6
14086 Lancaster 13,056 .... C5
14882 Lansing 3,039 .... H5
10538 Larchmont 6,308 .... P7
12110 Latham 11,182 .... N5
†11560 Lattingtown 1,749 .... R6
11559 Lawrence 6,175 .... P7
14482 Le Roy 4,900 .... E5
11756 Levittown 57,045 .... R7
14092 Lewiston 3,326 .... B4
12754 Liberty 4,293 .... L7
14485 Lima 2,025 .... E5
11757 Lindenhurst 26,919 .... O9
13365 Little Falls 6,156 .... L4
14755 Little Valley⊙ 1,203 .... C6
13088 Liverpool 2,849 .... H4
12758 Livingston Manor 1,436 .... L7
†11743 Lloyd Harbor 3,405 .... R6
14094 Lockport⊙ 24,844 .... C4
†11791 Locust Grove 9,670 .... R6
11561 Long Beach 34,073 .... R7
13367 Lowville⊙ 3,364 .... J3
11563 Lynbrook 20,424 .... P7
14489 Lyons⊙ 4,160 .... F4
14502 Macedon 1,400 .... F4
10541 Mahopac 7,681 .... N8
12953 Malone⊙ 7,668 .... M1
11565 Malverne 9,262 .... R7
10543 Mamaroneck 17,616 .... P7
14504 Manchester 1,698 .... F5
11030 Manhasset 8,485 .... P7
*10001 Manhattan (borough) 1,428,285 .... M9
13104 Manlius 5,241 .... J5
13108 Marcellus 1,870 .... H5
12542 Marlboro 2,275 .... M7
11758 Massapequa 24,454 .... R7
11762 Massapequa Park 19,779 .... R7
13662 Massena 12,851 .... L1
11950 Mastic Beach 8,318 .... P9
11952 Mattituck 3,923 .... P9
12543 Maybrook 2,007 .... M8
14757 Mayville⊙ 1,626 .... A6
12118 Mechanicville 5,500 .... N5
14103 Medina 6,392 .... D4
†13021 Melrose Park 2,171 .... G5
11746 Melville 8,139 .... O9
†12201 Menands 4,012 .... N5
11566 Merrick 24,478 .... R7
13114 Mexico 1,621 .... H4
12122 Middleburgh 1,358 .... M5
12550 Middle Hope 3,229 .... M7
14105 Middleport 1,995 .... C4
10940 Middletown 21,454 .... L8
†12020 Milton 2,063 .... N4
11501 Mineola⊙ 20,757 .... R7
13115 Minetto 1,629 .... H4
12956 Mineville-Witherbee 1,925 .... O2
13116 Minoa 3,640 .... H4
13407 Mohawk 2,956 .... L4
10950 Monroe 5,996 .... M8
10952 Monsey 12,380 .... J8
12549 Montgomery 2,316 .... M7
12701 Monticello⊙ 6,306 .... L7
14865 Montour Falls 1,791 .... G6
13118 Moravia 1,582 .... H5
12962 Morrisonville 1,721 .... N1
13408 Morrisville 2,707 .... J5
10549 Mount Kisco 8,025 .... N8
14510 Mount Morris 3,039 .... E5
*10550 Mount Vernon 66,713 .... O7
10954 Nanuet 12,578 .... K8
12123 Nassau 1,285 .... N5
Nassau-Suffolk‡ 2,605,813 R7
14513 Newark 10,017 .... G4
13411 New Berlin 1,392 .... K5
12550 Newburgh 23,438 .... M7
Newburgh-Middletown‡ 259,603 .... M7
10956 New City⊙ 35,859 .... K8
14108 Newfane 3,120 .... C4
13413 New Hartford 2,313 .... K4
11040 New Hyde Park 9,801 .... P7
12561 New Paltz 4,938 .... M7
*10801 New Rochelle 70,794 .... P7
†10901 New Square 1,750 .... K8
12550 New Windsor 7,812 .... N8
*10001 New York⊙ 7,071,639 .... M9
New York‡ 9,119,737 .... M9
13417 New York Mills 3,549 .... K4
*14301 Niagara Falls 71,384 .... C4
†12301 Niskayuna 5,223 .... N5
13667 Norfolk 1,599 .... K1
14110 North Boston 2,743 .... C5
14111 North Collins 1,496 .... C5
11768 Northport 7,651 .... O9
13212 North Syracuse 7,970 .... H4
10591 North Tarrytown 7,994 .... O6
14120 North Tonawanda 35,760 .... C4
12134 Northville 1,304 .... M4
13815 Norwich⊙ 8,082 .... J5
13668 Norwood 1,902 .... L1
10960 Nyack 6,428 .... K8

14125 Oakfield 1,791 .... D4
11572 Oceanside 33,639 .... R7
13669 Ogdensburg 12,375 .... K1
14126 Olcott 1,571 .... C4
14760 Olean 18,207 .... D6
13421 Oneida 10,810 .... J4
13820 Oneonta 14,933 .... K6
14127 Orchard Park 3,671 .... C5
13424 Oriskany 1,680 .... K4
10562 Ossining 20,196 .... N8
13126 Oswego⊙ 19,793 .... G4
14521 Ovid⊙ 666 .... G5
13827 Owego⊙ 4,364 .... H6
13830 Oxford 1,765 .... J6
11771 Oyster Bay 6,497 .... R6
14870 Painted Post 2,196 .... F6
14522 Palmyra 3,729 .... F4
11772 Patchogue 11,291 .... P9
12564 Pawling 1,996 .... N7
10965 Pearl River 15,893 .... K8
10566 Peekskill 18,236 .... N8
10803 Pelham 6,848 .... O7
†10803 Pelham Manor 6,130 .... O7
14527 Penn Yan⊙ 5,242 .... F5
14530 Perry 4,198 .... D5
12972 Peru 1,716 .... N1
14532 Phelps 2,004 .... F5
12565 Philmont 1,539 .... N6
13135 Phoenix 2,357 .... H4
10968 Piermont 2,269 .... K8
12567 Pine Plains 1,303 .... N7
14534 Pittsford 1,568 .... E4
11803 Plainview 28,037 .... R7
12901 Plattsburgh⊙ 21,057 .... O1
10570 Pleasantville 6,749 .... N8
13140 Port Byron 1,400 .... G4
10573 Port Chester 23,565 .... P7
†13901 Port Dickinson 1,974 .... J6
12466 Port Ewen 2,813 .... N7
12974 Port Henry 1,450 .... O2
11777 Port Jefferson 6,731 .... P9
12771 Port Jervis 8,699 .... L8
11050 Port Washington 14,521 .... R6
13676 Potsdam 10,635 .... K1
*12601 Poughkeepsie⊙ 29,757 .... N7
Poughkeepsie‡ 245,055 .... N7
14873 Prattsburg○ 1,657 .... F5
13142 Pulaski 2,415 .... H3
10579 Putnam Valley○ 8,994 .... N8
*11101 Queens (borough) 1,891,325 .... N9
14772 Randolph 1,398 .... C6
14131 Ransomville 1,401 .... C4
12143 Ravena 3,091 .... N6
12571 Red Hook 1,692 .... N7
†12601 Red Oaks Mill 5,236 .... N7
12144 Rensselaer 9,047 .... N5
12572 Rhinebeck 2,542 .... N7
13439 Richfield Springs 1,561 .... K5
*10301 Richmond (Staten Island) (borough) 352,121 .... M9
11901 Riverhead⊙ 6,339 .... P9
*14601 Rochester⊙ 241,741 .... E4
Rochester‡ 971,879 .... E4
*11570 Rockville Centre 25,412 .... R7
13440 Rome 43,826 .... J4
11575 Roosevelt 14,109 .... R7
11576 Roslyn 2,134 .... R6
12979 Rouses Point 2,266 .... O1
10580 Rye 15,083 .... P6
11963 Sag Harbor 2,581 .... R8
11780 Saint James 12,122 .... O9
13452 Saint Johnsville 1,974 .... L5
14779 Salamanca 6,890 .... C6
†13132 Sand Ridge 1,293 .... H4
†11050 Sands Point 2,742 .... P6
12983 Saranac Lake 5,578 .... M2
12866 Saratoga Springs 23,906 .... N4
12477 Saugerties 3,882 .... M6
13146 Savannah○ 1,905 .... G4
11782 Sayville 12,013 .... O9
10583 Scarsdale 17,650 .... P6
*12301 Schenectady⊙ 67,972 .... M5
12157 Schoharie⊙ 1,016 .... M5
12871 Schuylerville 1,256 .... N4
12302 Scotia 7,280 .... N5
14546 Scottsville 1,789 .... E4
11579 Sea Cliff 5,364 .... R6
11783 Seaford 16,117 .... R7
13148 Seneca Falls 7,466 .... G5
13460 Sherburne 1,561 .... K5
13461 Sherrill 2,830 .... J4
14548 Shortsville 1,669 .... F5
13838 Sidney 4,861 .... K6
14136 Silver Creek 3,088 .... B5
13152 Skaneateles 2,789 .... H5
†14201 Sloan 4,529 .... C5
10974 Sloatsburg 3,154 .... M8
11787 Smithtown 30,906 .... O9
14551 Sodus 1,790 .... G4
14555 Sodus Point 1,334 .... G4
13209 Solvay 7,140 .... H4
11968 Southampton 4,000 .... R9
12779 South Fallsburg 2,196 .... L7
†12801 South Glens Falls 3,714 .... N4
†10960 South Nyack 3,602 .... K8
11971 Southold 4,770 .... P8
†14901 Southport 8,329 .... G6
14559 Spencerport 3,424 .... E4
10977 Spring Valley 20,537 .... K8
14141 Springville 4,285 .... C5
*10301 Staten Island (borough) 352,121 .... M9
12170 Stillwater 1,572 .... N5
11790 Stony Brook 16,155 .... O9
10980 Stony Point 8,686 .... M8
12172 Stottville 1,387 .... N6
10901 Suffern 10,794 .... J8
11791 Syosset 9,818 .... R6
*13201 Syracuse⊙ 170,105 .... H4
Syracuse‡ 642,375 .... H4
10983 Tappan 8,267 .... K8
10591 Tarrytown 10,648 .... O6
†11020 Thomaston 2,684 .... P7
12883 Ticonderoga 2,938 .... N3
12486 Tillson 1,529 .... M7
14150 Tonawanda 18,693 .... B4

*12180 Troy⊙ 56,638 .... N5
14886 Trumansburg 1,722 .... G5
10707 Tuckahoe 6,076 .... O7
12986 Tupper Lake 4,478 .... M2
13849 Unadilla 1,367 .... K6
11553 Uniondale 20,016 .... R7
*13501 Utica⊙ 75,632 .... K4
Utica-Rome‡ 320,180 .... K4
12184 Valatie 1,492 .... N6
10989 Valley Cottage 8,214 .... K8
*11580 Valley Stream 35,769 .... P7
13850 Vestal○ 27,238 .... H6
14564 Victor 2,370 .... F5
†10901 Viola 5,340 .... J8
12186 Voorheesville 3,320 .... M5
12586 Walden 5,659 .... M7
12589 Wallkill 2,064 .... M7
13856 Walton 3,329 .... K6
13163 Wampsville⊙ 569 .... J4
11793 Wantagh 19,817 .... R7
12590 Wappingers Falls 5,110 .... N7
12885 Warrensburg 2,834 .... N3
14569 Warsaw⊙ 3,619 .... D5
10990 Warwick 4,320 .... M8
10992 Washingtonville 2,380 .... M8
12188 Waterford 2,405 .... N5
13165 Waterloo⊙ 5,303 .... G5
13601 Watertown⊙ 27,861 .... J3
13480 Waterville 1,672 .... K5
12189 Watervliet 11,354 .... N5
14891 Watkins Glen⊙ 2,440 .... G6
14892 Waverly 4,738 .... G7
14572 Wayland 1,846 .... E5
14580 Webster 5,499 .... F4
13166 Weedsport 1,952 .... G4
14895 Wellsville 5,769 .... E6
11590 Westbury 13,871 .... R7
†13619 West Carthage 1,824 .... J3
†14901 West Elmira 5,485 .... G6
14787 Westfield 3,446 .... A6
†12801 West Glens Falls 5,331 .... N4
11977 Westhampton 2,774 .... P9
11978 Westhampton Beach 1,629 P9
12491 West Hurley 2,382 .... M6
10994 West Nyack 8,553 .... K8
14788 Westons Mills 1,837 .... D6
10996 West Point 8,105 .... M8
11796 West Sayville 8,185 .... O9
14224 West Seneca 51,210 .... C5
12887 Whitehall 3,241 .... O3
*10601 White Plains⊙ 46,999 .... P6
13492 Whitesboro 4,460 .... K4
14588 Willard 1,339 .... G5
14589 Williamson 1,768 .... F4
14221 Williamsville 6,017 .... C5
11596 Williston Park 8,216 .... R7
13865 Windsor 1,155 .... J6

13697 Winthrop-Brasher Falls 1,454 .... L1
12998 Witherbee-Mineville 1,925 .... N2
14590 Wolcott 1,496 .... G4
11598 Woodmere 17,205 .... P7
12498 Woodstock 2,280 .... M6
12790 Wurtsboro 1,128 .... L7
11798 Wyandanch 13,215 .... N9
*10701 Yonkers 195,351 .... O6
10598 Yorktown Heights 7,696 .... N8
13495 Yorkville 3,115 .... K4
14174 Youngstown 2,191 .... C4

OTHER FEATURES

Adirondack (mts.) M3
Algonquin (peak) M2
Allegany Ind. Res. 1,243 .... C6
Allegheny (res.) C7
Allegheny (riv.) C6
Ashokan (res.) M7
Ausable (riv.) N2
Batten Kill (riv.) O4
Beaver (riv.) K3
Big Moose (lake) L3
Black (lake) J1
Black (riv.) K3
Block Island (sound) S8
Blue Mountain (lake) M3
Bonaparte (lake) K2
Brandreth (lake) L3
Brant (lake) N3
Brookhaven Nat'l Lab. P9
Butterfield (lake) J2
Canandaigua (lake) F5
Canisteo (riv.) F6
Cannonsville (res.) K6
Catskill (mts.) L6
Cattaraugus (creek) C6
Cattaraugus Ind. Res. 1,994 .... C5
Cayuga (lake) G5
Champlain (lake) O1
Chateaugay, Upper (lake) M1
Chautauqua (lake) A6
Chazy (lake) N1
Chenango (riv.) J6
Cohocton (riv.) F6
Conesus (lake) E5
Conewango (creek) B6
Cranberry (lake) L2
Deer (riv.) J3
Deer (riv.) L1
Delaware (riv.) K7
East (riv.) N9
Erie (lake) A5
Fire Island Nat'l Seashore P9
Fishers (isl.) S8

Forked (lake) L3
Fort Drum J2
Fort Niagara C4
Fort Stanwix Nat'l Mon. J4
Fulton Chain (lkes) K3
Galloo (isl.) H3
Gardiners (bay) R8
Gardiners (isl.) R8
Gateway Nat'l Rec. Area M9
Genesee (riv.) E5
George (lake) N4
Grand (isl.) B5
Grass (riv.) K1
Great Sacandaga (lake) M4
Great South (bay) O9
Great South (beach) O9
Greenwood (lake) M8
Grenadier (isl.) H2
Griffiss A.F.B. K4
Haystack (mt.) N2
Hemlock (lake) E5
Hinckley (res.) K4
Honeoye (lake) F5
Honnedaga (lake) L3
Hudson (riv.) N7
Hunter (mt.) M6
Indian (lake) M3
Jones (beach) R7
Keuka (lake) F5
Lila (lake) L2
Little Tupper (lake) L2
Long (isl.) P9
Long (lake) M2
Long Island (sound) P9
Manhattan (isl.) M9
Marcy (mt.) N2
Martin Van Buren Nat'l Hist. Site N6
Meacham (lake) M1
Mohawk (riv.) L5
Montauk (pt.) S8
Moose (riv.) K3
Neversink (res.) L7
New York State Barge (canal) C4
Niagara (riv.) B4
Oil Spring Ind. Res. 6 .... D6
Oneida (lake) J4
Onondaga Ind. Res. 596 .... H5
Ontario (lake) F3
Orient (pt.) R8
Oswegatchie (riv.) K2
Oswego (riv.) H4
Otisco (lake) H5
Otsego (lake) L5
Otselic (riv.) J5
Owasco (lake) G5
Peconic (bay) R9

Peninsula (pt.) H3
Pepacton (res.) L6
Piseco (lake) M4
Placid (lake) N2
Plattsburgh A.F.B. 5,905 .... N1
Pleasant (lake) M4
Plum (isl.) R8
Poosepatuck Ind. Res. 203 .... P9
Raquette (lake) L3
Rondout (res.) M7
Round (lake) L2
Sacandaga (lake) L3
Sackets (harb.) H3
Sagamore Hill Nat'l Hist. Site R6
Saint Lawrence (lake) K1
Saint Lawrence (riv.) J2
Saint Regis (riv.) L1
Saint Regis Ind. Res. 1,802 .... M1
Salmon (res.) J3
Salmon (riv.) H3
Salmon (riv.) M1
Saranac (lkes) M2
Saranac (riv.) N1
Saratoga (lake) N4
Saratoga Nat'l Hist. Park N4
Schoharie (res.) M6
Schroon (lake) N3
Seneca (lake) G5
Seneca (riv.) G5
Shelter (isl.) R8
Shinnecock Ind. Res. 297 .... R9
Silver (lake) N1
Skaneateles (lake) H5
Skylight (mt.) M2
Slide (mt.) L6
Staten (isl.) M9
Statue of Liberty Nat'l Mon. M9
Stony (isl.) H3
Stony (pt.) H3
Susquehanna (riv.) H6
Thousand (isls.) H2
Tioughnioga (riv.) H6
Titus (lake) M1
Tomhannock (res.) O5
Tonawanda Ind. Res. 467 .... D4
Toronto (res.) L7
Tupper (lake) M2
Tuscarora Ind. Res. 921 .... B4
Unadilla (riv.) K5
Upper Chateaugay (lake) M1
Valcour (isl.) N1
Wallkill (riv.) L8
Whiteface (mt.) N2
Whitney Point (lake) J6
Woodhull (lake) L3

⊙County seat.
‡Population of metropolitan area.
○Population of town or township.
† Zip of nearest p.o. * Multiple zips.

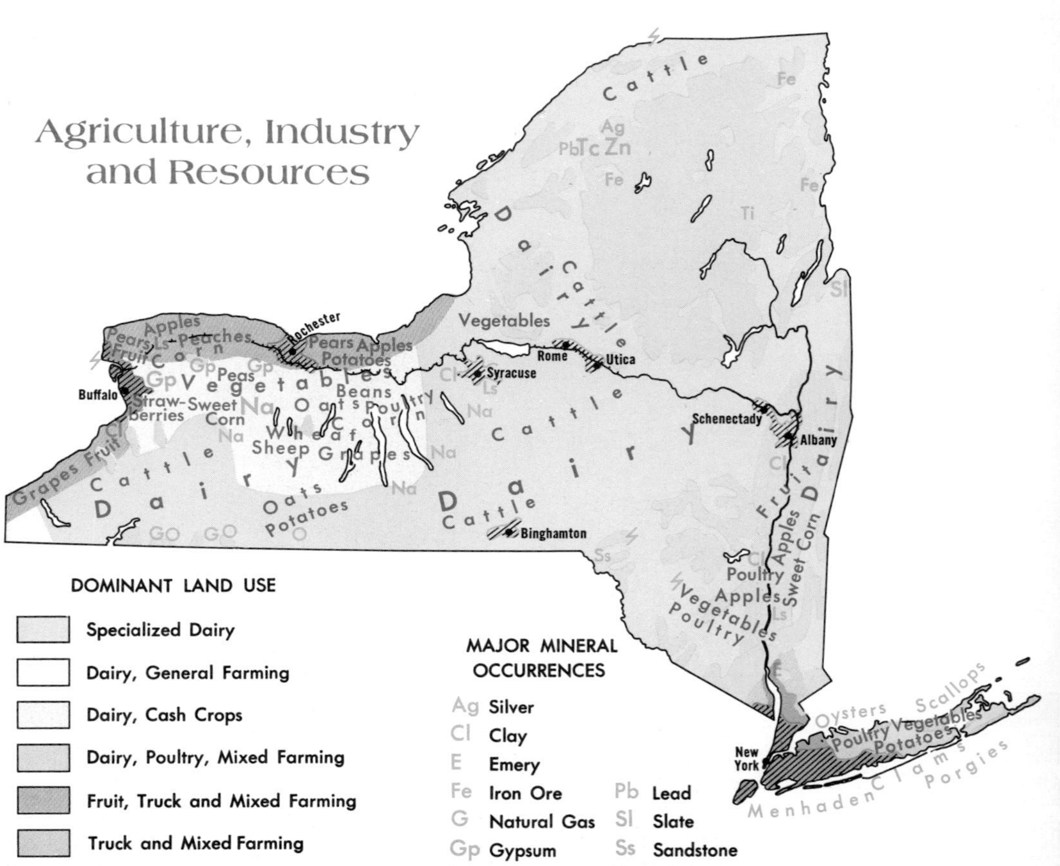

Agriculture, Industry and Resources
Cattle
Dairy
Vegetables
Pears Apples Peaches
Pears Apples Potatoes
Fruit
Peas
Straw-Sweet berries
Corn
Oats
Poultry
Beans
Wheat
Sheep
Grapes
Grapes Fruit
Potatoes
Apples Sweet Corn
Poultry Apples Vegetables Poultry
Oysters Scallops
Poultry Vegetables Potatoes
Clams Porgies
Menhaden
Rochester
Buffalo
Syracuse
Rome
Utica
Schenectady
Albany
Binghamton
New York
DOMINANT LAND USE
Specialized Dairy
Dairy, General Farming
Dairy, Cash Crops
Dairy, Poultry, Mixed Farming
Fruit, Truck and Mixed Farming
Truck and Mixed Farming
Forests
Urban Areas
MAJOR MINERAL OCCURRENCES
Ag Silver
Cl Clay
E Emery
Fe Iron Ore
G Natural Gas
Gp Gypsum
Ls Limestone
Na Salt
O Petroleum
Pb Lead
Sl Slate
Ss Sandstone
Tc Talc
Ti Titanium
Zn Zinc
Water Power
Major Industrial Areas

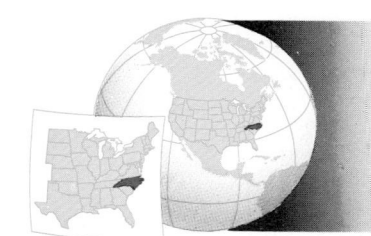

AREA 52,669 sq. mi. (136,413 sq. km.)
POPULATION 5,881,813
CAPITAL Raleigh
LARGEST CITY Charlotte
HIGHEST POINT Mt. Mitchell 6,684 ft. (2037 m.)
SETTLED IN 1650
ADMITTED TO UNION November 21, 1789
POPULAR NAME Tarheel State
STATE FLOWER Flowering Dogwood
STATE BIRD Cardinal

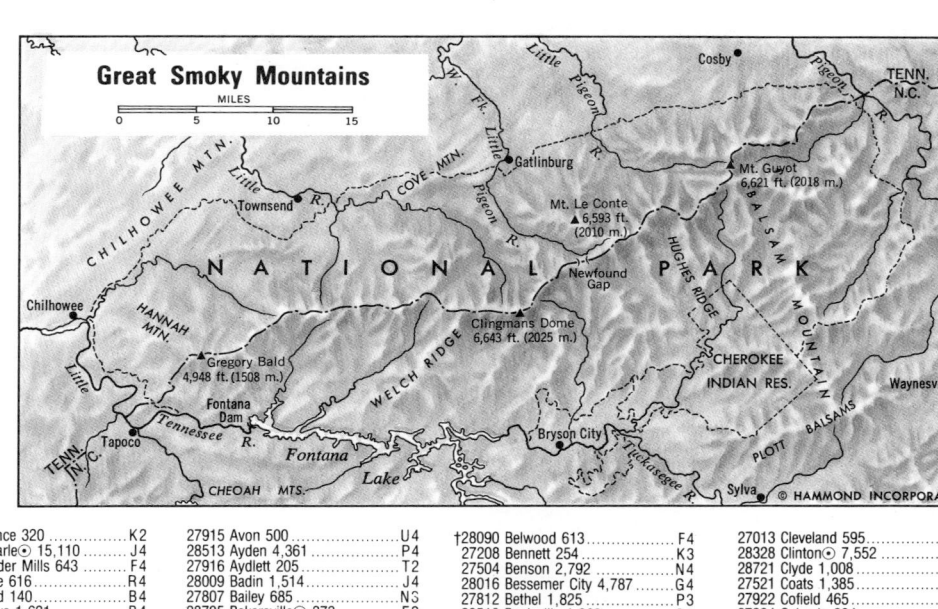

Great Smoky Mountains

COUNTIES

Alamance 99,319	L3
Alexander 24,999	G3
Alleghany 9,587	G1
Anson 25,649	J4
Ashe 22,325	F2
Avery 14,409	F2
Beaufort 40,355	R4
Bertie 21,024	P2
Bladen 30,491	M5
Brunswick 35,777	N6
Buncombe 160,934	D3
Burke 72,504	F3
Cabarrus 85,895	H4
Caldwell 67,746	F3
Camden 5,829	S2
Carteret 41,092	R5
Caswell 20,705	L2
Catawba 105,208	G3
Chatham 33,415	L3
Cherokee 18,933	A4
Chowan 12,558	R2
Clay 6,619	B4
Cleveland 83,435	F4
Columbus 51,037	M6
Craven 71,043	P4
Cumberland 247,160	M4
Currituck 11,089	S2
Dare 13,377	T3
Davidson 113,162	J3
Davie 24,599	H3
Duplin 40,952	O5
Durham 152,785	M3
Edgecombe 55,988	O3
Forsyth 243,683	J2
Franklin 30,055	N2
Gaston 162,568	G4
Gates 8,875	R2
Graham 7,217	B4
Granville 34,043	M2
Greene 16,117	O3
Guilford 317,154	K3
Halifax 55,286	O2
Harnett 59,570	M4
Haywood 46,495	C3
Henderson 58,580	D4
Hertford 23,368	P2
Hoke 20,383	L4
Hyde 5,873	S3
Iredell 82,538	H3
Jackson 25,811	C4
Johnston 70,599	N4
Jones 9,705	P4

Lee 36,718	L4
Lenoir 59,819	O4
Lincoln 42,372	G3
Macon 20,178	B4
Madison 16,827	D3
Martin 25,948	P3
McDowell 35,135	E3
Mecklenburg 404,270	H4
Mitchell 14,428	E2
Montgomery 22,469	K4
Moore 50,505	L4
Nash 67,153	O2
New Hanover 103,471	O6
Northampton 22,584	P2
Onslow 112,784	P5
Orange 77,055	L2
Pamlico 10,398	R4
Pasquotank 28,462	S2
Pender 22,215	O5
Perquimans 9,486	S2
Person 29,164	M2
Pitt 90,146	P3
Polk 12,984	E4
Randolph 91,728	K3
Richmond 45,481	K4
Robeson 101,610	L5
Rockingham 83,426	K2
Rowan 99,186	H3
Rutherford 53,787	E4
Sampson 49,687	N4
Scotland 32,273	L5
Stanly 48,517	H4
Stokes 33,086	J2
Surry 59,449	H2
Swain 10,283	B3
Transylvania 23,417	D4
Tyrrell 3,975	S3
Union 70,380	H4
Vance 36,748	N2
Wake 301,327	M3
Warren 16,232	N2
Washington 14,801	R3
Watauga 31,666	F2
Wayne 97,054	N4
Wilkes 58,657	G2
Wilson 63,132	O3
Yadkin 28,439	H2
Yancey 14,934	E3

CITIES and TOWNS

Zip	Name/Pop.	Key
28315	Aberdeen 1,945	L4
27910	Ahoskie 4,887	P2
27201	Alamance 320	K2
28001	Albemarle⊙ 15,110	J4
†28043	Alexander Mills 643	F4
28509	Alliance 616	R4
28702	Almond 140	B4
28901	Andrews 1,621	B4
27501	Angier 1,709	M4
28007	Ansonville 794	J4
27502	Apex 2,847	M3
28510	Arapahoe 467	R4
27263	Archdale 5,326	K3
†28642	Arlington 872	H2
28420	Ash 141	N6
27203	Asheboro⊙ 15,252	K3
*28801	Asheville⊙ 53,583	D3
	Asheville‡ 177,761	D3
†27983	Askewville 227	R2
28421	Atkinson 298	N5
28512	Atlantic Beach 941	R5
27805	Aulander 1,214	P2
27806	Aurora 698	R4
28318	Autryville 228	M4

Zip	Name/Pop.	Key
27915	Avon 500	U4
28513	Ayden 4,361	P4
27916	Aydlett 205	T2
28009	Badin 1,514	J4
27807	Bailey 685	N3
28705	Bakersville⊙ 373	E2
28706	Balfour 1,772	E4
28707	Balsam 200	C4
28604	Banner Elk 1,087	F2
†27030	Bannertown 1,028	H1
27008	Barber 155	H3
†28739	Barker Heights 1,267	D4
28710	Bat Cave 450	E4
27808	Bath 207	R4
27809	Battleboro 632	O2
28515	Bayboro⊙ 759	R4
†27892	Beargrass 82	P3
28516	Beaufort⊙ 3,826	R5
27810	Belhaven 2,430	R3
27811	Bellarthur 350	P4
28012	Belmont 4,607	H4
†28451	Belville 102	N6

Zip	Name/Pop.	Key
†28090	Belwood 613	F4
27208	Bennett 254	K3
27504	Benson 2,792	N4
28016	Bessemer City 4,787	G4
27812	Bethel 1,825	P3
28518	Beulaville 1,060	O5
†28803	Biltmore Forest 1,499	E3
27209	Biscoe 1,334	K4
27813	Black Creek 523	O3
28711	Black Mountain 4,083	E3
28320	Bladenboro 1,428	M5
27212	Blanch 200	L2
28605	Blowing Rock 1,337	F2
28092	Boger City 2,252	G4
28461	Boiling Spring Lakes 998	N7
28017	Boiling Springs 2,381	F4
28422	Bolivia⊙ 252	N6
28423	Bolton 563	N6
27213	Bonlee 300	L3
28606	Boomer 250	G2
28607	Boone⊙ 10,191	F2
27011	Boonville 1,028	H2
28322	Bowdens 200	N4
28712	Brevard⊙ 5,323	D4
28519	Bridgeton 461	R4
27505	Broadway 908	L4
†28601	Brookford 467	G3
28424	Brunswick 283	M6
28713	Bryson City⊙ 1,556	C4
27506	Buies Creek 1,939	M4
27507	Bullock 525	M2
27508	Bunn 505	N3
28425	Burgaw⊙ 1,738	N5
27215	Burlington 37,266	K2
	Burlington‡ 99,136	F2
28714	Burnsville⊙ 1,452	E3
27509	Butner 4,240	M2
27312	Bynum 350	L3
†29566	Calabash 128	M7
28325	Calypso 689	N4
27921	Camden⊙ 300	S2
28326	Cameron 225	L4
27229	Candor 868	K4
28716	Canton 4,631	D3
†28584	Cape Carteret 944	P5
28428	Carolina Beach 2,000	O6
27510	Carrboro 7,336	L3
28327	Carthage⊙ 925	K4
27511	Cary 21,763	M3
28020	Casar 346	F3
28717	Cashiers 553	C4
27816	Castalia 358	O2
28429	Castle Hayne 1,087	O6
†28461	Caswell Beach 110	N7
28609	Catawba 509	G3
27230	Cedar Falls 400	K3
27231	Cedar Grove 250	L2
28520	Cedar Island 310	S5
†27549	Centerville 135	N2
28430	Cerro Gordo 325	M6
28431	Chadbourn 1,975	M6
†28445	Chadwick Acres 15	P6
27514	Chapel Hill 32,421	L3
*28201	Charlotte⊙ 314,447	H4
	Charlotte-Gastonia‡ 637,218	H4
28021	Cherryville 4,844	G4
28023	China Grove 2,081	H3
28521	Chinquapin 280	O5
27817	Chocowinity 644	P4
28610	Claremont 880	G3
28433	Clarkton 664	M6
27520	Clayton 4,091	N3
27012	Clemmons 7,401	J2

Zip	Name/Pop.	Key
27013	Cleveland 595	H3
28328	Clinton⊙ 7,552	N5
28721	Clyde 1,008	D3
27521	Coats 1,385	M4
27922	Cofield 465	R2
27924	Colerain 284	R2
27925	Columbia⊙ 758	S3
28722	Columbus⊙ 727	E4
28522	Comfort 325	O5
27818	Como 89	P1
28025	Concord⊙ 16,942	H4
27819	Conetoe 215	O3
28613	Conover 4,245	G3
27820	Conway 678	P2
27014	Cooleemee 1,448	H3
28031	Cornelius 1,460	H4
27927	Corolla 158	T2
28523	Cove City 500	P4
28032	Cramerton 1,869	G4
27522	Creedmoor 1,641	M2
28524	Creswell 426	S3
27852	Crisp 435	O3
28616	Crossnore 297	F2
28331	Cumberland 400	M5
27237	Cumnock 200	L3
27929	Currituck⊙ 700	T2
28034	Dallas 3,340	G4
27016	Danbury⊙ 140	J2
28036	Davidson 3,241	H4
28524	Davis 612	R5
27239	Denton 949	J3
28725	Dillsboro 179	C4
27017	Dobson⊙ 1,222	H2
†27801	Dortches 885	O2
28526	Dover 600	P4
28619	Drexel 1,392	F3
28332	Dublin 477	M5
28334	Dunn 8,962	M4
*27701	Durham⊙ 100,538	M2
	Durham-Raleigh‡ 530,673	M2
27242	Eagle Springs 280	K4
28038	Earl 206	F4
†28434	East Arcadia 461	N6
27018	East Bend 602	H2
28726	East Flat Rock 3,365	E4
†28723	East Laport 150	C4
28352	East Laurinburg 536	L5
†28752	East Marion 1,851	F3
28039	East Spencer 2,150	J3
27288	Eden 15,672	K1
27932	Edenton⊙ 5,357	R2
27909	Elizabeth City⊙ 14,004	S2
28337	Elizabethtown⊙ 3,551	M5
28621	Elkin 2,858	H2
28622	Elk Park 535	E2
28040	Ellenboro 560	F4
28338	Ellerbe 1,415	K4
27822	Elm City 1,561	O3
27244	Elon College 2,873	L2
†28557	Emerald Isle 865	P5
28021	Cherryville 4,844	G4
28728	Enka 5,567	D3
28339	Erwin 2,828	M4
27247	Ether 425	K4
27935	Eure 300	R2
27830	Eureka 303	O3
27825	Everetts 213	P3
28438	Evergreen 310	M6
28439	Fair Bluff 1,095	M6
27826	Fairfield 900	S3
28340	Fairmont 2,658	L6
28730	Fairview 1,122	D3
28341	Faison 636	N4
28041	Faith 552	J3

(continued on following page)

Agriculture, Industry and Resources

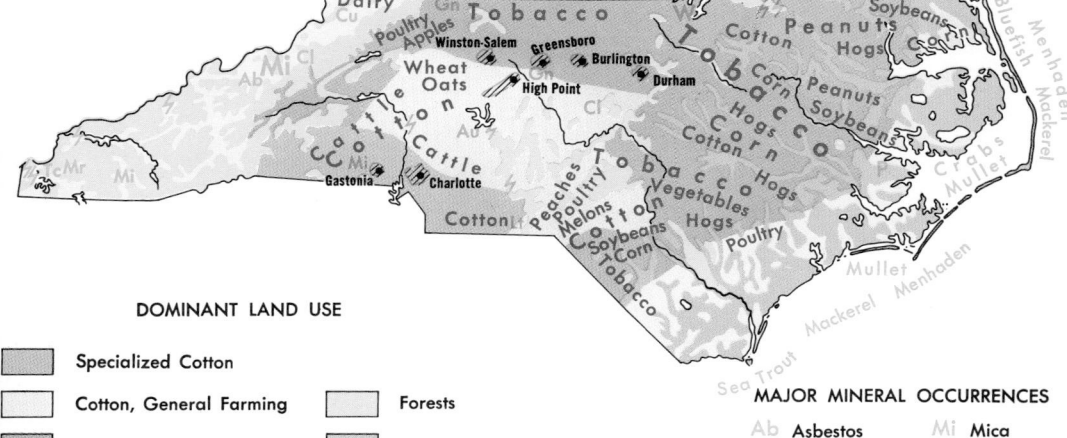

DOMINANT LAND USE

▢	Specialized Cotton
▢	Cotton, General Farming
▢	Cotton and Tobacco
▢	Tobacco, General Farming
▢	Peanuts, General Farming
▢	General Farming, Livestock, Fruit, Tobacco
▢	General Farming, Truck Farming, Tobacco, Livestock

▢	Forests
▢	Swampland, Limited Agriculture
▢	Nonagricultural Land
⚡	Water Power
▨	Major Industrial Areas

MAJOR MINERAL OCCURRENCES

Ab	Asbestos		Mi	Mica
Au	Gold		Mr	Marble
Cl	Clay		P	Phosphates
Cu	Copper		Tc	Talc
Gn	Granite		W	Tungsten
Lt	Lithium			

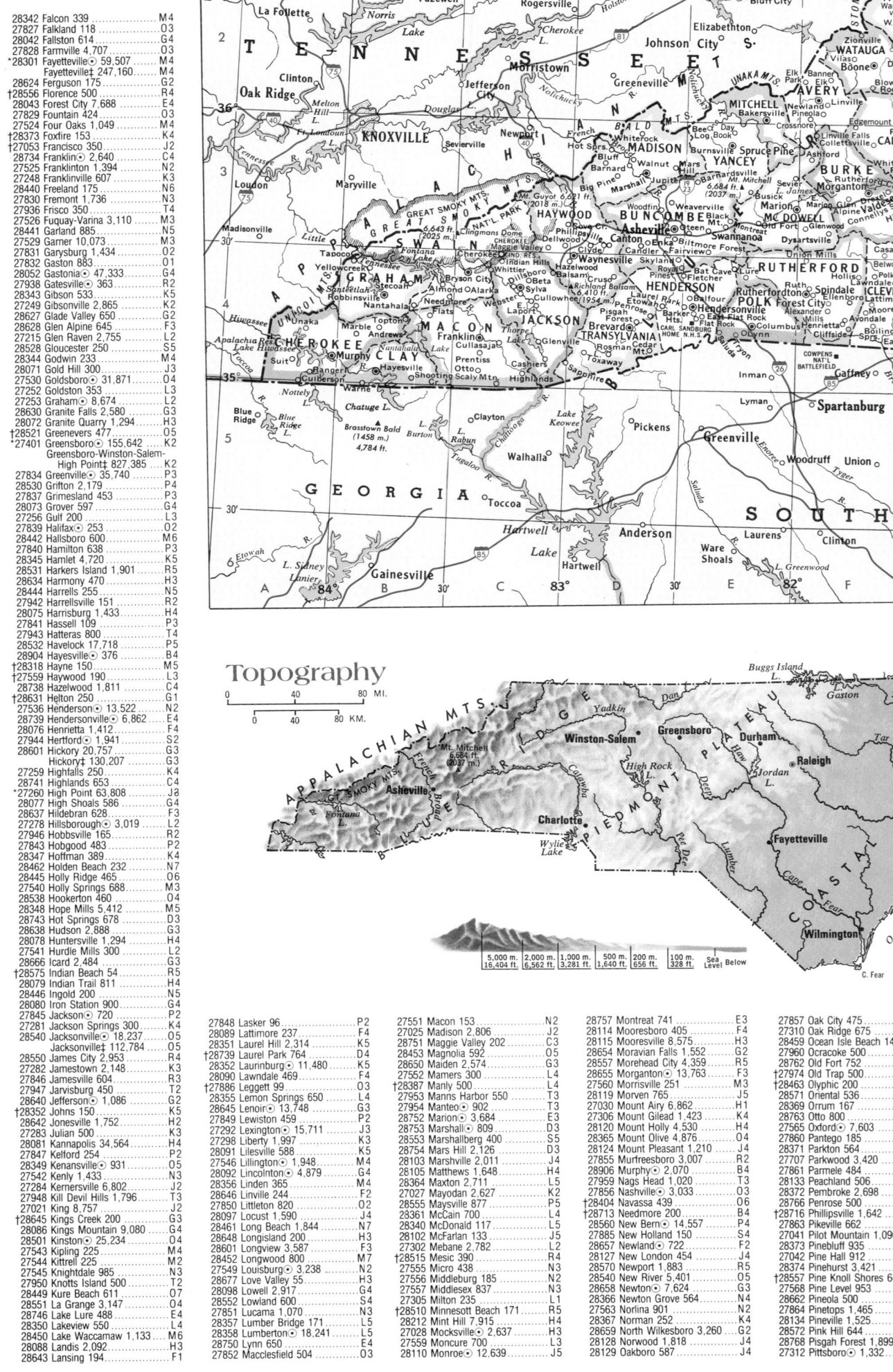

Topography

5,000 m. / 16,404 ft.   2,000 m. / 6,562 ft.   1,000 m. / 3,281 ft.   500 m. / 1,640 ft.   200 m. / 656 ft.   100 m. / 328 ft.   Sea Level   Below

North Carolina

SCALE
0 5 10 20 30 40 50MI.
0 5 10 20 30 40 50 KM.
State Capitals........................⊛
County Seats..........................◉
Canals
Major Limited Access Hwys.————
Scale 1:2,070,000
© Copyright HAMMOND INCORPORATED, Maplewood, N.J.

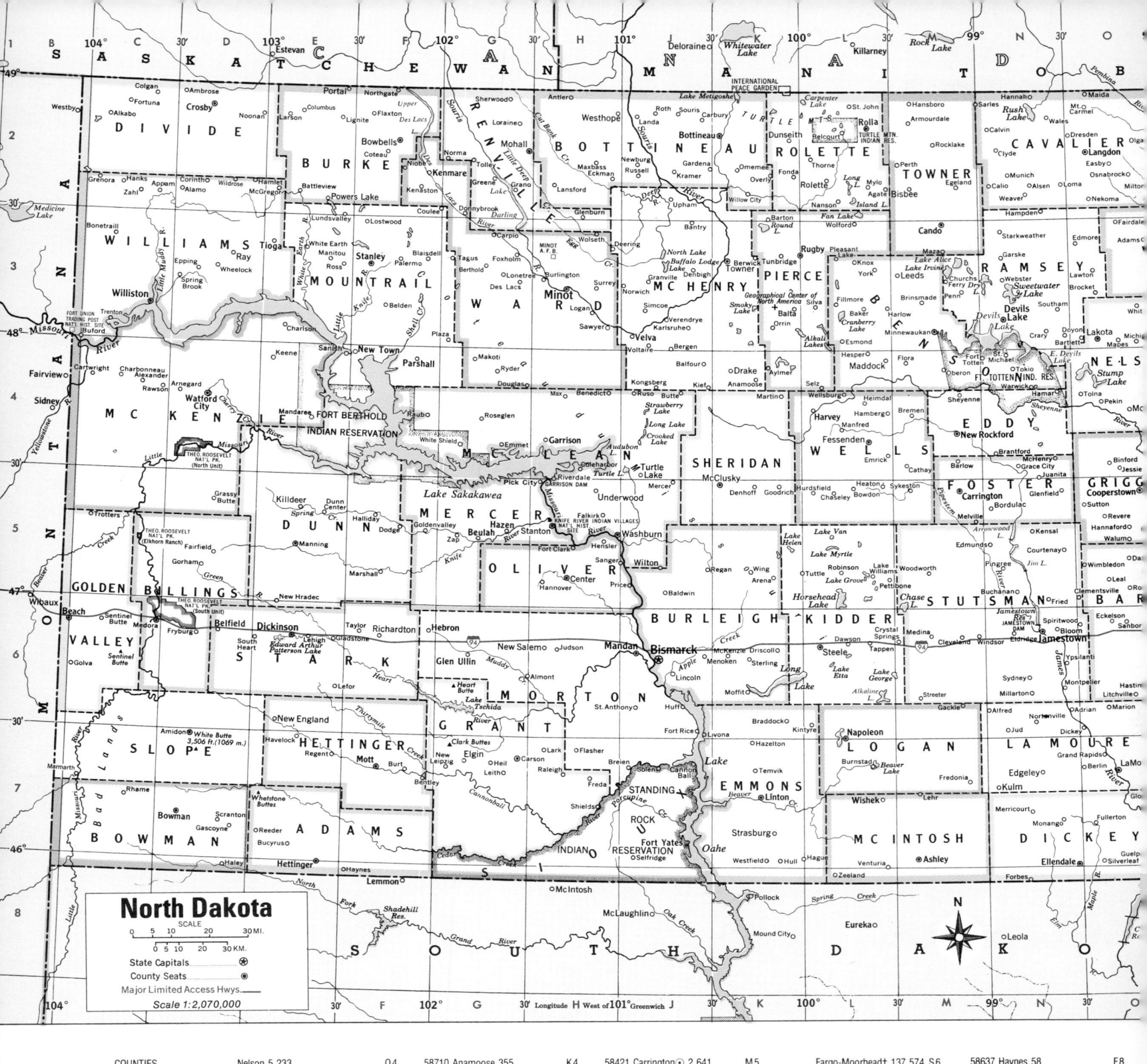

North Dakota

SCALE
0 5 10   20   30 MI.
0 5 10   20   30 KM.

⊛ State Capitals
◉ County Seats
Major Limited Access Hwys.

Scale 1:2,070,000

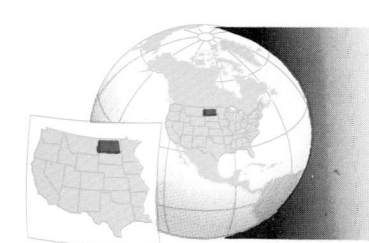

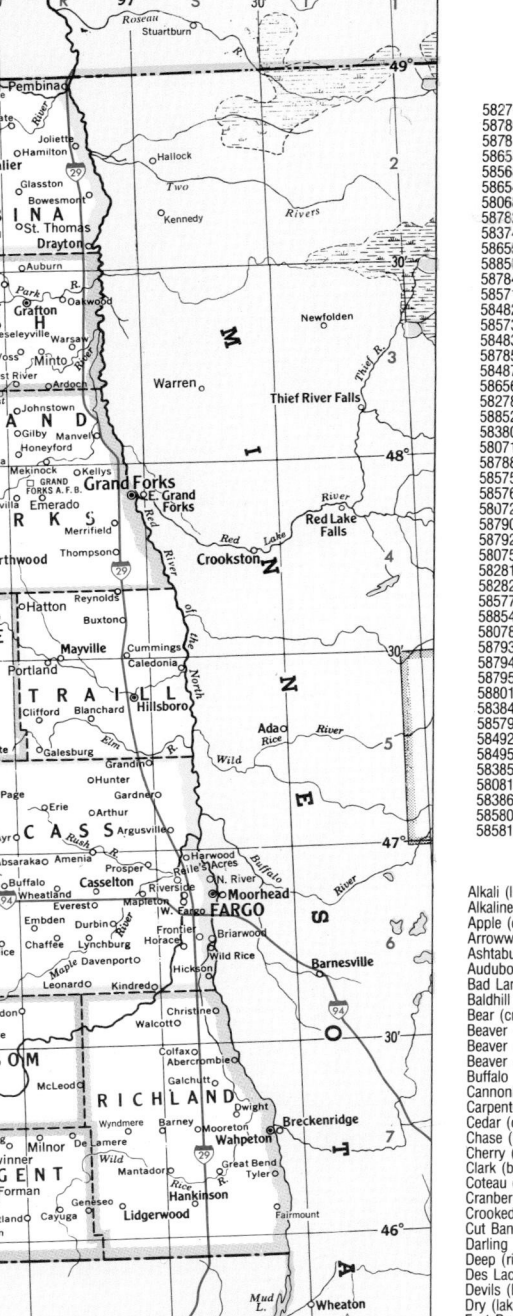

58276 Saint Thomas 528 ....R2
58780 Sanish............................E4
58781 Sawyer 417 ....H3
58653 Scranton 415 ....D7
58568 Selfridge 273 ....J7
58654 Sentinel Butte 86 ....C6
58068 Sheldon 173 ....P6
58782 Sherwood 294 ....G2
58374 Sheyenne 307 ....M4
58655 South Heart 294 ....D6
58850 Spring Brook 52 ....D3
58784 Stanley⊙ 1,631 ....F3
58571 Stanton⊙ 623 ....H5
58482 Steele⊙ 796 ....L6
58573 Strasburg 623 ....K7
58483 Streeter 264 ....M6
58785 Surrey 999 ....H3
58487 Tappen 271 ....L6
58656 Taylor 239 ....F6
58278 Thompson 785 ....R4
58852 Tioga 1,597 ....E3
58380 Tolna 241 ....O4
58071 Tower City 293 ....P6
58788 Towner⊙ 867 ....K3
58575 Turtle Lake 802 ....J4
58576 Underwood 1,329 ....H5
58072 Valley City⊙ 7,774 ....P6
58790 Velva 1,101 ....J3
58792 Voltaire 65 ....J3
58075 Wahpeton⊙ 9,064 ....S7
58281 Wales 74 ....N2
58282 Walhalla 1,429 ....P2
58577 Washburn⊙ 1,767 ....J5
58854 Watford City⊙ 2,119 ....D4
58078 West Fargo 10,099 ....S6
58793 Westhope 741 ....H2
58794 White Earth 98 ....E3
58795 Wildrose 214 ....D2
58801 Williston⊙ 13,336 ....C3
58384 Willow City 329 ....K2
58579 Wilton 950 ....J5
58492 Wimbledon 330 ....O5
58495 Wishek 1,345 ....L7
58385 Wolford 76 ....L3
58081 Wyndmere 550 ....R7
58386 York 69 ....L3
58580 Zap 511 ....G5
58581 Zeeland 253 ....L8

OTHER FEATURES

Alkali (lkes) L3
Alkaline (lake) L6
Apple (creek) J6
Arrowwood (lake) N5
Ashtabula (lake) P5
Audubon (lake) H4
Bad Lands (reg.) C7
Baldhill (Ashtabula) (res.) P5
Bear (creek) O7
Beaver (creek) B5
Beaver (creek) K7
Beaver (creek) L7
Buffalo Lodge (lake) J3
Cannonball (riv.) G7
Carpenter (lake) L2
Cedar (creek) G7
Chase (lake) M5
Cherry (creek) D4
Clark (buttes) G7
Coteau du Missouri (plain) G3
Cranberry (lake) L3
Crooked (lake) J4
Cut Bank (creek) H2
Darling (lake) G2
Deep (riv.) J1
Des Lacs (riv.) G3
Devils (lake) N3
Dry (lake) M3
East Devils (lake) N4
Egg (creek) H3
Elm (riv.) N8
Elm (riv.) R5
Etta (lake) L6

Fan (lake) L2
Forest (riv.) P3
Fort Berthold Ind. Res. E4
Fort Totten Ind. Res. N4
Fort Union Trading Post Nat'l Hist.
  Site B3
Garrison (dam) H5
George (lake) L6
Goose (riv.) P4
Grand, North Fork (riv.) E8
Grand Forks A.F.B. 9,390 ....R4
Green (riv.) D5
Grove (lake) L5
Heart (lake) G6
Heart (riv.) F6
Helen (lake) K5
Horsehead (lake) L5
International Peace Garden K1
Irvine (lake) M3
Island (lake) L2
James (riv.) N6
Jamestown (res.) N6
Jim (riv.) N5
Knife (riv.) G5
Knife R. Indian Villages Nat'l Hist.
  Site H5
Little Deep (creek) G2
Little Knife (riv.) F3

Little Missouri (riv.) D4
Little Muddy (riv.) C3
Long (lake) J4
Long (lake) K6
Long (lake) L2
Maple (riv.) O8
Maple (riv.) R6
Metigoshe (lake) K2
Minot A.F.B. 9,880 ....H3
Missouri (riv.) H5
Muddy (creek) G6
Myrtle (lake) L5
North (lake) J3
Oahe (lake) J7
Oak (creek) J8
Park (riv.) R3
Patterson, Edward A. (lake) E6
Pembina (riv.) O1
Pipestem (riv.) M5
Porcupine (creek) J7
Red River of the North (riv.) S4
Round (lake) K3
Rush (lake) N2
Rush (riv.) R5
Sakakawea (lake) G5
Sentinel (butte) C6
Shell (creek) F3
Sheyenne (riv.) O6

Smoky (lake) K3
Souris (riv.) J2
Spring (creek) E5
Standing Rock Ind. Res. J7
Strawberry (lake) J4
Stump (lake) O4
Sweetwater (lake) N3
Theodore Roosevelt Nat'l Mem. Park
  ....C5, D4, D6
Thirty Mile (creek) F6
Tongue (riv.) P2
Tschida (lake) G6
Turtle (lake) H4
Turtle (mts.) K2
Turtle Mountain Ind. Res. L2
Upper Des Lacs (lake) F2
Van (lake) L5
Whetstone (buttes) E7
White (butte) D7
White Butte (mt.) D7
White Earth (riv.) E3
Wild Rice (riv.) R7
Yellowstone (riv.) B4

⊙County seat.
‡Population of metropolitan area.
† Zip of nearest p.o.
* Multiple zips.

AREA 70,702 sq. mi. (183,118 sq. km.)
POPULATION 652,717
CAPITAL Bismarck
LARGEST CITY Fargo
HIGHEST POINT White Butte 3,506 ft.
  (1069. m.)
SETTLED IN 1780
ADMITTED TO UNION November 2, 1889
POPULAR NAME Flickertail State; Sioux
  State
STATE FLOWER Wild Prairie Rose
STATE BIRD Western Meadowlark

Topography

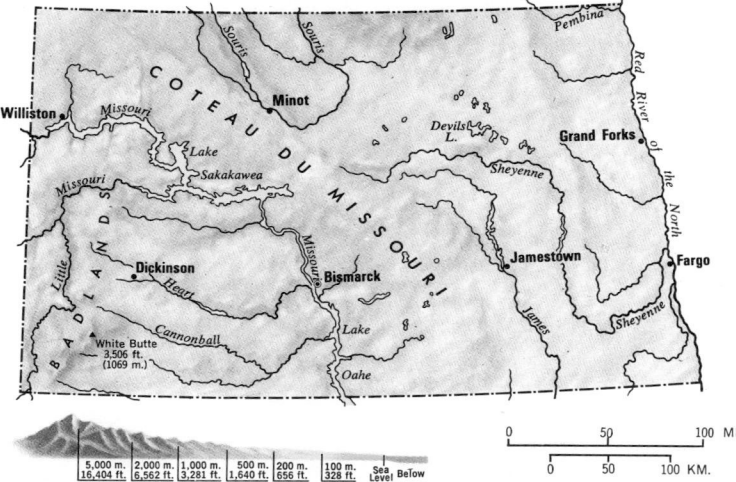

†58501 Lincoln 656 ....J6
58552 Linton⊙ 1,561 ....K7
58054 Lisbon⊙ 2,283 ....P7
58461 Litchville 251 ....O6
58056 Luverne 65 ....P5
58348 Maddock 677 ....L4
58554 Mandan⊙ 15,513 ....J6
58642 Manning⊙ 75 ....E5
58058 Mantador 76 ....R7
58256 Manvel 308 ....R3
58059 Mapleton 306 ....R6
58643 Marmarth 190 ....B7
58759 Max 317 ....H4
58257 Mayville 2,255 ....R4
58463 McClusky⊙ 658 ....K4
58254 McVille 626 ....O4
58467 Medina 521 ....M6
58645 Medora⊙ 94 ....C6
58259 Michigan 502 ....O3
58060 Milnor 716 ....R7
58351 Minnewaukan⊙ 461 ....M3
58701 Minot⊙ 32,843 ....H3
58261 Minto 592 ....R3
58761 Mohall⊙ 1,049 ....G2
58471 Monango 59 ....N7
58472 Montpelier 96 ....N6
58646 Mott⊙ 1,315 ....F7
58352 Munich 300 ....N2
58561 Napoleon⊙ 1,103 ....L6
58265 Neche 471 ....P2
58647 New England 825 ....E6
58562 New Leipzig 352 ....G7
58356 New Rockford⊙ 1,791 ....N4

58563 New Salem 1,081 ....G6
58763 New Town 1,335 ....F4
58266 Niagara 76 ....P4
58765 Noonan 283 ....D2
†58102 North River 65 ....S6
58267 Northwood 1,240 ....P4
58474 Oakes 2,112 ....O7
58063 Oriska 125 ....P6
58064 Page 329 ....P5
58769 Palermo 97 ....F3
58270 Park River 1,844 ....P3
58770 Parshall 1,059 ....F4
58271 Pembina 673 ....R2
58476 Pingree 88 ....N5
58772 Portal 238 ....E2
58274 Portland 627 ....R5
58773 Powers Lake 466 ....E2
58849 Ray 766 ....D3
58649 Reeder 355 ....E7
58477 Regan 71 ....K5
58650 Regent 297 ....E7
58275 Reynolds 309 ....R4
58651 Rhame 222 ....C7
58652 Richardton 699 ....F6
†58078 Riverside 465 ....S6
58365 Rocklake 287 ....M2
58479 Rogers 68 ....O5
58366 Rolette 667 ....L2
58367 Rolla⊙ 1,538 ....L2
58368 Rugby⊙ 3,335 ....L3
58067 Rutland 250 ....P7
58369 Saint John 401 ....L2

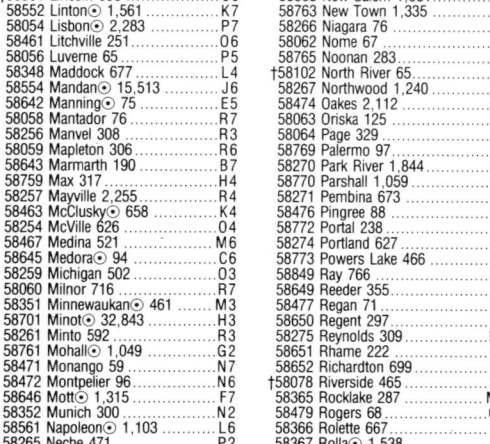

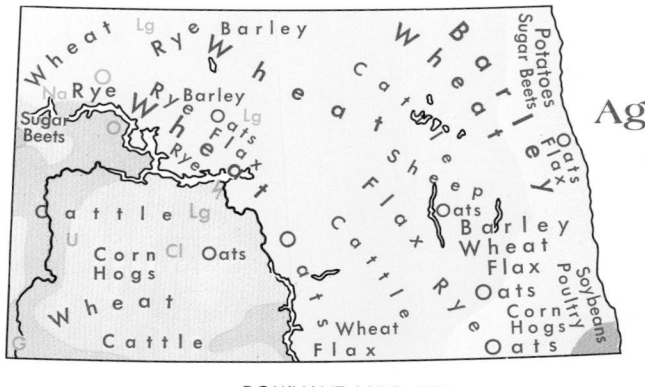

Agriculture, Industry and Resources

DOMINANT LAND USE

- Specialized Wheat
- Wheat, General Farming
- Wheat, Range Livestock
- Livestock, Cash Grain
- Sugar Beets, Dry Beans, Livestock, General Farming
- Range Livestock
- ⚡ Water Power

MAJOR MINERAL OCCURRENCES

Cl Clay
G Natural Gas
Lg Lignite
Na Salt
O Petroleum
U Uranium

Copyright HAMMOND INCORPORATED, Maplewood, N.J.

Ohio

SCALE

0 5 10 20 30 40 MI.

0 5 10 20 30 40 KM.

State Capitals..............⊛

County Seats..............⊛

Major Limited Access Hwys.————

Scale 1:1,800,000

© Copyright HAMMOND INCORPORATED, Maplewood, N.J.

AREA 41,330 sq. mi. (107,045 sq. km.)
POPULATION 10,797,624
CAPITAL Columbus
LARGEST CITY Cleveland
HIGHEST POINT Campbell Hill 1,550 ft. (472 m.)
SETTLED IN 1788
ADMITTED TO UNION March 1, 1803
POPULAR NAME Buckeye State
STATE FLOWER Scarlet Carnation
STATE BIRD Cardinal

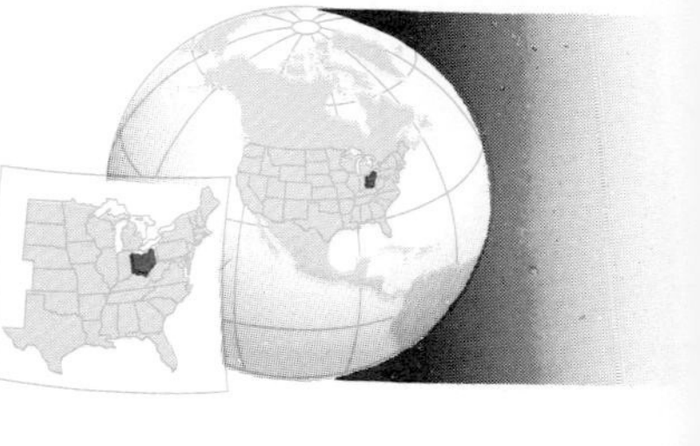

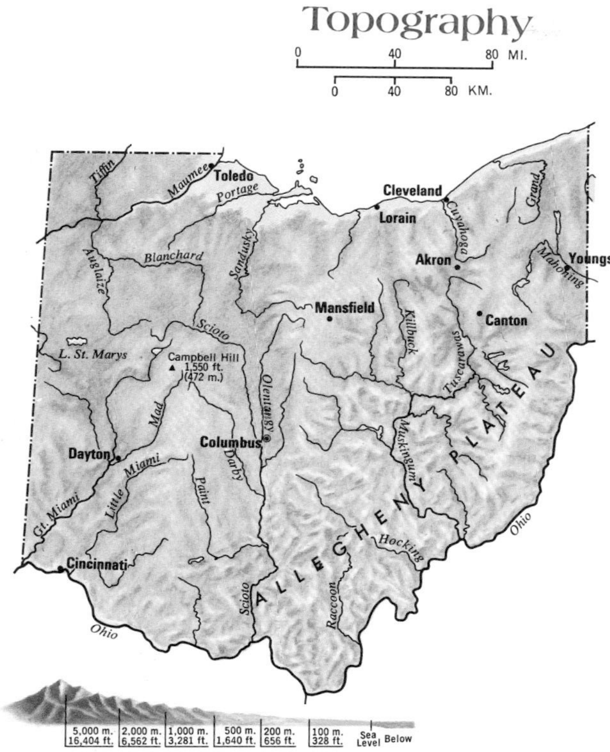

COUNTIES

Adams 24,328 .... D8
Allen 112,241 .... B4
Ashland 46,178 .... F4
Ashtabula 104,215 .... J2
Athens 56,399 .... F7
Auglaize 42,554 .... B4
Belmont 82,569 .... J5
Brown 31,920 .... C8
Butler 258,787 .... A7
Carroll 25,598 .... H4
Champaign 33,649 .... C5
Clark 150,236 .... C6
Clermont 128,483 .... B7
Clinton 34,603 .... C7
Columbiana 113,572 .... J4
Coshocton 36,024 .... G5
Crawford 50,075 .... E4
Cuyahoga 1,498,400 .... G3
Darke 55,096 .... A5
Defiance 39,987 .... A3
Delaware 53,840 .... D5
Erie 79,655 .... E3
Fairfield 93,678 .... E6
Fayette 27,467 .... D6
Franklin 869,126 .... E5
Fulton 37,751 .... B2
Gallia 30,098 .... F8
Geauga 74,474 .... H3
Greene 129,769 .... C6
Guernsey 42,024 .... H5
Hamilton 873,224 .... A7
Hancock 64,581 .... C3
Hardin 32,719 .... C4
Harrison 18,152 .... H5
Henry 28,383 .... B3
Highland 33,477 .... C7
Hocking 24,304 .... F6
Holmes 29,416 .... G4
Huron 54,608 .... E3
Jackson 30,592 .... E7
Jefferson 91,564 .... J5
Knox 46,304 .... F5
Lake 212,801 .... H2
Lawrence 63,849 .... E8
Licking 120,981 .... F5
Logan 39,155 .... C5
Lorain 274,909 .... F3
Lucas 471,741 .... C2
Madison 33,004 .... D6
Mahoning 289,487 .... J4
Marion 67,974 .... D4
Medina 113,150 .... G3
Meigs 23,641 .... F7
Mercer 38,334 .... A4
Miami 90,381 .... B5
Monroe 17,382 .... H6
Montgomery 571,697 .... B6
Morgan 14,241 .... G6
Morrow 26,480 .... E4
Muskingum 83,340 .... G5
Noble 11,310 .... G6
Ottawa 40,076 .... D2
Paulding 21,302 .... A3
Perry 31,032 .... F6
Pickaway 43,662 .... D6
Pike 22,802 .... D7
Portage 135,856 .... H3
Preble 38,223 .... A6
Putnam 32,991 .... B3
Richland 131,205 .... E4
Ross 65,004 .... D7
Sandusky 63,267 .... D3
Scioto 84,545 .... D8
Seneca 61,901 .... D3
Shelby 43,089 .... B5
Stark 378,823 .... H4
Summit 524,472 .... G3
Trumbull 241,863 .... J3
Tuscarawas 84,614 .... H5
Union 29,536 .... D5
Van Wert 30,458 .... A4
Vinton 11,584 .... E7
Warren 99,276 .... B7
Washington 64,266 .... H7
Wayne 97,408 .... G4
Williams 36,369 .... A2
Wood 107,372 .... C3
Wyandot 22,651 .... D4

CITIES and TOWNS

Zip Name/Pop. Key

45101 Aberdeen 1,566 .... C8
45810 Ada 5,669 .... C4
45001 Addyston 1,195 .... B9
43101 Adelphi 472 .... E7
43901 Adena 1,062 .... J5
*44301 Akron⊙ 237,177 .... G3
Akron‡ 660,328 .... G3
45710 Albany 905 .... F7
43001 Alexandria 489 .... E5
45812 Alger 992 .... C4
44601 Alliance 24,315 .... H4
43102 Amanda 720 .... E6
†45201 Amberley 3,442 .... C9
45102 Amelia 1,108 .... D10
44001 Amherst 10,638 .... F3
43903 Amsterdam 783 .... J5
44003 Andover 1,205 .... J2
45302 Anna 1,038 .... B5
45303 Ansonia 1,267 .... A5
45813 Antwerp 1,765 .... A3
44606 Apple Creek 741 .... G4
44804 Arcadia 580 .... D3
45304 Arcanum 2,002 .... A6
43502 Archbold 3,318 .... B2
45814 Arlington 1,187 .... C4
†45201 Arlington Heights 1,082 .... C9
44805 Ashland⊙ 20,326 .... F4
43003 Ashley 1,057 .... E5
44004 Ashtabula 23,449 .... J2
43103 Ashville 2,046 .... E6
45701 Athens⊙ 19,743 .... F7
44807 Attica 865 .... E3
44201 Atwater 975 .... H3
44202 Aurora 8,177 .... H3
44010 Austinburg 900 .... J2
44515 Austintown 33,636 .... J3
44011 Avon 7,241 .... F3
44012 Avon Lake 13,222 .... F2
†43512 Ayersville 950 .... B3
†44805 Bailey Lakes 397 .... F4
45612 Bainbridge 1,042 .... D7
43804 Baltic 563 .... G5
43105 Baltimore 2,689 .... E6
44203 Barberton 29,751 .... G4
43713 Barnesville 4,633 .... H6
43905 Barton 1,039 .... J5
45103 Batavia⊙ 1,896 .... B7
†44870 Bay View 804 .... E3
44140 Bay Village 17,846 .... G9
44608 Beach City 1,083 .... G4
44122 Beachwood 9,983 .... J9
43716 Beallsville 601 .... J6
45808 Beaverdam 492 .... C4
44146 Bedford 15,056 .... H9
†44146 Bedford Heights 13,214 .... J9
43906 Bellaire 8,241 .... J5
45305 Bellbrook 5,174 .... C6
43310 Belle Center 930 .... C4
43311 Bellefontaine⊙ 11,888 .... C5
44811 Bellevue 8,187 .... E3
44813 Bellville 1,714 .... E4
43718 Belmont 714 .... J5
44609 Beloit 1,093 .... J4
45714 Belpre 7,193 .... G7
44017 Berea 19,567 .... G10
43908 Bergholz 914 .... J4
44814 Berlin Heights 756 .... F3
45106 Bethel 2,231 .... B8
43719 Bethesda 1,429 .... H5
44815 Bettsville 752 .... D3
45715 Beverly 1,471 .... G6
43209 Bexley 13,405 .... E6
45107 Blanchester 3,202 .... B7
44817 Bloomdale 744 .... D3
43106 Bloomingburg 869 .... D6
44818 Bloomville 1,019 .... D3
†45242 Blue Ash 9,506 .... C9
45817 Bluffton 3,310 .... C4
44512 Boardman 39,161 .... J3
44612 Bolivar 989 .... G4
†44264 Boston Heights 781 .... J10
45306 Botkins 1,372 .... B5
44695 Bowerston 487 .... H5
43402 Bowling Green⊙ 25,728 .... C3
45308 Bradford 2,166 .... B5
43406 Bradner 1,175 .... C3
44211 Brady Lake 470 .... H3
†44101 Bratenahl 1,485 .... H9
44141 Brecksville 10,132 .... H10
43107 Bremen 1,432 .... F6
44613 Brewster 2,321 .... G4
43912 Bridgeport 2,642 .... J5
†45211 Bridgetown 11,460 .... B9
43913 Brilliant 1,751 .... J5
†44240 Brimfield 3,161 .... H3
44402 Bristolville 900 .... J3
†44141 Broadview Heights 10,920 .... H10
44403 Brookfield 1,527 .... J3
44144 Brooklyn 12,342 .... H9
†44131 Brooklyn Heights 1,653 .... H9
44142 Brook Park 26,195 .... G9
†43912 Brookside 887 .... J5
45309 Brookville 4,322 .... B6
44212 Brunswick 28,104 .... G3
43506 Bryan⊙ 7,879 .... A3
45716 Buchtel 585 .... F7
43008 Buckeye Lake F6
44820 Bucyrus⊙ 13,433 .... E4
†45680 Burlington 900 .... F9
44021 Burton 1,401 .... H3
44822 Butler 991 .... F4
43723 Byesville 2,572 .... G6
43907 Cadiz⊙ 4,058 .... J5
45820 Cairo 596 .... B4
43920 Calcutta 1,121 .... J4
43724 Caldwell⊙ 1,935 .... G6
43314 Caledonia 759 .... D4
43725 Cambridge⊙ 13,573 .... G5
45311 Camden 1,971 .... A6
44405 Campbell 11,619 .... J3
45111 Camp Dennison 625 .... D9
44614 Canal Fulton 3,481 .... H4
43110 Canal Winchester 2,749 .... E6
44406 Canfield 5,535 .... J3
*44701 Canton⊙ 93,077 .... H4
Canton‡ 404,421 .... H4
43315 Cardington 1,665 .... E5
43316 Carey 3,674 .... D4
45005 Carlisle 4,276 .... B6
43112 Carroll 641 .... E6
44615 Carrollton⊙ 3,065 .... J4
44824 Castalia 973 .... E3
45314 Cedarville 2,799 .... C6
45822 Celina⊙ 9,137 .... A4
43011 Centerburg 1,275 .... E5
45459 Centerville 18,886 .... B6
44022 Chagrin Falls 4,335 .... J9
†45631 Chambersburg F8
44024 Chardon⊙ 4,434 .... H2
45719 Chauncey 1,050 .... F7
†45202 Cherry Grove 850 .... C10
45619 Chesapeake 1,370 .... E9
44026 Chesterland 2,301 .... H2
†45211 Cheviot 9,888 .... B9
45601 Chillicothe⊙ 23,420 .... E7
45389 Christiansburg 593 .... C5
*45201 Cincinnati⊙ 385,457 .... B9
Cincinnati‡ 1,401,403 .... B9
43113 Circleville⊙ 11,700 .... D6
43915 Clarington 558 .... J6
43115 Clarksburg 483 .... D7
45113 Clarksville 525 .... C7
45315 Clayton 752 .... B6
*44101 Cleveland⊙ 573,822 .... H9
Cleveland‡ 1,898,720 .... H9
44118 Cleveland Heights 56,438 .... H9
45002 Cleves 2,094 .... B9
44216 Clinton 1,277 .... G4
43410 Clyde 5,489 .... E3
†45638 Coal Grove 2,602 .... E9
45621 Coalton 639 .... E7
45828 Coldwater 4,220 .... A5
†44034 Colebrook 700 .... J2
44028 Columbia Station 518 .... G10
44408 Columbiana 4,987 .... J4
*43201 Columbus (cap.)⊙ 565,032 .... E6
Columbus‡ 1,093,293 .... E6
45830 Columbus Grove 2,313 .... B4
43811 Conesville 451 .... G5
44030 Conneaut 13,835 .... J2
45831 Continental 1,179 .... B3
45832 Convoy 1,140 .... A4
45723 Coolville 649 .... G7
43730 Corning 789 .... F6
44410 Cortland 5,011 .... J3
43812 Coshocton⊙ 13,405 .... G5
†45238 Covedale 5,830 .... B10
45318 Covington 2,610 .... B5
†44429 Craig Beach 1,657 .... H3
44827 Crestline 5,406 .... E4
44217 Creston 1,828 .... G4
45806 Cridersville 1,843 .... B4
43731 Crooksville 2,766 .... F6
45623 Crown City 513 .... F8
†45341 Crystal Lakes 1,463 .... C6
*44221 Cuyahoga Falls 43,890 .... G3
†44101 Cuyahoga Heights 739 .... H9
43413 Cygnet 646 .... C3
44618 Dalton 1,357 .... G4
43014 Danville 1,127 .... F5
†43123 Darbydale 825 .... D6
*45401 Dayton⊙ 193,444 .... B6
Dayton‡ 830,070 .... B6
44411 Deerfield 800 .... H3
45236 Deer Park 6,745 .... C9
43512 Defiance⊙ 16,810 .... B3
43318 Degraff 1,358 .... C5
43015 Delaware⊙ 18,780 .... E5
45833 Delphos 7,314 .... B4
43515 Delta 2,831 .... B2
44621 Dennison 3,398 .... H5
†45202 Dent 800 .... B9
43516 Deshler 1,870 .... C3
45750 Devola 2,708 .... H7
43917 Dillonvale 912 .... J5
44622 Dover 11,782 .... G4
44230 Doylestown 2,493 .... G4
43821 Dresden 1 646 .... G5
43017 Dublin 3,855 .... D5
43734 Duncan Falls 900 .... G6
45836 Dunkirk 954 .... C4
44730 East Canton 1,721 .... H4
44112 East Cleveland 36,957 .... H9
†44094 Eastlake 22,104 .... J8
43920 East Liverpool 16,687 .... J4
44413 East Palestine 5,306 .... J4
44626 East Sparta 868 .... H4
45320 Eaton⊙ 6,839 .... A6
†44035 Eaton Estates 1,806 .... G3
43517 Edgerton 1,813 .... A3
†44004 Edgewood 3,099 .... J2
43320 Edison 504 .... E4
43314 Edon 947 .... A2
45321 Eldorado 509 .... A6
45807 Elida 1,349 .... B4
43416 Elmore 1,271 .... D3
45216 Elmwood Place 2,840 .... B9
*44035 Elyria⊙ 57,538 .... F3
45322 Englewood 11,329 .... B6
45323 Enon 2,597 .... C6
44117 Euclid 59,999 .... J9
†45201 Evendale 1,954 .... C9
45042 Excello 900 .... B7
45324 Fairborn 29,702 .... B6
†45201 Fairfax 2,222 .... C9
45014 Fairfield 30,777 .... A7
44313 Fairlawn 6,100 .... G3
44077 Fairport Harbor 3,357 .... H2
44126 Fairview Park 19,311 .... G9
45325 Farmersville 950 .... A6
43521 Fayette 1,222 .... B2
45120 Felicity 929 .... B8
45840 Findlay⊙ 35,594 .... C3
45326 Fletcher 498 .... B5
43977 Flushing 1,266 .... J5
45843 Forest 1,633 .... C4
45405 Forest Park 18,675 .... B9
45230 Forestville 950 .... C10
45844 Fort Jennings 538 .... B4
45845 Fort Loramie 977 .... B5
†45426 Fort McKinley B6
45846 Fort Recovery 1,370 .... A5
†45801 Fort Shawnee 4,541 .... B4
44830 Fostoria 15,743 .... D3
45628 Frankfort 1,008 .... D7
45005 Franklin 10,711 .... B6
45629 Franklin Furnace 1,093 .... E8
43822 Frazeysburg 1,025 .... F5
44627 Fredericksburg 511 .... G4
43019 Fredericktown 2,299 .... F5
43973 Freeport 525 .... H5
43420 Fremont⊙ 17,834 .... D3
45630 Friendship 900 .... D8
43230 Gahanna 18,001 .... E5
44833 Galion 12,391 .... E4
45631 Gallipolis⊙ 5,576 .... F8
43022 Gambier 2,056 .... F5
44125 Garfield Heights 34,938 .... J9
44231 Garrettsville 1,769 .... H3
44040 Gates Mills 2,236 .... J9
44041 Geneva 6,655 .... J2
44043 Geneva-on-the-Lake 1,634 .... H2
43430 Genoa 2,213 .... D2
45121 Georgetown⊙ 3,467 .... C8
45327 Germantown 5,015 .... B6
45328 Gettysburg 545 .... A5
43431 Gibsonburg 2,479 .... D3
44420 Girard 12,517 .... J3
45848 Glandorf 746 .... B3
45246 Glendale 2,368 .... C9
†44139 Glenwillow 492 .... J10
45732 Glouster 2,211 .... F6
44629 Gnadenhutten 1,320 .... G5
†45201 Golf Manor 4,317 .... C9
45122 Goshen B7
44044 Grafton 2,231 .... F3
43522 Grand Rapids 962 .... C3
44045 Grand River 412 .... H2
†43212 Grandview Heights 7,420 .... D6
43023 Granville 3,851 .... E5
45330 Gratis 809 .... A6
43322 Green Camp 475 .... D4
45123 Greenfield 5,150 .... D7
45218 Greenhills 4,927 .... B9
44232 Greensburg 950 .... G4
44836 Green Springs 1,568 .... E3
44630 Greentown 300 .... H4
45331 Greenville⊙ 12,999 .... A5
44837 Greenwich 1,458 .... E3
43123 Grove City 16,816 .... D6
43125 Groveport 3,286 .... E6
45849 Grover Hill 486 .... B3
45634 Hamden 1,010 .... F7
45130 Hamersville 688 .... C8
*45011 Hamilton⊙ 63,189 .... A7
Hamilton-Middletown‡ 258,787 .... A7
43524 Hamler 625 .... B3
43931 Hannibal 550 .... J6
†43055 Hanover 926 .... F5
43126 Harrisburg 363 .... D6
45030 Harrison 5,855 .... A9
45850 Harrod 506 .... C4
†44085 Hartsgrove 200 .... J2
44632 Hartville 1,772 .... H4
43525 Haskins 568 .... C3
43127 Haydenville 395 .... F7
44838 Hayesville 518 .... F4
43055 Heath 6,969 .... F5
43025 Hebron 2,035 .... E6
43526 Hicksville 3,929 .... A3
†44143 Highland Heights 5,739 .... J9
43026 Hilliard 8,008 .... D5
45133 Hillsboro⊙ 6,356 .... C7
44234 Hiram 1,360 .... H3
43527 Holgate 1,315 .... B3
43528 Holland 1,048 .... C2
45033 Hooven 550 .... A9
43976 Hopedale 857 .... J5
44425 Hubbard 9,245 .... J3
45424 Huber Heights 35,480 .... B6
44236 Hudson 4,615 .... H3
†44022 Hunting Valley 786 .... J9
44839 Huron 7,123 .... E3
44131 Independence 6,607 .... H9
†45201 Indian Hill 5,521 .... C9
43932 Irondale 535 .... J4
45638 Ironton⊙ 14,290 .... E8
45640 Jackson⊙ 6,675 .... E7
45334 Jackson Center 1,310 .... B5
45740 Jacksonville 651 .... F7
45335 Jamestown 1,702 .... C6
44047 Jefferson⊙ 2,952 .... J2
†43162 Jefferson (West Jefferson) 4,448 .... D6
43128 Jeffersonville 1,252 .... C6
44840 Jeromesville 582 .... F4
43437 Jerry City 512 .... C3
43986 Jewett 972 .... H5
43031 Johnstown 3,158 .... E5
43748 Junction City 754 .... F6
45853 Kalida 1,019 .... B4
44240 Kent 26,164 .... H3
43326 Kenton⊙ 8,605 .... C4
45429 Kettering 61,186 .... B6
44637 Killbuck 937 .... G5
45034 Kings Mills 500 .... B7
45644 Kingston 1,208 .... E7
44048 Kingsville J2
44428 Kinsman 900 .... J3
43033 Kirkersville 626 .... E6
†44094 Kirtland 5,969 .... H2
43951 Lafferty 855 .... H5
44050 Lagrange 1,258 .... F3
44250 Lakemore 2,744 .... H3
43440 Lakeside 850 .... E2
43331 Lakeview 1,089 .... C4
44107 Lakewood 61,963 .... G9
43130 Lancaster⊙ 34,953 .... E6
43934 Lansing 950 .... J5
43332 La Rue 861 .... D4
43135 Laurelville 591 .... E7
†45501 Lawrenceville 307 .... C6
45036 Lebanon⊙ 9,636 .... B7
45135 Leesburg 1,019 .... D7
44431 Leetonia 2,121 .... J4
45856 Leipsic 2,171 .... C3
45338 Lewisburg 1,450 .... A6
44904 Lexington 3,823 .... E4
43532 Liberty Center 1,111 .... B3
*45801 Lima⊙ 47,381 .... B4
Lima‡ 218,244 .... B4
†45201 Lincoln Heights 5,259 .... C9
43442 Lindsey 571 .... D3
44432 Lisbon⊙ 3,159 .... J4
44253 Litchfield 650 .... F3
43136 Lithopolis 652 .... E6
45742 Little Hocking 800 .... G7
45215 Lockland 4,292 .... C9
44254 Lodi 2,942 .... F3
43138 Logan⊙ 6,557 .... F6
43140 London⊙ 6,958 .... C6
*44052 Lorain 75,416 .... F3
Lorain-Elyria‡ 274,909 .... F3
†44481 Lordstown 3,280 .... J3
44842 Loudonville 2,945 .... F4
44641 Louisville 7,996 .... H4
45140 Loveland 9,106 .... D9
45744 Lowell 729 .... H6
44436 Lowellville 1,558 .... J3
44843 Lucas 753 .... F4
45648 Lucasville 3,349 .... E8
43443 Luckey 895 .... D3
45142 Lynchburg 1,205 .... C7
44124 Lyndhurst 18,092 .... J9
43533 Lyons 596 .... B2
44056 Macedonia 6,571 .... J10
†45202 Mack B9
45243 Madeira 9,341 .... C9
44057 Madison 2,291 .... H2
44643 Magnolia 986 .... H4
43758 Malta 956 .... G6
44644 Malvern 1,032 .... H4
45144 Manchester 2,313 .... C8
*44901 Mansfield⊙ 53,927 .... F4
Mansfield‡ 131,205 .... F4
44255 Mantua 1,041 .... H3
44137 Maple Heights 29,735 .... H9
†43440 Marblehead 679 .... E2
45860 Maria Stein 950 .... A5

(continued on following page)

Agriculture, Industry and Resources

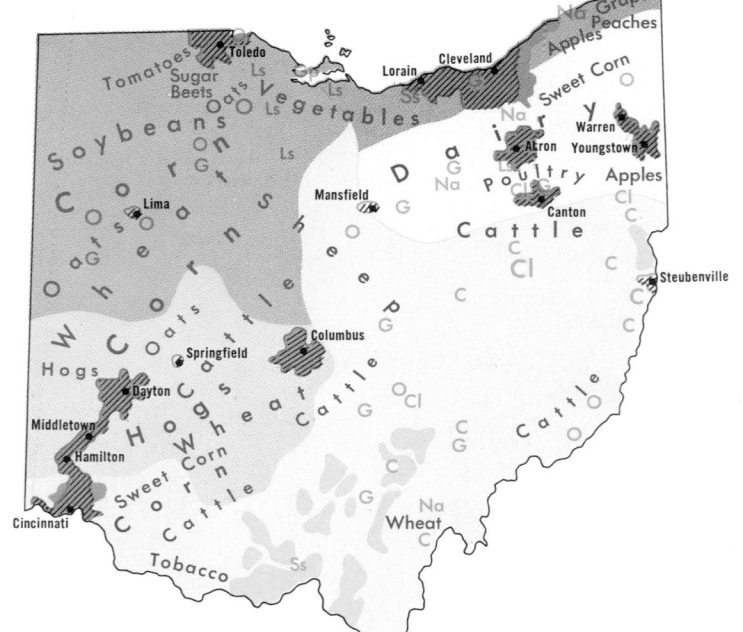

DOMINANT LAND USE

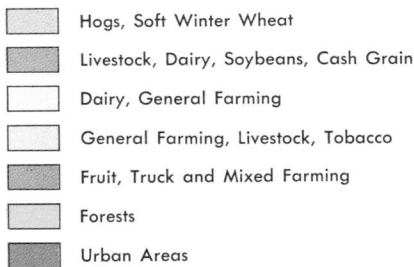

- Hogs, Soft Winter Wheat
- Livestock, Dairy, Soybeans, Cash Grain
- Dairy, General Farming
- General Farming, Livestock, Tobacco
- Fruit, Truck and Mixed Farming
- Forests
- Urban Areas

MAJOR MINERAL OCCURRENCES

- C Coal
- Cl Clay
- G Natural Gas
- Gp Gypsum
- Ls Limestone
- Na Salt
- O Petroleum
- Ss Sandstone
- Major Industrial Areas

45227 Mariemont 3,295 ....C9
45750 Marietta⊙ 16,467 ....G7
43302 Marion⊙ 37,040.............D4
44645 Marshallville 788 ....G4
43935 Martins Ferry 9,331 .... J5
45146 Martinsville 539 ....C7
43040 Marysville⊙ 7,414 ....D5
45040 Mason 8,692 ....B7
44646 Massillon 30,557 ....H4
44438 Masury 1,836 .... J3
†45069 Maud 800 ....B7
43537 Maumee 15,747 ....C2
44124 Mayfield 3,577 .... J9
44124 Mayfield Heights 21,550.... J9
45651 McArthur⊙ 1,912 .... F7
43534 McClure 694 ....C3
45858 McComb 1,608 ....C3
43756 McConnelsville⊙ 2,018.....G6
44437 McDonald 3,744 .... J3
45859 McGuffey 646 ....C4
43044 Mechanicsburg 1,792.......D5
44256 Medina⊙ 15,268 ....G3
45862 Mendon 749 ....A4
44060 Mentor 42,065 ....H2
44060 Mentor-on-the-Lake 7,919 .G2
43540 Metamora 556.................C2
45342 Miamisburg 15,304 ....B6
45041 Miamitown 800...............A9
44652 Middlebranch 300............H4
†44017 Middleburg Heights 16,218 G10
44062 Middlefield 1,997 ....H3
45863 Middle Point 709.............B4
45760 Middleport 2,971 .... F7
45042 Middletown 43,719..........A6
44653 Midvale 654....................H5
44846 Milan 1,569.....................E3
45150 Milford 5,232..................D9
43045 Milford Center 764...........D5
43447 Millbury 955 ....D2
44654 Millersburg⊙ 3,247 .... F4
43046 Millersport 844 ....E6
†45011 Millville 809 ....A7
44656 Mineral City 884 ....H4
44657 Minerva 4,549..................H4
†43201 Minerva Park 1,618 ....E5
43938 Mingo Junction 4,834 ...... J5
45865 Minster 2,557 ....B5
44260 Mogadore 4,190 ....H3
45050 Monroe 4,256 ....B7
44847 Monroeville 1,329 ....E3
45242 Montgomery 10,088 ....C9
43543 Montpelier 4,431..............A2
†45439 Moraine 5,325.................B6
†44022 Moreland Hills 3,083........ J9
45152 Morrow 1,254..................B7
43338 Mount Gilead⊙ 2,911 ......E4
45231 Mount Healthy 7,562........B9
45154 Mount Orab 1,573............C7
43939 Mount Pleasant 616......... J5
43143 Mount Sterling 1,623 ....D6
43050 Mount Vernon⊙ 14,323 ...E5
43340 Mount Victory 667...........D4
44262 Munroe Falls 4,731..........H3
43144 Murray City 579.............. F6
43545 Napoleon⊙ 8,614 ....B3
44662 Navarre 1,343 ....H4
43940 Neffs 1,106 .... J5
44441 Negley 917 .... J4
45764 Nelsonville 4,567............. F7
44849 Nevada 945 ....D4
43055 Newark⊙ 41,200 .... F5
Newark‡ 120,981............ F5
45662 New Boston 3,188............E8
45869 New Bremen 2,393...........B5
†44101 Newburgh Heights 2,678...H9
†45201 New Burlington 900 ....B9
45344 New Carlisle 6,498 ....C6
43832 Newcomerstown 3,986 .....G5
43762 New Concord 1,860..........G6
43145 New Holland 783 ....D6
45871 New Knoxville 760............B5
45345 New Lebanon 4,501..........B6
43764 New Lexington⊙ 5,179 .... F6
44851 New London 2,449.......... F3
45346 New Madison 1,008.........A6
45767 New Matamoras.............. J6
45011 New Miami 2,980.............A7
44442 New Middletown 2,195 ..... J4
45347 New Paris 1,709 ....A6
44663 New Philadelphia⊙ 16,883 G5
45768 Newport 975....................H7
45157 New Richmond 2,769.......B8
43766 New Straitsville 937 .... F6
44444 Newton Falls 4,960.......... J3
45244 Newtown 1,817 .... C10
45159 New Vienna 1,133...........C7
44854 New Washington 1,213.....E4
44445 New Waterford 1,314 .... J4
44446 Niles 23,088 .... J3
45872 North Baltimore 3,127 ......C3
45052 North Bend 546 ....B9
44450 North Bloomfield 650 .... J3
44720 North Canton 14,228.........H4
45239 North College Hill 11,114 ..B9
44855 North Fairfield 525...........E3
44067 Northfield 3,913..............J10
44707 North Industry H4
44068 North Kingsville 2,939 ...... J2
43060 North Lewisburg 1,072 .....C5
44452 North Lima 800 .... J4
†44057 North Madison 8,741 ....H2
44070 North Olmsted 36,486 ......G9
†44081 North Perry 897 ....H2
†44101 North Randall 1,054.........H9
45414 Northridge 9,720..............B6
44039 North Ridgeville 21,522 .... F3
44133 North Royalton 17,671 ... H10
†43619 Northwood 5,495 ....D2
†43701 North Zanesville 2,166......G6
44203 Norton 12,242..................G3
44857 Norwalk⊙ 14,358 ....E3
45212 Norwood 26,342...............C9
43449 Oak Harbor 2,678 ....D2
45656 Oak Hill 1,713 ....E8
†45419 Oakwood 9,372 ....B6
†44146 Oakwood 3,786 ....H9
45873 Oakwood 886...................B3
44074 Oberlin 8,660.................. F3
†43201 Obetz 3,095.....................E6
45874 Ohio City 881 ....A4
44138 Olmsted Falls 5,868 ....G9
44862 Ontario 4,123...................E4
†44101 Orange 2,376 .... J9
43616 Oregon 18,675 ....D2
44667 Orrville 7,511 ....G4
44076 Orwell 1,067 .... J2
45875 Ottawa⊙ 3,874 ....B3
†43601 Ottawa Hills 4,065 ....C2
45876 Ottoville 833 ....B4
45160 Owensville 858 ....B7
45056 Oxford 17,655 ....A6
44077 Painesville⊙ 16,391 ....H2
45877 Pandora 977 ....C4
44080 Parkman 600 ....H3
44129 Parma 92,548 ....H9
†44130 Parma Heights 23,112......G9
43062 Pataskala 2,284 ....E5
45879 Paulding⊙ 2,754 ....A3
45880 Payne 1,399 ....A3
45660 Peebles 1,790 ....D8
43450 Pemberville 1,321 ....C3
44264 Peninsula 604 ....G3
†44124 Pepper Pike 6,177 .... J9
44081 Perry 961.........................H2
43551 Perrysburg 10,215............C2
44864 Perrysville 836................ F4
45354 Phillipsburg 705..............B6
43771 Philo 799 ....G6
43147 Pickerington 3,917 ....E6
45661 Piketon 1,726...................E7
43554 Pioneer 1,133 ....A2
45356 Piqua 20,480 ....B5
43064 Plain City 2,102...............D5
43772 Pleasant City 481 ....G6
45359 Pleasant Hill 1,051 ....B5
43148 Pleasantville 780 .... F6
44865 Plymouth 1,939 ....E4
44514 Poland 3,084 .... J3
45769 Pomeroy⊙ 2,728............G7
43452 Port Clinton⊙ 7,223 ....E2
45770 Portland 150...................G7
45662 Portsmouth⊙ 25,943.......D8
43837 Port Washington 622 ....G5
43942 Powhatan Point 2,181 ...... J6
45669 Proctorville 975 .... F9
43342 Prospect 1,159................D5
43456 Put-in-Bay 146 ....E2
43773 Quaker City 698...............H6
43343 Quincy 633......................C5
45771 Racine 908......................G8
44265 Randolph 900 ....H3
44266 Ravenna⊙ 11,987............H3
43943 Rayland 566 .... J5
45215 Reading 12,843 ....C9
†44202 Reminderville 1,960 ....J10
†45202 Remington 600.................C9
45773 Reno 576.........................H7
†43412 Reno Beach D2
44867 Republic 656....................D3
43068 Reynoldsburg 20,661 .... E6
44286 Richfield 3,437 ....G3
43944 Richmond 624.................. J5
†44045 Richmond (Grand River) 412..................H2
45673 Richmond Dale 950 .... E7
44143 Richmond Heights 10,095 .H9
43344 Richwood 2,181 ....D5
45674 Rio Grande 864 .... F8
45167 Ripley 2,174 ....C8
43457 Risingsun 698 ....C3
44270 Rittman 6,063 ....G4
†43085 Riverlea 528 ....D5
44670 Robertsville 600...............H4
44084 Rock Creek 652 .... J2
45882 Rockford 1,245 ....A4
44116 Rocky River 21,084 ....G9
44085 Rome 210........................ J2
44272 Rootstown 900.................H3
†45662 Rosemount 1,747............D8
43777 Roseville 1,915............... F6
45061 Ross 2,767 ....B9
43460 Rossford 5,978 ....C2
45236 Rossmoyne C9
†43943 Rush Run 560.................. J5
43347 Rushsylvania 610 ....C5
43348 Russells Point 1,156 ....C5
45775 Rutland 635.................... F7
45169 Sabina 2,799 ....C7
†44067 Sagamore Hills J10
45217 Saint Bernard 5,396.........B9
43950 Saint Clairsville⊙ 5,452 .... J5
45883 Saint Henry 1,596 ....A5
45885 Saint Marys 8,414............B4
43072 Saint Paris 1,742 ....C5
44460 Salem 12,869 .... J4
43945 Salineville 1,629.............. J4
44870 Sandusky⊙ 31,360 ....E3
44671 Sandyville 500.................H4
45171 Sardinia 826 ....C7
43946 Sardis 865 .... J6
43988 Scio 1,003 ....H5
†45662 Sciotodale 1,191 ....E8
45679 Seaman 1,039..................C8
44672 Sebring 5,078 ....H4
†44131 Seven Hills 13,650 ....H9
45062 Seven Mile 841................A7
44273 Seville 1,568....................G3
43947 Shadyside 4,315 .... J6
44120 Shaker Heights 32,487 .....H9
45241 Sharonville 10,108...........C9
43782 Shawnee 924 .... F6
†44052 Sheffield 1,886 .... F3
44054 Sheffield Lake 10,484....... F3
44875 Shelby 9,646 ....E4
43556 Sherwood 915.................A3
44878 Shiloh 857 ....E4
44676 Shreve 1,608 .... F4
45365 Sidney⊙ 17,657 ....B5
†44221 Silver Lake 2,915 ....G3
†45201 Silverton 6,172................C9
43948 Smithfield 1,308 .... J5
44677 Smithville 1,467..............G4
44139 Solon 14,341 .... J9
43783 Somerset 1,432............... F6
†44001 South Amherst 1,848 .... F3
†43103 South Bloomfield 934 ....D6
45368 South Charleston 1,682 ....C6
44121 South Euclid 25,713 ....H9
45065 South Lebanon 2,700........B7
45680 South Point 3,918 ....E9
†44022 South Russell 2,784.........H3
45369 South Vienna 464.............C6
45682 South Webster 886...........E8
43701 South Zanesville 1,739 ..... F6
44275 Spencer 764 .... F3
45887 Spencerville 2,184 ....B4
45066 Springboro 4,962 ....B6
45246 Springdale 10,111 ....B9
*45501 Springfield⊙ 72,563 ....C6
Springfield‡ 183,885........C6
45370 Spring Valley 541 ....C6
44276 Sterling 600.....................G4
43952 Steubenville⊙ 26,400....... J5
Steubenville-Weirton‡ 163,099.................... J5
43787 Stockport 558 ....G6
43154 Stoutsville 537.................E6
44224 Stow 25,303....................H3
44680 Strasburg 2,091...............G4
44240 Streetsboro 9,055 ....H3
44136 Strongsville 28,577 .... G10
44471 Struthers 13,624.............. J3
43557 Stryker 1,423 ....B3
†44260 Suffield 650 ....H3
44681 Sugarcreek 1,966 ....G5
43074 Sunbury 2,101 ....E5
43558 Swanton 3,424 ....C2
44882 Sycamore 1,059 ....D4
43560 Sylvania 15,527 ....C2
45779 Syracuse 946 ....G7
44278 Tallmadge 15,269.............H3
†43771 Taylorsville (Philo) 799......G6
45174 Terrace Park 2,044 ....D9
45780 The Plains 2,044....... ..... F7
43076 Thornville 838 .... F6
44883 Tiffin⊙ 19,549 ....D3
43963 Tiltonsville 1,750.............. J5
†44094 Timberlake 885................ J8
45371 Tipp City 5,595................B6
†45245 Tobasco 950 .... C10
*43601 Toledo⊙ 354,635 ....D2
Toledo‡ 791,599 ....D2
43964 Toronto 6,934 .... J5
45067 Trenton 6,401 ....B7
45782 Trimble 579 .... F7
45426 Trotwood 7,802................B6
45373 Troy⊙ 19,086..................B5
44682 Tuscarawas 917...............H5
44087 Twinsburg 7,632.............J10
44683 Uhrichsville 6,130.............H5
45322 Union 5,219 ....B6
†47390 Union City 1,716..............A5
44685 Uniontown 875 ....H4
44118 University Heights 15,401..H9
43221 Upper Arlington 35,648.....D6
43351 Upper Sandusky⊙ 5,967 ..D4
43078 Urbana⊙ 10,762 ....C5
†43123 Urbancrest 880................D6
43080 Utica 2,238 .... F5
†43201 Valley View 730 . ...D6
†44101 Valleyview 1,576..............H9
45377 Vandalia 13,161 ....B6
45890 Vanlue 390.......................C4
45891 Van Wert⊙ 11,035............A4
44089 Vermilion 11,012 .... F3
45378 Verona 571......................A6
45380 Versailles 2,384 ....A5
44473 Vienna 900 .... J3
44281 Wadsworth 15,166 ....G3
†44094 Waite Hill 529 ....H2
45687 Wakefield 300 ....E8
44889 Wakeman 906 .... F3
43465 Walbridge 2,900 ....C2
44687 Walnut Creek 550.............G4
†44146 Walton Hills 2,199............J10
45895 Wapakoneta⊙ 8,402........B4
45785 Warner 250 ....H6
*44481 Warren⊙ 56,629 .... J3
44128 Warrensville Heights 16,565 ....H9
43844 Warsaw 765 ....G5
43160 Washington Court House⊙ 12,682..........D6
44490 Washingtonville 865......... J4
45786 Waterford 600 ....G6
43566 Waterville 3,884...............C3
43567 Wauseon⊙ 6,173 ....B2
45690 Waverly⊙ 4,603 ....D7
43466 Wayne 894.......................C3
44688 Waynesburg 1,160 ....H4
45896 Waynesfield 826 ....C4
45068 Waynesville 1,796 ....B6
44090 Wellington 4,146.............. F3
45692 Wellston 6,016 .... F7
43968 Wellsville 5,095 .... J4
45381 West Alexandria 1,313......A6
45449 West Carrollton 13,148 .....B6
43081 Westerville 23,414............D5
44491 West Farmington 563 .... J3
44251 Westfield Center 791 ....G3
43162 West Jefferson 4,448 ....D6
43845 West Lafayette 2,225 ....G5
44145 Westlake 19,483 ....G9
43357 West Liberty 1,653 ....C5
43358 West Mansfield 716 ....C5
45383 West Milton 4,119.............B6
43569 Weston 1,708 ....C3
†45662 West Portsmouth 4,095 ....D8
44287 West Salem 1,357............ F4
45693 West Union⊙ 2,791 ....C8
43570 West Unity 1,639 ....B2
45694 Wheelersburg 4,796......... E8
43213 Whitehall 21,299.............. E6
43571 Whitehouse 2,137 ....C2
44092 Wickliffe 16,790............... J9
44890 Willard 5,720 ....E3
45176 Williamsburg 1,952...........B7
44093 Williamsfield 950.............. J2
43164 Williamsport 792..............D6
44094 Willoughby 19,329 .... J8
†44094 Willoughby Hills 8,612...... J9
44094 Willowick 17,834 .... J8
45898 Willshire 564...................A4
45177 Wilmington⊙ 10,431 ....C7
45697 Winchester 1,080.............C8
44288 Windham 3,721 ....H3
43952 Wintersville 4,724............ J5
45245 Withamsville 975........... C10
†45201 Woodlawn 2,715..............C9
†44101 Woodmere 877 .... J9
43793 Woodsfield⊙ 3,145 ....H6
43469 Woodville 2,050................D3
44691 Wooster⊙ 19,289............G4
43085 Worthington 15,016......... E5
45215 Wyoming 8,282................C9
45385 Xenia⊙ 24,653 ....C6
45387 Yellow Springs 4,077 ....C6
43971 Yorkville 1,447 .... J5
*44501 Youngstown⊙ 115,436 .... J3
Youngstown-Warren‡ 531,350.................... J3
43701 Zanesville⊙ 28,655 ....G6
44697 Zoar 264.........................H4
44698 Zoarville 125 ....H4

OTHER FEATURES

Atwood (lake) H4
Auglaize (riv.) B4
Berlin (lake) H4
Big Walnut (creek) E5
Black (riv.)............................. F3
Black Fork, Mohican (riv.)........... F4
Blanchard (riv.) C4
Blennerhassett (isl.)..................G7
Buckeye (lake) F6
Campbell (hill) C5
Captina (creek)........................J6
Cedar (pt.)..............................D2
Chagrin (riv.)........................... J8
Clear Fork (res.) E4
Clear Fork, Mohican (riv.) F4
Clendening (lake).....................H5
Cleveland-Hopkins Mun. Airport G9
Cuyahoga (riv.) H10
Darby (creek) D5
Deer (creek) D6
Delaware (lake) E5
Dillon (lake) F5
Dover (lake) H4
Duck (creek) H6
Erie (lake)..............................H1
Eufaula (res.).......................... L4
Grand (riv.)............................H2
Great Miami (riv.) A7
Hocking (riv.) F7
Hoover (res.)........................... E5
Huron (riv.)............................ E3
Indian (lake)...........................C5
James A. Garfield Nat'l Hist. Site G2
Kelleys (isl.) E2
Keystone (res.) K2
Killbuck (creek) G4
Kokosing (riv.)......................... E5
Leesville (lake) H5
Licking (riv.) F5
Little Beaver (creek).................. J4
Little Miami (riv.).....................B6
Little Miami, East Fork (riv.) C7
Little Muskingum (riv.)...............H6
Loramie (lake) B5
Mad (riv.)...............................C6
Maumee (bay) D2
Maumee (riv.)..........................A3
Middle Bass (isl.) E2
Mohican (riv.)........................... F4
Mosquito Creek (lake) J3
Mound City Group Nat'l Mon. E7
Muskingum (riv.)......................G6
North Bass (isl.)....................... E2
Ohio (riv.) B8
Ohio Brush (creek)....................D8
Olentangy (riv.) D4
Paint (creek)...........................D7
Perry's Victory and Int'l Peace Mem. E2
Piedmont (lake)........................H5
Portage (riv.)..........................D3
Pymatuning (res.)..................... J2
Raccoon (creek) F8
Rattlesnake (creek)...................C7
Rickenbacker Air Force Base 1,763. E6
Rocky (riv.).............................G9
Rocky, West Branch (riv.).......... G10
Rocky Fork (lake) D7
Saint Joseph (riv.) A3
Saint Marys (lake).....................A4
Saint Marys (riv.) A4
Salt Fork (creek).......................H5
Sandusky (bay) E3
Sandusky (riv.) D3
Scioto (riv.) D8
Senecaville (lake) H6
Sevenmile (creek) A6
South Bass (isl.) E2
Stillwater (riv.)........................B5
Symmes (creek)....................... F8
Tappan (lake) H5
Tiffin (riv.) B3
Tuscarawas (riv.).....................H5
Vermilion (riv.)........................ F3
Wabash (riv.) A5
West Sister (isl.) D2
Whiteoak (creek) C7
William H. Taft Nat'l Hist. Site ... C10
Wills (creek)...........................G5
Wills Creek (lake).....................G5
Wright-Patterson Air Force Base 9,155 ....B6
Yellow (creek).........................J4

⊙County seat.
‡Population of metropolitan area.
† Zip of nearest p.o. * Multiple zips

AREA 69,956 sq. mi. (181,186 sq. km.)
POPULATION 3,025,290
CAPITAL Oklahoma City
LARGEST CITY Oklahoma City
HIGHEST POINT Black Mesa 4,973 ft. (1516 m.)
SETTLED IN 1889
ADMITTED TO UNION November 16, 1907
POPULAR NAME Sooner State
STATE FLOWER Mistletoe
STATE BIRD Scissor-tailed Flycatcher

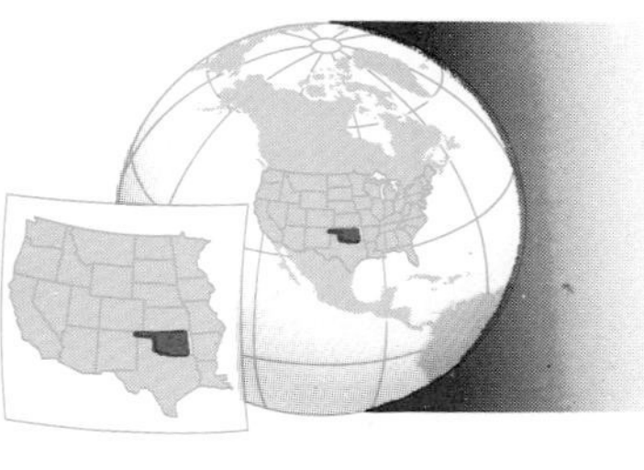

COUNTIES

Adair 18,575 S3
Alfalfa 7,077 K1
Atoka 12,748 O6
Beaver 6,806 E1
Beckham 19,243 G4
Blaine 13,443 K3
Bryan 30,535 O7
Caddo 30,905 K4
Canadian 56,452 K3
Carter 43,610 M6
Cherokee 30,684 R3
Choctaw 17,203 P6
Cimarron 3,648 A1
Cleveland 133,173 M4
Coal 6,041 O5
Comanche 112,456 K5
Cotton 7,338 K6
Craig 15,014 R1
Creek 59,016 O3
Custer 25,995 H3
Delaware 23,946 S2
Dewey 5,922 H2
Ellis 5,596 G2
Garfield 62,820 L2
Garvin 27,856 M5
Grady 39,490 L5
Grant 6,518 L1
Greer 7,028 G5
Harmon 4,519 G5
Harper 4,715 G1
Haskell 11,010 R4
Hughes 14,338 O4
Jackson 30,356 H5
Jefferson 8,183 L6
Johnston 10,356 N6
Kay 49,852 M1
Kingfisher 14,187 L3
Kiowa 12,711 J5
Latimer 9,840 R5
Le Flore 40,698 S5
Lincoln 26,601 N3
Logan 26,881 M3
Love 7,469 M7
Major 8,772 K2
Marshall 10,550 N6
Mayes 32,261 R2
McClain 20,291 L5
McCurtain 36,151 S6
McIntosh 15,562 P4
Murray 12,147 M6
Muskogee 66,939 R3
Noble 11,573 M2
Nowata 11,486 P1
Okfuskee 11,125 O3
Oklahoma 568,933 M3
Okmulgee 39,169 P3
Osage 39,327 O1
Ottawa 32,870 S1
Pawnee 15,310 N2
Payne 62,435 N2
Pittsburg 40,524 P5
Pontotoc 32,598 N5
Pottawatomie 55,239 N4
Pushmataha 11,773 R6
Roger Mills 4,799 G3
Rogers 46,436 P2
Seminole 27,473 N4
Sequoyah 30,749 S3
Stephens 43,419 L6
Texas 17,727 C1
Tillman 12,398 J6
Tulsa 470,593 P2
Wagoner 41,801 P3
Washington 48,113 P1
Washita 13,798 J4
Woods 10,923 J1
Woodward 21,172 H2

CITIES and TOWNS

Zip Name/Pop. Key

74720 Achille 480 O7
74820 Ada⊙ 15,902 N5
74330 Adair 508 R2
73901 Adams 150 D1
73520 Addington 141 L6
74331 Afton 1,174 S1
74824 Agra 354 N3
74721 Albany 65 O7
73001 Albert 100 K4
74521 Albion 165 R5
74522 Alderson 366 P5
73002 Alex 769 L5
73716 Aline 313 K1
74825 Allen 998 O5
73521 Altus⊙ 23,101 H5
73717 Alva⊙ 6,416 J1
73004 Amber 416 L4
73718 Ames 314 K2
73719 Amorita 66 K1
73005 Anadarko⊙ 6,378 K4
74523 Antlers⊙ 2,989 P6
73006 Apache 1,560 K5
73620 Arapaho⊙ 851 H3
73401 Ardmore⊙ 23,689 M6
74901 Arkoma 2,175 T4
73832 Arnett⊙ 714 G2
74826 Asher 659 N5
74524 Ashland 72 O5
74525 Atoka⊙ 3,409 O6
74827 Atwood 225 O5
74001 Avant 461 O2
†73860 Avard 51 J1
73930 Baker 70 D1
74002 Barnsdall 1,501 O1
†74965 Baron 300 S3
74003 Bartlesville⊙ 34,568 O1
74722 Battiest 250 S6
73932 Beaver⊙ 1,939 F1
74421 Beggs 1,428 P3
†74966 Bengal 300 R5
74723 Bennington 302 P7
74331 Bernice 318 S1
73622 Bessie 245 H4
73008 Bethany 22,130 L3
74724 Bethel 350 S6
†74801 Bethel Acres 2,314 M4
74332 Big Cabin 252 R1
74630 Billings 632 M1
73009 Binger 791 K4
73720 Bison 103 L2
74008 Bixby 6,969 P3
74058 Blackburn 114 N2
74631 Blackwell 8,400 M1
73526 Blair 1,092 H5
73010 Blanchard 1,688 L4
74528 Blanco 215 P5
74529 Blocker 135 P4
†74701 Blue 150 O7
74333 Bluejacket 247 R1
73933 Boise City⊙ 1,761 B1
74726 Bokchito 628 O6
74930 Bokoshe 556 S4
74829 Boley 423 O4
74727 Boswell 702 P6
74830 Bowlegs 522 N4
74009 Bowring 115 O1
74422 Boynton 518 P3
73011 Bradley 284 L5
74423 Braggs 351 R3
74632 Braman 355 M1
73012 Bray 591 L5
73721 Breckinridge 261 L2
†73047 Bridgeport 115 K3
74010 Bristow 4,702 O3
74012 Broken Arrow 35,761 P2
74728 Broken Bow 3,965 S7
74530 Bromide 180 N6
†74873 Brooksville 46 M4
†74437 Bryant 74 P4
73834 Buffalo⊙ 1,381 G1
74931 Bunch 64 S3
74633 Burbank 161 N1
73722 Burlington 206 K1
73430 Burneyville 150 M7
73624 Burns Flat 2,431 H4
73625 Butler 388 H3
74831 Byars 353 N5
†74820 Byng 833 N5
73723 Byron 67 K1
73527 Cache 1,661 J5
74729 Caddo 923 O6
74730 Calera 1,390 O7
73014 Calumet 469 K3
74531 Calvin 315 O5
73835 Camargo 264 H2
74932 Cameron 365 T4
74425 Canadian 279 P4
74533 Caney 147 O6
73724 Canton 854 J2
73626 Canute 676 H4
73725 Capron 54 J1
74335 Cardin 500 S1
73726 Carmen 516 J1
73015 Carnegie 2,016 J4
74832 Carney 622 N3
73727 Carrier 259 K2
73627 Carter 367 H4
74934 Cartersville 79 S4
73016 Cashion 547 L3
74833 Castle 130 O4
74015 Catoosa 1,561 P2
73017 Cement 884 K5
74534 Centrahoma 166 O5
74834 Chandler⊙ 2,926 N3
73528 Chattanooga 403 J6
74426 Checotah 3,454 R4
74016 Chelsea 1,754 P1
73728 Cherokee⊙ 2,105 K1
73838 Chester 104 J2
73628 Cheyenne⊙ 1,207 G3
73018 Chickasha⊙ 15,828 L4
74635 Chilocco 400 M1
73020 Choctaw 7,520 M3
74337 Chouteau 1,559 R2
†74965 Christie 375 S3
73111 Cimarron L3
74017 Claremore⊙ 12,085 R2
74535 Clarita 72 O6
74536 Clayton 833 R5
74835 Clearview 250 O4
73729 Cleo Springs 514 K2
74020 Cleveland 2,972 O2
73601 Clinton 8,796 H3
74538 Coalgate⊙ 2,001 O5
74733 Colbert 1,122 O7
74338 Colcord 530 S2
†73010 Cole 309 L5
73432 Coleman 200 O6
74021 Collinsville 3,556 P2
73021 Colony 185 J4
73529 Comanche 1,937 L6
74339 Commerce 2,556 R1
73022 Concho 300 L3
†73041 Cooperton 31 J5
74022 Copan 960 P1
73632 Cordell⊙ 3,301 H4
73024 Corn 542 J4
†73456 Cornish 115 L6
74428 Council Hill 141 P3
73025 Countyline 550 L6
73730 Covington 715 L2
74429 Coweta 4,554 P3
†74934 Cowlington 546 S4
73027 Coyle 345 M3
73638 Crawford 53 G3
73028 Crescent 1,651 L3
74837 Cromwell 337 N4
74430 Crowder 431 P4
†73446 Cumberland 100 N6
74023 Cushing 7,720 N3
73639 Custer City 530 J3
73029 Cyril 1,220 K5
73731 Dacoma 226 J1
74838 Dale 160 M4
74026 Davenport 974 N3
73530 Davidson 501 J6
73030 Davis 2,782 M5
74636 Deer Creek 174 L1
74027 Delaware 544 P1
73115 Del City 28,523 L4
74028 Depew 682 O3
73531 Devol 186 J6
74431 Dewar 1,048 P4
74029 Dewey 3,545 P1
73031 Dibble 348 L4
†73401 Dickson 996 M6
73641 Dill City 649 H4
74340 Disney 464 S2
73032 Dougherty 210 M6
73733 Douglas 89 L2
74341 Douthat 30 S1
73734 Dover 570 L3
73735 Drummond 482 L2
74030 Drumright 3,162 N3
73533 Duncan⊙ 22,517 L5
74701 Durant⊙ 11,972 O6
73642 Durham 30 G3
74839 Dustin 498 O4
74734 Eagletown 650 S6
73033 Eakly 452 K4
74840 Earlsboro 266 N4
†73532 East Duke 484 H5
73034 Edmond 34,637 M3
73537 Eldorado 688 G6
73538 Elgin 1,003 K5
73644 Elk City 9,579 G4
73539 Elmer 131 H6
73035 Elmore City 582 M5
73935 Elmwood 300 F1
73036 El Reno⊙ 15,486 K3
†73529 Empire City 13 L6
73701 Enid⊙ 50,363 L2
73645 Erick 1,375 G4
74342 Eucha 210 S2
74432 Eufaula⊙ 3,159 P4
74637 Fairfax 1,949 N1
74343 Fairland 1,073 S1
73736 Fairmont 419 L2
†74080 Fair Oaks 346 P2
73737 Fairview⊙ 3,370 J2
†74881 Fallis 22 M3
74935 Fanshawe 416 S5
73840 Fargo 409 G2
73540 Faxon 140 J6
73646 Fay 140 J3
73937 Felt 120 A1
74543 Finley 350 R6
74842 Fittstown 500 N5
74843 Fitzhugh 150 N5
†73569 Fleetwood 12 L7
73541 Fletcher 1,074 K5
74652 Foraker 34 O1
†73101 Forest Park 1,148 M3
73938 Forgan 611 E1
73038 Fort Cobb 760 K4
74434 Fort Gibson 2,477 R3
73841 Fort Supply 559 G1
74735 Fort Towson 789 R7
73647 Foss 188 H4
73039 Foster 100 M5
73435 Fox 400 M6
74031 Foyil 191 R2
74844 Francis 365 N5
73542 Frederick⊙ 6,153 H6
73842 Freedom 339 H1
73843 Gage 667 G2
74936 Gans 346 S4
73738 Garber 1,215 M2
74736 Garvin 162 S7
73844 Gate 146 F1
73040 Geary 1,700 K3
73436 Gene Autry 178 N6
73543 Geronimo 726 K6
†74531 Gerty 149 O5
74032 Glencoe 490 M2
74033 Glenpool 2,706 P3
74737 Golden 300 S6
†73093 Goldsby 603 L4
73739 Goltry 305 K1
†74740 Goodwater 240 S7
73939 Goodwell 1,186 C1
74435 Gore 445 R3
73041 Gotebo 457 J4
73544 Gould 318 G5
74545 Gowen 75 R5
73042 Gracemont 503 K4
73545 Grady 85 L6
73437 Graham 200 M6
†74652 Grainola 67 N1
73546 Grandfield 1,445 J6
†74349 Grand Lake Towne 36 S1
73547 Granite 1,617 H5
†74437 Grayson 150 P3
73043 Greenfield 233 K3
74344 Grove 3,378 S1
73044 Guthrie⊙ 10,312 M3
73942 Guymon⊙ 8,492 D1
74546 Haileyville 832 P5
74034 Hallett 186 N2
†73069 Hall Park 577 M4
73650 Hammon 866 H3
74845 Hanna 157 P4
74846 Harden City 250 N5
73944 Hardesty 243 D1
73832 Harmon 27 G2
73045 Harrah 2,897 M4
†74740 Harris 192 S7
74547 Hartshorne 2,380 R5
74436 Haskell 1,953 P3
73548 Hastings 246 K6
74740 Haworth 341 S7
73549 Headrick 223 H5
73438 Healdton 3,769 M6
74937 Heavener 2,776 S5
73741 Helena 710 K1
74741 Hendrix 106 O7
73046 Hennepin 300 M5
73742 Hennessey 2,287 L2
74437 Henryetta 6,432 O4
†73086 Hickory 95 N5
73743 Hillsdale 110 K1
73047 Hinton 1,432 K4
73744 Hitchcock 172 K3
74438 Hitchita 126 P3
73651 Hobart⊙ 4,735 J5
74439 Hoffman 407 P4
74848 Holdenville⊙ 5,469 O4
73550 Hollis⊙ 2,958 G5
73551 Hollister 82 J6
74035 Hominy 3,130 O2
74549 Honobia 80 R5
73945 Hooker 1,788 D1
†74366 Hoot Owl 3 R2
73746 Hopeton 42 J1
74940 Howe 562 S5
74440 Hoyt 160 R4
74743 Hugo⊙ 7,172 P7
74441 Hulbert 633 R3
74640 Hunter 276 L1
73048 Hydro 938 J3
74745 Idabel⊙ 7,622 S7
73552 Indiahoma 364 J5
74442 Indianola 254 P4
74036 Inola 1,550 P2
73747 Isabella 113 K2
74346 Jay⊙ 2,100 S2
†73759 Jefferson 92 L1
74037 Jenks 5,876 P2
74038 Jennings 395 N2
73749 Jet 352 K1
73049 Jones 2,270 M3
74347 Kansas 491 S2
74641 Kaw City 283 N1
74039 Kellyville 960 O3

(continued on following page)

Agriculture, Industry and Resources

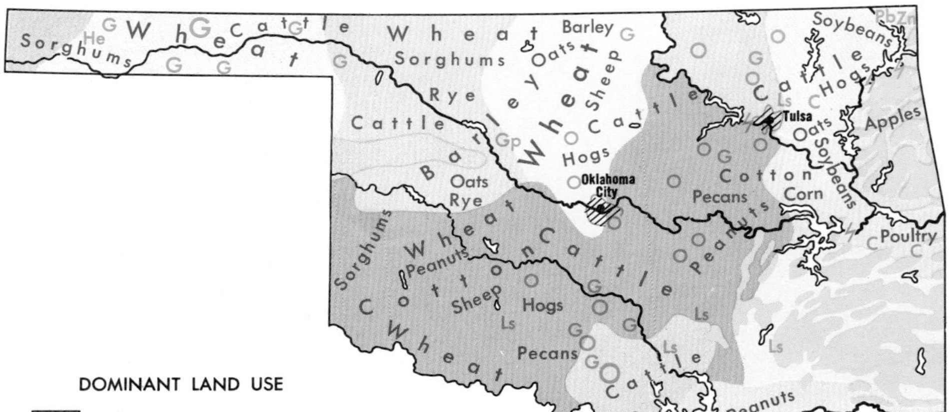

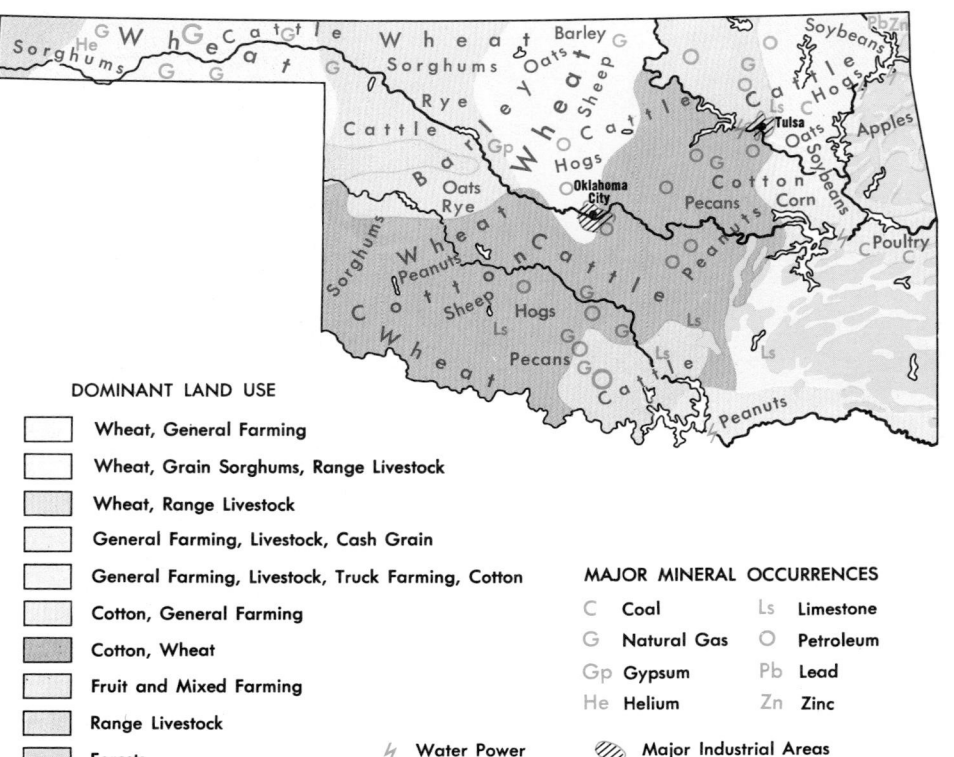

DOMINANT LAND USE

- Wheat, General Farming
- Wheat, Grain Sorghums, Range Livestock
- Wheat, Range Livestock
- General Farming, Livestock, Cash Grain
- General Farming, Livestock, Truck Farming, Cotton
- Cotton, General Farming
- Cotton, Wheat
- Fruit and Mixed Farming
- Range Livestock
- Forests

MAJOR MINERAL OCCURRENCES

- C Coal
- G Natural Gas
- Gp Gypsum
- He Helium
- Ls Limestone
- O Petroleum
- Pb Lead
- Zn Zinc

Water Power

Major Industrial Areas

Oklahoma

SCALE
0 5 10   20   30   40 MI.
0 5 10 20   30   40 KM.

State Capitals .... ⊛
County Seats .... ⊙
Major Limited Access Hwys.

Scale 1:2,040,000

© Copyright HAMMOND INCORPORATED, Maplewood, N. J.

Topography

0   50   100 MI.
0   50   100 KM.

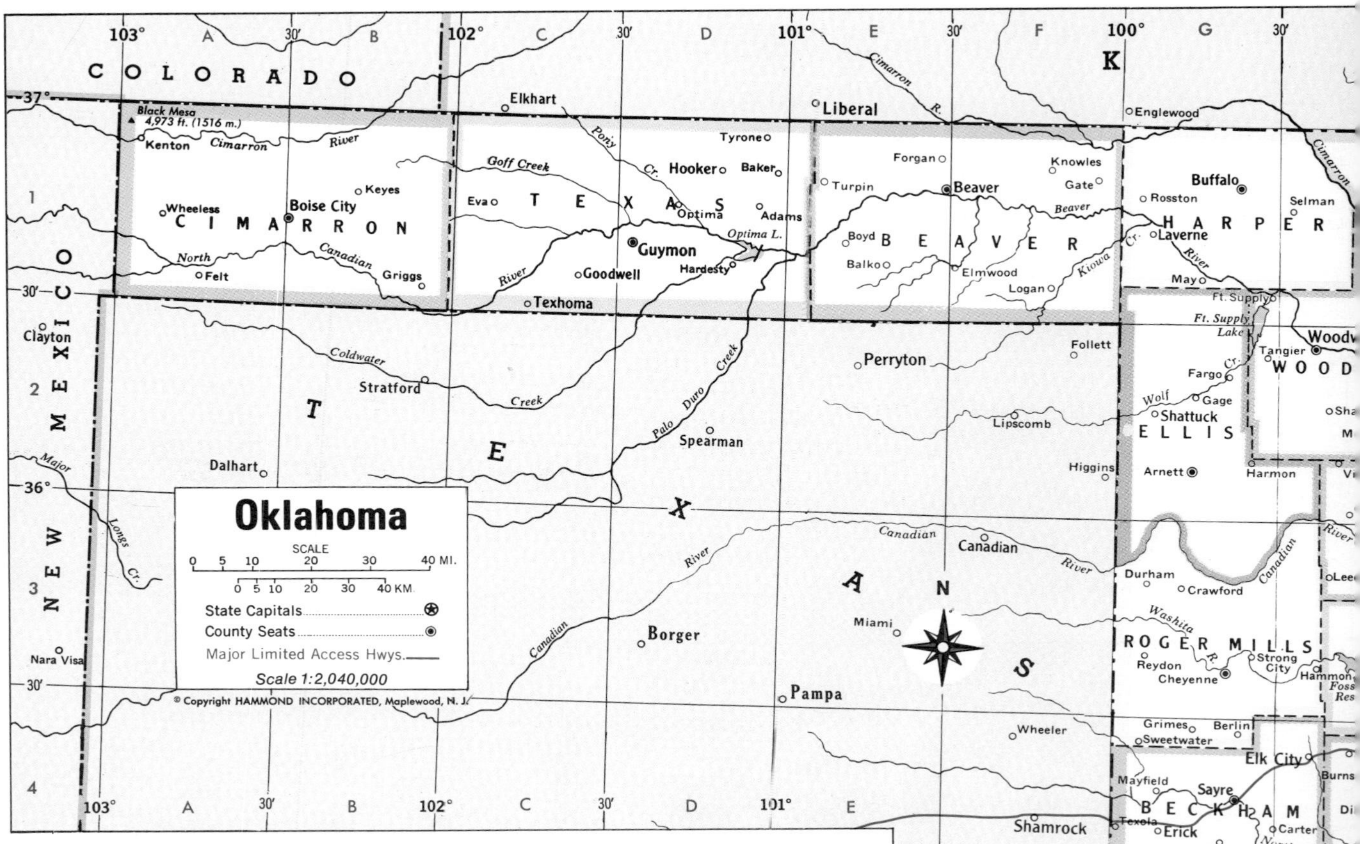

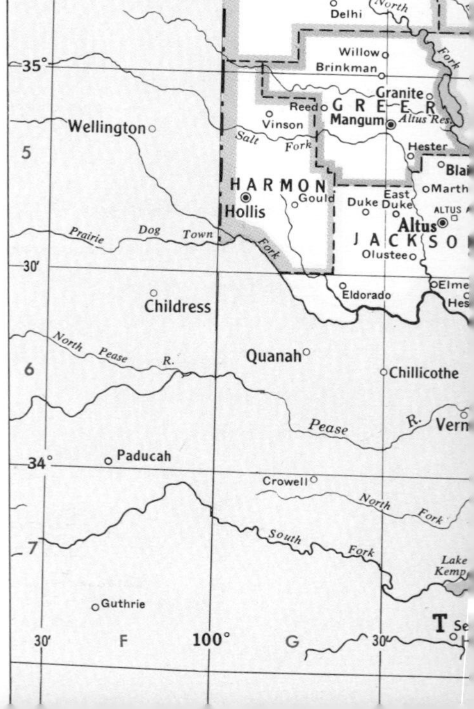

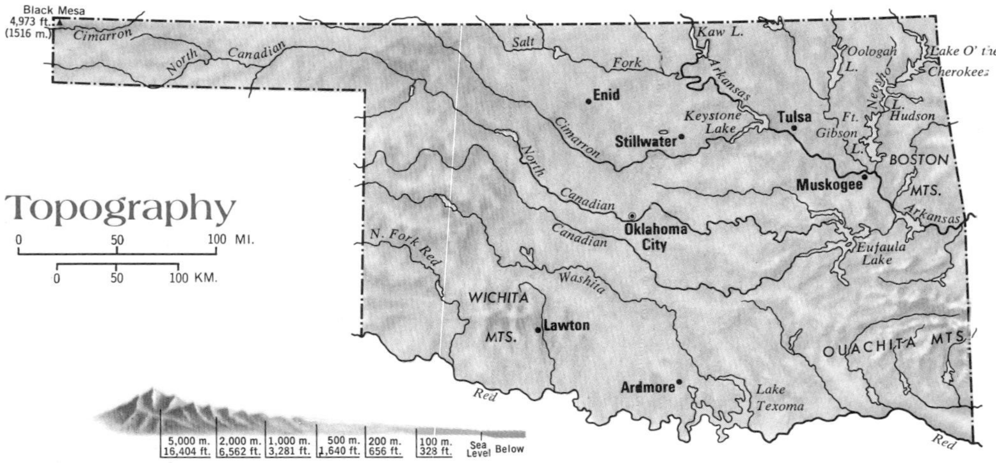

COUNTIES

Baker 16,134		K3
Benton 68,211		D3
Clackamas 241,911		E2
Clatsop 32,489		D1
Columbia 35,646		D2
Coos 64,047		C4
Crook 13,091		G3
Curry 16,992		C5
Deschutes 62,142		F4
Douglas 93,748		D4
Gilliam 2,057		G2
Grant 8,210		J3
Harney 8,314		H4
Hood River 15,835		F2
Jackson 132,456		E5
Jefferson 11,599		F3
Josephine 58,855		D5
Klamath 59,117		F5
Lake 7,532		G5
Lane 275,226		E4
Lincoln 35,264		D3
Linn 89,495		E3
Malheur 26,896		K4
Marion 204,692		E3
Morrow 7,519		H2
Multnomah 562,640		E2
Polk 45,203		D3
Sherman 2,172		G2
Tillamook 21,164		D2
Umatilla 58,861		J2
Union 23,921		J2
Wallowa 7,273		K2
Wasco 21,732		G2
Washington 245,860		D2
Wheeler 1,513		G3
Yamhill 55,332		D2

CITIES and TOWNS

Zip	Name/Pop.	Key
†97330	Adair Village 589	D3
97810	Adams 240	J2
97620	Adel 24	H5
97901	Adrian 162	K4
†97365	Agate Beach 975	C3
97406	Agness 150	C5
97321	Albany⊙ 26,678	D3
97407	Allegany 300	D4
97005	Aloha 28,353	A2
97324	Alsea 125	D3
†97601	Altamont 19,805	F5
97409	Alvadore 800	D3
97101	Amity 1,092	D2
97001	Antelope 39	G3
97530	Applegate 150	D5
97812	Arlington 521	G2
97520	Ashland 14,943	E5
97103	Astoria⊙ 9,998	D1
97813	Athena 965	J2
97325	Aumsville 1,432	E3
97002	Aurora 523	B2
97817	Austin 19	J3
†97601	Baker⊙ 9,471	K3
†97378	Ballston 150	D2
97411	Bandon 2,311	C4
97106	Banks 489	A1
†97013	Barlow 105	B2
†97009	Barton 100	B2
†97136	Bar View 170	C2
97420	Barview 1,462	C4
97305	Bates 56	J3
97817	Beatty 350	F5
97107	Bay City 986	D2
97621	Beatty 350	F5
97108	Beaver 350	D2
97004	Beavercreek 708	D3
97005	Beaverton 30,582	A2
97701	Bend⊙ 17,263	F4
†97058	Biggs 50	G2
97412	Blachly 80	D3
97108	Blaine 38	D2
97326	Blodgett 250	D3
97413	Blue River 318	E4
97622	Bly 800	F5
97818	Boardman 1,261	H2
97623	Bonanza 270	F5
97008	Bonneville 80	F2
97009	Boring 150	E2
97010	Bridal Veil 20	F2
†97458	Bridge 200	D4
†97136	Brighton 150	C2
97001	Brightwood 200	E2
97414	Broadbent 400	C4
97903	Brogan 130	K3
97415	Brookings 3,384	C5
97305	Brooks 490	A3
†97524	Brownsboro 150	E5
97327	Brownsville 1,261	E3
†97351	Buena Vista 130	D3
†97420	Bunker Hill 1,555	C4
97720	Burns⊙ 3,579	H4
97109	Buxton 80	D2
†97002	Butteville 20	A2
97522	Butte Falls 428	E5
†97010	Canby 7,659	B2
97110	Cannon Beach 1,187	D2
97820	Canyon City⊙ 639	J3
97417	Canyonville 1,288	D5
97111	Carlton 1,302	D2
97014	Cascade Locks 838	E2
97329	Cascadia 250	E3
†97523	Cave Junction 1,023	D5
97821	Cayuse 200	J2
97225	Cedar Hills 9,619	A2
†97058	Cedar Mill 900	A2
97058	Celilo 50	G2
97502	Central Point 6,357	D5
97420	Charleston 500	C4
97306	Chemawa 400	A3
97731	Chemult 800	F4
†97058	Chenoweth 2,820	F2
†97055	Cherry Grove 350	D2
†97055	Cherryville 75	E2
97419	Cheshire 300	D3
97624	Chiloquin 778	F5
97015	Clackamas	B2
97016	Clatskanie 1,648	D1
97112	Cloverdale 260	C2
97401	Coburg 699	E3
97017	Colton 305	B3
97018	Columbia City 678	E2
97823	Condon⊙ 783	G2
97113	Cornelius 4,462	A2
97330	Corvallis⊙ 40,960	D3
97424	Cottage Grove 7,148	D4

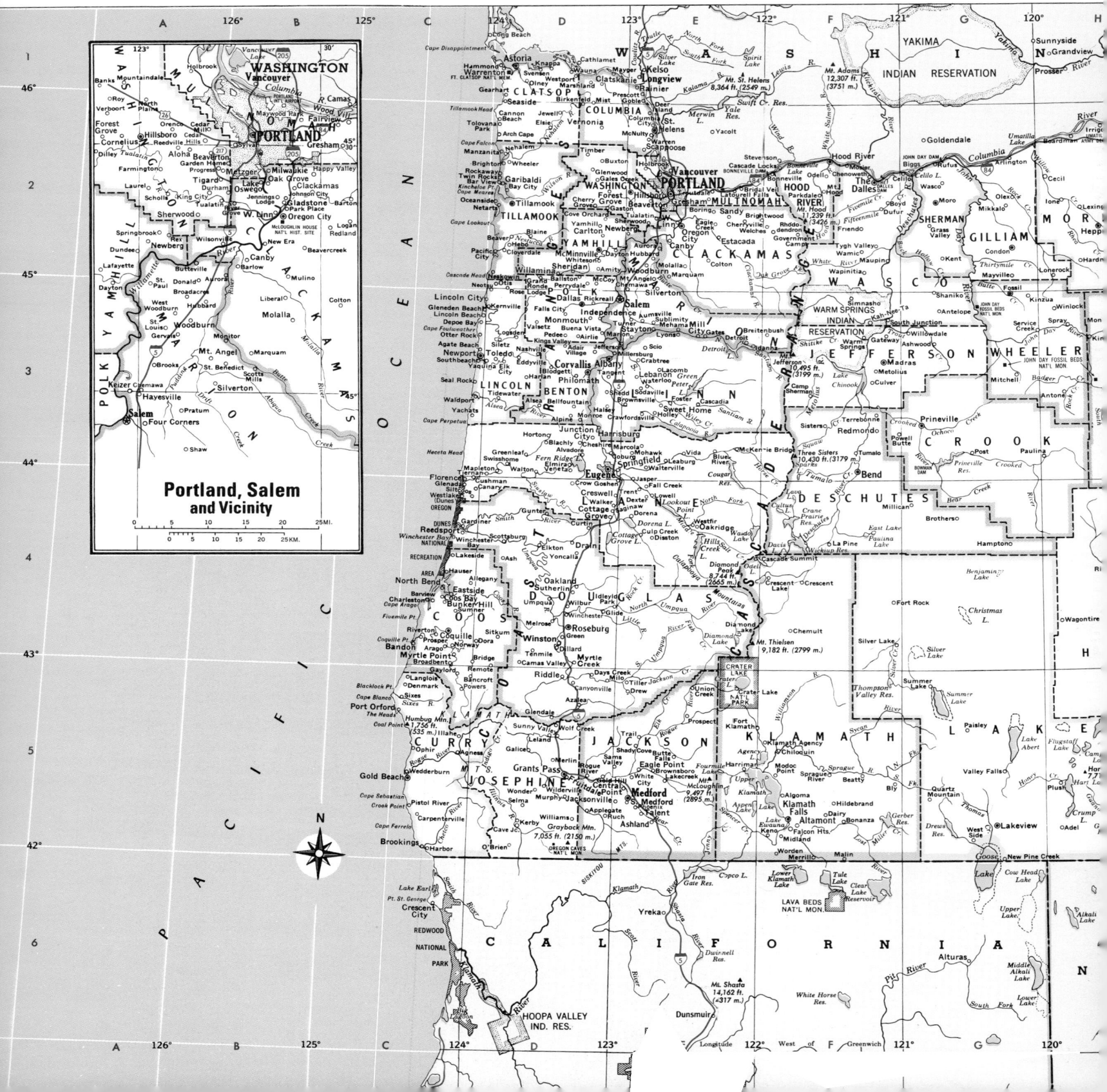

97824 Cove 451 ....K2
97335 Crabtree 200 ....E3
97732 Crane 84 ....J4
97336 Crawfordsville 350 ....E3
97733 Crescent 750 ....F4
97425 Crescent Lake 120 ....F4
97426 Creswell 1,770 ....D4
†97401 Crow 200 ....D4
97427 Culp Creek 600 ....E4
97734 Culver 514 ....D4
97428 Curtin 350 ....D4
†97439 Cushman 175 ....D4
97625 Dairy 80 ....F5
97338 Dallas⊙ 8,530 ....D3
97058 Dalles, The⊙ 10,820 ..F2
97429 Days Creek 550 ....D5
97114 Dayton 1,409 ....A3
97825 Dayville 199 ....H3
97054 Deer Island 225 ....E2
97341 Depoe Bay 723 ....C3
97342 Detroit 367 ....E3
97431 Dexter 500 ....E4
97432 Dillard 602 ....D4
†97116 Dilley 250 ....A2

†97427 Disston 123 ....E4
97020 Donald 267 ....A3
97434 Dorena 200 ....E4
97435 Drain 1,148 ....D4
97021 Dufur 560 ....F2
97115 Dundee 1,223 ....A2
97233 Durham 707 ....A2
97905 Durkee 158 ....K3
97022 Eagle Creek 250 ....E2
97524 Eagle Point 2,764 .....E5
97420 Eastside 1,601 ....C4
97826 Echo 624 ....H2
97343 Eddyville 564 ....D3
97827 Elgin 1,701 ....K2
97436 Elkton 155 ....D4
97437 Elmira 900 ....D3
97828 Enterprise⊙ 2,003 .....K2
97023 Estacada 1,419 ....E2
*97401 Eugene⊙ 105,624 ......D3
        Eugene-Springfield‡
        275,226 ....D3
97024 Fairview 1,749 ....B2
†97601 Falcon Heights F5

97344 Falls City 804 ....D3
97710 Fields 150 ....J5
97439 Florence 4,411 ....C4
97116 Forest Grove 11,499 ..A2
97626 Fort Klamath 200 .....E5
97735 Fort Rock 150 ....G4
97830 Fossil⊙ 535 ....G2
97345 Foster 850 ....E3
97301 Four Corners 11,331 ..A3
97831 Fox 30 ....H3
†97526 Fruitdale-Harbeck 4,733 ...D5
97117 Gales Creek 150 ......D2
97223 Garden Home-
        Whitford 6,926 ....A2
97441 Gardiner 750 ....C4
97118 Garibaldi 999 ....D2
97119 Gaston 471 ....D2
97346 Gates 455 ....E3
†97441 Gateway 108 ....F3
97458 Gaylord 80 ....C5
97138 Gearhart 967 ....C1
97026 Gervais 799 ....A3
†97810 Gibbon 100 ....J2
97027 Gladstone 9,500 ....B2

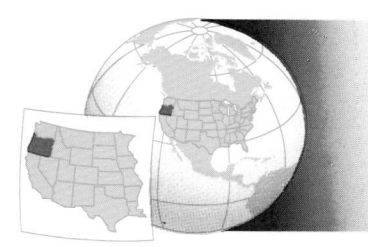

AREA 97,073 sq. mi. (251,419 sq. km.)
POPULATION 2,633,149
CAPITAL Salem
LARGEST CITY Portland
HIGHEST POINT Mt. Hood 11,239 ft.
        (3426 m.)
SETTLED IN 1810
ADMITTED TO UNION February 14, 1859
POPULAR NAME Beaver State
STATE FLOWER Oregon Grape
STATE BIRD Western Meadowlark

Topography

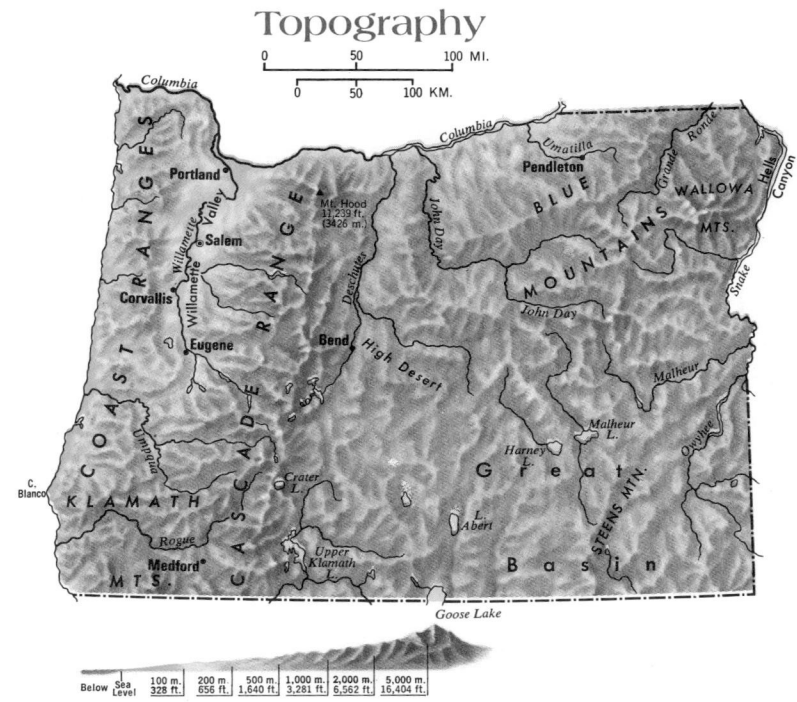

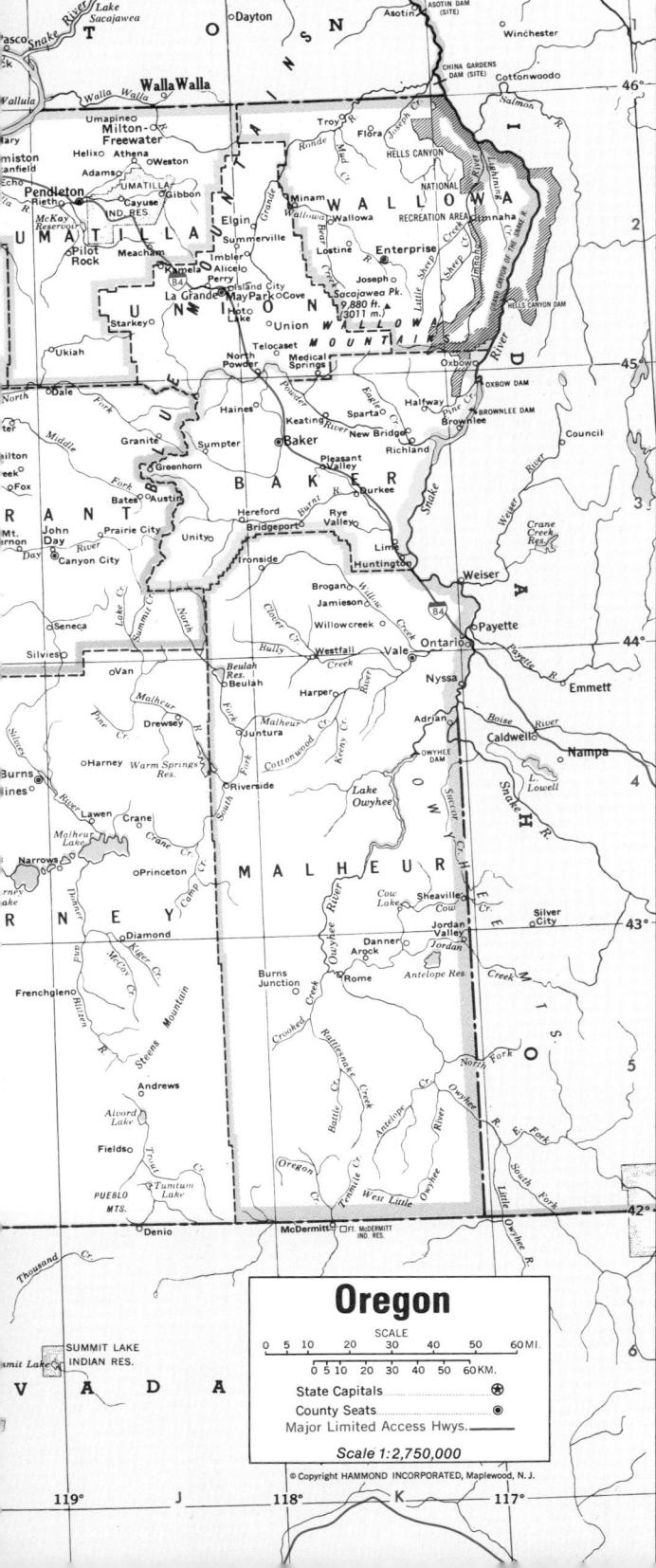

Oregon

SCALE
0 5 10 20 30 40 50 60 MI.
0 5 10 20 30 40 50 60 KM.

State Capitals ....⊛
County Seats ....⊙
Major Limited Access Hwys. ..━━

Scale 1:2,750,000

© Copyright HAMMOND INCORPORATED, Maplewood, N.J.

†97439 Glenada 300 ....C4
97442 Glendale 712 ....D5
97388 Gleneden Beach 400 ...C3
97120 Glenwood 225 ....D2
97443 Glide 470 ....D4
97048 Goble 108 ....E1
97444 Gold Beach⊙ 1,515 ....C5
97525 Gold Hill 904 ....D5
97401 Goshen 200 ....D4
97028 Government Camp 230 ..F2
97347 Grand Ronde 289 ......D2
†97877 Granite 17 ....J3
97526 Grants Pass⊙ 15,032 ..D5
97029 Grass Valley 164 ......G2
†97470 Green 3,897 ....D4
97030 Gresham 33,005 ....B2
97833 Haines 341 ....J3
97834 Halfway 150 ....K3
97348 Halsey 693 ....D3
97121 Hammond 516 ....C1
†97222 Happy Valley 1,499 ...B2
97415 Harbor 2,856 ....C5
97906 Harper 400 ....K4
†97601 Harriman 250 ....E5
97446 Harrisburg 1,881 ......D3
†97459 Hauser 400 ....C4
†97301 Hayesville 9,213 ......A3
97122 Hebo 400 ....D2
97835 Heix 155 ....J2
97836 Heppner⊙ 1,498 ....H2
97837 Hereford 128 ....K3
97838 Hermiston 9,408 ......H2
†97123 Hillsboro⊙ 27,664 .....B2
97738 Hines 1,632 ....H4
†97208 Holbrook 494 ....A1
†97386 Holley 75 ....E3
97031 Hood River⊙ 4,329 ....F2
97032 Hubbard 1,640 ....A3
97907 Huntington 539 ....K3
97350 Idanha 319 ....E3
97447 Idleyld Park 300 ......D4
97841 Imbler 292 ....J2
97351 Independence 4,024 ...D3
97843 Ione 345 ....H2
97844 Irrigon 700 ....H2
97851 Island City 477 ....K2
97530 Jacksonville 2,030 ....D5
97909 Jamieson 120 ....K3
97401 Jasper 231 ....E3
97352 Jefferson 1,702 ....D3
†97845 John Day 2,012 ....J3
†97027 Johnson City 378 ......B2
97910 Jordan Valley 473 .....K5
97846 Joseph 999 ....K2
97448 Junction City 3,320 ...D3
97911 Juntura K4
97303 Keizer 18,592 ....A3

97627 Keno 500 ....F5
97033 Kent 200 ....G2
97531 Kerby 650 ....D5
97223 King City 1,853 ....A2
†97361 Kings Valley 50 ....D3
97849 Kinzua 2 ....H3
97601 Klamath Falls⊙ 16,661 ..F5
†97103 Knappa 950 ....D1
†97355 Lacomb 250 ....E3
97127 Lafayette 1,215 ....A2
97850 La Grande⊙ 11,354 ....J2
†97524 Lakecreek 160 ....E5
97034 Lake Oswego 22,527 ...B2
97449 Lakeside 1,453 ....C4
97630 Lakeview⊙ 2,770 ......G5
97450 Langlois 150 ....C5
97739 La Pine 850 ....F4
97401 Leaburg 150 ....E3
97355 Lebanon 10,413 ....E3
†97839 Lexington 307 ....H2
†97042 Liberal 300 ....B3
†97341 Lincoln Beach 275 .....C3
97367 Lincoln City 5,469 ....C3
97405 Logan 450 ....D4
97823 Lonerock 26 ....H2
97856 Long Creek 252 ....H3
97857 Lostine 250 ....K2
97452 Lowell 661 ....E4
97358 Lyons 877 ....E3
97741 Madras⊙ 2,235 ....F3
97632 Malin 539 ....F5
97130 Manzanita 443 ....C2
97453 Mapleton 950 ....C3
97454 Marcola 900 ....E3
97359 Marion 300 ....D3
97037 Maupin 495 ....F2
†97850 May Park J2
97220 Maywood Park 1,083 ..B2
97401 McKenzie Bridge 500 ..E3
97128 McMinnville⊙ 14,080 ..D2
97858 McNary 330 ....H2
†97053 McNulty 1,805 ....E2
97859 Meacham 150 ....J2
97501 Medford⊙ 39,603 ......E5
        Medford‡ 132,456 .....E5
97384 Mehama 250 ....E3
97532 Merlin 500 ....D5
†97741 Metolius 451 ....F3
†97223 Midland 520 ....F5
97634 Midland 520 ....F5
97360 Mill City 1,565 ....E3
97321 Millersburg 562 ....D3
†97417 Milo 600 ....E5
97862 Milton-Freewater 5,086 ..J2
97222 Milwaukie 17,931 .....B2
97038 Molalla 2,992 ....B3
97361 Monmouth 5,594 ......D3
97456 Monroe 412 ....D3

97864 Monument 192 ....H3
97039 Moro⊙ 336 ....G2
97040 Mosier 340 ....F2
97362 Mount Angel 2,876 ....B3
97041 Mount Hood 200 ......F2
97865 Mount Vernon 569 ....H3
97042 Mulino 720 ....B2
97533 Murphy 500 ....D5
97457 Myrtle Creek 3,365 ...D4
97458 Myrtle Point 2,859 ...C4
97131 Nehalem 258 ....D2
97364 Neotsu 300 ....C3
97149 Neskowin 250 ....D2
97143 Netarts 975 ....C2
97132 Newberg 10,394 ......A2
97635 New Pine Creek 400 ..G5
97365 Newport⊙ 7,519 ......C3
97459 North Bend 9,779 ....C4
97133 North Plains 715 .....A2
97867 North Powder 430 ....K2
97460 Norway 150 ....C4
97913 Nyssa 2,862 ....K4
97268 Oak Grove 11,640 ....B2
97462 Oakland 886 ....D4
97463 Oakridge 3,729 ....E4
97534 O'Brien 850 ....D5
97134 Oceanside 300 ....C2
97044 Odell 450 ....F2
97914 Ontario 8,814 ....K3
97464 Ophir 275 ....C5
97045 Oregon City⊙ 14,673 ..B2
†97123 Orenco 220 ....A2
97368 Otis 200 ....D2
97369 Otter Rock 450 ....C3
97840 Oxbow 100 ....L2
97135 Pacific City 500 ......C2
97636 Paisley 343 ....G5
97041 Parkdale 350 ....F2
†97045 Park Place 500 ....B2
97801 Pendleton⊙ 14,521 ....J2
†97101 Perrydale 200 ....D2
97370 Philomath 2,673 ......D3
97535 Phoenix 2,309 ....E5
97868 Pilot Rock 1,630 ......J2
*97201 Portland⊙ 366,383 ....B2
        Portland‡ 1,242,187 ..B2
97465 Port Orford 1,061 ....C5
97753 Powell Butte 350 .....G3
97466 Powers 819 ....D5
97869 Prairie City 1,106 ....J3
†97048 Prescott 73 ....D1
97721 Princeton 5 ....J4
97754 Prineville⊙ 5,276 ....G3
†97233 Progress 100 ....A2
97536 Prospect 200 ....E5
†97411 Prosper 110 ....C4
†97048 Rainier 1,655 ....E1
†97045 Redland 700 ....B2
97756 Redmond 6,452 ....F3
97467 Reedsport 4,984 ......C4

(continued on following page)

Agriculture, Industry and Resources

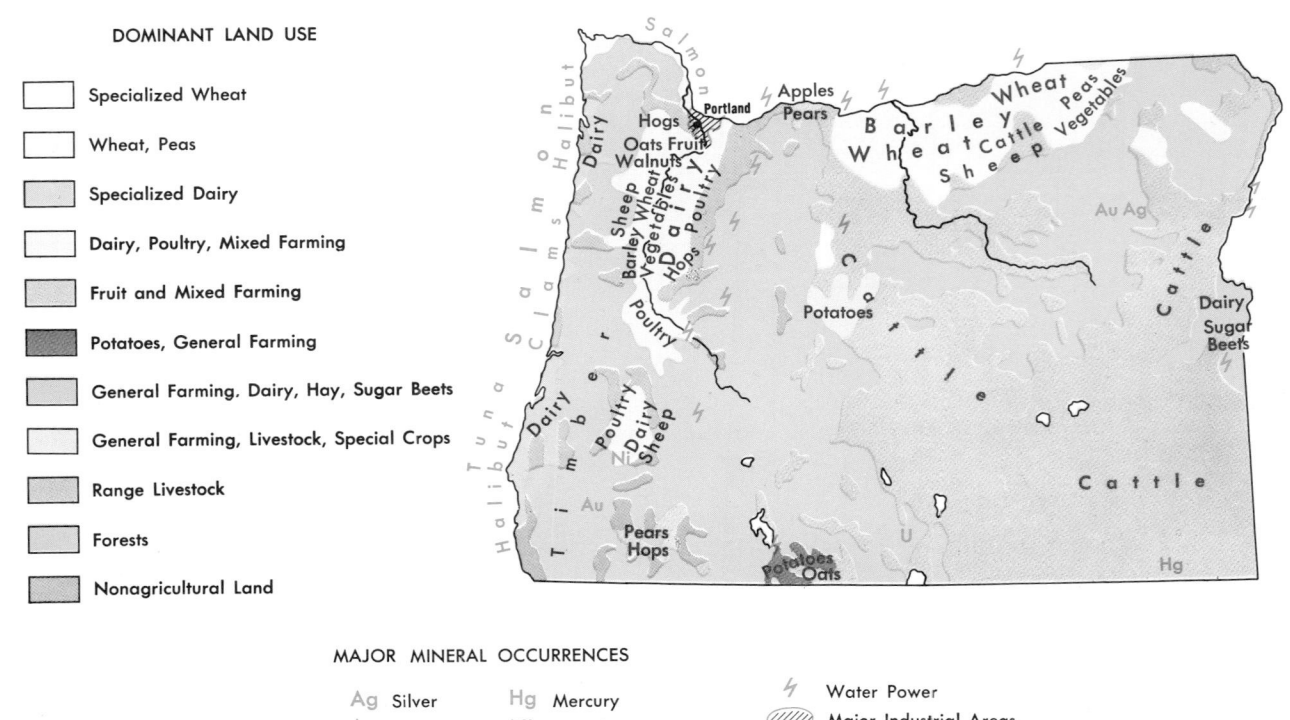

DOMINANT LAND USE

- Specialized Wheat
- Wheat, Peas
- Specialized Dairy
- Dairy, Poultry, Mixed Farming
- Fruit and Mixed Farming
- Potatoes, General Farming
- General Farming, Dairy, Hay, Sugar Beets
- General Farming, Livestock, Special Crops
- Range Livestock
- Forests
- Nonagricultural Land

MAJOR MINERAL OCCURRENCES

Ag Silver	Hg Mercury	⚡ Water Power
Au Gold	Ni Nickel	⧄ Major Industrial Areas
	U Uranium	

AREA 45,308 sq. mi. (117,348 sq. km.)
POPULATION 11,863,895
CAPITAL Harrisburg
LARGEST CITY Philadelphia
HIGHEST POINT Mt. Davis 3,213 ft. (979 m.)
SETTLED IN 1682
ADMITTED TO UNION December 12, 1787
POPULAR NAME Keystone State
STATE FLOWER Mountain Laurel
STATE BIRD Ruffed Grouse

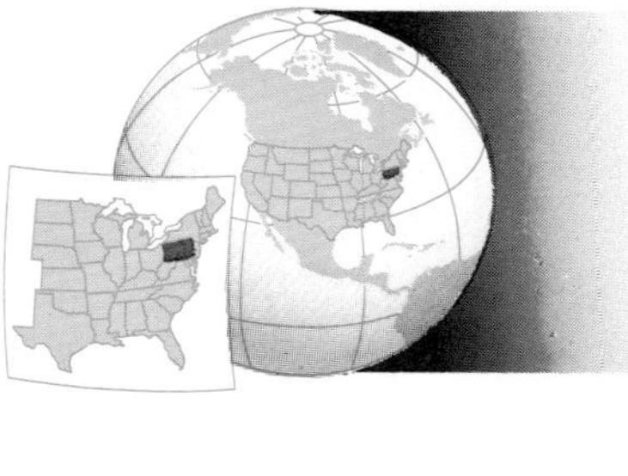

DOMINANT LAND USE

- Specialized Dairy
- Dairy, General Farming
- Fruit and Mixed Farming
- Fruit, Truck and Mixed Farming
- General Farming, Livestock, Tobacco
- General Farming, Livestock, Fruit, Tobacco
- Forests
- Urban Areas

MAJOR MINERAL OCCURRENCES

C Coal
Cl Clay
Co Cobalt
Fe Iron Ore
G Natural Gas
Ls Limestone
O Petroleum
Sl Slate
Ss Sandstone
Zn Zinc

Water Power
Major Industrial Areas

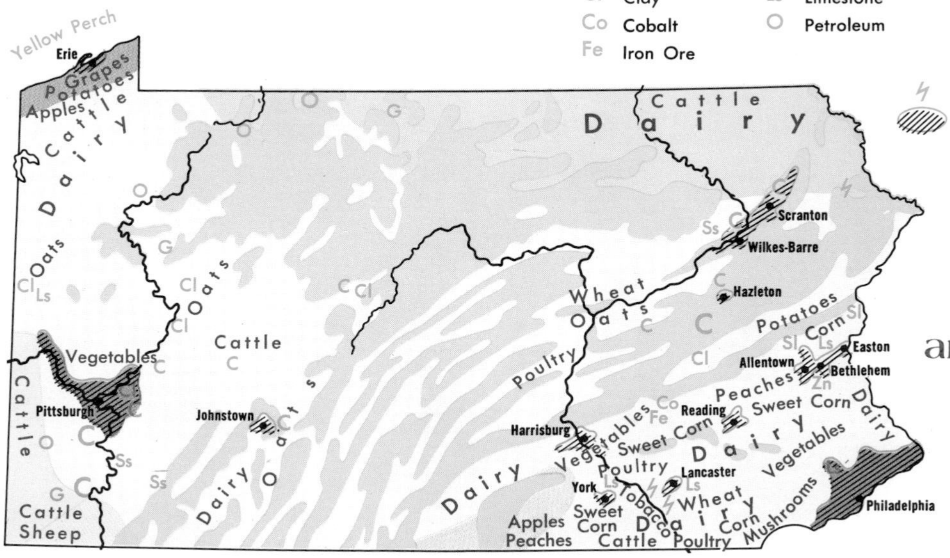

Agriculture, Industry and Resources

COUNTIES

Adams 68,292 .... H6
Allegheny 1,450,085 .... B5
Armstrong 77,768 .... D4
Beaver 204,441 .... B4
Bedford 46,784 .... E6
Berks 312,509 .... K5
Blair 136,621 .... F4
Bradford 62,919 .... J2
Bucks 479,211 .... M5
Butler 147,912 .... C4
Cambria 183,263 .... E4
Cameron 6,674 .... F3
Carbon 53,285 .... L4
Centre 112,760 .... G4
Chester 316,660 .... L6
Clarion 43,362 .... D3
Clearfield 83,578 .... F3
Clinton 38,971 .... G3
Columbia 61,967 .... K3
Crawford 88,869 .... B2
Cumberland 178,541 .... H5
Dauphin 232,317 .... J5
Delaware 555,007 .... M6
Elk 38,338 .... E3
Erie 279,780 .... B2
Fayette 159,417 .... C6
Forest 5,072 .... D2
Franklin 113,629 .... G6
Fulton 12,842 .... F6
Greene 40,476 .... B6
Huntingdon 42,253 .... F5
Indiana 92,281 .... D4
Jefferson 48,303 .... D3
Juniata 19,188 .... H4
Lackawanna 227,908 .... L3
Lancaster 362,346 .... K5
Lawrence 107,150 .... B4
Lebanon 108,582 .... K5
Lehigh 272,349 .... L4
Luzerne 343,079 .... L3
Lycoming 118,416 .... H3
McKean 50,635 .... E2
Mercer 128,299 .... B3
Mifflin 46,908 .... G4
Monroe 69,409 .... M3
Montgomery 643,621 .... M5
Montour 16,675 .... J3
Northampton 225,418 .... M4
Northumberland 100,381 .... J4
Perry 35,718 .... H5
Philadelphia (city county) 1,688,210 .... M6
Pike 18,271 .... M3
Potter 17,726 .... G2
Schuylkill 160,630 .... K4
Snyder 33,584 .... H4
Somerset 81,243 .... D6
Sullivan 6,349 .... J3
Susquehanna 37,876 .... L2
Tioga 40,973 .... H2
Union 32,870 .... H4
Venango 64,444 .... C3
Warren 47,449 .... D2
Washington 217,074 .... B5
Wayne 35,237 .... M2
Westmoreland 392,294 .... D5
Wyoming 26,433 .... L2
York 312,963 .... J6

CITIES and TOWNS

Zip Name/Pop. Key

19001 Abington○ 59,084 .... M5
19501 Adamstown 1,119 .... K5
17501 Akron 3,471 .... K5
16401 Albion 1,818 .... B2
18011 Alburtis 1,428 .... L5
†19018 Aldan 4,671 .... M7
15001 Aliquippa 17,094 .... B4
*18101 Allentown⊙ 103,758 .... L4
Allentown-Bethlehem-Easton‡ 636,714 .... L4
15101 Allison Park 10,000 .... C4
*16601 Altoona 57,078 .... F4
Altoona‡ 136,621 .... F4
19002 Ambler 6,628 .... M5
15003 Ambridge 9,575 .... B4
17003 Annville 4,493 .... J5
15613 Apollo 2,212 .... C4
18403 Archbald 6,295 .... F6
19003 Ardmore M6
15068 Arnold 6,853 .... C4
17921 Ashland 4,235 .... K4
18706 Ashley 3,512 .... E7
15215 Aspinwall 3,284 .... C6
18810 Athens 3,622 .... K2
17851 Atlas 1,162 .... K4
15202 Avalon 6,240 .... B6
15312 Avella 900 .... B5
17721 Avis 1,718 .... H3
18641 Avoca 3,536 .... F7
19311 Avondale 891 .... L6
15618 Avonmore 1,234 .... C4
15005 Baden 5,318 .... B4
19004 Bala-Cynwyd N6
†15208 Baldwin 24,598 .... B7
19503 Bally 1,051 .... L5
18013 Bangor 5,006 .... M4
15714 Barnesboro 2,741 .... E4
18014 Bath 1,953 .... M4
15009 Beaver⊙ 5,441 .... B4
15921 Beaverdale 1,187 .... E5
15010 Beaver Falls 12,525 .... B4
18216 Beaver Meadows 1,078 .... L4
15522 Bedford⊙ 3,326 .... F5
16823 Bellefonte⊙ 6,300 .... G4
15012 Belle Vernon 1,489 .... C5
17004 Belleville 1,689 .... G4
15202 Bellevue 10,128 .... B6
16617 Bellwood 2,114 .... F4
†15202 Ben Avon 2,314 .... B6
15314 Bentleyville 2,525 .... B5
15530 Berlin 1,999 .... E6
19506 Bernville 798 .... K5
18603 Berwick 11,850 .... K3
19312 Berwyn 5,246 .... L5
16112 Bessemer 1,293 .... B4
15102 Bethel Park 34,755 .... B7
*18015 Bethlehem 70,419 .... M4
19508 Birdsboro 3,481 .... L5
15716 Black Lick 1,313 .... D4
15717 Blairsville 4,166 .... D5
18447 Blakely 7,438 .... F6
15238 Blawnox 1,653 .... C6
17068 Bloomfield (New Bloomfield)⊙ 1,109 .... H5
17815 Bloomsburg⊙ 11,717 .... J3
16912 Blossburg 1,757 .... H2
16827 Boalsburg 2,295 .... G4
15315 Bobtown 1,008 .... B6
17007 Boiling Springs 2,223 .... H5
15923 Bolivar 706 .... D5
15531 Boswell 1,480 .... E5
18030 Bowmanstown 1,078 .... L4
19512 Boyertown 3,979 .... L5
15014 Brackenridge 4,297 .... C4
15104 Braddock 5,634 .... C7
16701 Bradford 11,211 .... E2
15227 Brentwood 11,907 .... B7
19405 Bridgeport 4,843 .... M5
15017 Bridgeville 6,154 .... B5
19007 Bristol 10,867 .... N5
19007 Bristol○ 58,733 .... N5
15824 Brockway 2,376 .... E3
19015 Brookhaven 7,912 .... M7
15825 Brookville⊙ 4,568 .... D3
19008 Broomall M6
15417 Brownsville 4,043 .... C5
19010 Bryn Mawr M5
15021 Burgettstown 1,867 .... A5
17009 Burnham 2,457 .... H4
16001 Butler⊙ 17,026 .... C4
15924 Cairnbrook 1,081 .... E5
15419 California 5,703 .... C5
16403 Cambridge Springs 2,102 .... C2
17011 Camp Hill 8,422 .... H5
15317 Canonsburg 10,459 .... B5
17724 Canton 1,959 .... J2
18407 Carbondale 11,255 .... L2
17013 Carlisle⊙ 18,314 .... H5
15106 Carnegie 10,099 .... B7
15722 Carrolltown 1,395 .... E4
15234 Castle Shannon 10,164 .... B7
18032 Catasauqua 6,711 .... M4
17820 Catawissa 1,568 .... K4
16404 Centerville 4,207 .... B6
15926 Central City 1,496 .... E5
17927 Centralia 1,017 .... K4
16828 Centre Hall 1,233 .... G4
18914 Chalfont 2,802 .... M5
17201 Chambersburg⊙ 16,174 .... G6
15022 Charleroi 5,717 .... C5
19012 Cheltenham○ 35,509 .... M5
*19013 Chester 45,794 .... L7
19017 Chester Heights 1,302 .... L7
†16866 Chester Hill 1,054 .... F4
15024 Cheswick 2,336 .... C6
16025 Chicora 1,192 .... C4
17509 Christiana 1,183 .... K6
†15235 Churchill 4,285 .... C7
15025 Clairton 12,188 .... C7
16214 Clarion⊙ 6,664 .... D3
†18411 Clarks Green 1,862 .... F6
18411 Clarks Summit 5,272 .... F6
16625 Claysburg 1,346 .... F5
15323 Claysville 1,029 .... B5
16830 Clearfield⊙ 7,580 .... F3
19018 Clifton Heights 7,320 .... M7
15728 Clymer 1,761 .... E4
18218 Coaldale 2,762 .... L4
19320 Coatesville 10,698 .... L5
16314 Cochranton 1,240 .... B2
19426 Collegeville 3,406 .... M5
19023 Collingdale 9,539 .... N7
17512 Columbia 10,466 .... K5
15927 Colver 1,165 .... E4
†19023 Colwyn 2,851 .... N7
15425 Connellsville 10,319 .... C5
19428 Conshohocken 8,475 .... M5
15027 Conway 2,747 .... B4
18219 Conyngham 2,242 .... K3
18036 Coopersburg 2,595 .... M4
18037 Coplay 3,130 .... L4
15108 Coraopolis 7,308 .... B4
17016 Cornwall 2,653 .... K5
16407 Corry 7,149 .... C2
16915 Coudersport⊙ 2,791 .... G2
15624 Crabtree 900 .... D5
15205 Crafton 7,623 .... B7
16630 Cresson 2,184 .... E5
17929 Cressona 1,810 .... K4
16833 Curwensville 3,116 .... E4
†15901 Dale 1,906 .... E5
18612 Dallas 2,679 .... E7
17313 Dallastown 3,949 .... J6
18414 Dalton 1,383 .... L2
17821 Danville⊙ 5,239 .... J4
19023 Darby 11,513 .... M7
18327 Delaware Water Gap 597 .... M4
15626 Delmont 2,159 .... D5
17517 Denver 2,018 .... K5
15627 Derry 3,072 .... D5
18519 Dickson City 6,699 .... F7
17019 Dillsburg 1,733 .... J5
15033 Donora 7,524 .... C5
15216 Dormont 11,275 .... B7
17315 Dover 1,910 .... J6
19335 Downingtown 7,650 .... L5
18901 Doylestown⊙ 8,717 .... M5
15034 Dravosburg 2,511 .... C7
19026 Drexel Hill M6
18221 Drifton 1,786 .... L3
18917 Dublin 1,565 .... M5
15801 DuBois 9,290 .... E3
†17701 Duboistown 1,218 .... H3
15431 Dunbar 1,369 .... C6
17020 Duncannon 1,645 .... H5
16635 Duncansville 1,355 .... F5
18512 Dunmore 16,781 .... F7
18641 Dupont 3,460 .... F7
15110 Duquesne 10,094 .... C7
18642 Duryea 5,415 .... F7
17316 East Berlin 1,054 .... J6
†18603 East Berwick 2,324 .... K3
16028 East Brady 1,153 .... C3
15909 East Conemaugh 2,128 .... E5
†17701 East Faxon 3,951 .... J3
18041 East Greenville 2,456 .... L5
†19050 East Lansdowne 2,806 .... M7
18042 Easton⊙ 26,027 .... M4
17520 East Petersburg 3,600 .... K5
18301 East Stroudsburg 8,039 .... M4
†15301 East Washington 2,241 .... B5
15931 Ebensburg⊙ 4,096 .... E5
†15005 Economy 9,538 .... B4
†19013 Eddystone 2,555 .... M7
†15218 Edgewood 4,382 .... B7
†15143 Edgeworth 1,738 .... B4
16412 Edinboro 6,324 .... B2
18704 Edwardsville 5,729 .... E7
16731 Eldred 965 .... F2
15037 Elizabeth 1,892 .... C5
17022 Elizabethtown 8,233 .... J5
17023 Elizabethville 1,531 .... J4
16920 Elkland 1,974 .... H1
15331 Ellsworth 1,228 .... B5
16117 Ellwood City 9,998 .... B4
17824 Elysburg 1,447 .... K4
17318 Emigsville 2,413 .... J5
16373 Emlenton 807 .... C3
18049 Emmaus 11,001 .... M4
15834 Emporium⊙ 2,837 .... F2
15202 Emsworth 3,074 .... B6
17025 Enola J5
17522 Ephrata 11,095 .... K5
*16501 Erie⊙ 119,123 .... B1
Erie‡ 279,780 .... B1
17815 Espy 1,571 .... K4
15223 Etna 4,534 .... B6
16033 Evans City 2,299 .... B4
15537 Everett 1,828 .... F5
15631 Everson 1,032 .... C5
15632 Export 1,143 .... C5
15436 Fairchance 2,106 .... C6
19030 Fairless Hills 16,000 .... N5
16415 Fairview 1,855 .... B1
15840 Falls Creek 1,208 .... E3
16121 Farrell 8,645 .... A3
17222 Fayetteville 3,202 .... G6
18921 Ferndale 2,204 .... E5
19522 Fleetwood 3,422 .... L5
†17745 Flemington 1,416 .... G3
19032 Folcroft 8,231 .... M7
16226 Ford City 3,923 .... D4
18421 Forest City 1,924 .... L2
†15221 Forest Hills 8,198 .... C7
18704 Forty Fort 5,590 .... F7
†18015 Fountain Hill 4,805 .... L4
†15238 Fox Chapel 5,049 .... C6
17931 Frackville 5,308 .... K4
16323 Franklin⊙ 8,146 .... C3
†16335 Fredericksburg 1,202 .... B2
15333 Fredericktown 1,052 .... C6
15042 Freedom 2,272 .... B4
18224 Freeland 4,285 .... L3
†18017 Freemansburg 1,879 .... M4
16229 Freeport 2,381 .... C4
16922 Galeton 1,462 .... G2
16641 Gallitzin 2,315 .... E4
†17701 Garden View 2,777 .... H3
15904 Geistown 3,304 .... E5
17325 Gettysburg⊙ 7,194 .... H6
17934 Gilberton 1,096 .... K4
16417 Girard 2,615 .... B2
17935 Girardville 2,268 .... K4
15045 Glassport 6,242 .... C7
18617 Glen Lyon 2,352 .... E7
19036 Glenolden 7,633 .... M7
17327 Glen Rock 1,662 .... J6
19038 Glenside M5
15634 Grapeville C5
18821 Great Bend 740 .... L2
17225 Greencastle 3,679 .... G6
15601 Greensburg⊙ 17,558 .... C5
15242 Greentree 5,722 .... B7
16125 Greenville 7,730 .... B3
16127 Grove City 8,162 .... B3
17032 Halifax 909 .... J5
17406 Hallam 1,428 .... J6
18822 Hallstead 1,280 .... L2
19526 Hamburg 4,011 .... L4
17331 Hanover 14,890 .... J6
16037 Harmony 1,334 .... B4
*17101 Harrisburg (cap.)⊙ 53,264 .... H5
Harrisburg‡ 446,072 .... H5
16038 Harrisville 1,033 .... B3
18618 Harveys Lake 2,318 .... E7
16646 Hastings 1,574 .... E4
19040 Hatboro 7,579 .... M5
19440 Hatfield 2,533 .... M5
19041 Haverford○ 52,349 .... M6
19083 Havertown M6
16840 Hawk Run 1,960 .... F4
18428 Hawley 1,181 .... M3
18201 Hazleton 27,318 .... L4
15106 Heidelberg 1,606 .... B7
17406 Hellam (Hallam) 1,428 .... J6
18055 Hellertown 6,025 .... M4
17033 Hershey 13,249 .... J5
†17044 Highland Park 1,879 .... H4
17034 Highspire 2,959 .... J5
16648 Hollidaysburg⊙ 5,892 .... F5
15748 Homer City 2,248 .... D4
15120 Homestead 5,092 .... B7
18431 Honesdale⊙ 5,128 .... M2
19344 Honey Brook 1,164 .... L5
15936 Hooversville 863 .... E5
15445 Hopwood 2,420 .... C6
15342 Houston 1,568 .... B5
16651 Houtzdale 1,222 .... F4
†18640 Hughestown 1,783 .... F7
17737 Hughesville 2,174 .... J3
17036 Hummelstown 4,267 .... J5
16652 Huntingdon⊙ 7,042 .... G5
16843 Hyde 1,791 .... F4
15545 Hyndman 1,106 .... E6
15126 Imperial 3,207 .... B5
15701 Indiana⊙ 16,051 .... D4
15052 Industry 2,417 .... B4
†15205 Ingram 4,346 .... B7
15642 Irwin 4,995 .... C5
17407 Jacobus 1,396 .... J6
15644 Jeannette 13,106 .... C5
†15025 Jefferson 8,643 .... B7
19046 Jenkintown 4,942 .... M5
18433 Jermyn 2,411 .... L2
15937 Jerome 1,196 .... D5
17740 Jersey Shore 4,631 .... H3
18434 Jessup 4,974 .... F6
18229 Jim Thorpe⊙ 5,263 .... L4
15845 Johnsonburg 3,938 .... E3
*15901 Johnstown 35,496 .... D5
Johnstown‡ 264,506 .... D5
16735 Kane 4,916 .... E2
†19607 Kenhorst 3,187 .... L5
19348 Kennett Square 4,715 .... L6
18704 Kingston 15,681 .... F7
16201 Kittanning⊙ 5,432 .... D4
16232 Knox 1,364 .... C3
16136 Koppel 1,146 .... B4
17834 Kulpmont 3,675 .... J4
19530 Kutztown 4,040 .... L4
16423 Lake City 2,384 .... B1
*17601 Lancaster⊙ 54,725 .... K5
Lancaster‡ 362,346 .... K5

(continued on following page)

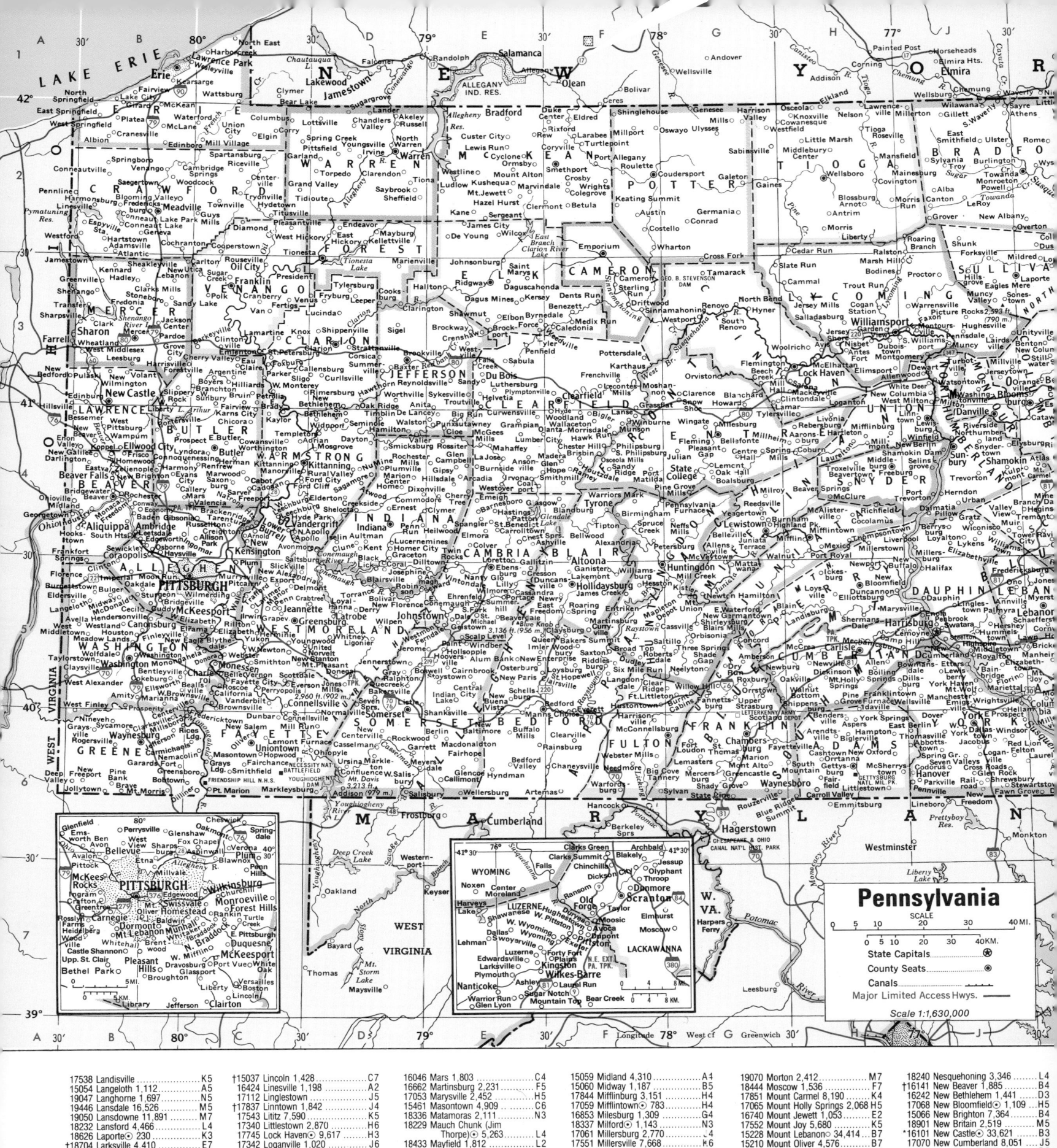

Pennsylvania

SCALE

State Capitals .... ⊛
County Seats .... ◉
Canals ....
Major Limited Access Hwys. ———

Scale 1:1,630,000

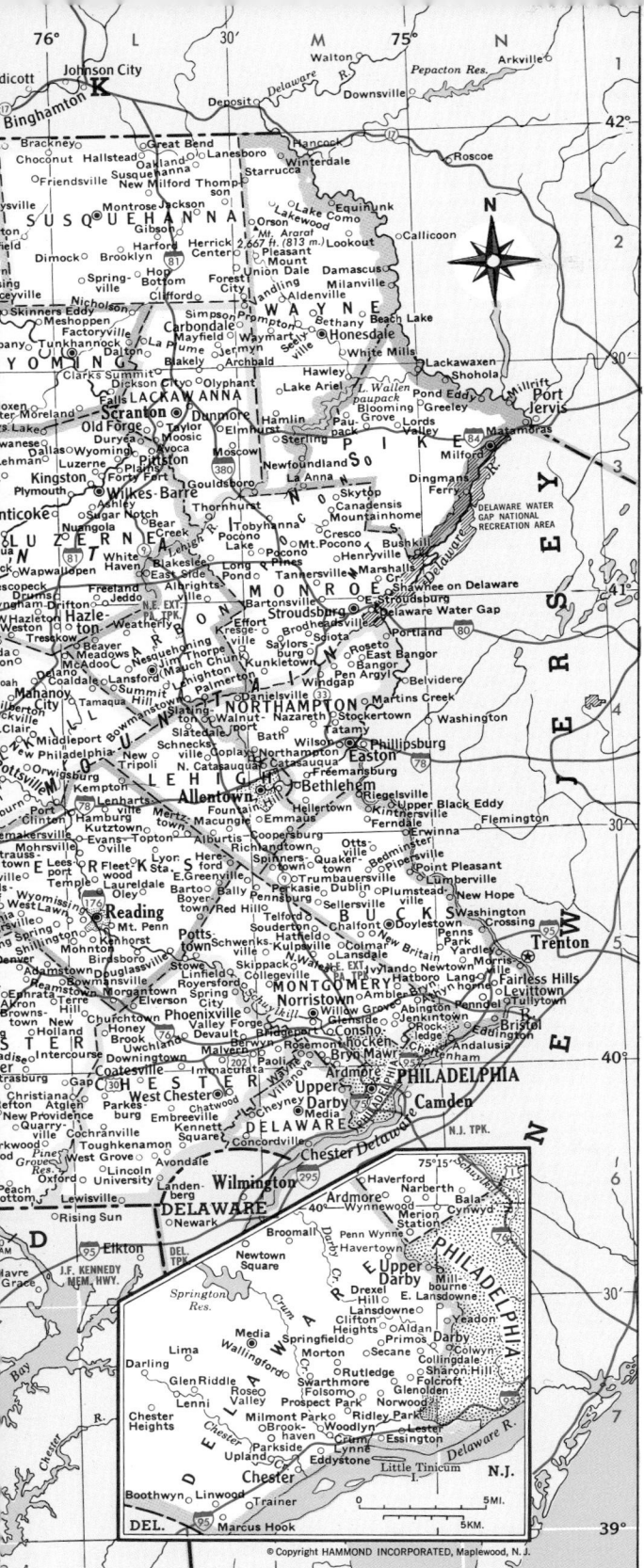

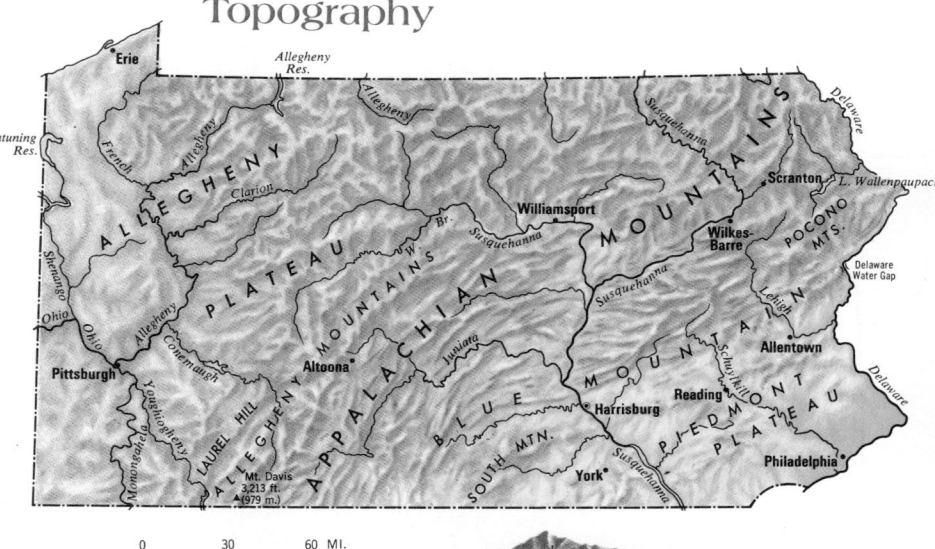

Topography

16823 Pleasant Gap 1,859 ....G4	17701 South Williamsport 6,581 ..J3	18644 West Wyoming 3,288.......E7
15236 Pleasant Hills 9,676 ....B7	15775 Spangler 2,399 ....E4	†17401 West York 4,526.........J6
16341 Pleasantville 1,099 ....C2	19475 Spring City 3,389 ......L5	15120 Whitaker 1,615 ....C7
15239 Plum 25,390 ....C5	15144 Springdale 4,418 ....C5	†15234 Whitehall 15,206 ....B7
18651 Plymouth 7,605 ....E7	19064 Springfield 25,326 ......M7	18661 White Haven 1,921 ....L3
15474 Point Marion 1,642 ....C6	17362 Spring Grove 1,832 .....J6	15131 White Oak 9,480 ....C7
16342 Polk 1,884 ....C3	16801 State College 36,130 ....G4	17097 Wiconisco 1,321 ....J4
15946 Portage 3,510 ....E5	State College‡ 112,760...G4	*18701 Wilkes-Barre⊙ 51,551 ...F7
16743 Port Allegany 2,593 ......F2	17263 State Line 1,253 ....G6	15221 Wilkinsburg 23,669 ......C7
17965 Port Carbon 2,576 ....K4	17113 Steelton 6,484 ....J5	16693 Williamsburg 1,400 ......F5
†15133 Port Vue 5,316 ....C7	17363 Stewartstown 1,072 .....K6	17701 Williamsport⊙ 33,401 ....H3
19464 Pottstown 22,729 ....L5	16153 Stoneboro 1,177 ....B3	Williamsport‡ 118,416...H3
17901 Pottsville⊙ 18,195 ....K4	19464 Stowe 3,860 ....L5	17098 Williamstown 1,664 ......J4
19076 Prospect Park 6,593 ......M7	17579 Strasburg 1,999 ....K6	19090 Willow Grove M5
15767 Punxsutawney 7,479 ......D4	18360 Stroudsburg⊙ 5,148 .....M4	15148 Wilmerding 2,421 ....C5
18951 Quakertown 8,867 ....M5	15082 Sturgeon 1,312 ....B5	15025 Wilson 7,564 ....M4
17566 Quarryville 1,558 ....K6	†16323 Sugar Creek 5,954 ......C3	15963 Windber 5,585 ....E5
†15104 Rankin 2,892 ....C7	18706 Sugar Notch 1,191 ......E7	18091 Windgap 2,651 ....M4
*19601 Reading⊙ 78,686 ....L5	18250 Summit Hill 3,418 ......L4	19567 Womelsdorf 1,827 ......K5
Reading‡ 312,509 ....L5	17801 Sunbury⊙ 12,292 ....J4	19094 Woodlyn M7
17567 Reamstown 1,308 ....K5	18847 Susquehanna 1,994 .....L2	17368 Wrightsville 2,365 ......J5
18076 Red Hill 1,727 ....L5	19081 Swarthmore 5,950 ......M7	18644 Wyoming 3,655 ....E7
17356 Red Lion 5,824 ....J6	18704 Swoyersville 5,795 ......E7	19610 Wyomissing 6,551 ......K5
17084 Reedsville 1,023 ....G4	15865 Sykesville 1,537 ....E3	19067 Yardley 2,533 ....N5
17764 Renovo 1,812 ....G3	18252 Tamaqua 8,843 ....L4	19050 Yeadon 11,727 ....N7
15851 Reynoldsville 3,016 ......D3	15084 Tarentum 6,419 ....C4	17099 Yeagertown 1,305 ......G4
17087 Richland 1,470 ....K5	18517 Taylor 7,246 ....F7	*17401 York⊙ 44,619 ....J6
18955 Richlandtown 1,180 .....M5	18969 Telford 3,507 ....M5	York‡ 381,255 ....J6
15853 Ridgway⊙ 5,604 ....E3	19560 Temple 1,486 ....L5	16371 Youngsville 2,006 ......D2
19078 Ridley Park 7,889 ....M7	17581 Terre Hill 1,217 ....L5	15697 Youngwood 3,749 ......D5
18077 Riegelsville 993 ....M4	18512 Throop 4,166 ....F7	16063 Zelienople 3,502 ....B4
16248 Rimersburg 1,096 ....D3	16351 Tidioute 844 ....D2	
17868 Riverside 2,266 ....J4	16353 Tionesta⊙ 659 ....D2	OTHER FEATURES
16673 Roaring Spring 2,962 ....F5	16684 Tipton 1,348 ....F4	
9551 Robesonia 1,748 ....K5	16354 Titusville 6,884 ....C2	Allegheny (res.) E2
15074 Rochester 4,759 ....B4	19562 Topton 1,818 ....L5	Allegheny (riv.) D2
19101 Rockledge 2,538 ....M5	19374 Toughkenamon 1,111 ...L6	Allegheny Front (mts.) E5
15557 Rockwood 1,058 ....D6	18848 Towanda⊙ 3,526 ....J2	Appalachian (mts.) H4
15477 Roscoe 1,123 ....C5	17980 Tower City 1,667 ......J4	Ararat (mt.) M2
18013 Roseto 1,484 ....M4	15085 Trafford 3,662 ....C5	Arthur (lake) C4
†19065 Rose Valley 1,038 ....L7	†19013 Trainer 2,056 ....L7	Beaver (riv.) B4
17250 Rouzerville 1,371 ....G6	17981 Tremont 1,796 ....K4	Blue (riv.) B3
19468 Royersford 4,243 ....L5	18254 Trescow 1,128 ....K4	Blue Knob (mt.) E5
16249 Rural Valley 1,033 ......D4	17881 Trevorton 2,192 ....J4	Casselman (riv.) D6
15076 Russellton 1,878 ....C4	16947 Troy 1,381 ....J2	Clarion (riv.) D3
17970 Saint Clair 4,037 ....K4	19007 Tullytown 2,277 ......N5	Conemaugh (riv.) D5
15857 Saint Marys⊙ 6,417 .....E3	18657 Tunkhannock⊙ 2,144 ...L2	Conemaugh River (lake) ...D4
15951 Saint Michael 1,445 .....E5	15145 Turtle Creek 6,959 .....C7	Conewango (creek) D1
15681 Saltsburg 964 ....C4	16686 Tyrone 6,346 ....F4	Davis (mt.) D6
†15801 Sandy 1,835 ....E3	16438 Union City 3,623 ......C2	Delaware (riv.) N3
16056 Saxonburg 1,336 ....C4	15401 Uniontown⊙ 14,510 ....C6	Delaware Water Gap Nat'l Rec.
18840 Sayre 6,951 ....K2	†19013 Upland 3,458 ....L7	Area N3
†15963 Scalp Level 1,186 ....E5	†19082 Upper Darby 84,054 ....M6	Erie (lake) B1
17972 Schuylkill Haven 5,977 ...K4	15241 Upper Saint Clair⊙ 19,023 B7	Fort Necessity Nat'l
19473 Schwenksville 1,041 .....L5	19481 Valley Forge 400 ......L5	Battlefield C6
15683 Scottdale 5,833 ....C5	17983 Valley View 1,722 .....J4	George B. Stevenson (dam) .G3
*18501 Scranton⊙ 88,117 ......F7	15690 Vandergrift 6,823 .....D4	Gettysburg Nat'l Mil. Park ..H6
Scranton (Northeast	15147 Verona 3,179 ....C6	Glendale (lake) F4
Pa.)‡ 640,396 ....F7	15132 Versailles 2,150 ....C7	Juniata (riv.) G5
17870 Selinsgrove 5,227 ......J4	19085 Villanova M6	Laurel Hill (mt.) D5
18960 Sellersville 3,143 ....M5	18088 Walnutport 2,007 .....L4	Lehigh (riv.) L3
15143 Sewickley 4,778 ....B4	16365 Warren⊙ 12,146 ......D2	Letterkenny Army Depot ...G6
17872 Shamokin 10,357 ......J4	15301 Washington⊙ 18,363 ...B5	Licking (creek) F6
17876 Shamokin Dam 1,622 ...J4	16441 Waterford 1,568 ......B2	Little Tinicum (isl.) M7
16146 Sharon 19,057 ....B3	17777 Watsontown 2,366 ....J3	Lycoming (creek) H3
Sharon‡ 128,299 ......B3	17268 Waynesboro 9,726 ....G6	Monongahela (riv.) C6
19079 Sharon Hill 6,221 ......N7	15370 Waynesburg⊙ 4,482 ...B6	North (mt.) K3
15215 Sharpsburg 4,351 ......B6	18255 Weatherly 2,891 ......L4	Ohio (riv.) A4
16150 Sharpsville 5,375 ......A3	16901 Wellsboro⊙ 3,805 .....H2	Oil (creek) C2
16347 Sheffield 1,471 ....D2	16510 Wesleyville 3,998 .....C1	Pine (creek) H2
17976 Shenandoah 7,589 .....K4	15417 West Brownsville 1,433 ..C5	Pine Grove (res.) K6
18655 Shickshinny 1,192 ......K3	19380 West Chester⊙ 17,435 ..L6	Pocono (mts.) M3
19607 Shillington 5,601 ......K5	16950 Westfield 1,268 ......H2	Pymatuning (res.) A2
16748 Shinglehouse 1,310 ....F2	19390 West Grove 1,820 .....L6	Redbank (creek) E3
17257 Shippensburg 5,261 ....H5	18201 West Hazleton 4,871 ...K4	Schuylkill (riv.) M5
19555 Shoemakersville 1,391 ..K4	16201 West Kittanning 1,591 ..C4	Shenango River (lake) B3
17361 Shrewsbury 2,688 .....J6	15656 West Leechburg 1,395 ..C4	Sinnemahoning (creek) F3
19608 Sinking Spring 2,617 ...K5	16159 West Middlesex 1,064 ..B3	South (mt.) H6
18080 Slatington 4,277 ......L4	15122 West Mifflin 26,279 ....C7	Susquehanna (riv.) K6
15684 Slickville 1,178 ....C5	†15905 Westmont 6,113 ......E5	Tioga (riv.) H1
16057 Slippery Rock 3,047 ....B3	15089 West Newton 3,387 ....C5	Tionesta Creek (lake) D3
16749 Smethport⊙ 1,797 .....F2	16160 West Pittsburg 1,133 ...B3	Towanda (creek) J2
15478 Smithfield 1,084 ......C6	18643 West Pittston 5,980 ...F7	Tuscarora (mt.) G5
15501 Somerset⊙ 6,474 ......D6	15229 West View 7,648 .....B6	Wallenpaupack (lake) M3
18964 Souderton 6,657 ......M5		Youghiogheny River (riv.) .D6
15425 South Connellsville 2,296 .C6		⊙County seat.
15956 South Fork 1,401 ......E5		‡Population of metropolitan area.
†18840 South Waverly 1,176 ...J2		⊙Population of town or township.
		† Zip of nearest p.o. * Multiple zips.

18067 Northampton 8,240 ....M4	17562 Paradise 1,107 ....K5
15673 North Apollo 1,487 ....D4	19365 Parkesburg 2,578 ....L6
15104 North Braddock 8,711 ....C7	†19013 Parkside 2,464 ....M7
†18032 North Catasauqua 2,554 ..L4	17331 Parkville 5,009 ....J6
16428 North East 4,568 ....C1	16668 Patton 2,441 ....E4
17857 Northumberland 3,636 ....J4	18072 Pen Argyl 3,388 ....M4
19454 North Wales 3,391 ....M5	17103 Penbrook 3,006 ....J5
†16365 North Warren 1,232 ......D2	19047 Penndel 2,703 ....N5
15074 Norvelt 2,541 ....D5	18073 Pennsburg 2,339 ....M5
19074 Norwood 6,647 ....M7	†17331 Pennville 1,398 ....J6
15071 Oakdale 1,955 ....B5	19151 Penn Wynne M6
15139 Oakmont 7,039 ....C6	18944 Perkasie 5,241 ....M5
6301 Oil City 13,881 ....C3	15473 Perryopolis 2,139 ....C5
18518 Old Forge 9,304 ....F7	*19101 Philadelphia⊙ 1,688,210 .N6
15472 Oliver 3,777 ....C6	Philadelphia‡ 4,716,818 .N6
18447 Olyphant 5,204 ....F7	16866 Philipsburg 3,533 ....F4
17961 Orwigsburg 2,700 ....K4	19460 Phoenixville 14,165 .....L5
16666 Osceola Mills 1,466 ...F4	17963 Pine Grove 2,244 ......K4
19363 Oxford 3,633 ....K6	16868 Pine Grove Mills 1,030 .G4
†15963 Paint 1,177 ....E5	15140 Pitcairn 4,175 ....C5
18071 Palmerton 5,455 .....L4	*15201 Pittsburgh⊙ 423,938 ...B7
17078 Palmyra 7,228 ......J5	Pittsburgh‡ 2,263,894 .B7
19301 Paoli 5,277 ....M5	*18640 Pittston 9,930 ....F7
	18701 Plains 5,455 ....F7

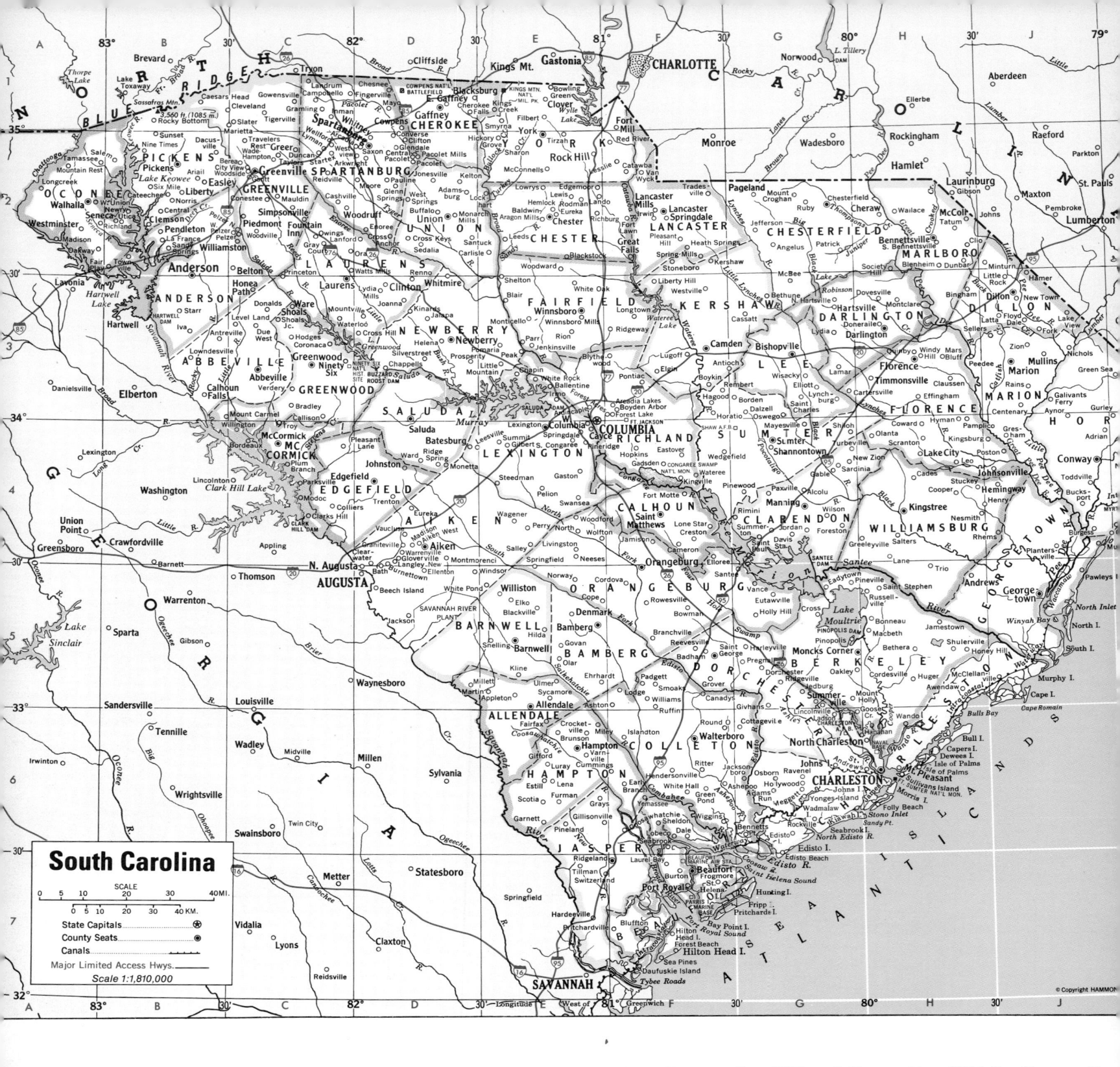

South Carolina

SCALE
0 5 10 20 30 40MI.
0 5 10 20 30 40 KM.

State Capitals............⊛
County Seats............⊙
Canals............

Major Limited Access Hwys.............
Scale 1:1,810,000

© Copyright HAMMOND

COUNTIES		
Abbeville 22,627	B3
Aiken 105,625	D4
Allendale 10,700	E6
Anderson 133,235	B2
Bamberg 18,118	E5
Barnwell 19,868	E5
Beaufort 65,364	F7
Berkeley 94,727	G5
Calhoun 12,206	F4
Charleston 276,974	H6
Cherokee 40,983	D1
Chester 30,148	E2
Chesterfield 38,161	G2
Clarendon 27,464	G4
Colleton 31,776	F6
Darlington 62,717	H3
Dillon 31,083	J3
Dorchester 58,761	G5
Edgefield 17,528	D4
Fairfield 20,700	E3
Florence 110,163	H3
Georgetown 42,461	J5
Greenville 287,913	C2
Greenwood 57,847	C3
Hampton 18,159	E6
Horry 101,419	J4
Jasper 14,504	E6
Kershaw 39,015	F3

Lancaster 53,361	F2
Laurens 52,214	D2
Lee 18,929	G3
Lexington 140,353	E4
Marion 34,179	J3
Marlboro 31,634	H2
McCormick 7,797	C4
Newberry 31,242	D3
Oconee 48,611	A2
Orangeburg 82,276	F5
Pickens 79,292	B2
Richland 269,735	E4
Saluda 16,150	D3
Spartanburg 201,861	C2
Sumter 88,243	G4
Union 30,764	D2
Williamsburg 38,226	H4
York 106,720	E2

CITIES and TOWNS

Zip	Name/Pop.	Key
29620	Abbeville⊙ 5,833	C3
29801	Aiken⊙ 14,978	D4
†29801	Aiken West 3,083	D4
29810	Allendale⊙ 4,400	E5
*29621	Anderson⊙ 27,965	B2
	Anderson‡ 133,235	B2
29510	Andrews 3,129	H5
29320	Arcadia 2,088	C2

†29201	Arcadia Lakes 611	F3
†29640	Arial 2,419	B2
29301	Arkwright 2,623	C2
†29582	Atlantic Beach 289	K4
29511	Aynor 643	J3
29003	Bamberg⊙ 3,672	E5
29812	Barnwell⊙ 5,572	E5
29006	Batesburg 4,023	D4
29816	Bath 2,242	D5
29902	Beaufort⊙ 8,634	F7
29627	Belton 5,312	C2
29512	Bennettsville⊙ 8,774	H2
29611	Berea 13,164	C2
29009	Bethune 481	G3
29010	Bishopville⊙ 3,429	G3
29702	Blacksburg 1,873	D1
29817	Blackville 2,840	E5
29516	Blenheim 202	H2
29910	Bluffton 541	F7
29016	Blythewood 92	E3
29431	Bonneau 401	H5
29432	Branchville 1,769	F5
29911	Brunson 590	E6
29527	Bucksport 1,125	J4
29321	Buffalo 1,641	D2
†29834	Burnettown 359	D5
29628	Calhoun Falls 2,491	B3
29020	Camden⊙ 7,462	F3

29030	Cameron 536	F4
29322	Campobello 472	C1
29031	Carlisle 503	D2
29169	Cayce 11,701	E4
29519	Centenary 700	J3
29630	Central 1,914	B2
29042	Chapin 311	E3
29037	Chappells 109	D3
*29401	Charleston⊙ 69,510	G6
	Charleston-North
	Charleston‡ 430,301	G6
29520	Cheraw 5,654	H2
29323	Chesnee 1,069	D1
29706	Chester⊙ 6,820	E2
29709	Chesterfield⊙ 1,432	G2
29611	City View 1,662	C2
29822	Clearwater 3,967	D4
29631	Clemson 8,118	B2
29635	Cleveland 800	C1
29324	Clifton 950	D2
29325	Clinton 8,596	D3
29525	Clio 1,031	H2
29710	Clover 3,451	E1
*29201	Columbia (cap.)⊙ 100,385	F4
	Columbia‡ 408,176	F4
29329	Converse 1,173	D2
29526	Conway⊙ 10,240	J4
29038	Cope 167	E5
29039	Cordova 202	F5

29435	Cottageville 371	G6
29530	Coward 428	H4
29330	Cowpens 2,023	D1
29332	Cross Hill 604	D3
29532	Darlington⊙ 7,989	H3
29042	Denmark 4,434	E5
29536	Dillon⊙ 7,060	J3
29638	Donalds 366	C3
29639	Due West 1,366	C3
29334	Duncan 1,259	C2
29640	Easley⊙ 14,264	B2
29044	Eastover 899	F4
29824	Edgefield⊙ 2,713	D4
†29438	Edisto Beach 193	G7
29438	Edisto Island 900	G6
29081	Ehrhardt 353	E5
29045	Elgin 595	F3
29826	Elko 329	E5
29047	Elloree 909	F4
29335	Enoree 1,108	D2
29918	Estill 2,308	E6
†29706	Eureka 1,627	E2
29048	Eutawville 615	G5
29827	Fairfax 2,154	E6
29501	Florence⊙ 29,176	H3
	Florence‡ 110,163	H3
29439	Folly Beach 1,478	H6
29206	Forest Acres 6,071	E3

29714	Fort Lawn 471	F2
29715	Fort Mill 4,162	F1
29050	Fort Motte 700	F4
29644	Fountain Inn 4,226	C2
29921	Furman 348	E6
29340	Gaffney⊙ 13,453	D1
†29609	Gantt 13,719	C2
29053	Gaston 960	E4
29440	Georgetown⊙ 10,144	J5
29923	Gifford 385	E6
29054	Gilbert 211	E4
29346	Glendale 1,049	D2
29828	Gloverville 2,619	D4
29445	Goose Creek 17,811	H6
†29843	Govan 109	E5
29829	Graniteville 1,158	D4
29645	Gray Court 988	C2
29055	Great Falls 2,601	F2
29056	Greeleyville 593	H4
*29601	Greenville⊙ 58,242	C2
	Greenville-Spartanburg‡
	568,758	C2
29646	Greenwood⊙ 21,613	C3
29651	Greer 10,525	C2
29924	Hampton⊙ 3,143	E6
29410	Hanahan 13,224	H6
29927	Hardeeville 1,250	E7
29448	Harleyville 606	G5
29550	Hartsville 7,631	G3
29058	Heath Springs 979	F2

Agriculture, Industry and Resources

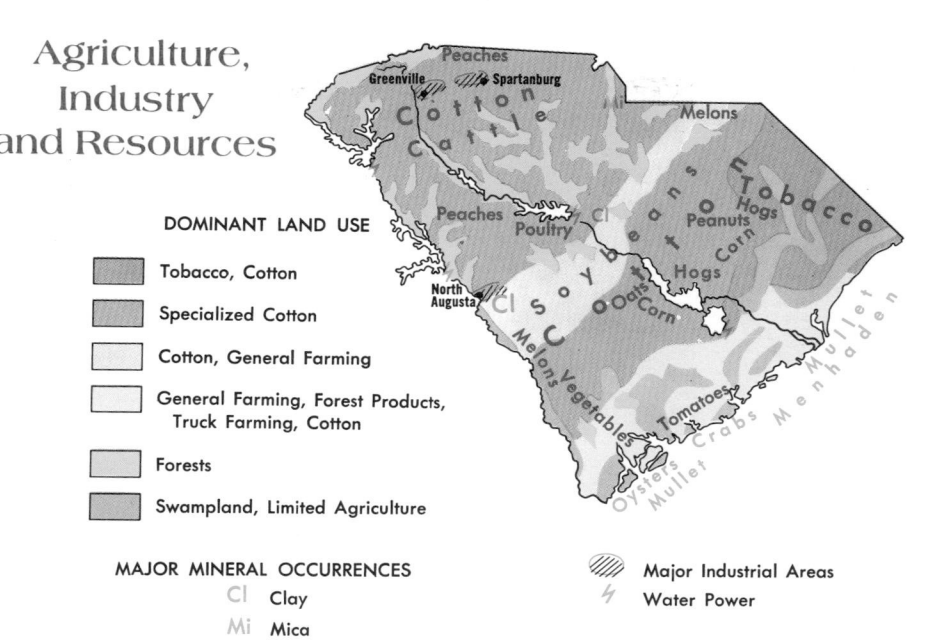

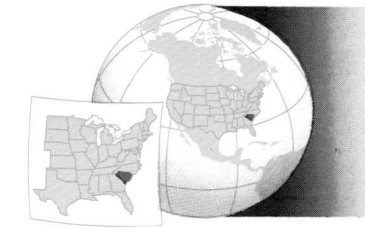

DOMINANT LAND USE

- Tobacco, Cotton
- Specialized Cotton
- Cotton, General Farming
- General Farming, Forest Products, Truck Farming, Cotton
- Forests
- Swampland, Limited Agriculture

MAJOR MINERAL OCCURRENCES

Cl Clay
Mi Mica

- Major Industrial Areas
- Water Power

AREA 31,113 sq. mi. (80,583 sq. km.)
POPULATION 3,121,833
CAPITAL Columbia
LARGEST CITY Columbia
HIGHEST POINT Sassafras Mtn. 3,560 ft. (1085 m.)
SETTLED IN 1670
ADMITTED TO UNION May 23, 1788
POPULAR NAME Palmetto State
STATE FLOWER Carolina (Yellow) Jessamine
STATE BIRD Carolina Wren

†29720 Lancaster Mills 2,096 ...... F2
29356 Landrum 2,141 .... C1
29564 Lane 554 .... H5
29834 Langley 1,714 .... D4
29565 Latta 1,804 .... J3
29902 Laurel Bay 5,238 .... F7
29360 Laurens⊙ 10,587 .... C3
29070 Leesville 2,296 .... E4
†29730 Lesslie 1,102 .... E2
29072 Lexington 2,131 .... E4
29657 Liberty 3,167 .... B2
†29483 Lincolnville 808 .... G6
29075 Little Mountain 282 .... E3
29076 Livingston 166 .... E4
29364 Lockhart 85 .... E2
29082 Lodge 145 .... F5
29569 Loris 2,193 .... K3
29659 Lowndesville 197 ...... B3
†29706 Lowrys 225 .... E2
29078 Lugoff 2,939 .... F3
29932 Luray 149 .... E6
29325 Lydia Mills 925 .... D3
29365 Lyman 1,067 .... C2
29080 Lynchburg 534 .... G3
†29829 Madison 1,150 .... D4
29102 Manning⊙ 4,746 ...... G4
29661 Marietta-Slater 1,834 .. C1
29571 Marion⊙ 7,700 .... J3
29662 Mauldin 8,143 .... C2
29104 Mayesville 663 .... G4
29101 McBee 774 .... G3
29458 McClellanville 436 ..... H5
29570 McColl 2,677 .... H2
29726 McConnells 171 .... E2
29835 McCormick⊙ 1,725 .... C4
29460 Meggett 249 .... G6
†29379 Monarch Mills 2,353 .. D2
29461 Moncks Corner⊙ 3,699 . G5
29105 Monetta 167 .... D4
29840 Mount Carmel 182 .... C3
29727 Mount Croghan 146 ... G2
29464 Mount Pleasant 14,209 . H6
29574 Mullins 6,068 .... J3
29576 Murrells Inlet 2,410 ... K4
29577 Myrtle Beach 18,446 .. K4
29107 Neeses 557 .... E4
29108 Newberry⊙ 9,866 ..... D3
29809 New Ellenton 2,628 ... D5
†29536 New Town 950 .... J3
29581 Nichols 606 .... J3
29666 Ninety Six 2,249 ...... C3
29667 Norris 903 .... B2
29112 North 1,304 .... E4
29841 North Augusta 13,593 . C5
29406 North Charleston 62,534 . G6
†29550 North Hartsville 2,650 . G3
29582 North Myrtle Beach 3,960 . K4
29113 Norway 518 .... E5
29114 Olanta 699 .... H4
29843 Olar 381 .... E5
29115 Orangeburg⊙ 14,933 .. F4
29372 Pacolet 1,556 .... D2
29373 Pacolet Mills 1,051 ... D2
29728 Pageland 2,113 .... G2
29583 Pamplico 1,213 .... H4
29844 Parksville 157 .... C4
29102 Paxville 244 .... G4
29122 Peak 82 .... E3
29123 Pelion 213 .... E4
29669 Pelzer 130 .... B2
29670 Pendleton 3,154 ...... B2
29124 Perry 273 .... E4
29671 Pickens⊙ 3,199 ...... B2
29673 Piedmont 2,992 .... C2
29934 Pineland 800 .... E6
29169 Pineridge 1,287 ...... E4
29125 Pinewood 689 .... G4
29469 Pinopolis 788 .... G5
29845 Plum Branch 73 ...... C4
29126 Pomaria 271 .... E3
29935 Port Royal 2,977 ..... F7
29127 Prosperity 803 .... D3
†29501 Quinby 952 .... H3
29470 Ravenel 1,655 .... G6

29471 Reevesville 241 .... F5
29729 Richburg 269 .... E2
29936 Ridgeland⊙ 1,143 .... E7
29129 Ridge Spring 969 ..... D4
29472 Ridgeville 603 .... G5
29130 Ridgeway 343 .... F3
29730 Rock Hill 35,344 ..... E2
        Rock Hill‡ 106,720 ... E2
29133 Rowesville 388 .... F5
29741 Ruby 256 .... G2
29407 Saint Andrews 9,908 .. G6
29477 Saint George⊙ 2,134 .. F5
29135 Saint Matthews⊙ 2,496 . F4
29479 Saint Stephen 1,850 .. H5
29676 Salem 194 .... A2
29137 Salley 584 .... E4
29138 Saluda⊙ 2,752 .... D4
29142 Santee 612 .... E4
†29301 Saxon 4,383 .... D2
29939 Scotia 72 .... E6
29591 Scranton 861 .... H4
29592 Sellers 388 .... H3
29678 Seneca 7,436 .... A2
29742 Sharon 323 .... E2
29145 Silverstreet 200 ...... D3
29681 Simpsonville 9,037 .... C2
29682 Six Mile 470 .... B2
29683 Slater-Marietta 1,834 .. C1
29481 Smoaks 165 .... F5
29743 Smyrna 47 .... E1
†29812 Snelling 111 .... E5
29593 Society Hill 848 ..... H2
†29512 South Bennettsville 1,065 . H2
†29169 South Congaree 2,113 . E4
*29301 Spartanburg⊙ 43,826 . C1
29169 Springdale 2,985 ..... E4
†29720 Springdale 2,570 .... E4
29146 Springfield 604 ...... E4
†29067 Spring Mills 1,419 ... F2
29684 Starr 241 .... B3
29377 Startex 1,006 .... C2
29554 Stuckey 222 .... H4
29482 Sullivans Island 1,867 . H6
29148 Summerton 1,173 ..... G4
29483 Summerville 6,706 .... G5
†29054 Summit 172 .... E4
29150 Sumter⊙ 24,890 ...... G4
29577 Surfside Beach 2,522 .. K4
29160 Swansea 888 .... E4
29846 Sycamore 261 .... E5
29594 Tatum 101 .... H2
29687 Taylors 15,801 .... C2
29688 Tigerville 975 .... C1
29161 Timmonsville 2,112 ... H3
29690 Travelers Rest 3,017 .. C2
29847 Trenton 404 .... D4
29848 Troy 705 .... C4
29162 Turbeville 549 .... G4
29849 Ulmer 91 .... E5
29379 Union⊙ 10,523 ...... D2
†29678 Utica 1,501 .... B2
29163 Vance 89 .... G5
29944 Varnville 1,948 ...... E6
†29607 Wade-Hampton 20,180 . C2
29164 Wagener 903 .... E4
29691 Walhalla⊙ 3,801 ..... A2
29488 Walterboro⊙ 6,209 ... F6
29166 Ward 98 .... D4
29692 Ware Shoals 2,370 ... C3
29851 Warrenville 1,029 .... D4
29384 Waterloo 200 .... C3
†29360 Watts Mills 1,324 .... D2
29385 Wellford 2,143 .... C2
29169 West Columbia 10,409 . E4
29693 Westminster 3,114 .... A2
29669 West Pelzer 944 ...... B2
29696 West Union 300 ...... B2
†29301 Westview 1,999 ...... C2
29178 Whitmire 2,038 ...... D3
29303 Whitney 4,052 .... D1
29493 Williams 205 .... F5
29697 Williamston 4,310 .... B2
29853 Williston 3,173 ...... E5
29856 Windsor 55 .... E5
†29501 Windy Hill 1,622 .... H3
29180 Winnsboro⊙ 2,919 ... E3

†29180 Winnsboro Mills 1,890 .. E3
29112 Woodford 206 .... E4
29388 Woodruff 5,171 ...... D2
29945 Yemassee 789 .... F6
29745 York⊙ 6,412 .... E1

OTHER FEATURES

Ashepoo (riv.) F6
Ashley (riv.) G6
Bay Point (isl.) F7
Beaufort Marine Air Sta. F7
Big Black (creek) G2
Black (riv.) H4
Blue Ridge (mts.) B1
Broad (riv.) E2
Broad (riv.) F7
Buck (creek) J3
Bull (isl.) H6
Bullock (creek) E2
Bulls (bay) H6
Bush (riv.) D3
Buzzard Roost (dam) D3
Cape (isl.) J5
Capers (isl.) H6
Catawba (riv.) F2
Catfish (creek) J3
Charleston A.F.B. G6
Chattooga (riv.) A2
Clark Hill (dam) C4
Clark Hill (lake) C4
Combahee (riv.) F6
Congaree (riv.) F4
Congaree Nat'l. Mon. F4
Cooper (riv.) H6
Coosaw (riv.) G7
Coosawhatchie (riv.) E6
Cowpens Nat'l Battlefield D1
Crooked (creek) H2
Deep (creek) B2
Dewees (isl.) H6
Donaldson A.F.B. C2

Edisto (isl.) G6
Edisto (riv.) G7
Enoree (riv.) C2
Fort Jackson F4
Fort Sumter Nat'l Mon. H6
Four Hole Swamp (creek) F5
Fripp (isl.) G7
Great Pee Dee (riv.) J4
Greenwood (lake) D3
Hartwell (dam) B3
Hartwell (lake) A3
Hilton Head (isl.) F7
Hunting (isl.) G7
Intracoastal Waterway H5
James (isl.) H6
Johns (isl.) G6
Juniper (creek) H2
Keowee (lake) B2
Keowee (riv.) B2
Kiawah (isl.) G6
Kings Mountain Nat'l Mil. Park . E1
Little (riv.) C3
Little (riv.) K4
Little Lynches (riv.) G3
Little Pee Dee (riv.) J4
Little River (inlet) L4
Lumber (riv.) J3
Lynches (riv.) H3
Marion (lake) G5
Morris (isl.) H6
Moultrie (lake) G5
Murphy (isl.) J5
Murray (lake) D4
Myrtle Beach A.F.B. K4
Naval Base H6
New (riv.) E6
Ninety Six Nat'l Hist. Site ... C3
North (inlet) J5
North (isl.) J5
North Edisto (riv.) G6
Pacolet (riv.) D1
Palms, Isle of (isl.) H6

Parris Island Marine Base F7
Pee Dee (riv.) H2
Pinopolis (dam) G5
Pocotaligo (riv.) G4
Port Royal (sound) F7
Pritchards (isl.) G7
Reedy (riv.) C2
Robinson (lake) G3
Romain (cape) J6
Saint Helena (isl.) F7
Saint Helena (sound) G7
Salkehatchie (riv.) E5
Saluda (riv.) D3
Sandy (pt.) H6
Sandy (riv.) E2
Santee (dam) G4
Santee (riv.) H5
Sassafras (mt.) B1
Savannah (riv.) D5
Savannah River Plant D5
Sea (isls.) G7
Seabrook (isl.) G6
Seneca (riv.) B2
Shaw A.F.B. 6,939 .... F4
South (isl.) J5
Stevens (creek) C4
Stono (riv.) H6
Thompsons (creek) G2
Tugaloo (riv.) A2
Turkey (creek) E2
Tybee Roads (chan.) F7
Tyger (riv.) D2
Waccamaw (riv.) J5
Wadmalaw (isl.) G6
Wando (riv.) H6
Wateree (lake) F3
Wateree (riv.) F3
Winyah (bay) J5
Wylie (lake) E1

⊙County seat.
‡Population of metropolitan area.
† Zip of nearest p.o. * Multiple zips.

29554 Hemingway 853 .... J4
†29706 Hemlock (Eureka) 1,627 .. E2
29717 Hickory Grove 344 .... E2
29813 Hilda 355 .... E5
29928 Hilton Head Island 11,344 . F7
29653 Hodges 154 .... C3
29059 Holly Hill 1,785 .... G5
29449 Hollywood 729 .... G6
29654 Honea Path 4,114 .... C3
29349 Inman 1,554 .... C1
29063 Irmo 3,957 .... E3
†29720 Irwin 1,373 .... F2
29451 Isle of Palms 3,421 ..... H6
29655 Iva 1,369 .... B3
29831 Jackson 1,771 .... D5
29453 Jamestown 193 .... H5
†29483 Jedburg 900 .... G5
29718 Jefferson 651 .... G2
29351 Joanna 1,839 .... D3
29555 Johnsonville 1,421 ...... J4
29832 Johnston 2,624 .... D4
29353 Jonesville 1,201 .... D2
29067 Kershaw 1,993 .... F2
29556 Kingstree⊙ 4,147 ...... H4
29814 Kline 315 .... E5
29456 Ladson 13,246 .... G6
29560 Lake City 6,731 .... H4
29563 Lake View 939 .... J3
29069 Lamar 1,333 .... G3
29720 Lancaster⊙ 9,703 ...... F2

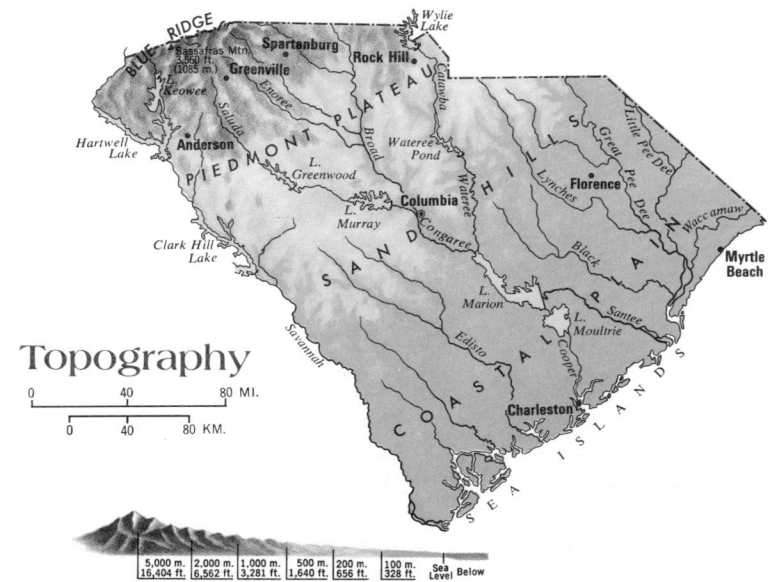

Topography

0 ___ 40 ___ 80 MI.
0 ___ 40 ___ 80 KM.

| 5,000 m. 16,404 ft. | 2,000 m. 6,562 ft. | 1,000 m. 3,281 ft. | 500 m. 1,640 ft. | 200 m. 656 ft. | 100 m. 328 ft. | Sea Level | Below |

COUNTIES

Aurora 3,628 ....M6
Beadle 19,195 ....N5
Bennett 3,044 ....F7
Bon Homme 8,059 ....O7
Brookings 24,332 ....R5
Brown 36,962 ....N2
Brule 5,245 ....L6
Buffalo 1,795 ....L5
Butte 8,372 ....B4
Campbell 2,243 ....J2
Charles Mix 9,680 ......M7
Clark 4,894 ....O4
Clay 13,689 ....P8
Codington 20,885 ......P4
Corson 5,196 ....G2
Custer 6,000 ....B6
Davison 17,820 ....N6
Day 8,133 ....O3
Deuel 5,289 ....R4
Dewey 5,366 ....G3
Douglas 4,181 ....N7
Edmunds 5,159 ....L3
Fall River 8,439 ....B7
Faulk 3,327 ....L3
Grant 9,013 ....R3
Gregory 6,015 ....L7
Haakon 2,794 ....F5
Hamlin 5,261 ....P4
Hand 4,948 ....L4
Hanson 3,415 ....O6
Harding 1,700 ....B2
Hughes 14,220 ....J5
Hutchinson 9,350 ....O7
Hyde 2,069 ....K4
Jackson 3,437 ....F6
Jerauld 2,929 ....M5
Jones 1,463 ....H6
Kingsbury 6,679 ....O5
Lake 10,724 ....P5
Lawrence 18,339 ....B5
Lincoln 13,942 .....R7

Lyman 3,864 ....J6
Marshall 5,404 ....O2
McCook 6,444 ....P6
McPherson 4,027 ....L2
Meade 20,717 ....D5
Mellette 2,249 ....H6
Miner 3,739 ....O5
Minnehaha 109,435 ....R6
Moody 6,692 ....R5
Pennington 70,361 ....C6
Perkins 4,700 ....D3
Potter 3,674 ....J3
Roberts 10,991 ....P2
Sanborn 3,213 ....N5
Shannon 11,323 .....D7
Spink 9,201 ....N4
Stanley 2,533 ....H5
Sully 1,990 ....J4
Todd 7,328 ....H7
Tripp 7,268 ....K7
Turner 9,255 ....P7
Union 10,938 ....R8
Walworth 7,011 ......J3

Yankton 18,952 ....P7
Ziebach 2,308 ....F4

CITIES and TOWNS

Zip Name/Pop.   Key
57401 Aberdeen⊙ 25,851 ....M3
57310 Academy 10 ....M7
57520 Agar 139 ....J4
57420 Akaska 49 ....J3
57001 Alcester 885 ....R7
57311 Alexandria⊙ 588 ...O6
57714 Allen 300 ....F7
57312 Alpena 288 ....N5
57211 Altamont 58 ....R4
57421 Amherst 75 ....O2
57422 Andover 139 ....O3
57715 Ardmore 16 ....B7
57212 Arlington 991 .....P5
57313 Armour⊙ 819 ......N7
57423 Artas 43 ....K2
57314 Artesian 227 ......O6

57424 Ashton 154 ....N3
57213 Astoria 154 ....S4
57425 Athol 38 ....M3
57002 Aurora 507 ....R5
57315 Avon 576 ....N8
57214 Badger 99 ....P5
57003 Baltic 679 ....R6
57316 Bancroft 41 ....O4
57426 Barnard 65 ....N2
57716 Batesland 163 ......E7
57427 Bath 175 ....S3
57214 Belvidere 80 ....G6
57215 Bemis 37 ....R4
57004 Beresford 1,865 ....R8
57713 Black Hawk 1,608 ...C5
57522 Blunt 424 ....J4
57317 Bonesteel 358 ......M7
57428 Bowdle 644 ....K3
57719 Box Elder 3,186 ....D5

57217 Bradley 135 ....O3
57005 Brandon 2,589 ....R6
57218 Brandt 129 ....R4
57429 Brentford 91 ....N3
57319 Bridgewater 653 ....P6
57219 Bristol 445 ....O3
57430 Britton⊙ 1,590 ....O2
57006 Brookings⊙ 14,951 ..R5
57220 Bruce 254 ....P4
57221 Bryant 388 ....O4
57720 Buffalo⊙ 453 ....B2
57722 Buffalo Gap 186 ....C6
57621 Bullhead 400 ....G2
57010 Burbank 92 ....R8
57523 Burke⊙ 859 ....L7
57276 Bushnell 76 ....R5
57222 Butler 22 ....O3
57724 Camp Crook 100 .....B2
57012 Canistota 626 ......P6
57321 Canova 194 ....O6
57013 Canton⊙ 2,886 .....R7
57725 Caputa 50 ....D5

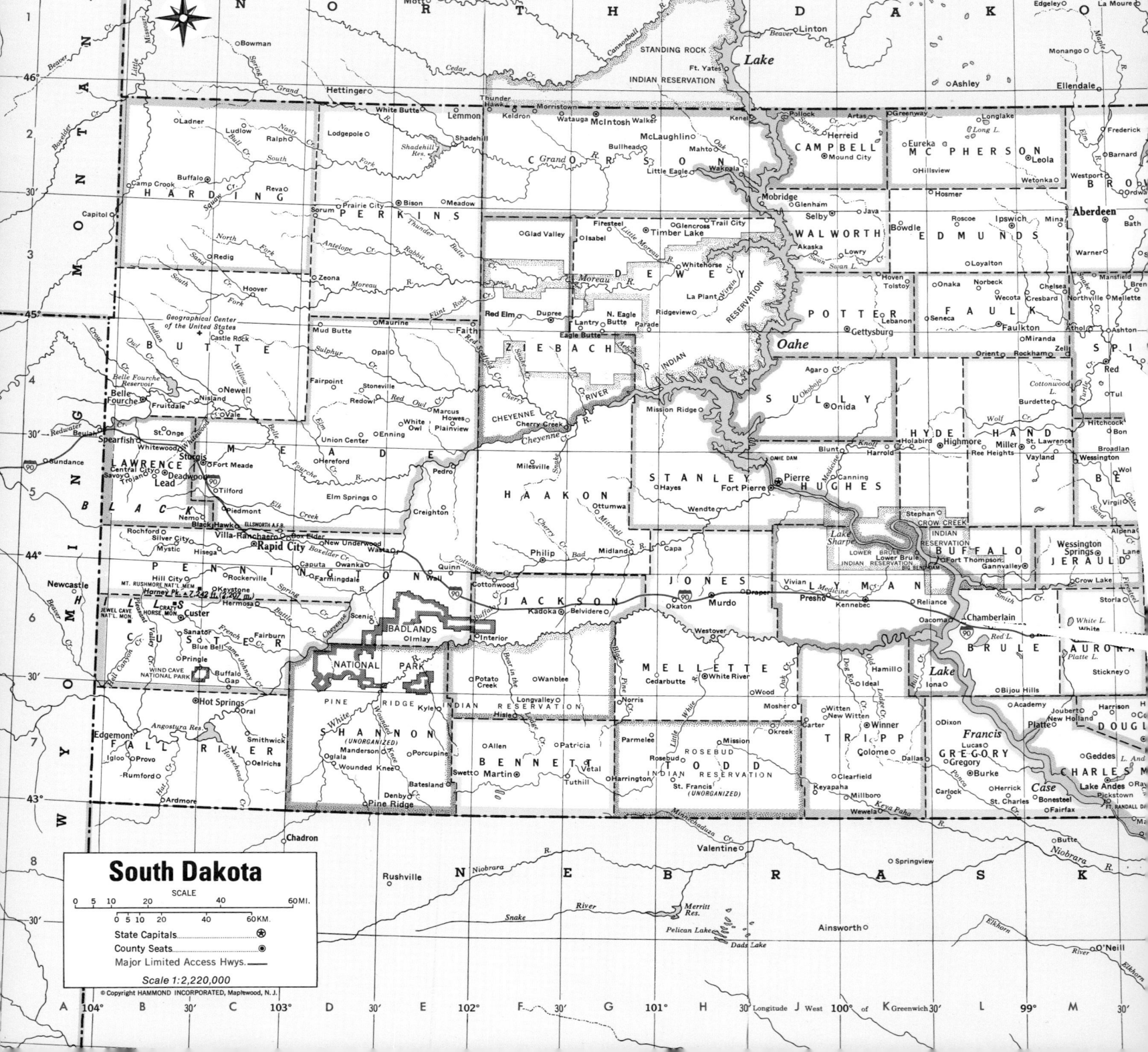

South Dakota

SCALE
0 5 10   20   40   60MI.
0 5 10   20   40   60KM.

State Capitals ....⊛
County Seats ....⊙
Major Limited Access Hwys. ___

Scale 1:2,220,000

© Copyright HAMMOND INCORPORATED, Maplewood, N.J.

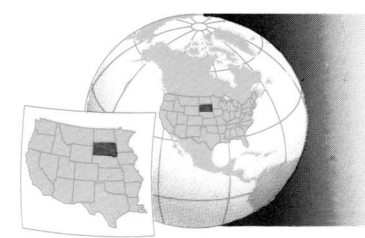

AREA 77,116 sq. mi. (199,730 sq. km.)
POPULATION 690,768
CAPITAL Pierre
LARGEST CITY Sioux Falls
HIGHEST POINT Harney Pk. 7,242 ft.
  (2207 m.)
SETTLED IN 1856
ADMITTED TO UNION November 2, 1889
POPULAR NAME Coyote State; Sunshine
  State
STATE FLOWER Pasqueflower
STATE BIRD Ring-necked Pheasant

Topography

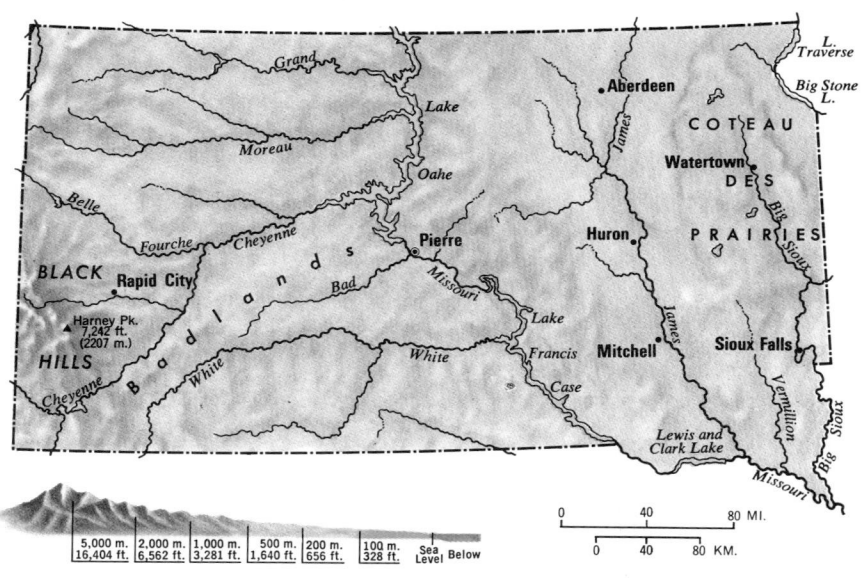

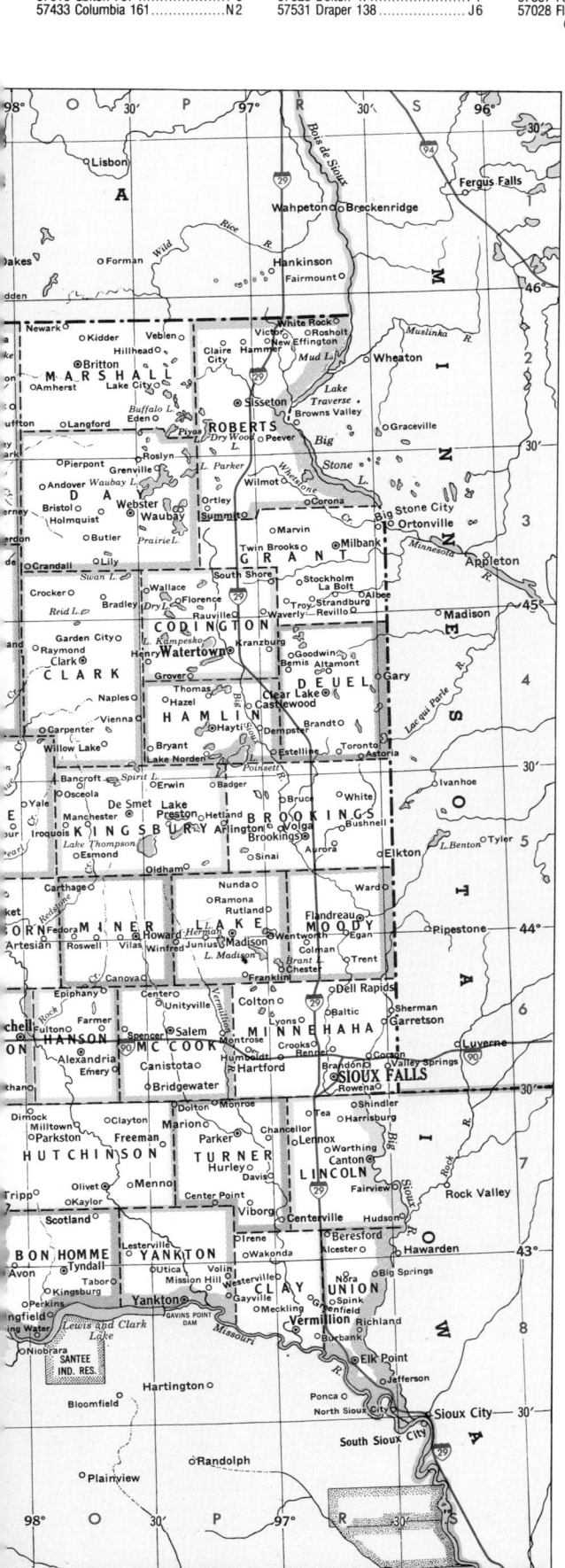

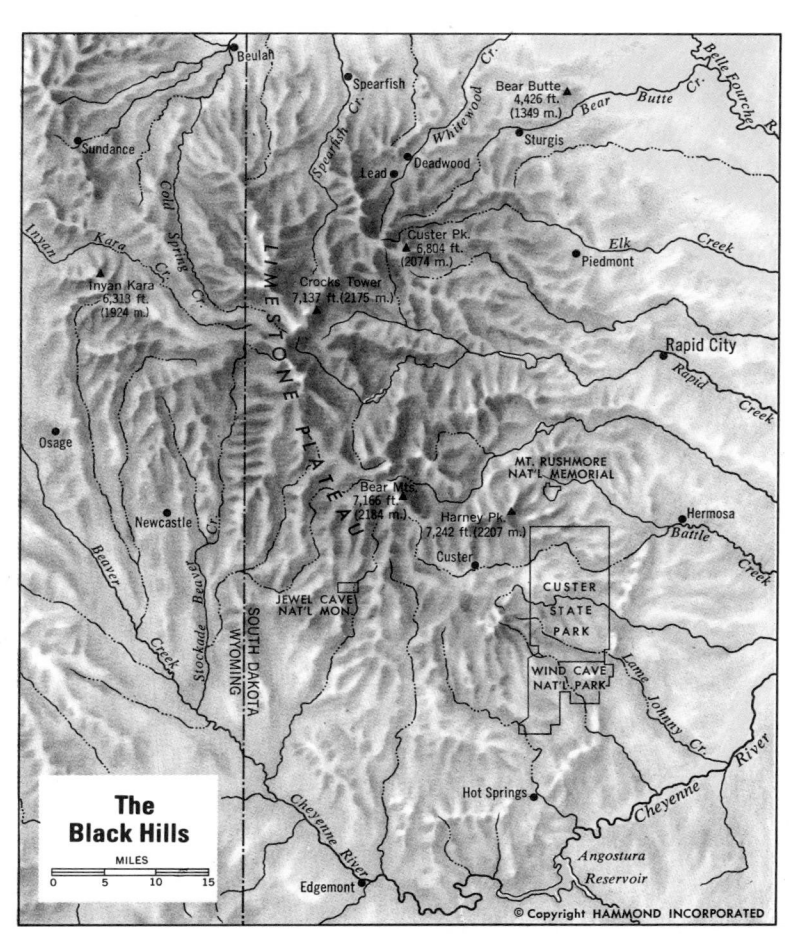

The Black Hills

MILES
0 5 10 15

© Copyright HAMMOND INCORPORATED

Agriculture, Industry and Resources

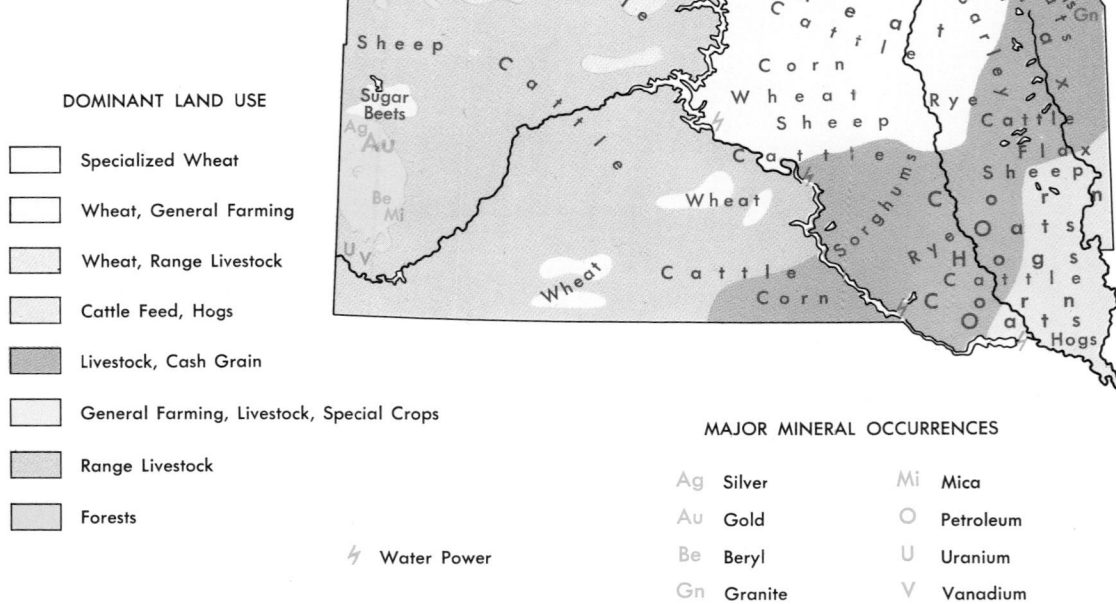

DOMINANT LAND USE

- Specialized Wheat
- Wheat, General Farming
- Wheat, Range Livestock
- Cattle Feed, Hogs
- Livestock, Cash Grain
- General Farming, Livestock, Special Crops
- Range Livestock
- Forests

⚡ Water Power

MAJOR MINERAL OCCURRENCES

Ag	Silver	Mi	Mica
Au	Gold	O	Petroleum
Be	Beryl	U	Uranium
Gn	Granite	V	Vanadium

COUNTIES

Anderson 38,381 J6
Andrews 13,323 B5
Angelina 64,172 K6
Aransas 14,260 H10
Archer 7,266 F4
Armstrong 1,994 C3
Atascosa 25,055 F9
Austin 17,726 H8
Bailey 8,168 B3
Bandera 7,084 E8
Bastrop 24,726 G7
Baylor 4,919 E4
Bee 26,030 G9
Bell 157,820 G6
Bexar 988,798 F8
Blanco 4,681 F8
Borden 859 C5
Bosque 13,401 G6
Bowie 75,301 K4
Brazoria 169,587 J8
Brazos 93,588 H7
Brewster 7,573 A8
Briscoe 2,579 C3
Brooks 8,428 F11
Brown 33,057 F6
Burleson 12,313 H7
Burnet 17,803 F7
Caldwell 23,637 G8
Calhoun 19,574 H9
Callahan 10,992 E5
Cameron 209,727 G11
Camp 9,275 K5
Carson 6,672 C2
Cass 29,430 K4
Castro 10,556 B3
Chambers 18,538 K8
Cherokee 38,127 J6
Childress 6,950 D3
Clay 9,582 F4
Cochran 4,825 B4
Coke 3,196 D6
Coleman 10,439 E6
Collin 144,576 H4
Collingsworth 4,648 D3
Colorado 18,823 H8
Comal 36,446 F8
Comanche 12,617 F5
Concho 2,915 E6
Cooke 27,656 G4
Coryell 56,767 G6
Cottle 2,947 D3
Crane 4,600 B6
Crockett 4,608 C7
Crosby 8,859 C4
Culberson 3,315 C11
Dallam 6,531 B1
Dallas 1,556,390 H5
Dawson 16,184 C5
Deaf Smith 21,165 B3
Delta 4,839 J4
Denton 143,126 G4
De Witt 18,903 G9
Dickens 3,539 D4
Dimmit 11,367 E9
Donley 4,075 D2
Duval 12,517 F10
Eastland 19,480 F5
Ector 115,374 B6
Edwards 2,033 D7
Ellis 59,743 H5
El Paso 479,899 A10
Erath 22,560 F5
Falls 17,946 H6
Fannin 24,285 H4
Fayette 18,832 H8
Fisher 5,891 D5
Floyd 9,834 C3
Foard 2,158 E3
Fort Bend 130,846 J8
Franklin 6,893 J4
Freestone 14,830 H6
Frio 13,785 E9
Gaines 13,150 B5
Galveston 195,940 K8
Garza 5,336 C4
Gillespie 13,532 F7
Glasscock 1,304 C6
Goliad 5,193 G9
Gonzales 15,949 G8
Gray 26,386 D2
Grayson 89,796 H4
Gregg 99,495 K5
Grimes 13,580 J7
Guadalupe 46,708 G8
Hale 37,592 C3
Hall 5,594 D3
Hamilton 8,297 F6
Hansford 6,209 C1
Hardeman 6,368 E3
Hardin 40,721 K7
Harris 2,409,547 J8
Harrison 52,265 K5
Hartley 3,987 B2
Haskell 7,725 E4
Hays 40,594 F7
Hemphill 5,304 D2
Henderson 42,606 J5
Hidalgo 283,323 F11
Hill 25,024 G5
Hockley 23,230 B4
Hood 17,714 G5
Hopkins 25,247 J4
Houston 22,299 J6
Howard 33,142 C5
Hudspeth 2,728 B10
Hunt 55,248 H4
Hutchinson 26,304 C2
Irion 1,386 C6
Jack 7,408 F4
Jackson 13,352 H9
Jasper 30,781 K7
Jeff Davis 1,647 C11
Jefferson 250,938 K8
Jim Hogg 5,168 F11
Jim Wells 36,498 F10
Johnson 67,649 G5
Jones 17,268 E5
Karnes 13,593 G9
Kaufman 39,029 H5
Kendall 10,635 F8
Kenedy 543 G11
Kent 1,145 D4
Kerr 28,780 E7
Kimble 4,063 E7
King 425 D4
Kinney 2,279 D8
Kleberg 33,358 G10
Knox 5,329 E4
Lamar 42,156 J4
Lamb 18,669 B3
Lampasas 12,005 F6
La Salle 5,514 E9
Lavaca 19,004 H8
Lee 10,952 H7
Leon 9,594 J6
Liberty 47,088 K7
Limestone 20,224 H6
Lipscomb 3,766 D1
Live Oak 9,606 F9
Llano 10,144 F7
Loving 91 A6
Lubbock 211,651 C4
Lynn 8,605 C4
Madison 10,649 J6
Marion 10,360 K5
Martin 4,684 C5
Mason 3,683 E7
Matagorda 37,828 H9
Maverick 31,398 D9
McCulloch 8,735 E6
McLennan 170,755 G6
McMullen 789 F9
Medina 23,164 E8
Menard 2,346 E7
Midland 82,636 B6
Milam 22,732 H7
Mills 4,477 F6
Mitchell 9,088 D5
Montague 17,410 G4
Montgomery 128,487 J7
Moore 16,575 C2
Morris 14,629 K4

AREA 266,807 sq. mi. (691,030 sq. km.)
POPULATION 14,229,288
CAPITAL Austin
LARGEST CITY Houston
HIGHEST POINT Guadalupe Pk. 8,749 ft. (2667 m.)
SETTLED IN 1686
ADMITTED TO UNION December 29, 1845
POPULAR NAME Lone Star State
STATE FLOWER Bluebonnet
STATE BIRD Mockingbird

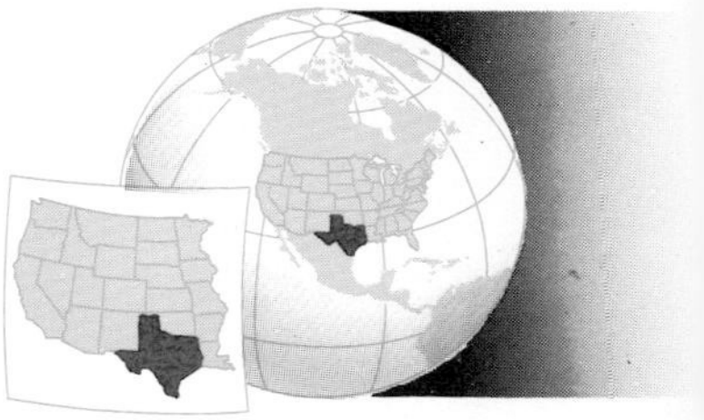

Motley 1,950 D3
Nacogdoches 46,786 K6
Navarro 35,323 H5
Newton 13,254 L7
Nolan 17,359 D5
Nueces 268,215 G10
Ochiltree 9,588 D1
Oldham 2,283 B2
Orange 83,838 L7
Palo Pinto 24,062 F5
Panola 20,724 K5
Parker 44,609 G5
Parmer 11,038 B3
Pecos 14,618 B7
Polk 24,407 K7
Potter 98,637 C2
Presidio 5,188 C12
Rains 4,839 J5
Randall 75,062 C2
Reagan 4,135 C6
Real 2,469 E8
Red River 16,101 J4
Reeves 15,801 D11
Refugio 9,289 G9
Roberts 1,187 D2
Robertson 14,653 H6
Rockwall 14,528 H5
Runnels 11,872 E6
Rusk 41,382 K5
Sabine 8,702 L6
San Augustine 8,785 K6
San Jacinto 11,434 J7
San Patricio 58,013 G10
San Saba 6,204 F6
Schleicher 2,820 D7
Scurry 18,192 D5
Shackelford 3,915 E5
Shelby 23,084 K6
Sherman 3,174 C1
Smith 128,366 J5
Somervell 4,154 G5
Starr 27,266 F11
Stephens 9,926 F5
Sterling 1,206 C6
Stonewall 2,406 D4
Sutton 5,130 D7
Swisher 9,723 C3
Tarrant 860,880 G5
Taylor 110,932 E5
Terrell 1,595 B7
Terry 14,581 B4
Throckmorton 2,053 E4
Titus 21,442 K4
Tom Green 84,784 D6
Travis 419,573 G7
Trinity 9,450 J6
Tyler 16,223 K7
Upshur 28,595 K5
Upton 4,619 B6
Uvalde 22,441 E8
Val Verde 35,910 C8
Van Zandt 31,426 J5
Victoria 68,807 H9
Walker 41,789 J7
Waller 19,798 J8
Ward 13,976 A6
Washington 21,998 H7
Webb 99,258 E10
Wharton 40,242 H8
Wheeler 7,137 D2
Wichita 121,082 F3
Wilbarger 15,931 E3
Willacy 17,495 G11
Williamson 76,507 G7
Wilson 16,756 F8
Winkler 9,944 A6
Wise 26,575 G4
Wood 24,697 J5
Yoakum 8,299 B4
Young 19,083 F4
Zapata 6,628 E11
Zavala 11,666 E9

CITIES and TOWNS

Zip *Name/Pop.* *Key*

*79601 Abilene⊙ 98,315 E5
Abilene‡ 139,192 E5
78516 Alamo 5,831 F11
78209 Alamo Heights 6,252 K10
76430 Albany⊙ 2,450 E5
78332 Alice⊙ 20,961 F10
75002 Allen 8,314 H1
79830 Alpine⊙ 5,465 D12
77511 Alvin 16,515 J3
*79101 Amarillo⊙ 149,230 C2
Amarillo‡ 173,699 C2
77514 Anahuac⊙ 1,840 K8
77830 Anderson⊙ 500 J7
79714 Andrews⊙ 11,061 B5
77515 Angleton⊙ 13,929 J8
79501 Anson⊙ 2,831 E5
78336 Aransas Pass 7,173 G10
76351 Archer City⊙ 1,862 F4
*76010 Arlington 160,123 F2
79502 Aspermont⊙ 1,357 D4
75751 Athens⊙ 10,197 J5
75551 Atlanta 6,272 K4
*78701 Austin (cap.)⊙ 345,496 G7
Austin‡ 536,450 G7
76020 Azle 5,822 E2
77518 Bacliff 4,851 K2
79504 Baird⊙ 1,696 E5
75180 Balch Springs 13,746 H2
†78201 Balcones Heights 2,511 J10
76821 Ballinger⊙ 4,207 E6
78003 Bandera⊙ 947 F8
77532 Barrett 3,183 K1
78602 Bastrop⊙ 3,789 G7
77414 Bay City⊙ 17,837 H9
77520 Baytown 56,923 L2
*77701 Beaumont⊙ 118,102 K7
Beaumont-Port Arthur-Orange‡ 375,497 K7
76021 Bedford 20,821 F2
78102 Beeville⊙ 14,574 G9
77401 Bellaire 14,950 J2
76704 Bellmead 7,569 H6
77418 Bellville⊙ 2,860 H8
76513 Belton⊙ 10,660 G7
76126 Benbrook 13,579 E2
79505 Benjamin⊙ 257 E4
76932 Big Lake⊙ 3,404 C6
79720 Big Spring⊙ 24,804 C5
78006 Boerne⊙ 3,229 J10
75418 Bonham⊙ 7,338 H4
79007 Borger 15,837 C2
75557 Boston⊙ 400 K4
76230 Bowie 5,610 G4
78832 Brackettville⊙ 1,676 D8
76825 Brady⊙ 5,969 E6
77422 Brazoria 3,025 J9
76024 Breckenridge⊙ 6,921 F5
77833 Brenham⊙ 10,966 H7
77611 Bridge City 7,667 L7
79316 Brownfield⊙ 10,387 B4
*78520 Brownsville⊙ 84,997 G12
Brownsville-Harlingen-San Benito‡ 209,680 G12
76801 Brownwood⊙ 19,396 F6
77801 Bryan⊙ 44,337 H7
Bryan-College Station‡ 93,588 H7
76354 Burkburnett 10,668 F3
76028 Burleson 11,734 F3
78611 Burnet⊙ 3,410 F7
77836 Caldwell⊙ 2,953 H7
76520 Cameron⊙ 5,721 H7
79014 Canadian⊙ 3,491 D2
75103 Canton⊙ 2,845 J5
79015 Canyon⊙ 10,724 C3
78834 Carrizo Springs⊙ 6,886 E9
*75006 Carrollton 40,595 G2
75633 Carthage⊙ 6,447 K5
†78213 Castle Hills 4,773 J10
75104 Cedar Hill 6,849 G3
75935 Center⊙ 5,827 K6
75833 Centerville⊙ 799 H6
77530 Channelview 17,471 K1
79018 Channing⊙ 304 B2
79201 Childress⊙ 5,817 D3
76437 Cisco 4,517 E5
79226 Clarendon⊙ 2,220 C3
75426 Clarksville⊙ 4,917 K4
79019 Claude⊙ 1,112 C2
†77565 Clear Lake Shores 755 K2
76031 Cleburne⊙ 19,218 G5
77327 Cleveland 5,977 K7
77531 Clute 9,577 J9
77331 Coldspring⊙ 569 J7
76834 Coleman⊙ 5,960 E6
77840 College Station 37,272 H7
76034 Colleyville 6,700 F2
79512 Colorado City⊙ 5,405 C5
78934 Columbus⊙ 3,923 H8
76442 Comanche⊙ 4,075 F6
75428 Commerce 8,136 J4
*77301 Conroe⊙ 18,034 J7
78109 Converse 5,150 K11
75432 Cooper⊙ 2,338 J4
76522 Copperas Cove 19,469 G6
*78401 Corpus Christi⊙ 231,999 G10
Corpus Christi‡ 326,228 G10
75110 Corsicana⊙ 21,712 H5
78014 Cotulla⊙ 3,912 E9
79731 Crane⊙ 3,622 B6
75835 Crockett⊙ 7,405 J6
79322 Crosbyton⊙ 2,289 C4
79227 Crowell⊙ 1,509 E4
76036 Crowley 5,852 E3
78839 Crystal City⊙ 8,334 E9
77954 Cuero⊙ 7,124 G8
75638 Daingerfield⊙ 3,030 K4
79022 Dalhart⊙ 6,854 B1
*75201 Dallas⊙ 904,078 G2
Dallas-Ft. Worth‡ 2,974,878 G2
77535 Dayton 4,908 J7
76234 Decatur⊙ 4,104 G4
77536 Deer Park 22,648 K2
76444 De Leon 2,478 F5
78840 Del Rio⊙ 30,034 D8
75020 Denison 23,884 H4
76201 Denton⊙ 48,063 G4

(continued on following page)

Agriculture, Industry and Resources

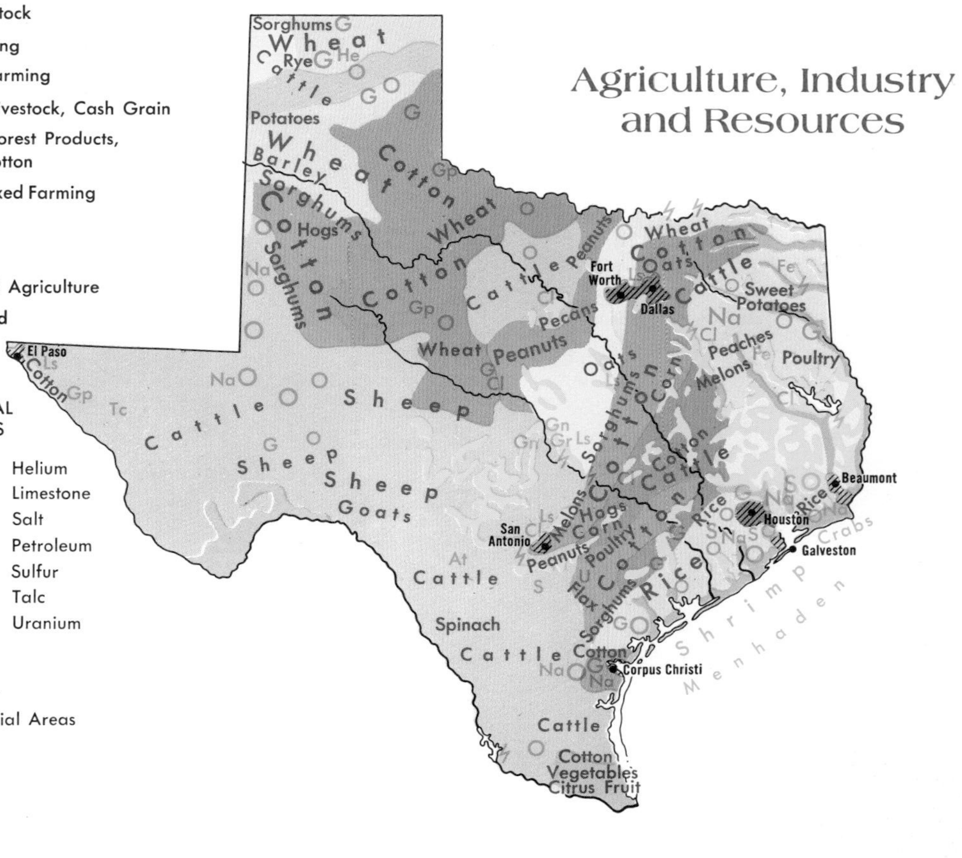

DOMINANT LAND USE

- Wheat, Grain Sorghums, Range Livestock
- Cotton, Wheat
- Specialized Cotton
- Cotton, General Farming
- Cotton, Forest Products
- Cotton, Range Livestock
- Rice, General Farming
- Peanuts, General Farming
- General Farming, Livestock, Cash Grain
- General Farming, Forest Products, Truck Farming, Cotton
- Fruit, Truck and Mixed Farming
- Range Livestock
- Forests
- Swampland, Limited Agriculture
- Nonagricultural Land
- Urban Areas

MAJOR MINERAL OCCURRENCES

At Asphalt
Cl Clay
Fe Iron Ore
G Natural Gas
Gn Granite
Gp Gypsum
Gr Graphite
He Helium
Ls Limestone
Na Salt
O Petroleum
S Sulfur
Tc Talc
U Uranium

Water Power
Major Industrial Areas

79323 Denver City 4,704 .... B4
75115 De Soto 15,538 .... G3
78016 Devine 3,756 .... E8
75941 Diboll 5,227 .... K6
79229 Dickens⊙ 409 .... D4
77539 Dickinson 7,505 .... K3
79027 Dimmitt⊙ 5,019 .... B3
78537 Donna 9,952 .... F11
79029 Dumas⊙ 12,194 .... C2
75116 Duncanville 27,781 .... G3
78852 Eagle Pass⊙ 21,407 .... D9
76448 Eastland⊙ 3,747 .... F5
78539 Edinburg⊙ 24,075 .... F11
77957 Edna⊙ 5,650 .... H9
77437 El Campo 10,462 .... H8
76936 Eldorado⊙ 2,061 .... D7
78621 Elgin 4,535 .... G7
*79901 El Paso⊙ 425,259 .... A10
El Paso‡ 479,899 .... A10
78543 Elsa 5,061 .... G11
75440 Emory⊙ 813 .... J5
75119 Ennis 12,110 .... H5
76039 Euless 24,002 .... F2
76140 Everman 5,387 .... F3
79838 Fabens 4,285 .... B10
75840 Fairfield⊙ 3,505 .... H6
78355 Falfurrias⊙ 6,103 .... F10
75234 Farmers Branch 24,863 .... G2
79325 Farwell⊙ 1,354 .... A3
78114 Floresville⊙ 4,381 .... K11
†75067 Flower Mound 4,402 .... F1
79235 Floydada⊙ 4,193 .... C3
†76119 Forest Hill 11,684 .... F2
79734 Fort Davis⊙ 900 .... D11
79735 Fort Stockton⊙ 8,688 .... A7
*76101 Fort Worth⊙ 385,164 .... F2
77856 Franklin⊙ 1,349 .... H7
78624 Fredericksburg⊙ 6,412 .... E7
76842 Fredonia 50 .... E7
77541 Freeport 13,444 .... J9
77546 Friendswood 10,719 .... J2
79035 Friona 3,809 .... B3
75034 Frisco 3,499 .... H4
79738 Gail⊙ 171 .... C5
76240 Gainesville⊙ 14,081 .... G4
77547 Galena Park 9,879 .... J1
*77550 Galveston⊙ 61,902 .... L3
Galveston-Texas
City‡ 195,940 .... L3
79739 Garden City⊙ 350 .... C6
*75040 Garland 138,857 .... H2
76528 Gatesville⊙ 6,260 .... G6
78626 Georgetown⊙ 9,468 .... G7
78022 George West⊙ 2,627 .... F9
78942 Giddings⊙ 3,950 .... H7
75644 Gilmer⊙ 5,167 .... J5
75647 Gladewater 6,548 .... K5
76043 Glen Rose⊙ 2,075 .... G5
76844 Goldthwaite⊙ 1,783 .... F6
77963 Goliad⊙ 1,990 .... G9
78629 Gonzales⊙ 7,152 .... G8
76046 Graham⊙ 9,170 .... F4
76048 Granbury⊙ 3,332 .... G5
*75050 Grand Prairie 71,462 .... G2
76051 Grapevine 11,801 .... F2
75401 Greenville⊙ 22,161 .... H4
76642 Groesbeck⊙ 3,373 .... H6
77619 Groves 17,090 .... L8
75845 Groveton⊙ 1,262 .... J7
79236 Guthrie⊙ 170 .... D4
77964 Hallettsville⊙ 2,865 .... G8
76117 Haltom City 29,014 .... F2
76531 Hamilton⊙ 3,189 .... G6
78550 Harlingen 43,543 .... G11
79521 Haskell⊙ 3,782 .... E4
77859 Hearne 5,418 .... H7
78361 Hebbronville⊙ 4,684 .... F10
75948 Hemphill⊙ 1,353 .... L6
77445 Hempstead⊙ 3,456 .... J7
75652 Henderson⊙ 11,473 .... K5
76365 Henrietta⊙ 3,149 .... F4
79045 Hereford⊙ 15,853 .... B3
†75201 Highland Park 8,909 .... G2
77562 Highlands 6,467 .... K1
76645 Hillsboro⊙ 7,397 .... G5
77563 Hitchcock 6,655 .... K3
78861 Hondo⊙ 6,057 .... E8
*77001 Houston⊙ 1,595,138 .... J2
Houston‡ 2,905,350 .... J2
*77338 Humble 6,729 .... J7
†77001 Hunters Creek
Village 4,215 .... J1
77340 Huntsville⊙ 23,936 .... J7
76053 Hurst 31,420 .... F2
76367 Iowa Park 6,184 .... F4
*75061 Irving 109,943 .... G2
77029 Jacinto City 8,953 .... J1
76056 Jacksboro⊙ 4,000 .... F4
75766 Jacksonville 12,264 .... J5
75951 Jasper⊙ 6,959 .... L7
79528 Jayton⊙ 638 .... D4
75657 Jefferson⊙ 2,643 .... K5
†77001 Jersey Village 4,084 .... J1
78636 Johnson City⊙ 872 .... F7
78026 Jourdanton⊙ 2,743 .... F9
76849 Junction⊙ 2,593 .... E7
78118 Karnes City⊙ 3,296 .... G9
77450 Katy 5,660 .... J8
75142 Kaufman⊙ 4,658 .... H5
76248 Keller 4,156 .... F2
78119 Kenedy 4,356 .... G9
79745 Kermit⊙ 8,015 .... B6
78028 Kerrville⊙ 15,276 .... E7
75662 Kilgore 11,006 .... K5
76541 Killeen 46,296 .... G6
Killeen-Temple‡ 214,656 .... G6
78363 Kingsville⊙ 28,808 .... G10
†78109 Kirby 6,435 .... K11
77625 Kountze⊙ 2,716 .... K7
78945 La Grange⊙ 3,768 .... G8
77566 Lake Jackson 19,102 .... J8
76135 Lake Worth 4,394 .... E2
77568 La Marque 15,372 .... K3
79331 Lamesa⊙ 11,790 .... C5
76550 Lampasas⊙ 6,165 .... F6
*75146 Lancaster 14,807 .... G3
77571 La Porte 14,062 .... K2

*78040 Laredo⊙ 91,449 .... E10
Laredo‡ 99,258 .... E10
77573 League City 16,578 .... K2
78873 Leakey⊙ 468 .... E8
†78201 Leon Valley 9,088 .... J10
79336 Levelland⊙ 13,809 .... B4
*75067 Lewisville 24,273 .... G1
77575 Liberty⊙ 7,945 .... K7
75563 Linden⊙ 2,443 .... K4
79056 Lipscomb⊙ 52 .... D1
79339 Littlefield⊙ 7,409 .... B4
†78201 Live Oak 8,183 .... K10
77351 Livingston⊙ 4,928 .... K7
78643 Llano⊙ 3,071 .... F7
78644 Lockhart⊙ 7,953 .... G8
79241 Lockney 2,334 .... C3
*75601 Longview⊙ 62,762 .... K5
Longview-Marshall‡
151,752 .... K5
*79401 Lubbock⊙ 173,979 .... C4
Lubbock‡ 211,651 .... C4
75901 Lufkin⊙ 28,562 .... K6
78648 Luling 5,039 .... G8
77864 Madisonville⊙ 3,660 .... J7
76063 Mansfield 8,092 .... F3
77578 Manvel 3,549 .... J3
79843 Marfa⊙ 2,466 .... C12
76661 Marlin⊙ 7,099 .... H6
75670 Marshall⊙ 24,921 .... K5
76856 Mason⊙ 2,153 .... E7
79244 Matador⊙ 1,052 .... D3
78368 Mathis 5,667 .... G9
78501 McAllen 66,281 .... F11
McAllen-Pharr-Edinburg‡
283,229 .... F11
76657 McGregor 4,513 .... G6
75069 McKinney⊙ 16,256 .... H4
†77520 McNair K1
79245 Memphis⊙ 3,352 .... D3
76859 Menard⊙ 1,697 .... E7
79754 Mentone⊙ 50 .... D10
78570 Mercedes 11,851 .... F12
76665 Meridian⊙ 1,330 .... G6
76941 Mertzon⊙ 687 .... C6
*75149 Mesquite 67,053 .... H2
76667 Mexia 7,094 .... H6
79059 Miami⊙ 813 .... D2
*79701 Midland⊙ 70,525 .... C6
Midland‡ 82,636 .... C6
76065 Midlothian 3,219 .... G5
75773 Mineola 4,346 .... J5
76067 Mineral Wells 14,468 .... F5
78572 Mission 22,653 .... F11
77459 Missouri City 24,533 .... J2
79756 Monahans⊙ 8,397 .... B6
76251 Montague⊙ 1,253 .... G4
79346 Morton⊙ 2,674 .... B4
75455 Mount Pleasant⊙ 11,003 .... K4
75457 Mount Vernon⊙ 2,025 .... J4
79347 Muleshoe⊙ 4,842 .... B3
75961 Nacogdoches⊙ 27,149 .... J6
†77598 Nassau Bay 4,526 .... K2
77868 Navasota 5,971 .... J7
77627 Nederland 16,855 .... K8
75570 New Boston 4,628 .... K4
78130 New Braunfels⊙ 22,402 .... K10
75966 Newton⊙ 1,620 .... L7
76118 North Richland
Hills 30,592 .... F2
79760 Odessa⊙ 90,027 .... B6
Odessa‡ 115,374 .... B6
76374 Olney 4,060 .... F4
77630 Orange⊙ 23,628 .... L7
76943 Ozona⊙ 3,766 .... C7
79248 Paducah⊙ 2,216 .... D4
76866 Paint Rock⊙ 256 .... E6
77465 Palacios 4,667 .... H9
75801 Palestine⊙ 15,948 .... J6
76072 Palo Pinto⊙ 350 .... F5
79065 Pampa⊙ 21,396 .... D2
79068 Panhandle⊙ 2,226 .... C2
75460 Paris⊙ 25,498 .... J4
*77501 Pasadena 112,560 .... J2
77581 Pearland 13,248 .... J2
78061 Pearsall⊙ 7,383 .... E9
79772 Pecos⊙ 12,855 .... D10
79070 Perryton⊙ 7,991 .... D1
78577 Pharr 21,381 .... F11
75686 Pittsburg⊙ 4,245 .... J4
79355 Plains⊙ 1,457 .... B4
79072 Plainview⊙ 22,187 .... C3
75074 Plano 72,331 .... G1
78064 Pleasanton 6,346 .... F9
77640 Port Arthur 61,251 .... K8
78578 Port Isabel 3,769 .... G11
78374 Portland 12,023 .... G10
77979 Port Lavaca⊙ 10,911 .... H9
77651 Port Neches 13,944 .... K7
79356 Post⊙ 3,961 .... C4
78065 Poteet 3,086 .... F8
77445 Prairie View 3,993 .... J7
79845 Presidio 1,723 .... C12
79252 Quanah⊙ 3,890 .... E3
76470 Ranger 3,142 .... F5
79778 Rankin⊙ 1,216 .... B6
78580 Raymondville⊙ 9,493 .... G11
78377 Refugio⊙ 3,898 .... G9
75080 Richardson 72,496 .... G2
76118 Richland Hills 7,977 .... F2
77469 Richmond⊙ 9,692 .... J8
78582 Rio Grande City⊙ 8,930 .... F11
77019 River Oaks 6,890 .... E2
76945 Robert Lee⊙ 1,202 .... D6
78380 Robstown 12,100 .... G10
79543 Roby⊙ 814 .... D5
76567 Rockdale 5,611 .... G7
78382 Rockport⊙ 3,686 .... H9
78880 Rocksprings⊙ 1,317 .... D8
75087 Rockwall⊙ 5,939 .... H5
78584 Roma-Los Saenz 3,384 .... E11
77471 Rosenberg 17,995 .... J8
78664 Round Rock 12,740 .... G7
75088 Rowlett 7,522 .... H2
75785 Rusk⊙ 4,681 .... J6
76179 Saginaw 5,736 .... E2
*76901 San Angelo⊙ 73,240 .... D6
San Angelo‡ 84,784 .... D6

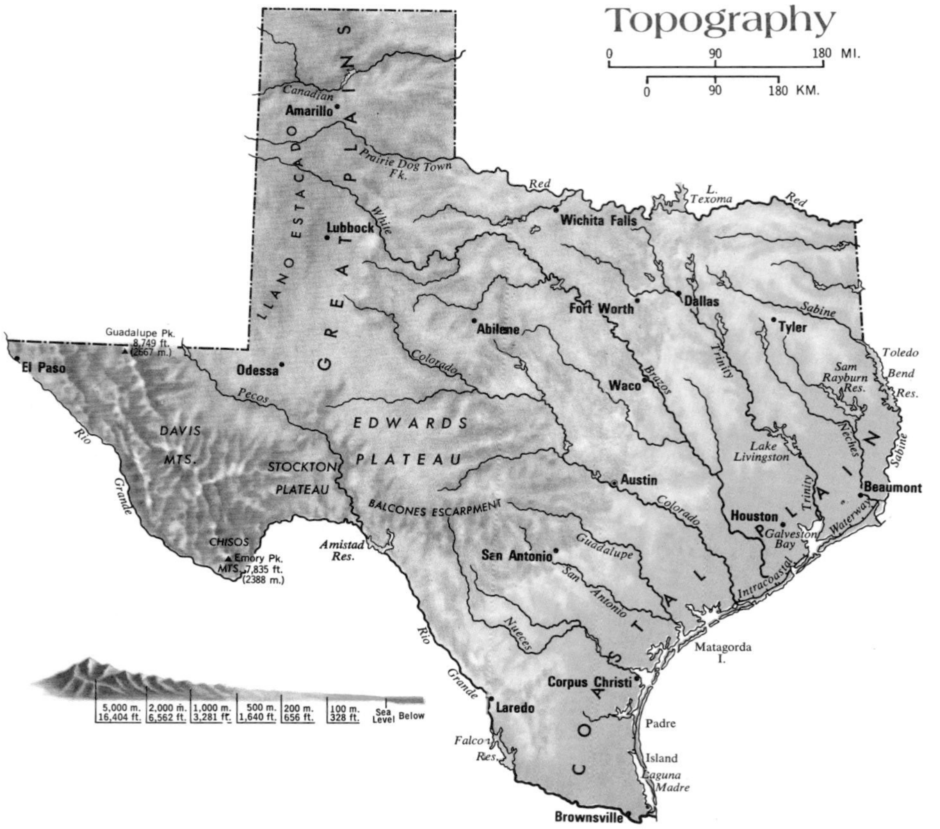

Topography
0
90
180 MI.
0
90
180 KM.
Canadian
Amarillo
Prairie Dog Town Fk.
Red
L. Texoma
Red
Wichita Falls
Lubbock
White
LLANO ESTACADO
GREAT PLAINS
Fort Worth
Dallas
Sabine
Tyler
Abilene
Guadalupe Pk. 8,749 ft. (2667 m.)
El Paso
Odessa
Colorado
Waco
Brazos
Trinity
Toledo Bend Res.
Sam Rayburn Res.
Pecos
EDWARDS PLATEAU
DAVIS MTS.
STOCKTON PLATEAU
Lake Livingston
Neches
Sabine
Austin
Rio Grande
BALCONES ESCARPMENT
Colorado
Beaumont
Houston
Galveston Bay
Intracoastal Waterway
CHISOS MTS.
Emory Pk. 7,835 ft. (2388 m.)
Amistad Res.
San Antonio
Guadalupe
San Antonio
Nueces
COASTAL PLAIN
Matagorda I.
Corpus Christi
Rio Grande
Laredo
Padre Island
Falcon Res.
Laguna Madre
Brownsville
5,000 m. 16,404 ft.
2,000 m. 6,562 ft.
1,000 m. 3,281 ft.
500 m. 1,640 ft.
200 m. 656 ft.
100 m. 328 ft.
Sea Level
Below

*78201 San Antonio⊙ 786,023 .... J11
San Antonio‡ 1,071,954 .... J11
75972 San Augustine⊙ 2,930 .... K6
78586 San Benito 17,988 .... G12
79848 Sanderson⊙ 1,241 .... B7
78384 San Diego⊙ 5,225 .... F10
76266 Sanger 2,574 .... G4
78589 San Juan 7,608 .... F11
78666 San Marcos⊙ 23,420 .... F8
76877 San Saba⊙ 2,847 .... F6
†76101 Sansom Park Village 3,921 .... E2
†77510 Santa Fe 6,172 .... K3
78385 Sarita⊙ 200 .... G10
78154 Schertz 7,262 .... K10
77586 Seabrook 4,670 .... K2
75159 Seagoville 7,304 .... H3
77474 Sealy 3,875 .... H8
78155 Seguin⊙ 17,854 .... G8
79360 Seminole⊙ 6,080 .... B5
†78357 Seven Sisters 2 .... F9
76380 Seymour⊙ 3,657 .... E4
75090 Sherman⊙ 30,413 .... H4
Sherman-Denison‡ 89,796 .... H4
79851 Sierra Blanca⊙ 800 .... B11
77656 Silsbee 7,684 .... K7
79257 Silverton⊙ 918 .... C3
78387 Sinton⊙ 6,044 .... G9
79364 Slaton 6,804 .... C4
78957 Smithville 3,470 .... G7
79549 Snyder⊙ 12,705 .... D5
76950 Sonora⊙ 3,856 .... D7
77587 South Houston 13,293 .... J2
79081 Spearman⊙ 3,413 .... C1
*77373 Spring J7
†77001 Spring Valley 3,353 .... J1
77477 Stafford 4,755 .... J2
79553 Stamford 4,542 .... E5
79782 Stanton⊙ 2,314 .... C5
76401 Stephenville⊙ 11,881 .... F5
76951 Sterling City⊙ 915 .... D6
79083 Stinnett⊙ 2,222 .... C2
79084 Stratford⊙ 1,917 .... C1
77478 Sugar Land 8,826 .... J8
75482 Sulphur Springs⊙ 12,804 .... J4
77480 Sweeny 3,538 .... J8
79556 Sweetwater⊙ 12,242 .... D5
78390 Taft 3,686 .... G9
79373 Tahoka⊙ 3,262 .... C4
76574 Taylor 10,619 .... G7
†77586 Taylor Lake Village 3,669 .... K2
75860 Teague 3,390 .... H6
76501 Temple 42,354 .... G6
79852 Terlingua 100 .... D12
75160 Terrell 13,269 .... H5
†78201 Terrell Hills 4,644 .... K11
*75501 Texarkana 31,271 .... L4
Texarkana, Tex.-Texarkana,
Ark.‡ 27,019 .... L4
77590 Texas City 41,403 .... K3
73949 Texhoma 358 .... C1
The Colony 11,586 .... G1
76083 Throckmorton⊙ 1,174 .... F4
78072 Tilden⊙ 450 .... F9
77375 Tomball 3,996 .... J7
75862 Trinity 2,620 .... J7
79088 Tulia⊙ 5,033 .... C3
*75701 Tyler⊙ 70,508 .... J5
Tyler‡ 128,366 .... J5
78148 Universal City 10,720 .... K10
†75205 University Park 22,254 .... G2
78801 Uvalde⊙ 14,178 .... E8
75095 Van Alstyne 1,860 .... H4

79855 Van Horn⊙ 2,772 .... C11
79092 Vega⊙ 900 .... B2
76384 Vernon⊙ 12,695 .... E3
77901 Victoria⊙ 50,695 .... H9
Victoria‡ 68,807 .... H9
77662 Vidor 11,834 .... L7
*76701 Waco⊙ 101,261 .... G6
Waco‡ 170,755 .... G6
75501 Wake Village 3,865 .... K4
75165 Waxahachie⊙ 14,624 .... H5
76086 Weatherford⊙ 12,049 .... G5
79095 Wellington⊙ 3,043 .... D3
78596 Weslaco 19,331 .... F11
77486 West Columbia 4,109 .... J8
77630 West Orange 4,610 .... L7
†77005 West University
Place 12,010 .... J2
†76101 Westworth 3,651 .... E2
77488 Wharton⊙ 9,033 .... J8
79096 Wheeler⊙ 1,584 .... D2
75693 White Oak 4,415 .... K5
76273 Whitesboro 3,197 .... H4
76108 White Settlement 13,508 .... E2
*76301 Wichita Falls⊙ 94,201 .... F4
Wichita Falls‡ 130,664 .... F4
†78201 Windcrest 5,332 .... K11
75494 Winnsboro 3,458 .... J5
79567 Winters 3,061 .... E6
75979 Woodville⊙ 2,821 .... K7
75098 Wylie 3,152 .... H1
78076 Zapata⊙ 3,831 .... E11

OTHER FEATURES

Amistad (res.) C8
Amistad Nat'l Rec. Area D8
Angelina (riv.) K6
Apache (mts.) C11
Aransas (passage) H10
Arlington (lake) F2
Baffin (bay) G10
Balcones Escarpment (plat.) E8
Beals (creek) C5
Benbrook (lake) E3
Bergstrom A.F.B. G7
Big Bend Nat'l Park A8
Bolivar (pen.) K8
Brazos (riv.) H7
Brownwood (lake) E6
Buchanan (lake) F7
Buck (creek) C3
Caddo (lake) L5
Canadian (riv.) D1
Carrizo (creek) A1
Carswell A.F.B. E2
Cathedral (mt.) D12
Cavallo (passage) H9
Cedar (lake) B5
Cerro Alto (mt.) B10
Chamizal Nat'l Mem. A10
Chase N.A.S. G9
Chinati (mts.) C12
Chinati (peak) C12
Chisos (mts.) A8
Cibolo (creek) K11
Clear Fork, Brazos (riv.) D5
Coldwater (creek) B1
Colorado (riv.) F7
Copano (bay) G9
Corpus Christi (lake) F9

Corpus Christi N.A.S. G10
Cottonwood Draw (dry riv.) C10
Davis (mts.) C11
Deep (creek) C5
Delaware (creek) C10
Delaware (mts.) C10
Denison (dam) H4
Devils (riv.) D7
Diablo, Sierra (mts.) C10
Double Mountain Fork, Brazos
(riv.) C4
Dyess A.F.B. D5
Eagle (peak) C11
Eagle Mountain (lake) E2
Edwards (plat.) C7
Elephant (mt.) D12
Ellington A.F.B. K2
Elm Fork, Trinity (riv.) G2
Emory (peak) A8
Falcon (res.) E11
Finlay (mts.) B10
Fort Bliss 12,687 .... A10
Fort Davis Nat'l Hist. Site D11
Fort Hood 31,250 .... G6
Frio (riv.) E8
Galveston (bay) L2
Galveston (isl.) K8
Glass (mts.) A7
Goodfellow A.F.B. D6
Grapevine (lake) F2
Guadalupe (mts.) C10
Guadalupe (peak) B10
Guadalupe (riv.) G8
Guadalupe Mts. Nat'l Park C10
Houston (lake) J8
Houston Ship (chan.) K2
Howard (creek) C7
Hubbard Creek (lake) F5
Hueco (mts.) B10
Intracoastal Waterway J9
Johnson Draw (dry riv.) C7
Kelly A.F.B. J11
Kemp (lake) E4
Kingsville N.A.S. G10
Kiowa (creek) D1
Lackland A.F.B. 14,459 .... J11
Lake Meredith Nat'l Rec. Area C2
Lampasas (riv.) G6
Laughlin A.F.B. 2,994 .... D8
Lavon (lake) H1
Leon (riv.) F6
Livermore (mt.) C11
Livingston (lake) K7
Llano (riv.) D7
Llano Estacado (plain) B4
Locke (mt.) D11
Los Olmos (creek) F10
Los Olmos (creek) F11
Lyndon B. Johnson Nat'l Hist.
Site F7
Lyndon B. Johnson Space Ctr. K2
Madre (lag.) G11
Maravillas (creek) A7
Matagorda (bay) H9
Matagorda (isl.) H9
Matagorda (pen.) J9
Matagorda Isl. Bombing and Gunnery
Range H9
Medina (lake) E8
Medina (riv.) J11
Mexico (gulf) K9
Middle Concho (riv.) C6

Mountain Creek (lake) G2
Mustang (creek) A1
Mustang (isl.) G10
Mustang Draw (dry riv.) B5
Navasota (riv.) H7
Navidad (riv.) H8
Neches (riv.) K6
North Concho (riv.) C6
North Pease (riv.) D3
Nueces (riv.) F9
Padre (isl.) G10
Padre Island Nat'l Seashore G11
Palo Duro (creek) B2
Palo Duro (creek) C1
Pease (riv.) D3
Pecos (riv.) C7
Pedernales (riv.) F7
Possum Kingdom (lake) F5
Prairie Dog Town Fork, Red (riv.) C3
Quitman (mts.) B11
Red (riv.) F3
Red Bluff (lake) A6
Reese A.F.B. 1,934 .... B4
Rio Grande (riv.) D9
Rita Blanca (creek) B2
Sabine (riv.) L7
Salt Fork, Red (riv.) D3
Sam Rayburn (res.) K6
San Antonio (bay) H9
San Antonio (mt.) B10
San Antonio Missions Nat'l Hist.
Park J11
San Francisco (creek) B8
San Luis (passage) K8
San Martine Draw (dry riv.) C11
San Saba (riv.) D7
Santa Isabel (creek) E10
Santiago (mts.) A8
Santiago (peak) D12
Sheppard A.F.B. F3
Sierra Diablo (mts.) C10
Sierra Vieja (mts.) C11
Staked (Llano Estacado) (plain) B4
Stamford (lake) E4
Stockton (plat.) B7
Sulphur (riv.) J4
Sulphur Draw (dry riv.) B4
Sulphur Springs (creek) B4
Tenmile (creek) G3
Terlingua (creek) D12
Texoma (lake) H3
Tierra Blanca (creek) B3
Toledo Bend (res.) L6
Toyah (creek) D11
Toyah (lake) A6
Travis (lake) G7
Trinity (bay) L2
Trinity (riv.) H5
Trinity, West Fork (riv.) G2
Trujillo (creek) A2
Vieja, Sierra (mts.) C11
Walnut (creek) F3
Washita (riv.) D2
West (bay) K3
White (riv.) C3
White River (lake) C4
White Rock (creek) G2
Wichita (riv.) F4
Wolf (creek) D1
Worth (lake) E2

⊙County seat.
‡Population of metropolitan area.
† Zip of nearest p.o. * Multiple zips.

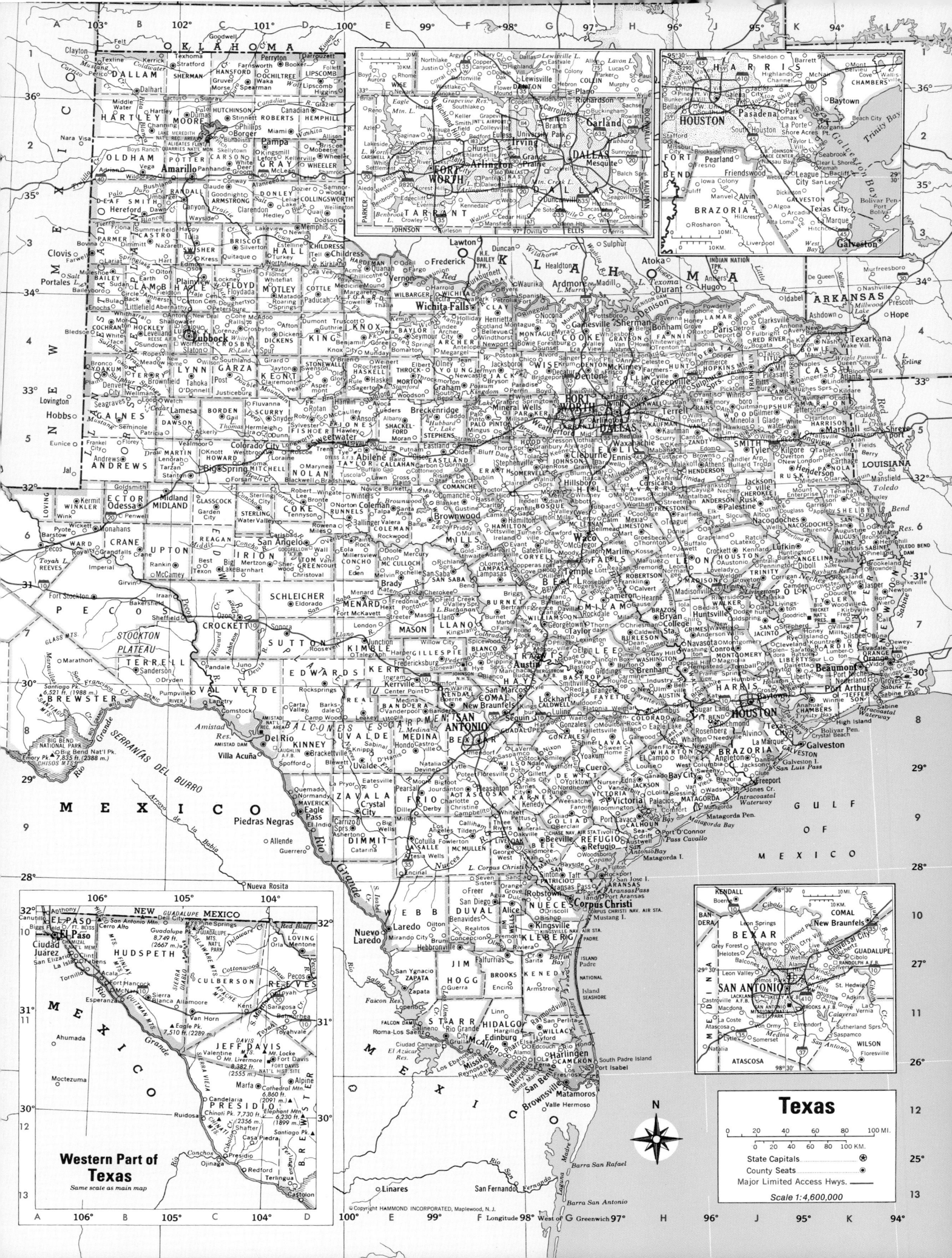

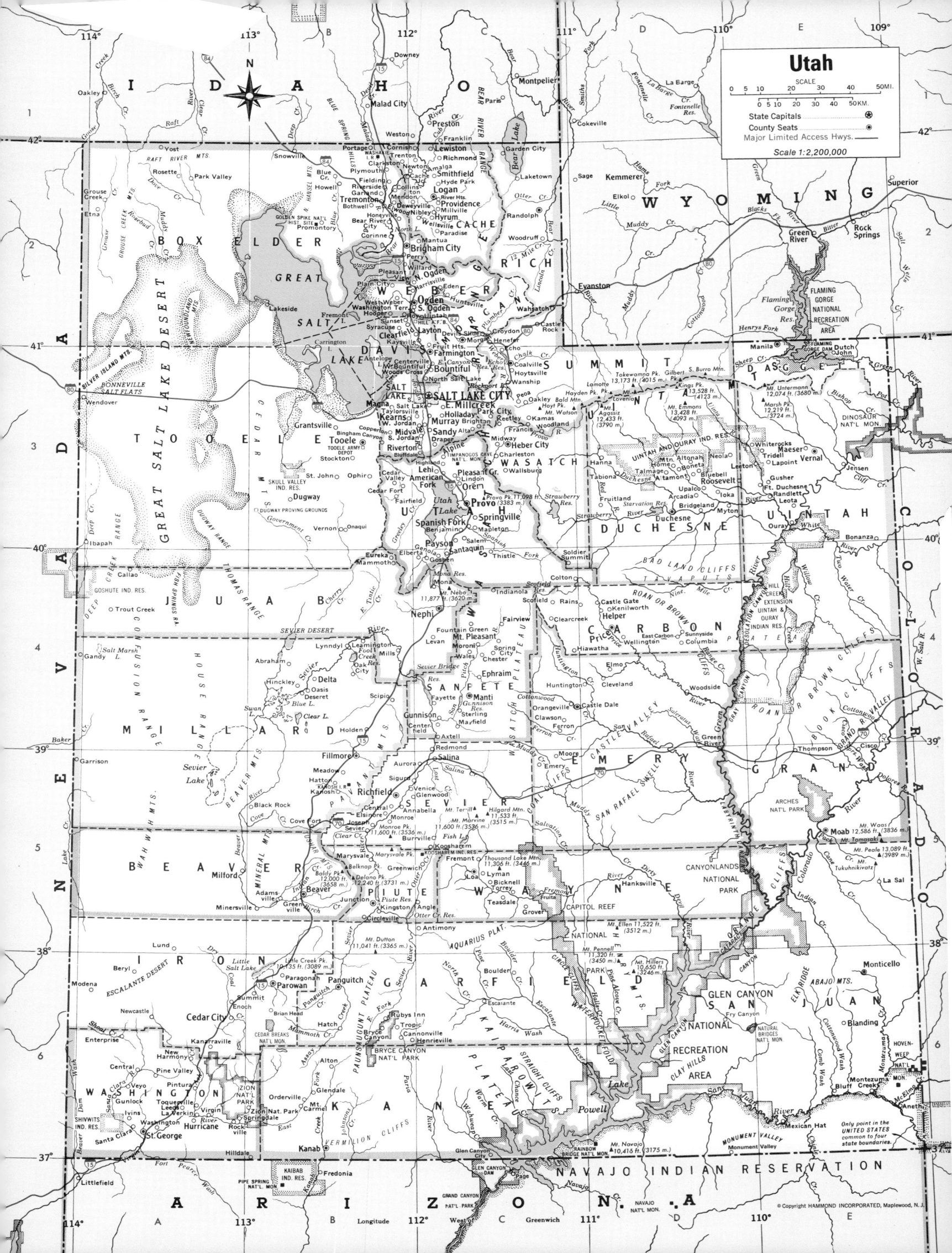

AREA 84,899 sq. mi. (219,888 sq. km.)
POPULATION 1,461,037
CAPITAL Salt Lake City
LARGEST CITY Salt Lake City
HIGHEST POINT Kings Pk. 13,528 ft. (4123 m.)
SETTLED IN 1847
ADMITTED TO UNION January 4, 1896
POPULAR NAME Beehive State
STATE FLOWER Sego Lily
STATE BIRD Sea Gull

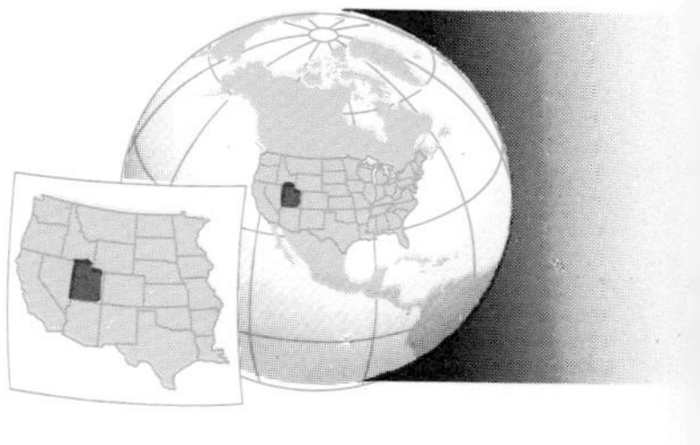

COUNTIES

Beaver 4,378 ... A5
Box Elder 33,222 ... A2
Cache 57,176 ... C2
Carbon 22,179 ... D4
Daggett 769 ... E3
Davis 146,540 ... B3
Duchesne 12,565 ... D3
Emery 11,451 ... D4
Garfield 3,673 ... C6
Grand 8,241 ... E5
Iron 17,349 ... A6
Juab 5,530 ... A4
Kane 4,024 ... B6
Millard 8,970 ... A4
Morgan 4,917 ... C2
Piute 1,329 ... B5
Rich 2,100 ... C2
Salt Lake 619,066 ... B3
San Juan 12,253 ... E6
Sanpete 14,620 ... C4
Sevier 14,727 ... C5
Summit 10,198 ... D3
Tooele 26,033 ... A3
Uintah 20,506 ... E3
Utah 218,106 ... C3
Wasatch 8,523 ... C3
Washington 26,065 ... A6
Wayne 1,911 ... C5
Weber 144,616 ... B2

CITIES and TOWNS

Zip *Name/Pop.* *Key*

†84003 Alpine 2,649 ... C3
84003 American Fork 12,693 ... C3
84713 Beaver⊙ 1,792 ... B5
84511 Blanding 3,118 ... E6
†84065 Bluffdale 1,300 ... B3
84010 Bountiful 32,877 ... C3
84302 Brigham City⊙ 15,596 ... C2
†84101 Brighton 150 ... C3
84513 Castle Dale⊙ 1,910 ... D4
84720 Cedar City 10,972 ... A6
84014 Centerville 8,069 ... C3
84015 Clearfield 17,982 ... B2
84017 Coalville⊙ 1,031 ... C3
84624 Delta 1,930 ... B4
84020 Draper 5,521 ... C3
84021 Duchesne⊙ 1,677 ... D3
84022 Dugway 1,646 ... B3
84520 East Carbon 1,942 ... D4
84109 East Millcreek 24,150 ... C3
84627 Ephraim 2,810 ... C4
84025 Farmington⊙ 4,691 ... C3
84523 Ferron 1,718 ... C4
84631 Fillmore⊙ 2,083 ... B5
†84037 Fruit Heights 2,728 ... C2
84312 Garland 1,405 ... B2
84029 Grantsville 4,419 ... B3
84525 Green River 1,048 ... D4
84634 Gunnison 1,255 ... C4
†84401 Harrisville 1,371 ... C2
84032 Heber City⊙ 4,362 ... C3
84526 Helper 2,724 ... D4
†84043 Highland 2,435 ... C3
†84767 Hilldale 1,009 ... A6
84117 Holladay 22,189 ... C3
84528 Huntington 2,316 ... C4
84737 Hurricane 2,361 ... A6
84318 Hyde Park 1,495 ... C2
84319 Hyrum 3,952 ... C2
84740 Junction⊙ 151 ... B5
84036 Kamas 1,064 ... C3
84741 Kanab⊙ 2,148 ... B6
84037 Kaysville 9,811 ... B2
84118 Kearns 21,353 ... B3
84745 La Verkin 1,174 ... A6
84041 Layton 22,862 ... C2
84043 Lehi 6,848 ... C3
84320 Lewiston 1,438 ... C2
†84062 Lindon 2,796 ... C3
84747 Loa⊙ 364 ... C5
84321 Logan⊙ 26,844 ... C2
†84078 Maeser 2,216 ... E3
84044 Magna 13,138 ... B3
84046 Manila⊙ 272 ... E3
84642 Manti⊙ 2,080 ... C4
†84663 Mapleton 2,726 ... C3
84531 Mexican Hat 250 ... E6
84047 Midvale 10,146 ... B3
84049 Midway 1,194 ... C3
84751 Milford 1,293 ... A5
84532 Moab⊙ 5,333 ... E5
84754 Monroe 1,476 ... B5
84535 Monticello⊙ 1,929 ... E6
84050 Morgan⊙ 1,896 ... C2
84646 Moroni 1,086 ... C4
84647 Mount Pleasant 2,049 ... C4
84107 Murray 25,750 ... C3
84648 Nephi⊙ 3,285 ... C4
†84321 Nibley 1,036 ... C2
†84404 North Ogden 9,309 ... C2
†84010 North Salt Lake 5,548 ... C3
*84401 Ogden⊙ 64,407 ... C2
Ogden-Salt Lake City‡ 936,255 ... C4
84537 Orangeville 1,309 ... C4
84057 Orem 52,399 ... C3
Orem-Provo‡ 218,106 ... C3
84759 Panguitch⊙ 1,343 ... B6
84060 Park City 2,823 ... C3
84761 Parowan⊙ 1,836 ... B6
84651 Payson 8,246 ... C3
†84302 Perry 1,084 ... C2
†84401 Plain City 2,379 ... B2
84062 Pleasant Grove 10,833 ... C3
†84401 Pleasant View 3,983 ... B2
84501 Price⊙ 9,086 ... D4
84332 Providence 2,675 ... C2
84601 Provo⊙ 74,108 ... C3
Provo-Orem‡ 218,106 ... C3
84064 Randolph⊙ 659 ... C2
84701 Richfield⊙ 5,482 ... B5
84333 Richmond 1,705 ... C2
†84321 River Heights 1,211 ... C2
84065 Riverton 7,293 ... B3
84066 Roosevelt 3,842 ... D3
84067 Roy 19,694 ... C2
Saint George⊙ 11,350 ... A6
84653 Salem 2,233 ... C3
84654 Salina 1,992 ... C5
*84101 Salt Lake City (cap)⊙ 163,697 ... C3
Salt Lake City-Ogden‡ 936,255 ... C3
*84070 Sandy 52,210 ... C3
84765 Santa Clara 1,091 ... A6
84655 Santaquin 2,175 ... C4
84335 Smithfield 4,993 ... C2
†84065 South Jordan 7,492 ... B3
†84403 South Ogden 11,366 ... C2
84115 South Salt Lake 9,884 ... C3
84660 Spanish Fork 9,825 ... C3
84663 Springville 12,101 ... C3
†84015 Sunset 5,733 ... B2
†84041 Syracuse 3,702 ... B2
†84101 Taylorsville 17,448 ... B3
84074 Tooele⊙ 14,335 ... B3
84337 Tremonton 3,464 ... B2
84078 Vernal⊙ 6,600 ... E3
84780 Washington 3,092 ... A6
†84403 Washington Terrace 8,212 ... B2
84542 Wellington 1,406 ... D4
84339 Wellsville 1,952 ... C2
84083 Wendover 1,099 ... A3
†84087 West Bountiful 3,556 ... B3
84084 West Jordan 27,192 ... B3
84340 Willard 1,241 ... C2
84087 Woods Cross 4,263 ... B3

OTHER FEATURES

Abajo (mts.) ... E6
Agassiz (mt.) ... D3
Antelope (isl.) ... B3
Aquarius (plat.) ... C5
Arches Nat'l Park ... E5
Assay (creek) ... B6
Bad Land (cliffs) ... D4
Baldy (peak) ... B5
Bear (lake) ... C2
Bear (riv.) ... B2
Beaver (mts.) ... A5
Beaver (riv.) ... A5
Beaver Dam Wash (creek) ... A6
Birch (creek) ... B5
Blue (creek) ... B2
Bonneville (salt flats) ... A3
Book (cliffs) ... E4
Brown (Roan) (cliffs) ... E4
Bryce Canyon Nat'l Park ... B6
Canyonlands Nat'l Park ... D5
Capitol Reef Nat'l Park ... C5
Castle (valley) ... D4
Cedar (mts.) ... B3
Cedar Breaks Nat'l Mon. ... B6
Chalk (creek) ... C3
Chinle (creek) ... E6
Clear (lake) ... B4
Cliff (creek) ... E3
Coal (cliffs) ... C5
Colorado (riv.) ... E5
Confusion (range) ... A4
Cottonwood (creek) ... C4
Cub (creek) ... C1
Deep (creek) ... B1
Deep Creek (range) ... A4
Delano (peak) ... B5
Desolation (canyon) ... E4
Dinosaur Nat'l Mon. ... E3
Dirty Devil (riv.) ... D5
Dolores (riv.) ... E5
Dry Coal (creek) ... A6
Duchesne (riv.) ... D3
Dugway (range) ... A3
Dugway Proving Grounds ... B3
Dutton (mt.) ... B5
East Canyon (res.) ... C3
Echo (res.) ... C3
Elk (ridge) ... E6
Ellen (mt.) ... D5
Emmons (mt.) ... D3
Escalante (des.) ... A6
Escalante (riv.) ... C6
Fish (lake) ... C5
Fish Springs (range) ... A4
Flaming Gorge (res.) ... E3
Flaming Gorge Nat'l Rec. Area ... E2
Fool Creek (res.) ... B4
Fremont (isl.) ... B2
Fremont (riv.) ... C5
Glen Canyon Nat'l Rec. Area ... D6
Golden Spike Nat'l Hist. Site ... B2
Goshute Ind. Res. ... A4
Government (creek) ... B3
Gray (canyon) ... D4
Great Salt (lake) ... B2
Great Salt Lake (des.) ... A3
Greeley (creek) ... B3
Green (riv.) ... D4
Grouse (creek) ... A2
Grouse Creek (mts.) ... A2
Gunnison (res.) ... C4
Henry (mts.) ... D6
Hilgard (mt.) ... C5
Hill (creek) ... E4
Hill A.F.B. ... C2
Hill Creek Ext., Uintah and Ouray Ind. Res. ... E4
Hillers (mt.) ... D6
House (range) ... A4
Hovenweep Nat'l Mon. ... E6
Huntington (creek) ... C4
Indian (creek) ... B5
Jordan (riv.) ... C3
Kaiparowits (plat.) ... C6
Kanab (creek) ... B7
Kanosh Ind. Res. ... B5
Kings (peak) ... D3
Koosharem Ind. Res. ... C5
Little Creek (peak) ... B6
Little Salt (lake) ... A6
Malad (riv.) ... B1
Marsh (peak) ... E3
Marvine (mt.) ... C5
Mineral (mts.) ... B5
Mona (res.) ... C4
Monroe (peak) ... B5
Montezuma (creek) ... E6
Monument (valley) ... D6
Muddy (creek) ... C4
Natural Bridges Nat'l Mon. ... E6
Navajo (mt.) ... D6
Navajo Ind. Res. ... D7
Nebo (mt.) ... C4
Newfoundland (mts.) ... A2
Nine Mile (creek) ... D4
North (lake) ... B2
Orange (cliffs) ... D5
Otter (creek) ... C5
Otter Creek (res.) ... C5
Paria (riv.) ... B6
Paunsaugunt (plat.) ... B6
Pavant (mts.) ... B5
Peale (mt.) ... E5
Pennell (mt.) ... D6
Piute (res.) ... B5
Plumber (creek) ... C2
Powell (lake) ... D6
Price (riv.) ... D4
Provo (peak) ... C3
Provo (riv.) ... C3
Raft River (mts.) ... A2
Rainbow Bridge Nat'l Mon. ... C6
Roan (cliffs) ... E4
Rockport (lake) ... C3
Salvation (creek) ... C5
San Juan (riv.) ... D6
San Pitch (riv.) ... C4
San Rafael (riv.) ... D4
San Rafael Swell (mts.) ... D5
Santa Clara (riv.) ... A6
Sevier (des.) ... B4
Sevier (lake) ... A5
Sevier (riv.) ... B4
Sevier Bridge (res.) ... C4
Shivwits Ind. Res. ... A6
Silver Island (mts.) ... A3
Skull Valley Ind. Res. ... B3
Spanish Fork (riv.) ... C3
Strait (cliffs) ... C6
Strawberry (res.) ... C3
Strawberry (riv.) ... D3
Swan (lake) ... B4
Tavaputs (plat.) ... D4
Thomas (range) ... A4
Thousand Lake (mt.) ... C5
Timpanogos Cave Nat'l Mon. ... C3
Tokewamna (peak) ... D3
Tooele Army Depot ... B3
Two Water (creek) ... E4
Uinta (mts.) ... D3
Uinta (riv.) ... D3
Uintah and Ouray Ind. Res. ... D3
Utah (lake) ... C3
Virgin (riv.) ... A6
Waas (mt.) ... E5
Wah Wah (mts.) ... A5
Wahweap (creek) ... C6
Wasatch (range) ... C3
Washakie Ind. Res. ... B2
Waterpocket Fold (cliffs) ... D6
Weber (riv.) ... C3
White (riv.) ... E3
Willow (creek) ... E4
Zion Nat'l Park ... A6

⊙County seat.
‡Population of metropolitan area.
† Zip of nearest p.o.
* Multiple zips.

Agriculture, Industry and Resources

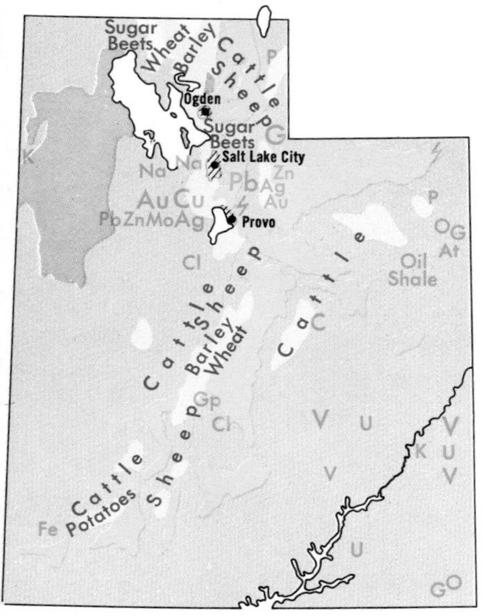
Sugar Beets
Wheat
Barley
Cattle
Sheep
Ogden
Sugar Beets
Salt Lake City
Provo
Oil Shale
Cattle
Sheep
Barley
Wheat
Cattle
Sheep
Cattle
Potatoes
Na
Pb Ag
Zn
Au
Au Cu
PbZnMoAg
Cl
P
OG
At
C
Gp
Cl
V
U
V
K
U
V
Fe
U
GO

DOMINANT LAND USE

Wheat, General Farming
General Farming, Livestock, Special Crops
Range Livestock
Forests
Nonagricultural Land

MAJOR MINERAL OCCURRENCES

Ag	Silver	Fe	Iron Ore	O	Petroleum
At	Asphalt	G	Natural Gas	P	Phosphates
Au	Gold	Gp	Gypsum	Pb	Lead
C	Coal	K	Potash	U	Uranium
Cl	Clay	Mo	Molybdenum	V	Vanadium
Cu	Copper	Na	Salt	Zn	Zinc

Water Power
Major Industrial Areas

Topography

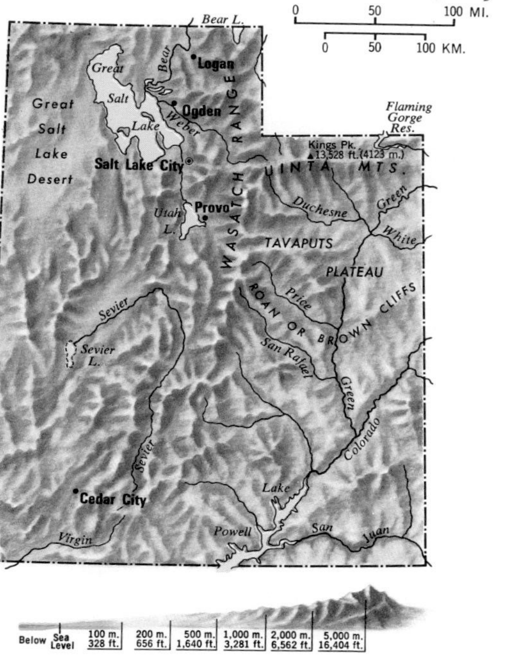
0 50 100 MI.
0 50 100 KM.
Bear L.
Logan
Great
Salt
Lake
Bear
Ogden
Weber
Great Salt Lake Desert
Salt Lake City
Kings Pk. 13,528 ft. (4123 m.)
Flaming Gorge Res.
UINTA MTS.
Utah L.
Provo
WASATCH RANGE
Duchesne
Green
White
TAVAPUTS PLATEAU
Price
ROAN OR BROWN CLIFFS
Sevier
Sevier L.
San Rafael
Green
Colorado
Sevier
Cedar City
Lake
Powell
San Juan
Virgin
Below Sea Level
100 m. 328 ft.
200 m. 656 ft.
500 m. 1,640 ft.
1,000 m. 3,281 ft.
2,000 m. 6,562 ft.
5,000 m. 16,404 ft.

Topography

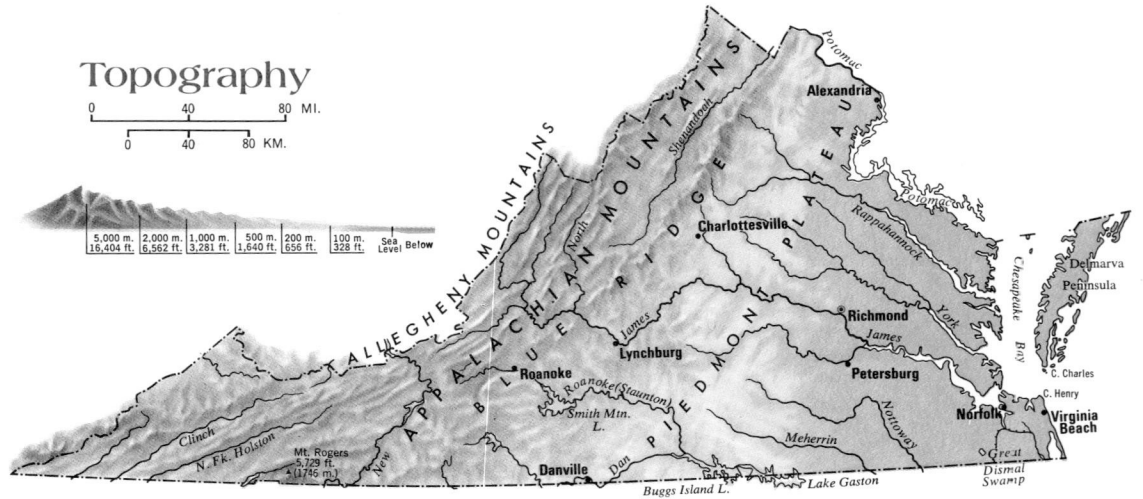

0   40   80 MI.

0   40   80 KM.

5,000 m. | 2,000 m. | 1,000 m. | 500 m. | 200 m. | 100 m. | Sea
16,404 ft. | 6,562 ft. | 3,281 ft. | 1,640 ft. | 656 ft. | 328 ft. | Level Below

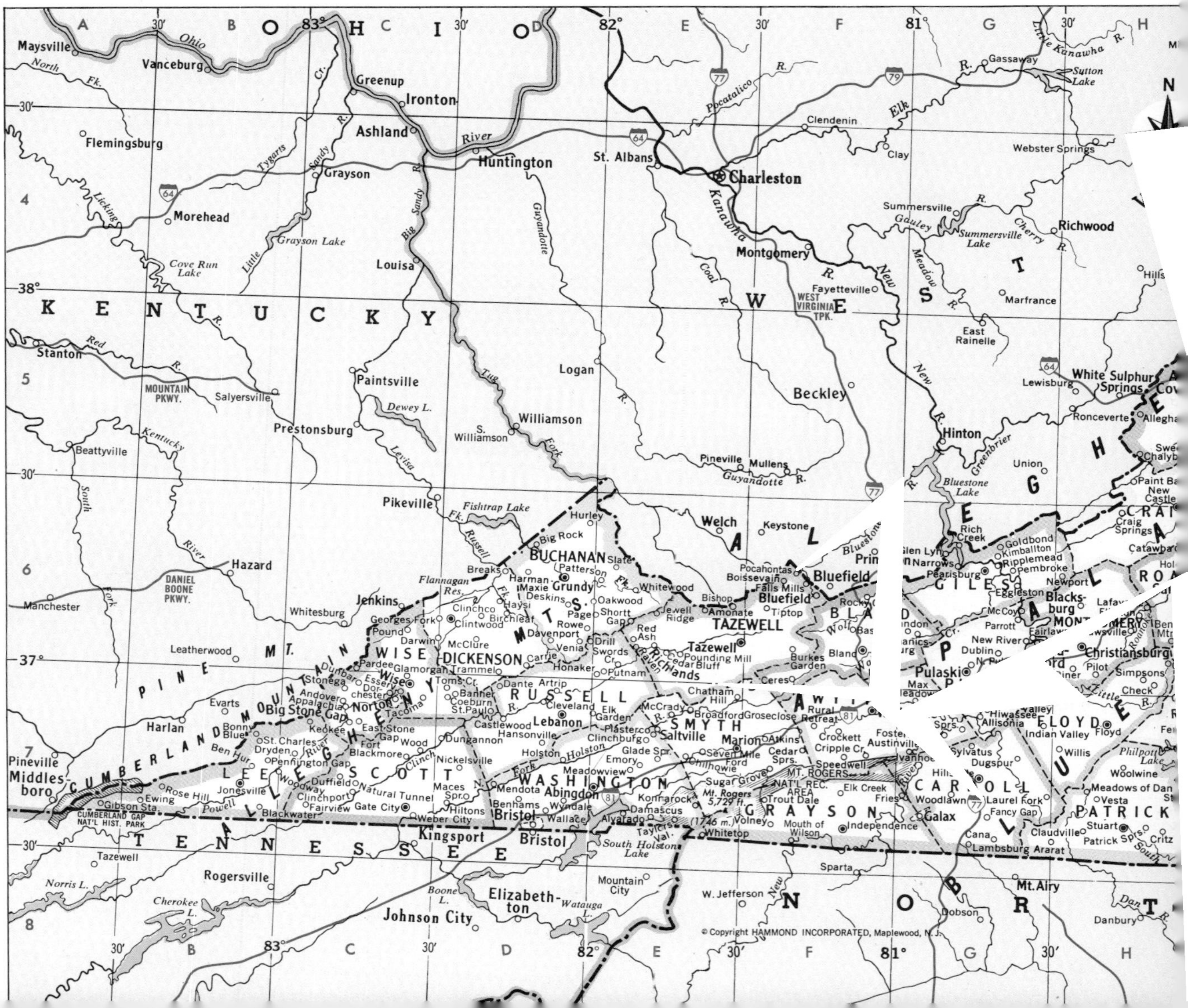

(continued on following page)

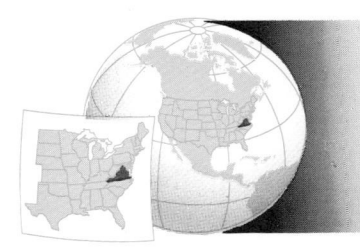

AREA 40,767 sq. mi. (105,587 sq. km.)
POPULATION 5,346,818
CAPITAL Richmond
LARGEST CITY Norfolk
HIGHEST POINT Mt. Rogers 5,729 ft. (1746 m.)
SETTLED IN 1607
ADMITTED TO UNION June 26, 1788
POPULAR NAME Old Dominion
STATE FLOWER Dogwood
STATE BIRD Cardinal

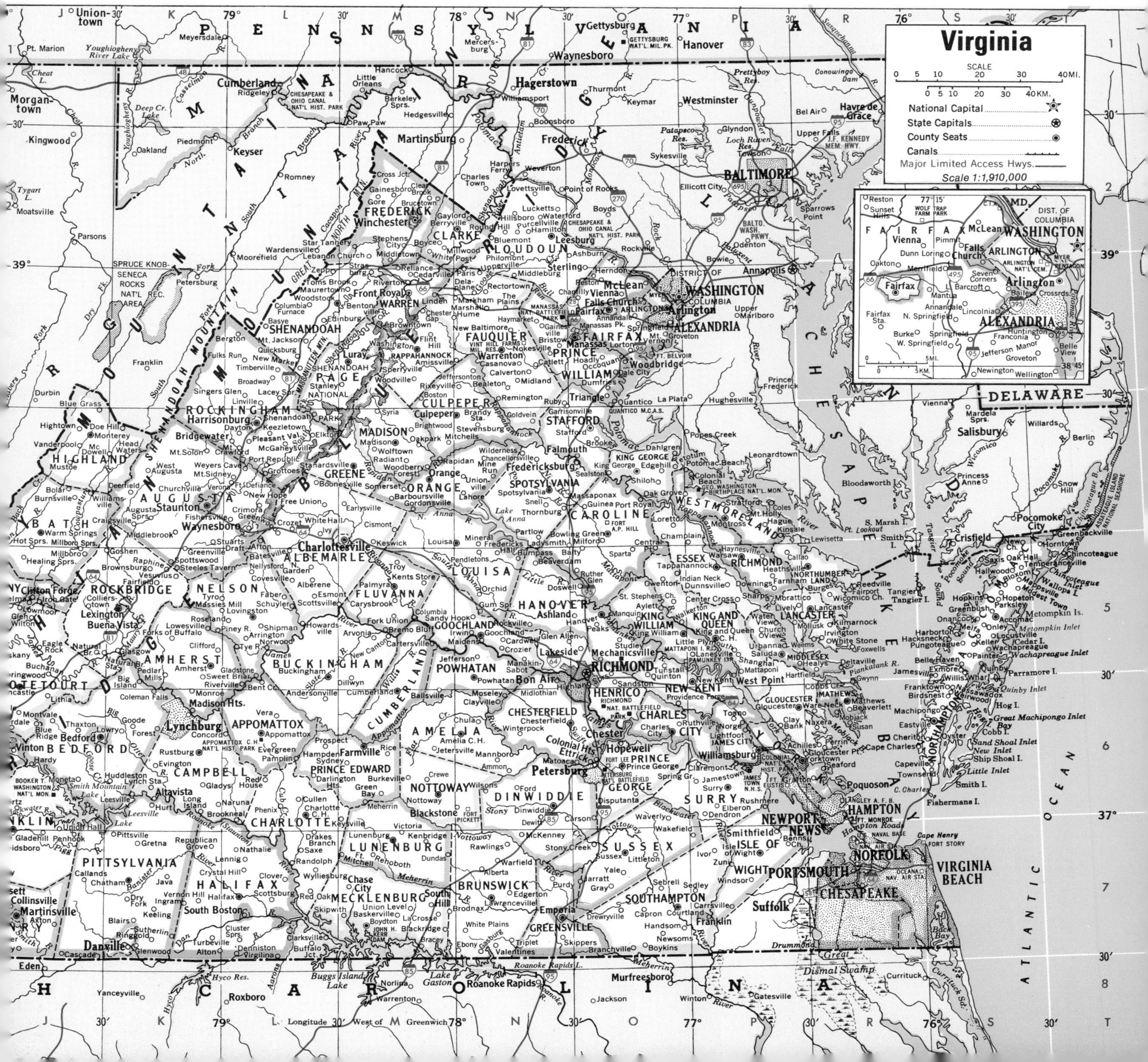

Virginia

SCALE
0 5 10 20 30 40 MI.
0 5 10 20 30 40 KM.

National Capital ★
State Capitals ⊛
County Seats ⊙
Canals
Major Limited Access Hwys.
Scale 1:1,910,000

Agriculture, Industry and Resources

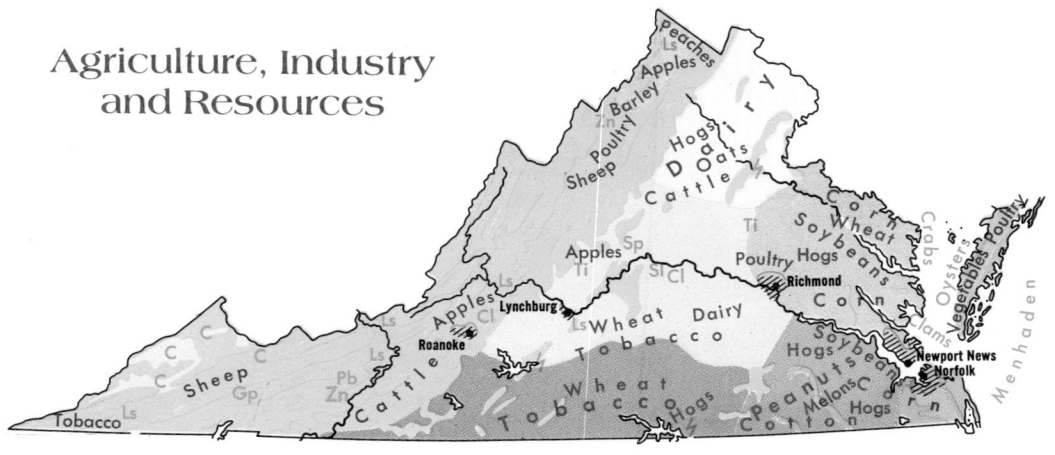

MAJOR MINERAL OCCURRENCES

C Coal
Cl Clay
Gp Gypsum
Ls Limestone
Pb Lead
Sl Slate
Sp Soapstone
Ti Titanium
Zn Zinc

Water Power
Major Industrial Areas

DOMINANT LAND USE

Dairy, General Farming
General Farming, Livestock, Dairy
General Farming, Livestock, Tobacco
General Farming, Livestock, Fruit, Tobacco
General Farming, Truck Farming, Tobacco, Livestock
Tobacco, General Farming
Peanuts, General Farming
Fruit and Mixed Farming
Truck and Mixed Farming
Forests
Swampland, Limited Agriculture

22639 Hume 350 .... N3
†22301 Huntington 5,813 .... S3
24620 Hurley 850 .... D6
24563 Hurt 1,481 .... K6
24348 Independence⊙ 1,112 .... F7
24105 Indian Valley 300 .... G7
24448 Iron Gate 620 .... J5
22480 Irvington 567 .... R5
23397 Isle of Wight⊙ 185 .... P7
24350 Ivanhoe 900 .... G7
23866 Ivor 403 .... P7
22945 Ivy 900 .... L4
23081 Jamestown 12 .... P6
23398 Jamesville 500 .... S5
23867 Jarratt 614 .... O7
22303 Jefferson Manor S3
22724 Jeffersonton 300 .... N3
24622 Jewell Ridge 600 .... E6
24263 Jonesville⊙ 874 .... B7
24566 Keeling 680 .... K7
22832 Keezletown 975 .... L4
23401 Keller 236 .... S5
23944 Kenbridge 1,352 .... M7
24265 Keokee 300 .... C7
22947 Keswick 300 .... M4
23947 Keysville 704 .... M6
22482 Kilmarnock 945 .... R5
23085 King and Queen Court House⊙ 500 .... P5
22485 King George⊙ 575 .... O4
23086 King William⊙ 100 .... O5
22488 Kinsale 250 .... P4
23950 La Crosse 734 .... M7
22501 Ladysmith 360 .... N4
24108 Lafayette-Elliston 1,172 .... H6
†22041 Lake Barcroft 8,725 .... S3
23228 Lakeside 12,289 .... N5
24351 Lambsburg 800 .... G7
22503 Lancaster⊙ 110 .... R5
24352 Laurel Fork 300 .... G7
23868 Lawrenceville⊙ 1,484 .... N7
24266 Lebanon⊙ 3,206 .... D7
22641 Lebanon Church 300 .... L2
22075 Leesburg⊙ 8,357 .... N2
24450 Lexington (I.C.)⊙ 7,292 .... J5
†22313 Lincolnia 10,350 .... S3
22642 Linden 320 .... M3
22834 Linville 500 .... L3
22507 Lively 400 .... P5
22079 Lorton 5,813 .... O3
23093 Louisa⊙ 932 .... M4

22080 Lovettsville 613 .... N2
22949 Lovingston⊙ 600 .... L5
22951 Lowesville 500 .... K5
24457 Lowmoor 700 .... J5
†22075 Lucketts 500 .... N2
23952 Lunenburg⊙ 13 .... M7
22835 Luray⊙ 3,584 .... M3
*24501 Lynchburg (I.C.) 66,743 .... K6
Lynchburg‡ 153,260 .... K6
24571 Lynch Station 500 .... K6
23405 Machipongo 400 .... S6
22727 Madison⊙ 267 .... M4
24572 Madison Heights 14,146 .... K6
23103 Manakin-Sabot 200 .... N5
22110 Manassas (I.C.)⊙ 15,438 .... O3
22110 Manassas Park (I.C.) 6,524 .... O3
23106 Manquin 576 .... O5
†22030 Mantua 6,523 .... S3
23407 Mappsville 700 .... T5
24354 Marion⊙ 7,029 .... E7
22643 Markham 300 .... N3
22115 Marshall 800 .... N3
24112 Martinsville (I.C.)⊙ 18,149 .... J7
22954 Massies Mill 225 .... K5
23109 Mathews⊙ 500 .... R6
23803 Matoaca 1,967 .... N6
23110 Mattaponi 300 .... P5
24360 Max Meadows 782 .... G6
24269 McClure 300 .... D6
24111 McCoy 600 .... G6
22840 McGaheysville 600 .... L4
23872 McKenney 473 .... N7
*22101 McLean 35,664 .... S2
24361 Meadowview-Emory 2,292 .... D7
†24315 Mechanicsburg 350 .... G6
23111 Mechanicsville 9,269 .... O5
23954 Meherrin 400 .... M6
23410 Melfa 391 .... S5
24270 Mendota 375 .... D7
22116 Merrifield 7,525 .... S3
22117 Middleburg 619 .... N3
22645 Middletown 841 .... M2
22728 Midland 600 .... N3
23113 Midlothian 950 .... N6
22514 Milford 650 .... O4
24460 Millboro 400 .... J5
24460 Millboro Springs 200 .... J4
22646 Millwood 400 .... N2
23117 Mineral 399 .... N4

22568 Mine Run 450 .... N4
23118 Mobjack 210 .... R6
23412 Modest Town 225 .... T5
22517 Mollusk 800 .... P5
24121 Moneta 300 .... J6
24574 Monroe 500 .... K6
24465 Monterey⊙ 247 .... K4
22520 Montross⊙ 456 .... P4
24122 Montvale 900 .... J6
22523 Morattico 225 .... P5
23120 Moseley 210 .... N6
22841 Mount Crawford 315 .... L4
22524 Mount Holly 200 .... P4
22842 Mount Jackson 1,419 .... L3
24467 Mount Sidney 500 .... K4
22121 Mount Vernon 24,058 .... O3
24363 Mouth of Wilson 400 .... F7
24124 Narrows 2,516 .... G6
23413 Nassawadox 630 .... S6
24577 Nathalie 200 .... L7
24578 Natural Bridge 200 .... J5
24579 Natural Bridge Sta. 450 .... K5
23122 Naxera 300 .... R6
22958 Nellysford 290 .... L5
24127 New Castle⊙ 213 .... H5
23415 New Church 427 .... S5
24469 New Hope 200 .... L4
22122 Newington 8,313 .... S3
23124 New Kent⊙ 25 .... P5
22844 New Market 1,118 .... L3
24128 Newport 600 .... H6
*23601 Newport News (I.C.) 144,903 .... P6
Newport News-Hampton‡ 364,449 .... P6
24129 New River 500 .... G6
23874 Newsoms 368 .... O7
24271 Nickelsville 464 .... D7
22123 Nokesville 520 .... N3
24272 Nora 550 .... D6
*23501 Norfolk (I.C.) 266,979 .... R7
Norfolk-Virginia Beach-Portsmouth ‡ 806,691 .... R7
23127 Norge 750 .... P6
22959 North Garden 200 .... L5
†24301 North Pulaski 1,405 .... G6
22151 North Springfield 9,538 .... S3
24273 Norton (I.C.) 4,757 .... C7
23955 Nottoway⊙ 170 .... M6
23416 Oak Hall 221 .... S5
22124 Oakton 19,150 .... R3
24631 Oakwood 715 .... E6
22125 Occoquan 241 .... O3
23417 Onancock 1,461 .... S5
23418 Onley 526 .... S5
22960 Orange⊙ 2,631 .... M4
23419 Oyster 200 .... S6
24131 Paint Bank 235 .... H5
23420 Painter 321 .... S5
22963 Palmyra⊙ 250 .... M5
23958 Pamplin 273 .... L6
23421 Parksley 979 .... S5
24132 Parrott 750 .... G6
24133 Patrick Springs 800 .... H7
†23069 Peaks 500 .... O5
24134 Pearisburg⊙ 2,128 .... G6
24136 Pembroke 1,302 .... G6
24137 Penhook 500 .... J7
24277 Pennington Gap 1,716 .... C7
23803 Petersburg (I.C.) 41,055 .... N6
Petersburg-Colonial Heights-Hopewell‡ 129,296 .... N6
23959 Phenix 250 .... L6
22131 Philomont 265 .... N2

24138 Pilot 360 .... H6
22043 Pimmit 6,658 .... S2
22964 Piney River 778 .... L5
24139 Pittsville 600 .... K7
24635 Pocahontas 708 .... F6
23662 Poquoson (I.C.) 8,726 .... R6
22535 Port Royal 291 .... O4
*23701 Portsmouth (I.C.) 104,577 .... R7
24279 Pound 1,086 .... C6
24637 Pounding Mill 399 .... E6
23139 Powhatan⊙ 600 .... N5
23875 Prince George⊙ 150 .... O6
23960 Prospect 275 .... L6
23140 Providence Forge 500 .... P6
24301 Pulaski⊙ 10,106 .... G6
23422 Pungoteague 500 .... S5
22132 Purcellville 1,567 .... N2
†23847 Purdy 350 .... N7
22134 Quantico 621 .... O3
23423 Quinby 350 .... S5
24141 Radford (I.C.) 13,225 .... G6
22732 Radiant 250 .... M4
24472 Raphine 500 .... K5
24639 Raven 4,000 .... E6
23876 Rawlings 200 .... N7
22140 Rectortown 225 .... N3
24640 Red Ash 300 .... E6
23964 Red Oak 250 .... L7
22539 Reedville 400 .... R5
22734 Remington 425 .... N3
22090 Reston 36,407 .... R2
24147 Rich Creek 746 .... G6
24641 Richlands 5,796 .... E5
*23201 Richmond (cap.) (I.C.)⊙ 219,214 .... O5
Richmond‡ 632,015 .... O5
24148 Ridgeway 858 .... J7
24149 Riner 360 .... H6
24150 Ripplemead 600 .... G6
22651 Riverton 500 .... M3
*24001 Roanoke (I.C.) 100,220 .... H6
Roanoke‡ 224,341 .... H6
23146 Rockville 290 .... N5
24366 Rocky Gap 200 .... F6
24151 Rocky Mount⊙ 4,198 .... J7
24280 Rosedale 760 .... E7
24281 Rose Hill 700 .... B7
22967 Roseland 300 .... K5
22141 Round Hill 510 .... N2
24368 Rural Retreat 1,083 .... F7
†23430 Rushmere 1,070 .... P6
24588 Rustburg⊙ 650 .... K6
22546 Ruther Glen 200 .... O5
23147 Ruthville 300 .... P6
24282 Saint Charles 241 .... B7
24283 Saint Paul 973 .... D7
23148 St. Stephens Church 500 .... O5
24153 Salem (I.C.)⊙ 23,958 .... H6
24370 Saltville 2,376 .... E7
23149 Saluda⊙ 150 .... P5
23150 Sandston O5
23153 Sandy Hook 700 .... M5
23427 Saxis 415 .... S5
22969 Schuyler 250 .... L5
24589 Scottsburg 335 .... L7
24590 Scottsville 250 .... L5
23696 Seaford R6
22547 Sealston 200 .... O4
23878 Sedley 523 .... P7
24474 Selma 500 .... J5
22044 Seven Corners 6,058 .... S3
24373 Seven Mile Ford 425 .... E7
24162 Shawsville 950 .... H6
22849 Shenandoah 1,861 .... L4

22971 Shipman 350 .... L5
23430 Smithfield 3,718 .... P7
22553 Snell 300 .... N4
22972 Somerset 200 .... M4
24592 South Boston (I.C.) 7,093 .... L7
23970 South Hill 4,347 .... M7
22552 Sparta 485 .... O4
24374 Speedwell 650 .... F8
24165 Spencer 500 .... J7
22740 Sperryville 500 .... M3
22553 Spotsylvania⊙ 350 .... N4
*22150 Springfield 21,435 .... S3
22554 Stafford⊙ 750 .... O4
22973 Stanardsville⊙ 284 .... L4
22851 Stanley 1,204 .... L3
24168 Stanleytown 1,761 .... H7
22654 Star Tannery 500 .... L2
24401 Staunton (I.C.)⊙ 21,857 .... K4
24476 Steeles Tavern 200 .... K5
22655 Stephens City 1,179 .... M2
22170 Sterling 16,080 .... O2
24285 Stonega 275 .... C7
23882 Stony Creek 329 .... N7
22657 Strasburg 2,311 .... M3
24171 Stuart⊙ 1,131 .... H7
24477 Stuarts Draft 1,776 .... L4
23162 Studley 500 .... O5
*23432 Suffolk (I.C.) 47,621 .... P7
24375 Sugar Grove 1,027 .... E7
22090 Sunset Hills R2
23883 Surry⊙ 237 .... P6
23163 Susan 500 .... R6
23884 Sussex⊙ 75 .... O7
24595 Sweet Briar 900 .... K5
24649 Swords Creek 315 .... E6
†24343 Sylvatus 200 .... G7
23602 Tabb R6
23440 Tangier 771 .... R5
22560 Tappahannock⊙ 1,821 .... O5
24651 Tazewell⊙ 4,468 .... E6
23442 Temperanceville 400 .... T5
24174 Thaxton 450 .... K6
22171 The Plains 382 .... N3
22853 Timberville 1,510 .... L3
23168 Toano 950 .... P6
22660 Toms Brook 226 .... L3
23443 Townsend 525 .... R6
24289 Trammel 450 .... D6
22172 Triangle 4,770 .... O3
23886 Triplet 300 .... N7
24378 Trout Dale 248 .... F7
24175 Troutville 496 .... J6
22567 Unionville 500 .... N4
22176 Upperville 250 .... N2
23175 Urbanna 518 .... P5
23887 Valentines 400 .... N7
24656 Vansant 2,708 .... D6
24597 Vernon Hill 250 .... K7
24482 Verona 2,782 .... K4
24177 Vesta 350 .... H7
24483 Vesuvius 500 .... K5
23974 Victoria 2,004 .... M6
22180 Vienna 15,469 .... R2
24179 Vinton 8,027 .... J6
*23450 Virginia Beach (I.C.) 262,199 .... S7
23480 Wachapreague 404 .... S5
23888 Wakefield 1,355 .... O7
23177 Walkerton 985 .... O5
24484 Warm Springs⊙ 325 .... J4
22186 Warrenton⊙ 3,907 .... N3
22572 Warsaw⊙ 771 .... P5
22747 Washington⊙ 247 .... M3
22190 Waterford 350 .... N2
23180 Water View 265 .... P5
23890 Waverly 2,284 .... O6
22980 Waynesboro (I.C.) 15,329 .... K4
24251 Weber City 1,543 .... C7
22576 Weems 500 .... P5
23484 Weirwood 300 .... S6
24485 West Augusta 325 .... K4
23181 West Point 2,726 .... P5
22153 West Springfield 25,012 .... S3
24486 Weyers Cave 300 .... L4
22987 White Hall 250 .... L4
22578 White Stone 409 .... R5
24292 Whitetop 860 .... E7
24657 Whitewood 350 .... E6
22579 Wicomico Church 500 .... R5
†22553 Wilderness 200 .... N4
23185 Williamsburg (I.C.)⊙ 9,870 .... P6
23486 Willis Wharf 360 .... S5
22601 Winchester (I.C.)⊙ 20,217 .... M2
23487 Windsor 985 .... P7
24184 Wirtz 500 .... J6
24293 Wise⊙ 3,894 .... C7
22748 Wolftown 350 .... M4
22989 Woodberry Forest 450 .... M4
*22191 Woodbridge 24,004 .... O3
24381 Woodlawn 1,689 .... G7
22664 Woodstock⊙ 2,627 .... L3
†24277 Woodway 400 .... C7
23976 Wylliesburg 213 .... L7
24382 Wytheville⊙ 7,135 .... G7
23690 Yorktown⊙ 550 .... R6
23898 Zuni 300 .... P7

OTHER FEATURES

Aarons (creek) L7
Allegheny (mts.) H5
Anna (lake) N4
Appalachian (mts.) J5
Appomattox (riv.) M6
Appomattox Court House Nat'l Hist. Park K6
Arlington Nat'l Cemetery T3
Assateague Island Nat'l Seashore T4
Back (bay) S7
Back (creek) J4
Banister (riv.) K7
Big Otter (riv.) K6
Blackwater (riv.) J6
Blackwater (riv.) O6
Blue Ridge (mts.) J6
Bluestone (lake) G5
Booker T. Washington Nat'l Mon. J6
Buggs Island (lake) L8
Bull Run (creek) N3
Cedar (isl.) S5
Central Intelligence Agency (C.I.A.) S2
Charles (cape) R6
Chesapeake (bay) R5
Chesapeake and Ohio Canal Nat'l Mon. O2
Chincoteague (bay) T4
Chincoteague (inlet) T5
Claytor (lake) G6
Clinch (riv.) C7
Cobb (isl.) S6
Colonial Nat'l Hist. Park P6
Cowpasture (riv.) J4
Craig (creek) H5
Cub (creek) L6
Cumberland (mt.) B7
Cumberland Gap Nat'l Hist. Pk. A7
Dan (riv.) K7
Drummond (lake) P7
Fishermans (isl.) S6
Flannagan (res.) C6
Flat (creek) M6
Fort Belvoir 7,726 .... O3
Fort Eustis P6
Fort A.P. Hill O4
Fort Lee 9,784 .... O6
Fort Monroe R6
Fort Myer T2
Fort Pickett N6
Fort Story S7
Gaston (lake) M8
George Washington Birthplace Nat'l Mon. P4
Goose (creek) J6
Goose (creek) N3
Great Machipongo (inlet) S6
Great North (mt.) L2
Hampton Roads (est.) R7
Henry (cape) R7
Hog (isl.) S6
Hog Island (bay) S6
Holston, North Fork (riv.) D7
Hyco (riv.) K8
Jackson (riv.) J4
James (riv.) O6
Jamestown Nat'l Hist. Site P6
John H. Kerr (dam) M7
Langley A.F.B. R6
Leesville (lake) K6
Levisa Fork (riv.) C5
Little (inlet) S6
Little (riv.) N5
Little (riv.) H7
Manassas Nat'l Battlefield Pk. K3
Massanutten (mt.) L3
Mattaponi (riv.) O5
Mattaponi Ind. Res. P5
Maury (riv.) K5
Meherrin (riv.) M7
Metompkin (inlet) T5
Metompkin (isl.) T5
Mobjack (bay) R6
Mount Rogers Nat'l Rec. Area F7
Naval Air Station R7
New (inlet) S6
New (riv.) F8
Ni (riv.) N4
North Anna (riv.) M4
Nottoway (riv.) O7
Oceana N.A.S. S7
Pamunkey (riv.) O5
Pamunkey Ind. Res. P5
Parramore (isl.) S5
Pentagon T3
Petersburg Nat'l Battlefield O6
Philpott (lake) H7
Piankatank (riv.) R5
Pigg (riv.) J7
Po (riv.) N4
Pocomoke (sound) S5
Potomac (riv.) O4
Powell (riv.) B7
Quantico Marine Corps Air Sta. 7,121 .... O4
Quinby (inlet) S6
Rapidan (riv.) M4
Rappahannock (riv.) P4
Richmond Nat'l Battlefield Pk. O6
Rivanna (riv.) M5
Roanoke (riv.) N8
Rogers (mt.) E7
Russell Fork (riv.) C5
Sand Shoal (inlet) S6
Shenandoah (mt.) K3
Shenandoah (riv.) N2
Shenandoah Nat'l Park L3
Ship Shoal (isl.) S6
Slate (riv.) L5
Smith (isl.) S6
Smith (riv.) J7
Smith Mountain (lake) J6
South Anna (riv.) N5
South Holston (lake) E7
South Mayo (riv.) H7
Staunton (Roanoke) (riv.) K6
Stony (creek) N6
Swift (creek) O6
Tangier (isl.) R5
Tangier (sound) S5
Tug Fork (riv.) D5
U.S. Naval Base R7
Vint Hill Farms Mil. Res. N3
Wachapreague (inlet) T6
Walker (creek) F6
Wallops (isl.) T5
Willis (riv.) M5
Wolf (creek) F6
Wolf Trap Farm Park S2
York (riv.) P6

I.C. Independent City.
⊙County seat.
‡Population of metropolitan area.
† Zip of nearest p.o * Multiple zips

AREA 68,139 sq. mi. (176,480 sq. km.)
POPULATION 4,132,180
CAPITAL Olympia
LARGEST CITY Seattle
HIGHEST POINT Mt. Rainier 14,410 ft. (4392 m.)
SETTLED IN 1811
ADMITTED TO UNION November 11, 1889
POPULAR NAME Evergreen State
STATE FLOWER Western Rhododendron
STATE BIRD Willow Goldfinch

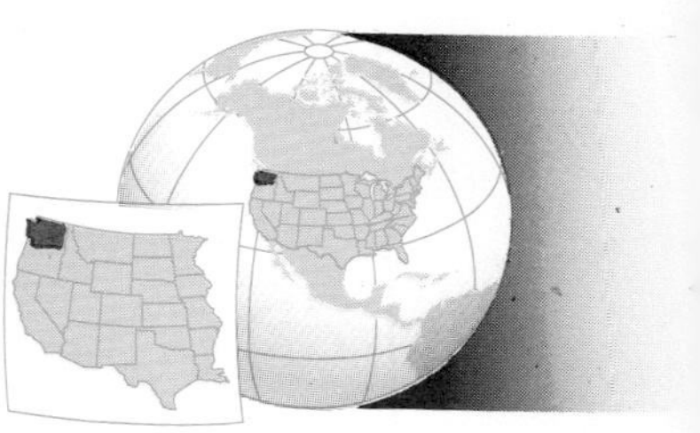

COUNTIES

Adams 13,267 .... G3
Asotin 16,823 .... H4
Benton 109,444 .... F4
Chelan 45,061 .... E3
Clallam 51,648 .... B2
Clark 192,227 .... C5
Columbia 4,057 .... H4
Cowlitz 79,548 .... C4
Douglas 22,144 .... F3
Ferry 5,811 .... G2
Franklin 35,025 .... G4
Garfield 2,468 .... H4
Grant 48,522 .... F3
Grays Harbor 66,314 .... B3
Island 44,048 .... C2
Jefferson 15,965 .... B3
King 1,269,749 .... D3
Kitsap 147,152 .... C3
Kittitas 24,877 .... E3
Klickitat 15,822 .... E5
Lewis 56,028 .... C4
Lincoln 9,604 .... G3
Mason 31,184 .... B3
Okanogan 30,639 .... F2
Pacific 17,237 .... B4
Pend Oreille 8,580 .... H2
Pierce 485,667 .... C3
San Juan 7,838 .... C2
Skagit 64,138 .... D2
Skamania 7,919 .... D5
Snohomish 337,720 .... D2
Spokane 341,835 .... H3
Stevens 28,979 .... H2
Thurston 124,264 .... C4
Wahkiakum 3,832 .... B4
Walla Walla 47,435 .... G4
Whatcom 106,701 .... D2
Whitman 40,103 .... H4
Yakima 172,508 .... E4

CITIES and TOWNS

Zip *Name/Pop.* *Key*

98520 Aberdeen 18,739 .... B3
98220 Acme 500 .... C2
99001 Airway Heights 1,730 .... H3
99102 Albion 631 .... H4
†98328 Alder 300 .... C4
98002 Algona 1,467 .... C3
98524 Allyn 850 .... C3
99103 Almira 330 .... G3
98526 Amanda Park 495 .... A3
98601 Amboy 480 .... C5
98221 Anacortes 9,013 .... C2
98603 Ariel 386 .... C5
98223 Arlington 3,282 .... C2
98304 Ashford 300 .... C4
99402 Asotin⊙ 943 .... H4
98002 Auburn 26,417 .... C3
98110 Bainbridge Island-Winslow (Winslow) 2,196 .... A2
98604 Battle Ground 2,774 .... C5
†98004 Beaux Arts Village 328 .... B2
98305 Beaver 450 .... A2
98528 Belfair 500 .... C3
*98004 Bellevue 73,903 .... B2
98225 Bellingham⊙ 45,794 .... C2
Bellingham‡ 106,701 .... C2
99320 Benton City 1,980 .... F4
98605 Bingen 644 .... D5
98010 Black Diamond 1,170 .... D3
98230 Blaine 2,363 .... C2
†98390 Bonney Lake 5,328 .... C3
98011 Bothell 7,943 .... B1
98310 Bremerton 36,208 .... A2
Bremerton‡ 146,609 .... A2
98812 Brewster 1,337 .... F2
98813 Bridgeport 1,174 .... F3
†98036 Brier 2,915 .... C3
98320 Brinnon 500 .... B3
†98101 Bryn Mawr-Skyway 11,754 B2
98321 Buckley 3,143 .... C3
98530 Bucoda 519 .... C4
98921 Buena 590 .... E4
98166 Burien 23,189 .... A2
98233 Burlington 3,894 .... C2
98013 Burton 650 .... C3
98607 Camas 5,681 .... C5
98323 Carbonado 456 .... D3
98324 Carlsborg 500 .... B2
98814 Carlton 410 .... F2
98014 Carnation 913 .... D3
98610 Carson 500 .... D5
98815 Cashmere 2,240 .... E3
98611 Castle Rock 2,162 .... B4
98612 Cathlamet⊙ 635 .... B4
98531 Centralia 11,555 .... C4
98520 Central Park 2,709 .... B3
98532 Chehalis⊙ 6,100 .... C4
98816 Chelan 2,802 .... E3
99004 Cheney 7,630 .... H3
99109 Chewelah 1,888 .... H2
98614 Chinook 928 .... B4
98326 Clallam Bay 600 .... A2
99403 Clarkston 6,903 .... H4
98235 Clearlake 750 .... C2
98922 Cle Elum 1,773 .... E3
98236 Clinton 900 .... C3
†98004 Clyde Hill 3,229 .... B2
†98055 Coalfield 500 .... B2
99111 Colfax⊙ 2,780 .... H4
99324 College Place 5,771 .... G4
99113 Colton 307 .... H4
†98632 Columbia Heights 2,515 .... C4
99114 Colville⊙ 4,510 .... H2
98819 Conconully 157 .... F2
98237 Concrete 592 .... D2
99326 Connell 1,981 .... G4
98535 Copalis Beach 600 .... A3
98536 Copalis Crossing 500 .... B3
98537 Cosmopolis 1,575 .... B4
99115 Coulee City 510 .... F3
99116 Coulee Dam 1,412 .... G3
98239 Coupeville⊙ 1,006 .... C2
99117 Creston 309 .... G3
99119 Cusick 246 .... H2
98240 Custer 300 .... C2
98617 Dallesport 600 .... D5
98241 Darrington 1,064 .... D2
99122 Davenport⊙ 1,559 .... G3
99328 Dayton⊙ 2,565 .... H4
98243 Deer Harbor 400 .... B2
99006 Deer Park 2,140 .... H3
98188 Des Moines 7,378 .... B2
99213 Dishman 10,169 .... H3
99329 Dixie 210 .... G4
98821 Dryden 500 .... E3
†98382 Dungeness 675 .... B2
98327 Du Pont 559 .... C3
98019 Duvall 729 .... D3
98245 Eastsound 800 .... B2
98801 East Wenatchee 1,640 .... E3
98328 Eatonville 998 .... C4
98020 Edmonds 27,679 .... C3
99123 Electric City 927 .... F3
98926 Ellensburg⊙ 11,752 .... E3
98541 Elma 2,720 .... B4
99124 Elmer City 312 .... G2
99125 Endicott 290 .... H4
†98310 Enetai 2,638 .... A2
98822 Entiat 445 .... E3
98022 Enumclaw 5,427 .... D3
98823 Ephrata⊙ 5,359 .... F3
†98310 Erlands Point 1,254 .... A2
*98201 Everett⊙ 54,413 .... C3
98247 Everson 898 .... C2
99012 Fairfield 582 .... H3
†98901 Fairview-Sumach 2,788 .... E4
98024 Fall City 1,528 .... D3
99128 Farmington 176 .... H3
98248 Ferndale 3,855 .... C2
98424 Fife 1,823 .... C3
98466 Fircrest 5,477 .... C3
†98531 Fords Prairie 2,582 .... B4
98331 Forks 3,060 .... A3
99014 Four Lakes 500 .... H3
98250 Friday Harbor⊙ 1,200 .... B2
†98901 Fruitvale 3,967 .... E4
99130 Garfield 599 .... H3
†99362 Garrett 1,134 .... G4
98824 George 261 .... F3
98335 Gig Harbor 2,429 .... C3
98336 Glenoma 500 .... C4
98619 Glenwood 626 .... D4
98251 Gold Bar 794 .... D3
98620 Goldendale⊙ 3,575 .... E5
98337 Gorst 750 .... C3
99133 Grand Coulee 1,180 .... G3
98930 Grandview 5,615 .... F4
98932 Granger 1,812 .... E4
98252 Granite Falls 911 .... D2
98547 Grayland 750 .... A4
98621 Grays River 350 .... B4
98253 Greenbank 600 .... C2
98339 Hadlock-Irondale 1,752 .... C2
98255 Hamilton 268 .... D2
†98366 Harper 300 .... A2
98933 Harrah 343 .... E4
99134 Harrington 507 .... G3
99135 Hartline 165 .... F3
99332 Hatton 81 .... G4
98025 Hobart 500 .... D3
98548 Hoodsport 500 .... B3
98550 Hoquiam 9,719 .... A3
†98004 Hunts Point 480 .... B2
98624 Ilwaco 604 .... A4
98256 Index 147 .... D3
98342 Indianola 800 .... A1
99139 Ione 594 .... H2
98027 Issaquah 5,536 .... C3
98343 Joyce 375 .... B2
98033 Juanita 17,232 .... B1
99335 Kahlotus 203 .... G4
98625 Kalama 1,216 .... C4
98344 Kapowsin 500 .... C4
98626 Kelso⊙ 11,129 .... C4
98028 Kenmore 7,281 .... B1
99336 Kennewick 34,397 .... F4
98031 Kent 23,152 .... C3
99141 Kettle Falls 1,087 .... H2
98345 Keyport 900 .... A2
98346 Kingston 950 .... C3
98033 Kirkland 18,779 .... B2
98934 Kittitas 782 .... E4
98628 Klickitat 750 .... D5
†98832 Krupp (Marlin) 83 .... F3
98629 La Center 439 .... C5
98503 Lacey 13,940 .... C3
98257 La Conner 633 .... C2
99143 Lacrosse 373 .... H4
†98101 Lake Forest Park 2,485 .... B1
98258 Lake Stevens 1,660 .... D3
99017 Lamont 101 .... H3
98260 Langley 650 .... C2
98350 La Push 500 .... A3
99018 Latah 155 .... H3
98826 Leavenworth 1,522 .... E3
99019 Liberty Lake 1,599 .... J3
98555 Lilliwaup 75 .... B3
99341 Lind 567 .... G4
98556 Littlerock 850 .... B4
98631 Long Beach 1,199 .... A4
98351 Longbranch 640 .... C3
98632 Longview 31,052 .... B4
99148 Loon Lake 500 .... H2
98262 Lummi Island 675 .... C2
98635 Lyle 580 .... D5
98263 Lyman 285 .... D2
98264 Lynden 4,022 .... C2
98036 Lynnwood 22,641 .... C3
98935 Mabton 1,248 .... E4
99149 Malden 200 .... H3
98829 Malott 350 .... F2
98353 Manchester 400 .... A2
98830 Mansfield 315 .... F3
98266 Maple Falls 300 .... D2
98038 Maple Valley 900 .... C3
99151 Marcus 174 .... H2
98268 Marietta-Alderwood 2,324 .... C2
98832 Marlin 83 .... F3
98270 Marysville 5,080 .... C2
99344 Mattawa 299 .... F4
98557 McCleary 1,419 .... B3
99022 Medical Lake 3,600 .... H3
98039 Medina 3,220 .... B2
98040 Mercer Island (city) 21,522 .... B2
99343 Mesa 278 .... G4
99152 Metaline 190 .... H2
99153 Metaline Falls 296 .... H2
†99210 Millwood 1,717 .... H3
98354 Milton 3,162 .... C3
98355 Mineral 550 .... C4
98562 Moclips 500 .... A3
98836 Monitor 650 .... E3
98272 Monroe 2,869 .... D3
98563 Montesano⊙ 3,247 .... B4
98356 Morton 1,264 .... C4
98837 Moses Lake 10,629 .... F3
98564 Mossyrock 463 .... C4
98043 Mountlake Terrace 16,534 . B1
98273 Mount Vernon⊙ 13,009 .... C2
98936 Moxee City 687 .... E4
98275 Mukilteo 1,426 .... C3
98937 Naches 644 .... E4
98565 Napavine 611 .... C4
98638 Naselle 500 .... B4
†98310 Navy Yard City 2,594 .... A2
98357 Neah Bay 800 .... A2
99155 Nespelem 284 .... G2
†98283 Newhalem 350 .... D2
99156 Newport⊙ 1,665 .... H2
†98501 Nisqually 500 .... C3
98276 Nooksack 429 .... C2
98358 Nordland 706 .... C2
†98100 Normandy Park 4,268 .... A2
98045 North Bend 1,701 .... D3
98639 North Bonneville 394 .... C5
99157 Northport 368 .... H2
99158 Oakesdale 444 .... H3
98277 Oak Harbor 12,271 .... C2
98568 Oakville 537 .... B4
98569 Ocean City 350 .... A3
98640 Ocean Park 918 .... A4
98551 Ocean Shores 1,692 .... A3
†98520 Ocosta 369 .... B4
99159 Odessa 1,009 .... G3
98840 Okanogan⊙ 2,302 .... F2
98359 Olalla 500 .... A2
*98501 Olympia (cap.)⊙ 27,447 .... C3
Olympia‡ 124,264 .... C3
98841 Omak 4,007 .... F2
98570 Onalaska 600 .... C4
99214 Opportunity 21,241 .... H3
98662 Orchards 8,828 .... C5
98844 Oroville 1,483 .... F2
98360 Orting 1,787 .... C3
99344 Othello 4,454 .... F4
99027 Otis Orchards-East Farms 4,597 .... H3
98938 Outlook 300 .... E4
98047 Pacific 2,261 .... C3
98571 Pacific Beach 900 .... A3
98361 Packwood 800 .... D4
99161 Palouse 1,005 .... H4
98939 Parker 500 .... E4
98444 Parkland 23,355 .... C3
99301 Pasco⊙ 18,425 .... F4
98846 Pateros 555 .... E2
98572 Pe Ell 617 .... B4
98847 Peshastin 500 .... E3
98281 Point Roberts 500 .... B2
99347 Pomeroy⊙ 1,716 .... H4
98362 Port Angeles⊙ 17,311 .... B2
†98101 Port Blakely 600 .... A2
98366 Port Orchard⊙ 4,787 .... A2
98368 Port Townsend⊙ 6,067 .... C2
†98584 Potlach 100 .... B3
98370 Poulsbo 3,453 .... A1
99348 Prescott 341 .... G4
98050 Preston 500 .... D3
99350 Prosser⊙ 3,896 .... F4
99163 Pullman 23,579 .... H4
98371 Puyallup 18,251 .... C3
98376 Quilcene 900 .... B3
98575 Quinault 450 .... B3
98848 Quincy 3,525 .... F3
98576 Rainier 891 .... C4

(continued on following page)

Agriculture, Industry and Resources

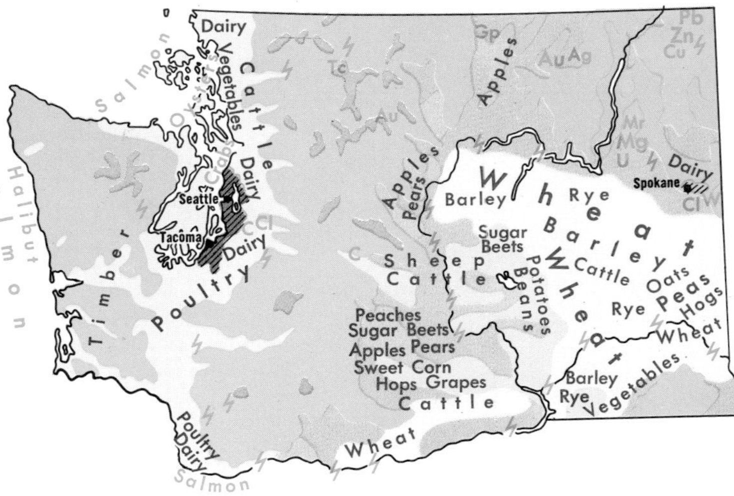

DOMINANT LAND USE

- Specialized Wheat
- Wheat, Peas
- Dairy, Poultry, Mixed Farming
- Fruit and Mixed Farming
- General Farming, Dairy, Range Livestock
- General Farming, Livestock, Special Crops
- Range Livestock
- Forests
- Urban Areas
- Nonagricultural Land

MAJOR MINERAL OCCURRENCES

Ag	Silver	Mr	Marble
Au	Gold	Pb	Lead
C	Coal	Tc	Talc
Cl	Clay	U	Uranium
Cu	Copper	W	Tungsten
Gp	Gypsum	Zn	Zinc
Mg	Magnesium		

Water Power
Major Industrial Areas

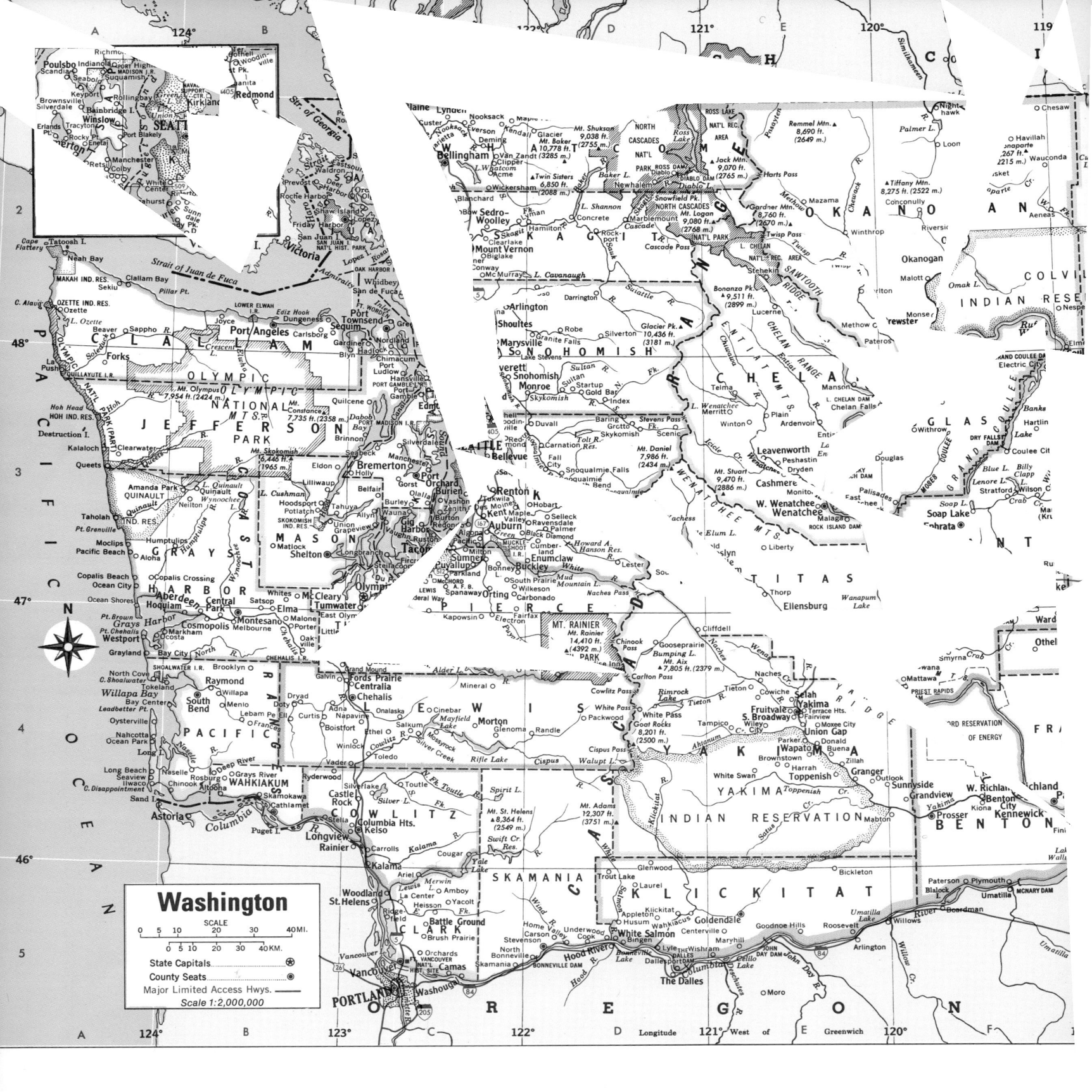

Washington

SCALE
0 5 10 20 30 40 MI.
0 5 10 20 30 40 KM.

State Capitals .... ⊛
County Seats .... ◉
Major Limited Access Hwys. _____
Scale 1:2,000,000

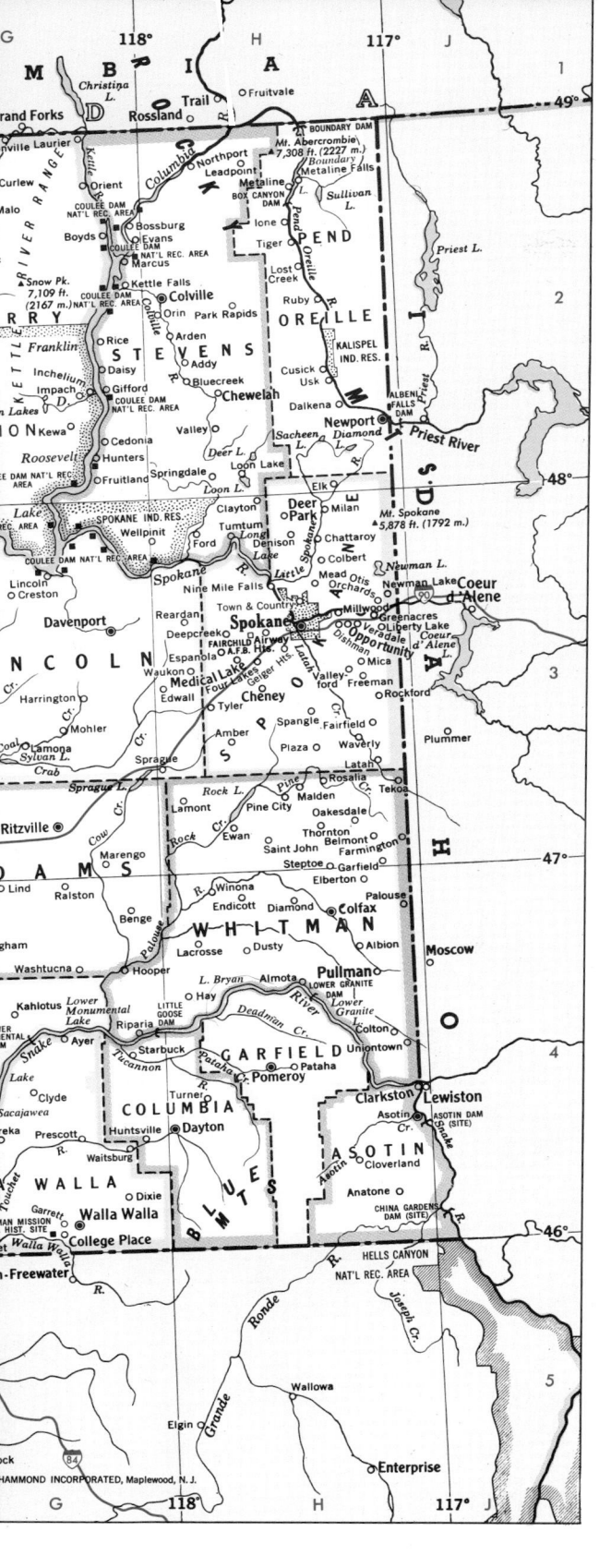

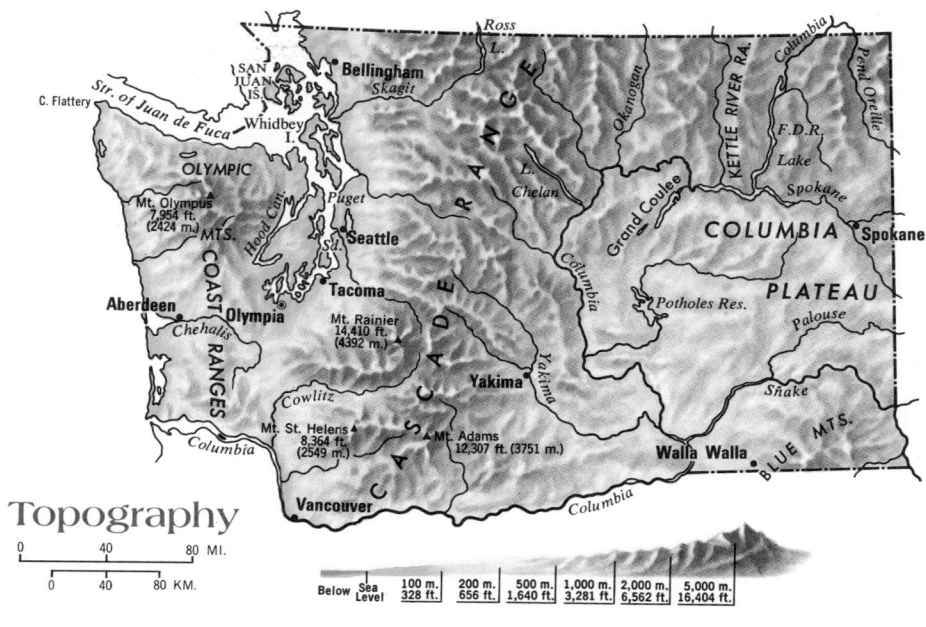

Topography

```
        0    40    80 MI.
        0    40    80 KM.
```

Below Sea Level	100 m. 328 ft.	200 m. 656 ft.	500 m. 1,640 ft.	1,000 m. 3,281 ft.	2,000 m. 6,562 ft.	5,000 m. 16,404 ft.

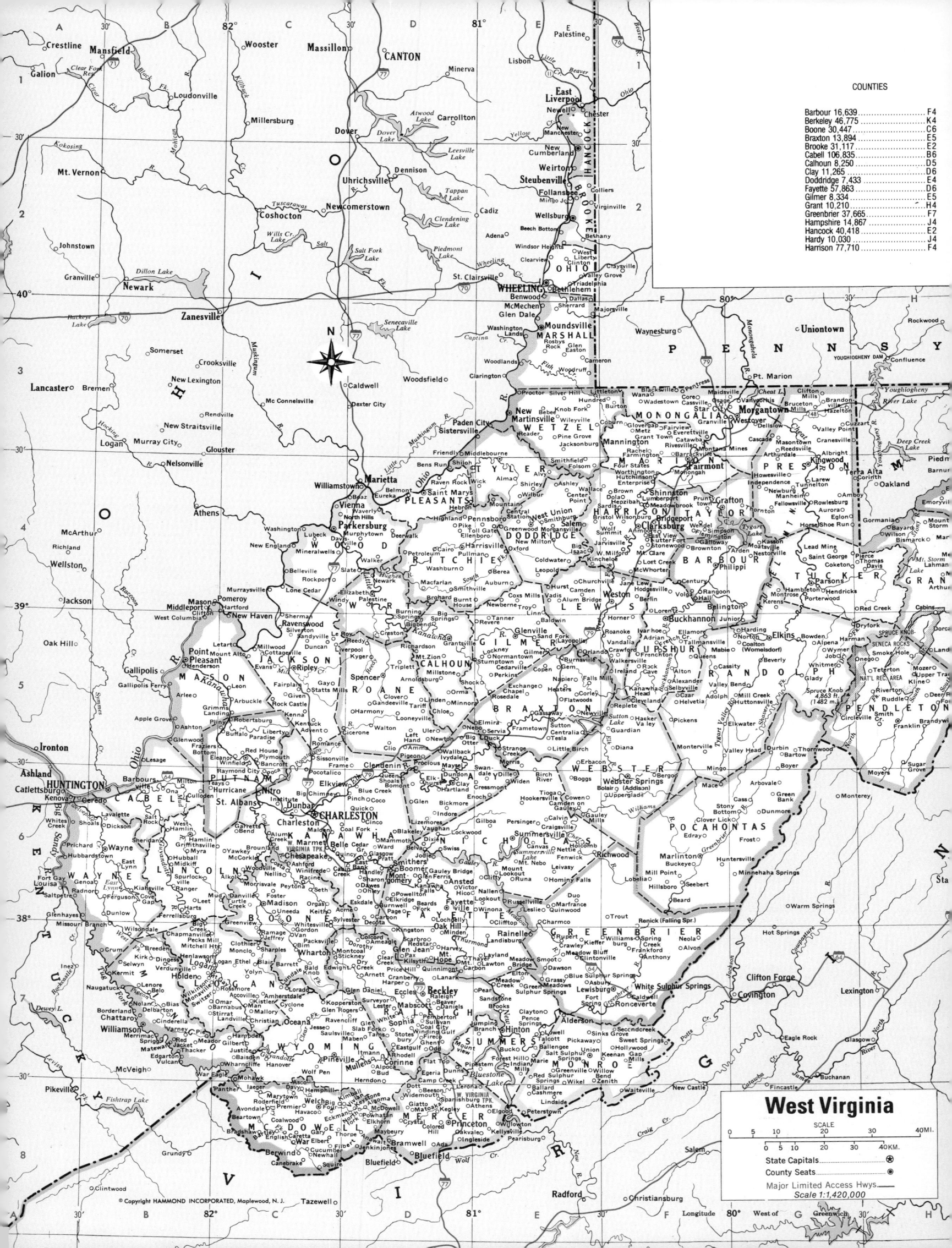

West Virginia

SCALE

0 5 10   20   30   40 MI.

0 5 10   20   30   40 KM.

State Capitals .... ⊛

County Seats .... ⊙

Major Limited Access Hwys. _____

Scale 1:1,420,000

© Copyright HAMMOND INCORPORATED, Maplewood, N.J.

Jackson 25,794	C5
Jefferson 30,302	L4
Kanawha 231,414	C6
Lewis 18,813	E4
Lincoln 23,675	B6
Logan 50,679	C7
Marion 65,789	F4
Marshall 41,608	E3
Mason 27,045	B5
McDowell 49,899	C8
Mercer 73,942	D8
Mineral 27,234	J4
Mingo 37,336	B7
Monongalia 75,024	F3
Monroe 12,873	E7
Morgan 10,711	K3
Nicholas 28,126	E6
Ohio 61,389	E2
Pendleton 7,910	H5
Pleasants 8,236	D4
Pocahontas 9,919	F6
Preston 30,460	G4
Putnam 38,181	C6
Raleigh 86,821	D7
Randolph 28,734	G5
Ritchie 11,442	D4
Roane 15,952	D5
Summers 15,875	E7
Taylor 16,584	F4
Tucker 8,675	F4
Tyler 11,320	E4
Upshur 23,427	F5
Wayne 46,021	B6
Webster 12,245	F6
Wetzel 21,874	E3
Wirt 4,922	D4
Wood 93,648	D4
Wyoming 35,993	C7

AREA 24,231 sq. mi. (62,758 sq. km.)
POPULATION 1,950,279
CAPITAL Charleston
LARGEST CITY Charleston
HIGHEST POINT Spruce Knob 4,863 ft. (1482 m.)
SETTLED IN 1774
ADMITTED TO UNION June 20, 1863
POPULAR NAME Mountain State
STATE FLOWER Big Rhododendron
STATE BIRD Cardinal

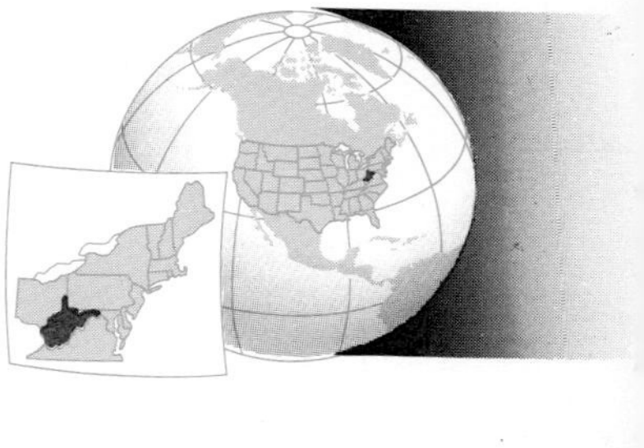

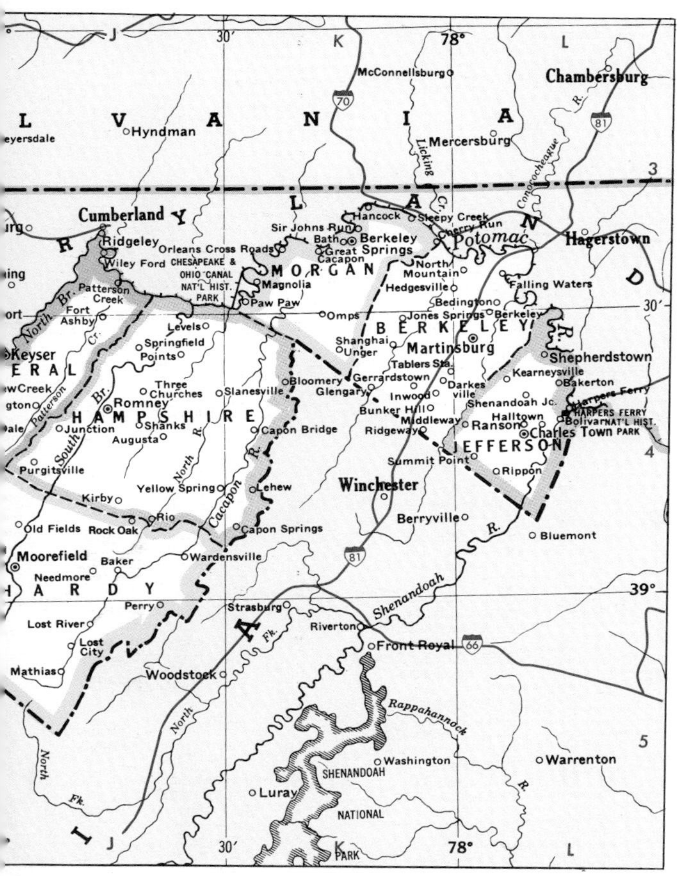

McConnellsburg
Chambersburg
Hyndman
Mercersburg
Cumberland
Hancock
Sleepy Creek
Cherry Run
Hagerstown
Ridgeley
Wiley Ford
Orleans Cross Roads
Sir Johns Run
Bath
Berkeley
Great Springs
Cacapon
Potomac
MORGAN
North Mountain
Magnolia
Paw Paw
Hedgesville
Falling Waters
Bedington
Patterson Creek
Fort Ashby
Omps
Jones Springs
BERKELEY
Martinsburg
Shepherdstown
Keyser
Springfield
Points
Shanghai
Unger
Tablers Sta.
Kearneysville
Three Churches
Slanesville
Bloomery
Gerrardstown
Glengary
Darkesville
Bakerton
Harpers Ferry
Romney
HAMPSHIRE
Inwood
Bunker Hill
Shenandoah Jc.
Halltown
Bolivar
Junction
Shanks
Augusta
Capon Bridge
Middleway
Ridgeway
Ranson
Charles Town
JEFFERSON
Summit Point
Purgitsville
Yellow Spring
Lehew
Winchester
Rippon
Kirby
Rio
Old Fields
Rock Oak
Capon Springs
Berryville
Bluemont
Moorefield
Baker
Wardensville
Needmore
HARDY
Perry
Strasburg
Lost River
Riverton
Front Royal
Lost City
Mathias
Woodstock
Rappahannock
Washington
Warrenton
SHENANDOAH
NATIONAL
PARK
Luray

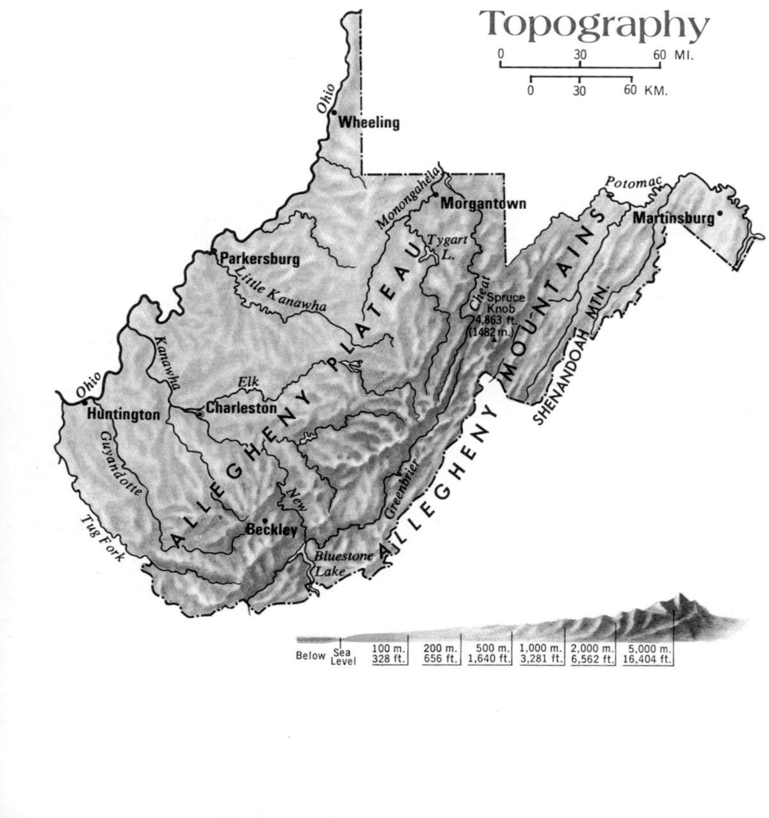

Topography
0 30 60 MI.
0 30 60 KM.
Ohio
Wheeling
Monongahela
Morgantown
Potomac
Martinsburg
Parkersburg
Little Kanawha
Tygart L.
Spruce Knob 4,863 ft. (1482 m.)
ALLEGHENY PLATEAU
ALLEGHENY MOUNTAINS
SHENANDOAH MTN.
Kanawha
Elk
Charleston
Huntington
Guyandotte
Tug Fork
New
Greenbrier
Beckley
Bluestone Lake
ALLEGHENY
Below Sea Level
100 m. 328 ft.
200 m. 656 ft.
500 m. 1,640 ft.
1,000 m. 3,281 ft.
2,000 m. 6,562 ft.
5,000 m. 16,404 ft.

CITIES and TOWNS

Zip	Name/Pop.	Key
25606	Accoville 975	C7
†26288	Addison (Webster Springs)⊙ 939	F6
26210	Adrian 510	F5
26519	Albright 357	G3
24910	Alderson 1,375	E7
24807	Algoma 200	D8
25501	Alkol 500	C6
26320	Alma 197	E4
24710	Alpoca 200	D7
26321	Alum Bridge 150	E4
25003	Alum Creek 900	C6
26322	Alvy 150	E4
25004	Ameagle 230	D7
25607	Amherstdale 1,075	C7
25005	Amma 200	D5
24808	Anawalt 652	D8
26323	Anmoore 865	F4
25812	Ansted 1,952	D6
25502	Apple Grove 900	B5
24915	Arbovale 610	G6
26816	Arthur 350	H4
26520	Arthurdale 1,063	G3
24916	Asbury 280	E7
24809	Asco 175	C8
25009	Ashford 400	C6
25503	Ashton 259	B5
24712	Athens 1,147	E8
26325	Auburn 116	E4
26704	Augusta 750	J4
26705	Aurora 250	G4
24811	Avondale 250	C8
25608	Baisden 500	C7
26801	Baker 200	J4
25410	Bakerton 125	L4
25010	Bald Knob 356	C7
26326	Baldwin 92	E5
25011	Bancroft 528	C5
25504	Barboursville 2,871	B6
25609	Barnabus 750	C7
26559	Barrackville 1,815	F3
25013	Barrett 950	C7
24813	Bartley 900	C8
24920	Bartow 500	G5
†25411	Bath (Berkeley Springs) 789	K3
26707	Bayard 540	H4
25014	Beards Fork 400	D6
25813	Beaver (Glen Hedrick) 1,122	D7
25801	Beckley⊙ 20,492	D7
26030	Beech Bottom 507	E2
24714	Beeson 300	D8
26250	Belington 2,038	F4
25015	Belle 1,621	C6
26133	Belleville 105	C4
26134	Belmont 887	D4
26656	Belva 275	D6
26135	Bens Run 85	D4
26031	Benwood 1,994	E2
26298	Bergoo 220	F6
25411	Berkeley Springs (Bath)⊙ 789	K3
24815	Berwind 615	C8
26032	Bethany 1,336	E2
†26003	Bethlehem 3,045	E2
26253	Beverly 475	G5
25019	Bickmore 300	D6
26136	Bigbend 120	D5
25302	Big Chimney 450	C6
25505	Big Creek 500	B7
26137	Big Springs 485	D5
25021	Bim 500	C7
26610	Birch River 650	E6
26521	Blacksville 248	F3
25022	Blair 800	C7
26817	Bloomery 200	K4
25026	Blue Creek 650	D6
24701	Bluefield 16,060	D8
26288	Bolair 450	F6
†25425	Bolivar 672	L4
25030	Bomont 170	D6
25031	Boomer 1,051	D6
24817	Bradshaw 1,002	C8
24715	Bramwell 989	D8
26523	Brandonville 92	G3
26802	Brandywine 300	H5
25666	Breeden 600	B7
26330	Bridgeport 6,604	F4
26138	Brohard 80	D4
25957	Brooks 196	E7
26334	Brownton 400	F4
26525	Bruceton Mills 296	G3
24924	Buckeye 125	F6
26201	Buckhannon⊙ 6,820	F5
24716	Bud 400	D7
25033	Buffalo 1,034	C5
25413	Bunker Hill 600	K4
26710	Burlington 300	J4
26335	Burnsville 531	E5
26336	Burnt House 175	D4
26562	Burton 200	F3
25035	Cabin Creek 900	C6
26337	Cairo 428	D4
24925	Caldwell 795	F7
26660	Calvin 400	E6
26208	Camden on Gauley 236	E6
26033	Cameron 1,474	E3
24819	Canebrake 300	C8
26662	Canvas 300	E6
26711	Capon Bridge 191	K4
26823	Capon Springs 580	K4
25037	Carbon 300	D6
24821	Caretta 650	C8
24927	Cass 148	G6
26527	Cassville 800	F3
25039	Cedar Grove 1,479	D6
26339	Center Point 250	E4
26612	Centralia 100	E5
26340	Central Station 200	E4
26214	Century 250	F4
25507	Ceredo 2,255	B6
25508	Chapmanville 1,164	B7
*25301	Charleston (cap.)⊙ 63,968	C6
	Charleston‡ 269,595	C6
25414	Charles Town⊙ 2,857	L4
25958	Charmco 800	E6
25667	Chattaroy 1,383	B7
25418	Cherry Run 120	L3
†25301	Chesapeake 2,364	C6
26034	Chester 3,297	E1
26301	Clarksburg⊙ 22,371	F4
25043	Clay⊙ 940	D6
25044	Clear Creek 300	D7
†26003	Clearview 740	E2
25045	Clendenin 1,373	D5
26215	Cleveland 74	F5
25822	Clifftop 100	E6
25237	Clifton 325	B5
24928	Clintonville 250	E7
25046	Clio 300	D5
25047	Clothier 900	C7
25823	Coal City 2,324	D7
25306	Coal Fork 2,775	D6
26257	Coalton 306	G5
24824	Coalwood 650	C8
25048	Colcord 600	D7
26035	Colliers 864	E2
26615	Copen 50	E5
25826	Corinne 900	D7
25051	Costa 250	C6
25239	Cottageville 300	C5
25509	Cove Gap 650	B6
26206	Cowen 723	E6
26342	Coxs Mills 275	E4
26205	Craigsville 1,562	E6
25828	Cranberry 315	D7
24931	Crawley 395	E7
25669	Crum 500	B7
24826	Cucumber 274	C8
25510	Culloden 2,931	B6
24827	Cyclone 500	C7
26036	Dallas 450	E2
25832	Daniels 1,959	D7
25053	Danville 727	C6
†25428	Darkesville 150	L4
26260	Davis 979	H4
24828	Davy 882	C8
25054	Dawes 800	D6
24932	Dawson 300	E7
25670	Delbarton 981	B7
26531	Dellslow 300	G3
26217	Diana 300	F5
26617	Dille 300	E6
25671	Dingess 600	B7
25059	Dixie 985	D6
25060	Dorothy 400	D7
24721	Dott 100	D8
25062	Dry Creek 441	D7
26263	Dryfork 425	H5
25063	Duck 500	E5
25064	Dunbar 9,285	C6
24934	Dunmore 280	G6
26264	Durbin 379	G5
25067	East Bank 1,155	D6
25835	Eastgulf 300	D7
25512	East Lynn 150	B6
†26301	East View 1,222	F4
25836	Eccles 1,162	D7
24829	Eckman 750	C8
25672	Edgarton 415	B7
26716	Eglon 70	G4
24830	Elbert 400	C8
25070	Eleanor 1,282	C5
26143	Elizabeth⊙ 856	D4
26717	Elk Garden 291	H4
26241	Elkins⊙ 8,536	G5
25071	Elkview 1,161	C6
26267	Ellamore 250	F5
26346	Ellenboro 357	D4
25965	Elton 200	E7
24832	English 500	C8
26568	Enterprise 1,110	F4
25075	Eskdale 400	D6
25076	Ethel 450	C7
26144	Eureka 125	D4
25241	Evans 400	C5
26533	Everettville 175	F3
26554	Fairmont 23,863	F4
26570	Fairview 759	F3
†24966	Falling Spring (Renick) 240	F6
26571	Farmington 583	F3
25840	Fayetteville⊙ 2,366	D6
26202	Fenwick 500	E6
24835	Filbert 130	D8
26818	Fisher 500	H4
25841	Flat Top 550	D7
26621	Flatwoods 405	E5
26347	Flemington 452	F4
26037	Follansbee 3,994	E2
26348	Folsom 360	E4
24935	Forest Hill 314	E7
26719	Fort Ashby 1,205	J4
25514	Fort Gay 886	A6
26806	Fort Seybert 200	H5
24936	Fort Spring 250	E7
25081	Foster 500	C6
26572	Four States 500	F4
25071	Frame 76	C5
26623	Frametown 150	E5
26807	Franklin⊙ 780	H5
25082	Fraziers Bottom 250	B5
26219	Frenchton 102	F5
26146	Friendly 242	D3
25515	Gallipolis Ferry 325	B5
26349	Galloway 500	F4
25243	Gandeeville 150	D5
24941	Gap Mills 300	F7
24836	Gary 2,233	C8
26624	Gassaway 1,225	E5
25085	Gauley Bridge 1,177	D6
26240	Gauley Mills 165	E6
25244	Gay 300	C5
25420	Gerrardstown 240	K4
25843	Ghent 500	D7
25621	Gilbert 757	C7
26671	Gilboa 500	E6
26350	Gilmer 110	E5
26268	Glady 175	G5
25086	Glasgow 1,031	D6
25088	Glen 175	D6
26038	Glen Dale 1,875	E3
26039	Glen Easton 100	E3
25090	Glen Ferris 200	D6
25421	Glengary 250	K4
†25813	Glen Hedrick (Beaver) 1,122	D7
25846	Glen Jean	D7
25848	Glen Rogers 500	D7
26351	Glenville⊙ 2,155	E5
25849	Glen White 300	D7
25520	Glenwood 400	B5
†26585	Glovergap 100	F3
25093	Gordon 300	C7
26720	Gormania 100	H4
26354	Grafton⊙ 6,845	G4
26147	Grantsville⊙ 788	D5
26574	Grant Town 987	F3
26534	Granville 992	F3
24943	Grassy Meadows 100	E7
25422	Great Cacapon 750	K3
24944	Green Bank 115	G6
25966	Green Sulphur Springs 225	E7
24945	Greenville 125	E7
26360	Greenwood 750	E4
25095	Grimms Landing 350	B5
26221	Guardian 175	F5
26222	Hacker Valley 440	F5
25423	Halltown 375	L4
26269	Hambleton 403	G4
25523	Hamlin⊙ 1,219	B6
25623	Hampden 300	C7
25424	Hancock 175	K3
25102	Handley 633	D6
†26250	Harding 100	G5
26270	Harman 181	G5
25246	Harmony 600	D5
25851	Harper 400	D7
25425	Harpers Ferry 361	L4
26362	Harrisville⊙ 1,673	E4
25247	Hartford 556	C4
25524	Harts 400	B6
25852	Harvey 300	D7
24841	Havaco 350	C8
26627	Heaters 440	E5
25427	Hedgesville 217	K3
26224	Helvetia 130	F5
24842	Hemphill 700	C8
25106	Henderson 604	B5
26271	Hendricks 390	G4
25624	Henlawson 900	B7
26369	Hepzibah 600	F4
24726	Herndon 500	D7
25854	Hico 750	D6
24946	Hillsboro 276	F6
25951	Hinton⊙ 4,622	E7
25625	Holden 2,036	B7
26372	Horner 125	F5
26769	Horse Shoe Run 500	G4
†25506	Hubball 145	B6
26575	Hundred 485	E3
*25701	Huntington⊙ 63,684	A6
	Huntington-Ashland‡ 311,350	A6
25526	Hurricane 3,751	C6
26273	Huttonsville 242	G5
24844	Iaeger 833	C8
26374	Independence 200	G4
24949	Indian Mills 150	E7
25111	Indore 300	D6
25112	Institute	C6
25428	Inwood 1,159	K4
24847	Itmann 600	D7
25113	Ivydale 800	D5
26377	Jacksonburg 400	E3
26378	Jane Lew 406	F4
25114	Jeffrey 900	C7
24848	Jenkinjones 750	D8
24849	Jesse 400	C7
26674	Jodie 440	D6
25969	Jumping Branch 700	E7
26824	Junction 75	J4

(continued on following page)

Agriculture, Industry and Resources

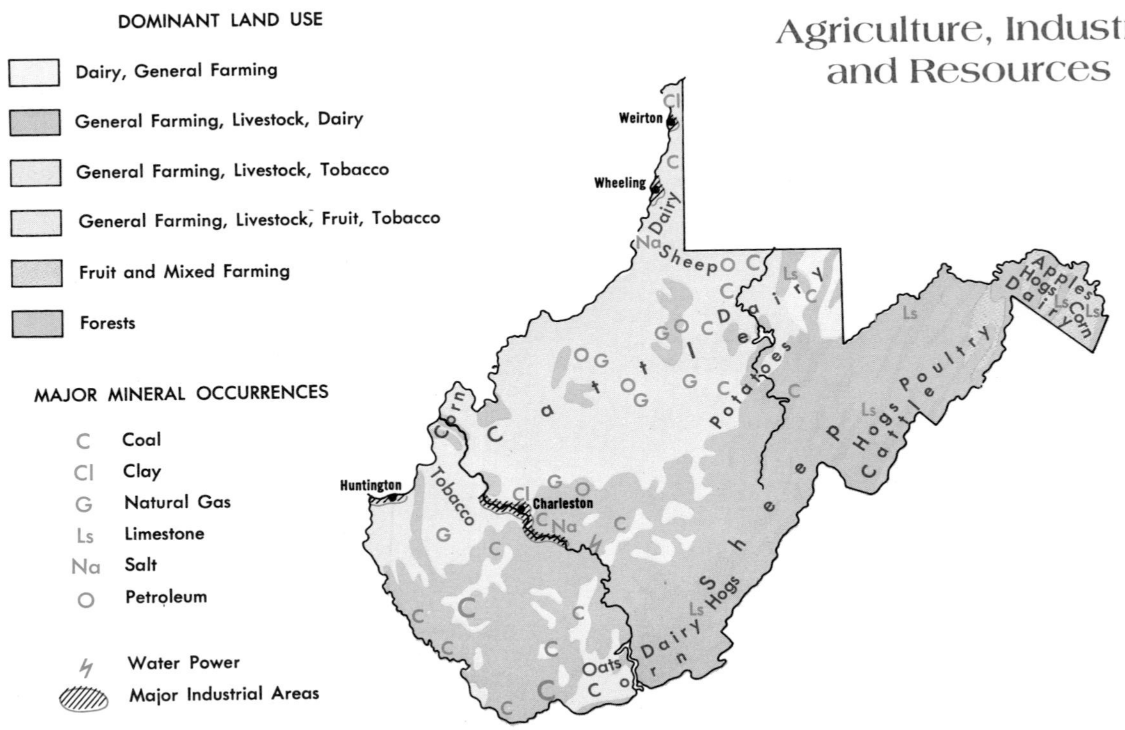
DOMINANT LAND USE
Dairy, General Farming
General Farming, Livestock, Dairy
General Farming, Livestock, Tobacco
General Farming, Livestock, Fruit, Tobacco
Fruit and Mixed Farming
Forests
MAJOR MINERAL OCCURRENCES
C Coal
Cl Clay
G Natural Gas
Ls Limestone
Na Salt
O Petroleum
Water Power
Major Industrial Areas
Weirton
Wheeling
Huntington
Charleston
Dairy
Sheep
Poultry
Apples
Hogs
Corn
Cattle
Potatoes
Tobacco
Oats

26275 Junior 591 .... G5
24851 Justice 600 .... C7
25115 Kanawha Falls 105 .... D6
25430 Kearneysville 250 .... L4
24731 Kegley 900 .... D8
24732 Kellysville 165 .... E8
25248 Kenna 150 .... C5
25530 Kenova 4,454 .... A6
25249 Kentuck 200 .... C5
25674 Kermit 705 .... B7
26726 Keyser⊙ 6,569 .... J4
24852 Keystone 902 .... D8
24950 Kieffer 135 .... E7
25859 Kilsyth 200 .... D7
24853 Kimball 871 .... C8
25120 Kingston 189 .... D7
26537 Kingwood⊙ 2,877 .... G4
26729 Kirby 110 .... J4
25628 Kistler 200 .... C7
26579 Knob Fork 106 .... E3
24854 Kopperston 700 .... C7
26731 Lahmansville 200 .... H4
25860 Lanark 559 .... D7
25629 Landville 400 .... C7
25535 Lavalette 600 .... B6
25863 Lawton 100 .... E7
25864 Layland 500 .... E7
†26430 Layopolis (Sand Fork) 280 .... E5
25251 Left Hand 700 .... D5
26676 Leivasy 200 .... E6
25676 Lenore 800 .... B7
25123 Leon 228 .... C5
25971 Lerona 550 .... D8
25537 Lesage 600 .... B5
25972 Leslie 350 .... E6
25865 Lester 626 .... D7
25253 Letart 350 .... C5
25431 Levels 180 .... J4
24901 Lewisburg⊙ 3,065 .... E7
26384 Linn 165 .... E4
26629 Little Birch 400 .... E5
26581 Littleton 335 .... F3
25125 Lizemores 400 .... D6
25866 Lochgelly 250 .... D6
25258 Lockney 190 .... E5
25601 Logan⊙ 3,029 .... B7
25630 Lorado 400 .... C7
†26201 Lorentz 200 .... F4
26810 Lost City 130 .... J5
26385 Lost Creek 604 .... F4
26811 Lost River 500 .... J5
†26101 Lubeck 1,356 .... C4
26386 Lumberport 939 .... F4
25631 Lundale 525 .... C7
25870 Maben 450 .... D7
26278 Mabie 550 .... F5
25871 Mabscott 1,668 .... D7
26148 Macfarlan 436 .... D4
25130 Madison⊙ 3,228 .... C6
26541 Maidsville 500 .... F3
25306 Malden 900 .... C6
25634 Mallory 1,330 .... C7
25132 Mammoth 563 .... D6
25635 Man 1,333 .... C7
26582 Mannington 3,036 .... F3
25975 Marfrance 225 .... E6
24954 Marlinton⊙ 1,352 .... F6
25315 Marmet 2,196 .... C6
25401 Martinsburg⊙ 13,063 .... K4
25260 Mason 1,432 .... B4
26542 Masontown 1,052 .... G3

25678 Matewan 822 .... B7
24736 Matoaka 613 .... D8
24861 Maybeury 300 .... D8
26833 Maysville 150 .... H4
24858 McDowell 500 .... D8
26040 McMechen 2,402 .... E3
26401 McWhorter 150 .... F4
24958 Meadow Bluff 250 .... E7
25976 Meadow Bridge 530 .... E7
26404 Meadowbrook 500 .... F4
25977 Meadow Creek 300 .... E7
26585 Metz 150 .... F3
26149 Middlebourne⊙ 941 .... E3
25540 Midkiff 650 .... B6
26280 Mill Creek 801 .... G5
24959 Mill Point 148 .... F6
25261 Millstone 850 .... D5
25262 Millwood 800 .... C5
25541 Milton 2,178 .... B6
25879 Minden 800 .... D7
26150 Mineralwells 325 .... C4
26281 Mingo 350 .... F5
25263 Minnora 500 .... D5
26405 Moatsville 150 .... G4
25636 Monaville 950 .... B7
26554 Monongah 1,132 .... F4
26586 Montana Mines 200 .... F3
25135 Montcoal 150 .... D7
26282 Monterville 250 .... F5
25136 Montgomery 3,104 .... D6
26283 Montrose 129 .... G4
26836 Moorefield⊙ 2,257 .... J4
26505 Morgantown⊙ 27,605 .... G3
25542 Morrisvale 450 .... C6
26041 Moundsville⊙ 12,419 .... E3
26407 Mountain 200 .... E4
25264 Mount Alto 200 .... C5
25139 Mount Carbon 450 .... D7
26408 Mount Clare 950 .... F4
25637 Mount Gay 4,366 .... C7
25880 Mount Hope 1,849 .... D7
26678 Mount Lookout 500 .... E6
26679 Mount Nebo 535 .... E6
26739 Mount Storm 500 .... H4
25882 Mullens 2,919 .... D7
26680 Nallen 250 .... E6
26631 Napier 158 .... E5
25685 Naugatuck 500 .... B7
25141 Nebo 200 .... D5
25142 Nellis 600 .... C6
24961 Neola 300 .... F7
26681 Nettie 500 .... E6
26410 Newburg 418 .... G4
26047 New Cumberland⊙ 1,752 .... E2
26050 Newell 2,032 .... E1
26154 New England 335 .... C4
24866 Newhall 400 .... C8
25265 New Haven 1,723 .... C5
26056 New Manchester 800 .... E1
26155 New Martinsville⊙ 7,109 .... E3
25266 Newton 390 .... D5
26632 Newville 160 .... E5
25143 Nitro 8,074 .... C6
25687 Nolan 250 .... B7
25267 Normantown 112 .... E5
24868 Northfork 1,105 .... D8
†26101 North Hills 940 .... D4
26285 Norton 400 .... G5
26301 Nutter Fort 2,078 .... F4
25901 Oak Hill 7,120 .... D6
24739 Oakvale 208 .... D8
24870 Oceana 2,143 .... C7

25902 Odd 500 .... D7
25147 Ohley 450 .... D6
25638 Omar 900 .... C7
26886 Onego 400 .... H5
25148 Orgas 500 .... C6
26412 Orlando 700 .... E5
25268 Orma D5
26543 Osage 285 .... F3
25151 Packsville 225 .... C7
26159 Paden City 3,671 .... D3
25152 Page 600 .... D6
26160 Palestine 110 .... D4
24872 Panther 450 .... C8
26101 Parkersburg⊙ 39,967 .... D4
Parkersburg-Marietta‡ 162,836 .... D4
26287 Parsons⊙ 1,937 .... G4
26746 Patterson Creek 157 .... J3
25434 Paw Paw 644 .... K3
25904 Pax 274 .... D7
†25955 Pear 100 .... E7
25547 Pecks Mill 350 .... B7
25905 Pemberton 300 .... D7
24962 Pence Springs 300 .... E7
26415 Pennsboro 1,652 .... E4
26544 Pentress 250 .... F3
26847 Petersburg⊙ 2,084 .... H5
24963 Peterstown 648 .... E8
25154 Peytona 175 .... C6
26416 Philippi⊙ 3,194 .... G4
24964 Pickaway 225 .... E7
26230 Pickens 240 .... F5
25689 Pie 250 .... B7
26750 Piedmont 1,491 .... H4
25156 Pinch 800 .... D6
26419 Pine Grove 767 .... E3
24874 Pineville⊙ 1,140 .... C7
25158 Pliny 900 .... B5
25159 Poca 1,142 .... C6
†25301 Pocotalico 2,420 .... C6
25550 Point Pleasant⊙ 5,682 .... B5
25437 Points 250 .... J4
25161 Powellton 1,339 .... D6
24877 Powhatan 400 .... D8
25162 Pratt 821 .... D6
24878 Premier 400 .... C8
†25880 Price Hill 175 .... D7
25555 Prichard 500 .... A6
24740 Princeton⊙ 7,493 .... D8
25164 Procious 600 .... D5
26055 Proctor 350 .... E3
26421 Pullman 196 .... D4
26852 Purgitsville 450 .... J4
25045 Quick 400 .... D6
†25015 Quincy 150 .... C6
25981 Quinwood 460 .... E6
26587 Rachel 550 .... F3
25165 Racine 725 .... C6
25556 Radnor 300 .... A6
25962 Rainelle 1,983 .... E7
25911 Raleigh 900 .... D7
25166 Ramage 350 .... C7
25557 Ranger 300 .... B6
25438 Ranson 2,471 .... L4
25913 Ravencliff 350 .... C7
26164 Ravenswood 4,126 .... C5
26167 Reader 950 .... E3
26289 Red Creek 125 .... H4
25168 Red House 600 .... C5
25692 Red Jacket 850 .... B7
26547 Reedsville 564 .... G3
25270 Reedy 338 .... D5

24966 Renick 240 .... F6
25915 Rhodell 472 .... D7
26261 Richwood 3,568 .... F6
26753 Ridgeley 994 .... J3
25440 Ridgeway 200 .... K4
26755 Rio 140 .... J4
25271 Ripley⊙ 3,464 .... C5
25441 Rippon 500 .... L4
26588 Rivesville 1,327 .... F3
26234 Rock Cave 400 .... F5
24881 Roderfield 900 .... C8
26757 Romney⊙ 2,094 .... J4
24970 Ronceverte 2,312 .... F7
26636 Rosedale 400 .... E5
25643 Rossmore 200 .... C7
26425 Rowlesburg 966 .... G4
26688 Runa 150 .... E6
25984 Rupert 1,276 .... E7
26689 Russellville 280 .... E6
25177 Saint Albans 12,402 .... C6
26290 Saint George 150 .... G4
26170 Saint Marys⊙ 2,219 .... D4
26426 Salem 2,706 .... E4
25559 Salt Rock 350 .... B6
26430 Sand Fork 280 .... E5
25985 Sandstone 300 .... E7
25275 Sandyville 500 .... C5
25876 Saulsville 250 .... C7
25917 Scarbro 800 .... D7
24975 Seebert 100 .... F6
25181 Seth 950 .... C6
26761 Shanks 500 .... J4
25182 Sharon 450 .... D6
25183 Sharples 250 .... C7
25443 Shepherdstown 1,791 .... L4
26173 Sherman 104 .... C5
26431 Shinnston 3,059 .... F4
26434 Shirley 275 .... E4
25562 Shoals 150 .... B6
26638 Shock 200 .... D5
†26164 Silverton 250 .... C5
26435 Simpson 250 .... F4
24976 Sinks Grove 156 .... F7
25320 Sissonville 450 .... C5
26175 Sistersville 2,367 .... D3
25920 Slab Fork 210 .... D7
25444 Slanesville 250 .... K4
26436 Smithburg 130 .... E4
25186 Smithers 1,482 .... D6
26437 Smithfield 278 .... E4
26178 Smithville 200 .... D4
24977 Smoot 300 .... E7
25921 Sophia 1,216 .... D7
25303 South Charleston 15,968 .... C6
25922 Spanishburg 550 .... D8
25276 Spencer⊙ 2,799 .... D5
25693 Sprigg 225 .... B7
26763 Springfield 250 .... J4
25565 Spurlockville 250 .... B6
24884 Squire 900 .... C8
26505 Star City 1,464 .... F3
25279 Statts Mills 400 .... C5
25188 Stickney 150 .... D7
25645 Stirrat 250 .... C7
26301 Stonewood 2,058 .... F4
24979 Stony Bottom 50 .... F6
25280 Stumptown 125 .... E5
26651 Summersville⊙ 2,972 .... E6
25446 Summit Point 455 .... K4
25932 Surveyor 300 .... D7
26601 Sutton⊙ 1,192 .... E5
26690 Swiss 500 .... D6

25647 Switzer 1,034 .... B7
25193 Sylvester 256 .... C6
24981 Talcott 800 .... E7
26237 Tallmansville 140 .... F5
26179 Tanner 375 .... E5
26764 Terra Alta 1,946 .... H4
26640 Tesla 300 .... E5
25694 Thacker 525 .... B7
26292 Thomas 747 .... H4
26440 Thornton 200 .... G4
24888 Thorpe 600 .... D8
26765 Three Churches 350 .... J4
25936 Thurmond 67 .... D7
26691 Tioga 825 .... E6
26059 Triadelphia 1,461 .... E2
26443 Troy 110 .... E4
26444 Tunnelton 510 .... G4
25203 Turtle Creek 566 .... C6
25205 Uneeda 700 .... C6
25447 Unger 300 .... K4
24983 Union⊙ 743 .... E7
26266 Upperglade 750 .... F6
26866 Upper Tract 155 .... H5
26445 Vadis 130 .... E4
26293 Valley Bend 950 .... F5
26060 Valley Grove 597 .... E2
26294 Valley Head 900 .... G5
25206 Van 800 .... C7
25696 Varney 750 .... B7
25649 Verdunville 950 .... B7
25938 Victor 500 .... D6
26105 Vienna 11,618 .... D4
24891 Vivian 500 .... D8
26238 Volga 125 .... F4
25697 Vulcan 130 .... B7
26589 Wadestown 300 .... F3
24984 Waiteville 230 .... F8
26180 Walker 100 .... D4
26448 Wallace 325 .... E4
25286 Walton 550 .... D5
26590 Wana 150 .... F3
24892 War 2,158 .... C8
26851 Wardensville 241 .... J4
26181 Washington 450 .... C4
26184 Waverly 500 .... D4
25570 Wayne⊙ 1,495 .... B6
26288 Webster Springs⊙ 939 .... F6
26062 Weirton 25,371 .... E2
Weirton-Steubenville‡ 163,099 .... E2
24801 Welch⊙ 3,885 .... C8
26070 Wellsburg⊙ 3,963 .... E2
25287 West Columbia 245 .... B5
25571 West Hamlin 643 .... B6
26074 West Liberty 744 .... E2
25601 West Logan 630 .... C7
26451 West Milford 510 .... F4
26452 Weston⊙ 6,250 .... F4
26505 Westover 4,884 .... G3
26456 West Union⊙ 1,090 .... E4
25651 Wharncliffe 900 .... C7
25208 Wharton 450 .... C7
26003 Wheeling⊙ 43,070 .... E2
Wheeling‡ 185,566 .... E2
24986 White Sulphur Springs 3,371 .... F7
25209 Whitesville 689 .... C6
26296 Whitmer 400 .... G5
25211 Widen 230 .... E6
26767 Wiley Ford 1,224 .... J3
26186 Wileyville 175 .... E3
25653 Wilkinson 975 .... B7

24991 Williamsburg 350 .... F7
25661 Williamson⊙ 5,219 .... B7
26187 Williamstown 3,095 .... C4
26461 Wilsonburg 350 .... F4
25699 Wilsondale 250 .... B7
26075 Windsor Heights 800 .... E2
25213 Winfield⊙ 329 .... C5
25214 Winifrede 750 .... C6
25942 Winona 250 .... E6
26462 Wolf Summit 750 .... F4
†26257 Womelsdorf (Coalton) 306 .... G5
25572 Woodville 300 .... C6
26591 Worthington 329 .... F4
25573 Yawkey 985 .... C6
26865 Yellow Spring 280 .... J4
25654 Yolyn 400 .... C7

OTHER FEATURES

Big Sandy (riv.) A6
Bluestone (lake) E7
Buckhannon (riv.) F5
Cacapon (riv.) J4
Cheat (riv.) G3
Cherry (riv.) E6
Chesapeake and Ohio Canal Nat'l Hist. Pa J3
Clear Fork, Guyandotte (riv.) C7
Coal (riv.) C6
Dry Fork (riv.) C8
Dry Fork (riv.) G5
East Lynn (lake) B6
Elk (riv.) D6
Fish (creek) E3
Gauley (riv.) D6
Greenbrier (riv.) F6
Guyandotte (riv.) B6
Harpers Ferry Nat'l Hist. Park L4
Hughes (riv.) D4
Kanawha (riv.) C5
Little Kanawha (riv.) D5
Meadow (riv.) E6
Mill (creek) C5
Monongahela (riv.) G3
Mount Storm (lake) H4
Mud (riv.) B6
New (riv.) E7
North (riv.) J4
Ohio (riv.) B5
Patterson (creek) J4
Pigeon (creek) B7
Pocatalico (riv.) C5
Pond Fork (riv.) C6
Potomac (riv.) L3
Potts (creek) F7
Reedy (creek) D5
Shavers Fork (riv.) G5
Shenandoah (riv.) K4
Spruce Knob (mt.) G5
Spruce Knob-Seneca Rocks Nat'l Rec. Area H5
Stony (riv.) H4
Summersville (lake) E6
Sutton (lake) F5
Tug Fork (riv.) B7
Twelvepole (creek) A6
Tygart (lake) G4
Tygart Valley (riv.) F5
West Fork (riv.) E5
Williams (riv.) F6

⊙County seat.
‡Population of metropolitan area.
† Zip of nearest p.o. * Multiple zips.

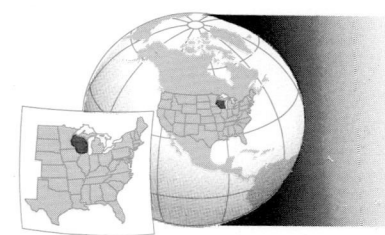

AREA 56,153 sq. mi. (145,436 sq. km.)
POPULATION 4,705,521
CAPITAL Madison
LARGEST CITY Milwaukee
HIGHEST POINT Timms Hill 1,951 ft. (595 m.)
SETTLED IN 1670
ADMITTED TO UNION May 29, 1848
POPULAR NAME Badger State
STATE FLOWER Wood Violet
STATE BIRD Robin

COUNTIES

Adams 13,457 .... G7
Ashland 16,783 .... E3
Barron 38,730 .... C5
Bayfield 13,822 .... D3
Brown 175,280 .... L7
Buffalo 14,309 .... C7
Burnett 12,340 .... B4
Calumet 30,867 .... K7
Chippewa 52,127 .... D5
Clark 32,910 .... E6
Columbia 43,222 .... H9
Crawford 16,556 .... E9
Dane 323,545 .... H9
Dodge 75,064 .... J9
Door 25,029 .... M6
Douglas 44,421 .... C3
Dunn 34,314 .... C6
Eau Claire 78,805 .... D6
Florence 4,172 .... K4
Fond du Lac 88,964 .... K8
Forest 9,044 .... J4
Grant 51,736 .... E10
Green 30,012 .... G10
Green Lake 18,370 .... H8
Iowa 19,802 .... F9
Iron 6,730 .... F3
Jackson 16,831 .... E7
Jefferson 66,152 .... J9
Juneau 21,039 .... F8
Kenosha 123,137 .... K10
Kewaunee 19,539 .... L6
La Crosse 91,056 .... D8
Lafayette 17,412 .... F10
Langlade 19,978 .... H5
Lincoln 26,555 .... G5
Manitowoc 82,918 .... L7
Marathon 111,270 .... G6
Marinette 39,314 .... K5
Marquette 11,672 .... H8
Menominee 3,373 .... J5
Milwaukee 964,988 .... L9
Monroe 35,074 .... E8
Oconto 28,947 .... K6
Oneida 31,216 .... G4
Outagamie 128,799 ...... K7
Ozaukee 66,981 .... L9
Pepin 7,477 .... C6
Pierce 31,149 .... B6
Polk 32,351 .... B5
Portage 57,420 .... G6
Price 15,788 .... F4
Racine 173,132 .... K10
Richland 17,476 ...... F9
Rock 139,420 .... H10
Rusk 15,589 .... D5
Saint Croix 43,262 .. B5
Sauk 43,469 .... G9
Sawyer 12,843 ...... D4
Shawano 35,928 .... J6
Sheboygan 100,935 . L8
Taylor 18,817 ...... E5
Trempealeau 26,158 . D7
Vernon 25,642 ...... E8
Vilas 16,535 .... G3
Walworth 71,507 ... J10
Washburn 13,174 .. C4
Washington 84,848 . K9
Waukesha 280,080 . K9
Waupaca 42,831 ... J6
Waushara 18,526 .. H7
Winnebago 131,722 . J8
Wood 72,799 ...... F7

CITIES and TOWNS

Zip   Name/Pop.   Key

54405 Abbotsford 1,901 .... F6
53910 Adams 1,744 .... G8
53001 Adell 545 .... L8
53501 Afton 225 .... H10
53502 Albany 1,051 .... G10
†53534 Albion 300 .... H10
54201 Algoma 3,656 .... M6
53002 Allenton 915 .... K9
†54301 Allouez 14,882 ..... L7
54610 Alma⊙ 876 .... C7
54611 Alma Center 454 ... E7
54805 Almena 526 .... B5
54909 Almond 477 .... G7
54720 Altoona 4,393 ..... C6
54102 Amberg 875 ...... K5
54001 Amery 2,404 ..... B5
54406 Amherst 701 .... H7
54407 Amherst Junction 225 . H7
54408 Aniwa 273 .... H6
54409 Antigo⊙ 8,653 ... H5
54911 Appleton⊙ 58,913 . J7
   Appleton-Oshkosh‡ 291,325 J7
†54568 Arbor Vitae 900 .. G4
54612 Arcadia 2,109 .... D7
53503 Arena 451 .... G9
54511 Argonne 600 ..... J4
53504 Argyle 720 ...... G10
54721 Arkansaw 400 ... B6

53911 Arlington 440 .... H9
54103 Armstrong Creek 615 ... K4
54410 Arpin 361 .... G6
53003 Ashippun 750 .... H1
54806 Ashland⊙ 9,115 ...... E2
54304 Ashwaubenon 14,486 . K7
54411 Athens 988 .... G5
54412 Auburndale 641 ..... F6
54722 Augusta 1,560 ...... D6
53506 Avoca 505 .... F9
†53520 Avon 120 .... H10
54413 Babcock 250 ...... F7
53801 Bagley 317 .... D10
54202 Baileys Harbor 250 . M5
54002 Baldwin 1,620 .... B6
54810 Balsam Lake⊙ 749 . B5
54921 Bancroft 355 ..... G7
54614 Bangor 1,012 .... E8
53913 Baraboo⊙ 8,081 . G9
53507 Barneveld 579 ... F10
54812 Barron⊙ 2,595 .. C5
†53001 Batavia 125 .... K8
54723 Bay City 543 ... B6
54814 Bayfield 778 ... E2
†53201 Bayside 4,724 . M1
54922 Bear Creek 454 . J6
53916 Beaver Dam 14,149 . J9
53802 Beetown 150 .... E10
53004 Belgium 892 .... L8
†54631 Bell Center 124 . E9
53508 Belleville 1,302 . G10
53510 Belmont 826 ... F10
53511 Beloit 35,207 .. H10
53803 Benton 983 .... F10
54923 Berlin 5,478 .. H8
†54410 Bethel 210 ... F6
54440 Bevent 200 .. H6
53103 Big Bend 1,345 . K2
54926 Big Falls 107 . H6
54817 Birchwood 437 . C4
54414 Birnamwood 688 . H6
†54494 Biron 698 .... G7
54106 Black Creek 1,097 . K7
53515 Black Earth 1,145 . G9
54615 Black River Falls⊙ 3,434 . E7
†54541 Blackwell 550 . J4
54616 Blair 1,142 .... D7
53516 Blanchardville 803 . G10
54617 Bloom City 167 . E8
54724 Bloomer 3,342 . D5
53804 Bloomington 743 . E10
53517 Blue Mounds 387 . G9
53518 Blue River 412 . E9
†53581 Boaz 161 ..... E9
†53105 Bohners Lake 1,507 . K10
54107 Bonduel 1,160 .. K6
53805 Boscobel 2,662 .. E9
54512 Boulder Junction 780 . G3
54416 Bowler 339 .... J6
54725 Boyceville 862 . C5
54726 Boyd 660 ...... E6
54203 Branch 300 .... L7
53919 Brandon 862 ... J8
54513 Brantwood 500 . F4
53920 Briggsville 250 . H8
54110 Brillion 2,907 .. L7
53520 Brodhead 3,153 . G10
54417 Brokaw 298 .... G5
53005 Brookfield 34,035 . K1
53521 Brooklyn 627 ... H10
53209 Brown Deer 12,921 . L1
†53105 Brown's Lake 1,648 . K3
53006 Brownsville 433 . J8
53522 Browntown 284 . G10
54819 Bruce 905 ..... D5
54820 Brule 335 ..... C2
54204 Brussels 500 .. L6
54622 Buffalo 894 ... C7
†53105 Burlington 8,385 . K10
53922 Burnett 260 .. J9
53007 Butler 2,059 . K1
54514 Butternut 438 . E3
53009 Byron 40 ..... K8
54821 Cable 227 ... D3
54727 Cadott 1,247 . D6
53923 Cambria 680 . H8
53523 Cambridge 844 . H9
54822 Cameron 1,115 . C5
†53019 Campbellsport 1,740 . K8
54618 Camp Douglas 589 . F8
53109 Camp Lake 2,060 . K10
54823 Canton 100 ... C5
54928 Caroline 450 . J6
53011 Cascade 615 . K8
54205 Casco 484 ... L6
54619 Cashton 827 . E8
54806 Cassville 1,270 . E10
54620 Cataract 200 . E7
54515 Catawba 205 . E4
54206 Cato 85 ..... L7
53924 Cazenovia 259 . F8
54111 Cecil 445 ... K6
53012 Cedarburg 9,005 . L9
53013 Cedar Grove 1,420 . L8
54824 Centuria 711 . A5

54621 Chaseburg 279 .... D8
54419 Chelsea 120 .... F5
†53029 Chenequa 532 .... J1
54728 Chetek 1,931 .... C5
54420 Chili 185 .... F6
53014 Chilton⊙ 2,965 .. K7
54729 Chippewa Falls⊙ 12,270 . D6
54004 Clayton 425 ..... B5
54005 Clear Lake 899 .. B5
53015 Cleveland 1,270 . L8
53525 Clinton 1,751 .. J10
54929 Clintonville 4,567 . J6
53016 Clyman 317 .... J9
53526 Cobb 409 ..... F10
54622 Cochrane 512 . C7
54421 Colby 1,496 .. F6
54112 Coleman 852 . L5
54730 Colfax 1,149 . C6
54930 Coloma 367 . H7
53925 Columbus 4,049 . H9
54113 Combined Locks 2,573 . K7
†53147 Como 1,376 ..... K10
54519 Conover 480 ... H3
54731 Conrath 86 .... E5
54623 Coon Valley 758 . E8
54732 Cornell 1,583 . D5
54827 Cornucopia 250 . D2
54520 Crandon⊙ 1,969 . H4
54114 Crivitz 1,041 . L5
53528 Cross Plains 2,156 . G9
53807 Cuba City 2,129 . F10
53110 Cudahy 19,547 . M2
54829 Cumberland 1,983 . C4
54422 Curtiss 127 .. F6
54006 Cushing 150 . A4
54931 Dale 410 .... J7
54733 Dallas 477 .. C5
53926 Dalton 300 . H8
53529 Dane 518 ... G9
53114 Darien 1,152 . J10
53530 Darlington⊙ 2,300 . F10
53531 Deerfield 1,466 . H9
54007 Deer Park 232 . B5
53532 De Forest 3,367 . H9
53018 Delafield 4,083 . J1
53115 Delavan 5,684 . J10
†53115 Delavan Lake 2,082 . J10
†54856 Delta 35 .... D3
54208 Denmark 1,475 . L7
54115 De Pere 14,892 . K7
†54663 De Soto 318 . D9
54014 Diamond Bluff 100 . A6
53808 Dickeyville 1,156 . E10
54625 Dodge 185 .. D7
53533 Dodgeville⊙ 3,458 . F10
54425 Dorchester 613 . F5
53118 Dousman 1,153 . J1
54734 Downing 242 . B5
54735 Downsville 200 . C6
53928 Doylestown 294 . H9
54009 Dresser 670 . A5
54832 Drummond 200 . D3
54736 Durand⊙ 2,047 . C6
53119 Eagle 1,008 . H2
54521 Eagle River⊙ 1,326 . H4
54626 Eastman 371 . D9
53120 East Troy 2,385 . J2
54701 Eau Claire⊙ 51,509 . D6
   Eau Claire‡ 130,507 . D6
53019 Eden 534 ... K8
54426 Edgar 1,194 . G6
53534 Edgerton 4,335 . H10
54209 Egg Harbor 238 . M5
54427 Eland 230 .. H6
54428 Elcho 500 .. H5
54429 Elderon 191 . H6
54932 Eldorado 200 . J8
54738 Eleva 593 .. D6
53020 Elkhart Lake 1,054 . L8
53121 Elkhorn⊙ 4,605 . J10
54739 Elk Mound 737 . C6
54210 Ellison Bay 112 . M5
54011 Ellsworth⊙ 2,143 . A6
53122 Elm Grove 6,735 . K1
54011 Elmwood 885 . B6
†53401 Elmwood Park 483 . M3
53929 Elroy 1,504 . F8
54430 Elton 150 .. J5
54933 Embarrass 496 . J6
53930 Endeavor 335 . G8
54211 Ephraim 319 . M5
54627 Ettrick 462 . D7
53536 Evansville 2,835 . H10
54835 Exeland 219 . D4
54741 Fairchild 577 . D6
53931 Fair Water 310 . J8
54742 Fall Creek 1,148 . D6
53932 Fall River 850 . H9
54840 Falun 95 ... A4
54206 Fence 200 . K4
53809 Fennimore 2,212 . E9
54431 Fenwood 165 . F6
54628 Ferryville 227 . D9
54524 Fifield 310 . F4
54212 Fish Creek 119 . M5
54121 Florence⊙ 780 . K4

54935 Fond du Lac⊙ 35,863 ...... K8
53125 Fontana 1,764 .... J10
53537 Footville 794 .... H10
54123 Forest Junction 140 . K7
54213 Forestville 455 ..... L6
53538 Fort Atkinson 9,785 . J10
54629 Fountain City 963 ... C7
54836 Foxboro 360 .... B2
53933 Fox Lake 1,373 .... J8
†53117 Fox Point 7,649 ... M1
54214 Francis Creek 589 . L7
53132 Franklin 16,871 ... L2
54837 Frederic 1,039 .... B4
53021 Fredonia 1,437 ... L8
54940 Fremont 510 ..... J7
53934 Friendship⊙ 744 . G8
53935 Friesland 267 ... H8
54630 Galesville 1,239 . D7
54631 Gays Mills 627 .. E9
53127 Genesee Depot 350 . J2
54632 Genoa 283 ...... D9
53128 Genoa City 1,202 . K11
53022 Germantown 10,729 . K1
54124 Gillett 1,356 ... K6

54433 Gilman 436 .... E5
54743 Gilmanton 300 ..... C7
54435 Gleason 200 ...... G5
53023 Glenbeulah 423 .. L8
†53209 Glendale 13,882 . M1
54526 Glen Flora 83 .. E4
53810 Glen Haven 160 . E10
54013 Glenwood City 950 . B5
54527 Glidden 940 .... E3
54125 Goodman 875 ... K4
54838 Gordon 600 ..... C3
53540 Gotham 250 .... F9
53024 Grafton 8,381 .. L9
53936 Grand Marsh 725 . G8
54839 Grand View 447 . D3
54436 Granton 399 .... E6
54840 Grantsburg⊙ 1,153 . A4
53541 Gratiot 280 .... F10
*54301 Green Bay⊙ 87,899 . K6
   Green Bay‡ 175,280 . K6
53129 Greendale 16,928 . L2
53220 Greenfield 31,467 . L2
54941 Green Lake⊙ 1,208 . H8
54126 Greenleaf 300 ... L7

54942 Greenville 900 .... J7
54437 Greenwood 1,124 ..... E6
54128 Gresham 534 .... J6
54014 Hager City 110 .... A6
53130 Hales Corners 7,110 . K2
54015 Hammond 991 .... A6
54943 Hancock 419 ..... H7
54529 Harshaw 87 ...... G4
53027 Hartford 7,046 .. K9
53029 Hartland 5,559 .. J1
54440 Hatley 300 ..... H6
54841 Haugen 251 .... C4
54530 Hawkins 407 ... E4
54842 Hawthorne 200 . C3
54843 Hayward⊙ 1,698 . D3
53811 Hazel Green 1,282 . F11
54531 Hazelhurst 630 . G4
†53538 Hebron 450 .... J10
53137 Helenville 300 . J10
54844 Herbster 100 .. D2
54441 Hewitt 470 .... F6
53543 Highland 860 .. F9
54129 Hilbert 1,176 . K7
†54511 Hiles 350 .... J4

(continued on following page)

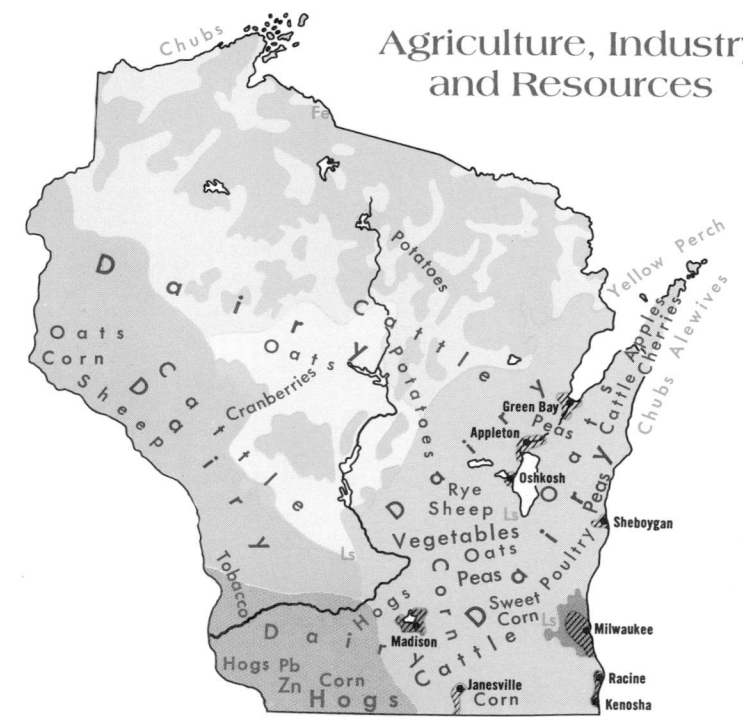

Agriculture, Industry and Resources

DOMINANT LAND USE

- Specialized Dairy
- Dairy, Hay, Potatoes
- Dairy, General Farming
- Hogs, Dairy
- Dairy, Livestock
- Forests
- Urban Areas

MAJOR MINERAL OCCURRENCES

Fe Iron Ore   Pb Lead
Ls Limestone   Zn Zinc

 Major Industrial Areas

54634 Hillsboro 1,263 F8
53031 Hingham 250 K8
54635 Hixton 364 E7
54745 Holcombe 200 D5
53544 Hollandale 271 G10
54636 Holmen 2,411 D8
53138 Honey Creek 300 J3
53032 Horicon 3,584 J9
54944 Hortonville 2,016 J7
†55082 Houlton 915 A5
54303 Howard 8,240 K6
53081 Howards Grove-Millersville 1,838 L8
53033 Hubertus 600 K1
54016 Hudson⊙ 5,434 A6
54746 Humbird 190 E6
54534 Hurley⊙ 2,015 F3
53034 Hustisford 874 J9
54637 Hustler 170 F8
54747 Independence 1,180 D7
54945 Iola 957 H6
54536 Iron Belt 300 F3
53035 Iron Ridge 766 K9
54847 Iron River 878 D2
†53941 Ironton 206 F8
53036 Ixonia 525 H1
53037 Jackson 1,817 K9
†54235 Jacksonport 150 M6
53545 Janesville⊙ 51,071 H10
Janesville-Beloit‡ 139,420 H10
53549 Jefferson⊙ 5,647 J10
54748 Jim Falls 100 D5
53038 Johnson Creek 1,136 J9
53550 Juda 500 H10
54443 Junction City 523 G6
53039 Juneau⊙ 2,045 J9
53139 Kansasville 150 L3
54130 Kaukauna 11,310 K7
†53050 Kekoskee 224 J8
54215 Kellnersville 369 L7
54638 Kendall 486 F8
54537 Kennan 194 F5
*53140 Kenosha⊙ 77,685 M3
Kenosha‡ 123,137 M3
54135 Keshena⊙ 980 J6
53040 Kewaskum 2,381 K8
54216 Kewaunee⊙ 2,801 M7
53042 Kiel 3,083 L8
53812 Kieler 800 E10
54136 Kimberly 5,881 K7
53939 Kingston 328 H8
54749 Knapp 419 B6
†54455 Knowlton 127 G6
53044 Kohler 1,651 L8
53147 Krakow 345 K6
54538 Lac du Flambeau 500 G4
†53066 Lac La Belle 289 H1
54601 La Crosse⊙ 48,347 D8
La Crosse‡ 91,056 D8
54848 Ladysmith⊙ 3,826 D5
54639 La Farge 746 E8
53940 Lake Delton 1,158 G8
53147 Lake Geneva 5,612 K10
53551 Lake Mills 3,670 H9
54849 Lake Nebagamon 780 C3
54539 Lake Tomahawk 660 H4
†54494 Lake Wazeecha 2,176 G7
†54729 Lake Wissota 1,788 D6
54138 Lakewood 425 K5
53813 Lancaster⊙ 4,076 E10
54540 Land O'Lakes 786 H3
53046 Lannon 987 K1
53941 La Valle 412 F8
53047 Lebanon 250 H1
54139 Lena 585 K6
†54656 Leon 100 E8
54948 Leopolis 200 J6
54851 Lewis 200 B4
53942 Limeridge 191 F9
53553 Linden 395 F10
54140 Little Chute 7,907 K7
53554 Livingston 642 E10
53555 Lodi 1,959 G9
53943 Loganville 239 F9
†54970 Lohrville 336 H7
53048 Lomira 1,446 J8
53556 Lone Rock 577 F9
54542 Long Lake 150 J4
53557 Lowell 326 J9
54446 Loyal 1,252 E6
54447 Lublin 142 E5
54853 Luck 997 B4
54217 Luxemburg 1,040 L6
53944 Lyndon Station 375 F8
54640 Lynxville 174 D9
53148 Lyons 550 K10
*53701 Madison (cap.)⊙ 170,616 H9
Madison‡ 323,545 H9
54750 Maiden Rock 172 B6
54949 Manawa 1,205 J7
54220 Manitowoc⊙ 32,547 L7
54226 Maplewood 200 M6
54448 Marathon 1,552 G6
54855 Marengo 130 E3
54227 Maribel 363 L7
54143 Marinette⊙ 11,965 L5
54950 Marion 1,348 J6
53946 Markesan 1,446 J8
53947 Marquette 204 H8
53559 Marshall 2,363 H9
54449 Marshfield 18,290 F6
54856 Mason 102 D3
54450 Mattoon 382 J5
53948 Mauston⊙ 3,284 F8
53050 Mayville 4,333 K9
53560 Mazomanie 1,248 G9
53558 McFarland 3,783 H10
54543 McNaughton 450 H4
54451 Medford⊙ 4,035 F5
54546 Mellen 1,046 E3
54642 Melrose 507 E7
54619 Melvina 117 E8
54952 Menasha 14,728 J7
53051 Menomonee Falls 27,845 K1
54751 Menomonie⊙ 12,769 C6
53092 Mequon 16,193 L1
54452 Merrill⊙ 9,578 G5
54754 Merrillan 587 E7
53561 Merrimac 365 G9
53056 Merton 1,045 K1
53562 Middleton 11,848 G9
54857 Mikana 200 C4
54453 Milan 153 F6
†53038 Milford 35 J9
54454 Milladore 250 G6
54643 Millston 110 E7
54858 Milltown 732 B4
53563 Milton 4,092 J10
*53201 Milwaukee⊙ 636,236 M1
Milwaukee‡ 1,397,143 M1
54644 Mindoro 200 D7
53565 Mineral Point 2,259 F10
54548 Minocqua 950 G4
54859 Minong 557 C3
54228 Mishicot 1,503 L7
54755 Mondovi 2,545 C6
54549 Monico 250 H4
53716 Monona 8,809 H9
53566 Monroe⊙ 10,027 G10
53949 Montello⊙ 1,273 H8
53569 Montfort 616 E10
53570 Monticello 1,021 G10
54550 Montreal 887 F3
53571 Morrisonville 375 G9
54455 Mosinee 3,015 G6
54149 Mountain 250 K5
53057 Mount Calvary 585 K8
53816 Mount Hope 197 D10
53572 Mount Horeb 3,251 G10
54645 Mount Sterling 223 D9
†53572 Mount Vernon 138 G10
53149 Mukwonago 4,014 J2
53573 Muscoda 1,331 F9
53150 Muskego 15,277 K2
53058 Nashotah 513 J1
54646 Necedah 773 F7
54956 Neenah 22,432 J7
54456 Neillsville⊙ 2,780 E6
54457 Nekoosa 2,519 G7
54756 Nelson 389 C7
54458 Nelsonville 199 H7
54150 Neopit 1,065 J6
53059 Neosho 575 J9
54960 Neshkoro 386 H8
54551 Newald 375 J4
54757 New Auburn 466 D5
53151 New Berlin 30,529 K2
53060 Newburg 783 K9
†61075 New Diggings 65 F10
54229 New Franken 150 L6
53574 New Glarus 1,763 G10
53061 New Holstein 3,412 K8
53950 New Lisbon 1,390 F8
54961 New London 6,210 J7
54017 New Richmond 4,306 A5
54151 Niagara 2,079 K4
54152 Nichols 267 K6
†53401 North Bay 219 M3
†54935 North Fond du Lac 3,844 J8
53951 North Freedom 616 G9
†54016 North Hudson 2,218 A5
53064 North Lake 400 J1
53217 North Shore 14,930 M1
54648 Norwalk 517 E8
53154 Oak Creek 16,932 M2
54649 Oakdale 150 F8
53065 Oakfield 990 J8
53066 Oconomowoc 9,909 H1
†53066 Oconomowoc Lake 524 H1
54153 Oconto⊙ 4,505 L6
54154 Oconto Falls 2,500 K6
54962 Ogdensburg 214 J7
54459 Ogema 238 F5
53069 Okauchee 3,958 J1
†53555 Okee 250 H9
†54880 Oliver 253 B2
54963 Omro 2,763 J7
54650 Onalaska 9,249 D8
54155 Oneida 900 K7
54651 Ontario 398 E8
53070 Oostburg 1,647 L8
53575 Oregon 3,876 H10
53576 Orfordville 1,143 H10
54020 Osceola 1,581 A5
54901 Oshkosh⊙ 49,620 J8
54758 Osseo 1,474 D6
54460 Owen 998 F6
53952 Oxford 432 H8
53953 Packwaukee 271 G8
†53168 Paddock Lake 2,207 K10
53156 Palmyra 1,515 H2
53954 Pardeeville 1,594 H8
54552 Park Falls 3,192 F4
†54481 Park Ridge 643 H6
53817 Patch Grove 259 D10
53157 Pell Lake 1,826 K10
54553 Pence 234 F3
54759 Pepin 890 B7
54157 Peshtigo 2,807 L5
53072 Pewaukee 4,637 K1
54554 Phelps 950 H3
54555 Phillips⊙ 1,522 E4
54464 Phlox 150 J5
54465 Pickerel 107 J5
54760 Pigeon Falls 338 D7
54466 Pittsville 810 F7
53577 Plain 676 F9
54966 Plainfield 813 G7
†53017 Plat 120 K1
53818 Platteville 9,580 F10
53158 Pleasant Prairie 950 L10
54467 Plover 5,310 G7
54761 Plum City 505 B6
53073 Plymouth 6,027 L8
†54423 Polonia 200 H6
54864 Poplar 569 C2
53901 Portage⊙ 7,896 G8
54469 Port Edwards 2,077 G7
53074 Port Washington⊙ 8,612 L9
54865 Port Wing 290 D2
53820 Potosi 736 E10
54160 Potter 330 K7
54161 Pound 407 L5
53955 Poynette 1,447 G9
54967 Poy Sippi 425 J7
53821 Prairie du Chien⊙ 5,859 D9
53578 Prairie du Sac 2,145 G9
54762 Prairie Farm 387 C5
54556 Prentice 605 F4
54021 Prescott 2,654 A6
54968 Princeton 1,479 H8
54162 Pulaski 1,875 K6
54164 Pulcifer 35 K6
*53401 Racine⊙ 85,725 M3
Racine‡ 173,132 M3
54867 Radisson 280 D4
53956 Randolph 1,691 H8
53075 Random Lake 1,287 K8
†53126 Raymond 300 L2
54652 Readstown 396 E9
54970 Redgranite 976 J7
53959 Reedsburg 5,038 G8
54230 Reedsville 1,134 L7
53579 Reeseville 649 J9
53580 Rewey 233 F10
54501 Rhinelander⊙ 7,873 H4
54470 Rib Lake 945 F5
54868 Rice Lake 7,691 C5
53581 Richland Center⊙ 4,997 F9
54763 Ridgeland 300 B5
53582 Ridgeway 503 F10
53960 Rio 785 H9
54971 Ripon 7,111 J8
54022 River Falls 9,019 A6
†53201 River Hills 1,642 M1
54023 Roberts 833 A6
53167 Rochester 746 K3
†53523 Rockdale 200 J10
53077 Rockfield 200 L1
54653 Rockland 383 D8
53961 Rock Springs 426 F8
†53178 Rome 200 H1
54974 Rosendale 725 J8
54473 Rosholt 520 H6
54474 Rothschild 3,338 G6
†53583 Roxbury 260 G9
54475 Rudolph 392 G7
†54751 Rusk 40 C6
53079 Saint Cloud 560 K8
54024 Saint Croix Falls 1,497 A5
†53207 Saint Francis 10,042 M2
†54601 Saint Joseph Ridge 450 D8
54232 Saint Nazianz 738 L7
54765 Sand Creek 225 C5
53583 Sauk City 2,703 G9
53080 Saukville 3,494 L9
54559 Saxon 375 F3
54977 Scandinavia 292 H7
54476 Schofield 2,226 H6
†54843 Seeley 68 D3
54654 Seneca 235 E9
53584 Sextonville 225 F9
54165 Seymour 2,530 K6
53585 Sharon 1,280 J11
54166 Shawano⊙ 7,013 J6
53081 Sheboygan⊙ 48,085 L8
Sheboygan‡ 100,935 L8
53085 Sheboygan Falls 5,253 L8
54766 Sheldon 292 D5
54871 Shell Lake⊙ 1,135 C4
54169 Sherwood 372 K7
54170 Shiocton 805 K7
53211 Shorewood 14,327 M1
†53701 Shorewood Hills 1,837 G9
53586 Shullsburg 1,484 F10
53170 Silver Lake 1,598 K10
54872 Siren 896 B4
54234 Sister Bay 564 M5
53086 Slinger 1,612 K9
54655 Soldiers Grove 622 E9
54873 Solon Springs 590 C3
54025 Somerset 860 A5
53172 South Milwaukee 21,069 M2
53587 South Wayne 495 G10
54656 Sparta⊙ 6,934 E8
54479 Spencer 1,754 F6
54801 Spooner 2,365 B4
53588 Spring Green 1,265 G9
54767 Spring Valley 982 B6
54768 Stanley 2,095 E6
54026 Star Prairie 420 A5
54480 Stetsonville 487 F5
54657 Steuben 175 E9
54481 Stevens Point⊙ 22,970 G7
54172 Stiles 300 L6
53825 Stitzer 190 E10
53088 Stockbridge 567 K7
54769 Stockholm 104 B7
54658 Stoddard 762 D8
54876 Stone Lake 210 C4
53589 Stoughton 7,589 H10
54484 Stratford 1,385 F6
54770 Strum 944 D6
54235 Sturgeon Bay⊙ 8,847 M6
53177 Sturtevant 4,130 M3
54173 Suamico 900 K6
53178 Sullivan 434 H1
54485 Summit Lake 250 H5
53590 Sun Prairie 12,931 H9
54880 Superior⊙ 29,571 C2
Superior-Duluth‡ 266,650 C2
†54880 Superior Village 580 B2
54174 Suring 581 K5
53089 Sussex 3,482 K1
53090 Taycheedah 350 K8
54659 Taylor 411 E7
†53820 Tennyson 476 E10
53091 Theresa 766 K8
53092 Thiensville 3,341 L1
54771 Thorp 1,635 E6
54562 Three Lakes 950 H4
54486 Tigerton 865 H6
54240 Tisch Mills 315 L7
54660 Tomah 7,204 F8
54487 Tomahawk 3,527 G5
54563 Tony 146 E5
54888 Trego 280 C4
54661 Trempealeau 956 C8
54662 Tunnel City 200 E7
54889 Turtle Lake 762 B5
53181 Twin Lakes 3,474 K11

Topography

54241 Two Rivers 13,354 M7
53962 Union Center 216 F8
53182 Union Grove 3,517 L3
54488 Unity 418 F6
54245 Valders 984 L7
53593 Verona 3,336 G9
54489 Vesper 554 F7
54664 Viola 696 E8
54665 Viroqua⊙ 3,716 D8
54566 Wabeno 800 J5
53093 Waldo 416 L8
53183 Wales 1,992 J1
53184 Walworth 1,607 J10
54666 Warrens 300 E7
54890 Wascott 70 C3
54891 Washburn⊙ 2,080 D2
54246 Washington Island 550 M5
53185 Waterford 2,051 K3
53594 Waterloo 2,393 J9
53094 Watertown 18,113 J9
53021 Waubeka 450 L9
53186 Waukesha⊙ 50,365 K1
53597 Waunakee 3,866 G9
54981 Waupaca⊙ 4,472 H7
53963 Waupun 8,132 J8
54401 Wausau⊙ 32,426 G6
Wausau‡ 111,270 G6
54177 Wausaukee 648 K5
54982 Wautoma⊙ 1,629 H7
53226 Wauwatosa 51,308 L1
53826 Wauzeka 580 E9
†54126 Wayside 140 L7
54893 Webster 610 B4
53214 West Allis 63,982 L1
†53913 West Baraboo 846 G9
53095 West Bend⊙ 21,484 K9
54490 Westboro 750 F5
54667 Westby 1,797 E8
53964 Westfield 1,033 H8
†53201 West Milwaukee 3,535 L1
†54476 Weston 8,775 G6
54669 West Salem 3,276 D8
54983 Weyauwega 1,549 H7
54895 Weyerhaeuser 313 D5
54896 Wheeler 221 C5
54773 Whitehall⊙ 1,530 D7
54491 White Lake 309 J5
54247 Whitelaw 649 L7
53190 Whitewater 11,520 J10
†54481 Whiting 2,050 H7
54984 Wild Rose 741 H7
53191 Williams Bay 1,763 J10
54027 Wilson 155 B6
54670 Wilton 465 F8
54567 Winchester 300 G3
53185 Wind Lake 900 K2
†53401 Wind Point 1,695 M2
53598 Windsor 827 H9
54985 Winnebago 1,433 J8
54986 Winneconne 1,935 J7
54896 Winter 376 E4
53965 Wisconsin Dells 2,521 G8
54494 Wisconsin Rapids⊙ 17,995 G7
54498 Withee 509 E6
54499 Wittenberg 997 H6
53968 Wonewoc 842 F8
53827 Woodman 116 E9
54568 Woodruff 850 G4
54028 Woodville 725 B6
54180 Wrightstown 1,169 K7
54671 Wyeville 163 F7
53969 Wyocena 548 H9
54182 Zachow 135 K6

OTHER FEATURES

Apostle (isls.) F2
Apostle Islands Nat'l Lakeshore E1
Apple (riv.) A5
Bad River Ind. Res. E2
Bardon (lake) C3
Bear (isl.) E1
Beaver Dam (lake) J9
Beulah (lake) J2
Big Eau Pleine (res.) G6
Big Muskego (lake) L2
Big Rib (riv.) G5
Black (riv.) E7
Butternut (lake) J4
Castle Rock (lake) G8
Cat (isl.) E1
Chambers (isl.) M5
Chequamegon (bay) E2
Chetac (lake) D4
Chippewa (lake) D4
Chippewa (riv.) B7
Clam (lake) B4
Clam (riv.) A4
Dells, The (valley) G8
Denoon (lake) K2
Du Bay (lake) G6
Eagle (lake) H2
Eagle (lake) L6
Eau Claire (riv.) D6
Flambeau (riv.) E4
Flambeau Flowage (res.) F3
Fox (riv.) K2
Fox (riv.) L6
General Mitchell Field M2
Geneva (lake) K10
Golden (lake) H1
Green (bay) L6
Grindstone (lake) C4
Holcombe Flowage (res.) D5
Jump (riv.) E5
Kegonsa (lake) H10
Kickapoo (riv.) E9
Koshkonong (lake) H10
La Belle (lake) H1
Lac Court Oreilles Ind. Res. D4
Lac du Flambeau Ind. Res. G3
Long (lake) C4
Madeline (isl.) E2
Mendota (lake) H9
Menominee (riv.) L5
Metonga (lake) J4
Michigan (isl.) F2
Michigan (lake) M9
Mississippi (riv.) D10
Montreal (riv.) F2
Moose (lake) E3
Moose (lake) F3
Nagawicka (lake) J1
Namekagon (lake) D3
Namekagon (riv.) C3
North (lake) J1
Oak (isl.) E2
Oconomowoc (lake) H1
Oconto (riv.) K5
Okauchee (lake) J1
Outer (isl.) F1
Owen (lake) D3
Pecatonica (riv.) H11
Pelican (lake) H4
Pepin (lake) B7
Peshtigo (riv.) K5
Petenwell (lake) G7
Pewaukee (lake) K1
Phantom (lake) J2
Pine (lake) J1
Porte des Morts (str.) N5
Poygan (lake) J7
Puckaway (lake) H8
Red Cedar (riv.) C5
Red Cliff Ind. Res. E2
Rib (mt.) G6
Rock (riv.) J9
Round (lake) F4
Round (lake) D3
Saint Croix (lake) A6
Saint Croix (riv.) A4
Saint Croix Flowage (res.) C3
Saint Louis (riv.) A2
Sand (isl.) D2
Shawano (lake) K6
Shell (lake) C4
Spider (lake) D3
Stockbridge Ind. Res. J6
Stockton (isl.) F2
Sugar (riv.) H10
Sugarbush Hill (mt.) J4
Superior (lake) F1
Thunder (lake) H4
Tichigan (lake) K2
Timms Hill (mt.) F5
Trempealeau (riv.) C7
Trout (lake) G3
Vieux Desert (lake) J3
Washington (isl.) M5
Willow (res.) F4
Wind (lake) K2
Winnebago (lake) K7
Wisconsin (riv.) E9
Wolf (riv.) J5
Yellow (lake) B4
Yellow (riv.) F7

⊙County seat.
‡Population of metropolitan area.
† Zip of nearest p.o. * Multiple zips.

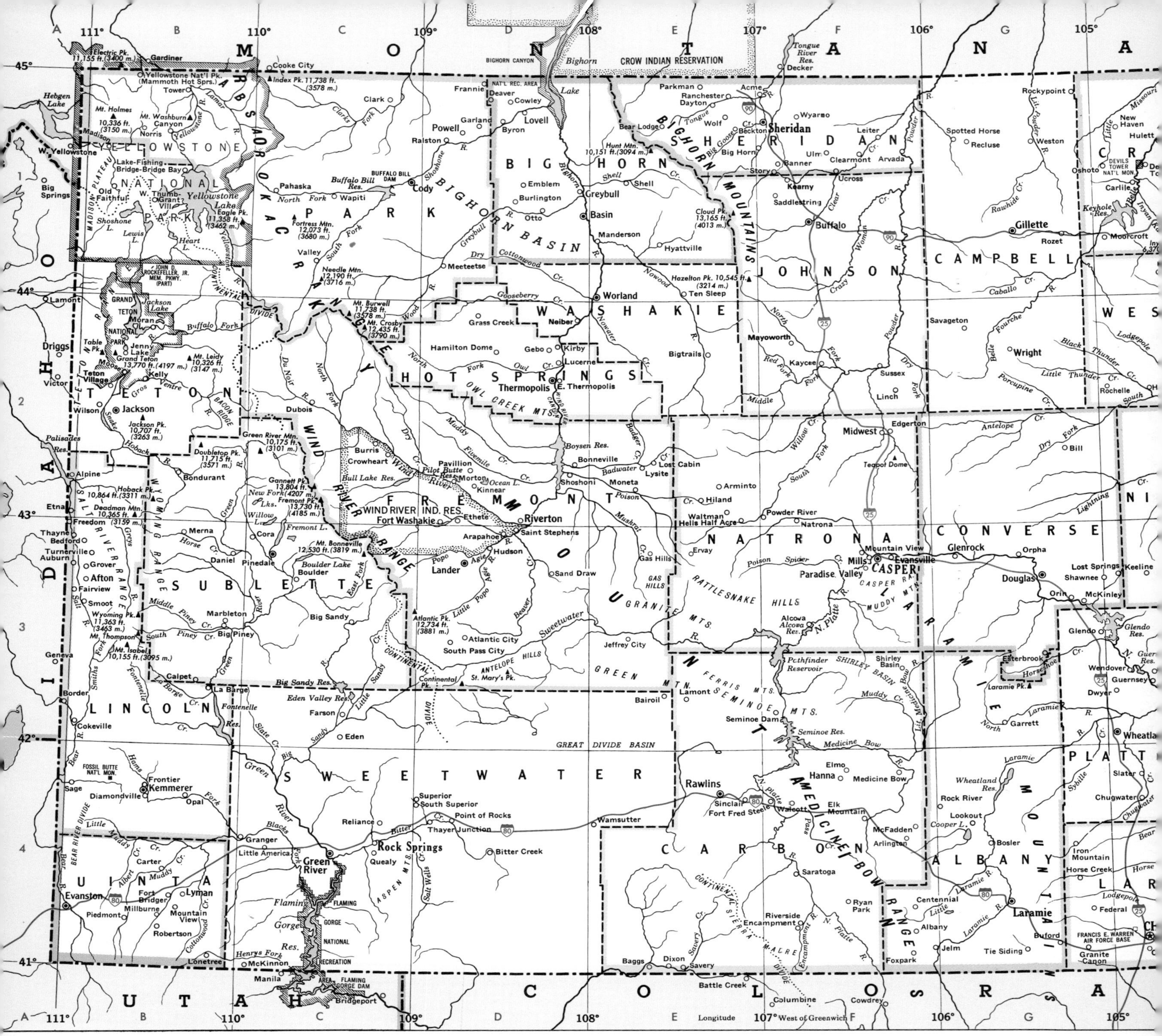

Agriculture, Industry and Resources

DOMINANT LAND USE

- ☐ Specialized Wheat
- ☐ Specialized Dairy
- ☐ General Farming, Livestock, Special Crops
- ☐ Sugar Beets, Dry Beans, Livestock, General Farming
- ☐ Range Livestock
- ☐ Forests
- ☐ Nonagricultural Land

MAJOR MINERAL OCCURRENCES

C Coal	G Natural Gas	So Soda Ash
Cl Clay	O Petroleum	U Uranium
Fe Iron Ore	P Phosphates	V Vanadium
	⚡ Water Power	

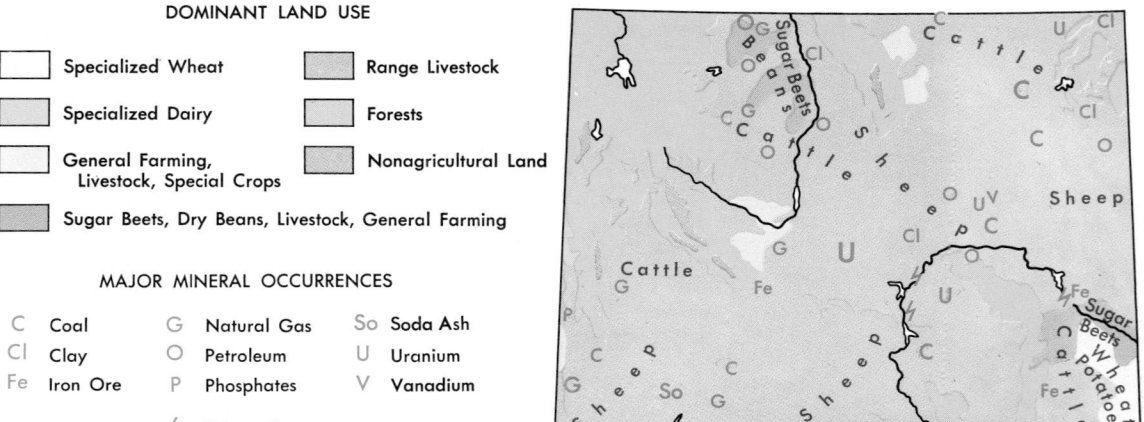

COUNTIES

Albany 29,062	G4
Big Horn 11,896	E1
Campbell 24,367	G1
Carbon 21,896	F4
Converse 14,069	G3
Crook 5,308	H1
Fremont 38,992	D2
Goshen 12,040	H4
Hot Springs 5,710	D2
Johnson 6,700	F1
Laramie 68,649	H4
Lincoln 12,177	B3
Natrona 71,856	F3
Niobrara 2,924	H2
Park 21,639	C1
Platte 11,975	H4
Sheridan 25,048	F1
Sublette 4,548	C3
Sweetwater 41,723	D4
Teton 9,355	B2
Uinta 13,021	B4
Washakie 9,496	E2
Weston 7,106	H2

CITIES and TOWNS

Zip	Name/Pop.	Key
83110	Afton 1,481	B3
82050	Albin 128	H4
82620	Alcova 275	F3

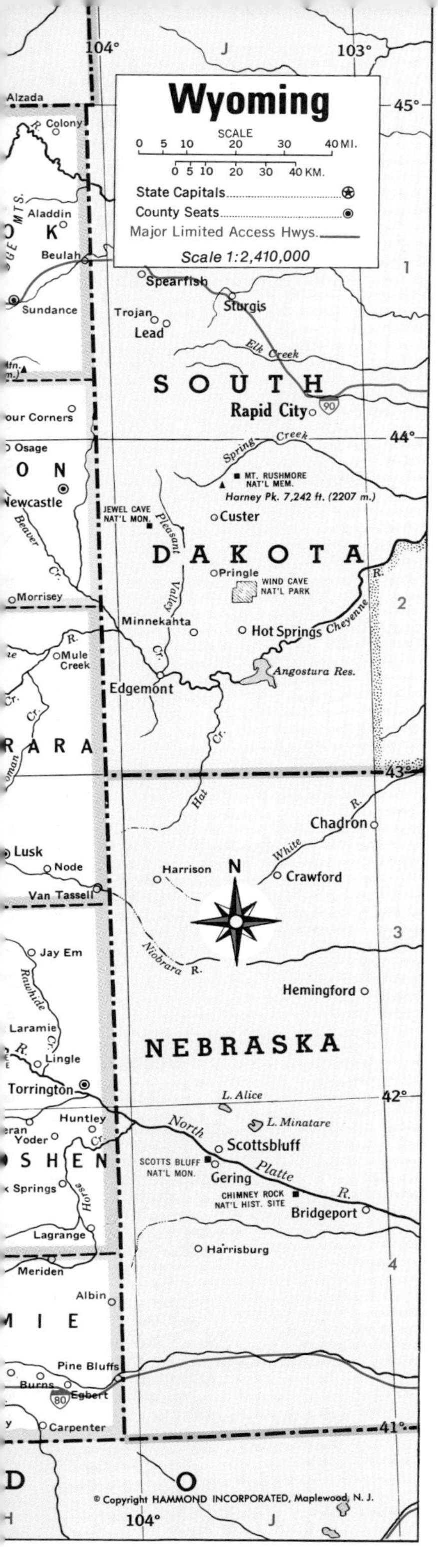
Wyoming
SCALE
0 5 10 20 30 40 MI.
0 5 10 20 30 40 KM.
State Capitals
County Seats
Major Limited Access Hwys.
Scale 1:2,410,000
104°
J
103°
45°
44°
43°
42°
41°
SOUTH DAKOTA
NEBRASKA
Spearfish
Sturgis
Lead
Rapid City
Custer
Hot Springs
Edgemont
Chadron
Crawford
Harrison
Scottsbluff
Gering
Bridgeport
Harrisburg
Newcastle
Sundance
Beulah
Lusk
Torrington
Pine Bluffs
MT. RUSHMORE NAT'L MEM.
Harney Pk. 7,242 ft. (2207 m.)
JEWEL CAVE NAT'L MON.
WIND CAVE NAT'L PARK
Angostura Res.
SCOTTS BLUFF NAT'L MON.
CHIMNEY ROCK NAT'L HIST. SITE
© Copyright HAMMOND INCORPORATED, Maplewood, N. J.

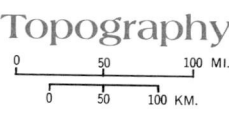

AREA 97,809 sq. mi. (253,325 sq. km.)
POPULATION 469,557
CAPITAL Cheyenne
LARGEST CITY Casper
HIGHEST POINT Gannett Pk. 13,804 ft. (4207 m.)
SETTLED IN 1834
ADMITTED TO UNION July 10, 1890
POPULAR NAME Equality State
STATE FLOWER Indian Paintbrush
STATE BIRD Meadowlark

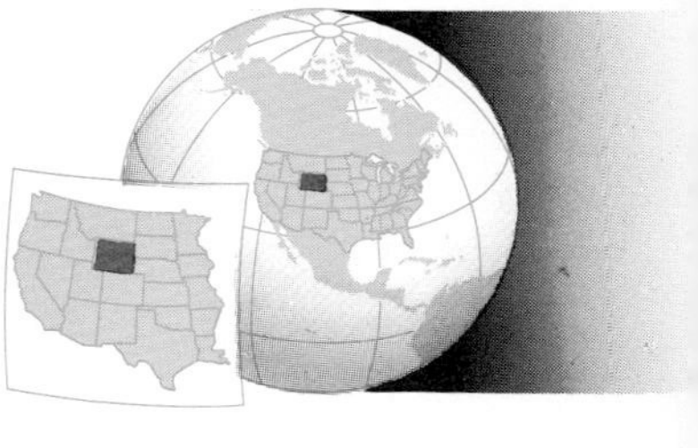

Topography

0 50 100 MI.
0 50 100 KM.

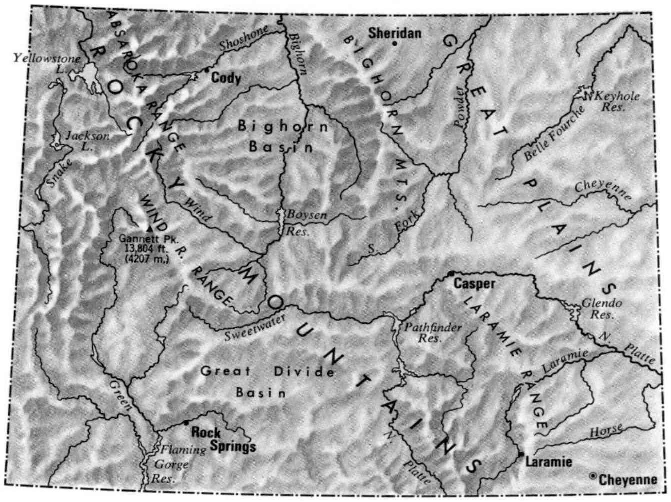
Sheridan
Cody
Yellowstone L.
Jackson L.
ABSAROKA RANGE
ROCKY
BIGHORN MTS.
Bighorn Basin
Boysen Res.
WIND R. RANGE
Gannett Pk. 13,804 ft. (4207 m.)
GREAT PLAINS
Keyhole Res.
Belle Fourche
Cheyenne
Powder
Casper
Glendo Res.
Pathfinder Res.
LARAMIE RANGE
Sweetwater
Great Divide Basin
MOUNTAINS
Rock Springs
Flaming Gorge Res.
Laramie
Cheyenne
N. Platte
Snake
Green
Wind

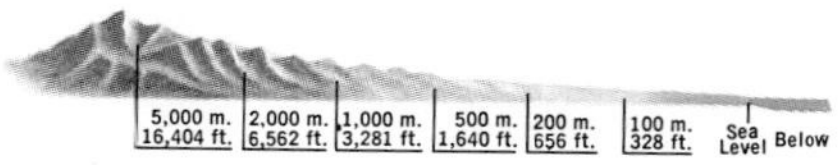
5,000 m. 16,404 ft.
2,000 m. 6,562 ft.
1,000 m. 3,281 ft.
500 m. 1,640 ft.
200 m. 656 ft.
100 m. 328 ft.
Sea Level
Below

82510 Arapahoe 682 ..... D3
83111 Auburn 360 ..... A3
82321 Baggs 433 ..... E4
82322 Bairoil 300 ..... E3
82410 Basin⊙ 1,349 ..... E1
†82801 Beckton 110 ..... E1
83112 Bedford 350 ..... A3
82712 Beulah 184 ..... H1
82833 Big Horn 350 ..... E1
83113 Big Piney 530 ..... B3
82051 Bosler 195 ..... G4
82834 Buffalo⊙ 3,799 ..... F1
82411 Burlington 300 ..... D1
82053 Burns 268 ..... H4
82412 Byron 633 ..... D1
82601 Casper⊙ 51,016 ..... F3
82055 Centennial 140 ..... F4
82001 Cheyenne (cap.)⊙ 47,283 . H4
82210 Chugwater 282 ..... H4
82835 Clearmont 191 ..... F1
82414 Cody⊙ 6,790 ..... D1
83114 Cokeville 515 ..... B3
82420 Cowley 455 ..... D1
82512 Crowheart 200 ..... C2
83115 Daniel 130 ..... B3
82836 Dayton 701 ..... E1
82421 Deaver 178 ..... D1
83116 Diamondville 1,000 ..... B4
82323 Dixon 82 ..... E4
82633 Douglas⊙ 6,030 ..... G3
82513 Dubois 1,067 ..... C2
†82443 East Thermopolis 359 ..... D2
82926 Eden 198 ..... C3
82635 Edgerton 510 ..... F2
82324 Elk Mountain 338 ..... F4
82325 Encampment 611 ..... F4
83118 Etna 200 ..... A2
82930 Evanston⊙ 6,421 ..... B4
82636 Evansville 2,335 ..... F3
83119 Fairview 150 ..... B3
82932 Farson 350 ..... C3
82933 Fort Bridger 300 ..... B4
82212 Fort Laramie 356 ..... H3
82514 Fort Washakie 400 ..... C2
†82001 Fox Farm 2,850 ..... H4
82423 Frannie 138 ..... D1
83120 Freedom 400 ..... B3
83121 Frontier 150 ..... B4
82501 Gas Hills 150 ..... E3
82716 Gillette⊙ 12,134 ..... G1
82213 Glendo 367 ..... G3
82637 Glenrock 2,736 ..... G3
82934 Granger 177 ..... C4
82425 Grass Creek 152 ..... D2
82935 Green River⊙ 12,807 ..... C4
82426 Greybull 2,277 ..... E1
83122 Grover 425 ..... B3
82214 Guernsey 1,512 ..... H3
82327 Hanna 2,288 ..... F4
82215 Hartville 149 ..... H3
82060 Hillsdale 160 ..... H4
82061 Horse Creek 225 ..... G4
82515 Hudson 514 ..... D3
82720 Hulett 291 ..... H1
83001 Jackson⊙ 4,511 ..... B2
82310 Jeffrey City 1,882 ..... E3
82639 Kaycee 271 ..... F2
83011 Kelly 100 ..... B2
83101 Kemmerer⊙ 3,273 ..... B4
82516 Kinnear 145 ..... D2
82430 Kirby 129 ..... D2
83123 La Barge 302 ..... B3
82221 Lagrange 232 ..... H4
82520 Lander⊙ 7,867 ..... D3
82070 Laramie⊙ 24,410 ..... G4
82640 Linch 187 ..... F2
82223 Lingle 475 ..... H3
82929 Little America 175 ..... C4
†82642 Lost Cabin 25 ..... E2
82224 Lost Springs 9 ..... G3
82431 Lovell 2,447 ..... D1
†82443 Lucerne 240 ..... D2
82225 Lusk⊙ 1,650 ..... H3
82937 Lyman 2,284 ..... B4
82642 Lysite 175 ..... E2
†82190 Mammoth Hot Springs (Yellowstone Nat'l Park 350 ..... B1
82432 Manderson 174 ..... E1
82227 Manville 94 ..... H3
†83113 Marbleton 537 ..... B3
82938 McKinnon 135 ..... C4
82329 Medicine Bow 953 ..... F4
82433 Meeteetse 512 ..... D1
82643 Midwest 638 ..... F2
82644 Mills 2,139 ..... F3
82721 Moorcroft 1,014 ..... H1
83012 Moose 150 ..... B2
83013 Moran 200 ..... B2
†82601 Mountain View F3
82939 Mountain View 628 ..... B4
82701 Newcastle⊙ 3,596 ..... H2
82190 Old Faithful 75 ..... B1
†82001 Orchard Valley 3,327 ..... H4
82723 Osage 500 ..... H2
†82601 Paradise Valley F3
82523 Pavillion 287 ..... D2
82082 Pine Bluffs 1,077 ..... H4
82941 Pinedale⊙ 1,066 ..... C3
82942 Point of Rocks 425 ..... D4
82435 Powell 5,310 ..... D1
82839 Ranchester 655 ..... E1
82301 Rawlins⊙ 11,547 ..... E4
82725 Recluse 225 ..... G1
82943 Reliance 325 ..... C4
†82325 Riverside 55 ..... F4
82501 Riverton 9,247 ..... D2
82944 Robertson 142 ..... B4
82083 Rock River 415 ..... G4
82901 Rock Springs 19,458 ..... C4
82331 Saratoga 2,410 ..... F4
82801 Sheridan⊙ 15,146 ..... F1
82615 Shirley Basin 400 ..... F3
82649 Shoshoni 879 ..... D2
82334 Sinclair 586 ..... E4
83126 Smoot 310 ..... B3
†82945 South Superior 586 ..... D4
82842 Story 637 ..... F1
82729 Sundance⊙ 1,087 ..... H1
82945 Superior 500 ..... D4
82442 Ten Sleep 407 ..... E1
83127 Thayne 256 ..... A3
82443 Thermopolis⊙ 3,852 ..... D2
82240 Torrington⊙ 5,441 ..... H3
82730 Upton 1,193 ..... H1
82242 Van Tassell 10 ..... H3
82335 Walcott 200 ..... F4
82336 Wamsutter 681 ..... E4
82201 Wheatland⊙ 5,816 ..... H3
83014 Wilson 480 ..... B2
82401 Worland⊙ 6,391 ..... E1
82732 Wright 1,117 ..... G2
82190 Yellowstone Nat'l Pk. 350 .. B1
82244 Yoder 110 ..... H4

OTHER FEATURES

Absaroka (range) C1
Antelope (creek) G2
Antelope (hills) D3
Aspen (mts.) C4
Atlantic (peak) D3
Badwater (creek) E2
Bear (creek) H4
Bear (riv.) B4
Bear Lodge (mts.) H1
Bear River Divide (mts.) B4
Beaver (creek) D3
Beaver (creek) H2
Belle Fourche (riv.) H1
Big Goose (creek) E1
Bighorn (basin) D1
Bighorn (lake) D1
Bighorn (mts.) E1
Bighorn (riv.) D1
Bighorn Canyon Nat'l Rec. Area D1
Big Sandy (riv.) C3
Bitter (creek) C4
Blacks Fork, Green (riv.) C4
Black Thunder (creek) G2
Bonneville (mt.) C3
Boysen (res.) D2
Buffalo Bill (dam) C1
Buffalo Bill (res.) C1
Buffalo Fork, Snake (riv.) B2
Burwell (mt.) C2
Caballo (creek) G1
Casper (range) F3
Cheyenne (riv.) H2
Chugwater (creek) H4
Clarks Fork (riv.) C1
Clear (creek) F1
Cloud (peak) E1
Cottonwood (creek) B4
Crazy Woman (creek) F1
Crosby (mt.) C2
Crow (creek) H4
Deadman (mt.) B2
Devils Tower Nat'l Mon. H1
Doubletop (peak) B2
Dry (creek) C2
Dry Cottonwood (creek) D1
Eagle (peak) B1
Fivemile (creek) D2
Flaming Gorge (res.) C4
Flaming Gorge Nat'l Rec. Area C4
Fontenelle (creek) B3
Fontenelle (res.) B3
Fort Laramie Nat'l Hist. Site H3
Fortress (mt.) C1
Fossil Butte Nat'l Mon. B4
Francis E. Warren A.F.B. 3,627 ..... G4
Fremont (lake) C3
Fremont (peak) C2
Gannett (peak) C2
Gas (hills) E3
Glendo (res.) H3
Gooseberry (creek) D1
Grand Teton (mt.) B2
Grand Teton Nat'l Park B2
Granite (mts.) E3
Great Divide (basin) E3
Green (mt.) E3
Green (riv.) C4
Green, East Fork (riv.) C3
Green River (mt.) C2
Greybull (riv.) D1
Greys (riv.) B3
Gros Ventre (riv.) B2
Guernsey (res.) H3
Hams Fork (riv.) B4
Hazelton (peak) E1
Henrys Fork, Green (riv.) C4
Hoback (peak) B2
Hoback (riv.) B2
Holmes (mt.) B1
Horse (creek) H4
Horseshoe (creek) G3
Hunt (mt.) E1
Index (peak) C1
Inyan Kara (creek) H1
Inyan Kara (mt.) H1
Isabel (mt.) B3
Jackson (lake) B2
Jackson (peak) B2
John D. Rockefeller, Jr., Mem. Pkwy. B1
Keyhole (res.) H1
Lamar (riv.) B1
Lance (creek) H2
Laramie (mts.) G3
Laramie (peak) G3
Laramie (riv.) G4
Leidy (mt.) B2
Lewis (lake) B1
Lightning (creek) G2
Little Missouri (riv.) H1
Little Muddy (creek) B4
Little Powder (riv.) G1
Little Sandy (creek) C3
Little Thunder (creek) G2
Lodgepole (creek) H2
Lodgepole (creek) H4
Madison (plat.) B1
Medicine Bow (range) F4
Medicine Bow (riv.) F3
Middle Piney (creek) B3
Muddy (creek) D2
Muskrat (creek) E2
Needle (mt.) C1
Niobrara (riv.) J3
North Laramie (riv.) G3
North Platte (riv.) H3
Nowater (creek) E2
Nowood (riv.) E1
Owl, North Fork (creek) D2
Owl Creek (mts.) D2
Palisades (res.) A2
Pass (creek) F4
Pathfinder (res.) F3
Poison (creek) E2
Poison Spider (creek) F3
Popo Agie (riv.) D3
Powder (riv.) F2
Rattlesnake (range) E3
Rawhide (creek) G1
Rawhide (creek) H3
Rocky (mts.) C1
Salt (riv.) B3
Salt River (range) B3
Salt Wells (creek) D4
Seminoe (mts.) E3
Seminoe (res.) F3
Shell (creek) E1
Shirley (basin) F3
Shoshone (lake) B1
Shoshone (riv.) D1
Sierra Madre (mts.) E4
Slate (creek) C3
Smiths Fork (riv.) B3
Snake (riv.) B2
South Cheyenne (riv.) H2
South Piney (creek) B3
Sweetwater (riv.) D3
Sybille (creek) G4
Teapot Dome (mt.) F2
Teton (range) B2
Tongue (riv.) E1
Washburn (mt.) B1
Wheatland (res.) G4
Willow (creek) F2
Wind (riv.) C2
Wind River (canyon) D2
Wind River (range) C2
Wind River Ind. Res. C2
Wood (riv.) C2
Wyoming (peak) B3
Wyoming (range) B2
Yellowstone (lake) B1
Yellowstone (riv.) B1
Yellowstone Nat'l Park B1

⊙County seat.
† Zip of nearest p.o. * Multiple zips.

Acquisitions of Territory

OREGON COUNTRY
OREGON 1846 Treaty with Great Britain

LOUISIANA 1803 Purchased from France

RED RIVER Title Established 1818

MEXICAN CESSION 1848

GADSDEN PURCHASE 1853

TEXAS Annexed in 1845

ALASKA 1867 Purchased from Russia

UNITED STATES 1783

FLORIDA 1819 Treaty with Spain

HAWAII Annexed in 1898

The United States in 1783 comprised the thirteen original states and included lands acquired by conquest during the Revolution and by the Treaty of 1783.

YEAR OF ADMISSION TO THE UNION

State	Year
DELAWARE ☆	1787
PENNSYLVANIA ☆	
NEW JERSEY ☆	
GEORGIA ☆	1788
CONNECTICUT ☆	
MASSACHUSETTS ☆	
MARYLAND ☆	
SOUTH CAROLINA ☆	
NEW HAMPSHIRE ☆	
VIRGINIA ☆	
NEW YORK ☆	
NORTH CAROLINA ☆	1789
RHODE ISLAND ☆	1790
VERMONT ☆	1791
KENTUCKY ☆	1792
TENNESSEE ☆	1796
OHIO ☆	1803
LOUISIANA ☆	1812
INDIANA ☆	1816
MISSISSIPPI ☆	1817
ILLINOIS ☆	1818
ALABAMA ☆	1819
MAINE ☆	1820
MISSOURI ☆	1821

Rank by Area

Rank by Population

1959 ☆ HAWAII ☆ ALASKA

1912 ☆ ARIZONA ☆ NEW MEXICO

1907 ☆ OKLAHOMA

☆ NORTH DAKOTA
☆ SOUTH DAKOTA
UTAH ☆ ☆ MONTANA
IDAHO ☆ ☆ WASHINGTON
WYOMING

COLORADO ☆

NEBRASKA

WEST VIRGINIA ☆
NEVADA ☆
KANSAS ☆
OREGON ☆
MINNESOTA ☆

CALIFORNIA ☆
WISCONSIN ☆
IOWA ☆
FLORIDA ☆
TEXAS ☆

ARKANSAS ☆
MICHIGAN ☆

| 1896 | 1889 | 1876 | 1867 | 1864 | 1861 | 1858 | 1848 | 1845 | 1836 |
| 1890 | | | | 1863 | 1859 | | 1850 | 1846 | 1837 |

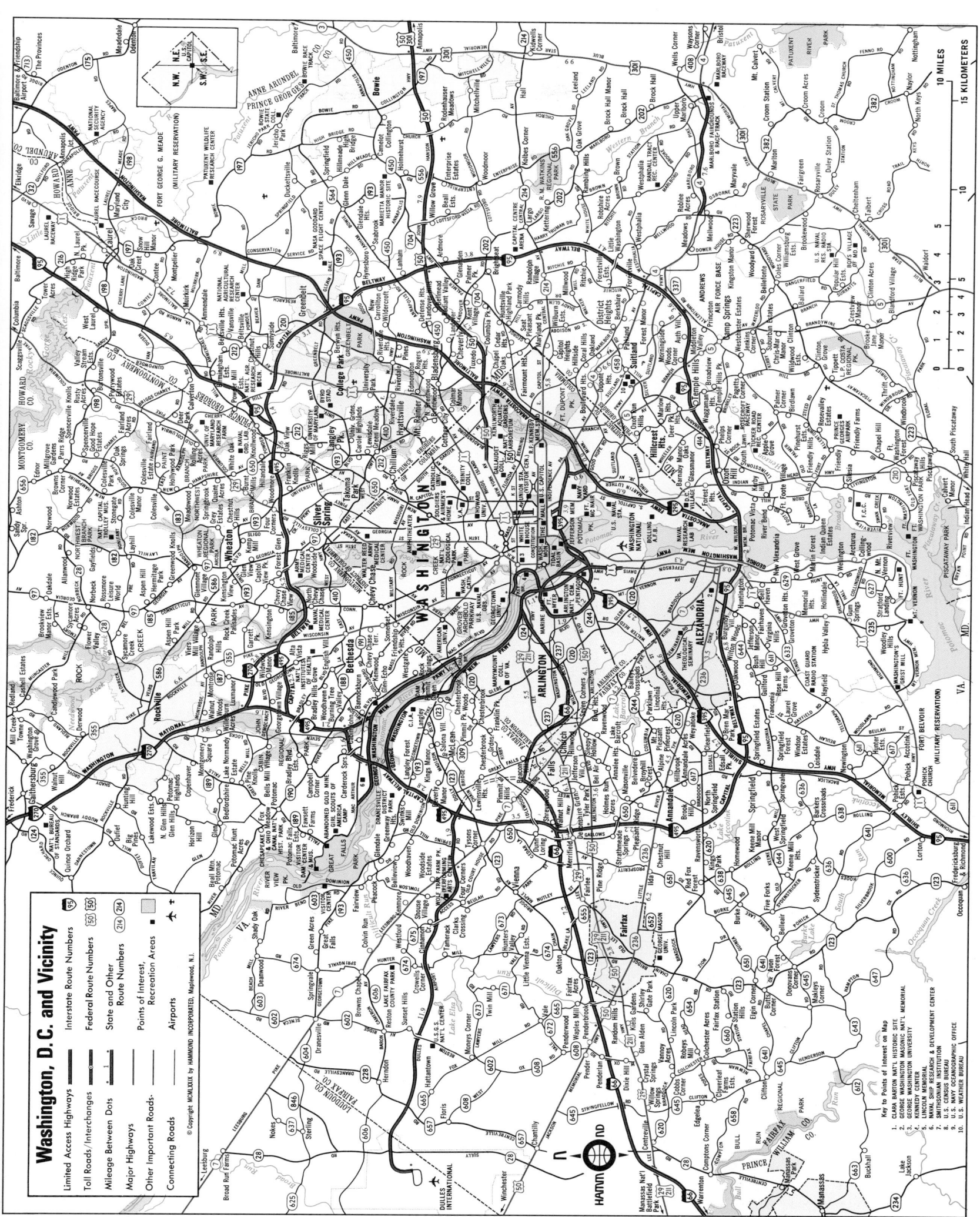

Washington, D.C. and Vicinity

Limited Access Highways
Toll Roads/Interchanges
Mileage Between Dots
Major Highways
Other Important Roads
Connecting Roads

Interstate Route Numbers
Federal Route Numbers
State and Other Route Numbers
Points of Interest, Recreation Areas
Airports

© Copyright MCMLXIX by HAMMOND INCORPORATED, Maplewood, N.J.

Key to Points of Interest on Map

1. CLARA BARTON NAT'L HISTORIC SITE
2. GEORGE WASHINGTON MASONIC NAT'L MEMORIAL
3. GEORGE WASHINGTON UNIVERSITY
4. KENNEDY CENTER
5. LINCOLN MEMORIAL
6. NAVAL SHIP RESEARCH & DEVELOPMENT CENTER
7. SMITHSONIAN INSTITUTION
8. U.S. CENSUS BUREAU
9. U.S. NAVY OCEANOGRAPHIC OFFICE
10. U.S. WEATHER BUREAU

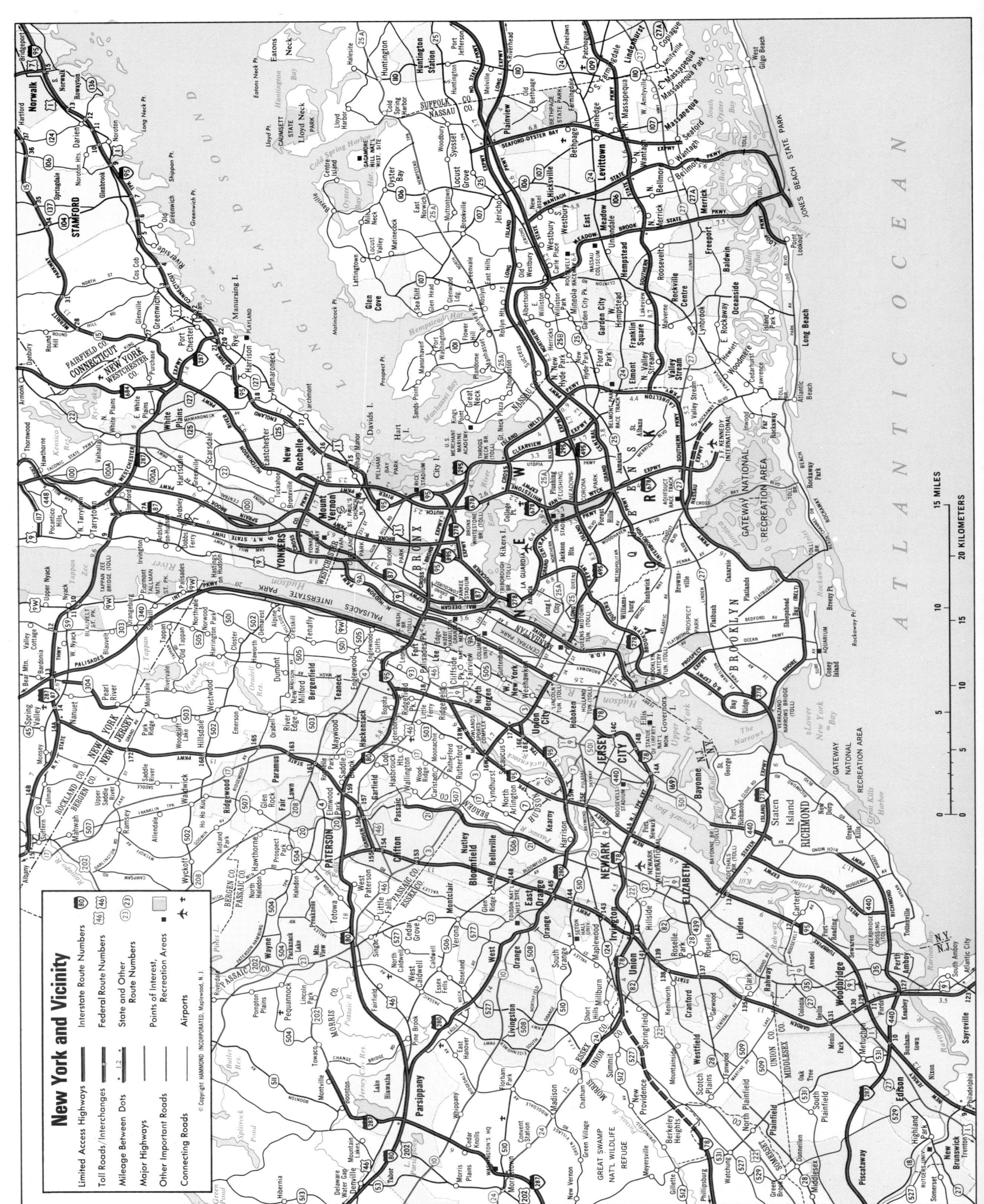

New York and Vicinity

Limited Access Highways	Interstate Route Numbers
Toll Roads/Interchanges	Federal Route Numbers
Mileage Between Dots	State and Other Route Numbers
Major Highways	Points of Interest, Recreation Areas
Other Important Roads	Airports
Connecting Roads	

© Copyright HAMMOND INCORPORATED, Maplewood, N.J.

15 MILES

20 KILOMETERS

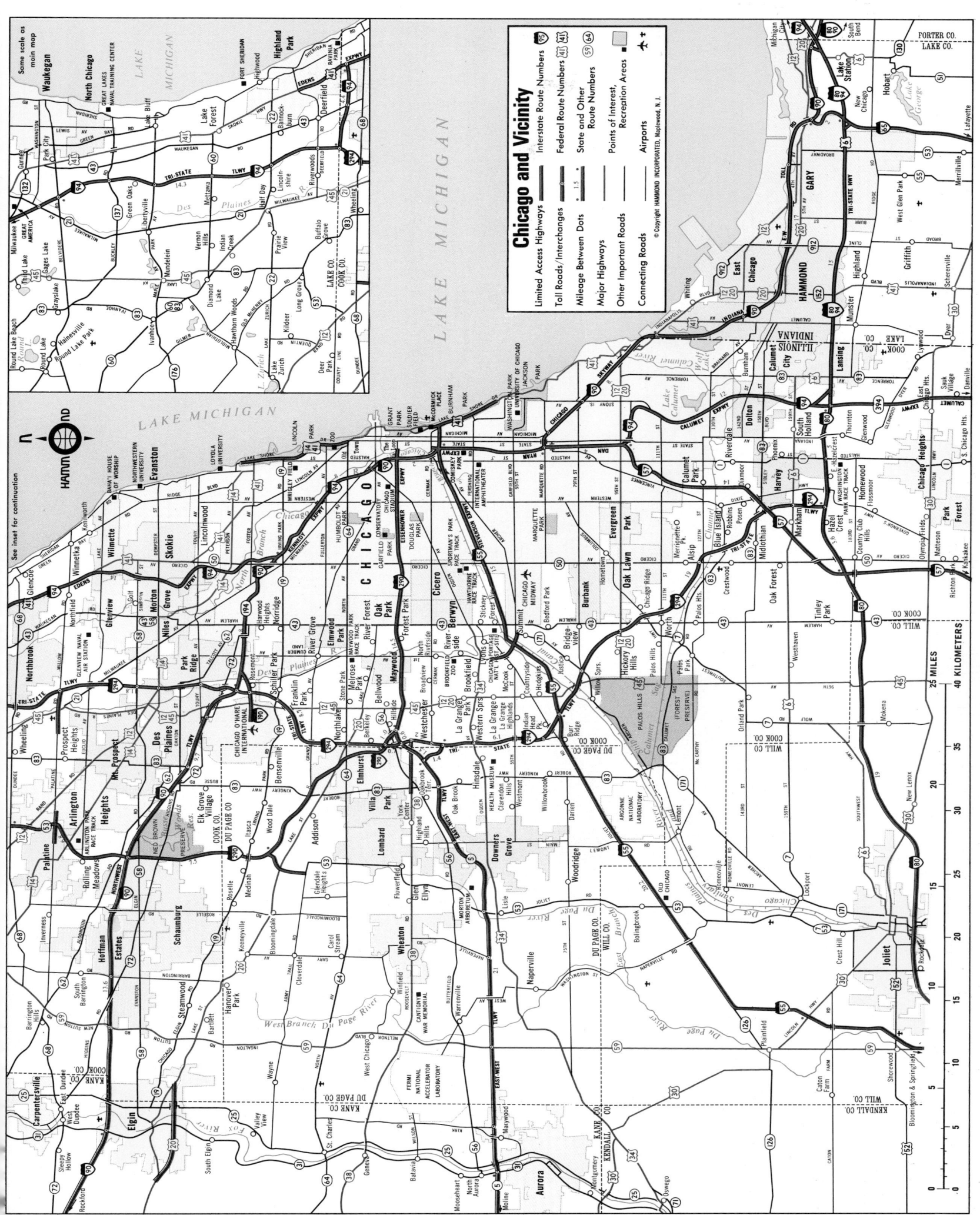

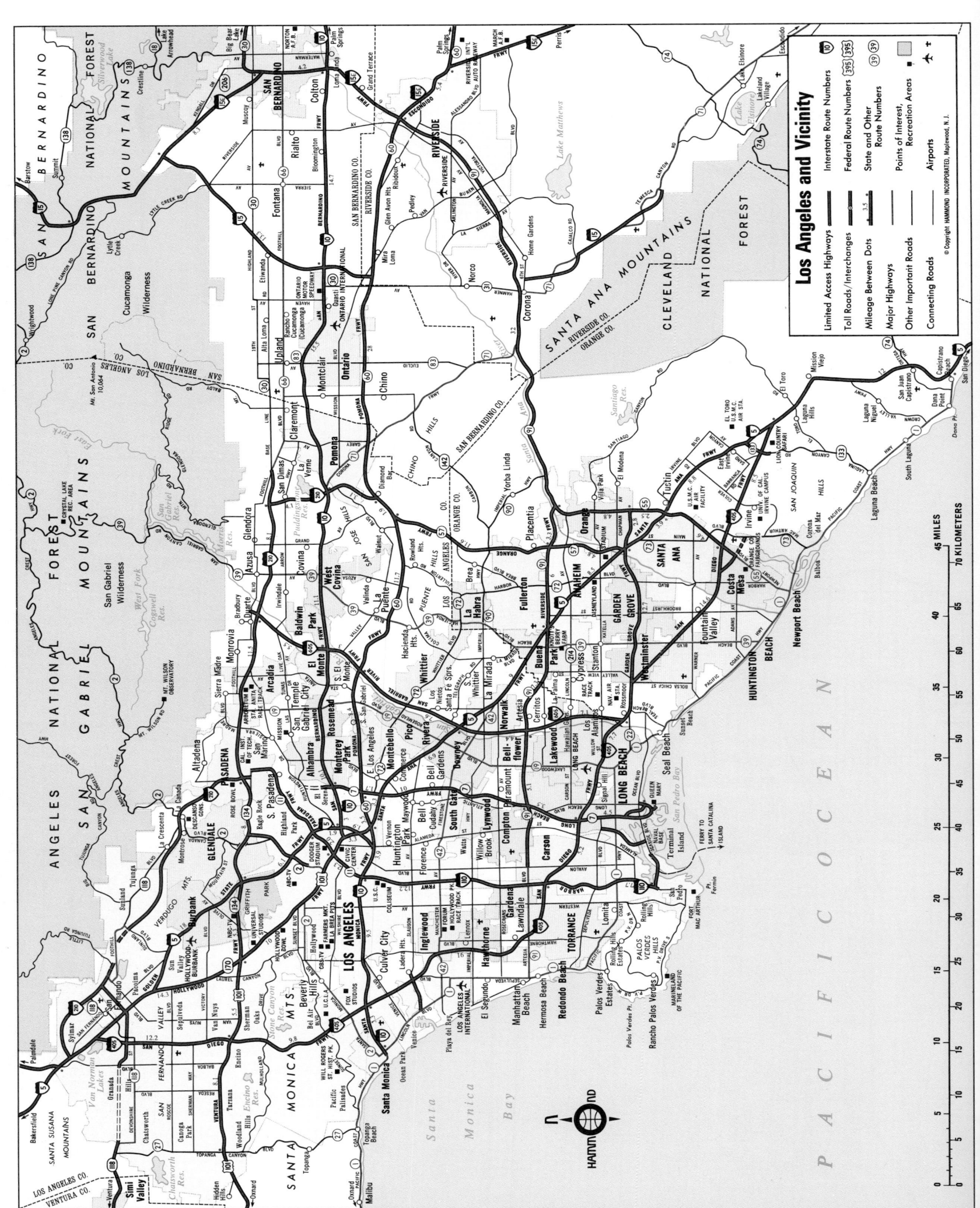

Los Angeles and Vicinity

Limited Access Highways	Interstate Route Numbers
Toll Roads/Interchanges	Federal Route Numbers
Mileage Between Dots	State and Other Route Numbers
Major Highways	Points of Interest, Recreation Areas
Other Important Roads	Airports
Connecting Roads	

© Copyright HAMMOND INCORPORATED, Maplewood, N.J.

INDEX OF THE WORLD

Introduction

This index is a directory to the atlas as a whole. It contains an alphabetical listing of the major political divisions (countries and administrative subdivisions, i.e., states, provinces, departments), principal cities and towns, and geographical features, such as mountains, rivers, bays, islands, shown on the maps contained in this atlas.

Entries are generally indexed to the map or inset having the largest scale, but in some cases, where the entry has equal coverage or is important to its surroundings on more than one map, more than one reference is given.

Each entry gives the political division in which it is located, or in the case of certain geographical features the appropriate continent or regional name, and the page number of the map on which the name will be found. The user who is unfamiliar with a place name will thus be able to identify the political division to which it belongs and to locate quickly the appropriate map or maps.

Once having found the map listed in this index, the user will easily find the place name on the map by first locating it in the accompanying map index. Here the user will find the necessary index key reference. When there is more than one place of the same name on the same map, only one reference is given. The individual map index will give the multiple listings of names and key references. A glance at adjacent pages will show whether there are additional maps on which the place name may be found, by referring to the accompanying index or by looking in the same relative location on the map.

The abbreviations for the political division names and geographical terms are explained in the glossary in the front of the atlas. In some cases place names have been shortened here. The full name will be found in the individual index accompanying the map itself.

A

B

G

GEOGRAPHICAL TERMS

A. = Arabic Burm. = Burmese Camb. = Cambodian Ch. = Chinese Czech. = Czechoslovakian Dan. = Danish Du. = Dutch Finn. = Finnish Fr. = French Ger. = German Ice. = Icelandic It. = Italian Jap. = Japanese Mong. = Mongol Nor. = Norwegian Per. = Persian Port. = Portuguese Russ. = Russian Sp. = Spanish Sw. = Swedish Turk. = Turkish

Å	Nor., Sw.	Stream
Aas	Dan., Nor.	Hills
Abajo	Sp	Lower
Ada, Adasi	Turk	Island
Altipiano	It	Plateau
Altiplano	Sp	Plateau
Alv, Alf, Elf	Sw	River
Arrecife	Sp	Reef
Asa	Nor., Sw	Hill
Asaga	Turk	Lower
Austral	Sp	Southern
Baai	Du	Bay
Bab	Arabic	Gate or Strait
Bahia	Sp	Bay
Bahr	Arabic	Marsh, Lake, Sea, River
Baia	Port	Bay
Baie	Fr	Bay, Gulf
Baizo	Port	Low
Bakke	Dan	Hill
Bana	Jap	Cape
Bañados	Sp	Marshes
Band	Per	Mt. Range
Bandao	Ch	Peninsula
Bandar	Per	Harbor
Barra	Sp	Reef
Bel	Turk	Pass
Belt	Ger	Strait
Ben	Gaelic	Mountain
Bera	Du	Mountain
Berg	Ger., Du	Mountain
Bir	Arabic	Well
Boca	Sp	Gulf, Inlet
Boğhaz	Turk	Strait
Bolshoi, Bolshaya	Russ	Big
Bolson	Sp	Depression
Bong	Korean	Mountain
Boreal	Sp	Northern
Breen	Nor	Glacier
Bro	Dan., Nor., Sw.	Bridge
Bucht	Ger	Bay
Bugt	Dan	Bay
Bukhta	Russ	Bay
Bukit	Malay	Hill, Mountain
Bukt	Nor., Sw	Bay, Gulf
Burnu, Burun	Turk	Cape, Point
By	Dan., Nor., Sw	Town
Cabo	Port., Sp	Cape
Campos	Port	Plains
Canal	Port., Sp	Channel
Cap, Capo	Fr., It	Cape
Cataratas	Sp	Falls
Catena	It	Mt. Range
Catingas	Port.	Open Woodlands
Cayos	Sp	Islands
Central, Centrale	Fr., It	Middle
Cerrito, Cerro	Sp	Hill
Cerros	Sp	Hills, Mountains
Chai	Turk	River
Chott	Arabic	Salt Lake
Ciénaga	Sp	Swamp
Ciudad	Sp	City
Col	Fr	Pass
Cordillera	Sp	Mt. Range, Mts.
Côte	Fr	Coast
Csatoria	Magyar	Canal
Cuchilla	Sp	Mt. Range
Curiche	Sp	Swamp
Dağ, Daği	Turk	Mountain, Peak
Dağlari	Turk	Mt. Range
Dal	Nor., Sw	Valley
Dar	Arabic	Land
Dar'ya	Russ	River
Daryacheh	Per	Marshy Lake
Dasht	Per	Desert, Plain
Deniz, Denizi	Turk	Sea, Lake
Desierto	Sp	Desert
Détroit	Fr	Strait
Djeziret	Arabic, Turk	Island
Do	Korean	Island
Doi	Thai	Mountain
Eiland	Du	Island
Elv	Dan., Nor	River
Embalse	Sp	Reservoir
Emi	Berber	Mountain
Erg	Arabic	Dune, Desert
Eski	Turk	Old
Est, Este	Fr., Port., Sp	East
Estero	Sp	Estuary, Creek
Estrecho, Estreito	Sp., Port	Strait
Etang	Fr	Pond, Lagoon, Lake
Feng	Ch	Mountain
Fiume	It	River
Fjäll	Sw	Mountain
Fjeld, Fjell	Nor	Hills, Mountain
Fjord	Dan., Nor., Sw	Fiord
Fleuve	Fr	River
Fljót	Ice	Stream
Fluss	Ger	River
Fors	Sw	Waterfall
Fos, Foss	Dan., Nor	Waterfall
Gamla	Nor	Old
Gamle	Dan	Old
Gata	Jap	Lake
Gawa	Jap	River
Gebel	Arabic	Mountain
Gebergte	Du	Mt. Range
Gebirge	Ger	Mt. Range
Gobi	Mongol	Desert
Goe	Jap	Pass
Gol	Mongol, Turk	Lake, Stream
Golf	Ger., Du	Gulf
Golfe	Fr	Gulf
Golfo	Sp., It., Port	Gulf
Gölü	Turk	Lake
Gora	Russ	Mountain
Grand, Grande	Fr., Sp	Big
Groot	Du	Big
Gross	Ger	Big
Grosso	It., Port	Big
Guba	Russ	Bay, Gulf
Gunto	Jap	Archipelago
Gunung	Malay	Mountain
Hai	Ch	Sea
Haixia	Ch	Strait
Halbinsel	Ger	Peninsula
Hamáda, Hammada	Arabic.	Rocky Plateau
Hamn	Sw	Harbor
Hamún	Per	Marsh
Hanto	Jap	Peninsula
Has, Hassi	Arabic	Well
Hav	Dan., Nor., Sw	Sea, Ocean
Havet	Nor	Bay
Havn	Dan., Nor	Harbor
Havre	Fr	Harbor
He	Ch	River, Stream
Higashi, Higasi	Jap	East
Hochebene	Ger	Plateau
Hoek	Du	Cape
Hoku	Jap	North
Holm	Dan., Nor., Sw	Island
Hory	Czech	Mountains
Hoved	Dan., Nor	Cape, Promontory
Hu	Ch	Lake
Huang	Ch	Yellow
Huk	Dan., Nor., Sw	Point
Hus, Huus	Dan., Nor., Sw	House
Idehan	Arabic	Desert
Ile	Fr	Island
Ilet	Fr	Islet
Ilot	Fr	Islet
Indre	Dan., Nor	Inner
Inferieur, Inferiore	Fr., It	Lower
Inner, Inre	Sw	Inner
Insel	Ger	Island
Irmak	Turk	River
Isla	Sp	Island
Isola	It	Island
Jabal, Jebel	Arabic	Mountains
Järvi	Finn	Lake
Jaure	Sw	Lake
Jiang	Ch	River, Stream
Jima	Jap	Island
Joki	Finn	River
Kaap	Du	Cape
Kabir, Kebir	Arabic	Big
Kai	Jap	Sea
Kaikyo	Jap	Strait
Kami	Turk	Upper
Kanaal	Du	Canal
Kanal	Russ., Ger	Canal, Channel
Kao	Thai	Mountain
Kap, Kapp	Nor., Sw., Ice	Cape
Kaupunki	Finn	Town
Kawa	Jap	River
Khao	Thai	Mountain
Khrebet	Russ	Mt. Range
Kita	Jap	North
Klein	Du., Ger	Small
Klint	Dan	Promontory
Kô	Jap	Lake
Ko	Thai	Island
Koh	Camb., Khmer	Island
Kop	Du	Peak, Head
Köping	Sw	Market, Borough
Körfez, Körfezi	Turk	Gulf
Kosa	Russ	Spit
Kosui	Jap	Lake
Kraal	Du	Native Village
Kuchuk	Turk	Small
Kuh, Kuhha	Per	Mt. Range, Mts.
Kul	Sinkiang Turki	Lake
Kum	Turk	Desert
Kuro	Jap	Black
Laag	Du	Low
Lac	Fr	Lake
Lago	Port., Sp., It	Lake
Lagoa	Port	Lagoon
Laguna	Sp	Lagoon
Lagune	Fr	Lagoon
Lahti	Finn	Bay, Bight
Län	Sw	County
Liedao	Ch	Islands, Archipelago
Lilla	Sw	Small
Lille	Dan., Nor	Small
Ling	Ch	Mountain
Llanos	Sp	Plains
Mae Nam	Thai	River
Mali, Malaya	Russ	Small
Man	Korean	Bay
Mar	Sp., Port	Sea
Mare	It	Sea
Medio	Sp	Middle
Meer	Du	Lake
Meer	Ger	Sea
Mer	Fr	Sea
Meridionale	It	Southern
Meseta	Sp	Plateau
Middelst, Midden	Du	Middle
Minami	Jap	Southern
Mis	Russ	Cape
Misaki	Jap	Cape
Mittel	Ger	Middle
Mont	Fr	Mountain
Montagne	Fr	Mountain
Montaña	Sp	Mountains
Monte	Sp., It., Port.	Mountain
More	Russ	Sea
Mörön	Mong	Stream
Morro	Port., Sp	Mountain, Promontory
Morue	Fr	Hill
Moyen	Fr	Middle
Muang	Siamese	Town
Mui	Vietnamese	Cape, Point
Mys	Russ	Cape
Nada	Jap	Sea
Naka	Jap	Middle
Nam	Burm., Lao	River
Namakzar	Per	Salt Waste
Nan	Jap	South
Nes	Nor	Cape, Point
Nevado	Sp	Snow-covered Peak
Nieder	Ger	Lower
Nishi, Nisi	Jap	West
Nizhni, Nizhnyaya	Russ	Lower
Njarga	Finn	Peninsula, Promontory
Nong	Thai	Lake
Noord	Du	North
Nord	Fr., Ger	North
Norte	Sp., It., Port	North
Nos	Russ	Cape
Novi, Novaya	Russ	New
Nur, Nuur	Ch., Mong	Lake
Nuruu	Mong	Mountains
Nusa	Malay	Island
Ny, Nya	Nor., Sw	New
O	Jap	Big
ö	Nor., Sw	Island
Ober	Ger	Upper
Occidental, Occidentale	Sp., It	Western
Odde	Dan	Point
Oeste	Port	West
Ooster	Du	Eastern
Opper, Over	Du	Upper
Oriental	Sp., Fr	Eastern
Orientale	It	Eastern
Orta	Turk	Middle
Ost	Ger	East
Ostrov	Russ	Island
Ouest	Fr	West
öy	Nor	Island
Ozero	Russ	Lake
Pampa	Sp	Plain
Pas	Fr	Channel, Strait
Paso	Sp	Pass
Passo	It., Port	Pass
Peña	Sp	Rock, Mountain
Pendi	Ch	Basin
Penisola	It	Peninsula
Pequeño	Sp	Small
Pereval	Russ	Pass
Peski	Russ	Desert
Petit, Petite	Fr	Small
Phu	Lao, Annamese	Mtn.
Pic	Fr	Mountain
Piccolo	It	Small
Pico	Port., Sp	Mountain, Peak
Pik	Russ	Mountain, Peak
Piton	Fr	Mountain, Peak
Planalto	Port	Plateau
Plato	Russ	Plateau
Pointe	Fr	Point
Poluostrov	Russ	Peninsula
Ponta	Port	Point
Presa	Sp	Reservoir
Presqu'île	Fr	Peninsula
Proliv	Russ	Strait
Pulou, Pulo	Malay	Island
Punt	Du	Point
Punta	Sp., It., Port	Point
Qiryat	Hebrew	City, Settlement
Qum	Turk	Desert
Qundao	Ch	Islands
Rada	Sp	Inlet
Rade	Fr	Bay, Inlet
Ras	Arabic	Cape
Reka	Russ	River
Retto	Jap	Archipelago
Ria	Sp	Estuary
Río	Sp	River
Rivier, Rivière	Du., Fr	River
Rud	Per	River
Sai	Jap	West
Saki	Jap	Cape
Salar, Salina	Sp	Salt Deposit
Salto	Sp., Port	Falls
San	Jap., Korean	Hill
Sanmaek	Korean	Mt. Range
Schiereiland	Du	Peninsula
Se	Camb., Khmer	River
See	Ger	Sea, Lake
Selvas	Sp., Port	Woods, Forest
Seno	Sp	Bay, Gulf
Serra	Port	Mts.
Serranía	Sp	Mts.
Seto	Jap	Strait
Settentrionale	It	Northern
Severni, Severnaya	Russ	North
Shamo	Ch	Desert
Shan	Ch., Jap	Hill, Mts.
Shankou	Ch	Pass
Shatt	Arabic	River
Shima	Jap	Island
Shimo	Jap	Lower
Shin	Jap	Land
Shiro	Jap	White
Shoto	Jap	Islands
Si	Ch	West
Sierra	Sp	Mt. Range, Mts.
Sjö	Nor., Sw	Lake, Sea
Sok, Suk, Souk	Arabic	Market
Song	Annamese	River
Sopka	Russ	Volcano
Spitze	Ger	Mt. Peak
Sredni, Srednyaya	Russ	Middle
Stad	Dan., Nor., Sw	City
Stari, Staraya	Russ	Old
Step	Russ	Treeless Plain
Straat	Du	Strait
Strasse	Ger	Strait
Stretto	It	Strait
Ström	Dan., Nor., Sw	Sound
Stung	Camb., Khmer	River
Su	Turk	River
Sud, Süd	Sp., Fr., Ger	South
Suido	Jap	Strait, Channel
Sul	Port	South
Sund	Dan., Nor., Sw.	Sound
Sungei	Malay	River
Supérieur	Fr	Upper
Superior, Superiore	Sp., It	Upper
Sur	Sp	South
Suyu	Turk	River
Ta	Ch	Big
Tafelland	Du	Plateau
Tagh	Turk	Mt. Range
Take	Jap	Peak, Ridge
Takht	Arabic	Lower
Tal	Ger	Valley
Tanjung	Malay	Cape, Point
Tell	Arabic	Hill
Thale	Thai	Sea, Lake
Tind	Nor	Peak
Tö	Jap	East
To	Jap	Island
Toge	Jap	Pass
Trask	Finn	Lake
Tugh	Somali	Dry River
Ujung	Malay	Point
Umi	Jap	Bay
Unter	Ger	Lower
Ura	Jap	Inlet
Uul	Mong	Mountain
Val	Fr	Valley
Vatn	Nor	Lake
Vecchio	It	Old
Veld	Du	Plain, Field
Velho	Port	Old
Verkhni	Russ	Upper
Vesi	Finn	Lake
Viejo	Sp	Old
Vik	Nor., Sw	Bay
Vishni, Vishnyaya	Russ	High
Vodokhranilishche	Russ	Reservoir
Volcán	Sp	Volcano
Vostochni, Vostochnaya	Russ	East, Eastern
Wadi	Arabic	Dry River
Wald	Ger	Forest
Wan	Jap	Bay
Westersch	Du	Western
Wüste	Ger	Desert
Yama	Jap	Mountain
Yug, Yuzhni, Yuzhnaya	Russ.	South, Southern
Zaki	Jap	Cape
Zaliv	Russ	Bay, Gulf
Zangbo	Tibetan	River, Stream
Zapadni, Zapadnaya	Russ	Western
Zee	Du	Sea
Zemlya	Russ	Land
Zizhiqu	Ch	Autonomous Region
Zuid	Du	South

Between Principal Cities in the United States

FROM/TO	Albuquerque, N. Mex.	Atlanta, Ga.	Baltimore, Md.	Boise, Idaho	Boston, Mass.	Brownsville, Tex.	Buffalo, N. Y.	Chicago, Ill.	Cincinnati, Ohio	Cleveland, Ohio	Denver, Colo.	Des Moines, Iowa	Detroit, Mich.	El Paso, Tex.	Fargo, N. Dak.	Fort Worth, Tex.	Galveston, Tex.	Hastings, Nebr.	Hot Springs, Ark.	Houghton, Mich.
Albuquerque, N. Mex.	....	1273	1670	774	1967	838	1577	1126	1248	1417	332	833	1360	228	968	561	803	588	773	1252
Atlanta, Ga.	1273	....	575	1830	933	960	695	583	368	550	1208	738	595	1293	1112	750	688	901	498	947
Baltimore, Md.	1670	575	....	2055	358	1525	273	603	423	305	1505	913	398	1750	1143	1239	1245	1154	964	808
Boise, Idaho	774	1830	2055	....	2266	1610	1872	1453	1663	1754	637	1155	1671	969	975	1263	1538	934	1384	1367
Boston, Mass.	1967	933	358	2266	....	1881	398	849	737	550	1766	1159	613	2067	1304	1574	1598	1415	1302	922
Brownsville, Tex.	838	960	1525	1610	1881	....	1575	1234	1184	1402	1047	1102	1398	682	1445	471	287	1013	650	1543
Buffalo, N. Y.	1577	695	273	1872	398	1575	....	454	392	175	1368	762	218	1690	923	1221	1289	1019	956	560
Chicago, Ill.	1126	583	603	1453	849	1234	454	....	249	307	918	310	236	1249	571	820	954	566	585	367
Cincinnati, Ohio	1248	368	423	1663	737	1184	392	249	....	218	1090	509	234	1333	818	839	897	742	569	589
Cleveland, Ohio	1417	550	305	1754	550	1402	175	307	218	....	1223	617	94	1521	838	1046	1116	871	787	518
Denver, Colo.	332	1208	1505	637	1766	1047	1368	918	1090	1223	....	607	1153	554	642	643	925	353	749	970
Des Moines, Iowa	833	738	913	1155	1159	1102	762	310	509	617	607	....	545	980	397	640	851	256	488	458
Detroit, Mich.	1360	595	398	1671	613	1398	218	236	234	94	1153	545	....	1475	745	1018	1111	800	761	427
El Paso, Tex.	228	1293	1750	969	2067	682	1690	1249	1333	1521	554	980	1475	....	1161	543	723	757	802	1422
Fargo, N. Dak.	968	1112	1143	975	1304	1445	923	571	818	838	642	397	745	1161	....	973	1218	440	875	393
Fort Worth, Tex.	561	750	1239	1263	1574	471	1221	820	839	1046	643	640	1018	543	973	....	283	544	273	1093
Galveston, Tex.	803	688	1245	1538	1598	287	1289	954	897	1116	925	851	1111	723	1218	283	....	808	375	1277
Hastings, Nebr.	588	901	1154	934	1415	1013	1019	566	742	871	353	256	800	757	440	544	808	....	513	666
Hot Springs, Ark.	773	498	964	1384	1302	650	956	585	569	787	749	488	761	802	875	273	375	513	....	901
Houghton, Mich.	1252	947	808	1367	922	1543	560	367	589	518	970	458	427	1422	393	1093	1277	666	901	....
Jacksonville, Fla.	1492	286	682	2098	1015	1025	880	861	628	768	1468	1024	832	1481	1400	943	799	1178	728	1216
Kansas City, Mo.	717	675	962	1158	1250	923	862	413	541	700	555	180	643	836	548	460	677	226	326	633
Los Angeles, Calif.	663	1935	2313	663	2590	1370	2195	1741	1892	2044	828	1433	1976	702	1426	1212	1423	1177	1437	1787
Louisville, Ky.	1174	317	498	1623	823	1093	483	268	92	309	1035	477	315	1253	818	751	807	693	480	636
Memphis, Tenn.	938	335	792	1506	1133	777	802	481	410	627	878	485	621	978	882	448	492	591	176	830
Miami, Fla.	1710	610	958	2368	1258	1100	1184	1190	957	1088	1732	1338	1156	1662	1721	1150	941	1468	983	1545
Minneapolis, Minn.	980	905	948	1140	1125	1335	733	356	603	632	699	235	542	1156	219	870	1087	399	722	272
Missoula, Mont.	895	1790	1947	252	2124	1706	1740	1348	1578	1640	670	1074	1552	1115	819	1312	1595	891	1385	1208
Nashville, Tenn.	1117	218	597	1631	941	952	626	394	239	456	1018	523	468	1169	900	643	666	697	370	760
New Orleans, La.	1030	427	1001	1713	1359	536	1087	831	708	922	1079	825	938	986	1221	470	288	870	358	1187
New York, N. Y.	1810	747	170	2153	188	1695	291	711	568	404	1628	1023	483	1902	1213	1398	1415	1275	1125	849
Norfolk, Va.	1696	507	167	2137	467	1465	435	696	474	429	1562	983	522	1755	1258	1226	1195	1216	955	946
Oklahoma, Okla.	518	753	1173	1138	1490	659	1117	689	755	946	503	469	905	578	786	188	456	357	260	926
Omaha, Nebr.	718	815	1026	1044	1280	1061	883	432	620	738	485	122	666	875	390	590	828	135	490	547
Philadelphia, Pa.	1748	663	90	2113	268	1614	278	664	501	343	575	972	444	1834	1186	1324	1335	1222	1051	827
Phoenix, Ariz.	330	1592	2002	733	2295	1023	1904	1451	1578	1745	585	1154	1685	347	1225	858	1065	901	1094	1550
Pittsburgh, Pa.	1498	520	194	1863	478	1424	178	411	258	115	1320	718	208	1592	952	1097	1140	967	825	530
Portland, Me.	2015	1022	446	2282	100	1961	438	892	802	603	1803	1197	657	2126	1313	1642	1678	1454	1371	924
Portland, Oreg.	1107	2172	2367	349	2553	1944	2167	1765	1987	2063	985	1479	1975	1286	1248	1612	1885	1271	1733	1638
Richmond, Va.	1628	470	128	2060	471	1428	375	618	399	353	1488	905	445	1695	1180	1170	1154	1142	897	870
St. Louis, Mo.	938	467	731	1389	1036	975	662	259	308	490	793	270	452	1033	658	568	697	455	325	591
Salt Lake City, Utah	483	1580	1858	292	2099	1317	1701	1260	1450	1567	372	952	1490	689	865	977	1249	708	1116	1242
San Francisco, Calif.	893	2133	2451	516	2696	1675	2298	1855	2037	2163	946	1547	2087	993	1447	1454	1693	1297	1648	1833
Schenectady, N. Y.	1823	840	278	2120	150	1770	249	702	605	408	1618	1012	467	1930	1157	1445	1487	1267	1175	776
Seattle, Wash.	1178	2180	2341	405	2508	2015	2130	1743	1974	2035	1020	1470	1945	1373	1206	1658	1938	1288	1759	1588
Shreveport, La.	764	548	1064	1433	1410	510	1080	725	688	904	799	624	891	752	1002	209	233	615	142	1043
Spokane, Wash.	1028	1960	2110	290	2279	1852	1900	1514	1746	1804	827	1243	1715	1238	976	1470	1753	1061	1552	1360
Springfield, Mass.	1889	863	282	2196	79	1805	325	774	659	473	1692	1085	540	1990	1240	1495	1524	1340	1224	860
Vermillion, S. Dak.	742	917	1083	973	1314	1161	916	479	694	785	468	187	705	920	284	689	938	167	605	510
Washington, D. C.	1648	542	33	2045	392	1493	290	594	403	303	1490	895	397	1726	1141	1210	1214	1139	936	813

FROM/TO	Jacksonville, Fla.	Kansas City, Mo.	Los Angeles, Calif.	Louisville, Ky.	Memphis, Tenn.	Miami, Fla.	Minneapolis, Minn.	Missoula, Mont.	Nashville, Tenn.	New Orleans, La.	New York, N. Y.	Norfolk, Va.	Oklahoma, Okla.	Omaha, Nebr.	Philadelphia, Pa.	Phoenix, Ariz.	Pittsburgh, Pa.	Portland, Me.
Albuquerque, N. Mex.	1492	717	663	1174	938	1710	980	895	1117	1030	1810	1696	518	718	1748	330	1498	2015
Atlanta, Ga.	286	675	1935	317	335	610	905	1790	218	427	747	507	753	815	663	1592	520	1022
Baltimore, Md.	682	962	2313	498	792	958	948	1947	597	1001	170	167	1173	1026	90	2002	194	446
Boise, Idaho	2098	1158	663	1623	1506	2368	1140	252	1631	1713	2153	2137	1138	1044	2113	733	1863	2282
Boston, Mass.	1015	1250	2590	823	1133	1258	1125	2124	941	1359	188	467	1490	1280	268	2295	478	100
Brownsville, Tex.	1025	923	1370	1093	777	1100	1335	1706	952	536	1695	1465	659	1061	1614	1023	1424	1961
Buffalo, N. Y.	880	862	2195	483	802	1184	733	1740	626	1087	291	435	1117	883	278	1904	178	438
Chicago, Ill.	861	413	1741	268	481	1190	356	1348	394	831	711	696	689	432	664	1451	411	892
Cincinnati, Ohio	628	541	1892	92	410	957	603	1578	239	708	568	474	755	620	501	1578	258	802
Cleveland, Ohio	768	700	2044	309	627	1088	632	1640	456	922	404	429	946	738	343	1745	115	603
Denver, Colo.	1468	555	828	1035	878	1732	699	670	1018	1079	1628	1562	503	485	1575	585	1320	1803
Des Moines, Iowa	1024	180	1433	477	485	1338	235	1074	523	825	1023	983	469	122	972	1154	718	1197
Detroit, Mich.	832	643	1976	315	621	1156	542	1552	468	938	483	522	905	666	444	1685	208	657
El Paso, Tex.	1481	836	702	1253	973	1662	1156	1115	1169	986	1902	1755	578	875	1834	347	1592	2126
Fargo, N. Dak.	1400	548	1426	818	882	1721	219	819	900	1221	1213	1258	786	390	1186	1225	952	1313
Fort Worth, Tex.	943	460	1212	751	448	1150	870	1312	643	470	1398	1226	188	590	1324	858	1097	1642
Galveston, Tex.	799	677	1423	807	492	941	1087	1595	666	288	1415	1195	456	828	1336	1065	1140	1078
Hastings, Nebr.	1178	226	1177	693	591	1468	399	891	697	870	1275	1216	357	135	1222	901	967	1454
Hot Springs, Ark.	728	326	1437	480	176	983	722	1385	370	358	1125	955	260	490	1051	1094	825	1371
Houghton, Mich.	1216	633	1787	636	830	1545	272	1208	760	1187	849	946	926	547	827	1550	630	924
Jacksonville, Fla.	....	952	2153	595	591	328	1192	2070	502	511	838	548	988	1098	758	1800	703	1113
Kansas City, Mo.	952	....	1352	480	370	1247	413	1117	472	678	1097	1009	293	165	1037	1045	784	1300
Los Angeles, Calif.	2153	1352	....	1825	1602	2355	1522	910	1777	1675	2446	2352	1182	1312	2388	357	2135	2631
Louisville, Ky.	595	480	1825	....	319	923	605	1550	153	623	650	528	675	579	580	1512	345	892
Memphis, Tenn.	591	370	1602	319	....	878	700	1483	195	358	953	778	422	529	878	1264	660	1205
Miami, Fla.	328	1247	2355	923	878	....	1516	2359	821	681	1095	802	1233	1402	1023	1998	1014	1357
Minneapolis, Minn.	1192	413	1522	605	700	1516	....	1010	695	1050	1019	1047	692	291	985	1279	745	1145
Missoula, Mont.	2070	1117	910	1550	1483	2359	1010	....	1582	1733	2030	2045	1162	978	1997	932	1754	2133
Nashville, Tenn.	502	472	1777	153	195	821	695	1582	....	470	758	586	602	604	683	1445	472	1015
New Orleans, La.	511	678	1675	623	358	681	1050	1733	470	....	1173	932	575	845	1090	1318	923	1445
New York, N. Y.	838	1097	2446	650	953	1095	1019	2030	758	1173	....	293	1324	1144	83	2142	313	277
Norfolk, Va.	548	1009	2352	528	778	802	1047	2045	586	932	293	....	1186	1095	220	2027	316	565
Oklahoma, Okla.	988	293	1182	675	422	1233	692	1162	602	575	1324	1186	....	405	1256	843	1013	1550
Omaha, Nebr.	1098	165	1312	579	529	1402	291	978	604	845	1144	1095	405	....	1094	1032	837	1318
Philadelphia, Pa.	758	1037	2388	580	878	1023	985	1997	683	1090	83	220	1256	1094	....	2079	254	360
Phoenix, Ariz.	1800	1045	357	1512	1264	1998	1279	932	1445	1318	2142	2027	843	1032	2079	....	1829	2345
Pittsburgh, Pa.	703	784	2135	345	660	1014	745	1754	472	923	313	316	1013	837	254	1829	....	545
Portland, Me.	1113	1300	2631	892	1205	1357	1145	2133	1015	1445	277	565	1550	1318	360	2345	545	....
Portland, Oreg.	2442	1397	825	1953	1852	2716	1435	430	1970	2063	2455	2458	1488	1373	2419	1007	2174	2563
Richmond, Va.	953	937	2283	457	722	831	968	1967	526	899	287	79	1122	1020	205	1960	242	565
St. Louis, Mo.	755	238	1585	242	242	1067	464	1331	253	599	873	771	456	352	808	1270	561	1094
Salt Lake City, Utah	1840	922	577	1400	1250	2098	988	435	1390	1433	1972	1925	862	833	1923	504	1670	2127
San Francisco, Calif.	2375	1500	345	1983	1800	2603	1585	762	1958	1923	2568	2510	1386	1425	2518	652	2264	2725
Schenectady, N. Y.	960	1107	2445	695	1010	1229	975	1978	820	1259	142	426	1354	1133	205	2152	350	197
Seattle, Wash.	2450	1505	956	1945	1867	2740	1403	395	1973	2098	2419	2440	1523	1372	2388	1112	2145	2513
Shreveport, La.	733	326	1420	598	279	950	859	1457	470	280	1230	1037	297	617	1153	1067	939	1484
Spokane, Wash.	2239	1286	939	1720	1652	2528	1173	170	1752	1898	2190	2211	1324	1149	2159	1020	1918	2285
Springfield, Mass.	957	1173	2515	745	1055	1210	1056	2060	863	1287	120	411	1412	1205	201	2220	400	159
Vermillion, S. Dak.	1203	280	1291	663	642	1510	238	887	704	960	1189	1166	502	115	1143	1043	891	1345
Washington, D. C.	647	943	2295	473	763	927	936	1940	567	968	204	145	1150	1012	122	1980	188	480

Between Principal Cities of Europe

	Amsterdam	Athens	Baku	Barcelona	Belgrade	Berlin	Brussels	Bucharest	Budapest	Cologne	Copenhagen	Istanbul	Dresden	Dublin	Frankfort	Hamburg	Leningrad
Amsterdam	....	1340	2218	770	875	365	105	1100	710	128	381	1360	385	468	228	232	1090
Athens	1340	....	1395	1160	500	1112	1292	460	698	1200	1320	350	1022	1765	1113	1250	1535
Baku	2218	1395	....	2427	1487	1867	2240	1220	1562	2127	1980	1070	1837	2490	2055	2020	1570
Barcelona	770	1160	2427	....	998	925	658	1210	924	692	1085	1380	860	919	665	910	1740
Belgrade	875	500	1487	998	....	618	850	295	205	750	840	502	530	1327	652	760	1165
Berlin	365	1112	1867	925	618	....	401	798	425	300	225	1068	95	815	268	165	815
Brussels	105	1292	2240	658	850	401	....	1110	700	110	475	1345	407	480	198	301	1175
Bucharest	1100	460	1220	1210	295	798	1110	....	295	982	970	272	725	1560	890	950	1080
Budapest	710	698	1562	924	205	425	700	295	....	590	629	650	345	1176	504	572	965
Cologne	128	1200	2127	692	750	300	110	982	590	....	400	1240	292	585	93	228	1090
Copenhagen	381	1320	1960	1085	840	225	475	970	629	400	....	1240	315	768	412	180	708
Istanbul	1360	350	1070	1380	502	1068	1345	272	650	1240	1240	....	995	1830	1150	1222	1292
Dresden	385	1022	1837	860	530	95	407	725	345	292	315	995	....	852	236	238	885
Dublin	468	1765	2490	919	1327	815	480	1560	1176	585	768	1830	852	....	671	668	1440
Frankfort	228	1113	2055	665	652	268	198	890	504	93	412	1150	236	671	....	250	1075
Hamburg	232	1250	2020	910	760	165	301	950	572	228	180	1222	238	668	250	....	880
Leningrad	1090	1535	1570	1740	1165	815	1175	1080	965	1090	708	1292	885	1440	1075	880	....
Lisbon	1140	1770	3050	610	1555	1410	998	1842	1515	1126	1520	2005	1380	1015	1160	1301	2235
London	220	1476	2435	707	1040	575	202	1285	900	308	590	1540	592	300	392	448	1300
Lyon	458	1100	2238	327	752	601	352	1025	680	370	760	1238	540	720	350	580	1420
Madrid	912	1463	2742	316	1235	1149	807	1518	1214	875	1272	1690	1100	902	888	1098	1980
Marseilles	627	1025	2238	211	750	730	521	1020	718	528	906	1205	655	875	492	730	1540
Milan	517	900	2028	450	540	570	435	819	476	390	720	1030	435	880	323	570	1315
Moscow	1325	1388	1175	1852	1160	995	1392	920	965	1285	970	1180	1200	1728	1240	1100	391
Munich	415	925	1912	648	475	310	372	725	350	282	520	975	227	855	193	378	1100
Oslo	568	1610	2118	1330	1112	520	672	1245	920	635	303	1505	620	786	675	445	670
Paris	257	1300	2335	518	890	540	170	1152	770	250	634	1390	523	480	295	459	1335
Riga	820	1310	1590	1440	855	520	900	870	685	805	453	1115	585	1210	780	600	300
Rome	808	650	1900	530	440	730	730	700	500	675	948	840	630	1175	698	810	1440
Sofia	1073	335	1360	1072	231	810	945	194	395	945	1010	315	730	1525	860	954	1218
Stockholm	695	1495	1862	1410	1005	503	793	1080	820	722	330	1340	598	1010	730	502	435
Toulouse	625	1215	2425	156	930	815	515	1210	883	875	962	1400	762	761	560	780	1635
Warsaw	673	990	1555	1150	510	320	720	580	342	602	415	852	325	1130	550	462	640
Vienna	580	795	1700	830	300	322	568	520	128	460	538	790	235	1040	370	460	975
Zurich	375	1000	2050	513	590	410	312	855	498	259	595	1090	342	768	193	432	1225

	Lisbon	London	Lyon	Madrid	Marseilles	Milan	Moscow	Munich	Oslo	Paris	Riga	Rome	Sofia	Stockholm	Toulouse	Warsaw	Vienna	Zurich
Amsterdam	1140	220	458	912	627	517	1325	415	568	257	820	808	1073	695	625	673	580	375
Athens	1770	1476	1100	1463	1025	900	1388	925	1610	1300	1310	650	335	1495	1215	990	795	1000
Baku	3050	2435	2238	2742	2238	2028	1175	1912	2118	2335	1590	1900	1360	1862	2425	1555	1700	2050
Barcelona	610	707	327	316	211	450	1852	648	1330	518	1440	530	1072	1410	156	1150	830	513
Belgrade	1555	1040	752	1235	750	540	1160	475	1112	890	855	440	231	1005	930	510	300	590
Berlin	1410	575	601	1149	730	570	995	310	520	540	520	730	810	503	815	320	322	410
Brussels	998	202	352	807	521	435	1392	372	672	170	900	730	945	793	515	720	568	312
Bucharest	1842	1285	1025	1518	1020	819	920	725	1245	1152	870	700	194	1080	1210	580	520	855
Budapest	1515	900	680	1214	718	476	965	350	920	770	685	500	395	820	883	342	128	498
Cologne	1126	308	370	875	528	390	1285	282	635	250	805	675	945	722	875	602	460	259
Copenhagen	1520	590	760	1272	906	720	970	520	303	634	453	948	1010	330	962	415	538	595
Istanbul	2005	1540	1238	1690	1205	1030	1180	975	1505	1390	1115	840	315	1340	1400	852	790	1090
Dresden	1380	592	540	1100	655	435	1200	227	620	523	585	630	730	598	762	325	235	342
Dublin	1015	300	720	902	875	880	1728	855	786	480	1210	1175	1525	1010	761	1130	1040	768
Frankfort	1160	392	350	888	492	323	1240	193	675	295	780	698	860	730	560	550	370	193
Hamburg	1301	448	580	1098	730	570	1100	378	445	459	600	810	954	502	780	462	460	432
Leningrad	2235	1300	1420	1980	1540	1315	391	1100	670	1335	300	1440	1218	435	1635	640	975	1225
Lisbon	....	975	850	313	810	1350	430	1208	1690	890	1940	1150	1685	1848	640	1700	1415	1058
London	975	....	455	777	620	595	1540	526	720	210	1035	890	1235	885	550	890	762	480
Lyon	850	455	....	577	170	210	1560	352	1005	248	1122	462	928	1080	228	850	562	206
Madrid	313	777	557	....	394	728	2120	910	1474	645	1670	840	1385	1598	344	1410	1110	765
Marseilles	810	620	170	394	....	238	1642	445	1165	410	1238	372	895	1225	196	950	620	318
Milan	1350	595	210	728	238	....	1408	215	1000	400	1010	295	715	1020	400	705	385	137
Moscow	430	1540	1560	2120	1642	1408	....	1220	1030	1538	520	1462	1100	770	1770	710	1028	1350
Munich	1208	526	352	910	445	215	1220	....	810	425	800	430	672	811	570	500	222	158
Oslo	1690	720	1005	1474	1165	1000	1030	810	....	830	531	1242	1295	267	1140	653	835	869
Paris	890	210	248	645	410	400	1538	425	830	....	1050	690	1080	950	431	845	770	295
Riga	1940	1035	1122	1670	1238	1010	520	800	531	1050	....	1155	985	276	1335	350	685	930
Rome	1150	890	462	840	372	295	1462	430	1242	690	1155	....	545	1220	569	810	470	421
Sofia	1685	1235	928	1385	895	715	1100	672	1295	1080	985	545	....	1170	1080	662	500	780
Stockholm	1848	885	1080	1598	1225	1020	770	811	267	950	276	1220	1170	....	1281	500	770	908
Toulouse	640	550	228	344	196	400	1770	570	1140	431	1335	569	1080	1281	....	1062	725	425
Warsaw	1700	890	850	1410	950	705	710	500	653	845	350	810	662	500	1062	....	345	640
Vienna	1415	762	562	1110	620	385	1028	222	835	770	685	470	500	770	725	345	....	365
Zurich	1058	480	206	765	318	137	1350	158	869	295	930	421	780	908	425	640	365	....

Portland, Oreg.	Richmond, Va.	St. Louis, Mo.	Salt Lake City, Utah	San Francisco, Calif.	Schenectady, N. Y.	Seattle, Wash.	Shreveport, La.	Spokane, Wash.	Springfield, Mass.	Vermillion, S. Dak.	Washington, D.
1107	1628	938	483	893	1823	1178	764	1028	1889	742	1648
2172	470	467	1580	2133	840	2180	548	1960	863	917	542
2367	128	731	1858	2451	278	2341	1064	2110	282	1083	33
349	2060	1389	292	516	2120	405	1433	290	2196	973	2045
2553	471	1036	2099	2696	150	2508	1410	2279	79	1314	392
1944	1428	975	1317	1675	1770	2015	510	1852	1805	1161	1493
2167	375	662	1701	2298	249	2130	1080	1900	325	916	290
1765	618	259	1260	1855	702	1743	725	1514	774	479	594
1987	399	308	1450	2037	605	1974	688	1746	659	694	403
2063	353	490	1567	2163	408	2035	904	1804	478	785	303
985	1488	793	372	946	1618	1020	799	827	1692	468	1490
1479	905	270	952	1547	1012	1470	624	1243	1085	187	895
1975	445	452	1490	2087	467	1945	891	1715	540	705	397
1286	1695	1033	689	993	1930	1373	752	1238	1990	920	1726
1248	1180	658	865	1447	1157	1206	1002	976	1240	284	1141
1612	1170	568	977	1454	1445	1658	209	1470	1495	689	1210
1885	1154	697	1249	1693	1487	1938	233	1753	1524	938	1214
1271	1142	455	708	1297	1267	1288	615	1061	1340	167	1139
1733	897	325	1116	1648	1175	1759	142	1552	1224	605	936
1638	870	591	1242	1833	776	1588	1043	1360	860	510	813
2442	953	755	1840	2375	960	2450	733	2239	957	1203	647
1397	937	238	922	1500	1107	1505	326	1286	1173	280	943
825	2283	1585	577	345	2445	956	1420	939	2515	1291	2295
1953	457	242	1400	1983	695	1945	598	1720	745	663	473
1852	722	242	1250	1800	1010	1867	279	1652	1055	642	763
2716	831	1067	2098	2603	1229	2740	950	2528	1210	1510	927
1435	968	464	988	1585	975	1403	859	1173	1056	238	936
430	1967	1331	435	762	1978	395	1457	170	2060	887	1940
1970	526	253	1390	1958	820	1973	470	1752	863	704	567
2063	899	599	1433	1923	1259	2098	280	1898	1287	960	968
2455	287	873	1972	2568	142	2419	1230	2190	120	1189	204
2458	79	771	1925	2510	426	2440	1037	2211	411	1166	145
1488	1122	456	862	1386	1354	1523	297	1324	1412	502	1150
1373	1020	352	833	1425	1133	1372	617	1149	1205	115	1012
2419	205	808	1923	2518	205	2388	1153	2159	201	1143	122
1007	1960	1270	504	652	2152	1112	1067	1020	2220	1043	1980
2174	242	561	1670	2264	350	2145	939	1918	400	891	188
2563	565	1094	2127	2725	197	2513	1484	2285	159	1345	480
....	2381	1723	636	536	2405	143	1783	295	2488	1293	2360
2381	....	699	1850	2436	406	2362	985	2133	407	1089	96
1723	699	....	1158	1738	898	1722	466	1500	958	450	710
636	1850	1158	....	592	1950	697	1155	548	2027	785	1845
536	2436	1738	592	....	2548	680	1655	730	2625	1383	2437
2405	406	898	1950	2548	....	2363	1290	2139	86	1165	313
143	2362	1722	697	680	2363	....	1820	229	2445	1282	2335
1783	985	466	1155	1655	1290	1820	....	1621	1333	726	1035
295	2133	1500	548	730	2139	229	1621	....	2216	1055	2105
2488	407	958	2027	2625	86	2445	1333	2216	....	1242	321
1293	1089	450	785	1383	1165	1282	726	1055	1242	....	1073
2360	96	710	1845	2437	313	2335	1035	2105	321	1073	....

NEW YORK TO	Miles	SAN FRANCISCO TO	Miles	SEATTLE TO	Miles	WASHINGTON TO	Miles
Buenos Aires	5,295	Buenos Aires	6,487	Buenos Aires	6,956	Buenos Aires	5,205
Bogota	2,474	Bogota	3,863	Bogota	4,166	Bogota	2,344
Caracas	2,100	Caracas	3,900	Caracas	4,100	Caracas	2,040
Guatemala City	2,060	Guatemala City	2,525	Guatemala City	2,930	Guatemala City	1,835
Havana	1,302	Havana	2,600	Havana	2,805	Havana	1,110
La Paz	3,905	La Paz	5,080	La Paz	5,110	La Paz	3,780
Panama	2,211	Panama	3,349	Panama	3,680	Panama	2,020
Para	3,281	Para	5,430	Para	5,550	Para	3,270
Managua	2,100	Managua	2,860	Managua	3,240	Managua	1,920
Rio de Janeiro	4,810	Rio de Janeiro	6,655	Rio de Janeiro	6,945	Rio de Janeiro	4,710
San Jose	2,200	San Jose	3,070	San Jose	3,430	San Jose	2,030
Santiago	5,134	Santiago	5,960	Santiago	6,466	Santiago	4,965
Tampico	1,880	Tampico	1,790	Tampico	2,200	Tampico	1,665

Between Representative Cities of the United States and Latin America

CHICAGO TO	Miles	DENVER TO	Miles	LOS ANGELES TO	Miles	NEW ORLEANS TO	Miles
Buenos Aires	5,598	Buenos Aires	5,935	Buenos Aires	6,148	Buenos Aires	4,902
Bogota	2,691	Bogota	3,100	Bogota	3,515	Bogota	1,996
Caracas	2,480	Caracas	3,105	Caracas	3,610	Caracas	1,990
Guatemala City	1,870	Guatemala City	1,935	Guatemala City	2,190	Guatemala City	1,050
Havana	1,315	Havana	1,760	Havana	2,320	Havana	672
La Paz	4,130	La Paz	4,445	La Paz	4,805	La Paz	3,480
Panama	2,320	Panama	2,620	Panama	3,025	Panama	1,600
Para	3,820	Para	4,580	Para	5,110	Para	3,470
Managua	2,060	Managua	2,230	Managua	2,540	Managua	1,250
Rio de Janeiro	5,320	Rio de Janeiro	5,900	Rio de Janeiro	6,330	Rio de Janeiro	4,798
San Jose	2,100	San Jose	2,420	San Jose	2,725	San Jose	1,425
Santiago	5,320	Santiago	5,495	Santiago	5,595	Santiago	4,553
Tampico	1,460	Tampico	1,240	Tampico	1,470	Tampico	720

TABLES OF AIRLINE DISTANCES

All Distances in Statute Miles

Between Principal Cities of the World

FROM/TO	Azores	Bagdad	Berlin	Bombay	Buenos Aires	Callao	Cairo	Cape Town	Chicago	Istanbul
Azores	....	3906	2148	5930	5385	4825	3325	5670	3305	2880
Bagdad	3906	....	2040	2022	8215	8618	785	4923	6490	1085
Berlin	2148	2040	....	3947	7411	6937	1823	5949	4458	1068
Bombay	5930	2022	3947	....	9380	10530	2698	5133	8144	3043
Buenos Aires	5385	8215	7411	9380	....	1982	7428	4332	5598	7638
Callao	4825	8618	6937	10530	1982	....	7870	6195	3765	7666
Cairo	3325	785	1823	2698	7428	7870	....	4476	6231	780
Cape Town	5670	4923	5949	5133	4332	6195	4476	....	8551	5210
Chicago	3305	6490	4458	8144	5598	3765	6231	8551	....	5530
Istanbul	2880	1085	1068	3043	7638	7666	780	5210	5530	....
Guam	8985	6380	7158	4831	10516	9760	7175	8918	7510	7015
Honolulu	7421	8445	7384	8172	7653	5993	8925	11655	4315	8200
Juneau	4715	6180	4638	6992	7964	5806	6352	10382	2310	5665
London	1562	2568	575	4526	6919	6376	2218	5975	4015	1540
Los Angeles	5034	7695	5849	8810	6148	4155	7675	10165	1741	6895
Melbourne	12190	8150	9992	6140	7336	8196	8720	6510	9837	9189
Mexico City	4584	8155	6119	9818	4609	2619	7807	8620	1690	7160
Montreal	2548	5814	3776	7582	5619	3954	5502	7975	750	4825
New Orleans	3718	7212	5182	8952	4902	2990	6862	8390	827	6220
New York	2604	6066	4026	7875	5295	3633	5701	7845	727	5060
Panama	3918	7807	5902	9832	3319	1450	7230	7090	2320	6797
Paris	1617	2385	540	4391	6891	6455	2020	5762	4219	1390
Rio de Janeiro	4312	7012	6246	8438	1230	2400	6242	3850	5320	6420
San Francisco	5114	7521	5744	8523	6487	4500	7554	10340	1875	6770
Santiago	5718	8876	7842	10127	731	1548	8100	5080	5325	8230
Seattle	4720	6848	5121	7830	6956	4964	6915	10305	1753	6124
Shanghai	7324	4468	5323	3219	12295	10760	5290	8179	7155	5084
Singapore	8338	4443	6226	2425	9940	11700	5152	6025	9475	5440
Tokyo	7370	5242	5623	4247	11601	9740	6005	9234	6410	5649
Wellington	11475	9782	11384	7752	6341	6696	10360	7149	8465	10790

FROM/TO	Guam	Honolulu	Juneau	London	Los Angeles	Melbourne	Mexico City	Montreal	New Orleans	New York
Azores	8985	7421	4715	1562	5034	12190	4584	2548	3718	2604
Bagdad	6380	8445	6180	2568	7695	8150	8155	5814	7212	6066
Berlin	7158	7384	4638	575	5849	9992	6119	3776	5182	4026
Bombay	4831	8172	6992	4526	8810	6140	9818	7582	8952	7875
Buenos Aires	10516	7653	7964	6919	6148	7336	4609	5619	4902	5295
Callao	9760	5993	5806	6376	4155	8196	2619	3954	2990	3633
Cairo	7175	8925	6352	2218	7675	8720	7807	5502	6862	5701
Cape Town	8918	11655	10382	5975	10165	6510	8620	7975	8390	7845
Chicago	7510	4315	2310	4015	1741	9837	1690	750	827	727
Istanbul	7015	8200	5665	1540	6895	9189	7160	4825	6220	5060
Guam	....	3896	5225	7605	6255	3497	7690	7840	7895	8115
Honolulu	3896	....	2825	7320	2620	5581	3846	4992	4305	5051
Juneau	5225	2825	....	4496	1835	8162	3210	2647	2860	2874
London	7605	7320	4496	....	5496	10590	5605	3370	4656	3500
Los Angeles	6255	2620	1835	5496	....	8098	1445	2468	1695	2466
Melbourne	3497	5581	8162	10590	8098	....	8599	10553	9455	10541
Mexico City	7690	3846	3210	5605	1445	8599	....	2247	940	2110
Montreal	7840	4992	2647	3370	2468	10553	2247	....	1390	340
New Orleans	7895	4305	2860	4656	1695	9455	940	1390	....	1161
New York	8115	5051	2874	3500	2466	10541	2110	340	1161	....
Panama	9220	5347	4456	5310	3025	9211	1532	2545	1600	2211
Paris	7675	7525	4700	210	5711	10500	5800	3490	4846	3600
Rio de Janeiro	11710	8400	7611	5747	6330	8340	4810	5110	4798	4810
San Francisco	5952	2407	1530	5440	345	7970	1870	2557	1960	2606
Santiago	9946	6935	7320	7275	5595	7130	4122	5461	4553	5134
Seattle	5785	2707	870	4850	961	8330	2339	2309	2137	2440
Shanghai	1945	5009	4968	5841	6598	4967	8120	7141	7830	7460
Singapore	2990	6874	7375	6818	8955	3768	10495	9280	10255	9617
Tokyo	1596	3940	4117	6050	5600	5172	7190	6546	6993	6846
Wellington	4206	4676	7501	11790	6806	1655	7003	9206	7950	9067

FROM/TO	Panama	Paris	Rio de Janeiro	San Francisco	Santiago	Seattle	Shanghai	Singapore	Tokyo	Wellington
Azores	3918	1617	4312	5114	5718	4720	7324	8338	7370	11475
Bagdad	7807	2385	7012	7521	8876	6848	4468	4443	5242	9782
Berlin	5902	540	6246	5744	7842	5121	5323	6226	5623	11384
Bombay	9832	4391	8438	8523	10127	7830	3219	2425	4247	7752
Buenos Aires	3319	6891	1230	6487	731	6956	12295	9940	11601	6341
Callao	1450	6455	2400	4500	1548	4964	10760	11700	9740	6696
Cairo	7230	2020	6242	7554	8100	6915	5290	5152	6005	10360
Cape Town	7090	5732	3850	10340	5080	10305	8179	6025	9234	7149
Chicago	2320	4219	5320	1875	5325	1753	7155	9475	6410	8465
Istanbul	6797	1390	6420	6770	8230	6124	5084	5440	5649	10790
Guam	9220	7675	11710	5952	9946	5785	1945	2990	1596	4206
Honolulu	5347	7525	8400	2407	6935	2707	5009	6874	3940	4676
Juneau	4456	4700	7611	1530	7320	870	4968	7375	4117	7501
London	5310	210	5747	5440	7275	4850	5841	6818	6050	11790
Los Angeles	3025	5711	6330	345	5595	961	6598	8955	5600	6806
Melbourne	9211	10500	8340	7970	7130	8330	4967	3768	5172	1655
Mexico City	1532	5800	4810	1870	4122	2339	8120	10495	7190	7003
Montreal	2545	3490	5110	2557	5461	2309	7141	9280	6546	9206
New Orleans	1600	4846	4798	1960	4553	2137	7830	10255	6993	7950
New York	2211	3600	4810	2606	5134	2440	7460	9617	6846	9067
Panama	....	5440	3311	3349	3000	3680	9430	11800	8560	7580
Paris	5440	....	5710	5680	7300	5080	5855	6730	6132	11865
Rio de Janeiro	3311	5710	....	6655	1852	6945	11510	9875	11600	7510
San Francisco	3349	5680	6655	....	5960	692	6245	8440	5250	6800
Santiago	3000	7300	1852	5960	....	6466	11850	10270	10850	5925
Seattle	3680	5080	6945	692	6466	....	5780	8200	4863	7310
Shanghai	9430	5855	11510	6245	11850	5780	....	2395	1095	6080
Singapore	11800	6730	9875	8440	10270	8200	2395	....	3350	5360
Tokyo	8560	6132	11600	5250	10850	4863	1095	3350	....	5730
Wellington	7580	11865	7510	6800	5925	7310	6080	5360	5730	......

WORLD STATISTICAL TABLES

Elements of the Solar System

	Mean Distance from Sun: in Miles	in Kilometers	Period of Revolution around Sun	Period of Rotation on Axis	Equatorial Diameter: in Miles	in Kilometers	Surface Gravity (Earth = 1)	Mass (Earth = 1)	Mean Density (Water = 1)	Number of Satellites
MERCURY	35,990,000	57,900,000	87.97 days	59 days	3,032	4,880	0.38	0.055	5.5	0
VENUS	67,240,000	108,200,000	224.70 days	243 days†	7,523	12,106	0.90	0.815	5.25	0
EARTH	93,000,000	149,700,000	365.26 days	23h 56m	7,926	12,755	1.00	1.00	5.5	1
MARS	141,730,000	228,100,000	687.00 days	24h 37m	4,220	6,790	0.38	0.107	4.0	2
JUPITER	483,880,000	778,700,000	11.86 years	9h 50m	88,750	142,800	2.87	317.9	1.3	16
SATURN	887,130,000	1,427,700,000	29.46 years	10h 14m	74,580	120,020	1.32	95.2	0.7	17
URANUS	1,783,700,000	2,870,500,000	84.01 years	10h 49m†	31,600	50,900	0.93	14.6·	1.3	5
NEPTUNE	2,795,500,000	4,498,800,000	164.79 years	15h 48m	30,200	48,600	1.23	17.2	1.8	3
PLUTO	3,667,900,000	5,902,800,000	247.70 years	6.39 days (?)	1,500	2,400	0.03 (?)	0.01(?)	0.7(?)	1

†Retrograde motion

Facts About the Sun

Equatorial diameter	865,000 miles	1,392,000 kilometers
Period of rotation on axis	25-35 days*	
Orbit of galaxy	every 225 million years	
Surface gravity (Earth = 1)	27.8	
Mass (Earth = 1)	333,000	
Density (Water = 1)	1.4	
Mean distance from Earth	93,000,000 miles	149,700,000 kilometers

*Rotation of 25 days at Equator, decreasing to about 35 days at the poles.

Facts About the Moon

Equatorial diameter	2,160 miles	3,476 kilometers
Period of rotation on axis	27 days, 7 hours, 43 minutes	
Period of revolution around Earth (sidereal month)	27 days, 7 hours, 43 minutes	
Phase period between new moons (synodic month)	29 days, 12 hours, 44 minutes	
Surface gravity (Earth = 1)	0.16	
Mass (Earth = 1)	0.0123	
Density (Water = 1)	3.34	
Maximum distance from Earth	252,710 miles	406,690 kilometers
Minimum distance from Earth	221,460 miles	356,400 kilometers
Mean distance from Earth	238,860 miles	384,400 kilometers

Dimensions of the Earth

	Area in Sq. Miles	Sq. Kilometers
Superficial area	197,751,000	512,175,090
Land surface	57,970,000	150,142,300
Water surface	139,781,000	362,032,790

	Miles	Kilometers
Equatorial circumference	24,902	40,075
Polar circumference	24,860	40,007
Equatorial diameter	7,926.68	12,756.4
Polar diameter	7,899.99	12,713.4
Equatorial radius	3,963.34	6,378.2
Polar radius	3,949.99	6,356.7
Volume of the Earth	2.6×10^{11} cubic miles	10.84×10^{11} cubic kilometers
Mass or weight	6.6×10^{21} short tons	6.0×10^{21} metric tons
Maximum distance from Sun	94,600,000 miles	152,000,000 kilometers
Minimum distance from Sun	91,300,000 miles	147,000,000 kilometers

The Continents

	Area in: Sq. Miles	Sq. Km.	Percent of World's Land
Asia	17,128,500	44,362,815	29.5
Africa	11,707,000	30,321,130	20.2
North America	9,363,000	24,250,170	16.2
South America	6,875,000	17,806,250	11.8
Antarctica	5,500,000	14,245,000	9.5
Europe	4,057,000	10,507,630	7.0
Australia	2,966,136	7,682,300	5.1

Oceans and Major Seas

	Area in: Sq. Miles	Sq. Km.	Greatest Depth in: Feet	Meters
Pacific Ocean	64,186,000	166,241,700	36,198	11,033
Atlantic Ocean	31,862,000	82,522,600	28,374	8,648
Indian Ocean	28,350,000	73,426,500	25,344	7,725
Arctic Ocean	5,427,000	14,056,000	17,880	5,450
Caribbean Sea	970,000	2,512,300	24,720	7,535
Mediterranean Sea	969,000	2,509,700	16,896	5,150
Bering Sea	875,000	2,266,250	15,800	4,800
Gulf of Mexico	600,000	1,554,000	12,300	3,750
Sea of Okhotsk	590,000	1,528,100	11,070	3,370
East China Sea	482,000	1,248,400	9,500	2,900
Sea of Japan	389,000	1,007,500	12,280	3,740
Hudson Bay	317,500	822,300	846	258
North Sea	222,000	575,000	2,200	670
Black Sea	185,000	479,150	7,365	2,245
Red Sea	169,000	437,700	7,200	2,195
Baltic Sea	163,000	422,170	1,506	459

Major Ship Canals

	Length in: Miles	Kms.	Minimum Feet	Depth in: Meters
Volga-Baltic, U.S.S.R.	225	362	—	—
Baltic-White Sea, U.S.S.R.	140	225	16	5
Suez, Egypt	100.76	162	42	13
Albert, Belgium	80	129	16.5	5
Moscow-Volga, U.S.S.R.	80	129	18	6
Volga-Don, U.S.S.R.	62	100	—	—
Göta, Sweden	54	87	10	3
Kiel (Nord-Ostsee), W. Ger.	53.2	86	38	12
Panama Canal, Panama	50.72	82	41.6	13
Houston Ship, U.S.A.	50	81	36	11

Largest Islands

	Area in: Sq. Mi.	Sq. Km.		Area in: Sq. Mi.	Sq. Km.		Area in: Sq. Mi.	Sq. Km.
Greenland	840,000	2,175,600	South I., New Zealand	58,393	151,238	Hokkaido, Japan	28,983	75,066
New Guinea	305,000	789,950	Java, Indonesia	48,842	126,501	Banks, Canada	27,038	70,028
Borneo	290,000	751,100	North I., New Zealand	44,187	114,444	Ceylon, Sri Lanka	25,332	65,610
Madagascar	226,400	586,376	Newfoundland, Canada	42,031	108,860	Tasmania, Australia	24,600	63,710
Baffin, Canada	195,928	507,454	Cuba	40,533	104,981	Svalbard, Norway	23,957	62,049
Sumatra, Indonesia	164,000	424,760	Luzon, Philippines	40,420	104,688	Devon, Canada	21,331	55,247
Honshu, Japan	88,000	227,920	Iceland	39,768	103,000	Novaya Zemlya (north isl.), U.S.S.R.	18,600	48,200
Great Britain	84,400	218,896	Mindanao, Philippines	36,537	94,631	Marajó, Brazil	17,991	46,597
Victoria, Canada	83,896	217,290	Ireland	31,743	82,214	Tierra del Fuego, Chile & Argentina	17,900	46,360
Ellesmere, Canada	75,767	196,236	Sakhalin, U.S.S.R.	29,500	76,405	Alexander, Antarctica	16,700	43,250
Celebes, Indonesia	72,986	189,034	Hispaniola, Haiti & Dom. Rep.	29,399	76,143			

Principal Mountains of the World

Mountain	Feet	Meters
Everest, Nepal-China	29,028	8,848
Godwin Austen (K2), Pakistan-China	28,250	8,611
Kanchenjunga, Nepal-India	28,208	8,598
Lhotse, Nepal-China	27,923	8,511
Makalu, Nepal-China	27,824	8,481
Dhaulagiri, Nepal	26,810	8,172
Nanga Parbat, Pakistan	26,660	8,126
Annapurna, Nepal	26,504	8,078
Gasherbrum, Pakistan-China	26,740	8,068
Nanda Devi, India	25,645	7,817
Rakaposhi, Pakistan	25,550	7,788
Kamet, India	25,447	7,756
Gurla Mandhada, China	25,355	7,728
Kongur Shan, China	25,325	7,719
Tirich Mir, Pakistan	25,230	7,690
Gongga Shan, China	24,790	7,556
Muztagata, China	24,757	7,546
Communism Peak, U.S.S.R.	24,599	7,498
Pobeda Peak, U.S.S.R.	24,406	7,439
Chomo Lhari, Bhutan-China	23,997	7,314
Muztag, China	23,891	7,282
Cerro Aconcagua, Argentina	22,831	6,959
Ojos del Salado, Chile-Argentina	22,572	6,880
Bonete, Chile-Argentina	22,541	6,870
Tupungato, Chile-Argentina	22,310	6,800
Pissis, Argentina	22,241	6,779
Mercedario, Argentina	22,211	6,770
Huascarán, Peru	22,205	6,768
Llullaillaco, Chile-Argentina	22,057	6,723
Nevada Ancohuma, Bolivia	21,489	6,550
Illampu, Bolivia	21,276	6,485
Chimborazo, Ecuador	20,561	6,267
McKinley, Alaska	20,320	6,194
Logan, Canada (Yukon)	19,524	5,951
Cotopaxi, Ecuador	19,347	5,897
Kilimanjaro, Tanzania	19,340	5,895
El Misti, Peru	19,101	5,822
Pico Cristóbal Colón, Colombia	19,029	5,800
Huila, Colombia	18,865	5,750
Citlaltépetl (Orizaba), Mexico	18,855	5,747
El'brus, U.S.S.R.	18,510	5,642
Damavand, Iran	18,376	5,601
St. Elias, Alaska-Canada (Yukon)	18,008	5,489
Vilcanota, Peru	17,999	5,486
Popocatépetl, Mexico	17,887	5,452
Dykhtau, U.S.S.R.	17,070	5,203
Kenya, Kenya	17,058	5,199
Ararat, Turkey	16,946	5,165
Vinson Massif, Antarctica	16,864	5,140
Margherita (Ruwenzori), Africa	16,795	5,119
Kazbek, U.S.S.R.	16,512	5,033
Puncak Jaya, Indonesia	16,503	5,030
Tyree, Antarctica	16,289	4,965
Blanc, France	15,771	4,807
Klyuchevskaya Sopka, U.S.S.R.	15,584	4,750
Fairweather (Br. Col., Canada)	15,300	4,663
Dufourspitze (Mte. Rosa), Italy-Switzerland	15,203	4,634
Ras Dashan, Ethiopia	15,157	4,620
Matterhorn, Switzerland	14,691	4,478
Whitney, California, U.S.A.	14,494	4,418
Elbert, Colorado, U.S.A.	14,433	4,399
Rainier, Washington, U.S.A.	14,410	4,392
Shasta, California, U.S.A.	14,162	4,350
Pikes Peak, Colorado, U.S.A.	14,110	4,301
Finsteraarhorn, Switzerland	14,022	4,274
Mauna Kea, Hawaii, U.S.A.	13,796	4,205
Mauna Loa, Hawaii, U.S.A.	13,677	4,169
Jungfrau, Switzerland	13,642	4,158
Cameroon, Cameroon	13,350	4,069
Grossglockner, Austria	12,457	3,797
Fuji, Japan	12,389	3,776
Cook, New Zealand	12,349	3,764
Etna, Italy	11,053	3,369
Kosciusko, Australia	7,310	2,228
Mitchell, North Carolina, U.S.A.	6,684	2,037

Longest Rivers of the World

River	Length in Miles	Length in Kms.
Nile, Africa	4,145	6,671
Amazon, S. Amer.	3,915	6,300
Chang Jiang (Yangtze), China	3,900	6,276
Mississippi-Missouri-Red Rock, U.S.A.	3,741	6,019
Ob'Irtysh-Black Irtysh, U.S.S.R.	3,362	5,411
Yenisey-Angara, U.S.S.R.	3,100	4,989
Huang He (Yellow), China	2,877	4,630
Amur-Shilka-Onon, Asia	2,744	4,416
Lena, U.S.S.R.	2,734	4,400
Congo (Zaire), Africa	2,718	4,374
Mackenzie-Peace-Finlay, Canada	2,635	4,241
Mekong, Asia	2,610	4,200
Missouri-Red Rock, U.S.A.	2,564	4,125
Niger, Africa	2,548	4,101
Paraná-La Plata, S. Amer.	2,450	3,943
Mississippi, U.S.A.	2,348	3,778
Murray-Darling, Australia	2,310	3,718
Volga, U.S.S.R.	2,194	3,531
Madeira, S. Amer.	2,013	3,240
Purus, S. Amer.	1,995	3,211
Yukon, Alaska-Canada	1,979	3,185
St. Lawrence, Canada-U.S.A.	1,900	3,058
Rio Grande, Mexico-U.S.A.	1,885	3,034
Syrdar'ya-Naryn, U.S.S.R.	1,859	2,992
São Francisco, Brazil	1,811	2,914
Indus, Asia	1,800	2,897
Danube, Europe	1,775	2,857
Salween, Asia	1,770	2,849
Brahmaputra, Asia	1,700	2,736
Euphrates, Asia	1,700	2,736
Tocantins, Brazil	1,677	2,699
Xi (Si), China	1,650	2,655
Amudar'ya, Asia	1,616	2,601
Nelson-Saskatchewan, Canada	1,600	2,575
Orinoco, S. Amer.	1,600	2,575
Zambezi, Africa	1,600	2,575
Paraguay, S. Amer.	1,584	2,549
Kolyma, U.S.S.R.	1,562	2,514
Ganges, Asia	1,550	2,494
Ural, U.S.S.R.	1,509	2,428
Japurá, S. Amer.	1,500	2,414
Arkansas, U.S.A.	1,450	2,334
Colorado, U.S.A.-Mexico	1,450	2,334
Negro, S. Amer.	1,400	2,253
Dnieper, U.S.S.R.	1,368	2,202
Orange, Africa	1,350	2,173
Irrawaddy, Burma	1,325	2,132
Brazos, U.S.A.	1,309	2,107
Ohio-Allegheny, U.S.A.	1,306	2,102
Kama, U.S.S.R.	1,262	2,031
Red, U.S.A.	1,222	1,966
Don, U.S.S.R.	1,222	1,967
Columbia, U.S.A.-Canada	1,214	1,953
Saskatchewan, Canada	1,205	1,939
Peace-Finlay, Canada	1,195	1,923
Tigris, Asia	1,181	1,901
Darling, Australia	1,160	1,867
Angara, U.S.S.R.	1,135	1,827
Sungari, Asia	1,130	1,819
Pechora, U.S.S.R.	1,124	1,809
Snake, U.S.A.	1,000	1,609
Churchill, Canada	1,000	1,609
Pilcomayo, S. Amer.	1,000	1,609
Magdalena, Colombia	1,000	1,609
Uruguay, S. Amer.	994	1,600
Platte-N. Platte, U.S.A.	990	1,593
Ohio, U.S.A.	981	1,578
Pecos, U.S.A.	926	1,490
Oka, U.S.S.R.	918	1,477
Canadian, U.S.A.	906	1,458
Colorado, Texas, U.S.A.	894	1,439
Dniester, U.S.S.R.	876	1,410

Principal Natural Lakes

Lake	Area Sq. Miles	Area Sq. Km.	Max. Depth Feet	Max. Depth Meters
Caspian Sea, U.S.S.R.-Iran	143,243	370,999	3,264	995
Lake Superior, U.S.A.-Canada	31,820	82,414	1,329	405
Lake Victoria, Africa	26,724	69,215	270	82
Aral Sea, U.S.S.R.	25,676	66,501	256	78
Lake Huron, U.S.A.-Canada	23,010	59,596	748	228
Lake Michigan, U.S.A.	22,400	58,016	923	281
Lake Tanganyika, Africa	12,650	32,764	4,700	1,433
Lake Baykal, U.S.S.R.	12,162	31,500	5,316	1,620
Great Bear Lake, Canada	12,096	31,328	1,356	413
Lake Nyasa (Malawi), Africa	11,555	29,928	2,320	707
Great Slave Lake, Canada	11,031	28,570	2,015	614
Lake Erie, U.S.A.-Canada	9,940	25,745	210	64
Lake Winnipeg, Canada	9,417	24,390	60	18
Lake Ontario, U.S.A.-Canada	7,540	19,529	775	244
Lake Ladoga, U.S.S.R.	7,104	18,399	738	225
Lake Balkhash, U.S.S.R.	7,027	18,200	87	27
Lake Maracaibo, Venezuela	5,120	13,261	100	31
Lake Chad, Africa	4,000-10,000	10,360-25,900	25	8
Lake Onega, U.S.S.R.	3,710	9,609	377	115
Lake Eyre, Australia	3,500-0	9,000-0	—	—
Lake Titicaca, Peru-Bolivia	3,200	8,288	1,000	305
Lake Nicaragua, Nicaragua	3,100	8,029	230	70
Lake Athabasca, Canada	3,064	7,936	400	122
Reindeer Lake, Canada	2,568	6,651	—	—
Lake Turkana (Rudolf), Africa	2,463	6,379	240	73
Issyk-Kul', U.S.S.R.	2,425	6,281	2,303	702
Lake Torrens, Australia	2,230	5,776	—	—
Vänern, Sweden	2,156	5,584	328	100
Nettilling Lake, Canada	2,140	5,543	—	—
Lake Winnipegosis, Canada	2,075	5,374	38	12
Lake Mobutu Sese Seko (Albert), Africa	2,075	5,374	160	49
Kariba Lake, Zambia-Zimbabwe	2,050	5,310	295	90
Lake Nipigon, Canada	1,872	4,848	540	165
Lake Mweru, Zaire-Zambia	1,800	4,662	60	18
Lake Manitoba, Canada	1,799	4,659	12	4
Lake Taymyr, U.S.S.R.	1,737	4,499	85	26
Lake Khanka, China-U.S.S.R.	1,700	4,403	33	10
Lake Kioga, Uganda	1,700	4,403	25	8

MAP PROJECTIONS

by Erwin Raisz

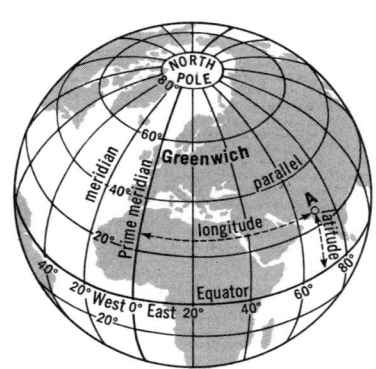

Our earth is rotating around its *axis* once a day. The two end points of its axis are the *poles;* the line circling the earth midway between the poles is the *equator.* The arc from either of the poles to the equator is divided into 90 *degrees.* The distance, expressed in degrees, from the equator to any point is its *latitude* and circles of equal latitude are the *parallels.* On maps it is customary to show parallels of evenly-spaced degrees such as every fifth or every tenth.

The equator is divided into 360 degrees. Lines circling from pole to pole through the degree points on the equator are called *meridians.* They are all equal in length but by international agreement the meridian passing through the Greenwich Observatory in London has been chosen as *prime meridian.* The distance, expressed in degrees, from the prime meridian to any point is its *longitude.* While meridians are all equal in length, parallels become shorter and shorter as they approach the poles. Whereas one degree of latitude represents everywhere approximately 69 miles, one degree of longitude varies from 69 miles at the equator to nothing at the poles.

Each degree is divided into 60 minutes and each minute into 60 seconds. One minute of latitude equals a nautical mile.

The map is flat but the earth is nearly spherical. Neither a rubber ball nor any part of a rubber ball may be flattened without stretching or tearing unless the part is very small. To present the curved surface of the earth on a flat map is not difficult as long as the areas under consideration are small, but the mapping of countries, continents, or the whole earth requires some kind of *projection.* Any regular set of parallels and meridians upon which a map can be drawn makes a map projection. Many systems are used.

In any projection only the parallels or the meridians or some other set of lines can be *true* (the same length as on the globe of corresponding scale); all other lines are too long or too short. Only on a globe is it possible to have both the parallels and the meridians true. The scale given on a flat map cannot be true everywhere. The construction of the various projections begins usually with laying out the parallels or meridians which have true lengths.

RECTANGULAR PROJECTION — This is a set of evenly-placed meridians and horizontal parallels. The central or *standard parallel* and all meridians are true. All other parallels are either too long or too short. The projection is used for simple maps of small areas, as city plans, etc.

Rectangular Projection

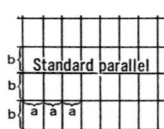

MERCATOR PROJECTION — In this projection the meridians are evenly-spaced vertical lines. The parallels are horizontal, spaced so that their length has the same relation to the meridians as on a globe. As the meridians converge at higher latitudes on the globe, while on the map they do not, the parallels have to be drawn also farther and farther apart to maintain the correct relationship. When every very small area has the same shape as on a globe we call the projection *conformal.* The most interesting quality of this projection is that all *compass directions* appear as straight lines. For this reason it is generally used for marine charts. It is also frequently used for world maps in spite of the fact that the high latitudes are very much exaggerated in size. Only the equator is true to scale; all other parallels and meridians are too long. The Mercator projection did *not* derive from projecting a globe upon a cylinder.

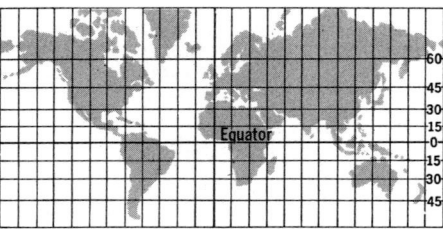

Mercator Projection

SINUSOIDAL PROJECTION — The parallels are truly-spaced horizontal lines. They are divided truly and the connecting curves make the meridians. It does not make a good world map because the outer regions are distorted, but the

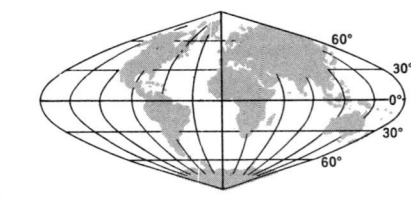

Sinusoidal Projection

central portion is good and this part is often used for maps of Africa and South America. Every part of the map has the same area as the corresponding area on the globe. It is an *equal-area* projection.

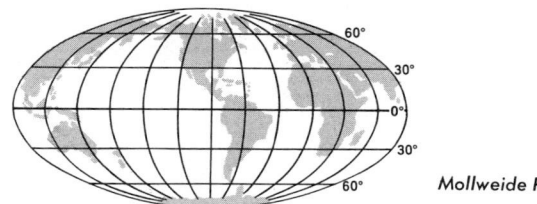

Mollweide Projection

MOLLWEIDE PROJECTION — The meridians are equally-spaced ellipses; the parallels are horizontal lines spaced so that every belt of latitude should have the same area as on a globe. This projection is popular for world maps, especially in European atlases.

GOODE'S INTERRUPTED PROJECTIONS—Only the good central part of the Mollweide or sinusoidal (or both) projection is used and the oceans are cut. This makes an equal-area map with little distortion of shape. It is commonly used for world maps.

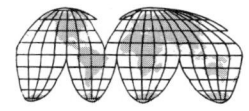

Goode's Interrupted Projection

Eckert Projection

ECKERT PROJECTIONS — These are similar to the sinusoidal or the Mollweide projections, but the poles are shown as lines half the length of the equator. There are several variants; the meridians are either sine curves or ellipses; the parallels are horizontal and spaced either evenly or so as to make the projection equal area. Their use for world maps is increasing. The figure shows the elliptical equal-area variant.

CONIC PROJECTION — The original idea of the conic projection is that of capping the globe by a cone upon which both the parallels and meridians are projected from the center of the globe. The cone is then cut open and laid flat. A cone can be made tangent to any chosen *standard parallel.*

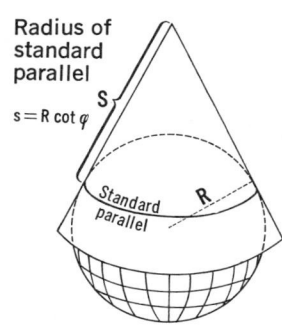

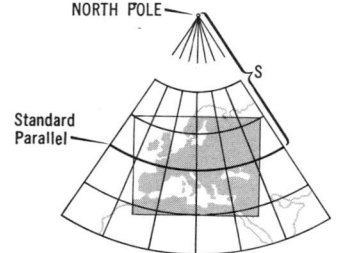

Conic Projection

The actually-used conic projection is a modification of this idea. The radius of the standard parallel is obtained as above. The meridians are straight radiating lines spaced truly on the standard parallel. The parallels are concentric circles spaced at true distances. All parallels except the standard are too long. The projection is used for maps of countries in middle latitudes, as it presents good shapes with small scale error.

There are several variants: The use of *two standard parallels,* one near the top, the other near the bottom of the map, reduces the scale error. In the *Albers projection* the parallels are spaced unevenly, to make the projection equal-area. This is a good projection for the United States. In the *Lambert conformal conic projection* the parallels are spaced so that any small quadrangle of the grid should have the same shape as on the globe. This is the best projection for air-navigation charts as it has relatively straight azimuths.

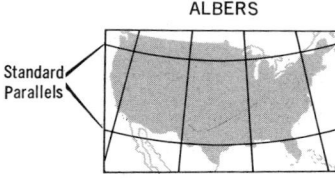

Albers Projection

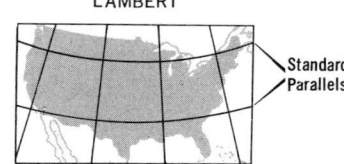

Lambert Conformal Conic Projection

An *azimuth* is a great-circle direction reckoned clockwise from north. A *great-circle direction* points to a place along the shortest line on the earth's surface. This is not the same as compass direction. The center of a great circle is the center of the globe.

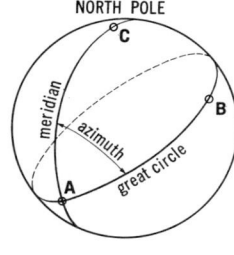

BONNE PROJECTION — The parallels are laid out exactly as in the conic projection. All parallels are divided truly and the connecting curves make the meridians. It is an equal-area projection. It is used for maps of the northern continents, as Asia, Europe, and North America.

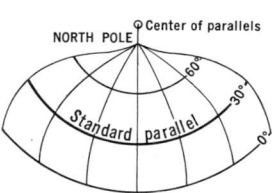

Bonne Projection

POLYCONIC PROJECTION — The central meridian is divided truly. The parallels are non-concentric circles, the radii of which are obtained by drawing tangents to the globe as though the globe were covered by several cones rather than by only one. Each parallel is divided truly and the connecting curves make the meridians. All meridians except the central one are too long. This projection is used for large-scale topographic sheets — less often for countries or continents.

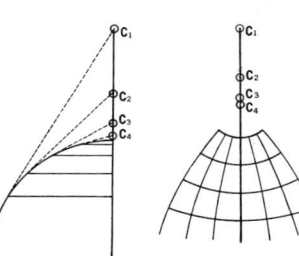

Polyconic Projection

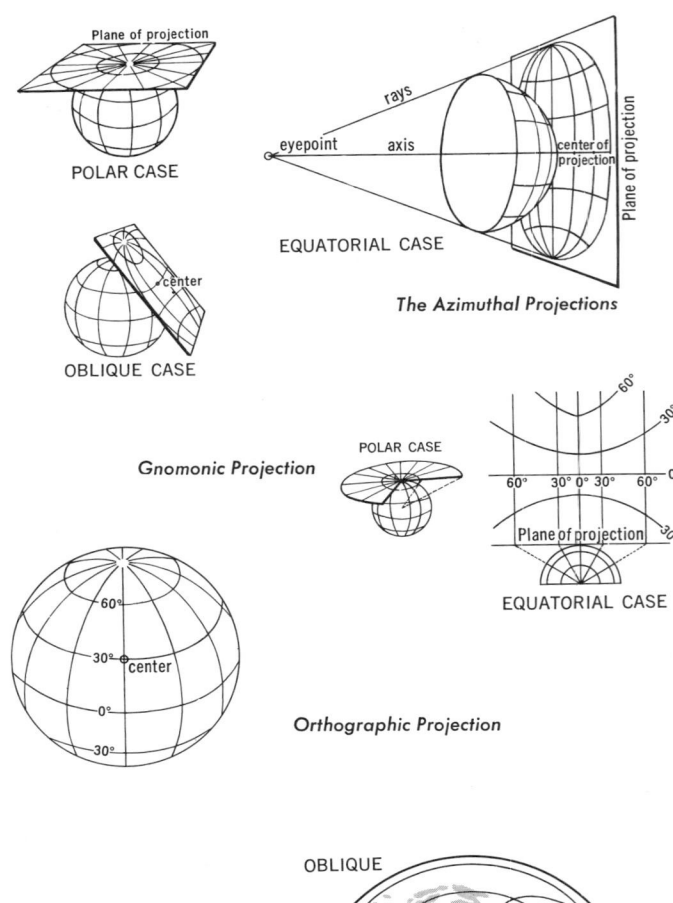

Plane of projection

POLAR CASE

OBLIQUE CASE

rays

eyepoint   axis

center of projection

Plane of projection

EQUATORIAL CASE

The Azimuthal Projections

Gnomonic Projection

POLAR CASE

60°

30°

60° 30° 0° 30° 60° 0°

Plane of projection

30°

EQUATORIAL CASE

60°

30° center

0°

30°

Orthographic Projection

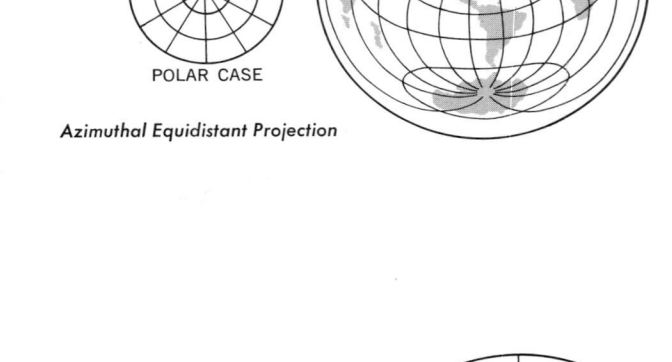

OBLIQUE

center

POLAR CASE

Azimuthal Equidistant Projection

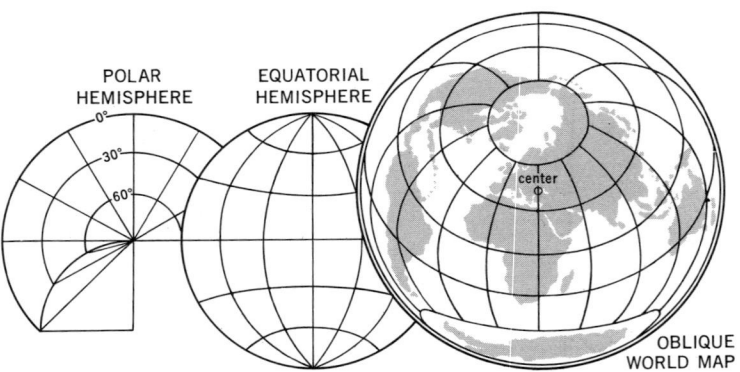

POLAR
HEMISPHERE

0°

30°

60°

EQUATORIAL
HEMISPHERE

center

OBLIQUE
WORLD MAP

Lambert Azimuthal Equal-Area Projection

THE AZIMUTHAL PROJECTIONS — In this group a part of the globe is projected from an eyepoint onto a plane. The eyepoint can be at different distances, making different projections. The plane of projection can be tangent at the equator, at a pole, or at any other point on which we want to focus attention. The most important quality of all azimuthal projections is that they show every point at its true direction (azimuth) from the center point, and all points equally distant from the center point will be equally distant on the map also.

GNOMONIC PROJECTION — This projection has the eyepoint at the center of the globe Only the central part is good; the outer regions are badly distorted. Yet the projection has one important quality, all great circles being shown as straight lines. For this reason it is used for laying out the routes for long range flying or trans-oceanic navigation.

ORTHOGRAPHIC PROJECTION — This projection has the eyepoint at infinite distance and the projecting rays are parallel. The polar or equatorial varieties are rare but the oblique case became very popular on account of its visual quality. It looks like a picture of a globe. Although the distortion on the peripheries is extreme, we see it correctly because the eye perceives it not as a map but as a picture of a three-dimensional globe. Obviously only a hemisphere (half globe) can be shown.

Some azimuthal projections do not derive from the actual process of projecting from an eyepoint, but are arrived at by other means:

AZIMUTHAL EQUIDISTANT PROJECTION — This is the only projection in which every point is shown both at true great-circle direction and at true distance from the center point, but all other directions and distances are distorted. The principle of the projection can best be understood from the polar case. Most polar maps are in this projection. The oblique case is used for radio direction finding, for earthquake research, and in long-distance flying. A separate map has to be constructed for each central point selected.

LAMBERT AZIMUTHAL EQUAL-AREA PROJECTION — The construction of this projection can best be understood from the polar case. All three cases are widely used. It makes a good polar map and it is often extended to include the southern continents. It is the most common projection used for maps of the Eastern and Western Hemispheres, and it is a good projection for continents as it shows correct areas with relatively little distortion of shape. Most of the continent maps in this atlas are in this projection.

IN THIS ATLAS, on almost all maps, parallels and meridians have been marked because they are useful for the following:

(a) They show the north-south and east-west directions which appear on many maps at oblique angles especially near the margins.

(b) With the help of parallels and meridians every place can be exactly located; for instance, New York City is at 41° N and 74° W on any map.

(c) They help to measure distances even in the distorted parts of the map. The scale given on each map is true only along certain lines which are specified in the foregoing discussion for each projection. One degree of latitude equals nearly 69 statute miles or 60 nautical miles. The length of one degree of longitude varies (1° long. = 1° lat. × cos lat.).